OXFORD PAPERBACK THESAURUS

Oxford Paperback Thesaurus

THIRD EDITION

Edited by
Maurice Waite

with Lucy Hollingworth
and Duncan Marshall

OXFORD
UNIVERSITY PRESS

Great Clarendon Street, Oxford OX2 6DP

Oxford University Press is a department of the University of Oxford.
It furthers the University's objective of excellence in research, scholarship,
and education by publishing worldwide in

Oxford New York

Auckland Cape Town Dar es Salaam Hong Kong Karachi
Kuala Lumpur Madrid Melbourne Mexico City Nairobi
New Delhi Shanghai Taipei Toronto

With offices in

Argentina Austria Brazil Chile Czech Republic France Greece
Guatemala Hungary Italy Japan Poland Portugal Singapore
South Korea Switzerland Thailand Turkey Ukraine Vietnam

Oxford is a registered trade mark of Oxford University Press
in the UK and in certain other countries

© Oxford University Press 1994, 2001, 2006

Database right Oxford University Press (maker)

First published 1994
Second edition 2001
Third edition 2006

British Library Cataloguing in Publication Data
Data available

Library of Congress Cataloging in Publication Data
Data available

ISBN 0-19-861425-X
ISBN 978-0-19-861425-8

10 9 8 7 6 5 4 3 2 1

Typeset in Frutiger and Parable
by Laserwords Pvt. Ltd., Chennai, India
Printed in Great Britain
by Clays Ltd, Bungay, Suffolk

Contents

Preface

A thesaurus (from the Greek for 'storehouse' or 'treasure') helps you to express yourself more accurately and in more interesting and varied ways. By listing groups of words that have similar meanings to each other, it offers a choice of alternative words (synonyms) that can be used in place of one that you already have in mind.

This new edition of the *Oxford Paperback Thesaurus* is based on the latest language research from Oxford: we have added thousands of new examples from the Oxford English Corpus, a database containing a billion words of English, making it even easier to find the meanings that you want.

A new Wordfinder section has also been added in the centre of this edition. This provides you with still further sources of vocabulary: extensive but handy lists of different animals, items of food and drink, parts of the body, plants, forms of transport, and many other categories. These lists are ideal for helping you solve crosswords and other puzzles or just reminding you of a word that is on the tip of your tongue.

The *Oxford Paperback Thesaurus* is an invaluable tool for writing memos and reports at work, essays and dissertations at school or college, letters to friends or potential employers, or in creative writing for a living or for pleasure.

Guide to the thesaurus entry

headword

numbered sense of the headword

air noun **1** *hundreds of birds hovered in the air:* **sky**, atmosphere; heavens, ether. **2** *open the windows to get some air into the room:* **breeze**, draught, wind; breath/blast of air, gust/puff of wind. **3** *he upended his glass with an air of defiance:* **expression**, appearance, look, impression, aspect, aura, mien, countenance, manner, bearing, tone. **4** (**airs**) *he'd no patience with women putting on airs:* **affectations**, pretension, pretentiousness, affectedness, posing, posturing, airs and graces; Brit. informal side. verb **1** *this is a chance for you to air your views:* **express**, voice, make public, ventilate, articulate, state, declare, give expression/voice to, have one's say. **2** *the windows were opened to air the room:* **ventilate**, freshen, refresh, cool. **3** *the film was aired nationwide:* **broadcast**, transmit, screen, show, televise, telecast.

core synonym—the closest synonym to the headword

form of the headword for which synonyms are given

example of use, to help distinguish different senses

forward slash used to show more than one possibility

part of speech of the headword

label indicating the region of the world in which the following synonym is used (*see opposite for abbreviations*)

luxurious adjective *a luxurious Mayfair apartment:* **opulent**, sumptuous, de luxe, grand, palatial, splendid, magnificent, well appointed, extravagant, fancy; Brit. upmarket; informal plush, posh, classy, ritzy, swanky; Brit. informal swish; N. Amer. informal swank.
– OPPOSITES plain, basic.

label indicating the level or style of English in which the following synonyms are used (*see opposite for explanations*)

words meaning the opposite of the headword; most have entries of their own, where a wider choice will be found

brackets to show more than one possibility

night noun night-time; (hours of) darkness, dark.
– OPPOSITES day.
■ **night and day** all the time, around the clock; (morning, noon, and night); (day in, day out), ceaselessly, endlessly, incessantly, unceasingly, interminably, constantly, perpetually, continually, relentlessly; informal 24-7.

phrase for which synonyms are given

brackets around a phrase, to avoid confusion

Most of the synonyms given are part of standard English, but some are used only in certain styles or situations. These are grouped at the end of their sense and have labels in front of them:

informal, e.g. *swig* as a synonym for *drink*: normally used only in speech or informal writing.

formal, e.g. *dwelling* as a synonym for *home*: normally used only in writing such as official documents.

technical, e.g. *neonate* as a synonym for *baby*: normally used only in technical and specialist language. Words used in specific fields are labelled Medicine, Nautical, etc.

literary, e.g. *strand* as a synonym for *beach*: found only or mainly in literature.

dated, e.g. *miffy* as a synonym for *bad-tempered*: no longer used by most, but still sometimes by older people.

historical, e.g. *privateer*, a type of *pirate*: only used today to refer to things that are no longer part of modern life.

humorous, e.g. *libation* as a synonym for *drink*: used with the intention of sounding funny or playful.

archaic, e.g. *meat* as a synonym for any kind of *food*: not used today except for old-fashioned effect.

Synonyms used exclusively or mainly in a particular part of the world are also labelled British (abbreviated to Brit.), Northern English (N. English), Scottish, Irish, North American (N. Amer.), Australian (Austral.), or New Zealand (NZ).

NOTE ON TRADEMARKS AND PROPRIETARY STATUS

Aa

aback

■ **take someone aback** surprise, shock, stun, stagger, astound, astonish, startle, take by surprise; dumbfound, nonplus, stop someone in their tracks; shake (up), jolt, throw, unnerve, disconcert, unsettle, bewilder; informal flabbergast, knock sideways, floor; Brit. informal knock for six.

abandon verb **1** *the party abandoned policies which made it unelectable:* **renounce**, relinquish, dispense with, disclaim, disown, disavow, discard, wash one's hands of; give up, drop, jettison, do away with, axe; informal ditch, scrap, scrub, junk; formal forswear. **2** *by that stage, she had abandoned painting:* **give up**, stop, cease, drop, forgo, desist from, have done with, abstain from, discontinue, break off, refrain from, set aside; informal cut out, kick, pack in, quit; Brit. informal jack in; formal abjure. **3** *he abandoned his wife and children:* **desert**, leave, leave high and dry, turn one's back on, cast aside; jilt, strand, leave stranded, leave in the lurch, throw over; informal walk out on, run out on, dump, ditch. **4** *the skipper gave the order to abandon ship:* **vacate**, leave, depart from, withdraw from, quit, evacuate. **5** *a vast expanse of territory was abandoned to the invaders:* **relinquish**, surrender, give up, cede, yield, leave.
– OPPOSITES keep, retain, continue.
noun *she sings and sways with total abandon:* **uninhibitedness**, lack of restraint, recklessness, wildness, impulsiveness, impetuosity, immoderation, wantonness.
– OPPOSITES self-control.

abandoned adjective **1** *a home for orphan and abandoned boys:* **deserted**, forsaken, cast aside/off; jilted, stranded, rejected; informal dumped, ditched. **2** *an abandoned tin mine:* **unused**, disused, neglected, idle; deserted, unoccupied, uninhabited, empty. **3** *a wild, abandoned dance:* **uninhibited**, reckless, unrestrained, wild, unbridled, impulsive, impetuous; immoderate, wanton.

abase verb *I watched my colleagues abasing themselves before the dean:* **humble**, humiliate, belittle, demean, lower, degrade, debase, cheapen, discredit, bring low; (**abase oneself**) grovel, kowtow, bow and scrape, toady, fawn; informal crawl, suck up to someone, lick someone's boots.

abashed adjective *Harriet looked slightly abashed:* **embarrassed**, ashamed, shamefaced, remorseful, conscience-stricken, mortified, humiliated, humbled, chagrined, crestfallen, sheepish, red-faced, discountenanced, with one's tail between one's legs.

abate verb **1** *the storm had abated:* **subside**, die down/away/out, lessen, ease (off), let up, decrease, diminish, moderate, decline, fade, dwindle, recede, tail off, peter out, taper off, wane, ebb, weaken, come to an end. **2** *nothing abated his crusading zeal:* **decrease**, lessen, diminish, reduce, moderate, ease, soothe, dampen, calm, tone down, allay, temper.
– OPPOSITES intensify, increase.

abatement noun **1** *the storm still rages with no sign of abatement:* **subsiding**, dying down/away/out, lessening, easing (off), let-up, decrease, moderation, decline, ebb. **2** *noise abatement:* **decrease**, reduction, lowering.

abattoir noun **slaughterhouse**; Brit. butchery.

abbey noun **monastery**, **convent**, priory, cloister, friary, nunnery.

abbreviate verb *'network' is often abbreviated to 'net':* **shorten**, reduce, cut, contract, condense, compress, abridge, truncate, pare down, prune, shrink, telescope; summarize, abstract, precis, synopsize, digest, edit.
– OPPOSITES lengthen, expand.

abbreviated adjective **shortened**, reduced, cut, condensed, abridged, concise, compact, succinct; summary, thumbnail, synoptic.
– OPPOSITES long.

abbreviation noun **short form**, contraction, acronym, initialism, symbol, diminutive; elision.

abdicate verb **1** *the king abdicated in 1936:* **resign**, retire, stand down, step down, bow out, renounce the throne. **2** *Ferdinand abdicated the throne:* **resign from**, relinquish, renounce, give up, surrender, vacate, cede; formal abjure. **3** *the state abdicated all responsibility for their welfare:* **disown**, reject, renounce, give up, refuse, relinquish, repudiate, abandon, turn one's back on, wash one's hands of; formal abjure.

abdication noun **1** *Edward VIII's abdication:* **resignation**, retirement; relinquishment, renunciation, surrender; formal abjuration.

2 *an abdication of responsibility:* **disowning**, renunciation, rejection, refusal, relinquishment, repudiation, abandonment.

abdomen noun **stomach**, belly, gut, middle, intestines; informal tummy, tum, insides, guts, maw, breadbasket, pot, paunch; Austral. informal bingy.

abdominal adjective *abdominal pain:* **gastric**, intestinal, stomach, stomachic, enteric, duodenal, visceral, coeliac, ventral.

abduct verb *she was abducted by two men and held for 36 hours:* **kidnap**, carry off, seize, capture, run away/off with, make off with, spirit away, hold hostage, hold to ransom; informal snatch.

aberrant adjective *Mrs Casper appears to be responsible for Billy's aberrant behaviour:* **deviant**, deviating, divergent, abnormal, atypical, anomalous, irregular, rogue; strange, odd, peculiar, uncommon, freakish; twisted, warped, perverted.
– OPPOSITES normal, typical.

aberration noun *economists said the figures were a statistical aberration:* **anomaly**, deviation, departure from the norm, divergence, abnormality, irregularity, variation, freak, rarity, oddity, peculiarity, curiosity; mistake.

abet verb *several villagers are accused of aiding and abetting the smugglers:* **assist**, aid, help, lend a hand, support, back, encourage; cooperate with, collaborate with, work with, collude with, be in collusion with, be hand in glove with, side with; second, endorse, sanction; promote, champion, further, expedite, connive at.
– OPPOSITES hinder.

abeyance noun *the project was left in abeyance for the time being:* **suspension**, a state of suspension, a state of uncertainty, remission; (**in abeyance**) pending, suspended, deferred, postponed, put off, put to one side, unresolved, up in the air; informal in cold storage, on ice, on the back burner, hanging fire.

abhor verb *he abhorred sexism in every form:* **detest**, hate, loathe, despise, execrate, regard with disgust, shrink from, recoil from, shudder at; formal abominate.
– OPPOSITES love, admire.

abhorrence noun **hatred**, loathing, detestation, execration, revulsion, abomination, disgust, repugnance, horror, odium, aversion.

abhorrent adjective *racial discrimination was abhorrent to us all:* **detestable**, hateful, loathsome, despicable, abominable, execrable, repellent, repugnant, repulsive, revolting, disgusting, distasteful, horrible, horrid, horrifying, awful, heinous, reprehensible, obnoxious, odious, nauseating, offensive, contemptible.
– OPPOSITES admirable.

abide verb **1** *he expected everybody to abide by the rules:* **comply with**, obey, observe, follow, keep to, hold to, conform to, adhere to, stick to, stand by, act in accordance with, uphold, heed, accept, go along with, acknowledge, respect, defer to. **2** (informal) *I can't abide the smell of cigarettes:* **tolerate**, bear, stand, put up with, endure, take, countenance; informal stomach; Brit. informal stick; formal brook. **3** *at least one memory will abide:* **continue**, remain, survive, last, persist, linger, stay, live on.
– OPPOSITES flout, disobey, vanish, dissipate.

abiding adjective *he had an abiding respect for her:* **enduring**, lasting, persisting, long-lasting, lifelong, continuing, remaining, surviving, standing, durable, everlasting, perpetual, eternal, unending, constant, permanent, unchanging, steadfast, immutable.
– OPPOSITES short-lived, ephemeral.

ability noun **1** *he was proud of his daughter's ability to read and write:* **capacity**, capability, power, faculty, aptness, facility; wherewithal, means. **2** *they criticized the president's leadership ability:* **talent**, skill, expertise, adeptness, aptitude, skilfulness, savoir faire, prowess, mastery, accomplishment; competence, proficiency; dexterity, adroitness, deftness; informal know-how.

abject adjective **1** *many families are living in abject poverty:* **wretched**, miserable, hopeless, pathetic, pitiful, pitiable, piteous, sorry, woeful, lamentable, appalling, atrocious, awful. **2** *an abject sinner:* **contemptible**, base, low, vile, worthless, debased, degraded, despicable, ignominious, mean, unworthy, ignoble. **3** *an abject apology:* **obsequious**, grovelling, fawning, toadyish, servile, cringing, sycophantic, submissive, craven.

ablaze adjective **1** *several vehicles were ablaze:* **on fire**, alight, aflame, in flames, flaming, burning, blazing. **2** *every window was ablaze with light:* **lit up**, alight, gleaming, glowing, aglow, illuminated, bright, shining, radiant, shimmering, sparkling, flashing, dazzling, luminous, incandescent.

able adjective **1** *he will soon be able to resume his duties:* **capable of**, competent to, equal to, up to, fit to, prepared to, qualified to; allowed to, free to, in a position to. **2** *an able student:* **intelligent**, clever, talented, skilful, skilled, accomplished, gifted; proficient, good, adroit, adept; capable, competent.
– OPPOSITES incompetent, incapable.

able-bodied adjective *every able-bodied man was required to serve in the armed forces:* **healthy**, fit, in good health, robust, strong, sound, sturdy, vigorous, hardy, hale and hearty, strapping, lusty; in good shape, in good trim, in fine fettle, fighting fit, as fit as a fiddle, as fit as a flea; informal husky; dated stalwart.
– OPPOSITES infirm, frail, disabled.

abnormal adjective *the illness is recognizable*

from the patient's abnormal behaviour: **unusual**, uncommon, atypical, untypical, non-typical, unrepresentative, rare, isolated, irregular, anomalous, deviant, divergent, aberrant, freakish; **strange**, odd, peculiar, curious, bizarre, weird, queer; eccentric, idiosyncratic, quirky; unexpected, unfamiliar, unconventional, surprising, unorthodox, singular, exceptional, extraordinary, out of the ordinary, out of the way; unnatural, perverse, perverted, twisted, warped, unhealthy, distorted; Brit. out of the common; informal funny, freaky.
– OPPOSITES normal, typical, common.

abnormality noun **1** *babies born with physical or mental abnormalities:* **malformation**, deformity, irregularity, flaw, defect. **2** *the abnormality of his behaviour was a cause for concern:* **unusualness**, uncommonness, atypicality, irregularity, anomalousness, deviation, divergence, aberrance, aberration; strangeness, oddness, peculiarity, singularity.

abolish verb *a bill to abolish the council tax:* **end**, get rid of, scrap, put an end to, stop, terminate, axe, eradicate, eliminate, exterminate, destroy, annihilate, stamp out, obliterate, wipe out, extinguish, quash, expunge, extirpate; annul, cancel, dissolve; rescind, repeal, revoke, overturn; discontinue, remove, excise, drop, jettison; informal do away with, ditch, junk, scrub, dump, chop, give something the chop, knock something on the head; formal abrogate.
– OPPOSITES retain, create.

abolition noun **scrapping**, ending, termination, eradication, elimination, extermination, destruction, annihilation, obliteration, extirpation; annulment, cancellation, dissolution; revocation, repeal, rescindment, discontinuation, removal; formal abrogation.

abominable adjective *the uprising was suppressed with abominable cruelty:* **loathsome**, detestable, hateful, odious, obnoxious, despicable, contemptible, damnable, diabolical; disgusting, revolting, repellent, repulsive, offensive, repugnant, abhorrent, reprehensible, atrocious, horrifying, execrable, foul, vile, wretched, base, horrible, awful, dreadful, appalling, nauseating; horrid, nasty, unpleasant; informal terrible, shocking, God-awful; Brit. informal beastly; dated cursed, accursed.
– OPPOSITES good, admirable.

abomination noun *in both wars, internment was an abomination:* **atrocity**, disgrace, horror, obscenity, outrage, evil, crime, monstrosity, anathema.

aboriginal adjective *the area's aboriginal inhabitants:* **indigenous**, native; original, earliest, first; ancient, primitive, primeval, primordial.
noun *the social structure of the aboriginals:* **native**, aborigine, original inhabitant.

abort verb **1** *I decided not to abort the pregnancy:* **terminate**, end. **2** *the organism can cause pregnant ewes to abort:* **miscarry**, have a miscarriage. **3** *the crew aborted the take-off:* **halt**, stop, end, axe, call off, cut short, discontinue, terminate, arrest; informal pull the plug on.

abortion noun **termination**, miscarriage.

abortive adjective *the rebels who led the abortive coup were shot:* **unsuccessful**, failed, vain, thwarted, futile, useless, worthless, ineffective, ineffectual, to no effect, inefficacious, fruitless, unproductive, unavailing, to no avail.
– OPPOSITES successful, fruitful.

abound verb **1** *cafes and bars abound in the narrow streets:* **be plentiful**, be abundant, be numerous, proliferate, be thick on the ground; informal grow on trees, be two/ten a penny. **2** *a stream which abounded with trout and eels:* **be full of**, overflow with, teem with, be packed with, be crowded with, be thronged with; be alive with, be crawling with, be overrun by/with, swarm with, bristle with, be infested with, be thick with; informal be lousy with, be stuffed with, be jam-packed with, be chock-a-block with, be chock-full of.

about preposition **1** *a book about ancient Greece:* **regarding**, concerning, with reference to, referring to, with regard to, with respect to, respecting, relating to, on, touching on, dealing with, relevant to, connected with, in connection with, on the subject of, in the matter of, apropos, re. **2** *two hundred people were milling about the room:* **around**, round, throughout, over, through, on every side of.
adverb **1** *there were babies crawling about in the grass:* **around**, here and there, to and fro, back and forth, from place to place, hither and thither, in all directions. **2** *I knew he was about somewhere:* **near**, nearby, around, hereabouts, not far off/away, close by, in the vicinity, in the neighbourhood. **3** *the car cost about £15,000:* **approximately**, roughly, around, round about, in the region of, circa, of the order of, something like; or so, more or less, give or take a few, not far off; Brit. getting on for; informal as near as dammit; N. Amer. informal in the ballpark of. **4** *there's a lot of flu about:* **around**, in circulation, in existence, current, going on, prevailing, prevalent, happening, in the air, abroad.
▪ **about to** (just) going to, ready to, all set to, preparing to, intending to, soon to; on the point of, on the verge of, on the brink of, within an ace of.

about-turn (Brit.) noun **1** *he saluted and did an about-turn:* **about-face**, turnaround, turnabout, U-turn; informal U-ey, one-eighty. **2** *the government was forced to make an about-turn:* **volte-face**, U-turn, reversal, retraction; change of heart, change of mind, sea change.

a

above preposition **1** *light filtered through a tiny window above the door:* **over**, higher (up) than; on top of, atop, on, upon. **2** *those above the rank of Colonel:* **superior to**, senior to, over, higher (up) than, more powerful than; in charge of, commanding. **3** *you must be above suspicion:* **beyond**, not liable to, not open to, not vulnerable to, out of reach of; immune to, exempt from. **4** *the Chinese valued pearls above gold:* **more than**, over, before, rather than, in preference to, instead of. **5** *an increase above the rate of inflation:* **greater than**, more than, higher than, exceeding, in excess of, over, over and above, beyond, surpassing, upwards of.
– OPPOSITES below, under, beneath.
adverb **1** *in the darkness above, something moved:* **overhead**, on/at the top, high up, on high, up above, (up) in the sky, high above one's head, aloft. **2** *the two cases described above:* **earlier**, previously, before, formerly.
adjective *the above example was chosen to illustrate the underlying problem:* **preceding**, previous, earlier, former, foregoing, prior, above-stated, aforementioned, aforesaid.
■ **above all** primarily, before everything, beyond everything, first of all, most of all, chiefly, most importantly, in the first place, first and foremost, mainly, principally, predominantly, especially, essentially, basically, in essence, at bottom; informal at the end of the day, when all is said and done.
■ **above oneself** *ever since her promotion she'd been getting above herself:* conceited, proud, arrogant, self-important, cocky, haughty, disdainful, snobbish, snobby, supercilious; informal stuck-up, high and mighty, snooty, uppity, big-headed, swollen-headed, too big for one's boots.

above board adjective *the proceedings were completely above board:* **legitimate**, lawful, legal, licit, honest, fair, open, frank, straight, overt, candid, forthright, unconcealed, trustworthy, unequivocal; informal legit, kosher, pukka, by the book, fair and square, square, on the level, on the up and up, upfront.
– OPPOSITES dishonest, shady.

abrade verb *the paintwork had been abraded over the years by the weather:* **wear away**, wear down, erode, scrape away, corrode, eat away at, gnaw away at.

abrasion noun **1** *he had abrasions to his forehead:* **graze**, cut, scrape, scratch, gash, laceration, injury, contusion; sore, ulcer. **2** *the metal is resistant to abrasion:* **erosion**, wearing away/down, corrosion.

abrasive adjective **1** *don't use abrasive kitchen cleaners:* **corrosive**, corroding, erosive; caustic, harsh, coarse. **2** *she was a tough girl with an abrasive manner:* **caustic**, cutting, biting, acerbic; rough, harsh, hard, tough, sharp, curt, brusque, stern, severe; wounding, nasty, cruel, callous, insensitive, unfeeling, unsympathetic, inconsiderate; N. Amer. acerb.
– OPPOSITES kind, gentle.

abreast adverb **1** *they walked three abreast:* **in a row**, side by side, alongside, level, beside each other, shoulder to shoulder. **2** *try to keep abreast of current affairs:* **up to date with**, up with, in touch with, informed about, acquainted with, knowledgeable about, conversant with, familiar with, au courant with, au fait with.

abridge verb **shorten**, cut, cut short/down, curtail, truncate, trim, crop, clip, pare down, prune; abbreviate, condense, contract, compress, reduce, decrease, shrink; summarize, sum up, abstract, precis, synopsize, give a digest of, put in a nutshell, edit.
– OPPOSITES lengthen.

abridged adjective *an abridged text of his speech:* **shortened**, cut, cut down, concise, condensed, abbreviated; summary, outline, thumbnail; bowdlerized, censored, expurgated; informal potted.

abridgement noun **summary**, abstract, synopsis, precis, outline, résumé, sketch, digest.

abroad adverb **1** *he regularly travels abroad:* **overseas**, out of the country, to/in foreign parts, to/in a foreign country/land. **2** *rumours were abroad:* **in circulation**, circulating, widely current, everywhere, in the air, {here, there, and everywhere}; about, around; at large.

abrupt adjective **1** *the car came to an abrupt halt | I was surprised by the abrupt change of subject:* **sudden**, unexpected, without warning, unanticipated, unforeseen, precipitate, surprising, startling; quick, swift, rapid, hurried, hasty, immediate, instantaneous. **2** *he spoke in a very abrupt manner:* **curt**, brusque, blunt, short, sharp, terse, brisk, crisp, gruff, rude, discourteous, uncivil, snappish, unceremonious, offhand, rough, harsh; informal snappy. **3** *he tends to write in abrupt, epigrammatic paragraphs:* **disjointed**, jerky, uneven, disconnected, inelegant. **4** *an abrupt slope:* **steep**, sheer, precipitous, bluff, sharp, sudden; perpendicular, vertical.
– OPPOSITES gradual, gentle.

abscess noun **ulcer**, ulceration, cyst, boil, blister, sore, pustule, carbuncle, pimple, wen, whitlow, canker; inflammation, infection, eruption.

abscond verb *176 detainees absconded:* **run away**, escape, bolt, flee, make off, take flight, take off, decamp; make a break for it, take to one's heels, make a quick getaway, beat a hasty retreat, show a clean pair of heels, run for it, make a run for it; disappear, vanish, slip away, steal away, sneak away; informal do a moonlight flit, clear out, cut and run, skedaddle, skip, head for the hills, do a disappearing act, fly the coop, take

French leave, scarper, vamoose; Brit. informal do a bunk, do a runner; N. Amer. informal take a powder.

absence noun **1** *he felt that everything had changed during his brief absence from school:* **non-attendance**, non-appearance, absenteeism; **truancy**, playing truant; leave, holiday, vacation, sabbatical. **2** *she found his total absence of facial expression disconcerting:* **lack**, want, non-existence, unavailability, deficiency, dearth; need.
– OPPOSITES presence.

absent adjective **1** *she was absent from work:* **away**, off, out, non-attending, truant; off duty, on holiday, on leave; gone, missing, lacking, unavailable, non-existent; informal AWOL. **2** *she looked up with an absent smile:* **distracted**, preoccupied, inattentive, vague, absorbed, abstracted, unheeding, oblivious, distrait, absent-minded, dreamy, far away, in a world of one's own, lost in thought, in a brown study; blank, empty, vacant; informal miles away.
– OPPOSITES present, attentive, alert.
verb *Rose absented herself from the occasion:* **stay away**, be absent, withdraw, retire, take one's leave, remove oneself.

absent-minded adjective *an absent-minded boffin:* **forgetful**, distracted, preoccupied, inattentive, vague, abstracted, unheeding, oblivious, distrait, in a brown study, wool-gathering; lost in thought, pensive, thoughtful, brooding; informal scatterbrained, miles away, having a mind/memory like a sieve.

absolute adjective **1** *there was absolute silence in the house | an absolute disgrace:* **complete**, total, utter, out-and-out, outright, entire, perfect, pure, decided; thorough, thoroughgoing, undivided, unqualified, unadulterated, unalloyed, unmodified, unreserved, downright, undiluted, consummate, unmitigated, sheer, arrant, rank, dyed-in-the-wool. **2** *everything I have told you is the absolute truth:* **definite**, certain, positive, unconditional, categorical, unquestionable, incontrovertible, undoubted, unequivocal, decisive, conclusive, confirmed, infallible. **3** *no one dare challenge her absolute authority:* **unlimited**, unrestricted, unrestrained, unbounded, boundless, infinite, ultimate, total, supreme, unconditional. **4** *an absolute monarch:* **autocratic**, despotic, dictatorial, tyrannical, tyrannous, authoritarian, arbitrary, autonomous, sovereign, autarchic, omnipotent. **5** *absolute moral standards:* **universal**, fixed, independent, non-relative, non-variable, absolutist.
– OPPOSITES partial, qualified, limited, conditional.

absolutely adverb *you're absolutely right:* **completely**, totally, utterly, perfectly, entirely, wholly, fully, quite, thoroughly, unreservedly; definitely, certainly, positively, unconditionally,

categorically, unquestionably, undoubtedly, without (a) doubt, without question, surely, unequivocally; exactly, precisely, decisively, conclusively, manifestly, in every way/respect, one hundred per cent, every inch, to the hilt; informal dead.
exclamation (informal) *'Have I made myself clear?' 'Absolutely!'* **yes**, indeed, of course, definitely, certainly, quite, without (a) doubt, without question, unquestionably; affirmative, by all means.

absolution noun **forgiveness**, pardon, exoneration, remission, dispensation, indulgence, clemency, mercy; discharge, acquittal; freedom, deliverance, release; informal let-off; formal exculpation.

absolve verb **1** *this fact does not absolve you from responsibility:* **exonerate**, discharge, acquit, vindicate; release, relieve, liberate, free, deliver, clear, exempt, let off. **2** (Christianity) *I absolve you from your sins:* **forgive**, pardon.
– OPPOSITES blame, condemn.

absorb verb **1** *a sponge-like material which absorbs water:* **soak up**, suck up, draw up/in, take up/in, blot up, mop up, sop up. **2** *she absorbed the information in silence:* **assimilate**, digest, take in. **3** *the company was absorbed into the new concern:* **incorporate**, assimilate, integrate, take in, subsume, include, co-opt, swallow up. **4** *she was totally absorbed in her book:* **engross**, captivate, occupy, preoccupy, engage, rivet, grip, hold, interest, intrigue, immerse, involve, enthral, spellbind, fascinate.

absorbent adjective *absorbent kitchen paper:* **porous**, spongy, sponge-like, permeable, pervious, absorptive.

absorbing adjective *an absorbing and informative book:* **fascinating**, interesting, captivating, gripping, engrossing, compelling, compulsive, enthralling, riveting, spellbinding, intriguing, thrilling, exciting; informal unputdownable.
– OPPOSITES boring, uninteresting.

absorption noun **1** *the absorption of water:* **soaking up**, sucking up. **2** *the company's absorption into a larger concern:* **incorporation**, assimilation, integration, inclusion. **3** *her total absorption in the music:* **involvement**, immersion, raptness, engrossment, occupation, preoccupation, engagement, captivation, fascination.

abstain verb **1** *Benjamin abstained from wine:* **refrain**, desist, hold back, forbear; give up, renounce, avoid, shun, eschew, forgo, go without, do without; refuse, decline; informal cut out. **2** *most pregnant women abstain, or drink very little:* **be teetotal**, take the pledge; informal be on the wagon. **3** *262 voted against, 38 abstained:* **not vote**, decline to vote.

abstemious adjective *he seems to have led an abstemious, not to say ascetic life:* **self-denying**, temperate, abstinent, moderate, self-disciplined, restrained, self-restrained,

a

sober, austere, ascetic, puritanical, spartan, self-abnegating, hair-shirt.
– OPPOSITES self-indulgent.

abstinence noun *I started drinking again after six years of abstinence:* **teetotalism**, temperance, sobriety, abstemiousness, abstention; **self-denial**, self-restraint.

abstract adjective **1** *abstract concepts such as love or beauty:* **theoretical**, conceptual, notional, intellectual, metaphysical, philosophical, academic. **2** *abstract art:* **non-representational**, non-pictorial.
– OPPOSITES actual, concrete.
verb **1** *the staff abstract material for an online database:* **summarize**, precis, abridge, condense, compress, shorten, cut down, abbreviate, synopsize. **2** *a scheme to abstract more water from the river:* **extract**, pump, draw (off), withdraw, remove, take out/away; separate, isolate.
noun *an abstract of her speech:* **summary**, synopsis, precis, résumé, outline, abridgement, digest, summation; N. Amer. wrap-up.

abstracted adjective *she seemed abstracted and unaware of her surroundings:* **preoccupied**, distracted, absent-minded, in a world of one's own, with one's head in the clouds, daydreaming, dreamy, inattentive, thoughtful, pensive, lost in thought, deep in thought, immersed in thought, wool-gathering, in a brown study, musing, brooding, absent, distrait; informal miles away.
– OPPOSITES attentive.

abstraction noun **1** *his style of writing focuses on facts rather than abstractions:* **concept**, idea, notion, thought, theory, hypothesis. **2** *she sensed his momentary abstraction:* **preoccupation**, distraction, absent-mindedness, dreaminess, inattentiveness, inattention, wool-gathering; thoughtfulness, pensiveness.

abstruse adjective *he was unable to follow the abstruse arguments put forward:* **obscure**, arcane, esoteric, little known, recherché, rarefied, recondite, difficult, hard, puzzling, perplexing, cryptic, Delphic, complex, complicated, involved, over/above one's head, incomprehensible, unfathomable, impenetrable, mysterious.

absurd adjective *what an absurd idea!* **preposterous**, ridiculous, ludicrous, farcical, laughable, risible, idiotic, stupid, foolish, silly, inane, imbecilic, insane, hare-brained; unreasonable, irrational, illogical, nonsensical, pointless, senseless; informal crazy; Brit. informal barmy, daft.
– OPPOSITES reasonable, sensible.

absurdity noun **preposterousness**, ridiculousness, ludicrousness, risibility, idiocy, stupidity, foolishness, folly, silliness, inanity, insanity; unreasonableness, irrationality, illogicality, pointlessness, senselessness; informal craziness.

abundance noun *the island boasts an abundance of wildlife:* **profusion**, plentifulness, profuseness, copiousness, amplitude, lavishness, bountifulness; host, cornucopia, riot; plenty, quantities, scores, multitude; informal millions, sea, ocean(s), wealth, lot(s), heap(s), mass(es), stack(s), pile(s), load(s), bags, bucketload(s), mountain(s), ton(s), slew, scads, oodles; Brit. informal shedload; N. Amer. informal gobs; formal plenitude.
– OPPOSITES lack, scarcity.

abundant adjective *an abundant supply of food:* **plentiful**, copious, ample, profuse, rich, lavish, liberal, generous, bountiful, large, huge, great, bumper, overflowing, prolific, teeming; in plenty, in abundance; informal a gogo, galore.
– OPPOSITES scarce, sparse.
■ **be abundant** abound, be plentiful, be numerous, be in abundance, proliferate, be thick on the ground; informal grow on trees, be two/ten a penny.

abuse verb **1** *the judge abused his power:* **misuse**, misapply, misemploy; exploit, take advantage of. **2** *he was accused of abusing children:* **mistreat**, maltreat, ill-treat, treat badly; molest, interfere with, indecently assault, sexually abuse, sexually assault; injure, hurt, harm, damage. **3** *the referee was abused by players from both teams:* **insult**, be rude to, swear at, curse, call someone names, taunt, shout at, revile, inveigh against, vilify, slander, cast aspersions on; Brit. informal slag off.
noun **1** *the abuse of power:* **misuse**, misapplication, misemployment; exploitation. **2** *the abuse of children:* **mistreatment**, maltreatment, ill-treatment; molestation, interference, indecent assault, sexual abuse, sexual assault; injury, hurt, harm, damage. **3** *the scheme is open to administrative abuse:* **corruption**, injustice, wrongdoing, wrong, misconduct, misdeed(s), offence(s), crime(s), sin(s). **4** *torrents of abuse:* **insults**, curses, jibes, expletives, swear words; swearing, cursing, name-calling; invective, vilification, vituperation, slander; Brit. informal verbal(s); N. Amer. informal trash talk.

abusive adjective *he was fined for making abusive comments to officials:* **insulting**, rude, vulgar, offensive, disparaging, belittling, derogatory, disrespectful, denigratory, uncomplimentary, pejorative; defamatory, slanderous, libellous; informal bitchy.

abut verb *the eight US states abutting the Great Lakes:* **adjoin**, be adjacent to, border, neighbour, join, touch, meet, reach, be contiguous with.

abysmal adjective (informal) *some of the teaching was abysmal:* **very bad**, dreadful, awful, terrible, frightful, atrocious, disgraceful, deplorable, shameful, hopeless, lamentable, laughable; informal rotten, appalling, crummy, pathetic, pitiful, woeful, useless, lousy, dire, poxy, the pits; Brit. informal chronic, shocking, pants.

abyss noun **chasm**, gorge, ravine, canyon, fissure, rift, crevasse, hole, gulf, pit, cavity, void, bottomless pit.

academic adjective **1** *an academic institution:* **educational**, scholastic, instructional, pedagogical. **2** *he has a distinctly academic turn of mind:* **scholarly**, studious, literary, well read, intellectual, clever, erudite, learned, educated, cultured, bookish, highbrow, pedantic, donnish, cerebral; informal brainy. **3** *the debate has been largely academic:* **theoretical**, conceptual, notional, philosophical, hypothetical, speculative, conjectural, suppositional, putative; impractical, unrealistic, ivory-tower.
– OPPOSITES vocational, practical.
noun *a group of Russian academics:* **scholar**, lecturer, don, teacher, tutor, professor, fellow, man/woman of letters, thinker, bluestocking; informal egghead, bookworm; formal pedagogue.

academy noun **school**, college, university, institute, seminary, conservatory, conservatoire.

accede verb (formal) *he acceded to the government's demands:* **agree to**, consent to, accept, assent to, acquiesce in, comply with, go along with, concur with, surrender to, yield to, give in to, give way to, defer to.

accelerate verb **1** *the car accelerated down the hill:* **speed up**, go faster, gain momentum, increase speed, pick up speed, gather speed, put on a spurt. **2** *inflation started to accelerate:* **increase**, rise, go up, leap up, surge, escalate, spiral. **3** *the university accelerated the planning process:* **hasten**, expedite, precipitate, speed up, quicken, make faster, step up, advance, further, forward, promote, give a boost to, stimulate, spur on; informal crank up.
– OPPOSITES decelerate, delay.

acceleration noun **1** *the acceleration of the industrial process:* **hastening**, precipitation, speeding up, quickening, stepping up, advancement, furtherance, boost. **2** *an acceleration in the divorce rate:* **increase**, rise, leap, surge, escalation.

accent noun **1** *a Scottish accent:* **pronunciation**, intonation, enunciation, articulation, inflection, tone, modulation, cadence, timbre, manner of speaking, delivery; brogue, burr, drawl, twang. **2** *the accent is on the first syllable:* **stress**, emphasis, accentuation, force, prominence; beat. **3** *the accent is on comfort:* **emphasis**, stress, priority; importance, prominence. **4** *an acute accent:* **mark**, diacritic, diacritical mark.
verb *fabrics which accent the background colours in the room:* **highlight**, focus attention on, draw attention to, point up, underline, underscore, accentuate, spotlight, foreground, feature, play up, bring to the fore, heighten, stress, emphasize.

accentuate verb *the simple outfit accentuated her long legs:* **highlight**, focus attention on, draw attention to, point up, underline, underscore, accent, spotlight, foreground, feature, play up, bring to the fore, heighten, stress, emphasize.

accept verb **1** *he accepted a pen as a present:* **receive**, take, get, gain, obtain, acquire. **2** *he accepted the job immediately:* **take on**, undertake, assume, take responsibility for. **3** *she accepted an invitation to lunch:* **say yes to**, reply in the affirmative, agree to. **4** *she was accepted as one of the family:* **welcome**, receive, embrace, adopt. **5** *he accepted Ellen's explanation:* **believe**, regard as true, give credence to, credit, trust; informal buy, swallow. **6** *we have agreed to accept his decision:* **go along with**, agree to, consent to, acquiesce in, concur with, assent to, comply with, abide by, follow, adhere to, act in accordance with, defer to, yield to, surrender to, bow to, give in to, submit to, respect; formal accede to. **7** *she will just have to accept the consequences:* **tolerate**, endure, put up with, bear, take, submit to, stomach, swallow; reconcile oneself to, resign oneself to, get used to, adjust to, learn to live with, make the best of; face up to.
– OPPOSITES refuse, reject.

acceptable adjective **1** *an acceptable standard of living:* **satisfactory**, adequate, reasonable, quite good, fair, decent, good enough, sufficient, sufficiently good, fine, not bad, all right, average, tolerable, passable, middling, moderate; informal OK, so-so, fair-to-middling. **2** *a most acceptable present:* **welcome**, appreciated; pleasing, agreeable, delightful, desirable, satisfying, gratifying, to one's liking. **3** *the risk had seemed acceptable at the time:* **bearable**, tolerable, allowable, admissible, sustainable, justifiable, defensible.

acceptance noun **1** *the acceptance of an award:* **receipt**, receiving, taking, obtaining. **2** *the acceptance of responsibility:* **undertaking**, assumption. **3** *her acceptance as one of the family:* **welcome**, favourable reception, adoption. **4** *his acceptance of Matilda's explanation:* **belief**, credence, trust, faith. **5** *their acceptance of the decision:* **compliance**, acquiescence, agreement, consent, concurrence, assent, adherence, deference, surrender, submission, respect.

accepted adjective *he wasn't handsome in the accepted sense:* **established**, traditional, acknowledged, recognized, orthodox; usual, customary, common, normal, general, prevailing, accustomed, familiar, wonted, popular, expected, routine, standard, stock.

access noun **1** *the building has a side access:* **entrance**, entry, way in, means of entry; approach, means of approach. **2** *they were denied access to the stadium:* **admission**, admittance, entry, entrée, ingress, right of entry. **3** *students have access to a* *photocopier:* **(the) use of**, permission to use. verb *the program used to access the data:* **retrieve**, gain access to, obtain; read.

accessible adjective **1** *the village is only accessible on foot | an easily accessible reference tool:* **reachable**, attainable, approachable; obtainable, available; informal get-at-able. **2** *his accessible style of writing:* **understandable**, comprehensible, easy to understand, intelligible. **3** *Professor Cooper is very accessible:* **approachable**, friendly, agreeable, obliging, congenial, affable, cordial, welcoming, easy-going, pleasant.

accession noun **1** *the Queen's accession to the throne:* **succession**, assumption, inheritance. **2** *accession to the Treaty of Rome was effected in 1971:* **assent**, consent, agreement; acceptance, acquiescence, compliance, concurrence. **3** *recent accessions to the museum:* **addition**, acquisition, new item, gift, purchase.

accessorize verb *there was no hat to accessorize this dress:* **complement**, enhance, set off, show off; go with, accompany; decorate, adorn, ornament, trim.

accessory noun **1** *camera accessories such as tripods and flashguns:* **attachment**, extra, addition, add-on, adjunct, appendage, appurtenance, fitment, supplement. **2** *fashion accessories:* **adornment**, embellishment, ornament, ornamentation, decoration; frills, trimmings. **3** *she was charged as an accessory to murder:* **accomplice**, partner in crime, associate, collaborator, fellow conspirator; henchman.

accident noun **1** *he was involved in an accident at work:* **mishap**, misadventure, unfortunate incident, mischance, misfortune, disaster, tragedy, catastrophe, calamity. **2** *there was an accident on the motorway:* **crash**, collision, smash, bump, car crash, road traffic accident, RTA; derailment; N. Amer. wreck; informal smash-up, pile-up; Brit. informal prang, shunt. **3** *it is no accident that there is a similarity between them:* **chance**, mere chance, coincidence, twist of fate, freak, fluke, bit of luck, serendipity; fate, fortuity, fortune, providence, happenstance.

accidental adjective **1** *an accidental meeting | the damage might have been accidental:* **chance**, fortuitous, adventitious, fluky, coincidental, casual, serendipitous, random; unexpected, unforeseen, unanticipated, unlooked-for, unintentional, unintended, inadvertent, unplanned, unpremeditated, unthinking, unwitting. **2** *the location is accidental and contributes nothing to the poem:* **incidental**, unimportant, by the way, by the by, supplementary, subsidiary, subordinate, secondary, accessory, peripheral, tangential, extraneous, extrinsic, irrelevant, non-essential, inessential. – OPPOSITES intentional, deliberate.

accidentally adverb *we met accidentally:* **by chance**, by mere chance, by accident, by a twist of fate, as luck would have it, fortuitously, by a fluke, by happenstance, coincidentally, adventitiously; unexpectedly, unintentionally, inadvertently, unwittingly.

acclaim verb *the booklet has been widely acclaimed by teachers:* **praise**, applaud, cheer, commend, approve, welcome, pay tribute to, speak highly of, eulogize, compliment, celebrate, sing the praises of, rave about, heap praise on, wax lyrical about, lionize, exalt, admire, hail, extol, honour, hymn; informal crack someone/something up; N. Amer. informal ballyhoo; formal laud. – OPPOSITES criticize. noun *she has won acclaim for her commitment to democracy:* **praise**, applause, cheers, ovation, tribute, accolade, acclamation, salutes, plaudits, bouquets; approval, approbation, admiration, congratulations, commendation, welcome, homage; compliment, a pat on the back. – OPPOSITES criticism.

acclaimed adjective *an acclaimed public figure:* **celebrated**, admired, highly rated, lionized, honoured, esteemed, exalted, well thought of, well received, acknowledged; eminent, great, renowned, distinguished, prestigious, illustrious, pre-eminent.

acclamation noun **praise**, applause, cheers, ovation, tribute, accolade, acclaim, salutes, plaudits, bouquets; approval, admiration, approbation, congratulations, commendation, homage; compliment, a pat on the back. – OPPOSITES criticism.

acclimatization noun **adjustment**, adaptation, accommodation, habituation, acculturation, familiarization, inurement; naturalization; N. Amer. acclimation.

acclimatize verb *the need to acclimatize to life at 3,000 metres:* **adjust**, adapt, accustom, accommodate, habituate, acculturate; get used, become inured, reconcile oneself, resign oneself; familiarize oneself; find one's feet, get one's bearings, become seasoned, become naturalized; N. Amer. acclimate.

accolade noun **1** *he received the accolade of knighthood:* **honour**, privilege, award, gift, title; prize, laurels. **2** *the hotel won a top accolade from the inspectors:* **tribute**, commendation, praise, testimonial, compliment, pat on the back; salutes, plaudits, congratulations, bouquets; informal rave.

accommodate verb **1** *refugees were accommodated in army camps:* **lodge**, house, put up, billet, quarter, board, take in, shelter, give someone a roof over their head; harbour. **2** *the cottages accommodate up to six people:* **hold**, take, have room for. **3** *our staff will make every effort to accommodate you:* **help**, assist, aid, oblige; meet the needs/wants of, cater for, fit in with, satisfy. **4** *she tried to accommodate herself to her new situation:* **adjust**, adapt, accustom, habituate, acclimatize, acculturate, get accustomed, get used, come to terms with; N. Amer. acclimate. **5** *the bank would be glad to accommodate you with a loan:* **provide**, supply, furnish, grant.

accommodating adjective *it's good of you to be so accommodating:* **obliging**, cooperative, helpful, eager to help, adaptable, amenable, considerate, unselfish, generous, willing, kindly, hospitable, neighbourly, kind, friendly, pleasant, agreeable; Brit. informal decent.

accommodation noun **1** *they were living in temporary accommodation:* **housing**, lodging(s), living quarters, quarters, rooms; home, residence, place to stay, billet; shelter, a roof over one's head; informal digs, pad; formal abode, place of residence, dwelling, dwelling place, habitation. **2** *there was lifeboat accommodation for 1,178 people:* **space**, room, seating; places. **3** *an accommodation between the two parties was reached:* **arrangement**, understanding, settlement, accord, deal, bargain, compromise. **4** *their accommodation to changing economic circumstances:* **adjustment**, adaptation, habituation, acclimatization, acculturation; inurement; N. Amer. acclimation.

accompaniment noun **1** *a musical accompaniment:* **backing**, support, background, soundtrack. **2** *the wine makes a superb accompaniment to cheese:* **complement**, supplement, addition, adjunct, appendage, companion, accessory.

accompany verb **1** *the driver accompanied her to the door:* **go with**, travel with, keep someone company, tag along with, partner, escort, chaperone, attend, show, see, usher, conduct. **2** *the illness is often accompanied by nausea:* **occur with**, co-occur with, coexist with, go with, go together with, go hand in hand with, appear with, attend by. **3** *he accompanied the choir on the piano:* **back**, play with, play for, support.

accomplice noun **partner in crime**, associate, accessory, confederate, collaborator, fellow conspirator; henchman; informal sidekick.

accomplish verb *the planes accomplished their mission:* **fulfil**, achieve, succeed in, realize, attain, manage, bring about/off, carry out/through, execute, effect, perform, do, discharge, complete, finish, consummate, conclude.

accomplished adjective *an accomplished pianist:* **skilled**, skilful, expert, masterly, virtuoso, master, consummate, complete, proficient, talented, gifted, adept, adroit, deft, dexterous, able, good, competent, capable, efficient, experienced, seasoned, trained, practised, professional, polished, ready, apt; informal great, mean, nifty, crack, ace, wizard; Brit. informal a dab hand at; N. Amer. informal crackerjack.

accomplishment noun **1** *the reduction of inflation was a remarkable accomplishment:*

achievement, act, deed, exploit, performance, attainment, effort, feat, move, coup. **2** *typing was another of her accomplishments:* **talent**, skill, gift, ability, attainment, achievement, forte, knack. **3** *a poet of considerable accomplishment:* **expertise**, skill, skilfulness, talent, adeptness, adroitness, deftness, dexterity, ability, prowess, mastery, competence, capability, proficiency, aptitude, artistry, art; informal know-how.

accord verb **1** *the national assembly accorded him more power:* **give**, grant, present, award, vouchsafe; confer on, bestow on, vest in, invest with. **2** *his views accorded with mine:* **correspond**, agree, tally, match, concur, be consistent, harmonize, be in harmony, be compatible, be in tune, correlate; conform to; informal square.
– OPPOSITES withhold, disagree, differ.
noun **1** *a peace accord:* **pact**, treaty, agreement, settlement, deal, entente, concordat, protocol, contract, convention. **2** *the two sides failed to reach accord:* **agreement**, consensus, unanimity, harmony, unison, unity; formal concord.
■ **of one's own accord** voluntarily, of one's own free will, of one's own volition, by choice; willingly, freely, readily.
■ **with one accord** unanimously, in complete agreement, with one mind, without exception, as one, of one voice, to a man.

accordance
■ **in accordance with** *a ballot held in accordance with trade union rules:* in agreement with, in conformity with, in line with, true to, in the spirit of, observing, following, heeding.

according
■ **according to 1** *she had a narrow escape, according to the doctors:* as stated by, as claimed by, on the authority of, in the opinion of. **2** *cook the rice according to the instructions:* as specified by, as per, in accordance with, in compliance with, in agreement with. **3** *salary will be fixed according to experience:* in proportion to, proportional to, commensurate with, in relation to, relative to, in line with, corresponding to.

accordingly adverb **1** *they appreciated the danger and acted accordingly:* **appropriately**, correspondingly, suitably. **2** *accordingly, he returned home to Yorkshire:* **therefore**, for that reason, consequently, so, as a result, as a consequence, in consequence, hence, thus, that being the case, ergo.

accost verb *reporters accosted him in the street:* **speak to**, call to, shout to, hail, address; approach, confront, detain, stop; informal buttonhole, collar; Brit. informal nobble.

account noun **1** *he gave them his account of the incident:* **description**, report, version, story, narration, narrative, statement,

explanation, exposition, delineation, portrayal, tale; chronicle, history, record, log, weblog, blog; view, impression. **2** *the firm's quarterly accounts:* **financial record**, ledger, balance sheet, financial statement; (**accounts**) books. **3** *I pay the account off in full each month:* **bill**, invoice, tally; debt, charges; N. Amer. check; informal tab. **4** *his background is of no account:* **importance**, import, significance, consequence, substance, note; formal moment. verb *her visit could not be accounted a success:* **consider**, regard as, reckon, hold to be, think, look on as, view as, see as, judge, adjudge, count, deem, rate.
■ **account for 1** *they must account for the delay:* explain, answer for, give reasons for, rationalize, justify. **2** *excise duties account for over half the price of Scotch:* constitute, make up, comprise, form, compose, represent.
■ **on account of** because of, owing to, due to, as a consequence of, thanks to, by/in virtue of, in view of.
■ **on no account** never, under no circumstances, not for any reason.

accountable adjective **1** *the government was held accountable for the food shortage:* **responsible**, liable, answerable; to blame. **2** *the game's popularity is barely accountable:* **explicable**, explainable; understandable, comprehensible.

accoutrements plural noun *the accoutrements of religious ritual:* **equipment**, paraphernalia, stuff, things, apparatus, tackle, kit, implements, material(s), rig, outfit, regalia, appurtenances, impedimenta, odds and ends, bits and pieces, bits and bobs, trappings, accessories.

accredit verb **1** *he was accredited with being one of the world's fastest sprinters:* **recognize as**, credit with. **2** *the discovery of distillation is usually accredited to the Arabs:* **ascribe**, attribute. **3** *professional bodies accredit these research degrees:* **authorize**, recognize, approve, certify, license.

accredited adjective **official**, appointed, recognized, authorized, approved, certified, licensed.

accretion noun **1** *the accretion of sediments in coastal mangroves:* **accumulation**, formation, collecting, cumulation, accrual; growth, increase. **2** *the city has a historic core surrounded by recent accretions:* **addition**, extension, appendage, add-on, supplement.

accrue verb **1** *financial benefits will accrue from restructuring:* **result**, arise, follow, ensue; be caused by. **2** *interest is added to the account as it accrues:* **accumulate**, collect, build up, mount up, grow, increase.

accumulate verb *investigators have yet to accumulate enough evidence:* **gather**, collect, amass, stockpile, pile up, heap up, store (up), hoard, cumulate, lay in/up; increase, multiply, accrue; run up.

accumulation noun **mass**, build-up, pile, heap, stack, collection, stock, store, stockpile, reserve, hoard; amassing, gathering, cumulation, accrual, accretion.

accuracy noun *we have confidence in the accuracy of the statistics:* **correctness**, precision, exactness; factuality, literalness, fidelity, faithfulness, truth, truthfulness, veracity, authenticity, realism, verisimilitude.

accurate adjective **1** *accurate information | an accurate representation of the situation:* **correct**, precise, exact, right, error-free, perfect; **factual**, fact-based, literal, faithful, true, truthful, true to life, authentic, realistic; informal on the mark, on the beam, on the nail; Brit. informal spot on, bang on; N. Amer. informal on the money, on the button; formal veracious. **2** *an accurate shot:* **well aimed**, on target, unerring, deadly, lethal, sure, true, on the mark.

accusation noun *accusations of bribery:* **allegation**, charge, claim, assertion, imputation; indictment, arraignment; suit, lawsuit.

accuse verb **1** *four people were accused of assault:* **charge with**, indict for, arraign for; summons, cite, prefer charges against; N. Amer. impeach for. **2** *the companies were accused of causing job losses:* **blame for**, lay the blame on, hold responsible for, hold accountable for; condemn for, criticize for, denounce for; informal lay at the door of, point the finger at, stick on, pin on.
– OPPOSITES absolve, exonerate.

accustom verb *I accustomed my eyes to the lenses:* **adapt**, adjust, acclimatize, habituate, accommodate, acculturate; reconcile oneself, become reconciled, get used to, come to terms with, learn to live with, become inured; N. Amer. acclimate.

accustomed adjective *the money would not have kept Nicholas in his accustomed lifestyle:* **customary**, usual, normal, habitual, regular, routine, ordinary, typical, traditional, established.

acerbic adjective *his acerbic wit:* **sharp**, sarcastic, sardonic, mordant, trenchant, cutting, razor-edged, biting, stinging, searing, scathing, caustic, astringent, abrasive; N. Amer. acerb; Brit. informal sarky; N. Amer. informal snarky.

ache noun **1** *a stomach ache:* **pain**, cramp, twinge, pang; gnawing, stabbing, stinging, smarting; soreness, tenderness, irritation, discomfort. **2** *the ache in her heart:* **sorrow**, sadness, misery, grief, anguish, suffering, pain, agony, torture, hurt.
verb **1** *my legs were aching:* **hurt**, be sore, be painful, be in pain, throb, pound, twinge; smart, burn, sting; informal give someone gyp; Brit. informal play up. **2** *her heart ached for poor Philippa:* **grieve**, sorrow, be in distress, be miserable, be in anguish, bleed. **3** *Marie ached for his affection:* **long**, yearn, hunger,

thirst, hanker, pine, itch; crave, desire.

achieve verb *we hope that our goals will be achieved:* **attain**, reach, arrive at; realize, bring off/about, pull off, accomplish, carry out/through, fulfil, execute, perform, engineer, conclude, complete, finish, consummate; earn, win, gain, acquire, obtain, come by, get, secure, clinch, net; informal wrap up, wangle, swing.

achievement noun **1** *the achievement of a high rate of economic growth:* **attainment**, realization, accomplishment, fulfilment, implementation, execution, performance; conclusion, completion, close, consummation. **2** *they felt justifiably proud of their achievement:* **accomplishment**, attainment, feat, performance, undertaking, act, action, deed, effort, exploit; work, handiwork.

Achilles heel noun *the cost of the process may prove to be its Achilles heel:* **weakness**, weak point, weak spot, soft underbelly, shortcoming, failing, imperfection, flaw, defect, chink in one's armour.
– OPPOSITES strength.

aching adjective **1** *he had an aching back:* **painful**, achy, sore, stiff, hurt, tender, uncomfortable; hurting, in pain, throbbing, pounding, smarting, burning, stinging. **2** *she's nursing an aching heart:* **sorrowful**, sad, miserable, grieving, upset, distressed, anguished, grief-stricken, heavy.

acid adjective **1** *a juicy fruit with a slightly acid flavour:* **sour**, tart, bitter, sharp, acidic, acrid, pungent, acerbic, vinegary, acetic, acetous. **2** *acid remarks:* **acerbic**, sarcastic, sharp, sardonic, scathing, cutting, razor-edged, biting, stinging, caustic, trenchant, mordant, bitter, acrimonious, astringent, harsh, abrasive, wounding, hurtful, unkind, vitriolic, venomous, waspish, spiteful, malicious; N. Amer. acerb; informal bitchy, catty; Brit. informal sarky; N. Amer. informal snarky.
– OPPOSITES sweet, pleasant.

acknowledge verb **1** *the government acknowledged the need to begin talks:* **admit**, accept, grant, allow, concede, confess, own, recognize. **2** *he did not acknowledge Colin, but hurried past:* **greet**, salute, address; nod to, wave to, raise one's hat to, say hello to. **3** *few people acknowledged my letters:* **answer**, reply to, respond to.
– OPPOSITES reject, deny, ignore.

acknowledged adjective *he is the acknowledged leader of the Turkish community:* **recognized**, accepted, approved, accredited, confirmed, declared, confessed, avowed.

acknowledgement noun **1** *there was acknowledgement of the need to take new initiatives:* **acceptance**, admission, concession, confession, recognition. **2** *Travis gave a smile of acknowledgement:* **greeting**, welcome, salutation. **3** *she left without a word of acknowledgement:* **thanks**, gratitude, appreciation, recognition.

4 *I sent off the form, but there was no acknowledgement:* **answer**, reply, response.

acolyte noun *he found himself surrounded by eager acolytes:* **assistant**, helper, attendant, minion, underling, lackey, henchman; follower, disciple, supporter, votary; informal sidekick, groupie, hanger-on.

acquaint verb *he will need to acquaint himself with the regulations:* **familiarize**, make familiar, make aware of, inform of, advise of, apprise of, let know, get up to date; brief, prime; informal fill in on, bring up to speed on.

acquaintance noun **1** *he was no more than a business acquaintance:* **contact**, associate, colleague. **2** *she had prospered from her acquaintance with the sergeant:* **association**, relationship, contact. **3** *the pupils had little acquaintance with the language:* **familiarity with**, knowledge of, experience of, awareness of, understanding of, comprehension of, grasp of.

acquainted adjective *she was well acquainted with Gothic literature:* **familiar**, conversant, at home, up to date, abreast, au fait, au courant, well versed, knowledgeable, well informed; informed, apprised; informal up to speed, clued in; formal cognizant.

acquiesce verb *he acquiesced in the cover-up:* **accept**, consent to, agree to, allow, concede, assent to, concur with, give the nod to; comply with, cooperate with, give in to, bow to, yield to, submit to; informal go along with.

acquiescence noun **consent**, agreement, acceptance, concurrence, assent, leave; compliance, concession, cooperation; submission.

acquiescent adjective **compliant**, cooperative, willing, obliging, agreeable, amenable, tractable, persuadable, pliant, unprotesting; submissive, yielding, biddable, docile.

acquire verb *I rapidly acquired the confidence of the leadership:* **obtain**, come by, get, receive, gain, earn, win, come into, be given; buy, purchase, procure, possess oneself of, secure, pick up; informal get one's hands on, get hold of, land, bag, score.
– OPPOSITES lose.

acquisition noun **1** *the gallery's Bronze Room will house a new acquisition:* **purchase**, buy, gain, accession, addition, investment, possession. **2** *the acquisition of funds:* **obtaining**, gaining, earning, winning, procurement, collection.

acquisitive adjective *he had the acquisitive instinct of a magpie:* **greedy**, covetous, avaricious, possessive, grasping, grabbing, predatory, avid, rapacious, mercenary, materialistic; informal money-grubbing.

acquisitiveness noun **greed**, covetousness, cupidity, possessiveness, avarice, avidity, rapaciousness, rapacity, materialism.

acquit verb **1** *the jury acquitted her:* **clear**,

a

exonerate, find innocent, absolve; discharge, release, free, set free; informal let off (the hook). **2** *the boys acquitted themselves well:* **behave**, conduct oneself, perform, act.
– OPPOSITES convict.

acquittal noun *the acquittal of the defendants:* **clearing**, exoneration; discharge, release, freeing; informal let-off.
– OPPOSITES conviction.

acrid adjective *the acrid smell of smoke:* **pungent**, bitter, sharp, sour, tart, harsh, acid, acidic, vinegary, acetic, acetous; stinging, burning.

acrimonious adjective *they had a heated and acrimonious discussion:* **bitter**, angry, rancorous, caustic, acerbic, acid, harsh, sharp, cutting; virulent, spiteful, vicious, vitriolic, hostile, venomous, nasty, bad-tempered, ill-natured, mean, malign, malicious, malignant, waspish; informal bitchy, catty.

acrimony noun **bitterness**, anger, rancour, resentment, ill feeling, ill will, bad blood, animosity, hostility, enmity, antagonism, waspishness, spleen, malice, spitefulness, venom.
– OPPOSITES goodwill.

act verb **1** *the Government must act to remedy the situation:* **take action**, take steps, take measures, move, react. **2** *he was acting on the orders of the party leader:* **follow**, act in accordance with, obey, heed, comply with; fulfil, meet, discharge. **3** *an estate agent acting for a prospective buyer:* **represent**, act on behalf of; stand in for, fill in for, deputize for, take the place of. **4** *Alison began to act oddly:* **behave**, conduct oneself, react. **5** *the scents act as a powerful aphrodisiac:* **operate**, work, function, serve. **6** *the drug acted directly on the blood vessels:* **affect**, have an effect on, work on; have an impact on, impact on, influence. **7** *he acted in a highly successful film:* **perform**, play a part, take part, appear; informal tread the boards. **8** *we laughed, but most of us were just acting:* **pretend**, play-act, put it on, fake it, feign it. noun **1** *acts of kindness | a criminal act:* **deed**, action, feat, exploit, move, gesture, performance, undertaking, stunt, operation; achievement, accomplishment. **2** *the act raised the tax on tobacco:* **law**, decree, statute, bill, act of Parliament, enactment, resolution, edict, dictum, ruling, measure; N. Amer. formal ordinance. **3** *the first act of the play:* **section**, subsection, division, part, segment. **4** *a music hall act:* **performance**, turn, routine, number, sketch, skit. **5** *it was all just an act:* **pretence**, show, front, facade, masquerade, charade, posture, pose, affectation, sham, fake; informal a put-on.

acting noun *the theory and practice of acting:* **drama**, the theatre, the stage, the performing arts, thespianism, dramatics, dramaturgy, stagecraft, theatricals; informal treading the boards.
adjective *the bank's acting governor:*

temporary, interim, caretaker, pro tem, provisional, stopgap; deputy, stand-in, fill-in; N. Amer. informal pinch-hitting.
– OPPOSITES permanent.

action noun **1** *there can be no excuse for their actions:* **deed**, act, move, undertaking, exploit, manoeuvre, endeavour, effort, exertion; behaviour, conduct, activity. **2** *the need for local community action:* **measures**, steps, activity, movement, work, operation. **3** *a man of action:* **energy**, vitality, vigour, forcefulness, drive, initiative, spirit, liveliness, vim, pep; activity; informal get-up-and-go. **4** *the action of hormones on the pancreas:* **effect**, influence, working; power. **5** *he missed all the action while he was away:* **excitement**, activity, happenings, events, incidents; informal goings-on. **6** *twenty-nine men died in the action:* **fighting**, hostilities, battle, conflict, combat, warfare; engagement, clash, encounter, skirmish. **7** *a civil action for damages:* **lawsuit**, legal action, suit (at law), case, prosecution, litigation, proceedings.

activate verb *Mark pressed the button which activated the machine:* **operate**, switch on, turn on, start (up), set going, trigger (off), set in motion, actuate, energize, boot (up), spin up; trip.

active adjective **1** *despite her illness she remained active:* **energetic**, lively, sprightly, spry, mobile, vigorous, vital, dynamic, sporty; busy, occupied; informal on the go, full of beans. **2** *an active member of the union:* **hard-working**, busy, industrious, diligent, tireless, contributing, effective, enterprising, involved, enthusiastic, keen, committed, devoted, zealous. **3** *the watermill was active until 1960:* **operative**, working, functioning, functional, operating, operational, in action, in operation; live; informal up and running.
– OPPOSITES listless, passive.

activity noun **1** *there was a lot of activity in the area:* **bustle**, hustle and bustle, busyness, action, liveliness, movement, life, stir, flurry; happenings, occurrences, proceedings, events, incidents; informal toing and froing, comings and goings. **2** *the school offers a wide range of activities:* **pursuit**, occupation, interest, hobby, pastime, recreation, diversion; venture, undertaking, enterprise, project, scheme, business, entertainment; act, action, deed, exploit.

actor, actress noun **performer**, player, trouper, thespian; film star, matinee idol, star, starlet; informal ham; Brit. informal luvvy; N. Amer. informal hambone.

actual adjective *the estimate was much less than the actual cost:* **real**, true, genuine, authentic, verified, attested, confirmed, definite, hard, plain, veritable; existing, existent, manifest, substantial, factual, de facto, bona fide; informal real live.
– OPPOSITES notional.

actuality noun *the journalistic debate about actuality and fiction:* **reality**, fact, truth, real life.

actually adverb *I looked upset but actually I was terribly excited:* **really**, in (actual) fact, in point of fact, as a matter of fact, in reality, in actuality, in truth, if truth be told, to tell the truth.

actuate verb **1** *the sprinkler system was actuated by the fire:* **activate**, operate, switch on, turn on, start (up), set going, trigger (off), trip, set in motion, energize. **2** *the defendant was actuated by malice:* **motivate**, prompt, stimulate, move, drive, influence, incite, spur on, impel.

acumen noun *a gullible young man with little or no business acumen:* **astuteness**, shrewdness, acuity, sharpness, sharp-wittedness, cleverness, smartness, brains; judgement, understanding, awareness, sense, common sense, canniness, discernment, wisdom, wit, sagacity, perspicacity, insight, perception, penetration; informal nous, savvy, know-how, horse sense; N. Amer. informal smarts.

acute adjective **1** *the acute food shortages:* **severe**, critical, drastic, dire, dreadful, terrible, awful, grave, bad, serious, desperate, parlous, dangerous. **2** *acute stomach pains:* **sharp**, severe, stabbing, excruciating, agonizing, racking, searing. **3** *his acute mind:* **astute**, shrewd, sharp, sharp-witted, razor-sharp, rapier-like, quick, quick-witted, agile, nimble, clever, intelligent, brilliant, smart, canny, discerning, perceptive, perspicacious, penetrating, insightful, incisive, piercing, discriminating, sagacious, wise, judicious; informal on the ball, quick off the mark, quick on the uptake, streetwise, savvy; N. Amer. informal heads-up. **4** *an acute sense of smell:* **keen**, sharp, good, penetrating, discerning, sensitive.
– OPPOSITES mild, dull.

acutely adverb *Lucy looked acutely embarrassed:* **extremely**, exceedingly, very, markedly, severely, intensely, deeply, profoundly, keenly, painfully, desperately, tremendously, enormously, thoroughly, heartily; informal awfully, terribly.
– OPPOSITES slightly.

adage noun *it is vital for every pilot to remember the old adage 'safety first':* **saying**, maxim, axiom, proverb, aphorism, apophthegm, saw, dictum, precept, motto, truism, platitude, cliché, commonplace.

adamant adjective *he is adamant that he is not going to resign:* **unshakeable**, immovable, inflexible, unwavering, unswerving, uncompromising, resolute, resolved, determined, firm, steadfast; stubborn, unrelenting, unyielding, unbending, rigid, obdurate, intransigent, dead set.

adapt verb **1** *we've adapted the hotels to*

suit their needs: **modify**, alter, change, adjust, convert, redesign, restyle, refashion, remodel, reshape, revamp, rework, rejig, redo, reconstruct, reorganize; customize, tailor; improve, amend, refine; informal tweak. **2** *he has adapted well to his new home:* **adjust**, acclimatize oneself, accommodate oneself, habituate oneself, become habituated, get used, orient oneself, reconcile oneself, come to terms, get one's bearings, find one's feet, acculturate, assimilate, blend in, fit in; N. Amer. acclimate.

adaptable adjective **1** *an adaptable workforce capable of acquiring new skills:* **flexible**, versatile, cooperative, accommodating, amenable. **2** *an adaptable piece of furniture:* **versatile**, modifiable, convertible, alterable, adjustable, changeable; multi-purpose, all-purpose.

adaptation noun **1** *the adaptation of old buildings:* **conversion**, alteration, modification, redesign, remodelling, revamping, reconstruction. **2** *the adaptation of an ethnic community to British society:* **adjustment**, acclimatization, accommodation, habituation, acculturation, assimilation, integration; N. Amer. acclimation.

add verb **1** *the front porch was added in 1751:* **attach**, build on, join, append, affix, connect, annex; include, incorporate. **2** *they added all the figures up:* **total**, count (up), compute, reckon up, tally; Brit. tot up. **3** *her decision just added to his woe:* **increase**, magnify, amplify, augment, intensify, heighten, deepen; exacerbate, aggravate, compound, reinforce; add fuel to the fire, fan the flames. **4** *she added that she had every confidence in Laura:* **go on to say**, state further, continue, carry on.
– OPPOSITES subtract.

■ **add up** (informal) *the situation just didn't add up:* make sense, stand to reason, hold up, hold water, ring true, be convincing.

■ **add up to 1** *the subsidies added up to £1700:* amount to, come to, run to, make, total, equal, number. **2** *the recent riots add up to a deepening crisis:* amount to, constitute; signify, signal, mean, indicate, denote, point to, be evidence of, be symptomatic of; informal spell.

addendum noun *each chapter ends with a short addendum entitled 'Further Reading':* **appendix**, codicil, postscript, afterword, tailpiece, rider, coda, supplement; adjunct, appendage, addition, add-on, attachment.

addict noun *a heroin addict:* **abuser**, user; informal junkie, druggy, -freak, -head, pill-popper; N. Amer. informal hophead.

addicted adjective **1** *he was addicted to tranquillizers:* **dependent on**; informal hooked on. **2** *she became addicted to the theatre:* **devoted to**, obsessed with, fixated on, fanatical about, passionate about, a slave to; informal hooked on, mad on, crazy about.

addiction noun **1** *his heroin addiction:*

a

dependency, habit; informal monkey. **2** *a slavish addiction to fashion:* **devotion to**, dedication to, obsession with, infatuation with, passion for, mania for, enslavement to.

addictive adjective *crack cocaine is highly addictive:* **habit-forming**; compulsive; Brit. informal moreish.

addition noun **1** *the soil is improved by the addition of compost:* **adding**, incorporation, inclusion, introduction. **2** *an addition to the existing regulations:* **supplement**, adjunct, addendum, appendage, add-on, extra; rider. ∎ **in addition 1** *conditions were harsh, and in addition some soldiers fell victim to snipers:* also, additionally, as well, what's more, furthermore, moreover, into the bargain, to boot. **2** *there were eight presidential candidates in addition to the General:* besides, as well as, on top of, plus, over and above.

additional adjective *beach towels are provided without additional charge:* **extra**, added, supplementary, supplemental, further, auxiliary, ancillary; more, other, another, new, fresh.

additionally adverb *the organization relied additionally on a vast network of informers:* **also**, in addition, as well, too, besides, on top (of that), moreover, further, furthermore, what's more, over and above that, into the bargain, to boot.

additive noun *the marmalade is free from any artificial additives:* **addition**, added ingredient; preservative, colouring; Brit. informal E-number.

addled adjective *his brain was fairly addled with hallucinogenic drugs:* **muddled**, confused, muzzy, fuddled, befuddled, dazed, disoriented, disorientated, fuzzy; informal woozy.

address noun **1** *Juliet looked at the address on the envelope:* inscription, superscription; directions. **2** *our officers called at the address:* **house**, flat, apartment, home, residence. **3** *the president's address received lukewarm applause:* **speech**, lecture, talk, monologue, dissertation, discourse, oration, peroration; sermon, homily, lesson.
verb **1** *the preacher addressed a crowded congregation:* **talk to**, give a talk to, speak to, make a speech to, give a lecture to, lecture, hold forth to; **preach to**, give a sermon to. **2** *she addressed my father as 'Mr Stevens':* **call**, name, designate; speak to, write to. **3** *correspondence should be addressed to the Banking Ombudsman:* **direct**, send, communicate, convey, remit. **4** *the minister failed to address the issue of subsidies:* **attend to**, apply oneself to, tackle, see to, deal with, confront, get to grips with, get down to, turn one's hand to, take in hand, undertake, concentrate on, focus on, devote oneself to.

adduce verb *facts and figures have been adduced to bolster the argument:* **cite**, quote, name, mention, instance, point out, refer

to; put forward, present, offer, advance, propose, proffer.

adept adjective *an adept negotiator:* **expert**, proficient, accomplished, skilful, talented, masterly, consummate, virtuoso; adroit, dexterous, deft, artful; brilliant, splendid, marvellous, formidable, outstanding, first-rate, first-class, excellent, fine; informal great, top-notch, tip-top, A1, ace, mean, hotshot, crack, nifty, deadly; N. Amer. informal crackerjack.
– OPPOSITES inept.

adequacy noun **1** *questions were raised about the adequacy of the existing services:* **satisfactoriness**, acceptability, acceptableness; sufficiency. **2** *he had deep misgivings about his own adequacy:* **capability**, competence, ability, aptitude, suitability; effectiveness, fitness; formal efficacy.

adequate adjective **1** *he lacked adequate financial resources:* **sufficient**, enough, requisite. **2** *the company provides an adequate service:* **acceptable**, passable, reasonable, satisfactory, tolerable, fair, decent, quite good, pretty good, goodish, moderate, unexceptional, unremarkable, undistinguished, ordinary, average, not bad, all right, middling; informal OK, so-so, fair-to-middling, nothing to write home about. **3** *the workstations were small but seemed adequate to the task:* **equal to**, up to, capable of, suitable for, able to do, fit for, sufficient for.

adhere verb **1** *a dollop of cream adhered to her nose:* **stick (fast)**, cohere, cling, bond, attach; be stuck, be fixed, be glued. **2** *they adhere scrupulously to Judaic law:* **abide by**, stick to, hold to, comply with, act in accordance with, conform to, submit to; follow, obey, heed, observe, respect, uphold, fulfil.
– OPPOSITES flout, ignore.

adherent noun *an adherent of the Catholic religion:* **follower**, supporter, upholder, defender, advocate, disciple, votary, devotee, partisan, member, friend, sectary; believer, worshipper.
– OPPOSITES opponent.

adhesive noun *a spray adhesive:* **glue**, fixative, gum, paste, cement; N. Amer. mucilage; N. Amer. informal stickum.
adjective *adhesive mortar:* **sticky**, tacky, gluey, gummed; viscous, viscid; informal icky.

ad infinitum adverb *the tradition will be maintained ad infinitum:* **forever**, for ever and ever, evermore, always, for all time, until the end of time, in perpetuity, until hell freezes over; perpetually, eternally, endlessly, interminably, unceasingly, unendingly; Brit. for evermore; informal until the cows come home, until the twelfth of never, until doomsday, until kingdom come.

adjacent adjective *they were given adjacent rooms:* **adjoining**, neighbouring, next-door, abutting, contiguous, proximate; (**adjacent**

to) close to, near, next to, by, by the side of, bordering on, beside, alongside, attached to, touching, cheek by jowl with.

adjoin verb *my office adjoined the doctor's surgery:* **be next to**, be adjacent to, border (on), abut, be contiguous with, communicate with, extend to; join, conjoin, connect with, touch, meet.

adjoining adjective *the two women had adjoining bedrooms:* **connecting**, connected, interconnecting, adjacent, neighbouring, bordering, next-door; contiguous; attached, touching.

adjourn verb **1** *the hearing was adjourned:* **suspend**, break off, discontinue, interrupt, prorogue, stay, recess. **2** *sentencing was adjourned until June 9:* **postpone**, put off/back, defer, delay, hold over, shelve. **3** *they adjourned to the sitting room for liqueurs:* **withdraw**, retire, retreat, take oneself; formal repair.

adjournment noun **suspension**, discontinuation, interruption, postponement, deferment, deferral, stay, prorogation; break, pause, recess.

adjudge verb *he was adjudged guilty of the offence of obstruction:* **judge**, deem, find, pronounce, proclaim, rule, hold, determine; consider, think, rate, reckon, perceive, regard as, view as, see as, believe to be.

adjudicate verb *the case was adjudicated in the High Court:* **judge**, try, hear, examine, arbitrate; pronounce on, give a ruling on, pass judgement on, decide, determine, settle, resolve.

adjudication noun **judgement**, decision, pronouncement, ruling, settlement, resolution, arbitration, finding, verdict, sentence.

adjudicator noun **judge**, arbitrator, arbiter; referee, umpire.

adjunct noun *surveys are a useful adjunct to other methods of data collection:* **supplement**, addition, extra, add-on, accessory, accompaniment, complement, appurtenance; attachment, appendage, addendum.

adjust verb **1** *Kate had adjusted to her new life:* **adapt**, become accustomed, get used, accommodate, acclimatize, orient oneself, reconcile oneself, habituate oneself, assimilate; come to terms with, blend in with, fit in with, find one's feet in; N. Amer. acclimate. **2** *he adjusted the brakes:* **modify**, alter, regulate, tune, fine-tune, calibrate, balance; adapt, rearrange, change, rejig, rework, revamp, remodel, reshape, convert, tailor, improve, enhance, customize; repair, correct, rectify, overhaul, put right; informal tweak.

adjustable adjective *the pilots sit on adjustable seats:* **alterable**, adaptable, modifiable, convertible, variable, multiway, versatile.

adjustment noun **1** *new teachers face*

a challenging period of adjustment: **adaptation**, accommodation, acclimatization, habituation, acculturation, naturalization, assimilation; N. Amer. acclimation. **2** *the car will run on unleaded petrol with no adjustment:* **modification**, alteration, regulation, adaptation, rearrangement, change, reconstruction, customization, refinement; repair, correction, amendment, overhaul, improvement.

ad-lib verb *she ad-libbed half the speech:* **improvise**, extemporize, speak impromptu; play it by ear, make it up as one goes along; informal busk it, wing it.
▸ adverb *she spoke ad lib:* **impromptu**, extempore, without preparation, without rehearsal, extemporaneously; informal off the cuff, off the top of one's head.
▸ adjective *a live, ad-lib commentary:* **impromptu**, extempore, extemporaneous, extemporary, improvised, unprepared, unrehearsed, unscripted; informal off-the-cuff, spur-of-the-moment.

administer verb **1** *the union is administered by a central executive:* **manage**, direct, control, operate, regulate, conduct, handle, run, organize, supervise, superintend, oversee, preside over, govern, rule, lead, head, steer; be in control of, be in charge of, be responsible for, be at the helm of; informal head up. **2** *the lifeboat crew administered first aid:* **dispense**, issue, give, provide, apply, allot, distribute, hand out, dole out, disburse. **3** *a gym shoe was used to administer punishment:* **inflict**, mete out, deal out, deliver.

administration noun **1** *the day-to-day administration of the company:* **management**, direction, control, command, charge, conduct, operation, running, leadership, government, governing, superintendence, supervision, regulation, overseeing. **2** *the previous Labour administration:* **government**, cabinet, ministry, regime, executive, authority, directorate, council, leadership, management; parliament, congress, senate; rule, term of office, incumbency. **3** *the administration of anti-inflammatory drugs:* **provision**, issuing, issuance, application, dispensing, dispensation, distribution, disbursement.

administrative adjective *administrative staff:* **managerial**, management, directorial, executive, organizational, supervisory, regulatory.

administrator noun **manager**, director, executive, controller, head, chief, leader, governor, superintendent, supervisor; informal boss.

admirable adjective *the player has done an admirable job for the team:* **commendable**, praiseworthy, laudable, estimable, meritorious, creditable, exemplary, honourable, worthy, deserving, respectable,

worthwhile, good, sterling, fine, masterly, great.
– OPPOSITES deplorable.

admiration noun *his patience and good nature commanded widespread admiration:* **respect**, approval, approbation, appreciation, regard, (high) regard, esteem; commendation, acclaim, applause, praise, compliments, tributes, accolades, plaudits.
– OPPOSITES scorn.

admire verb **1** *I admire your courage:* **respect**, approve of, esteem, think highly of, rate highly, hold in high regard, applaud, praise, commend, acclaim. **2** *Simon had admired her for a long time:* **adore**, love, worship, dote on, be enamoured of, be infatuated with, be taken with, be attracted to, find attractive; informal carry a torch for, have a thing about.
– OPPOSITES despise.

admirer noun **1** *he was a great admirer of Henry James:* **fan**, devotee, enthusiast, aficionado; supporter, adherent, follower, disciple. **2** *a handsome admirer of hers:* **suitor**, wooer, sweetheart, lover, boyfriend, young man.

admissible adjective *the tape recording was admissible as evidence:* **valid**, allowable, allowed, permissible, permitted, acceptable, satisfactory, justifiable, defensible, supportable, well founded, tenable, sound; legitimate, lawful, legal, licit; informal OK, legit, kosher, pukka.

admission noun **1** *membership entitles you to free admission:* **admittance**, entry, entrance, right of entry, access, right of access, ingress; entrée. **2** *a written admission of liability:* **confession**, acknowledgement, acceptance, concession, disclosure, divulgation.

admit verb **1** *he unlocked the door to admit her:* **let in**, allow entry, permit entry, take in, usher in, show in, receive, welcome. **2** *he was admitted as a scholar to Winchester College:* **accept**, take on, receive, enrol, enlist, register, sign up. **3** *Paul admitted that he was angry:* **confess**, acknowledge, own, concede, grant, accept, allow; reveal, disclose, divulge. **4** *he admitted three offences of reckless driving:* **confess (to)**, plead guilty to, own up to.
– OPPOSITES exclude, deny.

admittance noun *people were unable to gain admittance to the hall:* **entry**, right of entry, admission, entrance, access, right of access, ingress; entrée.
– OPPOSITES exclusion.

admonish verb **1** *he was severely admonished by his father:* **reprimand**, rebuke, scold, reprove, reproach, upbraid, chastise, chide, berate, criticize, take to task, pull up, read the Riot Act to, haul over the coals; informal tell off, dress down, bawl out, rap over the knuckles, give someone hell; Brit. informal tick off, give someone a rocket, have a go at, carpet, tear someone

off a strip; N. Amer. informal chew out; formal castigate. **2** *she admonished him to drink less:* **advise**, recommend, counsel, urge, exhort, bid, enjoin, warn.

admonition noun **1** *a breach of the rules which led to an admonition:* **reprimand**, rebuke, reproof, remonstrance, reproach, reproval, stricture, criticism, recrimination, scolding, censure; informal telling-off, dressing-down, talking-to, tongue-lashing, rap over the knuckles, slap on the wrist, flea in one's ear, earful; Brit. informal rocket, rollicking, wigging, ticking-off; formal castigation. **2** *an admonition to proceed carefully:* **exhortation**, warning, piece of advice, recommendation, counsel.

ado noun *this is much ado about almost nothing:* **fuss**, trouble, bother, upset, agitation, commotion, stir, hubbub, confusion, excitement, hurly-burly, flurry; palaver, rigmarole, brouhaha; N. Amer. fuss and feathers; informal hassle, to-do, hoo-ha, ballyhoo, song and dance, performance, kerfuffle; Brit. informal carry-on.

adolescence noun *they spent their adolescence hanging out together:* **teenage years**, teens, youth; pubescence, puberty.

adolescent noun *an awkward adolescent:* **teenager**, youngster, young person, youth, boy, girl; juvenile, minor; informal teen, tween, teeny-bopper.
adjective **1** *an adolescent boy:* **teenage**, pubescent, young; juvenile; informal teen. **2** *adolescent silliness:* **immature**, childish, juvenile, infantile, puerile, jejune.
– OPPOSITES adult, mature.

adopt verb **1** *they adopted local customs:* **espouse**, take on/up, embrace, assume; appropriate, arrogate. **2** *the people adopted him as their patron saint:* **choose**, select, pick, vote for, elect, settle on, decide on, opt for; name, nominate, appoint.
– OPPOSITES abandon.

adorable adjective *I have four adorable Siamese cats:* **lovable**, appealing, charming, cute, sweet, enchanting, bewitching, captivating, engaging, endearing, dear, darling, delightful, lovely, beautiful, attractive, gorgeous, winsome, winning, fetching; Scottish & N. English bonny.
– OPPOSITES hateful.

adoration noun **1** *the girl gazed at him with adoration:* **love**, devotion, care, fondness; admiration, high regard, awe, idolization, worship, hero-worship, adulation. **2** *the Mass begins our day of prayer and adoration:* **worship**, glory, glorification, praise, thanksgiving, homage, exaltation, extolment, veneration, reverence.

adore verb **1** *he adored his mother:* **love**, love dearly, be devoted to, dote on, hold dear, cherish, treasure, prize, think the world of; admire, hold in high regard, look up to, idolize, worship; informal put on a pedestal. **2** *the people had come to pray and adore God:* **worship**, glorify, praise, revere, reverence,

exalt, extol, venerate, pay homage to.
– OPPOSITES hate.

adorn verb *the public rooms were adorned with tapestries:* **decorate**, embellish, ornament, enhance; beautify, prettify, grace, bedeck, deck (out), dress (up), trim, swathe, wreathe, festoon, garland, array, emblazon.
– OPPOSITES disfigure.

adornment noun **decoration**, embellishment, ornamentation, ornament, enhancement; beautification, prettification; frills, accessories, trimmings, finishing touches.

adrift adjective **1** *their empty boat was spotted adrift:* **drifting**, unmoored, unanchored. **2** *the pipe of my breathing apparatus came adrift:* **loose**, free; detached, unsecured, unfastened, untied, unknotted, undone. **3** *he was adrift in a strange country:* **lost**, off course; disorientated, disoriented, confused, (all) at sea; drifting, rootless, unsettled, directionless, aimless, purposeless, without purpose.

adroit adjective *he showed himself to be an adroit politician:* **skilful**, adept, dexterous, deft, nimble, able, capable, skilled, expert, masterly, masterful, master, practised, polished, slick, proficient, accomplished, gifted, talented; quick-witted, quick-thinking, clever, smart, sharp, cunning, wily, resourceful, astute, shrewd, canny; informal nifty, crack, mean, wizard, demon, ace, A1, on the ball, savvy; N. Amer. informal crackerjack.
– OPPOSITES inept, clumsy.

adroitness noun **skill**, skilfulness, prowess, expertise, adeptness, dexterity, deftness, nimbleness, ability, capability, mastery, proficiency, accomplishment, artistry, art, facility, aptitude, flair, finesse, talent; quick-wittedness, cleverness, sharpness, cunning, astuteness, shrewdness, resourcefulness, savoir faire; informal know-how, savvy.

adulation noun *he is remarkably unspoilt by all the adulation he has received:* **hero-worship**, idolization, adoration, admiration, veneration, awe, devotion, glorification, praise, flattery, blandishments.

adult adjective **1** *an adult woman:* **mature**, grown-up, fully grown, full-grown, fully developed, of age. **2** *an adult movie:* **pornographic**, obscene, smutty, dirty, rude, erotic, sexually explicit, sexy, suggestive, titillating; informal porn, porno, naughty, blue, X-rated, skin.

adulterate verb *the brewer is said to adulterate his beer:* **make impure**, degrade, debase, spoil, taint, contaminate; doctor, tamper with, dilute, water down, weaken; bastardize, corrupt; informal cut, spike, dope.
– OPPOSITES purify.

adulterer noun **philanderer**, deceiver, womanizer, ladies' man, Don Juan, Casanova, Lothario; informal cheat, two-timer, love rat; formal fornicator.

adulterous adjective *British women are the most adulterous in Europe:* **unfaithful**, faithless, disloyal, untrue, inconstant, false, false-hearted, deceiving, deceitful, treacherous; extramarital; informal cheating, two-timing.
– OPPOSITES faithful.

adultery noun **infidelity**, unfaithfulness, falseness, disloyalty, cuckoldry, extramarital sex; affair, liaison, amour; informal carryings-on, hanky-panky, a bit on the side, playing around; formal fornication.
– OPPOSITES fidelity.

advance verb **1** *the battalion advanced rapidly:* **move forward**, proceed, press on, push on, push forward, make progress, make headway, gain ground, approach, come closer, draw nearer, near. **2** *the court may advance the date of the hearing:* **bring forward**, put forward, move forward. **3** *the move advanced his career:* **promote**, further, forward, help, aid, assist, boost, strengthen, improve, benefit, foster. **4** *our technology has advanced in the last few years:* **progress**, make progress, make headway, develop, evolve, make strides, move forward (in leaps and bounds), move ahead; improve, thrive, flourish, prosper. **5** *the hypothesis I wish to advance in this article:* **put forward**, present, submit, suggest, propose, introduce, offer, adduce, moot. **6** *a relative advanced him some money:* **lend**, loan, put up, come up with; Brit. informal sub.
– OPPOSITES retreat, hinder, postpone, retract, borrow.
noun **1** *the advance of the aggressors:* **progress**, forward movement; approach. **2** *a significant medical advance:* **breakthrough**, development, step forward, step in the right direction, (quantum) leap; find, finding, discovery, invention. **3** *the writer is going to be given a huge advance:* **down payment**, retainer, prepayment, deposit, front money, money up front. **4** *unwelcome sexual advances:* **pass**, proposition.
adjective **1** *an advance party of settlers:* **preliminary**, sent (on) ahead, first, exploratory; pilot, test, trial. **2** *advance warning:* **prior**, early, beforehand.
■ **in advance** beforehand, before, ahead of time, earlier, previously; in readiness.

advanced adjective **1** *advanced manufacturing techniques:* **state-of-the-art**, new, modern, up to date, up to the minute, the newest, the latest; progressive, avant-garde, ahead of the times, pioneering, innovatory, sophisticated. **2** *advanced further-education courses:* **higher-level**, higher, tertiary.
– OPPOSITES primitive.

advancement noun **1** *the advancement of computer technology:* **development**, progress, evolution, growth, improvement, advance, furtherance; headway. **2** *employees must be offered opportunities for advancement:* **promotion**, preferment, career development, upgrading, a step

a

up the ladder, progress, improvement, betterment, growth.

advantage noun **1** *the advantages of belonging to a union:* **benefit**, value, good point, strong point, asset, plus, bonus, boon, blessing, virtue; beauty, usefulness, convenience, profit. **2** *they appeared to be gaining the advantage over their opponents:* **upper hand**, edge, lead, whip hand, trump card; superiority, dominance, ascendancy, supremacy, power, mastery. **3** *there is no advantage to be gained from delaying the process:* **benefit**, profit, gain, good; informal mileage, percentage.
– OPPOSITES disadvantage, drawback, detriment.

advantageous adjective **1** *at the end of the war, farmers were in a relatively advantageous position:* **superior**, dominant, powerful; good, fortunate, lucky, favourable. **2** *the arrangement is advantageous to both sides:* **beneficial**, of benefit, helpful, of assistance, useful, of use, of value, of service, profitable, fruitful; expedient, in someone's interest.
– OPPOSITES disadvantageous, detrimental.

advent noun *operative techniques greatly improved with the advent of anaesthesia:* **arrival**, appearance, emergence, materialization, occurrence, dawn, birth, rise, development; approach, coming.
– OPPOSITES disappearance.

adventure noun **1** *stories of astonishing miracles and heroic adventures:* **exploit**, escapade, deed, feat, experience; stunt. **2** *they set off in search of adventure:* **excitement**, thrill, stimulation; risk, danger, hazard, peril, uncertainty.

adventurous adjective **1** *an adventurous traveller:* **daring**, daredevil, intrepid, venturesome, bold, fearless, brave, unafraid, unshrinking, dauntless; informal gutsy, spunky. **2** *adventurous activities:* **risky**, dangerous, perilous, hazardous, precarious, uncertain; exciting, thrilling.
– OPPOSITES cautious.

adversary noun **opponent**, rival, enemy, antagonist, combatant, challenger, contender, competitor, opposer; opposition, competition.
– OPPOSITES ally, supporter.

adverse adjective **1** *the plane crashed into a lake in adverse weather conditions:* **unfavourable**, disadvantageous, inauspicious, unpropitious, unfortunate, unlucky, untimely, untoward. **2** *the drug's adverse side effects:* **harmful**, dangerous, injurious, detrimental, hurtful, deleterious. **3** *the military feared an adverse response from the public:* **hostile**, unfavourable, antagonistic, unfriendly, ill-disposed, negative.
– OPPOSITES favourable, auspicious, beneficial.

adversity noun *they remain steadfast in the face of adversity:* **misfortune**, ill luck,

bad luck, trouble, difficulty, hardship, distress, disaster, suffering, affliction, sorrow, misery, tribulation, woe, pain, trauma; mishap, misadventure, accident, upset, reverse, setback, crisis, catastrophe, tragedy, calamity, trial, cross, burden, blow, vicissitude; hard times, trials and tribulations.

advertise verb *the booklets are designed to advertise the hotel:* **publicize**, promote, market, trail, make public, make known, announce, broadcast, proclaim, trumpet, call attention to, bill; informal push, plug, hype, boost; N. Amer. huckster; N. Amer. informal ballyhoo, flack.

advertisement noun *she placed an advertisement in a Canadian newspaper:* **notice**, announcement, bulletin; commercial, promotion, blurb, write-up; poster, leaflet, pamphlet, flyer, bill, handbill, handout, circular, brochure, sign, placard; informal ad, push, plug, puff, bumf; Brit. informal advert.

advice noun *the charity offers support and advice to people with mental illness:* **guidance**, counselling, counsel, help, direction; information, recommendations, guidelines, suggestions, hints, tips, pointers.

advisability noun *the advisability of sticking to a low-fat diet:* **wisdom**, desirability, preferability, prudence, sense, appropriateness, aptness, fitness, suitability, judiciousness; expediency, advantageousness, advantage, benefit, profit.

advisable adjective *it is advisable to book a table in advance:* **wise**, desirable, preferable, well, best, sensible, prudent, proper, appropriate, apt, suitable, fitting, judicious, recommended, suggested; expedient, politic, advantageous, beneficial, profitable, in one's (best) interests.

advise verb **1** *her grandmother advised her about marriage:* **counsel**, give guidance, guide, offer suggestions, give hints/tips/pointers. **2** *he advised caution:* **advocate**, recommend, suggest, urge, encourage, enjoin. **3** *you will be advised of the requirements:* **inform**, notify, give notice, apprise, warn, forewarn; acquaint with, make familiar with, make known to, update about; informal fill in on.

adviser noun **counsellor**, mentor, guide, consultant, confidant, confidante; coach, teacher, tutor, guru.

advisory adjective *she agreed to serve the committee in an advisory role:* **consultative**, consultatory, advising.
– OPPOSITES executive.

advocacy noun *his outspoken advocacy of the agreement has won him no friends:* **support for**, backing, promotion, championing; recommendation, prescription; N. Amer. boosterism.

advocate noun *she was a powerful advocate*

of children's rights: **champion**, upholder, supporter, backer, promoter, proponent, exponent, spokesman, spokeswoman, spokesperson, campaigner, fighter, crusader; propagandist, apostle, apologist; N. Amer. booster.
– OPPOSITES critic.
verb *heart specialists advocate a diet low in cholesterol:* **recommend**, prescribe, advise, urge; support, back, favour, uphold, subscribe to, champion, campaign on behalf of, speak for, argue for, lobby for, promote.

aegis noun *the negotiations were conducted under the aegis of the UN:* **protection**, backing, support, patronage, sponsorship, charge, care, guidance, guardianship, trusteeship, agency, safeguarding, shelter, umbrella, aid, assistance; auspices.

aeons plural noun *piracy was stamped out aeons ago:* **ages**, an age, an eternity, a long time, a lifetime; years; informal donkey's years; Brit. informal yonks.

aesthetic adjective *the law applies to both functional and aesthetic objects:* **artistic**, tasteful, in good taste; graceful, elegant, exquisite, beautiful, attractive, pleasing, lovely.

affability noun **friendliness**, amiability, geniality, congeniality, cordiality, warmth, pleasantness, likeability, good humour, good nature, kindliness, kindness, courtesy, courteousness, civility, approachability, amenability, sociability, gregariousness, neighbourliness.

affable adjective *Murray was in a most affable mood:* **friendly**, amiable, genial, congenial, cordial, warm, pleasant, nice, likeable, personable, charming, agreeable, sympathetic, good-humoured, good-natured, kindly, kind, courteous, civil, gracious, approachable, accessible, amenable, sociable, outgoing, gregarious, clubbable, neighbourly, welcoming, hospitable, obliging; Scottish couthy.
– OPPOSITES unfriendly.

affair noun **1** *what you do is your affair:* **business**, concern, matter, responsibility, province, preserve; problem, worry; Brit. informal lookout. **2** (**affairs**) *his financial affairs:* **transactions**, concerns, matters, activities, dealings, undertakings, ventures, business. **3** *the board admitted responsibility for the affair:* **event**, incident, happening, occurrence, eventuality, episode; case, matter, business. **4** *his affair with Anthea was over:* **relationship**, love affair, affaire (de cœur), romance, fling, flirtation, dalliance, liaison, involvement, intrigue, amour; informal hanky-panky; Brit. informal carry-on.

affect¹ verb **1** *this development may have affected the judge's decision:* **influence**, act on, work on, have an effect on, have an impact on; change, alter, modify, transform, form, shape, sway, bias. **2** *he was visibly affected by the experience:* **move**, touch,

make an impression on, hit (hard), tug at someone's heartstrings; **upset**, trouble, distress, disturb, agitate, shake (up). **3** *the disease affected his lungs:* **attack**, infect; hit, strike.

affect² verb **1** *he deliberately affected a republican stance:* **assume**, take on, adopt, embrace, espouse. **2** *Paul affected an air of injured innocence:* **pretend**, feign, fake, simulate, make a show of, make a pretence of, sham; informal put on; N. Amer. informal make like.

affectation noun **1** *George had always abhorred affectation:* **pretension**, pretentiousness, affectedness, artificiality, posturing, posing; airs (and graces); informal la-di-da; Brit. informal side. **2** *nothing would shake his affectation of calm:* **facade**, front, show, appearance, pretence, simulation, posture, pose.

affected adjective *the gesture appeared both affected and stagy:* **pretentious**, artificial, contrived, unnatural, stagy, studied, mannered, ostentatious; insincere, unconvincing, feigned, false, fake, sham, simulated; informal la-di-da, phoney, pretend, put on.
– OPPOSITES natural, unpretentious, genuine.

affecting adjective *their fumbling onstage shyness is oddly affecting:* **touching**, moving, emotive, emotional; stirring, soul-stirring, heart-warming; poignant, pathetic, pitiful, piteous, tear-jerking, heart-rending, heartbreaking, disturbing, distressing, upsetting, sad, haunting.

affection noun *they greeted each other with obvious affection:* **fondness**, love, liking, tenderness, warmth, devotion, endearment, care, caring, attachment, friendship; warm feelings.

affectionate adjective *an affectionate hug:* **loving**, fond, adoring, devoted, caring, doting, tender, warm, warm-hearted, soft-hearted, friendly; demonstrative, cuddly; informal touchy-feely, lovey-dovey.
– OPPOSITES cold.

affiliate verb *the college is affiliated with the University of Wisconsin:* **associate**, unite, combine, join (up), join forces, link up, ally, align, federate, amalgamate, merge; attach to, annex to, incorporate into, integrate into.

affiliated adjective **associated**, allied, related, federated, confederated, amalgamated, unified, connected, linked; in league, in partnership.

affiliation noun **association**, connection, alliance, alignment, link, attachment, tie, relationship, fellowship, partnership, coalition, union; amalgamation, incorporation, integration, federation, confederation.

affinity noun **1** *she has a natural affinity with animals and birds:* **empathy**, rapport, sympathy, accord, harmony, relationship, bond, fellow feeling, like-mindedness,

a

closeness, understanding; liking, fondness; informal chemistry. **2** *the semantic affinity between the two words:* **similarity**, resemblance, likeness, kinship, relationship, association, link, analogy, similitude, correspondence.
– OPPOSITES aversion, dislike, dissimilarity.

affirm verb **1** *he affirmed that they would lend military assistance:* **declare**, state, assert, proclaim, pronounce, attest, swear, avow, guarantee, pledge, give an undertaking. **2** *the referendum affirmed the republic's right to secede:* **uphold**, support, confirm, ratify, endorse.
– OPPOSITES deny.

affirmation noun **1** *an affirmation of faith:* **declaration**, statement, assertion, proclamation, pronouncement, attestation; oath, avowal, guarantee, pledge; deposition. **2** *the poem ends with an affirmation of pastoral values:* **confirmation**, ratification, endorsement.
– OPPOSITES denial.

affirmative adjective *an affirmative answer:* **positive**, assenting, consenting, corroborative, favourable.
– OPPOSITES negative.
noun *she took his grunt as an affirmative:* **agreement**, acceptance, assent, acquiescence, concurrence; OK, yes.
– OPPOSITES disagreement.

afflict verb *he was afflicted with chilblains:* **trouble**, burden, distress, cause suffering to, beset, harass, worry, oppress; torment, plague, blight, bedevil, rack, smite, curse.

affliction noun **1** *a herb reputed to cure a variety of afflictions:* **disorder**, disease, malady, complaint, ailment, illness, indisposition, handicap; scourge, plague, trouble. **2** *he bore his affliction with great dignity:* **suffering**, distress, pain, trouble, misery, wretchedness, hardship, misfortune, adversity, sorrow, torment, tribulation, woe.

affluence noun *the affluence of the higher social classes:* **wealth**, prosperity, fortune; riches, money, resources, assets, substance, means.
– OPPOSITES poverty.

affluent adjective **wealthy**, rich, prosperous, well off, moneyed, well-to-do; propertied, substantial, of means, of substance, plutocratic; informal well heeled, rolling in it, made of money, filthy rich, stinking rich, loaded, on easy street, worth a packet.
– OPPOSITES poor, impoverished.

afford verb **1** *I can't afford a new car:* **pay for**, bear the expense of, have the money for, spare the price of; run to, stretch to, manage. **2** *it took more time than he could afford:* **spare**, allow (oneself). **3** *the terrace affords beautiful views:* **provide**, supply, furnish, offer, give, make available, yield.

affront noun *the paintings, in his view, were an affront to public morality:* **insult**, offence, indignity, slight, snub, put-down,

provocation, injury; outrage, atrocity, scandal; informal slap in the face, kick in the teeth.
verb *she was affronted by his familiarity:* **insult**, offend, mortify, provoke, pique, wound, hurt; put out, irk, displease, bother, rankle, vex, gall; outrage, scandalize, disgust; informal put someone's back up, needle.

aficionado noun **connoisseur**, expert, authority, specialist, pundit; enthusiast, devotee; informal buff, freak, nut, fiend, maniac, fanatic, addict.

afloat adverb & adjective *the canoes were still afloat:* **buoyant**, floating, buoyed up, on/above the surface, (keeping one's head) above water.

afoot adjective & adverb *evil plans are afoot:* **happening**, going on, around, about, abroad, stirring, circulating, in circulation, at large, in the air/wind; brewing, looming, in the offing, on the horizon.

afraid adjective **1** *they ran away because they were afraid:* **frightened**, scared, terrified, fearful, scared witless, scared to death, terror-stricken, terror-struck, frightened/scared out of one's wits, shaking in one's shoes, shaking like a leaf; intimidated, alarmed, panicky; faint-hearted, cowardly; informal scared stiff, in a (blue) funk, in a cold sweat; N. Amer. informal spooked. **2** *don't be afraid to ask awkward questions:* **reluctant**, hesitant, unwilling, disinclined, loath, slow, chary, shy. **3** *I'm afraid that your daughter is ill:* **sorry**, sad, distressed, regretful, apologetic.
– OPPOSITES brave, confident.

afresh adverb *she left the job to start afresh:* **anew**, again, over/once again, once more, another time.

after preposition **1** *he made a speech after the performance:* **following**, subsequent to, at the close/end of, in the wake of. **2** *Guy shut the door after them:* **behind**, following. **3** *they asked after Dad:* **about**, concerning, regarding, with regard/respect/reference to. **4** *the village was named after a Roman officer:* **in honour of**, as a tribute to; with the name of. **5** *animal studies after Bandinelli:* **in the style of**, in the manner of, in imitation of; similar to, like, characteristic of.
– OPPOSITES before, preceding.
adverb **1** *the week after, we went to Madrid:* **later**, afterwards, after this/that, subsequently. **2** *porters were following on after with their bags:* **behind**, in the rear, at the back, in someone's wake.
– OPPOSITES previously, before, ahead, in front.
■ **after all** *I had to come—after all, I am your brother:* most importantly, above all, beyond everything, ultimately; informal when all's said and done, at the end of the day, when push comes to shove.

after-effect noun *she was suffering the*

after-effects of a hip injury: **repercussion**, aftermath, consequence.

afterlife noun *most Christians believe in an afterlife:* **life after death**, the next world, the hereafter, the afterworld; immortality.

aftermath noun *the bleak aftermath of war:* **repercussions**, after-effects, consequences, effects, results, fruits.

afterwards adverb *we all celebrated afterwards at a pub:* **later**, later on, subsequently, then, next, after this/that; at a later time/date, in due course.

again adverb *her spirits lifted again:* **once more**, another time, afresh, anew.
■ **again and again** repeatedly, over and over (again), time and (time) again, many times, many a time; often, frequently, continually, constantly.

against preposition 1 *a number of delegates were against the motion:* **opposed to**, in opposition to, hostile to, averse to, antagonistic towards, inimical to, unsympathetic to, resistant to, at odds with, in disagreement with, dead set against; informal anti, agin. 2 *he was swimming against the tide:* **counter to**, in opposition to, contrary to, in the opposite direction to. 3 *his age is against him:* **disadvantageous to**, unfavourable to, damaging to, detrimental to, prejudicial to, deleterious to, harmful to, injurious to, a drawback for. 4 *she leaned against the wall:* **touching**, in contact with, up against, on.
– OPPOSITES in favour of, pro.

age noun 1 *her hearing had deteriorated with age:* **elderliness**, old age, oldness, senescence, seniority, maturity; one's advancing/advanced/declining years. 2 *the Elizabethan age:* **era**, epoch, period, time. 3 (**ages**) (informal) *you haven't been in touch with me for ages:* **a long time**, days/months/years on end, an eternity; informal ages and ages, donkey's years, a month of Sundays; Brit. informal yonks.
verb *Cabernet Sauvignon ages well | the experience has aged her:* **mature**, mellow, ripen; grow/become/make old, (cause to) decline.

aged adjective *many people look after aged parents:* **elderly**, old, mature, older, senior, ancient, senescent, advanced in years, in one's dotage, long in the tooth, as old as the hills, past one's prime, not as young as one used to be; informal getting on, over the hill, no spring chicken.
– OPPOSITES young.

agency noun 1 *an advertising agency:* **business**, organization, company, firm, office, bureau. 2 *the infection is caused by the agency of insects:* **action**, activity, means, effect, influence, force, power, vehicle, medium.

agenda noun *a meeting with a fixed agenda:* **list of items**, schedule, programme, timetable, line-up, list, plan.

agent noun 1 *the sale was arranged through an agent:* **representative**, emissary, envoy, go-between, proxy, negotiator, broker, spokesperson, spokesman, spokeswoman; informal rep. 2 *a travel agent:* **agency**, business, organization, company, firm, bureau. 3 *a CIA agent:* **spy**, secret agent, undercover agent, operative, fifth columnist, mole, Mata Hari; N. Amer. informal spook, G-man. 4 *the agents of destruction:* **performer**, author, executor, perpetrator, producer, instrument, catalyst. 5 *a cleansing agent:* **medium**, means, instrument, vehicle.

agglomeration noun *the suburb is an agglomeration of houses, shops, and offices:* **collection**, mass, cluster, lump, clump, pile, heap; accumulation, build-up; miscellany, jumble, hotchpotch, mixed bag.

aggravate verb 1 *the new law could aggravate the situation:* **worsen**, make worse, exacerbate, inflame, compound; add fuel to the fire/flames, add insult to injury, rub salt in the wound. 2 (informal) *you don't have to aggravate people to get what you want:* **annoy**, irritate, exasperate, put out, nettle, provoke, antagonize, get on someone's nerves, ruffle (someone's feathers), try someone's patience; Brit. rub up the wrong way; informal peeve, needle, bug, miff, hack off, get someone's goat, get under someone's skin, get up someone's nose; Brit. informal wind up, nark, get at, get across, get on someone's wick; N. Amer. informal tick off.
– OPPOSITES alleviate, improve.

aggravation noun 1 *the recession led to the aggravation of unemployment problems:* **worsening**, exacerbation, compounding. 2 (informal) *no amount of money is worth the aggravation:* **nuisance**, annoyance, irritation, hassle, trouble, difficulty, inconvenience, bother; informal aggro.

aggregate noun 1 *the specimen is an aggregate of rock and mineral fragments:* **collection**, mass, agglomeration, assemblage; mixture, mix, combination, blend; compound, alloy, amalgam. 2 *he won with an aggregate of 325:* **total**, sum total, sum, grand total.
adjective *an aggregate score:* **total**, combined, gross, overall, composite.

aggression noun 1 *an act of aggression:* **hostility**, aggressiveness, belligerence, bellicosity, force, violence; pugnacity, pugnaciousness, militancy, warmongering. 2 *he played the game with unceasing aggression:* **confidence**, self-confidence, boldness, determination, forcefulness, vigour, energy, dynamism, zeal.

aggressive adjective 1 *aggressive and disruptive behaviour:* **violent**, confrontational, antagonistic, truculent, pugnacious, macho; quarrelsome, argumentative. 2 *aggressive foreign policy:* **warmongering**, warlike, warring, belligerent, bellicose, hawkish, militaristic;

a

offensive, expansionist; informal gung-ho.
3 *an aggressive promotional drive:* **assertive**,
pushy, forceful, vigorous, energetic,
dynamic; bold, audacious; informal in-your-
face, feisty.
– OPPOSITES peaceable, peaceful.

aggressor noun **attacker**, assaulter,
assailant; invader.

aggrieved adjective **1** *the manager looked
aggrieved at the suggestion:* **resentful**,
affronted, indignant, disgruntled,
discontented, upset, offended, piqued, riled,
nettled, vexed, irked, irritated, annoyed,
put out, chagrined; informal peeved, miffed,
in a huff; Brit. informal cheesed off; N. Amer.
informal sore, steamed. **2** *the aggrieved party:*
wronged, injured, harmed.
– OPPOSITES pleased.

aghast adjective *she winced, aghast at his
cruelty:* **horrified**, appalled, dismayed,
thunderstruck, stunned, shocked, staggered;
informal flabbergasted; Brit. informal gobsmacked.

agile adjective **1** *she was as agile as a monkey:*
nimble, lithe, supple, limber, acrobatic,
fleet-footed, light-footed, light on one's
feet; informal nippy, twinkle-toed. **2** *she had
an agile mind:* **alert**, sharp, acute, shrewd,
astute, perceptive, quick-witted.
– OPPOSITES clumsy, stiff.

agitate verb **1** *any mention of Clare agitates
my grandmother:* **upset**, perturb, fluster,
ruffle, disconcert, unnerve, disquiet,
disturb, worry, distress, unsettle; informal
rattle, faze; N. Amer. informal discombobulate.
2 *she agitated for the appointment of more
women:* **campaign**, strive, battle, fight,
struggle, push, press. **3** *agitate the water
to disperse the oil:* **stir**, whisk, beat.

agitated adjective *I could see that he
was agitated and edgy:* **upset**, perturbed,
flustered, ruffled, disconcerted, unnerved,
disquieted, disturbed, anxious, worried,
unsettled; nervous, jumpy, on edge, tense,
keyed up; informal rattled, fazed, in a dither,
in a flap, in a state, in a lather, jittery, in
a tizz/tizzy; Brit. informal having kittens, in a
(flat) spin; N. Amer. informal discombobulated.
– OPPOSITES calm, relaxed.

agitation noun **1** *Freddie gritted his teeth
in agitation:* **anxiety**, perturbation, disquiet,
distress, concern, alarm, worry. **2** *an upsurge
in nationalist agitation:* **campaigning**,
striving, battling, fighting, struggling.
3 *the vigorous agitation of the components:*
stirring, whisking, beating.

agitator noun **troublemaker**, rabble-rouser,
agent provocateur, demagogue, incendiary;
revolutionary, firebrand, rebel, insurgent,
subversive; informal stirrer.

agnostic noun **sceptic**, doubter, doubting
Thomas; unbeliever, disbeliever, non-
believer; rationalist.
– OPPOSITES believer, theist.

ago adverb *my husband died nearly fifteen*

years ago: **in the past**, before, earlier, back,
since, previously.

agog adverb *everyone was agog to hear what
he would say:* **eager**, excited, impatient,
keen, anxious, avid, in suspense, on
tenterhooks, on the edge of one's seat,
waiting with bated breath.

agonize verb *all the way home she agonized
about what she should do:* **worry**, fret, fuss,
brood, upset oneself, rack one's brains,
wrestle with oneself, be worried/anxious,
feel uneasy, exercise oneself; informal stew.

agonizing adjective *he died after suffering
months of agonizing pain:* **excruciating**,
harrowing, racking, searing, extremely
painful, acute, severe, torturous,
tormenting, piercing; informal hellish, killing.

agony noun *he was screaming in agony:* **pain**,
hurt, suffering, torture, torment, anguish,
affliction, trauma.

agrarian adjective *Brazil is diversifying
its agrarian economy:* **agricultural**, rural,
rustic, pastoral, countryside, farming.

agree verb **1** *I agree with you:* **concur**, be
of the same mind/opinion, see eye to eye,
be in sympathy, be united, be as one man.
2 *they had agreed to a ceasefire:* **consent**,
assent, acquiesce, accept, approve, say
yes, give one's approval, give the nod;
formal accede. **3** *the plan and the drawing
do not agree with each other:* **match (up)**,
accord, correspond, conform, coincide,
fit, tally, be in harmony/agreement, be
consistent/equivalent; informal square. **4** *they
agreed on a price:* **settle**, decide, arrive at,
negotiate, reach an agreement, come to
terms, strike a bargain, make a deal, shake
hands.
– OPPOSITES differ, contradict, reject.

agreeable adjective **1** *an agreeable
atmosphere of rural tranquillity:* **pleasant**,
pleasing, enjoyable, pleasurable, nice, to
one's liking, appealing, charming, delightful.
2 *the policeman was an agreeable fellow:*
likeable, charming, amiable, affable,
pleasant, nice, friendly, good-natured,
sociable, genial, congenial. **3** *we should
get together for a talk, if you're agreeable:*
willing, amenable, in accord/agreement.
– OPPOSITES unpleasant.

agreement noun **1** *all heads nodded in
agreement:* **accord**, concurrence, consensus;
assent, acceptance, consent, acquiescence,
endorsement. **2** *an agreement on military
cooperation:* **contract**, compact, treaty,
covenant, pact, accord, concordat, protocol.
3 *there is some agreement between my view
and that of the author:* **correspondence**,
consistency, compatibility, accord;
similarity, resemblance, likeness, similitude.
– OPPOSITES discord.

agricultural adjective **1** *an agricultural
labourer:* **farm**, farming, agrarian; rural,
rustic, pastoral, countryside. **2** *agricultural*

land: **farmed**, farm, agrarian, cultivated, tilled.
– OPPOSITES urban.

agriculture noun **farming**, cultivation, tillage, tilling, husbandry, land/farm management; agribusiness, agronomy.

aground adverb & adjective *a year later, the tanker was still aground:* **grounded**, ashore, beached, stuck, shipwrecked, high and dry, on the rocks, on the ground/bottom.

ahead adverb **1** *he peered ahead, but could see nothing:* **forward(s)**, towards the front, frontwards. **2** *he had ridden on ahead:* **in front**, at the head, in the lead, at the fore, in the vanguard, in advance. **3** *she was preparing herself for what lay ahead:* **in the future**, in time, in time to come, in the fullness of time, at a later date, after this, henceforth, later on, in due course, next. **4** *they are ahead by six points:* **leading**, winning, in the lead, (out) in front, first.
– OPPOSITES behind, at the back, in the past.
■ **ahead of 1** *Blanche went ahead of the others:* in front of, before. **2** *we have a demanding trip ahead of us:* in store for, waiting for. **3** *the motorway was finished two months ahead of schedule:* in advance of, before, earlier than. **4** *in terms of these amenities, Britain is ahead of other European countries:* more advanced than, further on than, superior to, surpassing, exceeding, better than.

aid noun **1** *with the aid of his colleagues he prepared a manifesto:* **assistance**, support, help, backing, cooperation, succour; a helping hand. **2** *humanitarian aid:* **relief**, charity, financial assistance, donations, contributions, subsidies, handouts, subvention; debt remission.
– OPPOSITES hindrance.
verb **1** *he provided an army to aid the King of England:* **help**, assist, abet, come to someone's aid, give assistance, lend a hand, be of service. **2** *essences can aid restful sleep:* **facilitate**, promote, encourage, help, further, boost; speed up, hasten, accelerate, expedite.
– OPPOSITES hinder.

aide noun **assistant**, helper, adviser, right-hand man, man/girl Friday, adjutant, deputy, second (in command); subordinate, junior, underling, acolyte; N. Amer. cohort.

ailing adjective **1** *I went to see my ailing mother:* **ill**, unwell, sick, sickly, poorly, weak, indisposed, in poor/bad health, infirm, debilitated, delicate, below par; Brit off colour; informal laid up, under the weather. **2** *the country's ailing economy:* **failing**, in poor condition, weak, poor, deficient.
– OPPOSITES healthy.

ailment noun *a mysterious stomach ailment left me very shaky:* **illness**, disease, disorder, affliction, malady, complaint, infirmity; informal bug, virus; Brit. informal lurgy.

aim verb **1** *he aimed the rifle:* **point**, direct, train, sight, line up. **2** *she aimed at the*

target: **zero in on**, fix on, draw a bead on. **3** *undergraduates aiming for a first degree:* **work towards**, be after, set one's sights on, try for, strive for, aspire to, endeavour to achieve; formal essay. **4** *this system is aimed at the home entertainment market:* **target**, intend, destine, direct, design, tailor, market, pitch. **5** *we aim to give you the best possible service:* **intend**, mean, have in mind/view; plan, resolve, propose, design.
noun *our aim is to develop gymnasts to the top level:* **objective**, object, goal, end, target, design, desire, desired result, intention, intent, plan, purpose, raison d'être, object of the exercise; ambition, aspiration, wish, dream, hope.

aimless adjective *Flavia set out on an aimless walk:* **purposeless**, objectless, goalless, without purpose, without goal.
– OPPOSITES purposeful.

air noun **1** *hundreds of birds hovered in the air:* **sky**, atmosphere; heavens, ether. **2** *open the windows to get some air into the room:* **breeze**, draught, wind; breath/blast of air, gust/puff of wind. **3** *he upended his glass with an air of defiance:* **expression**, appearance, look, impression, aspect, aura, mien, countenance, manner, bearing, tone. **4** (**airs**) *he'd no patience with women putting on airs:* **affectations**, pretension, pretentiousness, affectedness, posing, posturing, airs and graces; Brit. informal side.
verb **1** *this is a chance for you to air your views:* **express**, voice, make public, ventilate, articulate, state, declare, give expression/voice to; have one's say. **2** *the windows were opened to air the room:* **ventilate**, freshen, refresh, cool. **3** *the film was aired nationwide:* **broadcast**, transmit, screen, show, televise, telecast.

airily adverb *the doctor had dismissed his troubles airily:* **lightly**, breezily, flippantly, casually, nonchalantly, heedlessly, without consideration.
– OPPOSITES seriously.

airing noun **1** *give the bedroom a good airing:* **ventilating**, ventilation, freshening, refreshing, cooling. **2** *the airing of different views:* **expression**, voicing, venting, ventilation, articulation, stating, declaration, communication. **3** *I hope the BBC gives the play another airing:* **broadcast**, transmission, screening, showing, televising, telecast.

airless adjective *a hot, airless room:* **stuffy**, close, stifling, suffocating, oppressive; unventilated, badly/poorly ventilated.
– OPPOSITES airy, ventilated.

airport noun airfield, airstrip; Brit. aerodrome; N. Amer. airdrome; informal drome.

airtight adjective *an airtight container:* **sealed**, hermetically sealed, closed/shut tight.

airy adjective **1** *the conservatory is light and airy:* **well ventilated**, fresh; spacious, uncluttered; light, bright. **2** *an airy gesture:*

a

nonchalant, casual, breezy, flippant, insouciant, heedless.
– OPPOSITES stuffy.

aisle noun **passage**, passageway, gangway, walkway.

ajar adjective & adverb *the door to the sitting room was ajar:* **slightly open**, half open, agape.
– OPPOSITES closed, wide open.

akin adjective *something akin to gratitude overwhelmed her:* **similar**, related, close, near, corresponding, comparable, equivalent; analogous.
– OPPOSITES unlike.

alacrity noun *she accepted with alacrity:* **eagerness**, willingness, readiness; enthusiasm, ardour, fervour, keenness; promptness, haste, swiftness, dispatch, speed.

alarm noun **1** *the girl spun round in alarm:* **fear**, anxiety, apprehension, trepidation, nervousness, unease, distress, agitation, consternation, disquiet, perturbation, fright, panic. **2** *a smoke alarm:* **siren**, audible warning, danger/distress signal; warning device.
– OPPOSITES calmness, composure.
verb *the news had alarmed her:* **frighten**, scare, panic, unnerve, distress, agitate, upset, disconcert, shock, dismay, disturb; informal rattle, spook, scare the living daylights out of; Brit. informal put the wind up.

alarming adjective *infant mortality is rising at an alarming rate:* **frightening**, unnerving, shocking; distressing, upsetting, disconcerting, perturbing, dismaying, disquieting, disturbing; informal scary.
– OPPOSITES reassuring.

alarmist adjective *the newspapers were filled with alarmist propaganda:* **scaremongering**, pessimistic.
– OPPOSITES optimistic.

alchemy noun *they were involved with the quest for immortality through alchemy:* **chemistry**; magic, sorcery, witchcraft.

alcohol noun **liquor**, intoxicating liquor, strong/alcoholic drink, drink, spirits; informal booze, hooch, the hard stuff, firewater, rotgut, moonshine, grog, tipple, the demon drink, the bottle; Brit. informal gut-rot; N. Amer. informal juice.

alcoholic adjective *alcoholic drinks:* **intoxicating**, inebriating, containing alcohol; strong, hard, stiff.
noun *he is an alcoholic:* **dipsomaniac**, drunk, drunkard, heavy/hard/serious drinker, problem drinker, alcohol-abuser, person with a drink problem; tippler, sot, inebriate; informal boozer, lush, alky, dipso, soak, tosspot, wino, sponge, barfly; Austral./NZ informal hophead.

alcove noun **recess**, niche, nook, inglenook, bay.

alert adjective **1** *police have asked neighbours to keep alert:* **vigilant**, watchful, attentive, observant, wide awake, circumspect; on the lookout, on one's guard/toes, on the qui vive; informal keeping one's eyes open/peeled. **2** *he was over eighty, yet he was as mentally alert as a man half his age:* **quick-witted**, sharp, bright, quick, keen, perceptive, wide awake, on one's toes; informal on the ball, quick on the uptake, all there, with it.
– OPPOSITES inattentive.
noun **1** *the army called for a state of alert:* **vigilance**, watchfulness, attentiveness, alertness, circumspection. **2** *a flood alert has been issued:* **warning**, notification, notice; siren, alarm, signal, danger/distress signal.
verb *police were alerted by a phone call:* **warn**, notify, apprise, forewarn, put on one's guard, put on the qui vive; informal tip off, clue in.

alias noun *he is known under several aliases:* **assumed name**, false name, pseudonym, sobriquet, incognito; pen/stage name, nom de plume/guerre.
adverb *Cassius Clay, alias Muhammad Ali:* **also known as**, aka, also called, otherwise known as.

alibi noun *we've both got a good alibi for last night:* **defence**, justification, explanation, reason; informal story, line.

alien adjective **1** *alien cultures:* **foreign**, overseas, non-native. **2** *an alien landscape:* **unfamiliar**, unknown, strange, peculiar; exotic, foreign. **3** *a vicious role alien to his nature:* **incompatible**, opposed, conflicting, contrary, in conflict, at variance. **4** *alien beings:* **extraterrestrial**, unearthly.
– OPPOSITES native, familiar, earthly.
noun **1** *an illegal alien:* **foreigner**, non-native, immigrant, emigrant, émigré, incomer. **2** *the alien's spaceship crashed:* **extraterrestrial**, ET; informal little green man.

alienate verb *his homosexuality alienated him from his conservative father:* **estrange**, divide, distance, put at a distance, isolate, cut off; set against, turn away, drive apart, disunite, set at variance/odds, drive a wedge between.

alienation noun *she also shared my deep sense of alienation:* **isolation**, detachment, estrangement, distance, separation, division; cutting off, turning away.

alight[1] verb **1** *he alighted from the train:* **get off**, step off, disembark, pile out. **2** *a swallow alighted on a branch:* **land**, come to rest, settle, perch.
– OPPOSITES get on, board.

alight[2] adjective **1** *the bales of hay were alight:* **burning**, ablaze, aflame, on fire, in flames, blazing. **2** *her face was alight with laughter:* **lit up**, gleaming, glowing, aglow, ablaze, bright, shining, radiant.

align verb **1** *the desks are aligned in straight rows:* **line up**, put in order, put in rows/columns, place, position, situate, set, range. **2** *he aligned himself with the workers:*

ally, affiliate, associate, join, side, unite, combine, join forces, form an alliance, team up, band together, throw in one's lot, make common cause.

alike adjective *all the doors looked alike:* **similar**, (much) the same, indistinguishable, identical, uniform, interchangeable, cut from the same cloth, like (two) peas in a pod, (like) Tweedledum and Tweedledee; informal much of a muchness.
– OPPOSITES different.
adverb *great minds think alike:* **similarly**, (just) the same, in the same way/manner/fashion, identically.

alimony noun *his ex-wife has been trying to track him down for alimony:* **financial support**, maintenance, support; child support.

alive adjective **1** *he was last seen alive on Boxing Day:* **living**, live, breathing, animate, sentient; informal alive and kicking. **2** *the synagogue has kept the Jewish faith alive:* **active**, existing, in existence, existent, functioning, in operation; on the map. **3** *the thrills that kept him really alive:* **animated**, lively, full of life, alert, active, energetic, vigorous, spry, sprightly, vital, vivacious, buoyant, exuberant, ebullient, zestful, spirited; informal full of beans, bright-eyed and bushy-tailed, chirpy, chipper, peppy, full of vim and vigour. **4** *teachers need to be alive to their pupils' backgrounds:* **alert**, awake, aware, conscious, mindful, heedful, sensitive, familiar; informal wise.
– OPPOSITES dead, inanimate, inactive, lethargic.

all determiner **1** *all the children went:* **each of**, each/every one of, every single one of; every (single), each and every. **2** *the sun shone all week:* **the whole of the**, every bit of the, the complete, the entire. **3** *in all honesty | with all speed:* **complete**, entire, total, full; greatest (possible), maximum.
– OPPOSITES no, none of.
pronoun **1** *all are welcome:* **everyone**, everybody, each/every person. **2** *all of the cups were broken:* **each one**, the sum, the total, the whole lot. **3** *they took all of it:* **everything**, every part, the whole/total amount, the (whole) lot, the entirety.
– OPPOSITES none, nobody, nothing.
adverb *he was dressed all in black:* **completely**, fully, entirely, totally, wholly, absolutely, utterly; in every respect, in all respects, without reservation/exception.
– OPPOSITES partly.

allay verb *this should help to allay your fears:* **reduce**, diminish, decrease, lessen, assuage, alleviate, ease, relieve, soothe, soften, calm, take the edge off.
– OPPOSITES increase, intensify.

allegation noun *he made allegations of corruption against the administration:* **claim**, assertion, charge, accusation, declaration, statement, contention, argument, affirmation, attestation.

allege verb *he alleged that he had been assaulted:* **claim**, assert, charge, accuse, declare, state, contend, argue, affirm, attest, testify, swear.

alleged adjective *the alleged conspirators:* **supposed**, so-called, claimed, professed, purported, ostensible, putative, unproven.

allegedly adverb *he allegedly stabbed the girl:* **reportedly**, supposedly, reputedly, purportedly, ostensibly, apparently, by all accounts, so the story goes.

allegiance noun *those wishing to receive citizenship must swear allegiance to the republic:* **loyalty**, faithfulness, fidelity, obedience, adherence, homage, devotion.
– OPPOSITES disloyalty, treachery.

allegorical adjective *an allegorical painting:* **symbolic**, metaphorical, figurative, representative, emblematic.

allegory noun *'Pilgrim's Progress' is an allegory of the spiritual journey:* **parable**, analogy, metaphor, symbol, emblem.

allergic adjective *she was allergic to nuts:* **hypersensitive**, sensitive, sensitized.

allergy noun *she developed an allergy to feathers:* **hypersensitivity**, sensitivity, allergic reaction.

alleviate verb *he couldn't prevent her pain, only alleviate it:* **reduce**, ease, relieve, take the edge off, deaden, dull, diminish, lessen, weaken, lighten, attenuate, allay, assuage, palliate, damp, soothe, help, soften, temper.
– OPPOSITES aggravate.

alley noun **passage**, passageway, alleyway, back alley, backstreet, lane, path, pathway, walk.

alliance noun **1** *a defensive alliance:* **association**, union, league, confederation, federation, confederacy, coalition, consortium, affiliation, partnership. **2** *an alliance between medicine and morality:* **relationship**, affinity, association, connection.

allied adjective **1** *a group of allied nations:* **federated**, confederated, associated, in alliance, in league, in partnership; unified, united, amalgamated, integrated. **2** *agricultural and allied industries:* **associated**, related, connected, interconnected, linked; similar, like, comparable, equivalent.
– OPPOSITES independent, unrelated.

allocate verb *the authorities allocated 50,000 places to refugees:* **allot**, assign, distribute, apportion, share out, portion out, deal out, dole out, give out, dish out, parcel out, ration out, divide out/up; informal divvy up.

allocation noun **1** *the efficient allocation of resources:* **allotment**, assignment, distribution, apportionment, sharing out, handing out, dealing out, doling out, giving out, dishing out, parcelling out, rationing out, dividing out/up; informal divvying up.

a

2 *our annual allocation of funds:* **allowance**, allotment, quota, share, ration, grant, slice; informal cut; Brit. informal whack.

allot verb *an extra £3 billion has been allotted to the health service:* **allocate**, assign, apportion, distribute, issue, grant; earmark for, designate for, set aside for; hand out, deal out, dish out, dole out, give out; informal divvy up.

allow verb **1** *the police allowed him to go home:* **permit**, let, authorize, give permission/authorization/leave, sanction, grant someone the right, license, enable, entitle; consent, assent, give one's consent/assent/blessing, give the nod, acquiesce, agree, approve; informal give the go-ahead, give the thumbs up, OK, give the OK, give the green light. **2** *allow an hour or so for driving:* **set aside**, allocate, allot, earmark, designate, assign. **3** *the house was demolished to allow for road widening:* **provide**, get ready, cater, take into consideration, take into account, make provision, make preparations, prepare, plan, make plans.
– OPPOSITES prevent, forbid.

allowable adjective *the maximum allowable number of users:* **permissible**, permitted, allowed, admissible, acceptable, legal, lawful, legitimate, licit, authorized, sanctioned, approved, in order; informal OK, legit.
– OPPOSITES forbidden.

allowance noun **1** *your baggage allowance:* **quota**, allocation, allotment, permitted amount, share, ration, grant, limit, portion, slice. **2** *her father gave her an allowance:* **payment**, pocket money, sum of money, contribution, grant, subsidy, maintenance, financial support. **3** *a tax allowance:* **concession**, reduction, decrease, discount.
■ **make allowance(s) for 1** *you must make allowances for delays:* take into consideration, take into account, bear in mind, have regard to, plan for, get ready for, cater for, allow for, make provision for, prepare for. **2** *she made allowances for his faults:* excuse, make excuses for, forgive, pardon, overlook.

alloy noun **mixture**, mix, amalgam, fusion, meld, blend, compound, combination, composite, union.

all right adjective **1** *the tea was all right:* **satisfactory**, acceptable, adequate, fairly good, passable, reasonable; informal so-so, OK. **2** *are you all right?* **unhurt**, uninjured, unharmed, unscathed, in one piece, safe (and sound); well, fine, alive and well; informal OK. **3** *it's all right for you to go now:* **permissible**, permitted, allowed, allowable, admissible, acceptable, legal, lawful, legitimate, licit, authorized, sanctioned, approved, in order; informal OK, legit.
– OPPOSITES unsatisfactory, hurt, forbidden.
adverb **1** *the system works all right:* **satisfactorily**, adequately, fairly well,

passably, acceptably, reasonably; informal OK. **2** *it's him all right:* **definitely**, certainly, unquestionably, undoubtedly, indubitably, undeniably, assuredly, without (a) doubt, beyond (any) doubt, beyond the shadow of a doubt.
exclamation *all right, I'll go:* **very well (then)**, right (then), fine, good, yes, agreed, wilco; informal OK, okey-dokey, roger; Brit. informal righto.

allude verb *we will allude briefly to the main points:* **refer**, touch on, suggest, hint, imply, mention (in passing), make an allusion to.

allure noun *the allure of Paris:* **attraction**, lure, draw, pull, appeal, allurement, enticement, temptation, charm, seduction, fascination.

alluring adjective *the town offers alluring shops and restaurants:* **enticing**, tempting, attractive, appealing, inviting, captivating, fetching, seductive; enchanting, charming, fascinating; informal come-hither.

allusion noun *an allusion to Shakespeare:* **reference**, mention, suggestion, hint, comment, remark.

ally noun *close political allies:* **associate**, colleague, friend, confederate, partner, supporter.
– OPPOSITES enemy, opponent.
verb **1** *he allied his racing experience with business acumen:* **combine**, marry, couple, merge, amalgamate, join, fuse. **2** *the Catholic powers allied with Philip II:* **unite**, combine, join (up), join forces, band together, team up, collaborate, side, align oneself, form an alliance, throw in one's lot, make common cause.
– OPPOSITES split.

almighty adjective **1** *I swear by almighty God:* **all-powerful**, omnipotent, supreme, pre-eminent. **2** (informal) *an almighty explosion:* **very great**, huge, enormous, immense, colossal, massive, prodigious, stupendous, tremendous, monumental, mammoth, vast, gigantic, giant, mighty, Herculean, epic; very loud, deafening, ear-splitting, ear-piercing, booming, thundering, thunderous; informal whopping, thumping, astronomical, mega, monster, humongous, jumbo; Brit. informal whacking, ginormous.
– OPPOSITES powerless, insignificant.

almost adverb *lunch is almost ready:* **nearly**, (just) about, more or less, practically, virtually, all but, as good as, close to, near, not quite, not far from/off, to all intents and purposes; approaching, bordering on, verging on; informal pretty nearly/much/well.

aloft adjective & adverb **1** *he hoisted the Cup aloft:* **upwards**, up, high, into the air/sky, skyward, heavenward. **2** *the airships stayed aloft for many hours:* **in the air**, in the sky, high up, up (above), on high, overhead.
– OPPOSITES down.

alone adjective & adverb **1** *she was alone in the house:* **by oneself**, on one's own, all

alone, solitary, single, singly, solo, solus; unescorted, partnerless, companionless; Brit. informal on one's tod, on one's lonesome, on one's Jack Jones; Austral./NZ informal on one's Pat Malone. **2** *he managed alone:* **unaided**, unassisted, without help/assistance, single-handedly, solo, on one's own. **3** *she felt terribly alone:* **lonely**, isolated, solitary, deserted, abandoned, forlorn, friendless. **4** *a house standing alone:* **apart**, by itself/oneself, separate, detached, isolated. **5** *you alone can inspire me:* **only**, solely, just; and no one else, and nothing else, no one but, nothing but.
– OPPOSITES in company, with help, among others.

along preposition **1** *she walked along the corridor:* **down**, from one end of ... to the other. **2** *trees grew along the river bank:* **beside**, by the side of, on the edge of, alongside. **3** *they'll stop along the way:* **on**, at a point on, in the course of.
adverb **1** *Maurice moved along past the other exhibits:* **onwards**, on, ahead, forward(s). **2** *I invited a friend along:* **as company**, with one, to accompany one, as a partner.
▪ **along with** together with, accompanying, accompanied by; at the same time as; as well as, in addition to, plus, besides.

aloof adjective *an aloof and somewhat austere figure:* **distant**, detached, unfriendly, unsociable, remote, unapproachable, formal, stiff, austere, withdrawn, reserved, unforthcoming, uncommunicative; informal stand-offish.
– OPPOSITES familiar, friendly.

aloud adverb *he read the letter aloud:* **audibly**, out loud, for all to hear.
– OPPOSITES silently.

already adverb **1** *Anna had suffered a great deal already:* **by this/that time**, by now/then, thus/so far, before now/then, until now/then, up to now/then. **2** *is it 3 o'clock already?* **as early as this/that**, as soon as this/that, so soon.

also adverb *he's also very good at sport:* **too**, as well, besides, in addition, additionally, furthermore, further, moreover, into the bargain, on top of (that), what's more, to boot, equally; informal and all.

alter verb **1** *Eliot was persuaded to alter the passage:* **change**, make changes to, make different, make alterations to, adjust, make adjustments to, adapt, amend, modify, revise, revamp, rework, redo, refine, vary, transform; informal tweak. **2** *the state of affairs has altered:* **change**, become different, undergo a (sea) change, adjust, adapt, transform, evolve.
– OPPOSITES preserve, stay the same.

alteration noun *he made an alteration to the text:* **change**, adjustment, adaptation, modification, variation, revision, amendment; rearrangement, reordering, restyling, rejigging, reworking, revamping;

sea change, transformation; humorous transmogrification.

altercation noun *I had an altercation with the ticket collector:* **argument**, quarrel, squabble, fight, shouting match, disagreement, difference of opinion, falling-out, dispute, disputation, wrangle, war of words; informal tiff, run-in, slanging match, spat, scrap; Brit. informal row, barney, ding-dong, bust-up, bit of argy-bargy; N. Amer. informal rhubarb.

alternate verb **1** *rows of trees alternate with dense shrub:* **be interspersed**, occur in turn/rotation, rotate, follow one another; take turns, take it in turns, work/act in sequence. **2** *we could alternate the groups so that no one felt they had been left out:* **give turns to**, take in turn, rotate, take in rotation; swap, exchange, interchange.
adjective **1** *she attended on alternate days·* **every other**, every second. **2** *place the leeks and pasta in alternate layers:* **interchanging**, sequential, following in sequence, alternating, occurring in turns. **3** (N. Amer.) *an alternate plan.* See ALTERNATIVE adjective sense 1.

alternative adjective **1** *an alternative route:* **different**, other, another, second, possible, substitute, replacement; standby, emergency, reserve, backup, auxiliary, fallback; N. Amer. alternate. **2** *an alternative lifestyle:* **unorthodox**, unconventional, non-standard, unusual, uncommon, out of the ordinary, radical, revolutionary, nonconformist, avant-garde; informal off the wall, oddball, offbeat, way-out.
noun *we have no alternative:* **option**, choice, other possibility; substitute, replacement.

alternatively adverb *alternatively, you may telephone us direct if you wish:* **on the other hand**, as an alternative, or; otherwise, instead, if not, then again; N. Amer. alternately.

although conjunction *although the sun was shining it wasn't that warm:* **in spite of the fact that**, despite the fact that, notwithstanding (the fact) that, even though/if, for all that, while, whilst.

altitude noun *we are now flying at an altitude of 40,000 feet:* **height**, elevation.

altogether adverb **1** *he wasn't altogether happy:* **completely**, totally, entirely, absolutely, wholly, fully, thoroughly, utterly, perfectly, one hundred per cent, in all respects. **2** *we have five offices altogether:* **in all**, all told, in toto. **3** *altogether it was a great evening:* **on the whole**, overall, all in all, all things considered, on balance, on average, for the most part, in the main, in general, generally, by and large.

altruism noun *they supported the measures not out of altruism but out of self-interest:* **unselfishness**, selflessness, compassion, kindness, public-spiritedness; charity, benevolence, beneficence, philanthropy,

humanitarianism.
– OPPOSITES selfishness.

always adverb **1** *he's always late:* **every time**, each time, at all times, all the time, without fail, consistently, invariably, regularly, habitually, unfailingly. **2** *she's always complaining:* **continually**, continuously, constantly, forever, perpetually, incessantly, ceaselessly, unceasingly, endlessly, the entire time; informal 24-7. **3** *the place will always be dear to me:* **forever**, for always, for good (and all), for evermore, for ever and ever, until the end of time, eternally, for eternity, until hell freezes over; informal for keeps, until the cows come home.
– OPPOSITES never, seldom, sometimes.

amalgamate verb *the two departments were amalgamated:* **combine**, merge, unite, fuse, blend, meld; join (together), join forces, band (together), link (up), team up, go into partnership.
– OPPOSITES separate.

amalgamation noun **combination**, union, blend, mixture, fusion, coalescence, synthesis, composite, amalgam.

amass verb *he amassed a large fortune:* **gather**, collect, assemble; accumulate, stockpile, store (up), cumulate, accrue, lay in/up, garner; informal stash (away).
– OPPOSITES dissipate.

amateur noun **1** *the crew were all amateurs:* **non-professional**, non-specialist, layman, layperson; dilettante. **2** *what a bunch of amateurs:* **bungler**, incompetent, clown, bumbler; Brit. informal bodger.
– OPPOSITES professional, expert.
adjective **1** *an amateur sportsman:* **non-professional**, non-specialist, lay; dilettante. **2** *their amateur efforts:* **incompetent**, inept, unskilful, inexpert, amateurish, clumsy, maladroit, bumbling; Brit. informal bodged.

amaze verb *it never ceases to amaze me:* **astonish**, astound, surprise, stun, stagger, nonplus, shock, startle, stupefy, stop someone in their tracks, leave open-mouthed, leave aghast, take someone's breath away, dumbfound; informal bowl over, flabbergast; Brit. informal knock for six; (**amazed**) thunderstruck, at a loss for words, speechless; Brit. informal gobsmacked.

amazement noun **astonishment**, surprise, shock, stupefaction, incredulity, disbelief, speechlessness, awe, wonder, wonderment.

amazing adjective *yet another amazing coincidence:* **astonishing**, astounding, surprising, stunning, staggering, shocking, startling, stupefying, breathtaking, awesome, awe-inspiring, sensational, remarkable, spectacular, stupendous, phenomenal, extraordinary, incredible, unbelievable; informal mind-blowing, flabbergasting.

ambassador noun **1** *the American ambassador:* **envoy**, plenipotentiary, emissary, (papal) nuncio, representative,

diplomat. **2** *a great ambassador for the sport:* **campaigner**, representative, promoter, champion, supporter, backer; N. Amer. booster.

ambience noun *the relaxed ambience of the cocktail lounge:* **atmosphere**, air, aura, climate, mood, feel, feeling, vibrations, character, quality, impression, flavour, look, tone; informal vibes.

ambiguity noun *the plot revolves around the ambiguity in the title:* **ambivalence**, equivocation; obscurity, vagueness, abstruseness, doubtfulness, uncertainty.

ambiguous adjective *the judge agreed that the law was ambiguous:* **equivocal**, ambivalent, open to debate/argument, arguable, debatable; obscure, unclear, vague, abstruse, doubtful, dubious, uncertain.
– OPPOSITES clear.

ambition noun **1** *young people with ambition:* **drive**, determination, enterprise, initiative, eagerness, motivation, enthusiasm, zeal, commitment, a sense of purpose; informal get-up-and-go. **2** *her ambition was to become a model:* **aspiration**, intention, goal, aim, objective, object, purpose, intent, plan, desire, wish, design, target, dream.

ambitious adjective **1** *an energetic and ambitious politician:* **aspiring**, determined, forceful, pushy, enterprising, motivated, enthusiastic, energetic, zealous, committed, purposeful, power-hungry; informal go-ahead, go-getting. **2** *he was ambitious to make it to the top:* **eager**, determined, intent on, enthusiastic, anxious, hungry, impatient, striving. **3** *an ambitious task:* **difficult**, exacting, demanding, formidable, challenging, hard, arduous, onerous, tough.
– OPPOSITES laid-back.

ambivalent adjective *the public has a rather ambivalent attitude toward science:* **equivocal**, uncertain, unsure, doubtful, indecisive, inconclusive, irresolute, in two minds, undecided, torn, in a dilemma, on the horns of a dilemma, in a quandary, on the fence, hesitating, wavering, vacillating, equivocating, blowing hot and cold; informal iffy.
– OPPOSITES unequivocal, certain.

amble verb *they ambled along the riverbank:* **stroll**, saunter, wander, ramble, promenade, walk, go for a walk, take a walk; informal mosey, tootle; Brit. informal pootle, mooch.

ambush noun *the soldiers were killed in an ambush:* **surprise attack**, trap.
verb *twenty youths ambushed their patrol car:* **pounce on**, surprise, attack by surprise, lay a trap for, set an ambush for, lie in wait for, waylay; N. Amer. bushwhack.

ameliorate verb *any move that ameliorates the situation is welcome:* **improve**, make better, better, make improvements to, enhance, help, benefit, boost, amend; relieve, ease, mitigate.
– OPPOSITES worsen.

amenable adjective **1** *an amenable child:* **compliant**, acquiescent, biddable, manageable, controllable, governable, persuadable, tractable, responsive, pliant, malleable, complaisant, easily handled. **2** *many cancers are amenable to treatment:* **susceptible**, receptive, responsive.
– OPPOSITES uncooperative.

amend verb *the rule was amended to apply only to non-members:* **revise**, alter, change, modify, qualify, adapt, adjust; edit, copy-edit, rewrite, redraft, rephrase, reword, rework, revamp.

amends
■ **make amends** atone, make restitution, make good; (**make amends to**) compensate, recompense, indemnify, make it up to; (**make amends for**) atone for, make up for, expiate.

amenity noun **1** *the older type of housing lacks basic amenities:* **facility**, service, convenience, resource, appliance, aid, comfort, benefit, advantage. **2** *a loss of amenity:* **pleasantness**, agreeableness, niceness.

amiable adjective *the amiable young man greeted me enthusiastically:* **friendly**, affable, amicable, cordial; warm, warm-hearted, good-natured, nice, pleasant, agreeable, likeable, genial, good-humoured, charming, easy to get on/along with, companionable, sociable, personable; informal chummy; Brit. informal matey; N. Amer. informal regular.
– OPPOSITES unfriendly, disagreeable.

amicable adjective *the meeting was relatively amicable:* **friendly**, good-natured, cordial, easy, easy-going, neighbourly, harmonious, cooperative, civilized.
– OPPOSITES unfriendly.

amid preposition **1** *the jeep was concealed amid pine trees:* **in the middle of**, surrounded by, among, amongst. **2** *the truce collapsed amid fears of a revolt:* **at a time of**, in an atmosphere of, against a background of; as a result of.

amiss adjective *an inspection revealed nothing amiss:* **wrong**, awry, faulty, out of order, defective, unsatisfactory, incorrect; inappropriate, improper.
– OPPOSITES right, in order.
■ **not come/go amiss** be welcome, be appropriate, be useful.
■ **take something amiss** be offended, take offence, be upset.

amity noun *this will bring greater amity between our peoples:* **friendship**, friendliness, harmony, understanding, accord, cooperation, amicableness, goodwill, cordiality, warmth; formal concord.
– OPPOSITES animosity, enmity.

ammunition noun *police seized arms and ammunition:* **bullets**, shells, projectiles, missiles, rounds, shot, slugs, cartridges, munitions; informal ammo.

amnesty noun *an amnesty for political prisoners:* **pardon**, reprieve; release, discharge; informal let-off.

amok
■ **run amok** go berserk, get out of control, rampage, riot, run riot, go on the rampage, behave like a maniac, behave wildly/uncontrollably, become violent/destructive; informal raise hell.

among, amongst preposition **1** *you're among friends:* **surrounded by**, in the company of, amongst, amid, in the middle of. **2** *a child was among the injured:* **included in**, one/some of, in the group/number of. **3** *he distributed the proceeds among his creditors:* **between**, to each of.
■ **among ourselves/yourselves/themselves** jointly, with one another, together, mutually, reciprocally.

amoral adjective *an amoral attitude to sex:* **unprincipled**, without standards/morals/scruples, unethical.
– OPPOSITES principled.

amorous adjective *she rejected his amorous advances:* **lustful**, sexual, erotic, amatory, ardent, passionate, impassioned; in love, enamoured, lovesick; informal lovey-dovey, kissy, smoochy, goo-goo, hot; Brit. informal randy.
– OPPOSITES unloving.

amorphous adjective *an amorphous grey mass:* **shapeless**, formless, structureless, indeterminate.
– OPPOSITES shaped, definite.

amount noun *a substantial amount of money:* **quantity**, number, total, aggregate, sum, quota, group, size, mass, weight, volume, bulk, quantum.
■ **the full amount** the grand total, the total, the aggregate; informal the whole caboodle/shebang, the full nine yards.
■ **amount to 1** *the bill amounted to £50:* add up to, come to, run to, be, make, total; Brit. tot up to. **2** *the delays amounted to maladministration:* constitute, comprise, be tantamount to, come down to, boil down to; signify, signal, mean, indicate, suggest, denote, point to, be evidence of, be symptomatic of. **3** *her relationships had never amounted to anything significant:* become, grow/develop into, prove to be, turn out to be.

ample adjective **1** *there is ample time for discussion:* **enough**, sufficient, adequate, plenty of, more than enough, enough and to spare. **2** *an ample supply of wine:* **plentiful**, abundant, copious, profuse, rich, lavish, liberal, generous, bountiful, large, huge, great, bumper. **3** *his ample tunic:* **spacious**, capacious, roomy, sizeable; voluminous, loose-fitting, baggy, sloppy; formal commodious.
– OPPOSITES insufficient, meagre.

amplify verb **1** *many frogs amplify*

a

their voices: **make louder,** louden, turn up, magnify, intensify, increase, boost, step up, raise. **2** *these notes amplify our statement:* **expand,** enlarge on, elaborate on, add to, supplement, develop, flesh out, add detail to, go into detail about.
– OPPOSITES reduce, quieten.

amplitude noun *the amplitude of the signal was remarkably constant:* **magnitude,** size, volume; extent, range, compass; breadth, width.

amputate verb *they had to amputate his leg:* **cut off,** sever, surgically remove, saw/chop off.

amulet noun **lucky charm,** charm, talisman, fetish, mascot, totem, idol, juju.

amuse verb **1** *her annoyance simply amused him:* **entertain,** make laugh, delight, divert, cheer (up), please, charm, tickle; informal tickle pink, crack up; Brit. informal crease up. **2** *he amused himself by writing poetry:* **occupy,** engage, busy, employ, distract, absorb, engross, hold someone's attention; interest, entertain, divert.
– OPPOSITES bore.

amusement noun **1** *we looked with amusement at the cartoon:* **mirth,** merriment, light-heartedness, hilarity, glee, delight, gaiety, joviality, fun; enjoyment, pleasure, high spirits, cheerfulness. **2** *I read the book for amusement:* **entertainment,** pleasure, leisure, relaxation, fun, enjoyment, interest, diversion; informal R & R; N. Amer. informal rec. **3** *a wide range of amusements:* **activity,** entertainment, diversion; game, sport.

amusing adjective *behind that incident there lies an amusing story:* **entertaining,** funny, comical, humorous, light-hearted, jocular, witty, mirthful, hilarious, droll, diverting; informal wacky, side-splitting, rib-tickling.
– OPPOSITES boring, solemn.

anaemic adjective **1** *his anaemic face:* **colourless,** bloodless, pale, pallid, wan, ashen, grey, sallow, pasty-faced, whey-faced, peaky, sickly. **2** *an anaemic description of her feelings:* **feeble,** weak, insipid, wishy-washy, vapid, bland; lame, tame, lacklustre, spiritless, lifeless, ineffective, ineffectual, etiolated; informal pathetic.

anaesthetic noun **narcotic,** painkiller, painkilling drug, pain reliever, sedative, anodyne, analgesic; general, local.

analgesic adjective *an analgesic drug:* **painkilling,** pain-relieving, anodyne, narcotic, palliative.

analogous adjective *sleep had always been regarded as being in some way analogous to death:* **comparable,** parallel, similar, like, corresponding, related, kindred, equivalent.
– OPPOSITES unrelated.

analogy noun **similarity,** parallel, correspondence, likeness, resemblance, correlation, relation, kinship, equivalence, similitude.

– OPPOSITES dissimilarity.

analyse verb *DNA can be analysed by various methods:* **examine,** inspect, survey, study, scrutinize, look over; investigate, explore, probe, research, go over (with a fine-tooth comb), review, evaluate, break down, dissect, anatomize.

analysis noun *analysis of the pottery fragments confirmed their Mediterranean origin:* **examination,** investigation, inspection, survey, study, scrutiny; exploration, probe, research, review, evaluation, interpretation, anatomization, dissection.

analytical, analytic adjective *a more analytical approach was needed:* **systematic,** logical, scientific, methodical, organized, ordered, orderly, meticulous, rigorous.
– OPPOSITES unsystematic.

anarchic adjective *an anarchic and bitter civil war:* **lawless,** without law and order, in disorder/turmoil, unruly, chaotic, turbulent.
– OPPOSITES ordered.

anarchist noun **nihilist,** insurgent, agitator, subversive, terrorist, revolutionary, insurrectionist.

anarchy noun **lawlessness,** nihilism, mobocracy, revolution, insurrection, disorder, chaos, tumult, turmoil.
– OPPOSITES government, order.

anathema noun *racial hatred was anathema to her:* **abhorrent,** hateful, repugnant, repellent, offensive; **abomination,** outrage, bane, bugbear, bête noire.

anatomy noun **1** *a cat's anatomy:* **structure,** make-up, composition, constitution, form. **2** *an anatomy of society:* **analysis,** examination, inspection, survey, study, investigation, review, evaluation.

ancestor noun **1** *he could trace his ancestors back to King James I:* **forebear,** forefather, predecessor, antecedent, progenitor, primogenitor. **2** *the instrument is an ancestor of the lute:* **forerunner,** precursor, predecessor.
– OPPOSITES descendant, successor.

ancestral adjective *the family's ancestral home:* **inherited,** hereditary, familial.

ancestry noun **ancestors,** forebears, forefathers, progenitors, antecedents; family tree; lineage, genealogy, roots.

anchor noun **1** *the anchor of the new coalition:* **mainstay,** cornerstone, linchpin, bulwark, foundation. **2** *a CBS news anchor:* **presenter,** announcer, anchorman, anchorwoman, broadcaster.
verb **1** *the ship was anchored in the bay:* **moor,** berth, be at anchor. **2** *the fish anchors itself to the coral:* **secure,** fasten, attach, affix, fix.

anchorage noun **moorings,** roads, roadstead, harbour, bay.

ancient adjective **1** *ancient civilizations:* **early,** prehistoric, primeval, primordial, primitive, of long ago. **2** *an ancient custom:*

old, very old, age-old, archaic, antediluvian, time-worn, time-honoured. **3** *I feel positively ancient:* **antiquated**, aged, elderly, decrepit, antediluvian, in one's dotage; old-fashioned, out of date, outmoded, démodé, passé; informal out of the ark; Brit. informal past its/one's sell-by date.
– OPPOSITES recent, contemporary.

ancillary adjective *ancillary staff:* **additional**, auxiliary, supporting, helping, extra, supplementary, accessory.

and conjunction *bread and butter:* **together with**, along with, with, as well as, in addition to, also, too; besides, furthermore; informal plus.

anecdotal adjective *anecdotal evidence:* **unscientific**, unreliable, based on hearsay.
– OPPOSITES factual, reliable.

anecdote noun **story**, tale, narrative; urban myth; informal yarn.

angel noun **1** *God sent an angel:* **messenger of God**, divine/heavenly messenger, divine being. **2** *she's an absolute angel:* **saint**, paragon of virtue; gem, treasure, darling, dear; informal star.
– OPPOSITES devil.

angelic adjective **1** *angelic beings:* **divine**, heavenly, celestial, holy, seraphic. **2** *Sophie's angelic appearance:* **innocent**, pure, virtuous, good, saintly, wholesome.
– OPPOSITES demonic, infernal.

anger noun *his face was livid with anger:* **annoyance**, vexation, exasperation, crossness, irritation, irritability, indignation, pique; rage, fury, wrath, outrage, irascibility, ill temper/humour; informal aggravation.
– OPPOSITES pleasure, good humour.
verb *she was angered by his terse reply:* **annoy**, irritate, exasperate, irk, vex, put out; enrage, incense, infuriate, make someone's hackles rise; Brit. rub up the wrong way; informal make someone's blood boil, get someone's back up, make someone see red, get someone's dander up, rattle someone's cage; aggravate, get someone, rile, hack off; Brit. informal wind up, nark; N. Amer. informal tee off, tick off, burn up, gravel.
– OPPOSITES pacify, placate.

angle[1] noun **1** *the wall is sloping at an angle of 33°:* **gradient**, slant, inclination. **2** *the angle of the roof:* **corner**, intersection, point, apex. **3** *consider the problem from a different angle:* **perspective**, point of view, viewpoint, standpoint, position, aspect, slant, direction.
verb **1** *Anna angled her camera towards the tree:* **tilt**, slant, direct, turn. **2** *angle your answer so that it is relevant:* **present**, slant, orient, twist, bias.

angle[2] verb *he was angling for an invitation:* **try to get**, seek to obtain, fish for, hope for, be after.

angler noun **fisherman**, rod.

angry adjective **1** *Vivienne got angry:* **irate**, annoyed, cross, vexed, irritated, indignant,

irked; furious, enraged, infuriated, in a temper, incensed, raging, incandescent, fuming, seething, beside oneself, outraged; informal (hopping) mad, wild, livid, apoplectic, as cross as two sticks, hot under the collar, up in arms, foaming at the mouth, steamed up, in a lather/paddy, fit to be tied; Brit. informal aerated, shirty; N. Amer. informal sore, bent out of shape, teed off, ticked off; Austral./NZ informal ropeable, snaky. **2** *an angry debate:* **heated**, passionate, stormy, 'lively'; bad-tempered, ill-tempered, acrimonious, bitter. **3** *angry sores:* **inflamed**, red, swollen, sore, painful.
– OPPOSITES pleased, good-humoured.
■ **get angry** lose one's temper, become enraged, go into a rage, go berserk, flare up; informal go mad/crazy/wild, go bananas, hit the roof, go through the roof, go up the wall, see red, go off the deep end, fly off the handle, blow one's top, blow a fuse/gasket, lose one's rag, flip (one's lid), have a fit, foam at the mouth, explode, go non-linear, go ballistic; Brit. informal go spare, do one's nut; N. Amer. informal flip one's wig, blow one's lid/stack, have a conniption fit.

angst noun *teenage angst:* **anxiety**, fear, apprehension, worry, foreboding, trepidation, malaise, disquiet, disquietude, unease, uneasiness.
– OPPOSITES confidence, peace of mind.

anguish noun *a cry of anguish:* **agony**, pain, torment, torture, suffering, distress, angst, misery, sorrow, grief, heartache, desolation, despair.
– OPPOSITES happiness.

anguished adjective **agonized**, tormented, tortured; grief-stricken, wretched, heartbroken, desolate, devastated; informal cut up.

angular adjective **1** *an angular shape:* **sharp-cornered**, pointed, V-shaped, Y-shaped. **2** *an angular face:* **bony**, raw-boned, lean, rangy, spare, thin, gaunt.
– OPPOSITES rounded, curving.

animal noun **1** *endangered animals:* **creature**, beast, living thing; N. Amer. informal critter; (**animals**) wildlife, fauna. **2** *the man was an animal:* **brute**, beast, monster, devil, demon, fiend; informal swine, bastard, pig.
adjective **1** *animal life:* **zoological**, animalistic. **2** *a grunt of animal passion:* **carnal**, fleshly, bodily, physical; brutish, unrefined, uncultured, coarse.

animate verb *a sense of excitement animated the whole school:* **enliven**, vitalize, breathe (new) life into, energize, invigorate, revive, vivify, liven up; inspire, inspirit, exhilarate, thrill, excite, fire, arouse, rouse; N. Amer. light a fire under; informal buck up, pep up, give someone a buzz.
– OPPOSITES depress.
adjective *an animate being:* **living**, alive, live, breathing.
– OPPOSITES inanimate.

animated adjective *an animated discussion:* **lively**, spirited, high-spirited, energetic, full

a

of life, excited, enthusiastic, eager, alive, active, vigorous, vibrant, vital, vivacious, buoyant, exuberant, ebullient, effervescent, bouncy, bubbly, perky; informal bright-eyed and bushy-tailed, full of beans, bright and breezy, chirpy, chipper, peppy.
– OPPOSITES lethargic, lifeless.

animosity noun *there was considerable animosity between him and his brother:* **antipathy**, hostility, friction, antagonism, enmity, animus, bitterness, rancour, resentment, dislike, ill feeling/will, bad blood, hatred, hate, loathing; malice, spite.
– OPPOSITES goodwill, friendship.

annals plural noun **records**, archives, chronicles, accounts, registers.

annex verb **1** *ten amendments were annexed to the constitution:* **add**, append, attach, tack on, tag on. **2** *Charlemagne annexed northern Italy:* **take over**, take possession of, appropriate, seize, conquer, occupy. noun (also **annexe**) **extension**, addition; wing; N. Amer. ell.

annexation noun *Hitler's annexation of Austria:* **seizure**, occupation, invasion, conquest, takeover, appropriation.

annihilate verb *this was an attempt to annihilate a whole people:* **destroy**, wipe out, obliterate, wipe off the face of the earth; kill, slaughter, exterminate, eliminate, liquidate; informal take out, rub out, snuff out, waste.
– OPPOSITES create.

annotate verb *the text was annotated with explanatory notes:* **comment on**, add notes/footnotes to, gloss, interpret.

annotation noun **note**, comment, gloss, footnote; commentary, explanation, interpretation.

announce verb **1** *their financial results were announced:* **make public**, make known, report, declare, state, give out, notify, publicize, broadcast, publish, advertise, circulate, proclaim, blazon abroad. **2** *Victor announced the guests:* **introduce**, present, name. **3** *strains of music announced her arrival:* **signal**, indicate, give notice of, herald, proclaim.

announcement noun **1** *an announcement by the Minister is expected this afternoon:* **statement**, report, declaration, proclamation, pronouncement; bulletin, communiqué; N. Amer. advisory. **2** *the announcement of the decision:* **declaration**, notification, reporting, publishing, broadcasting, proclamation.

announcer noun **presenter**, anchorman, anchorwoman, anchor; newsreader, newscaster, broadcaster.

annoy verb *such remarks never failed to annoy him:* **irritate**, vex, make angry/cross, anger, exasperate, irk, gall, pique, put out, antagonize, get on someone's nerves, ruffle someone's feathers, make someone's hackles rise, nettle; Brit. rub up the wrong way; informal aggravate, peeve, hassle, miff, rile, needle,

get (to), bug, hack off, get up someone's nose, get someone's goat, get someone's back up, give someone the hump, drive mad/crazy, drive round the bend/twist, drive up the wall; Brit. informal wind up, nark, get on someone's wick; N. Amer. informal tee off, tick off, burn up, rankle, gravel.
– OPPOSITES please, gratify.

annoyance noun **1** *much to his annoyance, Louise didn't even notice:* **irritation**, exasperation, vexation, indignation, anger, displeasure, chagrin; informal aggravation. **2** *they found him an annoyance:* **nuisance**, pest, bother, irritant, inconvenience, thorn in one's flesh; informal pain (in the neck), bind, bore, hassle; N. Amer. informal nudnik, burr in/under someone's saddle; Austral./NZ informal nark.

annoyed adjective **irritated**, cross, angry, vexed, exasperated, irked, piqued, displeased, put out, disgruntled, nettled, in a bad mood, in a temper; informal aggravated, peeved, miffed, miffy, riled, hacked off, hot under the collar; Brit. informal narked, shirty; N. Amer. informal teed off, ticked off, sore, bent out of shape; Austral./NZ informal snaky, crook.

annoying adjective **irritating**, infuriating, exasperating, maddening, trying, tiresome, troublesome, bothersome, irksome, vexing, vexatious, galling; informal aggravating, pesky.

annual adjective *an annual report:* **yearly**, once-a-year; year-long, twelve-month.

annually adverb **yearly**, once a year, each year, per annum.

annul verb *the European Court annulled the decision:* **nullify**, declare null and void, declare invalid, invalidate, void; repeal, reverse, rescind, revoke.
– OPPOSITES restore, enact.

anodyne adjective *the conversation was anodyne:* **bland**, inoffensive, innocuous, neutral, unobjectionable.

anoint verb *he was anointed and crowned:* **consecrate**, bless, ordain; formal hallow.

anomalous adjective *anomalous results:* **abnormal**, atypical, irregular, aberrant, exceptional, freak, freakish, odd, bizarre, peculiar, unusual, out of the ordinary.
– OPPOSITES normal, typical.

anomaly noun *there are a number of anomalies in the present system:* **oddity**, peculiarity, abnormality, irregularity, inconsistency, incongruity, aberration, quirk.

anonymous adjective **1** *an anonymous donor:* **unnamed**, nameless, incognito, unidentified, unknown. **2** *an anonymous letter:* **unsigned**, unattributed. **3** *an anonymous housing estate:* **characterless**, nondescript, impersonal, faceless.
– OPPOSITES known, identified.

another determiner **1** *have another drink:* **one more**, a further, an additional; an extra, a spare. **2** *she left him for another man:* **a different**, some other, an alternative.

– OPPOSITES the same.

answer noun 1 *her answer was unequivocal:* **reply**, response, rejoinder, reaction; retort, riposte; informal comeback. 2 *the answer is 150:* **solution**, key. 3 *a new filter is the answer:* **solution**, remedy, way out.
– OPPOSITES question.

verb 1 *Steve was about to answer:* **reply**, respond, make a rejoinder, rejoin; retort, riposte. 2 *he has yet to answer the charges:* **rebut**, refute, defend oneself against. 3 *a man answering this description:* **match**, fit, correspond to, be similar to. 4 *we're trying to answer the needs of our audience:* **satisfy**, meet, fulfil, fill, measure up to. 5 *I answer to the Commissioner:* **report**, work for/under, be subordinate, be accountable, be answerable, be responsible.
■ **answer someone back** respond cheekily to, be cheeky to, be impertinent to, talk back to, cheek; N. Amer. informal sass.
■ **answer for 1** *he will answer for his crime:* pay for, be punished for, suffer for; make amends for, make reparation for, atone for. 2 *the government has a lot to answer for:* be accountable for, be responsible for, be liable for, take the blame for; informal take the rap for.

answerable adjective *the Attorney General is answerable only to Parliament:* **accountable**, responsible, liable; subject.

antagonism noun *the overt antagonism between her and Susan:* **hostility**, friction, enmity, antipathy, animus, opposition, dissension, rivalry; acrimony, bitterness, rancour, resentment, aversion, dislike, ill/bad feeling, ill will; Brit. informal needle.
– OPPOSITES rapport, friendship.

antagonist noun **adversary**, opponent, enemy, rival; (**antagonists**) opposition, competition.
– OPPOSITES ally.

antagonistic adjective 1 *he was antagonistic to the reforms:* **hostile**, against, (dead) set against, opposed, inimical, antipathetic, ill-disposed, resistant, in disagreement; informal anti. 2 *an antagonistic group of bystanders:* **hostile**, aggressive, belligerent, bellicose, pugnacious.
– OPPOSITES pro.

antagonize verb *he seemed to be deliberately trying to antagonize her:* **anger**, annoy, provoke, vex, irritate; arouse hostility in, alienate; Brit. rub up the wrong way; informal aggravate, rile, needle, rattle someone's cage, get someone's back up, get someone's dander up; Brit. informal nark, get on someone's wick.
– OPPOSITES pacify, placate.

antecedent noun 1 *her antecedents have been traced:* **ancestor**, forefather, forebear, progenitor, primogenitor; (**antecedents**) ancestry, family tree, lineage, genealogy, roots. 2 *the guitar's antecedent:* **precursor**, forerunner, predecessor.
– OPPOSITES descendant.

antedate verb *a civilization that antedated the Roman Empire:* **precede**, predate, come/go before.

antediluvian adjective 1 *antediluvian animals:* **prehistoric**, primeval, primordial, primal, ancient, early. 2 *his antediluvian attitudes:* **out of date**, outdated, outmoded, old-fashioned, antiquated, behind the times, passé.

anthem noun **hymn**, song, chorale, psalm, paean.

anthology noun *an anthology of poetry:* **collection**, selection, compendium, treasury, miscellany.

anticipate verb 1 *the police did not anticipate trouble:* **expect**, foresee, predict, be prepared for, bargain on, reckon on; N. Amer. informal figure on. 2 *Elaine anticipated her meeting with Will:* **look forward to**, await. 3 *warders can't always anticipate the actions of prisoners:* **pre-empt**, forestall, second-guess; informal beat someone to the punch.

anticipation noun 1 *my anticipation is that we will see a rise in rates:* **expectation**, prediction, forecast. 2 *her eyes sparkled with anticipation:* **expectancy**, expectation, excitement, suspense.
■ **in anticipation of** in the expectation of, in preparation for, ready for.

anticlimax noun *the rest of the journey was an anticlimax by comparison:* **let-down**, disappointment, comedown, non-event; disillusionment; Brit. damp squib; informal washout.

antics plural noun *she laughed, recalling her son's antics:* **capers**, pranks, larks, high jinks, skylarking; Brit. informal monkey tricks.

antidote noun 1 *the antidote to this poison:* **antitoxin**, antiserum, antivenin. 2 *laughter is a good antidote to stress:* **remedy**, cure, nostrum.

antipathetic adjective **hostile**, against, (dead) set against, opposed, antagonistic, ill-disposed, unsympathetic; informal anti, down on.
– OPPOSITES pro.

antipathy noun *she felt a violent antipathy to Emily:* **hostility**, antagonism, animosity, aversion, animus, enmity, dislike, distaste, hatred, hate, abhorrence, loathing.
– OPPOSITES liking, affinity.

antiquated adjective *antiquated attitudes:* **outdated**, out of date, outmoded, outworn, behind the times, old-fashioned, anachronistic, old-fangled, passé, démodé; informal out of the ark, mouldy; N. Amer. informal horse-and-buggy, mossy, clunky.
– OPPOSITES modern, up to date.

antique noun **collector's item**, period piece, antiquity, object of virtu, objet d'art.
adjective 1 *antique furniture:* **old**, antiquarian, collectable. 2 *statues of antique gods:* **ancient**, of long ago.
– OPPOSITES modern, state-of-the-art.

antiquity noun **1** *the civilizations of antiquity:* **ancient times**, the ancient past, classical times, the distant past. **2** *Islamic antiquities:* **antique**, period piece, collector's item. **3** *a church of great antiquity:* **age**, oldness, ancientness.

antiseptic adjective **1** *an antiseptic substance:* **disinfectant**, germicidal, bactericidal. **2** *antiseptic bandages:* **sterile**, aseptic, germ-free, uncontaminated, disinfected. **3** *their antiseptic surroundings:* **characterless**, colourless, soulless; clinical, institutional.
– OPPOSITES contaminated.
noun **disinfectant**, germicide, bactericide.

antisocial adjective **1** *antisocial behaviour:* **objectionable**, offensive, unacceptable, distasteful, disruptive; sociopathic. **2** *I'm feeling a bit antisocial:* **unsociable**, unfriendly, uncommunicative, reclusive, misanthropic.

antithesis noun *love is the antithesis of selfishness:* **(direct) opposite**, converse, reverse, inverse, obverse, the other side of the coin; informal the flip side.

antithetical adjective **(directly) opposed**, contrasting, contrary, contradictory, conflicting, incompatible, irreconcilable, inconsistent, poles apart, at variance/odds.
– OPPOSITES identical, like.

anxiety noun **1** *his anxiety grew:* **worry**, concern, apprehension, apprehensiveness, uneasiness, unease, fearfulness, fear, disquiet, disquietude, perturbation, agitation, angst, nervousness, nerves, tension, tenseness; informal butterflies (in one's stomach), jitteriness, twitchiness, collywobbles, jim-jams. **2** *an anxiety to please:* **eagerness**, keenness, desire.
– OPPOSITES serenity.

anxious adjective **1** *I'm anxious about her:* **worried**, concerned, apprehensive, fearful, uneasy, perturbed, troubled, bothered, disturbed, distressed, fretful, agitated, nervous, edgy, unquiet, on edge, tense, overwrought, worked up, keyed up, jumpy, worried sick, with one's stomach in knots, with one's heart in one's mouth; informal uptight, on tenterhooks, with butterflies in one's stomach, like a cat on a hot tin roof, jittery, twitchy, in a stew/twitter, all of a dither/lather, in a tizz/tizzy, het up; Brit. informal strung up, windy, having kittens, in a (flat) spin, like a cat on hot bricks; N. Amer. informal antsy, spooky, squirrelly, in a twit; Austral./NZ informal toey. **2** *she was anxious for news:* **eager**, keen, desirous, impatient.
– OPPOSITES carefree, unconcerned.

any determiner **1** *is there any cake left?* **some**, a piece/part/bit of. **2** *it doesn't make any difference:* **the slightest bit of**, a scrap/shred/jot/whit of, an iota of. **3** *any job will do:* **whichever**, no matter which, never mind which; informal any old.
pronoun *you don't know any of my friends:* **a single one**, (even) one; anyone, anybody.

adverb *is your father any better?* **at all**, in the least, to any extent, in any degree.

anyhow adverb **1** *anyhow, it doesn't really matter:* **anyway**, in any case/event, at any rate; however, be that as it may; N. Amer. informal anyways. **2** *her clothes were strewn about anyhow:* **haphazardly**, carelessly, heedlessly, negligently, in a muddle; informal all over the place; Brit. informal all over the shop; N. Amer. informal all over the lot.

apart adverb **1** *the villages are two miles apart:* **away/distant from each other**. **2** *Isabel stood apart:* **to one side**, aside, separately, alone, by oneself/itself. **3** *his parents are living apart:* **separately**, independently, on one's own. **4** *the car was blown apart:* **to pieces/bits**, up.
■ **apart from** except for, but for, aside from, with the exception of, excepting, excluding, bar, barring, besides, other than; informal outside of; formal save.

apartment noun **1** *a rented apartment:* **flat**, penthouse; Austral. home unit; N. Amer. informal crib. **2** *the royal apartments:* **suite (of rooms)**, rooms, living quarters, accommodation.

apathetic adjective *the workforce was described as apathetic and demoralized:* **uninterested**, indifferent, unconcerned, unmoved, uninvolved, unemotional, emotionless, dispassionate, lukewarm, unmotivated; informal couldn't-care-less.

apathy noun *there was widespread apathy amongst the electorate:* **indifference**, lack of interest/enthusiasm/concern, unconcern, unresponsiveness, impassivity, dispassion, lethargy, languor, ennui, accidie.
– OPPOSITES enthusiasm, passion.

ape noun **primate**, simian; monkey.
verb *he aped Barbara's accent:* **imitate**, mimic, copy, do an impression of; informal take off, send up.

aperture noun **opening**, hole, gap, slit, slot, vent, crevice, chink, crack, interstice.

apex noun **1** *the apex of a pyramid:* **tip**, peak, summit, pinnacle, top, vertex. **2** *the apex of his career:* **climax**, culmination, apotheosis; peak, pinnacle, zenith, acme, apogee, high(est) point.
– OPPOSITES bottom, nadir.

aphorism noun **saying**, maxim, axiom, adage, epigram, dictum, gnome, proverb, saw, tag.

aphrodisiac noun **love potion**, philtre.
adjective *the aphrodisiac effects of ylang-ylang oil:* **erotic**, sexy, sexually arousing.

apiece adverb *the largest stones weigh over fifty tons apiece:* **each**, respectively, per item; informal a throw.

aplenty adjective *the town has museums and galleries aplenty:* **in abundance**, in profusion, galore, in large quantities/numbers, by the dozen; informal a gogo, by the truckload.

aplomb noun *he handled the crisis*

with surprising aplomb: **poise**, self-assurance, self-confidence, calmness, composure, collectedness, level-headedness, sangfroid, equilibrium, equanimity; informal unflappability.

apocryphal adjective *an apocryphal story:* **fictitious**, made-up, untrue, fabricated, false, spurious; unverified, unauthenticated, unsubstantiated.
– OPPOSITES authentic.

apologetic adjective *she was very apologetic about the whole incident:* **regretful**, sorry, contrite, remorseful, penitent, repentant; conscience-stricken, shamefaced, ashamed.
– OPPOSITES unrepentant.

apologia noun *Norbrook offers a spirited apologia for his methodology:* **defence**, justification, vindication, explanation; argument, case.

apologist noun *an apologist for hard-line government policies:* **defender**, supporter, upholder, advocate, proponent, exponent, propagandist, champion, campaigner.
– OPPOSITES critic.

apologize verb *I must apologize for disturbing you like this:* **say sorry**, express regret, be apologetic, make an apology, ask forgiveness, ask for pardon, eat humble pie.

apology noun **1** *I owe you an apology:* **expression of regret**, one's regrets; Austral./NZ informal beg-pardon. **2** (informal) *an apology for a flat:* **travesty**, inadequate/poor example; informal excuse.

apostle noun **1** *the 12 apostles:* **disciple**, follower. **2** *an apostle of capitalism:* **advocate**, apologist, proponent, exponent, promoter, supporter, upholder, champion; N. Amer. booster.

appal verb *civil-rights activists were appalled by the police brutality:* **horrify**, shock, dismay, distress, outrage, scandalize; disgust, repel, revolt, sicken, nauseate, offend, make someone's blood run cold.

appalling adjective **1** *an appalling crime:* **shocking**, horrific, horrifying, horrible, terrible, awful, dreadful, ghastly, hideous, horrendous, frightful, atrocious, abominable, abhorrent, outrageous, gruesome, grisly, monstrous, heinous, egregious. **2** (informal) *your schoolwork is appalling:* **dreadful**, awful, terrible, frightful, atrocious, disgraceful, deplorable, hopeless, lamentable; informal rotten, crummy, pathetic, pitiful, woeful, useless, lousy, abysmal, dire; Brit. informal chronic, shocking, pants.

apparatus noun **1** *laboratory apparatus:* **equipment**, gear, rig, tackle, gadgetry; appliance, instrument, machine, mechanism, device, contraption. **2** *the apparatus of government:* **structure**, system, framework, organization, network.

apparent adjective **1** *their relief was all too apparent:* **evident**, plain, obvious, clear, manifest, visible, discernible, perceptible; unmistakable, crystal clear, palpable, patent, blatant, as plain as a pikestaff, writ large; informal as plain as the nose on one's face, written all over one's face. **2** *his apparent lack of concern:* **seeming**, ostensible, outward, superficial; supposed, alleged, professed.
– OPPOSITES unclear.

apparently adverb *apparently, he had a mild heart attack:* **seemingly**, evidently, it seems/appears (that), as far as one knows, by all accounts; ostensibly, outwardly, on the face of it, so the story goes, so I'm told; allegedly, reputedly.

apparition noun **1** *a monstrous apparition:* **ghost**, phantom, spectre, spirit, wraith; vision, hallucination; informal spook. **2** *the apparition of a strange man:* **appearance**, manifestation, materialization, emergence; visitation.

appeal verb **1** *police are appealing for information:* **plead**, make an urgent/earnest request, call, make a plea, ask urgently/earnestly. **2** *Andrew appealed to me to help them:* **implore**, beg, entreat, call on, plead with, exhort, ask, request, petition. **3** *the thought of travelling appealed to me:* **attract**, be attractive to, interest, take someone's fancy, fascinate, tempt, entice, allure, lure, draw, whet someone's appetite; informal float someone's boat.
noun **1** *an appeal for help:* **plea**, urgent/earnest request, entreaty, cry, call, petition, supplication, cri de cœur. **2** *the cultural appeal of the island:* **attraction**, attractiveness, allure, charm; fascination, magnetism, drawing power, pull. **3** *the court allowed the appeal:* **retrial**, re-examination.

appealing adjective *she's such an appealing girl:* **attractive**, engaging, alluring, enchanting, captivating, bewitching, fascinating, tempting, enticing, seductive, irresistible, winning, winsome, charming, desirable.
– OPPOSITES disagreeable, off-putting.

appear verb **1** *a cloud of dust appeared on the horizon:* **become visible**, come into view/sight, materialize, pop up. **2** *fundamental differences were beginning to appear:* **be revealed**, emerge, surface, manifest itself, become apparent/evident, come to light; arise, crop up. **3** *Bill still hadn't appeared:* **arrive**, turn up, put in an appearance, come, get here/there; informal show (up), pitch up, fetch up, roll in, blow in. **4** *they appeared to be completely devoted:* **seem**, look, give the impression, come across as, strike someone as.
– OPPOSITES vanish.

appearance noun **1** *she was conscious of her dishevelled appearance:* **look(s)**, air, aspect, mien. **2** *Martha took care to keep up an appearance of respectability:* **impression**, air, (outward) show; semblance, facade, veneer, front, pretence. **3** *the sudden appearance of her daughter:* **arrival**, advent, coming, emergence, materialization.

appease verb *an attempt to appease his critics:* **conciliate**, placate, pacify, propitiate, reconcile, win over; informal sweeten.
– OPPOSITES provoke, inflame.

appeasement noun *a policy of appeasement:* **conciliation**, placation, pacification, propitiation, reconciliation; peacemaking, peace-mongering.
– OPPOSITES provocation.

append verb *the results of the survey are appended to this chapter:* **add**, attach, affix, tack on, tag on.

appendage noun **1** *I am not just an appendage to the family:* **addition**, attachment, adjunct, addendum, appurtenance, accessory. **2** *a pair of feathery appendages:* **protuberance**, projection.

appendix noun *the list was published as an appendix to the report:* **supplement**, addendum, postscript, codicil; coda, epilogue, afterword, tailpiece, back matter.

appertain
■ **appertain to** *in those days, the laws appertaining to hygiene were much slacker:* pertain to, apply to, relate to, concern, be concerned with, have to do with, be relevant to, have reference to, have a bearing on, bear on.

appetite noun **1** *a walk sharpens the appetite:* **hunger**, ravenousness; taste, palate. **2** *my appetite for learning:* **craving**, longing, yearning, hankering, hunger, thirst, passion; enthusiasm, keenness, eagerness, desire; informal yen.

appetizer noun **starter**, first course, hors d'oeuvre, amuse-gueule, antipasto.

appetizing adjective **1** *an appetizing lunch:* **mouth-watering**, inviting, tempting; tasty, delicious, flavoursome, toothsome, delectable; informal scrumptious, scrummy, yummy, moreish. **2** *the least appetizing part of election campaigns:* **appealing**, attractive, inviting, alluring.
– OPPOSITES bland, unappealing.

applaud verb **1** *the audience applauded:* **clap**, put one's hands together; show one's appreciation; informal give someone a big hand. **2** *police have applauded the decision:* **praise**, commend, acclaim, salute, welcome, celebrate, express admiration for, express approval of, look on with favour, approve of, sing the praises of, pay tribute to, speak highly of, take one's hat off to, express respect for.
– OPPOSITES boo, criticize.

applause noun **1** *a massive round of applause:* **clapping**, handclapping; acclamation. **2** *the museum's design won general applause:* **praise**, acclaim, acclamation, admiration, commendation, adulation, favour, approbation, approval, respect; compliments, accolades, tributes.

appliance noun **1** *domestic appliances:* **device**, machine, instrument, gadget, contraption, apparatus, utensil, implement, tool, mechanism, contrivance, labour-saving device; informal gizmo, mod con. **2** *the appliance of science:* **application**, use, exercise, employment, implementation, utilization, practice, applying, discharge, execution, prosecution, enactment; formal praxis.

applicable adjective *the laws applicable to the dispute:* **relevant**, appropriate, pertinent, appurtenant, apposite, germane, material, significant, related, connected; fitting, suitable, apt, befitting, to the point, useful, helpful.
– OPPOSITES inappropriate, irrelevant.

applicant noun *admissions tutors vet applicants for places at university:* **candidate**, interviewee, competitor, contestant, contender, entrant; claimant, suppliant, supplicant, petitioner, postulant; prospective student/employee, job-seeker, job-hunter, auditioner.

application noun **1** *an application for an overdraft:* **request**, appeal, petition, entreaty, plea, solicitation, supplication, requisition, suit, approach, claim, demand. **2** *the application of anti-inflation policies:* **implementation**, use, exercise, employment, utilization, practice, applying, discharge, execution, prosecution, enactment; formal praxis. **3** *the argument is clearest in its application to the theatre:* **relevance**, relevancy, bearing, significance, pertinence, aptness, appositeness, germaneness, importance. **4** *the application of make-up:* **putting on**, rubbing in, applying. **5** *an application to relieve muscle pain:* **ointment**, lotion, cream, rub, salve, emollient, preparation, liniment, embrocation, balm, unguent, poultice. **6** *the job takes a great deal of application:* **diligence**, industriousness, industry, assiduity, commitment, dedication, devotion, conscientiousness, perseverance, persistence, tenacity, doggedness, sedulousness; concentration, attention, attentiveness, steadiness, patience, endurance; effort, hard work, labour, endeavour. **7** *a vector graphics application:* **program**, software, routine.

apply verb **1** *300 people applied for the job:* **put in**, try, bid, appeal, petition, sue, register, audition; request, seek, solicit, claim, ask, try to obtain. **2** *the Act did not apply to Scotland:* **be relevant**, have relevance, have a bearing, appertain, pertain, relate, concern, affect, involve, cover, deal with, touch; be pertinent, be appropriate, be significant. **3** *she applied some ointment:* **put on**, rub in, work in, spread, smear. **4** *a steady pressure should be applied:* **exert**, administer, implement, use, exercise, employ, utilize, bring to bear.
■ **apply oneself** *if he applied himself he could be the best in the world:* be diligent, be industrious, be assiduous, show

commitment, show dedication; work hard, exert oneself, make an effort, try hard, do one's best, give one's all, buckle down, put one's shoulder to the wheel, keep one's nose to the grindstone; strive, endeavour, struggle, labour, toil; pay attention, commit oneself, devote oneself; persevere, persist; informal put one's back in it, knuckle down, get stuck in.

appoint verb **1** *he was appointed chairman:* **nominate**, name, designate, install as, commission, engage, co-opt; select, choose, elect, vote in. **2** *the arbitrator shall appoint a date for the meeting:* **specify**, determine, assign, designate, allot, set, fix, arrange, choose, decide on, establish, settle, ordain, prescribe, decree.
– OPPOSITES reject.

appointed adjective **1** *I reported to HQ at the appointed time:* **scheduled**, arranged, pre-arranged, specified, decided, agreed, determined, assigned, designated, allotted, set, fixed, chosen, established, settled, preordained, ordained, prescribed, decreed. **2** *a well appointed room:* **furnished**, decorated, outfitted, fitted out, provided, supplied.

appointment noun **1** *she failed to keep a six o'clock appointment:* **meeting**, engagement, interview, arrangement, consultation, session; date, rendezvous, assignation; commitment, fixture. **2** *the appointment of directors:* **nomination**, naming, designation, installation, commissioning, engagement, co-option; selection, choosing, election, voting in. **3** *he held an appointment at the university:* **job**, post, position, situation, employment, place, office.

apportion verb *in many households, domestic work is not apportioned equally between partners:* **share**, divide, allocate, distribute, allot, assign, give out, hand out, mete out, deal out, dish out, dole out; ration, measure out; split; informal divvy up.

apposite adjective *each chapter is prefaced by an apposite quotation:* **appropriate**, suitable, fitting, apt, befitting; relevant, pertinent, appurtenant, to the point, applicable, germane, material, congruous, felicitous.
– OPPOSITES inappropriate.

appraisal noun **1** *an objective appraisal of the book:* **assessment**, evaluation, estimation, judgement, rating, gauging, sizing up, summing-up, consideration. **2** *a free insurance appraisal:* **valuation**, estimate, estimation, quotation, pricing; survey.

appraise verb **1** *they appraised their handiwork:* **assess**, evaluate, judge, rate, gauge, review, consider; informal size up. **2** *his goods were appraised at £1,800:* **value**, price, estimate, quote; survey.

appreciable adjective *tea and coffee both contain appreciable amounts of caffeine:* **considerable**, substantial, significant, sizeable, goodly, fair, reasonable, marked; perceptible, noticeable, visible; informal tidy.
– OPPOSITES negligible.

appreciate verb **1** *I'd appreciate your advice:* **be grateful for**, be thankful for, be obliged for, be indebted for, be in your debt for, be appreciative of. **2** *the college appreciated her greatly:* **value**, treasure, admire, respect, hold in high regard, think highly of, think much of. **3** *we appreciate the problems:* **recognize**, acknowledge, realize, know, be aware of, be conscious of, be sensitive to, understand, comprehend; informal be wise to. **4** *a home that will appreciate in value:* **increase**, gain, grow, rise, go up, escalate, soar, rocket.
– OPPOSITES disparage, depreciate, decrease.

appreciation noun **1** *he showed his appreciation:* **gratitude**, thanks, gratefulness, thankfulness, recognition, sense of obligation. **2** *her appreciation of literature:* **valuing**, treasuring, admiration, respect, regard, esteem, high opinion. **3** *an appreciation of the value of teamwork:* **acknowledgement**, recognition, realization, knowledge, awareness, consciousness, understanding, comprehension. **4** *an appreciation of the professor's work:* **review**, critique, criticism, critical analysis, assessment, evaluation, judgement, rating; Brit. informal crit. **5** *the appreciation of the franc against the pound:* **increase**, gain, growth, rise, inflation, escalation.
– OPPOSITES ingratitude, unawareness, depreciation, decrease.

appreciative adjective **1** *children may not seem terribly appreciative at the time:* **grateful**, thankful, obliged, indebted, in someone's debt. **2** *an appreciative audience:* **supportive**, encouraging, sympathetic, responsive; enthusiastic, admiring, approving, complimentary.
– OPPOSITES ungrateful, disparaging.

apprehend verb **1** *the thieves were quickly apprehended:* **arrest**, catch, capture, seize; take prisoner, take into custody, detain, put in jail, put behind bars, imprison, incarcerate; informal collar, nab, nail, run in, pinch, bust, pick up, pull in, feel someone's collar; Brit. informal nick, do. **2** *they are slow to apprehend danger:* **appreciate**, recognize, discern, perceive, make out, take in, realize, grasp, understand, comprehend; informal get the picture; Brit. informal twig, suss (out).

apprehension noun **1** *he was filled with apprehension:* **anxiety**, worry, unease, nervousness, nerves, misgivings, disquiet, concern, tension, trepidation, perturbation, consternation, angst, dread, fear, foreboding; informal butterflies, the willies, the heebie-jeebies. **2** *the apprehension of a perpetrator:* **arrest**, capture, seizure; detention, imprisonment, incarceration; informal collar, nabbing, bust.
– OPPOSITES confidence.

a

apprehensive adjective *I'm a bit apprehensive about seeing her again:* **anxious**, worried, uneasy, nervous, concerned, agitated, tense, afraid, scared, frightened, fearful; informal on tenterhooks, trepidatious.
– OPPOSITES confident.

apprentice noun **trainee**, learner, probationer, novice, beginner, starter; pupil, student; N. Amer. tenderfoot; informal rookie; N. Amer. informal greenhorn.
– OPPOSITES veteran.

apprenticeship noun **traineeship**, training period, studentship, novitiate.

apprise verb *I thought it right to apprise Chris of what had happened:* **inform**, tell, notify, advise, brief, make aware, enlighten, update, keep posted; informal clue in, fill in, put wise, put in the picture.

approach verb **1** *she approached the altar:* **move towards**, come/go towards, advance towards, go/come/draw/move nearer, go/come/draw/move closer, near; close in, gain on; reach, arrive at. **2** *the trade deficit is approaching £20 million:* **border on**, verge on, approximate, touch, nudge, get on for, near, come near to, come close to. **3** *she approached him about leaving his job:* **speak to**, talk to; make advances, make overtures, make a proposal, sound out, proposition. **4** *he approached the problem in the best way:* **tackle**, set about, address oneself to, undertake, get down to, launch into, embark on, go about, get to grips with.
– OPPOSITES leave.
noun **1** *the dog barked at the approach of any intruder:* **advance**, coming, nearing; arrival, appearance; advent. **2** *the approach to the castle:* **driveway**, drive, access road, road, avenue; way. **3** *the traditional British approach:* **method**, procedure, technique, modus operandi, MO, style, way, manner; strategy, tactic, system, means, line of action. **4** *he considered an approach to the High Court:* **proposal**, proposition, submission, application, appeal, plea, request.

approachable adjective **1** *students found the staff approachable:* **friendly**, welcoming, pleasant, agreeable, congenial, affable, cordial; obliging, communicative, helpful. **2** *the south landing is approachable by boat:* **accessible**, attainable, reachable; informal get-at-able.
– OPPOSITES aloof, inaccessible.

approbation noun *he yearned for popular approbation:* **approval**, acceptance, endorsement, appreciation, respect, admiration, commendation, praise, congratulations, acclaim, esteem, applause.
– OPPOSITES criticism.

appropriate adjective *this isn't the appropriate time:* **suitable**, proper, fitting, apt, right; relevant, pertinent, apposite; convenient, opportune; seemly, befitting.
– OPPOSITES unsuitable.

verb **1** *the barons appropriated church lands:* **seize**, commandeer, expropriate, annex, arrogate, sequestrate, sequester, take over, hijack; steal, take; informal swipe, nab, bag; Brit. informal pinch, half-inch, nick. **2** *his images have been appropriated by advertisers:* **plagiarize**, copy; poach, steal; informal rip off. **3** *we are appropriating funds for these expenses:* **allocate**, assign, allot, earmark, set aside, devote, apportion.

approval noun **1** *their proposals went to the ministry for approval:* **acceptance**, agreement, consent, assent, permission, leave, the nod; rubber stamp, sanction, endorsement, ratification, authorization, validation; support, backing; informal the go-ahead, the green light, the OK, the thumbs up. **2** *Lily looked at him with approval:* **approbation**, appreciation, favour, liking, admiration, regard, esteem, respect, praise. **3** *we will send you the goods on approval:* **trial**, sale or return; Brit. informal appro.
– OPPOSITES refusal, dislike.

approve verb **1** *his boss doesn't approve of his lifestyle:* **agree with**, hold with, endorse, support, back, uphold, subscribe to, recommend, advocate, be in favour of, favour, think well of, like, appreciate, take kindly to; be pleased with, admire, applaud, praise. **2** *the government approved the proposals:* **accept**, agree to, consent to, assent to, give one's blessing to, bless, rubber-stamp, give the nod; ratify, sanction, endorse, authorize, validate, pass; support, back; informal give the go-ahead, give the green light, give the OK, give the thumbs-up.
– OPPOSITES condemn, refuse.

approximate adjective *all measurements are approximate:* **estimated**, rough, imprecise, inexact, indefinite, broad, loose; N. Amer. informal ballpark.
– OPPOSITES precise.
verb *this scenario probably approximates to the truth:* **be/come close to**, be/come near to, approach, border on, verge on; resemble, be similar to, be not unlike.

approximately adverb *there are guided tours lasting approximately an hour:* **roughly**, about, around, circa, round about, more or less, in the neighbourhood of, in the region of, of the order of, something like, give or take (a few); near to, close to, nearly, almost, approaching; Brit. getting on for; informal pushing; N. Amer. informal in the ballpark of.
– OPPOSITES precisely.

approximation noun **1** *the figure is only an approximation:* **estimate**, estimation, guess, rough calculation; informal guesstimate; N. Amer. informal ballpark figure. **2** *an approximation to the truth:* **semblance**, resemblance, likeness, similarity, correspondence.

a priori adjective *a priori reasoning:* **theoretical**, deduced, deductive, inferred, postulated, suppositional; scientific.

– OPPOSITES empirical.
adverb *the results cannot be predicted a priori:* **theoretically**, deductively, scientifically.

apron noun **pinafore**, overall; informal **pinny**.

apropos preposition *he was asked a question apropos his resignation:* **with reference to**, with regard to, with respect to, regarding, concerning, on the subject of, connected with, about, re.
adjective *the word 'conglomerate' was decidedly apropos:* **appropriate**, pertinent, relevant, apposite, apt, applicable, suitable, germane, material.
– OPPOSITES inappropriate.
■ **apropos of nothing** irrelevantly, arbitrarily, at random, for no reason, illogically.

apt adjective **1** *it was a very apt description of how I felt:* **suitable**, fitting, appropriate, befitting, relevant, applicable, apposite; Brit. informal **spot on**. **2** *they are apt to get a mite slipshod:* **inclined**, given, likely, liable, disposed, predisposed, prone. **3** *an apt pupil:* **clever**, quick, bright, sharp, smart, intelligent, able, gifted, adept, astute.
– OPPOSITES inappropriate, unlikely, slow.

aptitude noun *he showed an aptitude for skiing:* **talent**, gift, flair, bent, skill, knack, facility, ability, capability, potential, capacity, faculty, genius.

aquatic adjective *aquatic plants:* **marine**, water, saltwater, freshwater, seawater, sea, oceanic, river.

aqueduct noun **conduit**, race, channel, watercourse, sluice, sluiceway, spillway; bridge, viaduct.

aquiline adjective *he had an aquiline nose:* **hooked**, curved, bent, angular; beak-like.

arable adjective *acres of arable land:* **farmable**, cultivable, cultivatable; fertile, productive, fecund.

arbiter noun **1** *he believed Britain could play a major role as arbiter between Moscow and Washington.* See **ARBITRATOR**. **2** *the great arbiter of fashion:* **authority**, judge, controller, director; master, expert, pundit.

arbitrary adjective **1** *an arbitrary decision:* **capricious**, whimsical, random, chance, unpredictable; casual, wanton, unmotivated, motiveless, unreasoned, unsupported, irrational, illogical, groundless, unjustified. **2** *the arbitrary power of a prince:* **autocratic**, dictatorial, autarchic, undemocratic, despotic, tyrannical, authoritarian; absolute, uncontrolled, unlimited, unrestrained.
– OPPOSITES reasoned, democratic.

arbitrate verb *the board has the power to arbitrate in disputes:* **adjudicate**, judge, referee, umpire; mediate, conciliate, intervene, intercede; settle, decide, resolve, pass judgement.

arbitration noun *the council called for arbitration to settle the dispute:* **adjudication**, judgement; mediation, mediatorship, conciliation, intervention.

arbitrator noun *the facts of the case were put to an independent arbitrator:* **adjudicator**, arbiter, judge, referee, umpire; mediator, conciliator, intervenor, intercessor, go-between.

arbour noun **bower**, alcove, grotto, recess, pergola, gazebo.

arc noun *the arc of a circle:* **curve**, arch, crescent, semicircle, half-moon; curvature, convexity.
verb *I sent the ball arcing out over the river:* **curl**, curve; arch.

arcade noun **1** *a classical arcade:* **gallery**, colonnade, cloister, loggia, portico, peristyle, stoa. **2** (Brit.) *she went to a cafe in the arcade:* **shopping centre**, shopping precinct; N. Amer. plaza, mall, shopping mall.

arcane adjective *the arcane world of the legal profession:* **mysterious**, secret, covert, clandestine; enigmatic, esoteric, obscure, abstruse, recondite, recherché, impenetrable, opaque.

arch¹ noun *the arch of his spine:* **curve**, bow, bend, arc, curvature, convexity; hunch, crook.
verb *she arched her eyebrows:* **curve**, arc; raise.

arch² adjective *an arch grin:* **mischievous**, teasing, saucy, knowing, playful, roguish, impish, cheeky, tongue-in-cheek.

arch- combining form *his arch-enemy:* **chief**, principal, foremost, leading, main, major, prime, premier, greatest; informal **number one**.
– OPPOSITES minor.

archaic adjective *'smite' is an archaic word:* **obsolete**, out of date, old-fashioned, outmoded, behind the times, bygone, anachronistic, antiquated, superannuated, antediluvian, olde worlde; ancient, old, extinct, defunct; informal out of the ark.
– OPPOSITES modern.

arched adjective *a great arched ceiling:* **vaulted**, domed, curved, bowed.

archetypal adjective *Blackpool is the archetypal British seaside resort:* **quintessential**, classic, most typical, representative, model, exemplary, textbook, copybook; stock, stereotypical, prototypical.
– OPPOSITES atypical.

archetype noun **quintessence**, essence, typification, representative, model, embodiment, prototype, stereotype; original, pattern, standard, paradigm.

architect noun **1** *the architect of Durham Cathedral:* **designer**, planner, draughtsman. **2** *the architect of the National Health Service:* **originator**, author, creator, founder, (founding) father; engineer, inventor, mastermind.

architecture noun **1** *modern architecture:* **building design**, building style, planning, building, construction. **2** *the architecture of a computer system:* **structure**, construction,

a

organization, layout, design, build, anatomy, make-up; informal set-up.

archive noun 1 *she delved into the family archives:* **records**, annals, chronicles, accounts; papers, documents, files; history. 2 *the National Sound Archive:* **record office**, registry, repository, museum, chancery. verb *the videos are archived for future use:* **file**, log, catalogue, document, record, register; store, cache.

arctic adjective *arctic weather conditions:* **freezing**, wintry, bitterly cold, frozen, icy, glacial, gelid, sub-zero, polar, Siberian.
– OPPOSITES tropical.

ardent adjective *an ardent feminist:* **passionate**, fervent, zealous, wholehearted, vehement, intense, fierce; enthusiastic, keen, eager, avid, committed, dedicated.
– OPPOSITES apathetic.

ardour noun *she was unaccustomed to being kissed with such ardour:* **passion**, fervour, zeal, vehemence, intensity, fire, emotion; enthusiasm, eagerness, gusto, keenness, dedication.
– OPPOSITES apathy.

arduous adjective *an arduous journey:* **onerous**, taxing, difficult, hard, heavy, laborious, burdensome, strenuous, vigorous, back-breaking; demanding, tough, challenging, formidable; exhausting, tiring, punishing, gruelling; informal killing; Brit. informal knackering.
– OPPOSITES easy.

area noun 1 *an inner-city area:* **district**, region, zone, sector, quarter; locality, locale, neighbourhood, parish, patch; tract, belt; informal neck of the woods; Brit. informal manor; N. Amer. informal turf, hood. 2 *specific areas of scientific knowledge:* **field**, sphere, discipline, realm, domain, sector, province, territory, line. 3 *the dining area:* **section**, space; place, room. 4 *the area of a circle:* **expanse**, extent, size, scope, compass; dimensions, proportions.

arena noun 1 *an ice-hockey arena:* **stadium**, amphitheatre, coliseum; ground, field, ring, rink, pitch, court; N. Amer. bowl, park. 2 *the political arena:* **scene**, sphere, realm, province, domain, sector, forum, territory, world.

argot noun *a word borrowed from the argot of criminals:* **jargon**, slang, idiom, cant, parlance, vernacular, patois; dialect, speech, language; informal lingo.

arguable adjective 1 *he had an arguable claim for asylum:* **tenable**, defendable, defensible, supportable, sustainable, able to hold water; reasonable, viable, acceptable. 2 *it is arguable whether these routes are worthwhile:* **debatable**, questionable, open to question, controversial, contentious, doubtful, uncertain, moot.
– OPPOSITES untenable, certain.

arguably adverb *she is arguably the greatest female tennis player of all time:* **possibly**,

conceivably, feasibly, plausibly, probably, maybe, perhaps.

argue verb 1 *they argued that the government was to blame:* **contend**, assert, maintain, insist, hold, claim, reason, swear, allege; Law depose; formal opine. 2 *the children are always arguing:* **quarrel**, disagree, row, squabble, fall out, bicker, fight, wrangle, dispute, feud, have words, cross swords, lock horns, be at each other's throats. 3 *it is hard to argue the point:* **dispute**, debate, discuss, controvert.

argument noun 1 *he had an argument with Tony:* **quarrel**, disagreement, squabble, fight, dispute, wrangle, clash, altercation, feud, contretemps, disputation, falling-out; informal tiff, barney, slanging match; Brit. informal row. 2 *arguments for the existence of God:* **reasoning**, justification, explanation, rationalization; case, defence, vindication; evidence, reasons, grounds.

argumentative adjective *he was argumentative, opinionated, and outspoken:* **quarrelsome**, disputatious, captious, contrary, cantankerous, contentious; belligerent, bellicose, combative, antagonistic, truculent, pugnacious.

arid adjective 1 *an arid landscape:* **dry**, dried up, waterless, moistureless, parched, scorched, baked, thirsty, droughty, desert; barren, infertile. 2 *this town has an arid, empty feel:* **dreary**, dull, drab, dry, sterile, colourless, unstimulating, uninspiring, flat, boring, uninteresting, lifeless.
– OPPOSITES wet, fertile, vibrant.

arise verb 1 *many problems arose:* **come to light**, become apparent, appear, emerge, crop up, turn up, surface, spring up; occur. 2 *injuries arising from defective products:* **result**, proceed, follow, ensue, derive, stem, originate; be caused by.

aristocracy noun *members of the aristocracy:* **nobility**, peerage, gentry, upper class, ruling class, elite, high society, establishment, haut monde; aristocrats, lords, ladies, peers (of the realm), nobles, noblemen, noblewomen; informal upper crust, top drawer, aristos; Brit. informal nobs, toffs.
– OPPOSITES working class.

aristocrat noun *nobleman*, noblewoman, lord, lady, peer (of the realm), peeress, grandee; informal aristo; Brit. informal toff, nob.
– OPPOSITES commoner.

aristocratic adjective 1 *an aristocratic family:* **noble**, titled, upper-class, blue-blooded, high-born, well born, elite; Brit. upmarket; informal upper crust, top drawer; Brit. informal posh. 2 *he had a stately, aristocratic manner:* **refined**, polished, courtly, dignified, decorous, gracious, fine, gentlemanly, ladylike; haughty, proud.
– OPPOSITES working-class, vulgar.

arm[1] noun 1 *an arm of the sea:* **inlet**, creek, cove, fjord, bay, voe; estuary, firth, strait(s), sound, channel. 2 *the political arm of the group:* **branch**, section, department, division, wing, sector, detachment, offshoot, extension.

arm[2] verb **1** *he armed himself with a revolver:* **equip**, provide, supply, furnish, issue, fit out. **2** *you have to arm yourself against criticism:* **prepare**, forearm, make ready, brace, steel, fortify.

armada noun *an armada of forty-five warships:* **fleet**, flotilla, squadron.

armaments plural noun **arms**, weapons, weaponry, firearms, guns, ordnance, artillery, munitions, materiel.

armistice noun *an armistice was concluded between the warring countries:* **truce**, ceasefire, peace, suspension of hostilities.

armour noun **protective covering**, armour plate; historical chain mail.

armoured adjective *an armoured vehicle:* **armour-plated**, steel-plated, ironclad; bulletproof, bombproof; reinforced, toughened.

armoury noun **arsenal**, arms depot, arms cache, ordnance depot, magazine, ammunition dump.

arms plural noun **1** *the illegal export of arms:* **weapons**, weaponry, firearms, guns, ordnance, artillery, armaments, munitions, materiel. **2** *the family arms:* **crest**, emblem, coat of arms, heraldic device, insignia, escutcheon, shield.

army noun **1** *the invading army:* **armed force**, military force, land force, military, soldiery, infantry, militia; troops, soldiers. **2** *an army of tourists:* **crowd**, swarm, multitude, horde, mob, gang, throng, mass, flock, herd, pack.

aroma noun *the tantalizing aroma of fresh coffee:* **smell**, odour, fragrance, scent, perfume, bouquet, nose.

aromatic adjective *an aromatic herb:* **fragrant**, scented, perfumed, fragranced, odoriferous.

around adverb **1** *there were houses scattered around:* **on every side**, on all sides, throughout, all over (the place), everywhere; about, here and there. **2** *he turned around:* **in the opposite direction**, to face the other way, backwards, to the rear. **3** *there was no one around:* **nearby**, near, about, close by, close (at hand), at hand, in the vicinity, at close range. preposition **1** *the palazzo is built around a courtyard:* **on all sides of**, about, encircling, surrounding. **2** *they drove around town:* **about**, all over, in/to all parts of. **3** *around three miles:* **approximately**, about, round about, circa, roughly, something like, more or less, in the region of, in the neighbourhood of, give or take (a few); nearly, close to, approaching; Brit. getting on for; N. Amer. informal in the ballpark of.

arouse verb **1** *they had aroused his suspicion:* **induce**, prompt, trigger, stir up, bring out, kindle, fire, spark off, provoke, engender, cause, foster. **2** *his ability to arouse the masses:* **stir up**, rouse, galvanize, excite,

electrify, stimulate, inspire, inspirit, move, fire up, whip up, get going, inflame, agitate, goad, incite. **3** *his touch aroused her:* **excite**, stimulate (sexually), titillate; informal turn on, get going, give a thrill to, light someone's fire.
– OPPOSITES allay, pacify, turn off.

arraign verb **1** *he was arraigned for murder:* **indict**, prosecute, put on trial, bring to trial, take to court, lay/file/prefer charges against, summons, cite; accuse of, charge with; N. Amer. impeach; informal do. **2** *they bitterly arraigned the government:* **criticize**, censure, attack, condemn, chastise, lambaste, rebuke, admonish, remonstrate with, take to task, berate, reproach; informal knock, slam, blast, lay into; Brit. informal slate, slag off; formal castigate, excoriate.
– OPPOSITES acquit, praise.

arrange verb **1** *she arranged the flowers:* **order**, set out, lay out, array, position, dispose, present, display, exhibit; group, sort, organize, tidy. **2** *they hoped to arrange a meeting:* **organize**, fix (up), plan, schedule, pencil in, contrive, settle on, decide, determine, agree. **3** *he arranged the piece for a full orchestra:* **adapt**, set, score, orchestrate.

arrangement noun **1** *the arrangement of the furniture:* **positioning**, disposition, order, presentation, display; grouping, organization, alignment. **2** *how are the arrangements for your trip going?* **preparation**, plan, provision; planning, groundwork. **3** *we had an arrangement:* **agreement**, deal, understanding, bargain, settlement, pact, modus vivendi. **4** *an arrangement of Beethoven's symphonies:* **adaptation**, orchestration, instrumentation.

array noun *a huge array of cars met our eyes:* **range**, collection, selection, assortment, diversity, variety; arrangement, assemblage, line-up, formation; display, exhibition, exposition. verb **1** *a buffet was arrayed on the table:* **arrange**, assemble, group, order, range, place, position, set out, lay out, dispose; display. **2** *he was arrayed in grey flannel:* **dress**, attire, clothe, garb, deck (out), outfit, get up, turn out.

arrears plural noun *rent arrears:* **debts**, money owing, outstanding payment(s), liabilities, dues.
– OPPOSITES credit.
■ **in arrears** behind, behindhand, late, overdue, in the red, in debt.

arrest verb **1** *police arrested him for murder:* **apprehend**, take into custody, take prisoner, detain, put in jail; informal pick up, pull in, pinch, bust, nab, do, collar; Brit. informal nick, feel someone's collar. **2** *the spread of the disease can be arrested:* **stop**, halt, check, block, hinder, restrict, limit, inhibit, impede, curb; prevent, obstruct.
– OPPOSITES release, start.
noun **1** *a warrant for your arrest:* **detention**,

a

apprehension, seizure, capture. **2** *a cardiac arrest:* **stoppage**, halt, interruption.

arresting adjective *an arresting image:* **striking**, eye-catching, conspicuous, engaging, impressive, imposing, spectacular, dramatic, breathtaking, dazzling, stunning, awe-inspiring; remarkable, outstanding, distinctive.
– OPPOSITES inconspicuous.

arrival noun **1** *they awaited Ruth's arrival:* **coming**, appearance, entrance, entry, approach. **2** *the arrival of democracy:* **emergence**, appearance, advent, coming, dawn, onset, inauguration, origin, birth.
– OPPOSITES departure, end.

arrive verb **1** *more police arrived:* **come**, turn up, get here/there, make it, appear, enter, present oneself, come along, materialize; informal show (up), roll in/up, blow in, show one's face. **2** *we arrived at his house:* **reach**, get to, come to, make, make it to, gain, end up at; informal wind up at. **3** *they arrived at an agreement:* **reach**, achieve, attain, gain, accomplish; work out, draw up, put together, strike, settle on; informal clinch. **4** *the wedding finally arrived:* **happen**, occur, take place, come about; present itself, crop up. **5** *quadraphony had arrived:* **emerge**, appear, surface, dawn, be born, come into being, arise.
– OPPOSITES depart, leave.

arrogant adjective *he's arrogant and opinionated:* **haughty**, conceited, self-important, egotistic, full of oneself, superior; overbearing, pompous, bumptious, imperious, overweening; proud, immodest; informal high and mighty, too big for one's boots, big-headed.
– OPPOSITES modest.

arrow noun **1** *a bow and arrow:* **shaft**, bolt, dart. **2** *the arrow pointed right:* **pointer**, indicator, marker, needle.

arsenal noun **1** *Britain's nuclear arsenal:* **weapons**, weaponry, arms, armaments. **2** *mutineers broke into the arsenal:* **armoury**, arms depot, arms cache, ordnance depot, magazine, ammunition dump.

arson noun *the fire is being treated as arson:* **incendiarism**, pyromania; Brit. fire-raising.

arsonist noun **incendiary**, pyromaniac; Brit. fire-raiser; informal firebug, pyro; N. Amer. informal torch.

art noun **1** *the art of writing:* **skill**, craft, technique, knack, facility, ability. **2** *she uses art to achieve her aims:* **cunning**, artfulness, slyness, craftiness, guile; deceit, duplicity, artifice, wiles.

artful adjective *an artful political ruse:* **sly**, crafty, cunning, wily, scheming, devious, Machiavellian, sneaky, tricky, conniving, designing, calculating; canny, shrewd; deceitful, duplicitous, disingenuous, underhand; informal foxy, shifty.
– OPPOSITES ingenuous.

article noun **1** *small household articles:*

object, thing, item, artefact, commodity, product. **2** *an article in The Times:* **report**, account, story, write-up, feature, item, piece (of writing), column, review, commentary. **3** *the crucial article of the treaty:* **clause**, section, subsection, point, item, paragraph, division, subdivision, part, portion.

articulate adjective *an articulate speaker:* **eloquent**, fluent, effective, persuasive, lucid, expressive, silver-tongued; intelligible, comprehensible, understandable.
– OPPOSITES unintelligible.
verb *they were unable to articulate their emotions:* **express**, voice, vocalize, put in words, communicate, state; air, ventilate, vent, pour out; utter, say, speak, enunciate, pronounce; informal come out with.

articulated adjective *an articulated lorry:* **hinged**, jointed, segmented.

artifice noun *an industry dominated by artifice:* **trickery**, deceit, deception, duplicity, guile, cunning, artfulness, wiliness, craftiness, slyness, chicanery; fraud, fraudulence.

artificial adjective **1** *artificial flowers:* **synthetic**, fake, faux, imitation, mock, ersatz, substitute, replica, reproduction; man-made, manufactured, fabricated; plastic; informal pretend. **2** *an artificial smile:* **insincere**, feigned, false, unnatural, contrived, put-on, exaggerated, forced, laboured, strained, hollow; informal pretend, phoney.
– OPPOSITES natural, genuine.

artillery noun **ordnance**, (big) guns, cannon(s), cannonry.

artisan noun **craftsman**, craftswoman, craftsperson; skilled worker, technician; smith, wright, journeyman.

artist noun **1** *a Belfast mural artist:* **designer**, creator, originator, producer; old master. **2** *the surgeon is an artist with the knife:* **expert**, master, maestro, past master, virtuoso, genius; informal pro, ace; Brit. informal dab hand.
– OPPOSITES novice.

artiste noun **entertainer**, performer, showman, artist; player, musician, singer, dancer, actor, actress; star.

artistic adjective **1** *he's very artistic:* **creative**, imaginative, inventive, expressive; sensitive, perceptive, discerning. **2** *artistic dances:* **aesthetic**, aesthetically pleasing, beautiful, attractive, fine; decorative, ornamental; tasteful, stylish, elegant, exquisite.
– OPPOSITES unimaginative, inelegant.

artistry noun *all four perform with innate artistry:* **creative skill**, creativity, art, skill, talent, genius, brilliance, flair, proficiency, virtuosity, finesse, style; craftsmanship, workmanship.

artless adjective *artless sincerity:* **natural**, ingenuous, naive, simple, innocent,

childlike, guileless; candid, open, sincere, unaffected.
– OPPOSITES scheming.

as conjunction **1** *she saw him as he disappeared:* **while,** just as, even as, just when, at the time that, at the moment that. **2** *we all felt as Frank did:* **in the (same) way that,** the (same) way; informal like. **3** *do as you're told:* **what,** that which. **4** *they were free, as the case had not been proved:* **because,** since, seeing that/as, in view of the fact that, owing to the fact that; informal on account of. **5** *relatively short distances, as Paris to Lyons:* **such as,** like, for instance, for example, e.g. **6** *I'm away a lot, as you know:* **which,** a fact which.
preposition **1** *he was dressed as a policeman:* **like,** in the guise of, so as to appear to be. **2** *I'm speaking to you as your friend:* **in the role of,** being, acting as.
■ **as for/to** concerning, with respect to, on the subject of, in the matter of, as regards, with regard to, regarding, with reference to, re, in re, apropos, vis-à-vis.
■ **as it were** so to speak, in a manner of speaking, to some extent, so to say; informal sort of.
■ **as yet** so far, thus far, yet, still, up till now, up to now.

ascend verb *she ascended the stairs:* **climb,** go up/upwards, move up/upwards, rise (up); mount, scale, conquer; take to the air, take off.
– OPPOSITES descend.

ascendancy noun *the ascendancy of good over evil:* **dominance,** domination, supremacy, superiority, paramountcy, predominance, primacy, dominion, hegemony, authority, control, command, power, rule, sovereignty, lordship, leadership, influence.
– OPPOSITES subordination.

ascendant
■ **in the ascendant** *the communist parties of the republics were in the ascendant:* rising (in power), on the rise, on the way up, up-and-coming, flourishing, prospering, burgeoning.

ascent noun **1** *the first ascent of the Matterhorn:* **climb,** scaling, conquest. **2** *a balloon ascent:* **rise,** climb, launch, take-off, lift-off, blast-off. **3** *the ascent grew steeper:* **(upward) slope,** incline, rise, upward gradient, inclination.
– OPPOSITES descent, drop.

ascertain verb *we ascertained the exact location of the vehicle:* **find out,** discover, get to know, work out, make out, fathom (out), learn, deduce, divine, discern, see, understand, comprehend; establish, determine, verify, confirm; informal figure out; Brit. informal suss (out).

ascetic adjective *an ascetic life:* **austere,** self-denying, abstinent, abstemious, self-disciplined, self-abnegating; simple,

puritanical, monastic; reclusive, eremitic, hermitic; celibate, chaste.
– OPPOSITES sybaritic.
noun *a desert ascetic:* **abstainer,** puritan, recluse, hermit, solitary; fakir, Sufi, dervish, sadhu, muni; historical anchorite.
– OPPOSITES sybarite.

ascribe verb *he ascribed Jane's short temper to her upset stomach:* **attribute,** assign, put down, accredit, credit, chalk up, impute; blame on, lay at the door of; connect with, associate with.

ashamed adjective **1** *she felt ashamed that she had hit him:* **sorry,** shamefaced, abashed, sheepish, guilty, contrite, remorseful, repentant, penitent, regretful, rueful, apologetic; embarrassed, mortified. **2** *he was ashamed to admit it:* **reluctant,** loath, unwilling, disinclined, indisposed, afraid.
– OPPOSITES proud, pleased.

ashen adjective *his ashen face:* **pale,** wan, pasty, grey, colourless, pallid, white, waxen, ghostly, bloodless.

ashore adverb *the seals came ashore to breed:* **on to (the) land,** on to the shore; shorewards, landwards; on to the shore, on (dry) land.

aside adverb **1** *they stood aside:* **to one side,** to the side, on one side; apart, away, separately. **2** *that aside, he seemed a nice man:* **apart,** notwithstanding.
noun *'Her parents died,' said Mrs Manton in an aside:* **whispered remark,** confidential remark, stage whisper; digression, incidental remark, obiter dictum, deviation.
■ **aside from** apart from, besides, in addition to, not counting, barring, other than, but (for), excluding, not including, except (for), excepting, leaving out, save (for).

asinine adjective *Lydia ignored his asinine remark:* **foolish,** stupid, brainless, mindless, senseless, idiotic, imbecilic, ridiculous, ludicrous, absurd, nonsensical, fatuous, silly, inane, witless, empty-headed; informal half-witted, dumb, moronic; Brit. informal daft; Scottish & N. English informal glaikit.
– OPPOSITES intelligent, sensible.

ask verb **1** *he asked what time we opened:* **enquire,** query, want to know; question, interrogate, quiz. **2** *they want to ask a few questions:* **put (forward),** pose, raise, submit; get an answer to. **3** *don't be afraid to ask for advice:* **request,** demand; solicit, seek, crave, apply, petition, call, appeal, sue. **4** *let's ask them to dinner:* **invite,** bid, summon, have someone over/round.
– OPPOSITES answer.

askance adverb *they look askance at anything foreign:* **suspiciously,** sceptically, cynically, mistrustfully, distrustfully, doubtfully, dubiously; disapprovingly, contemptuously, scornfully, disdainfully.
– OPPOSITES approvingly.

askew adjective *her hat was slightly askew:*

crooked, lopsided, tilted, angled, at an angle, skew, skewed, slanted, aslant, awry, squint, out of true, to/on one side, uneven, off-centre, asymmetrical; informal cockeyed, wonky; Brit. informal skew-whiff.
– OPPOSITES straight.

asleep adjective *she was asleep in bed:* **sleeping**, in a deep sleep, napping, catnapping, dozing, drowsing; informal snoozing, dead to the world; Brit. informal kipping; humorous in the land of Nod.
– OPPOSITES awake.

aspect noun **1** *the photos depict every aspect of life:* **feature**, facet, side, characteristic, particular, detail; angle, slant. **2** *his face had a sinister aspect:* **appearance**, look, air, cast, mien, demeanour, expression; atmosphere, mood, quality, ambience, feeling. **3** *a summer house with a southern aspect:* **outlook**, view, exposure; situation, position, location. **4** *the front aspect of the hotel:* **face**, elevation, facade, side.

aspersions plural noun *he claimed he could prove the aspersions groundless:* **vilification**, disparagement, denigration, defamation, condemnation, criticism, denunciation, slander, libel, calumny; slurs, smears, insults, slights; informal mud-slinging, bad-mouthing; Brit. informal slagging off; formal castigation.
▪ **cast aspersions on** vilify, disparage, denigrate, defame, run down, impugn, belittle, criticize, condemn, decry, denounce, pillory; malign, slander, libel, discredit; informal pull apart, throw mud at, knock, bad-mouth; Brit. informal rubbish, slate, slag off.

asphyxiate verb *they were asphyxiated by the carbon monoxide fumes:* **suffocate**, choke to death, smother, stifle; throttle, strangle.

aspiration noun *the needs and aspirations of the people:* **desire**, hope, dream, wish, longing, yearning; aim, ambition, expectation, goal, target.

aspire verb *other people will aspire to be like you:* **desire**, hope, dream, long, yearn, set one's heart on, wish, want, be desirous of; aim, seek, pursue, set one's sights on.

aspiring adjective *advice to aspiring writers:* **would-be**, aspirant, hopeful, budding; potential, prospective, future; ambitious, determined; informal wannabe.

ass noun **donkey**, jackass, jenny; Scottish cuddy; Brit. informal moke, neddy.

assail verb **1** *the army moved in to assail the enemy:* **attack**, assault, pounce on, set upon/about, fall on, charge, rush, storm; informal lay into, tear into, pitch into. **2** *she was assailed by doubts:* **plague**, torment, rack, beset, dog, trouble, disturb, worry, bedevil, nag, vex. **3** *critics assailed the policy:* **criticize**, censure, attack, condemn, pillory, revile; informal knock, slam; Brit. informal slate, slag off; formal castigate.

assailant noun **attacker**, mugger, assaulter.

assassin noun **murderer**, killer, gunman; executioner; informal hit man, hired gun.

assassinate verb *John F. Kennedy was assassinated in 1963:* **murder**, kill, slaughter; eliminate, execute; N. Amer. terminate; informal hit.

assassination noun **murder**, killing, slaughter, homicide; political execution, elimination; N. Amer. termination; informal hit.

assault verb **1** *he assaulted a police officer:* **attack**, hit, strike, punch, beat up, thump; pummel, pound, batter; informal clout, wallop, belt, clobber, bop, biff, sock, deck, slug, plug, lay into, do over, rough up; Austral. informal quilt. **2** *they left to assault the hill:* **attack**, assail, pounce on, set upon, strike, fall on, swoop on, rush, storm, besiege.
noun **1** *he was charged with assault:* **battery**, violence; sexual assault, rape; Brit. grievous bodily harm, GBH, actual bodily harm, ABH. **2** *an assault on the city:* **attack**, strike, onslaught, offensive, charge, push, thrust, invasion, bombardment, sortie, incursion, raid, blitz, campaign.

assay noun *new plate was brought for assay:* **evaluation**, assessment, appraisal, analysis, examination, tests, inspection, scrutiny.
verb *gold is assayed to determine its purity:* **evaluate**, assess, appraise, analyse, examine, test, inspect, scrutinize, probe.

assemble verb **1** *a crowd had assembled:* **gather**, collect, get together, congregate, convene, meet, muster, rally; formal foregather. **2** *he assembled the suspects:* **bring/call together**, gather, collect, round up, marshal, muster, summon. **3** *how to assemble the kite:* **construct**, build, fabricate, manufacture, erect, set up, put/piece together, connect, join.
– OPPOSITES disperse, dismantle.

assembly noun **1** *an assembly of dockers:* **gathering**, meeting, congregation, convention, rally, convocation, assemblage, group, body, crowd, throng, company; informal get-together. **2** *the labour needed in car assembly:* **construction**, manufacture, building, fabrication, erection.

assent noun *they are likely to give their assent:* **agreement**, acceptance, approval, approbation, consent, acquiescence, compliance, concurrence, the nod; sanction, endorsement, confirmation; permission, leave, blessing; informal the go-ahead, the green light, the OK, the thumbs up.
– OPPOSITES dissent, refusal.
verb *he assented to the change:* **agree to**, accept, approve, consent to, acquiesce in, concur in, give one's blessing to, give the nod; sanction, endorse, confirm; informal give the go-ahead, give the green light, give the OK, OK, give the thumbs up; formal accede to.
– OPPOSITES refuse.

assert verb **1** *they asserted that all aboard were safe:* **declare**, maintain, contend, argue, state, claim, propound, proclaim, announce,

pronounce, swear, insist, avow. **2** *we find it difficult to assert our rights:* **insist on**, stand up for, uphold, defend, contend, establish, press/push for, stress.
■ **assert oneself** behave/speak confidently, be assertive, put oneself forward, make one's presence felt; informal put one's foot down.

assertion noun **1** *I questioned his assertion:* **declaration**, contention, statement, claim, opinion, proclamation, announcement, pronouncement, protestation, avowal. **2** *an assertion of the right to march:* **defence**, upholding; insistence on.

assertive adjective *the job may call for assertive behaviour:* **confident**, self-confident, bold, decisive, assured, self-assured, self-possessed; authoritative, strong-willed, forceful, insistent, determined, commanding, pushy; informal feisty.
– OPPOSITES timid.

assess verb **1** *the committee's power is hard to assess:* **evaluate**, judge, gauge, rate, estimate, appraise, get the measure of, determine, weigh up, analyse; informal size up. **2** *the damage was assessed at £5 billion:* **value**, calculate, work out, determine, fix, cost, price, estimate.

assessment noun **1** *a teacher's assessment of the pupil's abilities:* **evaluation**, judgement, rating, estimation, appraisal, analysis, opinion. **2** *some assessments valued the estate at £2 million:* **valuation**, calculation, costing, pricing, estimate.

asset noun **1** *he sees his age as an asset:* **benefit**, advantage, blessing, good point, strong point, strength, forte, virtue, recommendation, attraction, resource, boon, merit, bonus, plus, pro. **2** *the seizure of all their assets:* **property**, resources, estate, holdings, possessions, effects, goods, valuables, belongings, chattels.
– OPPOSITES liability.

assiduous adjective *she was assiduous in pointing out every feature:* **diligent**, careful, meticulous, thorough, sedulous, attentive, conscientious, punctilious, painstaking, rigorous, particular; persevering.

assign verb **1** *a young doctor was assigned the task:* **allocate**, allot, give, set; charge with, entrust with. **2** *she was assigned to a new post:* **appoint**, promote, delegate, commission, post, co-opt; select for, choose for, install in. **3** *we assign large sums of money to travel budgets:* **earmark**, designate, set aside, reserve, appropriate, allot, allocate, apportion. **4** *he may assign the money to a third party:* **transfer**, make over, give, pass, hand over/down, convey, consign.

assignation noun *he and Jane arranged a secret assignation in town:* **rendezvous**, date, appointment, meeting.

assignment noun **1** *I'm going to finish this assignment tonight:* **task**, piece of work, job, duty, chore, mission, errand, undertaking, exercise, business, endeavour, enterprise; project, homework. **2** *the assignment of tasks:* **allocation**, allotment, issuance, designation; sharing out, apportionment, distribution, handing out, dispensation. **3** *the assignment of property:* **transfer**, making over, giving, handing down, consignment.

assimilate verb **1** *the amount of information he can assimilate:* **absorb**, take in, acquire, pick up, grasp, comprehend, understand, learn, master; digest, ingest. **2** *many tribes were assimilated by Turkic peoples:* **subsume**, incorporate, integrate, absorb, engulf, acculturate; co-opt, adopt, embrace, admit.

assist verb **1** *I spend my time assisting the chef:* **help**, aid, abet, lend a (helping) hand to, oblige, accommodate, serve; collaborate with, work with; support, back (up), second; informal pitch in with; Brit. informal muck in with. **2** *the exchange rates assisted the firm's expansion:* **facilitate**, aid, ease, expedite, spur, promote, boost, benefit, foster, encourage, stimulate, precipitate, accelerate, advance, further, forward.
– OPPOSITES hinder, impede.

assistance noun *they said that they could manage and did not need assistance:* **help**, aid, support, backing, reinforcement, succour, relief, intervention, cooperation, collaboration; a (helping) hand, a good turn; informal a break, a leg up.
– OPPOSITES hindrance.

assistant noun **1** *a photographer's assistant:* **subordinate**, deputy, second (in command), number two, right-hand man/woman, aide, personal assistant, PA, attendant, mate, apprentice, junior, auxiliary; hired hand, hired help, helper, man/girl Friday; informal sidekick, gofer; Brit. informal dogsbody, skivvy. **2** *Judy was an assistant in the local shop:* **sales assistant**, salesperson, saleswoman/girl, salesman, server, checkout operator; seller, vendor; N. Amer. clerk; informal counter-jumper.

associate verb **1** *the colours that we associate with fire:* **link**, connect, relate, identify, equate, bracket, set side by side. **2** *I was forced to associate with them:* **mix**, keep company, mingle, socialize, go around, rub shoulders, fraternize, consort, have dealings; N. Amer. rub elbows; informal hobnob, hang out/around/round, be thick with; Brit. informal hang about. **3** *the firm is associated with a local charity:* **affiliate**, align, connect, join, attach, team up, be in league, ally; merge, integrate, confederate.
noun *his business associate:* **partner**, colleague, co-worker, workmate, mate, comrade, ally, confederate; connection, contact, acquaintance; collaborator; informal crony; Austral./NZ informal offsider.

associated adjective **1** *salaries and associated costs:* **related**, connected, linked, correlated,

similar, corresponding; attendant, accompanying, incidental. **2** *they share in the results and net assets of their associated company:* **affiliated**, allied, integrated, amalgamated, federated, confederated, syndicated, connected, related.
– OPPOSITES unrelated.

association noun **1** *a trade association:* **alliance**, consortium, coalition, union, league, guild, syndicate, federation, confederation, confederacy, conglomerate, cooperative, partnership, affiliation. **2** *the association between man and environment:* **relationship**, relation, interrelation, connection, interconnection, link, bond, union, tie, attachment, interdependence, affiliation.

assorted adjective *assorted artefacts were recovered from the site:* **various**, miscellaneous, mixed, varied, varying, diverse, eclectic, multifarious, sundry.
– OPPOSITES uniform, similar.

assortment noun *the alcove held an assortment of books:* **mixture**, variety, array, mixed bag, mix, miscellany, selection, medley, diversity, ragbag, pot-pourri, salmagundi, farrago, gallimaufry.

assuage verb **1** *a pain that could never be assuaged:* **relieve**, ease, alleviate, soothe, mitigate, allay, palliate, abate, suppress, subdue, tranquillize; moderate, lessen, diminish, reduce. **2** *her hunger was quickly assuaged:* **satisfy**, gratify, appease, fulfil, indulge, relieve, slake, sate, satiate, quench, check.
– OPPOSITES aggravate, intensify.

assume verb **1** *I assumed he wanted me to keep the book:* **presume**, suppose, take it (as given), take for granted, take as read, conjecture, surmise, conclude, deduce, infer, reckon, reason, think, fancy, believe, understand, gather; N. Amer. figure. **2** *he assumed a Southern accent:* **affect**, adopt, impersonate, put on, simulate, feign, fake. **3** *the disease may assume epidemic proportions:* **acquire**, take on, come to have. **4** *they are to assume more responsibility:* **accept**, shoulder, bear, undertake, take on/up, manage, handle, deal with. **5** *he assumed control of their finances:* **seize**, take (over), appropriate, commandeer, expropriate, hijack, wrest, usurp.

assumed adjective *he may have travelled under an assumed name:* **false**, fictitious, invented, made-up, fake, bogus, sham, spurious, make-believe, improvised, adopted; informal pretend, phoney; Brit. informal cod.
– OPPOSITES genuine.

assumption noun **1** *an informed assumption:* **supposition**, presumption, belief, expectation, conjecture, speculation, surmise, guess, premise, hypothesis; conclusion, deduction, inference, notion, impression. **2** *the assumption of power by revolutionaries:* **seizure**,

arrogation, appropriation, expropriation, commandeering, confiscation, hijacking, wresting.

assurance noun **1** *her calm assurance:* **self-confidence**, confidence, self-assurance, self-possession, nerve, poise, aplomb, level-headedness; calmness, composure, sangfroid, equanimity; informal cool, unflappability. **2** *you have my assurance:* **word (of honour)**, promise, pledge, vow, avowal, oath, bond, undertaking, guarantee, commitment. **3** *there is no assurance of getting one's money back:* **guarantee**, certainty, certitude, surety, confidence. **4** *life assurance:* **insurance**, indemnity, indemnification, protection, security, cover.
– OPPOSITES self-doubt, uncertainty.

assure verb **1** *we must assure him of our loyal support:* **reassure**, convince, satisfy, persuade, guarantee, promise, tell; affirm, pledge, swear, vow. **2** *they guarantee to assure your life:* **insure**, provide insurance, cover, indemnify.

assured adjective **1** *an assured voice:* **confident**, self-confident, self-assured, self-possessed, poised, phlegmatic, level-headed; calm, composed, equanimous, imperturbable, unruffled; informal unflappable, together. **2** *an assured supply of weapons:* **guaranteed**, certain, sure, secure, reliable, dependable, sound; infallible, unfailing; informal sure-fire.
– OPPOSITES doubtful, uncertain.

astonish verb *it astonished her that he was so anxious:* **amaze**, astound, stagger, surprise, startle, stun, confound, dumbfound, stupefy, daze, nonplus, take aback, leave open-mouthed, leave aghast; informal flabbergast, bowl over; Brit. informal knock for six.

astonished adjective **amazed**, astounded, staggered, surprised, startled, stunned, thunderstruck, aghast, taken aback, dumbfounded, dumbstruck, stupefied, dazed, nonplussed, awestruck; informal flabbergasted; Brit. informal gobsmacked.

astonishing adjective **amazing**, astounding, staggering, surprising, breathtaking; remarkable, extraordinary, incredible, unbelievable, phenomenal; informal mind-boggling.

astonishment noun **amazement**, surprise, stupefaction, incredulity, disbelief, speechlessness, awe, wonder.

astound verb *Kate was astounded by his arrogance:* **amaze**, astonish, stagger, surprise, startle, stun, confound, dumbfound, stupefy, daze, nonplus, take aback, leave open-mouthed, leave aghast; informal flabbergast, bowl over; Brit. informal knock for six.

astounding adjective **amazing**, astonishing, staggering, surprising, breathtaking; remarkable, extraordinary, incredible, unbelievable, phenomenal; informal mind-boggling.

astray adverb **1** *the shots went astray:* **off target**, wide of the mark, awry, off course. **2** *the older boys lead him astray:* **into wrongdoing**, into sin, away from the straight and narrow.

astringent adjective **1** *the lotion has an astringent effect on pores:* **constricting**, constrictive, contracting; styptic. **2** *her astringent words:* **severe**, sharp, stern, harsh, acerbic, acidulous, caustic, mordant, trenchant; scathing, cutting, incisive, waspish; N. Amer. acerb.
– OPPOSITES kind.

astronaut noun **spaceman/woman**, cosmonaut, taikonaut, space traveller, space cadet; N. Amer. informal jock.

astronomical adjective *astronomical alignments:* **planetary**, stellar; celestial.

astute adjective *he had a reputation as an astute businessman:* **shrewd**, sharp, acute, quick, clever, intelligent, bright, smart, canny, intuitive, perceptive, insightful, incisive, sagacious, wise; informal on the ball, quick on the uptake, savvy; Brit. informal suss; N. Amer. informal heads-up.
– OPPOSITES stupid.

asylum noun **1** *he appealed for political asylum:* **refuge**, sanctuary, shelter, safety, protection, security, immunity; a safe haven. **2** *his father was confined to an asylum:* **psychiatric hospital**, mental hospital, mental institution, mental asylum; informal madhouse, loony bin, funny farm; N. Amer. informal bughouse.

asymmetrical adjective *the church has an asymmetrical plan with a single southern aisle:* **lopsided**, unsymmetrical, uneven, unbalanced, crooked, awry, askew, skew, squint, misaligned; disproportionate, unequal, irregular; informal cockeyed; Brit. informal skew-whiff, wonky.

atheism noun *Wordsworth swung from atheism to orthodox Christianity:* **non-belief**, disbelief, unbelief, scepticism, doubt, agnosticism; nihilism.

atheist noun *although an atheist he takes an interest in religion:* **non-believer**, disbeliever, unbeliever, sceptic, doubter, doubting Thomas, agnostic; nihilist.
– OPPOSITES believer.

athlete noun **sportsman**, sportswoman, sportsperson; Olympian; runner; N. Amer. informal jock.

athletic adjective **1** *his athletic physique:* **muscular**, muscly, sturdy, strapping, well built, strong, powerful, robust, able-bodied, vigorous, hardy, lusty, hearty, brawny, burly, broad-shouldered, Herculean; fit, in good shape, in trim; informal sporty, husky, hunky, beefy. **2** *athletic events:* **sporting**, sports; Olympic.
– OPPOSITES puny.

atmosphere noun **1** *the gases present in the atmosphere:* **air**, aerospace; sky. **2** *the hotel has a relaxed atmosphere:* **ambience**, air, mood, feel, feeling, character, tone, tenor, aura, quality, undercurrent, flavour; informal vibes.

atom noun **1** *they build tiny circuits atom by atom:* **particle**, molecule, bit, piece, fragment, fraction. **2** *there wasn't an atom of truth in the allegations:* **grain**, iota, jot, whit, mite, scrap, shred, ounce, scintilla; Irish stim; informal smidgen.

atone verb *a human sacrifice to atone for the sin:* **make amends**, make reparation, make up for, compensate, pay, recompense, expiate, make good, offset; do penance.

atrocious adjective **1** *atrocious cruelties:* **brutal**, barbaric, barbarous, savage, vicious, wicked, cruel, nasty, heinous, monstrous, vile, inhuman, black-hearted, fiendish, ghastly, horrible; abominable, outrageous, hateful, disgusting, despicable, contemptible, loathsome, odious, abhorrent, sickening, horrifying, unspeakable, execrable, egregious. **2** *the weather was atrocious:* **appalling**, dreadful, terrible, very bad, unpleasant, miserable; informal abysmal, dire, rotten, lousy, God-awful; Brit. informal shocking, chronic, pants.
– OPPOSITES admirable, superb.

atrocity noun **1** *press reports detailed a number of atrocities:* **abomination**, cruelty, enormity, outrage, horror, monstrosity, obscenity, violation, crime, abuse. **2** *conflict and atrocity around the globe:* **barbarity**, barbarism, brutality, savagery, inhumanity, cruelty, wickedness, evil, iniquity, horror.

atrophy verb *muscles atrophy in microgravity:* **waste away**, become emaciated, wither, shrivel (up), shrink; decay, decline, deteriorate, degenerate, weaken.
– OPPOSITES strengthen, grow.
noun *muscular atrophy:* **wasting**, emaciation, withering, shrivelling, shrinking; decay, decline, deterioration, degeneration, weakening, debilitation, enfeeblement.
– OPPOSITES strengthening.

attach verb **1** *a lead weight is attached to the cord:* **fasten**, fix, affix, join, connect, link, secure, make fast, tie, bind, chain; stick, adhere, glue, fuse; append. **2** *he attached himself to the Liberal Party:* **affiliate**, associate, align, ally, unite, integrate, join; be in league with, form an alliance with. **3** *they attached importance to research:* **ascribe**, assign, attribute, accredit, impute. **4** *the medical officer attached to HQ:* **assign**, appoint, allocate, second.
– OPPOSITES detach, separate.

attached adjective **1** *I'm not interested in you—I'm attached:* **married**, engaged, promised in marriage; going out, spoken for, involved; informal hitched, spliced, shackled, going steady; formal wed, wedded. **2** *she was very attached to her brother:* **fond of**, devoted to; informal mad about, crazy about.

a

– OPPOSITES single.

attachment noun **1** *he has a strong attachment to his mother:* **bond**, closeness, devotion, loyalty; fondness for, love for, affection for, feeling for; relationship with. **2** *the shower had a massage attachment:* **accessory**, fitting, fitment, extension, add-on, appendage. **3** *the attachment of safety restraints:* **fixing**, fastening, linking, coupling, connection. **4** *he was on attachment from another regiment:* **assignment**, appointment, secondment, transfer. **5** *his family's Conservative attachment:* **affiliation**, association, alliance, alignment, connection; links, ties, sympathies.

attack verb **1** *Chris had been brutally attacked:* **assault**, assail, set upon, beat up; batter, pummel, punch; N. Amer. beat up on; informal do over, work over, rough up; Brit. informal duff up. **2** *the French had still not attacked:* **strike**, charge, pounce; bombard, shell, blitz, strafe, fire. **3** *the clergy attacked government policies:* **criticize**, censure, condemn, pillory, savage, revile, vilify; informal knock, slam, bash, lay into; Brit. informal slate, slag off, rubbish; N. Amer. informal pummel. **4** *they have to attack the problem soon:* **address**, attend to, deal with, confront, apply oneself to, get to work on, undertake, embark on; informal get stuck into, get cracking on, get weaving on. **5** *the virus attacks the liver:* **affect**, have an effect on, strike; infect, damage, injure.

– OPPOSITES defend, praise, protect.

noun **1** *an attack on their home:* **assault**, onslaught, offensive, strike, blitz, raid, charge, rush, invasion, incursion. **2** *she wrote a hostile attack on him:* **criticism**, censure, rebuke, admonishment, reprimand, reproval; condemnation, denunciation, revilement, vilification; tirade, diatribe, polemic; informal roasting, caning; Brit. informal slating, rollicking, blast. **3** *an asthmatic attack:* **fit**, seizure, spasm, convulsion, paroxysm, outburst, bout.

– OPPOSITES defence, commendation.

attacker noun **assailant**, assaulter, aggressor; mugger, rapist, killer, murderer.

attain verb *they help the child attain his or her full potential:* **achieve**, accomplish, reach, obtain, gain, procure, secure, get, hook, net, win, earn, acquire; realize, fulfil; informal clinch, bag, wrap up.

attainable adjective *a challenging but attainable target:* **achievable**, obtainable, accessible, within reach, securable, realizable; practicable, workable, realistic, reasonable, viable, feasible, possible; informal doable, get-at-able.

attainment noun **1** *the attainment of common goals:* **achievement**, accomplishment, realization, fulfilment, completion; formal effectuation, reification. **2** *educational attainment:* **achievement**, accomplishment, proficiency, competence;

qualification; skill, aptitude, ability.

attempt verb *I attempted to answer the question:* **try**, strive, aim, venture, endeavour, seek, undertake, make an effort; have a go at, try one's hand at; informal go all out, bend over backwards, bust a gut, have a crack at, have a shot at, have a stab at; formal essay.

noun *an attempt to put the economy to rights:* **effort**, endeavour, try, venture, trial; informal crack, go, shot, stab; formal essay.

attend verb **1** *they attended a carol service:* **be present at**, sit in on, take part in; appear at, present oneself at, turn up at, visit, go to; informal show up at, show one's face at. **2** *he had not attended to the regulations:* **pay attention**, pay heed, be attentive, listen; concentrate, take note, bear in mind, take into consideration, heed, observe, mark. **3** *the wounded were attended to nearby:* **care for**, look after, minister to, see to; tend, treat, nurse, help, aid, assist, succour; informal doctor. **4** *he attended to the boy's education:* **deal with**, see to, manage, organize, sort out, handle, take care of, take charge of, take in hand, tackle. **5** *the queen was attended by an usher:* **escort**, accompany, chaperone, squire, guide, lead, conduct, usher, shepherd; assist, help, serve, wait on.

– OPPOSITES miss, disregard, ignore, neglect.

attendance noun **1** *you requested the attendance of a doctor:* **presence**, appearance; attention. **2** *their gig attendances grew:* **audience**, turnout, house, gate; crowd, congregation, gathering; Austral. informal muster.

– OPPOSITES absence.

■ **in attendance** present, here, there, near, nearby, at hand, available; assisting, supervising.

attendant noun **1** *a sleeping car attendant:* **steward**, waiter, waitress, garçon, porter, servant; N. Amer. waitperson. **2** *a royal attendant:* **escort**, companion, retainer, aide, lady-in-waiting, equerry, chaperone; servant, manservant, valet, gentleman's gentleman, maidservant, maid; N. Amer. houseman; Brit. informal skivvy.

adjective *new discoveries and the attendant excitement:* **accompanying**, associated, related, connected, concomitant; resultant, resulting, consequent.

attention noun **1** *the issue needs further attention:* **consideration**, contemplation, deliberation, thought, study, observation, scrutiny, investigation, action. **2** *he tried to attract the attention of a policeman:* **awareness**, notice, observation, heed, regard, scrutiny, surveillance. **3** *adequate medical attention:* **care**, treatment, ministration, succour, relief, aid, help, assistance. **4** *he was effusive in his attentions:* **overtures**, approaches, suit, wooing, courting; compliments, flattery.

attentive adjective **1** *a bright and attentive scholar:* **perceptive**, observant, alert,

acute, aware, heedful, vigilant; intent, focused, committed, studious, diligent, conscientious, earnest; informal not missing a trick, on the ball. **2** *the most attentive of husbands:* **conscientious**, considerate, thoughtful, kind, caring, solicitous, understanding, sympathetic, obliging, accommodating, gallant, chivalrous; dutiful, responsible.
– OPPOSITES inconsiderate.

attenuated adjective **1** *attenuated fingers:* **thin**, slender, narrow, slim, skinny, spindly, bony. **2** *his muscle activity was much attenuated:* **weakened**, reduced, lessened, decreased, diminished, impaired.
– OPPOSITES plump, broad, strengthened.

attest verb *previous experience is attested by a certificate:* **certify**, corroborate, confirm, verify, substantiate, authenticate, evidence, demonstrate, show, prove; endorse, support, affirm, bear out, give credence to, vouch for.
– OPPOSITES disprove.

attic noun **loft**, roof space; garret, mansard.

attire noun *Thomas preferred formal attire:* **clothing**, clothes, garments, dress, wear, outfits, garb, costume; informal gear, togs, duds, get-up; Brit. informal clobber; N. Amer. informal threads; formal apparel.
verb *she was attired in black crêpe:* **dress (up)**, clothe, garb, robe, array, costume, swathe, deck (out), turn out, fit out, trick out/up, rig out; informal get up.

attitude noun **1** *you seem ambivalent in your attitude:* **view**, viewpoint, outlook, perspective, stance, standpoint, position, inclination, orientation, approach, reaction; opinion, ideas, convictions, feelings, thinking. **2** *an attitude of prayer:* **position**, posture, pose, stance.

attorney noun **lawyer**, legal practitioner, legal executive, legal representative, member of the bar, counsel, barrister, Queen's Counsel, QC; Scottish advocate; N. Amer. counselor(-at-law); informal brief.

attract verb **1** *positive ions are attracted to the negatively charged terminal:* **draw**, pull, magnetize. **2** *he was attracted by her smile:* **entice**, allure, lure, tempt, charm, win over, woo, engage, enchant, entrance, captivate, beguile, bewitch, seduce; excite, titillate, arouse; informal turn on.
– OPPOSITES repel.

attraction noun **1** *the stars are held together by gravitational attraction:* **pull**, draw; magnetism. **2** *she had lost whatever attraction she had ever had:* **appeal**, attractiveness, desirability, seductiveness, seduction, allure, animal magnetism; charisma, charm, beauty, good looks; informal come-on. **3** *the fair offers sideshows and other attractions:* **entertainment**, activity, diversion, interest.
– OPPOSITES repulsion.

attractive adjective **1** *a more attractive career:* **appealing**, inviting, tempting, irresistible; agreeable, pleasing, interesting. **2** *she has no idea how attractive she is:* **good-looking**, beautiful, pretty, handsome, lovely, stunning, striking, arresting, gorgeous, prepossessing, fetching, captivating, bewitching, beguiling, engaging, charming, enchanting, appealing, delightful; sexy, seductive, alluring, tantalizing, irresistible, ravishing, desirable; Scottish & N. English bonny; informal fanciable, tasty, hot, easy on the eye, drop-dead gorgeous; Brit. informal fit; N. Amer. informal cute, foxy; Austral./NZ informal spunky.
– OPPOSITES uninviting, ugly.

attribute verb *they attributed their success to him:* **ascribe**, assign, accredit, credit, impute; put down, chalk up, hold responsible, pin on; connect with, associate with.
noun *he has all the attributes of a top player:* **quality**, characteristic, trait, feature, element, aspect, property, sign, hallmark, mark, distinction.

attrition noun **1** *a gradual attrition of the market economy:* **wearing down/away**, weakening, debilitation, enfeebling, sapping, attenuation. **2** *the attrition of the edges of the teeth:* **abrasion**, friction, erosion, corrosion, grinding, wearing (away); deterioration, damaging; rare detrition.

attune verb *a society more attuned to consumerism than ideology:* **accustom**, adjust, adapt, acclimatize, condition, accommodate, assimilate; N. Amer. acclimate.

atypical adjective *a lack of social relationships is atypical:* **unusual**, untypical, uncommon, unconventional, unorthodox, irregular, abnormal, aberrant, deviant, unrepresentative; strange, odd, peculiar, bizarre, weird, queer, freakish; exceptional, singular, rare, out of the way, out of the ordinary, extraordinary; Brit. out of the common; informal funny, freaky.
– OPPOSITES normal.

auburn adjective *auburn hair:* **reddish-brown**, red-brown, Titian (red), tawny, russet, chestnut, copper, coppery, rufous.

audacious adjective **1** *his audacious exploits:* **bold**, daring, fearless, intrepid, brave, courageous, valiant, heroic, plucky; daredevil, devil-may-care, death-or-glory, reckless, madcap; venturesome, mettlesome; informal gutsy, spunky, ballsy. **2** *an audacious remark:* **impudent**, impertinent, insolent, presumptuous, cheeky, irreverent, discourteous, disrespectful, insubordinate, ill-mannered, unmannerly, rude, brazen, shameless, pert, defiant, cocky, bold (as brass); informal brass-necked, fresh, lippy, mouthy, saucy; N. Amer. informal sassy, nervy.
– OPPOSITES timid, polite.

audacity noun **1** *a traveller of extraordinary audacity:* **boldness**, daring, fearlessness, intrepidity, bravery, courage, heroism, pluck, grit; recklessness; spirit, mettle;

informal **guts**, **gutsiness**, **spunk**; Brit. informal
bottle; N. Amer. informal **moxie**. **2** *he had the
audacity to contradict me:* **impudence**,
impertinence, insolence, presumption,
cheek, bad manners, effrontery, nerve,
gall, defiance, temerity; informal **brass** (neck),
chutzpah; Brit. informal **sauce**; N. Amer. informal
sass.

audible adjective *her voice was weak and
barely audible:* **hearable**, perceptible,
discernible, detectable, appreciable; clear,
distinct, loud.
– OPPOSITES faint.

audience noun **1** *the audience applauded:*
spectators, **listeners**, viewers, onlookers,
patrons; crowd, throng, congregation,
turnout; house, gallery, stalls; Brit. informal
punters. **2** *the radio station has a teenage
audience:* **market**, **public**, following, fans;
listenership, viewership. **3** *an audience with
the Pope:* **meeting**, consultation, conference,
hearing, reception, interview.

audit noun *an audit of the party accounts:*
inspection, examination, scrutiny, probe,
investigation, assessment, appraisal,
evaluation, review, analysis; informal
going-over, once-over.
verb *we audited their accounts:* **inspect**,
examine, survey, go through, scrutinize,
check, probe, vet, investigate, enquire into,
assess, appraise, evaluate, review, analyse,
study; informal give something a/the
once-over, give something a going-over.

auditorium noun **theatre**, hall, assembly
room; chamber, room.

au fait adjective *he was au fait with all the
latest technology:* **familiar**, acquainted,
conversant, at home, up to date, au courant,
in touch; abreast, apprised, in the know,
well informed, knowledgeable, well versed,
enlightened; informal clued up, wise to, hip to.

augment verb *Aubrey's arrival had
augmented their difficulties:* **increase**, add
to, supplement, top up, build up, enlarge,
expand, extend, raise, multiply, swell;
magnify, amplify, escalate; improve, boost;
informal up, jack up, hike up, bump up.
– OPPOSITES decrease.

augur verb *these successes augur well for
the future:* **bode**, portend, herald, be a sign,
warn, forewarn, foreshadow, be an omen,
presage, indicate, signify, signal, promise,
threaten, spell, denote; predict, prophesy.

august adjective *she was in august company:*
distinguished, respected, eminent,
venerable, hallowed, illustrious, prestigious,
renowned, celebrated, honoured, acclaimed,
esteemed, exalted; great, important, lofty,
noble; imposing, impressive, awe-inspiring,
stately, grand, dignified.

aura noun *the ceremony retains an aura
of mystery:* **atmosphere**, ambience, air,
quality, character, mood, feeling, feel,
flavour, tone, tenor; emanation, vibration;
informal **vibe**.

auspices plural noun *the talks were to be held
under the auspices of the UN:* **patronage**,
aegis, umbrella, protection, keeping, care;
support, backing, guardianship, trusteeship,
guidance, supervision.

auspicious adjective *an auspicious day
was chosen for the wedding:* **favourable**,
propitious, promising, rosy, good,
encouraging; opportune, timely, lucky,
fortunate, providential, felicitous,
advantageous.

austere adjective **1** *an outwardly austere
man:* **severe**, stern, strict, harsh, steely,
flinty, dour, grim, cold, frosty, unemotional,
unfriendly; formal, stiff, reserved, aloof,
forbidding; grave, solemn, serious,
unsmiling, unsympathetic, unforgiving;
hard, unyielding, unbending, inflexible,
illiberal; informal hard-boiled. **2** *an austere
life:* **ascetic**, self-denying, self-disciplined,
non-indulgent, frugal, spartan, puritanical,
abstemious, abstinent, self-sacrificing,
strict, temperate, sober, simple, restrained;
celibate, chaste. **3** *the buildings were austere:*
plain, simple, basic, functional, modest,
unadorned, unembellished, unfussy,
restrained; stark, bleak, bare, clinical,
spartan, ascetic; informal no frills.
– OPPOSITES genial, immoderate, ornate.

authentic adjective **1** *an authentic document:*
genuine, real, bona fide, true, veritable,
simon-pure; legitimate, lawful, legal, valid;
informal the real McCoy, the real thing,
pukka, kosher; Austral./NZ informal dinkum. **2** *an
authentic depiction of the situation:* **reliable**,
dependable, trustworthy, authoritative,
honest, faithful; accurate, factual, true,
truthful; formal veridical, veracious.
– OPPOSITES fake, unreliable.

authenticate verb *the evidence will
authenticate his claim:* **verify**, validate,
prove, substantiate, corroborate, confirm,
support, back up, attest to, give credence to.

authenticity noun **1** *the authenticity
of the painting:* **genuineness**, bona
fides; legitimacy, legality, validity. **2** *the
authenticity of this account:* **reliability**,
dependability, trustworthiness, credibility,
accuracy, truth, veracity, fidelity.

author noun **1** *modern Canadian authors:*
writer, wordsmith; novelist, playwright,
poet, essayist, biographer; columnist,
reporter; informal penman, penwoman,
scribe, scribbler. **2** *the author of the peace
plan:* **originator**, creator, instigator,
founder, father, architect, designer, deviser,
producer; cause, agent.

authoritarian adjective *his authoritarian
manner:* **autocratic**, dictatorial, despotic,
tyrannical, draconian, oppressive,
repressive, illiberal, undemocratic;
disciplinarian, domineering, overbearing,
high-handed, peremptory, imperious, strict,
rigid, inflexible; informal bossy.
– OPPOSITES democratic, liberal.
noun *the army is dominated by*

authoritarians: *autocrat*, despot, dictator, tyrant; disciplinarian, martinet.

authoritative adjective **1** *authoritative information:* **reliable**, dependable, trustworthy, sound, authentic, valid, attested, verifiable, accurate. **2** *the authoritative edition:* **definitive**, most reliable, best; authorized, accredited, recognized, accepted, approved. **3** *his authoritative manner:* **assured**, confident, assertive; commanding, masterful, lordly; domineering, imperious, overbearing, authoritarian; informal bossy.
– OPPOSITES unreliable, timid.

authority noun **1** *a rebellion against those in authority:* **power**, jurisdiction, command, control, charge, dominance, rule, sovereignty, supremacy; influence; informal clout. **2** *military forces have the legal authority to arrest drug traffickers:* **authorization**, right, power, mandate, prerogative, licence. **3** *the money was spent without parliamentary authority:* **authorization**, permission, consent, leave, sanction, licence, dispensation, assent, acquiescence, agreement, approval, endorsement, clearance; informal the go-ahead, the thumbs up, the OK, the green light. **4** *the authorities:* **officials**, officialdom; government, administration, establishment; police; informal the powers that be. **5** *an authority on the stock market:* **expert**, specialist, aficionado, pundit, doyen(ne), guru, sage; informal boffin. **6** *he cites the nuns' testimony as an authority:* **source**, reference, citation, quotation, passage. **7** *I have it on good authority that you were there:* **evidence**, testimony, witness, attestation, word, avowal.

authorization noun *they will require authorization from the Law Society or another regulator:* **permission**, consent, leave, sanction, licence, dispensation, clearance, the nod; assent, agreement, approval, endorsement; authority, right, power, mandate; informal the go-ahead, the thumbs up, the OK, the green light.
– OPPOSITES refusal.

authorize verb **1** *they authorized further action:* **sanction**, permit, allow, approve, consent to, assent to; ratify, endorse, validate; informal give the green light, give the go-ahead, OK, give the thumbs up. **2** *the troops were authorized to fire:* **empower**, mandate, commission; entitle.
– OPPOSITES forbid.

authorized adjective *authorized financial institutions:* **approved**, recognized, sanctioned; accredited, licensed, certified; official, lawful, legal, legitimate.
– OPPOSITES unofficial.

autobiography noun **memoirs**, life story, personal history.

autocracy noun **absolutism**, totalitarianism, dictatorship, despotism, tyranny, monocracy, autarchy.

– OPPOSITES democracy.

autocrat noun **absolute ruler**, dictator, despot, tyrant, monocrat.

autocratic adjective *an autocratic government:* **despotic**, tyrannical, dictatorial, totalitarian, autarchic; undemocratic, one-party, monocratic; domineering, draconian, overbearing, high-handed, peremptory, imperious; harsh, rigid, inflexible, illiberal, oppressive.

autograph noun *fans pestered him for his autograph:* **signature**; N. Amer. informal John Hancock.
verb *Jack autographed copies of his book:* **sign**.

automatic adjective **1** *automatic garage doors:* **mechanized**, mechanical, automated, computerized, electronic, robotic; self-activating. **2** *an automatic reaction:* **instinctive**, involuntary, unconscious, reflex, knee-jerk, instinctual, subconscious; spontaneous, impulsive, unthinking; mechanical; informal gut. **3** *he is the automatic choice for the team:* **inevitable**, unavoidable, inescapable; certain, definite, undoubted, assured.
– OPPOSITES manual, deliberate.

autonomous adjective *an autonomous republic:* **self-governing**, self-ruling, self-determining, independent, sovereign, free.

autonomy noun **self-government**, self-rule, home rule, self-determination, independence, sovereignty, freedom.

autopsy noun **post-mortem**, PM, necropsy.

auxiliary adjective **1** *an auxiliary power source:* **additional**, supplementary, supplemental, extra, reserve, backup, emergency, fallback, other **2** *auxiliary nursing staff:* **ancillary**, assistant, support.
noun *a nursing auxiliary:* **assistant**, helper, ancillary.

avail verb **1** *guests can avail themselves of the facilities:* **use**, take advantage of, utilize, employ. **2** *his arguments cannot avail him:* **help**, aid, assist, benefit, profit, be of service.
■ **to no avail** in vain, without success, unsuccessfully, fruitlessly, for nothing.

available adjective **1** *refreshments will be available:* **obtainable**, accessible, to/at hand, at one's disposal, handy, convenient; on sale, procurable; untaken, unengaged, unused; informal up for grabs, on tap, gettable. **2** *I'll see if he's available:* **free**, unoccupied; present, in attendance; contactable.
– OPPOSITES busy, engaged.

avalanche noun **1** **icefall**; rockslide, landslide, landslip; Brit. snow-slip; N. Amer. snowslide. **2** *an avalanche of press comment:* **barrage**, volley, flood, deluge, torrent, tide, shower, wave.

avant-garde adjective *her tastes were too avant-garde for her contemporaries:* **innovative**, innovatory, original, experimental, left-field, inventive, ahead of the times, new, modern, advanced,

forward-looking, state-of-the-art, trendsetting, pioneering, progressive, groundbreaking, trailblazing, revolutionary; unfamiliar, unorthodox, unconventional; informal offbeat, way-out.
– OPPOSITES conservative.

avarice noun *he had a reputation for ruthlessness and avarice:* **greed**, acquisitiveness, cupidity, covetousness, rapacity, materialism, mercenariness, Mammonism; informal money-grubbing.
– OPPOSITES generosity.

avenge verb *his determination to avenge the murder of his brother:* **requite**, punish, repay, pay back, take revenge for, get even for.

avenue noun **1** *tree-lined avenues:* **road**, street, drive, parade, boulevard, broadway, thoroughfare. **2** *possible avenues of research:* **line**, path; method, approach.

average noun *the price is above the national average:* **mean**, median, mode; norm, standard, rule, par.
adjective **1** *the average temperature in May:* **mean**, median, modal. **2** *a woman of average height:* **ordinary**, standard, normal, typical, regular. **3** *a very average director:* **mediocre**, second-rate, undistinguished, ordinary, middle-of-the-road, unexceptional, unexciting, unremarkable, unmemorable, indifferent, pedestrian, lacklustre, forgettable, amateurish; informal OK, so-so, fair-to-middling, no great shakes, not up to much; Brit. informal not much cop; N. Amer. informal bush-league; NZ informal half-pie.
– OPPOSITES exceptional, outstanding.
■ **on average** normally, usually, ordinarily, generally, in general, for the most part, as a rule, typically; overall, by and large, on the whole.

averse adjective *many manufacturing firms remain averse to innovation and risk-taking:* **opposed**, against, antipathetic, hostile, ill-disposed, resistant; disinclined, reluctant, loath; informal anti.
– OPPOSITES keen.

aversion noun *their deep-seated aversion to the use of force:* **dislike of**, antipathy, distaste for, abhorrence, hatred, loathing, detestation, hostility; reluctance, disinclination.
– OPPOSITES liking.

avert verb **1** *she averted her head:* **turn aside**, turn away. **2** *an attempt to avert political chaos:* **prevent**, avoid, stave off, ward off, forestall, preclude.

avid adjective *an avid reader of science fiction:* **keen**, eager, enthusiastic, ardent, passionate, zealous; devoted, dedicated, wholehearted, earnest; Brit. informal as keen as mustard.
– OPPOSITES apathetic.

avoid verb **1** *I avoid situations that stress me:* **keep away from**, steer clear of, give a wide berth to, fight shy of. **2** *he is trying to*

avoid responsibility: **evade**, dodge, sidestep, escape, run away from; informal duck, wriggle out of, get out of, cop out of; Austral./NZ informal duck-shove. **3** *she moved to avoid a blow:* **dodge**, duck, get out of the way of. **4** *you've been avoiding me all evening:* **shun**, stay away from, evade, keep one's distance, elude, hide from; ignore. **5** *he should avoid drinking alcohol:* **refrain from**, abstain from, desist from, eschew.
– OPPOSITES confront, face up to, seek out.

avoidable adjective *such fatalities are frequently avoidable:* **preventable**, stoppable, avertable, escapable.
– OPPOSITES inescapable.

avowed adjective *an avowed Marxist:* **self-confessed**, self-declared, acknowledged, admitted; open, overt.

await verb **1** *Peter was awaiting news:* **wait for**, expect, anticipate. **2** *many dangers await them:* **be in store for**, lie ahead of, lie in wait for, be waiting for.

awake verb **1** *she awoke the following morning:* **wake (up)**, awaken, stir, come to, come round. **2** *the alarm awoke him at 7.30:* **wake (up)**, awaken, rouse, arouse; Brit. informal knock up. **3** *they finally awoke to the extent of the problem:* **realize**, become aware of, become conscious of; informal get wise to.
adjective **1** *she was still awake:* **wakeful**, sleepless, restless, restive. **2** *too few are awake to the dangers:* **aware of**, conscious of, mindful of, alert to; formal cognizant of.
– OPPOSITES asleep, oblivious.

awaken verb **1** *I awakened early | the jolt awakened her.* See AWAKE senses 1, 2. **2** *he had awakened strong emotions in her:* **arouse**, rouse, bring out, engender, evoke, trigger, stir up, stimulate, kindle.

award verb *the society awarded him a silver medal:* **give**, grant, accord, assign; confer on, bestow on, present to, endow with, decorate with.
noun **1** *an award for high-quality service:* **prize**, trophy, medal, decoration; reward; informal gong. **2** *a libel award:* **payment**, settlement, compensation. **3** *the Arts Council gave him an award of £1,500:* **grant**, scholarship, endowment; Brit. bursary. **4** *the award of an honorary doctorate:* **conferral**, conferment, bestowal, presentation.

aware adjective **1** *she is aware of the dangers:* **conscious of**, mindful of, informed about, acquainted with, familiar with, alive to, alert to; informal wise to, in the know about, hip to; formal cognizant of. **2** *we need to be more environmentally aware:* **knowledgeable**, enlightened, well informed, au fait; informal clued up, genned up; Brit. informal switched-on.
– OPPOSITES ignorant.

awareness noun **consciousness**, recognition, realization; understanding, grasp, appreciation, knowledge, insight; familiarity; formal cognizance.

awash adjective **1** *the road was awash:* **flooded**, under water, submerged. **2** *the city was awash with journalists:* **inundated**, flooded, swamped, teeming, overflowing, overrun; informal knee-deep in.

away adverb **1** *she began to walk away:* **off**, from here, from there, aside, to one side. **2** *stay away from the trouble:* **at a distance from**, apart from. **3** *we'll be away for two weeks:* **elsewhere**, abroad; gone, absent; on holiday, on vacation.

awe noun *the sight filled me with awe:* **wonder**, wonderment; admiration, reverence, respect; dread, fear.

awe-inspiring adjective. See AWESOME.

awesome adjective *an awesome achievement:* **breathtaking**, awe-inspiring, magnificent, amazing, stunning, staggering, imposing, stirring, impressive; formidable, fearsome; informal mind-boggling, mind-blowing.
– OPPOSITES unimpressive.

awestruck adjective *Caroline was too awestruck by her surroundings to reply:* **amazed**, wonderstruck, awed, lost for words, open-mouthed; reverential; terrified, afraid, fearful.

awful adjective **1** *the place smelled awful:* **disgusting**, nasty, terrible, dreadful, ghastly, horrible, vile, foul, revolting, repulsive, repugnant, odious, sickening, nauseating; informal yucky, sick-making, gross; Brit. informal beastly. **2** *an awful book:* **dreadful**, terrible, frightful, atrocious, execrable; inadequate, inferior, substandard, lamentable; informal crummy, pathetic, rotten, woeful, lousy, appalling, abysmal, dire, poxy; Brit. informal duff, rubbish, pants. **3** *an awful accident:* **serious**, grave, bad, terrible, dreadful. **4** *you look awful—go and lie down:* **ill**, unwell, sick, peaky, queasy, nauseous; Brit. off colour, poorly; informal rough, lousy, rotten, terrible, dreadful; Brit. informal grotty, ropy; Scottish informal wabbit, peely-wally; Austral./NZ informal crook. **5** *I felt awful for getting so angry:* **remorseful**, guilty, ashamed, contrite, sorry, regretful, repentant, self-reproachful.
– OPPOSITES wonderful.

awfully adverb **1** (informal) *an awfully nice man:* **very**, extremely, really, immensely, exceedingly, thoroughly, dreadfully, exceptionally, remarkably, extraordinarily; N. English right; informal terrifically, terribly, devilishly, seriously, majorly; Brit. informal well, jolly, ever so, dead; N. Amer. informal real, mighty, awful; informal, dated frightfully. **2** (informal) *thanks awfully:* **very much**, a lot; informal a million. **3** *we played awfully:* **very badly**, terribly, dreadfully, atrociously, appallingly, execrably; informal abysmally, pitifully, diabolically.

awhile adverb *stand here awhile:* **for a moment**, for a (little) while, for a short time; informal for a bit.

awkward adjective **1** *the box was awkward to carry:* **difficult**, tricky; cumbersome, lumbersome, unwieldy; Brit. informal fiddly. **2** *I'm sorry to call at such an awkward time:* **inconvenient**, inappropriate, inopportune, unseasonable, difficult. **3** *he put her in a very awkward position:* **embarrassing**, uncomfortable, unpleasant, delicate, tricky, problematic(al), troublesome, thorny; humiliating, compromising; informal sticky, dicey, hairy; Brit. informal dodgy. **4** *she felt awkward alone with him:* **uncomfortable**, uneasy, tense, nervous, edgy, unquiet; self-conscious, embarrassed. **5** *his awkward movements:* **clumsy**, ungainly, uncoordinated, graceless, inelegant, gauche, gawky, wooden, stiff; unskilful, maladroit, inept, blundering; informal clodhopping, ham-fisted, ham-handed, cack-handed; Brit. informal all (fingers and) thumbs. **6** (Brit.) *you're being damned awkward:* **unreasonable**, uncooperative, unhelpful, disobliging, difficult, obstructive; contrary, perverse; stubborn, obstinate; Brit. informal bloody-minded, bolshie; N. Amer. informal balky; formal refractory.
– OPPOSITES easy, convenient, at ease, graceful, amenable.

awning noun **canopy**, shade, sunshade, shelter, cover; Brit. blind, sunblind.

awry adjective **1** *something was awry:* **amiss**, wrong; informal up. **2** *his wig looked awry:* **askew**, crooked, lopsided, tilted, skewed, skew, squint, to one side, off-centre, uneven; informal cockeyed; Brit. informal skew-whiff, wonky.
– OPPOSITES straight.

axe noun **hatchet**, cleaver, tomahawk, adze, poleaxe; Brit. chopper; historical battleaxe.
verb **1** *the show was axed:* **cancel**, withdraw, drop, scrap, discontinue, terminate, end; informal ditch, dump, pull the plug on. **2** *500 staff were axed:* **dismiss**, make redundant, lay off, let go, discharge, get rid of; informal sack, fire, give someone the sack, give someone the bullet, give someone their marching orders; Brit. informal give someone their cards.

axiom noun **accepted truth**, general truth, dictum, truism; maxim, adage, aphorism, apophthegm, gnome.

axis noun **1** *the earth revolves on its axis:* **centre line**, vertical, horizontal. **2** *the Anglo-American axis:* **alliance**, coalition, bloc, union, confederation, confederacy, league.

axle noun **shaft**, spindle, rod, arbor, mandrel, pivot.

azure adjective **sky-blue**, bright blue, blue.

Bb

babble verb 1 *Betty babbled away, ignoring the look on his face:* **prattle**, rattle on, gabble, chatter, jabber, twitter, go on, run on, ramble, burble, blather, blether; informal gab, yak, yabber, yatter, yammer, blabber; Brit. informal witter, rabbit, chunter, natter, waffle. 2 *just out of sight, a brook babbled gently:* **burble**, murmur, gurgle, purl, tinkle.
noun *a stream of continuous and incomprehensible babble:* **prattle**, gabble, chatter, jabber, rambling, blather, blether; informal gab, yak, yabbering, yatter; Brit. informal wittering, waffle, natter, chuntering.

babel noun *I stood, silent amid the babel of discordant voices:* **clamour**, din, racket, tumult, uproar, hubbub; babble, babbling, shouting, yelling, screaming; informal hullabaloo; Brit. informal row.

baby noun *she's expecting a baby in March:* **infant**, child, tot, little one; Scottish & N. English bairn; informal sprog, tiny; literary babe, babe in arms; technical neonate.
adjective *baby carrots:* **miniature**, mini, little, small; small-scale, scaled-down, toy, pocket, midget, dwarf; Scottish wee; N. Amer. vest-pocket; informal teeny, teeny-weeny, teensy, teensy-weensy, itsy-bitsy, itty-bitty, tiddly; Brit. informal titchy; N. Amer. informal little-bitty.
– OPPOSITES giant.

babyish adjective *he thinks toys are babyish and wants a computer:* **childish**, immature, infantile; juvenile, puerile, adolescent, young.
– OPPOSITES mature.

back noun 1 *she's broken her back in three places:* **spine**, backbone, spinal column, vertebral column. 2 *the back of the house was in the shade:* **rear**, rear side, other side; Nautical stern. 3 *get to the back of the queue:* **end**, tail end, rear end, tail; N. Amer. tag end. 4 *a few notes written on the back of an envelope:* **reverse**, other side; informal flip side.
– OPPOSITES front, head, face.
adverb 1 *he pushed his chair back and got to his feet:* **backwards**, behind one, to one's rear, rearwards; away. 2 *a few months back she visited Chicago:* **ago**, earlier, previously, before, in the past.
– OPPOSITES forward.
verb 1 *the scheme was backed by the English Tourist Board:* **sponsor**, finance, fund, subsidize, underwrite, support; N. Amer. informal bankroll. 2 *most people backed the*

idea of reform: **support**, endorse, sanction, approve of, give one's blessing to, smile on, favour, advocate, promote, uphold, champion; vote for, ally oneself with, stand behind, side with, be on the side of, defend, take up the cudgels for; second; informal throw one's weight behind. 3 *he backed Helter Skelter at 33–1:* **bet on**, gamble on, put money on. 4 *he took a step towards her and she backed away:* **reverse**, draw back, step back, move backwards, back off, pull back, retreat, withdraw, give ground, backtrack.
– OPPOSITES oppose, advance.
adjective 1 *the back seats were all taken:* **rear**, rearmost, hind, hindmost, posterior. 2 *I thumbed through some back copies of 'Homes and Gardens':* **past**, old, previous, earlier, former, out of date.
– OPPOSITES front, forthcoming.
■ **back down** *Shell was forced to back down and dismantle the platform:* give in, concede defeat, surrender, yield, submit, climb down, concede, reconsider; backtrack, back-pedal.
■ **back out of** *Sir Arthur Bliss unexpectedly backed out of the project:* renege on, go back on, withdraw from, pull out of, retreat from, fail to honour, abandon, default on, back-pedal on.
■ **back something up** *he makes a startling claim, then he backs it up with some evidence:* substantiate, corroborate, confirm, support, bear out, endorse, bolster, reinforce, lend weight to.
■ **back someone up** *if you need anyone to back you up I will be only too happy:* support, stand by, give one's support to, side with, be on someone's side, take someone's side, take someone's part; vouch for.
■ **behind someone's back** *he was saying terrible things about me behind my back:* secretly, without someone's knowledge, on the sly, sneakily, covertly, surreptitiously, furtively.

backbiting noun *all the backbiting and prejudice have shattered her confidence:* **malicious talk**, slander, libel, defamation, abuse, character assassination, disparagement, denigration; slurs, aspersions; informal bitching, bitchiness, cattiness, mud-slinging, bad-mouthing; Brit. informal slagging off, rubbishing.

backbone noun 1 *the rib-eye muscle lies on each side of the cow's backbone:* **spine**, spinal column, vertebral column, vertebrae; back; Anatomy dorsum, rachis. **2** *small businesses are the backbone of many rural communities*: **mainstay**, cornerstone, foundation, keystone, buttress. **3** *he has enough backbone to see us through this difficult period*: **strength of character**, firmness, resolution, resolve, grit, determination, fortitude, mettle, spirit; informal guts, spunk; Brit. informal bottle.

back-breaking adjective *it took eight days of back-breaking effort*: **gruelling**, arduous, strenuous, onerous, punishing, crushing, demanding, exacting, taxing, exhausting; informal killing; Brit. informal knackering.
– OPPOSITES easy.

backer noun *£3 million was provided by the project's backers*: **sponsor**, investor, underwriter, financier, patron, benefactor, benefactress; informal angel.

backfire verb *Bernard's plan backfired on him*: **rebound**, boomerang, come back; fail, miscarry, go wrong; informal blow up in someone's face.

background noun **1** *the sculpture is set against a background of high buildings*: **backdrop**, backcloth, surrounding(s), setting, scene. **2** *a mix of students from many different backgrounds*: **circumstances**; environment, class, culture, tradition; upbringing. **3** *her nursing background was an advantage*: **experience**, record, history, past, training, education, grounding, knowledge. **4** *an understanding of the political background of the dispute*: **circumstances**, context, conditions, situation, environment, milieu, scene, scenario.
– OPPOSITES foreground.
■ **in the background** *this tactic allows him to remain in the background*: behind the scenes, out of the public eye, out of the spotlight, out of the limelight, backstage; inconspicuous, unobtrusive, unnoticed.

backhanded adjective *his coach Steve Alford offered him a backhanded compliment*: **ambiguous**, indirect, oblique, equivocal; double-edged, two-edged, barbed; tongue-in-cheek.
– OPPOSITES direct.

backing noun **1** *he has the full backing of his colleagues*: **support**, help, assistance, aid; approval, endorsement, sanction, blessing. **2** *you can't always get that sort of financial backing*: **sponsorship**, funding, patronage, money, investment, funds, finance; grant, contribution, subsidy. **3** *uptempo classical music played against a disco backing*: **accompaniment**; harmony, obbligato.

backlash noun *the backlash against feminism in society*: **adverse reaction**, counterblast, comeback; retaliation, reprisal.

backlog noun **accumulation**, logjam, pile-up.

back-pedal verb *the government has back-pedalled on its plans*: **change one's mind**, go into reverse, backtrack, back down, climb down, do an about-face, do a U-turn, renege, go back on, back out of, withdraw, take back, default on; Brit. do an about-turn.

backslide verb *many things can cause slimmers to backslide*: **relapse**, lapse, regress, retrogress, weaken, lose one's resolve, give in to temptation, go astray, leave the straight and narrow.
– OPPOSITES persevere.

backup noun *there is always backup available in case violence erupts*: **help**, support, assistance, aid; reinforcements, reserves, additional resources.

backward adjective **1** *he left without a backward glance*: **rearward**, to/towards the rear, to/towards the back, behind one, reverse. **2** *the court decision was a backward step for the UK*: **retrograde**, retrogressive, regressive, for the worse, in the wrong direction, downhill, negative. **3** *a war-torn, backward country*: **underdeveloped**, undeveloped; primitive, benighted.
– OPPOSITES forward, progressive, advanced. adverb *the car rolled slowly backward*. See **BACKWARDS**.

backwards adverb **1** *he walked backwards off the stage and fell into the orchestra pit*: **towards the rear**, rearwards, backward, behind one. **2** *count backwards from twenty to ten*: **in reverse**, in reverse order.
– OPPOSITES forwards.

backwash noun **1** *there was a lot of backwash and the sea was hard to get out of*: **wake**, wash, slipstream, backflow. **2** *the backwash from the Cuban Missile Crisis*: **repercussions**, reverberations, after-effects, aftermath, fallout.

backwoods plural noun *the backwoods of south-west Virginia*: **the back of beyond**, remote areas, the wilds, the hinterlands, a backwater; N. Amer. the backcountry, the backland; informal the middle of nowhere, the sticks; N. Amer. informal the boondocks, the boonies; Austral./NZ informal beyond the black stump.
adjective *some backwoods hick who thinks he's a hero*: **provincial**, rural, hillbilly, country, primitive, crude, simple.

bacteria plural noun **micro-organisms**, microbes, germs, bacilli, pathogens; informal bugs.

bad adjective **1** *the bad roads that criss-crossed the plains*: **substandard**, poor, inferior, second-rate, second-class, unsatisfactory, inadequate, unacceptable, not up to scratch, not up to par, deficient, imperfect, defective, faulty, shoddy; informal crummy, rotten, pathetic, useless, woeful, bum, lousy, ropy, not up to snuff; Brit. informal duff, rubbish, pants. **2** *the alcohol had a really bad effect on me*: **harmful**, damaging, detrimental, injurious, hurtful, inimical, destructive,

b

ruinous, negative; unhealthy, unwholesome. **3** *we debated whether human nature is good or bad:* **wicked**, sinful, immoral, evil, corrupt. **4** *he's not a bad person, really:* base, black-hearted, reprobate, amoral; criminal, villainous, nefarious, iniquitous, dishonest, dishonourable, unscrupulous, unprincipled; informal crooked, bent, dirty. **5** *you bad girl!* **naughty**, badly behaved, disobedient, wayward, wilful, self-willed, defiant, unruly, insubordinate, undisciplined. **6** *I'm afraid I've got some bad news:* **unpleasant**, disagreeable, unwelcome; unfortunate, unlucky, unfavourable; terrible, dreadful, awful, grim, distressing. **7** *it was a bad time to arrive:* **inauspicious**, unfavourable, inopportune, unfortunate, disadvantageous, adverse, inappropriate, unsuitable, untoward. **8** *a bad accident had closed both lanes of the A74:* **severe**, serious, grave, critical, acute; formal grievous. **9** *the meat's gone bad:* **rotten**, off, decayed, decomposed, decomposing, putrid, putrefied, mouldy; sour, rancid, rank, unfit for human consumption. **10** *if you feel bad, stay in bed.* See **ILL** adjective sense 1. **11** *a bad knee:* **injured**, wounded, diseased, damaged, stiff, sore; Brit. informal gammy, knackered; Austral./NZ informal crook. **12** *I felt bad about leaving them:* **guilty**, conscience-stricken, remorseful, guilt-ridden, ashamed, uncomfortable. **13** *all these bad cheques cost us money:* **invalid**, worthless; counterfeit, fake, false, bogus, fraudulent; informal phoney, dud. **14** *sex, violence, and bad language:* **offensive**, vulgar, crude, foul, obscene, rude, coarse, smutty, dirty, filthy, indecent; blasphemous, profane.
– OPPOSITES good, beneficial, virtuous, well behaved, minor, slight, fresh, unrepentant.
■ **not bad** *500 points is not bad for a beginner:* all right, adequate, good enough, reasonable, fair, decent, average, tolerable, acceptable, passable, middling, moderate, fine; informal OK, so-so, fair-to-middling.

badge noun **1** *a red plastic name badge:* pin, brooch; N. Amer. button. **2** *the ponytail became a badge of masculinity:* **sign**, symbol, indication, signal, mark; hallmark, trademark.

badger verb *we should badger our MP about it:* **pester**, harass, bother, plague, torment, hound, nag, chivvy, harry, keep on at, go on at; informal hassle, bug.

badly adverb **1** *a series of badly written, boring articles:* **poorly**, incompetently, ineptly, inexpertly, inefficiently, defectively, unsatisfactorily, inadequately, incorrectly, faultily, shoddily, amateurishly, carelessly, negligently; informal crummily, pitifully, woefully. **2** *try not to think badly of me:* **unfavourably**, ill, critically, disapprovingly. **3** *men behaving badly:* **naughtily**, disobediently, reprehensibly, mischievously. **4** *he had been badly treated by his employer:* **cruelly**, wickedly,

unkindly, harshly, shamefully; unfairly, unjustly, wrongly, improperly. **5** *things were going badly for Charles:* **unsuccessfully**, unfavourably, adversely, unfortunately, unhappily, unluckily. **6** *the mosque was badly damaged in an earthquake:* **severely**, seriously, gravely, acutely, critically; formal grievously. **7** *I was missing him badly and couldn't wait to get home:* **desperately**, sorely intensely, seriously, very much, greatly, exceedingly.
– OPPOSITES well, slightly.

bad-tempered adjective **irritable**, irascible, tetchy, testy, grumpy, grouchy, crotchety, in a (bad) mood, cantankerous, curmudgeonly, ill-tempered, ill-humoured, peevish, having got out of bed on the wrong side, cross, as cross as two sticks, fractious, pettish, crabby; informal snappish, on a short fuse; Brit. informal shirty, stroppy, ratty; N. Amer. informal cranky, ornery; Austral./NZ informal snaky; informal, dated miffy.
– OPPOSITES good-humoured, affable.

baffle verb *this decision has baffled the cast and crew of the film:* **perplex**, puzzle, bewilder, mystify, bemuse, confuse, confound, nonplus; informal flummox, faze, stump, beat, fox, be all Greek to, floor; N. Amer. informal discombobulate, buffalo.
– OPPOSITES enlighten.

baffled adjective **puzzled**, bewildered, confused, perplexed, mystified, bemused, confounded, flummoxed, fazed, nonplussed; N. Amer. informal discombobulated.

baffling adjective **puzzling**, bewildering, perplexing, mystifying, bemusing, confusing, unclear; inexplicable, incomprehensible, impenetrable, cryptic, opaque.
– OPPOSITES clear, comprehensible.

bag noun **1** *I searched in my bag for my lipstick:* **handbag**, shoulder bag, clutch bag, evening bag, pochette; N. Amer. pocketbook, purse. **2** *she began to unpack her bags:* **suitcase**, case, valise, portmanteau, holdall, grip, overnighter; backpack, rucksack, knapsack, haversack, kitbag, duffel bag; satchel; (**bags**) luggage, baggage.

baggage noun **luggage**, suitcases, cases, bags.

baggy adjective **loose-fitting**, loose, roomy, generously cut, full, ample, voluminous, billowing; oversized, shapeless, ill-fitting, tent-like, sack-like.
– OPPOSITES tight.

bail noun *he was released on bail:* **surety**, security, assurance, indemnity, indemnification; bond, guarantee, pledge; archaic gage.
■ **bail out 1** *the pilot bailed out:* eject, parachute to safety. **2** *if you don't bail out now, it could well be the sack:* leave, quit, get out, withdraw, move (on), make a move.
■ **bail someone/something out** rescue,

save, relieve; finance, help (out), assist, aid; informal save someone's bacon/neck/skin.

bait noun **1** *the fish are ready to bite as soon as they see the bait:* **lure**, fly, worm; troll, jig, plug. **2** *she was the bait to lure him into a trap:* **enticement**, lure, snare, trap, carrot, attraction, draw, magnet, incentive, temptation, inducement.
verb *it was childish of them to continually bait Chapman:* **taunt**, tease, goad, pick on, torment, persecute, plague, harry, harass, hound; informal needle; Brit. informal wind up.

bake verb **1** *bake the fish for 15–20 minutes:* **cook**, oven-bake, roast, dry-roast, pot-roast. **2** *the earth was baked by the burning sun:* **scorch**, burn, sear, parch, dry (up), desiccate; N. Amer. broil.

balance noun **1** *I tripped and lost my balance:* **stability**, equilibrium; footing. **2** *the importance of balance in broadcasting:* **fairness**, justice, impartiality; parity, equity, equilibrium, evenness, even-handedness, symmetry, correspondence, equality, equivalence, comparability. **3** *we need to maintain the proper balance of nutrients in the soil:* **proportion(s)**, ratio, combination, mix, mixture; interaction, relationship. **4** *I will pay you the balance on Thursday:* **remainder**, outstanding amount, rest, difference.
– OPPOSITES instability.
verb **1** *she balanced the vase on a pile of books:* **steady**, stabilize, level; rest, position, arrange, perch. **2** *we manage forests in a way that balances profitability and environmental sustainability:* **combine**, mix, bring together, offset, even out/up; juggle. **3** *romantic music that will balance the harshness of the story:* **counterbalance**, offset, even out/up, counteract, compensate for, make up for. **4** *you need to balance the costs against the benefits:* **weigh**, weigh up, compare, evaluate, consider, assess, appraise, judge.
■ **(to hang) in the balance** *the fate of the firm hung in the balance:* uncertain, undetermined, unsettled, unresolved, unsure, in limbo, up in the air, at a turning point, critical, at a critical stage, at a crisis point.
■ **on balance** *on balance, people still perform better than machines:* overall, all in all, all things considered, taking everything into consideration/account, by and large, on average, at the end of the day.

balanced adjective **1** *a balanced point of view:* **fair**, equitable, just, unbiased, unprejudiced, objective, impartial, dispassionate. **2** *you need to eat a balanced diet:* **mixed**, varied; healthy, sensible.
– OPPOSITES partial, unhealthy.

balcony noun **1** *the balcony of the villa faced south:* veranda, loggia, terrace, patio. **2** *the applause from the balcony was deafening:* **gallery**, upper circle; informal the gods.

bald adjective **1** *his bald head glistened with*

sweat: **hairless**, smooth, shaven, depilated; bald-headed. **2** *a bald patch on the front tyre:* **bare**, worn, smooth. **3** *a bald statement of intent:* **plain**, simple, unadorned, unvarnished, stark, severe, austere, brutal, harsh; blunt, direct, forthright, straight, straightforward, frank, upfront.
– OPPOSITES hairy, vague.

balderdash noun. See NONSENSE sense 1.

baldness noun **hair loss**, hairlessness; Medicine alopecia.

bale[1] noun *a bale of hay:* **bundle**, truss, bunch, pack, package, parcel.

bale[2] noun
■ **bale out.** See BAIL.

baleful adjective *Bill shot a baleful glance in her direction:* **menacing**, threatening, unfriendly, hostile, antagonistic, evil, vindictive, malevolent, malicious, malignant, malign, sinister; harmful, injurious, dangerous, noxious, pernicious, deadly, venomous, poisonous.
– OPPOSITES benevolent, friendly.

balk verb. See BAULK.

ball[1] noun *a ball of clay:* **sphere**, globe, orb, globule, spheroid, ovoid.

ball[2] noun *a fancy-dress ball:* **dance**, dinner dance, masked ball, masquerade; N. Amer. hoedown, prom; informal hop, disco, bop.

ballad noun **song**, folk song, shanty, ditty; poem, tale.

balloon noun hot-air balloon, barrage balloon; airship, dirigible, Zeppelin; informal blimp.
verb **1** *her long skirt ballooned in the wind:* **swell (out)**, puff out/up, bulge (out), bag, belly (out), fill (out), billow (out). **2** *the company's debts have ballooned:* **increase rapidly**, soar, rocket, shoot up, escalate, mount, surge, spiral; informal go through the roof, skyrocket.
– OPPOSITES plummet.

ballot noun **vote**, poll, election, referendum, plebiscite, show of hands.

ballyhoo noun (informal) *after all the ballyhoo, the film was a flop:* **publicity**, advertising, promotion, marketing, propaganda, puffery, build-up, boosting; fuss, excitement; informal hype, spiel, hoo-ha, hullabaloo, splash.

balm noun **1** *more men are now using a skin balm after shaving:* **ointment**, lotion, cream, salve, liniment, embrocation, rub, gel, emollient, unguent, balsam, moisturizer. **2** *the lapping water of the great river was a balm to the spirit:* **relief**, comfort, ease, succour, consolation, cheer, solace.
– OPPOSITES astringent, misery.

balmy adjective *the hot, balmy days of late summer:* **mild**, gentle, temperate, summery, calm, tranquil, clement, fine, pleasant, soothing, soft.
– OPPOSITES harsh, wintry.

ban verb **1** *smoking has been banned in public places:* **prohibit**, forbid, veto, proscribe,

b

disallow, outlaw, make illegal, embargo, bar, debar, block, stop, suppress. **2** *Gary was banned from the King George:* **exclude**, banish, bar, forbid.
– OPPOSITES permit, admit.
noun 1 *a ban on smoking:* **prohibition**, veto, proscription, embargo, bar, suppression, stoppage, interdict, interdiction, moratorium, injunction. **2** *a lifelong ban from driving:* **exclusion**, banishment.
– OPPOSITES permission, admission.

banal adjective *books with trivial content and banal style, so they're easier to read:* **trite**, hackneyed, clichéd, platitudinous, vapid, commonplace, ordinary, common, stock, conventional, stereotyped, overused, overdone, overworked, stale, worn out, tired, threadbare, hoary, hack, unimaginative, unoriginal, uninteresting, dull; informal old hat, corny, played out; N. Amer. informal cornball, dime-store.
– OPPOSITES original.

banality noun triteness, platitudinousness, vapidity, staleness, unimaginativeness, lack of originality, prosaicness, dullness; informal corniness.
– OPPOSITES originality.

band¹ noun *a long, narrow band of cloud:* **stripe**, strip, streak, line, bar, belt, swathe; technical striation.

band² noun **1** *the band played a few old favourite numbers:* **group**, pop group, ensemble, orchestra; informal combo. **2** *a band of volunteer drivers provides transport:* **group**, gang, mob, pack, troop, troupe, company, party, crew, body, posse; team, side, line-up; association, society, club, circle, fellowship, partnership, union, alliance, affiliation, institution, league, federation, clique, set, coterie; informal bunch.
verb *local people banded together and bought the mill:* **join (up)**, team up, join forces, pool resources, club together, get together; unite.
– OPPOSITES split up.

bandage noun *she had a bandage on her foot:* **dressing**, covering, gauze, compress, plaster, tourniquet; trademark Elastoplast, Band-Aid.
verb *she bandaged my knee:* **bind**, bind up, dress, cover, wrap, strap (up).

bandit noun *I'm a target for every bandit and assassin out there:* **robber**, thief, raider, mugger; outlaw, hijacker, looter, marauder, gangster; dated desperado; historical rustler.

bandy¹ adjective *I had buck teeth and bandy legs:* **bowed**, curved, bent; bow-legged, bandy-legged.
– OPPOSITES straight.

bandy² verb **1** *a lot of facts and figures were bandied about:* **spread (about/around)**, put about, toss about, discuss, rumour, mention, repeat. **2** *I'm not here to bandy words with you:* **exchange**, swap, trade.

bane noun *these adolescents were the bane of the long-suffering manager, Len:* **scourge**,

plague, curse, blight, burden, thorn in one's flesh/side.

bang noun **1** *the door slammed with a loud bang:* **thud**, thump, bump, crack, crash, smack, boom, clang, clap, knock, clunk, clonk; report, explosion, detonation; informal wham. **2** *he got a nasty bang on the head:* **blow**, knock, thump, bump, hit, smack, crack; informal bash, whack, thwack.
verb **1** *he banged the table with his fist:* **hit**, strike, beat, thump, hammer, knock, rap, pound, thud, punch, bump, smack, crack, slap, slam, pummel, buffet; informal bash, whack, thwack, clobber, clout, wallop, belt, biff, bop; Brit. informal slosh; N. Amer. informal boff, bust, slug, whale. **2** *the door banged shut:* **go bang**, thud, thump, boom, clap, pound, crack, crash; burst.

bangle noun **bracelet**, wristlet, anklet, armlet.

banish verb **1** *Weber was eventually banished on a trumped-up charge:* **exile**, expel, deport, eject, transport; cast out, oust, evict, throw out, exclude, shut out, ban. **2** *I banished all thought of illness from my mind:* **dispel**, dismiss, disperse, scatter, dissipate, drive away, chase away, shut out.
– OPPOSITES admit, engender.

banister noun **handrail**, railing, rail; baluster; balustrade.

bank¹ noun **1** *the banks of Lake Michigan:* **edge**, side; embankment, levee, border, verge, margin. **2** *we lay on a grassy bank:* **slope**, rise, incline, gradient, ramp; mound, ridge, hillock, hummock, knoll; bar, reef, shoal, shelf; accumulation, pile, heap, mass, drift. **3** *he gestured towards a bank of switches:* **array**, row, line, tier, group, series.
verb *Mike's aircraft banked sharply to the left:* **tilt**, lean, tip, slant, incline, angle, slope, list, camber, pitch, dip, cant.

bank² noun **1** *the banks have raised the rate of interest:* **financial institution**, merchant bank, savings bank, finance company, finance house; Brit. building society; N. Amer. savings and loan (association), thrift. **2** *the name will be on a file in the data bank:* **store**, reserve, stockpile, pool, fund, cache, hoard, deposit; library, archive, storehouse, reservoir, repository, depository.
verb **1** *I banked the money straight away:* **deposit**, pay in. **2** *they bank with Barclays:* **have an account**, use, be a customer.
■ **bank on** *it might arouse some interest, but don't bank on it:* rely on, depend on, count on, plan on, reckon on; anticipate, expect; be confident of, be sure of, pin one's hopes/faith on; N. Amer. informal figure on.

banknote noun **note**; N. Amer. bill; US informal greenback; (**banknotes**) paper money.

bankrupt adjective **1** *the company was declared bankrupt:* **insolvent**, failed, ruined; in debt, in the red, in arrears; Brit. in administration, in receivership; informal

bust, belly up, gone to the wall, broke. **2** *this government is bankrupt of ideas:* **bereft**, devoid, empty; (completely) lacking, without.
– OPPOSITES solvent, teeming with.
verb *the strike nearly bankrupted the union:* **ruin**, bring someone to their knees, wipe out, break, finish (off), destroy.

bankruptcy noun **insolvency**, liquidation, failure, (financial) ruin; Brit. administration, receivership.
– OPPOSITES solvency.

banner noun **1** *students waved banners:* **placard**, sign, poster, notice. **2** *the Star Spangled Banner:* **flag**, standard, ensign.

banquet noun **feast**, dinner; informal spread, blowout; Brit. informal nosh-up, slap-up meal.
– OPPOSITES snack.

banter noun *a brief exchange of harmless banter:* **repartee**, conversation, wordplay, cut and thrust, badinage; chat; Irish informal the crack; N. Amer. informal josh.
verb *sightseers were bantering with the guards:* **joke**, jest; chat; informal josh, wisecrack.

baptism noun **1** *the baptism ceremony:* **christening**, naming. **2** *his baptism as a politician:* **initiation**, debut, introduction, inauguration, launch, rite of passage.

baptize verb **1** *he was baptized as a baby:* **christen**; rare lustrate. **2** *they were baptized into the church:* **admit**, initiate, enrol, recruit, convert. **3** *he was baptized Enoch:* **name**, give the name, call, dub; formal denominate.

bar noun **1** *an iron bar:* **rod**, pole, stick, batten, shaft, rail, spar, strut, crosspiece, beam. **2** *a bar of chocolate:* **block**, slab, cake, tablet, brick, loaf, wedge, ingot. **3** *your drinks are standing on the bar:* **counter**, table, buffet, stand; worktop. **4** *she had a drink in a posh bar:* **hostelry**, tavern, inn, taproom; cafe, bistro; Brit. pub, public house; informal watering hole; Brit. informal local, boozer; N. Amer. historical saloon.
verb **1** *they have barred the door:* **bolt**, lock, fasten, secure, block, barricade. **2** *he was barred from seeking re-election:* **prohibit**, debar, preclude, forbid, ban; exclude, keep out; obstruct, hinder, block.
– OPPOSITES open, admit.
preposition *everyone bar me.* See EXCEPT preposition.

barb noun **1** *the hook has a nasty barb:* **spike**, prong, spur, thorn, needle, prickle, spine, quill. **2** *celebrity interviews full of barbs and innuendo:* **insult**, sneer, jibe, cutting remark, slight, brickbat, slur, jeer, taunt; (**barbs**) abuse, disparagement, scoffing, scorn, sarcasm, goading; informal dig, put-down.

barbarian noun *these people are terrorists, animals, and barbarians:* **savage**, animal, brute, beast; boor, thug, lout, vandal, hoodlum, hooligan; informal roughneck; Brit. informal yobbo, yob.

barbaric adjective *their barbaric medical practices sickened him:* **brutal**, barbarous, brutish, bestial, savage, vicious, wicked, cruel, ruthless, merciless, villainous, murderous, heinous, monstrous, vile, inhuman, infernal, dark, fiendish, diabolical.
– OPPOSITES civilized, compassionate.

barbarity noun **1** *words are insufficient to describe the barbarity of this act:* **brutality**, brutalism, cruelty, bestiality, barbarism, barbarousness, savagery, viciousness, wickedness, inhumanity. **2** *the barbarities of the war had driven him mad:* **atrocity**, act of brutality/savagery, crime, outrage.
– OPPOSITES benevolence, compassion.

barbarous adjective. See BARBARIC.

barbecue noun ... roast; N. Amer. cookout; informal barbie, BBQ.
verb grill, spit-roast; N. Amer. broil, charbroil; tandoori.

barbed adjective *Wilder's scripts were littered with barbed jokes:* **hurtful**, wounding, cutting, stinging, mean, spiteful, nasty, cruel, vicious, unkind, snide, scathing, pointed, bitter, acid, caustic, sharp, vitriolic, venomous, hostile, malicious, malevolent, vindictive; informal bitchy, catty.
– OPPOSITES kindly.

bare adjective **1** *the dust clung to her bare legs:* **naked**, exposed, unclothed, uncovered, stripped, nude. **2** *the stage was bare except for a few stools:* **empty**, unfurnished, clear; unadorned, unembellished, unornamented, plain. **3** *a little hill, bare of shrubbery but covered with grass:* **empty**, devoid, bereft; without, lacking, free from/of. **4** *paint was applied to the bare metal:* **uncovered**, exposed, stripped; naked. **5** *the report limited itself to stating the bare facts:* **basic**, essential, fundamental, plain, straightforward, simple, pure, stark, bald, cold, hard, brutal, harsh.
– OPPOSITES clothed, furnished, embellished, lush.
verb *I opened my shirt and bared my chest:* **uncover**, strip, lay bare, expose.
– OPPOSITES cover.

barefaced adjective *that's a barefaced lie and you know it:* **flagrant**, blatant, glaring, obvious, undisguised, unconcealed, naked; shameless, unabashed, unashamed, impudent, audacious, unblushing, brazen, brass-necked.

barely adverb *he sped away, his feet barely touching the road:* **hardly**, scarcely, just, only just; narrowly, by the skin of one's teeth, by a hair's breadth; informal by a whisker.
– OPPOSITES easily.

bargain noun **1** *how can I be certain that you'll keep your side of the bargain?* **agreement**, arrangement, understanding, deal; contract, pact, compact; pledge, promise. **2** *he's got an eye for a bargain:* **good buy**, cheap buy; (good) value for

b

b

money, surprisingly cheap; informal snip, steal, giveaway.
– OPPOSITES rip-off.
verb *he spent time haggling and bargaining in the market:* **haggle**, negotiate, discuss terms, hold talks, deal, barter.
adjective *most of the stuff is available at bargain prices:* **low**, reduced, cheap; informal rock-bottom.
■ **bargain for** *the hot-headed Frenchman got more than he bargained for:* expect, anticipate, be prepared for, allow for, plan for, reckon with, take into account/consideration, contemplate, imagine, envisage, foresee, predict.
■ **into the bargain** also, as well, in addition, additionally, besides, on top (of that), over and above that, to boot, for good measure; N. Amer. in the bargain.

barge noun lighter, canal boat; Brit. narrowboat, wherry; N. Amer. scow.
verb *Will barged between them, thrusting Gerry aside:* **push**, shove, thrust, ram.
■ **barge in** *don't you come barging in here and order me around:* burst in, break in, butt in, cut in, interrupt; intrude, encroach; informal horn in.

bark[1] noun *it was Lucky's bark that woke us up:* **woof**, yap, yelp, howl.
verb **1** *dogs barked, birds sang, ducks quacked:* **woof**, yap, yelp, howl, bay. **2** *'Okay, everyone outside!' he barked:* snap; shout, cry, yell, roar, bellow, thunder; informal holler.
– OPPOSITES whisper.

bark[2] noun *a milky white liquid oozes out of the bark:* **rind**, skin, peel, covering; cork; technical cortex.

barmy adjective (Brit. informal). See **FOOLISH**.

barn noun **outbuilding**, shed, outhouse, shelter; stable, stall; Brit. byre; archaic grange.

baron noun *the wife of a media baron:* **magnate**, tycoon, mogul, captain of industry.

baroque adjective *a complex world of fantasy and baroque imagery:* **ornate**, fancy, elaborate, extravagant, fussy, busy, ostentatious, showy.

barrack verb (Brit. & Austral./NZ) *Tony Blair was barracked on Friday by angry firefighters:* **jeer**, heckle, shout at/down; interrupt, boo, hiss.
– OPPOSITES applaud.

barracks plural noun **garrison**, camp, depot, billet, quarters, fort.

barrage noun **1** *an overnight artillery barrage killed at least four people:* **bombardment**; shelling; salvo, volley. **2** *Drummond faces a barrage of criticism following his appointment:* **deluge**, stream, storm, torrent, flood, tide, avalanche, hail, blaze.

barrel noun **1** *we have exported 15,000 oak barrels to France:* **cask**, keg, butt, vat, drum. **2** *I felt the cold metal of the barrel against my temple:* muzzle.

barren adjective **1** *peasants struggling to*

survive on barren ground: **unproductive**, infertile, unfruitful, sterile, arid; desert. **2** *we plodded on through the barren desert:* **empty**, arid, sterile, dead, bleak, featureless, deserted, lifeless.
– OPPOSITES fertile.

barricade noun *barricades went up and the riot police moved in:* **barrier**, roadblock, blockade; obstacle, obstruction.
verb *I barricaded the door, but they broke it down:* **seal (up)**, close up, block off, shut off/up.

barrier noun **1** *the barrier across the entrance:* **fence**, railing, barricade, blockade, roadblock. **2** *a barrier to international trade:* **obstacle**, obstruction, hurdle, stumbling block, bar, block, impediment, hindrance.

barring preposition *barring St John's, they have beaten everyone:* **except for**, with the exception of, excepting, bar, discounting, apart from, but for, other than, aside from, excluding, save for, saving; informal outside of.

barrister noun **counsel**, Queen's Counsel, QC, lawyer; Scottish advocate; N. Amer. attorney, counselor(-at-law); informal brief; (**barristers**) Brit. the Bar.

barter verb **1** *T-shirts were bartered for bread:* **trade**, swap, exchange, sell. **2** *she bartered tirelessly with the carpet sellers:* **haggle**, bargain, negotiate.
noun *an economy based on barter:* **trading**, trade, exchange, business, commerce, buying and selling, dealing.

base noun **1** *the base of the tower:* **foundation**, bottom, foot, support, stand, pedestal, plinth. **2** *the company needs to expand its client base:* **pool**, database, reserve, reservoir, platform, range. **3** *the Kharkov base had become a hive of activity:* **headquarters**, camp, site, station, settlement, post, centre.
– OPPOSITES top.
verb **1** *these allegations are based on good evidence:* **found**, build, construct, form, ground, root; use as a basis; (**be based on**) derive from, spring from, stem from, originate in, have its origin in, issue from. **2** *the company was based in London:* **locate**, situate, position, install, station, site, establish, garrison.

baseless adjective *she's already said that those rumours are baseless:* **groundless**, unfounded, ill-founded, without foundation; unsubstantiated, unproven, unsupported, uncorroborated, unconfirmed, unverified, unattested; unjustified, unwarranted; speculative, conjectural; unsound, unreliable, spurious, specious, trumped up, fabricated, untrue.
– OPPOSITES valid.

basement noun **cellar**, vault, crypt, undercroft; Brit. lower ground floor; Scottish dunny.

bashful adjective *many men are bashful about*

discussing their feelings: **shy**, reserved, diffident, inhibited, retiring, reticent, reluctant, shrinking; hesitant, timid, apprehensive, nervous, wary.
– OPPOSITES bold, confident.

basic adjective **1** *the need to maintain a level of basic fitness:* **fundamental**, essential, primary, principal, cardinal, elementary, elemental, quintessential, intrinsic, central, pivotal, critical, key, focal; vital, necessary, indispensable. **2** *although a bit basic, the apartments are all spotlessly clean:* **plain**, simple, unsophisticated, straightforward, adequate; unadorned, undecorated, unornamented, without frills; spartan, stark, severe, austere, limited, meagre, rudimentary, patchy, sketchy, minimal; rough (and ready), crude, makeshift; informal bog-standard.
– OPPOSITES secondary, unimportant, elaborate.

basically adverb *basically I have just put everything on hold:* **fundamentally**, essentially, in essence; firstly, first of all, first and foremost, primarily; at heart, at bottom; principally, chiefly, above all, most of all, mostly, mainly, on the whole, by and large, substantially; informal at the end of the day, when all is said and done.

basics plural noun *the basics of vegetarian cookery:* **fundamentals**, essentials, rudiments, (first) principles, foundations, preliminaries, groundwork; essence, basis, core; informal nitty-gritty, brass tacks, nuts and bolts, ABC.

basin noun **bowl**, dish, pan.

basis noun **1** *off-road riding is still the basis of his training programme:* **foundation**, support, base. **2** *the information used as the basis for her decision:* **rationale**, reasoning; reason, grounds, justification. **3** *we now have the basis of a new trade agreement:* **starting point**, base, point of departure, beginning, premise, fundamental point/principle, principal constituent, main ingredient, cornerstone, core, heart, thrust, essence, kernel, nub. **4** *he was employed on a part-time basis:* **footing**, condition, status, position; arrangement, system, method.

bask verb **1** *cats basked on the stone window sills:* **laze**, lie, lounge, relax, sprawl, loll; sunbathe, sun oneself. **2** *Christie refused to bask in the glory of his Olympic victory:* **revel**, delight, luxuriate, wallow, rejoice, glory; enjoy, relish, savour, lap up.

basket noun hamper, creel, pannier, punnet, trug.

bass adjective **low**, deep, low-pitched, resonant, sonorous, rumbling, booming, resounding; baritone.
– OPPOSITES high.

bastardize verb *he spoke franglais, bastardizing both languages:* **adulterate**, corrupt, contaminate, weaken, dilute, taint, pollute, debase, distort.

bastardized adjective *the bastardized Vivaldi that played all day in the reception area:* **bowdlerized**, adulterated, mutant, debased, cheap, poor man's, cheap and nasty, substandard, plastic; ersatz, phoney, pseudo, pretend, tacky.

bastion noun *Augusta has always been a Republican bastion:* **stronghold**, bulwark, defender, supporter, guard, protection, protector, defence, prop, mainstay.

batch noun **group**, quantity, lot, bunch, mass, cluster, raft, set, collection, bundle, pack; consignment, shipment.

bath noun **1** *he lay soaking in the bath:* **bathtub**, tub, hot tub, whirlpool, sauna, steam bath, Turkish bath; trademark jacuzzi. **2** *she had a bath, then got ready:* **wash**, soak, dip, scrub; shower.
verb *have you bathed?* | *he would bath the baby every night:* **bathe**, have/take a bath, give someone a bath, wash; shower.

bathe verb **1** *she bathed and dressed.* See BATH verb. **2** *it is not safe for children to bathe here:* **swim**, go swimming, take a dip. **3** *they bathed his wounds in warm water:* **clean**, wash, rinse, wet, soak, immerse.

bathing costume noun (Brit.) **swimsuit**, bathing suit; swimming trunks, bikini; swimwear; Brit. swimming costume; informal cossie; Austral./NZ informal bathers.

baton noun **1** *the conductor raised his baton:* **stick**, rod, staff, wand. **2** *he was hit by a police baton:* **truncheon**, club, cudgel, bludgeon, stick, mace; N. Amer. nightstick, blackjack; Brit. informal cosh.

battalion noun force, contingent, regiment, brigade, division, squadron, squad, company, section, detachment, legion, corps, cohort.

batten noun *the blinds can be fitted onto a wooden batten:* **bar**, bolt, rail, shaft; board, strip.

batter verb **pummel**, pound, buffet, belabour, thrash, beat up; informal knock about/around, beat the living daylights out of, give someone a good hiding, lay into, do over, rough up.

battered adjective **damaged**, shabby, run down, worn out, falling to pieces, falling apart, dilapidated, rickety, ramshackle, crumbling, the worse for wear, on its last legs.

battery noun **1** *change the battery at least once a year:* **cell**, accumulator. **2** *the cabinet housed a battery of fluorescent tubes:* **array**, set, bank, group, row, line, line-up, collection. **3** *I was subjected to a battery of medical tests:* **series**, sequence, cycle, string, succession. **4** *the closure left only one air defence battery in Wales:* **emplacement**, artillery unit.

battle noun **1** *the largest naval battle of all time:* **fight**, conflict, clash, struggle, skirmish, engagement, fray; war, campaign, crusade; fighting, warfare, combat, action,

b

hostilities, firefight; informal, dogfight, shoot-out. **2** *Guinness acquired Bell's whisky after a takeover battle in 1985:* **conflict**, clash, contest, competition, struggle, duel; dispute, controversy.

verb 1 *conservation groups battled to save the house from demolition:* **fight**, struggle, strive, work, campaign, lobby; war, feud. **2** *the company was battling lawsuits alleging copyright infringement:* **contest**, combat, contend with, resist, withstand, stand up to, confront. **3** *Mark battled his way to victory against enormous odds:* **force**, push, elbow, shoulder, fight; struggle, claw.

battle cry noun *the battle cry of the feminist movement:* **slogan**, motto, watchword, catchphrase, rallying cry; mantra.

battlement noun **parapet**, rampart, wall.

bauble noun *we were not impressed by all his silly baubles:* **trinket**, knick-knack, ornament, frippery, gewgaw, gimcrack, bibelot; N. Amer. kickshaw; N. Amer. informal tchotchke.

baulk verb *he baulked at having Mrs Lopatina as his mother-in-law:* **be unwilling to**, draw the line at, jib at, be reluctant to; eschew, resist, refuse to, take exception to; shrink from, recoil from, demur from.

bawdy adjective *Mark would sing bawdy songs in the bath:* **ribald**, indecent, risqué, racy, rude, spicy, sexy, suggestive, titillating, naughty, improper, indelicate, indecorous, off colour, earthy, broad, locker-room; pornographic, obscene, vulgar, crude, coarse, gross, lewd, dirty, filthy, smutty, unseemly, salacious, prurient, lascivious, licentious, near the bone, near the knuckle; informal X-rated, blue, raunchy, nudge-nudge; euphemistic adult.
– OPPOSITES clean, innocent.

bawl verb **1** *'Come on!' he bawled:* **shout**, yell, roar, bellow, screech, scream, shriek, howl, whoop, bark, trumpet, thunder; informal yammer, holler. **2** *the children continued to bawl:* **cry**, sob, weep, wail, whine, howl; Scottish informal greet.
– OPPOSITES whisper.
noun *he addressed every class in a terrifying bawl:* **shout**, yell, roar, bellow, screech, scream; voice.
– OPPOSITES whisper.
■ **bawl someone out** (informal). See REPRIMAND.

bay[1] noun *seven German warships were anchored in the bay:* **cove**, inlet, gulf, bight, basin, fjord, arm; anchorage.

bay[2] noun *the satellite was finally released from the shuttle's cargo bay:* **compartment**, area; space, cavity, recess; hold, room; deck.

bay[3] verb **1** *we ran for the car, dogs baying at our heels:* **howl**, bark, yelp, cry, bellow, roar. **2** *the opposition benches were baying for his blood:* **clamour**, shout, call, press, yell, scream, shriek, roar; demand.
■ **at bay** *the overuse of antibiotics to*

keep disease at bay: at a distance, away, off, at arm's length.

bayonet noun *he was stabbed by a man armed with a bayonet:* **sword**, knife; blade, spear, lance, pike, javelin.
verb *some prisoners protested and were bayoneted by the guards:* **stab**, spear, knife, spike, stick, impale, run through, transfix, gash, slash.

bazaar noun **1** *the bazaars and cafes of Baghdad:* **market**, market place, souk. **2** *we all helped with the bazaars and fund-raising:* **fête**, fair, jumble sale, bring-and-buy sale, car boot sale, carnival; fund-raiser; N. Amer. tag sale.

beach noun *a sandy beach lapped by the warm ocean:* **seaside**, seashore, shore, coast, coastline, littoral, seaboard, foreshore, water's edge; sands, lido; literary strand.
verb **1** *they beached the boat and walked up to the house:* **land**, ground, run aground, run ashore. **2** *65 dolphins have been beached on Cornish shores so far this year:* **ground**, strand, maroon, wash up/ashore.

beachcomber noun **scavenger**, forager, collector; informal scrounger.

beached adjective **1** *rows of beached fishing boats lay along the shore:* **grounded**; aground, ashore. **2** *she lay sprawled on the double bed like a beached whale:* **stranded** marooned, high and dry, stuck.

beacon noun **signal**, light, flare, fire; transmitter, aerial, mast, buoy, marker; sign, symbol.

bead noun **1** *her costume was made entirely of feathers and beads:* **ball**, pellet, globule, sphere, orb, round; (**beads**) necklace, rosary, chaplet. **2** *a bead of sweat ran down the side of his face:* **droplet**, drop, blob, dot.

beak noun **bill**, nib; Scottish & N. English neb.

beaker noun **cup**, tumbler, glass, mug, drinking vessel.

beam noun **1** *the two bells hung from a stout oak beam:* **joist**, lintel, rafter; spar, girder, baulk, timber, plank; support, strut; transom. **2** *a beam of light from the window lit up the path:* **ray**, shaft, stream, streak, pencil, finger; flash, gleam, glow, glimmer, glint, flare.
verb **1** *the message is beamed worldwide by satellite:* **broadcast**, transmit, relay, send/put out, disseminate; direct, aim. **2** *the sun beamed down and I lay on the bench:* **shine**, burn, glare; gleam. **3** *he beamed broadly and shook my hand:* **grin**, smile, smirk; informal be all smiles.
– OPPOSITES frown.

bear verb **1** *she arrived bearing gifts for everyone:* **carry**, bring, convey, take; informal tote. **2** *the bag clearly bore his name:* **display**, exhibit, be marked with, show, carry, have. **3** *the bridge was unable to bear her weight:* **support**, carry, hold, sustain. **4** *they can't bear the cost alone:* **sustain**, carry, support, shoulder, absorb, take on. **5** *she bore no* grudges: **harbour**, foster, entertain, cherish, nurse. **6** *such a solution does not bear close scrutiny:* **withstand**, stand up to, stand, put up with, take, cope with, handle, sustain, accept. **7** *I can't bear having him around:* **endure**, tolerate, put up with, stand, abide, go through with, countenance, brave, weather, stomach, support; Scottish thole; informal hack, swallow; Brit. informal stick, wear, be doing with; archaic suffer. **8** *the antelope bears one large calf each year:* **give birth to**, bring forth, deliver, be delivered of, have, produce; N. Amer. birth; informal drop. **9** *a shrub that bears waxy yellow berries:* **produce**, yield, give forth, give, grow, provide, supply. **10** *bear left at the junction:* **veer**, curve, swerve, fork, diverge, deviate, turn, bend.

■ **bear down on** *the Chinese intend to bear down on environmental lawbreakers:* advance on, close in on, move in on, converge on, put pressure on.

■ **bear fruit** *it would be many years before the scheme would bear fruit:* yield results, succeed, pay dividends, be successful, be effective, be profitable, work; informal pay off.

■ **bear something in mind** *please bear in mind that these plans can be revised:* take into account, take into consideration, remember, consider, be mindful, mind, mark, heed.

■ **bear on** *points of view which bear on the issue of taxation:* be relevant to, appertain to, pertain to, relate to, have a bearing on, have relevance to, apply to, be pertinent to.

■ **bear something out** *do the statistics bear out these fears?* confirm, corroborate, substantiate, endorse, vindicate, support, ratify, warrant, uphold, justify, prove, authenticate, verify.

■ **bear up** *the parents were brave, and they were trying to bear up, but it was hard:* remain cheerful, grin and bear it; cope, manage, get by, muddle through.

■ **bear with** *please bear with me while I explain the details:* be patient with, show forbearance towards, make allowances for, tolerate, put up with, endure.

■ **bear witness/testimony to** *these ruined churches bear witness to the island's turbulent past:* testify to, be evidence of, be proof of, attest to, evidence, prove; demonstrate, show, establish, indicate, reveal, bespeak.

bearable adjective **tolerable**, endurable, supportable, sustainable.

beard noun **facial hair**, whiskers, stubble, designer stubble, five o'clock shadow, bristles; goatee.

bearded adjective **unshaven**, whiskered, whiskery, bewhiskered; stubbly, bristly.
– OPPOSITES clean shaven.

bearer noun **1** *all regiments include a standard bearer:* **carrier**, porter. **2** *I'm sorry to be the bearer of bad news:* **messenger**, agent, conveyor, carrier, bringer. **3** *the*

cheque should be crossed and made payable to the bearer: **holder**, possessor, owner.

bearing noun **1** *he was a large and imposing presence, with a rather military bearing:* **posture**, stance, carriage, gait; Brit. deportment; formal comportment. **2** *there was something majestic about his bearing:* **demeanour**, manner, air, aspect, attitude, behaviour, mien, style. **3** *this has no bearing on the matter in hand:* **relevance**, pertinence, connection, appositeness, importance, significance, application. **4** *continue on a bearing of 190 degrees for another 50m:* **direction**, orientation, course, trajectory, heading, tack, path, line, run. **5** (**bearings**) *I lost my bearings in the forest:* **orientation**, sense of direction; whereabouts, location, position.

beast noun **1** *this beast was believed to be the offspring of a panther and a camel:* **animal**, creature; N. Amer. informal critter. **2** *you filthy beast:* **animal**, brute, monster, swine, pig, devil; ogre, fiend, sadist, savage.

beastly adjective (Brit. informal) **1** *Tweed had nothing to do with that beastly murder:* **awful**, horrible, rotten, nasty, vile, hateful, detestable; informal terrible, God-awful. **2** *every time her father was beastly to her, she got her own back:* **unkind**, mean, nasty, unpleasant, unfriendly, spiteful, cruel; informal horrible, horrid, rotten.
– OPPOSITES pleasant, kind.

beat verb **1** *she called the police after being beaten by her ex-husband:* **hit**, strike, batter, thump, bang, hammer, punch, knock, thrash, pound, pummel, slap; assault, attack, abuse; club, birch; informal wallop, belt, bash, whack, clout, clobber, slug, tan, biff, bop, sock, deck, plug, beat the living daylights out of, give someone a good hiding. **2** *the waves beat against the cliffs:* **break on/against**, dash against; lash, strike, lap, wash; splash, roll. **3** *the metal is beaten into a narrow strip:* **hammer**, forge, form, shape, mould, work, stamp, fashion, model. **4** *her heart was beating furiously:* **pulsate**, pulse, palpitate, vibrate, throb; pump, pound, thump, thud, hammer, drum; pitter-patter, go pit-a-pat. **5** *the tiny bird beat its wings frantically against the bars:* **flap**, flutter, thresh, thrash, wave, vibrate. **6** *beat the cream into the rest of the mixture:* **whisk**, mix, blend, whip. **7** *South Korea beat Italy:* **defeat**, conquer, win against, get the better of, vanquish, trounce, rout, overpower, overcome, subdue; informal lick, thrash, whip, wipe the floor with, clobber. **8** *he beat the previous record by over five seconds:* **surpass**, exceed, better, improve on, go one better than, eclipse, top, trump, cap.
noun **1** *a pounding, relentless techno beat filled the air:* **rhythm**, pulse, metre, time, measure, cadence; stress, accent. **2** *he felt the beat of her heart against his chest:* **pulse**, pulsation, vibration, throb, palpitation, reverberation; pounding, thump, thud,

b

hammering, drumming; pit-a-pat. **3** *a community policeman on his inner-city beat:* **circuit**, round, route, way, path.

■ **beat someone/something off** *Thompson successfully beat off the German challenge and retained his title:* repel, fight off, fend off, stave off, repulse, drive away/back, force back, beat back, push back, put to flight.

■ **beat someone up** *he watched his drunken father beat up his mother:* assault, attack, mug, thrash; informal knock about/around, do over, work over, rough up, fill in, lay into, beat the living daylights out of, let someone have it; Brit. informal duff someone up; N. Amer. informal beat up on.

beatific adjective *Adam looked up, a beatific smile on his face:* **rapturous**, joyful, ecstatic, seraphic, blissful, serene, happy, beaming.

beautiful adjective **attractive**, pretty, handsome, good-looking, alluring, prepossessing; lovely, charming, delightful, appealing, engaging, winsome; ravishing, gorgeous, stunning, arresting, glamorous, bewitching, beguiling; graceful, elegant, exquisite, artistic, magnificent; Scottish & N. English bonny; informal tasty, divine, knockout, drop-dead gorgeous, fanciable; Brit. informal smashing; N. Amer. informal cute, foxy; Austral./NZ informal beaut, spunky.
– OPPOSITES ugly.

beautify verb *he can grow flowers to beautify the garden:* **adorn**, embellish, enhance, decorate, ornament, garnish, gild, smarten, prettify, enrich, glamorize, spruce up, deck (out), trick out, grace; informal get up, do up, do out, tart up.
– OPPOSITES spoil, uglify.

beauty noun **1** *several people remarked on the beauty of the surroundings:* **attractiveness**, prettiness, good looks, comeliness, allure; loveliness, charm, appeal; winsomeness, grace, elegance, exquisiteness; splendour, magnificence, grandeur, impressiveness, decorativeness; gorgeousness, glamour; Scottish & N. English bonniness. **2** *the 21-year old beauty already has a string of achievements to her name:* **beautiful woman**, belle, vision, Venus, goddess, beauty queen, English rose; informal looker, good-looker, lovely, stunner, knockout, bombshell, dish, cracker, peach, eyeful, bit of all right; Brit. informal smasher. **3** *the beauty of this plan lay in its simplicity:* **advantage**, attraction, strength, benefit, boon, blessing, good thing, strong point, virtue, merit, selling point.
– OPPOSITES ugliness, drawback.

beaver
■ **beaver away** (informal). See **SLOG** verb sense1.

becalmed adjective **motionless**, still, at a standstill, at a halt, unmoving, stuck.

because conjunction **since**, as, in view of the fact that, owing to the fact that, seeing that/as; informal on account of.
– OPPOSITES despite.
■ **because of** on account of, as a result of, as

a consequence of, owing to, due to; thanks to, by/in virtue of; formal by reason of.

beckon verb **1** *the guard beckoned to Benny:* **gesture**, signal, wave, gesticulate, motion. **2** *rows of sunbeds beckon you to unwind beside the pool:* **invite**, tempt, coax, lure, charm, attract, draw, call.

become verb **1** *she became depressed and started drinking:* **grow**, get, turn, come to be, get to be. **2** *Germany became Poland's main trading partner:* **turn into**, change into, be transformed into, be converted into. **3** *he became Foreign Secretary:* **be appointed (as)**, be assigned as, be nominated, be elected (as), be made. **4** *she wears a violet robe which becomes her well:* **suit**, flatter, look good on; set off, show to advantage; informal do something for.
■ **become of** *what in the world has become of her?* happen to, be the fate of, be the lot of, overtake; literary befall, betide.

becoming adjective *I always think that curls look very becoming:* **flattering**, fetching; attractive, lovely, pretty, handsome; stylish, elegant, chic, fashionable, tasteful; archaic comely.

bed noun **1** *she sighed and got into bed:* couch, cot, cradle, berth, billet; informal the sack, the hay; Brit. informal one's pit; Scottish informal one's kip. **2** *a south-facing flower bed:* **patch**, plot, border, strip. **3** *before the mould is made, the figures are laid on a bed of clay:* **base**, foundation, support, prop, substructure, substratum. **4** *sunlight glints through the trees, illuminating the river bed:* **bottom**, floor.
■ **bed down**. See GO TO BED.
■ **go to bed** *after supper I went to bed:* retire, call it a day; go to sleep, have/take a nap, have a doze, get some sleep; informal hit the sack, hit the hay, turn in, snatch forty winks, get some shut-eye; Brit. informal have a kip, get some kip, hit the pit; N. Amer. informal catch some Zs.

bedclothes plural noun **bedding**, sheets and blankets; bed linen; bedcovers, covers.

bedeck verb *the Christmas tree which we bedeck with gifts each year:* **decorate**, adorn, ornament, embellish, furnish, garnish, trim, deck, grace, enrich, dress up, trick out; swathe, wreathe, festoon; informal get up, do out.

bedevil verb *the long-term debts that bedevil many fourth-division clubs:* **afflict**, torment, beset, assail, beleaguer, plague, blight, rack, oppress, curse, dog; harass, distress, trouble, worry, torture.

bedlam noun *as he was led in, there was bedlam in the courtroom:* **uproar**, pandemonium, commotion, mayhem, confusion, disorder, chaos, anarchy, lawlessness; furore, upheaval, hubbub, hurly-burly, turmoil, riot, ruckus, rumpus, tumult; informal hullabaloo, ructions.
– OPPOSITES calm.

bedraggled adjective *a bedraggled group of men eventually arrived at the base camp:* **dishevelled**, disordered, untidy, unkempt, tousled, disarranged, in a mess; N. Amer. informal mussed.
– OPPOSITES neat, clean, dry.

bedridden adjective *Liz is bedridden with severe bronchitis:* **confined to bed**, immobilized; informal laid up, flat on one's back.

bedrock noun *in all civilized countries, the bedrock of democracy is the justice system:* **core**, basis, base, foundation, roots, heart, backbone, principle, essence, nitty-gritty; informal nuts and bolts.

bedspread noun **bedcover**, coverlet, quilt, throw-over, blanket; Brit. eiderdown; N. Amer. throw, spread, comforter; dated counterpane.

beef (informal) noun *I have no beef about people earning an honest living:* **complaint**, criticism, objection, cavil, quibble, grievance, grumble, grouse; informal gripe, grouch, moan, whinge.
verb *the security budget includes money to beef up airport security:* **toughen up**, strengthen, build up, reinforce, consolidate, invigorate, improve.

beefy adjective (informal) **1** *a big, beefy man in a Harley Davidson T-shirt:* **muscular**, brawny, hefty, burly, hulking, strapping, well built, solid, strong, heavy, sturdy; informal hunky, husky. **2** *those beefy tyres deliver plenty of traction in all conditions:* **strong**, robust, heavy-duty, heavy, solid, hefty, powerful, chunky, muscular.
– OPPOSITES puny.

beer noun **ale**, brew; Brit. informal wallop, pint, jar; lager, bitter; Austral./NZ informal hop, sherbet.

beetle verb (informal) *they beetled down to the campsite followed by hordes of scruffy children:* **scurry**, scamper, scuttle, bustle, hurry, hasten, rush, dash; informal scoot, zip.

befall verb (literary) *this is the latest tragedy to befall young people travelling in Australia:* **happen to**, overtake, come upon, be visited on.

befitting adjective *he couldn't have chosen a more befitting slogan:* **appropriate**, apt, fit, suitable, suited, proper, right.
preposition **in keeping with**, as befits, appropriate to, fit for, suitable for, suited to, proper to, right for, compatible with, consistent with, in character with; archaic meet for.

before preposition **1** *he had a quick drink before going out:* **prior to**, previous to, earlier than, preparatory to, in preparation for, preliminary to, in anticipation of, in expectation of, in advance of, ahead of, leading up to, on the eve of; rare anterior to. **2** *he appeared before the magistrate on Tuesday morning:* **in front of**, in the presence of, in the sight of. **3** *these men are loyal to God before anything else:* **in**

preference to, rather than, sooner than.
– OPPOSITES after.
adverb **1** *he had lied under oath before and would do so again:* **previously**, before now/then, until now/then, up to now/then; earlier, formerly, hitherto, in the past, in days gone by. **2** *a small party went on before to set up camp:* **ahead**, in front, in advance.
– OPPOSITES behind.

beforehand adverb *I'd like to spend some time with Sarah beforehand:* **in advance**, in readiness, ahead of time; before, before now/then, earlier (on), previously, already, sooner.
– OPPOSITES afterwards.

befriend verb *I only made things worse for myself by befriending Ian:* **make friends with**, get to know.

befuddled adjective *her reaction was one of befuddled astonishment:* **confused**, muddled, addled, bewildered, disorientated, all at sea, fazed, perplexed, dazed, dizzy, stupefied, groggy, muzzy, foggy, fuzzy, dopey, woozy; informal mixed up; N. Amer. informal discombobulated.
– OPPOSITES clear.

beg verb **1** *he was reduced to begging on the streets:* **ask for money**; informal sponge, cadge, scrounge, bum; Brit. informal scab; N. Amer. informal mooch; Austral./NZ informal bludge. **2** *we begged for more time:* **ask for**, plead for, appeal for, call for, sue for, solicit, seek, press for. **3** *he begged her not to go into the army:* **implore**, entreat, plead with, appeal to, supplicate, pray to, importune; ask, request, call on, petition; literary beseech.

beget verb *violence begets violence:* **cause**, give rise to, lead to, result in, bring about, create, produce, generate, engender, spawn, occasion, bring on, precipitate, prompt, provoke, kindle, trigger, spark off, touch off, stir up, whip up, induce, inspire.

beggar noun **1** *if you stop on the street for a moment, the beggars tug at your arms:* **tramp**, vagrant, vagabond; N. Amer. hobo; informal scrounger, sponger, cadger, freeloader; Brit. informal dosser; N. Amer. informal bum, moocher, mooch, schnorrer; Austral./NZ informal bagman, bludger. **2** (informal) *you lucky beggar!* See PERSON.

begin verb **1** *we began work first thing in the morning:* **start**, commence, set about, go about, embark on, launch into, get down to, take up; initiate, set in motion, institute, inaugurate, get ahead with; informal get cracking on, get going on. **2** *he began by saying hello to everyone:* **open**, lead off, get under way, get going, get off the ground, start (off), go ahead, commence; informal start the ball rolling, kick off, get the show on the road. **3** *when did the illness actually begin?* **appear**, arise, become apparent, make an appearance, spring up, crop up, turn up, come into existence, come into being, originate, start, commence, develop; literary come to pass.

b

– OPPOSITES finish, end, disappear.

beginner noun **novice**, starter, (raw) recruit, newcomer, tyro, fledgling, neophyte, initiate, fresher, freshman, cub, probationer; N. Amer. tenderfoot; informal rookie, new kid (on the block), newie, newbie; N. Amer. informal greenhorn, probie.
– OPPOSITES expert, veteran.

beginning noun **1** *this change in attitude signified the beginning of socialism:* **dawn**, birth, inception, conception, origination, genesis, emergence, rise, start, commencement, starting point, onset, outset; day one; informal kick-off. **2** *I've read the beginning of the article:* **opening**, start, commencement, first part, introduction, preamble, opening statement. **3** *the therapy has its beginnings in China:* **origin**, source, roots, starting point, birthplace, fons et origo, cradle, spring, early stages, fountainhead; genesis, creation.
– OPPOSITES end, conclusion.

begrudge verb **1** *it was obvious she begrudged Brian his affluence:* **envy**, grudge; resent, be jealous of, be envious of. **2** *I don't begrudge the support we've been given:* **resent**, feel aggrieved about, feel bitter about, be annoyed about, be resentful of, grudge, mind, object to, take exception to, regret.

beguile verb **1** *she was beguiled by his charming manner:* **charm**, attract, enchant, entrance, win over, woo, captivate, bewitch, spellbind, dazzle, hypnotize, mesmerize, seduce. **2** *the show has been beguiling children for years:* **entertain**, amuse, delight, please, occupy, absorb, engage, distract, divert, fascinate, enthral, engross.
– OPPOSITES repel, bore.

beguiling adjective *he spoke to her in that soft, beguiling voice:* **charming**, enchanting, entrancing, charismatic, captivating, bewitching, spellbinding, hypnotizing, mesmerizing, magnetic, alluring, enticing, tempting, inviting, seductive, irresistible.
– OPPOSITES unappealing.

behalf
■ **on behalf of/on someone's behalf 1** *I am writing to you on behalf of my client:* for, in the name of, in place of, on the authority of, at the behest of. **2** *he campaigned tirelessly on behalf of cyclists:* in the interests of, in support of, for, for the benefit of, for the good of, for the sake of.

behave verb **1** *she behaved abominably last night:* **conduct oneself**, act, acquit oneself, bear oneself. **2** *for once, the children behaved and we had a lovely afternoon:* **act correctly**, act properly, be well behaved, be good; be polite, mind one's manners, mind one's Ps and Qs.
– OPPOSITES misbehave.

behaviour noun **1** *his behaviour yesterday was inexcusable:* **conduct**, deportment, bearing; actions, doings; manners, ways; formal comportment. **2** *we examined the structure and behaviour of these organisms:* **functioning**, action, performance, operation, working, reaction, response.

behead verb **decapitate**, cut someone's head off, guillotine.

behest noun (literary) *Mary signed away her kingdom at the behest of King Henry:* **instruction**, requirement, demand, insistence, bidding, request, wish, desire, will; command, order, decree, ruling, directive; informal say-so.

behind preposition **1** *he hid behind a tree and waited:* **at the back/rear of**, beyond, on the far/other side of; N. Amer. in back of. **2** *a policeman walked behind him all the way to the office:* **after**, following, at the back/rear of, hard on the heels of, in the wake of. **3** *you are behind the rest of the class:* **less advanced than**, slower than, weaker than. **4** *the group was behind the bombings in the capital:* **responsible for**, at the bottom of; to blame for, guilty of. **5** *they know they have the team behind them:* **supporting**, backing, for, on the side of, in agreement with; financing; informal rooting for.
– OPPOSITES in front of, ahead of.
adverb **1** *a man followed behind with a placard:* **after**, afterwards, at the back/end, in the rear. **2** *I looked behind and saw a grey Mercedes:* **over one's shoulder**, to/towards the back, to/towards the rear, backwards. **3** *we're a bit behind, so don't stop:* **late**, running late, behind schedule, behindhand, not on time, behind time. **4** *he was behind with his rent:* **in arrears**, overdue; late, behindhand.
– OPPOSITES in front, ahead.
noun (informal) *he landed on his behind with a bump.* See **BOTTOM** noun sense 6.
■ **put something behind one** *the team have to put last night's result behind them:* consign to the past, put down to experience, regard as water under the bridge, forget about, ignore.

behold verb (literary) *after fourteen years here, this spring I beheld my garden with astonishment:* **see**, observe, view, look at, watch, survey, gaze at/upon, regard, contemplate, inspect, eye; catch sight of, glimpse, spot, spy, notice; informal clap eyes on, clock; N. Amer. informal eyeball; literary espy.

beige adjective **fawn**, pale brown, buff, sand, sandy, oatmeal, biscuit-coloured, coffee-coloured, café au lait, camel, ecru.

being noun **1** *I hate this man with my entire being:* **existence**, living, life, reality, lifeblood, vital force. **2** *we are all spiritual beings at heart:* **creature**, life form, living entity, living thing, (living) soul, individual, person, human (being).

belabour verb **1** *he belaboured the driver about the head with his fists:* **beat**, hit, strike, smack, batter, pummel, pound, buffet, thrash; N. Amer. beat up on; informal wallop, whack, clout, clobber, bop, biff, sock, plug; N. Amer. informal whale; archaic smite. **2** *he was*

primarily concerned with belabouring the failings of the previous generation: **criticize**, attack, berate, censure, condemn, denounce, denigrate, revile, pillory, flay, lambaste, savage, tear/pull to pieces, run down; informal knock, slam, pan, bash, take apart, crucify, hammer, lay into, roast; Brit. informal slate, rubbish, slag off; N. Amer. informal pummel, cut up; formal castigate, excoriate.
– OPPOSITES praise, understate.

belated adjective Gilman makes her belated New York debut this summer: **late**, overdue, behindhand, behind time, behind schedule, delayed, tardy, unpunctual.
– OPPOSITES early.

belch verb 1 onions always make me belch: bring up wind; informal **burp**; Scottish & N. English informal rift. 2 the furnace belched smoke and flames: **emit**, give off, give out, pour out, discharge, disgorge, spew out, spit out, vomit, cough up.
noun he gave a loud belch: informal **burp**; Scottish & N. English informal rift; formal eructation.

beleaguered adjective an effort by a beleaguered Congress to answer criticisms of the legal system: **hard-pressed**, troubled, in difficulties, under pressure, under stress, with one's back to the wall, in a tight corner, in a tight spot; informal up against it.

belie verb 1 the look in his eyes belied his easy manner: **contradict**, be at odds with, call into question, give the lie to, disprove, debunk, discredit; formal confute. 2 this light-hearted speech belies his deep disappointment: **conceal**, cover, disguise.
– OPPOSITES testify to, reveal.

belief noun 1 it's my belief that party politics is becoming increasingly irrelevant: **opinion**, view, conviction, judgement, thinking, way of thinking, idea, theory, conclusion, notion. 2 my belief in God has been a tremendous source of comfort: **faith**, trust, reliance, confidence, credence. 3 he spoke out against traditional religious beliefs: **ideology**, principle, ethic, tenet, canon; doctrine, teaching, dogma, creed, credo.
– OPPOSITES disbelief, doubt.

believable adjective **credible**, plausible, tenable, able to hold water, conceivable, likely, probable, possible, feasible, reasonable, with a ring of truth.
– OPPOSITES inconceivable.

believe verb 1 I'm afraid I don't believe you any more: **be convinced by**, trust, have confidence in. 2 if you believe that, you must be mad: **accept**, be convinced by, give credence to, credit, trust; informal swallow, buy, go for. 3 I believed that my phone was being tapped: **think**, be of the opinion that, imagine, suspect, suppose, assume, presume, take it, surmise, conclude, deduce, understand, be given to understand, gather, fancy, guess, dare say; informal reckon, figure.
– OPPOSITES doubt.
■ **believe in** I believe in a varied diet and lots of exercise: have faith in, pin one's faith on, trust in, have every confidence in, cling to, set (great) store by, value, be convinced by, be persuaded by; subscribe to, approve of; informal swear by, rate.

believer noun plays which told Bible stories to illiterate believers in medieval times: **devotee**, adherent, disciple, follower, supporter, upholder, worshipper; Christian, Muslim.
– OPPOSITES infidel, sceptic.

belittle verb the opposition constantly belittled the government's achievements: **disparage**, denigrate, run down, deprecate, depreciate, downgrade, play down, trivialize, minimize, make light of, treat lightly; informal do down, pooh-pooh.
– OPPOSITES praise, magnify.

bellicose adjective the extreme right adopted a bellicose attitude to Europe: **belligerent**, aggressive, hostile, antagonistic, pugnacious, truculent, confrontational, contentious, militant, combative; informal spoiling for a fight; Brit. informal stroppy, bolshie; N. Amer. informal scrappy.
– OPPOSITES peaceable.

belligerent adjective she stared round in a belligerent manner: **hostile**, aggressive, threatening, antagonistic, pugnacious, bellicose, truculent, confrontational, contentious, militant, combative; informal spoiling for a fight; Brit. informal stroppy, bolshie; N. Amer. informal scrappy.
– OPPOSITES peaceable.

bellow verb he cringed as she bellowed in his ear: **roar**, shout, bawl, thunder, trumpet, boom, bark, yell, shriek, howl, scream; informal holler.
– OPPOSITES whisper.
noun he gave a bellow of pain: **roar**, shout, bawl, bark, yell, yelp, shriek, howl, scream; informal holler.
– OPPOSITES whisper.

belly noun he scratched his hairy belly: **stomach**, abdomen, paunch, middle, midriff, girth; informal tummy, tum, gut, guts, insides, pot, pot belly, beer belly, beer gut, bread basket; Scottish informal kyte; N. Amer. informal bay window; dated corporation.
verb her skirt bellied out in the wind: **billow (out)**, bulge (out), balloon (out), bag (out), fill (out); distend.
– OPPOSITES sag, flap.

belong verb 1 the house belongs to his mother: **be owned by**, be the property of, be the possession of, be held by, be in the hands of. 2 I no longer belong to a trade union: **be a member of**, be in, be affiliated to, be allied to, be associated with. 3 the garden belongs to the basement flat: **be part of**, be attached to, go with. 4 these creatures belong with the insects: **be classed**, be classified, be categorized, be included, have a place, be located, be situated, be found, lie. 5 she feels she doesn't belong here: **fit in**, be suited to, have a rightful place, have a home; informal go, click.

b

belonging noun *the club helps give people a sense of belonging:* **affiliation**, acceptance, association, attachment, integration, closeness; rapport, fellow feeling, fellowship.
– OPPOSITES alienation.

belongings plural noun *she carried a canvas bag containing all her belongings:* **possessions**, effects, worldly goods, property; paraphernalia; informal gear, tackle, kit, things, stuff, bits and pieces, bits and bobs; Brit. informal clobber, gubbins.

beloved adjective *she wrote regularly to her beloved brother:* **darling**, dear, dearest, precious, adored, much loved, cherished, treasured, prized, highly regarded, admired, esteemed, revered, venerated.
– OPPOSITES hated.
noun *he watched his beloved from the end of the garden:* **sweetheart**, love, darling, dearest, lover, girlfriend, boyfriend, young lady, young man, lady friend; informal steady, baby, angel, honey, pet.

below preposition **1** *the water rushed below them:* **beneath**, under, underneath, further down than, lower than. **2** *their income is below the national average:* **less than**, lower than, under, not as much as, smaller than. **3** *a captain is below a major in rank:* **lower than**, under, inferior to, subordinate to, subservient to.
– OPPOSITES above, over, more than.
adverb **1** *I looked out to see what was happening below:* **further down**, lower down, in a lower position, underneath, beneath. **2** *please answer the questions below:* **underneath**, following.

belt noun **1** *the belt of her coat had come undone:* **girdle**, sash, strap, cummerbund, band. **2** *the farmers in the cotton belt are doing very well:* **region**, area, district, zone, sector, territory; tract, strip, stretch.
verb **1** *she belted the children in:* **fasten**, tie, bind; secure. **2** (informal) *he belted down the hill.* See SPEED verb sense 1.
■ **below the belt** *she thinks what they have done is a bit below the belt:* unfair, unjust, unacceptable, inequitable; unethical, unprincipled, immoral, unscrupulous, unsporting, sneaky, dishonourable, dishonest, underhand; informal low-down, dirty; Brit. informal out of order, off, a bit thick, not cricket.

bemoan verb *they were bemoaning the recent decline in moral standards:* **lament**, bewail, mourn, cry over; deplore, complain about.
– OPPOSITES rejoice at, applaud.

bemused adjective *they wandered about with bemused expressions on their faces:* **bewildered**, confused, puzzled, perplexed, baffled, mystified, nonplussed, muddled, dumbfounded, at sea, at a loss, taken aback, disoriented, disconcerted; informal flummoxed, bamboozled, clueless, fazed; N. Amer. informal discombobulated.

bemusement noun **bewilderment**, confusion, puzzlement, perplexity, bafflement, befuddlement, stupefaction, mystification, disorientation; informal bamboozlement; N. Amer. informal discombobulation.

bench noun **1** *he sat on a bench at the front of the hall:* **pew**, form, stall, settle. **2** *in the centre of the laboratory was a huge bench:* **workbench**, work table, worktop, work surface, counter. **3** *the bench has now heard the evidence and must make a decision:* **judges**, magistrates, judiciary; court.

benchmark noun *the agreement was used as a benchmark in all further negotiations:* **standard**, point of reference, gauge, criterion, specification, canon, convention, guide, guideline, guiding principle, norm, touchstone, yardstick, barometer, indicator, measure, model, exemplar, pattern.

bend verb **1** *the spectacle frames can be bent to fit your face:* **curve**, crook, flex, angle, hook, bow, arch, buckle, warp, contort, distort, deform. **2** *the highway bent to the left up ahead:* **turn**, curve, incline, swing, veer, deviate, diverge, fork, curl, loop. **3** *he bent down to tie his shoe:* **stoop**, bow, crouch, hunch, lean down/over.
– OPPOSITES straighten.
noun *he came to a bend in the road:* **curve**, turn, corner, kink, angle, arc, crescent, twist, crook, deviation, deflection, loop; dog-leg, oxbow, zigzag; Brit. hairpin bend, hairpin.
– OPPOSITES straight.
■ **bend over backwards** (informal) *they have bent over backwards to ensure a fair trial:* try hard, do one's best, do one's utmost, do all one can, give one's all, make every effort; informal do one's damnedest, go all out, pull out all the stops, bust a gut, move heaven and earth.

beneath preposition **1** *we sat in the shade beneath the trees:* **under**, underneath, below, at the foot of, at the bottom of; lower than. **2** *the rank beneath his is that of major:* **inferior to**, below, not so important as, lower in status than, subordinate to, subservient to. **3** *she thought such an attitude was beneath her:* **unworthy of**, unbecoming to, degrading to, below.
– OPPOSITES above.
adverb *the floor was wooden, with concrete beneath:* **underneath**, below, further down, lower down.
– OPPOSITES above.

benediction noun *the priest said a benediction:* **blessing**, prayer, invocation; grace.

benefactor, benefactress noun *they erected a statue to their benefactor:* **patron**, supporter, backer, sponsor; donor, contributor, subscriber; informal angel.

beneficent adjective *a bid to contrast their beneficent rule with that of their bigoted and intolerant predecessors:* **benevolent**, charitable, altruistic, humanitarian, neighbourly, public-spirited, philanthropic;

generous, magnanimous, munificent,
unselfish, open-handed, liberal, lavish,
bountiful; literary bounteous.
– OPPOSITES unkind, mean.

beneficial adjective *alcohol in moderation
can be beneficial:* **advantageous**, favourable,
helpful, useful, of use, of benefit, of
assistance, valuable, of value, profitable,
rewarding, gainful.
– OPPOSITES disadvantageous.

beneficiary noun *she was the major
beneficiary of her uncle's will:* **heir**, heiress,
inheritor, legatee; recipient; Law devisee;
Scottish Law heritor.

benefit noun **1** *a life lived for the benefit
of others:* **good**, sake, welfare, well-being,
advantage, comfort, ease, convenience; help,
aid, assistance, service. **2** *the numerous
benefits of working for a large firm:*
advantage, reward, merit, boon, blessing,
virtue; bonus; value; informal perk. **3** *there is
new hope for those who are dependent on
benefit:* **social security**, welfare; charity,
donations, gifts, financial assistance; informal
the dole; Scottish informal the buroo, the broo.
– OPPOSITES detriment, disadvantage.
verb **1** *the deal benefited them both:* **be
advantageous to**, be beneficial to, be of
advantage to, profit, do good to, be of service
to, serve, be useful to, be of use to, be helpful
to, be of help to, help, aid, assist, be of
assistance to; better, improve, strengthen,
boost, advance, further. **2** *they may benefit
from grants that are now available:* **profit**,
gain, reap benefits, reap reward, make
money; make the most of, exploit, turn to
one's advantage, put to good use, do well
out of; informal cash in, make a killing.
– OPPOSITES damage, suffer.

benevolence noun **kindness**,
kind-heartedness, big-heartedness,
goodness, goodwill, charity, altruism,
humanitarianism, compassion,
philanthropism; generosity, magnanimity,
munificence, unselfishness, open-
handedness, beneficence; literary bounty,
bounteousness.
– OPPOSITES spite, miserliness.

benevolent adjective *they thought
him a benevolent and conscientious
guardian:* **kind**, kindly, kind-hearted,
big-hearted, good-natured, good, benign,
compassionate, caring, altruistic,
humanitarian, philanthropic; generous,
magnanimous, munificent, unselfish, open-
handed, beneficent; literary bounteous.
– OPPOSITES unkind, tight-fisted.

benighted adjective *we are healthier and
generally better off than our poor benighted
ancestors:* **ignorant**, unenlightened,
uneducated, uninformed, backward, simple;
primitive, uncivilized, unsophisticated,
philistine, barbarian, barbaric, barbarous.
– OPPOSITES enlightened.

benign adjective **1** *he adopted a benign,
grandfatherly role:* **kindly**, kind,

warm-hearted, good-natured, friendly,
warm, affectionate, agreeable, genial,
congenial, cordial, approachable,
tender-hearted, gentle, sympathetic,
compassionate, caring, well disposed,
benevolent. **2** *the climate becomes more
benign nearer the Black Sea:* **temperate**,
mild, gentle, balmy, soft, pleasant; healthy,
wholesome, salubrious. **3** (Medicine) *a benign
tumour:* **harmless**, non-malignant, non-
cancerous; Medicine benignant.
– OPPOSITES unfriendly, hostile, unhealthy,
unfavourable, malignant.

bent adjective **1** *the bucket was dented and had
a bent handle:* **twisted**, crooked, warped,
contorted, deformed, misshapen, out of
shape, irregular; bowed, arched, curved,
angled, hooked, kinked; N. Amer. informal
pretzeled. **2** (Brit. informal) *he hates drug dealers
and bent coppers.* See **CORRUPT** adjective sense 1.
– OPPOSITES straight, law-abiding.
noun *she has an artistic bent:* **inclination**,
leaning, tendency; talent, gift, flair,
aptitude, facility, skill, capability, capacity;
predisposition, disposition, instinct,
orientation, predilection, proclivity,
propensity.
■ **bent on** *she's bent on going and nothing
will stop her:* **intent on**, determined on, set
on, insistent on, resolved on, hell-bent on;
committed to.

benumbed adjective *he knew nothing of
this—his mind was benumbed:* **numb**,
unfeeling, insensible, stupefied, groggy,
foggy, fuzzy, muzzy, dazed, dizzy;
befuddled, fuddled, disoriented, confused,
bewildered, all at sea; informal dopey, woozy,
mixed up; N. Amer. informal discombobulated.
– OPPOSITES perceptive.

bequeath verb *he bequeathed his artworks
to the city of Philadelphia:* **leave (in one's
will)**, will, make over, pass on, hand
on/down, entrust, grant, transfer; donate,
give; bestow on, confer on, endow with; Law
demise, devise, convey.

bequest noun *they received a bequest of over
£300,000:* **legacy**, inheritance, endowment,
settlement; estate, heritage; bestowal,
bequeathal; Law devise.

berate verb *Tom berated Mary for being
a scatterbrained idiot:* **scold**, rebuke,
reprimand, reproach, reprove, admonish,
chide, criticize, upbraid, take to task, pull
up, read someone the Riot Act, haul over
the coals; informal tell off, give someone a
talking-to, give someone a telling-off, give
someone a dressing-down, give someone
a roasting, rap over the knuckles, send
someone away with a flea in their ear, bawl
out, come down on, tear into, put on the
mat, slap down, blast; Brit. informal tick off,
have a go at, carpet, give someone a rocket,
give someone a rollicking, tear someone
off a strip; Brit. informal, dated give someone a
wigging; N. Amer. informal chew out, ream out,
take to the woodshed; Austral. informal monster;

formal castigate; dated call down, rate.
– OPPOSITES praise.

bereaved adjective orphaned, widowed;
mourning, grieving.

bereft adjective *the poor were bereft of any
opportunity for advancement:* **deprived**,
wanting, in need of, lacking, without; informal
minus, sans, clean out of.

berry noun **fruit**, currant.

berserk adjective *she went berserk, calling
him names, screaming and crying:* **mad**,
crazy, insane, out of one's mind, hysterical,
wild, out of control, amok, on the rampage;
informal off one's head, off the deep end, ape,
bananas, bonkers, nuts, hyper; Brit. informal
spare, crackers, barmy; N. Amer. informal postal.

berth noun **1** *a 4-berth cabin:* **bunk**, bed, cot,
couch, hammock. **2** *the vessel has now left its
berth:* **mooring**, dock.
▶ verb *the ship berthed in London Docks:* **dock**,
moor, land, tie up, make fast.
■ **give someone/something a wide berth**
*the public was outraged and gave the film
a wide berth:* avoid, shun, keep away from,
stay away from, steer clear of, keep at arm's
length, have nothing to do with; dodge,
sidestep, circumvent, skirt round.

beseech verb (literary) *a dozen well-heeled
widows beseeched him to manage their funds:*·
implore, beg, entreat, plead with, appeal to,
call on, supplicate, importune, pray to, ask,
request, petition.

beset verb *he is beset by fears of failure:*
plague, bedevil, assail, beleaguer, afflict,
torment, rack, oppress, trouble, worry,
harass, dog.

beside preposition **1** *Kate walked beside
him:* **alongside**, by/at the side of, next to,
parallel to, abreast of, at someone's elbow;
adjacent to, next door to, cheek by jowl
with; bordering, abutting, neighbouring.
2 *beside Paula, she felt clumsy and useless:*
compared with/to, in comparison with/to,
by comparison with, next to, against,
contrasted with, in contrast to/with.
■ **beside oneself** *Ursula was beside herself
with worry:* distraught, overcome, out of
one's mind, frantic, desperate, distracted,
at one's wits' end, frenzied, wound up,
worked up; hysterical, unhinged, mad,
crazed, berserk, demented.
■ **beside the point**. See POINT¹.

besides preposition *who did you ask besides
Mary?* **in addition to**, as well as, over and
above, above and beyond, on top of; apart
from, other than, aside from, but for, save
for, not counting, excluding, not including,
except, with the exception of, excepting,
leaving aside; N. Amer. informal outside of.
▶ adverb **1** *there's the stuff in the attic and a
lot more besides:* **in addition**, as well, too,
also, into the bargain, on top of that, to
boot. **2** *besides, he's a man, so he wouldn't
understand:* **furthermore**, moreover,
further; anyway, anyhow, in any case, be

that as it may; informal what's more; N. Amer.
informal anyways.

besiege verb **1** *the army unit which besieged
and shelled the Croatian city of Vukovar:*
lay siege to, beleaguer, blockade, surround.
2 *motorists throughout the country were
besieging petrol stations:* **surround**, mob,
crowd round, swarm round, throng round,
ring round, encircle. **3** *during the study
we were besieged with requests for help:*
overwhelm, inundate, deluge, flood,
swamp, snow under; bombard.

besotted adjective *she won't listen—she's
besotted with him:* **infatuated**, smitten,
in love, head over heels in love, obsessed;
doting on, greatly enamoured of; informal
struck on, crazy about, mad about, wild
about, gone on, carrying a torch for; Brit.
informal potty about.

bespeak verb *this literal-mindedness
bespeaks a lack of imagination on his part:*
indicate, be evidence of, be a sign of,
denote, point to, testify to, evidence, reflect,
demonstrate, show, manifest, display,
signify; reveal, betray; informal spell.
– OPPOSITES belie.

best adjective **1** *the best hotel in Paris:*
finest, greatest, top, foremost, leading,
pre-eminent, premier, prime, first, chief,
principal, supreme, superlative, par
excellence, second to none, without
equal, unsurpassed, peerless, matchless,
unparalleled, unbeaten, unbeatable,
optimum, optimal, ultimate, incomparable,
ideal, perfect; highest, record-breaking;
informal star, number-one, a cut above the
rest, top-drawer. **2** *do whatever you think
best:* **most advantageous**, most useful, most
suitable, most fitting, most appropriate;
most prudent, most sensible, most advisable.
– OPPOSITES worst.
▶ adverb *the food he likes best is curry:* **most
(of all)**, above all, more than anything.
– OPPOSITES worst, least.
▶ noun *only the best will do:* **finest**, choicest,
top, cream, choice, prime, elite, crème de
la crème, flower, jewel in the crown; informal
tops, pick of the bunch.
■ **at one's best** *Lily was not at her best
yesterday evening:* on top form, at one's
peak, in one's prime, in the pink, in the best
of health.
■ **do one's best** *Caroline had done her
best to help him:* do one's utmost, try one's
hardest, make every effort, do all one can,
give one's all; informal bend over backwards,
do one's damnedest, go all out, pull out all
the stops, bust a gut, break one's neck, move
heaven and earth.

bestial adjective **1** *Oric is a war criminal
of the most bestial kind:* **savage**, brutish,
brutal, barbarous, barbaric, cruel, vicious,
violent, inhuman, subhuman; depraved,
degenerate, perverted, immoral, warped. **2** *I
was stunned by the bestial grunting noises*

that emerged from the shed: **animal**, beast-like, animalistic.
– OPPOSITES civilized, humane.

bestir
■ **bestir oneself** *his friends urged him to bestir himself:* exert oneself, make an effort, rouse oneself, get going, get moving, get on with it; informal shake a leg, look lively, get cracking, get weaving, get one's finger out, get off one's backside; Brit. informal, dated stir one's stumps.

bestow verb *many favours were bestowed on him by the new king:* **confer on**, grant, accord, afford, endow someone with, vest in, present, award, give, donate, entrust with, vouchsafe.

bestride verb **1** *the oilfield bestrides the border between the two countries:* **extend across**, lie on both sides of, straddle, span, bridge. **2** *he bestrode his horse with an easy grace:* **straddle**, sit/stand astride.

best-seller noun great success, brand leader; informal hit, smash (hit), blockbuster, chart-topper, chartbuster.
– OPPOSITES failure, flop.

best-selling adjective **very successful**, very popular; informal number-one, chart-topping, hit, smash.

bet verb **1** *he bet £10 on Liverpool to win the championship:* **wager**, gamble, stake, risk, venture, hazard, chance; put/lay money, speculate; informal punt; Brit. informal have a flutter, chance one's arm. **2** (informal) *I bet it was your idea:* **be certain**, be sure, be convinced, be confident; expect, predict, forecast, guess.
noun **1** *a £20 bet:* **wager**, gamble, stake, ante, Brit. informal flutter, punt. **2** (informal) *your best bet is to go early and avoid the traffic:* **option**, choice, alternative, course of action, plan.

betray verb **1** *he was betrayed by a crooked French cop:* be disloyal to, be unfaithful to, break faith with, play someone false; inform on/against, give away, denounce, sell out, stab in the back; informal split on, rat on, peach on, stitch up, do the dirty on, sell down the river, squeal on; Brit. informal grass on, shop, sneak on; N. Amer. informal rat out, drop a/the dime on, finger; Austral./NZ informal dob on, point the bone at. **2** *his expression betrays nothing, except a kind of resignation:* **reveal**, disclose, divulge, tell, give away, leak; expose, bring out into the open; let slip, let out, let drop, blurt out; informal blab, spill.
– OPPOSITES be loyal to, hide.

betrayal noun **disloyalty**, treachery, bad faith, faithlessness, falseness, Punic faith; duplicity, deception, double-dealing; breach of faith, breach of trust, stab in the back; double-cross, sell-out; literary perfidy.
– OPPOSITES loyalty.

better adjective **1** *he is clearly a better player than Thompson:* **superior**, finer, of higher quality; preferable; informal a cut

above, streets ahead, head and shoulders above, ahead of the pack/field. **2** *there couldn't be a better time to invest:* **more advantageous**, more suitable, more fitting, more appropriate, more useful, more valuable, more desirable. **3** *I'm feeling better than I was | are you better?* **healthier**, fitter, stronger; well, cured, healed, recovered; recovering, on the road to recovery, making progress, improving; informal on the mend.
– OPPOSITES worse, inferior.
verb *a score bettered by only one other athlete:* **surpass**, improve on, beat, exceed, top, cap, trump, eclipse.

betterment noun *his selfless devotion to the betterment of his country:* **improvement**, amelioration, advancement, development, upgrading, enhancement.

between preposition **1** *Philip stood between his parents:* **in the middle of**. **2** *the bond between her and her mother:* **connecting**, linking, joining; uniting, allying.

bevelled adjective *the new skis have rust-free bevelled edges:* **angled**, slanted, chamfered, sloping, mitred.

beverage noun **drink**, liquid refreshment; humorous libation.

bevy noun *he was always surrounded by a bevy of Hollywood starlets:* **group**, crowd, herd, flock, horde, army, galaxy, gathering, band, body, pack; knot, cluster; informal bunch, gaggle, posse.

bewail verb *many experts bewail the decline of standards:* **lament**, bemoan, mourn, sorrow over, cry over; deplore, complain about.
– OPPOSITES rejoice at, applaud.

beware verb *beware of holding confidential conversations where you may be easily overheard:* **be on your guard**, watch out, look out, mind out, be alert, be on the lookout, keep your eyes open/peeled, keep an eye out, keep a sharp lookout; take care, be careful, be cautious, have a care, watch your step.

bewilder verb *all these big words bewildered Sally:* **baffle**, mystify, bemuse, perplex, puzzle, confuse, confound, nonplus; informal flummox, faze, stump, beat, fox, make someone scratch their head, be all Greek to, floor; N. Amer. informal discombobulate, buffalo.
– OPPOSITES enlighten.

bewildered adjective *Mark looked completely bewildered:* **baffled**, mystified, bemused, perplexed, puzzled, confused, nonplussed, at sea, at a loss, disorientated, taken aback; informal flummoxed, bamboozled; N. Amer. informal discombobulated.

bewildering adjective *the bewildering complexity of local politics:* **baffling**, perplexing, puzzling, mystifying, mysterious, confusing; complex, labyrinthine, convoluted, Byzantine; N. Amer. informal discombobulating.

bewitch verb **1** *his relatives were convinced*

b

he had been bewitched: **cast/put a spell on**, enchant; possess, witch, curse; N. Amer. hex, hoodoo; Austral. point the bone at. **2** *she was bewitched by her surroundings:* **captivate**, enchant, entrance, enrapture, charm, beguile, delight, fascinate, enthral. – OPPOSITES repel.

beyond preposition **1** *the farm buildings were visible beyond the trees:* **on the other side of**, behind, past, after. **2** *nobody ever worked beyond six o'clock:* **later than**, past, after. **3** *inflation was running at way beyond 10 per cent:* **greater than**, more than, exceeding, in excess of, above, over and above, above and beyond, upwards of. **4** *there was little vegetation beyond a few stunted bushes:* **apart from**, except, other than, besides; informal outside of; formal save.
adverb *I could see the house and Mount Wellington beyond:* **further away**, further off.

bias noun **1** *the chairman accused the media of bias:* **prejudice**, partiality, partisanship, favouritism, unfairness, one-sidedness; bigotry, intolerance, discrimination; leaning, tendency, inclination, predilection. **2** *a dress cut on the bias:* **diagonal**, cross, slant, angle.
– OPPOSITES impartiality.
verb *their recollections may be biased by discussions with other people:* **prejudice**, influence, colour, sway, weight, predispose; distort, skew, slant.

biased adjective *that's a very biased view, I must say:* **prejudiced**, partial, partisan, one-sided, blinkered; bigoted, intolerant, discriminatory; jaundiced, distorted, warped, twisted, skewed.
– OPPOSITES impartial.

Bible noun **1** *he read the Bible every day:* **the (Holy) Scriptures**, the Good Book, God's Word; the Gospel(s). **2** (informal) *the taxi driver's bible:* **handbook**, manual, ABC, companion, guide.

bicker verb *he bled to death while the others bickered about who sold them out:* **squabble**, argue, quarrel, wrangle, fight, disagree, dispute, spar, have words; informal scrap, argufy, spat.
– OPPOSITES agree.

bicycle noun **cycle**, two-wheeler, pedal cycle; informal bike, pushbike.

bid¹ verb **1** *United bid £1 million for the Everton striker:* **offer**, make an offer of, put in a bid of, put up, tender, proffer, propose. **2** *she is bidding for a place in the England team:* **try**, make a pitch, make a bid; go. noun **1** *a bid of £3,000:* **offer**, tender, proposal. **2** *a frantic bid to cut crime before the election:* **attempt**, effort, endeavour, try; informal crack, go, shot, stab; formal essay.

bid² verb **1** *she turned and bid him farewell:* **wish**; utter. **2** (literary) *I did as he bade me:* **order**, command, tell, instruct, direct, enjoin, charge. **3** (literary) *he bade*

his companions enter: **invite to**, ask to, request to.

biddable adjective *she was a pretty, biddable child, with none of her brother's temper:* **obedient**, acquiescent, compliant, tractable, amenable, complaisant, cooperative, dutiful, submissive.
– OPPOSITES disobedient, uncooperative.

bidding noun *Williams was arrested and led away at Belville's bidding:* **command**, order, instruction, decree, injunction, demand, mandate, direction, summons, call; wish, desire; request; literary behest.

big adjective **1** *a big Victorian building:* **large**, sizeable, substantial, great, huge, immense, enormous, extensive, colossal, massive, mammoth, vast, tremendous, gigantic, giant, monumental, mighty, gargantuan, elephantine, titanic, mountainous, Brobdingnagian; towering, tall, high, lofty; outsize, oversized; goodly; capacious, voluminous, spacious; king-size(d), man-size, family-size(d), economy-size(d); informal jumbo, whopping, thumping, bumper, mega, humongous, monster, astronomical, almighty, dirty great; Brit. informal whacking, ginormous; formal commodious. **2** *a big man with a red face:* **well built**, sturdy, brawny, burly, broad-shouldered, muscular, muscly, rugged, lusty, Herculean, bulky, hulking, strapping, thickset, stocky, solid, hefty; tall, huge, gigantic; fat, stout, portly, plump, fleshy, paunchy, corpulent, obese; informal hunky, beefy. **3** *I fell out with my big brother:* **grown-up**, adult, mature, grown; elder, older. **4** *it's a big decision, so don't rush it:* **important**, significant, major, momentous, weighty, consequential, far-reaching, key, vital, critical, crucial. **5** (informal) *a big man in the government:* **powerful**, important, prominent, influential, high-powered, leading; N. Amer. major-league. **6** *she's got a big heart:* **generous**, kind, kindly, caring, compassionate, loving; magnanimous, sporting. **7** (informal) *African bands are big in Britain right now:* **popular**, successful, in demand, sought-after, all the rage; informal hot, in, cool, trendy, now, hip.
– OPPOSITES small, minor, modest.

big-headed adjective (informal) *local councils should act against these big-headed developers:* **conceited**, full of oneself, cocky, arrogant, cocksure, above oneself, self-important; vain, self-satisfied, pleased with oneself, smug, complacent; informal swollen-headed, too big for one's boots.
– OPPOSITES modest.

bigot noun **dogmatist**, partisan, sectarian; racist, sexist, chauvinist, jingoist.

bigoted adjective *they're nothing but a bigoted group of reactionaries:* **prejudiced**, biased, partial, one-sided, sectarian, discriminatory; opinionated, dogmatic, intolerant, narrow-minded, blinkered, illiberal; racist, sexist, chauvinistic, jingoistic, xenophobic, homophobic,

misogynistic; jaundiced, warped, twisted, distorted.
– OPPOSITES open-minded.

bigotry noun **prejudice**, bias, partiality, partisanship, sectarianism, discrimination; dogmatism, intolerance, narrow-mindedness; racism, sexism, chauvinism, jingoism.
– OPPOSITES open-mindedness.

bigwig noun (informal) *he arrived at the town hall with all the local politicians and bigwigs in attendance:* **VIP**, important person, notable, dignitary, grandee; celebrity; informal somebody, heavyweight, big shot, big noise, big gun, big cheese, big fish; N. Amer. informal big wheel.
– OPPOSITES nonentity.

bilious adjective **1** *I woke up feeling bilious and with a raging headache:* **nauseous**, sick, queasy, nauseated, green about the gills; N. Amer. informal barfy. **2** *his bilious disposition made him few friends:* **bad-tempered**, irritable, irascible, tetchy, testy, crotchety, ill-tempered, ill-natured, ill-humoured, peevish, fractious, pettish, crabby, waspish, prickly, crusty, shrewish, quick-tempered; N. Amer. informal cranky, ornery. **3** *a bilious green and pink colour scheme:* **lurid**, garish, loud, violent; sickly, nauseating.
– OPPOSITES well, good-humoured, muted.

bill[1] noun **1** *the bill came to £69:* **invoice**, account, statement, list of charges; N. Amer. check; informal, humorous the damage; N. Amer. informal tab. **2** *a bill to ban smoking would receive a lot of support:* **draft law**, proposal, measure. **3** (N. Amer.) *a $10 bill:* **banknote**, note; US informal greenback. **4** *he had been hard at work posting bills:* **poster**, advertisement, public notice, announcement; flyer, leaflet, handbill; Brit. fly-poster; N. Amer. dodger; informal ad; Brit. informal advert.
verb **1** *please bill me for the work:* **invoice**, charge, debit. **2** *the concert went ahead as billed:* **advertise**, announce; schedule, programme, timetable; N. Amer. slate. **3** *he was billed as the new Sean Connery:* **describe**, call, style, label, dub; promote, publicize, talk up; informal hype.

bill[2] noun *one of the swans had a fishing hook caught in its bill:* **beak**; Scottish & N. English neb; technical mandibles.

billet noun *the troops returned to their billets:* **quarters**, rooms; accommodation, lodging, housing; barracks, cantonment.
verb *two German soldiers were billeted here:* **accommodate**, quarter, put up, lodge, house; station, garrison.

billow noun *he was puffing billows of smoke from his cigar:* **cloud**, mass.
verb **1** *her dress billowed out around her:* **puff up/out**, balloon (out), swell, fill (out), belly out. **2** *smoke billowed from the chimney:* **swirl**, spiral, roll, undulate, eddy; pour, flow, issue (forth).

billowing adjective *her silhouette was visible behind a billowing green bedroom curtain:* **rolling**, swirling, undulating, surging, heaving, billowy, swelling, rippling.

bin noun *the beans are stored in round metal bins:* **container**, receptacle, holder; drum, canister, caddy, can, tin.

bind verb **1** *they bound her hands and feet:* **tie (up)**, fasten (together), hold together, secure, make fast, attach; rope, strap, lash, truss, tether. **2** *Shelley bound up the wound with a clean dressing:* **bandage**, dress, cover, wrap; strap up, tape up. **3** *the experience had bound them together:* **unite**, join, bond, knit together, draw together. **4** *the edges are bound in a contrasting colour:* **trim**, hem, edge, border, fringe; finish. **5** *they are bound by the terms of the agreement:* **constrain**, restrict, restrain, trammel, tie (down), shackle, limit; hamper, hinder, inhibit.
– OPPOSITES untie, separate.
noun (informal) **1** *having to start so early is a bind:* **nuisance**, annoyance, inconvenience, bore, bother, irritant, trial; informal pain, pain in the neck/backside, headache, hassle, drag; N. Amer. informal pain in the butt. **2** *these simple precautions may help you avoid getting into a bind:* **predicament**, difficult/awkward situation, quandary, dilemma, plight, cleft stick; informal spot, tight spot, hole.

binding adjective *for the sake of everyone, we need a binding international treaty:* **irrevocable**, unalterable, inescapable, unbreakable, contractual; compulsory, obligatory, mandatory.

binge noun (informal) *the lads went on a two-day binge in London:* **bout**, debauch; informal bender, session, booze-up, blind; Scottish informal skite; N. Amer. informal jag, toot, drunk.

biography noun **life story**, life history, life, memoir; informal bio, biog.

bird noun **fowl**; chick, fledgling, nestling; **(birds)** avifauna; informal feathered friend, birdie.

birth noun **1** *I was present at the birth of our son:* **childbirth**, delivery, nativity, birthing. **2** *the birth of science in the Victorian era:* **beginning(s)**, emergence, genesis, dawn, dawning, rise, start. **3** *he claims he is of noble birth:* **ancestry**, lineage, blood, descent, parentage, family, extraction, origin, genealogy, heritage, stock, kinship.
– OPPOSITES death, demise, end.
■ **give birth to** *Sally gave birth to a beautiful eight-pound baby boy:* **have**, bear, produce, be delivered of, bring into the world; N. Amer. birth; informal drop.

birthmark noun **naevus**, mole, blemish.

birthright noun *freedom is the birthright of every human being:* **right**, due, prerogative, privilege; primogeniture; inheritance, heritage.

biscuit noun (Brit.) **cracker**, wafer; N. Amer. cookie; informal bicky.

bisect verb *Kenya, a nation which is bisected by the Equator:* **cut in half**, halve, divide/cut/split in two, split down the middle; cross, intersect.

bisexual adjective **1** *individual flowers develop from a bisexual state:* **hermaphrodite**, hermaphroditic, intersex; androgynous, epicene; technical monoclinous, gynandrous, gynandromorphic. **2** *how I see life as a bisexual woman:* **ambisexual**; informal AC/DC, bi, swinging both ways, ambidextrous; N. Amer. informal switch-hitting.

bit noun **1** *a bit of bread | add a bit of salt:* **piece**, portion, segment, section, part; chunk, lump, hunk, slice; fragment, scrap, shred, crumb, grain, speck; spot, drop, pinch, dash, soupçon, modicum; morsel, mouthful, bite, sample; iota, jot, whit, atom, particle, trace, touch, suggestion, hint, tinge; snippet, snatch; informal smidgen, tad. **2** *wait a bit:* **moment**, minute, second, (little) while; informal sec, jiffy; Brit. informal mo, tick.
– OPPOSITES lot.
■ **a bit** *he looked a bit annoyed:* rather, fairly, slightly, somewhat, quite, moderately; informal pretty, sort of, kind of.
■ **bit by bit** *bit by bit the truth emerged:* gradually, little by little, in stages, step by step, piecemeal, slowly.
■ **in a bit** *I'll see you in a bit:* soon, in a (little) while, in a second, in a minute, in a moment, shortly; informal anon, in a jiffy, in two shakes; Brit. informal in a tick, in two ticks, in a mo; N. Amer. informal in a snap.

bitch noun (informal) **1** *she's such a cheeky bitch:* informal **cow**, mare; devil, minx. **2** *a bitch of a job:* **nightmare**; informal bastard, bummer, ... from hell, swine, pig, bugger, sod, stinker. verb **1** *businessmen bitched about the price of oil:* **complain**, whine, grumble, grouse; informal whinge, moan, grouch, gripe. **2** *he's always bitching about colleagues:* **criticize**, run down, speak ill of, slander, malign; informal knock, pull to pieces, take apart, bad-mouth, do a hatchet job on; N. Amer. informal trash; Brit. informal slag off.

bitchy adjective (informal). See SPITEFUL.

bite verb **1** *the dog bit his arm:* **sink one's teeth into**, chew, munch, crunch, champ, tear at. **2** *my wheels couldn't bite on the snow:* **grip**, hold, get a purchase/grip. **3** *the free-market measures are beginning to bite:* **take effect**, have an effect, be effective, work, act, have results.
noun **1** *he took a bite at his sandwich:* **chew**, munch, nibble, gnaw, nip, snap. **2** *he ate the whole thing in two bites:* **mouthful**, piece, bit, morsel. **3** *do you fancy a bite?* **snack**, mouthful; refreshments, something to eat; informal a little something. **4** *the appetizer had a fiery bite to it:* **piquancy**, pungency, spiciness, tang, zest, sharpness, tartness; informal kick, punch, zing.

biting adjective **1** *his biting comments on political life:* **vicious**, harsh, cruel, savage, cutting, sharp, bitter, scathing, caustic, acid, acerbic, stinging; vitriolic, hostile, spiteful, venomous, mean, nasty; informal bitchy, catty.

2 *the biting wind that blew from the east:* **freezing**, icy, arctic, glacial; bitter, piercing, penetrating, raw, wintry.
– OPPOSITES mild.

bitter adjective **1** *a tepid cup of thick, bitter coffee:* **sharp**, acid, acidic, acrid, tart, sour, biting, unsweetened, vinegary; N. Amer. acerb; technical acerbic. **2** *Carla is a frustrated, bitter woman:* **resentful**, embittered, aggrieved, begrudging, rancorous, spiteful, jaundiced, ill-disposed, sullen, sour, churlish, morose, petulant, peevish, with a chip on one's shoulder. **3** *today's decision has come as a bitter blow:* **painful**, unpleasant, disagreeable, nasty, cruel, awful, distressing, upsetting, heartbreaking, heart-rending, agonizing, traumatic, tragic, chilling; formal grievous. **4** *we were chilled by a bitter north wind:* **freezing**, icy, arctic, glacial; biting, piercing, penetrating, raw, wintry. **5** *a bitter row broke out:* **acrimonious**, virulent, angry, rancorous, spiteful, vicious, vitriolic, savage, ferocious, hate-filled, venomous, poisonous, acrid, nasty, ill-natured.
– OPPOSITES sweet, magnanimous, content, welcome, warm, amicable.

bitterness noun **1** *the bitterness of the medicine made him splutter:* **sharpness**, acidity, acridity, tartness, sourness, harshness, vinegariness; technical acerbity. **2** *his bitterness against his parents grew:* **resentment**, rancour, indignation, grudge, spite, sullenness, sourness, churlishness, moroseness, petulance, pique, peevishness. **3** *there was no bitterness between them:* **acrimony**, hostility, antipathy, antagonism, enmity, animus, friction, rancour, vitriol, hatred, loathing, venom, poison, nastiness, ill feeling, ill will, bad blood.
– OPPOSITES sweetness, magnanimity, contentment, warmth, goodwill.

bitty adjective (informal) *a bitty, scrappy match with only the occasional brilliant rally:* **disjointed**, incoherent, fragmented, fragmentary, scrappy, piecemeal; inconsistent, unsystematic, jumbled; uneven, erratic, patchy.
– OPPOSITES coherent.

bizarre adjective *Satie's music consists mostly of short piano pieces with bizarre titles:* **strange**, peculiar, odd, funny, curious, outlandish, outré, eccentric, unconventional, unorthodox, queer, extraordinary; informal weird, wacky, oddball, way out, freaky, off the wall, offbeat; Brit. informal rum; N. Amer. informal wacko.
– OPPOSITES normal.

black adjective **1** *a black horse:* **dark**, pitch-black, jet-black, coal-black, inky; Heraldry sable. **2** *a black night:* **unlit**, dark, starless, moonless. **3** *the blackest days of the war:* **tragic**, disastrous, calamitous, catastrophic, cataclysmic, fateful, wretched, woeful, awful, terrible, grim. **4** *Mary was in a black mood:* **miserable**, wretched, anguished,

desolate, despairing, disconsolate, downcast, dejected, cheerless, melancholy, morose, gloomy, glum, mournful, doleful, bleak, dismal, forlorn, woeful. **5** *black humour:* **cynical**, macabre, weird, unhealthy, ghoulish, morbid, perverted, gruesome; informal sick. **6** *a black look.* See **ANGRY** sense 1.
– OPPOSITES white, clear, bright, joyful.
■ **black out** *he tightened his grip and she felt herself begin to black out:* **faint**, lose consciousness, pass out, swoon; informal flake out, go out.
■ **in the black** *all bar one of its factories are in the black:* **in credit**, debt-free, out of debt, solvent, (financially) sound, able to pay one's debts, creditworthy.
■ **black and white 1** *on the wall hung a framed black and white print:* **monochrome**, greyscale. **2** *I wish to see the proposals in black and white:* **in print**, printed, written down, set down, on paper, recorded, on record, documented. **3** *in black-and-white terms:* **categorical**, unequivocal, absolute, uncompromising, heightened, unqualified, unambiguous, clear, clear-cut.

blackball verb *two committee members intended to blackball me in the ballot:* **reject**, debar, bar, ban, vote against, blacklist, exclude, shut out.
– OPPOSITES admit.

blacken verb **1** *the pollutants blackening the air over Mexico City:* **darken**; dirty, stain, pollute, soil. **2** *we stood watching the sky blacken in the west:* **grow/become black**, darken, dim, grow dim, cloud over. **3** *the whole incident had been contrived to blacken my name:* **sully**, tarnish, besmirch, drag through the mud/mire, stain, taint, smear, disgrace, dishonour, bring discredit to, damage, ruin; slander, defame.
– OPPOSITES whiten, clean, lighten, brighten, clear.

blacklist verb *200 suspected Communists were blacklisted by the major studios:* **boycott**, ostracize, avoid, embargo, steer clear of, ignore; snub, send to Coventry.

black magic noun **sorcery**, witchcraft, wizardry, necromancy, the black arts, devilry; malediction, voodoo, witching, witchery.

blackout noun **1** *a generator would power the computer in the event of a blackout:* **power cut**, power failure; brown-out. **2** *the authorities imposed a news blackout:* **suppression**, silence, censorship, reporting restrictions. **3** *he had a blackout in the street:* **fainting fit**, faint, loss of consciousness, passing out, swoon, collapse; Medicine syncope.

blame verb **1** *the inquiry blamed the driver of the train:* **hold responsible**, hold accountable, condemn, accuse, find/consider guilty, assign fault/liability/guilt to. **2** *they blame youth crime on unemployment:* **ascribe to**, attribute to, impute to, lay at the door of, put down to; informal pin.

– OPPOSITES absolve.
noun *he was cleared of all blame for the incident:* **responsibility**, guilt, accountability, liability, culpability, fault.

blameless adjective *he led a blameless life:* **innocent**, guiltless, above reproach, irreproachable, unimpeachable, in the clear, exemplary, perfect, virtuous, pure, impeccable.
– OPPOSITES blameworthy.

blameworthy adjective *in what way do you consider him blameworthy?* **culpable**, guilty, criminal, delinquent, wrong; to blame, at fault, reproachable, responsible, answerable, erring, errant, in the wrong.
– OPPOSITES blameless.

blanch verb **1** *fronds of seaweed began to stiffen and blanch in the sun:* **turn pale**, whiten, lighten, fade, blench, etiolate, bleach. **2** *people who have children may blanch at the idea of a cream sofa:* **pale**, turn pale, turn white, whiten, lose its colour, blench. **3** *blanch the spinach leaves in boiling water for about 30 seconds:* **scald**, boil briefly.
– OPPOSITES colour, darken.

bland adjective **1** *over-processed, bland convenience foods:* **tasteless**, flavourless, insipid, weak, watery, spiceless, wishy-washy. **2** *the channel specializes in innocuous romances and bland dramas:* **uninteresting**, dull, boring, tedious, monotonous, dry, drab, dreary, wearisome; unexciting, unimaginative, uninspiring, uninspired, lacklustre, vapid, flat, stale, trite, vacuous, wishy-washy. **3** *when he turned round, his face was as bland as ever:* **unemotional**, emotionless, dispassionate, passionless; unexpressive, cool, impassive; expressionless, blank, wooden, stony, deadpan, hollow, undemonstrative, imperturbable.
– OPPOSITES tangy, interesting, emotional.

blandishments plural noun *he soon learned that such bribes and blandishments would not help his case:* **flattery**, cajolery, coaxing, wheedling, persuasion, honeyed words, smooth talk, blarney; informal sweet talk, soft soap, buttering up.

blank adjective **1** *he still had to put his own words on this blank sheet of paper:* **empty**, unmarked, unused, clear, free, bare, clean, plain. **2** *Jack continued to gaze down at Ken's blank face:* **expressionless**, deadpan, wooden, stony, impassive, unresponsive, poker-faced, vacuous, empty, glazed, fixed, lifeless, inscrutable. **3** *'What?' said Maxim, looking blank:* **baffled**, mystified, puzzled, perplexed, stumped, at a loss, stuck, bewildered, nonplussed, bemused, lost, uncomprehending, (all) at sea, confused; informal flummoxed, bamboozled.
– OPPOSITES full, expressive, clear.
noun **space**, gap, lacuna.

blanket noun *a thick grey blanket of cloud:* **covering**, layer, coating, carpet, overlay,

b

cloak, mantle, veil, pall, shroud.
adjective *a blanket ban on tobacco advertising:* **complete**, total, comprehensive, overall, general, mass, umbrella, inclusive, all-inclusive, all-round, wholesale, outright, across the board, sweeping, indiscriminate, thorough; universal, global, worldwide, international, nationwide, countrywide, coast-to-coast.
– OPPOSITES partial, piecemeal.
verb *a heavy fall of snow blanketed the mountains:* **cover**, coat, carpet, overlay; cloak, shroud, swathe, envelop.
– OPPOSITES reveal.

blare verb *sirens blared all around:* **blast**, sound, trumpet, clamour, boom, roar, thunder, bellow, resound.
– OPPOSITES murmur.
noun *the blare of the siren made him jump:* **blast**, trumpeting, clamour, boom, roar, thunder, bellow.
– OPPOSITES murmur.

blasé adjective *she was becoming quite blasé about the dangers:* **indifferent**, unconcerned, uncaring, casual, nonchalant, offhand, uninterested, apathetic, unimpressed, unmoved, unresponsive, phlegmatic; informal laid-back.
– OPPOSITES concerned, responsive.

blaspheme verb *how could you blaspheme in church?* **swear**, curse, take the Lord's name in vain; informal cuss.

blasphemous adjective *a blasphemous book that should be banned:* **sacrilegious**, profane, irreligious, irreverent, impious, ungodly, godless.
– OPPOSITES reverent.

blasphemy noun *he has been accused of blasphemy:* **profanity**, sacrilege, irreligion, irreverence; taking the Lord's name in vain, swearing, curse, cursing, impiety, desecration.
– OPPOSITES reverence.

blast noun **1** *the blast from the bomb:* **shock wave**; aftershock, impact, percussion.
2 *Friday's blast killed two people:* **explosion**, detonation, discharge, burst. **3** *a sudden blast of cold air:* **gust**, rush, gale, squall, wind, draught, waft, puff, flurry. **4** *the shrill blast of the trumpets:* **blare**, wail, roar, screech, shriek, hoot, honk, beep.
verb **1** *bombers were blasting enemy airfields:* **blow up**, bomb, blow (to pieces), dynamite, explode; shell, strafe, bombard. **2** *the big guns were blasting away:* **fire**, shoot, blaze, let fly, discharge. **3** *he blasted his horn in frustration:* **honk**, beep, toot, sound. **4** *radios blasting out pop music:* **blare**, boom, roar, thunder, bellow, pump, shriek, screech.
■ **blast off** *a rocket blasted off to rendezvous with the space station:* take off, lift off, leave the ground, become airborne, take to the air.

blasted adjective (informal). See DAMNED sense 2.

blast-off noun **launch**, lift-off, take-off, ascent, firing.
– OPPOSITES touchdown.

blatant adjective *that is a blatant lie:* **flagrant**, glaring, obvious, undisguised, unconcealed, open; shameless, barefaced, unabashed, unashamed, unblushing, brazen, brass-necked.
– OPPOSITES inconspicuous, shamefaced.

blather verb *he just blathered on about nothing:* **prattle**, babble, chatter, twitter, prate, go on, run on, rattle on, yap, jabber, maunder, ramble, burble, drivel; informal yak, yatter; Brit. informal witter, rabbit, chunter, waffle.
noun *sick of listening to their mindless blather:* **prattle**, chatter, twitter, babble, prating, gabble, rambling; informal yatter, twaddle; Brit. informal wittering, chuntering.

blaze noun **1** *firemen fought the blaze all night:* **fire**, flames, conflagration, inferno, holocaust. **2** *a blaze of light:* **glare**, gleam, flash, burst, flare, streak, radiance, brilliance, beam.
verb **1** *the fire blazed merrily in the hearth:* **burn**, flame; be on fire, be in flames. **2** *headlights blazed:* **shine**, flash, flare, glare, gleam, glint, dazzle, glitter, glisten.

blazon verb **1** *the sponsor's name is blazoned across the sails:* **display**, exhibit, present, spread, emblazon, plaster. **2** *the newspapers blazoned the news abroad:* **publicize**, make known, make public, announce, report, communicate, spread, circulate, give out, publish, broadcast, trumpet, proclaim, promulgate.

bleach verb **1** *her hair had been bleached by the sun:* **turn white**, whiten, turn pale, blanch, lighten, fade, decolour, peroxide. **2** *they saw bones bleaching in the sun:* **turn white**, whiten, turn pale, pale, blanch, lose its colour, fade.
– OPPOSITES darken.

bleak adjective **1** *a bleak, rocky landscape lay before them:* **bare**, exposed, desolate, stark, desert, lunar, open, empty, windswept; treeless, without vegetation, denuded. **2** *the future looks pretty bleak:* **unpromising**, unfavourable, unpropitious, inauspicious; discouraging, disheartening, depressing, dim, gloomy, black, dark, grim, hopeless.
– OPPOSITES lush, promising.

bleary adjective *he tried to focus his bleary eyes:* **blurred**, blurry, unfocused; fogged, clouded, dull, misty, watery, rheumy.
– OPPOSITES clear.

bleat verb **1** *the sheep were bleating frantically:* **baa**; N. Amer. informal blat. **2** *don't bleat to me about fairness:* **complain**, grouse, carp, fuss, snivel; Scottish & Irish gurn; informal gripe, beef, whinge, bellyache, moan, go on; N. English informal mither; N. Amer. informal kvetch.

bleed verb **1** *his arm was bleeding badly:* **lose blood**, haemorrhage. **2** *one colour bled into* *another:* **flow**, run, seep, filter, percolate, leach.

blemish noun *not a single blemish marred her skin:* **imperfection**, flaw, defect, fault, deformity, discoloration, disfigurement; bruise, scar, pit, pock, scratch, cut, gash; mark, streak, spot, smear, speck, blotch, smudge; birthmark; Medicine stigma.
− OPPOSITES virtue.
verb *his reputation has been blemished by the controversy:* **sully**, tarnish, besmirch, blacken, blot, taint; spoil, mar, ruin, disgrace, damage, undermine, degrade.
− OPPOSITES enhance.

blench verb *she blenched at the size of the bill:* **flinch**, start, shy (away), recoil, shrink, pull back, cringe, wince, quail, cower.

blend verb **1** *blend the ingredients until smooth:* **mix**, mingle, combine, merge, fuse, meld, coalesce, integrate, intermix; stir, whisk, fold in; literary commingle. **2** *the new buildings blend well with the older ones:* **harmonize**, go (well), fit (in), be in tune, be compatible; coordinate, match, complement.
noun *a blend of bananas, raisins, and ginger:* **mixture**, mix, combination, amalgamation, amalgam, union, marriage, fusion, meld, synthesis; technical admixture.

bless verb **1** *the Cardinal blessed the memorial plaque:* **consecrate**, sanctify, dedicate (to God); formal hallow. **2** *God has blessed us with special gifts:* **endow**, bestow, furnish, accord, give, favour, grace; confer on. **3** *the government refused to bless the undertaking:* **sanction**, consent to, endorse, agree to, approve, back, support; informal give the thumbs up to, give the green light to, OK.
− OPPOSITES curse, trouble, rue, oppose.

blessing noun **1** *may God give us his blessing:* **protection**, favour. **2** *a special blessing from the priest:* **benediction**, invocation, prayer, intercession; grace. **3** *she gave the plan her blessing:* **sanction**, endorsement, approval, approbation, favour, consent, assent, agreement; backing, support; informal the thumbs up. **4** *it was a blessing they didn't have far to go:* **boon**, godsend, advantage, benefit, help, bonus, plus; stroke of luck, windfall.
− OPPOSITES condemnation, affliction.

blight noun **1** *the whole region has been afflicted with potato blight:* **disease**, canker, infestation, fungus, mildew, mould. **2** *the blight of aircraft noise has driven many people from the area:* **affliction**, scourge, bane, curse, plague, menace, misfortune, woe, trouble, ordeal, trial, nuisance, pest.
− OPPOSITES blessing.
verb **1** *a tree blighted by leaf curl:* **infect**, mildew; kill, destroy. **2** *scandal blighted the careers of several politicians:* **ruin**, wreck, spoil, mar, frustrate, disrupt, undo, end, scotch, destroy, shatter, devastate, demolish; informal mess up, foul up, put paid to, put the kibosh on, stymie; Brit. informal scupper.

blind adjective **1** *he has been blind since birth:*

sightless, unsighted, visually impaired, unseeing; partially sighted, purblind; informal as blind as a bat. **2** *she was ignorant, but not blind:* **imperceptive**, unperceptive, insensitive, slow, obtuse, uncomprehending, stupid, unintelligent; informal dense, dim, thick, dumb, dopey; Brit. informal dozy; Scottish & N. English informal glaikit. **3** *the blind acceptance of conventional opinion:* **uncritical**, unreasoned, unthinking, unconsidered, mindless, undiscerning, indiscriminate. **4** *a blind rage:* **wild**, uncontrolled, uncontrollable, unrestrained, furious, towering.
− OPPOSITES sighted, perceptive, discerning.
verb **1** *he was blinded in a car crash:* **make blind**, deprive of sight, render sightless; put someone's eyes out. **2** *they try to blind you with statistics:* **overawe**, intimidate, confuse, bewilder, confound, perplex, overwhelm; informal faze, psych out.
noun **1** *I pulled the blind down:* **screen**, shade, sunshade, curtain, awning, canopy; louvre, shutter. **2** *some crook had sent the card as a blind:* **deception**, camouflage, smokescreen, front, facade, cover, pretext, masquerade, feint; trick, ploy, ruse, machination.

blindly adverb **1** *he stared blindly ahead:* **sightlessly**, unseeingly. **2** *they blindly followed US policy:* **uncritically**, unthinkingly, mindlessly, indiscriminately.

blink verb **1** *his eyes did not blink:* **flutter**, flicker, wink, bat. **2** *several red lights began to blink:* **flash**, flicker, wink. **3** *no one even blinks at the 'waitresses' in drag:* **be surprised**, look twice, bat an eyelid, turn a hair; informal boggle.

blinkered adjective *we should not be quite so blinkered and xenophobic:* **narrow-minded**, inward-looking, parochial, provincial, insular, small-minded, close-minded, short-sighted; hidebound, inflexible, entrenched, prejudiced, bigoted.
− OPPOSITES broad-minded.

bliss noun *she gave a sigh of bliss:* **joy**, happiness, pleasure, delight, ecstasy, elation, rapture, euphoria.
− OPPOSITES misery.

blissful adjective **ecstatic**, euphoric, joyful, elated, rapturous, on cloud nine, in seventh heaven; delighted, thrilled, overjoyed, joyous; informal over the moon, on top of the world; Austral. informal wrapped.

blister noun **1** *she had a blister on each heel:* bleb; Medicine pustule, vesicle. **2** *check for blisters in the roofing felt:* **bubble**, swelling, bulge, protuberance.

blistering adjective **1** *we sweated in the blistering heat:* **intense**, extreme, ferocious, fierce; **scorching**, searing, blazing, burning, fiery; informal boiling, baking, roasting, sweltering. **2** *a blistering attack on the government:* **savage**, vicious, fierce, bitter, harsh, scathing, devastating, caustic, searing, vitriolic.
− OPPOSITES mild.

b

blithe adjective *he shows a blithe disregard for the rules:* **casual**, indifferent, unconcerned, unworried, untroubled, uncaring, careless, heedless, thoughtless; nonchalant, blasé.
– OPPOSITES thoughtful.

blitz noun *election year heralds an ad blitz by the main parties:* **campaign**, onslaught, attack.
verb *I had some posters made, and I blitzed the town with them:* **fill**, bombard, cover, saturate, hit.

blizzard noun **snowstorm**, white-out.

bloated adjective *a black pond where a bloated rat floated belly-up:* **swollen**, distended, tumefied, bulging, inflated, enlarged, expanded, dilated.

blob noun **1** *a blob of cold gravy stuck to his tie:* **drop**, droplet, globule, bead, bubble; informal glob. **2** *a blob of ink:* **spot**, dab, blotch, blot, dot, smudge; informal splotch, splodge.

bloc noun *all five parties moved towards forming a political bloc:* **alliance**, coalition, federation, confederation, league, union, partnership, axis, body, association, group.

block noun **1** *a block of cheese:* **chunk**, hunk, lump, wedge, cube, brick, slab, piece; Brit. informal wodge. **2** *an apartment block:* **building**, complex, structure, development. **3** *a block of shares:* **batch**, group, set, quantity, tranche. **4** *a sketch block:* **pad**, notepad, sketch pad, jotter, tablet. **5** *a block to Third World development:* **obstacle**, bar, barrier, impediment, hindrance, check, hurdle, stumbling block, handicap, deterrent.
– OPPOSITES aid.
verb **1** *weeds can block the drainage ditches:* **clog (up)**, stop up, choke, plug, obstruct, gum up, dam up, congest, jam, close; informal bung up; Brit. informal gunge up; technical occlude. **2** *picket lines blocked access to the factory:* **hinder**, hamper, obstruct, impede, inhibit, restrict, limit; halt, stop, bar, check, prevent. **3** *he blocked a shot on the goal line:* **parry**, stop, deflect, fend off, hold off, repel, repulse.
– OPPOSITES facilitate.
■ **block something off** *one van was enough to block off a street:* close up, shut off, seal off, barricade, bar, obstruct.
■ **block something out** *the trees blocked out the light:* conceal, keep out, blot out, exclude, obliterate, blank out, stop.

blockade noun **1** *a naval blockade of the island:* **siege**. **2** *rioters erected blockades in the streets:* **barricade**, barrier, roadblock; obstacle, obstruction.
verb *rebels blockaded the capital:* **barricade**, block off, shut off, seal; besiege, surround.

blockage noun *there's a blockage in the main drain:* **obstruction**, stoppage, block, occlusion, congestion.

bloke noun (Brit. informal). See FELLOW sense 1.

blonde, blond adjective *her blonde hair tumbled about her face:* **fair**, light, yellow,

flaxen, tow-coloured, golden, platinum, ash blonde, strawberry blonde; bleached, peroxide.
– OPPOSITES dark.

blood noun *a woman of noble blood:* **ancestry**, lineage, bloodline, descent, parentage, family, birth, extraction, origin, genealogy, heritage, stock, kinship.

blood-curdling adjective *he let out a blood-curdling scream:* **terrifying**, frightening, spine-chilling, chilling, hair-raising, horrifying, alarming; eerie, sinister, horrible; Scottish eldritch.

bloodless adjective **1** *a bloodless revolution:* **non-violent**, peaceful, peaceable. **2** *his face was bloodless:* **anaemic**, pale, wan, pallid, ashen, colourless, chalky, waxen, white, grey, pasty, drained, drawn, deathly. **3** *a shrewd and bloodless Hollywood mogul:* **heartless**, unfeeling, cruel, ruthless, merciless, pitiless, uncharitable; cold, hard, stony-hearted, cold-blooded, callous.
– OPPOSITES bloody, ruddy, charitable.

bloodshed noun *the chance to avoid further bloodshed in Kashmir:* **slaughter**, massacre, killing, wounding; carnage, butchery, bloodletting; violence, fighting, warfare, battle.

bloodthirsty adjective *the most bloodthirsty of the Celtic warriors:* **murderous**, homicidal, violent, vicious, barbarous, barbaric, savage, brutal, cut-throat; fierce, ferocious, inhuman.

bloody adjective **1** *he held his bloody nose:* **bleeding**, dripping. **2** *a pile of bloody bandages:* **bloodstained**, blood-soaked, gory. **3** *a bloody civil war threatened to erupt:* **vicious**, ferocious, savage, fierce, brutal, murderous, gory. **4** (Brit. informal) *he's a bloody nuisance!* See DAMNED.

bloody-minded adjective (Brit. informal) *he was a combative, bloody-minded old fool:* **uncooperative**, awkward, disobliging, recalcitrant, unaccommodating, inflexible, uncompromising, contrary, perverse, obstinate, stubborn; difficult; informal pig-headed; Brit. informal bolshie, stroppy.
– OPPOSITES compliant.

bloom noun **1** *a display of gorgeous orchid blooms:* **flower**, blossom, floweret, floret. **2** *a girl in the bloom of youth:* **prime**, perfection, acme, peak, height, heyday; salad days. **3** *the bloom of her skin:* **radiance**, lustre, sheen, glow, freshness; **blush**, rosiness, pinkness, colour.
verb **1** *the geraniums finally bloomed:* **flower**, blossom, open; mature. **2** *the children bloomed in the Devonshire air:* **flourish**, thrive, prosper, progress, burgeon.
– OPPOSITES wither, decline.

blossom noun *pink blossoms covered the branches:* **flower**, bloom, floweret, floret.
verb **1** *the snowdrops have blossomed:* **bloom**, flower, open, unfold; mature. **2** *the whole region had blossomed:* **develop**, grow,

mature, progress, evolve; flourish, thrive, prosper, bloom, burgeon.
– OPPOSITES fade, decline.

■ **in blossom** *the cherry trees are all in blossom at this time of year:* in flower, flowering, blossoming, blooming, in (full) bloom, open, out.

blot noun 1 *a shape emerged from the gloom, a blot of black in the greyness:* **spot**, dot, mark, blotch, smudge, patch, dab; informal splotch; Brit. informal splodge. 2 *the one blot on their record was their treatment of ethnic minorities in Georgia:* **blemish**, taint, stain, blight, flaw, fault; disgrace, dishonour.
verb *blot any excess water with a paper towel:* **soak up**, absorb, sponge up, mop up; dry up/out; dab, pat.

■ **a blot on the landscape** *modern buildings that are a blot on the landscape:* eyesore, monstrosity, carbuncle, mess; informal sight.

■ **blot something out 1** *clouds were starting to blot out the stars:* conceal, hide, obscure, exclude, obliterate; shadow, eclipse. 2 *he urged her to blot out the memory:* erase, efface, eradicate, expunge, wipe out.

blotch noun 1 *pink flowers with dark blotches:* **patch**, smudge, dot, spot, blot, dab, daub; informal splotch; Brit. informal splodge. 2 *his face was covered in blotches:* **patch**, mark, freckle, birthmark, discoloration, eruption, naevus.
verb *her face was blotched and swollen:* **spot**, mark, smudge, streak, blemish.

blotchy adjective **mottled**, dappled, blotched, patchy, spotty, spotted, smudged, marked; informal splotchy; Brit. informal splodgy.

blow[1] verb 1 *the icy wind blew around our ankles:* **gust**, puff, blast, roar, bluster, rush, storm. 2 *his ship was blown on to the rocks:* **sweep**, carry, toss, drive, push, force. 3 *leaves blew across the road:* **drift**, flutter, waft, float, glide, whirl, move. 4 *he blew a huge smoke ring and the students gasped in awe:* **exhale**, puff, emit, expel, discharge, produce. 5 *Uncle Albert was soon puffing and blowing like a steam train:* **wheeze**, puff, pant, gasp. 6 *he blew his trumpet and everyone went quiet:* **sound**, blast, toot, pipe, trumpet; play. 7 *a rear tyre had blown:* **burst**, explode, blow out, split, rupture, puncture. 8 *the bulb had blown again:* **fuse**, short-circuit, burn out, break, go. 9 (informal) *he blew a lot of his money on gambling:* **squander**, waste, spend, throw away, fritter away, go through, lose, lavish, dissipate, use up; spend recklessly; informal splurge. 10 (informal) *if you blow this opportunity you might never get another chance:* **spoil**, ruin, bungle, mess up, fudge, muff; **waste**, lose, squander; informal botch, screw up, foul up; Brit. informal cock up, bodge.
noun *James wanted a blow on the guard's whistle:* **toot**, blast, blare; whistle.

■ **blow out 1** *these matches will not blow out*

even in a strong wind: be extinguished, go out, be put out, stop burning. 2 *the front tyre blew out.* See **BLOW**[1] verb sense 7. 3 *there was an enormous explosion and the windows blew out:* shatter, rupture, crack, smash, splinter, disintegrate; burst, explode, fly apart; informal bust.

■ **blow something out** *Sam was allowed to blow out the altar candles after Mass:* extinguish, put out, snuff, douse, quench, smother.

■ **blow over** *she wants all of this to blow over and life to return to normal:* calm down, go away, fade (away), disappear, recede, dwindle, peter out, pass, die down, fizzle out.

■ **blow up 1** *a lorryload of shells blew up in the mountains:* explode, detonate, go off, ignite, erupt. 2 *he blows up at whoever's in his way:* lose one's temper, get angry, rant and rave, go berserk, flare up, erupt; informal go mad, go crazy, go wild, go ape, hit the roof, fly off the handle. 3 *if it wasn't to blow up into a row, she'd have to compromise:* break out, erupt, flare up, boil over; emerge, arise.

■ **blow something up 1** *the hijackers had threatened to blow up the aircraft:* bomb, blast, destroy; explode, detonate. 2 *we blew up all the balloons ourselves:* inflate, pump up, fill up, puff up, swell, expand, aerate. 3 *things sometimes get blown up out of all proportion:* exaggerate, overstate, overstress, overestimate, magnify, amplify; aggrandize. 4 *I blew the picture up on a photocopier:* enlarge, magnify, expand, increase.

blow[2] noun 1 *death was due to a blow on the head:* **knock**, **bang**, hit, punch, thump, smack, crack, rap; informal whack, thwack, bash, clout, sock, wallop. 2 *losing his wife must have been a severe blow:* **shock**, surprise, bombshell, thunderbolt, jolt; calamity, catastrophe, disaster, upset, setback.

blowout noun 1 *the steering is automatic in the event of blowouts:* **puncture**, flat tyre, burst tyre; informal flat. 2 (informal) *this meal is our last real blowout:* **feast**, banquet, celebration, party; informal shindig, do, binge; Brit. informal beanfeast, bunfight, nosh-up.

blowsy adjective *a loud, blowsy woman wearing Bermuda shorts:* **untidy**, sloppy, scruffy, messy, dishevelled, unkempt, frowzy, slovenly; coarse; **red-faced**, ruddy, florid, raddled.
– OPPOSITES tidy, respectable.

blowy adjective *it's a bit blowy outside!* **windy**, windswept, blustery, gusty, breezy; stormy, squally.
– OPPOSITES still.

blubber[1] noun *body heat is retained by a layer of blubber under the skin:* **fat**, fatty tissue; insulation, padding.

blubber[2] verb (informal) *she started to blubber:*

cry, sob, weep, howl, snivel; informal blub, boohoo.

bludgeon noun *he had a formidable-looking bludgeon loaded with lead:* **cudgel**, club, stick, truncheon, baton; N. Amer. nightstick, blackjack; Brit. informal cosh.
verb **1** *he was bludgeoned to death by his captors:* **batter**, cudgel, club, beat, thrash; informal clobber. **2** *I let him bludgeon me into a loveless marriage:* **coerce**, force, compel, pressurize, pressure, bully, browbeat, hector, dragoon, steamroller; informal strong-arm, railroad.

blue adjective **1** *bright blue eyes:* sky-blue, azure, cobalt, sapphire, navy, Oxford blue, Cambridge blue, ultramarine, aquamarine, cyan; literary cerulean. **2** (informal) *Mum was feeling a bit blue:* **depressed**, down, sad, unhappy, melancholy, miserable, gloomy, dejected, downhearted, downcast, despondent, low, glum; informal down in the dumps, down in the mouth, fed up. **3** (informal) *a blue movie:* **pornographic**, racy, risqué, naughty, spicy; indecent, dirty, lewd, smutty, filthy, obscene, sordid; erotic, arousing, sexy, titillating, explicit; informal porn, porno, X-rated, raunchy; euphemistic adult.
– OPPOSITES happy, clean.

blueprint noun **1** *he produced blueprints of the aircraft:* **plan**, design, diagram, drawing, sketch, map, layout, representation. **2** *this is a blueprint for similar measures in other countries:* **model**, plan, template, framework, pattern, example, guide, prototype, pilot.

blues plural noun (informal) *many of the winners were suffering from post-championship blues:* **depression**, sadness, unhappiness, melancholy, misery, sorrow, gloom, dejection, despondency, despair; the doldrums.

bluff¹ noun *this offer was denounced as a bluff:* **deception**, subterfuge, pretence, sham, fake, deceit, feint, hoax, fraud, charade; trick, ruse, scheme, machination; informal put-on, kidology.
verb **1** *they are bluffing to hide their guilt:* **pretend**, sham, fake, feign, lie, hoax, pose, posture, masquerade, dissemble. **2** *I managed to bluff the board into believing me:* **deceive**, delude, mislead, trick, fool, hoodwink, dupe, hoax, beguile, gull; informal con, kid, have on.

bluff² adjective *Thomas had been a bluff hearty man with no finesse:* **plain-spoken**, straightforward, blunt, direct, no-nonsense, frank, open, candid, forthright, unequivocal; hearty, genial, good-natured; informal upfront.

bluff³ noun *he was standing on the edge of a bluff about fifty feet high:* **cliff**, promontory, headland, crag, bank, peak, escarpment, scarp.

blunder noun *he shook his head at his blunder:* **mistake**, error, gaffe, slip,

oversight, faux pas; informal botch, slip-up, boo-boo; Brit. informal clanger, boob; N. Amer. informal blooper.
verb **1** *the government admitted it had blundered:* **make a mistake**, err, miscalculate, bungle, trip up, be wrong; informal slip up, screw up, blow it, goof; Brit. informal boob. **2** *she blundered down the steps to the cellar:* **stumble**, lurch, stagger, flounder, struggle, fumble, grope.

blunt adjective **1** *a blunt knife:* **unsharpened**, dull, worn, edgeless. **2** *the leaf is broad with a blunt tip:* **rounded**, flat, obtuse, stubby. **3** *he delivered a blunt message to home owners:* **straightforward**, frank, plain-spoken, candid, direct, bluff, forthright, unequivocal; **brusque**, abrupt, curt, terse, bald, brutal, harsh; stark, undisguised, unvarnished; informal upfront.
– OPPOSITES sharp, pointed, subtle.
verb **1** *ebony blunts tools very rapidly:* **dull**, wear, take the edge off. **2** *age hasn't blunted my passion for life:* **dull**, deaden, dampen, numb, weaken, sap, cool, temper, allay, abate; diminish, reduce, decrease, lessen, deplete.
– OPPOSITES sharpen, intensify.

blur verb **1** *she felt tears blur her vision:* **cloud**, fog, obscure, dim, make hazy, unfocus, soften. **2** *these films blur the difference between villains and victims:* **obscure**, make vague, confuse, muddle, muddy, obfuscate, cloud, weaken. **3** *memories of the picnic had blurred in my mind:* **become dim**, dull, numb, deaden, mute; lessen, decrease, diminish.
– OPPOSITES sharpen, focus.
noun *I could make out a blur on the horizon:* **shape**, smudge; form, outline.

blurred adjective *all he saw was a blurred grey oval:* **indistinct**, blurry, fuzzy, hazy, misty, foggy, shadowy, faint; unclear, vague, indefinite, unfocused, obscure, nebulous.

blurt
■ **blurt something out** *a man like Sterne wasn't likely to blurt out a confession of guilt:* **burst out with**, exclaim, call out; divulge, disclose, reveal, betray, let slip, give away; informal blab, gush.

blush verb *Joan blushed at the compliment:* **redden**, turn/go pink, turn/go red, flush, colour, burn up; feel shy, feel embarrassed.
noun *the darkness hid her fiery blush:* **flush**, rosiness, pinkness, bloom, high colour.

bluster verb **1** *he started blustering about the general election:* **rant**, thunder, bellow, sound off; be overbearing; informal throw one's weight about/around. **2** *storms bluster in from the sea:* **blast**, gust, storm, roar, rush.
noun *his bluster turned to cooperation:* **ranting**, thundering, hectoring, bullying; bombast, bumptiousness, braggadocio.

blustery adjective **stormy**, gusty, blowy, windy, squally, wild, tempestuous, turbulent; howling, roaring.
– OPPOSITES calm.

board noun 1 *a wooden board:* **plank**, beam, panel, slat, batten, timber, lath. 2 *the board of directors:* **committee**, council, panel, directorate, commission, group. 3 *your room and board will be free:* **food**, meals, provisions, refreshments, diet, table, bread; keep, maintenance; informal grub, nosh, eats, chow; Brit. informal scoff.
verb 1 *he turned and boarded the aircraft:* **get on**, go aboard, enter, mount, ascend; embark, emplane, entrain; catch; informal hop on. 2 *a number of students boarded with them:* **lodge**, live, reside, be housed; N. Amer. room; informal put up, have digs. 3 *they run a facility for boarding dogs:* **accommodate**, lodge, take in, put up, house; keep, feed, cater for.
■ **board something up/over** *they're coming to board up the windows:* cover up/over, close up, shut up, seal (up).

boast verb 1 *his mother had been boasting about him:* **brag**, crow, swagger, swank, gloat, show off; exaggerate, overstate; informal talk big, lay it on thick; Austral./NZ informal skite. 2 *the hotel boasts two fine restaurants:* **possess**, have, own, enjoy, pride oneself/itself on, offer.
noun *a boast that Britain's tap water is the best in Europe:* **claim**, assertion; allegation, suggestion.

boastful adjective *he's always so boastful that people rarely believe him:* **bragging**, swaggering, bumptious, puffed up, full of oneself; cocky, conceited, arrogant, egotistical; informal swanky, big-headed; N. Amer. informal blowhard; literary vainglorious.
– OPPOSITES modest.

boat noun *a rowing boat:* **vessel**, craft, ship; literary barque.

bob verb 1 *their yacht bobbed about on the waves:* **move up and down**, bounce, toss, skip, dance, jounce; wobble, jiggle, joggle, jolt, jerk. 2 *the bookie's head bobbed:* **nod**, incline, dip; wag, waggle. 3 *the maid bobbed and left the room:* **curtsy**, bow.
noun 1 *he agreed with a bob of his head:* **nod**, inclination, dip; wag, waggle. 2 *the maid scurried away with a bob:* **curtsy**, bow.

bode verb *this does not bode well for the development of cricket in Zimbabwe | the 12 per cent interest rate bodes dark times for retailers:* **augur**, portend, herald, be a sign of, warn of, foreshadow, be an omen of, presage, indicate, signify, promise, threaten, spell, denote.

bodily adjective *bodily sensations:* **physical**, corporeal, corporal, somatic, fleshly; concrete, real, actual, tangible.
– OPPOSITES spiritual, mental.
adverb *he hauled her bodily from the van:* **forcefully**, forcibly, violently; wholly, completely, entirely.

body noun 1 *drawings of the human body:* **figure**, frame, form, physique, anatomy, skeleton; soma; informal bod. 2 *he was hit by shrapnel in the head and body:* **torso**, trunk.
3 *the bodies were dumped in a hole in the ground:* **corpse**, carcass, skeleton, remains; informal stiff; Medicine cadaver. 4 *the body of the article:* **main part**, central part, core, heart, hub. 5 *the body of the aircraft:* **bodywork**, hull; fuselage. 6 *a body of water:* **expanse**, mass, area, stretch, tract, sweep, extent. 7 *a growing body of evidence:* **quantity**, amount, volume, collection, mass, corpus. 8 *the representative body of the employers:* **association**, organization, group, party, company, society, circle, syndicate, guild, corporation, contingent. 9 *a heavenly body:* **object**, entity. 10 *add body to your hair:* **fullness**, thickness, substance, bounce, lift, shape.

bodyguard noun **minder**, guard, protector, guardian, defender; informal heavy.

boffin noun (Brit. informal) *a 15-year-old computer boffin from New York:* **expert**, specialist, authority, genius, mastermind; **scientist**, technician, inventor; informal egghead, Einstein.

bog noun **marsh**, swamp, mire, quagmire, morass, slough, fen, wetland; Brit. carr; Scottish & N. English moss.
■ **get bogged down** *we don't want to get bogged down in academic arguments | the funeral car got bogged down in a snow drift:* mire, stick, entangle, ensnare, embroil; hamper, hinder, impede, delay, stall, detain; swamp, overwhelm.

bogey noun 1 *he thinks if no one mentions the bogey of recession, it will go away:* **gremlin**, spectre, phantom, hobgoblin, demon, monster. 2 *the guild is the bogey of bankers:* **bugbear**, pet hate, bane, anathema, abomination, nightmare, horror, dread, curse; N. Amer. bugaboo.

boggy adjective *the plant grows in boggy areas:* **marshy**, swampy, miry, fenny, muddy, waterlogged, wet, soggy, sodden, squelchy; spongy, heavy, sloughy.

bogus adjective *the bogus officers were dressed in full police uniform:* **fake**, spurious, false, fraudulent, sham, deceptive, counterfeit, forged, feigned, make-believe, dummy, pseudo; informal phoney, pretend.
– OPPOSITES genuine.

bohemian noun *he is an artist and a real bohemian:* **nonconformist**, avant-gardist, free spirit, dropout; hippy, beatnik.
– OPPOSITES conservative.
adjective *he lived a bohemian student life:* **unconventional**, nonconformist, unorthodox, avant-garde, irregular, alternative; artistic; informal arty-farty, way-out, offbeat.
– OPPOSITES conventional.

boil¹ verb 1 *boil and mash the potatoes:* **cook**, simmer, braise; bring to the boil. 2 *the soup is boiling, so let's eat:* **simmer**, bubble. 3 *a huge cliff with the sea boiling below:* **churn**, seethe, froth, foam.
■ **boil down to** *the issues boil down to*

b

b

questions about corporate finance: come down to, amount to, add up to, be in essence.

boil² noun a boil on her neck: **swelling**, **spot**, pimple, blister, pustule, eruption, carbuncle, wen, abscess, ulcer; technical furuncle.

boiling adjective 1 boiling water: at boiling point, scalding; very hot, piping hot; bubbling. 2 (informal) it was absolutely boiling in the afternoon: **very hot**, scorching, blistering, sweltering, sultry, torrid; informal roasting, baking.
– OPPOSITES freezing.

boisterous adjective a boisterous game of handball: **lively**, animated, exuberant, spirited; rowdy, unruly, wild, uproarious, unrestrained, undisciplined, uninhibited, uncontrolled, rough, disorderly, riotous; noisy, loud, clamorous; Brit. informal rumbustious, Tiggerish.
– OPPOSITES restrained.

bold adjective 1 this is a bold and innovative move: **daring**, brave, courageous, valiant, fearless, audacious, daredevil; adventurous, heroic, plucky, spirited, confident, assured; informal gutsy, spunky, feisty. 2 the bold colours and designs employed in Caucasian rugs: **striking**, vivid, bright, strong, eye-catching, prominent; gaudy, lurid, garish. 3 the departure times are in bold: **heavy type**, thick type, black type.
– OPPOSITES timid, pale.

bolster noun the bed was strewn with bolsters: **pillow**, cushion, pad.
verb a break would bolster her morale: **strengthen**, reinforce, boost, fortify, renew; support, buoy up, shore up, maintain, aid, help; augment, increase.
– OPPOSITES undermine.

bolt noun 1 the bolt on the shed door had been forced: **bar**, **lock**, catch, latch, fastener. 2 tins of nuts and bolts: **rivet**, pin, peg, screw. 3 a bolt of lightning: **flash**, shaft, streak, burst, flare. 4 Mark made a bolt for the door: **dash**, dart, run, sprint, leap, bound.
verb 1 he bolted the door: **lock**, bar, latch, fasten, secure. 2 the lid was bolted down: **rivet**, pin, peg, screw; fasten, fix. 3 Anna bolted from the room: **dash**, dart, run, sprint, hurtle, rush, fly, shoot, bound; flee; informal tear, scoot, leg it. 4 he bolted down his breakfast: **gobble**, gulp, wolf, guzzle, devour; informal demolish, polish off, shovel down; Brit. informal shift, gollop, scoff; N. Amer. informal scarf, snarf.
■ **a bolt from/out of the blue** the Mishcon job offer came like a bolt from the blue: shock, surprise, bombshell, thunderbolt, revelation; informal turn-up for the books.
■ **bolt upright** she sat bolt upright in bed: straight, rigidly, stiffly.

bomb noun 1 they saw bombs bursting on the runway: **explosive**, incendiary (device); missile, projectile. 2 the world has to live with the bomb: **nuclear weapons**, the nuclear bomb, the atom bomb, the A-bomb; weapons of mass destruction, WMD. 3 (Brit.

informal) a new superstore will cost a bomb. See FORTUNE sense 5.
verb 1 their headquarters were bombed by separatists: **bombard**, blast, shell, blitz, strafe, pound; attack, assault; blow up, destroy, demolish, flatten, devastate. 2 (Brit. informal) she bombed across Texas. See SPEED verb sense 1. 3 (informal) the film bombed at the box office. See FAIL sense 1.

bombard verb 1 gun batteries bombarded the islands: **shell**, pound, blitz, strafe, bomb; assail, attack, assault, batter, blast, pelt. 2 we were bombarded with information: **inundate**, swamp, flood, deluge, snow under; besiege, overwhelm.

bombast noun his bombast concealed political shrewdness and commercial acumen: **bluster**, pomposity, empty talk, humbug, turgidity, verbosity, verbiage; pretentiousness, ostentation, grandiloquence; informal hot air; rare fustian.

bombastic adjective he spoke in the bombastic tones of a man accustomed to a respectful audience: **pompous**, blustering, turgid, verbose, orotund, high-flown, high-sounding, overwrought, pretentious, ostentatious, grandiloquent; informal highfalutin.

bona fide adjective it is questionable whether or not all such bodies were bona fide trade unions: **authentic**, genuine, real, true, actual; legal, legitimate, lawful, valid, proper; informal legit, pukka, the real McCoy.
– OPPOSITES bogus.

bonanza noun the bosses' bonanza has continued into the recession: **windfall**, bonus, stroke of luck; informal jackpot, gravy train, freebie, cash cow.

bond noun 1 the women forged a close bond: **friendship**, relationship, fellowship, partnership, association, affiliation, alliance, attachment. 2 the prisoner struggled in vain with his bonds: **chains**, fetters, shackles, manacles, irons, restraints. 3 a gentleman's word is his bond: **promise**, pledge, vow, oath, word (of honour), guarantee, assurance; agreement, contract, pact, bargain, deal.
verb the extensions are bonded to your hair: **join**, fasten, fix, affix, attach, secure, bind, stick, fuse.

bondage noun they saw themselves as releasing Protestants from Catholic bondage: **slavery**, enslavement, servitude, subjugation, subjection, oppression, domination, exploitation, persecution.
– OPPOSITES liberty.

bonhomie noun he exuded an aura of cheerful bonhomie: **geniality**, affability, conviviality, cordiality, amiability, sociability, friendliness, warmth, joviality.
– OPPOSITES coldness.

bonny adjective (Scottish & N. English) did you ever see such a bonny baby? **beautiful**, attractive, pretty, gorgeous, fetching, prepossessing; lovely, nice, sweet, cute,

appealing, endearing, adorable, lovable, charming, winsome; informal **beaut**; archaic **fair**, comely.
– OPPOSITES unattractive.

bonus noun **1** *the work's fun, and coming back to Ireland is a real bonus:* **benefit**, advantage, boon, blessing, asset, plus, pro, attraction, extra; informal perk. **2** *she's on a good salary and she gets a bonus:* **gratuity**, handout, gift, present, reward, prize; incentive, inducement; informal perk, sweetener.
– OPPOSITES disadvantage.

bon viveur, bon vivant noun *he was a bon viveur, savouring his food and especially his wine:* **hedonist**, pleasure-seeker, sensualist, sybarite, voluptuary; epicure, gourmet, gastronome.
– OPPOSITES puritan.

bony adjective *his pale, bony face was half hidden by hair:* **gaunt**, **angular**, skinny, thin, lean, spare, spindly, skin-and-bones, skeletal, emaciated, underweight; informal like a bag of bones.
– OPPOSITES plump.

book noun **1** *he published his first book in 1610:* **volume**, tome, publication, title; novel, storybook, treatise, manual; paperback, hardback, softback. **2** *he scribbled a few notes in his book:* **notepad**, notebook, pad, memo pad, exercise book; logbook, ledger, journal, diary; Brit. jotter, pocketbook; N. Amer. scratch pad. **3** *the council had to balance its books:* **accounts**, records; account book, record book, ledger, balance sheet.
verb **1** *Steven booked a table at their favourite restaurant:* **reserve**, pre-arrange, order; informal bag. **2** *we've booked a jazz band for the evening do:* **arrange**, programme, schedule, timetable, line up, lay on; N. Amer. slate.
■ **by the book** *he does all his police work strictly by the book:* according to the rules, lawfully, legally, legitimately; honestly, fairly; informal on the level, fair and square.
■ **book in** *he booked in at the St Francis Hotel:* register, check in, enrol.

booking noun *we made a provisional booking for Friday afternoon:* **reservation**, pre-arrangement; appointment, date.

bookish adjective *he was considerably more bookish than his fellow students:* **studious**, scholarly, academic, intellectual, highbrow, erudite, learned, educated, knowledgeable; cerebral, serious.

booklet noun **pamphlet**, brochure, leaflet, handbill, flyer, tract; N. Amer. folder, mailer.

boom noun **1** *Mary could hear the boom of the waves on the rocks below:* **reverberation**, resonance, thunder, echoing, crashing, drumming, pounding, roar, rumble. **2** *retailers are cashing in on an unprecedented boom in sales:* **upturn**, upsurge, upswing, increase, advance, growth, boost, escalation, improvement.
– OPPOSITES slump.
verb **1** *thunder boomed in the sky overhead:* **reverberate**, resound, resonate; rumble,

thunder, blare, echo; crash, roll, clap, explode, bang. **2** *a voice boomed at her from a small doorway:* **bellow**, roar, thunder, shout, bawl; informal holler. **3** *the property market continued to boom:* **flourish**, burgeon, thrive, prosper, progress, improve, pick up, expand, mushroom, snowball.
– OPPOSITES whisper, slump.

booming adjective **1** *he had a booming voice that contradicted his diminutive stature:* **resonant**, sonorous, ringing, resounding, reverberating, carrying, thunderous; strident, stentorian, strong, powerful. **2** *shops are reporting booming business:* **flourishing**, burgeoning, thriving, prospering, prosperous, successful, strong, buoyant; profitable, fruitful, lucrative; expanding.

boon noun *his offer of rent-free accommodation was such a boon:* **blessing**, godsend, bonus, plus, benefit, advantage, help, aid, asset; stroke of luck.
– OPPOSITES curse.

boor noun *he is such a boor when he's had a few drinks:* **lout**, oaf, ruffian, thug, yahoo, barbarian, Neanderthal, brute, beast; informal pig; Brit. informal yobbo, yob, oik.

boorish adjective **coarse**, uncouth, rude, ill-bred, ill-mannered, uncivilized, unrefined, common, rough, thuggish, loutish; vulgar, unsavoury, gross, brutish, Neanderthal; informal plebby; Brit. informal yobbish; Austral. informal ocker.
– OPPOSITES refined.

boost noun **1** *it's a boost to our morale to know that people care:* **uplift**, lift, spur, encouragement, help, inspiration, stimulus, fillip. **2** *the economy will benefit from a boost in sales:* **increase**, expansion, upturn, upsurge, upswing, rise, escalation, improvement, advance, growth, boom; informal hike.
– OPPOSITES decrease.
verb **1** *he phones her regularly to boost her confidence:* **improve**, raise, uplift, increase, enhance, encourage, heighten, help, promote, foster, stimulate, invigorate, revitalize; informal buck up. **2** *they used radio advertising to boost sales:* **increase**, raise, escalate, improve, strengthen, inflate, push up, promote, advance, foster, stimulate; facilitate, help, assist, aid; informal hike, bump up.
– OPPOSITES decrease.

boot¹ noun **1** *don't come in here in those muddy boots!* **gumboot**, wellington, wader, walking boot, riding boot, moon boot, thigh boot, ankle boot, pixie boot, desert boot; informal welly; trademark Doc Martens. **2** (informal) *he got a boot in the stomach:* **kick**, blow, knock.
verb **1** *his shot was booted away by the goalkeeper:* **kick**, punt, bunt, tap; propel, drive, knock. **2** *the menu is ready as soon as you boot up your computer:* **start up**, fire up, activate.

b

■ **boot someone out** (informal). See DISMISS sense 1.

■ **give someone the boot** (informal). See DISMISS sense 1.

boot²
■ **to boot** *I am the father of four children, and a grandfather to boot:* as well, also, too, besides, into the bargain, in addition, additionally, on top, what's more, moreover, furthermore; informal and all.

booth noun *the market place was covered in booths for different traders:* **stall**, stand, kiosk.

bootleg adjective *he had a stall selling bootleg CDs:* **illegal**, illicit, unlawful, unauthorized, unlicensed, pirated; contraband, smuggled, black-market.

booty noun *among the vast quantities of booty are treasures plundered from Buddhist monasteries:* **loot**, plunder, pillage, haul, spoils, stolen goods, ill-gotten gains, pickings; informal swag.

bordello noun (N. Amer.) **brothel**, whorehouse; Law disorderly house; Brit. informal knocking shop; N. Amer. informal cathouse; euphemistic massage parlour; archaic bawdy house, house of ill repute.

border noun **1** *the designs decorating the border of a medieval manuscript:* **edge**, **margin**, perimeter, circumference, periphery; rim, fringe, verge; sides. **2** *the road runs from Kabul to the border:* **frontier**, boundary, borderline, perimeter; marches, bounds.
verb **1** *the fields were bordered by hedges and trees:* **surround**, enclose, encircle, circle, edge, fringe, bound, flank. **2** *years ago, the forest bordered on Broadmoor:* **adjoin**, abut, be next to, be adjacent to, be contiguous with, touch, join, meet, reach.
■ **border on** *he looked at her with something that bordered on contempt:* verge on, approach, come close to, be comparable to, approximate to, be tantamount to, be similar to, resemble.

borderline noun *the item in question is on the borderline between old and antique:* **dividing line**, divide, division, demarcation line, line, cut-off point; threshold, margin, border, boundary.
adjective *the moderators discussed student grades, especially borderline cases:* **marginal**, uncertain, indefinite, unsettled, undecided, doubtful, indeterminate, unclassifiable, equivocal; questionable, debatable, controversial, contentious, problematic; informal iffy.

bore¹ verb *bore a hole in the ceiling to pass the cable through:* **drill**, punch, cut; tunnel, burrow, mine, dig, gouge, sink.
noun *the anti-tank cannon has a bore of 88 millimetres:* **calibre**, diameter, gauge.

bore² verb *the television news bored Philip:* **stultify**, pall on, stupefy, weary, tire, fatigue, send to sleep, leave cold; informal turn off.
– OPPOSITES interest.
noun *you can be such a bore sometimes:* **tedious person/thing**, bother, nuisance, pest, annoyance, trial, vexation, thorn in one's flesh/side; informal drag, pain (in the neck), headache, hassle; N. Amer. informal nudnik.

boredom noun **weariness**, ennui, apathy, unconcern, accidie; frustration, dissatisfaction, restlessness, restiveness; tedium, dullness, monotony, repetitiveness, flatness, dreariness; informal deadliness.

boring adjective **tedious**, dull, monotonous, repetitive, unrelieved, unvaried, unimaginative, uneventful; characterless, featureless, colourless, lifeless, insipid, uninteresting, unexciting, uninspiring, unstimulating, jejune, flat, bland, dry, stale, tired, banal, lacklustre, stodgy, dreary, humdrum, mundane; mind-numbing, soul-destroying, wearisome, tiring, tiresome, irksome, trying, frustrating; informal deadly, not up to much; Brit. informal samey; N. Amer. informal dullsville.

borrow verb **1** *we borrowed a lot of money from the bank:* **loan**; lease, hire; informal cadge, scrounge, bum; Brit. informal scab; N. Amer. informal mooch; Austral./NZ informal bludge. **2** *adventurous chefs often borrow foreign techniques where appropriate:* **adopt**, take on, acquire, embrace, use.
– OPPOSITES lend.

bosom noun **1** *the gown was set low over her bosom:* **bust**, chest; breasts, mammary glands, mammae; informal boobs, knockers, bubbies; Brit. informal bristols, charlies, baps; N. Amer. informal bazooms. **2** (literary) *the family took Gillian into its bosom:* **protection**, shelter, safety, refuge; heart, core; literary midst. **3** *the flame of love was eventually kindled within his bosom:* **heart**, breast, soul, core, spirit.

boss (informal) noun *he is the boss of a large trading company:* **head**, chief, principal, director, president, chief executive, chair, manager(ess); supervisor, foreman, overseer, controller; employer, owner, proprietor, patron; Brit. gangmaster; informal number one, kingpin, top dog, bigwig; Brit. informal gaffer, governor; N. Amer. informal head honcho, padrone, sachem, big kahuna.
verb *you have no right to boss me about:* **order about/around**, dictate to, lord it over, bully, push around/about, domineer, dominate, browbeat; call the shots, lay down the law; informal bulldoze, walk all over, railroad.

bossy (informal) adjective **domineering**, pushy, overbearing, imperious, officious, high-handed, authoritarian, dictatorial, controlling; informal high and mighty.
– OPPOSITES submissive.

botch (informal) verb *examiners botched the marking of 1,000 A level papers:* **bungle**, mismanage, mishandle, make a mess of; informal mess up, make a hash of, muff, fluff,

foul up, screw up; Brit. informal bodge, cock up; N. Amer. informal flub.
noun *I've made a botch of things, haven't I?* **mess**, blunder, failure, wreck, fiasco, debacle; informal hash; Brit. informal bodge, cock-up, pig's ear.
– OPPOSITES success.

bother verb **1** *she had her own life, and no one bothered her:* **disturb**, trouble, inconvenience, pester, badger, harass, molest, plague, nag, hound, harry, annoy, upset, irritate; informal hassle, bug, get up someone's nose, get in someone's hair; N. English informal mither; N. Amer. informal ride. **2** *the incident with the waiter was too small to bother about:* **mind**, care, concern oneself, trouble oneself, worry oneself; informal give a damn, give a hoot. **3** *there was something in her voice that bothered him:* **worry**, trouble, concern, perturb, disturb, disquiet, disconcert, unnerve; fret, upset, distress, agitate, gnaw at, weigh down; informal rattle.
noun **1** *I don't want to put you to any bother:* **trouble**, effort, exertion, inconvenience, fuss, pains; informal hassle. **2** *the food was such a bother to cook:* **nuisance**, pest, palaver, rigmarole, job, trial, bind, bore, drag, inconvenience, trouble, problem; informal hassle, headache, pain (in the neck). **3** *he went to sort out a spot of bother in the public bar:* **disorder**, trouble, ado, disturbance, agitation, commotion, uproar; NZ bobsy-die; informal hoo-ha, aggro, argy-bargy, kerfuffle.

bothersome adjective *I have had a lot of bothersome letters from former students:* **annoying**, irritating, vexatious, maddening, exasperating; tedious, wearisome, tiresome; troublesome, trying, taxing, awkward; informal aggravating, pesky.

bottle noun **1** *Gareth opened a bottle of whisky:* carafe, flask, decanter, pitcher, flagon, carboy, demijohn. **2** (informal) *a world blurred by the bottle.* See **ALCOHOL**.
■ **bottle something up** *you've been bottling up your feelings for too long:* suppress, repress, restrain, withhold, hold in, rein in, inhibit, smother, stifle, contain, conceal, hide; informal keep a lid on.

bottleneck noun **traffic jam**, jam, congestion, hold-up, gridlock, tailback; constriction, narrowing, restriction, obstruction, blockage; informal snarl-up.

bottom noun **1** *she reached the bottom of the stairs, then stopped:* **foot**, lowest part, lowest point, base; foundation, substructure, underpinning. **2** *the police examined the bottom of the car:* **underside**, underneath, undersurface, undercarriage, underbelly. **3** *the boat sank to the bottom of Lake Ontario:* **floor**, bed, depths. **4** *there's a little log cabin at the bottom of his garden:* **farthest point**, far end, extremity. **5** *Mark was right at the bottom of his class:* **lowest level**, lowest position. **6** (Brit.) *I've got a butterfly tattoo on my bottom:* **rear (end)**, rump, backside, seat; buttocks, cheeks; informal behind, BTM,

sit-upon, derrière; Brit. informal bum, botty, jacksie; N. Amer. informal butt, fanny, tush, tail, buns, booty, heinie; humorous fundament, posterior, stern; Anatomy nates.
– OPPOSITES top, surface.
adjective *she sat on the bottom step holding a glass of champagne:* **lowest**, last, bottommost.
– OPPOSITES top.

bottomless adjective *you are doomed to burn in the bottomless pits of hell:* **fathomless**, unfathomable, endless, infinite, immeasurable.
– OPPOSITES limited.

bough noun **branch**, limb, arm, offshoot.

boulder noun **rock**, stone; Austral./NZ gibber.

boulevard noun **avenue**, street, road, drive, lane, parade, broadway, thoroughfare.

bounce verb **1** *the ball hit the ground and bounced:* **rebound**, spring back, ricochet, jounce; N. Amer. carom. **2** *William bounced down the stairs grinning:* **bound**, leap, jump, spring, bob, hop, skip, trip, prance.
noun **1** *the pitch's uneven bounce deceived many less experienced batsmen:* **springiness**, resilience, elasticity, give. **2** *she had lost a good deal of her bounce:* **vitality**, vigour, energy, vivacity, liveliness, animation, sparkle, verve, spirit, enthusiasm, dynamism; cheerfulness, happiness, buoyancy, optimism; informal get-up-and-go, pep, zing.
■ **bounce back** *skipper McAllister is confident that Leeds will bounce back:* recover, revive, rally, pick up, be on the mend; perk up, cheer up, brighten up, liven up; informal buck up.

bouncing adjective *a bouncing baby boy:* **vigorous**, thriving, flourishing, blooming; **healthy**, strong, robust, fit, in fine fettle; informal in the pink.

bouncy adjective **1** *they crossed a bouncy bridge of narrow wooden planks:* **springy**, flexible, resilient, elastic, stretchy, rubbery. **2** *the car gives a rather bouncy ride:* **bumpy**, jolting, jerky, jumpy, jarring, rough. **3** *she was always bouncy, and rarely lost for words:* **lively**, energetic, perky, frisky, jaunty, dynamic, vital, vigorous, vibrant, animated, spirited, buoyant, bubbly, sparkling, vivacious; enthusiastic, upbeat; informal peppy, zingy, chirpy.

bound¹ adjective **1** *he raised his bound ankles and kicked the door:* **tied**, chained, fettered, shackled, secured. **2** *she was so far ahead that she seemed bound to win:* **certain**, sure, destined. **3** *you're bound by the Official Secrets Act to keep this to yourselves:* **obligated**, obliged, compelled, required, constrained. **4** *religion and morality are bound up with one another:* **connected**, linked, tied, united, allied.

bound² verb *hares bound and skip in the warm sunshine:* **leap**, jump, spring, bounce, hop; skip, bob, dance, prance, gambol, gallop.

b

b

noun *he crossed the room with a single bound:*
leap, jump, spring, bounce, hop.

bound³ verb **1** *corporate freedom of action
is bounded by law:* **limit**, restrict, confine,
circumscribe, demarcate, delimit. **2** *the
heath is bounded by a hedge of conifers:*
enclose, surround, encircle, circle, border;
close in/off, hem in. **3** *the garden was
bounded to the east by Mill Lane:* **border**,
adjoin, abut; be next to, be adjacent to.

boundary noun **1** *the river marks the
boundary between Israel and Jordan:*
border, frontier, borderline, partition.
2 *the boundary between art and advertising:*
dividing line, divide, division, borderline,
cut-off point. **3** *guards patrolled the
boundary of his estate:* **bounds**, confines,
limits, margins, edges, fringes; border,
periphery, perimeter. **4** *the pupils probed
the boundaries of accepted behaviour:*
limits, parameters, bounds, confines; ambit,
compass.

boundless adjective *children have
boundless curiosity and enthusiasm:*
limitless, unlimited, unbounded, untold,
immeasurable, abundant; inexhaustible,
endless, infinite, interminable, unfailing,
ceaseless, everlasting.
– OPPOSITES limited.

bounds plural noun **1** *landlords are managing
to keep rents within reasonable bounds:*
limits, confines, proportions. **2** *they owned
land within the forest bounds:* **borders**,
boundaries, confines, limits, margins, edges;
periphery, perimeter.
■ **out of bounds** *we had planned to go from
Switzerland through to Italy, but it looks
like Austria is out of bounds:* off limits,
restricted; forbidden, banned, proscribed,
illegal, illicit, unlawful, unacceptable, taboo;
informal no go.

bountiful adjective **1** *he was exceedingly
bountiful to people in distress:* **generous**,
magnanimous, munificent, open-handed,
unselfish, unstinting, lavish; benevolent,
beneficent, charitable. **2** *the ocean provided
a bountiful supply of fresh food:* **abundant**,
plentiful, ample, copious, bumper,
superabundant, inexhaustible, prolific,
profuse; lavish, generous, handsome, rich;
literary plenteous.
– OPPOSITES mean, meagre.

bounty noun **1** *the cartel's leader paid a
bounty for each policeman killed:* **reward**,
prize, award, commission, premium,
dividend, bonus, gratuity, tip, donation,
handout; incentive, inducement; money;
informal perk, sweetener. **2** (literary) *I thank the
Lord for all his bounty to me:* **generosity**,
magnanimity, munificence, bountifulness,
largesse, lavishness; benevolence,
beneficence, charity, goodwill; blessings,
favours.

bouquet noun **1** *she wanted orchids for her
bridal bouquet:* **bunch of flowers**, posy,
nosegay, tussie-mussie, spray, corsage. **2** *the*

Chardonnay has a fine bouquet: **aroma**, nose,
smell, fragrance, perfume, scent, odour.

bourgeois adjective **1** *she came from a
bourgeois family:* **middle-class**, propertied;
conventional, conservative, conformist;
provincial, suburban, small-town. **2** *foreign
ideas were denounced as bourgeois
decadence:* **capitalistic**, materialistic,
money-oriented, commercial.
– OPPOSITES proletarian, communist.

bout noun **1** *a short bout of exercise can
ease insomnia:* **spell**, period, time, stretch,
stint, session; burst, flurry, spurt. **2** *her
breathlessness sparked off a coughing bout:*
attack, fit, spasm, paroxysm, convulsion,
eruption, outburst. **3** *he is fighting only
his fifth professional bout:* **contest**, match,
round, heat, competition, event, meeting,
fixture; fight.

bovine adjective **1** *she gazed at me with
her large, bovine eyes:* **cow-like**, calf-like,
taurine. **2** *his jaw dropped in an expression of
bovine amazement:* **stupid**, slow, ignorant,
unintelligent, imperceptive, half-baked,
vacuous, mindless, witless, doltish; informal
dumb, dense, dim, dim-witted, dopey,
birdbrained, pea-brained; Brit. informal dozy,
daft; Scottish & N. English informal glaikit.

bow¹ verb **1** *the officers bowed and removed
their caps:* **nod**, salaam, curtsy, bob;
genuflect, kowtow. **2** *the government
reluctantly bowed to foreign pressure:*
yield, submit, give in, surrender, succumb,
capitulate, defer, conform; comply with,
accept, heed, cave in, observe.
noun *a perfunctory bow:* **obeisance**, salaam,
bob, curtsy, nod.
■ **bow out** *Christie will bow out as the
undisputed No 1 sprinter in the world:*
withdraw, resign, retire, step down, pull
out, back out; give up, quit, leave; informal
pack in, chuck (in); Brit. informal jack in.

bow² noun *the bow of the tanker swept
by them:* **prow**, front, stem, nose, head,
cutwater; Brit. humorous sharp end.

bow³ noun **1** *thread the ribbon through
the hole and tie it in a bow:* **loop**, knot.
2 *swifter than an arrow from an archer's
bow:* longbow, crossbow; Archery recurve.

bowdlerize verb **expurgate**, censor, cut,
edit; sanitize, water down.

bowdlerized adjective *Plato was made
available only in bowdlerized and misleading
translations:* **expurgated**, censored, edited,
cut, sanitized, watered down.

bowel noun **1** *he had trouble with his
bowels:* **intestine(s)**, small intestine, large
intestine, colon; informal guts, insides. **2** *the
skipper emerged from the bowels of the ship:*
interior, inside, core, belly; depths, recesses;
informal innards.

bowl¹ verb **1** *he bowled a hundred or so balls:*
pitch, throw, propel, hurl, toss, lob, loft,
fling, launch, deliver; spin, roll; informal chuck,
sling, bung, heave. **2** *the car bowled along the*

country roads: **hurtle**, speed, shoot, sweep, career, hare, fly; informal belt, tear, scoot; Brit. informal bomb; N. Amer. informal clip.

■ **bowl someone over 1** *the explosion bowled us over:* knock down/over, fell, floor, prostrate. **2** *I have been bowled over by your generosity:* overwhelm, astound, astonish, overawe, dumbfound, stagger, stun, daze, shake, take aback, leave aghast; informal knock sideways, flabbergast, blow away; Brit. informal knock for six.

bowl² noun **1** *she cracked two eggs into a bowl:* **dish**, basin, pot, crock, crucible; container, vessel, receptacle. **2** *the town lay in a shallow bowl:* **valley**, hollow, dip, depression, trough, crater. **3** (N. Amer.) *the Hollywood Bowl:* **stadium**, arena, amphitheatre, colosseum; enclosure, ground; informal park.

box¹ noun **1** *he produced a box of cigars:* **carton**, pack, packet; case, crate, chest, coffer, casket; container, receptacle. **2** *she left her purse in a telephone box:* **booth**, cubicle, kiosk, cabin, hut; compartment, carrel, alcove, bay, recess.
verb *Muriel boxed up Christopher's clothes:* **package**, pack, parcel, wrap, bundle, bale, crate.

■ **box something/someone in** *he got boxed in by members of the press:* hem in, fence in, close in, shut in; trap, confine, imprison, intern; surround, enclose, encircle, circle.

box² verb **1** *he began boxing professionally before his 15th birthday:* **fight**, prizefight, spar; battle, brawl; informal scrap. **2** *he boxed my ears and stalked out:* **cuff**, smack, strike, hit, thump, slap, swat, punch, jab, wallop; Scottish & N. English skelp; informal belt, bop, biff, sock, clout, clobber, whack, plug, slug; Brit. informal slosh, dot; N. Amer. informal boff, bust.
noun *he sent him away with a box on the ear:* **cuff**, hit, thump, slap, smack, swat, punch, jab, hook; Scottish & N. English skelp; informal belt, bop, biff, sock, clout, whack, plug, slug.

boxer noun **fighter**, pugilist, ringster, prizefighter, kick-boxer; informal bruiser, scrapper.

boxing noun **pugilism**, the noble art, fighting, sparring, fisticuffs; kick-boxing, prizefighting; the ring.

boy noun **lad**, schoolboy, (male) child, youth, young man, stripling; Scottish & N. English laddie; derogatory brat. See also **CHILD**.

boycott verb *the main opposition parties boycotted the elections:* **spurn**, snub, shun, avoid, abstain from, wash one's hands of, turn one's back on, reject, veto.
– OPPOSITES support.
noun *they called for a boycott on the use of tropical timbers:* **ban**, veto, embargo, prohibition, sanction, restriction; avoidance, rejection, refusal.

boyfriend noun **lover**, sweetheart, beloved, darling, dearest, young man, man friend, man, escort, suitor; **partner**, significant other; informal fella, flame, fancy man, toy

boy, sugar daddy; N. Amer. informal squeeze; dated beau; archaic paramour.

boyish adjective *his gleaming smile, his chunky good looks, and his boyish charm:* **youthful**, young, childlike; immature, juvenile, infantile, childish, babyish, puerile.

brace noun **1** *the saw is best used with a brace:* **vice**, clamp, press. **2** *the aquarium is supported by wooden braces:* **prop**, beam, joist, batten, rod, post, strut, stay, support, stanchion, bracket. **3** *he has to wear a brace on his right leg:* **support**, caliper. **4** *he killed a brace of partridges:* **pair**, couple, duo, twosome; two.
verb **1** *the plane's wing is braced by a system of rods:* **support**, shore up, prop up, hold up, buttress, underpin; strengthen, reinforce. **2** *he braced his hand on the railing:* **steady**, secure, stabilize, fix, poise; tense, tighten. **3** *you'd better brace yourself for disappointment:* **prepare**, get ready, gear up, nerve, steel, galvanize, gird, strengthen, fortify; informal psych oneself up.

bracelet noun **bangle**, band, circlet, armlet, wristlet; manilla, rakhi, kara.

bracing adjective *we spent a bracing day in the Welsh countryside:* **invigorating**, refreshing, stimulating, energizing, exhilarating, reviving, restorative, rejuvenating, revitalizing, rousing, fortifying, strengthening; **fresh**, brisk, keen.

bracket noun **1** *each speaker is fixed on a separate bracket:* **support**, prop, stay, batten, joist; rest, mounting, rack, frame. **2** *put these words in brackets:* **parenthesis**; Printing brace. **3** *I'm now in a higher tax bracket:* **group**, category, grade, band, stratum, set, division, order.
verb *women were bracketed with children for the purposes of wage assessment:* **group**, **classify**, class, categorize, grade, list, sort, place, assign; couple, pair, twin; liken, compare, stratify.

brag verb *she listened to him brag about his business connections:* **boast**, crow, swagger, swank, bluster, gloat, show off; blow one's own trumpet, sing one's own praises; informal talk big, lay it on thick; Austral./NZ informal skite.

braggart noun *he was a braggart and a liar:* **boaster**, bragger, swaggerer, poser, poseur, egotist; informal big-head, loudmouth, show-off, swank; N. Amer. informal showboat, blowhard; Austral./NZ informal skite.

braid noun **1** *the shoulder straps were bordered with gold braid:* **cord**, bullion, thread, tape, binding, rickrack, ribbon; Military slang scrambled egg. **2** *his long hair was worn in braids and tied at the back of his neck:* **plait**, pigtail, twist; cornrows, dreadlocks.
verb **1** *she began to braid her long hair:* **plait**, entwine, intertwine, interweave, weave, twist, twine. **2** *the sleeves are braided in scarlet and lined with ermine:* **trim**, edge, border, pipe, hem, fringe.

brain noun **1** *the disease attacks certain cells*

b

in the brain: **cerebrum**, cerebral matter, encephalon. **2** *success requires brains as well as brawn:* **intelligence**, intellect, brainpower, cleverness, wit(s), reasoning, wisdom, acumen, discernment, judgement, understanding, sense; informal nous, grey matter, savvy; N. Amer. informal smarts.

brainless adjective *they behave as if they are totally brainless:* **stupid**, **foolish**, witless, unintelligent, ignorant, idiotic, simple-minded, empty-headed, half-baked; informal dumb, half-witted, brain-dead, moronic, cretinous, thick, dopey, dozy, birdbrained, pea-brained, dippy, wooden-headed; Brit. informal divvy; Scottish & N. English informal glaikit; N. Amer. informal dumb-ass, chowderheaded.
– OPPOSITES clever.

brainwash verb *women have been brainwashed into thinking they should go out to work:* **indoctrinate**, condition, persuade, influence, programme.

brainy adjective (informal) *he's incredibly brainy and speaks seven languages:* **clever**, intelligent, bright, brilliant, gifted; intellectual, erudite, academic, scholarly, studious, bookish; informal smart; Brit. informal swotty.
– OPPOSITES stupid.

brake verb *she braked at the traffic lights:* **slow (down)**, decelerate, reduce speed.
– OPPOSITES accelerate.

branch noun **1** *the branches of the tree creaked in the wind:* **bough**, limb, arm, offshoot. **2** *a branch of the river flows through Jonestown:* **tributary**, feeder, side stream. **3** *the judicial branch of government is completely independent:* **division**, subdivision, section, subsection, department, sector, part, side, wing. **4** *the corporation's New York branch was doing rather well:* **office**, bureau, agency; subsidiary, offshoot, satellite.
verb **1** *turn right where the road branches:* **fork**, bifurcate, divide, subdivide, split. **2** *several narrow paths branched off the road:* **diverge from**, deviate from, split off from; fan out from, radiate from.
■ **branch out** *the company is branching out into Europe:* expand, open up, extend; diversify, broaden one's horizons.

brand noun **1** *a new brand of low-fat spread:* **make**, line, label, marque; type, kind, sort, variety; trade name, trademark, proprietary name. **2** *I don't care for her particular brand of humour:* **type**, kind, sort, variety, class, category, genre, style, ilk; N. Amer. stripe.
verb **1** *the letter M was branded on each animal:* **mark**, stamp, burn, sear. **2** *the media branded us as communists:* **stigmatize**, mark out; denounce, discredit, vilify; label.

brandish verb *an old man approached me, brandishing a stick:* **wave**, flourish, shake, wield; swing, swish; display, flaunt.

brash adjective **1** *he was a brash, noisy little man:* **self-assertive**, pushy, cocksure, cocky,

self-confident, arrogant, bold, audacious, brazen; forward, impudent, insolent, rude. **2** *Magalluf is a resort full of bustle and a brash sort of charm:* **garish**, gaudy, loud, flamboyant, showy, tasteless; informal flashy, tacky.
– OPPOSITES meek, muted.

brat noun (derogatory) *Sarah had everything a child could possibly want, and was a spoilt, ungrateful brat:* **rascal**, wretch, imp; minx, chit; informal monster, horror, whippersnapper.

bravado noun *despite all his bravado, he was actually very sensitive:* **boldness**, swagger, bluster; machismo; boasting, bragging, bombast, braggadocio.

brave adjective *all those brave Hungarians who tried to fight the Russians:* **courageous**, plucky, valiant, valorous, intrepid, heroic, lionhearted, bold, fearless, daring, audacious; unflinching, unshrinking, unafraid, dauntless, doughty, mettlesome, stout-hearted, spirited; informal game, gutsy, spunky.
– OPPOSITES cowardly.
verb *around 400 fans braved freezing temperatures to see them play:* **endure**, put up with, bear, withstand, weather, suffer, go through; face, confront, defy.

bravery noun **courage**, pluck, valour, intrepidity, nerve, daring, fearlessness, audacity, boldness, dauntlessness, stout-heartedness, heroism; backbone, grit, spine, spirit, mettle; informal guts, spunk; Brit. informal bottle; N. Amer. informal moxie.

bravo exclamation *Bravo Toshiba for finally introducing a sensible electronic notebook:* **well done**, congratulations; encore.

bravura noun *Zelensky danced with technical bravura, but put the choreography and music first:* **skill**, brilliance, virtuosity, expertise, artistry, talent, ability, flair.
adjective *as in the earlier books, the bravura set pieces dominate everything else:* **virtuoso**, masterly, outstanding, excellent, superb, brilliant, first-class; informal mean, ace, A1.

brawl noun *three footballers have been accused of assault after a brawl in a nightclub:* **fight**, skirmish, scuffle, tussle, fray, melee, free-for-all, scrum; fisticuffs; informal scrap, dust-up, set-to; Brit. informal punch-up, ruck; Scottish informal rammy; N. Amer. informal rough house, brannigan; Law, dated affray.
verb *he ended up brawling with photographers at the airport:* **fight**, skirmish, scuffle, tussle, exchange blows, grapple, wrestle; informal scrap; N. Amer. informal rough-house.

brawn noun *the Hazard Team is sent on missions typically requiring more brawn than brain:* **(physical) strength**, muscle(s); burliness, toughness, power, might; informal beef, beefiness.

brawny adjective **strong**, muscular, muscly,

well built, powerful, mighty, Herculean, strapping, burly, sturdy, husky, rugged; bulky, hefty, meaty, solid; informal beefy, hunky, hulking.
– OPPOSITES puny, weak.

bray verb **1** *a donkey brayed loudly in the street:* **neigh**, whinny, hee-haw. **2** *Billy brayed with laughter at the thought of this:* **roar**, bellow, trumpet.

brazen adjective *this year the pickpockets seemed more brazen than ever:* **bold**, **shameless**, unashamed, unabashed, unembarrassed; defiant, impudent, impertinent, cheeky; barefaced, blatant, flagrant.
– OPPOSITES timid.
■ **brazen it out** *we wanted a product recall, but the marketing people tried to brazen it out:* put on a bold front, stand one's ground, be defiant, be unrepentant, be unabashed.

breach noun **1** *this is a clear breach of the regulations:* **contravention**, violation, infringement, infraction, transgression, neglect. **2** *there is a widening breach between government and Church:* **rift**, schism, division, gulf, chasm; disunion, estrangement, discord, dissension, disagreement; split, break, rupture, scission; Brit. informal bust-up. **3** *there were a number of breaches in the sea wall:* **break**, rupture, split, crack, fracture; opening, gap, hole, fissure.
verb **1** *on Tuesday the river breached its banks:* **break (through)**, burst, rupture; informal bust. **2** *the changes clearly breached union rules:* **break**, contravene, violate, infringe; defy, disobey, flout, fly in the face of.

breadth noun **1** *the human heart is about three and a half inches in breadth:* **width**, broadness, wideness, thickness; span; diameter. **2** *nowhere else can you get the same breadth of experience in a single place:* **range**, extent, scope, depth, reach, compass, scale, degree.

break verb **1** *the mirror fell to the floor and broke:* **shatter**, smash, crack, snap, fracture, fragment, splinter, fall to bits, fall to pieces; split, burst; informal bust. **2** *she had broken her leg in two places:* **fracture**, crack. **3** *the bite had barely broken the skin:* **pierce**, puncture, penetrate, perforate; cut. **4** *the coffee machine has broken again:* **stop working**, break down, give out, go wrong, malfunction, crash; informal go kaput, conk out, be on the blink, give up the ghost; Brit. informal pack up. **5** *traders who break the law will be prosecuted:* **contravene**, violate, infringe, breach; defy, flout, disobey, fly in the face of. **6** *his concentration was broken by a sound in the hall:* **interrupt**, disturb, interfere with. **7** *at mid-morning they broke for coffee:* **stop**, pause, have a rest; N. Amer. recess; informal knock off, take five. **8** *fortunately, a pile of carpets broke his fall:* **cushion**, soften, take the

edge off. **9** *the second film broke all box-office records:* **exceed**, surpass, beat, better, cap, top, outdo, outstrip, eclipse; informal leave standing. **10** *these habits are very difficult to break:* **give up**, relinquish, drop; informal kick, shake, pack in, quit. **11** *the strategies used to break the union:* **destroy**, crush, quash, defeat, vanquish, overcome, overpower, overwhelm, suppress, cripple, smash; weaken, subdue, cow, undermine, wear/grind down; bankrupt, bring to its knees. **12** *her self-control finally broke:* **give way**, crack, cave in, yield, go to pieces. **13** *he tried to break the news gently:* **reveal**, disclose, divulge, impart, tell; announce, release. **14** *Krycek managed to break the encryption code:* **decipher**, decode, decrypt, unravel, work out; informal crack, figure out. **15** *the day broke fair and cloudless:* **dawn**, begin, start, emerge, appear. **16** *another political scandal broke in mid 1991:* **erupt**, break out. **17** *overnight the weather broke:* **change**, alter, shift. **18** *huge waves broke against the rocks:* **crash**, dash, beat, pound, lash. **19** *her voice broke as she relived the experience:* **falter**, quaver, quiver, tremble, shake.
– OPPOSITES repair, keep, resume.
noun **1** *the magazine has been published without a break since 1950:* **interruption**, interval, gap, hiatus; discontinuation, suspension, disruption, cut-off; stop, stoppage, cessation. **2** *we're hoping for a break in the weather:* **change**, alteration, variation. **3** *let's have a break and get something to eat:* **rest**, respite, recess; stop, pause; interval, intermission; informal breather, time out, down time. **4** *a weekend break for two in Amsterdam:* **holiday**; N. Amer. vacation; Brit. informal vac. **5** (informal) *the actress got her first break in 1951:* **opportunity**, chance, opening.
■ **break away 1** *she attempted to break away from his grip:* escape, get away, run away, flee, make off; break free, break loose, get out of someone's clutches; informal leg it, cut and run. **2** *a group broke away from the main party:* leave, secede from, split off from, separate from, part company with, defect from; form a splinter group.
■ **break down 1** *his van broke down on the M6.* See BREAK verb sense 4. **2** *pay negotiations with the management broke down:* fail, collapse, founder, fall through, disintegrate; informal fizzle out. **3** *Vicky broke down, sobbing loudly:* burst into tears; lose control, be overcome, go to pieces, crumble, disintegrate; informal crack up, lose it.
■ **break something down 1** *the police broke the door down:* knock down, kick down, smash in, pull down, tear down, demolish. **2** *break big tasks down into smaller parts:* divide, separate. **3** *graphs show how the information can be broken down:* analyse, categorize, classify, sort out, itemize, organize; dissect.
■ **break in 1** *thieves broke in and took*

b

her cheque book: break and enter; force one's way in, burst in, get in. **2** *'I don't want to interfere,' Mrs Hendry broke in:* interrupt, butt in, cut in, interject, interpose, intervene, chime in; Brit. informal chip in.
■ **break into 1** *thieves broke into a house in Perth Street:* burgle, rob; force one's way into, burst into, get into. **2** *he broke into a German drinking song:* burst into, launch into.
■ **break off** *the fuselage had broken off just behind the cockpit:* snap off, come off, detach, separate.
■ **break something off 1** *I broke off a branch from the tree:* snap off, pull off, sever, detach. **2** *they threatened to break off diplomatic relations:* end, terminate, stop, cease, call a halt to, finish, dissolve; suspend, discontinue; informal pull the plug on.
■ **break out 1** *two suspected terrorists broke out of the detention centre:* escape from, abscond from, flee from; get free. **2** *fighting broke out between rival army units:* flare up, start suddenly, erupt, burst out.
■ **break up 1** *after about an hour, the meeting broke up:* end, finish, stop, terminate; adjourn; N. Amer. recess. **2** *gradually the crowd began to break up:* disperse, scatter, disband; disintegrate. **3** *Danny and I broke up last year:* split up, separate, part (company), go one's separate ways; divorce.
■ **break something up 1** *police tried to break up the demonstration:* disperse, scatter, disband. **2** *I'm not going to let you break up my marriage:* wreck, ruin, destroy.

breakable adjective *you can always use clothes as packing material in between breakable items:* **fragile**, delicate, flimsy, insubstantial; formal frangible.

breakaway adjective *a breakaway nationalist group had claimed responsibility:* **separatist**, secessionist, schismatic, splinter; rebel, renegade.

breakdown noun **1** *the breakdown of the negotiations was inevitable:* **failure**, collapse, disintegration, foundering. **2** *on the death of her father she suffered a breakdown:* **nervous breakdown**; informal crack-up. **3** *we need a breakdown of the figures:* **analysis**, classification, examination, investigation, dissection.

breaker noun **wave**, roller, comber, white horse; informal boomer; N. Amer. informal kahuna.

break-in noun **burglary**, robbery, theft, raid; informal smash-and-grab.

breakneck adjective *the breakneck pace of technological change:* **extremely fast**, rapid, speedy, high-speed, lightning, whirlwind.
■ **at breakneck speed** *a 2-3 hour film that moves along at breakneck speed:* extremely fast, at full tilt, flat out; informal hell for leather, like the wind, like a bat out of hell, like greased lightning; Brit. informal like the clappers.

breakthrough noun *a major breakthrough in the fight against Aids:* **advance**, development, step forward, success, improvement; discovery, innovation, revolution.
– OPPOSITES setback.

break-up noun **1** *the break-up of the peace negotiations:* **end**, dissolution; breakdown, failure, collapse, disintegration. **2** *their break-up was very amicable:* **separation**, split, parting, divorce; estrangement, rift; Brit. informal bust-up. **3** *the break-up of the former Soviet Union:* **division**, partition.

breakwater noun **sea wall**, jetty, mole, groyne, pier.

breast noun **1** *the gentle curve of her breasts:* mammary gland, mamma; (**breasts**) **bosom(s)**, bust, chest; informal boobs, knockers, bubbies; Brit. informal bristols, charlies, baps; N. Amer. informal bazooms. **2** *feelings of frustration were rising up in his breast:* **heart**, bosom, soul, core.

breath noun **1** *I took a deep breath:* **inhalation**, gulp (of air); exhalation, expiration; Medicine respiration. **2** *I had barely enough breath left to reply:* **wind**; informal puff. **3** *the night was still, with barely a breath of wind:* **puff**, waft, faint breeze.
■ **take someone's breath away** *Hoad's ruthless efficiency would take my breath away:* astonish, astound, amaze, stun, startle, stagger, shock, take aback, dumbfound, jolt, shake up; awe, overawe, thrill; informal knock sideways, flabbergast, blow away, bowl over; Brit. informal knock for six.

breathe verb **1** *she breathed deeply before replying:* inhale and exhale, respire, draw breath; puff, pant, blow, gasp, wheeze. **2** *'Together at last,' she breathed:* **whisper**, murmur, purr, sigh, say.

breathless adjective **1** *Will ran back, arriving flushed and breathless:* **out of breath**, panting, puffing, gasping, wheezing; winded, puffed out, short of breath; informal out of puff. **2** *the crowd waited, breathless with anticipation:* **agog**, open-mouthed, on the edge of one's seat, on tenterhooks, in suspense; excited, impatient.

breathtaking adjective *visually, the movie is nothing short of breathtaking:* **spectacular**, magnificent, wonderful, awe-inspiring, awesome, astounding, astonishing, amazing, stunning, incredible; thrilling, exciting; informal sensational, out of this world; literary wondrous.

breed verb **1** *Asian elephants breed readily in captivity:* **reproduce**, procreate, multiply; mate. **2** *she was born and bred in the village:* **bring up**, rear, raise, nurture. **3** *the political system bred massive discontent:* **cause**, bring about, give rise to, lead to, produce, generate, foster, result in; stir up; literary beget.
noun **1** *a breed of cow that is now*

disappearing: **variety**, stock, strain; type, kind, sort. **2** *he is one of a new breed of journalists:* **type**, kind, sort, variety, class, genre, generation; N. Amer. stripe.

breeding noun **1** *individual birds pair late in the season for breeding:* **reproduction**, procreation; mating. **2** *the breeding of rats for scientific experiments:* **rearing**, raising, nurturing, production. **3** *her aristocratic breeding was never far from the surface:* **upbringing**, rearing; parentage, family, pedigree, blood, birth. **4** *people of rank and breeding should know better than this:* **(good) manners**, gentility, refinement, cultivation, polish, urbanity; informal class.

breeding ground noun *the school is a breeding ground for progressive ideas:* **nursery**, cradle, nest, den; hotbed.

breeze noun *a slight breeze ruffled the leaves:* **wind**, puff (of air), gust; literary zephyr.
verb (informal) *Roger breezed into her office:* **saunter**, stroll, sail, cruise, sweep.

breezy adjective **1** *it's 9 p.m. on a breezy February night:* **windy**, fresh, brisk, airy; blowy, blustery, gusty. **2** *this is a breezy comedy that gets a lot of mileage out of its top-flight cast:* **jaunty**, **cheerful**, cheery, brisk, carefree, easy, casual, relaxed, informal, light-hearted, lively, buoyant, sunny; Brit. Tiggerish; informal upbeat.

brevity noun **1** *the report is notable for its clarity and brevity:* **conciseness**, concision, succinctness, economy of language, pithiness, incisiveness, shortness, compactness. **2** *the brevity of human life is all too apparent here:* **shortness**, briefness, transience, ephemerality, impermanence.
– OPPOSITES verbosity.

brew verb **1** *this beer is brewed in Frankfurt:* **ferment**, make. **2** *I'll go and brew some tea:* **prepare**, infuse, make, stew; Brit. informal mash. **3** *there's trouble brewing, I can feel it:* **develop**, loom, impend, be imminent, be on the horizon, be in the offing, be just around the corner.
noun **1** *she took a sip of the hot, reviving brew:* **drink**, beverage; tea, coffee. **2** *a dangerous brew of political turmoil and violent conflict:* **mixture**, mix, blend, combination, amalgam.

bribe verb *he used his considerable wealth to bribe officials:* **buy off**, pay off, suborn; informal grease someone's palm, keep someone sweet, fix, square; Brit. informal nobble.
noun *he accepted bribes from lobbyists:* **inducement**, incentive, douceur; informal backhander, pay-off, kickback, sweetener; Brit. informal bung; N. Amer. informal schmear.

bribery noun *the company faces charges of bribery over a dam project in Lesotho:* **subornation**, corruption; N. Amer. payola; informal palm-greasing, graft, hush money.

bric-a-brac noun *the Victorians crammed their homes with furniture, bric-a-brac, and pianos:* **ornaments**, knick-knacks, trinkets; bits and pieces, bits and bobs, odds and ends, things, stuff; informal junk, paraphernalia.

brick noun *a brick of ice cream:* **block**, cube, bar, cake.

bridal adjective *the bridal party was actually on time:* **wedding**, nuptial, marriage, matrimonial, marital, conjugal.

bride noun **wife**, marriage partner, newly-wed, fiancée.

bridge noun *the Romans built a bridge over the river:* **viaduct**, flyover, overpass, aqueduct.
verb *an attempt to bridge the gap between the two cultures:* **join**, link, connect, unite; straddle; overcome, reconcile.

bridle verb **1** *President Mkapa bridled at the idea of any interference in Zimbabwe's affairs:* **bristle**, take offence, take umbrage, be affronted, be offended, get angry. **2** *Maura's disappointment could not be bridled:* **curb**, restrain, hold back, control, check, rein in/back; suppress, stifle; informal keep a/the lid on.

brief adjective **1** *he gave a brief account of what had happened:* **concise**, succinct, short, pithy, incisive, abridged, condensed, compressed, abbreviated, compact, thumbnail, potted; formal compendious. **2** *a flight to Kuala Lumpur, with a brief stop in Dubai:* **short**, flying, fleeting, hasty, hurried, quick, cursory, perfunctory; temporary, short-lived, momentary, transient; informal quickie. **3** *a pair of extremely brief black shorts:* **skimpy**, scanty, short; revealing.
– OPPOSITES lengthy.
noun **1** *in his brief, the federal prosecutor accused the six men of being terrorists:* **summary**, case, argument, contention; dossier. **2** *the brief given to Ford's designers was to take a Fiesta and make it chic:* **outline**, summary, synopsis, precis, sketch, digest; plan, job description.
verb *council employees were briefed about the decision:* **inform**, tell, update, notify, advise, apprise; prepare, prime, instruct; informal fill in, clue in, put in the picture.

briefing noun **1** *the daily press briefings at the White House:* **conference**, meeting, interview, session; N. Amer. backgrounder. **2** *sign up here to get the briefing emailed to you by 9 a.m.* **information**, rundown, guidance; instructions, directions, guidelines, summary.

briefly adverb **1** *Henry paused briefly to catch his breath:* **momentarily**, temporarily, for a moment, fleetingly. **2** *briefly, the plot is as follows:* **in short**, in brief, to cut a long story short, in a word, in sum, in a nutshell, in essence.

briefs plural noun **underpants**, pants, knickers, Y-fronts, G-string; N. Amer. shorts, undershorts; informal panties, undies, frillies; Brit. informal kecks, smalls.

brigade noun **1** *there were two regiments per brigade, each with a strength of around 4,000:* **unit**, battalion, regiment, division,

b

squadron, company, platoon, section, corps, troop. **2** *the volunteer ambulance brigade:* **squad**, team, group, band, party, crew, force, outfit. **3** (informal) *the 'it's all in the mind' brigade have ridiculed sufferers of chronic fatigue syndrome for years:* **group**, contingent; school; informal crowd, lot, gang, squad, bunch, crew; Brit. informal mob.

bright adjective **1** *she stood blinking in the bright sunlight* | *the bright surface of the metal:* **shining**, brilliant, dazzling, beaming, glaring; sparkling, flashing, glittering, scintillating, gleaming, glowing, luminous, radiant; shiny, lustrous, glossy. **2** *it was a cold, bright morning:* **sunny**, sunshiny, cloudless, clear, fair, fine. **3** *he loved bright colours:* **vivid**, brilliant, intense, strong, bold, glowing, rich; gaudy, lurid, garish. **4** *a bright guitar sound:* **clear**, vibrant, ringing; sharp. **5** *he is a bright young man who should go far:* **clever**, intelligent, quick-witted, smart, canny, astute, intuitive, perceptive; ingenious, resourceful; gifted, brilliant; informal brainy. **6** *he felt remarkably bright and cheerful:* **happy**, cheerful, cheery, jolly, merry, sunny, beaming; lively, exuberant, buoyant, bubbly, bouncy, perky, chirpy; Brit. Tiggerish. **7** *she had a bright future ahead of her:* **promising**, rosy, optimistic, hopeful, favourable, propitious, auspicious, encouraging, good, golden.
– OPPOSITES dull, dark, stupid.

brighten verb **1** *the morning sunshine brightened the room:* **illuminate**, light up, lighten, make bright, make brighter, cast/shed light on. **2** *with the right shrubs you can brighten up the shadiest of corners:* **enhance**, embellish, enrich, dress up, prettify, beautify; informal jazz up. **3** *Sarah brightened up as she thought of Emily's words:* **cheer up**, perk up, rally; be enlivened, feel heartened, be uplifted, be encouraged, take heart; informal buck up, pep up.

brilliance noun **1** *he was a philosopher of great brilliance:* **genius**, talent, ability, prowess, skill, expertise, aptitude, flair, finesse, panache; greatness, distinction; intelligence, wisdom, sagacity, intellect. **2** *I was blinded by the brilliance of the sunshine:* **brightness**, vividness, intensity; sparkle, glitter, glittering, glow, blaze, beam, luminosity, radiance.

brilliant adjective **1** *Marshall was a brilliant student:* **gifted**, talented, able, adept, skilful; bright, intelligent, clever, smart, astute, intellectual; elite, superior, first-class, first-rate, excellent; informal brainy. **2** *an artist whose brilliant reputation had gone before him:* **superb**, glorious, illustrious, impressive, remarkable, exceptional; glittering, stellar. **3** *there are brilliant halogen lamps in the conference room to keep the delegates awake:* **bright**, shining, blazing, dazzling, vivid, intense, gleaming, glaring, luminous, radiant. **4** *brilliant pink bougainvillea covered the old stone walls*

of the cottage: **vivid**, intense, bright, bold, dazzling.
– OPPOSITES stupid, bad, dark.

brim noun **1** *the rector fingered the brim of his hat:* peak, visor, shield, shade. **2** *the cup was filled to its brim with cocoa:* **rim**, lip, brink, edge, top.
verb **1** *the pan was brimming with water:* **be full (up)**, be filled to the top; overflow, run over. **2** *her eyes were brimming with tears:* **fill**, fill up; overflow.

brimful adjective *it was a beautiful smile, brimful of wisdom, understanding, and compassion:* **full**, brimming, filled, replete, bursting, radiating, oozing; informal chock-full.
– OPPOSITES empty.

brindle, brindled adjective *some said that the Galloway breed had originally been brindle with a white stripe:* **tawny**, brownish, brown; **dappled**, streaked, mottled, speckled, flecked.

bring verb **1** *he brought over a tray with coffee on it:* **carry**, fetch, bear, take; convey, transport; move, haul, shift. **2** *Philip brought his young bride to his mansion:* **escort**, conduct, guide, lead, usher, show, shepherd. **3** *that evening, the wind changed and brought rain:* **cause**, produce, create, generate, precipitate, lead to, give rise to, result in; stir up, whip up, promote. **4** *the police contemplated bringing charges of assault:* **put forward**, prefer, lay, submit, present, initiate, institute. **5** *this job brings him a regular salary and few worries:* **earn**, make, fetch, bring in, yield, net, gross, return, produce; command, attract.

■ **bring something about 1** *the war brought about a large increase in government debt:* cause, produce, give rise to, result in, lead to, occasion, bring to pass; provoke, generate, engender, precipitate. **2** *he brought the ship about:* turn (round/around), reverse, swing round.

■ **bring something back 1** *the smell brought back memories of her misspent youth:* remind one of, put one in mind of, bring/call to mind, conjure up, evoke, summon up; take one back. **2** *the conference voted to bring back capital punishment:* reintroduce, reinstate, re-establish, revive, resurrect.

■ **bring someone down 1** *he was brought down by a clumsy challenge:* trip, knock over/down; foul. **2** *she was in such a good mood that I couldn't bear to bring her down:* depress, sadden, upset, get down, dispirit, dishearten, discourage.

■ **bring something down 1** *we will bring down the price of CDs:* decrease, reduce, lower, cut, drop; informal slash. **2** *the unrest eventually brought down the government:* unseat, overturn, topple, overthrow, depose, oust.

■ **bring something forward** *we intend to bring forward proposals for new Sunday* *trading legislation:* propose, suggest, advance, raise, table, present, move, submit, lodge.

■ **bring someone in** *it was nice of him to bring me in on the deal so early:* involve, include, count in.

■ **bring something in 1** *he brought in a private member's bill:* introduce, launch, inaugurate, initiate, institute, put in place. **2** *the event brings in one million pounds each year.* See **BRING** sense 5.

■ **bring something off** *they knew he could bring off brilliant business coups:* achieve, accomplish, attain, bring about, pull off, manage, realize, complete, finish; execute, perform, discharge.

■ **bring something on**. See **BRING SOMETHING ABOUT** sense 1.

■ **bring something out 1** *they were bringing out a new teenage magazine for girls:* launch, establish, begin, start, found, set up, instigate, inaugurate, market; publish, print, issue, produce. **2** *the shawl brings out the colour of your eyes:* accentuate, highlight, emphasize, accent, set off.

■ **bring someone round 1** *she administered artificial respiration and brought him round:* wake up, return to consciousness, rouse, bring to. **2** *we would have brought him round when he got to know the situation a bit better:* persuade, convince, talk round, win over, sway, influence.

■ **bring oneself to** *she could not bring herself to pull the trigger:* force oneself to, make oneself, bear to.

■ **bring someone up** *she was brought up by her grandmother:* rear, raise, care for, look after, nurture, provide for.

■ **bring something up** *later that evening he casually brought up the subject of money:* mention, allude to, touch on, raise, broach, introduce, voice, air, suggest, propose, submit, put forward, bring forward, table.

brink noun *the two countries were on the brink of war:* **verge**, threshold, point, edge.

brio noun *Biddulph gave us Weber's A flat Sonata, played with brio and wit:* **vigour**, vivacity, gusto, verve, zest, enthusiasm, vitality, dynamism, animation, spirit, energy; informal pep, vim, get-up-and-go.

brisk adjective **1** *he set off at a brisk pace:* **quick**, rapid, fast, swift, speedy, hurried; energetic, lively, vigorous; informal nippy. **2** *the bar was already doing a brisk trade:* **busy**, bustling, lively, hectic; good. **3** *his tone suddenly became brisk and businesslike:* **nononsense**, decisive, businesslike, brusque, abrupt, short, sharp, curt, blunt, terse, gruff; informal snappy. **4** *there was a brisk breeze blowing in from the sea:* **bracing**, fresh, crisp, invigorating, refreshing, stimulating, energizing; biting, keen, chilly, cold; informal nippy.
– OPPOSITES slow, quiet.

bristle noun *Curtis smoothed the bristles on*

his chin: **hair**, whisker; (**bristles**) stubble, five o'clock shadow.
verb **1** *Corbett sensed the danger, and the hair on the back of his neck bristled:* **rise**, stand up, stand on end. **2** *she swivelled round, bristling at his tone:* **bridle**, take offence, take umbrage, be affronted, be offended; get angry, be irritated. **3** *the roof of the outhouse bristled with antennae:* **abound**, overflow, be full, be packed, be crowded, be jammed, be covered; informal be thick, be jam-packed, be chock-full.

bristly adjective **1** *the dunes were dotted with bristly little bushes:* **prickly**, spiky, thorny, scratchy, brambly. **2** *she rubbed the bristly skin of his cheek with the back of her hand:* **stubbly**, hairy, fuzzy, unshaven, whiskered, whiskery; scratchy, rough, coarse, prickly.
– OPPOSITES smooth.

Britain noun **the United Kingdom**, the UK, Great Britain, the British Isles; Brit. informal Blighty; literary Albion.

brittle adjective **1** *glass is a very brittle material:* **breakable**, fragile, delicate; splintery; formal frangible. **2** *she began to speak in a brittle, staccato voice:* **harsh**, hard, sharp, grating. **3** *a brittle, asexual young woman in a cream linen suit:* **edgy**, nervy, anxious, unstable, highly strung, tense, excitable, jumpy, skittish, neurotic; informal uptight.
– OPPOSITES flexible, resilient, soft, relaxed.

broach verb *I made up my mind to broach the issue over lunch:* **bring up**, raise, introduce, talk about, mention, touch on, air.

broad adjective **1** *they descended a broad flight of steps:* **wide**. **2** *the leaves are six inches long and two inches broad:* **wide**, across, in breadth, in width, from side to side. **3** *the area consisted of broad open meadows, which frequently flooded:* **extensive**, vast, immense, great, spacious, expansive, sizeable, sweeping, rolling. **4** *we offer a broad range of opportunities for young entrepreneurs:* **comprehensive**, inclusive, extensive, wide, all-embracing, eclectic, unlimited. **5** *this report gives a broad outline of our environmental performance:* **general**, non-specific, unspecific, rough, approximate, basic; loose, vague. **6** *he dropped a broad hint about the likely outcome of the negotiations:* **obvious**, unsubtle, explicit, direct, plain, clear, straightforward, bald, patent, transparent, undisguised, overt. **7** *he spoke in a broad Somerset accent:* **pronounced**, noticeable, strong, thick.
– OPPOSITES narrow, limited, detailed, subtle.

broadcast verb **1** *the show will be broadcast worldwide:* **transmit**, relay, air, beam, show, televise, telecast, screen. **2** *it suits the police for their community role to be broadcast in this way:* **report**, announce, publicize, proclaim; spread, circulate, air, blazon, trumpet.

b

b

noun *at the time of the broadcast Iraqi forces were not in control of Kuwait City:* **programme**, show, production, transmission, telecast, screening; informal prog.

broaden verb **1** *porches have been added in order to broaden the building at its centre | he let his expression broaden into a smile:* **widen**, expand, stretch (out), draw out, spread; deepen. **2** *Mr Gould is to assess how Labour can broaden its appeal at the next election:* **expand**, enlarge, extend, widen, swell; increase, augment, add to, amplify; develop, enrich, improve, build on.

broadly adverb **1** *the pattern of illness is broadly similar for men and women:* **in general**, on the whole, as a rule, in the main, mainly, predominantly; loosely, roughly, approximately. **2** *he smiled broadly, shaking his head:* **widely**, openly.

broad-minded adjective *in Europe, music fans are usually more broad-minded:* **liberal**, tolerant, open-minded, freethinking, indulgent, progressive, permissive, unshockable; unprejudiced, unbiased, unbigoted.
– OPPOSITES intolerant.

broadside noun *the BBC reported on the latest broadside from the Ayatollah in Paris:* **criticism**, censure, polemic, diatribe, tirade; attack, onslaught.

brochure noun **booklet**, prospectus, catalogue; pamphlet, leaflet, handbill, handout; N. Amer. folder.

broil verb (N. Amer.) *I have also had broiled rabbit and rabbit stew:* **grill**, toast, barbecue, bake; cook.

broke adjective (informal). See **PENNILESS**.

broken adjective **1** *she was staring across the farmyard at the broken stable door:* **smashed**, shattered, fragmented, splintered, crushed, snapped; in bits, in pieces; destroyed, disintegrated; cracked, split; informal in smithereens. **2** *she suffered a broken arm in the attack:* **fractured**, damaged, injured. **3** *he said the toilet was broken and had been for some time:* **damaged**, faulty, defective, not working, malfunctioning, in disrepair, inoperative, out of order, broken-down, down; informal on the blink, kaput, bust, busted, conked out, acting up, done for; Brit. informal knackered. **4** *after three broken marriages, he's found some stability with his fourth wife:* **failed**, unsuccessful. **5** *send a letter to the President about all his broken promises:* **flouted**, violated, infringed, contravened, disregarded, ignored. **6** *it was an enormous humiliation and he was left a broken man:* **defeated**, beaten, subdued; **demoralized**, dispirited, discouraged, crushed, humbled; dishonoured, ruined. **7** *we endured a long, noisy night of broken sleep:* **interrupted**, disturbed, fitful, disrupted, discontinuous, intermittent, unsettled, troubled. **8** *he*

pressed on gingerly over the broken ground: **uneven**, rough, irregular, bumpy; rutted, pitted. **9** *they expressed themselves in broken English with much arm waving:* **halting**, hesitating, disjointed, faltering, imperfect.
– OPPOSITES whole, working, uninterrupted, smooth, perfect.

broken-down adjective **1** *the family disembarked at a broken-down council estate covered in rubbish:* **dilapidated**, run down, ramshackle, tumbledown, in disrepair, battered, crumbling, deteriorated, gone to rack and ruin. **2** *a broken-down Land Rover parked by the roadside had its windows broken:* **defective**, broken, faulty; not working, malfunctioning, inoperative, non-functioning; informal kaput, conked out, clapped out, done for; Brit. informal knackered.
– OPPOSITES smart.

broken-hearted adjective *pupils at the school were broken-hearted when thieves stole two of their computers:* **heartbroken**, grief-stricken, desolate, devastated, inconsolable, miserable, depressed, melancholy, wretched, sorrowful, forlorn, heavy-hearted, woeful, doleful, downcast, woebegone.
– OPPOSITES overjoyed.

broker noun *the broker is looking for pre-tax profits of about £1.2m:* **dealer**, broker-dealer, agent; middleman, intermediary, mediator; factor, liaison; stockbroker.
verb *Pakistan initiated efforts to broker a plan for a peaceful transfer of power:* **arrange**, organize, orchestrate, work out, settle, clinch, bring about; negotiate, mediate.

bronzed adjective *with their youthful good looks and bronzed faces they were an attractive couple:* **tanned**, suntanned, tan, bronze, brown, reddish-brown.

brooch noun **breastpin**, pin, clip, badge.

brood noun *the male then returns to his mate and helps her raise the brood:* **offspring**, young, progeny; family, hatch, clutch.
verb *he slumped in his armchair, brooding on how life had let him down:* **worry**, fret, agonize, mope, sulk; think, ponder, contemplate, meditate, muse, ruminate.

brook[1] noun *silent except for the gurgle of a small brook as it splashed down some rocks:* **stream**, streamlet, rill, brooklet, runnel, runlet, gill; N. English beck; Scottish & N. English burn; S. English bourn; N. Amer. & Austral./NZ creek.

brook[2] verb (formal) *he was not, one gathers, a man to brook opposition:* **tolerate**, allow, stand, bear, abide, put up with, endure, accept, permit, countenance; informal stomach, stand for, hack; Brit. informal stick; archaic suffer.

brothel noun **whorehouse**; N. Amer. bordello; Brit. informal knocking shop; N. Amer. informal cathouse, creepjoint; euphemistic massage parlour; Law disorderly house; archaic bawdy house, house of ill fame, house of ill repute.

brother noun **1** *my eldest brother was a lot*

older than me: informal bro; sibling. **2** *they often depicted her less favourably than their German brothers:* **colleague**, associate, partner, comrade, fellow, friend; informal pal, chum; Brit. informal mate. **3** *brothers of the Carmelite order who had returned from the crusades:* **monk**, cleric, friar.

brotherhood noun **1** *the ideals of justice and brotherhood:* **comradeship**, fellowship, brotherliness, fraternalism, kinship; camaraderie, friendship. **2** *he'd be a loss to the Brotherhood if we expelled him:* **society**, fraternity, association, alliance, union, league, guild, order, body, community, club, lodge, circle.

brotherly adjective **1** *in this endeavour Chapman was to meet some brotherly rivalry:* **fraternal**, sibling. **2** *religions which preach brotherly love to all mankind:* **friendly**, comradely; affectionate, amicable, kind, devoted, loyal; loving.

brow noun **1** *the doctor wiped his brow with a large handkerchief:* **forehead**, temple. **2** *his eyes were deep set beneath heavy black brows:* **eyebrow**. **3** *the beagles tumbled over brow of the hill:* **summit**, peak, top, crest, crown, head, pinnacle, apex.

browbeat verb *Newbury Council managed to browbeat the Department of the Environment into accepting the plan:* **bully**, hector, intimidate, force, coerce, compel, dragoon, bludgeon, pressure, pressurize, tyrannize, terrorize, menace; harass, harry, hound; informal bulldoze, railroad.

brown adjective **1** *two pairs of brown gloves:* hazel, chocolate-coloured, coffee-coloured, cocoa-coloured, nut-brown; brunette; sepia, mahogany, umber, burnt sienna; beige, buff, tan, fawn, camel, café au lait, caramel, chestnut. **2** *her plump, jolly, brown face:* **tanned**, suntanned, browned, bronze, bronzed; dark, swarthy, dusky. **3** *brown bread:* **wholemeal**; unrefined.
verb *the grill browns food evenly as it turns:* **grill**, toast, singe, sear, crisp (up); barbecue, bake, cook.

browse verb **1** *you can browse and compare price and quality, without pressure to buy:* **look around/round**, window-shop, peruse. **2** *Stella browsed through the newspaper:* **scan**, skim, glance, look, peruse; thumb, leaf, flick; dip into. **3** *three cows were browsing at the far end of the meadow:* **graze**, feed, crop; ruminate.
noun *this brochure is well worth a browse:* **scan**, read, skim, glance, look.

bruise noun *she had a nasty bruise across her forehead:* **contusion**, lesion, mark, injury; swelling, lump, bump, welt.
verb **1** *she grabbed his arm, hard enough to bruise it:* **contuse**, injure, mark, discolour. **2** *potatoes bruise easily, so treat them with care:* **mark**, discolour, blemish; damage, spoil.

brunette adjective **brown-haired**, dark, dark-haired.

brunt noun *car dealers are bearing the brunt of the recession:* **(full) force**, impact, shock, burden, pressure, weight; effect, repercussions, consequences.

brush[1] noun **1** *a barmaid emerged with a brush and shovel:* **broom**, sweeper, besom, whisk. **2** *he gave the seat a brush with the back of his hand:* **clean**, sweep, wipe, dust. **3** *she longed for the brush of his lips against her cheek:* **touch**, stroke, skim, graze, nudge, contact; kiss. **4** *Mario's unfortunate and ill-timed brush with the law:* **encounter**, clash, confrontation, conflict, altercation, incident; informal run-in, to-do; Brit. informal spot of bother.
verb **1** *he spent most of his day brushing the floors:* **sweep**, clean, buff, scrub. **2** *she brushed her long auburn hair:* **groom**, comb, neaten, tidy, smooth, arrange, fix, do; curry. **3** *she felt his lips lightly brush her cheek:* **touch**, stroke, caress, skim, sweep, graze, contact; kiss. **4** *she brushed a wisp of hair away from her face:* **push**, move, sweep, clear.
■ **brush something aside** *they thought they could brush aside the difficulties of women in science with a series of bright, appealing images:* disregard, ignore, dismiss, shrug off, wave aside; overlook, pay no attention to, take no notice of, neglect, forget about, turn a blind eye to; reject, spurn; laugh off, make light of, trivialize; informal pooh-pooh.
■ **brush someone off** *somehow Meredith knew he wouldn't be as easy to brush off as the other young men:* rebuff, dismiss, spurn, reject; slight, scorn, disdain; ignore, disregard, snub, cut, turn one's back on, give someone the cold shoulder, freeze out; jilt, cast aside, discard, throw over, drop, leave; informal knock back.
■ **brush up (on)** *I've been brushing up my Italian:* revise, read up, go over, relearn, cram, study; improve, sharpen (up), polish up; hone, refine, perfect; informal bone up; Brit. informal swot up, gen up.

brush[2] noun *the area was covered in dense brush:* **undergrowth**, underwood, scrub, brushwood, shrubs, bushes; N. Amer. underbrush, chaparral.

brusque adjective *he was disliked because of his brusque manner:* **curt**, abrupt, blunt, short, sharp, terse, brisk, peremptory, gruff, bluff; offhand, discourteous, impolite, rude; informal snappy.
– OPPOSITES polite.

brutal adjective **1** *a brutal attack on an elderly man:* **savage**, cruel, vicious, ferocious, barbaric, barbarous, wicked, murderous, bloodthirsty, cold-blooded, callous, heartless, merciless, sadistic; heinous, monstrous, abominable, atrocious. **2** *he replied with brutal honesty:* **unsparing**, unstinting, unembellished, unvarnished, bald, naked, stark, blunt, direct, straightforward, frank, outspoken, forthright, plain-spoken; complete, total.

b

– OPPOSITES gentle.

brutalize verb **1** *the men were brutalized by their experiences in the trenches:* **desensitize**, dehumanize, harden, toughen, inure. **2** *the prison staff brutalized and tortured those in their custody:* **attack**, assault, beat, batter; abuse.

brute noun **1** *she had a husband, a great brawny brute who knocked her about:* **savage**, beast, monster, animal, barbarian, fiend, ogre; sadist; thug, lout, ruffian; informal swine, pig. **2** *you want to take that brute for a walk?* **animal**, beast, creature, monster; N. Amer. informal critter.
adjective *most break-ins are committed by people who rely on brute force to gain entry:* **physical**, bodily; sheer; crude, violent.

bubble noun **1** *he watched the bubbles in his mineral water:* globule, bead, blister; air pocket; (**bubbles**) sparkle, fizz, effervescence, froth. **2** *hardware companies that survived the 1980s bubble are more soundly based:* **illusion**, delusion, fantasy, dream, chimera; surge, blip.
verb **1** *this wine bubbles nicely on the tongue:* **sparkle**, fizz, effervesce, foam, froth. **2** *the milk was bubbling above the flame:* **boil**, simmer, seethe, gurgle. **3** *I was bubbling with ideas, desperate to get things to happen:* **overflow**, brim over, be filled, gush; burst.

bubbly adjective **1** *I could see patches of bubbly froth along the edge of the river:* **bubbling**, fizzy, effervescent, gassy, foaming, frothy, foamy. **2** *Mary was a petite young woman with sparkling eyes and a bubbly personality:* **vivacious**, animated, ebullient, lively, high-spirited, zestful; sparkling, bouncy, buoyant, carefree; merry, happy, cheerful, perky, sunny, bright; Brit. Tiggerish; informal upbeat, chirpy.
– OPPOSITES still, listless.

buccaneer noun (archaic) *Holmes had a touch of the buccaneer about him, and delighted in taking risks:* **pirate**, marauder, raider, freebooter, plunderer, cut-throat, privateer.

buck verb *the £10bn investment has bucked the trend and returned over 50 per cent to investors:* **resist**, oppose, defy, fight, kick against.

bucket noun *order was only restored when the manager doused them with a bucket of water:* **pail**, scuttle, can, tub.

buckle noun *a broad leather belt with a brass buckle:* **clasp**, clip, catch, hasp, fastener.
verb **1** *he buckled the seat belt round his waist:* **fasten**, do up, hook, strap, secure, clasp, clip. **2** *his knees buckled and he fell to the pavement:* **give (way)**, crumple; collapse. **3** *the pillars were put in to stop the walls buckling:* **bend**, twist, curve, distort, deform; bulge, arc, arch.
■ **buckle down** *it is time to stop making promises and buckle down to building a 21st-century health service:* get (down) to work, set to work, get down to business; work hard, apply oneself, make an effort, focus;

informal pull one's finger out; Brit. informal get stuck in.

bucolic adjective *the church is lovely, both in itself and for its bucolic setting:* **rustic**, rural, pastoral, country, countryside; literary Arcadian, sylvan.

bud noun *the uppermost bud is the one that will appear first:* **sprout**, shoot.
verb *the daffodils are about to bud:* **sprout**, shoot, germinate, swell.

budding adjective *budding musicians are being given a chance to shine with the launch of the Ulster Schools Jazz Orchestra:* **promising**, up-and-coming, rising, in the making, aspiring, future, prospective, potential, fledgling, developing; informal would-be, wannabe.

budge verb **1** *the horses wouldn't budge: it was as if something was holding them to the road:* **move**, shift, stir, go. **2** *even with my back against the door I couldn't budge it:* **dislodge**, shift, move; open. **3** *I tried to persuade him out of it but he wouldn't budge:* **give way**, give in, yield, change one's mind, acquiesce, compromise.

budget noun **1** *your personal budget for the week:* **plan**, forecast; accounts, statement. **2** *proposed cuts in the defence budget:* **allowance**, allocation, quota; grant, award, funds, resources, capital.
verb **1** *Adidas has budgeted $88m for World Cup promotions:* **allocate**, allot, allow, earmark, designate, set aside. **2** *it was initially budgeted at $100m, but that had doubled by the time filming had ended:* **cost**, price; value; estimate, schedule. **3** *in this business you should budget for periods of unemployment:* **allow**, plan, be ready/prepared, make allowances. **4** *it's important for your mother to budget her expenses:* **schedule**, plan, cost, estimate; organize, rationalize.
adjective *a complete kit, ideal for budget home cinema:* **cheap**, inexpensive, economy, low-cost, low-price, cut-price, discount, bargain.
– OPPOSITES expensive.

buff¹ adjective *a plain buff envelope lay on the table:* **beige**, yellowish, yellowish-brown, light brown, fawn, sandy, wheaten, biscuit, camel.
verb *some manicurists will then buff the nails with a chamois pad:* **polish**, burnish, shine, clean, rub.

buff² noun (informal) *Mr Woodward was something of a railway buff:* **enthusiast**, fan, devotee, lover, admirer; expert, aficionado, authority, pundit; informal freak, nut, fanatic, addict.

buffer noun *family, friends, and colleagues can provide a buffer against the stressful effects of change:* **cushion**, bulwark, shield, barrier, guard, safeguard.
verb *corals provide homes for sea creatures and buffer coastal areas from storms:*

cushion, absorb, soften, lessen, diminish, moderate, allay.
– OPPOSITES intensify.

buffet[1] noun 1 *the occasion concluded with a buffet in the parish hall:* **cold table**, self-service meal, smorgasbord. 2 *he was waiting in the buffet at Madrid Station:* **cafe**, cafeteria, snack bar, canteen, restaurant.

buffet[2] verb 1 *rough seas and wild winds buffeted the coast for most of the year:* **batter**, pound, lash, strike, hit. 2 *most ordinary citizens have been buffeted by price rises:* **afflict**, trouble, harm, burden, bother, beset, harass, torment, blight, bedevil.

buffoon noun *DC Comics plan to turn the Caped Crusader into a drunken buffoon:* **fool**, idiot, dunce, ignoramus, simpleton, jackass; informal chump, blockhead, nincompoop, numbskull, dope, twit, nitwit, halfwit, clot, birdbrain, twerp; Brit. informal muppet.

bug noun 1 *bugs and spiders conceal themselves in the bark:* **insect**, mite; informal creepy-crawly, beastie. 2 (informal) *Tranmere striker Tommy Coyne has been sidelined by a flu bug:* **illness**, ailment, disorder, infection, disease, sickness, complaint, upset, condition; bacterium, germ, virus; Brit. informal lurgy. 3 (informal) *the travel bug had truly taken a firm hold:* **obsession**, enthusiasm, craze, fad, mania, passion, fixation. 4 *the bug must have been put in my case before I left Helsinki:* **listening device**, microphone; wire, wiretap, tap. 5 *install the program in a separate subdirectory in case it has a hidden bug:* **fault**, error, defect, flaw; virus; informal glitch, gremlin.
verb 1 *Wilson's offices had been bugged by security men:* **wire (up)**; informal mike (up); tap; monitor. 2 *the phone call made by Prince Charles must have been bugged:* **record**, overhear; tap, monitor. 3 (informal) *she really bugs me.* See ANNOY.

bugbear noun *dusting was a particular bugbear of Murti's, rarely attempted:* **pet hate**, bête noire, bogey; bane, irritation, vexation, anathema, thorn in one's flesh/side; nightmare, horror; informal hang-up; N. Amer. bugaboo.

build verb 1 *a supermarket had been built on Gallowhill Road:* **construct**, erect, put up, assemble. 2 *the kids were building a snowman:* **make**, construct, form, create, fashion, model, shape. 3 *they are building a business strategy for the next decade:* **establish**, found, set up, institute, inaugurate, initiate.
noun *police are looking for a man of slim build:* **physique**, frame, body, figure, form, shape, stature, proportions; informal vital statistics.
■ **build something in/into** *environmental priorities must be built into all aspects of government policy:* incorporate in/into, include in, absorb into, subsume into, assimilate into.
■ **build on** *a new study will be undertaken*

to build on existing research: expand on, enlarge on, develop, elaborate, flesh out, embellish, amplify; refine, improve, perfect.
■ **build up** *the traffic is steadily building up:* increase, grow, mount up, intensify, escalate; strengthen.
■ **build something up** 1 *he built up a huge export business:* establish, set up, found, institute, start, create; develop, expand, enlarge. 2 *he built up his stamina by playing football:* boost, strengthen, increase, improve, augment, raise, enhance, swell; informal beef up. 3 *I have built up a collection of around 1,700 prints:* accumulate, amass, collect, gather; stockpile, hoard.

builder noun 1 *Thomas Telford was a canal builder:* **designer**, planner, architect, deviser, creator, maker, constructor. 2 *the builders had better finish the job in time:* **(construction) worker**, bricklayer, labourer; Brit. ganger.

building noun 1 *the church is a plain red brick building:* **structure**, construction, edifice, erection, pile; property, premises, establishment. 2 *they are calling for a moratorium on the building of power stations:* **construction**, erection, fabrication, assembly.

build-up noun 1 *this build-up of military strength is worrying many experts:* **increase**, growth, expansion, escalation, development, proliferation. 2 *the build-up of carbon dioxide in the atmosphere:* **accumulation**, accretion. 3 *the build-up for the next World Cup has already begun:* **publicity**, promotion, advertising, marketing; informal hype, ballyhoo.

built-in adjective 1 *there's a built-in cupboard in the corner:* **fitted**, integral, integrated, incorporated. 2 *television has built-in advantages for advertisers:* **inherent**, intrinsic, inbuilt; essential, implicit, basic, fundamental, deep-rooted.

bulb noun **tuber**, corm, rhizome.

bulbous adjective *he had a large bulbous red nose:* **bulging**, protuberant, round, fat, rotund; swollen, tumid, distended, bloated.

bulge noun 1 *the money made a fat bulge in his pocket:* **swelling**, bump, lump, protuberance, prominence. 2 (informal) *a bulge in the prison population:* **surge**, upsurge, rise, increase, escalation.
verb *he leaned forward, his forearms bulging beneath the rolled-up sleeves of his shirt:* **swell**, stick out, puff out, balloon (out), fill out, belly, distend; project, protrude, stand out.

bulging adjective *when the working day was over, he carried his bulging briefcase home:* **huge**, distended, swollen, protuberant, bulbous, protruding, fat, rounded.

bulk noun 1 *the sheer bulk of the bags made them hard to carry:* **size**, volume, dimensions, proportions, mass, scale, magnitude, immensity, vastness. 2 *not*

b

surprisingly, the bulk of entrants were British: **majority**, generality, main part, major part, lion's share, preponderance; most, almost all.
– OPPOSITES minority.
verb *some takeaway meals are bulked out with fat:* **expand**, pad out, fill out, eke out; augment, increase.

bulky adjective **1** *bulky items of household refuse:* **large**, big, huge, sizeable, substantial, massive; king-size, outsize, oversized, considerable, **cumbersome**, unmanageable, unwieldy, ponderous, heavy, weighty; informal jumbo, whopping, hulking; Brit. informal ginormous. **2** *he was a bulky man, not good at climbing:* **heavily built**, stocky, thickset, sturdy, well built, burly, strapping, solid, heavy, hefty, meaty; stout, fat, plump, chubby, portly, rotund, round, chunky; overweight, obese, fleshy, corpulent; informal tubby, pudgy, roly-poly, beefy, porky, blubbery; Brit. informal podgy.
– OPPOSITES small, slight.

bulldoze verb **1** *they plan to bulldoze the park and build flats:* **demolish**, knock down, tear down, pull down, flatten, level, raze, clear. **2** *Williams bulldozed his way through to score the equalizer:* **force**, push, shove, barge, elbow, shoulder, jostle; plunge, crash, sweep, bundle. **3** (informal) *she tends to bulldoze everyone, operating by overpowering others:* **bully**, hector, browbeat, intimidate, steamroller, dragoon, bludgeon, domineer, pressurize, tyrannize, strong-arm; informal railroad, lean on, boss.

bullet noun ball, shot; informal slug; (**bullets**) lead.

bulletin noun **1** *our next bulletin is at 10.30 p.m.* **report**, dispatch, story, press release, newscast, flash; statement, announcement, message, communication, communiqué. **2** *the Society produces a monthly bulletin:* **newsletter**, news-sheet, proceedings; newspaper, magazine, digest, gazette, review.

bullish adjective *Karan was in bullish mood about the future of his company:* **confident**, positive, assertive, self-assertive, assured, self-assured, bold, determined; optimistic, buoyant, sanguine; informal feisty, upbeat.

bully noun *whisky turned him into a savage bully:* **persecutor**, oppressor, tyrant, tormentor, intimidator; tough guy, bully boy, thug.
verb **1** *I allowed William Ash to bully me for most of my life:* **persecute**, oppress, tyrannize, browbeat, intimidate, strong-arm, dominate; informal push around/about. **2** *Alice would coax or bully her into making all sorts of concessions:* **coerce**, pressure, pressurize, press, push; force, compel; badger, goad, prod, browbeat, bludgeon, intimidate, dragoon, strong-arm; informal bulldoze, railroad, lean on.

bulwark noun **1** *alterations have included cutting off part of the north bulwark:*

wall, rampart, fortification, parapet, stockade, palisade, barricade, embankment, earthwork. **2** *the security forces remain the ultimate bulwark against the breakdown of society:* **protector**, defender, protection, guard, defence, supporter, buttress; mainstay, bastion, stronghold.

bum[1] noun (Brit. informal). See BOTTOM noun sense 6.

bum[2] (informal) noun **1** (N. Amer.) *the bums sleeping on the sidewalk.* See TRAMP noun sense 1. **2** *out of bed, you lazy bum:* **idler**, loafer, good-for-nothing, ne'er-do-well, layabout, lounger, shirker; informal waster, loser, scrounger.
verb **1** *he bummed around Florida for a few months:* **loaf**, lounge, idle, moon, amble, wander, drift, meander, dawdle; informal mooch; N. Amer. informal lollygag. **2** *they tried to bum money off him:* **beg**, borrow; informal scrounge, cadge, sponge; Brit. informal scab; N. Amer. informal mooch; Austral./NZ informal bludge.
adjective *it's probably all bum advice, but it's the best I can offer:* **bad**, poor, second-rate, third-rate, second-class, unsatisfactory, inadequate, unacceptable; dreadful, awful, terrible, deplorable, lamentable; informal crummy, rotten, pathetic, lousy, pitiful, dire, poxy; Brit. informal duff, rubbish.
– OPPOSITES excellent.

bumble verb *they bumbled around the house, still half asleep:* **blunder**, lurch, stumble, stagger, lumber, flounder, totter.

bumbling adjective *Sherlock Holmes' bumbling sidekick Doctor Watson:* **blundering**, bungling, inept, clumsy, maladroit, awkward, muddled; oafish, clodhopping, lumbering; crude; informal botched, ham-fisted, cack-handed.
– OPPOSITES efficient.

bump noun **1** *I landed on the floor with a bump:* **jolt**, crash, smash, smack, crack, bang, thud, thump; informal whack, thwack, bash, wallop. **2** *I was woken from my daydream by a loud bump:* **bang**, crack, boom, clang, knock, thud, thump, clunk, crash, smash; stomp, clump, clomp; informal whump. **3** *my front wheel hit a bump in the road:* **hump**, lump, ridge, bulge, knob, protuberance. **4** *the police wanted to know how he got the bump on his head:* **swelling**, lump, bulge, injury, contusion; outgrowth, growth, carbuncle, protuberance.
verb **1** *all those cars bumped into each other in the fog:* **hit**, crash, smash, slam, bang, knock, run, plough; ram, collide with, strike; N. Amer. impact. **2** *we swerved round a cart bumping along the road:* **bounce**, jolt, jerk, rattle, shake.
▪ **bump into** (informal) *he returned to his workshop, hoping to bump into her on the way:* **meet**, encounter, run into/across, come across, chance on, happen on.

bumper adjective *Jacques was speaking enthusiastically about grapes, and was prophesying a bumper harvest:* **abundant**,

rich, bountiful, good, fine; large, big, huge, plentiful, profuse, copious; informal whopping; literary plenteous, bounteous.
– OPPOSITES meagre.

bumpkin noun *Voight plays a country bumpkin who comes to Chicago and gets shot by mobsters:* **yokel**, peasant, provincial, rustic, country cousin, countryman/woman; N. Amer. informal hayseed, hillbilly, hick; Austral. informal bushy; Irish informal culchie.

bumptious adjective *a bumptious and opinionated ass who took any opportunity to further his own interests:* **self-important**, conceited, arrogant, self-assertive, pushy, swollen-headed, pompous, overbearing, cocky, swaggering; proud, haughty, overweening, egotistical; informal snooty, uppity.
– OPPOSITES modest.

bumpy adjective **1** *the main street was a narrow, bumpy lane piled up with rubble:* **uneven**, rough, rutted, pitted, potholed, holey; lumpy, rocky. **2** *after a very bumpy ride they arrived at the top of Thorpe Street:* **bouncy**, rough, uncomfortable, jolting, lurching, jerky, jarring, bone-shaking. **3** *the season got off to a bumpy start:* **inconsistent**, variable, irregular, fluctuating, intermittent, erratic, patchy; rocky, unsettled, unstable, turbulent, chaotic, full of ups and downs.
– OPPOSITES smooth.

bunch noun **1** *he produced a bunch of flowers:* **bouquet**, posy, nosegay, tussie-mussie, spray, corsage; wreath, garland. **2** *a bunch of keys | a bunch of bananas:* **cluster**, clump, knot; group. **3** (informal) *what a great bunch of people:* **group**, set, circle, company, collection, bevy, band; informal gang, crowd, load. **4** (N. Amer. informal) *a whole bunch of things.* See LOT pronoun.
verb **1** *he bunched the reins in his hands:* **bundle**, clump, cluster, group, gather; pack. **2** *the runners bunched up behind him:* **cluster**, huddle, gather, congregate, collect, amass, group, crowd.

bundle noun *a bundle of clothes:* **bunch**, roll, clump, wad, parcel, sheaf, bale, bolt; pile, stack, heap, mass; informal load, wodge.
verb **1** *she bundled up her things:* **tie**, pack, parcel, wrap, roll, fold, bind, truss, bale. **2** (informal) *he was bundled into a van:* **hustle**, manhandle, frogmarch, hurry, rush; shove, push, thrust.

bung noun **stopper**, plug, cork, spigot, spile, seal; N. Amer. stopple.

bungle verb *the four prisoners bungled their escape bid:* **mishandle**, mismanage, mess up, spoil, ruin; informal botch, muff, fluff, make a hash of, foul up, screw up; Brit. informal make a pig's ear of, cock up; N. Amer. informal flub, goof up.

bungler noun *his frequent mistakes have caused him to be branded a bungler:* **incompetent**, amateur, bumbler, blunderer, clown; informal botcher, butterfingers; Brit. informal bodger; N. Amer. informal jackleg.

– OPPOSITES expert.

bungling adjective *this is obviously the work of a bungling amateur:* **incompetent**, blundering, amateurish, inept, unskilful, clumsy, awkward, bumbling; informal ham-fisted, cack-handed.

bunk¹ noun **berth**, cot, bed.

bunk² (Brit. informal) verb *he bunked off school every Thursday afternoon:* **(play) truant from**, skip, avoid, shirk; Brit. informal skive off; N. Amer. informal play hookey from, goof off, cut; Austral./NZ informal wag.
■ **do a bunk.** See ABSCOND.

bunk³ noun (informal). See NONSENSE sense 1.

buoy noun *the channel is marked by red and green buoys:* **float**, marker, beacon.
verb *the party was buoyed by an election victory:* **cheer (up)**, hearten, rally, invigorate, uplift, lift, encourage, stimulate, inspirit; informal pep up, perk up, buck up.
– OPPOSITES depress.

buoyancy noun **1** *the drum's buoyancy forced it to the surface:* **lightness**, floatability. **2** *her natural buoyancy helped her cope:* **cheerfulness**, happiness, light-heartedness, joy, bounce, sunniness, breeziness, jollity, liveliness, ebullience, high spirits, vivacity, vitality, verve, sparkle, zest; optimism; informal pep. **3** *greater buoyancy in overseas markets has boosted UK exports:* **vigour**, strength, resilience, growth, improvement, expansion.
– OPPOSITES depression.

buoyant adjective **1** *a buoyant substance:* **light**, floatable. **2** *it takes a very buoyant personality to cope with constant rejection:* **cheerful**, cheery, happy, light-hearted, carefree, bright, merry, joyful, bubbly, bouncy, sunny, jolly; lively, jaunty, high-spirited, perky; optimistic, confident, positive; informal peppy, upbeat. **3** *in the US, demand has been buoyant:* **booming**, strong, vigorous, thriving; improving, expanding, mushrooming, snowballing.
– OPPOSITES depressed.

burble verb **1** *the exhaust was burbling as only a twin-pipe V8 can:* **gurgle**, bubble, murmur, purr, whirr, drone, hum, rumble. **2** *he burbled on about annuities:* **prattle**, blather, blether, babble, gabble, prate, drivel, rattle, ramble, maunder, go on, run on; informal jabber, blabber, yatter, gab; Brit. informal rabbit, witter, waffle, chunter; N. Amer. informal run off at the mouth.

burden noun **1** *the porters shouldered their burdens and we set off:* **load**, cargo, weight; pack, bundle. **2** *he took on a huge financial burden:* **responsibility**, onus, charge, duty, obligation, liability; trouble, care, problem, worry, difficulty, strain, encumbrance. **3** *the burden of his message was as follows:* **gist**, substance, drift, thrust, meaning, significance, essence, import, message.
verb **1** *he was burdened with a heavy pack:* **load**, charge, weigh down, encumber,

b

hamper; overload, overburden. **2** *we should avoid burdening our parents with guilt:* **oppress**, trouble, worry, harass, upset, distress; haunt, afflict, strain, stress, tax, overwhelm.

burdensome adjective *complying with the legislation can be burdensome:* **onerous**, oppressive, troublesome, weighty, worrisome, stressful; vexatious, irksome, trying, difficult; arduous, strenuous, hard, laborious, exhausting, tiring, taxing, demanding, punishing, gruelling.

bureau noun **1** *a beautiful oak bureau:* **desk**, writing table, secretaire, escritoire; Brit. davenport. **2** *reservations can be made through the accommodation bureau's free room-finding service:* **agency**, service, office, business, company, firm. **3** *the Bureau is in close touch with key people in Brussels:* **department**, division, branch, section.

bureaucracy noun **1** *the higher ranks of the bureaucracy:* **civil service**, government, administration; establishment, system, powers that be; ministries, authorities. **2** *unnecessary bureaucracy in local government:* **red tape**, rules and regulations, protocol, officialdom, paperwork.

bureaucrat noun *the faceless bureaucrats who make the rules:* **official**, administrator, civil servant, minister, functionary, mandarin; Brit. jack-in-office; derogatory apparatchik.

bureaucratic adjective **1** *bureaucratic structure of the Council:* **administrative**, official, governmental, ministerial, state, civic. **2** *current procedures are far too bureaucratic:* **rule-bound**, rigid, inflexible, complicated.

burgeon verb *the popularity of snowboarding continues to burgeon:* **flourish**, thrive, prosper, improve; expand, escalate, swell, grow, boom, mushroom, snowball, rocket, go from strength to strength.

burgeoning adjective *they are the undisputed leaders of the burgeoning downtown scene:* **flourishing**, thriving, growing, expanding, booming.

burglar noun **housebreaker**, robber, cat burglar, thief, raider, looter, safe-breaker/cracker; intruder; N. Amer. informal yegg.

burglary noun **1** *a two-year sentence for burglary:* **housebreaking**, breaking and entering, theft, stealing, robbery, larceny, thieving, looting. **2** *a series of burglaries has made residents very nervous indeed:* **break-in**, theft, robbery, raid; informal smash-and-grab.

burgle verb *her house was burgled again last night:* **rob**, loot, steal from, plunder, rifle, pillage; break into; informal do.

burial noun *the body was flown home for burial:* **burying**, interment, committal, inhumation, entombment; funeral,

obsequies.
– OPPOSITES exhumation.

burial ground noun **cemetery**, graveyard, churchyard, necropolis, garden of remembrance; Scottish kirkyard; N. Amer. memorial park; informal boneyard; archaic God's acre; historical potter's field.

burlesque noun *new poems are indebted to past literature, by imitation or even burlesque of a preceding form:* **parody**, caricature, satire, lampoon, skit; informal send-up, take-off, spoof.

burly adjective *two burly bodyguards stood beside him:* **strapping**, well built, sturdy, brawny, strong, muscular, muscly, thickset, big, hefty, bulky, stocky, Herculean; informal hunky, beefy, husky, hulking.
– OPPOSITES puny.

burn verb **1** *by nightfall, the whole city was burning:* **be on fire**, be alight, be ablaze, blaze, go up (in smoke), be in flames, be aflame; smoulder, glow. **2** *he burned all her letters:* **set fire to**, set on fire, set alight, set light to, light, ignite, touch off; incinerate; informal torch. **3** *I left the iron on and burned my dress:* **scorch**, singe, sear, char, blacken; brand; scald. **4** *her lip burned where her teeth had pierced it:* **be hot**, be warm, be feverish, be on fire; blush, redden, go red, flush, colour. **5** *by this time, Martha was burning with curiosity:* **be consumed**, be eaten up, be obsessed, be tormented, be beside oneself. **6** *Meredith burned to know what the secret was:* **yearn**, long, ache, desire, want, wish, hanker, crave, hunger, thirst; informal have a yen, yen, itch, be dying. **7** *people differ considerably in the energy they burn up:* **consume**, use up, expend, get/go through, eat up; dissipate.

burning adjective **1** *a burning building:* **blazing**, flaming, fiery, ignited, glowing, red-hot, smouldering; raging, roaring. **2** *the burning desert sands:* **hot**, red-hot, fiery, blistering, scorching, searing, sweltering, torrid; informal baking, boiling (hot), roasting, sizzling. **3** *a burning desire to win:* **intense**, passionate, deep-seated, profound, wholehearted, strong, ardent, fervent, urgent, fierce, eager, frantic, consuming, uncontrollable. **4** *the burning issues of the day:* **vital**, crucial, significant, important, essential, pivotal; urgent, pressing, compelling, critical.

burnish verb *marks can be removed by scraping and burnishing the metal:* **polish (up)**, shine, buff (up), rub (up).

burp (informal) verb *he couldn't help burping:* **belch**, bring up wind; Scottish & N. English informal rift.
noun *Cranston let out a loud burp:* **belch**; Scottish & N. English informal rift; formal eructation.

burrow noun *ferrets are released into the burrow:* **warren**, tunnel, hole, dugout; lair, set, den, earth.
verb *the termites burrow downwards and*

start laying eggs: **tunnel**, dig, excavate, grub, mine, bore, channel.

burst verb 1 *one balloon burst | he burst my balloon:* **split (open)**, rupture, break, tear. 2 *a shell burst a short distance away:* **explode**, blow up, detonate, go off. 3 *smoke and heat burst through the hole:* **break**, erupt, surge, gush, rush, stream, flow, pour, spill; spout, spurt, jet, spew. 4 *he burst into the room without knocking:* **plunge**, charge, barge, plough, hurtle, career, rush, dash, tear. 5 *she burst into tears:* **break out in**, erupt in, have a fit of.
noun 1 *damage to tyres by punctures and bursts:* **rupture**, puncture, breach, split, blowout. 2 *the mortar bursts were further away than before:* **explosion**, detonation, blast, eruption, discharge, bang, report. 3 *a burst of gunfire shattered the stillness:* **volley**, salvo, fusillade, barrage, discharge; hail, rain. 4 *a sudden burst of activity | a burst of anger:* **outbreak**, eruption, flare-up, blaze, attack, fit, rush, gale, storm, surge, upsurge, spurt; informal splurt.
■ **burst out** *'I don't care!' she burst out angrily:* exclaim, blurt, cry, shout, yell.

bury verb 1 *the crew were buried at Stonefall cemetery:* **inter**, lay to rest, entomb; informal put six feet under, plant. 2 *she buried her face in her hands:* **hide**, conceal, cover, enfold, engulf, tuck, cup, sink. 3 *the bullet buried itself in the wall:* **embed**, sink, implant, submerge; drive into. 4 *he buried himself in his work:* **absorb**, engross, immerse, occupy, engage, busy, involve.
– OPPOSITES exhume.

bush noun 1 *we planted a rose bush in her memory:* **shrub**; (**bushes**) undergrowth, shrubbery. 2 *it's easy to get lost in the bush:* **wilds**, wilderness; backwoods, hinterland(s); N. Amer. backcountry, backland(s); Austral./NZ outback, backblocks, booay; N. Amer. informal boondocks, tall timbers; Austral./NZ informal Woop Woop, beyond the black stump.

bushy adjective *Harry's eyes went back and forth under his bushy eyebrows:* **thick**, shaggy, fuzzy, bristly, fluffy, woolly; luxuriant.
– OPPOSITES sleek, wispy.

busily adverb *folk songs that scholars were busily collecting in Europe and America:* **energetically**, vigorously, enthusiastically; industriously, purposefully, diligently.

business noun 1 *she has to smile a lot in her business:* **work**, line of work, occupation, profession, career, employment, job, position; vocation, calling; field, sphere, trade, craft; informal racket, game. 2 *who do you do business with in Manila?* **trade**, trading, commerce, dealing, traffic, merchandising; dealings, transactions, negotiations. 3 *she was running her own business:* **firm**, company, concern, enterprise, venture, organization, operation, undertaking; office, agency, franchise,

practice; informal outfit, set-up. 4 *that's none of your business:* **concern**, affair, responsibility, duty, function, obligation; problem, worry; informal pigeon, bailiwick; Brit. informal lookout. 5 *the odd business with the keys remained unexplained:* **affair**, matter, thing, case, circumstance, situation, event, incident, happening, occurrence; episode.

businesslike adjective 1 *investors have been heartened by this new businesslike approach:* **professional**, efficient, slick, competent, methodical, disciplined, systematic, orderly, organized, structured, practical, pragmatic. 2 *his presentation style was abrupt and businesslike:* **impersonal**, clinical, mechanical, efficient, perfunctory, emotionless; cold, distant, detached, soulless.

businessman, businesswoman
noun **entrepreneur**, business person, industrialist, manufacturer, tycoon, magnate, employer; dealer, trader, broker, merchant, buyer, seller, marketeer, merchandiser, vendor, tradesman, retailer, supplier.

bust[1] noun 1 *a woman with a large bust:* **chest**, bosom; breasts, mammary glands, mammae; informal boobs, knockers, bubbies; Brit. Informal bristols, charlies; N. Amer. informal bazooms. 2 *a bust of Julius Caesar:* **sculpture**, carving, effigy, statue.

bust[2] (informal) verb 1 *the lock has bust | he bust the clip that held the lid down:* **break**, crack, snap, smash, fracture, shatter, disintegrate; split, burst. 2 *he promised to bust the mafia:* **overthrow**, destroy, topple, bring down, ruin, break, overturn, overcome, defeat, get rid of, oust, dislodge. 3 *two roadies were busted for possession of marijuana.* See ARREST verb sense 1. 4 (N. Amer.) *my apartment got busted.* See RAID verb sense 3.
■ **go bust** *his haulage business went bust in 1996:* fail, collapse, fold, go under, founder; go bankrupt, go into receivership, go into liquidation, be wound up; informal crash, go broke, go to the wall, go belly up, flop.

bustle verb *people clutching clipboards bustled about:* **rush**, dash, hurry, scurry, scuttle, scamper, scramble; run, tear, charge; informal scoot, beetle, buzz, zoom.
noun *I loved the bustle of the market:* **activity**, action, liveliness, hustle and bustle, excitement; tumult, hubbub, whirl; informal toing and froing, comings and goings.

bustling adjective *the bustling streets of Kowloon:* **busy**, crowded, swarming, teeming, thronged; buzzing, hectic, lively; informal buzzy.
– OPPOSITES deserted.

busy adjective 1 *he's always busy with some scheme or other:* **occupied (in)**, engaged in, involved in, employed in, working at, hard at work (on); rushed off one's feet, hard-pressed; on the job, absorbed, engrossed, immersed, preoccupied; informal (as) busy as a bee, on the go, hard at it; Brit. informal on the

b

hop. **2** *Mr Jenkins is busy at the moment:* **unavailable**, engaged, occupied; working, in a meeting, on duty; informal tied up. **3** *I've had a busy day:* **hectic**, active, lively, full, eventful; energetic, tiring. **4** *the town centre was unusually busy:* **crowded**, bustling, hectic, swarming, teeming, full, thronged; informal buzzy. **5** *the frame should be plain to balance the rather busy design:* **ornate**, over-elaborate, overblown, overwrought, overdone, fussy, cluttered, overworked.
– OPPOSITES idle, free, quiet.
verb *he busied himself with paperwork:* **occupy**, involve, engage, concern, absorb, engross, immerse, preoccupy; distract, divert.

busybody noun *others considered him an interfering busybody:* **meddler**, interferer, mischief-maker, troublemaker; gossip, scandalmonger; eavesdropper, gawker; informal nosy parker, snoop, snooper, rubberneck; Brit. informal gawper.

butch adjective informal **1** *big, butch rappers like LL Cool J and Public Enemy:* **masculine**, manly, macho. **2** *my jeans and short hair etc. were the traditional butch look:* **lesbian**, dyke(y); mannish, unfeminine, unladylike, masculine.
– OPPOSITES effeminate, feminine.

butcher noun **1** *he used to work in a butcher's shop:* **meat seller**, meat trader; slaughterer; Scottish flesher. **2** *the butcher of Baghdad:* **murderer**, slaughterer, killer, assassin; N. Amer. terminator; literary slayer; dated cut-throat.
verb **1** *the goat was butchered and skinned:* **slaughter**, cut up, carve up, joint. **2** *they butchered 150 people:* **massacre**, murder, slaughter, kill, destroy, exterminate, assassinate; N. Amer. terminate; informal dispose of; literary slay. **3** *the film was butchered by the studio:* **spoil**, ruin, mutilate, mangle, mess up, wreck; informal make a hash of, screw up.

butchery noun **1** *organic meat needs experienced butchery:* **slaughtering**, processing, treatment. **2** (Brit.) *the truck careered through the traffic lights before virtually demolishing a butchery:* **butcher's (shop)**, meat market, meat counter; slaughterhouse, abattoir. **3** *futile uprisings ending in butchery and defeat for the rebels:* **slaughter**, massacre, (mass) murder, bloodletting; genocide; literary slaying.

butt[1] verb *she butted him in the chest:* **ram**, headbutt, bunt; bump, buffet, push, shove; N. English tup.
■ **butt in** *David Harthorne butted in and asked about payment:* interrupt, break in, cut in, chime in, interject, intervene, interfere; informal poke one's nose in, put one's oar in; Brit. informal chip in.

butt[2] noun *she had been made the butt of a joke:* **target**, victim, object, subject; laughing stock.

butt[3] noun **1** *Taff prodded me with the butt of the Bren gun:* **stock**, end, handle, hilt, haft,

helve. **2** *a cigarette butt:* **stub**, end, stump, remnant; informal fag end, dog-end. **3** (N. Amer. informal) *arching her back made her butt stick out.* See BUTTOCKS.

butt[4] noun *your water butt is full of bacteria:* **barrel**, cask, keg, vat; tub, bin, drum, canister.

butter
■ **butter someone up** (informal) *she was good at buttering up advertisers:* flatter, court, wheedle, persuade, blarney, coax, get round, prevail on; toady to, fawn on, make up to, play up to, ingratiate oneself with, rub up the right way, curry favour with; informal suck up to, be all over, keep someone sweet, sweet-talk, soft-soap.

buttocks plural noun **cheeks**; rear (end), rump, backside, seat; Brit. bottom; informal behind, BTM, sit-upon, derrière; Brit. informal bum, botty, jacksie; N. Amer. informal butt, fanny, tush, tail, buns, booty, heinie; humorous fundament, posterior, stern; Anatomy nates.

button noun **1** *he did up his shirt buttons:* **fastener**, stud, toggle; hook, catch, clasp. **2** *press the start button:* **switch**, knob, control; lever, handle.

buttonhole verb (informal) *I was tired of being buttonholed in the street by worried investors.* See ACCOST.

buttress noun **1** *the wall was supported by stone buttresses:* **prop**, support, abutment, shore, pier, reinforcement, stanchion. **2** *a buttress against social collapse:* **safeguard**, defence, protection, guard; support, prop; bulwark.
verb *at that time, authority was buttressed by religion:* **strengthen**, reinforce, fortify, support, bolster, shore up, underpin, cement, uphold, defend, back up.

buxom adjective *a buxom young woman in a tight dress:* **large-breasted**, big-breasted, bosomy, big-bosomed; shapely, ample, plump, rounded, full-figured, voluptuous, curvaceous, Rubenesque; informal busty, chesty, well endowed, curvy.

buy verb **1** *they bought a new house:* **purchase**, acquire, obtain, get, pick up, snap up; take, procure, pay for; invest in; informal get hold of, score. **2** *he was a man who could not be bought:* **bribe**, buy off, suborn, corrupt; informal grease someone's palm, get at, fix; Brit. informal nobble.
– OPPOSITES sell.
noun (informal) *salmon is a good buy at the moment:* **purchase**, investment, acquisition, gain; deal, bargain.

buyer noun *a way of satisfying the buyer's concerns about reliability:* **purchaser**, customer, consumer, shopper, investor; (**buyers**) clientele, patronage, market; Law vendee.

buzz noun **1** *the buzz of the bees filled the air:* **hum**, humming, buzzing, murmur, drone; Brit. informal zizz. **2** *there was an insistent buzz from her control panel:* **noise**, purr,

ring, note, tone, beep, bleep, warble, alarm.
3 (informal) *give me a buzz.* See **CALL** noun sense
3. **4** (informal) *the buzz is that he's gone.* See
RUMOUR. **5** (informal) *I get a buzz out of stunt
flying:* **thrill**, glow, tingle; informal kick, hit,
lift, high; N. Amer. informal charge.
verb **1** *bees buzzed in the clover:* **hum**, drone,
bumble, murmur; Brit. informal zizz. **2** *the
intercom on her desk buzzed:* **sound**, go
off, warble, purr, ring, beep, bleep. **3** *the
club is buzzing with excitement:* **hum**, throb,
vibrate, pulse, bustle.

bygone adjective *those are the values of a
bygone age:* **past**, former, olden, earlier,
previous, one-time, long-ago, of old, ancient,
antiquated; departed, dead, extinct, defunct,
out of date, outmoded; literary of yore.
–OPPOSITES present, recent.

bypass noun *traffic will get heavier when
the new bypass opens:* **ring road**, detour,
diversion, alternative route; Brit. relief road.

verb **1** *bypass the farm and continue to the
main road:* **go round**, go past, make a detour
round; avoid. **2** *anyone can bypass their GP
and go straight to a clinic:* **ignore**, pass over,
omit, neglect, go over the head of; informal
short-circuit.

by-product noun *he saw poverty as the
by-product of colonial prosperity:* **side
effect**, consequence, entailment, corollary;
ramification, repercussion, spin-off, fallout;
fruits; Brit. knock-on effect.

bystander noun *the police had shot an
innocent bystander:* **onlooker**, looker-
on, passer-by, non-participant, observer,
spectator, eyewitness, witness, watcher;
informal gawper, rubberneck.

byword noun *the Court had become was a
byword for administrative delay:* **perfect
example**, classic case, model, exemplar,
embodiment, incarnation, personification,
epitome, typification.

b

Cc

cab noun **1** *she hailed a cab:* **taxi**, taxi cab; Brit minicab, hackney carriage; N. Amer. hack. **2** *a truck driver's cab:* **(driver's) compartment**, cabin.

cabal noun *a cabal of dissidents:* **clique**, faction, coterie, cell, sect, camarilla; pressure group; Brit. ginger group.

cabaret noun **1** *the evening's cabaret:* **entertainment**, (floor) show, performance. **2** *the cabarets of Montreal:* **nightclub**, club, boîte; N. Amer. cafe; informal nightspot, niterie, clip joint; N. Amer. informal honky-tonk.

cabin noun **1** *a first-class cabin:* **berth**, stateroom, deckhouse. **2** *a cabin by the lake:* **hut**, log cabin, shanty, shack; chalet; Scottish bothy; N. Amer. cabana; Austral. mia-mia. **3** *the driver's cabin:* **cab**, compartment.

cabinet noun **1** *a walnut cabinet:* **cupboard**, bureau, chest of drawers. **2** *the new cabinet:* **senior ministers**, ministry, council, executive.

cable noun **1** *a thick cable moored the ship:* **rope**, cord, line, guy; Nautical hawser, stay, shroud, bridle; N. Amer. choker. **2** *electric cables:* **wire**, lead, power line; Brit. flex; N. Amer. cord.

cache noun **1** *a cache of arms:* **hoard**, store, stockpile, stock, supply, reserve; arsenal; informal stash. **2** *a niche used as a cache:* **hiding place**, secret place; informal hidey-hole.

cachet noun *no other shipping company had quite the cachet of Cunard:* **prestige**, prestigiousness, status, standing, kudos, snob value, stature, pre-eminence, eminence; street credibility.

cackle verb **1** *the geese cackled at him:* **squawk**, cluck. **2** *Noel cackled with glee:* **guffaw**, crow, chortle, chuckle.

cacophonous adjective *cacophonous rock music blared from the speakers:* **loud**, noisy, ear-splitting, raucous, discordant, dissonant, inharmonious, unmelodious, unmusical, tuneless.
– OPPOSITES harmonious.

cacophony noun *a cacophony of deafening alarm bells:* **din**, racket, noise, discord, dissonance, discordance.

cadaverous adjective *his cadaverous face:* **(deathly) pale**, pallid, ashen, grey, whey-faced, etiolated, corpse-like; as thin as a rake, bony, skeletal, emaciated, skin-and-bones, haggard, gaunt, drawn, pinched, hollow-cheeked, hollow-eyed; informal like a bag of bones, anorexic.
– OPPOSITES rosy, plump.

cadence noun *there is a biblical cadence in the last words he utters:* **rhythm**, tempo, metre, beat, pulse; intonation, modulation, lilt.

cadge verb (informal) *can I cadge a lift?* **scrounge**, borrow; informal bum, touch someone for, sponge; Brit. informal scab; N. Amer. informal mooch; Austral./NZ informal bludge.

cadre noun *a cadre of professional managers:* **corps**, body, team, group.

cafe noun **snack bar**, cafeteria, buffet; coffee bar/shop, tea room/shop; bistro, brasserie; N. Amer. diner; informal eatery; Brit. informal caff.

cafeteria noun **self-service restaurant**, canteen, cafe, buffet.

cage noun *animals in cages:* **enclosure**, pen, pound; coop, hutch; birdcage, aviary; N. Amer. corral.
verb *many animals are caged:* **confine**, shut in/up, pen, coop up, immure, impound; N. Amer. corral.

cagey adjective (informal) *he was rather cagey about his plans:* **secretive**, guarded, non-committal, tight-lipped, reticent, evasive; informal playing one's cards close to one's chest.
– OPPOSITES open.

cahoots
■ **in cahoots** (informal) **in league**, colluding, in collusion, conspiring, collaborating, hand in glove.

cajole verb *he had been cajoled into escorting Nadia to a concert:* **persuade**, wheedle, coax, talk into, prevail on, blarney; informal sweet-talk, soft-soap, twist someone's arm.

cajolery noun **persuasion**, wheedling, coaxing, inveiglement, cajolement; blandishments, blarney; informal sweet talk, soft soap, arm-twisting.

cake noun **1** *cream cakes:* **bun**, pastry, gateau. **2** *a cake of soap:* **bar**, tablet, block, slab, lump.
verb **1** *boots caked with mud:* **coat**, encrust, plaster, cover. **2** *the blood was beginning to cake:* **clot**, congeal, coagulate, solidify, set, inspissate.

calamitous adjective *the consequences of his decision were calamitous:* **disastrous**, catastrophic, cataclysmic, devastating, dire, tragic.

calamity noun *the fire was only the latest calamity to strike the area:* **disaster**, catastrophe, tragedy, cataclysm, adversity, tribulation, affliction, misfortune, misadventure.
– OPPOSITES godsend.

calculate verb **1** *the interest is calculated on a daily basis:* **compute**, work out, reckon, figure; add up/together, count up, tally, total; Brit. tot up. **2** *his words were calculated to wound her:* **intend**, mean, design.

calculated adjective *victims of vicious and calculated assaults:* **deliberate**, premeditated, planned, pre-planned, preconceived, intentional, intended.
– OPPOSITES unintentional.

calculating adjective *he was a coolly calculating, ruthless man:* **cunning**, crafty, wily, shrewd, scheming, devious, designing, Machiavellian; informal foxy.
– OPPOSITES ingenuous.

calculation noun **1** *the calculation of the overall cost:* **computation**, reckoning, adding up, counting up, working out, figuring; Brit. totting up. **2** *the government's political calculations:* **assessment**, judgement; forecast, projection, prediction.

calendar noun **1** almanac. **2** *my social calendar:* **schedule**, programme, diary.

calibre noun **1** *they could ill afford to lose a man of his calibre:* **quality**, merit, distinction, stature, excellence, pre-eminence; ability, expertise, talent, capability, capacity, proficiency. **2** *if only they could play rugby of this calibre every week:* **standard**, level, quality. **3** *the calibre of a gun:* **bore**, diameter, gauge.

call verb **1** *'Wait for me!' she called:* **cry (out)**, shout, yell, bellow, roar, bawl, scream, vociferate; informal holler. **2** *Mum called me in the morning:* **wake (up)**, awaken, rouse; Brit. informal knock up. **3** *I'll call you tomorrow:* **phone**, telephone, get someone on the phone; Brit. ring (up), give someone a ring; informal call up, give someone a buzz; Brit. informal give someone a bell/tinkle, get someone on the blower; N. Amer. informal get someone on the horn. **4** *Rose called a taxi:* **summon**, send for, order. **5** *he called at Ashgrove Cottage:* **pay a (brief) visit to**, visit, pay a call on, call/drop/look in on, drop/stop by, pop into. **6** *the prime minister called a meeting:* **convene**, summon, assemble; formal convoke. **7** *they called their daughter Hannah:* **name**, christen, baptize; designate, style, term, dub. **8** *I would call him a friend:* **describe as**, regard as, look on as, consider to be.

noun **1** *I heard calls from the auditorium:* **cry**, shout, yell, roar, scream, exclamation, vociferation; informal holler. **2** *the call of the water rail:* **cry**, song, sound. **3** *I'll give you a call tomorrow:* **phone call**, telephone call;

Brit. ring; informal buzz; Brit. informal bell, tinkle. **4** *he paid a call on Harold:* **visit**, social call. **5** *a call for party unity:* **appeal**, request, plea, entreaty. **6** *the last call for passengers on flight BA701:* **summons**, request. **7** *there's no call for that kind of language:* **need**, necessity, reason, justification, excuse. **8** *there's no call for expensive wine here:* **demand**, desire, market. **9** *the call of the Cairngorms:* **attraction**, appeal, lure, allure, spell, pull, draw.
■ **call for 1** *desperate times call for desperate measures:* require, need, necessitate; justify, warrant. **2** *I'll call for you around seven:* pick up, collect, fetch.
■ **call something off** *the proposed tour of Australia was called off:* cancel, abandon, scrap, drop, axe; informal scrub, nix; N. Amer. informal redline.
■ **call on 1** *I might call on her later:* visit, pay a call on, go and see, look/drop in on; N. Amer. visit with; informal look up, pop in on. **2** *he called on the government to hold a plebiscite:* appeal to, ask, request, petition, urge. **3** *we are able to call on qualified staff:* have recourse to, avail oneself of, draw on, make use of.
■ **call someone up 1** (informal) *Roland called me up.* See CALL verb sense 3. **2** *they called up the reservists:* enlist, recruit, conscript; US draft. **3** *he was called up for the England team:* select, pick, choose; Brit. cap.
■ **on call** on duty, on standby, available.

call girl noun **prostitute**, whore, sex worker, fille de joie; informal tart, pro, working girl; N. Amer. informal hooker, hustler; euphemistic escort, masseuse.

calling noun *he considered engineering one of the highest possible callings:* **profession**, occupation, vocation, career, work, employment, job, business, trade, craft, line (of work).

callous adjective *his callous disregard for the feelings and wishes of others:* **heartless**, unfeeling, uncaring, cold, cold-hearted, hard, as hard as nails, hard-hearted, stony-hearted, insensitive, lacking compassion, hardbitten, unsympathetic.
– OPPOSITES kind, compassionate.

callow adjective *a callow youth:* **immature**, inexperienced, juvenile, adolescent, naive, green, raw, untried, unworldly, unsophisticated; informal wet behind the ears.
– OPPOSITES mature.

calm adjective **1** *she seemed very calm:* **serene**, tranquil, relaxed, unruffled, unperturbed, unflustered, untroubled; equable, even-tempered; placid, unexcitable, unemotional, phlegmatic; composed, {cool, calm, and collected}, cool-headed, self-possessed; informal unflappable, unfazed. **2** *the night was calm:* **windless**, still, tranquil, quiet. **3** *the calm waters of the lake:* **tranquil**, still, smooth, glassy, like a millpond.
– OPPOSITES excited, nervous, stormy.
noun **1** *calm prevailed:* **tranquillity**, stillness,

C

calmness, quiet, quietness, quietude, peace, peacefulness. **2** *his usual calm deserted him:* **composure**, coolness, calmness, self-possession, sangfroid; serenity, tranquillity, equanimity, equability, placidness, placidity; informal cool, unflappability.
verb **1** *I tried to calm him down:* **soothe**, pacify, placate, mollify, appease, conciliate; Brit. quieten (down); Austral. square off. **2** *she forced herself to calm down:* **compose oneself**, recover/regain one's composure, control oneself, pull oneself together, simmer down, cool down/off, take it easy; Brit. quieten down; informal get a grip, keep one's shirt on, wind down; N. Amer. informal chill out, hang/stay loose, decompress.
– OPPOSITES excite, upset.

calumny noun *a bitter struggle marked by calumny and litigation:* **slander**, defamation (of character), character assassination, libel; vilification, traducement, obloquy, verbal abuse, revilement; informal mud-slinging.

camaraderie noun *he enjoyed the camaraderie of army life:* **friendship**, comradeship, fellowship, companionship; mutual support, team spirit, esprit de corps.

camouflage noun **1** *pieces of turf served for camouflage:* **disguise**, concealment. **2** *her indifference was merely camouflage:* **facade**, (false) front, smokescreen, cover-up, mask, blind, screen, masquerade, dissimulation, pretence.
verb *the caravan was camouflaged with branches:* **disguise**, hide, conceal, keep hidden, mask, screen, cover (up).

camp¹ noun **1** *an army camp:* **bivouac**, encampment; campsite, camping ground. **2** *the liberal and conservative camps:* **faction**, wing, group, lobby, caucus, bloc, coterie, sect, cabal.
verb *they camped in a field:* **pitch tents**, set up camp, encamp, bivouac.

camp² (informal) adjective **1** *a highly camp actor:* **effeminate**, effete, mincing; informal campy, limp-wristed; Brit. informal poncey. **2** *camp humour:* **exaggerated**, theatrical, affected; informal over the top, OTT, camped up.
– OPPOSITES macho.
■ **camp it up** posture, behave theatrically/affectedly, overact; informal ham it up.

campaign noun **1** *Napoleon's Russian campaign:* **military operation(s)**, manoeuvre(s); crusade, war, battle, offensive, attack. **2** *the campaign to reduce vehicle emissions:* **crusade**, drive, push, struggle; operation, strategy, battle plan.
verb **1** *they are campaigning for political reform:* **crusade**, fight, battle, push, press, strive, struggle, lobby. **2** *she campaigned as a political outsider:* **run/stand for office**, canvass, electioneer; N. Amer. stump.

campaigner noun **crusader**, fighter, activist; champion, advocate, promoter.

can noun **tin**, canister, jerrycan.

canal noun **1** *barges chugged up the canal:* **inland waterway**. **2** *the ear canal:* **duct**, tube, passage.

cancel verb **1** *the match was cancelled:* **call off**, abandon, scrap, drop, axe; informal scrub, nix; N. Amer. informal redline. **2** *his visa has been cancelled:* **annul**, invalidate, nullify, declare null and void, void; revoke, rescind, retract, countermand, withdraw. **3** *rising unemployment cancelled out earlier economic gains:* **neutralize**, counterbalance, counteract, balance (out), countervail; negate, nullify, wipe out, negative.

cancer noun **1** *most skin cancers are curable:* **malignant growth**, cancerous growth, tumour, malignancy. **2** *racism is a cancer:* **evil**, blight, scourge, poison, canker, plague.

candid adjective **1** *his responses were remarkably candid:* **frank**, outspoken, forthright, blunt, open, honest, truthful, sincere, direct, plain-spoken, bluff; informal upfront, on the level; N. Amer. informal on the up and up. **2** *it's better to let the photographer mingle and take candid shots:* **unposed**, informal, uncontrived, impromptu, natural.
– OPPOSITES guarded.

candidate noun **1** *candidates should be computer-literate:* **(job) applicant**, job-seeker, interviewee; contender, nominee, possible; Brit. informal runner. **2** *A-level candidates:* **examinee**, entrant.

candour noun *a man of refreshing candour:* **frankness**, openness, honesty, candidness, truthfulness, sincerity, forthrightness, directness, plain-spokenness, bluffness, bluntness, outspokenness; informal telling it like it is.

candy noun (N. Amer.). See CONFECTIONERY.

cane noun **1** *a silver-topped cane:* **(walking) stick**, staff; alpenstock; crook; Austral./NZ waddy. **2** *tie the shoot to a cane:* **stick**, stake, upright, pole. **3** *he was been beaten with a cane:* **stick**, rod, birch; N. Amer. informal paddle.
verb *Matthew was caned for bullying:* **beat**, strike, hit, flog, thrash, lash, birch, flagellate; informal give someone a hiding, larrup; N. Amer. informal whale.

canker noun **1** *this plant is susceptible to canker:* **fungal disease**, plant rot; blight. **2** *ear cankers:* **ulcer**, ulceration, infection, sore, abscess. **3** *racism remains a canker.* See CANCER sense 2.

cannabis noun **marijuana**, hashish, bhang, hemp, kif, ganja, sinsemilla, skunkweed; informal hash, dope, grass, skunk, pot, blow, draw, the weed, reefer; Brit. informal wacky baccy; N. Amer. informal locoweed.

cannibal noun **maneater**, people-eater.

cannon noun **mounted gun**, field gun, piece of artillery; mortar, howitzer.
verb *the couple behind cannoned into us:* **collide with**, hit, run into, crash into, plough into.

canny adjective *canny investors:* **shrewd**, astute, smart, sharp, sharp-witted,

discerning, penetrating, discriminating, perceptive, perspicacious, wise, sagacious; cunning, crafty, wily; N. Amer. as sharp as a tack; informal savvy; Brit. informal suss, sussed; N. Amer. informal heads-up.
– OPPOSITES foolish.

canoe noun **kayak**, dugout, outrigger, bidarka, pirogue, waka.

canon noun **1** *the canons of fair play and equal opportunity:* **principle**, rule, law, tenet, precept; standard, convention, criterion, measure. **2** *a set of ecclesiastical canons:* **law**, decree, edict, statute, dictate, decretal. **3** *the Shakespeare canon:* **(list of) works**, writings, oeuvre.

canonical adjective **1** *the canonical method:* **recognized**, authoritative, authorized, accepted, sanctioned, approved, established, orthodox. **2** *canonical rites:* **according to ecclesiastical law**, official, sanctioned.
– OPPOSITES unorthodox.

canopy noun **awning**, shade, sunshade; baldachin, tester, chuppah, velarium.

cant[1] noun **1** *religious cant:* **hypocrisy**, sanctimoniousness, sanctimony, humbug, pietism. **2** *thieves' cant:* **slang**, jargon, idiom, argot, patois, speech, terminology, language; informal lingo, -speak, -ese.

cant[2] verb *the deck canted some twenty degrees:* **tilt**, lean, slant, slope, incline; tip, list, bank, heel.
noun *the cant of the walls:* **slope**, slant, tilt, angle, inclination.

cantankerous adjective *a cantankerous old man:* **bad-tempered**, irascible, irritable, grumpy, grouchy, crotchety, tetchy, testy, crusty, curmudgeonly, ill-tempered, ill-humoured, peevish, cross, fractious, pettish, crabbed, crabby, prickly, touchy; informal snappish, snappy, chippy; Brit. informal shirty, stroppy, narky, ratty; N. Amer. informal cranky, ornery; Austral./NZ informal snaky.
– OPPOSITES affable.

canteen noun **1** *the staff canteen:* **restaurant**, cafeteria, refectory, mess hall; Brit. Military NAAFI; N. Amer. lunchroom. **2** *a canteen of water:* **container**, flask, bottle.

canvass verb **1** *he's canvassing for the Green Party:* **campaign**, electioneer; N. Amer. stump; Brit. informal doorstep. **2** *they promised to canvass all members:* **poll**, question, ask, survey, interview. **3** *they're canvassing support:* **seek**, try to obtain. **4** *early retirement was canvassed as a solution:* **propose**, suggest, discuss, debate, consider.

canyon noun **ravine**, gorge, gully, defile, couloir; chasm, abyss, gulf; N. Amer. gulch, coulee.

cap noun **1** *a small bottle with a white plastic cap:* **lid**, top, stopper, cork, bung, spile; N. Amer. stopple. **2** *the cap on spending:* **(upper) limit**, ceiling; curb, check.
verb **1** *mountains capped with snow:* **top**, crown, cover, coat. **2** *his innings capped a*

great day: **round off**, crown, be a fitting climax to. **3** *they tried to cap each other's stories:* **beat**, better, improve on, surpass, outdo, outshine, top, upstage. **4** (Brit.) *he was capped for England:* **choose**, select, pick, give someone the nod. **5** *budgets will be capped:* **set a limit on**, limit, restrict; curb, control, peg.

capability noun *the company's capability to increase productivity:* **ability**, capacity, power, potential; competence, proficiency, accomplishment, adeptness, aptitude, faculty, experience, skill, skilfulness, talent, flair; informal know-how.

capable adjective *a very capable young woman:* **competent**, able, efficient, effective, proficient, accomplished, adept, handy, experienced, skilful, skilled, talented, gifted; informal useful.
– OPPOSITES incompetent.
■ **be capable of 1** *I'm quite capable of looking after myself:* have the ability to, be equal to (the task of), be up to; informal have what it takes to. **2** *the strange events are capable of rational explanation:* be open/susceptible to, admit of, allow of.

capacious adjective *she rummaged in her capacious handbag:* **roomy**, spacious, ample, big, large, sizeable, generous.
– OPPOSITES cramped, small.

capacity noun **1** *the capacity of the freezer:* **volume**, size, magnitude, dimensions, measurements, proportions. **2** *his capacity to inspire trust.* See **CAPABILITY**. **3** *in his capacity as Commander-in-Chief:* **position**, post, job, office; role, function.

cape[1] noun *a woollen cape:* **cloak**, mantle, cope, wrap, stole, tippet, poncho.

cape[2] noun *the ship rounded the cape:* **headland**, promontory, point, head, foreland; horn, hook, bill, ness, mull.

caper verb *children were capering about:* **skip**, dance, romp, frisk, gambol, cavort, prance, frolic, leap, hop, jump.
noun **1** *she did a little caper:* **dance**, skip, hop, leap, jump, curvet, gambado. **2** (informal) *I'm too old for this kind of caper:* **escapade**, stunt, prank, trick, mischief, antics, high jinks, skylarking; informal lark, shenanigans.

capital noun **1** *Warsaw is the capital of Poland:* **first city**, seat of government, metropolis. **2** *he had enough capital to pull off the deal:* **money**, finance(s), funds, the wherewithal, the means, assets, wealth, resources, investment capital; informal dough, bread, loot; Brit. informal dosh, brass, lolly, spondulicks; US informal greenbacks; N. Amer. informal bucks; Austral./NZ informal Oscar. **3** *he wrote the name in capitals:* **capital letter**, upper-case letter, block capital; informal cap.

capitalism noun **private enterprise**, free enterprise, the free market.
– OPPOSITES communism.

capitalist noun **financier**, investor, industrialist; magnate, tycoon.

capitalize verb *the capacity to capitalize new ventures:* **finance**, fund, underwrite, provide capital for, back; N. Amer. informal bankroll, stake.
■ **capitalize on** take advantage of, profit from, make the most of, exploit; informal cash in on.

capitulate verb *the patriots had to capitulate to the enemy forces:* **surrender**, give in, yield, concede defeat, give up the struggle, submit; lay down one's arms, raise/show the white flag, throw in the towel/sponge.
– OPPOSITES resist, hold out.

caprice noun **1** *his wife's caprices and demands made his life impossible:* **whim**, whimsy, vagary, fancy, fad, quirk, eccentricity, foible. **2** *the staff tired of his caprice:* **fickleness**, changeableness, volatility, capriciousness, unpredictability.

capricious adjective *the capricious workings of fate:* **fickle**, inconstant, changeable, variable, mercurial, volatile, unpredictable, temperamental; whimsical, fanciful, flighty, quirky, faddish.
– OPPOSITES consistent.

capsize verb *the craft capsized in heavy seas:* **overturn**, turn over, turn upside down, upend, flip/tip/keel over, turn turtle.
– OPPOSITES right.

capsule noun **1** *he swallowed a capsule:* **pill**, tablet, lozenge, pastille, drop; informal tab. **2** *a space capsule:* **module**, craft, probe.

captain noun **1** *the ship's captain:* **commander**, master; informal skipper. **2** *the team's captain:* **leader**, head; informal boss, skipper. **3** *a captain of industry:* **magnate**, tycoon, industrialist; chief, head, leader, principal; informal boss, number one, bigwig, big shot/gun, honcho, top dog; N. Amer. informal kahuna, top banana.
verb *a vessel captained by a cut-throat:* **command**, run, be in charge of, control, manage, govern; informal skipper.

caption noun **title**, heading, wording, head, legend, rubric, slogan.

captious adjective *a captious teacher:* **critical**, fault-finding, quibbling, cavilling; hypercritical, pedantic, hair-splitting; informal nit-picking, pernickety.
– OPPOSITES forgiving.

captivate verb *he was captivated by her beauty:* **enthral**, charm, enchant, bewitch, fascinate, beguile, entrance, enrapture, delight, attract, allure.
– OPPOSITES repel, bore.

captive noun *release the captives:* **prisoner**, convict, detainee, inmate; prisoner of war, POW, internee; informal jailbird, con; Brit. informal (old) lag; N. Amer. informal yardbird.
adjective *captive wild animals:* **confined**, caged, incarcerated, locked up; jailed, imprisoned, in prison, interned, detained, in captivity, under lock and key, behind bars.

captivity noun *the third month of their captivity passed:* **imprisonment**, confinement, internment, incarceration, detention.
– OPPOSITES freedom.

captor noun **jailer**, guard, incarcerator, keeper.

capture verb **1** *the spy was captured in Moscow:* **catch**, apprehend, seize, arrest; take prisoner/captive, imprison, detain, put/throw in jail, put behind bars, put under lock and key, incarcerate; informal nab, collar, lift, pick up, pull in; Brit. informal nick. **2** *guerrillas captured a strategic district:* **occupy**, invade, conquer, seize, take (possession of). **3** *the music captured the atmosphere of a summer morning:* **express**, reproduce, represent, encapsulate. **4** *the tales of pirates captured the children's imaginations:* **engage**, attract, catch, seize, hold.
– OPPOSITES free.
noun *he tried to evade capture:* **arrest**, apprehension, seizure, being taken prisoner/captive, imprisonment.

car noun **1** *he drove up in his car:* **motor (car)**, automobile; informal wheels; N. Amer. informal auto. **2** *the dining car:* **carriage**, coach; Brit. saloon.

carafe noun **flask**, jug, pitcher, decanter, flagon.

caravan noun **1** *a fishing holiday in a caravan:* **mobile home**, camper, caravanette; N. Amer. trailer; Brit. trademark Dormobile. **2** *a gypsy caravan:* **wagon**, covered cart. **3** *a refugee caravan:* **convoy**, procession, column, train.

carbuncle noun **boil**, sore, abscess, pustule, wen, whitlow.

carcass noun **corpse**, (dead) body, remains; Medicine cadaver; informal stiff.

card noun **1** *a piece of stiff card:* **cardboard**, pasteboard, board. **2** *I'll send her a card:* **greetings card**, postcard. **3** *she produced her card:* **identification**, ID, credentials; business card. **4** *she paid with her card:* **credit card**, debit card, cash card, swipe card; informal plastic. **5** *the cards were dealt:* **playing card**, (cards) pack of cards.

cardinal adjective *one of the cardinal rules of the sea was to stay by your boat:* **fundamental**, basic, main, chief, primary, prime, principal, paramount, pre-eminent, highest, key, essential.
– OPPOSITES unimportant.

care noun **1** *foster-parents had the care of the child:* **safe keeping**, supervision, custody, charge, protection, control, responsibility; guardianship, wardship. **2** *handle with care:* **caution**, carefulness, heedfulness, heed, attention, attentiveness. **3** *she chose her words with care:* **discretion**, judiciousness, forethought, thought, regard, heed, mindfulness; accuracy, precision. **4** *a place where you can escape from the cares of the day:* **worry**, anxiety, trouble, concern, stress, pressure, strain; sorrow, woe, hardship. **5** *a*

*life of unblemished virtue and constant care
for others:* **concern**, consideration, thought,
regard, solicitude.
– OPPOSITES neglect, carelessness.
verb *the teachers didn't care about our
work:* **be concerned**, worry (oneself),
trouble/concern oneself, bother, mind, be
interested; informal give a damn/hoot/rap.
■ **care for** *he obviously cares for his
children:* love, be fond of, be devoted to,
treasure, adore, dote on, think the world of,
worship, idolize. *2 would you care for a cup
of coffee?* like, want, desire, fancy, feel like.
3 *the hospice cares for the terminally ill:* look
after, take care of, tend, attend to, minister
to, nurse; be responsible for, keep safe, keep
an eye on.

career noun **1** *a business career:* **profession**,
occupation, vocation, calling, employment,
line (of work), walk of life, métier. **2** *a
chequered career:* **existence**, life, course,
passage, path.
adjective *a career politician:* **professional**,
permanent, full-time.
verb *they careered down the hill:* **rush**, hurtle,
streak, shoot, race, bolt, dash, speed, run,
whizz, zoom, flash, blast, charge, hare, fly,
pelt, go like the wind; informal belt, scoot, tear,
zap, zip, whip, go like a bat out of hell; Brit.
informal bomb, bucket; N. Amer. informal hightail,
clip.

carefree adjective *we were young and
carefree:* **unworried**, untroubled, blithe,
airy, nonchalant, insouciant, happy-go-
lucky, free and easy, easy-going, relaxed;
informal laid-back.
– OPPOSITES careworn.

careful adjective **1** *be careful when you
go up the stairs:* **cautious**, heedful, alert,
attentive, watchful, vigilant, wary, on
guard, circumspect. **2** *his mother had always
been careful with money:* **prudent**, thrifty,
economical, sparing, frugal, scrimping,
abstemious; informal stingy. **3** *careful
consideration of the facts:* **attentive**,
conscientious, painstaking, meticulous,
diligent, assiduous, sedulous, scrupulous,
punctilious, methodical; informal pernickety.
– OPPOSITES careless, extravagant.

careless adjective **1** *careless motorists:*
inattentive, incautious, negligent, remiss;
heedless, irresponsible, impetuous,
reckless. **2** *careless work:* **shoddy**, slapdash,
slipshod, scrappy, slovenly, negligent,
lax, slack, disorganized, hasty, hurried;
informal sloppy, slap-happy. **3** *a careless
remark:* **thoughtless**, insensitive, indiscreet,
unguarded, incautious, inadvertent.
4 *careless masculine grace:* **unstudied**,
artless, casual, effortless, nonchalant,
insouciant, languid.
– OPPOSITES careful, meticulous.

caress verb *she caressed the girl's forehead:*
stroke, touch, fondle, brush, skim, nuzzle.

caretaker noun **janitor**, attendant,
porter, custodian, concierge; N. Amer.

superintendent.
adjective *the caretaker manager:* **temporary**,
short-term, provisional, substitute, acting,
interim, pro tem, stand-in, fill-in, stopgap;
N. Amer. informal pinch-hitting.
– OPPOSITES permanent.

careworn adjective *a careworn expression:*
worried, anxious, harassed, strained,
stressed; drained, drawn, gaunt, haggard;
informal hassled.
– OPPOSITES carefree.

cargo noun **freight**, load, haul, consignment,
delivery, shipment; goods, merchandise.

caricature noun *a caricature of the Prime
Minister:* **cartoon**, parody, satire, lampoon,
burlesque; informal send-up, take-off.
verb *she has turned to caricaturing her fellow
actors:* **parody**, satirize, lampoon, make fun
of, burlesque; informal send up, take off.

caring adjective *his friend was a bright
student and a caring person:* **kind**,
kind-hearted, warm-hearted, tender;
concerned, attentive, thoughtful, solicitous,
considerate; affectionate, loving, doting,
fond; sympathetic, understanding,
compassionate, feeling.
– OPPOSITES cruel.

carnage noun *the carnage of the First
World War:* **slaughter**, massacre, mass
murder, butchery, bloodbath, bloodletting;
holocaust, pogrom, ethnic cleansing.

carnal adjective *carnal desire:* **sexual**, sensual,
erotic, lustful, lascivious, libidinous,
lecherous, licentious; physical, bodily,
corporeal, fleshly.
– OPPOSITES spiritual.

carnival noun **1** *the town's carnival:* **festival**,
fiesta, fête, gala, jamboree, celebration. **2** (N.
Amer.) *he worked at a carnival:* **funfair**, circus,
fair, amusement show.

carnivorous adjective *a carnivorous lizard:*
meat-eating, predatory, of prey.
– OPPOSITES herbivorous.

carol noun *children sang carols:* **Christmas
song**, hymn, canticle.
verb *Boris carolled happily:* **sing**, trill, warble,
chirp.

carouse verb *they danced and caroused until
the drink ran out:* **drink and make merry**,
go on a drinking bout, go on a spree; revel,
celebrate, roister; informal booze, go boozing,
binge, go on a binge, go on a bender, paint
the town red, party, rave, make whoopee,
whoop it up; Brit. informal go on the bevvy.

carp verb *the opposition parties constantly
carp about the level of pensions in Britain:*
complain, cavil, grumble, grouse, whine,
bleat, nag; informal gripe, grouch, beef,
bellyache, moan, bitch, whinge; Brit. informal
be on at someone; N. English informal mither;
N. Amer. informal kvetch.
– OPPOSITES praise.

carpenter noun **woodworker**, joiner,
cabinet-maker; Brit. informal chippy.

carpet noun **1** *a Turkish carpet:* **rug**, mat,

c

matting, floor covering. **2** *a carpet of wild flowers:* **covering**, blanket, layer, cover, cloak, mantle.
verb **1** *the gravel was carpeted in moss:* **cover**, coat, overlay, overspread, blanket. **2** (Brit. informal) *an officer was carpeted for leaking information.* See **REPRIMAND** verb.

carriage noun **1** *a railway carriage:* **coach**, car; Brit. saloon. **2** *a horse and carriage:* **wagon**, hackney, hansom, gig, landau, trap. **3** *the carriage of bikes on trains:* **transport**, transportation, conveyance, carrying, movement, shipment.

carrier noun **bearer**, conveyor, transporter; porter, courier, haulier.

carry verb **1** *she carried the box into the kitchen:* **convey**, transfer, move, take, bring, bear, lug, fetch; informal cart, hump. **2** *a coach operator carrying 12 million passengers a year:* **transport**, convey, move, handle. **3** *satellites carry the signal over the Atlantic:* **transmit**, conduct, relay, communicate, convey, dispatch, beam. **4** *the dinghy can carry the weight of the baggage:* **support**, sustain, stand; prop up, shore up, bolster. **5** *managers carry most responsibility:* **undertake**, accept, assume, bear, shoulder, take on (oneself). **6** *she was carrying his baby:* **be pregnant with**, bear, expect. **7** *she carried herself with assurance:* **conduct**, bear, hold; act, behave, acquit; formal comport. **8** *a resolution was carried:* **approve**, vote for, accept, endorse, ratify; agree to, assent to, rubber-stamp; informal OK, give the thumbs up to. **9** *I carried the whole audience:* **win over**, sway, convince, persuade, influence; motivate, stimulate. **10** *today's paper carried an article on housing policy:* **publish**, print, communicate, distribute; broadcast, transmit. **11** *his voice carried across the quay:* **be audible**, travel, reach.
■ **be/get carried away** lose self-control, get overexcited, go too far; informal flip, lose it.
■ **carry someone off** kill (off), cause the death of, take/end the life of, finish off; informal do in.
■ **carry something off 1** *she carried off four awards:* win, secure, gain, achieve, collect; informal land, net, bag, scoop. **2** *he has carried it off:* succeed, triumph, be victorious, be successful, do well, make good; informal crack it.
■ **carry on 1** *they carried on arguing:* continue, keep (on), go on; persist in, persevere in; informal stick with/at. **2** (informal) *she was carrying on with other men:* have an affair, commit adultery, have a fling; informal play around, mess about/around; Brit. informal play away; N. Amer. informal fool around.
■ **carry something on** *a bank carrying on a bona fide business:* engage in, conduct, undertake, be involved in, carry out, perform.
■ **carry something out 1** *they carried out a Caesarean:* conduct, perform, implement, execute. **2** *I carried out my promise to her:*

fulfil, carry through, honour, redeem, make good; keep, observe, abide by, comply with, adhere to, stick to, keep faith with.

cart noun **1** *a horse-drawn cart:* **wagon**, carriage, dray. **2** *a man with a cart took their luggage:* **handcart**, pushcart, trolley, barrow.

carton noun **box**, package, cardboard box, container, pack, packet.

cartoon noun **1** *a cartoon of the Prime Minister:* **caricature**, parody, lampoon, satire; informal take-off, send-up. **2** *he was reading cartoons:* **comic strip**, comic, graphic novel. **3** *they watched cartoons on television:* **animated film**, animation.

cartridge noun **1** *a toner cartridge:* **cassette**, magazine, canister, container. **2** *a rifle cartridge:* **bullet**, round, shell, charge, shot.

carve verb **1** *he carved horn handles:* **sculpt**, sculpture; cut, hew, whittle; form, shape, fashion. **2** *I carved my initials on the tree:* **engrave**, etch, incise, score. **3** *he carved the roast chicken:* **slice**, cut up, chop.
■ **carve something up** divide, partition, apportion, subdivide, split up, break up; share out, dole out; informal divvy up.

carving noun **sculpture**, model, statue, statuette, figure, figurine.

cascade noun **waterfall**, cataract, falls, rapids, white water.
verb *rain cascaded from the roof:* **pour**, gush, surge, spill, stream, flow, issue, spurt, jet.

case¹ noun **1** *a classic case of overreaction:* **instance**, occurrence, manifestation, demonstration, exposition, exhibition; example, illustration, specimen, sample, exemplification. **2** *if that is the case I will have to find somebody else:* **situation**, position, state of affairs, the lie of the land; circumstances, conditions, facts, how things stand; Brit. state of play; informal score. **3** *the officers on the case:* **investigation**, enquiry, examination, exploration, probe, search, inquest. **4** *urgent cases were turned away from the hospital:* **patient**, sick person, invalid, sufferer, victim. **5** *he lost his case and was ordered to pay £1.5 million in damages:* **lawsuit**, (legal) action, legal dispute, suit, trial, legal/judicial proceedings, litigation. **6** *the book makes a strong case for new research methods:* **argument**, contention, reasoning, logic, defence, justification, vindication, exposition, thesis.

case² noun **1** *a cigarette case:* **container**, box, canister, receptacle, holder. **2** *a seed case:* **casing**, cover, covering, sheath, sheathing, envelope, sleeve, jacket, integument. **3** (Brit.) *she threw some clothes into a case:* **suitcase**, (travelling) bag, valise, portmanteau; (**cases**) luggage, baggage. **4** *a case of wine:* **crate**, box, pack, twelve bottles. **5** *a glass display case:* **cabinet**, cupboard.
verb **1** *the rifle is cased in wood:* **cover**, surround, encase, sheathe, envelop. **2** (informal) *a thief casing the joint:*

reconnoitre, inspect, examine, survey, explore; informal recce, check out.

cash noun **1** *a wallet stuffed with cash:* **money**, currency, hard cash; (bank) notes, coins, change; N. Amer. bills; informal dough, bread, loot, readies, moolah; Brit. informal dosh, brass, lolly, spondulicks; US informal greenbacks; N. Amer. informal bucks, dinero; Austral./NZ informal Oscar. **2** *a lack of cash:* **finance**, money, resources, funds, assets, the means, the wherewithal.
– OPPOSITES cheque, credit.
verb *the bank cashed her cheque:* **exchange**, change, convert into cash/money; honour, pay, accept; Brit. encash.
■ **cash in on** take advantage of, exploit, milk; make money from, profit from; informal make a killing out of.

cashier noun **clerk**, bank clerk, teller, banker, treasurer, bursar, purser.

casing noun **cover**, case, shell, envelope, sheath, sheathing, sleeve, jacket, housing.

casino noun **gambling house**, gambling club, gambling den.

cask noun **barrel**, keg, butt, tun, vat, drum, hogshead; historical firkin.

casket noun **1** *a small casket:* **box**, chest, case, container, receptacle. **2** (N. Amer.) *the casket of a dead soldier:* **coffin**; informal box; humorous wooden overcoat.

cast verb **1** *he cast the stone into the stream:* **throw**, toss, fling, pitch, hurl, lob; informal chuck, sling, bung. **2** *fishermen cast their nets:* **spread**, throw, open out. **3** *she cast a fearful glance over her shoulder:* **direct**, shoot, throw, send. **4** *each citizen cast a vote:* **register**, record, enter, file, vote. **5** *the fire cast a soft light:* **emit**, give off, send out, radiate. **6** *the figures cast shadows:* **form**, create, produce; project, throw. **7** *a figure cast by hand:* **mould**, fashion, form, shape, model; sculpt, sculpture, forge. **8** *they were cast as extras:* **choose**, select, pick, name, nominate.
noun **1** *a cast of the writer's hand:* **mould**, die, matrix, shape, model. **2** *a cast of the dice:* **throw**, toss, fling, pitch, hurl, lob; informal chuck, sling, bung. **3** *the cast of 'The Barber of Seville':* **actors**, performers, players, company; dramatis personae, characters.
■ **cast something aside** discard, reject, throw away/out, get rid of, dispose of, abandon.
■ **cast someone away** shipwreck, wreck; strand, leave stranded, maroon.
■ **cast down** depressed, downcast, unhappy, sad, miserable, gloomy, down, low; dejected, dispirited, discouraged, disheartened, downhearted, demoralized, disconsolate, crestfallen, despondent; informal blue.

caste noun **(social) class**, social order, rank, level, stratum, echelon, status.

castigate verb (formal) *he was castigated for not setting a good example:* **reprimand**, rebuke, admonish, chastise, chide, upbraid,

reprove, reproach, scold, berate, take to task, lambaste, give someone a piece of one's mind, haul over the coals, censure; informal tell off, give someone an earful, give someone a roasting, rap someone on the knuckles, slap someone's wrist, dress down, bawl out, give someone hell, blow up at, pitch into, lay into, blast; Brit. informal tick off, have a go at, carpet, tear someone off a strip, give someone what for, give someone a rocket; N. Amer. informal chew out, ream out; Austral. informal monster.
– OPPOSITES praise, commend.

castle noun **fortress**, fort, stronghold, fortification, keep, citadel.

castrate verb *many of these colts are castrated:* **neuter**, geld, cut, desex, sterilize, fix; N. Amer. & Austral. alter; Brit. informal doctor.

casual adjective **1** *a casual attitude to life:* **indifferent**, apathetic, uncaring, unconcerned; lackadaisical, blasé, nonchalant, insouciant, offhand, flippant; easy-going, free and easy, blithe, carefree, devil-may-care; informal laid-back. **2** *a casual remark:* **offhand**, spontaneous, unpremeditated, unthinking, unconsidered, impromptu, throwaway, unguarded; informal off-the-cuff. **3** *a casual glance:* **cursory**, perfunctory, superficial, passing, fleeting; hasty, brief, quick. **4** *a casual acquaintance:* **slight**, superficial. **5** *casual work:* **temporary**, part-time, freelance, impermanent, irregular, occasional. **6** *casual sex:* **promiscuous**, recreational, extramarital, free. **7** *a casual meeting changed his life:* **chance**, accidental, unplanned, unintended, unexpected, unforeseen, unanticipated, fortuitous, serendipitous, adventitious. **8** *a casual shirt:* **informal**, comfortable, leisure, sportif, everyday; informal sporty. **9** *the inn's casual atmosphere:* **relaxed**, friendly, informal, unceremonious, easy-going, free and easy; informal laid-back.
– OPPOSITES careful, planned, formal.
noun *we employ ten casuals:* **temporary worker**, part-timer, freelance, freelancer; informal temp.

casualty noun **victim**, fatality, loss, missing (in action), MIA, dead or injured.

casuistry noun *the moral law had been covered with casuistry and hypocrisy:* **sophistry**, specious reasoning, speciousness.

cat noun **feline**, tomcat, tom, kitten, mouser; informal pussy (cat), puss; Brit. informal moggie, mog.

cataclysm noun *their homeland was destroyed by a great cataclysm:* **disaster**, catastrophe, calamity, tragedy, devastation, holocaust, ruin, ruination, upheaval, convulsion.

cataclysmic adjective *a cataclysmic earthquake:* **disastrous**, catastrophic, calamitous, tragic, devastating, ruinous, terrible, violent, awful.

catacombs plural noun **underground cemetery**, crypt, vault, tomb, ossuary.

catalogue noun **1** *a library catalogue:* **directory**, register, index, list, listing, record, archive, inventory. **2** *a mail-order catalogue:* **brochure**, magalogue, mailer; N. Amer. informal wish book.
verb *the collection is fully catalogued:* **classify**, categorize, systematize, index, list, archive, make an inventory of, inventory, record, itemize.

catapult noun *a boy fired the catapult:* **sling**, slingshot; Austral./NZ shanghai.
verb *Sam was catapulted into the sea:* **propel**, launch, hurl, fling, send flying, fire, blast, shoot.

cataract noun **waterfall**, cascade, falls, rapids, white water.

catastrophe noun *an environmental catastrophe:* **disaster**, calamity, cataclysm, holocaust, ruin, ruination, tragedy; adversity, blight, trouble, trial, tribulation.

catastrophic adjective *a catastrophic earthquake:* **disastrous**, calamitous, cataclysmic, ruinous, tragic, fatal, dire, awful, terrible, dreadful.

catcall noun **whistle**, boo, hiss, jeer, raspberry, hoot, taunt; (**catcalls**) scoffing, abuse, taunting, derision.

catch verb **1** *he caught the ball:* **seize**, grab, snatch, seize/grab/take hold of, grasp, grip, clutch, clench; receive, get, intercept. **2** *we've caught the thief:* **capture**, seize; apprehend, arrest, take prisoner/captive, take into custody; trap, snare, ensnare; net, hook, land; informal nab, collar, run in, bust; Brit. informal nick. **3** *her heel caught in a hole:* **become trapped**, become entangled, snag. **4** *she caught the 7.45 bus:* **be in time for**, make, get; board, get on, step aboard. **5** *they were caught siphoning petrol:* **discover**, find, come upon/across, stumble on, chance on; surprise, catch red-handed, catch in the act. **6** *it caught his imagination:* **engage**, capture, attract, draw, grab, grip, seize; hold, absorb, engross. **7** *she caught a trace of aftershave:* **perceive**, notice, observe, discern, detect, note, make out; Brit. informal clock. **8** *I couldn't catch what she was saying:* **hear**, perceive, discern, make out; understand, comprehend, grasp, apprehend; informal get, get the drift of, figure out; Brit. informal twig, suss (out). **9** *it caught the flavour of the sixties:* **evoke**, conjure up, call to mind, recall, encapsulate, capture. **10** *the blow caught her on the side of her face:* **hit**, strike, slap, smack, bang. **11** *he caught malaria:* **contract**, become infected with, get, be taken ill with, develop, come down with, be struck down with; Brit. go down with; informal take ill with; N. Amer. informal take sick with. **12** *the kindling wouldn't catch:* **ignite**, start burning, catch fire, kindle.
– OPPOSITES drop, release, miss.
noun **1** *he inspected the catch:* **haul**, net, bag, yield. **2** (informal) *Giles is a good catch:* **eligible man/woman**, marriage prospect. **3** *he slipped the catch:* **latch**, lock, fastener, clasp, hasp. **4** *he is always looking for the catch:* **snag**, disadvantage, drawback, stumbling block, hitch, fly in the ointment, pitfall, complication, problem, hiccup, difficulty; trap, trick, snare; informal con.
▪ **catch on 1** *radio soon caught on:* **become popular/fashionable**, take off, boom, flourish, thrive. **2** *I caught on fast:* **understand**, comprehend, learn, see the light; informal cotton on, latch on, get the picture/message, get wise.
▪ **catch (someone) up** draw level (with), reach; gain on.

catching adjective (informal) *Huntington's disease isn't catching:* **infectious**, contagious, communicable, transmittable, transmissible; dated infective.

catchphrase noun **saying**, quotation, quote, slogan, catchword; N. Amer. informal tag line.

catchword noun **motto**, watchword, slogan, byword, catchphrase; informal buzzword.

catchy adjective *a catchy tune:* **memorable**, unforgettable; appealing, popular; singable, melodious, tuneful.

categorical adjective *a categorical assurance that the government will not raise VAT:* **unqualified**, unconditional, unequivocal, absolute, explicit, unambiguous, definite, direct, downright, outright, emphatic, positive, point-blank, conclusive, without reservations, out-and-out.
– OPPOSITES qualified, equivocal.

categorize verb *silk is categorized as a luxury import:* **classify**, class, group, grade, rate, designate; order, arrange, sort, rank; file, catalogue, list, index.

category noun *weedkillers fall into five broad categories:* **class**, classification, group, grouping, bracket, heading, set; type, sort, kind, variety, species, breed, brand, make, model; grade, order, rank.

cater
▪ **cater for 1** *we cater for vegetarians:* **provide food for**, feed, serve, cook for. **2** *a resort catering for older holidaymakers:* **serve**, provide for, meet the needs/wants of, accommodate. **3** *he seemed to cater for all tastes:* **take into account/consideration**, allow for, consider, bear in mind, make provision for, have regard for.
▪ **cater to** *he catered to her every whim:* **satisfy**, indulge, pander to, gratify, accommodate, minister to, give in to, fulfil.

caterwaul verb *it wasn't until afterwards I realized it was cats caterwauling:* **howl**, wail, bawl, cry, yell, scream, screech, yowl.

catharsis noun *this process of catharsis can bring improvements in both physical and mental health:* **purging**, purgation, purification, cleansing, (emotional) release, relief.

catholic adjective *her tastes are pretty catholic:* **diverse**, diversified, wide,

broad, broad-based, eclectic, liberal; comprehensive, all-encompassing, all-embracing, all-inclusive.
– OPPOSITES narrow.

cattle plural noun **cows**, bovines, oxen, bulls; stock, livestock.

caucus noun 1 (in North America & NZ) *caucuses will be held in eleven states:* **meeting**, assembly, gathering, congress, conference, convention, rally, convocation. 2 (in the UK) *the right-wing caucus:* **faction**, camp, bloc, group, set, band, ring, cabal, coterie, pressure group; Brit. ginger group.

cause noun 1 *the cause of the fire is not known:* **source**, root, origin, beginning(s), starting point; mainspring, base, basis, foundation, fountainhead; originator, author, creator, producer, agent. 2 *there is no cause for alarm:* **reason**, grounds, justification, call, need, necessity, occasion, excuse, pretext. 3 *the cause of human rights | a good cause:* **principle**, ideal, belief, conviction; object, end, aim, objective, purpose; charity. 4 *he went to plead his cause:* **case**, suit, lawsuit, action, dispute.
– OPPOSITES effect, result.
verb *this disease can cause blindness:* **bring about**, give rise to, lead to, result in, create, produce, generate, engender, spawn, bring on, precipitate, prompt, provoke, trigger, make happen, induce, inspire, promote, foster.
– OPPOSITES result from.

caustic adjective 1 *a caustic cleaner:* **corrosive**, corroding, mordant, acid. 2 *a caustic comment:* **sarcastic**, cutting, biting, mordant, sharp, bitter, scathing, derisive, sardonic, ironic, scornful, trenchant, acerbic, vitriolic, acidulous; Brit. informal sarky.

caution noun 1 *proceed with caution:* **care**, carefulness, heedfulness, heed, attention, attentiveness, alertness, watchfulness, vigilance, circumspection, discretion, prudence. 2 *a first offender may receive a caution:* **warning**, admonishment, injunction; reprimand, rebuke, reproof, scolding; informal telling-off, dressing-down, talking-to; Brit. informal ticking-off, carpeting.
verb 1 *advisers cautioned against tax increases:* **advise**, warn, counsel, urge. 2 *he was cautioned by the police:* **warn**, admonish; reprimand, rebuke, reprove, scold; informal tell off, give someone a dressing-down, give someone a talking-to; Brit. informal give someone a ticking-off, carpet.

cautious adjective *a cautious driver:* **careful**, heedful, attentive, alert, watchful, vigilant, circumspect, prudent.
– OPPOSITES reckless.

cavalcade noun *a royal cavalcade proceeded through the city:* **procession**, parade, motorcade, cortège; Brit. march past.

cavalier adjective *a cavalier disregard for danger:* **offhand**, indifferent, casual, dismissive, insouciant, unconcerned; supercilious, patronizing, condescending,

disdainful, scornful, contemptuous; informal couldn't care less.

cave noun **cavern**, grotto, pothole, underground chamber.
■ **cave in** 1 *the roof caved in:* collapse, fall in/down, give (way), crumble, subside. 2 *the manager caved in to their demands:* yield, surrender, capitulate, give in, back down, make concessions, throw in the towel/sponge.

caveat noun *he added the caveat that the results still had to be corroborated:* **warning**, caution, admonition; proviso, condition, stipulation, provision, clause, rider, qualification.

caveman, cavewoman noun cave-dweller, troglodyte, primitive man/woman, prehistoric man/woman.

cavern noun large cave, grotto, underground chamber/gallery.

cavernous adjective *he led them into a dismal cavernous hall:* **vast**, huge, large, immense, spacious, roomy, airy, capacious, voluminous, extensive, deep; hollow, gaping, yawning.
– OPPOSITES small.

cavil verb *they cavilled at the cost:* **complain**, carp, grumble, grouse, whine, bleat, quibble, niggle; informal gripe, grouch, beef, bellyache, moan, bitch, whinge, kick up a fuss; Brit. informal chunter, create; N. English informal mither; N. Amer. informal kvetch.

cavity noun *customs officers found a secret cavity in the car:* **space**, chamber, hollow, hole, pocket, pouch; orifice, aperture; socket, gap, crater, pit.

cavort verb *the children were cavorting in the snow:* **skip**, dance, romp, jig, caper, frisk, gambol, prance, frolic, lark; bounce, trip, leap, jump, bound, spring, hop.

cease verb 1 *hostilities had ceased:* **end**, come to a halt, come to an end, halt, stop, conclude, terminate, finish, draw to a close, be over. 2 *they ceased all military activity:* **bring to an end**, bring to a halt, end, halt, stop, conclude, terminate, finish, wind up, discontinue, suspend, break off; informal leave off.
– OPPOSITES start, continue.
■ **without cease** continuously, incessantly, unendingly, unremittingly, without a pause/break, on and on.

ceaseless adjective *the fort was subjected to ceaseless bombardment:* **continual**, constant, continuous; incessant, unceasing, unending, endless, never-ending, interminable, non-stop, uninterrupted, unremitting, relentless, unrelenting, unrelieved, sustained, persistent, eternal, perpetual.
– OPPOSITES intermittent.

cede verb *Cuba was ceded by Spain to the United States:* **surrender**, concede, relinquish, yield, part with, give up; hand over, deliver up, give over, make over, transfer; abandon, forgo, sacrifice.

c

ceiling noun *the government imposed a wage ceiling of 3 per cent:* **upper limit**, maximum, limitation.

celebrate verb **1** *they were celebrating their wedding anniversary:* **commemorate**, observe, mark, keep, honour, remember, memorialize. **2** *let's all celebrate!* **enjoy oneself**, make merry, have fun, have a good time, have a party, revel, roister, carouse; N. Amer. step out; informal party, go out on the town, paint the town red, whoop it up, make whoopee, live it up, have a ball. **3** *the priest celebrated mass:* **perform**, observe, officiate at. **4** *he was celebrated for his achievements:* **praise**, extol, glorify, eulogize, reverence, honour, pay tribute to.

celebrated adjective *a celebrated photographer:* **acclaimed**, admired, highly rated, lionized, revered, honoured, esteemed, exalted, vaunted, well thought of; eminent, great, distinguished, prestigious, illustrious, pre-eminent, estimable, notable, of note, of repute.
– OPPOSITES unsung.

celebration noun **1** *the celebration of his 50th birthday:* **commemoration**, observance, marking, keeping. **2** *a cause for celebration:* **jollification**, merrymaking, enjoying oneself, carousing, revelry, revels, festivities; informal partying. **3** *a birthday celebration:* **party**, function, gathering, festivities, festival, fête, carnival, jamboree; informal do, bash, rave; Brit. informal rave-up, knees-up, beanfeast, bunfight, beano. **4** *the celebration of the Eucharist:* **observance**, performance, officiation, solemnization.

celebrity noun **1** *his celebrity grew:* **fame**, prominence, renown, eminence, pre-eminence, stardom, popularity, distinction, note, notability, prestige, stature, repute, reputation. **2** *a sporting celebrity:* **famous person**, VIP, very important person, personality, (big) name, famous/household name, star, superstar; informal celeb, somebody, someone, megastar.
– OPPOSITES obscurity.

celestial adjective **1** *a celestial body:* **(in) space**, heavenly, astronomical, extraterrestrial, stellar, planetary. **2** *celestial beings:* **heavenly**, holy, saintly, divine, godly, godlike, ethereal; immortal, angelic, seraphic, cherubic.
– OPPOSITES earthly, hellish.

celibate adjective *a celibate priest:* **unmarried**, single, unwed, spouseless, chaste, virginal, virgin, maidenly, maiden, intact, abstinent, self-denying.

cell noun **1** *a prison cell:* **room**, cubicle, chamber; dungeon, oubliette, lock-up. **2** *each cell of the honeycomb:* **compartment**, cavity, hole, hollow, section. **3** *terrorist cells:* **unit**, faction, arm, section, coterie, group.

cellar noun **basement**, vault, underground room, lower ground floor; crypt, undercroft.
– OPPOSITES attic.

cement noun *polystyrene cement:* **adhesive**, glue, fixative, gum, paste; superglue, epoxy resin; N. Amer. mucilage; N. Amer. informal stickum.
verb *he cemented the sample to a microscope slide:* **stick**, bond; fasten, fix, affix, attach, secure, bind, glue, gum, paste.

cemetery noun **graveyard**, churchyard, burial ground, necropolis; informal boneyard; historical potter's field.

censor noun *the film censors:* **expurgator**, bowdlerizer; examiner, inspector, editor.
verb *letters home were censored:* **cut**, delete parts of, make cuts in, blue-pencil; edit, expurgate, bowdlerize, sanitize; informal clean up.

censorious adjective *she used not to be so censorious of others' behaviour:* **hypercritical**, overcritical, disapproving, condemnatory, denunciatory, deprecatory, disparaging, reproachful, reproving, censuring, captious.
– OPPOSITES complimentary.

censure verb *he was censured for his conduct.* See **REPRIMAND** verb.
noun *a note of censure:* **condemnation**, criticism, attack, abuse; reprimand, rebuke, admonishment, reproof, reproval, upbraiding, disapproval, reproach, reprehension, obloquy.
– OPPOSITES approval.

central adjective **1** *a Roman basilica always occupied a central position:* **middle**, centre, halfway, midway, mid, median, medial, mean. **2** *central London:* **inner**, innermost, middle, mid. **3** *their central campaign issue:* **main**, chief, principal, primary, leading, foremost, first, most important, predominant, dominant, key, crucial, vital, essential, basic, fundamental, core, prime, premier, paramount, major, overriding; informal number-one.
– OPPOSITES side, outer, subordinate.

centralize verb *the minister intends to centralize tax collection:* **concentrate**, consolidate, amalgamate, condense, unify, streamline, focus, rationalize.
– OPPOSITES devolve.

centre noun *the centre of the town:* **middle**, nucleus, heart, core, hub; middle point, midpoint, halfway point, mean, median.
– OPPOSITES edge.
verb *the story centres on a doctor:* **focus**, concentrate, pivot, revolve, be based.

centrepiece noun *the tower is the centrepiece of the park:* **highlight**, main feature, high point/spot, best part, climax; focus of attention, focal point, centre of attention/interest, magnet, cynosure.

ceramics plural noun **pottery**, pots, china.

ceremonial adjective *a ceremonial occasion:* **formal**, official, state, public; ritual, ritualistic, prescribed, stately, courtly, solemn.
– OPPOSITES informal.

noun *diplomatic ceremonial:* **ritual**, ceremony, rite, formality, pomp, protocol.

ceremonious adjective *he rose from his desk to take a ceremonious farewell:* **dignified**, majestic, imposing, impressive, solemn, stately, formal, courtly; regal, imperial, elegant, grand, glorious, splendid, magnificent, resplendent, portentous; informal starchy.

ceremony noun **1** *a wedding ceremony:* **rite**, ritual, ceremonial, observance; service, sacrament, liturgy, worship, celebration. **2** *the new Queen was proclaimed with due ceremony:* **pomp**, protocol, formalities, niceties, decorum, etiquette, punctilio, politesse.

certain adjective **1** *I'm certain he's guilty:* **sure**, confident, positive, convinced, in no doubt, satisfied, assured, persuaded. **2** *it is certain that more changes are in the offing:* **unquestionable**, sure, definite, beyond question, not in doubt, indubitable, undeniable, irrefutable, indisputable; obvious, evident, recognized, confirmed, accepted, acknowledged, undisputed, undoubted, unquestioned, as sure as eggs is eggs. **3** *they are certain to win:* **sure**, very likely, bound, destined. **4** *certain defeat:* **inevitable**, assured, destined, predestined; unavoidable, inescapable, inexorable, ineluctable. **5** *there is no certain cure for this:* **reliable**, dependable, trustworthy, foolproof, tried and tested, effective, guaranteed, sure, unfailing, infallible; informal sure-fire; dated sovereign. **6** *a certain sum of money:* **determined**, definite, fixed, established, precise. **7** *a certain lady that you know:* **particular**, specific, individual, special. **8** *to a certain extent that is true:* **moderate**, modest, medium, middling; limited, small.
– OPPOSITES doubtful, possible, unlikely.

certainly adverb **1** *this is certainly a late work:* **unquestionably**, surely, assuredly, definitely, beyond/without question, without doubt, indubitably, undeniably, irrefutably, indisputably; obviously, patently, evidently, plainly, clearly, unmistakably, undisputedly, undoubtedly, as sure as eggs is eggs. **2** *our revenues are certainly lower:* **admittedly**, without question, definitely, undoubtedly, without a doubt.
– OPPOSITES possibly.
exclamation *'Shall we eat now?' 'Certainly.'* **yes**, definitely, absolutely, sure, by all means, indeed, of course, naturally; affirmative.

certainty noun **1** *she knew with certainty that he was telling the truth:* **confidence**, sureness, positiveness, conviction, certitude, assurance. **2** *he accepted defeat as a certainty:* **inevitability**, foregone conclusion; informal sure thing; Brit. informal cert, dead cert.
– OPPOSITES doubt, possibility.

certificate noun **guarantee**, certification,

document, authorization, authentication, credentials, accreditation, licence, diploma.

certify verb **1** *the aircraft was certified as airworthy:* **verify**, guarantee, attest, validate, confirm, substantiate, endorse, vouch for, testify to; provide evidence, give proof, prove, demonstrate. **2** *a certified hospital:* **accredit**, recognize, license, authorize, approve, warrant.

certitude noun *the question may never be answered with certitude:* **certainty**, confidence, sureness, positiveness, conviction, assurance.
– OPPOSITES doubt.

cessation noun *the cessation of hostilities:* **end**, ending, termination, stopping, halting, ceasing, finish, finishing, stoppage, conclusion, winding up, discontinuation, abandonment, suspension, breaking off, cutting short.
– OPPOSITES start, resumption.

cession noun *the cession of twenty important towns:* **surrender**, surrendering, ceding, concession, relinquishment, yielding, giving up; handing over, transfer; abandonment, sacrifice.

chafe verb **1** *the collar chafed his neck:* **abrade**, graze, rub against, gall, scrape, scratch. **2** *I chafed her feet:* **rub**, warm (up). **3** *material chafed by the rock:* **wear away/down**, erode, abrade, scour, scrape away. **4** *the bank chafed at the restrictions:* **be angry**, be annoyed, be irritated, fume, be exasperated, be frustrated.

chaff[1] noun **1** *separating the chaff from the grain:* **husks**, hulls, pods, shells, bran; N. Amer. shucks. **2** *the proposals were so much chaff:* **rubbish**, dross; N. Amer. garbage, trash; Austral./NZ mullock; informal junk.

chaff[2] noun *good-natured chaff:* **banter**, repartee, teasing, ragging, joking, jesting, raillery, badinage, wisecracks, witticism(s); informal kidding, ribbing.
verb *the pleasures of chaffing your mates:* **tease**, make fun of, poke fun at, rag; informal take the mickey out of, rib, josh, kid, have on, pull someone's leg; Brit. informal wind up; N. Amer. informal goof on, rag on, razz; Austral./NZ informal poke mullock at, poke borak at.

chagrin noun *to my chagrin, he was nowhere to be seen:* **annoyance**, irritation, vexation, exasperation, displeasure, dissatisfaction, discontent; anger, rage, fury, wrath, indignation, resentment; embarrassment, mortification, humiliation, shame.
– OPPOSITES delight.

chain noun **1** *he was held in chains:* **fetters**, shackles, irons, leg irons, manacles, handcuffs; informal cuffs, bracelets. **2** *a chain of events:* **series**, succession, string, sequence, train, course. **3** *a chain of shops:* **group**, multiple shop/store, multiple.
verb *she chained her bicycle to the railings:* **secure**, fasten, tie, tether, hitch; restrain, shackle, fetter, manacle, handcuff.

C

chair noun 1 *he sat down on a chair:* **seat**.
2 *the chair of the committee.* See **CHAIRMAN**.
3 *a university chair:* **professorship**.
verb *she chairs the economic committee:*
preside over, take the chair of; lead, direct,
run, manage, control, be in charge of.

chairman, chairwoman noun **chair**,
chairperson, president, leader, convener;
spokesperson, spokesman, spokeswoman.

chalk
■ **chalk something up** 1 *he has chalked up
another success:* achieve, attain, accomplish,
gain, earn, win, succeed in making, make,
get, obtain, notch up, rack up. 2 *I forgot
completely—chalk it up to age:* attribute,
assign, ascribe, put down; blame on, pin on,
lay at the door of.

chalky adjective 1 *chalky skin:* **pale**,
bloodless, pallid, colourless, wan, ashen,
white, pasty. 2 *chalky bits at the bottom of
the glass:* **powdery**, gritty, granular.

challenge noun 1 *he accepted the challenge:*
dare, provocation; summons. 2 *a challenge
to his leadership:* **test**, questioning, dispute,
stand, opposition, confrontation. 3 *it was
proving quite a challenge:* **problem**, difficult
task, test, trial.
verb 1 *we challenged their statistics:*
question, disagree with, dispute, take issue
with, protest against, call into question,
object to. 2 *he challenged one of my men
to a duel:* **dare**, summon, throw down the
gauntlet to. 3 *changes that would challenge
them:* **test**, tax, strain, make demands on;
stretch, stimulate, inspire, excite.

challenging adjective *an interesting,
worthwhile, and challenging job:*
demanding, testing, taxing, exacting;
stretching, exciting, stimulating, inspiring;
difficult, tough, hard, formidable, onerous,
arduous, strenuous, gruelling.
– OPPOSITES easy, uninspiring.

chamber noun 1 *a debating chamber:* **room**,
hall, assembly room, auditorium. 2 *the left
chamber of the heart:* **compartment**, cavity;
Anatomy auricle, ventricle.

champagne noun **sparkling wine**;
mousseux, spumante, cava; informal champers,
bubbly, fizz.

champion noun 1 *the world champion:*
winner, title-holder, defending champion,
gold medallist; prizewinner, victor
(ludorum); informal champ, number one. 2 *a
champion of change:* **advocate**, proponent,
promoter, supporter, defender, upholder,
backer, exponent; campaigner, lobbyist,
crusader, apologist; N. Amer. booster.
verb *championing the rights of tribal
peoples:* **advocate**, promote, defend, uphold,
support, back, stand up for, take someone's
part; campaign for, lobby for, fight for,
crusade for, stick up for.
– OPPOSITES oppose.

chance noun 1 *there was a chance he might be
released:* **possibility**, prospect, probability,

likelihood, likeliness, expectation,
anticipation; risk, threat, danger. 2 *I gave
her a chance to answer:* **opportunity**,
opening, occasion, turn, time, window
(of opportunity); N. Amer. & Austral./NZ show;
informal shot, look-in. 3 *Nigel took an awful
chance:* **risk**, gamble, venture, speculation,
long shot, leap in the dark. 4 *it was pure
chance that made me notice the writing:*
accident, coincidence, serendipity, fate,
destiny, fortuity, providence, happenstance;
good fortune, (good) luck, fluke.
adjective *a chance discovery:* **accidental**,
fortuitous, adventitious, fluky, coincidental,
serendipitous; unintentional, unintended,
inadvertent, unplanned.
– OPPOSITES intentional.
verb 1 *I chanced to meet him:* **happen**.
2 (informal) *she chanced another look:* **risk**,
hazard, venture, try.
■ **by chance** fortuitously, by
accident, accidentally, coincidentally,
serendipitously; unintentionally,
inadvertently.
■ **chance on/upon** come across/upon, run
across/into, happen on, light on, stumble
on, find by chance, meet (by chance); informal
bump into.

chancy adjective (informal) **risky**, unpredictable,
uncertain, precarious; unsafe, insecure,
tricky, high-risk, hazardous, perilous,
parlous; informal dicey, hairy; Brit. informal dodgy.
– OPPOSITES predictable.

change verb 1 *this could change the face
of Britain | things have changed:* **alter**,
make/become different, adjust, adapt, amend,
amend, modify, revise, refine; reshape,
refashion, redesign, restyle, revamp,
rework, remodel, reorganize, reorder;
vary, transform, transfigure, transmute,
metamorphose, evolve; informal tweak. 2 *he's
changed his job:* **exchange**, substitute, swap,
switch, replace, alternate, interchange.
– OPPOSITES preserve, keep.
noun 1 *a change of plan:* **alteration**,
modification, variation, revision,
amendment, adjustment, adaptation;
remodelling, reshaping, rearrangement,
reordering, restyling, reworking;
metamorphosis, transformation, evolution,
mutation; humorous transmogrification.
2 *a change of government:* **exchange**,
substitution, swap, switch, replacement,
alternation, interchange. 3 *I've no change:*
coins, loose/small change, (hard) cash,
silver, coppers, specie.
■ **have a change of heart.** See **HEART**.

changeable adjective 1 *the weather will be
changeable | changeable moods:* **variable**,
inconstant, varying, changing, fluctuating,
irregular; erratic, inconsistent, unstable,
unsettled, turbulent, changeful, protean;
fickle, capricious, temperamental, volatile,
mercurial, unpredictable, blowing hot and
cold; informal up and down. 2 *the colours
are changeable:* **alterable**, adjustable,

modifiable, variable, mutable, exchangeable, interchangeable, replaceable.
– OPPOSITES constant.

changeless adjective *changeless truths:* **unchanging**, unvarying, timeless, static, fixed, permanent, constant, unchanged, consistent, uniform, undeviating; stable, steady, unchangeable, unalterable, invariable, immutable.
– OPPOSITES variable.

channel noun 1 *the English Channel:* **strait(s)**, sound, narrows, (sea) passage. 2 *the water ran down a channel:* **duct**, gutter, conduit, trough, culvert, sluice, spillway, race, drain. 3 *a channel for their extraordinary energy:* **use**, medium, vehicle, way of harnessing; release (mechanism), safety valve, vent. 4 *a channel of communication:* **means**, medium, instrument, mechanism, agency, vehicle, route, avenue.
▶ verb 1 *she channelled out a groove:* **hollow out**, gouge (out), cut (out). 2 *many countries channel their aid through charities:* **convey**, transmit, conduct, direct, guide, relay, pass on, transfer.

chant noun 1 *the protesters' chants:* **shout**, cry, (rallying) call, slogan. 2 *the melodious chant of the monks:* **incantation**, intonation, singing, song, recitative.
▶ verb 1 *protesters were chanting slogans:* **shout**, chorus, repeat. 2 *the choir chanted Psalm 118:* **sing**, intone, incant.

chaos noun *snow caused chaos in the region:* **disorder**, disarray, disorganization, confusion, mayhem, bedlam, pandemonium, havoc, turmoil, tumult, commotion, disruption, upheaval, uproar; a muddle, a mess, a shambles; anarchy, lawlessness; informal hullabaloo, all hell broken loose.
– OPPOSITES order.

chaotic adjective *the political situation was chaotic:* **disorderly**, disordered, in disorder, in chaos, in disarray, disorganized, topsy-turvy, in pandemonium, in turmoil, in uproar; in a muddle, in a mess, messy, in a shambles; anarchic, lawless; Brit. informal shambolic.

chap verb *my skin chapped in the wind:* **become raw**, become sore, become inflamed, chafe, crack.

chaperone noun *Aunt Millie went as chaperone:* **companion**, duenna, escort, protectress, protector, minder.
▶ verb *she was chaperoned by her mother:* **accompany**, escort, attend, watch over, keep an eye on, protect, mind.

chapter noun 1 *the first chapter of the book:* **section**, division, part, portion. 2 *a new chapter in our history:* **period**, phase, page, stage, epoch, era. 3 (N. Amer.) *a local chapter of the American Cancer Society:* **branch**, division, subdivision, section, department, lodge, wing, arm. 4 *the cathedral chapter:* **governing body**, council, assembly, convocation, synod, consistory.

char verb *a region charred by bush fires:* **scorch**, burn, singe, sear, blacken; informal toast.

character noun 1 *Jenny had a forceful character | the character of a town:* **personality**, nature, disposition, temperament, temper, mentality, make-up; features, qualities, properties, traits; spirit, essence, identity, ethos, complexion, tone, feel, feeling. 2 *a woman of character:* **integrity**, honour, moral strength/fibre, rectitude, uprightness; fortitude, strength, backbone, resolve, grit, will power; informal guts, gutsiness; Brit. informal bottle. 3 *a stain on his character:* **reputation**, (good) name, standing, stature, position, status. 4 (informal) *John was a bit of a character:* **eccentric**, oddity, madcap, crank, individualist, nonconformist, rare bird; informal oddball; Brit. informal odd bod. 5 *a boorish character:* **person**, man, woman, soul, creature, individual, customer; informal cookie; Brit. informal bod, guy. 6 *the characters develop throughout the play:* **persona**, role, part; (**characters**) dramatis personae. 7 *the file name must not exceed thirty characters:* **letter**, figure, symbol, sign, mark.

characteristic noun *these men have some interesting characteristics:* **attribute**, feature, (essential) quality, property, trait, aspect, element, facet; mannerism, habit, custom, idiosyncrasy, peculiarity, quirk, oddity, foible.
▶ adjective *his characteristic eloquence:* **typical**, usual, normal, predictable, habitual; distinctive, particular, special, especial, peculiar, idiosyncratic, singular, unique.

characterize verb 1 *the period was characterized by scientific advancement:* **distinguish**, make distinctive, mark, typify, set apart. 2 *the women are characterized as prophets of doom:* **portray**, depict, present, represent, describe; categorize, class, style, brand.

charade noun *the race for the presidential nomination has been a shameless charade:* **farce**, pantomime, travesty, mockery, parody, act, masquerade.

charge verb 1 *he didn't charge much:* **ask (in payment)**, levy, demand, exact; bill, invoice. 2 *the subscription will be charged to your account:* **bill**, debit from, take from. 3 *two men were charged with affray:* **accuse**, indict, arraign; prosecute, try, put on trial; N. Amer. impeach. 4 *they charged him with reforming the system:* **entrust**, burden, encumber, saddle, tax. 5 *the cavalry charged the tanks:* **attack**, storm, assault, assail, fall on, swoop on, descend on; informal lay into, tear into. 6 *we charged into the crowd:* **rush**, storm, stampede, push, plough, launch oneself, go headlong; informal steam; N. Amer. informal barrel. 7 *his work was charged with energy:* **suffuse**, pervade, permeate, saturate, infuse, imbue, fill.
▶ noun 1 *all customers pay a charge:* **fee**,

c

payment, price, tariff, amount, sum, fare, levy. **2** *he pleaded guilty to the charge:* **accusation**, allegation, indictment, arraignment; N. Amer. impeachment. **3** *an infantry charge:* **attack**, assault, offensive, onslaught, drive, push, thrust. **4** *the child was in her charge:* **care**, protection, safe keeping, control; custody, guardianship, wardship; hands. **5** *I am concerned for the safety of my charge:* **ward**, protégé, dependant.
■ **in charge of** responsible for, in control of, at the helm/wheel of; managing, running, administering, directing, supervising, overseeing, controlling; informal running the show.

charisma noun *she enchanted guests with her charisma:* **charm**, presence, (force of) personality, strength of character; (animal) magnetism, attractiveness, appeal, allure.

charismatic adjective *he was a charismatic figure with great appeal to the public:* **charming**, fascinating, strong in character; magnetic, captivating, beguiling, attractive, appealing, alluring.

charitable adjective **1** *charitable activities:* **philanthropic**, humanitarian, altruistic, benevolent, public-spirited; non-profit-making. **2** *charitable people:* **big-hearted**, generous, open-handed, free-handed, munificent, bountiful, beneficent. **3** *he was charitable in his judgements:* **magnanimous**, generous, liberal, tolerant, easy-going, broad-minded, considerate, sympathetic, lenient, indulgent, forgiving.

charity noun **1** *an Aids charity:* **fund**, trust, foundation; non-profit-making organization, voluntary organization, charitable institution. **2** *we don't need charity:* **financial assistance**, aid, welfare, (financial) relief; handouts, gifts, presents, largesse; historical alms. **3** *his actions are motivated by charity:* **philanthropy**, humanitarianism, humanity, altruism, public-spiritedness, social conscience, benevolence, beneficence, munificence. **4** *show a bit of charity:* **goodwill**, compassion, consideration, concern, kindness, kind-heartedness, tenderness, tender-heartedness, sympathy, indulgence, tolerance, leniency.

charlatan noun *they denounced him as a corrupt charlatan:* **quack**, mountebank, sham, fraud, fake, impostor, hoodwinker, hoaxer, cheat, deceiver, double-dealer, (confidence) trickster, swindler, fraudster; informal phoney, shark, con man/artist, flimflammer; Brit. informal twister; N. Amer. informal bunco artist, gold brick, chiseller; Austral. informal magsman, illywhacker.

charm noun **1** *people were captivated by her charm:* **attractiveness**, beauty, glamour, loveliness; appeal, allure, desirability, seductiveness, sexual/animal magnetism, charisma; informal pulling power. **2** *these traditions retain a lot of charm:* **appeal**, drawing power, attraction, allure, fascination. **3** *magical charms:* **spell**, incantation, conjuration, rune, magic formula/word; N. Amer. mojo, hex. **4** *a lucky charm:* **talisman**, fetish, amulet, mascot, totem, juju.
verb **1** *he charmed them with his singing:* **delight**, please, win (over), attract, captivate, allure, lure, dazzle, fascinate, enchant, enthral, enrapture, seduce, spellbind. **2** *he charmed his mother into agreeing:* **coax**, cajole, wheedle; informal sweet-talk, soft-soap.

charming adjective *he stayed with a French family and their charming daughter:* **delightful**, pleasing, pleasant, agreeable, likeable, endearing, lovely, lovable, adorable, appealing, attractive, good-looking, prepossessing; alluring, delectable, ravishing, winning, winsome, fetching, captivating, enchanting, entrancing, fascinating, seductive; informal heavenly, divine, gorgeous, easy on the eye; Brit. informal smashing.
– OPPOSITES repulsive.

chart noun **1** *check your ideal weight on the chart:* **graph**, table, diagram, histogram; bar chart, pie chart, flow chart; Computing graphic. **2** *the pop charts:* **top twenty**, list, listing. verb **1** *the changes were charted accurately:* **tabulate**, plot, graph, record, register, represent; make a chart/diagram of. **2** *the book charted his progress:* **follow**, trace, outline, describe, detail, record, document, chronicle, log.

charter noun **1** *a Royal charter:* **authority**, authorization, sanction, dispensation, consent, permission; permit, licence, warrant, franchise. **2** *the UN Charter:* **constitution**, code, canon; fundamental principles, rules, laws. **3** *the charter of a yacht:* **hire**, hiring, lease, leasing, rent, rental, renting; booking, reservation, reserving.
verb *they chartered a bus:* **hire**, lease, rent; book, reserve.

chary adjective *she had been chary of telling the whole truth:* **wary**, cautious, circumspect, heedful, careful, on one's guard; distrustful, mistrustful, sceptical, suspicious, dubious, hesitant, reluctant, leery, nervous, apprehensive, uneasy; informal cagey, iffy.

chase[1] verb **1** *the dogs chased the fox:* **pursue**, run after, give chase to, follow; hunt, track, trail; informal tail. **2** *Jim had been chasing young girls for years:* **woo**, pursue, run after, make advances to, flirt with, pay court to; informal chat up, come on to. **3** *she chased away the donkeys:* **drive**, send, scare; informal send packing. **4** *photographers chased on to the runway:* **rush**, dash, race, speed, streak, shoot, charge, scramble, scurry, hurry, fly, pelt; informal scoot, belt, tear, zip, whip; N. Amer. informal boogie, hightail, clip.

noun *they gave up the chase:* **pursuit**, hunt, trail.

■ **chase someone/something up** pester, harass, harry, nag; seek out, find, go after; informal hassle.

chase² verb *the figures are chased on the dish:* **engrave**, etch, carve, inscribe, cut, chisel.

chasm noun **1** *a deep chasm:* **gorge**, abyss, canyon, ravine, gully, gulf, defile, couloir, crevasse, fissure, crevice; N. Amer. gulch, coulee. **2** *the chasm between their views:* **breach**, gulf, rift; difference, separation, division, dissension, schism, scission.

chassis noun **framework**, frame, structure, substructure, shell, casing, bodywork, body.

chaste adjective **1** *chaste girlhood:* **virginal**, virgin, intact, maidenly, unmarried, unwed; celibate, abstinent, self-restrained, self-denying, continent; innocent, virtuous, pure (as the driven snow), sinless, undefiled, unsullied. **2** *a chaste kiss on the cheek:* **non-sexual**, platonic, innocent. **3** *the dark, chaste interior:* **plain**, simple, bare, unadorned, undecorated, unornamented, unembellished, functional, no-frills, austere.
– OPPOSITES promiscuous, passionate.

chasten verb *both men were chastened:* **subdue**, humble, cow, squash, deflate, flatten, take down a peg or two, put someone in their place; informal cut down to size, settle someone's hash.

chastise verb *the staff were chastised for arriving late:* **scold**, upbraid, berate, reprimand, reprove, rebuke, admonish, chide, censure, lambaste, lecture, give someone a piece of one's mind, take to task, haul over the coals; informal tell off, dress down, bawl out, blow up at, give someone an earful, give someone a roasting, come down on someone like a ton of bricks, have someone's guts for garters, slap someone's wrist, rap over the knuckles, give someone hell; Brit. informal carpet, tick off, have a go at, tear someone off a strip, give someone what for, give someone a rocket; N. Amer. informal chew out, ream out; Austral. informal monster.
– OPPOSITES praise.

chastity noun *vows of chastity:* **celibacy**, chasteness, virginity, abstinence, self-restraint, self-denial, continence; singleness, maidenhood; innocence, purity, virtue, morality.

chat noun *I popped in for a chat:* **talk**, conversation, gossip, chatter, heart-to-heart, tête-à-tête, blather; informal jaw, gas, confab; Brit. informal natter, chinwag, rabbit; N. Amer. informal rap, bull session.
verb *they chatted with their guests:* **talk**, gossip, chatter, speak, converse, engage in conversation, tittle-tattle, prattle, jabber, babble; informal gas, jaw, chew the rag/fat, yap, yak, yabber, yatter, yammer; Brit. informal natter, rabbit, chunter, have a chinwag; N. Amer. informal shoot the breeze/bull, visit; Austral./NZ informal mag.

■ **chat someone up** (informal) flirt with, make advances to; informal come on to.

chatter noun *she tired him with her chatter:* **chat**, talk, gossip, chit-chat, patter, jabbering, jabber, prattling, prattle, babbling, babble, tittle-tattle, blathering, blather; informal yabbering, yammering, yattering, yapping, jawing, chewing the rag/fat; Brit. informal nattering, chuntering, rabbiting on.
verb *they chattered excitedly.* See CHAT verb.

chatterbox noun (informal) **talker**, chatterer, prattler; N. Amer. blatherskite; informal windbag, gasbag, blabbermouth; Brit. informal natterer.

chatty adjective **1** *he was a chatty person:* **talkative**, communicative, expansive, unreserved, gossipy, gossiping, garrulous, loquacious, voluble, verbose; informal mouthy, gabby, gassy; Brit. informal able to talk the hind legs off a donkey. **2** *a chatty letter:* **conversational**, gossipy, informal, casual, familiar, friendly; informal newsy.
– OPPOSITES taciturn.

chauvinist adjective *chauvinist sentiments:* **jingoistic**, chauvinistic, excessively patriotic, excessively nationalistic, flag-waving, xenophobic, racist, racialist, ethnocentric; sexist, male chauvinist, anti-feminist, misogynist, woman-hating.
noun *he's a chauvinist:* **sexist**, anti-feminist, misogynist, woman-hater; informal male chauvinist pig, MCP.

cheap adjective **1** *cheap tickets:* **inexpensive**, low-priced, low-cost, economical, competitive, affordable, reasonable, reasonably priced, budget, economy, bargain, cut-price, reduced, discounted, discount, rock-bottom, giveaway, bargain-basement; informal dirt cheap. **2** *the dashboard is plain without looking cheap:* **poor-quality**, second-rate, third-rate, substandard, low-grade, inferior, vulgar, shoddy, trashy, tawdry, meretricious, cheap and nasty, cheapjack, gimcrack, Brummagem, pinchbeck; informal rubbishy, cheapo, junky, tacky, kitsch; Brit. informal naff, duff, ropy, grotty; N. Amer. informal two-bit, dime-store. **3** *that was a cheap joke:* **despicable**, contemptible, immoral, unscrupulous, unprincipled, unsavoury, distasteful, vulgar, ignoble, shameful. **4** *he made me feel cheap:* **ashamed**, humiliated, mortified, debased, degraded. **5** (N. Amer. informal) *he made the other guests look cheap.* See MEAN² sense 1.
– OPPOSITES expensive.

cheapen verb **1** *cheapening the cost of exports:* **reduce**, lower (in price), cut, mark down, discount; informal slash. **2** *Hetty never cheapened herself:* **demean**, debase, degrade, lower, humble, devalue, abase, discredit, disgrace, dishonour, shame, humiliate, mortify, prostitute.

cheat verb **1** *customers were cheated:* **swindle**, defraud, deceive, trick, dupe, hoodwink, double-cross, gull; informal diddle,

c

rip off, con, fleece, shaft, sting, bilk, rook, gyp, finagle, flimflam, put one over on, pull a fast one on; N. Amer. informal sucker, gold-brick, stiff; Austral. informal pull a swifty on. **2** *she cheated Ryan out of his fortune:* **deprive of**, deny, prevent from gaining; informal do out of. **3** *the boy cheated death:* **avoid**, escape, evade, elude; foil, frustrate, thwart. **4** *cheating husbands:* **commit adultery**, be unfaithful, stray; informal two-time, play about/around; Brit. informal play away.

noun 1 *he called the principal witness a liar and a cheat:* **swindler**, cheater, fraudster, (confidence) trickster, deceiver, hoaxer, hoodwinker, double-dealer, double-crosser, sham, fraud, fake, charlatan, quack, mountebank; informal con man/artist, shark, sharper, phoney, flimflammer; Brit. informal twister; N. Amer. informal grifter, bunco artist, gold brick, chiseller; Austral. informal magsman, illywhacker. **2** *a sure cheat for generating cash:* **swindle**, fraud, deception, deceit, hoax, sham, trick, ruse; informal con.

check verb **1** *troops checked all vehicles | I checked her background:* **examine**, inspect, look at/over, scrutinize, survey; study, investigate, research, probe, look into, enquire into; informal check out, give something a/the once-over. **2** *he checked that the gun was cocked:* **make sure**, confirm, verify. **3** *two defeats checked their progress:* **halt**, stop, arrest, cut short; bar, obstruct, hamper, impede, inhibit, frustrate, foil, thwart, curb, block, stall, hold up, retard, delay, slow down. **4** *her tears could not be checked:* **suppress**, repress, restrain, control, curb, rein in, stifle, hold back, choke back; informal keep a lid on.

noun 1 *a check of the records:* **examination**, inspection, scrutiny, scrutinization, perusal, study, investigation, probe, analysis; test, trial, monitoring; check-up; informal once-over, look-see. **2** *a check on the abuse of authority:* **control**, restraint, constraint, curb, limitation. **3** (N. Amer.) *the waitress arrived with the check:* **bill**, account, invoice, statement; N. Amer. informal tab.

■ **check in** report (one's arrival), book in, register.

■ **check out** leave, vacate, depart; pay the bill, settle up.

■ **keep something in check** curb, restrain, hold back, keep a tight rein on, rein in/back; control, govern, master, suppress, stifle; informal keep a lid on.

check-up noun *you should go to the hospital for a check-up:* **examination**, inspection, evaluation, analysis, survey, probe, test, appraisal; check, health check; informal once-over, going-over.

cheek noun *that's enough of your cheek!* **impudence**, impertinence, insolence, cheekiness, presumption, effrontery, gall, pertness, impoliteness, disrespect, bad manners, overfamiliarity, cockiness; answering back, talking back; informal

brass (neck), lip, mouth, chutzpah; Brit. informal sauce, backchat; N. Amer. informal sass, sassiness, nerviness, back talk.
verb *they were cheeking the dinner lady:* **answer back**, talk back, be cheeky, be impertinent; Brit. informal backchat; N. Amer. informal sass, be sassy.

cheeky adjective *a cheeky grin:* **impudent**, impertinent, insolent, presumptuous, forward, pert, bold (as brass), brazen, cocky, overfamiliar, discourteous, disrespectful, impolite, bad-mannered; informal brass-necked, lippy, mouthy, fresh, saucy; N. Amer. informal sassy, nervy.
– OPPOSITES respectful, polite.

cheep verb *the chicks cheeped loudly and paddled for shelter:* **chirp**, chirrup, twitter, tweet, peep, chitter, chirr, trill, warble, sing.

cheer noun **1** *the cheers of the crowd:* **hurrah**, hurray, whoop, bravo, shout; hosanna, alleluia; (**cheers**) acclaim, acclamation, clamour, applause, ovation. **2** *a time of cheer:* **happiness**, joy, joyousness, cheerfulness, cheeriness, gladness, merriment, gaiety, jubilation, jollity, jolliness, high spirits, joviality, jocularity, conviviality, light-heartedness; merrymaking, pleasure, rejoicing, revelry.
– OPPOSITES boo, sadness.
verb **1** *they cheered their team:* **acclaim**, hail, salute, shout for, hurrah, hurray, applaud, clap, put one's hands together for; bring the house down; informal holler for, give someone a big hand; N. Amer. informal ballyhoo. **2** *the bad weather did little to cheer me:* **raise someone's spirits**, make happier, brighten, buoy up, enliven, exhilarate, hearten, gladden, uplift, perk up, encourage, inspirit; informal buck up.
– OPPOSITES boo, depress.

■ **cheer someone on** encourage, urge on, spur on, drive on, motivate, inspire, fire (up), inspirit; N. Amer. light a fire under.

■ **cheer up** perk up, brighten (up), become more cheerful, liven up, rally, revive, bounce back, take heart; informal buck up.

■ **cheer someone up**. See CHEER verb sense 2.

cheerful adjective **1** *he arrived looking cheerful:* **happy**, jolly, merry, bright, glad, sunny, joyful, joyous, light-hearted, in good/high spirits, full of the joys of spring, sparkling, bubbly, exuberant, buoyant, ebullient, cock-a-hoop, elated, gleeful, breezy, cheery, jaunty, animated, radiant, smiling, jovial, genial, good-humoured; carefree, unworried, untroubled, without a care in the world; informal upbeat, chipper, chirpy, peppy, bright-eyed and bushy-tailed, full of beans. **2** *a cheerful room:* **pleasant**, attractive, agreeable, cheering, bright, sunny, happy, friendly, welcoming.
– OPPOSITES sad.

cheerio exclamation (Brit. informal) **goodbye**, farewell, adieu, au revoir, ciao, adios, auf Wiedersehen, sayonara; Austral./NZ hooray; informal bye, bye-bye, so long, see you (later),

later(s); Brit. informal cheers, ta-ta, ta-ra.

cheerless adjective *the corridors were ill-lit and cheerless:* **gloomy**, dreary, dull, dismal, bleak, drab, sombre, dark, dim, dingy, funereal; austere, stark, bare, comfortless, unwelcoming, uninviting; miserable, wretched, joyless, depressing, disheartening, dispiriting.

cheers exclamation (informal) *he raised his glass and said 'Cheers!'* **here's to you**, good health, your health, skol, prosit, salut; informal bottoms up, down the hatch; Brit. informal here's mud in your eye.

cheery adjective. See CHEERFUL sense 1.

chef noun **cook**, cordon bleu cook, food preparer; chef de cuisine, chef de partie; pastry cook, saucier; N. Amer. informal short-order cook.

chef-d'œuvre noun *his chef-d'œuvre was his biography of George Washington:* **masterpiece**, masterwork, finest work, magnum opus, pièce de résistance, tour de force.

chequered adjective **1** *a chequered tablecloth:* **checked**, multicoloured, many-coloured. **2** *a chequered history:* **varied**, mixed, full of ups and downs, vicissitudinous; unstable, irregular, erratic, inconstant; informal up and down.

cherish verb **1** *a woman he could cherish:* **adore**, hold dear, love, dote on, be devoted to, revere, esteem, admire; think the world of, set great store by, hold in high esteem; care for, look after, protect, preserve, keep safe. **2** *I cherish her letters:* **treasure**, prize, value highly, hold dear. **3** *they cherished dreams of glory:* **harbour**, entertain, possess, hold (on to), cling to, keep in one's mind, foster, nurture.

cherub noun *a cherub of 18 months:* **baby**, infant, toddler; pretty/loveable child, innocent child, little angel; informal (tiny) tot, tiny.

cherubic adjective *a round, cherubic face:* **angelic**, sweet, cute, adorable, appealing, loveable; innocent, seraphic, saintly.

chest noun **1** *he had several bullet wounds in his chest:* **breast**, upper body, torso, trunk. **2** *she had a large chest:* **bust**, bosom. **3** *an oak chest:* **box**, case, casket, crate, trunk, coffer, strongbox.

chew verb *Carolyn chewed a mouthful of toast:* **masticate**, munch, champ, crunch, nibble, gnaw, eat, consume.
 ■ **chew something over** meditate on, ruminate on, think about/over/through, mull over, consider, weigh up, ponder on, deliberate on, reflect on, muse on, dwell on, give thought to, turn over in one's mind; brood over, puzzle over, rack one's brains about; N. Amer. think on; informal kick around/about, bat around/about.
 ■ **chew the fat/rag** (informal). See CHAT verb.

chic adjective *she looked every inch the chic Frenchwoman:* **stylish**, smart, elegant, sophisticated, dressy, dapper, dashing, trim; fashionable, high fashion, in vogue, up to date, up to the minute, contemporary, à la mode; informal trendy, with it, snappy, snazzy, natty, swish; N. Amer. informal fly, spiffy, kicky, tony.
 – OPPOSITES unfashionable.

chicanery noun *political chicanery of all sorts goes on behind closed doors:* **trickery**, deception, deceit, deceitfulness, duplicity, dishonesty, deviousness, unscrupulousness, underhandedness, subterfuge, fraud, fraudulence, sharp practice, skulduggery, swindling, cheating, duping, hoodwinking; informal crookedness, monkey business, hanky-panky, shenanigans; Brit. informal jiggery-pokery; N. Amer. informal monkeyshines.

chide verb *she chided him for not replying to her letters:* **scold**, chastise, upbraid, berate, reprimand, reprove, rebuke, admonish, censure, lambaste, lecture, give someone a piece of one's mind, take to task, haul over the coals; informal tell off, dress down, bawl out, blow up at, give someone an earful, give someone a roasting, come down on someone like a ton of bricks, have someone's guts for garters, slap someone's wrist, rap over the knuckles, give someone hell; Brit. informal carpet, tick off, have a go at, tear someone off a strip, give someone what for, give someone a rocket; N. Amer. informal chew out, ream out; Austral. informal monster; formal castigate.
 – OPPOSITES praise.

chief noun **1** *a Highland chief:* **leader**, chieftain, head, headman, ruler, overlord, master, commander, seigneur, liege (lord), potentate. **2** *the chief of the central bank:* **head**, principal, chief executive, president, chair, chairman, chairwoman, chairperson, governor, director, manager, manageress; employer, proprietor; N. Amer. chief executive officer, CEO; informal skipper, numero uno, (head) honcho, boss; Brit. informal gaffer, guv'nor; N. Amer. informal padrone, sachem.
 adjective **1** *the chief rabbi:* **head**, leading, principal, premier, highest, foremost, supreme, arch. **2** *their chief aim:* **main**, principal, most important, primary, prime, first, cardinal, central, key, crucial, essential, predominant, pre-eminent, paramount, overriding; informal number-one.
 – OPPOSITES subordinate, minor.

chiefly adverb *he is remembered chiefly for his organ sonatas:* **mainly**, in the main, primarily, principally, predominantly, mostly, for the most part; usually, habitually, typically, commonly, generally, on the whole, largely, by and large, as a rule, almost always.

child noun **youngster**, little one, boy, girl; baby, newborn, infant, toddler; schoolboy, schoolgirl, minor, junior; son, daughter, descendant; (**children**) offspring, progeny; Scottish & N. English bairn, laddie, lassie, lass; informal kid, kiddie, kiddiewink, nipper, tiny,

(tiny) tot, shaver, young 'un, lad; Brit. informal sprog; N. Amer. informal rug rat; Austral./NZ informal ankle-biter; derogatory brat, guttersnipe.

childbirth noun **labour**, delivery, giving birth, birthing.

childhood noun *she had been writing poems since her childhood:* **youth**, early years/life, infancy, babyhood, boyhood, girlhood, pre-teens, pre-pubescence, minority; the springtime of life, one's salad days.
– OPPOSITES adulthood.

childish adjective **1** *childish behaviour:* **immature**, babyish, infantile, juvenile, puerile; silly, inane, jejune, foolish, irresponsible. **2** *a round childish face:* **childlike**, youthful, young, young-looking, girlish, boyish.
– OPPOSITES mature, adult.

childlike adjective **1** *grandmother looked almost childlike:* **youthful**, young, young-looking, girlish, boyish. **2** *geniuses tend to be rather childlike:* **innocent**, artless, guileless, unworldly, unsophisticated, naive, ingenuous, trusting, unsuspicious, unwary, credulous, gullible; unaffected, without airs, uninhibited, natural, spontaneous; informal wet behind the ears.

chill noun **1** *a chill in the air:* **coldness**, chilliness, coolness, iciness, rawness, bitterness, nip. **2** *he had a chill:* **cold**, dose of flu/influenza. **3** *the chill in their relations:* **unfriendliness**, lack of warmth/understanding, chilliness, coldness, coolness.
– OPPOSITES warmth.
verb **1** *the dessert is best chilled:* **make cold**, make colder, cool (down/off); refrigerate, ice. **2** *his quiet tone chilled Ruth:* **scare**, frighten, petrify, terrify, alarm; make someone's blood run cold, chill to the bone/marrow, make someone's flesh crawl; informal scare the pants off; Brit. informal put the wind up.
– OPPOSITES warm.
adjective *a chill wind:* **cold**, chilly, cool, fresh; wintry, frosty, icy, ice-cold, icy-cold, glacial, polar, arctic, raw, bitter, bitterly cold, biting, freezing, frigid, gelid; informal nippy; Brit. informal parky.

chilly adjective **1** *the weather had turned chilly:* **cold**, cool, crisp, fresh, wintry, frosty, icy, ice-cold, icy-cold, chill, glacial, polar, arctic, raw, bitter, bitterly cold, freezing, frigid, gelid; informal nippy; Brit. informal parky. **2** *I woke up feeling chilly:* **cold**, frozen (stiff), frozen to the marrow/core/bone, freezing (cold), bitterly cold, shivery, chilled. **3** *a chilly reception:* **unfriendly**, unwelcoming, cold, cool, frosty, gelid; informal stand-offish, offish.
– OPPOSITES warm.

chime verb **1** *the bells began to chime:* **ring**, peal, toll, sound; ding, dong, clang, boom. **2** *the clock chimed eight o'clock:* **strike**, sound.
noun *the chimes of the bells:* **peal**, pealing,

ringing, carillon, toll, tolling; ding-dong, clanging, tintinnabulation.
■ **chime in 1** *'Yes, you do that,' Doreen chimed in:* **interject**, interpose, interrupt, butt in, cut in, join in; Brit. informal chip in. **2** *his remarks chimed in with the ideas of Adam Smith:* **accord**, correspond, be consistent, be compatible, agree, be in agreement, fit in, be in tune, be consonant; informal square.

chimera noun *the economic sovereignty she claims to defend is a chimera:* **illusion**, fantasy, delusion, dream, fancy.

chimney noun stack, smokestack; flue, funnel, vent.

china noun *a table laid with the best china:* **dishes**, plates, cups and saucers, crockery, porcelain, tableware, dinner service, tea service; N. Amer. dinnerware.

chink[1] noun *a chink in the curtains:* **opening**, gap, space, hole, aperture, crack, fissure, crevice, cranny, cleft, split, slit, slot.

chink[2] verb *the glasses chinked:* **jingle**, jangle, clink, tinkle.

chip noun **1** *wood chips:* **fragment**, sliver, splinter, spell, shaving, paring, flake. **2** *a chip in the glass:* **nick**, crack, scratch; flaw, fault. **3** *fish and chips:* chipped potatoes, potato chips; Brit. French fried potatoes; N. Amer. (French) fries. **4** *gambling chips:* **counter**, token; N. Amer. check.
verb **1** *the teacup was chipped:* **nick**, crack, scratch; damage. **2** *the plaster had chipped:* **break (off)**, crack, crumble. **3** *chip the flint to the required shape:* **whittle**, hew, chisel.
■ **chip in 1** *'He's right,' Gloria chipped in:* **interrupt**, interject, interpose, cut in, chime in, butt in. **2** *parents and staff chipped in to raise the cash:* **contribute**, make a contribution/donation, club together, pay; informal fork out, shell out, cough up; Brit. informal stump up; N. Amer. informal kick in.

chirp verb *a canary chirped from a cage on the veranda:* **tweet**, twitter, chirrup, cheep, peep, chitter, chirr; sing, warble, trill.

chirpy adjective (informal) *a chirpy mood.* See CHEERFUL sense 1.

chivalrous adjective **1** *his chivalrous treatment of women:* **gallant**, gentlemanly, honourable, respectful, considerate; courteous, polite, gracious, well mannered, mannerly. **2** *chivalrous pursuits:* **knightly**, noble, chivalric; brave, courageous, bold, valiant, valorous, heroic, daring, intrepid.
– OPPOSITES rude, cowardly.

chivalry noun **1** *acts of chivalry:* **gallantry**, gentlemanliness, considerateness; courtesy, courteousness, politeness, graciousness, mannerliness, good manners. **2** *the values of chivalry:* **knight errantry**, courtly manners, knightliness, courtliness, nobility; bravery, courage, boldness, valour, heroism, daring.
– OPPOSITES rudeness.

chivvy verb *busy young mothers chivvied and scolded their children:* **nag**, badger, hound, harass, harry, pester, keep on at, go on at;

informal hassle, bug, breathe down someone's neck; N. Amer. informal ride.

choice noun **1** *their choice of candidate | freedom of choice:* **selection**, election, choosing, picking; decision, say, vote. **2** *you have no other choice:* **option**, alternative, possible course of action. **3** *an extensive choice of wines:* **range**, variety, selection, assortment.
adjective **1** *choice plums:* **superior**, first-class, first-rate, prime, premier, grade A, best, finest, excellent, select, quality, high-quality, top, top-quality, high-grade, prize, fine, special; hand-picked, carefully chosen; informal tip-top, A1, top-notch. **2** *a few choice words:* **rude**, abusive, insulting, offensive.
– OPPOSITES inferior.

choir noun **singers**, chorus, chorale.

choke verb **1** *Christopher started to choke:* **gag**, retch, cough, fight for breath. **2** *thick dust choked her:* **suffocate**, asphyxiate, smother, stifle. **3** *she had been choked to death:* **strangle**, throttle; asphyxiate, suffocate; informal strangulate. **4** *the guttering was choked with leaves:* **clog (up)**, bung up, stop up, block, obstruct, plug.
■ **choke something back** suppress, hold back, fight back, bite back, swallow, check, restrain, control, repress, smother, stifle; informal keep a/the lid on.

choose verb **1** *we chose a quiet country hotel:* **select**, pick (out), opt for, plump for, settle on, decide on, fix on; appoint, name, nominate, vote for. **2** *I'll stay as long as I choose:* **wish**, want, desire, feel/be inclined, please, like, see fit.

choosy adjective (informal) *she's become very choosy about the food she'll eat:* **fussy**, finicky, fastidious, over-particular, difficult/hard to please, exacting, demanding; informal picky, pernickety; N. Amer. informal persnickety; archaic nice.

chop verb **1** *chop the potatoes into pieces:* **cut up**, cut into pieces, chop up, cube, dice; N. Amer. hash. **2** *the sound of men chopping wood:* **chop up**, cut up, cut into pieces, hew, split. **3** *four fingers were chopped off:* **sever**, cut off, hack off, slice off, lop off, saw off, shear off. **4** *they chopped down large areas of rainforest:* **cut down**, fell, hack down.
■ **the chop** (Brit. informal) notice; informal the sack, the boot, the elbow, the push, one's marching orders; Brit. informal one's cards.

chopper noun (Brit.) **axe**, cleaver, hatchet.

choppy adjective *the choppy sea:* **rough**, turbulent, heavy, heaving, stormy, tempestuous, squally.
– OPPOSITES calm.

chore noun *daily household chores like shopping and cleaning:* **task**, job, duty, errand; (domestic) work.

chortle verb *pleased with his joke, Robert chortled and slapped his thigh:* **chuckle**, laugh, giggle, titter, tee-hee, snigger.

chorus noun **1** *the chorus sang powerfully:*

choir, ensemble, choral group, choristers, (group of) singers. **2** *they sang the chorus:* **refrain**.
■ **in chorus** in unison, together, simultaneously, as one; in concert, in harmony.

Christ noun **Jesus (Christ)**, the Messiah, the Son of God, the Lamb of God, the Prince of Peace, the Nazarene, the Galilean.

christen verb **1** *she was christened Sara:* **baptize**, name, give the name of, call. **2** *a group who were christened 'The Magic Circle':* **call**, name, dub, style, term, designate, label, nickname, give the name of; formal denominate.

Christmas noun **Noel**; informal Xmas; Brit. informal Chrimbo, Chrissie.

chronic adjective **1** *a chronic illness:* **persistent**, long-standing, long-term; incurable. **2** *chronic economic problems:* **constant**, continuing, ceaseless, unabating, unending, persistent, long-lasting; severe, serious, acute, grave, dire. **3** *a chronic liar:* **inveterate**, hardened, dyed-in-the-wool, incorrigible; compulsive; informal pathological. **4** (Brit. informal) *the film was chronic.* See SUBSTANDARD.
– OPPOSITES acute, temporary.

chronicle noun *a chronicle of the region's past:* **record**, written account, history, annals, archive(s); log, diary, journal.
verb *the events that followed have been chronicled:* **record**, put on record, write down, set down, document, register, report.

chronicler noun **annalist**, historian, archivist, diarist, recorder, reporter.

chronological adjective *the entries are in chronological order:* **sequential**, consecutive, in sequence, in order (of time).

chubby adjective *a pretty child with chubby cheeks:* **plump**, tubby, fat, rotund, portly, dumpy, chunky, well upholstered, well covered, well rounded; informal roly-poly, pudgy, blubbery; Brit. informal podgy; N. Amer. informal zaftig, corn-fed.
– OPPOSITES skinny.

chuck verb (informal) **1** *he chucked the letter onto the table:* **throw**, toss, fling, hurl, pitch, cast, lob; informal sling, bung, buzz; Austral. informal hoy; NZ informal bish. **2** *I chucked the rubbish:* **throw away/out**, discard, dispose of, get rid of, dump, bin, scrap, jettison; informal ditch, junk; N. Amer. informal trash. **3** *I've chucked my job:* **give up**, leave, resign from; informal quit, pack in; Brit. informal jack in. **4** *Mary chucked him for another guy:* **leave**, throw over, finish with, break off with, jilt; informal dump, ditch, give someone the elbow; Brit. informal give someone the push, give someone the big E.

chuckle verb *Adam chuckled to himself as he drove away:* **chortle**, giggle, titter, tee-hee, snicker, snigger.

chunk noun *huge chunks of masonry littered the street:* **lump**, hunk, wedge, block, slab,

c

square, nugget, brick, cube, bar, cake; informal wodge; N. Amer. informal gob.

chunky adjective 1 *a chunky young man:* **stocky**, sturdy, thickset, heavily built, well built, burly, bulky, brawny, solid, heavy; Austral./NZ nuggety; Brit. informal fubsy. 2 *a chunky sweater:* **thick**, bulky, heavy-knit.
– OPPOSITES slight, light.

church noun 1 *a village church:* **place of worship**, house of God; cathedral, minster, abbey, chapel, basilica; Scottish & N. English kirk. 2 *the Methodist Church:* **denomination**, sect, creed; faith.

churchyard noun **graveyard**, cemetery, necropolis, burial ground, garden of remembrance; Scottish kirkyard; N. Amer. memorial park.

churlish adjective *it seems churlish to complain:* **rude**, ill-mannered, ill-bred, discourteous, impolite, unmannerly, uncivil, unchivalrous; inconsiderate, uncharitable, surly, sullen; informal ignorant.
– OPPOSITES polite.

churn verb 1 *propellers churned up the water:* **stir**, agitate, disturb, beat, whip, whisk. 2 *the sea churned:* **heave**, boil, swirl, toss, seethe. ■ **churn something out** produce, make, turn out; informal crank out, bang out.

chute noun 1 *a refuse chute:* **channel**, slide, shaft, funnel, conduit. 2 *water chutes:* **(water) slide**, flume.

cigarette noun filter tip, king-size; informal ciggy, cig, smoke, cancer stick, coffin nail; Brit. informal fag, snout, roll-up.

cinch noun (informal) *winning is a cinch:* **easy task**, child's play, five-finger exercise, gift, walkover; informal doddle, piece of cake, picnic, breeze, low-hanging fruit, kids' stuff, cakewalk, pushover; Brit. informal doss; N. Amer. informal duck soup, snap; Austral./NZ informal bludge, snack.
– OPPOSITES challenge.

cinders plural noun **ashes**, ash, embers.

cinema noun 1 *the local cinema:* multiplex, cinematheque; N. Amer. movie theatre/house. 2 *I hardly ever go to the cinema:* **the pictures**, the movies; informal the flicks. 3 *British cinema:* **films**, movies, pictures, motion pictures.

cipher noun 1 *the information may be given in cipher:* **code**, secret writing; cryptograph. 2 *he has spent most of his life working as a cipher:* **nobody**, nonentity, unimportant person.

circa preposition *a survey by questionnaire of circa 100 companies:* **approximately**, (round) about, around, in the region of, roughly, something like, of the order of, or so, or thereabouts, more or less; informal as near as dammit; N. Amer. informal in the ballpark of.
– OPPOSITES exactly.

circle noun 1 *a circle of gold stars:* **ring**, band, hoop, circlet; halo, disc. 2 *her circle of friends:* **group**, set, company, coterie, clique;

crowd, band; informal gang, bunch, crew. 3 *I'm afraid I don't move in such illustrious circles:* **sphere**, world, milieu; society.
verb 1 *seagulls circled above:* **wheel**, move round, revolve, rotate, whirl, spiral. 2 *satellites circling the earth:* **go round**, travel round, circumnavigate; orbit, revolve round. 3 *the abbey was circled by a wall:* **surround**, encircle, ring, enclose, encompass.

circuit noun 1 *two circuits of the village green:* **lap**, turn, round, circle. 2 (Brit.) *a racing circuit:* **track**, racetrack, running track, course.

circuitous adjective 1 *a circuitous route:* **roundabout**, indirect, winding, meandering, serpentine. 2 *a circuitous discussion:* **indirect**, oblique, roundabout, circumlocutory, periphrastic.
– OPPOSITES direct.

circular adjective *a circular window:* **round**, disc-shaped, ring-shaped, annular.
noun *we send a circular out to members:* **leaflet**, pamphlet, handbill, flyer; N. Amer. mailer, folder, dodger.

circulate verb 1 *the news was widely circulated:* **spread (about/around)**, communicate, disseminate, make known, make public, broadcast, publicize, advertise; distribute, give out, pass around. 2 *fresh air circulates freely:* **flow**, course, move round. 3 *they circulated among their guests:* **socialize**, mingle.

circumference noun *the circumference of the pit:* **perimeter**, border, boundary, girth; edge, rim, verge, margin, fringe.

circumlocution noun *his admission came after years of circumlocution:* **periphrasis**, discursiveness, long-windedness, verbosity, verbiage, wordiness, prolixity, redundancy, pleonasm, tautology, repetitiveness, repetitiousness.

circumscribe verb *the power of the organization has until recently been severely circumscribed:* **restrict**, limit, keep within bounds, curb, confine, restrain; regulate, control.

circumspect adjective *she would have to be very circumspect in her dealings with Catherine:* **cautious**, wary, careful, chary, guarded, on one's guard; watchful, alert, attentive, heedful, vigilant, leery; informal cagey, playing one's cards close to one's chest.
– OPPOSITES unguarded.

circumstances plural noun 1 *favourable economic circumstances:* **situation**, conditions, state of affairs, position; (turn of) events, incidents, occurrences, happenings; factors, context, background, environment; informal circs. 2 *Jane explained the circumstances to him:* **the facts**, the details, the particulars, how things stand, the lie of the land; Brit. the state of play; N. Amer. the lay of the land; informal what's what, the score. **3** *a desire to improve their circumstances:* **financial position**, lot, lifestyle; resources, means, finances, income.

circumstantial adjective *they have only circumstantial evidence:* **indirect**, inferred, deduced, conjectural; inconclusive, unprovable.

circumvent verb *terrorists found the airport checks easy to circumvent:* **avoid**, get round/past, evade, bypass, sidestep, dodge; N. Amer. end-run; informal duck.

cistern noun **tank**, reservoir, container, butt.

citadel noun **fortress**, fort, stronghold, fortification, castle, burg.

citation noun **1** *a citation from an eighteenth-century text:* **quotation**, quote, extract, excerpt, passage, line; reference, allusion; N. Amer. cite. **2** *a citation for gallantry:* **commendation**, (honourable) mention.

cite verb **1** *cite the passage in full:* **quote**, reproduce. **2** *he cited the case of Leigh v. Gladstone:* **refer to**, make reference to, mention, allude to, adduce, instance; specify, name. **3** *he has been cited many times:* **commend**, pay tribute to, praise.

citizen noun **1** *a British citizen:* **subject**, national, passport holder, native. **2** *the citizens of Edinburgh:* **inhabitant**, resident, native, townsman, townswoman.

city noun **town**, municipality, metropolis, megalopolis; conurbation, urban area, metropolitan area; Scottish burgh; informal big smoke; N. Amer. informal burg.

civic adjective *civic buildings:* **municipal**, city, town, urban, metropolitan; public, civil, community.

civil adjective **1** *a civil marriage:* **secular**, non-religious, lay. **2** *civil aviation:* **non-military**, civilian. **3** *a civil war:* **internal**, domestic, interior, national. **4** *he behaved in a civil manner:* **polite**, courteous, well mannered, well bred, gentlemanly, chivalrous, gallant, ladylike; cordial, genial, pleasant, affable. – OPPOSITES religious, military, international, rude.

civilian noun *the slaughter of unarmed civilians:* **non-military person**, non-combatant person, ordinary/private citizen; informal civvy.

civility noun **1** *he treated me with civility:* **courtesy**, courteousness, politeness, good manners, graciousness, consideration, respect, politesse, comity. **2** *she didn't waste time on civilities:* **polite remark**, politeness, courtesy; formality. – OPPOSITES rudeness.

civilization noun **1** *a higher stage of civilization:* **human development**, advancement, progress, enlightenment, culture, refinement, sophistication. **2** *ancient civilizations:* **culture**, society, nation, people.

civilize verb *he built roads and attempted to civilize the people:* **enlighten**, edify,

improve, educate, instruct, refine, cultivate, polish, socialize, humanize.

civilized adjective *such an affront to civilized behaviour will no longer be tolerated:* **polite**, courteous, well mannered, civil, gentlemanly, ladylike, mannerly; cultured, cultivated, refined, polished, sophisticated; enlightened, educated, advanced, developed. – OPPOSITES rude, unsophisticated.

civil servant noun **public servant**, government official; bureaucrat, mandarin, official, administrator, functionary.

clad adjective *they were clad in T-shirts and shorts:* **dressed**, clothed, attired, got up, garbed, rigged out, costumed; wearing, sporting.

claim verb **1** *Davies claimed that she was lying:* **assert**, declare, profess, maintain, state, hold, affirm, avow; argue, contend, allege. **2** *no one claimed the items:* **assert ownership of**, lay claim to, formally request. **3** *you can claim compensation:* **request**, ask for, apply for; demand, exact. **4** *the fire claimed four lives:* **take**, cause/result in the loss of.
noun **1** *her claims that she was raped:* **assertion**, declaration, profession, affirmation, avowal, protestation; contention, allegation. **2** *a claim for damages:* **request**, application; demand, petition. **3** *we have first claim on their assets:* **entitlement to**, title to, right to.

claimant noun *benefit claimants:* **applicant**, candidate, supplicant; petitioner, plaintiff, litigant, appellant.

clairvoyance noun **second sight**, psychic powers, ESP, extrasensory perception, sixth sense; telepathy.

clairvoyant noun **psychic**, fortune-teller, crystal-gazer; medium, spiritualist; telepathist, telepath, mind-reader.
adjective *I'm not clairvoyant:* **psychic**, having second sight, having a sixth sense; telepathic.

clamber verb *I clambered out of the trench:* **scramble**, climb, scrabble, claw one's way.

clammy adjective **1** *his clammy hands:* **moist**, damp, sweaty, sticky; slimy, slippery. **2** *the clammy atmosphere:* **damp**, dank, wet; humid, close, muggy, heavy. – OPPOSITES dry.

clamorous adjective *a jostling, clamorous mob:* **noisy**, loud, vocal, vociferous, raucous, rowdy; importunate, demanding, insistent, vehement. – OPPOSITES quiet.

clamour noun **1** *her voice rose above the clamour:* **din**, racket, rumpus, loud noise, uproar, tumult, shouting, yelling, screaming, baying, roaring; commotion, brouhaha, hue and cry, hubbub; informal hullabaloo; Brit. informal row. **2** *the clamour for her resignation:* **demand(s)**, call(s), urging. **3** *the clamour of protectionists:* **protests**, complaints, outcry.

c

verb **1** *clamouring crowds:* **yell**, shout loudly, bay, scream, roar. **2** *scientists are clamouring for a ban:* **demand**, call, press, push, lobby.

clamp noun **1** *a clamp was holding the wood:* **brace**, vice, press, clasp. **2** *clamps had been fitted to the car:* **immobilizer**, wheel clamp; N. Amer. boot.
verb **1** *the sander is clamped on to the workbench:* **fasten**, secure, fix, attach; screw, bolt. **2** *a pipe was clamped between his teeth:* **clench**, grip, hold, press, clasp. **3** *his car was clamped:* **immobilize**, wheel-clamp; N. Amer. boot.
■ **clamp down on** *a new initiative to clamp down on software piracy:* suppress, prevent, stop, put a stop/end to, stamp out; crack down on, limit, restrict, control, keep in check.

clampdown noun *a clampdown on crime:* **suppression**, prevention, stamping out; crackdown, restriction, restraint, curb, check.

clan noun **1** *the Macleod clan:* **family**, house, dynasty, tribe. **2** *a clan of art collectors:* **group**, set, circle, clique, coterie; crowd, band; informal gang, bunch.

clandestine adjective *their clandestine meetings:* **secret**, covert, furtive, surreptitious, stealthy, cloak-and-dagger, hole-and-corner, closet, backstairs, hugger-mugger; informal hush-hush.

clang noun *the clang of the church bells:* **reverberation**, ringing, ring, ding-dong, bong, peal, chime, toll.
verb *the huge bells clanged:* **reverberate**, resound, ring, bong, peal, chime, toll.

clank noun *the clank of rusty chains:* **jangling**, clanging, rattling, clinking, jingling; clang, jangle, rattle, clangour, clink, jingle.
verb *I could hear the chain clanking:* **jangle**, rattle, clink, clang, jingle.

clannish adjective *he was regarded as an outsider in the clannish community:* **cliquey**, cliquish, insular, exclusive; unfriendly, unwelcoming.

clap verb **1** *the audience clapped:* **applaud**, clap one's hands, give someone a round of applause, put one's hands together; informal give someone a (big) hand; N. Amer. informal give it up. **2** *he clapped Owen on the back:* **slap**, strike, hit, smack, thump; pat; informal whack, thwack. **3** *the dove clapped its wings:* **flap**, beat, flutter.
noun **1** *everybody gave him a clap:* **round of applause**, handclap; informal hand. **2** *a clap on the shoulder:* **slap**, blow, smack, thump; pat; informal whack, thwack. **3** *a clap of thunder:* **crack**, crash, bang, boom; thunderclap.

clarify verb **1** *their report clarified the situation:* **make clear**, shed/throw light on, elucidate, illuminate; **explain**, explicate, define, spell out, clear up. **2** *clarified butter:* **purify**, refine; filter, fine.
– OPPOSITES confuse.

clarity noun **1** *the clarity of his account:*
lucidity, lucidness, clearness, coherence. **2** *the clarity of the image:* **sharpness**, clearness, crispness, definition. **3** *the crystal clarity of the water:* **limpidity**, limpidness, clearness, transparency, translucence, pellucidity.
– OPPOSITES vagueness, blurriness, opacity.

clash noun **1** *clashes between armed gangs:* **confrontation**, skirmish, fight, battle, engagement, encounter, conflict. **2** *an angry clash:* **argument**, altercation, confrontation, shouting match; contretemps, quarrel, disagreement, dispute; informal run-in, slanging match. **3** *a clash of tweeds and a striped shirt:* **mismatch**, discordance, discord, lack of harmony. **4** *a clash of dates:* **coincidence**, concurrence; conflict. **5** *the clash of cymbals:* **striking**, bang, clang, crash.
verb **1** *protesters clashed with police:* **fight**, skirmish, contend, come to blows, come into conflict; do battle. **2** *the prime minister clashed with union leaders:* **disagree**, differ, wrangle, dispute, cross swords, lock horns, be at loggerheads. **3** *her red coat clashed with her hair:* **be incompatible**, not match, not go, be discordant. **4** *the dates clash:* **conflict**, coincide, occur simultaneously. **5** *she clashed the cymbals together:* **bang**, strike, clang, crash.

clasp verb **1** *Ruth clasped his hand:* **grasp**, grip, clutch, hold tightly; take hold of, seize, grab. **2** *he clasped Joanne in his arms:* **embrace**, hug, enfold, fold, envelop; hold, squeeze.
noun **1** *a gold clasp:* **fastener**, fastening, catch, clip, pin; buckle, hasp. **2** *his tight clasp:* **embrace**, hug, cuddle; grip, grasp.

class noun **1** *a first-class hotel:* **category**, grade, rating, classification, group, grouping. **2** *a new class of heart drug:* **kind**, sort, type, variety, genre, brand; species, genus, breed, strain; N. Amer. stripe. **3** *the middle class:* **social division**, social stratum, rank, level, echelon, group, grouping; social status. **4** *there are 30 pupils in the class:* **form**, study group, set, stream. **5** *a Maths class:* **lesson**, period; seminar, tutorial, workshop. **6** *a woman of class:* **style**, stylishness, elegance, chic, sophistication, taste, refinement, quality, excellence.
verb *the 12-seater is classed as a commercial vehicle:* **classify**, categorize, group, grade; order, sort, codify; bracket, designate, label, pigeonhole.

classic adjective **1** *the classic work on the subject:* **definitive**, authoritative; outstanding, first-rate, first-class, best, finest, excellent, superior, masterly. **2** *a classic example of Norman design:* **typical**, archetypal, quintessential, vintage; model, representative, perfect, prime, textbook. **3** *a classic style which never dates:* **simple**, elegant, understated; traditional, timeless, ageless.
– OPPOSITES atypical.
noun *a classic of the genre:* **definitive**

example, model, epitome, paradigm, exemplar; great work, masterpiece.

classical adjective **1** *classical mythology:* ancient Greek, Hellenic, Attic; Latin, ancient Roman. **2** *classical music:* **traditional**, long-established; serious, highbrow, heavyweight. **3** *a classical style:* **simple**, pure, restrained, plain, austere; well proportioned, harmonious, balanced, symmetrical, elegant.
– OPPOSITES modern.

classification noun **1** *the classification of diseases:* **categorization**, categorizing, classifying, grouping, grading, ranking, organization, sorting, codification, systematization. **2** *a series of classifications:* **category**, class, group, grouping, grade, grading, ranking, bracket.

classify verb *we can classify the students into two groups:* **categorize**, group, grade, rank, rate, order, organize, range, sort, type, codify, bracket, systematize, systemize; catalogue, list, file, index.

classy adjective (informal) *a classy hotel:* **stylish**, high-class, superior, exclusive, chic, elegant, smart, sophisticated; Brit. upmarket; N. Amer. high-toned; informal posh, ritzy, plush, swanky; Brit. informal swish.

clatter verb *the cups clattered on the tray:* **rattle**, clank, clink, clunk, clang.

clause noun *a new clause in the treaty:* **section**, paragraph, article, subsection; stipulation, condition, proviso, rider.

claw noun **1** *a bird's claw:* **talon**, nail. **2** *a crab's claw:* **pincer**, nipper.
verb *her fingers clawed his shoulders:* **scratch**, lacerate, tear, rip, scrape, graze, dig into.

clean adjective **1** *keep the wound clean:* **washed**, scrubbed, cleansed, cleaned; spotless, unsoiled, unstained, unsullied, unblemished, immaculate, pristine, dirt-free, as clean as a whistle; hygienic, sanitary, disinfected, sterilized, sterile, aseptic, decontaminated; laundered; informal squeaky clean. **2** *a clean sheet of paper:* **blank**, empty, clear, plain; unused, new, pristine, fresh, unmarked. **3** *clean air:* **pure**, clear, fresh, crisp, refreshing; unpolluted, uncontaminated. **4** *a clean life:* **virtuous**, good, upright, upstanding; honourable, respectable, reputable, decent, righteous, moral, exemplary; innocent, pure, chaste; informal squeaky clean. **5** *the investigation demonstrated that the firm is clean:* **innocent**, guiltless, blameless, guilt-free, crime-free, above suspicion; informal squeaky clean. **6** *a good clean fight:* **fair**, honest, sporting, sportsmanlike, honourable, according to the rules; informal on the level. **7** *these secateurs give a clean cut:* **neat**, smooth, crisp, straight, precise. **8** *he is making a clean break with the past:* **complete**, thorough, total, absolute, conclusive, decisive, final, irrevocable. **9** *the clean lines of a good design:* **simple**, elegant,

graceful, streamlined, smooth.
– OPPOSITES dirty, polluted
verb **1** *Dad cleaned the windows:* **wash**, cleanse, wipe, sponge, scrub, mop, rinse, scour, swab, hose down, sluice (down), disinfect; shampoo. **2** *I got my clothes cleaned:* **launder**, dry-clean. **3** *she cleaned the fish:* **gut**, draw, dress.
– OPPOSITES dirty.

cleanse verb **1** *the wound was cleansed:* **clean (up)**, wash, bathe, rinse, disinfect. **2** *a plan to cleanse the environment of traces of lead:* **rid**, clear, free, purify, purge. **3** *only God can cleanse us from sin:* **purify**, purge, absolve, free; deliver.

clear adjective **1** *clear instructions:* **understandable**, comprehensible, intelligible, plain, uncomplicated, explicit, lucid, coherent, simple, straightforward, unambiguous, clear-cut, crystal clear; formal perspicuous. **2** *a clear case of harassment:* **obvious**, evident, plain, crystal clear; sure, definite, unmistakable, manifest, indisputable, patent, incontrovertible, irrefutable, beyond doubt, beyond question; palpable, visible, discernible, conspicuous, overt, blatant, glaring; as plain as a pikestaff, as plain as day; informal as plain as the nose on one's face. **3** *clear water:* **transparent**, limpid, pellucid, translucent, crystal clear; unclouded. **4** *a clear blue sky:* **bright**, cloudless, unclouded, without a cloud in the sky. **5** *her clear complexion:* **unblemished**, spot-free. **6** *Rosa's clear voice:* **distinct**, bell-like, as clear as a bell. **7** *the road was clear | a clear view:* **unobstructed**, unblocked, passable, open; unrestricted, unhindered. **8** *the algae were clear of toxins:* **free**, devoid, without, unaffected by; rid, relieved. **9** *a clear conscience:* **untroubled**, undisturbed, unperturbed, unconcerned, having no qualms; peaceful, at peace, tranquil, serene, calm, easy. **10** *two clear days' notice:* **whole**, full, entire, complete.
– OPPOSITES vague, opaque, cloudy, obstructed.
adverb **1** *stand clear of the doors:* **away from**, apart from, at a (safe) distance from, out of contact with. **2** *Tommy's voice came loud and clear:* **distinctly**, clearly, as clear as a bell, plainly, audibly. **3** *he has time to get clear away:* **completely**, entirely, fully, wholly, totally, utterly; informal clean.
verb **1** *the sky cleared briefly:* **brighten (up)**, lighten, clear up, become bright/brighter/lighter, become fine/sunny. **2** *the drizzle had cleared:* **disappear**, go away, end; peter out, fade, wear off, decrease, lessen, diminish. **3** *together they cleared the table:* **empty**, unload, unburden, strip. **4** *plumbers' tools for clearing drains:* **unblock**, unstop. **5** *staff cleared the building:* **evacuate**, empty; leave. **6** *Karen cleared the dirty plates:* **remove**, take away, carry away, tidy away/up. **7** *I'm clearing my debts:* **pay (off)**, repay, settle, discharge. **8** *I cleared the bar at my first attempt:* **go over**, pass

over, sail over; jump (over), vault (over), leap (over), hurdle. **9** *he was cleared by an appeal court:* **acquit**, declare innocent, find not guilty; absolve, exonerate; informal let off (the hook). **10** *I was cleared to work on the atomic project:* **authorize**, give permission, permit, allow, pass, accept, endorse, license, sanction, give approval/consent to; informal OK, give the OK, give the thumbs up, give the green light, give the go-ahead. **11** *I cleared £50,000 profit:* **net**, make/realize a profit of, take home, pocket; gain, earn, make, get, bring in, pull in.
■ **clear something out 1** *we cleared out the junk room:* empty (out); tidy (up), clear up. **2** *clear out the rubbish:* get rid of, throw out/away, discard, dispose of, dump, bin, scrap, jettison; informal chuck (out/away), ditch, get shut of; Brit. informal get shot of; N. Amer. informal trash.
■ **clear up.** See CLEAR verb sense 1.
■ **clear something up 1** *clear up the garden:* tidy (up), put in order, straighten up, clean up, spruce up. **2** *we've cleared up the problem:* solve, resolve, straighten out, find an/the answer to; get to the bottom of, explain; informal crack, figure out, suss out.

clearance noun **1** *slum clearance:* **removal**, clearing, demolition. **2** *you must have Home Office clearance:* **authorization**, permission, consent, approval, blessing, leave, sanction, licence, dispensation, assent, agreement, endorsement; informal the green light, the go-ahead, the thumbs up, the OK, the say-so. **3** *there is plenty of clearance:* **space**, room (to spare), margin, leeway.

clear-cut adjective *we now had a clear-cut objective:* **definite**, distinct, clear, well defined, precise, specific, explicit, unambiguous, unequivocal, black and white, cut and dried.
– OPPOSITES vague.

clearing noun **glade**, dell, gap, opening.

clearly adverb **1** *her ability to write clearly:* **intelligibly**, plainly, distinctly, comprehensibly, with clarity; legibly, audibly. **2** *clearly, substantial changes are needed:* **obviously**, evidently, patently, unquestionably, undoubtedly, without doubt, indubitably, plainly, undeniably, incontrovertibly, irrefutably, doubtless, it goes without saying, needless to say.

cleave verb **1** *the axe his father used to cleave wood for the fire:* **split (open)**, cut (up), hew, hack, chop up. **2** *cleaving a path through the traffic:* **plough**, drive, bulldoze, carve.

cleaver noun **chopper**, hatchet, axe, knife; butcher's knife, kitchen knife.

cleft noun **1** *a deep cleft in the rocks:* **split**, slit, crack, fissure, crevice, rift, break, fracture, rent, breach. **2** *the cleft in his chin:* **dimple**. adjective *a cleft tail:* **split**, divided, cloven.

clemency noun *an appeal for clemency:* **mercy**, mercifulness, leniency, lenience, mildness, indulgence, quarter; compassion,

humanity, pity, sympathy.
– OPPOSITES ruthlessness.

clench verb **1** *he stood there clenching his hands:* **squeeze together**, clamp together, close/shut tightly; make into a fist. **2** *he clenched the back of chair:* **grip**, grasp, grab, clutch, clasp, hold tightly, seize, press, squeeze.

clergy noun **clergymen**, clergywomen, churchmen, churchwomen, clerics, priests, ecclesiastics, men/women of God; ministry, priesthood, holy orders, the church, the cloth.
– OPPOSITES laity.

clergyman, clergywoman noun **priest**, churchman, churchwoman, man/woman of the cloth, man/woman of God; cleric, minister, preacher, chaplain, father, ecclesiastic, bishop, pastor, vicar, rector, parson, curate, deacon, deaconess; Scottish kirkman; N. Amer. dominie; informal reverend, padre, Holy Joe, sky pilot; Austral. informal josser.

clerical adjective **1** *clerical jobs:* **office**, desk, back-room; administrative, secretarial; white-collar. **2** *he was still in his clerical clothes:* **ecclesiastical**, church, priestly, religious, spiritual, sacerdotal; holy, divine.
– OPPOSITES secular.

clerk noun **office worker**, clerical worker, administrator; bookkeeper; cashier, teller; informal pen-pusher.

clever adjective **1** *a clever young woman:* **intelligent**, bright, smart, astute, quick-witted, shrewd; talented, gifted, brilliant, capable, able, competent, apt; educated, learned, knowledgeable, wise; informal brainy, savvy. **2** *a clever scheme:* **ingenious**, canny, cunning, crafty, artful, slick, neat. **3** *she was clever with her hands:* **skilful**, dexterous, adroit, adept, deft, nimble, handy; skilled, talented, gifted. **4** *a clever remark:* **witty**, amusing, droll, humorous, funny.
– OPPOSITES stupid.

cliché noun *it's a cliché that a trouble shared is a trouble halved:* **platitude**, hackneyed phrase, commonplace, banality, truism, stock phrase, trite phrase; informal old chestnut.

click noun *the door shut with a click:* **clack**, snick, snap, pop, tick; clink.
verb **1** *cameras clicked:* **clack**, snap, snick, tick, pop; clink. **2** (informal) *that night it clicked:* **become clear**, fall into place, come home, make sense, dawn, register, get through, sink in. **3** (informal) *we just clicked:* **take to each other**, get along, be compatible, be like-minded, feel a rapport, see eye to eye; informal hit it off, get on like a house on fire, be on the same wavelength.

client noun **customer**, buyer, purchaser, shopper, consumer, user; patient; patron, regular; **(clients)** clientele, patronage, public, market; Brit. informal punter.

cliff noun **precipice**, rock face, crag, bluff,

ridge, escarpment, scar, scarp, overhang.

climactic adjective *the movie's climactic scene:* **final**, ending, the closing, concluding, ultimate; exciting, thrilling, gripping, riveting, dramatic, hair-raising; crucial, decisive, critical.

climate noun **1** *a mild climate:* **weather conditions**, weather; atmospheric conditions. **2** *they come from colder climates:* **region**, area, zone, country, place. **3** *the political climate:* **atmosphere**, mood, feeling, ambience, tenor; tendency, ethos, attitude; milieu; informal vibe(s).

climax noun *the climax of his career:* **peak**, pinnacle, height, high(est) point, top; acme, zenith; culmination, crowning point, crown, crest; highlight, high spot, high water mark.
– OPPOSITES nadir.
verb *the event will climax with a concert:* **culminate**, peak, reach a pinnacle, come to a crescendo, come to a head.

climb verb **1** *we climbed the hill:* **ascend**, mount, scale, scramble up, clamber up, shin up; go up, walk up; conquer, gain. **2** *the plane climbed:* **rise**, ascend, go up, gain altitude. **3** *the road climbs steeply:* **slope upwards**, rise, go uphill, incline upwards. **4** *the shares climbed to 550 pence:* **increase**, rise, go up; shoot up, soar, rocket. **5** *he climbed through the ranks:* **advance**, rise, move up, progress, work one's way. **6** *he climbed out of his car:* **clamber**, scramble; step.
– OPPOSITES descend, drop, fall.
noun *a steep climb:* **ascent**, clamber.
– OPPOSITES descent.
■ **climb down 1** *Sandy climbed down the ladder:* **descend**, go/come down, move down, shin down. **2** *the Government had to climb down:* **back down**, admit defeat, surrender, capitulate, yield, give in, give way, submit; retreat, backtrack; eat one's words, eat humble pie; do a U-turn; Brit. do an about-turn; N. Amer. informal eat crow.

clinch verb **1** *he clinched the deal:* **secure**, settle, conclude, close, pull off, bring off, complete, confirm, seal, finalize; informal sew up, wrap up. **2** *these findings clinched the matter:* **settle**, decide, determine; resolve; informal sort out. **3** *they clinched the title:* **win**, secure; be victorious, come first, triumph, prevail.
– OPPOSITES lose.
noun *a passionate clinch:* **embrace**, hug, cuddle, squeeze, hold, clasp.

cling verb *rice grains tend to cling together:* **stick**, adhere, hold, cohere, bond, bind.
■ **cling (on) to 1** *she clung to him:* hold on, clutch, grip, grasp, clasp, attach oneself to, hang on; embrace, hug. **2** *they clung to their beliefs:* adhere to, hold to, stick to, stand by, abide by, cherish, remain true to, have faith in; informal swear by, stick with.

clinic noun **medical centre**, health centre, outpatients' department, surgery, doctor's.

clinical adjective **1** *he seemed so clinical:* **detached**, impersonal, dispassionate, objective, uninvolved, distant, remote, aloof, removed, cold, indifferent, neutral, unsympathetic, unfeeling, unemotional. **2** *the room was clinical:* **plain**, simple, unadorned, unembellished, stark, austere, spartan, bleak, bare; clean; functional, basic, institutional, impersonal, characterless.
– OPPOSITES emotional, luxurious.

clip[1] noun **1** *a briefcase clip:* **fastener**, clasp, hasp, catch, hook, buckle, lock. **2** *a diamanté clip:* **brooch**, pin, badge. **3** *his clip was empty:* **magazine**, cartridge, cylinder.
verb *he clipped the pages together:* **fasten**, attach, fix, join; pin, staple, tack.

clip[2] verb **1** *I clipped the hedge:* **trim**, prune, cut, snip, shorten, crop, shear, pare; lop; neaten, shape. **2** *clip the coupon below:* **remove**, cut out, snip out, tear out, detach. **3** *his lorry clipped a van:* **hit**, strike, touch, graze, glance off, run into. **4** *Mum clipped his ear:* **hit**, cuff, strike, smack, slap, box; informal clout, whack, wallop, clobber, biff, sock.
noun **1** *I gave him a full clip:* **trim**, cut, crop, haircut; shear. **2** *a film clip:* **extract**, excerpt, snippet, cutting, fragment; trailer. **3** (informal) *I'd give him a clip round the ear:* **smack**, cuff, slap, box; informal clout, whack, wallop, biff, sock.
■ **clip someone's wings** restrict someone's freedom, impose limits on, keep under control, stand in the way of; obstruct, impede, frustrate, thwart, fetter, hamstring.

clipping noun *friends are sending us newspaper clippings from the British press:* **cutting**, snippet, extract, excerpt.

clique noun *his flat became a haven for a clique of young men of similar tastes:* **coterie**, set, circle, ring, in-crowd, group; club, society, fraternity, sorority; cabal, caucus; informal gang.

cloak noun **1** *the cloak over his shoulders:* **cape**, robe, mantle, shawl, wrap, stole, tippet; poncho, serape, djellaba; cope. **2** *a cloak of secrecy:* **cover**, veil, mantle, shroud, screen, mask, shield, blanket.
verb *a peak cloaked in mist:* **conceal**, hide, cover, veil, shroud, mask, obscure, cloud; envelop, swathe, surround.

clock noun *a grandfather clock:* **timepiece**, timekeeper, timer; chronometer, chronograph.
verb (informal) *the UK clocked up record exports:* **register**, record, log, notch up; achieve, attain, accomplish, make; informal chalk up, bag.

clod noun *clods of earth:* **lump**, clump, chunk, hunk, wedge.

clog noun *a wooden clog:* **sabot**.
verb *the pipes were clogged:* **block**, obstruct, congest, jam, choke, bung up, plug, stop up, fill up; Brit. informal gunge up.

cloister noun *the convent cloisters:* **walkway**, covered walk, arcade, loggia, gallery.
verb *they were cloistered at home:* **confine**,

isolate, shut away, sequester, seclude, closet.

cloistered adjective *his cloistered life was devoted to writing:* **secluded**, sequestered, sheltered, protected, insulated; shut off, isolated, confined; solitary, monastic, reclusive.

close[1] adjective **1** *the town is close to Leeds:* **near**, adjacent; in the vicinity of, in the neighbourhood of, within reach of; neighbouring, adjoining, abutting, alongside, on the doorstep, a stone's throw away; nearby, at hand, at close quarters; informal within spitting distance. **2** *flying in close formation:* **dense**, compact, tight, close-packed, packed, solid; crowded, cramped, congested. **3** *I was close to tears:* **near**, on the verge of, on the brink of, on the point of. **4** *the race will be a close contest:* **evenly matched**, even, with nothing to choose between them, neck and neck; informal fifty-fifty, even-steven(s). **5** *not all elderly people have close relatives they might live with:* **immediate**, direct, near. **6** *they became close friends:* **intimate**, dear, bosom; close-knit, inseparable, attached, devoted, faithful; special, good, best, fast, firm; informal (as) thick as thieves. **7** *there is a close resemblance between them:* **strong**, marked, distinct, pronounced. **8** *their work deserves close examination:* **careful**, detailed, thorough, minute, searching, painstaking, meticulous, rigorous, scrupulous, conscientious; attentive, focused. **9** *a close translation:* **strict**, faithful, exact, precise, literal; word for word, verbatim. **10** *the weather was close:* **humid**, muggy, stuffy, airless, heavy, sticky, sultry, oppressive, stifling.
– OPPOSITES far, distant, one-sided, slight, loose, fresh.
noun (Brit.) *a small close of houses:* **cul-de-sac**, street, road; courtyard, quadrangle, enclosure.

close[2] verb **1** *she closed the door:* **shut**, pull to, push to, slam; fasten, secure. **2** *close the hole:* **block (up/off)**, stop up, plug, seal (up/off), shut up/off, cork, stopper, bung (up); clog (up), choke, obstruct. **3** *the enemy were closing fast:* **catch up**, creep up, near, approach, gain on someone. **4** *the gap is closing:* **narrow**, reduce, shrink, lessen, get smaller, diminish, contract. **5** *his arms closed around her:* **meet**, join, connect; form a circle. **6** *he closed the meeting:* **end**, conclude, finish, terminate, wind up, break off, halt, discontinue, dissolve; adjourn, suspend. **7** *the factory is to close:* **shut down**, close down, cease production, cease trading, be wound up, go out of business, go bankrupt, go into receivership, go into liquidation; informal fold, go to the wall, go bust. **8** *he closed a deal:* **clinch**, settle, secure, seal, confirm, establish; transact, pull off; complete, conclude, fix, agree, finalize; informal wrap up.
– OPPOSITES open, widen, begin.

noun *the close of the talks:* **end**, finish, conclusion, termination, cessation, completion, resolution; climax, denouement.
– OPPOSITES beginning.
■ **close down**. See CLOSE[2] verb sense 7.

closet noun *a clothes closet:* **cupboard**, wardrobe, cabinet, locker.
adjective *a closet gay:* **secret**, covert, private; surreptitious, clandestine, underground, furtive.
verb *David was closeted in his den:* **shut away**, sequester, seclude, cloister, confine, isolate.

closure noun *the closure of rural schools:* **closing down**, shutdown, winding up; termination, discontinuation, cessation, finish, conclusion; failure; informal folding.

clot noun **1** *blood clots:* **lump**, clump, mass; thrombus, thrombosis, embolus; informal glob; Brit. informal gob. **2** (Brit. informal) *a clumsy clot.* See FOOL noun sense 1.
verb *the blood is likely to clot:* **coagulate**, set, congeal, curdle, thicken, solidify.

cloth noun **1** *a maker of cloth:* **fabric**, material, textile(s); Brit. soft goods. **2** *a cloth to wipe the table:* **rag**, wipe, duster, sponge; flannel, towel; Austral. washer; UK trademark J-cloth.

clothe verb **1** *they were clothed in silk:* **dress**, attire, robe, garb, array, costume, swathe, deck (out), turn out, fit out, rig (out); informal get up. **2** *a valley clothed in conifers:* **cover**, blanket, carpet; envelop, swathe.

clothes plural noun **clothing**, garments, attire, garb, dress, wear, costume; informal gear, togs, duds, get-up; Brit. informal clobber; N. Amer. informal threads.

cloud noun *a cloud of exhaust smoke:* **mass**, billow; pall, mantle, blanket.
verb **1** *the sky clouded:* **become overcast**, cloud over, become cloudy, lour, blacken, darken. **2** *the sand is churned up, clouding the water:* **make cloudy**, make murky, dirty, darken, blacken. **3** *anger clouded my judgement:* **confuse**, muddle, obscure, fog, muddy, mar.

cloudy adjective **1** *a cloudy sky:* **overcast**, clouded; dark, grey, black, leaden, murky; sombre, dismal, heavy, gloomy; sunless, starless; hazy, misty, foggy. **2** *cloudy water:* **murky**, muddy, milky, dirty, opaque, turbid. **3** *his eyes grew cloudy:* **tearful**, teary, weepy, lachrymose; moist, watery; misty, blurred.
– OPPOSITES clear.

cloven adjective *cloven hooves:* **split**, divided, cleft.

clown noun **1** *a circus clown:* **comic entertainer**, comedian; historical jester, fool, zany. **2** *the class clown:* **joker**, comedian, comic, humorist, wag, wit, prankster, jester, buffoon; informal laugh, kidder, wisecracker; Austral./NZ informal hard case. **3** *bureaucratic clowns:* **fool**, idiot, dolt, ass, simpleton, ignoramus; bungler, blunderer;

informal **moron**, jackass, chump, numbskull, nincompoop, halfwit, bonehead, fathead, birdbrain; Brit. informal prat, berk, twit, nitwit, twerp, muppet.
verb *Harvey clowned around:* **fool around/about**, play the fool, play about/around, monkey about/around; joke, jest; informal mess about/around, lark (about/around), horse about/around; Brit. informal muck about/around.

cloy verb *the piece goes on a little too long and the sweetness can begin to cloy:* **sicken**, disgust; become sickening, become nauseating, pall; be excessive.

cloying adjective *a romantic, rather cloying story:* **sickly**, syrupy, saccharine, oversweet; sickening, nauseating; mawkish, sentimental; Brit. twee; informal over the top, OTT, mushy, slushy, sloppy, gooey, cheesy, corny; N. Amer. informal cornball, sappy.

club¹ noun **1** *a canoeing club:* **society**, association, organization, institution, group, circle, band, body, ring, crew; alliance, league, union. **2** *the city has great clubs:* **nightclub**, disco, discotheque, bar; informal niterie. **3** *the top club in the league:* **team**, squad, side, line-up.
■ **club together** pool resources, join forces, team up, band together, get together, pull together, collaborate, ally; informal have a whip-round.

club² noun *a wooden club:* **cudgel**, truncheon, bludgeon, baton, stick, mace, bat; N. Amer. blackjack, nightstick; Brit. informal cosh.
verb *he was clubbed with an iron bar:* **cudgel**, bludgeon, bash, beat, hit, strike, batter; informal clout, clobber; Brit. informal cosh.

clue noun **1** *police are searching for clues:* **hint**, indication, sign, signal, pointer, trace, indicator; lead, tip, tip-off; evidence, information. **2** *a crossword clue:* **question**, problem, puzzle, riddle, poser, conundrum.
■ **not have a clue** (informal) have no idea, be ignorant, not have an inkling; be baffled, be mystified, be at a loss; informal be clueless, not have the faintest.

clump noun *a clump of trees:* **cluster**, thicket, group, bunch, assemblage. **2** *a clump of earth:* **lump**, clod, mass, gobbet, wad; informal glob; Brit. informal gob.
verb **1** *galaxies clump together:* **cluster**, group, collect, gather, assemble, congregate, mass. **2** *they were clumping around upstairs:* **stamp**, stomp, clomp, tramp, lumber; thump, thud, bang; informal galumph.

clumsy adjective **1** *she was terribly clumsy:* **awkward**, uncoordinated, ungainly, graceless, inelegant; inept, maladroit, unskilful, unhandy, accident-prone, like a bull in a china shop, all fingers and thumbs; informal cack-handed, ham-fisted, butterfingered, having two left feet; N. Amer. informal klutzy. **2** *a clumsy contraption:* **unwieldy**, cumbersome, bulky, awkward. **3** *a clumsy remark:* **gauche**, awkward, graceless; unsubtle, uncouth, boorish,

crass; tactless, insensitive, thoughtless, undiplomatic, indelicate, ill-judged.
– OPPOSITES graceful, elegant, tactful.

cluster noun **1** *clusters of berries:* **bunch**, clump, mass, knot, group, clutch, bundle, truss. **2** *a cluster of spectators:* **crowd**, group, knot, huddle, bunch, throng, flock, pack, band; informal gang, gaggle.
verb *they clustered around the television:* **congregate**, gather, collect, group, assemble; huddle, crowd, flock.

clutch¹ verb *she clutched his arm:* **grip**, grasp, clasp, cling to, hang on to, clench, hold.
■ **clutch at** reach for, snatch at, make a grab for, catch at, claw at.

clutch² noun **1** *a clutch of eggs:* **group**, batch. **2** *the film won a clutch of awards:* **group**, collection; raft, armful; informal load, bunch.

clutches plural noun *Tom had fallen into Amanda's clutches:* **power**, control, domination, command, rule, tyranny; hands, hold, grip, grasp, claws, jaws; custody.

clutter noun **1** *a clutter of toys:* **mess**, jumble, litter, heap, tangle, muddle, hotchpotch. **2** *a desk full of clutter:* **disorder**, chaos, disarray, untidiness, mess, confusion; litter, rubbish.
verb *the garden was cluttered with tools:* **litter**, mess up, disarrange; be strewn, be scattered.

coach¹ noun **1** *a journey by coach:* **bus**, minibus. **2** *a railway coach:* **carriage**, wagon, compartment, van, Pullman; N. Amer. car. **3** *a coach and horses:* **horse-drawn carriage**, trap, hackney, hansom, gig, landau, brougham.

coach² noun *a football coach:* **instructor**, trainer; teacher, tutor, mentor, guru.
verb *he coached Richard in maths:* **instruct**, teach, tutor, school, educate; drill, cram; train.

coagulate verb *the heat causes the blood to coagulate:* **congeal**, clot, thicken, gel; solidify, harden, set, dry.

coalesce verb *some of the puddles had coalesced into shallow streams:* **merge**, unite, join together, combine, fuse, mingle, blend; amalgamate, consolidate, integrate, homogenize, converge.

coalition noun *a coalition between Conservatives and Liberals:* **alliance**, union, partnership, bloc, caucus; federation, league, association, confederation, consortium, syndicate; amalgamation, merger.

coarse adjective **1** *coarse blankets:* **rough**, scratchy, prickly, wiry. **2** *his coarse features:* **large**, rough, rough-hewn, heavy; ugly. **3** *a coarse boy:* **oafish**, loutish, boorish, uncouth, rude, impolite, ill-mannered, uncivil; vulgar, common, rough, uncultured, crass. **4** *a coarse innuendo:* **vulgar**, crude, rude, off colour, dirty, filthy, smutty, indelicate, improper, unseemly, crass, tasteless, lewd, prurient; informal blue, farmyard.
– OPPOSITES soft, delicate, refined.

coarsen verb **1** *hands coarsened by work:*

roughen, toughen, harden. **2** *I had been coarsened by the army:* **desensitize**, dehumanize; dull, deaden.
– OPPOSITES soften, refine.

coast noun *the west coast:* **seaboard**, coastal region, coastline, seashore, shore, foreshore, shoreline, seaside, waterfront, littoral.
verb *the car coasted down a hill:* **freewheel**, cruise, taxi, drift, glide, sail.

coat noun **1** *a winter coat:* **overcoat**, jacket. **2** *a animal's coat:* **fur**, hair, wool, fleece; hide, pelt, skin. **3** *a coat of paint:* **layer**, covering, coating, skin, film, wash; plating, glaze, varnish, veneer, patina; deposit.
verb *the tube was coated with wax:* **cover**, paint, glaze, varnish, wash; surface, veneer, laminate, plate, face; daub, smear, cake, plaster.

coax verb *the trainees were coaxed into doing boring work:* **persuade**, wheedle, cajole, get round; beguile, seduce, inveigle, manoeuvre; informal sweet-talk, soft-soap, butter up, twist someone's arm.

cobble
▪ **cobble something together** *she cobbled together a rough draft:* prepare roughly/hastily, make roughly/hastily, throw together; improvise, contrive, rig (up), whip up; informal rustle up; Brit. informal knock up.

cock noun **rooster**, cockerel, capon.
verb **1** *he cocked his head:* **tilt**, tip, angle, incline, dip. **2** *she cocked her little finger:* **bend**, flex, crook, curve. **3** *the dog cocked its leg:* **lift**, raise, hold up.

cocksure adjective *he made a change from the cocksure men she usually met:* **arrogant**, conceited, overweening, overconfident, cocky, proud, vain, self-important, swollen-headed, egotistical, presumptuous; smug, patronizing, pompous; informal high and mighty.
– OPPOSITES modest.

cocky adjective *I thought she was far too cocky:* **arrogant**, conceited, overweening, overconfident, cocksure, swollen-headed, self-important, egotistical, presumptuous, boastful, self-assertive; bold, forward, insolent, cheeky.
– OPPOSITES modest.

cocoon verb **1** *he cocooned her in a towel:* **wrap**, swathe, swaddle, muffle, cloak, enfold, envelop, cover, fold. **2** *he was cocooned in the upper classes:* **protect**, shield, shelter, screen, cushion, insulate, isolate, cloister.

coddle verb *I was coddled and cosseted:* **pamper**, cosset, mollycoddle; spoil, indulge, overindulge, pander to; wrap in cotton wool; baby, mother, wait on hand and foot.
– OPPOSITES neglect.

code noun **1** *a secret code:* **cipher**, key; hieroglyphics; cryptogram. **2** *a strict social code:* **morality**, convention, etiquette, protocol. **3** *the penal code:* **law(s)**, rules,

regulations; constitution, system.

codify verb *the bill codified these standards for the first time:* **systematize**, systemize, organize, arrange, order, structure; tabulate, catalogue, list, sort, index, classify, categorize, file, log.

coerce verb *he was coerced into giving evidence:* **pressure**, pressurize, press, push, constrain; force, compel, oblige, browbeat, bludgeon, bully, threaten, intimidate, dragoon, twist someone's arm; informal railroad, squeeze, lean on.

coercion noun **force**, compulsion, constraint, duress, oppression, enforcement, harassment, intimidation, threats, arm-twisting, pressure.

coffee noun N. Amer. informal joe, java.

coffer noun **1** *every church had a coffer:* **strongbox**, money box, cash box, money chest, treasure chest, safe; casket, box. **2** *the Imperial coffers:* **fund(s)**, reserves, resources, money, finances, wealth, cash, capital, purse; treasury, exchequer.

coffin noun sarcophagus; N. Amer. casket; informal box; humorous wooden overcoat.

cogent adjective *a cogent argument:* **convincing**, compelling, strong, forceful, powerful, potent, weighty, effective; valid, sound, plausible, telling; impressive, persuasive, eloquent, credible, influential; conclusive, authoritative; logical, reasoned, rational, reasonable, lucid, coherent, clear.

cognition noun *a theory of human cognition:* **perception**, discernment, apprehension, learning, understanding, comprehension, insight; reasoning, thinking, thought.

cohabit verb *Mary is now cohabiting with Paul:* **live together**, live with; informal shack up (with).

coherent adjective *a coherent argument:* **logical**, reasoned, reasonable, rational, sound, cogent, consistent; clear, lucid, articulate; intelligible, comprehensible.
– OPPOSITES muddled.

cohesion noun *rewarding individuals breaks the cohesion in the group:* **unity**, togetherness, solidarity, bond, coherence; connection, linkage.

cohort noun **1** *a Roman army cohort:* **unit**, force, corps, division, brigade, battalion, regiment, squadron, company, troop, contingent, legion. **2** *the 1940–4 birth cohort of women:* **group**, grouping, category, class, set, division, batch, list; age group, generation.

coil noun *coils of rope:* **loop**, twist, turn, curl, convolution; spiral, helix, corkscrew.
verb *he coiled her hair around his finger:* **wind**, loop, twist, curl, curve, bend, twine, entwine; spiral, corkscrew.

coin noun *a gold coin:* **piece**; (**coins**) coinage, specie; (loose) change, small change, silver, copper(s), gold.
verb **1** *guineas were coined:* **mint**, stamp,

strike, cast, punch, die, mould, forge, make.
2 *he coined the term:* **invent**, create, make
up, conceive, originate, think up, dream up.

coincide verb **1** *the events coincided:*
occur simultaneously, happen together,
be concurrent, concur, coexist. **2** *their
interests do not always coincide:* **tally**,
correspond, agree, accord, concur, match,
fit, be consistent, equate, harmonize, be
compatible, dovetail, correlate; informal
square.
– OPPOSITES differ.

coincidence noun **1** *the resemblances
are too close to be mere coincidence:*
accident, chance, serendipity, fortuity,
providence, happenstance, fate; a
fluke. **2** *the coincidence of inflation
and unemployment:* **co-occurrence**,
coexistence, conjunction, simultaneity,
contemporaneity, concomitance.

coincident adjective *algae blooms coincident
with dolphin deaths:* **concurrent**, coinciding,
simultaneous, contemporaneous,
concomitant, coexistent.

coincidental adjective *a coincidental
resemblance:* **accidental**, chance, fluky,
random; fortuitous, adventitious,
serendipitous; unexpected, unforeseen,
unintentional, inadvertent, unplanned.

cold adjective **1** *a cold day:* **chilly**, chill,
cool, freezing, icy, snowy, wintry, frosty,
frigid, gelid; bitter, biting, raw; informal
nippy, brass monkeys, arctic; Brit. informal
parky. **2** *I'm very cold:* **chilly**, chilled,
cool, freezing, frozen, shivery, numb,
benumbed; hypothermic. **3** *Rodrigo met with
a cold and scornful reception:* **unfriendly**,
inhospitable, unwelcoming, forbidding,
cool, frigid, frosty, glacial, lukewarm,
indifferent, unfeeling, unemotional, formal,
stiff.
– OPPOSITES hot, warm.

cold-blooded adjective *a cold-blooded
murder:* **cruel**, callous, sadistic, inhuman,
inhumane, pitiless, merciless, ruthless,
unforgiving, unfeeling, uncaring, heartless;
savage, brutal, barbaric, barbarous; cold,
cold-hearted, unemotional.

cold-hearted adjective *I don't want to
appear cold-hearted or stubborn:* **unfeeling**,
unloving, uncaring, unsympathetic,
unemotional, unfriendly, uncharitable,
unkind, insensitive; hard-hearted, stony-
hearted, heartless, hard, cold.

collaborate verb **1** *they collaborated
on the project:* **cooperate**, join forces,
team up, band together, work together,
participate, combine, ally; pool resources,
club together. **2** *they collaborated with
the enemy:* **fraternize**, conspire, collude,
cooperate, consort, sympathize.

collaborator noun **1** *his collaborator on
the book:* **co-worker**, partner, associate,
colleague, confederate; assistant. **2** *a
wartime collaborator:* **quisling**, fraternizer,

collaborationist, colluder, (enemy)
sympathizer; traitor, fifth columnist.

collapse verb **1** *the roof collapsed:* **cave
in**, fall in, subside, fall down, give (way),
crumple, sag, slump. **2** *he collapsed last
night:* **faint**, pass out, black out, lose
consciousness, keel over, swoon; informal
flake out, conk out. **3** *she collapsed in tears:*
break down, go to pieces, lose control,
be overcome, crumble; informal crack up.
4 *peace talks collapsed:* **break down**, fail,
fall through, fold, founder, miscarry, come
to grief, be unsuccessful; end; informal flop,
fizzle out.
noun **1** *the collapse of the roof:* **cave-
in**, subsidence. **2** *her collapse on stage:*
fainting fit, faint, blackout, loss of
consciousness, swoon. **3** *the collapse of the
talks:* **breakdown**, failure, disintegration;
end. **4** *he suffered a collapse:* **(nervous)
breakdown**, personal crisis, psychological
trauma; informal crack-up.

collar noun *a collar round the pipe:* **ring**,
band, collet, sleeve, flange.
verb (informal) **1** *he collared a thief:* **apprehend**,
arrest, catch, capture, seize; take prisoner,
take into custody, detain; informal nab, pinch,
bust, pick up, pull in, feel someone's collar;
Brit. informal nick. **2** *she collared me in the
street:* **accost**, waylay, hail, approach, detain,
stop, halt, catch, confront, importune; informal
buttonhole; Brit. informal nobble.

collate verb *the system is used to collate
information:* **collect**, gather, accumulate,
assemble; combine, aggregate, put together;
arrange, organize.

collateral noun *she put up her house as
collateral for the bank loan:* **security**, surety,
guarantee, guaranty, insurance, indemnity,
indemnification; backing.

colleague noun **co-worker**, fellow worker,
workmate, teammate, associate, partner,
collaborator, ally, confederate.

collect verb **1** *he collected the rubbish:*
gather, accumulate, assemble; amass,
stockpile, pile up, heap up, store (up), hoard,
save; mass, accrue. **2** *a crowd soon collected:*
gather, assemble, meet, muster, congregate,
convene, converge, flock together. **3** *I must
collect the children:* **fetch**, go/come to get,
call for, meet. **4** *they collect money for
charity:* **raise**, appeal for, ask for, solicit;
obtain, acquire, gather. **5** *he paused to collect
himself:* **recover**, regain one's composure,
pull oneself together, steady oneself; informal
get a grip (on oneself). **6** *she collected her
thoughts:* **muster**, summon (up), gather, get
together, marshal.
– OPPOSITES disperse, distribute.

collected adjective *outwardly they are
cool, calm, and collected:* **calm**, cool, self-
possessed, self-controlled, composed,
poised; serene, tranquil, relaxed, unruffled,
unperturbed, untroubled; placid, quiet,
sedate, phlegmatic; informal unfazed,
together, laid-back.

–OPPOSITES excited, hysterical.

collection noun **1** *a collection of stolen items:* **hoard**, pile, heap, stack, stock, store, stockpile; accumulation, reserve, supply, bank, pool, fund, mine, reservoir. **2** *a collection of shoppers:* **group**, crowd, body, assemblage, gathering, throng; knot, cluster; multitude, bevy, party, band, horde, pack, flock, swarm, mob; informal gang, load, gaggle. **3** *a collection of Victorian dolls:* **set**, series; array, assortment. **4** *a collection of short stories:* **anthology**, selection, compendium, treasury, compilation, miscellany, pot-pourri. **5** *a collection for the poor:* **donations**, contributions, gifts, subscription(s); informal whip-round. **6** *a church collection:* **offering**, offertory, tithe.

collective adjective *collective ownership of the means of production:* **common**, shared, joint, combined, mutual, communal, pooled; united, allied, cooperative, collaborative.
–OPPOSITES individual.

college noun **1** *a college of technology:* **school**, academy, university, polytechnic, institute, seminary, conservatoire, conservatory. **2** *the College of Heralds:* **association**, society, club, institute, body, fellowship, guild, lodge, order, fraternity, league, union, alliance.

collide verb **1** *the trains collided with each other:* **crash**, impact; hit, strike, run into, bump into, meet head-on, cannon into, plough into; N. Amer. informal barrel into. **2** *politics and metaphysics collide:* **conflict**, clash; differ, diverge, disagree, be at odds, be incompatible.

collision noun **1** *a collision on the ring road:* **crash**, accident, impact, smash, bump, hit; Brit. RTA (road traffic accident); N. Amer. wreck; informal pile-up; Brit. informal prang, shunt. **2** *a collision between two ideas:* **conflict**, clash; disagreement, incompatibility, contradiction.

colloquial adjective *some students have a good grasp of colloquial language:* **informal**, conversational, everyday, non-literary; unofficial, idiomatic, slangy, vernacular, popular, demotic.
–OPPOSITES formal.

collude verb *corrupt border officials colluded with the importers of dubious goods:* **conspire**, connive, collaborate, plot, scheme; informal be in cahoots.

colonist noun *European colonists of North America:* **settler**, colonizer, colonial, pioneer; immigrant, incomer, newcomer.
–OPPOSITES native.

colonize verb *the Germans colonized Tanganyika in 1885:* **settle (in)**, people, populate; occupy, take over, seize, capture, subjugate.

colonnade noun **row of columns**; portico, stoa, peristyle.

colony noun **1** *a French colony:* **territory**, dependency, protectorate, satellite, settlement, outpost, province. **2** *the*

British colony in New York: **population**, community. **3** *an artists' colony:* **community**, commune; quarter, district, ghetto.

colossal adjective *a colossal building:* **huge**, massive, enormous, gigantic, very big, giant, mammoth, vast, immense, monumental, prodigious, mountainous, titanic, towering, king-size(d); informal monster, whopping, humongous, jumbo; Brit. informal ginormous.
–OPPOSITES tiny.

colour noun **1** *the lights changed colour:* **hue**, shade, tint, tone, coloration. **2** *eight tubes of oil colour:* **paint**, pigment, colourant, dye, stain, tint, wash. **3** *the colour in her cheeks:* **redness**, pinkness, rosiness, ruddiness, blush, flush, bloom. **4** *people of every colour:* **skin colouring**, skin tone, colouring; race, ethnic group. **5** *anecdotes add colour to the text:* **vividness**, life, liveliness, vitality, excitement, interest, richness, zest, spice, piquancy, impact, force; informal oomph, pizzazz, punch, kick. **6** *the regimental colours.* See **FLAG**[1] noun.
verb **1** *the wood was coloured blue:* **tint**, dye, stain, paint, pigment, wash. **2** *she coloured up:* **blush**, redden, go pink, go red, flush. **3** *the experience coloured her outlook:* **influence**, affect, taint, warp, skew, distort, bias, prejudice. **4** *they colour evidence to make a story saleable:* **exaggerate**, overstate, embroider, embellish, dramatize, enhance, varnish; falsify, misreport, manipulate.

colourful adjective **1** *a colourful picture:* **brightly coloured**, vivid, vibrant, brilliant, radiant, rich; gaudy, glaring, garish; multicoloured, multicolour, rainbow, varicoloured, harlequin, polychromatic, psychedelic; informal jazzy. **2** *he regaled her with a colourful account of that afternoon's meeting:* **vivid**, graphic, lively, animated, dramatic, fascinating, interesting, stimulating, scintillating, evocative.

colourless adjective **1** *a colourless liquid:* **uncoloured**, white, bleached. **2** *her colourless face:* **pale**, pallid, wan, anaemic, bloodless, ashen, white, waxen, pasty, peaky, sickly, drained, drawn, ghostly, deathly. **3** *a colourless personality:* **uninteresting**, dull, boring, tedious, dry, dreary; unexciting, bland, weak, insipid, vapid, vacuous, feeble, wishy-washy, lame, lifeless, spiritless, anaemic, bloodless; nondescript, characterless.
–OPPOSITES colourful, rosy.

column noun **1** *arches supported by massive columns:* **pillar**, post, support, upright, baluster, pier, pile, pilaster, stanchion; obelisk, monolith. **2** *a column in the paper:* **article**, piece, item, story, report, account, write-up, feature, review, notice, editorial, leader. **3** *we walked in a column:* **line**, file, queue, procession, train, cavalcade, convoy; informal crocodile.

columnist noun *a columnist for the Irish Times:* **writer**, contributor, journalist, correspondent, newspaperman, newspaperwoman, newsman, newswoman; wordsmith, penman; critic, reviewer, commentator; informal scribbler, pen-pusher, hack(ette), journo.

coma noun **state of unconsciousness**; Medicine persistent vegetative state, PVS.

comatose adjective **1** *he was comatose after the accident:* **unconscious**, in a coma, insensible, insensate. **2** (informal) *she lay comatose in the sun:* **inert**, inactive, lethargic, sluggish, torpid, languid; somnolent, sleeping, dormant.

comb verb **1** *she combed her hair:* **groom**, brush, untangle, smooth, straighten, neaten, tidy, arrange; curry. **2** *the wool was combed:* **separate**, dress, card, tease, hackle, heckle. **3** *police combed the area:* **search**, scour, explore, sweep, probe, hunt through, forage through, poke about/around in, go over, go over with a fine-tooth comb; leave no stone unturned.

combat noun *he was killed in combat:* **battle**, fighting, action, hostilities, conflict, war, warfare.
verb *they tried to combat the disease:* **fight**, battle, tackle, attack, counter, resist, withstand; impede, block, thwart, inhibit; stop, halt, prevent, check, curb.

combatant noun *a combatant in the war:* **fighter**, soldier, serviceman/woman, warrior, trooper.
adjective *combatant armies:* **warring**, at war, opposing, belligerent, fighting, battling.

combative adjective *he made some enemies with his combative style:* **pugnacious**, aggressive, antagonistic, quarrelsome, argumentative, contentious, hostile, truculent, belligerent, bellicose, militant; informal spoiling for a fight.
– OPPOSITES conciliatory.

combination noun **1** *a combination of ancient and modern:* **amalgamation**, amalgam, merge, blend, mixture, mix, fusion, marriage, coalition, integration, incorporation, synthesis, composite. **2** *he acted in combination with his brother:* **cooperation**, collaboration, association, union, partnership, league.

combine verb **1** *he combines comedy with tragedy:* **amalgamate**, integrate, incorporate, merge, mix, fuse, blend; bind, join, marry, unify. **2** *teachers combined to tackle the problem:* **cooperate**, collaborate, join forces, get together, club together, unite, team up, throw in one's lot; informal gang up.

combustible adjective *a combustible gas:* **inflammable**, flammable, incendiary, ignitable.

combustion noun **burning**; kindling, ignition.

come verb **1** *come and listen:* **move nearer**, move closer, approach, advance, draw close/closer, draw near/nearer;

proceed. **2** *they came last night:* **arrive**, get here/there, make it, appear, come on the scene; approach, enter, turn up, come along, materialize; informal show (up), roll in/up, blow in, show one's face. **3** *they came to a stream:* **reach**, arrive at, get to, make it to, make, gain; come across, run across, happen on, chance on, come upon, stumble on; end up at; informal wind up at. **4** *the dress comes to her ankles:* **extend**, stretch, reach, come as far as. **5** *she comes from Belgium:* **be from**, be a native of, hail from, originate in; live in, reside in. **6** *attacks came without warning.* **happen**, occur, take place, come about, transpire, fall, present itself, crop up, materialize, arise, arrive, appear; ensue, follow.
– OPPOSITES go, leave.

■ **come about** happen, occur, take place, transpire, fall; crop up, materialize, arise, arrive, appear, surface; ensue, follow.

■ **come across 1** *they came across his friends:* meet/find by chance, meet, run into, run across, come upon, chance on, stumble on, happen on; discover, encounter, find, locate; informal bump into. **2** *the emotion comes across:* be communicated, be perceived, get across, be clear, be understood, register, sink in, strike home. **3** *she came across as cool:* seem, appear, look, sound, look to be; Brit. come over; N. Amer. come off.

■ **come along 1** *the puppies are coming along nicely:* progress, develop, shape up; come on, turn out; improve, get better, pick up, rally, recover. **2** *Come along!* hurry (up), be quick, get a move on, look lively, speed up, move faster; Brit. look smart; informal get moving, get cracking, step on it, move it, buck up, shake a leg, make it snappy; Brit. informal get your skates on; N. Amer. informal get a wiggle on.

■ **come apart** break up, fall to bits, fall to pieces, disintegrate, come unstuck, separate, split, tear.

■ **come back** return, get back, arrive home, come home; come again.

■ **come between** *nothing should come between brothers:* alienate, estrange, separate, divide, split up, break up, disunite, set at odds.

■ **come by** *good medical care was hard to come by:* obtain, acquire, gain, get, find, pick up, procure, secure; buy, purchase; informal get one's hands on, get hold of, bag, score, swing.

■ **come down** *the study comes down against kerbside collection:* decide, conclude, settle; choose, opt, plump.

■ **come down on.** See REPRIMAND verb.

■ **come down to** *it came down to her word against Guy's:* amount to, add up to, constitute, boil down to, be equivalent to.

■ **come down with** *I came down with flu:* fall ill with, fall sick with, be taken ill with, show symptoms of, become infected with, get, catch, develop, contract, fall victim to; Brit. go down with.

C

■ **come forward** *a local trader came forward to pay the fines:* volunteer, offer one's services, make oneself available.

■ **come in** enter, gain admission, cross the threshold.

■ **come into** *he came into money and set up his own business:* inherit, be left, be willed, be bequeathed.

■ **come in for** *he has come in for a lot of criticism:* receive, experience, sustain, undergo, go through, encounter, face, be subjected to, bear, suffer.

■ **come off 1** *this soufflé rarely comes off:* succeed, work, turn out well, work out, go as planned, produce the desired result, get results. **2** *she always came off worse:* end up, finish up.

■ **come on** progress, develop, shape up, take shape, come along, turn out; improve.

■ **come out 1** *it came out that he'd been to Rome:* become known, become apparent, come to light, emerge, transpire; get out, be discovered, be uncovered, be revealed, leak out, be disclosed. **2** *my book is coming out:* be published, be issued, be released, be brought out, be printed, go on sale. **3** *the flowers have come out:* bloom, flower, open. **4** *it will come out all right:* end, finish, conclude, work out, turn out; informal pan out.

■ **come out with** *she was puzzled that he should come out with this remark:* utter, say, let out, blurt out, burst out with.

■ **come round 1** *he has just come round from anaesthetic:* regain consciousness, come to, come to one's senses, recover, revive, awake, wake up. **2** *I came round to her view:* be converted, be won over (by), agree (with), change one's mind, be persuaded (by); give way, yield, relent. **3** *Friday the 13th comes round every few months:* occur, take place, happen, come up, crop up, arise; recur, reoccur, return, reappear. **4** *come round for a drink:* visit, call (in/round), look in, stop by, drop by/in/round/over, come over; informal pop in/round/over.

■ **come through** *his four shops came through the war intact:* survive, get through, ride out, weather, live through, pull through; withstand, stand up to, endure, surmount, overcome; informal stick out.

■ **come to 1** *the bill came to £17.50:* amount to, add up to, run to, total, equal; Brit. tot up to. **2** *I came to in the hospital:* regain consciousness, come round, come to one's senses, recover, revive, awake, wake up.

■ **come up** *when the opportunity came up again we didn't hesitate:* arise, occur, happen, come about, transpire, emerge, surface, crop up, turn up, pop up.

■ **come up to 1** *she came up to his shoulder:* reach, come to, be as tall as, extend to. **2** *he never came up to her expectations:* measure up to, match up to, live up to, fulfil, satisfy, meet, equal, compare with; be good enough; informal hold a candle to.

■ **come up with** *I needed to come up with a solution:* devise, produce, think up; propose,

put forward, submit, suggest, recommend, advocate, introduce, moot.

comeback noun *he made a determined comeback:* **resurgence**, recovery, return, rally, upturn; Brit. fightback.

comedian noun **1** *a famous comedian:* **comic**, comedienne, funny man/woman, humorist, gagster, stand-up; N. Amer. tummler. **2** *Dad was such a comedian:* **joker**, jester, wit, wag, comic, wisecracker, jokester; prankster, clown, fool, buffoon; informal laugh, hoot, case.

comedown noun (informal) **1** *a bit of a comedown for a sergeant:* **loss of status**, loss of face, humiliation, belittlement, demotion, degradation, disgrace. **2** *it's such a comedown after Christmas:* **anticlimax**, let-down, disappointment, disillusionment, deflation, decline.

comedy noun **1** *he excels in comedy:* **light entertainment**, comic play, comic film, farce, situation comedy, satire, pantomime, comic opera; burlesque, slapstick; informal sitcom. **2** *the comedy in their work:* **humour**, fun, funny side, comical aspect, absurdity, drollness, farce.
– OPPOSITES tragedy, gravity.

comeuppance noun *in those films the villain always got his comeuppance:* (informal) **just deserts**, just punishment, due, retribution, requital.

comfort noun **1** *travel in comfort:* **ease**, relaxation, repose, serenity, tranquillity, contentment, cosiness; luxury, opulence, prosperity; bed of roses. **2** *words of comfort:* **consolation**, solace, condolence, sympathy, commiseration; support, reassurance, cheer.
verb *a friend tried to comfort her:* **console**, solace, condole with, commiserate with, sympathize with; support, succour, ease, reassure, soothe, calm; cheer, hearten, uplift; informal buck up.
– OPPOSITES distress, depress.

comfortable adjective **1** *a comfortable lifestyle:* **pleasant**, free from hardship; affluent, well-to-do, luxurious, opulent. **2** *a comfortable room:* **cosy**, snug, warm, pleasant, agreeable; restful, homelike, homely; informal comfy. **3** *comfortable clothes:* **loose**, loose-fitting, casual; informal comfy. **4** *a comfortable pace:* **leisurely**, unhurried, relaxed, easy, gentle, sedate, undemanding, slow; informal laid-back. **5** *they feel comfortable with each other:* **at ease**, relaxed, secure, safe, unworried, contented, happy.
– OPPOSITES hard, spartan, tense.

comforting adjective *Anne gave her a comforting hug:* **consoling**, sympathetic, compassionate, solicitous, tender, warm, caring, loving; supportive, reassuring, soothing, calming; cheering, heartening, encouraging.

comfortless adjective **1** *a comfortless house:* **gloomy**, dreary, dismal, bleak, grim, sombre; joyless, cheerless, depressing,

disheartening, dispiriting, unwelcoming, uninviting; austere, spartan, institutional. **2** *he left her comfortless:* **miserable**, heartbroken, grief-stricken, unhappy, sad, distressed, desolate, devastated, inconsolable, disconsolate, downcast, downhearted, dejected, cheerless, depressed, melancholy, gloomy, glum; informal blue, down in the mouth, down in the dumps.
– OPPOSITES cosy, happy.

comic adjective *a comic play:* **humorous**, funny, droll, amusing, hilarious, uproarious, comical, farcical, silly, slapstick, zany; witty, jocular; informal priceless, side-splitting, rib-tickling.
– OPPOSITES serious.
noun **1** *a TV comic:* **comedian**, comedienne, funny man/woman, comedy actor/actress, humorist, wit; joker, clown; informal kidder, wisecracker. **2** *Tony read his comic:* **cartoon paper**, comic paper, comic book, graphic novel; informal funny.

comical adjective **1** *he could be quite comical:* **funny**, comic, humorous, droll, witty, jocular, hilarious, amusing, diverting, entertaining; informal jokey, wacky, waggish, side-splitting, rib-tickling, priceless, a scream, a laugh. **2** *they look comical in those suits:* **silly**, absurd, ridiculous, laughable, risible, ludicrous, preposterous, foolish; informal wacky, crazy.
– OPPOSITES sensible.

coming adjective *the coming election:* **forthcoming**, imminent, impending, approaching; future, expected, anticipated; close, at hand, in store, in the offing, in the pipeline, on the horizon, on the way; informal on the cards.
noun *the coming of spring:* **approach**, advance, advent, arrival, appearance, emergence, onset.

command verb **1** *he commanded his men to retreat:* **order**, tell, direct, instruct, call on, require. **2** *Jones commanded a tank squadron:* **be in charge of**, be in command of, be the leader of; head, lead, control, direct, manage, supervise, oversee; informal head up. **3** *they command great respect:* **receive**, get, gain, secure.
noun **1** *officers shouted commands:* **order**, instruction, directive, direction, commandment, injunction, demand, stipulation, requirement, exhortation, bidding, request. **2** *he had 160 men under his command:* **authority**, control, charge, power, direction, dominion, guidance; leadership, rule, government, management, supervision, jurisdiction. **3** *a brilliant command of English:* **knowledge**, mastery, grasp, comprehension, understanding.

commandeer verb *everything surrounding the base was commandeered by the army:* **seize**, take, requisition, appropriate, expropriate, sequestrate, sequester, confiscate, annex, take over, claim, pre-empt; hijack, arrogate, help oneself to; informal walk off with.

commander noun **leader**, head, chief, overseer, controller; commander-in-chief, C in C, commanding officer, CO, officer; informal boss, boss man, skipper, numero uno, number one, top dog, kingpin, head honcho; Brit. informal gaffer, guv'nor.

commanding adjective **1** *the world champion was in a commanding position:* **dominant**, dominating, controlling, superior, powerful, prominent, advantageous, favourable. **2** *his mother's voice was soft and commanding:* **authoritative**, masterful, assertive, firm, emphatic, insistent, imperative; peremptory, imperious, dictatorial; informal bossy.

commemorate verb *the event commemorated the courage of the villagers:* **celebrate**, pay tribute to, pay homage to, honour, salute, toast; remember, recognize, acknowledge, observe, mark.

commemorative adjective *veterans of the battle will attend commemorative services:* **memorial**, remembrance; celebratory.

commence verb *the headmaster commenced his tour of inspection:* **begin**, start; get the ball rolling, get going, get under way, get off the ground, set about; embark on, launch into, lead off; open, initiate, inaugurate; informal kick off, get the show on the road.
– OPPOSITES conclude.

commencement noun **beginning**, start, opening, outset, onset, launch, initiation, inception, origin; informal kick-off.

commend verb **1** *we should commend him:* **praise**, compliment, congratulate, applaud, salute, honour; sing the praises of, pay tribute to, take one's hat off to, pat on the back. **2** *I commend her to you without reservation:* **recommend**, suggest, propose; endorse, advocate, vouch for, speak for, support, back.
– OPPOSITES criticize.

commendable adjective *he tackled the tests with commendable zeal:* **admirable**, praiseworthy, creditable, laudable, estimable, meritorious, exemplary, noteworthy, honourable, respectable, fine, excellent.
– OPPOSITES reprehensible.

commendation noun **1** *letters of commendation:* **praise**, congratulation, appreciation; acclaim, credit, recognition, respect, esteem, admiration, homage, tribute. **2** *a commendation for bravery:* **award**, accolade, prize, honour, (honourable) mention, citation.

commensurate adjective **1** *they had privileges but commensurate duties:* **equivalent**, equal, corresponding, correspondent, comparable, proportionate, proportional. **2** *a salary commensurate with your qualifications:* **appropriate to**, in keeping with, in line with, consistent with, corresponding to, according to, relative to; dependent on, based on.

comment noun 1 *she was upset by their comments on her appearance:* **remark**, observation, statement, utterance; pronouncement, judgement, reflection, opinion, view; criticism. 2 *the story excited a great deal of comment:* **discussion**, debate; interest. 3 *a comment had been inserted in the register:* **note**, annotation, footnote, gloss, commentary, explanation.
verb 1 *they commented on the food:* **remark on**, speak about, talk about, discuss, mention. 2 *'It will soon be night,' he commented:* **remark**, observe, reflect, say, state, declare, announce; interpose, interject.

commentary noun 1 *the test match commentary:* **narration**, description, account, report, review. 2 *textual commentary:* **explanation**, elucidation, interpretation, exegesis, analysis; assessment, appraisal, criticism; notes, comments.

commentator noun 1 *a television commentator:* **narrator**, announcer, presenter, anchor, anchorman, anchorwoman; reporter, journalist, newscaster, sportscaster; informal talking head. 2 *a political commentator:* **analyst**, pundit, monitor, observer; blogger; writer, speaker.

commerce noun *the changes in taxation are of benefit to commerce:* **trade**, trading, buying and selling, business, dealing, traffic; (financial) transactions, dealings.

commercial adjective 1 *a vessel built for commercial purposes:* **trade**, trading, business, private enterprise, mercantile, sales. 2 *we turn good ideas into commercial products:* **lucrative**, moneymaking, money-spinning, profitable, remunerative, fruitful, gainful; viable, successful.
noun *a TV commercial:* **advertisement**, promotion, display; informal ad, plug; Brit. informal advert.

commercialized adjective *the art world became increasingly commercialized:* **profit-orientated**, money-orientated, commercial, materialistic, mercenary.

commiserate verb (**commiserate with**) *he commiserated with them for their sufferings:* **offer sympathy to**, be sympathetic to, offer condolences to, condole with, sympathize with, empathize with, feel pity for, feel sorry for, feel for; comfort, console.

commiseration noun **condolence(s)**, sympathy, pity, comfort, solace, consolation; compassion, understanding.

commission noun 1 *the dealer's commission:* **percentage**, brokerage, share, portion, dividend, premium, fee, consideration, bonus; informal cut, take, rake-off, slice; Brit. informal whack, divvy. 2 *the commission of*

building a palace: **task**, employment, job, project, mission, assignment, undertaking; duty, charge, responsibility. 3 *the plan requires approval by an independent commission:* **committee**, board, council, panel, directorate, delegation. 4 *the commission of an offence:* **perpetration**, committing, committal, execution.
verb 1 *he was commissioned to paint a portrait:* **engage**, contract, charge, employ, hire, recruit, retain, appoint, enlist, co-opt, book, sign up. 2 *they commissioned a sculpture:* **order**; authorize.
■ **in commission** in service, in use; working, functional, operative, up and running, in operation, in working order.
■ **out of commission** not in service, not in use, unserviceable; not working, inoperative, out of order; down.

commit verb 1 *he committed a murder:* **carry out**, do, perpetrate, engage in, enact, execute, effect, accomplish; be responsible for; informal pull off. 2 *she was committed to their care:* **entrust**, consign, assign, deliver, give, hand over, relinquish. 3 *they committed themselves to the project:* **pledge**, devote, apply, give, dedicate. 4 *the judge committed him to prison:* **consign**, send, deliver, confine. 5 *her husband had her committed:* **hospitalize**, confine, institutionalize, put away; certify.

commitment noun 1 *he resigned because of the pressure of other commitments:* **responsibility**, obligation, duty, tie, liability; task; engagement, arrangement. 2 *her commitment to her students continued undiminished:* **dedication**, devotion, allegiance, loyalty, faithfulness, fidelity. 3 *he made a commitment:* **vow**, promise, pledge, oath; contract, pact, deal; decision, resolution.

committed adjective *they are committed Christians:* **devout**, devoted, dedicated, loyal, faithful, staunch, firm, steadfast, unwavering, wholehearted, keen, passionate, ardent, fervent, sworn, pledged; dutiful, diligent; informal card-carrying, true blue, deep-dyed.
– OPPOSITES apathetic.

commodity noun *improving productivity will lower the cost of a commodity:* **item**, material, product, article, object; import, export.

common adjective 1 *a very common art form:* **usual**, ordinary, familiar, regular, frequent, recurrent, everyday; standard, typical, conventional, stock, commonplace, run-of-the-mill. 2 *it is a common belief that elephants have long memories:* **widespread**, general, universal, popular, mainstream, prevalent, prevailing, rife, established, conventional, traditional, orthodox, accepted. 3 *they work together for the common good:* **collective**, communal, community, public, popular, general; shared, combined. 4 *they are far too common:*

uncouth, vulgar, coarse, rough, boorish, unladylike, ungentlemanly, ill-bred, uncivilized, unsophisticated, unrefined; lowly, low-born, low-class, inferior, proletarian, plebeian; informal plebby; Brit. informal common as muck.
– OPPOSITES unusual, rare, individual, refined.
noun (Brit. informal) *use your common!* See **COMMON SENSE**.

commonly adverb *shift workers commonly complain of not being able to sleep:* **often**, frequently, regularly, repeatedly, time and (time) again, all the time, routinely, habitually, customarily; N. Amer. oftentimes; informal lots.

commonplace adjective **1** *a commonplace writing style:* **ordinary**, run-of-the-mill, unremarkable, unexceptional, average, mediocre, pedestrian, prosaic, lacklustre, dull, bland, uninteresting, mundane; hackneyed, trite, banal, clichéd, predictable, stale, tired, unoriginal; informal (plain) vanilla, bog-standard, a dime a dozen; Brit. informal common or garden; N. Amer. informal ornery, bush-league. **2** *a commonplace occurrence:* **common**, normal, usual, ordinary, familiar, routine, standard, everyday, daily, regular, frequent, habitual, typical.
– OPPOSITES original, unusual.
noun 1 *early death was a commonplace:* **everyday event**, routine. **2** *a great store of commonplaces:* **platitude**, cliché, truism, hackneyed phrase, trite phrase, old chestnut, banality.

common sense noun *he is quick to praise her professionalism and common sense:* **sensibleness**, (good) sense, (native) wit, judgement, level-headedness, prudence, discernment, canniness, astuteness, shrewdness, wisdom, insight, perception, perspicacity; practicality, capability, resourcefulness, enterprise; informal horse sense, gumption, nous, savvy; Brit. informal common; N. Amer. informal smarts.
– OPPOSITES folly.

commotion noun *a commotion broke out in the street behind us:* **disturbance**, uproar, tumult, rumpus, ruckus, brouhaha, furore, hue and cry, fuss, stir, storm; turmoil, disorder, confusion, chaos, mayhem, havoc, pandemonium; unrest, fracas, riot, breach of the peace; Irish, N. Amer., & Austral. donnybrook; informal ruction(s), ballyhoo, kerfuffle, hoo-ha, to-do, hullabaloo; Brit. informal carry-on, row, aggro, argy-bargy.

communal adjective **1** *the kitchen was communal:* **shared**, joint, common. **2** *they farm on a communal basis:* **collective**, cooperative, community, communalist, combined.
– OPPOSITES private, individual.

commune noun *she lives in a commune:* **collective**, cooperative, communal settlement, kibbutz.
verb 1 *we pray to commune with God:*

communicate, speak, talk, converse, interface. **2** *she likes to commune with nature:* **empathize**, identify, have a rapport, feel at one; relate to, feel close to.

communicable adjective *they are concerned about the spread of communicable diseases:* **contagious**, **infectious**, transmittable, transmissible, transferable, spreadable; informal catching.

communicate verb **1** *he communicated the news to his boss:* **convey**, tell, impart, relay, transmit, pass on, announce, report, recount, relate, present; divulge, disclose, mention; spread, disseminate, promulgate, broadcast. **2** *they communicate daily:* **liaise**, be in touch, be in contact, have dealings, interface, commune, meet; talk, speak, converse; informal have a confab, powwow. **3** *learn how to communicate better:* **get one's message across**, explain oneself, be understood, get through to someone. **4** *the disease is communicated easily:* **transmit**, transfer, spread, carry, pass on. **5** *each bedroom communicates with a bathroom:* **connect with**, join up with, open on to, lead into.

communication noun **1** *the communication of news:* **transmission**, conveyance, divulgence, divulgation, disclosure; dissemination, promulgation, broadcasting. **2** *there was no communication between them:* **contact**, dealings, relations, connection, association, socializing, intercourse; correspondence, dialogue, talk, conversation, discussion. **3** *an official communication:* **message**, statement, announcement, report, dispatch, communiqué, letter, bulletin, correspondence. **4** *road and rail communications:* **links**, connections, services, routes.

communicative adjective *she is always very pleasant and communicative:* **forthcoming**, expansive, expressive, unreserved, uninhibited, vocal, outgoing, frank, open, candid; talkative, chatty, loquacious; informal gabby.

communion noun **1** *a sense of communion with others:* **affinity**, fellowship, kinship, friendship, fellow feeling, togetherness, closeness, harmony, understanding, rapport, connection, communication, empathy, accord, unity. **2** *Christ's presence at Communion:* **Eucharist**, Holy Communion, Lord's Supper, Mass.

communiqué noun *the foreign ministry issued a communiqué:* **official communication**, press release, bulletin, message, missive, dispatch, statement, report, announcement, declaration, proclamation; N. Amer. advisory; informal memo.

communism noun **collectivism**, state ownership, (radical) socialism; Sovietism, Bolshevism, Marxism, Leninism, Trotskyism, Maoism.

communist noun & adjective *a French*

C

communist writer: **collectivist**, leftist, (radical) socialist; Soviet, Bolshevik, Bolshevist, Marxist, Leninist, Trotskyist, Trotskyite, Maoist; informal, derogatory Commie, Bolshie, red, lefty.

community noun 1 *work done for the community:* **population**, populace, people, citizenry, (general) public, collective; residents, inhabitants, citizens. 2 *a rural community:* **district**, region, zone, area, locality, locale, neighbourhood; informal neck of the woods, turf; Brit. informal manor; N. Amer. informal hood, nabe. 3 *gays are not one homogenous community:* **group**, body, set, circle, clique, faction; informal gang, bunch. 4 *a monastic community:* **brotherhood**, sisterhood, fraternity, sorority, sodality; colony, order. 5 *community of interests:* **similarity**, likeness, comparability, correspondence, agreement, closeness, affinity.

commute verb 1 *they commute on a train:* **travel to and from work**, travel to and fro, travel back and forth. 2 *his sentence was commuted:* **reduce**, lessen, lighten, shorten, cut, attenuate, moderate. 3 *knight service was commuted for a payment:* **exchange**, change, substitute, swap, trade, switch.
– OPPOSITES increase.

commuter noun **(daily) traveller**, traveller, passenger; informal straphanger.

compact¹ adjective 1 *a compact rug:* **dense**, close-packed, tightly packed; thick, tight, firm. 2 *a compact camera:* **small**, little, petite, miniature, mini, small-scale; Scottish wee; informal teeny, teeny-weeny; Brit. informal dinky; N. Amer. little-bitty.
– OPPOSITES loose, large.
verb *the snow has been compacted:* **compress**, condense, pack down, press down, tamp (down), flatten.

compact² noun *the warring states signed a compact:* **treaty**, pact, accord, agreement, contract, bargain, deal, settlement, covenant, concordat; pledge, promise, bond.

companion noun 1 *Harry and his companion:* **associate**, partner, escort, compatriot, confederate; friend, intimate, confidant(e), comrade; informal pal, chum, crony, sidekick; Brit. informal mate, oppo, china, mucker; N. Amer. informal buddy, amigo, compadre; Austral./NZ informal offsider. 2 *a lady's companion:* **attendant**, aide, helper, assistant, valet, equerry, lady-in-waiting; chaperone; carer, minder. 3 *the tape is a companion to the book:* **complement**, counterpart, twin, match; accompaniment, supplement, addition, adjunct, accessory.

companionable adjective *the most generous and companionable of men:* **friendly**, affable, cordial, genial, congenial, amiable, easy-going, good-natured, comradely; sociable, convivial, outgoing, gregarious; informal chummy, pally; Brit. informal matey; N. Amer. informal buddy-buddy, clubby.

companionship noun *she needed the companionship of like-minded young people:* **friendship**, fellowship, closeness, togetherness, amity, intimacy, rapport, camaraderie, brotherhood, sisterhood; company, society, social contact.

company noun 1 *an oil company:* **firm**, business, corporation, establishment, agency, office, bureau, institution, organization, concern, enterprise; conglomerate, consortium, syndicate, multinational; informal outfit. 2 *I enjoy his company:* **companionship**, friendship, fellowship, amity, camaraderie; society, association. 3 *I'm expecting company:* **guests**, visitors, callers, people; someone. 4 *a company of poets:* **group**, crowd, party, band, assembly, cluster, flock, herd, troupe, throng, congregation; informal bunch, gang. 5 *a company of infantry:* **unit**, section, detachment, troop, corps, squad, squadron, platoon, battalion, division.

comparable adjective 1 *comparable incomes:* **similar**, close, near, approximate, akin, equivalent, commensurate, proportional, proportionate; like, matching. 2 *nobody is comparable with him:* **equal to**, as good as, in the same league as, able to hold a candle to, on a par with, on a level with; a match for.

comparative adjective *they left the city for the comparative cool of the country:* **relative**; in/by comparison.

compare verb 1 *we compared the data sets:* **contrast**, juxtapose, collate, differentiate, weigh up. 2 *he was compared to Wagner:* **liken**, equate, analogize; class with, bracket with, set side by side with. 3 *the porcelain compares with Dresden's fine china:* **be as good as**, be comparable to, bear comparison with, be the equal of, match up to, be on a par with, be in the same league as, come close to, hold a candle to, be not unlike; match, resemble, emulate, rival, approach.
■ **beyond compare** without equal, second to none, in a class of one's own; peerless, matchless, unmatched, incomparable, inimitable, supreme, outstanding, consummate, unique, singular, perfect.

comparison noun 1 *a comparison of the results:* **juxtaposition**, collation, differentiation. 2 *there's no comparison between them:* **resemblance**, likeness, similarity, correspondence, correlation, parallel, parity, comparability.

compartment noun 1 *a secret compartment:* **section**, part, bay, recess, chamber, cavity; pocket. 2 *they put science and religion in separate compartments:* **domain**, field, sphere, department; category, pigeonhole, bracket, group, set.

compartmentalize verb *we need to compartmentalize the issues we're working on:* **categorize**, pigeonhole, bracket, group, classify, characterize, stereotype, label, brand; sort, rank, rate.

compass noun *faith cannot be defined within the compass of human thought:* **scope**, range, extent, reach, span, breadth, ambit, limits, parameters, bounds.

compassion noun *she gazed with compassion at the two dejected figures:* **pity**, sympathy, empathy, fellow feeling, care, concern, solicitude, sensitivity, warmth, love, tenderness, mercy, leniency, tolerance, kindness, humanity, charity.
– OPPOSITES indifference, cruelty.

compassionate adjective *they showed a compassionate concern for the victims:* **sympathetic**, empathetic, understanding, caring, solicitous, sensitive, warm, loving; merciful, lenient, tolerant, considerate, kind, humane, charitable, big-hearted.

compatibility noun *they felt the bond of true compatibility:* **like-mindedness**, similarity, affinity, closeness, fellow feeling, harmony, rapport, empathy, sympathy.

compatible adjective **1** *they were never compatible:* **(well) suited**, well matched, like-minded, in tune, in harmony; reconcilable. **2** *her bruising is compatible with a fall:* **consistent**, congruous, congruent; in keeping.

compatriot noun **fellow countryman/woman**, countryman, countrywoman, fellow citizen.

compel verb **1** *he compelled them to leave their land:* **force**, pressurize, pressure, press, push, urge; dragoon, browbeat, bully, intimidate; oblige, require, make; informal lean on, put the screws on. **2** *they can compel compliance:* **exact**, extort, demand, insist on, force, necessitate.

compelling adjective **1** *a compelling performance:* **enthralling**, captivating, gripping, riveting, spellbinding, mesmerizing, absorbing, irresistible. **2** *a compelling argument:* **convincing**, persuasive, cogent, irresistible, powerful, strong, weighty, plausible, credible, sound, valid, telling, conclusive, irrefutable, unanswerable.
– OPPOSITES boring, weak.

compendium noun *a compendium of useful information about language:* **collection**, compilation, anthology, treasury, digest; summary, synopsis, precis, outline.

compensate verb **1** *you must compensate for what you did:* **make amends**, make up, make reparation, recompense, atone, requite, pay; expiate, make good, rectify. **2** *we agreed to compensate him for his loss:* **recompense**, repay, pay back, reimburse, remunerate, recoup, requite, indemnify. **3** *his flair compensated for his faults:* **balance (out)**, counterbalance, counteract, offset, make up for, cancel out, neutralize, negative.

compensation noun *he is seeking compensation for injuries suffered at work:* **recompense**, repayment, reimbursement, remuneration, requital, indemnification, indemnity, redress; damages; N. Amer. informal comp.

compère noun **host**, presenter, anchor, anchorman/woman, master of ceremonies, MC, announcer; N. Amer. informal emcee.

compete verb **1** *they competed in a tennis tournament:* **take part**, participate, play, be a competitor, be involved; enter, go in for. **2** *they had to compete with other firms:* **contend**, vie, battle, wrangle, jockey, go head to head; strive against, pit oneself against; challenge, take on. **3** *no one can compete with him:* **rival**, challenge, keep up with, keep pace with, compare with, match, be in the same league as, come near to, come close to, touch; informal hold a candle to.

competence noun **1** *this area of research is beyond my technical competence:* **capability**, ability, competency, proficiency, accomplishment, expertise, adeptness, skill, prowess, mastery, talent; informal savvy, know-how. **2** *doubts arose over the competence of the system:* **adequacy**, appropriateness, suitability, fitness; effectiveness; formal efficacy. **3** *matters within the competence of the courts:* **authority**, power, control, jurisdiction, ambit, scope, remit.

competent adjective **1** *a competent carpenter:* **capable**, able, proficient, adept, adroit, accomplished, complete, skilful, skilled, gifted, talented, expert; good, excellent; informal great, mean, wicked, nifty, ace. **2** *she spoke competent French:* **adequate**, acceptable, satisfactory, reasonable, fair, decent, not bad, all right, average, tolerable, passable, moderate, middling; informal OK, okay, so-so. **3** *the court was not competent to hear the case:* **fit**, suitable, suited, appropriate; qualified, empowered, authorized.
– OPPOSITES inadequate, unfit.

competition noun **1** *Stephanie won the competition:* **contest**, tournament, match, game, heat, fixture, event; trials, stakes. **2** *I'm not interested in competition:* **rivalry**, competitiveness, vying; conflict, feuding, fighting; informal keeping up with the Joneses. **3** *we must stay ahead of the competition:* **opposition**, other side, field; enemy; challengers, opponents, rivals, adversaries.

competitive adjective **1** *a competitive player:* **ambitious**, zealous, keen, pushy, combative, aggressive; informal go-ahead. **2** *a highly competitive industry:* **ruthless**, aggressive, fierce; informal dog-eat-dog, cut-throat. **3** *competitive prices:* **reasonable**, moderate, keen; low, inexpensive, cheap, budget, bargain, reduced, discount; rock-bottom, bargain-basement.
– OPPOSITES apathetic, exorbitant.

competitor noun **1** *the competitors in the race:* **contestant**, contender, challenger, participant, entrant; runner, player. **2** *our European competitors:* **rival**, challenger,

c

opponent, adversary; competition, opposition.
– OPPOSITES ally.

compilation noun *there are thirty-three stories in this compilation:* **collection**, selection, anthology, treasury, compendium, album, corpus, collectanea; pot-pourri.

compile verb *he compiled a dossier of patients with tropical diseases:* **assemble**, put together, collate, compose, organize, arrange; gather, collect.

complacency noun *success brings with it the danger of complacency:* **smugness**, self-satisfaction, self-congratulation, self-regard; gloating, triumph, pride; satisfaction, contentment.

complacent adjective *no one in the industry can afford to stand still and be complacent:* **smug**, self-satisfied, self-congratulatory, self-regarding; gloating, triumphant, proud; pleased, satisfied, content, contented; informal like the cat that got the cream, I'm-all-right-Jack; N. Amer. informal wisenheimer.

complain verb *the neighbours complained about his singing:* **protest**, grumble, whine, bleat, carp, cavil, grouse, make a fuss; object to, speak out against, oppose, criticize, find fault with; informal whinge, kick up a fuss, bellyache, moan, beef, bitch, sound off; Brit. informal gripe, chunter, create; N. Amer. informal kvetch.

complaint noun **1** *they lodged a complaint:* **protest**, objection, grievance, grouse, cavil, quibble, grumble; charge, accusation, criticism; informal beef, gripe, whinge. **2** *there appears to be little cause for complaint:* **protestation**, objection, exception, grievance, grumbling; criticism, fault-finding, condemnation, disapproval, dissatisfaction; informal whingeing, grousing, bellyaching, nit-picking. **3** *a kidney complaint:* **disorder**, disease, infection, affliction, illness, ailment, sickness; condition, problem, upset, trouble; informal bug, virus.

complaisant adjective *he made drunken moves on complaisant chambermaids:* **willing**, acquiescent, agreeable, amenable, cooperative, accommodating, obliging; biddable, compliant, docile, obedient.

complement noun **1** *the perfect complement to the food:* **accompaniment**, companion, addition, supplement, accessory, trimming. **2** *a full complement of lifeboats:* **amount**, total, contingent, capacity, allowance, quota. verb *this sauce complements the dessert:* **accompany**, go with, round off, set off, suit, harmonize with; enhance, complete.

complementary adjective *neutral tones allow the widest choice of complementary furnishings and decoration:* **harmonious**, compatible, corresponding, matching, twin, complemental; supportive, reciprocal, interdependent.
– OPPOSITES incompatible.

complete adjective **1** *the complete interview will appear in next week's issue:* **entire**, whole, full, total; uncut, unabridged. **2** *their research was complete:* **finished**, ended, concluded, completed, finalized; accomplished, achieved, discharged, settled, done; informal wrapped up, sewn up, polished off. **3** *you're acting like a complete fool:* **absolute**, out-and-out, utter, total, real, downright, thoroughgoing, veritable, prize, perfect, unqualified, unmitigated, sheer, arrant; N. Amer. full-bore; Brit. informal right.
– OPPOSITES partial, unfinished.
verb **1** *he had to complete his training:* **finish**, end, conclude, finalize, wind up; informal wrap up, sew up, polish off. **2** *the outfit was completed with a veil:* **finish off**, round off, top off, crown, cap, complement. **3** *complete the application form:* **fill in/out**, answer.

completely adverb *he had always been completely honest with her:* **totally**, entirely, wholly, thoroughly, fully, utterly, absolutely, perfectly, unreservedly, unconditionally, quite, altogether, downright; in every way, in every respect, one hundred per cent, every inch, to the hilt; informal dead, deadly.

completion noun *the money ran out before the scheme's completion:* **realization**, accomplishment, achievement, fulfilment, consummation, finalization, resolution; finish, end, conclusion, close, cessation.

complex adjective **1** *a complex situation:* **complicated**, involved, intricate, convoluted, elaborate, impenetrable, Gordian; difficult, knotty, tricky, thorny; Brit. informal fiddly. **2** *a complex structure:* **compound**, composite, multiplex.
– OPPOSITES simple.
noun **1** *a complex of roads:* **network**, system, nexus, web, tissue; combination, aggregation. **2** (informal) *he had a complex about losing his hair:* **obsession**, fixation, preoccupation; neurosis; informal hang-up, thing, bee in one's bonnet.

complexion noun **1** *a pale complexion:* **skin**, skin colour, skin tone; pigmentation. **2** *this puts an entirely new complexion on things:* **perspective**, angle, slant, interpretation; appearance, light, look. **3** *governments of all complexions:* **type**, kind, sort; nature, character, stamp, ilk, kidney.

complexity noun *an issue of great complexity:* **complication**, problem, difficulty; twist, turn, intricacy.

compliance noun **1** *compliance with international law:* **obedience to**, observance of, adherence to, conformity to, respect for. **2** *he mistook her silence for compliance:* **acquiescence**, agreement, assent, consent, acceptance; complaisance, pliability, docility, meekness, submission.
– OPPOSITES violation, defiance.

compliant adjective *a compliant labour force:* **acquiescent**, amenable, biddable, tractable, complaisant, accommodating, cooperative;

obedient, docile, malleable, pliable, submissive, tame, yielding, controllable, unresisting, persuadable, persuasible.
– OPPOSITES recalcitrant.

complicate verb *choice will complicate matters for the consumer:* **make (more) difficult**, make complicated, mix up, confuse, muddle; informal mess up, screw up, snarl up.
– OPPOSITES simplify.

complicated adjective *a complicated problem:* **complex**, intricate, involved, convoluted, tangled, impenetrable, knotty, tricky, thorny, labyrinthine, tortuous, Gordian; confusing, bewildering, perplexing; Brit. informal fiddly.
– OPPOSITES straightforward.

complication noun **1** *a complication concerning ownership:* **difficulty**, problem, obstacle, hurdle, stumbling block; drawback, snag, catch, hitch; informal fly in the ointment, prob, headache, facer; Brit. informal spanner in the works. **2** *the complication of life in our society:* **complexity**, complicatedness, intricacy, convolutedness.

complicity noun *they were accused of complicity in the attempt to overthrow the government:* **collusion**, involvement, collaboration, connivance; conspiracy; informal being in cahoots.

compliment noun **1** *an unexpected compliment:* **flattering remark**, tribute, accolade, commendation, bouquet, pat on the back; **(compliments)** praise, acclaim, admiration, flattery, blandishments, honeyed words. **2** *my compliments on your cooking:* **congratulations**, commendations, praise. **3** *Margaret sends her compliments:* **greetings**, regards, respects, good wishes, best wishes, salutations, felicitations.
– OPPOSITES insult.
verb *they complimented his performance:* **praise**, pay tribute to, speak highly/well of, flatter, wax lyrical about, make much of, commend, acclaim, applaud, salute, honour; congratulate, pat on the back.
– OPPOSITES criticize.

complimentary adjective **1** *complimentary remarks:* **flattering**, appreciative, congratulatory, admiring, approving, commendatory, favourable, glowing, adulatory; informal rave. **2** *complimentary tickets:* **free (of charge)**, gratis, for nothing; courtesy; informal on the house.
– OPPOSITES derogatory.

comply verb *Myra complied with his wishes:* **abide by**, observe, obey, adhere to, conform to, follow, respect; agree to, assent to, go along with, yield to, submit to, defer to; satisfy, fulfil.
– OPPOSITES ignore, disobey.

component noun *the components of electronic devices:* **part**, piece, bit, element, constituent, ingredient; unit, module, section.
adjective *the molecule's component elements:*

constituent, integral; basic, essential.

compose verb **1** *a poem composed by Shelley:* **write**, formulate, devise, make up, think up, produce, invent, concoct; pen, author, draft. **2** *compose a still life:* **organize**, arrange, set out. **3** *the congress is composed of ten senators:* **make up**, constitute, form, comprise.
■ **compose oneself** calm down, control oneself, regain one's composure, pull oneself together, collect oneself, steady oneself, keep one's head; informal get a grip, keep one's cool; N. Amer. informal decompress.

composed adjective *a very talented and composed young player:* **calm**, collected, cool (as a cucumber), self-controlled, self-possessed; serene, tranquil, relaxed, at ease, unruffled, unperturbed, untroubled; equable, even-tempered, imperturbable; informal unflappable, together, laid-back.
– OPPOSITES excited.

composer noun melodist, symphonist, songwriter, songster, writer; informal tunesmith, songsmith.

composite adjective *a composite structure:* **compound**, complex; combined, blended, mixed.
noun *a composite of plastic and metal:* **amalgamation**, amalgam, combination, compound, fusion, synthesis, mixture, blend; alloy.
– OPPOSITES simple, homogeneous.

composition noun **1** *the composition of the council:* **make-up**, constitution, configuration, structure, formation, form, framework, fabric, anatomy, organization; informal set-up. **2** *a literary composition:* **work (of art)**, creation, opus, oeuvre, piece, arrangement. **3** *the composition of a poem:* **writing**, creation, formulation, invention, concoction, compilation. **4** *a school composition:* **essay**, paper, study, piece of writing; N. Amer. theme. **5** *the composition of the painting:* **arrangement**, disposition, layout; proportions, balance, symmetry. **6** *an adhesive composition:* **mixture**, compound, amalgam, blend, mix.

compost noun **fertilizer**, mulch, manure, bonemeal, fishmeal, guano; humus, peat; plant food, top-dressing.

composure noun *she was struggling to regain her composure:* **self-control**, self-possession, calm, equanimity, equilibrium, serenity, tranquillity; aplomb, poise, presence of mind, sangfroid; imperturbability, placidness, impassivity; informal cool.

compound noun *a compound of two elements:* **amalgam**, amalgamation, combination, composite, blend, mixture, mix, fusion, synthesis; alloy.
adjective *a compound substance:* **composite**, complex; blended, fused, combined.
– OPPOSITES simple.
verb **1** *a smell compounded of dust and mould:* **be composed of**, be made up of, be formed

from. **2** *soap compounded with disinfectant:* **mix**, combine, blend, amalgamate, fuse, synthesize. **3** *his illness compounds their problems:* **aggravate**, exacerbate, worsen, add to, augment, intensify, heighten, increase, magnify; complicate.
– OPPOSITES alleviate.

comprehend verb *Katie couldn't comprehend his message:* **understand**, grasp, take in, see, apprehend, follow, make sense of, fathom, get to the bottom of; unravel, decipher, interpret; informal work out, figure out, make head or tail of, get one's head around, take on board, get the drift of, catch on to, get; Brit. informal twig, suss (out).

comprehensible adjective *clear and comprehensible English:* **intelligible**, understandable, accessible; lucid, coherent, clear, plain, explicit, unambiguous, straightforward, fathomable.
– OPPOSITES opaque.

comprehension noun *the comprehension of spoken language:* **understanding**, grasp, conception, apprehension, cognition, ken, knowledge, awareness, perception; interpretation.
– OPPOSITES ignorance.

comprehensive adjective *a comprehensive review of UK defence policy:* **inclusive**, all-inclusive, complete; thorough, full, extensive, all-embracing, exhaustive, detailed, in-depth, encyclopedic, universal, catholic; far-reaching, radical, sweeping, across the board, wholesale; broad, wide-ranging; informal wall-to-wall.
– OPPOSITES limited.

compress verb **1** *the skirt can be compressed into a bag:* **squeeze**, press, squash, crush, cram, jam, stuff; tamp, pack, compact; constrict; informal scrunch. **2** *Polly compressed her lips:* **purse**, press together, pucker. **3** *the text was compressed:* **abridge**, condense, shorten, cut, abbreviate, truncate; summarize, precis.
– OPPOSITES expand.

comprise verb **1** *the country comprises twenty states:* **consist of**, be made up of, be composed of, contain, encompass, incorporate; include; formal comprehend. **2** *this breed comprises half the herd:* **make up**, constitute, form, compose; account for.

compromise noun **1** *they reached a compromise:* **agreement**, understanding, settlement, terms, deal, trade-off, bargain; middle ground, happy medium, balance. **2** *a happy marriage needs compromise:* **give and take**, concession, cooperation.
– OPPOSITES intransigence.
verb **1** *we compromised:* **meet each other halfway**, come to an understanding, make a deal, make concessions, find a happy medium, strike a balance; give and take. **2** *his actions could compromise his reputation:* **undermine**, weaken, damage, harm; jeopardize, prejudice; discredit, dishonour, shame, embarrass.

compulsion noun **1** *he is under no compulsion to go:* **obligation**, constraint, coercion, duress, pressure, intimidation. **2** *a compulsion to tell the truth:* **urge**, impulse, need, desire, drive; obsession, fixation, addiction; temptation.

compulsive adjective **1** *a compulsive desire:* **irresistible**, uncontrollable, compelling, overwhelming, urgent; obsessive. **2** *compulsive eating:* **obsessive**, obsessional, addictive, uncontrollable. **3** *a compulsive liar:* **inveterate**, chronic, incorrigible, incurable, hardened, hopeless, persistent; obsessive, addicted, habitual; informal pathological, hooked. **4** *it's compulsive viewing:* **fascinating**, compelling, gripping, riveting, engrossing, enthralling, captivating.

compulsory adjective *legislation which made the wearing of seat belts compulsory:* **obligatory**, mandatory, required, requisite, necessary, essential; imperative, unavoidable, enforced, demanded, prescribed.
– OPPOSITES optional.

compunction noun *she had no compunction about deceiving them:* **scruples**, misgivings, qualms, worries, unease, uneasiness, doubts, reluctance, reservations; guilt, regret, contrition, self-reproach.

compute verb *the hire charge is computed on a daily basis:* **calculate**, work out, reckon, determine, evaluate, quantify; add up, count up, tally, total, totalize; Brit. tot up.

comrade noun **companion**, friend; colleague, associate, partner, co-worker, workmate; informal pal, crony; Brit. informal mate, chum, oppo; N. Amer. informal buddy.

concatenation noun *a concatenation of events which had finally led to the murder:* **series**, sequence, succession, chain.

concave adjective **incurved**, curved inwards, hollow, depressed, sunken; indented, recessed.
– OPPOSITES convex.

conceal verb **1** *clouds concealed the sun:* **hide**, screen, cover, obscure, block out, blot out, mask, shroud, secrete. **2** *he concealed his true feelings:* **hide**, cover up, disguise, mask, veil; keep secret, keep dark, draw a veil over; suppress, repress, bottle up; informal keep a/the lid on, keep under one's hat.
– OPPOSITES reveal, confess.

concealed adjective **hidden**, not visible, out of sight, invisible, covered, disguised, camouflaged, obscured; private, secret.

concealment noun **1** *the concealment of his weapon:* **hiding**, secretion. **2** *he darted forwards from the concealment of the bushes:* **cover**, shelter, protection, screen; privacy, seclusion; secrecy. **3** *the deliberate concealment of facts:* **suppression**, hiding, cover-up, hushing up; whitewash.

concede verb **1** *I had to concede that I'd overreacted:* **admit**, acknowledge, accept,

allow, grant, recognize, own, confess; agree. **2** *he conceded the Auvergne to the king:* **surrender**, yield, give up, relinquish, cede, hand over.
– OPPOSITES deny, retain.
■ **concede defeat** capitulate, give in, surrender, yield, give up, submit, raise the white flag; back down, climb down, throw in the towel.

conceit noun **1** *Polly's eyes widened at his extraordinary conceit:* **vanity**, narcissism, conceitedness, egotism, self-admiration, self-regard; pride, arrogance, hubris, self-importance; self-satisfaction, smugness; informal big-headedness, swollen-headedness. **2** *the conceits of Shakespeare's verse:* **image**, imagery, metaphor, simile, trope.
– OPPOSITES humility.

conceited adjective *he's so conceited he'd never believe anyone would turn him down:* **vain**, narcissistic, self-centred, egotistic, egotistical, egocentric; proud, arrogant, boastful, full of oneself, self-important, immodest, swaggering; self-satisfied, smug; supercilious, haughty, snobbish; informal big-headed, too big for one's boots, stuck-up, high and mighty, uppity, snotty; Brit. informal toffee-nosed; N. Amer. informal chesty.

conceivable adjective *the body was photographed from every conceivable angle:* **imaginable**, possible; plausible, tenable, credible, believable, thinkable, feasible; understandable, comprehensible.

conceive verb **1** *she was unable to conceive:* **become pregnant**, become impregnated. **2** *the project was conceived in 1977:* **think up**, think of, dream up, devise, formulate, design, originate, create, develop; hatch; informal cook up. **3** *I could hardly conceive what it must be like:* **imagine**, envisage, visualize, picture, think, envision; grasp, appreciate, apprehend.

concentrate verb **1** *the government concentrated its efforts:* **focus**, direct, centre, centralize. **2** *she concentrated on the film:* **focus on**, pay attention to, keep one's mind on, devote oneself to; be absorbed in, be engrossed in, be immersed in; informal get stuck into. **3** *troops concentrated on the horizon:* **collect**, gather, congregate, converge, mass, cluster, rally. **4** *the liquid is filtered and concentrated:* **condense**, boil down, reduce, thicken.
– OPPOSITES disperse, dilute.
noun *a fruit concentrate:* **extract**, decoction, distillation.

concentrated adjective **1** *a concentrated effort:* **strenuous**, concerted, intensive, intense; informal all-out. **2** *a concentrated solution:* **condensed**, reduced, evaporated, thickened; undiluted, strong.
– OPPOSITES half-hearted, diluted.

concentration noun **1** *a task requiring concentration:* **close attention**, attentiveness, application, single-mindedness, absorption. **2** *the concentration*

of effort: **focusing**, centralization. **3** *Islay is famous for its concentrations of barnacle geese:* **gathering**, cluster, mass, flock, congregation, assemblage.
– OPPOSITES inattention.

concept noun *structuralism is a difficult concept:* **idea**, notion, conception, abstraction; theory, hypothesis; belief, conviction, opinion; image, impression, picture.

conception noun **1** *the fertility treatment resulted in conception:* **inception of pregnancy**, conceiving, fertilization, impregnation, insemination. **2** *the product's conception:* **inception**, genesis, origination, creation, invention; beginning, origin. **3** *the original conception involved a shopping complex run by local people:* **plan**, scheme, project, proposal; intention, aim, idea. **4** *my conception of democracy:* **idea**, concept, notion, understanding, abstraction; theory, hypothesis; perception, image, impression. **5** *they had no conception of our problems:* **understanding**, comprehension, appreciation, grasp, knowledge; idea, inkling; informal clue.

concern verb **1** *the report concerns the war:* **be about**, deal with, cover; discuss, go into, examine, study, review, analyse; relate to, pertain to. **2** *that doesn't concern you:* **affect**, involve, be relevant to, apply to, have a bearing on, impact on; be important to, interest. **3** *I won't concern myself with your affairs:* **involve oneself in**, take an interest in, busy oneself with, devote one's time to, bother oneself with. **4** *one thing still concerns me:* **worry**, disturb, trouble, bother, perturb, unsettle, make anxious.
noun **1** *a voice full of concern:* **anxiety**, worry, disquiet, apprehensiveness, unease, consternation. **2** *his concern for others:* **solicitude**, solicitousness, consideration, care, sympathy, regard. **3** *housing is the concern of the council:* **responsibility**, business, affair, charge, duty, job; province, preserve; problem, worry; informal pigeon, bag, bailiwick; Brit. informal lookout. **4** *issues that are of concern to women:* **interest**, importance, relevance, significance. **5** *Aboriginal concerns:* **affair**, issue, matter, question, consideration. **6** *a publishing concern:* **company**, business, firm, organization, operation, corporation, establishment, house, office, agency; informal outfit, set-up.
– OPPOSITES indifference.

concerned adjective **1** *her mother looked concerned:* **worried**, anxious, upset, perturbed, troubled, distressed, uneasy, apprehensive, agitated. **2** *he is concerned about your welfare:* **solicitous**, caring; attentive to, considerate of. **3** *all concerned parties:* **interested**, involved, affected; connected, related, implicated.

concerning preposition *further revelations concerning his role in the affair:* **about**, regarding, relating to, with reference to, referring to, with regard to, as regards, with respect to, respecting, dealing with, on the subject of, in connection with, re, apropos of.

concert noun **musical performance**, show, production, presentation; recital; informal gig. ■ **in concert** together, jointly, in combination, in collaboration, in cooperation, in league, side by side; in unison.

concerted adjective 1 *you must make a concerted effort to curb this*: **strenuous**, vigorous, intensive, intense, concentrated; informal all-out. 2 *there were calls for concerted action*: **joint**, united, collaborative, collective, combined, cooperative.
– OPPOSITES half-hearted, individual.

concession noun 1 *the government made several concessions*: **compromise**, allowance, exception, sop. 2 *a concession of failure*: **admission**, acknowledgement, acceptance, recognition, confession. 3 *the concession of territory*: **surrender**, relinquishment, sacrifice, handover. 4 *tax concessions*: **reduction**, cut, discount, deduction, decrease; rebate; informal break. 5 *a logging concession*: **right**, privilege; licence, permit, franchise, warrant, authorization.
– OPPOSITES denial, acquisition.

conciliate verb 1 *he tried to conciliate the peasantry*: **appease**, placate, pacify, mollify, assuage, soothe, humour, reconcile, win over, make peace with. 2 *he conciliated in the dispute*: **mediate**, act as peacemaker, arbitrate; pour oil on troubled waters.
– OPPOSITES provoke.

conciliation noun *he held his hands up in a gesture of conciliation*: **appeasement**, pacification, peacemaking, placation, propitiation, mollification, reconciliation.
– OPPOSITES provocation.

conciliator noun **peacemaker**, mediator, go-between, middleman, intermediary, intercessor; dove.
– OPPOSITES troublemaker.

conciliatory adjective *a conciliatory gesture*: **propitiatory**, placatory, appeasing, pacifying, pacific, mollifying, peacemaking.

concise adjective *a concise account*: **succinct**, pithy, incisive, brief, short and to the point, short and sweet; abridged, condensed, compressed, abbreviated, compact, potted; informal snappy.
– OPPOSITES lengthy, wordy.

conclave noun *a conclave of American, European, and Japanese business leaders*: **(private) meeting**, gathering, assembly, conference, council, summit; informal parley, powwow, get-together.

conclude verb 1 *the meeting concluded at ten*: **finish**, end, draw to a close, be over, stop, cease. 2 *he concluded the press conference*: **bring to an end**, close, wind up, terminate, dissolve; round off; informal wrap up. 3 *an*

attempt to conclude a ceasefire: **negotiate**, broker, agree, come to terms on, settle, clinch, finalize, tie up; bring about, arrange, effect, engineer; informal sew up. 4 *I concluded that he was rather unpleasant*: **deduce**, infer, gather, judge, decide, conjecture, surmise; N. Amer. figure; informal reckon.
– OPPOSITES commence.

conclusion noun 1 *the conclusion of his speech*: **end**, ending, finish, close, termination, wind-up, cessation; culmination, denouement, coda. 2 *the conclusion of a trade agreement*: **negotiation**, brokering, settlement, completion, arrangement, resolution. 3 *his conclusions have been verified*: **deduction**, inference, interpretation, reasoning; opinion, judgement, verdict; assumption, presumption, supposition.
– OPPOSITES beginning.
■ **in conclusion** finally, in closing, to conclude, last but not least; to sum up, in short.

conclusive adjective 1 *conclusive proof*: **incontrovertible**, undeniable, indisputable, irrefutable, unquestionable, unassailable, convincing, certain, decisive, definitive, definite, positive, categorical, unequivocal; airtight, watertight. 2 *a conclusive win*: **emphatic**, resounding, convincing.
– OPPOSITES unconvincing.

concoct verb 1 *she began to concoct her dinner*: **prepare**, make, assemble; informal fix, rustle up; Brit. informal knock up. 2 *his cronies concocted a simple plan*: **make up**, dream up, fabricate, invent, trump up; formulate, hatch, brew; informal cook up.

concoction noun 1 *a concoction containing gin and vodka*: **mixture**, brew, preparation, potion. 2 *a strange concoction of styles*: **blend**, mixture, mix, combination, hybrid. 3 *her story is an improbable concoction*: **fabrication**, invention, falsification; informal fairy story, fairy tale.

concourse noun *the station concourse*: **entrance**, foyer, lobby, hall.

concrete adjective 1 *concrete objects*: **solid**, material, real, physical, tangible, palpable, substantial, visible, existing. 2 *I haven't got any concrete proof*: **definite**, firm, positive, conclusive, definitive; real, genuine, bona fide.
– OPPOSITES abstract, imaginary.

concur verb 1 *we concur with this view*: **agree**, be in agreement, go along, fall in, be in sympathy; see eye to eye, be of the same mind, be of the same opinion. 2 *the two events concurred*: **coincide**, be simultaneous, be concurrent, coexist.
– OPPOSITES disagree.

concurrent adjective 1 *he was given nine concurrent life sentences*: **simultaneous**, coincident, contemporaneous, parallel. 2 *concurrent lines*: **convergent**, converging, meeting, intersecting.

concussion noun 1 *he suffered concussion:* temporary unconsciousness; brain injury. 2 *the concussion of the blast:* **force**, impact, shock, jolt.

condemn verb 1 *he condemned the suspended players:* **censure**, criticize, denounce, revile, blame, chastise, berate, reprimand, rebuke, reprove, take to task, find fault with; informal slam, blast, lay into; Brit. informal slate, slag off, have a go at; formal castigate. 2 *he was condemned to death:* **sentence**; convict, find guilty. 3 *the house has been condemned:* **declare unfit**, declare unsafe. 4 *her mistake had condemned her:* **incriminate**, implicate. 5 *his illness condemned him to a lonely life:* **doom**, destine, damn; consign, assign.
– OPPOSITES praise.

condemnation noun *a comment which provoked widespread condemnation:* **censure**, criticism, strictures, denunciation, vilification; reproof, disapproval; informal flak, a bad press; formal castigation.

condemnatory adjective **censorious**, critical, damning; reproving, reproachful, deprecatory, disapproving, unfavourable; formal castigatory.

condensation noun 1 *windows misty with condensation:* **moisture**, water droplets, steam. 2 *the condensation of the vapour:* **precipitation**, liquefaction, deliquescence. 3 *a condensation of recent literature:* **abridgement**, summary, synopsis, precis, digest. 4 *the condensation of the report:* **shortening**, abridgement, abbreviation, summarization.

condense verb 1 *the water vapour condenses:* **precipitate**, liquefy, become liquid, deliquesce. 2 *he condensed the play:* **abridge**, shorten, cut, abbreviate, compact; summarize, synopsize, precis; truncate, curtail.
– OPPOSITES vaporize, expand.

condensed adjective 1 *a condensed text:* **abridged**, shortened, cut, compressed, abbreviated, reduced, truncated, concise; outline, thumbnail; informal potted. 2 *condensed soup:* **concentrated**, evaporated, reduced; strong, undiluted.
– OPPOSITES diluted.

condescend verb 1 *don't condescend to your reader:* **patronize**, talk down to, look down one's nose at, look down on, put down. 2 *he condescended to see us:* **deign**, stoop, descend, lower oneself, demean oneself; vouchsafe, see fit, consent.

condescending adjective *she looked us up and down in a condescending manner:* **patronizing**, supercilious, superior, snobbish, snobby, disdainful, lofty, haughty; informal snooty, stuck-up; Brit. informal toffee-nosed.

condition noun 1 *check the condition of your wiring:* **state**, shape, order; Brit. informal nick. 2 *they lived in appalling conditions:*

circumstances, surroundings, environment, situation, set-up, setting, habitat; informal circs. 3 *she was in tip-top condition:* **fitness**, health, form, shape, trim, fettle. 4 *a liver condition:* **disorder**, problem, complaint, illness, disease, ailment, sickness, affliction, infection, upset; informal bug, virus; Brit. informal lurgy. 5 *it is a condition of employment that employees should be paid through a bank:* **stipulation**, constraint, prerequisite, precondition, requirement, rule, term, specification, provision, proviso.
verb 1 *their choices are conditioned by the economy:* **constrain**, control, govern, determine, decide; affect, touch, impact on; form, shape, guide, sway, bias. 2 *our minds are conditioned by habit:* **train**, teach, educate, guide; accustom, adapt, habituate, mould, inure. 3 *condition the boards with water:* **treat**, prepare, prime, temper, process, acclimatize, acclimate, season. 4 *a product to condition your skin:* **improve**, nourish, tone (up), moisturize.

conditional adjective 1 *their approval is conditional on success:* **subject to**, dependent on, contingent on, based on, determined by, controlled by, tied to. 2 *he was only made a conditional offer of a university place:* **contingent**, dependent, qualified, with reservations, limited, provisional, provisory.

condolences plural noun *we offer our sincere condolences to his widow:* **sympathy**, commiseration(s), compassion, pity, support, comfort, consolation, understanding.

condom noun **contraceptive**, sheath; N. Amer. prophylactic; Brit. trademark Durex, Femidom; Brit. informal johnny; N. Amer. informal rubber, safe.

condone verb *we cannot condone such dreadful behaviour:* **disregard**, accept, allow, let pass, turn a blind eye to, overlook, forget; forgive, pardon, excuse, let go.
– OPPOSITES condemn.

conducive adjective *an environment which is conducive to learning:* **favourable**, beneficial, advantageous, opportune, propitious, encouraging, promising, convenient, good, helpful, instrumental, productive, useful.
– OPPOSITES unfavourable.

conduct noun 1 *they complained about her conduct:* **behaviour**, performance, demeanour; actions, activities, deeds, doings, exploits; habits, manners. 2 *the conduct of the elections:* **management**, running, direction, control, supervision, regulation, administration, organization, coordination, orchestration, handling.
verb 1 *the election was conducted lawfully:* **manage**, direct, run, administer, organize, coordinate, orchestrate, handle, control, oversee, supervise, regulate, carry out/on. 2 *he was conducted through the corridors:* **escort**, guide, lead, usher, show; shepherd, see, bring, take, help. 3 *aluminium conducts heat:* **transmit**, convey, carry, transfer,

impart, channel, relay; disseminate, diffuse, radiate.
■ **conduct oneself** behave, act, acquit oneself, bear oneself.

conduit noun **channel**, duct, pipe, tube, gutter, trench, culvert, cut, sluice, spillway, flume, chute.

confectionery noun **sweets**, chocolates, bonbons; N. Amer. candy; informal sweeties.

confederacy noun *the Empire was a loosely organized confederacy of allies:* **federation**, confederation, alliance, league, association, coalition, consortium, syndicate, group, circle; bloc, axis.

confederate adjective *confederate councils:* **federal**, confederated, federated, allied, associated, united.
– OPPOSITES split.
noun *he met his confederate in the street:* **associate**, partner, accomplice, helper, assistant, ally, collaborator, colleague; Brit. informal oppo; Austral./NZ informal offsider.

confederation noun *a confederation of trade unions:* **alliance**, league, confederacy, federation, association, coalition, consortium, conglomerate, cooperative, syndicate, group, circle; society, union.

confer verb 1 *she conferred a knighthood on him:* **bestow on**, present to, grant to, award to, decorate with, honour with, give to, endow with, extend to, vouchsafe to. 2 *she went to confer with her colleagues:* **consult**, talk, speak, converse, have a chat, have a tête-à-tête, parley; informal have a confab, powwow.

conference noun 1 *an international conference:* **congress**, meeting, convention, seminar, colloquium, symposium, forum, summit. 2 *he gathered them for a conference:* **discussion**, consultation, debate, talk, conversation, dialogue, chat, tête-à-tête, parley; informal confab.

confess verb 1 *he confessed that he had done it:* **admit**, acknowledge, reveal, disclose, divulge, avow, declare, profess; own up, tell all. 2 *they would not make him confess:* **own up**, plead guilty, accept the blame; tell the truth, tell all, make a clean breast of it; informal come clean, spill the beans, let the cat out of the bag, get something off one's chest, let on; Brit. informal cough. 3 *I confess I don't know:* **acknowledge**, admit, concede, grant, allow, own, declare, affirm.
– OPPOSITES deny.

confession noun *the interrogators soon got a confession out of him:* **admission**, acknowledgement, profession; revelation, disclosure, divulgence, avowal; guilty plea.

confidant, confidante noun *he was her confidant and business adviser:* **close friend**, bosom friend, best friend; intimate, familiar; informal chum, pal, crony; Brit. informal mate, oppo, mucker; N. Amer. informal buddy.

confide verb 1 *he confided his fears to his mother:* **reveal**, disclose, divulge, lay bare,

betray, impart, declare, intimate, uncover, expose, vouchsafe, tell; confess, admit, give away; informal blab, spill. 2 *I need him to confide in:* **open one's heart to**, unburden oneself to, confess to, tell all to.

confidence noun 1 *I have little confidence in these figures:* **trust**, belief, faith, credence, conviction. 2 *she's brimming with confidence:* **self-assurance**, self-confidence, self-possession, assertiveness; poise, aplomb, phlegm; courage, boldness, mettle, nerve. 3 *the girls exchanged confidences:* **secret**, confidentiality, intimacy.
– OPPOSITES scepticism, doubt.

confident adjective 1 *we are confident that business will improve:* **optimistic**, hopeful, sanguine; sure, certain, positive, convinced, in no doubt, satisfied, assured, persuaded. 2 *a confident girl:* **self-assured**, assured, self-confident, positive, assertive, self-possessed, self-reliant, poised; cool-headed, phlegmatic, level-headed, unperturbed, imperturbable, unruffled, at ease; informal together.

confidential adjective *a confidential chat:* **private**, personal, intimate, quiet; secret, sensitive, classified, restricted, unofficial, unrevealed, undisclosed, unpublished; informal hush-hush, mum.

confidentially adverb **privately**, in private, in confidence, between ourselves/themselves, off the record, quietly, secretly, in secret, behind closed doors; formal sub rosa.

configuration noun *the configuration of the stars at the moment of your birth:* **arrangement**, layout, geography, design, organization, order, grouping, positioning, disposition, alignment; shape, form, appearance, formation, structure, format.

confine verb 1 *they were confined in the house:* **enclose**, incarcerate, imprison, intern, impound, hold captive, trap; shut in/up, keep, lock in/up, coop (up); fence in, hedge in, wall in/up. 2 *he confined his remarks to the weather:* **restrict**, limit.

confined adjective *her fear of confined spaces:* **cramped**, constricted, restricted, limited, small, narrow, compact, tight, poky, uncomfortable, inadequate.
– OPPOSITES roomy.

confinement noun 1 *he was being held in solitary confinement:* **imprisonment**, internment, incarceration, custody, captivity, detention, restraint; house arrest. 2 *the confinement of an animal:* **caging**, enclosure; quarantine.

confines plural noun *within the confines of the hall, escape was difficult:* **limits**, margins, extremities, edges, borders, boundaries, fringes, marches; periphery, perimeter.

confirm verb 1 *records confirm the latest evidence:* **corroborate**, verify, prove, validate, authenticate, substantiate, justify, vindicate; support, uphold, back up. 2 *he*

confirmed that help was on the way: **affirm**, reaffirm, assert, assure someone, repeat; promise, guarantee. **3** *his appointment was confirmed by the President:* **ratify**, validate, sanction, endorse, formalize, authorize, warrant, accredit, approve, accept.
– OPPOSITES contradict, deny.

confirmation noun **1** *there was no independent confirmation of the reported deaths:* **corroboration**, verification, proof, testimony, endorsement, authentication, substantiation, evidence. **2** *confirmation of your appointment is dependent upon satisfactory performance:* **ratification**, approval, authorization, validation, sanction, endorsement, formalization, accreditation, acceptance.

confirmed adjective *a confirmed bachelor:* **established**, long-standing, committed, dyed-in-the-wool, through and through; staunch, loyal, faithful, devoted, dedicated, steadfast; habitual, compulsive, persistent; unapologetic, unashamed, inveterate, chronic, incurable; informal deep-dyed, card-carrying.

confiscate verb *the guards confiscated his camera:* **impound**, seize, commandeer, requisition, appropriate, expropriate, sequester, sequestrate, take (away).
– OPPOSITES return.

confiscation noun **seizure**, requisition, appropriation, expropriation, sequestration.

conflict noun **1** *industrial conflicts:* **dispute**, quarrel, squabble, disagreement, dissension, clash; discord, friction, strife, antagonism, hostility, disputation, contention; feud, schism. **2** *the Vietnam conflict:* **war**, campaign, battle, fighting, (armed) confrontation, engagement, encounter, struggle, hostilities; warfare, combat. **3** *a conflict between his business and domestic life:* **clash**, incompatibility, incongruity, friction; mismatch, variance, difference, divergence, contradiction, inconsistency.
– OPPOSITES agreement, peace, harmony.
verb *their interests sometimes conflict:* **clash**, be incompatible, vary, be at odds, be in conflict, differ, diverge, disagree, contrast, collide.

conflicting adjective *there are conflicting accounts of what occurred:* **contradictory**, incompatible, inconsistent, irreconcilable, incongruous, contrary, opposite, opposing, antithetical, clashing, discordant, divergent; at odds.

confluence noun *the confluence of the Rhine and the Mosel:* **convergence**, meeting, junction, conflux, watersmeet.

conform verb **1** *visitors have to conform to our rules:* **comply with**, abide by, obey, observe, follow, keep to, stick to, adhere to, uphold, heed, accept, go along with, fall in with, respect, defer to; satisfy, meet, fulfil. **2** *they refuse to conform:* **follow convention**, be conventional, fit in, adapt, adjust, follow the crowd; comply, acquiesce, toe the line,

follow the rules; submit, yield; informal play it by the book, play by the rules. **3** *goods must conform to their description:* **match**, fit, suit, answer, agree with, be like, correspond to, be consistent with, measure up to, tally with, square with.
– OPPOSITES flout, rebel.

conformist noun *he was too much of a conformist to wear anything but a suit at work:* **conventionalist**, traditionalist, conservative, stickler, formalist, diehard, reactionary; informal stick-in-the-mud, stuffed shirt.
– OPPOSITES eccentric, rebel.

confound verb **1** *the figures confounded analysts:* **amaze**, astonish, dumbfound, stagger, surprise, startle, stun, nonplus; throw, shake, discompose, bewilder, baffle, mystify, bemuse, perplex, puzzle, confuse; take aback, shake up, catch off balance; informal flabbergast, blow someone's mind, blow away, flummox, faze, stump, beat, fox; N. Amer. informal discombobulate. **2** *he has always confounded expectations:* **contradict**, counter, invalidate, negate, go against, drive a coach and horses through; quash, explode, demolish, shoot down, destroy, disprove; informal shoot full of holes.

confront verb **1** *Jones confronted the burglar:* **challenge**, square up to, face (up to), come face to face with, meet, accost, waylay; stand up to, brave, beard, tackle; informal collar; Brit. informal nobble. **2** *the problems that confront us:* **trouble**, bother, burden, distress, worry, oppress, annoy, strain, stress, tax, torment, plague, blight, curse; face, beset. **3** *they must confront their problems:* **tackle**, address, face, get to grips with, grapple with, take on, attend to, see to, deal with, take care of, handle, manage; informal get stuck into. **4** *she confronted him with the evidence:* **present**, face.
– OPPOSITES avoid.

confrontation noun *a peaceful protest turned into a violent confrontation:* **conflict**, clash, fight, battle, encounter, head-to-head, face-off, engagement, skirmish; hostilities, fighting; informal set-to, run-in, dust-up, showdown.

confuse verb **1** *don't confuse students with too much detail:* **bewilder**, baffle, mystify, bemuse, perplex, puzzle, confound, nonplus; informal flummox, faze, stump, fox; N. Amer. informal discombobulate. **2** *the authors have confused the issue:* **complicate**, muddle, jumble, garble, blur, obscure, cloud. **3** *some confuse strokes with heart attacks:* **mix up**, muddle up, confound; mistake for.
– OPPOSITES enlighten, simplify.

confused adjective **1** *they are confused about what is going on:* **bewildered**, bemused, puzzled, perplexed, baffled, mystified, nonplussed, muddled, dumbfounded, at sea, at a loss, taken aback, disoriented, disconcerted; informal flummoxed, bamboozled, clueless, fazed;

N. Amer. informal discombobulated. **2** *her confused elderly mother:* **demented**, bewildered, muddled, addled, befuddled, disoriented, disorientated; unbalanced, unhinged; senile. **3** *a confused recollection:* **vague**, unclear, indistinct, imprecise, blurred, hazy, woolly, shadowy, dim; imperfect, sketchy. **4** *a confused mass of bones:* **disorderly**, disordered, disorganized, disarranged, out of order, untidy, muddled, jumbled, mixed up, chaotic, topsy-turvy; informal higgledy-piggledy; Brit. informal shambolic.
– OPPOSITES lucid, clear, precise, neat.

confusing adjective *the instructions are a little confusing:* **bewildering**, baffling, unclear, perplexing, puzzling, mystifying, disconcerting; ambiguous, misleading, inconsistent, contradictory; unaccountable, inexplicable, impenetrable, unfathomable; complex, complicated.

confusion noun **1** *there is confusion about the new system:* **uncertainty**, incertitude, unsureness, doubt, ignorance; formal dubiety. **2** *she stared in confusion:* **bewilderment**, bafflement, perplexity, puzzlement, mystification, befuddlement; shock, daze, wonder, wonderment, astonishment; informal bamboozlement; N. Amer. informal discombobulation. **3** *her life was in utter confusion:* **disorder**, disarray, disorganization, untidiness, chaos, mayhem; turmoil, tumult, disruption, upheaval, uproar, hurly-burly, muddle, mess; informal shambles. **4** *a confusion of boxes:* **jumble**, muddle, mess, heap, tangle; informal shambles.
– OPPOSITES certainty, order.

congeal verb *the blood had congealed around the cut:* **coagulate**, clot, thicken, gel, inspissate, cake, set, curdle.

congenial adjective **1** *I was working with a bunch of very congenial people:* **like-minded**, compatible, kindred, well suited; companionable, sociable, sympathetic, comradely, convivial, hospitable, genial, personable, agreeable, friendly, pleasant, likeable, amiable, nice. **2** *a congenial environment:* **pleasant**, pleasing, agreeable, enjoyable, pleasurable, nice, appealing, satisfying, gratifying, delightful, relaxing, welcoming, hospitable; suitable, well suited, favourable.
– OPPOSITES unpleasant.

congenital adjective **1** *congenital defects:* **inborn**, inherited, hereditary, innate, inbred, constitutional, inbuilt, natural, inherent. **2** *a congenital liar:* **inveterate**, compulsive, persistent, chronic, regular, habitual, obsessive, confirmed; incurable, incorrigible, irredeemable, hopeless; unashamed, shameless; informal pathological.
– OPPOSITES acquired.

congested adjective *more traffic will use the already congested road:* **crowded**, overcrowded, full, overflowing, packed, jammed, thronged, teeming, swarming; obstructed, blocked, clogged, choked; informal snarled up, gridlocked, jam-packed; Brit. informal like Piccadilly Circus.
– OPPOSITES clear.

congestion noun **crowding**, overcrowding; obstruction, blockage; traffic jam, bottleneck; informal snarl-up, gridlock.

conglomerate noun **1** *the conglomerate was broken up:* **corporation**, combine, group, consortium, partnership; firm, company, business, multinational. **2** *a conglomerate of disparate peoples:* **mixture**, mix, combination, amalgamation, union, marriage, fusion, composite, synthesis; miscellany, hotchpotch.
adjective *a conglomerate mass:* **aggregate**, agglomerate, amassed, combined.
verb *the debris conglomerated into planets:* **coalesce**, unite, join, combine, merge, fuse, consolidate, amalgamate, integrate, mingle, intermingle.

congratulate verb **1** *she congratulated him on his marriage:* **send one's best wishes to**, wish someone good luck, wish someone joy; drink someone's health, toast. **2** *they are to be congratulated:* **praise**, commend, applaud, salute, honour; pay tribute to, regard highly, pat on the back, take one's hat off to.
– OPPOSITES criticize.
■ **congratulate oneself** take pride, feel proud, flatter oneself, preen oneself, pat oneself on the back; feel satisfaction, take pleasure, glory, bask, delight.

congratulations plural noun **1** *her congratulations on their wedding:* **good wishes**, best wishes, compliments, felicitations. **2** *you all deserve congratulations:* **praise**, commendation, applause, salutes, honour, acclaim, cheers, bouquets; approval, admiration, compliments, kudos, adulation; a pat on the back.

congregate verb *some 4000 demonstrators had congregated at a border point:* **assemble**, gather, collect, come together, convene, rally, rendezvous, muster, meet, cluster, group.
– OPPOSITES disperse.

congregation noun **1** *the chapel congregation:* **parishioners**, parish, churchgoers, flock, faithful, followers, believers, fellowship, communicants, laity, brethren; throng, company, assemblage, audience. **2** *congregations of birds:* **gathering**, assembly, flock, swarm, bevy, pack, group, body, crowd, mass, multitude, horde, host, mob, throng.

congress noun **1** *a congress of mathematicians:* **conference**, convention, seminar, colloquium, symposium, forum, meeting, assembly, gathering, rally, summit. **2** *elections for the new Congress:* **legislature**, legislative assembly, parliament, convocation, diet, council, senate, chamber, house.

congruence noun *he took care that there should be congruence of meaning and sound*

in his music: **compatibility**, consistency, conformity, match, balance, consonance, congruity; agreement, accord, consensus, harmony, unity.
– OPPOSITES conflict.

conical adjective *a circular tower with a conical roof:* **cone-shaped**, tapered, tapering, pointed, funnel-shaped; informal pointy.

conjectural adjective *the evidence was deemed too conjectural:* **speculative**, suppositional, suppositious, theoretical, hypothetical, putative, notional; postulated, inferred, presumed, assumed, presupposed, tentative.

conjecture noun *the information is merely conjecture:* **speculation**, guesswork, surmise, fancy, presumption, assumption, theory, postulation, supposition; inference, extrapolation; estimate; informal guesstimate, a shot in the dark.
– OPPOSITES fact.
verb *I conjectured that the game was over:* **guess**, speculate, surmise, infer, fancy, imagine, believe, think, suspect, presume, assume, hypothesize, suppose.
– OPPOSITES know.

conjugal adjective *conjugal rights:* **marital**, matrimonial, nuptial, marriage, bridal.

conjunction noun *a conjunction of favourable political and economic circumstances:* **co-occurrence**, concurrence, coincidence, coexistence, simultaneity, contemporaneity, concomitance, synchronicity, synchrony.

conjure verb **1** *he conjured a cigarette out of the air:* **produce**, make something appear, materialize, magic, summon. **2** *the picture that his words conjured up:* **bring to mind**, call to mind, evoke, summon up, recall, recreate; echo, allude to, suggest, awaken.

conjuring noun *a demonstration of conjuring:* **magic**, illusion, sleight of hand, legerdemain.

conjuror noun **magician**, illusionist; formal prestidigitator.

connect verb **1** *electrodes were connected to the device:* **attach**, join, fasten, fix, affix, couple, link, secure, hitch; stick, adhere, fuse, pin, screw, bolt, clamp, clip, hook (up); add, append. **2** *there are lots of customs connected with Easter:* **associate**, link, couple; identify, equate, bracket, relate to.

connection noun **1** *the connection between commerce and art:* **link**, relationship, relation, interconnection, interdependence, association; bond, tie, tie-in, correspondence, parallel, analogy. **2** *a poor connection in the plug:* **attachment**, joint, fastening, coupling. **3** *he has the right connections:* **contact**, friend, acquaintance, ally, colleague, associate; relation, relative, kin.
■ **in connection with** regarding, concerning, with reference to, with regard to, with respect to, respecting, relating to,

in relation to, on, connected with, on the subject of, in the matter of, apropos, re, in re.

connivance noun *this infringement of the law had taken place with the connivance of officials:* **collusion**, complicity, collaboration, involvement, assistance; tacit consent, conspiracy, intrigue.

connive verb **1** *wardens connived at offences:* **deliberately ignore**, overlook, disregard, pass over, take no notice of, make allowances for, turn a blind eye to, wink at, excuse, condone, let go; look the other way, let something ride. **2** *the government connived with security forces:* **conspire**, collude, collaborate, intrigue, be hand in glove, plot, scheme; informal be in cahoots.

conniving adjective **scheming**, cunning, crafty, calculating, devious, wily, sly, tricky, artful, guileful; manipulative, Machiavellian, disingenuous, deceitful, underhand, treacherous; informal foxy.

connoisseur noun *a connoisseur of fine wines:* **expert**, authority, specialist, pundit, savant; arbiter of taste, aesthete; gourmet, epicure, gastronome; informal buff; N. Amer. informal maven.

connotation noun *the word 'discipline' has unhappy connotations of punishment and repression:* **overtone**, undertone, undercurrent, implication, hidden meaning, nuance, hint, echo, vibrations, association, intimation, suggestion, suspicion, insinuation.

connote verb *the British think that crying and showing emotion connote weakness:* **imply**, suggest, indicate, signify, hint at, give the impression of, smack of, be associated with, allude to.

conquer verb **1** *the Franks conquered the Visigoths:* **defeat**, beat, vanquish, trounce, triumph over, be victorious over, get the better of, worst; overcome, overwhelm, overpower, overthrow, subdue, subjugate, quell, quash, crush, rout; informal lick, best, hammer, clobber, thrash, paste, demolish, annihilate, wipe the floor with, walk all over, make mincemeat of, massacre, slaughter; Brit. informal stuff; N. Amer. informal cream, shellac, skunk. **2** *Peru was conquered by Spain:* **seize**, take (over), appropriate, subjugate, capture, occupy, invade, annex, overrun. **3** *the first men to conquer Mount Everest:* **climb**, ascend, mount, scale, top, crest. **4** *the only way to conquer fear is to face it:* **overcome**, get the better of, control, master, get a grip on, deal with, cope with, surmount, rise above, get over; quell, quash, beat, triumph over; informal lick.
– OPPOSITES lose.

conqueror noun **vanquisher**, conquistador; victor, winner, champion, conquering hero.

conquest noun **1** *the conquest of the Aztecs:* **defeat**, vanquishment, annihilation, overthrow, subjugation, rout, mastery,

C

crushing; victory over, triumph over. **2** *their conquest of the valley:* **seizure**, takeover, capture, occupation, invasion, acquisition, appropriation, subjugation, subjection. **3** *the conquest of Everest:* **ascent**. **4** *she's his latest conquest:* **catch**, acquisition, prize, slave; admirer, fan, worshipper; lover, boyfriend, girlfriend; informal fancy man, fancy woman.
– OPPOSITES victory, surrender.

conscience noun *her conscience wouldn't allow her to keep silent any longer:* **sense of right and wrong**, moral sense, inner voice; morals, standards, values, principles, ethics, beliefs; compunction, scruples, qualms.

conscience-stricken adjective *she was still conscience-stricken over her outburst:* **guilt-ridden**, remorseful, ashamed, shamefaced, apologetic, sorry; chastened, contrite, guilty, regretful, rueful, repentant, penitent, self-reproachful, abashed, sheepish.
– OPPOSITES unrepentant.

conscientious adjective *a conscientious man, he took his duties very seriously:* **diligent**, industrious, punctilious, painstaking, sedulous, assiduous, dedicated, careful, meticulous, thorough, attentive, hard-working, studious, rigorous, particular; religious, strict.
– OPPOSITES casual.

conscious adjective **1** *the patient was conscious:* **aware**, awake, alert, responsive, sentient, compos mentis. **2** *he became conscious of people talking:* **aware of**, alert to, mindful of, sensible of. **3** *he made a conscious effort to stop staring:* **deliberate**, intentional, intended, purposeful, purposive, knowing, considered, calculated, wilful, premeditated, planned.
– OPPOSITES unaware.

conscript verb *they were conscripted into the army:* **call up**, enlist, recruit; US draft.
noun *an army conscript:* **recruit**, compulsorily enlisted soldier; US draftee.
– OPPOSITES volunteer.

consecrate verb *the present Holy Trinity Church was consecrated in 1845:* **sanctify**, bless, make holy, make sacred; dedicate to God, devote, reserve, set apart; anoint, ordain.

consecutive adjective *share prices fell for three consecutive days:* **successive**, succeeding, following, in succession, running, in a row, one after the other, back-to-back, continuous, straight, uninterrupted; informal on the trot.

consensus noun **1** *there was consensus among delegates:* **agreement**, harmony, concurrence, accord, unity, unanimity, solidarity; formal concord. **2** *the consensus was that they should act:* **general opinion**, majority opinion, common view.
– OPPOSITES disagreement.

consent noun *a change in the rules requires the consent of all members:* **agreement**, assent, acceptance, approval, approbation; permission, authorization, sanction, leave; backing, endorsement, support; informal go-ahead, thumbs up, green light, OK.
– OPPOSITES dissent.
verb *she consented to surgery:* **agree**, assent, yield, give in, submit; allow, give permission for, sanction, accept, approve, go along with.
– OPPOSITES forbid.

consequence noun **1** *inflation is a consequence of a rapid growth in the money supply:* **result**, upshot, outcome, out-turn, effect, repercussion, ramification, corollary, concomitant, aftermath; fruit(s), product, by-product, end result; informal pay-off. **2** *the past is of no consequence:* **importance**, import, significance, account, substance, note, mark, prominence, value, concern, interest.
– OPPOSITES cause.

consequent adjective *if accurate measurements are not taken, there will be consequent errors in construction:* **resulting**, resultant, ensuing, consequential; following, subsequent, successive; attendant, accompanying, concomitant; collateral, associated, related.

consequential adjective **1** *a fire and the consequential smoke damage:* **resulting**, resultant, ensuing, consequent; following, subsequent; attendant, accompanying, concomitant; collateral, associated, related. **2** *one of his more consequential initiatives:* **important**, significant, major, momentous, weighty, material, appreciable, memorable, far-reaching, serious.
– OPPOSITES insignificant.

consequently adverb *many of the subjects available are not taught in school, and consequently may be unfamiliar:* **as a result**, as a consequence, so, thus, therefore, ergo, accordingly, hence, for this/that reason, because of this/that, on this/that account; inevitably, necessarily.

conservation noun *the conservation of tropical forests:* **preservation**, protection, safeguarding, safe keeping; care, guardianship, husbandry, supervision; upkeep, maintenance, repair, restoration; ecology, environmentalism.

conservative adjective **1** *the conservative wing of the party:* **right-wing**, reactionary, traditionalist; Brit. Tory, blimpish; US Republican; informal true blue. **2** *the conservative trade-union movement:* **traditionalist**, traditional, conventional, orthodox, old-fashioned, dyed-in-the-wool, hidebound, unadventurous, set in one's ways; moderate, middle-of-the-road; informal stick in the mud. **3** *a conservative suit:* **conventional**, sober, modest, plain, unobtrusive, restrained, subtle, low-key, demure; informal square, straight. **4** *a conservative estimate:* **low**, cautious, understated, moderate, reasonable.
– OPPOSITES socialist, radical, ostentatious.
noun *liberals and conservatives have found*

common ground: **right-winger**, reactionary, rightist, diehard; Brit. Tory, blimp; US Republican.

conservatory noun **1** *a frost-free conservatory:* **summer house**, belvedere; glasshouse, greenhouse, hothouse.
2 *a teaching job at the conservatory:* **conservatoire**, music school, drama school.

conserve verb *fossil fuel should be conserved:* **preserve**, protect, save, safeguard, keep, look after; sustain, prolong, perpetuate; store, reserve, husband.
– OPPOSITES squander.
noun *cherry conserve:* **jam**, preserve, jelly, marmalade, confiture.

consider verb **1** *Isabel considered her choices:* **think about**, contemplate, reflect on, examine, review; mull over, ponder, deliberate on, chew over, meditate on, ruminate on; assess, evaluate, weigh up, appraise; informal size up. **2** *I consider him irresponsible:* **deem**, think, believe, judge, adjudge, rate, count, find; regard as, hold to be, reckon to be, view as, see as. **3** *he considered the ceiling:* **look at**, contemplate, observe, regard, survey, view, scrutinize, scan, examine, inspect; informal check out; N. Amer. informal eyeball. **4** *the inquiry will consider those issues:* **take into consideration**, take account of, make allowances for, bear in mind, be mindful of, remember, mind, mark, respect, heed, note, make provision for.
– OPPOSITES ignore.

considerable adjective **1** *he escaped with a considerable amount of money:* **sizeable**, substantial, appreciable, significant; goodly, fair, hefty, handsome, decent, worthwhile; ample, plentiful, abundant, great, large, generous; informal tidy, not to be sneezed at. **2** *he turned professional and met with considerable success:* **much**, great, a lot of, lots of, a great deal of, plenty of, a fair amount of. **3** *a considerable cricketer:* **distinguished**, noteworthy, important, significant, prominent, eminent, influential, illustrious; renowned, celebrated, acclaimed.
– OPPOSITES paltry, minor.

considerably adverb *alcoholic drinks vary considerably in strength:* **greatly**, (very) much, a great deal, a lot, lots; significantly, substantially, appreciably, markedly, noticeably; informal plenty, seriously.

considerate adjective *she was unfailingly kind and considerate:* **attentive**, thoughtful, solicitous, mindful, heedful, obliging, accommodating, helpful, cooperative, patient; kind, unselfish, compassionate, sympathetic, caring, charitable, altruistic, generous; polite, sensitive, tactful.

consideration noun **1** *your case needs careful consideration:* **thought**, deliberation, reflection, contemplation, rumination, meditation; examination, inspection, scrutiny, analysis, discussion;

attention, regard. **2** *his health is the prime consideration:* **factor**, issue, matter, concern, detail, aspect, feature. **3** *firms should show more consideration:* **attentiveness**, concern, care, thoughtfulness, solicitude; kindness, understanding, respect, sensitivity, tact, discretion; compassion, charity, benevolence. **4** *I might do it, for a consideration:* **payment**, fee, premium, remuneration, compensation; commission, percentage, dividend; informal cut, slice, piece of the action.
▪ **take something into consideration** consider, give thought to, take into account, allow for, provide for, plan for, make provision for, accommodate, bargain for, reckon with; foresee, anticipate.

considering preposition *considering his size he was speedy:* **bearing in mind**, taking into consideration, taking into account, keeping in mind, in view of, in the light of.
adverb (informal) *he'd been lucky, considering:* **all things considered**, all in all, on the whole, at the end of the day, when all's said and done.

consign verb **1** *he was consigned to prison:* **send**, deliver, hand over, turn over, sentence; confine in, imprison in, incarcerate in, lock up in; informal put away, put behind bars; Brit. informal bang up. **2** *the picture was consigned for sale:* **assign**, allocate, place, put, remit, hand down. **3** *I consigned her picture to the bin:* **deposit**, commit, banish, relegate.

consignment noun *a consignment of goods:* **delivery**, shipment, load, boatload, truckload, cargo; batch; goods.

consist verb **1** *the exhibition consists of 180 drawings:* **be composed**, be made up, be formed; comprise, contain, include, incorporate. **2** *style consists in the choices that writers make:* **be inherent**, lie, reside, be present, be contained; be expressed by.

consistency noun **1** *the trend shows a degree of consistency:* **uniformity**, constancy, regularity, evenness, steadiness, stability, equilibrium; dependability, reliability. **2** *cream of pouring consistency:* **thickness**, density, viscosity, heaviness, texture; firmness, solidity.

consistent adjective **1** *there was consistent opinion-poll evidence that the ALP was likely to lose the next election:* **constant**, regular, uniform, steady, stable, even, unchanging, undeviating, unfluctuating; dependable, reliable, predictable. **2** *her injuries were consistent with a knife attack:* **compatible**, congruous, consonant, in tune, in line, reconcilable; corresponding to, conforming to.
– OPPOSITES irregular, incompatible.

consolation noun *I murmured some words of consolation:* **comfort**, solace, sympathy, compassion, pity, commiseration; relief, help, (moral) support, encouragement, reassurance.

C

console¹ verb *she tried to console him:* **comfort**, solace, condole with, sympathize with, commiserate with, show compassion for; help, support, cheer (up), hearten, encourage, reassure, soothe.
– OPPOSITES upset.

console² noun *a digital console:* **control panel**, instrument panel, dashboard, keyboard, keypad; informal dash.

consolidate verb **1** *we consolidated our position in the market:* **strengthen**, secure, stabilize, reinforce, fortify; enhance, improve. **2** *consolidate the results into an action plan:* **combine**, unite, merge, integrate, amalgamate, fuse, synthesize, bring together, unify.

consonance noun *a constitution in consonance with the customs of the people:* **agreement**, accord, harmony, unison; compatibility, congruity, congruence; formal concord.

consonant
■ **consonant with** *these findings are consonant with recent research:* in agreement with, consistent with, in accordance with, in harmony with, compatible with, congruous with, in tune with.

consort noun *the queen and her consort:* **partner**, companion, mate; spouse, husband, wife.
verb *he consorted with other women:* **associate**, keep company, mix, go around, spend time, socialize, fraternize, have dealings; informal run around, hang around/round, hang out, be thick; Brit. informal hang about.

conspicuous adjective *lots of birds have highly conspicuous plumage:* **easily seen**, clear, visible, noticeable, discernible, perceptible, detectable; obvious, manifest, evident, apparent, marked, pronounced, prominent, patent, crystal clear; striking, eye-catching, overt, blatant, writ large; distinct, recognizable, unmistakable, inescapable; informal as plain as the nose on one's face, standing out like a sore thumb, standing out a mile.

conspiracy noun **1** *a conspiracy to manipulate the race results:* **plot**, scheme, plan, machination, ploy, trick, ruse, subterfuge; informal racket. **2** *conspiracy to murder:* **plotting**, collusion, intrigue, connivance, machination, collaboration; treason.

conspirator noun *conspirators had planned to seize the state:* **plotter**, schemer, intriguer, colluder, collaborator, conniver, machinator.

conspire verb **1** *they admitted conspiring to steal cars:* **plot**, scheme, plan, intrigue, machinate, collude, connive, collaborate, work hand in glove; informal be in cahoots. **2** *circumstances conspired against them:* **act together**, work together, combine, unite, join forces; informal gang up.

constancy noun **1** *constancy between lovers:* **fidelity**, faithfulness, loyalty, commitment, dedication, devotion; dependability, reliability, trustworthiness. **2** *the constancy of Henry's views:* **steadfastness**, resolution, resolve, firmness, fixedness; determination, perseverance, tenacity, doggedness, staunchness, staying power, obstinacy. **3** *a constancy of human motive:* **consistency**, permanence, persistence, durability, endurance; uniformity, immutability, regularity, stability, steadiness.

constant adjective **1** *the constant background noise:* **continual**, continuous, persistent, sustained, round-the-clock; ceaseless, unceasing, perpetual, incessant, never-ending, eternal, endless, unabating, non-stop, unrelieved; interminable, unremitting, relentless. **2** *the disc revolves at a constant speed:* **consistent**, regular, steady, uniform, even, invariable, unvarying, unchanging, undeviating, unfluctuating. **3** *a constant friend:* **faithful**, loyal, devoted, true, fast, firm, unswerving; steadfast, staunch, dependable, trustworthy, trusty, reliable, dedicated, committed. **4** *there is a need for constant vigilance:* **steadfast**, steady, resolute, determined, tenacious, dogged, unwavering, unflagging.
– OPPOSITES fitful, variable, fickle.
noun *dread of cancer has been a constant:* **unchanging factor**, given.

constantly adverb *the English language is constantly in flux:* **always**, all the time, continually, continuously, persistently; round-the-clock, night and day, {morning, noon, and night}; endlessly, non-stop, incessantly, unceasingly, perpetually, eternally, forever; interminably, unremittingly, relentlessly; Scottish aye; informal 24-7.
– OPPOSITES occasionally.

consternation noun *much to the consternation of his detractors, he emerged as a management guru:* **dismay**, perturbation, distress, disquiet, discomposure; surprise, amazement, astonishment; alarm, panic, fear, fright, shock.
– OPPOSITES satisfaction.

constituent adjective *constituent parts:* **component**, integral; elemental, basic, essential, inherent.
noun **1** *MPs must listen to their constituents:* **voter**, elector, member of a constituency. **2** *the constituents of tobacco:* **component**, ingredient, element; part, piece, bit, unit; section, portion.

constitute verb **1** *farmers constituted 10 per cent of the population:* **amount to**, add up to, account for, form, make up, compose, comprise. **2** *this constitutes a breach of copyright:* **be equivalent to**, be, embody, be tantamount to, be regarded as. **3** *the courts were constituted in 1875:* **inaugurate**, establish, initiate, found, create, set up, start, form, organize, develop; commission, charter, invest, appoint, install, empower.

constitution noun **1** *the constitution guarantees our rights:* **charter**, social code, law; bill of rights; rules, regulations, fundamental principles. **2** *the chemical constitution of the dye:* **composition**, make-up, structure, construction, arrangement, configuration, formation, anatomy; informal set-up. **3** *she has the constitution of an ox:* **health**, physique, physical condition, shape, fettle.

constitutional adjective **1** *constitutional powers:* **legal**, lawful, legitimate, authorized, permitted; sanctioned, ratified, warranted, constituted, statutory, chartered, vested, official; by law. **2** *a constitutional weakness:* **inherent**, intrinsic, innate, fundamental, essential, organic; congenital, inborn, inbred.

constrain verb **1** *he felt constrained to explain:* **compel**, force, drive, impel, oblige, coerce, prevail on, require; press, push, pressure, pressurize. **2** *prices were constrained by state controls:* **restrict**, limit, curb, check, restrain, contain, rein in, hold back, keep down.

constrained adjective *his constrained manner:* **unnatural**, awkward, self-conscious, forced, stilted, strained; restrained, reserved, reticent, guarded. – OPPOSITES relaxed.

constraint noun **1** *financial constraints:* **restriction**, limitation, curb, check, restraint, control, damper, rein; hindrance, impediment, obstruction, handicap. **2** *they were able to talk without constraint:* **inhibition**, uneasiness, embarrassment; restraint, reticence, guardedness, formality; self-consciousness, forcedness, awkwardness.

constrict verb **1** *fat constricts the blood vessels:* **narrow**, make narrower, tighten, compress, contract, squeeze, strangle, strangulate. **2** *fear of crime constricts many people's lives:* **restrict**, impede, limit, inhibit, obstruct, interfere with, hinder, hamper. – OPPOSITES expand, dilate.

constriction noun *there was a constriction in her throat:* **tightness**, pressure, compression, contraction; obstruction, blockage, impediment.

construct verb **1** *a new motorway was being constructed:* **build**, erect, put up, set up, raise, establish, assemble, manufacture, fabricate, create, make. **2** *he constructed a faultless argument:* **formulate**, form, put together, create, devise, design, compose, work out; fashion, mould, shape, frame. – OPPOSITES demolish.

construction noun **1** *the construction of a new airport:* **building**, erection, putting up, setting up, establishment; assembly, manufacture, fabrication, creation. **2** *the station was a spectacular construction:* **structure**, building, edifice, pile. **3** *you*

could put an honest construction on their conduct: **interpretation**, reading, meaning, explanation, explication, construal; informal take.

constructive adjective *he described the talks as fruitful and constructive:* **useful**, helpful, productive, positive, encouraging; practical, valuable, profitable, worthwhile.

construe verb *his actions could be construed as an admission of guilt:* **interpret**, understand, read, see, take, take to mean, regard.

consul noun **ambassador**, diplomat, chargé d'affaires, attaché, envoy, emissary, plenipotentiary.

consult verb **1** *you need to consult a solicitor:* **seek advice from**, ask, take counsel from, call on/upon, speak to, turn to, have recourse to; informal pick someone's brains. **2** *the government must consult with interested parties:* **confer**, have discussions, talk things over, exchange views, communicate, parley, deliberate; informal put their heads together. **3** *she consulted her diary:* **refer to**, turn to, look at.

consultant noun **1** *an engineering consultant:* **adviser**, expert, specialist, authority, pundit. **2** *a consultant at Guy's hospital:* **senior doctor**, specialist.

consultation noun **1** *the need for further consultation with industry:* **discussion**, dialogue, discourse, debate, negotiation, deliberation. **2** *a 30-minute consultation:* **meeting**, talk, discussion, interview, audience, hearing; appointment, session; formal confabulation, colloquy.

consume verb **1** *vast amounts of food and drink were consumed:* **eat**, devour, ingest, swallow, gobble up, wolf down, guzzle, feast on, snack on; **drink**, gulp down, imbibe, sup; informal tuck into, put away, polish off, dispose of, pig oneself on, down, neck, sink, swill; Brit. informal scoff, gollop, shift; N. Amer. informal scarf (down/up), snarf (down/up). **2** *natural resources are being consumed at an alarming rate:* **use (up)**, utilize, expend; deplete, exhaust; waste, squander, drain, dissipate, fritter away. **3** *the fire consumed fifty houses:* **destroy**, demolish, lay waste, wipe out, annihilate, devastate, gut, ruin, wreck. **4** *Carolyn was consumed with guilt:* **eat up**, devour, obsess, grip, overwhelm; absorb, preoccupy.

consumer noun *at the moment the consumer is not prepared to pay higher prices for organically farmed food:* **purchaser**, buyer, customer, shopper; user, end-user; client; (**consumers** or **the consumer**) the public, the market.

consuming adjective *his lifetime's consuming interest:* **absorbing**, compelling, compulsive, besetting, obsessive, overwhelming; intense, ardent, strong, powerful, burning, raging, fervid, profound, deep-seated.

C

consummate verb *the deal was finally consummated:* **complete**, conclude, finish, accomplish, achieve; execute, carry out, perform; informal sew up, wrap up.
adjective *his consummate skill | a consummate politician:* **supreme**, superb, superlative, superior, accomplished, expert, proficient, skilful, skilled, masterly, master, first-class, talented, gifted, polished, practised, perfect, ultimate; complete, total, utter, absolute, pure.

consumption noun **1** *food unfit for human consumption:* **eating**, drinking, ingestion. **2** *the consumption of fossil fuels:* **use**, using up, utilization, expending, depletion; waste, squandering, dissipation.

contact noun **1** *a disease transmitted through direct contact with rats:* **touch**, touching; proximity, exposure. **2** *foreign diplomats were asked to avoid all contact with him:* **communication**, correspondence, touch; association, connection, intercourse, relations, dealings. **3** *he had many contacts in Germany:* **connection**, acquaintance, associate, friend.
verb *anyone with information should contact the police:* **get in touch with**, communicate with, make contact with, approach, notify; telephone, phone, call, ring up, speak to, talk to, write to; informal get hold of.

contagious adjective *a contagious disease:* **infectious**, communicable, transmittable, transmissible, spreadable; informal catching.

contain verb **1** *the archive contains much unpublished material:* **include**, comprise, take in, incorporate, involve, encompass, embrace; consist of, be made up of, be composed of. **2** *the boat contained four people:* **hold**, carry, accommodate, seat. **3** *he must contain his anger:* **restrain**, curb, rein in, suppress, repress, stifle, subdue, quell, swallow, bottle up, hold in, keep in check; control, master.

container noun **receptacle**, vessel, holder, repository.

contaminate verb *the site was found to be contaminated by radioactivity:* **pollute**, adulterate; defile, debase, corrupt, taint, infect, foul, spoil, soil, stain, sully; poison.
– OPPOSITES purify.

contemplate verb **1** *she contemplated her image in the mirror:* **look at**, view, regard, examine, inspect, observe, survey, study, scrutinize, scan, stare at, gaze at, eye. **2** *he contemplated his fate:* **think about**, ponder, reflect on, consider, mull over, muse on, dwell on, deliberate over, meditate on, ruminate on, chew over, brood on/about, turn over in one's mind. **3** *he was contemplating action for damages:* **consider**, think about, have in mind, intend, plan, propose; envisage, foresee.

contemplation noun **1** *the contemplation of beautiful objects:* **viewing**, examination, inspection, observation, survey, study,

scrutiny. **2** *the monks sat in quiet contemplation:* **thought**, reflection, meditation, consideration, rumination, deliberation, reverie, introspection, brown study.

contemplative adjective *a peaceful, contemplative mood:* **thoughtful**, pensive, reflective, meditative, musing, ruminative, introspective, brooding, deep/lost in thought, in a brown study.

contemporary adjective **1** *the event was recorded by a contemporary historian:* **of the time**, of the day, contemporaneous, concurrent, coeval, coexisting, coexistent. **2** *contemporary society:* **modern**, present-day, present, current, present-time. **3** *a very contemporary design:* **modern**, up to date, up to the minute, fashionable; modish, latest, recent; informal trendy, with it.
– OPPOSITES old-fashioned, out of date.
noun *Chaucer's contemporaries:* **peer**, fellow; formal compeer.

contempt noun **1** *she regarded him with contempt:* **scorn**, disdain, disrespect, scornfulness, contemptuousness, derision; disgust, loathing, hatred, abhorrence. **2** *he is guilty of contempt of court:* **disrespect**, disregard, slighting.
– OPPOSITES respect.

contemptible adjective *a display of contemptible cowardice:* **despicable**, detestable, hateful, reprehensible, deplorable, unspeakable, disgraceful, shameful, ignominious, abject, low, mean, cowardly, unworthy, discreditable, petty, worthless, shabby, cheap, beyond contempt, beyond the pale.
– OPPOSITES admirable.

contemptuous adjective *he spoke in a coldly contemptuous tone:* **scornful**, disdainful, disrespectful, insulting, insolent, derisive, mocking, sneering, scoffing, withering, scathing, snide; condescending, supercilious, haughty, proud, superior, arrogant, dismissive, aloof; informal high and mighty, snotty, sniffy.
– OPPOSITES respectful.

contend verb **1** *the pilot had to contend with torrential rain:* **cope with**, face, grapple with, deal with, take on, pit oneself against. **2** *three main groups were contending for power:* **compete**, vie, contest, fight, battle, tussle, go head to head; strive, struggle. **3** *he contends that the judge was wrong:* **assert**, maintain, hold, claim, argue, insist, state, declare, profess, affirm; allege.

content[1] adjective *she seemed content with life:* **contented**, satisfied, pleased, gratified, fulfilled, happy, cheerful, glad; unworried, untroubled, at ease, at peace, tranquil, serene.
– OPPOSITES discontented, dissatisfied.
verb *her reply seemed to content him:* **satisfy**, please; soothe, pacify, placate, appease, mollify.
noun *a time of content.* See **CONTENTMENT**.

content[2] noun **1** *foods with a high fibre content:* **amount**, proportion, quantity. **2** (**contents**) *the contents of a vegetarian sausage:* **constituents**, ingredients, components, elements. **3** (**contents**) *the book's list of contents:* **chapters**, sections, divisions. **4** *the content of the essay:* **subject matter**, subject, theme, argument, thesis, message, thrust, substance, matter, material, text, ideas.

contented adjective *a contented man.* See **CONTENT**[1] adjective.

contention noun **1** *a point of contention:* **disagreement**, dispute, disputation, argument, discord, conflict, friction, strife, dissension, disharmony. **2** *the Marxist contention that capitalism equals exploitation:* **argument**, claim, plea, submission, allegation, assertion, declaration; opinion, stand, position, view, belief, thesis, case.
– OPPOSITES agreement.
■ **in contention** in competition, competing, contesting, contending, vying; striving, struggling.

contentious adjective **1** *a contentious issue:* **controversial**, disputable, debatable, disputed, open to debate, moot, vexed. **2** *a contentious debate:* **heated**, vehement, fierce, violent, intense, impassioned. **3** *contentious people.* See **QUARRELSOME**.

contentment noun *he found contentment in living a basic life:* **contentedness**, content, satisfaction, gratification, fulfilment, happiness, pleasure, cheerfulness; ease, comfort, well-being, peace, equanimity, serenity, tranquillity.

contest noun **1** *a boxing contest:* **competition**, match, tournament, game, meet, event, trial, bout, heat, fixture, tie, race. **2** *the contest for the party leadership:* **fight**, battle, tussle, struggle, competition, race.
verb **1** *he intended to contest the seat:* **compete for**, contend for, vie for, fight for, try to win, go for, throw one's hat in the ring. **2** *we contested the decision:* **oppose**, object to, challenge, take a stand against, take issue with, question, call into question. **3** *the issues have been hotly contested:* **debate**, argue about, dispute, quarrel over.

contestant noun **competitor**, participant, player, contender, candidate, aspirant, entrant; rival, opponent, adversary, antagonist.

context noun **1** *the wider historical context:* **circumstances**, conditions, factors, state of affairs, situation, background, scene, setting. **2** *a quote taken out of context:* **frame of reference**, contextual relationship; text, subject, theme, topic.

contiguous adjective *the contiguous states of New Mexico, Arizona, Texas, and California:* **adjacent**, neighbouring, adjoining, bordering, next-door; abutting,

connecting, touching, in contact, proximate.

contingency noun *a detailed contract which attempts to provide for all possible contingencies:* **eventuality**, (chance) event, incident, happening, occurrence, juncture, possibility, fortuity, accident, chance, emergency.

contingent adjective **1** *the merger is contingent on government approval:* **dependent on**, conditional on, subject to, determined by, hinging on, resting on. **2** *contingent events:* **chance**, accidental, fortuitous, possible, unforeseeable, unpredictable, random, haphazard.
noun **1** *a contingent of Japanese businessmen:* **group**, party, body, band, company, cohort, deputation, delegation; *informal* bunch, gang. **2** *a contingent of marines:* **detachment**, unit, group.

continual adjective **1** *a service disrupted by continual breakdowns:* **frequent**, repeated, constant, recurrent, recurring, regular. **2** *she was in continual pain:* **constant**, continuous, unending, never-ending, unremitting, unabating, relentless, unrelenting, unrelieved, chronic, uninterrupted, unbroken, round-the-clock.
– OPPOSITES occasional, temporary.

continuation noun *the continuation of discussions:* **carrying on**, continuance, extension, prolongation, protraction, perpetuation.
– OPPOSITES end.

continue verb **1** *he was unable to continue with his job:* **carry on**, proceed, pursue, go on, keep on, persist, press on, persevere, keep at; *informal* stick at, soldier on. **2** *discussions continued throughout the year:* **go on**, carry on, last, extend, be prolonged, run on, drag on. **3** *we are keen to continue this relationship:* **maintain**, keep up, sustain, keep going, keep alive, preserve. **4** *his willingness to continue in office:* **remain**, stay, carry on, keep going. **5** *we continued our conversation after supper:* **resume**, pick up, take up, carry on with, return to, recommence.
– OPPOSITES stop, break off.

continuing adjective *a background of continuing civil war:* **ongoing**, continuous, sustained, persistent, steady, relentless, uninterrupted, unabating, unremitting, unrelieved, unceasing.
– OPPOSITES sporadic.

continuity noun *a breakdown in the continuity of care:* **continuousness**, uninterruptedness, flow, progression.

continuous adjective *for the past few days there had been continuous rain:* **continual**, uninterrupted, unbroken, constant, ceaseless, incessant, steady, sustained, solid, continuing, ongoing, unceasing, without a break, non-stop, round-the-clock, persistent, unremitting, relentless, unrelenting, unabating, unrelieved, without respite, endless, unending, never-

C

ending, perpetual, everlasting, eternal,
interminable; consecutive, running; N. Amer.
without surcease.
– OPPOSITES intermittent.

contort verb *chunks of contorted metal:*
twist, bend out of shape, distort, misshape,
warp, buckle, deform.

contour noun *the perfect contours of her
body:* **outline**, shape, form; lines, curves,
figure; silhouette, profile.

contraband adjective *contraband goods:*
smuggled, black-market, bootleg, under the
counter, illegal, illicit, unlawful; prohibited,
banned, proscribed, forbidden; informal hot.

contract noun *a legally binding contract:*
agreement, commitment, arrangement,
settlement, understanding, compact,
covenant, bond; deal, bargain.
verb **1** *the market for such goods began to
contract:* **shrink**, get smaller, decrease,
diminish, reduce, dwindle, decline. **2** *her
stomach muscles contracted:* **tighten**,
tense, flex, constrict, draw in, narrow.
3 *she contracted her brow:* **wrinkle**, knit,
crease, purse, pucker. **4** *his name was soon
contracted to 'Jack':* **shorten**, abbreviate,
cut, reduce; elide. **5** *the company contracted
to rebuild the stadium:* **undertake**, pledge,
promise, covenant, commit oneself, engage,
agree, enter an agreement, make a deal.
6 *she contracted German measles:* **develop**,
catch, get, pick up, come down with, be
struck down by, be stricken with, succumb
to; Brit. go down with. **7** *he contracted a debt
of £3,300:* **incur**, run up.
– OPPOSITES expand, relax, lengthen.
■ **contract something out** subcontract,
outsource, farm out.

contraction noun **1** *the contraction of the
industry:* **shrinking**, shrinkage, decline,
decrease, diminution, dwindling. **2** *the
contraction of muscles:* **tightening**, tensing,
flexing. **3** *my contractions started at
midnight:* **labour pains**, labour; cramps.
4 *'goodbye' is a contraction of 'God be with
you':* **abbreviation**, short form, shortened
form, elision, diminutive.

contradict verb **1** *he contradicted the
government's account of the affair:* **deny**,
refute, rebut, dispute, challenge, counter,
controvert; formal gainsay. **2** *nobody dared to
contradict him:* **argue against**, go against,
challenge, oppose. **3** *this research contradicts
previous computer models:* **conflict with**,
be at odds with, be at variance with, be
inconsistent with, run counter to, disagree
with.
– OPPOSITES confirm, agree with.

contradiction noun **1** *the contradiction
between his faith and his lifestyle:*
conflict, clash, disagreement, opposition,
inconsistency, mismatch, variance. **2** *the
second sentence appears to be a flat
contradiction of the first:* **denial**, refutation,
rebuttal, countering, counterstatement.
– OPPOSITES confirmation, agreement.

contradictory adjective *the two attitudes
are contradictory:* **opposed**, in opposition,
opposite, antithetical, contrary, contrasting,
conflicting, at variance, at odds, opposing,
clashing, divergent, discrepant, different;
inconsistent, incompatible, irreconcilable.

contraption noun *a newfangled contraption
for making coffee:* **device**, gadget, apparatus,
machine, appliance, mechanism, invention,
contrivance; informal gizmo, widget; Brit. informal
gubbins; Austral. informal bitzer.

contrary adjective **1** *contrary views:*
opposite, opposing, opposed, contradictory,
clashing, conflicting, antithetical,
incompatible, irreconcilable. **2** *she was sulky
and contrary:* **perverse**, awkward, difficult,
uncooperative, unhelpful, obstructive,
disobliging, recalcitrant, wilful, self-willed,
stubborn, obstinate, mulish, pig-headed,
intractable; informal cussed; Brit. informal bloody-
minded, bolshie, stroppy; N. Amer. informal
balky.
– OPPOSITES compatible, accommodating.
noun *in fact, the contrary is true:* **opposite**,
reverse, converse, antithesis.
■ **contrary to** in conflict with, against, at
variance with, at odds with, in opposition
to, counter to, incompatible with.

contrast noun **1** *the contrast between
rural and urban trends:* **difference**,
dissimilarity, disparity, distinction,
contradistinction, divergence, variance,
variation, differentiation; contradiction,
incongruity, opposition, polarity. **2** *Jane
was a complete contrast to Sarah:* **opposite**,
antithesis; foil, complement.
– OPPOSITES similarity.
verb **1** *a view which contrasts with his earlier
opinion:* **differ from**, be at variance with,
be contrary to, conflict with, go against, be
at odds with, be in opposition to, disagree
with, clash with. **2** *people contrasted her
with her sister:* **compare**, set side by side,
juxtapose; measure against; distinguish
from, differentiate from.
– OPPOSITES resemble, liken.

contravene verb **1** *he contravened the
Official Secrets Act:* **break**, breach, violate,
infringe; defy, disobey, flout. **2** *the
prosecution contravened the rights of the
individual:* **conflict with**, be in conflict with,
be at odds with, be at variance with, run
counter to.
– OPPOSITES comply with.

contravention noun *a contravention of EC
regulations:* **breach**, violation, infringement,
neglect, dereliction.

contretemps noun *her little contretemps
with Terry:* **argument**, quarrel, squabble,
disagreement, difference of opinion,
dispute; informal tiff, set-to, run-in, spat; Brit.
informal row, barney; Scottish informal rammy.

contribute verb **1** *the government
contributed a million pounds:* **give**, donate,
put up, subscribe, hand out, grant, bestow,
present, provide, supply, furnish; informal

chip in, pitch in, fork out, shell out, cough up; Brit. informal stump up; N. Amer. informal kick in, ante up, pony up. **2** *an article contributed by Dr Clouson:* **supply**, provide, submit. **3** *numerous factors contribute to job satisfaction:* **play a part in**, be instrumental in, be a factor in, have a hand in, be conducive to, make for, lead to, cause.

contribution noun **1** *voluntary financial contributions:* **donation**, gift, offering, present, handout, grant, subsidy, allowance, endowment, subscription. **2** *contributions from local authors:* **article**, piece, story, item, chapter, paper, essay.

contributor noun **1** *the magazine's regular contributors:* **writer**, columnist, correspondent. **2** *campaign contributors:* **donor**, benefactor, subscriber, supporter, backer, subsidizer, patron, sponsor.

contrite adjective *he looked so contrite that she relented:* **remorseful**, repentant, penitent, regretful, sorry, apologetic, rueful, sheepish, hangdog, ashamed, chastened, shamefaced, conscience-stricken, guilt-ridden, in sackcloth and ashes.

contrition noun **remorse**, remorsefulness, repentance, penitence, sorrow, sorrowfulness, regret, ruefulness, pangs of conscience; shame, guilt, compunction.

contrivance noun **1** *a mechanical contrivance:* **device**, gadget, machine, appliance, contraption, apparatus, mechanism, implement, tool, invention; informal gizmo, widget, Austral. informal bitzer. **2** *her matchmaking contrivances:* **scheme**, stratagem, tactic, manoeuvre, move, plan, ploy, gambit, wile, trick, ruse, plot, machination.

contrive verb *his opponents contrived a cabinet crisis:* **bring about**, engineer, manufacture, orchestrate, stage-manage, create, devise, concoct, construct, plan, fabricate, plot, hatch; informal wangle, set up.

contrived adjective *David replied with contrived joviality:* **forced**, strained, studied, artificial, affected, put-on, pretended, false, feigned, manufactured, unnatural; laboured, overdone, elaborate.
– OPPOSITES natural.

control noun **1** *China retained control over the region:* **jurisdiction**, sway, power, authority, command, dominance, government, mastery, leadership, rule, sovereignty, supremacy, ascendancy; charge, management, direction, supervision, superintendence. **2** *strict import controls:* **restraint**, constraint, limitation, restriction, check, curb, brake, rein; regulation. **3** *her control deserted her:* **self-control**, self-restraint, self-possession, composure, calmness; informal cool. **4** *easy-to-use controls:* **switch**, knob, button, dial, handle, lever, pedal. **5** *mission control:* **headquarters**, HQ, base, centre of operations, command post.
verb **1** *one family had controlled the company since its formation:* **be in charge of**, run, manage, direct, administer, head, preside over, supervise, superintend, steer; command, rule, govern, lead, dominate, hold sway over, be at the helm; informal head up, be in the driving seat, run the show. **2** *she struggled to control her temper:* **restrain**, keep in check, curb, check, contain, hold back, bridle, rein in, suppress, repress, master. **3** *public spending was controlled:* **limit**, restrict, curb, cap, constrain; informal put the brakes on.

controversial adjective *controversial issues such as abortion and hanging:* **contentious**, disputed, at issue, moot, disputable, debatable, arguable, vexed, tendentious.

controversy noun *he refused to be drawn into the political controversy:* **disagreement**, dispute, argument, debate, dissension, contention, disputation, altercation, wrangle, wrangling, quarrel, quarrelling, war of words, storm; cause célèbre; Brit. informal row.

contusion noun **bruise**, discoloration, black-and-blue mark, injury.

conundrum noun **1** *the conundrums facing policy-makers in the 1980s:* **problem**, difficult question, vexed question, difficulty, quandary, dilemma; informal poser, facer. **2** *Roderick enjoyed conundrums and crosswords:* **riddle**, puzzle, wordgame; informal brain-teaser.

convalesce verb *he went abroad to convalesce:* **recuperate**, get better, recover, get well, get back on one's feet.

convalescence noun **recuperation**, recovery, return to health, rehabilitation, improvement.

convalescent adjective *you're still convalescent and you need to rest:* **recuperating**, recovering, getting better, on the road to recovery, improving; informal on the mend.

convene verb **1** *he convened a secret meeting:* **summon**, call, call together, order. **2** *the committee convened for its final session:* **assemble**, gather, meet, come together, congregate.

convenience noun **1** *the convenience of the arrangement:* **expedience**, advantageousness, advantage, opportuneness, propitiousness, timeliness; suitability, appropriateness. **2** *for convenience, the handset is wall-mounted:* **ease of use**, usability, usefulness, utility, serviceability, practicality. **3** *the kitchen has all the modern conveniences:* **appliance**, (labour-saving) device, gadget; amenity, facility; informal gizmo, mod con.

convenient adjective **1** *try to agree on a mutually convenient time:* **suitable**, appropriate, fitting, fit, suited, opportune, timely, well timed, favourable, advantageous, seasonable, expedient. **2** *a hotel that's convenient for the beach:* **near**

(to), close to, within easy reach of, well situated for, handy for, not far from, just round the corner from; informal a stone's throw from, within spitting distance of.

convent noun **nunnery**, priory, abbey, religious community.

convention noun **1** *a social convention:* **custom**, usage, practice, tradition, way, habit, norm; rule, code, canon, punctilio; propriety, etiquette, protocol; formal praxis; (**conventions**) mores. **2** *a convention signed by 74 countries:* **agreement**, accord, protocol, compact, pact, treaty, concordat, entente; contract, bargain, deal. **3** *the party's biennial convention:* **conference**, meeting, congress, assembly, gathering, summit, convocation, synod, conclave.

conventional adjective **1** *the conventional wisdom of the day:* **orthodox**, traditional, established, accepted, received, mainstream, prevailing, prevalent, accustomed, customary. **2** *a cross between a monorail and a conventional railway:* **normal**, standard, regular, ordinary, usual, traditional, typical, common. **3** *Karen was a very conventional woman:* **conservative**, traditional, traditionalist, conformist, bourgeois, old-fashioned, of the old school, small-town, suburban; informal straight, square, stick-in-the-mud, fuddy-duddy. **4** *an unexciting and rather conventional compilation:* **unoriginal**, formulaic, predictable, stock, unadventurous, unremarkable.
– OPPOSITES unorthodox, original.

converge verb **1** *Oxford Circus, a station where three lines converge:* **meet**, intersect, cross, connect, link up, coincide, join, unite, merge. **2** *90,000 fans converged on Wembley:* **close in on**, bear down on, approach, move towards.
– OPPOSITES diverge, leave.

conversant adjective *he was fully conversant with the principles of word processing:* **familiar**, acquainted, au fait, au courant, at home, well versed, well informed, knowledgeable, informed, abreast, up to date; informal up to speed, clued up, genned up.

conversation noun *he must have overheard her conversation with Victoria:* **discussion**, talk, chat, gossip, tête-à-tête, heart-to-heart, head-to-head, exchange, dialogue; informal confab, jaw, chit-chat; Brit. informal chinwag, natter; N. Amer. informal gabfest, schmooze; Austral./NZ informal yarn.

conversational adjective **1** *conversational English:* **informal**, chatty, relaxed, friendly; colloquial, idiomatic. **2** *a conversational man:* **talkative**, chatty, communicative, forthcoming, expansive, loquacious, garrulous.

converse[1] verb *they conversed in low voices:* **talk**, speak, chat, have a conversation, discourse, communicate; informal chew the fat/rag, jaw; Brit. informal natter; N. Amer. informal visit, shoot the breeze/bull; Austral./NZ informal mag.

converse[2] noun *the converse is also true:* **opposite**, reverse, obverse, contrary, antithesis, other side of the coin; informal flip side.

conversion noun **1** *the conversion of waste into energy:* **change**, changing, transformation, metamorphosis, transfiguration, transmutation, sea change; humorous transmogrification. **2** *the conversion of the building:* **adaptation**, alteration, modification, reconstruction, rebuilding, redevelopment, redesign, renovation, rehabilitation. **3** *his religious conversion:* **rebirth**, regeneration, reformation.

convert verb **1** *plants convert the sun's energy into chemical energy:* **change**, turn, transform, metamorphose, transfigure, transmute; humorous transmogrify. **2** *the factory was converted into flats:* **adapt**, turn, change, alter, modify, rebuild, reconstruct, redevelop, refashion, redesign, restyle, revamp, renovate, rehabilitate; N. Amer. bring up to code; informal do up; N. Amer. informal rehab. **3** *they sought to convert sinners:* **proselytize**, evangelize, bring to God, redeem, save, reform, re-educate, cause to see the light. noun *Christian converts:* **proselyte**, neophyte, new believer; Christianity catechumen.

convey verb **1** *taxis conveyed guests to the station:* **transport**, carry, bring, take, fetch, bear, move, ferry, shuttle, shift, transfer. **2** *he conveyed the information to me:* **communicate**, pass on, make known, impart, relay, transmit, send, hand on, relate, tell, reveal, disclose. **3** *it's impossible to convey how I felt:* **express**, communicate, get across/over, put across/over, indicate, say. **4** *he conveys an air of competence:* **project**, exude, emit, emanate.

conveyance noun *the conveyance of agricultural produce:* **transportation**, transport, carriage, carrying, transfer, movement, delivery; haulage, portage, cartage, shipment, freightage.

convict verb *he was convicted of indecent assault:* **find guilty**, sentence; Brit. informal be done for.
– OPPOSITES acquit.
noun *two escaped convicts:* **prisoner**, inmate; trusty; criminal, offender, lawbreaker, felon; informal jailbird, con, (old) lag, crook; N. Amer. informal yardbird.

conviction noun **1** *his conviction for murder:* **declaration of guilt**, sentence, judgement. **2** *his political convictions:* **belief**, opinion, view, thought, persuasion, idea, position, stance, article of faith. **3** *she spoke with conviction:* **certainty**, certitude, assurance, confidence, sureness, no shadow of a doubt.
– OPPOSITES acquittal, uncertainty.

convince verb **1** *he convinced me that I was wrong:* **make certain**, persuade, satisfy, prove to; assure, put/set someone's mind at rest. **2** *I convinced her to marry me:* **persuade**, induce, prevail on, get, talk into, win over, cajole, inveigle.

convincing adjective **1** *a convincing argument:* **cogent**, persuasive, plausible, powerful, potent, strong, forceful, compelling, irresistible, telling, conclusive. **2** *a convincing 5–0 win:* **resounding**, emphatic, decisive, conclusive.

convivial adjective *he was always a convivial host:* **friendly**, genial, affable, amiable, congenial, agreeable, good-humoured, cordial, warm, sociable, outgoing, gregarious, clubbable, companionable, hail-fellow-well-met, cheerful, jolly, jovial, lively; enjoyable, festive; Scottish couthy.

conviviality noun **friendliness**, geniality, affability, amiability, bonhomie, congeniality, cordiality, warmth, good nature, sociability, gregariousness, cheerfulness, good cheer, joviality, jollity, gaiety, liveliness.

convocation noun **assembly**, gathering, meeting, conference, convention, congress, council, symposium, colloquium, conclave, synod.

convoluted adjective *an extraordinarily convoluted narrative:* **complicated**, complex, involved, elaborate, serpentine, labyrinthine, tortuous, tangled, Byzantine; confused, confusing, bewildering, baffling. – OPPOSITES straightforward.

convolution noun **1** *crosses adorned with elaborate convolutions:* **twist**, turn, coil, spiral, twirl, curl, helix, whorl, loop, curlicue. **2** *the convolutions of the plot:* **complexity**, intricacy, complication, twist, turn, entanglement.

convoy noun *a convoy of vehicles:* **group**, fleet, cavalcade, motorcade, cortège, caravan, line, train.
verb *the ship was convoyed by army gunboats:* **escort**, accompany, attend, flank; protect, defend, guard.

convulse verb *his whole body convulsed:* **shake uncontrollably**, go into spasms, shudder, jerk, thrash about.

convulsion noun **1** *she had convulsions:* **fit**, seizure, paroxysm, spasm, attack; throes. **2** (**convulsions**) *the audience collapsed in convulsions:* **fits of laughter**, paroxysms of laughter, uncontrollable laughter; informal hysterics. **3** *the political convulsions of the period:* **upheaval**, eruption, cataclysm, turmoil, turbulence, tumult, disruption, agitation, disturbance, unrest, disorder.

convulsive adjective *convulsive movements:* **spasmodic**, jerky, paroxysmal, violent, uncontrollable.

cook verb **1** *Iris had cooked dinner:* **prepare**, make, put together; informal fix, rustle up; Brit. informal knock up. **2** (informal) *he'd been cooking the books:* **falsify**, alter, doctor, tamper with, interfere with, massage, manipulate; Brit. informal fiddle.

cooking noun *authentic Italian cooking:* **cuisine**, cookery, baking; food.

cool adjective **1** *a cool breeze:* **chilly**, chill, cold, bracing, brisk, crisp, fresh, refreshing, invigorating; draughty; informal nippy; Brit. informal parky. **2** *a cool response:* **unenthusiastic**, lukewarm, tepid, indifferent, uninterested, apathetic, half-hearted; unfriendly, distant, remote, aloof, cold, chilly, frosty, unwelcoming, unresponsive, offhand, uncommunicative, undemonstrative; informal stand-offish. **3** *his ability to keep cool in a crisis:* **calm**, {cool, calm, and collected}, composed, as cool as a cucumber, collected, cool-headed, level-headed, self-possessed, controlled, self-controlled, poised, serene, tranquil, unruffled, unperturbed, unmoved, untroubled, imperturbable, placid, phlegmatic; informal unflappable, together, laid-back. **4** *a cool lack of morality:* **bold**, audacious, nerveless; brazen, shameless, unabashed. **5** (informal) *she thinks she's so cool:* **fashionable**, stylish, chic, up to the minute, sophisticated; informal trendy, funky, with it, hip, big, happening, groovy; N. Amer. informal kicky, tony, fly. **6** (informal) *a cool song.* See EXCELLENT.
– OPPOSITES warm, enthusiastic, agitated.
noun **1** *the cool of the evening:* **chill**, chilliness, coldness, coolness. **2** *Ken lost his cool:* **self-control**, control, composure, self-possession, calmness, equilibrium, calm; aplomb, poise, sangfroid, presence of mind.
– OPPOSITES warmth.
verb **1** *cool the sauce in the fridge:* **chill**, refrigerate. **2** *her reluctance did nothing to cool his interest:* **lessen**, moderate, diminish, reduce, dampen. **3** *Simpson's ardour had cooled:* **subside**, lessen, diminish, decrease, abate, moderate, die down, fade, dwindle, wane. **4** *after a while, she cooled off:* **calm down**, recover/regain one's composure, compose oneself, control oneself, pull oneself together, simmer down.
– OPPOSITES heat, inflame, intensify.

coop noun *a hen coop:* **pen**, run, cage, hutch, enclosure.
verb *he hates being cooped up at home:* **confine**, shut in/up, cage (in), pen up/in, keep, detain, trap, incarcerate, immure.

cooperate verb **1** *police and social services cooperated in the operation:* **collaborate**, work together, work side by side, pull together, band together, join forces, team up, unite, combine, pool resources, make common cause, liaise. **2** *he was happy to cooperate:* **be of assistance**, assist, help, lend a hand, be of service, do one's bit; informal play ball.

cooperation noun **1** *cooperation between management and workers:* **collaboration**, joint action, combined effort, teamwork, partnership, coordination, liaison, association, synergy, give and take, compromise. **2** *thank you for your*

C

cooperation: **assistance**, helpfulness, help, helping hand, aid.

cooperative adjective **1** *a cooperative effort:* **collaborative**, collective, combined, common, joint, shared, mutual, united, concerted, coordinated. **2** *pleasant and cooperative staff:* **helpful**, eager to help, glad to be of assistance, obliging, accommodating, willing, amenable, adaptable.

coordinate verb **1** *exhibitions coordinated by a team of international scholars:* **organize**, arrange, order, systematize, harmonize, correlate, synchronize, bring together, fit together, dovetail. **2** *care workers coordinate at a local level:* **cooperate**, liaise, collaborate, work together, negotiate, communicate, be in contact. **3** *floral designs coordinate with the decor:* **match**, complement, set off; harmonize, blend, fit in, go.

cope verb **1** *she couldn't cope on her own:* **manage**, survive, subsist, look after oneself, fend for oneself, shift for oneself, carry on, get by/through, bear up, hold one's own, keep one's end up, keep one's head above water; informal make it, hack it. **2** *his inability to cope with the situation:* **deal with**, handle, manage, address, face (up to), confront, tackle, get to grips with, get through, weather, come to terms with.

copious adjective *she listened to me and took copious notes:* **abundant**, superabundant, plentiful, ample, profuse, full, extensive, generous, bumper, lavish, fulsome, liberal, overflowing, in abundance, many, numerous; informal a gogo, galore.
– OPPOSITES sparse.

copse noun **thicket**, grove, wood, coppice, stand, clump, brake; Brit. spinney; N. Amer. & Austral./NZ brush.

copulate verb. See **HAVE SEX** at **SEX**.

copulation noun. See **SEX** sense 1.

copy noun **1** *copies of the report had been sent to the tribunal:* **duplicate**, facsimile, photocopy, carbon (copy), mimeograph, mimeo; transcript; reprint; trademark Xerox, photostat. **2** *a copy of a sketch by Leonardo da Vinci:* **replica**, reproduction, replication, print, imitation, likeness; counterfeit, forgery, fake; informal knock-off.
verb **1** *each form had to be copied:* **duplicate**, photocopy, xerox, photostat, mimeograph, run off, reproduce. **2** *portraits copied from original paintings by Reynolds:* **reproduce**, replicate; forge, fake, counterfeit. **3** *their sound was copied by a lot of jazz players:* **imitate**, reproduce, emulate, follow, echo, mirror, parrot, mimic, ape; plagiarize, steal; informal rip off.

coquettish adjective *she gave Dan a coquettish glance from beneath her eyelashes:* **flirtatious**, flirty, provocative, seductive, inviting, kittenish, coy, arch, teasing, playful; informal come-hither, vampish.

cord noun **string**, thread, thong, lace, ribbon, strap, tape, tie, line, rope, cable, wire, ligature; twine, yarn, elastic, braid.

cordial adjective *a cordial welcome:* **friendly**, warm, genial, affable, amiable, pleasant, fond, affectionate, warm-hearted, good-natured, gracious, hospitable, welcoming, hearty.
noun *fruit cordial:* **squash**, crush, concentrate.

cordon noun *the crowds had broken through the police cordon:* **barrier**, line, row, chain, ring, circle; picket line.
verb *troops cordoned off the area:* **close off**, shut off, seal off, fence off, separate off, isolate, enclose, surround.

core noun **1** *the earth's core:* **centre**, interior, middle, nucleus; recesses, bowels, depths; informal innards. **2** *the core of the argument:* **heart**, heart of the matter, nucleus, nub, kernel, marrow, meat, essence, quintessence, crux, gist, pith, substance, basis, fundamentals; informal nitty-gritty, brass tacks, nuts and bolts.
adjective *the core issue:* **central**, key, basic, fundamental, principal, primary, main, chief, crucial, vital, essential; informal number-one.
– OPPOSITES peripheral.

cork noun **stopper**, stop, plug, bung, peg, spigot, spile; N. Amer. stopple.

corn noun **grain**, cereal (crop); maize, wheat, barley, oats, rye.

corner noun **1** *the cart lurched round the corner:* **bend**, curve, crook, dog-leg; turn, turning, junction, fork, intersection; Brit. hairpin bend. **2** *a charming corner of Italy:* **district**, region, area, section, quarter, part; informal neck of the woods. **3** *he found himself in a tight corner:* **predicament**, plight, tight spot, mess, muddle, difficulty, problem, dilemma, quandary; informal pickle, jam, stew, fix, hole, hot water, bind.
verb **1** *he was eventually cornered by police dogs:* **hem in**, run to earth, bring to bay, cut off, block off, trap, pen in, surround, enclose; capture, catch. **2** *crime syndicates have cornered the stolen car market:* **gain control of**, take over, control, dominate, monopolize; capture; informal sew up.

cornerstone noun *the theory of natural selection is a cornerstone of biological thought:* **foundation**, basis, keystone, mainspring, mainstay, linchpin, bedrock, base, backbone, key, centrepiece, core, heart, centre, crux.

corny adjective (informal) *it sounds corny, but as soon as I saw her I knew she was the one:* **banal**, trite, hackneyed, commonplace, clichéd, predictable, stereotyped, platitudinous, tired, stale, overworked, overused, well worn; mawkish, sentimental, cloying, syrupy, sugary, saccharine; Brit. twee; informal cheesy, schmaltzy, mushy, slushy, sloppy, cutesy, toe-curling; Brit. informal soppy; N. Amer. informal cornball, hokey.

corollary noun *the corollary of increased car ownership has been a decline in public transport:* **consequence,** (end) result, upshot, effect, repercussion, product, by-product; Brit. knock-on effect.

coronet noun. See CROWN noun sense 1.

corporal adjective *corporal punishment:* **bodily,** fleshly, corporeal, somatic, carnal, physical, material.
– OPPOSITES spiritual.

corporation noun **1** *the chairman of the corporation:* **company,** firm, business, concern, operation, house, organization, agency, trust, partnership; conglomerate, group, chain, multinational; informal outfit, set-up. **2** (Brit.) *the corporation refused two planning applications:* **council,** town council, municipal authority.

corporeal adjective *he was frank about his corporeal appetites:* **bodily,** fleshly, carnal, corporal, human, mortal, earthly, physical, material, tangible, concrete, real, actual.

corps noun **1** *an army corps:* **unit,** division, detachment, section, company, contingent, squad, squadron, regiment, battalion, brigade, platoon. **2** *a corps of trained engineers:* **group,** body, band, cohort, party, gang, pack; team, crew.

corpse noun dead body, body, carcass, skeleton, remains; informal stiff; Medicine cadaver.

corpulent adjective *his corpulent figure seemed to fill the small pulpit:* **fat,** obese, overweight, plump, portly, stout, chubby, paunchy, beer-bellied, heavy, bulky, chunky, well upholstered, well padded, well covered, meaty, fleshy, rotund, broad in the beam; informal tubby, pudgy, beefy, porky, roly-poly, blubbery; Brit. informal podgy, fubsy; N. Amer. informal corn-fed.
– OPPOSITES thin.

correct adjective **1** *the correct answer:* **right,** accurate, true, exact, precise, unerring, faithful, strict, faultless, flawless, error-free, perfect, word-perfect; informal on the mark, on the beam, on the nail; Brit. informal spot on, bang on; N. Amer. informal on the money, on the button. **2** *correct behaviour:* **proper,** seemly, decorous, decent, respectable, right, suitable, fit, fitting, befitting, appropriate, apt; approved, accepted, conventional, customary, traditional, orthodox, comme il faut.
– OPPOSITES wrong, improper.
verb **1** *proof-read your work and correct any mistakes:* **rectify,** put right, set right, right, amend, emend, remedy, repair. **2** *an attempt to correct the trade imbalance:* **counteract,** offset, counterbalance, compensate for, make up for, neutralize. **3** *the brakes need correcting:* **adjust,** regulate, fix, set, standardize, normalize, calibrate, fine-tune.

correction noun **rectification,** rectifying, righting, amendment, emendation, repair, remedy.

corrective adjective *he agreed to undergo corrective surgery:* **remedial,** therapeutic, restorative, curative, reparatory, reparative, rehabilitative.

correctly adverb **1** *the questions were answered correctly:* **accurately,** right, unerringly, precisely, faultlessly, flawlessly, perfectly, without error. **2** *she behaved correctly at all times:* **properly,** decorously, with decorum, decently, suitably, fittingly, appropriately, well.

correlate verb **1** *socio-economic status often correlates with educational achievement:* **correspond,** match, parallel, agree, tally, tie in, be consistent, be compatible, be consonant, coordinate, dovetail, relate, conform; informal square; N. Amer. informal jibe. **2** *consumption of such foods was correlated with a decreased risk for certain cancers:* **connect,** establish a relationship/connection between, associate, relate.
– OPPOSITES contrast.

correlation noun *the correlation between smoking and lung cancer is well-known:* **connection,** association, link, tie-in, tie-up, relation, relationship, interrelationship, interdependence, interconnection, interaction; correspondence, parallel.

correspond verb **1** *their policies do not correspond with their statements:* **correlate,** agree, be in agreement, be consistent, be compatible, be consonant, accord, be in tune, concur, coincide, tally, tie in, dovetail, fit in; match, parallel; informal square; N. Amer. informal jibe. **2** *a rank corresponding to the British rank of sergeant:* **be equivalent,** be analogous, be comparable, equate. **3** *Debbie and I corresponded for years:* **exchange letters,** write, communicate, keep in touch/contact.

correspondence noun **1** *there is some correspondence between the two variables:* **correlation,** agreement, consistency, compatibility, consonance, conformity, similarity, resemblance, parallel, comparability, accord, concurrence, coincidence. **2** *his private correspondence:* **letters,** messages, missives, mail, post; communication.

correspondent noun *the paper's foreign correspondent:* **reporter,** journalist, columnist, writer, contributor, newspaperman, newspaperwoman, commentator; Brit. pressman; informal stringer, news hound, journo.
adjective *the price has been increased without any correspondent improvement in quality:* **corresponding,** parallel, matching, equivalent, comparable, similar, analogous, commensurate.

corresponding adjective *a change in money supply brings a corresponding change in expenditure:* **commensurate,** parallel, correspondent, matching, correlated, relative, proportional, proportionate, comparable, equivalent, analogous.

C

corridor noun **passage**, passageway, aisle, gangway, hall, hallway, gallery, arcade.

corroborate verb *the witness had corroborated the boy's account of the attack:* **confirm**, verify, endorse, ratify, authenticate, validate, certify; support, back up, uphold, bear out, bear witness to, attest to, testify to, vouch for, give credence to, substantiate, sustain.
– OPPOSITES contradict.

corrode verb **1** *the iron had corroded:* **rust**, become rusty, tarnish; wear away, disintegrate, crumble, perish, spoil; oxidize. **2** *acid rain corrodes buildings:* **wear away**, eat away (at), gnaw away (at), erode, abrade, destroy.

corrosive adjective *the workers are exposed to corrosive chemicals:* **caustic**, corroding, erosive, abrasive, burning, stinging; destructive, damaging, harmful, harsh.

corrugated adjective *the roof was made of corrugated iron:* **ridged**, fluted, grooved, furrowed, crinkled, crinkly, puckered, creased, wrinkled, wrinkly.

corrupt adjective **1** *a corrupt official | corrupt practices:* **dishonest**, unscrupulous, dishonourable, unprincipled, unethical, amoral, untrustworthy, venal, underhand, double-dealing, fraudulent, bribable, buyable; criminal, illegal, unlawful, nefarious; informal crooked, shady, dirty, mucky, sleazy; Brit. informal bent, dodgy. **2** *the earth was corrupt in God's sight:* **immoral**, depraved, degenerate, reprobate, vice-ridden, perverted, debauched, dissolute, dissipated, bad, wicked, evil, base, sinful, ungodly, unholy, irreligious, profane, impious, impure; informal warped. **3** *a corrupt text:* **impure**, bastardized, debased, adulterated.
– OPPOSITES honest, ethical, pure.
verb **1** *the fear of firms corrupting politicians in the search for contracts:* **bribe**, suborn, buy (off), pay off; informal grease someone's palm, give someone a backhander/sweetener, get at, square; Brit. informal nobble. **2** *a book that might corrupt its readers:* **deprave**, pervert, debauch, degrade, warp, lead astray, defile, pollute, sully. **3** *the apostolic writings had been corrupted:* **alter**, tamper with, interfere with, bastardize, debase, adulterate.

corruption noun **1** *political corruption:* **dishonesty**, unscrupulousness, double-dealing, fraud, fraudulence, misconduct, crime, criminality, wrongdoing; bribery, subornation, venality, extortion, profiteering, jobbery; N. Amer. payola; informal graft, crookedness, sleaze. **2** *his fall into corruption:* **immorality**, depravity, vice, degeneracy, perversion, pervertedness, debauchery, dissoluteness, decadence, wickedness, evil, sin, sinfulness, ungodliness. **3** *these figures have been subject to corruption:* **alteration**, bastardization, debasement, adulteration.

– OPPOSITES honesty, morality, purity.

corset noun **girdle**, panty girdle, foundation (garment), corselette; Brit. roll-on.

cortège noun **1** *the funeral cortège:* **procession**, parade, cavalcade, motorcade, convoy, caravan, train, column, file, line. **2** *the prince's cortège:* **entourage**, retinue, train, suite; attendants, companions, followers, retainers.

cosmetic adjective *most of the changes were merely cosmetic:* **superficial**, surface, skin-deep, outward, exterior, external.
– OPPOSITES fundamental.
noun (**cosmetics**) *a new range of cosmetics:* **make-up**, beauty products, maquillage, face paint; informal warpaint, paint, slap.

cosmic adjective **1** *cosmic bodies:* **extraterrestrial**, in space, from space. **2** *an epic of cosmic dimensions:* **vast**, huge, immense, enormous, massive, colossal, prodigious, immeasurable, incalculable, unfathomable, fathomless, measureless, infinite, limitless, boundless.

cosmonaut noun **astronaut**, spaceman/woman, taikonaut, space traveller, space cadet; N. Amer. informal jock.

cosmopolitan adjective **1** *the student body has a cosmopolitan character:* **multicultural**, multiracial, international, worldwide, global. **2** *a cosmopolitan audience:* **worldly**, worldly-wise, well travelled, experienced, unprovincial, cultivated, cultured, sophisticated, suave, urbane, glamorous, fashionable; informal jet-setting, cool.

cosset verb *before her papa died she had been spoiled and cosseted:* **pamper**, indulge, overindulge, mollycoddle, coddle, baby, pet, mother, nanny, nursemaid, pander to, feather-bed, spoil; wrap in cotton wool, wait on someone hand and foot.

cost noun **1** *there was a row over the cost of the equipment:* **price**, asking price, market price, selling price, fee, tariff, fare, toll, levy, charge, rental; value, valuation, quotation, rate, worth; informal, humorous damage. **2** *the human cost of the conflict:* **sacrifice**, loss, expense, penalty, toll, price. **3** (**costs**) *we need to make £10,000 to cover our costs:* **expenses**, outgoings, disbursements, overheads, running costs, operating costs, fixed costs; expenditure, spending, outlay.
verb **1** *the chair costs £186:* **be priced at**, sell for, be valued at, fetch, come to, amount to; informal set someone back, go for; Brit. informal knock someone back. **2** *the proposal has not yet been costed:* **put a price on**, price, value, put a value on, put a figure on.

costly adjective **1** *costly machinery:* **expensive**, dear, high-cost, highly priced, overpriced; Brit. over the odds; informal steep, pricey. **2** *a costly mistake:* **catastrophic**, disastrous, calamitous, ruinous; damaging, harmful, injurious, deleterious, woeful, awful, terrible, dreadful.

– OPPOSITES cheap.

costume noun **1** *Elizabethan costumes:* **(set of) clothes**, garments, robes, outfit, ensemble; dress, clothing, attire, garb, uniform, livery; informal get-up, gear, togs; Brit. informal clobber, kit; N. Amer. informal threads. **2** (Brit.) *if you'd like a dip, we can lend you a costume.* See **SWIMSUIT**.

cosy adjective **1** *a cosy country cottage:* **snug**, comfortable, warm, homelike, homey, homely, welcoming; safe, sheltered, secure; N. Amer. down-home, homestyle; informal comfy, snug as a bug (in a rug). **2** *a cosy chat:* **intimate**, relaxed, informal, friendly.

coterie noun *all prime ministers develop a small coterie of kindred spirits:* **clique**, set, circle, inner circle, crowd, in-crowd, band, community; informal gang.

cottage noun **small house**, lodge, chalet, cabin; shack, shanty; (in Russia) dacha; Scottish bothy, but and ben; Austral. informal weekender.

couch noun *she seated herself on the couch:* **settee**, sofa, divan, chaise longue, chesterfield, love seat, settle, ottoman; Brit. put-you-up; N. Amer. daybed, davenport, studio couch.
verb *his reply was couched in deferential terms:* **express**, phrase, word, frame, put, formulate, style, convey, say, state, utter.

cough verb *he coughed loudly:* **hack**, hawk, bark, clear one's throat, hem.
noun *a loud cough:* **hack**, bark; informal frog in one's throat.
■ **cough something up** (informal) *the tenants refused to cough up the rent:* pay (up), come up with, hand over, dish out, part with; informal fork out, shell out, lay out; Brit. informal stump up; N. Amer. informal ante up, pony up.

council noun **1** *the town council:* **local authority**, local government, municipal authority, administration, executive, chamber, assembly; Brit. corporation. **2** *the Schools Council:* **advisory body**, board, committee, commission, assembly, panel; synod, convocation. **3** *that evening, she held a family council:* meeting, gathering, conference, conclave, assembly.

counsel noun **1** *he no longer came to me for counsel:* **advice**, guidance, counselling, direction, information; recommendations, suggestions, guidelines, hints, tips, pointers. **2** *the counsel for the defence:* **barrister**, lawyer; Scottish advocate; N. Amer. attorney, counselor(-at-law); informal brief.
verb *he counselled the team to withdraw from the deal:* **advise**, recommend, direct, advocate, encourage, urge, warn, caution; guide, give guidance.

counsellor noun **adviser**, consultant, guide, mentor; expert, specialist.

count verb **1** *she counted the money again:* **add up**, add together, reckon up, figure up, total, tally, calculate, compute; Brit. tot up. **2** *a company with 250 employees, not counting overseas staff:* **include**, take into account,

take account of, take into consideration, allow for. **3** *I count it a privilege to be asked:* **consider**, think, feel, regard, look on as, view as, hold to be, judge, deem, account. **4** *it's your mother's feelings that count:* **matter**, be of consequence, be of account, be significant, signify, be important, carry weight; informal cut any ice.
noun **1** *at the last count, the committee had 579 members:* **calculation**, computation, reckoning, tally. **2** *her white blood cell count:* **amount**, number, total.
■ **count on/upon 1** *you can count on me:* rely on, depend on, bank on, trust (in), be sure of, have (every) confidence in, believe in, put one's faith in, take for granted, take as read. **2** *they hadn't counted on Rangers' indomitable spirit:* expect, reckon on, anticipate, envisage, allow for, be prepared for, bargain for/on; N. Amer. informal figure on.

countenance noun *his strikingly handsome countenance:* **face**, features, physiognomy, profile; (facial) expression, look, appearance, aspect, mien; informal mug; Brit. informal mush, phizog, phiz, clock, boat race; N. Amer. informal puss.
verb *he would not countenance the use of force:* **tolerate**, permit, allow, agree to, consent to, give one's blessing to, go along with, hold with, put up with, endure, stomach, swallow; Scottish thole; informal stand for.

counter[1] noun *the idea of the game is to collect the most counters:* **token**, chip, disc, jetton, plaque; piece, man, marker; N. Amer. check.

counter[2] verb **1** *workers countered accusations of dishonesty with claims of oppression:* **respond to**, parry, hit back at, answer, retort to. **2** *the second argument is more difficult to counter:* **oppose**, dispute, argue against/with, contradict, controvert, negate, counteract; challenge, contest.
– OPPOSITES support.
adjective *a counter bid:* **opposing**, opposed, opposite.
■ **counter to** against, in opposition to, contrary to, at variance with, in defiance of, in contravention of, in conflict with, at odds with.

counteract verb **1** *new measures to counteract drug trafficking:* **prevent**, thwart, frustrate, foil, impede, curb, hinder, hamper, check, put a stop/end to, defeat. **2** *a drug to counteract the possible effect on her heart:* **offset**, counterbalance, balance (out), cancel out, even out, counterpoise, countervail, compensate for, make up for, remedy; neutralize, nullify, negate, invalidate.
– OPPOSITES encourage, exacerbate.

counterbalance verb *the risk of failure tends to be counterbalanced by high rewards:* **compensate for**, make up for, offset, balance (out), even out, counterpoise, counteract, equalize, neutralize; nullify, negate, undo.

C

counterfeit adjective *counterfeit cassettes:* **fake**, faked, bogus, forged, imitation, spurious, substitute, ersatz; informal phoney.
– OPPOSITES genuine.
noun *the notes were counterfeits:* **fake**, forgery, copy, reproduction, imitation, fraud, sham; informal phoney, knock-off.
– OPPOSITES original.
verb *his signature was hard to counterfeit:* **fake**, forge, copy, reproduce, imitate.

countermand verb *an order to arrest the strike leaders had been countermanded:* **revoke**, rescind, reverse, undo, repeal, retract, withdraw, quash, overturn, overrule, cancel, annul, invalidate, nullify, negate.
– OPPOSITES uphold.

counterpart noun *the minister held talks with his French counterpart:* **equivalent**, opposite number, peer, equal, coequal, parallel, complement, analogue, match, twin, mate, fellow.

countless adjective *she'd apologized countless times before:* **innumerable**, numerous, untold, legion, without number, numberless, unnumbered, limitless, multitudinous, incalculable; informal umpteen, no end of, a slew of, loads of, stacks of, heaps of, masses of, oodles of, zillions of; N. Amer. informal gazillions of.
– OPPOSITES few.

countrified adjective *the countrified ambience was spoilt by the express trains:* **rural**, rustic, pastoral, bucolic, country; idyllic, unspoilt.
– OPPOSITES urban.

country noun **1** *foreign countries:* **nation**, (sovereign) state, kingdom, realm, territory, province, principality, palatinate, duchy. **2** *he risked his life for his country:* **homeland**, native land, fatherland, motherland, the land of one's fathers. **3** *the whole country took to the streets:* **people**, public, population, populace, citizenry, nation, body politic; electors, voters, taxpayers, grass roots; Brit. informal Joe Public. **4** *thickly forested country:* **terrain**, land, territory, parts; landscape, scenery, setting, surroundings, environment. **5** *she hated living in the country:* **countryside**, green belt, great outdoors; provinces, rural areas, backwoods, back of beyond, hinterland; Austral./NZ outback, bush, back country, backblocks, booay; informal sticks, middle of nowhere; N. Amer. informal boondocks, boonies, tall timbers; Austral. informal beyond the black stump.
adjective *country pursuits:* **rural**, countryside, outdoor, rustic, pastoral, bucolic.
– OPPOSITES urban.

countryman, countrywoman noun **1** *the traditions of his countrymen:* **compatriot**, fellow citizen. **2** *the countryman takes a great interest in the weather:* **country dweller**, country cousin, son/daughter of the soil, farmer; rustic, yokel, bumpkin,

peasant, provincial; Irish informal culchie; N. Amer. informal hayseed, hick, hillbilly, rube; Austral. informal bushy.

countryside noun **1** *beautiful unspoilt countryside:* **landscape**, scenery, surroundings, setting, environment; country, terrain, land. **2** *I was brought up in the countryside.* See **COUNTRY** noun sense 5.

county noun *the northern counties:* **shire**, province, territory, administrative unit, region, district, area.
adjective (Brit.) *a county lady:* **upper-class**, aristocratic, landed, landowning; informal upper-crust, top-drawer, {huntin', shootin', and fishin'}, tweedy.

coup noun **1** *a violent military coup:* **seizure of power**, coup d'état, putsch, overthrow, takeover, deposition; (palace) revolution, rebellion, revolt, insurrection, mutiny, insurgence, uprising. **2** *a major publishing coup:* **success**, triumph, feat, accomplishment, achievement, scoop, master stroke, stroke of genius.

coup de grâce noun *he administered the coup de grâce with a knife:* **death blow**, finishing blow, kiss of death; informal KO, kayo.

coup d'état noun. See **COUP** sense 1.

couple noun **1** *a couple of girls:* **pair**, duo, twosome, two, brace, span, yoke. **2** *a honeymoon couple:* **husband and wife**, twosome, partners, lovers; informal item.
verb **1** *a sense of hope is coupled with a sense of loss:* **combine**, accompany, mix, incorporate, link, associate, connect, ally; add to, join to. **2** *a cable is coupled to one of the wheels:* **connect**, attach, join, fasten, fix, link, secure, tie, bind, strap, rope, tether, truss, lash, hitch, yoke, chain, hook (up).
– OPPOSITES detach.

coupon noun **1** *money-off coupons:* **voucher**, token, ticket, slip; N. Amer. informal ducat, comp, rain check. **2** *fill in the coupon below:* **form**, tear-off slip.

courage noun *it takes courage to speak out against the tide of opinion:* **bravery**, courageousness, pluck, pluckiness, valour, fearlessness, intrepidity, nerve, daring, audacity, boldness, grit, hardihood, heroism, gallantry; informal guts, spunk; Brit. informal bottle; N. Amer. informal moxie, cojones, sand.
– OPPOSITES cowardice.

courageous adjective *her courageous human rights work:* **brave**, plucky, fearless, valiant, valorous, intrepid, heroic, lionhearted, bold, daring, daredevil, audacious, undaunted, unflinching, unshrinking, unafraid, dauntless, indomitable, doughty, mettlesome, venturesome, stout-hearted, gallant, death-or-glory; N. Amer. rock-ribbed; informal game, gutsy, spunky, ballsy, have-a-go.
– OPPOSITES cowardly.

courier noun **1** *the documents were sent by courier:* **messenger**, dispatch rider, runner.

2 *a courier for a package holiday company:* **representative**, (tour) guide; dragoman; N. Amer. tour director; informal rep.

course noun **1** *the island was not far off our course:* **route**, way, track, direction, tack, path, line, trail, trajectory, bearing, heading, orbit. **2** *a device which changed the course of history:* **progression**, development, progress, advance, evolution, flow, movement, sequence, order, succession, rise, march, passage, passing. **3** *what is the best course to adopt?* **procedure**, plan (of action), course/line of action, MO, modus operandi, practice, approach, technique, way, means, policy, strategy, programme. **4** *a waterlogged course:* **racecourse**, racetrack, track, ground. **5** *a French course:* **programme/course of study**, curriculum, syllabus; classes, lectures, studies. **6** *a course of antibiotics:* **programme**, series, sequence, system, schedule, regimen.
verb *tears coursed down her cheeks:* **flow**, pour, stream, run, rush, gush, cascade, flood, roll.
■ **in due course** at the appropriate time, when the time is ripe, in time, in the fullness of time, in the course of time, at a later date, by and by, sooner or later, in the end, eventually.
■ **of course** *there are, of course, exceptions to the rule:* naturally, as might be expected, as you/one would expect, needless to say, certainly, to be sure, as a matter of course, obviously, it goes without saying; informal natch.

court noun **1** *the court found him guilty:* **court of law**, law court, bench, bar, judicature, tribunal, chancery, assizes. **2** *walking in the castle court:* **courtyard**, quadrangle, square, close, enclosure, plaza, piazza, cloister; informal quad. **3** *he put on plays for the King's court:* **royal household**, retinue, entourage, train, suite, courtiers, attendants. **4** *she made her way to the Queen's court:* **royal residence**, palace, castle, chateau.
verb **1** *a newspaper editor who was courted by senior politicians:* **curry favour with**, cultivate, try to win over, make up to, ingratiate oneself with; informal suck up to, butter up; N. Amer. informal shine up to. **2** *he was busily courting public attention:* **seek**, pursue, go after, strive for, solicit. **3** *he's often courted controversy:* **risk**, invite, attract, bring on oneself.

courteous adjective *enquiries will be dealt with by our highly skilled courteous staff:* **polite**, well mannered, civil, respectful, well behaved, well bred, well spoken, mannerly; gentlemanly, chivalrous, gallant; gracious, obliging, considerate, pleasant, cordial, urbane, polished, refined, courtly, civilized.
– OPPOSITES rude.

courtesy noun *customers deserve to be treated with courtesy:* **politeness**, courteousness, good manners, civility, respect, respectfulness; chivalry, gallantry; graciousness, consideration, thought, thoughtfulness, cordiality, urbanity, courtliness.

courtier noun **attendant**, lord, lady, lady-in-waiting, steward, equerry, page, squire.

courtly adjective *he gave a courtly bow:* **refined**, polished, suave, cultivated, civilized, elegant, urbane, debonair; polite, civil, courteous, gracious, well mannered, well bred, chivalrous, gallant, gentlemanly, ladylike, aristocratic, dignified, decorous, formal, ceremonious, stately.
– OPPOSITES uncouth.

courtship noun **1** *a whirlwind courtship:* **romance**, (love) affair; engagement. **2** *his courtship of Emma:* **wooing**, courting, suit, pursuit.

courtyard noun **quadrangle**, cloister, square, plaza, piazza, close, enclosure, yard; informal quad.

cove noun *a small sandy cove:* **bay**, inlet, fjord, anchorage; Scottish (sea) loch; Irish lough.

covenant noun *a breach of the covenant:* **contract**, agreement, undertaking, commitment, guarantee, warrant, pledge, promise, bond, indenture; pact, deal, settlement, arrangement, understanding.
verb *the landlord covenants to repair the property:* **undertake**, contract, guarantee, pledge, promise, agree, engage, warrant, commit oneself, bind oneself.

cover verb **1** *she covered her face with a towel:* **protect**, shield, shelter; hide, conceal, veil. **2** *his car was covered in mud:* **cake**, coat, encrust, plaster, smother, daub, bedaub. **3** *snow covered the fields:* **blanket**, overlay, overspread, carpet, coat. **4** *a course covering all aspects of the business:* **deal with**, consider, take in, include, involve, comprise, incorporate, embrace. **5** *the trial was covered by a range of newspapers:* **report on**, write about, describe, commentate on, publish/broadcast details of. **6** *he turned on the radio to cover their conversation:* **mask**, disguise, hide, camouflage, muffle, stifle, smother. **7** *I'm covering for Jill:* **stand in for**, fill in for, deputize for, take over from, relieve, take the place of, sit in for, understudy, hold the fort; informal sub for; N. Amer. informal pinch-hit for. **8** *can you make enough to cover your costs?* **pay (for)**, be enough for, fund, finance; pay back, make up for, offset. **9** *your home is covered against damage and loss:* **insure**, protect, secure, underwrite, assure, indemnify. **10** *we covered ten miles each day:* **travel**, journey, go, do, traverse.
– OPPOSITES expose.
noun **1** *a protective cover:* **covering**, sleeve, wrapping, wrapper, envelope, sheath, housing, jacket, casing, cowling; awning, canopy, tarpaulin. **2** *a manhole cover:* **lid**, top, cap. **3** *a book cover:* **binding**, jacket, dust jacket, dust cover, wrapper. **4** *a thick cover of snow:* **coating**, coat, covering, layer, carpet, blanket, overlay, dusting, film, sheet,

veneer, crust, skin, cloak, mantle, veil, pall, shroud. **5** *panicking onlookers ran for cover:* **shelter**, protection, refuge, sanctuary, haven, hiding place. **6** *the company was a cover for an international swindle:* **front**, facade, smokescreen, screen, blind, camouflage, disguise, mask, cloak. **7** (Brit.) *your policy provides cover against damage by subsidence:* **insurance**, protection, security, assurance, indemnification, indemnity, compensation.

■ **cover something up** conceal, hide, keep secret/dark, hush up, draw a veil over, suppress, sweep under the carpet, gloss over; informal whitewash, keep a/the lid on.

coverage noun *they praised the newspaper's coverage of sport:* **reportage**, reporting, description, treatment, handling, presentation, investigation, commentary; reports, articles, pieces, stories.

covering noun **1** *a canvas covering:* **awning**, canopy, tarpaulin, cowling, casing, housing; wrapping, wrapper, cover, envelope, sheath, sleeve, jacket, lid, top, cap. **2** *a covering of snow:* **layer**, coating, coat, carpet, blanket, overlay, topping, dusting, film, sheet, veneer, crust, skin, cloak, mantle, veil.
adjective *a covering letter:* **accompanying**, explanatory, introductory, prefatory.

covert adjective *covert operations against the dictatorship:* **secret**, furtive, clandestine, surreptitious, stealthy, cloak-and-dagger, hole-and-corner, backstairs, hidden, under-the-table, hugger-mugger, concealed, private, undercover, underground; informal hush-hush.
– OPPOSITES overt.

cover-up noun *the officers were implicated in the cover-up rather than the massacre itself:* **whitewash**, concealment, false front, facade, camouflage, disguise, mask.
– OPPOSITES exposé.

covet verb *people still coveted things which didn't belong to them:* **desire**, yearn for, crave, have one's heart set on, want, wish for, long for, hanker after/for, hunger after/for, thirst for.

covetous adjective *the covetous man will never have enough:* **grasping**, greedy, acquisitive, desirous, possessive, envious, green with envy, green-eyed.

cow verb *has he cowed you with all his threats?* **intimidate**, daunt, browbeat, bully, tyrannize, scare, terrorize, frighten, dishearten, unnerve, subdue; informal psych out, bulldoze.

coward noun **weakling**, milksop, namby-pamby, mouse; informal chicken, scaredy-cat, yellow-belly, sissy, baby; Brit. informal big girl's blouse; N. Amer. informal candy-ass, pussy; Austral./NZ informal dingo, sook.
– OPPOSITES hero.

cowardly adjective *the cowardly little wretches were trying to keep out of his way:* **faint-hearted**, lily-livered, spineless,

chicken-hearted, craven, timid, timorous, fearful, pusillanimous; informal yellow, chicken, weak-kneed, gutless, yellow-bellied, wimpish, wimpy; Brit. informal wet.
– OPPOSITES brave.

cowboy noun **1** *cowboys on horseback:* **cattleman**, cowhand, cowman, cowherd, herder, herdsman, drover, stockman, rancher, gaucho, vaquero; N. Amer. informal cowpuncher, cowpoke, broncobuster; N. Amer. dated buckaroo. **2** (informal) *the builders were complete cowboys:* **rogue**, rascal, scoundrel, cheat, swindler, fraudster, fly-by-night.

cower verb *children cowered in terror as the shoot-out erupted:* **cringe**, shrink, crouch, recoil, flinch, pull back, draw back, tremble, shake, quake, blench, quail, grovel.

coy adjective *she treated him to a coy smile of invitation:* **arch**, simpering, coquettish, flirtatious, kittenish, skittish; demure, shy, modest, bashful, reticent, diffident, self-effacing, shrinking, timid.
– OPPOSITES brazen.

crabby adjective *she was regarded as crabby and reclusive:* **irritable**, cantankerous, irascible, bad-tempered, grumpy, grouchy, crotchety, tetchy, testy, crusty, curmudgeonly, ill-tempered, ill-humoured, peevish, cross, fractious, pettish, crabbed, prickly, waspish; informal snappish, snappy, chippy; Brit. informal shirty, stroppy, narky, ratty; N. Amer. informal cranky, ornery; Austral./NZ informal snaky.
– OPPOSITES affable.

crack noun **1** *a crack in the glass:* **split**, break, chip, fracture, rupture; crazing. **2** *a crack between two rocks:* **space**, gap, crevice, fissure, cleft, breach, rift, cranny, chink, interstice. **3** *the crack of a rifle:* **bang**, report, explosion, detonation, pop; clap, crash. **4** *a crack on the head:* **blow**, bang, hit, knock, rap, punch, thump, bump, smack, slap; informal bash, whack, thwack, clout, wallop, clip, biff, bop.
verb **1** *the glass cracked in the heat:* **break**, split, fracture, rupture, snap. **2** *she cracked him across the forehead:* **hit**, strike, smack, slap, beat, thump, knock, rap, punch; informal bash, whack, thwack, clobber, clout, clip, wallop, belt, biff, bop, sock; Brit. informal slosh; N. Amer. informal boff, bust, slug. **3** *the witnesses cracked:* **break down**, give way, cave in, go to pieces, crumble, lose control, yield, succumb.
adjective *a crack shot:* **expert**, skilled, skilful, formidable, virtuoso, masterly, consummate, excellent, first-rate, first-class, marvellous, wonderful, magnificent, outstanding, superlative; deadly; informal great, superb, fantastic, ace, hotshot, mean, demon; Brit. informal brilliant; N. Amer. informal crackerjack.
– OPPOSITES incompetent.

■ **crack down on** suppress, prevent, stop, put a stop to, put an end to, stamp out, eliminate, eradicate; clamp down on, get tough on, come down hard on, limit, restrain, restrict, check, keep in check, control, keep under control.

cracked adjective *a cracked cup:* **chipped**, broken, crazed, fractured, splintered, split; damaged, defective, flawed, imperfect.

crackle verb *the fire crackled and spat sparks:* **sizzle**, fizz, hiss, crack, snap, sputter, crepitate.

cradle noun 1 *the baby's cradle:* **crib**, bassinet, Moses basket, cot, carrycot. 2 *the cradle of democracy:* **birthplace**, fount, fountainhead, source, spring, fountain, origin, place of origin, seat.
verb *she cradled his head in her arms:* **hold**, support, pillow, cushion, shelter, protect; rest, prop (up).

craft noun 1 *the craft of cobbling:* **skill**, skilfulness, ability, capability, competence, art, talent, expertise, proficiency. 2 *the historian's craft:* **activity**, occupation, profession, work, line of work, pursuit. 3 *she used craft and diplomacy:* **cunning**, craftiness, guile, wiliness, artfulness, deviousness, slyness, trickery, duplicity, dishonesty, deceit, deceitfulness, deception, intrigue, subterfuge; wiles, ploys, ruses, schemes, stratagems, tricks. 4 *a sailing craft:* **vessel**, ship, boat.

craftsman, craftswoman noun **artisan**, artist, skilled worker; expert, master.

craftsmanship noun *one of the finest examples of early twentieth-century Russian craftsmanship:* **workmanship**, artistry, craft, art, handiwork, work; skill, skilfulness, expertise, technique.

crafty adjective *Mum knew them to be crafty rogues:* **cunning**, wily, guileful, artful, devious, sly, tricky, scheming, calculating, designing, sharp, shrewd, astute, canny; duplicitous, dishonest, deceitful; informal foxy.
– OPPOSITES honest.

crag noun **cliff**, bluff, ridge, precipice, height, peak, tor, escarpment, scarp.

craggy adjective 1 *the craggy cliffs:* **steep**, precipitous, sheer, perpendicular; rocky, rugged, ragged. 2 *his craggy face:* **rugged**, rough-hewn, strong, manly; weather-beaten, weathered.

cram verb 1 *wardrobes crammed with clothes:* **fill**, stuff, pack, jam, fill to overflowing, fill to the brim, overload; crowd, throng, overcrowd. 2 *they all crammed into the car:* **crowd**, pack, pile, squash, wedge oneself, force one's way. 3 *he crammed his clothes into a suitcase:* **thrust**, push, shove, force, ram, jam, stuff, pack, pile, squash, compress, squeeze, wedge. 4 *most of the students are cramming for exams:* **revise**; informal swot, mug up, bone up.

cramp noun *stomach cramps:* **spasm**, pain, shooting pain, pang, stitch.
verb *tighter rules will cramp economic growth:* **hinder**, impede, inhibit, hamper, constrain, hamstring, interfere with, restrict, limit, shackle; slow down, check, arrest, curb, retard.

cramped adjective 1 *cramped accommodation:* **poky**, uncomfortable, confined, restricted, constricted, small, tiny, narrow; crowded, packed, congested. 2 *cramped handwriting:* **small**, crabbed, illegible, unreadable, indecipherable.
– OPPOSITES spacious.

crane noun **derrick**, winch, hoist, davit, windlass; block and tackle.

cranium noun **skull**, head; N. Amer. informal brainpan.

crank[1] verb *you crank the engine by hand:* **start**, turn (over), get going.

crank[2] noun *they're nothing but a bunch of cranks:* **eccentric**, oddity, madman/madwoman, lunatic; informal oddball, freak, weirdo, crackpot, loony, nut, nutcase, head case, maniac; Brit. informal nutter, mentalist; N. Amer. informal screwball, kook.

cranky adjective 1 (informal) *a cranky diet:* **eccentric**, bizarre, weird, peculiar, odd, strange, unconventional, left-field, unorthodox, outlandish; silly, stupid, mad, crazy, idiotic; informal wacky, crackpot, nutty; Brit. informal daft, potty; N. Amer. informal wacko. 2 (N. Amer. informal) *the children were tired and cranky.* See IRRITABLE.

cranny noun *every little cranny was filled with drifted snow:* **chink**, crack, crevice, slit, split, fissure, rift, cleft, opening, gap, aperture, cavity, hole, hollow, niche, corner, nook, interstice.

crash verb 1 *the car crashed into a tree:* **smash into**, collide with, be in collision with, hit, strike, ram, cannon into, plough into, meet head-on, run into; N. Amer. impact. 2 *he crashed his car:* **smash**, wreck; Brit. write off; Brit. informal prang; N. Amer. informal total. 3 *waves crashed against the shore:* **dash**, batter, pound, lash, slam, be hurled. 4 *thunder crashed overhead:* **boom**, crack, roll, clap, explode, bang, blast, blare, resound, reverberate, rumble, thunder, echo.
noun 1 *a crash on the motorway:* **accident**, collision, smash, road traffic accident, RTA; derailment; N. Amer. wreck; informal pile-up; Brit. informal prang, shunt. 2 *a loud crash:* **bang**, smash, smack, crack, bump, thud, clatter, clunk, clonk, clang; report, detonation, explosion; noise, racket, clangour, din.
adjective *a crash course:* **intensive**, concentrated, rapid, short; accelerated-learning, total-immersion.

crass adjective *the crass assumptions that men make about women:* **stupid**, insensitive, mindless, thoughtless, witless, oafish, boorish, asinine, coarse, gross, graceless, tasteless, tactless, clumsy, heavy-handed, blundering; informal ignorant, pig-ignorant.
– OPPOSITES intelligent.

crate noun **case**, packing case, chest, tea

C

chest, box; container, receptacle.

crater noun **hollow**, bowl, basin, hole, cavity, depression.

crave verb *he craved professional recognition:* **long for**, yearn for, desire, want, wish for, hunger for, thirst for, sigh for, pine for, hanker after, covet, lust after, ache for, set one's heart on, dream of, be bent on; informal have a yen for, itch for, be dying for.

craven adjective *a craven surrender:* **cowardly**, lily-livered, faint-hearted, chicken-hearted, spineless, timid, timorous, fearful, pusillanimous, weak, feeble; informal yellow, chicken, weak-kneed, gutless, yellow-bellied, wimpish; contemptible, abject, ignominious; Brit. informal wet.
– OPPOSITES brave.

craving noun *a craving for chocolate:* **longing**, yearning, desire, want, wish, hankering, hunger, thirst, appetite, greed, lust, ache, need, urge; informal yen, itch.

crawl verb **1** *they crawled under the table:* **creep**, worm one's way, go on all fours, go on hands and knees, wriggle, slither, squirm, scrabble. **2** (informal) *I'm not going to go crawling to him:* **grovel to**, ingratiate oneself with, be obsequious to, kowtow to, pander to, toady to, truckle to, bow and scrape to, dance attendance on, curry favour with, make up to, fawn on/over; informal suck up to, lick someone's boots, butter up. **3** *the place was crawling with soldiers:* **be full of**, overflow with, teem with, be packed with, be crowded with, be alive with, be overrun with, swarm with, be bristling with, be infested with, be thick with; informal be lousy with, be stuffed with, be jam-packed with, be chock-a-block with, be chock-full of.

craze noun *the latest fitness craze to sweep the country:* **fad**, fashion, trend, vogue, enthusiasm, mania, passion, rage, obsession, compulsion, fixation, fetish, fancy, taste, fascination, preoccupation; informal thing.

crazed adjective *a crazed murderer:* **mad**, insane, out of one's mind, deranged, demented, certifiable, lunatic, psychopathic; wild, raving, berserk, manic, maniac, frenzied; informal crazy, mental, off one's head, out of one's head, raving mad. See also CRAZY sense 1.
– OPPOSITES sane.

crazy adjective (informal) **1** *a crazy old man:* **mad**, insane, out of one's mind, deranged, demented, not in one's right mind, crazed, lunatic, non compos mentis, unhinged, mad as a hatter, mad as a March hare; informal mental, off one's head, nutty (as a fruitcake), off one's rocker, not right in the head, round the bend, raving mad, bats, batty, bonkers, cuckoo, loopy, loony, bananas, loco, with a screw loose, touched, gaga, doolally, not all there, out to lunch, away with the fairies; Brit. informal barmy, crackers, barking, potty, round the twist, off one's trolley, not the full shilling;

N. Amer. informal **nutso**, out of one's tree, meshuga, wacko, gonzo; Austral./NZ informal bushed. **2** *a crazy idea:* **stupid**, foolish, idiotic, silly, absurd, ridiculous, ludicrous, preposterous, farcical, laughable, risible, nonsensical, imbecilic, hare-brained, half-baked, impracticable, unworkable, ill-conceived, senseless; informal cockeyed; Brit. informal barmy, daft. **3** *he's crazy about her:* **passionate about**, very keen on, enamoured of, infatuated with, smitten with, devoted to; very enthusiastic about, fanatical about; informal wild/mad/nuts about, gone on; Brit. informal potty about.
– OPPOSITES sane, sensible, apathetic.

creak verb *the floorboards creaked:* **squeak**, grate, rasp; groan, complain.

cream noun **1** *skin creams:* **lotion**, ointment, moisturizer, emollient, unguent, cosmetic; salve, rub, embrocation, balm, liniment. **2** *the cream of the world's photographers:* **best**, finest, pick, flower, crème de la crème, elite.
– OPPOSITES dregs.
adjective *a cream dress:* **off-white**, whitish, cream-coloured, creamy, ivory, yellowish-white.

creamy adjective **1** *mix the flour and milk into a creamy paste:* **smooth**, thick, velvety, whipped; rich, buttery. **2** *creamy flowers:* **off-white**, whitish, cream-coloured, cream, ivory, yellowish-white.
– OPPOSITES lumpy.

crease noun **1** *trousers with knife-edge creases:* **fold**, line, ridge; pleat, tuck; furrow, groove, corrugation. **2** *the creases at the corners of her eyes:* **wrinkle**, line, crinkle, pucker; (**creases**) crow's feet.
verb *her skirt was creased and stained:* **crumple**, wrinkle, crinkle, line, scrunch up, rumple, ruck up.

create verb **1** *she has created a work of stunning originality:* **produce**, generate, bring into being, make, fabricate, fashion, build, construct; design, devise, originate, frame, develop, shape, form, forge. **2** *regular socializing creates a good team spirit:* **bring about**, give rise to, lead to, result in, cause, breed, generate, engender, produce, make for, promote, foster, sow the seeds of, contribute to. **3** *the governments planned to create a free-trade zone:* **establish**, found, initiate, institute, constitute, inaugurate, launch, set up, form, organize, develop. **4** *she was created a life peer in 1990:* **appoint**, make; invest as, install as.
– OPPOSITES destroy.

creation noun **1** *the creation of a coalition government:* **establishment**, formation, foundation, initiation, institution, inauguration, constitution; production, generation, fabrication, fashioning, building, construction, origination, development. **2** *Dickens's literary creations:* **work**, work of art, production, opus, oeuvre; achievement.

– OPPOSITES destruction.

creative adjective *our pupils are encouraged to be creative:* **inventive**, imaginative, innovative, innovatory, experimental, original; artistic, expressive, inspired, visionary; enterprising, resourceful; informal blue-sky.

creativity noun **inventiveness**, imagination, imaginativeness, innovation, innovativeness, originality, individuality; artistry, inspiration, vision; enterprise, initiative, resourcefulness.

creator noun **1** *the creator of the series:* **author**, writer, designer, deviser, maker, producer; originator, inventor, architect, mastermind, prime mover. **2** *the Sabbath is kept to honour the Creator.* See **GOD** sense 1.

creature noun **1** *the earth and its creatures:* **animal**, beast, brute; living thing, living being; N. Amer. informal critter. **2** *she was denounced as a creature of the liberals:* **lackey**, minion, hireling, servant, puppet, tool, cat's paw, pawn; informal stooge, yes-man; Brit. informal poodle.

credence noun **1** *the government placed little credence in the scheme:* **belief**, faith, trust, confidence, reliance. **2** *later reports lent credence to this view:* **credibility**, plausibility.

credentials plural noun *the policemen went to check the driver's credentials:* **documents**, documentation, papers, identity papers, bona fides, ID, ID card, identity card, passport, proof of identity; certificates, diplomas, certification.

credibility noun **1** *the whole tale lacks credibility:* **plausibility**, believability, tenability, probability, feasibility, likelihood, credence; authority, cogency. **2** *the party lacked moral credibility:* **trustworthiness**, reliability, dependability, integrity.

credible adjective *very few people found his story credible:* **believable**, plausible, tenable, able to hold water, conceivable, likely, probable, possible, feasible, reasonable, with a ring of truth, persuasive.

credit noun **1** *he never got much credit for the show's success:* **praise**, commendation, acclaim, acknowledgement, recognition, kudos, glory, esteem, respect, admiration, tributes, thanks, gratitude, appreciation; informal bouquets, brownie points. **2** *the speech did his credit no good in the House of Commons:* **reputation**, repute, image, (good) name, character, prestige, standing, status, estimation, credibility.
verb **1** *the wise will seldom credit all they hear:* **believe**, accept, give credence to, trust, have faith in; informal buy, swallow, fall for, take something as gospel. **2** *the scheme's success can be credited to the team's frugality:* **ascribe**, attribute, assign, accredit, chalk up, put down.
▪ **on credit** on hire purchase, on (the) HP,

by instalments, on account; informal on tick, on the slate; Brit. informal on the never-never.

creditable adjective *the team worked hard and produced a creditable performance:* **commendable**, praiseworthy, laudable, admirable, honourable, estimable, meritorious, worthy, deserving, respectable.
– OPPOSITES deplorable.

credulous adjective *he sold 'miracle' cures to desperate and credulous clients:* **gullible**, naive, over-trusting, over-trustful, easily taken in, impressionable, unsuspecting, unsuspicious, unwary, unquestioning; innocent, ingenuous, inexperienced, unsophisticated, unworldly, wide-eyed; informal born yesterday, wet behind the ears.
– OPPOSITES suspicious.

creed noun **1** *people of many creeds and cultures:* **faith**, religion, religious belief, religious persuasion, faith community, Church, denomination, sect. **2** *his political creed:* **system of belief**, (set of) beliefs, principles, articles of faith, ideology, credo, doctrine, teaching, dogma, tenets, canons.

creek noun **inlet**, arm of the sea, bay, estuary, bight, fjord, sound; Scottish firth, frith; (in Orkney & Shetland) voe.

creep verb *Tim crept out of the house:* **tiptoe**, steal, sneak, slip, slink, sidle, pad, edge, inch; skulk, prowl.

creeper noun **climbing plant**, trailing plant; vine, climber, rambler.

creeps
▪ **give someone the creeps** (informal) **repel**, repulse, revolt, disgust, sicken, nauseate, make someone's flesh creep, make someone's skin crawl; scare, frighten, terrify, horrify; N. Amer. informal gross out.

creepy adjective (informal) *that deserted house is really creepy:* **frightening**, eerie, disturbing, sinister, weird, hair-raising, menacing, threatening; Scottish eldritch; informal spooky, scary.

crescent noun **half-moon**, sickle-shape, demilune, lunula, lunette; arc, curve, bow.

crest noun **1** *the bird's crest:* **comb**, plume, tuft of feathers. **2** *the crest of the hill:* **summit**, peak, top, tip, pinnacle, brow, crown, apex. **3** *the Duke of Wellington's crest:* **insignia**, regalia, badge, emblem, heraldic device, coat of arms, arms; Heraldry bearing, charge.

crestfallen adjective *he came back empty-handed and crestfallen:* **downhearted**, downcast, despondent, disappointed, disconsolate, disheartened, discouraged, dispirited, dejected, depressed, desolate, in the doldrums, sad, glum, gloomy, dismayed, doleful, miserable, unhappy, woebegone, forlorn; informal blue, down in the mouth, down in the dumps.
– OPPOSITES cheerful.

crevasse noun *the sled slipped sideways into the crevasse:* **chasm**, abyss, fissure, cleft, crack, split, breach, rift, hole, cavity.

crevice noun *birds nested in every crevice of the cliff:* **crack**, fissure, cleft, chink, interstice, cranny, nook, slit, split, rift, fracture, breach; opening, gap, hole.

crew noun 1 *the ship's crew:* **sailors**, mariners, hands, ship's company, ship's complement. 2 *a crew of cameramen and sound engineers:* **team**, group, company, unit, corps, party, gang.

crib noun 1 *the baby's crib:* **cot**, cradle, bassinet, Moses basket, carrycot. 2 *the oxen's cribs:* **manger**, stall, feeding trough, fodder rack.

crick verb *he cricked his neck during practice:* **strain**, twist, rick, sprain, pull, wrench; injure, hurt, damage.

crime noun 1 *kidnapping is a very serious crime:* **offence**, unlawful act, illegal act, felony, misdemeanour, misdeed, wrong. 2 *the increase in crime:* **lawbreaking**, delinquency, wrongdoing, criminality, misconduct, illegality, villainy; informal crookedness. 3 *a crime against humanity:* **sin**, evil, immoral act, wrong, atrocity, abomination, disgrace, outrage.

criminal noun *a convicted criminal:* **lawbreaker**, offender, villain, delinquent, felon, convict, malefactor, wrongdoer, culprit, miscreant; thief, burglar, robber, armed robber, gunman, gangster; informal crook, con, jailbird, (old) lag; N. Amer. informal hood, yardbird; Austral./NZ informal crim.
adjective 1 *criminal conduct:* **unlawful**, illegal, illicit, lawless, felonious, delinquent, fraudulent, actionable, culpable; villainous, nefarious, corrupt, wrong, bad, evil, wicked, iniquitous; informal crooked; Brit. informal bent. 2 (informal) *a criminal waste of taxpayer's money:* **deplorable**, shameful, reprehensible, disgraceful, inexcusable, unforgivable, unpardonable, outrageous, monstrous, shocking, scandalous, wicked.
– OPPOSITES lawful.

crimp verb *she crimped the edge of the pie:* **pleat**, flute, corrugate, ruffle, fold, crease, crinkle, pucker, gather; pinch, compress, press together, squeeze together.

crimped adjective *crimped blonde hair:* **curly**, wavy, curled, frizzy, ringlety.

cringe verb 1 *she cringed as he bellowed in her ear:* **cower**, shrink, recoil, shy away, flinch, blench, draw back; shake, tremble, quiver, quail, quake. 2 *it makes me cringe when I think of it:* **wince**, shudder, squirm, feel embarrassed/mortified.

crinkle verb *Rose's face crinkled in bewilderment:* **wrinkle**, crease, pucker, furrow, corrugate, line; rumple, scrunch up, ruck up.

crinkly adjective **wrinkled**, wrinkly, crinkled, creased, crumpled, rumpled, crimped, corrugated, fluted, puckered, furrowed; wavy.

cripple verb 1 *the accident crippled her:* **disable**, paralyse, immobilize, lame,

incapacitate, handicap. 2 *the company had been crippled by the recession:* **devastate**, ruin, destroy, wipe out; paralyse, hamstring, bring to a standstill, put out of action, put out of business, bankrupt, break, bring someone to their knees.

crippled adjective **disabled**, paralysed, incapacitated, physically handicapped, lame, immobilized, bedridden, confined to a wheelchair; euphemistic physically challenged.

crisis noun 1 *the situation had reached a crisis:* **critical point**, turning point, crossroads, climacteric, head, moment of truth, zero hour, point of no return, Rubicon, doomsday; informal crunch. 2 *the current economic crisis:* **emergency**, disaster, catastrophe, calamity; predicament, plight, mess, trouble, dire straits, difficulty, extremity.

crisp adjective 1 *crisp bacon:* **crunchy**, crispy, brittle, crumbly, friable, breakable; firm, dry. 2 *a crisp autumn day:* **invigorating**, bracing, brisk, fresh, refreshing, exhilarating, tonic, energizing; cool, chill, chilly, cold; informal nippy; Brit. informal parky. 3 *her answer was crisp:* **brisk**, decisive, businesslike, no-nonsense, incisive, to the point, matter of fact, brusque; terse, succinct, concise, brief, short, short and sweet, laconic; informal snappy. 4 *crisp white bedlinen:* **smooth**, uncreased, ironed; starched.
– OPPOSITES soft, sultry, rambling.

criterion noun *academic ability is not the sole criterion for allocating funds:* **standard**, specification, measure, gauge, test, scale, benchmark, yardstick, touchstone, barometer; principle, rule, law, canon.

critic noun 1 *a literary critic:* **reviewer**, commentator, evaluator, analyst, judge, pundit. 2 *critics of the government:* **detractor**, attacker, fault-finder.

critical adjective 1 *a highly critical report:* **censorious**, condemnatory, condemning, denunciatory, disparaging, disapproving, scathing, fault-finding, judgemental, negative, unfavourable; informal nit-picking, picky. 2 *a critical essay:* **evaluative**, analytical, interpretative, expository, explanatory. 3 *the situation is critical:* **grave**, serious, dangerous, risky, perilous, hazardous, precarious, touch-and-go, in the balance, uncertain, parlous, desperate, dire, acute, life-and-death. 4 *the choice of materials is critical for product safety:* **crucial**, vital, essential, of the essence, all-important, paramount, fundamental, key, pivotal, decisive, deciding, climacteric.
– OPPOSITES complimentary, unimportant.

criticism noun 1 *she was stung by his criticism:* **censure**, condemnation, denunciation, disapproval, disparagement, opprobrium, fault-finding, attack, broadside, brickbats, stricture, recrimination; informal flak, a bad press, panning; Brit. informal stick, slating. 2 *literary criticism:* **evaluation**, assessment, appraisal, analysis, judgement; commentary, interpretation, explanation, explication, elucidation.

criticize verb *the opposition criticized the government's failure to consult adequately:* **find fault with**, censure, denounce, condemn, attack, lambaste, pillory, rail against, inveigh against, arraign, cast aspersions on, pour scorn on, disparage, denigrate, give a bad press to, run down; informal knock, pan, slam, hammer, lay into, pull to pieces, pick holes in; Brit. informal slag off, slate, rubbish; N. Amer. informal pummel, trash; Austral./NZ informal bag, monster.
– OPPOSITES praise.

critique noun *he produced a critique of North American culture:* **analysis**, evaluation, assessment, appraisal, appreciation, criticism, review, study, commentary, exposition, exegesis.

crock noun **1** *a crock of honey:* **pot**, jar; jug, pitcher, ewer; container, receptacle, vessel. **2** (**crocks**) *a pile of dirty crocks.* See CROCKERY.

crockery noun **dishes**, crocks, china, tableware; plates, bowls, cups, saucers; N. Amer. dinnerware.

crook noun **1** (informal) *the crook got five years for swindling two families:* **criminal**, lawbreaker, villain, delinquent, felon, convict, malefactor, wrongdoer; rogue, scoundrel, cheat, swindler, racketeer; thief, robber, burglar; informal shark, con man, con; N. Amer. informal hood, yardbird; Austral./NZ informal crim. **2** *the crook of a tree branch:* **bend**, fork, curve, angle.
verb *he crooked his finger and called the waiter:* **cock**, flex, bend, curve, curl.

crooked adjective **1** *narrow, crooked streets:* **winding**, twisting, zigzag, meandering, tortuous, serpentine. **2** *a crooked spine:* **bent**, twisted, misshapen, deformed, malformed, contorted, out of shape, wry, warped, bowed, distorted; Scottish thrawn. **3** *the picture over the bed looked crooked:* **lopsided**, askew, awry, off-centre, uneven, out of true, out of line, asymmetrical, tilted, at an angle, aslant, slanting, squint; Scottish agley; informal cockeyed; Brit. informal skew-whiff, wonky.
– OPPOSITES straight.

croon verb *she was crooning to the child:* **sing softly**, hum, warble, trill.

crop noun **1** *some farmers lost their entire crop:* **harvest**, year's growth, yield; fruits, produce. **2** *a bumper crop of mail:* **batch**, lot, assortment, selection, collection, supply, intake. **3** *a rider's crop:* **whip**, switch, cane, stick.
verb **1** *she's had her hair cropped:* **cut short**, cut, clip, shear, shave, lop off, chop off, hack off; dock. **2** *a flock of sheep were cropping the turf:* **graze on**, browse on, feed on, nibble, eat. **3** *the hay was cropped several times this summer:* **harvest**, reap, mow; gather (in), collect, pick, bring home.
■ **crop up** *things kept cropping up to delay*

their work: happen, occur, arise, turn up, spring up, pop up, emerge, materialize, surface, appear, come to light, present itself.

cross noun **1** *a bronze cross:* **crucifix**, rood. **2** *we all have our crosses to bear:* **burden**, trouble, worry, trial, tribulation, affliction, curse, bane, misfortune, adversity, hardship, vicissitude; millstone, albatross, thorn in one's flesh/side; misery, woe, pain, sorrow, suffering; informal hassle, headache. **3** *a cross between a yak and a cow:* **hybrid**, hybridization, cross-breed, half-breed, mongrel; mixture, amalgam, blend, combination.
verb **1** *they crossed the hills on foot:* **travel across**, traverse, range over; negotiate, navigate, cover. **2** *a lake crossed by a fine stone bridge:* **span**, bridge; extend/stretch across, pass over. **3** *the point where the two roads cross:* **intersect**, meet, join, connect, criss-cross. **4** *no one dared cross him:* **oppose**, resist, defy, obstruct, impede, hinder, hamper; contradict, argue with, quarrel with, stand up to, take a stand against, take issue with. **5** *the breed was crossed with the similarly coloured Friesian:* **hybridize**, cross-breed, interbreed, cross-fertilize, cross-pollinate.
adjective *Jane was getting cross:* **angry**, annoyed, irate, irritated, in a bad mood, vexed, irked, piqued, out of humour, put out, displeased; irritable, short-tempered, bad-tempered, snappish, crotchety, grouchy, grumpy, fractious, testy, tetchy, crabby; informal mad, hot under the collar, peeved, riled, snappy, on the warpath, up in arms, steamed up, in a paddy; Brit. informal aerated, shirty, stroppy, ratty; N. Amer. informal sore, bent out of shape, teed off, ticked off; Austral./NZ informal ropeable, snaky, crook.
– OPPOSITES pleased.
■ **cross something out** *he crossed out several sentences:* delete, strike out, ink out, score out, edit out, blue-pencil, cancel, obliterate.

cross-examine verb *the witness did not wish to be cross-examined by the police:* **interrogate**, question, cross-question, quiz, catechize, give someone the third degree; informal grill, pump, put someone through the wringer/mangle.

crossing noun **1** *a busy road crossing:* **junction**, crossroads, intersection, interchange; level crossing. **2** *a short ferry crossing:* **journey**, passage, voyage.

crosswise, crossways adverb *there was just about room to lie crosswise in the bed:* **diagonally**, obliquely, transversely, aslant, cornerwise, at an angle, on the bias; N. Amer. cater-cornered, kitty-corner.

crotch noun **groin**, crutch; lap.

crotchety adjective *he was tired and crotchety:* **bad-tempered**, irascible, irritable, grumpy, grouchy, cantankerous, short-tempered, tetchy, testy, curmudgeonly, ill-tempered, ill-humoured,

peevish, cross, fractious, pettish, waspish, crabbed, crabby, crusty, prickly, touchy; informal snappish, snappy, chippy; Brit. informal shirty, stroppy, narky, ratty; N. Amer. informal cranky, ornery; Austral./NZ informal snaky.
– OPPOSITES good-humoured.

crouch verb *we all crouched behind the wall:* **squat**, bend (down), hunker down, hunch over, stoop, kneel (down); duck, cower.

crow verb 1 *a cock crowed:* **cry**, squawk, screech, caw. 2 *try to avoid crowing about your success:* **boast**, brag, trumpet, swagger, swank, gloat, show off, preen oneself, sing one's own praises; informal talk big, blow one's own trumpet, lay it on thick; Austral./NZ informal skite.

crowd noun 1 *a crowd of people:* **throng**, horde, mass, multitude, host, army, herd, flock, drove, swarm, sea, troupe, pack, press, crush, mob, rabble; collection, company, gathering, assembly, assemblage, congregation; informal gaggle, bunch, gang, posse. 2 *she wanted to stand out from the crowd:* **majority**, multitude, common people, populace, general public, masses, rank and file; Brit. informal Joe Public. 3 *he's been hanging round with Hurley's crowd:* **set**, group, circle, clique, coterie; camp; informal gang, crew, lot. 4 *the final attracted a capacity crowd:* **audience**, spectators, listeners, viewers; house, turnout, attendance, gate; congregation; Brit. informal punters.
verb 1 *reporters crowded round her:* **cluster**, flock, swarm, mill, throng, huddle, gather, assemble, congregate, converge. 2 *the guests all crowded into the dining room:* **surge**, push one's way, jostle, elbow one's way; squeeze, pile, cram. 3 *the quayside was crowded with holidaymakers:* **throng**, pack, jam, cram, fill. 4 *stop crowding me:* **pressurize**, pressure; harass, hound, pester, harry, badger, nag; informal hassle, lean on.

crowded adjective *the crowded streets of Southwark:* **packed**, full, filled to capacity, full to bursting, congested, overcrowded, overflowing, teeming, swarming, thronged, populous, overpopulated, busy; informal jam-packed, stuffed, chock-a-block, chock-full, bursting at the seams, full to the gunwales, wall-to-wall; Austral./NZ informal chocker.
– OPPOSITES deserted.

crown noun 1 *a jewelled crown:* **coronet**, diadem, circlet. 2 *the world heavyweight crown:* **title**, award, accolade, distinction; trophy, cup, medal, plate, shield, belt, prize; laurels, bays, palm. 3 *his family were loyal servants of the Crown:* **monarch**, sovereign, king, queen, emperor, empress; monarchy, royalty; informal royals.
verb 1 *David II was crowned in 1331:* **enthrone**, install; invest, induct. 2 *a teaching post at Harvard crowned his career:* **round off**, cap, be the climax of, be the culmination of, top off, consummate, perfect, complete, put the finishing

touch(es) to. 3 *a steeple crowned by a gilded weathercock:* **top**, cap, tip, head, surmount.

crucial adjective 1 *negotiations were at a crucial stage:* **pivotal**, critical, key, climacteric, decisive, deciding; life-and-death. 2 *confidentiality is crucial in this case:* **all-important**, of the utmost importance, of the essence, critical, pre-eminent, paramount, essential, vital.
– OPPOSITES unimportant.

crude adjective 1 *crude oil:* **unrefined**, unpurified, unprocessed, untreated; unmilled, unpolished; coarse, raw, natural. 2 *a crude barricade:* **primitive**, simple, basic, homespun, rudimentary, rough, rough and ready, rough-hewn, make-do, makeshift, improvised, unfinished. 3 *crude jokes:* **vulgar**, rude, naughty, suggestive, bawdy, off colour, indecent, obscene, offensive, lewd, salacious, licentious, ribald, coarse, uncouth, indelicate, tasteless, crass, smutty, dirty, filthy, scatological; informal blue.
– OPPOSITES refined, sophisticated.

cruel adjective 1 *a cruel man:* **brutal**, savage, inhuman, barbaric, barbarous, brutish, bloodthirsty, murderous, vicious, sadistic, wicked, evil, fiendish, diabolical, monstrous, abominable; callous, ruthless, merciless, pitiless, remorseless, uncaring, heartless, stony-hearted, hard-hearted, cold-blooded, cold-hearted, unfeeling, unkind, inhumane. 2 *her death was a cruel blow:* **harsh**, severe, bitter, harrowing, heartbreaking, heart-rending, painful, agonizing, traumatic; formal grievous.
– OPPOSITES compassionate.

cruelty noun *he treated her with extreme cruelty:* **brutality**, savagery, inhumanity, barbarity, barbarousness, brutishness, bloodthirstiness, viciousness, sadism, wickedness; callousness, ruthlessness, lack of compassion.

cruise noun *a cruise down the Nile:* **boat trip**, sea trip; voyage, journey.
verb 1 *she cruised across the Atlantic:* **sail**, voyage, journey. 2 *a taxi cruised past:* **drive slowly**, drift; informal mosey, tootle; Brit. informal pootle.

crumb noun *there was only one crumb of comfort:* **fragment**, bit, morsel, particle, speck, scrap, shred, sliver, atom, grain, trace, tinge, mite, iota, jot, whit, ounce, scintilla, soupçon; informal smidgen, tad.

crumble verb *his empire began to crumble around him:* **disintegrate**, fall apart, fall to pieces, fall down, break up, collapse, fragment; decay, fall into decay, deteriorate, degenerate, go to rack and ruin, decompose, rot, moulder, perish.

crumbly adjective *the cheese is crumbly and moist:* **brittle**, breakable, friable, powdery, granular; short; crisp, crispy.

crumple verb 1 *she crumpled the note in her fist:* **crush**, scrunch up, screw up, squash, squeeze; Brit. scrumple. 2 *his trousers were* *dirty and crumpled:* **crease**, wrinkle, crinkle, rumple, ruck up. **3** *her resistance crumpled:* **collapse**, give way, cave in, go to pieces, break down, crumble, be overcome.

crunch verb *she crunched the biscuit with relish:* **munch**, chomp, champ, scrunch, bite into.
noun (informal) *when the crunch comes, she'll be forced to choose:* **moment of truth**, critical point, crux, crisis, decision time, zero hour, point of no return; showdown.

crusade noun **1** *the medieval crusades:* **holy war**; Islam jihad. **2** *a crusade against crime:* **campaign**, drive, push, movement, effort, struggle; battle, war, offensive.
verb *she likes crusading for the cause of the underdog:* **campaign**, fight, do battle, battle, take up arms, take up the cudgels, work, strive, struggle, agitate, lobby, champion, promote.

crusader noun **campaigner**, fighter, champion, advocate; reformer.

crush verb **1** *essential oils are released when the herbs are crushed:* **squash**, squeeze, press, compress; pulp, mash, macerate, mangle; flatten, trample on, tread on; informal squidge, splat; N. Amer. informal smush. **2** *your dress will get crushed:* **crease**, crumple, rumple, wrinkle, crinkle, scrunch up, ruck up; Brit. scrumple up. **3** *crush the biscuits with a rolling pin:* **pulverize**, pound, grind, break up, smash, crumble; mill. **4** *he crushed her in his arms:* **hug**, squeeze, hold tight, embrace, enfold. **5** *the new regime crushed all popular uprisings:* **suppress**, put down, quell, quash, stamp out, put an end to, overcome, overpower, defeat, triumph over, break, repress, subdue, extinguish. **6** *Alan was crushed by her words:* **mortify**, humiliate, abash, chagrin, deflate, demoralize, flatten, squash; devastate, shatter, put someone in their place; informal shoot down in flames, cut down to size, knock the stuffing out of.
noun **1** *the crush of people:* **crowd**, throng, horde, swarm, sea, mass, pack, press, mob. **2** (informal) *a teenage crush:* **infatuation**, obsession, love, passion; informal pash, puppy love, calf love.

crust noun *a crust of ice:* **covering**, layer, coating, cover, coat, sheet, thickness, film, skin, topping; encrustation, scab.

crusty adjective **1** *crusty French bread:* **crisp**, crispy, well baked; crumbly, brittle, friable. **2** *a crusty old man:* **irritable**, cantankerous, irascible, bad-tempered, ill-tempered, grumpy, grouchy, crotchety, short-tempered, tetchy, testy, crabby, curmudgeonly, peevish, cross, fractious, pettish, crabbed, prickly, waspish, peppery, cross-grained; informal snappish, snappy, chippy; Brit. informal stroppy, narky, ratty; N. Amer. informal cranky, ornery; Austral./NZ informal snaky.
– OPPOSITES soft, good-natured.

crux noun *the crux of the matter is that attitudes have changed:* **nub**, heart, essence,

central point, main point, core, centre, nucleus, kernel; informal bottom line.

cry verb **1** *Mandy started to cry:* **weep**, shed tears, sob, wail, cry one's eyes out, bawl, howl, snivel, whimper, squall, mewl, bleat; lament, grieve, mourn, keen; Scottish greet; informal boohoo, blub, blubber, turn on the waterworks; Brit. informal grizzle. **2** *'Wait!' he cried:* **call**, shout, exclaim, sing out, yell, shriek, scream, screech, bawl, bellow, roar, vociferate, squeal, yelp; informal holler.
– OPPOSITES laugh, whisper.
noun **1** *Leonora had a good cry:* **sob**, weep, crying fit. **2** *a cry of despair:* **call**, shout, exclamation, yell, shriek, scream, screech, bawl, bellow, roar, howl, yowl, squeal, yelp, interjection; informal holler. **3** *fund-raisers have issued a cry for help:* **appeal**, plea, entreaty, cry from the heart, cri de cœur.

crypt noun **tomb**, vault, mausoleum, burial chamber, sepulchre, catacomb, ossuary, undercroft.

cryptic adjective *his cryptic comments taxed her powers of comprehension:* **enigmatic**, mysterious, confusing, mystifying, perplexing, puzzling, obscure, abstruse, arcane, oracular, Delphic, ambiguous, elliptical, oblique; informal as clear as mud.
– OPPOSITES clear.

cub noun **1** *a lioness and her cubs:* baby; (**cubs**) **young**, offspring. **2** *a cub reporter:* **trainee**, apprentice, probationer, novice, tyro, learner, beginner; N. Amer. tenderfoot; informal rookie, newbie; N. Amer. informal greenhorn, probie.
– OPPOSITES veteran.

cubbyhole noun **small room**, booth, cubicle; den, snug; N. Amer. cubby.

cube noun **1** *a shape that was neither a cube nor a sphere:* **hexahedron**, cuboid, parallelepiped. **2** *a cube of soap:* **block**, lump, chunk, brick.

cuddle verb **1** *she picked up the baby and cuddled it:* **hug**, embrace, clasp, hold tight, hold/fold in one's arms. **2** *the pair were kissing and cuddling:* **embrace**, hug, caress, pet, fondle; informal canoodle, smooch. **3** *I cuddled up to him:* **snuggle**, nestle, curl, nuzzle, burrow against.

cuddly adjective *she was short and cuddly:* **huggable**, cuddlesome; plump, curvaceous, rounded, buxom, soft, warm; attractive, endearing, lovable; N. Amer. informal zaftig.

cudgel noun *a thick wooden cudgel:* **club**, bludgeon, stick, truncheon, baton, blackthorn, shillelagh, mace; N. Amer. blackjack, billy, nightstick; Brit. life preserver; Brit. informal cosh.
verb *she was cudgelled to death:* **bludgeon**, club, beat, batter, bash; Brit. informal cosh.

cue noun *he looked at his watch and Sylvie knew it was a cue for her to leave:* **signal**, sign, indication, prompt, reminder; nod, word, gesture.

cuff verb *Cullam cuffed him on the head:*

hit, strike, slap, smack, thump, beat, punch; informal clout, wallop, belt, whack, thwack, bash, clobber, bop, biff, sock; Brit. informal slosh; N. Amer. informal boff, slug.

■ **off the cuff** (informal) **1** *an off-the-cuff remark:* impromptu, extempore, ad lib; unrehearsed, unscripted, unprepared, improvised, spontaneous, unplanned. **2** *I spoke off the cuff:* without preparation, without rehearsal, impromptu, ad lib; informal off the top of one's head.

cuisine noun *French cuisine:* **cooking**, cookery; haute cuisine, cordon bleu, nouvelle cuisine.

cul-de-sac noun **no through road**, blind alley, dead end.

cull verb **1** *anecdotes culled from Greek history:* **select**, choose, pick, take, obtain, glean. **2** *he sees culling deer as a necessity:* **slaughter**, kill, destroy.

culminate verb *the festival culminated in a dramatic fire-walking ceremony:* **come to a climax**, come to a head, peak, climax, reach a pinnacle; build up to, lead up to; end with, finish with, conclude with.

culmination noun **climax**, pinnacle, peak, high point, highest point, height, high water mark, top, summit, crest, zenith, crowning moment, apotheosis, apex, apogee; consummation, completion, finish, conclusion.
– OPPOSITES nadir.

culpable adjective *I hold you personally culpable:* **to blame**, guilty, at fault, in the wrong, answerable, accountable, responsible, blameworthy, censurable.
– OPPOSITES innocent.

culprit noun *the police are doing all they can to catch the culprit:* **guilty party**, offender, wrongdoer, miscreant; criminal, malefactor, lawbreaker, felon, delinquent; informal baddy, crook.

cult noun **1** *a religious cult:* **sect**, denomination, group, movement, church, faith community, persuasion, body, faction. **2** *the cult of youth in Hollywood:* **obsession with**, fixation on, mania for, passion for, idolization of, devotion to, worship of, veneration of.

cultivate verb **1** *the peasants cultivated the land:* **till**, plough, dig, hoe, farm, work, fertilize, mulch. **2** *they were encouraged to cultivate basic food crops:* **grow**, raise, rear, plant, sow. **3** *Tessa tried to cultivate him:* **win someone's friendship**, woo, court, pay court to, keep sweet, curry favour with, ingratiate oneself with; informal get in someone's good books, butter up, suck up to; N. Amer. informal shine up to. **4** *he wants to cultivate his mind:* **improve**, better, refine, elevate; educate, train, develop, enrich.

cultivated adjective *a remarkably cultivated man:* **cultured**, educated, well read, civilized, enlightened, discerning, discriminating, refined, polished; sophisticated, urbane, cosmopolitan.

cultural adjective **1** *cultural differences:* **ethnic**, racial, folk; societal, lifestyle. **2** *cultural achievements:* **aesthetic**, artistic, intellectual; educational, edifying, civilizing.

culture noun **1** *20th-century popular culture:* **the arts**, the humanities, intellectual achievement; literature, music, painting, philosophy. **2** *a man of culture:* **intellectual/artistic awareness**, education, cultivation, enlightenment, discernment, discrimination, good taste, taste, refinement, polish, sophistication. **3** *Afro-Caribbean culture:* **civilization**, society, way of life, lifestyle; customs, traditions, heritage, habits, ways, mores, values. **4** *the culture of crops:* **cultivation**, farming; agriculture, husbandry, agronomy.

cultured adjective *a sensitive, cultured man:* **cultivated**, intellectually/artistically aware, artistic, enlightened, civilized, educated, well educated, well read, well informed, learned, knowledgeable, discerning, discriminating, refined, polished, sophisticated; informal arty.
– OPPOSITES ignorant.

culvert noun **channel**, conduit, watercourse, trough; drain, gutter.

cumbersome adjective **1** *a cumbersome diving suit:* **unwieldy**, unmanageable, awkward, clumsy, inconvenient, incommodious; bulky, large, heavy, hefty, weighty, burdensome; informal hulking, clunky. **2** *cumbersome procedures:* **complicated**, complex, involved, inefficient, unwieldy, slow.
– OPPOSITES manageable, straightforward.

cumulative adjective *the cumulative effect of two years of drought:* **increasing**, accumulative, growing, mounting; collective, aggregate, amassed; Brit. knock-on.

cunning adjective *a cunning scheme:* **crafty**, wily, artful, guileful, devious, sly, scheming, designing, calculating, Machiavellian; shrewd, astute, clever, canny; deceitful, deceptive, duplicitous; informal foxy.
– OPPOSITES honest.
noun *his political cunning:* **guile**, craftiness, deviousness, slyness, trickery, duplicity; shrewdness, astuteness.

cup noun **1** *a cup and saucer:* teacup, coffee cup, demitasse; mug, beaker; historical chalice. **2** *the winner was presented with a silver cup:* **trophy**, award, prize.

cupboard noun **cabinet**, sideboard, dresser, armoire, credenza, buffet; Brit. chiffonier; informal glory hole.

cupidity noun *he was anxious to defend himself from charges of cupidity:* **greed**, avarice, avariciousness, acquisitiveness, covetousness, rapacity, materialism, mercenariness, Mammonism; informal money-grubbing, an itching palm.
– OPPOSITES generosity.

curable adjective *most skin cancers are completely curable:* **remediable**, treatable, medicable, operable.

curative adjective *the curative properties of herbs:* **healing**, therapeutic, medicinal, remedial, corrective, restorative, tonic, health-giving.

curator noun **custodian**, keeper, conservator, guardian, caretaker, steward.

curb noun *a curb on public spending:* **restraint**, restriction, check, brake, rein, control, limitation, limit, constraint; informal crackdown.
▶ verb *he tried to curb his temper:* **restrain**, hold back/in, keep back, repress, suppress, fight back, bite back, keep in check, check, control, rein in, contain, bridle, subdue; informal keep a/the lid on.

curdle verb *take care not to let the soup boil or it will curdle:* **clot**, coagulate, congeal, solidify, thicken; turn, sour, ferment.

cure verb **1** *he was cured of the disease:* **heal**, restore to health, make well/better. **2** *economic equality cannot cure all social ills:* **rectify**, remedy, put/set right, right, fix, mend, repair, heal, make better; solve, sort out, be the answer/solution to; eliminate, end, put an end to. **3** *some farmers cured their own bacon:* **preserve**, smoke, salt, dry, pickle.
▶ noun **1** *a cure for cancer:* **remedy**, medicine, medication, medicament, antidote, antiserum; treatment, therapy. **2** *interest rate cuts are not the cure for the problem:* **solution**, answer, antidote, nostrum, panacea, cure-all; informal quick fix, magic bullet.

cure-all noun *the antibiotic was supposed to be the great cure-all:* **panacea**, cure for all ills, sovereign remedy, heal-all, nostrum; informal magic bullet.

curio noun **trinket**, knick-knack, bibelot, ornament, bauble; objet d'art, collector's item, object of virtu, rarity, curiosity; N. Amer. kickshaw.

curiosity noun **1** *his evasiveness roused my curiosity:* **interest**, spirit of inquiry, inquisitiveness. **2** *the shop is a treasure trove of curiosities:* **oddity**, curio, conversation piece, object of virtu, collector's item.

curious adjective **1** *she was curious to know what had happened:* **intrigued**, interested, eager/dying to know, agog; inquisitive. **2** *her curious behaviour:* **strange**, odd, peculiar, funny, unusual, bizarre, weird, eccentric, queer, unexpected, unfamiliar, extraordinary, abnormal, out of the ordinary, anomalous, surprising, incongruous, unconventional, unorthodox; informal offbeat; Brit. out of the common; Scottish unco; Brit. informal rum.
– OPPOSITES uninterested, ordinary.

curl verb **1** *smoke curled up from his cigarette:* **spiral**, coil, wreathe, twirl, swirl; wind, curve, bend, twist (and turn), loop, meander,

snake, corkscrew, zigzag. **2** *Ruth curled her arms around his neck:* **wind**, twine, entwine, wrap. **3** *she washed and curled my hair:* **crimp**, perm, tong, wave. **4** *they curled up together on the sofa:* **nestle**, snuggle, cuddle; N. Amer. snug down.
– OPPOSITES straighten
▶ noun **1** *the tangled curls of her hair:* **ringlet**, corkscrew, kink; wave, kiss-curl. **2** *a curl of smoke:* **spiral**, coil, twirl, swirl, twist, corkscrew, curlicue, helix.

curly adjective *curly hair:* **wavy**, curling, curled, ringlety, crimped, permed, frizzy, kinky, corkscrew.
– OPPOSITES straight.

currency noun **1** *foreign currency:* **money**, legal tender, cash, banknotes, notes, coins, coinage, specie; N. Amer. bills. **2** *a term which has gained new currency:* **prevalence**, circulation, exposure; acceptance, popularity.

current adjective **1** *current events:* **contemporary**, present-day, modern, present, contemporaneous; topical, in the news, live, burning. **2** *the idea is still current:* **prevalent**, prevailing, common, accepted, in circulation, circulating, on everyone's lips, popular, widespread. **3** *a current driving licence:* **valid**, usable, up to date. **4** *the current prime minister:* **incumbent**, present, in office, in power; reigning.
– OPPOSITES past, out of date, former.
▶ noun **1** *a current of air:* **flow**, stream, backdraught, slipstream; airstream, thermal, updraught, draught; undercurrent, undertow, tide. **2** *the current of human life:* **course**, progress, progression, flow, tide, movement. **3** *the current of opinion:* **trend**, drift, direction, tendency.

curriculum noun **syllabus**, course/programme of study, subjects, modules.

curse noun **1** *she put a curse on him:* **malediction**, the evil eye; N. Amer. hex; Irish cess; informal jinx; formal imprecation. **2** *the curse of racism:* **evil**, blight, scourge, plague, cancer, canker, poison. **3** *the curse of unemployment:* **affliction**, burden, cross to bear, bane. **4** *muffled curses:* **swear word**, expletive, oath, profanity, four-letter word, dirty word, obscenity, blasphemy; informal cuss, cuss word.
▶ verb **1** *it seemed as if the family had been cursed:* **put a curse on**, put the evil eye on, hoodoo, anathematize, damn; N. Amer. hex; informal jinx. **2** *she was cursed with feelings of inadequacy:* **afflict**, trouble, plague, bedevil. **3** *drivers cursed and sounded their horns:* **swear**, blaspheme, take the Lord's name in vain; informal cuss, turn the air blue, eff and blind.

cursed adjective *a cursed city:* **ill-fated**, damned, doomed, ill-starred; informal jinxed.

cursory adjective *a cursory glance at the figures:* **perfunctory**, desultory, casual, superficial, token; hasty, quick, hurried,

rapid, brief, passing, fleeting.
– OPPOSITES thorough.

curt adjective *his reply was curt:* **terse**, brusque, abrupt, clipped, blunt, short, monosyllabic, summary; snappish, sharp, tart; gruff, offhand, unceremonious, ungracious, rude, impolite, discourteous, uncivil; informal snappy.
– OPPOSITES expansive, polite.

curtail verb **1** *economic policies designed to curtail spending:* **reduce**, cut, cut down, decrease, lessen, pare down, trim, retrench; restrict, limit, curb, rein in/back; informal slash. **2** *his visit was curtailed:* **shorten**, cut short, truncate.
– OPPOSITES increase, lengthen.

curtain noun *he drew the curtains:* **hanging**, screen, blind; N. Amer. drape.
verb *the bed was curtained off from the rest of the room:* **conceal**, hide, screen, shield; separate, isolate.

curtsy verb *she curtsied to the king:* **bend one's knee**, drop/bob a curtsy, genuflect.
noun *she made a curtsy:* **bob**, genuflection, obeisance.

curvaceous adjective *a curvaceous young woman:* **shapely**, voluptuous, sexy, full-figured, buxom, full-bosomed, bosomy, Junoesque; cuddly; informal curvy, well endowed, pneumatic, busty.
– OPPOSITES skinny.

curve noun *the serpentine curves of the river:* **bend**, turn, loop, curl, twist, hook; arc, arch, bow, half-moon, undulation, curvature.
verb *the road curved back on itself:* **bend**, turn, loop, wind, meander, undulate, snake, spiral, twist, coil, curl; arc, arch.

curved adjective *birds with long curved bills:* **bent**, arched, bowed, crescent, curving, wavy, sinuous, serpentine, meandering, undulating, curvilinear, curvy.
– OPPOSITES straight.

cushion noun *a cushion against inflation:* **protection**, buffer, shield, defence, bulwark.
verb **1** *she cushioned her head on her arms:* **support**, cradle, prop (up), rest. **2** *to cushion the blow, wages and pensions were increased:* **soften**, lessen, diminish, decrease, mitigate, temper, allay, alleviate, take the edge off, dull, deaden. **3** *residents are cushioned from the outside world:* **protect**, shield, shelter, cocoon.

custodian noun **curator**, keeper, conservator, guardian, overseer, superintendent; caretaker, steward, protector.

custody noun *the parent who has custody of the child:* **care**, guardianship, charge, keeping, safe keeping, wardship, responsibility, protection, tutelage; custodianship, trusteeship.
■ **in custody** in prison, in jail, imprisoned, incarcerated, locked up, under lock and key, interned, detained; on remand; informal behind bars, doing time, inside; Brit. informal banged up.

custom noun **1** *his unfamiliarity with the local customs:* **tradition**, practice, usage, observance, way, convention, formality, ceremony, ritual; shibboleth, sacred cow, unwritten rule; mores. **2** *it is our custom to visit the Lake District in October:* **habit**, practice, routine, way, wont; policy, rule. **3** (Brit.) *if you keep me waiting I will take my custom elsewhere:* **business**, patronage, trade.

customarily adverb *these discussions customarily take place in the evening:* **usually**, traditionally, normally, as a rule, generally, ordinarily, commonly; habitually, routinely.
– OPPOSITES occasionally.

customary adjective **1** *customary social practices:* **usual**, traditional, normal, conventional, familiar, accepted, routine, established, time-honoured, regular, prevailing. **2** *her customary good sense:* **usual**, accustomed, habitual, wonted.
– OPPOSITES unusual.

customer noun **consumer**, buyer, purchaser, patron, client; shopper; Brit. informal punter.

customs plural noun. See TAX noun sense 1.

cut verb **1** *the knife slipped and cut his finger:* **gash**, slash, lacerate, sever, slit, pierce, penetrate, wound, injure; scratch, graze, nick, snick, incise, score; lance. **2** *cut the pepper into small pieces:* **chop**, cut up, slice, dice, cube, mince; carve; N. Amer. hash. **3** *cut back the new growth to about half its length:* **trim**, snip, clip, crop, barber, shear, shave; pare; prune, pollard, poll, lop, dock; mow. **4** *I went to cut some flowers:* **pick**, pluck, gather. **5** *lettering had been cut into the stonework:* **carve**, engrave, incise, etch, score; chisel, whittle. **6** *the government cut public expenditure:* **reduce**, cut back/down on, decrease, lessen, retrench, trim, slim down; rationalize, downsize, slenderize; mark down, discount, lower; informal slash. **7** *the text has been substantially cut:* **shorten**, abridge, condense, abbreviate, truncate; edit; bowdlerize, expurgate. **8** *you need to cut at least ten lines per page:* **delete**, remove, take out, excise, blue-pencil. **9** *oil supplies to the area had been cut:* **discontinue**, break off, suspend, interrupt; stop, end, put an end to. **10** *the point where the line cuts the vertical axis:* **cross**, intersect, bisect; meet, join.
noun **1** *a cut on his jaw:* **gash**, slash, laceration, incision, wound, injury; scratch, graze, nick, snick. **2** *a cut of beef:* **joint**, piece, section. **3** *his hair was in need of a cut:* **haircut**, trim, clip, crop. **4** *he followed this with the unkindest cut of all:* **insult**, slight, affront, slap in the face, jibe, barb, cutting remark; informal put-down, dig. **5** *a cut in interest rates:* **reduction**, cutback, decrease, lessening; N. Amer. rollback. **6** *the elegant cut*

of his jacket: **style**, design; tailoring, lines, fit.

■ **cut back** *companies cut back on foreign investment:* reduce, cut, cut down on, decrease, lessen, retrench, economize on, trim, slim down, scale down; rationalize, downsize, pull/draw in one's horns, tighten one's belt; informal slash.

■ **cut someone/something down 1** *24 hectares of trees were cut down:* fell, chop down, hack down, saw down, hew. **2** *he was cut down in his prime:* kill, slaughter, shoot down, mow down, gun down; informal take out, blow away.

■ **cut and dried** definite, decided, settled, explicit, specific, precise, unambiguous, clear-cut, unequivocal, black and white, hard and fast.

■ **cut in** interrupt, butt in, break in, interject, interpose, chime in; Brit. informal chip in.

■ **cut someone/something off 1** *they cut off his finger:* sever, chop off, hack off; amputate. **2** *oil and gas supplies were cut off:* discontinue, break off, disconnect, suspend; stop, end, bring to an end. **3** *a community cut off from the mainland by the flood waters:* isolate, separate, keep apart; seclude, closet, cloister, sequester.

■ **cut out** *both the engines cut out:* stop working, stop, fail, give out, break down; informal die, give up the ghost, conk out; Brit. informal pack up.

■ **cut someone/something out 1** *cut out all the diseased wood:* remove, take out, excise, extract; snip out, clip out. **2** *it's best to cut out alcohol altogether:* give up, refrain from, abstain from, go without; informal quit, leave off, pack in, lay off, knock off. **3** *his mother cut him out of her will:* exclude, leave out, omit, eliminate.

■ **cut something short** *they decided to cut short their holiday:* break off, shorten, truncate, curtail, terminate, end, stop, abort, bring to an untimely end.

■ **cut someone short** *Peter cut him short:* interrupt, cut off, butt in on, break in on.

cutback noun *cutbacks in defence spending:* **reduction**, cut, decrease; economy, saving; N. Amer. rollback.
– OPPOSITES increase.

cute adjective *a picture of a cute kitten:* **endearing**, adorable, lovable, sweet, lovely, appealing, engaging, delightful, dear, darling, winning, winsome, attractive, pretty; informal cutesy, twee; Brit. informal dinky.

cut-price adjective *cut-price footwear:* **cheap**, marked down, reduced, on (special) offer, discount; N. Amer. cut-rate.

cut-throat adjective *cut-throat competition between rival firms:* **ruthless**, merciless, fierce, intense, aggressive, dog-eat-dog.

cutting noun **1** *a newspaper cutting:* **clipping**, clip, snippet; article, piece, column, paragraph. **2** *plant cuttings:* **scion**, slip; graft. **3** *fabric cuttings:* **piece**, bit, fragment; trimming.
▶ adjective **1** *a cutting remark:* **hurtful**, wounding, barbed, pointed, scathing, acerbic, mordant, caustic, acid, sarcastic, sardonic, snide, spiteful, malicious, mean, nasty, cruel, unkind; informal bitchy, catty; Brit. informal sarky; N. Amer. informal snarky. **2** *cutting winter winds:* **icy**, icy-cold, freezing, arctic, Siberian, glacial, bitter, chilling, chilly, chill; biting, piercing, penetrating, raw, keen, sharp.
– OPPOSITES friendly, warm.

cycle noun **1** *the cycle of birth, death, and rebirth:* **round**, rotation; pattern, rhythm. **2** *the painting is one of a cycle of seven:* **series**, sequence, succession, run; set. **3** *cycles may be hired from the station.* See BICYCLE.

cyclical adjective *the cyclical fluctuations in demand:* **recurrent**, recurring, regular, repeated; periodic, seasonal, circular.

cyclone noun **hurricane**, typhoon, tropical storm, storm, tornado, windstorm, whirlwind, tempest; Austral. willy-willy; N. Amer. informal twister.

cynic noun *some cynics thought the controversy was all a publicity stunt:* **sceptic**, doubter, doubting Thomas; pessimist, prophet of doom, doomsayer, Cassandra; informal doom (and gloom) merchant.
– OPPOSITES idealist.

cynical adjective *she was cynical about men:* **sceptical**, doubtful, distrustful, suspicious, disbelieving; pessimistic, negative, world-weary, disillusioned, disenchanted, jaundiced, sardonic.
– OPPOSITES idealistic.

cynicism noun **scepticism**, doubt, distrust, mistrust, suspicion, disbelief; pessimism, negativity, world-weariness, disenchantment.
– OPPOSITES idealism.

cyst noun **growth**, lump; abscess, wen, boil, carbuncle.

Dd

d

dab verb *she dabbed disinfectant on the cut:* **pat**, press, touch, blot, mop, swab; daub, apply, wipe, stroke.
noun **1** *a dab of glue:* **drop**, spot, smear, splash, speck, taste, trace, touch, hint, bit; informal smidgen, tad, lick. **2** *apply concealer with light dabs:* **pat**, touch, blot, wipe.

dabble verb **1** *they dabbled their feet in rock pools:* **splash**, dip, paddle, trail; immerse. **2** *he dabbled in politics:* **toy with**, dip into, flirt with, tinker with, trifle with, play with, dally with.

dabbler noun *he was a dabbler in psychology:* **amateur**, dilettante, layman, layperson; tinkerer, trifler.
– OPPOSITES professional.

daft adjective (Brit. informal) **1** *a daft idea:* **absurd**, preposterous, ridiculous, ludicrous, farcical, laughable; idiotic, stupid, foolish, silly, inane, fatuous, hare-brained, half-baked; informal crazy, cockeyed; Brit. informal barmy. **2** *are you daft?* **simple-minded**, stupid, idiotic, slow, witless, feeble-minded, empty-headed, vacuous, vapid; unhinged, insane, mad; informal thick, dim, dopey, dumb, dim-witted, half-witted, birdbrained, pea-brained, slow on the uptake, soft in the head, brain-dead, not all there, touched, crazy, mental, nuts, batty, bonkers; Brit. informal potty, not the full shilling, barmy, crackers; N. Amer. informal dumb-ass. **3** *she's daft about him:* **infatuated with**, enamoured of, smitten by, besotted by, very fond of; informal crazy, mad, nuts; Brit. informal potty.
– OPPOSITES sensible.

daily adjective *a daily event:* **everyday**, day-to-day, quotidian, diurnal, circadian.
adverb *the museum is open daily:* **every day**, once a day, day after day, diurnally.

dainty adjective **1** *a dainty china cup:* **delicate**, fine, neat, elegant, exquisite; Brit. informal dinky. **2** *a dainty morsel:* **tasty**, delicious, choice, palatable, luscious, mouth-watering, delectable, toothsome; appetizing, inviting, tempting; informal scrumptious, yummy, scrummy, finger-licking, moreish. **3** *a dainty eater:* **fastidious**, fussy, finicky, finical, faddish; particular, discriminating; informal choosy, pernickety, picky; Brit. informal faddy.
– OPPOSITES unwieldy, unpalatable, undiscriminating.
noun *home-made dainties:* **delicacy**, titbit,

fancy, luxury, treat; nibble, savoury, appetizer, confection, bonbon; informal goody.

dais noun **platform**, stage, podium, rostrum, stand, apron; soapbox, stump.

dale noun **valley**, vale; hollow, basin, gully, gorge, ravine; Brit. dene, combe; N. English clough; Scottish glen, strath.

dally verb **1** *don't dally on the way to work:* **dawdle**, delay, loiter, linger, waste time; lag, trail, straggle, fall behind; amble, meander, drift; informal dilly-dally. **2** *he likes dallying with film stars:* **trifle**, toy, amuse oneself, flirt, play fast and loose, philander, carry on; informal play around.
– OPPOSITES hurry.

dam noun *the dam burst:* **barrage**, barrier, wall, embankment, barricade, obstruction.
verb *the river was dammed:* **block (up)**, obstruct, bung up, close.

damage noun **1** *did the thieves do any damage?* **harm**, destruction, vandalism; injury, impairment, desecration, vitiation, detriment; ruin, havoc, devastation. **2** *she won £4,300 damages:* **compensation**, recompense, restitution, redress, reparation(s); indemnification, indemnity; N. Amer. informal comp.
verb *the parcel had been damaged:* **harm**, deface, mutilate, mangle, impair, injure, disfigure, vandalize; tamper with, sabotage; ruin, destroy, wreck; N. Amer. informal trash.
– OPPOSITES repair.

damaging adjective *new cars are less damaging to the environment:* **harmful**, detrimental, injurious, hurtful, inimical, dangerous, destructive, ruinous, deleterious; bad, malign, adverse, undesirable, prejudicial, unfavourable; unhealthy, unwholesome.
– OPPOSITES beneficial.

damn verb **1** *they were all damning him:* **curse**, put the evil eye on, hoodoo; anathematize; N. Amer. hex; informal jinx. **2** *we are not going to damn the new product:* **condemn**, censure, criticize, attack, denounce, revile; find fault with, give something a bad press, deprecate, disparage; informal slam, lay into, blast; Brit. informal slate, slag off, have a go at.
– OPPOSITES bless, praise.
noun (informal) *I don't care a damn:* **jot**, whit, iota, rap, scrap, bit; informal hoot, two hoots.

damnable adjective **1** *a damnable nuisance:*

unpleasant, disagreeable, objectionable, horrible, horrid, awful, nasty, dreadful, terrible; annoying, irritating, maddening, exasperating; hateful, detestable, loathsome, abominable; Brit. informal beastly. **2** *suicide was thought damnable:* **sinful**, wicked, evil, iniquitous, heinous, base, execrable.

damnation noun **condemnation to hell**, eternal punishment, perdition, doom, hellfire; curse, anathema; N. Amer. hex.

damned adjective **1** *damned souls:* **cursed**, doomed, lost, condemned to hell; anathematized. **2** (informal) *this damned car won't start:* **blasted**, damn, damnable, flaming, confounded, rotten, wretched; Brit. informal blessed, flipping, blinking, blooming, bloody, bleeding, ruddy.

damning adjective *in the face of such damning evidence Jakobs had little defence:* **incriminating**, condemnatory, damnatory; damaging, derogatory; conclusive, strong.

damp adjective *her hair was damp:* **moist**, moistened, wettish, dampened, dampish; humid, steamy, muggy, clammy, sweaty, sticky, dank, moisture-laden, wet, wetted, rainy, drizzly, showery, misty, foggy, vaporous, dewy.
– OPPOSITES dry.
noun *the damp in the air:* **moisture**, dampness, humidity, wetness, wet, water, condensation, steam, vapour; clamminess, dankness; rain, dew, drizzle, precipitation, spray; perspiration, sweat.
– OPPOSITES dryness.
verb **1** *sweat damped his hair.* See DAMPEN sense 1. **2** *nothing damped my enthusiasm.* See DAMPEN sense 2.

dampen verb **1** *the rain dampened her face:* **moisten**, damp, wet, dew, water. **2** *nothing could dampen her enthusiasm:* **lessen**, decrease, diminish, reduce, moderate, damp, put a damper on, throw cold water on, cool, discourage; suppress, extinguish, quench, stifle, curb, limit, check, restrain, inhibit, deter.
– OPPOSITES dry, heighten.

damper noun *this will put a damper on the liberal agenda:* **curb**, check, restraint, restriction, limit, limitation, constraint, rein, brake, control, impediment; chill, pall, gloom.

dampness noun. See DAMP noun.

dance verb **1** *he danced with her:* sway, trip, twirl, whirl, pirouette, gyrate; informal bop, disco, shake a leg, hoof it, cut a rug, trip the light fantastic; N. Amer. informal get down. **2** *little girls danced round me:* **caper**, cavort, frisk, frolic, skip, prance, gambol, jig; leap, jump, hop, bounce. **3** *flames danced in the fireplace:* **flicker**, leap, dart, play, flit, quiver; twinkle, shimmer.
noun *the school dance:* **ball**, discotheque; masquerade; N. Amer. prom, hoedown; informal disco, hop, bop.

dancer noun danseur, danseuse; informal bopper, hoofer.

dandle verb *he dandled his two-year-old son on his knee:* **bounce**, jiggle, dance, rock.

dandy noun *he became something of a dandy:* **fop**, man about town, bright young thing, glamour boy, rake; informal sharp dresser, snappy dresser, trendy, dude, pretty boy.
adjective (N. Amer. informal) *our trip was dandy.* See EXCELLENT.

danger noun **1** *there's an element of danger in the job:* **peril**, hazard, risk, jeopardy; perilousness, riskiness, precariousness, uncertainty, instability, insecurity. **2** *he is a danger to society:* **menace**, hazard, threat, risk. **3** *a serious danger of fire:* **possibility**, chance, risk, probability, likelihood, fear, prospect.
– OPPOSITES safety.

dangerous adjective **1** *a dangerous animal:* **menacing**, threatening, treacherous; savage, wild, vicious, murderous, desperate. **2** *dangerous wiring:* **hazardous**, perilous, risky, high-risk, unsafe, unpredictable, precarious, insecure, touch-and-go, chancy, treacherous; informal dicey, hairy; Brit. informal dodgy.
– OPPOSITES harmless, safe.

dangle verb **1** *a chain dangled from his belt:* **hang (down)**, droop, swing, sway, wave, trail, stream. **2** *he dangled the keys:* **wave**, swing, jiggle, brandish, flourish. **3** *he dangled money in front of the locals:* **offer**, hold out; entice someone with, tempt someone with.

dangling adjective **hanging**, drooping, droopy, suspended, pendulous, pendent, trailing, flowing, tumbling.

dank adjective *he shivered as he entered the dank cellar:* **damp**, musty, chilly, clammy, moist, wet, unaired, humid.
– OPPOSITES dry.

dapper adjective *Pablo looked very dapper in his best clothes:* **smart**, spruce, trim, debonair, neat, well dressed, besuited, well groomed, well turned out, elegant, chic, dashing; informal snazzy, snappy, natty, sharp; N. Amer. informal spiffy, fly.
– OPPOSITES scruffy.

dapple verb *fine rays of sunlight dappled the surface of a lake:* **dot**, spot, fleck, streak, speck, speckle, mottle, marble.

dappled adjective *the dappled purple carpet of flowers:* **speckled**, blotched, blotchy, spotted, spotty, dotted, mottled, marbled, flecked, freckled, piebald, pied, brindle, pinto, tabby, patchy, variegated; informal splotchy, splodgy.

dare verb **1** *nobody dared to say a word:* **be brave enough**, have the courage; venture, have the nerve, have the temerity, be so bold as, have the audacity; risk, hazard, take the liberty of; N. Amer. take a flyer; informal stick one's neck out, go out on a limb. **2** *she dared him to go:* **challenge**, defy, invite, bid, provoke, goad; throw down the gauntlet.

d

noun *she accepted the dare:* **challenge**, provocation, goad; gauntlet, invitation.

daredevil noun *a young daredevil crashed his car:* **madcap**, hothead, adventurer, exhibitionist, swashbuckler; stuntman; Brit. tearaway; informal show-off.
adjective *a daredevil skydiver:* **daring**, bold, audacious, intrepid, fearless, madcap, death-or-glory, dauntless; heedless, reckless, rash, impulsive, impetuous, foolhardy, incautious, imprudent; Brit. tearaway, harum-scarum.
– OPPOSITES cowardly, cautious.

daring adjective *a daring attack:* **bold**, audacious, intrepid, venturesome, fearless, brave, unafraid, undaunted, dauntless, valiant, valorous, heroic, dashing; madcap, rash, reckless, heedless; informal gutsy, spunky.
noun *his sheer daring:* **boldness**, audacity, temerity, fearlessness, intrepidity, bravery, courage, valour, heroism, pluck, spirit, mettle; recklessness, rashness, foolhardiness; informal nerve, guts, spunk, grit; Brit. informal bottle; N. Amer. informal moxie, sand.

dark adjective **1** *a dark night:* **black**, pitch-black, jet-black, inky; unlit, unilluminated; starless, moonless; dingy, gloomy, dusky, shadowy, shady. **2** *a dark secret:* **mysterious**, secret, hidden, concealed, veiled, covert, clandestine; enigmatic, arcane, esoteric, obscure, abstruse, impenetrable, incomprehensible, cryptic. **3** *dark hair:* **brunette**, dark brown, chestnut, sable, jet-black, ebony. **4** *dark skin:* **swarthy**, dusky, olive, black, ebony; tanned, bronzed. **5** *the dark days of the war:* **tragic**, disastrous, calamitous, catastrophic, cataclysmic; dire, awful, terrible, dreadful, horrible, horrendous, atrocious, nightmarish, harrowing; wretched, woeful. **6** *my mind is full of dark thoughts:* **gloomy**, dismal, pessimistic, negative, downbeat, bleak, grim, fatalistic, black, sombre; despairing, despondent, hopeless, cheerless, lugubrious, Eeyorish, melancholy, glum, grave, morose, mournful, doleful. **7** *Matthew flashed a dark look at her:* **moody**, brooding, sullen, dour, scowling, glowering, angry, forbidding, threatening, ominous.
– OPPOSITES bright, blonde, pale, happy.
noun **1** *he's afraid of the dark:* **darkness**, blackness, gloom, murkiness, shadow, shade; dusk, twilight, gloaming. **2** *she went out after dark:* **night**, night-time, darkness; nightfall, evening, twilight, sunset.
– OPPOSITES light, day.

darken verb **1** *the sky darkened:* **blacken**, grow dark, dim, cloud over, lour; shade, fog. **2** *his mood darkened:* **blacken**, become angry, become annoyed; sadden, become gloomy, become unhappy, become depressed, become dejected, become dispirited, become troubled.

darkness noun **1** *lights shone in the darkness:*

dark, blackness, gloom, dimness, murkiness, shadow, shade; dusk, twilight, gloaming. **2** *darkness fell:* **night**, night-time, dark.

darling noun **1** *good night, darling:* **dear**, dearest, love, lover, sweetheart, sweet, beloved; informal honey, angel, pet, sweetie, sugar, babe, baby, poppet, treasure. **2** *the darling of the media:* **favourite**, pet, idol, hero, heroine; informal blue-eyed boy/girl.
adjective **1** *his darling wife:* **dear**, dearest, precious, adored, loved, beloved, cherished, treasured, esteemed, worshipped. **2** *a darling little hat:* **adorable**, appealing, charming, cute, sweet, enchanting, bewitching, endearing, dear, delightful, lovely, beautiful, attractive, gorgeous, fetching; Scottish & N. English bonny.

darn verb *he was darning his socks:* **mend**, repair, reinforce; sew up, stitch, patch.

dart noun **1** *a poisoned dart:* **arrow**, flechette, bolt; missile, projectile. **2** *she made a dart for the door:* **dash**, rush, run, bolt, break, start, charge, sprint, bound, leap, dive; scurry, scamper, scramble.
verb **1** *Karl darted across the road:* **dash**, rush, tear, run, bolt, fly, shoot, charge, race, sprint, bound, leap, dive, gallop, scurry, scamper, scramble; informal scoot. **2** *he darted a glance at her:* **direct**, cast, throw, shoot, send, flash.

dash verb **1** *he dashed home:* **rush**, race, run, sprint, bolt, dart, gallop, career, charge, shoot, hurtle, hare, fly, speed, zoom, scurry, scuttle, scamper; informal tear, belt, pelt, scoot, zip, whip, hotfoot it, leg it; Brit. informal bomb, go like the clappers; N. Amer. informal barrel. **2** *he dashed the glass to the ground:* **hurl**, smash, crash, slam, throw, toss, fling, pitch, cast, project, propel, send; informal chuck, heave, sling, bung; N. Amer. informal peg. **3** *rain dashed against the walls:* **be hurled**, crash, smash; batter, strike, beat, pound, lash. **4** *her hopes were dashed:* **shatter**, destroy, wreck, ruin, crush, devastate, demolish, blight, overturn, scotch, spoil, frustrate, thwart, check; informal banjax, do for, blow a hole in, put paid to; Brit. informal scupper.
– OPPOSITES dawdle, raise.
noun **1** *they made a dash for the door:* **rush**, race, run, sprint, bolt, dart, leap, charge, bound, break; scramble. **2** *the soup needs a dash of salt:* **pinch**, touch, sprinkle, taste, spot, drop, dab, speck, smattering, sprinkling, splash, bit, modicum, little; informal smidgen, tad, lick. **3** *he led off with such dash:* **verve**, style, flamboyance, gusto, zest, confidence, self-assurance, elan, flair, vigour, vivacity, sparkle, brio, panache, éclat, vitality, dynamism; informal pizzazz, pep, oomph.

dashing adjective **1** *a dashing pilot:* **debonair**, devil-may-care, raffish, sporty, spirited, lively, dazzling, energetic, animated, exuberant, flamboyant, dynamic, bold, intrepid, daring, adventurous, plucky, swashbuckling; romantic, attractive, gallant. **2** *he looked exceptionally dashing:* **stylish**, smart, elegant, chic, dapper, spruce, trim, debonair; fashionable, modish, voguish; informal trendy, with it, hip, sharp, snazzy, classy, natty, swish; N. Amer. informal fly, spiffy.

data noun *there is a lack of data on the drug's effect on humans:* **facts**, figures, statistics, details, particulars, specifics; information, intelligence, material, input; informal info, gen.

date noun **1** *the only date he has to remember:* **day (of the month)**, occasion, time; year; anniversary. **2** *a later date is suggested for this bridge:* **age**, time, period, era, epoch, century, decade, year. **3** *a lunch date:* **appointment**, meeting, engagement, rendezvous, assignation; commitment. **4** (informal) *have you got a date for tonight?* **partner**, escort, girlfriend, boyfriend; informal steady, bird, fella.
▸verb **1** *the sculpture can be dated accurately:* **assign a date to**, ascertain the date of, put a date on. **2** *the building dates from the 16th century:* **was made in**, was built in, originates in, comes from, belongs to, goes back to. **3** *the best films don't date:* **become old-fashioned**, become outmoded, become dated, show its age. **4** (informal) *he's dating Jill:* **go out with**, take out, go around with, be involved with, see, woo; informal go steady with.
■ **to date** so far, thus far, yet, as yet, up to now, till now, until now, up to the present (time), hitherto.

dated adjective *the graphics are looking a little dated:* **old-fashioned**, outdated, outmoded, passé, behind the times, archaic, obsolete, antiquated; unfashionable, unstylish; crusty, olde worlde, prehistoric, antediluvian; informal old hat, out, out of the ark.
– OPPOSITES modern.

daub verb *he daubed a rock with paint:* **smear**, bedaub, plaster, splash, spatter, splatter, cake, cover, smother, coat.
▸noun *daubs of paint:* **smear**, smudge, splash, blot, spot, patch, blotch; informal splodge, splotch.

daunt verb *it will take more than December sleet and gales to daunt the crews:* **discourage**, deter, demoralize, put off, dishearten, dispirit; intimidate, abash, take aback, throw, cow, overawe, awe, frighten, scare, unman, dismay, disconcert, discompose, perturb, unsettle, unnerve; throw off balance; informal rattle, faze, shake up.
– OPPOSITES hearten.

dauntless adjective *an ambitious and dauntless woman who truckled to no man:* **fearless**, determined, resolute, indomitable, intrepid, doughty, plucky, spirited, mettlesome; undaunted, undismayed, unflinching, unshrinking, bold, audacious, valiant, brave, courageous, daring; informal gutsy, spunky, feisty.

dawdle verb **1** *they dawdled over breakfast:*

linger, dally, take one's time, be slow, waste time, idle, delay, procrastinate, stall; informal dilly-dally. **2** *Ruth dawdled home:* **amble**, stroll, trail, walk slowly, move at a snail's pace; informal mosey, tootle; Brit. informal pootle, mooch.
– OPPOSITES hurry.

dawn noun **1** *we got up at dawn:* **daybreak**, sunrise, first light, daylight, cockcrow; first thing in the morning; N. Amer. sunup. **2** *the dawn of civilization:* **beginning**, start, birth, inception, origination, genesis, emergence, advent, appearance, arrival, dawning, rise, origin, onset; unfolding, development, infancy; informal kick-off.
– OPPOSITES dusk, end.
▸verb **1** *Thursday dawned crisp and sunny:* **begin**, break, arrive, emerge. **2** *a bright new future has dawned:* **begin**, start, commence, be born, appear, arrive, emerge; arise, rise, break, unfold, develop. **3** *the reality dawned on him:* **occur to**, come to, strike, hit, enter someone's mind, register with, enter someone's consciousness, cross someone's mind, suggest itself.
– OPPOSITES end.

day noun **1** *I stayed for a day:* **twenty-four-hour period**, twenty-four hours. **2** *enjoy the beach during the day:* **daytime**, daylight; waking hours. **3** *the leading architect of the day:* **period**, time, age, era, generation. **4** *in his day he had great influence:* **heyday**, prime, time; peak, height, zenith, ascendancy; youth, springtime, salad days.
– OPPOSITES night, decline.
■ **day after day** repeatedly, again and again, over and over (again), time and (time) again, frequently, often, time after time; {day in, day out}, night and day, all the time; persistently, recurrently, constantly, continuously, continually, relentlessly, regularly, habitually, unfailingly, always; N. Amer. oftentimes; informal 24-7.
■ **day by day 1** *day by day they were forced to retreat:* gradually, slowly, progressively; bit by bit, inch by inch, little by little, inchmeal. **2** *they follow the news day by day:* daily, every day, day after day; diurnally.
■ **day in, day out**. See DAY AFTER DAY.

daybreak noun *they rested for the night and journeyed on at daybreak:* **dawn**, crack of dawn, sunrise, first light, first thing in the morning, cockcrow; daylight; N. Amer. sunup.
– OPPOSITES nightfall.

daydream noun **1** *she was lost in a daydream:* **reverie**, trance, fantasy, vision, fancy, brown study; inattentiveness, wool-gathering, preoccupation, absorption, self-absorption, absent-mindedness, abstraction. **2** *a big house was one of her daydreams:* **dream**, pipe dream, fantasy, castle in the air, castle in Spain, fond hope; wishful thinking; informal pie in the sky.
▸verb *stop daydreaming and get on with something useful!* **dream**, muse, stare into

d

d

space; fantasize, be in cloud cuckoo land, build castles in the air, build castles in Spain.

daydreamer noun **dreamer**, fantasist, fantasizer, romantic, wishful thinker, idealist; visionary, theorizer, utopian, Walter Mitty.

daylight noun **1** *do the test in daylight:* **natural light**, sunlight. **2** *she only went there in daylight:* **daytime**, day; broad daylight. **3** *police moved in at daylight:* **dawn**, daybreak, break of day, crack of dawn, sunrise, first light, first thing in the morning, early morning, cockcrow; N. Amer. sunup.
– OPPOSITES darkness, night-time, nightfall.
■ **see daylight 1** *Sam finally saw daylight:* **understand**, comprehend, realize, see the light; informal cotton on, catch on, latch on, get the picture, get the message, get it; Brit. informal twig. **2** *his project never saw daylight:* **be completed**, be accomplished, see (the) light of day.

day-to-day adjective *day-to-day expenditure such as food, household goods, and petrol:* **regular**, everyday, daily, routine, habitual, frequent, normal, standard, usual, typical.

daze verb **1** *he was dazed by his fall:* **stun**, stupefy; knock unconscious, knock out; informal knock the stuffing out of. **2** *she was dazed by the revelations:* **astound**, amaze, astonish, startle, dumbfound, stupefy, overwhelm, stagger, shock, confound, bewilder, take aback, nonplus, shake up; informal flabbergast, knock sideways, bowl over, blow away; Brit. informal knock for six.
noun *she is in a daze:* **stupor**, trance, haze; spin, whirl, muddle, jumble.

dazzle verb **1** *she was dazzled by the headlights:* **blind temporarily**, deprive of sight. **2** *I was dazzled by the exhibition:* **overwhelm**, overcome, impress, move, stir, affect, touch, awe, overawe, leave speechless, take someone's breath away; spellbind, hypnotize; informal bowl over, blow away, knock out.
noun **1** *dazzle can be a problem to sensitive eyes:* **glare**, brightness, brilliance, shimmer, radiance, shine. **2** *the dazzle of the limelight:* **sparkle**, glitter, brilliance, glory, splendour, magnificence, glamour; attraction, lure, allure, draw, appeal; informal razzle-dazzle, razzmatazz.

dazzling adjective **1** *the sunlight was dazzling:* **bright**, blinding, glaring, brilliant. **2** *a dazzling performance:* **impressive**, remarkable, extraordinary, outstanding, exceptional; incredible, amazing, astonishing, phenomenal, breathtaking, thrilling; excellent, wonderful, magnificent, marvellous, superb, first-rate, superlative, matchless; informal mind-blowing, out of this world, fabulous, fab, super, sensational, ace, A1, cool, awesome; Brit. informal smashing, brill.

dead adjective **1** *my parents are dead:* **passed on/away**, expired, departed, gone,

no more; late, lost, lamented; perished, fallen, slain, slaughtered, killed, murdered; lifeless, extinct; informal (as) dead as a doornail, six feet under, pushing up daisies; formal deceased; euphemistic with God, asleep. **2** *patches of dead ground:* **barren**, lifeless, bare, desolate, sterile. **3** *a dead language:* **obsolete**, extinct, defunct, disused, abandoned, discarded, superseded, vanished, forgotten; archaic, antiquated, ancient. **4** *the phone was dead:* **not working**, out of order, inoperative, inactive, in disrepair, broken, malfunctioning, defective; informal kaput, conked out, on the blink, bust; Brit. informal knackered. **5** *a dead leg:* **numb**, numbed, deadened, desensitized, unfeeling; paralysed, crippled, incapacitated, immobilized, frozen. **6** *she has dead eyes:* **emotionless**, unemotional, unfeeling, impassive, unresponsive, indifferent, dispassionate, inexpressive, wooden, stony, cold; deadpan, flat; blank, vacant. **7** *his affection for her was dead:* **extinguished**, quashed, stifled; finished, over, gone, no more; ancient history. **8** *a dead town:* **uneventful**, uninteresting, unexciting, uninspiring, dull, boring, flat, quiet, sleepy, slow, lacklustre, lifeless; informal one-horse, dead-and-alive; N. Amer. informal dullsville.
– OPPOSITES alive, fertile, modern, lively.
adverb **1** *he was dead serious:* **completely**, absolutely, totally, utterly, deadly, perfectly, entirely, quite, thoroughly; definitely, certainly, positively, categorically, unquestionably, undoubtedly, surely; in every way, one hundred per cent. **2** *flares were seen dead ahead:* **directly**, exactly, precisely, immediately, right, straight, due, squarely; informal bang, slap bang.

deaden verb **1** *surgeons tried to deaden the pain:* **numb**, dull, blunt, suppress; alleviate, mitigate, diminish, reduce, lessen, ease, soothe, relieve, assuage. **2** *the wood panelling deadened any noise:* **muffle**, mute, smother, stifle, dull, damp (down); silence, quieten, soften; cushion, buffer, absorb. **3** *laughing might deaden us to the moral issue:* **desensitize**, numb, anaesthetize; harden (one's heart), toughen.
– OPPOSITES intensify, amplify, sensitize.

deadline noun *they stipulated a deadline for the army's withdrawal:* **time limit**, limit, finishing date, target date, cut-off point.

deadlock noun **1** *the strike reached a deadlock:* **stalemate**, impasse, checkmate, stand-off; standstill, halt, (full) stop, dead end. **2** (Brit.) *the deadlock is opened with a key:* **bolt**, lock, latch, catch; Scottish sneck, snib.

deadly adjective **1** *these drugs can be deadly:* **fatal**, lethal, mortal, death-dealing, life-threatening; dangerous, injurious, harmful, detrimental, deleterious, unhealthy; noxious, toxic, poisonous. **2** *the two men became deadly enemies:* **mortal**, irreconcilable, implacable, unappeasable,

unforgiving, remorseless, merciless, pitiless; bitter, hostile, antagonistic. **3** *I noted their deadly seriousness:* **intense**, great, marked, extreme.
– OPPOSITES harmless, mild, inaccurate.
▸ adverb *her voice was deadly calm:* **completely**, absolutely, totally, utterly, perfectly, entirely, wholly, quite, dead, thoroughly; in every way, one hundred per cent, to the hilt.

deadpan adjective *he cracked jokes with a deadpan expression on his face:* **blank**, expressionless, unexpressive, impassive, inscrutable, poker-faced, straight-faced; stony, wooden, vacant, fixed, lifeless.
– OPPOSITES expressive.

deaf adjective **1** *she is deaf and blind:* **hard of hearing**, with impaired hearing; informal deaf as a post. **2** *she was deaf to their pleading:* **unmoved by**, untouched by, unaffected by, indifferent to, unresponsive to, unconcerned by; unaware of, oblivious to, impervious to.

deafening adjective *the guns started up with a deafening roar:* **very loud**, very noisy, ear-splitting, ear-shattering, overwhelming, almighty, mighty, tremendous; booming, thunderous, roaring, resounding, resonant, reverberating.
– OPPOSITES quiet.

deal noun *completion of the deal:* **agreement**, understanding, pact, bargain, covenant, contract, treaty; arrangement, compromise, settlement; terms; transaction, sale, account; Law indenture.
▸ verb **1** *they got advice on how to deal with difficult children:* **cope with**, handle, manage, treat, take care of, take charge of, take in hand, sort out, tackle, take on; control; act towards, behave towards. **2** *the article deals with advances in chemistry:* **concern**, be about, have to do with, discuss, consider, cover, pertain to; tackle, study, explore, investigate, examine, review, analyse. **3** *the company deals in high-tech goods:* **trade in**, buy and sell; sell, purvey, supply, stock, market, merchandise; traffic, smuggle; informal push; Brit. informal flog. **4** *the cards were dealt:* **distribute**, give out, share out, divide out, hand out, pass out, pass round, dole out, dispense, allocate; informal divvy up. **5** *the court dealt a blow to government reforms:* **deliver**, administer, dispense, inflict, give, impose; aim.
▪ **a great deal/a good deal** a lot, a large amount, a fair amount, much, plenty; informal lots, loads, heaps, bags, masses, tons; Brit. informal a shedload.

dealer noun *an antique dealer:* **trader**, tradesman, tradesperson, merchant, broker, agent; salesman/woman, seller, vendor, purveyor, pedlar, hawker; buyer, merchandiser, distributor, supplier, shopkeeper, retailer, wholesaler; Brit. stockist.

dealing noun **1** *dishonest dealing:* **business**

methods, business practices, business, commerce, trading, transactions; behaviour, conduct, actions. **2** *the UK's dealings with China:* **relations**, relationship, association, connections, contact, intercourse; negotiations, bargaining, transactions; trade, trading, business, commerce, traffic; informal truck, doings.

dean noun *students must have the consent of the dean:* **faculty head**, department head, college head, provost; chief, director, principal, president, governor.

dear adjective **1** *a dear friend:* **beloved**, loved, adored, cherished, precious; esteemed, respected, worshipped; close, intimate, bosom, boon, best. **2** *her pictures were too dear to part with:* **precious**, treasured, valued, prized, cherished, special. **3** *such a dear man:* **endearing**, adorable, lovable, appealing, engaging, charming, captivating, winsome, lovely, nice, pleasant, delightful, sweet, darling. **4** *the dining car served rather dear meals:* **expensive**, costly, high-priced, overpriced, exorbitant, extortionate; Brit. over the odds; informal pricey, steep, stiff.
– OPPOSITES hated, disagreeable, cheap.
▸ noun **1** *don't worry, my dear:* **darling**, dearest, love, beloved, sweetheart, sweet, precious, treasure; informal sweetie, sugar, honey, baby, pet, sunshine, poppet. **2** *he's such a dear:* **lovable person**, darling, sweetheart, pet, angel, gem, treasure; informal star.
▸ adverb *they buy cheaply and sell dear:* **at a high price**, at an exorbitant price, at high cost.

dearly adverb **1** *I love my son dearly:* **very much**, a great deal, greatly, deeply, profoundly, extremely; fondly, devotedly, tenderly. **2** *our freedom has been bought dearly:* **at great cost**, at a high price, with much suffering, with much sacrifice.

dearth noun *there is a dearth of evidence:* **lack**, scarcity, shortage, shortfall, want, deficiency, insufficiency, inadequacy, paucity, sparseness, scantiness, rareness; absence.
– OPPOSITES surfeit.

death noun **1** *she broke down when she learnt of her father's death:* **demise**, dying, end, passing, loss of life; eternal rest, quietus; murder, assassination, execution, slaughter, massacre; informal curtains; formal decease. **2** *the death of their dream:* **end**, finish, termination, extinction, extinguishing, collapse, destruction, eradication, obliteration. **3** *Death gestured towards a grave:* **the Grim Reaper**, the Dark Angel, the Angel of Death.
– OPPOSITES life, birth.
▪ **put someone to death** execute, hang, behead, guillotine, decapitate, electrocute, shoot, gas, crucify, stone; kill, murder, assassinate, eliminate, terminate, exterminate, destroy; informal bump off, polish off, do away with, do in, knock off, top, string up, take out, croak, stiff, blow

d

d

away; N. Amer. informal ice, rub out, waste, whack, smoke.

deathless adjective *the notion that animals have immaterial and deathless souls:* **immortal**, undying, imperishable, indestructible; enduring, everlasting, eternal; timeless, ageless.
– OPPOSITES mortal, ephemeral.

deathly adjective *the wounded soldiers had a deathly pallor:* **deathlike**, deadly, ghostly, ghastly; ashen, chalky, white, pale, pallid, bloodless, wan, anaemic, pasty.
– OPPOSITES healthy.

debacle noun *the coup attempt resulted in an embarrassing debacle:* **fiasco**, failure, catastrophe, disaster, mess, ruin; downfall, collapse, defeat; informal foul-up, screw-up, hash, botch, washout; Brit. informal cock-up, pig's ear, bodge; N. Amer. informal snafu.

debar verb **1** *women were debarred from the club:* **exclude**, ban, bar, disqualify, declare ineligible, preclude, shut out, lock out, keep out, reject, blackball; N. Amer. disfellowship. **2** *the unions were debarred from striking:* **prevent**, prohibit, proscribe, disallow, ban, interdict, block, stop; forbid to.
– OPPOSITES admit, allow.

debase verb **1** *the moral code has been debased:* **degrade**, devalue, demean, cheapen, prostitute, discredit, drag down, tarnish, blacken, blemish; disgrace, dishonour, shame; damage, harm, undermine. **2** *the added copper debases the silver:* **reduce in value**, reduce in quality, depreciate; contaminate, adulterate, pollute, taint, sully, corrupt; dilute, alloy.
– OPPOSITES enhance.

debased adjective **1** *their debased amusements:* **immoral**, debauched, dissolute, perverted, degenerate, wicked, sinful, vile, base, iniquitous, corrupt; lewd, lascivious, lecherous, prurient, indecent. **2** *the myth lives on in a debased form:* **corrupt**, corrupted, bastardized, adulterated, diluted, tainted, sullied.
– OPPOSITES honourable, original.

debatable adjective *the extent to which personality is inherited is debatable:* **arguable**, disputable, questionable, open to question, controversial, contentious; doubtful, dubious, uncertain, unsure, unclear; borderline, inconclusive, moot, unsettled, unresolved, unconfirmed, undetermined, undecided, up in the air; informal iffy.

debate noun *a debate on the reforms:* **discussion**, discourse, parley, dialogue; argument, dispute, wrangle, war of words; argumentation, disputation, dissension, disagreement, contention, conflict; negotiations, talks; informal confab, powwow.
verb **1** *MPs will debate our future:* **discuss**, talk over/through, talk about, thrash out, argue, dispute; informal kick around/about, bat around/about. **2** *he debated whether to call her:* **consider**, think over/about, chew over,

mull over, weigh up, ponder, deliberate, contemplate, muse, meditate.

debauch verb *public morals have been debauched:* **corrupt**, debase, deprave, warp, pervert, lead astray, ruin.

debauched adjective *a debauched lifestyle:* **dissolute**, dissipated, degenerate, corrupt, depraved, sinful, unprincipled, immoral; lascivious, lecherous, lewd, lustful, libidinous, licentious, promiscuous, loose, wanton, abandoned; decadent, profligate, intemperate, sybaritic.
– OPPOSITES wholesome.

debauchery noun **dissipation**, degeneracy, corruption, vice, depravity; immodesty, indecency, perversion, iniquity, wickedness, sinfulness, impropriety, immorality; lasciviousness, salaciousness, lechery, lewdness, lust, promiscuity, wantonness, profligacy; decadence, intemperance, sybaritism.

debilitate verb *she was severely debilitated by a stomach upset:* **weaken**, enfeeble, enervate, devitalize, sap, drain, exhaust, weary, fatigue, prostrate; undermine, impair, indispose, incapacitate, cripple, disable, paralyse, immobilize, lay low; informal knock out, do in.
– OPPOSITES invigorate.

debility noun *his chronic debility made it hard to do even the basic things:* **frailty**, weakness, enfeeblement, enervation, devitalization, lassitude, exhaustion, weariness, fatigue, prostration; incapacity, indisposition, infirmity, illness, sickness, sickliness; informal weediness.

debonair adjective *a debonair young man:* **suave**, urbane, sophisticated, cultured, self-possessed, self-assured, confident, charming, gracious, courteous, gallant, chivalrous, gentlemanly, refined, polished, well bred, genteel, dignified, courtly; well groomed, elegant, stylish, smart, dashing; informal smooth, swish, sharp, cool.
– OPPOSITES unsophisticated.

debrief verb *Soviet scientists were debriefed by the KGB:* **question**, quiz, interview, examine, cross-examine, interrogate, probe, sound out; informal grill, pump.

debris noun *the irrigation channels were blocked with debris:* **detritus**, refuse, rubbish, waste, litter, scrap, dross, chaff, flotsam and jetsam; lumber, rubble, wreckage; remains, scraps, dregs; N. Amer. trash, garbage; Austral./NZ mullock; informal dreck, junk.

debt noun **1** *he couldn't pay his debts:* **bill**, account, dues, arrears, charges; financial obligation, outstanding payment, money owing; N. Amer. check; informal tab. **2** *his debt to the author:* **indebtedness**, obligation; gratitude, appreciation, thanks.
■ **in debt** owing money, in arrears, behind with payments, overdrawn; insolvent, bankrupt, ruined; Brit. in liquidation; informal

in the red, in Queer Street, on the rocks.
■ **in someone's debt** indebted to, beholden
to, obliged to, duty-bound to, honour-
bound to, obligated to; grateful, thankful,
appreciative.

debtor noun **borrower**, mortgagor;
bankrupt, insolvent, defaulter.
– OPPOSITES creditor.

debunk verb *he debunked the myth that
savants rely on photographic memories:*
explode, deflate, quash, drive a coach
and horses through, discredit, disprove,
contradict, controvert, invalidate, negate;
challenge, call into question; informal shoot
full of holes, blow sky-high.
– OPPOSITES confirm.

debut noun *the new car made its debut at
the German Grand Prix:* **first appearance**,
first performance, launch, coming out,
entrance, premiere, introduction, inception,
inauguration; informal kick-off.

decadence noun *the decadence of
modern society:* **dissipation**, degeneracy,
debauchery, corruption, depravity, vice, sin,
moral decay, immorality; immoderateness,
intemperance, licentiousness, self-
indulgence, hedonism.
– OPPOSITES morality, rise.

decadent adjective *he turned his back on
decadent city life:* **dissolute**, dissipated,
degenerate, corrupt, depraved, sinful,
unprincipled, immoral; licentious,
abandoned, profligate, intemperate;
sybaritic, hedonistic, pleasure-seeking, self-
indulgent.

decamp verb *he decamped with the profits:*
abscond, make off, run off/away, flee, bolt,
take flight, disappear, vanish, steal away,
sneak away, escape, make a run for it, leave,
depart; informal split, scram, vamoose, cut and
run, do a disappearing act, head for the hills,
go AWOL; Brit. informal do a bunk, do a runner,
scarper; N. Amer. informal take a powder, go on
the lam.

decant verb *the wine was decanted into a
clean flask:* **pour out/off**, draw off, siphon
off, drain, tap; transfer.

decapitate verb *he was found guilty of high
treason and decapitated:* **behead**, guillotine.

decay verb **1** *the corpses had decayed:*
decompose, rot, putrefy, go bad, go off,
spoil, fester, perish, deteriorate; degrade,
break down, moulder, mortify, shrivel,
wither. **2** *the cities continue to decay:*
deteriorate, degenerate, decline, go
downhill, slump, slide, go to rack and ruin,
go to seed; disintegrate, fall to pieces, fall
into disrepair; fail, collapse; informal go to pot,
go to the dogs, go down the toilet; Austral./NZ
informal go to the pack.
noun **1** *the fish showed no signs of decay:*
decomposition, putrefaction, festering; rot,
mould, mildew, fungus. **2** *tooth decay:* **rot**,
corrosion, decomposition; caries, cavities,
holes. **3** *the decay of American values:*

deterioration, degeneration, debasement,
degradation, decline, weakening, atrophy;
crumbling, disintegration, collapse.

decayed adjective *she discovered his decayed
body:* **decomposed**, decomposing, rotten,
putrescent, putrid, bad, off, spoiled,
perished; mouldy, festering, fetid, rancid,
rank; maggoty, wormy, flyblown.

decaying adjective **1** *decaying fish:*
decomposing, decomposed, rotting, rotten,
putrescent, putrid, bad, off, perished;
mouldy, festering, fetid, rancid, rank;
maggoty, wormy, flyblown. **2** *a decaying city:*
declining, degenerating, dying, crumbling;
run down, tumbledown, ramshackle, shabby,
decrepit; in decline, in ruins; informal on the
way out.

deceit noun **1** *her endless deceit:* **deception**,
deceitfulness, duplicity, double-dealing,
fraud, cheating, trickery, chicanery,
deviousness, slyness, wiliness, guile,
bluff, lying, pretence, treachery; informal
crookedness, monkey business, jiggery-
pokery; N. Amer. informal monkeyshines. **2** *their
life is a deceit:* **sham**, fraud, pretence,
hoax, fake, blind, artifice; trick, stratagem,
device, ruse, scheme, dodge, machination,
deception, subterfuge; cheat, swindle; informal
con, set-up, scam, flimflam; N. Amer. informal
bunco.
– OPPOSITES honesty.

deceitful adjective **1** *a deceitful woman:*
dishonest, untruthful, mendacious,
insincere, false, disingenuous,
untrustworthy, unscrupulous, unprincipled,
two-faced, duplicitous, double-dealing,
underhand, crafty, cunning, sly, scheming,
calculating, treacherous, Machiavellian;
informal sneaky, tricky, foxy, crooked;
Brit. informal bent. **2** *a deceitful allegation:*
fraudulent, counterfeit, fabricated,
invented, concocted, made up, trumped
up, untrue, false, bogus, fake, spurious,
fallacious, deceptive, misleading; euphemistic
economical with the truth.
– OPPOSITES honest.

deceive verb **1** *she was deceived by a con man:*
swindle, defraud, cheat, trick, hoodwink,
hoax, dupe, take in, mislead, delude, fool,
outwit, lead on, inveigle, beguile, double-
cross, gull; informal con, bamboozle, do, gyp,
diddle, swizzle, rip off, shaft, pull a fast
one on, take for a ride, pull the wool over
someone's eyes, sell a pup to; N. Amer. informal
sucker, snooker, stiff. **2** *he deceived her with
another woman:* **be unfaithful to**, cheat on,
betray, play someone false; informal two-time.

decelerate verb *there is a whine from
the gearbox every time I decelerate:* **slow
down/up**, ease up, slack up, reduce speed,
brake.

decency noun **1** *TV companies need
to maintain standards of taste and
decency:* **propriety**, decorum, good taste,
respectability, dignity, correctness, good
form, etiquette; morality, virtue, modesty,

d

delicacy. **2** *he didn't have the decency to tell me:* **courtesy**, politeness, good manners, civility, respect; consideration, thoughtfulness, tact, diplomacy.

decent adjective **1** *I'd like them to have a decent Christian burial:* **proper**, correct, appropriate, apt, fitting, suitable; respectable, dignified, decorous, seemly; nice, tasteful; conventional, accepted, standard, traditional, orthodox; comme il faut; informal pukka. **2** (Brit. informal) *he was a very decent chap:* **honourable**, honest, trustworthy, dependable; respectable, upright, clean-living, virtuous, good; obliging, helpful, accommodating, unselfish, generous, kind, thoughtful, considerate; neighbourly, hospitable, pleasant, agreeable, amiable. **3** *a job with decent pay:* **satisfactory**, reasonable, fair, acceptable, adequate, sufficient, ample; not bad, all right, tolerable, passable, suitable; informal OK, okay, up to snuff.
– OPPOSITES unpleasant, unsatisfactory.

deception noun **1** *they obtained money by deception:* **deceit**, deceitfulness, duplicity, double-dealing, fraud, cheating, trickery, chicanery, deviousness, slyness, wiliness, guile, bluff, lying, pretence, treachery; informal crookedness, monkey business, jiggery-pokery; N. Amer. informal monkeyshines. **2** *it was all a deception:* **trick**, deceit, sham, fraud, pretence, hoax, fake, blind, artifice; stratagem, device, ruse, scheme, dodge, machination, subterfuge; cheat, swindle; informal con, kidology, set-up, scam, flimflam; N. Amer. informal bunco.

deceptive adjective **1** *distances are very deceptive:* **misleading**, illusory, illusionary, specious; ambiguous; distorted; literary illusive. **2** *deceptive practices:* **deceitful**, duplicitous, fraudulent, counterfeit, underhand, cunning, crafty, sly, guileful, scheming, treacherous, Machiavellian; disingenuous, untrustworthy, unscrupulous, unprincipled, dishonest, insincere, false; informal crooked, sharp, shady, sneaky, tricky, foxy; Brit. informal bent.

decide verb **1** *she decided to become a writer:* **resolve**, determine, make up one's mind, make a decision; elect, choose, opt, plan, aim, have the intention, have in mind, set one's sights on. **2** *research to decide a variety of questions:* **settle**, resolve, determine, work out, answer; informal sort out, figure out. **3** *the court is to decide the case:* **adjudicate**, arbitrate, adjudge, judge; hear, try, examine; sit in judgement on, pronounce on, give a verdict on, rule on.

decided adjective **1** *they have a decided advantage:* **distinct**, clear, marked, pronounced, obvious, striking, noticeable, unmistakable, patent, manifest; definite, certain, positive, emphatic, undeniable, indisputable, unquestionable; assured, guaranteed. **2** *he was very decided:*

determined, resolute, firm, strong-minded, strong-willed, emphatic, dead set, unwavering, unyielding, unbending, inflexible, unshakeable, unrelenting, obstinate, stubborn; N. Amer. rock-ribbed. **3** *our future is decided:* **settled**, established, resolved, determined, agreed, designated, chosen, ordained, prescribed; set, fixed; informal sewn up, wrapped up.

decidedly adverb *they were decidedly hostile to one another:* **distinctly**, clearly, markedly, obviously, noticeably, unmistakably, patently, manifestly; definitely, certainly, positively, absolutely, downright, undeniably, unquestionably; extremely, exceedingly, exceptionally, particularly, especially, very; N. English right; informal terrifically, devilishly, ultra, mega, majorly; Brit. informal jolly, ever so, dead, well; N. Amer. informal real, mighty, awful.

deciding adjective *taxes could be the deciding factor for millions of floating voters:* **determining**, decisive, conclusive, key, pivotal, crucial, critical, significant, major, chief, principal, prime.

decipher verb **1** *he deciphered the code:* **decode**, decrypt, break, work out, solve, interpret, translate; make sense of, get to the bottom of, unravel; informal crack, figure out; Brit. informal twig, suss (out). **2** *the writing was hard to decipher:* **make out**, discern, perceive, read, follow, fathom, make sense of, interpret, understand, comprehend, grasp.
– OPPOSITES encode.

decision noun **1** *they came to a decision:* **resolution**, conclusion, settlement, commitment, resolve, determination; choice, option, selection. **2** *they're delighted with the judge's decision:* **verdict**, finding, ruling, recommendation, judgement, pronouncement, adjudication, arbitrament; order, rule; findings, results; N. Amer. resolve. **3** *his order had a ring of decision:* **decisiveness**, determination, resolution, resolve, firmness; strong-mindedness, purpose, purposefulness.

decisive adjective **1** *a decisive man:* **resolute**, firm, strong-minded, strong-willed, determined; purposeful, forceful, dead set, unwavering, unyielding, unbending, inflexible, unshakeable, obstinate, stubborn; N. Amer. rock-ribbed. **2** *the decisive factor:* **deciding**, conclusive, determining; key, pivotal, critical, crucial, significant, influential, major, chief, principal, prime.

deck verb **1** *the street was decked with bunting:* **decorate**, bedeck, adorn, ornament, trim, trick out, garnish, cover, hang, festoon, garland, swathe, wreathe; embellish, beautify, prettify, enhance, grace, set off; informal get up, do up, do out, tart up. **2** *Ingrid was decked out in blue:* **dress (up)**, clothe, attire, garb, robe, drape, turn out, fit out, rig out, outfit, costume; informal doll up, get up, do up.

declaim verb **1** *a preacher declaiming from the pulpit:* **make a speech**, give an address, give a lecture, deliver a sermon; speak, hold forth, orate, preach, lecture, sermonize, moralize; informal sound off, spout, speechify, preachify. **2** *they loved to hear him declaim poetry:* **recite**, read aloud, read out loud, read out; deliver; informal spout. **3** *he declaimed against the evils of society:* **speak out**, rail, inveigh, fulminate, rage, thunder; rant, expostulate; condemn, criticize, attack, decry, disparage.

declamation noun *he delivered a passionate declamation:* **speech**, address, lecture, sermon, homily, discourse, oration, recitation, disquisition, monologue.

declaration noun **1** *they issued a declaration:* **announcement**, statement, communication, pronouncement, proclamation, communiqué, edict; N. Amer. advisory. **2** *the declaration of war:* **proclamation**, notification, announcement, revelation, disclosure, broadcasting. **3** *a declaration of faith:* **assertion**, profession, affirmation, acknowledgement, revelation, disclosure, manifestation, confirmation, testimony, validation, certification, attestation; pledge, avowal, vow, oath, protestation.

declare verb **1** *she declared her political principles:* **proclaim**, announce, state, reveal, air, voice, articulate, express, vent, set forth, publicize, broadcast; informal come out with, shout from the rooftops. **2** *he declared that they were guilty:* **assert**, maintain, state, affirm, contend, argue, insist, hold, profess, claim, avow, swear. **3** *his speech declared him a gentleman:* **show to be**, reveal as, confirm as, prove to be, attest to someone's being.

decline verb **1** *she declined all invitations:* **turn down**, reject, brush aside, refuse, rebuff, spurn, repulse, dismiss; forgo, deny oneself, pass up; abstain from, say no; informal give the thumbs down to, give something a miss, give someone the brush-off; Brit. informal knock back. **2** *the number of traders has declined:* **decrease**, reduce, lessen, diminish, dwindle, contract, shrink, fall off, tail off; drop, fall, go down, slump, plummet; informal nosedive, take a header, crash. **3** *standards steadily declined:* **deteriorate**, degenerate, decay, crumble, collapse, slump, slip, slide, go downhill, worsen; weaken, wane, ebb; informal go to pot, go to the dogs, go down the toilet; Austral./NZ informal go to the pack.
– OPPOSITES accept, increase, rise.
noun **1** *a decline in profits:* **reduction**, decrease, downturn, downswing, devaluation, depreciation, diminution, ebb, drop, slump, plunge; informal nosedive, crash. **2** *forest decline:* **deterioration**, degeneration, degradation, shrinkage; death, decay.
■ **in decline** declining, decaying, crumbling, collapsing, failing; disappearing, dying,

moribund; informal on its last legs, on the way out.

decode verb *battle plans sent out on Germany's Enigma machine were quickly decoded:* **decipher**, decrypt, work out, solve, interpret, translate; make sense of, get to the bottom of, unravel, find the key to; informal crack, figure out; Brit. informal twig, suss (out).

decompose verb *the chemical prevents corpses decomposing:* **decay**, rot, putrefy, go bad, go off, spoil, fester, perish, deteriorate; degrade, break down, moulder, mortify, shrivel, wither.

decomposition noun *the body is in an advanced state of decomposition:* **decay**, putrefaction, putrescence, putridity.

decontaminate verb *they tried to decontaminate nearby villages:* **sanitize**, sterilize, disinfect, clean, cleanse, purify; fumigate.

decor noun *inside, the decor is elegant and traditional:* **decoration**, furnishing, ornamentation; colour scheme.

decorate verb **1** *the door was decorated with a wreath:* **ornament**, adorn, trim, embellish, garnish, furnish, enhance, grace, prettify; festoon, garland, bedeck. **2** *he started to decorate his home:* **paint**, **wallpaper**, paper; refurbish, furbish, renovate, redecorate; informal do up, spruce up, do over, fix up, give something a facelift. **3** *he was decorated for courage:* **give a medal to**, honour, cite, reward.

decoration noun **1** *a ceiling with rich decoration:* **ornamentation**, adornment, trimming, embellishment, garnishing, gilding; beautification, prettification; enhancements, enrichments, frills, accessories, trimmings, finery, frippery. **2** *internal decoration.* See DECOR. **3** *a Christmas tree decoration:* **ornament**, bauble, trinket, knick-knack, spangle; trimming, tinsel. **4** *a decoration won on the battlefield:* **medal**, award, star, ribbon; laurel, trophy, prize; Military slang fruit salad; Brit. informal gong.

decorative adjective *mirrors were used as decorative features:* **ornamental**, embellishing, garnishing; fancy, ornate, attractive, pretty, showy.
– OPPOSITES functional.

decorous adjective *he always behaves towards her in a decorous way:* **proper**, seemly, decent, becoming, befitting, tasteful; correct, appropriate, suitable, fitting; tactful, polite, well mannered, genteel, respectable; formal, restrained, modest, demure, gentlemanly, ladylike.
– OPPOSITES unseemly.

decorum noun **1** *he had acted with decorum:* **propriety**, seemliness, decency, good taste, correctness; politeness, courtesy, good manners; dignity, respectability, modesty, demureness. **2** *a breach of decorum:* **etiquette**, protocol, good form, custom,

convention; formalities, niceties, punctilios, politeness.
– OPPOSITES impropriety.

decoy noun *a decoy to distract their attention:* **lure**, bait, red herring; enticement, inducement, temptation, attraction, carrot; snare, trap.
verb *he was decoyed to the mainland:* **lure**, entice, tempt; entrap, snare, trap.

decrease verb **1** *pollution levels decreased:* **lessen**, reduce, drop, diminish, decline, dwindle, fall off; die down, abate, subside, tail off, ebb, wane; plummet, plunge.
2 *decrease the amount of fat in your body:* **reduce**, lessen, lower, cut, curtail; slim down, tone down, deplete, minimize; informal slash.
– OPPOSITES increase.
noun *a decrease in crime:* **reduction**, drop, decline, downturn, cut, cutback, diminution, ebb, wane.
– OPPOSITES increase.

decree noun **1** *a presidential decree:* **order**, edict, command, commandment, mandate, proclamation, dictum, fiat; law, statute, act. **2** *a court decree:* **judgement**, verdict, adjudication, ruling, resolution, decision.
verb *he decreed that a stadium should be built:* **order**, command, rule, dictate, pronounce, proclaim, ordain; direct, decide, determine.

decrepit adjective **1** *a decrepit old man:* **feeble**, infirm, weak, weakly, frail; disabled, incapacitated, crippled, doddering, tottering; old, elderly, aged, ancient, senile; informal past it, over the hill, no spring chicken. **2** *a decrepit house:* **dilapidated**, rickety, run down, tumbledown, ramshackle, derelict, ruined, in (a state of) disrepair, gone to rack and ruin; battered, decayed, crumbling, deteriorating.
– OPPOSITES strong, sound.

decry verb *they decried human rights abuses:* **denounce**, condemn, criticize, censure, attack, rail against, run down, pillory, lambaste, vilify, revile; disparage, deprecate, cast aspersions on; informal slam, blast, knock; Brit. informal slate.
– OPPOSITES praise.

dedicate verb **1** *she dedicated her life to the sick:* **devote**, commit, pledge, give, surrender, sacrifice; set aside, allocate, consign. **2** *a book dedicated to a noblewoman:* **inscribe**, address; assign. **3** *the chapel was dedicated to the Virgin Mary:* **devote**, assign; bless, consecrate, sanctify.

dedicated adjective **1** *a dedicated socialist:* **committed**, devoted, staunch, firm, steadfast, resolute, unwavering, loyal, faithful, true, dyed-in-the-wool; wholehearted, single-minded, enthusiastic, keen, earnest, zealous, ardent, passionate, fervent; informal card-carrying, deep-dyed.
2 *data is accessed by a dedicated machine:* **exclusive**, custom built, customized.
– OPPOSITES indifferent.

dedication noun **1** *sport requires*

dedication: **commitment**, application, diligence, industry, resolve, enthusiasm, zeal, conscientiousness, perseverance, persistence, tenacity, drive, staying power; hard work, effort. **2** *her dedication to the job:* **devotion**, commitment, loyalty, adherence, allegiance. **3** *the book has a dedication to his wife:* **inscription**, address, message. **4** *the dedication of the church:* **blessing**, consecration, sanctification, benediction.
– OPPOSITES apathy.

deduce verb *little can be safely deduced from these figures:* **conclude**, reason, work out, infer; glean, divine, intuit, understand, assume, presume, conjecture, surmise, reckon; informal figure out; Brit. informal suss out.

deduct verb *any tax due will be deducted from the pension:* **subtract**, take away, take off, debit, dock, discount; abstract, remove; informal knock off.
– OPPOSITES add.

deduction noun **1** *the deduction of tax:* **subtraction**, removal, debit, abstraction. **2** *gross pay, before deductions:* **stoppage**, subtraction. **3** *she was right in her deduction:* **conclusion**, inference, supposition, hypothesis, assumption, presumption; suspicion, conviction, belief, reasoning.

deed noun **1** *knightly deeds:* **act**, action; feat, exploit, achievement, accomplishment, endeavour, undertaking, enterprise. **2** *unity must be established in deed and word:* **fact**, reality, actuality. **3** *the mortgage deeds are kept at the bank:* **legal document**, contract, indenture, instrument.

deem verb *the event was deemed a great success:* **consider**, regard as, judge, adjudge, hold to be, view as, see as, take for, class as, count, find, esteem, suppose, reckon; think, believe, feel.

deep adjective **1** *a deep ravine:* **cavernous**, yawning, gaping, huge, extensive; bottomless, fathomless, unfathomable.
2 *a puddle about two inches deep:* **in depth**, downwards, inwards, in vertical extent. **3** *deep affection:* **intense**, heartfelt, wholehearted, deep-seated, deep-rooted; sincere, genuine, earnest, enthusiastic, great. **4** *Laura drifted into a deep sleep:* **sound**, heavy, intense. **5** *a deep thinker:* **profound**, serious, philosophical, complex, weighty; abstruse, esoteric, recondite, mysterious, obscure; intelligent, intellectual, learned, wise, scholarly; discerning, penetrating, perceptive, insightful. **6** *he was deep in concentration:* **rapt**, absorbed, engrossed, preoccupied, immersed, lost, gripped, intent, engaged.
7 *a deep mystery:* **obscure**, mysterious, secret, unfathomable, opaque, abstruse, recondite, esoteric, enigmatic, arcane; puzzling, baffling, mystifying, inexplicable.
8 *his deep voice:* **low-pitched**, low, bass, rich, powerful, resonant, booming, sonorous. **9** *a*

deep red: **dark**, intense, rich, strong, bold, warm.
– OPPOSITES shallow, superficial, high, light.
noun *the deep of night:* **the middle**, the midst; the depths, the dead, the thick.
adverb **1** *I dug deep:* **far down**, way down, to a great depth. **2** *he brought them deep into woodland:* **far**, a long way, a great distance.

deepen verb **1** *his love for her had deepened:* **grow**, increase, intensify, strengthen, heighten, amplify, augment; informal step up; Brit. informal hot up. **2** *they deepened the hole:* **dig out**, dig deeper, excavate.

deeply adverb *she was deeply hurt:* **profoundly**, greatly, enormously, extremely, very much; strongly, powerfully, intensely, keenly, acutely; thoroughly, completely, entirely; informal well, seriously, majorly.

deep-rooted adjective *her deep-rooted fears and anxieties:* **deep-seated**, deep, profound, fundamental, basic; established, ingrained, entrenched, unshakeable, inveterate, inbuilt; secure; persistent, abiding, lingering.
– OPPOSITES superficial.

deface verb *a graffiti artist who defaced buildings and motorway bridges:* **vandalize**, disfigure, mar, spoil, ruin, sully, damage, blight, impair; N. Amer. informal trash.

de facto adverb *the republic is de facto two states:* **in practice**, in effect, in fact, in reality, really, actually.
adjective *they took de facto control of the land:* **actual**, real, effective.

defamation noun *he sued the newspaper for defamation:* **libel**, slander, calumny, character assassination, vilification; scandalmongering, malicious gossip, aspersions, muckraking, abuse; disparagement, denigration; smear, slur; informal mud-slinging.

defamatory adjective *there were defamatory statements in the book:* **libellous**, slanderous, calumnious, calumniatory, scandalmongering, malicious, vicious, backbiting, muckraking; abusive, disparaging, denigratory, insulting; informal mud-slinging, bitchy, catty.

defame verb *they were horribly defamed by the allegations:* **libel**, slander, malign, cast aspersions on, smear, traduce, give someone a bad name, run down, speak ill of, vilify, besmirch, stigmatize, disparage, denigrate, discredit, decry; informal do a hatchet job on, drag through the mud; N. Amer. slur; informal bad-mouth; Brit. informal slag off.
– OPPOSITES compliment.

default noun **1** *the incidence of defaults on loans:* **non-payment**, failure to pay, non-remittance. **2** *I became a teacher by default:* **inaction**, omission, lapse, neglect, negligence, disregard; absence, non-appearance.
verb **1** *the customer defaulted:* **fail to pay**, not

pay, renege, back out; go back on one's word; informal welsh, bilk. **2** *the program will default to its own style:* **revert**, select automatically.

defaulter noun *a mortgage defaulter:* **non-payer**, debt-dodger; tax-dodger; N. Amer. delinquent.

defeat verb **1** *the army which defeated the Scots:* **beat**, conquer, win against, triumph over, get the better of, vanquish; rout, trounce, overcome, overpower, crush, subdue; informal lick, thrash, whip, wipe the floor with, make mincemeat of, clobber, slaughter, demolish, cane; Brit. informal stuff; N. Amer. informal cream, skunk. **2** *these complex plans defeat their purpose:* **thwart**, frustrate, foil, ruin, scotch, debar, snooker, derail; obstruct, impede, hinder, hamper; informal put the kibosh on, put paid to, stymie; Brit. informal scupper, nobble. **3** *the motion was defeated:* **reject**, overthrow, throw out, dismiss, outvote, turn down; informal give the thumbs down. **4** *how to make it work defeats me:* **baffle**, perplex, bewilder, mystify, bemuse, confuse, confound, throw; informal beat, flummox, faze, stump, fox.
noun **1** *a crippling defeat:* **loss**, conquest, vanquishment; rout, trouncing; downfall; informal thrashing, hiding, drubbing, licking, pasting, massacre, slaughter. **2** *the defeat of his plans:* **failure**, downfall, collapse, ruin; rejection, frustration, abortion, miscarriage; undoing, reverse.
– OPPOSITES victory, success.

defeatist adjective *a defeatist attitude:* **pessimistic**, fatalistic, negative, cynical, despondent, despairing, hopeless, bleak, gloomy.
– OPPOSITES optimistic.
noun **pessimist**, fatalist, cynic, prophet of doom, doomster; misery, killjoy, worrier; informal quitter, wet blanket.
– OPPOSITES optimist.

defecate verb **excrete (faeces)**, have a bowel movement, evacuate one's bowels, relieve oneself, go to the lavatory; informal do number two, do a pooh.

defect¹ noun *he spotted a defect in my work:* **fault**, flaw, imperfection, deficiency, weakness, weak spot, inadequacy, shortcoming, limitation, failing; kink, deformity, blemish; mistake, error; informal glitch, gremlin; Computing bug.

defect² verb *his chief intelligence officer defected:* **desert**, change sides, turn traitor, rebel, renege; abscond, quit, escape; break faith; secede from, revolt against; informal rat on; Military go AWOL.

defection noun **desertion**, absconding, decamping, flight; apostasy, secession; treason, betrayal, disloyalty.

defective adjective **1** *a defective seat belt:* **faulty**, flawed, imperfect, shoddy, inoperative, malfunctioning, out of order, unsound; in disrepair, broken; informal on the blink; Brit. informal knackered, duff. **2** *these*

methods are defective: **lacking**, wanting, deficient, inadequate, insufficient.
– OPPOSITES perfect.

defector noun **deserter**, turncoat, traitor, renegade, Judas, quisling; informal rat.

defence noun **1** *the defence of the fortress:* **protection**, guarding, security, fortification; resistance, deterrent. **2** *the enemy's defences:* **barricade**, fortification; fortress, keep, rampart, bulwark, bastion. **3** *he spoke in defence of his boss:* **vindication**, justification, support, advocacy, endorsement; apology, explanation, exoneration. **4** *more spending on defence:* **armaments**, weapons, weaponry, arms; the military, the armed forces. **5** *the prisoner's defence:* **vindication**, explanation, mitigation, justification, rationalization, excuse, alibi, reason; plea, pleading; testimony, declaration, case.

defenceless adjective **1** *defenceless animals:* **vulnerable**, helpless, powerless, impotent, weak, susceptible. **2** *the country is wholly defenceless:* **undefended**, unprotected, unguarded, unshielded, unarmed; vulnerable, assailable, exposed, insecure, pregnable.
– OPPOSITES resilient.

defend verb **1** *a fort built to defend Ireland:* **protect**, guard, safeguard, secure, shield; fortify, garrison, barricade; uphold, support, watch over. **2** *he defended his policy:* **justify**, vindicate, argue for, support, make a case for, plead for; excuse, explain. **3** *the manager defended his players:* **support**, back, stand by, stick up for, stand up for, argue for, champion, endorse; informal throw one's weight behind.
– OPPOSITES attack, criticize.

defendant noun *the defendant was charged with murder:* **accused**, prisoner (at the bar); appellant, litigant, respondent; suspect.
– OPPOSITES plaintiff.

defender noun **1** *defenders of the environment:* **protector**, guard, guardian, preserver; custodian, watchdog, keeper, overseer, superintendent, caretaker. **2** *a defender of colonialism:* **supporter**, upholder, backer, champion, advocate, apologist, proponent, exponent, promoter; adherent, believer. **3** *he passed two defenders and scored:* **fullback**, back, sweeper; (**defenders**) back four.

defensible adjective **1** *a defensible attitude:* **justifiable**, arguable, tenable, defendable, supportable; plausible, sound, sensible, reasonable, rational, logical; acceptable, valid, legitimate; excusable, pardonable, understandable. **2** *a defensible territory:* **secure**, safe, fortified; invulnerable, impregnable, impenetrable, unassailable.
– OPPOSITES untenable, vulnerable.

defensive adjective **1** *troops in defensive positions:* **defending**, protective; wary, watchful. **2** *a defensive response:* **self-justifying**, oversensitive, prickly, paranoid,

neurotic; informal uptight, twitchy.

defer[1] verb *the committee will defer their decision:* **postpone**, put off, delay, hold over/off, put back; shelve, suspend, stay, mothball; N. Amer. put over, table, take a rain check on; informal put on ice, put on the back burner, put in cold storage.

defer[2] verb *they deferred to Joseph's judgement:* **yield**, submit, give way, give in, surrender, capitulate, acquiesce; respect, honour.

deference noun *he addressed her with the deference due to age:* **respect**, respectfulness, dutifulness; submissiveness, submission, obedience, surrender, accession, capitulation, acquiescence, complaisance, obeisance.
– OPPOSITES disrespect.

deferential adjective *people were always deferential to him:* **respectful**, humble, obsequious; dutiful, obedient, submissive, subservient, yielding, acquiescent, complaisant, compliant, tractable, biddable, docile.

deferment noun **postponement**, deferral, suspension, delay, adjournment, interruption, pause; respite, stay, moratorium, reprieve, grace.

defiance noun *he wasn't used to such outspoken defiance:* **resistance**, opposition, non-compliance, disobedience, insubordination, dissent, recalcitrance, subversion, rebellion; contempt, disregard, scorn, insolence, truculence.
– OPPOSITES obedience.

defiant adjective **intransigent**, resistant, obstinate, uncooperative, non-compliant, recalcitrant; obstreperous, truculent, dissenting, disobedient, insubordinate, subversive, rebellious, mutinous; informal feisty; Brit. informal stroppy, bolshie.
– OPPOSITES cooperative.

deficiency noun **1** *a vitamin deficiency:* **insufficiency**, lack, shortage, want, dearth, inadequacy, deficit, shortfall; scarcity, paucity, absence, undersupply, deprivation, shortness. **2** *the team's big deficiency:* **defect**, fault, flaw, imperfection, weakness, weak point, inadequacy, shortcoming, limitation, failing.
– OPPOSITES surplus, strength.

deficient adjective **1** *a diet deficient in vitamin A:* **lacking**, wanting, inadequate, insufficient, limited, poor, scant; short of/on, low on. **2** *deficient leadership:* **defective**, faulty, flawed, inadequate, imperfect, shoddy, weak, inferior, unsound, substandard, second-rate, poor; Brit. informal duff.

deficit noun *there was a large, continuing deficit in the federal budget:* **shortfall**, deficiency, shortage, undersupply; debt, arrears; negative amount, loss.
– OPPOSITES surplus.

defile verb **1** *her capacity for love had been*

defiled: **spoil**, sully, mar, impair, debase, degrade; poison, taint, tarnish; destroy, ruin. **2** *the sacred bones were defiled:* **desecrate**, profane, violate; contaminate, pollute, debase, degrade, dishonour.
– OPPOSITES sanctify.

definable adjective *Aunt Emily wasn't ill, or at least she had no definable complaint:* **determinable**, ascertainable, known, definite, clear-cut, precise, exact, specific.

define verb **1** *the dictionary defines it succinctly:* **explain**, expound, interpret, elucidate, describe, clarify; give the meaning of, put into words. **2** *he defined the limits of the middle class:* **determine**, establish, fix, specify, designate, decide, stipulate, set out; demarcate, delineate. **3** *he could see the farm buildings defined against the fields:* **outline**, delineate, silhouette.

definite adjective **1** *I need a definite answer:* **explicit**, specific, precise, exact, clear-cut, direct, plain, outright; fixed, established, confirmed, concrete. **2** *definite evidence:* **certain**, sure, positive, conclusive, decisive, firm, concrete, unambiguous, unequivocal, clear, unmistakable, proven; guaranteed, assured, cut and dried. **3** *she had a definite dislike for Robert:* **unmistakable**, unequivocal, unambiguous, certain, undisputed, decided, marked, distinct. **4** *a definite geographical area:* **fixed**, marked, demarcated, delimited, stipulated, particular.
– OPPOSITES vague, ambiguous, indeterminate.

definitely adverb *I shall definitely be at the airport to meet you:* **certainly**, surely, for sure, unquestionably, without doubt, without question, undoubtedly, indubitably, positively, absolutely; undeniably, unmistakably, plainly, clearly, obviously, patently, palpably, transparently, unequivocally, as sure as eggs is eggs.

definition noun **1** *there is no agreed definition of 'intelligence':* **meaning**, denotation, sense; interpretation, explanation, elucidation, description, clarification, illustration. **2** *the definition of the picture can be aided by using computer graphics:* **clarity**, visibility, sharpness, crispness, acuteness; resolution, focus, contrast.

definitive adjective **1** *a definitive decision:* **conclusive**, final, ultimate; unconditional, unqualified, absolute, categorical, positive, definite. **2** *the definitive guide to the movies:* **authoritative**, exhaustive, best, finest, consummate; classic, standard, recognized, accepted, official.

deflate verb **1** *he deflated the tyres:* **let down**, flatten, void; puncture. **2** *the balloon deflated:* **go down**, collapse, shrink, contract. **3** *the news had deflated him:* **subdue**, humble, cow, chasten; dispirit, dismay, discourage, dishearten; squash, crush, bring down, take the wind out of someone's sails;

informal knock the stuffing out of. **4** *the budget deflated the economy:* **reduce**, slow down, diminish; devalue, depreciate, depress.
– OPPOSITES inflate.

deflect verb **1** *she wanted to deflect attention from herself:* **turn aside/away**, divert, avert, sidetrack; distract, draw away; block, parry, fend off, stave off. **2** *the ball deflected off the wall:* **bounce**, glance, ricochet; diverge, deviate, veer, swerve, slew.

deform verb **disfigure**, bend out of shape, contort, buckle, warp; damage, impair.

deformed adjective *a deformed skeleton:* **misshapen**, distorted, malformed, contorted, out of shape; twisted, crooked, warped, buckled, gnarled; crippled, humpbacked, hunchbacked, disfigured, grotesque; injured, damaged, mutilated, mangled.

deformity noun **malformation**, misshapenness, distortion, crookedness; imperfection, abnormality, irregularity; disfigurement; defect, flaw, blemish.

defraud verb *the men were alleged to have defrauded thousands of investors:* **swindle**, cheat, rob; deceive, dupe, hoodwink, double-cross, trick; informal con, do, sting, diddle, rip off, shaft, bilk, rook, gyp, pull a fast one on, put one over on, sell a pup to; N. Amer. informal sucker, snooker, stiff; Austral. informal pull a swifty on.

defray verb *the rest of the money was used to defray the costs of restoring the house:* **pay (for)**, cover, meet, square, settle, clear, discharge; foot the bill for; N. Amer. informal pick up the tab for.

deft adjective *a deft piece of footwork:* **skilful**, adept, adroit, dexterous, agile, nimble, handy; able, capable, skilled, proficient, accomplished, expert, polished, slick, professional, masterly; clever, shrewd, astute, canny, sharp; informal nifty, nippy.
– OPPOSITES clumsy.

defunct adjective *the now defunct local paper mill:* **disused**, unused, inoperative, non-functioning, unusable, obsolete; no longer existing, discontinued; extinct.
– OPPOSITES working, extant.

defuse verb **1** *he tried to defuse the grenade:* **deactivate**, disarm, disable, make safe. **2** *officers are taught how to defuse potentially explosive situations:* **ease**, calm, cool, smooth over, take the heat out of, restore order in/to; settle, resolve, patch up, sort out, iron out, put to rights, remedy, rectify; get control of, get a grip on; pour oil on troubled waters.
– OPPOSITES activate, inflame.

defy verb **1** *he defied European law:* **disobey**, go against, flout, fly in the face of, disregard, ignore; break, violate, contravene, breach, infringe; informal cock a snook at. **2** *his actions*

d

defy belief: **elude**, escape, defeat; frustrate, thwart, baffle. **3** *he glowered, defying her to mock him:* **challenge**, dare.
– OPPOSITES obey.

degeneracy noun *an attack on the sexual degeneracy of the time:* **decadence**, corruption, moral decay, dissipation, dissolution, profligacy, vice, immorality, sin, sinfulness, ungodliness; debauchery.

degenerate adjective **1** *a degenerate form of classicism:* **debased**, degraded, corrupt, impure; formal vitiated. **2** *her degenerate brother:* **decadent**, corrupt, dissolute, dissipated, debauched, reprobate, profligate; sinful, ungodly, immoral, unprincipled, amoral, dishonourable, disreputable, unsavoury, sordid, low, ignoble.
– OPPOSITES pure, moral.
noun *a group of degenerates:* **reprobate**, debauchee, profligate, libertine, roué, loose-liver.
verb **1** *their quality of life had degenerated:* **deteriorate**, decline, slip, slide, worsen, lapse, slump, go downhill, regress, retrogress; go to rack and ruin; informal go to pot, go to the dogs, hit the skids, go down the toilet. **2** *the muscles started to degenerate:* **waste (away)**, atrophy, weaken.
– OPPOSITES improve.

degradation noun **1** *poverty brings with it degradation:* **humiliation**, shame, loss of self-respect, abasement, indignity, ignominy. **2** *the degradation of women:* **demeaning**, debasement, discrediting. **3** *the degradation of the tissues:* **deterioration**, degeneration, atrophy, decay; breakdown.

degrade verb **1** *prisons should not degrade prisoners:* **demean**, debase, cheapen, devalue; shame, humiliate, humble, mortify, abase, dishonour; dehumanize, brutalize. **2** *the polymer will not degrade:* **break down**, deteriorate, degenerate, decay.
– OPPOSITES dignify.

degrading adjective *claiming benefit can be a degrading experience:* **humiliating**, demeaning, shameful, mortifying, ignominious, undignified, inglorious, wretched; informal infra dig.

degree noun *the high degree of risk involved:* **level**, standard, grade, mark; amount, extent, measure; magnitude, intensity, strength; proportion, ratio.
■ **by degrees** gradually, little by little, bit by bit, inch by inch, step by step, slowly; piecemeal.
■ **to a degree** to some extent, to a certain extent, up to a point.

dehydrate verb **1** *alcohol dehydrates the skin:* **dry (out)**, desiccate, dehumidify, effloresce. **2** *frogs can dehydrate quickly:* **dry up/out**, lose water.
– OPPOSITES hydrate.

deify verb **1** *she was deified by the early Romans:* **worship**, revere, venerate, reverence, hold sacred; immortalize. **2** *he*

was deified by the press: **idolize**, lionize, hero-worship, extol; idealize, glorify, aggrandize; informal put on a pedestal.
– OPPOSITES demonize.

deign verb *I'm not going to hang around here waiting until you deign to come back to me:* **condescend**, stoop, lower oneself, demean oneself, humble oneself; consent, vouchsafe; informal come down from one's high horse.

deity noun **god**, goddess, divine being, supreme being, divinity, immortal; creator, demiurge; godhead.

dejected adjective *he stood in the street looking dejected:* **downcast**, downhearted, despondent, disconsolate, dispirited, crestfallen, disheartened; depressed, crushed, desolate, heartbroken, in the doldrums, sad, unhappy, doleful, melancholy, miserable, woebegone, forlorn, fed up, wretched, glum, gloomy; informal blue, down in the mouth, down in the dumps; Brit. informal brassed off, cheesed off.
– OPPOSITES cheerful.

delay verb **1** *we were delayed by the traffic:* **detain**, hold up, make late, slow up/down, bog down; hinder, hamper, impede, obstruct. **2** *they delayed no longer:* **linger**, dally, drag one's feet, be slow, hold back, dawdle, waste time; procrastinate, stall, hang fire, mark time, temporize, hesitate, dither, shilly-shally; informal dilly-dally. **3** *he may delay the cut in interest rates:* **postpone**, put off, defer, hold over, shelve, suspend, stay; reschedule; N. Amer. put over, table; informal put on ice, put on the back burner, put in cold storage.
– OPPOSITES hurry, advance.
noun **1** *drivers will face lengthy delays:* **hold-up**, wait, detainment; hindrance, impediment, obstruction, setback. **2** *the delay of his trial:* **postponement**, deferral, deferment, stay, respite; adjournment. **3** *I set off without delay:* **procrastination**, stalling, hesitation, dithering, dallying, dawdling.

delectable adjective **1** *a delectable meal:* **delicious**, mouth-watering, appetizing, flavoursome, flavourful, toothsome, palatable; succulent, luscious, tasty; informal scrumptious, delish, scrummy, yummy; Brit. informal moreish; N. Amer. informal finger-licking, nummy. **2** *the delectable Ms Davis:* **delightful**, lovely, captivating, charming, enchanting, appealing, beguiling; beautiful, attractive, ravishing, gorgeous, stunning, alluring, sexy, seductive, desirable, luscious; informal divine, heavenly, dreamy; Brit. informal tasty.
– OPPOSITES unpalatable, unattractive.

delectation noun (humorous) *they had all manner of goodies for our delectation:* **enjoyment**, gratification, delight, pleasure, satisfaction, relish; entertainment, amusement, titillation.

delegate noun *trade union delegates:* **representative**, envoy, emissary, commissioner, agent, deputy, commissary;

spokesperson, spokesman/woman; ambassador, plenipotentiary.
verb **1** *she must delegate routine tasks:* **assign**, entrust, pass on, hand on/over, turn over, devolve, depute, transfer. **2** *they were delegated to negotiate with the States:* **authorize**, commission, depute, appoint, nominate, mandate, empower, charge, choose, designate, elect.

delegation noun **1** *the delegation from South Africa:* **deputation**, delegacy, legation, (diplomatic) mission, commission; delegates, representatives, envoys, emissaries, deputies. **2** *the delegation of tasks to others:* **assignment**, entrusting, giving, devolution, deputation, transference.

delete verb *the offending paragraph was deleted from the letter:* **remove**, cut out, take out, edit out, expunge, excise, eradicate, cancel; cross out, strike out, blue-pencil, ink out, scratch out, obliterate, white out; rub out, erase, efface, wipe out, blot out.
– OPPOSITES add.

deleterious adjective *these policies are having a deleterious effect on British industry:* **harmful**, damaging, detrimental, injurious; bad, adverse, disadvantageous, unfavourable, unfortunate, undesirable.
– OPPOSITES beneficial.

deliberate adjective **1** *a deliberate attempt to provoke him:* **intentional**, calculated, conscious, intended, planned, studied, knowing, wilful, wanton, purposeful, purposive, premeditated, pre-planned; voluntary, volitional. **2** *small, deliberate steps:* **careful**, cautious; measured, regular, even, steady. **3** *a careful and deliberate worker:* **methodical**, systematic, careful, painstaking, meticulous, thorough.
– OPPOSITES accidental, hasty, careless.
verb *she deliberated on his words:* **think about/over**, ponder, consider, contemplate, reflect on, muse on, meditate on, ruminate on, mull over, give thought to, weigh up; brood over, dwell on; N. Amer. think on.

deliberately adverb **1** *he deliberately hurt me:* **intentionally**, on purpose, purposely, by design, knowingly, wittingly, consciously, purposefully; wilfully, wantonly. **2** *he walked deliberately down the aisle:* **carefully**, cautiously, slowly, steadily, evenly.

deliberation noun **1** *after much deliberation, I accepted:* **thought**, consideration, reflection, contemplation, meditation, rumination. **2** *he replaced the glass with deliberation:* **care**, carefulness, caution, steadiness.

delicacy noun **1** *the fabric's delicacy:* **fineness**, exquisiteness, delicateness, daintiness, airiness; flimsiness, gauziness, floatiness, silkiness. **2** *the children's delicacy:* **sickliness**, ill health, frailty, fragility, weakness, debility; infirmity. **3** *the delicacy of the situation:* **difficulty**, trickiness; sensitivity, ticklishness, awkwardness.

4 *treat this matter with delicacy:* **care**, sensitivity, tact, discretion, diplomacy, subtlety, sensibility. **5** *the crabs are an Australian delicacy:* **choice food**, gourmet food, dainty, treat, luxury, bonne bouche; speciality.

delicate adjective **1** *delicate embroidery:* **fine**, exquisite, intricate, dainty; flimsy, gauzy, filmy, floaty, diaphanous, wispy, insubstantial. **2** *a delicate shade of blue:* **subtle**, soft, muted; pastel, pale, light. **3** *delicate china cups:* **fragile**, breakable, frail. **4** *his wife is delicate:* **sickly**, unhealthy, frail, feeble, weak, debilitated; unwell, infirm. **5** *a delicate issue:* **difficult**, tricky, sensitive, ticklish, awkward, problematical, touchy, prickly; embarrassing; informal sticky, dicey. **6** *the matter required delicate handling:* **careful**, sensitive, tactful, diplomatic, discreet, kid-glove, softly-softly. **7** *his delicate palate:* **discriminating**, discerning; **fastidious**, fussy, finicky, dainty; informal picky, choosy, pernickety. **8** *a delicate mechanism:* **sensitive**, precision, precise.
– OPPOSITES coarse, lurid, strong, robust, clumsy.

delicious adjective **1** *a delicious meal:* **delectable**, mouth-watering, appetizing, tasty, flavoursome, flavourful, toothsome, palatable; succulent, luscious; informal scrumptious, delish, scrummy, yummy; Brit. informal moreish; N. Amer. informal finger-licking, nummy. **2** *a delicious languor stole over her:* **delightful**, exquisite, lovely, pleasurable, pleasant; informal heavenly, divine.
– OPPOSITES unpalatable, unpleasant.

delight verb **1** *her manners delighted him:* **please greatly**, charm, enchant, captivate, entrance, thrill; gladden, gratify, appeal to; entertain, amuse, divert; informal send, tickle pink, bowl over. **2** *Fabia delighted in his touch:* **take pleasure**, revel, luxuriate, wallow, glory; adore, love, relish, savour, lap up; informal get a kick out of, get a buzz out of, get a thrill out of, dig; N. Amer. informal get a charge out of.
– OPPOSITES dismay, disgust, dislike.
noun *she squealed with delight:* **pleasure**, happiness, joy, glee, gladness; excitement, amusement; bliss, rapture, elation, euphoria.
– OPPOSITES displeasure.

delighted adjective *we're delighted to have him back:* **pleased**, glad, happy, thrilled, overjoyed, ecstatic, elated; on cloud nine, walking on air, in seventh heaven, jumping for joy; enchanted, charmed; amused, diverted; gleeful, cock-a-hoop; informal over the moon, tickled pink, as pleased as Punch, on top of the world, as happy as Larry, blissed out; Brit. informal chuffed; N. English informal made up; Austral. informal wrapped.

delightful adjective **1** *a delightful evening:* **pleasant**, lovely, pleasurable, enjoyable; amusing, entertaining, diverting; gratifying, satisfying; marvellous, wonderful, splendid,

d

sublime, thrilling; informal great, super, fabulous, fab, terrific, heavenly, divine, grand; Brit. informal brilliant, brill, smashing; N. Amer. informal peachy, ducky; Austral./NZ informal beaut, bonzer. **2** *the delightful Sally:* **charming**, enchanting, captivating, bewitching, appealing; sweet, endearing, cute, lovely, adorable, delectable, delicious, gorgeous, ravishing, beautiful, pretty; Scottish & N. English bonny; informal dreamy, divine.

delimit verb *their responsibilities will be more strictly delimited:* **determine**, establish, set, fix, demarcate, define, delineate.

delineate verb **1** *the aims of the study as delineated by the boss:* **describe**, set forth/out, present, outline, depict, represent; map out, define, specify, identify. **2** *a section delineated in red marker pen:* **outline**, trace, block in, mark (out/off), delimit.

delinquency noun *teenage delinquency:* **crime**, wrongdoing, lawbreaking, lawlessness, misconduct, misbehaviour; misdemeanours, offences, misdeeds.

delinquent adjective *delinquent teenagers:* **lawless**, lawbreaking, criminal; errant, badly behaved, troublesome, difficult, unruly, disobedient, uncontrollable.
– OPPOSITES dutiful.
noun *teenage delinquents:* **offender**, wrongdoer, malefactor, lawbreaker, culprit, criminal; hooligan, vandal, ruffian, hoodlum; young offender; informal tearaway.

delirious adjective **1** *she was delirious but had lucid intervals:* **incoherent**, raving, babbling, irrational; feverish, frenzied; deranged, demented, unhinged, mad, insane, out of one's mind. **2** *the delirious crowd:* **ecstatic**, euphoric, elated, thrilled, overjoyed, beside oneself, walking on air, on cloud nine, in seventh heaven, carried away, transported, rapturous; hysterical, wild, frenzied; informal blissed out, over the moon, on a high.

delirium noun **1** *she had fits of delirium:* **derangement**, dementia, madness, insanity; incoherence, irrationality, hysteria, feverishness, hallucination. **2** *the delirium of desire:* **ecstasy**, rapture, transports, wild emotion, passion, wildness, excitement, frenzy, feverishness, fever; euphoria, elation.
– OPPOSITES lucidity.

deliver verb **1** *the parcel was delivered to his house:* **bring**, take, convey, carry, transport; send, dispatch, remit. **2** *the money was delivered up to the official:* **hand over**, turn over, make over, sign over, surrender, give up, yield, cede; consign, commit, entrust, trust. **3** *he was delivered from his enemies:* **save**, rescue, free, liberate, release, extricate, emancipate, redeem. **4** *the court delivered its verdict:* **utter**, give, make, read, broadcast; pronounce, announce, declare, proclaim, hand down, return, set forth. **5** *she*

delivered a blow to his head: **administer**, deal, inflict, give; informal land. **6** *he delivered the first ball:* **bowl**, pitch, hurl, throw, cast, lob. **7** *she returned home to deliver her child:* **give birth to**, bear, be delivered of, have, bring into the world; N. Amer. birth; informal drop.

deliverance noun **1** *their deliverance from prison:* **liberation**, release, delivery, discharge, rescue, emancipation; salvation. **2** *the tone he adopted for such deliverances:* **utterance**, statement, announcement, pronouncement, declaration, proclamation; lecture, speech.

delivery noun **1** *the delivery of the goods:* **conveyance**, carriage, transportation, transport, distribution; dispatch, remittance; freightage, haulage, shipment. **2** *we get several deliveries a day:* **consignment**, load, shipment. **3** *the deliveries take place in hospital:* **birth**, childbirth; formal parturition. **4** *her delivery was stilted:* **speech**, pronunciation, enunciation, articulation, elocution; utterance, recitation, recital, execution.

delude verb *you're lying—why do you persist in trying to delude me?* **mislead**, deceive, fool, take in, trick, dupe, hoodwink, gull, lead on; informal con, pull the wool over someone's eyes, lead up the garden path, take for a ride; N. Amer. informal sucker, snooker; Austral. informal pull a swifty on.

deluge noun **1** *homes were swept away by the deluge:* **flood**, torrent; Brit. spate. **2** *the deluge turned the pitch into a swamp:* **downpour**, torrential rain; thunderstorm, rainstorm, cloudburst. **3** *a deluge of complaints:* **barrage**, volley; flood, torrent, avalanche, stream, spate, rush, outpouring.
verb **1** *homes were deluged by the rains:* **flood**, inundate, submerge, swamp, drown. **2** *we have been deluged with calls:* **inundate**, overwhelm, overrun, flood, swamp, snow under, engulf, bombard.

delusion noun **1** *a common male delusion:* **misapprehension**, misconception, misunderstanding, mistake, error, misinterpretation, misconstruction, misbelief; fallacy, illusion, fantasy. **2** *a web of delusion:* **deception**, trickery.

de luxe adjective *a de luxe hotel:* **luxurious**, luxury, sumptuous, palatial, opulent, lavish; grand, high-class, quality, exclusive, choice, fancy; expensive, costly; Brit. upmarket; informal plush, posh, classy, ritzy, swanky, pricey; Brit. informal swish; N. Amer. informal swank.
– OPPOSITES basic, cheap.

delve verb **1** *she delved in her pocket:* **rummage**, search, hunt, scrabble about/around, root about/around, ferret, fish about/around in, dig; go through, rifle through; Brit. informal rootle around in. **2** *we must delve deeper into the matter:* **investigate**, enquire, probe, explore, research, look into, go into.

demand noun **1** *I gave in to her demands:* **request**, call, command, order, dictate, ultimatum, stipulation. **2** *the demands of a young family:* **requirement**, need, desire, wish, want; claim, imposition. **3** *the big demand for such toys:* **market**, call, appetite, desire; run on, rush on.
verb **1** *workers demanded wage increases:* **call for**, ask for, request, push for, hold out for; insist on, stipulate, claim. **2** *Harvey demanded that I tell him the truth:* **order**, command, enjoin, urge. **3** *'Where is she?' he demanded:* **ask**, inquire, question, interrogate; challenge. **4** *an activity demanding detailed knowledge:* **require**, need, necessitate, call for, involve, entail.
■ **in demand** sought-after, desired, coveted, wanted, requested; marketable, desirable, popular, all the rage, at a premium, like gold dust; informal big, trendy, hot.

demanding adjective **1** *a demanding task:* **difficult**, challenging, taxing, exacting, tough, hard, onerous, burdensome, formidable; arduous, uphill, rigorous, gruelling, back-breaking, punishing. **2** *a demanding child:* **nagging**, clamorous, importunate, insistent; trying, tiresome, hard to please.
– OPPOSITES easy.

demarcate verb *plots of land demarcated by barbed wire:* **separate**, divide, mark (out/off), delimit, delineate; bound.

demarcation noun **1** *clear demarcation of function:* **separation**, distinction, differentiation, division, delimitation, definition. **2** *territorial demarcations:* **boundary**, border, borderline, frontier; dividing line, divide.

demean verb *his actions only served to demean him in the eyes of the public:* **discredit**, lower, degrade, debase, devalue; cheapen, abase, humble, humiliate, disgrace, dishonour.
– OPPOSITES dignify.

demeaning adjective *a demeaning experience:* **degrading**, humiliating, shameful, mortifying, abject, ignominious, undignified, inglorious; informal infra dig.

demeanour noun *his normally calm demeanour:* **manner**, air, attitude, appearance, look; bearing, carriage; behaviour, conduct.

demented adjective *the ravings of a demented old man:* **mad**, insane, deranged, out of one's mind, crazed, lunatic, unbalanced, unhinged, disturbed, non compos mentis; informal crazy, mental, off one's head, off one's rocker, nutty, round the bend, raving mad, batty, cuckoo, loopy, loony, bananas, screwy, touched, gaga, not all there, out to lunch; Brit. informal barmy, bonkers, crackers, barking, round the twist, off one's trolley, not the full shilling; N. Amer. informal buggy, nutso, squirrelly, wacko.
– OPPOSITES sane.

dementia noun **mental illness**, madness, insanity, derangement, lunacy; Alzheimer's (disease).

demise noun **1** *her tragic demise:* **death**, dying, passing, loss of life, end, quietus. **2** *the demise of the Ottoman empire:* **end**, break-up, disintegration, fall, downfall, collapse.
– OPPOSITES birth.

demobilize verb *the militia were demobilized:* **disband**, decommission, discharge; Brit. informal demob.

democracy noun *a capitalist system of parliamentary democracy:* **representative government**, elective government, constitutional government; self-government, autonomy; republic, commonwealth.
– OPPOSITES dictatorship.

democratic adjective *a democratic government:* **elected**, representative, parliamentary, popular; egalitarian, classless; self-governing, autonomous, republican.

demolish verb **1** *they demolished a block of flats:* **knock down**, pull down, tear down, bring down, destroy, flatten, raze (to the ground), level, bulldoze, topple; blow up; dismantle, disassemble. **2** *he demolished her credibility:* **destroy**, ruin, wreck; refute, disprove, discredit, overturn, explode, drive a coach and horses through; informal shoot full of holes, do for.
– OPPOSITES construct, strengthen.

demolition noun **1** *the demolition of the building:* **destruction**, levelling, bulldozing, clearance; obliteration. **2** *the demolition of his theory:* **destruction**, refutation.

demon noun **1** *the demons from hell:* **devil**, fiend, evil spirit, cacodemon; incubus, succubus; hellhound. **2** *the man was a demon:* **monster**, ogre, fiend, devil, brute, savage, beast, barbarian, animal. **3** *Surrey's fast-bowling demon:* **genius**, expert, master, virtuoso, maestro, past master, marvel; star; informal hotshot, whizz, buff, pro, ace.
– OPPOSITES angel, saint.

demonic, demoniac, demoniacal adjective **1** *demonic powers:* **devilish**, fiendish, diabolical, satanic, Mephistophelean, hellish, infernal; evil, wicked. **2** *the demonic intensity of his playing:* **frenzied**, wild, feverish, frenetic, frantic, furious, manic, like one possessed.

demonstrable adjective *there are demonstrable links between French and American art:* **verifiable**, provable, attestable; verified, proven, confirmed; obvious, clear, clear-cut, evident, apparent, manifest, patent, distinct, noticeable; unmistakable, undeniable.

demonstrate verb **1** *his findings demonstrate that boys commit more crimes:* **show**, indicate, determine, establish, prove, confirm, verify, corroborate, substantiate. **2** *she was asked to demonstrate quilting:* **give**

a demonstration of, show how something is done; display, show, illustrate, exemplify. **3** *his work demonstrated an analytical ability:* **reveal**, bespeak, indicate, signify, signal, denote, show, display, exhibit; bear witness to, testify to; imply, intimate, give away. **4** *they demonstrated against the Government:* **protest**, rally, march; stage a sit-in, picket, strike, walk out; mutiny, rebel.

demonstration noun **1** *there is no demonstration of God's existence:* **proof**, substantiation, confirmation, affirmation, corroboration, verification, validation; evidence, indication, witness, testament. **2** *a demonstration of woodcarving:* **exhibition**, presentation, display, exposition, teaching; informal demo, expo, taster. **3** *his paintings are a demonstration of his talent:* **manifestation**, indication, sign, mark, token, embodiment; expression. **4** *an anti-racism demonstration:* **protest**, march, rally, lobby, sit-in; stoppage, strike, walkout, picket (line); informal demo.

demonstrative adjective **1** *a very demonstrative family:* **expressive**, open, forthcoming, communicative, unreserved, emotional, effusive, gushing; affectionate, cuddly, loving, warm; informal touchy-feely, lovey-dovey. **2** *the successes are demonstrative of their skill:* **indicative**, indicatory, suggestive, illustrative.
– OPPOSITES reserved.

demoralize verb *they kept wages low, which demoralized the staff:* **dishearten**, dispirit, deject, cast down, depress, dismay, daunt, discourage, unman, unnerve, crush, shake, throw, cow, subdue; break someone's spirit; informal knock the stuffing out of, knock sideways; Brit. informal knock for six.
– OPPOSITES hearten.

demoralized adjective **dispirited**, disheartened, downhearted, dejected, downcast, low, depressed, despairing; disconsolate, crestfallen, disappointed, dismayed, daunted, discouraged; crushed, humbled, subdued.

demote verb *she was demoted after a rift with her boss:* **downgrade**, relegate, declass, reduce in rank; depose, unseat, displace, oust.
– OPPOSITES promote.

demotic adjective *a demotic idiom:* **popular**, vernacular, colloquial, idiomatic, vulgar, common; informal, everyday, slangy.
– OPPOSITES formal.

demur verb *Steed demurred when the suggestion was made:* **object**, take exception, take issue, protest, cavil, dissent; voice reservations, be unwilling, be reluctant, baulk, think twice; drag one's heels, refuse; informal boggle, kick up a fuss.
noun *they accepted without demur:* **objection**, protest, protestation, complaint, dispute, dissent, opposition, resistance; reservation, hesitation, reluctance,

disinclination; doubts, qualms, misgivings, second thoughts; a murmur, a word.

demure adjective *the paintings show a demure Victorian miss:* **modest**, unassuming, meek, mild, reserved, retiring, quiet, shy, bashful, diffident, reticent, timid, shrinking, coy; decorous, decent, seemly, ladylike, respectable, proper, virtuous, pure, innocent, chaste; sober, sedate, staid, prim, goody-goody, strait-laced; informal butter-wouldn't-melt.
– OPPOSITES brazen.

den noun **1** *the mink left its den:* **lair**, sett, earth, drey, burrow, hole, dugout, covert, shelter, hiding place, hideout. **2** *a notorious drinking den:* **haunt**, site, hotbed, nest, pit, hole; informal joint, dive. **3** *the poet scribbled in his den:* **study**, studio, library; sanctum, retreat, sanctuary, hideaway, snug, cubbyhole; informal hidey-hole.

denial noun **1** *the reports met with a denial:* **contradiction**, refutation, rebuttal, repudiation, disclaimer; negation, dissent. **2** *the denial of insurance to certain people:* **refusal**, withholding; rejection, rebuff, repulse, veto, turndown; informal knock-back. **3** *the denial of worldly values:* **renunciation**, eschewal, repudiation, disavowal, rejection, abandonment, surrender, relinquishment.

denigrate verb *doom and gloom merchants who denigrate their own country:* **disparage**, belittle, deprecate, decry, cast aspersions on, criticize, attack; speak ill of, give someone a bad name, defame, slander, libel; run down, abuse, insult, revile, malign, vilify; N. Amer. slur; informal bad-mouth, pull to pieces; Brit. informal rubbish, slate, slag off.
– OPPOSITES extol.

denomination noun **1** *a Christian denomination:* **religious group**, faith community, sect, cult, movement, body, branch, persuasion, order, school; Church. **2** *banknotes in a number of denominations:* **value**, unit, size.

denote verb **1** *the headdresses denoted warriors:* **designate**, indicate, be a mark of, signify, signal, symbolize, represent, mean; typify, characterize, distinguish, mark, identify. **2** *his manner denoted an inner strength:* **suggest**, point to, smack of, indicate, show, reveal, intimate, imply, convey, betray, bespeak; informal spell.

denouement noun **1** *the film's denouement:* **finale**, final scene, epilogue, coda, end, ending, finish, close; culmination, climax, conclusion, resolution, solution. **2** *the debate had an unexpected denouement:* **outcome**, upshot, consequence, result, end; informal pay-off.
– OPPOSITES beginning, origin.

denounce verb **1** *the Pope denounced abortion:* **condemn**, criticize, attack, censure, decry, revile, vilify, discredit, damn, reject; proscribe; malign, rail against, run down; N. Amer. slur; informal knock, slam, hit out at, lay into; Brit. informal slate, slag

off; formal castigate. **2** *he was denounced as a traitor:* **expose**, betray, inform on; incriminate, implicate, cite, name, accuse.
– OPPOSITES praise.

dense adjective **1** *a dense forest:* **thick**, close-packed, tightly packed, closely set, crowded, compact, solid, tight; overgrown, jungly, impenetrable, impassable. **2** *dense smoke:* **thick**, heavy, opaque, soupy, murky, smoggy; concentrated, condensed. **3** (informal) *they were dense enough to believe me:* **stupid**, unintelligent, ignorant, brainless, mindless, foolish, slow, witless, simple-minded, empty-headed, vacuous, vapid, idiotic, imbecilic; informal thick, dim, moronic, dumb, dopey, dozy, wooden-headed, lamebrained, birdbrained, pea-brained; Brit. informal daft.
– OPPOSITES sparse, thin, clever.

density noun *vitamin D deficiency causes a lack of bone density:* **solidity**, solidness, denseness, thickness, substance, mass; compactness, tightness, hardness.

dent noun **1** *I made a dent in his car:* **indentation**, dint, dimple, dip, depression, hollow, crater, pit, trough. **2** *lawyer's fees will make a nasty dent in their finances:* **reduction**, depletion, deduction, cut.
– OPPOSITES increase.
verb **1** *Jamie dented his bike:* **dint**, indent, mark. **2** *the experience dented her confidence:* **diminish**, reduce, lessen, shrink, weaken, erode, undermine, sap, shake, damage, impair.

dentist noun **dental surgeon**, orthodontist, periodontist, paedodontist.

denude verb *the island had been denuded of trees:* **strip**, clear, deprive, bereave, rob; lay bare, uncover, expose; deforest, defoliate.
– OPPOSITES cover.

deny verb **1** *the report was denied by witnesses:* **contradict**, repudiate, challenge, contest, oppose; disprove, debunk, explode, discredit, refute, rebut, invalidate, negate, nullify, quash; informal shoot full of holes. **2** *he denied the request:* **refuse**, turn down, reject, rebuff, repulse, decline, veto, dismiss; informal knock back, give the thumbs down to, give the red light to. **3** *she had to deny her parents:* **renounce**, eschew, repudiate, disavow, disown, wash one's hands of, reject, discard, cast aside, abandon, give up.
– OPPOSITES confirm, accept.

deodorant noun *an underarm deodorant:* **antiperspirant**, body spray, perfume, scent.

deodorize verb *the sewage waters were deodorized without chemicals:* **freshen**, sweeten, purify, disinfect, sanitize, sterilize; fumigate, aerate, air, ventilate.

depart verb **1** *James departed after lunch:* **leave**, go (away), withdraw, absent oneself, abstract oneself, quit, exit, decamp, retreat, retire; make off, run off/away; set off/out, get under way, be on one's way; informal make tracks, up sticks, clear off/out, take off, split; Brit. informal sling one's hook. **2** *the*

budget departed from the norm: **deviate**, diverge, digress, drift, stray, veer; differ, vary; contrast with.
– OPPOSITES arrive.

departed adjective *he saw the ghost of his departed wife:* **dead**, expired, gone, no more, passed on/away; perished, fallen; informal six feet under, pushing up daisies; euphemistic with God, asleep.

department noun **1** *the public health department:* **division**, section, sector, unit, branch, arm, wing; office, bureau, agency, ministry. **2** *the various departments of France:* **district**, canton, province, territory, state, county, shire, parish; region, area. **3** *the food is Kay's department:* **domain**, territory, province, area, line; responsibility, duty, function, business, affair, charge, task, concern; informal pigeon, baby, bag, bailiwick.

departure noun **1** *he tried to delay her departure:* **leaving**, going, leave-taking, withdrawal, exit, egress, retreat. **2** *a departure from normality:* **deviation**, divergence, digression, shift; variation, change. **3** *the film represents an exciting departure for film-makers:* **change**, innovation, novelty, rarity.

depend verb **1** *her career depends on a good reference:* **be contingent on**, be conditional on, be dependent on, hinge on, hang on, rest on, rely on; be decided by. **2** *my family depends on me:* **rely on**, lean on; count on, bank on, trust (in), have faith in, believe in; pin one's hopes on.

dependable adjective *he was a solid and dependable person:* **reliable**, trustworthy, trusty, faithful, loyal, unfailing, sure, steadfast, stable; honourable, sensible, responsible.

dependant noun **child**, minor; ward, charge, protégé; relative; (**dependants**) family, offspring, progeny.

dependency noun **1** *her dependency on her husband:* **dependence**, reliance; need for. **2** *the association of retirement with dependency:* **helplessness**, dependence, weakness, defencelessness, vulnerability. **3** *drug dependency:* **addiction**, dependence, reliance; craving, compulsion, fixation, obsession; abuse. **4** *a British dependency:* **colony**, protectorate, province, outpost, satellite state; holding, possession.
– OPPOSITES independence.

dependent adjective **1** *your placement is dependent on her decision:* **conditional**, contingent, based; subject to, determined by, influenced by. **2** *the army is dependent on volunteers:* **reliant on**, relying on, counting on; sustained by. **3** *she is dependent on drugs:* **addicted to**, reliant on; informal hooked on. **4** *he is ill and dependent:* **reliant**, needy; helpless, weak, infirm, invalid, incapable, debilitated, disabled. **5** *a UK dependent territory:* **subsidiary**, subject; satellite, ancillary; puppet.

d

d

depict verb **1** *the painting depicts the Last Supper:* **portray**, represent, picture, illustrate, delineate, reproduce, render; draw, paint. **2** *the process depicted by Darwin's theory:* **describe**, detail, relate; present, set forth, set out, outline, delineate; represent, portray, characterize.

depiction noun **1** *a depiction of Aphrodite:* **picture**, painting, portrait, drawing, sketch, study, illustration; image, likeness. **2** *the film's depiction of women:* **portrayal**, representation, presentation, characterization.

deplete verb *clan warfare has severely depleted the food supply:* **exhaust**, use up, consume, expend, drain, empty, milk; reduce, decrease, diminish; slim down, cut back.
– OPPOSITES augment.

depletion noun **exhaustion**, use, consumption, expenditure; reduction, decrease, diminution; impoverishment.

deplorable adjective **1** *your conduct is deplorable:* **disgraceful**, shameful, dishonourable, unworthy, inexcusable, unpardonable, unforgivable; reprehensible, despicable, abominable, contemptible, execrable, heinous, beyond the pale. **2** *the garden is in a deplorable state:* **lamentable**, regrettable, unfortunate, wretched, atrocious, awful, terrible, dreadful, diabolical; sorry, poor, inadequate; informal appalling, dire, abysmal, woeful, lousy.
– OPPOSITES admirable.

deplore verb **1** *we deplore violence:* **abhor**, find unacceptable, frown on, disapprove of, take a dim view of, take exception to; detest, despise; condemn, denounce. **2** *he deplored their lack of flair:* **regret**, lament, mourn, rue, bemoan, bewail, complain about, grieve over, sigh over.
– OPPOSITES applaud.

deploy verb **1** *forces were deployed at strategic points:* **position**, station, post, place, install, locate, situate, site, establish; base; distribute, dispose. **2** *she deployed all her skills:* **use**, utilize, employ, take advantage of, exploit; bring into service, call on, turn to, resort to.

deport verb *they were fined and deported:* **expel**, banish, exile, transport, expatriate, extradite, repatriate; evict, oust, throw out; informal kick out, boot out, send packing; Brit. informal turf out.
– OPPOSITES admit.

deportment noun **1** (Brit.) *poise is concerned with good deportment:* **posture**, carriage, bearing, stance, gait. **2** (N. Amer.) *unprofessional deportment:* **behaviour**, conduct, performance; manners, practices, actions.

depose verb *the president was deposed:* **overthrow**, unseat, dethrone, topple, remove, supplant, displace; dismiss, oust,

drum out, throw out, expel, eject; informal chuck out, boot out, get rid of, show someone the door; Brit. informal turf out.

deposit noun **1** *a thick deposit of ash:* **accumulation**, sediment; layer, covering, coating, blanket. **2** *a copper deposit:* **seam**, vein, lode, layer, stratum, bed. **3** *they paid a deposit:* **down payment**, advance payment, prepayment, instalment, retainer, stake.
verb **1** *she deposited her books on the table:* **put (down)**, place, set (down), unload, rest; drop; informal dump, park, plonk; N. Amer. informal plunk. **2** *the silt deposited by flood water:* **leave (behind)**, precipitate, dump; wash up, cast up. **3** *the gold was deposited at the bank:* **lodge**, bank, house, store, stow, put away; informal stash, squirrel away.

deposition noun **1** *a commissioner is to take depositions from witnesses:* **statement**, sworn statement, affidavit, attestation, affirmation, submission, declaration; testimony, evidence. **2** *the barons plotted the King's deposition:* **overthrow**, downfall, removal, dethronement, displacement, dismissal, expulsion, ejection; N. Amer. ouster.

depository noun *the burial chamber was used as a depository for a coin hoard:* **repository**, cache, store, storeroom, storehouse, warehouse; vault, strongroom, safe, treasury; container, receptacle; informal lock-up.

depot noun **1** *the bus depot:* **terminal**, terminus, station, garage; headquarters, base. **2** *an arms depot:* **storehouse**, warehouse, store, repository, depository, cache, dump; arsenal, magazine, armoury.

deprave verb *they have been depraved by pornography:* **corrupt**, lead astray, warp, subvert, pervert, debauch, debase, degrade, defile, sully, pollute.

depraved adjective **corrupt**, perverted, deviant, degenerate, debased, immoral, unprincipled; debauched, dissolute, licentious, lecherous, prurient, indecent, sordid; wicked, sinful, vile, iniquitous, nefarious; informal warped, twisted, pervy, sick.

depravity noun **corruption**, vice, perversion, deviance, degeneracy, immorality, debauchery, dissipation, profligacy, licentiousness, lechery, prurience, obscenity, indecency; wickedness, sin, iniquity; informal perviness.

deprecate verb **1** *the school deprecates this behaviour:* **deplore**, abhor, disapprove of, frown on, take a dim view of, take exception to, detest, despise; criticize, censure. **2** *he deprecates the value of television:* **belittle**, disparage, denigrate, run down, discredit, decry, play down, trivialize, underrate, undervalue, underestimate, depreciate; scoff at, sneer at, scorn, disdain; informal pooh-pooh.
– OPPOSITES praise, overrate.

deprecatory adjective **1** *deprecatory*

remarks: **disapproving**, censorious, critical, scathing, damning, condemnatory, denunciatory, disparaging, denigratory, derogatory, negative, unflattering; disdainful, derisive, snide. **2** *a deprecatory smile:* **apologetic**, rueful, regretful, sorry, remorseful, contrite, penitent, repentant; shamefaced, sheepish.

depreciate verb **1** *new cars depreciate quickly:* **decrease in value**, lose value, fall in price. **2** *the decision to depreciate property:* **devalue**, cheapen, reduce, lower in price, mark down, cut, discount; informal slash. **3** *they depreciate the importance of art:* **belittle**, disparage, denigrate, decry, deprecate, underrate, undervalue, underestimate, diminish, trivialize; disdain, sneer at, scoff at, scorn; informal knock, badmouth, sell short, pooh-pooh, do down; Brit. informal rubbish.

depredation noun *few survived the depredation of the barbarian invasion:* **plundering**, plunder, looting, pillaging, robbery; devastation, destruction, damage, rape; ravages, raids.

depress verb **1** *the news depressed him:* **sadden**, dispirit, cast down, get down, dishearten, demoralize, crush, shake, desolate, weigh down, oppress; upset, distress, grieve, haunt, harrow; informal give someone the blues, make someone fed up. **2** *new economic policies depressed sales:* **slow down**, reduce, lower, weaken, impair; limit, check, inhibit, restrict. **3** *imports will depress farm prices:* **reduce**, lower, cut, cheapen, keep down, discount, deflate, depreciate, devalue, diminish, axe; informal slash. **4** *depress each key in turn:* **press**, push, hold down; thumb, tap; operate, activate.
– OPPOSITES encourage, raise.

depressant noun *the drug is a stimulant rather than a depressant:* **sedative**, tranquillizer, calmative, sleeping pill, soporific, opiate, hypnotic; informal downer, trank, sleeper, dope.
– OPPOSITES stimulant.

depressed adjective **1** *he felt lonely and depressed:* **sad**, unhappy, miserable, gloomy, glum, melancholy, dejected, disconsolate, downhearted, downcast, down, despondent, dispirited, low, heavy-hearted, morose, dismal, desolate; tearful, upset; informal blue, down in the dumps, down in the mouth, fed up. **2** *a depressed economy:* **weak**, enervated, devitalized, impaired; inactive, flat, slow, slack, sluggish, stagnant. **3** *depressed prices:* **reduced**, low, cut, cheap, marked down, discounted, discount; informal slashed. **4** *a depressed town:* **poverty-stricken**, poor, disadvantaged, deprived, needy, distressed; run down; informal slummy. **5** *a depressed area of the skull:* **sunken**, hollow, concave, indented, recessed.
– OPPOSITES cheerful, strong, inflated, prosperous, raised.

depressing adjective **1** *depressing*

thoughts: **upsetting**, distressing, painful, heartbreaking; dismal, bleak, black, sombre, gloomy, grave, unhappy, melancholy, sad; wretched, doleful; informal morbid, blue. **2** *a depressing room:* **gloomy**, bleak, dreary, grim, drab, sombre, dark, dingy, funereal, cheerless, joyless, comfortless, uninviting.

depression noun **1** *she ate to ease her depression:* **unhappiness**, sadness, melancholy, melancholia, misery, sorrow, woe, gloom, despondency, low spirits, heavy heart, despair, desolation, hopelessness; upset, tearfulness; informal the dumps, the doldrums, the blues, one's black dog, a (blue) funk. **2** *an economic depression:* **recession**, slump, decline, downturn, standstill; stagnation. **3** *a depression in the ground:* **hollow**, indentation, dent, dint, cavity, concavity, dip, pit, hole, sinkhole, trough, crater; basin, bowl.

deprivation noun *unemployment and deprivation:* **poverty**, impoverishment, penury, privation, hardship, destitution; need, want, distress, indigence, beggary, ruin; straitened circumstances.
– OPPOSITES wealth.

deprive verb *she was deprived of her royal privileges:* **dispossess**, strip, divest, relieve, bereave, deny, rob; cheat out of; informal do out of.

deprived adjective *the most deprived sections of society:* **disadvantaged**, underprivileged, poverty-stricken, impoverished, poor, destitute, needy, unable to make ends meet; Brit. on the bread line.

depth noun **1** *the depth of the caves:* **deepness**, distance downwards, distance inwards; drop, vertical extent. **2** *the depth of his knowledge:* **extent**, range, scope, breadth, width; magnitude, scale, degree. **3** *her lack of depth:* **profundity**, deepness, wisdom, understanding, intelligence, sagacity, discernment, penetration, insight, astuteness, acumen, shrewdness. **4** *a work of great depth:* **complexity**, intricacy; profundity, gravity, weight. **5** *depth of colour:* **intensity**, richness, deepness, vividness, strength, brilliance. **6** *the depths of the sea:* **deepest part**, bottom, floor, bed; abyss.
– OPPOSITES shallowness, triviality, surface.
■ **in depth** thoroughly, extensively, comprehensively, rigorously, exhaustively, completely, fully; meticulously, scrupulously, painstakingly.

deputation noun *the prime minister agreed to receive a deputation of bankers:* **delegation**, delegacy, legation, commission, committee, (diplomatic) mission; contingent, group, party.

depute verb **1** *he was deputed to handle negotiations:* **appoint**, designate, nominate, assign, commission, charge, choose, select, elect; empower, authorize. **2** *the judge deputed smaller cases to others:* **delegate**,

d

d

transfer, hand over, pass on, consign, assign, entrust, give.

deputize verb *the assistant's task is to deputize for the account executive:* **stand in**, sit in, fill in, cover, substitute, replace, take someone's place, understudy, be a locum, relieve, take over; hold the fort, step into the breach; act for, act on behalf of; informal sub.

deputy noun *he handed over to his deputy:* **second (in command)**, number two, subordinate, junior, assistant, personal assistant, PA, aide, helper, right-hand man/woman, underling, man/girl Friday; substitute, stand-in, fill-in, relief, understudy, locum tenens; representative, proxy, agent, spokesperson; Scottish depute; informal sidekick, locum, temp.
adjective *her deputy editor:* **assistant**, substitute, stand-in, acting, reserve, fill-in, caretaker, temporary, provisional, stopgap, surrogate; pro tempore, ad interim; informal second-string.

deranged adjective *five schoolchildren were shot by a deranged gunman:* **insane**, mad, disturbed, unbalanced, unhinged, unstable, irrational; crazed, demented, berserk, frenzied, lunatic, certifiable; non compos mentis; informal touched, crazy, mental; Brit. informal barmy, barking (mad), round the twist.
– OPPOSITES rational.

derelict adjective **1** *a derelict building:* **dilapidated**, ramshackle, run down, tumbledown, in ruins, falling apart; rickety, creaky, deteriorating, crumbling; neglected, untended, gone to rack and ruin. **2** *a derelict airfield:* **disused**, abandoned, deserted, discarded, rejected, neglected, untended. **3** (N. Amer.) *he was derelict in his duty:* **negligent**, neglectful, remiss, lax, careless, sloppy, slipshod, slack, irresponsible, delinquent.
noun *the derelicts who survive on the streets:* **tramp**, vagrant, vagabond, down and out, homeless person, drifter; beggar, mendicant; outcast; informal dosser, bag lady; N. Amer. informal hobo, bum.

dereliction noun **1** *buildings were reclaimed from dereliction:* **dilapidation**, disrepair, deterioration, ruin, rack and ruin; abandonment, neglect, disuse. **2** *dereliction of duty:* **negligence**, neglect, delinquency, failure; carelessness, laxity, sloppiness, slackness, irresponsibility; oversight, omission.

deride verb *the decision was derided by environmentalists:* **ridicule**, mock, scoff at, jibe at, make fun of, poke fun at, laugh at, hold up to ridicule, pillory; disdain, disparage, denigrate, dismiss, slight; sneer at, scorn, insult; informal knock, pooh-pooh, take the mickey out of.
– OPPOSITES praise.

de rigueur adjective **1** *straight hair was de rigueur:* **fashionable**, in fashion, in vogue, modish, up to date, up to the minute, all the rage; informal trendy, with it. **2** *an address is de rigueur for business cards:* **customary**, standard, conventional, normal, orthodox, usual, comme il faut; compulsory; informal done.

derision noun *my stories were greeted with disbelief and derision:* **mockery**, ridicule, jeers, sneers, taunts; disdain, disparagement, denigration, disrespect, insults; scorn, contempt; lampooning, satire.

derisive adjective *he gave a harsh, derisive laugh:* **mocking**, jeering, scoffing, teasing, derisory, snide, sneering; disdainful, scornful, contemptuous, taunting, insulting; scathing, sarcastic; informal snidey; Brit. informal sarky.

derisory adjective **1** *a derisory sum:* **inadequate**, insufficient, tiny, small; trifling, paltry, pitiful, miserly, miserable; negligible, token, nominal; ridiculous, laughable, ludicrous, preposterous, insulting; informal measly, stingy, lousy, pathetic, piddling, piffling, mingy, poxy. **2** *derisory calls from the crowd.* See DERISIVE.

derivation noun **1** *the derivation of theories from empirical observation:* **deriving**, induction, deduction, inference; extraction, eliciting. **2** *the derivation of a word:* **origin**, etymology, root, etymon, provenance; source; origination, beginning, foundation, basis, cause; development, evolution.

derivative adjective *her poetry was derivative:* **imitative**, unoriginal, uninventive, unimaginative, uninspired; copied, plagiarized, plagiaristic, second-hand; trite, hackneyed, clichéd, stale, stock, banal; informal copycat, cribbed, old hat.
– OPPOSITES original.
noun **1** *a derivative of opium:* **by-product**, subsidiary product; spin-off. **2** *a derivative of a verb:* **derived word**.

derive verb **1** *he derives consolation from his poetry:* **obtain**, get, take, gain, acquire, procure, extract, attain, glean. **2** *'coffee' derives from the Turkish 'kahveh':* **originate in**, stem from, descend from, spring from, be taken from. **3** *his fortune derives from property:* **originate in**, be rooted in; stem from, come from, spring from, proceed from, issue from.

derogatory adjective *a derogatory remark:* **disparaging**, denigratory, deprecatory, disrespectful, demeaning; critical, pejorative, negative, unfavourable, uncomplimentary, unflattering, insulting; offensive, personal, abusive, rude, nasty, mean, hurtful; defamatory, slanderous, libellous; informal bitchy, catty.
– OPPOSITES complimentary.

descend verb **1** *the plane started descending:* **go down**, come down; drop, fall, sink, dive, plummet, plunge, nosedive. **2** *she descended the stairs:* **climb down**, go down, come down; shin down. **3** *the road descends to a village:* **slope**, dip, slant, go down, fall away.

4 *she saw Leo descend from the bus:* **alight**, disembark, get down, get off, dismount. **5** *they would not descend to such mean tricks:* **stoop**, lower oneself, demean oneself, debase oneself; resort, be reduced, go as far as. **6** *they descended on the pub:* **come in force**, arrive in hordes; attack, assail, assault, storm, invade, swoop on, charge. **7** *he is descended from a Flemish family:* **be a descendant of**, originate from, issue from, spring from, derive from.
– OPPOSITES ascend, climb, board.

descendant noun *a descendant of Charles Darwin:* **successor**, scion; heir; (**descendants**) offspring, progeny, family, lineage.
– OPPOSITES ancestor.

descent noun **1** *the plane began its descent:* **dive**, drop; fall, pitch. **2** *their descent of the mountain:* **downward climb**, way down. **3** *a steep descent:* **slope**, incline, dip, drop, gradient, declivity, slant; hill. **4** *his descent into alcoholism:* **decline**, slide, fall, degeneration, deterioration, regression. **5** *she is of Italian descent:* **ancestry**, parentage, ancestors, family, antecedents; extraction, origin, derivation, birth; lineage, line, genealogy, heredity, stock, pedigree, blood, bloodline; roots, origins.

describe verb **1** *he described his experiences:* **report**, recount, relate, tell of, set out, chronicle; detail, catalogue, give a rundown of; explain, illustrate, discuss, comment on. **2** *she described him as a pathetic figure:* **designate**, pronounce, call, label, style, dub; characterize, class; portray, depict, brand, paint. **3** *the pen described a circle:* **delineate**, mark out, outline, trace, draw.

description noun **1** *a description of my travels:* **account**, report, rendition, explanation, illustration; chronicle, narration, narrative, story, commentary; portrayal, portrait; details. **2** *the description of coal as 'bottled sunshine':* **designation**, labelling, naming, dubbing, pronouncement; characterization, classification, branding; portrayal, depiction. **3** *vehicles of every description:* **sort**, variety, kind, type, category, order, breed, class, designation, specification, genre, genus, brand, make, character, ilk; N. Amer. stripe.

descriptive adjective *his style uses colourful descriptive language:* **illustrative**, expressive, graphic, detailed, lively, vivid, striking; explanatory, elucidatory, explicative.

desecrate verb *invaders desecrated the temple:* **violate**, profane, defile, debase, degrade, dishonour; vandalize, damage, destroy, deface.

desert[1] verb **1** *his wife deserted him:* **abandon**, leave, turn one's back on; throw over, jilt, break up with; leave high and dry, leave in the lurch, leave behind, strand, maroon; informal walk out on, run out on, drop, dump, ditch. **2** *his allies were deserting*

the cause: **renounce**, repudiate, relinquish, wash one's hands of, abandon, turn one's back on, betray, disavow. **3** *soldiers deserted in droves:* **abscond**, defect, run away, make off, decamp, flee, turn tail, take French leave, depart, quit; Military go AWOL.

desert[2] noun *an African desert:* **wasteland**, wastes, wilderness, wilds, barren land; dust bowl.
adjective **1** *desert conditions:* **arid**, dry, moistureless, parched, scorched, hot; barren, bare, stark, infertile, unfruitful, dehydrated, sterile. **2** *a desert island:* **uninhabited**, empty, lonely, desolate, bleak; wild, uncultivated.
– OPPOSITES fertile.

deserted adjective **1** *a deserted wife:* **abandoned**, thrown over, jilted, cast aside; neglected, stranded, marooned; forlorn, bereft; informal dumped, ditched, dropped. **2** *a deserted village:* **empty**, uninhabited, unoccupied, unpeopled, abandoned, evacuated, vacant; untenanted, tenantless, neglected; desolate, lonely, godforsaken.
– OPPOSITES populous.

deserter noun *a deserter from the Foreign Legion:* **absconder**, runaway, fugitive, truant, escapee; renegade, defector, turncoat, traitor.

desertion noun **1** *his wife's desertion of him:* **abandonment**, leaving, jilting. **2** *the desertion of the president's colleagues:* **defection**; betrayal, renunciation, repudiation, apostasy. **3** *soldiers were executed for desertion:* **absconding**, running away, truancy, going absent without leave, taking French leave, escape; defection, treason; Military going AWOL.

deserve verb *everyone involved with the book deserves the greatest praise:* **merit**, earn, warrant, rate, justify, be worthy of, be entitled to, have a right to, be qualified for.

deserved adjective **well earned**, merited, warranted, justified, justifiable; rightful, due, right, just, fair, fitting, appropriate, suitable, proper, apt.

deserving adjective **1** *the deserving poor:* **worthy**, meritorious, commendable, praiseworthy, admirable, estimable, creditable; respectable, decent, honourable, righteous. **2** *a lapse deserving of punishment:* **meriting**, warranting, justifying, suitable for, worthy of.

desiccated adjective *desiccated coconut:* **dried**, dry, dehydrated, powdered.
– OPPOSITES moist.

desideratum noun *integrity was a desideratum:* **requirement**, prerequisite, need, indispensable thing, sine qua non, essential, requisite, necessary.

design noun **1** *a design for the offices:* **plan**, blueprint, drawing, sketch, outline, map, plot, diagram, draft, representation, scheme, model. **2** *tableware with a gold design:* **pattern**, motif, device; style, composition,

d

d

make-up, layout, construction, shape, form. **3** *his design of reaching the top:* **intention**, aim, purpose, plan, intent, objective, object, goal, end, target; hope, desire, wish, dream, aspiration, ambition.
▶ verb **1** *the church was designed by Hicks:* **plan**, outline, map out, draft, draw. **2** *they designed a new engine:* **invent**, originate, create, think up, come up with, devise, formulate, conceive; make, produce, develop, fashion; informal dream up. **3** *this paper is designed to provoke discussion:* **intend**, aim; devise, contrive, purpose, plan; tailor, fashion, adapt, gear; mean, destine.
▪ **by design** deliberately, intentionally, on purpose, purposefully; knowingly, wittingly, consciously, calculatedly.

designate ▶ verb **1** *some firms designate a press officer:* **appoint**, nominate, depute, delegate; select, choose, pick, elect, name, identify, assign. **2** *the rivers are designated 'Sites of Special Scientific Interest':* **classify**, class, label, tag; name, call, entitle, term, dub.

designation ▶ noun **1** *the designation of a leader:* **appointment**, nomination, naming, selection, election. **2** *the designation of nature reserves:* **classification**, specification, definition, earmarking, pinpointing. **3** *the designation 'Generalissimo':* **title**, name, epithet, tag; nickname, byname, sobriquet; informal moniker, handle.

designer ▶ noun **1** *a designer of farmhouses:* **creator**, planner, deviser, inventor, originator; maker; architect, builder. **2** *young designers made the dress:* **couturier**, tailor, costumier, dressmaker.

desirability ▶ noun **1** *the desirability of the property:* **appeal**, attractiveness, allure; agreeableness, worth, excellence. **2** *the desirability of a different economy:* **advisability**, advantage, expedience, benefit, merit, value, profit, profitability. **3** *her obvious desirability:* **attractiveness**, sexual attraction, beauty, good looks; charm, seductiveness; informal sexiness.

desirable ▶ adjective **1** *a desirable location:* **attractive**, sought-after, in demand, popular, desired, covetable, enviable; appealing, agreeable, pleasant; valuable, good, excellent; informal to die for. **2** *it is desirable that they should meet:* **advantageous**, advisable, wise, sensible, recommendable; helpful, useful, beneficial, worthwhile, profitable, preferable. **3** *a very desirable woman:* **(sexually) attractive**, beautiful, pretty, appealing; seductive, alluring, enchanting, beguiling, captivating, bewitching, irresistible; informal sexy, beddable.
– OPPOSITES unattractive, unwise.

desire ▶ noun **1** *a desire to see the world:* **wish**, want, aspiration, fancy, inclination, impulse; yearning, longing, craving, hankering, hunger; eagerness, enthusiasm, determination; informal yen, itch. **2** *his*

eyes glittered with desire: **lust**, sexual attraction, passion, sensuality, sexuality; lasciviousness, lechery, salaciousness, libidinousness; informal the hots, raunchiness, horniness; Brit. informal randiness.
▶ verb **1** *they desired peace:* **want**, wish for, long for, yearn for, crave, hanker after, be desperate for, be bent on, covet, aspire to; fancy; informal have a yen for, yen for. **2** *she desired him:* **be attracted to**, lust after, burn for, be infatuated by; informal fancy, have the hots for, have a crush on, be mad about.

desired ▶ adjective **1** *cut the cloth to the desired length:* **required**, necessary, proper, right, correct; appropriate, suitable; preferred, chosen, selected. **2** *the desired results:* **wished for**, wanted, coveted; sought-after, longed for, yearned for.

desirous ▶ adjective *he became restless and desirous of change:* **eager**, desiring, anxious, keen, craving, yearning, longing, hungry; ambitious, aspiring; covetous, envious; informal dying, itching.

desist ▶ verb *we must desist from any industrial action that may disturb national unity:* **abstain**, refrain, forbear, hold back, keep; stop, cease, discontinue, suspend, give up, break off, drop, dispense with, eschew; informal lay off, give over, quit, pack in.
– OPPOSITES continue.

desk ▶ noun **writing table**, bureau, escritoire, secretaire; Brit. davenport.

desolate ▶ adjective **1** *desolate moorlands:* **bleak**, stark, bare, dismal, grim; wild, inhospitable; deserted, uninhabited, godforsaken, abandoned, unpeopled, untenanted, empty; unfrequented, unvisited, isolated, remote. **2** *she is desolate at such appalling news:* **miserable**, despondent, depressed, disconsolate, devastated, despairing, inconsolable, broken-hearted, grief-stricken, crushed, bereft; sad, unhappy, downcast, down, dejected, forlorn, upset, distressed; informal blue, cut up.
– OPPOSITES populous, joyful.
▶ verb **1** *droughts desolated the plains:* **devastate**, ravage, ruin, lay waste to; level, raze, demolish, wipe out, obliterate. **2** *she was desolated by the loss of her husband:* **dishearten**, depress, sadden, cast down, make miserable, weigh down, crush, upset, distress; informal shatter.

desolation ▶ noun **1** *the desolation of the Gobi desert:* **bleakness**, starkness, barrenness, sterility; wildness; isolation, loneliness, remoteness. **2** *a feeling of utter desolation:* **misery**, sadness, unhappiness, despondency, sorrow, depression, grief, woe; broken-heartedness, wretchedness, dejection, devastation, despair, anguish, distress.

despair ▶ noun *a voice full of self-hatred and despair:* **hopelessness**, disheartenment, discouragement, desperation, distress, anguish, unhappiness; despondency, depression, disconsolateness, melancholy,

misery, wretchedness; defeatism, pessimism.
– OPPOSITES hope, joy.
verb *she despaired of finding a good restaurant nearby:* **lose hope**, abandon hope, give up, lose heart, be discouraged, be despondent, be demoralized, resign oneself; be pessimistic, look on the black side.
■ **be the despair of** be the bane of, be the scourge of, be a burden on, be a trial to, be a thorn in the flesh/side of.

despairing adjective *her mother gave me a despairing look:* **hopeless**, in despair, dejected, depressed, despondent, disconsolate, gloomy, miserable, wretched, desolate, inconsolable; disheartened, discouraged, demoralized, devastated; defeatist, pessimistic.

despatch verb & noun. See DISPATCH.

desperate adjective **1** *he gave me a desperate look:* **despairing**, hopeless, anguished, distressed, wretched, desolate, forlorn, distraught, fraught; out of one's mind, at one's wits' end, beside oneself, at the end of one's tether. **2** *a desperate attempt to escape:* **last-ditch**, last-gasp, eleventh-hour, do-or-die, final; frantic, frenzied, wild; futile, hopeless, doomed. **3** *a desperate shortage of teachers:* **grave**, serious, critical, acute, risky, precarious; dire, awful, terrible, dreadful; urgent, pressing, crucial, vital, drastic, extreme; informal chronic. **4** *they were desperate for food:* **in great need of**, urgently requiring, in want of; eager, longing, yearning, hungry, crying out; informal dying. **5** *a desperate act:* **violent**, dangerous, lawless; reckless, rash, hasty, impetuous, foolhardy, incautious, hazardous, risky; death-or-glory, do-or-die.

desperately adverb **1** *he screamed desperately for help:* **in desperation**, in despair, despairingly, in anguish, in distress; wretchedly, hopelessly, desolately, forlornly. **2** *they are desperately ill:* **seriously**, critically, gravely, severely, acutely, dangerously, perilously; very, extremely, dreadfully; hopelessly, irretrievably; informal terribly. **3** *he desperately wanted to talk:* **urgently**, pressingly; intensely, eagerly.

desperation noun *he became a thief out of sheer desperation:* **hopelessness**, despair, distress; anguish, agony, torment, misery, wretchedness; disheartenment, discouragement.

despicable adjective *these were particularly despicable crimes:* **contemptible**, loathsome, hateful, detestable, reprehensible, abhorrent, abominable, awful, heinous; odious, vile, low, mean, abject, shameful, ignominious, shabby, ignoble, disreputable, discreditable, unworthy; informal dirty, rotten, low-down; Brit. informal beastly.
– OPPOSITES admirable.

despise verb *he despised weakness in any form:* **detest**, hate, loathe, abhor, execrate,

deplore, dislike; scorn, disdain, look down on, deride, sneer at, revile; spurn, shun.
– OPPOSITES adore.

despite preposition *he remains a great leader despite age and infirmity:* **in spite of**, notwithstanding, regardless of, in the face of, for all, even with.

despoil verb **1** *a village despoiled by invaders:* **plunder**, pillage, rob, ravage, raid, ransack, rape, loot, sack; devastate, lay waste, ruin. **2** *the robbers despoiled him of all he had:* **rob**, strip, deprive, dispossess, denude, divest, relieve, clean out.

despondency noun *the mood became one of gloom and despondency:* **hopelessness**, despair, disheartenment, discouragement, low spirits, wretchedness; melancholy, gloom, misery, desolation, disappointment, dejection, sadness, unhappiness; informal the blues, heartache.

despondent adjective **disheartened**, discouraged, dispirited, downhearted, downcast, crestfallen, down, low, disconsolate, despairing, wretched; melancholy, gloomy, morose, lugubrious, Eeyorish, dismal, woebegone, miserable, depressed, dejected, sad; informal blue, down in the mouth, down in the dumps.
– OPPOSITES hopeful, cheerful.

despot noun *we must not support such despots by arming them:* **tyrant**, oppressor, dictator, absolute ruler, totalitarian, autocrat.

despotic adjective *a despotic regime:* **autocratic**, dictatorial, totalitarian, absolutist, undemocratic, unaccountable; one-party, autarchic, monocratic; tyrannical, tyrannous, oppressive, repressive, draconian, illiberal.
– OPPOSITES democratic.

despotism noun **tyranny**, dictatorship, totalitarianism, absolute rule, absolutism; oppression, repression; autocracy, monocracy, autarchy.

dessert noun **pudding**, sweet, second course, last course; Brit. informal afters, pud.

destabilize verb *the tsar's isolation helped to destabilize the regime:* **undermine**, weaken, damage, subvert, sabotage, unsettle, upset, disrupt.
– OPPOSITES strengthen.

destination noun *at around 1 p.m. we arrived at our destination:* **journey's end**, end of the line; terminus, stop, stopping place, port of call; goal, target, end.

destined adjective **1** *he is destined to lead a troubled life:* **fated**, ordained, predestined, meant; certain, sure, bound, assured, likely; doomed. **2** *computers destined for Pakistan:* **heading**, bound, en route, scheduled; intended, meant, designed, designated, allotted, reserved.

destiny noun **1** *man is master of his own destiny:* **future**, fate, fortune, doom; lot. **2** *she was sent by destiny:* **fate**, providence;

d

predestination; divine decree, God's will, kismet, the stars; luck, fortune, chance; karma.

destitute adjective **1** *she was left destitute:* **penniless**, poor, impoverished, poverty-stricken, impecunious, without a penny to one's name; needy, in straitened circumstances, distressed, badly off; Brit. on the breadline; informal hard up, (flat) broke, strapped (for cash), cash-strapped, without a brass farthing, without two pennies to rub together, without a bean; Brit. informal stony broke, skint; N. Amer. informal stone broke, without a red cent. **2** *we were destitute of clothing:* **devoid**, bereft, deprived, in need; lacking, without, deficient in, wanting.
– OPPOSITES rich.

destitution noun **poverty**, impoverishment, penury, pennilessness, privation, pauperism; hardship, need, want, straitened circumstances, dire straits, deprivation, (financial) distress.

destroy verb **1** *their offices were destroyed by bombing:* **demolish**, knock down, level, raze (to the ground), fell; wreck, ruin, shatter; blast, blow up, dynamite, explode, bomb. **2** *traffic would destroy the conservation area:* **spoil**, ruin, wreck, disfigure, blight, mar, impair, deface, scar, injure, harm, devastate, damage, wreak havoc on. **3** *illness destroyed his career chances:* **wreck**, ruin, spoil, disrupt, undo, upset, put an end to, put a stop to, terminate, frustrate, blight, crush, quash, dash, scotch; devastate, demolish, sabotage; informal mess up, muck up, foul up, put paid to, put the kibosh on, do for, queer, blow a hole in; Brit. informal scupper, throw a spanner in the works of. **4** *the horse had to be destroyed:* **kill**, put down, put to sleep, slaughter, terminate, exterminate. **5** *we had to destroy the enemy:* **annihilate**, wipe out, obliterate, wipe off the face of the earth, eliminate, eradicate, liquidate, finish off, erase; kill, slaughter, massacre, exterminate; informal take out, rub out, snuff out; N. Amer. informal waste.
– OPPOSITES build, preserve, raise, spare.

destruction noun **1** *the destruction by allied bombers:* **demolition**, wrecking, ruination, blasting, bombing; wreckage, ruins. **2** *the destruction of the countryside:* **spoliation**, devastation, ruination, blighting, disfigurement, impairment, scarring, harm, desolation. **3** *the destruction of cattle:* **slaughter**, killing, putting down, extermination, termination. **4** *the destruction of the enemies' forces:* **annihilation**, obliteration, elimination, eradication, liquidation; killing, slaughter, massacre, extermination.

destructive adjective **1** *the most destructive war:* **devastating**, ruinous, disastrous, catastrophic, calamitous, cataclysmic; harmful, damaging, detrimental, deleterious, injurious, crippling; violent, savage, fierce, brutal, deadly, lethal.

2 *destructive criticism:* **negative**, hostile, vicious, unfriendly; unhelpful, obstructive, discouraging.

desultory adjective *a few people were left, dancing in a desultory fashion:* **casual**, cursory, superficial, token, perfunctory, half-hearted, lukewarm; random, aimless, erratic, unmethodical, unsystematic, chaotic, inconsistent, irregular, intermittent, sporadic, fitful.
– OPPOSITES keen.

detach verb **1** *he detached the lamp from its bracket:* **unfasten**, disconnect, disengage, separate, uncouple, remove, loose, unhitch, unhook, free, disunite; pull off, cut off, break off. **2** *he detached himself from the crowd:* **free**, separate, segregate; move away, split off; leave, abandon. **3** *he has detached himself from his family:* **dissociate**, divorce, alienate, separate, segregate, isolate, cut off, delink; break away, disaffiliate, defect; leave, quit, withdraw from, break with.
– OPPOSITES attach, join.

detached adjective **1** *a detached collar:* **unfastened**, disconnected, separated, separate, loosened; untied, unhitched, undone, unhooked, unbuttoned; free, severed, cut off. **2** *a detached observer:* **dispassionate**, disinterested, objective, uninvolved, outside, neutral, unbiased, unprejudiced, impartial, non-partisan; indifferent, aloof, remote, distant, impersonal. **3** *a detached house:* **standing alone**, separate.

detachment noun **1** *she looked on everything with detachment:* **objectivity**, dispassion, disinterest, open-mindedness, neutrality, impartiality; indifference, aloofness. **2** *a detachment of soldiers:* **unit**, detail, squad, troop, contingent, outfit, task force, patrol, crew; platoon, company, corps, regiment, brigade, battalion. **3** *the detachment of the wallpaper:* **loosening**, disconnection, disengagement, separation; removal.

detail noun **1** *the picture is correct in every detail:* **particular**, respect, feature, characteristic, attribute, specific, aspect, facet, part, unit, component, constituent; fact, piece of information, point, element, circumstance, consideration. **2** *that's just a detail:* **unimportant point**, trivial fact, triviality, technicality, nicety, subtlety, trifle, fine point, incidental, inessential, nothing. **3** *records with a considerable degree of detail:* **precision**, exactness, accuracy, thoroughness, carefulness, scrupulousness, particularity. **4** *a guard detail:* **unit**, detachment, squad, troop, contingent, outfit, task force, patrol. **5** *I got the toilet detail:* **duty**, task, job, chore, charge, responsibility, assignment, function, mission, engagement, occupation, undertaking, errand.
verb **1** *the report details our objections:* **describe**, explain, expound, relate, catalogue, list, spell out, itemize,

particularize, identify, specify; state, declare, present, set out, frame; cite, quote, instance, mention, name. **2** *troops were detailed to prevent the escape:* **assign**, allocate, appoint, delegate, commission, charge; send, post; nominate, vote, elect, co-opt.

■ **in detail** thoroughly, in depth, exhaustively, minutely, closely, meticulously, rigorously, scrupulously, painstakingly, carefully; completely, comprehensively, fully, extensively.

detailed adjective *he was able to give the police a detailed description of his attacker:* **comprehensive**, full, complete, thorough, exhaustive, all-inclusive; elaborate, minute, intricate; explicit, specific, precise, exact, accurate, meticulous, painstaking; itemized, blow-by-blow.
– OPPOSITES general.

detain verb **1** *they were detained for questioning:* **hold**, take into custody, take (in), confine, imprison, lock up, put in jail, intern; arrest, apprehend, seize; informal pick up, run in, haul in, nab, collar; Brit. informal nick. **2** *don't let me detain you:* **delay**, hold up, make late, keep, slow up/down; hinder, hamper, impede, obstruct.
– OPPOSITES release.

detect verb **1** *no one detected the smell of diesel:* **notice**, perceive, discern, be aware of, note, make out, spot, recognize, distinguish, remark, identify, diagnose; catch, sense, see, smell, scent, taste; Brit. informal clock. **2** *they are responsible for detecting fraud:* **discover**, uncover, find out, turn up, unearth, dig up, root out, expose, reveal. **3** *help the police to detect crime:* **solve**, clear up, get to the bottom of, find the person behind; informal crack. **4** *the hackers were detected:* **catch**, hunt down, track down, find, expose, reveal, unmask, smoke out; apprehend, arrest; informal nail.

detection noun **1** *the detection of methane:* **discernment**, perception, awareness, recognition, identification, diagnosis; sensing, sight, smelling, tasting. **2** *the detection of insider dealing:* **discovery**, uncovering, unearthing, exposure, revelation. **3** *the detection rate for burglary:* **solving**, clear-up. **4** *he managed to escape detection:* **capture**, identification, exposure; apprehension, arrest.

detective noun **investigator**, private investigator, private detective, operative; Brit. enquiry agent; informal private eye, PI, sleuth, snoop; N. Amer. informal shamus, gumshoe.

detention noun *she was released after spending over a year in police detention:* **custody**, imprisonment, confinement, incarceration, internment, detainment, captivity; arrest, house arrest; quarantine.

deter verb **1** *the high cost deterred many:* **discourage**, dissuade, put off, scare off; dishearten, demoralize, daunt, intimidate.

2 *the presence of a caretaker deters crime:* **prevent**, stop, avert, fend off, stave off, ward off, block, halt, check; hinder, impede, hamper, obstruct, foil, forestall, counteract, inhibit, curb.
– OPPOSITES encourage.

detergent noun *washing detergent:* **cleaner**, cleanser; washing powder, washing-up liquid; soap.
adjective *detergent action:* **cleaning**, cleansing; surface-active.

deteriorate verb **1** *his health deteriorated:* **worsen**, decline, degenerate; fail, slump, slip, go downhill, go backwards, wane, ebb; informal go to pot. **2** *these materials deteriorate if stored wrongly:* **decay**, degrade, degenerate, break down, decompose, rot, go off, spoil, perish; break up, disintegrate, crumble, fall apart.
– OPPOSITES improve.

deterioration noun **1** *a deterioration in law and order:* **decline**, collapse, failure, drop, downturn, slump, slip, retrogression. **2** *deterioration of the roof structure:* **decay**, degradation, degeneration, breakdown, decomposition, rot; atrophy, weakening; break-up, disintegration, dilapidation.

determinate adjective *a determinate hierarchy of authority:* **fixed**, settled, specified, established, defined, explicit, known, determined, definitive, conclusive, express, precise, categorical, positive, definite.

determination noun **1** *it took great determination to win:* **resolution**, resolve, will power, strength of character, single-mindedness, purposefulness, intentness; staunchness, perseverance, persistence, tenacity, staying power; strong-mindedness, backbone; stubbornness, doggedness, obstinacy; spirit, courage, pluck, grit, stout-heartedness; informal guts, spunk. **2** *the determination of the rent:* **setting**, specification, settlement, designation, arrangement, establishment, prescription. **3** *the determination of the speed of light:* **calculation**, discovery, ascertainment, establishment, deduction, divination, diagnosis, discernment, verification, confirmation.

determine verb **1** *chromosomes determine the sex of the embryo:* **control**, decide, regulate, direct, dictate, govern; affect, influence, mould. **2** *he determined to sell up:* **resolve**, decide, make up one's mind, choose, elect, opt. **3** *the rent shall be determined by an accountant:* **specify**, set, fix, decide on, settle, assign, designate, arrange, choose, establish, ordain, prescribe, decree. **4** *determine the composition of the fibres:* **ascertain**, find out, discover, learn, establish, calculate, work out, make out, deduce, diagnose, discern; check, verify, confirm; informal figure out.

determined adjective **1** *he was determined to have his way:* **intent on**, bent on,

d

set on, insistent on, resolved to, firm about, committed to; single-minded about, obsessive about. **2** *a very determined man:* **resolute**, purposeful, purposive, adamant, single-minded, unswerving, unwavering, undaunted, intent, insistent; steadfast, staunch, stalwart; persevering, persistent, indefatigable, tenacious; strong-minded, strong-willed, unshakeable, steely, four-square, dedicated, committed; stubborn, dogged, obstinate, inflexible, intransigent, unyielding, immovable; N. Amer. rock-ribbed.

determining adjective *the size of your house may be the determining factor:* **deciding**, decisive, conclusive, final, definitive, key, pivotal, crucial, critical, major, chief, prime.

deterrent noun *complications of this nature are a deterrent to investors:* **disincentive**, discouragement, damper, curb, check, restraint; obstacle, hindrance, impediment, obstruction, block, barrier, inhibition.
– OPPOSITES incentive.

detest verb *she really did detest his mockery:* **abhor**, hate, loathe, despise, shrink from, be unable to bear, find intolerable, dislike, disdain, have an aversion to.
– OPPOSITES love.

detestable adjective *all terrorist crime is detestable:* **abhorrent**, hateful, loathsome, despicable, abominable, execrable, repellent, repugnant, repulsive, revolting, disgusting, distasteful, horrible, horrid, awful; heinous, reprehensible, obnoxious, odious, offensive, contemptible.

dethrone verb *he had hoped to dethrone the king:* **depose**, unseat, uncrown, oust, topple, overthrow, bring down, dislodge, displace, supplant, usurp, eject, drum out.
– OPPOSITES crown.

detonate verb **1** *the charge detonated under the engine:* **explode**, go off, blow up, shatter, erupt; ignite; bang, blast, boom. **2** *they detonated the bomb:* **set off**, explode, discharge, let off, touch off, trigger; ignite, kindle.

detonation noun **explosion**, discharge, blowing up, ignition; blast, bang, report.

detour noun *visiting Bagley meant a detour of only a mile or so:* **diversion**, roundabout route, indirect route, scenic route; digression, deviation.

detract verb **1** *my reservations should not detract from the book's excellence:* **belittle**, take away from, diminish, reduce, lessen, minimize, play down, trivialize, decry, depreciate, devalue, deprecate. **2** *the patterns will detract attention from each other:* **divert**, distract, draw away, deflect, avert, shift one's attention.

detractor noun *detractors complained about the display's confused nature:* **critic**, disparager, denigrator, deprecator, belittler, attacker, fault-finder, backbiter; slanderer, libeller; informal knocker.

detriment noun *he is engrossed in his work*

to the detriment of his married life: **harm**, damage, injury, hurt, impairment, loss, disadvantage, disservice, mischief.
– OPPOSITES benefit.

detrimental adjective *the erosion will have a detrimental effect on water quality:* **harmful**, damaging, injurious, hurtful, inimical, deleterious, destructive, ruinous, disastrous, bad, malign, adverse, undesirable, unfavourable, unfortunate; unhealthy, unwholesome.
– OPPOSITES benign.

detritus noun *large areas of land are now littered with military detritus:* **debris**, waste, refuse, rubbish, litter, scrap, flotsam and jetsam, lumber, rubble; remains, remnants, fragments, scraps, dregs, leavings, sweepings, dross, scum; N. Amer. trash, garbage; Austral./NZ mullock; informal dreck.

devalue verb *our culture devalues the reasons for getting married:* **belittle**, depreciate, disparage, denigrate, decry, deprecate, treat lightly, discredit, underrate, undervalue, underestimate, deflate, diminish, trivialize, run down; informal knock, sell short, put down, pooh-pooh, do down, pick holes in; Brit. informal rubbish.

devastate verb **1** *the city was devastated by an earthquake:* **destroy**, ruin, wreck, lay waste, ravage, demolish, raze (to the ground), level, flatten. **2** *he was devastated by the news:* **shatter**, shock, stun, daze, dumbfound, traumatize, crush, overwhelm, overcome, distress; informal knock sideways; Brit. informal knock for six.

devastating adjective **1** *a devastating cyclone:* **destructive**, ruinous, disastrous, catastrophic, calamitous, cataclysmic; harmful, damaging, injurious, detrimental; crippling, violent, savage, fierce, dangerous, fatal, deadly, lethal. **2** *devastating news:* **shattering**, shocking, traumatic, overwhelming, crushing, distressing, terrible; informal gut-wrenching. **3** (informal) *he presented devastating arguments:* **incisive**, highly effective, penetrating, cutting; withering, blistering, searing, scathing, fierce, savage, stinging, biting, caustic, harsh, unsparing.

devastation noun **1** *the hurricane left a trail of devastation:* **destruction**, ruin, desolation, havoc, wreckage; ruins, ravages. **2** *the devastation of Prussia:* **destruction**, wrecking, ruination, despoliation; demolition, annihilation. **3** *the devastation you have caused the family:* **shock**, trauma, distress, stress, strain, pain, anguish, suffering, upset, agony, misery, heartache.

develop verb **1** *the industry developed rapidly:* **grow**, expand, spread; advance, progress, evolve, mature; prosper, thrive, flourish, blossom. **2** *a plan was developed:* **initiate**, instigate, set in motion; originate, invent, form, establish, generate. **3** *children should develop their talents:* **expand**, augment, broaden, supplement, reinforce;

enhance, refine, improve, polish, perfect. **4** *a row developed:* **start**, begin, emerge, erupt, break out, burst out, arise, break, unfold, happen.

development noun **1** *the development of the firm:* **evolution**, growth, maturation, expansion, enlargement, spread, buildout, progress; success. **2** *the development of an idea:* **forming**, establishment, initiation, instigation, origination, invention, generation. **3** *keep abreast of developments:* **event**, occurrence, happening, circumstance, incident, situation, issue. **4** *a housing development:* **estate**, complex, site.

deviant adjective *deviant behaviour:* **aberrant**, abnormal, atypical, anomalous, irregular, non-standard; nonconformist, perverse, uncommon, unusual; freakish, strange, odd, peculiar, bizarre, eccentric, idiosyncratic, unorthodox, exceptional; informal kinky, quirky.
– OPPOSITES normal.
noun *we were seen as deviants:* **nonconformist**, eccentric, maverick, individualist; outsider, misfit; informal oddball, weirdo, freak; N. Amer. informal screwball, kook.

deviate verb *you must not deviate from the agreed route:* **diverge**, digress, drift, stray, slew, veer, swerve; get sidetracked, branch off; differ, vary, run counter to, contrast with.

deviation noun **divergence**, digression, departure; difference, variation, variance; aberration, abnormality, irregularity, anomaly, inconsistency, discrepancy.

device noun **1** *a device for measuring pressure:* **implement**, gadget, utensil, tool, appliance, apparatus, instrument, machine, mechanism, contrivance, contraption; informal gizmo, widget. **2** *an ingenious legal device:* **ploy**, tactic, move, stratagem, scheme, plot, trick, ruse, manoeuvre, machination, contrivance, expedient, dodge, wile; Brit. informal wheeze. **3** *their shields bear his device:* **emblem**, symbol, logo, badge, crest, insignia, coat of arms, escutcheon, seal, mark, design, motif; monogram, hallmark, trademark.

devil noun **1** *God and the Devil:* **Satan**, Beelzebub, Lucifer, the Lord of the Flies, the Prince of Darkness; informal Old Nick. **2** *they drove out the devils from their bodies:* **evil spirit**, demon, cacodemon, fiend, bogie; informal spook. **3** *look what the cruel devil has done:* **brute**, beast, monster, fiend; villain, sadist, barbarian, ogre. **4** *he's a naughty little devil:* **rascal**, rogue, imp, fiend, monkey, wretch; informal monster, horror, scamp, tyke; Brit. informal perisher; N. Amer. informal varmint.

devilish adjective **1** *a devilish grin:* **diabolical**, fiendish, demonic, satanic, demoniac, demoniacal; hellish, infernal. **2** *a devilish torture:* **wicked**, evil, iniquitous, vile, foul, abominable, unspeakable, loathsome, monstrous, atrocious, heinous,

hideous, odious, horrible, appalling, dreadful, awful, terrible, ghastly, abhorrent, despicable, depraved, dark, black, immoral; vicious, cruel, savage, barbaric. **3** *a devilish job:* **difficult**, tricky, ticklish, troublesome, thorny, awkward, problematic.

devil-may-care adjective *those devil-may-care young pilots:* **reckless**, rash, incautious, heedless, impetuous, impulsive, daredevil, hot-headed, wild, foolhardy, audacious, death-or-glory; nonchalant, casual, breezy, flippant, insouciant, happy-go-lucky, easy-going, unworried, untroubled, unconcerned, harum-scarum; Brit. tearaway.

devilry, deviltry noun **1** *some devilry was afoot:* **wickedness**, evil, sin, iniquity, vileness, badness, wrongdoing, dishonesty, unscrupulousness, villainy, delinquency, devilishness, fiendishness; informal crookedness, shadiness. **2** *she had a perverse sense of devilry:* **mischief**, mischievousness, naughtiness, badness, perversity, impishness; misbehaviour, troublemaking, misconduct; pranks, tricks, roguery, devilment; informal monkey business, shenanigans. **3** *they dabbled in devilry:* **black magic**, sorcery, witchcraft, wizardry, necromancy, enchantment, spell-working, incantation; the supernatural, occultism, the occult, the black arts, divination, voodoo, witchery; N. Amer. mojo, orenda.

devious adjective **1** *the devious ways in which they bent the rules:* **underhand**, deceitful, dishonest, dishonourable, unethical, unprincipled, immoral, unscrupulous, fraudulent, dubious, unfair, treacherous, duplicitous; crafty, cunning, calculating, artful, conniving, scheming, sly, wily; sneaky, furtive, secret, clandestine, surreptitious, covert; N. Amer. snide, snidey; informal crooked, shady, dirty, low-down; Brit. informal dodgy. **2** *a devious route around the coast:* **circuitous**, roundabout, indirect, meandering, tortuous.

devise verb *scientists have devised a method of recycling oil contaminated with PCBs:* **conceive**, think up, dream up, work out, formulate, concoct; design, invent, coin, originate; compose, construct, fabricate, create, produce, develop; discover, hit on; hatch, contrive; informal cook up.

devoid adjective (**devoid of**) lacking, without, wanting; informal minus.

devolution noun *the devolution of power to the regions:* **decentralization**, delegation; redistribution, transfer; surrender, relinquishment.

devolve verb *the move would devolve responsibility to local units:* **delegate**, depute, pass (down/on), hand down/over/on, transfer, transmit, assign, consign, convey, entrust, turn over, give, cede, surrender, relinquish, deliver; bestow, grant.

devote verb *they need to devote considerable*

d

time to career planning: **allocate**, assign, allot, commit, give (over), apportion, consign, pledge; dedicate, consecrate; set aside, earmark, reserve, designate.

devoted adjective *a devoted follower:* **loyal**, faithful, true (blue), staunch, steadfast, constant, committed, dedicated, devout; fond, loving, affectionate, caring, admiring.

devotee noun **1** *a devotee of rock music:* **enthusiast**, fan, lover, aficionado, admirer; informal buff, freak, nut, fiend, fanatic, addict. **2** *devotees thronged the temple:* **follower**, adherent, supporter, advocate, disciple, votary, member, stalwart, fanatic, zealot; believer, worshipper.

devotion noun **1** *her devotion to her husband:* **loyalty**, faithfulness, fidelity, constancy, commitment, adherence, allegiance, dedication; fondness, love, admiration, affection, care. **2** *a life of devotion:* **devoutness**, piety, religiousness, spirituality, godliness, holiness, sanctity. **3** *morning devotions:* **(religious) worship**, religious observance; prayers, vespers, matins; prayer meeting, church service.

devotional adjective *the devotional paintings of the period:* **religious**, sacred, spiritual, divine, church, ecclesiastical.
– OPPOSITES secular.

devour verb **1** *he devoured his meal:* **eat hungrily**, eat greedily, gobble (up/down), guzzle, gulp (down), bolt (down), cram down, gorge oneself on, wolf (down), feast on, consume, eat up; informal pack away, demolish, dispose of, make short work of, polish off, shovel down, stuff oneself with, pig oneself on, put away, get outside of; Brit. informal scoff. **2** *flames devoured the house:* **consume**, engulf, envelop; destroy, demolish, lay waste, devastate; gut, ravage, ruin, wreck.

devout adjective **1** *a devout Christian:* **pious**, religious, devoted, dedicated, reverent, God-fearing; holy, godly, saintly, faithful, dutiful, righteous, churchgoing, orthodox. **2** *a devout soccer fan:* **dedicated**, devoted, committed, loyal, faithful, staunch, genuine, firm, steadfast, unwavering, sincere, wholehearted, keen, enthusiastic, zealous, passionate, ardent, fervent, active, sworn, pledged; informal card-carrying, true blue, deep-dyed.

dexterity noun **1** *painting china demanded dexterity:* **deftness**, adeptness, adroitness, agility, nimbleness, handiness, ability, talent, skill, proficiency, expertise, experience, efficiency, mastery, delicacy, knack, artistry, finesse. **2** *his political dexterity:* **shrewdness**, astuteness, sharp-wittedness, acumen, acuity, intelligence; ingenuity, inventiveness, cleverness, smartness; canniness, sense, discernment, insight, understanding, penetration, perception, perspicacity, discrimination; cunning, artfulness, craftiness; informal nous, horse sense, savvy.

dexterous, dextrous adjective **1** *a dexterous flick of the wrist:* **deft**, adept, adroit, agile, nimble, neat, handy, able, capable, skilful, skilled, proficient, expert, practised, polished; efficient, effortless, slick, professional, masterly; informal nifty, mean, ace. **2** *his dexterous accounting abilities:* **shrewd**, ingenious, inventive, clever, intelligent, brilliant, smart, sharp, acute, astute, canny, intuitive, discerning, perceptive, insightful, incisive, judicious; cunning, artful, crafty, wily; informal on the ball, quick off the mark, quick on the uptake, brainy, savvy; Brit. informal suss.
– OPPOSITES clumsy, stupid.

diabolical, diabolic adjective **1** *his diabolical skill:* **devilish**, fiendish, satanic, demonic, demoniacal, hellish, infernal, evil, wicked, ungodly, unholy. **2** (informal) *a diabolical performance:* **very bad**, dreadful, awful, terrible, disgraceful, shameful, lamentable, deplorable, appalling, atrocious; inferior, substandard, unsatisfactory, inadequate, second-rate, third-rate, shoddy, inept; informal crummy, dire, dismal, God-awful, abysmal, rotten, pathetic, pitiful, lousy; Brit. informal duff, rubbish, ropy, pants.

diagnose verb *the neurologist diagnosed a possible brain haemorrhage:* **identify**, determine, distinguish, recognize, detect, pinpoint.

diagnosis noun **1** *the diagnosis of coeliac disease:* **identification**, detection, recognition, determination, discovery, pinpointing. **2** *the results confirmed his diagnosis:* **opinion**, judgement, verdict, conclusion.

diagonal adjective *a diagonal line:* **crosswise**, crossways, slanting, slanted, aslant, squint, oblique, angled, at an angle, cornerways, cornerwise; N. Amer. cater-cornered, kitty-cornered.

diagram noun **drawing**, line drawing, sketch, representation, draft, illustration, picture, plan, outline, delineation, figure.

diagrammatic adjective *the information is presented in diagrammatic form:* **graphic**, graphical, representational, representative, schematic, simplified.

dial verb *she dialled her parents:* **phone**, telephone, call, ring, make/place a call (to); informal buzz; Brit. informal get on the blower; N. Amer. informal get someone on the horn.

dialect noun *Hilary found it hard to understand the moorland dialect:* **regional language**, local language, local speech, vernacular, patois, idiom; regionalisms, localisms; informal lingo.

dialectic noun *feminism has contributed a great deal to this dialectic:* **discussion**, debate, dialogue, logical argument, reasoning, argumentation, polemics.

dialogue noun **1** *a book consisting of a series of dialogues:* **conversation**, talk, discussion, interchange, discourse; chat, tête à tête;

informal confab. **2** *they called for a serious political dialogue:* **discussion**, exchange, debate, exchange of views, talk, head-to-head, consultation, conference, parley; talks, negotiations; informal powwow; N. Amer. informal skull session.

diameter noun *the pipe has a diameter of 14mm:* **breadth**, width, thickness; calibre, bore, gauge.

diametrical, diametric adjective *they set themselves in diametrical opposition to their society:* **direct**, absolute, complete, exact, extreme, polar, antipodal.

diaphanous adjective *she wore a diaphanous dress of pale gold:* **sheer**, fine, delicate, light, thin, insubstantial, floaty, flimsy, filmy, silken, chiffony, gossamer, gossamer-thin, gauzy; translucent, transparent, see-through.
– OPPOSITES thick, opaque.

diarrhoea noun loose motions; informal the runs, the trots, gippy tummy, holiday tummy, Delhi belly, Montezuma's revenge; Brit. informal the squits; N. Amer. informal turista.
– OPPOSITES constipation.

diary noun **1** *he put the date in his diary:* **appointment book**, engagement book, personal organizer; trademark Filofax. **2** *her World War II diaries:* **journal**, memoir, chronicle, log, weblog, blog, logbook, history, annal, record; N. Amer. daybook.

diatribe noun *he launched into a diatribe against the Catholic Church:* **tirade**, harangue, onslaught, attack, polemic, denunciation, broadside, fulmination, condemnation, censure, criticism; informal blast.

dicey adjective (informal) *refuelling at sea is a bit dicey in bad weather:* **risky**, uncertain, unpredictable, touch-and-go, precarious, unsafe, dangerous, fraught with danger, hazardous, perilous, high-risk, difficult; informal chancy, hairy, iffy; Brit. informal dodgy; N. Amer. informal gnarly.
– OPPOSITES safe.

dichotomy noun *there is a great dichotomy between social theory and practice:* **contrast**, difference, polarity, conflict; gulf, chasm, division, separation, split; rare contrariety.

dictate verb **1** *the tsar's attempts to dictate policy:* **prescribe**, lay down, impose, set down, order, command, decree, ordain, direct, determine, decide, control, govern. **2** *you are in no position to dictate to me:* **give orders to**, order about/around, lord it over; lay down the law; informal boss about/around, push around/about, throw one's weight about/around. **3** *choice is often dictated by availability:* **determine**, control, govern, decide, influence, affect.
noun *the dictates of his superior:* **order**, command, commandment, decree, edict, ruling, dictum, diktat, directive, direction, instruction, pronouncement, mandate,

requirement, stipulation, injunction, demand.

dictator noun **autocrat**, absolute ruler, despot, tyrant, oppressor, autarch.

dictatorial adjective **1** *a dictatorial regime:* **autocratic**, undemocratic, totalitarian, authoritarian, autarchic, despotic, tyrannical, tyrannous, absolute, unrestricted, unlimited, unaccountable, arbitrary. **2** *his dictatorial manner:* **domineering**, autocratic, authoritarian, oppressive, imperious, officious, overweening, overbearing, peremptory, dogmatic, high and mighty; severe, strict; informal bossy, high-handed.
– OPPOSITES democratic, meek.

dictatorship noun *an entire generation grew up in the shadow of dictatorship:* **absolute rule**, undemocratic rule, despotism, tyranny, autocracy, autarchy, authoritarianism, totalitarianism, Fascism; oppression, repression.
– OPPOSITES democracy.

diction noun *his careful diction:* **enunciation**, articulation, elocution, locution, pronunciation, speech, intonation, inflection; delivery.

dictionary noun **lexicon**, wordbook, word list, glossary.

dictum noun **1** *he received the head's dictum with evident reluctance:* **pronouncement**, proclamation, direction, injunction, dictate, command, commandment, order, decree, edict, mandate, diktat. **2** *the old dictum 'might is right':* **saying**, maxim, axiom, proverb, adage, aphorism, saw, precept, epigram, motto, truism, commonplace; expression, phrase.

didactic adjective *the inmates preferred social rather than didactic activities:* **instructive**, instructional, educational, educative, informative, informational, edifying, improving, preceptive, pedagogic, moralistic.

die verb **1** *her father died last year:* **pass away**, pass on, lose one's life, expire, breathe one's last, meet one's end, meet one's death, lay down one's life, perish, go the way of all flesh, go to one's last resting place, go to meet one's maker, cross the great divide; informal give up the ghost, kick the bucket, croak, buy it, turn up one's toes, cash in one's chips, shuffle off this mortal coil; Brit. informal snuff it, peg out, pop one's clogs; N. Amer. informal bite the big one, buy the farm. **2** *the wind had died down:* **abate**, subside, drop, lessen, ease (off), let up, moderate, fade, dwindle, peter out, wane, ebb, relent, weaken; melt away, dissolve, vanish, disappear.
– OPPOSITES live, intensify.

diehard adjective *the committee was full of diehard Stalinists:* **hard-line**, reactionary, ultra-conservative, conservative, traditionalist, dyed-in-the-wool, deep-dyed,

d

d

intransigent, inflexible, uncompromising, rigid, entrenched, set in one's ways; staunch, steadfast; informal blimpish.

diet noun *health problems related to your diet:* **selection of food**, food, foodstuffs; informal grub, nosh.
verb *she dieted for most of her life:* **be on a diet**, eat sparingly; slim, lose weight, watch one's weight; N. Amer. reduce; informal weight-watch; N. Amer. informal slenderize.

differ verb **1** *the second set of data differed from the first:* **contrast with**, be different/dissimilar to, be unlike, vary from, diverge from, deviate from, conflict with, run counter to, be incompatible with, be at odds with, go against, contradict. **2** *the two sides differed over this issue:* **disagree**, conflict, be at variance/odds, be in dispute, not see eye to eye.
– OPPOSITES resemble, agree.

difference noun **1** *the difference between the two sets of data:* **dissimilarity**, contrast, distinction, differentiation, variance, variation, divergence, disparity, deviation, polarity, gulf, gap, imbalance, contradiction, contradistinction. **2** *we've had our differences in the past:* **disagreement**, difference of opinion, dispute, argument, quarrel, wrangle, contretemps, altercation; informal tiff, set-to, run-in, spat; Brit. informal row. **3** *I am willing to pay the difference:* **balance**, remainder, rest, remaining amount, residue.
– OPPOSITES similarity.

different adjective **1** *people with different lifestyles:* **dissimilar**, unalike, unlike, contrasting, contrastive, divergent, differing, varying, disparate; poles apart, incompatible, mismatched, conflicting, clashing; informal like chalk and cheese. **2** *suddenly everything in her life was different:* **changed**, altered, transformed, new, unfamiliar, unknown, strange. **3** *two different occasions:* **distinct**, separate, individual, discrete, independent. **4** *he wanted to try something different:* **unusual**, out of the ordinary, unfamiliar, novel, new, fresh, original, unconventional, exotic, uncommon.
– OPPOSITES similar, related, ordinary.

differentiate verb **1** *he was unable to differentiate between fantasy and reality:* **distinguish**, discriminate, make/draw a distinction, tell the difference, tell apart. **2** *this differentiates their business from all other booksellers:* **make different**, distinguish, set apart, single out, separate, mark off.

differentiation noun **distinction**, distinctness, difference; separation, demarcation, delimitation.

difficult adjective **1** *a very difficult job:* **hard**, strenuous, arduous, laborious, tough, onerous, burdensome, demanding, punishing, gruelling, back-breaking, exhausting, tiring, fatiguing, wearisome; informal hellish, killing, no picnic.

2 *she found maths very difficult:* **hard**, complicated, complex, involved, impenetrable, unfathomable, over/above one's head, beyond one, puzzling, baffling, perplexing, confusing, mystifying; problematic, intricate, knotty, thorny, ticklish. **3** *a difficult child:* **troublesome**, tiresome, trying, exasperating, awkward, demanding, perverse, contrary, recalcitrant, unmanageable, obstreperous, unaccommodating, unhelpful, uncooperative, disobliging; hard to please, fussy, finicky. **4** *you've come at a difficult time:* **inconvenient**, awkward, inopportune, unfavourable, unfortunate, inappropriate, unsuitable, untimely, ill-timed.
– OPPOSITES easy, simple, accommodating.

difficulty noun **1** *the difficulty of balancing motherhood with a career:* **strain**, trouble, problems, toil, struggle, laboriousness, arduousness; informal hassle, stress. **2** *practical difficulties:* **problem**, complication, snag, hitch, pitfall, handicap, impediment, hindrance, obstacle, hurdle, stumbling block, obstruction, barrier; informal fly in the ointment, headache, hiccup; Brit. informal spanner in the works. **3** *Charles got into difficulties:* **trouble**, predicament, plight, hard times, dire straits; quandary, dilemma; informal deep water, a fix, a jam, a spot, a scrape, a stew, a hole, a pickle.
– OPPOSITES ease.

diffidence noun *he regretted his diffidence and awkwardness in larger groups:* **shyness**, bashfulness, modesty, self-effacement, meekness, unassertiveness, timidity, humility, hesitancy, reticence, insecurity, self-doubt, uncertainty, self-consciousness.

diffident adjective **shy**, bashful, modest, self-effacing, unassuming, meek, unconfident, unassertive, timid, timorous, humble, shrinking, reticent, hesitant, insecure, self-doubting, doubtful, uncertain, unsure, self-conscious; informal mousy.
– OPPOSITES confident.

diffuse verb *such ideas were diffused widely in the 1970s:* **spread**, spread around, send out, disseminate, scatter, disperse, distribute, put about, circulate, communicate, purvey, propagate, transmit, broadcast, promulgate.
adjective **1** *a diffuse community centred on the church:* **spread out**, scattered. **2** *a diffuse narrative:* **verbose**, wordy, prolix, long-winded, long-drawn-out, discursive, rambling, wandering, meandering, maundering, digressive, circuitous, roundabout, circumlocutory, periphrastic; Brit. informal waffly.

diffusion noun *the diffusion of Marxist ideas:* **spread**, dissemination, scattering, dispersal, distribution, circulation, propagation, transmission, broadcasting, promulgation.

dig verb **1** *she began to dig the heavy clay soil:* **turn over**, work, break up; till, harrow, plough. **2** *he took a spade and dug a hole:*

excavate, dig out, quarry, hollow out, scoop out, gouge out; cut, bore, tunnel, burrow, mine. **3** *the bodies were hastily dug up:* **exhume**, disinter, unearth. **4** *Winnie dug her elbow into his ribs:* **poke**, prod, jab, stab, shove, ram, push, thrust, drive. **5** *he'd been digging into my past:* **delve**, probe, search, inquire, look, investigate, research, examine, scrutinize, check up on; informal check out. **6** *I dug up some disturbing information:* **uncover**, discover, find (out), unearth, dredge up, root out, ferret out, turn up, reveal, bring to light, expose.
noun **1** *a dig in the ribs:* **poke**, prod, jab, stab, shove, push. **2** (informal) *they're always making digs at each other:* **snide remark**, cutting remark, jibe, jeer, taunt, sneer, insult, barb, insinuation; informal wisecrack, crack, put-down.

digest verb *Liz digested this information:* **assimilate**, absorb, take in, understand, comprehend, grasp; consider, think about, reflect on, ponder, contemplate, mull over.
noun *a digest of their findings:* **summary**, synopsis, abstract, precis, résumé, summation; compilation; N. Amer. informal wrap-up.

digit noun *the door code has ten digits:* **numeral**, number, figure, integer.

dignified adjective *the butler was dignified and courteous:* **stately**, noble, courtly, majestic, distinguished, proud, august, lofty, exalted, regal, lordly, imposing, impressive, grand; solemn, serious, grave, formal, proper, ceremonious, decorous, reserved, composed, sedate.

dignify verb *they dignified their departure with a ceremony:* **ennoble**, enhance, distinguish, add distinction to, honour, grace, exalt, magnify, glorify, elevate.

dignitary noun *there are many foreign dignitaries attending today's ceremony:* **worthy**, personage, VIP, grandee, notable, notability, pillar of society, luminary, leading light, big name; informal heavyweight, bigwig, top brass, top dog, big gun, big shot, big noise, big cheese, big chief, supremo; N. Amer. informal big wheel, big kahuna, big enchilada, top banana.

dignity noun **1** *the dignity of the Crown:* **stateliness**, nobility, majesty, regality, courtliness, augustness, loftiness, lordliness, grandeur; solemnity, gravity, gravitas, formality, decorum, propriety, sedateness. **2** *he had lost his dignity:* **self-respect**, pride, self-esteem, self-worth, amour propre.

digress verb *I have digressed a little from my original plan:* **deviate**, go off at a tangent, get off the subject, get sidetracked, lose the thread, diverge, turn aside/away, depart, drift, stray, wander.

digression noun **deviation**, detour, diversion, departure, divergence, excursus; aside, incidental remark.

dilapidated adjective *a terrace of dilapidated*

Edwardian houses: **run down**, tumbledown, ramshackle, broken-down, in disrepair, shabby, battered, rickety, shaky, unsound, crumbling, in ruins, ruined, decayed, decaying, decrepit; neglected, uncared-for, untended, the worse for wear, falling to pieces, falling apart, gone to rack and ruin, gone to seed.

dilate verb *her nostrils dilated:* **enlarge**, widen, expand, distend.
– OPPOSITES contract.

dilatory adjective **1** *he had been dilatory in appointing a solicitor:* **slow**, tardy, unhurried, sluggish, sluggardly, snail-like, tortoise-like, lazy. **2** *dilatory procedural tactics:* **delaying**, stalling, temporizing, procrastinating, time-wasting, Fabian.
– OPPOSITES fast.

dilemma noun *a discussion with a colleague resolved her dilemma:* **quandary**, predicament, catch-22, vicious circle, plight, mess, muddle; difficulty, problem, trouble, perplexity, confusion, conflict; informal no-win situation, fix, tight spot/corner; Brit. informal sticky wicket.
■ **on the horns of a dilemma** between the devil and the deep blue sea, between Scylla and Charybdis; informal between a rock and a hard place.

dilettante noun *there is no room for the dilettante in this business:* **dabbler**, amateur, non-professional, non-specialist, layman, layperson.
– OPPOSITES professional.

diligence noun *they set about their assigned jobs with diligence:* **conscientiousness**, assiduousness, assiduity, hard work, application, concentration, effort, care, industriousness, rigour, meticulousness, thoroughness; perseverance, persistence, tenacity, dedication, commitment, tirelessness, indefatigability, doggedness.

diligent adjective *skilled and diligent nursing staff:* **industrious**, hard-working, assiduous, conscientious, particular, punctilious, meticulous, painstaking, rigorous, careful, thorough, sedulous, earnest; persevering, persistent, tenacious, zealous, dedicated, committed, unflagging, untiring, tireless, indefatigable, dogged.
– OPPOSITES lazy.

dilly-dally verb (informal) *the board can't afford to dilly-dally over this issue:* **waste time**, dally, dawdle, loiter, linger, take one's time, delay, temporize, stall, procrastinate, pussyfoot around, drag one's feet; dither, hesitate, falter, vacillate, waver; Brit. haver, hum and haw; informal shilly-shally, let the grass grow under one's feet.
– OPPOSITES hurry.

dilute verb **1** *strong bleach can be diluted with water:* **make weaker**, weaken, water down; thin out, thin; doctor, adulterate; informal cut. **2** *the original plans have been diluted:* **weaken**, moderate, tone down, water down.

d

diluted adjective *wash the brushes in diluted bleach:* **weak**, dilute, thin, watered down, watery; adulterated.
– OPPOSITES concentrated.

dim adjective **1** *the dim light:* **faint**, weak, feeble, soft, pale, dull, subdued, muted, wishy-washy. **2** *long dim corridors:* **dark**, badly lit, ill-lit, dingy, dismal, gloomy, murky; literary tenebrous. **3** *a dim figure:* **indistinct**, ill-defined, unclear, vague, shadowy, nebulous, obscured, blurred, blurry, fuzzy. **4** *dim memories:* **vague**, imprecise, imperfect, unclear, indistinct, sketchy, hazy, blurred, shadowy. **5** (informal) *I'm awfully dim.* See **STUPID** sense 1. **6** *their prospects for the future looked dim:* **gloomy**, unpromising, unfavourable, discouraging, disheartening, depressing, dispiriting, hopeless.
– OPPOSITES bright, distinct, encouraging.
verb **1** *the lights were dimmed:* **turn down**, lower, dip, soften, subdue, mute. **2** *my memories have not dimmed with time:* **fade**, become vague, dwindle, blur. **3** *the fighting dimmed hopes of peace:* **diminish**, reduce, lessen, weaken, undermine.
– OPPOSITES brighten, sharpen, intensify.

dimension noun **1** *the dimensions of the room:* **size**, measurements, proportions, extent; length, width, breadth, depth, area, volume, capacity; footage, acreage. **2** *the dimension of the problem:* **size**, scale, extent, scope, magnitude; importance, significance. **3** *the cultural dimensions of the problem:* **aspect**, feature, element, facet, side.

diminish verb **1** *the pain will gradually diminish:* **decrease**, lessen, decline, reduce, subside, die down, abate, dwindle, fade, slacken off, moderate, let up, ebb, wane, recede, die away/out, peter out. **2** *new legislation diminished the courts' authority:* **reduce**, decrease, lessen, curtail, cut, cut down/back, constrict, restrict, limit, curb, check; weaken, blunt, erode, undermine, sap.
– OPPOSITES increase.

diminution noun *a gradual diminution in mental faculties:* **reduction**, decrease, lessening, decline, dwindling, moderation, fading, weakening, ebb.

diminutive adjective *a diminutive breed of parrot:* **tiny**, small, little, petite, elfin, minute, miniature, mini, minuscule, compact, pocket, toy, midget, undersized, short; Scottish wee; informal teeny, weeny, teeny-weeny, teensy-weensy, itty-bitty, itsy-bitsy, tiddly, dinky, baby, pint-sized, knee-high to a grasshopper; Brit. informal titchy; N. Amer. informal little-bitty.
– OPPOSITES enormous.

dimple noun **indentation**, hollow, cleft, dint.

dimwit noun (informal). See **FOOL** noun sense 1.

dim-witted adjective (informal). See **STUPID** senses 1, 2.

din noun *he shouted above the din:* **noise**, racket, rumpus, cacophony, babel, hubbub, tumult, uproar, commotion, clangour, clatter; shouting, yelling, screaming, caterwauling, clamour, outcry; Scottish & N. English stramash; informal hullabaloo; Brit. informal row.
– OPPOSITES silence.
verb **1** *she had had the evils of drink dinned into her:* **instil**, inculcate, drive, drum, hammer, drill, ingrain; indoctrinate, brainwash. **2** *the sound dinning in my ears:* **blare**, blast, clang, clatter, crash, clamour.

dine verb **1** *we dined at a restaurant:* **have dinner**, have supper, eat. **2** *they dined on lobster:* **eat**, feed on, feast on, banquet on, partake of; informal tuck into.

dingy adjective *a dingy bed-sitting room:* **gloomy**, dark, dull, badly/poorly lit, murky, dim, dismal, dreary, drab, sombre, grim, cheerless; dirty, grimy, shabby, faded, worn, dowdy, seedy, run down.
– OPPOSITES bright.

dinner noun **evening meal**, supper, main meal; lunch; feast, banquet, dinner party; Brit. tea; informal spread, blowout; Brit. informal nosh-up, slap-up meal.

dint noun *the dints and holes were the work of arrows:* **dent**, indentation, hollow, depression, dip, dimple, cleft, pit.
■ **by dint of** by means of, by virtue of, on account of, as a result of, as a consequence of, owing to, on the strength of, due to, thanks to, by; formal by reason of.

diocese noun **bishopric**, see.

dip verb **1** *he dipped a rag in the water:* **immerse**, submerge, plunge, duck, dunk, lower, sink. **2** *the sun dipped below the horizon:* **sink**, set, drop, go/drop down, fall, descend; disappear, vanish. **3** *the president's popularity has dipped:* **decrease**, fall, drop, fall off, decline, diminish, dwindle, slump, plummet, plunge; informal hit the floor. **4** *the road dipped:* **slope down**, descend, go down; drop away, fall, sink. **5** *he dipped his headlights:* **dim**, **lower**, turn down.
– OPPOSITES rise, increase.
noun **1** *a relaxing dip in the pool:* **swim**, bathe; paddle. **2** *give the fish a ten-minute dip in a salt bath:* **immersion**, plunge, ducking, dunking. **3** *chicken satay with peanut dip:* **sauce**, relish, dressing. **4** *the hedge at the bottom of the dip:* **slope**, incline, decline, descent; hollow, concavity, depression, basin, indentation. **5** *a dip in sales:* **decrease**, fall, drop, downturn, decline, falling-off, slump, reduction, diminution, ebb.

diplomacy noun **1** *diplomacy failed to win them independence:* **statesmanship**, statecraft, negotiation(s), discussion(s), talks, dialogue; international relations, foreign affairs. **2** *Jack's quiet diplomacy:* **tact**, tactfulness, sensitivity, discretion, subtlety, finesse, delicacy, savoir faire, politeness, thoughtfulness, care, judiciousness, prudence.

diplomat noun **ambassador**, attaché,

consul, chargé d'affaires, envoy, emissary, plenipotentiary.

diplomatic adjective *he tried to be diplomatic:* **tactful**, sensitive, subtle, delicate, polite, discreet, thoughtful, careful, judicious, prudent, politic, clever, skilful.
– OPPOSITES tactless.

dire adjective **1** *the dire economic situation:* **terrible**, dreadful, appalling, frightful, awful, atrocious, grim, alarming; grave, serious, disastrous, ruinous, hopeless, irretrievable, wretched, desperate, parlous; formal grievous. **2** *he was in dire need of help:* **urgent**, desperate, pressing, crying, sore, grave, serious, extreme, acute, drastic. **3** *dire warnings of fuel shortages:* **ominous**, gloomy, grim, dismal, unpropitious, inauspicious, unfavourable, pessimistic. **4** (informal) *the concert was dire.* See AWFUL sense 2.

direct adjective **1** *the most direct route:* **straight**, undeviating, unswerving; shortest, quickest. **2** *a direct flight:* **non-stop**, unbroken, uninterrupted, through. **3** *he is very direct:* **frank**, candid, straightforward, honest, open, blunt, plain-spoken, outspoken, forthright, downright, no-nonsense, matter-of-fact, not afraid to call a spade a spade; informal upfront. **4** *direct contact with the president:* **face to face**, personal, head-on, immediate, first-hand, tête-à-tête. **5** *the direct opposite:* **exact**, absolute, complete, diametrical.
verb *an economic elite directed the nation's affairs:* **manage**, govern, run, administer, control, conduct, handle, be in charge/control of, preside over, lead, head, rule, be at the helm of; supervise, superintend, oversee, regulate, orchestrate, coordinate; informal run the show, call the shots/tune, be in the driving seat. **2** *was that remark directed at me?* **aim at**, target at, address to, intend for, mean for, design for. **3** *a man in uniform directed them to the hall:* **give directions**, show the way, guide, lead, conduct, accompany, usher, escort. **4** *the judge directed the jury to return a not guilty verdict:* **instruct**, tell, command, order, charge, require.

direction noun **1** *a northerly direction:* **way**, route, course, line, run, bearing, orientation. **2** *the newspaper's political direction:* **orientation**, inclination, leaning, tendency, bent, bias, preference; drift, tack, attitude, tone, tenor, mood, current, trend. **3** *his direction of the project:* **administration**, management, conduct, handling, running, supervision, superintendence, regulation, orchestration; control, command, rule, leadership, guidance. **4** *explicit directions about nursing care:* **instruction**, order, command, prescription, rule, regulation, requirement.

directive noun *an EU directive on drinking water:* **instruction**, direction, command, order, charge, injunction, prescription, rule, ruling, regulation, law, dictate, decree, dictum, edict, mandate, fiat.

directly adverb **1** *they flew directly to New York:* **straight**, right, as the crow flies, by a direct route. **2** *I went directly after breakfast:* **immediately**, at once, instantly, right away, straight away, post-haste, without delay, without hesitation, forthwith; quickly, speedily, promptly; informal pronto. **3** *the houses directly opposite:* **exactly**, right, immediately; diametrically; informal bang. **4** *she spoke simply and directly:* **frankly**, candidly, openly, bluntly, forthrightly, without beating around the bush.

director noun *the director of a major British museum:* **administrator**, manager, chairman, chairwoman, chairperson, chair, head, chief, principal, leader, governor, president; managing director, MD, chief executive, CEO; supervisor, controller, overseer; informal boss, kingpin, top dog, gaffer, head honcho, numero uno; N. Amer. informal Mister Big.

directory noun **index**, list, listing, register, catalogue, record, archive, inventory.

dirge noun *he wrote dirges for funerals:* **elegy**, lament, threnody, requiem, dead march; Irish keen; Irish & Scottish coronach.

dirt noun **1** *his face was streaked with dirt:* **grime**, filth; dust, soot, smut; muck, mud, mire, sludge, slime, ooze, dross; smudges, stains; informal crud, yuck, grunge; Brit. informal grot, gunge. **2** *the packed dirt of the road:* **earth**, soil, loam, clay, silt; ground.

dirty adjective **1** *a dirty sweatshirt* | *dirty water:* **soiled**, grimy, grubby, filthy, mucky, stained, unwashed, greasy, smeared, smeary, spotted, smudged, cloudy, muddy, dusty, sooty, unclean, sullied, impure, tarnished, polluted, contaminated, defiled, foul, unhygienic, insanitary, unsanitary; informal cruddy, yucky, icky; Brit. informal manky, gungy, grotty. **2** *a dirty joke:* **indecent**, obscene, rude, naughty, vulgar, smutty, coarse, crude, filthy, bawdy, suggestive, ribald, racy, salacious, risqué, offensive, off colour, lewd, pornographic, explicit, X-rated; informal blue; euphemistic adult. **3** *dirty tricks:* **dishonest**, deceitful, unscrupulous, dishonourable, unsporting, ungentlemanly, below the belt, unfair, unethical, unprincipled; crooked, double-dealing, underhand, sly, crafty, devious, sneaky; Brit. informal out of order, not cricket. **4** *a dirty look:* **malevolent**, resentful, hostile, black, dark; angry, cross, indignant, annoyed, disapproving; informal peeved.
– OPPOSITES clean, innocent, honourable, friendly.
verb *the dog had dirtied her dress:* **soil**, stain, muddy, blacken, mess up, mark, spatter, bespatter, smudge, smear, splatter, sully, pollute, foul.
– OPPOSITES clean.

disability noun *my disability makes getting into bed rather difficult:* **handicap**,

d

disablement, incapacity, impairment, infirmity, defect, abnormality; condition, disorder, affliction.

disable verb **1** *an injury that could disable somebody for life:* **incapacitate**, put out of action, debilitate; handicap, cripple, lame, maim, immobilize, paralyse. **2** *the bomb squad disabled the device:* **deactivate**, defuse, disarm.

disabled adjective *they design computer aids for disabled people:* **handicapped**, incapacitated; debilitated, infirm, out of action; crippled, lame, paralysed, immobilized, bedridden; euphemistic physically challenged, differently abled.
– OPPOSITES able-bodied.

disabuse verb *he thought he was good enough to become a professional, but Dinah had disabused him:* **disillusion**, set straight, open someone's eyes, correct, enlighten, disenchant, shatter someone's illusions.

disadvantage noun *price is probably the biggest disadvantage of rail travel:* **drawback**, snag, downside, stumbling block, fly in the ointment, catch, hindrance, obstacle, impediment; flaw, defect, weakness, fault, handicap, con, trouble, difficulty, problem, complication, nuisance; Brit. disbenefit; informal minus, spanner in the works.
– OPPOSITES benefit.

disadvantaged adjective *a disadvantaged rural area:* **deprived**, underprivileged, depressed, in need, needy, poor, impoverished, indigent, hard up; Brit. on the breadline.

disadvantageous adjective *a very disadvantageous position:* **unfavourable**, adverse, unfortunate, unlucky, bad; detrimental, prejudicial, deleterious, harmful, damaging, injurious, hurtful; inconvenient, inopportune, ill-timed, untimely, inexpedient.

disaffected adjective *a plot by disaffected elements in the army:* **dissatisfied**, disgruntled, discontented, malcontent, frustrated, alienated; disloyal, rebellious, mutinous, seditious, dissident, up in arms; hostile, antagonistic, unfriendly.
– OPPOSITES contented.

disagree verb **1** *no one was willing to disagree with him:* **take issue**, challenge, contradict, oppose; be at variance/odds, not see eye to eye, differ, dissent, be in dispute, debate, argue, quarrel, wrangle, clash, be at loggerheads, cross swords, lock horns. **2** *their accounts disagree on details:* **differ**, be dissimilar, be different, vary, diverge; contradict each other, conflict, clash, contrast. **3** *the spicy food disagreed with her:* **make ill**, make unwell, nauseate, sicken, upset.

disagreeable adjective **1** *a disagreeable smell:* **unpleasant**, displeasing, nasty, offensive, off-putting, obnoxious, objectionable, horrible, horrid, dreadful, frightful, abominable, odious, repugnant, repulsive, repellent, revolting, disgusting, foul, vile, nauseating, sickening, unpalatable. **2** *a disagreeable man:* **bad-tempered**, ill-tempered, curmudgeonly, cross, crabbed, irritable, grumpy, peevish, sullen, prickly; unfriendly, unpleasant, nasty, mean, mean-spirited, rude, surly, discourteous, impolite, brusque, abrupt, churlish, disobliging.
– OPPOSITES pleasant.

disagreement noun **1** *there was some disagreement over possible solutions:* **dissent**, dispute, difference of opinion, variance, controversy, disaccord, discord, contention, division. **2** *a heated disagreement:* **argument**, debate, quarrel, wrangle, squabble, falling-out, altercation, dispute, disputation, war of words, contretemps; informal tiff, barney, set-to, spat, ding-dong; Brit. informal row; Scottish informal rammy. **3** *the disagreement between the results of the two assessments:* **difference**, dissimilarity, variation, variance, discrepancy, disparity, divergence, deviation, nonconformity; incompatibility, contradiction, conflict, clash, contrast.

disallow verb *if the registration officer disallows your application he will let you know:* **reject**, refuse, dismiss, say no to; ban, bar, block, debar, forbid, prohibit; cancel, invalidate, overrule, quash, overturn, countermand, reverse, throw out, set aside; informal give the thumbs down to.

disappear verb **1** *by 4 o'clock the mist had disappeared:* **vanish**, pass from sight, be lost to view/sight, recede from view; fade (away), melt away, clear, dissolve, disperse, evaporate, dematerialize; literary evanesce. **2** *this way of life has disappeared:* **die out**, die, cease to exist, come to an end, end, pass away, pass into oblivion, perish, vanish.
– OPPOSITES materialize.

disappoint verb *I'm sorry to have disappointed you:* **let down**, fail, dissatisfy, dash someone's hopes; upset, dismay, sadden, disenchant, disillusion, shatter someone's illusions, disabuse.
– OPPOSITES fulfil.

disappointed adjective *thousands of disappointed customers were kept waiting:* **upset**, saddened, let down, cast down, disheartened, downhearted, downcast, depressed, dispirited, discouraged, despondent, dismayed, crestfallen, distressed, chagrined; disenchanted, disillusioned; displeased, discontented, dissatisfied, frustrated, disgruntled; informal choked, miffed, cut up; Brit. informal gutted, as sick as a parrot.
– OPPOSITES pleased.

disappointing adjective *it was disappointing that there were relatively few possibilities:* **regrettable**, unfortunate, sorry, discouraging, disheartening, dispiriting, depressing, dismaying, upsetting, saddening; dissatisfactory, unsatisfactory; informal not all it's cracked up to be.

disappointment noun **1** *she tried to hide her disappointment:* **sadness**, regret, dismay, sorrow; dispiritedness, despondency, distress, chagrin; disenchantment, disillusionment; displeasure, dissatisfaction, disgruntlement. **2** *the trip was a bit of a disappointment:* **let-down**, non-event, anticlimax; Brit. damp squib; informal washout, lead balloon.
– OPPOSITES satisfaction.

disapproval noun *they expressed their strong disapproval of the law:* **disapprobation**, objection, dislike; dissatisfaction, disfavour, displeasure, distaste, exception; criticism, censure, condemnation, denunciation, deprecation; informal the thumbs down.

disapprove verb **1** *he disapproved of gamblers:* **object to**, have a poor opinion of, look down one's nose at, take exception to, dislike, take a dim view of, look askance at, frown on, be against, not believe in; deplore, criticize, censure, condemn, denounce, decry, deprecate. **2** *the board disapproved the plan:* **reject**, veto, refuse, turn down, disallow, throw out, dismiss, rule against; informal give the thumbs down to.

disapproving adjective *he cast a disapproving glance at Bridget:* **reproachful**, reproving, critical, censorious, condemnatory, disparaging, denigratory, deprecatory, unfavourable; dissatisfied, displeased, hostile.

disarm verb **1** *the UN must disarm the country:* **demilitarize**, demobilize. **2** *the militia refused to disarm:* **lay down one's arms**, demilitarize. **3** *police disarmed the bomb:* **defuse**, disable, deactivate, put out of action, make harmless. **4** *the warmth in his voice disarmed her:* **win over**, charm, persuade, thaw; mollify, appease, placate, pacify, conciliate, propitiate.

disarmament noun **demilitarization**, demobilization, decommissioning; arms reduction, arms limitation, arms control; the zero option.

disarming adjective *a disarming smile:* **winning**, charming, irresistible, persuasive, beguiling; conciliatory, mollifying.

disarrange verb *it's amazing how quickly my few possessions become disarranged:* **disorder**, throw into disarray/disorder, put out of place, disorganize, disturb, displace; mess up, make untidy, make a mess of, jumble, mix up, muddle, turn upside-down, scatter; dishevel, tousle, rumple; informal turn topsy-turvy, make a shambles of; N. Amer. informal muss up.

disarray noun *the room was in disarray:* **disorder**, confusion, chaos, untidiness, disorganization, dishevelment, mess,

muddle, clutter, jumble, tangle, hotchpotch, shambles.
– OPPOSITES tidiness.
verb *her clothes were disarrayed.* See **DISARRANGE**.

disassemble verb *the furniture was disassembled for transport:* **dismantle**, take apart, take to pieces, take to bits, deconstruct, break up, strip down.

disaster noun **1** *a railway disaster:* **catastrophe**, calamity, cataclysm, tragedy, act of God, holocaust; accident. **2** *a string of personal disasters:* **misfortune**, mishap, misadventure, mischance, setback, reversal, stroke of bad luck, blow. **3** (informal) *the film was a disaster:* **failure**, fiasco, catastrophe, debacle; informal flop, dud, washout, dead loss.
– OPPOSITES success.

disastrous adjective *a disastrous fire:* **catastrophic**, calamitous, cataclysmic, tragic; devastating, ruinous, harmful, dire, terrible, awful, shocking, appalling, dreadful; black, dark, unfortunate, unlucky, ill-fated, ill-starred, inauspicious.

disavow verb *the chairman publicly disavowed the press release:* **deny**, disclaim, disown, wash one's hands of, repudiate, reject, renounce.

disavowal noun **denial**, rejection, repudiation, renunciation, disclaimer.

disband verb *the unit was scheduled to disband:* **break up**, disperse, demobilize, dissolve, scatter, separate, go separate ways, part company.
– OPPOSITES assemble.

disbelief noun *she stared at him in disbelief:* **incredulity**, incredulousness, scepticism, doubt, doubtfulness, dubiousness; cynicism, suspicion, distrust, mistrust.

disbelieve verb *he totally disbelieved her:* **not believe**, give no credence to, discredit, discount, doubt, distrust, mistrust, be incredulous, be unconvinced; reject, repudiate, question, challenge; informal take with a pinch of salt.

disbeliever noun *as a disbeliever I can still read the Bible for the beauty of its prose:* **unbeliever**, non-believer, atheist, irreligionist, nihilist; sceptic, doubter, agnostic, doubting Thomas, cynic.

disbelieving adjective *he gave a disbelieving laugh:* **incredulous**, doubtful, dubious, unconvinced; distrustful, mistrustful, suspicious, cynical, sceptical.

disburden verb *I decided to disburden myself of the task:* **relieve**, free, liberate, unburden, disencumber, discharge, excuse, absolve.

disburse verb *the officers disbursed some £1.8 million on behalf of the fund:* **pay out**, spend, expend, dole out, dish out, hand out, part with, donate, give; informal fork out, shell out, lay out; Brit. informal stump up; N. Amer. informal ante up, pony up.

disc noun *the sun was a huge scarlet disc:*

circle, round, saucer, discus, ring. See also DISK.

discard verb *his old suit had been discarded:* **dispose of**, throw away/out, get rid of, toss out, jettison, scrap, dispense with, cast aside/off, throw on the scrap heap; reject, repudiate, abandon, drop, have done with, shed; informal chuck (away/out), dump, ditch, bin, junk, get shut of; Brit. informal get shot of; N. Amer. informal trash.
– OPPOSITES keep.

discern verb *in the dim light he could discern a handful of ghostly figures:* **perceive**, make out, pick out, detect, recognize, notice, observe, see, spot; identify, determine, distinguish.

discernible adjective *the figure was scarcely discernible in the pale moonlight:* **visible**, detectable, noticeable, perceptible, observable, distinguishable, recognizable, identifiable; apparent, evident, distinct, appreciable, clear, obvious, manifest, conspicuous.

discerning adjective *we have some real treasures for the discerning collector:* **discriminating**, judicious, shrewd, clever, astute, intelligent, sharp, selective, sophisticated, tasteful, sensitive, perceptive, percipient, perspicacious, wise, aware, knowing.

discharge verb **1** *he was discharged from the RAF:* **dismiss**, eject, expel, throw out, give someone notice, make redundant; release, let go; Military cashier; informal sack, give someone the sack, fire, boot out, give someone the boot, turf out, give someone their cards, give someone their marching orders, give someone the push. **2** *he was discharged from prison:* **release**, free, set free, let go, liberate, let out. **3** *oil is routinely discharged from ships:* **send out**, release, eject, let out, pour out, void, give off. **4** *the swelling will burst and discharge pus:* **emit**, exude, ooze, leak. **5** *he accidentally discharged a pistol:* **fire**, shoot, let off; set off, loose off, trigger, explode, detonate. **6** *the ferry was discharging passengers:* **unload**, offload, put off; remove. **7** *they discharged their duties efficiently:* **carry out**, perform, execute, conduct, do; fulfil, accomplish, achieve, complete.
– OPPOSITES recruit, imprison, absorb.
noun **1** *his discharge from the service:* **dismissal**, release, removal, ejection, expulsion, congé; Military cashiering; informal the sack, the boot. **2** *her discharge from prison:* **release**, liberation. **3** *a discharge of diesel oil into the river:* **leak**, leakage, emission, release, flow. **4** *a watery discharge from the eyes:* **emission**, secretion, excretion, seepage, suppuration; pus, matter. **5** *a single discharge of his gun:* **shot**, firing, blast; explosion, detonation. **6** *the discharge of their duties:* **carrying out**, performance, performing, execution, conduct; fulfilment, accomplishment,

completion.

disciple noun **1** *the disciples of Jesus:* **apostle**, follower. **2** *a disciple of Rousseau:* **follower**, adherent, believer, admirer, devotee, acolyte, votary; pupil, student, learner; upholder, supporter, advocate, proponent, apologist.

disciplinarian noun *a strict disciplinarian:* **martinet**, hard taskmaster, authoritarian, stickler for discipline; tyrant, despot; N. Amer. ramrod; informal slave-driver.

discipline noun **1** *a lack of proper parental discipline:* **control**, training, teaching, instruction, regulation, direction, order, authority, rule, strictness, a firm hand; routine, regimen, drill, drilling. **2** *he was able to maintain discipline among his men:* **good behaviour**, orderliness, control, obedience; self-control, self-discipline, self-government, self-restraint. **3** *sociology is a fairly new discipline:* **field (of study)**, branch of knowledge, subject, area; speciality, specialty.
verb **1** *she had disciplined herself to ignore the pain:* **train**, drill, teach, school, coach; regiment. **2** *she learned to discipline her emotions:* **control**, restrain, regulate, govern, keep in check, check, curb, keep a tight rein on, rein in, bridle, tame, bring into line. **3** *he was disciplined by the management:* **punish**, penalize, bring to book; reprimand, rebuke, reprove, chastise, upbraid; informal dress down, give someone a dressing-down, rap over the knuckles, give someone a roasting; Brit. informal carpet.

disclaim verb *the school disclaimed responsibility for his death:* **deny**, refuse to accept/acknowledge, reject, wash one's hands of.
– OPPOSITES accept.

disclose verb **1** *the information must not be disclosed to anyone:* **reveal**, make known, divulge, tell, impart, communicate, pass on, vouchsafe; release, make public, broadcast, publish, report, unveil; leak, betray, let slip, let drop, give away; informal let on, blab, spill the beans, let the cat out of the bag; Brit. informal blow the gaff. **2** *exploratory surgery disclosed an aneurysm:* **uncover**, reveal, show, bring to light.
– OPPOSITES conceal.

disclosure noun **1** *she was embarrassed by this unexpected disclosure:* **revelation**, declaration, announcement, news, report; exposé, leak. **2** *the disclosure of official information:* **publishing**, broadcasting; revelation, communication, release, uncovering, unveiling, exposure; leakage.

discoloration noun *a brown discoloration on the skin:* **mark**, stain, patch, soiling, streak, spot, blotch, tarnishing; blemish, flaw, defect, bruise, contusion; birthmark, naevus; liver spot, age spot; informal splodge, splotch.

discolour verb *smoke from the coal fire had discoloured the original paintwork:* **stain**, mark, soil, dirty, streak, smear, spot, tarnish, sully, spoil, mar, blemish; blacken, char; fade, bleach.

discoloured adjective **stained**, marked, spotted, dirty, soiled, tarnished, blackened; bleached, faded, yellowed.

discomfit verb *she kissed Sir John on the cheek, which discomfited him even more:* **embarrass**, abash, disconcert, nonplus, discompose, discomfort, take aback, set someone back on their heels, unsettle, unnerve, put someone off their stroke, ruffle, confuse, fluster, agitate, disorientate, upset, disturb, perturb, distress; chagrin, mortify; informal faze, rattle; N. Amer. informal discombobulate.

discomfiture noun **embarrassment**, unease, uneasiness, awkwardness, discomfort, discomposure, abashment, confusion, agitation, nervousness, disorientation, perturbation, distress; chagrin, mortification, shame, humiliation; N. Amer. informal discombobulation.

discomfort noun **1** *abdominal discomfort:* **pain**, aches and pains, soreness, tenderness, irritation, stiffness; ache, twinge, pang, throb, cramp; Brit. informal gyp. **2** *the discomforts of life at sea:* **inconvenience**, difficulty, bother, nuisance, vexation, drawback, disadvantage, trouble, problem, trial, tribulation, hardship; informal hassle. **3** *Ruth flushed and Thomas noticed her discomfort:* **embarrassment**, discomfiture, unease, uneasiness, awkwardness, discomposure, confusion, nervousness, flusteredness, perturbation, distress, anxiety; chagrin, mortification, shame, humiliation.
verb *his purpose was to discomfort the Prime Minister.* See **DISCOMFIT**.

discomposure noun *she laughed to cover her discomposure:* **agitation**, discomfiture, discomfort, uneasiness, unease, confusion, disorientation, perturbation, distress, nervousness; anxiety, worry, consternation, disquiet, disquietude; embarrassment, abashment, chagrin, loss of face; N. Amer. informal discombobulation.

disconcert verb *the abrupt change of subject disconcerted her:* **unsettle**, nonplus, discomfit, throw/catch off balance, take aback, rattle, set someone back on their heels, unnerve, disorient, perturb, disturb, perplex, confuse, bewilder, baffle, fluster, ruffle, shake, upset, agitate, worry, dismay, discountenance; surprise, take by surprise, startle, put someone off (their stroke/stride), distract; informal throw, faze; N. Amer. informal discombobulate.

disconcerting adjective **unsettling**, unnerving, discomfiting, disturbing, perturbing, troubling, upsetting, worrying, alarming, distracting, off-putting; confusing, bewildering, perplexing.

disconnect verb **1** *the trucks were*

disconnected from the train: **detach**, disengage, uncouple, decouple, unhook, unhitch, undo, unfasten, unyoke. **2** *she felt as if she had been disconnected from the real world:* **separate**, cut off, divorce, sever, isolate, delink, divide, part, disengage, dissociate, remove. **3** *an engineer disconnected the appliance:* **deactivate**, shut off, turn off, switch off, unplug.
– OPPOSITES attach.

disconnected adjective **1** *a world that seemed disconnected from reality:* **detached**, separate, separated, divorced, cut off, isolated, dissociated, disengaged; apart. **2** *a disconnected narrative:* **disjointed**, incoherent, garbled, confused, jumbled, mixed up, rambling, wandering, disorganized, uncoordinated, ill-thought-out.

disconsolate adjective *Giles was looking increasingly disconsolate:* **sad**, unhappy, doleful, woebegone, dejected, downcast, downhearted, despondent, dispirited, crestfallen, cast down, depressed, down, fed up, disappointed, disheartened, discouraged, demoralized, low-spirited, forlorn, in the doldrums, melancholy, miserable, long-faced, glum, gloomy; informal blue, choked, down in the mouth, down in the dumps.
– OPPOSITES cheerful.

discontent noun *there were reports of growing discontent among the military:* **dissatisfaction**, disaffection, discontentment, discontentedness, disgruntlement, grievances, unhappiness, displeasure, bad feelings, resentment, envy; restlessness, unrest, uneasiness, unease, frustration, irritation, annoyance; informal a chip on one's shoulder.
– OPPOSITES satisfaction.

discontented adjective **dissatisfied**, disgruntled, fed up, disaffected, discontent, malcontent, unhappy, aggrieved, displeased, resentful, envious; restless, frustrated, irritated, annoyed; informal fed up to the (back) teeth, browned off, hacked off; Brit. informal cheesed off, brassed off; N. Amer. informal teed off, ticked off.
– OPPOSITES satisfied.

discontinue verb *the ferry service was discontinued:* **stop**, end, terminate, put an end to, put a stop to, wind up, finish, call a halt to, cancel, drop, abandon, dispense with, do away with, get rid of, axe, abolish; suspend, interrupt, break off, withdraw; informal cut, pull the plug on, scrap, knock something on the head.

discontinuity noun *the discontinuity of policy frustrated industrialists and investors:* **disconnectedness**, disconnection, break, disruption, interruption, disjointedness.

discontinuous adjective *a person with a discontinuous employment record:* **intermittent**, sporadic, broken, fitful,

d

interrupted, on and off, disrupted, erratic, disconnected.

discord noun 1 *stress resulting from family discord:* **strife**, conflict, friction, hostility, antagonism, antipathy, enmity, bad feeling, ill feeling, bad blood, argument, quarrelling, squabbling, bickering, wrangling, feuding, contention, disagreement, dissension, dispute, difference of opinion, disunity, division, opposition. 2 *the music faded in discord:* **dissonance**, discordance, disharmony, cacophony, jangling.
– OPPOSITES accord, harmony.

discordant adjective 1 *the messages from Washington and London were discordant:* **different**, in disagreement, at variance, at odds, divergent, discrepant, contradictory, contrary, in conflict, conflicting, opposite, opposed, opposing, clashing; incompatible, inconsistent, irreconcilable. 2 *discordant sounds:* **inharmonious**, tuneless, off-key, dissonant, harsh, jarring, grating, jangling, jangly, strident, shrill, screeching, screechy, cacophonous; sharp, flat.
– OPPOSITES harmonious.

discount noun *students get a 10 per cent discount:* **reduction**, deduction, markdown, price cut, cut, concession; rebate.
verb 1 *I'd heard rumours, but discounted them:* **disregard**, pay no attention to, take no notice of, take no account of, dismiss, ignore, overlook, disbelieve, reject; informal take with a pinch of salt, pooh-pooh. 2 *the recommended price is discounted in many stores:* **reduce**, mark down, cut, lower; informal knock down.
– OPPOSITES believe, increase.

discountenance verb *she was not discountenanced by the accusation:* **disconcert**, discomfit, unsettle, nonplus, throw/catch off balance, take aback, unnerve, disorient, perturb, disturb, perplex, fluster, ruffle, shake, upset, agitate, worry, dismay, discompose, abash; informal throw, faze, rattle; N. Amer. informal discombobulate.

discourage verb 1 *we want to discourage children from smoking:* **deter**, dissuade, disincline, put off, talk out of; advise against, urge against. 2 *she was discouraged by his hostile tone:* **dishearten**, dispirit, demoralize, cast down, depress, disappoint, dash someone's hopes; put off, unnerve, daunt, intimidate, cow, crush. 3 *he sought to discourage further conversation:* **prevent**, stop, put a stop to, avert, fend off, stave off, ward off; inhibit, hinder, check, curb, put a damper on, throw cold water on.
– OPPOSITES encourage.

discouraged adjective *Doug must be feeling pretty discouraged:* **disheartened**, dispirited, demoralized, deflated, disappointed, let down, disconsolate, despondent, fed up, dejected, cast down, downcast, depressed, crestfallen, dismayed, low-spirited, gloomy, glum,

pessimistic, unenthusiastic; put off, daunted, intimidated, cowed, crushed; informal down in the mouth, down in the dumps, unenthused.

discouraging adjective **depressing**, demoralizing, disheartening, dispiriting, disappointing, gloomy, off-putting; unfavourable, unpromising, inauspicious.
– OPPOSITES encouraging.

discourse noun 1 *they prolonged their discourse outside the door:* **discussion**, conversation, talk, dialogue, conference, debate, consultation; parley, powwow, chat; informal confab. 2 *a discourse on critical theory:* **essay**, treatise, dissertation, paper, study, critique, monograph, disquisition, tract; lecture, address, speech, oration; sermon, homily.
verb 1 *he discoursed at length on his favourite topic:* **hold forth**, expatiate, pontificate; talk, give a talk, give a speech, lecture, sermonize, preach; informal spout, sound off. 2 *Edward was discoursing with his friends:* **converse**, talk, speak, debate, confer, consult, parley, chat.

discourteous adjective *it would be discourteous to ignore her:* **rude**, impolite, ill-mannered, bad-mannered, disrespectful, uncivil, unmannerly, unchivalrous, ungentlemanly, unladylike, ill-bred, churlish, boorish, crass, ungracious, graceless, uncouth; insolent, impudent, cheeky, audacious, presumptuous; curt, brusque, blunt, offhand, unceremonious, short, sharp; informal ignorant.
– OPPOSITES polite.

discourtesy noun **rudeness**, impoliteness, ill manners, bad manners, incivility, disrespect, ungraciousness, churlishness, boorishness, ill breeding, uncouthness, crassness; insolence, impudence, impertinence; curtness, brusqueness, abruptness.

discover verb 1 *firemen discovered a body in the debris:* **find**, locate, come across/upon, stumble on, chance on, light on, bring to light, uncover, unearth, turn up; track down, run to earth, run to ground. 2 *eventually, I discovered the truth:* **find out**, learn, realize, recognize, see, ascertain, work out, fathom out, dig up/out, ferret out, root out; informal figure out, tumble to; Brit. informal twig, rumble, suss out; N. Amer. informal dope out. 3 *scientists discovered a new way of dating fossil crustaceans:* **hit on**, come up with, invent, originate, devise, design, contrive, conceive of; pioneer, develop.

discoverer noun **originator**, inventor, creator, deviser, designer; pioneer.

discovery noun 1 *the discovery of the body:* **finding**, location, uncovering, unearthing. 2 *the discovery that she was pregnant:* **realization**, recognition; revelation, disclosure. 3 *the discovery of new drugs:* **invention**, origination, devising; pioneering. 4 *he failed to take out a patent* *on his discoveries:* **find**, finding; invention, breakthrough, innovation.

discredit verb **1** *an attempt to discredit him and his company:* **bring into disrepute**, disgrace, dishonour, damage the reputation of, blacken the name of, put/show in a bad light, reflect badly on, compromise, stigmatize, smear, tarnish, taint; N. Amer. slur. **2** *that theory has been discredited:* **disprove**, invalidate, explode, drive a coach and horses through, refute; informal debunk, shoot full of holes, blow sky-high.
noun **1** *crimes which brought discredit on the administration:* **dishonour**, disrepute, disgrace, shame, humiliation, ignominy, infamy, notoriety; censure, blame, reproach, opprobrium; stigma. **2** *the ships were a discredit to the country:* **disgrace**, source of shame, reproach, blot on the escutcheon.
– OPPOSITES honour, glory.

discreditable adjective *his discreditable conduct:* **dishonourable**, reprehensible, shameful, deplorable, disgraceful, disreputable, blameworthy, ignoble, shabby, objectionable, regrettable, unacceptable, unworthy.
– OPPOSITES praiseworthy.

discreet adjective **1** *the police made discreet enquiries in the area:* **careful**, circumspect, cautious, wary, chary, guarded; tactful, diplomatic, prudent, judicious, strategic, politic, delicate, sensitive, kid-glove; informal softly-softly. **2** *discreet lighting shows off fine furnishings:* **unobtrusive**, inconspicuous, subtle, low-key, understated, subdued, muted, soft, restrained.

discrepancy noun *the discrepancy between the two sets of figures:* **difference**, disparity, variance, variation, deviation, divergence, disagreement, inconsistency, dissimilarity, mismatch, discordance, incompatibility, conflict.
– OPPOSITES correspondence.

discrete adjective *speech sounds are produced as a continuous signal rather than discrete units:* **separate**, distinct, individual, detached, unattached, disconnected, discontinuous, disjunct, disjoined.
– OPPOSITES connected.

discretion noun **1** *you can rely on his discretion:* **circumspection**, carefulness, caution, wariness, chariness, guardedness; **tact**, tactfulness, diplomacy, delicacy, sensitivity, prudence, judiciousness. **2** *honorary fellowships awarded at the discretion of the council:* **choice**, option, preference, disposition, volition; pleasure, liking, wish, will, inclination, desire.

discretionary adjective *a 12.5 per cent discretionary service charge:* **optional**, voluntary, at one's discretion, elective.
– OPPOSITES compulsory.

discriminate verb **1** *he cannot discriminate between fact and opinion:* **differentiate**, distinguish, draw a distinction, tell the difference, tell apart; separate, separate the sheep from the goats, separate the wheat from the chaff. **2** *existing employment policies discriminate against women:* **be biased**, be prejudiced; treat differently, treat unfairly, put at a disadvantage, disfavour; victimize.

discriminating adjective *a discriminating collector and patron of the arts:* **discerning**, perceptive, astute, shrewd, judicious, perspicacious, insightful, keen; selective, fastidious, tasteful, refined, sensitive, cultivated, cultured, artistic, aesthetic.
– OPPOSITES indiscriminate.

discrimination noun **1** *racial discrimination:* **prejudice**, bias, bigotry, intolerance, narrow-mindedness, unfairness, inequity, favouritism, one-sidedness, partisanship; sexism, chauvinism, racism, racialism, anti-Semitism, heterosexism, ageism, classism; positive discrimination. **2** *a man with no discrimination:* **discernment**, judgement, perception, perceptiveness, perspicacity, acumen, astuteness, shrewdness, judiciousness, insight; selectivity, (good) taste, fastidiousness, refinement, sensitivity, cultivation, culture.
– OPPOSITES impartiality.

discriminatory adjective *discriminatory employment practices:* **prejudicial**, biased, prejudiced, preferential, unfair, unjust, invidious, inequitable, weighted, one-sided, partisan; sexist, chauvinistic, chauvinist, racist, racialist, ageist, classist.
– OPPOSITES impartial.

discursive adjective **1** *dull, discursive prose:* **rambling**, digressive, meandering, wandering, maundering, diffuse, long, lengthy, wordy, verbose, long-winded, prolix; circuitous, roundabout, circumlocutory; Brit. informal waffly. **2** *an elegant discursive style:* **fluent**, flowing, fluid, eloquent, expansive.
– OPPOSITES concise, terse.

discuss verb **1** *I discussed the matter with my wife:* **talk over**, talk about, talk through, converse about, debate, confer about, deliberate about, chew over, consider, weigh up, consider the pros and cons of, thrash out; informal kick around/about, bat around/about. **2** *chapter three discusses this topic in detail:* **examine**, explore, study, analyse, go into, deal with, treat, consider, concern itself with, tackle.

discussion noun **1** *after a long discussion with her husband, she came to a decision:* **conversation**, talk, dialogue, discourse, conference, debate, exchange of views, consultation, deliberation; powwow, chat, tête-à-tête, heart-to-heart; negotiations, parley; informal confab, chit-chat, rap; N. Amer. informal skull session, bull session. **2** *the book's candid discussion of sexual matters:* **examination**, exploration, analysis, study; treatment, consideration.

d

disdain noun *she looked at him with disdain:* **contempt**, scorn, scornfulness, contemptuousness, derision, disrespect; disparagement, condescension, superciliousness, hauteur, haughtiness, arrogance, snobbishness, indifference, dismissiveness; distaste, dislike, disgust.
– OPPOSITES respect.
verb **1** *she disdained such vulgar exhibitionism:* **scorn**, deride, pour scorn on, regard with contempt, sneer at, sniff at, curl one's lip at, look down one's nose at, look down on; despise; informal turn up one's nose at, pooh-pooh. **2** *she disdained his invitation:* **spurn**, reject, refuse, rebuff, disregard, ignore, snub; decline, turn down, brush aside.

disdainful adjective *she gave him a disdainful look:* **contemptuous**, scornful, derisive, sneering, withering, slighting, disparaging, disrespectful, condescending, patronizing, supercilious, haughty, superior, arrogant, proud, snobbish, lordly, aloof, indifferent, dismissive; informal high and mighty, hoity-toity, sniffy, snotty.
– OPPOSITES respectful.

disease noun **illness**, sickness, ill health; infection, ailment, malady, disorder, complaint, affliction, condition, indisposition, upset, problem, trouble, infirmity; pestilence, plague, cancer, canker, blight; informal bug, virus; Brit. informal lurgy.

diseased adjective *the dogs were painfully thin and many were diseased:* **unhealthy**, ill, sick, unwell, ailing, sickly, unsound; infected, septic, contaminated, blighted, rotten, bad, abnormal.

disembark verb *the passengers began to disembark:* **get off**, step off, leave, pile out; go ashore, debark, detrain; land, arrive; Brit. alight; N. Amer. deplane.

disembodied adjective *a disembodied ghost:* **bodiless**, incorporeal, discarnate, spiritual; intangible, insubstantial, impalpable; ghostly, spectral, phantom, wraithlike.

disembowel verb **gut**, draw, remove the guts from.

disenchanted adjective *disenchanted with politics, he retired from the foreign service:* **disillusioned**, disappointed, disabused, let down, fed up, dissatisfied, discontented; cynical, soured, jaundiced, sick, out of love, indifferent.

disenchantment noun **disillusionment**, disappointment, dissatisfaction, discontent, discontentedness, rude awakening; cynicism.

disengage verb **1** *I disengaged his hand from mine:* **remove**, detach, disentangle, extricate, separate, release, free, loosen, loose, disconnect, unfasten, unclasp, uncouple, undo, unhook, unhitch, untie, unyoke, disentwine. **2** *American forces disengaged from the country:* **withdraw**, leave, pull out of, quit, retreat from.
– OPPOSITES attach, enter.

disentangle verb **1** *Allen was disentangling a coil of rope:* **untangle**, unravel, untwist, unwind, undo, untie, straighten out, smooth out; comb, card. **2** *he disentangled his fingers from her hair:* **extricate**, extract, free, remove, disengage, untwine, disentwine, release, loosen, detach, unfasten, unclasp, disconnect.

disfavour noun *the headmaster regarded her with disfavour:* **disapproval**, disapprobation; dislike, displeasure, distaste, dissatisfaction, low opinion.

disfigure verb *litter disfigures the countryside:* **mar**, spoil, deface, scar, blemish, uglify; damage, injure, impair, blight, mutilate, deform, maim, ruin; vandalize.
– OPPOSITES adorn.

disfigurement noun **1** *the disfigurement of Victorian buildings:* **defacement**, spoiling, scarring, uglification, mutilation, damage, vandalizing, ruin. **2** *a permanent facial disfigurement:* **blemish**, flaw, defect, imperfection, discoloration, blotch; scar, pockmark; deformity, malformation, abnormality, injury, wound.

disgorge verb *the combine disgorged a stream of grain:* **pour out**, discharge, eject, throw out, emit, expel, spit out, spew out, belch forth, spout; vomit, regurgitate.

disgrace noun **1** *he brought disgrace on the family:* **dishonour**, shame, discredit, ignominy, degradation, disrepute, ill-repute, infamy, scandal, stigma, opprobrium, obloquy, condemnation, vilification, contempt, disrespect; humiliation, embarrassment, loss of face; Austral. strife. **2** *the unemployment figures are a disgrace:* **scandal**, outrage; discredit, reproach, affront, insult; stain, blemish, blot, blot on the escutcheon, black mark; informal crime, sin.
– OPPOSITES honour.
verb **1** *you have disgraced the family name:* **bring shame on**, shame, dishonour, discredit, bring into disrepute, degrade, debase, defame, stigmatize, taint, sully, tarnish, besmirch, stain, blacken, drag through the mud/mire. **2** *he was publicly disgraced:* **discredit**, dishonour, stigmatize; humiliate, cause to lose face, chasten, humble, demean, put someone in their place, take down a peg or two, cut down to size.
– OPPOSITES honour.
■ **in disgrace** out of favour, unpopular, in bad odour, under a cloud, disgraced; informal in someone's bad/black books, in the doghouse; NZ informal in the dogbox.

disgraceful adjective *a disgraceful waste of money:* **shameful**, shocking, scandalous, deplorable, despicable, contemptible, beyond contempt, beyond the pale, dishonourable, discreditable, reprehensible, base, mean, low, blameworthy, unworthy, ignoble, shabby, inglorious, outrageous,

abominable, atrocious, appalling, dreadful, terrible, disgusting, shameless, vile, odious, monstrous, heinous, iniquitous, unspeakable, loathsome.
– OPPOSITES admirable.

disgruntled adjective *judges receive letters from disgruntled members of the public:* **dissatisfied**, discontented, aggrieved, resentful, fed up, displeased, unhappy, disappointed, disaffected; angry, irate, annoyed, cross, exasperated, indignant, vexed, irritated, piqued, irked, put out; informal peeved, miffed, aggravated, hacked off, browned off, riled, peed off, hot under the collar, in a huff; Brit. informal cheesed off, shirty, narked; N. Amer. informal sore, teed off, ticked off.

disguise verb *his controlled voice disguised his true feelings:* **camouflage**, conceal, hide, cover up, dissemble, mask, screen, shroud, veil, cloak; paper over, gloss over, put up a smokescreen.
– OPPOSITES expose.
■ **disguise oneself as** dress up as, pretend to be, pass oneself of as, impersonate, pose as.

disguised adjective *a disguised police officer:* **in disguise**, camouflaged; incognito, under cover.

disgust noun *a look of disgust:* **revulsion**, repugnance, aversion, distaste, nausea, abhorrence, loathing, detestation, odium, horror; contempt, outrage.
– OPPOSITES delight.
verb **1** *the hospital food disgusted me:* **revolt**, repel, repulse, sicken, nauseate, turn someone's stomach, make someone's gorge rise; informal turn off; N. Amer. informal gross out.
2 *Toby's behaviour disgusted her:* **outrage**, shock, horrify, appal, scandalize, offend.

disgusting adjective **1** *the food was disgusting:* **revolting**, repellent, repulsive, sickening, nauseating, stomach-churning, stomach-turning, off-putting, unpalatable, distasteful, foul, nasty; N. Amer. vomitous; informal yucky, icky, gross, sick-making.
2 *I find racism disgusting:* **abhorrent**, loathsome, offensive, appalling, outrageous, objectionable, shocking, horrifying, scandalous, monstrous, unspeakable, shameful, vile, odious, obnoxious, detestable, hateful, sickening, contemptible, despicable, deplorable, abominable, beyond the pale; informal gross, ghastly, sick.
– OPPOSITES delicious, appealing.

dish noun **1** *a china dish:* **bowl**, plate, platter, salver, paten; container, receptacle.
2 *vegetarian dishes:* **recipe**, meal, course; (**dishes**) food, fare.
■ **dish something out** *the waitress was dishing out free glasses of wine:* distribute, dispense, issue, hand out/round, give out, pass out/round; deal out, dole out, share out, allocate, allot, apportion.
■ **dish something up** *Mrs Mackay dished*

up the porridge: serve (up), spoon out, ladle out, scoop out.

disharmony noun *they hope he will heal the racial disharmony in their city:* **discord**, friction, strife, conflict, hostility, acrimony, bad blood, bad feeling, enmity, dissension, disagreement, feuding, quarrelling; disunity, division, divisiveness.

dishearten verb **discourage**, dispirit, demoralize, cast down, depress, disappoint, dismay, dash someone's hopes; put off, deter, unnerve, daunt, intimidate, cow, crush.
– OPPOSITES encourage.

disheartened adjective *the weather got worse and he felt cold and disheartened:* **discouraged**, dispirited, demoralized, deflated, disappointed, let down, disconsolate, despondent, fed up, dejected, cast down, downcast, depressed, crestfallen, dismayed, low-spirited, gloomy, glum, pessimistic, unenthusiastic; daunted, intimidated, cowed, crushed; informal down in the mouth, down in the dumps, unenthused.

dishevelled adjective *a man with long dishevelled hair:* **untidy**, unkempt, scruffy, messy, in a mess, disordered, disarranged, rumpled, bedraggled; uncombed, tousled, tangled, tangly, knotted, knotty, shaggy, straggly, windswept, wind-blown, wild; slovenly, slatternly, blowsy, frowzy, informal ratty; N. Amer. informal mussed (up).
– OPPOSITES tidy.

dishonest adjective *he is accused of dishonest business practices:* **fraudulent**, corrupt, swindling, cheating, double-dealing; underhand, crafty, cunning, devious, treacherous, unfair, unjust, dirty, unethical, immoral, dishonourable, untrustworthy, unscrupulous, unprincipled, amoral; criminal, illegal, unlawful; false, untruthful, deceitful, deceiving, lying, mendacious; informal crooked, shady, tricky, sharp, shifty; Brit. informal bent, dodgy; Austral./NZ informal shonky.

dishonesty noun *he lost money as a result of his solicitor's dishonesty:* **fraud**, fraudulence, sharp practice, corruption, cheating, chicanery, double-dealing, deceit, deception, duplicity, lying, falseness, falsity, falsehood, untruthfulness; craft, cunning, trickery, artifice, underhandedness, subterfuge, skulduggery, treachery, untrustworthiness, unscrupulousness, criminality, misconduct; informal crookedness, dirty tricks, shenanigans; Brit. informal jiggery-pokery.
– OPPOSITES probity.

dishonour noun *the incident brought dishonour upon the police profession:* **disgrace**, shame, discredit, humiliation, degradation, ignominy, scandal, infamy, disrepute, ill repute, loss of face, disfavour, ill favour, debasement, opprobrium, obloquy; stigma.
verb *his family name has been dishonoured:*

d

disgrace, shame, discredit, bring into disrepute, humiliate, degrade, debase, lower, cheapen, drag down, drag through the mud, blacken the name of, give a bad name to; sully, stain, taint, besmirch, smear, mar, blot, stigmatize.

dishonourable adjective *he is accused of dishonourable conduct:* **disgraceful**, shameful, disreputable, discreditable, degrading, ignominious, ignoble, blameworthy, contemptible, despicable, reprehensible, shabby, shoddy, sordid, sorry, base, low, improper, unseemly, unworthy; unprincipled, unscrupulous, corrupt, untrustworthy, treacherous, traitorous; informal shady, dirty.

disillusion verb **disabuse**, enlighten, set straight, open someone's eyes; disenchant, shatter someone's illusions, disappoint, make sadder and wiser.
– OPPOSITES deceive.

disillusioned adjective *his experience at the club left him disillusioned:* **disenchanted**, disabused, disappointed, let down, discouraged; cynical, sour, negative, world-weary.

disincentive noun *high interest rates are a disincentive to investment:* **deterrent**, discouragement, damper, brake, curb, check, restraint, inhibitor; obstacle, impediment, hindrance, obstruction, block, barrier.

disinclination noun *they show a disinclination to face up to these issues:* **reluctance**, unwillingness, lack of enthusiasm, indisposition, hesitancy; aversion, dislike, distaste; objection, demur, resistance, opposition.
– OPPOSITES enthusiasm.

disinclined adjective **reluctant**, unwilling, unenthusiastic, unprepared, indisposed, ill-disposed, not in the mood, hesitant; loath, averse, antipathetic, resistant, opposed.
– OPPOSITES willing.

disinfect verb *use bleach to disinfect your kitchen surfaces:* **sterilize**, sanitize, clean, cleanse, purify, decontaminate; fumigate.
– OPPOSITES contaminate.

disinfectant noun **antiseptic**, bactericide, germicide, sterilizer, cleanser, decontaminant; fumigant.

disingenuous adjective *this journalist was being somewhat disingenuous as well as cynical:* **insincere**, dishonest, untruthful, false, deceitful, duplicitous, lying, mendacious; hypocritical.

disinherit verb *the Duke is seeking to disinherit his eldest son:* **cut someone out of one's will**, cut off, dispossess; disown, repudiate, reject, cast off/aside, wash one's hands of, have nothing more to do with, turn one's back on; informal cut off without a penny.

disintegrate verb *the plane caught fire and disintegrated in the air:* **break up**, break apart, fall apart, fall to pieces, fragment,

fracture, shatter, splinter; explode, blow up, blow apart, fly apart; crumble, deteriorate, decay, decompose, rot, moulder, perish, dissolve, collapse, go to rack and ruin, degenerate; informal bust, be smashed to smithereens.

disinter verb *his corpse was disinterred and reburied in another grave:* **exhume**, unearth, dig up, disentomb.

disinterest noun **1** *scholarly disinterest:* **impartiality**, neutrality, objectivity, detachment, disinterestedness, lack of bias, lack of prejudice; open-mindedness, fairness, fair-mindedness, equity, balance, even-handedness. **2** *he looked at us with complete disinterest:* **indifference**, lack of interest, unconcern, impassivity; boredom, apathy.
– OPPOSITES bias.

disinterested adjective **1** *tax inspectors should give disinterested advice:* **unbiased**, unprejudiced, impartial, neutral, non-partisan, detached, uninvolved, objective, dispassionate, impersonal, clinical; open-minded, fair, just, equitable, balanced, even-handed, with no axe to grind, without fear or favour. **2** *he looked at her with disinterested eyes:* **uninterested**, indifferent, incurious, unconcerned, unmoved, unresponsive, impassive, passive, detached, unenthusiastic, lukewarm, bored, apathetic; informal couldn't-care-less.

disjointed adjective *a disjointed series of impressions in her mind:* **unconnected**, disconnected, disunited, discontinuous, fragmented, disorganized, disordered, muddled, mixed up, jumbled, garbled, incoherent, confused; rambling, wandering.

disk noun *download the files to disk:* **diskette**, floppy disk, floppy; hard disk, hard drive; CD, CD-ROM, DVD. See also **DISC**.

dislike verb *a man she had always disliked:* **find distasteful**, regard with distaste, be averse to, have an aversion to, have no liking/taste for, disapprove of, object to, take exception to; hate, detest, loathe, abhor, despise, be unable to bear/stand, shrink from, shudder at, find repellent; informal be unable to stomach.
noun *she viewed the other woman with dislike:* **distaste**, aversion, disfavour, disapproval, disapprobation, enmity, animosity, hostility, antipathy, antagonism; hate, hatred, detestation, loathing, disgust, repugnance, abhorrence, disdain, contempt.

dislocate verb **1** *she dislocated her hip:* **put out of joint**; informal put out. **2** *trade was dislocated by a famine:* **disrupt**, disturb, throw into disarray, throw into confusion, play havoc with, interfere with, disorganize, upset; informal mess up.

dislodge verb **1** *replace any stones you dislodge:* **displace**, knock out of place/position, move, shift; knock over, upset. **2** *economic sanctions failed to dislodge the dictator:* **remove**, force out, drive out, oust, eject, get rid of, evict, unseat, depose, topple, drum out; informal kick out, boot out; Brit. informal turf out.

disloyal adjective *many of her colleagues judged her disloyal:* **unfaithful**, faithless, false, false-hearted, untrue, inconstant, untrustworthy, unreliable, undependable, fickle; treacherous, traitorous, subversive, seditious, unpatriotic, two-faced, double-dealing, double-crossing, deceitful; dissident, renegade; adulterous; informal back-stabbing, two-timing.

disloyalty noun **unfaithfulness**, infidelity, inconstancy, faithlessness, fickleness, unreliability, untrustworthiness, betrayal, falseness; duplicity, double-dealing, treachery, treason, subversion, sedition, dissidence; adultery; informal back-stabbing, two-timing.

dismal adjective **1** *he had a dismal look in his eyes:* **gloomy**, glum, melancholy, morose, doleful, woebegone, forlorn, dejected, depressed, dispirited, downcast, despondent, disconsolate, miserable, sad, unhappy, sorrowful, desolate, wretched; informal blue, fed up, down in the dumps/mouth. **2** *a dismal hall:* **dingy**, dim, dark, gloomy, dreary, drab, dull, bleak, cheerless, depressing, uninviting, unwelcoming. **3** (informal) *a dismal performance.* See **POOR** sense 2.
– OPPOSITES cheerful, bright.

dismantle verb *he began to dismantle the revolver:* **take apart**, take to pieces/bits, pull apart, pull to pieces, disassemble, break up, strip (down); knock down, pull down, demolish.
– OPPOSITES assemble, build.

dismay verb *he was dismayed by the change in his friend:* **appal**, horrify, shock, shake (up); disconcert, take aback, alarm, unnerve, unsettle, throw off balance, discompose; disturb, upset, distress; informal rattle, faze, knock sideways; Brit. informal knock for six.
– OPPOSITES encourage, please.
noun *they greeted his decision with dismay:* **alarm**, shock, surprise, consternation, concern, perturbation, disquiet, discomposure, distress.
– OPPOSITES pleasure, relief.

dismember verb *a stag carcass was in the process of being dismembered:* **disjoint**, joint; pull apart, cut up, chop up, butcher.

dismiss verb **1** *the president dismissed five ministers:* **give someone their notice**, get rid of, discharge; lay off, make redundant; informal sack, give someone the sack, fire, boot out, give someone the boot/elbow/push, give someone their marching orders, show someone the door; Brit. informal give someone their cards. **2** *the guards were dismissed:* **send away**, let go; disband, dissolve, discharge. **3** *he dismissed all morbid thoughts:* **banish**, set aside, disregard, brush off, shrug off, put out of one's mind; reject, deny, repudiate, spurn.

– OPPOSITES engage.

dismissal noun **1** *the threat of dismissal:* **one's notice**, discharge; redundancy, laying off; informal the sack, sacking, firing, the push, the boot, the axe, the elbow, one's marching orders; Brit. informal one's cards, the chop. **2** *a condescending dismissal of ancient systems of thought:* **rejection**, repudiation, repulse, non-acceptance.
– OPPOSITES recruitment.

dismissive adjective *she often talked of him in dismissive terms:* **contemptuous**, disdainful, scornful, sneering, snide, disparaging, negative; informal sniffy.
– OPPOSITES admiring.

dismount verb *the postman slowed his bicycle and dismounted:* **alight**, get off/down.

disobedient adjective *the slave masters punished anyone who became disobedient:* **insubordinate**, unruly, wayward, badly behaved, naughty, delinquent, disruptive, troublesome, rebellious, defiant, mutinous, recalcitrant, uncooperative, wilful, intractable, obstreperous; Brit. informal bolshie.

disobey verb *the king severely chastised those who disobeyed his orders:* **defy**, go against, flout, contravene, infringe, transgress, violate; disregard, ignore, pay no heed to.

disobliging adjective *we have such disobliging neighbours:* **unhelpful**, uncooperative, unaccommodating, unamenable, unreasonable, awkward, difficult; discourteous, uncivil, unfriendly.
– OPPOSITES helpful.

disorder noun **1** *he hates disorder:* **untidiness**, disorderliness, mess, disarray, chaos, confusion; clutter, jumble; a muddle, a shambles. **2** *incidents of public disorder:* **unrest**, disturbance, disruption, upheaval, turmoil, mayhem, pandemonium; violence, fighting, rioting, lawlessness, anarchy; breach of the peace, fracas, rumpus, melee; informal aggro. **3** *a blood disorder:* **disease**, infection, complaint, condition, affliction, malady, sickness, illness, ailment, infirmity, irregularity.
– OPPOSITES tidiness, peace.

disordered adjective **1** *her grey hair was disordered:* **untidy**, unkempt, messy, in a mess; disorganized, chaotic, confused, jumbled, muddled; N. Amer. informal mussed (up); Brit. informal shambolic. **2** *a disordered digestive system:* **dysfunctional**, disturbed, unsettled, unbalanced, upset, poorly.

disorderly adjective **1** *a disorderly desk:* **untidy**, disorganized, messy, cluttered; in disarray, in a mess, in a jumble, in a muddle, at sixes and sevens; informal like a bomb's hit it, higgledy-piggledy; Brit. informal shambolic. **2** *disorderly behaviour:* **unruly**, boisterous, rough, rowdy, wild, riotous; disruptive, troublesome, undisciplined, lawless, unmanageable, uncontrollable, out of hand, out of control.

d

–OPPOSITES tidy, peaceful.

disorganized adjective **1** *a disorganized tool box:* **disorderly**, disordered, unorganized, jumbled, muddled, untidy, messy, chaotic, topsy-turvy, haphazard; in disorder, in disarray, in a mess, in a muddle, in a shambles; informal higgledy-piggledy; Brit. informal shambolic. **2** *my boss decided that I was unproductive and disorganized:* **unmethodical**, unsystematic, undisciplined, badly organized, inefficient; haphazard, careless, slapdash; informal sloppy, hit-or-miss.
–OPPOSITES orderly.

disorientated, disoriented adjective *when he emerged into the street he was completely disorientated:* **confused**, bewildered, (all) at sea; lost, adrift, off-course, having lost one's bearings; informal not knowing whether one is coming or going.

disown verb *he has been disowned by his parents:* **reject**, cast off/aside, abandon, renounce, deny; turn one's back on, wash one's hands of, have nothing more to do with.

disparage verb *it has become fashionable to disparage Lawrence and his achievements:* **belittle**, denigrate, deprecate, play down, trivialize, make light of, undervalue, underrate; ridicule, deride, mock, scorn, scoff at, sneer at; run down, defame, discredit, speak badly of, cast aspersions on, impugn, vilify, traduce, criticize; N. Amer. slur; informal do down, pick holes in, knock, slam, pan, bad-mouth, pooh-pooh; Brit. informal rubbish, slate.
–OPPOSITES praise, overrate.

disparaging adjective *disparaging comments just antagonize him:* **derogatory**, deprecatory, denigratory, belittling; critical, scathing, negative, unfavourable, uncomplimentary, uncharitable; contemptuous, scornful, snide, disdainful; informal bitchy, catty.
–OPPOSITES complimentary.

disparate adjective *the document is made up from several disparate chunks:* **contrasting**, different, differing, dissimilar, unalike, poles apart; varying, various, diverse, diversified, heterogeneous, distinct, separate, divergent.
–OPPOSITES homogen(e)ous.

disparity noun *there was a disparity between the two sets of figures:* **discrepancy**, inconsistency, imbalance; variance, variation, divergence, gap, gulf; difference, dissimilarity, contrast.
–OPPOSITES similarity.

dispassionate adjective **1** *he dealt with life's disasters in a calm, dispassionate way:* **unemotional**, emotionless, impassive, cool, calm, {cool, calm, and collected}, unruffled, unperturbed, composed, self-possessed, self-controlled, unexcitable; informal laid-back. **2** *a dispassionate analysis:* **objective**, detached,

neutral, disinterested, impartial, non-partisan, unbiased, unprejudiced; scientific, analytical.
–OPPOSITES emotional, biased.

dispatch verb **1** *all the messages were dispatched:* **send (off)**, post, mail, forward, transmit. **2** *the business was dispatched in the morning:* **deal with**, finish, conclude, settle, discharge, perform; expedite, push through; informal make short work of. **3** *the good guy dispatched a host of villains:* **kill**, put to death, take/end the life of; slaughter, butcher, massacre, wipe out, exterminate, eliminate; murder, assassinate, execute; informal bump off, do in, do away with, top, take out, blow away; N. Amer. informal ice, rub out, waste.
noun **1** *goods ready for dispatch:* **sending**, posting, mailing. **2** *he carries out his duties with efficiency and dispatch:* **promptness**, speed, speediness, swiftness, rapidity, briskness, haste, hastiness. **3** *she read out the latest dispatch from the front:* **communication**, communiqué, bulletin, report, statement, letter, message; news, intelligence; informal memo, info, low-down. **4** *the capture and dispatch of the wolf:* **killing**, slaughter, massacre, extermination, elimination; murder, assassination, execution.

dispel verb *the sunshine did nothing to dispel her feelings of dejection:* **banish**, eliminate, drive away/off, get rid of; relieve, allay, ease, quell.

dispensable adjective *he regards all of his lieutenants as highly dispensable:* **expendable**, disposable, replaceable, inessential, non-essential; unnecessary, redundant, superfluous, surplus to requirements.

dispensation noun **1** *the dispensation of supplies:* **distribution**, supply, supplying, issue, issuing, handing out, doling out, dishing out, sharing out, dividing out; division, allocation, allotment, apportionment. **2** *the dispensation of justice:* **administration**, administering, delivery, discharge, dealing out, meting out. **3** *dispensation from National Insurance contributions:* **exemption**, immunity, exception, exoneration, reprieve, remission; informal a let-off.

dispense verb **1** *servants dispensed the drinks:* **distribute**, pass round, hand out, dole out, dish out, share out; allocate, supply, allot, apportion. **2** *the soldiers dispensed summary justice:* **administer**, deliver, issue, discharge, deal out, mete out. **3** *dispensing medicines:* **prepare**, make up; supply, provide, sell.
■ **dispense with 1** *let's dispense with the formalities:* **waive**, omit, drop, leave out, forgo; do away with; informal give something a miss. **2** *he dispensed with his crutches:* get rid of, throw away/out, dispose of, discard; manage without, cope without; informal ditch,

scrap, dump, chuck out/away, get shut of; Brit. informal get shot of.

disperse verb 1 *the crowd began to disperse | police dispersed the demonstrators*: **break up**, split up, disband, scatter, leave, go their separate ways; drive away/off, chase away. 2 *the fog finally dispersed*: **dissipate**, dissolve, melt away, fade away, clear, lift. 3 *the seeds get dispersed by birds*: **scatter**, disseminate, distribute, spread, broadcast.
– OPPOSITES assemble, gather.

dispirited adjective *she was tired and dispirited after her long journey*: **disheartened**, discouraged, demoralized, downcast, low, low-spirited, dejected, downhearted, depressed, disconsolate; informal fed up; Brit. informal cheesed off.
– OPPOSITES heartened.

dispiriting adjective **disheartening**, depressing, discouraging, daunting, demoralizing.

displace verb 1 *roof tiles displaced by gales*: **dislodge**, dislocate, move, shift, reposition; move out of place, knock out of place/position. 2 *the minister was displaced*: **depose**, dislodge, unseat, remove (from office), dismiss, eject, oust, expel, force out, drive out; overthrow, topple, bring down; informal boot out, give someone the boot, show someone the door; Brit. informal turf out. 3 *English displaced the local language*: **replace**, take the place of, supplant, supersede.
– OPPOSITES replace, reinstate.

display noun 1 *a display of dolls and puppets | a motorcycle display*: **exhibition**, exposition, array, arrangement, presentation, demonstration; spectacle, show, parade, pageant. 2 *they vied to outdo each other in display*: **ostentation**, ostentatiousness, showiness, extravagance, flamboyance, lavishness, splendour; informal swank, flashiness, glitziness. 3 *his display of concern*: **manifestation**, expression, show.
verb 1 *the Crown Jewels are displayed in London*: **exhibit**, show, put on show/view; arrange, array, present, lay out, set out. 2 *the play displays his many theatrical talents*: **show off**, parade, flaunt, reveal; publicize, make known, call/draw attention to; informal hype. 3 *she displayed a vein of sharp humour*: **manifest**, show evidence of, reveal; demonstrate, show.
– OPPOSITES conceal.

displease verb *he was plainly displeased by Jenny's decision*: **annoy**, irritate, anger, irk, vex, pique, gall, nettle; put out, upset; informal aggravate, peeve, needle, bug, rile, miff, hack off; N. Amer. informal tee off, tick off.

displeasure noun **annoyance**, irritation, crossness, anger, vexation, pique, rancour; dissatisfaction, discontent, discontentedness, disgruntlement, disapproval; informal aggravation.
– OPPOSITES satisfaction.

disposable adjective 1 *disposable plates*:

throwaway, expendable, one-use. 2 *disposable income*: **available**, usable, spendable.

disposal noun 1 *rubbish ready for disposal*: **throwing away**, discarding, jettisoning, scrapping; informal dumping, ditching, chucking (out/away). 2 *we have twenty copies for disposal*: **distribution**, handing out, giving out/away, allotment, allocation. 3 *the disposal of the troops in two lines*: **arrangement**, arranging, positioning, placement, lining up, disposition, grouping.
■ **at someone's disposal** for use by, in reserve for, in the hands of, in the possession of.

dispose verb 1 *he disposed his attendants in a circle*: **arrange**, place, put, position, array, set up, form; marshal, gather, group; Military dress. 2 *the experience disposed him to be kind*: **incline**, encourage, persuade, predispose, make willing, prompt, lead, motivate; sway, influence.
■ **dispose of 1** *the waste was disposed of*: throw away/out, get rid of, discard, jettison, scrap; informal dump, ditch, chuck (out/away), get shut of; Brit. informal get shot of; N. Amer. informal trash. 2 *he had disposed of all his assets*: part with, give away, hand over, deliver up, transfer; sell, auction; informal get shut of; Brit. informal get shot of.

disposed adjective 1 *they are philanthropically disposed*: **inclined**, predisposed, minded. 2 *we are not disposed to argue*: **willing**, inclined, prepared, ready, minded, in the mood. 3 *he was disposed to be cruel*: **liable**, apt, inclined, likely, predisposed, prone, tending; capable of.

disposition noun 1 *the book is not recommended to readers of a nervous disposition*: **temperament**, nature, character, constitution, make-up, mentality. 2 *his disposition to clemency*: **inclination**, tendency, proneness, propensity, proclivity. 3 *the disposition of the armed forces*: **arrangement**, positioning, placement, configuration; set-up, line-up, layout, array; marshalling, mustering, grouping.
■ **at someone's disposition** at the disposal of, for use by, in reserve for, in the hands of, in the possession of.

dispossess verb *the peasants have been dispossessed of their land*: **divest**, strip, rob, cheat out of, deprive; informal do out of.

disproportionate adjective *the sentences are disproportionate to the offences they have committed*: **out of proportion to**, not appropriate to, not commensurate with, relatively too large/small for; inordinate, unreasonable, excessive, undue.

disprove verb *new forensic evidence disproved the allegations*: **refute**, prove false, rebut, falsify, debunk, negate, invalidate, contradict, confound, controvert, negative, discredit; informal shoot full of holes, blow out of the water.

disputable adjective *some of these*

figures are disputable: **debatable**, open to debate/question, arguable, contestable, moot, questionable, doubtful, controvertible; informal iffy.

disputation noun *religious disputation:* **debate**, discussion, dispute, argument, arguing, altercation, dissension, disagreement, controversy; polemics.

dispute noun **1** *the extent of the king's powers was the subject of constant dispute:* **debate**, discussion, disputation, argument, controversy, disagreement, quarrelling, dissension, conflict, friction, strife, discord. **2** *they have settled their dispute:* **quarrel**, argument, altercation, squabble, falling-out, disagreement, difference of opinion, clash, wrangle; informal tiff, spat, scrap; Brit. informal row, barney, ding-dong; N. Amer. informal rhubarb.
– OPPOSITES agreement.
verb **1** *George disputed with him:* **debate**, discuss, exchange views; quarrel, argue, disagree, clash, fall out, wrangle, bicker, squabble; informal have words, have a tiff/spat. **2** *they disputed his proposals:* **challenge**, contest, question, call into question, impugn, quibble over, contradict, controvert, argue about, disagree with, take issue with.
– OPPOSITES accept.

disqualified adjective *he admitted driving while disqualified:* **banned**, barred, debarred; ineligible.
– OPPOSITES allowed.

disquiet noun *there has been grave disquiet about the state of the prisons:* **unease**, uneasiness, worry, anxiety, anxiousness, concern, disquietude; perturbation, consternation, upset, malaise, angst; agitation, restlessness, fretfulness; informal jitteriness.
– OPPOSITES calm.
verb *I was disquieted by the news:* **perturb**, agitate, upset, disturb, unnerve, unsettle, discompose, disconcert; make uneasy, worry, make anxious; trouble, concern, make fretful, make restless.
– OPPOSITES reassure.

disregard verb *Annie disregarded the remark:* **ignore**, take no notice of, pay no attention/heed to; overlook, turn a blind eye to, turn a deaf ear to, shut one's eyes to, gloss over, brush off/aside, shrug off.
– OPPOSITES heed.
noun *he drove with blithe disregard for the rules of the road:* **indifference**, non-observance, inattention, heedlessness, neglect.
– OPPOSITES attention.

disrepair noun *a building in a state of disrepair:* **dilapidation**, decrepitude, shabbiness, ricketiness, collapse, ruin; abandonment, neglect, disuse.

disreputable adjective **1** *he fell into disreputable company:* **with a bad reputation**, infamous, notorious, louche;

dishonourable, dishonest, untrustworthy, unwholesome, villainous, corrupt, immoral; unsavoury, slippery, seedy, sleazy; informal crooked, shady, shifty; Brit. informal dodgy. **2** *they looked filthy and disreputable:* **scruffy**, shabby, down at heel, seedy, untidy, unkempt, dishevelled.
– OPPOSITES respectable, smart.

disrepute noun *Beth had shamed herself and brought the family name into disrepute:* **disgrace**, shame, dishonour, infamy, notoriety, ignominy, bad reputation; humiliation, discredit, ill repute, low esteem, opprobrium, obloquy.
– OPPOSITES honour.

disrespect noun **1** *there is a growing disrespect for authority:* **contempt**, lack of respect, scorn, disregard, disdain. **2** *he meant no disrespect to anybody:* **discourtesy**, rudeness, impoliteness, incivility, ill/bad manners; insolence, impudence, impertinence.
– OPPOSITES esteem.

disrespectful adjective **discourteous**, rude, impolite, uncivil, ill-mannered, bad-mannered; insolent, impudent, impertinent, cheeky, flippant, insubordinate.
– OPPOSITES polite.

disrobe verb *she began to disrobe before retiring to bed:* **undress**, strip, take off one's clothes, remove one's clothes; Brit. informal peel off.

disrupt verb *the strike disrupted public transport:* **throw into confusion/disorder/disarray**, cause confusion/turmoil in, play havoc with; disturb, interfere with, upset, unsettle; obstruct, impede, hold up, delay, interrupt, suspend; Brit. informal throw a spanner in the works of; N. Amer. informal throw a monkey wrench in the works of.

disruptive adjective *a very disruptive child:* **troublesome**, unruly, badly behaved, rowdy, disorderly, undisciplined, wild; unmanageable, uncontrollable, uncooperative, out of control/hand, obstreperous, truculent.
– OPPOSITES well behaved.

dissatisfaction noun *polls revealed widespread dissatisfaction with the new law:* **discontent**, discontentment, disaffection, disquiet, unhappiness, malaise, disgruntlement, vexation, annoyance, irritation, anger; disapproval, disapprobation, disfavour, displeasure.

dissatisfied adjective *a dissatisfied customer:* **discontented**, malcontent, unsatisfied, disappointed, disaffected, unhappy, displeased; disgruntled, aggrieved, vexed, annoyed, irritated, angry, exasperated, fed up; informal cheesed off; Brit. informal brassed off.
– OPPOSITES contented.

dissect verb **1** *the body was dissected:* **anatomize**, cut up/open, dismember;

vivisect. **2** *the text of the gospels was dissected:* **analyse**, examine, study, scrutinize, pore over, investigate, go over with a fine-tooth comb.

dissection noun **1** *the dissection of corpses:* **cutting up/open**, dismemberment; autopsy, post-mortem, necropsy, anatomy, vivisection. **2** *a thorough dissection of their policies:* **analysis**, examination, study, scrutiny, scrutinization, investigation; evaluation, assessment.

dissemble verb *she is an honest, sincere person who has no need to dissemble:* **dissimulate**, pretend, feign, act, masquerade, sham, fake, bluff, posture, hide one's feelings, put on a false front.

dissembler noun **liar**, dissimulator; humbug, bluffer, fraud, impostor, actor, hoaxer, charlatan.

disseminate verb *health authorities should foster good practice by disseminating information:* **spread**, circulate, distribute, disperse, promulgate, propagate, publicize, communicate, pass on, put about, make known.

dissension noun *there was dissension within the cabinet over these policies:* **disagreement**, difference of opinion, dispute, dissent, conflict, friction, strife, discord, antagonism; argument, debate, controversy, disputation, contention.

dissent verb *two members dissented:* **differ**, disagree, demur, fail to agree, be at variance/odds, take issue; decline/refuse to support, protest, object, dispute, challenge, quibble.
– OPPOSITES agree.
noun *murmurs of dissent:* **disagreement**, difference of opinion, argument, dispute; disapproval, objection, protest, opposition, defiance; conflict, friction, strife.
– OPPOSITES agreement.

dissenter noun **dissident**, dissentient, objector, protester, disputant; rebel, renegade, maverick, independent; apostate, heretic.

dissentient adjective *dissentient voices started to be heard:* **dissenting**, dissident, disagreeing, differing, discordant, contradicting, contrary, anti-; opposing, objecting, protesting, complaining, rebellious, revolutionary; nonconformist, recusant, unorthodox, heterodox, heretical.

dissertation noun **essay**, thesis, treatise, paper, study, discourse, disquisition, tract, monograph.

disservice noun *not checking your headlines does your readers a disservice:* **unkindness**, bad/ill turn, disfavour; injury, harm, hurt, damage, wrong, injustice.
– OPPOSITES favour.

dissidence noun *the chairman was faced by dissidence within his own party:* **disagreement**, dissent, discord, discontent; opposition, resistance, protest, sedition.

dissident noun *a jailed dissident:* **dissenter**, objector, protester; rebel, revolutionary, recusant, subversive, agitator, insurgent, insurrectionist, refusenik.
– OPPOSITES conformist.
adjective *dissident intellectuals:* **dissenting**, dissentient, disagreeing; opposing, objecting, protesting, rebellious, rebelling, revolutionary, recusant, nonconformist.
– OPPOSITES conforming.

dissimilar adjective *contact between dissimilar cultures:* **different**, differing, unlike, variant, diverse, divergent, heterogeneous, disparate, unrelated, distinct, contrasting.

dissimilarity noun **difference(s)**, variance, diversity, heterogeneity, disparateness, disparity, distinctness, contrast, non-uniformity, divergence.

dissimulate verb *now they have power, they no longer need to dissimulate:* **pretend**, deceive, feign, act, dissemble, masquerade, pose, posture, sham, fake, bluff, hide one's feelings, be dishonest, put on a false front, lie.

dissimulation noun **pretence**, dissembling, deceit, dishonesty, duplicity, lying, guile, subterfuge, feigning, shamming, faking, bluff, bluffing, posturing, hypocrisy.

dissipate verb **1** *his anger dissipated:* **disappear**, vanish, evaporate, dissolve, melt away, melt into thin air, be dispelled; disperse, scatter. **2** *he dissipated his fortune:* **squander**, fritter (away), misspend, waste, be prodigal with, spend recklessly/freely, spend like water; expend, use up, consume, run through, go through; informal blow, splurge.

dissipated adjective *the new heir was a dissipated youth:* **dissolute**, debauched, decadent, intemperate, profligate, self-indulgent, wild, depraved; licentious, promiscuous; drunken.
– OPPOSITES ascetic.

dissipation noun **1** *drunken dissipation:* **debauchery**, decadence, dissoluteness, dissolution, intemperance, excess, profligacy, self-indulgence, wildness; depravity, degeneracy; licentiousness, promiscuity; drunkenness. **2** *the dissipation of our mineral wealth:* **squandering**, frittering (away), waste, misspending; expenditure, draining, depletion.
– OPPOSITES asceticism.

dissociate verb *the word 'spiritual' has become dissociated from religion:* **separate**, detach, disconnect, sever, cut off, divorce; isolate, alienate.
– OPPOSITES relate.
■ **dissociate oneself from 1** *he dissociated himself from the Church of England:* break away from, end relations with, sever connections with; withdraw from, delink from, quit, leave, disaffiliate from, resign from, pull out of, drop out of, defect from.

d

d

2 *he dissociated himself from the statement:* disown, reject, disagree with, distance oneself from.

dissociation noun **separation**, disconnection, detachment, severance, divorce, split; segregation, division.
– OPPOSITES union.

dissolute adjective *a dissolute, disreputable rogue:* **dissipated**, debauched, decadent, intemperate, profligate, self-indulgent, wild, depraved; licentious, promiscuous; drunken.
– OPPOSITES ascetic.

dissolution noun **1** *the dissolution of parliament:* **cessation**, conclusion, end, ending, termination, winding up/down, discontinuation, suspension, disbanding; prorogation, recess. **2** *the dissolution of the empire:* **disintegration**, breaking up; decay, collapse, demise, extinction. **3** *a life of dissolution.* See **DISSIPATION** sense 1.

dissolve verb **1** *sugar dissolves in water:* **go into solution**, break down; liquefy, deliquesce, disintegrate. **2** *his hopes dissolved:* **disappear**, vanish, melt away, evaporate, disperse, dissipate, disintegrate; dwindle, fade (away), wither. **3** *the crowd dissolved:* **disperse**, disband, break up, scatter, go in different directions. **4** *the assembly was dissolved:* **disband**, disestablish, bring to an end, end, terminate, discontinue, close down, wind up/down, suspend; prorogue, adjourn. **5** *their marriage was dissolved:* **annul**, nullify, void, invalidate, overturn, revoke.
▪ **dissolve into/in** burst into, break (down) into, be overcome with.

dissonant adjective **1** *dissonant sounds:* **inharmonious**, discordant, unmelodious, atonal, off-key, cacophonous. **2** *harmonious and dissonant colours:* **incongruous**, anomalous, clashing; disparate, different, dissimilar.
– OPPOSITES harmonious.

dissuade verb *I tried to dissuade him from telling that story:* **discourage**, deter, prevent, divert, stop; talk out of, persuade against, advise against, argue out of.
– OPPOSITES encourage.

distance noun **1** *they measured the distance:* **interval**, space, span, gap, extent; length, width, breadth, depth; range, reach. **2** *our perception of distance:* **remoteness**; closeness. **3** *a mix of warmth and distance:* **aloofness**, remoteness, detachment, unfriendliness; reserve, reticence, restraint, formality; informal stand-offishness.
verb *he distanced himself from her:* **withdraw**, detach; separate, dissociate, isolate, put at a distance.
▪ **in the distance** far away/off, afar, just in view; on the horizon.

distant adjective **1** *distant parts of the world:* **faraway**, far-off, far-flung, remote, out of the way, outlying. **2** *the distant past:* **long ago**, bygone, olden; ancient, prehistoric. **3** *half a mile distant:* **away**,

off, apart. **4** *a distant memory:* **vague**, faint, dim, indistinct, unclear, indefinite, sketchy, hazy. **5** *a distant family connection:* **remote**, indirect, slight. **6** *father was always distant:* **aloof**, reserved, remote, detached, unapproachable; withdrawn, reticent, taciturn, uncommunicative, undemonstrative, unforthcoming, unresponsive, unfriendly; informal stand-offish. **7** *he had a distant look in his eyes:* **distracted**, absent-minded, faraway, detached, distrait, vague.
– OPPOSITES near, close, recent.

distaste noun *Harry nurtured a distaste for all things athletic:* **dislike**, aversion, disinclination, disapproval, disapprobation, disdain, repugnance, hatred, loathing.
– OPPOSITES liking.

distasteful adjective *distasteful behaviour:* **unpleasant**, disagreeable, displeasing, undesirable; objectionable, offensive, unsavoury, unpalatable, obnoxious; disgusting, repellent, repulsive, revolting, repugnant, abhorrent, loathsome, vile.
– OPPOSITES agreeable.

distended adjective *a grossly distended belly:* **swollen**, bloated, dilated, engorged, enlarged, inflated, expanded, extended, bulging, protuberant.

distil verb **1** *the water was distilled:* **purify**, refine, filter, treat, process; evaporate and condense. **2** *whisky is distilled from barley:* **brew**, ferment. **3** *the solvent is distilled to leave the oil:* **boil off**, remove, separate.

distinct adjective **1** *the gallery is divided into five distinct spaces:* **discrete**, separate, different, unconnected; precise, specific, distinctive, contrasting. **2** *the tail has distinct black tips:* **clear**, well defined, unmistakable, easily distinguishable; recognizable, visible, obvious, pronounced, prominent, striking.
– OPPOSITES overlapping, indefinite.

distinction noun **1** *class distinctions:* **difference**, contrast, dissimilarity, variance, variation; distinction, differentiation, dividing line, gulf, gap. **2** *a painter of distinction:* **importance**, significance, note, consequence; renown, fame, celebrity, prominence, eminence, pre-eminence, repute, reputation; merit, worth, greatness, excellence, quality. **3** *he had served with distinction:* **honour**, credit, excellence, merit.
– OPPOSITES similarity, mediocrity.

distinctive adjective *each subculture developed a distinctive dress style:* **distinguishing**, characteristic, typical, individual, particular, peculiar, unique, exclusive, special.
– OPPOSITES common.

distinctly adverb **1** *there's something distinctly odd about him:* **decidedly**, markedly, definitely; clearly, noticeably, obviously, plainly, evidently, unmistakably,

manifestly, patently; Brit. informal
dead. **2** *Laura spoke quite distinctly:*
clearly, plainly, intelligibly, audibly,
unambiguously.

distinguish verb **1** *the child is perfectly
capable of distinguishing reality from
fantasy:* **differentiate**, tell apart,
discriminate between, tell the difference
between. **2** *he could distinguish shapes in
the dark:* **discern**, see, perceive, make out;
detect, recognize, identify. **3** *this is what
distinguishes history from other disciplines:*
separate, set apart, make distinctive, make
different; single out, mark off, characterize.
■ **distinguish oneself** attain distinction, be
successful, bring fame/honour to oneself,
become famous.

distinguishable adjective **discernible**,
recognizable, identifiable, detectable.

distinguished adjective *a distinguished
physicist:* **eminent**, famous, renowned,
prominent, well known; esteemed,
respected, illustrious, acclaimed, celebrated,
great; notable, important, influential.
– OPPOSITES unknown, obscure.

distinguishing adjective *a distinguishing
feature of British society:* **distinctive**,
differentiating, characteristic, typical,
peculiar, singular, unique.

distorted adjective **1** *a distorted face:*
twisted, warped, contorted, buckled,
deformed, malformed, misshapen,
disfigured, crooked, awry, out of shape.
2 *a distorted version of Freud's ideas:*
misrepresented, perverted, twisted,
falsified, misreported, misstated, garbled,
inaccurate; biased, prejudiced, slanted,
coloured, loaded, weighted, altered,
changed.

distract verb *don't let me distract you from
what you were saying:* **divert**, sidetrack,
draw away, disturb, put off.

distracted adjective *he glanced at me with a
distracted smile:* **preoccupied**, inattentive,
vague, abstracted, distrait, absent-minded,
faraway, in a world of one's own; bemused,
confused, bewildered; troubled, harassed,
worried; informal miles away, not with it.
– OPPOSITES attentive.

distracting adjective *some people find even
the slightest noise distracting:* **disturbing**,
unsettling, intrusive, disconcerting,
bothersome, off-putting.

distraction noun **1** *a distraction from
the real issues:* **diversion**, interruption,
disturbance, interference, hindrance.
2 *frivolous distractions:* **amusement**,
entertainment, diversion, recreation, leisure
pursuit, divertissement. **3** *he was driven
to distraction:* **frenzy**, hysteria, mental
distress, madness, insanity, mania; agitation,
perturbation.

distrait, distraite adjective *he was
unusually distrait as he ate his breakfast:*
distracted, preoccupied, absorbed,

abstracted, distant, faraway; absent-minded,
vague, inattentive, in a brown study, wool-
gathering, with one's head in the clouds, in
a world of one's own; informal miles away, not
with it.
– OPPOSITES alert.

distraught adjective *the poor child was
distraught:* **worried**, upset, distressed,
fraught; overcome, overwrought, beside
oneself, out of one's mind, desperate,
hysterical, worked up, at one's wits' end;
informal in a state.

distress noun **1** *she concealed her
distress:* **anguish**, suffering, pain, agony,
torment, heartache, heartbreak; misery,
wretchedness, sorrow, grief, woe, sadness,
unhappiness, desolation, despair. **2** *a
ship in distress:* **danger**, peril, difficulty,
trouble, jeopardy, risk. **3** *the poor in
distress:* **hardship**, adversity, poverty,
deprivation, privation, destitution,
indigence, impoverishment, penury, need,
dire straits.
– OPPOSITES happiness, safety, prosperity.
verb *he was distressed by the trial:* **cause
anguish/suffering to**, pain, upset, make
miserable; trouble, worry, bother, perturb,
disturb, disquiet, agitate, harrow, torment;
informal cut up.
– OPPOSITES calm, please.

distressing adjective *it was distressing
to hear her talking like that:* **upsetting**,
worrying, disturbing, disquieting, painful,
traumatic, agonizing, harrowing; sad,
saddening, heartbreaking, heart-rending;
informal gut-wrenching.
– OPPOSITES comforting.

distribute verb **1** *the proceeds were
distributed among his creditors:* **give out**,
deal out, dole out, dish out, hand out/round;
allocate, allot, apportion, share out, divide
out/up, parcel out. **2** *the newsletter is
distributed free:* **circulate**, issue, hand out,
deliver. **3** *a hundred and thirty different
species are distributed worldwide:* **disperse**,
scatter, spread.
– OPPOSITES collect.

distribution noun **1** *the distribution of
charity:* **giving out**, dealing out, doling
out, handing out/round, issue, issuing,
dispensation; allocation, allotment,
apportioning, sharing out, dividing
up/out, parcelling out. **2** *the geographical
distribution of plants:* **dispersal**,
dissemination, spread; placement, position,
location, disposition. **3** *centres of food
distribution:* **supply**, supplying, delivery,
transport, transportation. **4** *the statistical
distribution of the problem:* **frequency**,
prevalence, incidence, commonness.

district noun *the business district of Manila:*
neighbourhood, area, region, locality,
locale, community, quarter, sector, zone,
territory; administrative division, ward,
parish; informal neck of the woods.

distrust noun *the general distrust of*

d

authority: **mistrust**, suspicion, wariness, chariness, leeriness, lack of trust, lack of confidence; scepticism, doubt, doubtfulness, cynicism; misgivings, qualms, disbelief.
verb *Louise distrusted him:* **mistrust**, be suspicious of, be wary/chary of, be leery of, regard with suspicion, suspect; be sceptical of, have doubts about, doubt, be unsure of/about, have misgivings about, wonder about, disbelieve (in).

disturb verb 1 *somewhere where we won't be disturbed:* **interrupt**, intrude on, butt in on, barge in on; distract, disrupt, bother, trouble, pester, harass; informal hassle. **2** *don't disturb his papers:* **disarrange**, muddle, rearrange, disorganize, disorder, mix up, interfere with, throw into disorder/confusion, turn upside down. **3** *waters disturbed by winds:* **agitate**, churn up, stir up. **4** *he wasn't disturbed by the allegations:* **perturb**, trouble, concern, worry, upset; agitate, fluster, discomfit, disconcert, dismay, distress, discompose, unsettle, ruffle.

disturbance noun 1 *we are concerned about the disturbance to local residents:* **disruption**, distraction, interference; bother, trouble, inconvenience, upset, annoyance, irritation, intrusion, harassment; informal hassle. **2** *disturbances among the peasantry:* **riot**, fracas, upheaval, brawl, street fight, melee, free-for-all, ruckus, rumpus; informal ruction. **3** *emotional disturbance:* **trouble**, perturbation, distress, worry, upset, agitation, discomposure, discomfiture; neurosis, illness, sickness, disorder, complaint.

disturbed adjective 1 *disturbed sleep:* **disrupted**, interrupted, fitful, intermittent, broken. **2** *disturbed children:* **troubled**, distressed, upset, distraught; unbalanced, unstable, disordered, dysfunctional, maladjusted, neurotic, unhinged; informal screwed up, mixed up.

disturbing adjective *this is disturbing news:* **worrying**, perturbing, troubling, upsetting; distressing, discomfiting, disconcerting, disquieting, unsettling, dismaying, alarming, frightening; informal gut-wrenching.

disunite verb *these nations are never to be disunited:* **break up**, separate, divide, split up, partition, dismantle.
– OPPOSITES unify.

disunity noun *there was disunity within the administration:* **disagreement**, dissent, dissension, argument, arguing, quarrelling, feuding; conflict, strife, friction, discord.

disuse noun *many of the mills fell into disuse:* **non-use**, non-employment, lack of use; neglect, abandonment, desertion, obsolescence.

disused adjective *a disused building:* **unused**, no longer in use, unemployed, idle;

abandoned, deserted, vacated, unoccupied, uninhabited.

ditch noun *she rescued an animal from a ditch:* **trench**, trough, channel, dyke, drain, gutter, gully, watercourse, conduit.
verb 1 (informal) *she decided to ditch her old curtains:* **throw out**, throw away, discard, get rid of, dispose of, do away with, shed; abandon, drop, shelve, scrap, jettison; informal dump, junk, scrub, axe, chuck (away/out); Brit. informal get shot of; N. Amer. informal trash. **2** (informal) *she ditched her husband.* See THROW SOMEONE OVER. **3** *they started ditching the coastal areas:* **trench**, dig a ditch in, excavate, drain.

dither verb *they wasted several minutes while she dithered:* **hesitate**, falter, waver, vacillate, change one's mind, be in two minds, be indecisive, be undecided; Brit. haver; informal shilly-shally, dilly-dally.

divan noun **settee**, sofa, couch; sofa bed; Brit. put-you-up; N. Amer. studio couch.

dive verb 1 *they dived into the clear water | the plane was diving towards the ground:* **plunge**, nosedive, jump head first, bellyflop; plummet, fall, drop, pitch. **2** *the islanders dive for oysters:* snorkel, scuba dive. **3** *they dived for cover:* **leap**, jump, lunge, launch oneself, throw oneself, go headlong, duck.
noun 1 *a dive into the pool:* **plunge**, nosedive, jump, bellyflop; plummet, fall, drop, swoop, pitch. **2** *a sideways dive:* **lunge**, spring, jump, leap. **3** (informal) *John got into a fight in some dive:* **sleazy bar/nightclub**, seedy bar/nightclub, drinking den; informal drinking joint.

diverge verb 1 *the two roads diverged:* **separate**, part, fork, divide, split, bifurcate, go in different directions. **2** *areas where our views diverge:* **differ**, be different, be dissimilar; disagree, be at variance/odds, conflict, clash. **3** *he diverged from his text:* **deviate**, digress, depart, veer, stray; stray from the point, get off the subject.
– OPPOSITES converge, agree.

divergence noun 1 *the divergence of the human and ape lineages:* **separation**, dividing, parting, forking, bifurcation. **2** *a marked political divergence:* **difference**, dissimilarity, variance, disparity; disagreement, incompatibility, mismatch. **3** *divergence from standard behaviour:* **deviation**, digression, departure, shift, straying; variation, change, alteration.

divergent adjective *they adopted divergent approaches to almost every issue:* **differing**, varying, different, dissimilar, unalike, disparate, contrasting, contrastive; conflicting, incompatible, contradictory, at odds, at variance.
– OPPOSITES similar.

diverse adjective *the company has to manage data from diverse databases:* **various**, sundry, manifold, multiple; varied, varying, miscellaneous, assorted, mixed, diversified, divergent, heterogeneous, a mixed bag of; different, differing, distinct, unlike, dissimilar.

diversify verb **1** *farmers looking for ways to diversify:* **branch out**, expand, extend operations. **2** *a plan aimed at diversifying the economy:* **vary**, bring variety to; modify, alter, change, transform; expand, enlarge.

diversion noun **1** *the diversion of 19 rivers:* **re-routing**, redirection, deflection, deviation, divergence. **2** *traffic diversions:* **detour**, deviation, alternative route. **3** *the noise created a diversion:* **distraction**, disturbance, smokescreen. **4** *a city full of diversions:* **entertainment**, amusement, pastime, delight, divertissement; fun, recreation, rest and relaxation, pleasure; informal R & R.

diversity noun *a diversity of abstract design styles:* **variety**, miscellany, assortment, mixture, mix, melange, range, array, multiplicity; variation, variance, diverseness, diversification, heterogeneity, difference, contrast.
– OPPOSITES uniformity.

divert verb **1** *a plan to divert Siberia's rivers:* **re-route**, redirect, change the course of, deflect, channel. **2** *he diverted her from her studies:* **distract**, sidetrack, disturb, draw away, be a distraction, put off. **3** *the story diverted them:* **amuse**, entertain, distract, delight, enchant, interest, fascinate, absorb, engross, rivet, grip, hold the attention of.

diverting adjective *a diverting comedy about two New York kids:* **entertaining**, amusing, enjoyable, pleasing, agreeable, delightful, appealing; interesting, fascinating, intriguing, absorbing, riveting, compelling; humorous, funny, witty, comical.
– OPPOSITES boring.

divest verb *he intends to divest you of all your power:* **deprive**, strip, dispossess, rob, cheat/trick out of.

divide verb **1** *he divided his kingdom into four:* **split (up)**, cut up, carve up; dissect, bisect, halve, quarter. **2** *a curtain divided her cabin from the galley:* **separate**, segregate, partition, screen off, section off, split off. **3** *the stairs divide at the mezzanine:* **diverge**, separate, part, branch (off), fork, split (in two), bifurcate. **4** *Jack divided up the cash:* **share out**, allocate, allot, apportion, portion out, ration out, parcel out, deal out, dole out, dish out, distribute, dispense; informal divvy up. **5** *he aimed to divide his opponents:* **disunite**, drive apart, break up, split up, set at variance/odds; separate, isolate, estrange, alienate. **6** *living things are divided into three categories:* **classify**, sort (out), categorize, order, group, grade, rank.
– OPPOSITES unify, join, converge.
noun *the sectarian divide:* **breach**, gulf, gap, split; borderline, boundary, dividing line.

dividend noun **1** *an annual dividend:* **share**, portion, premium, return, gain, profit; informal cut, rake-off; Brit. informal divvy. **2** *the research*

will produce dividends in the future: **benefit**, advantage, gain; bonus, extra, plus.

divination noun *she looked to divination for guidance when important decisions loomed:* **fortune-telling**, divining, prophecy, prediction, soothsaying, augury; clairvoyance, second sight.

divine[1] adjective **1** *a divine being:* **godly**, angelic, seraphic, saintly, beatific; heavenly, celestial, holy. **2** *divine worship:* **religious**, holy, sacred, sanctified, consecrated, blessed, devotional.
– OPPOSITES mortal.

divine[2] verb **1** *Fergus divined how afraid she was:* **guess**, surmise, conjecture, deduce, infer; discern, intuit, perceive, recognize, see, realize, appreciate, understand, grasp, comprehend; informal figure (out), savvy; Brit. informal twig, suss. **2** *they divined that this was an auspicious day:* **foretell**, predict, prophesy, forecast, foresee, prognosticate. **3** *he divined water supplies:* **dowse**.

diviner noun **fortune-teller**, clairvoyant, crystal-gazer, psychic, seer, soothsayer, prognosticator, prophesier, oracle, sibyl.

divinity noun **1** *they denied Christ's divinity:* **divine nature**, divineness, godliness, deity, godhead, holiness. **2** *the study of divinity:* **theology**, religious studies, religion, scripture. **3** *a female divinity:* **deity**, god, goddess, divine/supreme being.

division noun **1** *the division of the island | cell division:* **dividing (up)**, breaking up, break-up, carving up, splitting, dissection, bisection; partitioning, separation, segregation. **2** *the division of his estates:* **sharing out**, dividing up, parcelling out, dishing out, allocation, allotment, apportionment; splitting up, carving up; informal divvying up. **3** *the division between nomadic and urban cultures:* **dividing line**, divide, boundary, borderline, border, demarcation line. **4** *each class is divided into nine divisions:* **section**, subsection, subdivision, category, class, group, grouping, set, family. **5** *an independent division of the executive:* **department**, branch, arm, wing, sector, section, subsection, subdivision, subsidiary. **6** *the causes of social division:* **disunity**, disunion, conflict, discord, disagreement, dissension, disaffection, estrangement, alienation, isolation.

divisive adjective *the divisive effects of government policy:* **alienating**, estranging, isolating, schismatic.
– OPPOSITES unifying.

divorce noun **1** *she wants a divorce:* **dissolution**, annulment, (official/judicial) separation. **2** *a growing divorce between the church and people:* **separation**, division, split, disunity, estrangement, alienation; schism, gulf, chasm.
– OPPOSITES marriage, unity.
verb **1** *her parents have divorced:* **dissolve**

d

one's marriage, annul one's marriage, end one's marriage, get a divorce. **2** *religion cannot be divorced from morality:* **separate**, disconnect, divide, dissociate, detach, isolate, alienate, set apart, cut off.

divulge verb *he refused to divulge Father O'Neill's whereabouts:* **disclose**, reveal, tell, communicate, pass on, publish, broadcast, proclaim; expose, uncover, make public, give away, let slip; informal spill the beans about, let on about.
– OPPOSITES conceal.

dizzy adjective **1** *she felt dizzy:* **giddy**, light-headed, faint, unsteady, shaky, muzzy, wobbly; informal woozy. **2** *dizzy heights:* **causing dizziness**, causing giddiness, vertiginous. **3** (informal) *a dizzy blond.* See EMPTY-HEADED.

do verb **1** *she does most of the manual work:* **carry out**, undertake, discharge, execute, perform, accomplish, achieve; bring about, engineer; informal pull off. **2** *they can do as they please:* **act**, behave, conduct oneself, acquit oneself. **3** *regular coffee will do:* **suffice**, be adequate, be satisfactory, fill/fit the bill, serve one's purpose, meet one's needs. **4** *the boys will do the dinner:* **prepare**, make, get ready, see to, arrange, organize, be responsible for, be in charge of; informal fix. **5** *the company are doing a new range | a portrait I am doing:* **make**, create, produce, turn out, design, manufacture; paint, draw, sketch; informal knock up/off. **6** *each room was done in a different colour:* **decorate**, furnish, ornament, deck out, trick out; informal do up. **7** *her maid did her hair:* **style**, arrange, adjust; brush, comb, wash, dry, cut; informal fix. **8** *I am doing a show to raise money:* **put on**, present, produce; perform in, act in, take part in, participate in. **9** *you've done me a favour:* **grant**, pay, render, give. **10** *show me how to do these equations:* **work out**, figure out, calculate; solve, resolve. **11** *she's doing archaeology:* **study**, read, learn, take a course in. **12** *what does he do?* **have as a job**, have as a profession, be employed at, earn a living at. **13** *he is doing well at college:* **get on/along**, progress, fare, manage, cope; succeed, prosper. **14** *he was doing 80 mph:* **drive at**, travel at, move at. **15** *the cyclists do 30 miles per day:* **travel (over)**, journey, cover, traverse, achieve, notch up, log; informal chalk up.
■ **do away with** *they want to do away with the old customs:* abolish, get rid of, discard, remove, eliminate, discontinue, stop, end, terminate, put an end/stop to, dispense with, drop, abandon, give up; informal scrap, ditch, dump.
■ **do someone/something in** (informal) *the long walk home did me in:* wear out, tire out, exhaust, fatigue, weary, overtire, drain; informal shatter, take it out of; Brit. informal knacker.
■ **do someone out of something** (informal) swindle out of, cheat out of, trick out of,

deprive of; informal con out of, diddle out of.
■ **do something up 1** *she did her bootlace up:* fasten, tie (up), lace, knot; make fast, secure. **2** (informal) *he's had his house done up:* renovate, refurbish, refit, redecorate, decorate, revamp, make over, modernize, improve, spruce up, smarten up; informal give something a facelift; N. Amer. informal rehab.
■ **do without** forgo, dispense with, abstain from, refrain from, eschew, give up, cut out, renounce, manage without.

docile adjective *a cheap and docile workforce:* **compliant**, obedient, pliant, dutiful, submissive, deferential, unassertive, cooperative, amenable, accommodating, biddable, malleable.
– OPPOSITES disobedient, wilful.

dock[1] noun *his boat was moored at the dock:* **harbour**, marina, port, anchorage; wharf, quay, pier, jetty, landing stage.
verb *the ship docked:* **moor**, berth, put in, tie up, anchor.

dock[2] verb **1** *they docked the money from his salary:* **deduct**, subtract, remove, debit, take off/away; informal knock off. **2** *workers had their pay docked:* **reduce**, cut, decrease. **3** *the dog's tail was docked:* **cut off**, cut short, shorten, crop, lop; remove, amputate, detach, sever, chop off, take off.

docket noun (Brit.) *you need to fill in a docket for every transaction:* **document**, chit, coupon, voucher, certificate, counterfoil, bill, receipt; Brit. informal chitty.

doctor noun *Tim went to see a doctor:* **physician**, medical practitioner, clinician; general practitioner, GP, consultant, registrar, medical officer, MO; Brit. house officer, houseman; N. Amer. intern, extern; informal doc, medic, medico; Brit. informal quack.
verb **1** *he doctored Stephen's drinks:* **adulterate**, contaminate, tamper with, lace; informal spike, dope. **2** *the reports have been doctored:* **falsify**, tamper with, interfere with, alter, change; forge, fake; informal cook; Brit. informal fiddle (with).

doctrinaire adjective *democratic socialism was feared by doctrinaire Marxists:* **dogmatic**, rigid, inflexible, uncompromising; authoritarian, intolerant, fanatical, zealous, extreme.

doctrine noun *they rejected the doctrine of the Trinity:* **creed**, credo, dogma, belief, teaching, ideology; tenet, maxim, canon, principle, precept.

document noun *their solicitor drew up a document:* **(official/legal) paper**, certificate, deed, contract, legal agreement.
verb *many aspects of school life have been documented:* **record**, register, report, log, chronicle, archive, put on record, write down; detail, note, describe.

documentary adjective **1** *documentary evidence:* **recorded**, documented, registered, written, chronicled, archived, on record/paper, in writing. **2** *a documentary*

film: **factual**, non-fictional.
noun *a documentary about rural England:* **factual programme/film**; programme, film, broadcast.

dodder verb *the old couple doddered out of the hotel lounge:* **totter**, teeter, toddle, hobble, shuffle, shamble, falter.

doddery adjective **tottering**, tottery, staggering, shuffling, shambling, faltering, shaky, unsteady, wobbly; feeble, frail, weak.

dodge verb **1** *she dodged into a telephone booth:* **dart**, bolt, dive, lunge, leap, spring. **2** *he could easily dodge the two coppers:* **elude**, evade, avoid, escape, run away from, lose, shake (off); informal give someone the slip. **3** *the minister tried to dodge the debate:* **avoid**, evade, get out of, back out of, sidestep; N. Amer. end-run; informal duck, wriggle out of; Austral./NZ informal duck-shove.
noun **1** *a dodge to the right:* **dart**, bolt, dive, lunge, leap, spring. **2** *a clever dodge | a tax dodge:* **ruse**, ploy, scheme, tactic, stratagem, subterfuge, trick, hoax, wile, cheat, deception, blind; swindle, fraud; informal scam, con (trick); Brit. informal wheeze; N. Amer. informal bunco, grift; Austral. informal lurk, rort.

dodgy adjective (Brit. informal) **1** *a dodgy second-hand car salesman.* See DISHONEST. **2** *the champagne was dodgy:* **second-rate**, third-rate, substandard, low-quality; awful, terrible, dreadful, dire; N. Amer. cheapjack; informal not up to much, woeful; Brit. informal ropy, grotty.

doer noun **1** *the doer of unspeakable deeds:* **performer**, perpetrator, executor, accomplisher, agent. **2** *Daniel is a thinker more than a doer:* **worker**, organizer, man/woman of action; informal mover and shaker, busy bee.

dog noun *she went for a walk with her dog:* **hound**, canine, mongrel; pup, puppy; informal doggy, pooch; Austral. informal bitzer.
verb **1** *they dogged him the length of the country:* **pursue**, follow, track, trail, shadow, hound; informal tail. **2** *the scheme was dogged by bad weather:* **plague**, beset, bedevil, beleaguer, blight, trouble.

dogged adjective *success required dogged determination:* **tenacious**, determined, resolute, resolved, purposeful, persistent, persevering, single-minded, tireless; strong-willed, steadfast, staunch.
– OPPOSITES half-hearted.

dogma noun *a dogma of the Sikh religion:* **teaching**, belief, tenet, principle, precept, maxim, article of faith, canon; creed, credo, set of beliefs, doctrine, ideology.

dogmatic adjective *he criticized the Prime Minister's strident, dogmatic style:* **opinionated**, peremptory, assertive, insistent, emphatic, adamant, doctrinaire, authoritarian, imperious, dictatorial, uncompromising, unyielding, inflexible, rigid.

dogsbody noun (Brit. informal) **drudge**, menial (worker), factotum, servant, slave, lackey, minion, man/girl Friday; informal gofer; Brit. informal skivvy; N. Amer. informal peon.

doing noun **1** *the doing of the act constitutes the offence:* **performance**, performing, carrying out, execution, implementation, implementing, achievement, accomplishment, realization, completion. **2** *an account of his doings in Paris:* **exploit**, activity, act, action, deed, feat, achievement, accomplishment; informal caper.

doldrums plural noun *don't give in to winter doldrums:* **depression**, melancholy, gloom, gloominess, downheartedness, dejection, despondency, low spirits, despair; inertia, apathy, listlessness; N. Amer. blahs; informal blues.
■ **in the doldrums** inactive, quiet, slow, slack, sluggish, stagnant.

dole noun (Brit. informal) *he was on the dole:* **unemployment benefit**, social security, welfare.
■ **dole something out** *Dad began to dole out the sweets:* deal out, share out, divide up, allocate, allot, distribute, dispense, hand out, give out, dish out/up; informal divvy up.

doleful adjective *she regarded him with doleful eyes:* **mournful**, woeful, sorrowful, sad, unhappy, depressed, gloomy, morose, melancholy, miserable, forlorn, wretched, woebegone, despondent, dejected, disconsolate, downcast, crestfallen, downhearted; informal blue, down in the mouth/dumps, heartsick.
– OPPOSITES cheerful.

doll noun *the child was hugging a doll:* **figure**, figurine, model; toy, plaything; informal dolly.

dollop noun (informal) *she had a little dollop of cream on her nose:* **blob**, gobbet, lump, ball; informal glob; Brit. informal gob, wodge.

domain noun **1** *they extended their domain:* **realm**, kingdom, empire, dominion, province, territory, land. **2** *the domain of art:* **field**, area, sphere, discipline, province, world.

dome noun **cupola**, vault, arched roof.

domestic adjective **1** *domestic commitments:* **family**, home, household. **2** *she was not at all domestic:* **housewifely**, domesticated, homely, houseproud. **3** *small domestic animals:* **domesticated**, tame, pet, household. **4** *the domestic car industry:* **national**, state, home, internal.
noun *they worked as domestics:* **servant**, domestic worker/help, home help, maid, housemaid, cleaner, housekeeper; Brit. informal daily (help).

domesticated adjective **1** *domesticated animals:* **tame**, tamed, pet, domestic, trained. **2** *domesticated crops:* **cultivated**, naturalized. **3** *I'm quite domesticated really:* **housewifely**, home-loving, homely, houseproud.

d

– OPPOSITES wild.

dominance noun **supremacy**, superiority, ascendancy, pre-eminence, predominance, domination, dominion, mastery, power, authority, rule, command, control, sway.

dominant adjective **1** *the dominant classes:* **presiding**, ruling, governing, controlling, commanding, ascendant, supreme, authoritative. **2** *he has a dominant personality:* **assertive**, authoritative, forceful, domineering, commanding, controlling, pushy. **3** *the dominant issues in psychology:* **main**, principal, prime, premier, chief, foremost, primary, predominant, paramount, prominent; central, key, crucial, core; informal number-one.
– OPPOSITES subservient.

dominate verb **1** *the Russians dominated Iran in the nineteenth century:* **control**, influence, exercise control over, command, be in command of, be in charge of, rule, govern, direct, have ascendancy over, have mastery over; informal head up, be in the driver's seat, be at the helm, rule the roost; Brit. informal wear the trousers; N. Amer. informal have someone in one's hip pocket. **2** *the Puritan work ethic still dominates:* **predominate**, prevail, reign, be prevalent, be paramount, be pre-eminent. **3** *the village is dominated by the viaduct:* **overlook**, command, tower above/over, loom over.

domination noun *they believed that Communists were aiming for world domination:* **rule**, government, sovereignty, control, command, authority, power, dominion, dominance, mastery, supremacy, superiority, ascendancy, sway.

domineer verb *all her life she was domineered by Granny:* **browbeat**, bully, intimidate, push around/about, order about/around, lord it over; dictate to, be overbearing, have under one's thumb, rule with a rod of iron; informal boss about/around, walk all over.

domineering adjective *he was brought up by a cold, domineering father:* **overbearing**, authoritarian, imperious, high-handed, autocratic; masterful, dictatorial, despotic, oppressive, iron-fisted, strict, harsh; informal bossy.

dominion noun **1** *France had dominion over Laos:* **supremacy**, ascendancy, dominance, domination, superiority, predominance, pre-eminence, hegemony, authority, mastery, control, command, power, sway, rule, government, jurisdiction, sovereignty, suzerainty. **2** *a British dominion:* **dependency**, colony, protectorate, territory, province, possession.

don[1] noun *an Oxford don:* **university teacher**, (university) lecturer, fellow, professor, reader, academic, scholar.

don[2] verb *he donned an overcoat:* **put on**, get dressed in, dress (oneself) in, get into, slip into/on.

donate verb *he donated his fee to charity:* **give**, give/make a donation of, contribute, make a contribution of, gift, subscribe, grant, bestow; informal chip in, pitch in; Brit. informal stump up; N. Amer. informal kick in.

donation noun *his employer also made a donation to the fund:* **gift**, contribution, subscription, present, handout, grant, offering; charity.

done adjective **1** *the job is done:* **finished**, ended, concluded, complete, completed, accomplished, achieved, fulfilled, discharged, executed; informal wrapped up, sewn up, polished off. **2** *is the meat done?* **cooked (through)**, ready. **3** *those days are done:* **over (and done with)**, at an end, finished, ended, concluded, terminated, no more, dead, gone, in the past. **4** (informal) *that's just not done:* **proper**, seemly, decent, respectable, right, correct, in order, fitting, appropriate, acceptable, the done thing.
– OPPOSITES incomplete, underdone, ongoing.
exclamation *Done!* **agreed**, all right, very well; informal you're on, OK, okey-dokey; Brit. informal righto, righty-ho.
■ **be/have done with** be/have finished with, be through with, want no more to do with.

Don Juan noun **womanizer**, philanderer, Casanova, Lothario, flirt, ladies' man, playboy, seducer, rake, roué, libertine; informal skirt-chaser, ladykiller, wolf.

donkey noun *the cart was drawn by a donkey:* **ass**, jackass, jenny; mule, hinny; Brit. informal moke.

donnish adjective *you can never talk with these quiet, donnish types:* **scholarly**, studious, academic, bookish, intellectual, learned, highbrow; informal egghead.

donor noun *the cost has been met by a generous donor:* **giver**, contributor, benefactor, benefactress, subscriber; supporter, backer, patron, sponsor; informal angel.

doom noun *his impending doom:* **destruction**, downfall, ruin, ruination; extinction, annihilation, death.
verb *we were doomed to fail:* **destine**, fate, predestine, preordain, foredoom, mean; condemn, sentence.

doomed adjective *a doomed friendship:* **ill-fated**, ill-starred, cursed, jinxed, foredoomed, damned.

doorkeeper noun **doorman**, commissionaire, concierge.

dope verb **1** *the horse was doped:* **drug**, administer drugs/narcotics to, tamper with, interfere with; sedate; Brit. informal nobble. **2** *they doped his drink:* **add drugs to**, tamper with, adulterate, contaminate, lace; informal spike, doctor.

dopey adjective (informal) *he became dopey and fell into a deep sleep:* **stupefied**, confused, muddled, befuddled, disorientated, groggy,

muzzy; informal woozy, not with it.
– OPPOSITES alert.

dormant adjective *the bacteria may lie dormant in the bird:* **asleep**, sleeping, resting; **inactive**, passive, inert, latent, quiescent.
– OPPOSITES awake, active.

dose noun *a dose of cough mixture:* **measure**, portion, dosage, drench; informal hit.

dossier noun *we have a dossier on him:* **file**, report, case history; account, notes, document(s), documentation, data, information, evidence.

dot noun *a pattern of tiny dots:* **spot**, speck, fleck, speckle; full stop, decimal point.
verb **1** *spots of rain dotted his shirt:* **spot**, fleck, mark, stipple, freckle, sprinkle. **2** *restaurants are dotted around the site:* **scatter**, pepper, sprinkle, strew; spread, disperse, distribute.

dotage noun *Uncle Henry was in his dotage:* **declining years**, winter/autumn of one's life; advanced years, old age.

dote
■ **dote on** *she doted on the boy:* adore, love dearly, be devoted to, idolize, treasure, cherish, worship, hold dear; indulge, spoil, pamper.

doting adjective **adoring**, loving, besotted, infatuated; affectionate, fond, devoted, caring.

dotty adjective (informal). See **MAD** sense 1.

double adjective **1** *a double garage:* **dual**, duplex, twin, binary, duplicate, in pairs, coupled, twofold. **2** *a double helping:* **twofold**, doubled. **3** *a double meaning:* **ambiguous**, equivocal, dual, two-edged, double-edged, ambivalent, cryptic, enigmatic. **4** *he led a double life:* **deceitful**, double-dealing, two-faced, dual; hypocritical, false, duplicitous, insincere, deceiving, dissembling, dishonest.
– OPPOSITES single, unambiguous.
adverb *we had to pay double:* **twice (over)**, twice the amount, doubly.
noun **1** *if it's not her, it's her double:* **lookalike**, twin, clone, duplicate, exact likeness, replica, copy, facsimile, Doppelgänger; informal spitting image, dead ringer, dead spit. **2** *she used a double for the stunts:* **stand-in**, substitute.
verb **1** *they doubled his salary:* **multiply by two**, increase twofold. **2** *the bottom sheet had been doubled up:* **fold (back/up/down/over/under)**, turn back/up/down/over/under, tuck back/up/down/under. **3** *the kitchen doubles as a dining room:* **function**, do, (also) serve.
■ **at/on the double** very quickly, as fast as one's legs can carry one, at a run, at a gallop, fast, swiftly, rapidly, speedily, at (full) speed, at full tilt, as fast as possible; informal double quick, like (greased) lightning, like the wind, like a scalded cat, like a bat out of hell; Brit. informal like the clappers, at a rate of knots; N. Amer. informal lickety-split.

double-cross verb *he was blackmailed into double-crossing his own government:* **betray**, cheat, defraud, trick, hoodwink, mislead, deceive, swindle, be disloyal to, be unfaithful to, play false; informal do the dirty on, sell down the river.

double-dealing noun *one day his double-dealing would be discovered:* **duplicity**, treachery, betrayal, double-crossing, unfaithfulness, untrustworthiness, infidelity, bad faith, disloyalty, breach of trust, fraud, underhandedness, cheating, dishonesty, deceit, deceitfulness, deception, falseness; informal crookedness.
– OPPOSITES honesty.

double entendre noun *he was unable to resist a smutty double entendre:* **ambiguity**, double meaning, innuendo, play on words.

doubly adverb *we have to be doubly careful:* **twice as**, in double measure, even more, especially, extra.

doubt noun **1** *there was some doubt as to the caller's identity:* **uncertainty**, unsureness, indecision, hesitation, dubiousness, suspicion, confusion; queries, questions; formal dubiety. **2** *a weak leader racked by doubt:* **indecision**, hesitation, uncertainty, insecurity, unease, uneasiness, apprehension; hesitancy, vacillation, irresolution. **3** *there is doubt about their motives:* **scepticism**, distrust, mistrust, doubtfulness, suspicion, cynicism, uneasiness, apprehension, wariness, chariness, leeriness; reservations, misgivings, suspicions.
– OPPOSITES certainty, conviction.
verb **1** *they doubted my story:* **disbelieve**, distrust, mistrust, suspect, have doubts about, be suspicious of, have misgivings about, feel uneasy about, query, question, challenge. **2** *I doubt whether he will come:* **think something unlikely**, have (one's) doubts about, question, query, be dubious. **3** *stop doubting and believe!* **be undecided**, have doubts, be irresolute, be ambivalent, be doubtful, be unsure, be uncertain, be in two minds, hesitate, shilly-shally, waver, vacillate.
– OPPOSITES trust.
■ **in doubt 1** *the issue was in doubt:* **doubtful**, uncertain, open to question, unconfirmed, unknown, undecided, unresolved, in the balance, up in the air; informal iffy. **2** *if you are in doubt, ask for advice:* irresolute, hesitant, vacillating, dithering, wavering, ambivalent; doubtful, unsure, uncertain, in two minds, shilly-shallying, undecided, in a quandary/dilemma; informal sitting on the fence.
■ **no doubt** doubtless, undoubtedly, indubitably, doubtlessly, without (a) doubt; unquestionably, undeniably, incontrovertibly, irrefutably; unequivocally, clearly, plainly, obviously, patently.

doubter noun *this is his chance to confound the doubters:* **sceptic**, doubting Thomas, non-believer, unbeliever, disbeliever, cynic, scoffer, questioner, challenger, dissenter.
– OPPOSITES believer.

doubtful adjective **1** *I was doubtful about going:* **irresolute**, hesitant, vacillating, dithering, wavering, in doubt, unsure, uncertain, in two minds, shilly-shallying, undecided, in a quandary/dilemma, blowing hot and cold. **2** *it is doubtful whether he will come:* **in doubt**, uncertain, open to question, unsure, unconfirmed, not definite, unknown, undecided, unresolved, debatable, in the balance, up in the air; informal iffy. **3** *the whole trip is looking rather doubtful:* **unlikely**, improbable, dubious, impossible. **4** *they are doubtful of the methods used:* **distrustful**, mistrustful, suspicious, wary, chary, leery, apprehensive; sceptical, unsure, ambivalent, dubious, cynical. **5** *this decision is of doubtful validity:* **questionable**, arguable, debatable, controversial, contentious; informal iffy; Brit. informal dodgy.
– OPPOSITES confident, certain, probable, trusting.

doubtless adverb *Henry was doubtless glad of the opportunity:* **undoubtedly**, indubitably, doubtlessly, no doubt; unquestionably, indisputably, undeniably, incontrovertibly, irrefutably; certainly, surely, of course, indeed.

doughty adjective *a doughty fighter:* **fearless**, dauntless, determined, resolute, indomitable, intrepid, plucky, spirited, bold, valiant, brave, stout-hearted, courageous; informal gutsy, spunky, feisty.

dour adjective *they were barely acknowledged by the dour receptionist:* **stern**, unsmiling, unfriendly, severe, forbidding, gruff, surly, grim, sullen, solemn, austere, stony.
– OPPOSITES cheerful, friendly.

douse verb **1** *a mob doused the thieves with petrol:* **drench**, soak, saturate, wet, splash, slosh. **2** *a guard doused the flames:* **extinguish**, put out, quench, smother, dampen down.

dovetail verb **1** *the ends of the logs were dovetailed:* **joint**, join, fit together, splice, mortise, tenon. **2** *this will dovetail well with the division's existing activities:* **fit in**, go together, be consistent, match, conform, harmonize, be in tune, correspond; informal square; N. Amer. informal jibe.

dowdy adjective *she had serviceable but dowdy clothes:* **unfashionable**, frumpy, old-fashioned, inelegant, shabby, scruffy, frowzy; Brit. informal mumsy; Austral./NZ informal daggy.
– OPPOSITES fashionable.

down[1] adjective **1** *I'm feeling a bit down:* **depressed**, sad, unhappy, melancholy, miserable, wretched, sorrowful, gloomy, dejected, downhearted, despondent, dispirited, low; informal blue, down in the dumps/mouth, fed up. **2** *the computer is down:* **not working**, inoperative, malfunctioning, out of order, broken; not in service, out of action, out of commission; informal conked out, bust, (gone) kaput; N. Amer. informal on the fritz.
– OPPOSITES elated, working.
noun *the ups and downs of running a business:* **setbacks**, upsets, reverses, reversals, mishaps, vicissitudes; informal glitches.

down[2] noun *goose down:* **soft feathers**, fine hair; fluff, fuzz, floss, lint.

down and out adjective *a novel about being down and out on the streets of London:* **destitute**, poverty-stricken, impoverished, penniless, insolvent, impecunious; needy, in straitened circumstances, distressed, badly off; homeless, on the streets, vagrant, sleeping rough; informal hard up, (flat) broke, strapped (for cash), cash-strapped, without a brass farthing, without two pennies to rub together; Brit. informal stony broke, skint; N. Amer. informal without a red cent, stone broke, on skid row.
– OPPOSITES wealthy.
noun (**down-and-out**) *he gave his packed lunch to a down-and-out:* **poor person**, pauper, indigent; beggar, homeless person, vagrant, tramp, drifter, derelict, vagabond; N. Amer. hobo; Austral. bagman; informal have-not, dosser, bag lady; N. Amer. informal bum.

down at heel adjective **1** *the resort looks down at heel:* **run down**, dilapidated, neglected, uncared-for; seedy, insalubrious, squalid, slummy, wretched; informal scruffy, scuzzy; Brit. informal grotty; N. Amer. informal shacky. **2** *a down-at-heel labourer:* **scruffy**, shabby, ragged, tattered, mangy, sorry; unkempt, bedraggled, dishevelled, ungroomed, seedy, untidy, slovenly; informal tatty, scuzzy, grungy; Brit. informal grotty; N. Amer. informal raggedy.
– OPPOSITES smart.

downbeat adjective **1** *the mood is decidedly downbeat:* **pessimistic**, gloomy, negative, defeatist, cynical, bleak, fatalistic, dark, black; despairing, despondent, depressed, dejected, demoralized, hopeless, melancholy, glum. **2** *his downbeat joviality:* **relaxed**, easy-going, easy, casual, informal, nonchalant, insouciant; low-key, subtle, unostentatious, cool; informal laid-back.
– OPPOSITES upbeat.

downcast adjective *Morgan was understandably downcast following Scotland's defeat:* **despondent**, disheartened, discouraged, dispirited, downhearted, crestfallen, down, low, disconsolate, despairing; sad, melancholy, gloomy, glum, morose, doleful, dismal, woebegone, miserable, depressed, dejected; informal blue, down in the mouth, down in the dumps.
– OPPOSITES elated.

downfall noun *the crisis led to the downfall of the government:* **undoing**, ruin, ruination; defeat, conquest, deposition, overthrow; nemesis, destruction, annihilation, elimination; end, collapse, fall, crash, failure; debasement, degradation, disgrace; Waterloo.
– OPPOSITES rise.

downgrade verb **1** *plans to downgrade three workers:* **demote**, lower, reduce/lower in rank; relegate. **2** *I won't downgrade their achievement:* **disparage**, denigrate, detract from, run down, belittle; informal bad-mouth.
– OPPOSITES promote, praise.

downhearted adjective *fans must not be downhearted even though we lost:* **despondent**, disheartened, discouraged, dispirited, downcast, crestfallen, down, low, disconsolate, wretched; melancholy, gloomy, glum, morose, doleful, dismal, woebegone, miserable, depressed, dejected, sorrowful, sad; informal blue, down in the mouth, down in the dumps.
– OPPOSITES elated.

downmarket adjective (Brit.) *the quality papers and the downmarket tabloids:* **cheap**, cheap and nasty, inferior; low-class, lowbrow, unsophisticated, rough, insalubrious; informal tacky, rubbishy, dumbed down.

downpour noun *the drizzle was becoming a downpour:* **rainstorm**, cloudburst, deluge; thunderstorm; torrential/pouring rain.

downright adjective **1** *downright lies:* **complete**, total, absolute, utter, thorough, out-and-out, outright, sheer, arrant, pure, real, veritable, categorical, unmitigated, unadulterated, unalloyed, unequivocal; Brit. informal proper. **2** *her downright attitude:* **frank**, straightforward, direct, blunt, plain-spoken, forthright, uninhibited, unreserved; no-nonsense, matter-of-fact, bluff, undiplomatic; explicit, clear, plain, unequivocal, unambiguous; honest, candid, open, sincere; informal upfront.
adverb *that's downright dangerous:* **thoroughly**, utterly, positively, profoundly, really, completely, totally, entirely; unquestionably, undeniably, in every respect, through and through; informal plain.

downside noun *the downside is that getting a patent costs big money:* **drawback**, disadvantage, snag, stumbling block, catch, pitfall, fly in the ointment; handicap, limitation, trouble, difficulty, problem, complication, nuisance; hindrance; weak spot/point; informal minus, flip side.
– OPPOSITES advantage.

down-to-earth adjective *she seemed a good down-to-earth type:* **practical**, sensible, realistic, matter-of-fact, responsible, reasonable, rational, logical, balanced, sober, pragmatic, level-headed, commonsensical, sane.
– OPPOSITES idealistic.

downtrodden adjective *a downtrodden proletarian struggling for social justice:* **oppressed**, subjugated, persecuted, repressed, tyrannized, crushed, enslaved, exploited, victimized, bullied; disadvantaged, underprivileged, powerless, helpless; abused, maltreated.

downward adjective *the downward flow of water:* **descending**, downhill, falling, sinking, dipping; earthbound, earthward.

downy adjective *I stroked the downy hair on my tiny son's head:* **soft**, velvety, smooth, fleecy, fluffy, fuzzy, feathery, furry, woolly, silky.

dowry noun **marriage settlement**, (marriage) portion.

doze verb *he dozed but woke with a start:* **catnap**, nap, drowse, sleep lightly, rest; informal snooze, snatch forty winks, get some shut-eye; Brit. informal kip; N. Amer. informal catch some Zs.
noun *she had a short doze before work:* **catnap**, nap, siesta, light sleep, drowse, rest; informal snooze, forty winks; Brit. informal kip, zizz.
■ **doze off** fall asleep, go to sleep, drop off; informal nod off, drift off; N. Amer. informal sack out, zone out.

dozy adjective *he grew dozy at the end of a long day:* **drowsy**, sleepy, half asleep, heavy-eyed, somnolent; lethargic, listless, enervated, inactive, languid, weary, tired, fatigued; N. Amer. logy; informal dopey, yawny.

drab adjective **1** *a drab interior:* **colourless**, grey, dull, washed out, muted, lacklustre; dingy, dreary, dismal, cheerless, gloomy, sombre. **2** *a drab existence:* **uninteresting**, dull, boring, tedious, monotonous, dry, dreary; unexciting, unimaginative, uninspiring, insipid, lacklustre, flat, stale, wishy-washy, colourless; lame, tired, sterile, anaemic, barren, tame; middle-of-the-road, run-of-the-mill, mediocre, nondescript, characterless, mundane, unremarkable, humdrum.
– OPPOSITES bright, cheerful, interesting.

draconian adjective *collaborators suffered draconian reprisals:* **harsh**, severe, strict, extreme, drastic, stringent, tough; cruel, oppressive, ruthless, relentless, punitive; authoritarian, despotic, tyrannical, repressive; Brit. swingeing.
– OPPOSITES lenient.

draft noun **1** *the draft of his speech:* **preliminary version**, rough outline, plan, skeleton, abstract; main points, bare bones. **2** *a banker's draft:* **cheque**, order, money order, bill of exchange, postal order.

drag verb **1** *she dragged the chair backwards:* **haul**, pull, tug, heave, lug, draw; trail, trawl, tow; informal yank. **2** *the day dragged:* **become tedious**, pass slowly, creep along, hang heavy, wear on, go on too long, go on and on.

d

d

noun *the drag of the air brakes:* **pull**, resistance, tug.
■ **drag on** *the war dragged on:* persist, continue, go on, carry on, extend, run on, be protracted, endure, prevail.
■ **drag something out** *the procedure was bound to drag out the negotiations:* prolong, protract, draw out, spin out, string out, extend, lengthen, carry on, keep going, continue.

dragoon verb *he dragooned his friends into participating:* **coerce**, pressure, pressurize, press, push; force, compel, impel; hound, harass, nag, harry, badger, goad, pester; browbeat, bludgeon, bully, twist someone's arm, strong-arm; informal railroad.

drain verb **1** *a valve for draining the tank:* **empty (out)**, void, clear (out), evacuate, unload. **2** *drain off any surplus liquid:* **draw off**, extract, withdraw, remove, siphon off, pour out, pour off; milk, bleed, tap, void, filter, discharge. **3** *the water drained away to the sea:* **flow**, pour, trickle, stream, run, rush, gush, flood, surge; leak, ooze, seep, dribble, issue, filter, bleed, leach. **4** *more people would just drain our resources:* **use up**, exhaust, deplete, consume, expend, get through, sap, strain, tax; milk, bleed. **5** *he drained his drink:* **drink (up/down)**, gulp (down), guzzle, quaff, down, imbibe, sup, swallow, finish off, toss off, slug; informal sink, swig, swill (down), polish off, knock back, put away.
– OPPOSITES fill.
noun **1** *the drain filled with water:* **sewer**, channel, conduit, ditch, culvert, duct, pipe, gutter, trough; sluice, spillway, race, flume, chute. **2** *a drain on the battery:* **strain**, pressure, burden, load, tax, demand.

dram noun *Menzies offered the man a dram from his flask:* **drink**, nip, tot, sip, drop, finger, splash, little, spot, taste.

drama noun **1** *a television drama:* **play**, show, piece, theatrical work, dramatization. **2** *he is studying drama:* **acting**, the theatre, the stage, the performing arts, dramatic art, stagecraft. **3** *she liked to create a drama:* **incident**, scene, spectacle, crisis; excitement, thrill, sensation; disturbance, row, commotion, turmoil; dramatics, theatrics.

dramatic adjective **1** *dramatic art:* **theatrical**, theatric, thespian, stage, dramaturgical. **2** *a dramatic increase in speed:* **considerable**, substantial, sizeable, goodly, fair, marked, noticeable, measurable, perceptible, obvious, appreciable; significant, notable, noteworthy, remarkable, extraordinary, exceptional, phenomenal; informal tidy. **3** *there were dramatic scenes in the city:* **exciting**, stirring, action-packed, sensational, spectacular; startling, unexpected, tense, gripping, riveting, fascinating, thrilling, hair-raising; rousing, lively, electrifying, impassioned, moving. **4** *dramatic headlands:*

striking, impressive, imposing, spectacular, breathtaking, dazzling, sensational, awesome, awe-inspiring, remarkable, outstanding, incredible, phenomenal. **5** *a dramatic gesture:* **exaggerated**, theatrical, ostentatious, actressy, stagy, showy, melodramatic, overdone, histrionic, affected, mannered, artificial; informal hammy, ham, campy.
– OPPOSITES insignificant, boring.

dramatist noun **playwright**, writer, scriptwriter, screenwriter, scenarist, dramaturge.

dramatize verb **1** *the novel was dramatized for television:* **turn into a play/film**, adapt for the stage/screen. **2** *the tabloids dramatized the event:* **exaggerate**, overdo, overstate, hyperbolize, magnify, amplify, inflate; sensationalize, embroider, colour, aggrandize, embellish, elaborate; informal blow up (out of all proportion).

drape verb **1** *she draped a shawl round her:* **wrap**, wind, swathe, sling, hang. **2** *the chair was draped with blankets:* **cover**, envelop, swathe, shroud, deck, festoon, overlay, cloak, wind, enfold, sheathe. **3** *he draped one leg over the arm of his chair:* **dangle**, hang, suspend, droop, drop.

drastic adjective *drastic measures were necessary:* **extreme**, serious, desperate, radical, far-reaching, momentous, substantial; heavy, severe, harsh, rigorous; oppressive, draconian.
– OPPOSITES moderate.

draught noun **1** *the draught made Robyn shiver:* **current of air**, rush of air; waft, wind, breeze, gust, puff, blast; informal blow. **2** *he took a deep draught of his beer:* **gulp**, drink, haul, swallow, mouthful, slug; informal swig, swill.

draw verb **1** *he drew the house:* **sketch**, make a drawing (of), delineate, outline, draft, rough out, illustrate, render, represent, trace; portray, depict. **2** *she drew her chair in to the table:* **pull**, haul, drag, tug, heave, lug, trail, tow; informal yank. **3** *the train drew into the station:* **move**, go, come, proceed, progress, travel, advance, pass, drive; inch, roll, glide, cruise; forge, sweep; back. **4** *she drew the curtains:* **close**, shut, pull to, lower; open, part, pull back, pull open, fling open, raise. **5** *he drew some fluid off the knee joint:* **drain**, extract, withdraw, remove, suck, pump, siphon, milk, bleed, tap. **6** *he drew his gun:* **pull out**, take out, produce, fish out, extract, withdraw; unsheathe. **7** *I drew £50 out of the bank:* **withdraw**, take out. **8** *while I draw breath:* **breathe in**, inhale, inspire, respire. **9** *she was drawing huge audiences:* **attract**, interest, win, capture, catch, engage, lure, entice; absorb, occupy, rivet, engross, fascinate, mesmerize, spellbind, captivate, enthral, grip. **10** *what conclusion can we draw?* **deduce**, infer, conclude, derive, gather, glean.
noun **1** *she won the Christmas draw:* **raffle**,

lottery, sweepstake, sweep, tombola, ballot; N. Amer. lotto. **2** *the match ended in a draw:* **tie**, dead heat, stalemate. **3** *the draw of central London:* **attraction**, lure, allure, pull, appeal, glamour, enticement, temptation, charm, seduction, fascination, magnetism.

■ **draw on** *we can draw on centuries of experience:* call on, have recourse to, avail oneself of, turn to, look to, fall back on, rely on, exploit, use, employ, utilize, bring into play.

■ **draw something out 1** *he drew out a gun.* See **DRAW** verb sense 6. **2** *they always drew their parting out:* prolong, protract, drag out, spin out, string out, extend, lengthen.

■ **draw someone out** encourage to talk, put at ease.

■ **draw up** *a car drew up beside us:* stop, pull up, halt, come to a standstill, brake, park; arrive.

■ **draw something up** *we drew up a list:* compose, formulate, frame, write down, draft, prepare, think up, devise, work out; create, invent, design.

drawback noun *the major drawback to this method is that it can be very time-consuming:* **disadvantage**, snag, downside, stumbling block, catch, hitch, pitfall, fly in the ointment; weak spot/point, weakness, imperfection; handicap, limitation, trouble, difficulty, problem, complication; hindrance, obstacle, impediment, obstruction, inconvenience, discouragement; informal minus, hiccup; Brit. informal spanner in the works.
– OPPOSITES benefit.

drawing noun *he did a pencil drawing of the house:* **sketch**, picture, illustration, representation, portrayal, delineation, depiction, composition, study; diagram, outline, design, plan.

drawl verb *'Can't do that,' he drawled lazily:* **say slowly**, speak slowly, drone.

drawn adjective *she looked pale and drawn:* **pinched**, haggard, drained, wan, hollow-cheeked; fatigued, tired, exhausted; tense, stressed, strained, worried, anxious, harassed, fraught; informal hassled.

dread verb *I used to dread going to school:* **fear**, be afraid of, worry about, be anxious about, have forebodings about; be terrified by, tremble/shudder at, shrink from, quail from, flinch from; informal get cold feet about.
noun *she was filled with dread:* **fear**, apprehension, trepidation, anxiety, worry, concern, foreboding, disquiet, unease, angst; fright, panic, alarm; terror, horror; informal the jitters, the heebie-jeebies.
– OPPOSITES confidence.
adjective *a dread secret:* **awful**, frightful, terrible, horrible, dreadful; feared, frightening, alarming, terrifying, dire, dreaded.

dreadful adjective **1** *a dreadful accident:* **terrible**, frightful, horrible, grim, awful, dire; horrifying, alarming, shocking, distressing, appalling, harrowing; ghastly, fearful, horrendous; tragic, calamitous; formal grievous. **2** *a dreadful meal:* **unpleasant**, disagreeable, nasty; frightful, shocking, awful, abysmal, atrocious, disgraceful, deplorable, very bad, repugnant; poor, inadequate, inferior, unsatisfactory, distasteful; informal pathetic, woeful, crummy, rotten, sorry, third-rate, lousy, ropy, God-awful; Brit. informal duff, chronic, rubbish, pants. **3** *you're a dreadful flirt:* **outrageous**, shocking; inordinate, immoderate, unrestrained.
– OPPOSITES pleasant, agreeable.

dreadfully adverb **1** *I'm dreadfully hungry:* **extremely**, very, really, exceedingly, tremendously, exceptionally, extraordinarily; decidedly, most, particularly; N. English right; informal terrifically, terribly, desperately, awfully, devilishly, mega, seriously, majorly; Brit. informal jolly, ever so, dead, well; N. Amer. informal real, mighty, awful. **2** *she missed James dreadfully:* **very much**, much, lots, a lot, a great deal, intensely, desperately. **3** *the company performed dreadfully:* **terribly**, awfully, very badly, atrociously, appallingly, abominably, poorly; informal abysmally, pitifully, diabolically.

dream noun **1** *I awoke from my dreams:* REM sleep; nightmare; vision, fantasy, hallucination. **2** *she went around in a dream:* **daydream**, reverie, trance, daze, stupor, haze. **3** *he realized his childhood dream:* **ambition**, aspiration, hope; goal, aim, objective, grail, intention, intent, target; desire, wish, yearning; daydream, fantasy, pipe dream. **4** *he's an absolute dream:* **delight**, joy, marvel, wonder, gem, treasure; beauty, vision.
verb **1** *I dreamt of making the Olympic team:* **fantasize about**, daydream about; wish for, hope for, long for, yearn for, hanker after, set one's heart on; aspire to, aim for, set one's sights on. **2** *she's always dreaming:* **daydream**, be in a trance, be lost in thought, be preoccupied, be abstracted, stare into space, be in cloud cuckoo land; muse. **3** *I wouldn't dream of being late:* **think**, consider, contemplate, conceive.
adjective *his dream home:* **ideal**, perfect, fantasy.

■ **dream something up** think up, invent, concoct, devise, hatch, contrive, create, work out, come up with; informal cook up.

dreamer noun *you're just a bunch of naive dreamers:* **fantasist**, daydreamer; romantic, sentimentalist, idealist, wishful thinker, Don Quixote; Utopian, visionary.
– OPPOSITES realist.

dreamlike adjective *the gardens have a special dreamlike quality:* **unreal**, illusory, imaginary, unsubstantial, chimerical, ethereal, phantasmagorical, trance-like; surreal; nightmarish, Kafkaesque; hazy, shadowy, faint, indistinct, unclear.

d

d

dreamy adjective **1** *a dreamy expression:* **daydreaming**, dreaming; pensive, thoughtful, reflective, meditative, ruminative; lost in thought, preoccupied, distracted, rapt, inattentive, wool-gathering, vague, absorbed, absent-minded, with one's head in the clouds, in a world of one's own; informal miles away. **2** *he was dreamy as a child:* **idealistic**, romantic, starry-eyed, impractical, unrealistic, Utopian, quixotic; Brit. informal airy-fairy. **3** *a dreamy recollection:* **dreamlike**, vague, dim, hazy, shadowy, faint, indistinct, unclear.
– OPPOSITES alert, practical, clear.

dreary adjective **1** *a dreary day at school:* **dull**, drab, uninteresting, flat, tedious, wearisome, boring, unexciting, unstimulating, uninspiring, soul-destroying; humdrum, monotonous, uneventful, unremarkable, featureless. **2** *she thought of dreary things:* **sad**, miserable, depressing, gloomy, sombre, grave, mournful, melancholic, joyless, cheerless. **3** *a dreary day:* **gloomy**, dismal, dull, dark, dingy, murky, overcast; depressing, sombre.
– OPPOSITES exciting, cheerful, bright.

dregs plural noun **1** *the dregs from a bottle of wine:* **sediment**, deposit, residue, accumulation, sludge, lees, grounds, settlings; remains. **2** *the dregs of humanity:* **scum**, refuse, riff-raff, outcasts, deadbeats; the underclass, the untouchables, the lowest of the low, the great unwashed, the hoi polloi; informal trash, dossers.

drench verb *rain was falling fast, drenching the countryside:* **soak**, saturate, wet through, permeate, douse, souse; drown, swamp, inundate, flood; steep, bathe.

dress verb **1** *he dressed quickly:* **put on clothes**, clothe oneself, get dressed. **2** *she was dressed in a suit:* **clothe**, attire, garb, deck out, trick out/up, costume, array, robe; informal get up, doll up. **3** *they dress for dinner every day:* **wear formal clothes**, wear evening dress, dress up. **4** *they dressed his wounds:* **bandage**, cover, bind, wrap, swathe.
noun **1** *a long blue dress:* **frock**, gown, robe, shift. **2** *full evening dress:* **clothes**, clothing, garments, attire; costume, outfit, ensemble, garb, turnout; informal gear, get-up, togs, duds, glad rags; Brit. informal clobber; N. Amer. informal threads.
■ **dress down** dress informally, dress casually; informal slob around.
■ **dress up 1** *Angela loved dressing up:* dress smartly, dress formally, wear evening dress; informal doll oneself up, put on one's glad rags. **2** *Hugh dressed up as Santa Claus:* disguise oneself, dress; put on fancy dress, put on a costume.
■ **dress something up** *tabloids make money by dressing up the prejudices of their readers as informed opinion:* present, represent, portray, depict, characterize; embellish, enhance, touch up, embroider.

dressing noun **1** *salad dressing:* **sauce**, relish, condiment, dip. **2** *they put fresh dressings on her burns:* **bandage**, covering, plaster, gauze, lint, compress.

dressmaker noun **tailor**, seamstress, needlewoman; outfitter, costumier, clothier; couturier, designer.

dressy adjective *nobody changes into anything dressy for dinner:* **smart**, formal; elaborate, ornate; stylish, elegant, chic, fashionable; informal snappy, snazzy, natty, trendy.
– OPPOSITES casual.

dribble verb **1** *the baby started to dribble:* **drool**, slaver, slobber, salivate, drivel, water at the mouth; Scottish & Irish slabber. **2** *rainwater dribbled down her face:* **trickle**, drip, fall, drizzle; ooze, seep.
noun **1** *there was dribble on his chin:* **saliva**, spittle, spit, slaver, slobber, drool. **2** *a dribble of sweat:* **trickle**, drip, driblet, stream, drizzle; drop, splash.

dried adjective *dried fruit:* **dehydrated**, desiccated, dry, dried up, moistureless.

drift verb **1** *his raft drifted down the river:* **be carried**, be borne; float, bob, waft, meander. **2** *the guests drifted away:* **wander**, meander, stray, potter, dawdle; Brit. informal mooch. **3** *don't allow your attention to drift:* **stray**, digress, deviate, diverge, veer, get sidetracked. **4** *snow drifted over the path:* **pile up**, bank up, heap up, accumulate, gather, amass.
noun **1** *a drift from the country to urban areas:* **movement**, shift, flow, transfer, relocation, gravitation. **2** *the pilot had not noticed any drift:* **deviation**, digression. **3** *he caught the drift of her thoughts:* **gist**, essence, meaning, sense, substance, significance; thrust, import, tenor; implication, intention; direction, course. **4** *a drift of deep snow:* **pile**, heap, bank, mound, mass, accumulation.

drifter noun **wanderer**, traveller, transient, roamer, tramp, vagabond, vagrant; N. Amer. hobo.

drill noun **1** *a hydraulic drill:* **boring tool**, drilling tool, auger, (brace and) bit, gimlet, awl, bradawl. **2** *they learned military discipline and drill:* **training**, instruction, coaching, teaching; (physical) exercises, workout; informal square-bashing. **3** *Estelle knew the drill:* **procedure**, routine, practice, regimen, programme, schedule; method, system.
verb **1** *drill the piece of wood:* **bore a hole in**, make a hole in; bore, pierce, puncture, perforate. **2** *a sergeant drilling new recruits:* **train**, instruct, coach, teach, discipline; exercise, put someone through their paces. **3** *his mother had drilled politeness into him:* **instil**, hammer, drive, drum, din, implant, ingrain; teach, indoctrinate, brainwash.

drink verb **1** *she drank her coffee:* **swallow**, gulp down, quaff, guzzle, sup; imbibe, sip, consume; drain, toss off, slug; informal swig, down, knock back, put away, neck, sink, swill. **2** *he never drank:* **drink alcohol**, tipple, indulge; carouse; informal hit the bottle, booze, knock a few back, have one over the eight, get tanked up, go on a bender; Brit. informal bevvy; N. Amer. informal bend one's elbow. **3** *let's drink to success:* **toast**, salute.

noun 1 *he took a sip of his drink:* **beverage**, liquid refreshment; dram, bracer, nightcap, nip, tot; pint; Brit. informal bevvy; humorous libation. **2** *she turned to drink:* **alcohol**, (intoxicating) liquor, alcoholic drink; informal booze, hooch, the hard stuff, firewater, rotgut, moonshine, the bottle, the sauce, grog, Dutch courage. **3** *she took a drink of her wine:* **swallow**, gulp, sip, draught, slug; informal swig, swill.

■ **drink something in** *he drank in the details of the crime:* absorb, assimilate, digest, ingest, take in; be rapt in, be lost in, be fascinated by, pay close attention to.

drinkable adjective **fit to drink**, palatable; pure, clean, safe, unpolluted, untainted, uncontaminated; formal potable.

drinker noun *he was a notorious drinker and womanizer:* **drunkard**, drunk, inebriate, imbiber, tippler, sot; alcoholic, dipsomaniac, alcohol-abuser; informal boozer, soak, lush, wino, alky, sponge, barfly; Austral./NZ informal hophead.
– OPPOSITES teetotaller.

drip verb **1** *there was a tap dripping:* **dribble**, drop, leak. **2** *sweat dripped from his chin:* **drop**, dribble, trickle, drizzle, run, splash, plop; leak, emanate, issue.
noun *a bucket to catch the drips:* **drop**, dribble, spot, trickle, splash.

drive verb **1** *I can't drive a car:* **operate**, handle, manage; pilot, steer. **2** *he drove to the police station:* **travel by car**, motor. **3** *I'll drive you to the airport:* **chauffeur**, run, give someone a lift, take, ferry, transport, convey, carry. **4** *the engine drives the front wheels:* **power**, propel, move, push. **5** *he drove a nail into the boot:* **hammer**, screw, ram, sink, plunge, thrust, propel, knock. **6** *she drove her cattle to market:* **impel**, urge; herd, round-up, shepherd. **7** *a desperate mother driven to crime:* **force**, compel, prompt, precipitate; oblige, coerce, pressure, goad, spur, prod. **8** *he drove his staff extremely hard:* **work**, push, tax, exert.
noun 1 *an afternoon drive:* **excursion**, outing, trip, jaunt, tour; ride, run, journey; informal spin. **2** *the house has a long drive:* **driveway**, approach, access road. **3** *sexual drive:* **urge**, appetite, desire, need; impulse, instinct. **4** *she lacked the drive to succeed:* **motivation**, ambition, single-mindedness, will power, dedication, doggedness, tenacity; enthusiasm, zeal, commitment, aggression, spirit; energy, vigour, verve, vitality, pep; informal get-up-and-go. **5** *an anti-corruption drive:* **campaign**, crusade, movement, effort, push, appeal. **6** (Brit.)

a whist drive: **tournament**, competition, contest, event, match.

■ **drive at** *I can see what you're driving at but you're quite wrong:* suggest, imply, hint at, allude to, intimate, insinuate, indicate; refer to, mean, intend; informal get at.

drivel noun *he was talking complete drivel:* **nonsense**, twaddle, claptrap, balderdash, gibberish, rubbish, mumbo-jumbo; N. Amer. garbage; informal rot, poppycock, phooey, piffle, tripe, bosh, bull, hogwash, baloney; Brit. informal cobblers, codswallop, waffle, tosh, double Dutch; N. Amer. informal flapdoodle, bushwa.
verb *you always drivel on:* **talk nonsense**, talk rubbish, babble, ramble, gibber, blather, blether, prattle, gabble; Brit. informal waffle, witter.

driver noun **motorist**, chauffeur; pilot, operator.

drizzle noun **1** *they shivered in the drizzle:* **fine rain**, light shower, spray; N. English mizzle. **2** *a drizzle of sour cream:* **trickle**, dribble, drip, stream, rivulet; sprinkle, sprinkling.
verb 1 *it's beginning to drizzle:* **rain lightly**, shower, spot; Brit. spit; N. English mizzle; N. Amer. sprinkle. **2** *drizzle the cream over the jelly:* **trickle**, drip, dribble, pour, splash, sprinkle.

droll adjective *a droll comment:* **funny**, humorous, amusing, comic, comical, mirthful, hilarious; clownish, farcical, zany, quirky; jocular, light-hearted, facetious, witty, whimsical, wry, tongue-in-cheek; informal waggish, wacky, side-splitting, rib-tickling.
– OPPOSITES serious.

drone verb **1** *a plane droned overhead:* **hum**, buzz, whirr, vibrate, murmur, rumble, purr. **2** *he droned on about right and wrong:* **speak boringly**, go on and on, talk at length; intone, pontificate; informal spout, sound off, jaw, spiel, speechify.
noun 1 *the drone of aircraft taking off:* **hum**, buzz, whirr, vibration, murmur, purr. **2** *drones supported by tax-payers' money:* **hanger-on**, parasite, leech, passenger; idler, loafer, layabout, good-for-nothing, do-nothing; informal lazybones, scrounger, sponger, cadger, freeloader, bloodsucker, waster, slacker.

drool verb *his mouth was drooling:* **salivate**, dribble, slaver, slobber; Scottish & Irish slabber.
noun *a fine trickle of drool:* **saliva**, spit, spittle, dribble, slaver, slobber.

droop verb **1** *the dog's tail is drooping:* **hang (down)**, dangle, sag, flop; wilt, sink, slump, drop, drape. **2** *his eyelids were drooping:* **close**, shut, fall.

droopy adjective **hanging (down)**, dangling, falling, dropping, draped; bent, bowed, stooping; sagging, flopping, wilting.

drop verb **1** *Eric dropped the box:* **let fall**, let go of, lose one's grip on; release, unhand, relinquish. **2** *drop the gun on the ground:*

d

d

put, place, deposit, set, lay, leave; informal pop, plonk. **3** *stalactites are formed when water drops from a cave roof:* **drip**, fall, dribble, trickle, run, plop, leak. **4** *a plane dropped out of the sky:* **fall**, descend, plunge, plummet, dive, nosedive, tumble, pitch. **5** *she dropped to her knees:* **fall**, sink, collapse, slump, tumble. **6** *the track dropped from the ridge:* **slope downwards**, slant downwards, descend, go down, fall away, sink, dip. **7** *the exchange rate dropped:* **decrease**, lessen, reduce, diminish, depreciate; fall, decline, dwindle, sink, slump, plunge, plummet. **8** *pupils can drop history if they wish:* **give up**, finish with, withdraw from; discontinue, end, stop, cease, halt; abandon, forgo, relinquish, dispense with, have done with; informal pack in, quit. **9** *he was dropped from the team:* **exclude**, discard, expel, oust, throw out, leave out; dismiss, discharge, let go; informal boot out, kick out, turf out. **10** *he dropped his unsuitable friends:* **abandon**, desert, throw over; renounce, disown, turn one's back on, wash one's hands of; reject, give up, cast off; neglect, shun. **11** *he dropped all reference to compensation:* **omit**, leave out, eliminate, take out, miss out, delete, cut, erase. **12** *the taxi dropped her off:* **deliver**, bring, take, convey, carry, transport; leave, unload.
– OPPOSITES lift, rise, increase, keep, win.
noun **1** *a drop of water:* **droplet**, blob, globule, bead, bubble, tear, dot; informal glob. **2** *it needs a drop of oil:* **small amount**, little, bit, dash, spot; dribble, driblet, sprinkle, trickle, splash; dab, speck, smattering, sprinkling, modicum; informal smidgen, tad. **3** *a small drop in profits:* **decrease**, reduction, decline, fall-off, downturn, slump; cut, cutback, curtailment; depreciation. **4** *I walked to the edge of the drop:* **cliff**, abyss, chasm, gorge, gully, precipice; slope, descent, incline.
– OPPOSITES increase.
■ **drop back/behind** fall back/behind, get left behind, lag behind; straggle, linger, dawdle, dally, hang back, loiter, bring/take up the rear; informal dilly-dally.
■ **drop off 1** *trade dropped off sharply.* See DROP verb sense 7. **2** *she kept dropping off:* fall asleep, doze (off), nap, catnap, drowse; informal nod off, drift off, snooze, take forty winks.
■ **drop out of** *he dropped out of his studies.* See DROP verb sense 3.

dropout noun *long hair was the trademark of the dropout:* **nonconformist**, hippy, beatnik, bohemian, free spirit, rebel; idler, layabout, loafer; informal oddball, deadbeat, waster.

droppings plural noun **excrement**, excreta, faeces, stools, dung, ordure, manure; informal pooh.

dross noun *there are bargains if you have the patience to sift through the dross:* **rubbish**, junk; debris, chaff, detritus, flotsam and jetsam; N. Amer. garbage, trash; informal dreck.

drought noun **dry spell**, lack of rain, shortage of water.

drove noun **1** *a drove of cattle:* **herd**, flock, pack. **2** *they came in droves:* **crowd**, swarm, horde, multitude, mob, throng, host, mass, army, herd.

drown verb **1** *he nearly drowned:* **suffocate in water**, inhale water; go to a watery grave. **2** *the valleys were drowned:* **flood**, submerge, immerse, inundate, deluge, swamp, engulf. **3** *his voice was drowned out by the footsteps:* **make inaudible**, overpower, overwhelm, override; muffle, deaden, stifle, extinguish.

drowse verb *they like to drowse in the sun:* **doze**, nap, catnap, rest; informal snooze, get forty winks, get some shut-eye; Brit. informal kip; N. Amer. informal catch some Zs.
noun *she had been woken from her drowse:* **doze**, light sleep, nap, catnap, rest; informal snooze, forty winks, shut-eye; Brit. informal kip.

drowsy adjective **1** *the tablet made her drowsy:* **sleepy**, dozy, heavy-eyed, groggy, somnolent; tired, weary, fatigued, exhausted, yawning, nodding; lethargic, sluggish, torpid, listless, languid; informal snoozy, dopey, yawny, dead beat, all in, dog-tired; Brit. informal knackered. **2** *a drowsy afternoon:* **soporific**, sleep-inducing, sleepy, somniferous; narcotic, sedative, tranquillizing; lulling, soothing.
– OPPOSITES alert, invigorating.

drubbing noun *I gave him a good drubbing:* **beating**, thrashing, walloping, thumping, battering, pounding, pummelling, slapping, punching, pelting; informal hammering, licking, clobbering, belting, bashing, pasting, tanning, hiding, kicking.

drudge noun *a household drudge:* **menial worker**, slave, lackey, servant, labourer, worker, maid/man of all work; informal dogsbody, gofer, runner; Brit. informal skivvy.

drudgery noun *the housewives were left alone with their drudgery:* **hard work**, menial work, donkey work, toil, labour; chores; informal skivvying; Brit. informal graft; Austral./NZ informal (hard) yakka.

drug noun **1** *drugs prescribed by doctors:* **medicine**, medication, medicament; remedy, cure, antidote. **2** *she was under the influence of drugs:* **narcotic**, stimulant, hallucinogen; informal dope, gear, downer, upper.
verb **1** *he was drugged:* **anaesthetize**, narcotize; poison; knock out, stupefy; informal dope. **2** *she drugged his coffee:* **add drugs to**, tamper with, adulterate, contaminate, lace, poison; informal dope, spike, doctor.

drugged adjective *he was obviously drunk or drugged when he wrote it:* **stupefied**, insensible, befuddled; delirious, hallucinating, narcotized; anaesthetized, knocked out; informal stoned, high (as a kite), doped, tripping, spaced out, wasted, wrecked, off one's head.
– OPPOSITES sober.

drum noun **1** *the beat of a drum:* percussion instrument; bongo, tom-tom, snare drum, kettledrum. **2** *the steady drum of raindrops:* **beat**, rhythm, patter, tap, pounding, thump, thud, rattle, pitter-patter, pit-a-pat, rat-a-tat, thrum. **3** *a drum of radioactive waste:* **canister**, barrel, cylinder, tank, bin, can.
verb **1** *she drummed her fingers on the desk:* **tap**, beat, rap, thud, thump; tattoo, thrum. **2** *the rules were drummed into us at school:* **instil**, drive, din, hammer, drill, drub, implant, ingrain, inculcate.
■ **drum someone out** *he was drummed out of office:* expel, dismiss, throw out, oust; drive out, get rid of; exclude, banish; informal give someone the boot, boot out, kick out, give someone their marching orders, give someone the push, show someone the door, send packing.
■ **drum something up** *he was drumming up business for his new investment company:* round up, gather, collect; summon, attract; canvass, solicit, petition.

drunk adjective *they went to a pub and got drunk:* **intoxicated**, inebriated, drunken, incapable, tipsy, the worse for drink, under the influence; informal tight, merry, in one's cups, three sheets to the wind, pie-eyed, plastered, smashed, wrecked, wasted, sloshed, soused, sozzled, blotto, stewed, pickled, tanked (up), off one's face, out of one's head, ratted; Brit. informal legless, bevvied, paralytic, Brahms and Liszt, half cut, out of it, bladdered, trolleyed, squiffy, tiddly; N. Amer. informal loaded, trashed, juiced, sauced, out of one's gourd, in the bag, zoned; euphemistic tired and emotional.
– OPPOSITES sober.
noun *a drunk lay slumped against the wall:* **drunkard**, inebriate, drinker, tippler, imbiber, sot; heavy drinker, problem drinker, alcoholic, dipsomaniac; informal boozer, soak, lush, wino, alky, sponge, barfly, tosspot; Austral./NZ informal hophead, metho.
– OPPOSITES teetotaller.

drunken adjective **1** *a drunken driver.* See **DRUNK** adjective. **2** *a drunken all-night party:* **debauched**, dissipated, carousing, roistering, intemperate, unrestrained, uninhibited, abandoned; bacchanalian, bacchic; informal boozy.

drunkenness noun **intoxication**, inebriation, insobriety, tipsiness; intemperance, overindulgence, debauchery; heavy drinking, alcoholism, alcohol abuse, dipsomania.

dry adjective **1** *the dry desert:* **arid**, parched, droughty, scorched, baked; waterless, moistureless, rainless; dehydrated, desiccated, thirsty, bone dry. **2** *dry leaves:* **parched**, dried, withered, shrivelled, wilted, wizened; crisp, crispy, brittle; dehydrated, desiccated. **3** *the hamburgers were dry:* **hard**, stale, old; off. **4** *a dry well:* **waterless**, empty. **5** *I'm really dry:* **thirsty**, dehydrated; informal parched, gasping. **6** *dry*

toast: **unbuttered**, butterless, plain. **7** *the dry facts:* **bare**, simple, basic, fundamental, stark, bald, hard, straightforward. **8** *a dry debate:* **dull**, uninteresting, boring, unexciting, tedious, tiresome, wearisome, dreary, monotonous; unimaginative, sterile, flat, bland, lacklustre, stodgy, prosaic, humdrum, mundane; informal deadly. **9** *a dry sense of humour:* **wry**, subtle, laconic, sharp; ironic, sardonic, sarcastic, cynical; satirical, mocking, droll; informal waggish; Brit. informal sarky. **10** *this is a dry state:* **teetotal**, prohibitionist, alcohol-free, non-drinking, abstinent, sober; informal on the wagon. **11** *dry white wine:* **crisp**, sharp, piquant, tart, bitter.
– OPPOSITES wet, moist, fresh, lively, sweet.
verb **1** *the sun dried the ground:* **parch**, scorch, bake; dehydrate, desiccate, dehumidify. **2** *dry the leaves completely:* **dehydrate**, desiccate; wither, shrivel. **3** *he dried the dishes:* **towel**, rub; mop up, blot up, soak up, absorb. **4** *she dried her eyes:* **wipe**, rub, dab.
– OPPOSITES moisten.
■ **dry out** give up drinking, give up alcohol, become teetotal, take the pledge; informal go on the wagon.
■ **dry up 1** (informal) *he dried up and didn't say another thing:* stop speaking, stop talking, fall silent, shut up; forget one's words. **2** *investment may dry up:* dwindle, subside, peter out, wane, taper off, ebb, come to a halt/end, run out, give out, disappear, vanish.

dual adjective *their dual role at work and home:* **double**, twofold, binary; duplicate, twin, matching, paired, coupled.
– OPPOSITES single.

dub verb **1** *he was dubbed 'the world's sexiest man'* **nickname**, call, name, label, christen, term, tag, entitle, style; designate, characterize, nominate. **2** *she dubbed a new knight:* **knight**, invest.

dubious adjective **1** *I was rather dubious about the idea:* **doubtful**, uncertain, unsure, hesitant; undecided, indefinite, unresolved, up in the air; vacillating, irresolute; sceptical, suspicious; informal iffy. **2** *a dubious businessman:* **suspicious**, suspect, untrustworthy, unreliable, questionable; informal shady, fishy; Brit. informal dodgy.
– OPPOSITES certain, trustworthy.

duck verb **1** *he ducked behind the wall:* **bob down**, bend (down), stoop (down), crouch (down), squat (down), hunch down, hunker down; cower, cringe. **2** *she was ducked in the river:* **dip**, dunk, plunge, immerse, submerge, lower, sink.

duct noun *a ventilation duct:* **tube**, channel, canal, vessel; conduit, culvert; pipe, pipeline, outlet, inlet, flue, shaft, vent.

ductile adjective *ductile metals:* **pliable**, pliant, flexible, supple, plastic, tensile; soft, malleable, workable, bendable; informal bendy.
– OPPOSITES brittle.

d

dudgeon

■ **in high dudgeon** *Kirsty swept out the room in high dudgeon:* indignantly, resentfully, angrily, furiously; in a temper, in anger, with displeasure; informal in a huff, in a paddy, as cross as two sticks, seeing red.

due adjective **1** *their fees were due:* **owing**, owed, payable; outstanding, overdue, unpaid, unsettled, undischarged; N. Amer. delinquent. **2** *the chancellor's statement is due today:* **expected**, anticipated, scheduled for, awaited; required. **3** *the respect due to a great artist:* **deserved by**, merited by, warranted by; appropriate to, fit for, fitting for, right for, proper to. **4** *he drove without due care:* **proper**, correct, rightful, suitable, appropriate, apt; adequate, sufficient, enough, satisfactory, requisite.
noun **1** *he attracts more criticism than is his due:* **rightful treatment**, fair treatment, just punishment; right, entitlement; just deserts; informal comeuppance. **2** *members have paid their dues:* **fee**, subscription, charge; payment, contribution.
adverb *he hiked due north:* **directly**, straight, exactly, precisely, dead.
■ **due to 1** *her death was due to an infection:* attributable to, caused by, ascribed to, because of, put down to. **2** *the train was cancelled due to staff shortages:* because of, owing to, on account of, as a consequence of, as a result of, thanks to, in view of; formal by reason of.

duel noun **1** *he was killed in a duel:* **mano-a-mano**, single combat; fight, confrontation, head-to-head; informal face-off, shoot-out. **2** *a snooker duel:* **contest**, match, game, meet, encounter.
verb *they duelled with swords:* **fight**, battle, combat, contend.

duff adjective (Brit. informal). See **BAD** sense 1.

dulcet adjective *the Grand Duchess Anna spoke in dulcet tones:* **sweet**, soothing, mellow, honeyed, mellifluous, euphonious, pleasant, agreeable; melodious, melodic, lilting, lyrical, silvery, golden.
– OPPOSITES harsh.

dull adjective **1** *a dull novel:* **uninteresting**, boring, tedious, monotonous, unrelieved, unvaried, unimaginative, uneventful; characterless, featureless, colourless, lifeless, insipid, unexciting, uninspiring, unstimulating, jejune, flat, bland, dry, stale, tired, banal, lacklustre, stodgy, dreary, humdrum, mundane; mind-numbing, soul-destroying, wearisome, tiring, tiresome, irksome; informal deadly, not up to much; Brit. informal samey; N. Amer. informal dullsville. **2** *it was a miserably dull Saturday morning:* **overcast**, cloudy, gloomy, dark, dismal, dreary, sombre, grey, murky, sunless. **3** *dull colours:* **drab**, dreary, sombre, dark, subdued, muted, lacklustre, faded, washed out, muddy. **4** *a dull sound:* **muffled**, muted, quiet, soft, faint, indistinct; stifled, suppressed. **5** *the chisel became dull:* **blunt**, unsharpened, edgeless, worn down.
– OPPOSITES interesting, bright, loud, resonant, sharp.
verb **1** *the pain was dulled by drugs:* **lessen**, decrease, diminish, reduce, dampen, blunt, deaden, allay, ease, soothe, assuage, alleviate. **2** *sleep dulled her mind:* **numb**, benumb, deaden, desensitize, stupefy, daze. **3** *the leaves are dulled by mildew:* **fade**, bleach, decolorize, decolour, etiolate. **4** *rain dulled the sky:* **darken**, blacken, dim, veil, obscure, shadow, fog. **5** *the sombre atmosphere dulled her spirit:* **dampen**, lower, depress, crush, sap, extinguish, smother, stifle.
– OPPOSITES intensify, enliven, enhance, brighten.

duly adverb **1** *the document was duly signed:* **properly**, correctly, appropriately, suitably, fittingly. **2** *he duly arrived to collect Alice:* **at the right time**, on time, punctually.

dumb adjective *she stood dumb while he shouted:* **mute**, speechless, tongue-tied, silent, at a loss for words; taciturn, uncommunicative, untalkative, tight-lipped, close-mouthed; informal mum.
– OPPOSITES clever.

dumbfound verb **astonish**, astound, amaze, stagger, surprise, startle, stun, confound, stupefy, daze, nonplus, take aback, stop someone in their tracks, strike dumb, leave open-mouthed, leave aghast; informal flabbergast, floor, knock sideways, bowl over; Brit. informal knock for six.

dumbfounded adjective *when you told me I had won I was dumbfounded:* **astonished**, astounded, amazed, staggered, surprised, startled, stunned, confounded, nonplussed, stupefied, dazed, dumbstruck, open-mouthed, speechless, thunderstruck; taken aback, disconcerted; informal flabbergasted, flummoxed; Brit. informal gobsmacked.

dummy noun **1** *a shop-window dummy:* **mannequin**, model, figure. **2** *the book is just a dummy:* **mock-up**, imitation, likeness, lookalike, representation, substitute, sample; replica, reproduction; counterfeit, sham, fake, forgery; informal dupe.
adjective *a dummy attack on the airfield:* **simulated**, feigned, pretended, practice, trial, mock, make-believe; informal pretend, phoney.
– OPPOSITES real.

dump noun **1** *take the rubbish to the dump:* **tip**, rubbish dump, rubbish heap, dumping ground, landfill, recycling centre. **2** (informal) *the house is a dump:* **hovel**, shack, slum; mess; informal hole, pigsty.
verb **1** *he dumped his bag on the table:* **put down**, set down, deposit, place, shove, unload; drop, throw down; informal stick, park, plonk; Brit. informal bung; N. Amer. informal plunk. **2** *they will dump asbestos at the site:* **dispose of**, get rid of, throw away/out, discard, bin, jettison; informal ditch, junk.

dumpy adjective *that skirt makes you look*

dumpy and middle-aged: **short**, squat, stubby; **plump**, stout, chubby, chunky, portly, fat, bulky; informal tubby, roly-poly, pudgy, porky; Brit. informal podgy.
– OPPOSITES tall, slender.

dun[1] adjective *a dun cow:* **greyish-brown**, brownish, mousy, muddy, khaki, umber.

dun[2] verb *you can't dun me for her debts:* **importune**, press, plague, pester, nag, harass, hound, badger; informal hassle, bug; N. English informal mither.

dunce noun *they all called him a dunce at school:* **fool**, idiot, stupid person, simpleton, ignoramus, dullard; informal dummy, dumbo, clot, thickhead, nitwit, dimwit, halfwit, moron, cretin, imbecile, dope, duffer, booby, chump, numbskull, nincompoop, fathead, airhead, birdbrain, pea-brain, ninny, ass; Brit. informal wally, berk, divvy, muppet; N. Amer. informal doofus, goof, schmuck, bozo, lummox; Austral./NZ informal galah.
– OPPOSITES genius.

dune noun *sand dunes:* **bank**, mound, hillock, hummock, knoll, ridge, heap, drift.

dung noun **manure**, muck; excrement, faeces, droppings, ordure, cowpats.

dungeon noun **prison**, oubliette; cell, jail, lock-up.

dupe verb *they were duped by a con man:* **deceive**, trick, hoodwink, hoax, swindle, defraud, cheat, double-cross; gull, mislead, take in, fool, inveigle; informal con, do, rip off, diddle, shaft, bilk, rook, pull the wool over someone's eyes, pull a fast one on, sell a pup to; N. Amer. informal sucker, snooker; Austral. informal pull a swifty on.
noun *an innocent dupe in her game:* **victim**, gull, pawn, puppet, instrument; fool, innocent; informal sucker, stooge, sitting duck, muggins, fall guy; Brit. informal mug; N. Amer. informal pigeon, patsy, sap.

duplicate noun *a duplicate of the invoice:* **copy**, carbon copy, photocopy, facsimile, mimeograph, reprint; replica, reproduction, clone; informal dupe; trademark Xerox, photostat.
adjective *duplicate keys:* **identical**, matching, twin, corresponding, equivalent.
verb **1** *she will duplicate the newsletter:* **copy**, photocopy, photostat, xerox, mimeograph, reproduce, replicate, reprint, run off. **2** *a feat difficult to duplicate:* **repeat**, do again, redo, replicate.

duplicity noun *his conscience would not allow him to enter into duplicity:* **deceitfulness**, deceit, deception, double-dealing, underhandedness, dishonesty, fraud, fraudulence, sharp practice, chicanery, trickery, subterfuge, skulduggery, treachery; informal crookedness, shadiness, dirty tricks, shenanigans, monkey business.
– OPPOSITES honesty.

durability noun **imperishability**, durableness, longevity; resilience, strength, sturdiness, toughness, robustness.

– OPPOSITES fragility.

durable adjective **1** *durable carpets:* **hard-wearing**, long-lasting, heavy-duty, tough, resistant, imperishable, indestructible, strong, sturdy. **2** *a durable peace:* **lasting**, long-lasting, long-term, enduring, persistent, abiding; stable, secure, firm, deep-rooted, permanent, undying, everlasting.
– OPPOSITES delicate, short-lived.

duration noun *the student's fees will be paid for the duration of their course:* **full length**, time, time span, time scale, period, term, span, fullness, length, extent, continuation.

duress noun *their confessions were extracted under duress:* **coercion**, compulsion, force, pressure, intimidation, constraint; threats; informal arm-twisting.

during preposition *the exhibit attracted 5,000 visitors during January:* **throughout**, through, in, in the course of, for the time of.

dusk noun **twilight**, nightfall, sunset, sundown, evening, close of day; semi-darkness, gloom, murkiness.
– OPPOSITES dawn.

dusky adjective *the dusky countryside:* **shadowy**, dark, dim, gloomy, murky, shady; unlit, unilluminated; sunless, moonless.
– OPPOSITES bright.

dust noun *the desk was covered in dust:* **dirt**, grime, filth, smut, soot; fine powder.
verb **1** *she dusted her mantelpiece:* **wipe**, clean, brush, sweep, mop. **2** *dust the cake with icing sugar:* **sprinkle**, scatter, powder, dredge, sift, cover, strew.

dusty adjective **1** *the floor was dusty:* **dirty**, grimy, grubby, unclean, soiled, mucky, sooty; undusted; informal grungy, cruddy; Brit. informal grotty. **2** *dusty sandstone:* **powdery**, crumbly, chalky, friable; granular, gritty, sandy. **3** *a dusty pink:* **muted**, dull, faded, pale, pastel, subtle; greyish, darkish, dirty.
– OPPOSITES clean, bright.

dutiful adjective *she helped out, as a dutiful daughter should:* **conscientious**, responsible, dedicated, devoted, attentive, obedient, compliant, submissive, biddable; deferential, reverent, reverential, respectful, good.
– OPPOSITES remiss.

duty noun **1** *she was free of any duty:* **responsibility**, obligation, commitment; allegiance, loyalty, faithfulness, fidelity, homage. **2** *it was his duty to attend the king:* **job**, task, assignment, mission, function, charge, place, role, responsibility, obligation. **3** *the duty was raised on alcohol:* **tax**, levy, tariff, excise, toll, fee, payment, rate; dues.
■ **off duty** not working, at leisure, on holiday, on leave, off (work), free.
■ **on duty** working, at work, busy, occupied, engaged; informal on the job, tied up.

dwarf noun **1 person of restricted growth**, small person, short person; midget, pygmy,

d

manikin, homunculus. **2** *the wizard captured the dwarf:* **gnome**, goblin, hobgoblin, troll, hobbit, imp, elf, brownie, leprechaun.
adjective *dwarf conifers:* **miniature**, small, little, tiny, toy, pocket, diminutive, baby, pygmy, stunted, undersized, undersize; Scottish wee; informal mini, teeny, teeny-weeny, itsy-bitsy, tiddly, pint-sized; Brit. informal titchy; N. Amer. informal little-bitty.
– OPPOSITES giant.
verb **1** *the buildings dwarf the trees:* **dominate**, tower over, loom over, overshadow, overtop. **2** *her progress was dwarfed by her sister's success:* **overshadow**, outshine, surpass, exceed, outclass, outstrip, outdo, top, trump, transcend; diminish, minimize.

dwell
■ **dwell on** *she had no time to dwell on her disappointment:* linger over, mull over, muse on, brood about/over, think about; be preoccupied by, be obsessed by, eat one's heart out over; harp on about, discuss at length.

dwindle verb **1** *the population dwindled:* **diminish**, decrease, reduce, lessen, shrink; fall off, tail off, drop, fall, slump, plummet; disappear, vanish, die out; informal nosedive. **2** *her career dwindled:* **decline**, deteriorate, fail, slip, slide, fade, go downhill, go to rack and ruin; informal go to pot, go to the dogs, hit the skids, go down the toilet; Austral./NZ informal go to the pack.
– OPPOSITES increase, flourish.

dye noun *a blue dye:* **colourant**, colouring, colour, dyestuff, pigment, tint, stain, wash.
verb *the gloves were dyed:* **colour**, tint, pigment, stain, wash.

dyed-in-the-wool adjective *she's a dyed-in-the-wool Conservative:* **inveterate**, confirmed, entrenched, established, long-standing, deep-rooted, diehard; complete, absolute, thorough, thoroughgoing, out-and-out, true blue; firm, unshakeable, staunch, steadfast, committed, devoted,

dedicated, loyal, unswerving; N. Amer. full-bore; informal deep-dyed, card-carrying.

dying adjective **1** *his dying aunt:* **terminally ill**, at death's door, on one's deathbed, near death, fading fast, expiring, moribund, not long for this world, in extremis; informal on one's last legs, having one foot in the grave. **2** *a dying art form:* **declining**, vanishing, fading, ebbing, waning; informal on the way out. **3** *her dying words:* **final**, last; deathbed.
– OPPOSITES thriving, first.
noun *he took her dying very hard:* **death**, demise, passing, loss of life, quietus; formal decease.

dynamic adjective *he was eclipsed by his more dynamic colleagues:* **energetic**, spirited, active, lively, zestful, vital, vigorous, forceful, powerful, positive; high-powered, aggressive, bold, enterprising; magnetic, passionate, fiery, high-octane; informal go-getting, peppy, full of get-up-and-go, full of vim and vigour, gutsy, spunky, feisty, go-ahead.
– OPPOSITES half-hearted.

dynamism noun **energy**, spirit, liveliness, zestfulness, vitality, vigour, forcefulness, power, potency, positivity; aggression, drive, ambition, enterprise; magnetism, passion, fire; informal pep, get-up-and-go, vim and vigour, guts, feistiness.

dynasty noun *he was the fourth king of the Shang dynasty:* **bloodline**, line, ancestral line, lineage, house, family, ancestry, descent, succession, genealogy, family tree; regime, rule, reign, empire, sovereignty.

dyspeptic adjective *a rather dyspeptic senator put the blame on his European counterpart:* **bad-tempered**, short-tempered, irritable, snappish, testy, tetchy, touchy, crabby, crotchety, grouchy, cantankerous, peevish, cross, disagreeable, waspish, prickly; informal snappy, on a short fuse; Brit. informal stroppy, ratty, eggy, like a bear with a sore head; N. Amer. informal cranky, ornery.

Ee

each pronoun *there are 5000 books and each must be cleaned:* **every one**, each one, each and every one, all, the whole lot.
determiner *he visited each month:* **every**, each and every, every single.
adverb *they gave a tenner each:* **apiece**, per person, per capita, from each, individually, respectively, severally.

eager adjective **1** *small eager faces:* **keen**, enthusiastic, avid, fervent, ardent, motivated, wholehearted, dedicated, committed, earnest; informal mad keen, (as) keen as mustard. **2** *we were eager for news:* **anxious**, impatient, longing, yearning, wishing, hoping, hopeful; desirous of, hankering after; on the edge of one's seat, on tenterhooks, on pins and needles; informal itching, gagging, dying.
– OPPOSITES apathetic.

eagerness noun **keenness**, enthusiasm, avidity, fervour, zeal, wholeheartedness, earnestness, commitment, dedication; impatience, desire, longing, yearning, hunger, appetite, ambition; informal yen.

ear noun **1** *an infection of the ear:* inner ear, middle ear, outer ear. **2** *he had the ear of the president:* **attention**, notice, heed, regard, consideration. **3** *he has an ear for a good song:* **appreciation**, discrimination, perception.
■ **play it by ear** improvise, extemporize, ad lib; make it up as one goes along, think on one's feet; informal busk it, wing it.

early adjective **1** *early copies of the book:* **advance**, forward; initial, preliminary, first; pilot, trial. **2** *an early death:* **untimely**, premature, unseasonable, before time. **3** *early man:* **primitive**, ancient, prehistoric, primeval. **4** *an early official statement:* **prompt**, timely, quick, speedy, rapid, fast.
– OPPOSITES late, modern, overdue.
adverb **1** *Rachel has to get up early:* **in the early morning**, in the small hours; at dawn, at daybreak, at cockcrow, with the lark. **2** *they hoped to leave school early:* **before the usual time**; prematurely, too soon, ahead of time, ahead of schedule, in advance.
– OPPOSITES late.

earmark verb *the cash had been earmarked for the firm:* **set aside**, keep (back), reserve; designate, assign, mark; allocate, allot, devote, pledge, give over.

earn verb **1** *they earned £20,000:* **be paid**, take home, gross; receive, get, make, obtain, collect, bring in; informal pocket, bank, rake in, net, bag. **2** *he has earned their trust:* **deserve**, merit, warrant, justify, be worthy of; gain, win, secure, establish, obtain, procure, get, acquire; informal clinch.
– OPPOSITES lose.

earnest adjective **1** *he is dreadfully earnest:* **serious**, solemn, grave, sober, humourless, staid, intense; committed, dedicated, keen, diligent, zealous; thoughtful, cerebral, deep, profound. **2** *earnest prayer:* **devout**, heartfelt, wholehearted, sincere, impassioned, fervent, ardent, intense, urgent.
– OPPOSITES frivolous, half-hearted.
■ **in earnest 1** *we are in earnest about stopping burglaries:* serious, sincere, wholehearted, genuine; committed, firm, resolute, determined. **2** *he started writing in earnest:* zealously, purposefully, determinedly, resolutely; passionately, wholeheartedly.

earnestly adverb **seriously**, solemnly, gravely, intently; sincerely, resolutely, firmly, ardently, fervently, eagerly.

earnings plural noun *they lived off his wife's earnings:* **income**, wages, salary, stipend, pay, payment, fees; revenue, yield, profit, takings, proceeds, dividends, return, remuneration.

earth noun **1** *the moon orbits the earth:* **world**, globe, planet. **2** *a trembling of the earth:* **land**, ground, terra firma; floor. **3** *he ploughed the earth:* **soil**, clay, loam; dirt, sod, turf; ground. **4** *the fox's earth:* **den**, lair, sett, burrow, warren, hole; retreat, shelter, hideout, hideaway; informal hidey-hole.

earthenware noun **pottery**, crockery, stoneware; china, porcelain; pots.

earthly adjective **1** *the earthly environment:* **terrestrial**, telluric. **2** *the promise of earthly delights:* **worldly**, temporal, mortal, human; material; carnal, fleshly, bodily, physical, corporeal, sensual. **3** (informal) *there is no earthly explanation for this:* **feasible**, possible, likely, conceivable, imaginable.
– OPPOSITES extraterrestrial, heavenly.

earthquake noun **(earth) tremor**, shock, foreshock, aftershock, convulsion; informal quake, shake, trembler.

earthy adjective **1** *the earthy Calvinistic tradition:* **down-to-earth**, unsophisticated, unrefined, simple, plain, unpretentious, natural. **2** *Emma's earthy language:* **bawdy**, ribald, off colour, racy, rude, vulgar, lewd, crude, foul, coarse, uncouth, unseemly, indelicate, indecent, obscene; informal blue, locker-room, X-rated; Brit. informal fruity, near the knuckle.

ease noun **1** *he defeated them all with ease:* **effortlessness**, no trouble, simplicity; deftness, adroitness, proficiency, mastery. **2** *his ease of manner:* **naturalness**, casualness, informality, amiability, affability; unconcern, composure, nonchalance, insouciance. **3** *he couldn't find any ease:* **peace**, calm, tranquillity, serenity; repose, restfulness, quiet, security, comfort. **4** *a life of ease:* **affluence**, wealth, prosperity, luxury, plenty; comfort, contentment, enjoyment, well-being.
– OPPOSITES difficulty, formality, trouble, hardship.
verb **1** *the alcohol eased his pain:* **relieve**, alleviate, mitigate, soothe, palliate, moderate, dull, deaden, numb; reduce, lighten, diminish. **2** *the rain eased off:* **abate**, subside, die down, let up, slacken off, diminish, lessen, peter out, relent, come to an end. **3** *work helped to ease her mind:* **calm**, quieten, pacify, soothe, comfort, console; hearten, gladden, uplift, encourage. **4** *we want to ease their adjustment:* **facilitate**, expedite, assist, help, aid, advance, further, forward, simplify. **5** *he eased out the cork:* **guide**, manoeuvre, inch, edge; slide, slip, squeeze.
– OPPOSITES aggravate, worsen, hinder.
■ **at ease/at one's ease** relaxed, calm, serene, tranquil, unworried, contented, content, happy; comfortable.

easily adverb **1** *I overcame this problem easily:* **effortlessly**, comfortably, simply; with ease, without difficulty, without a hitch, smoothly; skilfully, deftly, smartly; informal no sweat. **2** *he's easily the best:* **undoubtedly**, without doubt, without question, indisputably, undeniably, definitely, certainly, clearly, obviously, patently; by far, far and away, by a mile.

east adjective **eastern**, easterly, oriental.

easy adjective **1** *the task was very easy:* **uncomplicated**, undemanding, unchallenging, effortless, painless, trouble-free, facile, simple, straightforward, elementary, plain sailing; informal easy as pie, a piece of cake, child's play, kids' stuff, a cinch, no sweat, a doddle, a breeze; Brit. informal easy-peasy; N. Amer. informal duck soup, a snap. **2** *easy babies:* **docile**, manageable, amenable, tractable, compliant, pliant, acquiescent, obliging, cooperative, easy-going. **3** *an easy target:* **vulnerable**, susceptible, defenceless; naive, gullible, trusting. **4** *Vic's easy manner made everyone feel at home:* **natural**, casual, informal, unceremonious, unreserved, uninhibited, unaffected, easy-going, amiable, affable, genial, good-humoured; carefree, nonchalant, unconcerned; informal

laid-back. **5** *an easy life:* **calm**, tranquil, serene, quiet, peaceful, untroubled, contented, relaxed, comfortable, secure, safe; informal cushy. **6** *the walkers set off at an easy pace:* **leisurely**, unhurried, comfortable, undemanding, easy-going, gentle, sedate, moderate, steady.
– OPPOSITES difficult, demanding, formal.

easy-going adjective *Fred was easy-going and a pleasure to work with:* **relaxed**, even-tempered, placid, mellow, mild, happy-go-lucky, carefree, free and easy, nonchalant, insouciant, imperturbable; amiable, considerate, undemanding, patient, tolerant, lenient, broad-minded, understanding; good-natured, pleasant, agreeable; informal laid-back, unflappable.
– OPPOSITES intolerant.

eat verb **1** *we ate a hearty breakfast:* **consume**, devour, ingest, partake of; gobble (up/down), bolt (down), wolf (down); swallow, chew, munch, chomp; informal guzzle, nosh, put away, tuck into, demolish, dispose of, polish off, get stuck into, pig out on, get outside of; Brit. informal scoff, gollop; N. Amer. informal scarf, snarf. **2** *we ate at a local restaurant:* **have a meal**, consume food, feed, snack; breakfast, lunch, dine; feast, banquet; informal graze, nosh. **3** *acidic water can eat away at pipes:* **erode**, corrode, wear away/down/through, burn through, consume, dissolve, disintegrate, crumble, decay; damage, destroy.

eatable adjective *the cake's not perfect but it's eatable:* **edible**, palatable, digestible; fit to eat, fit for consumption.

eavesdrop verb *we tried to eavesdrop on his telephone conversation:* **listen in**, spy; monitor, tap, wiretap, record, overhear; informal snoop, bug.

ebb verb **1** *the tide ebbed:* **recede**, go out, retreat, flow back, fall back/away, subside. **2** *his courage began to ebb:* **diminish**, dwindle, wane, fade away, peter out, decline, flag, let up, decrease, weaken, disappear.
– OPPOSITES increase.
noun **1** *the ebb of the tide:* **receding**, retreat, subsiding. **2** *the ebb of the fighting:* **abatement**, subsiding, easing, dying down, de-escalation, decrease, decline, diminution.

ebony adjective *he stared at her with his ebony eyes:* **black**, jet black, pitch black, coal black, sable, inky, sooty, raven, dark.

ebullience noun *the director's ebullience is a fantastic morale booster for the cast:* **exuberance**, buoyancy, cheerfulness, cheeriness, merriment, jollity, sunniness, jauntiness, light-heartedness, high spirits, elation, euphoria, jubilation; animation, sparkle, vivacity, enthusiasm, perkiness; informal bubbliness, chirpiness, bounciness, pep.

ebullient adjective **exuberant**, buoyant, cheerful, joyful, cheery, merry, jolly, sunny, jaunty, light-hearted, elated; animated, sparkling, vivacious, irrepressible; Brit.

Tiggerish; informal bubbly, bouncy, peppy, upbeat, chirpy, smiley, full of beans.
– OPPOSITES depressed.

eccentric adjective *eccentric behaviour:* **unconventional**, uncommon, abnormal, irregular, aberrant, anomalous, odd, queer, strange, peculiar, weird, bizarre, outlandish, freakish, extraordinary; idiosyncratic, quirky, nonconformist, outré; informal way out, offbeat, freaky, oddball, wacky, cranky; Brit. informal rum; N. Amer. informal kooky, wacko.
– OPPOSITES conventional.
noun *he was something of an eccentric:* **oddity**, odd fellow, character, individualist, individual, free spirit; misfit; informal oddball, queer fish, weirdo, freak, nut, head case, crank; Brit. informal one-off, odd bod, nutter, mentalist; N. Amer. informal wacko, screwball.

eccentricity noun **unconventionality**, singularity, oddness, strangeness, weirdness, quirkiness, freakishness; peculiarity, foible, idiosyncrasy, caprice, whimsy, quirk; informal nuttiness, screwiness, freakiness; N. Amer. informal kookiness.

ecclesiastical adjective *his ecclesiastical duties:* **priestly**, ministerial, clerical, ecclesiastic, canonical, sacerdotal; church, churchly, religious, spiritual, holy, divine; informal churchy.

echelon noun *he reached the upper echelons of government:* **level**, rank, grade, step, rung, tier, position, order.

echo noun 1 *the hills sent back a faint echo of my shout:* **reverberation**, reflection, ringing, repetition, repeat. 2 *the scene she described was an echo of the photograph:* **duplicate**, copy, replica, imitation, mirror image, double, match, parallel; informal lookalike, spitting image, dead ringer. 3 *was there even the slightest echo of the love they had known?* **trace**, vestige, remnant, ghost, memory, recollection, remembrance; reminder, sign, mark, token, indication, suggestion, hint; evidence.
verb 1 *his laughter echoed round the room:* **reverberate**, resonate, resound, reflect, ring, vibrate. 2 *Bill echoed Rex's words:* **repeat**, restate, reiterate; copy, imitate, parrot, mimic; reproduce, recite, quote, regurgitate; informal recap.

éclat noun *he finished his recital with great éclat:* **style**, flamboyance, confidence, elan, dash, flair, vigour, gusto, verve, zest, sparkle, brio, panache, dynamism, spirit; informal pizzazz, pep, oomph.

eclectic adjective *they played an eclectic mix of party music:* **wide-ranging**, broad-based, extensive, comprehensive, encyclopedic; varied, diverse, catholic, all-embracing, multifaceted, multifarious, heterogeneous, miscellaneous, assorted.

eclipse noun 1 *the eclipse of the sun:* **blotting out**, blocking, covering, obscuring, concealing, darkening. 2 *the eclipse of*

the empire: **decline**, fall, failure, decay, deterioration, degeneration, weakening, collapse.
verb 1 *the sun was eclipsed by the moon:* **blot out**, block, cover, obscure, hide, conceal, obliterate, darken; shade. 2 *the system was eclipsed by new methods:* **outshine**, overshadow, surpass, exceed, outclass, outstrip, outdo, top, trump, transcend, upstage.

economic adjective 1 *economic reform:* **financial**, monetary, budgetary, fiscal; commercial. 2 *the firm cannot remain economic:* **profitable**, moneymaking, lucrative, remunerative, fruitful, productive; solvent, viable, cost-effective.
– OPPOSITES unprofitable.

economical adjective 1 *an economical car:* **cheap**, inexpensive, low-cost, budget, economy, economic; cut-price, discount, bargain. 2 *a very economical shopper:* **thrifty**, provident, prudent, sensible, frugal, sparing, abstemious; mean, parsimonious, penny-pinching, miserly; N. Amer. forehanded; informal stingy.
– OPPOSITES expensive, spendthrift.

economize verb *they economized by growing their own vegetables:* **save (money)**, cut costs; cut back, make cutbacks, retrench, budget, make economies, be thrifty, be frugal, scrimp, cut corners, tighten one's belt, draw in one's horns, watch the/your pennies.

economy noun 1 *the nation's economy:* **wealth**, (financial) resources; financial system, financial management. 2 *one can combine good living with economy:* **thrift**, thriftiness, providence, prudence, careful budgeting, economizing, saving, scrimping, restraint, frugality, abstemiousness; N. Amer. forehandedness.
– OPPOSITES extravagance.

ecstasy noun *there was a look of ecstasy on his face:* **rapture**, bliss, elation, euphoria, transports, rhapsodies; joy, jubilation, exultation.
– OPPOSITES misery.

ecstatic adjective *ecstatic fans filled the stadium:* **enraptured**, elated, in raptures, euphoric, rapturous, joyful, overjoyed, blissful; on cloud nine, in seventh heaven, beside oneself with joy, jumping for joy, delighted, thrilled, exultant; informal over the moon, on top of the world, blissed out.

ecumenical adjective *an ecumenical church service:* **non-denominational**, universal, catholic, all-embracing, all-inclusive.
– OPPOSITES denominational.

eddy noun *small eddies at the river's edge:* **swirl**, whirlpool, vortex, maelstrom.
verb *cold air eddied around her:* **swirl**, whirl, spiral, wind, circulate, twist; flow, ripple, stream, surge, billow.

edge noun 1 *the edge of the lake:* **border**, boundary, extremity, fringe, margin, side;

e

lip, rim, brim, brink, verge; perimeter,
circumference, periphery, limits, bounds.
2 *she had an edge in her voice:* **sharpness**,
severity, bite, sting, asperity, acerbity,
acidity, trenchancy; sarcasm, acrimony,
malice, spite, venom. **3** *they have an
edge over their rivals:* **advantage**, lead,
head start, the whip hand, the upper
hand; superiority, dominance, ascendancy,
supremacy, primacy.
– OPPOSITES middle, disadvantage.
▶ verb **1** *poplars edged the orchard:* **border**,
fringe, verge, skirt; surround, enclose,
encircle, circle, encompass, bound. **2** *a frock
edged with lace:* **trim**, pipe, band, decorate,
finish; border, fringe; bind, hem. **3** *he edged
closer to the fire:* **creep**, inch, work one's
way, pick one's way, ease oneself; sidle,
steal, slink.
■ **on edge** tense, nervous, edgy, anxious,
apprehensive, uneasy, unsettled; twitchy,
jumpy, nervy, keyed up, restive, skittish,
neurotic, insecure; informal uptight, wired; Brit.
informal strung up.

edgy adjective *she felt edgy, dreading
tomorrow:* **tense**, nervous, on edge, anxious,
apprehensive, uneasy, unsettled; twitchy,
jumpy, nervy, keyed up, restive, skittish,
neurotic, insecure; irritable, touchy, tetchy,
testy, crotchety, prickly; informal uptight,
wired, snappy; Brit. informal strung up.
– OPPOSITES calm.

edible adjective *are these mushrooms edible?*
safe to eat, fit for human consumption, good
to eat; consumable, digestible, palatable.

edict noun *oil exploration is prohibited by
government edict:* **decree**, order, command,
commandment, mandate, proclamation,
pronouncement, dictate, fiat, promulgation;
law, statute, act, bill, ruling, injunction.

edifice noun *an imposing edifice:* **building**,
structure, construction, erection, pile,
complex; property, development, premises.

edit verb **1** *she edited the text:* **correct**, check,
copy-edit, improve, emend, polish; modify,
adapt, revise, rewrite, reword, rework,
redraft; shorten, condense, cut, abridge;
informal clean up. **2** *this volume was edited
by a consultant:* **select**, choose, assemble,
organize, put together. **3** *he edited The
Times:* **be the editor of**, direct, run, manage,
head, lead, supervise, oversee, preside over;
informal be the boss of.

edition noun *the early editions of tomorrow's
papers:* **issue**, number, volume, impression,
publication; version, revision.

educate verb *they decided to educate Edward
at home:* **teach**, school, tutor, instruct,
coach, train, drill; guide, inform, enlighten;
inculcate, indoctrinate.

educated adjective *an educated workforce
learns how to exploit new technology:*
informed, literate, schooled, tutored, well
read, learned, knowledgeable, enlightened;
intellectual, academic, erudite, scholarly,
cultivated, cultured.

education noun **1** *the education of
young children:* **teaching**, schooling,
tuition, tutoring, instruction, coaching,
training, tutelage, guidance; indoctrination,
inculcation, enlightenment. **2** *a woman
of some education:* **learning**, knowledge,
literacy, scholarship, enlightenment.

educational adjective **1** *an educational
establishment:* **academic**, scholastic, school,
learning, teaching, pedagogic, tuitional,
instructional. **2** *an educational experience:*
instructive, instructional, educative,
informative, illuminating, pedagogic,
enlightening, didactic, heuristic.

educator noun **teacher**, tutor,
instructor, schoolteacher, schoolmaster,
schoolmistress; educationalist, educationist;
lecturer, professor; guide, mentor, guru; N.
Amer. informal schoolmarm; Brit. informal beak;
formal pedagogue.

eerie adjective *an eerie silence descended
over the house:* **uncanny**, sinister, ghostly,
unnatural, unearthly, supernatural, other-
worldly; strange, abnormal, odd, weird,
freakish; frightening, spine-chilling, hair-
raising, blood-curdling, terrifying; informal
creepy, scary, spooky, freaky.

efface verb **1** *the words were effaced by
the rain:* **erase**, eradicate, expunge, blot
out, rub out, wipe out, remove, eliminate;
delete, cancel, obliterate, blank out. **2** *he
attempted to efface himself:* **make oneself
inconspicuous**, keep out of sight, keep out
of the limelight, lie low, keep a low profile,
withdraw.

effect noun **1** *the effect of these changes:*
result, consequence, upshot, outcome,
out-turn, repercussions, ramifications; end
result, conclusion, culmination, corollary,
concomitant, aftermath; fruit(s), product,
by-product; informal pay-off. **2** *the effect of
the drug:* **impact**, action, effectiveness,
influence; power, potency, strength;
success; formal efficacy. **3** *with effect from
tomorrow:* **force**, operation, enforcement,
implementation, effectiveness; validity,
lawfulness, legality, legitimacy. **4** *he said
'See you later' or words to that effect:*
sense, meaning, theme, drift, import,
intent, intention, tenor, significance,
message; gist, essence, spirit. **5** *they went
through the dead man's effects:* **belongings**,
possessions, (worldly) goods, chattels;
property, paraphernalia; informal gear, tackle,
things, stuff, bits and pieces; Brit. informal
clobber.
– OPPOSITES cause.
▶ verb *they effected many changes:* **achieve**,
accomplish, carry out, realize, manage, bring
off, execute, conduct, engineer, perform,
do, perpetrate, discharge, complete,
consummate; cause, bring about, create,
produce, make; provoke, occasion, generate,
engender, actuate, initiate.
■ **in effect** really, in reality, in truth, in
(actual) fact, effectively, essentially, in

essence, practically, to all intents and purposes, all but, as good as, more or less, almost, nearly, just about; informal pretty much.

■ **take effect 1** *these measures will take effect in May:* come into force, come into operation, begin, become valid, become law, apply, be applied. **2** *the drug started to take effect:* work, act, be effective, produce results.

effective adjective **1** *an effective treatment:* **successful**, effectual, potent, powerful; helpful, beneficial, advantageous, valuable, useful. **2** *a more effective argument:* **convincing**, compelling, strong, forceful, potent, weighty, sound, valid; impressive, persuasive, plausible, credible, authoritative; logical, reasonable, lucid, coherent, cogent, eloquent; formal efficacious. **3** *the new law will be effective next week:* **operative**, in force, in effect; valid, official, lawful, legal, binding. **4** *Korea was under effective Japanese control:* **virtual**, practical, essential, actual, implicit, tacit.
– OPPOSITES weak, invalid, theoretical.

effectiveness noun *pupils' progress is a far better measure of a school's effectiveness:* **success**, productiveness, potency, power; benefit, advantage, value, virtue, usefulness.

effectual adjective *effectual political action:* **effective**, successful, productive, constructive; worthwhile, helpful, beneficial, advantageous, valuable, useful.

effeminate adjective *as his manicured fingers played with the gold medallion around his neck, he looked very effeminate:* **womanish**, effete, foppish, mincing; informal camp, campy, limp-wristed.
– OPPOSITES manly.

effervesce verb *heat the mixture until it effervesces:* **fizz**, sparkle, bubble; froth, foam.

effervescence noun **1** *wines of uniform effervescence:* **fizz**, fizziness, sparkle, gassiness, carbonation, aeration, bubbliness. **2** *his cheeky effervescence:* **vivacity**, liveliness, animation, high spirits, ebullience, exuberance, buoyancy, sparkle, gaiety, jollity, cheerfulness, perkiness, breeziness, enthusiasm, irrepressibility, vitality, zest, energy, dynamism; informal pep, bounce.

effervescent adjective **1** *an effervescent drink:* **fizzy**, sparkling, carbonated, aerated, gassy, bubbly; mousseux, pétillant, spumante. **2** *effervescent young people:* **vivacious**, lively, animated, high-spirited, bubbly, ebullient, buoyant, sparkling, scintillating, light-hearted, jaunty, happy, jolly, cheery, cheerful, perky, sunny, enthusiastic, irrepressible, vital, zestful, energetic, dynamic; Brit. Tiggerish; informal bright-eyed and bushy-tailed, peppy, bouncy, upbeat, chirpy, full of beans.
– OPPOSITES still, depressed.

effete adjective **1** *effete trendies:* **affected**,

pretentious, precious, mannered, over-refined; ineffectual; informal la-di-da, pseud; Brit. informal poncey. **2** *an effete young man:* **effeminate**, unmanly, girlish, feminine; soft, timid, cowardly, lily-livered, spineless, pusillanimous; informal sissy, wimpish, wimpy.
– OPPOSITES manly.

efficiency noun **1** *we need reforms to bring efficiency:* **organization**, order, orderliness, regulation, coherence; productivity, effectiveness. **2** *I compliment you on your efficiency:* **competence**, capability, ability, proficiency, adeptness, expertise, professionalism, skill, effectiveness.

efficient adjective **1** *efficient techniques:* **organized**, methodical, systematic, logical, orderly, businesslike, streamlined, productive, effective, cost-effective. **2** *an efficient secretary:* **competent**, capable, able, proficient, adept, skilful, skilled, effective, productive, organized, businesslike.
– OPPOSITES disorganized, incompetent.

effigy noun *they venerate an effigy of the saint:* **statue**, statuette, sculpture, model, dummy, figurine; guy; likeness, image; bust.

effluent noun **(liquid) waste**, sewage, effluvium, outflow, discharge, emission.

effort noun **1** *they made an effort to work together:* **attempt**, try, endeavour; informal crack, shot, stab, bash. **2** *his score was a fine effort:* **achievement**, accomplishment, attainment, result, feat; undertaking, enterprise, work; triumph, success, coup. **3** *the job requires little effort:* **exertion**, energy, work, endeavour, application, labour, power, muscle, toil, strain; informal sweat, elbow grease; Brit. informal graft; Austral./NZ informal (hard) yakka.

effortless adjective *Alexei rose to his feet in a single effortless movement:* **easy**, undemanding, unchallenging, painless, simple, uncomplicated, straightforward, elementary; fluent, natural; informal as easy as pie, child's play, kids' stuff, a cinch, no sweat, a doddle, a breeze; Brit. informal easy-peasy; N. Amer. informal duck soup, a snap.
– OPPOSITES difficult.

effrontery noun *one of the jurors had the effrontery to challenge the coroner's authority:* **impudence**, impertinence, cheek, insolence, cockiness, audacity, temerity, presumption, nerve, gall, shamelessness, impoliteness, disrespect, bad manners; informal brass (neck), face, chutzpah; Brit. informal sauce; N. Amer. informal sass.

effusion noun **1** *an effusion of poisonous gas:* **outflow**, outpouring, rush, current, flood, deluge, emission, discharge, emanation; spurt, surge, jet, stream, torrent, gush, flow. **2** *reporters' flamboyant effusions:* **outburst**, outpouring, gushing; wordiness, verbiage.

effusive adjective *a barrage of effusive compliments:* **gushing**, gushy, unrestrained, extravagant, fulsome, demonstrative, lavish,

enthusiastic, lyrical; expansive, wordy, verbose; informal over the top, OTT.
– OPPOSITES restrained.

egg noun **ovum**; gamete, germ cell; **(eggs)** roe, spawn, seed.
■ **egg someone on** *'Teach him a lesson,' shouted the boys, egging their friend on:* urge, goad, incite, provoke, push, drive, prod, prompt, induce, impel, spur on; encourage, exhort, motivate, galvanize.

ego noun *he needed a boost to his ego:* **self-esteem**, self-importance, self-worth, self-respect, self-image, self-confidence.

egocentric adjective *most children are unshakeably egocentric up to the age of seven:* **self-centred**, egomaniacal, self-interested, selfish, self-seeking, self-absorbed, self-obsessed; narcissistic, vain, self-important.
– OPPOSITES altruistic.

egotism, egoism noun *in his arrogance and egotism, he underestimated Gill:* **self-centredness**, egomania, egocentricity, self-interest, selfishness, self-seeking, self-serving, self-regard, self-obsession; self-love, narcissism, self-admiration, vanity, conceit, self-importance; boastfulness.

egotist, egoist noun *boxing is a sport that breeds egotists and exhibitionists:* **self-seeker**, egocentric, egomaniac, narcissist; boaster, brag, braggart; informal swank, show-off, big-head; N. Amer. informal showboat.

egotistic, egoistic adjective **self-centred**, selfish, egocentric, egomaniacal, self-interested, self-seeking, self-absorbed, self-obsessed; narcissistic, vain, conceited, self-important; boastful.

egregious adjective *an egregious error of judgement:* **shocking**, appalling, terrible, awful, horrendous, frightful, atrocious, abominable, abhorrent, outrageous, monstrous, heinous, dire, unspeakable, shameful, unforgivable, intolerable, dreadful.
– OPPOSITES marvellous.

egress noun **1** *the egress from the gallery was blocked:* **exit**, way out, escape route. **2** *a means of egress:* **departure**, exit, withdrawal, retreat, exodus; escape; vacation.
– OPPOSITES entrance.

ejaculate verb **1** **emit semen**, climax, orgasm; informal come. **2** *the sperm is ejaculated:* **emit**, eject, discharge, release, expel, disgorge; shoot out, squirt out, spurt out.

ejaculation noun **1** *the ejaculation of fluid:* **emission**, ejection, discharge, release, expulsion. **2** *premature ejaculation:* **emission of semen**, climax, orgasm.

eject verb **1** *the volcano ejected ash:* **emit**, spew out, discharge, give off, send out, belch, vent; expel, release, disgorge, spout, vomit, throw up. **2** *the pilot had time to eject:* **bail out**, escape, get out. **3** *they were ejected from the hall:* **expel**, throw out, turn out,

cast out, remove, oust; evict, banish; informal chuck out, kick out, turf out, boot out; N. Amer. informal give someone the bum's rush.
– OPPOSITES admit.

ejection noun **1** *the ejection of electrons:* **emission**, discharge, expulsion, release; elimination. **2** *their ejection from the ground:* **expulsion**, removal; eviction, banishment, exile.

eke verb *I had to eke out my remaining funds:* **husband**, use sparingly, be thrifty with, be frugal with, be sparing with, use economically; informal go easy on.
– OPPOSITES squander.
■ **eke out a living** subsist, survive, get by, scrape by, make ends meet, keep body and soul together, keep the wolf from the door, keep one's head above water.

elaborate adjective **1** *an elaborate plan:* **complicated**, complex, intricate, involved; detailed, painstaking, careful; tortuous, convoluted, serpentine, Byzantine. **2** *an elaborate plasterwork ceiling:* **ornate**, decorated, embellished, adorned, ornamented, fancy, fussy, busy, ostentatious, extravagant, showy, baroque, rococo, florid, wedding-cake.
– OPPOSITES simple, plain.
verb *both sides refused to elaborate on their reasons:* **expand on**, enlarge on, add to, flesh out, put flesh on the bones of, add detail to, expatiate on; develop, fill out, embellish, embroider, enhance, amplify.

elan noun *they performed with uncommon elan:* **flair**, style, panache, confidence, dash, éclat; energy, vigour, vitality, liveliness, brio, esprit, animation, vivacity, zest, verve, spirit, pep, sparkle, enthusiasm, gusto, eagerness, feeling, fire; informal pizzazz, zing, zip, vim, oomph.

elapse verb *a month elapsed before the appeal hearing began:* **pass**, go by/past, wear on, slip by/away/past, roll by/past, slide by/past, steal by/past, tick by/past.

elastic adjective **1** *elastic material:* **stretchy**, elasticated, stretchable, springy, flexible, pliant, pliable, supple, yielding, plastic, resilient. **2** *an elastic concept of nationality:* **adaptable**, flexible, adjustable, accommodating, variable, fluid, versatile.
– OPPOSITES rigid.

elasticity noun **1** *the skin's natural elasticity:* **stretchiness**, flexibility, pliancy, suppleness, plasticity, resilience, springiness; informal give. **2** *the elasticity of the term:* **adaptability**, flexibility, adjustability, fluidity, versatility.

elated adjective *I felt elated at beating Dennis:* **thrilled**, delighted, overjoyed, ecstatic, euphoric, very happy, joyous, gleeful, jubilant, beside oneself, exultant, rapturous, in raptures, walking on air, on cloud nine/seven, in seventh heaven, jumping for joy, in transports of delight; informal on top of the world, over the moon, on a high, tickled pink; Austral. informal wrapped.

– OPPOSITES miserable.

elation noun **euphoria**, ecstasy, happiness, delight, transports of delight, joy, joyousness, glee, jubilation, exultation, bliss, rapture.

elbow verb *he elbowed his way through the crowd:* **push**, shove, force, shoulder, jostle, barge, muscle, bulldoze.

elbow room noun *the province wants a little more elbow room within the federation:* **room to manoeuvre**, room, space, Lebensraum, breathing space, scope, freedom, play, free rein, licence, latitude, leeway.

elder adjective *his elder brother:* **older**, senior, big.
noun *the church elders:* **leader**, senior figure, patriarch, father.

elderly adjective *her elderly mother:* **aged**, old, advanced in years, ageing, long in the tooth, past one's prime; grey-haired, grey-bearded, grizzled, hoary; in one's dotage, decrepit, doddering, doddery, senescent; informal getting on, past it, over the hill, no spring chicken.
– OPPOSITES youthful.
noun (**the elderly**) **old people**, senior citizens, (old-age) pensioners, OAPs, retired people; geriatrics; N. Amer. seniors, retirees, golden agers; informal (golden) oldies, wrinklies; N. Amer. informal oldsters, woopies.

elect verb **1** *a new president was elected:* **vote in**, vote for, return, cast one's vote for; choose, pick, select. **2** *she elected to stay behind:* **choose**, decide, opt, vote.
adjective *the president elect:* **future**, -to-be, designate, chosen, elected, coming, next, appointed, presumptive.
noun (**the elect**) **the chosen**, the elite, the favoured; the crème de la crème.

election noun *he was defeated in the 1992 election:* **ballot**, vote, popular vote; poll; Brit. by-election; US primary.

electioneer verb *he accused the opposition of electioneering by raising the issue:* **campaign**, canvass, go on the hustings, doorstep; Brit. informal go out on the knocker.

elector noun *each elector has one vote:* **voter**, member of the electorate, constituent; selector.

electric adjective **1** *an electric kettle:* **electric-powered**, electrically operated, mains-operated, battery-operated. **2** *the atmosphere was electric:* **exciting**, charged, electrifying, thrilling, heady, dramatic, intoxicating, dynamic, stimulating, galvanizing, rousing, stirring, moving; tense, knife-edge, explosive, volatile.

electricity noun **power**, electric power, energy, current, static; Brit. mains; Canadian hydro; Brit. informal leccy.

electrify verb *both lecturers have for several years electrified students at Columbia University:* **excite**, thrill, stimulate,

arouse, rouse, inspire, stir (up), exhilarate, intoxicate, galvanize, move, fire (with enthusiasm), fire someone's imagination, invigorate, animate; startle, jolt, shock; N. Amer. light a fire under; informal give someone a buzz, give someone a kick; N. Amer. informal give someone a charge.

elegance noun **1** *he was attracted by her elegance:* **style**, stylishness, grace, gracefulness, taste, tastefulness, sophistication; refinement, dignity, beauty, poise, charm, culture; suaveness, urbanity, panache. **2** *the elegance of the idea:* **neatness**, simplicity; ingenuity, cleverness, inventiveness.

elegant adjective **1** *an elegant black outfit:* **stylish**, graceful, tasteful, sophisticated, classic, chic, smart, fashionable, modish; refined, dignified, poised, beautiful, lovely, charming, artistic, aesthetic; cultivated, polished, cultured; dashing, debonair, suave, urbane. **2** *an elegant solution:* **neat**, simple, effective; ingenious, clever, deft, intelligent, inventive.
– OPPOSITES gauche.

elegy noun *I wrote an elegy for my father:* **lament**, requiem, funeral poem/song, threnody, dirge, plaint; Irish keen; Irish & Scottish coronach.

element noun **1** *an essential element of the local community:* **component**, constituent, part, section, portion, piece, segment, bit; aspect, factor, feature, facet, ingredient, strand, detail, point; member, unit, module, item. **2** *there is an element of truth in this stereotype:* **trace**, touch, hint, smattering, soupçon. **3** (**elements**) *the elements of political science:* **basics**, essentials, principles, first principles; foundations, fundamentals, rudiments; informal nuts and bolts, ABC. **4** *I braved the elements:* **the weather**, the climate, meteorological conditions, atmospheric conditions; the wind, the rain.

elemental adjective **1** *the elemental principles of accountancy:* **basic**, primary, fundamental, essential, root, underlying; rudimentary. **2** *elemental forces:* **natural**, atmospheric, meteorological, environmental.

elementary adjective **1** *an elementary astronomy course:* **basic**, rudimentary, fundamental; preparatory, introductory, initiatory. **2** *a lot of the work is elementary:* **easy**, simple, straightforward, uncomplicated, undemanding, painless, child's play, plain sailing; informal as easy as falling off a log, as easy as pie, as easy as ABC, a piece of cake, no sweat, kids' stuff; Brit. informal easy-peasy.
– OPPOSITES advanced, difficult.

elevate verb **1** *a conveyor belt is used to elevate the grain into storage bins:* **raise**, lift (up), raise up/aloft, upraise; hoist, hike up, haul up. **2** *he was elevated to Secretary of State:* **promote**, upgrade, advance, move

up, raise, prefer; ennoble, exalt, aggrandize; informal kick upstairs, move up the ladder.
– OPPOSITES lower, demote.

elevated adjective **1** *an elevated motorway:* **raised**, upraised, high up, aloft; overhead. **2** *elevated language:* **lofty**, grand, exalted, fine, sublime; inflated, pompous, bombastic, orotund. **3** *the gentry's elevated status:* **high**, higher, high-ranking, of high standing, lofty, superior, exalted, eminent; grand, noble.
– OPPOSITES lowly.

elevation noun **1** *his elevation to the peerage:* **promotion**, upgrading, advancement, advance, preferment, aggrandizement; ennoblement; informal step up the ladder, kick upstairs. **2** *elevations in excess of 3000 metres:* **height**, altitude, hill, mountain, mount. **3** *elevation of thought:* **grandeur**, greatness, nobility, loftiness, majesty, sublimity.

elf noun **pixie**, fairy, sprite, imp, brownie; dwarf, gnome, goblin, hobgoblin; leprechaun, puck, troll, hobbit.

elfin adjective *her short hair accentuated her elfin face:* **elflike**, elfish, elvish, pixie-like; puckish, impish, playful, mischievous; dainty, delicate, small, petite, slight, little, tiny, diminutive.

elicit verb *I tried to elicit a smile from Joanna:* **obtain**, draw out, extract, bring out, evoke, call forth, bring forth, induce, prompt, generate, engender, trigger, provoke.

eligible adjective **1** *those people eligible to vote:* **entitled**, permitted, allowed, qualified, able. **2** *an eligible bachelor:* **desirable**, suitable; available, single, unmarried, unattached, unwed.

eliminate verb **1** *a policy that would eliminate inflation:* **remove**, get rid of, put an end to, do away with, end, stop, terminate, eradicate, destroy, annihilate, stamp out, wipe out, extinguish; informal knock something on the head. **2** *he was eliminated from the title race:* **knock out**, beat; exclude, rule out, disqualify.

elite noun *the party attracted the elite of London society:* **best**, pick, cream, crème de la crème, flower, nonpareil, elect; high society, jet set, beautiful people, beau monde, haut monde; aristocracy, nobility, upper class; N. Amer. four hundred.
– OPPOSITES dregs.

elixir noun *an elixir guaranteed to induce love:* **potion**, concoction, brew, philtre, decoction, mixture; medicine, tincture; extract, essence, concentrate, distillate, distillation.

elliptical adjective **1** *an elliptical shape:* **oval**, egg-shaped, elliptic, ovate, ovoid, oviform, ellipsoidal. **2** *elliptical phraseology:* **cryptic**, abstruse, ambiguous, obscure, oblique, Delphic; terse, concise, succinct, compact, economic, laconic, sparing.

elocution noun *she had lessons in singing and elocution:* **pronunciation**, enunciation,

articulation, diction, speech, intonation, vocalization, modulation; phrasing, delivery, public speaking.

elongate verb **1** *an exercise that elongates the muscles:* **lengthen**, extend, stretch (out). **2** *the high notes were elongated:* **prolong**, protract, draw out, sustain.
– OPPOSITES shorten.

eloquence noun *he was known for the eloquence of his sermons:* **fluency**, articulacy, articulateness, expressiveness, silver tongue, persuasiveness, forcefulness, power, potency, effectiveness; oratory, rhetoric, grandiloquence, magniloquence; informal gift of the gab, way with words, blarney.

eloquent adjective **1** *an eloquent speaker:* **fluent**, articulate, expressive, silver-tongued; persuasive, strong, forceful, powerful, potent, well expressed, effective, lucid, vivid, graphic; smooth-tongued, glib. **2** *her glance was more eloquent than words:* **expressive**, meaningful, suggestive, revealing, telling, significant, indicative.
– OPPOSITES inarticulate.

elsewhere adverb *the negatives are stored in one place, and the prints are stored elsewhere:* **somewhere else**, in/at/to another place, in/at/to a different place, hence; not here, not present, absent, away, abroad, out.
– OPPOSITES here.

elucidate verb *collections of letters can elucidate what was uppermost in an artist's mind:* **explain**, make clear, illuminate, throw/shed light on, clarify, clear up, sort out, unravel, spell out; interpret, explicate; gloss.
– OPPOSITES confuse.

elucidation noun **explanation**, clarification, illumination; interpretation, explication; gloss.

elude verb *the murderer managed to elude the police for several weeks:* **evade**, avoid, get away from, dodge, escape from, run (away) from; lose, shake off, give the slip to, slip away from, throw off the scent; informal slip through someone's fingers, slip through the net.

elusive adjective **1** *her elusive husband:* **difficult to find**; evasive, slippery; informal always on the move. **2** *an elusive quality:* **indefinable**, intangible, impalpable, unanalysable; fugitive; ambiguous.

Elysian adjective *an Elysian vision:* **heavenly**, paradisal, paradisiacal, celestial, superlunary, divine.

emaciated adjective *the captives were sick and emaciated:* **thin**, skeletal, bony, gaunt, wasted, thin as a rake; scrawny, skinny, scraggy, skin and bones, raw-boned, stick-like; starved, underfed, undernourished, underweight, half-starved; cadaverous, shrivelled, shrunken, withered; informal anorexic, like a bag of bones.
– OPPOSITES fat.

emanate verb **1** *warmth emanated from the fireplace:* **issue**, spread, radiate, be sent forth/out. **2** *the proposals emanated from a committee:* **originate**, stem, derive, proceed, spring, issue, emerge, flow, come. **3** *he emanated an air of power:* **exude**, emit, radiate, give off/out, send out/forth.

emanation noun **1** *the poem is an emanation of his tortured personality:* **product**, consequence, result, fruit. **2** *radon gas emanation:* **discharge**, emission, radiation, effusion, outflow, outpouring, flow, leak.

emancipate verb *the serfs privately owned by members of the nobility were emancipated:* **free**, liberate, set free, release, deliver, discharge; unchain, unfetter, unshackle, untie, unyoke.
– OPPOSITES enslave.

emancipated adjective **liberated**, independent, unconstrained, uninhibited; free.

emasculate verb *an Act which emasculated the House of Lords:* **weaken**, enfeeble, debilitate, erode, undermine, cripple; remove the sting from, pull the teeth of; informal water down.

embalm verb *his body had been embalmed:* **preserve**, mummify, lay out.

embankment noun **bank**, mound, ridge, earthwork, causeway, barrier, levee, dam, dyke.

embargo noun *an embargo on oil sales:* **ban**, bar, prohibition, stoppage, interdict, proscription, veto, moratorium; restriction, restraint, block, barrier, impediment, obstruction; boycott.
verb *arms sales were embargoed:* **ban**, bar, prohibit, stop, interdict, debar, proscribe, outlaw; restrict, restrain, block, obstruct; boycott.
– OPPOSITES allow.

embark verb **1** *he embarked at Dover:* **board ship**, go on board, go aboard, take ship; emplane; informal hop on, jump on. **2** *he embarked on a new career:* **begin**, start, commence, undertake, set about, take up, turn one's hand to, get down to; enter into, venture into, launch into, plunge into, engage in, settle down to; informal get cracking on, get going on, have a go/crack/shot at.

embarrass verb *she wouldn't embarrass either of them by making a scene:* **mortify**, shame, put someone to shame, humiliate, abash, chagrin, make uncomfortable, make self-conscious; discomfit, disconcert, discompose, upset, discountenance, distress; informal show up.

embarrassed adjective *I felt quite embarrassed whenever I talked to her:* **mortified**, red-faced, blushing, abashed, shamed, ashamed, shamefaced, humiliated, chagrined, awkward, self-conscious, uncomfortable, not knowing where to look, sheepish; discomfited, disconcerted, upset, discomposed, flustered, agitated,

discountenanced, distressed; shy, bashful, tongue-tied; informal with egg on one's face, wishing the earth would swallow one up.

embarrassing adjective *an embarrassing mistake:* **humiliating**, shaming, shameful, mortifying, ignominious; awkward, uncomfortable, compromising; disconcerting, discomfiting, upsetting, distressing; informal blush-making, cringeworthy, cringe-making, toe-curling.

embarrassment noun **1** *he was scarlet with embarrassment:* **mortification**, humiliation, shame, shamefacedness, chagrin, awkwardness, self-consciousness, sheepishness, discomfort, discomfiture, discomposure, agitation, distress; ignominy; shyness, bashfulness. **2** *his current financial embarrassment:* **difficulty**, predicament, plight, problem, mess; informal bind, jam, pickle, fix, scrape. **3** *an embarrassment of riches:* **surplus**, excess, overabundance, superabundance, glut, surfeit, superfluity; abundance, profusion, plethora.

embassy noun *the Italian embassy:* **consulate**, legation, ministry.

embed, imbed verb *the plaque was embedded in a wall at the rear of the house:* **implant**, plant, set, fix, lodge, root, insert, place; sink, drive in, hammer in, ram in.

embellish verb **1** *weapons embellished with precious metal:* **decorate**, adorn, ornament; beautify, enhance, grace; trim, garnish, gild; deck, bedeck, festoon, emblazon. **2** *the legend was embellished by an American academic:* **elaborate**, embroider, expand on, exaggerate.

embellishment noun **1** *architectural embellishments:* **decoration**, ornamentation, adornment; beautification, enhancement, trimming, trim, garnishing, gilding. **2** *we wanted the truth, not romantic embellishments:* **elaboration**, addition, exaggeration.

ember noun *the fire's dying embers:* **glowing coal**, live coal; cinder; (**embers**) ashes, residue.

embezzle verb *he was charged with embezzling money from a country club:* **misappropriate**, steal, thieve, pilfer, purloin, appropriate, abstract, defraud someone of, siphon off, pocket, help oneself to; put one's hand in the till; informal rob, rip off, skim, line one's pockets; Brit. informal pinch, nick, half-inch.

embezzlement noun **misappropriation**, theft, stealing, robbery, thieving, pilfering, purloining, pilferage, appropriation, swindling; fraud, larceny.

embittered adjective *he died an embittered man:* **bitter**, resentful, grudge-bearing, rancorous, jaundiced, aggrieved, sour, frustrated, dissatisfied, alienated, disaffected.

emblazon verb **1** *shirts emblazoned with the company name:* **adorn**, decorate, ornament, embellish; inscribe. **2** *a flag with a hammer and sickle emblazoned on it:* **display**, depict, show.

emblem noun *the white rose was the emblem of the Yorkist side:* **symbol**, representation, token, image, figure, mark, sign; crest, badge, device, insignia, stamp, seal, heraldic device, coat of arms, shield; logo, trademark.

emblematic, emblematical adjective **1** *a situation emblematic of the industrialized twentieth century:* **symbolic**, representative, demonstrative, suggestive, indicative. **2** *emblematic works of art:* **allegorical**, symbolic, metaphorical, parabolic, figurative.

embodiment noun *she was the living embodiment of '80s values:* **personification**, incarnation, realization, manifestation, expression, representation, actualization, symbol, symbolization; paradigm, epitome, paragon, soul, model; type, essence, quintessence, exemplification, example, exemplar, ideal.

embody verb **1** *Gradgrind embodies the spirit of industrial capitalism:* **personify**, realize, manifest, symbolize, represent, express, concretize, incarnate, epitomize, stand for, typify, exemplify. **2** *the changes in law embodied in the Children Act:* **incorporate**, include, contain, encompass; assimilate, consolidate, integrate, organize, systematize; combine.

embolden verb *emboldened by the brandy, he walked over to her table:* **fortify**, make brave/braver, encourage, hearten, strengthen, brace, stiffen the resolve of, lift the morale of; rouse, stir, stimulate, cheer, rally, fire, animate, inspirit, invigorate; informal buck up.
– OPPOSITES dishearten.

embrace verb **1** *he embraced her warmly:* **hug**, take/hold in one's arms, hold, cuddle, clasp to one's bosom, clasp, squeeze, clutch; caress; enfold, enclasp, encircle, envelop, entwine oneself around; informal canoodle, smooch. **2** *most western European countries have embraced the concept:* **welcome**, welcome with open arms, accept, take up, take to one's heart, adopt, espouse, support, back, champion. **3** *the faculty embraces a wide range of departments:* **include**, take in, comprise, contain, incorporate, encompass, cover, involve, embody, subsume, comprehend.
noun *a fond embrace:* **hug**, cuddle, squeeze, clinch, caress; bear hug.

embrocation noun **ointment**, lotion, cream, rub, salve, emollient, liniment, balm, unguent.

embroider verb **1** *a cushion embroidered with a pattern of golden keys:* **sew**, stitch; decorate, adorn, ornament, embellish. **2** *she embroidered her stories with colourful detail:* **elaborate**, embellish, enlarge on,

exaggerate, touch up, dress up, gild, colour; informal jazz up.

embroidery noun **1** *the girls were taught embroidery:* **needlework**, needlepoint, needlecraft, sewing, tatting, crewel work, tapestry. **2** *fanciful embroidery of the facts:* **elaboration**, embellishment, adornment, ornamentation, colouring, enhancement; exaggeration, overstatement, hyperbole.

embroil verb *she became embroiled in a dispute between the two women:* **involve**, entangle, ensnare, enmesh, catch up, mix up, bog down, mire.

embryo noun **1** *a human embryo:* **fetus**, fertilized egg, unborn child/baby. **2** *the embryo of a capitalist economy:* **germ**, nucleus, seed; rudimentary version, rudiments, basics, beginning, start.

embryonic adjective **1** *an embryonic chick:* **fetal**, unborn, unhatched. **2** *an embryonic pro-democracy movement:* **rudimentary**, undeveloped, unformed, immature, incomplete, incipient, inchoate; fledgling, budding, nascent, emerging, developing, early, germinal.
– OPPOSITES mature.

emend verb *the journalistic practice of emending quotations in the areas of grammar and syntax:* **correct**, rectify, repair, fix; improve, enhance, polish, refine, amend; edit, rewrite, revise, copy-edit, subedit, redraft, recast, rephrase, reword, rework, alter, change, modify.

emerge verb **1** *a policeman emerged from the alley:* **come out**, appear, come into view, become visible, surface, materialize, manifest oneself, issue, come forth. **2** *several unexpected facts emerged:* **become known**, become apparent, be revealed, come to light, come out, turn up, transpire, unfold, turn out, prove to be the case.

emergence noun *we are witnessing the emergence of a new generation of managers:* **appearance**, arrival, coming, materialization; advent, inception, dawn, birth, origination, start, development, rise.

emergency noun *a military emergency:* **crisis**, urgent situation, extremity, exigency; accident, disaster, catastrophe, calamity; difficulty, plight, predicament, danger; informal panic stations.
adjective **1** *an emergency meeting:* **urgent**, crisis; impromptu, extraordinary. **2** *emergency supplies:* **reserve**, standby, backup, fallback, in reserve.

emergent adjective *the emergent democracies of eastern Europe:* **emerging**, developing, rising, dawning, budding, embryonic, infant, fledgling, nascent, incipient.

emigrate verb *Rose's parents emigrated to Australia:* **move abroad**, move overseas, leave one's country, migrate; relocate, resettle; defect.
– OPPOSITES immigrate.

emigration noun **moving abroad**, moving overseas, expatriation, migration; exodus, diaspora; relocation, resettling; defection.

eminence noun *his eminence as a scientist:* **fame**, celebrity, illustriousness, distinction, renown, pre-eminence, notability, greatness, prestige, importance, reputation, repute, note; prominence, superiority, stature, standing.

eminent adjective **1** *an eminent man of letters:* **illustrious**, distinguished, renowned, esteemed, pre-eminent, notable, noteworthy, great, prestigious, important, influential, outstanding, noted, of note; famous, celebrated, prominent, well known, lionized, acclaimed, exalted, revered, august, venerable. **2** *the eminent reasonableness of their claims:* **obvious**, clear, conspicuous, marked, singular, signal; total, complete, utter, absolute, thorough, perfect, downright, sheer.
– OPPOSITES unknown.

eminently adverb *the car is eminently suitable for town driving:* **very**, greatly, highly, exceedingly, extremely, particularly, exceptionally, supremely, uniquely; obviously, clearly, conspicuously, markedly, singularly, signally, outstandingly, strikingly, notably, surpassingly; totally, completely, utterly, absolutely, thoroughly, perfectly, downright.

emissary noun *he sent an emissary to Constantinople for bilateral talks:* **envoy**, ambassador, delegate, attaché, consul, plenipotentiary; agent, representative, deputy; messenger, courier; nuncio.

emission noun *targets for reducing carbon dioxide emissions:* **discharge**, release, outpouring, outflow, outrush, leak, excretion, secretion, ejection; emanation, radiation, effusion, ejaculation, disgorgement; issuance.

emit verb **1** *the hydrocarbons emitted from vehicle exhausts:* **discharge**, release, give out/off, pour out, send forth, throw out, void, vent, issue; leak, ooze, excrete, disgorge, secrete, eject, ejaculate; spout, belch, spew out; emanate, radiate, exude. **2** *he emitted a loud cry:* **utter**, voice, let out, produce, give vent to, come out with, vocalize.
– OPPOSITES absorb.

emollient adjective **1** *a rich emollient shampoo:* **moisturizing**, soothing, softening. **2** *an emollient response:* **conciliatory**, conciliating, appeasing, soothing, calming, pacifying, assuaging, placating, mollifying, propitiatory.
noun *she applied an emollient:* **moisturizer**, cream, lotion, oil, rub, salve, unguent, balm.

emotion noun **1** *she was good at hiding her emotions:* **feeling**, sentiment; reaction, response. **2** *overcome by emotion, she turned away:* **passion**, strength of feeling, warmth of feeling. **3** *responses based purely on*

emotion: **instinct**, intuition, gut feeling; sentiment, the heart.

emotional adjective **1** *an emotional young man:* **passionate**, hot-blooded, ardent, fervent, excitable, temperamental, melodramatic, tempestuous; demonstrative, responsive, tender, loving, feeling, sentimental, sensitive. **2** *he paid an emotional tribute to his wife:* **poignant**, moving, touching, affecting, powerful, stirring, emotive, heart-rending, heart-warming, impassioned, dramatic; haunting, pathetic, sentimental; informal tear-jerking.
– OPPOSITES unfeeling.

emotionless adjective *a flat, emotionless voice:* **unemotional**, unfeeling, dispassionate, passionless, unexpressive, cool, cold, cold-blooded, impassive, indifferent, detached, remote, aloof; toneless, flat, dead, expressionless, blank, wooden, stony, deadpan, vacant.

emotive adjective *fox-hunting is an emotive issue:* **controversial**, contentious, inflammatory; sensitive, delicate, difficult, problematic, touchy, awkward, prickly, ticklish.

empathize verb *counsellors need to be able to empathize with people:* **identify**, sympathize, be in sympathy, understand, share someone's feelings, be in tune; be on the same wavelength as, talk the same language as; relate to, feel for, have insight into; informal put oneself in someone else's shoes.

emperor noun **ruler**, sovereign, king, monarch, potentate.

emphasis noun **1** *the curriculum gave more emphasis to reading and writing:* **prominence**, importance, significance, value; stress, weight, accent, attention, priority, pre-eminence, urgency, force. **2** *the emphasis is on the word 'little':* **stress**, accent, accentuation, weight, prominence; beat; Prosody ictus.

emphasize verb *the prime minister emphasized his commitment to reform:* **stress**, underline, highlight, focus attention on, point up, lay stress on, draw attention to, spotlight, foreground, play up, make a point of; bring to the fore, insist on, belabour; accent, accentuate, underscore; informal press home, rub it in.
– OPPOSITES understate.

emphatic adjective **1** *an emphatic denial:* **vehement**, firm, wholehearted, forceful, forcible, energetic, vigorous, direct, assertive, insistent; certain, definite, out-and-out, one hundred per cent; decided, determined, categorical, unqualified, unconditional, unequivocal, unambiguous, absolute, explicit, downright, outright, clear. **2** *an emphatic victory:* **conclusive**, decisive, decided, unmistakable; resounding, telling; informal thumping, thundering.
– OPPOSITES hesitant, narrow.

empire noun **1** *the Ottoman Empire:* **kingdom**, realm, domain, territory; commonwealth; power, world power, superpower. **2** *a worldwide shipping empire:* **organization**, corporation, multinational, conglomerate, consortium, company, business, firm, operation.

empirical adjective *they provided empirical evidence to support their argument:* **experiential**, practical, heuristic, first-hand, hands-on; observed, seen.
– OPPOSITES theoretical.

employ verb **1** *she employed a chauffeur:* **hire**, engage, recruit, take on, secure the services of, sign up, sign, put on the payroll, enrol, appoint; retain; indenture, apprentice. **2** *Sam was employed in carving a stone figure:* **occupy**, engage, involve, keep busy, tie up; absorb, engross, immerse. **3** *the team employed subtle psychological tactics:* **use**, utilize, make use of, avail oneself of; apply, exercise, practise, put into practice, exert, bring into play, bring to bear; draw on, resort to, turn to, have recourse to.
– OPPOSITES dismiss.

employed adjective *employed married women tend to delay their childbearing:* **working**, in work, in employment, holding down a job; earning, waged, breadwinning.

employee noun *the firm supports employees who show ambition:* **worker**, member of staff; blue-collar worker, white-collar worker, workman, labourer, (hired) hand; wage-earner, breadwinner; (**employees**) personnel, staff, workforce; informal liveware.

employer noun **1** *his employer gave him a glowing reference:* **manager**, manageress, proprietor, director, head man, head woman; informal boss, boss man, skipper; Brit. informal gaffer, governor, guv'nor; N. Amer. informal padrone, sachem. **2** *the largest private sector employer in Sheffield:* **firm**, company, business, organization, manufacturer.

employment noun **1** *she found employment as a clerk:* **work**, labour, service; job, post, position, situation, occupation, profession, trade, métier, business, line, line of work, calling, vocation, craft, pursuit. **2** *the employment of children:* **hiring**, hire, engagement, taking on; apprenticing.

emporium noun **shop**, store, outlet, retail outlet; department store, chain store, supermarket, hypermarket, superstore, megastore; establishment.

empower verb **1** *the Act empowered Henry to punish heretics:* **authorize**, entitle, permit, allow, license, sanction, warrant, commission, delegate, qualify, enable, equip. **2** *movements to empower the poor:* **emancipate**, unshackle, set free, liberate.
– OPPOSITES forbid.

empress noun **ruler**, sovereign, queen, monarch, potentate.

emptiness noun *she had filled an emptiness in his life:* **void**, vacuum, empty space, vacuity, gap, vacancy, hole.

empty adjective **1** *an empty house:* **vacant**, unoccupied, uninhabited, untenanted, bare, desolate, deserted, abandoned; clear, free. **2** *an empty threat:* **meaningless**, hollow, idle, vain, futile, worthless, useless, insubstantial, ineffective, ineffectual. **3** *without her my life is empty:* **futile**, pointless, purposeless, worthless, meaningless, valueless, of no value, useless, of no use, aimless, senseless, hollow, barren, insignificant, inconsequential, trivial.
– OPPOSITES full, serious, worthwhile.
verb **1** *I emptied the dishwasher:* **unload**, unpack, void; clear, evacuate. **2** *he emptied out the contents of the case:* **remove**, take out, extract, tip out, pour out.
– OPPOSITES fill.

empty-headed adjective *certain types of men treat me like some empty-headed bimbo:* **stupid**, foolish, silly, unintelligent, idiotic, brainless, witless, vacuous, vapid, feather-brained, birdbrained, scatterbrained, scatty, thoughtless; informal half-witted, dumb, dim, airheaded, brain-dead, dippy, dizzy, dopey, dozy, soft in the head, slow on the uptake; Brit. informal daft; N. Amer. informal ditsy, dumb-ass.
– OPPOSITES intelligent.

emulate verb *she tried to emulate Lucy's glowing performance:* **imitate**, copy, mirror, echo, follow, model oneself on, take a leaf out of someone's book; match, equal, parallel, be on a par with, be in the same league as, come close to; compete with, contend with, rival, surpass.

enable verb *the Act enabled ordinary citizens to operate radio stations:* **allow**, permit, let, give the means to, equip, empower, make able, fit; authorize, entitle, qualify.
– OPPOSITES prevent.

enact verb **1** *the Bill was enacted in 1963:* **pass**, make law, legislate; approve, ratify, sanction, authorize; impose, lay down. **2** *members of the church enacted a nativity play:* **act out**, act, perform, appear in, stage, mount, put on, present.
– OPPOSITES repeal.

enactment noun **1** *the enactment of a Bill of Rights:* **passing**; ratification, sanction, approval, authorization; imposition. **2** *parliamentary enactments:* **act**, law, by-law, ruling, rule, regulation, statute, measure; (**enactments**) legislation. **3** *the enactment of the play:* **acting**, performing, performance, staging, presentation.

enamoured adjective *she was secretly enamoured of the prince:* **in love with**, infatuated with, besotted with, smitten with, captivated by, enchanted by, fascinated by, bewitched by, beguiled by; keen on, taken with; informal mad about, crazy about, wild about, bowled over by, struck on, sweet on, carrying a torch for.

encampment noun *they planned an attack on the enemy's encampment:* **camp**, military camp, bivouac, cantonment; campsite, camping ground; tents.

encapsulate verb **1** *their conclusions are encapsulated in one sentence:* **summarize**, sum up, give the gist of, put in a nutshell; capture, express. **2** *seeds encapsulated in resin:* **enclose**, encase, contain, envelop, enfold, sheath, cocoon, surround.

enchant verb *the play continued to enchant all who watched it:* **captivate**, charm, delight, enrapture, entrance, enthral, beguile, bewitch, spellbind, fascinate, hypnotize, mesmerize, rivet, grip, transfix; informal bowl someone over.
– OPPOSITES bore.

enchanter noun **wizard**, witch, sorcerer, warlock, magician, necromancer, magus; witch doctor, medicine man, shaman.

enchanting adjective **captivating**, charming, delightful, bewitching, beguiling, adorable, lovely, attractive, appealing, engaging, winning, fetching, winsome, alluring, disarming, irresistible, fascinating.

enchantment noun **1** *a race of giants skilled in enchantment:* **magic**, witchcraft, sorcery, wizardry, necromancy; charms, spells, incantations; N. Amer. mojo. **2** *the enchantment of the garden by moonlight:* **allure**, delight, charm, beauty, attractiveness, appeal, fascination, irresistibility, magnetism, pull, draw, lure. **3** *being with him was sheer enchantment:* **bliss**, ecstasy, heaven, rapture, joy.

enchantress noun **witch**, sorceress, magician, fairy; Circe, siren.

encircle verb *medieval walls encircle the town:* **surround**, enclose, circle, girdle, ring, encompass; close in, shut in, fence in, wall in, hem in, confine.

enclose verb **1** *tall trees enclosed the garden:* **surround**, circle, ring, girdle, encompass, encircle; confine, close in, shut in, fence in, wall in, hedge in, hem in. **2** *please enclose a stamped addressed envelope:* **include**, insert, put in; send.

enclosure noun *they drove the donkeys into the enclosure:* **paddock**, fold, pen, compound, stockade, ring, yard; sty, coop; N. Amer. corral.

encompass verb **1** *the monument is encompassed by Hunsbury Park:* **contain**, have within; surround, enclose, encircle. **2** *debates encompassing a vast range of subjects:* **cover**, embrace, include, incorporate, take in, contain, comprise, involve, deal with.

encounter verb **1** *I encountered a girl I used to know:* **meet**, meet by chance, run into, come across/upon, stumble across/on, chance on, happen on; informal bump into. **2** *we encountered a slight problem:* **experience**, run into, come up against, face, be faced with, confront.

noun **1** *an unexpected encounter:* **meeting**, chance meeting. **2** *a violent encounter between police and demonstrators:* **battle**, fight, clash, confrontation, struggle, skirmish, engagement; informal run-in, set-to, dust-up, scrap.

encourage verb **1** *the players were encouraged by the crowd's response:* **hearten**, cheer, buoy up, uplift, inspire, motivate, spur on, stir, stir up, fire up, stimulate, invigorate, vitalize, revitalize, embolden, fortify, rally; informal buck up, pep up, give a shot in the arm to. **2** *she had encouraged him to go:* **persuade**, coax, urge, press, push, pressure, pressurize, prod, goad, egg on, prompt, influence, sway. **3** *the Government was keen to encourage local businesses:* **support**, back, champion, promote, further, foster, nurture, cultivate, strengthen, stimulate; help, assist, aid, boost, fuel.
– OPPOSITES discourage, dissuade, hinder.

encouragement noun **1** *she needed a bit of encouragement:* **heartening**, cheering up, inspiration, motivation, stimulation, fortification; morale-boosting; informal a shot in the arm. **2** *they required no encouragement to get back to work:* **persuasion**, coaxing, urging, pressure, pressurization, prodding, prompting; spur, goad, inducement, incentive, bait, motive; informal carrot. **3** *the encouragement of foreign investment:* **support**, backing, championship, championing, sponsoring, promotion, furtherance, furthering, fostering, nurture, cultivation; help, assistance; N. Amer. boosterism.

encouraging adjective **1** *an encouraging start:* **promising**, hopeful, auspicious, propitious, favourable, bright, rosy; heartening, reassuring, cheering, comforting, welcome, pleasing, gratifying. **2** *my parents were very encouraging:* **supportive**, understanding, helpful; positive, responsive, enthusiastic.

encroach verb *she didn't want to encroach on his privacy:* **intrude**, trespass, impinge, obtrude, impose oneself, invade, infiltrate, interrupt, infringe, violate, interfere with, disturb; tread/step on someone's toes; informal horn in on, muscle in on.

encroachment noun **intrusion**, trespass, invasion, infiltration, incursion, obtrusion, infringement, impingement.

encumber verb **1** *her movements were encumbered by her heavy skirts:* **hamper**, hinder, obstruct, impede, cramp, inhibit, restrict, limit, constrain, restrain, bog down, retard, slow (down); inconvenience, disadvantage, handicap. **2** *they are encumbered with debt:* **burden**, load, weigh down, saddle; overwhelm, tax, stress, strain, overload, overburden; Brit. informal lumber.

encumbrance noun **1** *he soon found the old equipment a great encumbrance:* **hindrance**, obstruction, obstacle, impediment, constraint, handicap, inconvenience, nuisance, disadvantage, drawback. **2** *she knew she was an encumbrance to him:* **burden**, responsibility, obligation, liability, weight, load, stress, strain, pressure, trouble, worry; millstone, albatross, cross to bear.

encyclopedic adjective *he has an encyclopedic knowledge of food:* **comprehensive**, complete, thorough, thoroughgoing, full, exhaustive, in-depth, wide-ranging, all-inclusive, all-embracing, all-encompassing, universal, vast.

end noun **1** *Laura's house was at the end of the row:* **extremity**, furthermost part, limit; margin, edge, border, boundary, periphery; point, tip, tail end; N. Amer. tag end. **2** *the end of the novel:* **conclusion**, termination, ending, finish, close, resolution, climax, finale, culmination, denouement; epilogue, coda, peroration. **3** *a cigarette end:* **butt**, stub, stump, remnant; informal fag end, dog-end. **4** *wealth is a means and not an end in itself:* **aim**, goal, purpose, objective, object, holy grail, target; intention, intent, design, motive; aspiration, wish, desire, ambition. **5** *his end might come at any time:* **death**, dying, demise, passing, expiry, quietus; doom, extinction, annihilation, extermination, destruction; downfall, ruin, ruination, Waterloo; informal curtains; formal decease.
– OPPOSITES beginning.
verb **1** *the show ended with a wedding scene:* **finish**, conclude, terminate, come to an end, draw to a close, close, stop, cease; culminate, climax. build up to, lead up to, come to a head. **2** *she ended their relationship:* **break off**, call off, bring to an end, put an end to, stop, finish, terminate, discontinue; dissolve, cancel, annul.
– OPPOSITES begin.

endanger verb *river pollution is likely to endanger fish:* **imperil**, jeopardize, risk, put at risk, put in danger; threaten, pose a threat to, be a danger to, be detrimental to, damage, injure, harm.

endearing adjective *hedgehogs are endearing creatures:* **lovable**, adorable, cute, sweet, dear, delightful, lovely, charming, appealing, attractive, engaging, winning, captivating, enchanting, beguiling, winsome.

endearment noun **1** *his murmured endearments:* **term of affection**, term of endearment, pet name; (**endearments**) sweet nothings, sweet talk. **2** *he spoke to her without endearment:* **affection**, fondness, tenderness, feeling, sentiment, warmth, love, liking, care.

endeavour verb *the company endeavoured to expand its activities:* **try**, attempt, seek, undertake, aspire, aim, set out; strive, struggle, labour, toil, work, exert oneself, apply oneself, do one's best, do one's utmost, give one's all, be at pains; informal have a go/shot/stab, give something one's best

shot, do one's damnedest, go all out, bend over backwards.
noun **1** *an endeavour to build a more buoyant economy:* **attempt**, try, bid, effort, venture; informal go, crack, shot, stab, bash. **2** *several days of endeavour:* **effort**, exertion, striving, struggling, labouring, struggle, labour, hard work, application, industry; pains; informal sweat, {blood, sweat, and tears}, elbow grease; Brit. informal graft; Austral./NZ informal (hard) yakka. **3** *an extremely unwise endeavour:* **undertaking**, enterprise, venture, exercise, activity, exploit, deed, act, action, move; scheme, plan, project; informal caper.

ending noun *the story has a happy ending:* **end**, finish, close, closing, conclusion, resolution, summing-up, denouement, finale; cessation, stopping, termination, discontinuation.
– OPPOSITES beginning.

endless adjective **1** *a woman with endless energy:* **unlimited**, limitless, infinite, inexhaustible, boundless, unbounded, untold, immeasurable, measureless, incalculable; abundant, abounding, great; ceaseless, unceasing, unending, without end, everlasting, constant, continuous, continual, interminable, unfading, unfailing, perpetual, eternal, enduring, lasting. **2** *as children we played endless games:* **countless**, innumerable, untold, legion, numberless, unnumbered, numerous, very many, manifold, multitudinous, multifarious; a great number of, infinite numbers of, a multitude of; informal umpteen, no end of, loads of, stacks of, heaps of, masses of, oodles of, scads of, zillions of; N. Amer. informal gazillions of.
– OPPOSITES limited, few.

endorse verb *they fully endorse a trade agreement:* **support**, back, agree with, approve (of), favour, subscribe to, recommend, champion, stick up for, uphold, affirm, sanction; informal throw one's weight behind.
– OPPOSITES oppose.

endorsement noun **support**, backing, approval, seal of approval, agreement, recommendation, championship, patronage, affirmation, sanction.

endow verb **1** *Henry II endowed a hospital for poor pilgrims:* **finance**, fund, pay for, subsidize, support financially, settle money on; establish, found, set up, institute. **2** *nature endowed the human race with intelligence:* **provide**, supply, furnish, equip, invest, favour, bless, grace, gift; give, bestow.

endowment noun **1** *the endowment of a Chair of Botany:* **funding**, financing, subsidizing; establishment, foundation, institution. **2** *a generous endowment:* **bequest**, legacy, inheritance; gift, present, grant, award, donation, contribution, subsidy, settlement. **3** *his natural* *endowments:* **quality**, characteristic, feature, attribute, facility, faculty, ability, talent, gift, strength, aptitude, capability, capacity.

endurable adjective *his confinement had gradually become endurable:* **bearable**, tolerable, supportable, manageable, sustainable.
– OPPOSITES unbearable.

endurance noun **1** *she pushed him beyond the limit of his endurance:* **toleration**, tolerance, sufferance, forbearance, patience, acceptance, resignation, stoicism. **2** *the race is a test of endurance:* **stamina**, staying power, fortitude, perseverance, persistence, tenacity, doggedness, grit, indefatigability, resolution, determination; informal stickability.

endure verb **1** *he endured years of pain:* **undergo**, go through, live through, experience, meet, encounter; cope with, deal with, face, suffer, tolerate, put up with, brave, bear, withstand, sustain, weather; Scottish thole. **2** *I cannot endure such behaviour:* **tolerate**, bear, put up with, suffer, take; informal hack, stand for, stomach, swallow, abide, hold with; Brit. informal stick, wear, be doing with. **3** *God's love will endure for ever:* **last**, live, live on, go on, survive, abide, continue, persist, remain, stay.
– OPPOSITES fade.

enduring adjective *an enduring commitment to democracy and human rights:* **lasting**, long-lasting, abiding, durable, continuing, persisting, eternal, perennial, permanent, unending, everlasting; constant, stable, steady, steadfast, fixed, firm, unwavering, unfaltering, unchanging.
– OPPOSITES short-lived.

enemy noun **opponent**, adversary, rival, antagonist, combatant, challenger, competitor, opposer, opposition, competition, other side.
– OPPOSITES ally.

energetic adjective **1** *an energetic woman:* **active**, lively, dynamic, zestful, spirited, animated, vital, vibrant, bouncy, bubbly, exuberant, perky, frisky, sprightly, tireless, indefatigable, enthusiastic; informal peppy, sparky, feisty, full of beans, full of the joys of spring, bright-eyed and bushy-tailed. **2** *energetic exercises:* **vigorous**, strenuous, brisk; hard, arduous, demanding, taxing, tough, rigorous. **3** *an energetic advertising campaign:* **forceful**, vigorous, high-powered, all-out, determined, bold, powerful, potent; intensive, hard-hitting, pulling no punches, aggressive, high-octane; informal punchy, in-your-face.
– OPPOSITES lethargic, gentle, half-hearted.

energize verb **1** *people are energized by his ideas:* **enliven**, liven up, animate, vitalize, invigorate, perk up, excite, electrify, stimulate, stir up, fire up, rouse, motivate, move, drive, spur on, encourage, galvanize; informal pep up, buck up, give a shot in the

arm to. **2** *floor sensors energized by standing passengers:* **activate**, trigger, trip, operate, actuate, switch on, turn on, start, start up, power.

energy noun *she set out feeling full of energy:* **vitality**, vigour, life, liveliness, animation, vivacity, spirit, spiritedness, verve, enthusiasm, zest, vibrancy, spark, sparkle, effervescence, exuberance, buoyancy, sprightliness; strength, stamina, forcefulness, power, dynamism, drive; fire, passion, ardour, zeal; informal zip, zing, pep, pizzazz, punch, bounce, oomph, go, get-up-and-go, vim and vigour; N. Amer. informal feistiness.

enervate verb *the scorching sun enervated her:* **exhaust**, tire, fatigue, weary, wear out, devitalize, drain, sap, weaken, enfeeble, debilitate, incapacitate, prostrate; informal knock out, do in, shatter, fag out; Brit. informal knacker.
– OPPOSITES invigorate.

enervation noun **fatigue**, exhaustion, tiredness, weariness, lassitude, weakness, feebleness, debilitation, indisposition, prostration.

enfeeble verb *the animal was enfeebled by lack of nutrition:* **weaken**, debilitate, incapacitate, indispose, lay low; drain, sap, exhaust, tire, fatigue, devitalize.
– OPPOSITES strengthen.

enfold verb **1** *the summit was enfolded in white cloud:* **envelop**, engulf, sheathe, swathe, swaddle, cocoon, shroud, veil, cloak, drape, cover; surround, enclose, encase, encircle. **2** *he enfolded her in his arms:* **clasp**, hold, fold, wrap, squeeze, clutch, gather; embrace, hug, cuddle.

enforce verb **1** *the sheriff enforced the law:* **impose**, apply, administer, implement, bring to bear, discharge, execute, prosecute. **2** *they cannot enforce cooperation between the parties:* **force**, compel, coerce, exact, extort.

enforced adjective *an enforced break from work:* **compulsory**, obligatory, mandatory, involuntary, forced, imposed, required, requisite, stipulated, prescribed, contractual, binding, necessary, unavoidable, inescapable.
– OPPOSITES voluntary.

enfranchise verb *women over thirty were enfranchised in 1918:* **give the vote to**, give/grant suffrage to.

engage verb **1** *tasks which engage children's interest:* **capture**, catch, arrest, grab, draw, attract, gain, win, hold, grip, captivate, engross, absorb, occupy. **2** *he engaged a nursemaid:* **employ**, hire, recruit, take on, secure the services of, put on the payroll, enrol, appoint. **3** *the chance to engage in many social activities:* **participate in**, take part in, join in, become involved in, go in for, partake in/of, share in, play a part/role in; have a hand in, be a party to, enter into. **4** *infantry units engaged the enemy:* **fight**,

do battle with, wage war on/against, attack, take on, set upon, clash with, skirmish with; encounter, meet.
– OPPOSITES lose, dismiss.

engaged adjective **1** *he's otherwise engaged:* **busy**, occupied, unavailable; informal tied up. **2** *she's engaged to an American guy:* promised/pledged in marriage; attached; informal spoken for.
– OPPOSITES free, unattached.

engagement noun **1** *they broke off their engagement:* **marriage contract**. **2** *a business engagement:* **appointment**, meeting, arrangement, commitment; date, assignation, rendezvous. **3** *Britain's continued engagement in open trading:* **participation**, involvement, association. **4** *his engagement as a curate:* **employment**, appointment; work, job, post, situation. **5** *the first engagement of the war:* **battle**, fight, clash, confrontation, encounter, conflict, skirmish; warfare, action, combat, hostilities; informal dogfight.

engaging adjective *she had such an engaging smile:* **charming**, appealing, attractive, pretty, delightful, lovely, pleasing, pleasant, agreeable, likeable, lovable, sweet, winning, winsome, fetching, captivating, enchanting, bewitching; Scottish & N. English bonny.
– OPPOSITES unappealing.

engender verb *his works engendered considerable controversy:* **cause**, be the cause of, give rise to, bring about, occasion, lead to, result in, produce, create, generate, arouse, rouse, inspire, provoke, kindle, trigger, spark, stir up, whip up, induce, incite, instigate, foment.

engine noun **1** *a car engine:* **motor**, machine, mechanism. **2** *the main engine of change:* **cause**, agent, instrument, originator, initiator, generator.

engineer noun **1** *a structural engineer:* designer, planner, builder. **2** *the ship's engineer:* **operator**, driver, controller. **3** *the prime engineer of the approach:* **originator**, deviser, designer, architect, inventor, developer, creator; mastermind.
verb *he engineered a takeover deal:* **bring about**, arrange, pull off, bring off, contrive, manoeuvre, manipulate, negotiate, organize, orchestrate, choreograph, mount, stage, mastermind, originate, manage, stage-manage, coordinate, control, superintend, direct, conduct; informal wangle.

England noun Brit. informal Blighty; Austral./NZ informal Old Dart.

engrained adjective. See INGRAINED.

engrave verb **1** *my name was engraved on the ring:* **carve**, inscribe, cut (in), incise, chisel, chase, score, notch, etch, imprint, impress. **2** *the image was engraved in his memory:* **fix**, set, imprint, stamp, brand, impress, embed, etch.

engraving noun *an engraving of a Georgian coffee house:* **etching**, print, impression,

lithograph; plate, dry point, woodcut, linocut.

engross verb *the notes totally engrossed him:* **absorb**, engage, rivet, grip, hold, interest, involve, occupy, preoccupy; fascinate, captivate, enthral, intrigue.

engrossed adjective *he was engrossed in his book:* **absorbed**, involved, interested, occupied, preoccupied, immersed, caught up, riveted, gripped, rapt, fascinated, intent, captivated, enthralled, intrigued.

engrossing adjective **absorbing**, interesting, riveting, gripping, captivating, compelling, compulsive, fascinating, intriguing, enthralling; informal unputdownable.

engulf verb *their new home was engulfed by stinking brown flood water:* **inundate**, flood, deluge, immerse, swamp, swallow up, submerge; bury, envelop, overwhelm.

enhance verb *his dramatic appearance enhanced his reputation:* **increase**, add to, intensify, heighten, magnify, amplify, inflate, strengthen, build up, supplement, augment, boost, raise, lift, elevate, exalt; improve, enrich, complement.
– OPPOSITES diminish.

enigma noun *how it works is a complete enigma to me:* **mystery**, puzzle, riddle, conundrum, paradox, problem; a closed book; informal poser.

enigmatic adjective *she smiled that enigmatic smile again:* **mysterious**, inscrutable, puzzling, mystifying, baffling, perplexing, impenetrable, unfathomable, sphinx-like, Delphic, oracular; cryptic, elliptical, ambiguous, equivocal, paradoxical, obscure, oblique, secret.

enjoin verb *the Code enjoined members to trade fairly and responsibly:* **urge**, encourage, admonish, press; instruct, direct, require, order, command, tell, call on, demand, charge.

enjoy verb **1** *he enjoys playing the piano:* **like**, love, be fond of, be entertained by, take pleasure in, be keen on, delight in, appreciate, relish, revel in, adore, lap up, savour, luxuriate in, bask in; informal get a kick out of, get a thrill out of, get a buzz out of, go a bundle on. **2** *she had always enjoyed good health:* **benefit from**, have the benefit of; be blessed with, be favoured with, be endowed with, be possessed of, possess, own, boast.
– OPPOSITES dislike, lack.
■ **enjoy oneself** have fun, have a good time, have the time of one's life; make merry, celebrate, revel; informal party, have a ball, have a whale of a time, whoop it up, let one's hair down.

enjoyable adjective *a most enjoyable film:* **entertaining**, amusing, diverting, delightful, to one's liking, pleasant, congenial, convivial, lovely, fine, good, great, agreeable, pleasurable, delicious, delectable, satisfying, gratifying; marvellous, wonderful, magnificent, splendid; informal super, fantastic, fabulous, fab, terrific, grand, magic; Brit. informal brilliant, brill, smashing.

enjoyment noun *he has brought enjoyment and happiness to millions:* **pleasure**, fun, entertainment, amusement, diversion, recreation, relaxation; delight, happiness, merriment, joy, gaiety, jollity; satisfaction, gratification, liking, relish, gusto; humorous delectation.

enlarge verb **1** *they enlarged the scope of their research:* **extend**, expand, grow, add to, amplify, augment, magnify, build up, supplement; widen, broaden, stretch, lengthen; elongate, deepen, thicken. **2** *the lymph glands had enlarged:* **swell**, distend, bloat, bulge, dilate, tumefy, blow up, puff up, balloon. **3** *he enlarged on this subject:* **elaborate on**, expand on, add to, build on, flesh out, put flesh on the bones of, add detail to, expatiate on; develop, fill out, embellish, embroider.
– OPPOSITES reduce, shrink.

enlargement noun *the modernization and enlargement of the factory:* **expansion**, extension, growth, amplification, augmentation, addition, magnification, widening, broadening, lengthening; elongation, deepening, thickening; swelling, distension, dilation, tumefaction.

enlighten verb *will you kindly enlighten me as to what this is?* **inform**, tell, make aware, open someone's eyes, notify, illuminate, apprise, brief, bring up to date; disabuse, set straight; informal put in the picture, clue in, fill in, put wise, bring up to speed.

enlightened adjective **informed**, well informed, aware, sophisticated, advanced, developed, liberal, open-minded, broad-minded, educated, knowledgeable, wise; civilized, refined, cultured, cultivated.
– OPPOSITES benighted.

enlightenment noun *the reader will be hoping for enlightenment from the text:* **insight**, understanding, awareness, wisdom, education, learning, knowledge; illumination, awakening, instruction, teaching; sophistication, advancement, development, open-mindedness, broad-mindedness; culture, refinement, cultivation, civilization.

enlist verb **1** *he enlisted in the Royal Engineers:* **join up**, join, enrol in, sign up for, volunteer for. **2** *he was enlisted in the army:* **recruit**, call up, enrol, sign up; conscript; US draft, induct. **3** *he enlisted the help of a friend:* **obtain**, engage, secure, win, get, procure.

enliven verb **1** *a meeting enlivened by her wit and vivacity:* **liven up**, spice up, add spice to, ginger up, vitalize, leaven; informal perk up, pep up. **2** *the visit had enlivened my mother:* **cheer up**, brighten up, liven up, raise someone's spirits, uplift, gladden, buoy up, animate, vivify, vitalize, invigorate, restore, revive, refresh, stimulate, rouse, boost, exhilarate; N. Amer. light a fire under; informal perk up, buck up, pep up.

en masse adverb *the Cabinet resigned en masse:* **(all) together**, as a group, as one, en bloc, as a whole, in a body, wholesale.

enmesh verb *the party became increasingly enmeshed in the parliamentary system:* **embroil**, entangle, ensnare, snare, trap, entrap, ensnarl, involve, catch up, mix up, bog down, mire.

enmity noun *a world free from enmity between nations and races:* **hostility**, animosity, antagonism, friction, antipathy, animus, acrimony, bitterness, rancour, resentment, aversion, ill feeling, bad feeling, ill will, bad blood, hatred, hate, loathing, odium; malice, spite, spitefulness, venom, malevolence; Brit. informal needle.
– OPPOSITES friendship.

ennoble verb *choreography tended to ennoble rustic figures:* **dignify**, honour, exalt, elevate, raise, enhance, add dignity to, distinguish; magnify, glorify, aggrandize.
– OPPOSITES demean.

enormity noun **1** *the enormity of the task:* **immensity**, hugeness; size, extent, magnitude, greatness. **2** *the enormity of his crimes:* **wickedness**, evil, vileness, baseness, depravity; outrageousness, monstrousness, hideousness, heinousness, horror, atrocity; villainy, cruelty, inhumanity, mercilessness, brutality, savagery, viciousness. **3** *the enormities of the regime:* **outrage**, horror, evil, atrocity, barbarity, abomination, monstrosity, obscenity, iniquity; crime, sin, violation, wrong, offence, disgrace, injustice, abuse.

enormous adjective *enormous sums of money:* **huge**, vast, immense, gigantic, very big, great, giant, massive, colossal, mammoth, tremendous, mighty, monumental, epic, prodigious, mountainous, king-size(d), titanic, towering, elephantine, gargantuan; informal mega, monster, whopping (great), humongous, jumbo, astronomical; Brit. informal whacking (great), ginormous.
– OPPOSITES tiny.

enormously adverb **1** *an enormously important factor:* **very**, extremely, really, exceedingly, exceptionally, tremendously, immensely, hugely; singularly, particularly, eminently; informal terrifically, awfully, terribly, seriously, desperately, ultra, damn, damned; Brit. informal ever so, well, dead, jolly; N. Amer. informal real, mighty, darned. **2** *prices vary enormously:* **considerably**, greatly, very much, a great deal, a lot.
– OPPOSITES slightly.

enough determiner *they had enough food for the journey:* **sufficient**, adequate, ample, the necessary; informal plenty of.

e

– OPPOSITES insufficient.

pronoun *there's enough for everyone:* **sufficient**, plenty, a sufficient amount, an adequate amount, as much as necessary; a sufficiency, an ample supply; one's fill.

enquire, inquire verb 1 *I enquired about part-time training courses:* **ask**, make enquiries, question someone, request information. 2 *the commission is to enquire into alleged illegal payments:* **investigate**, conduct an enquiry, probe, look into; research, examine, explore, delve into; informal check out.

enquiring, inquiring adjective *youngsters with enquiring minds:* **inquisitive**, curious, interested, questioning, probing, searching; investigative.

enquiry, inquiry noun 1 *telephone enquiries:* **question**, query. 2 *an enquiry into alleged security leaks:* **investigation**, probe, examination, exploration; inquest, hearing.

enrage verb *the scheme is bound to enrage farmers:* **anger**, infuriate, incense, madden, inflame; antagonize, provoke, exasperate; informal drive mad/crazy, drive up the wall, make someone see red, make someone's blood boil, make someone's hackles rise, get someone's back up, get someone's dander up; N. Amer. informal burn up.
– OPPOSITES placate.

enraged adjective **furious**, infuriated, very angry, irate, incensed, raging, incandescent, fuming, ranting, raving, seething, beside oneself; informal mad, hopping mad, wild, livid, boiling, apoplectic, hot under the collar, on the warpath, foaming at the mouth, steamed up, in a paddy, fit to be tied.
– OPPOSITES calm.

enrapture verb *all of us in the theatre were enraptured by the music:* **delight**, enchant, captivate, charm, enthral, entrance, bewitch, beguile, transport, thrill, excite, exhilarate, intoxicate, take someone's breath away; informal bowl someone over, blow someone's mind.

enrich verb *the fine arts can certainly enrich our society:* **enhance**, improve, better, add to, augment; supplement, complement; boost, elevate, raise, lift, refine.
– OPPOSITES spoil.

enrol verb 1 *they both enrolled for the course:* **register**, sign on/up, put one's name down, apply, volunteer; matriculate; enter, join. 2 *280 new members were enrolled:* **accept**, admit, take on, register, sign on/up, recruit, engage; matriculate; impanel.

en route adverb *he was en route from Paris to Bordeaux:* **on the way**, in transit, during the journey, along/on the road, on the move; coming, going, proceeding, travelling.

ensconce verb *Agnes ensconced herself in their bedroom:* **settle**, install, plant, position,

seat, sit, sit down; establish; informal park, plonk.

ensemble noun 1 *a Bulgarian folk ensemble:* **group**, band; company, troupe, cast, chorus, corps; informal combo. 2 *the buildings present a charming provincial ensemble:* **whole**, entity, unit, body, set, combination, composite, package; sum, total, totality, entirety, aggregate. 3 *a pink and black ensemble:* **outfit**, costume, suit; separates, coordinates; informal get-up.

enshrine verb *the following rights should be enshrined in the treaty:* **set down**, set out, spell out, express, lay down, set in stone, embody, realize, manifest, incorporate, represent, contain, include, preserve, treasure, immortalize, cherish.

ensign noun *the ship flew a British ensign:* **flag**, standard, colour(s), banner, pennant, pennon, streamer, banderole.

enslavement noun *the enslavement of Africans continued for most of the nineteenth century:* **slavery**, servitude, bondage, forced labour; exploitation, oppression, bonds, chains, fetters, shackles, yoke.
– OPPOSITES liberation.

ensnare verb *the larvae construct pits to ensnare their prey:* **capture**, catch, trap, entrap, snare, net; entangle, embroil, enmesh.

ensue verb *a fierce argument ensued from his remark:* **result**, follow, be consequent on, develop, proceed, succeed, emerge, stem, arise, derive, issue; occur, happen, take place, come next/after, transpire, supervene.

ensure verb 1 *ensure that the surface is completely clean:* **make sure**, make certain, see to it; check, confirm, establish, verify. 2 *legislation to ensure equal opportunities for all:* **secure**, guarantee, assure, certify, set the seal on, clinch.

entail verb *this proposal will entail additional expenditure:* **involve**, necessitate, require, need, demand, call for; mean, imply; cause, produce, result in, lead to, give rise to, occasion.

entangle verb 1 *their parachutes became entangled:* **twist**, intertwine, entwine, tangle, ravel, snarl, knot, coil, mat. 2 *the fish are easily entangled in fine nets:* **catch**, capture, trap, snare, ensnare, entrap, enmesh. 3 *he was entangled in a lawsuit:* **involve**, implicate, embroil, mix up, catch up, bog down, mire.

entanglement noun 1 *their entanglement in the war:* **involvement**, embroilment. 2 *romantic entanglements:* **affair**, relationship, love affair, romance, amour, fling, dalliance, liaison, involvement, intrigue; complication.

entente noun *the Foreign Office was reluctant to upset the entente with France:* **understanding**, agreement, arrangement, entente cordiale, settlement, deal; alliance, treaty, pact, accord, convention, concordat.

enter verb 1 *police entered the house:* **go in/into**, come in/into, get in/into, set foot in, cross the threshold of, gain access to. 2 *a bullet entered his chest:* **penetrate**, pierce, puncture, perforate. 3 *he entered politics in 1979:* **get involved in**, join, throw oneself into, engage in, embark on, take up; participate in, take part in, play a part/role in, contribute to. 4 *the planning entered a new phase:* **reach**, move into, get to, begin, start, commence. 5 *they entered the Army at eighteen:* **join**, become a member of, enrol in/for, enlist in, volunteer for, sign up for; take up. 6 *she entered a cookery competition:* **go in for**, put one's name down for, register for, enrol for, sign on/up for; compete in, take part in, participate in. 7 *the cashier entered the details in a ledger:* **record**, write, set down, put down, take down, note, jot down; put on record, minute, register, log. 8 *please enter your password:* **key (in)**, type (in), tap in.
– OPPOSITES leave.

enterprise noun 1 *a joint enterprise:* **undertaking**, endeavour, venture, exercise, activity, operation, task, business, proceeding; project, scheme, plan, programme, campaign. 2 *a woman with enterprise:* **initiative**, resourcefulness, entrepreneurialism, imagination, ingenuity, inventiveness, originality, creativity; quick-wittedness, native wit, cleverness; enthusiasm, dynamism, drive, ambition, energy; boldness, daring, courage; informal gumption, get-up-and-go, oomph. 3 *a profit-making enterprise:* **business**, company, firm, venture, organization, operation, concern, corporation, establishment, partnership; informal outfit, set-up.

enterprising adjective *some enterprising teachers have now started their own recycling scheme:* **resourceful**, entrepreneurial, imaginative, ingenious, inventive, creative; quick-witted, clever, bright, sharp, sharp-witted; enthusiastic, dynamic, ambitious, energetic; bold, daring, courageous, adventurous; informal go-ahead.
– OPPOSITES unimaginative.

entertain verb 1 *he wrote stories to entertain them:* **amuse**, divert, delight, please, charm, cheer, interest; engage, occupy, absorb, engross. 2 *he entertains foreign visitors:* **receive**, play host/hostess to, invite (round/over), throw a party for; wine and dine, feast, cater for, feed, treat, welcome, fête. 3 *we don't entertain much:* **receive guests**, have people round/over, have company, hold/throw a party. 4 *I would never entertain such an idea:* **consider**, give consideration to, contemplate, think about, give thought to; countenance, tolerate, support.
– OPPOSITES bore, reject.

entertainer noun **performer**, artiste, artist.

entertaining adjective *she found him a charming and entertaining companion:*

delightful, enjoyable, diverting, amusing, pleasing, agreeable, appealing, engaging, interesting, fascinating, absorbing, compelling; humorous, funny, comical; informal fun.

entertainment noun 1 *he read for entertainment:* **amusement**, pleasure, leisure, recreation, relaxation, fun, enjoyment, interest, diversion; N. Amer. informal rec. 2 *an entertainment for the emperor:* **show**, performance, presentation, production, extravaganza, spectacle.

enthral verb *last night he enthralled fans from six to sixty:* **captivate**, charm, enchant, bewitch, fascinate, beguile, entrance, delight; win, ensnare, absorb, engross, rivet, grip, transfix, hypnotize, mesmerize, spellbind.
– OPPOSITES bore.

enthralling adjective **fascinating**, entrancing, enchanting, bewitching, captivating, charming, beguiling, delightful; absorbing, engrossing, compelling, riveting, gripping, exciting, spellbinding; informal unputdownable.

enthuse verb 1 *I enthused about the idea:* **rave**, be enthusiastic, gush, wax lyrical, be effusive, get all worked up, rhapsodize; praise to the skies; informal go wild/mad/crazy; N. Amer. informal ballyhoo. 2 *he enthuses people and they get good results:* **motivate**, inspire, stimulate, encourage, spur (on), galvanize, rouse, excite, stir (up), fire, inspirit.

enthusiasm noun 1 *she worked with enthusiasm:* **eagerness**, keenness, ardour, fervour, passion, zeal, zest, gusto, energy, verve, vigour, vehemence, fire, spirit, avidity; wholeheartedness, commitment, willingness, devotion, earnestness; informal get-up-and-go. 2 *they put their enthusiasms to good use:* **interest**, passion, obsession, mania; inclination, preference, penchant, predilection, fancy; pastime, hobby, recreation, pursuit.
– OPPOSITES apathy.

enthusiast noun *a good present for a railway enthusiast:* **fan**, devotee, aficionado, lover, admirer, follower; expert, connoisseur, authority, pundit; informal buff, freak, fanatic, nut, fiend, addict, maniac.

enthusiastic adjective *an enthusiastic supporter of Scottish rugby:* **eager**, keen, avid, ardent, fervent, passionate, zealous, vehement; excited, wholehearted, committed, devoted, fanatical, earnest.

entice verb *the show should entice a new audience into the theatre:* **tempt**, lure, attract, appeal to; invite, persuade, convince, beguile, coax, woo; seduce, lead on; informal sweet-talk.

enticement noun *the enticement of power:* **lure**, temptation, allure, attraction, appeal, draw, pull, bait; charm, seduction, fascination; informal come-on.

enticing adjective *we caught enticing*

e

glimpses of tables laden with food: **tempting**, alluring, attractive, appealing, inviting, seductive, beguiling, charming; magnetic, irresistible.

entire adjective **1** *I devoted my entire life to him:* **whole**, complete, total, full; undivided. **2** *only one of the gates is entire:* **intact**, unbroken, undamaged, unimpaired, unscathed, unspoiled, perfect, in one piece. **3** *they are in entire agreement:* **absolute**, total, utter, out-and-out, thorough, wholehearted; unqualified, unreserved, outright.
– OPPOSITES partial, broken.

entirely adverb **1** *that's entirely out of the question:* **absolutely**, completely, totally, wholly, utterly, quite; altogether, in every respect, thoroughly, downright, one hundred per cent. **2** *a gift entirely for charitable purposes:* **solely**, only, exclusively, purely, merely, just, alone.

entirety noun *in the 1920s, cheap production constituted almost the entirety of British film-making:* **whole**, total, aggregate, totality, sum total.
– OPPOSITES part.
■ **in its entirety** completely, entirely, totally, fully, wholly; in every respect, in every way, one hundred per cent, all the way, every inch, to the hilt, to the core.

entitle verb **1** *this pass entitles you to visit the museum:* **qualify**, make eligible, authorize, allow, permit; enable, empower. **2** *a chapter entitled 'Comedy and Tragedy':* **title**, name, call, label, designate, dub.

entitlement noun **1** *their entitlement to benefits:* **right**, prerogative, claim; permission, dispensation, privilege. **2** *your holiday entitlement:* **allowance**, allocation, quota, ration, limit.

entity noun *a single entity:* **being**, creature, individual, organism, life form; person; body, object, article, thing.

entomb verb *mummified bodies were entombed in the Pyramids:* **inter**, lay to rest, bury; informal plant.

entourage noun *the king's entourage:* **retinue**, escort, cortège, train, suite; court, staff, bodyguard; attendants, companions, retainers.

entrails plural noun **intestines**, bowels, guts, viscera, internal organs, vital organs; offal; informal insides, innards.

entrance¹ noun **1** *the main entrance:* **entry**, way in, access, ingress, approach; door, portal, gate; opening, mouth; entrance hall, foyer, lobby, porch; N. Amer. entryway. **2** *the entrance of Mrs Knight:* **appearance**, arrival, entry, ingress, coming. **3** *he was refused entrance:* **admission**, admittance, (right of) entry, access, ingress.
– OPPOSITES exit, departure.

entrance² verb **1** *I was entranced by her beauty:* **enchant**, bewitch, beguile, captivate, mesmerize, hypnotize, spellbind;

enthral, engross, absorb, fascinate; stun, overpower, electrify; charm, delight; informal bowl over, knock out. **2** *Orpheus entranced the wild beasts:* **cast a spell on**, bewitch, hex, spellbind, hypnotize, mesmerize.

entrant noun **1** *university entrants:* **new member**, new arrival, beginner, newcomer, fresher, freshman, recruit; novice, neophyte; N. Amer. tenderfoot, greenhorn; informal rookie. **2** *a prize will be awarded to the best entrant:* **competitor**, contestant, contender, participant; candidate, applicant.

entrap verb **1** *fishing lines can entrap wildlife:* **trap**, snare, ensnare, entangle, enmesh; catch, capture. **2** *he was entrapped by an undercover policeman:* **entice**, lure, inveigle; bait, decoy, trap; lead on, trick, deceive, dupe, hoodwink; informal set up, frame; Brit. informal fit up.

entreat verb *his friends entreated him not to go:* **implore**, beg, plead with, pray, ask, request; bid, enjoin, appeal to, call on, petition, solicit.

entreaty noun *he ignored her entreaties:* **plea**, appeal, request, petition; suit, application, claim; solicitation, supplication; prayer.

entrée noun **1** *there are a dozen entrées on the menu:* **main course**, main dish. **2** *an excellent entrée into the profession:* **(means of) entry**, entrance, ingress; route, path, avenue, way, key, passport.

entrench, intrench verb **establish**, settle, lodge, set, root, install, plant, embed, seat; informal dig in.

entrenched, intrenched adjective *officials tended to cling to entrenched attitudes:* **ingrained**, established, confirmed, fixed, firm, deep-seated, deep-rooted; unshakeable, indelible, ineradicable, inexorable.

entrepreneur noun **businessman/woman**, enterpriser, speculator, tycoon, magnate, mogul; dealer, trader; promoter, impresario; informal wheeler-dealer, whizz-kid, mover and shaker, go-getter, high-flyer.

entrust verb **1** *he was entrusted with the task:* **charge**, invest, endow; burden, encumber, saddle. **2** *the powers entrusted to the Home Secretary:* **assign**, confer on, bestow on, vest in, consign; delegate, depute, devolve; give, grant, vouchsafe. **3** *she entrusted them to the hospital:* **hand over**, give custody of, turn over, commit, consign, deliver.

entry noun **1** *my moment of entry:* **appearance**, arrival, entrance, ingress, coming. **2** *the entry to the flats:* **entrance**, way in, access, ingress, approach; door, portal, gate; entrance hall, foyer, lobby; N. Amer. entryway. **3** *he was refused entry into the country:* **admission**, admittance, entrance, access, ingress. **4** *entries in the cash book:* **item**, record, note, listing; memo, memorandum; account. **5** *we must pick a winner from the entries:* **contestant**,

competitor, contender, entrant, participant; candidate, applicant; submission, entry form, application.
– OPPOSITES departure, exit.

entwine verb *her hair was entwined with ropes of pearls:* **wind round**, twist round, coil round; weave, intertwine, interlace, interweave; entangle, tangle; twine, braid, plait, knit.

enumerate verb *he enumerated four objectives:* **list**, itemize, set out, give; cite, name, specify, identify, spell out, detail, particularize.

enunciate verb **1** *she enunciated each word slowly:* **pronounce**, articulate; say, speak, utter, voice, vocalize, sound, mouth. **2** *a document enunciating the policy:* **express**, state, put into words, declare, profess, set forth, assert, affirm; put forward, air, proclaim.

envelop verb *the gases of the atmosphere that envelop the earth:* **surround**, cover, enfold, engulf, encircle, encompass, cocoon, sheathe, swathe, enclose; cloak, screen, shield, veil, shroud.

envelope noun **wrapper**, wrapping, sleeve, cover, covering, casing.

enviable adjective *this hotel has an enviable position in the main square:* **desirable**, desired, favoured, sought-after, admirable, covetable, attractive; fortunate, lucky; informal to die for.

envious adjective *she felt envious of her friend's beauty:* **jealous**, covetous, desirous; grudging, begrudging, resentful; bitter, green-eyed.

environment noun **1** *birds from many environments:* **habitat**, territory, domain; surroundings, conditions. **2** *proper research is impracticable in the hospital environment:* **situation**, **setting**, milieu, background, backdrop, scene, location; context, framework; sphere, world, realm; ambience, atmosphere. **3** *the impact of pesticides on the environment:* **the natural world**, nature, the earth, the ecosystem, the biosphere, Mother Nature; wildlife, flora and fauna, the countryside.

environmentalist noun *environmentalists are pressing for a ban on logging:* **conservationist**, preservationist, ecologist, nature-lover; informal ecofreak, tree hugger.

environs plural noun *the environs of London:* **surroundings**, surrounding area, vicinity; locality, neighbourhood, district, region; precincts; N. Amer. vicinage.

envisage verb **1** *it was envisaged that the hospital would open soon:* **foresee**, predict, forecast, anticipate, expect, think likely. **2** *I cannot envisage what the future holds:* **imagine**, contemplate, visualize, envision, picture; conceive of, think of.

envoy noun *he served as an envoy to France:* **ambassador**, emissary, diplomat, consul, attaché, chargé d'affaires, plenipotentiary;

nuncio; representative, delegate, proxy, surrogate, liaison, spokesperson; agent, intermediary, mediator; informal go-between.

envy noun **1** *a pang of envy:* **jealousy**, covetousness; resentment, bitterness, discontent; the green-eyed monster. **2** *the firm is the envy of Europe:* **finest**, best, pride, top, cream, jewel, flower, leading light, the crème de la crème.
verb **1** *I admired and envied her:* **be envious of**, be jealous of; begrudge, be resentful of. **2** *we envied her lifestyle:* **covet**, desire, aspire to, wish for, want, long for, yearn for, hanker after, crave.

ephemeral adjective *fashions are ephemeral:* **transitory**, transient, fleeting, passing, short-lived, momentary, brief, short; temporary, impermanent, short-term; fly-by-night.
– OPPOSITES permanent.

epic noun **1** *the epics of Homer:* **heroic poem**; story, saga, legend, romance, chronicle, myth, fable, tale. **2** *a big Hollywood epic:* **long film**; informal blockbuster.
adjective **1** *a traditional epic poem:* **heroic**, long, grand, monumental, Homeric, Miltonian. **2** *their epic journey:* **ambitious**, heroic, grand, great, Herculean; very long, monumental.

epicure noun *as an epicure, he is entranced by their new range of speciality foods:* **gourmet**, gastronome, gourmand, connoisseur; informal foodie.

epicurean noun *a generous, life-loving epicurean:* **hedonist**, sensualist, pleasure-seeker, sybarite, voluptuary, bon viveur; epicure, gourmet, gastronome, connoisseur, gourmand.
adjective *their careers have been undone by epicurean excess:* **hedonistic**, sensualist, pleasure-seeking, self-indulgent, sybaritic, voluptuary, lotus-eating; decadent, unrestrained, extravagant, intemperate, immoderate; gluttonous, gourmandizing.

epidemic noun **1** *an epidemic of typhoid:* **outbreak**, plague, pandemic, epizootic. **2** *a joyriding epidemic:* **spate**, rash, wave, eruption, outbreak, craze; flood, torrent; upsurge, upturn, increase, growth, rise.
adjective *investigative reporting seems epidemic in an election year:* **rife**, rampant, widespread, wide-ranging, extensive, pervasive; global, universal, ubiquitous; endemic, pandemic, epizootic.

epigram noun *a witty epigram:* **witticism**, quip, jest, pun, bon mot; saying, maxim, adage, aphorism, apophthegm, epigraph; informal one-liner, wisecrack, (old) chestnut.

epigrammatic adjective *her short, epigrammatic verses:* **concise**, succinct, pithy, aphoristic; incisive, short and sweet; witty, clever, quick-witted, piquant, sharp; informal snappy.
– OPPOSITES expansive.

e

epilogue noun *the body of the book is summarized in the epilogue:* **afterword**, postscript, PS, coda, codicil, appendix, tailpiece, supplement, addendum, postlude, rider, back matter; conclusion.
– OPPOSITES prologue.

episode noun **1** *the best episode of his career:* **incident**, event, occurrence, happening; occasion, interlude, chapter, experience, adventure, exploit; matter, affair, thing. **2** *the final episode of the series:* **instalment**, chapter, passage; part, portion, section, component; programme, show. **3** *an episode of illness:* **period**, spell, bout, attack, phase; informal dose.

episodic adjective **1** *episodic wheezing:* **intermittent**, sporadic, periodic, fitful, irregular, spasmodic, occasional. **2** *an episodic account of the war:* **in episodes**, in instalments, in sections, in parts.
– OPPOSITES continuous.

epistle noun (formal) **letter**, missive, communication, dispatch, note, line; correspondence, news.

epitaph noun *an epitaph on a tombstone:* **elegy**, commemoration, obituary; inscription, legend.

epithet noun *these works earned him the epithet 'the Spanish Heretic':* **sobriquet**, nickname, byname, title, name, label, tag; description, designation; informal moniker, handle.

epitome noun *he was the epitome of respectability:* **personification**, embodiment, incarnation, paragon; essence, quintessence, archetype, paradigm; typification; exemplar, model, soul, example; height.

epitomize verb *the town epitomizes the pioneer spirit:* **embody**, encapsulate, typify, exemplify, represent, manifest, symbolize, illustrate, sum up; personify; formal reify.

epoch noun *the Tudor epoch:* **era**, age, period, time, span, stage; aeon.

equable adjective **1** *an equable man:* **even-tempered**, calm, composed, collected, self-possessed, relaxed, easy-going; nonchalant, insouciant, mellow, mild, tranquil, placid, stable, level-headed; imperturbable, unexcitable, untroubled, well balanced; informal unflappable, together, laid-back. **2** *an equable climate:* **stable**, constant, uniform, unvarying, consistent, unchanging, changeless; moderate, temperate.
– OPPOSITES temperamental, extreme.

equal adjective **1** *lines of equal length:* **identical**, uniform, alike, like, the same, equivalent; matching, comparable, similar, corresponding. **2** *fares equal to a fortnight's wages:* **equivalent**, identical, amounting, proportionate to, commensurate with, on a par with. **3** *equal treatment before the law:* **unbiased**, impartial, non-partisan, fair, just, equitable; unprejudiced, non-discriminatory, egalitarian; neutral,

objective, disinterested. **4** *an equal contest:* **evenly matched**, even, balanced, level; on a par, on an equal footing; informal fifty-fifty, level pegging, neck and neck.
– OPPOSITES different, discriminatory.
noun *they did not treat him as their equal:* **equivalent**, peer, fellow, coequal, like; counterpart, match, parallel.
verb **1** *two plus two equals four:* **be equal to**, be equivalent to, be the same as; come to, amount to, make, total, add up to. **2** *he equalled the world record:* **match**, reach, parallel, be level with, measure up to. **3** *the fable equals that of any other poet:* **be as good as**, be a match for, measure up to, equate with; be in the same league as, rival, compete with.
■ **equal to** capable of, fit for, up to, good/strong enough for; suitable for, suited to, appropriate for; informal having what it takes.

equality noun **1** *we promote equality for women:* **fairness**, equal rights, equal opportunities, equitability, egalitarianism; impartiality, even-handedness; justice. **2** *equality between supply and demand:* **parity**, similarity, comparability, correspondence; likeness, resemblance; uniformity, evenness, balance, equilibrium, consistency, agreement, congruence, symmetry.

equalize verb **1** *attempts to equalize their earnings:* **make even**, make even, even out/up, level, regularize, standardize, balance, square, match; bring into line. **2** *Villa equalized in the second half:* **level the score**, draw.

equanimity noun *she was able to confront the daily crises with equanimity:* **composure**, calm, level-headedness, self-possession, cool-headedness, presence of mind; serenity, tranquillity, phlegm, imperturbability, equilibrium; poise, assurance, self-confidence, aplomb, sangfroid, nerve; informal cool.
– OPPOSITES anxiety.

equate verb **1** *he equates criticism with treachery:* **identify**, compare, bracket, class, associate, connect, link, relate, ally. **2** *the rent equates to £24 per square foot:* **correspond**, be equivalent, amount; equal. **3** *moves to equate supply and demand:* **equalize**, balance, even out/up, level, square, tally, match; make equal, make even, make equivalent.

equation noun **1** *a quadratic equation:* **mathematical problem**, sum, calculation, question. **2** *identification of success with riches:* **identification**, association, connection, matching; equivalence, correspondence, agreement, comparison. **3** *other factors came into the equation:* **situation**, problem, case, question; quandary, predicament.

equatorial adjective *the equatorial regions:* **tropical**, hot, humid, sultry.

– OPPOSITES polar.

equestrian adjective *an equestrian statue:* **on horseback**, mounted, riding.
noun *tracks for equestrians:* **(horse) rider**, horseman, horsewoman, jockey.

equilibrium noun **1** *the equilibrium of the economy:* **balance**, symmetry, equipoise, parity, equality; stability. **2** *his equilibrium was never shaken:* **composure**, calm, equanimity, sangfroid; level-headedness, cool-headedness, imperturbability, poise, presence of mind; self-possession, self-command; impassivity, placidity, tranquillity, serenity; informal cool.
– OPPOSITES imbalance, agitation.

equip verb **1** *the boat was equipped with a flare gun:* **provide**, furnish, supply, issue, kit out, stock, provision, arm, endow. **2** *the course will equip them for the workplace:* **prepare**, qualify, suit.

equipment noun *the museum has a collection of early sound-recording equipment:* **apparatus**, paraphernalia, articles, appliances, impedimenta; tools, utensils, implements, instruments, hardware, gadgets, gadgetry; stuff, things; kit, tackle; resources, supplies; trappings, appurtenances, accoutrements; informal gear.

equitable adjective *Parliament is to distribute the burden of tax in an equitable way:* **fair**, just, impartial, even-handed, unbiased, unprejudiced, egalitarian; disinterested, objective, neutral, non-partisan, open-minded; informal fair and square.
– OPPOSITES unfair.

equity noun **1** *the equity of Finnish society:* **fairness**, justness, impartiality, egalitarianism; objectivity, balance, open-mindedness. **2** *he owns 25% of the equity in the property:* **value**, worth; ownership, rights, proprietorship.

equivalence noun *equivalence of birth and death rates is rare in human populations:* **equality**, sameness, interchangeability, comparability, correspondence; uniformity, similarity, likeness, nearness.

equivalent adjective *a degree or equivalent qualification:* **equal**, identical; similar, parallel, analogous, comparable, corresponding, commensurate; approximate, near.
noun *Denmark's equivalent of the Daily Mirror:* **counterpart**, parallel, alternative, match, analogue, twin, opposite number; equal, peer.

equivocal adjective *an equivocal statement:* **ambiguous**, indefinite, non-committal, vague, imprecise, inexact, inexplicit, hazy; unclear, cryptic, enigmatic; ambivalent, uncertain, unsure, indecisive.
– OPPOSITES definite.

equivocated verb *the government have equivocated too often in the past:* **prevaricate**, be evasive, be non-committal, be vague, be ambiguous, dodge the issue, beat about the bush, hedge one's bets, pussyfoot around; vacillate, shilly-shally, waver; temporize, hesitate, stall; Brit. hum and haw; informal sit on the fence, duck the issue; rare tergiversate.

era noun *the Stalinist era:* **epoch**, age, period, time, span, aeon; generation.

eradicate verb *make sure that the lice have all been eradicated:* **get rid of**, remove, obliterate; exterminate, destroy, annihilate, kill, wipe out; abolish, stamp out, extinguish, quash; erase, efface, excise, expunge.

erase verb **1** *they erased his name from all lists:* **delete**, rub out, wipe off, blot out, blank out, cancel; efface, expunge, excise, remove, obliterate, eliminate. **2** *the old differences in style were erased:* **destroy**, wipe out, obliterate, eradicate, abolish, stamp out, quash.

erect adjective **1** *she held her body erect:* **upright**, straight, vertical, perpendicular; standing. **2** *an erect penis:* **engorged**, enlarged, swollen, tumescent; hard, stiff. **3** *the dog's fur was erect:* **bristling**, standing on end, upright.
– OPPOSITES bent, flaccid, flat.
verb **1** *the bridge was erected in 1973:* **build**, construct, put up; assemble, put together, fabricate. **2** *the party that erected the welfare state:* **establish**, form, set up, found, institute, initiate, create, organize.
– OPPOSITES demolish, dismantle, lower.

erection noun **1** *the erection of a house:* **construction**, building, assembly, fabrication, elevation. **2** *a bleak concrete erection:* **building**, structure, edifice, construction, pile. **3** *men who cannot get an erection:* **erect penis**, phallus; tumescence, tumidity.

ergo adverb *I'm a writer, ergo I write:* **therefore**, consequently, so, as a result, hence, thus, accordingly, for that reason, that being the case, on that account; formal whence.

erode verb *the soil has been eroded by the rainwater:* **wear away/down**, abrade, grind down, crumble; weather; eat away at, dissolve, corrode, rot, decay; undermine, weaken, deteriorate, destroy.

erosion noun *the erosion of the cliffs:* **wearing away**, abrasion, attrition; weathering; dissolution, corrosion, decay; deterioration, disintegration, destruction.

erotic adjective *erotic literature:* **sexually arousing**, sexually stimulating, titillating, suggestive; pornographic, sexually explicit, lewd, smutty, hard-core, soft-core, dirty, racy, risqué, ribald, naughty; sexual, sexy, sensual, amatory, seductive, alluring, tantalizing; informal blue, X-rated, steamy, raunchy; euphemistic adult.

err verb **1** *the judge had erred:* **make a mistake**, be wrong, be in error, be mistaken,

e

blunder, be incorrect, miscalculate, get it wrong; informal slip up, screw up, foul up, goof, make a boo-boo, bark up the wrong tree, get the wrong end of the stick; Brit. informal boob. **2** *she struck them when they erred:* **misbehave**, be bad, be naughty, get up to mischief, cause trouble; sin, transgress, lapse; clown about/around, fool about/around, act the goat; informal mess about/around, act up; Brit. informal play up.

errand noun *he ran errands for local shopkeepers:* **task**, job, chore, assignment; collection, delivery; mission, undertaking.

errant adjective *he fined the errant councillors:* **offending**, guilty, culpable, misbehaving, delinquent, lawbreaking; troublesome, unruly, disobedient.
– OPPOSITES innocent.

erratic adjective *there's no accounting for his erratic behaviour:* **unpredictable**, inconsistent, changeable, variable, inconstant, irregular, fitful, unstable, turbulent, unsettled, changing, varying, fluctuating, mutable; unreliable, undependable, volatile, mercurial, capricious, fickle, temperamental, moody.
– OPPOSITES consistent.

erring adjective *the court case resulted in a heavy fine for the erring skipper:* **offending**, guilty, culpable, misbehaving, errant, delinquent, lawbreaking, aberrant, deviant.

erroneous adjective *the report was based on an erroneous assumption:* **wrong**, incorrect, mistaken, in error, inaccurate, untrue, false, fallacious; unsound, specious, faulty, flawed; informal off beam, way out, full of holes.
– OPPOSITES correct.

error noun *the common error of calling schizophrenia a split personality:* **mistake**, inaccuracy, miscalculation, blunder, oversight; fallacy, misconception, delusion; misprint, erratum; informal slip-up, bloomer, boo-boo; Brit. informal boob.
■ **in error** wrongly, by mistake, mistakenly, incorrectly; accidentally, by accident, inadvertently, unintentionally, by chance.

ersatz adjective *ersatz coffee:* **artificial**, substitute, imitation, synthetic, fake, faux, false, mock, simulated; pseudo, sham, bogus, spurious, counterfeit; manufactured, man-made; informal phoney.
– OPPOSITES genuine.

erstwhile adjective *written in memory of the composer's erstwhile teacher:* **former**, old, past, one-time, sometime, ex-, late, then; previous.
– OPPOSITES present.

erudite adjective *he was so erudite that only people who were his equals in scholarship could understand him:* **learned**, scholarly, educated, knowledgeable, well read, well informed, intellectual; intelligent, clever, academic, literary; bookish, highbrow, cerebral; informal brainy.
– OPPOSITES ignorant.

erupt verb **1** *the volcano erupted:* **emit lava**, become active, flare up; explode. **2** *fighting erupted:* **break out**, flare up, start suddenly; ensue, arise, happen. **3** *a boil erupted on her temple:* **appear**, break out, flare up, come to a head, emerge.

eruption noun **1** *a volcanic eruption:* **discharge**, ejection, emission; explosion. **2** *an eruption of violence:* **outbreak**, flare-up, upsurge, outburst, breakout, explosion; wave, spate. **3** *a skin eruption:* **rash**, outbreak, inflammation.

escalate verb **1** *prices have escalated:* **increase rapidly**, soar, rocket, shoot up, mount, spiral, climb, go up; informal go through the roof, skyrocket. **2** *the dispute escalated:* **grow**, develop, mushroom, increase, heighten, intensify, accelerate.
– OPPOSITES plunge, shrink.

escalation noun **1** *an escalation in oil prices:* **increase**, rise, hike, growth, leap, upsurge, upturn, climb. **2** *an escalation of the conflict:* **intensification**, aggravation, exacerbation, magnification, amplification, augmentation; expansion, build-up; deterioration.

escapade noun *he is a paragliding fanatic famous for his flying escapades:* **exploit**, stunt, caper, antic(s), spree; adventure, venture, mission; deed, feat, trial, experience; incident, occurrence, event.

escape verb **1** *he escaped from prison:* **run away/off**, get out, break out, break free, make a break for it, bolt, flee, take flight, make off, take off, abscond, take to one's heels, make one's getaway, make a run for it; disappear, vanish, slip away, sneak away; informal cut and run, skedaddle, scarper, vamoose, do a vanishing act, fly the coop, take French leave, leg it; Brit. informal do a bunk, do a runner; N. Amer. informal go on the lam. **2** *he escaped his pursuers:* **get away from**, escape from, elude, avoid, dodge, shake off; informal give someone the slip. **3** *they escaped injury:* **avoid**, evade, dodge, elude, miss, cheat, sidestep, circumvent, steer clear of; shirk; informal duck. **4** *lethal gas escaped:* **leak (out)**, seep (out), discharge, emanate, issue, flow (out), pour (out), gush (out), spurt (out), spew (out).
noun **1** *his escape from prison:* **getaway**, breakout, bolt, flight; disappearance, vanishing act; Brit. informal flit. **2** *a narrow escape from death:* **avoidance of**, evasion of, circumvention of. **3** *a gas escape:* **leak**, leakage, spill, seepage, discharge, emanation, outflow, outpouring; gush, stream, spurt. **4** *an escape from boredom:* **distraction**, diversion.

escapee noun **runaway**, escaper, absconder; jailbreaker, fugitive; truant; deserter, defector.

escapism noun *musicals always do well in a recession because people want escapism:* **fantasy**, fantasizing, daydreaming, daydreams, reverie; imagination, flight(s) of fancy, pipe dreams, wishful thinking,

wool-gathering; informal pie in the sky.
– OPPOSITES realism.

eschew verb *he firmly eschewed political involvement:* **abstain from**, refrain from, give up, forgo, shun, renounce, steer clear of, have nothing to do with, fight shy of; relinquish, reject, disavow, abandon, spurn, wash one's hands of, drop; informal kick, pack in; Brit. informal jack in.

escort noun **1** *a police escort:* **guard**, bodyguard, protector, minder, custodian; attendant, chaperone; entourage, retinue, cortège; protection, defence, convoy. **2** *her escort for the evening:* **companion**, partner; informal date. **3** *an agency dealing with escorts:* **paid companion**, hostess, geisha; gigolo.
verb **1** *he was escorted home by the police:* **conduct**, accompany, guide, usher, shepherd, take. **2** *he escorted her in to dinner:* **accompany**, partner, take, bring.

esoteric adjective *the question is dominated by esoteric debate:* **abstruse**, obscure, arcane, recherché, rarefied, recondite, abstract; enigmatic, inscrutable, cryptic, Delphic, complex, complicated, incomprehensible, opaque, impenetrable, mysterious.

especial adjective **1** *especial care is required:* **particular**, (extra) special, superior, exceptional, extraordinary; unusual, out of the ordinary, uncommon, remarkable, singular. **2** *her especial brand of charm:* **distinctive**, individual, special, particular, distinct, peculiar, personal, own, unique, specific.

especially adverb **1** *work poured in, especially from Kent:* **mainly**, mostly, chiefly, principally, largely; substantially, particularly, primarily, generally, usually, typically. **2** *a committee especially formed for the purpose:* **expressly**, specially, specifically, exclusively, just, particularly, explicitly. **3** *he is especially talented:* **exceptionally**, particularly, specially, very, extremely, singularly, distinctly, unusually, extraordinarily, uncommonly, uniquely, remarkably, outstandingly, really; informal seriously, majorly; Brit. informal jolly, dead, well.

espionage noun *the shadowy world of espionage:* **spying**, infiltration; eavesdropping, surveillance, reconnaissance, intelligence.

espousal noun *his espousal of Western ideas:* **adoption**, embracing, acceptance; support, championship, encouragement, defence; sponsorship, promotion, endorsement, advocacy, approval.

espouse verb **adopt**, embrace, take up, accept, welcome; support, back, champion, favour, prefer, encourage; promote, endorse, advocate.
– OPPOSITES reject.

essay noun *he wrote an essay:* **article**, composition, study, paper, dissertation, thesis, discourse, treatise, disquisition;

monograph; commentary, critique; N. Amer. theme.

essence noun **1** *the very essence of economics:* **quintessence**, soul, spirit, nature; core, heart, crux, nucleus, substance; principle, fundamental quality, sum and substance, reality, actuality; informal nitty-gritty. **2** *essence of ginger:* **extract**, concentrate, distillate, elixir, decoction, juice, tincture; scent, perfume, oil.
■ **in essence** essentially, basically, fundamentally, primarily, principally, chiefly, predominantly, substantially; above all, first and foremost; effectively, virtually, to all intents and purposes; intrinsically, inherently.
■ **of the essence**. See ESSENTIAL adjective sense 1.

essential adjective **1** *it is essential to remove the paint:* **crucial**, necessary, key, vital, indispensable, important, all-important, of the essence, critical, imperative, mandatory, compulsory, obligatory; urgent, pressing, paramount, pre-eminent, high-priority. **2** *the essential simplicity of his style:* **basic**, inherent, fundamental, quintessential, intrinsic, underlying, characteristic, innate, primary, elementary, elemental; central, pivotal, vital. **3** *the essential English gentleman:* **ideal**, absolute, complete, perfect, quintessential.
– OPPOSITES unimportant, optional, secondary.
noun **1** *an essential for broadcasters:* **necessity**, prerequisite, requisite, requirement, need; condition, precondition, stipulation; sine qua non; informal must. **2** *the essentials of the job:* **fundamentals**, basics, rudiments, first principles, foundations, bedrock; essence, basis, core, kernel, crux, sine qua non; informal nitty-gritty, brass tacks, nuts and bolts.

establish verb **1** *they established an office in Moscow:* **set up**, start, initiate, institute, form, found, create, inaugurate; build, construct, install. **2** *evidence to establish his guilt:* **prove**, demonstrate, show, indicate, signal, exhibit, manifest, attest to, evidence, determine, confirm, verify, certify, substantiate.

established adjective **1** *this is established practice:* **accepted**, traditional, orthodox, habitual, set, fixed, official; usual, customary, common, normal, general, prevailing, accustomed, familiar, expected, routine, typical, conventional, standard. **2** *an established composer:* **well known**, recognized, esteemed, respected, famous, prominent, noted, renowned.

establishment noun **1** *the establishment of a democracy:* **foundation**, institution, formation, inception, creation, installation; inauguration, start, initiation. **2** *a dressmaking establishment:* **business**, firm, company, concern, enterprise, venture, organization, operation; factory, plant,

e

shop, office, practice; informal **outfit, set-up**.
3 *educational establishments:* **institution**,
place, premises, foundation, institute. **4** *they
dare to poke fun at the Establishment:* **the
authorities**, the powers that be, the system,
the ruling class; informal Big Brother.

estate noun **1** *the Balmoral estate:* **property**,
grounds, garden(s), park, parkland, land(s),
landholding, manor, territory. **2** *a housing
estate:* **area**, site, development, complex.
3 *a coffee estate:* **plantation**, farm, holding;
forest, vineyard; N. Amer. ranch. **4** *he left
an estate worth £610,000:* **assets**, capital,
wealth, riches, holdings, fortune; property,
effects, possessions, belongings.

estate agent noun **property agent**; Brit.
house agent; N. Amer. realtor.

esteem noun *she was held in high esteem:*
respect, admiration, acclaim, approbation,
appreciation, favour, recognition, honour,
reverence; estimation, regard, opinion.
verb *such ceramics are highly esteemed:*
respect, **admire**, value, regard, acclaim,
appreciate, like, prize, treasure, favour,
revere.

estimate verb **1** *estimate the cost:* **calculate
roughly**, approximate, guess; evaluate,
judge, gauge, reckon, rate, determine; informal
guesstimate. **2** *we estimate it to be worth
£50,000:* **consider**, believe, reckon, deem,
judge, rate, gauge.
noun **1** *an estimate of the cost:* **rough
calculation**, approximation, estimation,
rough guess; costing, quotation, valuation,
evaluation; informal guesstimate. **2** *his
estimate of Paul's integrity:* **evaluation**,
estimation, judgement, rating, appraisal,
opinion, view.

estimation noun **1** *an estimation of
economic growth:* **estimate**, approximation,
rough calculation, rough guess, evaluation;
informal guesstimate. **2** *he rated highly in
Carl's estimation:* **assessment**, evaluation,
judgement; esteem, opinion, view.

estrange verb *she realized that she had
estranged her favourite uncle:* **alienate**,
antagonize, turn away, drive away, distance;
sever, set at odds with, drive a wedge
between.

estrangement noun **alienation**,
antagonism, antipathy, disaffection,
hostility, unfriendliness; variance,
difference; parting, separation, divorce,
break-up, split, breach, schism.

estuary noun **(river) mouth**, firth; delta.

et cetera adverb *you need wellingtons,
raincoat, umbrella, et cetera:* **and so on**, and
so forth, and the rest, and/or the like, and
suchlike, among others, et al., etc.; informal
and what have you, and whatnot.

etch verb **1** *the metal is etched with acid:*
corrode, burn into; mark. **2** *a stone etched
with tiny designs:* **engrave**, carve, inscribe,
incise, chase, score, print, mark.

etching noun **engraving**, print, impression,
block, plate; woodcut, linocut.

eternal adjective **1** *eternal happiness:*
everlasting, never-ending, endless,
perpetual, undying, immortal, abiding,
permanent, enduring, infinite, boundless,
timeless. **2** *eternal vigilance:* **constant**,
continual, continuous, perpetual, persistent,
sustained, unremitting, relentless,
unrelieved, uninterrupted, unbroken, never-
ending, non-stop, round-the-clock, endless,
ceaseless.
– OPPOSITES transient, intermittent.

eternally adverb **1** *I shall be eternally
grateful:* **forever**, permanently, perpetually,
(for) evermore, for ever and ever, for
eternity, in perpetuity, enduringly; N.
Amer. forevermore; informal until doomsday,
until the cows come home. **2** *the tenants
complain eternally:* **constantly**, continually,
continuously, always, all the time,
persistently, repeatedly, regularly; day
and night, non-stop; endlessly, incessantly,
perpetually; interminably, relentlessly;
informal 24-7.

eternity noun **1** *the memory will remain
for eternity:* **ever**, all time, perpetuity.
2 *souls destined for eternity:* **the afterlife**,
everlasting life, life after death, the
hereafter, the afterworld, the next world;
heaven, paradise, immortality. **3** (informal) *I
waited an eternity for you:* **a long time**, an
age, ages, a lifetime; hours, years, aeons;
forever; informal donkey's years, a month of
Sundays; Brit. informal yonks.

ethereal adjective **1** *her ethereal beauty:*
delicate, exquisite, dainty, elegant, graceful;
fragile, airy, fine, subtle. **2** *theologians
discuss ethereal ideas:* **celestial**, heavenly,
spiritual, other-worldly, paradisal, Elysian.
– OPPOSITES substantial, earthly.

ethical adjective **1** *an ethical dilemma:* **moral**,
social, behavioural. **2** *an ethical investment
policy:* **morally correct**, right-minded,
principled, irreproachable; righteous, high-
minded, virtuous, good, moral; clean, lawful,
just, honourable, reputable, respectable,
noble, worthy; praiseworthy, commendable,
admirable, laudable; whiter than white,
saintly, impeccable; informal squeaky
clean.

ethics plural noun *the ethics of journalism:*
moral code, morals, morality, values, rights
and wrongs, principles, ideals, standards (of
behaviour), virtues.

ethnic adjective *a wide spectrum of ethnic
groups:* **racial**, race-related, ethnological;
cultural, national, tribal, ancestral,
traditional.

ethos noun *the governing body has
responsibility for the ethos of the school:*
spirit, character, atmosphere, climate,
mood, feeling, tenor, essence; disposition,
rationale, morality, moral code, principles,
standards, ethics.

etiquette noun *the club's brochure includes advice on etiquette:* **protocol**, manners, accepted behaviour, rules of conduct, decorum, good form; courtesy, propriety, formalities, niceties, punctilios; custom, convention; informal the done thing.

etymology noun **derivation**, word history, development, origin, source.

eulogize verb *the police eulogized the positive effect of speed cameras:* **extol**, acclaim, sing the praises of, praise to the skies, wax lyrical about, rhapsodize about, rave about, enthuse about; N. Amer. informal ballyhoo.
– OPPOSITES criticize.

eulogy noun *his lifelong collaborator delivered a graveside eulogy:* **accolade**, panegyric, paean, tribute, compliment, commendation; praise, acclaim; plaudits, bouquets.
– OPPOSITES attack.

euphemism noun *'downsizing' is often a euphemism for cuts:* **polite term**, indirect term, substitute, alternative, understatement, genteelism.

euphemistic adjective *euphemistic expressions for sacking someone, such as 'letting them go':* **polite**, substitute, mild, understated, indirect, neutral, evasive; diplomatic, inoffensive, genteel.

euphonious adjective *a stream of fine euphonious phrases:* **pleasant-sounding**, sweet-sounding, mellow, mellifluous, dulcet, sweet, honeyed, lyrical, silvery, golden, lilting, soothing; harmonious, melodious; informal easy on the ear.
– OPPOSITES cacophonous.

euphoria noun *they were swept up in the euphoria of victory:* **elation**, happiness, joy, delight, glee; excitement, exhilaration, jubilation, exultation; ecstasy, bliss, rapture.
– OPPOSITES misery.

euphoric adjective *the liberators received a euphoric welcome:* **elated**, happy, joyful, delighted, gleeful; excited, exhilarated, jubilant, exultant; ecstatic, blissful, rapturous, transported, on cloud nine, in seventh heaven; informal on the top of the world, over the moon, on a high.

euthanasia noun **mercy killing**, assisted suicide.

evacuate verb **1** *local residents were evacuated:* **remove**, clear, move out, take away. **2** *they evacuated the bombed town:* **leave**, vacate, abandon, desert, move out of, quit, withdraw from, retreat from, decamp from, flee, depart from, escape from. **3** *police evacuated the area:* **clear**, empty, depopulate. **4** *patients couldn't evacuate their bowels:* **empty (out)**, void, open, move, purge; defecate. **5** *he evacuated the contents of his stomach:* **expel**, eject, discharge, excrete, void, empty (out).

evacuation noun **1** *the evacuation of civilians:* **removal**, clearance, shifting; eviction, deportation. **2** *the evacuation of military bases:* **clearance**, depopulation; abandonment, vacation, desertion. **3** *involuntary evacuation of the bowels:* **emptying (out)**, voidance, opening, purging; defecation.

evade verb **1** *they evaded the guards:* **elude**, avoid, dodge, escape (from), steer clear of, keep at arm's length, sidestep; lose, leave behind, shake off; N. Amer. end-run; informal give someone the slip. **2** *he evaded the question:* **avoid**, dodge, sidestep, bypass, hedge, fence, skirt round, fudge, be evasive about; informal duck, cop out of.
– OPPOSITES confront.

evaluate verb *it is important to evaluate the results of surgery:* **assess**, judge, gauge, rate, estimate, appraise, analyse, weigh up, get the measure of; informal size up, check out.

evaluation noun **assessment**, appraisal, judgement, gauging, rating, estimation, consideration, analysis.

evangelical adjective **1** *evangelical Christianity:* **scriptural**, biblical; fundamentalist, orthodox. **2** *an evangelical preacher:* **evangelistic**, evangelizing, missionary, crusading, propagandist, propagandizing, proselytizing.

evangelist noun *people flocked to hear evangelists preach about Jesus:* **preacher**, missionary, gospeller, proselytizer, crusader, propagandist.

evangelistic adjective. See EVANGELICAL sense 2.

evangelize verb *some small groups have been evangelized by Protestant missionaries:* **convert**, proselytize, redeem, save, preach to, recruit; act as a missionary, crusade, campaign.

evaporate verb **1** *the water evaporated:* **vaporize**, become vapour, volatilize; dry up. **2** *the rock salt is washed and evaporated:* **dry out**, dehydrate, desiccate, dehumidify. **3** *the feeling has evaporated:* **end**, pass (away), fizzle out, peter out, wear off, vanish, fade, disappear, melt away.
– OPPOSITES condense, wet, materialize.

evasion noun **1** *the evasion of immigration control:* **avoidance**, elusion, circumvention, dodging, sidestepping. **2** *she grew tired of all the evasion:* **prevarication**, evasiveness, beating about the bush, hedging, pussyfooting, equivocation, vagueness, temporization; Brit. humming and hawing.

evasive adjective *she was undeterred by evasive replies:* **equivocal**, prevaricating, elusive, ambiguous, non-committal, vague, inexplicit, unclear; roundabout, indirect; informal cagey.

eve noun *the eve of the election:* **day before**, evening before, night before; the run-up to.

even adjective **1** *an even surface:* **flat**, smooth, uniform, featureless; unbroken, undamaged; level, plane. **2** *an even*

temperature: **uniform**, constant, steady, stable, consistent, unvarying, unchanging, regular. **3** *they all have an even chance:* **equal**, the same, identical, like, alike, similar, comparable, parallel. **4** *the score was even:* **level**, drawn, tied, all square, balanced; neck and neck; Brit. level pegging; informal even-steven(s). **5** *an even disposition:* **even-tempered**, balanced, stable, equable, placid, calm, composed, poised, cool, relaxed, easy, imperturbable, unexcitable, unruffled, untroubled; informal together, laid-back, unflappable.
– OPPOSITES bumpy, irregular, unequal, moody.
▶ verb **1** *the canal bottom was evened out:* **flatten**, level (off/out), smooth (off/out), plane; make uniform, make regular. **2** *the union wants to even up our wages:* **equalize**, make equal, level up, balance, square; standardize, regularize.
▶ adverb **1** *it got even colder:* **still**, yet, more, all the more. **2** *even the best hitters missed the ball:* **surprisingly**, unexpectedly, paradoxically. **3** *she is afraid, even ashamed, to ask for help:* **indeed**, you could say, veritably, in truth, actually, or rather, nay. **4** *she couldn't even afford food:* **so much as**.
■ **even as** while, whilst, as, just as, at the very time that, during the time that.
■ **even so** nevertheless, nonetheless, all the same, just the same, anyway, anyhow, still, yet, however, notwithstanding, despite that, in spite of that, for all that, be that as it may, in any event, at any rate.
■ **get even** have one's revenge, avenge oneself, take vengeance, even the score, settle the score, hit back, give as good as one gets, pay someone back, repay someone, reciprocate, retaliate, take reprisals, exact retribution; give someone their just deserts; informal get one's own back, give someone a taste of their own medicine, settle someone's hash.

even-handed adjective *teachers must have an even-handed approach:* **fair**, just, equitable, impartial, unbiased, unprejudiced, non-partisan, non-discriminatory; disinterested, detached, objective, neutral.
– OPPOSITES biased.

evening noun *he came over to see me one evening:* **night**, late afternoon, end of day, close of day; twilight, dusk, nightfall, sunset, sundown.

event noun **1** *an annual event:* **occurrence**, happening, proceeding, incident, affair, circumstance, occasion, phenomenon; function, gathering; informal bash, do. **2** *the team lost the event:* **competition**, contest, tournament, round, heat, match, fixture; race, game, bout.
■ **in any event/at all events** regardless, whatever happens, come what may, no matter what, at any rate, in any case, anyhow, anyway, even so, still, nevertheless,

nonetheless; N. Amer. informal anyways.
■ **in the event** as it turned out, as it happened, in the end; as a result, as a consequence.

even-tempered adjective *Russell was a gentle and even-tempered man:* **serene**, calm, composed, tranquil, relaxed, easy-going, mellow, unworried, untroubled, unruffled, imperturbable, placid, equable, stable, level-headed; informal unflappable, together, laid-back.
– OPPOSITES excitable.

eventful adjective *it had been a long and eventful day:* **busy**, action-packed, full, lively, active, hectic, strenuous; momentous, significant, important, historic, consequential, fateful.
– OPPOSITES dull.

eventual adjective *the eventual outcome of the competition:* **final**, ultimate, concluding, closing, end; resulting, ensuing, consequent, subsequent.

eventuality noun *it is impossible to anticipate every eventuality:* **event**, incident, occurrence, happening, development, phenomenon, situation, circumstance, case, contingency, chance, likelihood, possibility, probability; outcome, result.

eventually adverb *eventually we arrived at a small town:* **in the end**, in due course, by and by, in time, after some time, after a bit, finally, at last; ultimately, in the long run, at the end of the day, one day, some day, sometime, sooner or later.

ever adverb **1** *the best I've ever done:* **at any time**, at any point, on any occasion, under any circumstances, on any account; up till now, until now. **2** *he was ever the optimist:* **always**, forever, eternally, until hell freezes over; informal until the twelfth of never, until the cows come home, until doomsday. **3** *an ever increasing rate of crime:* **continually**, constantly, always, endlessly, perpetually, incessantly, unremittingly.

everlasting adjective **1** *everlasting love:* **eternal**, endless, never-ending, perpetual, undying, abiding, enduring, infinite, boundless, timeless. **2** *his everlasting complaints:* **constant**, continual, continuous, persistent, relentless, unrelieved, uninterrupted, unabating, endless, interminable, never-ending, non-stop, incessant.
– OPPOSITES transient, occasional.

every determiner **1** *he exercised every day:* **each**, each and every, every single. **2** *we make every effort to satisfy our clients:* **all possible**, the utmost.

everybody pronoun *everybody complains about taxes these days:* **everyone**, every person, each person, all, one and all, all and sundry, the whole world, the public; informal {every Tom, Dick, and Harry}, every man jack, every mother's son.

everyday adjective **1** *the everyday demands*

of a baby: **daily**, day-to-day, quotidian.
2 *everyday drugs like aspirin:* **commonplace**, ordinary, common, usual, regular, familiar, conventional, run-of-the-mill, standard, stock; household, domestic; Brit. common or garden; informal bog-standard.
– OPPOSITES unusual.

everyone pronoun *she didn't want everyone to know her business:* **everybody**, every person, each person, all, one and all, all and sundry, the whole world, the public; informal {every Tom, Dick, and Harry}, every man jack, every mother's son.

everything pronoun *the guards searched through everything:* **each item**, each thing, every single thing, the (whole) lot; all; informal the whole caboodle, the whole shebang; N. Amer. informal the whole ball of wax.
– OPPOSITES nothing.

everywhere adverb *I've looked everywhere:* **all over**, all around, in every nook and cranny, far and wide, near and far, high and low, {here, there, and everywhere}; throughout the land, the world over, worldwide; informal all over the place; Brit. informal all over the shop; N. Amer. informal all over the map.
– OPPOSITES nowhere.

evict verb *the police moved in and evicted the squatters:* **expel**, eject, oust, remove, dislodge, turn out, throw out, drive out; dispossess, expropriate; informal chuck out, kick out, boot out, bounce, give someone the (old) heave-ho, throw someone out on their ear; Brit. informal turf out; N. Amer. informal give someone the bum's rush.

eviction noun **expulsion**, ejection, ousting, removal, dislodgement, displacement, banishment; dispossession, expropriation.

evidence noun **1** *they found evidence of his plotting:* **proof**, confirmation, verification, substantiation, corroboration, affirmation, attestation. **2** *the court accepted her evidence:* **testimony**, statement, attestation, declaration, avowal, submission, claim, contention, allegation. **3** *evidence of a struggle:* **signs**, indications, pointers, marks, traces, suggestions, hints; manifestation.
verb *the rise of racism is evidenced here:* **indicate**, show, reveal, display, exhibit, manifest; testify to, confirm, prove, substantiate, endorse, bear out.
– OPPOSITES disprove.
■ **in evidence** noticeable, conspicuous, obvious, perceptible, visible, on view, plain to see; palpable, tangible, unmistakable, undisguised, prominent, striking, glaring; informal as plain as the nose on your face, sticking out like a sore thumb, sticking out a mile, staring someone in the face.

evident adjective *he regarded her with evident interest:* **obvious**, apparent, noticeable, conspicuous, perceptible, visible, discernible, clear, plain, manifest, patent; palpable, tangible, distinct, pronounced, marked, striking, glaring,

blatant; unmistakable, indisputable; informal as plain as the nose on your face, sticking out like a sore thumb, sticking out a mile, as clear as day.

evidently adverb **1** *he was evidently dismayed:* **obviously**, clearly, plainly, visibly, manifestly, patently, distinctly, markedly; unmistakably, undeniably, undoubtedly, as sure as eggs is eggs. **2** *evidently, she believed herself superior:* **seemingly**, apparently, as far as one can tell, from all appearances, on the face of it; it seems (that), it appears (that).

evil adjective **1** *an evil deed:* **wicked**, bad, wrong, immoral, sinful, foul, vile, dishonourable, corrupt, iniquitous, depraved, villainous, nefarious, vicious, malicious; malevolent, sinister, demonic, devilish, diabolical, fiendish, dark; monstrous, shocking, despicable, atrocious, heinous, odious, contemptible, horrible, execrable; informal low-down, dirty. **2** *an evil spirit:* **harmful**, hurtful, injurious, detrimental, deleterious, inimical, bad, mischievous, pernicious, malignant, malign, baleful; destructive, ruinous.
– OPPOSITES good, beneficial.
noun **1** *the evil in our midst:* **wickedness**, bad, badness, wrongdoing, sin, immorality, vice, iniquity, degeneracy, corruption, depravity, villainy, nefariousness, malevolence. **2** *nothing but evil would ensue:* **harm**, pain, misery, sorrow, suffering, trouble, disaster, misfortune, catastrophe, affliction, woe, hardship. **3** *the evils of war:* **abomination**, atrocity, obscenity, outrage, enormity, crime, monstrosity, barbarity.

evocative adjective *dark interiors are highly evocative of past centuries:* **reminiscent**, suggestive, redolent; expressive, vivid, graphic, powerful, haunting, moving, poignant.

evoke verb *the poems evoke a sense of desolate emptiness:* **bring to mind**, put one in mind of, conjure up, summon (up), invoke, elicit, induce, kindle, stimulate, stir up, awaken, arouse; recall, echo, capture.

evolution noun **1** *the evolution of Bolshevism:* **development**, advancement, growth, rise, progress, expansion, evolvement; transformation, adaptation, modification, revision. **2** *his interest in evolution:* **Darwinism**, natural selection.

evolve verb *the economies of all four nations evolved in different ways:* **develop**, progress, advance; mature, grow, expand, spread; alter, change, transform, adapt, metamorphose; humorous transmogrify.

exacerbate verb *political changes have exacerbated the conflict:* **aggravate**, worsen, inflame, compound; intensify, increase, heighten, magnify, add to, amplify, augment; informal add fuel to the fire/flames.
– OPPOSITES reduce.

exact adjective **1** *an exact description:* **precise**, accurate, correct, faithful, close, true;

e

literal, strict, faultless, perfect, impeccable; explicit, detailed, minute, meticulous, thorough; informal on the nail, on the mark; Brit. informal spot on, bang on; N. Amer. informal on the money, on the button. **2** *an exact manager:* **careful**, meticulous, painstaking, punctilious, conscientious, scrupulous, exacting; methodical, organized, orderly.
– OPPOSITES inaccurate, careless.
▸verb **1** *she exacted high standards from them:* **demand**, require, insist on, request, impose, expect; extract, compel, force, squeeze. **2** *they exacted a terrible vengeance on him:* **inflict**, impose, administer, apply.

exacting adjective **1** *an exacting training routine:* **demanding**, stringent, testing, challenging, onerous, arduous, laborious, taxing, gruelling, punishing, hard, tough. **2** *an exacting boss:* **strict**, stern, firm, demanding, tough, harsh; inflexible, uncompromising, unyielding, unsparing.
– OPPOSITES easy, easy-going.

exactly adverb **1** *it's exactly as I expected it to be:* **precisely**, entirely, absolutely, completely, totally, just, quite, in every way, in every respect, one hundred per cent, every inch, to the hilt; informal to a T; N. Amer. informal on the money. **2** *write the quotation out exactly:* **accurately**, precisely, correctly, unerringly, faultlessly, perfectly; verbatim, word for word, letter for letter, to the letter, faithfully.
▸exclamation *'She escaped?' 'Exactly.'* **precisely**, yes, that's right, just so, quite (so), indeed, absolutely; informal you got it.
■ **not exactly** by no means, not at all, in no way, certainly not; not really.

exaggerate verb *they often exaggerate for dramatic effect:* **overstate**, overemphasize, overestimate, magnify, amplify, aggrandize, inflate; embellish, embroider, elaborate, overplay, dramatize; hyperbolize, stretch the truth; Brit. overpitch; informal lay it on thick, make a mountain out of a molehill, blow out of all proportion, make a big thing of.
– OPPOSITES understate.

exaggerated adjective *I gave her an exaggerated account of my exploits:* **overstated**, inflated, magnified, amplified, aggrandized, excessive; hyperbolic, elaborate, overdone, overplayed, over-dramatized, highly coloured, melodramatic, sensational; informal over the top, OTT.

exaggeration noun **overstatement**, overemphasis, magnification, amplification, aggrandizement; dramatization, elaboration, embellishment, embroidery, hyperbole, overkill, gilding the lily.

exalt verb **1** *they exalted their hero:* **extol**, praise, acclaim, esteem; pay homage to, revere, venerate, worship, lionize, idolize, look up to; informal put on a pedestal. **2** *this power exalts the peasant:* **elevate**, promote, raise, advance, upgrade, ennoble, dignify, aggrandize. **3** *his works exalt the emotions:*

uplift, elevate, inspire, excite, stimulate, enliven, exhilarate.
– OPPOSITES disparage, lower, depress.

exaltation noun **1** *a heart full of exaltation:* **elation**, joy, rapture, ecstasy, bliss, happiness, delight, gladness. **2** *their exaltation of Shakespeare:* **praise**, extolment, acclamation, reverence, veneration, worship, adoration, idolization, lionization. **3** *the exaltation of Jesus to God's right hand:* **elevation**, rise, promotion, advancement, ennoblement.

exalted adjective **1** *his exalted office:* **high**, high-ranking, elevated, superior, lofty, eminent, prestigious, illustrious, distinguished, esteemed. **2** *his exalted aims:* **noble**, lofty, high-minded, elevated; inflated, pretentious. **3** *she felt spiritually exalted:* **elated**, exultant, jubilant, joyful, rapturous, ecstatic, blissful, transported, happy, exuberant, exhilarated; informal high.

exam noun **test**, examination, assessment; paper, oral, practical; Brit. viva (voce); N. Amer. quiz.

examination noun **1** *artefacts spread out for examination:* **scrutiny**, inspection, perusal, study, investigation, consideration, analysis, appraisal, evaluation. **2** *a medical examination:* **inspection**, check-up, assessment, appraisal; probe, test, scan; informal once-over, overhaul. **3** *a school examination:* **test**, exam, assessment; paper, oral, practical; Brit. viva (voce); N. Amer. quiz.

examine verb **1** *they examined the bank records:* **inspect**, scrutinize, investigate, look at, study, scan, sift, probe, appraise, analyse, review, survey; informal check out. **2** *students were examined after a year:* **test**, quiz, question; assess, appraise.

examiner noun **tester**, questioner, interviewer, assessor, appraiser, marker, inspector; auditor, analyst; adjudicator, judge, scrutineer.

example noun **1** *a fine example of Chinese porcelain:* **specimen**, sample, exemplar, exemplification, instance, case, illustration. **2** *we must follow their example:* **precedent**, lead, model, pattern, exemplar, ideal, standard; role model. **3** *he was hanged as an example to others:* **warning**, caution, lesson, deterrent, admonition; moral.
■ **for example** for instance, e.g., by way of illustration, such as, as, like; in particular, namely, viz.

exasperate verb *Smith's erratic behaviour exasperated him:* **infuriate**, incense, anger, annoy, irritate, madden, enrage, antagonize, provoke, irk, vex, get on someone's nerves, ruffle someone's feathers; Brit. rub up the wrong way; informal aggravate, rile, bug, needle, hack off, get up someone's nose, get someone's back up, get someone's goat, give someone the hump; Brit. informal nark, wind up, get on someone's wick; N. Amer. informal tee off, tick off.
– OPPOSITES please.

exasperating adjective **infuriating**, annoying, irritating, maddening, provoking, irksome, vexatious, trying, displeasing; informal aggravating.

exasperation noun **irritation**, annoyance, vexation, anger, fury, rage, ill humour, crossness, tetchiness, testiness; disgruntlement, discontent, displeasure; informal aggravation.

excavate verb **1** *she excavated a narrow tunnel:* **dig (out)**, bore, hollow out, scoop out; burrow, tunnel, sink, gouge. **2** *numerous artefacts have been excavated:* **unearth**, dig up, uncover, reveal; disinter, exhume.

excavation noun **1** *the excavation of a grave:* **unearthing**, digging up; disinterment, exhumation. **2** *the excavation of a moat:* **digging**, hollowing out, boring, channelling. **3** *implements found in the excavations:* **hole**, pit, trench, trough; archaeological site.

exceed verb **1** *the cost will exceed £400:* **be more than**, be greater than, be over, go beyond, overreach, top. **2** *Brazil exceeds America in fertile land:* **surpass**, outdo, outstrip, outshine, outclass, transcend, top, beat, better, eclipse, overshadow; informal best, leave standing, be head and shoulders above.

exceedingly adverb *an exceedingly comfortable home:* **extremely**, exceptionally, especially, tremendously, very, really, truly, most; informal terribly, awfully, seriously, mega, ultra; Brit. informal ever so, well, dead, jolly; N. Amer. informal real, mighty.

excel verb **1** *he excelled at football:* **shine**, be excellent, be outstanding, be skilful, be talented, be pre-eminent, reign supreme; stand out, be the best, be unparalleled, be unequalled, be second to none, be unsurpassed. **2** *she excelled him in her work:* **surpass**, outdo, outshine, outclass, outstrip, beat, top, transcend, better, pass, eclipse, overshadow; informal best, be head and shoulders above, be a cut above.

excellence noun *the children's hospital is a centre of medical excellence:* **distinction**, quality, superiority, brilliance, greatness, merit, calibre, eminence, pre-eminence, supremacy, peerlessness; skill, talent, virtuosity, accomplishment, mastery.

excellent adjective *their results are excellent:* **very good**, superb, outstanding, exceptional, marvellous, wonderful; pre-eminent, perfect, matchless, peerless, supreme, first-rate, first-class, superlative, splendid, fine; informal A1, ace, great, terrific, tremendous, fantastic, fabulous, fab, top-notch, class, awesome, magic, wicked, cool, out of this world; Brit. informal brilliant, brill, smashing; Austral. informal bonzer.
– OPPOSITES inferior.

except preposition *every day except Monday:* **excluding**, not including, excepting, omitting, not counting, but, besides, apart from, aside from, barring, bar, other

than, saving; with the exception of; informal outside of.
– OPPOSITES including.
verb *you're all crooks, present company excepted:* **exclude**, omit, leave out, count out, disregard.
– OPPOSITES include.

exception noun *this case is an exception:* **anomaly**, irregularity, deviation, special case, peculiarity, abnormality, oddity; misfit; informal freak.
■ **take exception** object, take offence, take umbrage, demur, disagree; resent, argue against, protest against, oppose, complain about; informal kick up a fuss, kick up a stink.
■ **with the exception of**. See EXCEPT preposition.

exceptionable adjective (formal). See OBJECTIONABLE.

exceptional adjective **1** *the drought was exceptional:* **unusual**, uncommon, abnormal, atypical, extraordinary, out of the ordinary, rare, unprecedented, unexpected, surprising; strange, odd, freakish, anomalous, peculiar; Brit. out of the common; informal weird, freaky, something else. **2** *her exceptional ability:* **outstanding**, extraordinary, remarkable, special, excellent, phenomenal, prodigious; unequalled, unparalleled, unsurpassed, peerless, matchless, first-rate, first-class; informal A1, top-notch.
– OPPOSITES normal, average.

exceptionally adverb **1** *it was exceptionally cold:* **unusually**, uncommonly, abnormally, atypically, extraordinarily, unexpectedly, surprisingly; strangely, oddly; informal weirdly, freakily. **2** *an exceptionally acute mind:* **exceedingly**, outstandingly, extraordinarily, remarkably, especially, phenomenally, prodigiously.

excerpt noun *he read an excerpt from his book:* **extract**, part, section, piece, portion, snippet, clip, bit; reading, citation, quotation, quote, line, passage; N. Amer. cite.

excess noun **1** *an excess of calcium:* **surplus**, surfeit, overabundance, superabundance, superfluity, glut; too much. **2** *the excess is turned into fat:* **remainder**, rest, residue; leftovers, remnants; surplus, extra, difference. **3** *a life of excess:* **overindulgence**, intemperance, immoderation, profligacy, lavishness, extravagance, decadence, self-indulgence.
– OPPOSITES lack, restraint.
adjective *excess skin oils:* **surplus**, superfluous, redundant, unwanted, unneeded, excessive; extra.
■ **in excess of** more than, over, above, upwards of, beyond.

excessive adjective **1** *excessive alcohol consumption:* **immoderate**, intemperate, imprudent, overindulgent, unrestrained, uncontrolled, lavish, extravagant; superfluous. **2** *the cost is excessive:* **exorbitant**, extortionate, unreasonable, outrageous, undue, uncalled for, extreme, inordinate, unwarranted, disproportionate, too much; informal over the top, OTT.

excessively adverb *her father had excessively high standards:* **inordinately**, unduly, unnecessarily, unreasonably, ridiculously, overly; very, extremely, exceedingly, exceptionally, impossibly; immoderately, intemperately, too much.

exchange noun **1** *the exchange of ideas:* **interchange**, trade, trading, swapping, traffic, trafficking. **2** *a broker on the exchange:* **stock exchange**, money market, bourse. **3** *an acrimonious exchange:* **conversation**, dialogue, chat, talk, discussion; debate, argument, altercation; Brit. informal confab, row, barney.
▶verb *we exchanged shirts:* **trade**, swap, switch, change, interchange.
■ **exchange blows** fight, brawl, scuffle, tussle, engage in fisticuffs; informal scrap, have a set-to; Brit. informal have a punch-up.
■ **exchange words** argue, quarrel, squabble, have an argument/disagreement; informal have a slanging match.

excise[1] noun *the excise on spirits:* **duty**, tax, levy, tariff.

excise[2] verb **1** *the tumours were excised:* **cut out/off/away**, take out, extract, remove. **2** *all unnecessary detail should be excised:* **delete**, cross out/through, strike out, score out, cancel, put a line through; erase.

excitable adjective *the horses were very excitable:* **temperamental**, mercurial, volatile, emotional, sensitive, highly strung, unstable, nervous, tense, edgy, jumpy, twitchy, uneasy, neurotic; informal uptight, wired.
– OPPOSITES placid.

excite verb **1** *the prospect of a holiday excited me:* **thrill**, exhilarate, animate, enliven, rouse, stir, stimulate, galvanize, electrify, inspirit; informal buck up, pep up, ginger up, give someone a buzz/kick; N. Amer. informal give someone a charge. **2** *she wore a chiffon nightgown to excite him:* **arouse (sexually)**, stimulate, titillate, inflame; informal turn someone on, get someone going, float someone's boat. **3** *his clothes excited envy:* **provoke**, stir up, rouse, arouse, kindle, trigger (off), spark off, incite, cause.
– OPPOSITES bore, depress.

excited adjective **1** *they were excited about the prospect:* **thrilled**, exhilarated, animated, enlivened, electrified; enraptured, intoxicated, feverish, enthusiastic; informal high (as a kite), fired up. **2** **(sexually) aroused**, stimulated, titillated, inflamed; informal turned on, hot, horny, sexed up; Brit. informal randy; N. Amer. informal squirrelly.

excitement noun **1** *the excitement of seeing a leopard in the wild:* **thrill**, pleasure, delight, joy; informal kick, buzz; N. Amer. informal charge. **2** *excitement in her eyes:* **exhilaration**, elation, animation, enthusiasm, eagerness,

anticipation, feverishness; informal pep, vim, zing. **3** **(sexual) arousal**, passion, stimulation, titillation.

exciting adjective **1** *an exciting story:* **thrilling**, exhilarating, stirring, rousing, stimulating, intoxicating, electrifying, invigorating; gripping, compelling, powerful, dramatic. **2** **(sexually) arousing**, (sexually) stimulating, titillating, erotic, sexual, sexy; informal raunchy, steamy.

exclaim verb *'Well I never!' she exclaimed:* **cry (out)**, declare, blurt out; call (out), shout, yell.

exclamation noun **cry**, call, shout, yell, interjection.

exclude verb **1** *women were excluded from many scientific societies:* **keep out**, deny access to, shut out, debar, disbar, bar, ban, prohibit. **2** *the clause excluded any judicial review:* **eliminate**, rule out, preclude. **3** *the price excludes postage:* **be exclusive of**, not include. **4** *he excluded his name from the list:* **leave out**, omit, miss out.
– OPPOSITES admit, include.

exclusion noun **1** *the exclusion of women from the society:* **barring**, keeping out, debarment, debarring, disbarring, banning, prohibition. **2** *the exclusion of other factors:* **elimination**, ruling out, precluding. **3** *the exclusion of pupils:* **expulsion**, ejection, throwing out; suspension.
– OPPOSITES acceptance, inclusion.

exclusive adjective **1** *an exclusive club:* **select**, chic, high-class, elite, fashionable, stylish, elegant, premier, grade A; expensive; Brit. upmarket; N. Amer. high-toned; informal posh, ritzy, classy; Brit. informal swish; N. Amer. informal tony. **2** *a room for your exclusive use:* **sole**, unshared, unique, only, individual, personal, private. **3** *prices exclusive of VAT:* **not including**, excluding, leaving out, omitting, excepting. **4** *mutually exclusive alternatives:* **incompatible**, irreconcilable.
– OPPOSITES inclusive.
▶noun *a six-page exclusive:* **scoop**, exposé, special, coup.

excrement noun **faeces**, excreta, stools, droppings; waste matter, ordure, dung; informal pooh, doings; Brit. informal cack, whoopsies, jobbies; N. Amer. informal poop.

excrescence noun **1** *an excrescence on his leg:* **growth**, lump, swelling, nodule, outgrowth. **2** *the new buildings were an excrescence:* **eyesore**, blot on the landscape, monstrosity.

excrete verb *the process by which waste products are excreted from the body:* **expel**, pass, void, discharge, eject, evacuate; defecate, urinate.
– OPPOSITES ingest.

excruciating adjective *an excruciating pain in her head:* **agonizing**, severe, acute, intense, violent, racking, searing, piercing, stabbing, raging; unbearable, unendurable; informal splitting, killing.

excursion noun *an excursion to Blackpool:* **trip**, outing, jaunt, expedition, journey, tour; day trip/out, drive, run, ride; informal junket, spin.

excusable adjective *an excusable mistake under the circumstances:* **forgivable**, pardonable, defensible, justifiable; venial.
– OPPOSITES unforgivable.

excuse verb **1** *eventually she excused him:* **forgive**, pardon, absolve, exonerate, acquit; informal let someone off (the hook). **2** *such conduct can never be excused:* **justify**, defend, condone, vindicate; forgive, overlook, disregard, ignore, tolerate, sanction. **3** *she has been excused from her duties:* **let off**, release, relieve, exempt, absolve, free.
– OPPOSITES punish, blame, condemn.
noun **1** *that's no excuse for stealing:* **justification**, defence, reason, explanation, mitigating circumstances, mitigation, vindication. **2** *an excuse to get away:* **pretext**, ostensible reason, pretence; Brit. get-out; informal story, alibi. **3** (informal) *that pathetic excuse for a man!* **travesty of**, poor specimen of; informal apology for.

execrable adjective *an execrable piece of work:* **appalling**, awful, dreadful, terrible, frightful, atrocious, lamentable, egregious; disgusting, deplorable, disgraceful, reprehensible, abhorrent, loathsome, odious, hateful, vile; informal abysmal, diabolical, lousy, God-awful; Brit. informal chronic, shocking, pants.
– OPPOSITES admirable.

execrate verb *the men were execrated as corrupt:* **revile**, denounce, decry, condemn, vilify; detest, loathe, abhor, despise.

execute verb **1** *he was convicted and executed:* **put to death**, kill; hang, behead, guillotine, electrocute, shoot, put before a firing squad, give someone a lethal injection; informal string up; N. Amer. send to the (electric) chair; N. Amer. informal fry. **2** *the corporation executed a series of financial deals:* **carry out**, accomplish, bring off/about, achieve, complete, engineer; informal pull off; formal effectuate. **3** *a well-executed act:* **perform**, present, render; stage.

execution noun **1** *the execution of the plan:* **implementation**, carrying out, accomplishment, bringing off/about, engineering, attainment, realization. **2** *the execution of the play:* **performance**, presentation, rendition, rendering, staging. **3** *thousands were sentenced to execution:* **capital punishment**, the death penalty; the gibbet, the gallows, the noose, the rope, the scaffold, the guillotine, the firing squad, a lethal injection; N. Amer. the (electric) chair.

executive adjective *executive powers:* **administrative**, decision-making, managerial; law-making.
noun **1** *top-level bank executives:* **chief**, head, director, senior official, senior manager, CEO, chief executive officer; informal boss, exec, suit. **2** *the executive has increased in number:* **administration**, management, directorate; government, legislative body.

exemplar noun *he was regarded as an exemplar of rationality and decorum:* **epitome**, perfect example, model, paragon, ideal, exemplification, textbook example, embodiment, essence, quintessence.

exemplary adjective **1** *her exemplary behaviour:* **perfect**, ideal, model, faultless, flawless, impeccable, irreproachable; excellent, outstanding, admirable, commendable, laudable, above/beyond reproach. **2** *exemplary jail sentences:* **cautionary**, warning, admonitory. **3** *her works are exemplary of certain feminist arguments:* **typical**, characteristic, representative, illustrative.
– OPPOSITES deplorable.

exemplify verb **1** *this story exemplifies current trends:* **typify**, epitomize, be a typical example of, be representative of, symbolize. **2** *he exemplified his point with an anecdote:* **illustrate**, give an example of, demonstrate.

exempt adjective *they are exempt from all charges:* **free**, not liable/subject, exempted, excepted, excused, absolved.
– OPPOSITES subject to.
verb *he had been exempted from military service:* **excuse**, free, release, exclude, give/grant immunity, spare, absolve; informal let off (the hook); N. Amer. informal grandfather.

exemption noun *exemption from the payment of road tax:* **immunity**, exception, dispensation, indemnity, exclusion, freedom, release, relief, absolution; informal let-off.

exercise noun **1** *exercise improves your heart:* **physical activity**, a workout, working-out; gymnastics, sports, games, physical education, PE, physical training, PT, aerobics, jogging, running; Brit. informal physical jerks. **2** *translation exercises:* **task**, piece of work, problem, assignment. **3** *the exercise of professional skill:* **use**, utilization, employment; practice, application. **4** *military exercises:* **manoeuvres**, operations; war games.
verb **1** *she exercised every day:* **work out**, do exercises, train; informal pump iron. **2** *he must learn to exercise patience:* **use**, employ, make use of, utilize; practise, apply. **3** *the problem continued to exercise him:* **worry**, trouble, concern, make anxious, bother, disturb, perturb, distress, preoccupy, prey on someone's mind, make uneasy; informal bug, do someone's head in.

exert verb **1** *he exerted considerable pressure on me:* **bring to bear**, apply, exercise, employ, use, utilize, deploy. **2** *he had been exerting himself:* **make an/every effort**, try hard, strive, endeavour, do one's best/utmost, give one's all, push oneself, drive oneself, work hard; informal go all out, pull out all the stops, bend/lean over backwards, do one's damnedest, move heaven and earth, work one's socks off; N. Amer. informal do one's darnedest, bust one's chops; Austral. informal go for the doctor.

exertion noun 1 *she was panting with the exertion:* **effort**, strain, struggle, toil, endeavour, hard work, labour; Brit. informal graft; Austral./NZ informal yakka. 2 *the exertion of pressure:* **use**, application, exercise, employment, utilization.

exhale verb 1 *she exhaled her cigarette smoke:* **breathe out**, blow out, puff out. 2 *the jungle exhaled mists of early morning:* **give off**, emanate, send forth, emit.
– OPPOSITES inhale.

exhaust verb 1 *the effort had exhausted him:* **tire (out)**, wear out, overtire, fatigue, weary, drain, run someone into the ground; informal do in, take it out of one, wipe out, knock out, shatter; Brit. informal knacker; N. Amer. informal poop, tucker out. 2 *the country has exhausted its reserves:* **use up**, run through, go through, consume, finish, deplete, spend, empty, drain; informal blow. 3 *we've exhausted the subject:* **treat thoroughly**, do to death, study in great detail.
– OPPOSITES invigorate, replenish.

exhausted adjective 1 *I'm exhausted:* **tired out**, worn out, weary, dog-tired, bone-tired, ready to drop, drained, fatigued, enervated; informal done in, all in, dead beat, shattered, bushed, knocked out, wiped out, bushwhacked; Brit. informal knackered, whacked (out), jiggered; N. Amer. informal pooped, tuckered out, fried, whipped; Austral./NZ informal stonkered. 2 *the personal wealth he accumulated is nearly exhausted:* **used up**, consumed, finished, spent, depleted; empty, drained.

exhausting adjective *a long and exhausting journey:* **tiring**, wearying, taxing, fatiguing, wearing, enervating, draining; arduous, strenuous, onerous, demanding, gruelling; informal killing, murderous; Brit. informal knackering.

exhaustion noun 1 *sheer exhaustion forced Paul to give up:* **extreme tiredness**, overtiredness, fatigue, weariness. 2 *the exhaustion of fuel reserves:* **consumption**, depletion, using up, expenditure; draining, emptying.

exhaustive adjective *an exhaustive study of the subject:* **comprehensive**, all-inclusive, complete, full, encyclopedic, thorough, in-depth; detailed, meticulous, painstaking.
– OPPOSITES perfunctory.

exhibit verb 1 *the paintings were exhibited at Sotheby's:* **put on display/show**, display, show, put on public view, showcase; set out, lay out, array, arrange. 2 *Luke exhibited signs of jealousy:* **show**, reveal, display, manifest; express, indicate, demonstrate, present.
noun *an exhibit at the British Museum:* **object on display**, item, piece.

exhibition noun 1 *an exhibition of French sculpture:* **(public) display**, show, showing, presentation, demonstration, exposition, showcase; N. Amer. exhibit. 2 *a convincing exhibition of concern:* **display**, show, demonstration, manifestation, expression.

exhibitionist noun **posturer**, poser, self-publicist; extrovert; informal show-off; N. Amer. informal showboat.

exhilarate verb *he was exhilarated by the boat's speed:* **thrill**, excite, intoxicate, elate, delight, enliven, animate, invigorate, energize, stimulate; informal give someone a thrill/buzz; N. Amer. informal give someone a charge.

exhilaration noun **elation**, euphoria, exultation, exaltation, joy, happiness, delight, joyousness, jubilation, rapture, ecstasy.

exhort verb *he exhorted delegates to fight corruption:* **urge**, encourage, call on, enjoin, charge, press; bid, appeal to, entreat, implore.

exhortation noun 1 *no amount of exhortation had any effect:* **urging**, encouragement, persuasion, pressure; admonishment, warning. 2 *the government's exhortations:* **entreaty**, appeal, call, charge, injunction; admonition, warning.

exhume verb *four years later his body was exhumed:* **disinter**, dig up, disentomb.
– OPPOSITES bury.

exigency noun 1 *the exigencies of the continuing war:* **need**, demand, requirement, necessity. 2 *financial exigency:* **urgency**, crisis, difficulty, pressure.

exile noun 1 *his exile from the land of his birth:* **banishment**, expulsion, expatriation, deportation. 2 *political exiles:* **émigré**, expatriate; displaced person, DP, refugee, deportee; informal expat.
verb *he was exiled from his country:* **expel**, banish, expatriate, deport, drive out, throw out, outlaw.

exist verb 1 *animals existing in the distant past:* **live**, be alive, be living; be, have being, have existence. 2 *the liberal climate that existed during his presidency:* **prevail**, occur, be found, be in existence; be the case. 3 *she had to exist on a low income:* **survive**, subsist, live, support oneself; manage, make do, get by, scrape by, make ends meet.

existence noun 1 *the industry's continued existence:* **actuality**, being, existing, reality; survival, continuation. 2 *her suburban existence:* **way of life/living**, life, lifestyle.
■ **in existence** 1 *there are several million unidentified species in existence:* alive, existing, extant. 2 *the only copy still in existence:* surviving, remaining, undestroyed, in circulation.

existent adjective *species that are no longer existent:* **in existence**, alive, existing, living, extant; surviving, remaining, undestroyed.

exit noun 1 *the fire exit:* **way out**, door, egress,

escape route; doorway, gate, gateway, portal. **2** *take the second exit:* **turning**, turn-off, turn; N. Amer. turnout. **3** *his sudden exit:* **departure**, leaving, withdrawal, going, decamping, retreat; flight, exodus, escape.
– OPPOSITES entrance, arrival.
verb *the doctor had just exited:* **leave**, go (out), depart, withdraw, retreat.
– OPPOSITES enter.

exodus noun *the exodus of refugees from Albania:* **mass departure**, withdrawal, evacuation, leaving; migration, emigration; flight, escape, fleeing.

exonerate verb **1** *the inquiry exonerated them:* **absolve**, clear, acquit, find innocent, discharge. **2** *the pope exonerated the king from his oath:* **release**, discharge, free, liberate; excuse, exempt, except, dispense; informal let off.
– OPPOSITES convict.

exorbitant adjective *the fees charged by the consultants were exorbitant:* **extortionate**, excessively high, excessive, prohibitive, outrageous, unreasonable, inflated, unconscionable, huge, enormous; Brit. over the odds; informal steep, stiff, over the top, a rip-off; Brit. informal daylight robbery.
– OPPOSITES reasonable.

exorcize verb **1** *exorcizing a spirit:* **drive out**, cast out, expel. **2** *they exorcized the house:* **purify**, cleanse, purge.

exotic adjective *exotic birds:* **foreign**, non-native, tropical. **2** *exotic places:* **foreign**, faraway, far-off, far-flung, distant. **3** *Linda's exotic appearance:* **striking**, colourful, eye-catching; unusual, unconventional, out of the ordinary, foreign-looking, extravagant, outlandish; informal offbeat, off the wall.
– OPPOSITES native, nearby, conventional.

expand verb **1** *metals expand when heated:* **increase in size**, become larger, enlarge; swell, dilate, inflate; lengthen, stretch, thicken, fill out; rare intumesce. **2** *the company is expanding:* **grow**, become/make larger, become/make bigger, increase in size/scope; extend, augment, broaden, widen, develop, diversify, build up; branch out, spread, proliferate. **3** *the minister expanded on the proposals:* **elaborate on**, enlarge on, go into detail about, flesh out, develop, expatiate on.
– OPPOSITES shrink, contract.

expanse noun *the wide expanse of grass:* **area**, stretch, sweep, tract, swathe, belt, region; sea, carpet, blanket, sheet.

expansion noun **1** *expansion and contraction:* **enlargement**, increase in size, swelling, dilation; lengthening, elongation, stretching, thickening. **2** *the expansion of the company:* **growth**, increase in size, enlargement, extension, development, buildout; spread, proliferation, multiplication.
– OPPOSITES contraction.

expansive adjective **1** *expansive moorland:*

extensive, sweeping, rolling. **2** *expansive coverage:* **wide-ranging**, extensive, broad, wide, comprehensive, thorough. **3** *Cara became engagingly expansive:* **communicative**, forthcoming, sociable, friendly, outgoing, affable, chatty, talkative, garrulous, loquacious, voluble.

expatiate verb *she expatiated on the subject:* **speak/write at length**, go into detail, expound, dwell, dilate, expand, enlarge, elaborate.

expatriate noun *expatriates working overseas:* **emigrant**, non-native, émigré, (economic) migrant; informal expat.
– OPPOSITES national.
adjective *expatriate workers:* **emigrant**, living abroad, non-native, émigré; informal expat.
– OPPOSITES indigenous.
verb **1** *he was not tempted to expatriate himself:* **settle abroad**, live abroad. **2** *he was expatriated:* **exile**, deport, banish, expel.

expect verb **1** *I expect she'll be late:* **suppose**, presume, think, believe, imagine, assume, surmise; informal guess, reckon; N. Amer. informal figure. **2** *a 10 per cent rise was expected:* **anticipate**, await, look for, hope for, look forward to; contemplate, bargain for/on, bank on; predict, forecast, envisage, envision. **3** *we expect total loyalty:* **require**, ask for, call for, want, insist on, demand.

expectancy noun **1** *an atmosphere of feverish expectancy:* **anticipation**, expectation, eagerness, excitement. **2** *life expectancy:* **likelihood**, probability, outlook, prospect.

expectant adjective **1** *expectant fans:* **eager**, excited, agog, waiting with bated breath, hopeful; in suspense, on tenterhooks. **2** *an expectant mother:* **pregnant**; informal expecting, in the family way, preggers; Brit. informal up the duff/spout, in the (pudding) club.

expectation noun **1** *her expectations were unrealistic:* **supposition**, assumption, presumption, conjecture, surmise, calculation, prediction. **2** *his body grew tense with expectation:* **anticipation**, expectancy, eagerness, excitement, suspense.

expedient adjective *a politically expedient strategy:* **convenient**, advantageous, in one's own interests, useful, of use, beneficial, of benefit, helpful; practical, pragmatic, politic, prudent, wise, judicious, sensible.
noun *a temporary expedient:* **measure**, means, method, stratagem, scheme, plan, move, tactic, manoeuvre, device, contrivance, ploy, machination, dodge; Austral. informal lurk.

expedite verb *he promised to expedite economic reforms:* **speed up**, accelerate, hurry, hasten, step up, quicken, precipitate, dispatch; advance, facilitate, ease, make easier, further, promote, aid, push through, urge on, boost, stimulate, spur on, help along.
– OPPOSITES delay.

expedition noun **1** *an expedition to the South Pole:* **journey**, voyage, tour, odyssey; exploration, safari, trek, hike. **2** (informal) *a shopping expedition:* **trip**, excursion, outing, jaunt.

expeditious adjective *an expeditious system for examining claims for refugee status:* **speedy**, swift, quick, rapid, fast, brisk, efficient; prompt, punctual, immediate, instant.
– OPPOSITES slow.

expel verb **1** *she was expelled from her party:* **throw out**, bar, ban, debar, drum out, oust, remove, get rid of, dismiss; Military cashier; informal chuck out, sling out, kick/boot out; Brit. informal turf out; N. Amer. informal give someone the bum's rush. **2** *he was expelled from the country:* **banish**, exile, deport, evict, expatriate, drive out, throw out. **3** *Dolly expelled a hiss:* **let out**, discharge, eject, issue, send forth.
– OPPOSITES admit.

expend verb **1** *they had already expended $75,000:* **spend**, pay out, disburse, dole out, dish out, get through, waste, fritter (away), dissipate; informal fork out, shell out, lay out, cough up, blow, splurge; Brit. informal splash out, stump up; N. Amer. informal ante up. **2** *children expend a lot of energy:* **use (up)**, utilize, consume, eat up, deplete, get through.
– OPPOSITES save, conserve.

expendable adjective **1** *an accountant decided he was expendable:* **dispensable**, replaceable, non-essential, inessential, unnecessary, not required, superfluous, disposable. **2** *an expendable satellite launcher:* **disposable**, throwaway, one-use, single-use.
– OPPOSITES indispensable.

expenditure noun **1** *the expenditure of funds:* **spending**, paying out, outlay, disbursement, doling out, waste, wasting, frittering (away), dissipation. **2** *reducing public expenditure:* **outgoings**, costs, payments, expenses, overheads, spending.
– OPPOSITES saving, income.

expense noun **1** *Nigel resented the expense:* **cost**, price, charge, outlay, fee, tariff, levy, payment; humorous damage. **2** *regular expenses:* **outgoing**, payment, outlay, expenditure, charge, bill, overhead. **3** *pollution controls come at the expense of jobs:* **sacrifice**, cost, loss.

expensive adjective *an expensive restaurant:* **costly**, dear, high-priced, overpriced, exorbitant, extortionate; informal steep, pricey, costing an arm and a leg, costing the earth, costing a bomb.
– OPPOSITES cheap, economical.

experience noun **1** *qualifications and experience:* **skill**, (practical) knowledge, understanding; background, record, history; maturity, worldliness, sophistication; informal know-how. **2** *an enjoyable experience:*

incident, occurrence, event, happening, episode; adventure, exploit, escapade. **3** *his first experience of business:* **involvement in**, participation in, contact with, acquaintance with, exposure to, observation of, awareness of, insight into.
verb *some policemen experience harassment:* **undergo**, encounter, meet, come into contact with, come across, come up against, face, be faced with.

experienced adjective **1** *an experienced pilot:* **knowledgeable**, skilful, skilled, expert, accomplished, adept, adroit, master, consummate; proficient, trained, competent, capable, well trained, well versed; seasoned, practised, mature, veteran. **2** *she deluded herself that she was experienced:* **worldly (wise)**, sophisticated, suave, urbane, mature, knowing; informal streetwise.
– OPPOSITES novice, naive.

experiment noun **1** *carrying out experiments:* **test**, investigation, trial, examination, observation; assessment, evaluation, appraisal, analysis, study. **2** *these results have been established by experiment:* **research**, experimentation, observation, analysis, testing.
verb *they experimented with new ideas:* **conduct experiments**, carry out trials/tests, conduct research; test, trial, do tests on, try out, assess, appraise, evaluate.

experimental adjective **1** *the experimental stage:* **exploratory**, investigational, trial, test, pilot; speculative, conjectural, hypothetical, tentative, preliminary, untested, untried. **2** *experimental music:* **innovative**, innovatory, new, original, radical, avant-garde, alternative, unorthodox, unconventional, left-field; informal way-out.

expert noun *he is an expert in kendo:* **specialist**, authority, pundit; adept, maestro, virtuoso, (past) master, wizard; connoisseur, aficionado; informal ace, buff, pro, whizz, hotshot; Brit. informal dab hand; N. Amer. informal maven, crackerjack.
adjective *an expert chess player:* **skilful**, skilled, adept, accomplished, talented, fine; master, masterly, brilliant, virtuoso, magnificent, outstanding, great, exceptional, excellent, first-class, first-rate, superb; proficient, good, able, capable, experienced, practised, knowledgeable; informal wizard, ace, crack, mean.
– OPPOSITES incompetent.

expertise noun *technical expertise:* **skill**, skilfulness, expertness, prowess, proficiency, competence; knowledge, mastery, ability, aptitude, facility, capability; informal know-how.

expiate verb *an attempt to expiate his sins:* **atone for**, make amends for, make up for, do penance for, pay for, redress, redeem, offset, make good.

expire verb **1** *my contract has expired:* **run out**, become invalid, become void, lapse; end, finish, stop, come to an end, terminate. **2** *the spot where he expired:* **die**, pass away/on, breathe one's last; informal kick the bucket, bite the dust, croak, buy it; Brit. informal snuff it, peg out, pop one's clogs.

expiry noun **1** *the expiry of the lease:* **lapse**, expiration. **2** *the expiry of his term of office:* **end**, finish, termination, conclusion.

explain verb **1** *a technician explained the procedure:* **describe**, give an explanation of, make clear/intelligible, spell out, put into words; elucidate, expound, explicate, clarify, throw light on; gloss, interpret. **2** *nothing could explain his new-found wealth:* **account for**, give an explanation for, give a reason for; justify, give a justification for, give an excuse for, vindicate, legitimize.

explanation noun **1** *an explanation of the ideas contained in the essay:* **clarification**, simplification; description, report, statement; elucidation, exposition, expounding, explication; gloss, interpretation, commentary, exegesis. **2** *I owe you an explanation:* **account**, reason; justification, excuse, alibi, defence, vindication.

explanatory adjective *explanatory notes:* **explaining**, descriptive, describing, illustrative, illuminative, elucidatory.

expletive noun *she let out an expletive and slammed the phone down:* **swear word**, oath, curse, obscenity, profanity, four-letter word, dirty word; informal cuss word, cuss; (**expletives**) bad language, foul language, strong language, swearing.

explicable adjective *differences in schools were not explicable in terms of differences in intake:* **explainable**, understandable, comprehensible, accountable, intelligible, interpretable.

explicate verb *scholars who have been devoted to explicating these stories:* **explain**, make explicit, clarify, make plain/clear, spell out; interpret, elucidate, expound, illuminate, throw light on.

explicit adjective **1** *explicit instructions:* **clear**, plain, straightforward, crystal clear, easily understandable; precise, exact, specific, unequivocal, unambiguous; detailed, comprehensive, exhaustive. **2** *sexually explicit material:* **uncensored**, graphic, candid, full-frontal.
– OPPOSITES vague.

explode verb **1** *a bomb has exploded:* **blow up**, detonate, go off, burst (apart), fly apart. **2** *Britain had not yet exploded her first atomic device:* **detonate**, set off, let off, discharge. **3** *he exploded in anger:* **lose one's temper**, blow up, get angry, become enraged; informal fly off the handle, hit the roof, blow one's cool/top, go wild, go bananas, see red, go off the deep end; Brit. informal go spare, go crackers; N. Amer. informal blow one's lid/stack. **4** *the city's exploding population:* **increase suddenly/rapidly**,

mushroom, snowball, escalate, multiply, burgeon, rocket. **5** *exploding the myths about men:* **disprove**, refute, rebut, invalidate, negate, negative, controvert, repudiate, discredit, debunk, belie, give the lie to; informal shoot full of holes, blow out of the water.
– OPPOSITES defuse.

exploit verb **1** *we should exploit this new technology:* **utilize**, use, make use of, turn/put to good use, make the most of, capitalize on, benefit from; informal cash in on. **2** *a ruling class which exploited the workers:* **take advantage of**, abuse, impose on, treat unfairly, misuse, ill-treat; informal walk (all) over, take for a ride, rip off.
noun *his exploits brought him notoriety:* **feat**, deed, act, adventure, stunt, escapade; achievement, accomplishment, attainment; informal lark, caper.

exploitation noun **1** *the exploitation of mineral resources:* **utilization**, use, making use of, making the most of, capitalization on; informal cashing in on. **2** *the exploitation of the poor:* **taking advantage**, abuse, misuse, ill-treatment, unfair treatment, oppression.

exploration noun **1** *the exploration of space:* **investigation**, study, survey, research, inspection, examination, scrutiny, observation; consideration, analysis, review. **2** *explorations into the mountains:* **expedition**, trip, journey, voyage; (**explorations**) travels.

exploratory adjective *surgeons performed an exploratory operation:* **investigative**, investigational, explorative, probing, fact-finding; experimental, trial, test, preliminary, provisional.

explore verb **1** *they explored all the possibilities:* **investigate**, look into, consider, examine, research, survey, scrutinize, study, review, go over with a fine-tooth comb; informal check out. **2** *exploring Iceland's north-west:* **travel over**, tour, range over; survey, take a look at, inspect, investigate, reconnoitre; informal recce, give something a/the once-over.

explorer noun **traveller**, discoverer, voyager, adventurer; surveyor, scout, prospector.

explosion noun **1** *Edward heard the explosion:* **detonation**, eruption, blowing up; bang, blast, boom. **2** *an explosion of anger:* **outburst**, flare-up, outbreak, eruption, storm, rush, surge; fit, paroxysm, attack. **3** *the explosion of human populations:* **sudden/rapid increase**, mushrooming, snowballing, escalation, multiplication, burgeoning, rocketing.

explosive adjective **1** *explosive gases:* **volatile**, inflammable, flammable, combustible, incendiary. **2** *Marco's explosive temper:* **fiery**, stormy, violent, volatile, angry, passionate, tempestuous, turbulent, touchy, irascible, hot-headed, short-tempered. **3** *an explosive situation:* **tense**, (highly) charged, overwrought; dangerous, perilous, hazardous, sensitive, delicate, unstable, volatile. **4** *explosive population growth:* **sudden**, dramatic, rapid; mushrooming, snowballing, escalating, rocketing, accelerating.

noun *stocks of explosives:* **bomb**, incendiary (device).

exponent noun **1** *an exponent of free-trade policies:* **advocate**, supporter, proponent, upholder, backer, defender, champion; promoter, propagandist, campaigner, fighter, crusader, enthusiast, apologist. **2** *a karate exponent:* **practitioner**, performer, player.

– OPPOSITES critic, opponent.

export verb **1** *exporting raw materials:* **sell overseas/abroad**, send overseas/abroad, trade internationally. **2** *he is trying to export his ideas to America:* **transmit**, spread, disseminate, circulate, communicate, pass on.

– OPPOSITES import.

expose verb **1** *at low tide the sands are exposed:* **reveal**, uncover, lay bare. **2** *he was exposed to asbestos:* **make vulnerable**, subject, lay open, put at risk, put in jeopardy. **3** *they were exposed to liberal ideas:* **introduce to**, bring into contact with, make aware of, familiarize with, acquaint with. **4** *he was exposed as a liar:* **uncover**, reveal, unveil, unmask, detect, find out; discover, bring to light, bring into the open, make known; denounce, condemn; informal spill the beans on, blow the whistle on.

– OPPOSITES cover.

■ **expose oneself** reveal one's genitals; informal flash.

exposé noun *a shocking exposé of a medical cover-up:* **revelation**, disclosure, exposure; report, feature, piece, column; informal scoop.

– OPPOSITES cover-up.

exposed adjective *the farm is on an exposed hillside:* **unprotected**, unsheltered, open to the elements/weather; vulnerable, defenceless, undefended, pregnable.

– OPPOSITES sheltered.

exposition noun **1** *a lucid exposition:* **explanation**, description, elucidation, explication, interpretation; account, commentary, appraisal, assessment, discussion, exegesis. **2** *the exposition will feature 200 exhibits:* **exhibition**, (trade) fair, display, show, presentation, demonstration; N. Amer. exhibit.

expository adjective *the film suffers from too obviously expository dialogue:* **explanatory**, descriptive, describing, elucidatory, explicatory, explicative, interpretative, exegetic.

expostulate verb *one of the prisoners expostulated with him:* **remonstrate**, disagree, argue, take issue, protest, reason, express disagreement, raise objections.

exposure noun **1** *the exposure of the lizard's vivid blue tongue:* **revealing**, revelation, uncovering, baring, laying bare. **2** *exposure to harmful chemicals:* **subjection**, vulnerability, laying open. **3** *suffering from exposure:* **frostbite**, cold, hypothermia. **4** *exposure to great literature:* **introduction to**, experience of, contact with, familiarity with, acquaintance with, awareness of. **5** *the exposure of a banking scandal:* **uncovering**, revelation, disclosure, unveiling, unmasking, discovery, detection; denunciation, condemnation. **6** *we're getting a lot of exposure:* **publicity**, publicizing, advertising, public interest/attention, media interest/attention; informal hype. **7** *the exposure is perfect:* **outlook**, aspect, view; position, setting, location.

expound verb **1** *he expounded his theories:* **present**, put forward, set forth, propose, propound; explain, give an explanation of, detail, spell out, describe. **2** *a treatise expounding Paul's teachings:* **explain**, interpret, explicate, elucidate; comment on, give a commentary on.

■ **expound on** elaborate on, expand on, expatiate on, discuss at length.

express¹ verb **1** *community leaders expressed their anger:* **communicate**, convey, indicate, show, demonstrate, reveal, make manifest, put across/over, get across/over; articulate, put into words, utter, voice, give voice to; state, assert, proclaim, profess, air, make public, give vent to. **2** *all the juice is expressed:* **squeeze out**, press out, extract.

■ **express oneself** communicate one's thoughts/opinions/views, put thoughts into words, speak one's mind, say what's on one's mind.

express² adjective *an express bus:* **rapid**, swift, fast, quick, speedy, high-speed; non-stop, direct.

– OPPOSITES slow.

noun *an overnight express:* fast train, direct train.

express³ adjective **1** *express reference to confidential matters:* **explicit**, clear, direct, obvious, plain, distinct, unambiguous, unequivocal; specific, precise, crystal clear, certain, categorical. **2** *one express purpose:* **sole**, specific, particular, exclusive, specified, fixed.

– OPPOSITES implied.

expression noun **1** *the free expression of opposition views:* **utterance**, uttering, voicing, pronouncement, declaration, articulation, assertion, setting forth; dissemination, circulation, communication, spreading, promulgation. **2** *an expression of sympathy:* **indication**, demonstration, show, exhibition, token; communication, illustration, revelation. **3** *an expression of harassed fatigue:* **look**, appearance, air, manner, countenance, mien. **4** *a time-worn expression:* **idiom**, phrase, idiomatic expression; proverb, saying, adage, maxim, axiom, aphorism, saw, motto, platitude, cliché. **5** *these pieces are very different in expression:* **emotion**, feeling, spirit, passion, intensity; style, intonation, tone.

expressionless adjective **1** *his face was expressionless:* **inscrutable**, deadpan, poker-faced; blank, vacant, emotionless, unemotional, inexpressive; glazed, stony, wooden, impassive. **2** *a flat, expressionless tone:* **dull**, dry, toneless, monotonous, boring, tedious, flat, wooden, unmodulated, unvarying, devoid of feeling/emotion.
– OPPOSITES expressive, lively.

expressive adjective **1** *an expressive shrug:* **eloquent**, meaningful, demonstrative, suggestive. **2** *an expressive song:* **emotional**, full of emotion/feeling, passionate, poignant, moving, stirring, evocative, powerful, emotionally charged. **3** *his diction is very expressive of his Englishness:* **indicative**, demonstrative, demonstrating, showing, suggesting.
– OPPOSITES expressionless, unemotional.

expressly adverb **1** *he was expressly forbidden to discuss the matter:* **explicitly**, clearly, directly, plainly, distinctly, unambiguously, unequivocally; absolutely; specifically, categorically, pointedly, emphatically. **2** *a machine expressly built for spraying paint:* **solely**, specifically, particularly, specially, exclusively, just, only, explicitly.

expropriate verb *legislation to expropriate land from absentee landlords:* **seize**, take (away/over), appropriate, take possession of, requisition, commandeer, claim, acquire, sequestrate, confiscate.

expulsion noun **1** *expulsion from the party:* **removal**, debarment, dismissal, exclusion, discharge, ejection, drumming out. **2** *the expulsion of bodily wastes:* **discharge**, ejection, excretion, voiding, evacuation, elimination, passing.
– OPPOSITES admission.

expunge verb *that moment can never be expunged from his memory:* **erase**, remove, delete, rub out, wipe out, efface; cross out, strike out, blot out, blank out; destroy, obliterate, eradicate, eliminate.

expurgate verb *a book which had been expurgated for use in schools:* **censor**, bowdlerize, blue-pencil, cut, edit; clean up, sanitize, make acceptable, make palatable, water down.

exquisite adjective **1** *exquisite antique glass:* **beautiful**, lovely, elegant, fine; magnificent, superb, excellent, wonderful, well-crafted, well-made, perfect; delicate, fragile, dainty, subtle. **2** *the garden was tended with exquisite taste:* **discriminating**, discerning, sensitive, selective, fastidious; refined, cultivated, cultured, educated. **3** *exquisite agony:* **intense**, acute, keen, piercing, sharp, severe, racking, excruciating, agonizing, harrowing, searing; unbearable, unendurable.

extant adjective *only one copy of Cavendish's book is still extant:* **still existing**, in existence, existent, surviving, remaining, undestroyed.

extempore adjective *an extempore speech:* **impromptu**, spontaneous, unscripted, ad lib, extemporary, extemporaneous; improvised, unrehearsed, unplanned, unprepared, off the top of one's head; informal off-the-cuff.
– OPPOSITES rehearsed.
adverb *he was speaking extempore:* **spontaneously**, extemporaneously, ad lib, without preparation, without rehearsal, off the top of one's head; informal off the cuff; formal ad libitum.

extemporize verb *in modern jazz, players extemporize in a very free manner:* **improvise**, ad lib, play it by ear, think on one's feet, do something off the top of one's head; informal busk it, wing it, do something off the cuff.

extend verb **1** *he attempted to extend his dominions:* **expand**, enlarge, increase, make larger/bigger; lengthen, widen, broaden. **2** *the garden extends down to the road:* **continue**, carry on, run on, stretch (out), reach, lead. **3** *we have extended our range of services:* **widen**, expand, broaden; augment, supplement, increase, add to, enhance, develop. **4** *extending the life of parliament:* **prolong**, lengthen, increase; stretch out, protract, spin out, string out. **5** *extend your arms and legs:* **stretch out**, spread out, reach out, straighten out. **6** *he extended a hand in greeting:* **hold out**, reach out, hold forth; offer, give, outstretch, proffer. **7** *we wish to extend our thanks to Mr Bayes:* **offer**, proffer, give, grant, bestow, accord.
– OPPOSITES reduce, narrow, shorten.
■ **extend to** include, take in, incorporate, encompass.

extended adjective *an extended legal battle:* **prolonged**, protracted, long-lasting, long-drawn-out, spun out, dragged out, strung out, lengthy, long.

extension noun **1** *they are planning an extension to their ground floor:* **addition**, add-on, adjunct, annexe, wing, supplementary building; N. Amer. ell. **2** *an extension of knowledge:* **expansion**, increase, enlargement, widening, broadening, deepening; augmentation, enhancement, development, growth, continuation. **3** *an extension of opening hours:* **prolongation**, lengthening, increase. **4** *I need an extension of time:* **postponement**, deferral, delay, more/extra time.

extensive adjective **1** *a mansion with extensive grounds:* **large**, large-scale, sizeable, substantial, considerable, ample, expansive, great, vast. **2** *extensive knowledge:* **comprehensive**, thorough, exhaustive; broad, wide, wide-ranging, catholic.

extent noun **1** *the garden was about two acres in extent:* **area**, size, expanse, length;

proportions, dimensions. **2** *the full extent of her father's illness:* **degree**, scale, level, magnitude, scope; size, breadth, width, reach, range.

extenuating adjective *there were extenuating circumstances:* **mitigating**, excusing, exonerative, palliating, palliative, justifying, justificatory, vindicating.

exterior adjective *the exterior walls:* **outer**, outside, outermost, outward, external.
– OPPOSITES interior.
noun *the exterior of the building:* **outside**, outer surface, external surface, outward appearance, facade.

exterminate verb *the invaders intended simply to exterminate any natives:* **kill**, put to death, take/end the life of, dispatch; slaughter, butcher, massacre, wipe out, eliminate, eradicate, annihilate; murder, assassinate, execute; informal do away with, bump off, do in, top, take out, blow away; N. Amer. informal ice, rub out, waste.

extermination noun **killing**, murder, assassination, putting to death, execution, dispatch, slaughter, massacre, liquidation, elimination, eradication, annihilation.

external adjective **1** *an external wall:* **outer**, outside, outermost, outward, exterior. **2** *an external examiner:* **outside**, independent, non-resident, from elsewhere.
– OPPOSITES internal, in-house.

extinct adjective **1** *an extinct species:* **vanished**, lost, died out, no longer existing, no longer extant, wiped out, destroyed, gone. **2** *an extinct volcano:* **inactive**.
– OPPOSITES extant, dormant.

extinction noun **dying out**, disappearance, vanishing; extermination, destruction, elimination, eradication, annihilation.

extinguish verb **1** *the fire was extinguished:* **douse**, put out, stamp out, smother, beat out, dampen down. **2** *all hope was extinguished:* **destroy**, end, finish off, put an end to, bring to an end, terminate, remove, annihilate, wipe out, erase, eliminate, eradicate, obliterate; informal take out, rub out.
– OPPOSITES light.

extol verb *nutritionists have long extolled the virtues of rice:* **praise enthusiastically**, go into raptures about/over, wax lyrical about, sing the praises of, praise to the skies, acclaim, eulogize, rhapsodize over, rave about, enthuse about/over; informal go wild about, go on about; N. Amer. informal ballyhoo; formal laud.
– OPPOSITES criticize.

extort verb *he was convicted of extorting money from local residents:* **obtain by force**, obtain by threat(s), blackmail someone for, extract, exact, wring, wrest, screw, squeeze; N. Amer. & Austral. informal put the bite on someone for.

extortion noun **demanding money with menaces**, blackmail, extraction; N. Amer. informal shakedown.

extortionate adjective **1** *extortionate prices:* **exorbitant**, excessively high, excessive, outrageous, unreasonable, inordinate, inflated; informal over the top, OTT. **2** *an unreasonable and extortionate clause in the contract:* **grasping**, bloodsucking, avaricious, greedy; exacting, harsh, severe, oppressive; informal money-grubbing.

extortionist noun **racketeer**, extortioner, extorter, blackmailer; informal bloodsucker.

extra adjective *extra income:* **additional**, more, added, supplementary, further, auxiliary, ancillary, subsidiary, secondary.
adverb **1** *working extra hard:* **exceptionally**, particularly, specially, especially, very, extremely; unusually, extraordinarily, uncommonly, remarkably, outstandingly, amazingly, incredibly, really; informal seriously, mucho, awfully, terribly; Brit. jolly, dead, well. **2** *postage is charged extra:* **in addition**, additionally, as well, also, too, besides, on top (of that).
noun **1** *an optional extra:* **addition**, supplement, adjunct, addendum, add-on. **2** *a film extra:* **walk-on**, supernumerary, spear-carrier.

extract verb **1** *he extracted the cassette:* **take out**, draw out, pull out, remove, withdraw; free, release, extricate. **2** *a promise was unfairly extracted from me:* **wrest**, exact, wring, screw, squeeze, obtain by force, obtain by threat(s), extort, blackmail someone for; N. Amer. & Austral. informal put the bite on someone for. **3** *the roots are crushed to extract the juice:* **squeeze out**, express, press out, obtain. **4** *the table is extracted from the report:* **excerpt**, select, reproduce, copy, take.
– OPPOSITES insert.
noun **1** *an extract from his article:* **excerpt**, passage, citation, quotation; (**excerpts**) analects. **2** *an extract of the ginseng root:* **decoction**, distillation, distillate, abstraction, concentrate, essence, juice.

extraction noun **1** *the extraction of gall bladder stones:* **removal**, taking out, drawing out, pulling out, withdrawal; freeing, release, extrication. **2** *a man of Irish extraction:* **descent**, ancestry, parentage, ancestors, family, antecedents; lineage, line, origin, derivation, birth; genealogy, heredity, stock, pedigree, blood, bloodline; roots, origins.
– OPPOSITES insertion.

extradite verb **1** *the government extradited him to Germany:* **deport**, send back, send home, repatriate. **2** *the government attempted to extradite suspects from Belgium:* **have someone deported**, have someone sent home, bring back.

extradition noun **deportation**, repatriation, expulsion.

extraneous adjective **1** *extraneous considerations:* **irrelevant**, immaterial, beside the point, unrelated, unconnected, inapposite, inapplicable. **2** *extraneous noise:* **external**, outside, exterior.

extraordinary adjective **1** *an extraordinary coincidence:* **remarkable**, exceptional, amazing, astonishing, astounding, sensational, stunning, incredible, unbelievable, phenomenal; striking, outstanding, momentous, impressive, singular, memorable, unforgettable, unique, noteworthy; out of the ordinary, unusual, uncommon, rare, surprising; informal fantastic, terrific, tremendous, stupendous, awesome. **2** *moving with extraordinary speed:* **very great**, tremendous, enormous, immense, prodigious, stupendous, monumental; informal almighty.

extravagance noun **1** *a fit of extravagance:* **profligacy**, unthriftiness, improvidence, wastefulness, prodigality, lavishness. **2** *the costliest brands are an extravagance:* **luxury**, indulgence, self-indulgence, treat, extra, non-essential. **3** *the extravagance of the decor:* **ornateness**, elaborateness, embellishment, ornamentation; ostentation, over-elaborateness. **4** *the extravagance of his compliments:* **excessiveness**, exaggeration, outrageousness, immoderation, excess.

extravagant adjective **1** *an extravagant lifestyle:* **spendthrift**, profligate, unthrifty, improvident, wasteful, prodigal, lavish. **2** *extravagant gifts:* **expensive**, costly, dear, high-priced, high-cost; valuable, precious; informal pricey, costing the earth, costing a bomb. **3** *extravagant prices:* **exorbitant**, extortionate, excessive, high, unreasonable. **4** *extravagant praise:* **excessive**, immoderate, exaggerated, gushing, unrestrained, effusive, fulsome. **5** *decorated in an extravagant style:* **ornate**, elaborate, decorated, ornamented, fancy; over-elaborate, ostentatious, exaggerated, baroque, rococo; informal flash, flashy.
– OPPOSITES thrifty, cheap, plain.

extravaganza noun *a live extravaganza featuring a host of stars:* **spectacular**, display, spectacle, show, pageant.

extreme adjective **1** *extreme danger:* **utmost**, very great, greatest (possible), maximum, maximal, highest, supreme, great, acute, enormous, severe, high, exceptional, extraordinary. **2** *extreme measures:* **drastic**, serious, desperate, dire, radical, far-reaching, momentous, consequential; heavy, sharp, severe, austere, harsh, tough, strict, rigorous, oppressive, draconian; Brit. swingeing. **3** *a person of very extreme views:* **radical**, extremist, immoderate, fanatical, revolutionary, rebel, subversive, militant. **4** *extreme sports:* **dangerous**, hazardous, risky, high-risk, adventurous. **5** *the extreme north-west:* **furthest**, farthest, furthermost, farthermost, very, utmost.
– OPPOSITES slight, moderate.
noun **1** *the two extremes:* **opposite**, antithesis, side of the coin, (opposite) pole, antipode.

2 *this attitude is taken to its extreme in the following quote:* **limit**, extremity, highest/greatest degree, maximum, height, top, zenith, peak.
■ **in the extreme**. See EXTREMELY.

extremely adverb *we are all extremely worried:* **very**, exceedingly, exceptionally, especially, extraordinarily, in the extreme, tremendously, immensely, vastly, hugely, intensely, acutely, singularly, uncommonly, unusually, decidedly, particularly, supremely, highly, remarkably, really, truly, mightily; informal terrifically, awfully, fearfully, terribly, devilishly, majorly, seriously, mega, ultra, damn, damned; Brit. informal ever so, well, hellish, dead, jolly; N. Amer. informal real, mighty, awful, darned.
– OPPOSITES slightly.

extremist noun *the attack was carried out by a group of right-wing extremists:* **fanatic**, radical, zealot, fundamentalist, hardliner, militant, activist; informal ultra.
– OPPOSITES moderate.

extremity noun **1** *the eastern extremity:* **limit**, end, edge, side, farthest point, boundary, border, frontier; perimeter, periphery, margin. **2** *she lost all feeling in her extremities:* **hands and feet**, fingers and toes, limbs. **3** *the extremity of the violence:* **intensity**, magnitude, acuteness, ferocity, vehemence, fierceness, violence, severity, seriousness, strength, power, powerfulness, vigour, force, forcefulness. **4** *in extremity he will send for her:* **dire straits**, trouble, difficulty, hard times, hardship, adversity, misfortune, distress; crisis, emergency, disaster, catastrophe, calamity; predicament, plight, mess, dilemma; informal fix, pickle, jam, spot, bind, scrape, hole, sticky situation, hot/deep water.

extricate verb *Deborah managed to extricate herself from the melee:* **extract**, free, release, disentangle, get out, remove, withdraw, disengage; informal get someone/oneself off the hook.

extrinsic adjective *the animal population is influenced by extrinsic factors like food supply and predation:* **external**, extraneous, exterior, outside, outward.
– OPPOSITES intrinsic.

extrovert noun *like most extroverts he was a good dancer:* **outgoing person**, sociable person, socializer, life and soul of the party.
– OPPOSITES introvert.
adjective *his extrovert personality:* **outgoing**, extroverted, sociable, gregarious, genial, affable, friendly, unreserved.
– OPPOSITES introverted.

extrude verb *lava that has been extruded under water:* **force out**, thrust out, express, eject, expel, release, emit.

exuberant adjective **1** *exuberant guests dancing on the terrace:* **ebullient**, buoyant, cheerful, jaunty, light-hearted, high-spirited, exhilarated, excited, elated, exultant, euphoric, joyful, cheery,

merry, jubilant, vivacious, enthusiastic, irrepressible, energetic, animated, full of life, lively, vigorous; Brit. Tiggerish; informal bubbly, bouncy, chipper, chirpy, full of beans. **2** *an exuberant coating of mosses:* **luxuriant**, lush, rich, dense, thick, abundant, profuse, plentiful, prolific. **3** *an exuberant welcome:* **effusive**, extravagant, fulsome, expansive, gushing, gushy, demonstrative.
– OPPOSITES gloomy, restrained.

exude verb **1** *milkweed exudes a milky sap:* **give off/out**, discharge, release, emit, issue; ooze, weep, secrete, excrete. **2** *slime exudes from the fungus:* **ooze**, seep, issue, escape, discharge, flow, leak. **3** *he exuded self-confidence:* **emanate**, radiate, ooze, emit; display, show, exhibit, manifest, transmit, embody.

exult verb **1** *her opponents exulted when she left:* **rejoice**, be joyful, be happy, be delighted, be elated, be ecstatic, be overjoyed, be cock-a-hoop, be jubilant, be rapturous, be in raptures, be thrilled, jump for joy, be on cloud nine, be in seventh heaven; celebrate, cheer; informal be over the moon, be on top of the world; Austral. informal be wrapped. **2** *he exulted in his triumph:* **rejoice at/in**, take delight in, find/take pleasure in, find joy in, enjoy, revel in, glory in, delight in, relish, savour; be/feel proud of, congratulate oneself on.
– OPPOSITES sorrow.

exultant adjective *the exultant winners waved to the crowd:* **jubilant**, thrilled, triumphant, delighted, exhilarated, happy, overjoyed, joyous, joyful, gleeful, cock-a-hoop, excited, rejoicing, ecstatic, euphoric, elated, rapturous, in raptures, enraptured, on cloud nine/seven, in seventh heaven; informal over the moon; N. Amer. informal wigged out.

exultation noun **jubilation**, rejoicing, happiness, pleasure, joy, gladness, delight,

glee, elation, cheer, euphoria, exhilaration, delirium, ecstasy, rapture, exuberance.

eye noun **1** *he rubbed his eyes:* **eyeball**; informal peeper. **2** *his sharp eyes had missed nothing:* **eyesight**, vision, sight, powers of observation, (visual) perception. **3** *the eye of a needle:* **hole**, opening, aperture, eyelet, slit, slot. **4** *the eye of the storm:* **centre**, middle, heart, core, hub, thick.
verb **1** *he eyed the stranger suspiciously:* **look at**, observe, view, gaze at, stare at, regard, contemplate, survey, scrutinize, consider, glance at; watch, keep an eye on, keep under observation; informal have/take a gander at, check out, size up; Brit. informal have/take a butcher's at, have/take a dekko at, have/take a shufti at, clock; N. Amer. informal eyeball. **2** *eyeing young women in the street:* **ogle**, leer at, stare at, make eyes at; informal eye up, give someone the glad eye; Brit. informal gawp at, gawk at; Austral./NZ informal perv on.
■ **see eye to eye** agree, concur, be in agreement, be of the same mind/opinion, be in accord, think as one; be on the same wavelength, get on/along.

eye-catching adjective *each pot is decorated with eye-catching designs:* **striking**, arresting, conspicuous, dramatic, impressive, spectacular, breathtaking, dazzling, amazing, stunning, sensational, remarkable, distinctive, unusual, out of the ordinary.

eyesight noun *he has poor eyesight:* **sight**, vision, faculty of sight, ability to see, (visual) perception.

eyesore noun *the rubbish tip is an eyesore:* **ugly sight**, blot (on the landscape), mess, scar, blight, disfigurement, blemish, monstrosity; informal sight.

eyewitness noun *eyewitnesses stated that one plane crashed in the harbour:* **observer**, onlooker, witness, bystander, spectator, watcher, viewer, passer-by.

Ff

fable noun **1** *the fable of the hare and the tortoise:* **tale**, parable, allegory. **2** *the fables of ancient Greece:* **myth**, legend, saga, epic, folk tale, folk story, fairy tale; folklore, mythology.

fabled adjective **1** *the fabled god-giant of Irish myth:* **legendary**, mythical, mythic, mythological, fabulous, folkloric, fairy-tale; fictitious, imaginary, imagined, made up. **2** *the fabled quality of French wine:* **celebrated**, renowned, famed, famous, well known, prized, noted, legendary, notable, acclaimed, esteemed, prestigious.

fabric noun **1** *they weave the finest silk fabrics in the world:* **cloth**, material, textile, tissue. **2** *the fabric of the building has deteriorated:* **structure**, framework, frame, form, composition, construction, foundations.

fabricate verb **1** *he was found to have fabricated research data:* **falsify**, fake, counterfeit, invent, make up. **2** *you will have to fabricate a new exhaust system:* **make**, create, manufacture, produce; construct, build, assemble, put together, form, fashion.

fabrication noun **1** *the story was a complete fabrication:* **invention**, concoction, (piece of) fiction, falsification, lie, untruth, falsehood, fib, myth, made-up story, fairy story/tale, cock-and-bull story; informal tall story, whopper; Brit. informal porky (pie). **2** *the lintels are galvanized after fabrication:* **manufacture**, creation, production; construction, building, assembly, forming, fashioning.

fabulous adjective **1** *they are paid fabulous salaries:* **tremendous**, stupendous, prodigious, phenomenal, remarkable, exceptional; astounding, amazing, fantastic, breathtaking, staggering, unthinkable, unimaginable, incredible, unbelievable, unheard of, untold, undreamed of, beyond one's wildest dreams; informal mind-boggling, mind-blowing. **2** (informal) *we had a fabulous time.* See EXCELLENT. **3** *a fabulous horse-like beast with a human head:* **mythical**, legendary, mythic, mythological, fabled, folkloric, fairy-tale; fictitious, imaginary, imagined, made up.

facade noun **1** *the house has a half-timbered facade:* **front**, frontage, face, elevation, exterior, outside. **2** *what lay behind their facade of bonhomie?* **show**, front, appearance, pretence, simulation, affectation, semblance, illusion, act, masquerade, charade, mask, cloak, veil, veneer.

face noun **1** *she has a beautiful face:* **countenance**, physiognomy, features; informal mug; Brit. informal mush, dial, clock, phiz, phizog, boat race; N. Amer. informal puss, pan; literary visage. **2** *her face grew sad again:* **(facial) expression**, look, appearance, air, manner, bearing, countenance, mien. **3** *he made a face at the sourness of the drink:* **grimace**, scowl, wince, frown, glower, pout. **4** *a cube has six faces:* **side**, aspect, flank, surface, plane, facet, wall, elevation. **5** *we are changing the face of the film industry:* **(outward) appearance**, aspect, nature, image. **6** *he put on a brave face for his audience:* **front**, show, display, act, appearance, facade, exterior, mask, masquerade, pretence, pose, veneer. **7** *criticism should never cause the recipient to lose face:* **respect**, honour, esteem, regard, admiration, approbation, acclaim, approval, favour, popularity, prestige, standing, status, dignity; self-respect, self-esteem.
verb **1** *the hotel faces the sea:* **look out on**, front on to, look towards, be facing, look over/across, overlook, give on to, be opposite (to). **2** *you'll just have to face facts:* **accept**, become reconciled to, get used to, become accustomed to, adjust to, acclimatize oneself to; learn to live with, cope with, deal with, come to terms with, become resigned to. **3** *he faces a humiliating rejection:* **be confronted by**, be faced with, encounter, experience, come into contact with, come up against. **4** *the problems facing our police force:* **beset**, worry, distress, trouble, bother, confront; torment, plague, blight, bedevil, curse. **5** *he faced this challenge boldly:* **brave**, face up to, encounter, meet (head-on), confront; oppose, resist, withstand. **6** *a low wall faced with flint:* **cover**, clad, veneer, overlay, surface, dress, put a facing on, laminate, coat, line.

■ **face to face** *the two men stood face to face:* facing (each other), opposite (each other), across from each other.

■ **on the face of it** *on the face of it, this decision is the height of folly:* ostensibly, to all appearances, to all intents and purposes, at first glance, on the surface, superficially; apparently, seemingly, outwardly, it seems (that), it would seem (that), it appears (that), it would appear (that), as far as one can see/tell, by all accounts.

facelift noun 1 *she's planning to have a facelift:* **cosmetic surgery**, plastic surgery. 2 (informal) *the theatre is reopening after a $20,000 facelift:* **renovation**, redecoration, refurbishment, revamp, makeover, overhaul, modernization, restoration, repair, redevelopment, rebuild, reconstruction, refit.

facet noun 1 *the large number of facets preserves the size of the gem:* **surface**, face, side, plane. 2 *she'd also seen other facets of his character:* **aspect**, feature, side, dimension, characteristic, detail, point, ingredient, strand; component, constituent, element.

facetious adjective *the crew greeted my arrival on board with facetious comments:* **flippant**, flip, glib, frivolous, tongue-in-cheek, joking, jokey, jocular, playful, sportive, teasing, mischievous; witty, amusing, funny, droll, comic, comical, light-hearted; formal jocose.
– OPPOSITES serious.

facile adjective *it is easy to fall into facile and unproductive stereotypes:* **simplistic**, superficial, oversimplified; shallow, glib, jejune, naive; N. Amer. dime-store.

facilitate verb *working in pairs appears to facilitate learning:* **make easy/easier**, ease, make possible, make smooth/smoother; enable, assist, help (along), aid, oil the wheels of, expedite, speed up, accelerate, forward, advance, promote, further, encourage.
– OPPOSITES impede.

facility noun 1 *there are ample car-parking facilities:* **provision**, space, room, means, potential, equipment. 2 *the camera has a zoom facility:* **feature**, option, setting; mode. 3 *a wealth of local facilities:* **amenity**, resource, service, advantage, convenience, benefit. 4 *they set up a medical facility deep in the jungle:* **establishment**, centre, place, station, location, premises, site, post, base; informal joint, outfit, set-up. 5 *his undoubted facility for drawing:* **aptitude**, talent, gift, flair, bent, skill, knack, genius; ability, proficiency, competence, capability, capacity, faculty.

facing noun 1 *a tartan jacket with green velvet facings:* **covering**, trimming, lining, interfacing. 2 *the bricks were used as a facing on a concrete core:* **cladding**, veneer, skin, surface, facade, front, coating, covering, dressing, overlay, lamination, plating; N. Amer. siding.

facsimile noun 1 *here's an extremely rare facsimile of the score for Beethoven's Fifth:* **copy**, reproduction, duplicate, replica, likeness; print, reprint. 2 *we are equipped with telephone, facsimile, and photocopying facilities:* **fax**.
– OPPOSITES original.

fact noun 1 *it is a fact that the water supply is polluted:* **reality**, actuality, certainty; truth, gospel. 2 *every fact in the report was double-checked:* **detail**, piece of information, particular, item, specific, element, point, factor, feature, characteristic, ingredient, circumstance, aspect, facet; (**facts**) information.
– OPPOSITES lie, fiction.
■ **in fact** actually, in actuality, in actual fact, really, in reality, in point of fact, as a matter of fact, in truth, to tell the truth.

faction noun 1 *he was supported by a faction of the Liberal Party:* **clique**, coterie, caucus, cabal, bloc, camp, group, grouping, sector, section, wing, arm, branch, set; ginger group, pressure group. 2 *the council was increasingly split by faction:* **infighting**, dissension, dissent, dispute, discord, strife, conflict, friction, argument, disagreement, controversy, quarrelling, wrangling, bickering, squabbling, disharmony, disunity, schism.

factious adjective *he had transformed a fragmented, factious movement into a united one:* **divided**, split, schismatic, discordant, quarrelling, warring, at loggerheads, at odds.
– OPPOSITES harmonious.

factitious adjective *the claim was, to a certain extent, factitious:* **bogus**, fake, specious, false, counterfeit, fraudulent, spurious, sham, mock, feigned, affected, pretended, contrived, engineered; informal phoney, pseudo, pretend; Brit. informal cod.
– OPPOSITES genuine.

factor noun *this had been a key factor in his decision to stand down:* **element**, part, component, ingredient, strand, constituent, point, detail, item, feature, facet, aspect, characteristic, consideration, influence, circumstance.

factory noun **works**, plant, yard, mill, industrial unit; workshop, shop.

factotum noun *in former times he might have been a nobleman's factotum:* **odd-job man**, handyman, jack of all trades, man/girl Friday; Austral. knockabout; informal (Mr) Fixit.

factual adjective *balanced, factual information about consumer products is very useful:* **truthful**, true, accurate, authentic, historical, genuine, fact-based; true-to-life, correct, exact, honest, faithful, literal, verbatim, word for word, unbiased, objective, unvarnished.
– OPPOSITES fictitious.

faculty noun 1 *he had quite lost the faculty of speech:* **power**, capability, capacity, facility, wherewithal, means; (**faculties**) senses, wits, reason, intelligence. 2 *he had a faculty for unearthing new contributors to the fund:* **ability**, proficiency, competence, capability, potential, capacity, facility; aptitude, talent, gift, flair, bent, skill, knack, genius; expertise, expertness, adeptness, adroitness, dexterity, prowess, mastery, artistry. **3** *the arts faculty of the university:* **department**, school, division, section.

fad noun *there is a general fad for see-through products:* **craze**, vogue, trend, fashion, mode, enthusiasm, passion, obsession, mania, rage, compulsion, fixation, fetish, fancy, whim, fascination; informal thing.

fade verb **1** *the paintwork has faded and peeled:* **pale**, bleach, lose colour, discolour; dull, dim. **2** *sunlight had faded the picture:* **bleach**, wash out, blanch, whiten, dim, dull. **3** *remove the flower heads as they fade:* **wither**, wilt, droop, shrivel, die. **4** *the afternoon light began to fade:* **(grow) dim**, grow faint, fail, dwindle, die away, wane, disappear, vanish, decline, melt away. **5** *the Communist movement was fading away:* **decline**, die out, diminish, deteriorate, decay, crumble, collapse, fail, fall, sink, slump, go downhill.
– OPPOSITES brighten, increase.

faeces plural noun **excrement**, bodily waste, waste matter, ordure, dung, manure; excreta, stools, droppings; ordure, filth, muck, mess, night soil; informal pooh, doo-doo, doings, turds; Brit. informal cack, whoopsies, jobbies; N. Amer. informal poop.

fail verb **1** *they could not explain why the enterprise had failed:* **be unsuccessful**, not succeed, fall through, fall flat, collapse, founder, backfire, meet with disaster, come to nothing/naught; informal flop, bomb. **2** *he failed all his exams:* **be unsuccessful in**, not pass, not make the grade, informal flunk. **3** *he felt his friends had failed him:* **let down**, disappoint; desert, abandon, betray, be disloyal to; literary forsake. **4** *the crops failed for the third year in a row:* **wither**, not grow. **5** *they went to bed when the daylight failed:* **fade**, dim, die away, wane, disappear, vanish. **6** *the ventilation system failed:* **break (down)**, stop working, cut out, crash; malfunction, go wrong, develop a fault; informal conk out, go on the blink; Brit. informal pack up, play up. **7** *Ceri's health was failing:* **deteriorate**, degenerate, decline, fade, wane, ebb. **8** *900 businesses are failing each week:* **collapse**, crash, go under, go bankrupt, go into receivership, go into liquidation, cease trading, be wound up; informal fold, flop, go bust, go broke, go to the wall.
– OPPOSITES succeed, pass, thrive, work.
■ **without fail** *she went to Mass every Sunday without fail:* **without exception**, unfailingly, regularly, invariably, predictably, conscientiously, religiously, come what may.

failing noun *Jeanne accepted him despite his failings:* **fault**, shortcoming, weakness, imperfection, defect, flaw, frailty; foible, idiosyncrasy, vice.
– OPPOSITES strength.
adjective *the dry climate would be good for his failing health:* **weak**, weakened, declining, ruined, damaged, fragile.

preposition *failing that, at least keep a detailed plan of your garden.* **in the absence of**, lacking, notwithstanding.

failure noun **1** *the failure of the assassination attempt improved police morale:* **lack of success**, non-fulfilment, defeat, collapse, foundering. **2** *every one of his schemes had been a failure:* **fiasco**, debacle, catastrophe, disaster; informal flop, washout, dead loss; N. Amer. informal snafu, clinker. **3** *she was regarded by everyone as a failure:* **loser**, underachiever, ne'er-do-well, disappointment; informal no-hoper, dead loss. **4** *he felt guilty for what seemed like a failure on his part:* **negligence**, dereliction; omission, oversight. **5** *the failure of the camera:* **breakdown**, malfunction; crash. **6** *the failure of several state-owned companies:* **collapse**, crash, bankruptcy, insolvency, liquidation, closure.
– OPPOSITES success.

faint adjective **1** *her skirt still had a faint mark on it:* **indistinct**, vague, unclear, indefinite, ill-defined, imperceptible, unobtrusive; pale, light, faded. **2** *the baby gave a faint cry:* **quiet**, muted, muffled, stifled; feeble, weak, whispered, murmured, indistinct; low, soft, gentle. **3** *the faint possibility of his returning to office:* **slight**, slender, slim, small, tiny, negligible, remote, vague, unlikely, improbable; informal minuscule. **4** *only faint praise was offered:* **unenthusiastic**, half-hearted, weak, feeble. **5** *I suddenly felt hot and faint:* **dizzy**, giddy, light-headed, unsteady; informal woozy.
– OPPOSITES clear, loud, strong.
verb *he was so pale she thought he would faint:* **pass out**, lose consciousness, black out, keel over, swoon; informal flake out, conk out, zonk out, go out like a light.
noun *she collapsed to the floor in a dead faint:* **blackout**, fainting fit, loss of consciousness, swoon; Medicine syncope.

faint-hearted adjective *the more faint-hearted tenants left after the raid:* **timid**, timorous, nervous, nervy, easily scared, fearful, afraid; cowardly, craven, spineless, pusillanimous, lily-livered; informal chicken-hearted, yellow-bellied, gutless, sissy, wimpy, wimpish.
– OPPOSITES brave.

faintly adverb **1** *Maria called his name faintly:* **indistinctly**, softly, gently, weakly, quietly, in a low voice. **2** *the new officer looked faintly bewildered:* **slightly**, vaguely, somewhat, quite, fairly, rather, a little, a bit, a touch, a shade; informal sort of, kind of.
– OPPOSITES loudly, extremely.

fair[1] adjective **1** *the courts were generally regarded as fair:* **just**, equitable, honest, upright, honourable, trustworthy; impartial, unbiased, unprejudiced, non-partisan, neutral, even-handed; informal legit, on the level; N. Amer. informal on the up and up. **2** *I am hoping for fair weather next week:* **fine**, dry, bright, clear, good, sunny; cloudless;

warm, balmy, clement, benign, pleasant. **3** *the voyage was helped by fair winds and calm seas:* **favourable**, advantageous, benign; on one's side, in one's favour. **4** *she had long fair hair:* **blond(e)**, yellowish, golden, flaxen, light, light brown, tow-coloured, ash blonde; fair-haired, light-haired, golden-haired. **5** *Belinda's skin was very fair:* **pale**, light, light-coloured, white, creamy. **6** *scoring twenty points was a fair achievement:* **reasonable**, passable, tolerable, satisfactory, acceptable, respectable, decent, all right, good enough, pretty good, not bad, average, middling; informal OK, so-so.
– OPPOSITES inclement, unfavourable, dark.
■ **fair and square** *I won the race fair and square:* honestly, fairly, by the book; lawfully, legally, legitimately; informal on the level; N. Amer. informal on the up and up.

fair² noun **1** *we visited the county fair:* **fête**, gala, festival, carnival. **2** *a local antiques fair:* **market**, bazaar, mart, exchange, sale. **3** *Manchester is to host a new British art fair:* **exhibition**, display, show, presentation, exposition; N. Amer. exhibit.

fairly adverb **1** *all pupils were treated fairly:* **justly**, equitably, impartially, without bias, without prejudice, even-handedly; lawfully, legally, legitimately, by the book; equally, the same. **2** *the pipes are in fairly good condition:* **reasonably**, passably, tolerably, adequately, moderately, quite, relatively, comparatively; informal pretty. **3** *he fairly hauled her along the street:* **positively**, really, actually, absolutely; practically, almost, nearly, all but; informal plain.

fair-minded adjective *he was respected as a fair-minded judge:* **fair**, just, even-handed, equitable, impartial, non-partisan, unbiased, unprejudiced; honest, honourable, trustworthy, upright, decent; informal on the level; N. Amer. informal on the up and up.

fairy noun **sprite**, pixie, elf, imp, brownie, puck, leprechaun, pishogue, nixie; literary faerie, fay.

fairy tale, fairy story noun **folk tale**, folk story, traditional story, myth, legend, fantasy, fable.

faith noun **1** *he justified his boss's faith in him:* **trust**, belief, confidence, conviction; optimism, hopefulness, hope. **2** *she gave her life for her faith:* **religion**, (religious) belief, church, sect, denomination, (religious) persuasion, ideology, creed, teaching, doctrine.
– OPPOSITES mistrust.
■ **break faith with** *any attempt to threaten us is an attempt to make us break faith with our customers:* be disloyal to, be unfaithful to, be untrue to, betray, play someone false, break one's promise to, fail, let down; double-cross, deceive, cheat, stab in the back; informal do the dirty on.
■ **keep faith with** *they must keep faith with their generation and not look back towards*

the old one: be loyal to, be faithful to, be true to, stand by, stick by, keep one's promise to.

faithful adjective **1** *she stayed faithful all her married life | his faithful assistant:* **loyal**, constant, true, devoted, true-blue, unswerving, staunch, steadfast, dedicated, committed; trusty, trustworthy, dependable, reliable. **2** *a faithful copy of a famous painting:* **accurate**, precise, exact, true, close, strict; realistic, authentic; informal on the mark, on the nail; Brit. informal spot on, bang on; N. Amer. informal on the money.
– OPPOSITES inaccurate.

faithless adjective **1** *the doomed Giselle and her faithless lover, Albrecht:* **unfaithful**, disloyal, inconstant, false, untrue, adulterous, traitorous; fickle, flighty, untrustworthy, unreliable, undependable; deceitful, two-faced, double-crossing; informal cheating, two-timing, back-stabbing; literary perfidious. **2** *they live undisciplined, faithless lives:* **unbelieving**, godless, irreligious, disbelieving, agnostic, atheistic.

fake noun **1** *the sculpture was found to be a fake:* **forgery**, counterfeit, copy, pirate copy, sham, fraud, hoax, imitation, mock-up, dummy, reproduction; informal phoney, rip-off. **2** *that so-called Doctor Dawes is a fake:* **charlatan**, quack, mountebank, sham, fraud, humbug, impostor, hoaxer, cheat, (confidence) trickster, fraudster; informal phoney, con man, con artist.
adjective **1** *he gave his wife fake banknotes:* **counterfeit**, forged, imitation, pirate(d), false, bogus; invalid; informal phoney, dud. **2** *they covered themselves in fake diamonds:* **imitation**, artificial, synthetic, simulated, reproduction, replica, ersatz, man-made, dummy, false, faux, mock, bogus; informal pretend, phoney, pseudo. **3** *she adopted a fake Liverpool accent:* **feigned**, faked, put-on, assumed, invented, affected, pseudo; unconvincing, artificial, mock; informal phoney, pseud; Brit. informal cod.
– OPPOSITES genuine, authentic.
verb **1** *the death certificate was faked:* **forge**, counterfeit, falsify, copy, pirate, reproduce, replicate; doctor, alter, tamper with. **2** *he faked a yawn and left:* **feign**, pretend (to), simulate, put on, make-believe, affect.

fall verb **1** *bombers droned above and bombs began to fall:* **drop**, descend, come down, go down; plummet, plunge, sink, dive, tumble; cascade. **2** *he tripped and fell:* **topple over**, tumble over, keel over, fall down/over, go head over heels, go headlong, collapse, take a spill, pitch forward; trip (over), stumble, slip; informal come a cropper; Brit. informal go for six. **3** *little by little, the water level began to fall:* **subside**, recede, fall away, go down, sink, drop. **4** *inflation is expected to fall in the spring:* **decrease**, decline, diminish, fall off, drop off, lessen, dwindle, plummet, plunge, slump, sink; depreciate, devalue; informal go through the floor, nosedive, take a header, crash. **5** *the Mogul empire fell several*

centuries later: **decline**, deteriorate, degenerate, go downhill, go to rack and ruin, decay, wither, fade, fail; informal go to the dogs, go to pot, go down the toilet; Austral./NZ informal go to the pack. **6** *a monument to those who fell in the war:* **die**, perish, lose one's life, be killed, be slain, be lost, meet one's death; informal bite the dust, croak, buy it; Brit. informal snuff it. **7** *the town fell to the Germans:* **be taken by**, be defeated by, be conquered by, be overwhelmed by, succumb; surrender, yield, submit, give in, capitulate. **8** *Easter falls on 23rd April:* **occur**, take place, happen, come about; arise. **9** *he waited for night to fall:* **come**, arrive, appear, arise, materialize. **10** *my grandmother has fallen ill:* **become**, grow, get, turn. **11** *more of the domestic chores may fall to him:* **be the responsibility of**, be the duty of, be borne by, be one's job; come someone's way.
– OPPOSITES rise, flood, increase, flourish.
noun 1 *he had a fall and broke his hip:* **tumble**, trip, spill, topple, slip; collapse; informal nosedive, header, cropper. **2** *September's figures showed a fall in sales:* **decline**, fall-off, drop, decrease, cut, dip, reduction, downswing; plummet, plunge, slump; informal nosedive, crash. **3** *the fall of the Roman Empire:* **downfall**, collapse, failure, decline, deterioration, degeneration; destruction, overthrow, demise. **4** *the fall of Saigon:* **surrender**, capitulation, yielding, submission; defeat. **5** *there is a steep fall down to the ocean:* **descent**, slope, slant, incline; N. Amer. downgrade. **6** *they went on rafting trips below the falls:* **waterfall**, cascade, cataract; rapids, white water.
– OPPOSITES increase, rise, ascent.
■ **fall apart** *my boots fell apart within weeks:* fall/come to pieces, fall/come to bits, come apart (at the seams); disintegrate, fragment, break up, break apart, crumble, decay, perish; informal bust.
■ **fall asleep** *Claire tried hard not to fall asleep:* doze off, drop off, go to sleep; informal nod off, go off, drift off, crash (out), flake out, conk out, go out like a light; N. Amer. informal sack out.
■ **fall away** *the ground fell away abruptly:* slope (down), slant down, go down, drop (away), descend, dip, sink, plunge.
■ **fall back** *the force of the blow caused him to fall back:* retreat, withdraw, back off, draw back, pull back, pull away, move away.
■ **fall back on** *you can always fall back on the support of your family:* resort to, turn to, look to, call on, have recourse to; rely on, depend on, lean on.
■ **fall behind 1** *the other walkers soon fell behind:* lag (behind), trail (behind), be left behind, drop back, bring up the rear; straggle, dally, dawdle, hang back. **2** *they fell behind on their HP instalments:* get into debt, get into arrears, default, be in the red.
■ **fall down 1** *I spin round and round till I fall down.* See FALL verb sense 2. **2** *for all its promises, the federation fell down in some*

areas: fail, be unsuccessful, not succeed, not make the grade, fall short, fall flat, disappoint; miss the mark; informal come a cropper, flop.
■ **fall for 1** *she fell for a younger man:* fall in love with, become infatuated with, lose one's heart to, take a fancy to, be smitten by, be attracted to; informal fancy, have the hots for. **2** *she is far too astute to fall for that trick:* be deceived by, be duped by, be fooled by, be taken in by, believe, trust, be convinced by; informal go for, buy, swallow, {swallow something hook, line, and sinker}.
■ **fall in 1** *the roof of our house fell in during the earthquake:* collapse, cave in, crash in, fall down; give way, crumble, disintegrate. **2** *he ordered the troops to fall in:* get in formation, get in line, line up, take one's position; Military dress.
■ **fall in with 1** *he fell in with a bad crowd and started drinking:* get involved with, take up with, join up with, go around with, string along with, make friends with; informal hang out/about with. **2** *he refused to fall in with their demands:* comply with, go along with, support, cooperate with, obey, yield to, submit to, bow to, defer to, adhere to, conform to; agree to, agree with, accept, concur with.
■ **fall off.** See FALL verb sense 4.
■ **fall on** *they fell on him the moment the key turned in the lock:* attack, assail, assault, fly at, set about, set upon; pounce upon, ambush, surprise, rush, storm, charge; informal jump, lay into, pitch into; Brit. informal have a go at.
■ **fall out** *let's not fall out over silly things:* quarrel, argue, row, fight, squabble, bicker, have words, disagree, be at odds, clash, wrangle, cross swords, lock horns, be at loggerheads, be at each other's throats; informal scrap, argufy.
■ **fall short of** *the results fall short of what was originally expected:* fail to meet, fail to reach, fail to live up to; be deficient, be inadequate, be insufficient, be wanting, be lacking, disappoint; informal not come up to scratch.
■ **fall through** *unfortunately, the sale fell through at the last minute:* fail, be unsuccessful, come to nothing, miscarry, abort, go awry, collapse, founder, come to grief; informal fizzle out, flop, fold, come a cropper, go down like a lead balloon.

fallacious adjective *the fallacious assumption underlying this reasoning:* **erroneous**, false, untrue, wrong, incorrect, flawed, inaccurate, mistaken, misinformed, misguided; groundless, unfounded, unproven, unsupported, uncorroborated; informal phoney, full of holes, off beam.
– OPPOSITES correct.

fallacy noun *the fallacy that we all work from nine to five:* **misconception**, misbelief, delusion, mistaken impression, misapprehension, error, mistake; untruth, myth.

f

fallen adjective *he attended a memorial service for his fallen comrades:* **dead**, slain, slaughtered, murdered; lost, late, lamented, departed, gone; formal deceased.

fallible adjective *all human beings are fallible, including Mr Darley:* **prone to error**; imperfect, flawed, weak.

fallow adjective **1** *this mix is used to improve the soil in fallow areas before planting:* **uncultivated**, unploughed, unplanted, unsown; unused, dormant, resting, empty, bare. **2** *trading is set to emerge from a fallow period:* **inactive**, dormant, quiet, slack, slow, stagnant; barren, unproductive.
– OPPOSITES cultivated, busy.

false adjective **1** *he gave a false account of his movements:* **incorrect**, untrue, wrong, erroneous, fallacious, flawed, distorted, inaccurate, imprecise; untruthful, fictitious, concocted, fabricated, invented, made up, trumped up, unfounded, spurious; counterfeit, forged, fraudulent. **2** *Briggs proved himself a false friend:* **faithless**, unfaithful, disloyal, untrue, inconstant, treacherous, traitorous, two-faced, double-crossing, deceitful, dishonest, duplicitous, untrustworthy, unreliable; untruthful; informal cheating, two-timing, back-stabbing; literary perfidious. **3** *she would never wear false pearls:* **fake**, artificial, imitation, synthetic, faux, simulated, reproduction, replica, ersatz, man-made, dummy, mock; informal phoney, pretend.
– OPPOSITES correct, truthful, faithful, genuine.

falsehood noun **1** *this is an exaggeration, if not a downright falsehood:* **lie**, untruth, fib, falsification, fabrication, invention, fiction, story, cock and bull story, flight of fancy; informal tall story, tall tale, fairy story, fairy tale, whopper; Brit. informal porky (pie); humorous terminological inexactitude. **2** *no one has ever accused me of falsehood before:* **lying**, mendacity, untruthfulness, fibbing, fabrication, invention, perjury, telling stories; deceit, deception, pretence, artifice, double-crossing, treachery; literary perfidy; informal kidology.
– OPPOSITES truth, honesty.

falsify verb *she falsified the accounts in an attempt to cover her tracks:* **forge**, fake, counterfeit, fabricate; alter, change, doctor, tamper with.

falsity noun *he was compelled to reveal the falsity of these assertions:* **untruthfulness**, untruth, fallaciousness, falseness, falsehood, fictitiousness, inaccuracy; mendacity, dishonesty.

falter verb **1** *when war seemed imminent the government faltered:* **hesitate**, delay, stall; waver, vacillate, blow hot and cold; Brit. haver, hum and haw; informal sit on the fence, dilly-dally, shilly-shally. **2** *only in the death scene did she falter:* **stumble**, flounder, hesitate, lose one's way; informal lose it.

fame noun *Stephen Bishop first shot to fame as a pianist:* **renown**, celebrity, stardom, popularity, prominence, greatness, eminence, prestige, stature, repute; notoriety, infamy.
– OPPOSITES obscurity.

famed adjective *he is famed for his grace and artistry:* **famous**, celebrated, well known, prominent, noted, notable, renowned, respected, esteemed, acclaimed; notorious, infamous.
– OPPOSITES unknown.

familiar adjective **1** *I see a lot of familiar faces | a familiar task:* **well known**, recognized, accustomed; common, commonplace, everyday, day-to-day, ordinary, habitual, usual, customary, routine, standard, stock, mundane, run-of-the-mill. **2** *are you familiar with this subject?* **acquainted**, conversant, versed, knowledgeable, well informed; skilled, proficient; at home, no stranger to, au fait; informal well up, in the know, genned up, clued up. **3** *he is too familiar with the teachers:* **overfamiliar**, presumptuous, disrespectful, forward, bold, impudent, impertinent.
– OPPOSITES formal.

familiarity noun **1** *he wants to gain greater familiarity with politics:* **acquaintance**, awareness, experience, insight; knowledge, understanding, comprehension, grasp. **2** *she was affronted by his familiarity:* **overfamiliarity**, presumption, presumptuousness, forwardness, boldness, audacity, cheek, impudence, impertinence, disrespect; liberties.

familiarize verb *I aim to familiarize students with a range of modern poets:* **acquaint**, make familiar; accustom, habituate, instruct, educate, school, prime, introduce; informal gen up, clue up, put in the picture, give the low-down, fill in.

family noun **1** *I finally met his family:* **relatives**, relations, (next of) kin, kinsfolk, kindred, one's (own) flesh and blood, nearest and dearest, people, connections; extended family; clan, tribe; informal folks. **2** *he came from the right kind of family:* **ancestry**, parentage, pedigree, genealogy, background, family tree, descent, lineage, bloodline, blood, extraction, stock; forebears, forefathers, antecedents, roots, origins. **3** *she is married with a family:* **children**, little ones, youngsters; offspring, progeny, descendants, scions, heirs; brood; Law issue; informal kids, kiddies, tots. **4** *the cat family:* **(taxonomic) group**, order, class, genus, species; stock, strain, line; Zoology phylum.

famine noun **1** *the nation is threatened by famine:* **food shortages**; starvation, malnutrition; hunger. **2** *the cotton famine of the 1860s:* **shortage**, scarcity, lack, dearth, deficiency, insufficiency, shortfall, scantiness, paucity, poverty, drought.
– OPPOSITES plenty.

famished adjective *the troops were exhausted and famished:* **ravenous**, hungry, starving, starved, empty, unfed; informal peckish.
– OPPOSITES full.

famous adjective *there were several famous artists in the exhibition:* **well known**, prominent, famed, popular; renowned, noted, eminent, distinguished, esteemed, celebrated, respected; of distinction, of repute; illustrious, acclaimed, great, legendary, lionized; notorious, infamous.
– OPPOSITES unknown.

fan¹ verb **1** *she fanned her face with a magazine:* **cool**, aerate, ventilate; freshen, refresh. **2** *the article fanned public fears regarding nuclear power:* **intensify**, increase, agitate, inflame, exacerbate; stimulate, stir up, whip up, fuel, kindle, spark, arouse. **3** *the police squad fanned out, weapons at the ready:* **spread**, branch; divide, split.

fan² noun *a basketball fan:* **enthusiast**, devotee, admirer, lover; supporter, follower, disciple, adherent, zealot; expert, connoisseur, aficionado; informal buff, fiend, freak, nut, addict, fanatic, groupie; N. Amer. informal jock.

fanatic noun **1** *a religious fanatic:* **zealot**, extremist, militant, dogmatist, devotee, adherent; sectarian, bigot, partisan, radical, diehard, ultra; informal maniac. **2** (informal) *a keep-fit fanatic.* See FAN².

fanatical adjective **1** *they are fanatical about their faith:* **zealous**, extremist, extreme, militant, dogmatic, radical, diehard; intolerant, single-minded, blinkered, inflexible, uncompromising. **2** *he was fanatical about cleanliness:* **enthusiastic**, eager, keen, fervent, ardent, passionate; obsessive, obsessed, fixated, compulsive; informal wild, gung-ho, nuts, crazy; Brit. informal potty.

fancier noun *a pigeon fancier:* **enthusiast**, lover, hobbyist; expert, connoisseur, aficionado; breeder; informal buff.

fanciful adjective **1** *some of these stories were pretty fanciful:* **fantastic**, far-fetched, unbelievable, extravagant; ridiculous, absurd, preposterous; imaginary, made-up, make-believe, mythical, fabulous; informal tall, hard to swallow. **2** *Maria is a fanciful girl:* **imaginative**; whimsical, impractical, dreamy, quixotic; out of touch with reality, in a world of one's own. **3** *the fanciful cornices and turrets of the imperial palace:* **ornate**, exotic, fancy, imaginative, extravagant, fantastic; curious, bizarre, eccentric, unusual.
– OPPOSITES literal, practical.

fancy verb **1** (Brit. informal) *I fancied a change of scene:* **wish for**, want, desire; long for, yearn for, crave, thirst for, hanker after, dream of, covet; informal have a yen for. **2** (Brit. informal) *she'd fancied him for ages:* **be attracted to**, find attractive, be infatuated with, be taken with; desire; lust after, burn for; informal have a crush on, have the hots for, be crazy about, have a thing about, have a soft spot for, carry a torch for. **3** *I fancied that I could see lights to the south:* **think**, imagine, believe, be of the opinion, be under the impression; informal reckon.
adjective *he's too hard up to buy fancy clothes:* **elaborate**, ornate, ornamental, decorative, intricate; ostentatious, showy, flamboyant; luxurious, lavish, extravagant, expensive; informal flash, flashy, jazzy, ritzy, snazzy, posh, classy; Brit. informal swish.
– OPPOSITES plain.
noun **1** *he was able to indulge his fancy to own a farm:* **desire**, urge, wish; inclination, whim, impulse, notion, whimsy; yearning, longing, hankering, craving; informal yen, itch. **2** *she had a vague fancy that it was cruel to leave the dolls in the dark:* **idea**, notion, thought, supposition, opinion, belief, impression, understanding; feeling, suspicion, hunch, inkling.

fanfare noun *the project was greeted with a great fanfare:* **fuss**, commotion, show, display; informal ballyhoo, hype, pizzazz, razzle-dazzle, glitz.

fantasize verb *I fantasized about London and what I'd do when I lived there:* **daydream**, dream, muse, think, wonder, imagine.

fantastic adjective **1** *it's a fantastic notion, but it would explain a lot:* **fanciful**, extravagant, extraordinary, irrational, wild, absurd, far-fetched, nonsensical, incredible, unbelievable, implausible, improbable, unlikely, doubtful, dubious; strange, peculiar, odd, queer, weird, eccentric, whimsical, capricious; visionary, romantic; informal crazy, cockeyed, off the wall. **2** *his fantastic accuracy when it came to target practice:* **tremendous**, remarkable, great, terrific, impressive, outstanding, phenomenal. **3** *the mountains assumed weird and fantastic shapes:* **strange**, weird, bizarre, outlandish, queer, peculiar, grotesque, freakish, surreal, exotic; elaborate, ornate, intricate. **4** (informal) *he's got this fantastic new car:* **marvellous**, wonderful, sensational, outstanding, superb, excellent, first-rate, first-class, dazzling, out of this world, breathtaking; informal great, terrific, fabulous, fab, mega, super, ace, magic, cracking, cool, wicked, awesome; Brit. informal brilliant, brill, smashing; Austral./NZ informal bonzer.
– OPPOSITES rational, ordinary.

fantasy noun **1** *the movie is an ambitious mix of fantasy and realism:* **imagination**, fancy, invention, make-believe; creativity, vision; daydreaming, reverie. **2** *his fantasy about appearing on television:* **dream**, daydream, pipe dream, fanciful notion, wish; fond hope, chimera, delusion, illusion; informal pie in the sky.
– OPPOSITES realism.

far adverb **1** *we are not far from the palace:* **a long way**, a great distance, a

good way; afar. **2** *the liveliness of the production far outweighs any flaws:* **much**, considerably, markedly, immeasurably, greatly, significantly, substantially, appreciably, noticeably; to a great extent, by a long way, by far, by a mile, easily.
– OPPOSITES near.
adjective *the department was on the far side of the campus:* **further**, (more) distant; other, opposite.
– OPPOSITES near.
■ **by far** *a compromise would be by far the best solution:* easily, by a long way, by a mile, far and away; undoubtedly, without doubt, without question, positively, absolutely; much; Brit. by a long chalk.
■ **far and away.** See BY FAR.
■ **far and wide** *the influence of the Chinese economy is being felt far and wide:* everywhere, {here, there, and everywhere}, all over (the world), throughout the land, worldwide; informal all over the place; Brit. informal all over the shop; N. Amer. informal all over the map.
■ **far from** *the staff were far from happy with this outcome:* not, not at all, nowhere near; the opposite of.
■ **go far** *she was the type of girl who would go far:* be successful, succeed, prosper, flourish, thrive, get on (in the world), make good, set the world on fire; informal make a name for oneself, make one's mark, go places, do all right for oneself.
■ **go too far** *in the end they sacked him because he went too far:* go over the top, go to extremes, go overboard.
■ **so far 1** *nobody has taken any notice of me so far:* until now, up to now, up to this point, as yet, thus far, hitherto, up to the present, to date. **2** *his liberalism only extends so far:* to a certain extent, up to a point, to a degree, within reason, within limits.

faraway adjective **1** *they spent their time jetting off to faraway places:* **distant**, far off, far, remote, far-flung, exotic; obscure, out of the way, off the beaten track. **2** *Noreen had that faraway look in her eyes:* **dreamy**, abstracted, absent-minded, distracted, preoccupied, vague; yearning, in a world of one's own; informal miles away.
– OPPOSITES nearby.

farce noun **1** *Mendes lightens the mood by playing the scene as farce rather than tragedy:* **slapstick (comedy)**, burlesque, vaudeville. **2** *the disarmament operation launched by NATO is a farce:* **mockery**, travesty, sham, pretence, masquerade, charade, joke, waste of time; informal shambles.
– OPPOSITES tragedy.

farcical adjective **1** *this is the honours system at its most farcical:* **ridiculous**, preposterous, ludicrous, absurd, laughable, risible, nonsensical; senseless, pointless, useless; silly, foolish, idiotic, stupid, hare-brained; informal crazy; Brit. informal barmy,

daft. **2** *the piece is farcical yet passionate, with music that is both witty and sensitive:* **madcap**, zany, slapstick, comic, comical, clownish, amusing; hilarious, uproarious; informal wacky.

fare noun **1** *we can't afford the air fare:* **ticket**; price, cost, charge, fee, toll, tariff. **2** *when at home, they eat simple fare:* **food**, meals, sustenance, nourishment, nutriment, foodstuffs, provender, eatables, provisions; cooking, cuisine; diet, table; informal grub, nosh, eats, chow; Brit. informal scoff; formal victuals.
verb *they went to see how their old friend was faring:* **get on**, get along, cope, manage, do; informal make out.

farewell exclamation *farewell, Patrick!* **goodbye**, so long, adieu; au revoir, ciao; informal bye, bye-bye, cheerio, see you (later), later; Brit. informal ta-ta, cheers.
noun *it was an emotional farewell:* **goodbye**, valediction, adieu; leave-taking, parting, departure; send-off.

far-fetched adjective *the storyline was a bit far-fetched, to say the least:* **improbable**, unlikely, implausible, unconvincing, dubious, doubtful, incredible, unbelievable, unthinkable; contrived, fanciful, unrealistic, ridiculous, absurd, preposterous; informal hard to swallow.
– OPPOSITES likely.

farm noun *he owned a small farm in Cumbria:* **smallholding**, farmstead, plantation, estate; Brit. grange, croft; Scottish steading; N. Amer. ranch; Austral./NZ station.
verb **1** *the marshes are being drained in order to farm the land:* **cultivate**, till, work, plough, dig, plant, exploit. **2** *the family farms sheep:* **breed**, rear, keep, raise, tend, grow.
■ **farm something out** *the job of building the models was farmed out to the Shawcroft division:* contract out, outsource, subcontract, delegate, give.

farmer noun **agriculturalist**, agronomist, smallholder; farmhand; Brit. crofter; N. Amer. rancher; historical yeoman.

farming noun **agriculture**, cultivation, land management, farm management; husbandry; agriscience, agronomy, agribusiness; Brit. crofting.

farrago noun *the whole business was a farrago of fantasies and errors:* **hotchpotch**, mishmash, ragbag, pot-pourri, jumble, mess, confusion, melange, hash, assortment, miscellany, mixture, conglomeration, medley; N. Amer. hodgepodge.

far-reaching adjective *this is a far-reaching change in consumer law:* **extensive**, wide-ranging; comprehensive, widespread, all-embracing, overarching, sweeping, blanket, wholesale; important, significant, radical, major, consequential.
– OPPOSITES limited.

far-sighted adjective *his far-sighted approach to resource management:*

prescient, visionary, percipient, shrewd, discerning, judicious, canny, prudent.

farther adverb & adjective. See **FURTHER**.

farthest adjective. See **FURTHEST**.

fascinate verb *he was fascinated by Laura's stories about Alaska:* **interest**, captivate, engross, absorb, enchant, enthral, entrance, transfix, rivet, mesmerize, engage, compel; lure, tempt, entice, draw; charm, attract, intrigue, divert, entertain.
– OPPOSITES bore.

fascinating adjective *it's a fascinating tale of fame, fortune, and human frailty:* **interesting**, captivating, engrossing, absorbing, enchanting, enthralling, spellbinding, riveting, engaging, compelling, compulsive, gripping, thrilling; alluring, tempting, irresistible; charming, attractive, intriguing, diverting, entertaining.

fascination noun *crime is a topic of endless fascination to most people:* **interest**, preoccupation, passion, obsession, compulsion; allure, lure, charm, attraction, intrigue, appeal, pull, draw.

fascism noun **authoritarianism**, totalitarianism, dictatorship, despotism, autocracy; Nazism, rightism; nationalism, xenophobia, racism, anti-Semitism, jingoism, isolationism; neo-fascism, neo-Nazism.

fascist noun *he was branded a fascist and an anti-Semite:* **authoritarian**, totalitarian, autocrat, extreme right-winger, rightist; Nazi, blackshirt; nationalist, xenophobe, racist, anti-Semite, jingoist; neo-fascist, neo-Nazi.
– OPPOSITES liberal.
adjective *fascist regimes in Europe:* **authoritarian**, totalitarian, dictatorial, autocratic, undemocratic, illiberal; Nazi, extreme right-wing, rightist, militarist; nationalist(ic), xenophobic, racist, jingoistic.
– OPPOSITES democratic.

fashion noun **1** *the current fashion for figure-hugging clothes:* **vogue**, trend, craze, rage, mania, fad; style, look; tendency, convention, custom, practice; informal thing. **2** *she was always interested in fashion:* **clothes**, clothing design, couture; informal the rag trade. **3** *it needs to be run in a sensible and organized fashion:* **manner**, way, method, mode, style; system, approach.
verb *the figure of Christ was fashioned from a tree trunk:* **construct**, produce, build, make, fabricate, contrive; cast, shape, form, mould, sculpt; forge, hew, carve.
■ **after a fashion** *the arrangement with the police worked after a fashion:* to a certain extent, in a way, in a manner of speaking, in its way, to some degree.
■ **in fashion** *the Seventies look is very much in fashion right now:* fashionable, in vogue, up to date, up to the minute, all the rage, chic, à la mode; informal trendy, with it, cool, in, the in thing, hot, big, hip, happening,

now, sharp, groovy; N. Amer. tony, fly.
■ **out of fashion** *such gallantry towards the opposite sex is now out of fashion:* unfashionable, dated, old-fashioned, out of date, outdated, outmoded, behind the times; unstylish, unpopular, passé, démodé; informal old hat, out, square.

fashionable adjective *a fashionable new wine bar has opened up:* **chic**, voguish, in fashion, popular, (bang) up to date, up to the minute, modern, all the rage, modish, à la mode, trendsetting; stylish; informal trendy, classy, with it, cool, in, the in thing, hot, big, hip, happening, now, sharp, groovy, snazzy; N. Amer. informal tony, fly.

fast[1] adjective **1** *it's a very fast car | the game is played at a fast pace:* **speedy**, quick, swift, rapid; fast-moving, high-speed, sporty; accelerated, express, blistering, breakneck, pell-mell; hasty, hurried; informal nippy, zippy, scorching, blinding, supersonic; Brit. informal cracking; literary fleet. **2** *he slammed the door and held it fast:* **secure**, tight, firm, closed, shut, to. **3** *the dyes are boiled to produce a fast colour:* **indelible**, lasting, permanent, stable. **4** *they remained fast friends for years:* **loyal**, devoted, faithful, firm, steadfast, staunch, true, boon, bosom, inseparable; constant, enduring, unswerving.
– OPPOSITES slow, loose, temporary.
adverb **1** *she drove fast down the drive towards the gates:* **quickly**, rapidly, swiftly, speedily, briskly, at speed, at full tilt; hastily, hurriedly, in a hurry, post-haste, pell-mell; like a shot, like a flash, on the double, at the speed of light; informal double quick, p.d.q. (pretty damn quick), like (greased) lightning, hell for leather, like mad, like the wind, like a scalded cat, like a bat out of hell; Brit. informal like the clappers, at a rate of knots, like billy-o; N. Amer. informal lickety-split; literary apace. **2** *his front wheels were stuck fast:* **securely**, firmly; well and truly. **3** *he's fast asleep:* **deeply**, sound, completely. **4** *she lived fast and died young:* **wildly**, dissolutely, intemperately, immoderately, recklessly, self-indulgently, extravagantly.
– OPPOSITES slowly.

fast[2] verb *we must fast and pray for forgiveness:* **eat nothing**, abstain, go without food, go hungry, starve oneself; go on hunger strike.
– OPPOSITES eat.
noun *a five-day fast:* **period of fasting**; hunger strike; diet.
– OPPOSITES feast.

fasten verb **1** *he fastened the door behind him:* **bolt**, lock, secure, make fast, chain, seal. **2** *they fastened splints to his leg:* **attach**, fix, affix, clip, pin, tack; stick, bond, join. **3** *he fastened his horse to a tree:* **tie (up)**, bind, tether, truss, fetter, lash, hitch, anchor, strap, rope. **4** *the dress fastens at the front:* **button (up)**, zip (up), do up, close. **5** *his gaze fastened on me:* **focus**, fix, be riveted, concentrate, zero in, zoom in, direct at.

– OPPOSITES unlock, remove, open, untie, undo.

fastidious adjective *he was fastidious about personal hygiene:* **scrupulous**, punctilious, painstaking, meticulous, fussy, finicky, over-particular; critical, overcritical, hypercritical, hard to please, exacting, demanding; informal pernickety, nit-picking, choosy, picky; N. Amer. informal persnickety.
– OPPOSITES lax.

fat adjective **1** *a fat man in a Black Sabbath T-shirt:* **plump**, stout, overweight, large, chubby, portly, flabby, paunchy, pot-bellied, beer-bellied, meaty; obese, corpulent, gross, fleshy; informal tubby, roly-poly, beefy, porky, blubbery, chunky; Brit. informal podgy, fubsy. **2** *a couple of rashers of fat bacon:* **fatty**, greasy, oily, oleaginous; formal pinguid. **3** *he produced a fat book from the shelf:* **thick**, big, chunky, substantial; long. **4** (informal) *a fat salary:* **large**, substantial, sizeable, considerable; generous, lucrative.
– OPPOSITES thin, lean, small, good.
noun **1** *whales are insulated by layers of fat:* **blubber**, fatty tissue, adipose tissue. **2** *fried bread swimming in fat:* **oil**, grease; lard, suet, butter, margarine.

fatal adjective **1** *a fatal disease:* **deadly**, lethal, mortal, death-dealing; terminal, incurable, untreatable, inoperable, malignant; literary deathly. **2** *he made a fatal mistake:* **disastrous**, devastating, ruinous, catastrophic, calamitous, dire; costly; formal grievous.
– OPPOSITES harmless, beneficial.

fatalism noun *a sense of fatalism prevented him from feeling any responsibility:* **acceptance**, resignation, stoicism; passivity.

fatality noun *there were hundreds of fatalities following the leak:* **death**, casualty, mortality, victim; fatal accident.

fate noun **1** *I was ready for whatever fate had in store for me:* **destiny**, providence, the stars, chance, luck, serendipity, fortune, karma. **2** *my fate was in their hands:* **future**, destiny, outcome, end, lot. **3** *a similar fate would befall other traitors:* **death**, demise, end; retribution, sentence.
verb *his daughter was fated to face the same dilemma:* **be predestined**, be preordained, be destined, be meant, be doomed.

fateful adjective *that fateful day when she met him:* **decisive**, critical, crucial, pivotal; momentous, important, key, significant, historic, portentous.
– OPPOSITES unimportant.

father noun **1** *his mother and father:* patriarch, paterfamilias; informal dad, daddy, pop, pa, old man. **2** (literary) *the religion of my fathers:* **ancestors**, forefathers, forebears, predecessors, antecedents, progenitors. **3** *he was the father of democracy:* **originator**, initiator, founder, inventor, creator, maker, author, architect. **4** *the city fathers:* **leader**, elder, patriarch, official. **5** *pray for me, Father:* **priest**, pastor, parson, clergyman,

cleric, minister, preacher; informal reverend, padre.
– OPPOSITES child, mother, descendant.
verb **1** *he fathered six children in as many years:* **be the father of**, sire, bring into the world, spawn, breed; literary beget. **2** *he fathered a new strand of applied economics:* **establish**, institute, originate, initiate, invent, found, create.

fatherland noun *they are traitors to the fatherland:* **native land**, native country, homeland, mother country, motherland, land of one's birth.

fatherly adjective *all he needs is some fatherly advice:* **paternal**, fatherlike; protective, supportive, encouraging, affectionate, caring, sympathetic, indulgent.

fathom verb *Charlie tried to fathom the expression on her face:* **understand**, comprehend, work out, make sense of, grasp, divine, puzzle out, get to the bottom of; interpret, decipher, decode; informal make head or tail of, tumble to, crack; Brit. informal twig, suss (out), savvy.

fatigue noun *his face was pale with fatigue:* **tiredness**, weariness, exhaustion, enervation, prostration.
– OPPOSITES energy.
verb *the troops were fatigued:* **tire (out)**, exhaust, wear out, drain, weary, wash out, overtire, prostrate; informal knock out, take it out of, do in, fag out, whack, poop, shatter, bush, wear to a frazzle; Brit. informal knacker.
– OPPOSITES invigorate.

fatness noun **plumpness**, stoutness, heaviness, chubbiness, portliness, rotundity, flabbiness, paunchiness; obesity, corpulence; informal tubbiness, podginess.
– OPPOSITES thinness.

fatten verb **1** *we are fattening the livestock for Christmas:* **make fat/fatter**, feed (up), build up. **2** *we're sending her home to fatten up:* **put on weight**, gain weight, fill out, bulk out.
– OPPOSITES slim.

fatty adjective *avoid fatty foods:* **greasy**, oily, fat, oleaginous.
– OPPOSITES lean.

fatuous adjective *she was irritated by this fatuous remark:* **silly**, foolish, stupid, inane, idiotic, vacuous, asinine; pointless, senseless, ridiculous, ludicrous, absurd; informal dumb, gormless; Brit. informal daft.
– OPPOSITES sensible.

fault noun **1** *he has his faults, but he's a good man:* **defect**, failing, imperfection, flaw, blemish, shortcoming, weakness, frailty, foible, vice. **2** *engineers have still not located the fault:* **defect**, flaw, imperfection, bug; error, mistake, inaccuracy; informal glitch, gremlin. **3** *it was my fault that we were late:* **responsibility**, liability, culpability, blameworthiness, guilt.
– OPPOSITES merit, strength.
verb *you couldn't fault any of the players:*

find fault with, criticize, attack, censure, condemn, reproach; complain about; informal knock, slam, gripe about, beef about, pick holes in; Brit. informal slag off, have a go at, slate.
■ **at fault** *the police say the driver of the car was not at fault:* to blame, blameworthy, culpable; responsible, guilty, in the wrong.
■ **to a fault** *Barry's generous to a fault:* excessively, unduly, immoderately, overly, needlessly.

faultless adjective *Professor Ruiperez had sent me a letter of invitation in faultless English:* **perfect**, flawless, error-free, impeccable, accurate, precise, exact, correct, exemplary.
– OPPOSITES flawed.

faulty adjective **1** *the fire was caused by a faulty electric blanket:* **malfunctioning**, broken, damaged, defective, out of order; informal on the blink, acting up, kaput, bust; Brit. informal knackered, playing up, duff; N. Amer. informal on the fritz. **2** *her logic is faulty at the best of times:* **defective**, flawed, unsound, inaccurate, incorrect, erroneous, fallacious, wrong.
– OPPOSITES working, sound.

faux pas noun *I committed a faux pas that they never let me forget:* **gaffe**, blunder, mistake, indiscretion, impropriety, solecism; informal boo-boo; Brit. informal boob; N. Amer. informal blooper.

favour noun **1** *will you do me a favour?* **good turn**, service, good deed, (act of) kindness, courtesy. **2** *she looked on him with favour:* **approval**, approbation, goodwill, kindness, benevolence. **3** *they accused the referee of showing favour to the home team:* **favouritism**, bias, partiality, partisanship.
– OPPOSITES disservice, disapproval.
verb **1** *the party favours electoral reform:* **advocate**, recommend, approve of, be in favour of, support, back, champion; campaign for, stand up for, press for, lobby for, promote; informal plug, push for. **2** *Robyn favours loose dark clothes:* **prefer**, go (in) for, choose, opt for, select, pick, plump for, be partial to, like. **3** *he was angry that his father always favoured George:* **show favouritism towards**, prefer, think more highly of. **4** *the conditions favoured the other team:* **benefit**, be to the advantage of, help, assist, aid, be of service to, do someone a favour. **5** *he favoured Lucy with a smile:* **oblige**, honour, gratify, humour, indulge.
– OPPOSITES oppose, dislike, hinder.
■ **in favour of** *two thirds of the staff were in favour of strike action:* on the side of, pro, (all) for, giving support to, approving of, sympathetic to.

favourable adjective **1** *we received a favourable assessment of his ability:* **approving**, commendatory, complimentary, flattering, glowing, enthusiastic; good, pleasing, positive; informal rave. **2** *in the hive where conditions are favourable:* **advantageous**, beneficial, in one's favour, good, right, suitable, fitting, appropriate; propitious, auspicious, promising, encouraging. **3** *he hoped for a favourable reply to this request:* **positive**, affirmative, assenting, agreeing, approving; encouraging, reassuring.
– OPPOSITES critical, disadvantageous, negative.

favourably adverb **positively**, approvingly, sympathetically, enthusiastically, appreciatively.

favoured adjective *he is the president's favoured candidate:* **preferred**, favourite, recommended, chosen, choice.

favourite adjective *Laura was his favourite aunt:* **best-loved**, most-liked, favoured, dearest; preferred, chosen, choice.
noun **1** *Brutus was always Caesar's favourite:* **(first) choice**, pick, preference, pet, darling, the apple of one's eye; informal blue-eyed boy, golden boy; N. Amer. informal fair-haired boy. **2** *the favourite fell at the first fence:* **expected winner**, front runner.

favouritism noun *we want one rule for everyone and no favouritism:* **partiality**, partisanship, preferential treatment, favour, prejudice, bias, inequality, unfairness, discrimination.

fawn[1] adjective *a hideous fawn carpet:* **beige**, yellowish-brown, pale brown, buff, sand, oatmeal, café au lait, camel, ecru, taupe, stone, mushroom.

fawn[2] verb *they were fawning over the President's wife:* **be obsequious to**, be sycophantic to, curry favour with, pay court to, play up to, crawl to, ingratiate oneself with, dance attendance on; informal suck up to, make up to, be all over, creep, grovel; Austral./NZ informal smoodge to.

fawning adjective *he was surrounded by a circle of fawning civil servants:* **obsequious**, servile, sycophantic, flattering, ingratiating, unctuous, oleaginous, grovelling, crawling; informal bootlicking, smarmy.

fear noun **1** *she felt fear at entering the house:* **terror**, fright, fearfulness, horror, alarm, panic, agitation, trepidation, dread, consternation, dismay, distress; anxiety, worry, unease, uneasiness, apprehension, apprehensiveness, nervousness, nerves, perturbation, foreboding; informal the creeps, the willies, the heebie-jeebies, jitteriness, twitchiness, butterflies (in the stomach), (blue) funk. **2** *she overcame her fears and made it to the top:* **phobia**, aversion, antipathy, dread, bugbear, bogey, nightmare, horror, terror; anxiety, neurosis; informal hang-up. **3** *there's no fear of me leaving you alone:* **likelihood**, likeliness, prospect, possibility, chance, probability; risk, danger.
verb **1** *she feared her ex-husband:* **be afraid of**, be fearful of, be scared of, be apprehensive of, dread, live in fear of, be terrified of; be anxious about, worry about,

feel apprehensive about. **2** *he feared to tell them what had happened:* **be too afraid**, be too scared, hesitate, dare not. **3** *doctors feared for his health:* **worry about**, feel anxious about, feel concerned about, have anxieties about. **4** *I fear that you may be right:* **suspect**, have a (sneaking) suspicion, be inclined to think, be afraid, have a hunch, think it likely.

fearful adjective **1** *they are fearful of being overheard:* **afraid**, frightened, scared (stiff), scared to death, terrified, petrified. **2** *the guards were ill-trained and fearful:* **nervous**, trembling, quaking, cowed, daunted; timid, timorous, faint-hearted; Brit. nervy; informal jittery, jumpy, twitchy, keyed up, in a cold sweat, trepidatious, a bundle of nerves, like a cat on a hot tin roof; Brit. informal having kittens, like a cat on hot bricks; N. Amer. informal spooky. **3** *there has been a fearful accident:* **terrible**, dreadful, awful, appalling, frightful, ghastly, horrific, horrible, horrifying, horrendous, terribly bad, shocking, atrocious, abominable, hideous, monstrous, gruesome.

fearfully adverb *she opened the door fearfully:* **apprehensively**, uneasily, nervously, timidly, timorously, hesitantly, with one's heart in one's mouth.

fearless adjective *he was cool and fearless in battle, and an excellent leader:* **unafraid**, brave, courageous, intrepid, valiant, valorous, gallant, plucky, heroic, daring, audacious, indomitable, doughty; bold, undaunted, unflinching.
– OPPOSITES timid, cowardly.

fearsome adjective *the crocodile's teeth are a fearsome sight:* **frightening**, horrifying, terrifying, menacing, chilling, spine-chilling, hair-raising, alarming, unnerving, daunting, formidable, forbidding, dismaying, disquieting, disturbing; informal scary.

feasible adjective *there is only one feasible solution:* **practicable**, practical, workable, achievable, attainable, realizable, viable, realistic, sensible, reasonable, within reason; suitable, possible, expedient, constructive; informal doable.
– OPPOSITES impractical.

feast noun **1** *the occasion was celebrated with a great feast:* **banquet**, meal, dinner; treat, entertainment; revels, festivities; informal blowout, spread; Brit. informal nosh-up, beanfeast, bunfight, beano, slap-up meal. **2** *the feast of St Stephen:* **(religious) festival**, feast day, saint's day, holy day, holiday.
verb *they feasted on lobster:* **dine on**, gorge on, eat, devour, consume, partake of; informal stuff one's face with, stuff oneself with, pig oneself on, pig out on.

feat noun *the bridge is an extraordinary feat of engineering:* **achievement**, accomplishment, attainment, coup, triumph; undertaking, enterprise, venture, operation, exercise, endeavour, effort, performance, exploit.

feather noun **plume**, quill, flight feather, tail feather; Ornithology covert, plumule; (**feathers**) plumage, feathering, down.

feature noun **1** *this is a typical feature of French music:* **characteristic**, attribute, quality, property, trait, hallmark, trademark; aspect, facet, factor, ingredient, component, element, theme; peculiarity, idiosyncrasy, quirk. **2** *his eyes swept over her delicate features:* **face**, countenance, physiognomy; informal mug, kisser; Brit. informal mush, phiz, phizog; N. Amer. informal puss, pan; literary visage. **3** *she made a feature of her garden sculptures:* **centrepiece**, (special) attraction, highlight, focal point, focus (of attention), conversation piece. **4** *a series of short features on the Vikings:* **article**, piece, item, report, story, column, review, commentary, write-up.
verb **1** *Radio Ulster is featuring a week of live concerts:* **present**, promote, focus on, spotlight, highlight. **2** *she is to feature in a major advertising campaign:* **star**, appear, participate, be.

febrile adjective *the patient was febrile, with severe abdominal pains:* **feverish**, hot, burning, flushed, sweating; informal having a temperature.

feckless adjective *the suggestion that armies of feckless teenagers should be supplied with free contraceptives:* **good-for-nothing**, worthless, incompetent, inept, useless, ne'er-do-well; lazy, idle, slothful, indolent, shiftless; informal no-good, no-account.

fecund adjective *a lush and fecund garden paradise:* **fertile**, fruitful, productive, high-yielding; rich, lush, flourishing, thriving.
– OPPOSITES barren.

federal adjective *Mrs Thatcher's warning about a federal Europe dominated by Germany:* **confederate**, federated; combined, allied, united, amalgamated, integrated.

federation noun *Switzerland is a federation of cantons:* **confederation**, confederacy, federacy, league; combination, alliance, coalition, union, syndicate, guild, consortium, partnership, cooperative, association, amalgamation.

fee noun *Cameron used his fee to finance an exhibition in London:* **payment**, price, cost, charge, tariff, rate; (**fees**) remuneration, dues, earnings, pay; formal emolument.

feeble adjective **1** *he was old and feeble:* **weak**, weakly, weakened, frail, infirm, delicate, sickly, ailing, unwell, poorly, enfeebled, enervated, debilitated, incapacitated, decrepit. **2** *this a pretty feeble argument:* **ineffective**, ineffectual, inadequate, unconvincing, implausible, unsatisfactory, poor, weak, flimsy. **3** *he's too feeble to stand up to his boss:* **cowardly**, craven, faint-hearted, spineless, spiritless, lily-livered; timid, timorous, fearful, unassertive, weak, ineffectual; informal wimpy, sissy, sissified,

gutless, chicken; Brit. informal wet. **4** *the lamp shed a feeble light:* **faint**, dim, weak, pale, soft, subdued, muted.
– OPPOSITES strong, brave.

feeble-minded adjective *she must be very tired to give room to such feeble-minded notions:* **stupid**, idiotic, imbecilic, foolish, witless, doltish, empty-headed, vacuous; informal half-witted, moronic, dumb, dim, dopey, dozy, dotty, dippy; Brit. informal daft.
– OPPOSITES clever, gifted.

feed verb **1** *she has a large family to feed:* **provide (food) for**, cater for, cook for; suckle, breastfeed, bottle-feed. **2** *the baby spends all day feeding:* **eat**, drink, snack; informal nosh, graze. **3** *there are too many cows feeding in such a small area:* **graze**, browse, crop, pasture. **4** *the birds feed on a diet of fish:* **live on**/off, exist on, subsist on, eat, consume. **5** *we all have ways of feeding our self-esteem:* **strengthen**, fortify, support, bolster, reinforce, boost, fuel, encourage. **6** *she fed secrets to the Russians for years:* **supply**, provide, give, deliver, furnish, issue.
noun *he sells feed for goats and sheep:* **fodder**, food, forage, pasturage, herbage, provender.

feel verb **1** *she encourages her customers to feel the fabrics:* **touch**, stroke, caress, fondle, finger, thumb, handle. **2** *she felt a breeze on her back:* **perceive**, sense, detect, discern, notice, be aware of, be conscious of. **3** *the patient does not feel any pain during the procedure:* **experience**, undergo, go through, bear, endure, suffer. **4** *he felt his way towards the door:* **grope**, fumble, scrabble, pick. **5** *feel the temperature of the water:* **test**, try (out), assess, gauge; establish, ascertain. **6** *he feels that he should go to the meeting:* **believe**, think, consider (it right), be of the opinion, hold, maintain, judge; informal reckon, figure. **7** *I feel that he is biding his time:* **sense**, have a (funny) feeling, get the impression, have a hunch, intuit. **8** *the air feels damp:* **seem**, appear, strike one as.
noun **1** *I liked the feel of the embossed wallpaper:* **texture**, surface, finish; weight, thickness, consistency, quality. **2** *a change in lighting can alter the feel of a room:* **atmosphere**, ambience, aura, mood, feeling, air, impression, character, tenor, spirit, flavour; informal vibrations, vibes. **3** *he has a feel for languages:* **aptitude**, knack, flair, bent, talent, gift, faculty, ability.
■ **feel for** *the press persecuted John, and I felt for him:* **sympathize with**, be sorry for, pity, feel pity for, feel sympathy for, feel compassion for, be moved by; commiserate with, condole with.
■ **feel like** *I feel like an ice cream:* **want**, would like, wish for, desire, fancy, feel in need of, long for; informal yen for, be dying for.

feeling noun **1** *she was overcome by a feeling of nausea:* **sensation**, sense, consciousness. **2** *I had a feeling that I would win:* **(sneaking)**

suspicion, notion, inkling, hunch, funny feeling, feeling in one's bones, fancy, idea; presentiment, premonition; informal gut feeling. **3** *he was amazed at the strength of her feeling for him:* **love**, affection, fondness, tenderness, warmth, warmness, emotion, sentiment; passion, ardour, desire. **4** *the government is hopelessly out of touch with public feeling:* **sentiment**, emotion; opinion, attitude, belief, ideas, views. **5** *Emma felt a rush of feeling for the child:* **compassion**, sympathy, empathy, fellow feeling, concern, solicitude, solicitousness, tenderness, (brotherly) love; pity, sorrow, commiseration. **6** *he hadn't meant to hurt her feelings:* **sensibilities**, sensitivities, self-esteem, pride. **7** *my feeling is that this claim is true:* **opinion**, belief, view, impression, intuition, instinct, hunch, estimation, guess. **8** *a feeling of peace prevailed in the garden:* **atmosphere**, ambience, aura, air, feel, mood, impression, spirit, quality, flavour; informal vibrations, vibes. **9** *he has a remarkable feeling for language:* **aptitude**, knack, flair, bent, talent, gift, faculty, ability.
adjective *he considers himself to be a feeling man:* **sensitive**, warm, warm-hearted, tender, tender-hearted, caring, sympathetic, kind, compassionate, understanding, thoughtful.

feign verb *she lay still and feigned sleep:* **simulate**, fake, sham, affect.

feigned adjective *he accepted the invitation with feigned enthusiasm:* **pretended**, simulated, affected, artificial, insincere, put-on, fake, false, sham; informal pretend, phoney.
– OPPOSITES sincere.

feint noun *his dismissal was a feint, a hollow gesture to allay public outrage:* **bluff**, blind, ruse, deception, subterfuge, hoax, trick, ploy, device, dodge, sham, pretence, cover, smokescreen, distraction, contrivance; informal red herring.

felicitous adjective **1** *the endings of his films may be happy, but they're seldom felicitous:* **apt**, well chosen, fitting, suitable, appropriate, apposite, pertinent, germane, relevant. **2** *by a felicitous coincidence, the club was directly opposite Coutts' head office in the Strand:* **favourable**, advantageous, good, pleasing.
– OPPOSITES inappropriate, unfortunate.

felicity noun **1** *these feelings are but shadows of our endless felicity in heaven:* **happiness**, joy, joyfulness, joyousness, bliss, delight, cheerfulness; contentedness, satisfaction, pleasure. **2** *David expressed his feelings with his customary felicity:* **eloquence**, aptness, appropriateness, suitability, suitableness, applicability, fitness, relevance, pertinence.
– OPPOSITES unhappiness, inappropriateness.

feline adjective *she moved with feline grace:* **catlike**, graceful, sleek, sinuous.
noun *her pet feline:* **cat**, kitten; informal puss, pussy (cat); Brit. informal moggie, mog.

f

fell verb **1** *all the dead sycamores had to be felled:* **cut down**, chop down, hack down, saw down, clear. **2** *she felled him with one well-aimed punch:* **knock down/over**, knock to the ground, strike down, bring down, bring to the ground, prostrate; knock out, knock unconscious; informal deck, floor, flatten, down, lay out, KO; Brit. informal knock for six.

fellow noun **1** (informal) *he seems like a decent sort of fellow:* **man**, boy; person, individual, soul; informal guy, geezer, lad, fella, character, customer, devil, bastard; Brit. informal chap, bloke; N. Amer. informal dude, hombre; Austral./NZ informal digger; informal, dated body, dog, cove. **2** *he exchanged glances with his fellows:* **companion**, friend, comrade, partner, associate, co-worker, colleague; informal chum, pal, buddy; Brit. informal mate.
■ **fellow feeling** *she felt a rush of fellow feeling for the unfortunate woman:* sympathy, empathy, feeling, compassion, care, concern, solicitude, solicitousness, warmth, tenderness, (brotherly) love; pity, sorrow, commiseration.

fellowship noun **1** *a community of brothers bound together in fellowship:* **companionship**, companionability, sociability, comradeship, camaraderie, friendship, mutual support; togetherness, solidarity; informal chumminess, palliness; Brit. informal mateyness. **2** *a new member of the church fellowship:* **association**, society, club, league, union, guild, affiliation, alliance, fraternity, brotherhood, sorority, sodality.

female adjective *these are typical female attributes:* **feminine**, womanly, ladylike.
– OPPOSITES male.
noun *the victim was an elderly female.* See WOMAN sense 1.

feminine adjective **1** *men who have some feminine tact and sensitivity:* **female**; womanly; yin, lunar. **2** *an attractive girl with a very feminine figure | his face was smooth, almost feminine:* **womanly**; girlish, girlie, womanish.
– OPPOSITES masculine, male, yang, solar, manly.

femme fatale noun *the sexual attraction between alluring femme fatale Matty and sleazy lawyer Ned:* **seductress**, temptress, siren; informal vamp.

fen noun **marsh**, marshland, salt marsh, fenland, wetland, (peat) bog, swamp, swampland; N. Amer. moor.

fence noun *she crept through a gap in the fence:* **barrier**, paling, railing, enclosure, barricade, stockade, palisade.
verb **1** *they intended to fence off many acres of prairie:* **enclose**, surround, encircle, separate off; circle, wall; encompass, isolate. **2** *he fenced in his chickens:* **confine**, pen in, coop up, shut in/up; enclose, surround; N. Amer. corral.

fend verb *they were unable to fend off a*

Viking invasion: **ward off**, head off, stave off, hold off, repel, repulse, resist, fight off, defend oneself against, prevent, stop, block, intercept, hold back.
■ **fend for oneself** *how could any mother leave a child to fend for itself?* take care of oneself, look after oneself, provide for oneself, shift for oneself, manage by oneself, cope by yourself, stand on one's own two feet.

feral adjective **1** *a pack of feral dogs:* **wild**, untamed, undomesticated, untrained. **2** *a feral snarl:* **savage**, ferocious, vicious, fierce, predatory, menacing, bloodthirsty; animal, bestial, atavistic.
– OPPOSITES tame, pet.

ferment verb **1** *the beer continues to ferment:* **brew**; effervesce, fizz, foam, froth. **2** *a brutalizing environment that ferments disorder:* **cause**, bring about, give rise to, generate, engender, spawn, instigate, provoke, incite, excite, stir up, whip up, foment; literary beget.
noun *in 1945 Korea was in a ferment of revolutionary upheaval:* **fever**, furore, frenzy, tumult, storm, rumpus; turmoil, upheaval, unrest, disquiet, uproar, agitation, turbulence, disruption, confusion, disorder, chaos, mayhem; informal kerfuffle, hoo-ha, to-do; Brit. informal aggro.

ferocious adjective **1** *bears are ferocious animals:* **fierce**, savage, wild, aggressive, dangerous. **2** *a ferocious attack on a policeman:* **brutal**, vicious, violent, bloody, barbaric, savage, sadistic, ruthless, cruel, merciless, heartless, bloodthirsty, murderous.
– OPPOSITES gentle, mild.

ferocity noun *detectives were shocked by the ferocity of the attack:* **savagery**, brutality, barbarity, fierceness, violence, bloodthirstiness, murderousness.

ferret verb **1** *she ferreted about in her handbag:* **rummage**, feel around, grope around, forage, fish (about/around), poke about/around; search through, hunt through, rifle through; Austral./NZ informal fossick through. **2** *the headmistress was adept at ferreting out misdemeanours:* **unearth**, uncover, discover, detect, search out, bring to light, track down, dig up, root out, nose out; informal get wise to; Brit. informal rumble.

ferry noun *we took the ferry from Dover to Calais:* **passenger boat/ship**, ferry boat, car ferry; ship, boat.
verb *we got the air force to ferry spare parts from Phnom Penh to Bangkok:* **transport**, convey, carry, ship, run, take, bring, shuttle.

fertile adjective **1** *the soil is moist and fertile:* **fecund**, fruitful, productive, rich, lush. **2** *even fertile couples may choose to adopt:* **able to conceive**, able to have children; childbearing, technical fecund. **3** *von Schlieffen had applied his fertile brain to this problem:* **imaginative**, inventive,

innovative, creative, visionary, original, ingenious; productive, prolific.
– OPPOSITES barren.

fertilization noun **conception**, impregnation, insemination; pollination, propagation.

fertilize verb **1** *the field was ploughed up and fertilized:* **feed**, mulch, compost, manure, dress, top-dress. **2** *these orchids are fertilized by insects:* **pollinate**, cross-pollinate, cross-fertilize.

fertilizer noun **manure**, plant food, compost, dressing, top dressing, dung.

fervent adjective *William is a fervent rugby supporter:* **impassioned**, passionate, intense, vehement, ardent, sincere, fervid, heartfelt; enthusiastic, zealous, fanatical, wholehearted, avid, eager, keen, committed, dedicated, devout; informal mad keen.
– OPPOSITES apathetic.

fervour noun *he preached with tremendous fervour to a packed hall:* **passion**, ardour, intensity, zeal, vehemence, emotion, warmth, earnestness, avidity, eagerness, keenness, enthusiasm, excitement, animation, vigour, energy, fire, spirit, zest, fervency, ardency.
– OPPOSITES apathy.

fester verb **1** *the deep wound in his neck had begun to fester:* **suppurate**, become septic, weep; Medicine maturate, be purulent. **2** *rubbish festered in the streets:* **rot**, moulder, decay, decompose, putrefy. **3** *they must not allow their resentment to fester:* **rankle**, eat/gnaw away at one's mind, brew, smoulder.

festival noun **1** *the town's annual arts festival:* **fête**, fair, gala (day), carnival, fiesta, jamboree, celebration(s), festivities, eisteddfod. **2** *forty days of fasting precede the festival:* **holy day**, feast day, saint's day.

festive adjective *everyone was in a festive mood despite the recession:* **jolly**, merry, joyous, joyful, happy, jovial, light-hearted, cheerful, jubilant, convivial, high-spirited, mirthful, uproarious; celebratory, holiday, carnival.

festivity noun **1** *food plays an important part in the festivities:* **celebration**, festival, entertainment, party, jamboree; merrymaking, feasting, revelry, jollification; revels, fun and games; informal bash, shindig, shindy; Brit. informal rave-up, knees-up, beanfeast, bunfight, beano. **2** *we joined in the festivity of the Last Night of the Proms:* **jollity**, merriment, gaiety, cheerfulness, cheer, joyfulness, jubilance, conviviality, high spirits, revelry.

festoon verb *the room was festooned with streamers:* **decorate**, adorn, ornament, trim, deck (out), hang, loop, drape, swathe, garland, wreathe, bedeck; informal do up/out, get up, trick out.

fetch verb **1** *he went to fetch a doctor from the nearby village:* **(go and) get**, go for, call

for, summon, pick up, collect, bring, carry, convey, transport. **2** *the estate in Caithness could fetch a million pounds:* **sell for**, bring in, raise, realize, yield, make, command, cost, be priced at; informal go for, set one back, pull in; Brit. informal knock someone back.

fetching adjective *she looked rather fetching in her nurse's uniform:* **attractive**, appealing, sweet, pretty, lovely, delightful, charming, prepossessing, captivating, enchanting, irresistible; Scottish & N. English bonny; informal divine, heavenly; Brit. informal fit, smashing; archaic comely, fair.

fête noun (Brit.) **gala (day)**, bazaar, fair, festival, fiesta, jubilee, carnival; fund-raiser, charity event.

fetid adjective *the fetid odour of damp refuse filled the air:* **stinking**, smelly, foul-smelling, malodorous, reeking, pungent, acrid, high, rank, foul, noxious; Brit. informal niffy, pongy, whiffy, humming; N. Amer. informal funky; literary noisome, miasmic.
– OPPOSITES fragrant.

fetish noun **1** *the Laney range has focused on solid state technology, resisting the current fetish for valves | he developed a rubber fetish:* **fixation**, obsession, compulsion, mania; weakness, fancy, fascination, fad; informal thing, hang-up. **2** *the thing is treated like a voodoo fetish:* **idol**, talisman, charm, amulet, totem, juju, image, effigy.

fetter verb **1** *the captive was branded and fettered:* **shackle**, manacle, handcuff, clap in irons, put in chains, chain (up); informal cuff. **2** *these obligations do not fetter the company's powers:* **restrict**, restrain, constrain, limit; hinder, hamper, impede, obstruct, hamstring, inhibit, check, curb, trammel.

fetters plural noun **shackles**, manacles, handcuffs, irons, leg irons, chains, restraints; informal cuffs, bracelets.

fettle noun *his best players were in fine fettle:* **shape**, trim, (physical) fitness, (state of) health; condition, form, (state of) repair, (working) order; Brit. informal nick.

feud noun *the region was riven by tribal feuds:* **vendetta**, conflict; rivalry, hostility, enmity, strife, discord; quarrel, argument, falling-out.
verb *he feuded constantly with his teammates:* **quarrel**, fight, argue, bicker, squabble, fall out, dispute, clash, differ, be at odds; informal scrap.

fever noun **1** *he developed a fever and was admitted to hospital:* **feverishness**, high temperature; Medicine pyrexia; informal temperature. **2** *Terry was in a fever of excitement:* **ferment**, frenzy, furore; ecstasy, rapture. **3** *the nation has been gripped by World Cup fever:* **excitement**, frenzy, agitation, passion.

fevered adjective **1** *Fernando soothed her fevered brow:* **feverish**, febrile, hot, burning. **2** *she wanted to see if the reality matched* *her fevered imagination:* **excited**, agitated, frenzied, overwrought, fervid.

feverish adjective **1** *she's really sick and feverish:* **febrile**, fevered, hot, burning; informal having a temperature; rare pyretic. **2** *he was thrown into a state of feverish excitement:* **frenzied**, frenetic, hectic, agitated, excited, restless, nervous, worked up, overwrought, frantic, furious, hysterical, wild, uncontrolled, unrestrained.

few determiner *police are revealing few details about the victim:* **not many**, hardly any, scarcely any; a small number of, a small amount of, one or two, a handful of; little.
– OPPOSITES many.
  adjective *though the car parks are few, they are well placed:* **scarce**, scant, meagre, insufficient, in short supply; thin on the ground, few and far between, infrequent, uncommon, rare.
– OPPOSITES plentiful.
  ■ **a few** *for a few, overcoming their fear of flying becomes a challenge:* a small number, a handful, one or two, a couple, two or three; not many, hardly any.

fiancée, fiancé noun **betrothed**, wife-to-be, husband-to-be, bride-to-be, future wife/husband, prospective spouse; informal intended.

fiasco noun *the whole evening was a total fiasco:* **failure**, disaster, catastrophe, debacle, shambles, farce, mess, wreck; informal flop, washout; Brit. informal cock-up; N. Amer. informal snafu; Austral./NZ informal fizzer.
– OPPOSITES success.

fib noun *I know you're telling a fib:* **lie**, untruth, falsehood, made-up story, invention, fabrication, deception, (piece of) fiction; (little) white lie, half-truth; informal tall story/tale, whopper; Brit. informal porky (pie).
– OPPOSITES truth.
  verb *she had bunked off school, fibbing about a sore throat:* **lie**, tell a fib, tell a lie, invent a story, make up a story; informal kid.

fibre noun **1** *fibres from his jumper were found on Lorraine's body:* **thread**, strand, filament. **2** *designer clothing in natural fibres:* **material**, cloth, fabric. **3** *a lack of fibre in his diet:* **roughage**, bulk.

fickle adjective *today's fickle fans demand instant success from their heroes:* **capricious**, changeable, variable, volatile, mercurial; inconstant, undependable, unsteady, unfaithful, faithless, flighty, giddy, skittish; literary mutable.
– OPPOSITES constant.

fiction noun **1** *the traditions of British detective fiction:* **novels**, stories, writing, literature. **2** *the president dismissed the allegation as absolute fiction:* **fabrication**, invention, lies, fibs, untruth, falsehood, fantasy, nonsense.
– OPPOSITES fact.

fictional adjective *a fictional character from*

a bad Victorian novel: **invented**, fictitious, imaginary, made up, make-believe, unreal, fabricated, mythical.
– OPPOSITES real.

fictitious adjective **1** *he used a fictitious name:* **false**, fake, fabricated, sham; bogus, spurious, assumed, affected, adopted, feigned, invented, made up; informal pretend, phoney. **2** *a fictitious character.* See FICTIONAL.
– OPPOSITES genuine.

fiddle (informal) noun *the men were involved in a major VAT fiddle:* **fraud**, swindle, confidence trick; informal racket, con trick, flimflam.
  verb **1** *he fiddled nervously with a beer mat:* **fidget**, play, toy, twiddle, fuss, fool about/around; finger, thumb, handle; informal mess about/around; Brit. informal muck about/around. **2** *he fiddled with some dials and knobs:* **adjust**, tinker; tweak, play about/around, meddle, interfere. **3** *the government is fiddling the figures:* **falsify**, manipulate, massage, rig, distort, misrepresent, doctor, alter, tamper with, interfere with; informal fix, cook (the books).

fidelity noun **1** *she was never tempted to stray from absolute fidelity to her husband:* **faithfulness**, loyalty, constancy; trustworthiness, dependability, reliability. **2** *the fidelity of the reproduction:* **accuracy**, exactness, precision, preciseness, correctness, strictness, closeness, faithfulness, authenticity.
– OPPOSITES disloyalty.

fidget verb **1** *during the second act, the audience began to fidget:* **wriggle**, squirm, twitch, jiggle, shuffle. **2** *she fidgeted with her scarf:* **play**, fuss, toy, twiddle, fool about/around; informal fiddle, mess about/around.

fidgety adjective *I get a bit fidgety around women:* **restless**, restive, on edge, uneasy, nervous, nervy, keyed up, anxious, agitated; informal jittery, twitchy.

field noun **1** *we crossed a large field full of cows:* **meadow**, pasture, paddock, grassland, pastureland, sward. **2** *a football field:* **pitch**, ground, sports field, playing field, recreation ground. **3** *the field of biotechnology:* **area**, sphere, discipline, province, department, domain, sector, branch, subject; informal bailiwick. **4** *the screen fills your field of vision:* **scope**, range, sweep, reach, extent. **5** *she is well ahead of the field:* **competitors**, entrants, competition; applicants, candidates.
  verb **1** *she could field a ball with the best of the boys:* **catch**, stop, retrieve; return, throw back. **2** *they should have been disqualified for fielding an ineligible player:* **put in**, send out, play, put up. **3** *he fielded some rather awkward questions:* **deal with**, handle, cope with, answer, reply to, respond to.

fiend noun **1** *a fiend bent on global domination:* **brute**, beast, villain, barbarian, monster, ogre, sadist, evil-doer; informal swine. **2** (informal) *I'm a bit of a curry fiend:* **enthusiast**, maniac; devotee, fan, lover; informal fanatic, addict, buff, freak, nut.

fiendish adjective **1** *the fiendish atrocities which have been perpetrated in Russia:* **wicked**, cruel, vicious, evil, villainous; brutal, savage, barbaric, barbarous, inhuman, murderous, ruthless, merciless. **2** *a fiendish plot by manufacturers to relieve the customers of their hard-earned cash:* **cunning**, clever, ingenious, crafty, canny, wily, devious, shrewd; informal foxy, sneaky. **3** *a fiendish puzzle that took hours to complete:* **difficult**, complex, challenging, complicated, intricate, involved, knotty, thorny.

fierce adjective **1** *a fierce black mastiff barred the way:* **ferocious**, savage, vicious, aggressive. **2** *they are facing fierce competition from the Americans:* **aggressive**, cut-throat, competitive; keen, intense, strong, relentless. **3** *a fierce, murderous jealousy filled his whole being:* **intense**, powerful, vehement, passionate, impassioned, fervent, fervid, ardent. **4** *a fierce wind coming in off the sea:* **powerful**, strong, violent, forceful; stormy, blustery, gusty, tempestuous. **5** *a fierce pain shot up his leg:* **severe**, extreme, intense, acute, awful, dreadful; excruciating, agonizing, piercing.
– OPPOSITES gentle, mild.

fiery adjective **1** *the fiery breath of the volcano:* **burning**, blazing, flaming; on fire, ablaze. **2** *she had blushed a fiery red:* **bright**, brilliant, vivid, intense, deep, rich. **3** *her fiery spirit:* **passionate**, impassioned, ardent, fervent, fervid, spirited; quick-tempered, volatile, explosive, aggressive, determined, resolute.

fiesta noun **festival**, carnival, holiday, celebration, party.

fight verb **1** *two men were fighting in the bar:* **brawl**, exchange blows, attack/assault each other, hit/punch each other; struggle, grapple, wrestle; informal scrap, have a dust-up, have a set-to; Brit. informal have a punch-up; N. Amer. informal rough-house; Austral./NZ informal stoush, go the knuckle. **2** *he fought in the First World War:* **(do) battle**, go to war, take up arms, be a soldier; engage, meet, clash, skirmish. **3** *a war fought for freedom:* **engage in**, wage, conduct, prosecute, undertake. **4** *she and her sister are always fighting:* **quarrel**, argue, row, bicker, squabble, fall out, have a row/fight, wrangle, be at odds, disagree, have words, be at each other's throats, be at loggerheads; informal scrap. **5** *textile workers are fighting against wage reductions:* **campaign**, strive, battle, struggle, contend, crusade, agitate, lobby, push, press. **6** *they will fight the decision tooth and nail:* **oppose**, contest, contend with, confront, challenge, combat, dispute, quarrel with, argue against/with, strive

against, struggle against. **7** *Donaldson fought the urge to put his tongue out:* **repress**, restrain, suppress, stifle, smother, hold back, fight back, keep in check, curb, control, rein in, choke back.
noun **1** *he'd got into a fight outside a club:* **brawl**, fracas, melee, rumpus, skirmish, sparring match, struggle, scuffle, altercation, scrum, clash, disturbance; fisticuffs; informal scrap, dust-up, set-to, shindy, shindig; Brit. informal punch-up, bust-up, ruck; N. Amer. informal rough house, brannigan; Austral./NZ informal stoush. **2** *a heavyweight championship fight:* **(boxing) match**, bout, contest. **3** *Britain's fight against German domination:* **battle**, engagement, clash, conflict, struggle; war, campaign, crusade, action, hostilities. **4** *I'd just had a fight with my girlfriend:* **argument**, quarrel, squabble, row, wrangle, disagreement, falling-out, contretemps, altercation, dispute; informal tiff, spat, scrap, slanging match; Brit. informal barney, ding-dong, bust-up. **5** *their long fight for control of the company:* **struggle**, battle, campaign, push, effort. **6** *she had no fight left in her:* **will**, resistance, spirit, courage, pluck, pluckiness, grit, strength, backbone, determination, resolution, resolve, resoluteness, aggression, aggressiveness; informal guts, spunk; Brit. informal bottle; N. Amer. informal sand, moxie.
▪ **fight back 1** *use your pent-up anger to fight back:* retaliate, counter-attack, strike back, hit back, respond, reciprocate, return fire, give tit for tat. **2** *she fought back her tears.* See **FIGHT** verb sense 7.
▪ **fight someone/something off** *he fought off a pit bull terrier that attacked him in the park:* repel, repulse, beat off/back, ward off, fend off, keep/hold at bay, drive away/back, force back.
▪ **fight shy of** *some people fight shy of taking out a personal loan:* flinch from, demur from, recoil from; have scruples about, have misgivings about, have qualms about, be averse to, be chary of, be loath to, be reluctant to, be disinclined to, be afraid to, hesitate to, baulk at; informal boggle at; archaic disrelish.

fightback noun (Brit.) *Hibs mounted a spirited fightback in the second half:* **counter-attack**, counter-offensive; rally, recovery; informal comeback.

fighter noun **1** *a guerrilla fighter:* **soldier**, warrior, combatant, serviceman, servicewoman, trooper; Brit. informal squaddie; archaic man-at-arms. **2** *the bout ends when the fighter is knocked to the ground:* **boxer**, pugilist, prizefighter; wrestler. **3** *he was shot down by enemy fighters:* **warplane**, plane.

fighting adjective *Hugh was always a fighting man:* **violent**, combative, aggressive, pugnacious, truculent, belligerent, bellicose.
– OPPOSITES peaceful.
noun *200 were injured in the fighting:*

violence, hostilities, conflict, action, combat; warfare, war, battles, skirmishing, rioting.
– OPPOSITES peace.

figment noun *all this nonsense about ghosts is just a figment of her imagination:* **invention**, creation, fabrication; hallucination, illusion, delusion, fancy, vision.

figurative adjective 1 *the role of figurative language in communication:* **metaphorical**, non-literal, symbolic, allegorical, representative, emblematic. 2 *his range of skills cover figurative work and other aspects of carving:* **representational**, pictorial; mimetic.
– OPPOSITES literal, abstract.

figure noun 1 *the production figures are down this month:* **statistic**, number, quantity, amount, level, total, sum; (**figures**) data, information. 2 *the second figure was 9:* **digit**, numeral, numerical symbol. 3 *her petite, curvaceous figure:* **physique**, build, frame, body, proportions, shape, form. 4 *a dark figure emerged from the shadows:* **silhouette**, outline, shape, form. 5 *a figure of authority:* **person**, personage, individual, man, woman, character, personality; representative, embodiment, personification, epitome. 6 *most of his sculptures are life-size figures:* **form**, shape, effigy. 7 *geometrical figures:* **shape**, pattern, design, motif. 8 *this is illustrated in figure 4:* **diagram**, illustration, drawing, picture, plate.
verb *an awesome beast that figured in Egyptian legend:* **feature**, appear, be featured, be mentioned, be referred to, have prominence.
■ **figure something out** (informal) *he tried to figure out how to switch on the lamp:* work out, make out, fathom, puzzle out, ascertain, make sense of, think through, get to the bottom of; understand, comprehend, see, grasp, get the hang of; Brit. informal suss out.

filament noun **fibre**, thread, strand; technical fibril.

file¹ noun 1 *he opened the file and began to read:* **folder**, portfolio, binder, document case. 2 *we have files on all the major companies:* **dossier**, document, record, report; data, information, documentation, annals, archives. 3 *the computer file was searched:* **document**, text; data bank, database.
verb 1 *make sure you file the documents correctly:* **categorize**, classify, organize, put in place/order, order, arrange, catalogue, record, store, archive. 2 *Debbie has filed for divorce:* **apply**, register, ask. 3 *two women have filed a civil suit against him:* **bring**, press, lodge, place; formal prefer.

file² noun *a file of boys in football kit crossed the field:* **line**, column, row, string, chain, procession; Brit. informal crocodile.

verb *we filed out into the car park:* **walk**, march, parade, troop.

file³ verb *she has nothing to do but file her nails:* **smooth**, buff, rub, polish, shape; scrape, abrade, rasp, sand(paper).

filial adjective *a display of filial affection:* **dutiful**, devoted, compliant, respectful, affectionate, loving.

filibuster verb *the opposition are filibustering:* **waste time**, stall, play for time, stonewall, procrastinate, buy time, use delaying tactics.

filigree noun *a bench decorated with gold filigree:* **tracery**, fretwork, latticework, scrollwork, lacework.

fill verb 1 *he filled a bowl with cereal:* **make/become full**, fill up, fill to the brim, top up, charge. 2 *guests filled the parlour:* **crowd into**, throng, pack (into), occupy, squeeze into, cram (into); overcrowd, overfill. 3 *he began filling his shelves:* **stock**, pack, load, supply, replenish, restock, refill. 4 *fill all the holes with a wood-repair compound:* **block up**, stop (up), plug, seal, pack, caulk. 5 *the perfume filled the room:* **pervade**, permeate, suffuse, penetrate, infuse.
– OPPOSITES empty.
■ **fill in** *I'm going to be filling in for Kim:* **substitute**, deputize, stand in, cover, take over, act as stand-in, take the place of; informal sub, step into someone's shoes/boots; N. Amer. informal pinch-hit.
■ **fill someone in** *Ian filled me in on what's been happening:* **inform of**, advise of, tell about, acquaint with, apprise of, brief on, update with; informal put in the picture about, bring up to speed on.
■ **fill something in** (Brit.) *he filled in all the forms:* **complete**, answer, fill up; N. Amer. fill out.
■ **fill out** *she had filled out since we last saw her:* **grow fatter**, become plumper, flesh out, put on weight, get heavier.
■ **fill something out** 1 *this account needs to be filled out by detailed evidence:* **expand**, enlarge, add to, elaborate on, flesh out; supplement, extend, develop, amplify. 2 (N. Amer.) *he filled out the forms.* See **FILL SOMETHING IN**.

filling noun *filling for cushions:* **stuffing**, padding, wadding, filler; contents, inside.
adjective *a cheap but filling meal:* **substantial**, hearty, ample, satisfying, square; heavy, stodgy.

fillip noun *this reduction in rates is a fillip to the housing market:* **stimulus**, stimulation, boost, incentive, impetus; tonic, spur, aid, help; informal shot in the arm.

film noun 1 *a film of sweat covered his face:* **layer**, coat, coating, covering, cover, sheet, patina, overlay. 2 *Emma was watching a film:* **movie**, picture, feature (film), motion picture; informal flick, pic, talkie. 3 *she would like to work in film:* **cinema**, movies; the

silver screen, celluloid.
verb 1 *he immediately filmed the next scene:*
record, shoot, capture, video. **2** *his eyes
had filmed over:* **cloud**, mist, haze; become
blurred, blur; archaic blear.

film star noun **(film) actor/actress**, movie
star, leading man/woman, leading lady,
lead; celebrity, star, starlet, superstar; informal
celeb; informal, dated matinee idol.

filmy adjective *she wore a filmy black blouse:*
diaphanous, transparent, see-through,
translucent, sheer, gossamer; delicate, fine,
light, thin, silky.
– OPPOSITES thick, opaque.

filter noun *the water passes through a carbon
filter:* **strainer**, sifter; sieve, riddle; gauze,
netting.
verb 1 *the farmers filter the water:* **sieve**,
strain, sift, filtrate, riddle; clarify, purify,
refine, treat. **2** *the rain had filtered through
her jacket:* **seep**, percolate, leak, trickle,
ooze.

filth noun **1** *stagnant pools of filth:* **dirt**,
muck, grime, mud, mire, sludge, slime, ooze;
excrement, excreta, dung, manure, ordure,
sewage; rubbish, refuse, dross; pollution,
contamination, filthiness, uncleanness,
foulness, nastiness; N. Amer. garbage; informal
crud, grunge; Brit. informal grot, gunge; N. Amer.
informal trash. **2** *I felt sick after reading that
filth:* **pornography**, dirty books, smut,
muck, indecency; informal porn, rubbish,
garbage.

filthy adjective **1** *the room was filthy:* **dirty**,
mucky, grimy, muddy, slimy, unclean;
foul, squalid, sordid, nasty, soiled, sullied;
polluted, contaminated, unhygienic,
unsanitary; informal cruddy, grungy; Brit. informal
grotty. **2** *his face was filthy:* **unwashed**,
unclean, dirty, grimy, smeared, grubby,
muddy, mucky, black, blackened, stained.
3 *she told a series of filthy jokes:* **obscene**,
indecent, dirty, smutty, rude, improper,
coarse, bawdy, vulgar, lewd, racy, off colour,
earthy, ribald, risqué, adult, pornographic,
explicit; informal blue, porn, porno, X-rated;
N. Amer. informal raw. **4** *he was in a filthy
mood:* **bad**, foul, bad-tempered, ill-tempered,
irritable, grumpy, grouchy, cross, fractious,
peevish; informal snappish, snappy; Brit. informal
shirty, stroppy, narky, ratty; N. Amer. informal
cranky, ornery.
– OPPOSITES clean.

final adjective **1** *the final year of study:*
last, closing, concluding, finishing, end,
terminating, ultimate, eventual. **2** *the
referee's decisions are final:* **irrevocable**,
unalterable, absolute, conclusive,
irrefutable, incontrovertible, indisputable,
unchallengeable, binding.
– OPPOSITES first, provisional.
noun *the FA Cup final:* **decider**, final
game/match.
– OPPOSITES qualifier.

finale noun *a firework display provided
a fitting finale to the weekend:* **climax**,

culmination; end, ending, finish, close,
conclusion, termination; denouement, last
act, last movement, final scene.
– OPPOSITES beginning.

finality noun *her voice had a finality
about it that made Roy's blood run cold:*
conclusiveness, decisiveness, decision,
definiteness, definitiveness, certainty,
certitude; irrevocability, irrefutability,
incontrovertibility.

finalize verb *the two countries have yet to
finalize a deal:* **conclude**, complete, clinch,
settle, work out, secure, wrap up, wind
up, put the finishing touches to; reach an
agreement on, agree on, come to terms on;
informal sew up.

finally adverb **1** *she finally got her man to
the altar:* **eventually**, ultimately, in the
end, after a long time, at (long) last; in the
long run, in the fullness of time. **2** *finally,
wrap the ribbon round the edge:* **lastly**,
last, in conclusion, to conclude, to end.
3 *this should finally dispel that common
misconception:* **conclusively**, irrevocably,
decisively, definitively, for ever, for good,
once and for all.

finance noun **1** *he knows all about
finance:* **financial affairs**, money,
economics, commerce, business, investment.
2 *companies seeking short-term finance:*
funds, assets, money, capital, resources,
cash, reserves, revenue, income; funding,
backing, sponsorship.
verb *the project was financed by grants:* **fund**,
pay for, back, capitalize, endow, subsidize,
invest in; underwrite, guarantee, sponsor,
support; N. Amer. informal bankroll.

financial adjective *a major financial
institution:* **monetary**, money, economic,
pecuniary, fiscal, banking, commercial,
business, investment.

financier noun **investor**, speculator, banker,
capitalist, industrialist, businessman,
businesswoman, stockbroker.

find verb **1** *I found the book I wanted:* **locate**,
spot, pinpoint, unearth, obtain; search
out, nose out, track down, root out; come
across/upon, run across/into, chance on,
light on, happen on, stumble on, encounter;
informal bump into; literary espy. **2** *they have
found a cure for rabies:* **discover**, invent,
come up with, hit on. **3** *amazingly, the
police found her purse:* **retrieve**, recover,
get back, regain, repossess. **4** *I hope you find
peace:* **obtain**, acquire, get, procure, come
by, secure, gain, earn, achieve, attain. **5** *I
found the courage to speak to her:* **summon
(up)**, gather, muster (up), screw up, call
up. **6** *caffeine is found in coffee and tea:*
be (present), occur, exist, be existent,
appear. **7** *you'll find that it's a lively area:*
discover, become aware, realize, observe,
notice, note, perceive, learn. **8** *I find their
decision strange:* **consider**, think, believe
to be, feel to be, look on as, view as, see
as, judge, deem, regard as. **9** *he was found*

f

guilty: **judge**, adjudge, adjudicate, deem, rule, declare, pronounce. **10** *she knew her barb had found its mark:* **arrive at**, reach, attain, achieve; hit, strike.
– OPPOSITES lose.
noun 1 *this exciting find dates from the second century:* **discovery**, acquisition. **2** *this table is a real find for anyone who's short of space:* **good buy**, bargain; godsend, boon.
■ **find out** *I found out my husband was having an affair* | *he finally found out the truth:* discover, become aware, learn, detect, discern, perceive, observe, notice, note, get/come to know, realize; bring to light, reveal, expose, unearth, disclose; informal figure out, cotton on, catch on, tumble, get wise, savvy; Brit. informal twig, rumble, suss.

finding noun 1 *the finding of the leak:* **discovery**, location, locating, detection, detecting, uncovering. **2** *he was appalled at the tribunal's findings:* **conclusion**, decision, verdict, pronouncement, judgement, ruling, rule, decree, order, recommendation; Law determination; N. Amer. resolve.

fine[1] **adjective 1** *a fine collection of Regency furniture:* **excellent**, first-class, first-rate, great, exceptional, outstanding, superior, splendid, magnificent, exquisite, supreme, superb, wonderful, superlative, second to none; informal A1, top-notch, splendiferous. **2** *fine wines:* **select**, choice, prime, superior, of distinction, quality, premium. **3** *the initiative is fine, but it's not enough on its own:* **all right**, acceptable, suitable, good (enough), passable, satisfactory, adequate, reasonable, tolerable; informal OK. **4** *I feel fine:* **in good health**, well, healthy, all right, (fighting) fit, as fit as a fiddle/flea, blooming, thriving, in good shape/condition, in fine fettle; informal OK, in the pink. **5** *it was a fine day:* **fair**, dry, bright, clear, sunny, without a cloud in the sky, warm, balmy, summery. **6** *she dressed him in fine clothes:* **elegant**, stylish, expensive, smart, chic, fashionable; fancy, sumptuous, lavish, opulent; informal flashy, swanky, ritzy, plush. **7** *fine china:* **delicate**, fragile, dainty. **8** *her fine golden hair:* **thin**, light, delicate, wispy, flyaway. **9** *she sharpened her pencil to a fine point:* **sharp**, keen, acute. **10** *the fine material of her dress:* **sheer**, light, lightweight, thin, flimsy; diaphanous, filmy, gossamer, silky, transparent, translucent, see-through. **11** *a beach of fine, golden sand:* **fine-grained**, powdery, powdered, dusty, ground, crushed; technical comminuted. **12** *for fine detailed work, you need a smaller brush:* **intricate**, delicate, detailed, elaborate, dainty, meticulous. **13** *a fine distinction:* **subtle**, nice, hair-splitting.
– OPPOSITES poor, unsatisfactory, ill, inclement, thick, coarse.

fine[2] **noun** *if convicted they face heavy fines:* **(financial) penalty**, sanction, fee, charge.
verb *they were fined for breaking environmental laws:* **penalize**, charge.

finery noun *she appeared, dressed in all her finery:* **regalia**, best clothes, (Sunday) best; informal glad rags, best bib and tucker.

finesse noun 1 *the comedy routine is performed with masterly finesse:* **skill**, skilfulness, expertise, subtlety, flair, panache, elan, polish, artistry, virtuosity, mastery. **2** *these situations call for a modicum of finesse:* **tact**, tactfulness, discretion, diplomacy, delicacy, sensitivity, perceptiveness, savoir faire.

finger noun *he wagged his finger at her:* **digit**, thumb, index finger, forefinger; informal pinkie.
verb *she fingered her brooch uneasily:* **touch**, feel, handle, stroke, rub, caress, fondle, toy with, play (about/around) with, fiddle with.

finicky adjective *birds are very temperamental, and finicky with their food at the best of times:* **fussy**, fastidious, punctilious, over-particular, difficult, exacting, demanding; informal picky, choosy, pernickety; N. Amer. informal persnickety.

finish verb 1 *Mrs Porter had just finished the task:* **complete**, end, conclude, stop, cease, terminate, bring to a conclusion/end/close, wind up; crown, cap, round off, put the finishing touches to; accomplish, discharge, carry out, do, get done, fulfil; informal wrap up, sew up, polish off. **2** *Hitch finished his dinner:* **consume**, eat, devour, drink, finish off, polish off, gulp (down); use (up), exhaust, empty, drain, get through, run through; informal down. **3** *the programme has finished:* **end**, come to an end, stop, conclude, come to a conclusion/end/close, cease. **4** *some items were finished in a black lacquer:* **varnish**, lacquer, veneer, coat, stain, wax, shellac, enamel, glaze.
– OPPOSITES start, begin, continue.
noun 1 *a party to celebrate the finish of filming:* **end**, ending, completion, conclusion, close, closing, cessation, termination; informal sewing up, polishing off. **2** *it was a real gallop to the finish:* **finishing line/post**, tape. **3** *the furniture has a mellow painted finish:* **veneer**, lacquer, lamination, glaze, coating, covering; surface, texture.
– OPPOSITES start, beginning.
■ **finish someone/something off 1** *the executioners finished them off:* kill, take/end the life of, execute, terminate, exterminate, liquidate, get rid of; informal wipe out, do in, bump off, take out, dispose of, do away with; N. Amer. informal ice, rub out, waste. **2** *financial difficulties finished off the business:* overwhelm, overcome, defeat, get the better of, worst, bring down; informal drive to the wall, best.

finished adjective 1 *he looked approvingly at the finished job:* **completed**, concluded, terminated, over (and done with), at an end; accomplished, executed, discharged, fulfilled, done; informal wrapped up, sewn up, polished off. **2** *a finished performance:* **accomplished**, polished, flawless, faultless,

perfect; expert, proficient, masterly, impeccable, virtuoso, skilful, skilled, professional. **3** *he knew he was finished:* **ruined**, defeated, beaten, wrecked, doomed, bankrupt, broken; informal washed up, through.
– OPPOSITES incomplete.

finite adjective *there is a finite amount of money available:* **limited**, restricted, determinate, fixed.

fire noun **1** *a fire broke out in the kitchen:* **blaze**, conflagration, inferno; flames, burning, combustion. **2** *he turned on an electric fire:* **heater**, radiator, convector. **3** *he lacked fire and animation:* **dynamism**, energy, vigour, animation, vitality, vibrancy, exuberance, zest, elan; passion, ardour, zeal, spirit, verve, vivacity, vivaciousness; enthusiasm, eagerness, gusto, fervour, fervency; informal pep, vim, go, get-up-and-go, oomph. **4** *rapid machine-gun fire:* **gunfire**, firing, flak, bombardment.
verb **1** *howitzers were firing shells from beyond the river:* **launch**, shoot, discharge, let fly with. **2** *someone fired a gun at me:* **shoot**, discharge, let off, set off. **3** (informal) *he was fired:* **dismiss**, discharge, give someone their notice, lay off, let go, get rid of, axe, cashier; informal sack, give someone the sack, boot out, give someone the boot/bullet, give someone the elbow/push, give someone their marching orders; Brit. informal give someone their cards. **4** *the engine fired and she put her foot down:* **start**, get started, get going. **5** *the stories fired my imagination:* **stimulate**, stir up, excite, awaken, arouse, rouse, inflame, animate, inspire, motivate.
■ **catch fire** *the driver got out before the car caught fire:* **ignite**, catch light, burst into flames, go up in flames.
■ **on fire 1** *the restaurant was on fire:* **burning**, alight, ablaze, blazing, aflame, in flames. **2** *she was on fire with passion:* **ardent**, passionate, fervent, excited, aflutter, eager, enthusiastic.

firearm noun **gun**, weapon; informal shooter; N. Amer. informal piece, rod, shooting iron.

firebrand noun *a political firebrand who loved to antagonize:* **radical**, revolutionary, agitator, rabble-rouser, incendiary, subversive, troublemaker.

fireproof adjective *he wore fireproof overalls:* **non-flammable**, incombustible, fire resistant, flame resistant, flame retardant, heatproof.
– OPPOSITES inflammable.

fireworks plural noun **1** *we went outside to watch the fireworks:* **pyrotechnics**. **2** *his stubbornness has produced some fireworks:* **uproar**, trouble, mayhem, fuss; tantrums, hysterics.

firm¹ adjective **1** *the ground is fairly firm:* **hard**, solid, unyielding, resistant; solidified, hardened, compacted, compressed, dense, stiff, rigid, frozen, set. **2** *firm foundations:* **secure**, secured, stable, steady, strong,

fixed, fast, set, taut, tight; immovable, irremovable, stationary, motionless. **3** *a firm handshake:* **strong**, vigorous, sturdy, forceful. **4** *I was very firm about what I wanted:* **resolute**, determined, decided, resolved, steadfast; adamant, emphatic, insistent, single-minded; sure, certain, definite. **5** *he's always been a firm Labour supporter:* **whole-hearted** unfaltering, unwavering, unflinching, unswerving, unbending; hard-line, committed, dyed-in-the-wool. **6** *they became firm friends:* **close**, good, boon, intimate, inseparable, dear, special, fast; constant, devoted, loving, faithful, long-standing, steady, steadfast. **7** *she had no firm plans:* **definite**, fixed, settled, decided, established, confirmed, agreed; unalterable, unchangeable, irreversible.
– OPPOSITES soft, unstable, limp, indefinite.

firm² noun *an accountancy firm:* **company**, business, concern, enterprise, organization, corporation, conglomerate, office, bureau, agency, consortium; informal outfit, set-up.

first adjective **1** *the first chapter of Genesis:* **earliest**, initial, opening, introductory. **2** *we decided to start from first principles:* **fundamental**, basic, rudimentary, primary; key, cardinal, central, chief, vital, essential. **3** *our first priority is law and order:* **foremost**, principal, highest, greatest, paramount, top, uppermost, prime, chief, leading, main, major; overriding, predominant, prevailing, central, core, dominant; informal number-one. **4** *he is hoping to win first prize:* **top**, best, prime, premier, winner's, winning.
– OPPOSITES last, closing.
adverb **1** *the room they had first entered:* **at first**, to begin with, first of all, at the outset, initially. **2** *she would eat first, then take a bath:* **before anything else**, first and foremost, now. **3** *she wouldn't go—she'd die first!* **in preference**, sooner, rather.
noun *from the first, surrealism was theatrical:* **the (very) beginning**, the start, the outset, the commencement; informal the word go, the off.

first-class adjective *this is a first-class hotel:* **superior**, first-rate, high-quality, top-quality, high-grade, five-star; prime, premier, premium, grade A, best, select, exclusive, excellent, superb; informal tip-top, A1, top-notch.
– OPPOSITES poor.

first-hand adjective *they have first-hand experience of bringing up children:* **direct**, immediate, personal, hands-on, experiential, empirical.
– OPPOSITES vicarious, indirect.

first name noun **forename**, Christian name, given name.
– OPPOSITES surname.

first-rate adjective *they have done a first-rate job:* **top-quality**, high-quality, top-grade, first-class, second to none, fine; superlative,

f

excellent, superb, outstanding, exceptional, exemplary, marvellous, magnificent, splendid; informal tip-top, top-notch, ace, A1, super, great, terrific, tremendous, fantastic; Brit. informal top-hole, smashing; informal, dated capital.

fiscal adjective *the government's fiscal policies:* **tax**, budgetary; financial, economic, monetary, money.

fish verb **1** *some people were fishing in the lake:* **go fishing**, angle, trawl. **2** *she opened her bag and fished for her purse:* **search**, delve, look, hunt; grope, fumble, ferret (about/around), root about/around, rummage (about/around/round). **3** *I'm not fishing for compliments:* **look**, solicit, angle, aim, hope, cast about/around/round, be after.
■ **fish someone/something out** *they eventually fished him out of the water:* **pull out**, haul out, remove, extricate, extract, retrieve; rescue from, save from.

fisherman noun **angler**, rod.

fishy adjective (informal) *there was something fishy going on.* See SUSPICIOUS.

fissure noun *fissures in the ocean floor:* **opening**, crevice, crack, cleft, breach, crevasse, chasm; break, fracture, fault, rift, rupture, split.

fist noun **clenched hand**; informal duke, meat hook; Brit. informal bunch of fives.

fit¹ adjective **1** *the house is not fit for human habitation | he is a fit subject for such a book:* **suitable**, good enough; relevant, pertinent, apt, appropriate, suited, apposite, fitting. **2** *is he fit to look after a child?* **competent**, able, capable; ready, prepared, qualified, trained, equipped. **3** *he looked tanned and fit:* **healthy**, well, in good health, in (good) shape, in (good) trim, in good condition, fighting fit, as fit as a fiddle/flea; athletic, muscular, strong, robust, hale and hearty.
– OPPOSITES unsuitable, incapable, unwell.
verb **1** *my overcoat should fit you:* **be the right/correct size (for)**, be big/small enough (for), fit like a glove. **2** *have your carpets fitted professionally:* **lay**, put in place/position, position, place, fix. **3** *cameras fitted with a backlight button:* **equip**, provide, supply, fit out, furnish. **4** *concrete slabs were fitted together:* **join**, connect, put together, piece together, attach, unite, link. **5** *a sentence that fits his crimes:* **be appropriate to**, suit, match, correspond to, tally with, go with, accord with, correlate to, be congruous with, be congruent with, be consonant with. **6** *an MSc fits you for a professional career:* **qualify**, prepare, make ready, train, groom.
noun *the degree of fit between a school's philosophy and practice:* **correlation**, correspondence, agreement, consistency, equivalence, match, similarity, compatibility, concurrence.
■ **fit in** *he made a big effort to fit in:* conform,

be in harmony, blend in, be in line, be assimilated into.
■ **fit someone/something out/up** *the carriage was fitted out with everything they could need:* equip, provide, supply, furnish, kit out, rig out.

fit² noun **1** *an epileptic fit:* **convulsion**, spasm, paroxysm, seizure, attack; Medicine ictus. **2** *a fit of the giggles:* **outbreak**, outburst, attack, bout, spell. **3** *my mother would have a fit if she knew:* **tantrum**, fit of temper, outburst of anger/rage, frenzy; informal paddy, stress; N. Amer. informal blowout.
■ **in/by fits and starts** *the government took little interest, and research continued in fits and starts:* spasmodically, intermittently, sporadically, erratically, irregularly, fitfully, haphazardly.

fitful adjective *I drifted off into a brief and fitful sleep:* **intermittent**, sporadic, spasmodic, broken, disturbed, disrupted, patchy, irregular, uneven, unsettled.

fitness noun **1** *polo requires tremendous fitness:* **good health**, strength, robustness, vigour, athleticism, toughness, physical fitness, muscularity; good condition, good shape, well-being. **2** *he was examined to assess his fitness for active service:* **suitability**, capability, competence, ability, aptitude; readiness, preparedness, eligibility.

fitted adjective **1** *a fitted sheet:* **shaped**, contoured. **2** *a fitted wardrobe:* **built-in**, integral, integrated, fixed. **3** *he wasn't fitted for the job:* **(well) suited**, right, suitable; equipped, fit; informal cut out.

fitting noun **1** *the light fitting in the centre of the ceiling:* **attachment**, connection, piece, component, accessory. **2** *a manufacturer of bathroom fittings:* **furnishings**, furniture, fixtures, fitments, equipment, appointments, appurtenances. **3** *the fitting of catalytic converters to vehicles:* **installation**, installing, putting in, fixing.
adjective *this is a fitting conclusion to the book:* **apt**, appropriate, suitable, apposite; fit, proper, right, seemly, correct.
– OPPOSITES unsuitable.

five cardinal number **quintet**, fivesome; quintuplets; Poetry pentameter; technical pentad.

fix verb **1** *new road signs were fixed to the lamp posts:* **fasten**, attach, affix, secure; join, connect, couple, link; install, implant, embed; stick, glue, pin, nail, screw, bolt, clamp, clip. **2** *his words are fixed in my memory:* **stick**, lodge, embed. **3** *his eyes were fixed on the ground:* **focus**, direct, level, point, train; glue. **4** *techniques of fixing the audience's attention:* **attract**, draw; hold, grip, engage, captivate, rivet. **5** *he fixed my washing machine:* **repair**, mend, put right, put to rights, get working, restore (to working order); overhaul, service, renovate, recondition. **6** *James fixed it for his parents to watch the show from the wings:* **arrange**,

organize, contrive, manage, engineer; informal swing, wangle. **7** *let's fix a date for the meeting:* **decide on**, select, choose, resolve on; determine, settle, set, arrange, establish, allot; designate, name, appoint, specify.
– OPPOSITES remove.
noun (informal) **1** *they are in a bit of a fix:* **predicament**, plight, difficulty, corner, tight spot; mess, mare's nest, dire straits; informal pickle, jam, hole, scrape, bind, sticky situation. **2** *there is no quick fix for the coal industry:* **solution**, answer, resolution, way out, remedy, cure; informal magic bullet.

fixated adjective *Bara was for a time fixated on oriental and Asian culture:* **obsessed**, preoccupied, obsessive; focused, keen, gripped, engrossed, immersed, wrapped up, enthusiastic, fanatical; informal hooked, wild, nuts, crazy; Brit. informal potty.

fixation noun *the modern fixation on fitness:* **obsession**, preoccupation, mania, addiction, compulsion; informal thing, bug, craze, fad.

fixed adjective *a fixed period of time:* **predetermined**, set, established, arranged, specified, decided, agreed, determined, confirmed, prescribed, definite, defined, explicit, precise.

fixture noun **1** *the hotel retains many of the original fixtures and fittings:* **appliance**, installation, unit; equipment, facility. **2** (Brit.) *their first fixture of the season:* **match**, race, game, competition, contest, event.

fizz verb **1** *the mixture fizzed like mad:* **effervesce**, sparkle, bubble, froth. **2** *all the screens were fizzing away:* **crackle**, buzz, hiss, fizzle, crepitate.
noun 1 *the process that puts the fizz in champagne:* **effervescence**, sparkle, fizziness, bubbles, bubbliness, gassiness, carbonation, froth. **2** (informal) *they all had another glass of fizz:* **sparkling wine**, champagne; informal bubbly, champers. **3** (informal) *their set is a little lacking in fizz:* **ebullience**, exuberance, liveliness, life, vivacity, animation, vigour, energy, verve, dash, spirit, sparkle, zest; informal pizzazz, pep, zip, oomph.

fizzle verb *the loudspeaker fizzled again:* **crackle**, buzz, hiss, fizz, crepitate.
■ **fizzle out** *their romance just fizzled out:* peter out, die off, ease off, cool off; tail off, wither away.

fizzy adjective *a fizzy drink:* **effervescent**, sparkling, carbonated, gassy, bubbly, frothy; mousseux, pétillant, spumante, frizzante.
– OPPOSITES still, flat.

flabbergasted adjective (informal). See ASTONISHED.

flabbiness noun *there was a little flabbiness in her lower belly:* **fat**, fatness, fleshiness, plumpness, chubbiness, portliness, obesity, corpulence; softness, looseness, flaccidity, droopiness, sag; informal flab, tubbiness.

flabby adjective **1** *his flabby stomach:* **soft**, loose, flaccid, slack, untoned, drooping,

sagging. **2** *a flabby woman:* **fat**, fleshy, overweight, plump, chubby, portly, rotund, broad in the beam, of ample proportions, obese, corpulent; informal tubby, roly-poly, well covered, well upholstered. **3** *flabby, colourless prose:* **sloppy**, lacklustre, lifeless, listless, uninspiring, tame, loose.
– OPPOSITES firm, thin.

flaccid adjective **1** *your muscles are sagging, they're flaccid:* **soft**, loose, flabby, slack, lax; drooping, sagging. **2** *his play seemed flaccid:* **lacklustre**, lifeless, listless, uninspiring, tame, loose.
– OPPOSITES firm, spirited.

flag¹ noun *the Irish flag:* **banner**, standard, ensign, pennant, banderole, streamer, jack, gonfalon; colours; Brit. pendant.
verb *a spelling checker can flag the misspelt words:* **indicate**, identify, point out, mark, label, tag, highlight.
■ **flag someone/something down** *she flagged down a police car:* hail, wave down, signal to stop, stop, halt.

flag² noun *stone flags.* See FLAGSTONE.

flag³ verb **1** *they were flagging towards the finish:* **tire**, grow tired/weary, weaken, grow weak, wilt, droop. **2** *my energy flags in the afternoon:* **fade**, decline, wane, ebb, diminish, decrease, lessen, dwindle; wither, melt away, peter out, die away/down.
– OPPOSITES revive.

flagon noun **jug**, vessel, bottle, carafe, flask, decanter, tankard, ewer, pitcher.

flagrant adjective *the regime has shown a flagrant disregard for human rights:* **blatant**, glaring, obvious, overt, conspicuous, barefaced, shameless, brazen, undisguised, unconcealed; outrageous, scandalous, shocking, disgraceful, dreadful, terrible, gross.

flagstone noun **paving slab**, paving stone, slab, flag, sett, tile.

flail verb **1** *he fell headlong, his arms flailing:* **wave**, swing, thrash about, flap about. **2** *I was flailing about in the water:* **flounder**, struggle, thrash, writhe, splash.

flair noun **1** *he had a real flair for publicity:* **aptitude**, talent, gift, instinct, (natural) ability, facility, skill, bent, feel. **2** *she dressed with flair:* **style**, stylishness, panache, dash, elan, poise, elegance; (good) taste, discernment, discrimination; informal class.

flak noun **1** *my aircraft had been damaged by flak:* **anti-aircraft fire**, shelling, gunfire; bombardment, barrage, salvo, volley. **2** (informal) *he has come in for a lot of flak:* **criticism**, censure, disapproval, disapprobation, hostility, complaints; opprobrium, obloquy, calumny, calumniation, vilification, abuse, brickbats; Brit. informal stick, verbal; formal castigation, excoriation.

flake¹ noun *flakes of pastry:* **sliver**, wafer, shaving, paring; chip, scale, spillikin; fragment, scrap, shred; technical lamina.

verb *the paint was flaking:* **peel (off)**, chip, blister, come off (in layers).

flake² verb
■ **flake out** (informal) *she flaked out in her chair:* fall asleep, go to sleep, drop off; collapse, faint, pass out, lose consciousness, black out, swoon; informal conk out, nod off; N. Amer. informal sack out, zone out.

flaky adjective *her skin had healed, though it was very flaky:* **flaking**, peeling, scaly, blistering, scabrous; dry, brittle.

flamboyant adjective **1** *her flamboyant personality:* **ostentatious**, exuberant, confident, lively, animated, vibrant, vivacious; larger than life. **2** *he sported a flamboyant cravat:* **colourful**, brightly coloured, bright, vibrant, vivid; dazzling, eye-catching, bold; showy, gaudy, garish, lurid, loud; informal jazzy, flashy. **3** *a flamboyant architectural style:* **elaborate**, ornate, fancy; baroque, rococo.
– OPPOSITES restrained.

flame noun *a sheet of flames engulfed the house:* **fire**; blaze, conflagration, inferno.
verb **1** *the logs crackled and flamed:* **burn**, blaze, be ablaze, be alight, be on fire, be in flames, be aflame; flare. **2** *Erica's cheeks flamed:* **become red**, go red, blush, flush, redden, grow pink/crimson/scarlet, colour, glow.
– OPPOSITES extinguish.
■ **in flames** *two ships are in flames, drifting towards the harbour:* on fire, burning, alight, flaming, blazing, ignited.

flameproof adjective *flameproof gloves:* **non-flammable**, non-inflammable, flame-resistant, fire-resistant, flame-retardant, uninflammable.
– OPPOSITES flammable.

flaming adjective **1** *a flaming bonfire:* **blazing**, ablaze, burning, on fire, in flames, aflame. **2** *a flaming row:* **furious**, violent, vehement, frenzied, angry, passionate. **3** *in a flaming temper:* **furious**, enraged, fuming, seething, incensed, infuriated, angry, raging; informal livid. **4** (informal) *where's that flaming ambulance?* **wretched**; informal damned, damnable, blasted, blessed, confounded; Brit. informal flipping, blinking, blooming, bleeding, effing; Brit. informal, dated ruddy.

flammable adjective *flammable liquids:* **inflammable**, burnable, combustible.

flank noun **1** *he touched the horse's flanks:* **side**, haunch, quarter, thigh. **2** *the southern flank of the Eighth Army:* **side**, wing; face, aspect.
verb *the garden is flanked by two rivers:* **edge**, bound, line, border, fringe.

flannel noun **1** (Brit.) *she dabbed her face with a flannel:* **facecloth**, cloth; N. Amer. washcloth, washrag; Austral. washer. **2** (Brit. informal) *don't accept any flannel from salespeople:* **smooth talk**, flattery, blarney, blandishments, honeyed words; prevarication, equivocation,

evasion, doublespeak; informal spiel, soft soap, sweet talk, baloney, hot air; Brit. informal waffle; Austral./NZ informal guyver.

flap verb **1** *the mallards flapped their wings angrily:* **beat**, flutter, agitate, wave, wag, swing. **2** *his shirt tails flapped in the breeze:* **flutter**, fly, blow, swing, sway, ripple, stir.
noun **1** *pockets with buttoned flaps:* **fold**, overlap, covering; lappet. **2** *the surviving bird made a few desperate flaps:* **flutter**; stroke, beat.

flare noun **1** *the flare of the match lit up his face:* **blaze**, flash, dazzle, burst, flicker. **2** *the helicopter spotted a flare set off by the crew:* **distress signal**, rocket, Very light, beacon, light, signal. **3** *Kelly felt a flare of anger within her:* **burst**, rush, eruption, explosion, spasm, access.
verb **1** *the match flared as he lit a cigarette:* **blaze**, flash, flare up, flame, burn; glow, flicker. **2** *her nostrils flared:* **spread**, broaden, widen; dilate.
■ **flare up 1** *the wooden houses flared up like matchsticks:* burn, blaze, go up in flames. **2** *his injury flared up again at the end of the year:* recur, reoccur, reappear; break out, start suddenly, erupt. **3** *how ridiculous of James to flare up and get sent off in a friendly match:* lose one's temper, become enraged, fly into a temper, go berserk; informal blow one's top, fly off the handle, go mad, go bananas, hit the roof, go up the wall, go off the deep end, lose one's rag, flip (one's lid), explode, have a fit; Brit. informal go spare, go crackers, do one's nut; N. Amer. informal flip one's wig, blow one's lid/stack, have a conniption fit. **4** *there are numerous disputes, any one of which might flare up into a major conflict:* erupt, explode, blow up, escalate, boil over; develop.

flash verb **1** *a torch flashed:* **light up**, shine, flare, blaze, gleam, glint, sparkle, burn; blink, wink, flicker, shimmer, twinkle, glimmer, glisten, scintillate. **2** (informal) *he was flashing his money about:* **wave**, flaunt, flourish, display, parade. **3** *racing cars flashed past:* **zoom**, streak, tear, shoot, dash, dart, fly, whistle, hurtle, rush, bolt, race, speed, career, whizz, whoosh, buzz; informal belt, zap; Brit. informal bomb, bucket; N. Amer. informal barrel.
noun **1** *a flash of light:* **flare**, blaze, burst; gleam, glint, sparkle, flicker, shimmer, twinkle, glimmer. **2** *he wore a plain uniform with no shoulder flashes:* **emblem**, insignia, badge; stripe, bar, chevron. **3** *a sudden flash of inspiration:* **burst**, outburst, wave, rush, surge, flush.
adjective (informal) *a flash sports car.* See FLASHY.
■ **in/like a flash** *it was all over in a flash:* instantly, suddenly, abruptly, immediately, all of a sudden; quickly, rapidly, swiftly, speedily; in an instant/moment, in a (split) second, in a trice, in the blink of an eye; informal in a jiffy, before you can say Jack Robinson.

flashy adjective (informal) *a big flashy car:* **ostentatious**, flamboyant, showy, conspicuous, extravagant, expensive; vulgar, tasteless, brash, lurid, garish, loud, gaudy; informal snazzy, fancy, swanky, flash, jazzy, glitzy.
– OPPOSITES discreet.

flask noun **bottle**, container; hip flask, vacuum flask; trademark Thermos.

flat¹ adjective **1** *a flat surface:* **level**, horizontal; smooth, even, uniform, regular, plane. **2** *a flat wooden box:* **shallow**, low-sided. **3** *flat sandals:* **low**, low-heeled, without heels. **4** *his voice was flat and without expression:* **monotonous**, toneless, droning, boring, dull, tedious, uninteresting, unexciting, soporific; bland, dreary, colourless, featureless, emotionless, expressionless, lifeless, spiritless, lacklustre. **5** *he felt flat, used-up, weary:* **depressed**, dejected, dispirited, despondent, downhearted, disheartened, low, low-spirited, down, unhappy, blue; without energy, enervated, sapped, weary, tired out, worn out, exhausted, drained; informal down in the mouth/dumps. **6** *the market was flat:* **slow**, inactive, sluggish, slack, quiet, depressed. **7** (Brit.) *a flat battery:* **expired**, dead, finished, used up, run out. **8** *a flat tyre:* **deflated**, punctured, burst. **9** *I charge a £30 flat fee:* **fixed**, set, regular, unchanging, unvarying, invariable. **10** *a flat denial of any impropriety:* **outright**, direct, absolute, definite, positive, straight, plain, explicit; firm, resolute, adamant, assertive, emphatic, categorical, unconditional, unqualified, unequivocal.
– OPPOSITES vertical, uneven.
adverb **1** *she lay down flat on the floor:* **stretched out**, outstretched, spreadeagled, sprawling, prone, supine, prostrate, recumbent. **2** (informal) *she turned me down flat:* **outright**, absolutely, firmly, resolutely, adamantly, emphatically, insistently, categorically, unconditionally, unequivocally.
■ **flat out** *I'd been working flat out all week:* hard, as hard as possible, for all one's worth, to the full/limit, all out; at full speed, as fast as possible, at full tilt; informal like crazy, like mad, like the wind, like a bomb; Brit. informal like billy-o, like the clappers.

flat² noun *a two-bedroom flat:* **apartment**, set of rooms, penthouse; rooms; Austral. home unit; N. Amer. informal crib.

flatten verb **1** *Tom flattened the crumpled paper:* **smooth (out)**, even (out), press, level (out/off). **2** *the cows flattened the grass:* **compress**, press down, crush, squash, compact, trample. **3** *tornadoes can flatten buildings in seconds:* **demolish**, raze (to the ground), tear down, knock down, destroy, wreck, devastate, obliterate; N. Amer. informal total. **4** (informal) *Flynn flattened him with a single punch:* **knock down/over**, knock to the ground, fell, prostrate; informal floor, deck; Brit. informal knock for six.

flatter verb **1** *it amused him to flatter her:* **compliment**, praise, express admiration for, say nice things about, pay court to, fawn on; cajole, humour, flannel, blarney; informal sweet-talk, soft-soap, butter up, play up to. **2** *I was flattered to be asked:* **honour**, gratify, please, delight; informal tickle pink. **3** *a hairstyle that flattered her:* **suit**, become, look good on, go well with; informal do something for.
– OPPOSITES insult, offend.

flatterer noun *the prince is surrounded by flatterers:* **sycophant**, lackey; informal crawler, toady, bootlicker, yes man, lickspittle, groupie.

flattering adjective **1** *these are very flattering remarks:* **complimentary**, praising, favourable, commending, admiring, applauding, appreciative, good; honeyed, sugary, silver-tongued, honey-tongued; fawning, oily, obsequious, ingratiating, servile, sycophantic; informal sweet-talking, soft-soaping, crawling, boot-licking; formal encomiastic. **2** *it was very flattering to be nominated:* **pleasing**, gratifying, honouring, gladdening. **3** *she wore her most flattering dress:* **becoming**, enhancing; attractive.

flattery noun *the old man sounded convinced by their flattery:* **praise**, adulation, compliments, blandishments, honeyed words; fawning, blarney, cajolery; informal sweet talk, soft soap, buttering up, toadying; Brit. informal flannel.

flatulence noun **(intestinal) gas**, wind; informal farting; formal flatus.

flaunt verb *he hated the way they flaunted their wealth:* **show off**, display ostentatiously, make a (great) show of, put on show/display, parade; brag about, crow about, vaunt; informal flash.

flavour noun **1** *the sweet flavour that paprika gives:* **taste**, savour, tang. **2** *salami can give extra flavour:* **flavouring**, seasoning, tastiness, tang, relish, bite, piquancy, pungency, spice, spiciness, zest; informal zing, zip. **3** *the tournament had a strong international flavour:* **character**, quality, feel, feeling, ambience, atmosphere, aura, air, mood, tone; spirit, essence, nature; informal vibe. **4** *this excerpt will give a flavour of the report:* **impression**, suggestion, hint, taste.
verb *spices for flavouring food:* **add flavour to**, season, spice (up), add piquancy to, ginger up, enrich; informal pep up.

flavouring noun **1** *this cheese is often combined with other flavourings:* **seasoning**, spice, herb, additive; condiment, dressing. **2** *vanilla flavouring:* **essence**, extract, concentrate, distillate.

flaw noun *he had a serious flaw in his character:* **defect**, blemish, fault, imperfection, deficiency, weakness, weak spot/point, inadequacy, shortcoming,

limitation, failing, foible; Computing bug; informal glitch.
– OPPOSITES strength.

flawed adjective **1** *a flawed mirror blurred the image still further:* **faulty**, defective, unsound, imperfect; broken, cracked, torn, scratched, deformed, distorted, warped, buckled; Brit. informal duff. **2** *the findings were fundamentally flawed:* **unsound**, defective, faulty, distorted, inaccurate, incorrect, erroneous, imprecise, fallacious, misleading.
– OPPOSITES flawless, sound.

flawless adjective **1** *her smooth, flawless skin:* **perfect**, unblemished, unmarked, unimpaired; whole, intact, sound, unbroken, undamaged, mint, pristine. **2** *a dazzling display of flawless virtuosity:* **consummate**, impeccable, immaculate, accurate, correct, faultless, error-free, unerring; exemplary, model, ideal, copybook.
– OPPOSITES flawed.

fleck noun *a grey colour interspersed with flecks of pale blue:* **spot**, mark, dot, speck, speckle, freckle, patch, smudge, streak, blotch, dab; informal splosh, splodge.
verb *the deer's flanks were flecked with white:* **spot**, mark, dot, speckle, bespeckle, freckle, stipple, stud, bestud, blotch, mottle, streak, splash, spatter, bespatter, scatter, sprinkle; Scottish & Irish slabber; informal splosh, splodge.

fledgling noun *a woodpecker fledgling:* **chick**, baby (bird), nestling.
adjective *fledgling industries in the developing world:* **emerging**, emergent, sunrise, dawning, embryonic, infant, nascent; developing, in the making, budding, up-and-coming, rising.
– OPPOSITES declining, mature.

flee verb **1** *she fled to her room:* **run (away/off)**, run (for it), make a run for it, take flight, be gone, make off, take off, take to one's heels, make a break for it, bolt, beat a (hasty) retreat, make a quick exit, make one's getaway, escape; informal beat it, clear off/out, vamoose, skedaddle, split, leg it, turn tail, scram; Brit. informal scarper; N. Amer. informal light out, bug out, cut out, peel out; Austral. informal shoot through; archaic fly. **2** *they fled the country:* **leave**, escape from; informal skip, quit; archaic fly.

fleece noun **wool**, coat.

fleecy adjective *he had on a fleecy green tracksuit:* **fluffy**, woolly, downy, soft, fuzzy, furry, velvety, shaggy; technical floccose, pilose.
– OPPOSITES coarse.

fleet noun **navy**, (naval) task force, armada, flotilla, squadron, convoy, column.

fleeting adjective *we caught a fleeting glimpse of him through the trees:* **brief**, short, short-lived, quick, momentary, cursory, transient, ephemeral, fugitive, passing, transitory.
– OPPOSITES lasting.

flesh noun **1** *you need more flesh on your bones:* **muscle**, meat, tissue, brawn; informal beef. **2** *she carries too much flesh:* **fat**, weight; Anatomy adipose tissue; informal blubber, flab. **3** *a fruit with juicy flesh:* **pulp**, marrow, meat. **4** *the pleasures of the flesh:* **the body**, human nature, physicality, carnality, animality; sensuality, sexuality.
■ **one's (own) flesh and blood** *the child was, after all, their own flesh and blood:* family, relative(s), relation(s), blood relation(s), kin, kinsfolk, kinsman, kinsmen, kinswoman, kinswomen, kindred, nearest and dearest, people; informal folks.
■ **flesh something out** *soon all three were back at Harvard to flesh out Yavlinsky's plan:* expand (on), elaborate on, add to, build on, add flesh to, put flesh on (the bones of), add detail to, expatiate on, supplement, reinforce, augment, fill out, enlarge on.
■ **in the flesh** *he's just as charming in the flesh as he is on TV:* in person, before one's (very) eyes, in front of one; in real life, live; physically, bodily, in bodily/human form, incarnate.

fleshly adjective *his laziness had made him prefer fleshly pleasures to work:* **carnal**, physical, animal, bestial; sexual, sensual, erotic, lustful.
– OPPOSITES spiritual, noble.

fleshy adjective *Rufus had curiously sharp features for so fleshy a man:* **plump**, chubby, portly, fat, obese, overweight, stout, corpulent, paunchy, well padded, well covered, well upholstered, rotund; informal tubby, pudgy, beefy, porky, roly-poly, blubbery; Brit. informal podgy, fubsy; N. Amer. informal corn-fed; Austral./NZ nuggety.
– OPPOSITES thin.

flex¹ verb **1** *you must flex your elbow:* **bend**, crook, hook, cock, angle, double up. **2** *Rachel flexed her cramped muscles:* **tighten**, tauten, tense (up), tension, contract.
– OPPOSITES straighten, relax.

flex² noun (Brit.) *an electric flex:* **cable**, wire, lead; N. Amer. cord.

flexibility noun **1** *the timbers give the boat flexibility:* **pliability**, suppleness, pliancy; plasticity; elasticity, stretchiness, springiness, spring, resilience, bounce; informal give. **2** *he prefers the flexibility of an endowment loan:* **adaptability**, adjustability, variability, versatility, open-endedness, freedom, latitude. **3** *the flexibility shown by the local authority regarding deadlines:* **willingness to compromise**, accommodation, amenability, cooperation, tolerance.
– OPPOSITES rigidity, inflexibility, intransigence.

flexible adjective **1** *the shoe is comfortable and flexible:* **pliable**, supple, bendable, pliant, plastic; elastic, stretchy, whippy, springy, resilient, bouncy; informal bendy. **2** *a flexible arrangement:* **adaptable**, adjustable, variable, versatile, open-ended, open, free.

3 *the need to be flexible towards tenants:* **accommodating**, amenable, willing to compromise, cooperative, tolerant, easy-going.
– OPPOSITES rigid, inflexible, intransigent.

flick noun *a flick of the wrist:* **jerk**, snap, flip, whisk.
verb **1** *he flicked the switch:* **click**, snap, flip, jerk. **2** *the horse flicked its tail:* **swish**, twitch, wave, wag, waggle, shake.
■ **flick through** *Christina flicked through her diary:* thumb (through), leaf through, flip through, skim through, scan, look through, browse through, dip into, glance at/through, peruse, run one's eye over.

flicker verb **1** *the lights flickered:* **glimmer**, glint, flare, dance, gutter; twinkle, sparkle, blink, wink, flash, scintillate, coruscate.
2 *her eyelids flickered in her sleep:* **flutter**, quiver, tremble, shiver, shudder, spasm, jerk, twitch.

flight noun **1** *the amazing history of flight:* **aviation**, flying, air transport, aerial navigation, aeronautics. **2** *the flight to Rome was rather turbulent:* **plane trip/journey**, air trip/journey, trip/journey by air. **3** *a flight of birds:* **flock**, skein, covey, swarm, cloud. **4** *his flight from England after the king's death:* **escape**, getaway, hasty departure, exit, exodus, breakout, bolt, disappearance; Brit informal flit. **5** *she ran up a flight of stairs:* **staircase**, set of steps/stairs.

flighty adjective *she was regarded as too flighty for such responsibility:* **fickle**, inconstant, mercurial, whimsical, capricious, skittish, volatile, impulsive; irresponsible, giddy, reckless, wild, careless, thoughtless.
– OPPOSITES steady, responsible.

flimsy adjective **1** *flimsy wooden buildings were swept away:* **insubstantial**, fragile, breakable, frail, shaky, unstable, wobbly, tottery, rickety, ramshackle, makeshift; jerry-built, shoddy, gimcrack. **2** *the flimsy material of her dress:* **thin**, light, fine, filmy, floaty, diaphanous, sheer, delicate, insubstantial, wispy, gossamer, gauzy. **3** *this is very flimsy evidence on which to base an accusation:* **weak**, feeble, poor, inadequate, insufficient, thin, unsubstantial, unconvincing, implausible, unsatisfactory.
– OPPOSITES sturdy, thick, sound.

flinch verb **1** *he flinched at the noise:* **wince**, start, shudder, quiver, jerk, shy. **2** *he never flinched from his duty:* **shrink from**, recoil from, shy away from, swerve from, demur from; dodge, evade, avoid, duck, baulk at, jib at, quail at, fight shy of.

fling verb *he flung the axe into the river:* **throw**, toss, sling, hurl, cast, pitch, lob; informal chuck, heave, bung, buzz; dated shy.
noun **1** *a birthday fling:* **good time**, spree, bit of fun, night out; fun and games, revels, larks; informal binge. **2** *she had a brief fling with him years ago:* **affair**, love affair, relationship, romance, affaire (de cœur),

flirtation, dalliance, liaison, entanglement, involvement, attachment.

flip verb **1** *the wave flipped the dinghy over | the plane flipped on to its back:* **overturn**, turn over, tip over, roll (over), upturn, capsize; upend, invert, knock over; keel over, topple over, turn turtle. **2** *he flipped the key through the air:* **throw**, flick, toss, fling, sling, pitch, cast, spin, lob; informal chuck, bung. **3** *I flipped the transmitter switch:* **flick**, click, snap.
■ **flip through** *he flipped through his address book:* thumb (through), leaf through, flick through, skim through, scan, look through, browse through, dip into, glance at/through, peruse, run one's eye over.

flippancy noun *I was upset by her flippancy on such a solemn occasion:* **frivolity**, levity, facetiousness; disrespect, irreverence, cheek, impudence, impertinence; Brit. informal sauce; N. Amer. informal sassiness; dated waggery.
– OPPOSITES seriousness, respect.

flippant adjective *a flippant remark:* **frivolous**, facetious, tongue-in-cheek; disrespectful, irreverent, cheeky, impudent, impertinent; informal flip, saucy, waggish; N. Amer. informal sassy.
– OPPOSITES serious, respectful.

flirt verb **1** *it amused him to flirt with her:* **trifle with**, toy with, tease, lead on. **2** *those conservatives who flirted with fascism:* **dabble in**, toy with, trifle with, amuse oneself with, play with, tinker with, dip into, scratch the surface of.
noun *Anna was quite a flirt:* **tease**, trifler, philanderer, coquette, heartbreaker.

flirtation noun **coquetry**, teasing, trifling, flirting.

flirtatious adjective **coquettish**, flirty, kittenish, teasing.

flit verb *butterflies flitted amongst the tall grasses:* **dart**, dance, skip, play, dash, trip, flutter, bob, bounce.

float verb **1** *oil floats on water:* **stay afloat**, be buoyant. **2** *the balloon floated in the air:* **hover**, levitate, be suspended, hang. **3** *a cloud floated across the moon:* **drift**, glide, sail, slip, slide, waft. **4** *they have just floated a number of new ideas:* **suggest**, put forward, come up with, submit, moot, propose, advance, test the popularity of; informal run something up the flagpole (to see who salutes). **5** *the company was floated on the Stock Exchange:* **launch**, get going, get off the ground, offer, sell, introduce.
– OPPOSITES sink, rush, withdraw.

floating adjective **1** *floating masses of seaweed:* **buoyant**, on the surface, afloat, drifting. **2** *floating gas balloons:* **hovering**, levitating, suspended, hanging, defying gravity. **3** *floating voters:* **uncommitted**, undecided, in two minds, torn, split, uncertain, unsure, wavering, vacillating, indecisive, blowing hot and

cold, undeclared; informal sitting on the fence. **4** *a floating population:* **unsettled**, transient, temporary, variable, fluctuating; migrant, wandering, nomadic, on the move, migratory, travelling, drifting, roving, roaming, itinerant, vagabond. **5** *a floating exchange rate:* **variable**, changeable, changing, fluid, fluctuating.
– OPPOSITES sunken, grounded, committed, settled, fixed.

flock noun **1** *a flock of sheep:* **herd**, drove. **2** *a flock of birds:* **flight**, congregation, covey, clutch. **3** *flocks of people descended on the restaurant:* **crowd**, throng, horde, mob, rabble, mass, multitude, host, army, pack, swarm, sea; informal gaggle.
verb **1** *people flocked around Jesus:* **gather**, collect, congregate, assemble, converge, mass, crowd, throng, cluster, swarm; formal foregather. **2** *tourists flock to the tiny village:* **stream**, go in large numbers, swarm, crowd, troop.

flog verb *the teenager was publicly flogged by a soldier:* **whip**, scourge, flagellate, lash, birch, switch, cane, thrash, beat, tan/whip someone's hide.

flood noun **1** *several villages were cut off by the flood:* **water(s)**, deluge; torrent, overflow, inundation, freshet; Brit. spate. **2** *she came home in a flood of tears:* **outpouring**, torrent, rush, stream, gush, surge, cascade. **3** *a flood of complaints:* **succession**, series, string, chain; barrage, volley, battery; avalanche, torrent, stream, tide, spate, storm, shower, cascade.
– OPPOSITES trickle.
verb **1** *the whole town was flooded:* **inundate**, swamp, deluge, immerse, submerge, drown, engulf. **2** *the river could flood at any time:* **overflow**, burst its banks, brim over, run over. **3** *imports are flooding the domestic market:* **glut**, swamp, saturate, oversupply. **4** *refugees flooded in:* **pour**, stream, flow, surge, swarm, pile, crowd.
– OPPOSITES trickle.

floor noun **1** *he sat on the floor:* **ground**, flooring. **2** *they live on the second floor:* **storey**, level, deck, tier.
verb **1** *he floored his attacker with a single punch:* **knock down**, knock over, bring down, fell, prostrate; informal lay out. **2** (informal) *the question floored him:* **baffle**, defeat, confound, perplex, puzzle, nonplus, mystify; informal beat, flummox, stump, fox; N. Amer. informal buffalo.

flop verb **1** *he flopped into a chair:* **collapse**, slump, crumple, subside, sink, drop. **2** *his hair flopped over his eyes:* **hang (down)**, dangle, droop, sag, loll. **3** (informal) *the play flopped:* **be unsuccessful**, fail, not work, fall flat, founder, misfire, backfire, be a disappointment; informal bomb, go to the wall, come a cropper, bite the dust, blow up in someone's face; N. Amer. informal tank.
– OPPOSITES succeed.

noun (informal) *the play was a flop:* **failure**, disaster, debacle, catastrophe, loser; Brit. damp squib; informal flopperoo, washout, also-ran, dog, lemon, non-starter; N. Amer. informal clinker.
– OPPOSITES success.

floppy adjective *Pongo shook his big floppy ears:* **limp**, flaccid, slack, flabby, relaxed; drooping, droopy; loose, flowing.
– OPPOSITES erect, stiff.

florid adjective **1** *a florid complexion:* **ruddy**, red, red-faced, rosy, rosy-cheeked, pink; flushed, blushing, high-coloured; archaic sanguine. **2** *the florid plasterwork that graces every ceiling:* **ornate**, fancy, elaborate, embellished, curlicued, extravagant, flamboyant, baroque, rococo, fussy, busy. **3** *a series of compliments expressed in florid English:* **flowery**, flamboyant, high-flown, high-sounding, grandiloquent, ornate, fancy, bombastic, elaborate, turgid, pleonastic; informal highfalutin.
– OPPOSITES pale, plain.

flotsam noun *bits of flotsam that were washed up on the beach | the room was cleared of all flotsam:* **wreckage**, lost cargo, (floating) remains; rubbish, debris, detritus, waste, dross, refuse, scrap; N. Amer. trash, garbage; informal dreck, junk; Brit. informal grot.

flounce[1] verb *she flounced off to her room:* **storm**, stride, sweep, stomp, stamp, march, strut, mince, stalk.

flounce[2] noun *a black suit with a little white flounce at the neckline:* **frill**, ruffle, ruff, peplum, jabot, furbelow, ruche.

flounder verb **1** *people were floundering about in the water:* **struggle**, thrash, flail, twist and turn, splash, stagger, stumble, reel, lurch, blunder, squirm, writhe. **2** *she floundered, not knowing quite what to say:* **struggle mentally**, be out of one's depth, have difficulty, be confounded, be confused; informal scratch one's head, be flummoxed, be clueless, be foxed, be fazed, be floored, be beaten. **3** *more firms are floundering:* **struggle financially**, be in dire straits, face ruin/bankruptcy, be in difficulties.
– OPPOSITES prosper.

flourish verb **1** *ferns flourish in the shade:* **grow**, thrive, prosper, do well, burgeon, increase, multiply, proliferate; spring up, shoot up, bloom, blossom, bear fruit, burst forth, run riot. **2** *the arts flourished in this period:* **thrive**, prosper, bloom, be in good health, be vigorous, be in its heyday; progress, make progress, advance, make headway, develop, improve; evolve, make strides, expand; informal be in the pink, go places, go great guns, get somewhere. **3** *he flourished the sword at them:* **brandish**, wave, shake, wield; swing, twirl, swish; display, exhibit, flaunt, show off.
– OPPOSITES die, wither, decline.

flout verb *retailers have been flouting the law for years:* **defy**, refuse to obey, disobey,

break, violate, contravene, infringe, breach, commit a breach of, transgress against; ignore, disregard; informal cock a snook at.
– OPPOSITES observe.

flow verb 1 *the water flowed down the channel she had dug:* **run**, course, glide, drift, circulate; trickle, seep, ooze, dribble, drip, drizzle, spill; stream, swirl, surge, sweep, gush, cascade, pour, roll, rush. **2** *many questions flow from today's announcement:* **result**, proceed, arise, follow, ensue, derive, stem, accrue; originate, emanate, spring, emerge; be caused by, be brought about by, be produced by, be consequent on.
noun *the pump produces a good flow of water:* **movement**, motion, current, flux, circulation; trickle, ooze, percolation, drip; stream, swirl, surge, gush, rush, spate, tide.

flower noun **bloom**, blossom, floweret, floret.

flowery adjective **1** *flowery fabrics:* **floral**, flower-patterned. **2** *his flowery language made no impression:* **florid**, flamboyant, ornate, fancy, convoluted; high-flown, high-sounding, magniloquent, grandiloquent, baroque, orotund, overblown, pleonastic; informal highfalutin, purple.
– OPPOSITES plain.

flowing adjective **1** *long flowing hair:* **loose**, free, unconfined, draping. **2** *the new model will have soft, flowing lines:* **sleek**, streamlined, aerodynamic, smooth, clean; elegant, graceful. **3** *he writes in an easy, flowing style:* **fluent**, fluid, free-flowing, effortless, easy, natural, smooth.
– OPPOSITES stiff, curly, jagged, halting.

fluctuate verb *the level of profit fluctuates from year to year:* **vary**, change, differ, shift, alter, waver, swing, oscillate, alternate, rise and fall, go up and down, see-saw, yo-yo, be unstable.

fluctuation noun *a series of fluctuations in the earth's temperature:* **variation**, change, shift, alteration, swing, movement, oscillation, alternation, rise and fall, instability, unsteadiness.
– OPPOSITES stability.

flue noun **duct**, tube, shaft, vent, pipe, passage, channel, conduit; funnel, chimney, smokestack.

fluent adjective **1** *a fluent introductory speech:* **articulate**, eloquent, expressive, communicative, coherent, cogent, illuminating, vivid. **2** *he soon became fluent in French:* **articulate**; at home, natural. **3** *he has a very fluent running style:* **free-flowing**, smooth, effortless, easy, natural, fluid; graceful, elegant; regular, rhythmic.
– OPPOSITES inarticulate, jerky.

fluff noun *there was fluff on her sleeve:* **fuzz**, lint, dust; N. Amer. dustballs, dust bunnies.
verb (informal) *Penney fluffed the shot:* **bungle**, make a mess of, fumble, miss, deliver badly, muddle up, forget; informal mess up, make a hash of, make a botch of, foul up, bitch up,

screw up; Brit. informal make a muck of, make a pig's ear of, cock up; N. Amer. informal flub, goof up.
– OPPOSITES succeed in.

fluffy adjective *a fluffy toy rabbit:* **fleecy**, woolly, fuzzy, hairy, feathery, downy, furry; soft.
– OPPOSITES rough.

fluid noun *the fluid seeps up the tube:* **liquid**, watery substance, solution; **gas**, gaseous substance, vapour.
– OPPOSITES solid.
adjective **1** *a fluid substance that allows the gas bubbles to expand:* **free-flowing**; liquid, liquefied, melted, molten, runny, running; gaseous, gassy. **2** *at this early stage his plans were still fluid:* **adaptable**, flexible, adjustable, open-ended, open, open to change, changeable, variable. **3** *the fluid state of affairs in the Middle East:* **fluctuating**, changeable, subject/likely to change, (ever-)shifting, inconstant; unstable, unsettled, turbulent, volatile, mercurial, protean. **4** *he stood up in one fluid movement:* **smooth**, fluent, flowing, effortless, easy, continuous; graceful, elegant.
– OPPOSITES solid, firm, static, jerky.

fluke noun *by a fluke, there was a cancellation:* **chance**, coincidence, accident, twist of fate; piece of luck, stroke of good luck/fortune.

fluky adjective *the goal was a bit fluky, to say the least:* **lucky**, fortunate, providential, timely, opportune, serendipitous, expedient, heaven-sent, auspicious, propitious, felicitous; chance, fortuitous, accidental, unintended; Brit. informal jammy.
– OPPOSITES planned.

flummox verb (informal) *I was completely flummoxed by the whole thing:* **baffle**, perplex, puzzle, bewilder, mystify, bemuse, confuse, confound, nonplus; informal faze, stump, beat, fox, floor; N. Amer. informal discombobulate, buffalo.

flunkey noun **1** *a flunkey brought us drinks:* **liveried servant**, lackey, steward, butler, footman, valet, attendant, page.
2 *government flunkeys searched his offices:* **minion**, lackey, hireling, subordinate, underling, servant; creature, instrument, cat's paw; informal stooge, gofer; Brit. informal poodle, dogsbody, skivvy.

flurried adjective *she hoped he didn't notice her pink cheeks and slightly flurried manner:* **agitated**, flustered, ruffled, in a panic, worked up, overwrought, perturbed, frantic; informal in a flap, in a state, in a twitter, in a fluster, in a dither, all of a dither, all of a lather, in a tizz/tizzy, in a tiz-woz; Brit. informal in a (flat) spin, having kittens; N. Amer. informal in a twit.
– OPPOSITES calm.

flurry noun **1** *a flurry of snow:* **swirl**, whirl, eddy, billow, shower, gust. **2** *a flurry of activity:* **burst**, outbreak, spurt, fit, spell,

f

bout, rash, eruption; fuss, stir, bustle, hubbub, commotion, disturbance, furore; informal to-do, flap. **3** *a flurry of imports:* **spate**, wave, flood, deluge, torrent, stream, tide, avalanche; series, succession, string, outbreak, rash, explosion, run, rush.
– OPPOSITES dearth, trickle.
▸ verb *snow flurried through the door:* **swirl**, whirl, eddy, billow, gust, blast, blow, rush.

flush¹ verb **1** *she flushed in embarrassment:* **blush**, redden, go pink, go red, go crimson, go scarlet, colour (up). **2** *fruit helps to flush toxins from the body:* **rinse**, wash, sluice, swill, cleanse, clean; Brit. informal **sloosh**. **3** *one of the beaters was flushing the birds from their hiding place:* **drive**, chase, force, dislodge, expel, frighten, scare.
– OPPOSITES pale.
▸ noun **1** *a flush crept over her face:* **blush**, reddening, high colour, colour, rosiness, pinkness, ruddiness, bloom. **2** *the first flush of manhood:* **bloom**, glow, freshness, radiance, vigour, rush.
– OPPOSITES paleness.

flush² adjective (informal) **1** *the company was flush with cash:* **well supplied**, well provided, well stocked, replete, overflowing, bursting, brimful, brimming, loaded, overloaded, teeming, stuffed, swarming, thick, solid; full of, abounding in, rich in, abundant in; informal **awash**, jam-packed, chock-full of; Austral./NZ informal **chocker**. **2** *the years when cash was flush:* **plentiful**, abundant, in abundance, copious, ample, profuse, superabundant; informal a gogo, galore; literary plenteous, bounteous.
– OPPOSITES lacking, low (on).

flushed adjective **1** *I looked at the children's flushed, happy faces:* **red**, pink, ruddy, glowing, reddish, pinkish, rosy, florid, high-coloured, healthy-looking, aglow, burning, feverish; blushing, red-faced, embarrassed, shamefaced. **2** *flushed with success, he was getting into his stride:* **elated**, excited, thrilled, exhilarated, happy, delighted, overjoyed, joyous, gleeful, jubilant, exultant, ecstatic, euphoric, rapturous; informal blissed out, over the moon, high, on a high; N. Amer. informal **wigged out**.
– OPPOSITES pale, dismayed.

fluster verb *she was flustered by his presence:* **unsettle**, make nervous, unnerve, agitate, ruffle, upset, bother, put on edge, disquiet, disturb, worry, perturb, disconcert, confuse, throw off balance, confound, nonplus; informal rattle, faze, put into a flap, throw into a tizzy; Brit. informal send into a spin; N. Amer. informal **discombobulate**.
– OPPOSITES calm.
▸ noun *the main thing is not to get all in a fluster:* **panic**, frenzy, fret; informal dither, flap, tizz, tizzy, tiz-woz, twitter, state, sweat; N. Amer. informal **twit**.

fluted adjective *the roof is supported by fluted columns:* **grooved**, channelled, furrowed, ribbed, corrugated, ridged.

– OPPOSITES smooth, plain.

flutter verb **1** *butterflies fluttered around:* **flit**, hover, dance. **2** *a tern was fluttering its wings:* **flap**, move up and down, beat, quiver, agitate, vibrate. **3** *she fluttered her eyelashes:* **flicker**, bat. **4** *flags fluttered in the gentle breeze:* **flap**, wave, ripple, undulate, quiver, fly. **5** *her heart fluttered:* **beat weakly**, beat irregularly, palpitate, miss/skip a beat, quiver, go pit-a-pat; Medicine exhibit arrhythmia; rare quop.
▸ noun **1** *the flutter of wings:* **beating**, flapping, quivering, agitation, vibrating. **2** *the flutter of the flags:* **flapping**, waving, rippling. **3** *a flutter of nervousness:* **tremor**, wave, rush, surge, flash, stab, flush, tremble, quiver, shiver, frisson, chill, thrill, tingle, shudder, ripple, flicker. **4** (Brit. informal) *he enjoys a flutter on the horses:* **bet**, wager, gamble; Brit. informal **punt**.

flux noun *things are in a state of flux:* **change**, changeability, variability, inconstancy, fluidity, instability, unsteadiness, fluctuation, variation, shift, movement, oscillation, alternation, rise and fall, see-sawing, yo-yoing.
– OPPOSITES stability.

fly verb **1** *a bird flew overhead:* **pass**, travel, wing its way, wing, glide, soar, wheel; hover, hang; take to the air, mount. **2** *they flew to Paris:* **travel**, jet. **3** *military planes flew in food supplies:* **transport**, airlift, lift, jet, drop. **4** *he pretended he couldn't fly the plane:* **pilot**, operate, control, manoeuvre, steer. **5** *the ship was flying a quarantine flag:* **display**, show, exhibit; have hoisted, have run up. **6** *flags flew in the town:* **flutter**, flap, wave. **7** *doesn't time fly?* **go quickly**, fly by/past, pass swiftly, slip past, rush past. **8** *the runners flew by.* See SPEED verb sense 1.
■ **fly at** *Robbie flew at him, fists clenched:* **attack**, assault, pounce on, set upon, set about, weigh into, let fly at, turn on, round on, lash out at, hit out at, belabour, fall on; informal lay into, tear into, lace into, sail into, pitch into, wade into, let someone have it, jump; Brit. informal have a go at; N. Amer. informal light into.
■ **let fly.** See LET.

flyer, flier noun **1** *we have increased the rewards for our most frequent flyers:* **air traveller**, air passenger, (airline) customer. **2** *the memorial was for flyers killed in the war:* **pilot**, airman, airwoman; N. Amer. informal jock; dated aviator, aeronaut. **3** *flyers promoting a new sandwich bar:* **handbill**, bill, handout, leaflet, circular, advertisement; N. Amer. dodger.

flying adjective **1** *a flying beetle:* **winged**; **airborne**, in the air, in flight. **2** *a flying visit:* **brief**, short, lightning, fleeting, hasty, rushed, hurried, quick, whistle-stop, cursory, perfunctory; informal quickie.
– OPPOSITES long.

foam noun *the foam on the waves:* **froth**,

spume, surf; fizz, effervescence, bubbles, head; lather, suds.

verb *the water foamed:* **froth**, spume; fizz, effervesce, bubble; lather; ferment, rise; boil, seethe, simmer.

foamy adjective *leave the yeast mixture until it is all foamy:* **frothy**, foaming, spumy, bubbly, aerated, bubbling; sudsy.

fob

■ **fob someone off** *I wasn't going to be fobbed off with excuses:* put off, stall, give someone the runaround, deceive; placate, appease.

■ **fob something off on** *he fobbed off the chairmanship on Clifford:* impose, palm off, unload, dump, get rid of, foist, offload; saddle someone with something, land someone with something, lumber someone with something.

focus noun **1** *schools are a focus of community life:* **centre**, focal point, central point, centre of attention, hub, pivot, nucleus, heart, cornerstone, linchpin, cynosure. **2** *the focus is on helping people find solutions:* **emphasis**, accent, priority, attention, concentration. **3** *the main focus of this chapter is local government:* **subject**, theme, concern, subject matter, topic, issue, thesis, point, thread; substance, essence, gist, matter. **4** *the light beams are brought to a focus at the eyepiece:* **focal point**, point of convergence.

verb **1** *he focused his binoculars on the distant tower:* **direct**; aim, point, turn, train. **2** *the investigation will focus on areas of social need:* **concentrate**, centre, zero in, zoom in; address itself to, pay attention to, pinpoint, revolve around, have as its starting point.

■ **in focus** *any photos will do as long as they're in focus:* sharp, crisp, distinct, clear, well defined, well focused.

■ **out of focus** *why are some of these shots out of focus?* blurred, unfocused, indistinct, blurry, fuzzy, hazy, misty, cloudy, lacking definition.

foe noun (literary) *Pakistan's neighbour and traditional foe, India:* **enemy**, adversary, opponent, rival, antagonist, combatant, challenger, competitor, opposer, opposition, competition.

– OPPOSITES friend.

fog noun *he lost his way in the fog:* **mist**, smog, murk, haze, haar; N. English (sea) fret; informal pea-souper.

verb **1** *the windscreen fogged up:* **steam up**, mist over, cloud over, film over, make/become misty. **2** *his brain was fogged with sleep:* **muddle**, daze, stupefy, fuddle, befuddle, bewilder, confuse, befog.

– OPPOSITES demist, clear.

foggy adjective **misty**, smoggy, hazy, murky.

– OPPOSITES clear.

foible noun *we have to tolerate each other's little foibles:* **weakness**, failing, shortcoming, flaw, imperfection, blemish, fault, defect, limitation; quirk, kink, idiosyncrasy, eccentricity, peculiarity.

– OPPOSITES strength.

foil[1] verb *their escape attempts were constantly foiled:* **thwart**, frustrate, counter, baulk, impede, obstruct, hamper, hinder, snooker, cripple, scotch, derail, smash; stop, block, prevent, defeat; informal do for, put paid to, stymie, cook someone's goose; Brit. informal scupper, nobble, queer, put the mockers on.

– OPPOSITES assist.

foil[2] noun *the red wine was a perfect foil to pasta:* **contrast**, complement, antithesis, relief.

foist verb *poor-quality lagers are constantly being foisted on the public:* **impose**, force, thrust, offload, unload, dump, palm off, fob off; pass off, get rid of; saddle someone with, land someone with, lumber someone with.

fold[1] verb **1** *I folded the cloth and put it away:* **double (over/up)**, crease, turn under/up/over, bend; tuck, gather, pleat. **2** *fold the cream into the chocolate mixture:* **mix**, blend, stir gently. **3** *he folded her in his arms:* **enfold**, wrap, envelop; take, gather, clasp, squeeze, clutch; embrace, hug, cuddle, cradle. **4** *the firm folded last year:* **fail**, collapse, founder; go bankrupt, become insolvent, cease trading, go into receivership, go into liquidation, be wound up, be closed (down), be shut (down); informal crash, go bust, go broke, go under, go to the wall, go belly up.

noun *there was a fold in the paper:* **crease**, knife-edge; wrinkle, crinkle, pucker, furrow; pleat, gather.

fold[2] noun **1** *the sheep were safely in their fold:* **enclosure**, pen, paddock, pound, compound, ring; N. Amer. corral. **2** *Lloyd George returned to the Liberal fold:* **community**, group, body, company, mass, throng, flock, congregation, assembly.

folder noun **file**, binder, ring binder, portfolio, document case, envelope, sleeve, wallet.

foliage noun *a garden bursting with green and gold foliage:* **leaves**, leafage; greenery, vegetation, verdure.

folk noun (informal) **1** *he doesn't work the same hours as ordinary folk:* **people**, individuals, {men, women, and children}, souls, mortals; citizenry, inhabitants, residents, populace, population; informal peeps; formal denizens. **2** *my folks come from Scotland:* **relatives**, relations, blood relations, family, nearest and dearest, people, kinsfolk, kinsmen, kinswomen, kin, kith and kin, kindred, flesh and blood.

folklore noun *he studies the local customs and folklore:* **mythology**, lore, oral history, tradition, folk tradition; legends, fables, myths, folk tales, folk stories, old wives' tales; mythos.

follow verb **1** *I'll go with you and we'll let the others follow:* **come behind**, come after, go behind, go after, walk behind. **2** *he was expected to follow his father* *into business:* **take the place of**, replace, succeed, take over from; informal step into someone's shoes, fill someone's shoes/boots. **3** *loads of people used to follow the band around:* **accompany**, go along with, go around with, travel with, escort, attend, trail around with, string along with; informal tag along with. **4** *the KGB man followed her everywhere:* **shadow**, trail, stalk, track, dog, hound; informal tail. **5** *always follow the manufacturer's instructions:* **obey**, comply with, conform to, adhere to, stick to, keep to, act in accordance with, abide by, observe, heed, pay attention to. **6** *severe penalties may follow from such behaviour:* **result**, arise, be a consequence of, be caused by, be brought about by, be a result of, come after, develop, ensue, emanate, issue, proceed, spring, flow, originate, stem. **7** *I couldn't follow what he was saying:* **understand**, comprehend, apprehend, take in, grasp, fathom, appreciate, see; informal make head or tail of, get, figure out, savvy, get one's head around, get one's mind around, get the drift of; Brit. informal suss out. **8** *he follows Manchester United:* **be a fan of**, be a supporter of, support, be a follower of, be an admirer of, be a devotee of, be devoted to.

– OPPOSITES lead, flout, misunderstand.

■ **follow something through** *they lack the resources to follow the project through to the end:* complete, see something through; continue with, carry on with, keep on with, keep going with, stay with; informal stick something out.

■ **follow something up** *I've got a hunch and I'm going to follow it up:* investigate, research, look into, dig into, delve into, make enquiries into, enquire about, ask questions about, pursue, chase up; informal check out; N. Amer. informal scope out.

follower noun **1** *the president summoned his closest followers:* **acolyte**, assistant, attendant, companion, henchman, minion, lackey, servant; informal hanger-on, sidekick. **2** *the picture was painted by a follower of Caravaggio:* **imitator**, emulator, copier, mimic; pupil, disciple; informal copycat. **3** *a follower of Christ:* **disciple**, apostle, supporter, defender, champion; believer, worshipper. **4** *followers of Scottish football will be disappointed:* **fan**, enthusiast, admirer, devotee, lover, supporter, adherent; N. Amer. informal rooter.

– OPPOSITES leader, opponent.

following noun *the nationalist cause retained a substantial following:* **admirers**, supporters, backers, fans, adherents, devotees, advocates, patrons, public, audience, circle, retinue, train.

– OPPOSITES opposition.

adjective **1** *he sent a reply the following day:* **next**, ensuing, succeeding, subsequent. **2** *please answer the following questions:* below, further on, underneath; these; formal hereunder, hereinafter.

– OPPOSITES preceding, aforementioned.

folly noun *he cursed himself for his folly:* **foolishness**, foolhardiness, stupidity, idiocy, lunacy, madness, rashness, recklessness, imprudence, injudiciousness, irresponsibility, thoughtlessness, indiscretion; informal craziness; Brit. informal daftness.

– OPPOSITES wisdom.

foment verb *the men were accused of fomenting civil unrest:* **instigate**, incite, provoke, agitate, excite, stir up, whip up, encourage, urge, fan the flames of.

fond adjective **1** *she was fond of dancing | I'm very fond of Chris:* **keen on**, partial to, addicted to, enthusiastic about, passionate about; attached to, attracted to, enamoured of, in love with, having a soft spot for; informal into, hooked on, gone on, sweet on, struck on. **2** *his fond father plied him with cakes:* **adoring**, devoted, doting, loving, caring, affectionate, warm, tender, kind, attentive. **3** *the fond hope that things might get better between them:* **unrealistic**, naive, foolish, over-optimistic, deluded, delusory, absurd, vain, Panglossian.

– OPPOSITES indifferent, unfeeling, realistic.

fondle verb *he fondled the Labrador's ears:* **caress**, stroke, pat, pet, finger, tickle, play with; maul, molest; informal paw, grope, feel up, touch up, cop a feel of.

fondness noun **1** *they look at each other with such fondness:* **affection**, love, liking, warmth, tenderness, kindness, devotion, endearment, attachment, friendliness. **2** *he has a fondness for spicy food:* **liking**, love, taste, partiality, keenness, inclination, penchant, predilection, relish, passion, appetite; weakness, soft spot; informal thing, yen.

– OPPOSITES hatred.

food noun **1** *he went three days without food:* **nourishment**, sustenance, nutriment, fare, bread, daily bread; cooking, cuisine; foodstuffs, edibles, provender, refreshments, meals, provisions, rations; solids; informal eats, eatables, nosh, grub, chow, nibbles; Brit. informal scoff, tuck; N. Amer. informal chuck; formal comestibles; dated victuals; archaic meat. **2** *food for the cattle and horses:* **fodder**, feed, provender, forage.

fool noun **1** *you've acted like a complete fool:* **idiot**, ass, halfwit, blockhead, dunce, dolt, dullard, simpleton, clod; informal dope, ninny, nincompoop, chump, dimwit, coot, goon, dumbo, dummy, dum-dum, fathead, numbskull, dunderhead, pudding-head, thickhead, airhead, lamebrain, cretin, moron, nerd, imbecile, pea-brain, birdbrain, jerk, dipstick, donkey, noodle; Brit. informal muppet, nit, nitwit, twit, clot, goat, plonker, berk, prat, pillock, wally, git, dork, twerp, charlie, mug; Scottish informal nyaff, balloon, sumph, gowk; N. Amer. informal schmuck, bozo, boob, turkey, schlepper, chowderhead, dumbhead, goofball, goof, goofus, galoot, lummox, klutz, putz, schlemiel, sap, meatball; Austral./NZ informal drongo, dill, alec, galah, boofhead. **2** *she made a fool of me again:* **laughing stock**, dupe, butt, gull; informal stooge, sucker, mug, fall guy; N. Amer. informal sap.

verb 1 *he found he'd been fooled by a schoolboy:* **deceive**, trick, hoax, dupe, take in, mislead, delude, hoodwink, bluff, gull; swindle, defraud, cheat, double-cross; informal con, bamboozle, pull a fast one on, take for a ride, pull the wool over someone's eyes, put one over on, have on, diddle, fiddle, rip off, do, sting, shaft; Brit. informal sell a pup to; N. Amer. informal sucker, snooker, stiff, euchre, hornswoggle; Austral. informal pull a swifty on; literary cozen. **2** *I'm not fooling, I promise you:* **pretend**, make believe, feign, put on an act, act, sham, fake; joke, jest; informal kid; Brit. informal have someone on.

■ **fool around 1** *someone's been fooling around with the controls:* fiddle, play (about/around), toy, trifle, meddle, tamper, interfere, monkey about/around; informal mess about/around; Brit. informal muck about/around. **2** (N. Amer. informal) *my husband's been fooling around:* philander, womanize, flirt, have an affair, commit adultery; informal play around, mess about/around, carry on, play the field, sleep around; Brit. informal play away.

foolery noun *we had to endure his foolery all afternoon:* **clowning**, fooling, tomfoolery, buffoonery, silliness, foolishness, stupidity, idiocy; antics, capers; informal larking around, larks, shenanigans; Brit. informal monkey tricks; N. Amer. informal didoes.

foolhardy adjective *obtaining such a large amount of credit could prove foolhardy in the extreme:* **reckless**, rash, irresponsible, impulsive, hot-headed, impetuous, daredevil, devil-may-care, death-or-glory, madcap, hare-brained, precipitate, hasty.
– OPPOSITES prudent.

foolish adjective *it horrified her to think how foolish she had been:* **stupid**, silly, idiotic, witless, brainless, mindless, unintelligent, thoughtless, half-baked, imprudent, incautious, injudicious, unwise; ill-advised, ill-considered, impolitic, rash, reckless, foolhardy; informal dumb, dim, dim-witted, half-witted, thick, gormless, hare-brained, crackbrained, pea-brained, wooden-headed; Brit. informal barmy, daft; Scottish & N. English informal glaikit; N. Amer. informal dumb-ass, chowderheaded.
– OPPOSITES sensible, wise.

foolishness noun *smiling at her own foolishness, she walked down the lane:* **folly**, stupidity, idiocy, imbecility, silliness, inanity, thoughtlessness, imprudence, injudiciousness, lack of caution/foresight/sense, irresponsibility, indiscretion, foolhardiness, rashness, recklessness; Brit. informal daftness.
– OPPOSITES sense, wisdom.

foolproof adjective *a foolproof guide to who does what:* **infallible**, dependable, reliable, trustworthy, certain, sure, guaranteed, safe, sound, tried and tested; watertight, airtight, flawless, perfect; informal sure-fire.
– OPPOSITES flawed.

foot noun **1** *my feet hurt:* informal tootsies, trotters, plates of meat; N. Amer. informal dogs. **2** *the animal's foot:* paw, hoof, trotter, pad. **3** *the foot of the hill:* **bottom**, base, lowest part; end; foundation.

■ **foot the bill** (informal) *ministers expected the taxpayer to foot the bill:* pay, settle up; informal pick up the tab, cough up, fork out, shell out, come across; N. Amer. informal pick up the check.

football noun (Brit.) **soccer**, Association football.

footing noun **1** *Jenny lost her footing and plunged into the river:* **foothold**, toehold, grip, purchase. **2** *the business was put on a solid financial footing:* **basis**, base, foundation.

footling adjective *she insisted on a few footling changes to the text:* **trivial**, trifling, petty, insignificant, inconsequential, unimportant, minor, small, time-wasting; informal piddling, piffling, fiddling.
– OPPOSITES important, large.

footnote noun **note**, annotation, comment, gloss; aside, incidental remark, digression.

footprint noun **footmark**, footstep, mark, impression; (**footprints**) track(s), spoor.

footstep noun **1** *he heard footsteps in the hall:* **footfall**, step, tread, stomp, stamp. **2** *I saw their footsteps in the sand:* **footprint**, footmark, mark, impression; (**footsteps**) track(s), spoor.

foppish adjective *he wore clothes that were less foppish than his usual attire:* **dandyish**, dandified, dapper, dressy; affected, preening, vain; effeminate, girlie, niminy-piminy, mincing; informal natty, sissy, camp, campy; Brit. informal poncey.

forage verb *the villagers were forced to forage for food:* **hunt**, search, look, rummage (about/around/round), ferret (about/around), root about/around, scratch about/around, nose around/about/round, scavenge; Brit. informal rootle around.
noun *a nightly forage for food:* **hunt**, search, look, quest, rummage, scavenge.

foray noun *this was to be their first foray into serious crime:* **venture**, outing, encounter, incursion; trip, visit, sortie, sally.

forbearance noun *through it all, the forbearance and good humour of the Peruvians was impressive:* **tolerance**, patience, resignation, endurance, fortitude, stoicism; leniency, clemency, indulgence; restraint, self-restraint, self-control.

forbearing adjective *he was tactful and forbearing when I got angry:* **patient**, tolerant, easy-going, lenient, clement, forgiving, understanding, accommodating,

f

indulgent; long-suffering, resigned, stoic; restrained, self-controlled.
– OPPOSITES impatient, intolerant.

forbid verb *the act forbids discrimination on the grounds of sex:* **prohibit**, ban, outlaw, make illegal, veto, proscribe, disallow, embargo, bar, debar, interdict; Law enjoin, restrain.
– OPPOSITES permit.

forbidding adjective **1** *he had a rather forbidding manner:* **hostile**, unwelcoming, unfriendly, off-putting, unsympathetic, unapproachable, grim, stern, hard, tough, frosty. **2** *in the dark everything looked unfamiliar and forbidding:* **threatening**, ominous, menacing, sinister, brooding, daunting, fearsome, frightening, chilling, disturbing, disquieting.
– OPPOSITES friendly, inviting.

force noun **1** *he pushed with all his force:* **strength**, power, energy, might, effort, exertion; impact, pressure, weight, impetus. **2** *they used force to achieve their aims:* **coercion**, compulsion, constraint, duress, oppression, harassment, intimidation, threats; informal arm-twisting. **3** *they couldn't deny the force of the argument:* **cogency**, weight, effectiveness, soundness, validity, strength, power, significance, influence, authority; informal punch; formal efficacy. **4** *the Bureau is undeniably a force for good:* **agency**, power, influence, instrument, vehicle, means. **5** *the government sent in a peace-keeping force:* **body**, group, outfit, party, team; detachment, unit, squad; informal bunch.
– OPPOSITES weakness.
verb **1** *he was forced to pay the full amount:* **compel**, coerce, make, constrain, oblige, impel, drive, pressurize, pressure, press, push, press-gang, bully, dragoon, bludgeon; informal, lean on, twist someone's arm. **2** *the door had to be forced:* **break open**, burst open, knock open, smash down, kick in. **3** *water was forced through a hole in the pipe:* **propel**, push, thrust, shove, drive, press, pump.
■ **in force 1** *the state of emergency is now in force:* effective, in operation, operative, operational, in action, valid. **2** *her fans were out in force:* in great numbers, in hordes, in full strength.

forced adjective **1** *a programme of forced repatriation:* **enforced**, compulsory, obligatory, mandatory, involuntary, imposed, required, stipulated, dictated, ordained, prescribed. **2** *Clara managed a forced smile:* **strained**, unnatural, artificial, false, feigned, simulated, contrived, laboured, stilted, studied, mannered, affected, unconvincing, insincere, hollow; informal phoney, pretend, put on.
– OPPOSITES voluntary, natural.

forceful adjective **1** *he had a forceful personality:* **dynamic**, energetic, assertive, authoritative, vigorous, powerful, strong, pushy, driving, determined, insistent, commanding, dominant, domineering; informal bossy, in-your-face, go-ahead, feisty. **2** *the board was persuaded by his forceful argument:* **cogent**, convincing, compelling, strong, powerful, potent, weighty, effective, well founded, telling, persuasive, irresistible, eloquent, coherent.
– OPPOSITES weak, submissive, unconvincing.

forcible adjective **1** *forcible entry:* **forced**, violent. **2** *forcible repatriation.* See **FORCED** sense 1. **3** *a forcible argument.* See **FORCEFUL** sense 2.

forebear noun *she speaks the language of her forebears:* **ancestor**, forefather, antecedent, progenitor, primogenitor.
– OPPOSITES descendant.

foreboding noun **1** *she was seized with a sense of foreboding:* **apprehension**, anxiety, trepidation, disquiet, unease, uneasiness, misgiving, suspicion, worry, fear, fearfulness, dread, alarm; informal the willies, the heebie-jeebies, the jitters. **2** *in the end their forebodings proved justified:* **premonition**, presentiment, bad feeling, sneaking suspicion, funny feeling, intuition; archaic presage.
– OPPOSITES calm.

forecast verb *they forecast record profits:* **predict**, prophesy, prognosticate, foretell, foresee, forewarn of.
noun *a gloomy forecast of the impact of global warming:* **prediction**, prophecy, forewarning, prognostication, augury, divination, prognosis.

forefather noun *they abandoned the customs of their forefathers:* **forebear**, ancestor, antecedent, progenitor, primogenitor.
– OPPOSITES descendant.

forefront noun *a cabinet post thrust him to the forefront of British politics:* **vanguard**, van, spearhead, head, lead, front, fore, front line, cutting edge.
– OPPOSITES rear, background.

forego verb. See **FORGO**.

foregoing adjective *despite the foregoing criticisms, we welcome the changes:* **preceding**, aforesaid, aforementioned, previously mentioned, earlier, above; previous, prior, antecedent.
– OPPOSITES following.

foregone
■ **a foregone conclusion** *they accepted the interest rate rise as a foregone conclusion:* certainty, inevitability, matter of course, predictable result; informal sure thing; Brit. informal cert, dead cert.

foreground noun *he retouched the figures in the foreground of the painting:* **front**, fore.
– OPPOSITES background.

forehead noun **brow**, temple.

foreign adjective **1** *foreign branches of UK banks:* **overseas**, exotic, distant, external, alien, non-native. **2** *the concept is very foreign to us in the West:* **unfamiliar**,

unknown, unheard of, strange, alien; novel, new.
– OPPOSITES domestic, native, familiar.

foreigner noun **alien**, non-native, stranger, outsider; immigrant, settler, newcomer, incomer.
– OPPOSITES native.

foreman, forewoman noun **supervisor**, overseer, superintendent, team leader; foreperson; Brit. chargehand, captain, ganger, gangmaster; Scottish grieve; N. Amer. informal ramrod, straw boss; Austral. informal pannikin boss; Mining overman.

foremost adjective *one of the foremost Spanish Renaissance artists:* **leading**, principal, premier, prime, top, top-level, greatest, best, supreme, pre-eminent, outstanding, most important, most prominent, most influential, most illustrious, most notable; N. Amer. ranking; informal number-one.
– OPPOSITES minor.

forerunner noun **1** *archosaurs were the forerunners of dinosaurs:* **predecessor**, precursor, antecedent, ancestor, forebear; prototype. **2** *headache may be the forerunner of other complaints:* **prelude**, herald, harbinger, precursor, sign, signal, indication, warning.
– OPPOSITES descendant.

foresee verb *Henry foresaw further problems for them:* **anticipate**, predict, forecast, expect, envisage, envision, see; foretell, prophesy; Scottish spae.

foreshadow verb *to what extent does the change in ministers foreshadow a change in policy?* **signal**, indicate, signify, mean, be a sign of, suggest, herald, be a harbinger of, warn of, portend, prefigure, presage, promise, point to, anticipate; informal spell; literary foretoken, betoken.

foresight noun *a little foresight might have saved them a lot of money:* **forethought**, planning, far-sightedness, vision, anticipation, prudence, care, caution, precaution, readiness, preparedness; N. Amer. forehandedness.
– OPPOSITES hindsight.

forest noun **wood(s)**, woodland, trees, plantation; jungle, rainforest; archaic greenwood.

forestall verb *the council resigned to forestall a vote of no confidence:* **pre-empt**, get in before, steal a march on; anticipate, second-guess; nip in the bud, thwart, frustrate, foil, stave off, ward off, fend off, avert, preclude, obviate, prevent; informal beat someone to it.

forestry noun **forest management**; technical arboriculture, silviculture.

foretaste noun *the opening parade gives a foretaste of the spectacle to come:* **sample**, taster, taste, preview, specimen, example; indication, suggestion, hint, whiff; warning, forewarning, omen.

foretell verb **1** *the locals can foretell a storm:*

predict, forecast, prophesy, prognosticate; foresee, anticipate, envisage, envision, see; Scottish spae. **2** *dreams really can foretell the future:* **indicate**, foreshadow, prefigure, anticipate, warn of, point to, signal, portend, augur, presage, be an omen of.

forethought noun *forethought is needed before you embark on such a project:* **anticipation**, planning, forward planning, provision, precaution, prudence, care, caution; foresight, far-sightedness, vision.
– OPPOSITES impulse, recklessness.

forever adverb **1** *their love would last forever:* **for always**, evermore, for ever and ever, for good, for all time, until the end of time, until hell freezes over, eternally; Brit. for evermore; N. Amer. forevermore; informal until the cows come home, until doomsday, until kingdom come. **2** *he was forever banging into things:* **always**, continually, constantly, perpetually, incessantly, endlessly, persistently, repeatedly, regularly; non-stop, day and night, {morning, noon, and night}; all the time, the entire time; Scottish aye; informal 24-7.
– OPPOSITES never, occasionally.

forewarn verb *he had been forewarned of a coup plot:* **warn**, warn in advance, give advance warning, give fair warning, give notice, apprise, inform; alert, caution, put someone on their guard; informal tip off; Brit. informal tip someone the wink.

forewarning noun *government officials confirmed that there had been some forewarning of the rebel attack:* **warning**, sign, indication, portent, presage, omen, harbinger, foreshadowing, augury, signal, threat, hint; literary foretoken.

foreword noun *he wrote the foreword to one of her books:* **preface**, introduction, prologue, preamble; informal intro; formal exordium, prolegomenon, proem.
– OPPOSITES conclusion.

forfeit verb *latecomers will forfeit their places:* **lose**, be deprived of, surrender, relinquish, sacrifice, give up, yield, renounce, forgo; informal pass up, lose out on.
– OPPOSITES retain.
noun *if they fail to obey they are liable to a forfeit:* **penalty**, sanction, punishment, penance; fine; confiscation, loss, relinquishment, forfeiture, surrender.

forfeiture noun *non-compliance may lead to forfeiture of the lease:* **confiscation**, loss; relinquishment, giving up, surrender, sacrifice; Law sequestration.

forge¹ verb **1** *the smith forged swords and knives:* **fashion**, beat, hammer, make. **2** *they forged a lifelong partnership:* **build**, construct, form, create, establish, set up. **3** *he forged her signature on the will:* **fake**, falsify, counterfeit, copy, imitate, reproduce, replicate, simulate; informal pirate.

forge² verb *they forged through the busy side*

streets: **advance**, press on, push on, soldier on, march on, push forward, make progress, make headway.
■ **forge ahead** *Jack's horse forged ahead and took the lead*: advance, make rapid progress, accelerate, put a spurt on.

forged adjective *he was charged with passing forged banknotes*: **fake**, faked, false, counterfeit, imitation, copied, pirate(d); sham, bogus; informal phoney, dud.
– OPPOSITES genuine.

forger noun **counterfeiter**, faker, copyist, imitator, pirate.

forgery noun **1** *he was found guilty of forgery*: **counterfeiting**, falsification, faking, copying, pirating. **2** *the painting was discovered to be a forgery*: **fake**, counterfeit, fraud, sham, imitation, replica, copy, pirate copy; informal phoney.

forget verb **1** *he forgot where he had parked his car*: **fail to remember**, fail to recall. **2** *I never forget my briefcase*: **leave behind**, fail to take/bring. **3** *I forgot to close the door*: **neglect**, fail, omit. **4** *you can forget that idea*: **stop thinking about**, put out of one's mind, shut out, blank out, pay no heed to, not worry about, ignore, overlook, discard, take no notice of, reject out of hand, abandon.
– OPPOSITES remember.
■ **forget oneself** *I'm sorry about that: I forgot myself*: misbehave, behave badly, be naughty, be disobedient, get up to mischief, get up to no good; be bad-mannered, be rude; informal carry on, act up.

forgetful adjective **1** *I'm so forgetful these days*: **absent-minded**, amnesic, amnesiac, vague, disorganized, dreamy, abstracted, with a mind/memory like a sieve; informal scatterbrained, scatty. **2** *she was forgetful of the time*: **heedless**, careless, unmindful; inattentive to, negligent about, oblivious to, unconcerned about, indifferent to, not bothered about.
– OPPOSITES reliable, heedful.

forgetfulness noun *his excuse was forgetfulness*: **absent-mindedness**, amnesia, poor memory, a lapse of memory, vagueness, abstraction; informal scattiness.

forgivable adjective *the odd lapse is forgivable*: **pardonable**, excusable, condonable, understandable, tolerable, permissible, allowable, justifiable.

forgive verb **1** *she would not forgive him*: **pardon**, excuse, exonerate, absolve; make allowances for, feel no resentment/malice towards, harbour no grudge against, bury the hatchet with; let bygones be bygones; informal let off (the hook); formal exculpate. **2** *you must forgive his rude conduct*: **excuse**, overlook, disregard, ignore, pass over, make allowances for, allow; turn a blind eye to, turn a deaf ear to, wink at, blink at, indulge, tolerate.
– OPPOSITES blame, resent, punish.

forgiveness noun *we beg your forgiveness*: **pardon**, absolution, exoneration, remission, dispensation, indulgence, clemency, mercy; reprieve, amnesty; informal let-off.
– OPPOSITES mercilessness, punishment.

forgiving adjective *Cromwell was not renowned for his forgiving nature*: **merciful**, lenient, compassionate, magnanimous, humane, soft-hearted, forbearing, tolerant, indulgent, understanding.
– OPPOSITES merciless, vindictive.

forgo, forego verb *Simon was prepared to forgo his lunch hour to help them*: **do without**, go without, give up, waive, renounce, surrender, relinquish, part with, drop, sacrifice, abstain from, refrain from, eschew, cut out; informal swear off; formal forswear, abjure.
– OPPOSITES keep.

forgotten adjective *Vivaldi's operas are largely forgotten*: **unremembered**, out of mind, consigned to oblivion; left behind; neglected, overlooked, ignored, disregarded, unrecognized.
– OPPOSITES remembered.

fork verb *where the road forks, bear left*: **split**, branch (off), divide, subdivide, separate, part, diverge, bifurcate.

forked adjective *the red kite has a forked tail*: **split**, branching, branched, bifurcate(d), Y-shaped, V-shaped, pronged, divided.
– OPPOSITES straight.

forlorn adjective **1** *he sounded so forlorn*: **unhappy**, sad, miserable, sorrowful, dejected, despondent, disconsolate, wretched, abject, down, downcast, dispirited, downhearted, crestfallen, depressed, melancholy, gloomy, glum, mournful, despairing, doleful, woebegone; informal blue, down in the mouth, down in the dumps, fed up. **2** *the house had a forlorn air of sagging decrepitude*: **desolate**, deserted, abandoned, forsaken, forgotten, neglected. **3** *his voice rose in a forlorn attempt to drown the racket*: **hopeless**, with no chance of success; useless, futile, pointless, purposeless, vain, unavailing, nugatory; archaic bootless.
– OPPOSITES happy, busy, cared for, hopeful, sure-fire.

form noun **1** *the general form of the landscape was established before the glaciers*: **shape**, configuration, formation, structure, construction, arrangement, appearance, exterior, outline, format, layout, design. **2** *the human form*: **body**, shape, figure, stature, build, frame, physique, anatomy; informal vital statistics. **3** *the infection takes different forms*: **manifestation**, appearance, embodiment, incarnation, semblance, shape, guise. **4** *sponsorship is a form of advertising*: **kind**, sort, type, class, classification, category, variety, genre, brand, style; species, genus, family. **5** *put the mixture into a form*: **mould**, cast, shape, matrix, die. **6** *what is the form here in London?* **etiquette**, social practice, custom, usage, use, modus

operandi, habit, wont, protocol, procedure, rules, convention, tradition, fashion, style; formal praxis. **7** *you have to fill in a form:* **questionnaire**, document, coupon, tear-off slip, paper. **8** *what form is your daughter in?* **class**, year; N. Amer. grade. **9** *he is in top form for the Olympics:* **fitness**, condition, fettle, shape, trim, health; Brit. informal nick.
– OPPOSITES content.

verb 1 *the pads are formed from mild steel:* **make**, construct, build, manufacture, fabricate, assemble, put together; create, produce, concoct, devise, contrive, frame, fashion, shape. **2** *he formed a plan:* **formulate**, devise, conceive, work out, think up, lay, draw up, put together, produce, fashion, concoct, forge, hatch, develop; informal dream up. **3** *they plan to form a company:* **set up**, establish, found, launch, float, create, bring into being, institute, start, get going, initiate, bring about, inaugurate. **4** *a mist was forming in the valley:* **materialize**, come into being/existence, crystallize, emerge, spring up, develop; take shape, appear, loom, show up, become visible. **5** *the horse may form bad habits:* **acquire**, develop, get, pick up, contract, slip into, get into. **6** *his men formed themselves into an arrowhead:* **arrange**, draw up, line up, assemble, organize, sort, order, range, array, dispose, marshal, deploy. **7** *the parts of society form an integrated whole:* **comprise**, make, make up, constitute, compose, add up to. **8** *the city formed a natural meeting point for traders:* **constitute**, serve as, act as, function as, perform the function of, do duty for, make. **9** *natural objects are most important in forming the mind of the child:* **develop**, mould, shape, train, teach, instruct, educate, school, drill, discipline, prime, prepare, guide, direct, inform, enlighten, inculcate, indoctrinate, edify.
– OPPOSITES dissolve, disappear, break.

formal adjective **1** *a formal dinner:* **ceremonial**, ceremonious, ritualistic, ritual, conventional, traditional; stately, courtly, solemn, dignified; elaborate, ornate, dressy. **2** *a very formal manner:* **aloof**, reserved, remote, detached, unapproachable; stiff, prim, stuffy, staid, ceremonious, correct, proper, decorous, conventional, precise, exact, punctilious, unbending, inflexible, strait-laced; informal stand-offish. **3** *a formal garden:* **symmetrical**, regular, orderly, arranged, methodical, systematic. **4** *formal permission is required:* **official**, legal, authorized, approved, validated, certified, endorsed, documented, sanctioned, licensed, recognized. **5** *she had received no formal education:* **conventional**, mainstream; school, institutional.
– OPPOSITES informal, casual, colloquial, unofficial.

formality noun **1** *he disliked the formality of the occasion:* **ceremony**, ceremoniousness, ritual, conventionality, red tape, protocol,

decorum; stateliness, courtliness, solemnity. **2** *his formality was off-putting:* **aloofness**, reserve, remoteness, detachment, unapproachability; stiffness, primness, stuffiness, staidness, correctness, decorum, punctiliousness, inflexibility; informal stand-offishness. **3** *we keep the formalities to a minimum:* **official procedure**, bureaucracy, red tape, paperwork.
– OPPOSITES informality.

format noun *the journal has been well received in its new format:* **design**, style, presentation, appearance, look; form, shape, size; arrangement, plan, structure, scheme, composition, configuration.

formation noun **1** *we managed to date the formation of the island's sand ridges:* **emergence**, coming into being, genesis, development, evolution, shaping, origination. **2** *the formation of a new government:* **establishment**, setting up, start, initiation, institution, foundation, inception, creation, inauguration, launch, flotation. **3** *the aircraft were flying in tight formation:* **configuration**, arrangement, pattern, array, alignment, positioning, disposition, order.
– OPPOSITES destruction, disappearance, dissolution.

formative adjective **1** *at a formative stage in the child's development:* **developmental**, developing, growing, malleable, impressionable, susceptible. **2** *the Fabians had a formative influence on British politics:* **determining**, controlling, influential, guiding, decisive, forming, shaping, determinative.

former adjective **1** *the former Bishop of London:* **one-time**, erstwhile, sometime, ex-, late; **previous**, foregoing, preceding, earlier, prior, past, last. **2** *in former times:* **earlier**, old, past, bygone, olden, long-ago, gone by, long past, of old. **3** *those who take the former view are mistaken:* **first-mentioned**, first.
– OPPOSITES future, next, latter.

formerly adverb *he was formerly the head of a large comprehensive school:* **previously**, earlier, before, until now/then, hitherto, once, once upon a time, at one time, in the past.

formidable adjective **1** *every man wore a formidable curved dagger:* **intimidating**, forbidding, daunting, disturbing, alarming, frightening, disquieting, brooding, awesome, fearsome, ominous, foreboding, sinister, menacing, threatening, dangerous. **2** *they face a formidable task:* **onerous**, arduous, taxing, difficult, hard, heavy, laborious, burdensome, strenuous, back-breaking, uphill, Herculean, monumental, colossal; demanding, tough, challenging, exacting. **3** *he is a formidable opponent:* **capable**, able, proficient, adept, adroit, accomplished, seasoned, skilful, skilled, gifted, talented, masterly, virtuoso, expert, knowledgeable, qualified; impressive,

f

powerful, mighty, terrific, tremendous, great, complete, redoubtable; informal mean, wicked, deadly, nifty, crack, ace, wizard, magic; N. Amer. informal crackerjack.
– OPPOSITES pleasant-looking, comforting, easy, poor, weak.

formless adjective *the tremors turned the house into a formless heap of rubble:* **shapeless**, amorphous, unshaped, indeterminate; structureless, unstructured.
– OPPOSITES shaped, definite.

formula noun **1** *a legal formula:* **form of words**, set expression, phrase, saying, aphorism. **2** *a peace formula:* **recipe**, prescription, blueprint, plan, method, procedure, technique, system. **3** *a formula for removing grease:* **preparation**, concoction, mixture, compound, creation, substance.

formulate verb **1** *the miners formulated a plan to keep the mines open:* **devise**, conceive, work out, think up, lay, draw up, put together, form, produce, fashion, concoct, contrive, forge, hatch, prepare, develop; informal dream up. **2** *this is how Marx formulated his question:* **express**, phrase, word, put into words, frame, couch, put, articulate, convey, say, state, utter.

fornication noun (formal) *the Act sought to punish those convicted of fornication with three months' imprisonment:* **extramarital sex**, extramarital relations, adultery, infidelity, unfaithfulness, cuckoldry; informal hanky-panky, a bit on the side.

forsake verb (literary) **1** *he forsook his wife:* **abandon**, desert, leave, leave high and dry, turn one's back on, cast aside, break (up) with; jilt, strand, leave stranded, leave in the lurch, throw over; informal walk out on, run out on, dump, ditch. **2** *I won't forsake my vegetarian principles:* **renounce**, abandon, relinquish, dispense with, disclaim, disown, disavow, discard, wash one's hands of; give up, drop, jettison, do away with, axe; informal ditch, scrap, scrub, junk; formal forswear.
– OPPOSITES keep to, adopt.

fort noun **fortress**, castle, citadel, blockhouse, burg; stronghold, redoubt, fortification, bastion; fastness.

forte noun *acting had always been her forte:* **strength**, strong point, speciality, strong suit, talent, special ability, skill, bent, gift, métier; informal thing.
– OPPOSITES weakness.

forth adverb **1** *smoke billowed forth:* **out**, outside, away, off, ahead, forward, into view; into existence. **2** *from that day forth:* **onwards**, onward, on, forward; for ever, into eternity; until now.

forthcoming adjective **1** *forthcoming events:* **imminent**, impending, coming, upcoming, approaching, future; close, (close) at hand, in store, in the wind, in the air, in the offing, in the pipeline, on the horizon, on the way, on us, about to happen. **2** *no*

reply was forthcoming: **available**, ready, at hand, accessible, obtainable, at someone's disposal, on offer; obtained, given, vouchsafed to someone; informal up for grabs, on tap. **3** *he was not very forthcoming about himself:* **communicative**, talkative, chatty, loquacious, vocal; expansive, expressive, unreserved, uninhibited, outgoing, frank, open, candid.
– OPPOSITES past, current, unavailable, uncommunicative.

forthright adjective *he was fearless and forthright in speaking out:* **frank**, direct, straightforward, honest, candid, open, sincere, outspoken, straight, blunt, plain-spoken, no-nonsense, bluff, matter-of-fact, to the point; informal upfront.
– OPPOSITES secretive, evasive.

forthwith adverb *the government insisted that all hostages be released forthwith:* **immediately**, at once, instantly, directly, right away, straight away, post-haste, without delay, with immediate effect; quickly, speedily, promptly; informal pronto.
– OPPOSITES sometime.

fortification noun **rampart**, wall, defence, bulwark, palisade, stockade, redoubt, earthwork, bastion, parapet, barricade.

fortify verb **1** *he rode in haste to fortify his castles and towns:* **secure**, strengthen, protect. **2** *the timber enclosure had been fortified by a stone wall:* **strengthen**, reinforce, toughen, consolidate, bolster, shore up, brace, buttress. **3** *he ordered a pot of coffee to fortify himself:* **invigorate**, strengthen, energize, enliven, liven up, animate, vitalize, rejuvenate, restore, revive, refresh; informal pep up, buck up, give a shot in the arm to.
– OPPOSITES weaken, sedate, subdue.

fortitude noun *he accepted his illness with fortitude:* **courage**, bravery, endurance, resilience, mettle, moral fibre, strength of mind, strength of character, strong-mindedness, backbone, spirit, grit, doughtiness, steadfastness; informal guts; Brit. informal bottle.
– OPPOSITES faint-heartedness.

fortress noun **fort**, castle, citadel, blockhouse, burg; stronghold, redoubt, fortification, bastion; fastness.

fortuitous adjective **1** *his success depended on entirely fortuitous events:* **chance**, adventitious, unexpected, unanticipated, unpredictable, unforeseen, unlooked-for, serendipitous, casual, incidental, coincidental, random, accidental, inadvertent, unintentional, unintended, unplanned, unpremeditated. **2** *United were saved by a fortuitous penalty:* **lucky**, fluky, fortunate, providential, advantageous, timely, opportune, serendipitous, heaven-sent; Brit. informal jammy.
– OPPOSITES predictable, unlucky.

fortunate adjective **1** *he was fortunate that the punishment was so slight:* **lucky**,

favoured, blessed, blessed with good luck, in luck, having a charmed life, charmed; informal sitting pretty; Brit. informal jammy. **2** *we find ourselves in a fortunate position:* **favourable**, advantageous, providential, auspicious, welcome, heaven-sent, beneficial, propitious, fortuitous, opportune, happy, felicitous.
– OPPOSITES unfortunate, unfavourable.

fortunately adverb *fortunately, no one was injured:* **luckily**, by good luck, by good fortune, as luck would have it, propitiously; mercifully, thankfully; thank goodness, thank God, thank heavens, thank the stars.

fortune noun **1** *fortune favoured him:* **chance**, accident, coincidence, serendipity, destiny, fortuity, providence; N. Amer. happenstance. **2** *a change of fortune:* **luck**, fate, destiny, predestination, the stars, serendipity, karma, kismet, lot. **3** *there should be an upswing in Sheffield's fortunes:* (**fortunes**) **circumstances**, state of affairs, condition, position, situation; plight, predicament. **4** *he made his fortune in steel:* **wealth**, riches, substance, property, assets, resources, means, possessions, treasure, estate. **5** (informal) *this dress cost a fortune:* **huge/vast amount**, king's ransom, millions, billions; informal packet, mint, bundle, pile, wad, arm and a leg, pretty penny, tidy sum, killing, big money; Brit. informal bomb, loadsamoney, shedloads; N. Amer. informal big bucks, gazillions.
– OPPOSITES pittance.

fortune-teller noun **clairvoyant**, crystal-gazer, psychic, prophet, seer, oracle, soothsayer, augur, diviner, sibyl; palmist, palm-reader; Scottish spaewife.

forum noun **1** *forums were held for staff to air grievances:* **meeting**, assembly, gathering, rally, conference, seminar, convention, symposium, colloquium; N. Amer. & NZ caucus; informal get-together; formal colloquy. **2** *the UN could provide a forum for discussion:* **setting**, place, scene, context, stage, framework, backdrop; medium, means, apparatus.

forward adverb **1** *the traffic moved slowly forward:* **ahead**, forwards, onwards, onward, on, further. **2** *the winner stepped forward:* **out**, up, forth, into view. **3** *from that day forward:* **onward**, onwards, on, forth.
– OPPOSITES backwards.
adjective **1** *in a forward direction:* **onward**, advancing, progressing, progressive. **2** *the fortress served as the Austrian army's forward base against the Russians:* **front**, advance, foremost, head, leading, frontal. **3** *forward planning:* **future**, forward-looking, for the future, prospective. **4** *the girls seemed very forward:* **bold**, **brazen**, brazen-faced, barefaced, brash, shameless, immodest, audacious, daring, presumptuous, familiar, overfamiliar, pert; informal brass-necked, fresh.
– OPPOSITES backward, rear, shy, late.
verb **1** *my mother forwarded me your letter:*

send on, post on, redirect, readdress, pass on. **2** *the goods were forwarded by sea:* **send**, dispatch, transmit, carry, convey, deliver, ship.

forward-looking adjective *meanwhile, the forward-looking countries of Europe forged ahead:* **progressive**, enlightened, dynamic, pushing, bold, enterprising, ambitious, pioneering, innovative, modern, avant-garde, positive, reforming, radical; informal go-ahead, go-getting.
– OPPOSITES backward-looking.

forwards adverb. See **FORWARD** adverb.

foster verb **1** *he was known for fostering the arts:* **encourage**, promote, further, stimulate, advance, forward, cultivate, nurture, strengthen, enrich; help, aid, abet, assist, contribute to, support, back. **2** *they have fostered a succession of children:* **bring up**, rear, raise, care for, take care of, look after, nurture, provide for; mother, parent.
– OPPOSITES neglect, suppress.

foul adjective **1** *skunks produce a foul stench:* **disgusting**, revolting, repulsive, repugnant, abhorrent, loathsome, offensive, sickening, nauseating, nauseous, stomach-churning, stomach-turning, distasteful, obnoxious, objectionable, odious, noxious; N. Amer. vomitous; informal ghastly, gruesome, gross, putrid, yucky, skanky, sick-making; Brit. informal beastly; Austral. informal on the nose; literary miasmic, noisome. **2** *get those foul clothes out of my bedroom:* **dirty**, filthy, mucky, grimy, grubby, muddy, muddied, unclean, unwashed; squalid, sordid, soiled, sullied, scummy; rotten, defiled, decaying, putrid, putrefied, smelly, fetid; informal cruddy, yucky, icky; Brit. informal manky, gungy, grotty; rare feculent. **3** *he had been foul to her:* **unkind**, malicious, mean, nasty, unpleasant, unfriendly, spiteful, cruel, vicious, base, malevolent, despicable, contemptible; informal horrible, horrid, rotten; Brit. informal beastly. **4** *foul weather:* **inclement**, unpleasant, disagreeable, bad; rough, stormy, squally, gusty, windy, blustery, wild, blowy, rainy, wet; Brit. informal filthy. **5** *foul drinking water was blamed for the outbreak:* **contaminated**, polluted, infected, tainted, impure, filthy, dirty, unclean; rare feculent. **6** *these foul deeds cannot go unpunished:* **evil**, wicked, bad, wrong, immoral, sinful, vile, dishonourable, corrupt, iniquitous, depraved, villainous, nefarious, vicious, malicious; malevolent, sinister, demonic, devilish, diabolical, fiendish, dark; monstrous, shocking, despicable, atrocious, heinous, odious, contemptible, horrible, execrable; informal low-down, dirty. **7** *foul language:* **vulgar**, crude, coarse, filthy, dirty, obscene, indecent, indelicate, naughty, lewd, suggestive, smutty, ribald, salacious, scatological, offensive, abusive; informal blue. **8** *a foul tackle:* **unfair**, illegal, unsporting, unsportsmanlike, below the belt, dirty.

f

– OPPOSITES pleasant, kind, fair, clean, righteous, mild, fair.

verb 1 *the river had been fouled with chemical waste:* **dirty**, infect, pollute, contaminate, poison, taint, sully, soil, stain, blacken, muddy, splash, spatter, smear, blight, defile, make filthy. **2** *the vessel had fouled her nets:* **tangle up**, entangle, snarl, catch, entwine, enmesh, twist.
– OPPOSITES clean up, disentangle.

foul-mouthed adjective **vulgar**, crude, coarse; obscene, rude, smutty, dirty, filthy, indecent, indelicate, offensive, lewd, X-rated, scatological, foul, abusive; informal blue.

found verb **1** *he founded his company in 1989:* **establish**, set up, start, begin, get going, institute, inaugurate, launch, float, form, create, bring into being, originate, develop. **2** *they abandoned Attica and founded a new city:* **build**, construct, erect, put up; plan, lay plans for. **3** *their relationship was founded on trust:* **base**, build, construct; ground in, root in; rest, hinge, depend.
– OPPOSITES dissolve, liquidate, abandon, demolish.

foundation noun **1** *the weight of the wall is transmitted to the foundations:* **foot**, base, substructure, underpinning; bottom, bedrock, substratum. **2** *good records are the foundation of any personnel system:* **basis**, starting point, base, point of departure, beginning, premise; principles, fundamentals, rudiments; cornerstone, core, heart, thrust, essence, kernel. **3** *there was no foundation for the claim:* **justification**, grounds, defence, reason, rationale, cause, basis, motive, excuse, call, pretext, provocation. **4** *in his will he set up an educational foundation:* **institution**, agency, charity.

founder[1] noun *the founder of modern physics:* **originator**, creator, (founding) father, prime mover, architect, engineer, designer, developer, pioneer, author, planner, inventor, mastermind; informal godfather.

founder[2] verb **1** *the ship foundered on a voyage to Holland:* **sink**, go to the bottom, go down, be lost at sea. **2** *the scheme foundered due to lack of funds:* **fail**, be unsuccessful, not succeed, fall flat, fall through, collapse, backfire, meet with disaster, come to nothing/naught; informal flop, bomb.
– OPPOSITES succeed.

fountain noun **1** *the fountain sprayed cool water into the air:* **jet**, spray, spout, well, fount, cascade. **2** *the head porter needs to be a fountain of knowledge:* **source**, fount, well; reservoir, fund, mass, mine.

four cardinal number **quartet**, foursome, tetralogy, quadruplets; technical tetrad; rare quadrumvirate.

foyer noun **entrance hall**, hall, hallway, entrance, entry, porch, reception area,

atrium, concourse, lobby; N. Amer. entryway.

fracas noun *officers were kicked and punched in a fracas earlier this week:* **disturbance**, brawl, melee, rumpus, skirmish, struggle, scuffle, scrum, clash, fisticuffs, altercation; informal scrap, dust-up, set-to, shindy, shindig; Brit. informal punch-up, bust-up, ruck; N. Amer. informal rough house, brannigan; Austral./NZ informal stoush; Law, dated affray.

fraction noun **1** *a fraction of the population:* **part**, subdivision, division, portion, segment, slice, section, sector; proportion, percentage, ratio, measure. **2** *this is only a fraction of the collection:* **tiny part**, fragment, snippet, snatch, smattering, selection. **3** *he moved a fraction closer:* **little**, bit, touch, soupçon, trifle, mite, shade, jot; informal smidgen, smidge, tad.
– OPPOSITES whole.

fractious adjective **1** *they squabble like fractious children:* **grumpy**, bad-tempered, irascible, irritable, crotchety, grouchy, cantankerous, short-tempered, tetchy, testy, curmudgeonly, ill-tempered, ill-humoured, peevish, cross, pettish, waspish, crabbed, crabby, crusty, prickly, touchy; informal snappish, snappy, chippy; Brit. informal shirty, stroppy, narky, ratty; N. Amer. informal cranky, ornery; Austral./NZ informal snaky. **2** *the fractious parliamentary party:* **wayward**, unruly, uncontrollable, unmanageable, out of hand, obstreperous, difficult, headstrong, recalcitrant, intractable; disobedient, insubordinate, disruptive, disorderly, undisciplined; contrary, wilful; formal refractory.
– OPPOSITES contented, affable, dutiful.

fracture noun **1** *fracture will occur at the point of greatest stress:* **breaking**, breakage, cracking, fragmentation, splintering, rupture. **2** *tiny fractures in the rock:* **crack**, split, fissure, crevice, break, rupture, breach, rift, cleft, chink, interstice; crazing.
verb *she fell and fractured her skull:* **break**, crack, shatter, splinter, split, rupture; informal bust.

fragile adjective **1** *she was anxious about her fragile porcelain:* **breakable**, easily broken; delicate, dainty, fine, flimsy; eggshell; formal frangible. **2** *moves to consolidate the fragile ceasefire:* **tenuous**, shaky, insecure, unreliable, vulnerable, flimsy. **3** *she is still very fragile after her ordeal:* **weak**, delicate, frail, debilitated; ill, unwell, ailing, poorly, sickly, infirm, enfeebled.
– OPPOSITES strong, durable, robust.

fragment noun **1** *meteorite fragments recovered from the desert:* **piece**, bit, particle, speck; chip, shard, sliver, splinter, shaving, paring, snippet, scrap, offcut, flake, shred, wisp, morsel; Scottish skelf. **2** *a fragment of conversation:* **snatch**, snippet, scrap, bit.
verb *explosions caused the chalk to fragment:* **break up**, break, break into pieces, crack open/apart, shatter, splinter, fracture; disintegrate, fall to pieces, fall apart.

fragmentary adjective *a few fragmentary descriptions are all we have:* **incomplete**, fragmented, disconnected, disjointed, broken, discontinuous, piecemeal, scrappy, bitty, sketchy, uneven, patchy.
– OPPOSITES integral, extensive.

fragrance noun **1** *the fragrance of spring flowers:* **sweet smell**, scent, perfume, bouquet; aroma, redolence, nose. **2** *a bottle of fragrance:* **perfume**, scent, eau de toilette, toilet water; eau de cologne, cologne; aftershave.

fragrant adjective *various fragrant herbs are used in aromatherapy:* **sweet-scented**, sweet-smelling, scented, perfumed, aromatic.
– OPPOSITES smelly.

frail adjective **1** *a frail old lady:* **weak**, delicate, feeble, enfeebled, debilitated; infirm, ill, ailing, unwell, sickly, poorly, in poor health. **2** *a frail structure of cardboard and plywood:* **fragile**, breakable, easily damaged, delicate, flimsy, insubstantial, unsteady, unstable, rickety; formal frangible.
– OPPOSITES strong, robust.

frailty noun **1** *the frailty of old age:* **infirmity**, weakness, enfeeblement, debility; fragility, delicacy; ill health, sickliness. **2** *his many frailties:* **weakness**, fallibility; weak point, flaw, imperfection, defect, failing, fault, shortcoming, deficiency, inadequacy, limitation.
– OPPOSITES strength.

frame noun **1** *a tubular metal frame:* **framework**, structure, substructure, skeleton, chassis, shell, casing, body, bodywork; support, scaffolding, foundation. **2** *his clothes clung to his tall, slender frame:* **body**, figure, form, shape, physique, build, size, proportions. **3** *the photograph hung in a polished frame:* **setting**, mount, mounting. verb **1** *he had the picture framed:* **mount**, set in a frame. **2** *the legislators who frame the regulations:* **formulate**, draw up, draft, plan, shape, compose, put together, form, devise, create, establish, conceive, think up, originate; informal dream up.
■ **frame of mind** *she was in a receptive frame of mind:* mood, state of mind, humour, temper, disposition.

framework noun **1** *a metal framework:* **frame**, substructure, structure, skeleton, chassis, shell, body, bodywork; support, scaffolding, foundation. **2** *the changing framework of society:* **structure**, shape, fabric, order, scheme, system, organization, construction, configuration, composition; informal make-up.

franchise noun **1** *the extension of the franchise to women:* **suffrage**, the vote, the right to vote, voting rights, enfranchisement. **2** *the company lost its TV franchise:* **warrant**, charter, licence, permit, authorization, permission, sanction.

frank¹ adjective **1** *he was quite frank with*

me: **candid**, direct, forthright, plain, plain-spoken, straight, straightforward, straight from the shoulder, explicit, to the point, matter-of-fact; open, honest, truthful, sincere; outspoken, bluff, blunt, unsparing, not afraid to call a spade a spade; informal upfront. **2** *she looked at Sam with frank admiration:* **open**, undisguised, unconcealed, naked, unmistakable, clear, obvious, transparent, patent, manifest, evident, perceptible, palpable; blatant, barefaced, flagrant.
– OPPOSITES evasive.

frank² verb *the envelope had not been franked:* **stamp**, postmark; imprint, print, mark.

frankly adverb **1** *frankly, I'm not very interested:* **to be frank**, to be honest, to tell you the truth, to be truthful, in all honesty, quite honestly. **2** *he stated the case quite frankly:* **candidly**, directly, plainly, straightforwardly, straight from the shoulder, forthrightly, openly, honestly, without beating about the bush, without mincing one's words, without prevarication, point-blank; bluntly, outspokenly, with no holds barred.

frantic adjective *Mary was frantic because she'd run out of matches:* **panic-stricken**, beside oneself, at one's wits' end, distraught, overwrought, worked up, agitated, distressed; frenzied, wild, frenetic, fraught, feverish, hysterical, desperate; informal in a state, in a tizzy/tizz, wound up, het up, in a flap, tearing one's hair out; Brit. informal having kittens, in a flat spin.
– OPPOSITES calm.

fraternity noun **1** *the meeting engendered a spirit of fraternity:* **brotherhood**, fellowship, kinship, friendship, (mutual) support, solidarity, community, union, togetherness; sisterhood. **2** *enthusiasts among the teaching fraternity:* **profession**, body of workers; band, group, set, circle. **3** (N. Amer.) *a college fraternity:* **society**, club, association; group, set.

fraternize verb *she forbade her musicians to fraternize with the dancers:* **associate**, mix, consort, socialize, keep company, rub shoulders; N. Amer. rub elbows; informal hang around/round, hang out, run around, knock about/around, hobnob.

fraud noun **1** *his business partner was arrested for fraud:* **fraudulence**, sharp practice, cheating, swindling, embezzlement, deceit, deception, double-dealing, chicanery. **2** *social security frauds:* **swindle**, racket, deception, trick, cheat, hoax; informal scam, con, con trick, rip-off, sting, gyp, diddle, fiddle; N. Amer. informal bunco, hustle, grift. **3** *they exposed him as a fraud:* **impostor**, fake, sham, charlatan, quack, mountebank; swindler, fraudster, cheat, confidence trickster, liar; informal phoney, con man, con artist.

fraudulent adjective *he was convicted*

of fraudulent share dealing: **dishonest**, cheating, swindling, corrupt, criminal, illegal, unlawful, illicit; deceitful, double-dealing, duplicitous, dishonourable, unscrupulous, unprincipled; informal crooked, shady, dirty; Brit. informal bent, dodgy; Austral./NZ informal shonky.
– OPPOSITES honest.

fraught adjective **1** *their world is fraught with danger:* **full of**, filled with, rife with; attended by, accompanied by. **2** *she sounded a bit fraught:* **anxious**, worried, stressed, upset, distraught, overwrought, worked up, agitated, distressed, distracted, desperate, frantic, panic-stricken, panic-struck, panicky; beside oneself, at one's wits' end, at the end of one's tether; informal wound up, in a state, in a flap, in a cold sweat, tearing one's hair out; Brit. informal having kittens, in a flat spin.

fray¹ verb **1** *cheap fabric soon frays:* **unravel**, wear, wear thin, wear out/through, shred. **2** *her nerves were frayed:* **strain**, tax, overtax, put on edge.

fray² noun *he launched himself into the fray:* **battle**, fight, engagement, conflict, clash, skirmish, altercation, tussle, struggle, scuffle, melee, brawl; informal scrap, dust-up, set-to; Brit. informal punch-up, bust-up; Scottish informal rammy; Law, dated affray.

frayed adjective **1** *a frayed shirt collar:* **worn**, well worn, threadbare, tattered, ragged, holey, moth-eaten, in holes, the worse for wear; informal tatty; N. Amer. informal raggedy. **2** *his frayed nerves couldn't take much more:* **strained**, fraught, tense, edgy, stressed.

freak noun **1** *the mouse was a genetically engineered freak:* **aberration**, abnormality, irregularity, oddity; monster, monstrosity, mutant. **2** *the accident was a complete freak:* **anomaly**, aberration, rarity, oddity, unusual occurrence; fluke. **3** (informal) *they were dismissed as a bunch of freaks:* **oddity**, eccentric, misfit; crank, lunatic; informal oddball, weirdo, nutcase, nut; Brit. informal nutter; N. Amer. informal wacko, kook. **4** (informal) *a fitness freak:* **enthusiast**, fan, devotee, lover, aficionado; informal fiend, nut, fanatic, addict, maniac, buff.
adjective *a freak result:* **unusual**, anomalous, aberrant, atypical, unrepresentative, irregular, fluky, exceptional, unaccountable, bizarre, queer, peculiar, odd, freakish; unpredictable, unforeseeable, unexpected, unanticipated, surprising; rare, singular, isolated.
– OPPOSITES normal.
verb (informal) *he freaked and started smashing the place up:* **go crazy**, go mad, go out of one's mind, go to pieces, crack, snap, lose control; panic, become hysterical; informal lose it, lose one's cool, crack up; N. Amer. informal go ape, go postal.

freakish adjective *freakish weather.* See **FREAK** adjective.

freaky adjective (informal). See **ODD** senses 1, 2.

free adjective **1** *admission is free:* **without charge**, free of charge, for nothing; complimentary, gratis; informal for free, on the house. **2** *she was free of any pressures:* **unencumbered by**, unaffected by, clear of, without, rid of; exempt from, safe from, immune to. **3** *I'm free this afternoon:* **unoccupied**, not busy, available, between appointments; off duty, off work, off, on holiday, on leave; at leisure, with time on one's hands, with time to spare. **4** *the bathroom's free now:* **vacant**, empty, available, unoccupied, not taken, not in use. **5** *a citizen of a proud free nation:* **independent**, self-governing, self-governed, self-ruling, self-determining, non-aligned, sovereign, autonomous; democratic. **6** *the killer is still free:* **on the loose**, at liberty, at large; on the run; loose, around, about, in circulation. **7** *after a few minutes of squirming, he was free:* **loose**, unconfined, unbound, untied, unchained, untethered, unshackled, unfettered, unrestrained. **8** *you are free to leave:* **able to**, in a position to, capable of; allowed, permitted, entitled. **9** *the free flow of water:* **unimpeded**, unobstructed, unrestricted, unhampered, clear, open, unblocked. **10** *she was always very free with her money:* **generous**, liberal, open-handed, unstinting, bountiful; lavish, extravagant, prodigal. **11** *Swedish traditional music leaves plenty of room for free interpretation:* **unconventional**, liberal, taking liberties, free and easy; natural, open, relaxed, uninhibited, unrestrained, unreserved; expressive, artistic, creative, communicative, demonstrative, eloquent, articulate, sensitive, lyrical; Music rubato.
– OPPOSITES busy, occupied, captive, mean, straight.
verb **1** *three of the hostages were freed:* **release**, set free, let go, liberate, discharge, deliver; set loose, let loose, turn loose, untie, unchain, unfetter, unshackle, unleash. **2** *the victims were freed by firefighters:* **extricate**, release, get out, pull out, pull free; rescue, set free. **3** *they wish to be freed from all legal ties:* **exempt**, except, excuse, relieve, unburden, disburden.
– OPPOSITES confine, trap.
■ **free and easy** *the restaurant has a free and easy atmosphere:* **easy-going**, relaxed, casual, informal, unceremonious, unforced, natural, open, spontaneous, uninhibited, friendly; tolerant, liberal; informal laid-back.

freedom noun **1** *the prisoners made a desperate bid for freedom:* **liberty**, liberation, release, deliverance, delivery, discharge. **2** *national revolution was the only path to freedom:* **independence**, self-government, self-determination, self-rule, home rule, sovereignty, non-alignment, autonomy; democracy. **3** *they want freedom from political accountability:* **exemption**, immunity, dispensation; impunity. **4** *patients have more freedom to choose who treats them:* **right**, entitlement,

privilege, prerogative; scope, latitude, leeway, flexibility, space, breathing space, room, elbow room; licence, leave, free rein, a free hand, carte blanche.
– OPPOSITES captivity, subjection, liability.

free-for-all noun *prompt action by staff prevented a violent free-for-all:* **brawl**, fight, scuffle, tussle, struggle, confrontation, clash, altercation, fray, fracas, melee, rumpus, disturbance; breach of the peace; informal dust-up, scrap, set-to, shindy; Brit. informal punch-up, bust-up, barney; Scottish informal rammy; Law, dated affray.

freely adverb **1** *may I speak freely?* **openly**, candidly, frankly, directly; truthfully, honestly, without beating about the bush, without mincing one's words. **2** *these workers gave their time and labour freely:* **voluntarily**, willingly, readily; of one's own volition, of one's own accord, of one's own free will, without compulsion.

freethinker noun *intellectuals, freethinkers, and radicals flourished in England:* **nonconformist**, individualist, independent, maverick; agnostic, atheist, non-believer, unbeliever.
– OPPOSITES conformist.

free will noun *enslaved by advertising, we were robbed of our free will:* **self-determination**, freedom (of choice), autonomy, liberty, independence.
■ **of one's own free will** *when he takes the drug, he takes it of his own free will:* voluntarily, willingly, readily, freely, of one's own accord, of one's own volition.

freeze verb **1** *the stream had frozen overnight:* **ice over**, ice up, solidify. **2** *the campers stifled in summer and froze in winter:* **be cold**, be numb (with cold), turn blue (with cold), shiver, be chilled to the bone/marrow. **3** *she froze in horror:* **stop dead**, stop in one's tracks, stop, stand (stock) still, go rigid. **4** *the prices of basic foodstuffs were frozen:* **fix**, hold, peg, set; limit, restrict, cap, confine, regulate; hold/keep down.
– OPPOSITES thaw.

freezing adjective **1** *a freezing wind:* **bitter**, bitterly cold, icy, chill, frosty, glacial, wintry, sub-zero; raw, biting, piercing, penetrating, cutting, numbing; arctic, polar, Siberian. **2** *you must be freezing:* **frozen**, cold, numb (with cold), chilled to the bone/marrow, frozen stiff/solid, shivery, shivering; informal frozen to death.
– OPPOSITES balmy, hot.

freight noun **1** *freight is generally carried by rail:* **goods**, cargo, load, consignment, delivery, shipment; merchandise. **2** *do not underestimate the importance of air freight:* **transportation**, transport, conveyance, freightage, carriage, portage, haulage.

frenetic adjective *Baker rushed from capital to capital at a frenetic pace:* **frantic**, wild, frenzied, hectic, fraught, feverish, fevered, mad, manic, hyperactive, energetic, intense, fast and furious, turbulent, tumultuous.

– OPPOSITES calm.

frenzied adjective *frenzied attempts to work off the festive flab can lead to injuries:* **frantic**, wild, frenetic, hectic, fraught, feverish, fevered, mad, crazed, manic, intense, furious, uncontrolled, out of control.
– OPPOSITES calm.

frenzy noun **1** *the crowd worked themselves into a state of frenzy:* **hysteria**, madness, mania, dementia, delirium, feverishness, fever, wildness, agitation, turmoil, tumult; wild excitement, euphoria, elation, ecstasy. **2** *a frenzy of anger:* **fit**, paroxysm, spasm, bout.

frequency noun *the frequency and severity of punishment was reduced:* **rate (of occurrence)**, incidence, amount, commonness, prevalence; Statistics distribution.

frequent adjective **1** *he has frequent bouts of chest infection:* **recurrent**, recurring, repeated, periodic, continual, one after another, successive; many, numerous, lots of, several. **2** *she's a frequent business traveller:* **habitual**, regular.
– OPPOSITES occasional.
verb *he frequented the most chic supper clubs:* **visit**, patronize, spend time in, visit regularly, be a regular visitor to, haunt; informal hang out at.

frequenter noun *he was known as a frequenter of public houses:* **habitué**, patron, regular, (regular) visitor, (regular) customer, (regular) client, familiar face.

frequently adverb *he frequently attended church:* **regularly**, often, very often, all the time, habitually, customarily, routinely; many times, many a time, lots of times, again and again, time and again, over and over again, repeatedly, recurrently, continually; N. Amer. oftentimes.

fresh adjective **1** *fresh fruit:* **newly picked**, garden-fresh, crisp; raw, natural, unprocessed. **2** *a fresh sheet of paper:* **clean**, blank, empty, clear, white; unused, new, pristine, unmarked, untouched. **3** *a fresh approach:* **new**, recent, latest, up-to-date, modern, ultra-modern; original, novel, different, innovative, unusual, unconventional, unorthodox; radical, revolutionary; informal offbeat. **4** *fresh recruits:* **young**, youthful; new, inexperienced, naive, untrained, unqualified, untried, raw; informal wet behind the ears. **5** *her fresh complexion:* **healthy**, healthy-looking, clear, bright, youthful, blooming, glowing, unblemished; fair, rosy, rosy-cheeked, pink, ruddy. **6** *the night air was clear and fresh:* **cool**, crisp, refreshing, invigorating, tonic; pure, clean, clear, uncontaminated, untainted. **7** *a fresh wind had sprung up from the east:* **chilly**, chill, cool, cold, brisk, bracing, invigorating; strong; informal nippy; Brit. informal parky.
– OPPOSITES stale, old, tired, warm.

f

freshen verb **1** *the cold water chilled his face and freshened him:* **refresh**, revitalize, restore, revive, wake up, rouse, enliven, liven up, energize, brace, invigorate; informal buck up, pep up. **2** *he opened a window to freshen the room:* **ventilate**, air, aerate, oxygenate; deodorize, purify, cleanse; refresh, cool. **3** *she went to freshen up before dinner:* **have a wash**, wash oneself, bathe, shower; tidy oneself (up), spruce oneself up, smarten oneself up, groom oneself, primp oneself; N. Amer. wash up; informal titivate oneself, do oneself up, doll oneself up; Brit. informal tart oneself up; formal or humorous perform one's ablutions. **4** (N. Amer.) *the waitress freshened their drinks:* **refill**, top up, fill up, replenish.

freshman, freshwoman noun **first-year student**; newcomer, new recruit, starter, probationer; beginner, learner, novice; N. Amer. tenderfoot; informal rookie; Brit. informal fresher; N. Amer. informal greenhorn.

fret verb *she was fretting about Jonathan:* **worry**, be anxious, feel uneasy, be distressed, be upset, upset oneself, concern oneself; agonize, sigh, pine, brood, eat one's heart out.

fretful adjective *the heat was making the child fretful:* **distressed**, upset, miserable, unsettled, uneasy, ill at ease, uncomfortable, edgy, agitated, worked up, tense, stressed, restive, fidgety; querulous, irritable, cross, fractious, peevish, petulant, out of sorts, bad-tempered, irascible, grumpy, crotchety, captious, testy, tetchy; N. Amer. informal cranky; informal het up, uptight, twitchy, crabby.

friable adjective *the soil was dark and friable:* **crumbly**, easily crumbled, powdery, dusty, chalky, soft; dry, crisp, brittle.

friar noun **monk**, brother, religious, coenobite, contemplative; prior, abbot.

friction noun **1** *a lubrication system which reduces friction:* **abrasion**, rubbing, chafing, grating, rasping, scraping; resistance, drag. **2** *there was considerable friction between father and son:* **discord**, strife, conflict, disagreement, dissension, dissent, opposition, contention, dispute, disputation, arguing, argument, quarrelling, bickering, squabbling, wrangling, fighting, feuding, rivalry; hostility, animosity, antipathy, enmity, antagonism, resentment, acrimony, bitterness, bad feeling, ill feeling, ill will, bad blood.
– OPPOSITES harmony.

friend noun **1** *a close friend of mine:* **companion**, boon companion, bosom friend, best friend, intimate, confidante, confidant, familiar, soul mate, playmate, playfellow, classmate, schoolmate, workmate; ally, associate; sister, brother; informal pal, chum, sidekick, crony, main man; Brit. informal mate, china, mucker; N. English informal marrow, marra; N. Amer. informal buddy, amigo, compadre, homeboy. **2** *friends of the Royal Botanic Garden:* **patron**, backer, supporter, benefactor, benefactress, sponsor; well-wisher, defender, champion.
– OPPOSITES enemy.

friendless adjective *she cared for those who were poor and friendless:* **alone**, all alone, by oneself, solitary, lonely, with no one to turn to, lone, without friends, unpopular, unwanted, unloved, abandoned, rejected, forsaken, shunned, spurned, forlorn; N. Amer. lonesome.
– OPPOSITES popular.

friendliness noun *she appreciated her host's friendliness:* **affability**, amiability, geniality, congeniality, bonhomie, cordiality, good nature, good humour, warmth, affection, conviviality, joviality, companionability, sociability, gregariousness, camaraderie, neighbourliness, hospitableness, approachability, accessibility, openness, kindness, kindliness, sympathy, amenability, benevolence.

friendly adjective **1** *she's very friendly and approachable:* **affable**, amiable, genial, congenial, cordial, warm, affectionate, demonstrative, convivial, companionable, sociable, gregarious, outgoing, clubbable, comradely, neighbourly, hospitable, approachable, easy to get on with, accessible, communicative, open, unreserved, easy-going, good-natured, kindly, benign, amenable, agreeable, obliging, sympathetic, well disposed, benevolent; Scottish couthy; informal chummy, pally, clubby; Brit. informal matey; N. Amer. informal buddy-buddy. **2** *she drew him into a friendly conversation:* **amicable**, congenial, cordial, pleasant, easy, relaxed, casual, informal, unceremonious; close, intimate, familiar.
– OPPOSITES hostile.

friendship noun **1** *lasting friendships are all too rare:* **relationship**, close relationship, attachment, mutual attachment, association, bond, tie, link, union. **2** *old ties of love and friendship:* **amity**, camaraderie, friendliness, comradeship, companionship, fellowship, fellow feeling, closeness, affinity, rapport, understanding, harmony, unity; intimacy, mutual affection.
– OPPOSITES enmity.

fright noun **1** *she was paralysed with fright:* **fear**, fearfulness, terror, horror, alarm, panic, dread, trepidation, dismay, nervousness, apprehension, apprehensiveness, perturbation, disquiet. **2** *the experience gave everyone a fright:* **scare**, shock, surprise, turn, jolt, start; the shivers, the shakes; informal the jitters, the heebie-jeebies, the willies, the creeps, the collywobbles, a cold sweat; Brit. informal the (screaming) abdabs, butterflies (in one's stomach).

frighten verb *she was frightened by the strange sounds outside:* **scare**, startle, alarm, terrify, petrify, shock, chill, panic, shake, disturb, dismay, unnerve, unman, intimidate, terrorize, cow, daunt; strike terror into, put the fear of God into, chill someone to the bone/marrow, make someone's blood run cold; informal scare the living daylights out of, scare stiff, scare someone out of their wits, scare witless, scare to death, scare the pants off, spook, make someone's hair stand on end, throw into a blue funk, make someone jump out of their skin; Brit. informal put the wind up, give someone the heebie-jeebies, make someone's hair curl; Irish informal scare the bejesus out of; archaic affright.

frightening adjective *it was a frightening ordeal:* **terrifying**, horrifying, alarming, startling, chilling, spine-chilling, hair-raising, blood-curdling, disturbing, unnerving, intimidating, daunting, dismaying, upsetting, harrowing, traumatic; eerie, sinister, fearsome, nightmarish, macabre, menacing; Scottish eldritch; informal scary, spooky, creepy, hairy.

frightful adjective **1** *an eerie place, full of strange sounds and things too frightful to contemplate:* **horrible**, horrific, ghastly, horrendous, serious, awful, dreadful, terrible, nasty, grim, dire, unspeakable; alarming, shocking, terrifying, harrowing, appalling, fearful; hideous, gruesome, grisly; informal horrid. **2** (informal) *her hair was a frightful mess:* **terrible**, awful, dreadful, appalling, ghastly, abominable; lamentable, deplorable, insufferable, unbearable; informal God-awful; Brit. informal beastly.

frigid adjective **1** *the frigid climate of the north:* **bitterly cold**, cold, freezing, frozen, frosty, icy, gelid, chilly, chill, wintry, bleak, sub-zero, arctic, Siberian, polar, glacial; informal nippy; Brit. informal parky. **2** *she addressed him with frigid politeness:* **stiff**, formal, stony, wooden, unemotional, passionless, unfeeling, indifferent, unresponsive, unenthusiastic, austere, distant, aloof, remote, reserved, unapproachable; frosty, cold, icy, cool, unsmiling, forbidding, unfriendly, unwelcoming, hostile; informal offish, stand-offish.
– OPPOSITES hot, friendly.

frill noun **1** *she wore a full skirt with a wide frill:* **ruffle**, flounce, ruff, furbelow, jabot, peplum, ruche, ruching, fringe. **2** *a comfortable flat with no frills:* **ostentation**, ornamentation, decoration, embellishment; trimmings, extras, additions, non-essentials, luxuries, extravagances, superfluities.

frilly adjective *she wore a white frilly apron:* **ruffled**, flounced, frilled, ruched, trimmed, lacy, frothy; fancy, ornate.

fringe noun **1** *he lived on the city's northern fringe:* **perimeter**, periphery, border, borderline, margin, rim, outer edge, edge, extremity, limit; outer limits, limits, borders, bounds, outskirts, marches. **2** *blue curtains with a yellow fringe:* **edging**, edge, border, trimming, frill, flounce, ruffle; tassels; archaic purfle.
– OPPOSITES middle.
adjective *fringe theatre:* **alternative**, avant-garde, experimental, left-field, radical; extreme, transgressive.
– OPPOSITES mainstream.
verb **1** *a robe of gold, fringed with black velvet:* **trim**, edge, hem, border, bind, braid; decorate, adorn, ornament, embellish, finish. **2** *the lake is fringed by a belt of trees:* **border**, edge, bound, skirt, line, surround, enclose, encircle, circle, girdle, encompass, ring.

frippery noun **1** *a functional building with not a hint of frippery:* **ostentation**, showiness, embellishment, adornment, ornamentation, ornament, decoration, trimming, gilding, prettification; informal bells and whistles. **2** *stalls full of charming fripperies:* **trinket**, bauble, knick-knack, gewgaw, gimcrack, bibelot, ornament, novelty, trifle; N. Amer. kickshaw.

frisk verb **1** *the spaniels frisked around my ankles:* **frolic**, gambol, cavort, caper, cut capers, scamper, skip, dance, romp, trip, prance, leap, spring, hop, jump, bounce. **2** *the officer frisked him:* **search**, body-search, check.

frisky adjective *the donkey was quite frisky and pranced around the field:* **lively**, bouncy, bubbly, perky, active, energetic, animated, zestful; playful, coltish, skittish, spirited, high-spirited, in high spirits, exuberant; Brit. Tiggerish; informal full of beans, sparky, zippy, peppy, bright-eyed and bushy tailed; literary frolicsome.

fritter verb *he frittered away the money his father left him:* **squander**, waste, dissipate; spend like water, be prodigal with, run through, get through; informal blow, splurge, pour/chuck something down the drain.
– OPPOSITES save.

frivolity noun *in such cases too much frivolity would be all wrong:* **light-heartedness**, levity, joking, jocularity, gaiety, fun, frivolousness, silliness, foolishness, flightiness, skittishness; superficiality, shallowness, vacuity, empty-headedness.

frivolous adjective **1** *all of the girls were idle and frivolous:* **skittish**, flighty, giddy, silly, foolish, superficial, shallow, light-minded, irresponsible, thoughtless, feather-brained, empty-headed, pea-brained, birdbrained, vacuous, vapid; informal dizzy, dippy; N. Amer. informal ditsy. **2** *frivolous remarks:* **flippant**, glib, facetious, joking, jokey, light-hearted; fatuous, inane, senseless, thoughtless; informal flip. **3** *new rules to stop frivolous lawsuits:* **time-wasting**, pointless, trivial, trifling, minor, petty, insignificant, unimportant.
– OPPOSITES sensible, serious.

frizzy adjective *she had frizzy blond hair:* **curly**, curled, corkscrew, ringlety, crimped, crinkly, kinky, frizzed; permed; N. Amer. informal nappy.
– OPPOSITES straight.

f

frock noun **dress**, gown, robe, shift; garment, costume.

frolic verb *children frolicked on the sand:* **play**, amuse oneself, romp, disport oneself, frisk, gambol, cavort, caper, cut capers, scamper, skip, dance, prance, leap about, jump about; dated sport.
noun *the youngsters enjoyed their frolic:* **antic**, caper, game, romp, escapade; (**frolics**) fun (and games), high jinks, merrymaking, amusement, skylarking.

frolicsome adjective (literary) *he encountered a group of frolicsome young ladies:* **playful**, frisky, fun-loving, jolly, merry, gleeful, light-hearted, exuberant, high-spirited, spirited, lively, perky, skittish, coltish, kittenish; mischievous, impish, roguish; informal peppy, zippy, full of beans.

front noun **1** *there was a little deck at the front of the boat:* **fore**, foremost part, forepart, anterior, forefront, nose, head; bow, prow; foreground. **2** *the car swerved and crashed into a shop front:* **frontage**, face, facing, facade; window. **3** *the battlefield surgeons who work at the front:* **front line**, firing line, vanguard, van; trenches. **4** *she pushed her way to the front of the queue:* **head**, beginning, start, top, lead. **5** *she kept up a brave front for most of the week:* **appearance**, air, face, manner, demeanour, bearing, pose, exterior, veneer, (outward) show, act, pretence, affectation. **6** *the shop was a front for dealing in stolen goods:* **cover**, cover-up, false front, blind, disguise, facade, mask, cloak, screen, smokescreen, camouflage.
– OPPOSITES rear, back.
adjective *the front runners had already finished:* **leading**, lead, first, foremost; in first place.
– OPPOSITES last.
verb *the houses fronted on a reservoir:* **overlook**, look out on/over, face (towards), lie opposite (to); have a view of, command a view of.
■ **in front** *he finished three lengths in front of me:* ahead, to/at the fore, at the head, up ahead, in the vanguard, in the van, in the lead, leading, coming first; at the head of the queue; informal up front.

frontier noun **border**, boundary, borderline, dividing line, demarcation line; perimeter, limit, edge, rim; marches, bounds.

frost noun *the hedges were covered with frost:* **ice crystals**, ice, rime, verglas; hoar frost, ground frost, black frost; informal Jack Frost; archaic hoar.

frosty adjective **1** *a cold and frosty morning:* **freezing**, cold, icy-cold, bitter, bitterly cold, chill, wintry, frigid, glacial, arctic; frozen, icy, gelid; informal nippy; Brit. informal parky; literary rimy. **2** *Mary fixed her frosty gaze on him:* **cold**, frigid, icy, glacial, unfriendly, inhospitable, unwelcoming, forbidding, hostile, stony, stern, hard.

froth noun *the froth on top of the beer:*

foam, head; bubbles, frothiness, fizz, effervescence; lather, suds; scum; literary spume.
verb *the liquid frothed up:* **bubble**, fizz, effervesce, foam, lather; churn, seethe; literary spume.

frothy adjective *a frothy liquid:* **foaming**, foamy, bubbling, bubbly, fizzy, sparkling, effervescent, gassy, carbonated; sudsy.

frown verb **1** *she frowned at him:* **scowl**, glower, glare, lour, make a face, look daggers, give someone a black look; knit/furrow one's brows; informal give someone a dirty look. **2** *public displays of affection were frowned on:* **disapprove of**, view with disfavour, dislike, look askance at, not take kindly to, take a dim view of, take exception to, object to, have a low opinion of.
– OPPOSITES smile.

frowsty adjective (Brit.) *the stench of the frowsty rooms left him pale:* **stuffy**, airless, unventilated, fusty, close, muggy, stifling; stale, musty, smelly; N. Amer. funky.
– OPPOSITES airy.

frozen adjective **1** *I've been digging in the frozen ground:* **icy**, ice-bound, frosty, frosted, gelid; frozen solid, hard, (as) hard as iron; literary rimy. **2** *his hands were frozen:* **freezing**, icy, very cold, chilled to the bone/marrow, numb, numbed, frozen stiff.
– OPPOSITES boiling.

frugal adjective **1** *a hard-working, frugal man:* **thrifty**, economical, careful, cautious, prudent, provident, unwasteful, sparing; abstemious, abstinent, austere, self-denying, ascetic, monkish, spartan; parsimonious, miserly, niggardly, cheese-paring, penny-pinching, close-fisted; N. Amer. forehanded; informal tight-fisted, tight, stingy. **2** *the boys finished their frugal breakfast:* **meagre**, scanty, scant, paltry, skimpy; plain, simple, spartan, inexpensive, cheap, economical.
– OPPOSITES extravagant, lavish.

fruit noun *the fruits of their labours:* **reward**, benefit, profit, product, return, yield, legacy, issue; result, outcome, upshot, consequence, effect.

fruitful adjective **1** *a fruitful tree:* **fertile**, fecund, prolific, high-yielding; fruit-bearing, fruiting. **2** *the two days of talks had been fruitful:* **productive**, constructive, useful, of use, worthwhile, helpful, beneficial, valuable, rewarding, profitable, advantageous, gainful, successful, effective, well spent.
– OPPOSITES barren, futile.

fruition noun *scientific projects need time to come to fruition:* **fulfilment**, realization, actualization, materialization, accomplishment, resolution; success, completion, consummation, conclusion, close, finish, perfection, maturity, maturation, ripening, ripeness.

fruitless adjective *the search proved fruitless:* **futile**, vain, in vain, to no avail, to no effect, idle; pointless, useless, worthless, wasted, hollow; ineffectual, ineffective, inefficacious; unproductive, unrewarding, profitless, unsuccessful, unavailing, barren, for naught; abortive.
– OPPOSITES productive.

fruity adjective **1** *he had a wonderfully fruity voice:* **deep**, rich, resonant, full, mellow, clear, strong, vibrant. **2** (Brit. informal) *a fruity story:* **bawdy**, racy, risqué, naughty, spicy, earthy, ribald, suggestive, titillating; rude, indelicate, vulgar, indecent, improper, dirty, smutty, coarse, off colour; N. Amer. gamy; euphemistic adult; informal blue, near the knuckle, nudge-nudge, raunchy; Brit. informal saucy.

frumpy adjective *her mother's frumpy brown and grey clothes:* **dowdy**, frumpish, unfashionable, old-fashioned; drab, dull, shabby, scruffy; Brit. informal mumsy.
– OPPOSITES fashionable.

frustrate verb **1** *his plans were frustrated by the weather:* **thwart**, defeat, foil, block, stop, put a stop to, counter, spoil, check, baulk, disappoint, forestall, dash, scotch, quash, crush, derail, snooker; obstruct, impede, hamper, hinder, hamstring, stand in the way of, spike someone's guns; informal stymie, foul up, screw up, put the kibosh on, banjax, do for; Brit. informal scupper. **2** *the delays frustrated him:* **exasperate**, infuriate, annoy, anger, vex, irritate, irk, try someone's patience; disappoint, discontent, dissatisfy, discourage, dishearten, dispirit; informal aggravate, bug, miff, hack off.
– OPPOSITES help, facilitate.

frustrating adjective *it is obviously very frustrating when something like this happens:* **exasperating**, infuriating, annoying, irritating, trying, irksome; disappointing, discouraging, disheartening, dispiriting; informal aggravating.

frustration noun **1** *he clenched his fists in frustration:* **exasperation**, annoyance, anger, vexation, irritation; disappointment, dissatisfaction, discontentment, discontent; informal aggravation. **2** *the frustration of his attempts to introduce changes:* **thwarting**, defeat, prevention, foiling, blocking, spoiling, circumvention, forestalling, disappointment, derailment; obstruction, hampering, hindering; failure, collapse.

fuddled adjective *she forced her weary fuddled brain to work:* **stupefied**, addled, befuddled, confused, muddled, bewildered, dazed, stunned, muzzy, groggy, foggy, fuzzy, vague, disorientated, disoriented, all at sea; informal dopey, woozy, woolly-minded, fazed, not with it; N. Amer. informal discombobulated.

fuddy-duddy noun (informal) *he is a bit younger, and probably thinks I'm an old fuddy-duddy:* **(old) fogey**, conservative, traditionalist, conformist; fossil, dinosaur,

troglodyte; Brit. museum piece; informal stick-in-the-mud, square, stuffed shirt.

fudge verb *the minister tried to fudge the issue:* **evade**, avoid, dodge, skirt, duck, gloss over; hedge, prevaricate, vacillate, be non-committal, stall, beat about the bush, equivocate; Brit. hum and haw; informal cop out, sit on the fence.
noun *the latest proposals are a fudge:* **compromise**, cover-up; spin, casuistry, sophistry; informal cop-out, whitewash.

fuel verb **1** *power stations fuelled by low-grade coal:* **power**, fire, run. **2** *the rumours fuelled anxiety among opposition backbenchers:* **fan**, feed, stoke up, inflame, intensify, stimulate, encourage, provoke, incite, whip up; sustain, keep alive.

fug noun (Brit. informal) *the blue fug of cigarette smoke in the flat:* **haze**; murk, fog, stuffiness, fustiness, frowstiness, staleness.

fugitive noun *the capture of Mafia fugitive Benedetto Santapaola:* **escapee**, runaway, deserter, absconder; refugee.
adjective **1** *the FBI proposed to kidnap the fugitive US financier from the Bahamas:* **runaway**, on the run, escaped, on the loose, at large; wanted; informal AWOL; N. Amer. informal on the lam. **2** *the fugitive nature of life:* **fleeting**, transient, transitory, ephemeral, fading, momentary, short-lived, short, brief, passing, impermanent, {here today, gone tomorrow}; literary evanescent.

fulfil verb **1** *he fulfilled a lifelong ambition to visit Israel:* **achieve**, attain, realize, actualize, make happen, succeed in, bring to completion, bring to fruition, satisfy. **2** *she failed to fulfil her duties:* **carry out**, perform, accomplish, execute, do, discharge, conduct; complete, finish, conclude, perfect. **3** *they fulfilled the criteria:* **meet**, satisfy, comply with, conform to, fill, answer.

fulfilled adjective *he's happier and more fulfilled than I've ever seen him before:* **satisfied**, content, contented, happy, pleased; serene, placid, untroubled, at ease, at peace.
– OPPOSITES discontented.

fulfilling adjective *the way to a prosperous and fulfilling career:* **satisfying**, rewarding, pleasing, gratifying, enjoyable, full, enriching; happy, pleasant, stimulating, interesting.

full adjective **1** *her glass was full:* **filled**, filled up, filled to capacity, filled to the brim, brimming, brimful. **2** *streets full of people:* **crowded**, packed, crammed, congested; teeming, swarming, thick, thronged, overcrowded, overrun; abounding, bursting, overflowing; informal jam-packed, wall-to-wall, stuffed, chock-a-block, chock-full, bursting at the seams, packed to the gunwales, awash. **3** *all the seats were full:* **occupied**, taken, in use, unavailable. **4** *he was too full to manage a dessert:* **replete**, full up, satisfied, well fed, sated,

satiated, surfeited; gorged, glutted; informal stuffed. **5** *she'd had a full life:* **eventful**, interesting, exciting, lively, fulfilled, action-packed, busy, energetic, active. **6** *a full list of available facilities:* **comprehensive**, thorough, exhaustive, all-inclusive, all-encompassing, all-embracing, in depth; complete, entire, whole, unabridged, uncut. **7** *a fire driven at full speed:* **maximum**, top, greatest, highest. **8** *she had a full figure:* **plump**, well rounded, rounded, buxom, shapely, ample, curvaceous, voluptuous, womanly, Junoesque; informal busty, curvy, well upholstered, well endowed; N. Amer. informal zaftig. **9** *the dress had a very full skirt:* **loose-fitting**, loose, baggy, voluminous, roomy, capacious, billowing. **10** *his full baritone voice:* **resonant**, rich, sonorous, deep, vibrant, full-bodied, strong, fruity, clear. **11** *the full flavour of a Bordeaux:* **rich**, intense, full-bodied, strong, deep.
– OPPOSITES empty, hungry, selective, thin.
adverb **1** *she looked full into his face:* **directly**, right, straight, squarely, square, dead, point-blank; informal bang, slap (bang), plumb. **2** *you knew full well I was leaving:* **very**, perfectly, quite; informal darn, damn, damned; Brit. informal jolly, bloody; N. Amer. informal darned.
■ **in full** *my letter was published in full:* in its entirety, in toto, in total, unabridged, uncut.
■ **to the full** *do your best to live life to the full:* fully, thoroughly, completely, to the utmost, to the limit, to the maximum, for all one's worth.

full-blooded adjective *the full-blooded aggression of ice hockey:* **uncompromising**, all-out, out and out, committed, vigorous, strenuous, intense; unrestrained, uncontrolled, unbridled, hard-hitting, pulling no punches, no-holds-barred; informal full-on.
– OPPOSITES half-hearted.

full-blown adjective *this problem could flare up into a full-blown crisis:* **fully developed**, full-scale, full-blooded, fully fledged, out and out, complete, total, thorough, entire; advanced.

full-bodied adjective *a rich, full-bodied claret:* **full-flavoured**, full, flavourful, flavoursome, full of flavour, rich, mellow, fruity, robust, strong, mature.
– OPPOSITES tasteless.

full-grown adjective *she was now a full-grown woman:* **adult**, mature, grown-up, of age; fully grown, fully developed, fully fledged, in one's prime, in full bloom, ripe.
– OPPOSITES infant.

fullness noun **1** *the honesty and fullness of the information they provide:* **comprehensiveness**, completeness, thoroughness, exhaustiveness, all-inclusiveness. **2** *the fullness of her body:* **plumpness**, roundedness, roundness, shapeliness, curvaceousness,

voluptuousness, womanliness; informal curviness. **3** *the recording has a fullness and warmth:* **resonance**, richness, intensity, depth, vibrancy, strength, clarity.
■ **in the fullness of time** in due course, when the time is ripe, eventually, in time, in time to come, one day, some day, sooner or later; ultimately, finally, in the end.

full-scale adjective **1** *a full-scale model:* **full-size**, life-size. **2** *a full-scale public inquiry:* **thorough**, comprehensive, extensive, exhaustive, complete, all-out, all-encompassing, all-inclusive, all-embracing, thoroughgoing, wide-ranging, sweeping, in-depth, far-reaching.
– OPPOSITES small-scale.

fully adverb **1** *I fully agree with him:* **completely**, entirely, wholly, totally, quite, utterly, perfectly, altogether, thoroughly, in all respects, in every respect, without reservation, without exception, to the hilt. **2** *fully two minutes must have passed:* **at least**, no less than, no fewer than, easily, without exaggeration.
– OPPOSITES partly, nearly.

fully fledged adjective *her ambition was to become a fully fledged teacher:* **proper**, real, (fully) trained, (fully) qualified, proficient, experienced; Brit. time-served.
– OPPOSITES novice.

fulminate verb *ministers fulminated against the new curriculum:* **protest**, rail, rage, rant, thunder, storm, declaim, inveigh, speak out, make/take a stand; denounce, decry, condemn, criticize, censure, disparage, attack, execrate, arraign; informal mouth off about, kick up a stink about.

fulmination noun *the fulminations of the media moralists:* **protest**, objection, complaint, rant, tirade, diatribe, harangue, invective, railing, obloquy; denunciation, condemnation, criticism, censure, attack, broadside, brickbats.

fulsome adjective *he paid fulsome tributes to his former secretary:* **excessive**, extravagant, overdone, immoderate, inordinate, over-appreciative, flattering, adulatory, fawning, unctuous, ingratiating, cloying, saccharine; enthusiastic, effusive, rapturous, glowing, gushing, profuse, generous, lavish; informal over the top, OTT, smarmy.

fumble verb **1** *he fumbled for his keys:* **grope**, fish, search, feel, scrabble (around). **2** *he fumbled about in the dark:* **stumble**, blunder, flounder, lumber, stagger, totter, lurch; feel (one's way), grope (one's way). **3** *the keeper fumbled the ball in the second half:* **miss**, drop, mishandle; misfield.
noun *a fumble from the goalkeeper gave Celtic the equalizer:* **slip**, mistake, error, gaffe; informal slip-up, boo-boo; Brit. informal cock-up, boob.

fume noun **1** *a fire giving off toxic fumes:* **smoke**, vapour, gas, effluvium; pollution. **2** *stale wine fumes:* **smell**, odour, stink, reek, stench; Brit. informal pong, niff; Scottish informal

guff; N. Amer. informal funk; literary miasma.
verb *Ella was still fuming at his arrogance:* **be furious**, be enraged, be very angry, seethe, be livid, be incensed, boil, be beside oneself, spit; rage, rant and rave; informal be hot under the collar, foam at the mouth, see red.

fumigate verb *we had to have the house fumigated:* **disinfect**, purify, sterilize, sanitize, decontaminate, cleanse, clean out.
– OPPOSITES soil.

fun noun **1** *I joined in with the fun:* **enjoyment**, entertainment, amusement, pleasure; jollification, merrymaking; recreation, diversion, leisure, relaxation; good time, great time; informal R & R (rest and recreation), living it up, a ball, beer and skittles. **2** *she's young, lively, and full of fun:* **merriment**, cheerfulness, cheeriness, jollity, joviality, jocularity, high spirits, gaiety, mirth, laughter, hilarity, glee, gladness, light-heartedness, levity. **3** *he became a figure of fun in the music press:* **ridicule**, derision, mockery, laughter, scorn, contempt.
– OPPOSITES boredom, misery.
■ **in fun** *some of the girls did go to extremes, but it was really all in fun:* playful, in jest, as a joke, tongue in cheek, light-hearted, for a laugh.
■ **make fun of** *the film does not set out to make fun of the Germans:* mock, poke fun at, ridicule, tease, laugh at, taunt, jeer at, scoff at, deride; parody, lampoon, caricature, satirize; informal take the mickey out of, send up.

function noun **1** *the main function of the machine:* **purpose**, task, use, role. **2** *my function was to select and train the recruits:* **responsibility**, duty, role, concern, province, activity, assignment, obligation, charge; task, job, mission, undertaking, commission; capacity, post, situation, office, occupation, employment, business. **3** *he was obliged to attend political functions:* **social event**, party, occasion, affair, gathering, reception, soirée, jamboree, gala; N. Amer. levee; informal do, bash, shindig; Brit. informal jolly, beanfeast.
verb **1** *the electrical system had ceased to function:* **work**, go, run, be in working/running order, operate, be operative. **2** *the museum functions as an educational and study centre:* **act**, serve, operate; perform, work, play the role of, do duty as.

functional adjective **1** *a small but functional kitchen:* **practical**, useful, utilitarian, utility, workaday, serviceable; minimalist, plain, simple, basic, modest, unadorned, unostentatious, no-frills; impersonal, characterless, soulless, institutional, clinical. **2** *the machine is now fully functional:* **working**, in working order, functioning, in service, in use; going, running, operative, operating; in operation, in commission, in action; informal

up and running.

functionary noun *Flores had been a leading party functionary in the province:* **official**, office-holder, public servant, civil servant, bureaucrat, administrator, apparatchik; Brit. jack-in-office.

fund noun **1** *an emergency fund for refugees:* **collection**, kitty, reserve, pool, purse; endowment, foundation, trust, grant, investment; savings, nest egg; informal stash. **2** *I was very short of funds:* **money**, cash, ready money; wealth, means, assets, resources, savings, capital, reserves, the wherewithal; informal dough, bread, loot, dosh, readies; Brit. informal lolly, spondulicks. **3** *his inexhaustible fund of stories:* **stock**, store, supply, accumulation, collection, bank, pool; mine, reservoir, storehouse, treasury, treasure house, hoard, repository.
verb *the agency was funded by the Treasury:* **finance**, pay for, back, sponsor, subsidize, underwrite, endow, support, maintain; informal foot the bill for, pick up the tab for; N. Amer. informal bankroll, stake.

fundamental adjective *fundamental political assumptions about the rights of the individual:* **basic**, underlying, core, foundational, rudimentary, elemental, elementary, basal, root; primary, prime, cardinal, first, principal, chief, key, central, vital, essential, important, indispensable, necessary, crucial, pivotal, critical; structural, organic, constitutional, inherent, intrinsic.
– OPPOSITES secondary, unimportant.

fundamentally adverb *she was, fundamentally, a good person:* **essentially**, in essence, basically, at heart, at bottom, deep down, au fond; primarily, above all, first and foremost, first of all; informal at the end of the day, when all is said and done, when you get right down to it.

fundamentals plural noun *I learned the fundamentals of financial accounting:* **basics**, essentials, rudiments, foundations, basic principles, first principles, preliminaries; crux, crux of the matter, heart of the matter, essence, core, heart, base, bedrock; informal nuts and bolts, nitty-gritty, brass tacks, ABC.

funeral noun **burial**, interment, entombment, committal, inhumation, laying to rest; cremation; obsequies, last offices.

funereal adjective *the funereal atmosphere of the place depressed him:* **sombre**, gloomy, mournful, melancholy, lugubrious, sepulchral, miserable, doleful, woeful, sad, sorrowful, cheerless, joyless, bleak, dismal, depressing, dreary; grave, solemn, serious; literary dolorous.
– OPPOSITES cheerful.

fungus noun **mushroom**, toadstool; mould, mildew, rust; Biology saprophyte.

funnel noun **1** *fluid was poured through a funnel:* **tube**, pipe, channel, conduit. **2** *smoke*

f

poured from the ship's funnels: **chimney**, flue, vent.
verb the money was funnelled back into Europe: **channel**, feed, direct, convey, move, pass; pour, filter.

funny adjective **1** it is certainly a very funny film: **amusing**, humorous, witty, comic, comical, droll, facetious, jocular, jokey; hilarious, hysterical, riotous, uproarious; entertaining, diverting, sparkling, scintillating; silly, farcical, slapstick; informal side-splitting, rib-tickling, laugh-a-minute, wacky, zany, waggish, off the wall, a scream, rich, priceless; informal, dated killing. **2** a funny coincidence: **strange**, peculiar, odd, queer, weird, bizarre, curious, freakish, freak, quirky; mysterious, mystifying, puzzling, perplexing; unusual, uncommon, anomalous, irregular, abnormal, exceptional, singular, out of the ordinary, extraordinary; Brit. informal, dated rum. **3** there's something funny about him: **suspicious**, odd, strange, peculiar, unsettling; suspect, dubious, untrustworthy, questionable; informal shady, fishy; Brit. informal dodgy.
– OPPOSITES serious, unsurprising, trustworthy.

fur noun **hair**, wool; coat, fleece, pelt; Zoology pelage.

furious adjective **1** he was furious when he learned about it: **enraged**, infuriated, very angry, irate, incensed, raging, incandescent, fuming, ranting, raving, seething, beside oneself, outraged; informal mad, hopping mad, wild, livid, boiling, apoplectic, hot under the collar, on the warpath, foaming at the mouth, steamed up, in a paddy, fit to be tied; literary wrathful. **2** a furious debate about the rights and wrongs of fox hunting: **heated**, hot, passionate, fiery; fierce, vehement, violent, wild, unrestrained, tumultuous, turbulent, tempestuous, stormy.
– OPPOSITES calm.

furnish verb **1** the bedrooms are elegantly furnished: **fit out**, appoint, outfit; Brit. informal do out. **2** grooms furnished us with horses for our journey: **supply**, provide, equip, provision, issue, kit out, present, give, offer, afford, purvey, bestow; informal fix up.

furniture noun **furnishings**, fittings, fitments, movables, appointments, effects; Law chattels; informal stuff, things.

furore noun the letter caused a furore in Britain: **commotion**, uproar, outcry, fuss, upset, brouhaha, palaver, pother, tempest, agitation, pandemonium, disturbance, hubbub, rumpus, tumult, turmoil; stir, excitement; informal song and dance, to-do, hoo-ha, hullabaloo, ballyhoo, kerfuffle, flap, stink; Brit. informal carry-on.

furrow noun **1** the long, neat furrows in a ploughed field: **groove**, trench, rut, trough, channel, hollow. **2** the furrows on either side of her mouth: **wrinkle**, line, crease, crinkle, crow's foot, corrugation.
verb his brow furrowed: **wrinkle**, crease,

line, crinkle, pucker, screw up, scrunch up, corrugate.

furry adjective **covered with fur**, hairy, downy, fleecy, soft, fluffy, fuzzy, woolly.

further adverb further, it gave him an excellent excuse not to attend: **furthermore**, moreover, what's more, also, additionally, in addition, besides, as well, too, to boot, on top of that, over and above that, into the bargain, by the same token; archaic withal.
adjective **1** the further side of the field: **more distant**, more remote, remoter, further away/off, farther (away/off); far, other, opposite. **2** for further information, phone our customer helpline: **additional**, more, extra, supplementary, supplemental, other; new, fresh.
verb an attempt to further his career: **promote**, advance, forward, develop, facilitate, aid, assist, help, help along, lend a hand to, abet; expedite, hasten, speed up, accelerate, step up, spur on, oil the wheels of, give a push to, boost, encourage, cultivate, nurture, foster.
– OPPOSITES impede.

furtherance noun he was acting in the furtherance of his business interests: **promotion**, furthering, advancement, forwarding, development, facilitation, aiding, assisting, helping; hastening, acceleration, boosting, encouragement, cultivation, nurturing, fostering.
– OPPOSITES hindrance.

furthermore adverb This program is simple to use. Furthermore, it can be used as a powerful document transmission system. **moreover**, further, what's more, also, additionally, in addition, besides, as well, too, to boot, on top of that, over and above that, into the bargain, by the same token; archaic withal.

furthest adjective the furthest limits of the universe: **most distant**, most remote, remotest, furthest/farthest away, farthest, furthermost, farthermost; outlying, outer, outermost, extreme, uttermost, ultimate; archaic outmost.
– OPPOSITES nearest.

furtive adjective they cast furtive glances at one another: **secretive**, secret, surreptitious, clandestine, hidden, covert, conspiratorial, cloak-and-dagger, hole-and-corner, backstairs, hugger-mugger; sly, sneaky, under-the-table; sidelong, sideways, oblique, indirect; informal hush-hush, shifty.
– OPPOSITES open.

fury noun **1** she exploded with fury: **rage**, anger, wrath, outrage, spleen, temper; crossness, indignation, umbrage, annoyance, exasperation; literary ire, choler. **2** the fury of the storm finally abated: **fierceness**, ferocity, violence, turbulence, tempestuousness, savagery; severity, intensity, vehemence, force, forcefulness, power, strength.
– OPPOSITES good humour, mildness.

fuse verb 1 *a band which fuses rap with rock:* **combine**, amalgamate, put together, join, unite, marry, blend, merge, meld, mingle, integrate, intermix, intermingle, synthesize; coalesce, compound, alloy; technical admix; literary commingle. **2** *metal fused to a base of coloured glass:* **bond**, stick, bind, weld, solder; melt, smelt. **3** (Brit.) *a light had fused:* **short-circuit**, stop working, trip; informal go, blow.
– OPPOSITES separate.

fusion noun *his novels are a disturbing fusion of metaphysics and politics:* **blend**, blending, combination, amalgamation, joining, union, marrying, bonding, merging, melding, mingling, integration, intermixture, intermingling, synthesis; coalescence.

fuss noun 1 *what's all the fuss about?* **excitement**, agitation, bother, stir, commotion, confusion, disturbance, brouhaha, uproar, furore, palaver, storm in a teacup; informal hoo-ha, to-do, ballyhoo, song and dance, performance, pantomime, kerfuffle; Brit. informal carry-on; N. Amer. informal fuss and feathers. **2** *they settled in with very little fuss:* **bother**, trouble, inconvenience, effort, exertion, labour; informal hassle. **3** *he didn't put up a fuss:* **protest**, complaint, objection, grumble, grouse; informal gripe.
verb *he was still fussing about his clothes:* **worry**, fret, be anxious, be agitated, make a big thing out of; make a mountain out of a molehill; informal flap, be in a tizzy, be in a stew, make a meal of.

fussy adjective 1 *he's very fussy about what he eats:* **finicky**, particular, over-particular, fastidious, discriminating, selective, dainty; hard to please, difficult, exacting, demanding; faddish; informal pernickety, choosy, picky, old womanish; Brit. informal faddy; N. Amer. informal persnickety. **2** *a fussy, frilly bridal gown:* **over-elaborate**, over-decorated, ornate, fancy, overdone; busy, cluttered.

fusty adjective *standing so close, he smelt the old man's fusty clothes:* **stale**, musty, dusty; stuffy, airless, unventilated; damp, mildewed, mildewy; Brit. frowsty.

– OPPOSITES fresh.

futile adjective *I wore my jacket in a futile attempt to keep dry:* **fruitless**, vain, pointless, useless, ineffectual, ineffective, inefficacious, to no effect, of no use, in vain, to no avail, unavailing; unsuccessful, failed, thwarted; unproductive, barren, unprofitable, abortive; impotent, hollow, empty, forlorn, idle, hopeless.
– OPPOSITES useful.

futility noun *he could see the futility of his actions:* **fruitlessness**, pointlessness, uselessness, vanity, ineffectiveness, inefficacy; failure, barrenness, unprofitability; impotence, hollowness, emptiness, forlornness, hopelessness; archaic bootlessness.

future noun 1 *his plans for the future:* **time to come**, time ahead; what lies ahead. **2** *she knew her future lay in acting:* **destiny**, fate, fortune; prospects, expectations, chances.
– OPPOSITES past.
adjective 1 *we arranged for repayment at a future date:* **later**, to come, following, ensuing, succeeding, subsequent, coming. **2** *his future wife:* **to be**, destined; intended, planned, prospective.
■ **in future** *this is certain to become a major issue in future:* from now on, after this, in the future, from this day forward, hence, henceforward, subsequently, in time to come; formal hereafter.

fuzz noun *the soft fuzz on his cheeks:* **hair**, down; fur, fluff, fleeciness.

fuzzy adjective 1 *I stroked the baby's fuzzy head:* **frizzy**, fluffy, woolly; downy, soft; N. Amer. informal nappy. **2** *a fuzzy picture of Mum at Blackpool:* **blurry**, blurred, indistinct, unclear, bleary, misty, distorted, out of focus, unfocused, lacking definition, nebulous; ill-defined, indefinite, vague, hazy, imprecise, inexact, loose, woolly. **3** *my mind was still fuzzy and unfocused:* **confused**, muddled, addled, fuddled, befuddled, groggy, disoriented, disorientated, mixed up, fazed, foggy, dizzy, stupefied, benumbed.

f

Gg

g

gabble verb *he gabbled on in a panicky way:* **jabber**, babble, prattle, rattle, blabber, gibber, blab, drivel, twitter, splutter; Brit. informal waffle, chunter, witter.
noun *the boozy gabble of the crowd:* **jabbering**, babbling, chattering, gibbering, babble, chatter, rambling; Brit. informal waffle, waffling, chuntering, wittering.

gad verb (informal) *she's been gadding about in Italy:* **gallivant**, flit around, run around, travel around, roam (around); Brit. informal swan about.

gadabout noun (informal) *she was an inveterate gadabout:* **pleasure-seeker**; traveller, globetrotter, wanderer, drifter, bird of passage; informal gallivanter.

gadget noun *the kitchen had every kind of modern gadget:* **appliance**, apparatus, instrument, implement, tool, utensil, contrivance, contraption, machine, mechanism, device, labour-saving device, convenience, invention; informal gizmo, gimmick, widget, mod con.

gaffe noun *I made some real gaffes at work:* **blunder**, mistake, error, slip, faux pas, indiscretion, impropriety, miscalculation, gaucherie, solecism; informal slip-up, howler, boo-boo, boner, fluff; Brit. informal boob, bloomer, clanger; N. Amer. informal blooper, goof.

gag verb **1** *a dirty rag was used to gag her mouth:* **stop up**, block, plug, stifle, smother, muffle. **2** *the government tried to gag its critics:* **silence**, muzzle, mute, muffle, suppress, stifle; censor, curb, check, restrain, fetter, shackle, restrict. **3** *the stench made her gag:* **retch**, heave, dry-heave; informal keck.
noun *his scream was muffled by the gag:* **muzzle**, tie, restraint.

gaiety noun **1** *I was struck by her gaiety:* **cheerfulness**, light-heartedness, happiness, merriment, glee, gladness, joy, joie de vivre, joyfulness, joyousness, delight, high spirits, good spirits, good humour, cheeriness, jollity, mirth, joviality, exuberance, elation, liveliness, vivacity, animation, effervescence, sprightliness, zest, zestfulness; informal chirpiness, bounce, pep. **2** *the hotel restaurant was a scene of gaiety:* **merrymaking**, festivity, fun, fun and games, frolics, revelry, jollification, celebration, pleasure; informal partying.
– OPPOSITES misery.

gaily adverb **1** *she skipped gaily along the path:* **merrily**, cheerfully, cheerily, happily, joyfully, joyously, light-heartedly, blithely, jauntily, gleefully. **2** *gaily painted boats:* **brightly**, colourfully, brilliantly. **3** *she plunged gaily into speculation on the stock market:* **heedlessly**, unthinkingly, thoughtlessly, without thinking, carelessly; casually, nonchalantly, airily, breezily, lightly.

gain verb **1** *he gained a scholarship to the college:* **obtain**, get, secure, acquire, come by, procure, attain, achieve, earn, win, capture, clinch, pick up, carry off, reap; informal land, net, bag, scoop, wangle, swing, walk away/off with. **2** *they stood to gain from the deal:* **profit**, make money, reap benefits, benefit, do well out of; informal make a killing, milk. **3** *she had gained weight:* **put on**, increase in. **4** *the others were gaining on us:* **catch up with/on**, catch someone up, catch, close in on, near. **5** *we gained the ridge:* **reach**, arrive at, get to, come to, make, attain, set foot on; informal hit.
– OPPOSITES lose.
noun **1** *his gain from the deal was negligible:* **profit**, advantage, benefit, reward; percentage, takings, yield, return, winnings, receipts, proceeds, dividend, interest; informal pickings, cut, take, rake-off, slice of the cake; Brit. informal whack, bunce. **2** *a price gain of 7.5 per cent:* **increase**, rise, increment, augmentation, addition.
– OPPOSITES loss, decrease.
■ **gain time** play for time, stall, procrastinate, delay, use delaying tactics, temporize, hold back, hang back, hang fire, dally, drag one's feet.

gainful adjective *they see no prospect of finding gainful employment:* **profitable**, paid, well paid, remunerative, lucrative, moneymaking; rewarding, fruitful, worthwhile, useful, productive, constructive, beneficial, advantageous, valuable.

gait noun *he had the gait of a professional soldier:* **walk**, step, stride, pace, tread, way of walking; bearing, carriage; Brit. deportment.

gala noun *the annual summer gala:* **fête**, fair, festival, carnival, pageant, jubilee, jamboree, party, garden party, celebration; festivities.
adjective *a gala occasion:* **festive**, celebratory, merry, joyous, joyful; diverting, entertaining, enjoyable, spectacular.

galaxy noun **1** *a distant galaxy:* **star system**, solar system, constellation; stars, heavens. **2** *a galaxy of the rock world's biggest stars:* **host**, multitude, array, gathering, assemblage, assembly, throng, crowd, company, flock, group.

gale noun **1** *a howling gale:* **strong wind**, high wind, hurricane, tornado, cyclone, whirlwind; storm, squall, tempest, typhoon; N. Amer. windstorm; informal burster, buster. **2** *gales of laughter:* **peal**, howl, hoot, shriek, scream, roar; outburst, burst, fit, paroxysm, explosion.

gall¹ noun **1** *she had the gall to ask for money:* **effrontery**, impudence, impertinence, cheek, cheekiness, insolence, audacity, temerity, presumption, cockiness, nerve, shamelessness, disrespect, bad manners; informal brass neck, face, chutzpah; Brit. informal sauce; N. Amer. informal sass. **2** *scholarly gall was poured on this work:* **bitterness**, resentment, rancour, bile, spleen, malice, spite, spitefulness, malignity, venom, vitriol, poison.

gall² verb *it galled him to have to sit in silence:* **irritate**, annoy, vex, anger, infuriate, exasperate, irk, pique, nettle, put out, displease, antagonize, get on someone's nerves, make someone's hackles rise; Brit. rub up the wrong way; informal aggravate, peeve, miff, rile, needle, get (to), bug, hack off, get up someone's nose, get someone's goat, get/put someone's back up, get someone's dander up, drive mad/crazy, drive round the bend/twist, drive up the wall; Brit. informal wind up, nark, get on someone's wick, give someone the hump; N. Amer. informal tee off, tick off, rankle.

gallant adjective **1** *his gallant countrymen:* **brave**, courageous, valiant, valorous, bold, plucky, daring, fearless, intrepid, heroic, lionhearted, stout-hearted, doughty, mettlesome, death-or-glory, dauntless, undaunted, unflinching, unafraid; informal gutsy, spunky. **2** *her gallant companion:* **chivalrous**, gentlemanly, honourable, courteous, polite, mannerly, attentive, respectful, gracious, considerate, thoughtful.
– OPPOSITES cowardly, discourteous.

gallantry noun **1** *he received medals for gallantry:* **bravery**, courage, courageousness, valour, pluck, pluckiness, nerve, daring, boldness, fearlessness, dauntlessness, intrepidity, heroism, stout-heartedness, mettle, grit; informal guts, spunk; Brit. informal bottle; N. Amer. informal moxie. **2** *she acknowledged his selfless gallantry:* **chivalry**, chivalrousness, gentlemanliness, courtesy, courteousness, politeness, good manners, attentiveness, graciousness, respectfulness, respect, considerateness.

gallery noun **1** *the National Portrait Gallery:* **exhibition**, museum, display, show. **2** *they sat up in the gallery:* **balcony**, circle, upper circle; informal gods. **3** *a long gallery with doors along each side:* **passage**, passageway, corridor, walkway, arcade.

galling adjective *his display of hypocrisy was extremely galling:* **annoying**, irritating, vexing, vexatious, infuriating, maddening, irksome, provoking, exasperating, trying, tiresome, troublesome, bothersome, displeasing, disagreeable; informal aggravating.

gallivant verb *she quit her job to go gallivanting around the world:* **flit**, jaunt, run; roam, wander, travel, rove; informal gad.

gallop verb *Paul galloped across the clearing:* **rush**, race, run, sprint, bolt, dart, dash, career, charge, shoot, hurtle, hare, fly, speed, zoom, streak; informal tear, belt, pelt, scoot, zip, whip, hotfoot it, leg it; Brit. informal bomb, go like the clappers; N. Amer. informal barrel.
– OPPOSITES amble.

gallows plural noun **1** *the wooden gallows:* **gibbet**, scaffold, gallows tree, Tyburn tree. **2** *they were condemned to the gallows:* **hanging**, being hanged, the noose, the rope, the gibbet, the scaffold, execution; informal the drop.

galore adjective *the shop contained fine furniture and paintings galore:* **aplenty**, in abundance, in profusion, in great quantities, in large numbers, by the dozen; to spare; everywhere, all over (the place); informal a gogo, by the truckload; Brit. informal by the shedload.

galvanize verb *the letter managed to galvanize him into action:* **jolt**, shock, startle, impel, stir, spur, prod, urge, motivate, stimulate, electrify, excite, rouse, arouse, awaken; invigorate, fire, animate, vitalize, energize, exhilarate, thrill, dynamize, inspire; N. Amer. light a fire under; informal give someone a shot in the arm.

gambit noun *the most ambitious financial gambit in history:* **stratagem**, scheme, plan, tactic, manoeuvre, move, course/line of action, device; machination, ruse, trick, ploy; Brit. informal wheeze, wangle.

gamble verb **1** *he started to gamble more often:* **bet**, place/lay a bet on something, stake money on something, back the horses, game; informal play the ponies; Brit. informal punt, have a flutter. **2** *investors are gambling that the pound will fall:* **take a chance**, take a risk; N. Amer. take a flier; informal stick one's neck out, go out on a limb; Brit. informal chance one's arm.
noun **1** *his grandfather enjoyed a gamble:* **bet**, wager, speculation; game of chance; Brit. informal flutter, punt. **2** *I took a gamble and it paid off:* **risk**, chance, hazard, leap in the dark; pig in a poke, pot luck.

gambol verb *the foal gambolled beside its mother:* **frolic**, frisk, cavort, caper, skip, dance, romp, prance, leap, hop, jump, spring, bound, bounce; play.

game noun **1** *the children invented a new game:* **pastime**, diversion, entertainment,

amusement, distraction, divertissement, recreation, sport, activity. **2** *the club haven't lost a game all season:* **match**, contest, fixture, tie, tournament; cup tie, final, cup final, play-off. **3** *we were only playing a game on him:* **practical joke**, prank, jest, trick, hoax; informal lark. **4** *he's in the banking game:* **business**, profession, occupation, trade, industry, line, line of work/business; informal racket. **5** *I spoiled his little game:* **scheme**, plot, ploy, stratagem, strategy, gambit, cunning plan, tactics; trick, device, manoeuvre, wile, dodge, ruse, machination, contrivance, subterfuge; informal scam; Brit. informal wheeze. **6** *he hunted game in Africa:* **wild animals**, wild fowl, big game.
adjective **1** *they weren't game enough to join in:* **brave**, courageous, plucky, bold, daring, intrepid, valiant, stout-hearted, mettlesome; fearless, dauntless, undaunted, unflinching; informal gutsy, spunky. **2** *I need a bit of help—are you game?* **willing**, prepared, ready, disposed, of a mind; eager, keen, enthusiastic.
verb *they were drinking and gaming all evening:* **gamble**, bet, place/lay bets.

gamut noun *the complete gamut of human emotion:* **range**, spectrum, span, scope, sweep, compass, area, breadth, reach, extent, catalogue, scale; variety.

gang noun **1** *a gang of teenagers:* **band**, group, crowd, pack, horde, throng, mob, herd, swarm, troop, crew; company, gathering; informal posse, bunch, gaggle, load. **2** (informal) *John was one of our gang:* **circle**, social circle, social set, group, clique, in-crowd, coterie, lot, ring; informal crew. **3** *a gang of workmen:* **crew**, team, group, squad, shift, detachment, unit.
verb *they all ganged up to put me down:* **conspire**, cooperate, work together, act together, combine, join forces, team up, get together, unite, ally.

gangling, gangly adjective *a gangling teenager:* **lanky**, rangy, tall, thin, skinny, spindly, stringy, bony, angular, scrawny, spare; awkward, uncoordinated, ungainly, gawky, inelegant, graceless, ungraceful.
– OPPOSITES squat.

gangster noun *they were held up at gunpoint by gangsters:* **hoodlum**, gang member, racketeer, robber, ruffian, thug, tough, villain, lawbreaker, criminal; gunman, terrorist; Mafioso; informal mobster, crook, hit man; N. Amer. informal hood.

gaol noun (Brit. dated). See JAIL.

gaoler noun (Brit. dated). See JAILER.

gap noun **1** *a gap in the shutters:* **opening**, aperture, space, breach, chink, slit, slot, vent, crack, crevice, cranny, cavity, hole, orifice, interstice, perforation, break, fracture, rift, rent, fissure, cleft, divide. **2** *a gap between meetings:* **pause**, intermission, interval, interlude, break, breathing space, breather, respite, hiatus; N. Amer. recess. **3** *a gap in our records:* **omission**, blank, lacuna, void,

vacuity. **4** *the gap between rich and poor:* **chasm**, gulf, rift, split, separation, breach; contrast, difference, disparity, divergence, imbalance.

gape verb **1** *she gaped at him in astonishment:* **stare**, stare open-mouthed, stare in wonder, goggle, gaze, ogle; informal rubberneck; Brit. informal gawk, gawp. **2** *a leather jerkin which gaped at every seam:* **open wide**, open up, yawn; part, split.

gaping adjective *a gaping hole:* **cavernous**, yawning, wide, broad; vast, huge, enormous, immense, extensive.

garb noun *men and women in riding garb:* **clothes**, clothing, garments, attire, dress, costume, outfit, wear, uniform, livery, regalia; informal gear, get-up, togs, rig-out, duds; Brit. informal clobber.
verb *both men were garbed in black:* **dress**, clothe, attire, fit out, turn out, deck (out), kit out, costume, robe; informal get up.

garbage (N. Amer.) noun **1** *the garbage is taken to landfill sites:* **rubbish**, refuse, waste, detritus, litter, junk, scrap; scraps, scourings, leftovers, remains, slops; N. Amer. trash; Austral./NZ mullock. **2** *most of what he says is garbage:* **rubbish**, nonsense, balderdash, claptrap, twaddle, blather; dross; informal hogwash, baloney, tripe, bilge, bull, bunk, poppycock, rot, bosh, piffle, dreck; Brit. informal tosh, codswallop, cobblers, stuff and nonsense.

garble verb *the message was garbled in transmission:* **mix up**, muddle, jumble, confuse, obscure, distort; misstate, misquote, misreport, misrepresent, mistranslate, misinterpret, misconstrue, twist.

gargantuan adjective *a gargantuan wedding cake:* **huge**, enormous, vast, gigantic, very big, giant, massive, colossal, mammoth, immense, mighty, monumental, mountainous, titanic, towering, tremendous, elephantine, king-size(d), prodigious; informal mega, monster, whopping, humongous, jumbo; Brit. informal whacking, ginormous.
– OPPOSITES tiny.

garish adjective *they wore silly hats in garish colours:* **gaudy**, lurid, loud, over-bright, harsh, glaring, violent, showy, glittering, brassy, brash; tasteless, in bad taste, vulgar, unattractive, bilious; informal flash, flashy, tacky.
– OPPOSITES drab.

garland noun *a garland of flowers:* **festoon**, lei, wreath, ring, circle, swag; coronet, crown, coronal, chaplet, fillet.
verb *gardens garlanded with coloured lights:* **festoon**, wreathe, swathe, hang; adorn, ornament, embellish, decorate, deck, trim, dress, bedeck, array.

garment noun *she wore a shapeless black garment:* **item of clothing**, article of clothing; (**garments**) clothes, clothing, dress, garb, outfit, costume, attire; informal get-up, rig-out, gear, togs, duds; N. Amer. informal threads.

garner verb *Edward garnered ideas from his travels:* **gather**, collect, accumulate, amass, get together, assemble.

garnish verb *garnish the dish with chopped parsley:* **decorate**, adorn, ornament, trim, dress, embellish; enhance, grace, beautify, prettify, add the finishing touch to.
noun *keep a few sprigs for a garnish:* **decoration**, adornment, trim, trimming, ornament, ornamentation, embellishment, enhancement, finishing touch; Cookery chiffonade.

garret noun attic, loft, roof space, cock loft, mansard.

garrison noun **1** *the English garrison had been burned alive:* **troops**, militia, soldiers, forces; armed force, military detachment, unit, platoon, brigade, squadron, battalion, corps. **2** *forces from three garrisons:* **fortress**, fort, fortification, stronghold, citadel, camp, encampment, cantonment, command post, base, station; barracks.
verb **1** *French infantry garrisoned the town:* **defend**, guard, protect, barricade, shield, secure; man, occupy. **2** *troops were garrisoned in various regions:* **station**, post, put on duty, deploy, assign, install; base, site, place, position; billet.

garrulous adjective **1** *a garrulous old man:* **talkative**, loquacious, voluble, verbose, chatty, chattering, gossipy; effusive, expansive, forthcoming, conversational, communicative; informal mouthy, gabby, gassy, windy, having the gift of the gab, having kissed the Blarney Stone; Brit. informal able to talk the hind legs off a donkey. **2** *his garrulous reminiscences:* **long-winded**, wordy, verbose, prolix, long, lengthy, rambling, wandering, maundering, meandering, digressive, diffuse, discursive; gossipy, chatty; informal windy, gassy.
– OPPOSITES taciturn, concise.

gash noun *a gash on his forehead:* **laceration**, cut, wound, injury, slash, tear, incision; slit, split, rip, rent; scratch, scrape, graze, abrasion; Medicine lesion.
verb *he gashed his hand on some broken glass:* **lacerate**, cut (open), wound, injure, hurt, slash, tear, gouge, puncture, slit, split, rend; scratch, scrape, graze, abrade.

gasp verb **1** *I gasped in surprise:* **catch one's breath**, draw in one's breath, gulp; exclaim, cry (out). **2** *he collapsed on the ground, gasping:* **pant**, puff, puff and pant, puff and blow, wheeze, breathe hard, choke, fight for breath.
noun *a gasp of dismay:* **drawing-in of breath**, gulp; exclamation, cry.

gastric adjective *gastric pain:* **stomach**, intestinal, enteric, duodenal, coeliac, abdominal, ventral.

gate noun **1** *heavy wooden gates:* **barrier**, wicket gate, lychgate, five-barred gate, turnstile; Brit. kissing gate. **2** *she went through the gate:* **gateway**, doorway, entrance, exit, egress, opening; door, portal; N. Amer. entryway.

gather verb **1** *we gathered in the hotel lobby:* **congregate**, assemble, meet, collect, come/get together, convene, muster, rally, converge; cluster together, crowd, mass, flock together. **2** *he gathered his family together:* **summon**, call together, bring together, assemble, convene, rally, round up, muster, marshal. **3** *knickknacks she had gathered over the years:* **collect**, accumulate, amass, garner, accrue; store, stockpile, hoard, put by/away, lay by/in; informal stash away, squirrel away. **4** *they gathered corn from the fields:* **harvest**, reap, crop; pick, pluck; collect. **5** *the show soon gathered a fanatical following:* **attract**, draw, pull, pull in, collect, pick up. **6** *I gather he's a keen footballer:* **understand**, be given to understand, believe, be led to believe, think, conclude, deduce, infer, assume, take it, surmise, fancy; hear, hear tell, learn, discover. **7** *he gathered her to his chest:* **clasp**, clutch, pull, embrace, enfold, hold, hug, cuddle, squeeze. **8** *his tunic was gathered at the waist:* **pleat**, shirr, pucker, tuck, fold, ruffle.
– OPPOSITES disperse.

gathering noun *she rose to address the gathering:* **assembly**, meeting, convention, rally, turnout, congress, convocation, conclave, council, synod, forum; congregation, audience, crowd, group, throng, mass, multitude; informal get-together.

gauche adjective *she grew from a gauche teenager into a poised young woman:* **awkward**, gawky, inelegant, graceless, ungraceful, ungainly, maladroit, inept; lacking in social grace(s), unsophisticated, uncultured, uncultivated, unrefined, raw, inexperienced, unworldly.
– OPPOSITES elegant, sophisticated.

gaudy adjective *he wears cheap, gaudy clothes:* **garish**, lurid, loud, over-bright, glaring, harsh, violent, showy, glittering, brassy, ostentatious; tasteless, in bad taste, vulgar, unattractive, bilious; informal flash, flashy, tacky.
– OPPOSITES drab, tasteful.

gauge noun **1** *the temperature gauge:* **measuring device**, measuring instrument, meter, measure; indicator, dial, scale, display. **2** *exports are an important gauge of economic activity:* **measure**, indicator, barometer, point of reference, guide, guideline, touchstone, yardstick, benchmark, criterion, test, litmus test. **3** *guitar strings of a different gauge:* **size**, diameter, thickness, width, breadth; measure, capacity, magnitude; bore, calibre.
verb **1** *astronomers can gauge the star's intrinsic brightness:* **measure**, calculate,

g

compute, work out, determine, ascertain; count, weigh, quantify, put a figure on. **2** *it is difficult to gauge how effective the ban was:* **assess**, evaluate, determine, estimate, form an opinion of, appraise, weigh up, get the measure of, judge, guess; informal guesstimate, size up.

gaunt adjective **1** *a gaunt, greying man:* **haggard**, drawn, thin, lean, skinny, spindly, spare, bony, angular, raw-boned, pinched, hollow-cheeked, scrawny, scraggy, as thin as a rake, cadaverous, skeletal, emaciated, skin-and-bones; wasted, withered; informal like a bag of bones. **2** *the gaunt ruin of Pendragon Castle:* **bleak**, stark, desolate, bare, gloomy, dismal, sombre, grim, stern, harsh, forbidding, uninviting, cheerless.
– OPPOSITES plump.

gauzy adjective *she wore a loose gauzy nightdress:* **translucent**, transparent, sheer, see-through, fine, delicate, flimsy, filmy, gossamer-like, diaphanous, chiffony, wispy, thin, light, insubstantial; Brit. floaty.
– OPPOSITES opaque, thick.

gawky adjective *she had been a thin, gawky adolescent:* **awkward**, ungainly, gangling, gauche, maladroit, clumsy, inelegant, uncoordinated, graceless, ungraceful; unsophisticated, unconfident.
– OPPOSITES graceful.

gay adjective *there is discrimination against gay men and women:* **homosexual**, lesbian; informal queer, camp, pink, swinging the other way, homo, dykey; Brit. informal bent, poofy.
– OPPOSITES heterosexual.
noun *in Denmark gays can marry in church:* **homosexual**, lesbian; informal queer, homo, queen, friend of Dorothy, pansy, nancy, dyke, les, lezzy, butch, femme; Brit. informal poof, ponce, woofter.

gaze verb *he gazed at her:* **stare**, look fixedly, gape, goggle, eye, look, study, scrutinize, take a good look; ogle, leer; informal gawk, rubberneck; Brit. informal gawp; N. Amer. informal eyeball.
noun *his piercing gaze:* **stare**, fixed look, gape, regard, inspection, scrutiny.

gazebo noun **summer house**, pavilion, belvedere; arbour, bower.

gazette noun *she put a notice in the local gazette:* **newspaper**, paper, journal, periodical, organ, news-sheet, newsletter, bulletin; informal rag.

gear noun (informal) **1** *his fishing gear:* **equipment**, apparatus, paraphernalia, articles, appliances, impedimenta; tools, utensils, implements, instruments, gadgets; stuff, things; kit, rig, tackle, odds and ends, bits and pieces, bits and bobs; trappings, appurtenances, accoutrements, regalia; Brit. informal clobber, gubbins, odds and sods. **2** *I'll go back to my hotel and pick up my gear:* **belongings**, possessions, effects, personal effects, property, paraphernalia, odds and ends, bits and pieces, bits and bobs, bags, baggage; Law chattels; informal things, stuff,

kit; Brit. informal clobber. **3** *the best designer gear:* **clothes**, clothing, garments, outfits, attire, garb; dress, wear; informal togs, duds, get-up; Brit. informal clobber, kit; N. Amer. informal threads.

gel, jell verb **1** *leave the mixture to gel:* **set**, stiffen, solidify, thicken, harden; cake, congeal, coagulate, clot. **2** *things started to gel very quickly:* **take shape**, fall into place, come together, take form, work out; crystallize.

gelatinous adjective *the grain is cooked until it becomes gelatinous:* **jelly-like**, glutinous, viscous, viscid, mucilaginous, ropy, sticky, gluey, gummy, slimy; informal gooey, gunky.

geld verb *it is best to geld a colt before it is one year old:* **castrate**, neuter, desex, fix; N. Amer. & Austral. alter; Brit. informal doctor.

gelid adjective *the gelid green spikes of the glacier:* **frozen**, freezing, icy, glacial, frosty, wintry, snowy; arctic, polar, Siberian.

gem noun **1** *rubies and other gems:* **jewel**, precious stone, semi-precious stone, stone; solitaire, brilliant, cabochon. **2** *the gem of the collection:* **best**, finest, pride, prize, treasure, flower, pearl, the jewel in the crown; pick, choice, cream, the crème de la crème, elite, acme; informal one in a million, the bee's knees.

genealogy noun *a lengthy genealogy of the kings of France:* **lineage**, line (of descent), family tree, bloodline; pedigree, ancestry, extraction, heritage, parentage, birth, family, dynasty, house, stock, blood, roots.

general adjective **1** *this is suitable for general use:* **widespread**, common, extensive, universal, wide, popular, public, mainstream; established, conventional, traditional, orthodox, accepted. **2** *a general pay increase:* **comprehensive**, overall, across the board, blanket, umbrella, mass, wholesale, sweeping, broad-ranging, inclusive, company-wide; universal, global, worldwide, nationwide. **3** *general knowledge:* **miscellaneous**, mixed, assorted, diversified, composite, heterogeneous. **4** *the general practice:* **usual**, customary, habitual, traditional, normal, conventional, typical, standard, regular; familiar, accepted, prevailing, routine, run-of-the-mill, established, everyday, ordinary, common. **5** *a general description:* **broad**, imprecise, inexact, rough, loose, approximate, unspecific, vague, woolly, indefinite; N. Amer. informal ballpark.
– OPPOSITES restricted, localized, specialist, exceptional, detailed.

generality noun **1** *the debate has moved on from generalities:* **generalization**, general statement, general principle, sweeping statement; abstraction, extrapolation. **2** *the generality of this principle:* **universality**, comprehensiveness, all-inclusiveness, broadness. **3** *the generality of people are kind:* **majority**, greater part/number,

best/better part; bulk, mass, preponderance, predominance; most.
– OPPOSITES specific, minority.

generally adverb **1** *summers were generally hot:* **normally**, in general, as a rule, by and large, more often than not, almost always, mainly, mostly, for the most part, predominantly, on the whole; usually, habitually, customarily, typically, ordinarily, commonly. **2** *France was moving generally to the left:* **overall**, in general terms, generally speaking, all in all, broadly, on average, basically, effectively. **3** *the method was generally accepted:* **widely**, commonly, extensively, universally, popularly.

generate verb **1** *moves to generate extra business:* **cause**, give rise to, lead to, result in, bring about, create, make, produce, engender, spawn, precipitate, prompt, provoke, trigger, spark off, stir up, induce, promote, foster. **2** *the male most likely to generate offspring:* **procreate**, breed, father, sire, spawn, create, produce, have.

generation noun **1** *people of the same generation:* **age**, age group, peer group. **2** *generations ago:* **ages**, years, aeons, a long time, an eternity; informal donkey's years; Brit. informal yonks. **3** *the next generation of computers:* **crop**, batch, wave, range. **4** *the generation of novel ideas:* **creation**, production, initiation, origination, inception, inspiration. **5** *human generation:* **procreation**, reproduction, breeding, creation.

generic adjective **1** *a generic term for two separate offences:* **general**, common, collective, non-specific, inclusive, all-encompassing, broad, comprehensive, blanket, umbrella. **2** *generic drugs are cheaper than branded ones:* **unbranded**, non-proprietary.
– OPPOSITES specific.

generosity noun **1** *the generosity of our host:* **liberality**, lavishness, magnanimity, munificence, open-handedness, free-handedness, unselfishness; kindness, benevolence, altruism, charity, big-heartedness, goodness. **2** *the generosity of the food portions:* **abundance**, plentifulness, copiousness, lavishness, liberality, largeness.

generous adjective **1** *she is generous with money:* **liberal**, lavish, magnanimous, munificent, giving, open-handed, free-handed, bountiful, unselfish, ungrudging, free, indulgent, prodigal. **2** *it was generous of them to offer:* **magnanimous**, kind, benevolent, altruistic, charitable, noble, big-hearted, honourable, good; unselfish, self-sacrificing. **3** *a generous amount of fabric:* **lavish**, plentiful, copious, ample, liberal, large, great, abundant, profuse, bumper, opulent, prolific; informal a gogo, galore.
– OPPOSITES mean, selfish, meagre.

genesis noun **1** *the hatred had its genesis in something dark:* **origin**, source, root, beginning, start. **2** *the genesis of neurosis:* **formation**, development, evolution, emergence, inception, origination, creation, formulation, propagation.

genial adjective *Fred is genial and well liked:* **friendly**, affable, cordial, amiable, warm, easy-going, approachable, sympathetic; good-natured, good-humoured, cheerful; neighbourly, hospitable, companionable, comradely, sociable, convivial, outgoing, gregarious; informal chummy, pally; Brit. informal matey.
– OPPOSITES unfriendly.

genitals plural noun **private parts**, genitalia, sexual organs, reproductive organs, pudenda; crotch, groin; informal naughty bits, privates; euphemistic nether regions.

genius noun **1** *the world knew of his genius:* **brilliance**, intelligence, intellect, ability, cleverness, brains, erudition, wisdom, fine mind; artistry, flair. **2** *he has a genius for organization:* **talent**, gift, flair, aptitude, facility, knack, bent, ability, expertise, capacity, faculty; strength, forte, brilliance, skill, artistry. **3** *he is a genius:* **brilliant person**, gifted person, mastermind, Einstein, intellectual, great intellect, brain; prodigy; informal egghead, bright spark; Brit. informal brainbox, clever clogs; N. Amer. informal brainiac, rocket scientist.
– OPPOSITES stupidity, dunce.

genocide noun *the killing of native Americans was the biggest genocide in world history:* **mass murder**, mass homicide, massacre; annihilation, extermination, elimination, liquidation, eradication, decimation, butchery, bloodletting; pogrom, ethnic cleansing, holocaust.

genre noun *a whole new genre of novels:* **category**, class, classification, group, set, list; type, sort, kind, variety, style, model, school, stamp, cast, ilk.

genteel adjective *an extremely genteel couple who have fallen on hard times:* **refined**, respectable, decorous, mannerly, well mannered, courteous, polite, proper, correct, seemly; well bred, cultured, sophisticated, ladylike, gentlemanly, dignified, gracious; affected; Brit. informal posh.
– OPPOSITES uncouth.

gentility noun *his grandmother's pretensions to gentility:* **social superiority**, respectability, punctiliousness, decorum, good manners, politeness, civility, courtesy, correctness; refinement, distinction, breeding, sophistication; graciousness, affectation, ostentation.

gentle adjective **1** *his manner was gentle:* **kind**, tender, sympathetic, considerate, understanding, compassionate, benevolent, good-natured; humane, lenient, merciful, clement; mild, placid, serene, sweet-tempered. **2** *a gentle breeze:* **light**, soft. **3** *a*

g

gentle slope: **gradual**, slight, easy.
– OPPOSITES brutal, strong, steep.

gentleman noun **man**; nobleman, honnête homme; informal gent.

gentlemanly adjective *the girls declined his gentlemanly offer to allow them to go first:* **chivalrous**, gallant, honourable, noble, courteous, civil, mannerly, polite, gracious, considerate, thoughtful; well bred, cultivated, cultured, refined, suave, urbane.
– OPPOSITES rude.

gentry noun *though of humble origins, she aspires to the gentry:* **upper classes**, privileged classes, elite, high society, haut monde, smart set; establishment; informal upper crust, top drawer; Brit. informal nobs, toffs.

genuine adjective **1** *a genuine Picasso:* **authentic**, real, actual, original, bona fide, true, veritable; attested, undisputed; informal pukka, the real McCoy, the real thing, kosher; Austral./NZ informal dinkum. **2** *a very genuine person:* **sincere**, honest, truthful, straightforward, direct, frank, candid, open; artless, natural, unaffected; informal straight, upfront, on the level; N. Amer. informal on the up and up.
– OPPOSITES bogus, insincere.

genus noun **1** (Biology) *a large genus of plants:* **subdivision**, division, group, subfamily. **2** *a new genus of music:* **type**, sort, kind, genre, style, variety, category, class; breed, brand, family, stamp, cast, ilk.

germ noun **1** *this detergent kills germs:* **microbe**, micro-organism, bacillus, bacterium, virus; informal bug. **2** *a fertilized germ:* **embryo**, bud; seed, spore, ovule; egg, ovum. **3** *the germ of an idea:* **start**, beginning(s), seed, embryo, bud, root, rudiment; origin, source, potential; core, nucleus, kernel, essence.

germane adjective *those factors are not germane to the present discussion:* **relevant**, pertinent, applicable, apposite, material; apropos, to the point, appropriate, apt, fitting, suitable; connected, related, akin.
– OPPOSITES irrelevant.

germinate verb **1** *the grain is allowed to germinate:* **sprout**, shoot (up), bud; develop, grow, spring up. **2** *the idea began to germinate:* **develop**, take root, grow, emerge, evolve, mature, expand, advance, progress.

gestation noun **1** *a gestation of thirty days:* **pregnancy**, incubation; development, maturation. **2** *the law underwent a period of gestation:* **development**, evolution, formation, emergence, origination.

gesticulate verb *they were gesticulating wildly and pointing at the tyres:* **gesture**, signal, motion, wave, sign.

gesticulation noun **gesturing**, gesture, hand movement, signals, signs; wave, indication; body language.

gesture noun **1** *a gesture of surrender:* **signal**, sign, motion, indication, gesticulation. **2** *a*

symbolic gesture: **action**, act, deed, move.
verb *he gestured to her:* **signal**, motion, gesticulate, wave, indicate, give a sign.

get verb **1** *where did you get that hat?* **acquire**, obtain, come by, receive, gain, earn, win, come into, take possession of, be given; buy, purchase, procure, secure; gather, collect, pick up, hook, net, land; achieve, attain; informal get one's hands on, get one's mitts on, get hold of, grab, bag, score. **2** *I got your letter:* **receive**, be sent, be in receipt of, be given. **3** *your tea's getting cold:* **become**, grow, turn, go. **4** *get the children from school:* **fetch**, collect, go for, call for, pick up, bring, deliver, convey, ferry, transport. **5** *the chairman gets £650,000 a year:* **earn**, be paid, take home, bring in, make, receive, collect, gross; informal pocket, bank, rake in, net, bag. **6** *have the police got their man?* **apprehend**, catch, arrest, capture, seize; take prisoner, take into custody, detain, put in jail, put behind bars, imprison, incarcerate; informal collar, grab, nab, nail, run in, pinch, bust, pick up, pull in, do, feel someone's collar; Brit. informal nick. **7** *I got a taxi:* **travel by/on/in**; take, catch, use. **8** *she got flu:* **succumb to**, develop, go/come down with, sicken for, fall victim to, be struck down with, be afflicted by/with; become infected with, catch, contract, fall ill with, be taken ill with; Brit. go down with; informal take ill with; N. Amer. informal take sick with. **9** *I got a pain in my arm:* **experience**, suffer, be afflicted with, sustain, feel, have. **10** *I got him on the radio:* **contact**, get in touch with, communicate with, make contact with, reach; phone, call, radio; speak to, talk to; Brit. get on to; informal get hold of. **11** *I didn't get what he said:* **hear**, discern, distinguish, make out, perceive, follow, take in. **12** *I don't get the joke:* **understand**, comprehend, grasp, see, fathom, follow, perceive, apprehend, unravel, decipher; informal get the drift of, catch on to, latch on to, figure out; Brit. informal twig, suss. **13** *we got there early:* **arrive**, reach, come, make it, turn up, appear, come on the scene, approach, enter, present oneself, come along, materialize, show one's face; informal show (up), roll in/up, blow in. **14** *we got her to go:* **persuade**, induce, prevail on, influence; wheedle into, talk into, cajole into. **15** *I'd like to get to meet him:* **contrive**, arrange, find a way, manage; succeed in, organize; informal work it, fix it. **16** *I'll get supper:* **prepare**, get ready, cook, make, assemble, muster, concoct; informal fix, rustle up; Brit. informal knock up. **17** (informal) *I'll get him for that:* **take revenge on**, exact/wreak revenge on, get one's revenge on, avenge oneself on, take vengeance on, get even with, pay back, get back at, exact retribution on, give someone their just deserts; Brit. informal get one's own back on. **18** *He scratched his head. 'You've got me there.'* **baffle**, nonplus, perplex, puzzle, bewilder, mystify, bemuse, confuse, confound; informal flummox, faze, stump,

beat, fox; N. Amer. informal discombobulate.
19 *what gets me is how neurotic she is:*
annoy, irritate, exasperate, anger, irk,
vex, provoke, incense, infuriate, madden,
try someone's patience, ruffle someone's
feathers; informal aggravate, peeve, miff,
rile, get to, needle, hack off, get someone's
back up, get on someone's nerves, get up
someone's nose, get someone's goat, drive
mad, make someone see red; Brit. informal wind
up, nark, get on someone's wick; N. Amer.
informal tee off, tick off.
– OPPOSITES give, send, take, leave.
■ **get about** *he has to rely on a wheelchair to
get about:* move about, move around, travel.
■ **get something across** *a photo will help
get the message across:* communicate, get
over, impart, convey, transmit, make clear,
express.
■ **get ahead** *people with ideas and the desire
to get ahead:* prosper, flourish, thrive, do
well; succeed, make it, advance, get on
in the world, go up in the world, make
good, become rich; informal go places, get
somewhere, make the big time.
■ **get along 1** *does he get along with his
family?* be friendly, be compatible, get on;
agree, see eye to eye, concur, be in accord;
informal hit it off, be on the same wavelength.
2 *he was getting along well at school:* fare,
manage, progress, advance, get on, get by,
do, cope; succeed.
■ **get around** *she certainly gets around:*
travel, circulate, socialize, do the rounds.
■ **get at 1** *it's difficult to get at the pipes:*
access, get to, reach, touch. **2** *he had been
got at by enemy agents:* corrupt, suborn,
influence, bribe, buy off, pay off; informal fix,
square; Brit. informal nobble.
■ **get away** *the prisoners get away:* escape,
run away/off, break out, break free, break
loose, bolt, flee, take flight, make off, take
off, decamp, abscond, make a run for it;
slip away, sneak away; informal cut and run,
skedaddle, do a disappearing act, scarper,
leg it; Brit. informal do a bunk, do a runner.
■ **get away with** *it's not our policy to let
kidnappers get away with their crime:* escape
blame for, escape punishment for.
■ **get back** *they should get back at dawn:*
return, come home, come back.
■ **get something back** *she got her gloves
back from the lost property office:* retrieve,
regain, win back, recover, recoup, reclaim,
repossess, recapture, redeem; find (again),
trace.
■ **get back at** *she made the story up to
get back at the teacher for punishing her:*
take revenge on, exact/wreak revenge on,
avenge oneself on, take vengeance on, get
even with, pay back, retaliate on/against,
exact retribution on, give someone their
just deserts; Brit. informal get one's own back
on.
■ **get someone down** *sometimes I can
laugh it off but inside it gets me down:*
depress, sadden, make unhappy, make

gloomy, dispirit, dishearten, demoralize,
discourage, crush, weigh down, oppress;
upset, distress; informal give someone the
blues, make someone fed up.
■ **get by** *he had just enough money to get by:*
manage, cope, survive, exist, subsist, muddle
through/along, scrape by, make ends meet,
make do, keep the wolf from the door; informal
make out.
■ **get off 1** *Sally got off the bus:* alight
(from), step off, dismount (from), descend
(from), disembark (from), leave, exit.
2 (informal) *he was arrested but got off:* escape
punishment, be acquitted, be absolved, be
cleared, be exonerated.
■ **get on** *we got on the train:* board, enter,
step aboard, climb on, mount, ascend, catch;
informal hop on, jump on. **2** *how are you getting
on?* fare, manage, progress, get along, do,
cope, get by, survive, muddle through/along;
succeed, prosper; informal make out. **3** *he got
on with his job:* continue, proceed, go ahead,
carry on, go on, press on, persist, persevere;
keep at; informal stick with/at. **4** *we don't get
on.* See GET ALONG sense 1.
■ **get out 1** *the prisoners got out.* See
GET AWAY. **2** *the news got out:* become known,
become common knowledge, come to light,
emerge, transpire; come out, be uncovered,
be revealed, be divulged, be disclosed, be
reported, be released, leak out.
■ **get out of** *he tried to get out of paying the
survivors any compensation:* evade, dodge,
shirk, avoid, escape, sidestep; informal duck
(out of), wriggle out of, cop out of; Austral./NZ
informal duck-shove.
■ **get over 1** *I have just got over flu:* recover
from, recuperate from, get better after,
shrug off, survive. **2** *we tried to get over this
problem:* overcome, surmount, get the better
of, master, get round, find an/the answer to,
get a grip on, deal with, cope with, sort out,
take care of, crack, rise above; informal lick.
■ **get something over.** See GET SOMETHING
ACROSS.
■ **get round someone** *he got round his
mother and she bought it for him:* cajole,
persuade, wheedle, coax, prevail on, win
over, bring round, sway, beguile, charm,
inveigle, influence, woo; informal sweet-talk,
soft-soap, butter up, twist someone's arm.
■ **get together 1** *get together the best
writers:* collect, gather, assemble, bring
together, rally, muster, marshal, congregate,
convene, amass. **2** *we must get together
soon:* meet (up), rendezvous, see each other,
socialize.
■ **get up** *Rose used to get up very early:* get
out of bed, rise, stir, rouse oneself; informal
surface.

getaway noun *guards spotted the gunman
as he tried to make his getaway:* **escape**,
breakout, bolt for freedom, flight;
disappearance, vanishing act; Brit. informal flit.

get-together noun *we're having a get-
together after work:* **party**, meeting,
gathering, social event; informal do, bash; Brit.

g

informal rave-up, knees-up, jolly, bunfight,
beano.

ghastly adjective **1** *there was a ghastly
stabbing in the town centre:* **terrible**,
frightful, horrible, grim, awful, dire;
frightening, terrifying, horrifying,
alarming; distressing, shocking, appalling,
harrowing; dreadful, horrendous,
monstrous, gruesome, grisly. **2** (informal) *that
ghastly building ought to be pulled down:*
unpleasant, objectionable, disagreeable,
distasteful, awful, terrible, dreadful,
frightful, detestable, insufferable, vile;
informal horrible, horrid. **3** *the patient feels
ghastly:* **ill**, unwell, peaky, poorly; sick,
queasy, nauseous; Brit. off colour; informal
rough, lousy, rotten, terrible, awful,
dreadful; Brit. informal grotty, ropy; Scottish
informal peely-wally; Austral./NZ informal crook.
4 *his face had a ghastly pallor:* **pale**, white,
pallid, pasty, wan, bloodless, peaky, ashen,
grey, waxy, blanched, drained, pinched,
green, sickly; informal like death warmed up.
– OPPOSITES pleasant, charming, healthy,
fine.

ghost noun *his ghost haunts the crypt:*
spectre, phantom, wraith, spirit, presence;
apparition; informal spook.

ghostly adjective *a ghostly figure appeared
at the end of the tunnel:* **spectral**,
ghostlike, phantom, wraithlike, phantasmal,
phantasmic; unearthly, unnatural,
supernatural; insubstantial, shadowy; eerie,
weird, uncanny; frightening, spine-chilling,
hair-raising, blood-curdling, terrifying,
chilling, sinister; informal creepy, scary,
spooky.

ghoulish adjective *the torchlight gave his
face a ghoulish appearance:* **macabre**, grisly,
gruesome, grotesque, ghastly; unhealthy,
horrible, unwholesome.

giant noun *the giant chased Jack down
the beanstalk:* **colossus**, man mountain,
behemoth, Brobdingnagian, mammoth,
monster; informal jumbo.
– OPPOSITES dwarf.
  adjective *a giant vacuum cleaner:* **huge**,
colossal, massive, enormous, gigantic,
very big, mammoth, vast, immense,
monumental, mountainous, titanic,
towering, elephantine, king-size(d),
gargantuan, Brobdingnagian; substantial,
hefty; informal mega, monster, whopping,
humongous, jumbo, hulking, bumper; Brit.
informal ginormous.
– OPPOSITES miniature.

gibber verb *what are you gibbering about?*
prattle, babble, ramble, drivel, jabber,
gabble, burble, twitter, flannel, mutter,
mumble; informal yammer, blabber, jibber-
jabber, blather, blether; Brit. informal witter,
chunter.

gibberish noun *he just stared at her as
if she was talking gibberish:* **nonsense**,
rubbish, balderdash, blather, blether; informal
drivel, gobbledegook, mumbo-jumbo, tripe,

hogwash, baloney, bilge, bosh, bull, bunk,
guff, eyewash, piffle, twaddle, poppycock;
Brit. informal cobblers, codswallop, double
Dutch, tosh, cack; N. Amer. informal garbage,
blathers, applesauce.

gibe noun & verb. See JIBE.

giddiness noun *I nearly fell down with
giddiness:* **dizziness**, light-headedness;
faintness, unsteadiness, shakiness,
wobbliness; informal wooziness, legs like jelly.

giddy adjective **1** *she felt giddy:* **dizzy**, light-
headed, faint, weak, vertiginous; unsteady,
shaky, wobbly, reeling; informal woozy.
2 *she was young and giddy:* **flighty**, silly,
frivolous, skittish, irresponsible, flippant,
whimsical, capricious; feather-brained,
scatty, thoughtless, heedless, carefree;
informal dippy; N. Amer. informal ditsy.
– OPPOSITES steady, sensible.

gift noun **1** *he gave the staff a gift:* **present**,
handout, donation, offering, bestowal,
bonus, award, endowment; tip, gratuity,
baksheesh; largesse; informal prezzie, freebie,
perk. **2** *he had a unique gift for melody:*
talent, flair, aptitude, facility, knack, bent,
ability, expertise, capacity, capability,
faculty; endowment, strength, genius,
brilliance, skill, artistry.
  verb *he gifted a composition to the orchestra:*
present, give, bestow, confer, donate,
endow, award, accord, grant; hand over,
make over.

gifted adjective *she was already a gifted artist:*
talented, skilful, skilled, accomplished,
expert, consummate, master(ly), first-rate,
able, apt, adept, proficient; intelligent,
clever, bright, brilliant; precocious; informal
crack, top-notch, ace.
– OPPOSITES inept.

gigantic adjective *the college is a gigantic
Victorian building:* **huge**, enormous,
vast, extensive, very big, very large,
giant, massive, colossal, mammoth,
immense, monumental, mountainous,
titanic, towering, elephantine, king-
size(d), gargantuan; informal mega, monster,
whopping, humongous, jumbo, hulking,
bumper; Brit. informal ginormous.
– OPPOSITES tiny.

giggle verb *he giggled at the picture:* **titter**,
snigger, snicker, tee-hee, chuckle, chortle,
laugh.
  noun *she suppressed a giggle:* **titter**, snigger,
snicker, tee-hee, chuckle, chortle, laugh.

gigolo noun *she frivolously whittled away
the family money on a succession of gigolos:*
playboy, (male) escort; admirer, lover;
informal fancy man; Brit. informal toy boy.

gild verb **1** *a gilded weathercock:* **cover with
gold**, paint gold. **2** *he tends to gild the
truth:* **elaborate**, embellish, embroider;
camouflage, disguise, dress up, colour,
exaggerate, expand on; informal jazz up.

gimcrack adjective *they lived in gimcrack
villas you'd be afraid to sneeze in:* **shoddy**,

jerry-built, flimsy, insubstantial, thrown together, makeshift; inferior, poor-quality, second-rate, cheap, cheapjack, tawdry, kitschy, trashy; informal tacky, junky, rubbishy.

gimmick noun *a quality newspaper shouldn't have to resort to gimmicks like bingo:* **publicity device**, stunt, contrivance, scheme, stratagem, ploy; informal shtick.

gingerly adverb *he stepped gingerly onto the ice:* **cautiously**, carefully, with care, warily, charily, circumspectly, delicately; heedfully, watchfully, vigilantly, attentively; hesitantly, timidly.
– OPPOSITES recklessly.

girdle noun **1** *a diamond-studded girdle:* **belt**, sash, cummerbund, waistband, strap, band, girth, cord. **2** *her stockings were held up by her girdle:* **corset**, corselet, foundation garment, panty girdle; truss.
verb *a garden girdled the house:* **surround**, enclose, encircle, circle, encompass, circumscribe, border, bound, skirt, edge.

girl noun **1** *a five-year-old girl:* **female child**, daughter; schoolgirl; Scottish & N. English lass, lassie; derogatory chit. See also **CHILD**. **2** *a tall dark girl:* **young woman**, young lady, miss, mademoiselle; Scottish lass, lassie; Irish colleen; informal chick, girlie, filly; Brit. informal bird, bint; N. Amer. informal gal, broad, dame, jane, babe; Austral./NZ informal sheila.

girlfriend noun *Richard's split up with his girlfriend:* **sweetheart**, lover, partner, significant other, girl, woman; fiancée; informal steady; Brit. informal bird; N. Amer. informal squeeze.

girlish adjective *her girlish giggles:* **girlie**, youthful, childlike, childish, immature; feminine.

girth noun **1** *a tree ten feet in girth:* **circumference**, perimeter; width, breadth. **2** *he tied the towel around his girth:* **stomach**, midriff, middle, abdomen, belly, gut; informal tummy, tum.

gist noun *the gist of his speech:* **essence**, substance, central theme, heart of the matter, nub, kernel, marrow, meat, burden, crux; thrust, drift, sense, meaning, significance, import; informal nitty-gritty.

give verb **1** *he gave them £2000:* **present with**, provide with, supply with, furnish with, let someone have; hand (over), offer, proffer, award, grant, bestow, accord, confer, make over; donate, contribute, put up. **2** *can I give him a message?* **convey**, pass on, impart, communicate, transmit, send, deliver, relay; tell. **3** *a baby given into their care:* **entrust**, commit, consign, assign. **4** *he gave his life for them:* **sacrifice**, give up, relinquish; devote, dedicate. **5** *he gave her time to think:* **allow**, permit, grant, accord; offer. **6** *he gave a party:* **organize**, arrange, lay on, throw, host, hold, have, provide. **7** *Dominic gave a bow:* **perform**, execute, make, do. **8** *she gave a shout:* **utter**, let out, emit, produce,

make. **9** *he gave Harry a beating:* **administer**, deliver, deal, inflict, impose. **10** *the door gave:* **give way**, cave in, collapse, break, fall apart; bend, buckle.
– OPPOSITES receive, take.
noun (informal) *there isn't enough give in the jacket:* **elasticity**, flexibility, stretch, stretchiness; slack, play.
■ **give someone away** *Luke would never forgive her if she gave him away:* betray, inform on; informal split on, rat on, peach on, do the dirty on, blow the whistle on, sell down the river; Brit. informal grass on, shop; N. Amer. informal rat out, finger; Austral./NZ informal dob on.
■ **give something away** *his face gave little away:* reveal, disclose, divulge, let slip, leak, let out.
■ **give in** *in the end, he was forced to give in:* capitulate, concede defeat, admit defeat, give up, surrender, yield, submit, back down, give way, defer, relent, throw in the towel/sponge.
■ **give something off/out** *a small fire burned, giving off more smoke than heat:* emit, produce, send out, throw out; discharge, release, exude, vent.
■ **give out** *his strength was giving out:* run out, be used up, be consumed, be exhausted, be depleted; fail, flag; dry up.
■ **give something out** *thousands of leaflets were given out:* distribute, issue, hand out, pass round, dispense; dole out, dish out, mete out; allocate, allot, share out.
■ **give up.** See **GIVE IN**.
■ **give something up** *I'm determined to give up smoking:* stop, cease, discontinue, desist from, abstain from, cut out, renounce, forgo; resign from, stand down from; informal quit, kick, swear off, leave off, pack in, lay off; Brit. informal jack in.

give and take noun *there has to be some give and take on both sides:* **compromise**, concession; cooperation, reciprocity, teamwork, interplay.

given adjective **1** *a given number of years:* **specified**, stated, designated, set, particular, specific; prescribed, agreed, appointed, pre-arranged, predetermined. **2** *she was given to fits of temper:* **prone**, liable, inclined, disposed, predisposed, apt, likely.
– OPPOSITES unspecified.
preposition *given the issue's complexity, a summary is difficult:* **considering**, in view of, bearing in mind, in the light of; assuming.
noun *his aggression is taken as a given:* **established fact**, reality, certainty.

giver noun **donor**, contributor, donator, benefactor, benefactress, provider; supporter, backer, patron, sponsor, subscriber.

glacial adjective **1** *glacial conditions:* **freezing**, cold, icy, ice-cold, sub-zero, frozen, gelid, wintry; arctic, polar, Siberian; bitter, biting, raw, chill. **2** *Polly's tone was glacial:*

g

unfriendly, hostile, unwelcoming; frosty, icy, cold, chilly.
– OPPOSITES tropical, hot, friendly.

glad adjective **1** *I'm really glad you're coming:* **pleased**, happy, delighted, thrilled, overjoyed, cock-a-hoop, elated, gleeful; gratified, grateful, thankful; informal tickled pink, over the moon; Brit. informal chuffed; N. English informal made up; Austral. informal wrapped. **2** *I'd be glad to help:* **willing**, eager, happy, pleased, delighted; ready, prepared. **3** *glad tidings:* **pleasing**, welcome, happy, joyful, cheering, heartening, gratifying.
– OPPOSITES dismayed, reluctant, distressing.

gladden verb *it gladdened him to see her again:* **delight**, please, make happy, elate; cheer (up), hearten, buoy up, give someone a lift, uplift; gratify; informal give someone a kick, tickle someone pink, buck up.
– OPPOSITES sadden.

gladly adverb *I would gladly have given him the money:* **with pleasure**, happily, cheerfully; willingly, readily, eagerly, freely, ungrudgingly.

glamorous adjective **1** *a glamorous woman:* **beautiful**, attractive, lovely, bewitching, enchanting, beguiling; elegant, chic, stylish, fashionable; charming, charismatic, appealing, alluring, seductive; informal classy, glam. **2** *a glamorous lifestyle:* **exciting**, thrilling, stimulating; dazzling, glittering, glossy, colourful, exotic; informal ritzy, glitzy, jet-setting.
– OPPOSITES dowdy, dull.

glamour noun **1** *she had undeniable glamour:* **beauty**, allure, attractiveness; elegance, chic, style; charisma, charm, magnetism, desirability. **2** *the glamour of show business:* **allure**, attraction, fascination, charm, magic, romance, mystique, exoticism, spell; excitement, thrill; glitter, the bright lights; informal glitz, glam.

glance verb **1** *Rachel glanced at him:* **look briefly**, look quickly, peek, peep; glimpse; Scottish keek; informal have a gander; Brit. informal take a dekko, have a shufti, have a butcher's; Austral./NZ informal squiz. **2** *I glanced through the report:* **read quickly**, scan, skim, leaf, flick, flip, thumb, browse; dip into. **3** *a bullet glanced off the ice:* **ricochet**, rebound, be deflected, bounce; graze, clip. **4** *sunlight glanced off her hair:* **reflect**, flash, gleam, glint, glitter, glisten, glimmer, shimmer.
noun *a glance at his watch:* **peek**, peep, brief look, quick look, glimpse; Scottish keek; informal gander; Brit. informal dekko, shufti, butcher's; Austral./NZ informal squiz, geek.
■ **at first glance** on the face of it, on the surface, at first sight, to the casual eye, to all appearances; apparently, seemingly, outwardly, superficially, it would seem, it appears, as far as one can see/tell; by all accounts.

glare verb *she glared at him:* **scowl**, glower, stare angrily, look daggers, frown, lour, give someone a black look, look threateningly;

informal give someone a dirty look.
noun **1** *a cold glare:* **scowl**, glower, angry stare, frown, black look, threatening look; informal dirty look. **2** *the harsh glare of the lights:* **blaze**, dazzle, shine, beam; radiance, brilliance, luminescence.

glaring adjective **1** *glaring lights:* **dazzling**, blinding, blazing, strong, bright, harsh. **2** *a glaring omission:* **obvious**, conspicuous, unmistakable, inescapable, unmissable, striking; flagrant, blatant, outrageous, gross; overt, patent, transparent, manifest; informal standing/sticking out like a sore thumb.
– OPPOSITES soft, minor.

glass noun **1** *a glass of water:* **tumbler**, drinking vessel; flute, schooner, balloon, goblet, chalice. **2** *we sell china and glass:* **glassware**, crystal, crystalware.

glasses plural noun **spectacles**; N. Amer. eyeglasses; informal specs.

glasshouse noun **greenhouse**, hothouse, conservatory.

glassy adjective **1** *the glassy surface of the lake:* **smooth**, mirror-like, gleaming, shiny, glossy, polished, vitreous; slippery, icy; clear, transparent, translucent; calm, still, flat. **2** *a glassy stare:* **expressionless**, glazed, blank, vacant, fixed, motionless; emotionless, impassive, lifeless, wooden, vacuous.
– OPPOSITES rough, expressive.

glaze verb **1** *the pots are glazed when dry:* **varnish**, enamel, lacquer, japan, shellac, paint; gloss. **2** *pastry glazed with caramel:* **cover**, coat; ice, frost. **3** *his eyes glazed over:* **become glassy**, go blank; mist over, film over.
noun **1** *pottery with a blue glaze:* **varnish**, enamel, lacquer, finish, coating; lustre, shine, gloss. **2** *a cake with an apricot glaze:* **coating**, topping; icing, frosting.

gleam verb *her eyes gleamed with satisfaction:* **shine**, glimmer, glint, glitter, shimmer, sparkle, twinkle, flicker, wink, glisten, flash.
noun **1** *a gleam of light:* **glimmer**, glint, shimmer, twinkle, sparkle, flicker, flash; beam, ray, shaft. **2** *the gleam of brass:* **shine**, lustre, gloss, sheen; glint, glitter, glimmer, sparkle; brilliance, radiance, glow. **3** *a gleam of hope:* **glimmer**, flicker, ray, spark, trace, suggestion, hint, sign.

glean verb *the information is gleaned from press cuttings:* **obtain**, get, take, draw, derive, extract, cull, garner, gather; learn, find out.

glee noun *Agnes clapped her hands with glee:* **delight**, pleasure, happiness, joy, gladness, elation, euphoria; amusement, mirth, merriment; excitement, gaiety, exuberance; triumph, jubilation, relish, satisfaction, gratification.
– OPPOSITES disappointment.

gleeful adjective *a gleeful chuckle:* **delighted**, pleased, joyful, happy, glad, overjoyed, elated, euphoric; amused, mirthful, merry, exuberant; cock-a-hoop, jubilant; informal over the moon.

glib adjective *the glib phrases rolled off his tongue:* **slick**, pat, plausible; smooth-talking, fast-talking, silver-tongued, smooth, urbane, having kissed the Blarney Stone; disingenuous, insincere, facile, shallow, superficial, flippant; informal flip, sweet-talking.
– OPPOSITES sincere.

glide verb 1 *a gondola glided past:* **slide**, slip, sail, float, drift, flow; coast, freewheel, roll; skim, skate. 2 *seagulls gliding over the waves:* **soar**, wheel, plane; fly. 3 *he glided out of the door:* **slip**, steal, slink.

glimmer verb *moonlight glimmered on the lawn:* **gleam**, shine, glint, flicker, shimmer, glisten, glow, twinkle, sparkle, glitter, wink, flash.
noun 1 *a glimmer of light:* **gleam**, glint, flicker, shimmer, glow, twinkle, sparkle, flash, ray. 2 *a glimmer of hope:* **gleam**, flicker, ray, trace, sign, suggestion, hint.

glimpse noun *a glimpse of her face:* **brief look**, quick look; glance, peek, peep; sight, sighting.
verb *he glimpsed a figure:* **catch sight of**, notice, discern, spot, spy, sight, pick out, make out; Brit. informal clock.

glint verb *the diamond glinted:* **shine**, gleam, catch the light, glitter, sparkle, twinkle, wink, glimmer, shimmer, glisten, flash.
noun *the glint of the silver:* **glitter**, gleam, sparkle, twinkle, glimmer, flash.

glisten verb *the sea glistened in the early morning light:* **shine**, sparkle, twinkle, glint, glitter, glimmer, shimmer, wink, flash.

glitter verb *crystal glittered in the candlelight:* **shine**, sparkle, twinkle, glint, gleam, shimmer, glimmer, wink, flash, catch the light.
noun 1 *the glitter of light on the water:* **sparkle**, twinkle, glint, gleam, shimmer, glimmer, flicker, flash; brilliance, luminescence. 2 *the glitter of show business:* **glamour**, excitement, thrills, attraction, appeal; dazzle; informal razzle-dazzle, razzmatazz, glitz, ritziness.

gloat verb *she gloated over his recent humiliation:* **delight**, relish, take great pleasure, revel, rejoice, glory, exult, triumph, crow; boast, brag, be smug, congratulate oneself, preen oneself, pat oneself on the back; rub one's hands together; informal rub it in.

global adjective 1 *the global economy:* **worldwide**, international, world, intercontinental. 2 *a global view of the problem:* **comprehensive**, overall, general, all-inclusive, all-encompassing, encyclopedic, universal, blanket; broad, far-reaching, extensive, sweeping.

globe noun 1 *every corner of the globe:* **world**, earth, planet. 2 *the sun is a globe:* **sphere**,

orb, ball, spheroid, round.

globular adjective *the plant's globular pinkish-green blooms:* **spherical**, spheric, spheroidal, round, globe-shaped, ball-shaped, orb-shaped, rounded, bulbous.

globule noun *globules of sweat:* **droplet**, drop, bead, tear, ball, bubble, pearl; informal blob, glob.

gloom noun 1 *she peered into the gloom:* **darkness**, dark, dimness, blackness, murkiness, shadows, shade; dusk, twilight, gloaming. 2 *his gloom deepened:* **despondency**, depression, dejection, downheartedness, melancholy, melancholia, unhappiness, sadness, glumness, gloominess, misery, sorrow, woe, wretchedness; despair, pessimism, hopelessness; informal the blues, the dumps.
– OPPOSITES light, happiness.

gloomy adjective 1 *a gloomy room:* **dark**, shadowy, sunless, dim, sombre, dingy, dismal, dreary, murky, unwelcoming, cheerless, comfortless, funereal. 2 *Joanna looked gloomy:* **despondent**, downcast, downhearted, dejected, dispirited, disheartened, discouraged, demoralized, crestfallen; depressed, desolate, low, sad, unhappy, glum, melancholy, miserable, fed up, woebegone, mournful, forlorn, morose, Eeyorish; informal blue, down in the mouth, down in the dumps. 3 *gloomy forecasts about the economy:* **pessimistic**, depressing, downbeat, disheartening, disappointing; unfavourable, bleak, bad, black, sombre, grim, cheerless, hopeless.
– OPPOSITES bright, cheerful, optimistic.

glorify verb 1 *they gather to glorify God:* **praise**, extol, exalt, worship, revere, reverence, venerate, pay homage to, honour, adore, thank, give thanks to. 2 *a poem to glorify the memory of the dead:* **ennoble**, exalt, elevate, dignify, enhance, augment, promote; praise, celebrate, honour, extol, lionize, acclaim, applaud, hail; glamorize, idealize, romanticize, enshrine, immortalize.
– OPPOSITES dishonour.

glorious adjective 1 *a glorious victory:* **illustrious**, celebrated, famous, acclaimed, distinguished, honoured; outstanding, great, magnificent, noble, triumphant. 2 *there are glorious views across the valley:* **wonderful**, marvellous, magnificent, superb, sublime, spectacular, lovely, fine, delightful; informal super, great, stunning, fantastic, terrific, tremendous, sensational, heavenly, divine, gorgeous, fabulous, fab, awesome, ace; Brit. informal smashing.
– OPPOSITES undistinguished, horrid.

glory noun 1 *a sport that won him glory:* **renown**, fame, prestige, honour, distinction, kudos, eminence, acclaim, praise; celebrity, recognition, reputation; informal bouquets. 2 *glory be to God:* **praise**, worship, adoration, veneration, honour, reverence, exaltation, extolment, homage, thanksgiving, thanks.

g

3 *a house restored to its former glory:*
magnificence, splendour, resplendence,
grandeur, majesty, greatness, nobility;
opulence, beauty, elegance. **4** *the glories of
Vermont:* **wonder**, beauty, delight, marvel,
phenomenon; sight, spectacle.
– OPPOSITES shame, obscurity, modesty.
verb *we gloried in our independence:* **take
pleasure in**, revel in, rejoice in, delight in;
relish, savour; congratulate oneself on, be
proud of; boast about; informal get a kick out
of, get a thrill out of.

gloss¹ noun **1** *the gloss of her hair:* **shine**,
sheen, lustre, gleam, patina, brilliance,
shimmer. **2** *beneath the gloss of success:*
facade, veneer, surface, show, camouflage,
disguise, mask, smokescreen; window
dressing.
verb **1** *she glossed her lips:* **make glossy**,
shine; glaze, polish, burnish. **2** *he tried to
gloss over his problems:* **conceal**, cover up,
hide, disguise, mask, veil; shrug off, brush
aside, play down, minimize, understate,
make light of; informal brush under the carpet.

gloss² noun *specialized terms have glosses in
the margin:* **explanation**, interpretation,
exegesis, explication, elucidation;
annotation, note, footnote, commentary,
comment; translation.
verb *difficult words are glossed in a footnote:*
explain, interpret, explicate, elucidate;
annotate; translate, paraphrase.

glossy adjective **1** *a glossy wooden floor:*
shiny, gleaming, lustrous, brilliant,
shimmering, glistening, satiny, sheeny,
smooth, glassy; polished, lacquered, glazed.
2 *a glossy magazine:* **expensive**, high-quality,
stylish, fashionable, glamorous; attractive,
artistic; Brit. upmarket, coffee-table; informal
classy, ritzy, glitzy.
– OPPOSITES dull, cheap.

glove noun **mitten**, mitt, gauntlet.

glow verb **1** *lights glowed from the windows:*
shine, radiate, gleam, glimmer, flicker, flare;
luminesce. **2** *a fire glowed in the hearth:*
radiate heat, smoulder, burn. **3** *she glowed
with embarrassment:* **flush**, blush, redden,
colour (up), go pink, go scarlet; burn. **4** *she
glowed with pride:* **tingle**, thrill; beam.
noun **1** *the glow of the fire:* **radiance**, light,
shine, gleam, glimmer, incandescence,
luminescence; warmth, heat. **2** *a glow
spread over her face:* **flush**, blush, rosiness,
pinkness, redness, high colour; bloom,
radiance. **3** *a warm glow deep inside
her:* **happiness**, contentment, pleasure,
satisfaction.
– OPPOSITES pallor.

glower verb *she glowered at him:* **scowl**,
glare, look daggers, frown, lour, give
someone a black look; informal give someone
a dirty look.
noun *the glower on his face:* **scowl**, glare,
frown, black look; informal dirty look.

glowing adjective **1** *glowing coals in the
grate:* **bright**, shining, radiant, glimmering,

flickering, twinkling, incandescent,
luminous, luminescent; lit (up), lighted,
illuminated, ablaze; aglow, smouldering.
2 *his glowing cheeks:* **rosy**, pink, red, flushed,
blushing; radiant, blooming, ruddy, florid;
hot, burning. **3** *glowing colours:* **vivid**,
vibrant, bright, brilliant, rich, intense,
strong, radiant, warm. **4** *his work received a
glowing report:* **complimentary**, favourable,
enthusiastic, commendatory, admiring,
lionizing, rapturous, rhapsodic, adulatory;
fulsome; informal rave.

glue noun *a tube of glue:* **adhesive**, fixative,
gum, paste, cement; epoxy (resin), size;
N. Amer. mucilage; N. Amer. informal stickum.
verb **1** *the planks were glued together:* **stick**,
gum, paste; affix, fix, cement. **2** (informal)
she was glued to the television: **be riveted
to**, be gripped by, be hypnotized by, be
mesmerized by.

glum adjective *Kenneth looked glum and
resentful:* **gloomy**, downcast, downhearted,
dejected, despondent, crestfallen,
disheartened; depressed, desolate, unhappy,
doleful, melancholy, miserable, woebegone,
mournful, forlorn, fed up, in the doldrums,
morose; informal blue, down in the mouth,
down in the dumps.
– OPPOSITES cheerful.

glut noun *a glut of cars:* **surplus**, excess,
surfeit, superfluity, overabundance,
superabundance, oversupply, plethora.
– OPPOSITES dearth.
verb *the factories are glutted:* **cram full**,
overfill, overload, oversupply, saturate,
flood, inundate, deluge, swamp; informal stuff.

glutinous adjective *a glutinous liquid:* **sticky**,
viscous, viscid, tacky, gluey, gummy, treacly;
adhesive; informal gooey, gloopy, cloggy; N.
Amer. informal gloppy.

glutton noun **gourmand**, overeater, big
eater, gorger, gobbler; informal (greedy) pig,
gannet, greedy guts, gutbucket, guzzler.

gluttonous adjective *a gluttonous appetite:*
greedy, gourmandizing, voracious,
insatiable, wolfish; informal piggish, piggy.

gluttony noun **greed**, greediness,
overeating, gourmandism, gourmandizing,
voracity, insatiability; informal piggishness.

gnarled adjective **1** *a gnarled tree trunk:*
knobbly, knotty, knotted, gnarly, lumpy,
bumpy, nodular; twisted, bent, crooked,
distorted, contorted. **2** *gnarled hands:*
twisted, bent, misshapen; arthritic; rough,
wrinkled, wizened.

gnash verb *she wailed and gnashed her teeth:*
grind, grate, rasp, grit.

gnaw verb **1** *the dog gnawed at a bone:* **chew**,
champ, chomp, bite, munch, crunch; nibble,
worry. **2** *the pressures are gnawing away
their independence:* **erode**, wear away, wear
down, eat away (at); consume, devour. **3** *the
doubts gnawed at her:* **nag**, plague, torment,
torture, trouble, distress, worry, haunt,

oppress, burden, hang over, bother, fret; niggle.

go verb **1** *he's gone into town:* **move**, proceed, make one's way, advance, progress, pass; walk, travel, journey. **2** *the road goes to London:* **extend**, stretch, reach; lead. **3** *it's time to go:* **leave**, depart, take oneself off, go away, withdraw, absent oneself, make an exit, exit; set off, start out, get under way, be on one's way; decamp, retreat, retire, make off, clear out, run off/away, flee; Brit. make a move; informal make tracks, push off, beat it, take off, skedaddle, scram, split, scoot; Brit. informal sling one's hook. **4** *three years went past:* **pass**, elapse, slip by/past, roll by/past, tick away; fly by/past. **5** *a golden age that has gone for good:* **disappear**, vanish, be no more, be over, run its course, fade away; finish, end, cease. **6** *all our money had gone:* **be used up**, be spent, be exhausted, be consumed, be drained, be depleted. **7** *I'd like to see my grandchildren before I go:* **die**, pass away, pass on, lose one's life, expire, breathe one's last, perish, go to meet one's maker; informal give up the ghost, kick the bucket, croak, buy it, turn up one's toes; Brit. informal snuff it, pop one's clogs; N. Amer. informal bite the big one, buy the farm. **8** *the bridge went suddenly:* **collapse**, give way, fall down, cave in, crumble, disintegrate. **9** *his hair had gone grey:* **become**, get, turn, grow. **10** *everything went well:* **turn out**, work out, develop, come out; result, end (up); informal pan out. **11** *those colours don't go:* **match**, be harmonious, harmonize, blend, be suited, be complementary, coordinate, be compatible. **12** *my car won't go:* **function**, work, run, operate.
– OPPOSITES arrive, come, return, clash.
noun **1** *his second go:* **attempt**, try, effort, bid, endeavour; informal shot, stab, crack, bash, whirl, whack. **2** *he has plenty of go in him:* **energy**, vigour, vitality, life, liveliness, spirit, verve, enthusiasm, zest, vibrancy, sparkle; stamina, dynamism, drive, push, determination; informal pep, punch, oomph, get-up-and-go.
■ **go about** *Ruth went about her tasks enthusiastically:* set about, begin, embark on, start, commence, address oneself to, get down to, get to work on, get going on, undertake; approach, tackle, attack; informal get cracking on/with.
■ **go along with** *he seemed happy enough to go along with your plans:* agree to/with, fall in with, comply with, cooperate with, acquiesce in, assent to, follow; submit to, yield to, defer to.
■ **go away**. See **go** verb sense 3.
■ **go back on** *she went back on her promise:* renege on, break, fail to honour, default on, repudiate, retract; do an about-face; informal cop out (of), rat on.
■ **go by** *we have to go by his decision:* obey, abide by, comply with, keep to, conform to, follow, heed, defer to, respect.
■ **go down 1** *the ship went down:* sink,

founder, go under. **2** *interest rates are going down:* decrease, get lower, fall, drop, decline; plummet, plunge, slump. **3** *his name will go down in history:* be remembered, be recorded, be commemorated, be immortalized.
■ **go down with** (Brit.) *she's gone down with flu:* fall ill with, get, develop, contract, pick up, succumb to, fall victim to, be struck down with, become infected with.
■ **go far** be successful, succeed, be a success, do well, get on, get somewhere, get ahead, make good; informal make a name for oneself, make one's mark.
■ **go for 1** *I went for the tuna:* choose, pick, opt for, select, plump for, decide on. **2** *the man went for her:* attack, assault, hit, strike, beat up, assail, set upon, rush at, lash out at; informal lay into, rough up; Brit. informal have a go at, duff up; N. Amer. informal beat up on. **3** *he goes for older women:* be attracted to, like, fancy; prefer, favour, choose; informal have a thing about.
■ **go in for** *we don't normally go in for this sort of thing:* take part in, participate in, engage in, get involved in, join in, enter into, undertake; practise, pursue; espouse, adopt, embrace.
■ **go into** *you'll need to go into the subject in greater detail:* investigate, examine, enquire into, look into, research, probe, explore, delve into; consider, review, analyse.
■ **go off 1** *the bomb went off:* explode, detonate, blow up. **2** (Brit.) *the milk's gone off:* go bad, go stale, go sour, turn, spoil, go rancid; decompose, go mouldy.
■ **go on 1** *the lecture went on for hours:* last, continue, carry on, run on, proceed; endure, persist; take. **2** *she went on about the sea:* talk at length, ramble, rattle on, chatter, prattle, gabble, blether, blather, twitter; informal gab, yak, yabber, yatter; Brit. informal witter, rabbit, natter, waffle, chunter; N. Amer. informal run off at the mouth. **3** *I'm not sure what went on:* happen, take place, occur, transpire; N. Amer. informal go down.
■ **go out 1** *the lights went out:* be turned off, be extinguished; stop burning. **2** *he's going out with Kate:* see, take out, be someone's boyfriend/girlfriend, be involved with; informal date, go steady with, go with.
■ **go over 1** *you'd better go over the figures:* examine, study, scrutinize, inspect, look at/over, scan, check; analyse, appraise, review. **2** *we are going over our lines:* rehearse, practise, read through, run through.
■ **go round 1** *the wheels were going round:* spin, revolve, turn, rotate, whirl. **2** *a nasty rumour going round:* be spread, be circulated, be put about, circulate, pass round, be broadcast.
■ **go through 1** *the terrible things she has gone through:* undergo, experience, face, suffer, be subjected to, live through, endure, brave, bear, tolerate, withstand, put up with, cope with, weather. **2** *he went through*

g

hundreds of pounds: spend, use up, run through, get through, expend, deplete; waste, squander, fritter away. **3** *he went through Susie's bag:* search, look, hunt, rummage, rifle; informal frisk. **4** *I have to go through the report:* examine, study, scrutinize, inspect, look over, scan, check; analyse, appraise, review. **5** *the deal has gone through:* be completed, be concluded, be brought off; be approved, be signed, be rubber-stamped.

■ **go under** go bankrupt, cease trading, go into receivership, go into liquidation, become insolvent, be liquidated, be wound up, be shut (down); fail; informal go broke, go to the wall, go belly up, fold.

■ **go without 1** *I went without breakfast:* abstain from, refrain from, forgo, do without, deny oneself. **2** *the children did not go without:* be deprived, be in want, go short, go hungry, be in need.

goad noun **1** *he applied his goad to the cows:* **prod**, spike, staff, crook, rod. **2** *a goad to political change:* **stimulus**, incentive, encouragement, inducement, fillip, spur, prod, prompt; motive, motivation.
verb *we were goaded into action:* **provoke**, spur, prod, egg on, hound, badger, incite, rouse, stir, move, stimulate, motivate, prompt, induce, encourage, urge, inspire; impel, pressure, pressurize, dragoon.

goal noun *our long-term goal is a nuclear-free world:* **objective**, aim, end, target, design, intention, intent, plan, purpose; (holy) grail; ambition, aspiration, wish, dream, desire, hope.

goat noun **1** *a herd of goats:* billy (goat), nanny (goat), kid. **2** *be careful of that old goat:* **lecher**, libertine, womanizer, seducer, Don Juan, Casanova, Lothario, Romeo; pervert, debauchee, rake; informal lech, dirty old man, ladykiller.

gobble verb *he paused only to gobble down his lunch:* **guzzle**, bolt, gulp, devour, wolf, cram, gorge (oneself) on; informal tuck into, put away, demolish, polish off, shovel down, stuff one's face (with), pig oneself (on); Brit. informal scoff, gollop, shift; N. Amer. informal scarf (down/up).

gobbledegook noun (informal) *the authority wrote him a letter full of legal gobbledegook:* **gibberish**, claptrap, nonsense, rubbish, balderdash, mumbo-jumbo, blather, blether; N. Amer. garbage; informal drivel, tripe, hogwash, baloney, bilge, bosh, bull, bunk, guff, eyewash, piffle, twaddle, poppycock, phooey, hooey; Brit. informal cobblers, codswallop, double Dutch, tosh; N. Amer. informal bushwa, applesauce.

go-between noun *an American firm acted as go-between in the transaction:* **intermediary**, middleman, agent, broker, liaison, linkman, contact; negotiator, interceder, intercessor, mediator.

goblet noun **wine glass**, chalice; glass, beaker, tumbler, cup.

goblin noun **hobgoblin**, gnome, dwarf, troll, imp, elf, brownie, fairy, pixie, leprechaun.

god noun **1** *a gift from God:* **the Lord**, the Almighty, the Creator, the Maker, the Godhead, the Father; Allah, Jehovah, Yahweh. **2** *sacrifices to appease the gods:* **deity**, goddess, divine being, celestial being, divinity, immortal, avatar. **3** *wooden gods:* **idol**, graven image, icon, totem, talisman, fetish, juju.

godforsaken adjective *what are you doing in this godforsaken place?* **wretched**, miserable, dreary, dismal, depressing, grim, cheerless, bleak, desolate, gloomy; deserted, neglected, isolated, remote, backward; Brit. informal grotty.
– OPPOSITES charming.

godless adjective **1** *a godless society:* **atheistic**, unbelieving, agnostic, sceptical, heretical, faithless, irreligious, ungodly, unholy, impious, profane; infidel, heathen, idolatrous, pagan; satanic, devilish. **2** *godless pleasures:* **immoral**, wicked, sinful, wrong, evil, bad, iniquitous, corrupt; irreligious, sacrilegious, profane, blasphemous, impious; depraved, degenerate, debauched, perverted, decadent; impure.
– OPPOSITES religious, virtuous.

godlike adjective *he is a noble figure of godlike magnanimity:* **divine**, godly, superhuman; angelic, seraphic; spiritual, heavenly, celestial; sacred, holy, saintly.

godly adjective *how to live the godly life:* **religious**, devout, pious, reverent, believing, God-fearing, saintly, holy, prayerful, churchgoing.
– OPPOSITES irreligious.

godsend noun *hire purchase was a godsend to thousands of people:* **boon**, blessing, bonus, plus, benefit, advantage, help, aid, asset; stroke of luck; informal perk.
– OPPOSITES curse.

goggle verb *they goggled at the well-stocked liquor stores:* **stare**, gape, gaze, ogle; informal gawk, rubberneck; Brit. informal gawp.

goings-on plural noun *all these disturbing goings-on:* **events**, happenings, affairs, business; mischief, misbehaviour, misconduct, funny business; informal monkey business, hanky-panky, shenanigans; Brit. informal jiggery-pokery, carry-on; N. Amer. informal monkeyshines.

golden adjective **1** *her golden hair:* **blond(e)**, yellow, fair, flaxen, tow-coloured. **2** *a golden opportunity:* **excellent**, fine, superb, splendid; special, unique; favourable, opportune, promising, bright, full of promise; advantageous, profitable, valuable, providential.
– OPPOSITES dark.

gone adjective **1** *I wasn't gone long:* **away**, absent, off, out; missing, unavailable. **2** *those days are gone:* **past**, over (and done with), no more, done, finished; ended; forgotten; dead and buried. **3** *the milk's all gone:* **used**

up, consumed, finished, spent, depleted; at an end. **4** *an aunt of mine, long since gone:* **dead**, expired, departed, no more, passed on/away; late, lost, lamented; perished, fallen; defunct, extinct; informal six feet under, pushing up daisies; euphemistic with God, asleep, at peace.
– OPPOSITES present, here, alive.

goo noun (informal) *the treacly goo that stuck to my jacket:* **sticky substance**, ooze, sludge, muck; informal gunk, crud, gloop; Brit. informal gunge; N. Amer. informal glop.

good adjective **1** *a good product:* **fine**, superior, quality; excellent, superb, outstanding, magnificent, exceptional, marvellous, wonderful, first-rate, first-class, sterling; satisfactory, acceptable, up to scratch, up to standard, not bad, all right; informal great, OK, A1, ace, terrific, fantastic, fabulous, fab, top-notch, class, awesome, wicked; informal, dated capital; Brit. informal smashing, brilliant, brill; Austral. informal beaut, bonzer. **2** *a good person:* **virtuous**, righteous, upright, upstanding, moral, ethical, high-minded, principled; exemplary, law-abiding, irreproachable, blameless, guiltless, unimpeachable, honourable, scrupulous, reputable, decent, respectable, noble, trustworthy; meritorious, praiseworthy, admirable; whiter than white, saintly, saintlike, angelic; informal squeaky clean. **3** *the children are good at school:* **well behaved**, obedient, dutiful, polite, courteous, respectful, deferential, compliant. **4** *it was a good thing to do:* **right**, correct, proper, decorous, seemly; appropriate, fitting, apt, suitable; convenient, expedient, favourable, opportune, felicitous, timely. **5** *she's a good driver:* **capable**, able, proficient, adept, adroit, accomplished, skilful, skilled, talented, masterly, expert; informal great, mean, wicked, nifty, ace; N. Amer. informal crackerjack. **6** *he's been a good friend to me:* **close**, intimate, dear, bosom, special, best, firm, valued, treasured; loving, devoted, loyal, faithful, constant, reliable, dependable, trustworthy, trusty, true, unfailing, staunch. **7** *the dogs are in good condition:* **healthy**, fine, sound, tip-top, hale and hearty, fit, robust, sturdy, strong, vigorous. **8** *a good time was had by all:* **enjoyable**, pleasant, agreeable, pleasurable, delightful, great, nice, lovely; amusing, diverting, jolly, merry, lively; informal super, fantastic, fabulous, fab, terrific, grand; Brit. informal brilliant, brill, smashing; N. Amer. informal peachy, ducky; Austral./NZ informal beaut, bonzer. **9** *it was good of you to come:* **kind**, kind-hearted, good-hearted, generous, charitable, magnanimous, gracious; altruistic, unselfish, selfless. **10** *tomorrow would be a good time to call:* **convenient**, suitable, appropriate, fitting, fit; opportune, timely, favourable, advantageous, expedient, felicitous, happy, providential. **11** *milk is good for you:* **wholesome**, healthy, healthful, nourishing, nutritious, nutritional, beneficial, salubrious. **12** *are these eggs still good?* **edible**, safe to eat, fit for human consumption; fresh, wholesome, consumable. **13** *give me one good reason why I should go:* **valid**, genuine, authentic, legitimate, sound, bona fide; convincing, persuasive, telling, potent, cogent, compelling. **14** *a good number of them:* **considerable**, sizeable, substantial, appreciable, significant; goodly, fair, reasonable; plentiful, abundant, great, large, generous; informal tidy. **15** *good weather:* **fine**, fair, dry; bright, clear, sunny, cloudless; calm, windless; warm, mild, balmy, clement, pleasant, nice.
– OPPOSITES bad, wicked, naughty, poor, terrible, inconvenient, small.

noun **1** *issues of good and evil:* **virtue**, righteousness, goodness, morality, integrity, rectitude; honesty, truth, honour, probity; propriety, worthiness, merit; blamelessness, purity. **2** *it's all for your good:* **benefit**, advantage, profit, gain, interest, welfare, well-being; enjoyment, comfort, ease, convenience; help, aid, assistance, service; behalf.
– OPPOSITES wickedness, disadvantage.

■ **for good** *those days are gone for good:* forever, permanently, for always, (for) evermore, for ever and ever, for eternity, until hell freezes over, never to return; N. Amer. forevermore; informal for keeps, until doomsday, until the cows come home.

■ **in good part** *she took the joke in good part:* good-naturedly, good-humouredly, without offence, amicably, favourably, tolerantly, indulgently, cheerfully, well.

■ **make good** succeed, be successful, be a success, do well, get ahead, reach the top; prosper, flourish, thrive; informal make it, make the grade, make a name for oneself, make one's mark, get somewhere, arrive.

■ **make something good 1** *he promised to make good any damage:* repair, mend, fix, put right, see to; restore, remedy, rectify. **2** *they made good their escape:* effect, conduct, perform, implement, execute, carry out; achieve, accomplish, succeed in, realize, attain, engineer, bring about, bring off. **3** *he will make good his promise:* fulfil, carry out, implement, discharge, honour, redeem; keep, observe, abide by, comply with, stick to, heed, follow, be bound by, live up to, stand by, adhere to.

goodbye exclamation *goodbye, safe journey!* **farewell**, adieu, au revoir, ciao, auf Wiedersehen, adios; Austral./NZ hooray; informal bye, bye-bye, so long, see you (later), later(s); Brit. informal cheers, cheerio, ta-ta; N. English informal ta-ra.

good-for-nothing adjective *a good-for-nothing layabout:* **useless**, worthless, incompetent, inefficient, inept, ne'er-do-well; lazy, idle, slothful, indolent, shiftless; informal no-good, lousy.
– OPPOSITES worthy.

g

noun *lazy good-for-nothings:* **ne'er-do-well**, layabout, do-nothing, idler, loafer, lounger, sluggard, shirker; informal waster, slacker, lazybones, couch potato; Brit. informal skiver.

good-humoured adjective *he was too good-humoured to be offended:* **genial**, affable, cordial, friendly, amiable, easy-going, approachable, good-natured, cheerful, cheery; companionable, comradely, sociable, convivial, company-loving; informal chummy, pally; Brit. informal matey; N. Amer. informal clubby.
– OPPOSITES grumpy.

good-looking adjective *she was still good-looking without her make-up:* **attractive**, beautiful, pretty, handsome, lovely, stunning, striking, arresting, gorgeous, prepossessing, fetching, captivating, bewitching, beguiling, engaging, charming, enchanting, appealing, delightful; sexy, seductive, alluring, tantalizing, irresistible, ravishing, desirable; Scottish & N. English bonny; informal fanciable, tasty, hot, easy on the eye, drop-dead gorgeous; Brit. informal fit; N. Amer. informal cute, foxy; Austral./NZ informal spunky.
– OPPOSITES ugly.

goodly adjective *a goodly number of our countrymen:* **large**, largish, sizeable, substantial, considerable, respectable, significant, decent, generous, handsome; informal tidy, serious.
– OPPOSITES paltry.

good-natured adjective *the crowd was rowdy but good-natured:* **warm-hearted**, friendly, amiable; neighbourly, benevolent, kind, kind-hearted, generous, unselfish, considerate, thoughtful, obliging, helpful, supportive, charitable; understanding, sympathetic, easy-going, accommodating; Brit. informal decent.
– OPPOSITES malicious.

goodness noun **1** *he had some goodness in him:* **virtue**, good, righteousness, morality, integrity, rectitude; honesty, truth, truthfulness, honour, probity; propriety, decency, respectability, nobility, worthiness, worth, merit, trustworthiness; blamelessness, purity. **2** *God's goodness towards us:* **kindness**, kindliness, tender-heartedness, humanity, mildness, benevolence, graciousness; tenderness, warmth, affection, love, goodwill; sympathy, compassion, care, concern, understanding, tolerance, generosity, charity, leniency, clemency, magnanimity. **3** *slow cooking retains the food's goodness:* **nutritional value**, nutrients, wholesomeness, nourishment.

goods plural noun **1** *he dispatched the goods:* **merchandise**, wares, stock, commodities, produce, products, articles; imports, exports. **2** *the dead man's goods:* **property**, possessions, effects, chattels, valuables; informal things, stuff, junk, gear, kit, bits and pieces; Brit. informal clobber. **3** (Brit.) *most goods went by train:* **freight**, cargo; load, consignment, delivery, shipment.

good-tempered adjective *he remained good-tempered in spite of being in such demand:* **equable**, even-tempered, imperturbable; unruffled, unflustered, untroubled, well balanced; easy-going, mellow, mild, calm, relaxed, cool, at ease; placid, stable, level-headed; cheerful, upbeat; informal unflappable, laid-back.
– OPPOSITES moody.

goodwill noun *the UN is dependent on the goodwill of its most powerful members:* **benevolence**, compassion, goodness, kindness, consideration, charity; cooperation, collaboration; friendliness, amity, thoughtfulness, decency, sympathy, understanding, neighbourliness.
– OPPOSITES hostility.

gore[1] noun *the film's gratuitous gore:* **blood**, bloodiness; bloodshed, slaughter, carnage, butchery.

gore[2] verb *he was gored by a bull:* **pierce**, stab, stick, impale, spear, horn.

gorge noun *the river runs through a gorge:* **ravine**, canyon, gully, defile, couloir; chasm, gulf; N. English clough, gill; N. Amer. gulch, coulee.
verb **1** *they gorged themselves on cakes:* **stuff**, cram, fill; glut, satiate, overindulge, overfill; informal pig. **2** *vultures gorged on the flesh:* **devour**, guzzle, gobble, gulp (down), wolf; informal tuck into, demolish, polish off, scoff (down), down, stuff one's face (with); Brit. informal gollop; N. Amer. informal scarf (down/up).

gorgeous adjective **1** *a gorgeous girl:* **good-looking**, attractive, beautiful, pretty, handsome, lovely, stunning, striking, arresting, prepossessing, fetching, captivating, bewitching, charming, enchanting, appealing, delightful; sexy, seductive, alluring, tantalizing, irresistible, ravishing, desirable; Scottish & N. English bonny; informal fanciable, tasty, hot, easy on the eye, drop-dead gorgeous; Brit. informal fit; N. Amer. informal cute, foxy; Austral./NZ informal spunky. **2** *a gorgeous view:* **spectacular**, splendid, superb, wonderful, grand, impressive, awe-inspiring, awesome, amazing, stunning, breathtaking, incredible; informal sensational, fabulous, fantastic. **3** *the soldiers were in gorgeous uniforms:* **resplendent**, magnificent, sumptuous, luxurious, elegant, opulent; dazzling, brilliant. **4** (informal) *gorgeous weather:* **excellent**, marvellous, superb, very good, first-rate, first-class, wonderful, magnificent, splendid; informal great, glorious, terrific, fantastic, fabulous, fab, ace; Brit. informal smashing, brilliant, brill; Austral./NZ informal bonzer.
– OPPOSITES ugly, drab, terrible.

gory adjective **1** *a gory ritual slaughter:* **grisly**, gruesome, violent, bloody, brutal, savage; ghastly, frightful, horrid, fearful, hideous, macabre, horrible, horrific; shocking, appalling, monstrous, unspeakable; informal blood-and-guts, sick-making. **2** *gory pieces of flesh:* **bloody**, bloodstained, bloodsoaked.

gospel noun 1 *the Gospel was spread by missionaries:* **Christian teaching**, Christian doctrine, Christ's teaching; the word of God, the New Testament. 2 *don't treat this as gospel:* **the truth**; fact, actual fact, reality, actuality, factuality, the case, a certainty. 3 *his gospel of non-violence:* **doctrine**, dogma, teaching, principle, ethic, creed, credo, ideology, ideal; belief, tenet, canon.

gossamer noun *her dress swirled like gossamer:* **cobwebs**; silk, gauze, chiffon.
adjective *a gossamer veil:* **gauzy**, gossamery, fine, diaphanous, delicate, filmy, floaty, chiffony, cobwebby, wispy, thin, light, insubstantial, flimsy; translucent, transparent, see-through, sheer.

gossip noun 1 *tell me all the gossip:* **tittle-tattle**, tattle, rumour(s), whispers, canards, titbits; scandal, hearsay; informal dirt, buzz; Brit. informal goss; N. Amer. informal scuttlebutt. 2 *they went for a gossip:* **chat**, talk, conversation, chatter, heart-to-heart, tête-à-tête, blether, blather; discussion, dialogue; informal chit-chat, jaw, gas, confab, goss; Brit. informal natter, chinwag; N. Amer. informal gabfest; Austral./NZ informal yarn. 3 *she's such a gossip:* **scandalmonger**, gossipmonger, tattler, busybody, muckraker.
verb 1 *she gossiped about his wife:* **spread rumours**, spread gossip, tittle-tattle, tattle, talk, whisper, tell tales; informal dish the dirt. 2 *people sat around gossiping:* **chat**, talk, converse, speak to each other, discuss things; informal gas, chew the fat, chew the rag, jaw, yak, yap; Brit. informal natter, chinwag; N. Amer. informal shoot the breeze, shoot the bull.

gouge verb *a tunnel had been gouged out of the mountain:* **scoop out**, hollow out, excavate; cut (out), dig (out), scrape (out), scratch (out).

gourmand noun *gourmands who care more for quantity than quality:* **glutton**, overeater, big eater, gobbler, gorger; informal (greedy) pig, gannet, greedy guts, gutbucket, guzzler.

gourmet noun *even the most demanding gourmets adore the restaurants on Lake Como:* **gastronome**, epicure, epicurean, connoisseur; informal foodie.

govern verb 1 *he governs the province:* **rule**, preside over, reign over, control, be in charge of, command, lead, dominate; run, head, administer, manage, regulate, oversee, supervise; informal be in the driving seat. 2 *the rules governing social behaviour:* **determine**, decide, control, regulate, direct, rule, dictate, shape; affect, influence, sway, act on, mould, modify, impact on.

governess noun **tutor**, instructress, duenna; teacher.

government noun 1 *the government announced cuts:* **administration**, executive, regime, authority, powers that be, directorate, council, leadership; cabinet, ministry; informal top brass. 2 *they help him in the government of the country:* **rule**, running, leadership, control, administration, regulation, management, supervision.

governor noun *the governor of the province:* **leader**, ruler, chief, head; premier, president, viceroy, chancellor; administrator, principal, director, chairman/woman, chair, superintendent, commissioner, controller; informal boss.

gown noun **dress**, frock, shift, robe.

grab verb *Dot grabbed his arm:* **seize**, grasp, snatch, take hold of, grip, clasp, clutch; take.
noun *she made a grab for his gun:* **lunge**, snatch.

grace noun 1 *the grace of a ballerina:* **elegance**, poise, gracefulness, finesse; suppleness, agility, nimbleness, light-footedness. 2 *he had the grace to look sheepish:* **courtesy**, decency, (good) manners, politeness, decorum, respect, tact. 3 *he fell from grace:* **favour**, approval, approbation, acceptance, esteem, regard, respect; goodwill. 4 *he lived there by grace of the king:* **favour**, goodwill, generosity, kindness, indulgence. 5 *they have five days' grace to decide:* **deferment**, deferral, postponement, suspension, adjournment, delay, pause; respite, stay, moratorium, reprieve. 6 *would you say grace?* **prayer of thanks**, thanksgiving, blessing, benediction.
– OPPOSITES inelegance, effrontery, disfavour.
verb 1 *the occasion was graced by the prince:* **dignify**, distinguish, honour, favour; enhance, ennoble, glorify, elevate, aggrandize, upgrade. 2 *a mosaic graced the floor:* **adorn**, embellish, decorate, ornament, enhance; beautify, prettify, enrich, bedeck.

graceful adjective *her simple, graceful clothes have won legions of devotees:* **elegant**, fluid, fluent, natural, neat; agile, supple, nimble, light-footed.

graceless adjective *a loud, graceless teenager:* **gauche**, maladroit, inept, awkward, unsure, unpolished, unsophisticated, uncultured, unrefined; clumsy, ungainly, ungraceful, inelegant, uncoordinated, gawky, gangling, bumbling; tactless, thoughtless, inconsiderate; informal cack-handed, ham-handed, ham-fisted.

gracious adjective 1 *a gracious hostess:* **courteous**, polite, civil, chivalrous, well mannered, mannerly, decorous; tactful, diplomatic; kind, benevolent, considerate, thoughtful, obliging, accommodating, indulgent, magnanimous; friendly, amiable, cordial, hospitable. 2 *gracious colonial buildings:* **elegant**, stylish, tasteful, graceful; comfortable, luxurious, sumptuous, opulent, grand, high-class; informal swanky, plush. 3 *God's gracious intervention:* **merciful**, compassionate, kind; forgiving, lenient, clement, forbearing, humane, tender-hearted, sympathetic; indulgent, generous, magnanimous, benign, benevolent.

g

–OPPOSITES rude, crude, cruel.

gradation noun **1** *a gradation of ability:*
range, scale, spectrum, compass, span;
progression, hierarchy, ladder, pecking
order. **2** *each pay band has a number of
gradations:* **level**, grade, rank, position,
status, stage, standard, echelon, rung, step,
notch; class, stratum, group, grouping, set.

grade noun **1** *hotels within the same grade:*
category, set, class, classification, grouping,
group, bracket. **2** *his job is of the lowest
grade:* **rank**, level, echelon, standing,
position, class, status, order; step, rung,
stratum, tier. **3** (N. Amer.) *the best grades in the
school:* **mark**, score; assessment, evaluation,
appraisal. **4** (N. Amer.) *they're all in the fifth
grade:* **year**, form, class.
verb **1** *eggs are graded by size:* **classify**, class,
categorize, bracket, sort, group, arrange,
pigeonhole; rank, evaluate, rate, value. **2** (N.
Amer.) *the essays have been graded:* **assess**,
mark, score, judge, evaluate, appraise. **3** *the
colours grade into one another:* **pass**, shade,
merge, blend.
■ **make the grade** (informal) come up to
standard, come up to scratch, qualify, pass,
pass muster, measure up; succeed, win
through; informal be up to snuff, cut it, cut
the mustard.

gradient noun **1** *a steep gradient:* **slope**,
incline, hill, rise, ramp, bank; acclivity,
declivity; N. Amer. grade. **2** *the gradient of
the line:* **steepness**, angle, slant, slope,
inclination.

gradual adjective **1** *a gradual transition:*
slow, measured, unhurried, cautious;
piecemeal, step-by-step, little-by-little, bit-
by-bit; progressive, continuous, systematic,
steady. **2** *a gradual slope:* **gentle**, moderate,
slight, easy.
–OPPOSITES abrupt, steep.

gradually adverb *you can begin to introduce
new ideas gradually:* **slowly**, slowly
but surely, cautiously, gently, gingerly;
piecemeal, little by little, bit by bit,
inch by inch, by degrees; progressively,
systematically; regularly, steadily.

graduate verb **1** *he wants to teach
when he graduates:* **qualify**, pass one's
exams, get one's degree, complete one's
studies. **2** *she wants to graduate to serious
drama:* **progress**, advance, move up. **3** *a
thermometer graduated in Fahrenheit:*
calibrate, mark off, measure out, grade.

graft¹ noun **1** *grafts may die from lack of
water:* **scion**, cutting, shoot, offshoot, bud,
sprout, sprig. **2** *a skin graft:* **transplant**,
implant.
verb **1** *graft a bud on to the stem:* **affix**, join,
insert, splice. **2** *tissue is grafted on to the
cornea:* **transplant**, implant. **3** *a mansion
grafted on to a farmhouse:* **attach**, add, join.

graft² noun *sweeping measures to curb
official graft:* **corruption**, bribery,
subornation, dishonesty, deceit, fraud,

unlawful practices, illegal means; N. Amer.
payola; informal palm-greasing, hush money,
kickbacks, crookedness, sharp practices.
–OPPOSITES honesty.

grain noun **1** *the local farmers grow grain:*
cereal, cereal crops. **2** *a grain of corn:*
kernel, seed, grist. **3** *grains of sand:* **granule**,
particle, speck, mote, mite; bit, piece; scrap,
crumb, fragment, morsel. **4** *a grain of truth:*
trace, hint, tinge, suggestion, shadow; bit,
soupçon; scintilla, ounce, iota, jot, whit,
scrap, shred; informal smidgen, smidge, tad.
5 *the grain of the timber:* **texture**, surface,
finish; weave, pattern.

grammar noun **syntax**, rules of language,
morphology; linguistics.

grammatical adjective **1** *the grammatical
structure of a sentence:* **syntactic**,
morphological; linguistic. **2** *a grammatical
sentence:* **well formed**, correct, proper;
acceptable, allowable.

grand adjective **1** *a grand hotel:* **magnificent**,
imposing, impressive, awe-inspiring,
splendid, resplendent, majestic,
monumental; palatial, stately, large;
luxurious, sumptuous, lavish, opulent; Brit.
upmarket; N. Amer. upscale; informal fancy,
posh, plush, classy, swanky; Brit. informal
swish. **2** *a grand scheme:* **ambitious**, bold,
epic, big, extravagant. **3** *a grand old lady:*
august, distinguished, illustrious, eminent,
esteemed, honoured, venerable, dignified,
respectable; pre-eminent, prominent,
notable, renowned, celebrated, famous;
aristocratic, noble, regal, blue-blooded,
high-born, patrician; informal upper-crust;
Brit. informal posh, upmarket. **4** *a grand total
of £2,000:* **complete**, comprehensive, all-
inclusive, inclusive; final. **5** *the grand
staircase:* **main**, principal, central, prime;
biggest, largest. **6** (informal) *you're doing a
grand job:* **excellent**, very good, marvellous,
splendid, first-class, first-rate, wonderful,
outstanding, sterling, fine; informal superb,
terrific, great, super, ace; Brit. informal
smashing, brilliant, brill.
–OPPOSITES inferior, humble, minor, poor.

grandeur noun *the grandeur of formal
royal occasions:* **splendour**, magnificence,
impressiveness, glory, resplendence,
majesty, greatness; stateliness, pomp,
ceremony.

grandfather noun **1** *his grandfather lives
here:* informal grandad, grandpa, gramps,
gramp, grandaddy. **2** *the grandfather of
modern liberalism:* **founder**, inventor,
originator, creator, initiator; father,
founding father, pioneer.

grandiloquent adjective *their
grandiloquent phrases failed to convince
me:* **pompous**, bombastic, magniloquent,
pretentious, ostentatious, high-flown,
orotund, florid, flowery; overwrought,
overblown, overdone; informal highfalutin,
purple.
–OPPOSITES understated.

grandiose adjective **1** *the court's grandiose facade:* **magnificent**, impressive, grand, imposing, awe-inspiring, splendid, resplendent, majestic, glorious, elaborate; palatial, stately, luxurious, opulent; informal plush, swanky, flash. **2** *a grandiose plan:* **ambitious**, bold, overambitious, extravagant, high-flown, flamboyant; informal over the top, OTT.
– OPPOSITES humble, modest.

grandmother noun informal grandma, granny, gran, nan, nanna.

grant verb **1** *he granted them leave of absence:* **allow**, accord, permit, afford, vouchsafe. **2** *he granted them £20,000:* **give**, award, bestow on, confer on, present with, provide with, endow with, supply with. **3** *I grant that the difference is not absolute:* **admit**, accept, concede, yield, allow, appreciate, recognize, acknowledge, confess; agree.
– OPPOSITES refuse, deny.
noun *a grant from the council:* **endowment**, subvention, award, donation, bursary, allowance, subsidy, contribution, handout, allocation, gift; scholarship.

granular adjective *this is plant food in a new granular form:* **powder**, powdered, powdery, grainy, granulated, gritty.

granulated adjective **powdered**, crushed, crumbed, ground, minced, grated, pulverized.

granule noun *minute granules of gold:* **grain**, particle, fragment, bit, crumb, morsel, mote, speck.

graph noun *use graphs to analyse your data:* **chart**, diagram; histogram, bar chart, pie chart, scatter diagram.

graphic adjective **1** *a graphic representation of language:* **visual**, symbolic, pictorial, illustrative, diagrammatic; drawn, written. **2** *a graphic account:* **vivid**, explicit, expressive, detailed; uninhibited, powerful, colourful, rich, lurid, shocking; realistic, descriptive, illustrative; telling, effective.
– OPPOSITES vague.
noun *this printer's good enough for graphics:* **picture**, illustration, image; diagram, graph, chart.

grapple verb **1** *the policemen grappled with him:* **wrestle**, struggle, tussle; brawl, fight, scuffle, battle. **2** *he grappled his prey:* **seize**, grab, catch (hold of), take hold of, grasp. **3** *she is grappling with the problems of exile:* **tackle**, confront, face, deal with, cope with, get to grips with; apply oneself to, devote oneself to.

grasp verb **1** *she grasped his hands:* **grip**, clutch, clasp, hold, clench; catch, seize, grab, snatch, latch on to. **2** *everybody grasped the important points:* **understand**, comprehend, follow, take in, perceive, see, apprehend, assimilate, absorb; informal get, catch on to, latch on to, figure out, get one's head around, take on board; Brit. informal twig, suss (out). **3** *he grasped the opportunity:* **take**

advantage of, act on; seize, leap at, snatch, jump at, pounce on.
– OPPOSITES release, overlook.
noun **1** *his grasp on her hand:* **grip**, hold; clutch, clasp, clench. **2** *his domineering mother's grasp:* **control**, power, clutches, command, domination, rule, tyranny. **3** *a prize lay within their grasp:* **reach**, scope, power, limits, range; sights. **4** *your grasp of history leaves a lot to be desired:* **understanding**, comprehension, perception, apprehension, awareness, grip, knowledge; mastery, command.

grasping adjective *a grasping corporate executive:* **avaricious**, acquisitive, greedy, rapacious, mercenary, materialistic; mean, miserly, parsimonious, niggardly, hoarding, selfish, possessive, close; informal tight-fisted, tight, stingy, money-grubbing; N. Amer. informal cheap, grabby.

grass noun *he sat down on the grass:* **turf**, sod; lawn, green.
verb *the hill is completely grassed:* **grass over**, turf.

grate verb **1** *she grated the cheese:* **shred**, pulverize, mince, grind, granulate, crush, crumble. **2** *her bones grated together:* **grind**, rub, rasp, scrape, jar, grit, creak. **3** *the tune grates slightly:* **irritate**, set someone's teeth on edge, jar; annoy, nettle, chafe, fret; informal aggravate, get on someone's nerves, get under someone's skin, get someone's goat.

grateful adjective *I was most grateful for your hospitality:* **thankful**, appreciative; indebted, obliged, obligated, in your debt, beholden.

gratification noun *ours is the civilization of instant gratification:* **satisfaction**, fulfilment, indulgence, relief, appeasement; pleasure, enjoyment, relish.

gratify verb **1** *it gratified him to be seen with her:* **please**, gladden, make happy, delight, make someone feel good, satisfy; informal tickle pink, give someone a kick, buck up. **2** *he gratified his desires:* **satisfy**, fulfil, indulge, comply with, pander to, cater to, give in to, satiate, feed, accommodate.
– OPPOSITES displease, frustrate.

grating[1] adjective **1** *the chair made a grating noise:* **scraping**, scratching, grinding, rasping, jarring. **2** *a grating voice:* **harsh**, raucous, strident, piercing, shrill, screechy; discordant, cacophonous; hoarse, rough, gravelly. **3** *it's written in grating language:* **irritating**, annoying, infuriating, irksome, maddening, displeasing, tiresome; jarring, discordant, inharmonious, unsuitable, inappropriate; informal aggravating.
– OPPOSITES harmonious, pleasing, appropriate.

grating[2] noun *a strong iron grating:* **grid**, grate, grille, lattice, trellis, mesh.

gratis adverb *a monthly programme was issued gratis to dancers:* **free (of charge)**, without charge, for nothing, at no cost,

g

gratuitously; informal on the house, for free.

gratitude noun *Maureen ought to show gratitude for the money:* **gratefulness**, thankfulness, thanks, appreciation, indebtedness; recognition, acknowledgement, credit.

gratuitous adjective *there's too much gratuitous violence on TV:* **unjustified**, uncalled for, unwarranted, unprovoked, undue; indefensible, unjustifiable; needless, unnecessary, inessential, unmerited, groundless, senseless, wanton, indiscriminate; excessive, immoderate, inordinate, inappropriate.
– OPPOSITES necessary, paid.

gratuity noun (formal) *gratuities are at the discretion of customers:* **tip**, pourboire, baksheesh, gift, present, donation, reward, handout; bonus, extra; informal perk; formal perquisite.

grave[1] noun *she left flowers at his grave:* **burying place**, tomb, sepulchre, vault, burial chamber, mausoleum, crypt; last resting place.

grave[2] adjective **1** *a grave matter:* **serious**, important, weighty, profound, significant, momentous; critical, acute, urgent, pressing; dire, terrible, awful, dreadful. **2** *Jackie looked grave:* **solemn**, serious, sober, unsmiling, grim, sombre; severe, stern, dour.
– OPPOSITES trivial, cheerful.

gravel noun **shingle**, grit, pebbles, stones.

gravelly adjective **1** *a gravelly beach:* **shingly**, pebbly, stony, gritty. **2** *his gravelly voice:* **husky**, gruff, throaty, deep, croaky, rasping, grating, harsh, rough.

gravestone noun **headstone**, tombstone, stone, monument, memorial.

graveyard noun **cemetery**, churchyard, burial ground, necropolis; informal boneyard.

gravitas noun *a man of gravitas:* **dignity**, seriousness, solemnity, gravity, sobriety.
– OPPOSITES frivolity.

gravitate verb *young western Europeans will gravitate towards Berlin:* **move**, head, drift, be drawn, be attracted; tend, lean, incline.

gravity noun **1** *the gravity of the situation:* **seriousness**, importance, significance, weight, consequence, magnitude; acuteness, urgency, exigence; awfulness, dreadfulness. **2** *the gravity of his demeanour:* **solemnity**, seriousness, sombreness, sobriety, soberness, severity, grimness, humourlessness, dourness; gloominess.

graze[1] verb *the deer grazed:* **feed**, eat, crop, nibble, browse.

graze[2] verb **1** *he grazed his knuckles on the box:* **scrape**, abrade, skin, scratch, chafe, bark, scuff, rasp; cut, nick. **2** *his shot grazed the far post:* **touch**, brush, shave, skim, kiss, scrape, clip, glance off.
noun *grazes on the skin:* **scratch**, scrape, abrasion, cut.

grease noun **1** *guns packed in grease:* **oil**, lubricant, lubricator, lubrication. **2** *the cooker was covered with grease:* **fat**, oil, cooking oil, animal fat; lard, suet. **3** *his hair was smothered with grease:* **gel**, lotion, cream; trademark Brylcreem.
verb *grease a baking dish:* **lubricate**, oil, smear with oil.

greasy adjective **1** *a greasy supper:* **fatty**, oily, buttery, oleaginous. **2** *the pitch was very greasy:* **slippery**, slick, slimy, slithery, oily; informal slippy, skiddy. **3** *a greasy little man:* **ingratiating**, obsequious, sycophantic, fawning, toadying, grovelling; effusive, gushing, gushy; unctuous, oily; informal smarmy, slimy, bootlicking, sucky.
– OPPOSITES lean, dry.

great adjective **1** *they showed great interest:* **considerable**, substantial, significant, appreciable, special, serious; exceptional, extraordinary. **2** *a great expanse of water:* **large**, big, extensive, expansive, broad, wide, sizeable, ample; vast, immense, huge, enormous, massive; informal humongous, whopping; Brit. informal ginormous. **3** *a great big house:* **very**, extremely, exceedingly, exceptionally, especially, really; informal dirty. **4** *you great fool!* **absolute**, total, utter, out-and-out, downright, thoroughgoing, complete; perfect, positive, prize, sheer, arrant, unqualified, consummate, veritable; informal thundering; Brit. informal right, proper. **5** *great writers:* **prominent**, eminent, important, distinguished, illustrious, celebrated, honoured, acclaimed, admired, esteemed, revered, renowned, notable, famous, famed, well known; leading, top, major, principal, first-rate, matchless, peerless, star. **6** *the country is now a great power:* **powerful**, dominant, influential, strong, potent, formidable, redoubtable; leading, important, foremost, major, chief, principal. **7** *the great castle of Montellana-Coronil:* **magnificent**, imposing, impressive, awe-inspiring, grand, splendid, majestic, sumptuous, resplendent. **8** *a great sportsman:* **expert**, skilful, skilled, adept, accomplished, talented, fine, masterly, master, brilliant, virtuoso, marvellous, outstanding, first class, superb; informal crack, ace, A1, class. **9** *a great fan of rugby:* **enthusiastic**, eager, keen, zealous, devoted, ardent, fanatical, passionate, dedicated, committed. **10** *we had a great time:* **enjoyable**, delightful, lovely, pleasant, congenial; exciting, thrilling, excellent, marvellous, wonderful, fine, splendid, very good; informal terrific, fantastic, fabulous, fab, super, grand, cool; Brit. informal smashing, brilliant, brill; Austral./NZ informal bonzer, beaut.
– OPPOSITES little, small, minor, modest, poor, unenthusiastic, bad.

greatly adverb *a frantic training programme greatly increases the risk of injury:* **very much**, considerably, substantially, appreciably, significantly, markedly, sizeably, seriously, materially,

profoundly; enormously, vastly, immensely, tremendously, mightily, abundantly, extremely, exceedingly; informal plenty, majorly.
– OPPOSITES slightly.

greatness noun **1** *a woman destined for greatness:* **eminence**, distinction, illustriousness, repute, high standing; importance, significance; celebrity, fame, prominence, renown. **2** *his greatness as a writer:* **brilliance**, genius, prowess, talent, expertise, mastery, artistry, virtuosity, skill, proficiency; flair, finesse; calibre, distinction.

greed, greediness noun **1** *human greed:* **avarice**, cupidity, acquisitiveness, covetousness, rapacity; materialism, mercenariness, Mammonism; informal money-grubbing, money-grabbing. **2** *her mouth watered with greed:* **gluttony**, hunger, voracity, insatiability; gourmandism, intemperance, overeating, self-indulgence; informal piggishness. **3** *their greed for power:* **desire**, appetite, hunger, thirst, craving, longing, yearning, hankering; avidity, eagerness; informal yen, itch.
– OPPOSITES generosity, temperance, indifference.

greedy adjective **1** *a greedy eater:* **gluttonous**, ravenous, voracious, intemperate, self-indulgent, insatiable, wolfish; informal piggish, piggy. **2** *a greedy millionaire:* **avaricious**, acquisitive, covetous, grasping, materialistic, mercenary, possessive; informal money-grubbing, money-grabbing; N. Amer. informal grabby. **3** *she is greedy for a title:* **eager**, avid, hungry, craving, longing, yearning, hankering; impatient, anxious; informal dying, itching, gagging.

green adjective **1** *a green scarf:* viridescent; olive green, pea green, emerald green, lime green, bottle green, Lincoln green, sea green, eau de Nil. **2** *a green island:* **verdant**, grassy, leafy, verdurous. **3** *he promotes Green issues:* **environmental**, ecological, conservation, eco-. **4** *a green alternative to diesel:* **environmentally friendly**, non-polluting; ozone-friendly. **5** *green bananas:* **unripe**, immature. **6** *the new lieutenant was very green:* **inexperienced**, unversed, callow, immature; new, raw, unseasoned, untried; inexpert, untrained, unqualified; ignorant; simple, unsophisticated, unpolished; naive, innocent, ingenuous, credulous, gullible, unworldly; informal wet behind the ears, born yesterday. **7** *he went green:* **pale**, wan, pallid, ashen, ashen-faced, pasty, pasty-faced, grey, whitish, washed out, whey-faced, waxen, waxy, blanched, drained, pinched, sallow; sickly, nauseous, ill, sick, unhealthy.
– OPPOSITES barren, ripe, experienced, ruddy.
noun **1** *a canopy of green over the road:* **foliage**, greenery, plants, leaves, leafage, vegetation. **2** *a village green:* **lawn**, common, grassy area, sward. **3** *they had*

roast beef and greens: **vegetables**, leaf vegetables; informal veg, veggies. **4** *Greens are against multinationals:* **environmentalist**, conservationist, preservationist, naturelover, eco-activist.

greenery noun *the hotel is surrounded by lush greenery:* **foliage**, vegetation, plants, green, leaves, leafage, undergrowth, plant life, flora, herbage, verdure.

greenhouse noun **hothouse**, glasshouse, conservatory.

greet verb **1** *she greeted Hank cheerily:* **say hello to**, address, salute, hail, halloo; welcome, meet, receive. **2** *the decision was greeted with outrage:* **receive**, acknowledge, respond to, react to, take.

greeting noun **1** *he shouted a greeting:* **hello**, salute, salutation, address; welcome; acknowledgement. **2** *birthday greetings:* **best wishes**, good wishes, congratulations, felicitations; compliments, regards, respects.
– OPPOSITES farewell.

gregarious adjective **1** *he was fun-loving and gregarious:* **sociable**, company-loving, convivial, companionable, outgoing, friendly, affable, amiable, genial, warm, comradely, clubbable; Scottish couthy; informal chummy, pally; Brit. informal matey. **2** *gregarious fish:* **social**, community, living in groups.
– OPPOSITES unsociable.

grey adjective **1** *a grey suit:* **silvery**, silver-grey, gunmetal, slate, charcoal, smoky. **2** *his grey hair:* **white**, silver, hoary. **3** *a grey day:* **cloudy**, overcast, dull, sunless, gloomy, dreary, dismal, sombre, bleak, murky. **4** *her face looked grey:* **ashen**, wan, pale, pasty, pallid, colourless, bloodless, white, waxen; sickly, peaky, drained, drawn, deathly. **5** *the grey daily routine:* **characterless**, colourless, nondescript, unremarkable, insipid, jejune, flat, bland, dry, stale; dull, uninteresting, boring, tedious, monotonous. **6** *a grey area:* **ambiguous**, doubtful, unclear, uncertain, indefinite, open to question, debatable. **7** *the grey economy:* **unofficial**, informal, irregular, back-door.
– OPPOSITES sunny, ruddy, lively, certain.
verb *the population greyed:* **age**, grow old, mature.

grid noun **1** *a metal grid:* **grating**, mesh, grille, gauze, lattice. **2** *the grid of streets:* **network**, matrix, reticulation.

grief noun **1** *he was overcome with grief:* **sorrow**, misery, sadness, anguish, pain, distress, heartache, heartbreak, agony, torment, affliction, suffering, woe, desolation, dejection, despair; mourning, mournfulness, bereavement, lamentation. **2** (informal) *the police gave me loads of grief:* **trouble**, annoyance, bother, irritation, vexation, harassment; informal aggravation, aggro, hassle.
– OPPOSITES joy.
■ **come to grief** fail, meet with disaster, miscarry, go wrong, go awry, fall through,

fall flat, founder, come to nothing, come to naught; informal come unstuck, come a cropper, flop, go phut; Brit. informal go pear-shaped.

grief-stricken adjective *a grief-stricken widow:* **sorrowful**, sorrowing, miserable, sad, heartbroken, broken-hearted, anguished, pained, distressed, tormented, suffering, woeful, doleful, desolate, despairing, devastated, upset, inconsolable, wretched; mourning, grieving, mournful, bereaved, lamenting.
– OPPOSITES joyful.

grievance noun **1** *social and economic grievances:* **injustice**, wrong, injury, ill, unfairness; affront, insult, indignity. **2** *students voiced their grievances:* **complaint**, criticism, objection, grumble, grouse; ill feeling, bad feeling, resentment, bitterness, pique; informal gripe, whinge, moan, grouch, niggle, beef, bone to pick.

grieve verb **1** *she grieved for her father:* **mourn**, lament, sorrow, be sorrowful; cry, sob, weep, shed tears, keen, weep and wail, beat one's breast. **2** *it grieved me to leave her:* **sadden**, upset, distress, pain, hurt, wound, break someone's heart, make someone's heart bleed.
– OPPOSITES rejoice, please.

grievous adjective (formal) **1** *his death was a grievous blow:* **serious**, severe, grave, bad, critical, dreadful, terrible, awful, crushing, calamitous; painful, agonizing, traumatic, wounding, damaging, injurious; sharp, acute. **2** *a grievous sin:* **heinous**, grave, deplorable, shocking, appalling, atrocious, gross, dreadful, egregious, iniquitous.
– OPPOSITES slight, trivial.

grim adjective **1** *his grim expression:* **stern**, forbidding, uninviting, unsmiling, dour, formidable, harsh, steely, flinty, stony; cross, churlish, crabbed, surly, sour, ill-tempered; fierce, ferocious, threatening, menacing, implacable, ruthless, merciless. **2** *grim humour:* **black**, dark, mirthless, bleak, cynical. **3** *the asylum holds some grim secrets:* **dreadful**, dire, ghastly, horrible, horrendous, horrid, terrible, awful, appalling, frightful, shocking, unspeakable, grisly, gruesome, hideous, macabre; depressing, distressing, upsetting, worrying, unpleasant. **4** *a grim little hovel:* **bleak**, dreary, dismal, dingy, wretched, miserable, depressing, cheerless, comfortless, joyless, gloomy, uninviting; informal God-awful. **5** *grim determination:* **resolute**, determined, firm, decided, steadfast, dead set; obstinate, stubborn, obdurate, unyielding, intractable, uncompromising, unshakeable, unrelenting, relentless, dogged, tenacious.
– OPPOSITES amiable, pleasant.

grimace noun *his mouth twisted into a grimace:* **scowl**, frown, sneer; face.
verb *Nina grimaced at Joe:* **scowl**, frown, sneer, glower, lour; make a face, make faces, pull a face; Brit. gurn.

– OPPOSITES smile.

grime noun *her skirt was smeared with grime:* **dirt**, smut, soot, dust, mud, filth, mire; informal muck, yuck, crud; Brit. informal grot, gunge.
verb *concrete grimed by diesel exhaust:* **blacken**, dirty, stain, soil.

grimy adjective *reporters in grimy anoraks:* **dirty**, grubby, mucky, soiled, stained, smeared, filthy, smutty, sooty, dusty, muddy; informal yucky, cruddy; Brit. informal manky, grotty, gungy; Austral./NZ scungy.
– OPPOSITES clean.

grin verb *he grinned at her:* **smile**, smile broadly, beam, smile from ear to ear, grin like a Cheshire cat; smirk; informal be all smiles.
noun *a silly grin:* **smile**, broad smile; smirk.
– OPPOSITES frown, scowl.

grind verb **1** *the sandstone is ground into powder:* **crush**, pound, pulverize, mill, granulate, crumble, smash, press. **2** *the sound of a knife being ground on a wheel:* **sharpen**, whet, hone, file, strop; smooth, polish, sand, sandpaper. **3** *one tectonic plate grinds against another:* **rub**, grate, scrape, rasp.
noun *the daily grind:* **drudgery**, toil, hard work, labour, donkey work, exertion, chores, slog; informal fag, sweat.
■ **grind away** labour, toil, work hard, slave (away), work one's fingers to the bone, work like a Trojan, work like a dog; informal slog, plug away, beaver away, work one's socks off; Brit. informal graft.
■ **grind someone down** oppress, crush, persecute, tyrannize, ill-treat, maltreat.

grip verb **1** *she gripped the edge of the table:* **grasp**, clutch, hold, clasp, take hold of, clench, grab, seize, cling to; squeeze, press. **2** *Harry was gripped by a sneezing fit:* **afflict**, affect, take over, beset, rack, convulse. **3** *we were gripped by the drama:* **engross**, enthral, absorb, rivet, spellbind, hold spellbound, bewitch, fascinate, hold, mesmerize, enrapture; interest.
– OPPOSITES release.
noun **1** *a tight grip:* **grasp**, hold. **2** *the wheels lost their grip on the road:* **traction**, purchase, friction, adhesion, resistance. **3** *he was in the grip of an obsession:* **control**, power, hold, stranglehold, clutches, command, mastery, influence. **4** *I had a pretty good grip on the situation:* **understanding**, comprehension, grasp, perception, awareness, apprehension, conception. **5** *a leather grip:* **travelling bag**, bag, holdall, overnight bag, flight bag, kitbag, Gladstone bag.
■ **come/get to grips with** deal with, cope with, handle, grasp, grasp the nettle of, tackle, undertake, take on, grapple with, face, face up to, confront.

gripping adjective *a gripping thriller:* **engrossing**, enthralling, absorbing, riveting, captivating, spellbinding, bewitching,

fascinating, compulsive, compelling, mesmerizing; thrilling, exciting, action-packed, dramatic, stimulating; informal unputdownable, page-turning.
– OPPOSITES boring.

grisly adjective *the town was shaken by a series of grisly crimes:* **gruesome**, ghastly, frightful, horrid, horrifying, fearful, hideous, macabre, spine-chilling, horrible, horrendous, grim, awful, dire, dreadful, terrible, horrific, shocking, appalling, abominable, loathsome, abhorrent, odious, monstrous, unspeakable, disgusting, repulsive, repugnant, revolting, repellent, sickening; informal sick-making, gross.

gristly adjective *a gristly piece of meat:* **stringy**, sinewy, fibrous; tough, leathery, chewy.

grit noun **1** *the grit from the paths:* **gravel**, pebbles, stones, shingle, sand; dust, dirt. **2** *the true grit of a seasoned campaigner:* **courage**, bravery, pluck, mettle, backbone, spirit, strength of character, strength of will, moral fibre, steel, nerve, fortitude, toughness, hardiness, resolve, resolution, determination, tenacity, perseverance, endurance; informal guts, spunk; Brit. informal bottle.
verb *Gina gritted her teeth:* **clench**, clamp together, shut tightly; grind, gnash.

gritty adjective **1** *a gritty floor:* **sandy**, gravelly, pebbly, stony; powdery, dusty. **2** *a gritty performance:* **courageous**, brave, plucky, mettlesome, stout-hearted, valiant, bold, spirited, intrepid, tough, determined, resolute, purposeful, dogged, tenacious; informal gutsy, spunky.

grizzled adjective *he tugged at his grizzled beard:* **grey**, greying, silver, silvery, snowy, white, salt-and-pepper; grey-haired, hoary.

groan verb **1** *she groaned and rubbed her stomach:* **moan**, whimper, cry, call out. **2** *they were groaning about the management:* **complain**, grumble, grouse; informal moan, niggle, beef, bellyache, bitch, whinge, gripe.
noun **1** *a groan of anguish:* **moan**, cry, whimper. **2** *their moans and groans:* **complaint**, grumble, grouse, objection, protest, grievance; informal grouch, moan, beef, whinge; informal gripe.

groggy adjective *she is still feeling groggy from the anaesthetic:* **dazed**, muzzy, stupefied, in a stupor, befuddled, fuddled, disoriented, disorientated, dizzy, punch-drunk, shaky, unsteady, wobbly, weak, faint; informal dopey, woozy, not with it.

groom verb **1** *she groomed her pony:* **curry**, brush, comb, clean, rub down. **2** *his dark hair was carefully groomed:* **brush**, comb, arrange, do; tidy, spruce up, smarten up, preen, primp; informal fix. **3** *they were groomed for stardom:* **prepare**, prime, ready, condition, tailor; coach, train, instruct, drill, teach, school.
noun **1** *a groom took his horse:* **stable hand**, stableman, stable lad, stable boy, stable

girl; historical equerry. **2** *the bride and groom:* **bridegroom**; newly married man, newly-wed.

groove noun *water had worn a groove in the surface of the rock:* **furrow**, channel, trench, trough, canal, gouge, hollow, indentation, rut, gutter, cutting, cut, fissure.

grooved adjective **furrowed**, fluted, corrugated, ribbed, ridged.

grope verb **1** *she groped for her glasses:* **fumble**, scrabble, fish, ferret, rummage, feel, search, hunt; Brit. informal rootle. **2** (informal) *one of the men started groping her:* **fondle**, touch; informal paw, maul, feel up, touch up.

gross adjective **1** *the man was pale and gross:* **obese**, corpulent, overweight, fat, big, large, fleshy, flabby, portly, bloated; informal porky, pudgy, tubby, blubbery, roly-poly; Brit. informal podgy, fubsy. **2** *men of gross natures:* **boorish**, coarse, vulgar, loutish, oafish, thuggish, brutish, philistine, uncouth, crass, common, unrefined, unsophisticated, uncultured, uncultivated; informal cloddish; Brit. informal yobbish. **3** (informal) *the place smelled gross:* **disgusting**, repellent, repulsive, abhorrent, loathsome, foul, nasty, obnoxious, sickening, nauseating, stomach-churning, unpalatable; N. Amer. vomitous; informal yucky, icky, sick-making, gut-churning. **4** *a gross distortion of the truth:* **flagrant**, blatant, glaring, obvious, overt, naked, barefaced, shameless, brazen, audacious, brass-necked, undisguised, unconcealed, patent, transparent, manifest, palpable; out and out, utter, complete. **5** *their gross income:* **total**, whole, entire, complete, full, overall, combined, aggregate; before deductions, before tax.
– OPPOSITES slender, refined, pleasant, net.
verb *he grosses over a million dollars a month:* **earn**, make, bring in, take, get, receive, collect; informal rake in.

grotesque adjective **1** *a grotesque creature:* **malformed**, deformed, misshapen, misproportioned, distorted, twisted, gnarled, mangled, mutilated; ugly, unsightly, monstrous, hideous, freakish, unnatural, abnormal, strange, odd, peculiar; informal weird, freaky. **2** *grotesque mismanagement of funds:* **outrageous**, monstrous, shocking, appalling, preposterous; ridiculous, ludicrous, farcical, unbelievable, incredible.
– OPPOSITES normal.

grotto noun **cave**, cavern, hollow; pothole, underground chamber.

grouchy adjective *the old man grew sulky and grouchy:* **grumpy**, cross, irritable, bad-tempered, crotchety, crabby, crabbed, cantankerous, curmudgeonly, testy, tetchy, huffy, snappish, waspish, prickly; informal snappy; Brit. informal narky, ratty, like a bear with a sore head, whingy; N. Amer. informal cranky, soreheaded; informal, dated miffy.

ground noun **1** *she collapsed on the ground:* **floor**, earth, terra firma; flooring; informal

deck. **2** *the soggy ground:* **earth**, soil, dirt, clay, loam, turf, clod, sod; land, terrain. **3** *the team's home ground:* **stadium**, pitch, field, arena, track; N. Amer. bowl; Brit. informal park. **4** *the mansion's grounds:* **estate**, gardens, lawns, park, parkland, land, acres, property, surroundings, holding, territory. **5** *grounds for dismissal:* **reason**, cause, basis, base, foundation, justification, rationale, argument, premise, occasion, excuse, pretext, motive, motivation. **6** *coffee grounds:* **sediment**, precipitate, settlings, dregs, lees, deposit, residue.
verb 1 *the boat grounded on a mud bank:* **run aground**, run ashore, beach, land. **2** *an assertion grounded on results of several studies:* **base**, found, establish, root, build, construct, form. **3** *they were grounded in classics and history:* **instruct**, coach, teach, tutor, educate, school, train, drill, prime, prepare; familiarize with, acquaint with.

groundless adjective *she dismissed their fears as groundless:* **baseless**, without basis, without foundation, ill-founded, unfounded, unsupported, uncorroborated, unproven, empty, idle, unsubstantiated, unwarranted, unjustified, unjustifiable, without cause, without reason, without justification, unreasonable, irrational, illogical, misguided.

groundwork noun *I had to do the groundwork for a revolutionary new project:* **preliminary work**, preliminaries, preparations, spadework, legwork, donkey work; planning, arrangements, organization, homework; basics, essentials, fundamentals, underpinning, foundation.

group noun **1** *the exhibits were divided into three distinct groups:* **category**, class, classification, grouping, set, lot, batch, bracket, type, sort, kind, variety, family, species, genus, breed; grade, grading, rank, status. **2** *a group of tourists:* **crowd**, party, body, band, company, gathering, congregation, assembly, collection, cluster, flock, pack, troop, gang; informal bunch. **3** *a coup attempt by a group within the parliament:* **faction**, division, section, clique, coterie, circle, set, ring, camp, bloc, caucus, cabal, fringe movement, splinter group. **4** *the women's group:* **association**, club, society, league, guild, circle, union. **5** *a small group of trees:* **cluster**, knot, collection, mass, clump. **6** *a local folk group:* **band**, ensemble, act; informal line-up, combo, outfit.
verb 1 *patients were grouped according to their symptoms:* **categorize**, classify, class, catalogue, sort, bracket, pigeonhole, grade, rate, rank. **2** *wooden chairs were grouped round the table:* **place**, arrange, assemble, organize, range, line up, dispose. **3** *the two parties grouped together:* **unite**, join together/up, team up, join forces, get together, ally, form an alliance, affiliate, combine; collaborate, work together, pull together, cooperate.

grouse verb *she groused about the food:* **grumble**, complain, protest, whine, bleat, carp, cavil, make a fuss; informal moan, bellyache, gripe, beef, bitch, grouch, whinge, sound off; Brit. informal chunter, create; N. Amer. informal kvetch.
noun *our biggest grouse was about the noise:* **grumble**, complaint, grievance, objection, cavil, quibble; informal moan, beef, gripe, grouch.

grove noun *a villa sited in an olive grove:* **copse**, wood, thicket, coppice; orchard, plantation; Brit. spinney.

grovel verb **1** *George grovelled at his feet:* **prostrate oneself**, lie, kneel, cringe. **2** *she was not going to grovel to him:* **be obsequious**, fawn on, kowtow, bow and scrape, toady, truckle, abase oneself, humble oneself; curry favour with, flatter, dance attendance on, make up to, play up to, ingratiate oneself with; informal crawl, creep, suck up to, lick someone's boots.

grow verb **1** *the boys had grown:* **get bigger**, get taller, get larger, increase in size. **2** *sales and profits continue to grow:* **increase**, swell, multiply, snowball, mushroom, balloon, build up, mount up, pile up; informal skyrocket. **3** *flowers grew among the rocks:* **sprout**, germinate, shoot up, spring up, develop, bud, burst forth, bloom, flourish, thrive, run riot. **4** *he grew vegetables:* **cultivate**, produce, propagate, raise, rear, nurture, tend; farm. **5** *the family business grew:* **expand**, extend, develop, progress, make progress; flourish, thrive, burgeon, prosper, succeed, boom. **6** *the fable grew from an ancient Indian source:* **originate**, stem, spring, arise, emerge, issue; develop, evolve. **7** *Leonora grew bored:* **become**, get, turn, begin to feel.
– OPPOSITES shrink, decline.

growl verb *the dog growled at him:* **snarl**, bark, yap, bay.

grown-up noun *she wanted to be treated like a grown-up:* **adult**, (grown) woman, (grown) man, mature woman, mature man.
– OPPOSITES child.
adjective *she has two grown-up daughters:* **adult**, mature, of age; fully grown, full-grown, fully developed.

growth noun **1** *population growth:* **increase**, expansion, augmentation, proliferation, multiplication, enlargement, mushrooming, snowballing, rise, escalation, build-up. **2** *the growth of plants:* **development**, maturation, growing, germination, sprouting; blooming. **3** *the marked growth of local enterprises:* **expansion**, extension, development, progress, advance, advancement, headway, spread, buildout; rise, success, boom, upturn, upswing. **4** *a growth on his jaw:* **tumour**, malignancy, cancer; lump, excrescence, outgrowth, swelling, nodule; cyst, polyp.
– OPPOSITES decrease, decline.

grub noun *a small black grub:* **larva**; maggot; caterpillar.
verb **1** *kids grubbing around in the dirt:* **dig**, poke, scratch. **2** *they grubbed up the old trees:* **dig up**, unearth, uproot, root up/out, pull up/out, tear out. **3** *he began grubbing about in the bin:* **rummage**, search, hunt, delve, dig, scrabble, ferret, root, rifle, fish, poke; Brit. informal rootle; Austral./NZ informal fossick through.

grubby adjective *grubby net curtains:* **dirty**, grimy, filthy, mucky, unwashed, stained, soiled, smeared, spotted, muddy, dusty, sooty; unhygienic, insanitary; informal cruddy, yucky; Brit. informal manky, grotty, gungy.
– OPPOSITES clean.

grudge noun *a former employee with a grudge:* **grievance**, resentment, bitterness, rancour, pique, umbrage, dissatisfaction, disgruntlement, bad feelings, hard feelings, ill feelings, ill will, animosity, antipathy, antagonism, enmity, animus; informal a chip on one's shoulder.
verb **1** *he grudged the time that the meetings involved:* **begrudge**, resent, feel aggrieved about, be resentful of, mind, object to, take exception to. **2** *I don't grudge you your success:* **envy**, begrudge, resent, be jealous of, be envious of, be resentful of.

grudging adjective *she offered a grudging apology:* **reluctant**, unwilling, forced, half-hearted, unenthusiastic, hesitant; begrudging, resentful.
– OPPOSITES eager.

gruelling adjective *he undertook a gruelling three-mile run:* **exhausting**, tiring, fatiguing, wearying, taxing, draining, debilitating; demanding, exacting, difficult, hard, arduous, strenuous, laborious, back-breaking, harsh, severe, stiff, punishing, crippling; informal killing, murderous, hellish; Brit. informal knackering.

gruesome adjective *the gruesome evidence of a recent massacre:* **grisly**, ghastly, frightful, horrid, horrifying, hideous, horrible, horrendous, grim, awful, dire, dreadful, terrible, horrific, shocking, appalling, disgusting, repulsive, repugnant, revolting, repellent, sickening; loathsome, abhorrent, odious, monstrous, unspeakable; informal sick, sick-making, gross.
– OPPOSITES pleasant.

gruff adjective **1** *a gruff reply | his gruff exterior:* **abrupt**, brusque, curt, short, blunt, bluff, no-nonsense; laconic, taciturn; surly, churlish, grumpy, crotchety, crabby, crabbed, cross, bad-tempered, short-tempered, ill-natured, crusty, tetchy, bearish, ungracious, unceremonious; informal grouchy. **2** *a gruff voice:* **rough**, guttural, throaty, gravelly, husky, croaking, rasping, raspy, growly, hoarse, harsh; low, thick.
– OPPOSITES friendly, soft.

grumble verb *they grumbled about the disruption:* **complain**, grouse, whine, mutter, bleat, carp, cavil, protest, make a

fuss; informal moan, bellyache, beef, bitch, grouch, whinge, sound off; Brit. informal gripe, chunter, create; N. English informal mither; N. Amer. informal kvetch.
noun *his customers' grumbles:* **complaint**, grouse, grievance, protest, cavil, quibble, criticism; informal grouch, moan, whinge, beef, bitch, gripe.

grumpy adjective *she can be grumpy first thing in the morning:* **bad-tempered**, crabby, ill-tempered, short-tempered, crotchety, tetchy, testy, crabbed, waspish, prickly, touchy, irritable, irascible, crusty, cantankerous, curmudgeonly, bearish, surly, ill-natured, churlish, ill-humoured, peevish, cross, fractious, disagreeable, pettish; informal grouchy, snappy, snappish; Brit. informal shirty, stroppy, narky, ratty, eggy, like a bear with a sore head; N. Amer. informal cranky, ornery, soreheaded.
– OPPOSITES good-humoured.

guarantee noun **1** *all repairs have a one-year guarantee:* **warranty**, warrant. **2** *a guarantee that the hospital will stay open:* **promise**, assurance, word (of honour), pledge, vow, oath, bond, commitment, covenant. **3** *banks usually demand a personal guarantee for loans:* **collateral**, security, surety, guaranty, earnest.
verb **1** *he agreed to guarantee the loan:* **underwrite**, put up collateral for. **2** *can you guarantee he wasn't involved?* **promise**, swear, swear to the fact, pledge, vow, undertake, give one's word, give an assurance, give an undertaking, take an oath.

guard verb **1** *infantry guarded the barricaded bridge:* **protect**, stand guard over, watch over, keep an eye on; cover, patrol, police, defend, shield, safeguard, keep safe, secure. **2** *the prisoners were guarded by armed men:* **keep under surveillance**, keep under guard, keep watch over, mind. **3** *forest wardens must guard against poachers:* **beware of**, keep watch for, be alert to, keep an eye out for, be on the alert/lookout for.
noun **1** *border guards:* **sentry**, sentinel, security guard, nightwatchman; protector, defender, guardian; lookout; watch; garrison. **2** *her prison guard:* **warder**, warden, keeper; jailer; informal screw. **3** *he let his guard slip and they escaped:* **vigilance**, vigil, watch, surveillance, watchfulness, caution, heed, attention, care, wariness. **4** *a metal guard keeps fingers out of the mechanism:* **safety guard**, safety device, protective device, shield, screen, fender; bumper, buffer.
■ **off (one's) guard** unprepared, unready, inattentive, unwary, with one's defences down, cold, unsuspecting; informal napping, asleep at the wheel, on the hop.
■ **on one's guard** vigilant, alert, on the alert, wary, watchful, cautious, careful, heedful, chary, circumspect, on the lookout, on the qui vive, on one's toes, prepared,

g

ready, wide awake, attentive, observant, keeping one's eyes peeled; informal keeping a weather eye out.

guarded adjective *he has given a guarded welcome to the idea:* **cautious**, careful, circumspect, wary, chary, on one's guard, reluctant, non-committal, reticent, restrained, reserved; informal cagey.

guardian noun *an indefatigable guardian of public morality:* **protector**, defender, preserver, custodian, warden, guard, keeper; conservator, curator, caretaker, steward, trustee.

guerrilla noun *there was fierce fighting between guerrillas and government troops:* **freedom fighter**, irregular, member of the resistance, partisan; rebel, radical, revolutionary, revolutionist; terrorist.

guess verb **1** *he guessed she was about 40:* **estimate**, hazard a guess, reckon, gauge, judge, calculate; hypothesize, postulate, predict, speculate, conjecture, surmise; informal guesstimate. **2** (informal) *I guess I owe you an apology:* **suppose**, think, imagine, expect, suspect, dare say; informal reckon, figure.
noun *my guess was right:* **hypothesis**, theory, prediction, postulation, conjecture, surmise, estimate, belief, opinion, reckoning, judgement, supposition, speculation, suspicion, impression, feeling; informal guesstimate.

guesswork noun *their estimates were based largely on guesswork:* **guessing**, conjecture, surmise, supposition, assumptions, presumptions, speculation, hypothesizing, theorizing, prediction; approximations, rough calculations; hunches; informal guesstimates.

guest noun **1** *I have two guests coming to dinner:* **visitor**, caller; company. **2** *hotel guests have free use of the swimming pool:* **resident**, boarder, lodger, paying guest, PG; patron, client; N. Amer. roomer.
– OPPOSITES host.

guest house noun **boarding house**, bed and breakfast, B&B, hotel; pension, pensione.

guffaw verb *he guffawed at his own punchline:* **roar with laughter**, laugh heartily/loudly, roar, bellow, cackle; informal laugh like a drain.

guidance noun **1** *she looked to her father for guidance:* **advice**, counsel, direction, instruction, enlightenment, information; recommendations, suggestions, tips, hints, pointers, guidelines. **2** *work continued under the guidance of a project supervisor:* **direction**, control, leadership, management, supervision, superintendence, charge; handling, conduct, running, overseeing.

guide noun **1** *our guide took us back to the hotel:* **escort**, attendant, courier, cicerone, dragoman; usher; chaperone. **2** *he is my inspiration and my guide:* **adviser**, mentor, counsellor; guru. **3** *the light acted as a guide*

for shipping: **pointer**, marker, indicator, signpost, mark, landmark; guiding light, sign, signal, beacon. **4** *the techniques outlined are meant as a guide:* **model**, pattern, blueprint, template, example, exemplar; standard, touchstone, measure, benchmark, yardstick, gauge. **5** *a pocket guide of Paris:* **guidebook**, travelogue, vade mecum; companion, handbook, directory, A to Z; informal bible.
verb **1** *he guided her to her seat:* **lead**, lead the way, conduct, show, show someone the way, usher, shepherd, direct, steer, pilot, escort, accompany, attend; see, take, help, assist. **2** *the chairman must guide the meeting:* **direct**, steer, control, manage, command, lead, conduct, run, be in charge of, have control of, govern, preside over, superintend, supervise, oversee; handle, regulate. **3** *he was always there to guide me:* **advise**, counsel, give advice to, direct, give direction to.

guidebook noun *they followed the tour in the museum guidebook:* **guide**, travel guide, travelogue, vade mecum; companion, handbook, directory, A to Z; informal bible.

guideline noun *the planning authorities have fairly strict guidelines:* **recommendation**, instruction, direction, suggestion, advice; regulation, rule, principle, guiding principle; standard, criterion, measure, gauge, yardstick, benchmark, touchstone; procedure, parameter.

guild noun *a member of the Women's Cooperative Guild:* **association**, society, union, league, organization, company, cooperative, fellowship, club, order, lodge, brotherhood, fraternity, sisterhood, sorority.

guile noun *they penetrated the city's defences by guile:* **cunning**, craftiness, craft, artfulness, art, artifice, wiliness, slyness, deviousness; wiles, ploys, schemes, stratagems, manoeuvres, subterfuges, tricks, ruses; deception, deceit, duplicity, underhandedness, double-dealing, trickery.
– OPPOSITES honesty.

guileless adjective *Paul's questioning had the guileless innocence of a child:* **artless**, ingenuous, naive, open, genuine, natural, simple, childlike, innocent, unsophisticated, unworldly, unsuspicious, trustful, trusting; honest, truthful, sincere, straightforward.
– OPPOSITES scheming.

guilt noun **1** *the proof of his guilt:* **culpability**, guiltiness, blameworthiness; wrongdoing, wrong, criminality, misconduct, sin. **2** *a terrible feeling of guilt:* **self-reproach**, self-condemnation, shame, a guilty conscience, pangs of conscience; remorse, remorsefulness, regret, contrition, contriteness, compunction.
– OPPOSITES innocence.

guiltless adjective *I am entirely guiltless in this matter:* **innocent**, blameless, not to blame, without fault, above reproach, above

suspicion, in the clear, unimpeachable, irreproachable, faultless, sinless, spotless, immaculate, unsullied, uncorrupted, undefiled, untainted, unblemished, untarnished, impeccable; informal squeaky clean, whiter than white, as pure as the driven snow.
- OPPOSITES guilty.

guilty adjective 1 *the guilty party must make restitution:* **culpable**, to blame, at fault, in the wrong, blameworthy, responsible; erring, errant, delinquent, offending, sinful, criminal. 2 *I still feel guilty about it:* **ashamed**, guilt-ridden, conscience-stricken, remorseful, sorry, contrite, repentant, penitent, regretful, rueful, abashed, shamefaced, sheepish, hangdog; in sackcloth and ashes.
- OPPOSITES innocent, unrepentant.

guise noun 1 *the god appeared in the guise of a swan:* **likeness**, outward appearance, appearance, semblance, form, shape, image; disguise. 2 *additional sums paid under the guise of consultancy fees:* **pretence**, disguise, front, facade, cover, blind, screen, smokescreen.

gulf noun 1 *our ship sailed into the gulf:* **inlet**, bay, creek, bight, cove, fjord, estuary, sound, arm of the sea; Scottish firth, frith. 2 *the ice gave way and a gulf widened slowly:* **hole**, crevasse, fissure, cleft, split, rift, pit, cavity, chasm, abyss, void; ravine, gorge, canyon, gully. 3 *a growing gulf between rich and poor:* **divide**, division, separation, gap, breach, rift, split, chasm, abyss; difference, contrast, polarity.

gull verb *she knew she wouldn't be able to gull him:* **hoodwink**, fool, dupe, deceive, delude, hoax, trick, mislead, lead on, take in, swindle, cheat, double-cross; informal pull the wool over someone's eyes, pull a fast one on, put one over on, sell a pup to, bamboozle, con, do; N. Amer. informal sucker, snooker; Austral. informal pull a swifty on.

gullet noun **oesophagus**, throat, maw, pharynx; crop, craw.

gullible adjective *the swindler preyed on gullible old women:* **credulous**, naive, over-trusting, over-trustful, easily deceived, easily taken in, exploitable, dupable, impressionable, unsuspecting, unsuspicious, unwary, ingenuous, innocent, inexperienced, unworldly, green; informal wet behind the ears, born yesterday.
- OPPOSITES suspicious.

gully noun 1 *a steep icy gully:* **ravine**, canyon, gorge, pass, defile, couloir; S. English chine; N. English clough, gill; N. Amer. gulch, coulee. 2 *water runs from the drainpipe into a gully:* **channel**, conduit, trench, ditch, drain, culvert, cut, gutter.

gulp verb 1 *she gulped her juice:* **swallow**, quaff, swill down, down; informal swig, knock back. 2 *he gulped down the rest of his meal:* **gobble**, guzzle, devour, bolt, wolf, cram,

stuff; informal put away, demolish, polish off, shovel down; Brit. informal scoff. 3 *Jenny gulped back her tears:* **choke back**, fight back, hold back/in, suppress, stifle, smother.
- OPPOSITES sip.
noun *a gulp of cold beer:* **mouthful**, swallow, draught; informal swig.

gum noun *photographs stuck down with gum:* **glue**, adhesive, fixative, paste, epoxy resin; N. Amer. mucilage.
verb *the receipts were gummed into a book:* **stick**, glue, paste; fix, affix, attach, fasten.
■ **gum something up** clog (up), choke (up), stop up, plug; obstruct; informal bung up; Brit. informal gunge up.

gummy adjective **sticky**, tacky, gluey, adhesive, resinous, viscous, viscid, glutinous, mucilaginous; informal gooey.

gumption noun (informal) *she had the gumption to go and make a better life for herself:* **initiative**, resourcefulness, enterprise, ingenuity, imagination; astuteness, shrewdness, acumen, sense, common sense, wit, mother wit, native wit, practicality; spirit, backbone, pluck, mettle, nerve, courage; informal get-up-and-go, spunk, oomph, nous, savvy, horse sense; N. Amer. informal smarts.

gun noun **firearm**, pistol, revolver, rifle, shotgun, automatic, handgun, machine gun; weapon; informal shooter; N. Amer. informal piece, shooting iron.

gunfire noun *they heard the distant sounds of gunfire:* **gunshots**, shots, shooting, firing, sniping; artillery fire, strafing, shelling.

gunman noun *the gunman broke into the bank through the roof:* **armed robber**, gangster, terrorist; sniper, gunfighter; assassin, murderer, killer; informal hit man, hired gun, gunslinger, mobster; N. Amer. informal shootist, hood.

gurgle verb *the water swirled and gurgled:* **babble**, burble, tinkle, bubble, ripple, murmur, purl, splash.
noun *the gurgle of a small brook:* **babbling**, tinkling, bubbling, rippling, trickling, murmur, murmuring, purling, splashing.

guru noun 1 *a Hindu guru and mystic:* **spiritual teacher**, teacher, tutor, sage, mentor, spiritual leader, leader, master; Hinduism swami, Maharishi. 2 *a management guru:* **expert**, authority, pundit, leading light, master, specialist; informal whizz.
- OPPOSITES disciple.

gush verb 1 *water gushed through the weir:* **surge**, burst, spout, spurt, jet, stream, rush, pour, spill, well out, cascade, flood, flow, run, issue; Brit. informal sloosh. 2 *everyone gushed about the script:* **enthuse**, rave, be enthusiastic, be effusive, rhapsodize, go into raptures, wax lyrical, praise to the skies; informal go mad/wild/crazy, go over the top; N. Amer. informal ballyhoo.
noun *a gush of water:* **surge**, stream, spurt,

jet, spout, outpouring, outflow, burst, rush, cascade, flood, torrent.

gushing, gushy adjective *the gushing praise of the New York critics:* **effusive**, enthusiastic, over-enthusiastic, unrestrained, extravagant, fulsome, lavish, rhapsodic, lyrical; informal over the top, OTT, laid on with a trowel.
– OPPOSITES restrained.

gust noun 1 *a sudden gust of wind:* **flurry**, blast, puff, blow, rush; squall. **2** *gusts of laughter:* **outburst**, burst, eruption, fit, paroxysm; gale, peal, howl, hoot, shriek, roar.
verb *wind gusted around the chimneys:* **blow**, bluster, flurry, roar.

gusto noun *he was attacking his breakfast with some gusto:* **enthusiasm**, relish, appetite, enjoyment, delight, glee, pleasure, satisfaction, appreciation, liking; zest, zeal, fervour, verve, keenness, avidity.
– OPPOSITES apathy, distaste.

gusty adjective *a gusty autumnal night:* **blustery**, windy, breezy; squally, stormy, tempestuous, wild, turbulent; informal blowy.
– OPPOSITES calm.

gut noun 1 *he had an ache in his gut:* **stomach**, belly, abdomen, solar plexus; intestines, bowels; informal tummy, tum, insides, innards. **2** *fish heads and guts:* **entrails**; intestines, viscera; offal; informal insides, innards.
verb 1 *clean, scale, and gut the sardines:* **remove the guts from**, disembowel, draw. **2** *the church was gutted by fire:* **devastate**, destroy, demolish, wipe out, lay waste, ravage, consume, ruin, wreck.

gutter noun **drain**, sluice, sluiceway, culvert, spillway, sewer; channel, conduit, pipe; trough, trench, ditch, furrow, cut.

guttersnipe noun (derogatory) **urchin**, ragamuffin, waif, stray.

guttural adjective *he heard guttural shouts in a foreign language:* **throaty**, husky, gruff, gravelly, growly, growling, croaky, croaking, harsh, rough, rasping, raspy; deep, low, thick.

guy noun (informal) *he's a handsome guy:* **man**, fellow, gentleman; youth, boy; informal lad, fella, geezer, gent; Brit. informal chap, bloke; N. Amer. informal dude, hombre.
verb *she guyed him about his weight:* **make fun of**, poke fun at, laugh at, mock, ridicule, jeer at, scoff at; satirize, lampoon; informal send up, take the mickey out of; N. Amer. informal goof on.

guzzle verb 1 *he guzzled his burger:* **gobble**, bolt, wolf, devour; informal tuck into, put away, pack away, demolish, polish off, stuff one's face with, pig oneself on, shovel down; Brit. informal snarf down/up, scarf down/up. **2** *she guzzled down the orange juice:* **gulp down**, swallow, quaff, down, swill; informal knock back, swig, slug down.

gypsy, gipsy noun **Romany**, Rom, chal, gitano, gitana, tzigane; traveller, nomad, rover, roamer, wanderer; dialect didicoi; Brit. derogatory tinker.

gyrate verb *flashing lights gyrate above the dance floor:* **rotate**, revolve, wheel, turn round, whirl, circle, pirouette, twirl, swirl, spin, swivel.

Hh

habit noun **1** *it was his habit to go for a run every morning:* **custom**, practice, routine, wont, pattern, convention, way, norm, tradition, rule, usage. **2** *he failed to notice her many irritating habits:* **mannerism**, way, quirk, foible, trick, trait, idiosyncrasy, peculiarity, singularity, oddity, eccentricity, feature; tendency, propensity, inclination, bent, proclivity, disposition, predisposition. **3** *his cocaine habit:* **addiction**, dependence, dependency, craving, fixation, compulsion, obsession; informal monkey on one's back; N. Amer. informal jones. **4** *a monk's habit:* **garments**, dress, garb, clothes, clothing, attire, outfit, costume; informal gear; formal apparel.
■ **in the habit of** *they were in the habit of phoning one another regularly:* accustomed to, used to, given to, wont to, inclined to.

habitable adjective *contractors worked around the clock to make the building habitable:* **fit to live in**, inhabitable, liveable-in.

habitat noun *the thrill of spotting wildlife in its natural habitat:* **environment**, surroundings, home, domain, haunt; formal habitation.

habitation noun **1** *a house fit for human habitation:* **occupancy**, occupation, residence, residency, living in, tenancy. **2** *the river turned through a wide bend and we could see no other habitation upstream:* **residence**, place of residence, house, home, quarters, living quarters, rooms, accommodation; informal pad, digs; formal dwelling, dwelling place, abode, domicile.

habitual adjective **1** *they get into shoplifting and drug-taking, becoming habitual criminals:* **inveterate**, confirmed, compulsive, obsessive, incorrigible, hardened, ingrained, dyed-in-the-wool, chronic, regular; addicted; informal pathological. **2** *the commuters assembled in their habitual positions on the platform:* **customary**, accustomed, regular, usual, normal, set, fixed, established, routine, common, ordinary, familiar, traditional, typical, general, characteristic, standard, time-honoured; literary wonted.
– OPPOSITES occasional, unaccustomed.

habituate verb *the school had habituated him to shabbiness and discomfort:* **accustom**, make used, familiarize, adapt, adjust, attune, acclimatize, acculturate, condition; inure, harden; N. Amer. acclimate.

habitué noun *the book should appeal to Vegas visitors and habitués alike:* **regular**, regular visitor/customer/client, familiar face, patron; frequenter, haunter.

hack[1] verb *I hacked the padlock off:* **cut**, chop, hew, lop, saw, slash.

hack[2] noun *he briefed the media's industry hacks before the party conference:* **journalist**, reporter, newspaperman, newspaperwoman, writer; informal journo, scribbler, hackette.

hackle
■ **make someone's hackles rise** *his impatient reply made her hackles rise:* annoy, irritate, exasperate, anger, incense, infuriate, irk, nettle, vex, put out, provoke, gall, antagonize, get on someone's nerves, ruffle someone's feathers, rankle with; Brit. rub up the wrong way; informal aggravate, peeve, needle, rile, make someone see red, make someone's blood boil, hack off, get someone's back up, get someone's goat, get up someone's nose, get someone's dander up, bug, miff; Brit. informal wind up, nark, get on someone's wick; N. Amer. informal tee off, tick off, burn up.

hackneyed adjective *New Jersey has started to shed its hackneyed image as the home of toxic dumps and second-class citizens:* **overused**, overdone, overworked, worn out, time-worn, platitudinous, vapid, stale, tired, threadbare; trite, banal, hack, clichéd, hoary, commonplace, common, ordinary, stock, conventional, stereotyped, predictable; unimaginative, unoriginal, uninspired, prosaic, dull, boring, pedestrian, run-of-the-mill, routine; informal old hat, corny, played out.
– OPPOSITES original.

Hades noun. See HELL sense 1.

haft noun **handle**, shaft, hilt, butt, stock, grip, handgrip, helve, shank.

hag noun *she's companion to that evil hag upstairs:* **crone**, old woman, gorgon; informal witch, (old) crow, (old) cow, old bag, old boot.

haggard adjective *he looked terrible, all grey and haggard:* **drawn**, tired, exhausted, drained, careworn, unwell, unhealthy, spent, washed out, rundown; gaunt, pinched, peaked, peaky, hollow-cheeked, hollow-

h

eyed, thin, emaciated, wasted, cadaverous; pale, wan, grey, ashen.
– OPPOSITES healthy.

haggle verb *Italian tourists haggled enthusiastically over exotic handicrafts:* **barter**, bargain, negotiate, dicker, quibble, wrangle; beat someone down.

hail¹ verb **1** *a friend hailed him from the upper deck:* **call out to**, shout to, halloo, address; greet, say hello to, salute. **2** *he stuck up his arm and hailed a cab:* **flag down**, wave down, signal to. **3** *critics hailed the film as a masterpiece:* **acclaim**, praise, applaud, rave about, extol, eulogize, hymn, lionize, sing the praises of, make much of, glorify, cheer, salute, toast; N. Amer. informal ballyhoo; black English big up; formal laud. **4** *Rick hails from Australia:* **come from**, be from, be a native of, have one's roots in.

hail² noun *he died in a hail of bullets:* **barrage**, volley, shower, rain, torrent, burst, stream, storm, avalanche, onslaught; bombardment, cannonade, battery, blast, salvo.
verb *tons of gravel hailed down on us:* **beat**, shower, rain, fall, pour; pelt, pepper, batter, bombard, assail.

hair noun **1** *her thick curly black hair:* **head of hair**, shock of hair, mane, mop; locks, tresses, curls, ringlets. **2** *I like your hair:* **hairstyle**, haircut, cut, coiffure; informal hairdo, do, coif. **3** *a dog with short, blue-grey hair:* **fur**, wool; coat, fleece, pelt; mane.
■ **a hair's breadth** *the American bison was saved from extinction by a hair's breadth:* the narrowest of margins, the skin of one's teeth, a split second, a nose; informal a whisker.
■ **let one's hair down** (informal) *visitors young and old let their hair down and enjoyed the entertainment:* enjoy oneself, have a good time, have fun, make merry, let oneself go; informal have a ball, whoop it up, paint the town red, live it up, have a whale of a time, let it all hang out.
■ **make someone's hair stand on end** horrify, shock, appal, stun; make someone's blood run cold; informal make someone's hair curl.
■ **split hairs** quibble, cavil, carp, niggle, chop logic; informal nit-pick.

hairdo noun (informal). See HAIRSTYLE.

hairdresser noun **hairstylist**, stylist, coiffeur, coiffeuse; barber; informal crimper.

hairless adjective **bald**, bald-headed; shaven, shaved, shorn, clean-shaven, beardless, smooth, smooth-faced, depilated; tonsured; informal baldy; technical glabrous; archaic bald-pated.
– OPPOSITES hairy.

hairpiece noun **wig**, toupee, periwig; merkin; informal rug.

hair-raising adjective *I thought skiing was pretty hair-raising, but rafting beats it:* **terrifying**, frightening, petrifying, alarming, chilling, horrifying, shocking, spine-chilling, blood-curdling, fearsome,

nightmarish; eerie, sinister, weird, ghostly, unearthly; Scottish eldritch; informal hairy, spooky, scary, creepy.

hair-splitting adjective *legal experts have a particularly hair-splitting mentality:* **pedantic**, pettifogging; quibbling, niggling, cavilling, carping, critical, overcritical, hypercritical; informal nit-picking, pernickety, picky; N. Amer. informal persnickety.

hairstyle noun **haircut**, cut, style, hair, coiffure; informal hairdo, do, coif.

hairy adjective **1** *animals with hairy coats and huge horns:* **shaggy**, bushy, long-haired; woolly, furry, fleecy, fuzzy. **2** *a grin appeared on his hairy face:* **bearded**, bewhiskered, mustachioed; unshaven, stubbly, bristly; formal hirsute. **3** (informal) *it got very hairy when we tried to cross the border:* **risky**, dangerous, perilous, hazardous, touch-and-go; tricky, ticklish, difficult, awkward; informal dicey, sticky, scary; Brit. informal dodgy.

halcyon adjective *the halcyon days of the 1960s:* **happy**, golden, idyllic, palmy, carefree, blissful, joyful, joyous, contented; flourishing, thriving, prosperous, successful; serene, calm, tranquil, peaceful.

hale adjective *only just sixty, he is very hale and hearty:* **healthy**, fit, fighting fit, well, in good health, bursting with health, in fine fettle, as fit as a fiddle/flea; strong, robust, vigorous, hardy, sturdy, hearty, lusty, able-bodied; informal in the pink, as right as rain.
– OPPOSITES unwell.

half adverb **1** *half-cooked chicken:* **partially**, partly; incompletely, inadequately, insufficiently; in part, part, slightly. **2** *I'm half inclined to believe you:* **almost**, to some extent/degree, (up) to a point, in part, partly.
– OPPOSITES fully.

half-baked adjective *half-baked theories about a parallel universe:* **ill-conceived**, hare-brained, ill-judged, impractical, unrealistic, unworkable, ridiculous, absurd; informal crazy, crackpot, cockeyed.

half-hearted adjective *the plan received a half-hearted welcome from the committee members:* **unenthusiastic**, cool, lukewarm, tepid, apathetic, indifferent, uninterested, unconcerned, languid, listless; perfunctory, cursory, superficial, desultory, feeble, lacklustre.
– OPPOSITES enthusiastic.

halfway adjective *we have reached the halfway point:* **midway**, middle, mid, central, centre, intermediate; Anatomy medial, mesial.
adverb **1** *he stopped halfway down the passage:* **midway**, in the middle, in the centre; part of the way, part-way. **2** *he seemed halfway friendly:* **to some extent/degree**, in some measure, relatively, comparatively, moderately, somewhat, (up) to a point; just about, almost, nearly.
■ **meet someone halfway** *I was willing to meet him halfway on privatization:*

compromise, come to terms, reach an agreement, make a deal, make concessions, find the middle ground, strike a balance; give and take.

halfwit noun (informal). See **FOOL** noun sense 1.

half-witted adjective (informal). See **STUPID** senses 1, 2.

hall noun **1** *hang your coat in the hall:* **entrance hall**, hallway, entry, entrance, lobby, foyer, vestibule; atrium, concourse; passageway, passage, corridor; N. Amer. entryway. **2** *we met in the village hall:* **assembly room**, meeting room, chamber; auditorium, concert hall, theatre.

hallmark noun **1** *the hallmark on my wedding ring:* **assay mark**, stamp. **2** *the tiny bubbles are the hallmark of fine champagnes:* **mark**, distinctive feature, characteristic, sign, sure sign, telltale sign, badge, stamp, trademark, indication, indicator.

hallowed adjective *bones which they have sworn to bury in hallowed ground:* **sacred**, holy, consecrated, sanctified, blessed; venerated, honoured, sacrosanct.

hallucinate verb *the tablets were making me hallucinate:* **have hallucinations**, see things, be delirious; informal trip.

hallucination noun *don't worry, it's only a hallucination:* **delusion**, illusion, figment of the imagination, vision, apparition, mirage, chimera, fantasy; (**hallucinations**) delirium, phantasmagoria; informal trip.

halo noun **ring of light**, nimbus, aureole, glory, crown of light, corona; technical halation; rare gloriole.

halt verb **1** *Len halted and turned round:* **stop**, come to a halt, come to a stop, come to a standstill; pull up, draw up. **2** *a further strike has halted production:* **stop**, bring to a stop, put a stop to, bring to an end, put an end to, terminate, end, wind up; suspend, break off, arrest, impede, check, curb, stem, staunch, block, stall, hold back; informal pull the plug on, put the kibosh on.
– OPPOSITES start, continue.
noun **1** *the car drew to a halt:* **stop**, standstill. **2** *a halt in production:* **stoppage**, break, suspension, pause, interval, interruption, hiatus; cessation, termination, close, end.

halter noun **harness**, head collar, bridle; N. Amer. headstall.

halting adjective **1** *he spoke to us in halting English:* **hesitant**, faltering, hesitating, stumbling, stammering, stuttering; broken, imperfect. **2** *the slow, halting train, eventually drew to a standstill at a drowsy country station:* **unsteady**, awkward, faltering, stumbling, limping, hobbling.
– OPPOSITES fluent.

ham-fisted adjective *his ham-fisted handling of the situation attracted much criticism:* **clumsy**, bungling, incompetent, amateurish, inept, unskilful, inexpert, maladroit, gauche, awkward, inefficient, bumbling, useless;

informal cack-handed, ham-handed; Brit. informal all fingers and thumbs.
– OPPOSITES expert.

hammer noun *a hammer and chisel:* mallet, beetle, gavel, sledgehammer.
verb **1** *the alloy is hammered into a circular shape:* **beat**, forge, shape, form, mould, fashion, make. **2** *Sally hammered at the door:* **batter**, pummel, beat, bang, pound; strike, hit, knock on, thump on; cudgel, bludgeon, club; informal bash, wallop, clobber, whack, thwack. **3** *they hammered away at their non-smoking campaign:* **work away**, labour, slog away, plod away/on, slave away, keep one's nose to the grindstone; persist with, persevere with, press on with; informal stick at, peg away, beaver away, plug away, soldier on; Brit. informal graft away. **4** *anti-racism had been hammered into her:* **drum**, instil, inculcate, knock, drive, din; drive home to, impress upon; ingrain. **5** (informal) *he got hammered for an honest mistake.* See **CHASTISE**. **6** (informal) *we've hammered them twice this season.* See **TROUNCE**.
■ **hammer something out** *the area committees have hammered out a national plan:* thrash out, work out, agree on, sort out, decide on, bring about, effect, produce, broker, negotiate, reach an agreement on.

hamper¹ noun *start saving now for your Christmas hamper:* **basket**, pannier, box, container, holder.

hamper² verb *the search was hampered by fog:* **hinder**, obstruct, impede, inhibit, retard, baulk, thwart, foil, curb, delay, set back, slow down, hold up, interfere with; restrict, constrain, trammel, block, check, curtail, frustrate, cramp, bridle, handicap, cripple, hamstring, shackle, fetter; informal stymie; Brit. informal throw a spanner in the works of; N. Amer. informal bork, throw a monkey wrench in the works of.
– OPPOSITES help.

hamstring verb *manufacturing companies were hamstrung by the economic chaos:* **handicap**, constrain, restrict, cripple, shackle, fetter, encumber, block, frustrate; hamper, hinder, obstruct, impede, trammel, inhibit, baulk, thwart, foil; informal stymie; N. Amer. informal bork.
– OPPOSITES help.

hand noun **1** *he had big, strong hands:* palm, fist; informal paw, mitt, duke, hook, meat hook; Zoology manus. **2** *the clock's second hand had stopped:* **pointer**, indicator, needle, arrow, marker. **3** *the frontier posts remained in government hands:* **control**, power, charge, authority; command, responsibility, guardianship, management, care, supervision, jurisdiction; possession, keeping, custody; clutches, grasp, thrall; disposal; informal say-so. **4** *a document written in his own hand:* **handwriting**, writing, script, calligraphy. **5** *he found work as a farm hand:* **worker**, factory worker, manual worker, unskilled worker, blue-collar

worker, workman, labourer, operative, hired hand, roustabout; N. Amer. peon; Austral./NZ rouseabout.
verb *he handed each man a glass:* **pass**, give, reach, let someone have, throw, toss; present to; informal chuck, bung.
■ **at hand 1** *keep the manual close at hand:* readily available, available, handy, to hand, within reach, accessible, close (by), near, nearby, at the ready, at one's fingertips, at one's disposal, convenient; informal get-at-able. **2** *the time for action is at hand:* imminent, approaching, coming, about to happen, on the horizon; impending.
■ **hand something down** *a secret recipe handed down from generation to generation:* pass on, pass down; bequeath, will, leave, make over, give, gift, transfer; Law demise, devise.
■ **hand in glove** *they were working hand in glove with the authorities:* in collaboration, in association, in cooperation, closely, in partnership, in league, in collusion; informal in cahoots.
■ **hand something on** *the drugs were then handed on to a dealer:* give, pass, hand, transfer, grant, cede, surrender, relinquish, yield; part with, let go of; bequeath, will, leave.
■ **hand something out** *the attendant handed out prayer books:* distribute, hand round, give out/round, pass out/round, share out, dole out, dish out, deal out, mete out, issue, dispense; allocate, allot, apportion, disburse; circulate, disseminate.
■ **hand something over** *it was suggested he might hand over power to his son:* yield, give, give up, pass, grant, entrust, surrender, relinquish, cede, turn over, deliver up, forfeit, sacrifice.
■ **to hand** *we pelted the police with whatever was to hand:* (readily) available, handy, at hand, within reach, accessible, ready, close (by), near, nearby, (lying) about/around, at the ready, at one's fingertips, at one's disposal, convenient; informal get-at-able.
■ **try one's hand** *I would like to try my hand at bonsai:* have a go, make an attempt, have a shot; attempt, try, try out, give something a try; informal have a stab, have a bash, give something a whirl.

handbag noun **bag**, shoulder bag, clutch bag, evening bag, pochette; N. Amer. purse, pocketbook.

handbill noun **notice**, advertisement, flyer, leaflet, circular, handout, pamphlet, brochure; N. Amer. dodger; informal ad; Brit. informal advert.

handbook noun **manual**, instructions, instruction manual, ABC, A to Z; almanac, companion, directory, compendium; guide, guidebook, vade mecum.

handcuff verb *he was handcuffed and led away:* **manacle**, shackle, fetter; restrain, clap/put someone in irons; informal cuff.

handcuffs plural noun **manacles**, shackles,

irons, fetters, bonds, restraints; informal cuffs, bracelets; archaic darbies, gyves.

handful noun **1** *we've received only a handful of letters on the subject:* **few**, small number, scattering, trickle, one or two, some, not many. **2** (informal) *she's a bit of a handful at the best of times:* **nuisance**, problem, bother, irritant, thorn in someone's flesh/side; informal pest, headache, pain, pain in the neck/backside; Scottish informal nyaff, skelf; N. Amer. informal pain in the butt.

handgun noun **pistol**, revolver, gun, side arm; N. Amer. informal piece, shooting iron, Saturday night special, rod; trademark Colt.

handicap noun **1** *he was born with a significant visual handicap:* **disability**, physical/mental abnormality, defect, impairment, affliction, deficiency. **2** *the legislation is a handicap to the competitiveness of the industry:* **impediment**, hindrance, obstacle, barrier, bar, obstruction, encumbrance, constraint, restriction, check, block, curb; disadvantage, drawback, stumbling block, difficulty, shortcoming, limitation; ball and chain, albatross, millstone round someone's neck.
– OPPOSITES benefit, advantage.
verb *chronic lack of funding handicapped the research:* **hamper**, impede, hinder, impair, hamstring; restrict, check, obstruct, block, curb, bridle, hold back, constrain, trammel, limit, encumber; informal stymie; N. Amer. informal bork.
– OPPOSITES help.

handicapped adjective **disabled**, incapacitated, disadvantaged; infirm, invalid; euphemistic physically challenged, differently abled.

handicraft noun **craft**, handiwork, craftwork; craftsmanship, workmanship, artisanship, art, skill.

handiwork noun *jewellery which is the handiwork of Chinese goldsmiths:* **creation**, product, work, achievement; handicraft, craft, craftwork.

handkerchief noun tissue; trademark Kleenex; informal hanky, nose rag, snot rag; literary kerchief.

handle verb **1** *the measuring equipment must be handled with care:* **hold**, pick up, grasp, grip, lift; feel, touch, finger; informal paw. **2** *a car which is fast and easy to handle:* **control**, drive, steer, operate, manoeuvre, manipulate. **3** *I think she handled the situation very well:* **deal with**, manage, tackle, take care of, take charge of, attend to, see to, sort out, apply oneself to, take in hand. **4** *the advertising company that is handling the account:* **administer**, manage, control, conduct, direct, guide, supervise, oversee, be in charge of, take care of, look after. **5** *the traders handled goods manufactured in the Rhineland:* **trade in**, deal in, buy, sell, supply, peddle, traffic in, purvey, hawk, tout, market.
noun *the knife's handle was damaged:* **haft**,

shank, stock, shaft, grip, handgrip, hilt, helve, butt; knob.

hand-me-down adjective *we threw in some hand-me-down clothes for Jeannie:* **second-hand**, used, nearly new, handed-down, cast-off, worn, old, pre-owned, hackneyed, trite, worn-out; Brit. informal reach-me-down.
– OPPOSITES new.
noun *her drab, close-fitting gown was a hand-me-down from a previous employer:* **cast-off**, reject; Brit. informal reach-me-down.

handout noun **1** *she existed on state handouts:* **charity**, aid, benefit, allowance, donations, subsidies. **2** *he produced a badly xeroxed handout:* **leaflet**, pamphlet, brochure; handbill, flyer, notice, circular, mailshot.

hand-picked adjective *the lecture was attended by a hand-picked audience of supporters:* **specially chosen**, selected, invited; select, elite; choice.

handsome adjective **1** *a handsome man:* **good-looking**, attractive, personable, striking; informal hunky, dishy, tasty, fanciable; Brit. informal fit; N. Amer. informal cute; Austral./NZ informal spunky. **2** *a handsome woman:* **striking**, imposing, prepossessing, elegant, stately, dignified, statuesque, good-looking, attractive, personable. **3** *we made a handsome profit:* **substantial**, considerable, sizeable, princely, large, big, ample, bumper; informal tidy, whopping, not to be sneezed at; Brit. informal whacking, ginormous.
– OPPOSITES ugly, meagre.

handwriting noun **writing**, script, hand, pen; penmanship, calligraphy, chirography; informal scrawl, scribble.

handy adjective **1** *it's a handy reference book to have on your shelf:* **useful**, convenient, practical, easy-to-use, well-designed, user-friendly, user-oriented, helpful, functional, serviceable. **2** *keep your credit card handy:* **(readily) available**, to hand, (near) at hand, within reach, accessible, (at the) ready, close (by), near, nearby, at one's fingertips; informal get-at-able. **3** *he's very handy with a needle:* **skilful**, skilled, dexterous, deft, nimble-fingered, adroit, able, adept, proficient, capable, accomplished; good (with one's hands); informal nifty.
– OPPOSITES inconvenient, inept.

handyman noun **odd-job man**, odd-jobber, factotum, jack of all trades, man of all work; DIY'er; informal Mr Fixit.

hang verb **1** *fairy lights hung from the trees:* **be suspended**, hang down, dangle, swing, sway. **2** *hang your pictures at eye level:* **put up**, fix, attach, affix, fasten, post, display, suspend, pin up, nail up. **3** *the room was hung with streamers:* **decorate**, adorn, drape, festoon, deck out, trick out, bedeck, array, garland, swathe, cover, ornament; literary bedizen. **4** *he was hanged for stealing a sheep:* **execute**, send to the gallows; informal string up. **5** *a pall of smoke hung over the city:* **hover**, float, drift, be suspended. **6** *the*

threat of budget cuts is still hanging over us: **be imminent**, threaten, be close, be impending, impend, loom, be on the horizon.
■ **hang about** (Brit. informal). See HANG AROUND.
■ **hang around/round** (informal) **1** *they spent their time hanging around in bars:* loiter, linger, wait around, waste time, kill time, mark time, while away the/one's time, kick/cool one's heels, twiddle one's thumbs; frequent, haunt; informal hang out in. **2** *she's hanging around with a bunch of hippies:* associate, mix, keep company, socialize, fraternize, consort, rub shoulders; N. Amer. rub elbows; informal hang out, run around, knock about/around, be thick, hobnob.
■ **hang fire** *I think we should hang fire until things have cooled off a bit:* delay, hang back, hold back, hold on, stall, pause; informal hang about/around, sit tight, hold one's horses.
■ **hang on 1** *he hung on to her coat as they pushed through the crowd:* hold on, hold fast, grip, clutch, grasp, hold tightly, cling. **2** *her future hung on this decision:* depend on, be dependent on, turn on, hinge on, rest on, be contingent on, be determined by, be decided by. **3** *I'll hang on as long as I possibly can:* persevere, hold out, hold on, go on, carry on, keep on, keep going, keep at it, continue, persist, stay with it, struggle on, plod on, plough on; informal soldier on, stick at it, stick it out, hang in there. **4** (informal) *hang on, let me think about this:* wait, wait a minute, hold on, stop; hold the line; informal hold your horses, sit tight; Brit. informal hang about.

hangdog adjective *the man's face brightened and he lost his hangdog expression:* **shamefaced**, sheepish, abashed, ashamed, guilty-looking, abject, cowed, dejected, downcast, crestfallen, woebegone, disconsolate.
– OPPOSITES unabashed.

hanger-on noun *having begun the journey as an interpreter, she felt she had become a mere hanger-on:* **follower**, flunkey, toady, camp follower, sycophant, parasite, leech; henchman, minion, lackey, vassal, dependant, retainer; acolyte; N. Amer. cohort; informal groupie, sponger, freeloader, passenger, sidekick.

hanging noun *Chinese silk wall hangings:* **drape**, curtain; drapery.
adjective *hanging fronds of honeysuckle:* **dangling**, trailing, tumbling; suspended.

hang-out noun *the place became a favourite student hang-out:* **haunt**, stamping ground, favourite spot, meeting place, territory; den, refuge, retreat, watering hole; N. Amer. stomping ground.

hang-up noun *people with hang-ups about their age:* **neurosis**, phobia, preoccupation, fixation, obsession, idée fixe; inhibition, mental block, psychological block, block, difficulty; informal complex, thing, bee in one's bonnet.

hank noun **coil**, skein, length, roll, loop, twist,

h

piece; lock, ringlet, curl.

hanker verb *they hankered for the bright lights of the capital:* **yearn**, long, crave, desire, wish, want, hunger, thirst, lust, ache, pant, be eager, be desperate, be eating one's heart out; pine for, have one's heart set on; informal be dying, have a yen, itch.
– OPPOSITES not miss, eschew.

hankering noun *he often confessed a certain hankering for normal family life:* **longing**, yearning, craving, desire, wish, hunger, thirst, urge, ache, lust, appetite, fancy; informal yen, itch.
– OPPOSITES aversion.

hanky-panky noun (informal) *the public takes a dim view of hanky-panky among public officials:* **goings-on**, funny business, mischief, misbehaviour, misconduct, chicanery, dishonesty, deception, deceit, trickery, intrigue, skulduggery, subterfuge, machinations; infidelity, unfaithfulness, adultery; informal monkey business, shenanigans, carryings-on; Brit. informal jiggery-pokery.

haphazard adjective *things were strewn around the room in a haphazard fashion:* **random**, unplanned, unsystematic, unmethodical, disorganized, disorderly, irregular, indiscriminate, chaotic, hit-and-miss, arbitrary, aimless, careless, casual, slapdash, slipshod; chance, accidental; informal higgledy-piggledy.
– OPPOSITES methodical.

hapless adjective *the hapless victims of exploitation:* **unfortunate**, unlucky, luckless, ill-starred, ill-fated, cursed, doomed; unhappy, forlorn, wretched, miserable, woebegone; literary star-crossed.
– OPPOSITES lucky.

happen verb 1 *remember what happened last time he was here:* **occur**, take place, come about; ensue, result, transpire, materialize, arise, crop up, come up, present itself, supervene; N. Amer. informal go down; formal eventuate; literary come to pass, betide. 2 *I wonder what happened to Susie?* **become of**; literary befall, betide. 3 *they just happened to be in London:* **chance**, have the good/bad luck. 4 *he happened on a bird's nest in the hedgerow:* **discover**, find, find by chance, come across, chance on, stumble on, hit on.

happening noun *he was a witness to these bizarre happenings:* **occurrence**, event, incident, proceeding, affair, circumstance, phenomenon, episode, experience, occasion, development, eventuality.

happily adverb 1 *the children played happily for hours:* **contentedly**, cheerfully, cheerily, merrily, delightedly, joyfully, joyously, gaily, gleefully. 2 *I will happily do as you ask:* **gladly**, willingly, readily, freely, cheerfully, ungrudgingly, with pleasure; archaic fain. 3 *happily, we are now living in more enlightened times:* **fortunately**, luckily, thankfully, mercifully, by good luck, by good fortune, as luck would have it; thank

goodness, thank God, thank heavens, thank the stars.

happiness noun *her eyes shone with happiness:* **pleasure**, contentment, satisfaction, cheerfulness, merriment, gaiety, joy, joyfulness, joviality, jollity, glee, delight, good spirits, light-heartedness, well-being, enjoyment; exuberance, exhilaration, elation, ecstasy, jubilation, rapture, bliss, blissfulness, euphoria, transports of delight.

happy adjective 1 *Melissa looked so happy and excited:* **cheerful**, cheery, merry, joyful, jovial, jolly, jocular, gleeful, carefree, untroubled, delighted, smiling, beaming, grinning, in good spirits, in a good mood, light-hearted, pleased, contented, content, satisfied, gratified, buoyant, radiant, sunny, blithe, joyous, beatific; thrilled, elated, exhilarated, ecstatic, blissful, euphoric, overjoyed, exultant, rapturous, in seventh heaven, on cloud nine, walking on air, jumping for joy, cock-a-hoop, jubilant; informal chirpy, over the moon, on top of the world, as happy as a sandboy, tickled pink, like a dog with two tails, as pleased as Punch, on a high; Brit. informal chuffed, as happy as Larry; N. English informal made up; N. Amer. informal as happy as a clam; Austral. informal wrapped; formal jocund; dated gay. 2 *I will be happy to advise you on your finances:* **glad**, pleased, delighted; willing, ready, disposed. 3 *by a happy coincidence, it was also Richard's birthday:* **fortunate**, lucky, favourable, advantageous, opportune, timely, well-timed, convenient.
– OPPOSITES sad, unwilling, unfortunate.

happy-go-lucky adjective *their casual, happy-go-lucky manner did not exactly inspire confidence:* **easy-going**, carefree, casual, free and easy, devil-may-care, blithe, nonchalant, insouciant, blasé, unconcerned, untroubled, unworried, light-hearted; informal laid-back.
– OPPOSITES anxious.

harangue noun *we were subjected to a ten-minute harangue about immigration:* **tirade**, diatribe, lecture, polemic, rant, fulmination, broadside, attack, onslaught; criticism, condemnation, censure, admonition, speech; informal blast.
verb *he harangued his erstwhile colleagues for their complacency:* **rant at**, hold forth to, lecture, shout at; berate, criticize, attack; informal earbash, sound off at, mouth off at.

harass verb *council tenants who harass their neighbours:* **persecute**, intimidate, hound, harry, plague, torment, bedevil, pressurize; pester, bother, worry, disturb, trouble, provoke, stress; informal hassle, bug, give someone a hard time; N. English informal mither; N. Amer. informal devil, ride.

harassed adjective *this scheme is a godsend for harassed parents:* **stressed**, strained, worn out, hard-pressed, careworn, worried, troubled, beleaguered, under pressure, at the end of one's tether; N. Amer. at the end of

one's rope; informal hassled.
– OPPOSITES carefree.

harassment noun *he knows how to make a noise and claim police harassment:* **persecution**, intimidation, pressure, pressurization, force, coercion, victimization; informal hassle.

harbinger noun *this victory was a harbinger of a new era in computer chess:* **herald**, sign, indication, signal, portent, omen, augury, forewarning, presage; forerunner, precursor, messenger; literary foretoken.

harbour noun *a picturesque harbour on the east coast:* **port**, dock, haven, marina; mooring, anchorage; waterfront.
verb **1** *he is harbouring a dangerous criminal:* **shelter**, conceal, hide, shield, protect, give sanctuary to; take in, put up, accommodate, house. **2** *Rose had harboured a grudge against him for years:* **bear**, nurse, nurture, cherish, entertain, foster, hold on to, cling to.

hard adjective **1** *the ground was cold and hard:* **firm**, solid, rigid, stiff, resistant, unbreakable, inflexible, impenetrable, unyielding, solidified, hardened, compact, compacted, dense, close-packed, compressed; steely, tough, strong, stony, rock-like, flinty, as hard as iron, as hard as stone; frozen. **2** *I'm not afraid of hard physical work:* **arduous**, strenuous, tiring, fatiguing, exhausting, wearying, back-breaking, gruelling, heavy, laborious; difficult, taxing, exacting, testing, challenging, demanding, punishing, tough, formidable, onerous, rigorous, uphill, Herculean; informal murderous, killing, hellish; Brit. informal knackering. **3** *they're hard workers and expect to be well paid:* **diligent**, hard-working, industrious, sedulous, assiduous, conscientious, energetic, keen, enthusiastic, zealous, earnest, persevering, persistent, unflagging, untiring, indefatigable; studious. **4** *a hard problem to deal with at such short notice:* **difficult**, puzzling, perplexing, baffling, bewildering, mystifying, knotty, thorny, problematic, complicated, complex, intricate, involved; insoluble, unfathomable, impenetrable, incomprehensible, unanswerable. **5** *times are hard and we have to make some tough decisions:* **harsh**, grim, difficult, bad, bleak, dire, tough, austere, unpleasant, uncomfortable, straitened, spartan; dark, distressing, painful, awful. **6** *Mr Gwilliam was a hard taskmaster:* **strict**, harsh, firm, severe, stern, tough, rigorous, demanding, exacting; callous, unkind, unsympathetic, cold, heartless, hard-hearted, unfeeling; intransigent, unbending, uncompromising, inflexible, implacable, stubborn, obdurate, unyielding, unrelenting, unsparing, grim, ruthless, merciless, pitiless, cruel; standing no nonsense, ruling with a rod of iron. **7** *it was a long, hard winter:* **cold**, bitter, harsh, severe, bleak, freezing, icy, icy-cold, arctic. **8** *he received a hard blow to the head:* **forceful**, heavy, strong, sharp, smart, violent, powerful, vigorous, mighty, hefty, tremendous. **9** *we need some hard facts, madam:* **reliable**, definite, true, confirmed, substantiated, undeniable, indisputable, unquestionable, verifiable. **10** *I had developed a liking for hard liquor:* **alcoholic**, strong, intoxicating, potent. **11** *he got into hard drugs:* **addictive**, habit-forming; strong, harmful.
– OPPOSITES soft, easy, lazy, gentle.
adverb **1** *George pushed her hard, making her stumble:* **forcefully**, forcibly, roughly, powerfully, strongly, heavily, sharply, vigorously, energetically, with all one's might, with might and main. **2** *they had worked hard all day:* **diligently**, industriously, assiduously, conscientiously, sedulously, busily, enthusiastically, energetically, doggedly, steadily; informal like mad, like crazy; Brit. informal like billy-o. **3** *this prosperity has been hard won:* **with difficulty**, with effort, after a struggle, painfully, laboriously. **4** *her death hit him hard:* **severely**, badly, acutely, deeply, keenly, seriously, profoundly, gravely; formal grievously. **5** *it was raining hard:* **heavily**, strongly, in torrents, in sheets, cats and dogs; steadily. **6** *my mother looked hard at me:* **closely**, attentively, intently, critically, carefully, keenly, searchingly, earnestly, sharply.
■ **hard and fast** *there are no hard and fast rules about personal taste:* **definite**, fixed, set, strict, rigid, binding, clear-cut, cast-iron; inflexible, immutable, unchangeable, incontestable.
■ **hard by** close to, right by, beside, near (to), nearby, not far from, a stone's throw from, on the doorstep of; informal within spitting distance of, {a hop, skip, and jump away from}.
■ **hard feelings** *I had no hard feelings about being made redundant:* **resentment**, animosity, ill feeling, ill will, bitterness, bad blood, resentfulness, rancour, malice, acrimony, antagonism, antipathy, animus, friction, anger, hostility, hate, hatred.

hardbitten adjective *even a hardbitten war reporter like him was shocked:* **hardened**, tough, cynical, unsentimental, hard-headed, case-hardened, as hard as nails; informal hard-nosed, hard-boiled.
– OPPOSITES sentimental.

hard-boiled adjective (informal) *a hard-boiled undercover agent.* See **HARDBITTEN**.

hard-core adjective *he had a hard-core following on the football terraces:* **diehard**, staunch, dedicated, committed, steadfast, dyed-in-the-wool, long-standing; hard-line, extreme, entrenched, radical, intransigent, uncompromising, rigid; informal deep-dyed.

harden verb **1** *this glue will harden in a matter of minutes:* **solidify**, set, congeal, clot, coagulate, stiffen, thicken, cake, inspissate; freeze, crystallize; ossify, petrify.

h

2 *their years of suffering had hardened them:* **toughen**, desensitize, inure, case-harden, harden someone's heart; deaden, numb, benumb, anaesthetize; brutalize.
– OPPOSITES liquefy, soften.

hardened adjective **1** *he was hardened to the violence he witnessed:* **inured**, desensitized, deadened; accustomed, habituated, acclimatized, used. **2** *we're dealing here with a hardened criminal:* **inveterate**, seasoned, habitual, chronic, compulsive, confirmed, dyed-in-the-wool; incorrigible, incurable, irredeemable, unregenerate.

hard-headed adjective *he was a hard-headed businessman, not a social worker:* **unsentimental**, practical, pragmatic, businesslike, realistic, sensible, rational, clear-thinking, cool-headed, down-to-earth, matter-of-fact, no-nonsense, with one's/both feet on the ground; tough, hardbitten; shrewd, astute, sharp, sharp-witted; informal hard-nosed, hard-boiled.
– OPPOSITES idealistic.

hard-hearted adjective *only the most hard-hearted man would have turned her away:* **unfeeling**, heartless, cold, hard, callous, unsympathetic, uncaring, unloving, unconcerned, indifferent, unmoved, unkind, uncharitable, unemotional, cold-hearted, cold-blooded, mean-spirited, stony-hearted, having a heart of stone, as hard as nails, cruel.
– OPPOSITES compassionate.

hard-hitting adjective *a hard-hitting TV campaign about drunk-driving:* **uncompromising**, blunt, forthright, frank, honest, direct, tough; critical, unsparing, strongly worded, straight-talking, pulling no punches, not mincing one's words, not beating about the bush.

hardiness noun *the breed is renowned for its hardiness:* **robustness**, strength, toughness, ruggedness, sturdiness, resilience, stamina, vigour; healthiness, good health.
– OPPOSITES frailty.

hard-line adjective *he is a hard-line nationalist:* **uncompromising**, strict, extreme, tough, diehard, inflexible, intransigent, intractable, unyielding.
– OPPOSITES moderate.

hardly adverb *we hardly know each other:* **scarcely**, barely, only just, slightly.

hard-nosed adjective (informal) *you'll need to convince a panel of hard-nosed financiers:* **tough-minded**, unsentimental, no-nonsense, hard-headed, hardbitten, pragmatic, realistic, down-to-earth, practical, rational, shrewd, astute, businesslike; informal hard-boiled.
– OPPOSITES sentimental.

hard-pressed adjective *a package to help the hard-pressed construction industry:* **in difficulties**, under pressure, troubled, beleaguered, harassed, with one's back to/against the wall, in a tight corner, in a

tight spot, between a rock and a hard place; overburdened, overworked, overloaded, rushed off one's feet; informal pushed, up against it.

hardship noun *the cuts caused severe hardship in some areas:* **privation**, deprivation, destitution, poverty, austerity, want, need, neediness; misfortune, distress, suffering, affliction, trouble, pain, misery, wretchedness, tribulation, adversity, trials, trials and tribulations, dire straits; literary travails.
– OPPOSITES prosperity, ease.

hardware noun *a shortage of military hardware:* **equipment**, apparatus, gear, paraphernalia, tackle, kit, machinery; tools, articles, implements, instruments, appliances.

hard-wearing adjective *a hard-wearing fabric that looks great:* **durable**, strong, tough, resilient, lasting, long-lasting, made to last, stout, well made, rugged, heavy-duty.
– OPPOSITES flimsy.

hard-working adjective *unlike Tom, Bobby was loyal and hard-working:* **diligent**, industrious, conscientious, assiduous, sedulous, painstaking, persevering, unflagging, untiring, tireless, indefatigable, studious; keen, enthusiastic, zealous, busy, with one's shoulder to the wheel, with one's nose to the grindstone.
– OPPOSITES lazy.

hardy adjective *they were a couple of hardy outdoor types:* **robust**, healthy, fit, strong, sturdy, tough, rugged, hearty, lusty, vigorous; dated stalwart.
– OPPOSITES delicate.

hare-brained adjective **1** *a hare-brained scheme to recycle industrial waste:* **ill-judged**, rash, foolish, foolhardy, reckless, madcap, wild, silly, stupid, ridiculous, absurd, idiotic, asinine, imprudent, impracticable, unworkable, unrealistic, unconsidered, half-baked, ill-thought-out, ill-advised, ill-conceived; informal crackpot, crackbrained, cockeyed, crazy; Brit. informal daft, barmy. **2** *a hare-brained young girl with no experience:* **foolish**, silly, idiotic, unintelligent, empty-headed, scatterbrained, feather-brained, birdbrained, pea-brained, brainless, giddy; informal dippy, dizzy, dopey, dotty, airheaded.
– OPPOSITES sensible, intelligent.

hark verb (literary) *'hark at him!' said Mrs Stocks:* **listen**, lend an ear, pay attention, attend, mark; archaic hearken, give ear.
■ **hark back to** *it is pointless to hark back to how things used to be:* recall, call/bring to mind, evoke, put one in mind of.

harm noun **1** *the voltage is not sufficient to cause harm:* **injury**, hurt, pain, trauma; damage, impairment, mischief. **2** *I can't see any harm in it, can you?* **wrong**, ill, wickedness, iniquity, sin; informal badness.
– OPPOSITES benefit.
verb **1** *he's never harmed anybody in his*

life: **injure**, hurt, wound, lay a finger on, maltreat, mistreat, misuse, ill-treat, ill-use, abuse, molest. **2** *this ban could harm his World Cup prospects:* **damage**, spoil, mar, do mischief to, impair.

harmful adjective *the harmful effects of smoking are well known:* **damaging**, injurious, detrimental, dangerous, deleterious, unfavourable, negative, disadvantageous, unhealthy, unwholesome, hurtful, baleful, destructive; noxious, hazardous, poisonous, toxic, deadly, lethal; bad, evil, malign, malignant, malevolent, corrupting, pernicious.
– OPPOSITES beneficial.

harmless adjective **1** *it is a harmless substance if taken in moderation:* **safe**, innocuous, benign, gentle, mild, wholesome, non-toxic; non-addictive. **2** *he seems harmless enough:* **inoffensive**, innocuous, unobjectionable, unexceptionable.
– OPPOSITES dangerous.

harmonious adjective **1** *their debut album is released today and keeps up the harmonious accordion tradition:* **tuneful**, melodious, melodic, sweet-sounding, mellifluous, dulcet, lyrical; informal easy on the ear. **2** *the harmonious relationship between Britain and Greece:* **friendly**, amicable, cordial, amiable, congenial, easy, peaceful, peaceable, cooperative; compatible, sympathetic, united. **3** *dishes providing a harmonious blend of colour, texture, flavour, and aroma:* **congruous**, coordinated, balanced, in proportion, compatible, well matched, well balanced.
– OPPOSITES discordant, hostile, incongruous.

harmonize verb **1** *colours which harmonize in a pleasing way:* **coordinate**, go together, match, blend, mix, balance, tone in; be compatible, be harmonious, suit each other, set each other off. **2** *the need to harmonize tax laws across Europe:* **coordinate**, systematize, correlate, integrate, synchronize, make consistent, bring in line, bring in tune.
– OPPOSITES clash.

harmony noun **1** *the quartet owes its air of tranquillity to the subtle harmony:* **euphony**, polyphony; tunefulness, melodiousness, mellifluousness. **2** *the simplicity of the individual parts focused attention on the harmony of the whole structure:* **balance**, symmetry, congruity, consonance, coordination, compatibility. **3** *the villagers live together in harmony:* **accord**, agreement, peace, peacefulness, amity, amicability, friendship, fellowship, cooperation, understanding, consensus, unity, sympathy, rapport, like-mindedness; unison, union, concert, oneness, synthesis; formal concord.
– OPPOSITES dissonance, disagreement.

harness noun *a horse's harness:* **tack**, tackle, equipment; trappings; yoke; archaic equipage.
verb **1** *he harnessed a horse and set it to work:* **hitch up**, put in harness, yoke, couple.

2 *attempts to harness solar energy:* **control**, exploit, utilize, use, employ, make use of, put to use; channel, mobilize, apply, capitalize on.

harp noun
■ **harp on about** *you simply cannot keep harping on about the past, what matters is now:* keep on about, go on about, keep talking about, dwell on, make an issue of; labour the point.

harpoon noun **spear**, trident, dart, barb, gaff, leister.

harridan noun *that dreadful old harridan Mrs Butler, who half-starved the poor rector:* **shrew**, virago, harpy, vixen, nag, hag, crone, dragon, ogress; fishwife, hellcat, she-devil, gorgon; martinet, tartar; informal old bag, old bat, old cow, bitch, battleaxe, witch.

harried adjective *he seemed like a different person, much older, worn and harried:* **harassed**, beleaguered, flustered, agitated, bothered, vexed, beset, plagued; informal hassled, up against it.

harrowing adjective *conditions for the refugees have been described in harrowing terms by UN officials:* **distressing**, distressful, traumatic, upsetting; shocking, disturbing, painful, haunting, appalling, horrifying; informal gut-wrenching.

harry verb **1** *as his depleted army made its way home it was harried by Dwarfs and Men:* **attack**, assail, assault; charge, rush, strike, set upon; bombard, shell, strafe. **2** *the government is being mercilessly harried by a new lobby group:* **harass**, hound, pressurize, bedevil, torment, pester, bother, worry, badger, nag, plague; informal hassle, bug, lean on, give someone a hard time, get on someone's back.

harsh adjective **1** *his shrill, harsh voice:* **grating**, jarring, rasping, strident, raucous, brassy, discordant; screeching, shrill; rough, coarse, hoarse, gruff, croaky. **2** *the garden was drenched by a harsh white light* | *harsh colours:* **glaring**, bright, dazzling; loud, garish, gaudy, lurid, bold. **3** *during his harsh rule, thousands were exiled:* **cruel**, savage, barbarous, despotic, dictatorial, tyrannical, tyrannous; ruthless, merciless, pitiless, relentless, unmerciful; severe, strict, intolerant, illiberal; hard-hearted, heartless, unkind, inhuman, inhumane. **4** *politicians are taking harsh measures to end the crisis:* **severe**, stringent, firm, stiff, hard, stern, rigorous, grim, uncompromising; punitive, cruel, brutal. **5** *harsh words were exchanged and tempers got frayed:* **rude**, discourteous, uncivil, impolite; unfriendly, sharp, bitter, abusive, unkind, disparaging; abrupt, brusque, curt, gruff, short, surly, offhand. **6** *the harsh conditions in the refugee camps:* **austere**, grim, spartan, hard, comfortless, inhospitable, stark, bleak, desolate. **7** *a harsh winter:* **hard**, severe, cold, bitter, bleak, freezing, icy; arctic, polar, Siberian. **8** *harsh cream cleaners can scratch stains away:*

h

abrasive, strong, caustic; coarse, rough.
– OPPOSITES soft, subdued, kind, friendly, comfortable, balmy, mild.

harvest noun **1** *we all helped with the harvest:* **harvesting**, reaping, picking, collecting. **2** *a poor harvest:* **yield**, crop, vintage; fruits, produce.
verb *once he's harvested the wheat crop, there are still the beans:* **gather (in)**, bring in, reap, pick, collect.

hash[1]
■ **make a hash of** (informal) *as long as I could ski down a slope without making a complete hash of it, I was happy:* bungle, fluff, mess up, make a mess of; mismanage, mishandle, ruin, wreck; informal botch, muff, muck up, foul up, screw up, blow; Brit. informal make a pig's ear of, cock up; N. Amer. informal flub.

hash[2] noun (informal) *she smokes a lot of hash.* See **CANNABIS**.

hassle (informal) noun **1** *parking is such a hassle:* **inconvenience**, bother, nuisance, problem, trouble, struggle, difficulty, annoyance, irritation, thorn in one's flesh/side, fuss; informal aggravation, aggro, stress, headache, pain (in the neck). **2** (N. Amer.) *she got into a hassle with some guy.* See **QUARREL** noun.
verb *they were hassling him to pay what he owed them:* **harass**, pester, nag, keep on at, badger, hound, harry, chivvy, bother, torment, plague; informal bug, give someone a hard time, get on someone's back, breathe down someone's neck; N. English informal mither.

hassled adjective (informal) *Gerry cast Nirvana's hassled tour manager Alex a sympathetic look:* **harassed**, agitated, stressed (out), harried, frayed, flustered; beleaguered, hounded, plagued, bothered, beset, tormented; under pressure, hot and bothered; informal up against it.
– OPPOSITES calm.

haste noun *we worked with feverish haste:* **speed**, hastiness, hurriedness, swiftness, rapidity, quickness, briskness; formal expedition.
– OPPOSITES delay.
■ **in haste** *she went in haste along the landing towards her son's room:* quickly, rapidly, fast, speedily, with urgency, in a rush, in a hurry.

hasten verb **1** *we hastened back to Paris:* **hurry**, rush, dash, race, fly, shoot; scurry, scramble, dart, bolt, sprint, run, gallop; go fast, go quickly, go like lightning, go hell for leather; informal tear, hare, pelt, scoot, zip, zoom, belt, hotfoot it, leg it; Brit. informal bomb, bucket; N. Amer. informal hightail, barrel; dated make haste. **2** *these chemicals can hasten the ageing process:* **speed up**, accelerate, quicken, precipitate, advance, hurry on, step up, spur on; facilitate, aid, assist, boost.
– OPPOSITES dawdle, delay.

hastily adverb **1** *Meg retreated hastily as the blades began to rotate:* **quickly**, hurriedly, fast, swiftly, rapidly, speedily, briskly,

without delay, post-haste; with all speed, as fast as possible, at breakneck speed, at a run, hotfoot, at the double; informal double quick, p.d.q. (pretty damn quick), nippily, like (greased) lightning, like the wind, like a scalded cat, like a bat out of hell; Brit. informal at a rate of knots, like the clappers; N. Amer. informal lickety-split. **2** *an agreement was hastily drawn up:* **hurriedly**, speedily, quickly; on the spur of the moment, prematurely.

hasty adjective **1** *Fran took several hasty steps backwards:* **quick**, hurried, fast, swift, rapid, speedy, brisk. **2** *we don't want to be trapped by hasty decisions:* **rash**, impetuous, impulsive, reckless, precipitate, spur-of-the-moment, premature, unconsidered, unthinking; literary temerarious.
– OPPOSITES slow, considered.

hat noun **cap**, beret, bonnet; Brit. informal titfer.

hatch verb **1** *the duck hatched a clutch of eggs:* **incubate**, brood, sit on. **2** *the little plot that you and Sylvia hatched last night:* **devise**, conceive, concoct, brew, invent, plan, design, formulate; think up, dream up; informal cook up.

hatchet noun **axe**, cleaver, mattock, tomahawk; Brit. chopper.

hate verb **1** *the boys hate each other:* **loathe**, detest, despise, dislike, abhor, execrate; be repelled by, be unable to bear/stand, recoil from, shrink from; formal abominate. **2** *I hate to bother you:* **be sorry**, be reluctant, be loath, be unwilling, be disinclined; regret, dislike.
– OPPOSITES love.
noun **1** *I was eaten up by feelings of hate and revenge:* **hatred**, loathing, detestation, dislike, distaste, abhorrence, abomination, execration, aversion; hostility, enmity, animosity, antipathy, revulsion, disgust, contempt, odium. **2** *his pet hate is filling in forms:* **bugbear**, bane, bête noire, bogey, aversion, thorn in one's flesh/side; N. Amer. bugaboo.
– OPPOSITES love.

hateful adjective *that hateful, arrogant old woman:* **detestable**, horrible, horrid, unpleasant, awful, nasty, disagreeable, despicable, objectionable, insufferable, revolting, loathsome, abhorrent, abominable, execrable, odious, disgusting, distasteful, obnoxious, offensive, vile, heinous; informal ghastly; Brit. informal beastly, God-awful.
– OPPOSITES delightful.

hatred noun *she was full of hatred and bitterness:* **loathing**, hate, detestation, dislike, distaste, abhorrence, abomination, execration; aversion, hostility, ill will, ill feeling, enmity, animosity, antipathy; revulsion, disgust, contempt, odium.

haughtiness noun **arrogance**, conceit, pride, hubris, hauteur, vanity, self-importance, pomposity, condescension, disdain, contempt; snobbishness, snobbery,

superciliousness; informal snootiness.
–OPPOSITES modesty.

haughty adjective *his bearing was haughty and disdainful:* **proud**, arrogant, vain, conceited, snobbish, superior, self-important, pompous, supercilious, condescending, patronizing; scornful, contemptuous, disdainful; full of oneself, above oneself; informal stuck-up, snooty, hoity-toity, uppity, uppish, big-headed, high and mighty, la-di-da; Brit. informal toffee-nosed; N. Amer. informal chesty.
–OPPOSITES humble.

haul verb *she hauled the basket up the slope:* **drag**, pull, tug, heave, lug, hump, draw, tow; informal yank.
noun *the thieves were forced to abandon their haul:* **booty**, loot, plunder; spoils, stolen goods, ill-gotten gains; informal swag, boodle.

haunches plural noun *he stopped dead and sat back on his haunches:* **rump**, hindquarters, rear (end), seat; buttocks, thighs, derrière; Brit. bottom; informal behind, backside; Brit. informal bum, botty; N. Amer. informal butt, fanny, tush, heinie; humorous fundament, posterior.

haunt verb **1** *a ghost haunts this eighteenth-century house:* **wander**, frequent, visit, patrol. **2** *he haunts street markets and bazaars:* **frequent**, patronize, visit regularly; loiter in, linger in; informal hang out in. **3** *the sight haunted me for years:* **torment**, disturb, trouble, worry, plague, burden, beset, beleaguer; prey on, weigh on, gnaw at, nag at, weigh heavily on, obsess; informal bug.
noun *the inn was a favourite haunt of artists of the time:* **hang-out**, stamping ground, meeting place; territory, domain, resort, retreat, spot; N. Amer. stomping ground; Brit. informal patch.

haunted adjective **1** *a haunted house:* **possessed**, cursed; ghostly, eerie; informal spooky, scary. **2** *his haunted eyes still stared at her:* **tormented**, anguished, troubled, tortured, worried, disturbed.

haunting adjective *the sweet and haunting sound of pan pipes:* **evocative**, emotive, affecting, moving, touching, stirring, powerful; poignant, nostalgic, wistful; memorable, unforgettable, indelible.

have verb **1** *he had a new car and a boat:* **possess**, own, be in possession of, be the owner of; be blessed with, boast, enjoy; keep, retain, hold, occupy. **2** *the flat has five rooms:* **comprise**, consist of, contain, include, incorporate, be composed of, be made up of; boast; encompass. **3** *they had tea together:* **eat**, consume, devour, take, partake of; drink, imbibe, quaff; informal demolish, dispose of, put away, get outside of, scoff (down); sink, knock back; N. Amer. informal scarf (down/up). **4** *we've decided to have a party:* **organize**, arrange, hold, give, host, throw, put on, lay on, set up, fix up. **5** *she's going to have a baby:* **give birth to**, bear, be delivered of, bring into the world; informal drop; archaic

beget. **6** *the taxi driver had trouble finding the restaurant:* **experience**, encounter, face, meet, find, run into, go through, undergo. **7** *I have a headache:* **be suffering from**, be afflicted by, be affected by, be troubled with; informal be a martyr to. **8** *many of them have doubts about the new computer system:* **harbour**, entertain, feel, nurse, nurture, sustain, maintain. **9** *he had little patience with instruction manuals:* **manifest**, show, display, exhibit, demonstrate. **10** *he had his bodyguards throw Chris out:* **make**, ask to, request to, get to, tell to, require to, induce to, prevail upon someone to; order to, command to, direct to, force to. **11** *I have to get up at six o'clock tomorrow morning:* **must**, be obliged to, be required to, be compelled to, be forced to, be bound to.
–OPPOSITES send, give, visit.

■ **have had it** (informal) **1** *in private they admit that they've had it:* have no chance, have no hope, have failed, be finished, be defeated, have lost; informal have flopped, have come a cropper. **2** *if you tell anyone, you've had it:* be in trouble; informal be for the high jump, be in hot water, be in (deep) shtook; Brit. informal be for it.

■ **have someone on** (Brit. informal) *that's just too neat—you're having me on:* play a trick on, play a joke on, joke with, trick, tease, rag, make a monkey (out) of, pull someone's leg; informal kid, rib, take for a ride, lead up the garden path; Brit. informal wind up; N. Amer. informal put on.

■ **have something on 1** *she had a blue dress on:* be wearing, be dressed in, be clothed in, be attired in, be decked out in, be robed in. **2** (Brit.) *I have a lot on at the moment:* be committed to, have arranged, have planned, have organized, have fixed up.

haven noun *a safe haven in times of trouble:* **refuge**, retreat, shelter, sanctuary, asylum; port in a storm, oasis, sanctum.

haversack noun **knapsack**, rucksack, backpack, pack.

havoc noun **1** *the hurricane ripped through Florida, causing havoc:* **devastation**, destruction, damage, desolation, ruination, ruin; disaster, catastrophe. **2** *hyperactive children create havoc wherever they go:* **disorder**, chaos, disruption, mayhem, bedlam, pandemonium, turmoil, tumult, uproar; commotion, furore; N. Amer. a three-ring circus; informal hullabaloo.

hawk verb *street traders were hawking bad costume jewellery:* **peddle**, sell, tout, vend, trade in, traffic in, push; Brit. informal flog.

hawk-eyed adjective *a hawk-eyed policeman saved the lives of dozens of shoppers:* **vigilant**, observant, alert, sharp-eyed, keen-eyed, eagle-eyed, attentive.
–OPPOSITES inattentive.

hay noun **forage**, dried grass, herbage, silage, fodder.

haywire adjective (informal) *a bug in the operating system that makes computers go*

haywire: out of control, erratic, faulty, malfunctioning, out of order; chaotic, confused, disorganized, disordered, topsy-turvy; informal on the blink; Brit. informal up the spout.

hazard noun *the hazards of radiation:* **danger**, risk, peril, threat, menace; problem, pitfall.
▸ verb **1** *he hazarded a guess:* **venture**, advance, put forward, volunteer; conjecture, speculate, surmise; formal opine. **2** *the shipping business is too risky to hazard money on:* **risk**, jeopardize, gamble, stake, bet, chance.

hazardous adjective *we work in extremely hazardous conditions:* **risky**, dangerous, unsafe, perilous, precarious, fraught with danger; unpredictable, uncertain, chancy, high-risk, insecure, touch-and-go; informal dicey, hairy; Brit. informal dodgy.
– OPPOSITES safe, certain.

haze noun **1** *a thick haze lay on the sea:* **mist**, fog, cloud; smoke, vapour, steam. **2** *the evening passed in a haze of euphoria:* **blur**, daze.

hazy adjective **1** *it was a beautiful day, but quite hazy:* **misty**, foggy, cloudy, overcast; smoggy, murky. **2** *hazy memories of early childhood:* **vague**, indistinct, unclear, faint, dim, nebulous, shadowy, blurred, fuzzy, confused.

head noun **1** *she was hurt when her head hit the ground:* **skull**, cranium, crown; informal nut, noodle, noggin, dome; Brit. informal bonce. **2** *this new job meant he had to use his head:* **brain(s)**, brainpower, intellect, intelligence; wit(s), wisdom, mind, sense, reasoning, common sense; informal nous, savvy, grey matter; Brit. informal loaf; N. Amer. informal smarts. **3** *the head of the Dutch Catholic Church:* **leader**, chief, controller, governor, superintendent, headman; commander, captain; director, manager; principal, president, premier; informal boss, boss man, kingpin, top dog, Mr Big, skipper, numero uno, head honcho; Brit. informal gaffer, guv'nor; N. Amer. informal sachem, big kahuna. **4** *the head of the queue:* **front**, beginning, start, fore, forefront; top.
– OPPOSITES back.
▸ adjective *the head waiter was very unfriendly:* **chief**, principal, leading, main, first, prime, premier, top, highest, supreme, top-ranking; N. Amer. ranking; informal top-notch.
– OPPOSITES subordinate.
▸ verb **1** *the procession was headed by the mayor:* **lead**, be at the front of; be first, lead the way. **2** *a team headed by a line manager:* **command**, control, lead, run, manage, direct, supervise, superintend, oversee, preside over, rule, govern, captain; informal be the boss of. **3** *last time I saw him, he was heading for the exit:* **move towards**, make for, aim for, go in the direction of, be bound for, make a beeline for; set out for, start out for.

■ **at the head of** *his years at the head of the company:* in charge of, controlling, commanding, leading, managing, running, directing, supervising, overseeing; at the wheel of, at the helm of.
■ **come to a head** *the violence came to a head following the deaths of six youths:* reach a crisis, come to a climax, reach a critical point, reach a crossroads.
■ **go to someone's head 1** *the wine has gone to my head:* intoxicate, befuddle, make drunk; informal make woozy; formal inebriate. **2** *her victory went to her head:* make someone full of themselves, turn someone's head, puff someone up.
■ **head someone/something off 1** *he ran up the road to head off the cars:* intercept, divert, deflect, redirect, re-route, draw away, turn away. **2** *they headed off a crisis by ordering a second investigation:* forestall, avert, ward off, fend off, stave off, hold off, nip in the bud, keep at bay; prevent, avoid, stop.
■ **keep one's head** *he takes chances but always keeps his head:* keep/stay calm, maintain one's composure; informal keep one's cool.
■ **lose one's head** *I lost my head and started a big argument about the bill:* lose control, lose one's composure, lose one's equilibrium, go to pieces; panic, get flustered, get confused, get hysterical; informal lose one's cool, freak out, crack up; Brit. informal go into a (flat) spin, throw a wobbly.

headache noun **pain in the head**, sore head, migraine; neuralgia; informal head.

head first adjective & adverb **1** *she dived head first into the water:* **headlong**, on one's head. **2** *don't plunge head first into a new relationship:* **without thinking**, precipitously, impetuously, rashly, recklessly, heedlessly, hastily, headlong.
– OPPOSITES cautiously.

heading noun **1** *the chapter headings are clearly laid out:* **title**, caption, legend, subtitle, sub-heading, rubric, headline. **2** *this topic falls under four main headings:* **category**, division, classification, class, section, group, grouping, subject, topic, area.

headland noun **cape**, promontory, point, head, foreland, peninsula, ness, bluff; Scottish mull.

headlong adverb **1** *he fell headlong into the tent:* **head first**, on one's head. **2** *those who rush headlong to join the latest craze:* **without thinking**, precipitously, impetuously, rashly, recklessly, carelessly, heedlessly, hastily, mindlessly.
– OPPOSITES cautiously.
▸ adjective *a headlong dash through the house:* **breakneck**, whirlwind; reckless, precipitate, precipitous, hasty, careless, heedless.
– OPPOSITES cautious.

headman noun *the father and mother talked it over and then told the headmen of the clan:* **chief**, chieftain, leader, head,

ruler, overlord, master, commander; lord, potentate; N. Amer. sachem.
– OPPOSITES underling.

headquarters plural noun **head office**, main office, HQ, base, nerve centre, mission control, command post.

headstone noun **gravestone**, tombstone, stone, monument, memorial.

headstrong adjective *she is rather headstrong and argumentative:* **wilful**, strong-willed, stubborn, obstinate, unyielding, obdurate; contrary, perverse, wayward, unruly; formal refractory.
– OPPOSITES tractable.

head teacher noun **head**, headmaster, headmistress, principal, director, president, governor; Brit. master.

headway
■ **make headway** *they appear to be making headway in bringing the rebels under control:* make progress, progress, make strides, gain ground, advance, proceed, move, get ahead, come along, take shape.

heady adjective **1** *several bottles of heady local wine:* **potent**, intoxicating, strong, powerful; alcoholic; formal spirituous. **2** *the heady days of my youth:* **exhilarating**, exciting, thrilling, stimulating, invigorating, electrifying, rousing; informal mind-blowing.
– OPPOSITES weak, boring.

heal verb **1** *his concern is to heal sick people:* **make well**, make better, cure, treat, restore to health. **2** *he had to wait until his knee had healed:* **get better**, get well, be cured, recover, mend, improve. **3** *time will eventually heal the pain of grief:* **alleviate**, ease, assuage, palliate, relieve, help, lessen, mitigate, attenuate, allay. **4** *we've been trying to heal the rift between them:* **put right**, set right, repair, remedy, resolve, correct, settle; conciliate, reconcile, harmonize; informal patch up.
– OPPOSITES aggravate, worsen.

healing adjective *this flower is said to have healing properties:* **curative**, therapeutic, medicinal, remedial, corrective, reparative; restorative, tonic, health-giving, healthful, beneficial.
– OPPOSITES harmful.

health noun **1** *he was restored to health:* **well-being**, healthiness, fitness, good condition, good shape, fine fettle; strength, vigour. **2** *bad health forced him to retire:* **physical state**, (physical) shape, condition, constitution.
– OPPOSITES illness.

healthful adjective *garlic was considered very healthful in winter:* **healthy**, health-giving, beneficial, good for one, salubrious; wholesome, nourishing, nutritious.
– OPPOSITES unhealthy.

healthy adjective **1** *we're all fit and healthy:* **well**, in good health, fine, fit, in good trim, in good shape, in fine fettle, in tip-top condition; blooming, thriving, hardy, robust, strong, vigorous, fighting fit, fit as a fiddle, the picture of health; Brit. in rude health; informal OK, in the pink, right as rain. **2** *a healthy balanced diet:* **health-giving**, healthful, good for one; wholesome, nutritious, nourishing; beneficial, salubrious.
– OPPOSITES ill, unwholesome.

heap noun **1** *a disordered heap of boxes lay in the middle of the floor:* **pile**, stack, mound, mountain, mass, quantity, load, lot, jumble; collection, accumulation, assemblage, store, hoard. **2** (informal) *we have heaps of room:* **a lot**, a fair amount, much, plenty, a good deal, a great deal, an abundance, a wealth, a profusion; (a great) many, a large number, numerous, scores; informal hundreds, thousands, millions, a load, loads, loadsa, a pile, piles, oodles, stacks, bucketloads, lots, masses, scads, reams, wads, pots, oceans, miles, tons, zillions; Brit. informal a shedload, lashings.
verb *she heaped logs on the fire:* **pile (up)**, stack (up); assemble, collect.
■ **heap something on/upon** *they heaped praise on her:* shower on, lavish on, load on; bestow on, confer on, give, grant, vouchsafe, favour with.

hear verb **1** *behind her she could hear men's voices:* **perceive**, make out, discern, catch, get, apprehend; overhear. **2** *they heard that I had moved:* **be informed**, be told, find out, discover, learn, gather, glean, ascertain, get word, get wind. **3** *a jury of twelve citizens heard the case:* **try**, judge; adjudicate (on), adjudge, pass judgement on.

hearing noun **1** *she moved out of hearing:* **earshot**, hearing distance, hearing/auditory range. **2** *I think I had a fair hearing:* **chance to speak**, opportunity to be heard; interview, audience. **3** *he gave evidence at the hearing:* **trial**, court case, inquiry, inquest, tribunal; investigation, inquisition.

hearsay noun *a story based entirely on hearsay:* **rumour**, gossip, tittle-tattle, tattle, idle talk; stories, tales, on dit; informal the grapevine; Brit. informal goss; N. Amer. informal scuttlebutt.

heart noun **1** *his heart had stopped beating:* informal ticker. **2** *he poured out his heart to me | she captured my heart that afternoon:* **emotions**, feelings, sentiments; soul, mind, bosom, breast; love, affection, passion. **3** *he has no heart:* **compassion**, sympathy, humanity, feeling(s); fellow feeling, brotherly love, tenderness, empathy, understanding; kindness, goodwill. **4** *they may lose heart as the work mounts up:* **enthusiasm**, keenness, eagerness, spirit, determination, resolve, purpose, courage, nerve, will power, fortitude; informal guts, spunk; Brit. informal bottle. **5** *right in the heart of the city:* **centre**, middle, hub, core, nucleus, eye, bosom. **6** *now we're getting to the heart of the matter:* **essence**, crux, core, nub, root, gist, meat, marrow, pith,

substance, kernel; informal nitty-gritty.
– OPPOSITES edge.

■ **after one's own heart** *now there's a man after my own heart:* like-minded, of the same mind, kindred, compatible, congenial, sharing one's tastes; informal on the same wavelength.

■ **at heart** *he's a good lad at heart:* deep down, basically, fundamentally, essentially, in essence, intrinsically; really, actually, truly, in fact; informal when you get right down to it.

■ **(off) by heart** *I know the entire poem by heart:* from memory, off pat, by rote, word for word, verbatim, parrot-fashion, word-perfect.

■ **from the heart** *she spoke from the heart:* sincerely, earnestly, fervently, passionately, truly, genuinely, heartily, with all sincerity.

■ **give/lose one's heart to** *he lost his heart to a French girl:* fall in love with, fall for, be smitten by; informal fall head over heels for, be swept off one's feet by, develop a crush on.

■ **have a change of heart** *you can get your money back if you have a change of heart:* change one's mind, change one's tune, have second thoughts, have a rethink, think again, think twice; informal get cold feet.

■ **heart and soul** *they had committed themselves heart and soul to the project:* wholeheartedly, enthusiastically, eagerly, zealously; absolutely, completely, entirely, fully, utterly, to the hilt, one hundred per cent.

■ **take heart** *Mary took heart from the encouragement that was offered:* be encouraged, be heartened, be comforted; cheer up, brighten up, perk up, liven up, revive; informal buck up.

■ **with one's heart in one's mouth** *she watched with her heart in her mouth as the plane lost height:* in alarm, in fear, fearfully, apprehensively, on edge, with trepidation, in suspense, in a cold sweat, with bated breath, on tenterhooks; informal with butterflies in one's stomach, in a state, in a stew, in a sweat; Brit. informal having kittens; N. Amer. informal in a twit.

heartache noun *some times of her life were filled with heartache and pain:* **anguish**, grief, suffering, distress, unhappiness, misery, sorrow, sadness, heartbreak, pain, hurt, agony, angst, despondency, despair, woe, desolation.
– OPPOSITES happiness.

heartbreak noun. See HEARTACHE.

heartbreaking adjective *it would be heartbreaking to see it all fall apart at this stage:* **tragic**, upsetting, disturbing, heart-rending, sad, painful, traumatic, agonizing, harrowing; pitiful, poignant, plaintive, moving, tear-jerking.
– OPPOSITES comforting.

heartbroken adjective *he was heartbroken when his wife died in 1849:* **anguished**, devastated, broken-hearted, heavy-hearted, grieving, grief-stricken, inconsolable, crushed, shattered, desolate, despairing; upset, distressed, miserable, sorrowful, sad, downcast, disconsolate, crestfallen, despondent; informal choked, down in the mouth, down in the dumps, cut up.

heartburn noun **indigestion**, dyspepsia, pyrosis.

hearten verb *their success greatly heartened him:* **cheer (up)**, encourage, raise someone's spirits, boost, buoy up, perk up, ginger up, inspirit, uplift, elate; comfort, reassure; informal buck up, pep up.

heartfelt adjective *our heartfelt thanks for all you have done:* **sincere**, genuine, from the heart; earnest, profound, deep, wholehearted, ardent, fervent, passionate, enthusiastic, eager; honest, bona fide.
– OPPOSITES insincere.

heartily adverb **1** *we heartily welcome the changes:* **wholeheartedly**, sincerely, genuinely, warmly, profoundly, with all one's heart; eagerly, enthusiastically, earnestly, ardently. **2** *they were heartily sick of her:* **thoroughly**, completely, absolutely, really, exceedingly, immensely, most, downright, utterly; N. Amer. quite; informal right, seriously; Brit. informal jolly, dead, well; N. Amer. informal real, mighty.

heartless adjective *the heartless thieves who stole the pushchair of a two-year old boy:* **unfeeling**, unsympathetic, unkind, uncaring, unconcerned, insensitive, inconsiderate, hard-hearted, stony-hearted, cold-hearted, mean-spirited; cold, callous, cruel, merciless, pitiless, inhuman.
– OPPOSITES compassionate.

heart-rending adjective *I heard a single heart-rending cry of torment:* **distressing**, upsetting, disturbing, heartbreaking, sad, tragic, painful, traumatic, harrowing; pitiful, poignant, plaintive, moving, tear-jerking.

heart-throb noun (informal) **idol**, pin-up, star, superstar, hero; informal dreamboat.

heart-to-heart adjective *we had a heart-to-heart chat about things:* **intimate**, personal, man-to-man, woman-to-woman; candid, honest, truthful, sincere.
noun *they had a long heart-to-heart:* **conversation**, tête-à-tête, one-to-one, head-to-head; chat, talk, word; informal confab, chinwag; Brit. informal natter.

heart-warming adjective *the conductor told me this heart-warming little story:* **touching**, moving, heartening, stirring, uplifting, pleasing, cheering, gladdening, encouraging, gratifying.
– OPPOSITES distressing.

hearty adjective **1** *a hearty and boisterous character:* **exuberant**, jovial, ebullient, cheerful, uninhibited, effusive, lively, loud, animated, vivacious, energetic, spirited, dynamic, enthusiastic, eager; warm, cordial, friendly, affable, amiable, good natured.

2 *he expressed his hearty agreement* | *hearty congratulations:* **wholehearted**, heartfelt, sincere, genuine, real, true; earnest, fervent, ardent, enthusiastic. **3** *a formidably hearty woman of sixty-five:* **robust**, healthy, hardy, fit, flourishing, blooming; vigorous, sturdy, strong; Brit. in rude health; informal full of vim. **4** *they end each day with a hearty meal:* **substantial**, large, ample, sizeable, filling, generous, square, solid; healthy.
– OPPOSITES introverted, half-hearted, frail, light.

heat noun **1** *a plant sensitive to heat and cold:* **warmth**, hotness, warmness, high temperature; hot weather, warm weather, sultriness, mugginess, humidity; heatwave, hot spell. **2** *he took some of the heat out of the dispute:* **passion**, intensity, vehemence, warmth, fervour, fervency, ardency; enthusiasm, excitement, agitation; anger, fury.
– OPPOSITES cold, apathy.
verb **1** *the room faces north and is difficult to heat* | *the food was heated over a fire:* **warm (up)**, heat up, make hot, make warm; reheat, cook; Brit. informal hot up. **2** *the pipes expand as they heat up:* **become hot**, become warm, get hotter, get warmer, increase in temperature; Brit informal hot up.
– OPPOSITES cool.

heated adjective **1** *she had a heated argument with one of the officials:* **vehement**, passionate, impassioned, animated, spirited, lively, intense, fiery, angry, bitter, furious, fierce, stormy, tempestuous. **2** *Robert grew quite heated as he spoke of the risks:* **excited**, animated, inflamed, worked up, wound up, keyed up; informal het up, in a state.

heater noun **radiator**, convector, fire, brazier, warmer.

heath noun (Brit.) **moor**, heathland, moorland, scrub; common land.

heathen noun *he preached the common humanity of Christians and heathens:* **pagan**; infidel, idolater; unbeliever, non-believer, disbeliever, atheist, agnostic, sceptic, heretic.
– OPPOSITES believer.
adjective *old heathen practices, such as offering food and wine at the tombs of ancestors:* **pagan**; infidel, idolatrous; unbelieving, non-believing, atheistic, agnostic, heretical, faithless, godless, irreligious, ungodly, unholy; barbarian, barbarous, uncivilized, uncultured, primitive, ignorant, philistine.

heave verb **1** *she heaved the sofa back into place:* **haul**, pull, lug, drag, draw, tug, heft; informal hump, yank. **2** *he heaved a sigh of relief:* **let out**, breathe, give, sigh; emit, utter. **3** *the sea heaved up and down beneath her:* **rise and fall**, roll, swell, surge, churn, seethe, swirl. **4** *she crawled up to the rail and heaved into the sea:* **vomit**, gag; retch, bring up, cough up; Brit. be sick; N. Amer. get sick; informal throw up, puke, chunder, chuck up,

hurl, spew; Brit. informal sick up; Scottish informal boke; N. Amer. informal barf, upchuck.

heaven noun **1** *the good will have a place in heaven:* **paradise**, nirvana, Zion; the hereafter, the next world, the next life, the afterworld; Elysium, the Elysian Fields, Valhalla. **2** *lying by the sea with a good book is my idea of heaven:* **bliss**, ecstasy, rapture, contentment, happiness, delight, joy, seventh heaven; paradise, Utopia, nirvana. **3** *Galileo used a telescope to observe the heavens:* **the sky**, the skies, the upper atmosphere, the stratosphere; literary the firmament, the blue, the (wide) blue yonder, the welkin.
– OPPOSITES hell, misery.
■ **in seventh heaven** *Fred Proctor was in seventh heaven after notching up yet another election success:* **ecstatic**, euphoric, thrilled, elated, delighted, overjoyed, on cloud nine, walking on air, jubilant, rapturous, jumping for joy, transported, delirious, blissful; informal over the moon, on top of the world, on a high, tickled pink, as pleased as Punch, cock-a-hoop; Brit. informal as happy as Larry; N. Amer. informal as happy as a clam; Austral. informal wrapped.
■ **move heaven and earth** *if members tell us they are in dire straits, then we will move heaven and earth to help them:* **try one's hardest**, do one's best, do one's utmost, do all one can, give one's all, spare no effort, put oneself out; strive, exert oneself, work hard; informal bend over backwards, do one's damnedest, go all out, bust a gut.

heavenly adjective **1** *they saw visions of angels and heavenly choirs:* **divine**, holy, celestial; angelic, seraphic, cherubic. **2** *the heavenly bodies that swept sedately across the night sky:* **celestial**, cosmic, stellar; planetary.
– OPPOSITES mortal, infernal, terrestrial.

heaven-sent adjective *she was so afraid of losing this heaven-sent opportunity:* **auspicious**, providential, propitious, felicitous, opportune, golden, favourable, advantageous, serendipitous, lucky, happy, good, fortunate.
– OPPOSITES inopportune.

heavily adverb **1** *Dad walked heavily towards the door:* **laboriously**, slowly, ponderously, woodenly, stiffly; with difficulty, painfully, awkwardly, clumsily. **2** *we were heavily defeated in the by-election:* **decisively**, conclusively, roundly, soundly; utterly, completely, thoroughly. **3** *he started drinking heavily:* **excessively**, to excess, immoderately, copiously, inordinately, intemperately, a great deal, too much, overmuch. **4** *I became heavily involved in politics:* **deeply**, very, extremely, greatly, exceedingly, tremendously, profoundly; informal terribly, seriously.
– OPPOSITES easily, narrowly, moderately.

heavy adjective **1** *the box was too heavy for me to carry:* **weighty**, hefty,

substantial, ponderous; solid, dense, leaden; burdensome; informal hulking, weighing a ton. **2** *he was a heavy man of about sixty:* **overweight**, fat, obese, corpulent, large, bulky, stout, stocky, portly, plump, paunchy, fleshy; informal hulking, tubby, beefy, porky; Brit. informal podgy. **3** *a heavy blow to the head:* **forceful**, hard, strong, violent, powerful, vigorous, mighty, hefty, sharp, smart, severe. **4** *a gardener comes in to do all the heavy work for me:* **arduous**, hard, physical, laborious, difficult, strenuous, demanding, tough, onerous, back-breaking, gruelling. **5** *the helicopter flew into heavy fog:* **dense**, thick, soupy, murky, impenetrable. **6** *we had heavy rain overnight:* **torrential**, relentless, copious, teeming, severe. **7** *we suffered heavy losses* | *a heavy fine:* **sizeable**, hefty, substantial, colossal, big, considerable; stiff; informal tidy, whopping, steep, astronomical. **8** *the boat encountered heavy seas:* **tempestuous**, turbulent, rough, wild, stormy, choppy, squally. **9** *the battalion has been involved in heavy fighting:* **intense**, fierce, vigorous, relentless, all-out, severe, serious. **10** *he's a heavy drinker:* **immoderate**, excessive, intemperate, overindulgent, unrestrained, uncontrolled.
– OPPOSITES light, thin, gentle, easy, small, calm, moderate.

heavy-handed adjective **1** *they tend to be a bit heavy-handed with the equipment:* **clumsy**, careless, awkward, maladroit, inept, unskilful; informal ham-handed, ham-fisted, cack-handed; Brit. informal all (fingers and) thumbs. **2** *heavy-handed policing did nothing to improve the atmosphere:* **insensitive**, oppressive, overbearing, harsh, stern, severe, tyrannical, despotic, ruthless, merciless; tactless, undiplomatic, inept.
– OPPOSITES dexterous, sensitive.

heckle verb *he was booed and heckled when he tried to address the crowd:* **jeer**, taunt, jibe at, shout down, boo, hiss, harass; Brit. & Austral./NZ barrack; informal give someone a hard time.
– OPPOSITES cheer.

hectic adjective *his hectic business schedule has taken its toll:* **frantic**, frenetic, frenzied, feverish, manic, busy, active, fast and furious; lively, brisk, bustling, buzzing.
– OPPOSITES leisurely.

hector verb *instead of hectoring the Americans, world leaders should just let the US get on with it:* **bully**, intimidate, browbeat, harass, torment, plague; coerce, pressurize, strong-arm; threaten, menace; informal bulldoze; N. Amer. informal bullyrag.

hedge noun **1** *the house was concealed behind high hedges:* **hedgerow**, bushes, fence; windbreak; Brit. quickset. **2** *he sees the fund as an excellent hedge against a fall in sterling:* **safeguard**, protection, shield, screen, guard, buffer, cushion; insurance, security. **3** *his analysis is full of hedges like 'probably' and 'perhaps':* **equivocation**, evasion, fudge, quibble, qualification; temporizing, uncertainty, prevarication, vagueness.
verb **1** *the fields were hedged with hawthorn:* **surround**, enclose, encircle, ring, border, edge, bound. **2** *she was hedged in by her imperfect education:* **confine**, restrict, limit, hinder, obstruct, impede, constrain, trap; hem in. **3** *the company hedged its position on the futures market:* **safeguard**, protect, shield, guard, cushion; cover, insure. **4** *he hedged at every new question:* **prevaricate**, equivocate, vacillate, quibble, hesitate, stall, dodge the issue, be non-committal, be evasive, be vague, beat about the bush, pussyfoot around, mince one's words; Brit. hum and haw; informal sit on the fence, duck the question.

hedonism noun *punk was a mix of idealism and hedonism:* **self-indulgence**, pleasure-seeking, self-gratification, lotus-eating, sybaritism; intemperance, immoderation, extravagance, luxury, high living.
– OPPOSITES self-restraint.

hedonist noun **sybarite**, sensualist, voluptuary, pleasure-seeker, bon viveur, bon vivant; epicure, gastronome.
– OPPOSITES ascetic.

hedonistic adjective *a shift towards a more casual, private, and hedonistic style of life:* **self-indulgent**, pleasure-seeking, sybaritic, lotus-eating, epicurean; unrestrained, intemperate, immoderate, extravagant, decadent.

heed verb *he should have heeded the warnings:* **pay attention to**, take notice of, take note of, pay heed to, attend to, listen to; bear in mind, be mindful of, mind, mark, consider, take into account, follow, obey, adhere to, abide by, observe, take to heart, be alert to.
– OPPOSITES disregard.
noun *if he heard, he paid no heed:* **attention**, notice, note, regard; consideration, thought, care.

heedful adjective *on every side they cast a heedful eye:* **attentive**, careful, mindful, cautious, prudent, circumspect; alert, aware, wary, chary, watchful, vigilant, on guard, on the alert.

heedless adjective *someone had stayed behind, heedless of the warnings:* **unmindful**, taking no notice, paying no heed, unheeding, disregardful, neglectful, oblivious, inattentive, blind, deaf; incautious, imprudent, rash, reckless, foolhardy, improvident, unwary.

heel verb *the ship heeled to starboard:* **lean over**, list, careen, tilt, tip, incline, keel over.

heft verb *Donald hefted a stone jar of whisky into position:* **lift (up)**, raise (up), heave, hoist, haul; carry, lug, tote; informal cart, hump.

hefty adjective **1** *a hefty young man:* **burly**,

heavy, sturdy, strapping, bulky, brawny, husky, strong, muscular, large, big, solid, well built; portly, stout; informal hulking, hunky, beefy. **2** *he aimed a hefty kick at the door:* **powerful**, violent, hard, forceful, heavy, mighty. **3** *the horses hauled hefty loads of timber:* **heavy**, weighty, bulky, big, large, substantial, massive, ponderous; unwieldy, cumbersome, burdensome; informal hulking. **4** *they face a hefty fine:* **substantial**, sizeable, considerable, stiff, extortionate, large, excessive; informal steep, astronomical, whopping.
– OPPOSITES slight, feeble, light, small.

height noun **1** *we measured the height of the wall:* **highness**, tallness, elevation, stature, altitude. **2** *they were at the height of their fame when they split up:* **highest point**, crowning moment, peak, acme, zenith, apogee, pinnacle, climax, high water mark. **3** *it would be the height of bad manners not to attend:* **epitome**, acme, zenith, quintessence, very limit; ultimate, utmost. **4** *he is terrified of heights:* **high places**, high ground; precipices, cliffs.
– OPPOSITES width, nadir.

heighten verb *her pleasure was heightened by a sense of guilt:* **intensify**, increase, enhance, add to, augment, boost, strengthen, deepen, magnify, amplify, reinforce.
– OPPOSITES lower, reduce.

heinous adjective *child abuse is considered a most heinous offence:* **odious**, wicked, evil, atrocious, monstrous, abominable, detestable, contemptible, reprehensible, despicable, egregious, horrific, terrible, awful, abhorrent, loathsome, hideous, unspeakable, execrable; iniquitous, villainous.
– OPPOSITES admirable.

heir, heiress noun **successor**, next in line, inheritor, beneficiary, legatee; descendant, scion; Law devisee; English Law coparcener; Scottish Law heritor.

helix noun **spiral**, coil, corkscrew, curl, twist, gyre, whorl, convolution.

hell noun **1** *they feared they would go to hell:* **the netherworld**, the Inferno, the infernal regions, the abyss; eternal damnation, perdition; hellfire, fire and brimstone; Hades, Acheron, Gehenna, Tophet, Sheol. **2** *for ten years he made her life hell:* **a misery**, torture, agony, a torment, a nightmare, an ordeal; anguish, wretchedness, woe.
– OPPOSITES heaven, paradise.

▪ **give someone hell** (informal) **1** *when I found out, I gave him hell:* reprimand, rebuke, admonish, chastise, chide, upbraid, reprove, scold, berate, remonstrate with, reprehend, take to task, lambaste; read someone the Riot Act, give someone a piece of one's mind, haul over the coals; informal tell off, dress down, give someone an earful, give someone a roasting, rap over the knuckles, let someone have it, bawl out, come down hard on, lay into, blast; Brit. informal tick

off, have a go at, carpet, give someone a rollicking, give someone a mouthful, tear someone off a strip, give someone what for; N. Amer. informal chew out; formal castigate. **2** *she gave me hell when I was working for her:* harass, hound, plague, harry, bother, trouble, bully, intimidate, pick on, victimize, terrorize; informal hassle, give someone a hard time.

▪ **raise hell** (informal) **1** *they were hollering and raising hell:* cause a disturbance, cause a commotion, be noisy, run riot, run wild, be out of control; informal raise the roof. **2** *he raised hell with the planners and developers:* remonstrate, expostulate, be angry, be furious; argue; informal kick up a fuss, kick up a stink.

hell-bent adjective *why are you hell-bent on leaving?* **intent**, bent, determined, (dead) set, insistent, fixed, resolved; single-minded, fixated.
– OPPOSITES half-hearted.

hellish adjective **1** *I saw the hellish face of Death:* **infernal**, Hadean; diabolical, fiendish, satanic, demonic; evil, wicked. **2** (informal) *it's been a hellish week:* **horrible**, rotten, awful, terrible, dreadful, ghastly, horrid, vile, foul, appalling, atrocious, horrendous, frightful; difficult, unpleasant, nasty, disagreeable; stressful, taxing, tough, hard, frustrating, fraught, traumatic, gruelling; informal murderous, lousy; Brit. informal beastly; N. Amer. informal hellacious.
– OPPOSITES angelic, wonderful.
adverb (Brit. informal) *it's hellish hard work:* **extremely**, very, exceedingly, exceptionally, tremendously, immensely, intensely, unusually, decidedly, particularly, really, truly, mightily; most, so; N. English right; informal terrifically, awfully, fearfully, terribly, devilishly, majorly, seriously, ultra, oh-so, damn, damned; Brit. informal ever so, well, bloody, dead; N. Amer. informal real, mighty, awful; archaic exceeding.
– OPPOSITES moderately.

helm noun *the second mate took the helm:* **tiller**, wheel; rudder.
▪ **at the helm** *a family-run business whose founder remains at the helm:* in charge, in command, in control, responsible, in authority, at the wheel, in the driving seat, in the saddle; informal holding the reins, running the show, calling the shots.

help verb **1** *they helped her with the washing up:* **assist**, aid, lend a (helping) hand to, give assistance to, come to the aid of; be of service to, be of use to; do someone a favour, do someone a service, do someone a good turn, bail someone out, come to the rescue, give someone a leg up; rally round, pitch in; informal get someone out of a tight spot, save someone's bacon, save someone's skin. **2** *using this credit card helps cancer research:* **support**, contribute to, give money to, donate to; promote, boost, back; further the interests of;

N. Amer. informal bankroll. **3** *sore throats are helped by lozenges:* **relieve**, soothe, ease, alleviate, make better, improve, assuage, lessen; remedy, cure, heal.
– OPPOSITES hinder, impede, worsen.
noun **1** *I asked for help from my neighbours | this could be of help to you:* **assistance**, aid, a helping hand, support, succour, advice, guidance; benefit, use, advantage, service, comfort; informal a shot in the arm. **2** *he sought help for his eczema:* **relief**, alleviation, improvement, assuagement, healing; a remedy, a cure, a restorative.
■ **cannot help** *when he saw her, he could not help laughing:* be unable to stop, be unable to refrain from, be unable to keep from.
■ **help oneself to** *he helped himself to the contents of her purse:* steal, take, appropriate, pocket, purloin, commandeer; informal swipe, nab, filch, snaffle, liberate, walk off with, run off with; Brit. informal nick, pinch, whip, knock off.

helper noun *there was no shortage of helpers to relieve us:* **assistant**, aide, helpmate, helpmeet, deputy, auxiliary, second, right-hand man/woman, attendant, acolyte; co-worker, workmate, teammate, associate, colleague, partner; informal sidekick.

helpful adjective **1** *the staff are friendly and helpful:* **obliging**, eager to please, kind, accommodating, supportive, cooperative; sympathetic, neighbourly, charitable. **2** *we found it helpful to receive your comments:* **useful**, of use, beneficial, valuable, profitable, fruitful, advantageous, worthwhile, constructive; informative, instructive. **3** *we recommend this helpful new power tool:* **handy**, useful, convenient, practical, easy-to-use, functional, serviceable; informal neat, nifty.
– OPPOSITES unsympathetic, useless, inconvenient.

helping noun *there will be enough for six to eight helpings:* **portion**, serving, piece, slice, share, ration, allocation; informal dollop.

helpless adjective *the cubs are born blind and helpless:* **dependent**, incapable, powerless, impotent, weak; defenceless, vulnerable, exposed, unprotected, open to attack; paralysed, disabled.
– OPPOSITES independent.

helter-skelter adverb *the children ran helter-skelter down the valley:* **headlong**, pell-mell, hotfoot, post-haste, hastily, hurriedly, at full pelt, at full tilt, hell for leather; recklessly, precipitately, heedlessly, wildly; informal like a bat out of hell, like the wind, like greased lightning, like a bomb; Brit. informal like the clappers, at a rate of knots; N. Amer. informal lickety-split.
adjective *the village was a helter-skelter collection of dwellings:* **disordered**, disorderly, chaotic, muddled, jumbled, untidy, haphazard, disorganized, topsy-turvy; informal higgledy-piggledy; Brit. informal shambolic.

– OPPOSITES orderly.

hem noun *the hem of her dress:* **edge**, edging, border, trim, trimming.
verb *Nan taught me to hem skirts:* **edge**, trim.
■ **hem someone/something in 1** *the bay was hemmed in by pine trees:* surround, border, edge, encircle, circle, ring, enclose, skirt, fringe, encompass. **2** *he was hemmed in by parked cars | we were hemmed in by the rules:* restrict, confine, trap, hedge in, fence in; constrain, restrain, limit, curb, check.

he-man noun (informal) *intensive offseason training turned Mike into a he-man:* **muscleman**, strongman, macho man, iron man; Hercules, Samson, Tarzan; informal hunk, tough guy, beefcake, bruiser.
– OPPOSITES wimp.

hence adverb *many vehicle journeys (and hence a lot of pollution) would be saved:* **consequently**, as a consequence, for this reason, therefore, ergo, thus, so, accordingly, as a result, because of that, that being so.

henceforth, henceforward adverb *henceforth the director will be responsible for the whole establishment:* **from now on**, as of now, from this (the) future, hence, subsequently, from this day on/forth; formal hereafter.

henchman noun *the local warlord arrived with a group of henchmen:* **right-hand man**, assistant, aide, helper; underling, minion, man Friday, lackey, flunkey, stooge; bodyguard, minder; informal sidekick, crony, heavy.

henpecked adjective *a henpecked husband at the end of his tether:* **browbeaten**, downtrodden, bullied, dominated, subjugated, oppressed, intimidated; meek, timid, cringing; informal under someone's thumb, led by the nose.
– OPPOSITES domineering.

herald verb **1** *screams and shouts heralded their approach:* **proclaim**, announce, broadcast, publicize, declare, trumpet, blazon, advertise. **2** *the speech heralded a major policy change:* **signal**, indicate, announce, spell, presage, augur, portend, promise, foretell; usher in, pave the way for, be a harbinger of; literary foretoken, betoken.

Herculean adjective **1** *this is a Herculean task that he has undertaken:* **arduous**, gruelling, laborious, back-breaking, onerous, strenuous, difficult, formidable, hard, tough, huge, massive, uphill; demanding, exhausting, taxing. **2** *he was a man of Herculean build:* **strong**, muscular, muscly, powerful, robust, solid, strapping, brawny, burly; informal hunky, beefy, hulking.
– OPPOSITES easy, puny.

herd noun **1** *a herd of cows blocked the road:* **drove**, flock, pack, fold; group, collection. **2** *I ran into a herd of movie actors:* **crowd**, group, bunch, horde, mob, host, pack, multitude, throng, swarm, company. **3** *they consider themselves above the herd:* **the**

common people, the masses, the rank and file, the crowd, the commonality, the commonalty, the plebeians; the hoi polloi, the mob, the proletariat, the rabble, the riff-raff, the great unwashed; informal the proles, the plebs.
verb **1** *we herded the sheep back into the pen*: **drive**, shepherd, guide; round up, gather, collect. **2** *we all herded into the waiting room*: **crowd**, pack, flock; cluster, huddle. **3** *they live by herding reindeer*: **tend**, look after, keep, watch (over), mind, guard.

herdsman, herdswoman noun **stockman**, herder, drover, cattleman, cowherd, cowhand, cowman, cowboy, rancher, shepherd; N. Amer. ranchero; N. Amer. informal cowpuncher, cowpoke.

here
■ **here and there 1** *a landscape of ferns with clumps of heather here and there*: in various places, in different places; at random. **2** *they darted here and there, adjusting the controls*: hither and thither, around, about, to and fro, back and forth, in all directions.

hereafter adverb (formal) *nothing I say hereafter is intended to offend*: **from now on**, after this, as of now, from this moment forth, from this day forth, from this day forward, subsequently, in (the) future, hence, henceforth, henceforward.
noun *our preparation for the hereafter*: **life after death**, the afterlife, the afterworld, the next world; eternity, heaven, paradise.

hereditary adjective **1** *their hereditary right to hunt on this land*: **inherited**; bequeathed, willed, handed-down, passed-down, passed-on, transferred; ancestral, family, familial. **2** *cystic fibrosis is a fatal hereditary disease*: **genetic**, genetical, congenital, inborn, inherited, inbred, innate; in the family, in the blood, in the genes.

heredity noun *the effects of heredity and environment*: **genes**, genetic make-up; ancestry, descent, extraction, parentage.

heresy noun *an old man called Walter Myln was burned for heresy at St Andrews*: **dissension**, dissent, nonconformity, heterodoxy, unorthodoxy, apostasy, blasphemy, freethinking; atheism; idolatry; iconoclasm.

heretic noun **dissenter**, nonconformist, apostate, freethinker, iconoclast; atheist, non-believer, unbeliever, idolater, pagan, heathen.
– OPPOSITES conformist, believer.

heretical adjective *Uhtred's opinion was denounced as heretical at Oxford in 1367*: **dissenting**, nonconformist, freethinking, idolatrous, godless; iconoclastic.

heritage noun **1** *Europe's varied cultural heritage*: **tradition**, history, past, background; culture, customs. **2** *he is proud of his Greek heritage*: **ancestry**, lineage, descent, extraction, parentage, roots, background, heredity.

hermaphrodite noun **androgyne**, intersex, epicene; Biology bisexual, gynandromorph.
adjective **androgynous**, intersex, hermaphroditic, hermaphroditical, epicene; Biology bisexual, gynandrous, gynandromorphic.

hermetic adjective **airtight**, tight, sealed; watertight, waterproof.

hermit noun *the tale of the English monk and hermit St Godric of Finchale*: **recluse**, solitary, loner, ascetic; historical anchorite, anchoress.

hermitage noun **retreat**, refuge, hideaway, hideout, shelter; informal hidey-hole.

hero noun **1** *his father was a hero*: **brave man**; man of the hour, lionheart, warrior; champion, victor, conqueror. **2** *a football hero*: **star**, superstar, megastar, idol, celebrity, luminary; ideal, paragon; favourite, darling; informal celeb. **3** *the hero of the film is a young pianist*: **male protagonist**, principal male character/role, starring role; male lead, lead (actor), leading man.
– OPPOSITES coward, loser, villain.

heroic adjective **1** *their heroic deeds | heroic rescuers*: **brave**, courageous, valiant, valorous, lionhearted, intrepid, bold, fearless, daring, audacious; unafraid, undaunted, dauntless, doughty, plucky, stout-hearted, mettlesome; gallant, chivalrous, noble; informal gutsy, spunky. **2** *black granite obelisks on a heroic scale*: **prodigious**, grand, enormous, huge, massive, titanic, colossal, monumental; epic; informal mega.

heroine noun **1** *she's a heroine—she saved my baby*: **brave woman**, hero, woman of the hour; victor, winner, conqueror. **2** *the literary heroine of Moscow*: **star**, superstar, megastar, idol, celebrity, luminary; ideal, paragon; favourite, darling; informal celeb. **3** *the film's heroine makes a stand against the crooks*: **female protagonist**, principal female character/role; female lead, lead (actress), leading lady; prima donna, diva.

heroism noun *many of the women distinguished themselves by great acts of heroism*: **bravery**, courage, valour, intrepidity, boldness, daring, audacity, fearlessness, dauntlessness, pluck, stout-heartedness, lionheartedness; backbone, spine, grit, spirit, mettle; gallantry, chivalry; informal guts, spunk; Brit. informal bottle; N. Amer. informal moxie.

hero-worship noun **idolization**, adulation, admiration, lionization, idealization, worship, adoration, veneration.

hesitancy noun. See HESITATION.

hesitant adjective **1** *clients are hesitant about buying*: **uncertain**, undecided, unsure, doubtful, dubious, sceptical; tentative, nervous, reluctant; indecisive, irresolute, hesitating, dithering, vacillating, blowing hot and cold; ambivalent, in two minds;

h

h

Brit. havering, humming and hawing; informal iffy. **2** *a timid and hesitant child:* **lacking confidence**, diffident, timid, shy, bashful, insecure.
– OPPOSITES certain, decisive, confident.

hesitate verb **1** *she hesitated, unsure of what to say:* **pause**, delay, wait, shilly-shally, dither, stall, temporize; be in two minds, be uncertain, be unsure, be doubtful, be indecisive, equivocate, vacillate, waver, blow hot and cold, have second thoughts; Brit. haver, hum and haw; informal dilly-dally. **2** *please don't hesitate to contact me:* **be reluctant**, be unwilling, be disinclined, scruple; have misgivings about, have qualms about, shrink from, demur from, think twice about, baulk at.

hesitation noun **1** *she answered without hesitation:* **hesitancy**, hesitance, uncertainty, unsureness, doubt, doubtfulness, dubiousness; irresolution, irresoluteness, indecision, indecisiveness; equivocation, vacillation, second thoughts; dithering, stalling, temporization, delay. **2** *I have no hesitation in recommending him:* **reluctance**, disinclination, unease, ambivalence, second thoughts.

heterodox adjective *the heterodox character of Egyptian Christianity:* **unorthodox**, nonconformist, dissenting, dissident, rebellious, renegade; heretical, blasphemous, apostate.
– OPPOSITES orthodox.

heterogeneous adjective *the collection of heterogeneous tasks that make up housework:* **diverse**, varied, varying, miscellaneous, assorted, mixed, sundry, disparate, different, differing, unrelated; motley; literary divers.
– OPPOSITES homogeneous.

heterosexual adjective informal **straight**, hetero, het.
– OPPOSITES homosexual, gay.

hew verb *master carpenters hewed the logs with axes:* **chop**, hack, cut, lop, axe, cleave; fell; carve, shape, fashion, sculpt, model.

heyday noun *the paper has lost millions of readers since its heyday in 1964:* **prime**, peak, height, pinnacle, acme, zenith; day, time, bloom; prime of life, salad days.

hiatus noun *there has been a hiatus in manned space exploration:* **pause**, break, gap, lacuna, interval, intermission, interlude, interruption, suspension, lull, respite, time out; N. Amer. recess; informal breather, let-up.

hibernate verb **lie dormant**, lie torpid, sleep; overwinter.

hidden adjective **1** *they watched the action via a hidden camera:* **concealed**, secret, invisible, unseen, out of sight; camouflaged, disguised, masked. **2** *what is the hidden meaning behind these words?* **obscure**, unclear, concealed, indistinct, indefinite, vague, unfathomable, inexplicable; cryptic, mysterious, secret, covert, abstruse, arcane;

ulterior, deep, subliminal, coded.
– OPPOSITES visible, obvious.

hide[1] verb **1** *he hid the money under the floor:* **conceal**, secrete, put out of sight; camouflage; lock up, stow away, cache; informal stash. **2** *they escaped after hiding in an air vent:* **conceal oneself**, secrete oneself, hide out, take cover, keep out of sight; lie low, go to ground, go to earth; informal hole up. **3** *clouds rolled across the sky and hid the moon:* **obscure**, block out, blot out, obstruct, cloud, shroud, veil, blanket, envelop, eclipse. **4** *he could not hide his dislike of this process:* **conceal**, keep secret, cover up, keep dark, keep quiet about, hush up, bottle up, suppress; disguise, mask, camouflage; informal keep under one's hat, keep a/the lid on.
– OPPOSITES flaunt, reveal.

hide[2] noun *a cow hide:* **skin**, pelt, coat; leather.

hideaway noun *a mass of shrubs has created a secluded hideaway:* **retreat**, refuge, hiding place, hideout, den, bolt-hole, shelter, sanctuary, sanctum; hermitage; informal hidey-hole.

hidebound adjective *hidebound traditionalists who refuse to accept change:* **conservative**, reactionary, conventional, orthodox; fundamentalist, diehard, hard-line, dyed-in-the-wool, set in one's ways; narrow-minded, small-minded, intolerant, uncompromising, rigid; prejudiced, bigoted; Brit. blimpish.
– OPPOSITES liberal.

hideous adjective **1** *his smile made him look more hideous than ever:* **ugly**, repulsive, repellent, unsightly, revolting, gruesome, grotesque, monstrous, ghastly, reptilian; informal as ugly as sin. **2** *hideous cases of torture have been reported:* **horrific**, terrible, appalling, awful, dreadful, frightful, horrible, horrendous, horrifying, shocking, sickening, gruesome, ghastly, unspeakable, abhorrent, monstrous, heinous, abominable, foul, vile, odious, execrable.
– OPPOSITES beautiful, pleasant.

hideout noun *the kidnappers did not want their hideout discovered:* **hiding place**, hideaway, retreat, refuge, shelter, bolt-hole, safe house, sanctuary, sanctum; informal hidey-hole.

hiding
▪ **in hiding** *the fugitive priest is currently in hiding:* **hidden**, concealed, lying low, gone to ground, gone to earth, in a safe house.

hiding place noun *the guards passed within inches of my hiding place:* **hideaway**, hideout, retreat, refuge, shelter, sanctuary, sanctum, bolt-hole, safe house; informal hidey-hole.

hierarchy noun *the initiative was with those lower down in the hierarchy:* **pecking order**, ranking, grading, ladder, scale.

hieroglyphic noun **1** *his exploits were*

recorded in hieroglyphics on a stone monument: **symbols**, signs, ciphers, code, cryptograms. **2** tattered notebooks filled with hieroglyphics: **scribble**, scrawl, illegible writing; shorthand.

higgledy-piggledy (informal) adjective a higgledy-piggledy mountain of papers: **disordered**, disorderly, disorganized, untidy, messy, chaotic, jumbled, muddled, confused, unsystematic, irregular; out of order, in disarray, in a mess, in a muddle, haphazard; informal all over the place; Brit. informal shambolic.
– OPPOSITES tidy.
adverb the cars were parked higgledy-piggledy: **in disorder**, in a muddle, in a jumble, in disarray, untidily, haphazardly, anyhow; informal all over the place, topsy-turvy, every which way, any old how; Brit. informal all over the shop; N. Amer. informal all over the map, all over the lot.

high adjective **1** the top of a high mountain: **tall**, lofty, towering, elevated, giant, big; multi-storey, high-rise. **2** he rose to a high position in the government: **high-ranking**, high-level, leading, top, top-level, prominent, pre-eminent, foremost, senior; influential, powerful, important, elevated, prime, premier, exalted; N. Amer. ranking; informal top-notch. **3** shop around to avoid high prices: **inflated**, excessive, unreasonable, expensive, dear, costly, exorbitant, extortionate, prohibitive; Brit. over the odds; informal steep, stiff, pricey. **4** I have always insisted on high standards: **excellent**, outstanding, exemplary, exceptional, admirable, fine, good, first-class, first-rate, superior, superlative, superb; impeccable, irreproachable, unimpeachable, perfect, flawless; informal A1, top-notch. **5** the voices rose to hit a high note: **high-pitched**, high-frequency; soprano, treble, falsetto, shrill, sharp, piercing, penetrating. **6** (informal) they are high on a cocktail of drugs: **intoxicated**, inebriated, drugged, stupefied, befuddled, delirious, hallucinating; informal high as a kite, stoned, tripping, hyped up, spaced out, wasted, wrecked, off one's head. **7** the partridges were pretty high: **gamy**, smelly, strong-smelling; stinking, reeking, rank, malodorous, bad, off, rotting; Brit. informal pongy, niffy, whiffy; N. Amer. informal funky.
– OPPOSITES short, lowly, cheap, low, deep, sober, fresh.
noun commodity prices were at a rare high: **high level**, high point, peak, maximum, high water mark; pinnacle, zenith, acme, height.
– OPPOSITES low.
adverb a jet flew high overhead: **high up**, far (up), way (up); (up) in the air, (up) in the sky, on high, aloft, overhead.
– OPPOSITES low.
■ **high and dry** the family was left high and dry by the death of the breadwinner: destitute, bereft, helpless, in the lurch, in difficulties; abandoned, stranded, marooned.

■ **high and low** we searched for her high and low: everywhere, all over, all around, far and wide, {here, there, and everywhere}, extensively, thoroughly, widely, in every nook and cranny; informal all over the place; Brit. informal all over the shop; N. Amer. informal all over the map.
■ **high and mighty** (informal) her family were all high and mighty and ignored me whenever they could: self-important, condescending, patronizing, disdainful, supercilious, superior, snobbish, snobby, haughty, conceited, above oneself; informal stuck-up, snooty, hoity-toity, la-di-da, uppity; Brit. informal toffee-nosed.
■ **on a high** (informal) he was on a high following his team's triumph: ecstatic, euphoric, delirious, elated, thrilled, overjoyed, beside oneself, walking on air, on cloud nine, in seventh heaven, jumping for joy, in raptures, exultant, jubilant; excited, overexcited; informal blissed out, over the moon, on top of the world; Austral./NZ informal wrapped.

high-born adjective he is from a high-born Portuguese family: **noble**, aristocratic, well born, titled, patrician, blue-blooded, upper-class; informal upper-crust, top-drawer; Brit. informal posh.
– OPPOSITES lowly.

highbrow adjective his art has a small, mostly highbrow following: **intellectual**, scholarly, bookish, academic, educated, donnish, bluestocking; sophisticated, erudite, learned; informal brainy, egghead.
– OPPOSITES lowbrow.
noun all those highbrows who squirm when they hear pop music: **intellectual**, scholar, academic, bluestocking, thinker; informal egghead, brain, bookworm; Brit. informal brainbox, boffin; N. Amer. informal brainiac.

high-class adjective she went to a high-class boarding school: **superior**, upper-class, first-rate; excellent, select, elite, choice, premier, top, top-flight; luxurious, de luxe, high-quality, top-quality; Brit. upmarket; informal top-notch, top-drawer, A1, classy, posh.

highfalutin adjective (informal). See PRETENTIOUS.

high-flown adjective his novels seem high flown and absurd: **grand**, extravagant, elaborate, flowery, ornate, overblown, overdone, overwrought, grandiloquent, magniloquent, grandiose, inflated, affected, pretentious, turgid; informal windy, purple, highfalutin, la-di-da.
– OPPOSITES plain.

high-handed adjective people are disenchanted by the government's high-handed approach: **imperious**, arbitrary, peremptory, arrogant, haughty, domineering, pushy, overbearing, heavy-handed, lordly; inflexible, rigid; autocratic, authoritarian, dictatorial, tyrannical; informal bossy, high and mighty.
– OPPOSITES liberal.

h

high jinks plural noun *they get up to all kinds of high jinks on their trips away:* **antics**, pranks, larks, escapades, stunts, practical jokes, tricks; fun (and games), skylarking, mischief, horseplay, tomfoolery, clowning; informal shenanigans, capers, monkey business; Brit. informal monkey tricks.

highland noun **upland**, highlands, uplands, mountains, hills, heights, moors; tableland, plateau; Brit. wolds.

highlight noun *he views this as the highlight of his career:* **high point**, high spot, best part, climax, peak, pinnacle, height, acme, zenith, summit, crowning moment, high water mark.
– OPPOSITES nadir.
verb *he has highlighted numerous shortcomings in the plan:* **spotlight**, call attention to, focus on, underline, feature, play up, show up, bring out, accentuate, accent, zero in on, stress, emphasize.

highly adverb **1** *a highly dangerous substance:* **very**, extremely, exceedingly, particularly, most, really, thoroughly, decidedly, distinctly, exceptionally, immensely, inordinately, singularly, extraordinarily; N. English right; informal terrifically, awfully, terribly, majorly, seriously, desperately, mega, ultra, oh-so, damn, damned; Brit. informal ever so, well, dead, jolly; N. Amer. informal real, mighty, awful; dated frightfully. **2** *he was highly regarded by everyone:* **favourably**, well, appreciatively, admiringly, approvingly, positively, glowingly, enthusiastically.
– OPPOSITES slightly, unfavourably.

highly strung adjective *a young Russian artist who was rather highly strung:* **nervous**, nervy, excitable, temperamental, sensitive, unstable; brittle, on edge, edgy, jumpy, restless, anxious, tense, stressed, overwrought, neurotic; informal uptight, twitchy, wired, wound up, het up.
– OPPOSITES easy-going.

high-minded adjective *so many academics affect high-minded seriousness:* **high-principled**, principled, honourable, moral, upright, upstanding, right-minded, noble, good, honest, decent, ethical, righteous, virtuous, worthy, idealistic.
– OPPOSITES unprincipled.

high-powered adjective *the women were all very high-powered and impressive:* **dynamic**, ambitious, energetic, assertive, enterprising, vigorous; forceful, aggressive, pushy, high-octane; informal go-ahead, go-getting; N. Amer. informal go-go.

high-pressure adjective *unscrupulous salesmen who use high-pressure tactics:* **forceful**, insistent, persistent, pushy; intensive, high-powered, aggressive, coercive, compelling, thrusting, not taking no for an answer.

high-spirited adjective *he is just an ordinary high-spirited little boy:* **lively**, spirited, full of fun, fun-loving, animated, zestful, bouncy, bubbly, sparkling, vivacious, buoyant, cheerful, joyful, exuberant, ebullient, jaunty, irrepressible; Brit. Tiggerish; informal chirpy, peppy, sparky, full of beans; literary frolicsome.

high spirits plural noun *they were young, strong, and bursting with high spirits:* **liveliness**, vitality, spirit, zest, energy, bounce, sparkle, vivacity, buoyancy, cheerfulness, good humour, joy, joyfulness, exuberance, ebullience, joie de vivre; informal pep, zing.

hijack verb *three armed men hijacked a white van:* **commandeer**, seize, take over; appropriate, expropriate; informal snatch.

hike noun *a five-mile hike on the Yorkshire moors:* **walk**, trek, tramp, trudge, slog, footslog, march; ramble; Brit. informal yomp.
verb *they hiked across the moors for miles:* **walk**, trek, tramp, trudge, slog, footslog, march; ramble; informal hoof it, leg it; Brit. informal yomp.
■ **hike something up** *the government hiked up the price of milk by 40 per cent:* increase, raise, up, put up, mark up, push up, inflate; informal jack up, bump up.

hilarious adjective *she told us a hilarious story about her friends:* **funny**, hysterical, uproarious, riotous, farcical, rib-tickling; humorous, comic, amusing, entertaining; informal side-splitting, priceless, a scream, a hoot.
– OPPOSITES sad, serious.

hilarity noun *his bemused expression was the cause of much hilarity:* **amusement**, mirth, laughter, merriment, light-heartedness, levity, fun, humour, jocularity, jollity, gaiety, delight, glee, exuberance, high spirits; comedy.

hill noun **high ground**, prominence, hillock, foothill, hillside, rise, mound, mount, mountains, knoll, hummock, tor, tump, fell, pike, mesa; bank, ridge, slope, incline, gradient; (**hills**) heights, downs; Scottish & Irish drum; Scottish brae; Geology drumlin; formal eminence.

hillock noun **mound**, small hill, prominence, elevation, rise, knoll, hummock, hump, tump, dune; bank, ridge; N. English howe; N. Amer. knob; formal eminence.

hilt noun *the sword's hilt was beautifully crafted:* **handle**, haft, handgrip, grip, shaft, shank, stock, helve.
■ **to the hilt** *we will support our elected leaders to the hilt:* completely, fully, wholly, totally, entirely, utterly, unreservedly, unconditionally, in every respect, in all respects, one hundred per cent, every inch, to the full, to the maximum extent, all the way, body and soul, heart and soul.

hind adjective *the horse neighed and stood up on its hind legs:* **back**, rear, hinder, hindmost, posterior.
– OPPOSITES fore, front.

hinder verb *various technical problems have hindered our progress:* **hamper**, obstruct, impede, inhibit, retard, baulk, thwart, foil, curb, delay, arrest, interfere with, set back, slow down, hold back, hold up, stop, halt; restrict, restrain, constrain, block, check, curtail, frustrate, cramp, handicap, cripple, hamstring; informal stymie; Brit. informal throw a spanner in the works.
– OPPOSITES facilitate.

hindrance noun *the bad weather was a major hindrance to the relief effort:* **impediment**, obstacle, barrier, bar, obstruction, handicap, block, hurdle, restraint, restriction, limitation, encumbrance; complication, delay, drawback, setback, difficulty, inconvenience, snag, catch, hitch, stumbling block; informal fly in the ointment, hiccup; Brit. informal spanner in the works.
– OPPOSITES help.

hinge verb *our future hinges on the outcome of next month's election:* **depend**, hang, rest, turn, centre, be contingent, be dependent, be conditional; be determined by, be decided by, revolve around.

hint noun **1** *he had given no hint that he would leave:* **clue**, inkling, suggestion, indication, indicator, sign, signal, pointer, intimation, insinuation, innuendo, mention, whisper. **2** *handy hints about what to buy:* **tip**, suggestion, pointer, clue, guideline, recommendation; advice, help; informal how-to; dos and don'ts, wrinkle. **3** *the wine had a fresh, crisp flavour with a hint of mint:* **trace**, touch, suspicion, suggestion, dash, soupçon, tinge, modicum, whiff, taste, undertone; informal smidgen, tad.
verb *he has hinted that his loyalties lie elsewhere:* **imply**, insinuate, intimate, suggest, indicate, signal; allude to, refer to, drive at, mean; informal get at.

hinterland noun *early settlers made their way from coastal areas into the hinterland:* **the backwoods**, a backwater, the wilds, the bush, the back of beyond; Austral./NZ the outback, the backblocks, the booay; informal the sticks, the middle of nowhere; N. Amer. informal the boondocks, the tall timbers.

hips plural noun **pelvis**, hindquarters, haunches, thighs.

hire verb **1** *we hired a car and drove to Wales:* **rent**, lease, charter. **2** *they hire and fire labour in line with demand:* **employ**, engage, recruit, appoint, take on, sign up, enrol, commission, enlist.
– OPPOSITES dismiss.
noun *the agreed rate for the hire of the machine:* **rental**, rent, hiring, lease, leasing, charter.

hire purchase noun **instalment plan**, deferred payment, HP, credit, finance, easy terms; Brit. informal the never-never.

hirsute adjective (formal) *the rest of his body was similarly hirsute:* **hairy**, shaggy, bushy, hair-covered; woolly, furry, fleecy, fuzzy; bearded, unshaven, bristly.

hiss verb **1** *the escaping gas hissed alarmingly:* **fizz**, fizzle, whistle, wheeze; rare sibilate. **2** *the audience hissed loudly at the mention of his name:* **jeer**, catcall, whistle, hoot; scoff, jibe.
noun **1** *the hiss of steam from the leaking valve:* **fizz**, fizzing, whistle, hissing, sibilance, wheeze; rare sibilation. **2** *the speaker received hisses and boos:* **jeer**, catcall, whistle; abuse, scoffing, taunting, derision.

historian noun **chronicler**, annalist, archivist, recorder; historiographer, antiquarian, chronologist.

historic adjective *it's a historic moment that will bring an end to 100 years of bloodshed | Northampton has a rich variety of historic buildings:* **significant**, notable, important, momentous, consequential, memorable, unforgettable, remarkable; famous, famed, celebrated, renowned; landmark, groundbreaking, epoch-making, red-letter, earth-shattering.
– OPPOSITES insignificant.

historical adjective **1** *historical evidence is sparse, to say the least:* **documented**, recorded, chronicled, archival; authentic, factual, actual, true. **2** *famous historical figures:* **past**, bygone, ancient, old, former; literary of yore.
– OPPOSITES contemporary.

history noun **1** *my interest in history gave me a new perspective on events:* **the past**, former times, historical events, the olden days, the old days, bygone days, yesterday, antiquity; literary days of yore, yesteryear. **2** *I was reading a history of the Civil War:* **chronicle**, archive, record, report, narrative, account, study, tale; memoir. **3** *Kirsty calmly related the details of her history:* **background**, past, life story, experiences; antecedents.

histrionic adjective *his histrionic reaction to the visitors' tackling rarely impressed the referee:* **melodramatic**, theatrical, dramatic, exaggerated, actressy, stagy, showy, affected, artificial, overacted, overdone; informal hammy, ham, camp.

histrionics plural noun *Anna was accustomed to her mother's histrionics:* **dramatics**, theatrics, tantrums, overreaction, melodrama; affectation, staginess, artificiality.

hit verb **1** *the woman hit her child for stealing sweets:* **strike**, slap, smack, cuff, punch, thump, swat; beat, thrash, batter, belabour, pound, welt, pummel, box someone's ears; whip, flog, cane; informal whack, wallop, bash, biff, bop, lam, clout, clip, clobber, sock, swipe, crown, beat the living daylights out of, give someone a (good) hiding, belt, tan, lay into, let someone have it, deck, floor; Brit. informal stick one on, dot, slosh; N. Amer. informal slug, boff; Austral./NZ informal dong; literary smite. **2** *a car hit the barrier and burst into flames:* **crash into**, run into,

smash into, smack into, knock into, bump into, cannon into, plough into, collide with, meet head-on; N. Amer. impact. **3** *the tragedy has hit her hard:* **devastate**, affect badly, hurt, harm, leave a mark on; upset, shatter, crush, shock, overwhelm, traumatize; informal knock sideways, knock the stuffing out of; Brit. informal knock for six. **4** (informal) *spending for this year will hit £1,800 million:* **reach**, touch, arrive at, rise to, climb to. **5** *it hit me that I had forgotten to get the information I needed:* **occur to**, strike, dawn on, come to; enter one's head, cross one's mind, come to mind, spring to mind.
– OPPOSITES miss, spare, escape.

noun **1** *he received a hit from behind:* **blow**, thump, punch, knock, bang, box, cuff, slap, smack, tap, crack, stroke, welt; impact, collision, bump, crash; informal whack, thwack, wallop, bash, belt, biff, clout, sock, swipe, clip; Brit. informal slosh; N. Amer. informal boff, slug; Austral./NZ dong. **2** *he directed many Broadway hits:* **success**, box-office success, sell-out, winner, triumph, sensation; best-seller; informal smash (hit), knockout, crowd-puller, wow, biggie; Brit. informal smasher.
– OPPOSITES failure.

■ **hit back** *prison officers have hit back at the critical report:* retaliate, respond, reply, react, counter, defend oneself.

■ **hit home** *she could see that her remark had hit home:* have the desired effect, strike home, hit the mark, register, be understood, get through, sink in.

■ **hit it off** (informal) *they're an unlikely pair, but they hit it off:* get on (well), get along, be friends, be friendly, be compatible, feel a rapport, see eye to eye, take to each other, warm to each other; informal click, get on like a house on fire, be on the same wavelength.

■ **hit on/upon** *Hannah hit on a novel idea for fund-raising:* discover, come up with, think of, conceive of, dream up, work out, invent, create, devise, design, pioneer; uncover, stumble on, chance on, light on, come upon.

■ **hit out at** *he hit out at the government's lack of action:* criticize, attack, censure, denounce, condemn, lambaste, pillory, rail against, inveigh against, arraign, cast aspersions on, pour scorn on, disparage, denigrate, give a bad press to, run down; informal knock, pan, slam, hammer, lay into, pull to pieces, pick holes in; Brit. informal slag off, slate, rubbish; N. Amer. informal pummel, trash; formal excoriate.

hitch verb **1** *she hitched the blanket around her:* **pull**, jerk, hike, lift, raise; informal yank. **2** *Tom hitched the pony to his cart:* **harness**, yoke, couple, fasten, connect, attach, tether.
noun *it all went without a hitch:* **problem**, difficulty, snag, setback, hindrance, obstacle, obstruction, complication, impediment, stumbling block, barrier; hold-up, interruption, delay; informal headache, glitch, hiccup.

hither adverb (literary) *a change of mind has brought me hither:* **here**, to this place, to here, over here; near, nearer, close, closer.

hitherto adverb *hitherto a part of French West Africa, Benin achieved independence in 1960:* **previously**, formerly, earlier, before, beforehand; so far, thus far, to date, as yet, until now, until then, till now, till then, up to now, up to then; formal heretofore.

hit-or-miss, hit-and-miss adjective *her work can be rather hit-or-miss at times:* **erratic**, haphazard, disorganized, undisciplined, unmethodical, uneven; careless, slapdash, slipshod, casual, cursory, lackadaisical, perfunctory, random, aimless, undirected, indiscriminate; informal sloppy, slap-happy.
– OPPOSITES meticulous.

hoard noun *they claimed to have uncovered a hoard of Nazi gold:* **cache**, stockpile, stock, store, collection, supply, reserve, reservoir, fund, accumulation; treasure house, treasure trove; informal stash.
verb *many of the boat people had hoarded their rations for weeks:* **stockpile**, store (up), stock up on, put aside, put by, lay in, lay up, set aside, stow away, buy up; cache, amass, collect, save, gather, garner, accumulate, squirrel away, put aside for a rainy day; informal stash away, salt away.
– OPPOSITES squander.

hoarse adjective *their voices were hoarse from shouting:* **rough**, harsh, croaky, throaty, gruff, husky, guttural, growly, gravelly, grating, rasping.
– OPPOSITES mellow, clear.

hoary adjective **1** *hoary cobwebs festooned the ceiling:* **greyish-white**, grey, white, silver, silvery; frosty; literary rimy. **2** *a solitary hoary mariner sat in repose outside the tavern:* **grey-haired**, white-haired, silver-haired, grizzled; elderly, aged, old. **3** *a hoary old adage favoured by Fleet Street editors:* **trite**, hackneyed, clichéd, banal, commonplace, predictable, overused, stale, time-worn, tired, unimaginative, unoriginal, uninspired; informal old hat, corny; N. Amer. informal cornball.
– OPPOSITES young, original.

hoax noun *the call was a hoax:* **practical joke**, joke, jest, prank, trick; ruse, deception, fraud, bluff, humbug, confidence trick; informal con, spoof, scam.
verb *on April 1, the radio station hoaxed its listeners:* **play a (practical) joke on**, trick, fool; deceive, hoodwink, delude, dupe, take in, lead on, bluff, gull, humbug; informal con, kid, have on, pull a fast one on, put one over on, take for a ride, lead up the garden path; N. Amer. informal sucker, snooker.

hoaxer noun **(practical) joker**, prankster, trickster; fraudster, hoodwinker, swindler; informal spoofer, con man.

hobble verb *he was still hobbling around on crutches:* **limp**, walk with difficulty, move unsteadily, walk haltingly; shamble, totter, dodder, stagger, stumble; Scottish & N. English hirple.

hobby noun **pastime**, leisure activity, leisure pursuit; sideline, diversion, avocation; recreation, entertainment, amusement, enthusiasm.

hobgoblin noun **goblin**, imp, sprite, elf, brownie, pixie, leprechaun, gnome; Scottish kelpie.

hobnob verb (informal) *he was in his element, hobnobbing with the rich and famous:* **associate**, mix, fraternize, socialize, keep company, spend time, go around, mingle, consort, rub shoulders; N. Amer. rub elbows; informal hang around/round/out, knock about/around, be thick with.

hocus-pocus noun *he is a master of legal hocus-pocus:* **jargon**, mumbo-jumbo, gibberish, balderdash, claptrap, nonsense, rubbish, twaddle, garbage; informal gobbledegook, double Dutch, hokum; N. Amer. informal flapdoodle.

hodgepodge noun (N. Amer.). See HOTCHPOTCH.

hog noun **pig**, sow, swine, porker, piglet, boar; informal piggy.
  verb (informal) *he always hogged the limelight:* **monopolize**, dominate, take over, corner, control.
  – OPPOSITES share.

hoi polloi noun *royalty seem reluctant to let the hoi polloi into their homes:* **the masses**, the common people, the populace, the public, the multitude, the rank and file, the lower orders, the third estate, the plebeians, the proletariat; the mob, the herd, the rabble, the riff-raff, the great unwashed; informal the plebs, the proles.

hoist verb *as we travelled north we hoisted the mainsail:* **raise**, lift (up), haul up, heave up, jack up, hike up, winch up, pull up, upraise, uplift, elevate, erect.
  – OPPOSITES lower.
  noun *a mechanical hoist used for firefighting purposes:* **lifting gear**, crane, winch, block and tackle, pulley, windlass, derrick.

hold verb **1** *she was holding a brown leather suitcase:* **clasp**, clutch, grasp, grip, clench, cling to, hold on to; carry, bear. **2** *I wanted to hold her in my arms:* **embrace**, hug, clasp, cradle, enfold, squeeze, fold in one's arms. **3** *do you hold a clean driving licence?:* **possess**, have, own, bear, carry, have to one's name. **4** *the branch seemed likely to hold my weight:* **support**, bear, carry, take, keep up, sustain, prop up, shore up. **5** *the police were holding him on a murder charge:* **detain**, hold in custody; imprison, lock up, put behind bars, put in prison, put in jail, incarcerate, keep under lock and key, confine, intern; informal put away, put inside. **6** *the costumes are a way to hold the audience's attention:* **maintain**, keep, occupy, engross, absorb, interest, captivate, fascinate, enthral, rivet; engage, catch, capture, arrest. **7** *he held a senior post in the Foreign Office:* **occupy**, have, fill; informal hold down. **8** *the tank held*

250 gallons | the church is big enough to hold 400 people: **take**, contain, accommodate, fit; have a capacity of, have room for. **9** *the court held that there was no evidence to support this assertion:* **maintain**, consider, take the view, believe, think, feel, deem, be of the opinion; judge, rule, decide; informal reckon; formal opine. **10** *let's hope the good weather holds for the rest of the week:* **persist**, continue, carry on, go on, hold out, keep up, last, endure, stay, remain. **11** *I'll have that coffee now, if the offer still holds:* **be available**, be valid, hold good, stand, apply, remain, exist, be the case, be in force, be in effect. **12** *the president held a meeting with party leaders:* **convene**, call, summon; conduct, have, organize, run; formal convoke.
  – OPPOSITES release, lose, end.
  noun **1** *she kept a firm hold on my hand:* **grip**, grasp, clasp, clutch. **2** *Tom had some kind of hold over his father:* **influence**, power, control, dominance, authority, leverage, sway, mastery. **3** *the military tightened their hold on the capital:* **control**, grip, power, stranglehold, dominion, authority.
  ■ **get hold of 1** *I just can't get hold of saffron at the moment:* obtain, acquire, get, find, come by, pick up, procure; buy, purchase; informal get one's hands on. **2** *I'll try to get hold of Mark Dawes:* contact, get in touch with, communicate with, make contact with, reach, notify; phone, call, speak to, talk to; Brit. ring (up), get on to.
  ■ **hold back** *he held back, remembering the mistake he had made before:* hesitate, pause, stop oneself, desist, forbear.
  ■ **hold someone back** *I felt that my lack of experience held me back:* hinder, hamper, impede, obstruct, check, curb, block, thwart, baulk, hamstring, restrain, frustrate, stand in someone's way.
  ■ **hold something back 1** *Jane struggled to hold back the tears:* suppress, fight back, choke back, stifle, smother, subdue, rein in, repress, curb, control, keep a tight rein on; informal keep a/the lid on. **2** *don't hold anything back from me:* withhold, hide, conceal, keep secret, keep hidden, keep quiet about, hush up; informal sit on, keep under one's hat.
  ■ **hold something down 1** *they are determined to hold down inflation:* keep down, keep low, freeze, fix. **2** (informal) *holding down two jobs was proving to be tiring:* occupy, hold, have, do, fill.
  ■ **hold forth** *Richard was holding forth about the qualities of good wine:* speak at length, talk at length, go on, sound off; declaim, spout, pontificate, orate, preach, sermonize; informal speechify, preachify, drone on.
  ■ **hold off** *fortunately, the rain held off until evening:* stay away, keep off, not come.
  ■ **hold something off** *he held off a late challenge by Vose to win by 13 seconds:* resist, repel, repulse, rebuff, parry, deflect, fend off, stave off, ward off, keep at bay.

h

■ **hold on 1** *hold on a minute, I'll be right back:* wait (a minute), just a moment, just a second; stay here, stay put; hold the line; informal hang on, sit tight, hold your horses; Brit. informal hang about. **2** *if only they could hold on a little longer:* keep going, persevere, survive, last, continue, struggle on, carry on, go on, hold out, see it through, stay the course; informal soldier on, stick at it, hang in there.

■ **hold on to 1** *he held on to the back of the chair:* clutch, hold, hang on to, clasp, grasp, grip, cling to. **2** *they can't hold on to their most experienced staff:* retain, keep, hang on to.

■ **hold one's own**. See OWN.

■ **hold out 1** *British troops held out against constant attacks:* resist, withstand, hold off, fight off, fend off, keep off, keep at bay, stand up to, stand firm against. **2** *we can stay here as long as our supplies hold out:* last, remain, be extant, continue.

■ **hold something out** *Celia held out her hand:* extend, proffer, offer, present; outstretch, reach out, stretch out, put out.

■ **hold something over** *the usual family gathering was held over until January:* postpone, put off, put back, delay, defer, suspend, shelve, hold in abeyance; N. Amer. put over, table, take a rain check on; informal put on ice, put on the back burner.

■ **hold up** *their argument just doesn't hold up:* be convincing, be logical, hold water, bear examination, be sound.

■ **hold something up 1** *they held up the trophy for all to see:* display, hold aloft, exhibit, show (off), flourish, brandish; informal flash. **2** *eight concrete pillars hold up the bridge:* support, hold, bear, carry, take, keep up, prop up, shore up, buttress. **3** *our flight was held up for three hours:* delay, detain, make late, set back, keep back, retard, slow up. **4** *a lack of cash has held up progress:* obstruct, impede, hinder, hamper, inhibit, baulk, thwart, curb, hamstring, frustrate, foil, interfere with, stop; informal stymie; Brit. informal throw a spanner in the works of. **5** *a masked raider held up the post office:* rob; informal stick up, mug.

■ **hold water**. See WATER.

■ **hold with** *I don't hold with all this violence:* approve of, agree with, be in favour of, endorse, accept, countenance, support, subscribe to, give one's blessing to, take kindly to; informal stand for; Brit. informal be doing with.

holder noun **1** *a large knife in a leather holder:* **container**, receptacle, case, casing, cover, covering, housing, sheath; stand, rest, rack. **2** *he is a British passport holder:* **bearer**, owner, possessor, keeper; custodian.

holdings plural noun *they have holdings in various offshore funds:* **assets**, funds, capital, resources, savings, investments, securities, equities, bonds, stocks and shares, reserves; property, possessions.

hold-up noun **1** *I ran into a series of hold-ups and nearly didn't get here:* **delay**, setback, hitch, snag, difficulty, problem, trouble; traffic jam, tailback, gridlock; informal snarl-up, glitch, hiccup. **2** *there has been another bank hold-up:* **(armed) robbery**, (armed) raid; theft, burglary, mugging; informal stick-up; N. Amer. informal heist.

hole noun **1** *there was a huge hole in the roof:* **opening**, aperture, gap, space, orifice, vent, chink, breach; crack, leak, rift, rupture; puncture, perforation, cut, split, gash, slit, crevice, fissure. **2** *they were digging a hole in the ground:* **pit**, ditch, trench, cavity, crater, depression, hollow; well, borehole, excavation, dugout; cave, cavern, pothole. **3** *four of them dug the badger out of its hole:* **burrow**, lair, den, earth, sett; retreat, shelter.
verb *a fuel tank was holed in the attack:* **puncture**, perforate, pierce, penetrate, rupture, split, rent, lacerate, gash.

■ **hole up 1** *the bears hole up in winter until it gets warmer:* hibernate, lie dormant. **2** (informal) *the snipers holed up in a nearby farmhouse:* hide (out), conceal oneself, secrete oneself, shelter, take cover, lie low, go to ground, go to earth.

holiday noun **1** *she took a ten-day holiday:* **vacation**, break, rest, recess; time off, time out, leave, furlough, sabbatical; trip, tour, journey, voyage; informal hols, vac; formal sojourn. **2** *the twenty-fourth of May is a holiday:* **public holiday**, bank holiday, festival, feast day, fête, fiesta, celebration, anniversary, jubilee; saint's day, holy day.

holier-than-thou adjective *they had a rather critical, holier-than-thou approach:* **sanctimonious**, self-righteous, smug, self-satisfied; priggish, pious, pietistic, Pharisaic; informal goody-goody, preachy.
– OPPOSITES humble.

hollow adjective **1** *each fibre has a hollow core that traps air:* **empty**, void, unfilled, vacant. **2** *her hollow cheeks and bony face:* **sunken**, deep-set, concave, depressed, indented. **3** *a hollow victory:* **meaningless**, empty, valueless, worthless, useless, pyrrhic, futile, fruitless, profitless, pointless. **4** *the women believed it was nothing but a hollow promise:* **insincere**, hypocritical, feigned, false, sham, deceitful, cynical, spurious, untrue, two-faced; informal phoney, pretend.
– OPPOSITES solid, full, worthwhile, sincere.
noun **1** *we found a hollow at the base of a large tree:* **hole**, pit, cavity, crater, trough, cave, cavern; depression, indentation, dip; niche, nook, cranny, recess. **2** *the village nestled in a hollow in the Cotswolds:* **valley**, vale, dale; Brit. dene, combe; N. English clough; Scottish glen, strath; literary dell.
verb *cut the top off the pumpkin and hollow it out:* **gouge**, scoop, dig, cut; excavate, channel.

holocaust noun *fears of a nuclear holocaust:* **cataclysm**, disaster, catastrophe;

destruction, devastation, annihilation; massacre, slaughter, mass murder, carnage, butchery; genocide, ethnic cleansing.

holy adjective **1** *holy men who are revered by pilgrims:* **saintly**, godly, saintlike, pious, pietistic, religious, devout, God-fearing, spiritual; righteous, good, virtuous, sinless, pure; canonized, beatified, ordained. **2** *a Jewish holy place:* **sacred**, consecrated, hallowed, sanctified, venerated, revered, divine, religious, blessed, dedicated.
– OPPOSITES sinful, irreligious, cursed.

homage noun **1** *the book was intended as an act of homage:* **respect**, honour, reverence, worship, admiration, esteem, adulation, acclaim. **2** *the building is clearly a homage to the Guggenheim Museum in Manhattan:* **tribute**, acknowledgement, recognition; accolade, panegyric, paean, salute.
■ **pay homage to** *they paid homage to the local boy who became president:* honour, acclaim, applaud, salute, praise, commend, pay tribute to, take one's hat off to; formal laud.

home noun **1** *the floods forced people to flee their homes:* **residence**, place of residence, house, flat, apartment, bungalow, cottage; accommodation, property, quarters, lodgings, rooms; a roof over one's head; address, place; informal pad, digs, semi; formal domicile, abode, dwelling (place), habitation. **2** *I am stuck here, far from my home:* **homeland**, native land, home town, birthplace, roots, fatherland, motherland, mother country, country of origin, the old country. **3** *a private home for the elderly:* **institution**, nursing home, retirement home, rest home, children's home; hospice, shelter, refuge, retreat, asylum, hostel. **4** *the home of fine wines:* **domain**, realm, origin, source, cradle, fount, fountainhead.
adjective **1** *we need to stimulate demand within the UK home market:* **domestic**, internal, local, national, interior. **2** *a sale of delicious home produce:* **home-made**, home-grown, local, family.
– OPPOSITES foreign, international.
■ **at home 1** *I was at home all day on Friday:* in, in one's house, present, available, indoors, inside, here. **2** *she felt very much at home in Milan:* at ease, comfortable, relaxed, content; in one's element. **3** *he is not particularly at home with mathematics:* confident with, conversant with, proficient in; used to, familiar with, au fait with, au courant with, skilled in, experienced in, well versed in; informal well up on.
■ **bring something home to someone** *Arthur's illness brought home to them the gravity of the situation:* make someone realize, make someone understand, make something clear to someone; drive home, press home, impress upon someone, draw attention to, focus attention on, underline, highlight, spotlight, emphasize, stress.
■ **hit home.** See HIT.

■ **home in on** *a teaching style which homes in on what matters most to each pupil:* focus on, concentrate on, zero in on, centre on, fix on; highlight, spotlight, underline, pinpoint; informal zoom in on.

homeland noun *he left his homeland to settle in London:* **native land**, country of origin, home, fatherland, motherland, mother country, land of one's fathers, the old country.

homeless adjective *the plight of young homeless people:* **without a roof over one's head**, on the streets, vagrant, sleeping rough; destitute, down and out, street.
noun *charities for the homeless:* **homeless people**, vagrants, down-and-outs, tramps, vagabonds, itinerants, transients, migrants, derelicts, drifters; N. Amer. hoboes; Austral. bagmen; informal bag ladies; Brit. informal dossers; N. Amer. informal bums.

homely adjective **1** *a modern hotel with a homely atmosphere:* **cosy**, homelike, homey, comfortable, snug, welcoming, friendly, congenial, intimate, warm, hospitable, informal, relaxed, pleasant, cheerful; informal comfy. **2** *a meal for those who enjoy the more homely delights of the table:* **unsophisticated**, everyday, ordinary, domestic, simple, modest, unpretentious, unassuming; homespun, folksy. **3** (N. Amer.) *she's rather homely and she needs a date:* **unattractive**, plain, unprepossessing, unlovely, ill-favoured, ugly; informal not much to look at; Brit. informal no oil painting.
– OPPOSITES uncomfortable, formal, sophisticated, attractive.

homespun adjective *he was a source of rural homespun philosophy:* **unsophisticated**, plain, simple, unpolished, unrefined, rustic, folksy; coarse, rough, crude, rudimentary.
– OPPOSITES sophisticated.

homey adjective **1** *the house is homey yet elegant:* **cosy**, homelike, homely, comfortable, snug, welcoming, informal, relaxed, intimate, warm, pleasant, cheerful; informal comfy. **2** *an idealized version of peasant life as simple and homey:* **unsophisticated**, homely, unrefined, unpretentious, plain, simple, modest.
– OPPOSITES uncomfortable, formal, sophisticated.

homicidal adjective *he had homicidal tendencies:* **murderous**, violent, brutal, savage, ferocious, vicious, bloody, bloodthirsty, barbarous, barbaric; deadly, lethal, mortal, death-dealing.

homicide noun **murder**, killing, slaughter, butchery, massacre; assassination, execution, extermination; patricide, matricide, infanticide; literary slaying.

homily noun *she delivered her homily about the need for patience:* **sermon**, lecture, discourse, address, lesson, talk, speech, oration.

homogeneous, homogenous adjective

h

1 *the elderly are a far from homogeneous group:* **uniform**, identical, unvaried, consistent, undistinguishable; alike, similar, (much) the same, all of a piece; informal much of a muchness. **2** *we must consider cost efficiency to compete with homogeneous products:* **similar**, comparable, equivalent, like, analogous, corresponding, parallel, matching, related; formal cognate.
– OPPOSITES different.

homogenize verb *they wanted to wipe out differences and homogenize society:* **standardize**, unite, integrate, fuse, merge, blend, meld, coalesce, amalgamate, combine.
– OPPOSITES diversify.

homosexual adjective **gay**, lesbian; informal queer, camp, pink, swinging the other way, homo, dykey; Brit. informal bent, poofy.
– OPPOSITES heterosexual.
noun **gay**, lesbian; informal queer, homo, queen, pansy, nancy, dyke, les, lezzy, butch, femme; Brit. informal poof, ponce, woofter.
– OPPOSITES heterosexual.

hone verb **1** *he was carefully honing the long curved blade:* **sharpen**, whet, strop, grind, file. **2** *this gave me a great opportunity to hone my skills as a singer:* **improve**, develop, enhance, sharpen; upgrade.
– OPPOSITES blunt.

honest adjective **1** *he is an honest man:* **upright**, honourable, moral, ethical, principled, righteous, right-minded, respectable; virtuous, good, decent, law-abiding, high-minded, upstanding, incorruptible, truthful, trustworthy, trusty, reliable, conscientious, scrupulous, reputable; informal on the level. **2** *I haven't been completely honest with you:* **truthful**, sincere, candid, frank, open, forthright, straight; straightforward, plain-speaking, matter-of-fact; informal upfront. **3** *he'd made an honest mistake:* **genuine**, real, authentic, actual, true, bona fide, legitimate, fair and square; informal legit, kosher, on the level, honest-to-goodness.
– OPPOSITES unscrupulous, insincere.

honestly adverb **1** *he earned the money honestly:* **fairly**, lawfully, legally, legitimately, honourably, decently, ethically, in good faith, by the book; informal on the level. **2** *we honestly believe this is for the best:* **sincerely**, genuinely, truthfully, truly, wholeheartedly; really, actually, to be honest, to tell you the truth, to be frank, in all honesty, in all sincerity; informal Scouts' honour.

honesty noun **1** *I can attest to his honesty:* **integrity**, uprightness, honourableness, honour, morality, morals, ethics, (high) principles, righteousness, right-mindedness; virtue, goodness, probity, high-mindedness, fairness, incorruptibility, truthfulness, trustworthiness, reliability, dependability. **2** *they spoke with honesty about their fears:* **sincerity**, candour, frankness, directness, truthfulness, truth, openness,

straightforwardness.

honeyed adjective *he woos her with honeyed words:* **sweet**, sugary, saccharine, pleasant, flattering, adulatory, unctuous; dulcet, soothing, soft, mellow, mellifluous.
– OPPOSITES harsh.

honorarium noun **fee**, payment, consideration, allowance; remuneration, pay, expenses, compensation, recompense, reward; formal emolument.

honorary adjective **1** *he received an honorary doctorate from Harvard University:* **titular**, nominal, in name only, unofficial, token. **2** (Brit.) *the honorary treasurer of the Society:* **unpaid**, unsalaried, voluntary, volunteer; N. Amer. pro bono (publico).

honour noun **1** *the general was a man of honour:* **integrity**, honesty, uprightness, ethics, morals, morality, (high) principles, righteousness, high-mindedness; virtue, goodness, decency, probity, scrupulousness, worth, fairness, justness, trustworthiness, reliability, dependability. **2** *he earned the honour of having the building named after him:* **distinction**, privilege, glory, kudos, cachet, prestige, merit, credit; importance, illustriousness, notability; respect, esteem, approbation. **3** *our national honour is at stake:* **reputation**, (good) name, character, repute, image, kudos, standing, stature, status. **4** *she had the honour of meeting the Queen:* **privilege**, pleasure, pride, joy; compliment, favour. **5** *the highest military honours:* **accolade**, award, reward, prize, decoration, distinction, medal, ribbon, star, laurel; Brit. informal gong.
– OPPOSITES unscrupulousness, shame.
verb **1** *we should love and honour our parents:* **esteem**, respect, admire, defer to; look up to; appreciate, value, cherish; reverence, revere, venerate, worship; informal put on a pedestal. **2** *they were honoured at a special ceremony:* **applaud**, acclaim, praise, salute, recognize, celebrate, commemorate, commend, hail, lionize, exalt, eulogize, pay homage to, pay tribute to, sing the praises of; formal laud. **3** *he made sure we honoured the contract in every respect:* **fulfil**, observe, keep, obey, heed, follow, carry out, discharge, implement, execute, effect; keep to, abide by, adhere to, comply with, conform to, be true to, live up to. **4** *the bank informed us that the cheque would not be honoured:* **accept**, take, clear, pass, cash; Brit. encash.
– OPPOSITES disgrace, criticize, disobey.

honourable adjective **1** *a thoroughly decent and honourable man:* **honest**, moral, ethical, principled, righteous, right-minded; decent, respectable, virtuous, good, upstanding, upright, worthy, noble, fair, just, truthful, trustworthy, trusty, law-abiding, reliable, reputable, dependable. **2** *a long and honourable career:* **illustrious**, distinguished, eminent, great, glorious, prestigious, noble, creditable.
– OPPOSITES crooked, deplorable.

hoodlum noun **hooligan**, thug, lout, delinquent, tearaway, vandal, ruffian; gangster, mobster, criminal, Mafioso; Austral. larrikin; informal tough, bruiser, roughneck, heavy, hit man; Brit. informal yob, yobbo, bovver boy, lager lout; N. Amer. informal hood.

hoodwink verb *he kept an eye out for the young man who had hoodwinked him:* **deceive**, trick, dupe, outwit, fool, delude, cheat, take in, hoax, mislead, lead on, defraud, double-cross, swindle, gull; informal con, bamboozle, do, have, sting, gyp, diddle, shaft, rip off, lead up the garden path, pull a fast one on, put one over on, take for a ride, pull the wool over someone's eyes; N. Amer. informal sucker, snooker; Austral. informal pull a swifty on; literary cozen.

hook noun **1** *she hung her jacket on the hook:* **peg**. **2** *the dress fastens with a hook and eye:* **fastener**, fastening, catch, clasp, hasp, clip, pin.
verb **1** *they hooked their baskets onto the ladder rungs:* **attach**, hitch, fasten, fix, secure, clasp. **2** *he hooked his thumbs in his belt:* **curl**, bend, crook, loop, curve. **3** *he hooked a 24 lb pike:* **catch**, land, net, take, bag, snare, trap.
■ **by hook or by crook** *the government intends, by hook or by crook, to hold on to the land:* by any means, somehow (or other), no matter how, in one way or another, by fair means or foul, whatever it takes.
■ **hook, line, and sinker** *he fell, hook, line and sinker, for this year's April Fool:* completely, totally, utterly, entirely, wholly, absolutely, through and through, one hundred per cent, {lock, stock, and barrel}.
■ **off the hook** (informal) *I admit I lied to get him off the hook:* out of trouble, in the clear, free; acquitted, cleared, reprieved, exonerated, absolved; informal let off.

hooked adjective **1** *he had a long hooked nose:* **curved**, hook-shaped, hook-like, aquiline, angular, bent; Biology falcate, falciform, uncinate. **2** (informal) *they are hooked on cocaine:* **addicted to**, dependent on; informal using; (**be hooked on**) N. Amer. informal have a jones for. **3** (informal) *he has been hooked on crosswords since his teens:* **keen on**, enthusiastic about, addicted to, obsessed with, fixated on, fanatical about; informal mad about, crazy about, wild about, nuts about; Brit. informal potty about.
– OPPOSITES straight.

hooligan noun **hoodlum**, thug, lout, delinquent, tearaway, vandal, ruffian, troublemaker; Austral. larrikin; informal tough, rough, bruiser, roughneck; Brit. informal yob, yobbo, bovver boy, lager lout; Scottish informal ned.

hoop noun **ring**, band, circle, circlet, loop; technical annulus.

hoot noun **1** *I heard the hoot of an owl:* **screech**, shriek, call, cry; tu-whit tu-whoo. **2** *the hoot of a horn was followed by the roar of an engine:* **beep**, honk, toot, blast, blare. **3** *there were hoots of derision from the audience:* **shout**, yell, cry, howl, shriek, whoop, whistle; boo, hiss, jeer, catcall.
verb **1** *in the stillness of the night an owl hooted:* **screech**, shriek, cry, call; tu-whit tu-whoo. **2** *a car horn hooted, frightening her:* **beep**, honk, toot, blare, blast, sound. **3** *the delegates hooted in disgust:* **shout**, yell, cry, howl, shriek, whistle; boo, hiss, jeer, catcall.

hop verb *he hopped along the road:* **jump**, bound, spring, bounce, skip, jig, leap; prance, dance, frolic, gambol.

hope noun **1** *I had high hopes of making the Olympic team:* **aspiration**, desire, wish, expectation, ambition, aim, plan; dream, daydream, pipe dream. **2** *most of us begin married life filled with hope:* **hopefulness**, optimism, expectation, expectancy; confidence, faith, trust, belief, conviction, assurance; promise.
– OPPOSITES pessimism.
verb **1** *he's hoping for a medal in the high jump:* **expect**, anticipate, look for, be hopeful of, pin one's hopes on, want; wish for, dream of. **2** *we're hoping to address this issue as soon as possible:* **aim**, intend, be looking, have the intention, have in mind, plan, aspire.

hopeful adjective **1** *he remained hopeful that something could be worked out:* **optimistic**, full of hope, confident, positive, buoyant, sanguine, bullish, cheerful; informal upbeat. **2** *there are some hopeful signs of recovery in the US market:* **promising**, encouraging, heartening, reassuring, auspicious, favourable, optimistic, propitious, bright, rosy.

hopefully adverb **1** *he rode on hopefully:* **optimistically**, full of hope, confidently, buoyantly, sanguinely; expectantly. **2** *hopefully it should be finished by next year:* **all being well**, if all goes well, God willing, with luck; most likely, probably; conceivably, feasibly; informal touch wood, fingers crossed.

hopeless adjective **1** *Jess looked at him, making a hopeless appeal:* **despairing**, desperate, wretched, forlorn, pessimistic, defeatist, resigned; dejected, downhearted, despondent, demoralized. **2** *she gave him up as a hopeless case:* **irremediable**, beyond hope, lost, beyond repair, irreparable, irreversible; past cure, incurable; impossible, no-win, futile, forlorn, unworkable, impracticable. **3** *Joseph was hopeless at maths:* **bad**, poor, awful, terrible, dreadful, appalling, atrocious; inferior, incompetent, unskilled; informal pathetic, useless, lousy, rotten; Brit. informal duff, rubbish, pants.

hopelessly adverb **1** *she began to cry hopelessly:* **despairingly**, in despair, in distress, desperately; dejectedly, downheartedly, despondently, wretchedly, miserably, forlornly. **2** *she realized she was hopelessly lost:* **utterly**, completely,

h

irretrievably, impossibly; extremely, very, desperately, totally, dreadfully; informal terribly.

horde noun **crowd**, mob, pack, gang, troop, army, swarm, mass; throng, multitude, host, band, flock; informal crew, tribe, load.

horizon noun **1** *the sun rose above the horizon:* **skyline. 2** *she wanted to leave home and broaden her horizons:* **outlook**, perspective, perception; range of experience, scope, orbit.

■ **on the horizon** *trouble could be on the horizon:* imminent, impending, close, near, approaching, coming, forthcoming, in prospect, at hand, on the way, about to happen, upon us, in the offing, in the pipeline, in the air, just around the corner; brewing, looming, threatening, menacing; informal on the cards.

horizontal adjective **1** *draw a horizontal line near the top of the wall:* level, flat, plane, smooth, even; straight, parallel. **2** *she was stretched horizontal on a sunbed:* **flat**, supine, prone, prostrate.
– OPPOSITES vertical.

horrendous adjective. See HORRIBLE.

horrible adjective **1** *there was a horrible murder here last year:* **dreadful**, awful, terrible, shocking, appalling, horrifying, horrific, horrendous, grisly, ghastly, gruesome, harrowing, heinous, vile, unspeakable; nightmarish, macabre, spine-chilling; loathsome, monstrous, abhorrent, hateful, execrable, abominable, atrocious, sickening. **2** (informal) *the tea tasted horrible | a horrible little man:* **nasty**, horrid, disagreeable, unpleasant, awful, dreadful, terrible, appalling, foul, repulsive, repellent, ghastly; obnoxious, hateful, odious, objectionable, insufferable, vile, loathsome, abhorrent; informal frightful, God-awful; Brit. informal beastly.
– OPPOSITES pleasant, agreeable.

horrid adjective. See HORRIBLE.

horrific adjective **dreadful**, horrendous, horrible, frightful, awful, terrible, atrocious; horrifying, shocking, appalling, harrowing, gruesome; hideous, grisly, ghastly, unspeakable, monstrous, nightmarish, sickening; informal gut-wrenching.

horrify verb **1** *she loved to horrify us with murder stories:* **frighten**, scare, terrify, petrify, alarm, panic, terrorize, fill with fear, scare someone out of their wits, frighten the living daylights out of, make someone's hair stand on end, make someone's blood run cold; informal scare the pants off; Brit. informal put the wind up; N. Amer. informal spook. **2** *he was horrified by her remarks:* **shock**, appal, outrage, scandalize, offend; disgust, revolt, nauseate, sicken.

horror noun **1** *children screamed in horror:* **terror**, fear, fright, alarm, panic; dread, trepidation. **2** *to her horror she found herself alone:* **dismay**, consternation, perturbation,

alarm, distress; disgust, outrage, shock. **3** *photographs revealed the full horror of the tragedy:* **awfulness**, frightfulness, savagery, barbarity, hideousness; atrocity, outrage. **4** (informal) *he's a little horror:* **rascal**, devil, imp, monkey; informal terror, scamp, scallywag, tyke; Brit. informal perisher; N. Amer. informal varmint.
– OPPOSITES delight, satisfaction.

horse noun **mount**, charger, cob, nag, hack; pony, foal, yearling, colt, stallion, gelding, mare, filly; N. Amer. bronco; Austral./NZ moke, yarraman; informal gee-gee; archaic steed.
■ **horse around/about** (informal) *they were shouting and horsing around in the garden:* fool around/about, play the fool, act the clown, clown about/around, monkey about/around; informal mess about/around, lark about/around; Brit. informal muck about/around; dated play the giddy goat.

horseman, horsewoman noun **rider**, equestrian, jockey; cavalryman, trooper; historical hussar, dragoon; archaic cavalier.

horseplay noun **tomfoolery**, fooling around, foolish behaviour, clowning, buffoonery; pranks, antics, high jinks; informal shenanigans, monkey business; Brit. informal monkey tricks.

horticulture noun **gardening**, floriculture, arboriculture, agriculture, cultivation.

hose noun **1** *a thirty-foot garden hose:* **pipe**, piping, tube, tubing, duct, outlet, pipeline, siphon. **2** *her hose had laddered.* See HOSIERY.

hosiery noun **stockings**, tights, stay-ups, hold-ups, nylons, hose; socks; N. Amer. pantyhose.

hospitable adjective *everyone was very hospitable when we first moved in:* **welcoming**, friendly, congenial, genial, sociable, convivial, cordial; gracious, well disposed, amenable, helpful, obliging, accommodating, neighbourly, warm, kind, generous, bountiful.

hospital noun **infirmary**, sanatorium, hospice, medical centre, health centre, clinic; Brit. cottage hospital; Military field hospital.

hospitality noun **1** *he is renowned for his hospitality:* **friendliness**, hospitableness, warm reception, helpfulness, neighbourliness, warmth, kindness, congeniality, geniality, cordiality, amenability, generosity. **2** *the delights of corporate hospitality:* entertainment; catering, food (and drink).

host¹ noun **1** *the host greeted the new guests:* **party-giver**, hostess, entertainer. **2** *he was the host of a half-hour TV series:* **presenter**, compère, anchor, anchorman, anchorwoman, announcer.
– OPPOSITES guest.
verb **1** *the Queen hosted a dinner for 600 guests:* **give**, have, hold, throw, put on, provide, arrange, organize. **2** *the show was hosted by some media celebrity:* **present**,

introduce, compère, front, anchor.

host² noun **1** *a host of memories rushed into her mind:* **multitude**, lot, abundance, wealth, profusion; informal load, heap, mass, pile, ton; Brit. informal shedload; literary myriad. **2** *a host of film stars:* **crowd**, throng, flock, herd, swarm, horde, mob, army, legion; assemblage, gathering.

hostage noun **captive**, prisoner, detainee, internee.

hostel noun **cheap hotel**, youth hostel, YMCA, YWCA, bed and breakfast, B&B, boarding house, guest house, pension.

hostile adjective **1** *he wrote an extremely hostile review:* **unfriendly**, unkind, bitter, unsympathetic, malicious, vicious, rancorous, venomous; antagonistic, aggressive, confrontational, belligerent, truculent. **2** *hostile climatic conditions:* **unfavourable**, adverse, bad, harsh, grim, hard, tough, inhospitable, forbidding. **3** *people are very hostile to the idea:* **opposed**, averse, antagonistic, ill-disposed, unsympathetic, antipathetic, opposing, against; informal anti, down on.
– OPPOSITES friendly, favourable.

hostility noun **1** *the boy glared at her with hostility:* **antagonism**, unfriendliness, malevolence, malice, unkindness, rancour, venom, hatred; aggression, belligerence. **2** *there is a great amount of hostility to the present regime:* **opposition**, antagonism, animosity, antipathy, ill will, ill feeling, resentment, aversion, enmity. **3** *we are hoping for a cessation of hostilities:* **fighting**, (armed) conflict, combat, warfare, war, bloodshed, violence.

hot adjective **1** *they provided plenty of hot food:* **heated**, piping (hot), sizzling, steaming, roasting, boiling (hot), searing, scorching, scalding, red-hot. **2** *it was a beautiful, hot day:* **warm**, balmy, summery, tropical, scorching, searing, blistering, sweltering, torrid, sultry, humid, muggy, close; informal boiling, baking, roasting. **3** *she felt very hot, and her throat was dry:* **feverish**, fevered, febrile; burning, flushed. **4** *a hot chilli sauce:* **spicy**, spiced, highly seasoned, peppery, fiery, strong; piquant. **5** (informal) *the hottest story in Fleet Street:* **new**, fresh, recent, late, up to date, up to the minute; just out, breaking. **6** (informal) *this band is seriously hot:* **popular**, in demand, sought-after, in favour; fashionable, in vogue, all the rage; informal big, in, now, hip, trendy, cool. **7** (informal) *she is hot on local history:* **knowledgeable about**, well informed about, au fait with, up on, well versed in, au courant with; informal clued up about, genned up about.
– OPPOSITES cold, chilly, mild, dispassionate, weak, old.
■ **blow hot and cold** *he had been stringing her along, blowing hot and cold:* vacillate, dither, shilly-shally, waver, be indecisive, change one's mind, be undecided, be uncertain, be unsure; Brit. haver, hum and haw; Scottish swither.

hot air noun (informal) *critics dismissed this theory as a load of hot air:* **nonsense**, rubbish, garbage, empty talk, wind, blather, claptrap, drivel, balderdash, gibberish; pomposity, bombast; informal guff, bosh, hogwash, poppycock, bilge, twaddle; Brit. informal cobblers, codswallop, tosh; N. Amer. informal flapdoodle.

hotbed noun *the place is a hotbed of political activity:* **breeding ground**, den, cradle, nest.

hot-blooded adjective *tips for hot-blooded lovers:* **passionate**, amorous, amatory, ardent, lustful, libidinous, lecherous, sexy; informal horny, randy.
– OPPOSITES cold.

hotchpotch noun *the house was a hotchpotch of styles, ancient and modern:* **mixture**, mix, mixed bag, assortment, random collection, jumble, ragbag, miscellany, medley, pot-pourri; melange, mishmash, confusion, farrago, gallimaufry; N. Amer. hodgepodge.

hotel noun **inn**, motel, boarding house, guest house, bed and breakfast, B&B, hostel; pension, auberge.

hotfoot adverb *he rushed hotfoot to the planning office to lodge an objection:* **hastily**, hurriedly, speedily, quickly, fast, rapidly, swiftly, without delay; at top speed, at full tilt, headlong, post-haste, pell-mell, helter-skelter; informal like the wind, like greased lightning, like blazes; Brit. informal like the clappers, like billy-o; N. Amer. informal lickety-split.
– OPPOSITES slowly.
■ **hotfoot it** (informal) *we hotfooted it after him:* hurry, dash, run, race, sprint, bolt, dart, career, charge, shoot, hurtle, hare, fly, speed, zoom, streak; informal tear, belt, pelt, scoot, clip, leg it, go like a bat out of hell; Brit. informal bomb; N. Amer. informal hightail it.

hot-headed adjective *a number of hot-headed youths started the trouble:* **impetuous**, impulsive, headstrong, reckless, rash, irresponsible, foolhardy, madcap; excitable, volatile, fiery, hot-tempered, quick-tempered, unruly, harum-scarum.

hothouse noun **greenhouse**, glasshouse, conservatory, orangery, vinery, winter garden.

hotly adverb **1** *the rumours were hotly denied:* **vehemently**, vigorously, strenuously, fiercely, passionately, heatedly; angrily, indignantly. **2** *he rushed out, hotly pursued by Boris:* **closely**, swiftly, quickly, hotfoot; eagerly, enthusiastically.
– OPPOSITES calmly.

hot-tempered adjective *he is arrogant, hot-tempered, and capable of violence:* **irascible**, quick-tempered, short-tempered, irritable, fiery, bad-tempered; touchy, volatile, testy, tetchy, fractious, prickly, peppery; informal snappish, snappy, chippy, on a short fuse; Brit. informal narky, ratty.

h

h

– OPPOSITES easy-going.

hound noun **(hunting) dog**, canine, mongrel, cur; informal doggy, pooch, mutt; Austral./NZ informal mong, bitzer.
verb **1** *she was hounded by the Italian press:* **pursue**, chase, follow, shadow, hunt (down), stalk, track, trail; harass, persecute, harry, pester, bother, badger, torment, bedevil; informal hassle, bug, give someone a hard time; N. Amer. informal devil. **2** *they hounded him out of office:* **force**, drive, pressure, pressurize, push, urge, coerce, impel, dragoon, strong-arm; nag, bully, browbeat, chivvy; informal bulldoze, railroad; Brit. informal bounce; N. Amer. informal hustle.

house noun **1** *an estate of 200 houses:* **residence**, home; homestead; a roof over one's head; formal habitation, dwelling (place), abode, domicile. **2** *the house of Stewart:* **family**, clan, tribe; dynasty, line, bloodline, lineage, ancestry, family tree. **3** *the publishing house soon became profitable:* **firm**, business, company, corporation, enterprise, establishment, institution, concern, organization, operation; informal outfit, set-up. **4** *the National Council is the country's upper house:* **legislative assembly**, legislative body, chamber, council, parliament, congress, senate, diet. **5** *the house burst into spontaneous applause:* **audience**, crowd, spectators, viewers; congregation; gallery, stalls; Brit. informal punters.
verb **1** *they converted a disused cinema to house twelve employees:* **accommodate**, provide accommodation for, give someone a roof over their head, lodge, quarter, board, billet, take in, sleep, put up; harbour, shelter. **2** *this panel houses the main switch:* **contain**, hold, store; cover, protect, enclose.
■ **on the house** (informal) *this round is on the house:* **free** (of charge), without charge, at no cost, for nothing, gratis; courtesy, complimentary; informal for free; N. Amer. informal comp.

household noun *the whole household was asleep:* **family**, house, occupants; clan; tribe; informal brood.
adjective *we sell all kinds of household goods:* **domestic**, family; everyday, workaday.

householder noun **homeowner**, owner, occupant, resident; tenant, leaseholder; proprietor, landlady, landlord, freeholder; Brit. occupier, owner-occupier.

house-trained adjective (Brit.) **domesticated**, trained; N. Amer. housebroken.

housing noun **1** *they invested heavily in housing:* **houses**, homes, residences, buildings; accommodation, living quarters; formal dwellings, dwelling places, habitations. **2** *the protective housing for the radio antennae:* **casing**, covering, case, cover, holder, sheath, jacket, shell, capsule.

hovel noun **shack**, slum, shanty, hut; informal dump, hole.

hover verb **1** *army helicopters hovered overhead:* **be suspended**, be poised, hang, levitate; fly. **2** *she hovered anxiously nearby:* **linger**, loiter, wait about; informal hang around, stick around; Brit. informal hang about.

however adverb **1** *people tend to put on weight in middle age; however, this is not inevitable:* **nevertheless**, nonetheless, but, still, yet, though, although, even so, for all that, despite that, in spite of that; anyway, anyhow, be that as it may, having said that, notwithstanding; informal still and all. **2** *however you look at it, it's a bit of a disaster:* **in whatever way**, regardless of how, no matter how.

howl noun **1** *she heard the howl of a wolf:* **baying**, howling, bay, cry, yowl, bark, yelp. **2** *he let out a howl of anguish:* **wail**, cry, yell, yelp, yowl; bellow, roar, shout, shriek, scream, screech.
verb **1** *dogs howled in the distance:* **bay**, cry, yowl, bark, yelp. **2** *somewhere nearby, a baby started to howl:* **wail**, cry, yell, yowl, bawl, bellow, shriek, scream, screech, caterwaul; informal holler. **3** *we howled with laughter at this suggestion:* **laugh**, guffaw, roar; be creased up, be doubled up, split one's sides; informal fall about, crack up, be in stitches, be rolling in the aisles.

hub noun **1** *spokes radiate from the hub of the wheel:* **pivot**, axis, fulcrum, centre, middle. **2** *the kitchen was the hub of family life:* **centre**, core, heart, focus, focal point, nucleus, kernel, nerve centre.
– OPPOSITES periphery.

hubbub noun *her voice was lost in the hubbub:* **noise**, din, racket, commotion, clamour, cacophony, babel, rumpus; Brit. informal row.

hubris noun *their downfall was caused by a mixture of hubris and muddled thinking:* **arrogance**, conceit, haughtiness, hauteur, pride, self-importance, pomposity, superciliousness, superiority; informal big-headedness.
– OPPOSITES humility.

huddle verb **1** *they huddled together for warmth:* **crowd**, cluster, gather, bunch, throng, flock, herd, collect, group, congregate; press, pack, squeeze. **2** *he huddled beneath the sheets:* **curl up**, snuggle, nestle, hunch up.
– OPPOSITES disperse.
noun *a huddle of passengers gathered round the information desk:* **crowd**, cluster, bunch, knot, group, throng, flock, press, pack; collection, assemblage; informal gaggle.

hue noun **1** *seaweeds are found in a variety of hues:* **colour**, shade, tone, tint. **2** *men of all political hues soon forgot their feuding:* **complexion**, type, kind, sort, cast, stamp, character, nature.

hue and cry noun *her relatives raised a hue and cry after the accident:* **commotion**, outcry, uproar, fuss, clamour, storm, stir, furore, ruckus, brouhaha, palaver, rumpus; informal hoo-ha, hullabaloo, ballyhoo, kerfuffle, to-do, song and dance; Brit. informal row, stink.

huff noun *she walked off in a huff:* **bad mood**, sulk, fit of pique, pet; temper, tantrum, rage; informal grump; Brit. informal strop, paddy; N. Amer. informal snit.

hug verb **1** *they kissed and hugged each other:* **embrace**, cuddle, squeeze, clasp, clutch, cling to, hold close, hold tight, take someone in one's arms, hold someone to one's bosom. **2** *I headed north, hugging the coastline:* **follow closely**, keep close to, stay near to, follow the course of.
noun *there were tears and hugs as we left:* **embrace**, cuddle, squeeze, bear hug, clinch.

huge adjective **enormous**, vast, immense, large, big, great, massive, colossal, prodigious, gigantic, gargantuan, mammoth, monumental; giant, towering, elephantine, mountainous, titanic; epic, Herculean, Brobdingnagian; informal jumbo, mega, monster, whopping, humongous, hulking, bumper, astronomical; Brit. informal ginormous.
– OPPOSITES tiny.

hugely adverb *they are fighting a hugely expensive legal battle:* **very**, extremely, exceedingly, most, really, particularly, tremendously, greatly, decidedly, exceptionally, immensely, inordinately, extraordinarily, vastly; very much, to a great extent; N. English right; informal terrifically, awfully, terribly, majorly, seriously, mega, ultra, oh-so, damn, damned; Brit. informal ever so, well, dead, jolly; N. Amer. informal real, mighty, awful; informal, dated frightfully; archaic exceeding.

hulk noun **1** *the rusting hulks of ships:* **wreck**, shipwreck, ruin, derelict; shell, skeleton, hull. **2** *a great clumsy hulk of a man:* **giant**, lump; oaf; informal clodhopper, ape, gorilla; N. Amer. informal lummox.

hull[1] noun *the ship's hull was damaged:* **framework**, body, shell, frame, skeleton, structure.

hull[2] noun *seed hulls:* **shell**, husk, pod, case, covering, integument, shuck; Botany pericarp, legume.
verb *the bird uses its beak to hull seeds:* **shell**, husk, peel, pare, skin, shuck; technical decorticate.

hullabaloo noun (informal) *there was a terrific hullabaloo over the by-election:* **fuss**, commotion, hue and cry, uproar, outcry, clamour, storm, furore, hubbub, ruckus, brouhaha; pandemonium, mayhem, tumult, turmoil, hurly-burly; informal hoo-ha, to-do, kerfuffle, song and dance; Brit. informal carry-on, row, stink.

hum verb **1** *the engine was humming and ready to go:* **purr**, drone, murmur, buzz, thrum, whirr, throb, vibrate. **2** *she hummed a tune to herself:* sing, croon, murmur, drone. **3** *the workshops are humming as the men set about their various tasks:* **be busy**, be active,

be lively, buzz, bustle, be a hive of activity, throb.
noun *a low hum of conversation:* **murmur**, drone, purr, buzz.
■ **hum and haw** (Brit.) *they wasted a lot of time humming and hawing before going into action:* hesitate, dither, vacillate, be indecisive, equivocate, prevaricate, waver, blow hot and cold; Brit. haver; Scottish swither; informal shilly-shally.

human adjective **1** *the survival of the human race:* **anthropoid**. **2** *they're only human, so mistakes do occur | human frailty:* **mortal**, flesh and blood; fallible; physical, bodily, fleshly. **3** *the human side of politics:* **compassionate**, humane, kind, considerate, understanding, sympathetic, tolerant; approachable, accessible.
– OPPOSITES infallible.
noun *the link between humans and animals:* **person**, human being, mortal, member of the human race; man, woman; individual, (living) soul, being; Homo sapiens; earthling.

humane adjective *regulations concerning the humane treatment of animals:* **compassionate**, kind, considerate, understanding, sympathetic, tolerant; lenient, forbearing, forgiving, merciful, mild, tender, clement, benign, humanitarian, benevolent, charitable.
– OPPOSITES cruel.

humanitarian adjective **1** *they sought his release on humanitarian grounds | a humanitarian act:* **compassionate**, humane; unselfish, altruistic, generous, magnanimous, benevolent, merciful, kind, sympathetic. **2** *a humanitarian organization:* **charitable**, philanthropic, public-spirited, socially concerned, welfare.
– OPPOSITES selfish.
noun **philanthropist**, altruist, benefactor, social reformer, good Samaritan; do-gooder; archaic philanthrope.

humanities plural noun **(liberal) arts**, literature; classics, classical studies, classical literature.

humanity noun **1** *humanity evolved from the higher apes:* **humankind**, mankind, man, people, the human race; Homo sapiens. **2** *the humanity of Christ:* **human nature**, humanness, mortality; physicality, corporeality; incarnation. **3** *he praised them for their humanity:* **compassion**, brotherly love, fellow feeling, humaneness, kindness, consideration, understanding, sympathy, tolerance; leniency, mercy, mercifulness, pity, tenderness; benevolence, charity.

humanize verb *Dr Santiago has been fighting to humanize the hospital environment and improve the quality of patient care:* **civilize**, improve, better; develop, refine, polish.

humankind noun **the human race**, the human species, humanity, human beings, mankind, man, people, mortals; Homo sapiens.

humble adjective **1** *her bearing was very humble and apologetic:* **meek**, deferential, respectful, submissive, self-effacing, unassertive; unpresuming, modest, unassuming, self-deprecating; Scottish mim. **2** *she came from a humble background:* **lowly**, working-class, lower-class, poor, undistinguished, mean, ignoble, low-born; common, ordinary, simple, inferior, unremarkable, insignificant, inconsequential.
– OPPOSITES proud, noble, grand.
verb **1** *he had humbled himself to ask for my help:* **humiliate**, abase, demean, lower, degrade, debase; mortify, shame, eat humble pie; take someone down a peg or two; informal cut down to size, settle someone's hash; N. Amer. informal make someone eat crow. **2** *Wales were humbled at Cardiff Arms Park by Romania:* **defeat**, beat, trounce, rout, overwhelm, get the better of, bring to one's knees; informal lick, clobber, slaughter, massacre, crucify, walk all over; N. Amer. informal shellac, cream.

humbug noun **1** *to dress it up as concern for the environment is sheer humbug:* **hypocrisy**, sanctimoniousness, posturing, cant, empty talk; insincerity, dishonesty, falseness, deceit, deception, fraud. **2** *you are a coward as well as a humbug:* **hypocrite**, fraud, fake, plaster saint; charlatan, cheat, deceiver, dissembler; informal phoney; literary whited sepulchre.

humdrum adjective *the humdrum routine of work stretched out before him:* **mundane**, dull, dreary, boring, tedious, monotonous, prosaic; unexciting, uninteresting, uneventful, unvaried, unremarkable; routine, ordinary, everyday, day-to-day, quotidian, run-of-the-mill, commonplace, workaday, pedestrian.
– OPPOSITES remarkable, exciting.

humid adjective *a hot and humid afternoon in July:* **muggy**, close, sultry, sticky, steamy, oppressive, airless, stifling, suffocating, stuffy, clammy, heavy.
– OPPOSITES fresh.

humiliate verb *you humiliated me in front of the whole school:* **embarrass**, mortify, humble, shame, put to shame, disgrace; discomfit, chasten, abash, deflate, crush, squash; abase, debase, demean, degrade; cause to feel small, cause to lose face, take down a peg or two; informal show up, put down, cut down to size, settle someone's hash; N. Amer. informal make someone eat crow.

humiliating adjective *a humiliating election defeat:* **embarrassing**, mortifying, humbling, ignominious, inglorious, shameful; discreditable, undignified, chastening, demeaning, degrading, deflating.

humiliation noun *only a few tenants have the humiliation of finding the bailiffs at the door:* **embarrassment**, mortification, shame, indignity, ignominy, disgrace,

dishonour, degradation, discredit, obloquy, opprobrium; loss of pride, loss of face; blow to one's pride, slap in the face, kick in the teeth.
– OPPOSITES honour.

humility noun *he lacks the humility to admit that he's wrong:* **modesty**, humbleness, meekness, diffidence, self-effacement.
– OPPOSITES pride.

hummock noun **hillock**, hump, mound, knoll, tump, prominence, elevation, rise, dune; N. Amer. knob; formal eminence.

humorist noun **comic writer**, wit, wag; comic, funny man/woman, comedian, comedienne, joker, jokester; clown.

humorous adjective *the novel is a humorous account of hospital life:* **amusing**, funny, comic, comical, entertaining, diverting, witty, jocular, light-hearted, tongue-in-cheek, wry; hilarious, uproarious, riotous, zany, farcical, droll; informal priceless, side-splitting, rib-tickling, a scream, a hoot, a barrel of laughs, waggish; informal, dated killing.
– OPPOSITES serious.

humour noun **1** *I can see the humour of the situation:* **comedy**, comical aspect, funny side, funniness, hilarity; absurdity, ludicrousness, drollness; satire, irony. **2** *the familiar stories are spiced up with humour:* **jokes**, jests, jesting, quips, witticisms, funny remarks, puns; wit, wittiness, comedy, drollery; informal gags, wisecracks, cracks, waggishness, one-liners. **3** *his good humour was infectious:* **mood**, temper, disposition, temperament, state of mind; spirits.
verb *she was always humouring him to prevent trouble:* **indulge**, accommodate, pander to, cater to, yield to, give way to, give in to, go along with; pamper, spoil, overindulge, mollify, placate, gratify, satisfy.

humourless adjective *she was thought of as a hard-working, humourless academic:* **serious**, solemn, sober, sombre, grave, grim, dour, unsmiling, stony-faced; gloomy, glum, sad, melancholy, dismal, joyless, cheerless, lugubrious.
– OPPOSITES jovial.

hump noun *his back rose into a hump at the base of the spine:* **protuberance**, prominence, lump, bump, knob, protrusion, projection, bulge, swelling, hunch; growth, outgrowth.
verb (informal) *he humped the boxes up the stairs:* **heave**, carry, lug, lift, hoist, heft, tote; informal schlep.
– OPPOSITES straighten.
■ **give someone the hump** (informal). See ANNOY.

hunch verb **1** *he thrust his hands in his pockets and hunched his shoulders:* **arch**, curve, hump, bow. **2** *I hunched up as small as I could:* **crouch**, huddle, curl; hunker down, bend, stoop, squat.
– OPPOSITES straighten.

noun **1** *he had a hunch on his back:* **protuberance**, hump, lump, bump, knob, protrusion, prominence, bulge, swelling; growth, outgrowth. **2** *my hunch is that he'll be back before long:* **feeling**, feeling in one's bones, guess, suspicion, impression, inkling, idea, notion, fancy, intuition; informal gut feeling.

hundred cardinal number century; informal ton.

hunger noun **1** *she was faint with hunger:* **lack of food**, hungriness, ravenousness, emptiness; starvation, malnutrition, malnourishment, undernourishment. **2** *there is a global hunger for news:* **desire**, craving, longing, yearning, hankering, appetite, thirst; want, need; informal itch, yen. ■ **hunger after/for** *all actors hunger for such a role:* desire, crave; long for, yearn for, pine for, ache for, hanker after, thirst for, lust for; want, need; informal have a yen for, itch for, be dying for, be gagging for.

hungry adjective **1** *I was feeling really hungry:* **ravenous**, empty; starving, starved, famished; malnourished, undernourished, underfed; informal peckish, able to eat a horse. **2** *the new team are hungry for success:* **eager**, keen, avid, longing, yearning, aching, greedy; craving, desirous of, hankering after; informal itching, dying, gagging, hot.
– OPPOSITES full.

hunk noun *soup was served with a hunk of bread:* **chunk**, wedge, block, slab, lump, square, gobbet; Brit. informal wodge.

hunt verb **1** *in the autumn they hunted deer:* **chase**, stalk, pursue, course, run down; track, trail, follow, shadow; informal tail. **2** *police are still hunting for her attacker:* **search**, look (high and low), scour the area; seek, try to find; cast about/around/round, rummage (about/around/round), root about/around, fish about/around.
noun **1** *the thrill of the hunt:* **chase**, pursuit. **2** *police have stepped up their hunt:* **search**, look, quest, campaign; efforts.

hunted adjective *his eyes had a hunted look:* **harassed**, persecuted, harried, hounded, beleaguered, troubled, stressed, tormented; careworn, haggard; distraught, desperate; informal hassled.
– OPPOSITES carefree.

hunter noun **huntsman**, huntswoman, trapper, stalker; nimrod; predator.

hunting noun **blood sports**, field sports, coursing, fox-hunting; trapping; the chase, shooting.

hurdle noun **1** *his leg hit a hurdle as he jumped:* **fence**, jump, barrier, barricade, bar, railing, rail. **2** *this was the final hurdle for the college to overcome:* **obstacle**, difficulty, problem, barrier, bar, snag, stumbling block, impediment, obstruction, complication, hindrance; informal headache, fly in the ointment; Brit. informal spanner in the works.

hurl verb *rioters hurled bricks at the police:* **throw**, toss, fling, pitch, cast, lob, bowl, launch, catapult; project, propel, let fly; informal chuck, heave, sling, bung; N. Amer. informal peg; Austral. & N. English informal hoy; NZ informal bish.

hurly-burly noun *they wanted to escape the hurly-burly of city life:* **bustle**, hustle and bustle, hubbub, confusion, disorder, uproar, tumult, pandemonium, mayhem, rumpus; informal hoo-ha, hullabaloo, ballyhoo, kerfuffle.
– OPPOSITES calm, order.

hurricane noun **cyclone**, typhoon, tornado, storm, tempest, windstorm, whirlwind, gale; Austral. willy-willy; N. Amer. informal twister.

hurried adjective **1** *a hurried search revealed the whereabouts of the envelope:* **quick**, fast, swift, rapid, speedy, brisk, hasty; cursory, perfunctory, brief, short, fleeting, passing, superficial. **2** *a hurried decision was reached:* **hasty**, rushed, speedy, quick; impetuous, impulsive, precipitate, precipitous, rash, incautious, imprudent, spur-of-the-moment.
– OPPOSITES slow, considered.

hurriedly adverb *she got up and dressed hurriedly:* **hastily**, speedily, quickly, fast, rapidly, swiftly, briskly; without delay, at top speed, at full tilt, at the double; headlong, hotfoot, post-haste; informal like the wind, like greased lightning, in double quick time; Brit. informal like the clappers, at a rate of knots, like billy-o; N. Amer. informal lickety-split.

hurry verb **1** *you'd better hurry or you'll be late:* **be quick**, hurry up, hasten, speed up, press on, push on; run, dash, rush, race, fly; scurry, scramble, scuttle, sprint; informal get a move on, step on it, get cracking, get moving, shake a leg, tear, hare, zip, zoom, hotfoot it, leg it; Brit. informal shift, get one's skates on, stir one's stumps; N. Amer. informal get the lead out, get a wiggle on; dated make haste. **2** *she hurried him across the landing:* **hustle**, hasten, push, urge, drive, spur, goad, prod, usher; informal gee up.
– OPPOSITES dawdle, delay.
noun *in all the hurry, we forgot the picnic:* **rush**, haste, flurry, hustle and bustle, confusion, commotion, hubbub, turmoil; race, scramble, scurry.

hurt verb **1** *my back hurts:* **be painful**, be sore, be tender, cause pain, cause discomfort; ache, smart, sting, burn, throb; informal be killing; Brit. informal be playing up. **2** *Dad hurt his leg:* **injure**, wound, damage, disable, incapacitate, maim, mutilate; bruise, cut, gash, graze, scrape, scratch, lacerate. **3** *his cruel words hurt her deeply:* **distress**, pain, wound, sting, upset, sadden, devastate, grieve, mortify; cut to the quick. **4** *high interest rates are hurting the local economy:* **harm**, damage, be detrimental to, weaken, blight, impede, jeopardize, undermine, ruin, wreck, sabotage, cripple.
– OPPOSITES heal, comfort, benefit.
noun **1** *knowing how to fall properly minimizes hurt:* **harm**, injury, wounding,

pain, suffering, discomfort, soreness; aching, smarting, stinging, throbbing.
2 *she loved him, in spite of all the hurt he had caused:* **distress**, pain, suffering, grief, misery, anguish, trauma, woe, upset, sadness, sorrow; harm, damage, trouble.
– OPPOSITES joy.
adjective **1** *the doctor looked at my hurt hand:* **injured**, wounded, bruised, grazed, cut, gashed, sore, painful, aching, smarting, throbbing. **2** *Anne's hurt expression spoke volumes:* **pained**, distressed, anguished, upset, sad, mortified, offended; informal miffed, peeved, sore.
– OPPOSITES pleased.

hurtful adjective **1** *no more hurtful comments about people's looks:* **upsetting**, distressing, wounding, painful; unkind, cruel, nasty, mean, malicious, spiteful; cutting, barbed; informal catty, bitchy. **2** *the law ought to prohibit only actions that are hurtful to society:* **detrimental**, harmful, damaging, injurious, disadvantageous, unfavourable, prejudicial, deleterious, ruinous.

hurtle verb *a speeding car hurtled towards them:* **speed**, rush, run, race, bolt, dash, career, whizz, zoom, charge, shoot, streak, gallop, hare, fly, scurry, go like the wind; informal belt, pelt, tear, scoot, go like a bat out of hell; Brit. informal bomb, bucket, go like the clappers; N. Amer. informal hightail, barrel.

husband noun **spouse**, partner, mate, consort, man, helpmate, helpmeet; groom, bridegroom; informal hubby, old man, one's better half; Brit. informal other half.
verb *oil and gas reserves should be husbanded:* **conserve**, preserve, save, safeguard, save for a rainy day, put aside, put by, lay in, reserve, stockpile, hoard; use economically, use sparingly, be frugal with.
– OPPOSITES squander.

husbandry noun **1** *farmers have no money to invest in new methods of husbandry:* **farm management**, land management, farming, agriculture, agronomy; cultivation; animal husbandry. **2** *the careful husbandry of their slender resources:* **conservation**, management; economy, thrift, thriftiness, frugality.

hush verb **1** *he placed a finger over his lips to hush her:* **silence**, quieten (down), shush; gag, muzzle; informal shut up. **2** *the lights dimmed and the crowd hushed:* **fall silent**, stop talking, quieten down, go quiet; informal pipe down, shut up. **3** *management took steps to hush up the dangers:* **keep secret**, conceal, hide, suppress, cover up, keep dark, keep quiet about; obscure, veil, sweep under the carpet; informal sit on, keep under one's hat.
– OPPOSITES disclose.
exclamation *Hush! Someone will hear you:* **be quiet**, keep quiet, quieten down, be silent, stop talking, hold your tongue; informal shut up, shut your mouth, shut your face, shut your trap, button your lip, pipe down, put a sock in it, give it a rest, save it, not another

word; Brit. informal shut your gob.
noun *a hush descended over the crowd:* **silence**, quiet, quietness; stillness, peace, peacefulness, calm, tranquillity.
– OPPOSITES noise.

husk noun **shell**, hull, pod, case, covering, integument, shuck; Botany pericarp, legume.

husky adjective **1** *his voice deepened to a husky growl:* **throaty**, gruff, gravelly, hoarse, croaky, rough, guttural, harsh, rasping, raspy. **2** *Paddy was a husky guy:* **strong**, muscular, muscly, muscle-bound, brawny, hefty, burly, hulking, chunky, strapping, thickset, solid, powerful, heavy, robust, sturdy, Herculean, well built; informal beefy, hunky.
– OPPOSITES shrill, soft, puny.

hustle verb **1** *they were hissed and hustled as they went out:* **jostle**, shove, push, bump, knock, nudge, elbow, shoulder. **2** *I was hustled away to a cold cell:* **manhandle**, push, shove, thrust, frogmarch; rush, hurry, whisk; informal bundle.
■ **hustle and bustle** *we were tired of the hustle and bustle of city life:* hurly-burly, bustle, tumult, hubbub, activity, action, liveliness, animation, excitement, agitation, flurry, whirl; informal toing and froing, comings and goings, ballyhoo, hoo-ha, hullabaloo.

hut noun **shack**, shanty, (log) cabin, shelter, shed, lean-to; hovel; Scottish bothy, shieling; N. Amer. cabana.

hybrid noun *a hybrid between a brown and albino mouse:* **cross**, cross-breed, half-breed; mixture, blend, amalgam, amalgamation, combination, composite, fusion.
adjective *hybrid varieties of rose:* **composite**, cross-bred, interbred, mongrel; mixed, blended, compound.

hybridize verb **cross-breed**, cross, interbreed, cross-fertilize, cross-pollinate; mix, blend, combine, amalgamate.

hygiene noun *poor standards of food hygiene:* **cleanliness**, sanitation, sterility, purity, disinfection; public health, environmental health.

hygienic adjective *this will leave the kitchen area clean and hygienic:* **sanitary**, clean, germ-free, disinfected, sterilized, sterile, antiseptic, aseptic, unpolluted, uncontaminated, salubrious, healthy, wholesome; informal squeaky clean.
– OPPOSITES insanitary.

hymn noun **song**, anthem, canticle, chorale, psalm, carol; spiritual.

hype (informal) noun *her work relies on hype and headlines:* **publicity**, advertising, promotion, marketing, propaganda, exposure; informal plugging, ballyhoo; Brit. informal puff.
verb *a publicity stunt to hype a new product:* **publicize**, advertise, promote, push, puff, boost, merchandise, build up, bang the drum for; informal plug.

hyperbole noun *the usual media hyperbole*

that accompanied the final: **exaggeration**, overstatement, magnification, embroidery, embellishment, excess, overkill; informal purple prose, puffery.
– OPPOSITES understatement.

hypercritical adjective he was a sarcastic, hypercritical man: **overcritical**, fault-finding, hair-splitting, carping, cavilling, captious, niggling, quibbling, pedantic, pettifogging, fussy, finicky; informal picky, nit-picking, pernickety; N. Amer. informal persnickety.

hypnosis noun **mesmerism**, hypnotism, hypnotic suggestion, auto-suggestion.

hypnotic adjective her voice had a hypnotic quality: **mesmerizing**, mesmeric, spellbinding, entrancing, bewitching, irresistible, compelling; soporific, sedative, numbing.

hypnotism noun **mesmerism**, hypnosis, hypnotic suggestion, auto-suggestion.

hypnotize verb **1** he had been hypnotized to enhance his memory: **mesmerize**, put into a trance. **2** they were hypnotized by the dancers: **entrance**, spellbind, enthral, transfix, captivate, bewitch, enrapture, grip, rivet, absorb, magnetize.

hypochondriac noun she is a hypochondriac who depends on pills for everything: **valetudinarian**, valetudinary; neurotic. adjective her hypochondriac husband: **valetudinarian**, valetudinary, hypochondriacal, malingering, health-obsessed, neurotic.

hypocrisy noun plain speaking was important to him: he hated hypocrisy: **sanctimoniousness**, sanctimony, pietism, piousness, false virtue, cant, posturing, speciousness, empty talk; insincerity, falseness, deceit, dishonesty, dissimulation, duplicity; informal phoneyness.
– OPPOSITES sincerity.

hypocrite noun he condemned her as superficial and a hypocrite: **liar**, pietist, plaster saint, humbug, deceiver, dissembler; informal phoney; literary whited sepulchre.

hypocritical adjective the hypocritical morality regarding sexual behaviour: **sanctimonious**, pietistic, pious, self-righteous, holier-than-thou, superior; insincere, specious, false; deceitful, dishonest, dissembling, two-faced; informal phoney.

hypodermic noun **needle**, syringe; informal hype, spike.

hypothesis noun many people recognize that the hypothesis is not merely unprovable, but false: **theory**, theorem, thesis, conjecture, supposition, postulation, postulate, proposition, premise, assumption; notion, concept, idea.

hypothetical adjective a hypothetical case | the hypothetical tenth planet: **theoretical**, speculative, conjectured, notional, suppositional, supposed, assumed; academic.
– OPPOSITES actual.

hysteria noun his voice had an edge of hysteria to it: **frenzy**, feverishness, hysterics, fit of madness, derangement, mania; panic, alarm, distress; Brit. informal the screaming abdabs.
– OPPOSITES calm.

hysterical adjective Janet became hysterical and began screaming: **overwrought**, overemotional, out of control, frenzied, frantic, wild, feverish; beside oneself, driven to distraction, agitated, berserk, manic, delirious, unhinged, deranged, out of one's mind, raving; informal in a state.

hysterics plural noun (informal) **1** she had a fit of hysterics: **hysteria**, wildness, feverishness, irrationality, frenzy, loss of control, delirium, derangement, mania; Brit. informal the screaming abdabs. **2** the girls collapsed in hysterics: **fits of laughter**, gales of laughter, convulsions, fits; informal stitches.

h

Ii

ice noun **1** *a lake covered with ice:* **frozen water**, icicles; black ice, verglas, frost, rime; N. Amer. glaze. **2** *assorted ices:* **ice cream**, water ice, sorbet; N. Amer. sherbet. **3** *the ice in her voice:* **coldness**, coolness, frostiness, iciness; hostility, unfriendliness.
verb **1** *the lake has iced over:* **freeze (over)**, turn into ice, harden, solidify. **2** *I'll ice the drinks:* **cool**, chill, refrigerate. **3** *she had iced the cake:* **cover with icing**, glaze; N. Amer. frost.
– OPPOSITES thaw, heat.
■ **on ice** (informal). See **PENDING** sense 1.

icing noun *a big cake with white icing:* **glaze**, sugar paste; N. Amer. frosting.

icon noun *an icon of the Madonna hangs on the wall:* **image**, idol, portrait, representation, symbol; figure, statue.

iconoclast noun *she is an iconoclast, called to shatter the myth of restaurants she feels are too popular:* **critic**, sceptic; heretic, unbeliever, dissident, dissenter; rebel, renegade, mutineer.

icy adjective **1** *take care on the icy roads tonight:* **frosty**, frozen (over), iced over, ice-bound, ice-covered, iced up; slippery. **2** *an icy wind blew up:* **freezing**, chill, chilly, biting, bitter, raw, arctic, glacial, Siberian, polar, gelid. **3** *an icy voice:* **unfriendly**, hostile, forbidding; cold, cool, chilly, frigid, frosty, glacial, gelid; haughty, stern, hard.

idea noun **1** *the idea of death scares her:* **concept**, notion, conception, thought; image, visualization; hypothesis, postulation. **2** *our idea is to open a new shop:* **plan**, scheme, design, proposal, proposition, suggestion; aim, intention, objective, object, goal, target. **3** *Liz had other ideas on the subject:* **thought**, theory, view, opinion, feeling, belief, conclusion. **4** *I had an idea that it might happen:* **sense**, feeling, suspicion, fancy, inkling, hunch, theory, notion, impression. **5** *could you give me some idea of the cost?* **estimate**, estimation, approximation, guess, conjecture, rough calculation; informal guesstimate.

ideal adjective **1** *ideal flying weather:* **perfect**, best possible, consummate, supreme, flawless, faultless, exemplary, classic, model, ultimate, quintessential. **2** *an ideal concept:* **abstract**, theoretical, conceptual, notional; hypothetical, speculative, conjectural, suppositional. **3** *the film-makers*

portray an ideal world: **unattainable**, unachievable, impracticable; unreal, fictitious, hypothetical, theoretical, ivory-towered, imaginary, idealized, Utopian, fairy-tale.
– OPPOSITES bad, concrete, real.
noun **1** *she tried to be his ideal:* **perfection**, paragon, epitome, ne plus ultra, nonpareil, dream; informal one in a million, the tops, the bee's knees. **2** *an ideal to aim at:* **model**, pattern, exemplar, example, paradigm, archetype; yardstick. **3** *liberal ideals:* **principle**, standard, value, belief, conviction, persuasion; (**ideals**) morals, morality, ethics, ideology, creed.

idealist noun *he came to power with the reputation of a left-wing idealist:* **Utopian**, visionary, fantasist, romantic, dreamer, daydreamer; Walter Mitty, Don Quixote; N. Amer. fantast.
– OPPOSITES realist.

idealistic adjective **Utopian**, visionary, romantic, quixotic, dreamy, unrealistic, impractical.

idealize verb *they tend to idealize the post-war years:* **romanticize**, be unrealistic about, look at something through rose-tinted spectacles, paint a rosy picture of, glamorize.

ideally adverb *ideally, everyone should have enough to live on:* **in a perfect world**; preferably, if possible, for preference, by choice, as a matter of choice, (much) rather; all things being equal, theoretically, hypothetically, in theory, in principle, on paper.

idée fixe noun *his other idée fixe was his belief in the existence of a ninth planet:* **obsession**, fixation, (consuming) passion, mania, compulsion, preoccupation, infatuation, addiction, fetish; phobia, complex, neurosis; informal bee in one's bonnet, hang-up, thing.

identical adjective **1** *the guides wore identical badges:* **similar**, (exactly) the same, indistinguishable, uniform, twin, interchangeable, undifferentiated, homogeneous, of a piece, cut from the same cloth; alike, like, matching, like (two) peas in a pod; informal much of a muchness. **2** *I used the identical technique:* **the (very) same**, the selfsame, the very, one and the same; aforementioned, aforesaid, aforenamed,

above, above-stated; foregoing, preceding.
– OPPOSITES different.

identifiable adjective *there are no easily identifiable features on the shoreline:* **distinguishable**, recognizable, known; noticeable, perceptible, discernible, appreciable, detectable, observable, perceivable, visible; distinct, marked, conspicuous, unmistakable, clear.
– OPPOSITES unrecognizable.

identification noun **1** *police have made some progress with the identification of the suspect:* **recognition**, singling out, pinpointing, naming; discerning, distinguishing; informal fingering. **2** *early identification of problems should save time later on:* **determination**, establishment, ascertainment, discovery, diagnosis, divination; verification, confirmation. **3** *may I see your identification?* **ID**, (identity/identification) papers, bona fides, documents, credentials; ID card, identity card, pass, badge, warrant, licence, permit, passport.

identify verb **1** *Gail identified her attacker:* **recognize**, single out, pick out, spot, point out, pinpoint, put one's finger on, put a name to, name, know; discern, distinguish; remember, recall, recollect; informal finger. **2** *I identified four problem areas:* **determine**, establish, ascertain, make out, diagnose, discern, distinguish; verify, confirm; informal figure out, get a fix on. **3** *we identify sport with glamour:* **associate**, link, connect, relate, bracket, couple; mention in the same breath as, set side by side with. **4** *Peter identifies with the hero:* **empathize**, be in tune, have a rapport, feel at one, sympathize; be on the same wavelength as, speak the same language as; understand, relate to, feel for.

identity noun **1** *the identity of the owner remained a mystery:* **name**; specification. **2** *she was afraid of losing her identity:* **individuality**, self, selfhood; personality, character, originality, distinctiveness, singularity, uniqueness. **3** *a case of mistaken identity:* **identification**, recognition, naming, singling out. **4** *we share an identity of interests:* **congruity**, congruence, sameness, oneness, interchangeability; likeness, uniformity, similarity, closeness, accordance, alignment.

ideology noun *the horrors spawned by Nazi ideology:* **beliefs**, ideas, ideals, principles, ethics, morals; doctrine, creed, credo, teaching, theory; tenets, canon(s); conviction(s), persuasion.

idiocy noun *the idiocy of decimating yew forests:* **stupidity**, folly, foolishness, foolhardiness; madness, insanity, lunacy; silliness, brainlessness, thoughtlessness, senselessness, irresponsibility, imprudence, ineptitude, inanity, absurdity, ludicrousness, fatuousness; informal craziness; Brit. informal daftness.

– OPPOSITES sense.

idiom noun **1** *a rather dated idiom:* **expression**, phrase, turn of phrase, locution. **2** *the poet's idiom is terse:* **language**, mode of expression, style, speech, locution, usage, phraseology, phrasing, vocabulary, parlance, jargon, patter; informal lingo.

idiomatic adjective *the texts have been translated from Italian into idiomatic English:* **vernacular**, colloquial, everyday, conversational; natural, grammatical, correct.

idiosyncrasy noun *his idiosyncrasies included the recycling of cigar butts:* **peculiarity**, oddity, eccentricity, mannerism, quirk, whim, vagary, caprice, kink; fetish, foible, crotchet, habit, characteristic; individuality; unconventionality, unorthodoxy.

idiosyncratic adjective *each researcher had his or her own idiosyncratic approach:* **distinctive**, individual, individualistic, characteristic, peculiar, typical, special, specific, unique, personal; eccentric, unconventional, irregular, anomalous, odd, quirky, queer, strange, weird, bizarre, freakish; informal freaky.

idiot noun *that idiot was driving far too fast:* **fool**, ass, halfwit, blockhead, dunce, dolt, ignoramus, simpleton; informal dope, ninny, nincompoop, chump, dimwit, dumbo, dummy, loon, dork, jackass, bonehead, fathead, numbskull, dunderhead, thickhead, woodenhead, airhead, pinhead, lamebrain, cretin, moron, imbecile, pea-brain, birdbrain, jerk, nerd, donkey; Brit. informal nit, nitwit, twit, clot, plonker, berk, prat, pillock, wally, divvy, twerp, charlie; Scottish informal nyaff, balloon; N. Amer. informal schmuck, bozo, turkey, chowderhead, dingbat; Austral./NZ informal drongo, dill, alec, galah.

– OPPOSITES genius.

idiotic adjective *I'm trying to stop Suzanne making an idiotic mistake:* **stupid**, silly, foolish, witless, brainless, mindless, thoughtless, unintelligent; imprudent, unwise, ill-advised, ill-considered, half-baked, foolhardy; absurd, senseless, pointless, nonsensical, inane, fatuous, ridiculous; informal dumb, dim, dim-witted, half-witted, dopey, gormless, hare-brained, pea-brained, wooden-headed, thickheaded; Brit. informal barmy, daft; Scottish & N. English informal glaikit; N. Amer. informal dumb-ass.

idle adjective **1** *an idle fellow:* **lazy**, indolent, slothful, work-shy, shiftless, inactive, sluggish, lethargic, listless; slack, lax, lackadaisical, good-for-nothing; informal bone idle. **2** *I was bored with being idle:* **unemployed**, jobless, out of work, redundant, between jobs, workless, unwaged, unoccupied; Brit. informal on the dole, 'resting'. **3** *they left the machine idle:* **inactive**, unused, unoccupied, unemployed, disused; out of action,

inoperative, out of service. **4** *their idle hours:* **unoccupied**, spare, empty, vacant, unfilled, available. **5** *he didn't indulge in idle remarks:* **frivolous**, trivial, trifling, minor, petty, lightweight, shallow, superficial, insignificant, unimportant, worthless, paltry, niggling, peripheral, inane, fatuous; unnecessary, time-wasting. **6** *she was not a woman to make idle threats:* **empty**, meaningless, pointless, worthless, vain, insubstantial, futile, ineffective, ineffectual; groundless, baseless.
– OPPOSITES industrious, employed, working, busy, serious.
verb **1** *Lily idled on the window seat:* **do nothing**, be inactive, vegetate, take it easy, mark time, kick one's heels, twiddle one's thumbs, kill time, languish, laze, lounge, loll, loaf, slouch; informal hang around, veg out; Brit. informal hang about; N. Amer. informal bum around, lollygag. **2** *Rob idled along the pavement:* **saunter**, stroll, dawdle, drift, potter, amble, maunder, wander, straggle; informal mosey, tootle; Brit. informal pootle, mooch. **3** *he let the engine idle:* **tick over**.

idler noun *you were not brought into this world to be an idler:* **loafer**, layabout, good-for-nothing, ne'er-do-well, lounger, shirker, sluggard; informal skiver, waster, slacker, slowcoach, slob, lazybones; N. Amer. informal slowpoke.
– OPPOSITES workaholic.

idol noun **1** *there was an idol in a shrine at the roadside:* **icon**, effigy, statue, figure, figurine, fetish, totem; graven image, false god, golden calf. **2** *the pop world's latest idol:* **hero**, heroine, star, superstar, icon, celebrity; favourite, darling; informal pin-up, heart throb, blue-eyed boy/girl, golden boy/girl.

idolatry noun **1** *he preached against idolatry:* **idol worship**, fetishism, iconolatry; paganism, heathenism. **2** *our idolatry of art:* **idolization**, fetishization, worship, adulation, adoration, reverence, glorification, lionization, hero-worshipping.

idolize verb *he idolized professional wrestlers:* **hero-worship**, worship, revere, venerate, deify, lionize; stand in awe of, reverence, look up to, admire, exalt; informal put on a pedestal.

idyll noun **1** *an idyll unspoilt by machines:* **perfect time**, ideal time, moment of bliss; paradise, heaven (on earth), Shangri-La, Utopia. **2** *the poem began as a two-part idyll:* **pastoral**, eclogue, georgic, rural poem.

idyllic adjective *their idyllic times together:* **perfect**, wonderful, blissful, halcyon, happy; ideal, idealized; heavenly, paradisal, Utopian, Elysian; peaceful, picturesque.

if conjunction **1** *if the weather is fine, we can walk:* **on condition that**, provided (that), providing (that), presuming (that), supposing (that), assuming (that), as long as, given that, in the event that. **2** *if I go out she gets nasty:* **whenever**, every time. **3** *I*

wonder if he noticed: **whether**, whether or not.

iffy adjective (informal) **1** *the windscreen's a bit iffy, but it's a good car:* **substandard**, second-rate, low-grade, low-quality; doubtful, dubious, questionable; informal not up to much; Brit. informal dodgy, ropy. **2** *that date is a bit iffy:* **tentative**, undecided, unsettled, unsure, unresolved, in doubt; informal up in the air.

ignite verb **1** *he got to safety moments before the petrol ignited:* **catch fire**, burst into flames; be set off, explode. **2** *a cigarette ignited the fumes:* **light**, set fire to, set on fire, set alight, kindle, touch off; informal set/put a match to. **3** *the campaign failed to ignite voter interest:* **arouse**, kindle, trigger, spark, instigate, excite, provoke, stimulate, stir up, whip up, incite, fuel.
– OPPOSITES go out, extinguish.

ignoble adjective *the war is being fought over an ignoble cause:* **dishonourable**, unworthy, base, shameful, contemptible, despicable, shabby, sordid; improper, unprincipled, discreditable.

ignominious adjective *the leader's ignominious defeat:* **humiliating**, undignified, embarrassing, ignoble, inglorious.
– OPPOSITES glorious.

ignominy noun *the ignominy of a public trial:* **shame**, humiliation, embarrassment; disgrace, dishonour, discredit, degradation, scandal, infamy, indignity, ignobility, loss of face.

ignoramus noun *he was a foul-mouthed ignoramus:* **fool**, ass, halfwit, blockhead, dunce, simpleton; informal dope, ninny, nincompoop, chump, dimwit, imbecile, moron, dumbo, dummy, fathead, numbskull, thickhead, woodenhead, airhead, birdbrain; Brit. informal nit, nitwit, twit, clot, plonker, berk, divvy; Scottish informal balloon; N. Amer. informal schmuck, bozo, turkey; Austral./NZ informal drongo.

ignorance noun **1** *his ignorance of economics:* **incomprehension**, unawareness, unconsciousness, unfamiliarity, inexperience, innocence, lack of knowledge; informal cluelessness. **2** *their attitudes are based on ignorance:* **lack of knowledge**, lack of education; unenlightenment, benightedness; lack of intelligence, stupidity, foolishness, idiocy.
– OPPOSITES knowledge, education.

ignorant adjective **1** *an ignorant country girl:* **uneducated**, unknowledgeable, untaught, unschooled, untutored, untrained, illiterate, unlettered, unlearned, unread, uninformed, unenlightened, benighted; inexperienced, unworldly, unsophisticated; informal pig-ignorant, thick. **2** *they were ignorant of working-class life:* **without knowledge**, unaware, unconscious, unfamiliar, unacquainted, uninformed, unenlightened, unconversant, inexperienced, naive,

innocent, green; informal in the dark, clueless.
– OPPOSITES educated, knowledgeable.

ignore verb **1** *he ignored the customers:*
disregard, take no notice of, pay no
attention to, pay no heed to; turn a blind
eye to, turn a deaf ear to. **2** *he was ignored by
the countess:* **snub**, slight, spurn, shun, look
right through, cold-shoulder, freeze out;
Brit. send to Coventry; informal give someone
the brush-off, cut (dead); Brit. informal blank.
3 *doctors ignored her husband's instructions:*
set aside, pay no attention to, take no
account of; break, contravene, fail to comply
with, fail to observe, disregard, disobey,
breach, defy, flout.
– OPPOSITES acknowledge, obey.

ilk noun *fascists, racists, and others of that
ilk:* **type**, sort, class, category, group, set,
bracket, genre, vintage, make, model, brand,
stamp, variety.

ill adjective **1** *she was feeling rather ill:* **unwell**,
sick, not (very) well, ailing, poorly, sickly,
peaky, indisposed, infirm; out of sorts,
not oneself, under/below par, bad, in a
bad way; bedridden, invalided, on the
sick list, valetudinarian; queasy, nauseous,
nauseated; Brit. off colour; informal under the
weather, laid up, lousy, rough; Brit. informal
ropy, grotty; Austral./NZ informal crook. **2** *the
ill effects of smoking:* **harmful**, damaging,
detrimental, deleterious, adverse, injurious,
hurtful, destructive, pernicious, dangerous;
unhealthy, unwholesome, poisonous,
noxious. **3** *the ill feeling between him
and the Woodvilles:* **hostile**, antagonistic,
acrimonious, inimical, antipathetic;
unfriendly, unsympathetic; resentful,
spiteful, malicious, vindictive, malevolent,
bitter.
– OPPOSITES well, healthy, beneficial,
benevolent.
noun **1** *the ills of society:* **problems**, troubles,
difficulties, misfortunes, trials, tribulations;
worries, anxieties, concerns; informal
headaches, hassles. **2** *he wished them no ill:*
harm, hurt, injury, damage, pain, trouble,
misfortune, suffering, distress. **3** *the
body's ills:* **illnesses**, ailments, disorders,
complaints, afflictions, sicknesses, diseases,
maladies, infirmities.
adverb **1** *such behaviour ill became the
king:* **poorly**, badly, imperfectly. **2** *the
look on her face boded ill:* **unfavourably**,
adversely, badly, inauspiciously. **3** *he can ill
afford the loss of income:* **barely**, scarcely,
hardly, only just, just possibly. **4** *we are ill
prepared:* **inadequately**, unsatisfactorily,
insufficiently, imperfectly, poorly, badly.
– OPPOSITES well, auspiciously, satisfactorily.
■ **ill at ease** awkward, uneasy,
uncomfortable, embarrassed, self-conscious,
out of place, inhibited, gauche; restless,
restive, fidgety, discomfited, worried,
anxious, on edge, edgy, nervous, tense;
informal twitchy, jittery; N. Amer. informal
discombobulated, antsy.

■ **speak ill of** denigrate, disparage, criticize,
be critical of, speak badly of, be malicious
about, blacken the name of, run down,
insult, abuse, attack, revile, malign, vilify;
N. Amer. slur; informal bad-mouth, bitch about,
pull to pieces; Brit. informal rubbish, slate, slag
off.

ill-advised adjective *an ill-advised business
venture:* **unwise**, injudicious, misguided,
imprudent, ill-considered, ill-judged;
foolhardy, hare-brained, rash, reckless;
informal crazy, crackpot.
– OPPOSITES judicious.

ill-assorted adjective *an ill-assorted
travelling party:* **mismatched**, incongruous,
ill-matched, incompatible; dissimilar,
unalike, varied, disparate.

ill-bred adjective *she was unlikely to be
amused by ill-bred behaviour:* **ill-mannered**,
bad-mannered, rude, impolite, discourteous,
uncivil; boorish, churlish, loutish, vulgar,
coarse, crass, uncouth, uncivilized,
ungentlemanly, indecorous, unseemly;
informal ignorant; Brit. informal yobbish.

ill-considered adjective *the government can
force through this ill-considered legislation:*
rash, ill-advised, ill-judged, injudicious,
imprudent, unwise, hasty; misjudged, ill-
conceived, badly thought out, hare-brained.
– OPPOSITES judicious.

ill-defined adjective *the boundary between
the two manors was rather ill-defined:* **vague**,
indistinct, unclear, imprecise; blurred,
fuzzy, hazy, woolly.

ill-disposed adjective *the court may be
ill-disposed to foreign companies:* **hostile**,
antagonistic, unfriendly, unsympathetic,
antipathetic, inimical, unfavourable, averse,
at odds; informal anti.
– OPPOSITES friendly.

illegal adjective *gangs operating illegal
gambling:* **unlawful**, illicit, illegitimate,
criminal, felonious; unlicensed,
unauthorized, unsanctioned; outlawed,
banned, forbidden, prohibited, proscribed;
contraband, black-market, bootleg; informal
crooked, shady; Brit. informal bent, dodgy.
– OPPOSITES lawful, legitimate.

illegible adjective *an illegible signature:*
unreadable, indecipherable, unintelligible;
scrawled, scribbled, crabbed.

illegitimate adjective **1** *illegitimate share
trading:* **illegal**, unlawful, illicit, criminal,
felonious; unlicensed, unauthorized,
unsanctioned; prohibited, outlawed,
banned, forbidden, proscribed; fraudulent,
corrupt, dishonest; informal crooked, shady;
Brit. informal bent, dodgy. **2** *an illegitimate
child:* **born out of wedlock**; archaic or derogatory
bastard.
– OPPOSITES legal, lawful.

ill-fated adjective *an ill-fated rebellion:*
doomed, blighted, damned, cursed, ill-
starred, jinxed.

ill-favoured adjective *an ill-favoured old*

woman: **unattractive**, plain, ugly; N. Amer. homely; informal not much to look at; Austral./NZ informal drack.
– OPPOSITES attractive.

ill-founded adjective *your faith in his expertise was ill-founded:* **baseless**, groundless, without foundation, unjustified; questionable, misinformed, misguided.

ill humour noun *the downward tilt to her mouth betrayed her ill humour:* **bad mood**, bad temper, irritability, irascibility, cantankerousness, petulance, peevishness, pettishness, pique, crabbiness, testiness, tetchiness, fractiousness, snappishness, waspishness, touchiness, moodiness, sullenness, sulkiness, surliness, annoyance, anger, crossness.

ill-humoured adjective **bad-tempered**, ill-tempered, short-tempered, in a (bad) mood, cross; irritable, irascible, tetchy, testy, crotchety, touchy, cantankerous, curmudgeonly, peevish, fractious, waspish, prickly, pettish; grumpy, grouchy, crabbed, crabby, splenetic, dyspeptic, choleric; informal snappish, snappy, chippy, on a short fuse; Brit. informal shirty, stroppy, ratty, like a bear with a sore head; N. Amer. informal cranky, ornery, peckish; Austral./NZ informal snaky.
– OPPOSITES amiable.

illiberal adjective *the government moved towards more illiberal policies:* **intolerant**, conservative, unenlightened, reactionary, undemocratic, authoritarian, repressive, totalitarian, despotic, tyrannical, oppressive.

illicit adjective **1** *illicit drugs:* **illegal**, unlawful, illegitimate, criminal, felonious; outlawed, banned, forbidden, prohibited, proscribed; unlicensed, unauthorized, unsanctioned; contraband, black-market, bootleg. **2** *an illicit love affair:* **taboo**, forbidden, impermissible, unacceptable, tapu, haram; secret, clandestine.
– OPPOSITES lawful, legal.

illimitable adjective *the great illimitable space we were in:* **limitless**, unlimited, unbounded; endless, unending, never-ending, infinite, immeasurable.

illiteracy noun **1** *illiteracy was widespread:* **illiterateness**, inability to read or write. **2** *economic illiteracy:* **ignorance**, unawareness, inexperience, unenlightenment, lack of knowledge/education.

illiterate adjective **1** *an illiterate peasant:* **unable to read or write**, unlettered. **2** *politically illiterate:* **ignorant**, unknowledgeable, uneducated, unschooled, untutored, untrained, uninstructed, uninformed.

ill-judged adjective *she flinched at his ill-judged choice of words:* **ill-considered**, unwise, ill-thought-out; imprudent, incautious, injudicious, misguided, ill-advised, impolitic, inexpedient; rash, hasty, thoughtless, careless, reckless.

– OPPOSITES judicious.

ill-mannered adjective *ill-mannered children may not have been shown how to behave:* **bad-mannered**, discourteous, rude, impolite, uncivil, abusive; insolent, impertinent, impudent, cheeky, presumptuous, disrespectful; badly behaved, ill-behaved, loutish, oafish, uncouth, uncivilized, ill-bred; informal ignorant.
– OPPOSITES polite.

ill-natured adjective *a disagreeable, ill-natured girl:* **mean**, nasty, spiteful, malicious, disagreeable; ill-tempered, bad-tempered, moody, irritable, irascible, surly, sullen, peevish, petulant, fractious, crabbed, crabby, tetchy, testy, grouchy.

illness noun *he was making a steady recovery from his recent illness:* **sickness**, disease, ailment, complaint, malady, affliction, infection, indisposition; ill health, poor health, infirmity; informal bug, virus; Brit. informal lurgy; Austral. informal wog.
– OPPOSITES good health.

illogical adjective *he drew a strange and illogical conclusion:* **irrational**, unreasonable, unsound, unreasoned, unjustifiable; incorrect, erroneous, invalid, spurious, faulty, flawed, fallacious, unscientific; specious, sophistic, casuistic; absurd, preposterous, untenable; informal off beam, way out.

ill-starred adjective *an ill-starred venture:* **ill-fated**, doomed, ill-omened, blighted, damned, cursed, jinxed; unlucky, luckless, unfortunate, hapless.
– OPPOSITES blessed.

ill temper noun **bad mood**, irritation, vexation, exasperation, indignation, huff, moodiness, pet, pique; anger, crossness, bad temper; irritability, irascibility, peevishness, tetchiness, testiness; informal grump; Brit. informal paddy, strop; N. Amer. informal blowout, hissy fit.

ill-tempered adjective *an ill-tempered woman:* **bad-tempered**, short-tempered, ill-humoured, moody; in a (bad) mood, cross, irritable, irascible, tetchy, testy, crotchety, touchy, cantankerous, curmudgeonly, peevish, fractious, waspish, prickly, pettish; grumpy, grouchy, crabbed, crabby, splenetic, dyspeptic, choleric; informal snappish, snappy, chippy, on a short fuse; Brit. informal shirty, stroppy, ratty; N. Amer. informal cranky, ornery, peckish; Austral./NZ informal snaky.

ill-timed adjective *their ill-timed foray into overseas property markets:* **untimely**, mistimed, badly timed; premature, early, hasty, inopportune.
– OPPOSITES timely.

ill-treat verb *her mother had ill-treated her when she was young:* **abuse**, mistreat, maltreat, ill-use, misuse; manhandle, handle roughly, molest; harm, injure, damage; informal knock about/around.

–OPPOSITES pamper.

ill-treatment noun **abuse**, mistreatment, maltreatment, ill use, ill usage, misuse; manhandling, rough treatment.

illuminate verb **1** *the cave was illuminated by candles:* **light (up)**, throw light on, brighten, shine on. **2** *the manuscripts were beautifully illuminated:* **decorate**, illustrate, embellish, adorn, ornament. **3** *documents often illuminate people's thought processes:* **clarify**, elucidate, explain, reveal, shed light on, give insight into.
–OPPOSITES darken, conceal.

illuminating adjective *an illuminating account of the writer's style:* **informative**, enlightening, revealing, explanatory, instructive, helpful, educational.

illumination noun **1** *a floodlamp provided illumination:* **light**, lighting, radiance, gleam, glow, glare; shining, gleaming, glowing. **2** *the illumination of a manuscript:* **decoration**, illustration, embellishment, adornment, ornamentation. **3** *these books give illumination on the subject:* **clarification**, elucidation, explanation, revelation, explication. **4** *moments of real illumination:* **enlightenment**, insight, understanding, awareness; learning, education, edification.

illusion noun **1** *he had destroyed her illusions:* **delusion**, misapprehension, misconception, false impression; fantasy, fancy, dream, chimera. **2** *the lighting increases the illusion of depth:* **appearance**, impression, semblance. **3** *it's just an illusion:* **mirage**, hallucination, apparition, figment of the imagination, trick of the light. **4** *magical illusions:* **(magic) trick**, conjuring trick; (**illusions**) magic, conjuring, sleight of hand, legerdemain.

illusory adjective *the comfort these theories give is illusory:* **delusory**, delusive; illusionary, imagined, imaginary, fanciful, fancied, unreal; sham, false, fallacious, fake, bogus, mistaken, erroneous, misguided, untrue.
–OPPOSITES genuine.

illustrate verb **1** *the photographs that illustrate the book:* **decorate**, adorn, ornament, accompany; add pictures/drawings to, provide artwork for. **2** *this can be illustrated through a brief example:* **explain**, elucidate, clarify, make plain, demonstrate, show, emphasize; informal get across/over. **3** *his wit was illustrated by his remark to Lucy:* **exemplify**, show, demonstrate, display, represent.

illustrated adjective *an illustrated weekly magazine:* **with illustrations**, with pictures, with drawings, pictorial.

illustration noun **1** *the illustrations in children's books:* **picture**, drawing, sketch, figure, plate, print. **2** *by way of illustration:* **exemplification**, demonstration, showing; example, typical case, case in point, analogy.

3 *a career in illustration:* **artwork**, (graphic) design; ornamentation, decoration, embellishment.

illustrative adjective *historians provide illustrative details and examples:* **exemplifying**, explanatory, elucidatory, elucidative, explicative, expository, illuminative, exegetic.

illustrious adjective *an illustrious general:* **eminent**, distinguished, acclaimed, notable, noteworthy, prominent, pre-eminent, foremost, leading, important, influential; renowned, famous, famed, well known, celebrated; esteemed, honoured, respected, venerable, august, highly regarded, well thought of, of distinction.
–OPPOSITES unknown.

ill will noun *he didn't bear his wife any ill will:* **animosity**, hostility, enmity, acrimony, animus, hatred, hate, loathing, antipathy; ill feeling, bad blood, antagonism, unfriendliness, dislike; spite, spitefulness, resentment, hard feelings, bitterness.
–OPPOSITES goodwill.

image noun **1** *an image of the Madonna:* **likeness**, resemblance; depiction, portrayal, representation; statue, statuette, sculpture, bust, effigy; painting, picture, portrait, drawing, sketch; photograph; reflection. **2** *the image of this country as democratic:* **conception**, impression, idea, perception, notion; mental picture, vision. **3** *his heart-throb image:* **public perception**, persona, profile, face, front, facade, mask, guise.

imaginable adjective *the most severe weather conditions imaginable:* **thinkable**, conceivable, supposable, believable, credible, creditable; possible.

imaginary adjective *the imaginary world of the novel:* **unreal**, non-existent, fictional, fictitious, pretend, make-believe, mythical, fabulous, fanciful, illusory; made-up, dreamed-up, invented, fancied.
–OPPOSITES real.

imagination noun **1** *a vivid imagination:* **creative power**, fancy; informal mind's eye. **2** *you need imagination in dealing with these problems:* **creativity**, imaginativeness, creativeness; vision, inspiration, inventiveness, invention, resourcefulness, ingenuity; originality, innovation, innovativeness. **3** *the album captured the public's imagination:* **interest**, fascination, attention, passion, curiosity.

imaginative adjective *she came up with an imaginative solution:* **creative**, visionary, inspired, inventive, resourceful, ingenious; original, innovative, innovatory, unorthodox, unconventional; fanciful, whimsical; informal blue-sky.

imagine verb **1** *one can imagine the cloud-capped castle:* **visualize**, envisage, envision, picture, see in the mind's eye; dream up, think up/of, conceive. **2** *I imagine he was at home:* **assume**, presume, expect, take it (as read), presuppose; suppose, think (it likely), dare say, surmise, believe, be of the view; N. Amer. figure; informal guess, reckon.

imbalance noun *the political imbalance between North and South:* **disparity**, variance, variation, polarity, contrast, lack of harmony; gulf, breach, gap.

imbed verb. See **EMBED**.

imbue verb *a society imbued with a sense of fairness:* **permeate**, saturate, diffuse, suffuse, pervade; impregnate, inject, inculcate, ingrain, inspire; fill.

imitate verb **1** *other artists have imitated his style:* **emulate**, copy, model oneself on, follow, echo, parrot; informal rip off. **2** *he imitated Winston Churchill:* **mimic**, do an impression of, impersonate, ape; parody, caricature, burlesque, travesty; informal take off, send up; N. Amer. informal make like.

imitation noun **1** *an imitation of a sailor's hat:* **copy**, simulation, reproduction, replica. **2** *learning by imitation:* **emulation**, copying, echoing, parroting. **3** *a perfect imitation of Francis:* **impersonation**, impression, parody, mockery, caricature, burlesque, travesty, lampoon, pastiche; mimicry, mimicking, imitating, aping; informal send-up, take-off, spoof.
adjective *imitation ivory:* **artificial**, synthetic, simulated, man-made, manufactured, ersatz, substitute; mock, sham, fake, false, faux, bogus; informal pseudo, phoney.
– OPPOSITES real, genuine.

imitative adjective **1** *news reports can lead to imitative crime:* **similar**, like, mimicking; informal copycat. **2** *I found the film empty and imitative:* **derivative**, unoriginal, unimaginative, uninspired, plagiarized, plagiaristic; clichéd, hackneyed, stale, trite, banal; informal cribbed, old hat.

imitator noun **1** *the show's success has sparked off many imitators:* **copier**, copyist, emulator, follower, mimic, plagiarist, ape, parrot; informal copycat. **2** *an Elvis imitator:* **impersonator**, impressionist, mimicker; parodist, caricaturist, lampooner.

immaculate adjective **1** *an immaculate white shirt:* **clean**, spotless, pristine, unsoiled, unstained, unsullied; shining, shiny, gleaming; neat, tidy, spick and span; informal squeaky clean. **2** *in immaculate condition:* **perfect**, pristine, mint; flawless, faultless, unblemished, unspoiled, undamaged; excellent, impeccable; informal tip-top, A1. **3** *his immaculate record:* **unblemished**, spotless, impeccable, unsullied, undefiled, untarnished, stainless; informal squeaky clean.
– OPPOSITES dirty, damaged.

immaterial adjective *the difference in our ages was immaterial:* **irrelevant**, unimportant, inconsequential, insignificant, of no matter/moment, of little account, beside the point, neither here nor there.
– OPPOSITES significant.

immature adjective **1** *an immature Stilton:* **unripe**, not mature, unmellowed; undeveloped, unformed, unfinished. **2** *an extremely immature girl:* **childish**, babyish, infantile, juvenile, puerile, jejune, callow, green, inexperienced, unsophisticated, unworldly, naive; informal wet behind the ears.
– OPPOSITES ripe.

immeasurable adjective *he dreamed of possessing immeasurable riches:* **incalculable**, inestimable, innumerable, untold; limitless, boundless, unbounded, unlimited, illimitable, infinite, never-ending, interminable, endless, inexhaustible; vast, immense, great, abundant; informal no end of.

immediate adjective **1** *the UN called for immediate action:* **instant**, instantaneous, swift, prompt, speedy, rapid, quick, expeditious; sudden, hurried, hasty, precipitate; informal snappy. **2** *their immediate concerns:* **current**, present, existing, actual; urgent, pressing. **3** *the immediate past:* **recent**, not long past, just gone; occurring recently. **4** *our immediate neighbours:* **nearest**, near, close, closest, next-door; adjacent, adjoining. **5** *the immediate cause of death:* **direct**, primary.
– OPPOSITES delayed, distant.

immediately adverb **1** *it was necessary to make a decision immediately:* **straight away**, at once, right away, instantly, now, directly, promptly, forthwith, this/that (very) minute, this/that instant, there and then, here and now, without delay, without further ado, post-haste; quickly, as fast as possible, speedily, as soon as possible, a.s.a.p.; informal pronto, in double-quick time, pretty damn quick, p.d.q., toot sweet. **2** *I sat immediately behind him:* **directly**, right, exactly, precisely, squarely, just, dead; informal slap bang; N. Amer. informal smack dab.

immense adjective *an immense brick church dominates the town:* **huge**, vast, massive, enormous, gigantic, colossal, great, very large/big, monumental, towering, tremendous; giant, elephantine, monstrous, mammoth, titanic, king-sized; informal mega, monster, whopping (great), thumping (great), humongous, jumbo; Brit. informal whacking (great), ginormous.
– OPPOSITES tiny.

immensely adverb *it was an immensely difficult decision:* **extremely**, very, exceedingly, exceptionally, extraordinarily, tremendously, hugely, singularly, distinctly, outstandingly, uncommonly, unusually, decidedly, particularly, eminently, supremely, highly, remarkably, really, truly, mightily, thoroughly, in the extreme; informal terrifically, awfully, fearfully, terribly, devilishly, seriously, mega, damn, damned; Brit. informal ever so, well, bloody, hellish, dead, jolly; N. Amer. informal real, mighty, powerful, awful, darned.

– OPPOSITES slightly.

immerse verb **1** *litmus paper turns red on being immersed in acid:* **submerge**, dip, dunk, duck, sink; soak, drench, saturate, wet. **2** *Elliot was immersed in his work:* **absorb**, engross, occupy, engage, involve, bury; busy, employ, preoccupy; informal lose oneself in.

immigrant noun **newcomer**, settler, incomer, migrant, emigrant; non-native, foreigner, alien.
– OPPOSITES native.

imminent adjective *there was speculation that a ceasefire was imminent:* **impending**, close (at hand), near, (fast) approaching, coming, forthcoming, on the way, in the offing, in the pipeline, on the horizon, in the air/wind, expected, anticipated, brewing, looming; informal on the cards.

immobile adjective **1** *she sat immobile for a long time:* **motionless**, without moving, still, stock-still, static, stationary; rooted to the spot, rigid, frozen, transfixed, like a statue, not moving a muscle. **2** *she dreaded being immobile:* **unable to move**, immobilized; paralysed, crippled.
– OPPOSITES moving.

immobilize verb *the officer wanted to immobilize the vehicle:* **put out of action**, disable, make inoperative, inactivate, deactivate, paralyse, cripple; bring to a standstill, halt, stop; clamp, wheel-clamp.

immoderate adjective *they were concerned about his immoderate drinking:* **excessive**, heavy, intemperate, unrestrained, unrestricted, uncontrolled, unlimited, unbridled, uncurbed, overindulgent, imprudent, reckless; undue, inordinate, unreasonable, unjustified, unwarranted, uncalled for, outrageous; extravagant, lavish, prodigal, profligate.

immodest adjective *her clothes and manner were most immodest:* **indecorous**, improper, indecent, indelicate, immoral; forward, bold, brazen, impudent, shameless, loose, wanton; informal fresh, cheeky, saucy.

immoral adjective *they deplored immoral behaviour:* **unethical**, bad, morally wrong, wrongful, wicked, evil, unprincipled, unscrupulous, dishonourable, dishonest, unconscionable, iniquitous, disreputable, corrupt, depraved, vile, villainous, nefarious, base, miscreant; sinful, impure, unchaste, unvirtuous, shameless, degenerate, debauched, dissolute, reprobate, lewd, licentious, wanton, promiscuous; informal shady, low-down; Brit. informal dodgy, crooked.
– OPPOSITES ethical, chaste.

immorality noun **wickedness**, immoral behaviour, badness, evil, vileness, corruption, dishonesty, dishonourableness; sinfulness, unchastity, sin, depravity, vice, degeneracy, debauchery, dissolution, perversion, lewdness, wantonness,

promiscuity; informal shadiness; Brit. informal crookedness.

immortal adjective **1** *our souls are immortal:* **undying**, deathless, eternal, everlasting, never-ending, endless, lasting, enduring; imperishable, indestructible, inextinguishable, immutable. **2** *an immortal children's classic:* **timeless**, perennial, classic, time-honoured, enduring; famous, famed, renowned, great, eminent, outstanding, acclaimed, celebrated.
noun **1** *Greek temples of the immortals:* **god**, goddess, deity, divine being, supreme being, divinity. **2** *one of the immortals of soccer:* **great**, hero, Olympian.

immortality noun **1** *the immortality of the gods:* **eternal life**, everlasting life, deathlessness; indestructibility, imperishability. **2** *the book has achieved immortality:* **timelessness**, legendary status, lasting fame/renown.

immortalize verb *the battle was immortalized in prose by Pushkin:* **commemorate**, memorialize, eternalize; celebrate, eulogize, pay tribute to, honour, salute, exalt, glorify.

immovable adjective **1** *lock your bike to something immovable:* **fixed**, secure, stable, moored, anchored, braced, set firm, set fast; stuck, jammed, stiff, unbudgeable. **2** *he sat immovable:* **motionless**, unmoving, stationary, still, stock-still, not moving a muscle, rooted to the spot; transfixed, paralysed, frozen. **3** *she was immovable in her loyalties:* **steadfast**, unwavering, unswerving, resolute, determined, firm, unshakeable, unfailing, dogged, tenacious, inflexible, unyielding, unbending, uncompromising, iron-willed; N. Amer. rock-ribbed.
– OPPOSITES mobile, moving.

immune adjective *they are immune to hepatitis B:* **resistant**, not subject, not liable, unsusceptible, not vulnerable; protected from, safe from, secure against, not in danger of.
– OPPOSITES susceptible.

immunity noun **1** *an immunity to malaria:* **resistance**, non-susceptibility; ability to fight off, protection against, defences against; immunization against, inoculation against. **2** *immunity from prosecution:* **exemption**, exception, freedom, release, dispensation; informal a let-off. **3** *diplomatic immunity:* **indemnity**, privilege, prerogative, right, liberty, licence; legal exemption, impunity, protection.

immunize verb *he immunized the children against measles:* **vaccinate**, inoculate, inject; protect from, safeguard against; informal give someone a jab/shot.

immutable adjective *a precise and immutable set of rules:* **fixed**, set, rigid, inflexible, permanent, established; unchanging, unchanged, unvarying,

i

unvaried, static, constant, lasting, enduring.
– OPPOSITES variable.

imp noun **1** *imps are thought to sprout from Satan:* **demon**, devil, fiend; hobgoblin, goblin, elf, sprite, puck, cacodemon. **2** *a cheeky young imp:* **rascal**, monkey, devil, troublemaker, wretch, urchin, tearaway; informal scamp, brat, monster, horror, tyke, whippersnapper; Brit. informal perisher; N. Amer. informal hellion, varmint.

impact noun **1** *the force of the impact:* **collision**, crash, smash, bump, bang, knock. **2** *the job losses will have a major impact:* **effect**, influence; consequences, repercussions, ramifications, reverberations.
verb **1** (N. Amer.) *a comet impacted the earth sixty million years ago:* **crash into**, smash into, collide with, hit, strike, smack into, bang into. **2** *high interest rates have impacted on retail spending:* **affect**, influence, have an effect, make an impression; hit, touch, change, alter, modify, transform, shape.

impair verb *even one drink can impair driving performance:* **have a negative effect on**, damage, harm, diminish, reduce, weaken, lessen, decrease, impede, hinder; undermine, compromise.
– OPPOSITES improve, enhance.

impaired adjective *they care for themselves despite being physically impaired:* **disabled**, handicapped, incapacitated; euphemistic challenged, differently abled.

impairment noun **disability**, handicap, abnormality, defect, dysfunction.

impale verb *his head was impaled on a pike for all to see:* **stick**, skewer, spear, spike, transfix; pierce, stab, run through.

impalpable adjective *a glimpse of an idea that remained as impalpable as a dream:* **intangible**, insubstantial, incorporeal; indefinable, elusive, undescribable.

impart verb **1** *she had news to impart:* **communicate**, pass on, convey, transmit, relay, relate, recount, tell, make known, make public, report, announce, proclaim, spread, disseminate, circulate, promulgate, broadcast; disclose, reveal, divulge; informal let on about, blab. **2** *the brush imparts a good sheen:* **give**, bestow, confer, grant, lend, afford, provide, supply.

impartial adjective *the referee is obliged to be impartial:* **unbiased**, unprejudiced, neutral, non-partisan, disinterested, detached, dispassionate, objective, open-minded, equitable, even-handed, fair, just.
– OPPOSITES biased, partisan.

impassable adjective *many roads were impassable after the flood:* **unpassable**, unnavigable, untraversable; closed, blocked.

impasse noun *the negotiations seemed to have reached an impasse:* **deadlock**, dead end, stalemate, checkmate, stand-off; standstill, halt, (full) stop.

impassioned adjective *she made an*

impassioned plea for the return of her abducted child: **emotional**, heartfelt, wholehearted, earnest, sincere, fervent, ardent, passionate, fervid.

impassive adjective *she smiled at him, but his features remained impassive:* **expressionless**, inexpressive, inscrutable, blank, deadpan, poker-faced, straight-faced; stony, wooden, unresponsive.
– OPPOSITES expressive.

impatience noun **1** *he was shifting in his seat with impatience:* **restlessness**, restiveness, agitation, nervousness; eagerness, keenness; informal jitteriness. **2** *a burst of impatience:* **irritability**, testiness, tetchiness, irascibility, querulousness, peevishness, frustration, exasperation, annoyance, pique.

impatient adjective **1** *Melissa grew impatient:* **restless**, restive, agitated, nervous, anxious, ill at ease, edgy, jumpy, keyed up; Brit. nervy; informal twitchy, jittery, uptight. **2** *they are impatient to get back home:* **anxious**, eager, keen, yearning, longing, aching; informal itching, dying. **3** *an impatient gesture:* **irritated**, annoyed, angry, testy, tetchy, snappy, cross, querulous, peevish, piqued, short-tempered; abrupt, curt, brusque, terse, short; informal peeved.
– OPPOSITES calm, reluctant.

impeach verb **1** *moves to impeach the president:* **indict**, charge, accuse, lay charges against, arraign, take to court, put on trial, prosecute. **2** *the headlines impeached their clean image:* **challenge**, question, call into question, raise doubts about.

impeccable adjective *a youth of impeccable character:* **flawless**, faultless, unblemished, spotless, stainless, perfect, exemplary; sinless, irreproachable, blameless, guiltless; informal squeaky clean.
– OPPOSITES imperfect, sinful.

impecunious adjective *she came from a respectable but impecunious family:* **penniless**, poor, impoverished, indigent, insolvent, hard up, poverty-stricken, needy, destitute; in straitened circumstances, unable to make ends meet; Brit. on the breadline; informal (flat) broke, strapped (for cash), cash-strapped, on one's uppers; Brit. informal skint, stony broke, in Queer Street; N. Amer. informal stone broke.
– OPPOSITES wealthy.

impede verb *the programme had been impeded by several problems:* **hinder**, obstruct, hamper, hold back/up, delay, interfere with, disrupt, retard, slow (down); block, check, stop, thwart, frustrate, baulk, foil, derail; informal stymie; Brit. informal scupper, throw a spanner in the works; N. Amer. informal bork, throw a monkey wrench in the works.
– OPPOSITES facilitate.

impediment noun **1** *an impediment to economic improvement:* **hindrance**, obstruction, obstacle, barrier, bar, block, check, curb, restriction, limitation; setback, difficulty, snag, hitch, stumbling block; informal fly in the ointment, hiccup; Brit. informal spanner in the works; N. Amer. informal monkey wrench in the works. **2** *a speech impediment:* **defect**; stammer, stutter, lisp.

impedimenta plural noun *all the tedious impedimenta of a teacher's working life:* **paraphernalia**, trappings, equipment, accoutrements, appurtenances, accessories, bits and pieces, tackle; informal stuff, gear; Brit. informal clobber, gubbins.

impel verb **1** *financial difficulties impelled her to seek work:* **force**, compel, constrain, oblige, require, make, urge, press, pressurize, drive, push, spur, prod, goad, incite, prompt, persuade. **2** *vital energies impel him in unforeseen directions:* **propel**, drive, move, get going, get moving.

impending adjective *she had a strange feeling of impending danger:* **imminent**, close (at hand), near, nearing, approaching, coming, forthcoming, upcoming, to come, on the way, about to happen, in store, in the offing, on the horizon, in the air/wind, brewing, looming, threatening, menacing.

impenetrable adjective **1** *impenetrable armoured plating:* **unbreakable**, indestructible, solid, thick, unyielding; impregnable, inviolable, unassailable, unpierceable. **2** *a dark, impenetrable forest:* **impassable**, unpassable, inaccessible, unnavigable, untraversable, dense, thick, overgrown. **3** *an impenetrable clique:* **exclusive**, closed, secretive, secret, private; restrictive, restricted, limited. **4** *impenetrable statistics:* **incomprehensible**, unfathomable, inexplicable, unintelligible, unclear, baffling, bewildering, puzzling, perplexing, confusing, abstruse, opaque; complex, complicated, difficult.

impenitent adjective *I am quite impenitent at having encouraged her rebellion:* **unrepentant**, unrepenting, uncontrite, remorseless, unashamed, unapologetic, unabashed.

imperative adjective **1** *it is imperative that you find him:* **vitally important**, of vital importance, all-important, vital, crucial, critical, essential, necessary, indispensable, urgent. **2** *the imperative note in her voice:* **peremptory**, commanding, imperious, authoritative, masterful, dictatorial, assertive, firm, insistent.
– OPPOSITES unimportant, submissive.

imperceptible adjective *the change was slow and imperceptible:* **unnoticeable**, undetectable, indistinguishable, indiscernible, invisible, inaudible, impalpable, unobtrusive; slight, small, subtle, faint, fine, negligible; indistinct, unclear, obscure, vague, indefinite, hard to make out.
– OPPOSITES noticeable.

imperfect adjective **1** *the goods were returned as imperfect:* **faulty**, flawed, defective, shoddy, unsound, inferior, second-rate, below standard, substandard; damaged, blemished, torn, broken, cracked, scratched; informal not up to scratch, tenth-rate, crummy; Brit. informal duff. **2** *an imperfect form of the manuscript:* **incomplete**, unfinished, half-done; unpolished, unrefined, rough. **3** *she spoke imperfect Arabic:* **broken**, faltering, halting, hesitant, rudimentary, limited.
– OPPOSITES flawless.

imperfection noun **1** *the glass is free from imperfections:* **defect**, fault, flaw, deformity, discoloration, disfigurement; crack, scratch, chip, dent, blemish, stain, spot, mark. **2** *he was aware of his imperfections:* **flaw**, fault, failing, deficiency, weakness, weak point, shortcoming, foible, inadequacy, limitation.
– OPPOSITES strength.

imperial adjective **1** *imperial banners:* **royal**, regal, monarchal, sovereign, kingly, queenly, princely. **2** *her imperial bearing:* **majestic**, grand, dignified, proud, stately, noble, aristocratic, regal; magnificent, imposing, impressive.

imperil verb *a radiation leak would imperil life and health:* **endanger**, jeopardize, risk, put in danger, put in jeopardy, expose to danger; threaten, pose a threat to.

imperious adjective *he spoke to her in a very imperious manner:* **peremptory**, high-handed, commanding, imperial, overbearing, overweening, domineering, authoritarian, dictatorial, authoritative, lordly, assertive, bossy, arrogant; informal pushy, high and mighty.

imperishable adjective *the fruits of his inspired labours are imperishable:* **enduring**, everlasting, undying, immortal, perennial, long-lasting; indestructible, inextinguishable, ineradicable, unfading, permanent, never-ending, never dying.

impermanent adjective *life has value precisely because it is impermanent:* **temporary**, transient, transitory, passing, fleeting, momentary, ephemeral, fugitive; short-lived, brief, {here today, gone tomorrow}.

impermeable adjective *the product is packaged in impermeable containers:* **watertight**, waterproof, damp-proof, airtight, (hermetically) sealed.

impersonal adjective **1** *the hand of fate is impersonal:* **neutral**, unbiased, non-partisan, unprejudiced, objective, detached, disinterested, dispassionate, without favouritism. **2** *he remained strangely impersonal:* **aloof**, distant, remote, reserved, withdrawn, unemotional, unsentimental, dispassionate, cold, cool, indifferent, unconcerned; formal, stiff, businesslike; informal starchy, stand-offish.
– OPPOSITES biased, warm.

i

impersonate verb *she tried to impersonate her boss:* **imitate**, mimic, do an impression of, ape; parody, caricature, burlesque, travesty, satirize, lampoon; masquerade as, pose as, pass oneself off as; informal take off, send up; N. Amer. informal make like.

impersonation noun **impression**, imitation; parody, caricature, burlesque, travesty, lampoon, pastiche; informal take-off, send-up.

impertinence noun **rudeness**, insolence, impoliteness, bad manners, discourtesy, discourteousness, disrespect, incivility; impudence, cheek, cheekiness, audacity, temerity, effrontery, nerve, gall, boldness, cockiness, brazenness; informal brass (neck); Brit. informal sauce; N. Amer. informal sass, sassiness, chutzpah.

impertinent adjective *she asked a lot of impertinent questions:* **rude**, insolent, impolite, ill-mannered, bad-mannered, uncivil, discourteous, disrespectful; impudent, cheeky, audacious, bold, brazen, brash, presumptuous, forward; tactless, undiplomatic; informal brass-necked, saucy; N. Amer. informal sassy.
– OPPOSITES polite.

imperturbable adjective *my father was a solid, imperturbable man:* **self-possessed**, composed, {cool, calm, and collected}, cool-headed, self-controlled, serene, relaxed, unexcitable, even-tempered, placid, phlegmatic; unperturbed, unflustered, unruffled; informal unflappable, unfazed, laid-back.
– OPPOSITES excitable.

impervious adjective **1** *he seemed impervious to the chill wind:* **unaffected**, untouched, immune, invulnerable, insusceptible, resistant, indifferent, heedless, oblivious; proof against. **2** *an impervious damp-proof course:* **impermeable**, impenetrable, impregnable, waterproof, watertight; (hermetically) sealed.
– OPPOSITES susceptible, permeable.

impetuous adjective *an impetuous decision:* **impulsive**, rash, hasty, overhasty, reckless, heedless, foolhardy, incautious, imprudent, injudicious, ill-considered, unthought-out; spontaneous, impromptu, spur-of-the-moment, precipitate, precipitous, hurried, rushed.
– OPPOSITES considered.

impetus noun **1** *the flywheel lost all its impetus:* **momentum**, propulsion, impulsion, motive force, driving force, drive, thrust; energy, force, power, push, strength. **2** *the sales force were given fresh impetus:* **motivation**, stimulus, incitement, incentive, inducement, inspiration, encouragement, boost; informal a shot in the arm.

impinge verb *these issues impinge on all of us:* **affect**, have an effect, touch, influence, make an impact, leave a mark.

impious adjective *the church was shamefully plundered by impious villains:* **godless**, ungodly, unholy, irreligious, sinful, immoral, unrighteous, sacrilegious, profane, blasphemous, irreverent; apostate, atheistic, agnostic, pagan, heathen, faithless, non-believing, unbelieving.

impish adjective **1** *he takes an impish delight in shocking the press:* **mischievous**, naughty, wicked, rascally, roguish, playful, sportive; mischief-making, full of mischief. **2** *an impish grin:* **elfin**, elflike, pixie-like, puckish; mischievous, roguish.

implacable adjective *he was their most implacable critic:* **unappeasable**, unpacifiable, unplacatable, unmollifiable, unforgiving; intransigent, inflexible, unyielding, unbending, uncompromising, unrelenting, ruthless, remorseless, merciless, heartless, pitiless, cruel, hard, harsh, stern, tough.

implant verb **1** *the collagen is implanted under the skin:* **insert**, embed, bury, lodge, place; graft. **2** *he implanted the idea in my mind:* **instil**, inculcate, insinuate, introduce, inject, plant, sow, root, lodge.
noun *a silicone implant:* **transplant**, graft, implantation, insert.

implausible adjective *they despaired of his adherence to implausible theories:* **unlikely**, improbable, questionable, doubtful, debatable; unrealistic, unconvincing, far-fetched, incredible, unbelievable, unimaginable, inconceivable, fantastic, fanciful, ridiculous, absurd, preposterous; informal cock and bull.
– OPPOSITES convincing.

implement noun *garden implements:* **tool**, utensil, instrument, device, apparatus, gadget, contraption, appliance, machine, contrivance; informal gizmo.
verb *the cost of implementing the new law:* **execute**, apply, put into effect/action, put into practice, carry out/through, perform, enact; fulfil, discharge, accomplish, bring about, achieve, realize.

implicate verb **1** *he had been implicated in a financial scandal:* **incriminate**, compromise; involve, connect, embroil, enmesh. **2** *viruses are implicated in the development of cancer:* **involve in**, concern with, associate with, connect with.

implication noun **1** *he was smarting at their implication:* **suggestion**, inference, insinuation, innuendo, hint, intimation, imputation. **2** *important political implications:* **consequence**, result, ramification, repercussion, reverberation, effect. **3** *his implication in the murder case:* **incrimination**, involvement, connection, entanglement, association.

implicit adjective **1** *comments seen as implicit criticism of the policies:* **implied**, inferred, understood, hinted at, suggested, deducible; unspoken, unexpressed, undeclared,

unstated, tacit, unacknowledged, taken for granted. **2** *assumptions implicit in the way questions are asked:* **inherent**, latent, underlying, inbuilt, incorporated. **3** *an implicit trust in human nature:* **absolute**, complete, total, wholehearted, perfect, utter; unqualified, unconditional; unshakeable, unquestioning, firm, steadfast.
– OPPOSITES explicit.

implicitly adverb *he trusted Sarah implicitly:* **completely**, absolutely, totally, wholeheartedly, utterly, unconditionally, unreservedly, without reservation.

implied adjective *there was implied criticism of the king's choice of commanders:* **implicit**, hinted at, suggested, insinuated, inferred, understood, deducible; unspoken, unexpressed, undeclared, unstated, tacit, unacknowledged, taken for granted.
– OPPOSITES explicit.

implore verb *his mother implored him to continue studying:* **plead with**, beg, entreat, beseech, appeal to, ask, request, call on; exhort, urge, enjoin, press, push, petition, bid.

imply verb **1** *are you implying he is mad?* **insinuate**, suggest, hint, intimate, say indirectly, indicate, give someone to understand, make out. **2** *the forecast traffic increase implies more roads:* **involve**, entail; mean, presuppose, point to, signify, indicate, signal; necessitate, require.

impolite adjective *it would have been impolite to leave in the middle:* **rude**, bad-mannered, ill-mannered, discourteous, uncivil, disrespectful, inconsiderate, boorish, churlish, ill-bred, ungentlemanly, unladylike, ungracious, insolent, impudent, impertinent, cheeky; loutish, rough, crude, indelicate, indecorous; informal ignorant, lippy.

impolitic adjective *it would be impolitic not to make amends:* **imprudent**, unwise, injudicious, incautious, irresponsible; ill-judged, ill-advised, misguided, rash, reckless, foolhardy, foolish, short-sighted; undiplomatic, tactless.
– OPPOSITES prudent.

import verb *the UK imports iron ore:* **buy from abroad**, bring in, buy in, ship in.
– OPPOSITES export.
noun **1** *a tax on imports:* **imported commodity**, foreign commodity. **2** *the import of foreign books:* **importation**, importing, bringing in, bringing from abroad, shipping in. **3** *a matter of great import:* **importance**, significance, consequence, momentousness, magnitude, substance, weight, note, gravity, seriousness. **4** *the full import of her words:* **meaning**, sense, essence, gist, drift, purport, message, thrust, substance, implication.
– OPPOSITES export, insignificance.

importance noun **1** *an event of immense importance:* **significance**, momentousness, import, consequence, note, noteworthiness,

substance; seriousness, gravity, weightiness, urgency. **2** *she had a fine sense of her own importance:* **power**, influence, authority, sway, weight, dominance; prominence, eminence, pre-eminence, notability, worth.
– OPPOSITES insignificance.

important adjective **1** *an important meeting:* **significant**, consequential, momentous, of great import, major; critical, crucial, vital, pivotal, decisive, urgent, historic; serious, grave, weighty, material. **2** *the important thing is that you do well in your exams:* **main**, chief, principal, key, major, salient, prime, foremost, paramount, overriding, crucial, vital, critical, essential, significant; central, fundamental; informal number-one. **3** *the school was important to the community:* **of value**, valuable, beneficial, necessary, essential, indispensable, vital; of concern, of interest, relevant, pertinent. **4** *he was an important man:* **powerful**, influential, of influence, well-connected, high-ranking; prominent, eminent, pre-eminent, notable, noteworthy, of note; distinguished, esteemed, respected, prestigious, celebrated, famous, great; informal major league.
– OPPOSITES trivial, insignificant.

importunate adjective *an importunate beggar:* **persistent**, insistent, tenacious, persevering, dogged, unrelenting, tireless, indefatigable; aggressive, high-pressure; informal pushy.

importune verb *he importuned her for some spare change:* **beg**, beseech, entreat, implore, plead with, appeal to, call on; harass, pester, press, badger, bother, nag, harry; informal hassle.

impose verb **1** *he imposed his ideas on the art director:* **foist**, force, inflict, press, urge; informal saddle someone with, land someone with. **2** *new taxes will be imposed:* **levy**, charge, apply, enforce; set, establish, institute, introduce, bring into effect. **3** *how dare you impose on me like this!* **take advantage of**, exploit, take liberties with, treat unfairly; bother, trouble, disturb, inconvenience, put out, put to trouble.
■ **impose oneself** force oneself, foist oneself; control, take charge of; informal call the shots/tune, be in the driving seat, be in the saddle, run the show.

imposing adjective *an imposing mansion:* **impressive**, striking, arresting, eye-catching, dramatic, spectacular, stunning, awesome, formidable, splendid, grand, majestic.
– OPPOSITES modest.

imposition noun **1** *the imposition of an alien culture:* **imposing**, foisting, forcing, inflicting. **2** *the imposition of VAT:* **levying**, charging, application, applying, enforcement, enforcing; setting, establishment, introduction, institution. **3** *it would be no imposition:* **burden**, encumbrance, strain, bother, worry; informal hassle.

impossible adjective **1** *gale force winds made fishing impossible:* **out of the question**, unfeasible, impractical, impracticable, non-viable, unworkable, unthinkable, unimaginable, inconceivable. **2** *an impossible dream:* **unattainable**, unachievable, unobtainable, hopeless, impractical, implausible, far-fetched, impracticable, unworkable. **3** (informal) *an impossible woman:* **unreasonable**, objectionable, difficult, awkward; intolerable, unbearable, unendurable; exasperating, maddening, infuriating.
– OPPOSITES attainable, bearable.

impostor noun **impersonator**, masquerader, pretender, deceiver, hoaxer, trickster, fraudster; fake, fraud, sham; informal phoney.

impotent adjective **1** *forces which man is impotent to control:* **unable**, incapable, powerless. **2** *an impotent opposition party:* **weak**, powerless, ineffective, feeble.
– OPPOSITES powerful, effective.

impound verb *officials began impounding documents:* **confiscate**, appropriate, take possession of, seize, commandeer, expropriate, requisition, sequester, sequestrate.

impoverish verb **1** *the widow had been impoverished:* **make poor**, make penniless, reduce to penury, bankrupt, ruin, make insolvent, pauperize. **2** *the trees were impoverishing the soil:* **weaken**, sap, exhaust, deplete.

impoverished adjective **1** *an impoverished peasant farmer:* **poor**, poverty-stricken, penniless, destitute, indigent, impecunious, needy, pauperized, down and out, on the breadline; bankrupt, ruined, insolvent; informal (flat) broke, stony broke, on one's uppers, hard up, without a bean, on skid row; Brit. informal skint; N. Amer. informal stone broke; formal penurious. **2** *the soil is impoverished:* **weakened**, exhausted, drained, sapped, depleted, spent; barren, unproductive, unfertile.
– OPPOSITES rich.

impracticable adjective *my colleagues thought it an impracticable plan:* **unworkable**, unfeasible, non-viable, unachievable, unattainable, unrealizable; impractical.
– OPPOSITES workable, feasible.

impractical adjective **1** *an impractical suggestion:* **unrealistic**, unworkable, unfeasible, non-viable, impracticable; ill-thought-out, impossible, absurd, wild; informal cockeyed, crackpot, crazy. **2** *impractical white ankle boots:* **unsuitable**, not sensible, inappropriate, unserviceable. **3** *an impractical scholar:* **idealistic**, unrealistic, romantic, dreamy, fanciful, quixotic; informal airy-fairy.

– OPPOSITES practical, sensible.

imprecise adjective **1** *a rather imprecise definition:* **vague**, loose, indefinite, inexplicit, indistinct, non-specific, unspecific, sweeping, broad, general; hazy, fuzzy, woolly, nebulous, ambiguous, equivocal, uncertain. **2** *an imprecise estimate:* **inexact**, approximate, estimated, rough; N. Amer. informal ballpark.
– OPPOSITES exact.

impregnable adjective **1** *an impregnable castle:* **invulnerable**, impenetrable, unassailable, inviolable, secure, strong, well fortified, well defended; invincible, unconquerable, unbeatable, indestructible. **2** *an impregnable parliamentary majority:* **unassailable**, unbeatable, undefeatable, unshakeable, invincible, unconquerable, invulnerable.
– OPPOSITES vulnerable.

impregnate verb **1** *a pad impregnated with natural oils:* **infuse**, soak, steep, saturate, drench. **2** *the woman he had impregnated:* **make pregnant**, inseminate, fertilize; informal put in the family way; Brit. informal get up the duff/spout, put in the club; N. Amer. informal knock up.

impresario noun *a theatrical impresario:* **organizer**, (stage) manager, producer; promoter, publicist, showman; director, conductor, maestro.

impress verb **1** *Hazel had impressed him mightily:* **make an impression on**, have an impact on, influence, affect, move, stir, rouse, excite, inspire; dazzle, awe, overawe, take someone's breath away, amaze, astonish; informal grab, stick in someone's mind. **2** *goldsmiths impressed his likeness on medallions:* **imprint**, print, stamp, mark, emboss, punch. **3** *you must impress upon her the need to save:* **emphasize to**, stress to, bring home to, instil in, inculcate into, drum into, knock into, din into.
– OPPOSITES disappoint.

impression noun **1** *he got the impression that she was hiding something:* **feeling**, feeling in one's bones, sense, fancy, (sneaking) suspicion, inkling, intuition, hunch; notion, idea, funny feeling; informal gut feeling. **2** *she had formed a favourable impression of him:* **opinion**, view, image, picture, perception, judgement, verdict, estimation. **3** *school made a profound impression on me:* **impact**, effect, influence. **4** *the cap had left a circular impression:* **indentation**, dent, mark, outline, imprint. **5** *he did a good impression of their science teacher:* **impersonation**, imitation; parody, caricature, burlesque, travesty, lampoon; informal take-off, send-up, spoof. **6** *an artist's impression of the gardens:* **representation**, portrayal, depiction, rendition, interpretation, picture, drawing. **7** *a revised impression of the 1981 edition:* **print run**, imprint, reprint, issue, edition.

impressionable adjective *an impressionable adolescent girl:* **easily influenced**, suggestible, susceptible, persuadable, pliable, malleable, pliant, ingenuous, trusting, naive, gullible.

impressive adjective **1** *an impressive building:* **magnificent**, majestic, imposing, splendid, spectacular, grand, awe-inspiring, stunning, breathtaking; stately, palatial. **2** *they played some impressive football:* **admirable**, masterly, accomplished, expert, skilled, skilful, consummate; excellent, outstanding, first-class, first-rate, fine; informal great, mean, nifty, cracking, ace, wizard; N. Amer. informal crackerjack.
– OPPOSITES ordinary, mediocre.

imprint verb **1** *patterns can be imprinted in the clay:* **stamp**, print, impress, mark, emboss. **2** *the image was imprinted on his mind:* **fix**, establish, stick, lodge, implant, embed.
noun **1** *her feet left imprints on the floor:* **impression**, print, mark, indentation. **2** *colonialism has left its imprint:* **impact**, lasting effect, influence, impression.

imprison verb *she was imprisoned for sedition:* **incarcerate**, send to prison, jail, lock up, put away, intern, detain, hold prisoner, hold captive; informal send down, put behind bars, put inside; Brit. informal bang up.
– OPPOSITES free, release.

imprisoned adjective **incarcerated**, in prison, in jail, jailed, locked up, interned, detained, held prisoner, held captive; informal sent down, behind bars, doing time, inside; Brit. informal doing porridge, doing bird, banged up.

imprisonment noun **incarceration**, internment, confinement, detention, captivity; informal time; Brit. informal porridge, bird.

improbability noun **unlikelihood**, implausibility; doubtfulness, uncertainty, dubiousness.

improbable adjective **1** *it seemed improbable that the hot weather should continue:* **unlikely**, doubtful, dubious, debatable, questionable, uncertain; unthinkable, inconceivable, unimaginable, incredible. **2** *an improbable exaggeration:* **unconvincing**, unbelievable, incredible, ridiculous, absurd, preposterous.
– OPPOSITES certain, believable.

impromptu adjective *an impromptu lecture:* **unrehearsed**, unprepared, unscripted, extempore, extemporized, extemporaneous, improvised, spontaneous, unplanned; informal off-the-cuff.
– OPPOSITES prepared, rehearsed.
adverb *they played the song impromptu:* **extempore**, spontaneously, extemporaneously, without preparation, without rehearsal; informal off the cuff, off the top of one's head.

improper adjective **1** *it is improper for policemen to accept gifts:* **inappropriate**,

unacceptable, unsuitable, unprofessional, irregular; unethical, corrupt, immoral, dishonest, dishonourable; informal not cricket. **2** *it was improper for young ladies to drive a young man home:* **unseemly**, indecorous, unfitting, unladylike, ungentlemanly, indelicate, impolite; indecent, immodest, immoral. **3** *an extremely improper poem:* **indecent**, risqué, off colour, suggestive, naughty, ribald, earthy, smutty, dirty, filthy, vulgar, crude, rude, obscene, lewd; informal blue, raunchy, steamy; Brit. informal fruity, saucy.
– OPPOSITES acceptable, decent.

impropriety noun **1** *a suggestion of impropriety on his part:* **wrongdoing**, misconduct, dishonesty, corruption, unscrupulousness, unprofessionalism, irregularity; unseemliness, indecorousness, indelicacy, indecency, immorality. **2** *the director was jailed for fiscal improprieties:* **transgression**, misdemeanour, offence, misdeed, crime; indiscretion, mistake, peccadillo.

improve verb **1** *ways to improve the service:* **make better**, ameliorate, upgrade, refine, enhance, boost, build on, raise; informal tweak. **2** *communications improved during the 18th century:* **get better**, advance, progress, develop; make headway, make progress, pick up, look up. **3** *the dose is not repeated if the patient improves:* **recover**, get better, recuperate, gain strength, rally, revive, get back on one's feet, get over something; be on the road to recovery, be on the mend; informal turn the corner, take a turn for the better. **4** *resources are needed to improve the offer:* **increase**, make larger, raise, augment, supplement, top up; informal up, hike up, bump up.
– OPPOSITES worsen, deteriorate.
■ **improve on** surpass, better, do better than, outdo, exceed, beat, top, cap.

improvement noun *many areas in the design could do with improvement:* **advance**, development, upgrade, refinement, enhancement, advancement, upgrading, amelioration; boost, augmentation, raising; rally, recovery, upswing.

improvident adjective *a feckless and improvident lifestyle:* **spendthrift**, thriftless, wasteful, prodigal, profligate, extravagant, free-spending, lavish, immoderate, excessive; imprudent, irresponsible, careless, reckless.
– OPPOSITES thrifty.

improvise verb **1** *she was improvising in front of the cameras:* **extemporize**, ad-lib, speak impromptu; informal speak off the cuff, speak off the top of one's head, busk it, wing it. **2** *she improvised a sandpit:* **contrive**, devise, throw together, cobble together, rig up; informal whip up, rustle up; Brit. informal knock up.

improvised adjective **1** *an improvised speech:* **impromptu**, unrehearsed, unprepared,

unscripted, extempore, extemporized, spontaneous, unplanned; informal off-the-cuff. **2** *an improvised shelter:* **makeshift**, thrown together, cobbled together, rough and ready, make-do.
– OPPOSITES prepared, rehearsed.

imprudent adjective *the banks were imprudent in making the loans:* **unwise**, injudicious, incautious, misguided, ill-advised; thoughtless, unthinking, improvident, irresponsible, short-sighted, foolish.
– OPPOSITES sensible.

impudence noun **impertinence**, insolence, effrontery, cheek, cockiness, brazenness; presumption, presumptuousness, disrespect, flippancy, bumptiousness, brashness; rudeness, impoliteness, ill manners, discourteousness, gall; informal brass neck, chutzpah, nerve; Brit. informal sauce; N. Amer. informal sassiness.

impudent adjective *these impudent youngsters need to be taught a lesson:* **impertinent**, insolent, cheeky, cocky, brazen; presumptuous, forward, disrespectful, insubordinate, flippant, bumptious, brash; rude, impolite, ill-mannered, discourteous, ill-bred; informal brass-necked, saucy, lippy; N. Amer. informal sassy.
– OPPOSITES polite.

impulse noun **1** *she had an impulse to run and hide:* **urge**, instinct, drive, compulsion, itch; whim, desire, fancy, notion. **2** *a man of impulse:* **spontaneity**, impetuosity, recklessness, rashness. **3** *impulses from the spinal cord to the muscles:* **pulse**, current, wave, signal.
■ **on (an) impulse** impulsively, spontaneously, on the spur of the moment, without forethought, without premeditation.

impulsive adjective **1** *he had an impulsive nature:* **impetuous**, spontaneous, hasty, passionate, emotional, uninhibited; rash, reckless, foolhardy, unwise, madcap, devil-may-care, daredevil. **2** *an impulsive decision:* **impromptu**, snap, spontaneous, unpremeditated, spur-of-the-moment, extemporaneous; impetuous, precipitate, hasty, rash; sudden, ill-considered, ill-thought-out.
– OPPOSITES cautious, premeditated.

impunity noun *the impunity enjoyed by military officers:* **immunity**, indemnity, exemption (from punishment), non-liability, licence; privilege, special treatment.
– OPPOSITES liability.
■ **with impunity** without punishment, scot-free, unpunished.

impure adjective **1** *impure gold:* **adulterated**, mixed, combined, blended, alloyed. **2** *the water was impure:* **contaminated**, polluted, tainted, unwholesome, poisoned; dirty, filthy, foul; unhygienic, unsanitary,

insanitary. **3** *impure thoughts:* **immoral**, sinful, wrongful, wicked; unchaste, lustful, lecherous, lewd, lascivious, prurient, obscene, indecent, ribald, risqué, improper, crude, coarse.
– OPPOSITES clean, chaste.

impurity noun **1** *the impurity of the cast iron:* **adulteration**, debasement, degradation. **2** *the impurity of the air:* **contamination**, pollution; dirtiness, filthiness, uncleanliness, foulness, unwholesomeness. **3** *the impurities in beer:* **contaminant**, pollutant, foreign body; dross, dirt, filth. **4** *a struggle to rid the soul of sin and impurity:* **immorality**, sin, sinfulness, wickedness; unchastity, lustfulness, lechery, lecherousness, lewdness, lasciviousness, prurience, obscenity, dirtiness, crudeness, indecency, ribaldry, impropriety, vulgarity, coarseness.

impute verb *he imputes selfish views to me:* **attribute**, ascribe, assign, credit; connect with, associate with.

inability noun *his inability to accept new ideas:* **lack of ability**, incapability, incapacity, powerlessness, impotence, helplessness; incompetence, ineptitude, unfitness.

inaccessible adjective **1** *an inaccessible woodland site:* **unreachable**, out of reach; cut-off, isolated, remote, in the back of beyond, out of the way, lonely, godforsaken. **2** *the book was elitist and inaccessible:* **esoteric**, obscure, abstruse, recondite, arcane; elitist, exclusive, pretentious.

inaccuracy noun **1** *the inaccuracy of recent opinion polls:* **incorrectness**, inexactness, imprecision, erroneousness, mistakenness, fallaciousness, faultiness. **2** *the article contained a number of inaccuracies:* **error**, mistake, fallacy, slip, oversight, fault, blunder, gaffe; erratum; Brit. literal; informal howler, boo-boo, typo; Brit. informal boob; N. Amer. informal blooper, goof.
– OPPOSITES correctness.

inaccurate adjective *the maps were notoriously inaccurate:* **inexact**, imprecise, incorrect, wrong, erroneous, faulty, imperfect, flawed, defective, unsound, unreliable; fallacious, false, mistaken, untrue; informal off beam; Brit. informal adrift.

inaction noun *wildlife is threatened by government inaction:* **inactivity**, non-intervention; neglect, negligence, apathy, inertia, indolence.

inactive adjective **1** *over the next few days I was horribly inactive:* **idle**, indolent, lazy, lifeless, slothful, lethargic, inert, sluggish, unenergetic, listless, torpid. **2** *the device remains inactive while the computer is started up:* **inoperative**, non-functioning, idle; not working, out of service, unused, not in use.

inactivity noun **1** *years of inactivity:* **idleness**, indolence, laziness, lifelessness,

slothfulness, lethargy, inertia, sluggishness, listlessness. **2** *government inactivity:* **inaction**, non-intervention; neglect, negligence, apathy.
– OPPOSITES action.

inadequacy noun **1** *the inadequacy of available resources:* **insufficiency**, deficiency, scarcity, scarceness, sparseness, dearth, paucity, shortage, want, lack, undersupply; paltriness, meagreness. **2** *her feelings of personal inadequacy:* **incompetence**, incapability, unfitness, ineffectiveness, inefficiency, inefficacy, inexpertness, ineptness, uselessness, impotence, powerlessness. **3** *the inadequacies of the present system:* **shortcoming**, defect, fault, failing, weakness, weak point, limitation, flaw, imperfection.
– OPPOSITES abundance, competence.

inadequate adjective **1** *inadequate water supplies:* **insufficient**, deficient, poor, scant, scanty, scarce, sparse, in short supply; paltry, meagre, niggardly, limited; informal measly, pathetic. **2** *I felt like a fraud, inadequate to the task:* **incompetent**, incapable, unsatisfactory, not up to scratch, unfit, ineffective, ineffectual, inefficient, unskilful, inexpert, inept, amateurish, substandard, poor, useless, inferior; informal not up to snuff; Brit. informal duff, not much cop, no great shakes.
– OPPOSITES sufficient, competent.

inadmissible adjective *inadmissible evidence:* **unallowable**, invalid, unacceptable, impermissible, disallowed, forbidden, prohibited, precluded.

inadvertent adjective *an inadvertent omission:* **unintentional**, unintended, accidental, unpremeditated, unplanned, innocent, uncalculated, unconscious, unthinking, unwitting, involuntary.
– OPPOSITES deliberate.

inadvertently adverb **unintentionally**, by accident, accidentally, unwittingly.

inadvisable adjective *an economically inadvisable move:* **unwise**, ill-advised, imprudent, ill-judged, ill-considered, injudicious, impolitic, foolish, misguided.
– OPPOSITES shrewd.

inane adjective *an inane remark:* **silly**, foolish, stupid, fatuous, idiotic, ridiculous, ludicrous, asinine, frivolous, vapid; childish, puerile; informal dumb, gormless, moronic; Brit. informal daft.
– OPPOSITES sensible.

inanimate adjective *inanimate objects such as cars:* **lifeless**, insentient, without life; dead, defunct.
– OPPOSITES living.

inapplicable adjective *this theory is inapplicable to asteroids:* **irrelevant**, immaterial, not germane, not pertinent, unrelated, unconnected, extraneous, beside the point.

– OPPOSITES relevant.

inappropriate adjective *inappropriate behaviour:* **unsuitable**, unfitting, unseemly, unbecoming, unbefitting, improper; incongruous, out of place/keeping, inapposite, inapt; informal out of order.
– OPPOSITES suitable.

inarticulate adjective **1** *an inarticulate young man:* **tongue-tied**, lost for words, unable to express oneself. **2** *an inarticulate reply:* **unintelligible**, incomprehensible, incoherent, unclear, indistinct, mumbled, muffled.
– OPPOSITES silver-tongued, fluent.

inattention noun **1** *a moment of inattention:* **distraction**, inattentiveness, preoccupation, absent-mindedness, daydreaming, abstraction. **2** *his inattention to duty:* **negligence**, neglect, disregard; forgetfulness, carelessness, thoughtlessness, heedlessness.
– OPPOSITES concentration.

inattentive adjective **1** *an inattentive pupil:* **distracted**, lacking concentration, preoccupied, absent-minded, daydreaming, dreamy, abstracted, distrait; informal miles away. **2** *we received very inattentive service in the restaurant:* **negligent**, neglectful, remiss, slack, sloppy, slapdash, lax; forgetful, careless, thoughtless, heedless.
– OPPOSITES alert.

inaudible adjective *Michelle's response was inaudible:* **unheard**, out of earshot; indistinct, faint, muted, soft, low, muffled, whispered, muttered, murmured, mumbled.

inaugural adjective *the inaugural meeting of the Geographical Society:* **first**, opening, initial, introductory, initiatory.
– OPPOSITES final.

inaugurate verb **1** *he inaugurated a new policy:* **initiate**, begin, start, institute, put in place, launch, start off, get going, get under way, establish, lay the foundations of; bring in, usher in; informal kick off. **2** *the new President will be inaugurated in January:* **admit to office**, install, instate, swear in; invest, ordain, crown. **3** *the museum was inaugurated in September:* **open**, declare open, unveil; dedicate, consecrate; N. Amer. hansel.

inauspicious adjective *an inauspicious start to the season:* **unpromising**, unpropitious, unfavourable, unfortunate, infelicitous, ominous; discouraging, disheartening, bleak.
– OPPOSITES promising.

inborn adjective *a child's inborn linguistic ability:* **innate**, congenital, connate, connatural; inherent, natural, inbred, inherited, hereditary, in one's genes.

inbred adjective. See **INBORN**.

inbuilt adjective **1** *an inbuilt CD-ROM drive:* **built-in**, integral, incorporated, internal. **2** *our inbuilt survival instinct:* **inherent**,

i

intrinsic, innate, congenital, natural, connatural, connate.

incalculable adjective *archaeological treasures of incalculable value:* **inestimable**, indeterminable, untold, immeasurable, incomputable; infinite, endless, limitless, boundless, measureless; enormous, immense, huge, vast, innumerable.

incandescent adjective **1** *incandescent fragments of lava:* **white-hot**, red-hot, burning, fiery, blazing, ablaze, aflame; glowing, aglow, radiant, bright, brilliant, luminous. **2** *the minister was incandescent at the accusation:* **furious**, enraged, raging, very angry, incensed, seething, infuriated, fuming, irate, in a temper, beside oneself; informal livid, foaming at the mouth, (hopping) mad, wild, apoplectic, steamed up, in a lather, in a paddy.

incantation noun *he muttered some weird incantations:* **chant**, invocation, conjuration, magic spell/formula, rune; N. Amer. hex, mojo; NZ makutu.

incapable adjective **1** *an incapable government:* **incompetent**, inept, inadequate, not good enough, leaving much to be desired, inexpert, unskilful, ineffective, ineffectual, inefficacious, feeble, unfit, unqualified, unequal to the task; informal out of one's depth, not up to it, not up to snuff, useless, hopeless, pathetic, a dead loss. **2** *he was mentally incapable:* **incapacitated**, helpless, powerless, impotent.
– OPPOSITES competent.

incapacitated adjective *Richard was temporarily incapacitated:* **disabled**, debilitated, indisposed, unfit; immobilized, out of action, out of commission, hors de combat; informal laid up.
– OPPOSITES fit.

incapacity noun **1** *mental incapacity:* **disability**, incapability, inability, debility, impairment, indisposition; impotence, powerlessness, helplessness; incompetence, inadequacy, ineffectiveness. **2** *legal incapacity:* **disqualification**, lack of entitlement.
– OPPOSITES capability.

incarcerate verb *he was incarcerated for expressing counter-revolutionary opinions:* **imprison**, put in prison, send to prison, jail, lock up, put under lock and key, put away, intern, confine, detain, hold, immure, put in chains, clap in irons, hold prisoner, hold captive; informal send down, put behind bars, put inside; Brit. informal bang someone up.
– OPPOSITES release.

incarceration noun **imprisonment**, internment, confinement, detention, custody, captivity, restraint; informal time; Brit. informal porridge.

incarnate adjective *she looked at me as though I were the devil incarnate:* **in human**

form, in the flesh, in physical form, in bodily form, made flesh; corporeal, physical, fleshly, embodied.

incarnation noun **1** *the incarnation of artistic genius:* **embodiment**, personification, exemplification, type, epitome; manifestation, bodily form, avatar. **2** *a previous incarnation:* **lifetime**, life, existence.

incautious adjective *his anger made him incautious:* **rash**, unwise, careless, heedless, thoughtless, reckless, unthinking, imprudent, misguided, ill-advised, ill-judged, injudicious, impolitic, unguarded, foolhardy, foolish; unwary, off-guard, inattentive; informal asleep on the job.
– OPPOSITES circumspect.

incendiary adjective **1** *an incendiary bomb:* **combustible**, flammable, inflammable. **2** *an incendiary speech:* **inflammatory**, rabble-rousing, provocative, seditious, subversive; contentious, controversial.

incense¹ verb *his taunts used to incense me:* **enrage**, infuriate, anger, madden, outrage, inflame, exasperate, antagonize, provoke; informal make someone see red, make someone's blood boil, make someone's hackles rise, drive mad/crazy; N. Amer. informal burn up.
– OPPOSITES placate, please.

incense² noun *a whiff of incense:* **perfume**, fragrance, scent.

incensed adjective *Leonora glared back at him, incensed:* **enraged**, very angry, furious, infuriated, irate, in a temper, raging, incandescent, fuming, seething, beside oneself, outraged; informal mad, hopping mad, wild, livid, apoplectic, hot under the collar, foaming at the mouth, steamed up, in a paddy, fit to be tied.

incentive noun *tax laws which give factories a financial incentive to reduce pollution:* **inducement**, motivation, motive, reason, stimulus, stimulant, spur, impetus, encouragement, impulse; incitement, goad, provocation; attraction, lure, bait; informal carrot, sweetener, come-on.
– OPPOSITES deterrent.

inception noun *the inception of the EEC in 1958:* **establishment**, institution, foundation, founding, formation, initiation, setting up, origination, constitution, inauguration, opening, day one; beginning, commencement, start, birth, dawn, genesis, origin; informal kick-off.
– OPPOSITES end.

incessant adjective *incessant rain fell for several days:* **ceaseless**, unceasing, constant, continual, unabating, interminable, endless, unending, never-ending, everlasting, eternal, perpetual, continuous, non-stop, uninterrupted, unbroken, unremitting, persistent, relentless, unrelenting, unrelieved, sustained.
– OPPOSITES intermittent.

incessantly adverb **constantly**, continually, all the time, non-stop, without stopping, without a break, round the clock, {morning, noon, and night}, interminably, unremittingly, ceaselessly, endlessly; informal 24-7.
– OPPOSITES occasionally.

incidence noun *an increased incidence of heart disease in women in their thirties:* **occurrence**, prevalence; rate, frequency; amount, degree, extent.

incident noun **1** *incidents in his youth:* **event**, occurrence, episode, experience, happening, occasion, proceeding, eventuality, affair, business; adventure, exploit, escapade; matter, circumstance, fact, development. **2** *police are investigating the incident:* **disturbance**, fracas, melee, commotion, rumpus, scene; fight, skirmish, clash, brawl, free-for-all, encounter, conflict, ruckus, confrontation, altercation, contretemps; informal ruction. **3** *the journey was not without incident:* **excitement**, adventure, drama; danger, peril.

incidental adjective **1** *these are just incidental details:* **less important**, secondary, subsidiary; minor, peripheral, background, by-the-way, by-the-by, non-essential, inessential, unimportant, insignificant, inconsequential, tangential, extrinsic, extraneous. **2** *an incidental discovery:* **chance**, accidental, random; fluky, fortuitous, serendipitous, adventitious, coincidental, unlooked-for.
– OPPOSITES essential, deliberate.

incidentally adverb **1** *incidentally, I haven't had a reply yet:* **by the way**, by the by(e), in passing, en passant, speaking of which; parenthetically; informal btw, as it happens. **2** *the infection was discovered incidentally:* **by chance**, by accident, accidentally, fortuitously, by a fluke, by happenstance; coincidentally, by coincidence.

incinerate verb *household waste should be incinerated to generate electricity:* **burn**, reduce to ashes, consume by fire, carbonize; cremate.

incise verb *an inscription incised in Roman letters:* **engrave**, etch, carve, cut, chisel, inscribe, score, chase.

incision noun *a surgical incision:* **cut**, opening, slit.

incisive adjective *an incisive political commentator:* **penetrating**, acute, sharp, sharp-witted, razor-sharp, keen, astute, trenchant, shrewd, piercing, perceptive, insightful, percipient, perspicacious, discerning, analytical, clever, smart, quick; concise, succinct, pithy, to the point, crisp, clear; informal punchy.
– OPPOSITES rambling, vague.

incite verb **1** *he was arrested for inciting racial hatred:* **stir up**, whip up, encourage, fan the flames of, stoke up, fuel, kindle, ignite, inflame, stimulate, instigate,

provoke, excite, arouse, awaken, inspire, trigger, spark off, ferment, foment. **2** *she incited him to commit murder:* **egg on**, encourage, urge, goad, provoke, spur on, drive, stimulate, push, prod, prompt, induce, impel; arouse, rouse, excite, inflame, sting, prick; informal put up to.
– OPPOSITES discourage, deter.

incivility noun *incivility on the part of staff will not be tolerated:* **rudeness**, discourtesy, discourteousness, impoliteness, bad manners, disrespect, boorishness, ungraciousness; insolence, impertinence, impudence.
– OPPOSITES politeness.

inclement adjective *the work was delayed by the inclement weather:* **cold**, chilly, bleak, wintry, freezing, snowy, icy; wet, rainy, drizzly, damp; stormy, blustery, wild, rough, squally, windy; unpleasant, bad, foul, nasty, filthy, severe, extreme, harsh.
– OPPOSITES fine.

inclination noun **1** *his political inclinations:* **tendency**, propensity, proclivity, leaning, predisposition, disposition, predilection, desire, wish, impulse, bent; liking, penchant, partiality, preference, appetite, fancy, interest, affinity; stomach, taste; informal yen; formal velleity. **2** *an inclination of his head:* **bowing**, bow, bending, nod, nodding, lowering.
– OPPOSITES aversion.

incline verb **1** *his prejudice inclines him to overlook obvious facts:* **predispose**, lead, make, make of a mind to, dispose, prejudice; prompt, induce, influence, sway; persuade, convince. **2** *I incline to the opposite view:* **prefer**, favour, go for; tend, lean, swing, veer, gravitate, be drawn. **3** *he inclined his head:* **bend**, bow, nod, bob, lower, dip. **4** *the columns incline away from the vertical:* **lean**, tilt, angle, tip, slope, slant, bend, curve, bank, cant, bevel; list, heel.
noun *a steep incline:* **slope**, gradient, pitch, ramp, bank, ascent, rise, acclivity, upslope, dip, descent, declivity, downslope; hill; N. Amer. grade, downgrade, upgrade.

inclined adjective **1** *I'm inclined to believe her:* **disposed**, minded, of a mind, willing, ready, prepared; predisposed. **2** *she's inclined to gossip:* **prone**, given, in the habit of, liable, likely, apt, wont.

include verb **1** *activities include sports, drama, music, and chess:* **incorporate**, comprise, encompass, cover, embrace, involve, take in, number, contain; consist of, be made up of, be composed of. **2** *don't forget to include the cost of repairs:* **allow for**, count, take into account, take into consideration, add.
– OPPOSITES exclude.

including preposition *a wide range of sports facilities, including squash, tennis, and badminton:* **inclusive of**, counting, embracing, covering.

inclusive adjective **1** *an inclusive price* |

i

an inclusive definition: **all-in,** all-inclusive, comprehensive, in toto, overall, full, all-round, umbrella, catch-all, all-encompassing. **2** *prices are inclusive of VAT:* **including,** incorporating, taking in, counting; comprising, covering.

incognito adverb & adjective *he travelled incognito:* **under an assumed name,** under a false name, in disguise, disguised, under cover, in plain clothes, camouflaged; secretly, anonymously.

incoherent adjective **1** *a long, incoherent speech:* **unclear,** confused, muddled, unintelligible, incomprehensible, hard to follow, disjointed, disconnected, disordered, mixed up, garbled, jumbled, scrambled; rambling, wandering, discursive, disorganized, illogical; inarticulate, mumbling, slurred. **2** *she was incoherent and shivering violently:* **delirious,** raving, babbling, hysterical, irrational.
– OPPOSITES lucid.

income noun *each spouse is responsible for paying tax on their own income:* **earnings,** salary, pay, remuneration, wages, stipend; revenue, receipts, takings, profits, gains, proceeds, turnover, yield, dividend, incomings; means; N. Amer. take.
– OPPOSITES expenditure, outgoings.

incoming adjective **1** *incoming flights are delayed:* **arriving,** entering; approaching, coming (in). **2** *the incoming president:* **newly elected,** newly appointed, succeeding, new, next, future; elect, to-be, designate.
– OPPOSITES outgoing.

incomparable adjective *the incomparable beauty of Venice:* **without equal,** beyond compare, unparalleled, matchless, peerless, unmatched, without parallel, beyond comparison, second to none, in a class of its own, unequalled, unrivalled, inimitable, nonpareil, par excellence; transcendent, superlative, surpassing, unsurpassed, unsurpassable, supreme, top, outstanding, consummate, singular, unique, rare, perfect; informal one-in-a-million.

incomparably adverb *this beach is incomparably superior to the others on the island:* **far and away,** by far, infinitely, immeasurably, easily; inimitably, supremely, superlatively, uniquely, transcendently.

incompatible adjective **1** *she and McBride are totally incompatible:* **unsuited,** mismatched, ill-matched, poles apart, worlds apart, like day and night; Brit. like chalk and cheese. **2** *incompatible economic objectives:* **irreconcilable,** conflicting, opposed, opposite, contradictory, antagonistic, antipathetic; clashing, inharmonious, discordant; mutually exclusive. **3** *a theory incompatible with that of his predecessor:* **inconsistent with,** at odds with, out of keeping with, at variance with, inconsonant with, different to, divergent from, contrary to, in conflict with, in opposition to,

(diametrically) opposed to, counter to, irreconcilable with.
– OPPOSITES well matched, harmonious, consistent.

incompetent adjective *he lost his job due to his incompetent performance:* **inept,** unskilful, unskilled, inexpert, amateurish, unprofessional, bungling, blundering, clumsy, inadequate, substandard, inferior, ineffective, deficient, inefficient, ineffectual, wanting, lacking, leaving much to be desired; incapable, unfit, unqualified; informal useless, pathetic, cack-handed, ham-fisted, not up to it, not up to scratch; Brit. informal not much cop.

incomplete adjective **1** *the project is still incomplete:* **unfinished,** uncompleted, partial, half-finished, half-done, half-completed. **2** *inaccurate or incomplete information:* **deficient,** insufficient, imperfect, defective, partial, patchy, sketchy, fragmentary, fragmented, scrappy, bitty; abridged, shortened; expurgated, bowdlerized.

incomprehensible adjective *April muttered something incomprehensible:* **unintelligible,** impossible to understand, impenetrable, unclear, indecipherable, beyond one's comprehension, beyond one, beyond one's grasp, complicated, complex, involved, baffling, bewildering, mystifying, puzzling, confusing, perplexing; abstruse, esoteric, recondite, arcane, mysterious, Delphic; informal over one's head, all Greek to someone; Brit. informal double Dutch.
– OPPOSITES intelligible, clear.

inconceivable adjective *it seemed inconceivable that the president had been unaware of what was going on:* **unbelievable,** beyond belief, incredible, unthinkable, unimaginable, extremely unlikely; impossible, beyond the bounds of possibility, out of the question, preposterous, ridiculous, ludicrous, absurd, incomprehensible; informal hard to swallow.
– OPPOSITES likely.

inconclusive adjective *their findings were inconclusive:* **indecisive,** proving nothing; indefinite, indeterminate, unresolved, unproved, unsettled, still open to question/doubt, debatable, unconfirmed; moot; vague, ambiguous; informal up in the air, left hanging.

incongruous adjective **1** *the women looked incongruous in their smart hats and fur coats:* **out of place,** out of keeping, inappropriate, unsuitable, unsuited; wrong, strange, odd, absurd, bizarre, off-key, extraneous. **2** *an incongruous collection of objects:* **ill-matched,** ill-assorted, mismatched, unharmonious, discordant, dissonant, conflicting, clashing, jarring, incompatible, different, dissimilar, contrasting, disparate.
– OPPOSITES appropriate, harmonious.

inconsequential adjective *inconsequential*

scraps of information: **insignificant**, unimportant, of little no/consequence, neither here nor there, incidental, inessential, non-essential, immaterial, irrelevant; negligible, inappreciable, inconsiderable, slight, minor, trivial, trifling, petty; informal piddling, piffling.
– OPPOSITES important.

inconsiderable adjective *a not inconsiderable amount of money:* **insignificant**, negligible, trifling, small, tiny, little, minuscule, nominal, token, petty, slight, minor, inappreciable, insubstantial, inconsequential; informal piffling.

inconsiderate adjective *his inconsiderate behaviour hurt her:* **thoughtless**, unthinking, insensitive, selfish, self-centred, unsympathetic, uncaring, heedless, unmindful, unkind, uncharitable, ungracious, impolite, discourteous, rude, disrespectful; tactless, undiplomatic, indiscreet, indelicate; informal ignorant.
– OPPOSITES thoughtful.

inconsistent adjective **1** *his inconsistent behaviour:* **erratic**, changeable, unpredictable, variable, varying, changing, changeful, inconstant, unstable, irregular, fluctuating, unsteady, unsettled, uneven; self-contradictory, contradictory, paradoxical; capricious, fickle, flighty, whimsical, unreliable, mercurial, volatile, blowing hot and cold, ever-changing, chameleon-like; informal up and down. **2** *he had done nothing inconsistent with his morality:* **incompatible with**, conflicting with, in conflict with, at odds with, at variance with, differing from, contrary to, in opposition to, (diametrically) opposed to, irreconcilable with, out of keeping with, out of step with; antithetical to.

inconsolable adjective *his widow, Jane, was inconsolable:* **heartbroken**, broken-hearted, grief-stricken, beside oneself with grief, devastated, wretched, sick at heart, desolate, despairing, distraught, comfortless; miserable, unhappy, sad.

inconspicuous adjective *Isabel tried to remain as inconspicuous as possible:* **unobtrusive**, unnoticeable, unremarkable, unspectacular, unostentatious, undistinguished, unexceptional, modest, unassuming, discreet, hidden, concealed; unseen, in the background, low-profile.
– OPPOSITES noticeable.

incontrovertible adjective *incontrovertible proof:* **indisputable**, incontestable, undeniable, irrefutable, unassailable, beyond dispute, unquestionable, beyond question, indubitable, beyond doubt, unarguable, undebatable; certain, sure, definite, definitive, proven, decisive, conclusive, demonstrable, emphatic, categorical, airtight, watertight.
– OPPOSITES questionable.

inconvenience noun **1** *we apologize for any inconvenience caused:* **trouble**, bother, problems, disruption, difficulty, disturbance; vexation, irritation, annoyance; informal aggravation, hassle. **2** *his early arrival was clearly an inconvenience:* **nuisance**, trouble, bother, problem, vexation, worry, trial, bind, bore, irritant, thorn in someone's flesh; informal headache, pain, pain in the neck, pain in the backside, drag, aggravation, hassle; N. Amer. informal pain in the butt.
verb *I don't want to inconvenience you:* **trouble**, bother, put out, put to any trouble, disturb, impose on, burden; vex, annoy, irritate; informal hassle.

inconvenient adjective *visitors often park their cars in inconvenient places:* **awkward**, difficult, inopportune, untimely, ill-timed, unsuitable, inappropriate, unfortunate; tiresome, irritating, annoying, vexing, bothersome; informal aggravating.

incorporate verb **1** *the region was incorporated into Moldavian territory:* **absorb**, include, subsume, assimilate, integrate, take in, swallow up. **2** *the model incorporates some advanced features:* **include**, contain, comprise, embody, embrace, build in, encompass. **3** *a small amount of salt is incorporated with the butter:* **blend**, mix, mingle, meld, combine; fold in, stir in.

incorrect adjective **1** *an incorrect answer:* **wrong**, erroneous, in error, mistaken, inaccurate, wide of the mark, off target; untrue, false, fallacious; informal off beam, out, way out, full of holes. **2** *incorrect behaviour:* **inappropriate**, wrong, unsuitable, inapt, inapposite; ill-advised, ill-considered, ill-judged, injudicious, unacceptable, unfitting, out of keeping, improper, unseemly, unbecoming, indecorous; informal out of order.

incorrigible adjective *she's an incorrigible flirt:* **inveterate**, habitual, confirmed, hardened, incurable, irredeemable, hopeless, beyond hope, beyond redemption; impenitent, uncontrite, unrepentant, unapologetic, unashamed.

incorruptible adjective *an incorruptible man:* **honest**, honourable, trustworthy, principled, high-principled, unbribable, moral, ethical, good, virtuous.
– OPPOSITES venal.

increase verb **1** *demand is likely to increase:* **grow**, get bigger, get larger, enlarge, expand, swell; rise, climb, escalate, soar, surge, rocket, shoot up, spiral; intensify, strengthen, extend, heighten, stretch, spread, widen; multiply, snowball, mushroom, proliferate, balloon, build up, mount up, pile up, accrue, accumulate. **2** *higher expectations will increase user demand:* **add to**, make larger, make bigger, augment, supplement, top up, build up, extend, raise, swell, inflate; magnify, intensify, strengthen, heighten, amplify; informal up, jack up, hike up, bump up, crank up.

i

– OPPOSITES decrease, reduce.

noun *the increase in size | an increase in demand:* **growth**, rise, enlargement, expansion, extension, multiplication, elevation, inflation; increment, addition, augmentation; magnification, intensification, amplification, step up, climb, escalation, surge, upsurge, upswing, spiral, spurt; informal hike.

increasingly adverb *the regime became increasingly draconian:* **more and more**, progressively, to an increasing extent, ever more.

incredible adjective 1 *I find his story incredible:* **unbelievable**, beyond belief, hard to believe, unconvincing, far-fetched, implausible, improbable, highly unlikely, dubious, doubtful; inconceivable, unthinkable, unimaginable, impossible; feeble, weak, thin, lame; informal hard to swallow/take, cock-and-bull. 2 *an incredible feat of engineering:* **magnificent**, wonderful, marvellous, spectacular, remarkable, phenomenal, prodigious, breathtaking, extraordinary, unbelievable, amazing, stunning, astounding, astonishing, awe-inspiring, staggering, formidable, impressive, supreme, great, awesome, superhuman; informal fantastic, terrific, tremendous, stupendous, mind-boggling, mind-blowing, out of this world.

incredulity noun *reports of UFO sightings were met with incredulity:* **disbelief**, incredulousness, scepticism, distrust, mistrust, suspicion, doubt, doubtfulness, dubiousness, lack of conviction; cynicism.

incredulous adjective *he was frankly incredulous when told the cost:* **disbelieving**, sceptical, unbelieving, distrustful, mistrustful, suspicious, doubtful, dubious, unconvinced; cynical.

increment noun *an annual salary increment:* **increase**, addition, supplement, gain, augmentation, boost; informal hike.
– OPPOSITES reduction.

incriminate verb *Drury persuaded one witness to incriminate Cooper:* **implicate**, involve, enmesh; blame, accuse, denounce, inform against, point the finger at; entrap; informal frame, set up, stick/pin the blame on, rat on; Brit. informal fit up, grass on.

inculcate verb 1 *the beliefs inculcated in him by his father:* **instil**, implant, fix, impress, imprint; hammer into, drum into, drive into, drill into, din into. 2 *they will try to inculcate you with a respect for culture:* **imbue**, infuse, inspire, teach.

incumbent adjective 1 *it is incumbent on the government to give a clear lead:* **necessary**, essential, required, imperative; compulsory, binding, obligatory, mandatory. 2 *the incumbent president:* **current**, present, in office, in power; reigning.
noun *the first incumbent of the post:* **holder**, bearer, occupant.

incur verb *kicking one's opponent incurs a 25-point penalty:* **bring upon oneself**, expose oneself to, lay oneself open to; run up; attract, invite, earn, arouse, cause, give rise to, be liable/subject to, meet with, sustain, experience.

incurable adjective 1 *an incurable illness:* **untreatable**, inoperable, irremediable; terminal, fatal, mortal; chronic. 2 *an incurable romantic:* **inveterate**, dyed-in-the-wool, confirmed, established, long-established, long-standing, absolute, complete, utter, thorough, thoroughgoing, out-and-out, through and through; unashamed, unapologetic, unrepentant, incorrigible, hopeless.

incursion noun *the first Ottoman incursion into Europe:* **attack**, assault, raid, invasion, storming, foray, blitz, sortie, sally, advance, push, thrust.
– OPPOSITES retreat.

indebted adjective *I shall always be indebted to them for their help:* **beholden**, under an obligation, obliged, obligated, grateful, thankful, in someone's debt, owing a debt of gratitude.

indecent adjective 1 *indecent photographs:* **obscene**, dirty, filthy, rude, coarse, naughty, vulgar, gross, crude, lewd, salacious, improper, smutty, off colour; pornographic, offensive, prurient, sordid, scatological; ribald, risqué, racy; informal blue, nudge-nudge, porn, porno, X-rated, raunchy, skin; Brit. informal saucy; euphemistic adult. 2 *indecent clothes:* **revealing**, short, brief, skimpy, scanty, low-cut, flimsy, thin, see-through; erotic, arousing, sexy, suggestive, titillating. 3 *indecent haste:* **unseemly**, improper, indecorous, unceremonious, indelicate, unbecoming, ungentlemanly, unladylike, unfitting, unbefitting; untoward, unsuitable, inappropriate; in bad taste, tasteless, unacceptable, offensive, crass.

indecipherable adjective *he scribbled something indecipherable on the back of a cigarette packet:* **illegible**, unreadable, hard to read, unintelligible, unclear; scribbled, scrawled, hieroglyphic, squiggly, cramped, crabbed.

indecision noun *she was rooted to the spot, torn by indecision:* **indecisiveness**, irresolution, hesitancy, hesitation, tentativeness; ambivalence, doubt, doubtfulness, uncertainty, incertitude; vacillation, equivocation, second thoughts; shilly-shallying, dithering, temporizing; Brit. humming and hawing; Scottish swithering; informal dilly-dallying, sitting on the fence; formal dubiety.

indecisive adjective 1 *an indecisive result:* **inconclusive**, proving nothing, settling nothing, open, indeterminate, undecided, unsettled, borderline, indefinite, unclear, ambiguous; informal up in the air. 2 *an indecisive leader:* **irresolute**, hesitant, tentative, weak; vacillating, equivocating, dithering, wavering, faltering, shilly-shallying; ambivalent, divided, blowing hot and cold, in two minds, in a dilemma, in a quandary, torn; doubtful, unsure, uncertain; undecided, uncommitted; informal iffy, sitting on the fence.

indeed adverb 1 *there was, indeed, quite a furore:* **as expected**, to be sure; in fact, in point of fact, as a matter of fact, in truth, actually, as it happens/happened, if truth be told. 2 *'May I join you?' 'Indeed you may.'* **yes**, certainly, assuredly, of course, naturally, without (a) doubt, without question, by all means; informal you bet, I'll say. 3 *Ian's future with us looked rosy indeed:* **very**, extremely, exceedingly, tremendously, immensely, singularly, decidedly, particularly, remarkably, really.

indefatigable adjective *he is one of those indefatigable researchers who won't take no for an answer:* **tireless**, untiring, unwearied, unwearying, unflagging; determined, tenacious, dogged, single-minded, assiduous, industrious, unswerving, unfaltering, unshakeable, indomitable; persistent, relentless, unremitting.

indefensible adjective 1 *indefensible cruelty:* **inexcusable**, unjustifiable, unjustified, unpardonable, unforgivable; uncalled for, unprovoked, gratuitous, unreasonable, unnecessary. 2 *an indefensible system of dual justice:* **untenable**, unsustainable, insupportable, unwarranted, unwarrantable, unjustifiable, unjustified, flawed, unacceptable. 3 *an indefensible island:* **defenceless**, vulnerable, exposed, open to attack, pregnable, undefended, unfortified, unguarded, unprotected, unarmed.

indefinable adjective *the curious, indefinable quality which sets his sculptures apart:* **hard to describe**, hard to define, indescribable, inexpressible, nameless; vague, obscure, impalpable, elusive.

indefinite adjective 1 *the project has been shelved for an indefinite period:* **indeterminate**, unspecified, unlimited, unrestricted, undecided, undetermined, undefined, unfixed, unsettled, unknown, uncertain; limitless, infinite, endless, immeasurable. 2 *an indefinite meaning:* **vague**, ill-defined, unclear, loose, general, imprecise, inexact, nebulous, blurred, fuzzy, hazy, obscure, ambiguous, equivocal. –OPPOSITES fixed, clear.

indefinitely adverb *the trial has been postponed indefinitely:* **for an unspecified period**, for an unlimited period, without limit, sine die.

indelible adjective *the story made an indelible impression on me:* **ineradicable**, permanent, lasting, persisting, enduring, unfading, unforgettable, haunting, never to be forgotten.

indelicate adjective 1 *an indelicate question:*

insensitive, tactless, undiplomatic, impolitic, indiscreet. 2 *an indelicate sense of humour:* **vulgar**, rude, crude, bawdy, racy, risqué, ribald, earthy, indecent, improper, naughty, indecorous, off colour, dirty, smutty, salacious; informal blue, nudge-nudge, raunchy; Brit. informal saucy.

indemnify verb 1 *he should be indemnified for his losses:* **reimburse**, compensate, recompense, repay, pay back, remunerate, recoup. 2 *they are indemnified against breach of contract:* **insure**, guarantee, protect, secure, underwrite.

indemnity noun 1 *no indemnity will be given for loss of cash:* **insurance**, assurance, protection, security, indemnification, surety, guarantee, warranty, safeguard. 2 *indemnity from prosecution:* **immunity**, exemption, dispensation, freedom; special treatment, privilege. 3 *the company was paid $100,000 in indemnity:* **compensation**, reimbursement, recompense, repayment, restitution, payment, redress, reparation(s), damages.

indent verb 1 *a coastline indented by many fjords:* **notch**, make an indentation in, scallop, groove, furrow. 2 *you'll have to indent for a new uniform:* **order**, put in an order for, requisition, apply for, put in for, request, ask for, claim, put in a request/claim for, call for.
noun (Brit.) *an indent for silk scarves:* **order**, requisition, purchase order, request, call, application; claim.

indentation noun *there was a slight indentation in his chin:* **hollow**, depression, dip, dent, dint, cavity, concavity, pit, trough; dimple, cleft; snick, nick, notch; recess, bay, inlet, cove.

independence noun 1 *the struggle for American independence:* **self-government**, self-rule, home rule, self-determination, sovereignty, autonomy, non-alignment, freedom, liberty. 2 *he valued his independence:* **self-sufficiency**, self-reliance. 3 *the adviser's independence:* **impartiality**, neutrality, disinterest, disinterestedness, detachment, objectivity. 4 *independence of spirit:* **freedom**, individualism, unconventionality, unorthodoxy.

independent adjective 1 *an independent country:* **self-governing**, self-ruling, self-determining, sovereign, autonomous, autarchic, free, non-aligned. 2 *two independent groups of biologists verified the results:* **separate**, different, unconnected, unrelated, dissociated, discrete. 3 *an independent school:* **private**, non-state-run, private-sector, fee-paying; privatized, denationalized. 4 *her grown-up, independent children:* **self-sufficient**, self-supporting, self-reliant, standing on one's own two feet. 5 *you should take independent advice:* **impartial**, unbiased, unprejudiced, neutral, disinterested, uninvolved, uncommitted, detached, dispassionate, objective,

non-partisan, non-discriminatory, with
no axe to grind, without fear or favour.
6 *an independent spirit:* **freethinking**,
free, individualistic, unconventional,
maverick, bold, unconstrained, unfettered,
untrammelled.
– OPPOSITES subservient, related, public,
biased.

independently adverb *he prefers to
work independently:* **alone**, on one's own,
separately, unaccompanied, solo; unaided,
unassisted, without help, by one's own
efforts, under one's own steam, single-
handed(ly), off one's own bat, on one's own
initiative.

indescribable adjective *the indescribable
thrill of the chase:* **inexpressible**,
indefinable, beyond words/description,
incommunicable, ineffable; unutterable,
unspeakable; intense, extreme, acute,
strong, powerful, profound; incredible,
extraordinary, remarkable, prodigious.

indestructible adjective *indestructible
plastic containers:* **unbreakable**,
shatterproof, durable; lasting, enduring,
everlasting, perennial, deathless, undying,
immortal, inextinguishable, imperishable.
– OPPOSITES fragile.

indeterminate adjective **1** *an indeterminate
period of time:* **undetermined**, uncertain,
unknown, unspecified, unstipulated,
indefinite, unfixed. **2** *some indeterminate
background noise:* **vague**, indefinite,
unspecific, unclear, nebulous, indistinct;
amorphous, shapeless, formless; hazy, faint,
shadowy, dim.

index noun **1** *the library's subject index:*
list, listing, inventory, catalogue, register,
directory. **2** *the Retail Price Index:* **measure**,
indicator, guide, signal, mark.

indicate verb **1** *sales indicate a growing
market for such art:* **point to**, be a sign
of, be evidence of, evidence, demonstrate,
show, testify to, bespeak, be a symptom of,
be symptomatic of, denote, connote, mark,
signal, signify, suggest, imply; manifest,
reveal, betray, display, reflect, represent;
formal evince. **2** *the president indicated his
willingness to use force:* **state**, declare, make
known, communicate, announce, mention,
reveal, divulge, disclose; put on record;
admit. **3** *please indicate your choice of prize
on the form:* **specify**, designate, stipulate;
show. **4** *he indicated the room with a sweep
of his arm:* **point to**, point out, gesture
towards.

indicated adjective *in such cases surgery
is indicated:* **advisable**, recommended,
suggested, desirable, preferable, best,
sensible, wise, commonsensical, prudent,
in someone's (best) interests; necessary,
needed, required, called for.

indication noun *pain may be an indication
of injury:* **sign**, signal, indicator, symptom,
mark, manifestation, demonstration,
show, evidence; pointer, guide, hint, clue,

intimation, omen, augury, portent, warning,
forewarning.

indicative adjective *the President's visit
was indicative of improving diplomatic
arrangements:* **symptomatic**, expressive,
suggestive, representative, emblematic,
symbolic; typical, characteristic.

indicator noun **1** *these tests are a reliable
indicator of performance:* **measure**, gauge,
barometer, guide, index, mark, sign, signal;
standard, touchstone, yardstick, benchmark,
criterion, point of reference, guideline, test,
litmus test. **2** *the depth indicator:* **meter**,
measuring device, measure, gauge, dial. **3** *a
position indicator:* **pointer**, needle, hand,
arrow, marker.

indict verb *he was indicted for murder:*
charge, accuse, arraign, take to court, put
on trial, prosecute; summons, cite, prefer
charges against; N. Amer. impeach.
– OPPOSITES acquit.

indictment noun **charge**, accusation,
arraignment; citation, summons; Brit. plaint;
N. Amer. impeachment.

indifference noun **1** *his apparent
indifference infuriated her:* **lack of concern**,
unconcern, disinterest, lack of interest,
lack of enthusiasm, apathy, nonchalance;
boredom, unresponsiveness, impassivity,
dispassion, detachment. **2** *the indifference
of the midfield players:* **mediocrity**, lack of
distinction, amateurism, amateurishness,
lack of inspiration.

indifferent adjective **1** *an indifferent shrug:*
unconcerned, uninterested, uncaring,
casual, nonchalant, offhand, uninvolved,
unenthusiastic, apathetic, lukewarm,
phlegmatic; unimpressed, bored, unmoved,
unresponsive, impassive, dispassionate,
detached, cool. **2** *an indifferent
performance:* **mediocre**, ordinary, average,
middling, middle-of-the-road, uninspired,
undistinguished, unexceptional, unexciting,
unremarkable, run-of-the-mill, pedestrian,
prosaic, lacklustre, forgettable, amateur,
amateurish; informal OK, so-so, fair-to-
middling, no great shakes, not up to much;
Brit. informal not much cop; N. Amer. informal bush-
league; NZ informal half-pie.
– OPPOSITES enthusiastic, brilliant.

indigenous adjective *indigenous peoples are
being slowly wiped out as prospectors invade
their lands:* **native**, original, aboriginal,
autochthonous; earliest, first.

indigestion noun *crisps give me indigestion:*
dyspepsia, heartburn, pyrosis, acidity,
stomach ache; (an) upset stomach, (a)
stomach upset; informal bellyache, tummy
ache.

indignant adjective *he was indignant at
the way he was being treated:* **aggrieved**,
resentful, affronted, disgruntled,
displeased, cross, angry, annoyed, offended,
exasperated, irritated, piqued, nettled, in
high dudgeon, chagrined; informal peeved,

vexed, irked, put out, miffed, aggravated, riled, in a huff; Brit. informal narked; N. Amer. informal sore.

indignation noun *she was filled with indignation at having been blamed so unjustly:* **resentment**, umbrage, affront, disgruntlement, displeasure, anger, annoyance, irritation, exasperation, vexation, offence, pique; informal aggravation.

indignity noun *Annie has suffered the indignity of being dumped by her husband:* **shame**, humiliation, loss of self-respect, loss of pride, loss of face, embarrassment, mortification; disgrace, dishonour, stigma, discredit; affront, insult, abuse, mistreatment, injury, offence, injustice, slight, snub, discourtesy, disrespect; informal slap in the face, kick in the teeth.

indirect adjective **1** *pay levels have an indirect effect on interest rates:* **incidental**, accidental, unintended, secondary, subordinate, ancillary, collateral, concomitant, contingent. **2** *the indirect route:* **roundabout**, circuitous, wandering, meandering, serpentine, winding, tortuous, zigzag. **3** *his speech was an indirect attack on the government:* **oblique**, inexplicit, implicit, implied, allusive.

indiscreet adjective **1** *an indiscreet remark:* **imprudent**, unwise, impolitic, injudicious, incautious, irresponsible, ill-judged, ill-advised, misguided, ill-considered, careless, rash, unwary, hasty, reckless, precipitate, impulsive, foolhardy, foolish, short-sighted; undiplomatic, indelicate, tactless, insensitive; inexpedient, untimely, infelicitous. **2** *her indiscreet behaviour:* **immodest**, indecorous, unseemly, improper, indecent, indelicate.

indiscretion noun **1** *he was prone to indiscretion:* **imprudence**, injudiciousness, incaution, irresponsibility; carelessness, rashness, recklessness, precipitateness, impulsiveness, foolhardiness, foolishness, folly; tactlessness, insensitivity. **2** *his past indiscretions:* **blunder**, lapse, gaffe, mistake, faux pas, error, slip, miscalculation, impropriety; misdemeanour, transgression, peccadillo, misdeed; informal slip-up.

indiscriminate adjective *the indiscriminate bombing of cities:* **non-selective**, unselective, undiscriminating, uncritical, aimless, hit-or-miss, haphazard, random, arbitrary, unsystematic, undirected; wholesale, general, sweeping, blanket; thoughtless, unthinking, unconsidered, casual, careless.
– OPPOSITES selective.

indispensable adjective *education is indispensable for the preservation of democracy:* **essential**, necessary, all-important, of the utmost importance, of the essence, vital, crucial, key, needed, required, requisite; invaluable.
– OPPOSITES superfluous.

indisposed adjective **1** *my wife is indisposed:* **ill**, unwell, sick, on the sick list, poorly, ailing, not (very) well, out of sorts, under/below par; out of action, hors de combat; Brit. off colour; informal under the weather. **2** *she was indisposed to help him:* **reluctant**, unwilling, disinclined, loath, unprepared, not disposed, not minded, averse.
– OPPOSITES well, willing.

indisposition noun *a mild indisposition:* **illness**, malady, ailment, disorder, sickness, disease, infection; condition, complaint, problem; informal bug, virus; Brit. informal lurgy.

indisputable adjective *there is indisputable evidence that terrorists are to blame:* **incontrovertible**, incontestable, undeniable, irrefutable, beyond dispute, unassailable, unquestionable, beyond question, indubitable, not in doubt, beyond doubt, beyond a shadow of a doubt, unarguable, undebatable, airtight, watertight; unequivocal, unmistakable, certain, sure, definite, definitive, proven, decisive, conclusive, demonstrable, self-evident, clear, clear-cut, plain, obvious, manifest, patent, palpable.
– OPPOSITES questionable.

indistinct adjective **1** *the distant shoreline was indistinct:* **blurred**, out of focus, fuzzy, hazy, misty, foggy, cloudy, shadowy, dim, nebulous; unclear, obscure, vague, faint, indistinguishable, barely perceptible, hard to see, hard to make out. **2** *the last two digits are indistinct:* **indecipherable**, illegible, unreadable, hard to read. **3** *indistinct sounds:* **muffled**, muted, low, quiet, soft, faint, inaudible, hard to hear; muttered, mumbled.
– OPPOSITES clear.

indistinguishable adjective **1** *the two girls were indistinguishable:* **identical**, difficult to tell apart, like (two) peas in a pod, like Tweedledum and Tweedledee, very similar, two of a kind. **2** *his words were indistinguishable in the crowd:* **unintelligible**, incomprehensible, hard to make out, indistinct, unclear; inaudible.
– OPPOSITES unalike, clear.

individual adjective **1** *exhibitions devoted to individual artists:* **single**, separate, discrete, independent; sole, lone, solitary, isolated. **2** *he had his own individual style of music:* **characteristic**, distinctive, distinct, typical, particular, peculiar, personal, personalized, special. **3** *a chic and highly individual apartment:* **original**, unique, exclusive, singular, idiosyncratic, different, unusual, novel, unorthodox, atypical, out of the ordinary.
noun **1** *Peter was a rather stuffy individual:* **person**, human being, mortal, soul, creature; man, boy, woman, girl; character, personage; informal type, sort, beggar, cookie, customer, guy, geezer, devil, bastard; Brit. informal bod, gent, punter. **2** *she was a real individual:* **individualist**, free spirit, nonconformist,

original, eccentric, character, maverick, rare bird; Brit. informal one-off.

individualist noun *horn players tend to be individualists:* **free spirit**, individual, nonconformist, original, eccentric, maverick, rare bird; Brit. informal one-off.
– OPPOSITES conformist.

individualistic adjective **unconventional**, unorthodox, atypical, singular, unique, original, nonconformist, independent, freethinking; eccentric, maverick, strange, odd, peculiar, idiosyncratic.

individuality noun *we are motivated by the need to assert our individuality:* **distinctiveness**, distinction, uniqueness, originality, singularity, particularity, peculiarity, differentness, separateness; personality, character, identity, self.

individually adverb *a panel will look at all the applications individually:* **one at a time**, one by one, singly, separately, severally, independently, apart.
– OPPOSITES together.

indoctrinate verb *they use alien dogmas to indoctrinate the masses:* **brainwash**, propagandize, proselytize, inculcate, re-educate, persuade, convince, condition, mould, discipline; instruct, teach, school, drill.

indolence noun *my failure is probably due to my own indolence:* **laziness**, idleness, slothfulness, sloth, shiftlessness, inactivity, inaction, inertia, sluggishness, lethargy, languor, languidness, torpor.

indolent adjective *he's too indolent to achieve anything worthwhile:* **lazy**, idle, slothful, loafing, work-shy, do-nothing, sluggardly, shiftless, lackadaisical, languid, inactive, inert, sluggish, lethargic, torpid; slack, lax, remiss, negligent, good-for-nothing, feckless; informal bone idle.
– OPPOSITES industrious, energetic.

indomitable adjective *these indomitable warriors have never been subjugated:* **invincible**, unconquerable, unbeatable, unassailable, invulnerable, unshakeable; indefatigable, unyielding, unbending, stalwart, stout-hearted, lionhearted, strong-willed, strong-minded, steadfast, staunch, resolute, firm, determined, intransigent, inflexible, adamant; unflinching, courageous, brave, valiant, heroic, intrepid, fearless, plucky, mettlesome, gritty, steely.
– OPPOSITES submissive.

indubitable adjective *he furnished indubitable evidence of his identity:* **unquestionable**, undoubtable, indisputable, unarguable, undebatable, incontestable, undeniable, irrefutable, incontrovertible, unmistakable, unequivocal, certain, sure, positive, definite, absolute, conclusive, watertight; beyond doubt, beyond the shadow of a doubt, beyond dispute, beyond question, not in question, not in doubt.

– OPPOSITES doubtful.

induce verb **1** *the pickets induced many workers to stay away:* **persuade**, convince, prevail upon, get, make, prompt, move, inspire, influence, encourage, motivate; coax into, wheedle into, cajole into, talk into, prod into; informal twist someone's arm. **2** *these activities induce a feeling of togetherness:* **bring about**, cause, produce, effect, create, give rise to, generate, instigate, engender, occasion, set in motion, lead to, result in, trigger off, spark off, whip up, stir up, kindle, arouse, rouse, foster, promote, encourage.
– OPPOSITES dissuade, prevent.

inducement noun *shopkeepers began offering free gifts as an inducement to trade:* **incentive**, encouragement, attraction, temptation, stimulus, bait, lure, pull, draw, spur, goad, impetus, motive, motivation, provocation; bribe, reward; informal carrot, come-on, sweetener.
– OPPOSITES deterrent.

induct verb **1** *the new ministers were inducted into the government:* **admit to**, allow into, introduce to, initiate into, install in, instate in, swear into; appoint to. **2** *he inducted me into the skills of magic:* **introduce to**, acquaint with, familiarize with, make conversant with; ground in, instruct in, teach in, educate in, school in.

indulge verb **1** *Sally indulged her passion for long walks:* **satisfy**, gratify, fulfil, feed, accommodate; yield to, give in to, give way to. **2** *she indulged in a fit of sulks:* **wallow in**, give oneself up to, give way to, yield to, abandon oneself to, give free rein to; luxuriate in, revel in, lose oneself in. **3** *she did not like her children to be indulged:* **pamper**, spoil, overindulge, coddle, mollycoddle, cosset, baby, pet, spoon-feed, feather-bed, wrap in cotton wool; pander to, wait on hand and foot, cater to someone's every whim, kill with kindness.
– OPPOSITES frustrate.
■ **indulge oneself** treat oneself, give oneself a treat; have a spree, splash out; informal go to town, splurge.

indulgence noun **1** *excess indulgence contributed to his ill-health:* **self-gratification**, self-indulgence, overindulgence, intemperance, immoderation, excess, excessiveness, lack of restraint, extravagance, decadence, pleasure-seeking, sybaritism. **2** *they viewed holidays as an indulgence:* **extravagance**, luxury, treat, non-essential, extra, frill. **3** *her indulgence left him spoilt:* **pampering**, coddling, mollycoddling, cosseting, babying. **4** *his parents view his lapses with indulgence:* **tolerance**, forbearance, understanding, kindess, compassion, sympathy, forgiveness, leniency.

indulgent adjective *she had a very indulgent father:* **generous**, permissive, easy-going,

liberal, tolerant, forgiving, forbearing, lenient, kind, kindly, soft-hearted, compassionate, understanding, sympathetic; fond, doting, soft; compliant, obliging, accommodating.
– OPPOSITES strict.

industrial adjective **1** *industrial areas of the city:* **manufacturing**, factory; commercial, business, trade. **2** (Brit.) *industrial action:* **strike**, protest.

industrialist noun *industrialists are on the lookout for takeover targets:* **manufacturer**, producer, factory owner; captain of industry, big businessman, magnate, tycoon, capitalist, financier; informal, derogatory fat cat.

industrious adjective *he was honest, sober, and industrious:* **hard-working**, diligent, assiduous, conscientious, steady, painstaking, sedulous, persevering, unflagging, untiring, tireless, indefatigable, studious; busy, as busy as a bee, active, bustling, energetic, on the go, vigorous, determined, dynamic, zealous, productive; with one's shoulder to the wheel, with one's nose to the grindstone.
– OPPOSITES indolent.

industry noun **1** *British industry:* **manufacturing**, production; construction. **2** *the publishing industry:* **business**, trade, field, line (of business); informal racket. **3** *the kitchen was a hive of industry:* **activity**, busyness, energy, vigour, productiveness; hard work, industriousness, diligence, application, dedication.

inebriated adjective *they helped to put the inebriated man to bed:* **drunk**, intoxicated, drunken, incapable, tipsy, the worse for drink, under the influence; informal tight, merry, in one's cups, three sheets to the wind, pie eyed, plastered, smashed, wrecked, wasted, sloshed, soused, sozzled, blotto, stewed, pickled, tanked (up), off one's face, out of one's head, ratted; Brit. informal legless, bevvied, paralytic, Brahms and Liszt, half cut, out of it, bladdered, trolleyed, squiffy, tiddly; N. Amer. informal loaded, trashed, juiced, sauced, out of one's gourd, in the bag, zoned; euphemistic tired and emotional.
– OPPOSITES sober.

inedible adjective *inedible fruit:* **uneatable**, indigestible, unsavoury, unpalatable, unwholesome; stale, rotten, off, bad.

ineffable adjective **1** *the ineffable beauty of the Everglades:* **indescribable**, inexpressible, beyond words; undefinable, unutterable, untold, unimaginable; overwhelming, breathtaking, awesome, staggering, amazing. **2** *the ineffable name of God:* **unutterable**, unmentionable; taboo, forbidden, off limits; informal no go.

ineffective adjective **1** *an ineffective scheme:* **unsuccessful**, unproductive, fruitless, unprofitable, abortive, futile, purposeless, useless, worthless, ineffectual,

inefficient, inefficacious, inadequate; feeble, inept, lame. **2** *an ineffective president:* **ineffectual**, inefficient, inefficacious, unsuccessful, powerless, impotent, inadequate, incompetent, incapable, unfit, inept, weak, poor; informal useless, hopeless.

inefficient adjective **1** *an inefficient worker:* **ineffective**, ineffectual, incompetent, inept, incapable, unfit, unskilful, inexpert, amateurish; disorganized, unprepared; negligent, lax, sloppy, slack, careless; informal lousy, useless. **2** *inefficient processes:* **uneconomical**, wasteful, unproductive, time-wasting, slow; deficient, disorganized, unsystematic.

inelegant adjective **1** *an inelegant bellow of laughter:* **unrefined**, uncouth, unsophisticated, unpolished, uncultivated; ill-bred, coarse, vulgar, rude, impolite, unmannerly. **2** *inelegant dancing:* **graceless**, ungraceful, ungainly, uncoordinated, awkward, clumsy, lumbering; inept, unskilful, inexpert; informal having two left feet.
– OPPOSITES refined, graceful.

ineligible adjective *we are ineligible for a grant:* **unqualified**, ruled out, disqualified, not entitled to.

inept adjective *my attempts at baking were inept, but I fumbled on:* **incompetent**, unskilful, unskilled, inexpert, amateurish; clumsy, awkward, maladroit, unhandy, bungling, blundering; unproductive, unsuccessful, ineffectual, not up to scratch; informal cack-handed, ham-fisted, butterfingered, klutzy; Brit. informal all (fingers and) thumbs.
– OPPOSITES competent.

inequality noun *a society without social inequality:* **imbalance**, inequity, inconsistency, variation, variability; divergence, polarity, disparity, discrepancy, dissimilarity, difference; bias, prejudice, discrimination, unfairness.

inequitable adjective *a crude and inequitable process for setting salary rates:* **unfair**, unjust, unequal, uneven, unbalanced, one-sided, discriminatory, preferential, biased, partisan, partial, prejudiced.
– OPPOSITES fair.

inert adjective *she lay inert in her bed:* **unmoving**, motionless, immobile, inanimate, still, stationary, static; dormant, sleeping; unconscious, comatose, lifeless, insensible, insensate, insentient; idle, inactive, sluggish, lethargic, stagnant, listless, torpid.
– OPPOSITES active.

inertia noun *he showed signs of lapsing into inertia:* **inactivity**, inaction, inertness; apathy, accidie, malaise, stagnation, enervation, lethargy, listlessness, torpor, idleness, sloth; motionlessness, immobility, lifelessness.

inescapable adjective *they concluded that political reform was inescapable:* **unavoidable**, inevitable, ineluctable, inexorable; assured, sure, certain; necessary, required, compulsory, mandatory .
– OPPOSITES avoidable.

inessential adjective *he cut out the inessential details:* **unnecessary**, nonessential, unwanted, uncalled-for, needless, redundant, superfluous, excessive, surplus, dispensable, expendable; unimportant, peripheral, minor, secondary.

inestimable adjective *he believes the diet brings inestimable benefits:* **immeasurable**, incalculable, innumerable, unfathomable, indeterminable, measureless, untold; limitless, boundless, unlimited, infinite, endless, inexhaustible; informal no end of.
– OPPOSITES few.

inevitable adjective *his resignation was inevitable:* **unavoidable**, inescapable, inexorable, ineluctable; assured, certain, sure; fated, predestined, predetermined.
– OPPOSITES uncertain.

inevitably adverb *the poor crop will inevitably affect the price of wine:* **naturally**, necessarily, automatically, as a matter of course, of necessity, inescapably, unavoidably, certainly, surely, definitely, undoubtedly; informal like it or not.

inexact adjective *his description of the procedure is inexact:* **imprecise**, inaccurate, approximate, rough, crude, general, vague; incorrect, erroneous, wrong, false; off, out; N. Amer. informal ballpark.

inexcusable adjective *Geoffrey's behaviour was inexcusable:* **indefensible**, unjustifiable, unwarranted, unpardonable, unforgivable; blameworthy, censurable, reprehensible, deplorable, unconscionable, unacceptable, unreasonable; uncalled-for, unprovoked, gratuitous.

inexhaustible adjective **1** *her patience is inexhaustible:* **unlimited**, limitless, illimitable, infinite, boundless, endless, never-ending, unfailing, everlasting; immeasurable, incalculable, inestimable, untold; copious, abundant. **2** *the dancers were inexhaustible:* **tireless**, indefatigable, untiring, unfaltering, unflagging, unremitting, persevering, persistent, dogged.
– OPPOSITES limited, weary.

inexorable adjective **1** *the inexorable advance of science:* **relentless**, unstoppable, inescapable, inevitable, unavoidable, irrevocable; persistent, continuous, non-stop, steady, interminable, incessant, unceasing, unremitting, unrelenting. **2** *inexorable creditors:* **intransigent**, unbending, unyielding, inflexible, adamant, obdurate, immovable, unshakeable; implacable, unappeasable, unforgiving, unsparing, uncompromising, ruthless, relentless, pitiless, merciless.

inexpensive adjective *a retail chain specializing in inexpensive furniture:* **cheap**, low-priced, low-cost, economical, competitive, affordable, reasonable, budget, economy, bargain, cut-price, reduced, discounted, discount, rock-bottom, giveaway, bargain-basement; informal dirt cheap.

inexperience noun **ignorance**, unworldliness, naivety, naiveness, innocence, greenness, immaturity.

inexperienced adjective *the new secretary was enthusiastic but inexperienced:* **inexpert**, unpractised, untrained, unschooled, unqualified, unskilled, amateur; ignorant, unversed, unseasoned; naive, unsophisticated, callow, immature, green; informal wet behind the ears, wide-eyed.

inexpert adjective *the crane was manoeuvred by inexpert operators:* **unskilled**, unskilful, amateur, amateurish, unprofessional, inexperienced; inept, incompetent, maladroit, clumsy, bungling, blundering, unhandy; informal cack-handed, ham-fisted, butterfingered.

inexplicable adjective *she had an inexplicable change of heart:* **unaccountable**, unexplainable, incomprehensible, unfathomable, impenetrable, insoluble; baffling, puzzling, perplexing, mystifying, bewildering; mysterious, strange.
– OPPOSITES understandable.

inexpressible adjective *he felt inexpressible gratitude towards her:* **indescribable**, undefinable, unutterable, unspeakable, ineffable, beyond words; unimaginable, inconceivable, unthinkable, untold.

inexpressive adjective *their faces were utterly inexpressive:* **expressionless**, impassive, emotionless; inscrutable, unreadable, blank, vacant, glazed, lifeless, deadpan, wooden, stony; poker-faced, straight-faced.

inextricable adjective **1** *our lives are inextricable:* **inseparable**, indivisible, entangled, tangled, mixed up. **2** *an inextricable situation:* **inescapable**, unavoidable, ineluctable.

infallible adjective **1** *an infallible sense of timing:* **unerring**, unfailing, faultless, flawless, impeccable, perfect, precise, accurate, meticulous, scrupulous; Brit. informal spot on. **2** *infallible cures:* **unfailing**, guaranteed, dependable, trustworthy, reliable, sure, certain, safe, foolproof, effective; informal sure-fire.

infamous adjective **1** *an infamous mass murderer:* **notorious**, disreputable; legendary, fabled. **2** *infamous misconduct:* **abominable**, outrageous, shocking, shameful, disgraceful, dishonourable, discreditable, unworthy; monstrous, atrocious, appalling, dreadful, terrible, heinous, egregious, detestable, loathsome,

hateful, vile, unspeakable, unforgivable, iniquitous, scandalous; informal dirty, filthy, low-down; Brit. informal beastly.
– OPPOSITES reputable, honourable.

infamy noun **1** *these acts brought him infamy:* **notoriety**, disrepute, ill fame, disgrace, discredit, shame, dishonour, ignominy, scandal, censure, blame, disapprobation, condemnation. **2** *she was punished for her infamy:* **wickedness**, evil, vileness, iniquity, depravity, degeneracy, immorality; sin, wrongdoing, offence, abuse.

infancy noun **1** *she died in infancy:* **babyhood**, early childhood. **2** *the infancy of broadcasting:* **beginnings**, early days, early stages; seeds, roots; start, commencement, launch, debut, rise, emergence, dawn, birth, inception.
– OPPOSITES end.

infant noun *a fretful infant:* **baby**, newborn, young child, (tiny) tot, little one; Scottish & N. English bairn, wean; informal tiny, sprog.
adjective *infant industries:* **developing**, emergent, emerging, embryonic, nascent, new, fledgling, budding, up-and-coming.

infantile adjective *he refused to play their infantile games:* **childish**, babyish, immature, puerile, juvenile, adolescent; silly, inane, fatuous.

infantry noun **infantrymen**, foot soldiers, foot guards; the ranks; cannon fodder; US GIs; Brit. informal Tommies.

infatuated adjective *Sarah seemed to be infatuated with John:* **besotted**, in love, head over heels, obsessed, taken; enamoured of, attracted to, devoted to, captivated by, enchanted by, bewitched by, under the spell of; informal smitten with, sweet on, keen on, gone on, mad about, crazy about, stuck on, bowled over by, carrying a torch for.

infatuation noun **passion**, love, adoration, desire, feeling, devotion; obsession, fixation; fancy; informal crush, thing, hang-up, pash.

infect verb **1** *the ill can infect their partners:* **pass infection to**, spread disease to, contaminate. **2** *nitrates were infecting rivers:* **contaminate**, pollute, taint, foul, dirty, blight, damage, ruin; poison. **3** *his high spirits infected everyone:* **affect**, influence, impact on, touch; excite, inspire, stimulate, animate.

infection noun *a kidney infection:* **disease**, virus; disorder, condition, affliction, complaint, illness, ailment, sickness, infirmity; informal bug; Brit. informal lurgy. **2** *the infection in his wounds:* **contamination**, poison; septicity, septicaemia, suppuration, inflammation; germs, bacteria.

infectious adjective **1** *an infectious disease:* **contagious**, communicable, transmittable, transmissible, transferable, spreadable; epidemic; informal catching. **2** *the dogs may still be infectious:* **contaminating**, germ-laden, polluting; poisonous, toxic, noxious. **3** *her laughter is infectious:* **irresistible**, compelling, contagious, catching.

infer verb *the judge inferred that the deceased was murdered:* **deduce**, conclude, conjecture, surmise, reason; gather, understand, presume, assume, take it; read between the lines; N. Amer. figure; Brit. informal suss (out).

inference noun **deduction**, conclusion, reasoning, conjecture, speculation, presumption, assumption, supposition, reckoning, extrapolation; guesswork.

inferior adjective **1** *she regards him as inferior:* **second-class**, lower-ranking, subordinate, second-fiddle, junior, minor, lowly, humble, menial, beneath one. **2** *inferior accommodation:* **second-rate**, substandard, low-quality, low-grade, unsatisfactory, shoddy, deficient; poor, bad, awful, dreadful, wretched; Brit. downmarket; informal crummy, dire, rotten, lousy, third-rate; Brit. informal duff, rubbish, ropy, dodgy.
– OPPOSITES superior, luxury.
noun *how dare she treat him as an inferior?* **subordinate**, junior, underling, minion.

infernal adjective **1** *the infernal regions:* **hellish**, lower, nether, subterranean, underworld, chthonic; Hadean, Tartarean. **2** (informal) *an infernal nuisance:* **damnable**, wretched; annoying, irritating, infuriating, exasperating; informal damned, damn, flaming, blasted, blessed, pesky, aggravating; Brit. informal blinking, blooming, flipping.

infertile adjective **1** *infertile soil:* **barren**, unfruitful, unproductive, uncultivatable; sterile, impoverished, arid. **2** *she was infertile:* **sterile**, barren; childless; Medicine infecund.

infest verb *her house is infested with cockroaches:* **overrun**, invade, infiltrate, pervade, permeate, inundate, overwhelm, plague; **(infested)** swarming, teeming, crawling, alive.

infidel noun *a holy war against the infidels:* **unbeliever**, disbeliever, non-believer, agnostic, atheist; heathen, pagan, idolater, idolatress, heretic, freethinker, dissenter, nonconformist.

infidelity noun *her husband never knew of her infidelity:* **unfaithfulness**, adultery, unchastity; faithlessness, disloyalty, treachery, double-dealing, duplicity, deceit; affair; informal playing around, fooling around, cheating, two-timing.

infiltrate verb *customs officers infiltrated the smuggling operation:* **insinuate oneself into**, worm one's way into, sneak into, invade, intrude on, butt into; informal gatecrash, muscle in on.

infiltrator noun *the constant vigilance needed to outwit enemy infiltrators:* **spy**, (secret) agent, plant, intruder, interloper, subversive, informant, informer, mole, entrist, entryist; N. Amer. informal spook.

infinite adjective **1** *the universe is infinite:* **boundless**, unbounded, unlimited, limitless,

i

never-ending, interminable; immeasurable, fathomless; extensive, vast. **2** *an infinite number of birds:* **countless**, uncountable, inestimable, innumerable, numberless, immeasurable, incalculable, untold; great, huge, enormous. **3** *she bathed him with infinite care:* **great**, immense, supreme, absolute, real; informal no end of.
– OPPOSITES limited, small.

infinitesimal adjective *a tiny fish with infinitesimal white scales:* **minute**, tiny, minuscule, very small; microscopic, imperceptible, indiscernible; Scottish wee; informal teeny, teeny-weeny, itsy-bitsy, tiddly; Brit. informal titchy; N. Amer. informal little-bitty.
– OPPOSITES huge.

infinity noun *the infinity of space:* **endlessness**, infinitude, infiniteness, boundlessness, limitlessness; vastness, immensity.

infirm adjective *she cares for infirm people:* **frail**, weak, feeble, debilitated, decrepit, disabled; ill, unwell, sick, sickly, poorly, indisposed, ailing.
– OPPOSITES healthy, strong.

infirmity noun **1** *they were excused due to infirmity:* **frailty**, weakness, feebleness, delicacy, debility, decrepitude; disability, impairment; illness, sickness, indisposition, poor health. **2** *the infirmities of old age:* **ailment**, malady, illness, disease, disorder, sickness, affliction, complaint, indisposition.

inflame verb **1** *the play inflames anti-semitism:* **incite**, arouse, rouse, provoke, stir up, whip up, kindle, ignite, touch off, foment, inspire, stimulate, agitate. **2** *he inflamed a sensitive situation:* **aggravate**, exacerbate, intensify, worsen, compound. **3** *his opinions inflamed his rival:* **enrage**, incense, anger, madden, infuriate, exasperate, provoke, antagonize, rile; informal make someone see red, make someone's blood boil.
– OPPOSITES calm, soothe, placate.

inflamed adjective *they treated her for inflamed skin:* **swollen**, puffed up; red, hot, burning, itchy; raw, sore, painful, tender; infected, septic.

inflammable adjective *inflammable gases:* **flammable**, combustible, incendiary, ignitable; volatile, unstable.
– OPPOSITES fireproof.

inflammation noun *inflammation of the gums:* **swelling**, puffiness; redness, heat, burning; rawness, soreness, tenderness; infection, festering, septicity.

inflammatory adjective *inflammatory language:* **provocative**, incendiary, stirring, rousing, rabble-rousing, seditious, mutinous; like a red rag to a bull; fiery, passionate; controversial, contentious.

inflate verb **1** *the mattress inflated:* **blow up**, fill up, fill with air, aerate, puff up/out, pump up; dilate, distend, swell. **2** *the demand inflated prices:* **increase**, raise,

boost, escalate, put up; informal hike up, jack up, bump up. **3** *the figures were inflated by the press:* **exaggerate**, magnify, overplay, overstate, enhance, embellish, touch up; increase, amplify, augment.
– OPPOSITES decrease, understate.

inflated adjective **1** *an inflated balloon:* **blown up**, aerated, filled, puffed up/out, pumped up; distended, expanded, engorged, swollen. **2** *inflated prices:* **high**, sky-high, excessive, unreasonable, prohibitive, outrageous, exorbitant, extortionate; Brit. over the odds; informal steep. **3** *an inflated opinion of himself:* **exaggerated**, magnified, aggrandized, immoderate, overblown, overstated. **4** *inflated language:* **high-flown**, extravagant, exaggerated, elaborate, flowery, ornate, overblown, overwrought, grandiloquent, magniloquent, lofty, grandiose; affected, pretentious; informal windy, highfalutin.

inflection noun *his voice was without inflection:* **stress**, cadence, rhythm, accentuation, intonation, emphasis, modulation, lilt.

inflexible adjective **1** *his inflexible attitude:* **stubborn**, obstinate, obdurate, intractable, intransigent, unbending, immovable, unaccommodating; hidebound, single-minded, pig-headed, mulish, uncompromising, adamant, firm, resolute, diehard, dyed-in-the-wool. **2** *inflexible rules:* **unalterable**, unchangeable, immutable, unvarying; firm, fixed, set, established, entrenched, hard and fast; stringent, strict. **3** *an inflexible structure:* **rigid**, stiff, unyielding, unbending, unbendable; hard, firm, inelastic.
– OPPOSITES accommodating, pliable.

inflict verb **1** *he inflicted an injury on Frank:* **impose**, exact, wreak; administer to, deal out to, mete out to, cause to, give to. **2** *I won't inflict my pain on my children:* **impose**, force, thrust, foist; saddle someone with, burden someone with.

infliction noun *the infliction of pain:* **administration**, delivery, application; imposition, perpetration; formal exaction.

influence noun **1** *the influence of parents on their children:* **effect**, impact; control, sway, hold, power, authority, mastery, domination, supremacy; guidance, direction; pressure. **2** *a bad influence on young girls:* **example to**, (role) model for, guide for, inspiration to. **3** *political influence:* **power**, authority, sway, leverage, weight, pull, standing, prestige, stature, rank; informal clout, muscle, teeth; N. Amer. informal drag.
verb **1** *bosses can influence our careers:* **affect**, have an impact on, determine, guide, control, shape, govern, decide; change, alter, transform. **2** *an attempt to influence the jury:* **sway**, bias, prejudice, suborn; pressurize, coerce; dragoon, intimidate, browbeat, brainwash; informal twist someone's arm, lean on; Brit. informal nobble.

influential adjective **1** *an influential leader:* **powerful**, dominant, controlling, strong, authoritative; important, prominent, distinguished. **2** *he was influential in shaping her career:* **instrumental**, significant, important, crucial, pivotal.

influx noun **1** *an influx of tourists:* **inundation**, rush, stream, flood, incursion; invasion, intrusion. **2** *influxes of river water:* **inflow**, inrush, flood, inundation.

inform verb **1** *she informed him that she was ill:* **tell**, notify, apprise, advise, impart to, communicate to, let someone know; brief, prime, enlighten, send word to; informal fill in, clue in/up. **2** *he informed on two villains:* **denounce**, give away, betray, incriminate, inculpate, report; sell out, stab in the back; informal rat, squeal, split, tell, blow the whistle, sell down the river, snitch, peach, stitch up; Brit. informal grass, shop, sneak; Scottish informal clype; N. Amer. informal rat out, finger; Austral./NZ informal dob. **3** *the articles were informed by feminism:* **suffuse**, pervade, permeate, infuse, imbue; characterize, typify.

informal adjective **1** *an informal discussion:* **unofficial**, casual, relaxed, easy-going, unceremonious; open, friendly, intimate; simple, unpretentious, easy, homely, cosy; informal unstuffy, laid-back, chummy, pally, matey. **2** *an informal speech style:* **colloquial**, vernacular, idiomatic, demotic, popular; familiar, everyday, unofficial; simple, natural, unpretentious; informal slangy, chatty, folksy. **3** *informal clothes:* **casual**, relaxed, comfortable, everyday, sloppy, leisure; informal comfy.
– OPPOSITES formal, official, literary, smart.

informality noun **lack of ceremony**, casualness, unceremoniousness, unpretentiousness; homeliness, cosiness, ease, naturalness, approachability.

information noun *for further information write to the address below:* **details**, particulars, facts, figures, statistics, data; knowledge, intelligence; instruction, advice, guidance, direction, counsel, enlightenment; news; informal info, gen, the low-down, the dope, the inside story.

informative adjective *an informative booklet:* **instructive**, instructional, illuminating, enlightening, revealing, explanatory; factual, educational, educative, edifying, didactic; informal newsy.

informed adjective *an informed society:* **knowledgeable**, enlightened, literate, educated; sophisticated, cultured; briefed, up to date, up to speed, in the picture, in the know, au courant, au fait; informal clued up, genned up; Brit. informal switched-on, sussed.
– OPPOSITES ignorant.

informer noun *the police had a good network of informers:* **informant**, betrayer, traitor, Judas, collaborator, stool pigeon, fifth columnist, spy, double agent, infiltrator, plant; telltale, taleteller; N. Amer. tattletale; informal rat, squealer, whistle-blower, snake in the grass, snitch; Brit. informal grass, supergrass, nark, snout; Scottish informal clype; N. Amer. informal fink, stoolie.

infrequent adjective *his infrequent trips abroad:* **rare**, uncommon, unusual, exceptional, few (and far between), like gold dust, as scarce as hens' teeth; unaccustomed, unwonted; isolated, scarce, scattered; sporadic, irregular, intermittent; informal once in a blue moon.
– OPPOSITES common.

infringe verb **1** *the bid infringed EU rules:* **contravene**, violate, transgress, break, breach; disobey, defy, flout, fly in the face of; disregard, ignore, neglect; go beyond, overstep, exceed; Law infract. **2** *surveillance could infringe personal liberties:* **undermine**, erode, diminish, weaken, impair, damage, compromise; limit, curb, check, encroach on.
– OPPOSITES obey, preserve.

infuriate verb *his arrogance was beginning to infuriate her:* **enrage**, incense, anger, madden, inflame; exasperate, antagonize, provoke, rile, annoy, irritate, nettle, gall, irk, vex, pique, get on someone's nerves, try someone's patience; N. Amer. rankle; informal aggravate, make someone see red, get someone's back up, make someone's blood boil, get up someone's nose, needle, hack off, brown off; Brit. informal wind up, get to, nark, cheese off; N. Amer. informal bug, tick off.
– OPPOSITES please.

infuriating adjective **exasperating**, maddening, annoying, irritating, irksome, vexatious, trying, tiresome; informal aggravating, pesky.

infuse verb **1** *she was infused with a sense of hope:* **fill**, suffuse, imbue, inspire, charge, pervade, permeate. **2** *he infused new life into the group:* **instil**, breathe, inject, impart, inculcate, introduce, add. **3** *infuse the dried leaves:* **steep**, brew, stew, soak, immerse, souse; Brit. informal mash.

ingenious adjective *an ingenious solution:* **inventive**, creative, imaginative, original, innovative, pioneering, resourceful, enterprising, inspired; clever, intelligent, smart, brilliant, masterly, talented, gifted, skilful; astute, sharp-witted, quick-witted, shrewd; elaborate, sophisticated.

ingenuous adjective *he looked at her with wide ingenuous eyes:* **naive**, innocent, simple, childlike, trusting, trustful, over-trusting, unwary; unsuspicious, unworldly, wide-eyed, inexperienced, green; open, sincere, honest, frank, candid, forthright, artless, guileless, genuine.
– OPPOSITES artful.

inglorious adjective *an inglorious retreat:* **shameful**, dishonourable, ignominious, discreditable, disgraceful, scandalous;

humiliating, mortifying, demeaning,
ignoble, undignified, wretched.

ingrained, engrained adjective
1 *ingrained attitudes:* **entrenched**,
established, deep-rooted, deep-seated, fixed,
firm, unshakeable, ineradicable; inveterate,
dyed-in-the-wool, abiding, enduring,
stubborn. **2** *ingrained dirt:* **ground-in**, fixed,
implanted, embedded; permanent, indelible,
ineradicable, inexpungible.
– OPPOSITES transient, superficial.

ingratiate
■ **ingratiate oneself** *he was determined to
ingratiate himself with Stephen:* curry favour
with, cultivate, win over, get in someone's
good books; toady to, crawl to, grovel to,
fawn over, kowtow to, play up to, pander to,
flatter, court; informal suck up to, rub up the
right way, lick someone's boots.

ingratiating adjective *he sidled up to her
with an ingratiating smile:* **sycophantic**,
toadying, fawning, unctuous, obsequious,
flattering, insincere; smooth-tongued,
silver-tongued, slick; greasy, oily,
saccharine; informal smarmy, slimy, creepy,
sucky.

ingratitude noun *Harry was fuming at her
ingratitude:* **ungratefulness**, thanklessness,
unthankfulness, non-recognition.

ingredient noun *investment is an essential
ingredient of corporate success:* **constituent**,
component, element; part, piece, bit, strand,
portion, unit, feature, aspect, attribute;
(**ingredients**) contents, makings.

inhabit verb *the greater part of this area is
inhabited by Kurds:* **live in**, occupy; settle
(in), people, populate, colonize; dwell in,
reside in, tenant, lodge in, have one's home
in.

inhabitable adjective *an inhabitable
apartment:* **habitable**, fit to live in, usable;
informal liveable-in.

inhabitant noun *the inhabitants of the
village:* **resident**, occupant, occupier,
dweller, settler; local, native; (**inhabitants**)
population, populace, people, public,
community, citizenry, townsfolk,
townspeople.

inhale verb *he inhaled smoke deeply:* **breathe
in**, inspire, draw in, suck in, sniff in, drink
in.

inherent adjective *his belief in the inherent
goodness of man:* **intrinsic**, innate,
connate, connatural, immanent, built-in,
inborn, ingrained, deep-rooted; essential,
fundamental, basic, structural, organic;
natural, instinctive, instinctual, congenital,
native.
– OPPOSITES acquired.

inherit verb **1** *she inherited his farm:* **become
heir to**, come into/by, be bequeathed, be
left, be willed; Law be devised. **2** *Richard
inherited the title:* **succeed to**, assume, take
over, come into.

inheritance noun **1** *a comfortable*

inheritance: **legacy**, bequest, endowment,
bestowal, bequeathal, provision; birthright,
heritage, patrimony. **2** *his inheritance of the
title:* **succession to**, accession to, assumption
of, elevation to.

inheritor noun **heir**, heiress, legatee;
successor, next in line; Law devisee, grantee;
Scottish Law heritor.

inhibit verb **1** *the obstacles which inhibit
change:* **impede**, hinder, hamper, hold
back, discourage, interfere with, obstruct,
slow down, retard; curb, check, suppress,
restrict, fetter, cramp, frustrate, stifle,
prevent, block, thwart, foil, stop, halt. **2** *she
feels inhibited from taking part:* **prevent**,
disallow, exclude, forbid, prohibit, preclude,
ban, bar, interdict.
– OPPOSITES assist, encourage, allow.

inhibited adjective *older people are
sometimes inhibited about discussing
the past:* **shy**, reticent, reserved, self-
conscious, diffident, bashful, coy; wary,
reluctant, hesitant, insecure, unconfident,
unassertive, timid; withdrawn, repressed,
undemonstrative; informal uptight.

inhibition noun *they overcame their
inhibitions:* **shyness**, reticence, self-
consciousness, reserve, diffidence;
wariness, hesitance, hesitancy, insecurity;
unassertiveness, timidity; repression,
reservation; psychological block; informal
hang-up.

inhospitable adjective **1** *the inhospitable
landscape:* **uninviting**, unwelcoming;
bleak, forbidding, cheerless, hostile,
harsh, inimical; uninhabitable, barren,
bare, desolate, stark. **2** *forgive me if
I seem inhospitable:* **unwelcoming**,
unfriendly, unsociable, unsocial, antisocial,
unneighbourly, uncongenial; aloof, cool,
cold, frosty, distant, remote, indifferent,
offhand; uncivil, discourteous, ungracious,
ungenerous, unkind, unsympathetic; informal
stand-offish.
– OPPOSITES welcoming.

inhuman adjective **1** *inhuman treatment:*
cruel, harsh, inhumane, brutal, callous,
sadistic, severe, savage, vicious, barbaric;
monstrous, heinous, egregious; merciless,
ruthless, pitiless, remorseless, cold-
blooded, heartless, hard-hearted; unkind,
inconsiderate, unfeeling, uncaring; Brit.
informal beastly. **2** *hellish and inhuman
shapes:* **non-human**, non-mortal, monstrous,
devilish, ghostly; subhuman, animal;
strange, odd, unearthly.
– OPPOSITES humane.

inimical adjective **1** *this is inimical to genuine
democracy:* **harmful**, injurious, detrimental,
deleterious, prejudicial, damaging, hurtful,
destructive, ruinous; antagonistic, contrary,
antipathetic, unfavourable, adverse,
opposed, hostile. **2** *he fixed her with
an inimical gaze:* **hostile**, unfriendly,
antagonistic, unkind, unsympathetic,
malevolent; unwelcoming, cold, frosty.

– OPPOSITES advantageous, friendly.

inimitable adjective *in his own inimitable style he provides sound advice:* **unique**, exclusive, distinctive, individual, special, idiosyncratic; incomparable, unparalleled, unrivalled, peerless, matchless, unequalled, unsurpassable, superlative, supreme, beyond compare, second to none, in a class of one's own.

iniquity noun *the iniquity of his conduct:* **wickedness**, sinfulness, immorality, impropriety; vice, evil, sin, crime, wrong, wrongdoing; villainy, criminality; odiousness, atrocity, egregiousness; monstrosity, obscenity, reprehensibility.
– OPPOSITES goodness, virtue.

initial adjective *the initial stages:* **beginning**, opening, commencing, starting, inceptive, embryonic, fledgling; first, early, primary, preliminary, elementary, foundational, preparatory; introductory, inaugural.
– OPPOSITES final.
plural noun *what do the initials stand for?* **abbreviation**, acronym, initialism.
verb **1** *he initialled the warrant:* **put one's initials on**, sign, countersign, autograph, endorse, inscribe, witness. **2** *they initialled a new agreement:* **ratify**, accept, approve, authorize, validate, recognize.

initially adverb *initially, Steve cleared tables and washed up:* **at first**, at the start, at the outset, in/at the beginning, to begin with, to start with, originally.

initiate verb **1** *the government initiated the scheme:* **begin**, start (off), commence; institute, inaugurate, launch, instigate, establish, put in place, set up, sow the seeds of, start the ball rolling; originate, pioneer; informal kick off. **2** *he was initiated into a cult:* **introduce**, admit, induct, install, incorporate, enlist, enrol, recruit, sign up, swear in; ordain, invest. **3** *they were initiated into the world of maths:* **teach about**, instruct in, tutor in, school in, prime in, ground in; familiarize with, acquaint with; indoctrinate, inculcate; informal show someone the ropes.
– OPPOSITES finish, expel.
noun *an initiate on the team:* **novice**, starter, beginner, newcomer; learner, student, pupil, trainee, apprentice; new boy, new girl, recruit, tyro, neophyte; postulant, novitiate; informal rookie, new kid (on the block), newie, newbie, greenhorn.

initiative noun **1** *employers are looking for initiative:* **enterprise**, resourcefulness, inventiveness, imagination, ingenuity, originality, creativity; drive, dynamism, ambition, motivation, spirit, energy, vision; informal get-up-and-go, pep, punch. **2** *he has lost the initiative:* **advantage**, upper hand, edge, lead, whip hand, trump card. **3** *a recent initiative on recycling:* **plan**, scheme, strategy, stratagem, measure, proposal, step, action, approach.

inject verb **1** *he injected a dose of codeine:*

administer, introduce; inoculate, vaccinate; informal shoot (up), mainline, fix (up). **2** *a pump injects air into the valve:* **insert**, introduce, feed, push, force, shoot. **3** *he injected new life into the team:* **introduce**, instil, infuse, imbue, breathe.

injection noun *an anti-tetanus injection:* **inoculation**, vaccination, vaccine, immunization, booster; dose; informal jab, shot, hype.

injudicious adjective *he will probably pay dearly for his injudicious comments:* **imprudent**, unwise, inadvisable, ill-advised, misguided; ill-considered, ill-judged, incautious, hasty, rash, foolish, foolhardy, hare-brained; inappropriate, impolitic, inexpedient; informal dumb.
– OPPOSITES prudent.

injunction noun *a High Court injunction to prevent Sunday trading:* **order**, ruling, direction, directive, command, instruction; decree, edict, dictum, dictate, fiat, mandate.

injure verb **1** *he injured his foot:* **hurt**, wound, damage, harm; cripple, lame, disable; maim, mutilate, deform, mangle, break; Brit. informal knacker. **2** *a libel injured her reputation:* **damage**, mar, spoil, ruin, blight, blemish, tarnish, blacken.

injured adjective **1** *his injured arm:* **hurt**, wounded, damaged, sore, bruised; crippled, lame, game, disabled; maimed, mutilated, deformed, mangled, broken, fractured; Brit. informal gammy. **2** *the injured party:* **wronged**, offended, maltreated, mistreated, ill-used, harmed; defamed, maligned, insulted, dishonoured. **3** *an injured tone:* **upset**, hurt, wounded, offended, reproachful, pained, aggrieved, unhappy, put out.
– OPPOSITES healthy, offending.

injurious adjective *food which is injurious to health:* **harmful**, damaging, deleterious, detrimental, hurtful; disadvantageous, unfavourable, undesirable, adverse, inimical, unhealthy, pernicious.

injury noun **1** *minor injuries:* **wound**, bruise, cut, gash, scratch, graze, abrasion, contusion, lesion. **2** *they escaped without injury:* **harm**, hurt, damage, pain, suffering, impairment, affliction, incapacity. **3** *the injury to her feelings:* **offence**, abuse; affront, insult, slight, snub; wrong, wrongdoing, injustice.

injustice noun **1** *the injustice of the world:* **unfairness**, unjustness, inequity; cruelty, tyranny, repression, exploitation, corruption; bias, prejudice, discrimination, intolerance. **2** *his sacking was an injustice:* **wrong**, offence, crime, sin, misdeed, outrage, atrocity, scandal, disgrace, affront.

inkling noun *I had an inkling of what was going on:* **idea**, notion, sense, impression, suggestion, indication, whisper, glimmer, (sneaking) suspicion, fancy, hunch; hint, clue, intimation, sign; informal the foggiest (idea), the faintest (idea).

inky adjective **1** *the inky darkness:* **black**,

jet-black, pitch-black; sable, ebony, dark.
2 *inky fingers:* **ink-stained**, stained, blotchy.

inlaid adjective *a plaque inlaid with mother of pearl:* **inset**, set, studded, lined, panelled; ornamented, decorated; mosaic, intarsia, marquetry.

inland adjective **1** *inland areas:* **interior**, inshore, central, internal, upcountry. **2** *inland trade:* **domestic**, internal, home, local.
– OPPOSITES coastal, international.
adverb *the goods were carried inland:* **upcountry**, inshore, to the interior.

inlet noun **1** *coastal inlets:* **cove**, bay, bight, creek, estuary, fjord, sound; Scottish firth. **2** *a fresh air inlet:* **vent**, flue, shaft, duct, channel, pipe, pipeline.

inmate noun **1** *the inmates of the hospital:* **patient**, inpatient; convalescent; resident, inhabitant, occupant. **2** *the prison's inmates:* **prisoner**, convict, captive, detainee, internee; informal jailbird, con; Brit. informal lag; N. Amer. informal yardbird.

inmost adjective. See **INNERMOST**.

inn noun **tavern**, bar, hostelry, taproom; hotel, guest house; Brit. pub, public house; Canadian beer parlour; informal watering hole.

innate adjective *people differ in terms of their innate abilities:* **inborn**, inbred, congenital, inherent, natural, intrinsic, instinctive, intuitive, unlearned; hereditary, inherited, in the blood, in the family; inbuilt, deep-rooted, deep-seated, connate, connatural.
– OPPOSITES acquired.

inner adjective **1** *inner London:* **central**, innermost, mid, middle. **2** *the inner gates:* **internal**, interior, inside, inmost, innermost, intramural. **3** *the Queen's inner circle:* **privileged**, restricted, exclusive, private, confidential, intimate. **4** *the inner meaning:* **hidden**, secret, deep, underlying, unapparent; veiled, esoteric, unrevealed. **5** *one's inner life:* **mental**, intellectual, psychological, spiritual, emotional.
– OPPOSITES external, apparent.

innermost adjective **1** *the innermost shrine:* **central**, middle, internal, interior. **2** *her innermost feelings:* **deepest**, deep-seated, inward, underlying, intimate, private, personal, secret, hidden, concealed, unexpressed, unrevealed, unapparent; true, real, honest.

innkeeper noun **landlord**, landlady, hotelier, hotel owner, proprietor, manager, manageress; licensee, barman, barmaid; Brit. publican.

innocence noun **1** *he protested his innocence:* **guiltlessness**, blamelessness, irreproachability. **2** *the youthfulness and innocence of his bride:* **virginity**, chastity, chasteness, purity; integrity, morality, decency. **3** *she took advantage of his innocence:* **naivety**, ingenuousness, credulity, inexperience, gullibility, simplicity, unworldliness, guilelessness, greenness.

innocent adjective **1** *he was entirely innocent:* **guiltless**, blameless, in the clear, unimpeachable, irreproachable, above suspicion, faultless; honourable, honest, upright, law-abiding; informal squeaky clean. **2** *a bit of innocent fun:* **harmless**, innocuous, safe, inoffensive. **3** *nice innocent girls:* **virtuous**, pure, moral, decent, righteous, upright, wholesome; demure, modest, chaste, virginal; impeccable, spotless, sinless, unsullied, incorrupt, undefiled; informal squeaky clean, whiter than white. **4** *she is innocent of guile:* **free from**, without, lacking (in), clear of, ignorant of, unaware of, untouched by. **5** *innocent foreigners were exploited:* **naive**, ingenuous, trusting, credulous, unsuspicious, unwary, unguarded; impressionable, gullible, easily led; inexperienced, unworldly, unsophisticated, green; simple, artless, guileless; informal wet behind the ears, born yesterday.
– OPPOSITES guilty, sinful, worldly, malignant.
noun *an innocent in a strange land:* **ingénue**, unworldly person; child; novice; N. Amer. informal greenhorn.

innocuous adjective **1** *an innocuous fungus:* **harmless**, safe, non-toxic, innocent; edible, eatable. **2** *an innocuous comment:* **inoffensive**, unobjectionable, unexceptionable, harmless, mild, tame; anodyne, unremarkable, commonplace, run-of-the-mill.
– OPPOSITES harmful, offensive.

innovation noun *they favoured the traditional approach and resisted innovation:* **change**, alteration, revolution, upheaval, transformation, metamorphosis; reorganization, restructuring, rearrangement, remodelling; new measures, new methods, modernization, modernism; novelty, newness; informal a shake up, a shakedown.

innovative adjective *the store's products are innovative and effective:* **original**, innovatory, innovational, new, novel, fresh, unusual, unprecedented, avant-garde, experimental, inventive, ingenious; advanced, modern, state-of-the-art, pioneering, groundbreaking, revolutionary, radical, newfangled.

innovator noun *the 19th century's prolific scientific innovators:* **pioneer**, trailblazer, pathfinder, groundbreaker; developer, modernizer, reformer, reformist, progressive; experimenter, inventor, creator.

innuendo noun *he became the butt for their smutty innuendoes:* **insinuation**, suggestion, intimation, implication, hint, overtone, undertone, allusion, reference; aspersion, slur.

innumerable adjective *she served on innumerable committees:* **countless**, numerous, untold, legion, without number, numberless, unnumbered, multitudinous, incalculable, limitless; informal umpteen, a slew of, no end of, loads of, stacks of, heaps of, masses of, oodles of, zillions of; N. Amer. informal gazillions of.
– OPPOSITES few.

inoculate verb *he inoculated his patients against smallpox:* **immunize**, vaccinate, inject; protect from, safeguard against; informal give someone a jab/shot.

inoculation noun **immunization**, vaccination, vaccine; injection, booster; informal jab, shot.

inoffensive adjective *the victim was an inoffensive law-abiding citizen:* **harmless**, innocuous, unobjectionable, unexceptionable; non-violent, non-aggressive, mild, peaceful, peaceable, gentle; tame, innocent.

inoperable adjective **1** *an inoperable tumour:* **untreatable**, incurable, irremediable; malignant; terminal, fatal, deadly, lethal. **2** *the airfield was left inoperable:* **unusable**, out of action, out of service, non-active. **3** *the agreement is now inoperable:* **impractical**, unworkable, unfeasible, unrealistic, non-viable, impracticable, unsuitable.
– OPPOSITES curable, workable.

inoperative adjective **1** *the fan is inoperative:* **out of order**, out of service, broken, out of commission, unserviceable, faulty, defective; down; informal bust, kaput, on the blink, acting up, shot; Brit. informal knackered. **2** *the contract is inoperative:* **void**, null and void, invalid, ineffective, non-viable; cancelled, revoked, terminated; worthless, valueless, unproductive, abortive.
– OPPOSITES working, valid.

inopportune adjective *she turned up at the most inopportune moment:* **inconvenient**, unsuitable, inappropriate, unfavourable, unfortunate, infelicitous, inexpedient; untimely, ill-timed, unseasonable; awkward, difficult.
– OPPOSITES convenient.

inordinate adjective *the job had taken an inordinate amount of time:* **excessive**, undue, unreasonable, unjustifiable, unwarrantable, disproportionate, unwarranted, unnecessary, needless, uncalled for, exorbitant, extreme; immoderate, extravagant; informal over the top, OTT.
– OPPOSITES moderate.

inorganic adjective *the spontaneous generation of life from inorganic matter:* **inanimate**, inert; lifeless, dead, defunct, extinct; mineral.

input noun *an error resulted from invalid input:* **data**, details, information, material; facts, figures, statistics, particulars, specifics; informal info.
verb *she input data into the file:* **feed in**, put in, load, insert; key in, type in; code, store.

inquest noun *they held an inquest into the death of her daughter:* **inquiry**, investigation, inquisition, probe, examination, review, analysis; hearing.

inquire, inquiring, inquiry See ENQUIRE etc.

inquisition noun *she sat down opposite him and started on her inquisition:* **interrogation**, questioning, quizzing, cross-examination; investigation, inquiry, inquest; informal grilling; Law examination.

inquisitive adjective *their inquisitive neighbours had gathered at the gate:* **curious**, interested, intrigued, agog; prying, spying, eavesdropping, intrusive, busybody, meddlesome; inquiring, questioning, probing; informal nosy, nosy-parker, snoopy.
– OPPOSITES uninterested.

insalubrious adjective *he moved from one insalubrious dwelling to another:* **seedy**, unsavoury, sordid, seamy, sleazy, unpleasant, dismal, wretched; slummy, squalid, shabby, ramshackle, tumbledown, dilapidated, neglected, crumbling, decaying; informal scruffy, scuzzy, crummy; Brit. informal grotty; N. Amer. informal shacky.
– OPPOSITES smart.

insane adjective **1** *she was declared insane:* **mentally ill**, mentally disordered, of unsound mind, certifiable; psychotic, schizophrenic; mad, deranged, demented, out of one's mind, non compos mentis, sick in the head, unhinged, unbalanced, unstable, disturbed, crazed; informal crazy, (stark) raving mad, not all there, bonkers, cracked, batty, cuckoo, loony, loopy, nuts, screwy, bananas, wacko, off one's rocker, off one's head, round the bend; Brit. informal crackers, barmy, barking (mad), off one's trolley, round the twist, not the full shilling; N. Amer. informal buggy, nutso, out of one's tree; Austral./NZ informal bushed. **2** *an insane suggestion:* **foolish**, idiotic, stupid, silly, senseless, nonsensical, absurd, ridiculous, ludicrous, preposterous, fatuous, inane, asinine, hare-brained, half-baked; impracticable, implausible, irrational, illogical; informal crazy, mad, cockeyed; Brit. informal daft, barmy.
– OPPOSITES sensible, calm.

insanitary adjective *disease spreads quickly in crowded and insanitary conditions:* **unhygienic**, unsanitary, unhealthy, insalubrious, dirty, filthy, unclean, impure, contaminated, polluted, foul; infected, infested, germ-ridden.
– OPPOSITES hygienic.

insanity noun **1** *insanity runs in her family:* **mental illness**, madness, dementia; lunacy, instability; mania, psychosis; informal craziness. **2** *it would be insanity to take this loan:* **folly**, foolishness, madness, idiocy, stupidity, lunacy, silliness; informal craziness.

insatiable adjective *Steve had an insatiable appetite for apple pudding:* **unquenchable**, unappeasable, uncontrollable; voracious, gluttonous, greedy, hungry, ravenous, wolfish; avid, eager, keen; informal piggy.

inscribe verb **1** *his name was inscribed above the door:* **carve**, write, engrave, etch, cut; imprint, stamp, impress, mark. **2** *a book inscribed to him by the author:* **dedicate**, address, name, sign.

inscription noun **1** *the inscription on the sarcophagus:* **engraving**, etching; wording, writing, lettering, legend, epitaph, epigraph. **2** *the book had an inscription:* **dedication**, message; signature, autograph.

inscrutable adjective **1** *her inscrutable face:* **enigmatic**, unreadable, mysterious; unexpressive, inexpressive, emotionless, unemotional, expressionless, impassive, blank, vacant, deadpan, dispassionate; informal poker-faced. **2** *God's ways are inscrutable:* **mysterious**, inexplicable, unexplainable, incomprehensible, impenetrable, unfathomable, opaque, abstruse, arcane, obscure, cryptic.
– OPPOSITES expressive, transparent.

insecure adjective **1** *an insecure young man:* **unconfident**, uncertain, unsure, doubtful, hesitant, self-conscious, unassertive, diffident, unforthcoming, shy, timid, retiring, timorous, inhibited, introverted; anxious, fearful, worried; informal mousy. **2** *insecure windows:* **unguarded**, unprotected, vulnerable, defenceless, unshielded, exposed, assailable, pregnable; unlocked, unsecured. **3** *an insecure footbridge:* **unstable**, rickety, rocky, wobbly, shaky, unsteady, precarious; weak, flimsy, unsound, unsafe; informal jerry-built; Brit. informal dicky, dodgy.
– OPPOSITES confident, stable.

insecurity noun **1** *he hid his insecurity:* **lack of confidence**, self-doubt, diffidence, unassertiveness, timidity, uncertainty, nervousness, inhibition; anxiety, worry, unease. **2** *the insecurity of our situation:* **vulnerability**, defencelessness, peril, danger; instability, fragility, frailty, shakiness, unreliability.

insensible adjective **1** *she was insensible on the floor:* **unconscious**, insensate, senseless, insentient, inert, comatose, knocked out, passed out, blacked out; stunned, numb, numbed; informal out (cold), out for the count, out of it, zonked (out), dead to the world; Brit. informal spark out. **2** *he was insensible to the risks:* **unaware of**, ignorant of, unconscious of, unmindful of, oblivious to; indifferent to, impervious to, deaf to, blind to, unaffected by; informal in the dark about. **3** *he scared even the most insensible person:* **insensitive**, dispassionate, cool, emotionless, unfeeling, unconcerned, detached, indifferent, hardened, tough; informal hard-boiled.

– OPPOSITES conscious, aware, sensitive.

insensitive adjective **1** *an insensitive bully:* **heartless**, unfeeling, inconsiderate, thoughtless, thick-skinned; hard-hearted, cold-blooded, uncaring, unconcerned, unsympathetic, unkind, callous, cruel, merciless, pitiless. **2** *he was insensitive to her feelings:* **impervious to**, oblivious to, unaware of, unresponsive to, indifferent to, unaffected by, unmoved by, untouched by; informal in the dark about.
– OPPOSITES compassionate.

inseparable adjective **1** *inseparable friends:* **devoted**, bosom, close, fast, firm, good, best, intimate, boon, faithful; informal as thick as thieves. **2** *the laws are inseparable:* **indivisible**, indissoluble, inextricable, entangled; (one and) the same.

insert verb **1** *he inserted a tape in the machine:* **put**, place, push, thrust, slide, slip, load, fit, slot, lodge, install; informal pop, stick, bung. **2** *she inserted a clause in the contract:* **enter**, introduce, incorporate, interpolate, interpose, interject.
– OPPOSITES extract, remove.
noun *the newspaper carried an insert:* **enclosure**, insertion, inlay, supplement; circular, advertisement, pamphlet, leaflet; informal ad.

inside noun *the inside of a volcano:* **interior**, inner part; centre, core, middle, heart.
– OPPOSITES exterior.
adjective **1** *his inside pocket:* **inner**, interior, internal, innermost. **2** *inside information:* **confidential**, classified, restricted, privileged, private, secret, exclusive; informal hush-hush.
– OPPOSITES outer, public.
adverb **1** *she ushered me inside:* **indoors**, within, in. **2** *how do you feel inside?* **inwardly**, within, secretly, privately, deep down, at heart, emotionally, intuitively, instinctively. **3** (informal) *if I burgle again I'll be back inside:* **in prison**, in jail, in custody; locked up, imprisoned, incarcerated; informal behind bars, doing time; Brit. informal banged up.

insider noun *a Home Office insider leaked the information:* **member**, worker, employee, representative; person in the know.

insidious adjective *the insidious erosion of rights and liberties:* **stealthy**, subtle, surreptitious, cunning, crafty, artful, sly, wily, underhand, backhanded, indirect; informal sneaky.

insight noun **1** *your insight has been invaluable:* **intuition**, discernment, perception, awareness, understanding, comprehension, apprehension, appreciation, penetration, acumen, perspicacity, judgement, acuity; vision, prescience, imagination; informal nous, savvy. **2** *an insight into the government:* **understanding of**, appreciation of, revelation about; introduction to; informal eye-opener.

insignia noun **badge**, crest, emblem, symbol,

sign, device, mark, seal, colours.

insignificant adjective *too many articles are devoted to insignificant details:* **unimportant**, trivial, trifling, negligible, inconsequential, of no account, inconsiderable; nugatory, paltry, petty, insubstantial, frivolous, pointless, worthless, irrelevant, immaterial, peripheral; informal piddling.

insincere adjective *she flashed him an insincere smile:* **false**, fake, hollow, artificial, feigned, pretended, put-on; disingenuous, hypocritical, cynical, deceitful, deceptive, duplicitous, double-dealing, two-faced, lying, untruthful, mendacious; informal phoney, pretend, pseud.

insinuate verb **1** *he insinuated that she lied:* **imply**, suggest, hint, intimate, indicate, let it be known, give someone to understand; informal make out, tip someone the wink. **2** *he insinuated his hand under hers:* **slide**, slip, manoeuvre, insert, edge.
■ **insinuate oneself into** worm one's way into, ingratiate oneself with, curry favour with; foist oneself on, introduce oneself into; infiltrate, invade, sneak into, intrude on, impinge on; informal muscle in on.

insinuation noun **implication**, inference, suggestion, hint, intimation, innuendo, reference, allusion, indication, undertone, overtone; aspersion, slur, allegation.

insipid adjective **1** *insipid coffee:* **tasteless**, flavourless, savourless, bland, weak, wishy-washy; unappetizing, unpalatable. **2** *insipid pictures:* **unimaginative**, uninspired, uninspiring, characterless, flat, uninteresting, lacklustre, dull, boring, dry (as dust), jejune, humdrum, run-of-the-mill, commonplace, pedestrian, trite, tired, hackneyed, stale, lame, tame, poor, inadequate, sterile, anaemic.
– OPPOSITES tasty, interesting.

insist verb **1** *be prepared to insist:* **stand firm**, stand one's ground, be resolute, be determined, hold out, be emphatic, not take no for an answer; persevere, persist; informal stick to one's guns. **2** *she insisted that they pay up:* **demand**, command, require, dictate, urge, exhort. **3** *he insisted that he knew nothing:* **maintain**, assert, hold, contend, argue, protest, claim, vow, swear, declare, stress, repeat, reiterate.

insistence noun **1** *she sat down at Anne's insistence:* **demand**, bidding, command, dictate, instruction, requirement, request, entreaty, exhortation; informal say-so. **2** *his insistence that he loved her:* **assertion**, declaration, contention, claim, pronouncement, assurance, affirmation, avowal, profession.

insistent adjective **1** *Tony's insistent questioning:* **persistent**, determined, adamant, importunate, tenacious, unyielding, dogged, unrelenting, inexorable; demanding, pushy, urgent; emphatic, firm, assertive. **2** *an insistent buzzing:* **incessant**,

constant, unremitting, repetitive; obtrusive, intrusive.

insobriety noun *he had a tendency to insobriety:* **drunkenness**, intoxication, inebriation, tipsiness; informal tightness.

insolent adjective *she hated the insolent tone of his voice:* **impertinent**, impudent, cheeky, ill-mannered, bad mannered, unmannerly, rude, impolite, uncivil, discourteous, disrespectful, insubordinate, contemptuous; audacious, bold, cocky, brazen; insulting, abusive; informal fresh, flip, lippy, saucy; N. Amer. informal sassy.
– OPPOSITES polite.

insoluble adjective **1** *some problems are insoluble:* **unsolvable**, unanswerable, unresolvable; unfathomable, impenetrable, unexplainable, inscrutable, inexplicable. **2** *these minerals are insoluble:* **indissoluble**.

insolvency noun *the firm is on the brink of insolvency:* **bankruptcy**, liquidation, failure, collapse, (financial) ruin; pennilessness, penury; Brit. receivership.

insolvent adjective **bankrupt**, ruined, liquidated, wiped out; penniless, impoverished, impecunious; Brit. in receivership, without a penny (to one's name); informal bust, (flat) broke, belly-up, gone to the wall, on the rocks, in the red, hard up, strapped for cash; Brit. informal skint, in Queer Street, stony broke, cleaned out; formal penurious, stone broke.

insomnia noun *Ann was suffering from anxiety and insomnia:* **sleeplessness**, wakefulness, restlessness.

insouciance noun *his anxieties increased, despite Jen's insouciance:* **nonchalance**, unconcern, indifference, heedlessness, calm, equanimity, composure, ease, airiness; informal cool.
– OPPOSITES anxiety.

insouciant adjective **nonchalant**, untroubled, unworried, unruffled, unconcerned, indifferent, blasé, heedless; relaxed, calm, equable, equanimous, serene, composed, easy, carefree, free and easy, happy-go-lucky, light-hearted; informal cool, laid back.

inspect verb *the safety equipment is inspected by officials each year:* **examine**, check, scrutinize, investigate, vet, test, monitor, survey, study, look over, scan, explore, probe; assess, appraise, review; informal check out, give something a/the once-over.

inspection noun **examination**, check-up, survey, scrutiny, probe, exploration, observation, investigation; assessment, appraisal, review, evaluation; informal once-over, going-over, look-see, overhaul.

inspector noun *the machinery was not acceptable to the factory inspector:* **examiner**, checker, scrutinizer, scrutineer, investigator, surveyor, assessor, appraiser, reviewer, analyst; observer, overseer,

i

supervisor, monitor, watchdog, ombudsman; auditor.

inspiration noun **1** *she's a real inspiration to others:* **stimulus**, stimulation, motivation, fillip, encouragement, influence, muse, spur, lift, boost, incentive, impulse, catalyst; example, model. **2** *his work lacks inspiration:* **creativity**, inventiveness, innovation, ingenuity, imagination, originality; artistry, insight, vision; finesse, flair. **3** *she had a sudden inspiration:* **bright idea**, revelation; informal brainwave; N. Amer. informal brainstorm.

inspire verb **1** *the landscape inspired him to write:* **stimulate**, motivate, encourage, influence, rouse, move, stir, energize, galvanize, incite; animate, fire, inspirit, incentivize. **2** *the film inspired a musical:* **give rise to**, lead to, bring about, cause, prompt, spawn, engender. **3** *Charles inspired awe in her:* **arouse**, awaken, prompt, induce, ignite, trigger, kindle, produce, bring out.

inspired adjective *an inspired performance:* **outstanding**, wonderful, marvellous, excellent, magnificent, fine, exceptional, first-class, first-rate, virtuoso, supreme, superlative; innovative, innovatory, innovational, ingenious, original; informal tremendous, superb, super, ace, wicked, awesome, out of this world; Brit. informal brilliant, brill.
– OPPOSITES poor.

inspiring adjective *he was an inspiring example to his pupils:* **inspirational**, encouraging, heartening, uplifting, stirring, rousing, stimulating, electrifying; moving, affecting, influential.

instability noun **1** *the instability of political life:* **unreliability**, uncertainty, unpredictability, insecurity, perilousness, riskiness; impermanence, inconstancy, changeability, variability, fluctuation, mutability. **2** *emotional instability:* **volatility**, unpredictability, variability, capriciousness, vacillation; frailty, infirmity, weakness, irregularity. **3** *the instability of the foundations:* **unsteadiness**, unsoundness, shakiness, frailty, fragility.
– OPPOSITES steadiness.

install verb **1** *a photocopier was installed in the office:* **put**, position, place, locate, situate, station, site, lodge; insert. **2** *they installed a new president:* **swear in**, induct, instate, inaugurate, invest; appoint, take on; ordain, consecrate, anoint; enthrone, crown. **3** *she installed herself behind the table:* **ensconce**, establish, position, settle, seat, lodge, plant; sit (down); informal plonk, park; Brit. informal take a pew.
– OPPOSITES remove.

installation noun **1** *the installation of radiators:* **installing**, fitting, putting in; insertion. **2** *the installation of the chancellor:* **swearing in**, induction, instatement, inauguration, investiture; ordination, consecration; enthronement, coronation. **3** *a*

new computer installation: **unit**, appliance, fixture; equipment, machinery.

instalment noun **1** *I pay by monthly instalments:* **part payment**; deferred payment; Brit. hire purchase, HP; Brit. informal the never-never. **2** *a story published in instalments:* **part**, portion, section, segment, bit; chapter, episode, volume, issue.

instance noun *an instance of racism:* **example**, exemplar, occasion, occurrence, case; illustration.
verb *as an example I would instance Jones's work:* **cite**, quote, refer to, mention, allude to, give; specify, name, identify, draw attention to, put forward, offer, advance.
■ **in the first instance** initially, at first, at the start, at the outset, in/at the beginning, to begin with, to start with, originally.

instant adjective **1** *the account gives you instant access to your money:* **immediate**, instantaneous, on-the-spot, prompt, swift, speedy, rapid, quick, express, lightning; sudden, precipitate, abrupt; informal snappy, p.d.q. (pretty damn quick). **2** *instant meals tend not to be very nutritious:* **pre-prepared**, pre-cooked, ready mixed, fast; microwaveable, convenience, TV.
– OPPOSITES delayed.
noun **1** *come here this instant!* **moment**, time, minute, second; juncture, point. **2** *it all happened in an instant:* **trice**, moment, minute, (split) second, twinkling of an eye, flash, no time (at all); informal sec, jiffy, the blink of an eye; Brit. informal mo; N. Amer. informal snap.

instantaneous adjective *such an instantaneous response was not likely to be considered authoritative:* **immediate**, instant, on-the-spot, prompt, swift, speedy, rapid, quick, express, lightning; sudden, hurried, precipitate; informal snappy, p.d.q. (pretty damn quick).
– OPPOSITES delayed.

instantly adverb *she fell asleep almost instantly:* **immediately**, at once, straight away, right away, instantaneously; suddenly, abruptly, all of a sudden; forthwith, there and then, here and now, this/that minute, this/that instant; quickly, rapidly, speedily, promptly; in an instant, in a moment, in a (split) second, in a trice, in/like a flash, like a shot, in the twinkling of an eye, in no time (at all), before you know it; informal in a jiffy, pronto, before you can say Jack Robinson, double quick, like (greased) lightning.

instead adverb *if you get car-sick, travel by train instead:* **as an alternative**, in lieu, alternatively; rather, by contrast, for preference, by/from choice; on second thoughts, all things being equal, ideally; N. Amer. alternately.
■ **instead of** as an alternative to, as a substitute for, as a replacement for, in place of, in lieu of, in preference to; rather than,

as opposed to, as against, as contrasted with, before.

instigate verb **1** *they instigated formal proceedings:* **set in motion**, get under way, get off the ground, start, commence, begin, initiate, launch, institute, set up, put in place, inaugurate, establish, organize; actuate, generate, bring about; start the ball rolling; informal kick off. **2** *he instigated men to refuse allegiance:* **incite**, encourage, urge, goad, provoke, spur on, push, press, prompt, induce, prevail upon, motivate, influence, persuade, sway; informal put up to.
– OPPOSITES halt, dissuade.

instigation noun **1** *they became involved at his instigation:* **prompting**, suggestion; request, entreaty, demand, insistence; wish, desire, persuasion. **2** *foreign instigation of the disorder:* **initiation**, incitement, provocation, fomentation, encouragement, inducement, inception.

instigator noun *the instigators of the revolt:* **initiator**, prime mover, motivator, architect, designer, planner, inventor, mastermind, originator, author, creator, agent; founder, pioneer, founding father; agitator, fomenter, troublemaker, ringleader.

instil verb **1** *we instil vigilance in our children:* **inculcate**, implant, ingrain, impress, imprint, introduce; engender, produce, generate, induce, inspire, promote, foster; drum into. **2** *he instilled Monet with a love of nature:* **imbue**, inspire, infuse, inculcate; indoctrinate; teach.

instinct noun **1** *birds have an instinct to build nests:* **natural tendency**, inherent tendency, inclination, urge, drive, compulsion, need; intuition, feeling, sixth sense, insight; nose. **2** *a good instinct for acting:* **talent**, gift, ability, aptitude, skill, flair, feel, genius, knack, bent.

instinctive adjective *his instinctive reaction is to blame someone else:* **intuitive**, natural, instinctual, innate, inborn, inherent; unconscious, subconscious, intuitional; automatic, reflex, knee-jerk, mechanical, spontaneous, involuntary, impulsive; informal gut.
– OPPOSITES learned, voluntary.

institute noun *a research institute:* **organization**, establishment, institution, foundation, centre; academy, school, college, university; society, association, federation, body, guild.
verb **1** *we instituted a search:* **initiate**, set in motion, get under way, get off the ground, start, commence, begin, launch; set up, inaugurate, found, establish, organize, generate, bring about; start the ball rolling; informal kick off. **2** *he will be instituted as vicar:* **install**, instate, induct, invest, inaugurate, swear in, initiate; ordain, consecrate, anoint; appoint, create.
– OPPOSITES end, dismiss.

institution noun **1** *an academic institution:* **establishment**, organization, institute, foundation, centre; academy, school, college, university; society, association, body, guild, consortium. **2** *they spent their lives in institutions:* **(residential) home**, hospital, asylum. **3** *the institution of the rector:* **installation**, instatement, induction, investiture, inauguration; ordination, consecration, anointing, appointment, creation. **4** *marriage is a wonderful institution:* **practice**, custom, convention, tradition; phenomenon, fact; procedure, usage, method, system, policy; idea, notion, concept. **5** *the institution of legal proceedings:* **initiation**, instigation, launch, start, commencement, beginning, inauguration, generation, origination.

institutional adjective **1** *an institutional framework for discussions:* **organized**, established, bureaucratic, conventional, procedural, prescribed, set, routine, formal, systematic, systematized, methodical, businesslike, orderly, coherent, structured, regulated. **2** *the rooms are rather institutional:* **impersonal**, formal, regimented, uniform, unvaried, monotonous; insipid, bland, uninteresting, dull; unappealing, uninviting, unattractive, unwelcoming, dreary, drab, colourless; stark, spartan, bare, clinical, sterile.

instruct verb **1** *the union instructed them to strike:* **order**, direct, command, tell, enjoin, require, call on, mandate, charge. **2** *nobody instructed him in how to operate it:* **teach**, school, coach, train, enlighten, inform, educate, tutor, guide, prepare, prime. **3** *she instructed a solicitor of her own choice:* **employ**, authorize, brief. **4** *the bank was instructed that money would be withdrawn:* **inform**, tell, notify, apprise, advise, brief, prime; informal put in the picture, fill in.

instruction noun **1** *do not disobey my instructions:* **order**, command, directive, direction, decree, edict, injunction, mandate, dictate, commandment, bidding; requirement, stipulation; informal sayso. **2** *read the instructions before use:* **directions**, key, specification; handbook, manual, guide. **3** *he gave instruction in demolition work:* **tuition**, teaching, coaching, schooling, tutelage; lessons, classes, lectures; training, drill, preparation, grounding, guidance.

instructive adjective *a recent study of cooperatives makes instructive reading:* **informative**, instructional, informational, illuminating, enlightening, explanatory; educational, educative, edifying, didactic, pedagogic, heuristic; improving, moralistic, homiletic; useful, helpful.

instructor noun *a flying instructor:* **trainer**, coach, teacher, tutor; adviser, counsellor, guide; educator.

instrument noun **1** *a wound made with a sharp instrument:* **implement**, tool, utensil; device, apparatus, contrivance, gadget. **2** *check all the cockpit instruments:* **measuring device**, gauge, meter; indicator, dial, display. **3** *an instrument of learning:* **agent**, agency, cause, channel, medium, means, mechanism, vehicle, organ.

instrumental adjective *he was instrumental in developing new diagnostic procedures:* **involved**, active, influential, contributory; helpful, useful, of service; significant, important; (**be instrumental in**) play a part in, contribute to, be a factor in, have a hand in; add to, help, promote, advance, further; be conducive to, make for, lead to, cause.

insubordinate adjective *he soon found a means of dealing with his insubordinate son:* **disobedient**, unruly, wayward, errant, badly behaved, disorderly, undisciplined, delinquent, troublesome, rebellious, defiant, recalcitrant, uncooperative, wilful, intractable, unmanageable, uncontrollable; awkward, difficult, perverse, contrary; Brit. informal **bolshie**.
– OPPOSITES obedient.

insubordination noun **disobedience**, unruliness, indiscipline, bad behaviour, misbehaviour, misconduct, delinquency, rebellion, defiance, mutiny, revolt; recalcitrance, wilfulness, awkwardness, perversity; informal acting-up.

insubstantial adjective **1** *an insubstantial structure:* **flimsy**, slight, fragile, breakable, weak, frail, unstable, shaky, wobbly, rickety, ramshackle, jerry-built. **2** *insubstantial evidence:* **weak**, flimsy, feeble, poor, inadequate, insufficient, tenuous, insignificant, inconsequential, unsubstantial, unconvincing, implausible, unsatisfactory, paltry.
– OPPOSITES sturdy, sound.

insufferable adjective **1** *the heat was insufferable:* **intolerable**, unbearable, unendurable, insupportable, unacceptable, oppressive, overwhelming, overpowering; more than flesh and blood can stand; informal too much. **2** *his win made him insufferable:* **conceited**, arrogant, boastful, cocky, cocksure, full of oneself, self-important, swaggering; vain, self-satisfied, self-congratulatory, smug; informal swollen-headed, big-headed, too big for one's boots.
– OPPOSITES bearable, modest.

insufficient adjective *there was insufficient time available:* **inadequate**, deficient, poor, scant, scanty; not enough, too little, too few, too small; scarce, sparse, in short supply, lacking, wanting; paltry, meagre, niggardly; incomplete, restricted, limited; informal measly, pathetic, piddling.

insular adjective **1** *such insular people are not going to be swayed overnight:* **narrow-minded**, small-minded, blinkered, inward-looking, parochial, provincial, small-town, short-sighted, hidebound, set in one's ways, inflexible, rigid, entrenched; illiberal, intolerant, prejudiced, bigoted, biased,

partisan, xenophobic; Brit. blimpish. **2** *monks are often said to lead an insular existence:* **isolated**, inaccessible, cut off, segregated, detached, solitary, lonely.
– OPPOSITES broad-minded, cosmopolitan.

insulate verb **1** *pipes must be insulated to prevent heat loss:* **wrap**, sheathe, cover, encase, enclose, envelop; lag, heatproof, soundproof; pad, cushion. **2** *they were insulated from the impact of the war:* **protect**, save, shield, shelter, screen, cushion, cocoon; isolate, segregate, sequester, detach, cut off.

insulation noun **1** *most new hot-water tanks come with a layer of insulation:* **lagging**; blanket, jacket, wrap. **2** *insulation from the rigours of city life:* **protection**, defence, shelter, screen, shield; isolation, segregation, separation, sequestration, detachment.

insult verb *he insulted my wife:* **abuse**, be rude to, call someone names, slight, disparage, discredit, libel, slander, malign, defame, denigrate, cast aspersions on; offend, affront, hurt, humiliate, wound; informal bad-mouth; Brit. informal slag off.
– OPPOSITES compliment.
noun *he hurled insults at us:* **abusive remark**, jibe, affront, slight, barb, slur, indignity; injury, libel, slander, defamation; abuse, disparagement, aspersions; informal dig, put-down, slap in the face, kick in the teeth.

insulting adjective *I would not put up with such insulting comments:* **abusive**, rude, offensive, disparaging, belittling, derogatory, deprecatory, disrespectful, denigratory, uncomplimentary, pejorative; disdainful, derisive, scornful, contemptuous; defamatory, slanderous, libellous, scurrilous, blasphemous; informal bitchy, catty.

insuperable adjective *insuperable financial problems:* **insurmountable**, invincible, unassailable; overwhelming, hopeless, impossible.

insupportable adjective **1** *this view is insupportable:* **unjustifiable**, indefensible, inexcusable, unwarrantable, unreasonable; baseless, groundless, unfounded, unsupported, unsubstantiated, unconfirmed, uncorroborated, invalid, untenable, implausible, weak, flawed, specious, defective. **2** *the heat was insupportable:* **intolerable**, insufferable, unbearable, unendurable; oppressive, overwhelming, overpowering, more than flesh and blood can stand; informal too much.
– OPPOSITES justified, bearable.

insurance noun **1** *insurance for his new car:* **indemnity**, indemnification, assurance, (financial) protection, assurance, cover. **2** *insurance against a third World War:* **protection**, defence, safeguard, security, precaution, provision; immunity; guarantee, warranty; informal backstop.

insure verb *they had failed to insure the*

building against fire: **provide insurance for,** indemnify, cover, assure, protect, underwrite; guarantee, warrant.

insurgent adjective *insurgent forces:* **rebellious,** rebel, revolutionary, mutinous, insurrectionist; renegade, seditious, subversive.
– OPPOSITES loyal.
noun *the troops are fighting insurgents:* **rebel,** revolutionary, revolutionist, mutineer, insurrectionist, agitator, subversive, renegade; guerrilla, freedom fighter, anarchist, terrorist.
– OPPOSITES loyalist.

insurmountable adjective *an insurmountable problem:* **insuperable,** unconquerable, invincible, unassailable; overwhelming, hopeless, impossible.

insurrection noun *the leaders of the insurrection surrendered:* **rebellion,** revolt, uprising, mutiny, revolution, insurgence, riot, sedition; civil disorder, unrest, anarchy; coup (d'état).

intact adjective *something struck the window but the glass stayed intact:* **whole,** entire, complete, unbroken, undamaged, unimpaired, faultless, flawless, unscathed, untouched, unspoiled, unblemished, unmarked, perfect, pristine, inviolate, undefiled, unsullied, in one piece; sound, solid.
– OPPOSITES damaged.

intangible adjective **1** *the moonlight made things seem intangible:* **impalpable,** untouchable, incorporeal, discarnate, abstract; ethereal, insubstantial, airy; ghostly, spectral, unearthly, supernatural. **2** *an intangible atmosphere of intrigue:* **indefinable,** indescribable, inexpressible, nameless; vague, obscure, unclear, indefinite, subtle, elusive, fugitive.

integral adjective **1** *an integral part of human behaviour:* **essential,** fundamental, basic, intrinsic, inherent, constitutive, innate, structural; vital, necessary, requisite. **2** *the dryer has integral cord storage:* **built-in,** inbuilt, integrated, incorporated, fitted. **3** *an integral approach to learning:* **unified,** integrated, comprehensive, composite, combined, aggregate; complete, whole.
– OPPOSITES peripheral, fragmented.

integrate verb *he proposes to integrate our reserve forces more closely with the regular forces:* **combine,** amalgamate, merge, unite, fuse, blend, mingle, coalesce, consolidate, meld, intermingle, mix; incorporate, unify, assimilate, homogenize; desegregate.
– OPPOSITES separate.

integrated adjective **1** *an integrated package of services:* **unified,** united, consolidated, amalgamated, combined, merged, fused, homogeneous, assimilated, cohesive. **2** *an integrated school benefits pupils, staff, and the local community:* **desegregated,** non-segregated, unsegregated, mixed.

integrity noun **1** *I never doubted his integrity:* **honesty,** probity, rectitude, honour, good character, principle(s), ethics, morals, righteousness, morality, virtue, decency, fairness, scrupulousness, sincerity, truthfulness, trustworthiness. **2** *the integrity of the federation:* **unity,** unification, coherence, cohesion, togetherness, solidarity. **3** *the structural integrity of the aircraft:* **soundness,** strength, sturdiness, solidity, durability, stability, stoutness, toughness.
– OPPOSITES dishonesty, division, fragility.

intellect noun **1** *a film that appeals to the intellect:* **mind,** brain(s), intelligence, reason, understanding, thought, brainpower, sense, judgement, wisdom, wits; informal nous, grey matter, brain cells, upper storey; Brit. informal loaf; N. Amer. informal smarts. **2** *he is one of the finest intellects of our age:* **thinker,** intellectual, sage; mind, brain.

intellectual adjective **1** *his intellectual capacity:* **mental,** cerebral, cognitive, psychological; rational, abstract, conceptual, theoretical, analytical, logical; academic. **2** *an intellectual man:* **intelligent,** clever, academic, educated, well read, erudite, cerebral, learned, knowledgeable, literary, bookish, donnish, highbrow, scholarly, studious, enlightened, sophisticated; informal brainy.
– OPPOSITES physical, stupid.
noun *intellectuals are appalled by television:* **highbrow,** intelligent person, learned person, academic, bookworm, man/woman of letters, bluestocking; thinker, brain, scholar, sage; genius, Einstein, polymath, mastermind; informal egghead, brains; Brit. informal brainbox, clever clogs, boffin; N. Amer. informal brainiac, rocket scientist.
– OPPOSITES dunce.

intelligence noun **1** *a man of great intelligence:* **intellectual capacity,** mental capacity, intellect, mind, brain(s), brainpower, judgement, reasoning, understanding, comprehension; acumen, wit, sense, insight, perception, penetration, discernment, quick-wittedness, smartness, canniness, astuteness, intuition, acuity, cleverness, brilliance, ability, talent; informal braininess. **2** *intelligence from our agents indicates a military build-up:* **information,** facts, details, particulars, data, knowledge, reports; informal info, gen, dope. **3** *military intelligence:* **information gathering,** surveillance, observation, reconnaissance, spying, espionage, infiltration, ELINT, Humint; informal recon.

intelligent adjective **1** *he's an intelligent writer:* **clever,** bright, brilliant, quick-witted, quick on the uptake, smart, canny, astute, intuitive, insightful, perceptive, perspicacious, discerning; knowledgeable; able, gifted, talented; informal brainy. **2** *an intelligent being from another world:*

i

rational, higher-order, capable of thought. **3** *intelligent machines may take over the world:* **self-regulating**, capable of learning, smart.

intelligentsia plural noun *there is a distrust of the intelligentsia and of theoretical learning:* **intellectuals**, intelligent people, academics, scholars, literati, culturati, cognoscenti, illuminati, highbrows, thinkers, brains; the intelligent; informal eggheads; Brit. informal boffins.

intelligible adjective *statutes were drafted so as to be intelligible only to lawyers:* **comprehensible**, understandable; accessible, digestible, user-friendly, penetrable, fathomable; lucid, clear, coherent, plain, explicit, precise, unambiguous, self-explanatory.

intemperance noun **1** *they were criticized for intemperance:* **overindulgence**, immoderation, excess, extravagance, prodigality, profligacy, lavishness; self-indulgence, self-gratification; debauchery, decadence, dissipation, dissolution. **2** *he said intemperance was a disease:* **drinking**, alcoholism, alcohol abuse, dipsomania; drunkenness, intoxication, inebriation, insobriety, tipsiness.

intemperate adjective *I drank, I confess, an intemperate amount of beer:* **immoderate**, excessive, undue, inordinate, extreme, unrestrained, uncontrolled; self-indulgent, overindulgent, extravagant, lavish, prodigal, profligate; imprudent, reckless, wild; dissolute, debauched, wanton, dissipated.
– OPPOSITES moderate.

intend verb *Charlie intends to buy a bungalow:* **plan**, mean, have in mind, have the intention, aim, propose; aspire, hope, expect, be resolved, be determined; want, wish; contemplate, think of, envisage; design, earmark, set aside.

intended adjective *the foul was not intended:* **deliberate**, intentional, calculated, conscious, planned, studied, knowing, wilful, wanton, purposeful, done on purpose, premeditated, pre-planned, preconceived.
– OPPOSITES accidental.

intense adjective **1** *intense heat:* **extreme**, great, acute, fierce, severe, high; exceptional, extraordinary; harsh, strong, powerful, potent, vigorous; informal serious. **2** *a very intense young man:* **passionate**, impassioned, ardent, fervent, zealous, vehement, fiery, emotional; earnest, eager, animated, spirited, vigorous, energetic, fanatical, committed.
– OPPOSITES mild, apathetic.

intensify verb *they had intensified their military campaign:* **escalate**, increase, step up, boost, raise, strengthen, augment, reinforce; pick up, build up, heighten, deepen, extend, expand, amplify, magnify; aggravate, exacerbate, worsen, inflame, compound.

– OPPOSITES abate.

intensity noun **1** *the intensity of the sun:* **strength**, power, potency, force; severity, ferocity, vehemence, fierceness, harshness; magnitude, greatness, acuteness, extremity. **2** *his eyes had a glowing intensity:* **passion**, ardour, fervour, zeal, vehemence, fire, heat, emotion; eagerness, animation, spirit, vigour, strength, energy; fanaticism.

intensive adjective *an intensive search of the area:* **thorough**, thoroughgoing, in-depth, rigorous, exhaustive, all-out; all-embracing, all-inclusive, comprehensive, complete, full; vigorous, strenuous, detailed, minute, close, meticulous, scrupulous, painstaking, methodical, careful; extensive, widespread, sweeping; determined, resolute, persistent.
– OPPOSITES cursory.

intent noun *he tried to divine his father's intent:* **aim**, intention, purpose, objective, object, goal, target; design, plan, scheme; wish, desire, ambition, idea, aspiration.
adjective **1** *he was intent on proving his point:* **bent**, set, determined, insistent, resolved, hell-bent, keen; committed to, obsessive about, fanatical about; determined to, anxious to, impatient to. **2** *an intent expression:* **attentive**, absorbed, engrossed, fascinated, enthralled, rapt; focused, earnest, concentrating, intense, studious, preoccupied; alert, watchful.
■ **to all intents and purposes** in effect, effectively, in essence, essentially, virtually, practically; more or less, just about, all but, as good as, in all but name, as near as dammit; almost, nearly; informal pretty much, pretty well.

intention noun **1** *it is his intention to be leader:* **aim**, purpose, intent, objective, object, goal, target; design, plan, scheme; resolve, resolution, determination; wish, desire, ambition, idea, dream, aspiration. **2** *he managed, without intention, to upset me:* **intent**, intentionality, deliberateness, design, calculation; premeditation, forethought, pre-planning.

intentional adjective *there shall be no intentional physical contact between teams:* **deliberate**, calculated, conscious, intended, planned, meant, studied, knowing, wilful, wanton, purposeful, purposive, done on purpose, premeditated, pre-planned, preconceived; Law aforethought.

intently adverb *she listened intently to Harry's story:* **attentively**, closely, keenly, earnestly, hard, carefully, fixedly, steadily.

inter verb *his remains were interred in the new cemetery:* **bury**, lay to rest, entomb, inurn; informal put six feet under, plant.
– OPPOSITES exhume.

intercede verb *several nations offered to intercede on the captives' behalf:* **mediate**, intermediate, arbitrate, conciliate, negotiate, moderate; intervene, interpose, step in, act; plead, petition.

intercept verb *an Italian naval vessel intercepted the gunrunners' boat:* **stop**, head off, cut off; catch, seize, grab, snatch; obstruct, impede, interrupt, block, check, detain; ambush, challenge, waylay.

intercession noun *he made contact with the Austrians through the intercession of the Serbs:* **mediation**, intermediation, arbitration, conciliation, negotiation; intervention, involvement; pleading, petition, entreaty, agency; diplomacy.

interchange verb **1** *they interchange ideas:* **exchange**, trade, swap, barter, bandy, reciprocate. **2** *the terms are often interchanged:* **substitute**, transpose, exchange, switch, swap (round), change (round), reverse, invert, replace.
noun **1** *the interchange of ideas:* **exchange**, trade, swap, barter, give and take, traffic, reciprocation, reciprocity. **2** *a motorway interchange:* **junction**, intersection, crossing; N. Amer. cloverleaf.

interchangeable adjective **1** *the gun has interchangeable barrels:* **exchangeable**, transposable, replaceable. **2** *two more or less interchangeable roads:* **similar**, identical, indistinguishable, alike, the same, uniform, twin, undifferentiated; corresponding, commensurate, equivalent, comparable, equal; informal much of a muchness.

intercourse noun **1** *social intercourse:* **dealings**, relations, relationships, association, connections, contact; interchange, communication, communion, correspondence; negotiations, bargaining, transactions; trade, traffic; informal truck, doings. **2** *she did not consent to intercourse:* **sexual intercourse**, sex, lovemaking, sexual relations, intimacy, coupling, mating, copulation; informal nooky; Brit. informal bonking, rumpy pumpy, how's your father.

interdict noun *they breached an interdict:* **prohibition**, ban, bar, veto, proscription, interdiction, embargo, moratorium, injunction.
– OPPOSITES permission.
verb **1** *they interdicted foreign commerce:* **prohibit**, forbid, ban, bar, veto, proscribe, embargo, disallow, debar, outlaw; stop, suppress; Law enjoin, estop. **2** *efforts to interdict asylum seekers:* **intercept**, stop, head off, cut off; obstruct, impede, block; detain.
– OPPOSITES permit.

interest noun **1** *we listened with interest:* **attentiveness**, attention, absorption; heed, regard, notice; curiosity, inquisitiveness; enjoyment, delight. **2** *places of interest:* **attraction**, appeal, fascination, charm, beauty, allure. **3** *this will be of interest to those involved:* **concern**, consequence, importance, import, significance, note, relevance, value, weight. **4** *her interests include reading:* **hobby**, pastime, leisure pursuit, recreation, diversion, amusement, relaxation; passion, enthusiasm; informal

thing, bag, cup of tea. **5** *he has a financial interest in the firm:* **stake**, share, claim, investment, stock, equity; involvement, concern. **6** *what is your interest in the case?* **involvement**, partiality, partisanship, preference, loyalty; bias, prejudice. **7** *his attorney guarded his interests:* **concern**, business, affair. **8** *her savings earned interest:* **dividends**, profits, returns; a percentage.
– OPPOSITES boredom.
verb **1** *a topic that interests you:* **appeal to**, be of interest to, attract, intrigue, fascinate; absorb, engross, rivet, grip, captivate; amuse, divert, entertain; arouse one's curiosity, whet one's appetite; informal float someone's boat, tickle someone's fancy. **2** *can I interest you in a drink?* persuade to have; sell.
– OPPOSITES bore.
■ **in someone's interests** of benefit to, to the advantage of; for the sake of, for the benefit of.

interested adjective **1** *an interested crowd:* **attentive**, intent, absorbed, engrossed, fascinated, riveted, gripped, captivated, rapt, agog; intrigued, inquisitive, curious; keen, eager; informal all ears, nosy, snoopy. **2** *the government consulted with interested bodies:* **concerned**, involved, affected, connected, related. **3** *no interested party can judge the contest:* **partisan**, partial, biased, prejudiced, one-sided, preferential.

interesting adjective *it is one of the most interesting novels of its time:* **absorbing**, engrossing, fascinating, riveting, gripping, compelling, compulsive, captivating, engaging, enthralling; appealing, attractive, amusing, entertaining, stimulating, thought-provoking, diverting, intriguing; informal unputdownable.

interfere verb **1** *don't let emotion interfere with duty:* **impede**, obstruct, stand in the way of, hinder, inhibit, restrict, constrain, hamper, handicap, cramp, check, block; disturb, disrupt, influence, affect, confuse. **2** *she tried not to interfere in his life:* **butt into**, barge into, pry into, nose into, intrude into, intervene in, get involved in, encroach on, impinge on; meddle in, tamper with; informal poke one's nose into, horn in on, muscle in on, stick one's oar in.

interference noun **1** *they resent state interference:* **intrusion**, intervention, intercession, involvement, trespass, obtrusion; meddling, prying. **2** *radio interference:* **disruption**, disturbance, static.

interfering adjective *they wanted to be free from their interfering relatives:* **meddlesome**, meddling, intrusive, prying, inquisitive, over-curious, busybody; informal nosy, nosy-parker, snoopy.

interim noun *in the interim they did more research:* **meantime**, meanwhile, intervening time.
adjective *an interim advisory body:* **provisional**, temporary, pro tem, stopgap,

short-term, fill-in, caretaker, acting, intervening, transitional, makeshift, improvised, impromptu.
– OPPOSITES permanent.

interior adjective **1** *the house has interior panelling:* **inside**, inner, internal, intramural. **2** *the interior deserts of the US:* **inland**, inshore, upcountry, inner, innermost, central. **3** *the country's interior affairs:* **internal**, home, domestic, national, state, civil, local. **4** *an interior monologue:* **inner**, mental, spiritual, psychological; private, personal, intimate, secret.
– OPPOSITES exterior, outer, foreign.
noun **1** *the interior of the yacht:* **inside**, inner part, depths, recesses, bowels, belly; centre, core, heart. **2** *the country's interior:* **centre**, heartland, hinterland, Middle....
– OPPOSITES exterior, outside.

interject verb **1** *she interjected a comment:* **interpose**, introduce, throw in, interpolate, add. **2** *he interjected before there was a fight:* **interrupt**, intervene, cut in, break in, butt in, chime in; put one's oar in; Brit. informal chip in; N. Amer. informal put in one's two cents.

interjection noun **1** *an astonished interjection from one of the audience:* **exclamation**; cry, shout, vociferation, utterance. **2** *the interjection of a question:* **interposition**, interpolation, insertion, addition, introduction.

interlock verb *the fixed panel should interlock with the sliding section:* **interconnect**, interlink, engage, mesh, intermesh, join, unite, connect, couple.

interloper noun *they were a close community and could not abide interlopers:* **intruder**, encroacher, trespasser, invader, infiltrator; uninvited guest; outsider, stranger, alien; informal gatecrasher.

interlude noun *a peaceful interlude in her busy day:* **interval**, intermission, break, recess, pause, respite, rest, breathing space, halt, gap, stop, stoppage, hiatus, lull; informal breather, let-up, time out, down time.

intermediary noun *they concluded the deal through an intermediary:* **mediator**, go-between, negotiator, intervenor, interceder, intercessor, arbitrator, arbiter, conciliator, peacemaker; middleman, broker, linkman.

intermediate adjective *an intermediate stage in the cell's development:* **halfway**, in-between, middle, mid, midway, median, medial, intermediary, intervening, transitional.

interment noun *his body was taken for interment:* **burial**, burying, committal, entombment, inhumation; funeral.

interminable adjective *Wednesday was a day of interminable meetings:* **endless**, never-ending, unending, non-stop, everlasting, ceaseless, unceasing, incessant, constant, continual, uninterrupted, sustained; monotonous, long-winded, overlong, rambling.

intermingle verb *the two species of finch rarely intermingle:* **mix**, intermix, mingle, blend, fuse, merge, combine, amalgamate; unite, affiliate, associate, fraternize.

intermission noun *after the first film there was an intermission:* **interval**, interlude, entr'acte, break, recess, pause, rest, respite, breathing space, lull, gap, stop, stoppage, halt; cessation, suspension; informal let-up, breather, time out, down time.

intermittent adjective *they heard intermittent bursts of gunfire:* **sporadic**, irregular, fitful, spasmodic, broken, fragmentary, discontinuous, isolated, random, patchy, scattered; occasional, periodic.
– OPPOSITES continuous.

intern verb *they were interned without trial:* **imprison**, incarcerate, impound, jail, put behind bars, detain, hold (captive), lock up, confine; informal put away, put inside, send down; Brit. informal bang up.
noun *an intern at a local firm:* **trainee**, apprentice, probationer, student, novice, beginner.

internal adjective **1** *an internal courtyard:* **inner**, interior, inside, intramural; central. **2** *the state's internal affairs:* **domestic**, home, interior, civil, local; national, state. **3** *she was waging an internal battle with herself:* **mental**, psychological, emotional; personal, private, secret, hidden.
– OPPOSITES external, foreign.

international adjective *the international business community:* **global**, worldwide, intercontinental, universal; cosmopolitan, multiracial, multinational.
– OPPOSITES national, local.

interplay noun *the interplay between military and civilian populations:* **interaction**, interchange; teamwork, cooperation, reciprocation, reciprocity, give and take.

interpolate verb *the illustrations were interpolated in the text:* **insert**, interpose, enter, add, incorporate, inset, put, introduce.

interpose verb **1** *he interposed himself between the girls:* **insinuate**, place, put. **2** *I must interpose a note of caution:* **introduce**, insert, interject, add. **3** *they interposed to suppress the custom:* **intervene**, intercede, step in, involve oneself; interfere, intrude, butt in, cut in; informal barge in, horn in, muscle in.

interpret verb **1** *the rabbis interpreted the Jewish laws:* **explain**, elucidate, expound, explicate, clarify, illuminate, shed light on. **2** *the remark was interpreted as an invitation:* **understand**, construe, take, see, regard. **3** *the symbols are difficult to interpret:* **decipher**, decode, make intelligible; understand, comprehend, make sense of; informal crack.

interpretation noun **1** *the interpretation of the Bible's teachings:* **explanation**, elucidation, expounding, exposition, explication, exegesis, clarification. **2** *she did not care what interpretation he put on her haste:* **meaning**, understanding, construal, connotation, explanation, inference. **3** *the interpretation of experimental findings:* **analysis**, evaluation, review, study, examination. **4** *his interpretation of the sonata:* **rendition**, rendering, execution, presentation, performance, reading, playing, singing.

interpreter noun **1** *a Japanese interpreter:* **translator**, dragoman. **2** *a vocal interpreter of his music:* **performer**, presenter, exponent; singer, player. **3** *interpreters of Soviet history:* **analyst**, evaluator, reviewer, commentator.

interrogate verb *the police wished to interrogate her:* **question**, cross-question, cross-examine, quiz; interview, examine, debrief, give someone the third degree; informal pump, grill.

interrogative adjective *he gazed at me with a hard interrogative stare:* **questioning**, inquiring, inquisitive, probing, searching, quizzing, quizzical, curious.

interrupt verb **1** *she opened her mouth to interrupt:* **cut in (on)**, break in (on), barge in (on), intervene (in), put one's oar in; Brit. put one's pennyworth in; N. Amer. put one's two cents in; informal butt in (on), chime in (on); Brit. informal chip in (on). **2** *the band had to interrupt their tour:* **suspend**, adjourn, discontinue, break off; stop, halt, cease, end, bring to an end/close; informal put on ice, put on a back burner. **3** *the coastal plain is interrupted by large lagoons:* **break (up)**, punctuate; pepper, strew, dot, scatter.

interruption noun **1** *he was not pleased at her interruption:* **cutting in**, barging in, intervention, intrusion; informal butting in. **2** *an interruption of the power supply:* **discontinuation**, breaking off, suspension, stopping, halting, cessation. **3** *an interruption in her career:* **interval**, interlude, break, pause, gap.

intersect verb **1** *the lines intersect at right angles:* **cross**, criss-cross. **2** *the cornfield is intersected by a track:* **bisect**, divide, cut in two/half, cut across/through; cross, traverse.

intersection noun **1** *the intersection of the two curves:* **crossing**, criss-crossing. **2** *the driver stopped at an intersection:* **(road) junction**, T-junction, interchange, crossroads; Brit. roundabout.

intersperse verb **1** *giant lobelia were interspersed among the rocks:* **scatter**, disperse, spread, strew, dot, sprinkle, pepper. **2** *the beech trees are interspersed with conifers:* **intermix**, mix, mingle, punctuate.

intertwine verb *a wreath of laurel intertwined with daffodils:* **entwine**, interweave, interlace, interwind, twist, coil.

interval noun **1** *a 15-minute interval:*

intermission, interlude, entr'acte, break, recess; half time. **2** *polling day was a week away and Baldwin made two speeches in the interval:* **interim**, interlude, intervening time/period, meantime, meanwhile. **3** *short intervals of still water:* **stretch**, distance, span, area.

intervene verb **1** *had the war not intervened, they might have married:* **occur**, happen, take place, arise, crop up, come about; result, ensue, follow. **2** *she intervened in the row:* **intercede**, involve oneself, get involved, interpose oneself, step in; interfere, intrude.

intervention noun *they would suffer no state intervention in their business:* **involvement**, intercession, interceding, interposing; interference, intrusion.

interview noun *all applicants will be called for an interview:* **meeting**, discussion, conference, examination, interrogation; audience, talk, dialogue, exchange; talks. verb *we interviewed seventy subjects for the survey:* **talk to**, have a discussion/dialogue with; question, interrogate, cross-examine; poll, canvass, survey, sound out; informal grill, pump.

interviewer noun **questioner**, interrogator, examiner, assessor, appraiser; journalist, reporter.

interweave verb **1** *the threads are interwoven:* **intertwine**, entwine, interlace, splice, braid, plait; twist together, weave together, wind together; Nautical marry. **2** *their fates were interwoven:* **interlink**, link, connect; intermix, mix, merge, blend, interlock, knit/bind together.

intestinal adjective *he died from an intestinal complaint:* **enteric**, gastro-enteric, duodenal, coeliac, gastric, ventral, stomach, abdominal.

intestines plural noun **gut**, guts, entrails, viscera; small intestine, large intestine; informal insides, innards.

intimacy noun **1** *the sisters re-established their old intimacy:* **closeness**, togetherness, affinity, rapport, attachment, familiarity, friendliness, amity, affection, warmth; informal chumminess, palliness; Brit. informal mateyness. **2** *the memory of their intimacy:* **sexual relations**, (sexual) intercourse, sex, lovemaking, copulation.

intimate[1] adjective **1** *an intimate friend:* **close**, bosom, boon, dear, cherished, faithful, fast, firm; informal chummy, pally. **2** *an intimate atmosphere:* **friendly**, warm, welcoming, hospitable, relaxed, informal; cosy, comfortable, snug; informal comfy. **3** *intimate thoughts:* **personal**, private, confidential, secret; innermost, inner, inward, unspoken, undisclosed. **4** *an intimate knowledge of the industry:* **detailed**, thorough, exhaustive, deep, in-depth, profound. **5** *intimate relations:* **sexual**, carnal, amorous, amatory.
– OPPOSITES distant, formal.

i

noun *his circle of intimates:* **close friend**, best friend, bosom friend, confidant, confidante; informal chum, pal, crony; Brit. informal mate; N. Amer. informal buddy.

intimate² verb **1** *he intimated his decision:* **announce**, state, proclaim, make known, make public, disclose, reveal, divulge. **2** *her feelings were subtly intimated:* **imply**, suggest, hint at, insinuate, indicate, signal, allude to, refer to, convey.

intimation noun **1** *the early intimation of session dates:* **announcement**, statement, communication, notification, notice, reporting, publishing; disclosure, revelation, divulging. **2** *the first intimation of discord:* **suggestion**, hint, indication, sign, signal, inkling, suspicion, impression; clue to, undertone of, whisper of.

intimidate verb *he paid them to intimidate his rivals:* **frighten**, menace, terrify, scare, terrorize, cow, subdue; threaten, browbeat, bully, pressure, pressurize, harass, harry, hound; informal lean on, bulldoze, steamroller, railroad, use strong-arm tactics on.

intolerable adjective *the drilling noise had become intolerable:* **unbearable**, insufferable, unsupportable, insupportable, unendurable, beyond endurance, more than flesh and blood can stand, too much to bear.
– OPPOSITES bearable.

intolerant adjective **1** *Sophia was intolerant in religious matters:* **bigoted**, narrow-minded, small-minded, parochial, provincial, illiberal, uncompromising; prejudiced, biased, partial, partisan, discriminatory. **2** *foods to which you are intolerant:* **allergic**, sensitive, hypersensitive.

intonation noun **1** *she read the sentence with the wrong intonation:* **inflection**, pitch, tone, timbre, cadence, cadency, lilt, modulation, speech pattern. **2** *the intonation of hymns:* **chanting**, incantation, recitation, singing.

intone verb *grace before the meal was intoned in Gaelic:* **chant**, sing, recite.

intoxicate verb **1** *one glass of wine intoxicated him:* **inebriate**, make drunk, make intoxicated, befuddle, go to someone's head; informal make legless, make woozy. **2** *he was intoxicated by the cinema:* **exhilarate**, thrill, elate, delight, captivate, enthral, entrance, enrapture, excite, stir, rouse, inspire, fire with enthusiasm; informal give someone a buzz, give someone a kick; N. Amer. informal give someone a charge.

intoxicated adjective *he was cautioned for being intoxicated while on duty:* **drunk**, inebriated, inebriate, drunken, tipsy, under the influence; informal tight, merry, the worse for wear, pie-eyed, in one's cups, three sheets to the wind, plastered, smashed, sloshed, sozzled, well oiled, wrecked, blotto, stewed, pickled, tanked up, soaked, off one's face, out of one's head/skull; Brit. informal paralytic, legless, Brahms and Liszt, half cut, bladdered, trolleyed, tiddly; N. Amer. informal

loaded, trashed, out of one's gourd; euphemistic tired and emotional.
– OPPOSITES sober.

intoxicating adjective **1** *intoxicating drink:* **alcoholic**, strong, hard, potent, stiff, intoxicant; formal spirituous. **2** *an intoxicating sense of freedom:* **heady**, exhilarating, thrilling, exciting, rousing, stirring, stimulating, invigorating, electrifying; strong, powerful, potent; informal mind-blowing.
– OPPOSITES non-alcoholic.

intoxication noun **drunkenness**, inebriation, insobriety, tipsiness; informal tightness.

intractable adjective **1** *intractable problems:* **unmanageable**, uncontrollable, difficult, awkward, troublesome, demanding, burdensome. **2** *an intractable man:* **stubborn**, obstinate, obdurate, inflexible, unadaptable, unbending, unyielding, uncompromising, unaccommodating, uncooperative, difficult, awkward, perverse, contrary, pig-headed; N. Amer. rock-ribbed; informal stiff-necked.
– OPPOSITES manageable, compliant.

intransigent adjective *his intransigent attitude led to quarrels with his friends:* **uncompromising**, inflexible, unbending, unyielding, unshakeable, unwavering, resolute, rigid, unaccommodating, uncooperative, stubborn, obstinate, obdurate, pig-headed, single-minded, iron-willed; informal stiff-necked.
– OPPOSITES compliant.

intrench verb. See ENTRENCH.

intrenched adjective. See ENTRENCHED.

intrepid adjective *our intrepid reporter:* **fearless**, unafraid, undaunted, unflinching, unshrinking, bold, daring, audacious, adventurous, heroic, dynamic, spirited, indomitable; brave, courageous, valiant, valorous, stout-hearted, stalwart, plucky, doughty; informal gutsy, spunky.
– OPPOSITES fearful.

intricate adjective *intricate Arabic patterns:* **complex**, complicated, convoluted, tangled, entangled, twisted; elaborate, ornate, detailed, involuted; Brit. informal fiddly.
– OPPOSITES simple.

intrigue verb **1** *her answer intrigued him:* **interest**, be of interest to, fascinate, arouse someone's curiosity, attract. **2** *the ministers intrigued to bring about a resignation:* **plot**, conspire, make secret plans, scheme, manoeuvre, connive, collude, machinate.
noun **1** *the intrigue that accompanied the selection of a new leader:* **plotting**, conspiracy, collusion, conniving, scheming, machination, trickery, sharp practice, double-dealing, underhandedness, subterfuge; informal dirty tricks. **2** *the king's intrigues with his nobles' wives:* **(love) affair**, affair of the heart, liaison, amour, fling, flirtation, dalliance; adultery,

infidelity, unfaithfulness; informal fooling around, playing around, hanky-panky; Brit. informal carryings-on.

intriguer noun *he was revealed as a political intriguer:* **conspirator**, co-conspirator, plotter, schemer, colluder, conniver, machinator, Machiavelli.

intriguing adjective *a wealth of intriguing stories appear in this book:* **interesting**, fascinating, absorbing, compelling, gripping, riveting, captivating, engaging, enthralling.

intrinsic adjective *pride was an intrinsic component of his personal make-up:* **inherent**, innate, inborn, inbred, congenital, connate, connatural, natural; deep-rooted, indelible, ineradicable; integral, basic, fundamental, essential.

introduce verb **1** *he has introduced a new system:* **institute**, initiate, launch, put in place, inaugurate, establish, found; bring in, set in motion, start, begin, commence, get going, get under way, originate, pioneer; informal kick off. **2** *you can introduce new ideas:* **propose**, put forward, suggest, table; raise, broach, bring up, mention, air, float. **3** *she introduced Lindsey to the young man:* **present (formally)**, make known, acquaint with. **4** *introducing nitrogen into canned beer:* **insert**, inject, put, force, shoot, feed. **5** *she introduced a note of severity into her voice:* **instil**, infuse, inject, add. **6** *the same presenter introduces the programme each week:* **announce**, present, give an introduction to; start off, begin, open.

introduction noun **1** *the introduction of democratic reforms:* **institution**, establishment, initiation, launch, inauguration, foundation; start, commencement, inception, origination, pioneering. **2** *he wished for an introduction to the king:* **(formal) presentation**; meeting, audience. **3** *an introduction to the catalogue:* **foreword**, preface, preamble, prologue, prelude; opening (statement), beginning; informal intro. **4** *the handbook will include an introduction to the history of the period:* **basic explanation/account of**; the basics, the rudiments, the fundamentals. **5** *a gentle introduction to the life of the school:* **initiation**, induction, inauguration.
– OPPOSITES afterword.

introductory adjective **1** *the introductory chapter:* **opening**, initial, starting, initiatory, first; prefatory, preliminary. **2** *an introductory course:* **elementary**, basic, rudimentary; initiatory, preparatory.
– OPPOSITES final, advanced.

introspection noun *he wasn't given to introspection:* **self-analysis**, soul-searching, introversion; contemplation, meditation, thoughtfulness, pensiveness, reflection; informal navel-gazing.

introspective adjective *a shy and introspective man:* **inward-looking**, self-analysing, introverted, introvert; contemplative, thoughtful, pensive,

meditative, reflective; informal navel-gazing.

introverted adjective *an introverted and thoughtful person:* **shy**, reserved, withdrawn, reticent, diffident, retiring, quiet; introspective, introvert, inward-looking, indrawn, self-absorbed; contemplative, thoughtful, pensive, meditative, reflective.
– OPPOSITES extroverted.

intrude verb **1** *intruding on people's privacy:* **encroach**, impinge, trespass, infringe, obtrude, invade, violate, disturb, disrupt; informal horn in, muscle in. **2** *he intruded his own personality into his work:* **force**, push, obtrude, impose, thrust.

intruder noun *the intruder had rifled through drawers:* **trespasser**, interloper, invader, infiltrator; burglar, housebreaker, thief.

intrusion noun *she didn't want his constant intrusion into her life:* **encroachment**, obtrusion; invasion, incursion, intervention, disturbance, disruption, infringement, impingement.

intrusive adjective **1** *an intrusive journalist:* **intruding**, invasive, obtrusive, unwelcome; inquisitive, prying; informal nosy. **2** *opinion polls play an intrusive role in elections:* **invasive**, high-profile, prominent; informal in one's face. **3** *intrusive questions:* **personal**, prying, forward, impertinent; informal nosy.

intuition noun **1** *he works according to intuition:* **instinct**, intuitiveness; sixth sense, clairvoyance, second sight. **2** *this confirms an intuition I had:* **hunch**, feeling (in one's bones), inkling, (sneaking) suspicion; premonition, presentiment; informal gut feeling.

intuitive adjective *he had an intuitive grasp of people's moods:* **instinctive**, intuitional, instinctual; innate, inborn, inherent, natural, congenital; unconscious, subconscious, involuntary; informal gut.

inundate verb **1** *many buildings were inundated:* **flood**, deluge, overrun, swamp, submerge, engulf. **2** *we have been inundated by complaints:* **overwhelm**, overrun, overload, bog down, swamp, besiege, snow under.

inundation noun **flood**, deluge, torrent, flash flood, freshet; Brit. spate.

inure verb *they became inured to poverty:* **harden**, toughen, season, temper, condition; accustom, habituate, familiarize, acclimatize, adjust, adapt.
– OPPOSITES sensitize.

invade verb **1** *the island was invaded by amphibious forces:* **occupy**, conquer, capture, seize, take (over), annex, win, gain, secure; march into, overrun, overwhelm, storm. **2** *someone had invaded our privacy:* **intrude on**, violate, encroach on, infringe on, trespass on, obtrude on, disturb, disrupt; informal horn in on, muscle in on. **3** *the feeling of betrayal invaded my being:* **permeate**,

pervade, spread through/over, diffuse through, imbue.
– OPPOSITES withdraw.

invader noun **attacker**, raider, marauder; occupier, conqueror; intruder.

invalid[1] noun *my mother is an invalid:* **ill person**, sick person, valetudinarian; patient, convalescent.
adjective *her invalid husband:* **ill**, sick, ailing, unwell, infirm, valetudinarian, in poor health; incapacitated, bedridden, frail, feeble, weak, debilitated, sickly, poorly.
– OPPOSITES healthy.
verb *an officer invalided by a chest wound:* **disable**, incapacitate, indispose, hospitalize, put out of action, lay up; injure, wound, hurt.

invalid[2] adjective **1** *the law was invalid:* **(legally) void**, null and void, unenforceable, not binding, illegitimate, inapplicable.
2 *the whole theory is invalid:* **false**, untrue, inaccurate, faulty, fallacious, spurious, unconvincing, unsound, weak, wrong, wide of the mark, off target; untenable, baseless, ill-founded, groundless; informal off beam, full of holes.
– OPPOSITES binding, true.

invalidate verb **1** *a low turnout invalidated the ballot:* **render invalid**, void, nullify, annul, negate, cancel, overturn, overrule.
2 *this case invalidates the general argument:* **disprove**, refute, explode, contradict, rebut, negate, belie, discredit, debunk; weaken, undermine, compromise; informal shoot full of holes.

invaluable adjective *an invaluable member of the organization:* **indispensable**, crucial, critical, key, vital, irreplaceable, all-important.
– OPPOSITES dispensable.

invariable adjective *his routine was invariable:* **unvarying**, unchanging, unvaried; constant, stable, set, steady, predictable, regular, consistent; unchangeable, unalterable, immutable, fixed.
– OPPOSITES varied.

invariably adverb *he is invariably described as 'down to earth':* **always**, on every occasion, at all times, without fail, without exception; everywhere, in all places, in all cases/instances; regularly, consistently, repeatedly, habitually, unfailingly.
– OPPOSITES sometimes, never.

invasion noun **1** *the invasion of the islands:* **occupation**, conquering, capture, seizure, annexation, annexing, takeover; overrunning, overwhelming, storming.
2 *an invasion of cars:* **influx**, inundation, inrush, flood, torrent, deluge, avalanche.
3 *an invasion of my privacy:* **violation**, infringement, interruption, intrusion, encroachment, obtrusion, disturbance, disruption, breach.
– OPPOSITES withdrawal.

invective noun *she poured forth a string of invective:* **abuse**, insults, vituperation, expletives, swear words, swearing, curses, bad/foul language, obloquy.
– OPPOSITES praise.

inveigh verb *he went on to inveigh against pornography and violence in the cinema:* **fulminate**, declaim, protest, rail, rage, remonstrate; denounce, censure, condemn, decry, criticize; disparage, denigrate, run down, abuse, vilify, impugn; informal kick up a fuss/stink about, bellyache about, sound off about.
– OPPOSITES support.

inveigle verb *he inveigled her back to his room:* **cajole**, wheedle, coax, persuade, talk; tempt, lure, entice, seduce, beguile; informal sweet-talk, soft-soap, con; N. Amer. informal sucker.

invent verb **1** *Louis Braille invented an alphabet to help blind people:* **originate**, create, innovate, design, devise, contrive, develop; conceive, think up, dream up, come up with, pioneer. **2** *they invented the story for a laugh:* **make up**, fabricate, concoct, hatch, dream up; informal cook up.

invention noun **1** *the invention of the telescope:* **origination**, creation, innovation, devising, contriving, development, design.
2 *medieval inventions:* **innovation**, creation, design, contraption, contrivance, construction, device, gadget; informal brainchild. **3** *a journalistic invention:* **fabrication**, concoction, (piece of) fiction, story, tale; lie, untruth, falsehood, fib; myth, fantasy; informal tall story, cock-and-bull story.

inventive adjective **1** *the most inventive composer of his time:* **creative**, original, innovational, innovative, imaginative, ingenious, resourceful. **2** *a fresh, inventive comedy:* **original**, innovative, unusual, fresh, novel, new; experimental, avant-garde, groundbreaking, unorthodox, unconventional.
– OPPOSITES unimaginative, hackneyed.

inventor noun **originator**, creator, innovator; designer, deviser, developer, maker, producer; author, architect; pioneer, mastermind, father.

inventory noun *a complete inventory of all their belongings:* **list**, listing, catalogue, record, register, checklist, log, archive.
verb *I inventoried his collection:* **list**, catalogue, record, register, log.

inverse adjective *inverse snobbery:* **reverse**, reversed, inverted, opposite, converse, contrary, counter, antithetical.
noun *alkalinity is the inverse of acidity:* **opposite**, converse, obverse, antithesis; informal flip side.

inversion noun *a hypocrite's inversion of the truth:* **reversal**, transposition, turning upside down; reverse, contrary, antithesis, converse.

invert verb *the crew inverted the yacht's mast:* **turn upside down**, upturn, upend, turn around/about, turn inside out, turn back to front, reverse, flip (over).

invest verb **1** *he invested in a cotton mill:* **put/plough money into**, provide capital for, fund, back, finance, underwrite; buy into, buy shares in. **2** *they invested £18 million:* **spend**, expend, put in, plough in; venture, speculate, risk; *informal* lay out. **3** *their words were invested with sarcasm:* **imbue**, infuse, charge, steep, suffuse, pervade, endow. **4** *bishops whom the king had invested:* **admit to office**, instate, install, induct, swear in; ordain, crown.

investigate verb *police are investigating the death of a man:* **enquire into**, look into, go into, probe, explore, scrutinize, conduct an investigation into, make inquiries about; inspect, analyse, study, examine, consider, research; *informal* check out, suss out; *N. Amer. informal* scope out.

investigation noun *this claim requires further investigation:* **examination**, inquiry, study, inspection, exploration, consideration, analysis, appraisal; research, scrutiny, scrutinization, perusal; probe, review, survey.

investigator noun *social security fraud investigators were called in:* **inspector**, examiner, inquirer, explorer, analyser; researcher, factfinder, scrutineer, scrutinizer, prober, searcher; detective.

investiture noun *the investiture of archbishops:* **inauguration**, appointment, installation, instatement, initiation, swearing in; ordination, consecration, crowning, enthronement.

investment noun **1** *you can lose money by bad investment:* **investing**, speculation; funding, backing, financing, underwriting; buying shares. **2** *it's a good investment:* **venture**, speculation, risk, gamble; asset, acquisition, holding, possession. **3** *the company folded, and his entire investment went down the drain:* **stake**, share, money/capital invested. **4** *a substantial investment of time:* **sacrifice**, surrender, loss, forfeiture.

inveterate adjective **1** *an inveterate gambler:* **confirmed**, hardened, incorrigible, addicted, compulsive, obsessive; *informal* pathological. **2** *an inveterate Democrat:* **staunch**, steadfast, committed, devoted, dedicated, dyed-in-the-wool, out-and-out, diehard. **3** *mankind's inveterate stupidity:* **ingrained**, deep-seated, deep-rooted, entrenched, ineradicable, incurable.

invidious adjective **1** *that put her in an invidious position:* **unpleasant**, awkward, difficult; undesirable, unenviable. **2** *an invidious comparison:* **unfair**, unjust, iniquitous, unwarranted; deleterious, detrimental.
– OPPOSITES pleasant, fair.

invigorate verb *we were invigorated by the fresh air:* **revitalize**, energize, refresh, revive, vivify, brace, rejuvenate, enliven, liven up, perk up, wake up, animate, galvanize, fortify, stimulate, rouse, exhilarate; *informal* buck up, pep up.
– OPPOSITES tire.

invincible adjective *an invincible warrior:* **invulnerable**, indestructible, unconquerable, unbeatable, indomitable, unassailable; impregnable, inviolable.
– OPPOSITES vulnerable.

inviolable adjective *the inviolable right to life:* **inalienable**, absolute, unalterable, unchallengeable; sacrosanct, holy, sacred.

inviolate adjective *his home remained inviolate:* **untouched**, undamaged, unhurt, unharmed, unscathed; unspoiled, unflawed, unsullied, unstained, undefiled, unprofaned, perfect, pristine, pure; intact, unbroken, whole, entire, complete.

invisible adjective *an invisible gas:* **impossible to see**; undetectable, indiscernible, inconspicuous, imperceptible; unseen, unnoticed, unobserved, hidden, obscured, out of sight.

invitation noun **1** *an invitation to dinner:* **request to attend**, call, summons; *informal* invite. **2** *an open door is an invitation to a thief:* **encouragement**, provocation, temptation, lure, magnet, bait, enticement, attraction, allure; *informal* come-on.

invite verb **1** *they invited us to Sunday lunch:* **ask**, summon, have someone over/round, request (the pleasure of) someone's company at. **2** *applications are invited for the posts:* **ask for**, request, call for, appeal for, solicit, seek, summon. **3** *airing such views invites trouble:* **cause**, induce, provoke, create, generate, engender, foster, encourage, lead to; incite, elicit, bring on oneself, arouse.

inviting adjective *an inviting smell of coffee wafted into the room:* **tempting**, enticing, alluring, beguiling; attractive, appealing, pleasant, agreeable, delightful; appetizing, mouth-watering; fascinating, enchanting, entrancing, captivating, intriguing, irresistible, seductive.
– OPPOSITES repellent.

invocation noun **1** *her invocation of new methodologies:* **citation**, mention, acknowledgement, reference to, allusion to. **2** *the invocation of rain by tribal people:* **summoning**, calling up, conjuring up. **3** *an invocation to the Holy Ghost:* **prayer**, intercession, supplication, entreaty, petition, appeal.

invoice noun *an invoice for the goods:* **bill**, account, statement (of charges); *N. Amer.* check; *informal* tab.
verb *we'll invoice you for the damage:* **bill**, charge, send an invoice/bill to.

invoke verb **1** *he invoked his statutory rights:* **cite**, refer to, adduce, instance; resort

i

to, have recourse to, turn to. **2** *I invoked the Madonna:* **pray to**, call on, appeal to, supplicate, entreat, solicit, beg, implore. **3** *invoking the spirits:* **summon**, call (up), conjure (up). **4** *middle-class moralities invoke peculiar anxieties:* **bring forth**, bring out, elicit, induce, cause, kindle.

involuntary adjective **1** *she gave an involuntary shudder:* **reflex**, automatic; spontaneous, instinctive, unconscious, unintentional, uncontrollable. **2** *the involuntary repatriation of immigrants:* **compulsory**, obligatory, mandatory, forced, coerced, compelled, imposed, required, prescribed; unwilling, unconsenting, against one's will.
– OPPOSITES deliberate, optional.

involve verb **1** *the inspection involved a lot of work:* **require**, necessitate, demand, call for; entail, mean, imply, presuppose. **2** *I try to involve everyone in key decisions:* **include**, count in, bring in, take into account, take note of; cover, incorporate, encompass, touch on, embrace, comprehend. **3** *many drug addicts involve themselves in crime:* **implicate**, incriminate, inculpate; associate, connect, concern; embroil, entangle, enmesh; informal mix up.
– OPPOSITES preclude, exclude.

involved adjective **1** *social workers involved in the case:* **associated**, connected, concerned. **2** *he had been involved in burglaries:* **implicated**, incriminated, inculpated, embroiled, entangled, caught up, mixed up. **3** *a long and involved story:* **complicated**, intricate, complex, elaborate; convoluted, impenetrable, unfathomable. **4** *they were totally involved in their work:* **engrossed**, absorbed, immersed, caught up, preoccupied, busy, engaged, intent.
– OPPOSITES unconnected, straightforward.

involvement noun **1** *his involvement in a plot to overthrow the government:* **participation**, action, hand; collaboration, collusion, complicity, implication, incrimination, inculpation; association, connection, attachment, entanglement. **2** *emotional involvement:* **attachment**, friendship, intimacy; relationship, relations, bond.

invulnerable adjective *no state in the region is invulnerable to attack:* **impervious**, insusceptible, immune; indestructible, impenetrable, impregnable, unassailable, inviolable, invincible, secure; proof against.

inward adjective **1** *our inward flight was delayed:* **towards the inside**, incoming, ingoing, inbound, return, homeward, coming in, going in, concave. **2** *an inward smile:* **internal**, inner, interior, innermost; private, personal, hidden, secret, veiled, masked, concealed, unexpressed.
– OPPOSITES outward.
adverb *the door opened inward.* See **INWARDS**.

inwardly adverb *inwardly, George blamed himself:* **inside**, internally, within, deep down (inside), in one's heart (of hearts); privately, secretly, confidentially.

inwards adverb *light spilled inwards from the porch:* **inside**, into the interior, inward, within.

iota noun *nothing she said seemed to make an iota of difference:* **(little) bit**, mite, speck, scrap, shred, ounce, scintilla, atom, jot (or tittle); informal smidgen.

irascible adjective *an irascible young man:* **irritable**, quick-tempered, short-tempered, snappish, tetchy, testy, touchy, edgy, crabby, waspish, dyspeptic; crusty, grouchy, cantankerous, curmudgeonly, ill-natured, peevish, querulous, fractious; informal prickly, ratty, snappy.

irate adjective *an irate customer:* **angry**, furious, infuriated, incensed, enraged, incandescent, fuming, seething, cross, mad; raging, ranting, raving, in a frenzy, beside oneself, outraged, up in arms; indignant, annoyed, irritated, irked, piqued; informal foaming at the mouth, hot under the collar.

Ireland noun Eire, the Republic of Ireland, the Irish Republic; Hibernia, the Emerald Isle.

iridescent adjective *the iridescent films of oil on top of puddles:* **shimmering**, glittering, sparkling, dazzling, shining, gleaming, glowing, lustrous, scintillating, opalescent.

irk verb *her reticence about certain things irked him:* **irritate**, annoy, gall, pique, nettle, exasperate, try someone's patience; anger, infuriate, madden, incense, get on someone's nerves; antagonize, provoke, ruffle someone's feathers, make someone's hackles rise; Brit. rub up the wrong way; informal get someone's goat, get/put someone's back up, make someone's blood boil, peeve, miff, rile, aggravate, needle, get (to), bug, hack off, brown off, get up someone's nose, give someone the hump, drive mad/crazy, drive up the wall, make someone see red; Brit. informal wind up, cheese off, nark, get on someone's wick; N. Amer. informal tee off, tick off, rankle, ride, gravel.
– OPPOSITES please.

irksome adjective *an irksome task:* **irritating**, annoying, vexing, vexatious, galling, exasperating, disagreeable; tiresome, wearisome, tedious, trying, troublesome, bothersome, awkward, difficult, boring, uninteresting; infuriating, maddening; informal infernal.

iron noun **1** *a soldering iron:* **tool**, implement, utensil, device. **2** *they were clapped in irons:* **manacles**, shackles, fetters, chains, handcuffs; informal cuffs, bracelets.
adjective **1** *an iron compound:* **ferrous**, ferric. **2** *an iron law of politics:* **inflexible**, unbreakable, absolute, unconditional, categorical, incontrovertible, infallible. **3** *an iron will:* **uncompromising**, unrelenting, unyielding, unbending, resolute, resolved,

determined, firm, rigid, steadfast, unwavering.
– OPPOSITES flexible.
verb *she irons his shirts:* **press**, smooth.
■ **iron something out** *John had ironed out all the minor snags:* resolve, straighten out, sort out, clear up, settle, put right, solve, remedy, rectify; eliminate, eradicate, erase, get rid of; informal fix, mend.

ironic adjective **1** *Edward's tone was ironic:* **sarcastic**, sardonic, dry, caustic, sharp, stinging, scathing, acerbic, acid, bitter, trenchant, mordant, cynical; mocking, satirical, scoffing, derisory, derisive, scornful; Brit. informal sarky. **2** *it's ironic that I've ended up writing for a living:* **paradoxical**, incongruous, odd, strange, peculiar, unexpected.
– OPPOSITES sincere.

irony noun **1** *that note of irony in her voice:* **sarcasm**, sardonicism, dryness, causticity, sharpness, acerbity, bitterness, trenchancy, mordancy, cynicism; mockery, satire, ridicule, derision, scorn; Brit. informal sarkiness. **2** *the irony of the situation:* **paradox**, incongruity, incongruousness, peculiarity.
– OPPOSITES sincerity.

irradiate verb *he was irradiated by a steady glow:* **illuminate**, light (up), cast light upon, brighten, shine on.

irrational adjective *she told herself that it was an irrational fear:* **unreasonable**, illogical, groundless, baseless, unfounded, unjustifiable; absurd, ridiculous, ludicrous, silly, foolish, senseless.
– OPPOSITES logical.

irreconcilable adjective **1** *irreconcilable views:* **incompatible**, at odds, at variance, conflicting, clashing, antagonistic, mutually exclusive, diametrically opposed; disparate, variant, dissimilar, poles apart; rare oppugnant. **2** *irreconcilable enemies:* **implacable**, unappeasable, uncompromising, inflexible; mortal, bitter, deadly, sworn, out-and-out.
– OPPOSITES compatible.

irrecoverable adjective *an irrecoverable bad debt:* **unrecoverable**, unreclaimable, irretrievable, irredeemable, unsalvageable, gone for ever; written off.

irrefutable adjective *there is irrefutable evidence that there will be a shortfall:* **indisputable**, undeniable, unquestionable, incontrovertible, incontestable, beyond question, beyond doubt; conclusive, definite, definitive, decisive, certain, positive.

irregular adjective **1** *he had irregular features | an irregular coastline:* **asymmetrical**, non-uniform, uneven, crooked, misshapen, lopsided, twisted; jagged, ragged, serrated, indented. **2** *the instrument does not read accurately on irregular surfaces:* **rough**, bumpy, uneven, pitted, rutted; lumpy, knobbly, gnarled. **3** *an irregular heartbeat:* **inconsistent**, unsteady, uneven, fitful,

patchy, variable, varying, changeable, changing, inconstant, erratic, unstable, unsettled, spasmodic, intermittent, fluctuating. **4** *irregular financial dealings:* **against the rules**, out of order, improper, illegitimate, unscrupulous, unethical, unprofessional, unacceptable, beyond the pale; informal shady; Brit. informal not cricket; Austral./NZ informal over the fence. **5** *an irregular army:* **guerrilla**, underground; paramilitary, partisan, mercenary.
– OPPOSITES straight, smooth.
noun *gun-toting irregulars:* **guerrilla**, underground fighter; paramilitary; resistance fighter, partisan, mercenary.

irregularity noun **1** *the irregularity of the coastline:* **asymmetry**, non-uniformity, unevenness, crookedness, lopsidedness; jaggedness, raggedness, indentation. **2** *the irregularity of the surface:* **roughness**, bumpiness, unevenness, lumpiness, knobbliness. **3** *the irregularity of the bus service:* **inconsistency**, unsteadiness, unevenness, fitfulness, patchiness, inconstancy, instability, variability, changeableness, fluctuation, unpredictability, unreliability. **4** *financial irregularities:* **impropriety**, wrongdoing, misconduct, dishonesty, corruption, immorality; informal shadiness, crookedness. **5** *staff noted any irregularity in operation:* **abnormality**, unusualness, strangeness, oddness, singularity, atypicality, anomaly, deviation, aberration, peculiarity, idiosyncrasy.

irregularly adverb **1** *the tower is in fact irregularly hexagonal:* **asymmetrically**, unevenly. **2** *his heart was beating irregularly:* **erratically**, intermittently, in/by fits and starts, fitfully, patchily, haphazardly, unsystematically, unmethodically, inconsistently, unsteadily, unevenly, variably, spasmodically, discontinuously, inconstantly.

irrelevance noun *he was frustrated by the irrelevance of much that is taught:* **inapplicability**, unrelatedness, inappropriateness, inappositeness; unimportance, inconsequentiality, insignificance.

irrelevant adjective *students must avoid wasting time on irrelevant detail:* **beside the point**, immaterial, not pertinent, not germane, off the subject, unconnected, unrelated, peripheral, extraneous, inapposite; unimportant, inconsequential, insignificant, trivial.

irreligious adjective *an irreligious world:* **atheistic**, unbelieving, non-believing, agnostic, heretical, faithless, godless, ungodly, impious, profane, infidel, barbarian, heathen, pagan.
– OPPOSITES pious.

irreparable adjective *if the pump runs dry, irreparable damage can be done:* **irreversible**, unrectifiable, irrevocable,

unrestorable, irrecoverable, unrepairable, beyond repair.
– OPPOSITES repairable.

irreplaceable adjective *if you make a mistake you may ruin an irreplaceable recording:* **unique**, unrepeatable, incomparable, unparalleled; treasured, prized, cherished.

irrepressible adjective **1** *the desire for freedom is irrepressible:* **inextinguishable**, unquenchable, uncontainable, uncontrollable, indestructible, undying, everlasting. **2** *his irrepressible personality:* **ebullient**, exuberant, buoyant, sunny, breezy, jaunty, light-hearted, high-spirited, vivacious, animated, full of life, lively; Brit. Tiggerish; informal bubbly, bouncy, peppy, chipper, chirpy, full of beans.

irreproachable adjective *his private life was irreproachable:* **impeccable**, exemplary, model, immaculate, outstanding, exceptional, admirable, perfect; above/beyond reproach, blameless, faultless, flawless, unblemished, untarnished, spotless; informal squeaky clean, whiter than white.
– OPPOSITES reprehensible.

irresistible adjective **1** *her irresistible smile:* **tempting**, enticing, alluring, inviting, seductive; attractive, desirable, fetching, appealing, captivating, beguiling, enchanting. **2** *an irresistible impulse:* **uncontrollable**, overwhelming, overpowering, compelling, compulsive, irrepressible, ungovernable, driving, forceful.

irresolute adjective *she stood irresolute outside his door:* **indecisive**, hesitant, vacillating, equivocating, dithering, wavering, shilly-shallying; ambivalent, blowing hot and cold, in two minds, in a dilemma, in a quandary, torn; doubtful, in doubt, unsure, uncertain, undecided; informal sitting on the fence.
– OPPOSITES decisive.

irresolution noun **indecisiveness**, indecision, irresoluteness, hesitancy, hesitation; doubt, doubtfulness, unsureness, uncertainty; vacillation, equivocation, wavering, shilly-shallying, blowing hot and cold, dithering, temporizing, temporization; Brit. havering, humming and hawing; informal dilly-dallying, sitting on the fence.

irrespective adjective *each member has one vote, irrespective of the number of shares held:* **regardless of**, without regard to/for, notwithstanding, whatever, no matter what, without consideration of; informal irregardless of.

irresponsible adjective **1** *irresponsible behaviour:* **reckless**, rash, careless, thoughtless, incautious, unwise, imprudent, ill-advised, injudicious, misguided, unheeding, hasty, overhasty, precipitate, precipitous, foolhardy, impetuous, impulsive, devil-may-care,

hot-headed, delinquent; N. Amer. derelict. **2** *an irresponsible teenager:* **immature**, naive, foolish, hare-brained; unreliable, undependable, untrustworthy, flighty, giddy, scatterbrained, harum-scarum.
– OPPOSITES sensible.

irretrievable adjective *the situation was now irretrievable:* **irreversible**, unrectifiable, irremediable, irrecoverable, irreparable, unrepairable, beyond repair.
– OPPOSITES reversible.

irreverent adjective *an irreverent attitude to tradition:* **disrespectful**, disdainful, scornful, contemptuous, derisive, disparaging; impertinent, cheeky, flippant, rude, discourteous.
– OPPOSITES respectful.

irreversible adjective *irreversible damage:* **irreparable**, unrepairable, beyond repair, unrectifiable, irremediable, irrevocable, permanent; unalterable, unchangeable, immutable; Law peremptory.

irrevocable adjective *an irrevocable step:* **irreversible**, unalterable, unchangeable, immutable, final, binding, permanent; Law peremptory.

irrigate verb *the scheme aims to divert water from the river to irrigate the land:* **water**, bring water to, soak, flood, inundate.

irritability noun *his irritability puts people off him:* **irascibility**, tetchiness, testiness, touchiness, grumpiness, moodiness, grouchiness, a (bad) mood, cantankerousness, curmudgeonliness, bad temper, short temper, ill humour, peevishness, crossness, fractiousness, pettishness, crabbiness, waspishness, prickliness; Brit. informal shirtiness, stroppiness, rattiness; N. Amer. informal crankiness, orneriness; Austral./NZ informal snakiness.

irritable adjective *being out of work made him irritable:* **bad-tempered**, short-tempered, irascible, tetchy, testy, touchy, grumpy, grouchy, moody, crotchety, in a (bad) mood, cantankerous, curmudgeonly, ill-tempered, ill-humoured, peevish, cross, fractious, pettish, crabby, waspish, prickly, splenetic, dyspeptic, choleric; informal on a short fuse; Brit. informal shirty, stroppy, ratty; N. Amer. informal cranky, ornery, peckish; Austral./NZ informal snaky.
– OPPOSITES good-humoured.

irritant noun *in 1966 Vietnam was becoming an irritant to the Labour government:* **annoyance**, (source of) irritation, thorn in someone's side/flesh, pest, bother, trial, torment, plague, inconvenience, nuisance; informal aggravation, peeve, pain (in the neck), headache; N. Amer. informal nudnik, burr in/under someone's saddle; Austral./NZ informal nark.

irritate verb **1** *the smallest things may irritate you:* **annoy**, vex, make angry, make cross, anger, exasperate, irk, gall, pique, nettle, put

out, antagonize, get on someone's nerves, try someone's patience, ruffle someone's feathers, make someone's hackles rise; infuriate, madden, provoke; Brit. rub up the wrong way; informal aggravate, miff, rile, needle, get to, bug, hack off, get under someone's skin, get/put someone's back up, get up someone's nose, give someone the hump, drive mad/crazy, drive round the bend/twist, drive up the wall; Brit. informal wind up, get on someone's wick; N. Amer. informal tee off, tick off, rankle, ride, gravel. **2** *some sand irritated my eyes:* **inflame**, aggravate, hurt, chafe, abrade, scratch, scrape, graze.
– OPPOSITES pacify, soothe.

irritated adjective *she was irritated with herself for behaving so pettily:* **annoyed**, cross, angry, vexed, exasperated, irked, piqued, nettled, put out, fed up, disgruntled, in a bad mood, in a temper, testy, huffy, in a huff, aggrieved; irate, infuriated, incensed; informal aggravated, peeved, miffed, mad, riled, hacked off, browned off, hot under the collar; Brit. informal cheesed off, brassed off, ratty, shirty; N. Amer. informal teed off, ticked off, sore; Austral./NZ informal snaky, crook.
– OPPOSITES good-humoured.

irritating adjective *an irritating habit:* **annoying**, infuriating, exasperating, maddening, trying, tiresome, vexing, vexatious, irksome, galling; informal aggravating.
– OPPOSITES pleasing.

irritation noun **1** *she tried not to show her irritation:* **annoyance**, exasperation, vexation, indignation, impatience, crossness, displeasure, chagrin, pique; anger, rage, fury, wrath; informal aggravation. **2** *I realize my presence is an irritation for you:* **irritant**, annoyance, thorn in someone's side/flesh, bother, trial, torment, plague, inconvenience, nuisance; informal aggravation, pain (in the neck), headache; N. Amer. informal nudnik, burr in/under someone's saddle; Austral./NZ informal nark.
– OPPOSITES delight.

island noun **isle**, islet, atoll; Brit. holm; (**islands**) archipelago.

isolate verb **1** *she isolated herself from her family* | *the contaminated area was isolated:* **separate**, set/keep apart, segregate, detach, cut off, shut away, divorce, alienate, distance; keep in solitude, cloister, seclude; cordon off, seal off, close off, fence off. **2** *the laser beam can isolate the offending vehicles:* **identify**, single out, pick out, point out, spot, recognize, distinguish, pinpoint, locate.
– OPPOSITES integrate.

isolated adjective **1** *isolated communities:* **remote**, out of the way, outlying, off the beaten track, secluded, lonely, in the back of beyond, godforsaken, inaccessible, cut-off; N. Amer. in the backwoods, lonesome; Austral./NZ

in the backblocks, in the booay; informal in the middle of nowhere, in the sticks; N. Amer. informal jerkwater, in the tall timbers; Austral./NZ informal Barcoo, beyond the black stump. **2** *he lived a very isolated existence:* **solitary**, lonely, companionless, friendless; secluded, cloistered, segregated, unsociable, reclusive, hermitic; N. Amer. lonesome. **3** *an isolated incident:* **unique**, lone, solitary; unusual, uncommon, exceptional, anomalous, abnormal, untypical, freak; informal one-off.
– OPPOSITES accessible, sociable, common.

isolation noun **1** *patients who need isolation:* **separation**, segregation, seclusion, keeping apart. **2** *their feeling of isolation:* **solitariness**, loneliness, friendlessness. **3** *the isolation of some mental hospitals:* **remoteness**, seclusion, inaccessibility.
– OPPOSITES contact.

issue noun **1** *the committee discussed the issue:* **matter (in question)**, question, point (at issue), affair, case, subject, topic; problem, bone of contention. **2** *the issue of a special stamp:* **issuing**, publication, publishing; circulation, distribution, supplying; appearance. **3** *the latest issue of our magazine:* **edition**, number, instalment, copy. **4** (Law) *she died without issue:* **offspring**, descendants, heirs, successors, children, progeny, family; informal kids. **5** *an issue of blood:* **discharge**, emission, release, outflow, outflowing, outflux; secretion, emanation, exudation, effluence.
verb **1** *the minister issued a statement:* **send out**, put out, release, deliver, publish, announce, broadcast, communicate, circulate, distribute, disseminate. **2** *the captain issued the crew with guns:* **supply**, provide, furnish, arm, equip, fit out, rig out, kit out; informal fix up. **3** *savoury smells issued from the kitchen:* **emanate**, emerge, exude, flow (out/forth), pour (out/forth); be emitted. **4** *large profits might issue from the deal:* **result**, follow, ensue, stem, spring, arise, proceed; be the result of, be brought on/about by, be produced by.
– OPPOSITES withdraw.
■ **at issue** in question, in dispute, under discussion, under consideration, for debate.
■ **take issue** disagree, be in dispute, be in contention, be at variance, be at odds, argue, quarrel; challenge, dispute, (call into) question.

itch noun *I have an itch on my back:* **irritation**, tingling, itchiness.
verb *my chilblains really itch:* **be itchy**, tingle, be irritated.

item noun **1** *there were several items for sale:* **thing**, article, object, artefact, piece, product. **2** *the main item in a badger's diet:* **element**, constituent, component, ingredient. **3** *the meeting discussed the item:* **issue**, matter, affair, case, situation, subject, topic, question, point. **4** *a news item:* **report**, story, account, article, piece, write-up, bulletin, feature. **5** *items in the profit and loss account:* **entry**, record, statement, listing.

itemize verb **1** *Steinburg itemized thirty-two design faults:* **list**, catalogue, inventory, record, document, register, detail, specify, identify; enumerate, number. **2** *most phone companies give you an itemized bill:* **analyse**, break down, split up.

iterate verb *the process is iterated until a convincing agreement is reached:* **repeat**, recapitulate, go over/through again; say again, restate, reiterate; informal recap.

itinerant adjective *itinerant traders:* **travelling**, peripatetic, wandering, roving, roaming, touring, nomadic, gypsy, migrant, vagrant, vagabond, of no fixed address/abode.
 noun *an itinerants' lodging house:* **traveller**, wanderer, roamer, rover, nomad, gypsy, migrant, transient, drifter, vagabond, vagrant, tramp.

itinerary noun *Cambridge should be on every visitor's itinerary:* **(planned) route**, journey, way, road; travel plan, schedule, timetable, programme, tour.

i

Wordfinder

Index

Index

Wordfinder

Animals

Amphibians

axolotl	fire salamander	horned toad	newt	tree frog
bullfrog	flying frog	marsh frog	salamander	
cane toad	frog	natterjack toad	toad	

Birds

adjutant bird	dipper	hen harrier	noddy	seagull
albatross	diver	heron	nuthatch	secretary bird
antbird	dodo	herring gull	ortolan	shag
Arctic tern	dotterel	hobby	osprey	shearwater
auk	dove	honeyguide	ostrich	shelduck
avocet	duck	hooded crow	ouzel	shoebill
bald eagle	dunlin	hoopoe	owl	shoveler
barnacle goose	dunnock	hornbill	oystercatcher	shrike
barn owl	eagle	horned owl	parakeet	siskin
bateleur eagle	eagle owl	house martin	parrot	skua
Bewick's swan	egret	house sparrow	partridge	skylark
bird of paradise	eider duck	hummingbird	peacock	snipe
bittern	emperor	ibis	peafowl	snow bunting
blackbird	penguin	jackdaw	peewit	snow goose
blackcap	emu	jay	pelican	snowy owl
black swan	falcon	kestrel	penguin	song thrush
bluebird	fantail	kingfisher	peregrine falcon	sparrow
blue tit	fieldfare	king penguin	petrel	sparrowhawk
booby	finch	kite	phalarope	spoonbill
bowerbird	flamingo	kittiwake	pheasant	starling
brambling	flycatcher	kiwi	pigeon	stonechat
broadbill	frigate bird	kookaburra	pilot bird	stone curlew
brown owl	fulmar	lammergeier	pintail	stork
budgerigar	gannet	lanner	pipit	storm petrel
bullfinch	godwit	lapwing	plover	sunbird
bunting	goldcrest	lark	ptarmigan	swallow
bustard	golden eagle	laughing jackass	puffin	swan
butcher-bird	goldfinch	linnet	quail	swift
buzzard	goose	little grebe	rail	tawny owl
Canada goose	goshawk	little owl	raven	teal
canary	great auk	long-tailed tit	razorbill	tern
capercaillie	great crested	lorikeet	red kite	thrush
caracara	grebe	lovebird	redpoll	tit
cassowary	great tit	lyrebird	redshank	titmouse
chaffinch	grebe	macaw	redstart	toucan
chicken	green	magpie	redwing	treecreeper
chiffchaff	woodpecker	mallard	reed bunting	turkey
chough	greenfinch	mandarin duck	reed warbler	turkey vulture
coal tit	greenshank	marabou stork	rhea	turtle dove
cockatiel	greylag goose	marsh harrier	rhinoceros bird	vulture
cockatoo	griffon vulture	martin	ringdove	wagtail
condor	grouse	meadowlark	ring ouzel	wallcreeper
coot	guillemot	merlin	roadrunner	warbler
cormorant	guineafowl	mistle thrush	robin	waxbill
corncrake	gull	moa	rook	waxwing
crane	gyrfalcon	mockingbird	ruddy duck	weaver bird
crossbill	harrier	moorhen	ruff	wheatear
crow	hawfinch	mute swan	sand martin	whinchat
cuckoo	hawk	mynah bird	sandpiper	whippoorwill
curlew	hawk owl	nighthawk	scops owl	whitethroat
dabchick	hedge sparrow	nightingale	screech owl	whooping crane
darter	hen	nightjar	sea eagle	whydah

wigeon	woodchat	woodlark	wood pigeon	wryneck
willow warbler	woodcock	woodpecker	wren	yellowhammer

Butterflies and Moths

Adonis blue	codlin/codling	hairstreak	noctuid	silver Y
argus	moth	hawkmoth	nymphalid	skipper
atlas moth	comma	heath	oak eggar	speckled wood
birdwing	common heath	io moth	old lady	sulphur
blue	copper	lackey	painted lady	swallowtail
brimstone	dagger	lappet	papilionid	swift
brown	death's head	leopard moth	peacock	tiger moth
buff-tip	hawkmoth	lobster moth	butterfly	tortoiseshell
burnet	drinker	luna moth	peppered moth	tortrix
cabbage moth	eggar	magpie moth	plume moth	tussock moth
cabbage white	emerald	marbled white	pug	underwing
Camberwell	emperor	meadow brown	purple emperor	vapourer
beauty	ermine	merveille du jour	puss moth	wall brown
chalkhill blue	fritillary	milkweed	pyralid	wax moth
cinnabar	gatekeeper	monarch	red admiral	white admiral
clearwing	goat moth	morpho	ringlet	white spot
clouded yellow	grayling	Mother Shipton	satyrid	yellow-tail
	gypsy moth	mourning cloak	silk moth	

Crustaceans

acorn barnacle	fiddler crab	horseshoe crab	lobster	spiny lobster
barnacle	fish louse	king crab	mitten crab	tiger prawn
crab	freshwater	king prawn	Norway lobster	woodlouse
crawfish	crayfish	krill	prawn	
crayfish	ghost crab	land crab	sandhopper	
crevette	goose barnacle	langouste	shrimp	
fairy shrimp	hermit crab	langoustine	spider crab	

Dinosaurs

allosaurus	coelurosaur	hadrosaur	pterodactyl	theropod
ankylosaur	deinonychus	iguanodon	raptor	triceratops
apatosaurus	diplodocus	megalosaurus	saurischian	tyrannosaurus
brachiosaurus	dromaeosaur	pliosaur	sauropod	velociraptor
brontosaurus	duck-billed	protoceratops	seismosaurus	
carnosaur	dinosaur	pteranodon	stegosaur	

Fish

albacore	blackfish	butterfly fish	damselfish	flying fish
alewife	bleak	butterfly ray	darter	flying gurnard
amberjack	blenny	carp	devil ray	frogfish
anchovy	blowfish	carpet shark	dogfish	garfish
anemone fish	bluefin	catfish	dorado	garpike
angelfish	bluefish	charr	dory	goatfish
angel shark	blue shark	chimera	Dover sole	goby
anglerfish	boarfish	chub	dragonfish	goldfish
archerfish	bonefish	climbing perch	eagle ray	goosefish
balloonfish	bonito	clingfish	eel	gourami
bandfish	bonnethead	clownfish	eelpout	grayling
barbel	bowfin	coalfish	electric eel	great white
barracouta	boxfish	cod	electric ray	shark
barracuda	bream	coelacanth	fighting fish	grenadier
barramundi	brill	coley	filefish	grey mullet
basking shark	brisling	conger eel	flatfish	grouper
bass	brown trout	crappie	flathead	grunion
beluga	bullhead	dab	flounder	gudgeon
bitterling	burbot	dace	fluke	guitarfish

gulper eel
gunnel
guppy
gurnard
haddock
hake
halfbeak
halibut
hammerhead
herring
hoki
humpback
  salmon
huss
icefish
John Dory
kingfish
koi carp
labyrinth fish
lamprey
lanternfish
leatherjacket
lemon sole
ling
loach
lumpsucker
lungfish
mackerel
mako
manta

marlin
megamouth
minnow
molly
monkfish
moonfish
moray eel
mudfish
mudminnow
mudskipper
mullet
needlefish
nurse hound
nurse shark
oarfish
orfe
parrotfish
perch
pickerel
pike
pikeperch
pilchard
pilotfish
pipefish
piranha
plaice
pollack
pomfret
porbeagle
porcupine fish

porgy
puffer fish
rabbitfish
rainbow trout
ray
redfish
red mullet
red snapper
ribbonfish
roach
rock bass
rockling
rudd
ruffe
sailfish
salmon
salmon trout
sand eel
sandfish
sand shark
sardine
sawfish
scad
scorpionfish
sea bass
sea bream
sea horse
sea perch
sea robin
sea trout

shad
shark
shark-sucker
sheepshead
shovelhead
silverside
skate
skipjack tuna
skipper
smelt
smooth hound
snake mackerel
snapper
snipefish
sockeye salmon
sole
sparling
spearfish
sprat
stargazer
stickleback
stingray
stonefish
sturgeon
sucker
sunfish
surgeonfish
swordfish
swordtail
tench

tetra
thornback
threadfin
thresher
tiger shark
tilapia
toadfish
tope
triggerfish
trout
tuna
tunny
turbot
walleye
weakfish
weever
whaler
whale shark
whitebait
whitefish
whiting
witch
wobbegong
wolf fish
wrasse
yellowfin
yellowtail
zander

Insects

alderfly
amazon ant
ant
ant lion
aphid
army ant
army worm
assassin bug
bark beetle
bedbug
bee
beetle
black ant
blackfly
blister beetle
blowfly
bluebottle
body louse
boll weevil
bombardier
  beetle
booklouse
borer
botfly
bulldog ant
bumblebee
bush cricket
butterfly
caddis fly
carpenter ant

carpenter bee
carpet beetle
carrion beetle
chafer
chigger
cicada
click beetle
cluster fly
cockchafer
cockroach
Colorado beetle
crab louse
crane fly
cricket
cuckoo bee
cuckoo wasp
daddy-long-legs
damselfly
darter
death-watch
  beetle
devil's coach-
  horse
dragonfly
driver ant
drone fly
dung beetle
dung fly
earwig
filaria

fire ant
firefly
flea
fluke
fly
froghopper
fruit fly
furniture beetle
gadfly
gall wasp
glow-worm
gnat
goliath beetle
grasshopper
greenbottle
greenfly
groundhopper
head louse
Hercules beetle
honey ant
honeybee
hornet
horsefly
housefly
hoverfly
jewel beetle
lacewing
ladybird
lantern fly
leafcutter ant

leafcutter bee
leafhopper
leaf miner
leatherjacket
leech
locust
longhorn beetle
louse
mantis
mason bee
May bug
mayfly
meal beetle
mealy bug
midge
mining bee
mosquito
moth
oil beetle
pharaoh ant
phylloxera
pond skater
praying mantis
rhinoceros
  beetle
robber fly
sandfly
sawfly
scale insect
scarab

scorpion fly
sexton beetle
silverfish
springtail
stag beetle
stick insect
stink bug
stonefly
termite
thrips
thunderbug
thunderfly
toxocara
treehopper
tsetse fly
velvet ant
warble fly
wasp
water beetle
water boatman
water scorpion
weevil
whirligig
white ant
whitefly
witchetty grub
woodwasp

Wordfinder

Mammals

aardvark
alpaca
angora
anteater
antelope
ape
armadillo
ass
aurochs
baboon
badger
baleen whale
Barbary ape
bat
beaked whale
bear
beaver
beluga
bison
black bear
blue whale
boar
bobcat
bottlenose
  dolphin
bottlenose
  whale
bowhead whale
brown bear
buffalo
bushbaby
camel
capuchin
  monkey
capybara
caracal
caribou
cat
chamois
cheetah
chimpanzee
chinchilla
chipmunk
civet
coati
colobus
colugo

cougar
cow
coyote
coypu
deer
dingo
dog
dolphin
donkey
dormouse
dromedary
duck-billed
  platypus
dugong
duiker
echidna
eland
elephant
elephant seal
elk
ermine
fallow deer
fennec
ferret
fin whale
flying fox
fox
fur seal
galago
gaur
gayal
gazelle
gemsbok
gerbil
gibbon
giraffe
gnu
goat
gopher
gorilla
grampus
grey seal
grizzly bear
guinea pig
hamadryas
hamster
hanuman langur

hare
harp seal
hartebeest
hedgehog
hippo
hog
honey bear
hooded seal
horse
howler monkey
humpback
  whale
hyena
hyrax
ibex
impala
jackal
jaguar
jaguarundi
killer whale
kinkajou
Kodiak bear
kudu
langur
laughing hyena
lemming
lemur
leopard
leopard seal
lion
llama
loris
lynx
macaque
manatee
mandrill
margay
marmoset
marsupial
marten
meerkat
mink
minke whale
mole
mongoose
monkey
monk seal

moose
mountain goat
mountain lion
mouse
mule
muntjac
musk deer
musk ox
narwhal
ocelot
okapi
onager
opossum
orang-utan
orca
oryx
otter
ox
panda
pangolin
panther
peccary
pig
pika
pilot whale
pine marten
pipistrelle
platypus
polar bear
polecat
porcupine
porpoise
possum
potto
proboscis
  monkey
puma
rabbit
raccoon
rat
red deer
red panda
reindeer
rhesus monkey
rhinoceros
right whale
roe deer

rorqual
sable
sea cow
sea elephant
seal
sea lion
sei whale
serval
sheep
shrew
skunk
sloth
sloth bear
snow leopard
spectacled bear
sperm whale
spider monkey
spiny anteater
springbok
squirrel
squirrel monkey
stoat
sun bear
tamarin
tapir
tarsier
tiger
toothed whale
vampire bat
vervet monkey
vole
walrus
wapiti
warthog
waterbuck
water buffalo
weasel
whale
white whale
wild boar
wildcat
wildebeest
wisent
wolverine
yak
zebra
zebu

Marsupials

antechinus
bandicoot
bettong
bilby
brushtail
brushtail possum
cuscus

dasyure
dibbler
dunnart
flying phalanger
glider
kangaroo
koala

mulgara
numbat
opossum
pademelon
phalanger
planigale
possum

potoroo
quokka
quoll
rat kangaroo
ringtail
Tasmanian devil
Tasmanian tiger

thylacine
wallaby
wallaroo
wombat
yapok

Reptiles

adder
alligator

anaconda
asp

axolotl
basilisk

bearded dragon
black mamba

blind snake
blindworm

boa constrictor
boomslang
bull snake
bushmaster
caiman
chameleon
coachwhip
cobra
colubrid
constrictor
copperhead
coral snake
corn snake
crocodile
death adder

diamondback
  terrapin
Egyptian cobra
fer de lance
flying lizard
frilled lizard
Gaboon viper
galliwasp
garter snake
gecko
gharial
giant tortoise
Gila monster
glass lizard
grass snake

green snake
green turtle
hamadryad
hawksbill
hognose snake
horned toad
iguana
indigo snake
king cobra
Komodo dragon
leatherback
lizard
loggerhead
  turtle
mamba

moloch
monitor lizard
pit viper
puff adder
python
rat snake
rattlesnake
reticulated
  python
rinkhals
sea snake
sidewinder
skink
slider
slow-worm

smooth snake
snake
taipan
terrapin
tokay
tortoise
tuatara
turtle
viper
water moccasin
water snake
whip snake

Shellfish and other Molluscs

abalone
angel wings
argonaut
auger shell
cephalopod
chiton
clam
cockle
conch
cone shell
cowrie
cuttlefish
dog whelk

dove shell
duck mussel
edible snail
gaper
gastropod
geoduck
giant clam
harp shell
helmet
jewel box
lamp shell
limpet
mitre

murex
mussel
nautilus
nerite
nudibranch
octopus
ormer
oyster
paper nautilus
paua
pearl oyster
periwinkle
piddock

pteropod
quahog
ramshorn snail
razor shell
scallop
sea butterfly
sea hare
sea slug
shipworm
slug
snail
softshell clam
squid

teredo
tooth shell
triton
turret shell
tusk shell
wedge shell
wentletrap
whelk
winkle

Spiders and other Arachnids

bird-eating
  spider
black widow
camel spider
chigger
crab spider

false scorpion
funnel-web
  spider
harvestman
harvest mite
itch mite

jigger
mite
money spider
raft spider
redback
red spider mite

scorpion
spider mite
sun spider
tarantula
tick
trapdoor spider

whip scorpion
wolf spider

Male and Female Animals

antelope: *buck,
  doe*
badger: *boar,
  sow*
bear: *boar, sow*
bird: *cock, hen*
buffalo: *bull,
  cow*
cat: *tom, queen*
cattle: *bull, cow*
chicken: *cock,
  hen*

deer: *stag, doe*
dog: *dog, bitch*
donkey: *jackass,
  jenny*
duck: *drake,
  duck*
elephant: *bull,
  cow*
ferret: *jack, gill*
fish: *cock, hen*
fox: *dog, vixen*

goat: *billy goat,
  nanny*
goose: *gander,
  goose*
hare: *buck, doe*
horse: *stallion,
  mare*
kangaroo: *buck,
  doe*
leopard:
  *leopard,
  leopardess*

lion: *lion, lioness*
lobster: *cock,
  hen*
otter: *dog, bitch*
peafowl:
  *peacock,
  peahen*
pheasant: *cock,
  hen*
pig: *boar, sow*
rabbit: *buck,
  doe*

seal: *bull, cow*
sheep: *ram, ewe*
swan: *cob, pen*
tiger: *tiger,
  tigress*
weasel: *boar,
  cow*
whale: *bull, cow*
wolf: *dog, bitch*
zebra: *stallion,
  mare*

Young Animals

calf (*antelope,
  buffalo, camel,
  cattle, elephant,
  elk, giraffe,
  rhinoceros,
  seal, whale*)

chick (*chicken,
  hawk,
  pheasant*)
colt (*male horse*)

cub (*badger,
  bear, fox,
  leopard, lion,
  tiger, walrus,
  wolf*)

cygnet (*swan*)
duckling (*duck*)
eaglet (*eagle*)
elver (*eel*)
eyas (*hawk*)

fawn (*caribou,
  deer*)
filly (*female
  horse*)
foal (*horse,
  zebra*)

Wordfinder

fry (*fish*)
gosling (*goose*)
joey (*kangaroo, wallaby, possum*)
kid (*goat, roe deer*)

kit (*beaver, ferret, fox, mink, weasel*)
kitten (*cat, cougar, rabbit, skunk*)

lamb (*sheep*)
leveret (*hare*)
owlet (*owl*)
parr (*salmon*)
peachick (*peafowl*)

pickerel (*pike*)
piglet (*pig*)
pup (*dog, rat, seal, wolf*)
puppy (*coyote, dog*)

smolt (*salmon*)
squab (*pigeon*)
tadpole (*frog, toad*)
whelp (*dog, wolf*)

Collective Names for Animals

band (*gorillas*)
bask (*crocodiles*)
bellowing (*bullfinches*)
bevy (*roe deer, quails, larks, pheasants*)
bloat (*hippopotami*)
brood (*chickens*)
bury (*rabbits*)
busyness (*ferrets*)
charm (*finches*)
cloud (*gnats*)
covey (*partridges*)
crash (*rhinoceros*)

cry (*hounds*)
descent (*woodpeckers*)
down (*hares*)
drove (*bullocks*)
exaltation (*larks*)
flight (*birds*)
flock (*sheep*)
gaggle (*geese on land*)
herd (*cattle, elephants*)
hive (*bees*)
hover (*trout*)
kennel (*dogs*)
kindle (*kittens*)
knot (*toads*)
labour (*moles*)
leap (*leopards*)

litter (*kittens, pigs*)
mob (*kangaroos*)
murder (*crows*)
murmuration (*starlings*)
muster (*peacocks, penguins*)
obstinacy (*buffalo*)
pack (*hounds, grouse*)
pandemonium (*parrots*)
parade (*elephants*)

parliament (*owls*)
pod (*seals*)
pride (*lions*)
rookery (*rooks*)
safe (*ducks*)
school (*whales, dolphins, porpoises*)
shoal (*fish*)
shrewdness (*apes*)
siege (*herons*)
skein (*geese in flight*)
skulk (*foxes*)
sloth (*bears*)
span (*mules*)
stare (*owls*)

string (*horses*)
stud (*mares*)
swarm (*bees, flies*)
tiding (*magpies*)
trip (*goats*)
troop (*baboons*)
turmoil (*porpoises*)
turn (*turtles*)
unkindness (*ravens*)
watch (*nightingales*)
yoke (*oxen*)
zeal (*zebras*)

Art

Art Schools, Styles, and Movements

abstract expressionism
Aesthetic Movement
Art Deco
art nouveau
Arts and Crafts
avant-garde
baroque
Beaux Arts
Blaue Reiter
Bloomsbury Group
classicism

conceptual art
constructivism
cubism
Dada
De Stijl
expressionism
fauvism
Florentine school
futurism
Grand Manner
Group of Seven
Impressionism
Jugendstil
magic realism

Mannerism
metaphysical painting
minimalism
modernism
naive art
naturalism
Nazarenes
neoclassicism
neo-Impressionism
neoplasticism
neo-realism

Neue Sachlichkeit
op art
performance art
photorealism
plein-air painting
pop art
post-Impressionism
postmodernism
Pre-Raphaelitism
primitive art
Purism
realism

Renaissance art
rococo
romanticism
socialist realism
social realism
Sturm und Drang
suprematism
surrealism
symbolism
tenebrism
ukiyo-e

Art Techniques and Media

acrylic
action painting
airbrushing
aquarelle
aquatint
batik
ceramics
cityscape
cloisonné
collage

colour wash
Conté
distemper
divisionism
drawing
emulsion
enamel
encaustic
engraving
etching

finger-painting
fresco
frottage
gesso
glaze
gouache
grisaille
impasto
intaglio
kakemono

lino cut
lithography
marbling
marquetry
metalwork
mezzotint
miniature
montage
mosaic
mural

oil painting
painting
pastel
photography
photogravure
photomontage
pointillism
polychromy
screen printing
sculpture

scumbling
secco
silk-screen
  printing

sketching
stained glass
sumi-e
tachism

tapestry
tempera
wall painting
watercolour

wood carving
woodcut
wood engraving

Body

Human Bones

ankle bone
anvil
backbone
breastbone
calcaneus
capitate
carpal
carpus
cheekbone
clavicle
collarbone
cranium
cuboid
cuneiform bone
ethmoid

femur
fibula
floating rib
frontal bone
hamate
hammer
heel bone
humerus
hyoid
ilium
incus
innominate
  bone
ischium
jawbone

kneecap
lacrimal
lunate bone
malleus
mandible
maxilla
metacarpal
metatarsal
navicular bone
occipital bone
palatine bone
parietal bone
patella
pelvis
phalanx

pisiform bone
pubis
rachis
radius
rib
ribcage
sacrum
scaphoid
scapula
shin bone
shoulder blade
skull
sphenoid
spinal column
spine

stapes
sternum
stirrup
talus
tarsal
tarsus
temporal bone
thigh bone
tibia
triquetral
ulna
vertebra
vertebral column
zygomatic bone

Organs of the Body

anus
appendix
bladder
brain
breast
colon
duodenum

ear
eye
gall bladder
genitals
heart
ileum
intestine

kidney
larynx
liver
lung
mouth
nose
oesophagus

ovary
pancreas
rectum
skin
spinal cord
spleen
stomach

testicle
tongue
tonsil
trachea
uterus
vagina

Human Teeth

bicuspid
canine
cuspid

eye tooth
incisor
milk tooth

molar
permanent
  tooth

premolar
primary tooth
tricuspid

wisdom tooth

Parts of the Ear

anvil
auditory canal
auditory nerve
auricle

cochlea
eardrum
Eustachian tube
hair cell

hammer
incus
inner ear
middle ear

organ of Corti
outer ear
pinna
stapes

stirrup
tympanic
  membrane
vestibule

Parts of the Eye

aqueous
  humour
blind spot
choroid
cone

conjunctiva
cornea
dilator muscle
eyeball
eyelash

eyelid
fovea
iris
lacrimal glands
lens

limbus
optic nerve
orbit
pupil
retina

rod
sclera
socket
tear glands
vitreous humour

Parts of the Heart

aortic valve
atrium
epicardium

mitral valve
myocardium
pericardium

pulmonary
  artery
pulmonary vein

semilunar valve
tricuspid valve
upper chamber

vena cava
ventricle

Clothing

Wordfinder

Clothes

aloha shirt
anorak
apron
ascot
baggies
ballgown
bandanna
bandeau
Barbour
(trademark)
basque
bathing costume
bedjacket
bell-bottoms
belt
Bermuda shorts
bib
biker jacket
bikini
blazer
bloomers
blouse
blouson
boa
board shorts
bodice
body
body stocking
bodysuit
body warmer
bolero
bolo tie
bomber jacket
boot
bootlace tie
bow tie
bra
braces
breeches
breeks
bumsters
Burberry
(trademark)
burka/burkha/
burqa
burnous
bustier
cagoule
cape
capri pants
cardigan
cargo pants
carpenter
trousers
catsuit
chador
chaparajos
chaps

chemise
cheongsam
chinos
churidars
clamdiggers
coat
coat dress
coatee
combat trousers
cords
corduroys
cravat
crew neck
crinoline
crop top
culottes
cummerbund
cut-offs
cutaway
dashiki
denim jacket
denims
dhoti
dinner jacket
dirndl
divided skirt
djellaba
djibba
dolman
domino
donkey jacket
doublet
dress
dressing gown
dress shirt
ducks
duffel coat
dungarees
fichu
flak jacket
flannels
flares
fleece
flying jacket
foulard
frock coat
fustanella
gabardine/
gabardine
gilet
glove
gown
grandad shirt
grass skirt
greatcoat
guernsey
gymslip
hacking jacket

haik
hair shirt
halter neck
harem pants
hat
hip-huggers
hipsters
hoody/hoodie
hose
hot pants
housecoat
hula skirt
hunting jacket
jacket
jeans
jellaba
jerkin
jersey
jibba
jilbab
jodhpurs
joggers
jogging pants
jumper
jumpsuit
kaftan
kagoul
kameez
kecks
kilt
kimono
knickers
leather jacket
leathers
lederhosen
leggings
leg warmers
leotard
loden
loincloth
loons
lumberjacket
lumberjack shirt
lungi
mac
macfarlane
mackintosh/
macintosh
maillot
mandarin jacket
mantilla
mantle
mantlet
Mao jacket
mask
maternity dress
matinee coat
maxi

maxidress
mess jacket
middy blouse
midi
mini
minidress
miniskirt
mitt
mitten
morning coat
muff
muffler
neckerchief
Nehru jacket
nightdress
nightshirt
nor'wester
Norfolk jacket
obi
oilskins
overalls
overcoat
overtrousers
Oxford bags
palazzo pants
pantaloons
panties
pants
pantyhose
parka
pedal pushers
peignoir
pelisse
pencil skirt
peplum
pinafore
pinafore dress
pinny
plastron
plus fours
polo neck
polo shirt
poncho
puffball skirt
pullover
pyjamas
raglan
rah-rah skirt
raincoat
redingote
reefer jacket
robe
roll-neck
ruff
sack dress
safari jacket
sailor suit
salopettes

salwar
Sam Browne
sandal
sari
sarong
sash
scarf
serape/sarape
shalwar
shawl
sheath dress
sheepskin
shell suit
shift dress
shirt dress
shirtwaister
shooting coat
shooting jacket
shorts
shrug
skinny-rib
ski pants
skirt
skivvy
skort
slacks
slip
slipover
sloppy joe
smock
smoking jacket
sock
sports jacket
stirrup pants
stock
stocking
stole
string tie
suit
sundress
surcoat
surtout
sweater
sweatpants
sweatshirt
swimming
costume
swimming
trunks
swimsuit
swing coat
T-shirt
tabard
tailcoat
tank top
tee
tent dress
tie

tights
tippet
toga
top
topcoat
toreador pants
tracksuit
trench coat

trews
trousers
trouser suit
trunks
tube dress
tunic
turtleneck
tutu

tux/tuxedo
tweeds
twinset
ulster
underpants
underskirt
veil
vest

V-neck
waistcoat
waterproof
waxed jacket
wedding dress
windbreaker
windcheater
woollens

woolly
wrap
yashmak
yukata

Footwear

ballet shoe
balmoral
boot
bootee
bovver boot
brogan
brogue
brothel creeper
buskin
carpet slipper
chappal
Chelsea boot
clog
court shoe
cowboy boot
Cuban heel

dap
deck shoe
Derby
desert boot
Dr Martens
   (trademark)
elevator shoe
espadrille
flip-flop
galosh
ghillie/gillie
gumboot
half-boot
Hessian boot
high heels
high-low

high-top
hobnail boot
jackboot
jelly shoe
kitten heel
lace-up
loafer
moccasin
moon boot
mukluk
mule
napoleon
overboot
overshoe
Oxford
patten

peep-toe
penny loafer
platform
plimsoll
pump
sabot
sandal
shoe
slingback
slip-on
slipper
sneaker
snow boot
snowshoe
step-in
stiletto

tap shoe
tennis shoe
thong
top boot
track shoe
trainer
Turkish slipper
wader
walking boot
wedge
wellington boot
winkle-picker
zori

Headgear

Alice band
balaclava
balmoral
bandeau
baseball cap
beanie
bearskin
beaver hat
beret
biretta
boater
bobble hat
bonnet
bowler
busby
calash
cap
chaplet
circlet
cloche

cloth cap
cocked hat
coif
coolie hat
coronet
cowl
crash helmet
crown
deerstalker
derby
diadem
Dolly Varden
dunce's cap
Dutch cap
earmuffs
fedora
fez
flat cap
garland
glengarry

hairband
hard hat
headband
headscarf
headtie
helmet
high hat
hijab
homburg
hood
jester's cap
jockey cap
Juliet cap
keffiyeh
kepi
mantilla
mitre
mob cap
mortar board
nightcap

opera hat
panama
peaked cap
picture hat
pillbox hat
pixie hat
poke bonnet
pork-pie hat
sailor hat
skullcap
slouch hat
snap-brim hat
snood
sola topi
sombrero
sou'wester
Stetson (trademark)
stocking cap
stovepipe hat
sun bonnet

sun hat
sun helmet
tam-o'-shanter
tarboosh
ten-gallon hat
tiara
top hat
topi
topper
toque
tricorne
trilby
triple crown
turban
veil
wideawake
wimple
wreath
zucchetto

Fabrics and Fibres

acetate
acrylic
alpaca
angora
asbestos
astrakhan
bafta
baize
barathea
barkcloth

batiste
Bedford cord
blanketing
bobbinet
bobbin lace
bombazine
Botany wool
bouclé
broadcloth
brocade

buckram
burlap
butter muslin
calico
cambric
camel hair
candlewick
canvas
cashmere
cavalry twill

challis
chambray
Chantilly lace
cheesecloth
chenille
cheviot
chiffon
chinchilla
chino
chintz

ciré
cloqué
coconut matting
coir
cord
corduroy
cotton
crêpe
crêpe de Chine
crépon

cretonne
crewel
crimplene
(trademark)
crinoline
crushed velvet
cupro
Dacron (trademark)
damask
denim
devoré
dimity
doeskin
Donegal tweed
drab
Dralon (trademark)
drill
duchesse lace
duchesse satin
duffel
dungaree
dupion
elastane
faille
felt
fishnet
flannel
flannelette
flax
fleece
flock
foulard
frieze
fustian
gaberdine/
gabardine
gauze
georgette
gimp
gingham
Gore-tex
(trademark)

gossamer
grasscloth
grenadine
grogram
grosgrain
gros point
guipure
haircloth
Harris tweed
(trademark)
hemp
herringbone
hessian
holland
Honiton lace
hopsack
horsehair
huckaback
ikat
jaconet
jacquard
jean
jersey
jute
kapok
kemp
Kendal Green
kersey
kerseymere
khadi
khaki
kikoi
lace
lambswool
lamé
lawn
leathercloth
leatherette
(trademark)
leno
Lincoln green

linen
linsey-woolsey
lint
lisle
loden
Lurex (trademark)
Lycra (trademark)
madras
marocain
marquisette
matting
melton
merino
microfibre
micromesh
mohair
moiré
moleskin
moquette
moreen
mousseline
mungo
muslin
nainsook
nankeen
needlecord
net
Nottingham lace
nylon
oakum
oilcloth
oilskin
organdie
organza
organzine
Orlon (trademark)
ottoman
paisley
panne velvet
pashmina
peau-de-soie

percale
petersham
pillow lace
pilot cloth
piqué
plaid
plush
plush velvet
point lace
polycotton
polyester
pongee
poplin
raffia
ramie
rayon
rep
ripstop
sackcloth
sacking
sailcloth
sarsenet
sateen
satin
satinette
saxony
sea-island cotton
seersucker
serge
shahtoosh
sharkskin
sheer
Shetland wool
shoddy
silk
sisal
slub
Spandex
(trademark)
spun silk
stockinet

suede
surah
swansdown
tabaret
taffeta
tapestry
tarlatan
tarpaulin
tattersall
tatting
terry
terylene
(trademark)
ticking
tiffany
toile
toile de Jouy
torchon
towelling
tricot
tulle
tussore
tweed
twill
Valenciennes
Velcro (trademark)
velour
velvet
velveteen
vicuña
viscose
Viyella (trademark)
voile
waxcloth
webbing
whipcord
wild silk
wincey
winceyette
wool
worsted

Religious Clothing

alb
amice
biretta
cassock
chasuble
clerical collar

cope
cotta
cowl
dalmatic
dog collar
frock

Geneva bands
habit
hood
mitre
pallium
rochet

scapular
shovel hat
skullcap
soutane
stole
surplice

tallith
tippet
tunicle
wimple
yarmulke
zucchetto

Drinks

Alcoholic Drinks

absinthe
advocaat
aguardiente
alcopop

ale
amaretto
amontillado
amoroso

anisette
applejack
aquavit
arak

Armagnac
arrack
Asti
Auslese

Bandol
Bardolino
barley wine
Barolo

Barsac
Beaujolais
Beaune
beer
Beerenauslese
bitter
Blanc de blancs
bock
bourbon
brandy
brown ale
Bull's Blood
burgundy
Côtes du Rhône
Cabernet Franc
Cabernet
  Sauvignon
cachaca
Calvados
canary wine
cask beer
cassis
catawba
cava
Chablis
champagne
Chardonnay
chartreuse
Chenin Blanc
cherry brandy
Chianti
cider
claret
cocktail
cognac
cream sherry

crème de cacao
crème de
  menthe
curaçao
draught beer
Eiswein
Entre-Deux-Mers
fine champagne
fino
fraise
framboise
Frascati
Gamay
genever
Gewürztraminer
gin
ginger wine
grain whisky
grappa
Graves
Grenache
hock
ice beer
Irish whiskey
Kabinett
keg beer
kirsch
kümmel
kvass
lager
Lambrusco
Liebfraumilch
light ale
liqueur
Madeira
Malbec

malmsey
malt
malt whisky
Malvasia
manzanilla
maraschino
Margaux
Marsala
mead
Médoc
Merlot
mescal
Meursault
mild
milk stout
Minervois
Monbazillac
Montepulciano
Montrachet
moscato
Moselle
Müller-Thurgau
Muscadet
muscat
muscatel
Niersteiner
noyau
Nuits St George
oloroso
Orvieto
ouzo
pale ale
palm wine
pastis
perry
Piesporter

Pils
Pilsner/Pilsener
Pinot Blanc
Pinot Grigio
Pinot Noir
port
porter
poteen
Pouilly-Fuissé
Pouilly-Fumé
raki
ratafia
real ale
retsina
Riesling
Rioja
Rosé d'Anjou
rum
rye
sack
Saint Émilion
sake
sambuca
Sancerre
Sangiovese
Saumur
Sauternes
Sauvignon
schnapps
Scotch whisky
scrumpy
Sekt
Sémillon
shandy
sherry
Shiraz

single malt
slivovitz
sloe gin
Soave
sour mash
Spätlese
spruce beer
Spumante
stout
Sylvaner
Syrah
Tavel
tequila
Tia Maria
Tokay
Traminer
Trebbiano
Trocken-
  beerenauslese
triple sec
Valpolicella
Verdelho
Verdicchio
vermouth
vinho verde
Viognier
vodka
Vouvray
whiskey
whisky
wine
Zinfandel

Non-alcoholic Drinks

arabica
Assam
barley water
bitter lemon
black tea
bohea
buttermilk
cafe au lait
cafe noir
caffè latte
caffè macchiato
camomile tea
cappuccino
carbonated
  water
Ceylon tea
cherryade
China tea
citron pressé

club soda
  (trademark)
cocoa
coffee
cola
cordial
cream soda
crush
dandelion and
  burdock
Darjeeling
decaf
decaffeinated
  coffee
drinking
  chocolate
Earl Grey
espresso
filter coffee
fruit juice

fruit tea
ginger ale
ginger beer
Greek coffee
green tea
gunpowder tea
herbal tea
horchata
hot chocolate
iced tea
Indian tea
infusion
instant coffee
isotonic drink
jasmine tea
Keemun
Lapsang
  Souchong
lassi
latte

lemon tea
lemonade
limeade
malted milk
maté
milkshake
mineral water
mint tea
mocha
mochaccino
oolong
orangeade
orange pekoe
orgeat
pekoe
peppermint tea
pouchong
prairie oyster
pressé
robusta

root beer
rosehip tea
Russian tea
sarsaparilla
seltzer
sherbet
smoothie
soda water
soya milk
sports drink
spring water
squash
St Clements
tea
tisane
tonic water
Turkish coffee
yerba maté

Cocktails and Mixed Drinks

Bellini   B52   Black Russian   black velvet   Bloody Mary

Wordfinder

blue lagoon
brandy
 Alexander
Bronx
Buck's Fizz
caipirinha
champagne
 cocktail
cobbler
cosmopolitan
Cuba libre
daiquiri
egg flip

eggnog
G and T
gimlet
gin sling
grog
Harvey
 Wallbanger
highball
Irish coffee
John Collins
Kir
Kir Royale

Long Island iced
 tea
mai tai
manhattan
margarita
Martini (trademark)
mint julep
mojito
negroni
nog
old-fashioned
pina colada
pink gin

pink lady
planter's punch
prairie oyster
punch
rattlesnake
rum and black
sangria
screwdriver
sea breeze
sex on the beach
sidecar
Singapore sling
slammer

snakebite
snowball
sour
spritzer
tequila slammer
tequila sunrise
toddy
Tom Collins
whisky mac
whisky sour
White Lady
White Russian
zombie

Food

Bread and Bread Rolls

bagel
baguette
bannock
bap
bara brith
barmbrack
barm cake
bloomer
bridge roll
brioche
bun

challah
chapatti
ciabatta
cob
cornbread
cottage loaf
crumpet
damper
farl
farmhouse loaf
flatbread

focaccia
French stick
fruit loaf
granary bread
 (trademark)
hoagie
kaiser
malt loaf
matzo
milk loaf
muffin

nan/naan
panettone
panino
paratha
petit pain
pikelet
pitta
pone
poppadom
pumpernickel
puri

quartern loaf
roti
rye
soda bread
sourdough
split tin
stollen

Cakes, Biscuits, and Desserts

angel cake
angel food cake
apfelstrudel
apple charlotte
apple pie
baba
baked Alaska
Bakewell tart
baklava
banana split
Banbury cake
banoffi/banoffee
 pie
Bath bun
Bath Oliver
Battenberg
beignet
Berliner
biscotti
Black Forest
 gateau
blàncmange
bombe
bourbon
brack
brandy snap
bread pudding

bread-and-
 butter pudding
Brown Betty
brownie
bun
butterfly cake
cabinet pudding
cassata
charlotte
charlotte russe
cheesecake
chocolate chip
clafoutis
cobbler
compote
cookie
cracknel
cream cracker
cream puff
crème brûlée
crème caramel
crêpe
crêpe Suzette
crispbread
croquembouche
crumble
crumpet
cupcake

custard cream
custard pie
custard tart
Danish pastry
death by
 chocolate
devil's food cake
digestive
doughnut
drop scone
dumpling
Dundee cake
Eccles cake
eclair
egg custard
Eskimo pie
 (trademark)
Eve's pudding
fairy cake
fancy
flapjack
floating island
Florentine
flummery
fool
fortune cookie
frangipane
fruit cocktail

fruit salad
funnel cake
garibaldi
gateau
gelato
Genoa cake
gingerbread
ginger nut
ginger snap
granita
halwa
hasty pudding
hokey-pokey
hot cross bun
ice cream
jelly
junket
Knickerbocker
 Glory
kulfi
lady's finger
langue de chat
lardy cake
layer cake
Lincoln biscuit
macaroon
Madeira cake
madeleine

maid of honour
marble cake
marie biscuit
marquise
matzo
meringue
milk pudding
millefeuille
mince pie
Mississippi mud
 pie
mousse
mousseline
muffin
Nice biscuit
oatcake
pancake
panettone
panforte
parfait
parkin
pashka
pavlova
peach Melba
petit beurre
petit four
plum duff
plum pudding

popover
pound cake
pretzel
profiterole
queen cake
queen of
  puddings
ratafia
rice pudding
rock cake
roly-poly
rusk
Sachertorte
sago pudding

Sally Lunn
saltine
sandwich
savarin
scone
seed cake
semolina
ship's biscuit
shoo-fly pie
shortbread
shortcake
simnel cake
singing hinny
sorbet

soufflé
sponge
sponge pudding
spotted dick
steamed
  pudding
stollen
streusel
strudel
suet pudding
summer
  pudding
sundae

sweetmeal
  biscuit
Swiss roll
syllabub
tart
tarte Tatin
tartlet
tartufo
tipsy cake
tiramisu
torte
treacle tart
trifle
turnover

tutti-frutti
upside-down
  cake
Victoria sponge
waffle
water biscuit
water ice
whip
yogurt
yule log
zabaglione

Cheeses

asiago
Bel Paese
  (trademark)
blue vinny
Boursin (trademark)
Brie
Caerphilly
Camembert
cantal
Chaumes
Cheddar
Cheshire
chèvre
cottage cheese

cream cheese
crowdie/crowdy
curd cheese
Danish blue
Derby
Dolcelatte
  (trademark)
Double
  Gloucester
Dunlop
Edam
Emmental
feta/fetta
fontina

fromage blanc
fromage frais
Gloucester
Gorgonzola
Gouda
Gruyère
halloumi
havarti
Jarlsberg
  (trademark)
Lancashire
Leicester
Limburger
Manchego

mascarpone
Monterey Jack
mozzarella
Neufchâtel
paneer/panir
Parmesan
Parmigiano
  Reggiano
pecorino
Pont l'Évêque
Port Salut
provolone
quark
Red Leicester

ricotta
Romano
Roquefort
  (trademark)
sage Derby
scamorza
Stilton
taleggio
Tilsit
Wensleydale

Fruit and Nuts

almond
apple
apricot
avocado
banana
betel nut
bilberry
blackberry
blackcurrant
blood orange
blueberry
boysenberry
Brazil nut
breadfruit
butternut
cantaloupe
Cape gooseberry
carambola
cashew
cashew apple
chayote
checkerberry
cherimoya
cherry
cherry plum
chestnut
chincapin
Chinese
  gooseberry

citron
clementine
cloudberry
cob
cobnut
coconut
cola nut
cowberry
crab apple
cranberry
currant
custard apple
damson
date
dewberry
durian
earthnut
elderberry
feijoa
fig
filbert
galia melon
gooseberry
gourd
granadilla
grape
grapefruit
greengage
groundnut

guava
hazelnut
hognut
honeydew
  melon
huckleberry
jackfruit
jujube
kiwi fruit
kumquat
lemon
lime
loganberry
longan
loquat
lychee
macadamia
mammee
mandarin
mango
mangosteen
medlar
melon
minneola
monkey nut
mulberry
musk melon
naseberry
navel orange

nectarine
olive
orange
ortanique
papaya
passion fruit
pawpaw
peach
peanut
pear
pecan
persimmon
pineapple
pine nut
piñon
pistachio
plantain
plum
pomegranate
pomelo
prickly pear
pumpkin
quince
rambutan
raspberry
redcurrant
salmonberry
sapodilla
satsuma

serviceberry
sharon fruit
sloesorb
soursop
star anise
star apple
starfruit
strawberry
sugar apple
sweet chestnut
sweetsop
tamarillo
tamarind
tangelo
tangerine
tayberry
thimbleberry
tiger nut
tomato
Ugli fruit
  (trademark)
Victoria plum
walnut
water chestnut
watermelon
white currant
whortleberry
wineberry
youngberry

Wordfinder

Herbs and Spices

ajowan
allspice
angelica
anise
aniseed
asafoetida
balsam
basil
bay leaf
bergamot
black pepper
borage
camomile
caper
caraway
cardamom
cassia

cayenne pepper
chervil
chicory
chilli
chives
cilantro
cinnamon
clary
clove
coriander
cumin
curry powder
damiana
dill
dittany
dong quai
echinacea

fennel
fenugreek
feverfew
five-spice
   powder
galangal
garam masala
garlic
ginger
ginseng
grains of
   Paradise
green pepper
hyssop
jalapeño
juniper berry
lavender

lemon balm
lemon grass
lemon mint
lovage
mace
marjoram
milk thistle
mint
mustard
nutmeg
oregano
paprika
parsley
pepper
peppermint
pimento
rosemary

rue
saffron
sage
savory
sorrel
spearmint
St John's wort
star anise
sumac
sweet balm
sweet cicely
tarragon
thyme
turmeric
vanilla
white pepper

Meals

afternoon tea
banquet
barbecue
barbie
breakfast
brunch
buffet

clambake
continental
   breakfast
cookout
cream tea
dinner
dinner party

elevenses
evening meal
feast
finger buffet
harvest supper
high tea
lunch

luncheon
meze
midday meal
packed lunch
picnic
safari supper
smorgasbord

supper
takeaway
tapas
tea
TV dinner
wedding
   breakfast

Pasta

agnolotti
angel hair
bucatini
cannelloni
capelli
capellini
cappelletti
conchiglie
ditalini

farfalle
farfalline
fedelini
fettuccine
fusilli
gramigna
lasagne
linguine
lumache

macaroni
maltagliati
manicotti
noodles
orecchiette
orzo
pappardelle
penne
pipe

radiatori
ravioli
rigatoni
rotelle
rotini
spaghetti
spaghettini
strozzapreti
tagliatelle

tagliolini
tortelli
tortellini
tortelloni
tortiglioni
trenette
vermicelli
ziti

Sauces

apple sauce
Béarnaise sauce
béchamel sauce
baba ganoush
barbecue sauce
black bean
   sauce
Bolognese sauce
bordelaise sauce
bread sauce
brown sauce
carbonara sauce

chasseur sauce
chaud-froid
cheese sauce
chilli sauce
cranberry sauce
curry sauce
demi-glace
fish sauce
gravy
hoisin sauce
hollandaise

horseradish
   sauce
jus
ketchup
mint sauce
mornay sauce
mousseline
   sauce
onion sauce
oyster sauce
parsley sauce
pepper sauce

pesto
pizzaiola sauce
puttanesca
   sauce
ragù
salsa
salsa verde
satay sauce
soubise
soy sauce
sweet-and-sour
   sauce

Tabasco
   (trademark)
tartare sauce
teriyaki sauce
tomato ketchup
tomato sauce
velouté
vinaigrette
white sauce
Worcester sauce

Sweets and Confectionery

acid drop
aniseed ball
barley sugar
boiled sweet
bonbon

brittle
bullseye
butterscotch
candy
candyfloss

caramel
chew
chewing gum
chocolate
chocolate drop

coconut ice
comfit
cracknel
crystallized fruit
dolly mixtures

dragée
Easter egg
fondant
fruit drop
fruit gum

fruit pastille	jelly baby	lolly	peppermint	toffee
fudge	jelly bean	marshmallow	cream	toffee apple
gobstopper	jujube	marzipan	Pontefract cake	truffle
gulab jamun	Kendal mint	mint	praline	Turkish delight
gumdrop	cake	nougat	rock	walnut whip
halva	laddu	pastille	sherbet	wine gum
humbug	liquorice	pear drop	sherbet dip	
jalebi	liquorice allsort	peppermint	sherbet lemon	
jelly	lollipop		sugared almond	

Vegetables

ackee	cardoon	French bean	onion	soybean
acorn squash	carrot	garbanzo	oyster plant	spinach
aduki/adzuki	cassava	garden pea	pak choi	spinach beet
bean	cauliflower	garlic	parsnip	spring greens
alfalfa	cavolo nero	gherkin	pea	spring onion
artichoke	celeriac	globe artichoke	pepper	squash
asparagus	celery	gourd	petits pois	string bean
aubergine	chard	greens	pimiento	sugar pea
bamboo shoots	chayote	haricot bean	pinto bean	sugar snap pea
bean	chervil	Jerusalem	plantain	swede
beet	chickpea	artichoke	potato	sweetcorn
beetroot	chicory	kale	pumpkin	sweet pepper
black bean	Chinese	kidney bean	puy lentil	sweet potato
black-eyed bean	cabbage	kohlrabi	radicchio	taro
borlotti bean	Chinese leaves	leek	radish	tiger nut
breadfruit	corn on the cob	lentil	red cabbage	tomato
broad bean	cos lettuce	lettuce	rocket	turnip
broccoli	courgette	lima bean	romaine	vegetable
Brussels sprout	cress	lollo rosso	runner bean	spaghetti
butter bean	cucumber	mangetout	rutabaga	wasabi
butterhead	curly kale	manioc	salsify	water chestnut
lettuce	cush-cush	marrow	samphire	watercress
butternut	custard marrow	marrowfat pea	savoy cabbage	waxpod
squash	eggplant	mooli	scallion	yam
cabbage	endive	mung bean	scarlet runner	zucchini
cabbage lettuce	escarole	mushroom	scorzonera	
calabrese	fava bean	mustard	sea kale	
cannellini bean	fennel	oak leaf lettuce	shallot	
capsicum	flageolet	okra	snow pea	

Language and Literature

Literary Schools, Movements, and Groups

Acmeism	Cavalier poets	Lake Poets	neo-realism	social realism
Aesthetic	classicism	Liverpool poets	neoclassicism	socialist realism
Movement	Dadaism	magic realism	Parnassians	structuralism
Angry Young	expressionism	magical realism	post-	Sturm und
Men	futurism	metaphysical	structuralism	Drang
Augustans	Georgian poets	poets	postmodernism	surrealism
beat generation	Harlem	minimalism	primitivism	symbolism
Bloomsbury	Renaissance	modernism	realism	Vorticism
Group	imagism	naturalism	romanticism	

Poetry Terms

alcaics	alexandrine	aubade	blank verse	clerihew
alcaic verse	verse	ballad	bucolic	couplet
alexandrine	anapaest	ballade	choriambus	dactyl

Wordfinder

dactylics
dactylic verse
decasyllabic
dimeter
distich
disyllable
dithyramb
doggerel
eclogue
elegiac couplet
elegy
epic
epigram
epithalamium
epode

epyllion
free verse
georgic
haiku
heptameter
heroic couplet
heroic verse
hexameter
Horatian ode
iamb
iambic
  pentameter
iambics
iambic verse
iambus

idyll
lay
Leonines
limerick
lyric
macaronics
macaronic verse
monody
nursery rhyme
ode
ottava rima
paeon
palinode
pastoral
pentameter

Petrarchan
  sonnet
poem
prothalamium
pyrrhic
rondeau
roundel
saga
sapphics
satire
sestina
sonnet
Spenserian
  stanza
spondee

terza rima
tetrameter
tribrach
trimeter
triolet
triplet
trisyllable
trochaics
trochaic verse
trochee
verse
villanelle
virelay

Types of Drama

burlesque
closet drama
closet play
comedy
comedy of
  manners
commedia
  dell'arte

docudrama
dumbshow
duologue
farce
Grand Guignol
Greek drama
improvisation
kabuki

kitchen-sink
  drama
masque
melodrama
mime
miracle play
monodrama
morality play

mummers' play
mystery play
nativity play
Noh
pantomime
passion play
play
romcom

soap opera
teleplay
tragedy
tragicomedy
two-hander

Types of Fiction

adventure story
Aga saga
allegory
antinovel
bedtime story
Bildungsroman
black comedy
blockbuster
bodice-ripper
bonkbuster
chick lit
cliffhanger
comedy

conte
crime story
detective story
dime novel
epic
epistolary novel
fable
fairy story
fairy tale
fanfic
fan fiction
fantasy
folk story

folk tale
ghost story
gothic novel
graphic novel
historical novel
horror story
legend
mystery
myth
noir
nouveau roman
novel
novelette

novella
parable
picaresque novel
police
  procedural
policier
roman-à-clef
romance
roman-fleuve
romantic novel
saga
science fiction
sci-fi

short story
spine-chiller
stream of
  consciousness
sword and
  sorcery
tear-jerker
thriller
urban myth
western
whodunnit

Phonetic Alphabet

Alpha
Bravo
Charlie
Delta
Echo
Foxtrot

Golf
Hotel
India
Juliet
Kilo
Lima

Mike
November
Oscar
Papa
Quebec
Romeo

Sierra
Tango
Uniform
Victor
Whisky
X-ray

Yankee
Zulu

Punctuation Marks

accent
apostrophe
asterisk
asterism
backslash
brace
bracket

caret
colon
comma
dagger
dash
diacritical mark
ellipsis

em dash
en dash
exclamation
  mark
full stop
hyphen
inverted comma

obelus
parenthesis
period
point
question mark
quotation mark
rule

semicolon
solidus
square bracket
stop
stroke
swung dash
virgule

Medicine

Branches of Medicine

allopathy
audiology
cardiology
chiropody
community
   medicine
dermatology
embryology
endocrinology
epidemiology
geriatrics
gynaecology
haematology
immunology
laryngology
nephrology
neurology
neurosurgery
nuclear medicine
obstetrics
oncology
ophthalmology
orthopaedics
orthotics
osteopathy
paediatrics
parasitology
pathology
pharmacology
physiotherapy
plastic surgery
proctology
prosthetics
psychiatry
psychosurgery
radiology
surgery
therapeutics
therapy
urology
venereology
veterinary
   medicine

Therapies

acupressure
acupuncture
Alexander
   technique
aromatherapy
art therapy
autogenic
   training
aversion therapy
Ayurveda
Bates method
behaviour
   therapy
behavioural
   therapy
bioenergetics
biofeedback
brachytherapy
bush medicine
chemotherapy
chiropractic
cognitive
   therapy
colour therapy
combination
   therapy
craniosacral
   therapy
crystal healing
cupping
drama therapy
eurhythmics
faith healing
family therapy
gene therapy
gestalt therapy
group therapy
heat treatment
herbalism
homeopathy
hormone
   replacement
   therapy
hydropathy
hydrotherapy
hypnotherapy
immunotherapy
McTimoney
   chiropractic
moxibustion
music therapy
naturopathy
neurolinguistic
   programming
occupational
   therapy
osteopathy
physiotherapy
psychotherapy
radiation
   therapy
radionics
radiotherapy
rebirthing
recreational
   therapy
reflexology
reiki
Rolfing
sex therapy
shiatsu
shock therapy
shock treatment
speech therapy
spiritual healing
zone therapy

Physical Illnesses

acne
ague
Aids
alopecia
altitude sickness
Alzheimer's
   disease
anaemia
angina
ankylosing
   spondylitis
ankylosis
anthrax
appendicitis
arthritis
asbestosis
asthma
ataxia
athlete's foot
avian flu
Bell's palsy
bends
beriberi
bilharzia
bird flu
blackwater fever
botulism
bronchitis
bubonic plague
bursitis
cachexia
cancer
carpal tunnel
   syndrome
cataract
cerebral palsy
chickenpox
cholera
chorea
chronic fatigue
   syndrome
cirrhosis
coeliac disease
cold
colic
colitis
common cold
consumption
coronary heart
   disease
cough
cowpox
Creutzfeldt-
   Jakob disease
   (CJD)
Crohn's disease
croup
cyanosis
cystic fibrosis
cystitis
decompression
   sickness
deep-vein
   thrombosis
   (DVT)
deficiency
   disease
dengue
dermatitis
dermatosis
diabetes
diabetes
   insipidus
diabetes mellitus
diarrhoea
diphtheria
diverticular
   disease
Down's
   syndrome
dysentery
Ebola
eclampsia
eczema
elephantiasis
emphysema
encephalitis
endocarditis
endometriosis
endometritis
enteritis
epilepsy
ergotism
erysipelas
fetal alcohol
   syndrome
fever
fibrositis
filariasis
flu
frozen shoulder
gangrene
gastric flu
gastritis
gastro-enteritis
German measles
gigantism
gingivitis
glandular fever
glaucoma
glue ear
glycaemia
goitre
gonorrhoea
gout
Gulf War
   syndrome
haemophilia
Hansen's disease
hay fever
heat stroke
hepatitis
hepatoma
hernia
herpes
herpes simplex
hives
Hodgkin's
   disease
hookworm
Huntington's
   disease

hydrocephalus
hydrophobia
hypertension
hypoglycaemia
hypothermia
hypoxia
impetigo
infantile
   paralysis
influenza
irritable bowel
   syndrome
ischaemia
jaundice
Kaposi's sarcoma
ketosis
kwashiorkor
laryngitis
Lassa fever
legionella
legionnaires'
   disease
leishmaniasis
leprosy
leptospirosis
leukaemia
listeria
listeriosis
lupus
lupus vulgaris
Lyme disease
lymphoma
malaria
mastitis
measles
meningitis
molluscum
   contagiosum

morning
   sickness
motor neuron
   disease
mountain
   sickness
multiple sclerosis
   (MS)
mumps
muscular
   dystrophy
myalgic
   encephalo-
   myelitis (ME)
narcolepsy
necrotizing
   fasciitis
nephritis
new variant
   Creutzfeldt-
   Jakob disease
   (nvCJD)
non-Hodgkin's
   lymphoma
oedema
ophthalmia
osteomyelitis
osteoporosis
pancreatitis
paratyphoid
Parkinson's
   disease
pellagra
pelvic
   inflammatory
   disease
pericarditis
peritonitis

pernicious
   anaemia
pertussis
phlebitis
pleurisy
pneumonia
poliomyelitis
porphyria
prickly heat
pruritus
psittacosis
psoriasis
puerperal fever
pulmonary
   emphysema
pyaemia
pyrexia
quinsy
rabies
radiation
   sickness
rash
repetitive strain
   injury (RSI)
retinitis
retinopathy
rheumatic fever
rheumatism
rheumatoid
   arthritis
rhinitis
rickets
ringworm
rubella
St Vitus's dance
salmonella
sarcoma
scabies

scarlet fever
schizophrenia
sciatica
scleritis
scleroderma
sclerosis
scrofula
scurvy
seasonal
   affective
   disorder (SAD)
sepsis
septicaemia
severe acute
   respiratory syn-
   drome (SARS)
sexually
   transmitted
   disease (STD)
shingles
sick building
   syndrome
sickle-cell
   anaemia
silicosis
sinusitis
sleeping sickness
smallpox
Spanish flu
spina bifida
spondylosis
strabismus
sunburn
sunstroke
Sydenham's
   chorea
syphilis
tendinitis

tenosynovitis
tetanus
thrombosis
thrush
tonsillitis
Tourette's
   syndrome
toxaemia
toxic shock
   syndrome
toxocariasis
toxoplasmosis
trench foot
trichinosis
tuberculosis (TB)
typhoid
typhus
undulant fever
urethritis
urticaria
vaginismus
venereal disease
   (VD)
viraemia
virus
vitiligo
Weil's disease
whooping
   cough
yaws
yellow fever

Psychological Illnesses and Conditions

anorexia nervosa
Asperger's
   syndrome
attention deficit
   hyperactivity
   disorder
   (ADHD)
autism
body
   dysmorphic
   disorder
bulimia nervosa
catatonia

clinical
   depression
combat fatigue
de Clerambault's
   syndrome
dementia
dysphoria
dysthymia
eating disorder
erotomania
false memory
   syndrome
gender
   dysphoria

hebephrenia
hyperactivity
hyperkinesis
hypomania
Korsakoff's
   syndrome
manic
   depression
megalomania
multiple-
   personality
   disorder
Munchausen's
   syndrome

Munchausen's
   syndrome by
   proxy
obsessive–
   compulsive
   disorder
panic disorder
paramnesia
paranoia
paraphilia
pica
post-natal
   depression

post-traumatic
   stress disorder
psychosis
schizo-affective
   disorder
schizophrenia
seasonal
   affective
   disorder (SAD)
shell shock

Phobias

air travel: *aerophobia*
American people and things:
   Americophobia
animals: *zoophobia*
beards: *pogonophobia*

beating: *mastigophobia*
bed: *clinophobia*
bees: *apiphobia*
birds: *ornithophobia*
blood: *haemophobia*

blushing: *erythrophobia*
bridges: *gephyrophobia*
burial alive: *taphephobia*
cancer: *carcinophobia*
cats: *ailurophobia*

childbirth: *tocophobia*
children: *paedophobia*
Chinese people and things: *Sinophobia*
clouds: *nephophobia*
coitus: *coitophobia*
cold: *cheimaphobia*
colour: *chromophobia*
comets: *cometophobia*
computers: *cyberphobia*
corpses: *necrophobia*
crowds: *demophobia*
dampness: *hygrophobia*
darkness: *scotophobia*
dawn: *eosophobia*
death: *thanatophobia*
depth: *bathophobia*
dirt: *mysophobia*
disease: *pathophobia*
dogs: *cynophobia*
dreams: *oneirophobia*
drink: *potophobia*
dust: *koniophobia*
electricity: *electrophobia*
English people and things: *Anglophobia*
everything: *panophobia*, *pantophobia*
eyes: *ommetaphobia*
faeces: *coprophobia*
fatigue: *kopophobia*
fear: *phobophobia*
feathers: *pteronophobia*
fever: *febriphobia*
fire: *pyrophobia*
fish: *ichthyophobia*
flesh: *selaphobia*
floods: *antlophobia*
flowers: *anthophobia*
food: *cibophobia, sitophobia*
foreigners: *xenophobia*
French people and things: *Francophobia, Gallophobia*
fur: *doraphobia*
German people and things: *Germanophobia*, *Teutophobia*
germs: *spermophobia*
ghosts: *phasmophobia*
giving birth to monsters: *teratophobia*
glass: *nelophobia*
God: *theophobia*
gold: *aurophobia*, *chrysophobia*
hair: *trichophobia*
heart disease: *cardiophobia*
heat: *thermophobia*
heaven: *uranophobia*
hell: *hadephobia*, *stygiophobia*

heredity: *patroiophobia*
high buildings: *batophobia*
high places: *hypsophobia*
home: *oikophobia*
homosexuals: *homophobia*
horses: *hippophobia*
ice: *cryophobia*
ideas: *ideophobia*
idleness: *thassophobia*
illness: *nosophobia*
imperfection: *atelophobia*
infinity: *apeirophobia*
inoculation: *trypanophobia*, *vaccinophobia*
insanity: *lyssophobia*, *maniphobia*
insects: *entomophobia*
insect stings: *cnidophobia*
Italian people and things: *Italophobia*
justice: *dikephobia*
lakes: *limnophobia*
leprosy: *leprophobia*
light: *photophobia*
lightning: *astrapophobia*
lists: *pinaciphobia*
loneliness: *autophobia*, *ermitophobia*
machinery: *mechanophobia*
magic: *rhabdophobia*
marriage: *gametophobia*
men: *androphobia*
metal: *metallophobia*
mice: *musophobia*
microbes: *bacillophobia*
mites: *acarophobia*
mobs: *ochlophobia*
motion: *kinetophobia*
music: *musicophobia*
names: *onomatophobia*
narrowness: *anginophobia*
needles: *belonephobia*
new things: *neophobia*
night: *nyctophobia*
nudity: *gymnophobia*
open places: *agoraphobia*
pain: *algophobia*
philosophy: *philosophobia*
pins: *enetophobia*
places: *topophobia*
pleasure: *hedonophobia*
poison: *toxiphobia*
Pope: *papaphobia*
poverty: *peniaphobia*
precipices: *cremnophobia*
priests: *hierophobia*
punishment: *poinephobia*
religious works of art: *iconophobia*
responsibility: *hypegiaphobia*
rivers: *potamophobia*

robbers: *harpaxophobia*
ruin: *atephobia*
Russian people and things: *Russophobia*
saints: *hagiophobia*
Satan: *Satanophobia*
scabies: *scabiophobia*
Scottish people and things: *Scotophobia*
sex: *erotophobia*
shadows: *sciophobia*
sharpness: *acrophobia*
shock: *hormephobia*
sin: *hamartophobia*
sleep: *hypnophobia*
slime: *blennophobia*
small things: *microphobia*
smell: *olfactophobia*, *osmophobia*
smothering: *pnigerophobia*
snakes: *ophidiophobia*
snow: *chionophobia*
solitude: *eremophobia*
sourness: *acerophobia*
speech: *glossophobia*, *phonophobia*
speed: *tachophobia*
spiders: *arachnophobia*
standing: *stasophobia*
stars: *siderophobia*
stealing: *kleptophobia*
string: *linonophobia*
stuttering: *laliophobia*, *lalophobia*
sun: *heliophobia*
swallowing: *phagophobia*
taste: *geumatophobia*
technology: *technophobia*
teeth: *odontophobia*
thunder: *brontophobia*, *keraunophobia*, *tonitrophobia*
time: *chronophobia*
touch: *haptophobia*
travel: *hodophobia*
tyrants: *tyrannophobia*
vehicles: *ochophobia*
venereal disease: *syphilophobia*
voids: *kenophobia*
vomiting: *emetophobia*
water: *hydrophobia*
waves: *cymophobia*
weakness: *asthenophobia*
wind: *anemophobia*
women: *gynophobia*
words: *logophobia*
work: *ergophobia*
writing: *graphophobia*

Wordfinder

Types and Forms of Medication

abortifacient
alpha blocker
anaesthetic
analeptic
analgesic
anaphrodisiac
anodyne
anovulant
antacid
anthelmintic
antibacterial
antibiotic
anticoagulant
antidote
anti-emetic
antihistamine
anti-infective
anti-inflammatory
antipruritic
antipsychotic
antipyretic

antiscorbutic
antiseptic
antispasmodic
antitussive
antiviral
anxiolytic
aperient
aphrodisiac
balsam
beta blocker
booster
cachet
calmative
caplet
capsule
carminative
contraceptive
convulsant
cream
curative
cure-all
decongestant

depressant
diaphoretic
digestive
dilator
diuretic
draught
drip
drops
ear drops
emetic
enema
euphoriant
evacuant
expectorant
eye drops
febrifuge
fungicide
gargle
germicide
hypodermic
inhalant
injectable

laxative
linctus
lotion
lozenge
mercurial
muscle relaxant
narcotic
nasal spray
nebulizer
nervine
neuroleptic
nootropic
ointment
painkiller
palliative
pastille
pessary
pill
placebo
poultice
powder
preventive

prophylactic
psychotropic
relaxant
restorative
rub
salve
sedative
sleeping pill
soporific
spray
steroid
stimulant
stupefacient
sudorific
suppository
suppressant
tablet
tonic
tranquillizer
vasodilator
vermifuge

Music and Dance

Musical Genres and Forms

acid house
acid jazz
acid rock
air
alt.country
ambient
anthem
AOR
aria
aubade
bagatelle
ballad
ballet
barbershop
barcarole
baroque
barrelhouse
bebop
berceuse
bhangra
bluegrass
blues
boogie-woogie
bop
breakbeat
Britpop
cabaletta
calypso
canon
canticle
Cantopop

canzone
canzonetta
capriccio
carol
catch
cavatina
chaconne
chamber music
chanson
chant
chorale
choral music
chorus
classical music
comic opera
concertino
concerto
concerto grosso
cool jazz
coronach
country
country and
    western
country rock
courante
crossover
crunk
cumbia
dancehall
dead march
death metal

descant
dirge
disco
ditty
Dixieland
doo-wop
drinking song
drum and bass
dub
duet
duo
easy listening
electro
electronica
emo
entr'acte
étude
Europop
fado
fanfare
fantasia
fantasy
finale
flamenco
flourish
folk
free jazz
fugato
fugue
funk
fusion

garage
glam rock
glee
go-go
gospel
Goth
gradual
grand opera
grime
grunge
gumbo
heavy metal
heavy rock
hip hop
honky-tonk
house
humoresque
hymn
impromptu
indie
interlude
intermezzo
introit
jazz
jazz funk
jingle
jit
jive
juju
jungle
klezmer

Krautrock
kwaito
kwela
lament
Lied
light opera
lullaby
madrigal
march
mariachi
mass
medley
mento
merengue
modern jazz
monody
MOR
motet
moto perpetuo
Motown
movement
musette
musique
    concrète
New Age
New Romantic
new wave
nocturne
nonet
octet
opera

opera buffa
opera seria
operetta
oratorio
overture
parang
part-song
partita
passacaglia
passion
pastoral
pibroch
plainsong
pop
popular music
postlude
prelude
progressive rock
psalm
psychedelic
punk

qawwali
quartet
quintet
rag
raga
ragga
ragtime
rai
rap
rave
recitative
refrain
reggae
requiem
reverie
rhapsody
rhythm and
  blues
ricercar
ritornello
rock

rockabilly
rock and roll
rocksteady
romance
rondo
round
roundelay
salsa
scena
scherzo
septet
serenade
serenata
setting
sextet
shanty
signature tune
sinfonia
sinfonia
  concertante
sinfonietta

Singspiel
ska
skiffle
soca
solo
sonata
sonatina
song
song cycle
soukous
soul
spiritual
Sprechgesang
study
suite
swing
symphonic
  poem
symphony
talking blues
techno

Tejano
terzetto
Tex-Mex
thrash
threnody
toccata
tone poem
trad jazz
trance
trio
trip hop
two-step
UK garage
variation
voluntary
world music
zouk
zydeco

Musical Instruments

accordion
acoustic guitar
aeolian harp
alpenhorn
althorn
American organ
autoharp
bagpipes
balalaika
banjo
barrel organ
bass clarinet
bass drum
basset horn
bass guitar
bassoon
bass tuba
bass viol
bell
bombarde
bombardon
bongos
bouzouki
bugle
carillon
castanet
celesta
cello
Celtic harp
chamber organ
chitarrone
cimbalom
cinema organ
citole
cittern
clarinet
clarion

clarsach
claves
clavichord
clavier
conga drum
contrabass
contrabassoon
cor anglais
cornet
cornetto
cymbal
didgeridoo
double bass
drum
dulcimer
electric guitar
electric organ
electronic organ
euphonium
fiddle
fife
fipple flute
flageolet
flugelhorn
flute
fortepiano
French horn
gamba
glockenspiel
gong
grand piano
guitar
Hammond
  organ (trademark)
handbell
harmonica
harmonium

harp
harpsichord
Hawaiian guitar
heckelphone
helicon
hi-hat
horn
hurdy-gurdy
Jew's harp
kazoo
kettledrum
kick drum
krummhorn
lute
lyre
mandola
mandolin
maraca
melodeon
melodica
mouth organ
oboe
oboe d'amore
ocarina
ondes martenot
organ
oud
pedal steel
  guitar
piano
piano accordion
pianoforte
pianola
piano organ
piccolo
pipe
pipe organ

player-piano
portative organ
post horn
psaltery
rattle
rebec
recorder
reed organ
reed pipe
sackbut
samisen
santoor
sarod
sarrusophone
saxhorn
saxophone
serpent
shawm
side drum
sitar
sleigh bell
slide guitar
slide trombone
snare drum
sousaphone
Spanish guitar
spinet
steel drum
string bass
synthesizer
tabla
tabor
tambour
tamboura
tambourine
tamburitza
tam-tam

temple block
tenor drum
tenor horn
theorbo
thumb piano
timpani
tin whistle
tom-tom
triangle
triple harp
trombone
trumpet
tuba
tubular bell
ukulele/ukelele
upright piano
vibraphone
vihuela
viol
viola
viola da gamba
viola d'amore
violin
violoncello
violone
virginals
Wagner tuba
washboard
Welsh harp
whistle
wobbleboard
wood block
Wurlitzer
  (trademark)
xylophone
zither

Wordfinder

Types of Singer

alto	choirgirl	falsetto	mezzo-soprano	soprano
balladeer	chorister	folk singer	minstrel	spinto
baritone	coloratura	gleeman	opera singer	tenor
bass	contralto	Heldentenor	pop singer	treble
basso profundo	countertenor	jongleur	pop star	troubadour
castrato	crooner	Meistersinger	prima donna	
choirboy	diva	mezzo	soloist	

Dances and Types of Dancing

ballet	conga	hoedown	morris dance	samba
ballroom	Cossack dance	hokey-cokey	mosh	shake
barn dance	cotillion	hornpipe	old-time	shimmy
beguine	country dance	hula-hula	one-step	shuffle
belly dance	cumbia	Irish jig	pas de deux	skank
body popping	disco	Irish reel	paso doble	slam dance
bolero	do-si-do	jazz dance	pas seul	snake dance
boogaloo	ecossaise	jig	Paul Jones	square dance
boogie	eightsome reel	jitterbug	pole dancing	stomp
bop	fan dance	jive	polka	strut
bossa nova	fandango	jota	polonaise	sun dance
Boston	farruca	lambada	quadrille	sword dance
break-dancing	flamenco	Lambeth Walk	quickstep	tango
cakewalk	fling	lap dancing	rain dance	tap dance
cancan	folk dance	limbo	reel	turkey trot
carioca	formation	line dancing	robotic dancing	twist
ceroc	dancing	mambo	rock and roll	twosome reel
cha-cha	foxtrot	maypole dance	ronde	two-step
cha-cha-cha	galop	mazurka	round dance	vogueing
charleston	gavotte	minuet	roundelay	waltz
circle dance	Gay Gordons	moonstomp	rumba	war dance
clog dance	Highland fling	moonwalk	salsa	

Plants

Flowering Plants and Shrubs

Aaron's rod	arum lily	bindweed	bulrush	ceanothus
abelia	asphodel	bird of paradise	burdock	celandine
acacia	aspidistra	flower	burnet	centaury
acanthus	aster	bird's-foot trefoil	busy Lizzie	chaffweed
aconite	astilbe	black-eyed	buttercup	chervil
African daisy	astrantia	Susan	butterfly bush	chickweed
African violet	aubretia	blackthorn	butterwort	chicory
agapanthus	avens	bleeding heart	cabbage rose	chinaberry
agave	azalea	bluebell	cactus	Chinese lantern
agrimony	balsam	bog asphodel	calceolaria	chives
aloe	baneberry	bog rosemary	calendula	choisya
alstroemeria	banksia	boneset	camellia	chokeberry
alyssum	barberry	borage	camomile	Christmas cactus
amaranth	barrenwort	bougainvillea	campanula	Christmas rose
amaryllis	bearberry	bramble	campion	chrysanthemum
anemone	bedstraw	broom	candytuft	cicely
angelica	begonia	bryony	canna lily	cinchona
angel's trumpet	belladonna	buckeye	Canterbury bell	cinquefoil
aquilegia	bellflower	buddleia	Cape primrose	clarkia
arabis	bergamot	bugbane	carnation	clematis
arnica	betony	bugle	catmint	cloudberry
arrowgrass	bilberry	bugloss	cattleya	clove pink

clover
cockscomb
coltsfoot
columbine
comfrey
coneflower
convolvulus
coreopsis
cornflower
corydalis
cotoneaster
cottonweed
cow parsley
cowslip
cranesbill
creeping Jenny
crocus
crowfoot
crown imperial
crown of thorns
cuckoo pint
cuckooflower
cyclamen
daffodil
dahlia
daisy
damask rose
dandelion
daphne
deadly
　nightshade
delphinium
dianthus
dill
dittany
dock
dogbane
dog rose
dog violet
dropwort
duckweed
echinacea
edelweiss
eglantine
elder
evening
　primrose
eyebright
feverfew
figwort
firethorn
flax
fleabane
forget-me-not
forsythia
foxglove
frangipani
fraxinella
freesia
fritillary
fuchsia
furze
gaillardia

gardenia
gazania
gentian
geranium
gerbera
gillyflower
gladiolus
globeflower
glory-of-the-
　snow
gloxinia
goat's beard
golden rod
goldilocks
gorse
grape hyacinth
grass of
　Parnassus
groundsel
guelder rose
gypsophila
harebell
hawkbit
hawksbeard
hawkweed
hawthorn
heartsease
heather
hebe
helianthemum
helianthus
heliotrope
hellebore
helleborine
hemlock
herb Christopher
herb Paris
herb Robert
heuchera
hibiscus
hogweed
holly
hollyhock
honesty
honeysuckle
hop
hosta
hyacinth
hydrangea
ice plant
iris
jacaranda
Jack-by-the-
　hedge
Jacob's ladder
japonica
jasmine
jonquil
juneberry
kalanchoe
kalmia
kerria
kingcup

knapweed
knotgrass
laburnum
lady's mantle
lady's slipper
lady's smock
lady's tresses
larkspur
lavatera
lavender
lemon balm
leopard lily
lilac
lily
lily of the valley
lobelia
London pride
loosestrife
lords and ladies
lotus
lovage
love-in-a-mist
love-lies-
　bleeding
lungwort
lupin
madonna lily
magnolia
mahonia
mallow
mandrake
marguerite
marigold
marsh marigold
marshwort
may
mayflower
mayweed
meadow rue
meadow saffron
meadowsweet
Michaelmas
　daisy
mignonette
milfoil
milkwort
mimosa
mint
mistletoe
mock orange
monkey flower
monkshood
montbretia
moonflower
morning glory
motherwort
musk rose
myrtle
narcissus
nasturtium
nemesia
nettle
nicotiana

nigella
night-scented
　stock
nightshade
old man's beard
oleander
orchid
ox-eye daisy
oxlip
oyster plant
pansy
Parma violet
parsley
pasque flower
passion flower
pelargonium
pennyroyal
penstemon
peony
peppermint
periwinkle
petunia
pheasant's eye
phlox
pimpernel
pink
pitcher plant
plantain
plumbago
poinsettia
polyanthus
poppy
potentilla
prickly pear
prickly poppy
primrose
primula
privet
pulsatilla
pyracantha
pyrethrum
ragweed
ragwort
rampion
ramsons
rape
red-hot poker
rhododendron
rock rose
rose
rosebay
　willowherb
rose of Sharon
safflower
St John's wort
salpiglossis
salvia
samphire
sandwort
saxifrage
scabious
scarlet
　pimpernel

scilla
sedum
shamrock
sheep's-bit
shrimp plant
skullcap
snapdragon
snow-in-summer
snowdrop
snowflake
soapwort
Solomon's seal
sorrel
sowthistle
speedwell
spider flower
spider plant
spiderwort
spikenard
spiraea
spurge
spurrey
squill
star of
　Bethlehem
starwort
stitchwort
stock
stonecrop
storksbill
strawflower
streptocarpus
sunflower
sweetbriar
sweet cicely
sweet pea
sweet rocket
sweet william
tansy
tea rose
teasel
thistle
thorn apple
thrift
tiger lily
toadflax
tormentil
tradescantia
traveller's joy
trefoil
tuberose
tulip
turnsole
valerian
Venus flytrap
verbena
veronica
vervain
vetch
viburnum
violet
viper's bugloss
wallflower

water lily	wintergreen	wolfsbane	wood sorrel	yarrow
water violet	wintersweet	wood anemone	woody	yerba buena
willowherb	wisteria	wood avens	nightshade	yucca
winter jasmine	witch hazel	woodruff	wormwood	zinnia

Trees and Shrubs

acacia	cassava	guava	magnolia	roseapple
acer	cassia	gum tree	mahogany	rosewood
ackee	casuarina	handkerchief	maidenhair tree	rowan
alder	cedar	tree	mandarin	royal palm
allspice	cherimoya	hawthorn	mango	rubber plant
almond	cherry	hazel	mangosteen	rubber tree
angelica	cherry laurel	hemlock fir	mangrove	sallow
anise	cherry plum	hickory	maple	sandalwood
annatto	chestnut	holly	mastic	sapele
apple	chinaberry	holly oak	maté	sapodilla
apricot	cinnamon	holm oak	may	sassafras
araucaria	citron	honey locust	mimosa	satinwood
ash	clove	honeysuckle	mirabelle	schefflera
aspen	coco de mer	hornbeam	monkey puzzle	Scots pine
avocado	coconut palm	horse chestnut	mountain ash	senna
azalea	coffee	hydrangea	mulberry	sequoia
balsa	cola	ilex	myrtle	service tree
balsam fir	coolibah	iroko	nectarine	silver birch
bamboo	copper beech	ironbark	Norway spruce	Sitka
banksia	coral tree	ironwood	nutmeg	slippery elm
banyan	cork oak	jacaranda	nux vomica	smoke tree
baobab	coromandel	jackfruit	oak	soapberry
basswood	cottonwood	jack pine	oleaster	spindle
bay tree	crab apple	japonica	olive	spruce
beech	cryptomeria	jasmine	osier	star anise
beefwood	curry leaf	jojoba	pagoda tree	stinkwood
bergamot	custard apple	jujube	palm	stone pine
birch	cypress	juniper	palmyra	storax
blackthorn	damson	kalmia	papaya	sugar maple
bluegum	dawn redwood	kapok	paper mulberry	sumac
bodh tree	dogwood	kermes oak	paperbark	sycamore
bog oak	Douglas fir	kola	pawpaw	tallow tree
bottlebrush	dragon tree	kumquat	pear	tamarind
bottle tree	ebony	laburnum	pedunculate oak	tamarisk
bo tree	elder	lacquer tree	persimmon	tangerine
box	elm	larch	pine	tea
box elder	eucalyptus	laurel	piñon	teak
breadfruit	euonymus	lemon	pistachio	tea tree
bristlecone pine	false acacia	Leyland cypress	pitch pine	thuja
broom	fever tree	leylandii	plane	tree of heaven
buckeye	ficus	lilac	plum	trembling poplar
buckthorn	fig	lime	pomegranate	tulip tree
bullace	filbert	linden	pomelo	tulipwood
bur oak	fir	liquidambar	poplar	umbrella tree
butternut	firethorn	live oak	privet	viburnum
cacao	flame tree	locust	pussy willow	walnut
calabash	frangipani	lodgepole pine	quassia	wattle
camellia	fuchsia	logwood	quince	weeping willow
camphor tree	gean	Lombardy poplar	rain tree	wellingtonia
candelabra tree	genipapo	London plane	rambutan	whitebeam
candleberry	ginkgo	loquat	redbud	willow
candlenut	gorse	lychee	red cedar	witch hazel
carambola	grapefruit	macadamia	redwood	wych elm
carob	greengage	macrocarpa	rhododendron	yew
cashew	guaiacum	madroño	robinia	ylang-ylang

Mushrooms, Toadstools, and Other Fungi

agaric
amethyst
  deceiver
armillaria
beefsteak
  fungus
bird's-nest
black bulgar
blewit
blusher
boletus

bracket fungus
button
  mushroom
cep
champignon
chanterelle
dead man's
  fingers
death cap
destroying angel
earthstar

ergot
fairies' bonnets
field mushroom
fly agaric
grisette
honey fungus
horn of plenty
horse mushroom
ink cap
Jew's ear
liberty cap

morel
mousseron
oyster
  mushroom
parasol
  mushroom
penny bun
polypore
porcini
portobello
puffball

reishi
russula
shiitake
sickener
stinkhorn
straw mushroom
tartufo
truffle

Science

Branches of Science

acoustics
aerodynamics
agriscience
anatomy
anthropology
astronomy
astrophysics
bacteriology
behavioural
  science
biochemistry
biology
botany
chemistry
climatology
computer
  science
cosmology
cryogenics
cybernetics
cytology
dendrology
dynamics

earth science
ecology
economics
electrical
  engineering
electronics
endocrinology
engineering
entomology
epidemiology
ethnology
ethology
exobiology
fluid mechanics
forensics
genetic
  engineering
genetics
geochemistry
geography
geology
geomorphology
geophysics

glaciology
haematology
herpetology
histology
holography
hydrodynamics
hydrology
hydrostatics
ichthyology
immunology
linguistics
marine biology
mathematics
mechanics
medicine
metallurgy
meteorology
microbiology
mineralogy
molecular
  biology
mycology
natural history

neurology
neuroscience
nuclear
  chemistry
nuclear physics
oceanography
oncology
ophthalmology
optics
ornithology
palaeobotany
palaeontology
parasitology
particle physics
pathology
petrology
pharmacology
physics
physiography
physiology
phytology
psychiatry
psychology

quantum
  mechanics
radiology
robotics
seismology
sociobiology
sociology
soil science
spectroscopy
statistics
stratigraphy
taxonomy
tectonics
toxicology
veterinary
  medicine
virology
volcanology/
  vulcanology
zoogeography
zoology
zymurgy

Chemical Elements *Metals

*actinium (Ac)
*aluminium (Al)
*americium (Am)
*antimony (Sb)
argon (Ar)
arsenic (As)
astatine (At)
*barium (Ba)
*berkelium (Bk)
*beryllium (Be)
*bismuth (Bi)
bohrium (Bh)
boron (B)
bromine (Br)
*cadmium (Cd)
*caesium (Cs)
*calcium (Ca)

*californium (Cf)
carbon (C)
*cerium (Ce)
chlorine (Cl)
*chromium (Cr)
*cobalt (Co)
*copper (Cu)
*curium (Cm)
darmstadtium
  (Ds)
dubnium (Db)
*dysprosium
  (Dy)
einsteinium (Es)
*erbium (Er)
*europium (Eu)
*fermium (Fm)

fluorine (F)
*francium (Fr)
*gadolinium
  (Gd)
*gallium (Ga)
germanium (Ge)
*gold (Au)
*hafnium (Hf)
hassium (Hs)
helium (He)
*holmium (Ho)
hydrogen (H)
*indium (In)
iodine (I)
*iridium (Ir)
*iron (Fe)
krypton (Kr)

*lanthanum (La)
*lawrencium (Lr)
*lead (Pb)
*lithium (Li)
*lutetium (Lu)
*magnesium
  (Mg)
*manganese
  (Mn)
*meitnerium
  (Mt)
*mendelevium
  (Md)
*mercury (Hg)
*molybdenum
  (Mo)

*neodymium
  (Nd)
neon (Ne)
*neptunium (Np)
*nickel (Ni)
*niobium (Nb)
nitrogen (N)
*nobelium (No)
*osmium (Os)
oxygen (O)
*palladium (Pd)
phosphorus (P)
*platinum (Pt)
*plutonium (Pu)
*polonium (Po)
*potassium (K)

Wordfinder

Wordfinder

*praseodymium (Pr)
*promethium (Pm)
*protactinium (Pa)
*radium (Ra)
radon (Rn)
*rhenium (Re)

*rhodium (Rh)
roentgenium (Rg)
*rubidium (Rb)
*ruthenium (Ru)
rutherfordium (Rf)
*samarium (Sm)
*scandium (Sc)

seaborgium (Sg)
selenium (Se)
silicon (Si)
*silver (Ag)
*sodium (Na)
*strontium (Sr)
sulphur (S)
*tantalum (Ta)
*technetium (Tc)

tellurium (Te)
*terbium (Tb)
*thallium (Tl)
*thorium (Th)
*thulium (Tm)
*tin (Sn)
*titanium (Ti)
*tungsten (W)
*uranium (U)

*vanadium (V)
xenon (Xe)
*ytterbium (Yb)
*yttrium (Y)
*zinc (Zn)
*zirconium (Zr)

Chemicals

acetic acid
acetone
acetylene
alcohol
alum
alumina
baking soda
baryta
bicarbonate of soda
boracic acid
borax
calomel

carbolic acid
carbon tetrachloride
carborundum
caustic potash
caustic soda
chloroform
chrome yellow
cinnabar
common salt
corundum
cream of tartar
cyanide

dry ice
Epsom salts
ether
ethyl alcohol
firedamp
folic acid
formaldehyde
formic acid
glycerine
gypsum
hydrochloric acid
jeweller's rouge
laughing gas

lithia
magnesia
marsh gas
nitric oxide
peroxide
plaster of Paris
potash
prussic acid
quicklime
red lead
salt
saltpetre
silica

slaked lime
soda
strontia
sugar
verdigris
vitriol
washing soda
white arsenic
xylene
zirconia

Rocks and Minerals

agate
alabaster
alexandrite
almandine
amber
amethyst
aquamarine
asbestos
balas ruby
baryte
basalt
beryl
bloodstone
Blue John
borax
breccia
cairngorm
calcite
carbuncle
carnelian
cat's-eye
chalcedony
chalk
chert
chromite

chrysolite
chrysoprase
cinnabar
cipolin
citrine
coal
conglomerate
cornelian
corundum
cryolite
diamond
diorite
dolerite
dolomite
emerald
emery
feldspar
fire opal
flint
fluorite
fluorspar
fool's gold
gabbro
galena
garnet

girasol
gneiss
granite
graphite
greenstone
gypsum
haematite
hornblende
hornfels
ironstone
jacinth
jade
jadeite
jasper
lapis lazuli
lava
limestone
magnetite
malachite
manganite
marble
marcasite
marl
mica
mica schist

moonstone
moss agate
mudstone
muscovite
natron
nephrite
obsidian
oil shale
olivine
onyx
oolite
opal
orpiment
pegmatite
peridot
peridotite
phosphorite
pitchblende
porphyry
pumice
pyrites
pyrope
quartz
quartzite
rag

rhyolite
rock salt
ruby
sandstone
sapphire
sardonyx
schist
serpentine
shale
slate
smoky quartz
spinel
steatite
sunstone
talc
topaz
tourmaline
tuff
turquoise
vermiculite
zeolite
zircon

Subatomic Particles

antiparticle
antiproton
antiquark
axion
baryon
boson

electron
fermion
gluon
hadron
Higgs boson
Higgs particle

hyperon
kaon
lambda particle
lepton
meson
muon

neutrino
neutron
nucleon
photon
pion
positron

proton
quark
tau particle
WIMP

Sports and Games

Sports

aerobatics
aerobics
American
  football
angling
aquaplaning
archery
Association
  Football
athletics
Australian Rules
  football
badminton
ballooning
base-jumping
baseball
basketball
beach volleyball
beagling
billiards
BMX
bobsleighing
boule/boules
bowling
bowls
boxing
bullfighting
bungee jumping
caber tossing
Canadian
  football
canoeing
canyoning
caving
clay-pigeon
  shooting
climbing
clock golf

coarse fishing
coursing
cricket
croquet
cross-country
  running
crown-green
  bowls
curling
cycle racing
cycling
cyclo-cross
darts
dinghy racing
diving
downhill skiing
Eton fives
falconry
fencing
field hockey
figure-skating
fishing
five-a-side
  football
fives
flat-green bowls
flat racing
fly-fishing
football
fowling
free skating
freestyling
French cricket
Gaelic football
game fishing
gliding
goalball
golf

greyhound
  racing
gymkhana
gymnastics
handball
hang-gliding
harness racing
heli-skiing
hiking
hockey
horse racing
hunting
hurling
hydrospeed
ice dancing
ice hockey
ice skating
jai alai
jet-skiing
kabaddi
kayaking
kiteboarding
kitesurfing
korfball
lacrosse
langlauf
lawn tennis
luge
match fishing
mountain biking
mountaineering
netball
ninepins
orienteering
parachuting
paragliding
parapenting
parasailing

parascending
pelota
pétanque
pigeon racing
pistol shooting
point-to-point
polo
pool
potholing
powerboat
  racing
quoits
rackets
racquetball
rafting
real tennis
rock climbing
roller skating
rollerblading
rounders
rowing
Rugby fives
rugby league
rugby union
sailing
scuba-diving
sculling
sea fishing
shinty
shooting
showjumping
skateboarding
skating
skeet
skiing
skijoring
ski jumping
skin-diving

skittles
skydiving
slalom
snooker
snorkelling
snowboarding
soccer
softball
speed skating
spelunking
sprinting
squash
surfing
swimming
synchronized
  swimming
table tennis
tennis
tenpin bowling
three-day
  eventing
tobogganing
trap shooting
trotting
volleyball
wakeboarding
walking
water polo
waterskiing
weightlifting
white-water
  rafting
wild-water
  racing
wildfowling
windsurfing
wrestling
yachting

Athletics Events

biathlon
cross-country
  running
decathlon
discus
field event
half-marathon

hammer
heptathlon
high jump
hurdles
javelin
long jump

long-distance
  race
marathon
middle-distance
  race
mile
pentathlon

pole vault
race
relay race
shot-put
sprint
steeplechase
tetrathlon

track event
triathlon
triple jump
tug of war
walking

Gymnastics Events

artistic
  gymnastics
asymmetric bars

beamfloor
  exercises
high bar

parallel bars
pommel horse

rhythmic
  gymnastics
rings

sports aerobics
uneven bars
vault

Martial Arts and Combat Sports

aikido

ba gua

boxing

budo

capoeira

fencing	judo	Krav Maga	sumo wrestling	ultimate fighting
hapkido	kalaripayattu	kung fu	tae kwon do	wing chun
jeet kune do	karate	pa kua	t'ai chi chu'an	wrestling
jousting	kendo	Shotokan	tang soo do	wushu
ju-jitsu	kick-boxing	Silat	Thai boxing	

Motor Sports

autocross	enduro	hill-climbing	motorcycle	scrambling
cross-country	F1	Indy	racing	sidecar racing
demolition derby	Formula One	Indycar	off-roading	speedway
dirt-track racing	go-karting	karting	rallycross	stock-car racing
drag racing	Grand Prix	motocross	rallying	trials

Games

Aunt Sally	cops and	housey-housey	Pac-Man	shovelboard
backgammon	robbers	hunt the thimble	(trademark)	Simon Says
bagatelle	craps	I spy	paintball	snakes and
battleships	darts	jacks	pass the parcel	ladders
billiards	deck quoits	jackstraws	pat-a-cake	snooker
bingo	dice	kabaddi	peekaboo	solitaire
blind man's buff	dominoes	King of the	piggy in the	spillikins
cards	draughts	Castle	middle	spin the bottle
catch	ducks and	kriegspiel	pinball	Subbuteo
cat's cradle	drakes	leapfrog	pitch-and-toss	(trademark)
charades	dungeons and	lotto	poker dice	table football
checkers	dragons	ludo	Poohsticks	tag
chess	fantasy football	mah-jong	pool	team game
chicken	fivestones	marbles	postman's knock	thimblerig
Chinese	follow-my-leader	Monopoly	prisoner's base	tic-tac-toe
chequers	forfeits	(trademark)	quoits	tiddlywinks
Chinese	frisbee (trademark)	murder in the	ring-a-ring o'	tig
whispers	go	dark	roses	treasure hunt
Cluedo (trademark)	halma	musical bumps	roulette	Trivial Pursuit
computer game	hangman	musical chairs	sardines	(trademark)
conkers	hide-and-seek	nim	Scrabble	tug of war
consequences	hoopla	noughts and	(trademark)	word game
	hopscotch	crosses	shove-halfpenny	

Ball Games

American	bowling	French cricket	pétanque	snooker
football	bowls	Gaelic football	polo	soccer
Association	cricket	golf	pool	softball
Football	croquet	handball	rackets	squash
Australian Rules	crown-green	hockey	real tennis	table tennis
football	bowls	hurling	rounders	tennis
baseball	Eton fives	lacrosse	rugby	tenpin bowling
basketball	five-a-side	lawn tennis	rugby league	volleyball
beach volleyball	football	mini rugby	rugby union	water polo
billiards	fives	netball	shinty	
boule/boules	football	ninepins	skittles	

Card Games

baccarat	bridge	fan-tan	old maid	skat
beggar-my-	canasta	faro	ombre	snap
neighbour	cheat	gin rummy	patience	solitaire
bezique	chemin de fer	happy families	pinochle	solo whist
blackjack	cribbage	loo	piquet	stud poker
Black Maria	duplicate bridge	monte	poker	twenty-one
Boston	écarté	nap	pontoon	vingt-et-un
brag	euchre	Newmarket	rummy	whist

Technology

Computing and Internet Terms

acoustic coupler
agent
alias
applet
application
assembler
backup
bar-code reader
BASIC
baud
BIOS
bit
bitmap
blog
blogger
board
bookmark
boot
bot
browser
buffer
bug
bulletin board
bus
byte
cache
cache memory
card
CD-R
CD-ROM
CD-RW
central
    processing unit
chat room
chip
click
client
code
compact disc
computer
console
control unit
coprocessor
CPU
crash
crawler
cursor
daemon

data
debugger
desktop
dialler
dialog box
digital
digitizer
disk
disk drive
diskette
display
domain
domain name
DOS
dot-matrix
    printer
download
drive
DVD
DVD-R
DVD-ROM
DVD-RW
e-tailer
editor
email
emoticon
Ethernet
expansion card
expert system
FAQ
fax modem
file
filename
filter
firewall
firmware
flash memory
floppy disk
format
freeware
FTP
games console
gateway
GIF
gigabit
graphics card
groupware
hacker

hard disk
hard drive
hardware
home page
host
HTML
HTTP
hyperlink
hypertext
icon
in-box
information
    technology
inkjet printer
input
interactive
interface
Internet service
    provider
intranet
ISP
joystick
JPEG
keyboard
keypad
kilobyte
laptop
laser printer
light pen
log in
log out
loop
macro
mailer
malware
manager
megabyte
megapixel
memory
menu
microchip
microcomputer
minicomputer
modem
monitor
motherboard
mouse
mouse mat

navigator
Net
network
newsgroup
notebook
offline
online
optical disk
output
palmtop
parser
PC
PDA
PDF
phishing
plug-in
podcast
pop-up
port
portal
printed circuit
printed circuit
    board
printer
printout
processor
program
RAM
random-access
    memory
read-only
    memory
register
rollerball
ROM
routine
scanner
screen saver
script
search engine
sequencer
serial port
server
servlet
shareware
shell program
silicon chip
sniffer

software
sound card
spam
spellchecker
spider
spreadsheet
spyware
surf
talkboard
telnet
terminal
text editor
toggle
tool
toolbar
touch pad
touch screen
trackball
transistor
Trojan Horse
upload
URL
user interface
utility
vaccine
VDU
video card
viewscreen
virtual reality
virus
visual display
    unit
wallpaper
Web
webcam
weblog
web page
website
wiki
word processor
workstation
World Wide
    Web
worm
XML
zip
zip file

Wordfinder

Energy and Fuels

acetylene
anthracite
atomic power
bio-diesel
biofuel
biogas
briquette

butane
Calor gas
    (trademark)
chemical energy
coal
coal gas
coke

derv
diesel
electricity
electromagnetic
    energy
firewood
fossil fuel

fuel oil
fusion energy
gas
gasoline
geothermal
    energy
heat

hydroelectric
    power
hydrogen
kerosene
leaded petrol
light
lignite

methane
natural gas
nuclear power
oil

paraffin
peat
petrol
petroleum

propane
renewable
  energy
solar energy

steam power
tidal power
turf
unleaded petrol

water power
wave power
wind power
wood

Engines

aero engine
beam engine
diesel engine
donkey engine
dynamo
electric motor
external-
  combustion
  engine
flat-four engine

four-stroke
gas turbine
generator
heat engine
inboard
inline engine
internal-
  combustion
  engine
jet engine

linear motor
magneto
oil engine
outboard
petrol engine
piston engine
prop jet
pulse jet
radial engine
ramjet

rocket engine
rotary engine
scramjet
steam engine
steam turbine
straight-eight
transverse
  engine
thruster
turbine

turbo diesel
turbofan
turbojet
turboprop
turboshaft
twin-cam engine
two-stroke
V6
V8
V12

Tools

adze
air gun
Allen key
  (trademark)
auger
awl
axe
bandsaw
beetle
bevel
billhook
blowlamp
blowtorch
bodkin
borer
bowsaw
brace
bradawl
burin
burnisher
burr
capstan lathe
centre bit
centre punch
chainsaw
chisel
chopper
circular saw
clamp
claw hammer
cleaver
compass saw

coping saw
cramp
cross peen/pein
crowbar
cultivator
cutter
dibber
dibble
diestock
dovetailer
drill
edge tool
edging shears
edging tool
file
flail
float
fork
former
frame saw
fretsaw
froe
fuller
gimlet
glass cutter
graver
grinder
grouter
hack
hacksaw
hammer
hammer drill

hatchet
hedge clipper
hoe
hole saw
jack
jackhammer
jemmy
jigsaw
jointer
keyhole saw
knife
lathe
lawnmower
loppers
mallet
marlinspike
mattock
mortar board
nail punch
nailer
needle
nippers
padsaw
paint gun
panel saw
peen/pein
  hammer
perforator
pestle
pick
pickaxe
pincers

pitchfork
plane
pliers
priest
pruning hook
punch
rake
ram
rasp
reamer
riddle
ripsaw
roller
roulette
router
rule
sander
sandpaper
saw
sawbench
scarifier
scraper
screwdriver
screw tap
scribe
scroll saw
scythe
secateurs
shears
shovel
sickle
slasher

sledgehammer
socket spanner
soldering iron
spade
spanner
spokeshave
square
staple gun
steam hammer
strickle
swage
swingle
tenon saw
tilt hammer
tinsnips
torque wrench
trimmer
trip hammer
trowel
tweezers
vice
wedge
wheel brace
whipsaw
wire cutter
wire stripper
woodcarver
wrench

Units

acre
age
air mile
ampere
angstrom
astronomical
  unit
atmosphere
atomic mass unit

bale
bar
barrel
baud
becquerel
bel
bit
brake
  horsepower

British thermal
  unit
bushel
byte
cable
calorie
candela
carat
centigram

centilitre
centimetre
century
chain
cord
coulomb
cubit
cup
cupful

curie
cycle
day
decade
decalitre
decametre
decibel
decilitre
decimetre

degree	hand	lumen	nanometre	roentgen
denier	hectare	lux	nanosecond	rood
dessertspoon	henry	Mach number	nautical mile	scruple
dioptre	hertz	maxwell	newton	second
drachm	hogshead	megabyte	noggin	siemens
dyne	horsepower	megaflop	ohm	sievert
electronvolt	hour	megahertz	ounce	span
ell	hundredweight	megaton	parsec	square
epoch	inch	megavolt	pascal	steradian
erg	joule	megawatt	peck	stone
farad	kelvin	metre	pennyweight	tablespoon
fathom	kilobyte	metric ton	perch	teaspoon
firkin	kilocalorie	microgram	period	terabyte
fluid drachm	kilogram	microlitre	pica	teraflop
fluid ounce	kilohertz	micrometre	pint	tesla
foot	kilojoule	micron	pipe	therm
furlong	kilolitre	microsecond	point	tog
gallon	kilometre	mile	poise	ton
gauss	kiloton	millennium	pole	tonne
gigabit	kilovolt	millibar	pound	troy ounce
gigabyte	kilowatt	milligram	quantum bit	volt
gigaflop	kilowatt-hour	millilitre	quart	watt
gigahertz	knot	millimetre	quarter	weber
gigawatt	league	millisecond	quintal	week
gill	light year	minim	rad	yard
grain	line	minute	radian	year
gram	link	mole	rem	
gray	litre	month	rod	

Transport

Motor Vehicles

all-terrain vehicle	DUKW	juggernaut	public service	station wagon
ambulance	dumper truck	kart	vehicle (PSV)	stock car
armoured car	dune buggy	kit car	quad bike	stretch limo
articulated lorry	dustcart	limousine	racing car	superbike
automobile	earth mover	lorry	ragtop	supercar
autorickshaw	estate	low-loader	rally car	supermini
battlebus	fastback	microcar	recreational	tank
beach buggy	fire engine	milk float	vehicle (RV)	tanker
Black Maria	flatbed	minelayer	refrigerated van	taxi
bowser (trademark)	float	minicab	removal van	taxicab
buggy	forklift truck	moped	roadroller	tourer
bulldozer	four-by-four	motorbike	roadster	touring car
bus	four-wheel drive	motor caravan	rover	tow truck
cab	(4WD)	motorcycle	runabout	tracklayer
cabriolet	go-kart	multi-purpose	saloon	tractor
camper	golf cart	vehicle (MPV)	scooter	trail bike
car	gritter	notchback	scrambler	trailer
car transporter	hackney cab	off-road vehicle	sedan	tram
charabanc	half-track	off-roader	shooting brake	transporter
coach	hardtop	omnibus	snowcat	trolleybus
concept car	hatchback	pantechnicon	snowmobile	troop carrier
convertible	hearse	passenger-	snowplough	truck
coupé	heavy goods	carrying	soft top	utility
dirt bike	vehicle (HGV)	vehicle	sports car	van
double-decker	horsebox	people carrier	sportster	wagon/waggon
bus	hot rod	personnel carrier	sport utility	wrecker
dragster	Jeep (trademark)	pickup	vehicle (SUV)	

Carriages and Carts

barouche	carriole	curricle	handcart	tilbury
brake	chaise	dog cart	hansom	trailer
breaking cart	chariot	dray	landau	trap
brougham	clarence	droshky	ox cart	trishaw
buggy	coach	fiacre	phaeton	tumbril
cab	coach-and-four	fly	postchaise	Victoria
cabriolet	coupé	gig	rickshaw	wagon/waggon
caravan	covered wagon	hackney	stagecoach	wagonette

Trains and Rolling Stock

armoured train	diesel	guard's van	observation car	steam
bogie	locomotive	handcar	pannier tank	locomotive
boxcar	diesel multiple	high-speed train	passenger train	steam train
brake van	unit	hopper	Pullman	stopping train
buffet car	dining car	hospital train	railcar	subway train
bullet train	double-header	locomotive	restaurant car	tank engine
cable car	electric train	maglev	saddle tank	tender
caboose	engine	mail coach	shunter	TGV
car	express	mail train	sleeper	underground
carriage	flatcar	metro	sleeping car	train
coach	freight train	milk train	smokebox	wagon-lit
couchette	goods train	monorail	smoker	
diesel-electric	goods wagon	motor coach		

Ships and Boats

airboat	coal ship	galliot	liner	powerboat
aircraft carrier	coaler	gig	longboat	pram
amphibious	coaster	gondola	longship	privateer
assault ship	cockleshell	gulet	lugger	proa
amphibious	collier	gunboat	mailboat	punt
landing craft	container ship	helicopter carrier	man-of-war	Q-ship
auxiliary	coracle	hermaphrodite	merchantman	quinquereme
barge	corvette	brig	merchant ship	raft
barque	cruiser	hospital ship	minehunter	RIB
barquentine	cruise ship	houseboat	minelayer	rigger
bateau mouche	cutter	hovercraft	minesweeper	riverboat
bathyscaphe	destroyer	hydrofoil	monitor	roll-on roll-off
bathysphere	dhow	hydroplane	monohull	rowing boat
battlecruiser	dinghy	iceboat	motor boat	rubber dinghy
battleship	diving bell	ice-breaker	motor torpedo	safety boat
bireme	dory	inboard	boat	sailing boat
boatel	dragon boat	Indiaman	motor yacht	sailing ship
brig	dreadnought	inflatable dinghy	multihull	sampan
brigantine	dredger	ironclad	narrowboat	schooner
bulk carrier	drifter	jetboat	oiler	scow
bumboat	dugout	jetfoil	oil tanker	scull
cabin cruiser	E-boat	jet ski (trademark)	outboard	sealer
cable ship	East Indiaman	jolly	outrigger	shallop
caique	factory ship	junk	paddle boat	shell
canal boat	felucca	kayak	paddle steamer	ship of the line
canoe	ferry	keelboat	pedal boat	showboat
capital ship	flag boat	ketch	pedalo	side-wheeler
car ferry	flagship	landing craft	pilot boat	single-hander
caravel	flatboat	launch	pink	skiff
cargo ship	freighter	liberty boat	pinnace	skipjack
carrack	frigate	lifeboat	pirogue	slaver
catamaran	full-rigger	life raft	pocket	sloop
catboat	galleon	lighter	battleship	sloop of war
clipper	galley	lightship	pontoon	smack

speedboat · submersible · training ship · tugboat · whaler
square-rigger · supertanker · tramp steamer · U-boat · wherry
stake boat · supply ship · trawler · vaporetto · windjammer
steamboat · tall ship · trimaran · warship · workboat
steamer · tanker · trireme · water bus · xebec
steamship · tender · troop carrier · water taxi · yacht
sternwheeler · torpedo boat · troopship · weekender · yawl
submarine · trader · tub · whaleboat

Aircraft

airliner · fighter · hydroplane · sailplane · tug
airship · fighter-bomber · interceptor · seaplane · turbofan
autogiro · floatplane · jet · ski-plane · turbojet
balloon · flying boat · jet plane · spaceplane · turboprop
biplane · freighter · jetliner · spotter · warplane
blimp · glider · jumbo jet · stealth bomber · water bomber
bomber · gunship · jump jet · stealth fighter · whirlybird
chopper · gyrocopter · microlight · swept-wing · widebody
delta-wing · gyroplane · minelayer · tanker · Zeppelin
dirigible · hang-glider · monoplane · towplane
dive bomber · helicopter · night fighter · triplane
drone · hot-air balloon · paraglider · troop carrier

War

Weapons

A-bomb · Browning · flick knife · intercontinental · missile
air gun · buckshot · flintlock · ballistic missile · Molotov cocktail
anti-aircraft gun · cannon · flying bomb · (ICBM) · mortar
arquebus · cannonball · forty-five · incendiary bomb · musket
Armalite · car bomb · fragmentation · incendiary · neutron bomb
(trademark) · carbine · bomb · device · nuclear bomb
artillery · case knife · fragmentation · jackknife · nulla-nulla
assault rifle · catapult · grenade · javelin · panga
atom/atomic · claymore · fusil · Kalashnikov · parang
bomb · club · fusion bomb · knife · parcel bomb
automatic · cluster bomb · Gatling gun · knobkerrie · pellet
axe · Colt (trademark) · gelignite · knuckleduster · petard
ballistic missile · cordite · grapeshot · kris · petrol bomb
baseball bat · cosh · grenade · kukri · pike
baton · cruise missile · guided missile · lance · pistol
baton round · cudgel · gun · landmine · plastic bullet
battleaxe · cutlass · guncotton · lathi · plastic explosive
bayonet · dagger · gunpowder · Lee-Enfield · Polaris
bazooka · daisy-cutter · H-bomb · letter bomb · poleaxe
bill · depth charge · halberd · Lewis gun · pom-pom
birdshot · derringer · hand grenade · life preserver · poniard
blackjack · dirk · handgun · limpet mine · pump-action
blade · dirty bomb · harpoon · Luger (trademark) · shotgun
bludgeon · doodlebug · harpoon gun · mace · quarterstaff
blunderbuss · duelling pistol · harquebus · machete · rapier
Bofors gun · dumdum bullet · hatchet · machine gun · revolver
bomb · dynamite · high explosive · magnetic mine · rifle
bowie knife · épée · horse pistol · mail bomb · rocket
brass knuckles · Exocet · howitzer · matchlock · rocket-propelled
breech-loader · express rifle · hydrogen bomb · Mauser (trademark) · grenade
Bren gun · firebomb · · Maxim gun · rubber bullet
broadsword · firelock · · Mills bomb · sabre

sawn-off
  shotgun
scimitar
Scud
semi-automatic
Semtex
sheath knife
shell
shillelagh
shotgun
sidearm

siege gun
six-shooter
sjambok
skean
skean-dhu
slug
slung shot
small arms
small sword

Smith and
  Wesson
  (trademark)
smoke bomb
smooth-bore
spear
staff
stave
Sten gun
stick
stiletto

sub-machine
  gun
switchblade
sword
swordstick
thirty-eight
time bomb
tomahawk
tommy gun
torpedo
tracer

trench mortar
Trident
truncheon
Uzi
warhead
Winchester
  (trademark)
yataghan
zip gun

Parts of a Suit of Armour

basinet
beaver
bracer
brassard
breastplate
brigandine
burgonet
camail
casque

chain mail
chausses
coif
corselet
coutere
cuirass
cuisse
gauntlet
gorget

greave
habergeon
hauberk
helmet
jambeau
lance rest
mail
morion
nasal

neck guard
nosepiece
pectoral
plastron
poleyn
pouldron
rerebrace
sabaton
sallet

solleret
tasses
vambrace
ventail
visor

Types of Soldier

archer
artilleryman
beefeater
blue helmet
bowman
cadet
cannoneer
carabineer
cavalier
cavalryman
centurion
commando
conscript
cuirassier
dragoon

drum major
enlisted man
ensign
evzone
foot soldier
freelance
fusilier
grenadier
guardsman
guerrilla
gunner
halberdier
havildar
hoplite
hussar

infantryman
irregular
janissary
klepht
knight
lancer
legionary
legionnaire
marine
mercenary
military
  policeman
militiaman
musketeer

non-
  commissioned
  officer (NCO)
officer
orderly
paratrooper
partisan
pistoleer
point man
ranger
ranker
recruit
redcap
redcoat
regular

reservist
rifleman
sabreur
samurai
sapper
scout
SEAL
sentinel
sentry
sepoy
spearman
swordsman
Territorial
trooper
yeoman

Military Ranks

Acting Pilot
  Officer
Admiral
Admiral of the
  Fleet
Air Chief
  Marshal
Air Commodore
Air Marshal
Air Vice-Marshal
Aircraftman
Aircraftwoman
Bombardier
Brigadier
Brigadier
  General

Captain
Chief of Staff
Chief Petty
  Officer
Colonel
Commander
Commodore
Corporal
Ensign
Field Marshal
First Lieutenant
Fleet Admiral
Flight Lieutenant
Flight Sergeant
Flying Officer
General

Group Captain
Gunner
Lance
  Bombardier
Lance Corporal
Leading
  Aircraftman
Lieutenant
Lieutenant
  Colonel
Lieutenant
  Commander
Lieutenant
  General
Lieutenant junior
  grade

Major
Major General
Marshal of the
  Royal Air Force
Master Chief
  Petty Officer
Midshipman
Petty Officer
Pilot Officer
Private
Private First Class
Rear Admiral
Seaman
Second
  Lieutenant

Senior
  Aircraftman
Senior Chief
  Petty Officer
Sergeant
Squadron Leader
Staff Sergeant
Sub Lieutenant
Vice Admiral
Warrant Officer
Wing
  Commander

Jj

jab verb *he jabbed the Englishman with his finger:* **poke**, prod, dig, nudge, butt, ram; thrust, stab, push.
noun *a jab in the ribs:* **poke**, prod, dig, nudge, butt; thrust, stab, push.

jabber verb *they jabbered away non-stop:* **prattle**, babble, chatter, twitter, prate, gabble, rattle on/away, blather; informal yak, yap, yabber, yatter, blab, blabber; Brit. informal witter, rabbit, natter.
noun *stop your jabber!* **prattle**, babble, chatter, chattering, twitter, twittering, gabble, blather; informal yabbering, yatter, blabber; Brit. informal wittering, rabbiting, nattering.

jack
▪ **jack something up** *they jacked up the car:* raise, hoist, lift (up), winch up, lever up, hitch up, elevate.

jacket noun *a jacket for your hot-water tank will save at least £15 a year:* **wrapping**, wrapper, wrap, sleeve, sheath, sheathing, cover, covering.

jackpot noun *this week's lottery jackpot:* **top prize**, first prize; pool, bonanza.
▪ **hit the jackpot** (informal) win a large prize, win a lot of money, strike it lucky/rich; informal clean up, hit the big time.

jaded adjective **1** *a jaded palate:* **satiated**, sated, surfeited, glutted; dulled, blunted, deadened. **2** *she felt really jaded:* **tired (out)**, weary, wearied, worn out, exhausted, fatigued, overtired, sapped, drained; informal all in, done (in), dead (beat), dead on one's feet, bushed; Brit. informal knackered, whacked; N. Amer. informal tuckered out.
– OPPOSITES fresh.

jag noun *a head of rye, all jags and bristles:* **sharp projection**, point, barb, thorn.

jagged adjective *the jagged end of a broken bone:* **spiky**, barbed, ragged, rough, uneven, irregular, broken; serrated, sawtooth, indented.
– OPPOSITES smooth.

jail noun *he was thrown into jail:* **prison**, penal institution, lock-up, detention centre; N. Amer. penitentiary, jailhouse, stockade, correctional facility; informal clink, slammer, inside, jug, brig; Brit. informal nick; N. Amer. informal can, pen, cooler, slam, pokey.
verb *she was jailed for killing her husband:* **imprison**, put in prison, send to prison, incarcerate, lock up, put away, intern, detain, hold (prisoner/captive), put into detention; informal send down, put behind bars, put inside; Brit. informal bang up.
– OPPOSITES acquit, release.

jailer noun **prison officer**, warder, wardress, warden, guard, captor; informal screw.

jam¹ verb **1** *he jammed a finger in each ear:* **stuff**, shove, force, ram, thrust, press, push, stick, squeeze, cram. **2** *hundreds of people jammed into the hall:* **crowd**, pack, pile, press, squeeze, cram; throng, mob, occupy, fill, overcrowd, obstruct, block, clog, congest. **3** *the rudder had jammed:* **stick**, become stuck, catch, seize (up), become trapped. **4** *dust can jam the mechanism:* **immobilize**, paralyse, disable, cripple, put out of action, bring to a standstill.
noun **1** *a traffic jam:* **tailback**, hold-up, congestion, bottleneck; N. Amer. gridlock; informal snarl-up. **2** (informal) *we are in a real jam:* **predicament**, plight, tricky situation, difficulty, problem, quandary, dilemma, muddle, mess, imbroglio, mare's nest, dire straits; informal pickle, stew, fix, hole, scrape, bind, (tight) spot, (tight) corner, hot/deep water; Brit. informal spot of bother.

jam² noun *raspberry jam:* **preserve**, conserve, jelly, marmalade.

jamb noun **post**, doorpost, upright, frame.

jamboree noun *the world Scout jamboree:* **rally**, gathering, convention, conference; festival, fête, fiesta, gala, carnival, celebration; informal bash, shindig, shindy, junket.

jangle verb **1** *keys jangled at his waist:* **clank**, clink, jingle, tinkle. **2** *the noise jangled her nerves:* **grate on**, jar on, irritate, disturb, fray, put/set on edge; informal get on.
noun *the jangle of his chains:* **clank**, clanking, clink, clinking, jangling, jingle, jingling, tintinnabulation.

janitor noun **caretaker**, custodian, porter, concierge, doorkeeper, doorman, warden; cleaner, maintenance man; N. Amer. superintendent.

jar¹ noun *a jar of honey:* **(glass) container**, pot, crock, receptacle.

jar² verb **1** *each step jarred my whole body:* **jolt**, jerk, shake, vibrate. **2** *her shrill voice jarred on him:* **grate**, set someone's teeth on edge, irritate, annoy, irk, exasperate, nettle, disturb, discompose; informal rile, aggravate, get on someone's nerves. **3** *the* play's symbolism *jarred with the realism of its setting:* **clash**, conflict, contrast, be incompatible, be at variance, be at odds, be inconsistent, be discordant; informal scream at.

jargon noun *the instructions are written in electrician's jargon:* **specialized language**, slang, cant, idiom, argot, patter, gobbledegook; informal -speak, -ese.

jarring adjective *the jarring juxtaposition of opposites:* **clashing**, conflicting, contrasting, incompatible, incongruous; discordant, dissonant, inharmonious, harsh, grating, strident, shrill, cacophonous.
– OPPOSITES harmonious.

jaundiced adjective *a jaundiced view of the world:* **bitter**, resentful, cynical, soured, disenchanted, disillusioned, disappointed, pessimistic, sceptical, distrustful, suspicious, misanthropic.

jaunt noun *his wife went off for a jaunt round Oxford:* **(pleasure) trip**, outing, excursion, day trip, day out, mini holiday, short break; tour, drive, ride, run; informal spin, tootle.

jaunty adjective *he wore a cap pushed to one side to give him a jaunty air:* **cheerful**, cheery, happy, merry, jolly, joyful; lively, perky, bright, buoyant, bubbly, bouncy, breezy, full of the joys of spring, in good spirits, exuberant, ebullient; carefree, blithe, airy, light-hearted, nonchalant, insouciant, happy-go-lucky; Brit. Tiggerish; informal bright-eyed and bushy-tailed, full of beans, chirpy.
– OPPOSITES depressed, serious.

javelin noun **spear**, harpoon, dart, gig, shaft, assegai.

jaw noun **1** *a broken jaw:* **jawbone**, lower/upper jaw; Anatomy mandible, maxilla. **2** *the whale seized a seal pup in its jaws:* **mouth**, maw, muzzle; informal chops.

jazz
■ **jazz something up** (informal) *why not jazz up your documents with a few unusual typefaces?* enliven, liven up, brighten up, make more interesting/exciting, add (some) colour to, ginger up, spice up; informal perk up, pep up.

jazzy adjective *jazzy ties:* **bright**, colourful, brightly coloured, striking, eye-catching, vivid, lively, vibrant, bold, flamboyant, showy, gaudy; informal flashy.
– OPPOSITES dull.

jealous adjective **1** *he was jealous of his brother's popularity:* **envious**, covetous, desirous; resentful, grudging, begrudging, green (with envy). **2** *a jealous lover:* **suspicious**, distrustful, mistrustful, doubting, insecure, anxious; possessive, proprietorial, overprotective. **3** *they are very jealous of their rights:* **protective**, vigilant, watchful, heedful, mindful, careful, solicitous.
– OPPOSITES proud, trusting.

jealousy noun **1** *he was consumed with*

jealousy: **envy**, covetousness; resentment, resentfulness, bitterness, spite; informal the green-eyed monster. **2** *the jealousy of his long-suffering wife:* **suspicion**, suspiciousness, distrust, mistrust, insecurity, anxiety; possessiveness, overprotectiveness. **3** *an intense jealousy of status:* **protectiveness**, vigilance, watchfulness, heedfulness, mindfulness, care, solicitousness.

jeans plural noun **denims**, blue jeans; trademark Levi's, Wranglers.

jeer verb *the demonstrators jeered the police:* **taunt**, mock, scoff at, ridicule, sneer at, deride, insult, abuse, jibe (at), scorn, shout disapproval (at); heckle, catcall (at), boo (at), hoot at, whistle at, hiss (at).
– OPPOSITES cheer.
noun *the jeers of the crowd:* **taunt**, sneer, insult, shout, jibe, boo, hiss, catcall; derision, teasing, scoffing, abuse, scorn, heckling, catcalling; Brit. & Austral./NZ barracking.
– OPPOSITES applause.

jejune adjective **1** *their jejune opinions:* **naive**, innocent, artless, guileless, unworldly, childlike, ingenuous, unsophisticated; credulous, gullible; childish, immature, juvenile, puerile, infantile. **2** *the following poem is rather jejune:* **boring**, dull, tedious, dreary; uninteresting, unexciting, uninspiring, unimaginative; humdrum, run-of-the-mill, mundane, commonplace; lacklustre, dry, sterile, lifeless, vapid, flat, bland, banal, trite, prosaic; Brit. informal samey; N. Amer. informal ornery.
– OPPOSITES sophisticated, fascinating.

jell verb. See GEL.

jeopardize verb *relocating outside London will jeopardize their competitiveness:* **threaten**, endanger, imperil, risk, put at risk, put in danger/jeopardy; leave vulnerable; compromise, prejudice, be prejudicial to; be a danger to, pose a threat to.
– OPPOSITES safeguard.

jeopardy noun *the peace talks are in jeopardy:* **danger**, peril; (**in jeopardy**) at risk.

jerk noun **1** *she gave the reins a jerk:* **yank**, tug, pull, wrench, tweak, twitch. **2** *he let the clutch in with a jerk:* **jolt**, lurch, bump, start, jar, jog, bang, bounce, shake, shock.
verb **1** *she jerked her arm free:* **yank**, tug, pull, wrench, wrest, drag, pluck, snatch, seize, rip, tear. **2** *the car jerked along:* **jolt**, lurch, bump, rattle, bounce, shake, jounce.

jerky adjective **1** *jerky movements:* **convulsive**, spasmodic, fitful, twitchy, shaky. **2** *the coach drew to a jerky halt:* **jolting**, lurching, bumpy, bouncy, jarring.
– OPPOSITES smooth.

jerry-built adjective *they lived in tents and jerry-built shacks:* **shoddy**, badly built, gimcrack, flimsy, insubstantial, rickety, ramshackle, crude, makeshift; inferior,

poor-quality, second-rate, third-rate, low-grade.
– OPPOSITES sturdy.

jersey noun **pullover**, sweater; Brit. jumper; informal woolly.

jest noun *jests were bandied about freely:* **joke**, witticism, funny remark, gag, quip, sally, pun; informal crack, wisecrack, one-liner.
verb **1** *surely you are jesting:* **joke**, quip, gag, pun; tell jokes, crack jokes; informal wisecrack. **2** *she feared that they had not been jesting:* **fool (about/around)**, play a practical joke, tease; informal kid, have someone on, pull someone's leg; N. Amer. informal pull someone's chain, fun; Brit. informal wind someone up.
■ **in jest** in fun, as a joke, tongue in cheek, playfully, jokingly, light-heartedly, facetiously, flippantly, frivolously, for a laugh.

jester noun *the class jester:* **joker**, comedian, comic, humorist, wag, wit, prankster, jokester, clown, buffoon; informal card, case, caution, hoot, scream, laugh, wisecracker, barrel of laughs; Austral./NZ informal hard case.

jet[1] noun **1** *a jet of water:* **stream**, spurt, squirt, spray, spout; gush, rush, surge, burst. **2** *carburettor jets:* **nozzle**, head, spout. **3** *an executive jet:* **jet plane**, jetliner; aircraft, plane; Brit. aeroplane.
verb **1** *they jetted out of Heathrow:* **fly**, travel/go by jet, travel/go by plane. **2** *puffs of gas jetted out:* **squirt**, spurt, shoot, spray; gush, pour, stream, rush, pump, surge, spew, burst.

jet[2] adjective *her glossy jet hair:* **black**, jet-black, pitch-black, ink-black, ebony, raven, sable, sooty.

jettison verb **1** *six aircraft jettisoned their loads:* **dump**, drop, ditch, discharge, throw out, tip out, unload, throw overboard. **2** *he jettisoned his unwanted papers | the scheme was jettisoned:* **discard**, dispose of, throw away/out, get rid of; reject, scrap, axe, abandon, drop; informal chuck (away/out), dump, ditch, bin, junk, get shut of; Brit. informal get shot of; N. Amer. informal trash.
– OPPOSITES retain.

jetty noun **pier**, landing (stage), quay, wharf, dock; breakwater, mole, groyne, dyke; N. Amer. dockominium, levee.

jewel noun **1** *priceless jewels:* **gem**, gemstone, (precious) stone, brilliant; baguette; informal sparkler, rock. **2** *the jewel of his collection:* **finest example/specimen**, showpiece, pride (and joy), cream, crème de la crème, jewel in the crown, nonpareil, glory, prize, boast, pick, ne plus ultra. **3** *the girl is a jewel:* **treasure**, angel, paragon, marvel, find, godsend; informal one in a million, a star, the tops.

jewellery noun **jewels**, gems, gemstones, precious stones, bijouterie, costume jewellery, diamanté.

jib verb **1** *the horse jibbed at the final fence:* **stop (short) at**, baulk at, shy at; refuse.

2 *some farmers jib at paying large veterinary bills:* **baulk at**, fight shy of, recoil from, shrink from; be unwilling, be reluctant, be loath, demur at; informal boggle at.
– OPPOSITES clear.

jibe noun *cruel jibes:* **snide remark**, cutting remark, taunt, sneer, jeer, insult, barb; informal dig, put-down.
verb *Simon jibed in a sarcastic way:* **jeer**, taunt, mock, scoff, sneer.

jig verb *Joan jigged about with excitement:* **bob**, jump, spring, skip, hop, prance, bounce, jounce.

jiggle verb **1** *Barrett jiggled his foot:* **shake**, joggle, waggle, wiggle. **2** *Thomas jiggled excitedly:* **fidget**, wriggle, squirm.

jilt verb *the man I thought loved me jilted me:* **leave**, walk out on, throw over, finish with, break up with; informal chuck, ditch, dump, drop, run out on, give someone the push/elbow, give someone the old heave-ho, give someone the big E.

jingle noun **1** *the jingle of money in the till:* **clink**, chink, tinkle, jangle. **2** *the jingle of the bell:* **tinkle**, ring, ding, ping, ting-a-ling, chime, tintinnabulation. **3** *advertising jingles:* **slogan**, catchphrase; ditty, song, rhyme, tune; N. Amer. informal tag line.
verb **1** *her bracelets jingled noisily:* **clink**, chink, tinkle, jangle. **2** *the bell jingled:* **tinkle**, ring, ding, ping, chime.

jingoism noun *the jingoism of Hollywood war films:* **militarism**, hawkishness, belligerence, bellicosity: chauvinism, xenophobia; nationalism, patriotism.

jinx noun *the jinx struck six days later:* **curse**, spell, hoodoo, malediction; the evil eye, black magic, voodoo, bad luck; N. Amer. hex.
verb *the family is jinxed:* **curse**, cast a spell on, put the evil eye on, hoodoo; Austral. point the bone at; N. Amer. hex; Austral. informal mozz, put the mozz on.

job noun **1** *my job involves a lot of travelling:* **position**, post, situation, appointment, employment; occupation, profession, trade, career, (line of) work, métier, craft; vocation, calling; vacancy, opening; Austral. informal grip. **2** *this job will take three months:* **task**, piece of work, assignment, project; chore, errand; undertaking, venture, operation, enterprise, business. **3** *it's your job to protect her:* **responsibility**, duty, charge, task; role, function, mission; informal department, pigeon.

jobless adjective *sixteen per cent of the town's workforce is jobless:* **unemployed**, out of work, out of a job, unwaged, between jobs, redundant, laid off; Brit. informal signing on, on the dole, 'resting'; Austral./NZ informal on the wallaby track.
– OPPOSITES employed.

jockey noun **rider**, horseman, horsewoman, equestrian; Austral. informal hoop.
verb **1** *he jockeyed himself into the team:* **manoeuvre**, ease, edge, work, steer;

inveigle, insinuate, ingratiate; informal finagle. **2** *ministers began jockeying for position:* **compete**, contend, vie; struggle, fight, scramble, jostle.

jocular adjective *some rather inappropriate jocular comments:* **humorous**, funny, witty, comic, comical, amusing, droll, jokey, hilarious, facetious, tongue-in-cheek, teasing, playful; light-hearted, jovial, cheerful, cheery, merry.
– OPPOSITES solemn.

jog verb **1** *he jogged along the road:* **run slowly**, jogtrot, dogtrot, trot, lope. **2** *things are jogging along quite nicely:* **continue**, proceed, go on, carry on. **3** *a hand jogged his elbow:* **nudge**, prod, poke, push, bump, jar. **4** *something jogged her memory:* **stimulate**, prompt, stir, activate, refresh. **5** *she jogged her foot up and down:* **joggle**, jiggle, bob, bounce, jolt, jerk.
noun *he set off along at a jog:* **run**, jogtrot, dogtrot, trot, lope.

joie de vivre noun *Mediterranean joie de vivre is not a quality found in the typical Briton:* **gaiety**, cheerfulness, cheeriness, light-heartedness, happiness, joy, joyfulness, high spirits, jollity, joviality, exuberance, ebullience, liveliness, vivacity, verve, effervescence, buoyancy, zest, zestfulness; informal pep, zing.
– OPPOSITES sobriety.

join verb **1** *the two parts of the mould are joined with clay:* **connect**, unite, couple, fix, affix, attach, fasten, stick, glue, fuse, weld, amalgamate, bond, append, link, merge, secure, make fast, tie, bind, chain. **2** *here the path joins a major road:* **meet**, touch, reach, extend to, abut, adjoin, border (on). **3** *I'm off to join the search party:* **become a member of**, help in, participate in, join in, get involved in, contribute to, have a hand in; enlist, join up, sign up, affiliate to; play a part, band together, get together, ally, team up, join forces.
– OPPOSITES separate, leave.
noun. See JOINT.

joint noun **1** *a leaky joint in the guttering:* **join**, junction, juncture, intersection, link, linkage, connection; weld, seam. **2** *the hip joint:* ball-and-socket joint, hinge joint, articulation. **3** (informal) *a classy joint:* **establishment**, restaurant, bar, club, nightclub. **4** (informal) *he rolled a joint:* **cannabis cigarette**, marijuana cigarette; informal spliff, reefer, bomb, bomber, stick.
adjective *matters of joint interest* | *a joint effort:* **common**, shared, communal, collective; mutual, cooperative, collaborative, concerted, combined, united.
– OPPOSITES separate.
verb *she jointed the carcass:* **cut up**, chop up, butcher, carve.

jointly adverb *a survey organized jointly by the WWF and the Forestry Commission:* **together**, in partnership, in cooperation, cooperatively, in conjunction,

in combination, mutually.

joke noun **1** *they were telling jokes:* **funny story**, jest, witticism, quip; pun, play on words; informal gag, wisecrack, crack, funny, one-liner, killer, rib-tickler, knee-slapper, thigh-slapper; N. Amer. informal boffola. **2** *playing stupid jokes:* **trick**, practical joke, prank, stunt, hoax, jape; informal leg-pull, spoof. **3** (informal) *he soon became a joke to us:* **laughing stock**, figure of fun, object of ridicule; Brit. Aunt Sally. **4** (informal) *the present system is a joke:* **farce**, travesty, waste of time; N. Amer. informal shuck.
verb **1** *she joked with the guests:* **tell jokes**, jest, banter, quip; informal wisecrack, josh. **2** *I'm only joking:* **fool (about/around)**, play a trick, play a (practical) joke, tease, hoax, pull someone's leg, mess about/around; informal kid; Brit. informal have someone on, wind someone up; N. Amer. informal fun, shuck, pull someone's chain.

joker noun *he had a reputation as the family joker:* **humorist**, comedian, comedienne, comic, wit, jester; prankster, practical joker, hoaxer, trickster, clown; informal card, wisecracker, wag.

jolly adjective *a big, jolly woman:* **cheerful**, happy, cheery, good-humoured, jovial, merry, sunny, joyful, joyous, light-hearted, in high spirits, bubbly, exuberant, ebullient, cock-a-hoop, gleeful, mirthful, genial, fun-loving; informal chipper, chirpy, perky, bright-eyed and bushy-tailed.
– OPPOSITES miserable.
verb (informal) *he tried to jolly her along:* **encourage**, urge, coax, cajole, persuade.

jolt verb **1** *the train jolted the passengers to one side:* **push**, thrust, jar, bump, knock, bang; shake, joggle, jog. **2** *the car jolted along:* **bump**, bounce, jerk, rattle, lurch, shudder, judder, jounce. **3** *she was jolted out of her reverie:* **startle**, surprise, shock, stun, shake, take aback; astonish, astound, amaze, stagger, stop someone in their tracks; informal rock, floor, knock sideways; Brit. informal knock for six.
noun **1** *a series of sickening jolts:* **bump**, bounce, shake, jerk, lurch. **2** *he woke up with a jolt:* **start**, jerk, jump. **3** *the sight of the dagger gave him a jolt:* **fright**, the fright of one's life, shock, scare, surprise; informal turn.

jostle verb **1** *she was jostled by noisy students:* **bump into/against**, knock into/against, bang into, cannon into, plough into, jolt; push, shove, elbow; mob. **2** *I jostled my way to the exit:* **push**, thrust, barge, shove, force, elbow, shoulder, bulldoze. **3** *people jostled for the best position:* **struggle**, vie, jockey, scramble.

jot verb *I've jotted down a few details:* **write**, note, make a note of, take down, put on paper; scribble, scrawl.
noun *not a jot of evidence:* **iota**, scrap, shred,

whit, grain, crumb, ounce, (little) bit, jot or tittle, speck, atom, particle, scintilla, trace, hint; informal smidgen, tad; Austral./NZ informal skerrick.

journal noun **1** *a medical journal:* **periodical**, magazine, gazette, digest, review, newsletter, news-sheet, bulletin; newspaper, paper; daily, weekly, monthly, quarterly. **2** *he keeps a journal:* **diary**, daily record, log, weblog, blog, logbook, chronicle; N. Amer. daybook.

journalism noun **1** *a career in journalism:* **the newspaper business**, the press, the fourth estate; Brit. Fleet Street. **2** *his incisive style of journalism:* **reporting**, writing, reportage, feature writing, news coverage; articles, reports, features, pieces, stories.

journalist noun **reporter**, correspondent, newspaperman, newspaperwoman, newsman, newswoman, columnist, writer, commentator, blogger, reviewer; investigative journalist; Brit. pressman; N. Amer. legman, wireman; Austral. roundsman; informal news hound, hack, hackette, stringer, journo; N. Amer. informal newsy.

journey noun *his journey round the world:* **trip**, expedition, tour, trek, voyage, cruise, ride, drive; crossing, passage, flight; travels, wandering, globetrotting; odyssey, pilgrimage.
verb *they journeyed south:* **travel**, go, voyage, sail, cruise, fly, hike, trek, ride, drive, make one's way; go on a trip/expedition, tour.

jovial adjective *his jovial manner:* **cheerful**, jolly, happy, cheery, good-humoured, convivial, genial, good-natured, friendly, amiable, affable, sociable, outgoing; smiling, merry, sunny, joyful, joyous, high-spirited, exuberant; informal chipper, chirpy, perky, bright-eyed and bushy-tailed.
– OPPOSITES miserable.

joy noun **1** *whoops of joy:* **delight**, great pleasure, joyfulness, jubilation, triumph, exultation, rejoicing, happiness, gladness, glee, exhilaration, exuberance, elation, euphoria, bliss, ecstasy, rapture; enjoyment, felicity, joie de vivre. **2** *it was a joy to be with her:* **pleasure**, delight, treat, thrill; informal buzz, kick.
– OPPOSITES misery, trial.

joyful adjective **1** *his joyful mood:* **cheerful**, happy, jolly, merry, sunny, joyous, light-hearted, in good spirits, bubbly, exuberant, ebullient, cock-a-hoop, cheery, smiling, mirthful, radiant; jubilant, overjoyed, thrilled, ecstatic, euphoric, blissful, on cloud nine/seven, elated, delighted, gleeful; jovial, genial, good-humoured, full of the joys of spring; informal chipper, chirpy, peppy, over the moon, on top of the world; Austral./NZ informal wrapped. **2** *joyful news:* **pleasing**, happy, good, cheering, gladdening, welcome, heart-warming. **3** *a joyful occasion:* **happy**, cheerful, merry, jolly, festive, joyous.
– OPPOSITES sad, distressing.

joyless adjective **1** *a joyless man:* **gloomy**,

melancholy, morose, lugubrious, glum, sombre, saturnine, sullen, dour, humourless. **2** *a joyless room:* **depressing**, cheerless, gloomy, dreary, bleak, dispiriting, drab, dismal, desolate, austere, sombre; unwelcoming, uninviting, inhospitable.
– OPPOSITES cheerful, welcoming.

joyous adjective. See JOYFUL senses 1, 3.

jubilant adjective *crowds of jubilant fans ran on to the pitch:* **overjoyed**, exultant, triumphant, joyful, rejoicing, cock-a-hoop, exuberant, elated, thrilled, gleeful, euphoric, ecstatic, enraptured, in raptures, walking on air, in seventh heaven, on cloud nine; informal over the moon, on top of the world, on a high; N. Amer. informal wigged out; Austral. informal wrapped.
– OPPOSITES despondent.

jubilation noun *Arlene was unable to conceal her jubilation:* **exultation**, joy, joyousness, elation, euphoria, ecstasy, rapture, glee, gleefulness, exuberance.

jubilee noun **anniversary**, commemoration; celebration, festival, jamboree; festivities, revelry.

Judas noun **traitor**, betrayer, back-stabber, double-crosser; turncoat, quisling, renegade.

judge noun **1** *the judge sentenced him to five years:* **justice**, magistrate, recorder, sheriff; N. Amer. jurist; Brit. informal beak. **2** *a panel of judges will select the winner:* **adjudicator**, arbiter, assessor, evaluator, appraiser, examiner, moderator, mediator.
verb **1** *I judged that she was simply exhausted:* **form the opinion**, conclude, decide; consider, believe, think, deem, view; deduce, gather, infer, gauge, estimate, guess, surmise, conjecture; regard as, look on as, take to be, rate as, class as; informal reckon, figure. **2** *the case was judged by a tribunal:* **try**, hear; adjudicate, decide, give a ruling/verdict on. **3** *she was judged innocent of murder:* **adjudge**, pronounce, decree, rule, find. **4** *the competition will be judged by Alan Amey:* **adjudicate**, arbitrate, moderate. **5** *entries were judged by a panel of experts:* **assess**, appraise, evaluate; examine, review.

judgement noun **1** *his temper could affect his judgement:* **discernment**, acumen, shrewdness, astuteness, (common) sense, perception, perspicacity, percipience, acuity, discrimination, wisdom, wit, judiciousness, prudence, canniness, sharpness, sharp-wittedness, powers of reasoning, reason, logic; informal nous, savvy, horse sense, gumption; Brit. informal common; N. Amer. informal smarts. **2** *a court judgement:* **verdict**, decision, adjudication, ruling, pronouncement, decree, finding; sentence. **3** *critical judgement:* **assessment**, evaluation, appraisal; review, analysis, criticism, critique.
■ **against one's better judgement** reluctantly, unwillingly, grudgingly.
■ **in my judgement** in my opinion, to my

mind, to my way of thinking, I believe, I think, as I see it, in my estimation.

judgemental adjective *I don't like to sound judgemental, but it really was a big mistake:* **critical**, censorious, condemnatory, disapproving, disparaging, deprecating, negative, overcritical, hypercritical.

judicial adjective *a judicial inquiry:* **legal**, juridical, judicatory; official.

judicious adjective *a judicious course of action:* **wise**, sensible, prudent, politic, shrewd, astute, canny, sagacious, commonsensical, sound, well advised, well judged, discerning, percipient, intelligent, smart; N. Amer. informal heads-up.
– OPPOSITES ill-advised.

jug noun **pitcher**, ewer, crock, jar, urn; carafe, flask, flagon, decanter; N. Amer. creamer.

juggle verb *defence chiefs juggled the figures on bomb tests:* **misrepresent**, tamper with, falsify, distort, alter, manipulate, rig, massage, fudge; informal fix, doctor; Brit. informal fiddle.

juice noun **1** *the juice from two lemons:* **liquid**, fluid, sap; extract. **2** *cooking juices:* **liquid**, liquor.

juicy adjective **1** *a juicy peach:* **succulent**, tender, moist; ripe. **2** (informal) *juicy gossip:* **very interesting**, fascinating, sensational, lurid; scandalous, racy, risqué, spicy; informal hot.
– OPPOSITES dry, dull.

jumble noun **1** *the books were in a jumble:* **untidy heap**, clutter, muddle, mess, confusion, disarray, disarrangement, tangle; hotchpotch, mishmash, miscellany, motley collection, mixed bag, medley, farrago; N. Amer. hodgepodge. **2** (Brit.) *bags of jumble:* **junk**, bric-a-brac; Brit. lumber.
verb *the photographs are all jumbled up:* **mix up**, muddle up, disarrange, disorganize, disorder, put in disarray.

jumbo adjective (informal). See HUGE.

jump verb **1** *the cat jumped off his lap | Flora began to jump about:* **leap**, spring, bound, hop; skip, caper, dance, prance, frolic, cavort. **2** *he jumped the fence:* **vault (over)**, leap over, clear, sail over, hop over, hurdle. **3** *pre-tax profits jumped:* **rise**, go up, shoot up, soar, surge, climb, increase; informal skyrocket. **4** *the noise made her jump:* **start**, jerk, jolt, flinch, recoil; informal jump out of one's skin. **5** *Polly jumped at the chance:* **accept eagerly**, leap at, welcome with open arms, seize on, snap up, grab, pounce on.
noun **1** *the short jump across the gully:* **leap**, spring, vault, bound, hop. **2** *the horse cleared the last jump:* **obstacle**, barrier; fence, hurdle. **3** *a jump in profits:* **rise**, leap, increase, upsurge, upswing; informal hike. **4** *I woke up with a jump:* **start**, jerk, involuntary movement, spasm.
■ **jump the gun** (informal) act prematurely, act too soon, be over-hasty, be precipitate; informal be ahead of oneself.

jumper noun (Brit.) **sweater**, pullover, jersey; informal woolly.

jumpy adjective **1** (informal) *he was tired and jumpy:* **nervous**, on edge, edgy, tense, anxious, ill at ease, uneasy, restless, fidgety, keyed up, overwrought, on tenterhooks; Brit. nervy; informal a bundle of nerves, jittery, like a cat on a hot tin roof, uptight, het up, in a tizz/tizzy; Brit. informal strung up, like a cat on hot bricks; N. Amer. informal spooky, squirrelly, antsy; Austral./NZ informal toey. **2** *jumpy black-and-white footage:* **jerky**, jolting, lurching, bumpy, jarring; fitful, convulsive.
– OPPOSITES calm.

junction noun **1** *the junction between the roof and the wall:* **join**, joint, intersection, bond, seam, connection, juncture. **2** *the junction of the two rivers:* **confluence**, convergence, meeting point, conflux, juncture. **3** *turn right at the next junction:* **crossroads**, intersection, interchange, T-junction; turn, turn-off, exit; Brit. roundabout; N. Amer. turnout, cloverleaf.

juncture noun *at this juncture, I am unable to tell you:* **point (in time)**, time, moment (in time); period, phase.

jungle noun **1** *the Amazon jungle:* **tropical forest**, (tropical) rainforest. **2** *a jungle of bureaucracy:* **complexity**, confusion, complication, chaos; labyrinth, maze, tangle, web.

junior adjective **1** *the junior members of the family:* **younger**, youngest. **2** *a junior minister:* **low-ranking**, lower-ranking, subordinate, lesser, lower, minor, secondary. **3** *John White Junior:* **the Younger**; Brit. minor; N. Amer. II.
– OPPOSITES senior, older.

junk (informal) noun *an attic full of junk:* **rubbish**, clutter, odds and ends, bits and pieces, bric-a-brac; refuse, litter, scrap, waste, debris, detritus, dross; Brit. lumber; N. Amer. garbage, trash; Austral./NZ mullock; Brit. informal odds and sods.
verb *junk all the rubbish:* **throw away/out**, discard, get rid of, dispose of, scrap, toss out, jettison; informal chuck (away/out), dump, ditch, bin, get shut of; Brit. informal get shot of.

junta noun *the military junta took power in a coup last February:* **faction**, cabal, clique, party, set, ring, gang, league, confederacy.

jurisdiction noun **1** *an area under French jurisdiction:* **authority**, control, power, dominion, rule, administration, command, sway, leadership, sovereignty, hegemony. **2** *foreign jurisdictions:* **territory**, region, province, district, area, domain, realm.

just adjective **1** *a just and democratic society:* **fair**, fair-minded, equitable, even-handed, impartial, unbiased, objective, neutral, disinterested, unprejudiced, open-minded, non-partisan; honourable, upright, decent, honest, righteous, moral, virtuous, principled. **2** *a just reward:* **(well) deserved**, (well) earned, merited; rightful, due, fitting,

appropriate, suitable. **3** *just criticism:* **valid**, sound, well founded, justified, justifiable, warranted, legitimate.
– OPPOSITES unfair, undeserved.
adverb 1 *I just saw him:* **a moment/second ago**, a short time ago, very recently, not long ago. **2** *she's just right for him:* **exactly**, precisely, absolutely, completely, totally, entirely, perfectly, utterly, wholly, thoroughly, in all respects; informal down to the ground, to a T, dead. **3** *we just made it:* **narrowly**, only just, by a hair's breadth; barely, scarcely, hardly; informal by the skin of one's teeth, by a whisker. **4** *she's just a child:* **only**, merely, simply, (nothing) but, no more than.
▪ **just about** (informal) nearly, almost, practically, all but, virtually, as good as, more or less, to all intents and purposes; informal pretty much.

justice noun **1** *I appealed to his sense of justice:* **fairness**, justness, fair play, fair-mindedness, equity, equitableness, even-handedness, impartiality, objectivity, neutrality, disinterestedness, honesty, righteousness, morals, morality. **2** *the justice of his case:* **validity**, justification, soundness, well-foundedness, legitimacy. **3** *an order made by the justices:* **judge**, magistrate, recorder, sheriff; N. Amer. jurist; Brit. informal beak.

justifiable adjective *justifiable criticism:* **valid**, legitimate, warranted, well founded, justified, just, reasonable; defensible, tenable, supportable, acceptable.
– OPPOSITES indefensible.

justification noun *the justification for government action:* **grounds**, reason, basis, rationale, premise, rationalization, vindication, explanation; defence, argument, apologia, apology, case.

justify verb **1** *directors must justify the expenditure:* **give grounds for**, give reasons for, give a justification for, explain, give an explanation for, account for; defend, answer for, vindicate. **2** *the situation justified further investigation:* **warrant**, be good reason for, be a justification for.

justly adverb **1** *he is justly proud of his achievement:* **justifiably**, with (good) reason, legitimately, rightly, rightfully, deservedly. **2** *they were treated justly:* **fairly**, with fairness, equitably, even-handedly, impartially, without bias, objectively, without prejudice; informal fairly and squarely.
– OPPOSITES unjustifiably, unfairly.

jut verb *a rock jutted out from the side of the bank:* **stick out**, project, protrude, bulge out, overhang, obtrude.

juvenile adjective **1** *juvenile offenders:* **young**, teenage, adolescent, junior, pubescent, pre-pubescent. **2** *juvenile behaviour:* **childish**, immature, puerile, infantile, babyish; jejune, inexperienced, callow, green, unsophisticated, naive, foolish, silly.
– OPPOSITES adult, mature.
noun *many victims are juveniles:* **young person**, youngster, child, teenager, adolescent, minor, junior; informal kid.
– OPPOSITES adult.

juxtapose verb *her work juxtaposes images from serious and popular art:* **place side by side**, set side by side, mix; compare, contrast.

j

Kk

kaleidoscopic adjective **1** *the branches refracted the light into kaleidoscopic shapes on the pavement:* **multicoloured**, many-coloured, multicolour, many-hued, variegated, particoloured, varicoloured, psychedelic, rainbow. **2** *the country's kaleidoscopic political landscape:* **ever-changing**, changeable, shifting, fluid, protean, variable, inconstant, fluctuating, unpredictable, impermanent. **3** *children's questions about the kaleidoscopic world they are living in:* **multifaceted**, varied; complex, intricate, complicated.
– OPPOSITES monochrome, constant.

keel noun *the upturned keel of the boat:* **base**, bottom (side), underside.
■ **keel over** *the slightest activity made him keel over:* collapse, faint, pass out, black out, lose consciousness, swoon.

keen adjective **1** *his publishers were keen to capitalize on his success:* **eager**, anxious, intent, impatient, determined, ambitious; informal raring, itching, dying. **2** *I have always been a keen birdwatcher:* **enthusiastic**, avid, eager, ardent, passionate, fervent, fervid, impassioned; conscientious, committed, dedicated, zealous. **3** *both his sisters are keen on horses | there was a girl in Kentucky he was keen on:* **enthusiastic**, interested, passionate; attracted to, fond of, taken with, smitten with, enamoured of, infatuated with; informal struck on, gone on, mad about, crazy about, nuts about. **4** *he was an able administrator with a keen mind:* **acute**, penetrating, astute, incisive, sharp, perceptive, piercing, razor-sharp, perspicacious, shrewd, discerning, clever, intelligent, brilliant, bright, smart, wise, canny, percipient, insightful. **5** *there is keen competition for places on the committee:* **intense**, acute, fierce, passionate, burning, fervent, ardent, strong, powerful.
– OPPOSITES reluctant, unenthusiastic.

keenness noun **1** *the company has signalled its keenness to sign a deal:* **eagerness**, willingness, readiness, impatience; enthusiasm, fervour, wholeheartedness, zest, zeal, ardour, passion, avidity. **2** *the keenness of his mind:* **acuity**, sharpness, incisiveness, astuteness, perspicacity, perceptiveness, shrewdness, insight, cleverness, discernment, intelligence, brightness, brilliance, canniness. **3** *the*

keenness of his sense of loss: **intensity**, acuteness, strength, power, ferocity.

keep[1] verb **1** *he kept the ticket stub as a souvenir | you should keep all the old forms:* **retain**, hold on to, keep hold of, not part with; save, store, put by/aside, set aside; N. Amer. set by; informal hang on to, stash away. **2** *I tried to keep calm:* **remain**, continue to be, stay, carry on being, persist in being. **3** *he keeps going on about the murder:* **persist in**, keep on, carry on, continue, do something constantly. **4** *I shan't keep you long:* **detain**, keep waiting, delay, hold up, retard, slow down. **5** *most people kept the rules | he had to keep his promise:* **comply with**, obey, observe, conform to, abide by, adhere to, stick to, heed, follow; fulfil, carry out, act on, make good, honour, keep to, stand by. **6** *I like to keep the old traditions:* **preserve**, keep alive/up, keep going, carry on, perpetuate, maintain, uphold, sustain. **7** *the stand where her umbrella was kept:* **store**, house, stow, put (away), place, deposit. **8** *he is forced to steal to keep his family:* **provide for**, support, feed, keep alive, maintain, sustain; take care of, look after. **9** *she keeps rabbits in the back garden:* **breed**, rear, raise, farm; own. **10** *today's consumers do not keep the Sabbath:* **observe**, respect, honour, hold sacred; celebrate, mark, commemorate.
– OPPOSITES throw away, break, abandon.
noun *he had no money to pay for his keep:* **maintenance**, upkeep, sustenance, board (and lodging), food, livelihood.
■ **keep at** *start work early and keep at it until lunchtime:* persevere with, persist with, keep going with, carry on with, press on with, work away at, continue with; informal stick at, peg away at, plug away at, hammer away at.
■ **keep something back 1** *every week she kept back some of the money he gave her:* (keep in) reserve, put by/aside, set aside; retain, hold back, keep, hold on to, not part with; N. Amer. set by; informal stash away. **2** *she kept back the gory details from Anne:* conceal, keep secret, keep hidden, withhold, suppress, keep quiet about. **3** *she could hardly keep back her tears:* suppress, stifle, choke back, fight back, hold back/in, repress, keep in check, contain, smother, swallow, bite back.
■ **keep from** *Dinah bit her lip to keep from screaming:* refrain from, stop oneself,

restrain oneself from, prevent oneself from, forbear from, avoid.

■ **keep someone from something 1** *he could hardly keep himself from laughing:* prevent, stop, restrain, hold back. **2** *keep them from harm:* preserve, protect, keep safe, guard, shield, shelter, safeguard, defend.

■ **keep something from someone** *now you know what your mother tried to keep from you:* keep secret, keep hidden, hide, conceal, withhold; informal keep dark.

■ **keep off 1** *tell him he'd better keep off my land:* stay off, not enter, keep/stay away from, not trespass on. **2** *Maud tried to keep off political subjects:* avoid, steer clear of, stay away from, evade, sidestep; informal duck. **3** *you should keep off alcohol for a while:* abstain from, do without, refrain from, give up, forgo, not touch; informal swear off; formal forswear. **4** *I hope the rain keeps off:* stay away, hold off, not start, not begin.

■ **keep on 1** *they preferred to keep on working:* continue, go on, carry on, persist in, persevere in; soldier on, struggle on, keep going. **2** *the commander kept on about the need for vigilance:* talk constantly, talk endlessly, keep talking, go on (and on), rant on; informal harp on, witter on, rabbit on.

■ **keep someone on** *the boss decided to keep him on:* continue to employ, retain in one's service, not dismiss, not sack.

■ **keep on at** *they kept on at him to hurry up:* nag, go on at, harp on at, badger, chivvy, harass, hound, pester; informal hassle.

■ **keep to 1** *I've got to keep to the speed limit:* obey, abide by, observe, follow, comply with, adhere to, respect, keep, stick to, be bound by. **2** *keep to the path at all times:* follow, stick to, stay on. **3** *please keep to the point:* stick to, restrict oneself to, confine oneself to.

■ **keep something up** *keep up the good work:* continue (with), keep on with, keep going, carry on with, persist with, persevere with.

■ **keep up with 1** *she walked fast to keep up with him:* keep pace with, keep abreast of; match, equal. **2** *even while travelling he kept up with events at home:* keep informed about, keep up to date with, keep abreast of; informal keep tabs on.

keep² noun *the king's forces stormed the keep:* **fortress**, fort, stronghold, tower, donjon, castle, citadel, bastion.

keeper noun **1** *he was made keeper of the archives:* **curator**, custodian, guardian, administrator, overseer, steward, caretaker. **2** *she's not a child and you're not her keeper:* **guardian**, protector, guard, minder, chaperon/chaperone; carer, nursemaid, nurse.

keeping noun *the document is in the keeping of the county archivist:* **safe keeping**, care, custody, charge, possession, trust, protection.

■ **in keeping with** *this trend was in keeping with the mood of the times:* consistent with, in harmony with, in accord with, in agreement with, in line with, in character with, compatible with; appropriate to, befitting, suitable for.

keepsake noun **memento**, souvenir, reminder, remembrance, token.

keg noun **barrel**, cask, vat, butt, tun, hogshead; historical firkin.

ken noun *their talk hinted at mysteries beyond my ken:* **knowledge**, awareness, perception, understanding, grasp, comprehension, realization, appreciation, consciousness.

kernel noun **1** *the delicious kernel of a Brazil nut:* seed, grain, core; nut. **2** *the foreword contained the kernel of the argument:* **essence**, core, heart, essentials, quintessence, fundamentals, basics, nub, gist, substance; informal nitty-gritty.

key noun **1** *the key to the mystery lay elsewhere:* **answer**, clue, solution, explanation. **2** *customer satisfaction is the key to success:* **route**, basis, foundation, requisite, precondition, means, way, path, passport, secret, formula. **3** (Music) *a song in a minor key:* **tone**; pitch, timbre.
adjective *he was a key figure in the resistance movement:* **crucial**, central, essential, indispensable, pivotal, critical, dominant, vital, principal, prime, chief, major, leading, main, important, significant.
– OPPOSITES peripheral.

keynote noun *the keynote of the paper was 'positive planning':* **theme**, salient point, gist, substance, burden, tenor, pith, marrow, essence, heart, core, basis, essential feature/element.

keystone noun *cooperation remains the keystone of the government's security policy:* **foundation**, basis, linchpin, cornerstone, base, (guiding) principle, core, heart, centre, crux, fundament.

kick verb **1** *her attacker punched and kicked her:* **boot**; Brit. informal put the boot into. **2** (informal) *he was struggling to kick his drug habit:* **give up**, break, abandon, end, stop, cease, desist from, renounce; informal shake, pack in, leave off, quit. **3** *the gun kicked so hard he stumbled back:* **recoil**, jump, spring back; twitch, judder, shake.
noun **1** *he received a kick on the knee:* **blow**; informal boot. **2** (informal) *I get a kick out of driving a racing car | he killed for kicks:* **thrill**, tingle; informal buzz, high, rush; N. Amer. informal charge. **3** (informal) *a drink with a powerful kick | the addition of mustard gives the bread a bit of a kick:* **effect**; tang, zest, bite, edge, pungency, piquancy; informal punch, hit. **4** (informal) *his parents were on a health kick:* **craze**, mania; fashion, vogue, trend; informal fad, trip.

■ **kick against** *young people are expected to kick against the establishment:* resist, rebel against, oppose, struggle/fight against; defy, disobey, reject, spurn.

■ **kick someone/something around** (informal) **1** *we feel we are undervalued and get kicked around:* abuse, mistreat, maltreat, push around/about, trample on, take for granted; informal boss about/around, walk all over. **2** *they began to kick a few ideas around:* discuss, talk over, debate, thrash out, consider, toy with, play with.

■ **kick back** (N. Amer. informal) *a chance to kick back and enjoy the scenery:* relax, unwind, take it easy, rest, slow down, let up, ease up/off, sit back; N. Amer. informal chill out, hang loose.

■ **kick off** (informal) *the festival kicks off on Monday* | *the exhibition kicks off a three-year research project:* start, commence, begin, get going, get off the ground, get under way; open, start off, set in motion, launch, initiate, introduce, inaugurate, usher in.

■ **kick someone out** (informal) *he was kicked out of the regiment:* expel, eject, throw out, oust, evict, get rid of, axe; dismiss, discharge; informal chuck out, send packing, boot out, give someone their marching orders, sack, fire; Brit. informal turf out; N. Amer. informal give someone the bum's rush.

kick-off noun (informal) **beginning**, start, commencement, outset, opening.

kid[1] noun (informal) *she has three kids:* **child**, youngster, little one, baby, toddler, tot, infant, boy/girl, young person, minor, juvenile, adolescent, teenager, youth, stripling; offspring, son/daughter; Scottish bairn; informal kiddie, nipper, kiddiewink, shaver, young 'un; Brit. informal sprog; N. Amer. informal rug rat; Austral./NZ ankle-biter; derogatory brat; literary babe.

kid[2] verb (informal) **1** *the village is called Hell—I'm not kidding:* **joke**, tease, jest, chaff, fool about/around; informal pull someone's leg, have on, rib; Brit. informal wind up; N. Amer. informal pull someone's chain, fun, shuck. **2** *why did I kid myself that I'd succeed?* **delude**, deceive, fool, trick, hoodwink, hoax, beguile, dupe, gull; informal con, pull the wool over someone's eyes; literary cozen.

kidnap verb **abduct**, carry off, capture, seize, snatch, take as hostage; Brit. informal nobble.

kill verb **1** *street gangs killed twenty-seven people:* **murder**, take the life of, make away with, assassinate, eliminate, terminate, dispatch, finish off, put to death, execute; slaughter, butcher, massacre, wipe out, annihilate, exterminate, liquidate, mow down, shoot down, cut down, cut to pieces; informal bump off, polish off, do away with, do in, knock off, top, take out, croak, stiff, blow away, dispose of; N. Amer. informal ice, rub out, waste, whack, scrag, smoke; literary slay. **2** *media hostility would kill all hopes of progress:* **destroy**, put an end to, end, extinguish, dash, quash, ruin, wreck, shatter, smash, crush, scotch, thwart; informal put paid to, put the kibosh on, stymie; Brit. informal scupper. **3** *we had to kill several hours at*

the airport: **while away**, fill (up), occupy, beguile, pass, spend, waste. **4** (informal) *it would kill me to walk four miles:* **exhaust**, wear out, tire out, overtax, overtire, fatigue, weary, sap, drain, enervate, prostrate; informal knock out, shatter; Brit. informal knacker. **5** (informal) *my feet were killing me:* **hurt**, torture, torment, cause discomfort to; be painful, be sore, be uncomfortable. **6** (informal) *the music kills me every time I hear it:* **overwhelm**, take someone's breath away, move, stir, stun, amaze, stagger; informal bowl over, blow away, knock sideways, blow someone's mind. **7** *the engines were kept at a low rev to kill the noise:* **muffle**, deaden, stifle, dampen, damp down, smother, reduce, diminish, decrease, suppress, tone down, moderate. **8** *a shot of morphine to kill the pain:* **alleviate**, assuage, soothe, allay, dull, blunt, deaden, stifle, suppress, subdue.

noun **1** *the successful hunter flings down his kill for the women to prepare:* **prey**, quarry, victim, bag. **2** *the wolf was moving in for the kill:* **death blow**, killing, dispatch, finish, end, coup de grâce.

killer noun *police are searching for the killer:* **murderer**, assassin, slaughterer, butcher, serial killer, gunman; exterminator, terminator, executioner; informal hit man; literary slayer.

killing noun *a brutal killing that shocked the community:* **murder**, assassination, homicide, manslaughter, elimination, putting/doing to death, execution; slaughter, massacre, butchery, carnage, bloodshed, extermination, annihilation; literary slaying.

adjective **1** *a killing blow:* **deadly**, lethal, fatal, mortal, death-dealing; murderous, homicidal; literary deathly. **2** (informal) *the Minister has a killing schedule:* **exhausting**, gruelling, punishing, taxing, draining, wearing, prostrating, crushing, tiring, fatiguing, debilitating, enervating, arduous, tough, demanding, onerous, strenuous, rigorous; informal murderous; Brit. informal knackering.

■ **make a killing** (informal) *investors are set to make a killing in the sell-off:* make a large profit, make a/one's fortune, make money; informal clean up, make a packet, make a pretty penny; Brit. informal make a bomb; N. Amer. informal make big bucks.

killjoy noun *sun worshippers regard the health lobby as killjoys:* **spoilsport**, prophet of doom; informal wet blanket, party-pooper, misery; Austral./NZ informal wowser.

kilter

■ **out of kilter** *air travel throws everyone's body clock out of kilter:* awry, off balance, unbalanced, out of order, disordered, confused, muddled, out of tune, out of step.

kin noun *they fell out with their own kin:* **relatives**, relations, family (members), kindred, kith and kin; kinsfolk, kinsmen, kinswomen, people; informal folks.

kind[1] noun **1** *she brought all kinds of gifts:*
sort, type, variety, style, form, class,
category, genre. **2** *he named the kinds of
bird that could be seen:* **species**, genus, race,
breed. **3** *the tests were different in kind from
any that preceded them:* **character**, nature,
essence, quality, disposition, make-up; type,
style, stamp, manner, description, mould,
cast, temperament, ilk; N. Amer. stripe.
■ **kind of** (informal) *it got kind of cosy with
us all on the back seat:* rather, quite, fairly,
somewhat, a little, slightly, a shade; informal
sort of, a bit, kinda, pretty, a touch, a tad.

kind[2] adjective *she is such a kind and caring
person:* **kindly**, good-natured, kind-hearted,
warm-hearted, caring, affectionate, loving,
warm; considerate, helpful, thoughtful,
obliging, unselfish, selfless, altruistic, good,
attentive; compassionate, sympathetic,
understanding, big-hearted, benevolent,
benign, friendly, neighbourly, hospitable,
well meaning, public-spirited; generous,
liberal, open-handed, bountiful, beneficent,
munificent; Brit. informal decent.
– OPPOSITES inconsiderate, mean.

kind-hearted adjective **kind**, caring, warm-
hearted, kindly, benevolent, good-natured,
tender, warm, compassionate, sympathetic,
understanding; indulgent, altruistic, benign,
beneficent, benignant.
– OPPOSITES nasty.

kindle verb **1** *he kindled a fire of dry grass:*
light, ignite, set alight, set light to, set
fire to, put a match to. **2** *it was Elvis who
kindled my interest in music:* **rouse**, arouse,
wake, awaken; stimulate, inspire, stir (up),
excite, evoke, provoke, fire, inflame, trigger,
activate, spark off; literary waken.
– OPPOSITES extinguish.

kindliness noun **kindness**, benevolence,
warmth, gentleness, tenderness, care,
humanity, sympathy, compassion,
understanding; generosity, charity,
kind-heartedness, warm-heartedness,
thoughtfulness, solicitousness.
– OPPOSITES unkindness, cruelty.

kindly adjective *the children were looked after
by a kindly old lady | he smiled in a kindly
manner:* **kind**, benevolent, kind-hearted,
warm-hearted, generous, good-natured;
gentle, warm, compassionate, caring, loving,
benign, well meaning; helpful, thoughtful,
considerate, good-hearted, nice, friendly,
neighbourly; Brit. informal decent.
– OPPOSITES unkind, cruel.
adverb **1** *'Welcome,' she said kindly:*
benevolently, good-naturedly, warmly,
affectionately, tenderly, lovingly,
compassionately. **2** *someone kindly lent
us a car:* **considerately**, thoughtfully,
helpfully, obligingly, generously, selflessly,
unselfishly, sympathetically. **3** *kindly
explain what you mean by that:* **please**, if
you please, if you wouldn't mind, have the
goodness to; archaic prithee, pray.
– OPPOSITES unkindly, harshly.

■ **not take kindly to** *she does not take
kindly to being criticized:* resent, object to,
take umbrage at, take exception to, take
offence at, be annoyed by, be irritated by,
feel aggrieved about, be upset by.

kindness noun **1** *he thanked her
for her kindness:* **kindliness**, kind-
heartedness, warm-heartedness,
affection, warmth, gentleness, concern,
care; consideration, considerateness,
helpfulness, thoughtfulness, unselfishness,
selflessness, altruism, compassion,
sympathy, understanding, big-heartedness,
benevolence, benignity, friendliness,
neighbourliness, hospitality, public-
spiritedness; generosity, magnanimity,
charitableness; Brit. informal decency. **2** *she
has done us many a kindness:* **kind act**, good
deed, good turn, favour, service.

kindred adjective **1** *the centre collects work
on industrial relations and kindred subjects:*
related, allied, connected, comparable,
similar, like, parallel, associated, analogous;
formal cognate. **2** *she was glad to find a
kindred spirit:* **like-minded**, in sympathy,
in harmony, in tune, of one mind, akin,
similar, like, compatible; informal on the same
wavelength.
– OPPOSITES unrelated, alien.

king noun **1** *Edward wanted to be crowned
king of France:* **ruler**, sovereign, monarch,
crowned head, Crown, emperor, prince,
potentate, lord. **2** (informal) *he has become the
king of world football:* **star**, leading light,
luminary, superstar, giant, master; informal
supremo, megastar.

kingdom noun *his kingdom stretched to the
Caspian Sea:* **realm**, domain, dominion,
country, empire, land, nation, (sovereign)
state, province, territory.

kingly adjective **1** *the appeal to kingly honour
was repeated on several occasions until
1294:* **royal**, regal, monarchical, sovereign,
imperial, princely. **2** *Warna had a liking for
hunting, falcons, horses, and rich and kingly
robes:* **regal**, majestic, stately, noble, lordly,
dignified, distinguished, courtly; splendid,
magnificent, grand, glorious, rich, gorgeous,
resplendent, princely, superb, sumptuous;
informal splendiferous.

kink noun **1** *your fishing line should have no
kinks in it:* **curl**, twist, twirl, loop, crinkle;
knot, tangle, entanglement. **2** *we went
round a kink in the road:* **bend**, corner, dog-
leg, twist, turn, curve; Brit. hairpin bend.
3 *we're making headway, but there are
still some kinks to iron out:* **flaw**, defect,
imperfection, problem, complication, hitch,
snag, shortcoming, weakness; informal hiccup,
glitch.

kinky adjective **1** (informal) *he was involved a
kinky relationship with two older women:*
perverted, abnormal, deviant, unnatural,
depraved, degenerate, perverse; odd,
bizarre, weird; informal pervy. **2** (informal) *she
likes to wear kinky underwear:* **provocative**,

k

sexy, sexually arousing, erotic, titillating, naughty, indecent, immodest; Brit. informal saucy. **3** *Catriona's long kinky hair:* **curly**, crimped, curled, curling, frizzy, frizzed, wavy.

kinship noun **1** *ties of descent and kinship:* **relationship**, being related, family ties, blood ties, common ancestry, kindred, consanguinity. **2** *she felt kinship with the others:* **affinity**, sympathy, rapport, harmony, understanding, empathy, closeness, fellow feeling, bond, compatibility; similarity, likeness, correspondence, concordance.

kiosk noun **booth**, stand, stall, counter, news-stand.

kiss verb **1** *he kissed her on the lips:* brush one's lips against, air-kiss; informal peck, give a smacker to, smooch, canoodle, neck, pet; Brit. informal snog; N. Amer. informal buss; dated spoon; formal osculate. **2** *allow your foot just to kiss the floor:* **brush (against)**, caress, touch gently, blow a kiss to, stroke, skim over.
noun **1** *she gave him a kiss on the cheek:* X; informal peck, smack, smacker, smooch; Brit. informal snog; N. Amer. informal buss; formal osculation. **2** *she felt the kiss of the flowers against her cheeks:* **gentle touch**, caress, brush, stroke.

kit noun **1** *he produced his tool kit:* **equipment**, tools, implements, instruments, gadgets, utensils, appliances, tools of the trade, gear, tackle, hardware, paraphernalia; Military accoutrements. **2** (Brit. informal) *the boys were in their football kit:* **clothes**, clothing, rig, outfit, dress, costume, garments, attire, garb, gear, get-up, rig-out; formal apparel. **3** *a model aircraft kit:* **set (of parts)**, self-assembly set, flat-pack. **4** (informal) *we packed up all our kit and set off:* **belongings**, luggage, baggage, paraphernalia, effects, impedimenta; informal things, stuff, gear; Brit. informal clobber.
■ **kit someone/something out** *the studio is kitted out with six cameras* | *we were all kitted out in life jackets:* equip, fit (out/up), furnish, supply, provide, issue; dress, clothe, array, attire, rig out, deck out; informal fix up.

kitchen noun **cooking area**, kitchenette, kitchen-diner, cookhouse; Nautical galley; N. Amer. cookery.

kittenish adjective *they were expected to be all kittenish and girlie:* **playful**, light-hearted, skittish, lively, coquettish, flirtatious, frivolous, flippant, superficial, trivial, shallow, silly; informal flirty, dizzy; literary frolicsome.
– OPPOSITES serious.

knack noun **1** *he has a knack for making money:* **gift**, talent, flair, genius, instinct, faculty, ability, capability, capacity, aptitude, aptness, bent, forte, facility. **2** *it takes practice to acquire the knack:* **technique**, method, trick, skill, art, expertise; informal the hang of something. **3** *he has a knack of getting injured at the*

wrong time: **tendency**, propensity, habit, proneness, liability, predisposition.

knead verb **1** *knead the dough for five minutes:* **pummel**, work, pound, squeeze, shape, mould. **2** *she kneaded the base of his neck:* **massage**, press, manipulate, rub.

kneel verb **fall to one's knees**, get down on one's knees, genuflect; be on one's knees; historical kowtow.

knickers plural noun (Brit.) **underpants**, briefs, French knickers, camiknickers; underwear, lingerie, underclothes, undergarments; Brit. pants; informal panties, undies; Brit. informal knicks, smalls; dated drawers; historical bloomers, pantalettes.

knick-knack noun *we bought a few knick-knacks while we were in Turkey:* **ornament**, novelty, gewgaw, bibelot, trinket, trifle, bauble, gimcrack, curio, memento, souvenir; N. Amer. kickshaw; N. Amer. informal tchotchke.

knife noun *you need a sharp knife:* **blade**, cutter, carver.
verb *the victims had been knifed:* **stab**, hack, gash, run through, slash, lacerate, cut, pierce, spike, impale, transfix, bayonet, spear.

knight noun *knights in armour:* **cavalier**, cavalryman, horseman; lord, noble, nobleman; historical chevalier, paladin, banneret.

knit verb **1** *these disparate regions began to knit together:* **unite**, unify, become closer, bond, fuse, coalesce, merge, meld, blend. **2** *we expect broken bones to knit:* **heal**, mend, join, fuse. **3** *Marcus knitted his brows:* **furrow**, tighten, contract, gather, wrinkle.

knob noun **1** *the drake has a black bill with a knob at the base:* **lump**, bump, protuberance, protrusion, bulge, swelling, knot, node, nodule, ball, boss. **2** *he fiddled with the knobs on the radio:* **dial**, button, control, switch. **3** *she turned the knob on the door:* **doorknob**, (door) handle. **4** *add a few knobs of butter:* **nugget**, lump, pat, ball, dollop, piece; N. Amer. informal gob.

knock verb **1** *he knocked on the door:* **bang**, tap, rap, thump, pound, hammer; strike, hit, beat. **2** *she knocked her knee painfully on the table:* **bump**, bang, hit, strike, crack; injure, hurt, bruise; informal bash, thwack. **3** *he knocked into an elderly man with a walking stick:* **collide with**, bump into, bang into, be in collision with, run into, crash into, smash into, plough into; N. Amer. impact; informal bash into. **4** (informal) *I'm not knocking the company.* See CRITICIZE.
noun **1** *there was a sharp knock at the door:* **tap**, rap, rat-tat, knocking, bang, banging, pounding, hammering, drumming, thump, thud. **2** *the casing is tough enough to withstand knocks:* **bump**, blow, bang, jolt, jar, shock; collision, crash, smash, impact. **3** *he got a nasty knock on the ear:* **blow**, bang, hit, slap, smack, crack, punch, cuff, thump, box; informal clip, clout, wallop,

k

thwack, belt, bash. **4** *the ability to deal with life's hard knocks:* **setback**, reversal, defeat, failure, difficulty, misfortune, bad luck, mishap, (body) blow, disaster, calamity, disappointment, sorrow, trouble, hardship; informal kick in the teeth.

■ **knock about/around** (informal) **1** *for a couple of years we knocked around the Mediterranean:* wander around, roam around, rove around, range over, travel around, journey around, voyage around, drift around, gallivant around, potter around; informal gad about. **2** *she knocks around with a bunch of weird artists:* associate, consort, keep company, go around, mix, socialize, be friends, be friendly; informal hobnob, hang out, run around, pal around.

■ **knock someone/something about/around** *her husband was an animal who use to knock her around:* beat (up), batter, hit, punch, thump, thrash, slap; maltreat, mistreat, abuse, ill-treat, assault, attack; N. Amer. beat up on; informal rough up, do over, give someone a hiding, clobber, clout, bash, belt, whack, wallop.

■ **knock something back** (informal) *she knocked back her gin and asked for another:* gulp down, drink up, quaff, guzzle, slug; informal down, swig, swill (down), toss off; N. Amer. informal scarf (down/up), snarf (down/up).

■ **knock someone down** *two men knocked him down | their son was knocked down by a car:* fell, floor, flatten, bring down, knock to the ground; knock over, run over/down.

■ **knock something down 1** *the building was knocked down in the late seventies:* demolish, pull down, tear down, destroy; raze (to the ground), level, flatten, bulldoze. **2** (informal) *the firm has knocked down the prices of its machines:* reduce, lower, cut, decrease, drop, put down, mark down; informal slash.

■ **knock off** (informal) *they knock off at 5 o'clock:* stop work, finish (working), clock off, leave work.

■ **knock someone off** (informal). See **KILL** verb sense 1.

■ **knock something off 1** (Brit. informal) *someone knocked off the video.* See **STEAL** verb sense 1. **2** (informal) *we expect you to knock off three stories a day:* produce, make, turn out, create, construct, assemble, put together; complete, finish. **3** (informal) *knock off 10% from the bill:* deduct, take off/away, subtract, dock.

■ **knock it off!** (informal) stop it; informal cut it out, give it a rest, leave off, pack it in, lay off; Brit. informal give over.

■ **knock someone out 1** *I hit him in the face and knocked him out:* knock unconscious, knock senseless; floor, prostrate; informal lay out, put out cold, KO, kayo. **2** *England was knocked out by Belgium:* eliminate, beat, defeat, vanquish, overwhelm, trounce. **3** (informal) *walking that far in one go has knocked her out:* exhaust, wear out, tire

(out), overtire, fatigue, weary, drain; informal do in, take it out of, fag out; Brit. informal knacker; N. Amer. informal poop. **4** (informal) *the view really knocked me out:* overwhelm, stun, stupefy, amaze, astound, astonish, stagger, take someone's breath away; impress, dazzle, enchant, entrance; informal bowl over, flabbergast, knock sideways, blow away; Brit. informal knock for six.

■ **knock someone up** (Brit. informal) *we were knocked up at five in the morning:* wake (up), awaken, call, rouse, arouse, get out of bed, get up; literary waken.

■ **knock something up** (Brit. informal) *I could knock up some picture frames for you:* produce, make, prepare, build, whip up, rig up, throw together, cobble together, improvise, contrive; informal rustle up.

knoll noun *she walked up the grassy knoll:* **hillock**, mound, rise, hummock, hill, hump, tor, bank, ridge, elevation; Scottish brae; formal eminence.

knot noun **1** *tie a small knot in the yarn:* **tie**, twist, loop, join, fastening, bond; tangle, entanglement. **2** *the saw caught on a knot in the wood:* **nodule**, gnarl, node; lump, knob, swelling, gall, protuberance, bump; archaic knar. **3** *a small knot of people gathered around Caroline:* **cluster**, group, band, huddle, bunch, circle, ring, gathering, company, crowd, throng.

verb *their scarves were knotted round their throats:* **tie (up)**, fasten, secure, bind, do up.

knotted adjective *her wild knotted hair stuck out crazily:* **tangled**, tangly, knotty, entangled, matted, snarled, unkempt, uncombed, tousled; informal mussed up.

knotty adjective **1** *a knotty legal problem regarding ownership:* **complex**, complicated, involved, intricate, convoluted, involuted; difficult, hard, thorny, taxing, awkward, tricky, problematic, troublesome. **2** *the knotty roots of gorse bushes:* **gnarled**, knotted, knurled, nodular, knobbly, lumpy, bumpy. **3** *a knotty piece of thread:* **knotted**, tangled, tangly, twisted, entangled, snarled, matted.

– OPPOSITES straightforward.

know verb **1** *she doesn't know I'm here:* **be aware**, realize, be conscious, be informed; notice, perceive, see, sense, recognize; informal savvy, latch on. **2** *I don't know his address:* **have knowledge of**, be informed of, be apprised of; formal be cognizant of. **3** *do you know the rules? | he asked whether I knew any French:* **be familiar with**, be conversant with, be acquainted with, have knowledge of, be versed in, have mastered, have a grasp of, understand, comprehend; have learned, have memorized; informal be clued up on. **4** *I don't know many people here:* **be acquainted with**, have met, be familiar with; be friends with, be friendly with, be on good terms with, be close to, be intimate with; Scottish ken; informal be thick with. **5** *a man who had known better times:* **experience**, go

k

through, live through, undergo, taste. **6** *my brothers don't know a saucepan from a frying pan:* **distinguish**, tell (apart), differentiate, discriminate; recognize, pick out, identify.

know-all noun (informal) *you're such a know-all—you tell me!* **wiseacre**; informal smart alec, wise guy, smarty, smarty-pants; Brit. informal clever clogs, clever Dick; N. Amer. informal know-it-all.

know-how noun (informal) *our financial advice is based on the extensive experience and know-how of our staff:* **knowledge**, expertise, skill, skilfulness, expertness, proficiency, understanding, mastery, technique; ability, capability, competence, capacity, adeptness, dexterity, deftness, aptitude, adroitness, ingenuity, faculty; informal savvy.

knowing adjective **1** *she gave a knowing smile:* **significant**, meaningful, eloquent, expressive, suggestive, **arch**, sly, mischievous, impish, teasing, playful. **2** *she's a very knowing child:* **sophisticated**, worldly, worldly-wise, urbane, experienced; knowledgeable, well informed, enlightened; shrewd, astute, canny, sharp, wily, perceptive. **3** *a knowing infringement of the rules can result in disqualification:* **deliberate**, intentional, conscious, calculated, wilful, done on purpose, premeditated, preconceived, planned.

knowingly adverb *the chairman denied that the company had knowingly misled the public:* **deliberately**, intentionally, consciously, wittingly, on purpose, by design, premeditatedly, wilfully.

knowledge noun **1** *his knowledge of history was limited | her technical knowledge is impressive:* **understanding**, comprehension, grasp, command, mastery; expertise, skill, proficiency, expertness, accomplishment, adeptness, capacity, capability; informal know-how. **2** *people anxious to display their knowledge:* **learning**, erudition, education, scholarship, schooling, wisdom. **3** *he slipped away without my knowledge:* **awareness**, consciousness, realization, cognition, apprehension, perception, appreciation;

formal cognizance. **4** *the staff develop an intimate knowledge of the countryside:* **familiarity**, acquaintance, conversance, intimacy. **5** *it is your duty to inform the police of your knowledge:* **information**, facts, intelligence, news, reports; informal info, gen.
– OPPOSITES ignorance.

knowledgeable adjective **1** *he proved to be a very knowledgeable old man:* **well informed**, learned, well read, (well) educated, erudite, scholarly, cultured, cultivated, enlightened. **2** *we need someone who is knowledgeable about modern art:* **acquainted**, familiar, conversant, au fait; having a knowledge of, up on, up to date with, abreast of; informal clued up, genned up; Brit. informal switched on.
– OPPOSITES ill-informed.

known adjective **1** *Davies is a known criminal | a known fact:* **recognized**, well known, widely known, noted, celebrated, notable, notorious; acknowledged, self-confessed, declared, overt. **2** *the known world:* **familiar**, known about, well known; studied, investigated.

knuckle
■ **knuckle under** *bombing does not always make the victims knuckle under:* surrender, submit, capitulate, give in/up, yield, give way, succumb, climb down, back down, admit defeat, lay down one's arms, throw in the towel/sponge; informal quit, raise the white flag.

kowtow verb *she didn't have to kowtow to a boss any more:* **grovel**, be obsequious, be servile, be sycophantic, fawn on, bow and scrape, toady, truckle, abase oneself, humble oneself; curry favour with, dance attendance on, make up to, ingratiate oneself with; informal crawl, creep, suck up, lick someone's boots; Austral./NZ informal smoodge to.

kudos noun *considerable kudos is attached to the position of captain:* **prestige**, cachet, glory, honour, status, standing, distinction, prestigiousness, fame, celebrity; admiration, respect, esteem, acclaim, praise, credit.

k

LI

label noun **1** *the price is clearly stated on the label:* **tag**, ticket, tab, sticker, marker, docket, chit, chitty. **2** *a designer label:* **brand (name)**, trade name, trademark, make, logo. **3** *I always resented the label the media came up with for me:* **designation**, description, tag; name, epithet, nickname, title, sobriquet, pet name, cognomen; informal monicker, handle; formal denomination, appellation.
verb **1** *label each jar with the date:* **tag**, tab, ticket, mark, docket. **2** *school tests labelled him an underachiever:* **categorize**, classify, class, describe, designate, identify; mark, stamp, brand, condemn, pigeonhole, stereotype, typecast; call, name, term, dub, nickname.

laborious adjective **1** *tunnelling was a dangerous and laborious job:* **arduous**, hard, heavy, difficult, strenuous, gruelling, punishing, exacting, tough, onerous, burdensome, back-breaking, trying, challenging; tiring, fatiguing, exhausting, wearying, wearing, taxing, demanding, wearisome; tedious, boring. **2** *Doug's slow, laborious style:* **laboured**, strained, forced, contrived, affected, stiff, stilted, unnatural, artificial, overwrought, heavy, ponderous, convoluted.
– OPPOSITES easy, effortless.

labour noun **1** *he had a disdain for manual labour:* **(hard) work**, toil, exertion, industry, drudgery, effort, donkey work, menial work; informal slog, grind, sweat, elbow grease; Brit. informal graft; literary travail, moil. **2** *the conflict between capital and labour:* **workers**, employees, workmen, workforce, staff, working people, blue-collar workers, labourers, labour force, proletariat. **3** *the labours of Hercules:* **task**, job, chore, mission, assignment, challenge. **4** *Gina had a long and difficult labour:* **childbirth**, birth, delivery, nativity; contractions, labour pains; formal parturition; literary travail; dated confinement.
– OPPOSITES rest, management.
verb **1** *a project on which he had laboured for many years:* **work (hard)**, toil, slave (away), grind away, struggle, strive, exert oneself, work one's fingers to the bone, work like a Trojan/slave; informal slog away, plug away, peg away; Brit. informal graft. **2** *Newcastle laboured to break down the home team's defence:* **strive**, struggle, endeavour, work, try hard, make every effort, do one's

best, do one's utmost, do all one can, give one's all, go all out, fight, put oneself out, apply oneself, exert oneself; informal bend/lean over backwards, pull out all the stops. **3** *there is no need to labour the point:* **overemphasize**, belabour, overstress, overdo, strain, overplay, make too much of, exaggerate, dwell on, harp on (about). **4** *Rex was labouring under a misapprehension:* **suffer from**, be a victim of, be deceived by, be misled by.

laboured adjective **1** *his harsh, laboured breathing:* **strained**, difficult, forced, laborious. **2** *it was a rather laboured joke:* **contrived**, strained, stilted, forced, unnatural, artificial, overdone, ponderous, over-elaborate, laborious, unconvincing, overwrought.
– OPPOSITES easy, natural.

labourer noun **workman**, worker, working man, manual worker, unskilled worker, blue-collar worker, (hired) hand, roustabout, drudge, menial, coolie; Austral./NZ rouseabout.

labyrinth noun **1** *a labyrinth of little streets:* **maze**, warren, network, complex, web. **2** *the labyrinth of conflicting laws and regulations:* **tangle**, web, morass, jungle, confusion, entanglement, convolution; jumble, mishmash.

labyrinthine adjective **1** *the stadium's labyrinthine corridors:* **maze-like**, winding, twisting, serpentine, meandering, wandering, rambling. **2** *a labyrinthine criminal justice system:* **complicated**, intricate, complex, involved, tortuous, convoluted, involuted, tangled, elaborate; confusing, puzzling, mystifying, bewildering, baffling, byzantine.
– OPPOSITES straight, straightforward.

lace noun *brown shoes with laces:* **shoelace**, bootlace, shoestring, lacing, thong, tie.
verb **1** *he laced up his running shoes:* **fasten**, do up, tie up, secure, knot. **2** *he laced his fingers into mine:* **entwine**, intertwine, twine, entangle, interweave, link; braid, plait. **3** *a mug of tea laced with rum:* **flavour**, mix (in), blend, fortify, strengthen, stiffen, season, spice (up), enrich, liven up; doctor, adulterate; informal spike.
– OPPOSITES untie.

lacerate verb *the jagged edges of the wall lacerated their arms:* **cut (open)**, gash, slash, tear, rip, rend, shred, score, scratch, scrape, graze; wound, injure, hurt.

laceration noun *there was a bleeding laceration on the animal's back:* **gash**, cut, wound, injury, tear, slash, scratch, scrape, abrasion, graze.

lack noun *we were hampered by a lack of cash:* **absence**, want, need, deficiency, dearth, insufficiency, shortage, shortfall, scarcity, paucity, unavailability, scarceness, deficit.
– OPPOSITES abundance.
verb *she's immature and lacks judgement:* **be without**, be in need of, need, be lacking, require, want, be short of, be deficient in, be bereft of, be low on, be pressed for, have insufficient.
– OPPOSITES have, possess.

lackadaisical adjective *I was lackadaisical about my first-aid training:* **careless**, lazy, lax, unenthusiastic, half-hearted, lukewarm, indifferent, unconcerned, casual, offhand, blasé, insouciant, relaxed; apathetic, lethargic, listless, sluggish, spiritless, passionless; informal laid back, couldn't-care-less, easy-going.
– OPPOSITES enthusiastic.

lackey noun *as the only no-strike nurses' union, it had often been accused of being a government lackey:* **toady**, flatterer, minion, doormat, stooge, hanger-on, lickspittle; tool, puppet, instrument, pawn, subordinate, underling; informal yes-man, bootlicker.

lacking adjective **1** *what was lacking was hard evidence:* **absent**, missing, non-existent, unavailable. **2** *the advocate-general found the government lacking on two counts:* **deficient**, defective, inadequate, wanting, flawed, faulty, insufficient, unacceptable, imperfect, inferior. **3** *the game was lacking in atmosphere:* **without**, devoid of, bereft of; deficient in, low on, short on, in need of.
– OPPOSITES present, plentiful.

lacklustre adjective *he delivered a limp and lacklustre speech:* **uninspired**, uninspiring, unimaginative, dull, humdrum, colourless, characterless, bland, insipid, vapid, flat, dry, lifeless, tame, prosaic, spiritless, lustreless; boring, monotonous, dreary, tedious.
– OPPOSITES inspired.

laconic adjective **1** *his laconic comments to his students:* **brief**, concise, terse, succinct, short, pithy; epigrammatic, aphoristic, gnomic. **2** *their laconic press officer was as unhelpful as ever:* **taciturn**, uncommunicative, reticent, quiet, reserved, silent, unforthcoming, brusque.
– OPPOSITES verbose, loquacious.

lad noun (informal) **1** *a young lad of eight:* **boy**, schoolboy, youth, youngster, juvenile, stripling; informal kid, nipper, whippersnapper; Scottish informal laddie; derogatory brat. **2** *a hard-working lad:* **(young) man**; informal guy, fellow, geezer; Brit. informal chap, bloke; N. Amer. informal dude, hombre; Austral./NZ informal digger.

ladder noun **1** *she climbed down the ladder:* **set of steps**. **2** *I had begun to edge my way up the academic ladder:* **hierarchy**, scale, grading, ranking, pecking order.

laden adjective *a tray laden with dinner plates:* **loaded**, burdened, weighed down, overloaded, piled high, fully charged; full, filled, packed, stuffed, crammed; informal chock-full, chock-a-block.

ladle verb *he was ladling out the contents of the pot:* **spoon**, scoop, dish, serve.
noun *a soup ladle:* **spoon**, scoop, dipper, bailer.

lady noun **1** *several ladies were interested in his offer:* **woman**, female. **2** *lords and ladies:* **noblewoman**, duchess, countess, peeress, viscountess, baroness; archaic gentlewoman.

ladylike adjective *her antics were not very ladylike:* **genteel**, polite, refined, well bred, cultivated, polished, decorous, proper, respectable, seemly, well mannered, cultured, sophisticated, elegant.
– OPPOSITES coarse.

lag verb *Elizabeth was not walking with the others, and had lagged behind:* **fall behind**, straggle, fall back, trail (behind), hang back, not keep pace, bring up the rear.
– OPPOSITES keep up.

lagoon noun inland sea, bay, lake, bight, pool; Scottish loch; Anglo-Irish lough; N. Amer. bayou.

laid-back adjective (informal) **relaxed**, easy-going, equable, free and easy, casual, nonchalant, insouciant, unexcitable, imperturbable, unruffled, blasé, cool, calm, {cool, calm, and collected}, unperturbed, unflustered, unworried, unconcerned; leisurely, unhurried; stoical, phlegmatic, tolerant; informal unflappable.
– OPPOSITES uptight.

lair noun **1** *each year seven beautiful maidens were sent in to the monster's lair:* **den**, burrow, hole, tunnel, cave. **2** *the patrol boat finally reached Kurtz's lair deep in the jungle:* **hideaway**, hiding place, hideout, refuge, sanctuary, haven, shelter, retreat; informal hidey-hole.

laissez-faire noun *laissez-faire is an economic system based on self-interest:* **free enterprise**, free trade, non-intervention, free-market capitalism.

lake noun **pond**, pool, tarn, reservoir, lagoon, waterhole, inland sea; Scottish loch, lochan; Anglo-Irish lough; N. Amer. bayou, pothole (lake); literary mere.

lambaste verb *the manager lambasted his sales team:* **criticize**, chastise, censure, take to task, harangue, rail at, rant at, fulminate against; upbraid, scold, reprimand, rebuke, chide, reprove, admonish, berate; informal lay into, pitch into, tear into, give someone a dressing-down, carpet, tell off, bawl out; Brit. informal tick off, have a go at; N. Amer. informal chew out; formal castigate, excoriate.

lame adjective **1** *the mare was lame:* **limping**,

hobbling; crippled, disabled, incapacitated. **2** *a lame excuse:* **feeble**, weak, thin, flimsy, poor; unconvincing, implausible, unlikely.
– OPPOSITES convincing.

lament noun **1** *the widow's laments filled the huge room:* **wail**, wailing, lamentation, moan, moaning, weeping, crying, sob, sobbing, keening. **2** *a lament for the dead of both world wars:* **dirge**, requiem, elegy, threnody, monody; Irish keen; Scottish & Irish coronach; formal epicedium.
verb **1** *the mourners lamented:* **mourn**, grieve, sorrow, wail, weep, cry, sob, keen, beat one's breast. **2** *he lamented the modernization of the palace buildings:* **bemoan**, bewail, complain about, deplore; protest against, object to, oppose, fulminate against, inveigh against, denounce.
– OPPOSITES celebrate.

lamentable adjective *they have shown a lamentable lack of commitment:* **deplorable**, regrettable, terrible, awful, wretched, woeful, dire, disastrous, desperate, grave, appalling, dreadful, egregious; intolerable, pitiful, shameful, sorrowful, unfortunate.
– OPPOSITES wonderful.

lamentation noun *a time for weeping and lamentation was announced:* **weeping**, wailing, crying, sobbing, moaning, lament, keening, grieving, mourning.

lamp noun **light**, lantern.

lampoon verb *he was mercilessly lampooned in the press:* **satirize**, mock, ridicule, make fun of, caricature, burlesque, parody, take off, guy, rag, tease; informal send up.
noun *a lampoon of student life in the twenties:* **satire**, burlesque, parody, skit, caricature, impersonation, travesty, mockery, squib, pasquinade; informal send-up, take-off, spoof.

lance noun *a knight armed with a lance:* **spear**, pike, javelin; harpoon.
verb *the boil was lanced to drain the pus:* **cut (open)**, slit, incise, puncture, prick, pierce.

land noun **1** *Lyme Park has 1323 acres of land | publicly owned land:* **grounds**, fields, open space; property, acres, acreage, estate, lands, real estate; country, countryside, rural area, green belt. **2** *Tunisia is a land of variety:* **country**, nation, (nation) state, realm, kingdom, province; region, area, domain. **3** *the lookout sighted land to the east:* **terra firma**, dry land; coast, coastline, shore.
verb **1** *Allied troops landed in France:* **disembark**, go ashore, debark, alight, get off. **2** *the ship landed at Le Havre:* **berth**, dock, moor, (drop) anchor, tie up, put in. **3** *their plane landed at Chicago:* **touch down**, make a landing, come in to land, come down. **4** *a bird landed on the end of branch:* **perch**, settle, come to rest, alight. **5** (informal) *Nick landed the job of editor:* **obtain**, get, acquire, secure, be appointed to, gain, net, win, achieve, attain, bag, carry off; informal swing; Brit. informal blag. **6** (informal) *that habit soon landed her in trouble:* **bring**, lead, get. **7** (informal) *they landed her with the*

bill: **burden**, saddle, encumber; informal dump something on someone; Brit. informal lumber. **8** (informal) *John landed a punch on Brian's chin:* **inflict**, deal, deliver, administer, dispense, mete out; informal fetch.
– OPPOSITES sail, take off.
■ **land up** *many of them land up in prison:* finish up, find oneself, end up; informal wind up, fetch up.

landing noun **1** *we made a forced landing:* **touchdown**; informal greaser. **2** *I walked down to the ferry landing:* **harbour**, berth, dock, jetty, landing stage, pier, quay, wharf, slipway.
– OPPOSITES take-off.

landlady, landlord noun **1** *the landlord of the pub was not amused:* **publican**, licensee, innkeeper, pub-owner, barkeeper; hotel-keeper, hotelier, restaurateur; manager, manageress. **2** *his landlady had objected to the noise:* **property owner**, proprietor, proprietress, lessor, householder, landowner.
– OPPOSITES tenant.

landmark noun **1** *the spire was once a landmark for ships:* **marker**, mark, indicator, beacon. **2** *one of London's most famous landmarks:* **monument**, distinctive feature, prominent feature. **3** *the ruling was hailed as a landmark by human rights activists:* **turning point**, milestone, watershed, critical point.

landscape noun **scenery**, countryside, topography, country, terrain; outlook, view, prospect, aspect, vista, panorama, perspective, sweep.

landslide noun **1** *floods and landslides killed several people:* **landslip**, mudslide; avalanche. **2** *the Labour landslide of 1997:* **(decisive) victory**, overwhelming majority, triumph.

lane noun **1** *she walked along the country lanes alone:* **byroad**, byway, track, road, street; alley, alleyway. **2** *cycle lanes | a three-lane highway:* **track**, way, course, path.

language noun **1** *the grammatical structure of language:* **speech**, writing, communication, conversation, speaking, talking, talk, discourse; words, vocabulary. **2** *the English language:* **tongue**, mother tongue, native tongue; informal lingo. **3** *the booklet is written in simple, everyday language:* **wording**, phrasing, phraseology, style, vocabulary, terminology, expressions, turns of phrase, parlance, form/mode of expression, usages, locutions, idiolect, choice of words; speech, dialect, patois, slang, idioms, jargon, argot, cant; informal lingo.

languid adjective **1** *he left with a languid wave of the hand:* **relaxed**, unhurried, languorous, slow; listless, lethargic, sluggish, lazy, idle, indolent, apathetic; informal laid back; archaic otiose. **2** *I longed for those languid days in the Italian sun:* **leisurely**, languorous, relaxed, restful, lazy.

3 *pale, languid individuals who never see daylight:* **sickly**, weak, faint, feeble, frail, delicate; tired, weary, fatigued.
– OPPOSITES energetic.

languish verb **1** *the plants languished and died:* **weaken**, deteriorate; decline; wither, droop, wilt, fade, waste away; informal go downhill. **2** *the general is now languishing in prison:* **waste away**, rot, be abandoned, be neglected, be forgotten, suffer, experience hardship.
– OPPOSITES thrive.

languor noun **1** *she fought the sultry languor that was stealing over her:* **lassitude**, lethargy, listlessness, torpor, fatigue, weariness, sleepiness, drowsiness; laziness, idleness, indolence, inertia, sluggishness, apathy. **2** *the languor of a hot, breezeless day:* **stillness**, tranquillity, calm, calmness; oppressiveness, heaviness.
– OPPOSITES vigour.

lank adjective *the man had lank, greasy hair:* **limp**, lifeless, lustreless, dull; straggling, straight, long.

lanky adjective *a pale, lanky youth:* **tall**, **thin**, slender, slim, lean, lank, skinny, spindly, spare, gangling, gangly, gawky, rangy.
– OPPOSITES stocky.

lap[1] noun *Henry sat on his gran's lap:* **knee**, knees, thighs.

lap[2] noun *a race of eight laps:* **circuit**, leg, circle, revolution, round.
verb *she easily lapped the other runners:* **overtake**, outstrip, leave behind, pass, go past; catch up with.

lap[3] verb **1** *waves lapped against the sea wall:* **splash**, wash, swish, slosh, break, beat, strike, dash, roll. **2** *the dog lapped water out of a puddle:* **drink**, lick up, sup, swallow, slurp, gulp.
■ **lap something up** *their brand of blues-tinged metal was lapped up by a capacity crowd:* relish, revel in, savour, delight in, wallow in, glory in, enjoy.

lapse noun **1** *a momentary lapse of concentration:* **failure**, failing, slip, error, mistake, blunder, fault, omission; informal slip-up. **2** *his lapse into petty crime:* **decline**, fall, falling, slipping, drop, deterioration, degeneration, backsliding, regression, retrogression, descent, sinking, slide. **3** *after this lapse of time I can look at it more calmly:* **interval**, gap, pause, interlude, lull, hiatus, break; passage, course, passing.
verb **1** *the planning permission has lapsed:* **expire**, become void, become invalid, run out. **2** *do not let special friendships lapse:* **(come to an) end**, cease, stop, terminate, pass, fade, wither, die. **3** *since the war, morality has lapsed:* **deteriorate**, decline, fall (off), drop, worsen, degenerate, backslide, regress, retrogress, get worse, sink, wane, slump; informal go downhill, go to pot, go to the dogs. **4** *during dinner she*

lapsed into silence: **revert**, relapse; drift, slide, slip, sink.

lapsed adjective *a lapsed Catholic:* **non-practising**, backsliding, apostate.
– OPPOSITES practising.

larceny noun **theft**, stealing, robbery, pilfering, thieving; burglary, housebreaking, breaking and entering; informal filching, swiping; Brit. informal nicking, pinching; formal peculation.

larder noun **pantry**, (food) store, (food) cupboard; cooler, scullery; Brit. buttery.

large adjective **1** *a large house* | *large numbers of people:* **big**, great, huge, sizeable, substantial, immense, enormous, colossal, massive, mammoth, vast, prodigious, tremendous, gigantic, giant, monumental, stupendous, gargantuan, elephantine, titanic, mountainous, monstrous; towering, tall, high; mighty, voluminous, king-size, giant-size; informal jumbo, whopping (great), thumping (great), mega, humongous, monster, astronomical; Brit. informal whacking (great), ginormous. **2** *a large, red-faced man:* **big**, burly, heavy, tall, bulky, thickset, chunky, strapping, hulking, hefty, muscular, brawny, solid, powerful, sturdy, strong, rugged; fat, plump, overweight, chubby, stout, meaty, fleshy, portly, rotund, flabby, paunchy, obese, corpulent; informal hunky, beefy, tubby, pudgy; Brit. informal podgy, fubsy; N. Amer. informal zaftig, corn-fed. **3** *a large supply of wool:* **abundant**, copious, plentiful, ample, liberal, generous, lavish, bountiful, bumper, boundless, good, considerable, superabundant; literary plenteous. **4** *the measure has large economic implications:* **wide-reaching**, far-reaching, wide, sweeping, large-scale, broad, extensive, comprehensive, exhaustive.
– OPPOSITES small, meagre.
■ **at large 1** *fourteen criminals are still at large:* at liberty, free, (on the) loose, on the run, fugitive; N. Amer. informal on the lam. **2** *what are the implications for society at large?* as a whole, generally, in general.
■ **by and large** *the children, by and large, treated him well:* on the whole, generally, in general, all things considered, all in all, for the most part, in the main, as a rule, overall, almost always, mainly, mostly; on average, on balance.

largely adverb *Jessop was largely responsible for this pioneering work:* **mostly**, mainly, to a large/great extent, chiefly, predominantly, primarily, principally, for the most part, in the main; usually, typically, commonly.

large-scale adjective **1** *a large-scale privatization programme:* **extensive**, wide-ranging, far-reaching, comprehensive, exhaustive; mass, nationwide, global. **2** *a large-scale map:* **enlarged**, blown-up, magnified.

largesse noun *Tupper took advantage of his friend's largesse:* **generosity**, liberality, munificence, bounty, bountifulness,

beneficence, altruism, charity, philanthropy, magnanimity, benevolence, charitableness, open-handedness.
– OPPOSITES meanness.

lark (informal) noun **1** *we were just having a bit of a lark:* **laugh**, fun, giggle, joke; escapade, prank, trick, jape, practical joke; informal leg-pull; (**larks**) antics, high jinks, horseplay, mischief, tomfoolery; informal shenanigans, monkey business; Brit. informal monkey tricks. **2** *I've got this snowboarding lark sussed:* **affair**, matter; nonsense; informal business, caper, thing; stuff, malarkey.
verb *he's always larking about:* **fool about/around**, play tricks, make mischief, monkey about/around, clown about/around, have fun, skylark; informal mess about/around; Brit. informal muck about/around.

lascivious adjective *there was a lascivious glint in his eye:* **lecherous**, lewd, lustful, licentious, libidinous, salacious, lubricious, prurient, dirty, smutty, naughty, suggestive, indecent, ribald; informal horny; Brit. informal randy.

lash verb **1** *he lashed the prisoner repeatedly across his back:* **whip**, flog, beat, thrash, horsewhip, scourge, birch, switch, belt, strap, cane; strike, hit; informal wallop, whack, lam, larrup, give someone a (good) hiding; N. Amer. informal whale. **2** *rain lashed the window panes:* **beat against**, dash against, pound, batter, strike, hit, knock. **3** *the tiger began to growl and lash his tail:* **swish**, flick, twitch, whip. **4** *fear lashed them into a frenzy:* **provoke**, incite, arouse, excite, agitate, stir up, whip up, work up. **5** *two boats were lashed together:* **fasten**, bind, tie (up), tether, hitch, knot, rope, make fast.
noun **1** *he brought the lash down heavily upon the man's back:* **whip**, switch, scourge, thong, flail, strap, birch, cane; historical knout, cat-o'-nine-tails, cat. **2** *he received twenty lashes:* **stroke**, blow, strike.
■ **lash out 1** *the president lashed out at the opposition for opposing the policy:* criticize, chastise, censure, attack, condemn, denounce, lambaste, harangue, pillory; berate, upbraid, rebuke, reproach; informal lay into; formal castigate. **2** *Norman lashed out at Terry with a chisel:* hit out, strike, let fly, take a swing; set upon/about, turn on, round on, attack; informal lay into, tear into, pitch into.

lass noun (Scottish & N. English) **girl**, young woman, young lady; Scottish lassie; Irish colleen; informal chick, girlie; Brit. informal bird, bint; N. Amer. informal dame, babe, doll, gal, broad; Austral./NZ informal sheila; literary maid, maiden, damsel; archaic wench.

lassitude noun *she ascribed her lassitude to the heat:* **lethargy**, listlessness, weariness, languor, sluggishness, tiredness, fatigue, torpor, lifelessness, apathy.
– OPPOSITES vigour.

last¹ adjective **1** *the last woman in the queue:* **rearmost**, hindmost, endmost, at the end, at the back, furthest (back), final, ultimate. **2** *Rembrandt spent his last years in Amsterdam:* **closing**, concluding, final, ending, end, terminal; later, latter. **3** *I'd be the last person to say anything against him:* **least likely**, most unlikely; least suitable, least appropriate. **4** *we met last year in Berlin:* **previous**, preceding; prior, former. **5** *this was his last chance to prove himself:* **final**, only remaining.
– OPPOSITES first, early, next.
adverb *the candidate coming last is eliminated:* **at the end**, at/in the rear.
noun *the most important business was left to the last:* **end**, ending, finish, close, conclusion, finale, termination.
– OPPOSITES beginning.
■ **at last** *at last the storm died away:* finally, in the end, eventually, ultimately, at long last, after a long time, in (the fullness of) time.
■ **the last word** *the spa is the last word in luxury and efficiency:* the best, the peak, the acme, the epitome, the latest; the pinnacle, the apex, the apogee, the ultimate, the height, the zenith, the nonpareil, the crème de la crème.

last² verb **1** *the hearing lasted for six days:* **continue**, go on, carry on, keep on/going, proceed, take; stay, remain, persist. **2** *how long will he last as manager?* **survive**, endure, hold on/out, keep going, persevere; informal stick it out, hang on, hack it. **3** *the car is built to last:* **endure**, wear well, stand up, bear up.

lasting adjective *a lasting peace:* **enduring**, long-lasting, long-lived, abiding, continuing, long-term, surviving, persisting, permanent; durable, constant, stable, established, secure, long-standing; unchanging, irreversible, immutable, eternal, undying, everlasting, unending, never-ending, unfading, changeless, indestructible, unceasing, unwavering, unfaltering.
– OPPOSITES ephemeral.

lastly adverb **finally**, in conclusion, to conclude, to sum up, to end, last, ultimately.
– OPPOSITES firstly.

latch noun *he carefully lifted the latch:* **fastening**, catch, fastener, clasp.
verb *Jess latched the back door:* **fasten**, secure, make fast.

late adjective **1** *the train was always late:* **behind time**, behind schedule, behindhand; tardy, running late, overdue, delayed. **2** *her late husband:* **dead**, departed, lamented, passed on/away; formal deceased.
– OPPOSITES punctual, early.
adverb **1** *she had arrived late, as usual:* **behind schedule**, behind time, behindhand, belatedly, tardily, at the last minute. **2** *I was working late that night:* **after hours**, overtime. **3** *I won't have you staying out late:* **late at night**; informal till all hours.
■ **of late** *she'd been drinking too much of late:* recently, lately, latterly.

lately adverb *he's had a bad press lately:* **recently**, of late, latterly, in recent times.

lateness noun **unpunctuality**, tardiness, delay.

latent adjective *they have a huge reserve of latent talent:* **dormant**, untapped, unused, undiscovered, hidden, concealed, invisible, unseen, undeveloped, unrealized, unfulfilled, potential.

later adjective *this question will be dealt with in a later chapter:* **subsequent**, following, succeeding, future, upcoming, to come, ensuing.
– OPPOSITES earlier.
adverb **1** *later, the film rights were sold:* **subsequently**, eventually, then, next, later on, after this/that, afterwards, at a later date, in due course, by and by, in a while, in time. **2** *two days later a letter arrived:* **afterwards**, later on, after (that), subsequently, following; formal thereafter.

lateral adjective **1** *lateral movements:* **sideways**, sidewise, sideward, edgewise, edgeways, oblique. **2** *lateral thinking:* **unorthodox**, inventive, creative, imaginative, original, innovative.

latest adjective *the latest fashions:* **most recent**, newest, just out, just released, fresh, (bang) up to date, up to the minute, state-of-the-art, current, modern, contemporary, fashionable, in fashion, in vogue; informal in, with it, trendy, hip, hot, happening, cool.
– OPPOSITES old.

lather noun *a rich, soapy lather:* **foam**, froth, suds, soapsuds, bubbles; literary spume.

latitude noun **1** *Toronto is on the same latitude as Nice:* **parallel**. **2** *he gave them a lot of latitude in their day-to-day operations:* **freedom**, scope, leeway, (breathing) space, flexibility, liberty, independence, free rein, licence, room to manoeuvre, freedom of action.
– OPPOSITES longitude, restriction.

latter adjective **1** *things improved in the latter half of the season:* **later**, closing, end, concluding, final; latest, most recent. **2** *Russia chose the latter option:* **last-mentioned**, second, last, later.
– OPPOSITES former.

latter-day adjective *he evangelized Whitehall like a latter-day John the Baptist:* **modern**, present-day, current, contemporary.

latterly adverb **1** *latterly, she has been in considerable pain:* **recently**, lately, of late, in recent times. **2** *latterly he worked as a political editor:* **ultimately**, finally, towards the end.

lattice noun **grid**, latticework, fretwork, open framework, openwork, trellis, trelliswork, network, mesh.

laud verb (formal) *the second single was lauded by the music press as a return to form:* **praise**, extol, hail, applaud, acclaim, commend, sing the praises of, speak highly of, lionize, eulogize, rhapsodize over/about; informal rave about.
– OPPOSITES criticize.

laudable adjective *a laudable attempt to get women into parliament:* **praiseworthy**, commendable, admirable, meritorious, worthy, deserving, creditable, estimable, exemplary.
– OPPOSITES shameful.

laugh verb **1** *he started to laugh hysterically:* **chuckle**, chortle, guffaw, giggle, titter, snigger, snicker, tee-hee, burst out laughing, roar/hoot with laughter, dissolve into laughter, split one's sides, be doubled up; informal be in stitches, be rolling in the aisles, crease up, fall about, crack up. **2** *people laughed at his theories:* **ridicule**, mock, deride, scoff at, jeer at, sneer at, jibe at, make fun of, poke fun at, scorn; lampoon, satirize, parody; informal send up, take the mickey out of, pooh-pooh; Austral./NZ informal poke mullock at.
noun **1** *he gave a short laugh:* **chuckle**, chortle, guffaw, giggle, titter, tee-hee, snigger, snicker, roar/hoot of laughter, shriek of laughter, belly laugh. **2** (informal) *he was a right laugh:* **joker**, wag, wit, clown, jester, prankster, character; informal card, case, caution, hoot, scream, riot; Austral./NZ informal hard case. **3** (informal) *I entered the contest for a laugh:* **joke**, prank, piece of fun, jest, escapade, caper, practical joke; informal lark.
■ **laugh something off** *she laughed off any criticism with characteristic good humour:* **dismiss**, make a joke of, make light of, shrug off, brush aside, scoff at; informal pooh-pooh.

laughable adjective **1** *the idea that nuclear power is safe is laughable:* **ridiculous**, ludicrous, absurd, risible, preposterous, foolish, silly, idiotic, stupid, nonsensical, crazy, insane, outrageous; informal cockeyed; Brit. informal daft. **2** *if it wasn't so tragic, it'd be laughable:* **funny**, amusing, humorous, hilarious, uproarious, comical, comic, farcical.

laughter noun **1** *the sound of conversation and laughter:* **laughing**, chuckling, chortling, guffawing, giggling, tittering, sniggering; informal hysterics. **2** *he has made himself a source of laughter:* **amusement**, entertainment, humour, mirth, merriment, gaiety, hilarity, jollity, jocularity, fun.

launch verb **1** *he ordered his men to launch the boat:* **set afloat**, put to sea. **2** *they've launched the shuttle:* **send into orbit**, blast off, take off, lift off. **3** *a chair was launched at him:* **throw**, hurl, fling, pitch, lob, let fly; fire, shoot; informal chuck, heave, sling. **4** *the government launched a new campaign:* **set in motion**, get going, get under way, start, commence, begin, embark on, initiate, inaugurate, set up, put in place, organize, introduce, bring into being; informal kick off. **5** *he launched into a tirade against the* *government:* **start**, commence, burst into, come out with.

laundry noun **1** *a big pile of laundry:* **(dirty) washing**, dirty clothes. **2** *the facilities include a laundry:* **washroom**, laundry room, launderette; N. Amer. trademark laundromat.

lavatory noun **toilet**, WC, water closet, (public) convenience, cloakroom, powder room, urinal, privy, latrine, jakes; N. Amer. washroom, bathroom, rest room, men's/ladies' room, commode, comfort station; Nautical heads; informal little girls'/boys' room, smallest room; Brit. informal loo, bog, the Ladies, the Gents, khazi, lav; N. Amer. informal can, john; Austral./NZ informal dunny.

lavish adjective **1** *he held lavish parties at his new home:* **sumptuous**, luxurious, gorgeous, costly, expensive, opulent, grand, splendid, rich, fancy; informal posh. **2** *he was lavish with his hospitality:* **generous**, liberal, bountiful, open-handed, unstinting, unsparing, free, munificent, extravagant, prodigal. **3** *lavish amounts of champagne were on offer:* **abundant**, copious, plentiful, liberal, prolific, generous; literary plenteous.
– OPPOSITES meagre, frugal.
verb *she lavished money on her children:* **give freely**, spend generously, heap, shower.

law noun **1** *the law of the land:* **rules and regulations**, body of laws, constitution, legislation, legal code. **2** *a new law was passed to make divorce easier:* **regulation**, statute, enactment, act, bill, decree, edict, rule, ruling, resolution, dictum, command, order, directive, pronouncement, proclamation, dictate, diktat, fiat, by-law; N. Amer. formal ordinance. **3** *a career in the law:* **the legal profession**, the bar. **4** *the laws of the game:* **rule**, regulation, principle, convention, instruction, guideline. **5** *a moral law by which he attempted to live his life:* **principle**, rule, precept, directive, injunction, commandment, belief, creed, credo, maxim, tenet, doctrine, canon.

law-abiding adjective *why should law-abiding citizens have to suffer?* **honest**, lawful, righteous, honourable, upright, upstanding, good, decent, virtuous, moral, dutiful, obedient, compliant, disciplined.
– OPPOSITES criminal.

lawbreaker noun **criminal**, felon, wrongdoer, malefactor, evil-doer, offender, transgressor, miscreant; villain, rogue, ruffian; Law malfeasant, infractor; informal crook, con, jailbird.

lawful adjective *it was an offence to carry a weapon in public without lawful authority:* **legitimate**, legal, licit, just, permissible, permitted, allowable, allowed, rightful, sanctioned, authorized, warranted, within the law; informal legit.
– OPPOSITES illegal.

lawless adjective *it was a wild, lawless town on the edge of the jungle:* **anarchic**, disorderly, ungovernable, unruly, disruptive, rebellious, insubordinate, riotous, mutinous.
– OPPOSITES orderly, legal.

lawlessness noun **anarchy**, disorder, chaos, unruliness, criminality, crime.

lawsuit noun **(legal) action**, suit (at law), case, (legal/judicial) proceedings, litigation, trial.

lawyer noun **solicitor**, legal practitioner, legal adviser, member of the bar, barrister, advocate, counsel, Queen's Counsel, QC; N. Amer. attorney, counselor(-at-law); informal brief.

lax adjective *lax discipline in schools has fostered a contempt for authority:* **slack**, slipshod, negligent, remiss, careless, heedless, unmindful, slapdash, offhand, casual; easy-going, lenient, permissive, liberal, indulgent, overindulgent; informal sloppy.
– OPPOSITES strict.

laxative noun **purgative**, evacuant; Medicine aperient, cathartic.

lay[1] verb **1** *Curtis laid the newspaper on the table:* **put (down)**, place, set (down), deposit, rest, situate, locate, position, stow, shove; informal stick, dump, park, plonk; Brit. informal bung. **2** *the act laid the foundation for the new system:* **set in place**, set out/up, establish. **3** *I'll lay money that Michelle will be there:* **bet**, wager, gamble, stake, risk, venture. **4** *they are going to lay charges:* **bring (forward)**, press, prefer, lodge, register, place, file. **5** *he laid the blame at the Prime Minister's door:* **assign**, attribute, ascribe, attach, allot. **6** *we laid plans for the next voyage:* **devise**, arrange, make (ready), prepare, work out, hatch, design, plan, scheme, plot, conceive, put together, draw up, produce, develop, formulate; informal cook up. **7** *this will lay a new responsibility on the court:* **impose**, apply, entrust, vest, place, put; inflict, encumber, saddle, charge, burden. **8** *the eagles laid two eggs:* **produce**.
■ **lay something aside 1** *farmers are laying aside areas for conservation:* put aside, put to one side, keep, save. **2** *producers must lay aside their conservatism:* abandon, cast aside, reject, renounce, repudiate, disregard, forget, discard. **3** *protesters led the government to lay the plans aside:* defer, shelve, suspend, put on ice, mothball, set aside, put off/aside; informal put on the back burner.
■ **lay something down 1** *he laid down his glass:* put down, set down, place down, deposit, rest; informal dump, plonk down; Brit. informal bung down. **2** *they were forced to lay down their weapons:* relinquish, surrender, give up, yield, cede; disarm, give in, submit, capitulate. **3** *the ground rules have been laid down:* formulate, stipulate, set down, draw up, frame; prescribe, ordain, dictate, decree; enact, pass, decide, determine, impose,

codify. **4** *I like to buy young wines and lay them down for a few years:* store, put into store, keep.

■ **lay something in** *Bill proposed that we should lay in a lot of meat for the winter:* stock up with/on, stockpile, store (up), amass, hoard, stow (away), put aside/away/by, garner, collect, squirrel away; informal salt away, stash (away).

■ **lay into** (informal) **1** *a policeman laying into a protestor.* See ASSAULT verb sense 1. **2** *he laid into her with a string of insults.* See CRITICIZE.

■ **lay off** (informal) *you really should lay off smoking:* give up, stop, refrain from, abstain from, desist from, cut out; informal pack in, leave off, quit.

■ **lay someone off** *cutbacks have forced the museum to lay off 200 staff:* make redundant, dismiss, let go, discharge, give notice to; informal sack, fire, give someone their cards, give someone their marching orders, give someone the boot/push, give someone the (old) heave-ho.

■ **lay something on** *refreshments had been laid on:* provide, supply, furnish, line up, organize, prepare, produce, make available; informal fix up.

■ **lay someone out** (informal) *he belted him and laid him out flat:* knock out/down, knock unconscious, fell, floor, flatten; informal KO, kayo; Brit. informal knock for six.

■ **lay something out 1** *Robyn laid the plans out on the desk:* spread out, set out, display, exhibit. **2** *we have issued a statement laying out our priorities:* outline, sketch out, rough out, detail, draw up, formulate, work out, frame, draft. **3** (informal) *he had to lay out £70.* See PAY verb sense 2.

lay² adjective **1** *a lay preacher:* non-clerical, unordained, secular, temporal. **2** *I cannot explain this in detail to a lay audience:* non-professional, amateur, non-specialist, non-technical, untrained, unqualified.

layabout noun **idler**, good-for-nothing, loafer, lounger, shirker, sluggard, laggard, slugabed, malingerer; informal skiver, waster, slacker, lazybones; Austral./NZ informal bludger; literary wastrel.

layer noun *the walls were topped by a layer of concrete:* **coating**, sheet, coat, film, covering, blanket, skin, thickness.

layman noun. See LAYPERSON.

lay-off noun **redundancy**, dismissal, discharge; informal sacking, firing, the sack, the boot, the axe, the elbow.
– OPPOSITES recruitment.

layout noun **1** *I found the layout of the house confusing:* **arrangement**, geography, design, organization; plan, map. **2** *we changed the magazine's layout:* **design**, arrangement, presentation, style, format; structure, organization, composition, configuration.

layperson noun **1** *a prayer book for laypeople:* **unordained person**, member of the congregation, layman, laywoman. **2** *engineering sounds highly specialized to the*

layperson: **non-expert**, layman, laywoman, non-professional, amateur, non-specialist.

laze verb *we were just lazing about on the beach:* **relax**, unwind, idle, do nothing, loaf (around/about), lounge (around/about), loll (around/about), lie (around/about), take it easy; informal hang around/round, veg (out); N. Amer. informal bum (around).

lazy adjective *he is too lazy to make a success of anything:* **(bone) idle**, indolent, slothful, work-shy, shiftless, inactive, sluggish, lethargic; remiss, negligent, slack, lax, lackadaisical; archaic otiose.
– OPPOSITES industrious.

leach verb *nitrate is leached from the soil by the rain:* **drain**, filter, percolate, filtrate, strain.

lead verb **1** *Michelle led them into the house:* **guide**, conduct, show (the way), lead the way, usher, escort, steer, pilot, shepherd, head; accompany, see, take. **2** *he led us to believe they were lying:* **cause**, induce, prompt, move, persuade, influence, drive, condition, make; incline, dispose, predispose. **3** *this reform might lead to job losses:* **result in**, cause, bring on/about, give rise to, be the cause of, make happen, create, produce, occasion, effect, generate, contribute to, promote; provoke, stir up, spark off, arouse, foment, instigate; involve, necessitate, entail; formal effectuate. **4** *she led a coalition of Republican radicals:* **be the leader of**, be the head of, preside over, head, command, govern, rule, be in charge of, be in command of, be in control of, run, control, be at the helm of, spearhead; administer, organize, manage; reign over, be in power over; informal head up. **5** *Rangers were leading at half-time:* **be ahead**, be winning, be (out) in front, be in the lead, be first. **6** *the champion was leading the field:* **be at the front of**, be first in, be ahead of, head; outrun, outstrip, outpace, leave behind, draw away from; outdo, outclass, beat; informal leave standing. **7** *I just want to lead a normal life:* **live**, have, experience, spend, pass.
– OPPOSITES follow.

noun **1** *I was in the lead early on:* **leading position**, first place, van, vanguard; (**in the lead**) ahead, in front, winning. **2** *they took the lead in the personal computer market:* **first position**, forefront, primacy, dominance, superiority, ascendancy, pre-eminence, supremacy, advantage, upper hand, whip hand. **3** *sixth-formers should give a lead to younger pupils:* **example**, (role) model, exemplar, paradigm. **4** *he's not accustomed to playing the lead:* **leading role**, star/starring role, title role, principal part; principal character, male lead, female lead, leading man, leading lady. **5** *fortunately, the Labrador was on a lead:* **leash**, tether, cord, rope, chain. **6** *detectives were following up a new lead:* **clue**, pointer, hint, tip, tip-

off, suggestion, indication, sign; (**leads**) evidence, information.
adjective *the lead position was occupied by an American:* **leading**, first, top, foremost, front, head; chief, principal, premier.
■ **lead someone on** *he knew she was leading him on, but he couldn't help himself:* deceive, mislead, delude, hoodwink, dupe, trick, fool, pull the wool over someone's eyes; tease; informal string along, lead up the garden path, take for a ride.
■ **lead the way 1** *he led the way to the kitchen:* guide, conduct, show the way. **2** *Britain is leading the way in aerospace technology:* take the initiative, break (new) ground, blaze a trail, prepare the way.
■ **lead up to** *the prosecution's description of events leading up to the fire was very detailed:* precede, happen before, go/come before; pave/prepare the way for, herald, introduce, set the scene for; cause.

leaden adjective **1** *he rose from the armchair, his eyes leaden with sleep:* **dull**, heavy, weighty; listless, lifeless. **2** *he avoids the leaden prose style of so many academics:* **boring**, dull, unimaginative, uninspired, monotonous, heavy, laboured, wooden. **3** *he moved on leaden feet back to the staircase:* **sluggish**, heavy, lumbering, slow. **4** *we looked out at a dour and leaden sky:* **grey**, greyish, black, dark; cloudy, gloomy, overcast, dull, murky, sunless, louring, oppressive, threatening.

leader noun **1** *the leader of the Democratic Party:* **chief**, head, principal; commander, captain; controller, superior, headman; chairman, chairwoman, chairperson, chair; (managing) director, MD, manager, superintendent, supervisor, overseer, administrator, employer, master, mistress; president, premier, governor; ruler, monarch, king, queen, sovereign, emperor; informal boss, skipper, gaffer, guv'nor, number one, numero uno, honcho; N. Amer. informal sachem, padrone. **2** *a world leader in the use of video conferencing:* **pioneer**, front runner, innovator, trailblazer, groundbreaker, trendsetter, torch-bearer; originator, initiator, founder, architect.
– OPPOSITES follower, supporter.

leadership noun **1** *she won the leadership of the Conservative Party:* **headship**, directorship, premiership, governorship, governance, administration, captaincy, control, ascendancy, rule, command, power, dominion. **2** *we need firm and committed leadership:* **guidance**, direction, control, management, superintendence, supervision; organization, government.

leading adjective **1** *he played the leading role in his team's narrow victory:* **main**, chief, major, prime, most significant, principal, foremost, key, central, focal, paramount, dominant, essential. **2** *the leading industrialized countries:* **most powerful**, most important, greatest,

chief, pre-eminent, principal, dominant. **3** *Bailey was last season's leading scorer:* **top**, highest, best, first; front, lead; unparalleled, matchless, star.
– OPPOSITES subordinate, minor.

leaf noun **1** *sycamore leaves:* **frond**, leaflet, flag; Botany cotyledon, blade, bract. **2** *as he handled the book, a sheaf of loose leaves fell from the back:* **page**, sheet, folio.
verb *he leafed through the pile of documents:* **flick**, flip, thumb, skim, browse, glance, riffle; scan, run one's eye over, peruse.
■ **turn over a new leaf** *I saw fatherhood as the chance to turn over a new leaf:* reform, improve, mend one's ways, make a fresh start, change for the better; informal go straight.

leaflet noun **pamphlet**, booklet, brochure, handbill, circular, flyer, handout, bulletin; N. Amer. folder, dodger.

league noun **1** *he tried to form a league of chieftains:* **alliance**, confederation, confederacy, federation, union, association, coalition, consortium, affiliation, guild, cooperative, partnership, fellowship, syndicate. **2** *the football league:* **championship**, competition, contest. **3** *the store is not in the same league as the major supermarkets:* **class**, group, category, level.
■ **in league with** *even officials not in league with the cattle thieves did little:* collaborating with, cooperating with, in alliance with, allied with, conspiring with, hand in glove with; informal in cahoots with.

leak verb **1** *oil was leaking from the tanker:* **seep (out)**, escape, ooze (out), emanate, issue, drip, dribble, drain, bleed. **2** *the tanks are leaking gasoline into the river:* **discharge**, exude, emit, release, drip, dribble, ooze, secrete. **3** *civil servants who leak information are disciplined:* **disclose**, divulge, reveal, make public, tell, impart, pass on, relate, communicate, expose, broadcast, publish, release, let slip, bring into the open; informal blab, let the cat out of the bag, spill the beans, blow the gaff.
noun 1 *check that there are no leaks in the bag:* **hole**, opening, puncture, perforation, gash, slit, nick, rent, break, crack, fissure, rupture. **2** *a gas leak was discovered:* **discharge**, leakage, leaking, seepage, drip, escape. **3** *a series of leaks to the media:* **disclosure**, revelation, exposé.

leaky adjective *vast amounts of water are lost through leaky pipes:* **leaking**, dripping; cracked, split, punctured, perforated.
– OPPOSITES watertight.

lean[1] verb **1** *Polly leaned against the door:* **rest**, recline, be supported. **2** *a line of palm trees leaning in the wind:* **slant**, incline, bend, tilt, be at an angle, slope, tip, list. **3** *he leans towards existentialist philosophy:* **tend**, incline, gravitate; have a preference for, have an affinity with. **4** *what I need is a strong shoulder to lean on:* **depend**, be dependent, rely, count, bank, have faith in, trust.

■ **lean on** (informal) *I got leaned on by villains:* intimidate, coerce, browbeat, bully, pressurize, threaten, put pressure on; informal twist someone's arm, put the frighteners on, put the screws on.

lean² adjective **1** *a tall, lean aristocratic man:* **slim**, thin, slender, spare, wiry, lanky. **2** *a lean harvest will mean less food and fewer jobs:* **meagre**, sparse, poor, mean, inadequate, insufficient, paltry, deficient, insubstantial. **3** *too often in lean times it is the poor who suffer most:* **unproductive**, unfruitful, arid, barren; hard, bad, difficult, tough, impoverished, poverty-stricken.
– OPPOSITES fat, abundant, prosperous.

leaning noun *his early leanings towards socialism are apparent in these articles:* **inclination**, tendency, bent, proclivity, propensity, penchant, predisposition, predilection, partiality, preference, bias, attraction, liking, fondness, taste.

leap verb **1** *he leapt over the gate:* **jump (over)**, vault (over), spring over, bound over, hop (over), hurdle, clear. **2** *Claudia leapt to her feet in alarm:* **spring**, jump (up), bound, dart. **3** *as soon as the phone rang, we leapt into action:* **rush**, hurry, hasten, jump, burst. **4** *she had leapt at the chance of a free holiday:* **grab**, grasp (with both hands), take advantage of, seize (on), jump at. **5** *she had leapt to conclusions which were hopelessly wide of the mark:* **rush**; hurry, hasten, jump. **6** *profits leapt by 55%:* **increase rapidly**, soar, rocket, skyrocket, shoot up, escalate. noun **1** *he had cleared the brook in one leap:* **jump**, vault, spring, bound, hop, skip. **2** *a leap of 33%:* **rise**, surge, upsurge, upswing, upturn.

■ **in/by leaps and bounds** *once Derek came back to work, productivity improved in leaps and bounds:* **rapidly**, swiftly, quickly, speedily, dramatically.

learn verb **1** *we encourage students to learn a foreign language:* **master**, become competent in, become proficient in, grasp, acquire, take in, absorb, assimilate, digest, familiarize oneself with; study, read up on, be taught, have lessons in; informal get the hang of. **2** *she learnt the poem by heart:* **memorize**, commit to memory, learn parrot-fashion, get off/down pat. **3** *he learnt that the school would shortly be closing:* **discover**, find out, become aware, be informed, hear (tell); gather, understand, ascertain, establish; informal get wind of the fact; Brit. informal suss out.

learned adjective *he was very learned, a formidable intellect | we consulted learned academic journals:* **scholarly**, erudite, well educated, knowledgeable, widely read, well informed, lettered, cultured, intellectual, academic, literary, bookish, highbrow, studious; informal brainy.
– OPPOSITES ignorant.

learner noun *the teacher must develop a good relationship with the learner:* **student**, trainee, apprentice, pupil; novice, newcomer, starter, probationer, tyro, fledgling, neophyte;
N. Amer. tenderfoot; N. Amer. informal greenhorn.
– OPPOSITES veteran.

learning noun **1** *the importance of the library as a centre of learning:* **study**, studying, education, schooling, tuition, teaching, academic work; research, investigation. **2** *the astonishing range of his learning:* **scholarship**, knowledge, education, erudition, intellect, understanding, wisdom.
– OPPOSITES ignorance.

lease noun *a 15-year lease:* **leasehold**, rental/hire agreement, charter; rental, tenancy, tenure, period of occupancy.
– OPPOSITES freehold.
verb **1** *the film crew leased a large hangar:* **rent**, hire, charter. **2** *they leased the mill to a reputable family:* **rent (out)**, let (out), hire (out), sublet, sublease.

leash noun *keep your dog on a leash:* **lead**, tether, rope, chain, strap, restraint.
verb *she leashed the dog:* **put the leash on**, put the lead on, tether, tie up, secure, restrain; control.

least determiner *I have not the least idea what this means:* **slightest**, smallest, minutest, tiniest, littlest.
■ **at least** *you should arrive at least an hour before take-off:* **at the minimum**, no/not less than, more than.

leather noun *a leather jacket:* **skin**, hide.

leathery adjective **1** *he had soulful eyes and brown leathery skin:* **rough**, rugged, wrinkled, wrinkly, furrowed, lined, wizened, weather-beaten, callous, gnarled. **2** *leathery slices of beef in lukewarm gravy:* **tough**, hard, gristly, chewy, stringy.

leave¹ verb **1** *I left the hotel:* **depart from**, go (away) from, withdraw from, retire from, take oneself off from, exit from, take one's leave of, pull out of, quit, be gone from, decamp from, disappear from, vacate, absent oneself from; say one's farewells/goodbyes, make oneself scarce; informal push off, shove off, clear out/off, cut and run, split, vamoose, scoot, make tracks, up sticks; Brit. informal sling one's hook. **2** *the next morning we left for Leicester:* **set off**, head, make; set sail. **3** *he's left his wife:* **abandon**, desert, cast aside/off, jilt, leave in the lurch, leave high and dry, throw over; informal dump, ditch, chuck, drop, walk/run out on; literary forsake. **4** *he left his job in November:* **resign from**, retire from, step down from, withdraw from, pull out of, give up; informal quit. **5** *she left her handbag on the bus:* **leave behind**, forget, lose, mislay. **6** *I thought I'd leave it to the experts:* **entrust**, hand over, pass on, refer; delegate. **7** *he left her £100,000 in his will:* **bequeath**, will, endow, hand down, make over.

– OPPOSITES arrive.

■ **leave off** (informal) *'Will you leave off nagging?' he snarled at her:* stop, cease, finish, desist from, keep from, break off, lay off, give up, discontinue, refrain from, eschew; informal quit, knock off, jack in, swear off.

■ **leave someone/something out 1** *Adam left out the address on the label:* miss out, omit, fail to include, overlook, forget; skip, miss, jump. **2** *he was left out of the England squad:* exclude, omit, drop, pass over.

leave² noun **1** *the judge granted leave to appeal:* **permission**, consent, authorization, sanction, warrant, dispensation, approval, clearance, blessing, agreement, backing, assent, acceptance, licence, acquiescence; informal the go-ahead, the green light, the OK, the rubber stamp. **2** *he was on leave from the Royal Engineers:* **holiday**, vacation, break, time off, furlough, sabbatical, leave of absence; informal hols, vac. **3** *I will now take my leave of you:* **departure**, leaving, leave-taking, parting, withdrawal, exit, farewell, goodbye.

leaven verb **1** *yeast leavens the bread:* **raise**, make rise, puff up, expand. **2** *the formal proceedings were leavened by a touch of humour:* **permeate**, infuse, pervade, imbue, suffuse; enliven, liven up, invigorate, energize, electrify, ginger up, perk up, brighten up, season, spice; informal buck up, pep up.

leavings plural noun *the leavings of their hasty meal were soon dealt with:* **residue**, remainder, remains, remnants, leftovers, scrapings, scraps, oddments, odds and ends, rejects, dregs, refuse, rubbish.

lecherous adjective *Walter tried to dissociate himself from his lecherous, spendthrift brother:* **lustful**, licentious, lascivious, libidinous, lewd, salacious, lubricious, debauched, dissolute, wanton, dissipated, degenerate, depraved, dirty, filthy; informal randy, horny, goatish.
– OPPOSITES chaste.

lecture noun **1** *a lecture on children's literature:* **speech**, talk, address, discourse, disquisition, presentation, oration, lesson. **2** *Dave got a severe lecture for wasting his money:* **scolding**, chiding, reprimand, rebuke, reproof, reproach, upbraiding, berating, admonishment; informal dressing-down, telling-off, talking-to, tongue-lashing.
verb **1** *he visited schools to lecture on the dangers of drugs:* **give a lecture/talk**, talk, make a speech, speak, give an address; discourse, hold forth, declaim, expatiate; informal spout, sound off. **2** *she lectures at Dublin University:* **teach**, tutor. **3** *he was lectured by the headmaster in front of the whole school:* **scold**, chide, reprimand, rebuke, reprove, reproach, upbraid, berate, chastise, admonish, lambaste, haul over the coals, take to task; informal give someone a

dressing-down, give someone a talking-to, tell off; Brit. informal tick off, carpet; N. Amer. informal bawl out.

lecturer noun **1** *the lecturer is a well-known journalist:* **speaker**, presenter, orator. **2** *a lecturer in economics:* **university/college teacher**, tutor, reader, scholar, don, professor, fellow; academic.

ledge noun **shelf**, sill, mantel, mantelpiece, shelving; projection, protrusion, overhang, ridge, prominence.

ledger noun **(account) book**, record book, register, log; records, books; balance sheet, financial statement.

lee noun *they sat in the lee of the wall:* **shelter**, protection, cover, refuge, safety, security.

leer verb *Henry leered at her and licked his lips:* **ogle**, look lasciviously, look suggestively, eye; informal give someone a/the once-over, lech after/over.

leeway noun *this has left the police with some leeway in interpreting the law:* **freedom**, scope, latitude, space, room, liberty, flexibility, licence, free hand, free rein.

left adjective **left-hand**; Nautical port; Heraldry sinister.
– OPPOSITES right, starboard.

leftover noun **1** *she looks like a leftover from the 60s:* **residue**, survivor, vestige, legacy. **2** *put the leftovers in the fridge for later:* **leavings**, remainder, scraps, remnants, remains; excess, surplus.
adjective *any leftover food went to the dog:* **remaining**, left, uneaten, unconsumed; excess, surplus, superfluous, unused, unwanted, spare.

left-wing adjective **socialist**, communist, leftist, Labour, Marxist–Leninist, Bolshevik, Trotskyite, Maoist; informal Commie, lefty, red, pink.
– OPPOSITES right-wing.

leg noun **1** *poor Lee broke his leg:* **(lower) limb**, shank; informal peg, pin. **2** *a table leg:* **upright**, support, prop. **3** *the first leg of a European tour:* **part**, stage, portion, segment, section, phase, stretch, lap.
■ **give someone a leg up** *most parents want to give their children a leg up:* help/assist someone, give someone assistance, lend someone a helping hand, give someone a flying start.
■ **on its last legs 1** *my car is on its last legs:* dilapidated, worn out, rickety, about to fall apart. **2** *he bought a foundry business that was on its last legs:* failing, about to go bankrupt, near to ruin, going to the wall; informal going bust.
■ **pull someone's leg** *it's all right, I was only pulling your leg:* tease, rag, make fun of, chaff, jest, joke with, play a (practical) joke on, play a trick on, make a monkey out of; hoax, fool, deceive, lead on, hoodwink, dupe, beguile, gull; informal kid, have on, rib, take for a ride, take the mickey out of; Brit. informal wind up; N. Amer. informal put on.

■ **stretch one's legs** go for a walk, take a stroll, walk, stroll, move about, get some exercise.

legacy noun **1** *a legacy from a great-aunt had paid for their house:* **bequest**, inheritance, bestowal, endowment, gift, patrimony, settlement, birthright; formal benefaction. **2** *the tragic legacy of the Vietnam War:* **consequence(s)**, effects, upshot, spin-off, repercussion(s), aftermath, by-product(s), result(s).

legal adjective **1** *all their actions were perfectly legal:* **lawful**, legitimate, licit, within the law, legalized, valid; permissible, permitted, allowable, allowed, above board, admissible, acceptable; authorized, sanctioned, licensed, constitutional; informal legit. **2** *the legal profession:* **judicial**, juridical.
– OPPOSITES criminal.

legality noun **lawfulness**, legitimacy, validity, admissibility, permissibility, constitutionality; justice.

legalize verb *the campaign to legalize cannabis:* **make legal**, decriminalize, legitimize, legitimatize, legitimate, permit, allow, authorize, sanction, license; regularize, normalize; informal OK, give the go-ahead to, give the thumbs up to, give the green light to.
– OPPOSITES prohibit.

legate noun *a legate to the papal court:* **envoy**, emissary, agent, ambassador, representative, commissioner, delegate, proxy, deputy, plenipotentiary, messenger.

legend noun **1** *the Arthurian legends have a universal appeal:* **myth**, saga, epic, (folk) tale, (folk) story, fairy tale, fable; folklore, lore, mythology, fantasy, oral history, folk tradition. **2** *pop legends like the Beatles:* **celebrity**, star, superstar, icon, phenomenon, luminary, giant; informal celeb, megastar. **3** *experimental conditions were described in the legend to figure 5:* **explanation**, key, guide.

legendary adjective **1** *the legendary warrior kings of Ireland:* **fabled**, heroic, traditional, fairy-tale, storybook, mythical, mythological. **2** *he was a legendary figure in the trades union movement:* **famous**, celebrated, famed, renowned, acclaimed, illustrious, esteemed, honoured, exalted, venerable, well known, popular, prominent, distinguished, great, eminent, pre-eminent.
– OPPOSITES historical.

legibility noun **readability**, clarity, clearness, neatness.

legible adjective *unlike her brother, she had large, legible handwriting:* **readable**, easy to read, easily deciphered, clear, plain, neat, intelligible.

legion noun **1** *the Roman legions that fought the Germanic tribes:* **brigade**, regiment, battalion, company, troop, division, squadron, squad, platoon, unit. **2** *there were legions of photographers and TV cameras:* **horde**, throng, multitude, crowd, mass, mob, gang, swarm, flock, herd, score, army. adjective *her fans, who are legion, will love this:* **numerous**, countless, innumerable, incalculable, many, abundant, plentiful; literary myriad.

legislate verb *the government is determined to legislate against this practice:* **make laws**, pass laws, enact laws, formulate laws.

legislation noun *the repeal of anti-union legislation | it will require legislation to change things:* **law**, body of laws, rules, rulings, regulations, acts, bills, statutes, enactments; N. Amer. formal ordinances.

legislative adjective *the legislative assembly is undecided:* **law-making**, judicial, juridical, parliamentary, governmental, policy-making.

legislator noun **lawmaker**, lawgiver, parliamentarian, Member of Parliament, MP, congressman, congresswoman, senator.

legitimate adjective **1** *these gaming halls are the only form of legitimate gambling in the area:* **legal**, lawful, licit, legalized, authorized, permitted, permissible, allowable, allowed, admissible, sanctioned, approved, licensed, statutory, constitutional; informal legit. **2** *I am the legitimate heir:* **rightful**, lawful, genuine, authentic, real, true, proper, authorized, sanctioned, acknowledged, recognized. **3** *these are legitimate grounds for unease:* **valid**, sound, admissible, acceptable, well founded, justifiable, reasonable, sensible, just, fair, bona fide.
– OPPOSITES illegal, invalid.

legitimize verb *joining a union legitimizes workers' employment rights:* **validate**, legitimate, permit, authorize, sanction, license, condone, justify, endorse, support; legalize.
– OPPOSITES outlaw.

leisure noun *the balance between leisure and work:* **free time**, spare time, time off; recreation, relaxation, inactivity, pleasure; informal R & R.
– OPPOSITES work.

■ **at your leisure** *wander at your leisure through the stunning selection of shops:* at your convenience, when it suits you, in your own (good) time, without haste, unhurriedly.

leisurely adjective *the journey was undertaken at a leisurely pace | a leisurely stroll:* **unhurried**, relaxed, easy, gentle, sedate, comfortable, restful, undemanding, slow, lazy.
– OPPOSITES hurried.

lend verb **1** *I'll lend you my towel:* **loan**, let someone use; advance; Brit. informal sub. **2** *these examples lend weight to his assertions:* **add**, impart, give, bestow, confer, provide, supply, furnish, contribute.
– OPPOSITES borrow.

■ **lend itself to** *the landscape here does not lend itself to walking:* be suitable for, be suited to, be appropriate for, be applicable for.

length noun **1** *they grow to a length of three or four metres:* **extent**, distance, linear measure, span, reach; stretch, range, scope. **2** *a considerable length of time:* **period**, duration, stretch, span. **3** *she bought a length of pale blue silk:* **piece**, swatch, measure. **4** *MPs criticized the length of the speech:* **protractedness**, lengthiness, extent, extensiveness; prolixity, wordiness, verbosity, verboseness, long-windedness.
■ **at length 1** *he spoke at length of his suitability for the job:* for a long time, for ages, for hours, protractedly, extensively, exhaustively, interminably, endlessly, ceaselessly, unendingly. **2** *his search led him, at length, to Seattle:* after a long time, eventually, in time, finally, at (long) last, in the end, ultimately.

lengthen verb **1** *he lengthened his stride to keep up with her:* **elongate**, make longer, extend; expand, widen, broaden, enlarge. **2** *throughout spring, the days are lengthening:* **grow/get longer**, draw out. **3** *you'll need to lengthen the cooking time:* **prolong**, make longer, increase, extend, expand, protract, stretch out.
– OPPOSITES shorten.

lengthy adjective **1** *a lengthy civil war:* **(very) long**, long-lasting, prolonged, extended. **2** *the board held lengthy discussions:* **protracted**, overlong, long-drawn-out; verbose, wordy, prolix, long-winded; tedious, boring, interminable.
– OPPOSITES short.

leniency noun **mercifulness**, mercy, clemency, forgiveness; tolerance, forbearance, humanity, charity, indulgence, mildness; pity, sympathy, compassion, understanding.

lenient adjective *the courts may be more lenient with female offenders:* **merciful**, forgiving, forbearing, tolerant, charitable, humane, indulgent, easy-going, magnanimous, sympathetic, compassionate.
– OPPOSITES severe.

lesbian noun **homosexual woman**; informal les, lesbo, lezzy, dyke.
– OPPOSITES heterosexual.
adjective **homosexual**; informal les, lesbo, lezzy, butch, dykey.
– OPPOSITES straight.

lesion noun **wound**, injury, bruise, abrasion, contusion; ulcer, ulceration, (running) sore, abscess; Medicine trauma.

less pronoun *the fare is less than £1:* **not so/as much as**, under, below.
– OPPOSITES more.
determiner *there was less noise now that Des had left:* **not so much**, smaller, slighter, shorter, reduced; fewer.
adverb *we must use the car less:* **not so/as much**, to a lesser degree, to a smaller extent.

preposition *you pay the list price less 10 per cent:* **minus**, subtracting, discounted by, excepting, without.
– OPPOSITES plus.

lessen verb **1** *exercise lessens the risk of heart disease:* **reduce**, make less/smaller, minimize, decrease; allay, assuage, alleviate, attenuate, ease, dull, deaden, blunt, moderate, mitigate, dampen, soften, tone down, dilute, weaken. **2** *the pain began to lessen:* **grow less**, grow smaller, decrease, diminish, decline, subside, abate; fade, die down/off, let up, ease off, tail off, drop (off/away), fall, dwindle, ebb, wane, recede. **3** *his behaviour lessened him in their eyes:* **diminish**, degrade, discredit, devalue, belittle.
– OPPOSITES increase.

lesser adjective **1** *his was a lesser offence:* **less important**, minor, secondary, subsidiary, marginal, ancillary, auxiliary, supplementary, peripheral; inferior, insignificant, unimportant, petty. **2** *you look down on us lesser mortals:* **subordinate**, minor, inferior, second-class, subservient, lowly, humble.
– OPPOSITES greater, superior.

lesson noun **1** *a maths lesson on Thursday afternoon:* **class**, session, seminar, tutorial, lecture, period. **2** *they should be industrious at their lessons:* **exercises**, assignments, schoolwork, homework. **3** *I was reading the lesson in assembly:* **Bible reading**, scripture, text. **4** *Stuart's accident should be a lesson to all parents:* **warning**, deterrent, caution; example, exemplar, message, moral.

lest conjunction *he cut the remark out of his speech, lest it should offend people:* **(just) in case**, for fear that, in order to avoid.

let verb **1** *let him sleep for now:* **allow**, permit, give permission to, give leave to, authorize, sanction, grant the right to, license, empower, enable, entitle; assent to, consent to, agree to, acquiesce in, tolerate, countenance, give one's blessing to, give assent to, give someone/something the nod; informal give the green light to, give the go-ahead to, give the thumbs up to, OK; formal accede to. **2** *Wilcox opened the door to let her through:* **allow (to go)**, permit to pass; make way for. **3** *they've let their flat:* **rent (out)**, let out, lease, hire (out), sublet, sublease.
– OPPOSITES prevent, prohibit.
■ **let someone down** *it's the other players who have let the team down:* **fail**, fall short, disappoint, disillusion; abandon, desert, leave stranded, leave in the lurch; N. Amer. bail on.
■ **let something down** *I put on a skirt that Sylvie had let down for me:* lengthen, make longer.
■ **let fly 1** *he let fly with a brick:* **hurl**, fling, throw, propel, pitch, lob, toss, launch; shoot, fire, blast; informal chuck, sling, heave. **2** *she suddenly let fly at Geoffrey:* **lose one's temper with**, lash out at, scold, chastise, chide, rant

at, inveigh against, rail against; explode, burst out, let someone have it; informal carpet, give someone a rocket, tear someone off a strip; formal excoriate.

■ **let go** *apply the brakes before you let go of the trolley:* release, loose/loosen one's hold on, relinquish; archaic unhand.

■ **let someone go** *I was sorry we had to let him go after such a short period:* make redundant, dismiss, discharge, lay off, give notice to, axe; informal sack, fire, give someone their cards, give someone their marching orders, send packing, give someone the boot/push, give someone the (old) heave-ho.

■ **let someone in** *a young lady came to the gate and let me in:* allow to enter, allow in, admit, open the door to; receive, welcome, greet.

■ **let someone in on something** *he asked to be let in on the joke:* include, count in, admit, allow to share in, let participate in, inform about, tell about.

■ **let something off** *the kids let off some fireworks in the garden:* detonate, discharge, explode, set off, light, fire off.

■ **let someone off 1** (informal) *I'll let you off this time, but don't do it again:* pardon, forgive; acquit, absolve, exonerate, clear, vindicate; informal let someone off the hook; formal exculpate. **2** *he let me off work early:* excuse from, exempt from, spare from.

■ **let on** (informal) **1** *I never let on that I felt so anxious:* reveal, make known, tell, disclose, mention, divulge, let slip, give away, make public; blab; informal let the cat out of the bag, give the game away. **2** *they all let on they didn't hear me:* pretend, feign, affect, make out, make believe, simulate.

■ **let something out 1** *I let out a cry of triumph:* utter, emit, give (vent to), produce, issue, express, voice, release. **2** *she let out that he'd given her a lift home:* reveal, make known, tell, disclose, mention, divulge, let slip, give away, let it be known, blurt out.

■ **let someone out** *they should never have let Caroline out of hospital in that state:* release, liberate, (set) free, let go, discharge; set/turn loose, allow to leave.

■ **let up** (informal) **1** *the rain had let up, so we went for a walk:* abate, lessen, decrease, diminish, subside, relent, slacken, die down/off, ease (off), tail off, ebb, wane, dwindle, fade; stop, cease, finish. **2** *you never let up, do you?* relax, ease up/off, slow down; pause, break (off), take a break, rest, stop; informal take a breather.

let-down noun **disappointment**, anticlimax, comedown, non-event, fiasco, setback, blow; informal washout, damp squib.

lethal adjective *in the wrong hands it can be a lethal weapon | the pills proved lethal:* **deadly**, fatal, mortal, death-dealing, life-threatening, murderous, killing; poisonous, toxic, noxious, venomous; literary deathly.
– OPPOSITES harmless, safe.

lethargic adjective *she became depressed and lethargic after he left:* **sluggish**, inert, inactive, slow, torpid, lifeless; languid, listless, lazy, idle, indolent, shiftless, slothful, apathetic, weary, tired, fatigued.

lethargy noun **sluggishness**, inertia, inactivity, inaction, slowness, torpor, torpidity, lifelessness, listlessness, languor, languidness, laziness, idleness, indolence, shiftlessness, sloth, apathy, passivity, weariness, tiredness, lassitude, fatigue.
– OPPOSITES vigour, energy.

letter noun **1** *her name was spelt out in half-inch letters on a gold chain:* **character**, sign, symbol, mark, figure, rune. **2** *she received a letter from Jerry:* **message**, (written) communication, note, line, missive, dispatch; correspondence, news, information, intelligence, word; post, mail; formal epistle. **3** *he is truly a man of letters:* **(book) learning**, scholarship, erudition, education, knowledge; intellect, intelligence, enlightenment, wisdom, sagacity, culture.

■ **to the letter** *he followed her instructions to the letter:* strictly, precisely, exactly, accurately, closely, faithfully, religiously, punctiliously, literally, verbatim, in every detail.

let-up noun (informal) *there can be no let-up in the war on drugs:* **abatement**, lessening, decrease, diminishing, diminution, decline, relenting, remission, slackening, weakening, relaxation, dying down, easing off, tailing off, dropping away/off; respite, break, interval, hiatus, suspension, cessation, stop, pause.

level adjective **1** *the wall coverings look best on a smooth and level surface:* **flat**, smooth, even, uniform, plane, flush, plumb. **2** *he did his best to keep his voice level:* **unchanging**, steady, unvarying, even, uniform, regular, constant, invariable, unaltering; calm, unemotional, composed, equable, unruffled, serene, tranquil. **3** *at half-time the scores were level:* **equal**, even, drawn, tied, all square, neck and neck, level pegging, on a par, evenly matched; informal even-steven(s). **4** *his eyes were level with hers:* **aligned**, on the same level as, on a level, at the same height as, in line.
– OPPOSITES uneven, unsteady, unequal.
noun **1** *the post is at a senior level:* **rank**, standing, status, position; echelon, degree, grade, gradation, stage, standard, rung; class, stratum, group, grouping, set, classification. **2** *a high level of employment:* **quantity**, amount, extent, measure, degree, volume, size, magnitude, intensity, proportion. **3** *the level of the water is rising:* **height**; altitude, elevation. **4** *the museum tour ends on the sixth level:* **floor**, storey, deck.
verb **1** *tilt the tin to level the mixture:* **make level**, level out/off, make even, even off/out, make flat, flatten, smooth (out), make uniform. **2** *bulldozers levelled the building:* **raze (to the ground)**, demolish, flatten,

topple, destroy; tear down, knock down, pull down, bulldoze. **3** *he levelled his opponent with a single blow:* **knock down/out**, knock to the ground, lay out, prostrate, flatten, floor, fell; informal KO, kayo. **4** *Carl levelled the score with a superb goal:* **equalize**, make equal, equal, even (up), make level. **5** *he levelled his pistol at me:* **aim**, point, direct, train, focus, turn. **6** (informal) *I knew you'd level with me:* **be frank**, be open, be honest, tell the truth, tell all, hide nothing, be straight; informal be upfront.
■ **on the level** (informal) *she was either on the level or a really good actress:* **genuine**, straight, honest, above board, fair, true, sincere, straightforward; informal upfront; N. Amer. informal on the up and up.

level-headed adjective *he's a calm level-headed guy:* **sensible**, practical, realistic, prudent, pragmatic, wise, reasonable, rational, mature, judicious, sound, sober, businesslike, no-nonsense, composed, calm, {cool, calm, and collected}, confident, well balanced, equable, cool-headed, self-possessed, having one's feet on the ground; informal unflappable, together.
– OPPOSITES excitable.

lever noun **1** *you can insert a lever and prise the rail off:* **crowbar**, bar, jemmy. **2** *he pulled the lever but nothing happened:* **handle**, grip, pull, switch.
verb *he levered the door open:* **prise**, force, wrench, pull, wrest, heave; N. Amer. pry; informal jemmy.

leverage noun **1** *the long handles provide increased leverage:* **grip**, purchase, hold; support, anchorage, force, strength. **2** *high levels of unionization gave the dockers significant leverage in negotiations:* **influence**, power, authority, weight, sway, pull, control, say, advantage, pressure; informal clout, muscle, teeth.

levitate noun **float**, rise (into the air), hover, be suspended, glide, hang, fly, soar up.

levity noun *he tried to inject a note of levity into the proceedings:* **light-heartedness**, high spirits, vivacity, liveliness, cheerfulness, cheeriness, humour, gaiety, fun, jocularity, hilarity, frivolity, frivolousness, amusement, mirth, laughter, merriment, glee, comedy, wit, wittiness, jollity, joviality.
– OPPOSITES seriousness.

levy verb *a proposal to levy VAT on fuel:* **impose**, charge, exact, raise, collect.
noun *the levy on spirits has risen:* **tax**, tariff, toll, excise, duty, imposition, impost; formal mulct.

lewd adjective **1** *a lewd old man:* **lecherous**, lustful, licentious, lascivious, dirty, prurient, salacious, lubricious, libidinous, debauched, depraved, degenerate, perverted; informal horny; Brit. informal randy. **2** *a lewd song:* **vulgar**, crude, smutty, dirty, filthy, obscene, pornographic, coarse, off colour, unseemly, indecent, salacious; rude,

racy, risqué, naughty, earthy, spicy, bawdy, ribald; informal blue, raunchy, X-rated, nudge-nudge, porno; N. Amer. informal raw; euphemistic adult.
– OPPOSITES chaste, clean.

lexicon noun **dictionary**, wordbook, vocabulary list, glossary, word-finder, thesaurus.

liability noun **1** *journalists' attempts to avoid liability for defamation:* **accountability**, (legal) responsibility, answerability; blame, blameworthiness, culpability. **2** *they have huge assets and some equally big liabilities:* **financial obligations**, debts, arrears, dues. **3** *she had come to be seen as an electoral liability:* **hindrance**, encumbrance, burden, handicap, nuisance, inconvenience, embarrassment; obstacle, impediment, disadvantage, weakness, shortcoming; millstone round one's neck, albatross, Achilles heel.
– OPPOSITES immunity, asset.

liable adjective **1** *the defendants are liable for negligence:* **(legally) responsible**, accountable, answerable, at fault, culpable, guilty. **2** *my income is liable to fluctuate wildly:* **likely**, inclined, tending, disposed, apt, predisposed, prone, given. **3** *low-lying areas may well be liable to flooding:* **exposed**, prone, subject, susceptible, vulnerable, in danger of, at risk of.

liaise verb **cooperate**, work together, collaborate; communicate, network, interface, link up.

liaison noun **1** *the Bank of England works in close liaison with the Treasury:* **cooperation**, contact, association, connection, collaboration, communication, alliance, partnership. **2** *Dave was my White House liaison and all-round troubleshooter:* **intermediary**, mediator, middleman, contact, link, linkman, linkwoman, linkperson, go-between, representative, agent. **3** *she became involved in a liaison with William:* **(love) affair**, relationship, romance, attachment, fling, amour, affair of the heart, (romantic) entanglement; informal hanky-panky.

liar noun **fibber**, deceiver, perjurer, false witness, fabricator; romancer, fabulist; informal storyteller.

libel noun *she sued two newspapers for libel | our reputation could be ruined by a libel like that:* **defamation (of character)**, character assassination, calumny, misrepresentation; aspersions, denigration, vilification, disparagement, derogation, insult, slander, malicious gossip, traducement; lie, slur, smear, untruth, false report; informal mud-slinging, bad-mouthing.
verb *she alleged that the magazine had libelled her:* **defame**, malign, slander, blacken someone's name, sully someone's reputation, traduce, smear, cast aspersions on, drag someone's name through the mud/mire, besmirch, tarnish, taint, tell lies about, stain, vilify,

denigrate, disparage, run down, stigmatize, discredit; N. Amer. slur.

libellous adjective **defamatory**, denigratory, vilifying, disparaging, derogatory, calumnious, slanderous, false, untrue, traducing, maligning, insulting, scurrilous.

liberal adjective **1** *the values that are characteristic of a liberal society:* **tolerant**, unprejudiced, broad-minded, open-minded, enlightened; permissive, free (and easy), easy-going, libertarian, indulgent, lenient. **2** *the Prime Minister launched a liberal social agenda:* **progressive**, advanced, modern, forward-looking, forward-thinking, enlightened, reformist, radical; informal go-ahead. **3** *a liberal education:* **wide-ranging**, broad-based, general. **4** *this is a liberal interpretation of the divorce laws:* **flexible**, broad, loose, rough, free, general, non-literal, non-specific, imprecise, vague, indefinite. **5** *apply liberal amounts of adhesive:* **abundant**, copious, ample, plentiful, generous, lavish, luxuriant, profuse, considerable, prolific, rich; literary plenteous. **6** *they were liberal with their cash:* **generous**, open-handed, unsparing, unstinting, ungrudging, lavish, free, munificent, bountiful, beneficent, benevolent, big-hearted, philanthropic, charitable, altruistic, unselfish; literary bounteous.
– OPPOSITES reactionary, strict, miserly.

liberate verb *Lincoln's proclamation finally liberated the slaves:* **(set) free**, release, let out/go, set/let loose, save, rescue; emancipate.
– OPPOSITES imprison, enslave.

liberation noun **1** *the liberation of prisoners was a high priority:* **freeing**, release, rescue, setting free; freedom, liberty; emancipation; historical manumission. **2** *the battle for women's liberation:* **freedom**, equality, equal rights, emancipation, enfranchisement.
– OPPOSITES confinement, oppression.

liberator noun **rescuer**, saviour, deliverer, emancipator.

liberty noun **1** *we enjoy the liberty to pursue our own interests:* **freedom**, independence, free rein, license, self-determination, free will, latitude. **2** *parliamentary government is the essence of British liberty:* **independence**, freedom, autonomy, sovereignty, self-government, self-rule, self-determination; civil liberties, human rights. **3** *one should have the liberty to go where one pleases:* **right**, prerogative, entitlement, privilege, permission, sanction, authorization, authority, licence.
– OPPOSITES constraint, slavery.
■ **at liberty 1** *he was at liberty for three months before being recaptured:* **free**, (on the) loose, at large, unconfined; escaped, out. **2** *your great-aunt was at liberty to divide her estate how she chose:* **free**, permitted, allowed, authorized, able, entitled, eligible.

libidinous adjective *he couldn't come to terms with his own libidinous impulses:* **lustful**, lecherous, lascivious, lewd, carnal, salacious, prurient, licentious, libertine, lubricious, dissolute, debauched, depraved, degenerate, decadent, dissipated, wanton, promiscuous; informal horny, goatish; Brit. informal randy.

libido noun **sex drive**, (sexual) appetite; (sexual) desire, passion, sexiness, sensuality, sexuality, lust.

licence noun **1** *a driving licence:* **permit**, certificate, document, documentation, authorization, warrant; certification, credentials; pass, papers. **2** *the teachers had licence to administer beatings:* **permission**, authority, right, a free hand, leave, authorization, entitlement, privilege, prerogative; liberty, freedom, power. **3** *they manufacture fashion footwear under licence:* **franchise**, permission, consent, sanction, warrant, warranty, charter. **4** *the army was given too much licence:* **freedom**, liberty, free rein, latitude, independence, scope, impunity, carte blanche.

license verb *he was licensed to sell spirits:* **permit**, allow, authorize, grant/give authority to, grant/give permission to; certify, empower, entitle, enable, give approval to, let, qualify.
– OPPOSITES ban.

licentious adjective *he was a puritan in a licentious age:* **dissolute**, dissipated, debauched, degenerate, immoral, naughty, wanton, decadent, depraved, sinful, corrupt; lustful, lecherous, lascivious, libidinous, prurient, lubricious, lewd, promiscuous.
– OPPOSITES moral.

lick verb **1** *the spaniel licked the gravy off his hand:* tongue; lap, slurp. **2** *she stared into the flames licking round the coal:* **flicker**, play, flit, dance.

lid noun *the lid of a saucepan:* **cover**, top, cap, covering.

lie[1] noun *loyalty had made him tell lies:* **untruth**, falsehood, fib, fabrication, deception, invention, (piece of) fiction, falsification; (little) white lie, half-truth, exaggeration; informal tall story, whopper; Brit. informal porky (pie).
– OPPOSITES truth.
verb *he had lied to the police:* **tell a lie**, fib, dissemble, dissimulate, tell a white lie, perjure oneself, commit perjury; informal lie through one's teeth.
■ **give the lie to** *the success of our exports gives the lie to claims about the state of manufacturing:* **disprove**, contradict, negate, deny, refute, belie, invalidate, discredit, debunk; challenge, call into question; informal shoot full of holes, shoot down (in flames); formal confute, gainsay.

lie[2] verb **1** *he was lying on his bed:* **recline**, lie down/back, be recumbent, be prostrate, be supine, be prone, be stretched out, sprawl, rest, repose, lounge, loll. **2** *her handbag lay on a chair at the other end of the room:*

be placed, be situated, be positioned, rest. **3** *a tiny principality lying on the border of Switzerland and Austria:* **be situated**, be located, be placed, be found, be sited. **4** *his body lies in a crypt below the cathedral:* **be buried**, be interred, be laid to rest, rest, be entombed. **5** *the difficulty lies in building real quality into the products:* **consist**, be inherent, be present, be contained, exist, reside.
– OPPOSITES stand.

■ **lie low** *we'll have to lie low and wait until dark:* hide (out), go into hiding, conceal oneself, keep out of sight, go to earth/ground; informal hole up.

lieutenant noun **deputy**, second in command, right-hand man/woman, number two, assistant, aide; informal sidekick.

life noun **1** *the joy of giving life to a child:* **existence**, being, living, animation; sentience, creation, viability. **2** *the numerous threats to life on this planet:* **living beings/creatures**, the living; human/animal/plant life, fauna, flora, the ecosystem, the biosphere, the environment; human beings, humanity, humankind, mankind, man. **3** *he had a miserable life:* **existence**, lifestyle, situation, fate, lot. **4** *we never spoke during the last nine months of his life:* **lifetime**, life span, days, time on earth. **5** *the life of a parliament is limited to five years:* **duration**, lifetime, existence. **6** *he is happy and full of life:* **vivacity**, animation, liveliness, vitality, verve, high spirits, exuberance, zest, buoyancy, enthusiasm, energy, vigour, dynamism, elan, gusto, brio, bounce, spirit, fire; (hustle and) bustle, movement; informal oomph, pizzazz, pep, zing, zip, vim. **7** *more than 1,500 lives were lost in the accident:* **person**, human being, individual, soul. **8** *I am reading a life of Chopin:* **biography**, autobiography, life story/history, profile, chronicle, account, portrait; informal biog, bio. **9** *I'll miss you, but that's life:* **the way of the world**, the way things go, the human condition; fate, destiny, providence, karma, fortune, luck, chance; informal the way the cookie crumbles.
– OPPOSITES death.

■ **come to life** *I heard the familiar sounds of a barracks coming to life:* become active, come alive, wake up, awaken, arouse, rouse, stir; literary waken.

■ **give one's life 1** *he's devoted to his queen and would give his life for her:* die, lay down one's life, sacrifice oneself, offer one's life. **2** *he gave his life to the company:* dedicate oneself, devote oneself, give oneself, surrender oneself.

life-and-death adjective *it was a life-and-death decision:* **vital**, of vital importance, crucial, critical, urgent, pivotal, momentous, important, key, serious, grave, significant; informal earth-shattering.
– OPPOSITES trivial.

lifeblood noun *information is the lifeblood of*

a successful economy: **life (force)**, essential constituent, driving force, vital spark, inspiration, stimulus, essence, crux, heart, soul, core.

life-giving adjective *the tiny strips of life-giving vegetation which made it possible for some birds and animals to exist:* **sustaining**, invigorating, stimulating; life-preserving, life-sustaining, vital.
– OPPOSITES death-dealing.

lifeless adjective **1** *they dropped the lifeless body onto the ground:* **dead**, stiff, cold, rigid, limp. **2** *a lifeless rag doll:* **inanimate**, without life, inert, insentient. **3** *a lifeless planet:* **barren**, sterile, bare, desolate, stark, arid, infertile, uncultivated, uninhabited; bleak, colourless, characterless, soulless. **4** *a lifeless performance:* **lacklustre**, spiritless, apathetic, torpid, lethargic; dull, monotonous, boring, tedious, dreary, unexciting, expressionless, emotionless, colourless, characterless.
– OPPOSITES alive, animate, lively.

lifelike adjective *an extremely lifelike sketch of a baby elephant:* **realistic**, true to life, representational, faithful, exact, precise, detailed, vivid, graphic, natural, naturalistic.
– OPPOSITES unrealistic.

lifelong adjective *this working relationship blossomed into a lifelong friendship:* **lasting**, long-lasting, long-term, constant, stable, established, steady, enduring, permanent.
– OPPOSITES ephemeral.

lifestyle noun *the privileged lifestyle of affluent New Yorkers:* **way of life/living**, life, situation, fate, lot; conduct, behaviour, customs, habits, ways, mores.

lifetime noun **1** *he made an exceptional contribution to conservation during his lifetime:* **lifespan**, life, days, duration of life, one's time (on earth), existence, one's career. **2** *the lifetime of workstations is between three and five years:* **duration**, (active) life, life expectancy, functioning period, period of effectiveness/usefulness. **3** *it would take a lifetime to do it properly:* **all one's life**, a very long time, an eternity, years, aeons; informal ages (and ages), an age.

lift verb **1** *try and lift the pack on to your back:* **raise**, hoist, heave, haul up, uplift, heft, raise up/aloft, elevate, hold high; pick up, grab, take up, scoop up, snatch up; winch up, jack up, lever up; informal hump. **2** *the news lifted his flagging spirits:* **boost**, raise, buoy up, elevate, cheer up, perk up, uplift, brighten up, ginger up, gladden, encourage, stimulate, revive; informal buck up. **3** *by noon, the fog had lifted:* **clear**, rise, disperse, dissipate, disappear, vanish, dissolve. **4** *the ban has finally been lifted:* **cancel**, remove, withdraw, revoke, rescind, annul, void, discontinue, end, stop, terminate.
– OPPOSITES drop, put down.

noun **1** *Alice went up in the lift:* **elevator**, paternoster (lift); dumb waiter. **2** *give me a lift up, Martha:* **push**, hoist, heave, thrust, shove. **3** *he gave me a lift to the airport:* **(car) ride**, run, drive. **4** *that goal will give his confidence a real lift:* **boost**, fillip, stimulus, impetus, encouragement, spur, push; improvement, enhancement; informal shot in the arm.

■ **lift off** take off, become airborne, take to the air, take wing; be launched, blast off.

light[1] noun **1** *the light of the candles filled the room:* **illumination**, brightness, luminescence, luminosity, shining, gleaming, gleam, brilliance, radiance, lustre, glowing, glow, blaze, glare, dazzle; sunlight, moonlight, starlight, lamplight, firelight; ray of light, beam of light; literary effulgence. **2** *there was a light on in the hall:* **lamp**; headlight, headlamp, sidelight; street light, floodlight; lantern; torch, flashlight. **3** *we'll be driving home in the light:* **daylight (hours)**, daytime, day; natural light, sunlight. **4** *after this, he saw the problem in a different light:* **aspect**, angle, slant, approach, interpretation, viewpoint, standpoint, context, hue, complexion.
– OPPOSITES darkness.

verb *Alan lit a fire in the hearth:* **set alight**, set light to, set burning, set on fire, set fire to, put/set a match to, ignite, kindle, spark (off).
– OPPOSITES extinguish.

adjective **1** *it's a very light room:* **bright**, full of light, well lit, well illuminated, sunny. **2** *I prefer light pastel shades for the walls:* **light-coloured**, light-toned, pale, pale-coloured, pastel. **3** *a young woman with light hair:* **fair**, light-coloured, blond(e), golden, flaxen.
– OPPOSITES dark, gloomy.

■ **bring something to light** *the irregularities were first brought to light by an internal audit:* reveal, disclose, expose, uncover, show up, unearth, dig up/out, bring to notice, identify, hunt out, nose out.

■ **come to light** *the thefts came to light last year:* be discovered, be uncovered, be unearthed, come out, become known, become apparent, appear, materialize, emerge.

■ **in the light of** *in the light of this report, I see no reason to continue:* taking into consideration/account, considering, bearing in mind, taking note of, in view of.

■ **light up** *the dashboard suddenly lit up:* become bright, brighten, lighten, shine, gleam, flare, blaze, glint, sparkle, shimmer, glisten, scintillate.

■ **light something up 1** *a flare lit up the night sky:* make bright, brighten, illuminate, lighten, throw/cast light on, shine on, irradiate; literary illumine. **2** *her enthusiasm lit up her face:* animate, irradiate, brighten, cheer up, enliven.

■ **throw/cast/shed light on** *no one could shed any light on this mysterious accident:* explain, elucidate, clarify, clear up, interpret.

light[2] adjective **1** *it's light, portable, and you can use it anywhere:* **easy to lift**, not heavy, lightweight; easy to carry, portable. **2** *she had on a light cotton robe:* **flimsy**, lightweight, summerweight, insubstantial, thin; delicate, floaty, gauzy, diaphanous. **3** *she is light on her feet:* **nimble**, agile, lithe, limber, lissom, graceful; light-footed, fleet-footed, quick, quick-moving, spry, sprightly; informal twinkle-toed; literary fleet. **4** *you need plenty of sun and a light soil:* **friable**, sandy, workable, crumbly, loose. **5** *we had a light dinner:* **small**, modest, simple. **6** *I was put on light duties:* **easy**, simple, undemanding, untaxing; informal cushy. **7** *light entertainment | light reading:* **entertaining**, lightweight, diverting, undemanding, middle-of-the-road; frivolous, superficial, trivial. **8** *I pitched in with a light heart:* **carefree**, light-hearted, cheerful, cheery, happy, merry, jolly, blithe, bright, sunny; buoyant, bubbly, jaunty, bouncy, breezy, optimistic, positive, upbeat, ebullient. **9** *he heard light footsteps:* **gentle**, delicate, soft, dainty.
– OPPOSITES heavy.

light[3] verb
■ **light on/upon** *presumably the author has lighted upon some new material in his research:* come across, chance on, hit on, happen on, stumble on/across, blunder on, find, discover, uncover, come up with.

lighten[1] verb **1** *the sky was beginning to lighten:* **become/grow lighter**, brighten. **2** *the first touch of dawn lightened the sky:* **light up**, brighten, illuminate, irradiate; literary illumine. **3** *he used lemon juice to lighten his hair:* **whiten**, make whiter, bleach, blanch, make paler; fade.
– OPPOSITES darken.

lighten[2] verb **1** *we are lightening the burden of taxation:* **make lighter**, lessen, reduce, decrease, diminish, ease, alleviate, mitigate, allay, relieve, palliate, assuage. **2** *I made an attempt to lighten her spirits:* **raise**, lift; brighten, gladden, hearten, perk up, ginger up, enliven, boost, buoy (up), uplift, revive, restore, revitalize.
– OPPOSITES increase, depress.

light-headed adjective *the fumes made him light-headed:* **dizzy**, giddy, faint, muzzy, vertiginous; informal woozy.

light-hearted adjective *a very light-hearted approach to music:* **carefree**, cheerful, cheery, happy, merry, glad, playful, jolly, jovial, joyful, gleeful, ebullient, high-spirited, lively, blithe, bright, sunny, buoyant, vivacious, bubbly, jaunty, bouncy, breezy; entertaining, amusing, diverting; informal chirpy, upbeat.
– OPPOSITES miserable.

lightly adverb **1** *Maisie kissed him lightly on the cheek:* **softly**, gently, faintly, delicately. **2** *season the stock very lightly:* **sparingly**, slightly, sparsely, moderately, delicately.
– OPPOSITES hard, heavily.

lightweight adjective **1** *a comfortable lightweight jacket:* **thin**, light, flimsy,

insubstantial; summerweight, summery.
2 *snobs will no doubt dismiss the show
as lightweight:* **trivial**, insubstantial,
superficial, shallow, unintellectual,
undemanding, frivolous.
– OPPOSITES heavy.

like¹ verb **1** *I rather like Colonel Maitland:*
be fond of, be attached to, have a soft
spot for, have a liking for, have regard
for, think well of, admire, respect, esteem;
be attracted to, fancy, find attractive, be
keen on, be taken with; informal rate. **2** *Mark
quite likes veal:* **enjoy**, have a taste for,
have a preference for, have a liking for,
be partial to, take pleasure in, be keen on,
have a penchant/passion for, find enjoyable;
appreciate, love, adore, relish; informal have a
thing about, be into, be mad about/for, be
hooked on, go a bundle on. **3** *feel free to say
what you like:* **choose**, please, wish, want,
see/think fit, care to, will.
– OPPOSITES hate.

like² preposition **1** *you're acting like a teacher:*
similar to, the same as, identical to. **2** *the
figure landed like a cat and scampered into
the shadows:* **in the same way/manner as**,
in the manner of, in a similar way to. **3** *cities
like Birmingham need our backing:* **such
as**, for example, for instance; in particular,
namely, viz. **4** *Richard sounded scared, which
isn't like him:* **characteristic of**, typical of,
in character with.
noun *we shan't see his like again:* **equal**,
match, equivalent, counterpart, twin,
parallel.
adjective *I have found myself in a like
situation:* **similar**, much the same,
comparable, corresponding, resembling,
alike, analogous, parallel, equivalent,
related, kindred; identical, same, matching.
– OPPOSITES dissimilar.

likeable adjective **pleasant**, nice, friendly,
agreeable, affable, amiable, genial,
personable, charming, popular, good-
natured, engaging, appealing, endearing,
convivial, congenial, winning, delightful,
enchanting, lovable, adorable, sweet; informal
darling, lovely.
– OPPOSITES unpleasant.

likelihood noun *the changes could increase
the likelihood of a miscarriage of justice:*
probability, chance, prospect, possibility,
likeliness, odds, feasibility; risk, threat,
danger; hope, promise.

likely adjective **1** *it seemed likely that a
scandal of some sort would eventually
break:* **probable**, (distinctly) possible, to be
expected, odds-on, plausible, imaginable;
expected, anticipated, predictable,
predicted, foreseeable; informal on the cards.
2 *a more likely explanation can be found
elsewhere:* **plausible**, reasonable, feasible,
acceptable, believable, credible, tenable,
conceivable. **3** *it didn't take long to find a
likely-looking place:* **suitable**, appropriate,

apposite, fit, fitting, acceptable, right;
promising, hopeful.
– OPPOSITES improbable, unbelievable.
adverb *he was most likely dead:* **probably**,
in all probability, presumably, no doubt,
doubtlessly; informal (as) like as not.

liken verb *the sculptures have been likened
to huge seashells:* **compare**, equate, draw an
analogy between, draw a parallel between;
link, associate, bracket together.
– OPPOSITES contrast.

likeness noun **1** *her likeness to Anne is
quite uncanny:* **resemblance**, similarity,
correspondence, analogy, uniformity,
conformity. **2** *the handle was carved in
the likeness of a naked woman:* **semblance**,
guise, appearance, (outward) form, shape,
image. **3** *few coins now bear the likeness of
the last president:* **image**, representation,
depiction, portrayal; picture, drawing,
sketch, painting, portrait, photograph,
study; statue, sculpture.
– OPPOSITES dissimilarity.

likewise adverb **1** *an ambush was out
of the question, likewise poison:* **also**, in
addition, too, as well; besides, moreover,
furthermore. **2** *encourage your family and
friends to do likewise:* **the same**, similarly,
correspondingly, in the same way, in similar
fashion.

liking noun *he had a liking for whisky:*
fondness, love, affection, penchant,
attachment; enjoyment, appreciation, taste,
passion; preference, partiality, predilection;
desire, fancy, inclination.

lilt noun *the Welsh lilt was gone and he talked
like a Londoner:* **cadence**, rise and fall,
inflection, intonation, rhythm, swing, beat,
pulse, tempo.

limb noun **1** *he rubbed his sore limbs:* **arm**, **leg**,
appendage; archaic member. **2** *the limbs of the
tree creaked in the wind:* **branch**, bough.
■ **out on a limb** *the portrayal of Scotland
as being out on a limb:* isolated, set apart,
separate, cut off, solitary.
■ **go out on a limb** *she has gone out on a
limb to support unglamorous causes like Aids
victims:* expose oneself, stand up (and be
counted); take a chance/risk/gamble; informal
stick one's neck out.

limber
■ **limber up** warm up, loosen up, get into
condition, get into shape, practise, train,
stretch.

limbo
■ **in limbo** *the measure has been in limbo
since Congress took a 10-day break:* in
abeyance, unattended to, unfinished;
suspended, deferred, postponed, put off,
pending, on ice, in cold storage; unresolved,
undetermined, up in the air; informal on the
back burner, on hold.

limelight noun *she couldn't conceal her
excitement at being back in the limelight:*
attention, public attention/interest,

the public eye, the glare of publicity, prominence, the spotlight.
– OPPOSITES obscurity.

limit noun 1 *the campus was outside the city limits:* **boundary (line)**, border, bound, partition line, frontier, edge, demarcation line; perimeter, outside, outline, confine, periphery, margin, rim. 2 *the police have set a limit of 4,500 supporters for Saturday's match:* **maximum**, ceiling, limitation, upper limit; restriction, check, control, restraint. 3 *our resources are stretched to the limit:* **utmost**, breaking point, greatest extent.
verb *the pressure to limit costs:* **restrict**, curb, cap, (hold in) check, restrain, put a brake on, freeze, peg; regulate, control, govern, delimit.

limitation noun 1 *there have been calls for a limitation on the number of newcomers:* **restriction**, curb, restraint, control, check; impediment, obstacle, obstruction, bar, barrier, block, deterrent, ceiling. 2 *he is aware of his own limitations:* **imperfection**, flaw, defect, failing, shortcoming, weak point, deficiency, failure, frailty, weakness, foible.
– OPPOSITES increase, strength.

limited adjective *the competition for limited resources:* **restricted**, finite, little, tight, slight, in short supply, short; meagre, scanty, sparse, insubstantial, deficient, inadequate, insufficient, paltry, poor, minimal.
– OPPOSITES ample, boundless.

limitless adjective *our funds are not limitless, so don't squander them:* **boundless**, unbounded, unlimited, illimitable; infinite, endless, never-ending, unending, everlasting, untold, immeasurable, bottomless, fathomless; unceasing, interminable, inexhaustible, constant, perpetual.

limp[1] verb *she limped out of the house:* **hobble**, walk with a limp, walk lamely/unevenly, walk haltingly, falter.
noun *he still walked with a limp:* **lameness**, hobble, uneven gait.

limp[2] adjective 1 *he greeted me with a limp handshake:* **soft**, flaccid, loose, slack, lax; floppy, drooping, droopy, sagging. 2 *we were all limp with exhaustion:* **weak**, dead, comatose, prostrate, dead on one's feet; informal flat out. 3 *he delivered a limp and lacklustre speech:* **uninspired**, uninspiring, insipid, flat, lifeless, vapid.
– OPPOSITES firm, energetic.

limpid adjective 1 *a limpid rock pool:* **clear**, transparent, glassy, crystal clear, crystalline, translucent, unclouded. 2 *his limpid prose style is to be admired:* **lucid**, clear, plain, understandable, intelligible, comprehensible, coherent, explicit, unambiguous, simple, vivid, sharp, crystal clear.
– OPPOSITES opaque.

line[1] noun 1 *he drew a line through the name:* dash, rule, bar, score; underline, underscore, stroke, slash, solidus; stripe, strip, band, belt; Brit. oblique. 2 *there were lines round her eyes:* **wrinkle**, furrow, crease, crinkle, crow's foot. 3 *the classic lines of the vehicle's exterior:* **contour**, outline, configuration, shape, figure, delineation, profile, silhouette. 4 *he headed the ball over the line:* **boundary (line)**, limit, border, borderline, bounding line, frontier, demarcation line, dividing line, edge, margin, perimeter. 5 *he put the washing on the line:* **cord**, rope, string, cable, wire, thread, twine, strand. 6 *a line of soldiers:* **file**, rank, column, string, train, procession; row, queue; Brit. informal crocodile. 7 *he was adding up a line of figures:* **column**, row. 8 *this is just the latest in a long line of crass decisions:* **series**, sequence, succession, chain, string, set, cycle. 9 *the line of flight of some bees:* **course**, route, track, path, trajectory, profile. 10 *they took a very tough line with the industry:* **course (of action)**, procedure, technique, tactic, tack; policy, practice, approach, plan, programme, position, stance, philosophy. 11 *she was intent on pursuing her own line of thought:* **course**, direction, drift, tack, tendency, trend. 12 *he couldn't remember his lines:* **words**, part, script, speech. 13 *he is from a noble line:* **ancestry**, family, parentage, birth, descent, lineage, extraction, genealogy, roots, origin, background; stock, bloodline, pedigree. 14 *the opening line of the poem:* **sentence**, phrase, clause, utterance; passage, extract, quotation, quote, citation.
verb 1 *her face was lined with age:* **furrow**, wrinkle, crease, mark with lines. 2 *the driveway was lined by poplars:* **border**, edge, fringe, bound, rim.
■ **draw the line at** *I draw the line at badger-baiting:* stop short of, refuse to accept, baulk at; object to, take issue with, take exception to.
■ **in line 1** *the poor stood in line for food:* in a queue, in a row, in a file. 2 *the adverts are in line with the editorial style:* in agreement, in accord, in accordance, in harmony, in step, in compliance. 3 *hold the front sight in line with the bullseye:* in alignment, aligned, level, at the same height; abreast, side by side. 4 *the referee certainly kept him in line:* under control, in order, in check.
■ **in line for** *he was now in line for promotion:* a candidate for, in the running for, on the shortlist for, being considered for.
■ **lay it on the line** *I'm going to have to lay it on the line and tell them what I really think:* speak frankly/honestly, pull no punches, be blunt, not mince one's words, call a spade a spade; informal give it to someone straight.
■ **line up** *we entered the building and lined up at the counter:* form a queue/line, get into rows/columns, queue up, fall in; Military dress; Brit. informal form a crocodile.

■ **line someone/something up 1** *they lined them up and shot them:* stand/put in lines, stand/put in rows, align, range; Military dress. **2** *we've lined up an all-star cast:* assemble, get together, organize, prepare, arrange, pre-arrange, fix up, lay on; book, schedule, timetable.

■ **on the line** *it's police officers whose lives are on the line:* at risk, in danger, endangered, in jeopardy.

■ **toe the line** *sooner or later he has to learn to toe the line:* conform, obey/observe the rules, comply with the rules, abide by the rules; informal knuckle down.

line² verb *a cardboard box lined with a blanket:* **cover**, put a lining in, interline, face, back, pad.

lineage noun *George V, George VI, and other naval officers of royal lineage:* **ancestry**, family, parentage, birth, descent, line, extraction, derivation, genealogy, roots, origin, background; stock, bloodline, breeding, pedigree.

lined¹ adjective **1** *I prefer to use lined paper:* **ruled**, feint, striped, banded. **2** *his lined, weather-beaten face:* **wrinkled**, wrinkly, furrowed, wizened.
– OPPOSITES plain, smooth.

lined² adjective *lined curtains will keep out the light:* **covered**, backed, interlined; faced, padded.

line-up noun **1** *a star-studded line-up:* **list of performers**, cast, bill, programme. **2** *United's line-up for the final:* **list of players**, team, side, squad.

linger verb **1** *the crowd lingered for a while:* **wait (around)**, stay (put), remain; loiter, dawdle, dally, take one's time; informal stick around, hang around/round, hang on; archaic tarry. **2** *the infection can linger for many years:* **persist**, continue, remain, stay, endure, carry on, last, keep on/up.
– OPPOSITES vanish.

lingerie noun **(women's) underwear**, (women's) underclothes, underclothing, undergarments; nightwear, nightclothes; informal undies, frillies, underthings, unmentionables; Brit. informal smalls.

lingering adjective **1** *there were still a few lingering doubts:* **remaining**, surviving, persisting, abiding, nagging, niggling. **2** *he died a slow, lingering death:* **protracted**, prolonged, long-drawn-out, long-lasting.

linguistic adjective **verbal**, rhetorical, semantic.

lining noun **backing**, interlining, facing, padding, liner.

link noun **1** *a chain of steel links:* **loop**, ring, connection, connector, coupling, joint. **2** *the links between transport and the environment:* **connection**, relationship, association, linkage, tie-up. **3** *their links with the labour movement:* **bond**, tie, attachment, connection, relationship, association, affiliation.

verb **1** *four boxes were linked together:* **join**, connect, fasten, attach, bind, unite, combine, amalgamate; clamp, secure, fix, tie, couple, yoke. **2** *the evidence linking him with the accident:* **associate**, connect, relate, join, bracket.

lionize verb *the band's leader has been lionized by the music press:* **celebrate**, fête, glorify, honour, exalt, acclaim, admire, praise, extol, applaud, hail, venerate, eulogize; formal laud.
– OPPOSITES vilify.

lip noun *we crawled to the lip of the crater:* **edge**, rim, brim, border, verge, brink.

liquefy verb **make/become liquid**, condense, liquidize, melt; deliquesce.

liquid adjective **1** *liquid fertilizer is easier to apply:* **fluid**, liquefied; melted, molten, thawed, dissolved; Chemistry hydrous. **2** *her dark liquid eyes:* **clear**, limpid, crystal clear, crystalline, pellucid, unclouded. **3** *the liquid song of the birds:* **pure**, clear, mellifluous, dulcet, mellow, sweet, sweet-sounding, soft, melodious, harmonious. **4** *liquid assets:* **convertible**, disposable, usable, spendable.
– OPPOSITES solid.
noun *a vat of dark liquid:* **fluid**, moisture, wet, wetness; liquor, solution, juice.

liquidate verb **1** *the company was liquidated:* **close down**, wind up, put into liquidation, dissolve, disband. **2** *he would normally have liquidated his share portfolio:* **convert (to cash)**, cash in, sell off/up. **3** *the fund was raided for purposes other than liquidating the public debt:* **pay (off)**, pay in full, settle, clear, discharge, square, honour. **4** (informal) *they were liquidated in a series of bloody purges.* See KILL verb sense 1.

liquidize verb **purée**, cream, liquefy, blend.

liquor noun **1** *it is illegal to sell liquor to anyone under the age of 18:* **alcohol**, spirits, (alcoholic) drink, intoxicating liquor, intoxicant; informal booze, the hard stuff, grog, hooch. **2** *strain the liquor into the sauce:* **stock**, broth, bouillon, juice, liquid.

list¹ noun *a list of the world's wealthiest people:* **catalogue**, inventory, record, register, roll, file, index, directory, listing, checklist.
verb *the accounts are listed alphabetically:* **record**, register, make a list of, enter; itemize, enumerate, catalogue, file, log, minute, categorize, inventory; classify, group, sort, rank, alphabetize, index.

list² verb *the boat listed to starboard:* **lean (over)**, tilt, tip, heel (over), careen, cant, pitch, incline, slant, slope, bank.

listen verb **1** *are you listening carefully?* **hear**, pay attention, be attentive, attend, concentrate; keep one's ears open, prick up one's ears; informal be all ears, pin back one's ears; literary hark. **2** *policy-makers should listen to popular opinion:* **pay attention**, take heed, heed, take notice, take note, mind, mark, bear in mind, take into consideration/account.

■ **listen in** *anyone with the right equipment can listen in:* eavesdrop, spy, overhear, tap, bug, monitor.

listless adjective *she was pale and listless:* **lethargic**, enervated, spiritless, lifeless, vigourless; languid, languorous, inactive, inert, sluggish, torpid.
– OPPOSITES energetic.

litany noun 1 *her lips moved, repeating the litany:* **prayer**, invocation, supplication, devotion. 2 *a litany of complaints soon followed:* **recital**, recitation, repetition, enumeration; list, listing, catalogue, inventory.

literacy noun **ability to read and write**, reading/writing skills; (book) learning, education, scholarship, schooling.

literal adjective 1 *the literal meaning of the word 'dreadful':* **strict**, factual, plain, simple, exact, straightforward; unembellished, undistorted; objective, correct, true, truthful, accurate, genuine, authentic. 2 *a literal translation:* **word-for-word**, verbatim, letter-for-letter; exact, precise, faithful, close, strict, accurate. 3 *his literal, unrhetorical manner:* **literal-minded**, down-to-earth, matter-of-fact, no-nonsense, unsentimental; prosaic, unimaginative, pedestrian, uninspired, uninspiring.
– OPPOSITES figurative, loose.

literally adverb *the name, translated literally, means 'river':* **verbatim**, word for word, letter for letter; exactly, precisely, faithfully, closely, strictly, accurately.

literary adjective 1 *a wide-ranging selection of literary works:* **written**, poetic, artistic, dramatic. 2 *her literary friends | a literary magazine:* **scholarly**, learned, intellectual, cultured, erudite, bookish, highbrow, lettered, academic, cultivated; well read, widely read, (well) educated.

literate adjective *having a literate, informed audience obviously makes discussion easier:* **(well) educated**, well read, widely read, scholarly, learned, knowledgeable, lettered, cultured, cultivated, sophisticated, well informed.
– OPPOSITES ignorant.

literature noun 1 *he studied English literature at university:* **(creative) writing**, literary texts, compositions. 2 *I've looked at the literature on prototype theory:* **publications**, published writings, texts, reports, studies. 3 *the noticeboards are covered in election literature:* **printed matter**, brochures, leaflets, pamphlets, circulars, flyers, handouts, handbills, mailshots, bulletins, documentation, publicity, blurb, notices; informal bumf, propaganda.

lithe adjective *his tall, lithe figure filled the screen:* **agile**, graceful, supple, limber, lithesome, loose-limbed, nimble, deft, flexible, lissom.

– OPPOSITES clumsy.

litigant noun **claimant**, opponent (in law), contender, disputant, plaintiff, complainant, petitioner, appellant, respondent.

litigation noun *he objected to some passages but did not resort to litigation:* **(legal/judicial) proceedings**, (legal) action, lawsuit, legal dispute, (legal) case, suit (at law), prosecution, indictment.

litter noun 1 *never drop litter in the street:* **rubbish**, refuse, junk, waste, debris, scraps, leavings, fragments, detritus; N. Amer. trash, garbage. 2 *she looked at the litter of glasses around her:* **clutter**, jumble, muddle, mess, heap, disorder, untidiness, confusion, disarray; informal shambles. 3 *a litter of kittens:* **brood**, family; young, offspring, progeny; Law issue. 4 *we obtained straw for use as litter:* **(animal) bedding**, straw.
verb *clothes and newspapers littered the floor:* **cover**, mess up, clutter up, be strewn about, be scattered about.

little adjective 1 *he sat at a little writing desk:* **small**, small-scale, compact; mini, miniature, tiny, minute, minuscule; toy, baby, pocket, undersized, dwarf, midget; Scottish wee; informal teeny-weeny, teensy-weensy, itsy-bitsy, tiddly, half-pint; Brit. informal titchy, dinky; N. Amer. informal vest-pocket. 2 *the smile vanished from the little man's face:* **short**, small, slight, diminutive, tiny; elfin, dwarfish, midget, pygmy, Lilliputian; Scottish wee; informal teeny-weeny, pint-sized. 3 *my little sister:* **young**, younger, junior, small, baby, infant. 4 *I was a bodyguard for a little while:* **brief**, short; fleeting, momentary, transitory, transient; fast, quick, hasty, cursory. 5 *this car does have a few little problems:* **minor**, unimportant, insignificant, trivial, trifling, petty, paltry, inconsequential, nugatory.
– OPPOSITES big, large, elder, important.
determiner *they have low status and little political influence:* **hardly any**, not much, slight, scant, limited, restricted, modest, little or no, minimal, negligible.
– OPPOSITES considerable.
adverb 1 *he is little known as a teacher:* **hardly**, barely, scarcely, not much, (only) slightly. 2 *this disease is little seen nowadays:* **rarely**, seldom, infrequently, hardly (ever), scarcely (ever), not much.
– OPPOSITES well, often.
■ **a little** 1 *if the mixture is too thick, add a little water:* **some**, a small amount of, a bit of, a touch of, a soupçon of, a dash of, a taste of, a spot of, a shade of, a suggestion of, a trace of, a hint of, a suspicion of; a dribble of, a splash of, a pinch of, a sprinkling of, a speck of; informal a smidgen of, a smidge of. 2 *after a little, Oliver came in:* **a short time**, a little while, a bit, an interval, a short period; a minute, a moment, a second, an instant; informal a sec, a mo, a jiffy. 3 *this reminds me a little of the Adriatic:* **slightly**, faintly,

remotely, vaguely; somewhat, a little bit, quite, to some degree.
■ **little by little** gradually, slowly, by degrees, by stages, step by step, bit by bit, progressively; subtly, imperceptibly.

liturgy noun *the liturgy and rites of the Church of England:* ritual, worship, service, ceremony, rite, observance, celebration, sacrament; tradition, custom, practice, rubric; formal ordinance.

live¹ verb **1** *the greatest mathematician who ever lived:* exist, be alive, be, have life; breathe, draw breath, walk the earth. **2** *I live in London:* reside, have one's home, have one's residence, be settled; be housed, lodge; inhabit, occupy, populate; Scottish stay; formal dwell. **3** *they lived quietly:* pass/spend one's life, have a lifestyle; behave, conduct oneself. **4** *she had lived a difficult life:* experience, spend, pass, lead, have, go through, undergo. **5** *Freddy lived by his wits:* survive, make/earn a living; subsist, support oneself, sustain oneself, make ends meet, keep body and soul together. **6** *you should live a little:* enjoy oneself, enjoy life, have fun, live life to the full.
– OPPOSITES die, be dead.
■ **live it up** (informal) *those two are now living it up in Hawaii:* enjoy oneself, live in the lap of luxury; carouse, revel, have a good time, roister; informal party, push the boat out, paint the town red, have a ball, make whoopee; N. Amer. informal live high on/off the hog.
■ **live off/on** *the seabirds live off discarded fish:* subsist on, feed on/off, eat, consume.

live² adjective **1** *we decided to use live bait:* living, alive, having life, breathing, animate, sentient. **2** *this is her first live performance in Britain:* in the flesh, personal, in person. **3** *he accidentally touched a live rail:* electrified, charged, powered, active. **4** *a live grenade:* unexploded, active; unstable, volatile. **5** *this is very much a live issue:* topical, current, controversial; burning, pressing, important.
– OPPOSITES dead, inanimate, recorded.
■ **live wire** (informal) *she's a real live wire:* informal fireball, human dynamo, powerhouse, life and soul of the party.

livelihood noun *many people relied on the airport for their livelihood:* (source of) income, means of support, living, subsistence, keep, maintenance, sustenance, nourishment, daily bread, bread and butter; job, work, employment, occupation.

lively adjective **1** *the bride was an attractive, lively young woman:* energetic, active, animated, dynamic, full of life, outgoing, spirited, high-spirited, vivacious, enthusiastic, vibrant, buoyant, exuberant, effervescent, cheerful; bouncy, bubbly, perky, sparkling, zestful; Brit. Tiggerish; informal full of beans, chirpy, chipper, peppy. **2** *a lively West End bar:* busy, crowded, bustling, buzzing; vibrant, boisterous, jolly, festive; informal hopping, buzzy. **3** *a*

lively debate: heated, vigorous, animated, spirited, enthusiastic, forceful; exciting, interesting, memorable. **4** *a lively portrait of the local community:* vivid, colourful, striking, graphic, bold, strong. **5** *he bowled at a lively pace:* brisk, quick, fast, rapid, swift, speedy, smart; informal nippy, snappy.
– OPPOSITES quiet, dull.

liven
■ **liven up** *at the mention of food, he livened up a bit:* brighten up, cheer up, perk up, revive, rally, pick up, bounce back; informal buck up.
■ **liven someone/something up** *he could do with a drink to liven him up:* brighten up, cheer up, enliven, animate, raise someone's spirits, perk up, spice up, ginger up, make lively, wake up, invigorate, revive, refresh, vivify, galvanize, stimulate, stir up, get going; informal buck up, pep up.

livery noun **1** *servants in the blue and gold livery of the Prince scurried round with silver plates:* uniform, regalia, costume, dress, attire, garb, clothes, clothing, outfit, suit, garments, ensemble; informal get-up, gear, kit; formal apparel. **2** *the locomotive has reverted to its original two-tone green livery:* colours, colouring; paintwork, design, format, specification, look; informal spec, paint job.

livid adjective **1** (informal) *Mum was absolutely livid.* See FURIOUS sense 1. **2** *he now had a livid bruise on the side of his jaw:* purplish, bluish, dark, discoloured, purple, greyish-blue; bruised; angry.

living noun **1** *she cleaned floors for a living:* livelihood, (source of) income, means of support, subsistence, keep, maintenance, sustenance, nourishment, daily bread, bread and butter; job, work, employment, occupation. **2** *making informed choices about healthy living | urban living:* way of life, lifestyle, life; conduct, behaviour, activities, habits.
adjective **1** *living organisms:* alive, live, animate, sentient; breathing, existing, existent; informal alive and kicking. **2** *a living language:* current, contemporary, present; in use, active, surviving, extant, persisting, remaining, existing, in existence.
– OPPOSITES dead, extinct.

living room noun sitting room, lounge, front room, reception room, family room.

load noun **1** *I've got a load to deliver:* cargo, freight, consignment, delivery, shipment, goods, merchandise; pack, bundle, parcel; lorryload, truckload, shipload, boatload, vanload. **2** (informal) *I bought a load of clothes:* a lot, a great deal, a large amount/quantity, an abundance, a wealth, a mountain; many, plenty; informal a heap, a mass, a pile, a stack, a ton, lots, heaps, masses, bucketloads, piles, stacks, tons. **3** *we have a heavy teaching load:* commitment, responsibility, duty, obligation, charge, burden; trouble, worry, strain, pressure.

verb 1 *we quickly loaded the van:* **fill (up)**, pack, lade, charge, stock, stack. **2** *Larry loaded boxes into the jeep:* **pack**, stow, store, stack, bundle; place, deposit, put, cram. **3** *loading the committee with responsibilities means less gets done:* **burden**, weigh down, saddle, charge; overburden, overwhelm, encumber, tax, strain, trouble, worry. **4** *Richard loaded Marshall with honours:* **reward**, ply, regale, shower. **5** *he had already loaded a gun:* **prime**, charge, prepare. **6** *load the cassette into the camcorder:* **insert**, put, place, slot, slide, slip, drop. **7** *the dice are loaded against him:* **bias**, rig, fix; weight.

loaded adjective 1 *a loaded freight train:* **full**, filled, laden, packed, crammed, brimming, stacked; informal chock-full, chock-a-block. **2** *a loaded gun:* **primed**, charged; live. **3** (informal) *they are all loaded.* See RICH sense 1. **4** *a politically loaded word:* **charged**, emotive, sensitive, delicate.

loaf verb *he was just loafing around:* **laze**, lounge, loll, idle, waste time; informal hang around/round; Brit. informal hang about, mooch about/around; N. Amer. informal bum around.

loafer noun idler, layabout, good-for-nothing, lounger, shirker, sluggard, laggard; informal skiver, slacker, slob, lazybones.

loan noun *a loan of £7,000:* **credit**, advance; mortgage, overdraft; Brit. informal sub.
verb *he loaned me his flat:* **lend**, advance; give on loan, lease, charter, hire; Brit. informal sub.
– OPPOSITES borrow.

loath adjective *the forwards were loath to take risks:* **reluctant**, unwilling, disinclined, ill-disposed; against, averse, opposed, resistant.
– OPPOSITES willing.

loathe verb *the staff at school loathed him:* **hate**, detest, abhor, execrate, not be able to bear/stand, be repelled by.
– OPPOSITES love.

loathing noun hatred, hate, detestation, abhorrence, abomination, execration, odium; antipathy, dislike, hostility, animosity, ill feeling, bad feeling, malice, animus, enmity, aversion; repugnance.

loathsome adjective hateful, detestable, abhorrent, repulsive, odious, repugnant, repellent, disgusting, revolting, sickening, abominable, despicable, contemptible, reprehensible, execrable, damnable; vile, horrible, nasty, obnoxious, gross, foul; informal horrid, yucky; literary noisome.

lob verb *they lobbed a grenade into the crowded street:* **throw**, toss, fling, pitch, hurl, pelt, sling, launch, propel; informal chuck, bung, heave.

lobby noun 1 *the hotel lobby was empty:* **entrance (hall)**, hallway, hall, vestibule, foyer, reception area. **2** *the anti-hunt lobby:* **pressure group**, interest group, movement, campaign, crusade, lobbyists, supporters; faction, camp; Brit. ginger group.
verb 1 *readers are urged to lobby their MPs:* **approach**, work on, bring pressure to bear

on, importune, sway; petition, solicit, appeal to, pressurize. **2** *a group lobbying for better rail services:* **campaign**, crusade, press, push, ask, call, demand; promote, advocate, champion.

local adjective 1 *I will inform the local council:* **community**, district, neighbourhood, regional, city, town, municipal, provincial, village, parish. **2** *we dined at a local restaurant:* **neighbourhood**, nearby, near, at hand, close by; accessible, handy, convenient. **3** *a local infection:* **confined**, restricted, contained, localized.
– OPPOSITES national, widespread.
noun 1 *the police had complaints from the locals:* **local person**, native, inhabitant, resident, parishioner. **2** (Brit. informal) *a pint in the local.* See PUB.
– OPPOSITES outsider.

locale noun *the photography conveys the beauty of the locale:* **place**, site, spot, area; position, location, setting, scene, venue, background, backdrop, environment; neighbourhood, district, region, locality.

locality noun *other schools in the locality were unaffected:* **vicinity**, neighbourhood, area, district, region; informal neck of the woods.

localize verb *medical teams are working to localize the outbreak:* **limit**, restrict, confine, contain, circumscribe, concentrate, delimit.
– OPPOSITES generalize, globalize.

locate verb 1 *spotter planes are used to locate the shoals:* **find**, discover, pinpoint, detect, track down, run to earth, unearth, sniff out, smoke out, search out, ferret out, uncover. **2** *a company located near Pittsburgh:* **situate**, site, position, place, base; put, build, establish, found, station, install, settle.

location noun position, place, situation, site, locality, locale, spot, whereabouts, point; scene, setting, area, environment; bearings, orientation; venue, address.

lock[1] noun *the lock on the door had been forced:* **bolt**, catch, fastener, clasp, bar, hasp, latch.
verb 1 *he closed and locked the door:* **bolt**, fasten, bar, secure, seal; padlock, latch, chain. **2** *pins are inserted to lock the rods together:* **join**, interlock, link, mesh, engage, unite, connect, yoke, mate; couple. **3** *the wheels locked and we careered across the road:* **jam**, stick, seize, go rigid. **4** *he locked her in an embrace:* **clasp**, clench, grasp, embrace, hug, squeeze.
– OPPOSITES unlock, open, separate, divide, release.
■ **lock someone out** *she was locked out of her office:* **keep out**, shut out, refuse entrance to, deny admittance to; exclude, bar, debar, ban.
■ **lock someone up** *he was locked up for stabbing someone:* **imprison**, jail, incarcerate, intern, send to prison, put behind bars, put under lock and key, put in chains, clap in

irons, cage, pen, coop up; informal send down, put away, put inside.

lock² noun *a lock of Elvis Presley's hair:* **tress**, tuft, curl, ringlet, hank, strand, wisp, snippet.

locker noun **cupboard**, cabinet, chest, safe, box, case, coffer; compartment, storeroom.

lock-up noun **1** *drunks were put in the lock-up overnight:* **jail**, prison, cell, detention centre; N. Amer. jailhouse; informal cooler, slammer, jug, can, nick, stir, clink, quod, chokey. **2** *they stored spare furniture in a lock-up:* **storeroom**, store, warehouse, depository; garage.

locomotion noun *many prey species have developed strange forms of locomotion:* **movement**, motion, moving; travel, travelling; mobility; walking, ambulation, running; progress, progression, passage; informal getting/moving about/around; formal perambulation.

lodge noun **1** *the porter's lodge:* **gatehouse**, cottage. **2** *a hunting lodge:* **house**, cottage, cabin, chalet; Brit. shooting box. **3** *a beaver's lodge:* **den**, lair, hole, sett; retreat, haunt, shelter. **4** *a Masonic lodge:* **section**, branch, wing; hall, clubhouse, meeting room; N. Amer. chapter.
verb **1** *William lodged at our house:* **reside**, board, stay, live, have lodgings, have rooms, put up, be quartered, stop; N. Amer. room; informal have digs; formal dwell, be domiciled, sojourn. **2** *they were lodged at a draughty old inn:* **accommodate**, put up, take in, house, board, billet, quarter, shelter. **3** *the government has lodged a protest:* **submit**, register, enter, put forward, advance, lay, present, tender, proffer, put on record, record, table, file. **4** *the money was lodged in a bank:* **deposit**, put, bank; stash, store, stow, put away, squirrel away. **5** *the bullet lodged in his back:* **stick**, embed itself, become embedded, get/become stuck, catch, become/get caught, wedge.

lodger noun **boarder**, paying guest, PG, tenant; N. Amer. roomer.

lodging noun **accommodation**, rooms, chambers, living quarters, place to stay, residence, a roof over one's head, housing, shelter; informal digs, pad; formal abode, dwelling.

lofty adjective **1** *the buildings have lofty towers and spires:* **tall**, high, giant, towering, soaring. **2** *we failed to live up to his lofty ideals:* **noble**, exalted, high, high-minded, worthy, grand, fine, elevated. **3** *he regarded us with lofty disdain:* **haughty**, arrogant, disdainful, supercilious, condescending, patronizing, scornful, contemptuous, self-important, conceited, snobbish; informal stuck-up, snooty, snotty; Brit. informal toffee-nosed.
– OPPOSITES low, short, base, lowly, modest.

log noun **1** *she tripped over a fallen log:* **branch**, trunk; piece of wood; (**logs**) timber,

firewood. **2** *we keep a log of phone calls:* **record**, register, logbook, journal, diary, minutes, chronicle, record book, ledger, account, tally.
verb **1** *all complaints are logged by staff:* **register**, record, make a note of, note down, write down, jot down, put in writing, enter, file, minute. **2** *the pilot had logged 95 hours:* **attain**, achieve, chalk up, make, do, go, cover.

logic noun **1** *this case appears to defy all logic:* **reason**, judgement, logical thought, rationality, wisdom, sense, good sense, common sense, sanity. **2** *the logic of their argument:* **reasoning**, line of reasoning, rationale, argument, argumentation.

logical adjective **1** *the information is displayed in a logical fashion:* **reasoned**, well reasoned, rational, sound, cogent, well thought out, valid; coherent, clear, well organized, systematic, orderly, methodical, analytical, consistent, objective; informal joined-up. **2** *further privatization seems to be the logical outcome:* **natural**, reasonable, sensible, understandable; predictable, unsurprising, only to be expected, most likely, likeliest, obvious.
– OPPOSITES illogical, irrational, unlikely, surprising.

logistics plural noun *we need to consider the logistics of deploying troops in the region:* **organization**, planning, plans, management, arrangement, administration, orchestration, coordination, execution, handling, running.

logo noun **emblem**, trademark, device, symbol, design, sign, mark; insignia, crest, seal, coat of arms, shield, badge, motif, monogram, colophon.

loiter verb **1** *five or six teenagers loitered in front of the newsagent, drinking shandy and smoking:* **stand about/around**, wait, skulk; loaf, lounge, idle, laze, waste time, linger; informal hang around/round; Brit. informal hang about, mooch about/around. **2** *the churchyard is a pleasant spot to loiter on a sunny afternoon:* **dawdle**, dally, stroll, amble, saunter, meander, drift, potter, take one's time; informal dilly-dally, mosey, tootle; Brit. informal mooch.

loll verb **1** *Louis lolled in an armchair by the window:* **lounge**, sprawl, drape oneself, stretch oneself; slouch, slump; laze, luxuriate, put one's feet up, lean back, recline, relax, take it easy. **2** *her head lolled to one side:* **hang (loosely)**, droop, dangle, sag, drop, flop.

lone adjective **1** *a lone police officer stood on the corner:* **solitary**, single, solo, unaccompanied, unescorted, alone, by oneself/itself, sole, companionless; detached, isolated, unique; lonely. **2** *the difficulties of being a lone parent:* **single**, unmarried, unattached; separated, divorced, widowed.

loneliness noun **1** *his loneliness was*

I

unbearable: **isolation,** friendlessness, abandonment, rejection, unpopularity; N. Amer. lonesomeness. **2** *the enforced loneliness of a prison cell:* **solitariness,** solitude, lack of company, aloneness, separation.

lonely adjective **1** *I felt very lonely:* **isolated,** alone, friendless, with no one to turn to, forsaken, abandoned, rejected, unloved, unwanted; N. Amer. lonesome. **2** *the lonely life of a writer:* **solitary,** unaccompanied, lone, by oneself/itself, companionless. **3** *a lonely road:* **deserted,** uninhabited, unfrequented, unpopulated, desolate, isolated, remote, out of the way, secluded, off the beaten track, in the back of beyond, godforsaken; informal in the middle of nowhere.
– OPPOSITES popular, sociable, crowded.

loner noun **recluse,** introvert, lone wolf, hermit, solitary, misanthrope, outsider; historical anchorite.

long[1] adjective *there was a long silence:* **lengthy,** extended, prolonged, extensive, protracted, long-lasting, long-drawn(-out), spun out, dragged out, seemingly endless, lingering, interminable.
– OPPOSITES short, brief.
■ **before long** *before long, others will follow:* soon, shortly, presently, in the near future, in a little while, by and by, in a minute, in a moment, in a second; informal anon, in a jiffy; Brit. informal in a tick, in two ticks, in a mo; dated directly.

long[2] verb *I longed for the holidays:* **yearn,** pine, ache, hanker for/after, hunger, thirst, itch, be eager, be desperate; crave, dream of, set one's heart on; informal have a yen, be dying.

longing noun *many city dwellers have a longing for the countryside:* **yearning,** pining, craving, ache, burning, hunger, thirst, hankering; informal yen, itch.
adjective *he gave her a longing look:* **yearning,** pining, craving, hungry, thirsty, hankering, wistful, covetous.

long-lasting adjective **enduring,** lasting, abiding, long-lived, long-running, long-established, long-standing, lifelong, deep-rooted, time-honoured, traditional, permanent.
– OPPOSITES short-lived, ephemeral.

long-lived adjective. See **LONG-LASTING**.

long-standing adjective **well established,** long-established; time-honoured, traditional, age-old; abiding, enduring, long-lived, surviving, persistent, prevailing, perennial, deep-rooted, long-term, confirmed.
– OPPOSITES new, recent.

long-suffering adjective **patient,** forbearing, tolerant, uncomplaining, stoical, resigned; easy-going, indulgent, charitable, accommodating, forgiving.
– OPPOSITES impatient, complaining.

long-winded adjective **verbose,** wordy, lengthy, long, overlong, prolix, prolonged,

protracted, long-drawn-out, interminable; discursive, diffuse, rambling, tortuous, meandering, repetitious; informal windy; Brit. informal waffly.
– OPPOSITES concise, succinct, laconic.

look verb **1** *Mrs Wright looked at him | I looked out of the window:* **glance,** gaze, stare, gape, peer; peep, peek, take a look; watch, observe, view, regard, examine, inspect, eye, scan, scrutinize, survey, study, contemplate, consider, take in, ogle; informal take a gander, rubberneck, give someone/something a/the once-over, get a load of; Brit. informal take a dekko, take a butcher's, take a shufti, clock, gawp; N. Amer. informal eyeball. **2** *her room looked out on Broadway:* **command a view of,** face, overlook, front. **3** *they looked shocked:* **seem (to be),** appear (to be), have the appearance/air of being, give the impression of being, give every appearance/indication of being.
– OPPOSITES ignore.
noun **1** *have a look at this report:* **glance,** view, examination, study, inspection, observation, scan, survey, peep, peek, glimpse, gaze, stare; informal eyeful, gander, look-see, once-over, squint, recce; Brit. informal shufti, dekko, butcher's. **2** *the look on her face:* **expression,** mien. **3** *little details that help to create that rustic look:* **appearance,** air, aspect, bearing, cast, manner, mien, demeanour, facade, impression, effect, feel; informal vibe. **4** *this season's look:* **fashion,** style, vogue, mode.
■ **look after** *I had to look after my brother while he was ill:* take care of, care for, attend to, minister to, tend, mind, keep an eye on, keep safe, be responsible for, protect; nurse, babysit, childmind.
■ **look back on** *I now look back on my teenage years with amazement:* reflect on, think back to, remember, recall, reminisce about.
■ **look down on** *my mother was a terrible snob and looked down on most of our neighbours:* disdain, scorn, regard with contempt, look down one's nose at, sneer at, despise.
■ **look for** *she looked for her comb:* search for, hunt for, try to find, seek, cast about/around/round for, try to track down, forage for, scout out, quest for/after.
■ **look forward to** *I'm looking forward to seeing Ted again:* await with pleasure, eagerly anticipate, lick one's lips over, be unable to wait for, count the days until.
■ **look into** *the authorities promised to look into the complaints:* investigate, enquire into, ask questions about, go into, probe, explore, follow up, research, study, examine; informal check out; N. Amer. informal scope out.
■ **look like** *in his overcoat he looks like an undertaker:* resemble, bear a resemblance to, look similar to, take after, have the look of, have the appearance of, remind one of, make one think of; informal be the spitting image of, be a dead ringer for.

■ **look on/upon** *people he looked on as friends took advantage of him:* regard, consider, think of, deem, judge, see, view, count, reckon.

■ **look out** *you'll be trampled on if you don't look out:* beware, watch out, mind out, be on (one's) guard, be alert, be wary, be vigilant, be careful, take care, be cautious, pay attention, take heed, keep one's eyes open/peeled, keep an eye out; watch your step.

■ **look something over** *he looked over the reports from the engineer:* inspect, examine, scan, cast an eye over, take stock of, vet, view, look through, peruse, run through, read through; informal take a dekko at, give something a/the once-over; N. Amer. check out; N. Amer. informal eyeball.

■ **look to 1** *we must look to the future:* consider, think about, turn one's thoughts to, focus on, take heed of, pay attention to, attend to, address, mind, heed. **2** *they look to the government for help:* turn to, resort to, have recourse to, fall back on, rely on.

■ **look up** *from that victory on, things looked up:* improve, get better, pick up, come along/on, progress, make progress, make headway, perk up, rally, take a turn for the better.

■ **look someone up** (informal) *I went to Leeds to look up some old friends:* visit, pay a visit to, call on, go to see, look in on; N. Amer. visit with, go see; informal drop in on.

■ **look up to** *Jerry has always looked up to me:* admire, have a high opinion of, think highly of, hold in high regard, regard highly, rate highly, respect, esteem, value.

lookalike noun **double**, twin, clone, duplicate, exact likeness, replica, copy, facsimile, Doppelgänger; informal spitting image, dead ringer, dead spit.

lookout noun **1** *the lookout sighted sails on the horizon:* **watchman**, watch, guard, sentry, sentinel, picket. **2** (Brit. informal) *I doubt if she'll fit in, but that's her own lookout:* **problem**, concern, business, affair, responsibility, worry; informal pigeon.

■ **be on the lookout/keep a lookout** *he kept a sharp lookout for enemy fighters:* keep watch, keep an eye out, keep one's eyes peeled, keep a vigil, be alert.

loom verb **1** *ghostly shapes loomed out of the fog:* **emerge**, appear, come into view, take shape, materialize, reveal itself. **2** *the church loomed above him:* **soar**, tower, rise, rear up; overshadow, dominate. **3** *without reforms, disaster looms:* **be imminent**, be on the horizon, impend, threaten, brew, be just around the corner.

loop noun *make a loop in the twine:* **coil**, hoop, ring, circle, noose, oval, spiral, curl, bend, curve, arc, twirl, whorl, twist, hook, zigzag, helix.
verb **1** *Dave looped the rope around their hands:* **coil**, wind, twist, snake, wreathe, spiral, curve, bend, turn. **2** *he looped the*

cables together: **fasten**, tie, join, connect, knot, bind.

loophole noun *they took advantage of a loophole in the regulations:* **flaw**, omission, ambiguity, inconsistency, discrepancy.

loose adjective **1** *a loose floorboard:* **unsecured**, unattached; detached, unfastened; wobbly, unsteady, movable. **2** *she wore her hair loose:* **untied**, unpinned, unbound, hanging down, free, down, flowing. **3** *there's a wolf loose in the woods:* **free**, at large, at liberty, on the loose, escaped; untied, unchained, wandering about, roaming about. **4** *a loose interpretation of the drug laws:* **vague**, indefinite, inexact, imprecise, approximate; broad, general, rough; liberal. **5** *a loose jacket:* **baggy**, generously cut, slack, roomy; oversized, shapeless, sagging, sloppy.
– OPPOSITES secure, literal, narrow, tight, chaste.
verb **1** *the hounds have been loosed:* **free**, set free, unloose, turn loose, set loose, let loose, let go, release; untie, unchain, unfasten, unleash. **2** *the fingers loosed their hold:* **relax**, slacken, loosen; weaken, lessen, reduce, diminish, moderate. **3** *Brian loosed off a shot:* **fire**, discharge, shoot, let go, let fly with.
– OPPOSITES confine, tighten.

■ **at a loose end** *why don't you stay and eat if you're at a loose end?* with nothing to do, unoccupied, unemployed, at leisure, idle, adrift, with time to kill; bored, twiddling one's thumbs, kicking one's heels.

■ **break loose** *the horses broke loose during the storm:* escape, make one's escape, get away, get free, break free, free oneself.

■ **let loose.** See LOOSE verb sense 1.

■ **on the loose** *a convicted killer was on the loose:* free, at liberty, at large, escaped; on the run, fugitive; N. Amer. informal on the lam.

loose-limbed adjective **supple**, limber, lithe, lissom, willowy; agile, nimble.

loosen verb **1** *you simply loosen two screws:* **slacken**, unstick; unfasten, detach, release, disconnect, undo, unclasp, unlatch, unbolt. **2** *her fingers loosened:* **slacken**, become loose, let go, ease; work loose, work free. **3** *Philip loosened his grip:* **weaken**, relax, slacken, loose, lessen, reduce, moderate, diminish.
– OPPOSITES tighten.

■ **loosen up** *you need to loosen up, get rid of your inhibitions:* relax, unwind, ease up/off; informal let up, hang loose, lighten up, go easy.

loot noun *he produced a bag full of loot:* **booty**, spoils, plunder, stolen goods, contraband; informal swag, ill-gotten gains, boodle.
verb *troops looted the cathedral:* **plunder**, pillage, despoil, ransack, sack, raid, rifle, rob, burgle; strip, clear out.

lop verb **cut**, chop, hack, saw, hew, slash, axe; prune, sever, clip, trim, snip, dock, crop.

lope verb **stride**, run, bound; lollop.

lopsided adjective **crooked**, askew, awry, off-centre, uneven, out of true, out of line, asymmetrical, tilted, at an angle, aslant, slanting, squint; Scottish agley; informal cockeyed; Brit. informal skew-whiff, wonky.
– OPPOSITES even, level, balanced.

loquacious adjective *he is the loquacious representative for New York's 13th congressional district:* **talkative**, voluble, communicative, expansive, garrulous, unreserved, chatty, gossipy, gossiping; informal having the gift of the gab, gabby, gassy; Brit. informal able to talk the hind legs off a donkey.
– OPPOSITES reticent, taciturn.

loquacity noun **talkativeness**, volubility, expansiveness, garrulousness, garrulity, chattiness; informal the gift of the gab.
– OPPOSITES reticence, taciturnity.

lord noun **1** *the lords and ladies were entertained in this hall:* **noble**, nobleman, peer, aristocrat, patrician, grandee. **2** *it is my duty to obey my lord's wishes:* **master**, ruler, leader, chief, superior, monarch, sovereign, king, emperor, prince, governor, commander.
– OPPOSITES commoner, servant, inferior.
■ **lord it over someone** *when we were at school, you used to love to lord it over us:* order about/around, dictate to, ride roughshod over, pull rank on, tyrannize, have under one's thumb; be overbearing, put on airs, swagger; informal boss about/around, walk all over, push around, throw one's weight about/around.

lore noun **1** *Arthurian legend and lore:* **mythology**, myths, legends, stories, traditions, folklore, oral tradition, mythos. **2** *cricket lore:* **knowledge**, learning, wisdom; informal know-how, how-tos.

lorry noun **truck**, wagon, van, juggernaut, trailer; articulated lorry, heavy-goods vehicle, HGV; dated pantechnicon.

lose verb **1** *I've lost my watch:* **mislay**, misplace, be unable to find, lose track of, leave (behind), fail to keep/retain, fail to keep sight of. **2** *he's lost a lot of blood:* **be deprived of**, suffer the loss of; no longer have. **3** *he managed to lose his pursuers:* **escape from**, evade, elude, dodge, avoid, give someone the slip, shake off, throw off, throw off the scent; leave behind, outdistance, outstrip, outrun. **4** *they always lose at football:* **be defeated**, be beaten, suffer defeat, be the loser, be conquered, be vanquished, be trounced, be worsted; informal come a cropper, go down, take a licking, be bested.
– OPPOSITES find, regain, seize, win.
■ **lose out** *the ramshackle negotiating machinery is the main reason why the ambulance workers have lost out:* be the loser, fail to benefit, be disadvantaged; informal miss out .
■ **lose out on** *the town has lost out on a major tourist opportunity:* fail to benefit

from; informal miss out on.
■ **lose out to** *Celtic have lost out to rivals Rangers by two points:* be defeated by, be beaten by, suffer defeat at the hands of, lose to, be beaten into second place by; informal go down to, be bested by.

loser noun **1** *the loser still gets the silver medal:* **runner-up**, also-ran. **2** (informal) *he's a complete loser:* **failure**, non-achiever, underachiever, ne'er-do-well, dead loss; write-off, has-been; informal flop, non-starter, no-hoper, washout, lemon.
– OPPOSITES winner, success.

loss noun **1** *the loss of the documents is highly embarrassing:* **mislaying**, misplacement. **2** *loss of earnings is covered by insurance:* **deprivation**, disappearance, privation, forfeiture, diminution, erosion, reduction, depletion. **3** *the loss of her husband:* **death**, dying, demise, passing (away/on), end, quietus; bereavement; formal decease; archaic expiry. **4** *British losses in the war:* **casualty**, fatality, victim; dead; missing; death toll, number killed/dead/wounded. **5** *we made a loss of £15,000:* **deficit**, debit, debt, indebtedness, deficiency.
– OPPOSITES recovery, profit.
■ **at a loss** *I'm at a loss to explain this state of affairs:* **baffled**, nonplussed, mystified, puzzled, perplexed, bewildered, bemused, at sixes and sevens, confused, dumbfounded, stumped, stuck, blank; informal clueless, flummoxed, bamboozled, fazed, floored, beaten; N. Amer. informal discombobulated.

lost adjective **1** *we were searching for her lost keys:* **missing**, mislaid, misplaced, vanished, disappeared, gone missing/astray, forgotten, nowhere to be found; absent, not present, strayed. **2** *I think we're lost:* **off course**, off track, disorientated, having lost one's bearings, going round in circles, adrift, at sea, astray. **3** *a lost opportunity:* **missed**, forfeited, neglected, wasted, squandered, gone by the board; informal down the drain. **4** *lost species and habitats:* **extinct**, died out, defunct, vanished, gone; **destroyed**, wiped out, ruined, wrecked, exterminated, eradicated. **5** *a lost cause:* **hopeless**, beyond hope, futile, forlorn, failed, beyond remedy, beyond recovery. **6** *Father Reynard was lost in thought:* **engrossed**, absorbed, rapt, immersed, deep, intent, engaged, wrapped up.
– OPPOSITES current, saved.

lot pronoun *a lot of money | lots of friends:* **a large amount**, a fair amount, a good/great deal, a great quantity, quantities, an abundance, a wealth, a profusion, plenty; many, a great many, a large number, a considerable number, numerous, scores; informal hundreds, thousands, millions, billions, loads, bucketloads, masses, heaps, a pile, piles, oodles, stacks, scads, reams, wads, pots, oceans, a mountain, mountains, miles, tons, zillions, more ... than one can shake a stick at; Brit. informal a shedload, lashings; N.

Amer. informal gobs, a bunch, gazillions.
– OPPOSITES a little, not much, a few, not many.

adverb *I work in pastels a lot:* **a great deal**, a good deal, to a great extent, much; often, frequently, regularly.
– OPPOSITES a little, not much.

noun 1 (informal) *what do your lot think?* **group**, set, crowd, circle, band, crew; informal bunch, gang, mob. **2** *the books were auctioned as a number of separate lots:* **item**, article; batch, set, collection, group, bundle, quantity, assortment, parcel. **3** *he was discontented with his lot in life:* **fate**, destiny, fortune; situation, circumstances, state, condition, position, plight, predicament. **4** (N. Amer.) *some youngsters playing ball in a vacant lot:* **plot**, area, tract, parcel; N. Amer. plat.
■ **draw/cast lots** *the players draw lots to decide who goes first:* spin/toss a coin, throw dice, draw straws.
■ **throw in one's lot** *he threw in his lot with the nationalists:* join forces, join up, form an alliance, ally, align oneself, link up, make common cause.

lotion noun **ointment**, cream, salve, balm, rub, emollient, moisturizer, lubricant, unguent, liniment, embrocation.

lottery noun **1** *a national lottery:* **raffle**, (prize) draw, sweepstake, sweep, tombola, pools. **2** *the race is something of a lottery:* **gamble**, speculation, matter of luck.

loud adjective **1** *there was loud music in the lounge:* **noisy**, blaring, booming, deafening, roaring, thunderous, thundering, ear-splitting, ear-piercing, piercing; carrying, clearly audible; lusty, powerful, forceful, stentorian; Music forte, fortissimo. **2** *the congestion led to loud complaints:* **vociferous**, clamorous, insistent, vehement, emphatic, urgent. **3** *a loud T-shirt:* **garish**, gaudy, flamboyant, lurid, glaring, showy, ostentatious; vulgar, tasteless; informal flash, flashy, naff, kitsch, tacky.
– OPPOSITES quiet, soft, gentle, sober, tasteful.

loudly adverb **at high volume**, at the top of one's voice; noisily, deafeningly, thunderously, piercingly; stridently, lustily, powerfully, forcefully; Music forte, fortissimo; informal as if to wake the dead.
– OPPOSITES quietly, softly.

loudmouth noun (informal) **braggart**, boaster, blusterer, swaggerer; informal blabbermouth, big mouth, motormouth; N. Amer. informal blowhard.

loudspeaker noun **speaker**, monitor, woofer, tweeter; loudhailer, megaphone; public address system, PA (system); informal squawk box.

lounge verb *he just lounges by the pool all day:* **laze**, lie, loll, lie back, lean back, recline, stretch oneself, drape oneself, relax, rest, repose, take it easy, put one's feet up, unwind, luxuriate; sprawl, slump, slouch, flop; loaf, idle, do nothing.

noun *she sat by herself in the lounge:* **living room**, sitting room, front room, drawing room, morning room, reception room, salon, family room.

lour, lower verb *Darley's statue lours at people in the infirmary:* **scowl**, frown, look sullen, glower, glare, give someone black looks, look daggers, look angry; informal give someone dirty looks.
– OPPOSITES smile.

louring, lowering adjective *we laboured on beneath a louring sky:* **overcast**, dark, leaden, grey, cloudy, clouded, gloomy, threatening, menacing.
– OPPOSITES sunny, bright.

lousy (informal) adjective **1** *a lousy film.* See AWFUL sense 2. **2** *the lousy, double-crossing snake!* See DESPICABLE. **3** *I felt lousy.* See ILL adjective sense 1.
■ **be lousy with.** See CRAWL sense 3.

lout noun **ruffian**, hooligan, thug, boor, oaf, hoodlum, rowdy; informal tough, roughneck, bruiser, yahoo, lug; Brit. informal yob, yobbo.
– OPPOSITES smoothie, gentleman.

loutish adjective *their loutish behaviour infuriates me:* **uncouth**, rude, impolite, unmannerly, ill-mannered, ill-bred, coarse; thuggish, boorish, oafish, uncivilized, wild, rough; informal slobbish; Brit. informal yobbish.
– OPPOSITES polite, well behaved.

lovable adjective **adorable**, dear, sweet, cute, charming, darling, lovely, likeable, delightful, captivating, enchanting, engaging, bewitching, pleasing, appealing, winsome, winning, fetching, endearing.
– OPPOSITES hateful, loathsome.

love noun **1** *his friendship with Helen grew into love:* **deep affection**, fondness, tenderness, warmth, intimacy, attachment, endearment; devotion, adoration, doting, idolization, worship; passion, ardour, desire, lust, yearning, infatuation, besottedness. **2** *her love of fashion:* **liking**, enjoyment, appreciation, taste, delight, relish, passion, zeal, appetite, zest, enthusiasm, keenness, fondness, soft spot, weakness, bent, leaning, proclivity, inclination, disposition, partiality, predilection, penchant. **3** *their love for their fellow human beings:* **compassion**, care, caring, regard, solicitude, concern, friendliness, friendship, kindness, charity, goodwill, sympathy, kindliness, altruism, unselfishness, philanthropy, benevolence, fellow feeling, humanity. **4** *he was her one true love:* **beloved**, loved one, love of one's life, dear, dearest, dear one, darling, sweetheart, sweet, angel, honey; lover. **5** *their love will survive:* **relationship**, love affair, romance, liaison, affair of the heart. **6** *my mother sends her love:* **best wishes**, regards, good wishes, greetings, kind/kindest regards.
– OPPOSITES hatred.

verb **1** *she loves him dearly:* **care for**, feel affection for, hold dear, adore, think the world of, be devoted to, dote on, idolize,

worship; be in love with, be infatuated with, be smitten with, be besotted with; informal be mad/crazy/nuts/wild/potty about, have a pash on, carry a torch for. **2** *Laura loved painting:* **like**, delight in, enjoy greatly, have a passion for, take pleasure in, derive pleasure from, relish, savour; have a weakness for, be partial to, have a soft spot for, have a taste for, be taken with; informal get a kick out of, have a thing about, be mad/crazy/nuts/wild/potty about, be hooked on, go a bundle on, get off on, get a buzz out of.
– OPPOSITES hate.
■ **fall in love with** *the moment they met he fell in love with her:* become infatuated with, give/lose one's heart to; informal fall for, be bowled over by, be swept off one's feet by, develop a crush on.
■ **in love with** *I'm in love with Gillian:* infatuated with, besotted with, enamoured of, smitten with, consumed with desire for; captivated by, bewitched by, enthralled by, entranced by; devoted to, doting on; informal mad/crazy/nuts/wild/potty about.

love affair noun **1** *he had a love affair with a teacher:* **relationship**, affair, romance, liaison, affair of the heart, affaire de cœur, intrigue, fling, amour, involvement, romantic entanglement; flirtation, dalliance; Brit. informal carry-on. **2** *our culture's love affair with the motor car:* **enthusiasm**, mania, devotion, passion, obsession, worship.

loveless adjective **passionless**, unloving, unfeeling, heartless, cold, icy, frigid.
– OPPOSITES loving, passionate.

lovelorn adjective **lovesick**, unrequited in love, crossed in love; spurned, jilted, rejected; pining, moping.

lovely adjective **1** *she's a lovely young woman:* **beautiful**, pretty, attractive, good-looking, appealing, handsome, adorable, exquisite, sweet, personable, charming; enchanting, engaging, winsome, seductive, gorgeous, alluring, ravishing, glamorous; Scottish & N. English bonny; informal tasty, knockout, stunning, drop-dead gorgeous; Brit. informal smashing, fit; N. Amer. informal cute, foxy; formal beauteous; archaic comely, fair. **2** *there's a lovely view across the town from up here:* **scenic**, picturesque, pleasing, easy on the eye; magnificent, stunning, splendid. **3** (informal) *we had a lovely day in Wales:* **delightful**, pleasant, nice, agreeable, marvellous, wonderful, sublime, superb, fine, magical; informal terrific, fabulous, heavenly, divine, amazing, glorious.
– OPPOSITES ugly, horrible.

lover noun **1** *she had a secret lover:* **boyfriend**, girlfriend, lady-love, beloved, love, darling, sweetheart; mistress; partner, significant other; informal bit on the side, bit of fluff, toy boy, fancy man, fancy woman. **2** *a great present for dog lovers everywhere:* **devotee**, admirer, fan, enthusiast, aficionado; informal buff, freak, nut.

lovesick adjective **lovelorn**, pining, languishing, longing, yearning, infatuated; frustrated.

loving adjective **affectionate**, fond, devoted, adoring, doting, solicitous, demonstrative; caring, tender, warm, warm-hearted, close; amorous, ardent, passionate, amatory.
– OPPOSITES cold, cruel.

low¹ adjective **1** *we hopped over a low fence:* **short**, small, little; squat, stubby, stunted, dwarf; shallow. **2** *she was wearing a dress with a rather low neckline:* **low-cut**, skimpy, revealing, plunging. **3** *the low price of electrical goods is good for consumers:* **cheap**, economical, moderate, reasonable, modest, bargain, bargain-basement, rock-bottom. **4** *fuel supplies were perilously low:* **scarce**, scanty, scant, skimpy, meagre, sparse, few, little, paltry; reduced, depleted, diminished. **5** *the low quality of workmanship:* **inferior**, substandard, poor, bad, low-grade, below par, second-rate, unsatisfactory, deficient, defective. **6** *a woman of low birth:* **humble**, lowly, low-ranking, plebeian, proletarian, peasant, poor; common, ordinary. **7** *they have very low expectations of their children:* **unambitious**, unaspiring, modest. **8** *most Americans have a low opinion of New York:* **unfavourable**, poor, bad, adverse, negative. **9** *the show thrives on cheap remarks and low comedy:* **uncouth**, uncultured, unsophisticated, rough, rough-hewn, unrefined, tasteless, crass, common, vulgar, coarse, crude. **10** *he spoke in a low voice:* **quiet**, soft, faint, gentle, muted, subdued, muffled, hushed, quietened, whispered, stifled, murmured. **11** *hitting those low notes is very hard:* **bass**, low-pitched, deep, rumbling, booming, sonorous. **12** *she was feeling very low over Christmas:* **depressed**, dejected, despondent, downhearted, downcast, low-spirited, down, fed up, morose, miserable, dismal, heavy-hearted, mournful, forlorn, woebegone, crestfallen, dispirited; without energy, enervated, flat, sapped, weary; informal down in the mouth, down in the dumps, blue.
– OPPOSITES high, expensive, plentiful, superior, noble, favourable, admirable, decent, exalted, loud, cheerful, lively.
noun *the dollar fell to an all-time low:* **nadir**, low point, lowest point, lowest level, depth, rock bottom.
– OPPOSITES high.

low² verb *cattle were lowing:* **moo**, bellow.

lowbrow adjective *they publish mainly lowbrow fiction:* **mass-market**, popular, intellectually undemanding, tabloid, lightweight, accessible, unpretentious; uncultured, unsophisticated, trashy, simplistic; Brit. downmarket; informal dumbed-down, rubbishy.
– OPPOSITES highbrow, intellectual.

low-down (informal) adjective *a low-down trick:* **unfair**, mean, despicable, reprehensible, contemptible, lamentable,

disgusting, shameful, low, unworthy, shabby, basc, dishonourable, unprincipled, sordid, underhand; informal rotten, dirty; Brit. informal beastly; dated dastardly.
– OPPOSITES kind, honourable.
noun *he gave us the low-down on his career as a top comedian:* **facts**, information, story, data, facts and figures, intelligence, news; informal info, rundown, the score, the gen, the latest, the word, the dope.

lower[1] adjective 1 *the lower house of parliament:* **subordinate**, inferior, lesser, junior, minor, secondary, lower-level, subsidiary, subservient. 2 *her lower lip was quivering as she answered:* **bottom**, bottommost, nether, under; underneath, further down, beneath.
– OPPOSITES upper, higher.

lower[2] verb 1 *she lowered the mask and smiled:* **move down**, let down, take down, haul down, drop, let fall. 2 *please lower your voice:* **soften**, modulate, quieten, hush, tone down, muffle, turn down, mute. 3 *they are lowering their prices this autumn:* **reduce**, decrease, lessen, bring down, mark down, cut, slash, axe, diminish, curtail, prune, pare (down). 4 *the water level slowly lowered:* **subside**, fall (off), recede, ebb, wane; abate, die down, let up, moderate, diminish, lessen. 5 *don't lower yourself to their level:* **degrade**, debase, demean, abase, humiliate, downgrade, discredit, shame, dishonour, disgrace; belittle, cheapen, devalue; (**lower oneself**) stoop, sink, descend.
– OPPOSITES raise, increase.

lower[3] verb *he lowered at her.* See LOUR.

low-grade adjective **poor-quality**, inferior, substandard, second-rate; shoddy, cheap, reject, trashy, gimcrack; Brit. informal duff, ropy, twopenny-halfpenny, rubbishy; N. Amer. informal two-bit, bum, cheapjack.
– OPPOSITES top-quality, first-class.

low-key adjective *the council's low-key approach saved a lot of bother:* **restrained**, modest, understated, muted, subtle, quiet, low-profile, inconspicuous, unostentatious, unobtrusive, discreet, toned-down.
– OPPOSITES ostentatious, obtrusive.

lowly adjective *he comes from a lowly background:* **humble**, low, low-born, low-bred, low-ranking, plebeian, proletarian; common, ordinary, plain, average, modest, simple; inferior, ignoble, subordinate, obscure.
– OPPOSITES aristocratic, exalted.

loyal adjective *a loyal and trusted servant:* **faithful**, true, devoted; constant, steadfast, staunch, dependable, reliable, trusted, trustworthy, trusty, dutiful, dedicated, unchanging, unwavering, unswerving; patriotic.
– OPPOSITES treacherous.

loyalty noun *I have not done this just to demonstrate my loyalty to the Prime Minister:* **allegiance**, faithfulness,

obedience, adherence, homage, devotion; steadfastness, staunchness, dependability, reliability, trustiness, trustworthiness, duty, dedication, commitment; patriotism.
– OPPOSITES treachery.

lozenge noun 1 *the pattern consists of overlapping lozenges:* **diamond**, rhombus. 2 *I sucked furiously on a lozenge:* **pastille**, drop; cough sweet.

lubricant noun **grease**, oil, lubrication, lubricator, emollient, lotion, unguent; informal lube.

lubricate verb *lubricate the washer with silicone grease:* **oil**, **grease**, wax, polish.
– OPPOSITES impede.

lucid adjective 1 *he gives a lucid description of this complex subject:* **intelligible**, comprehensible, understandable, cogent, coherent, articulate; clear, transparent; plain, simple, vivid, sharp, straightforward, unambiguous, graphic. 2 *he was not sufficiently lucid to explain what had happened:* **rational**, sane, in one's right mind, in possession of one's faculties, compos mentis, able to think clearly, balanced, clear-headed, sober, sensible; informal all there.
– OPPOSITES confusing, confused.

luck noun 1 *with luck you'll make it to Sheffield by this afternoon:* **good fortune**, good luck; fluke, stroke of luck; informal lucky break. 2 *I wish you luck:* **success**, prosperity, good fortune, good luck. 3 *it is a matter of luck whether it hits or misses:* **fortune**, fate, destiny, lot, stars, karma, kismet; fortuity, serendipity; chance, accident, a twist of fate; Austral./NZ informal mozzle.
– OPPOSITES bad luck, misfortune.
■ **in luck** fortunate, lucky, blessed with good luck, born under a lucky star; successful, having a charmed life; Brit. informal jammy.
■ **out of luck** unfortunate, unlucky, luckless, hapless, unsuccessful, cursed, jinxed, ill-fated; informal down on one's luck.

luckily adverb **fortunately**, happily, providentially, opportunely, by good fortune, as luck would have it, propitiously; mercifully, thankfully.
– OPPOSITES unfortunately.

luckless adjective **unlucky**, unfortunate, unsuccessful, hapless, out of luck, cursed, jinxed, doomed, ill-fated; informal down on one's luck; literary star-crossed.
– OPPOSITES lucky.

lucky adjective 1 *the lucky winner will receive a cheque for £1,000* | *I'm lucky to have such a loving family:* **fortunate**, in luck, blessed, blessed with good luck, favoured, born under a lucky star, charmed; successful, prosperous; born with a silver spoon in one's mouth; Brit. informal jammy. 2 *I had a lucky escape:* **providential**, fortunate, advantageous, timely, opportune,

serendipitous, expedient, heaven-sent, auspicious; chance, fortuitous, fluky, accidental.
– OPPOSITES unfortunate.

lucrative adjective *drug dealing is a lucrative business:* **profitable**, profit-making, gainful, remunerative, moneymaking, paying, high-income, well paid, bankable; rewarding, worthwhile; thriving, flourishing, successful, booming.
– OPPOSITES unprofitable.

ludicrous adjective *that's a ludicrous suggestion that I will not deign to refute:* **absurd**, ridiculous, farcical, laughable, risible, preposterous, foolish, mad, insane, idiotic, stupid, inane, silly, asinine, nonsensical; informal crazy; rare derisible.
– OPPOSITES sensible.

lug verb *they lugged the baskets of laundry upstairs:* **carry**, lift, bear, tote, heave, hoist, shoulder, manhandle; haul, drag, tug, tow, transport, move, convey, shift; informal hump, schlep; Scottish informal humph.

luggage noun **baggage**; bags, suitcases, cases, trunks. See also **BAG** noun sense 2.

lugubrious adjective *Sven's lugubrious face lit up in a brief smile:* **mournful**, gloomy, sad, unhappy, doleful, glum, melancholy, woeful, miserable, woebegone, forlorn, long-faced, sombre, solemn, serious, sorrowful, morose, dour, cheerless, joyless, dismal; Eeyorish; funereal, sepulchral; informal down in the mouth; literary dolorous.
– OPPOSITES cheerful.

lukewarm adjective **1** *a cup of lukewarm coffee:* **tepid**, warm, warmish, at room temperature. **2** *we received a lukewarm response from the committee:* **indifferent**, cool, half-hearted, apathetic, unenthusiastic, tepid, offhand, perfunctory, non-committal, lackadaisical; informal laid-back, unenthused, couldn't-care-less.
– OPPOSITES hot, cold, enthusiastic.

lull verb **1** *the sound of the bells lulled us to sleep:* **soothe**, calm, hush; rock to sleep. **2** *his suspicions were soon lulled:* **assuage**, allay, ease, alleviate, soothe, quiet, quieten; reduce, diminish; quell, banish, dispel.
– OPPOSITES waken, agitate, arouse, intensify.
noun *there was a brief lull in the fighting:* **pause**, respite, interval, break, hiatus, suspension, interlude, intermission, breathing space; informal let-up, breather.
– OPPOSITES agitation, activity.

lumber[1] verb *a herd of elephants lumbered past:* **lurch**, stumble, trundle, shamble, shuffle, waddle; trudge, clump, stump, plod, tramp; informal galumph.

lumber[2] noun **1** *a spare room packed with lumber:* **jumble**, clutter, odds and ends, bits and pieces, flotsam and jetsam, cast-offs; refuse, rubbish, litter; N. Amer. trash; informal junk, odds and sods, gubbins, clobber. **2** *he worked in the lumber trade:* **timber**, wood.
verb (Brit. informal) *she was lumbered with a*

useless husband and a sick child: **burden**, saddle, encumber, hamper; load, oppress, trouble, tax; informal land, dump something on someone.
– OPPOSITES free.

lumbering adjective **clumsy**, awkward, heavy-footed, slow, blundering, bumbling, inept, maladroit, uncoordinated, ungainly, ungraceful, gauche, lumpish, hulking, ponderous; informal clodhopping.
– OPPOSITES nimble, agile.

luminary noun *the luminaries of the art world gathered to pay homage:* **leading light**, guiding light, inspiration, role model, hero, heroine, leader, expert, master; legend, great, giant.
– OPPOSITES nobody.

luminous adjective **shining**, bright, brilliant, radiant, dazzling, glowing, gleaming, scintillating, lustrous; luminescent, phosphorescent, fluorescent, incandescent.
– OPPOSITES dark.

lump noun **1** *I picked up a lump of coal:* **chunk**, hunk, piece, mass, block, wedge, slab, cake, nugget, ball, brick, cube, pat, knob, clod, gobbet, dollop, wad; informal glob; N. Amer. informal gob. **2** *he had a nasty lump on his head:* **swelling**, bump, bulge, protuberance, protrusion, growth, outgrowth, nodule, hump.
verb *the media tend to lump women singer-songwriters together:* **combine**, put, group, bunch, aggregate, unite, pool, merge, collect, throw.

lumpish adjective **1** *a room full of ugly, lumpish furniture:* **cumbersome**, unwieldy, heavy, hulking, chunky, bulky, ponderous. **2** *she was a dull, lumpish young girl:* **stupid**, obtuse, dense, dim-witted, dull-witted, slow-witted, slow; lethargic, bovine, sluggish, listless; informal thick, dumb, dopey, slow on the uptake, moronic; Brit. informal dozy.
– OPPOSITES elegant, quick-witted, sharp.

lumpy adjective **1** *a lumpy mattress:* **bumpy**, knobbly, bulging, uneven, rough, gnarled. **2** *lumpy custard:* **clotted**, curdled, congealed, coagulated.

lunacy noun **1** *the survivors descended into despair and lunacy:* **insanity**, madness, dementia, mania, psychosis; informal craziness. **2** *such a policy would be sheer lunacy:* **folly**, foolishness, foolhardiness, stupidity, silliness, idiocy, madness, rashness, recklessness, imprudence, irresponsibility, injudiciousness; informal craziness; Brit. informal daftness.
– OPPOSITES sanity, sense, prudence.

lunatic noun *he drives like a lunatic:* **maniac**, madman, madwoman, imbecile, psychopath, psychotic; fool, idiot; informal loony, nut, nutcase, head case, psycho, moron; Brit. informal nutter, mentalist; N. Amer. informal screwball.

lunch noun **midday meal**, luncheon; Brit. dinner.

lunge noun *Darren made a lunge at his*

attacker: **thrust**, dive, rush, charge, grab.
verb *he lunged at Finn with a knife:* **thrust**, dive, spring, launch oneself, rush.

lurch verb **1** *he lurched into the kitchen:* **stagger**, stumble, wobble, sway, reel, roll, weave, pitch, totter, blunder. **2** *the ship lurched alarmingly to one side:* **sway**, reel, list, heel, rock, roll, pitch, toss, jerk, shake, judder, flounder, swerve.

lure verb *consumers are frequently lured into debt:* **tempt**, entice, attract, induce, coax, persuade, inveigle, allure, seduce, cajole, beguile, bewitch, ensnare.
– OPPOSITES deter, put off.
noun *Les could never resist the lure of the stage:* **temptation**, enticement, attraction, pull, draw, appeal; allure, fascination.

lurid adjective **1** *a lurid birthday card:* **bright**, brilliant, vivid, glaring, shocking, fluorescent, dazzling, intense, gaudy, loud. **2** *a lurid account of prostitution and addiction:* **sensational**, sensationalist, exaggerated, over-dramatized, extravagant, colourful; salacious, graphic, explicit, prurient, shocking; gruesome, gory, grisly; informal tacky, shock-horror, juicy, full-frontal, full-on.
– OPPOSITES muted, restrained.

lurk verb **skulk**, loiter, lie in wait, hide.

luscious adjective **delicious**, succulent, lush, juicy, mouth-watering, sweet, tasty, appetizing; informal scrumptious, moreish, scrummy, yummy; N. Amer. informal nummy.
– OPPOSITES unappetizing.

lush adjective **1** *the hills are covered in lush vegetation:* **luxuriant**, rich, abundant, profuse, riotous, prolific, vigorous; dense, thick, rampant. **2** *a lush apartment:* **luxurious**, de luxe, sumptuous, palatial, opulent, lavish, elaborate, extravagant, fancy; informal plush, ritzy, posh, swanky; Brit. informal swish; N. Amer. informal swank.
– OPPOSITES barren, sparse, austere.

lust noun **1** *he was watching her with undisguised lust:* **desire**, longing, ardour, passion; libido, sex drive, sexuality; lechery, lecherousness, lasciviousness; informal horniness, the hots; Brit. informal randiness.
2 *he was driven by a lust for power:* **greed**, desire, craving, covetousness, eagerness, avidity, cupidity, longing, yearning, hunger, thirst, appetite, hankering.
– OPPOSITES dread, aversion.
verb **1** *he lusted after his employer's wife:* **desire**, crave, ache for, burn for, pant for; informal have the hots for, lech after/over, fancy, have a thing about/for, drool over, have the horn for. **2** *she lusted after adventure:* **crave**, desire, covet, want, wish for, long for, yearn for, dream of, hanker for, hanker after, hunger for, thirst for, ache for.
– OPPOSITES dread, avoid.

lustful adjective **lecherous**, lascivious, libidinous, licentious, salacious; wanton, unchaste, impure, naughty, immodest,

indecent, dirty, prurient; passionate, sensual, sexy, erotic; informal horny, randy, raunchy; formal concupiscent.
– OPPOSITES chaste, pure.

lustily adverb **heartily**, vigorously, loudly, at the top of one's voice, powerfully, forcefully, strongly; informal like mad, like crazy.
– OPPOSITES feebly, quietly.

lustre noun *the lustre on his pots is produced by several layers of wax:* **sheen**, gloss, shine, glow, gleam, shimmer, polish, patina.
– OPPOSITES dullness.

lustreless adjective **dull**, lacklustre, matt, unpolished, tarnished, dingy, dim, dark.
– OPPOSITES lustrous, bright.

lustrous adjective **shiny**, shining, satiny, glossy, gleaming, shimmering, burnished, polished; radiant, bright, brilliant, luminous; dazzling, sparkling, glistening, twinkling.
– OPPOSITES dull, dark.

lusty adjective **1** *a throng of lusty young men:* **healthy**, strong, fit, vigorous, robust, hale and hearty, energetic; rugged, sturdy, muscular, muscly, strapping, hefty, husky, burly, powerful; informal beefy. **2** *he sang a few bars in a lusty baritone:* **loud**, vigorous, hearty, strong, powerful, forceful.
– OPPOSITES feeble, quiet.

luxuriant adjective *luxuriant vegetation:* **lush**, rich, abundant, profuse, exuberant, riotous, prolific, vigorous; dense, thick, rank, rampant.
– OPPOSITES barren, sparse.

luxuriate verb *he would go and run a hot bath, then luxuriate in it:* **revel**, bask, delight, take pleasure, wallow; (**luxuriate in**) enjoy, relish, savour, appreciate; informal get a kick out of, get a thrill out of.
– OPPOSITES dislike.

luxurious adjective *a luxurious Mayfair apartment:* **opulent**, sumptuous, de luxe, grand, palatial, splendid, magnificent, well appointed, extravagant, fancy; Brit. upmarket; informal plush, posh, classy, ritzy, swanky; Brit. informal swish; N. Amer. informal swank.
– OPPOSITES plain, basic.

luxury noun **1** *we'll live in luxury for the rest of our lives:* **opulence**, luxuriousness, sumptuousness, grandeur, magnificence, splendour, lavishness, the lap of luxury, milk and honey; informal the life of Riley. **2** *a TV is his only luxury:* **indulgence**, extravagance, self-indulgence, non-essential, treat, extra, frill.
– OPPOSITES simplicity, necessity.

lying noun *she was no good at lying:* **untruthfulness**, fabrication, fibbing, perjury, white lies; falseness, dishonesty, mendacity, telling stories, invention, misrepresentation, deceit, duplicity; informal kidology; literary perfidy.
– OPPOSITES honesty.
adjective *he was a lying womanizer:* **untruthful**, false, dishonest, mendacious,

deceitful, deceiving, duplicitous, double-dealing, two-faced; literary perfidious.
– OPPOSITES truthful.

lyrical adjective **1** *lyrical love poetry:* **expressive**, emotional, deeply felt, personal, subjective, passionate. **2** *she was lyrical about her success:* **enthusiastic**, rhapsodic, effusive, rapturous, ecstatic, euphoric, carried away.
– OPPOSITES unenthusiastic.
■ **wax lyrical** be enthusiastic, enthuse, rave, gush, get carried away.

lyrics plural noun **words**, libretto, book, text, lines.

Mm

macabre adjective **1** *black magic involves some macabre rituals:* **gruesome**, grisly, grim, gory, morbid, ghastly, unearthly, grotesque, hideous, horrific, shocking, dreadful, loathsome, repugnant, repulsive, sickening. **2** *a macabre joke:* **black**, weird, unhealthy; informal sick.

mace noun **club**, cudgel, stick, staff, shillelagh, bludgeon, truncheon; Brit. life preserver; N. Amer. nightstick, billy, billy club, blackjack; Brit. informal cosh.

macerate verb *macerate the seeds in a vinegar solution:* **pulp**, mash, squash, soften, liquefy, soak.

Machiavellian adjective *there were press accusations of Machiavellian deception:* **devious**, cunning, crafty, artful, wily, sly, scheming, treacherous, two-faced, tricky, double-dealing, unscrupulous, deceitful, dishonest; informal foxy.
– OPPOSITES straightforward, ingenuous.

machinations plural noun *they attributed the unrest to the machinations of the communists:* **scheming**, plotting, intrigues, conspiracies, ruses, tricks, wiles, stratagems, tactics, manoeuvring.

machine noun **1** *it is quicker done by machine:* **apparatus**, appliance, device, contraption, contrivance, mechanism, engine, gadget, tool. **2** *an efficient publicity machine:* **organization**, system, structure, arrangement, machinery; informal set-up.

machinery noun **1** *road-making machinery:* **equipment**, apparatus, plant, hardware, gear, tackle; mechanism; instruments, tools; gadgetry, technology. **2** *the machinery of local government:* **workings**, organization, system, structure, administration, institution; informal set-up.

machismo noun *a woman following her career can challenge her husband's machismo:* **(aggressive) masculinity**, toughness, male chauvinism, sexism, laddishness; virility, manliness.

macho adjective *a macho, non-caring image:* **(aggressively) male**, (unpleasantly) masculine; manly, virile, red-blooded; informal butch, laddish.
– OPPOSITES wimpish.
noun *he was a macho at heart:* **red-blooded male**, macho man, muscleman; informal he-man, tough guy.
– OPPOSITES wimp.

mad adjective **1** *he was killed by his mad brother:* **insane**, mentally ill, certifiable, deranged, demented, of unsound mind, out of one's mind, not in one's right mind, sick in the head, crazy, crazed, lunatic, non compos mentis, unhinged, disturbed, raving, psychotic, psychopathic, mad as a hatter, mad as a March hare, away with the fairies; informal mental, off one's head, off one's nut, nuts, nutty, off one's rocker, not right in the head, round the bend, stark staring/raving mad, bats, batty, bonkers, dotty, cuckoo, cracked, loopy, loony, doolally, bananas, loco, dippy, screwy, schizoid, touched, gaga, up the pole, not all there, not right upstairs; Brit. informal barmy, crackers, barking, barking mad, round the twist, off one's trolley, not the full shilling; N. Amer. informal nutso, out of one's tree, meshuga, wacko, gonzo; Austral./NZ informal bushed; NZ informal porangi; **(be mad)** informal have a screw loose, have bats in the/one's belfry; Austral. informal have kangaroos in the/one's top paddock; **(go mad)** lose one's reason, lose one's mind, take leave of one's senses; informal lose one's marbles, crack up. **2** *some mad scheme:* **foolish**, insane, stupid, lunatic, foolhardy, idiotic, senseless, absurd, impractical, silly, inane, asinine, wild, unwise, imprudent; informal crazy, crackpot, crackbrained; Brit. informal daft. **3** (informal) *he's mad about jazz:* **enthusiastic**, passionate; ardent, fervent, avid, fanatical; devoted to, infatuated with, in love with, hot for; informal crazy, dotty, nuts, wild, hooked on, gone on; Brit. informal potty; N. Amer. informal nutso. **4** *it was a mad dash to get ready:* **frenzied**, frantic, frenetic, feverish, hysterical, wild, hectic, manic.
– OPPOSITES sane, pleased, sensible, indifferent, calm.

madcap adjective **1** *he wanted me to invest in some madcap scheme:* **reckless**, rash, foolhardy, foolish, hare-brained, wild, hasty, imprudent, ill-advised; informal crazy, crackpot, crackbrained. **2** *a madcap comedy:* **zany**, eccentric, unconventional.
noun *she was a boisterous madcap:* **eccentric**, crank, madman/madwoman, maniac, lunatic; oddity, character, individual; informal crackpot, oddball, weirdo, loony, nut; Brit. informal nutter, mentalist; N. Amer. informal screwball.

madden verb **1** *what maddens people most is his vagueness:* **infuriate**, exasperate,

m

irritate; incense, anger, enrage, provoke, upset, agitate, vex, irk, make someone's hackles rise, make someone see red; informal aggravate, make someone's blood boil, make livid, get up someone's nose, get someone's goat, get someone's back up; Brit. informal nark; N. Amer. informal tee off, tick off. **2** *they were maddened with pain:* **drive mad**, drive insane, derange, unhinge, unbalance; informal drive round the bend.

made-up adjective *a made-up story:* **invented**, fabricated, trumped up, concocted, fictitious, fictional, false, untrue, specious, spurious, bogus, apocryphal, imaginary, mythical.

madhouse noun informal *the place was a total madhouse:* **bedlam**, mayhem, chaos, pandemonium, uproar, turmoil, disorder, madness, all hell broken loose; N. Amer. three-ring circus.

madly adverb **1** *she was smiling madly:* **insanely**, deliriously, wildly, like a lunatic; informal crazily, barmily. **2** *it was fun, hurtling madly downhill:* **fast**, furiously, hurriedly, quickly, speedily, hastily, energetically; informal like mad, like crazy. **3** (informal) *he loved her madly:* **intensely**, fervently, wildly, unrestrainedly, to distraction.
– OPPOSITES sanely, slowly, slightly.

madman, madwoman noun **lunatic**, maniac, psychotic, psychopath; informal loony, nut, nutcase, head case, psycho; Brit. informal nutter, mentalist; N. Amer. informal screwball.

madness noun **1** *today madness is called mental illness:* **insanity**, mental illness, dementia, derangement, lunacy, instability; mania, psychosis; informal craziness. **2** *it would be madness to do otherwise:* **folly**, foolishness, idiocy, stupidity, insanity, lunacy, silliness; informal craziness. **3** *it's absolute madness in here:* **bedlam**, mayhem, chaos, pandemonium, uproar, turmoil, disorder, all hell broken loose; N. Amer. three-ring circus.
– OPPOSITES sanity, common sense, good sense, calm.

maelstrom noun **1** *a maelstrom in the sea:* **whirlpool**, vortex, eddy, swirl. **2** *the maelstrom of war:* **turbulence**, tumult, turmoil, disorder, disarray, chaos, confusion, upheaval, pandemonium, bedlam, whirlwind.

maestro noun *a remarkable resemblance to the Italian singing maestro:* **virtuoso**, master, expert, genius, wizard, prodigy; informal ace, whizz, pro, hotshot.
– OPPOSITES tyro, beginner.

magazine noun **journal**, periodical, supplement, colour supplement; informal glossy, mag, 'zine.

magenta adjective **reddish-purple**, purplish-red, crimson, plum, carmine red, fuchsia.

maggot noun **grub**, larva.

magic noun **1** *do you believe in magic?*

sorcery, witchcraft, wizardry, necromancy, enchantment, the supernatural, occultism, the occult, black magic, the black arts, voodoo, shamanism; charm, hex, spell, jinx; N. Amer. mojo. **2** *he does magic at children's parties:* **conjuring tricks**, sleight of hand, legerdemain, illusion, prestidigitation. **3** *the magic of the stage:* **allure**, attraction, excitement, fascination, charm, glamour. adjective **1** *a magic spell:* **supernatural**, enchanted, occult. **2** *a magic place:* **fascinating**, captivating, charming, glamorous, magical, enchanting, entrancing, spellbinding, magnetic, irresistible, hypnotic.

magical adjective **1** *magical incantations:* **supernatural**, magic, occult, shamanistic, mystical, paranormal, preternatural, other-worldly. **2** *the news had a magical effect:* **extraordinary**, remarkable, exceptional, outstanding, incredible, phenomenal, unbelievable, amazing, astonishing, astounding, stunning, staggering, marvellous, magnificent, wonderful, sensational, breathtaking, miraculous; informal fantastic, fabulous, stupendous, out of this world, terrific, tremendous, brilliant, mind-boggling, mind-blowing, awesome. **3** *this magical small land:* **enchanting**, entrancing, spellbinding, bewitching, beguiling, fascinating, captivating, alluring, enthralling, charming, attractive, lovely, delightful, beautiful; informal dreamy, heavenly, divine, gorgeous.
– OPPOSITES predictable, boring.

magician noun **1 sorcerer**, sorceress, witch, wizard, warlock, enchanter, enchantress, necromancer, shaman. **2 conjuror**, illusionist, prestidigitator.

magisterial adjective **1** *a magisterial pronouncement:* **authoritative**, masterful, assured, lordly, commanding, assertive. **2** *his magisterial style of questioning:* **domineering**, dictatorial, autocratic, imperious, overbearing, peremptory, high-handed, arrogant, supercilious, patronizing; informal bossy.
– OPPOSITES untrustworthy, humble, hesitant, tentative.

magnanimity noun **generosity**, charity, benevolence, beneficence, big-heartedness, altruism, philanthropy, humanity, chivalry, nobility; clemency, mercy, leniency, forgiveness, indulgence.
– OPPOSITES meanness, selfishness.

magnanimous adjective *she was magnanimous in victory:* **generous**, charitable, benevolent, beneficent, big-hearted, handsome, princely, altruistic, philanthropic, chivalrous, noble; forgiving, merciful, lenient, indulgent, clement.
– OPPOSITES mean-spirited, selfish.

magnate noun *the real power lay in the hands of a few rich magnates and landowners:* **tycoon**, mogul, captain of industry, baron, lord, king; industrialist, proprietor; informal big shot, honcho; derogatory fat cat.

magnet noun **1** *you can tell steel by using a magnet:* **lodestone**; electromagnet, solenoid. **2** *a magnet for tourists:* **attraction**, focus, draw, lure.

magnetic adjective *a magnetic personality:* **alluring**, attractive, fascinating, captivating, enchanting, enthralling, appealing, charming, prepossessing, engaging, entrancing, seductive, inviting, irresistible, charismatic.

magnetism noun *crowds were drawn by his sheer magnetism:* **allure**, attraction, fascination, appeal, draw, drawing power, pull, charm, enchantment, seductiveness, magic, spell, charisma.

magnification noun *optical magnification:* **enlargement**, enhancement, increase, augmentation, extension, expansion, amplification, intensification.
– OPPOSITES reduction.

magnificence noun **splendour**, resplendence, grandeur, impressiveness, glory, majesty, nobility, pomp, stateliness, elegance, sumptuousness, opulence, luxury, lavishness, richness, brilliance, dazzle, skill, virtuosity.
– OPPOSITES modesty, tawdriness, weakness.

magnificent adjective **1** *a magnificent view of the mountains:* **splendid**, spectacular, impressive, striking, glorious, superb, majestic, awesome, awe-inspiring, breathtaking. **2** *a magnificent apartment overlooking the lake:* **sumptuous**, resplendent, grand, impressive, imposing, monumental, palatial, stately, opulent, luxurious, lavish, rich, dazzling, beautiful, elegant; informal splendiferous, ritzy, posh. **3** *a magnificent performance:* **masterly**, skilful, virtuoso, brilliant.
– OPPOSITES uninspiring, modest, tawdry, poor, weak.

magnify verb *the lens magnifies the image:* **enlarge**, boost, enhance, maximize, increase, augment, extend, expand, amplify, intensify; informal blow up.
– OPPOSITES reduce, minimize.

magnitude noun **1** *the magnitude of the task:* **immensity**, vastness, hugeness, enormity; size, extent, expanse, greatness, largeness, bigness. **2** *events of tragic magnitude:* **importance**, import, significance, weight, consequence, mark, notability, note. **3** *a change in magnitude on the Richter scale:* **value**, figure, number, measure, order, quantity, vector, index, indicator. **4** *a star of magnitude 4.2:* **brightness**, brilliance, radiance, luminosity.
– OPPOSITES smallness, triviality.
■ **of the first magnitude** of the utmost importance, of the greatest significance, very important, of great consequence; formal of great moment.

maid noun *the maid cleared the table:*

female servant, maidservant, housemaid, parlourmaid, lady's maid, chambermaid, maid-of-all-work, domestic; help, cleaner, cleaning woman/lady; Brit. informal daily, skivvy, Mrs Mop.

maiden adjective **1** *a maiden aunt:* **unmarried**, spinster, unwed, unwedded, single, husbandless, celibate. **2** *a maiden voyage:* **first**, initial, inaugural, introductory, initiatory.

maidenly adjective *her maidenly demeanour:* **virginal**, immaculate, intact, chaste, pure, virtuous; demure, reserved, retiring, decorous, seemly.
– OPPOSITES fast, slatternly.

mail noun *the mail arrived:* **post**, letters, correspondence; postal system, postal service, post office; delivery, collection; email; informal snail mail; N. Amer. the mails.
verb *we mailed the parcels:* **send**, post, dispatch, direct, forward, redirect, ship; email.

maim verb *they are prepared to kill and maim innocent people in pursuit of their cause:* **injure**, wound, cripple, disable, incapacitate, impair, mar, mutilate, lacerate, disfigure, deform, mangle.

main adjective *the main item:* **principal**, chief, head, leading, foremost, most important, major, ruling, dominant, central, focal, key, prime, master, premier, primary, first, fundamental, supreme, predominant, (most) prominent, pre-eminent, paramount, overriding, cardinal, crucial, critical, pivotal, salient, elemental, essential, staple.
– OPPOSITES subsidiary, minor.

mainly adverb *the people are mainly visitors:* **mostly**, for the most part, in the main, on the whole, largely, by and large, to a large extent, predominantly, chiefly, principally, primarily; generally, usually, typically, commonly, on average, as a rule, almost always.

mainspring noun *the mainspring of anti-communism:* **motive**, motivation, impetus, driving force, incentive, impulse, prime mover, reason, fountain, fount, root, generator.

mainstay noun *agriculture was the mainstay of the economy:* **central component**, central figure, centrepiece, prop, linchpin, cornerstone, pillar, bulwark, buttress, chief support, backbone, anchor, foundation, base, staple.

mainstream adjective *the author never strays far from mainstream physics:* **normal**, conventional, ordinary, orthodox, conformist, accepted, established, recognized, common, usual, prevailing, popular.
– OPPOSITES fringe.

maintain verb **1** *they wanted to maintain peace:* **preserve**, conserve, keep, retain, keep going, keep alive, keep up, prolong, perpetuate, sustain, carry on, continue. **2** *the*

m

council maintains the roads: **keep in good condition**, keep in (good) repair, keep up, service, care for, take good care of, look after. **3** the costs of maintaining a family: **support**, provide for, keep, sustain; nurture, feed, nourish. **4** he always maintained his innocence | he maintains that he is innocent: **insist (on)**, declare, assert, protest, affirm, avow, profess, claim, allege, contend, argue, swear (to), hold to.
– OPPOSITES break, discontinue, neglect, deny.

maintenance noun **1** the maintenance of peace is the UN's priority: **preservation**, conservation, keeping, prolongation, perpetuation, carrying on, continuation, continuance. **2** I can do a bit of car maintenance: **upkeep**, service, servicing, repair(s), care, aftercare. **3** the maintenance of his children: **support**, keeping, upkeep, sustenance; nurture, feeding, nourishment. **4** absent fathers are forced to pay maintenance: **financial support**, child support, alimony, provision; keep, subsistence, living expenses.
– OPPOSITES breakdown, discontinuation, neglect.

majestic adjective majestic mountain scenery: **stately**, dignified, distinguished, solemn, magnificent, grand, splendid, resplendent, glorious, sumptuous, impressive, august, noble, awe-inspiring, monumental, palatial; statuesque, Olympian, imposing, marvellous, sonorous, resounding, heroic.
– OPPOSITES modest, wretched.

majesty noun **1** the majesty of the procession: **stateliness**, dignity, distinction, solemnity, magnificence, pomp, grandeur, grandness, splendour, resplendence, glory, impressiveness, augustness, nobility. **2** the majesty invested in the monarch: **sovereignty**, authority, power, dominion, supremacy.
– OPPOSITES modesty, wretchedness.

major adjective **1** the major English poets: **greatest**, best, finest, most important, chief, main, prime, principal, capital, cardinal, leading, star, foremost, outstanding, first-rate, pre-eminent, arch-. **2** an issue of major importance: **crucial**, vital, great, considerable, paramount, utmost, prime. **3** a major factor: **important**, big, significant, weighty, crucial, key, sweeping, substantial. **4** major surgery: **serious**, radical, complicated, difficult.
– OPPOSITES minor, little, trivial.

majority noun **1** the majority of cases: **larger part/number**, greater part/number, best/better part, most, more than half; bulk, mass, weight, (main) body, preponderance, predominance, generality, lion's share. **2** Labour retained the seat by a large majority: **(winning) margin**, superiority of numbers/votes; landslide. **3** my son has reached his majority: **coming of age**, legal

age, adulthood, manhood/womanhood, maturity; age of consent.
– OPPOSITES minority.

make verb **1** he makes models: **construct**, build, assemble, put together, manufacture, produce, fabricate, create, form, fashion, model. **2** she made me drink it: **force**, compel, coerce, press, drive, pressure, pressurize, oblige, require; have someone do something, prevail on, dragoon, bludgeon, strong-arm, impel, constrain; informal railroad. **3** don't make such a noise: **cause**, create, give rise to, produce, bring about, generate, engender, occasion, effect, set up, establish, institute, found, develop, originate. **4** she made a little bow: **perform**, execute, give, do, accomplish, achieve, bring off, carry out, effect. **5** they made him chairman: **appoint**, designate, name, nominate, select, elect, vote in, install; induct, institute, invest, ordain. **6** I've made a mistake: **perpetrate**, commit, be responsible for, be guilty of, be to blame for. **7** he's made a lot of money: **acquire**, obtain, gain, get, realize, secure, win, earn; gross, net, clear; bring in, take (in). **8** he made tea: **prepare**, get ready, put together, concoct, cook, dish up, throw together, whip up, brew; informal fix; Brit. informal mash. **9** we've got to make a decision: **reach**, come to, settle on, determine on, conclude. **10** she made a short announcement: **utter**, give, deliver, give voice to, enunciate, recite, pronounce. **11** the sofa makes a good bed: **be**, act as, serve as, function as, constitute, do duty for.
– OPPOSITES destroy, lose.
noun what make is the car? **brand**, marque, label.
■ **make as if/though** feign, pretend, make a show/pretence of, affect, feint, make out; informal put it on.
■ **make away with 1** she decided to make away with him: kill, murder, dispatch, eliminate; informal bump off, do away with, do in, do for, knock off, top, croak, stiff, blow away; N. Amer. informal ice, rub out, smoke, waste. **2** they made away with the evidence: dispose of, get rid of, destroy, throw away, jettison, ditch, dump; informal do away with.
■ **make believe** pretend, fantasize, daydream, build castles in the air, build castles in Spain, dream, imagine, play-act, play.
■ **make do** scrape by, scrape along, get by/along, manage, cope, survive, muddle through/along, improvise, make ends meet, keep the wolf from the door, keep one's head above water; informal make out; (**make do with**) make the best of, get by on, put up with.
■ **make for 1** she made for the door: go for/towards, head for/towards, aim for, make one's way towards, move towards, direct one's steps towards, steer a course towards, be bound for, make a beeline for. **2** constant arguing doesn't make for a happy marriage: contribute to, be conducive to, produce, promote, facilitate, foster.

■ **make it 1** *he never made it as a singer:*
succeed, be a success, distinguish oneself,
get ahead, make good; informal make the
grade, arrive, crack it. **2** *she's very ill—is
she going to make it?* survive, come through,
pull through, get better, recover.

■ **make love.** See HAVE SEX at SEX.

■ **make off** *on seeing the police they made
off:* run away/off, take to one's heels, beat
a hasty retreat, flee, make one's getaway,
make a quick exit, run for it, make a run for
it, take off, take flight, bolt, make oneself
scarce, decamp, do a disappearing act; informal
clear off/out, beat it, leg it, cut and run,
skedaddle, vamoose, hightail it, hotfoot it,
show a clean pair of heels, fly the coop, split,
scoot, scram; Brit. informal scarper, do a runner;
N. Amer. informal take a powder.

■ **make off with** *he's made off with my
handbag!* take, steal, purloin, pilfer, abscond
with, run away/off with, carry off, snatch;
kidnap, abduct; informal walk away/off with,
swipe, filch, snaffle, nab, lift, liberate, snitch;
Brit. informal pinch, half-inch, nick, whip, knock
off; N. Amer. informal heist, glom.

■ **make something out 1** *I could just
make out a figure in the distance:* see,
discern, distinguish, perceive, pick out,
detect, observe, recognize. **2** *he couldn't
make out what he was saying:* understand,
comprehend, follow, grasp, fathom, work
out, make sense of, interpret, decipher,
make head or tail of, get, get the drift of,
catch. **3** *she made out that he was violent:*
allege, claim, assert, declare, maintain,
affirm, suggest, imply, hint, insinuate,
indicate, intimate, impute. **4** *he made out
a receipt for $20:* write out, fill out, fill in,
complete, draw up.

■ **make something over to someone**
transfer, sign over, turn over, hand
over/on/down, give, leave, bequeath,
bestow, pass on, assign, consign, entrust.

■ **make up** *let's kiss and make up:* be friends
again, bury the hatchet, declare a truce,
make peace, forgive and forget, shake hands,
become reconciled, settle one's differences,
mend fences, call it quits.

■ **make something up 1** *exports make up
42% of earnings:* comprise, form, compose,
constitute, account for. **2** *Gina brought a
friend to make up a foursome:* complete,
round off, finish. **3** *the pharmacist made up
the prescription:* prepare, mix, concoct, put
together. **4** *he made up an excuse:* invent,
fabricate, concoct, dream up, think up,
hatch, trump up; devise, manufacture,
formulate, coin; informal cook up. **5** *she made
up her face:* apply make-up/cosmetics to,
powder, rouge; (**make oneself up**) informal
put on one's face, do/paint one's face, apply
one's warpaint, doll oneself up.

■ **make up for 1** *she tried to make up for
what she'd said:* atone for, make amends
for, compensate for, make recompense
for, make reparation for, make redress
for, make restitution for, expiate. **2** *job

satisfaction can make up for low pay: offset,
counterbalance, counteract, compensate for;
balance, neutralize, cancel out, even up,
redeem.

■ **make up one's mind** decide, come to a
decision, make/reach a decision; settle on a
plan of action, come to a conclusion, reach a
conclusion; determine, resolve.

■ **make up to** (informal) *she spent the whole
evening making up to Adam:* curry favour
with, cultivate, try to win over, court,
ingratiate oneself with; informal suck up to,
butter up; N. Amer. informal shine up to.

■ **make way** *make way for the king:* move
aside, clear the way, make a space, make
room, stand back.

make-believe noun *that was sheer make-
believe:* **fantasy**, pretence, daydreaming,
imagination, invention, fancy, dream,
fabrication, play-acting, charade,
masquerade.
– OPPOSITES reality.
adjective *make-believe adventures:*
imaginary, imagined, made-up, fantasy,
dreamed-up, fanciful, fictitious, fictive,
feigned, fake, mock, sham, simulated; informal
pretend, phoney.
– OPPOSITES real, actual.

maker noun *the maker's name is stamped
on the back:* **creator**, manufacturer,
constructor, builder, producer, fabricator.

makeshift adjective *a huge makeshift
scaffold had been erected in front of the
palace:* **temporary**, provisional, stopgap,
standby, rough and ready, improvised, ad
hoc, extempore, thrown together, cobbled
together.
– OPPOSITES permanent.

make-up noun **1** *she used excessive make-
up:* **cosmetics**, maquillage; greasepaint;
face paint; informal warpaint, slap. **2** *the
cellular make-up of plants:* **composition**,
constitution, structure, configuration,
arrangement, organization, formation.
3 *jealousy isn't part of his make-
up:* **character**, nature, temperament,
personality, disposition, mentality, persona,
psyche; informal what makes someone tick.

making noun **1** *the making of cars:*
manufacture, mass production, building,
construction, assembly, production,
creation, putting together, fabrication,
forming, moulding, forging. **2** *she has
the makings of a champion:* **qualities**,
characteristics, ingredients; potential,
promise, capacity, capability; essentials,
essence, beginnings, rudiments, basics,
stuff.
– OPPOSITES destruction.

■ **in the making** *a hero in the making:*
budding, up and coming, emergent,
developing, nascent, potential, promising,
incipient.

maladjusted adjective *a school for
maladjusted pupils:* **disturbed**, unstable,
neurotic, unbalanced, unhinged,

m

dysfunctional; informal mixed up, screwed up, hung up, messed up.
– OPPOSITES normal, stable.

maladroit adjective *both men are unhappy about the maladroit way the matter has been handled:* **bungling**, awkward, inept, clumsy, bumbling, incompetent, unskilful, heavy-handed, gauche, tactless, inconsiderate, undiplomatic, impolitic; informal ham-fisted, cack-handed.
– OPPOSITES adroit, skilful.

malady noun *sea sickness, a malady with no respect for rank or courage:* **illness**, sickness, disease, infection, ailment, disorder, complaint, indisposition, affliction, infirmity; informal bug, virus; Brit. informal lurgy; Austral. informal wog.

malaise noun *a society affected by a deep cultural malaise:* **unhappiness**, uneasiness, unease, discomfort, melancholy, depression, despondency, dejection, angst, Weltschmerz, ennui; lassitude, listlessness, languor, weariness; indisposition, ailment, infirmity, illness, sickness, disease.
– OPPOSITES comfort, well-being.

malapropism noun **wrong word**, solecism, misuse, misapplication, infelicity, slip of the tongue.

malcontent noun *a group of malcontents started a protest:* **troublemaker**, mischief-maker, agitator, dissident, rebel; discontent, complainer, grumbler, moaner; informal stirrer, whinger, grouch, bellyacher; N. Amer. informal kvetch.
adjective *a malcontent employee:* **disaffected**, discontented, dissatisfied, disgruntled, fed up, unhappy, annoyed, irritated, displeased, resentful; rebellious, dissentient, troublemaking, grumbling, complaining; informal browned off, hacked off, peeved, bellyaching; Brit. informal cheesed off, brassed off; N. Amer. informal teed off, ticked off.
– OPPOSITES happy.

male adjective *male sexual jealousy:* **masculine**, virile, manly, macho, red-blooded.
– OPPOSITES female.
noun *two males walked past.* See MAN noun sense 1.

malediction noun *the simple villagers were terrified by his maledictions:* **curse**, damnation, oath; spell; N. Amer. hex.
– OPPOSITES blessing.

malefactor noun *most malefactors are the victims of their environment:* **wrongdoer**, miscreant, offender, criminal, culprit, villain, lawbreaker, felon, evil-doer, delinquent, sinner, transgressor; informal crook, baddy; Austral. informal crim.

malevolence noun **malice**, hostility, hate, hatred, ill will, enmity, ill feeling, balefulness, venom, rancour, malignity, vindictiveness, viciousness, vengefulness.
– OPPOSITES benevolence.

malevolent adjective *she shot a malevolent glare at her companion:* **malicious**, hostile, evil-minded, baleful, evil-intentioned, venomous, evil, malign, malignant, rancorous, vicious, vindictive, vengeful.
– OPPOSITES benevolent.

malformation noun *a congenital malformation of the larynx:* **deformity**, distortion, crookedness, misshapenness, disfigurement, abnormality, warp.

malformed adjective **deformed**, misshapen, misproportioned, ill-proportioned, disfigured, distorted, crooked, contorted, twisted, wry, warped; abnormal, grotesque, monstrous; Scottish thrawn.
– OPPOSITES perfect, normal, healthy.

malfunction verb *the computer has malfunctioned:* **crash**, go wrong, break down, fail, stop working; informal conk out, go kaput, fall over, act up; Brit. informal play up, pack up.
noun *a computer malfunction:* **crash**, breakdown, fault, failure, bug; informal glitch.

malice noun **spite**, malevolence, ill will, vindictiveness, vengefulness, revenge, malignity, evil intentions, animus, enmity, rancour; informal bitchiness, cattiness.
– OPPOSITES benevolence.

malicious adjective *he bore their malicious insults with dignity:* **spiteful**, malevolent, evil-intentioned, vindictive, vengeful, malign, mean, nasty, hurtful, mischievous, wounding, cruel, unkind; informal bitchy, catty.
– OPPOSITES benevolent.

malign adjective *a malign influence:* **harmful**, evil, bad, baleful, hostile, inimical, destructive, malignant, injurious.
– OPPOSITES beneficial.
verb *he maligned an innocent man:* **defame**, slander, libel, blacken someone's name/character, smear, vilify, speak ill of, cast aspersions on, run down, traduce, denigrate, disparage, slur, abuse, revile; informal bad-mouth, knock; Brit. informal rubbish, slag off.
– OPPOSITES praise.

malignant adjective **1** *a malignant disease:* **virulent**, very infectious, invasive, uncontrollable, dangerous, deadly, fatal, life-threatening. **2** *a malignant growth:* **cancerous**; technical metastatic. **3** *a malignant thought:* **spiteful**, malicious, malevolent, evil-intentioned, vindictive, vengeful, malign, mean, nasty, hurtful, mischievous, wounding, cruel, unkind; informal bitchy, catty.
– OPPOSITES benign, benevolent.

malinger verb *the doctor alleged that the plaintiff was malingering:* **pretend to be ill**, feign/fake illness, sham; shirk; informal put it on; Brit. informal skive, swing the lead; N. Amer. informal gold-brick.

malingerer noun *patients for whom no specific diagnosis can be made tend to be regarded as malingerers:* **shirker**, idler, layabout; informal slacker; Brit. informal skiver, lead swinger; N. Amer. informal gold brick.

mall noun **shopping precinct**, shopping centre, shopping complex, arcade, galleria; N. Amer. plaza.

malleable adjective **1** *a malleable substance:* **pliable**, ductile, plastic, pliant, soft, workable. **2** *a malleable young woman:* **easily influenced**, suggestible, susceptible, impressionable, pliable, amenable, compliant, tractable; biddable, complaisant, manipulable, persuadable, like putty in someone's hands.
– OPPOSITES hard, intractable.

malnutrition noun *there is a real danger of hunger and even malnutrition:* **undernourishment**, malnourishment, poor diet, inadequate diet, unhealthy diet, lack of food.

malpractice noun *victims of medical malpractice:* **wrongdoing**, professional misconduct, breach of ethics, unprofessionalism, unethical behaviour; negligence, carelessness, incompetence.

maltreat verb *Keith was a bully and occasionally maltreated his wife:* **ill-treat**, mistreat, abuse, ill-use, misuse, mishandle; knock about/around, hit, beat, strike, manhandle, harm, hurt, persecute, molest; informal beat up, rough up, do over.

maltreatment noun **ill-treatment**, mistreatment, abuse, ill use, ill usage, misuse, mishandling; violence, harm, persecution, molestation.

mammoth adjective *a mammoth task:* **huge**, enormous, gigantic, giant, colossal, massive, vast, immense, mighty, stupendous, monumental, Herculean, epic, prodigious, mountainous, monstrous, titanic, towering, elephantine, king-size(d), gargantuan, Brobdingnagian; informal mega, monster, whopping, humongous, bumper, jumbo, astronomical; Brit. informal whacking, whacking great, ginormous.
– OPPOSITES tiny.

man noun **1** *a handsome man:* **male**, adult male, gentleman; youth; informal guy, fellow, geezer, gent; Brit. informal bloke, chap, lad, cove; Scottish & Irish informal bodach; N. Amer. informal dude, hombre; Austral./NZ informal digger. **2** *all men are mortal:* **human being**, human, person, mortal, individual, personage, soul. **3** *the evolution of man:* **the human race**, the human species, Homo sapiens, humankind, humanity, human beings, humans, people, mankind.
verb **1** *the office is manned from 9 a.m. to 5 p.m.* **staff**, crew, occupy, people. **2** *firemen manned the pumps:* **operate**, work, use, utilize.
■ **man to man** frankly, openly, honestly, directly, candidly, plainly, forthrightly, without beating about the bush; woman to woman.
■ **to a man** without exception, with no exceptions, bar none, one and all, everyone,

each and every one, unanimously, as one.

manacle verb **shackle**, fetter, chain, put/clap in irons, handcuff, restrain; secure; informal cuff.

manacles plural noun **handcuffs**, shackles, chains, irons, fetters, restraints, bonds; informal cuffs, bracelets.

manage verb **1** *she manages a staff of 80 people:* **be in charge of**, run, be head of, head, direct, control, preside over, lead, govern, rule, command, superintend, supervise, oversee, administer, organize, conduct, handle, guide, be at the helm of; informal head up. **2** *how much work can you manage this week?* **accomplish**, achieve, do, carry out, perform, undertake, bring about/off, effect, finish; succeed in, contrive, engineer. **3** *will you be able to manage without him?* **cope**, get along/on, make do, be/fare/do all right, carry on, survive, get by, muddle through/along, fend for oneself, shift for oneself, make ends meet, weather the storm; informal make out, hack it. **4** *she can't manage that horse:* **control**, handle, master; cope with, deal with.

manageable adjective **1** *a manageable amount of work:* **achievable**, doable, practicable, possible, feasible, reasonable, attainable, viable. **2** *a manageable child:* **compliant**, tractable, pliant, pliable, malleable, biddable, docile, amenable, governable, controllable, accommodating, acquiescent, complaisant, yielding.
– OPPOSITES difficult, impossible.

management noun **1** *he's responsible for the management of the firm:* **administration**, running, managing, organization; charge, care, direction, leadership, control, governing, governance, ruling, command, superintendence, supervision, overseeing, conduct, handling, guidance, operation. **2** *workers are in dispute with the management:* **managers**, employers, directors, board of directors, board, directorate, executives, administrators, administration; owners, proprietors; informal bosses, top brass.

manager noun **1** *the works manager:* **executive**, head of department, line manager, supervisor, principal, administrator, head, director, managing director, employer, superintendent, foreman, forewoman, overseer; proprietor; informal boss, chief, head honcho, governor; Brit. informal gaffer, guv'nor. **2** *the band's manager:* **organizer**, controller, comptroller; impresario.

mandate noun **1** *he called an election to seek a mandate for his policies:* **authority**, approval, acceptance, ratification, endorsement, sanction, authorization. **2** *a mandate from the UN:* **instruction**, directive, decree, command, order, injunction, edict, charge, commission, bidding, ruling, fiat.

mandatory adjective *the concept of*

mandatory retirement: **obligatory**, compulsory, binding, required, requisite, necessary, essential, imperative.
– OPPOSITES optional.

manful adjective *his manful attempt to smile:* **brave**, courageous, bold, plucky, gallant, manly, heroic, intrepid, fearless, stout-hearted, valiant, valorous, dauntless, doughty; resolute, with gritted teeth, determined; informal gutsy, spunky.
– OPPOSITES cowardly.

manfully adverb **bravely**, courageously, boldly, gallantly, pluckily, heroically, intrepidly, fearlessly, valiantly, dauntlessly; resolutely, determinedly, hard, strongly, vigorously, with might and main, like a Trojan; with all one's strength, to the best of one's abilities, as best one can, desperately.

mangle verb **1** *the bodies were mangled beyond recognition:* **mutilate**, maim, disfigure, damage, injure, crush; hack, cut up, lacerate, tear apart, butcher, maul. **2** *he's mangling the English language:* **spoil**, ruin, mar, mutilate, make a mess of, wreck; informal murder, make a hash of, butcher.

mangy adjective **1** *a mangy cat:* **scabby**, scaly, scabious, diseased. **2** *a mangy old armchair:* **scruffy**, moth-eaten, shabby, worn; dirty, squalid, sleazy, seedy; informal tatty, the worse for wear, scuzzy; Brit. informal grotty.

manhandle verb **1** *he was manhandled by a gang of youths:* **push**, shove, jostle, hustle; maltreat, ill-treat, mistreat, maul, molest; informal paw, rough up; N. Amer. informal roust. **2** *we manhandled the piano down the stairs:* **heave**, haul, push, shove; pull, tug, drag, lug, carry, lift, manoeuvre; informal hump.

manhood noun **1** *the transition from boyhood to manhood:* **maturity**, sexual maturity, adulthood. **2** *an insult to his manhood:* **virility**, manliness, machismo, masculinity, maleness; mettle, spirit, strength, fortitude, determination, bravery, courage, intrepidity, valour, heroism, boldness.

mania noun **1** *he suffered from fits of mania:* **madness**, derangement, dementia, insanity, lunacy, psychosis, mental illness; delirium, frenzy, hysteria, raving, wildness. **2** *his mania for gadgets:* **obsession**, compulsion, fixation, fetish, fascination, preoccupation, passion, enthusiasm, desire, urge, craving; craze, fad, rage; informal thing, yen.

maniac noun *a homicidal maniac:* **lunatic**, madman, madwoman, psychopath; informal loony, fruitcake, nutcase, nut, psycho, head case, headbanger, sicko; Brit. informal nutter, mentalist; N. Amer. informal screwball, crazy, meshuggener.

manic adjective **1** *a manic grin:* **mad**, insane, deranged, demented, maniacal, lunatic, wild, crazed, demonic, hysterical, raving, unhinged, unbalanced; informal crazy. **2** *the threatened inspection caused manic activity:* **frenzied**, feverish, frenetic, hectic, intense;

informal hyper, mad.
– OPPOSITES sane, calm.

manifest verb **1** *she manifested signs of depression:* **display**, show, exhibit, demonstrate, betray, present, reveal. **2** *strikes manifest bad industrial relations:* **be evidence of**, be a sign of, indicate, show, attest, reflect, bespeak, prove, establish, evidence, substantiate, corroborate, confirm.
– OPPOSITES hide, mask.
adjective *his manifest lack of interest:* **obvious**, clear, plain, apparent, evident, patent, palpable, distinct, definite, blatant, overt, glaring, barefaced, explicit, transparent, conspicuous, undisguised, unmistakable, noticeable, perceptible, visible, recognizable.
– OPPOSITES secret.

manifestation noun **1** *the manifestation of anxiety:* **display**, demonstration, show, exhibition, presentation. **2** *manifestations of global warming:* **sign**, indication, evidence, token, symptom, testimony, proof, substantiation, mark, reflection, example, instance. **3** *a supernatural manifestation:* **apparition**, appearance, materialization, visitation.

manifesto noun **policy statement**, mission statement, platform, programme, declaration, proclamation, pronouncement, announcement.

manifold adjective *the implications of this decision were manifold:* **many**, numerous, multiple, multifarious, legion, diverse, various, several, varied, different, miscellaneous, assorted, sundry.

manipulate verb **1** *he manipulated some knobs and levers:* **operate**, work; turn, pull. **2** *she manipulated the muscles of his back:* **massage**, rub, knead, feel, palpate. **3** *the government tried to manipulate the situation:* **control**, influence, use/turn to one's advantage, exploit, manoeuvre, engineer, steer, direct; twist someone round one's little finger. **4** *they accused him of manipulating the data:* **falsify**, rig, distort, alter, change, doctor, massage, juggle, tamper with, tinker with, interfere with, misrepresent; informal cook, fiddle.

manipulative adjective *a ruthlessly manipulative woman:* **scheming**, calculating, cunning, crafty, wily, shrewd, devious, designing, conniving, Machiavellian, artful, guileful, slippery, slick, sly, unscrupulous, disingenuous; informal foxy.

manipulator noun *a ruthless political manipulator:* **exploiter**, user, manoeuvrer, conniver, puppet master, wheeler-dealer; informal operator, thimblerigger.

mankind noun **the human race**, man, humanity, human beings, humans, Homo sapiens, humankind, people, men and women.

manly adjective **1** *his manly physique:* **virile**, masculine, strong, all-male, muscular, muscly, strapping, well built, sturdy, robust, rugged, tough, powerful, brawny, red-blooded, vigorous; informal hunky. **2** *their manly deeds:* **brave**, courageous, bold, valiant, valorous, fearless, plucky, macho, manful, intrepid, daring, heroic, lionhearted, gallant, chivalrous, swashbuckling, adventurous, stout-hearted, dauntless, doughty, resolute, determined, stalwart; informal gutsy, spunky.
– OPPOSITES effeminate, cowardly.

man-made adjective *a blend of 80% wool and 20% man-made fibres:* **artificial**, synthetic, manufactured; imitation, ersatz, simulated, mock, fake, false, faux, plastic.
– OPPOSITES natural, real.

mannequin noun **1** *mannequins in a shop window:* **dummy**, model, figure. **2** *mannequins on the catwalk:* **model**, fashion model, supermodel; informal clothes horse.

manner noun **1** *it was dealt with in a very efficient manner:* **way**, fashion, mode, means, method, system, style, approach, technique, procedure, process, methodology, modus operandi, form. **2** *her rather unfriendly manner:* **demeanour**, air, aspect, attitude, bearing, cast, behaviour, conduct; mien. **3** *the life and manners of Victorian society:* **customs**, habits, ways, practices, conventions, usages. **4** *it's bad manners to stare:* **behaviour**, conduct, way of behaving; form. **5** *you ought to teach him some manners:* **correct behaviour**, etiquette, social graces, good form, protocol, politeness, decorum, propriety, gentility, civility, Ps and Qs, breeding; informal the done thing.

mannered adjective *inane dialogue and mannered acting:* **affected**, pretentious, unnatural, artificial, contrived, stilted, stiff, forced, put-on, theatrical, precious, stagy, camp; informal pseudo.
– OPPOSITES natural.

mannerism noun *he has the mannerisms of a bishop without actually having become one:* **idiosyncrasy**, quirk, oddity, foible, trait, peculiarity, habit, characteristic.

mannerly adjective. See POLITE sense 1.

mannish adjective *her gruff, mannish exterior:* **unfeminine**, unwomanly, masculine, unladylike, Amazonian; informal butch.
– OPPOSITES feminine, girlish.

manoeuvre verb **1** *I manoeuvred the car into the space:* **steer**, guide, drive, negotiate, navigate, pilot, direct, manipulate, move, work, jockey. **2** *he manoeuvred things to suit himself:* **manipulate**, contrive, manage, engineer, devise, plan, fix, organize, arrange, set up, orchestrate, choreograph, stage-manage; informal wangle. **3** *he began manoeuvring for the party leadership:* **intrigue**, plot, scheme, plan, lay plans, conspire, pull strings.
noun **1** *a tricky parking manoeuvre:* **operation**, exercise, activity, move, movement, action. **2** *diplomatic manoeuvres resulted in the trio's release:* **stratagem**, tactic, gambit, ploy, trick, dodge, ruse, plan, scheme, operation, device, plot, machination, artifice, subterfuge, intrigue. **3** *military manoeuvres:* **training exercises**, exercises, war games, operations.

manse noun **minister's house**, vicarage, parsonage, rectory, deanery.

manservant noun **valet**, attendant, retainer, equerry, gentleman's gentleman, man, Jeeves; steward, butler, footman, flunkey, page, houseboy, lackey; N. Amer. houseman.

mansion noun **stately home**, hall, seat, manor, manor house, country house; informal palace, pile.
– OPPOSITES hovel.

mantle noun **1** *a dark green velvet mantle:* **cloak**, cape, shawl, wrap, stole. **2** *a thick mantle of snow:* **covering**, layer, blanket, sheet, veil, curtain, canopy, cover, cloak, pall, shroud. **3** *the mantle of leadership:* **role**, burden, onus, duty, responsibility.
verb *heavy mists mantled the forest:* **cover**, envelop, veil, cloak, curtain, shroud, swathe, wrap, blanket, conceal, hide, disguise, mask, obscure, surround, clothe.

manual adjective **1** *manual work makes a change from reading:* **done with one's hands**, labouring, physical, blue-collar. **2** *a manual typewriter:* **hand-operated**, hand, non-automatic.
noun *a training manual:* **handbook**, instruction book, instructions, guide, companion, ABC, guidebook; informal bible.

manufacture verb **1** *the company manufactures laser printers:* **make**, produce, mass-produce, build, construct, assemble, put together, create, fabricate, prefabricate, turn out, process, engineer. **2** *a story manufactured by the press:* **make up**, invent, fabricate, concoct, hatch, dream up, think up, trump up, devise, formulate, frame, contrive; informal cook up.
noun *the manufacture of aircraft engines:* **production**, making, manufacturing, mass production, construction, building, assembly, creation, fabrication, prefabrication, processing.

manufacturer noun **maker**, producer, builder, constructor, creator; factory owner, industrialist, captain/baron of industry.

manure noun **dung**, muck, excrement, droppings, ordure, guano, cowpats; fertilizer; N. Amer. informal cow chips, horse apples.

manuscript noun **document**, text, script, paper, typescript; codex, palimpsest, scroll; autograph, holograph.

many determiner, pronoun, & adjective *many*

m

animals were killed: **numerous**, a great/good deal of, a lot of, plenty of, countless, innumerable, scores of, crowds of, droves of, an army of, a horde of, a multitude of, a multiplicity of, multitudinous, multiple, untold; several, various, multifarious; copious, abundant, profuse, an abundance of, a profusion of; frequent; informal lots of, umpteen, loads of, masses of, stacks of, scads of, heaps of, piles of, bags of, bucketloads of, tons of, oodles of, dozens of, hundreds of, thousands of, millions of, billions of, zillions of, a slew of, more ... than one can shake a stick at; Brit. informal a shedload of; N. Amer. informal gazillions of; Austral./NZ informal a swag of.
– OPPOSITES few.

noun *sacrificing the individual for the sake of the many:* **the people**, the common people, the masses, the multitude, the populace, the public, the rank and file; derogatory the hoi polloi, the common herd, the mob, the proletariat, the riff-raff, the great unwashed, the proles.
– OPPOSITES few.

map noun **plan**, chart, cartogram; road map, A to Z, street plan, guide; atlas, globe; sketch map, relief map, contour map; Mercator projection, Peters projection; N. Amer. plat, plot.
verb *the region was mapped from the air:* **chart**, plot, delineate, draw, depict, portray.
■ **map something out** *he mapped out a plan of campaign:* **outline**, set out, lay out, sketch out, trace out, rough out, block out, delineate, detail, draw up, formulate, work out, frame, draft, plan, plot out, arrange, design, programme.

mar verb **1** *an ugly scar marred his features:* **spoil**, impair, disfigure, detract from, blemish, scar; mutilate, deface, deform. **2** *the celebrations were marred by violence:* **spoil**, ruin, impair, damage, wreck; harm, hurt, blight, taint, tarnish, sully, stain, pollute; informal foul up.
– OPPOSITES enhance.

marauder noun *they placed chains across the river mouth to keep out marauders:* **raider**, plunderer, pillager, looter, robber, pirate, freebooter, bandit, highwayman, rustler.

marauding adjective *reservists are being called up to protect civilians from marauding gunmen:* **predatory**, rapacious, thieving, plundering, pillaging, looting, freebooting, piratical.

march verb **1** *the men marched past:* **stride**, walk, troop, step, pace, tread; footslog, slog, tramp, hike, trudge; parade, file, process; Brit. informal yomp. **2** *she marched in without even knocking:* **stalk**, stride, strut, flounce, storm, stomp, sweep. **3** *time marches on:* **advance**, progress, move on, roll on.
noun **1** *a 20-mile march:* **hike**, trek, tramp, slog, footslog, walk; route march, forced march; Brit. informal yomp. **2** *police sought to ban the march:* **parade**, procession,

march past, cortège; demonstration; informal demo. **3** *the march of technology:* **progress**, advance, progression, development, evolution; passage.

margin noun **1** *the margin of the lake:* **edge**, side, verge, border, perimeter, brink, brim, rim, fringe, boundary, limits, periphery, bound, extremity. **2** *there's no margin for error:* **leeway**, latitude, scope, room, room for manoeuvre, space, allowance, extra, surplus. **3** *they won by a narrow margin:* **gap**, majority, amount, difference.

marginal adjective **1** *the difference is marginal:* **slight**, small, tiny, minute, insignificant, minimal, negligible. **2** *a very marginal case:* **borderline**, disputable, questionable, doubtful.

marijuana noun **cannabis**, hashish, bhang, hemp, kif, ganja, sinsemilla, skunkweed; informal dope, hash, grass, pot, blow, draw, the weed, skunk; Brit. informal wacky baccy; N. Amer. informal locoweed.

marinate verb *marinate the fruit in the rum for 30 minutes:* **souse**, soak, steep, immerse, marinade.

marine adjective **1** *marine plants:* **seawater**, sea, saltwater, oceanic; aquatic; technical pelagic, thalassic. **2** *a marine insurance company:* **maritime**, nautical, naval; seafaring, seagoing, ocean-going.

mariner noun **sailor**, seaman, seafarer; informal Jack tar, tar, sea dog, salt, bluejacket, matelot; N. Amer. informal shellback.

marital adjective *she wanted to talk about their marital problems:* **matrimonial**, married, wedded, conjugal, nuptial, marriage, wedding.

maritime adjective **1** *maritime law:* **naval**, marine, nautical; seafaring, seagoing, sea, ocean-going. **2** *maritime regions:* **coastal**, seaside, littoral.

mark noun **1** *a dirty mark:* **blemish**, streak, spot, fleck, dot, blot, stain, smear, speck, speckle, blotch, smudge, smut, fingermark, fingerprint; bruise, discoloration; birthmark; informal splotch, splodge. **2** *a punctuation mark:* **symbol**, sign, character; diacritic. **3** *books bearing the mark of a well-known bookseller:* **logo**, seal, stamp, imprint, symbol, emblem, device, insignia, badge, brand, trademark, monogram, hallmark, logotype, watermark. **4** *unemployment passed the three million mark:* **point**, level, stage, degree. **5** *a mark of respect:* **sign**, token, symbol, indication, badge, emblem; symptom, evidence, proof. **6** *the war left its mark on him:* **impression**, imprint, traces; effect, impact, influence. **7** *the mark of a civilized society:* **characteristic**, feature, trait, attribute, quality, hallmark, badge, stamp, property, indicator. **8** *he got good marks for maths:* **grade**, grading, rating, score, percentage. **9** *the bullet missed its mark:* **target**, goal, aim, bullseye; objective, object, end.

m

verb **1** *be careful not to mark the paintwork:* **discolour**, stain, smear, smudge, streak, blotch, blemish; dirty, pockmark, bruise; informal splotch, splodge. **2** *her possessions were clearly marked:* **put one's name on**, name, initial, label; hallmark, watermark, brand. **3** *I've marked the relevant passages:* **indicate**, label, flag, tick; show, identify, designate, delineate, denote. **4** *a festival to mark the town's 200th anniversary:* **celebrate**, observe, recognize, acknowledge, keep, honour, solemnize, pay tribute to, salute, commemorate, remember, memorialize. **5** *his style is marked by simplicity and concision:* **characterize**, distinguish, identify, typify, brand, signalize, stamp. **6** *I have a pile of essays to mark:* **assess**, evaluate, appraise, correct; N. Amer. grade.
■ **make one's mark** be successful, distinguish oneself, succeed, be a success, prosper, get ahead/on, make good; informal make it, make the grade, find a place in the sun.
■ **mark something down** *prices have been marked down for quick sale:* reduce, decrease, lower, cut, put down, discount; informal slash.
■ **mark someone out 1** *his honesty marked him out from the rest:* set apart, separate, single out, differentiate, distinguish. **2** *she is marked out for fame:* destine, ordain, predestine, preordain.
■ **mark something up** *they marked up the price by 66%:* increase, raise, up, put up, hike (up), escalate; informal jack up.
■ **quick off the mark** alert, quick, quick-witted, bright, clever, perceptive, sharp, sharp-witted, observant, wide awake, on one's toes; informal on the ball, quick on the uptake.
■ **wide of the mark** inaccurate, incorrect, wrong, erroneous, off target, off beam, out, mistaken, misguided, misinformed.

marked adjective *a marked deterioration in her health:* **noticeable**, pronounced, decided, distinct, striking, clear, glaring, blatant, unmistakable, obvious, plain, manifest, patent, palpable, prominent, signal, significant, conspicuous, notable, recognizable, identifiable, distinguishable, discernible, apparent, evident; written all over one.
– OPPOSITES imperceptible.

market noun **1** **shopping centre**, marketplace, mart, flea market, bazaar, souk, fair. **2** *there's no market for such goods:* **demand**, call, want, desire, need, requirement. **3** *the market is sluggish:* **trade**, trading, business, commerce, buying and selling, dealing.
verb *the product was marketed worldwide:* **sell**, retail, vend, merchandise, trade, peddle, hawk; advertise, promote.
■ **on the market** on sale, (up) for sale, on offer, available, obtainable; N. Amer. on the block.

marksman, markswoman noun **sniper**, sharpshooter, good shot; informal crack shot; N. Amer. informal deadeye, shootist.

maroon verb *a novel about schoolboys marooned on a desert island:* **strand**, cast away, cast ashore; abandon, leave behind, leave, leave in the lurch, desert; informal leave high and dry.

marriage noun **1** *a proposal of marriage:* **(holy) matrimony**, wedlock. **2** *the marriage took place at St Margaret's:* **wedding**, wedding ceremony, marriage ceremony, nuptials, union. **3** *a marriage of jazz, pop, and gospel:* **union**, alliance, fusion, mixture, mix, blend, amalgamation, combination, merger.
– OPPOSITES divorce, separation.

married adjective **1** *a married couple:* **wedded**, wed; informal spliced, hitched. **2** *married bliss:* **marital**, matrimonial, conjugal, nuptial; Law spousal.
– OPPOSITES single.

marry verb **1** *the couple married last year:* **get/be married**, wed, be wed, become man and wife, plight/pledge one's troth; informal tie the knot, walk down the aisle, take the plunge, get spliced, get hitched, say 'I do'. **2** *John wanted to marry her:* **wed**, take to wife/husband; informal make an honest woman of. **3** *the show marries poetry with art:* **join**, unite, combine, fuse, mix, blend, merge, amalgamate, link, connect, couple, knit, yoke.
– OPPOSITES divorce, separate.

marsh noun **swamp**, marshland, bog, peat bog, swampland, morass, mire, quagmire, slough, fen, fenland, wetland; N. Amer. bayou; Scottish & N. English moss.

marshal verb **1** *the king marshalled an army:* **assemble**, gather together, collect, muster, call together, draw up, line up, align, array, organize, group, arrange, deploy, position, order, dispose; mobilize, rally, round up. **2** *guests were marshalled to their seats:* **usher**, guide, escort, conduct, lead, shepherd, steer, take.

marshy adjective **boggy**, swampy, muddy, squelchy, soggy, waterlogged, miry, fenny; Scottish & N. English mossy.
– OPPOSITES dry, firm.

martial adjective *their martial exploits:* **military**, soldierly, soldier-like, army, naval; warlike, fighting, combative, militaristic; informal gung-ho.

martinet noun *the general was known to be a martinet to his men:* **disciplinarian**, slave-driver, stickler for discipline, (hard) taskmaster, authoritarian, tyrant.

martyr verb *she was martyred for her faith:* **put to death**, kill, martyrize; burn, burn at the stake, immolate, stone to death, throw to the lions, crucify.

martyrdom noun **death**, suffering, torture, torment, agony, ordeal; killing, sacrifice, crucifixion, immolation, burning, auto-da-fé;

m

Christianity Passion.

marvel verb *she marvelled at their courage:* **be amazed**, be astonished, be surprised, be awed, stand in awe, wonder, stare, gape, goggle, not believe one's eyes/ears, be dumbfounded; informal be flabbergasted.
noun *the marvels of technology:* **wonder**, miracle, sensation, spectacle, phenomenon; informal something else, something to shout about, eye-opener.

marvellous adjective **1** *his solo climb was marvellous:* **amazing**, astounding, astonishing, awesome, breathtaking, sensational, remarkable, spectacular, stupendous, staggering, stunning; phenomenal, prodigious, miraculous, extraordinary, incredible, unbelievable. **2** *marvellous weather:* **excellent**, splendid, wonderful, magnificent, superb, glorious, sublime, lovely, delightful, too good to be true; informal super, great, amazing, fantastic, terrific, tremendous, sensational, heavenly, divine, gorgeous, grand, fabulous, fab, awesome, to die for, magic, ace, wicked, mind-blowing, far out, out of this world; Brit. informal smashing, brilliant, brill; N. Amer. informal boss; Austral./NZ informal beaut, bonzer.
– OPPOSITES commonplace, awful.

masculine adjective **1** *a masculine trait:* **male**, man's, men's; male-oriented. **2** *a powerfully masculine man:* **virile**, macho, manly, all-male, muscular, muscly, strong, strapping, well built, rugged, robust, brawny, powerful, red-blooded, vigorous; informal hunky. **3** *a rather masculine woman:* **mannish**, unfeminine, unwomanly, unladylike, Amazonian; informal butch.
– OPPOSITES feminine, effeminate.

masculinity noun **virility**, manliness, maleness, machismo, vigour, strength, muscularity, ruggedness, robustness.

mash verb *mash the potatoes:* **pulp**, crush, purée, cream, smash, squash, pound, beat.
noun *first pound the garlic to a mash:* **pulp**, purée, mush, paste.

mask noun *he dropped his mask of good humour:* **pretence**, semblance, veil, screen, front, false front, facade, veneer, blind, false colours, disguise, guise, concealment, cover, cover-up, cloak, camouflage.
verb *poplar trees masked the factory:* **hide**, conceal, disguise, cover up, obscure, screen, cloak, camouflage, veil.

masquerade noun *he couldn't keep up the masquerade much longer:* **pretence**, deception, pose, act, front, facade, disguise, dissimulation, cover-up, bluff, play-acting, make-believe; informal put-on.
verb *a woman masquerading as a man:* **pretend to be**, pose as, pass oneself off as, impersonate, disguise oneself as.

Mass noun *a Roman Catholic Mass:* **Eucharist**, Holy Communion, Communion, the Lord's Supper.

mass noun **1** *a soggy mass of fallen leaves:* **pile**, heap; accumulation, aggregation, accretion, concretion, build-up. **2** *a mass of cyclists:* **crowd**, horde, large group, throng, host, troop, army, herd, flock, drove, swarm, mob, pack, press, crush, flood, multitude. **3** *the mass of the population don't care about this at all:* **majority**, greater part/number, best/better part, major part, most, bulk, main body, lion's share. **4** *I am not interested in writing for the masses:* **the common people**, the populace, the public, the people, the rank and file, the crowd, the third estate; derogatory the hoi polloi, the mob, the proletariat, the common herd, the great unwashed. **5** (informal) *masses of food.* See LOT pronoun.
adjective *mass hysteria:* **widespread**, general, wholesale, universal, large-scale, extensive, pandemic.
verb *they began massing troops in the region:* **assemble**, marshal, gather together, muster, round up, mobilize, rally.

massacre noun *a cold-blooded massacre of innocent civilians:* **slaughter**, wholesale/mass slaughter, indiscriminate killing, mass murder, mass execution, annihilation, liquidation, decimation, extermination; carnage, butchery, bloodbath, bloodletting, pogrom, genocide, ethnic cleansing, holocaust, Shoah, night of the long knives.
verb *thousands were brutally massacred:* **slaughter**, butcher, murder, kill, annihilate, exterminate, execute, liquidate, eliminate, decimate, wipe out, mow down, cut down, put to the sword, put to death.

massage noun *a massage will help loosen you up:* **rub**, rub-down, rubbing, kneading, palpation, manipulation, pummelling; shiatsu, reflexology, acupressure, hydromassage.
verb **1** *he massaged her tired muscles:* **rub**, knead, palpate, manipulate, pummel, work. **2** *the statistics have been massaged:* **alter**, tamper with, manipulate, doctor, falsify, juggle, fiddle with, tinker with, distort, change, rig, interfere with, misrepresent; informal fix, cook, fiddle.

massive adjective *these burial chambers were massive structures:* **huge**, enormous, vast, immense, large, big, mighty, great, colossal, tremendous, prodigious, gigantic, gargantuan, mammoth, monstrous, monumental, giant, towering, elephantine, mountainous, titanic; epic, Herculean, Brobdingnagian; informal monster, jumbo, mega, whopping, humongous, hulking, bumper, astronomical; Brit. informal whacking, ginormous.
– OPPOSITES tiny.

mast noun *the mast on top of the building:* **flagpole**, flagstaff, pole, post, rod, upright; aerial, transmitter, pylon.

master noun **1** *he acceded to his master's wishes:* **lord**, overlord, lord and master, ruler, sovereign, monarch, liege (lord),

suzerain. **2** *the dog's master:* **owner**, keeper.
3 *he was a real master at depicting light and
shade:* **expert**, adept, genius, past master,
maestro, virtuoso, professional, doyen,
authority; informal ace, pro, wizard, whizz,
hotshot; Brit. informal dab hand; N. Amer. informal
maven, crackerjack. **4** *the master of the ship:*
captain, commander; informal skipper. **5** *the
geography master:* **teacher**, schoolteacher,
schoolmaster, tutor, instructor, preceptor.
6 *their spiritual master:* **guru**, teacher,
leader, guide, mentor; swami, Maharishi;
Roshi.
– OPPOSITES servant, amateur, pupil.
▶ verb **1** *I managed to master my fears:*
overcome, conquer, beat, quell, quash,
suppress, control, overpower, triumph over,
subdue, vanquish, subjugate, prevail over,
govern, curb, check, bridle, tame, defeat,
get the better of, get a grip on, get over;
informal lick. **2** *it took ages to master the
technique:* **learn**, become proficient in, know
inside out, know backwards; pick up, grasp,
understand; informal get the hang of.
▶ adjective **1** *a master craftsman:* **expert**, adept,
proficient, skilled, skilful, deft, dexterous,
adroit, practised, experienced, masterly,
accomplished, complete, demon, brilliant;
informal crack, ace, mean, wizard; N. Amer.
informal crackerjack. **2** *the master bedroom:*
principal, main, chief; biggest.

masterful adjective **1** *a masterful man:*
commanding, powerful, imposing,
magisterial, lordly, authoritative;
dominating, domineering, overbearing,
overweening, imperious. **2** *their masterful
handling of the situation:* **expert**, adept,
clever, masterly, skilful, skilled, adroit,
proficient, deft, dexterous, accomplished,
polished, consummate; informal crack, ace.
– OPPOSITES weak, inept.

mastermind verb *he masterminded the
whole campaign:* **plan**, control, direct, be in
charge of, run, conduct, organize, arrange,
preside over, orchestrate, stage-manage,
engineer, manage, coordinate; conceive,
devise, originate, initiate, think up, frame,
hatch, come up with; informal be the brains
behind.
▶ noun *the mastermind behind the project:*
genius, mind, intellect, author, architect,
organizer, originator, prime mover,
initiator, inventor; informal brain, brains,
bright spark.

masterpiece noun *a great literary
masterpiece:* **chef-d'œuvre**, pièce de
résistance, masterwork, magnum opus,
finest/best work, tour de force.

master stroke noun *the takeover was hailed
as a master stroke:* **stroke of genius**, coup,
triumph, coup de maître, tour de force.

mastery noun **1** *her mastery of the language:*
proficiency, ability, capability; knowledge,
understanding, comprehension, familiarity,
command, grasp, grip. **2** *they played with
tactical mastery:* **skill**, skilfulness, expertise,

dexterity, finesse, adroitness, virtuosity,
prowess, deftness, proficiency; informal
know-how. **3** *man's mastery over nature:*
control, domination, command, ascendancy,
supremacy, pre-eminence, superiority;
triumph, victory, the upper hand, the
whip hand, rule, government, power,
sway, authority, jurisdiction, dominion,
sovereignty.

masticate verb *this lizard eats a wide variety
of plants but does not masticate the food:*
chew, munch, champ, chomp, crunch, eat;
ruminate, chew the cud.

mat noun **1** *she shut the front door behind her
and stood dripping on the mat:* **rug**, runner,
carpet, drugget; doormat, welcome mat,
hearthrug; dhurrie, numdah; kilim, flokati;
N. Amer. floorcloth. **2** *a beer mat:* **coaster**,
doily; Brit. drip mat. **3** *a thick mat of hair:*
mass, tangle, knot, mop, thatch, shock,
mane.
▶ verb *his hair was matted with blood:* **tangle**,
entangle, knot, ravel, snarl up.

match noun **1** *a football match | a boxing
match:* **contest**, competition, game,
tournament, tie, cup tie, event, fixture,
trial, test, meet, bout, fight; friendly, (local)
derby; play-off, replay, rematch. **2** *he was
no match for the champion:* **equal**, rival,
equivalent, peer, counterpart. **3** *the vase
was an exact match of the one she already
owned:* **lookalike**, double, twin, duplicate,
mate, fellow, companion, counterpart, pair;
replica, copy; informal spitting image, spit
and image, dead spit, dead ringer. **4** *a love
match:* **marriage**, betrothal, relationship,
partnership, union.
▶ verb **1** *the curtains matched the duvet cover:*
go with, coordinate with, complement,
suit; be the same as, be similar to. **2** *did
their statements match?* **correspond**, be in
agreement, tally, agree, match up, coincide,
accord, conform, square. **3** *no one can match
him at chess:* **equal**, be a match for, measure
up to, compare with, parallel, be in the same
league as, be on a par with, touch, keep pace
with, keep up with, emulate, rival, vie with,
compete with, contend with; informal hold a
candle to.
■ **match up to** *the film didn't match up to
my expectations:* measure up to, come up to,
meet with, be equal to, be as good as, satisfy,
fulfil, answer to.

matching adjective *he picked up a cup
and identified the matching saucer:*
corresponding, equivalent, parallel,
analogous; coordinating, complementary,
toning; paired, twin, identical, like, like
(two) peas in a pod, alike.
– OPPOSITES different, clashing.

matchless adjective *her sister's matchless
beauty:* **incomparable**, unrivalled,
inimitable, beyond compare/comparison,
unparalleled, unequalled, without equal,
peerless, second to none, unsurpassed,
unsurpassable, nonpareil, unique,

m

consummate, perfect, rare, transcendent, surpassing.

matchmaker noun **marriage broker**, shadchan; marriage bureau, dating agency; go-between.

mate noun **1** *she's finally found her ideal mate:* **partner**, husband, wife, spouse, lover, live-in lover, significant other, companion, helpmate, helpmeet, consort; informal better half, hubby, missus; Brit. informal other half, dutch, trouble and strife. **2** *a plumber's mate:* **assistant**, helper, apprentice.
verb *pandas rarely mate in captivity:* **breed**, couple, copulate.

material noun **1** *the decomposition of organic material:* **matter**, substance, stuff, medium. **2** *the materials for a new building:* **constituent**, raw material, element, component. **3** *cleaning materials:* **things**, items, articles, stuff, necessaries; Brit. informal gubbins. **4** *curtain material:* **fabric**, cloth, textiles. **5** *they were gathering material for a magazine article:* **information**, data, facts, facts and figures, statistics, evidence, details, particulars, background, notes; informal info, gen, dope, low-down.
adjective **1** *the material world:* **physical**, corporeal, tangible, non-spiritual, mundane, worldly, earthly, secular, temporal, concrete, real, solid, substantial. **2** *she was too fond of material pleasures:* **sensual**, physical, carnal, corporal, fleshly, bodily. **3** *information that could be material to the inquiry:* **relevant**, pertinent, applicable, germane; apropos, to the point; vital, essential, key. **4** *the storms caused material damage:* **significant**, major, important.
– OPPOSITES spiritual, aesthetic, irrelevant.

materialistic adjective *a materialistic society that worships consumer goods:* **consumerist**, acquisitive, money-oriented, greedy; worldly, capitalistic, bourgeois.

materialize verb **1** *the forecast investment boom did not materialize:* **happen**, occur, come about, take place, come into being, transpire; informal come off. **2** *Harry materialized at the door:* **appear**, turn up, arrive, make/put in an appearance, present oneself/itself, emerge, surface, reveal oneself/itself, show one's face, pop up; informal show up, fetch up, pitch up.

materially adverb *this will materially affect our plans:* **significantly**, greatly, much, very much, to a great extent, considerably, substantially, a great deal, appreciably, markedly, fundamentally, seriously, gravely.

maternal adjective **1** *her maternal instincts:* **motherly**, protective, caring, nurturing, loving, devoted, affectionate, fond, warm, tender, gentle, kind, kindly, comforting. **2** *his maternal grandparents:* **on one's mother's side**, on the distaff side.

mathematical adjective **1** *mathematical symbols:* **arithmetical**, numerical; statistical, algebraic, geometric,

trigonometric. **2** *mathematical precision:* **rigorous**, meticulous, scrupulous, punctilious, scientific, strict, precise, exact, accurate, pinpoint, correct, careful, unerring.

matrimonial adjective *the matrimonial home:* **marital**, conjugal, married, wedded; nuptial.

matrimony noun **marriage**, wedlock, union; nuptials.
– OPPOSITES divorce.

matted adjective *his greasy, matted hair:* **tangled**, tangly, knotted, knotty, tousled, dishevelled, uncombed, unkempt, ratty; black English natty.

matter noun **1** *decaying vegetable matter:* **material**, substance, stuff. **2** *the heart of the matter:* **affair**, business, proceeding, situation, circumstance, event, happening, occurrence, incident, episode, experience; subject, topic, issue, question, point, point at issue, case, concern. **3** *it is of little matter now:* **importance**, consequence, significance, note, import, weight. **4** *what's the matter?* **problem**, trouble, difficulty, complication; upset, worry. **5** *the matter of the sermon:* **content**, subject matter, text, argument, substance. **6** *an infected wound full of matter:* **pus**, suppuration, purulence, discharge.
verb *it doesn't matter what you wear:* **be important**, make any/a difference, be of importance, be of consequence, signify, be relevant, count; informal cut any ice.
■ **as a matter of fact** actually, in (actual) fact, in point of fact, as it happens, really, believe it or not, in reality, in truth, to tell the truth.
■ **no matter** it doesn't matter, it makes no difference/odds, it's not important, never mind, don't worry about it.

matter-of-fact adjective *she tried to keep her tone light and matter-of-fact:* **unemotional**, practical, down-to-earth, sensible, realistic, rational, sober, unsentimental, pragmatic, businesslike, commonsensical, level-headed, hard-headed, no-nonsense, factual, literal, straightforward, plain, unembellished, unvarnished, unadorned.

mature adjective **1** *a mature woman:* **adult**, grown-up, grown, fully grown, full-grown, of age, fully developed, in one's prime. **2** *he's very mature for his age:* **sensible**, responsible, adult, level-headed, reliable, dependable; wise, discriminating, shrewd, sophisticated. **3** *mature cheese:* **ripe**, ripened, mellow; ready to eat/drink. **4** *on mature reflection, he decided not to go:* **careful**, thorough, deep, considered.
– OPPOSITES adolescent, childish.
verb **1** *kittens mature when they are about a year old:* **be fully grown**, be full-grown; come of age, reach adulthood, reach maturity. **2** *he's matured since he left home:* **grow up**, become more sensible/adult; blossom. **3** *leave the cheese to mature:* **ripen**,

m

mellow; age. **4** *their friendship didn't have time to mature:* **develop**, grow, evolve, bloom, blossom, flourish, thrive.

maturity noun **1** *her progress from childhood to maturity:* **adulthood**, majority, coming-of-age, manhood/womanhood. **2** *he displayed a maturity beyond his years:* **responsibility**, sense, level-headedness; wisdom, discrimination, shrewdness, sophistication.

maudlin adjective **1** *whatever has happened, don't succumb to maudlin self-pity:* **sentimental**, over-sentimental, emotional, over-emotional, tearful, lachrymose; informal weepy. **2** *a maudlin ballad:* **mawkish**, sentimental, over-sentimental; Brit. twee; informal mushy, slushy, sloppy, schmaltzy, cheesy, corny, toe-curling; Brit. informal soppy; N. Amer. informal cornball, three-hankie.

maul verb **1** *he had been mauled by a lion:* **savage**, attack, tear to pieces, lacerate, claw, scratch. **2** *she hated being mauled by men:* **molest**, feel, fondle, manhandle; informal grope, paw, touch up. **3** *his book was mauled by the critics.* See CRITICIZE.

maunder verb **1** *he maundered on about his problems:* **ramble**, prattle, blather, blether, rattle, chatter, jabber, babble; informal yak, yatter; Brit. informal rabbit, witter, waffle, natter, chunter. **2** *she maundered across the road:* **wander**, drift, meander, amble, potter; Brit. informal mooch.

mausoleum noun **tomb**, sepulchre, crypt, vault, charnel house, burial chamber, catacomb, undercroft.

maverick noun *he was too much of a maverick to fit into any formal organization:* **individualist**, nonconformist, free spirit, unorthodox person, original, eccentric; rebel, dissenter, dissident.
– OPPOSITES conformist.

maw noun *a gigantic wolfhound with a fearful, gaping maw:* **mouth**, jaws, muzzle; throat, gullet; informal trap, chops, kisser; Brit. informal gob.

mawkish adjective *a long and mawkish poem:* **sentimental**, over-sentimental, maudlin, cloying, sickly, saccharine, sugary, syrupy, nauseating; Brit. twee; informal mushy, slushy, sloppy, schmaltzy, weepy, cutesy, lovey-dovey, cheesy, corny, sick-making, toe-curling; Brit. informal soppy; N. Amer. informal cornball, hokey, three-hankie.

maxim noun *'You are what you eat' is a favourite maxim:* **saying**, adage, aphorism, proverb, motto, saw, axiom, apophthegm, dictum, precept, epigram; truism, cliché.

maximum adjective *the maximum amount:* **greatest**, highest, biggest, largest, top, topmost, most, utmost, maximal.
– OPPOSITES minimum.
noun *production levels are near their maximum:* **upper limit**, limit, utmost, uttermost, greatest, most, extremity, peak, height, ceiling, top.

– OPPOSITES minimum.

maybe adverb *maybe I won't go back:* **perhaps**, possibly, conceivably, it could be, it is possible, for all one knows; N. English happen.

mayhem noun *complete mayhem broke out:* **chaos**, disorder, havoc, bedlam, pandemonium, tumult, uproar, turmoil, commotion, all hell broken loose, maelstrom, trouble, disturbance, confusion, riot, anarchy, violence; informal madhouse.

maze noun *a maze of corridors:* **labyrinth**, complex network, warren; web, tangle, jungle, snarl.

meadow noun **field**, paddock; pasture, pastureland.

meagre adjective **1** *their meagre earnings:* **inadequate**, scanty, scant, paltry, limited, restricted, modest, insufficient, sparse, deficient, negligible, skimpy, slender, poor, miserable, pitiful, puny, miserly, niggardly, beggarly; informal measly, stingy, pathetic, piddling. **2** *a tall, meagre man:* **thin**, lean, skinny, spare, scrawny, scraggy, gangling, gangly, spindly, stringy, bony, raw-boned, gaunt, underweight, underfed, undernourished, emaciated, skeletal, cadaverous.
– OPPOSITES abundant, fat.

meal noun snack; feast, banquet; informal bite (to eat), spread, blowout, feed; Brit. informal nosh-up.

mean[1] verb **1** *flashing lights mean the road is blocked:* **signify**, convey, denote, designate, indicate, connote, show, express, spell out; stand for, represent, symbolize; imply, suggest, intimate, hint at, insinuate, drive at, refer to, allude to. **2** *she didn't mean to break it:* **intend**, aim, plan, design, have in mind, contemplate, purpose, propose, set out, aspire, desire, want, wish, expect. **3** *he was hit by a bullet meant for a soldier:* **intend**, design; destine, predestine. **4** *the closures will mean a rise in unemployment:* **entail**, involve, necessitate, lead to, result in, give rise to, bring about, cause, engender, produce. **5** *this means a lot to me:* **matter**, be important, be significant. **6** *a red sky in the morning usually means rain:* **presage**, portend, foretell, augur, promise, foreshadow, herald, signal, bode.

mean[2] adjective **1** *he's too mean to leave a tip:* **miserly**, niggardly, close-fisted, parsimonious, penny-pinching, cheese-paring, Scrooge-like; informal tight-fisted, stingy, tight, mingy, money-grubbing; N. Amer. informal cheap. **2** *a mean trick:* **unkind**, nasty, unpleasant, spiteful, malicious, unfair, cruel, shabby, foul, despicable, contemptible, obnoxious, vile, odious, loathsome, base, low; informal horrible, horrid, hateful, rotten, low-down; Brit. informal beastly. **3** *the truth was obvious to even the meanest intelligence:* **inferior**, poor, limited, restricted. **4** *a man of mean*

m

birth: **lowly**, humble, ordinary, low, low-born, modest, common, base, proletarian, plebeian, obscure, undistinguished, ignoble. **5** (informal) *he's a mean cook.* See **EXCELLENT**.
– OPPOSITES generous, kind, noble.

mean³ noun *we all need to find a mean between saving and splashing out:* **middle course**, middle way, midpoint, happy medium, golden mean, compromise, balance; median, norm, average.
adjective *the mean temperature:* **average**, median, middle, medial, medium, normal, standard.

meander verb **1** *the river meandered gently:* **zigzag**, wind, twist, turn, curve, curl, bend, snake. **2** *we meandered along the path:* **stroll**, saunter, amble, wander, ramble, drift, maunder; Scottish stravaig; informal mosey, tootle.

meandering adjective **1** *a meandering stream:* **winding**, windy, zigzag, twisting, turning, curving, serpentine, sinuous, twisty. **2** *meandering reminiscences:* **rambling**, maundering, circuitous, roundabout, digressive, discursive, indirect, tortuous, convoluted.
– OPPOSITES straight, succinct.

meaning noun **1** *the meaning of his remark:* **significance**, sense, signification, import, gist, thrust, drift, implication, tenor, message, essence, substance, purport, intention. **2** *the word has several different meanings:* **definition**, sense, explanation, denotation, connotation, interpretation. **3** *my life has no meaning:* **value**, validity, worth, consequence, account, use, usefulness, significance, point. **4** *his smile was full of meaning:* **expressiveness**, significance, eloquence, implications, insinuations.

meaningful adjective **1** *a meaningful remark:* **significant**, relevant, important, consequential, telling, material, valid, worthwhile. **2** *a meaningful relationship:* **sincere**, deep, serious, in earnest, significant, important. **3** *a meaningful glance:* **expressive**, eloquent, pointed, significant, meaning; pregnant, speaking, telltale, revealing, suggestive.
– OPPOSITES inconsequential.

meaningless adjective **1** *a jumble of meaningless words:* **unintelligible**, incomprehensible, incoherent. **2** *she felt her life was meaningless:* **futile**, pointless, aimless, empty, hollow, vain, purposeless, valueless, useless, of no use, worthless, senseless, trivial, trifling, unimportant, insignificant, inconsequential.
– OPPOSITES worthwhile.

means plural noun **1** *the best means to achieve your goal:* **method**, way, manner, mode, measure, technique, expedient, agency, medium, instrument, channel, vehicle, avenue, course, process, procedure. **2** *she doesn't have the means to support herself:* **money**, resources, capital, income, finance,

funds, cash, the wherewithal, assets; informal dough, bread; Brit. informal dosh, brass, lolly, spondulicks, ackers. **3** *a man of means:* **wealth**, riches, affluence, substance, fortune, property, money, capital.
■ **by all means** of course, certainly, definitely, surely, absolutely, with pleasure; N. Amer. informal sure thing.
■ **by means of** *the load was raised by means of a crane:* using, utilizing, employing, through, with the help of; as a result of, by dint of, by way of, by virtue of.
■ **by no means** *the result is by no means certain:* not at all, in no way, not in the least, not in the slightest, not the least bit, not by a long shot, certainly not, absolutely not, definitely not, on no account, under no circumstances; Brit. not by a long chalk; informal no way.

meanwhile adverb **1** *meanwhile, I'll stay here:* **for now**, for the moment, for the present, for the time being, meantime, in the meantime, in the interim, in the interval. **2** *cook for a further half hour; meanwhile, make the stuffing:* **at the same time**, simultaneously, concurrently, the while.

measurable adjective **1** *a measurable amount:* **quantifiable**, assessable, gaugeable, computable. **2** *a measurable improvement:* **appreciable**, noticeable, significant, visible, perceptible, definite, obvious.

measure verb **1** *they measured the length of the room:* **calculate**, compute, count, meter, quantify, weigh, size, evaluate, assess, gauge, plumb, determine. **2** *I had better measure my words:* **choose carefully**, consider, plan. **3** *she did not need to measure herself against some ideal:* **compare with**, pit against, set against, test against, judge by.
noun **1** *cost-cutting measures:* **action**, act, course (of action), deed, proceeding, procedure, step, means, expedient; manoeuvre, initiative, programme, operation. **2** *the Senate passed the measure:* **statute**, act, bill, law, legislation. **3** *the original dimensions were in imperial measure:* **system**, standard, units, scale. **4** *use a measure to check the size:* **ruler**, tape measure, rule, gauge, meter, scale, level, yardstick. **5** *a measure of egg white:* **quantity**, amount, portion. **6** *the states retain a measure of independence:* **certain amount**, degree; some. **7** *sales are the measure of the company's success:* **yardstick**, test, standard, barometer, touchstone, litmus test, criterion, benchmark. **8** *poetic measure:* **metre**, cadence, rhythm; foot.
■ **beyond measure** *it irritates him beyond measure that she is nearly always right:* immensely, extremely, vastly, greatly, excessively, immeasurably, incalculably, infinitely.
■ **for good measure** *she added a couple of*

chilli peppers for good measure: as a bonus, as an extra, into the bargain, to boot, in addition, besides, as well.

■ **get/have the measure of** evaluate, assess, gauge, judge, weigh up; understand, fathom, read, be wise to, see through; informal have someone's number.

■ **measure something off** measure off six lengths of timber for the supports: mark off, measure out, demarcate, delimit, delineate, outline, describe, define, stake out.

■ **measure up** he was sacked because he didn't measure up: pass muster, match up, come up to standard, fit/fill the bill, be acceptable; informal come up to scratch, make the grade, cut the mustard, be up to snuff.

■ **measure someone up** the two men shook hands and silently measured each other up: evaluate, rate, assess, appraise, judge, weigh up; informal size up.

■ **measure up to** we didn't measure up to the standards they set: meet, come up to, equal, match, bear comparison with, be on a level with; achieve, satisfy, fulfil.

measured adjective **1** his measured tread: **regular**, steady, even, rhythmic, rhythmical, unfaltering; slow, dignified, stately, sedate, leisurely, unhurried. **2** his measured tones belied the turmoil in his mind: **thoughtful**, careful, carefully chosen, studied, calculated, planned, considered, deliberate, restrained.

measureless adjective Otto turned out to have measureless charm: **boundless**, limitless, unlimited, unbounded, untold, immense, vast, endless, inexhaustible, infinite, illimitable, immeasurable, incalculable.
– OPPOSITES limited.

measurement noun **1** measurement of the effect is difficult: **quantification**, computation, calculation, mensuration; evaluation, assessment, gauging. **2** all measurements are given in metric form: **size**, dimension, proportions, magnitude; amplitude; mass, bulk, volume, capacity, extent; value, amount, quantity, area, length, height, depth, weight, width, range.

meat noun **1** **flesh**, muscle. **2** the meat of the matter: **substance**, pith, marrow, heart, kernel, core, nucleus, nub, essence, essentials, gist, fundamentals, basics; informal nitty-gritty.

meaty adjective **1** a tall, meaty young man: **beefy**, brawny, burly, muscular, muscly, powerful, sturdy, strapping, well built, solidly built, thickset; fleshy, stout. **2** a good, meaty story: **interesting**, thought-provoking, three-dimensional, stimulating; substantial, satisfying, meaningful, deep, profound.

mechanical adjective **1** a mechanical device: **mechanized**, machine-driven, automated, automatic, power-driven, robotic. **2** a mechanical response: **automatic**, unthinking, robotic, involuntary, reflex,

knee-jerk, habitual, routine, unemotional, unfeeling, lifeless; perfunctory, cursory, careless, casual.
– OPPOSITES manual, conscious.

mechanism noun **1** an electrical mechanism: **machine**, piece of machinery, appliance, apparatus, device, instrument, contraption, gadget; informal gizmo. **2** the train's safety mechanism: **machinery**, workings, works, movement, action, gears, components. **3** a formal mechanism for citizens to lodge complaints: **procedure**, process, system, operation, method, technique, means, medium, agency, channel.

mechanize verb agriculture started to become mechanized: **automate**, industrialize, motorize, computerize.

medal noun he won his first gold medal in 1998: **decoration**, ribbon, star, badge, laurel, palm, award; honour; Military slang fruit salad; Brit. informal gong.

meddle verb **1** don't meddle in my affairs: **interfere**, butt in, intrude, intervene, pry; informal poke one's nose in, horn in on, muscle in on, snoop, put/stick one's oar in; N. Amer. informal kibitz. **2** someone had been meddling with her things: **fiddle**, interfere, tamper, tinker, finger; Brit. informal muck about/around.

meddlesome adjective a growing demand for more efficient and less meddlesome government: **interfering**, meddling, intrusive, prying, busybody; informal nosy, nosy-parker.

mediate verb **1** Austria tried to mediate between the belligerents: **arbitrate**, conciliate, moderate, act as peacemaker, make peace; intervene, step in, intercede, act as an intermediary, liaise. **2** a tribunal was set up to mediate disputes: **resolve**, settle, arbitrate in, umpire, reconcile, referee; mend, clear up; informal patch up. **3** he attempted to mediate a solution to the conflict: **negotiate**, bring about, effect; formal effectuate.

mediation noun **arbitration**, conciliation, reconciliation, intervention, intercession, good offices; negotiation, shuttle diplomacy.

mediator noun **arbitrator**, arbiter, negotiator, conciliator, peacemaker, go-between, middleman, intermediary, moderator, intervenor, intercessor, broker, honest broker, liaison officer; umpire, referee, adjudicator, judge.

medicinal adjective medicinal herbs: **curative**, healing, remedial, therapeutic, restorative, corrective, health-giving; medical.

medicine noun your doctor will be able to prescribe medicines: **medication**, medicament, drug, prescription, dose, treatment, remedy, cure; nostrum, panacea, cure-all.

medieval adjective **1** medieval times: **of the Middle Ages**, of the Dark Ages,

m

Dark-Age; Gothic. **2** (informal) *the plumbing's a bit medieval:* **primitive**, antiquated, archaic, antique, antediluvian, old-fashioned, out of date, outdated, outmoded, anachronistic, passé, obsolete; informal out of the ark; N. Amer. informal horse-and-buggy, clunky.
– OPPOSITES modern.

mediocre adjective *he is an enthusiastic if mediocre painter:* **ordinary**, average, middling, middle-of-the-road, uninspired, undistinguished, indifferent, unexceptional, unexciting, unremarkable, run-of-the-mill, pedestrian, prosaic, lacklustre, forgettable, amateur, amateurish; informal OK, so-so, (plain) vanilla, fair-to-middling, no great shakes, not up to much; Brit. informal not much cop; N. Amer. informal bush-league; NZ informal half-pie.
– OPPOSITES excellent.

meditate verb **contemplate**, think, consider, ponder, muse, reflect, deliberate, ruminate, chew the cud, brood, mull over; be in a brown study, be deep/lost in thought, debate with oneself; pray; informal put on one's thinking cap.

meditation noun *cultivating the presence of God in meditation and prayer:* **contemplation**, thought, thinking, musing, pondering, consideration, reflection, deliberation, rumination, brooding, reverie, brown study, concentration; prayer.

meditative adjective *meditative techniques:* **pensive**, thoughtful, contemplative, reflective, musing, ruminative, introspective, brooding, deep/lost in thought, in a brown study; prayerful.

medium noun **1** *using technology as a medium for job creation:* **means**, method, way, form, agency, avenue, channel, vehicle, organ, instrument, mechanism. **2** *organisms growing in their natural medium:* **habitat**, element, environment, surroundings, milieu, setting, conditions. **3** *she consulted a medium:* **spiritualist**, spiritist, necromancer. **4** *a happy medium:* **middle way**, middle course, middle ground, middle, mean, median, midpoint; compromise, golden mean.
adjective *the suspect is of medium height:* **average**, middling, medium-sized, middle-sized, moderate, normal, standard.

medley noun *a medley of Beatles songs:* **assortment**, miscellany, mixture, melange, variety, mixed bag, mix, collection, selection, pot-pourri, patchwork; motley collection, ragbag, gallimaufry, mishmash, hotchpotch, jumble; N. Amer. hodgepodge.

meek adjective *she brought her meek little husband along:* **submissive**, yielding, obedient, compliant, tame, biddable, tractable, acquiescent, deferential, timid, unprotesting, unresisting, like a lamb to the slaughter; quiet, mild, gentle, docile, lamblike, shy, diffident, unassuming, self-effacing.
– OPPOSITES assertive.

meet verb **1** *I met an old friend on the train:* **encounter**, meet up with, come face to face with, run into, run across, come across/upon, chance on, happen on, light on, stumble across/on; informal bump into. **2** *she first met Paul at a party:* **get to know**, be introduced to, make the acquaintance of. **3** *the committee met on Saturday:* **assemble**, gather, come together, get together, congregate, convene; formal foregather. **4** *the place where three roads meet:* **converge**, connect, touch, link up, intersect, cross, join. **5** *he met death bravely:* **face**, encounter, undergo, experience, go through, suffer, endure, bear; cope with, handle. **6** *the announcement was met with widespread hostility:* **greet**, receive, answer, treat. **7** *he does not meet the job's requirements:* **fulfil**, satisfy, fill, measure up to, match (up to), conform to, come up to, comply with, answer. **8** *shipowners would meet the cost of oil spills:* **pay**, settle, clear, honour, discharge, pay off, square.
noun *an athletics meet.* See **MEETING** sense 5.
■ **meet someone halfway.** See **HALFWAY**.

meeting noun **1** *he stood up to address the meeting:* **gathering**, assembly, conference, congregation, convention, summit, forum, convocation, conclave, council of war, rally; N. Amer. caucus; informal get-together. **2** *she demanded a meeting with the minister:* **consultation**, audience, interview. **3** *he intrigued her on their first meeting:* **encounter**, contact; appointment, assignation, rendezvous. **4** *the meeting of land and sea:* **convergence**, coming together, confluence, conjunction, union, junction, abutment; intersection, T-junction, crossing. **5** *an athletics meeting:* **event**, tournament, meet, rally, competition, match, game, contest.

megalomania noun *demanding changes in the script was an example of the star's megalomania:* **delusions of grandeur**, folie de grandeur, thirst for power; self-importance, egotism, conceit, conceitedness.

melancholy adjective *a melancholy expression:* **sad**, sorrowful, unhappy, desolate, mournful, lugubrious, gloomy, despondent, dejected, depressed, downhearted, downcast, disconsolate, glum, miserable, wretched, dismal, morose, woeful, woebegone, doleful, joyless, heavy-hearted; informal down in the dumps, down in the mouth, blue.
– OPPOSITES cheerful.
noun *a feeling of melancholy:* **sadness**, sorrow, unhappiness, woe, desolation, melancholia, dejection, depression, despondency, gloom, gloominess, misery; informal the dumps, the blues.

melange noun *the population is a melange of different cultures:* **mixture**, medley, assortment, blend, variety, mixed bag, mix, miscellany, selection, pot-pourri, patchwork; motley collection, ragbag, gallimaufry, mishmash, hotchpotch, jumble; N. Amer. hodgepodge.

melee, mêlée noun *a number of people were trampled to death during the subsequent melee:* **fracas**, disturbance, rumpus, tumult, commotion, disorder, fray; brawl, fight, scuffle, struggle, skirmish, free-for-all, tussle; informal scrap, set-to, ruction; N. Amer. informal rough house.

mellifluous adjective *his low, mellifluous voice was instantly recognizable:* **sweet-sounding**, dulcet, honeyed, mellow, soft, liquid, silvery, soothing, rich, smooth, euphonious, harmonious, tuneful, musical.
– OPPOSITES cacophonous.

mellow adjective **1** *the mellow tone of his voice:* **dulcet**, sweet-sounding, tuneful, melodious, mellifluous; soft, smooth, warm, full, rich. **2** *a mellow wine:* **full-bodied**, mature, well matured, full-flavoured, rich, smooth. **3** *a mellow mood:* **genial**, affable, amiable, good-humoured, good-natured, amicable, pleasant, relaxed, easy-going; jovial, jolly, cheerful, happy, merry.

melodious adjective *the melodious chant of the monks:* **tuneful**, melodic, musical, mellifluous, dulcet, sweet-sounding, silvery, silvery-toned, harmonious, euphonious, lyrical; informal easy on the ear.
– OPPOSITES discordant.

melodramatic adjective *he flung the door open with a melodramatic flourish:* **exaggerated**, histrionic, extravagant, over-dramatic, overdone, over-sensational, sensationalized, over-emotional, sentimental; theatrical, stagy, actressy; informal hammy.

melody noun **1** *the concert started with some familiar melodies:* **tune**, air, strain, theme, song, refrain, piece of music. **2** *his unique gift for melody:* **melodiousness**, tunefulness, lyricism, musicality, euphony.

melt verb **1** *the snow was beginning to melt:* **liquefy**, thaw, defrost, soften, dissolve, deliquesce. **2** *his smile melted her heart:* **soften**, disarm, touch, affect, move. **3** *his anger melted away:* **vanish**, disappear, fade away, dissolve, evaporate.

member noun **1** *a member of the club:* **subscriber**, associate, fellow, life member, founder member, card-carrying member. **2** *a member of a mathematical set:* **constituent**, element, component, part, portion, piece, unit.

membrane noun **layer**, sheet, skin, film, tissue, integument, overlay.

memento noun *you can purchase a memento of your visit:* **souvenir**, keepsake, reminder, remembrance, token, memorial; trophy, relic.

memoir noun **1** *a touching memoir of her childhood:* **account**, history, record, chronicle, narrative, story, portrayal, depiction, sketch, portrait, profile, biography, monograph. **2** *he published his memoirs in 1955:* **autobiography**, life story, life, memories, recollections, reminiscences; journal, diary.

memorable adjective *he recalled memorable moments in his life:* **unforgettable**, indelible, catchy, haunting; momentous, significant, historic, notable, noteworthy, important, consequential, remarkable, special, signal, outstanding, extraordinary, striking, vivid, arresting, impressive, distinctive, distinguished, famous, celebrated, renowned, illustrious, glorious.

memorandum noun **1** *a memorandum from the managing director:* **message**, communication, note, memo, email, letter, missive. **2** *hasty memoranda and jottings-down:* **record**, minute, note, aide-memoire, reminder.

memorial noun **1** *the war memorial:* **monument**, cenotaph, mausoleum; statue, plaque, cairn; shrine; tombstone, gravestone, headstone. **2** *the Festschrift is a memorial to his life's work:* **tribute**, testimonial; remembrance, memento.
adjective *a memorial service:* **commemorative**, remembrance, commemorating; monumental.

memorize verb *Paula listened, memorizing every detail:* **commit to memory**, remember, learn by heart, get off by heart, learn, learn by rote, become word-perfect in, get off pat.

memory noun **1** *she is losing her memory:* **ability to remember**, powers of recall. **2** *happy memories of her young days:* **recollection**, remembrance, reminiscence; impression. **3** *the town built a statue in memory of him:* **commemoration**, remembrance; honour, tribute, recognition, respect. **4** *a computer's memory:* **memory bank**, store, cache, disk, RAM, ROM.

menace noun **1** *an atmosphere full of menace:* **threat**, ominousness, intimidation, warning, ill omen. **2** *a menace to British society:* **danger**, peril, risk, hazard, threat. **3** *that child is a menace:* **nuisance**, pest, annoyance, plague, torment, troublemaker, mischief-maker, thorn in someone's side/flesh.
verb **1** *the elephants are still menaced by poaching:* **threaten**, be a danger to, put at risk, jeopardize, imperil. **2** *a gang of skinheads menaced local residents:* **intimidate**, threaten, terrorize, frighten, scare, terrify.

menacing adjective *she shot him a menacing look:* **threatening**, ominous, intimidating, frightening, terrifying, alarming, forbidding, black, thunderous, glowering, unfriendly, hostile, sinister, baleful, warning.
– OPPOSITES friendly.

mend verb **1** *workmen were mending faulty cabling:* **repair**, fix, put back together, piece together, restore; sew (up), stitch, darn, patch, cobble; rehabilitate, renew, renovate; informal patch up. **2** *'How's Walter?' 'He'll mend.'* **get better**, get well, recover,

m

recuperate, improve; be well, be cured, heal. **3** *quarrels could be mended by talking:* **put/set right**, set straight, straighten out, sort out, rectify, remedy, cure, right, resolve, square, settle, put to rights, correct, retrieve, improve, make better.
– OPPOSITES break, worsen.

mendacious adjective *mendacious propaganda:* **lying**, untruthful, dishonest, deceitful, false, dissembling, insincere, disingenuous, hypocritical, fraudulent, double-dealing, two-faced, two-timing, duplicitous, perjured; untrue, fictitious, falsified, fabricated, fallacious, invented, made up; euphemistic economical with the truth.
– OPPOSITES truthful.

menial adjective *a menial job:* **unskilled**, lowly, humble, low-grade, low-status, inferior, degrading; routine, humdrum, boring, dull.
noun *they were treated like menials:* **servant**, drudge, minion, factotum, lackey; informal wage slave, gofer; Brit. informal dogsbody, skivvy; N. Amer. informal peon.

menstruation noun **periods**, menses, menorrhoea, menstrual cycle; menarche; informal the curse, monthlies, one's/the time of the month.

mental adjective **1** *mental faculties:* **intellectual**, cerebral, brain, rational, cognitive. **2** *a mental disorder:* **psychiatric**, psychological, psychogenic.
– OPPOSITES physical.

mentality noun **1** *I can't understand the mentality of these people:* **way of thinking**, mind set, cast of mind, frame of mind, turn of mind, mind, psychology, mental attitude, outlook, disposition, make-up. **2** *a person of limited mentality:* **intellect**, intellectual capabilities, intelligence, IQ, (powers of) reasoning, rationality.

mentally adverb **in one's mind**, in one's head, inwardly, intellectually, cognitively.

mention verb **1** *don't mention the war:* **allude to**, refer to, touch on/upon; bring up, raise, broach, introduce, moot. **2** *Jim mentioned that he'd met them before:* **state**, say, indicate, let someone know, disclose, divulge, reveal. **3** *I'll gladly mention your work to my friends:* **recommend**, commend, put in a good word for, speak well of.
noun **1** *he made no mention of your request:* **reference**, allusion, remark, statement, announcement, indication. **2** *a mention in dispatches:* **tribute**, citation, acknowledgement, recognition. **3** *my book got a mention on the show:* **recommendation**, commendation, a good word.
■ **don't mention it** don't apologize, it doesn't matter, it makes no difference/odds, it's not important, never mind, don't worry.
■ **not to mention** in addition to, as well as; not counting, not including, to say nothing of, aside from, besides.

mentor noun **1** *his political mentors:* **adviser**, guide, guru, counsellor, consultant; confidant(e). **2** *regular meetings between mentor and trainee:* **trainer**, teacher, tutor, instructor.

menu noun **bill of fare**, tariff, carte du jour, table d'hôte.

mercantile adjective *the mercantile community of Bordeaux:* **commercial**, trade, trading, business, merchant, sales.

mercenary adjective **1** *mercenary self-interest:* **money-oriented**, grasping, greedy, acquisitive, avaricious, covetous, bribable, venal, materialistic; informal money-grubbing. **2** *mercenary soldiers:* **hired**, paid, bought, professional.
noun *a group of mercenaries:* **soldier of fortune**, professional soldier, hired soldier; informal hired gun.

merchandise noun *a wide range of merchandise:* **goods**, wares, stock, commodities, lines, produce, products.
verb *a new product that can be easily merchandised:* **promote**, market, sell, retail; advertise, publicize, push; informal hype (up), plug.

merchant noun **trader**, dealer, wholesaler, broker, agent, seller, buyer, buyer and seller, vendor, distributor.

merciful adjective **1** *God is merciful:* **forgiving**, compassionate, clement, pitying, forbearing, lenient, humane, mild, kind, tender-hearted, gracious, sympathetic, humanitarian, liberal, tolerant, indulgent, generous, magnanimous, benign, benevolent. **2** *a merciful silence fell:* **welcome**, blessed.
– OPPOSITES cruel.
■ **be merciful to** have mercy on, have pity on, show mercy to, spare, pardon, forgive, be lenient on/to; informal go/be easy on, let off.

mercifully adverb *mercifully, the event passed off without incident:* **luckily**, fortunately, happily, thank goodness/God/heavens.

merciless adjective *Mithra was merciless to his enemies:* **ruthless**, remorseless, pitiless, unforgiving, unsparing, implacable, inexorable, relentless, inflexible, inhumane, inhuman, unsympathetic, unfeeling, intolerant, rigid, severe, cold-blooded, hard-hearted, stony-hearted, heartless, harsh, callous, cruel, brutal, barbarous, cut-throat.
– OPPOSITES compassionate.

mercy noun **1** *he showed no mercy to the others:* **leniency**, clemency, compassion, grace, pity, charity, forgiveness, forbearance, quarter, humanity; soft-heartedness, tender-heartedness, kindness, sympathy, liberality, indulgence, tolerance, generosity, magnanimity, beneficence. **2** *we must be thankful for small mercies:* **blessing**, godsend, boon, favour, piece/stroke of luck.
– OPPOSITES ruthlessness, cruelty.
■ **at the mercy of 1** *they found themselves*

at the mercy of the tyrant: in the power of, under/in the control of, in the clutches of, under the heel of, subject to. **2** *he was at the mercy of the elements:* defenceless against, vulnerable to, exposed to, susceptible to, prey to, (wide) open to.

mere adjective *I was a mere boy at the time:* **no more than**, just, only, merely; no better than.

merely adverb *they were merely exercising their rights:* **only**, purely, solely, simply, just, but.

meretricious adjective *the meretricious glitter of the whole charade:* **worthless**, valueless, cheap, tawdry, trashy, Brummagem, tasteless, kitsch; false, artificial, fake, imitation; informal tacky.

merge verb **1** *the company merged with a European firm:* **join (together)**, join forces, amalgamate, unite, affiliate, team up, link (up). **2** *the two organizations were merged:* **amalgamate**, bring together, join, consolidate, conflate, unite, unify, combine, incorporate, integrate, link (up), knit, yoke. **3** *the two colours merged:* **mingle**, blend, fuse, mix, intermix, intermingle, coalesce.
– OPPOSITES separate.

merger noun *a merger between two supermarket chains:* **amalgamation**, combination, union, fusion, coalition, affiliation, unification, incorporation, consolidation, link-up, alliance.
– OPPOSITES split.

merit noun **1** *composers of outstanding merit:* **excellence**, quality, calibre, worth, worthiness, credit, value, distinction, eminence. **2** *the merits of the scheme:* **good point**, strong point, advantage, benefit, value, asset, plus.
– OPPOSITES inferiority, fault, disadvantage.
verb *the accusation did not merit a response:* **deserve**, earn, be deserving of, warrant, rate, justify, be worthy of, be worth, be entitled to, have a right to, have a claim to/on.

meritorious adjective *the captain was awarded a medal for meritorious conduct:* **praiseworthy**, laudable, commendable, admirable, estimable, creditable, worthy, deserving, excellent, exemplary, good.
– OPPOSITES discreditable.

merriment noun *her eyes were dancing with merriment:* **high spirits**, high-spiritedness, exuberance, cheerfulness, gaiety, fun, effervescence, verve, buoyancy, levity, zest, liveliness, cheer, joy, joyfulness, joyousness, jolliness, jollity, happiness, gladness, jocularity, conviviality, festivity, merrymaking, revelry, mirth, glee, gleefulness, laughter, hilarity, light-heartedness, amusement, pleasure.
– OPPOSITES misery.

merry adjective *merry throngs of students:* **cheerful**, cheery, in high spirits, high-spirited, bright, sunny, smiling, light-hearted, buoyant, lively, carefree, without a care in the world, joyful, joyous, jolly, convivial, festive, mirthful, gleeful, happy, glad, laughing; informal chirpy; formal jocund.
– OPPOSITES miserable.
■ **make merry** have fun, have a good time, enjoy oneself, have a party, celebrate, carouse, feast, {eat, drink, and be merry}, revel, roister; informal party, have a ball.

merry-go-round noun **carousel**; Brit. roundabout.

mesh noun **1** *wire mesh:* **netting**, net, network; web, webbing, lattice, latticework. **2** *a mesh of political intrigue:* **entanglement**, net, tangle, web.
verb **1** *one gear meshes with the input gear:* **engage**, connect, lock, interlock. **2** *don't get meshed in the weeds:* **entangle**, enmesh, snare, trap, catch. **3** *our ideas just do not mesh:* **harmonize**, fit together, match, dovetail.

mesmerize verb *they were mesmerized by his performance:* **enthral**, spellbind, entrance, dazzle, bewitch, charm, captivate, enchant, fascinate, transfix, grip, hypnotize.

mess noun **1** *please clear up the mess:* **untidiness**, disorder, disarray, clutter, shambles, jumble, muddle, chaos; Brit. informal tip. **2** *cat mess:* **excrement**, muck, faeces, excreta. **3** *I've got to get out of this mess:* **plight**, predicament, tight spot/corner, difficulty, trouble, quandary, dilemma, problem, muddle, mix-up, imbroglio; informal jam, fix, pickle, stew, hole, scrape. **4** *the project is a complete mess:* **muddle**, bungle; informal botch, hash, foul-up; Brit. informal cock-up; N. Amer. informal snafu.
■ **make a mess of** mismanage, mishandle, bungle, fluff, spoil, ruin, wreck; informal mess up, botch, make a hash of, muck up, foul up; Brit. informal make a pig's ear of, make a Horlicks of, cock up.
■ **mess about/around** *he loves messing about in boats:* potter about, pass the time, fiddle about/around, footle about/around, play about/around, fool about/around; fidget, toy, trifle, tamper, tinker, interfere, meddle, monkey (about/around); informal piddle about/around; Brit. informal muck about/around, lark (about/around).
■ **mess something up 1** *he messed up my kitchen:* dirty; clutter up, disarrange, jumble, dishevel, rumple; N. Amer. informal muss up. **2** (informal) *Eddie messed things up.* See **MAKE A MESS OF**.

message noun **1** *are there any messages for me?* **communication**, piece of information, news, note, memorandum, memo, email, letter, missive, report, bulletin, communiqué, dispatch. **2** *the message of his teaching:* **meaning**, sense, import, idea; point, thrust, gist, essence, content, subject (matter), substance, implication, drift, lesson.

messenger noun **message-bearer**, postman, courier, runner, dispatch rider, envoy, emissary, agent, go-between; historical herald.

m

messy adjective **1** *messy oil spills* | *messy hair:* **dirty**, filthy, grubby, soiled, grimy; mucky, muddy, slimy, sticky, sullied, spotted, stained, smeared, smudged; dishevelled, scruffy, unkempt, rumpled, matted, tousled, bedraggled, tangled; informal yucky; Brit. informal gungy. **2** *a messy kitchen:* **disorderly**, disordered, in a muddle, chaotic, confused, disorganized, in disarray, disarranged; untidy, cluttered, in a jumble; informal like a bomb's hit it; Brit. informal shambolic. **3** *a messy legal battle:* **complex**, intricate, tangled, confused, convoluted; unpleasant, nasty, bitter, acrimonious.
– OPPOSITES clean, tidy.

metallic adjective **1** *a metallic sound:* **tinny**, jangling, jingling; grating, harsh, jarring, dissonant. **2** *metallic paint:* **metallized**, burnished; shiny, glossy, lustrous.

metamorphose verb *in the painting, Queen Maria Luisa is metamorphosed into a barn owl:* **transform**, change, mutate, transmute, transfigure, convert, alter, modify, remodel, recast, reconstruct; humorous transmogrify.

metamorphosis noun **transformation**, mutation, transmutation, change, alteration, conversion, modification, remodelling, reconstruction; humorous transmogrification.

metaphor noun **figure of speech**, image, trope, analogy, comparison, symbol, word painting/picture.

metaphorical adjective *there is no clear line between literal and metaphorical senses:* **figurative**, allegorical, symbolic; imaginative, extended.
– OPPOSITES literal.

metaphysical adjective **1** *metaphysical questions:* **abstract**, theoretical, conceptual, notional, philosophical, speculative, intellectual, academic. **2** *Good and Evil are inextricably linked in a metaphysical battle:* **transcendental**, spiritual, supernatural, paranormal.

mete
▪ **mete something out** *the judges were unwilling to mete out harsh punishment:* dispense, hand out, allocate, allot, apportion, issue, deal out, dole out, dish out, assign, administer.

meteor noun **falling star**, shooting star, meteorite, meteoroid, bolide.

meteoric adjective *her meteoric rise to fame:* **rapid**, lightning, swift, fast, quick, speedy, accelerated, instant, sudden, spectacular.
– OPPOSITES gradual.

meteorologist noun **weather forecaster**, met officer, weatherman, weatherwoman.

method noun **1** *they use very old-fashioned methods:* **procedure**, technique, system, practice, routine, modus operandi, process; strategy, tactic, plan. **2** *there's method in his madness:* **order**, orderliness, organization, structure, form, system, logic, planning, design.
– OPPOSITES disorder.

methodical adjective *a methodical approach to the evaluation of computer systems:* **orderly**, well ordered, well organized, (well) planned, efficient, businesslike, systematic, structured, logical, analytic, disciplined; meticulous, punctilious.

meticulous adjective *meticulous attention to detail:* **careful**, conscientious, diligent, scrupulous, punctilious, painstaking, accurate; thorough, studious, rigorous, detailed, perfectionist, fastidious, methodical, particular.
– OPPOSITES careless.

métier noun **1** *he had another métier besides the priesthood:* **occupation**, job, work, profession, business, employment, career, vocation, trade, craft, line (of work); N. Amer. specialty. **2** *television is more my métier:* **forte**, strong point, strength, speciality, talent, bent; informal thing, cup of tea.

metropolis noun *their trip to London gave them nine days in the metropolis:* **capital (city)**, chief town, county town; big city, conurbation, megalopolis; informal big smoke.

mettle noun **1** *a man of mettle:* **spirit**, fortitude, strength of character, moral fibre, steel, determination, resolve, resolution, backbone, grit, courage, courageousness, bravery, valour, fearlessness, daring; informal guts, spunk; Brit. informal bottle. **2** *Frazer was of a very different mettle:* **calibre**, character, disposition, nature, temperament, personality, make-up, stamp.

mew verb **1** *the cat mewed plaintively:* **miaow**, mewl, cry. **2** *above them, seagulls mewed:* **cry**, screech.

mewl verb *the baby fretted and mewled:* **whimper**, cry, whine; informal grizzle.

microbe noun *microbes which cause dangerous diseases:* **micro-organism**, bacillus, bacterium, virus, germ; informal bug.

microscopic adjective *microscopic algae:* **tiny**, very small, minute, infinitesimal, minuscule; little, micro, diminutive; Scottish wee; informal teeny, weeny, teeny-weeny, teensy-weensy, itsy-bitsy; Brit. informal titchy, tiddly.
– OPPOSITES huge.

midday noun **noon**, twelve noon, high noon, noontide, noonday.
– OPPOSITES midnight.

middle noun **1** *a shallow dish with a spike in the middle:* **centre**, midpoint, halfway point, dead centre, focus, hub; eye, heart, core, kernel. **2** *he had a towel round his middle:* **midriff**, waist, belly, stomach, abdomen; informal tummy, tum.
– OPPOSITES outside.
adjective *a small hole is drilled through the quill below its middle point:* **central**, mid, mean, medium, medial, median, midway, halfway, intermediate.

middleman noun *we give value for money by cutting out the middleman and selling direct:* **intermediary**, go-between; dealer, broker, agent, factor, wholesaler, distributor.

middling adjective *a spa town of the middling kind, neither rich nor poor:* **average**, standard, normal, middle-of-the-road; moderate, ordinary, commonplace, everyday, workaday, tolerable, passable; run-of-the-mill, fair, mediocre, undistinguished, unexceptional, unremarkable; informal OK, so-so, bog-standard, fair-to-middling, (plain) vanilla; NZ informal half-pie.

midget noun *the inhabitants must have been midgets:* **small person**, dwarf, homunculus, Lilliputian, manikin, gnome, pygmy; informal shrimp.
adjective **1** *a story about midget matadors:* **diminutive**, dwarfish, petite, very small, pygmy; informal pint-sized; N. Amer. informal sawn-off. **2** *a midget submarine:* **miniature**, pocket, dwarf, baby.
– OPPOSITES giant.

midnight noun **the middle of the night**, twelve midnight, twenty-four hundred hours, the witching hour.
– OPPOSITES midday.

midst (literary) noun **middle**, centre, heart, core, midpoint, kernel, nub; depth(s), thick; **(in the midst of)** in the course of, halfway through, at the heart/core of.
▪ **in our midst** among us, amid us, in our group, with us.

midway adverb *Peter came to a halt midway down the street:* **halfway**, in the middle, at the midpoint, in the centre; part-way, at some point.

mien noun *a low-browed, frowning mien:* **appearance**, look, expression, countenance, aura, demeanour, attitude, air, manner, bearing.

might noun *she hit him with all her might:* **strength**, force, power, vigour, energy, brawn, powerfulness, forcefulness.
▪ **with might and main** with all one's strength, as hard as one can, as hard as possible, (with) full force, forcefully, powerfully, strongly, vigorously.

mightily adverb **1** *he is mightily impressive:* **extremely**, exceedingly, enormously, immensely, tremendously, hugely, dreadfully, very (much); informal awfully, majorly, mega; N. Amer. informal mighty, plumb. **2** *Ann and I laboured mightily:* **strenuously**, energetically, powerfully, hard, with all one's might, with might and main, all out, heartily, vigorously, diligently, assiduously, persistently, indefatigably; informal like mad, like crazy; Brit. informal like billy-o.

mighty adjective **1** *a mighty blow:* **powerful**, forceful, violent, vigorous, hefty, thunderous. **2** *a mighty warrior:* **fearsome**, ferocious, big, tough, robust, muscular, strapping. **3** *mighty industrial countries:* **dominant**, influential, strong, powerful, important, predominant. **4** *mighty oak trees:* **huge**, enormous, massive, gigantic, big,

large, giant, colossal, mammoth, immense; informal monster, whopping (great), thumping (great), humongous, jumbo(-sized); Brit. informal whacking (great), ginormous.
– OPPOSITES feeble, puny, tiny.

migrant noun *economic migrants:* **immigrant**, emigrant; nomad, itinerant, traveller, vagrant, transient, rover, wanderer, drifter.
adjective *migrant workers:* **travelling**, wandering, drifting, nomadic, roving, roaming, itinerant, vagrant, transient.

migrate verb **1** *rural populations migrated to urban areas:* **relocate**, resettle, move (house); emigrate, go abroad, go overseas; N. Amer. pull up stakes; Brit. informal up sticks. **2** *wildebeest migrate across the Serengeti:* **roam**, wander, drift, rove, travel (around).

migratory adjective *migratory birds:* **migrant**, migrating, moving, travelling.

mild adjective **1** *a mild tone of voice:* **gentle**, tender, soft-hearted, tender-hearted, sensitive, sympathetic, warm, placid, calm, tranquil, serene, peaceable, good-natured, amiable, affable, genial, easy-going. **2** *a mild punishment:* **lenient**, light; compassionate, merciful, humane. **3** *he was eyeing her with mild interest:* **slight**, faint, vague, minimal, nominal, token, feeble. **4** *mild weather:* **warm**, balmy, temperate, clement.
– OPPOSITES harsh, strong, severe.

milieu noun *the social, political, and artistic milieu in Britain:* **environment**, sphere, background, backdrop, setting, context, atmosphere; location, conditions, surroundings, environs.

militant adjective *militant supporters:* **aggressive**, violent, belligerent, bellicose, vigorous, forceful, active, fierce, combative, pugnacious; radical, extremist, extreme, zealous, fanatical.
noun *the demands of the militants:* **activist**, extremist, radical, Young turk, zealot.

militaristic adjective *the militaristic image of the current leadership:* **warmongering**, warlike, martial, hawkish, pugnacious, combative, aggressive, belligerent, bellicose; informal gung-ho.
– OPPOSITES peaceable.

military adjective *military activity:* **fighting**, service, army, armed, defence, martial.
– OPPOSITES civilian.
noun *the military took power:* **(armed) forces**, services, militia; army, navy, air force, marines.

militate verb *anger may militate against success in the negotiations:* **tend to prevent**, work against, hinder, discourage, prejudice, be detrimental to.

milk verb **1** *Pam was milking the cows:* **draw milk from**, express milk from. **2** *milk a little of the liquid:* **draw off**, siphon (off), pump off, tap, drain, extract. **3** *phoney psychics can milk their rich clients for years:* **exploit**, take advantage of, cash in on, suck dry; informal

m

bleed, squeeze, fleece.

milky adjective *not a blemish marred her milky skin:* **pale**, white, milk-white, whitish, off-white, cream, creamy, chalky, pearly, nacreous, ivory, alabaster.
– OPPOSITES swarthy.

mill noun **1** *workers from the steel mill:* **factory**, (processing) plant, works, workshop, shop, foundry, industrial unit. **2** *a pepper mill:* **grinder**, quern, crusher.
verb *the wheat is milled into flour:* **grind**, pulverize, powder, granulate, pound, crush, press.
■ **mill around/about** *people were milling about in the streets:* throng, swarm, seethe, crowd.

millstone noun *she had become a millstone round his neck:* **burden**, encumbrance, dead weight, cross to bear, albatross; duty, obligation, liability, misfortune.

mime noun *a mime of someone fencing:* **dumb show**, pantomime.
verb *she mimed picking up a phone:* **act out**, pantomime, gesture, simulate, represent, indicate by dumb show.

mimic verb **1** *she mimicked his accent:* **imitate**, copy, impersonate, do an impression of, ape, caricature, parody, lampoon, burlesque; informal send up, take off, spoof. **2** *most hoverflies mimic wasps:* **resemble**, look like, have the appearance of, simulate; N. Amer. informal make like.
noun *he was a superb mimic:* **impersonator**, impressionist, imitator, mimicker; parodist, caricaturist, lampooner, lampoonist; informal copycat.

mimicry noun **imitation**, imitating, impersonation, copying, aping.

mince verb **1** *mince the meat and onions:* **grind**, chop up, cut up, dice; N. Amer. hash. **2** *she minced out of the room:* **walk affectedly**; N. Amer. informal sashay.
■ **not mince (one's) words** talk straight, not beat about the bush, call a spade a spade, speak straight from the shoulder, pull no punches; informal tell it like it is; N. Amer. informal talk turkey.

mincing adjective *he had a strange, mincing walk, his hips slightly swaying:* **affected**, dainty, effeminate, niminy-piminy; pretentious; informal camp, sissy; Brit. informal poncey.

mind noun **1** *a good teacher must stretch pupils' minds:* **brain**, intelligence, intellect, intellectual capabilities, brains, brainpower, wits, understanding, reasoning, judgement, sense, head; informal grey matter, brainbox, brain cells; Brit. informal loaf; N. Amer. informal smarts. **2** *he kept his mind on the job:* **attention**, thoughts, concentration, attentiveness. **3** *the tragedy affected her mind:* **sanity**, mental faculties, senses, wits, reason, reasoning, judgement; informal marbles. **4** *his words stuck in her mind:* **memory**, recollection. **5** *a great mind:*

intellect, thinker, brain, scholar, academic. **6** *I've a mind to complain:* **inclination**, desire, wish, urge, notion, fancy, intention, will. **7** *of the same mind:* **opinion**, way of thinking, outlook, attitude, view, viewpoint, point of view.
verb **1** *do you mind if I smoke?* **care**, object, be bothered, be annoyed, be upset, take offence, disapprove, dislike it, look askance; informal give/care a damn, give/care a toss, give/care a hoot, give/care a rap. **2** *mind the step!* **be careful of**, watch out for, look out for, beware of, be on one's guard for, be wary of. **3** *mind you wipe your feet:* **be/make sure (that)**, see (that); remember to, don't forget to. **4** *her husband was minding the baby:* **look after**, take care of, keep an eye on, attend to, care for, tend. **5** *mind what your mother says:* **pay attention to**, heed, pay heed to, attend to, take note/notice of, note, mark, listen to, be mindful of; obey, follow, comply with.
■ **be in two minds** be undecided, be uncertain, be unsure, hesitate, waver, vacillate, dither; Brit. haver, hum and haw; informal dilly-dally, shilly-shally.
■ **bear/keep in mind** remember, note, be mindful of, take note of.
■ **cross one's mind** occur to one, enter one's mind/head, strike one, hit one, dawn on one.
■ **give someone a piece of one's mind**. See REPRIMAND verb.
■ **have something in mind** think of, contemplate; intend, plan, propose, desire, want, wish.
■ **mind out** take care, be careful, watch out, look out, beware, be on one's guard, be wary.
■ **never mind 1** *never mind the cost:* don't bother about, don't worry about, disregard, forget. **2** *never mind, it's all right now:* don't apologize, forget it, don't worry about it, it doesn't matter.
■ **out of one's mind 1** *you must be out of your mind!* See MAD sense 1. **2** *I've been out of my mind with worry:* frantic, beside oneself, distraught, in a frenzy.
■ **put someone in mind of** remind of, recall, conjure up, suggest; resemble, look like.
■ **to my mind** in my opinion, in my view, as I see it, personally, in my estimation, in my book, if you ask me.

mindful adjective *he was mindful of the difficulties involved:* **aware**, conscious, sensible, alive, alert, acquainted, heedful, wary, chary; informal wise, hip.
– OPPOSITES heedless.

mindless adjective **1** *a mindless idiot:* **stupid**, idiotic, brainless, imbecilic, imbecile, asinine, witless, foolish, empty-headed, slow-witted, obtuse, feather-brained, doltish; informal dumb, pig-ignorant, brain-dead, cretinous, moronic, thick, birdbrained, pea-brained, dopey, dim, half-witted, dippy, fat-headed, boneheaded; N. Amer. informal chowderheaded.

2 *mindless acts of vandalism:* **unthinking**, thoughtless, senseless, gratuitous, wanton, indiscriminate, unreasoning. **3** *a mindless task:* **mechanical**, automatic, routine; tedious, boring, monotonous, brainless, mind-numbing.
■ **mindless of** indifferent to, heedless of, unaware of, unmindful of, careless of, blind to.

mine noun **1** *a coal mine:* **pit**, excavation, quarry, workings, diggings; strip mine; Brit. opencast mine; N. Amer. open-pit mine. **2** *the book is a mine of information:* **rich source**, repository, store, storehouse, reservoir, gold mine, treasure house, treasury, reserve, fund, wealth, stock. **3** *he was killed by a mine:* **explosive**, landmine, limpet mine, magnetic mine, depth charge.
verb **1** *the iron ore was mined from shallow pits:* **quarry**, excavate, dig (up), extract, remove; strip-mine. **2** *medical data was mined for relevant statistics:* **search**, delve into, scour, scan, read through, survey.

miner noun **pitman**, digger, collier, faceworker, haulier; tinner.

mingle verb **1** *fact and fiction are skilfully mingled in his novels:* **mix**, blend, intermingle, intermix, interweave, interlace, combine, merge, fuse, unite, join, amalgamate, meld, mesh. **2** *wedding guests mingled in the marquee:* **socialize**, circulate, fraternize, get together, associate with others; informal hobnob.
– OPPOSITES separate.

miniature adjective *a miniature railway:* **small-scale**, mini, tiny, little, small, minute, baby, toy, pocket, dwarf, midget, pygmy, minuscule, diminutive; Scottish wee; N. Amer. vest-pocket; informal teeny, teeny-weeny, teensy, teensy-weensy, itsy-bitsy, eensy, eensy-weensy; Brit. informal titchy, tiddly.
– OPPOSITES giant.

minimal adjective *the committee approved the report with minimal alteration:* **very little**, minimum, the least (possible); nominal, token, negligible.
– OPPOSITES maximum.

minimize verb **1** *the aim is to minimize costs:* **keep down**, keep at/to a minimum, reduce, decrease, cut down, lessen, curtail, diminish, prune; informal slash. **2** *we should not minimize his contribution:* **belittle**, make light of, play down, underestimate, underrate, downplay, undervalue, understate; informal pooh-pooh.
– OPPOSITES maximize, exaggerate.

minimum noun *costs will be kept to the minimum:* **lowest level**, lower limit, bottom level, rock bottom; least, lowest, slightest.
– OPPOSITES maximum.
adjective *the minimum amount of effort:* **minimal**, least, smallest, least possible, slightest, lowest, minutest.

minion noun *Inspector Cotton and his minion Sergeant Mack:* **underling**, henchman, flunkey, lackey, hanger-on, follower, servant, hireling, vassal, stooge; informal yes-man, bootlicker; Brit. informal poodle; N. Amer. informal suck-up.

minister noun **1** *a government minister:* **member of the government**, cabinet minister, secretary of state, undersecretary. **2** *a minister of religion:* **clergyman**, clergywoman, cleric, ecclesiastic, pastor, vicar, rector, priest, parson, father, man/woman of the cloth, man/woman of God, churchman, churchwoman; curate, chaplain; informal reverend, padre, Holy Joe, sky pilot; Austral. informal josser. **3** *the British minister in Egypt:* **ambassador**, chargé d'affaires, plenipotentiary, envoy, emissary, diplomat, consul, representative.
verb *doctors were ministering to the injured:* **tend**, care for, take care of, look after, nurse, treat, attend to, see to, administer to, help, assist.

ministrations plural noun *her mother's anxious ministrations:* **attention**, treatment, help, assistance, aid, care, services.

ministry noun **1** *the ministry for foreign affairs:* **(government) department**, bureau, agency, office. **2** *he's training for the ministry:* **holy orders**, the priesthood, the cloth, the church. **3** *the ministry of Jesus:* **teaching**, preaching, evangelism. **4** *Gladstone's first ministry:* **period of office**, term (of office), administration.

minor adjective **1** *a minor problem:* **slight**, small; unimportant, insignificant, inconsequential, inconsiderable, subsidiary, negligible, trivial, trifling, paltry, petty; N. Amer. nickel-and-dime; informal piffling, piddling. **2** *a minor poet:* **little known**, unknown, lesser, unimportant, insignificant, obscure; N. Amer. minor-league; informal small-time; N. Amer. informal two-bit.
– OPPOSITES major, important.
noun *the heir to the throne was a minor:* **child**, infant, youth, adolescent, teenager, boy, girl; informal kid, kiddie.
– OPPOSITES adult.

minstrel noun (historical) *minstrels accompanied the banquet:* **musician**, singer, balladeer; historical troubadour, jongleur; literary bard.

mint noun (informal) *the bank made a mint out of the deal:* **a vast sum of money**, a king's ransom, millions, billions; informal a (small) fortune, a tidy sum, a bundle, a packet, a pile; Brit. informal a bomb, big money; N. Amer. informal big bucks; Austral. informal big bickies, motser.
adjective *in mint condition:* **brand new**, pristine, perfect, immaculate, unblemished, undamaged, unmarked, unused, first-class, excellent.
verb **1** *the shilling was minted in 1742:* **coin**, stamp, strike, cast, forge, manufacture. **2** *the slogan had been freshly minted:* **create**, invent, make up, think up, dream up.

minuscule adjective *the newsroom was minuscule, not much more than a cubbyhole:* **tiny**, minute, microscopic, very small, little,

m

micro, diminutive, miniature, baby, dwarf; Scottish wee; informal teeny, teeny-weeny, teensy, teensy-weensy, itsy-bitsy, eensy, eensy-weensy, tiddly; Brit. informal titchy.
– OPPOSITES huge.

minute¹ noun **1** *it'll only take a minute:* **moment**, short time, little while, second, bit, instant; informal sec, jiffy; Brit. informal tick, mo, two ticks. **2** *at that minute, Tony walked in:* **point (in time)**, moment, instant, juncture. **3** *their objection was noted in the minutes:* **record(s)**, proceedings, log, notes; transcript, summary, résumé.
■ **at the minute** (Brit. informal) at present, at the moment, now, currently.
■ **in a minute** very soon, in a moment/second/instant, in a trice, shortly, any minute (now), in a short time, in (less than) no time, before long; N. Amer. momentarily; informal anon, in a jiffy, in two shakes, before you can say Jack Robinson; Brit. informal in a tick, in a mo, in two ticks; N. Amer. informal in a snap.
■ **this minute** at once, immediately, directly, this second, instantly, straight away, right away/now, forthwith; informal pronto, straight off, right off, toot sweet.
■ **up to the minute** latest, newest, up to date, modern, fashionable, smart, chic, stylish, all the rage, in vogue; informal trendy, with it, in.

minute² adjective **1** *minute particles:* **tiny**, minuscule, microscopic, very small, little, micro, diminutive, miniature, baby, toy, dwarf, pygmy, Lilliputian; Scottish wee; informal teeny, teeny-weeny, teensy, teensy-weensy, itsy-bitsy, eensy, eensy-weensy; Brit. informal titchy, tiddly. **2** *a minute chance of success:* **negligible**, slight, infinitesimal, minimal, insignificant, inappreciable. **3** *considering the proposal in minute detail:* **exhaustive**, painstaking, meticulous, rigorous, scrupulous, punctilious, detailed.
– OPPOSITES huge.

minutely adverb *every document was examined minutely:* **exhaustively**, painstakingly, meticulously, rigorously, scrupulously, punctiliously, in detail.

minutiae plural noun *the captain cannot be concerned with the minutiae of shipboard life:* **details**, niceties, finer points, particulars, trivia, trivialities.

minx noun *she's a little minx—I should keep away from her:* **tease**, seductress, coquette, slut, Lolita; informal floozie, tart, vamp; Brit. informal scrubber, slapper; N. Amer. informal tramp.

miracle noun **1** *Christ's first miracle:* **supernatural phenomenon**, mystery, prodigy. **2** *Germany's economic miracle:* **wonder**, marvel, sensation, phenomenon.

miraculous adjective **1** *the miraculous help of St Blaise:* **supernatural**, preternatural, inexplicable, unaccountable, magical. **2** *a miraculous escape:* **amazing**, astounding, remarkable, extraordinary, incredible,

unbelievable, sensational; informal mind-boggling, mind-blowing.

mirage noun **optical illusion**, hallucination, phantasmagoria, apparition, fantasy, chimera, vision, figment of the imagination.

mire noun **1** *the land became a mire with all the recent rain:* **swamp**, bog, morass, quagmire, slough; swampland, wetland, marshland. **2** *her horse was spattered with mire:* **mud**, slime, dirt, filth, muck. **3** *struggling to pull Russia out of the mire:* **mess**, difficulty, plight, predicament, tight spot, trouble, quandary, muddle; informal jam, fix, pickle, hot water.
verb **1** *Frank's horse got mired in a bog:* **bog down**, sink (down). **2** *he has become mired in lawsuits:* **entangle**, tangle up, embroil, catch up, mix up, involve.

mirror noun **1** *a quick look in the mirror:* **looking glass**, reflecting surface; full-length mirror, hand mirror, wing mirror, rear-view mirror; Brit. glass. **2** *the Frenchman's life was a mirror of his own:* **reflection**, twin, replica, copy, match, parallel.
verb *pop music mirrored the mood of desperation:* **reflect**, match, reproduce, imitate, simulate, copy, mimic, echo, parallel, correspond to.

mirth noun *she giggled, making an effort to control her mirth:* **merriment**, high spirits, mirthfulness, cheerfulness, cheeriness, hilarity, glee, laughter, gaiety, buoyancy, blitheness, euphoria, exhilaration, light-heartedness, joviality, joy, joyfulness, joyousness.
– OPPOSITES misery.

mirthful adjective **merry**, high-spirited, gleeful, cheerful, cheery, jocular, buoyant, euphoric, exhilarated, elated, light-hearted, jovial, joyous, jolly, festive.

mirthless adjective **humourless**, unamused, grim, sour, surly, dour, sullen, sulky, gloomy, mournful, melancholy, doleful, miserable, grumpy.
– OPPOSITES cheerful.

miry adjective *the roads were miry and troublesome in winter:* **muddy**, slushy, slimy, swampy, marshy, boggy, squelchy, waterlogged.

misadventure noun *a series of misadventures:* **accident**, problem, difficulty, misfortune, mishap; setback, reversal (of fortune), stroke of bad luck, blow; failure, disaster, tragedy, calamity, woe, trial, tribulation, catastrophe.

misanthrope noun *Scrooge wasn't the mean-spirited misanthrope most of us believe him to be:* **hater of mankind**, cynic; recluse, hermit; informal grouch, grump; historical anchorite.

misanthropic adjective *his misanthropic gloom:* **antisocial**, unsociable, unfriendly, reclusive, uncongenial, cynical, jaundiced.

misapply verb *the idea of permissiveness has been overstated, exaggerated, or* *misapplied:* **misuse**, mishandle, misemploy, abuse; distort, garble, warp, misinterpret, misconstrue, misrepresent.

misapprehension noun **misunderstanding**, misinterpretation, misreading, misjudgement, misconception, misbelief, the wrong idea, false impression, delusion.

misappropriate verb *he confessed to having misappropriated $2.2bn from his clients' portfolios:* **embezzle**, expropriate, steal, thieve, pilfer, pocket, help oneself to, make off with; informal swipe, filch, rip off, snitch; Brit. informal pinch, nick, whip, knock off.

misappropriation noun **embezzlement**, expropriation, stealing, theft, thieving, pilfering.

misbegotten adjective *a misbegotten scheme:* **ill-conceived**, ill-advised, badly planned, badly thought-out, hare-brained.

misbehave verb *parents are summoned to the school if their children misbehave:* **behave badly**, be misbehaved, be naughty, be disobedient, get up to mischief, get up to no good; be bad-mannered, be rude; informal carry on, act up.

misbehaviour noun **bad behaviour**, misconduct, naughtiness, disobedience, mischief, mischievousness; bad/poor manners, rudeness; informal acting-up.

misbelief noun *it is a misbelief that alcohol problems require a specialist response:* **false belief**, delusion, illusion, fallacy, error, mistake, misconception, misapprehension.

miscalculate verb *he had grossly miscalculated the time it would take:* **misjudge**, make a mistake (about), calculate wrongly, estimate wrongly, overestimate, underestimate, overvalue, undervalue; go wrong, err, be wide of the mark.

miscalculation noun **error of judgement**, misjudgement, mistake, overestimate, underestimate.

miscarriage noun **1** *she's had a miscarriage:* **(spontaneous) abortion**, stillbirth. **2** *the miscarriage of the project:* **failure**, foundering, ruin, ruination, collapse, breakdown, thwarting, frustration, undoing, non-fulfilment, mismanagement.

miscarry verb **1** *the shock caused her to miscarry:* **lose one's baby**, have a miscarriage, abort, have a (spontaneous) abortion. **2** *our plan miscarried:* **go wrong**, go awry, go amiss, be unsuccessful, be ruined, fail, misfire, abort, founder, come to nothing, fall through, fall flat; informal flop, go up in smoke.
– OPPOSITES succeed.

miscellaneous adjective *a variety of miscellaneous tasks:* **various**, varied, different, assorted, mixed, sundry, diverse, disparate; diversified, motley, multifarious, heterogeneous.

miscellany noun *a miscellany of poems by several hands:* **assortment**, mixture,

melange, blend, variety, mixed bag, mix, medley, diversity, collection, selection, assemblage, pot-pourri, mishmash, hotchpotch, ragbag, salmagundi, gallimaufry, omnium gatherum; N. Amer. hodgepodge.

mischance noun *we lost it by mischance:* **accident**, misfortune, mishap, misadventure, setback, disaster, tragedy, calamity, catastrophe, reversal, upset, blow; bad luck, ill fortune.

mischief noun **1** *the boys are always getting up to mischief:* **naughtiness**, bad behaviour, misbehaviour, mischievousness, misconduct, disobedience; pranks, tricks, larks, capers, nonsense, devilry, funny business; informal monkey business, shenanigans, hanky-panky; Brit. informal monkey tricks, carryings-on, jiggery-pokery. **2** *the mischief in her eyes:* **impishness**, roguishness, devilment. **3** (informal) *you'll do yourself a mischief:* **harm**, hurt, injury, damage.

mischievous adjective **1** *a mischievous child:* **naughty**, badly behaved, misbehaving, disobedient, troublesome, full of mischief; rascally, roguish. **2** *a mischievous smile:* **playful**, teasing, wicked, impish, roguish, arch. **3** *a mischievous allegation:* **malicious**, malevolent, spiteful, venomous, poisonous, evil-intentioned, evil, baleful, vindictive, vengeful, vitriolic, rancorous, malign, malignant, pernicious, mean, nasty, harmful, hurtful, cruel, unkind; informal bitchy, catty.
– OPPOSITES well behaved.

misconceive verb *many lawyers misconceive their own role:* **misunderstand**, misinterpret, misconstrue, misapprehend, mistake, misread; miscalculate, err, be mistaken, get the wrong idea.

misconception noun *a popular misconception about science:* **misapprehension**, misunderstanding, mistake, error, misinterpretation, misconstruction, misreading, misjudgement, misbelief, miscalculation, false impression, illusion, fallacy, delusion.

misconduct noun **1** *allegations of misconduct:* **wrongdoing**, unlawfulness, lawlessness, crime, felony, criminality, sin, sinfulness; unprofessionalism, unethical behaviour, malpractice, negligence, impropriety. **2** *misconduct in the classroom:* **misbehaviour**, bad behaviour, misdeeds, misdemeanours, disorderly conduct, mischief, naughtiness, rudeness.

misconstrue verb *his indifference can easily be misconstrued as arrogance:* **misunderstand**, misinterpret, misconceive, misapprehend, mistake, misread; be mistaken about, get the wrong idea about, get it/someone wrong.

miscreant noun *the village stocks, where miscreants of olden days were pelted with rotten garbage:* **criminal**,

m

culprit, wrongdoer, malefactor, offender, villain, lawbreaker, evil-doer, delinquent, reprobate.

misdeed noun *he repented of his misdeeds and vowed to change his ways:* **wrongdoing**, wrong, evil deed, crime, felony, misdemeanour, misconduct, offence, error, transgression, sin.

misdemeanour noun *he preferred to turn a blind eye to his son's misdemeanours:* **wrongdoing**, evil deed, crime, felony; misdeed, misconduct, offence, error, peccadillo, transgression, sin.

miser noun *a typical miser, he hid his money in the house in various places:* **penny-pincher**, pinchpenny, niggard, cheese-parer, Scrooge; informal skinflint, meanie, money-grubber, cheapskate; N. Amer. informal tightwad.
– OPPOSITES spendthrift.

miserable adjective 1 *I'm too miserable to eat:* **unhappy**, sad, sorrowful, dejected, depressed, downcast, downhearted, down, despondent, disconsolate, wretched, glum, gloomy, dismal, melancholy, woebegone, doleful, forlorn, heartbroken; informal blue, down in the mouth/dumps. 2 *their miserable surroundings:* **dreary**, dismal, gloomy, drab, wretched, depressing, grim, cheerless, bleak, desolate; poor, shabby, squalid, seedy, dilapidated. 3 *miserable weather:* **unpleasant**, disagreeable, depressing; wet, rainy, stormy; informal rotten. 4 *a miserable old grouch:* **grumpy**, sullen, gloomy, bad-tempered, ill-tempered, dour, surly, sour, glum, moody, unsociable, saturnine, lugubrious, irritable, churlish, cantankerous, crotchety, cross, crabby, grouchy, testy, peevish, crusty, waspish. 5 *miserable wages:* **inadequate**, meagre, scanty, paltry, small, poor, pitiful, niggardly; informal measly, stingy, pathetic. 6 *all that fuss about a few miserable pounds:* **wretched**, confounded; informal blithering, flaming, blessed, damned, blasted.
– OPPOSITES cheerful, lovely.

miserliness noun **meanness**, niggardliness, close-fistedness, closeness, parsimony, parsimoniousness; informal stinginess, tight-fistedness; N. Amer. cheapness.

miserly adjective 1 *his miserly great-uncle:* **mean**, niggardly, parsimonious, close, close-fisted, penny-pinching, cheese-paring, grasping, Scrooge-like; informal stingy, tight, tight-fisted; N. Amer. informal cheap. 2 *the prize is a miserly £300:* **meagre**, inadequate, paltry, negligible, miserable, pitiful, niggardly, beggarly; informal measly, stingy, pathetic.
– OPPOSITES generous.

misery noun 1 *periods of intense misery:* **unhappiness**, distress, wretchedness, suffering, anguish, anxiety, angst, torment, pain, grief, heartache, heartbreak, despair, despondency, dejection, depression, desolation, gloom, melancholy, melancholia, woe, sadness, sorrow; informal the dumps,

the blues. 2 *the miseries of war:* **affliction**, misfortune, difficulty, problem, ordeal, trouble, hardship, deprivation; pain, sorrow, trial, tribulation, woe. 3 (Brit. informal) *he's a real old misery:* **killjoy**, dog in the manger, spoilsport; informal sourpuss, grouch, grump, party-pooper.
– OPPOSITES contentment, pleasure.

misfire verb *his plan had misfired:* **go wrong**, go awry, be unsuccessful, fail, founder, fall through/flat; backfire; informal flop, go up in smoke.

misfit noun *a refuge for failures, freeloaders, and misfits:* **nonconformist**, eccentric, maverick, individualist, square peg in a round hole; informal oddball, weirdo, freak; N. Amer. informal screwball.

misfortune noun *they endured many misfortunes:* **problem**, difficulty, setback, trouble, adversity, stroke of bad luck, reversal (of fortune), misadventure, mishap, blow, failure, accident, disaster; sorrow, misery, woe, trial, tribulation.

misgiving noun *despite occasional misgivings, he was optimistic:* **qualm**, doubt, reservation; suspicion, distrust, mistrust, lack of confidence, second thoughts; trepidation, scepticism, unease, uneasiness, anxiety, apprehension, disquiet.

misguided adjective 1 *the policy is misguided:* **erroneous**, fallacious, unsound, misplaced, misconceived, ill-advised, ill-considered, ill-judged, inappropriate, unwise, injudicious, imprudent. 2 *you are quite misguided:* **misinformed**, misled, labouring under a misapprehension, wrong, mistaken, deluded.

mishandle verb 1 *the officer mishandled the situation:* **bungle**, fluff, make a mess of, mismanage, spoil, ruin, wreck; informal botch, make a hash of, mess up, muck up; Brit. informal make a pig's ear of, make a Horlicks of. 2 *he mishandled his wife:* **bully**, persecute, ill-treat, mistreat, maltreat, abuse, knock about/around, hit, beat; informal beat up. 3 *the equipment could be dangerous if mishandled:* **misuse**, abuse, handle/treat roughly.

mishap noun *the event passed without mishap:* **accident**, trouble, problem, difficulty, setback, adversity, reversal (of fortune), misfortune, blow; failure, disaster, tragedy, catastrophe, calamity.

mishmash noun *a bizarre mishmash of colours and patterns:* **jumble**, confusion, hotchpotch, ragbag, patchwork, farrago, assortment, medley, miscellany, mixture, melange, blend, mix, pot-pourri, conglomeration, gallimaufry, omnium gatherum, salmagundi; N. Amer. hodgepodge.

misinform verb *I'm afraid you have been misinformed:* **mislead**, misguide, give wrong information, delude, take in, deceive, lie to, hoodwink; informal lead up the garden path, take for a ride; N. Amer. informal give someone a bum steer.

misinformation noun *a lot of misinformation was received:* **disinformation**, false/misleading information; lie, fib; informal kidology; N. Amer. informal bum steer.

misinterpret verb *he explained that his proposal had been misinterpreted:* **misunderstand**, misconceive, misconstrue, misapprehend, mistake, misread; confuse, take amiss, be mistaken, get the wrong idea.

misjudge verb *I have misjudged Doris—she didn't tell anyone:* **get the wrong idea about**, get wrong, judge incorrectly, estimate wrongly, be wrong about, miscalculate, misread; overestimate, underestimate, overvalue, undervalue, underrate.

mislay verb *I seem to have mislaid my driving licence:* **lose**, misplace, put in the wrong place, be unable to find, forget the whereabouts of.
– OPPOSITES find.

mislead verb *it seemed that Caroline had deliberately misled her:* **deceive**, delude, take in, lie to, fool, hoodwink, throw off the scent, pull the wool over someone's eyes, misguide, misinform, give wrong information to; informal lead up the garden path, take for a ride; N. Amer. informal give someone a bum steer.

misleading adjective *the leaflet was full of misleading statements:* **deceptive**, confusing, deceiving, equivocal, ambiguous, fallacious, specious, spurious, false.

mismanage verb *the campaign had been badly mismanaged:* **bungle**, fluff, make a mess of, mishandle, misconduct, spoil, ruin, wreck; informal botch, make a hash of, mess up, muck up; Brit. informal make a pig's ear of, make a Horlicks of.

mismatch noun *there is still a mismatch between policy and practice:* **discrepancy**, inconsistency, contradiction, incongruity, incongruousness, conflict, discord, irreconcilability.

mismatched adjective *mismatched kitchen units:* **ill-assorted**, ill-matched, incongruous, unsuited, incompatible, inconsistent, at odds; out of keeping, clashing, dissimilar, unalike, different, at variance, disparate, unrelated, divergent, contrasting.
– OPPOSITES matching.

misogynist noun *a bachelor and renowned misogynist:* **woman-hater**, anti-feminist, (male) chauvinist, sexist; informal male chauvinist pig, MCP.

misplace verb *he had misplaced the tickets:* **lose**, mislay, put in the wrong place, be unable to find, forget the whereabouts of.
– OPPOSITES find.

misplaced adjective *his comments were misplaced:* **misguided**, unwise, ill-advised, ill-considered, ill-judged, inappropriate.

misprint noun *the book is full of misprints:* **mistake**, error, typographical mistake/error, typing mistake/error, corrigendum, erratum; Brit. literal; informal typo.

misquote verb *my original statement has been misquoted:* **misreport**, misrepresent, misstate, take/quote out of context, distort, twist, slant, bias, put a spin on, falsify.

misrepresent verb *you are misrepresenting the views of the government:* **misstate**, misreport, misquote, quote/take out of context, misinterpret, put a spin on, falsify, distort.

misrule noun **1** *the misrule of Edward IV:* **bad government**, misgovernment, mismanagement, malpractice, incompetence. **2** *there is sometimes complete misrule at football games:* **lawlessness**, anarchy, disorder, chaos, mayhem.
– OPPOSITES order.

miss verb **1** *the shot missed her by inches:* **fail to hit**, be/go wide of, fall short of. **2** *Mandy missed the catch:* **fail to catch**, drop, fumble, fluff, mishandle, misfield, mishit. **3** *I've missed my bus:* **be too late for**, fail to catch/get. **4** *I missed what you said:* **fail to hear**, mishear. **5** *you can't miss the station:* **fail to see/notice**, overlook. **6** *she never missed a meeting:* **fail to attend**, be absent from, play truant from, cut, skip; Brit. informal skive off. **7** *don't miss this exciting opportunity!* **let slip**, fail to take advantage of, let go/pass, pass up. **8** *I left early to miss the rush-hour traffic:* **avoid**, beat, evade, escape, dodge, sidestep, elude, circumvent, steer clear of, find a way round, bypass. **9** *she missed him when he was away:* **pine for**, yearn for, ache for, long for, long to see.
– OPPOSITES hit, catch.
noun *one hit and three misses:* **failure**, omission, slip, blunder, error, mistake.
■ **miss someone/something out** leave out, exclude, miss (off), fail to mention, pass over, skip; Brit. informal give something a miss.

misshapen adjective *his bowed legs and misshapen feet:* **deformed**, malformed, distorted, crooked, twisted, warped, out of shape, bent, asymmetrical, irregular, misproportioned, ill-proportioned, disfigured, grotesque.

missing adjective **1** *his wallet is missing:* **lost**, mislaid, misplaced, absent, gone (astray), unaccounted for. **2** *passion was missing from her life:* **absent**, not present, lacking, wanting.
– OPPOSITES present.

mission noun **1** *a mercy mission to Romania:* **assignment**, commission, expedition, journey, trip, undertaking, operation; task, job, labour, work, duty, charge, trust. **2** *her mission in life:* **vocation**, calling, goal, aim, quest, purpose, function. **3** *a trade mission:* **delegation**, deputation, commission, legation, delegacy. **4** *a teacher in a mission:* **missionary post**, missionary station. **5** *a bombing mission:* **sortie**, operation, raid.

missionary noun *methods employed by*

Christian missionaries to convert Hindus:
evangelist, apostle, proselytizer, preacher, minister, priest.

missive noun *a missive from the Foreign Office:* **message**, communication, letter, word, note, memorandum, line, communiqué, dispatch, news; informal memo.

misspent adjective *his misspent youth:* **wasted**, dissipated, squandered, thrown away, frittered away, misused, misapplied.

misstate verb *they were accused of misstating the underlying purpose of the transaction:* **misreport**, misrepresent, take/quote out of context, distort, twist, put a spin on, falsify.

mist noun *the mist was clearing:* **haze**, fog, smog, murk, cloud, Scotch mist.
■ **mist over/up** steam up, become misty, fog over/up, film over, cloud over.

mistake noun **1** *I assumed it had been a mistake:* **error**, fault, inaccuracy, omission, slip, blunder, miscalculation, misunderstanding, oversight, misinterpretation, gaffe, faux pas, solecism; informal slip-up, boo-boo, howler, boner; Brit. informal boob, clanger, bloomer; N. Amer. informal goof. **2** *spelling mistakes:* **misprint**, typographical error/mistake, typing error/mistake, corrigendum, erratum; Brit. literal; informal typo.
verb **1** *men are apt to mistake their own feelings:* **misunderstand**, misinterpret, get wrong, misconstrue, misread. **2** *children often mistake vitamin pills for sweets:* **confuse with**, mix up with, take for, misinterpret as.
■ **be mistaken** be wrong, be in error, be under a misapprehension, be misinformed, be misguided; informal be barking up the wrong tree, get the wrong end of the stick.
■ **make a mistake** go wrong, err, make an error, blunder, miscalculate; informal slip up, make a boo-boo, make a howler; Brit. informal boob; N. Amer. informal drop the ball, goof (up).

mistaken adjective *she wondered whether she'd been mistaken about his intentions:* **wrong**, erroneous, inaccurate, incorrect, off beam, false, fallacious, unfounded, misguided, misinformed.
– OPPOSITES correct.

mistakenly adverb **1** *we often mistakenly imagine that when a problem is diagnosed it is solved:* **wrongly**, in error, erroneously, incorrectly, falsely, fallaciously, inaccurately. **2** *Matt mistakenly opened the letter:* **by accident**, accidentally, inadvertently, unintentionally, unwittingly, unconsciously, by mistake.
– OPPOSITES correctly, intentionally.

mistimed adjective *his mistimed floral tribute upset her greatly:* **ill-timed**, badly timed, inopportune, inappropriate, untimely, unseasonable.
– OPPOSITES opportune.

mistreat verb *foreign nationals held hostage*

in the country had been mistreated: **ill-treat**, maltreat, abuse, knock about/around, hit, beat, strike, molest, injure, harm, hurt; misuse, mishandle; informal beat up, rough up.

mistreatment noun **ill-treatment**, maltreatment, abuse, beating, molestation, injury, harm; mishandling, manhandling.

mistress noun *his wife never found out about his mistress:* **lover**, girlfriend, kept woman; courtesan, concubine; informal fancy woman, bit on the side.

mistrust verb **1** *I mistrust his motives:* **be suspicious of**, be mistrustful of, be distrustful of, be sceptical of, be wary of, be chary of, distrust, have doubts about, have misgivings about, have reservations about, suspect. **2** *don't mistrust your impulses:* **question**, challenge, doubt, have no confidence/faith in.
noun **1** *mistrust of Russia was widespread:* **suspicion**, distrust, doubt, misgivings, wariness. **2** *their mistrust of David's competence:* **questioning**, lack of confidence/faith in, doubt about.

mistrustful adjective *he wondered if he had been unduly mistrustful of her:* **suspicious**, chary, wary, distrustful, doubtful, dubious, uneasy, sceptical, leery.

misty adjective **1** *misty weather:* **hazy**, foggy, cloudy; smoggy. **2** *a misty figure:* **blurry**, fuzzy, blurred, dim, indistinct, unclear, vague. **3** *misty memories:* **vague**, unclear, indefinite, hazy, nebulous.
– OPPOSITES clear.

misunderstand verb *she misunderstood his motives:* **misapprehend**, misinterpret, misconstrue, misconceive, mistake, misread; be mistaken, get the wrong idea, receive a false impression; informal be barking up the wrong tree, get (hold of) the wrong end of the stick.

misunderstanding noun **1** *a fundamental misunderstanding of juvenile crime:* **misinterpretation**, misconstruction, misreading, misapprehension, misconception, the wrong idea, false impression. **2** *we have had some misunderstandings:* **disagreement**, difference (of opinion), dispute, falling-out, quarrel, argument, altercation, squabble, wrangle, row, clash; informal spat, scrap, tiff.

misuse verb **1** *misusing public funds:* **put to wrong use**, misemploy, embezzle, use fraudulently; abuse, squander, waste. **2** *she had been misused by her husband:* **ill-treat**, maltreat, mistreat, abuse, knock about/around, hit, beat, strike, molest, injure, harm, hurt; mishandle, manhandle; informal beat up, rough up.
noun **1** *a misuse of company assets:* **wrong use**, embezzlement, fraud; squandering, waste. **2** *the misuse of drugs:* **illegal use**, abuse.

mitigate verb *drugs which mitigated the*

worst symptoms of the disease: **alleviate**, reduce, diminish, lessen, weaken, lighten, attenuate, take the edge off, allay, ease, assuage, palliate, relieve, tone down.
– OPPOSITES aggravate.

mitigating adjective *he would have faced a prison sentence but for mitigating circumstances:* **extenuating**, exonerative, justificatory, justifying, vindicatory, vindicating, qualifying.

mitigation noun **1** *the mitigation of the problems:* **alleviation**, reduction, diminution, lessening, easing, weakening, assuagement, palliation, relief. **2** *what did she say in mitigation?* **extenuation**, explanation, excuse.

mix verb **1** *mix all the ingredients together:* **blend**, mix up, mingle, combine, put together, jumble; fuse, unite, unify, join, amalgamate, incorporate, meld, marry, coalesce, homogenize, intermingle, intermix. **2** *she mixes with all sorts:* **associate**, socialize, fraternize, keep company, consort; mingle, circulate; N. Amer. rub elbows; informal hang out/around, knock about/around, hobnob; Brit. informal hang about. **3** *we just don't mix:* **be compatible**, get along/on, be in harmony, see eye to eye, agree; informal hit it off, click, be on the same wavelength.
– OPPOSITES separate.
noun *a mix of ancient and modern:* **mixture**, blend, mingling, combination, compound, fusion, alloy, union, amalgamation, medley, melange, collection, selection, assortment, variety, mixed bag, miscellany, pot-pourri, jumble, hotchpotch, ragbag, patchwork, farrago, gallimaufry, omnium gatherum, salmagundi; N. Amer. hodgepodge.
■ **mix something up 1** *mix up the rusk with milk.* See **MIX** verb sense 1. **2** *I mixed up the dates:* confuse, get confused, muddle (up), get muddled up, mistake.
■ **mixed up in** *I'm sure he was mixed up in this business:* involved in, embroiled in, caught up in.

mixed adjective **1** *a mixed collection:* **assorted**, varied, variegated, miscellaneous, disparate, diverse, diversified, motley, sundry, jumbled, heterogeneous. **2** *chickens of mixed breeds:* **hybrid**, half-caste, cross-bred, interbred. **3** *mixed reactions:* **ambivalent**, equivocal, contradictory, conflicting, confused, muddled.
– OPPOSITES homogeneous.

mixer noun **1** *a kitchen mixer:* **blender**, food processor, liquidizer, beater, churn. **2** *she was never really a mixer:* **sociable person**, socializer, extrovert, socialite.

mixture noun **1** *the pudding mixture:* **blend**, mix, brew, combination, concoction; composition, compound, alloy, amalgam. **2** *a strange mixture of people:* **assortment**, miscellany, medley, melange, blend, variety, mixed bag, mix, diversity, collection, selection, pot-pourri,

mishmash, hotchpotch, ragbag, patchwork, farrago, gallimaufry, omnium gatherum, salmagundi; N. Amer. hodgepodge. **3** *the animals were a mixture of genetic strands:* **cross**, cross-breed, mongrel, hybrid, half-breed, half-caste.

mix-up noun *there's been a mix-up over the tickets:* **confusion**, muddle, misunderstanding, mistake, error.

moan verb **1** *he moaned in agony:* **groan**, wail, whimper, sob, cry. **2** *the wind moaned in the trees:* **sough**, sigh, murmur.

mob noun **1** *troops dispersed the mob:* **crowd**, horde, multitude, rabble, mass, throng, group, gang, gathering, assemblage. **2** *the mob were excluded from political life:* **the common people**, the masses, the rank and file, the commonality, the commonalty, the third estate, the plebeians, the proletariat; the hoi polloi, the lower classes, the rabble, the riff-raff, the great unwashed; informal the proles, the plebs. **3** *(Brit. informal) he stood out from the rest of the mob:* **group**, set, crowd, lot, circle, coterie, clan, faction, pack, band, ring; informal gang, bunch.
verb **1** *the Chancellor was mobbed when he visited Berlin:* **surround**, swarm around, besiege, jostle. **2** *reporters mobbed her hotel:* **crowd (into)**, fill, pack, throng, press into, squeeze into.

mobile adjective **1** *both patients are mobile:* **able to move (around)**, moving, walking; Medicine ambulant. **2** *her mobile face:* **expressive**, eloquent, revealing, animated. **3** *a mobile library:* **travelling**, transportable, portable, movable; itinerant, peripatetic. **4** *highly mobile young people:* **adaptable**, flexible, versatile, adjustable.
– OPPOSITES motionless, static.

mobility noun **1** *restricted mobility:* **ability to move**, movability. **2** *the mobility of Billy's face:* **expressiveness**, eloquence, animation. **3** *mobility in the workforce:* **adaptability**, flexibility, versatility, adjustability.

mobilize verb **1** *the government mobilized most of its trained troops:* **marshal**, deploy, muster, rally, call up, assemble, mass, organize, prepare. **2** *mobilizing support for the party:* **generate**, arouse, awaken, excite, incite, provoke, foment, prompt, stimulate, stir up, galvanize, encourage, inspire, whip up.

mock verb **1** *the local children mocked the old people:* **ridicule**, jeer at, sneer at, deride, scorn, make fun of, laugh at, scoff at, tease, taunt; informal take the mickey out of, josh; N. Amer. informal goof on, rag on, pull someone's chain; Austral./NZ informal poke mullock at, sling off at. **2** *they mocked the way he speaks:* **parody**, ape, take off, satirize, lampoon, imitate, mimic; informal send up.
adjective *mock leather:* **imitation**, artificial, man-made, simulated, synthetic, ersatz, fake, reproduction, dummy, sham, false, faux, spurious, bogus, counterfeit, pseudo; informal pretend, phoney.

m

-OPPOSITES genuine.

mockery noun 1 *the mockery in his voice:* **ridicule**, derision, jeering, sneering, contempt, scorn, scoffing, teasing, taunting, sarcasm. 2 *the trial was a mockery:* **travesty**, charade, farce, parody.

mocking adjective *a mocking smile:* **sneering**, derisive, contemptuous, scornful, sardonic, ironic, sarcastic.

mode noun 1 *an informal mode of policing:* **manner**, way, fashion, means, method, system, style, approach, technique, procedure, process, practice. 2 *the camera is in manual mode:* **function**, position, operation. 3 *the mode for active wear:* **fashion**, vogue, style, look, trend; craze, rage, fad.

model noun 1 *a working model:* **replica**, copy, representation, mock-up, dummy, imitation, duplicate, reproduction, facsimile. 2 *the American model of airline deregulation:* **prototype**, stereotype, archetype, type, version; mould, template, framework, pattern, design, blueprint. 3 *she was a model as a teacher:* **ideal**, paragon, perfect example/specimen; perfection, acme, epitome, nonpareil, crème de la crème. 4 *a top model:* **fashion model**, supermodel, mannequin; informal clothes horse. 5 *an artist's model:* **sitter**, poser, subject. 6 *the latest model of car:* **version**, type, design, variety, kind, sort. 7 *this dress is a model:* **original (design)**, exclusive; informal one-off.
adjective 1 *model trains:* **replica**, toy, miniature, dummy, imitation, duplicate, reproduction, facsimile. 2 *model farms:* **prototypical**, prototypal, archetypal. 3 *a model teacher:* **ideal**, perfect, exemplary, classic, flawless, faultless.

moderate adjective 1 *moderate success:* **average**, modest, medium, middling, ordinary, common, commonplace, everyday, workaday; tolerable, passable, adequate, fair; mediocre, indifferent, unexceptional, unremarkable, run-of-the-mill; informal OK, so-so, bog-standard, fair-to-middling, (plain) vanilla, no great shakes, not up to much; NZ informal half-pie. 2 *moderate prices:* **reasonable**, acceptable; inexpensive, low, fair, modest. 3 *a man of moderate views:* **middle-of-the-road**, non-extreme, non-radical. 4 *moderate behaviour:* **restrained**, controlled, sober; tolerant, lenient.
-OPPOSITES great, unreasonable, extreme.
verb 1 *the wind has moderated:* **die down**, abate, let up, calm down, lessen, decrease, diminish; recede, weaken, subside. 2 *you can help to moderate her anger:* **curb**, control, check, temper, restrain, subdue; repress, tame, lessen, decrease, lower, reduce, diminish, alleviate, allay, appease, assuage, ease, soothe, calm, tone down. 3 *the Speaker moderates the assembly:* **chair**, take the chair of, preside over.
-OPPOSITES increase.

moderately adverb *the event was* *moderately successful:* **somewhat**, quite, rather, fairly, reasonably, comparatively, relatively, to some extent; tolerably, passably, adequately; informal pretty.

moderation noun 1 *he urged them to show moderation:* **self-restraint**, restraint, self-control, self-discipline; moderateness, temperance, leniency, fairness. 2 *a moderation of their confrontational style:* **relaxation**, easing (off), reduction, abatement, weakening, slackening, tempering, softening, diminution, diminishing, lessening; decline, modulation, modification, mitigation, allaying; informal let-up.
■ **in moderation** in moderate quantities/amounts, within (sensible) limits; moderately.

modern adjective 1 *modern times:* **present-day**, contemporary, present, current, twenty-first-century, latter-day, recent. 2 *her clothes are very modern:* **fashionable**, in fashion, in style, in vogue, up to date, all the rage, trendsetting, stylish, voguish, modish, chic, à la mode; the latest, new, newest, newfangled, modernistic, advanced; informal trendy, cool, in, with it, now, hip, happening; N. Amer. informal tony.
-OPPOSITES past, old-fashioned.

modernity noun **contemporaneity**, contemporaneousness, modernness, modernism; fashionableness, vogue; informal trendiness.

modernize verb 1 *they are modernizing their manufacturing facilities:* **update**, bring up to date, streamline, rationalize, overhaul; renovate, remodel, refashion, revamp. 2 *we must modernize to survive:* **get up to date**, move with the times, innovate; informal get in the swim, get with it.

modest adjective 1 *she was modest about her poetry:* **self-effacing**, self-deprecating, humble, unpretentious, unassuming, unostentatious; shy, bashful, self-conscious, diffident, reserved, reticent, coy. 2 *a period of modest success:* **moderate**, fair, limited, tolerable, passable, adequate, satisfactory, acceptable, unexceptional. 3 *a modest house:* **small**, ordinary, simple, plain, humble, inexpensive, unostentatious, unpretentious. 4 *her modest dress:* **decorous**, decent, seemly, demure, proper.
-OPPOSITES conceited, great, grand.

modesty noun 1 *Hannah's modesty cloaks many talents:* **self-effacement**, humility, unpretentiousness; shyness, bashfulness, self-consciousness, reserve, reticence, timidity. 2 *the modesty of his aspirations:* **limited scope**, moderation. 3 *the modesty of his home:* **unpretentiousness**, simplicity, plainness. 4 *her maidenly modesty:* **decorum**, decorousness, decency, seemliness, demureness.

modicum noun *people with only a modicum of scientific knowledge:* **small amount**, particle, speck, fragment, scrap, crumb, grain, morsel, shred, dash, drop, pinch, jot, iota, whit, atom, smattering, scintilla, hint, suggestion; informal smidgen, tad.

modification noun **1** *the design is undergoing modification:* **alteration**, adjustment, change, adaptation, refinement, revision. **2** *some minor modifications were made:* **revision**, refinement, improvement, amendment, adaptation, adjustment, change, alteration. **3** *the modification of his views:* **softening**, moderation, tempering, qualification.

modify verb **1** *their economic policy has been modified:* **alter**, change, adjust, adapt, amend, revise, reshape, refashion, restyle, revamp, rework, remodel, refine; informal tweak. **2** *he modified his more extreme views:* **moderate**, revise, temper, soften, tone down, qualify.

modish adjective *a modish new restaurant:* **fashionable**, stylish, chic, modern, contemporary, all the rage, in vogue, voguish, up to the minute, à la mode; informal trendy, cool, with it, in, now, hip, happening; N. Amer. informal kicky, tony.

modulate verb **1** *the cells modulate the body's response:* **regulate**, adjust, set, modify, moderate. **2** *she modulated her voice:* **adjust**, change the tone of.

modus operandi noun *every killer has his own special modus operandi:* **method (of working)**, way, MO, manner, technique, style, procedure, approach, methodology, strategy, plan, formula.

mogul noun *Hollywood movie moguls:* **magnate**, tycoon, VIP, notable, personage, baron, captain, king, lord, grandee, nabob; informal bigwig, big shot, big noise, top dog; N. Amer. informal top banana, big enchilada.

moist adjective **1** *the air was moist:* **damp**, dampish, steamy, humid, muggy, clammy, dank, wet, wettish, soggy, sweaty, sticky. **2** *a moist fruitcake:* **succulent**, juicy, soft. **3** *her eyes grew moist:* **tearful**, watery, misty.
– OPPOSITES dry.

moisten verb *the compost should be moistened before use:* **dampen**, wet, damp, water, humidify.

moisture noun *dehumidifiers will remove moisture from the air:* **wetness**, wet, water, liquid, condensation, steam, vapour, dampness, damp, humidity, clamminess, mugginess, dankness, wateriness.

moisturizer noun **lotion**, cream, balm, emollient, salve, unguent, lubricant.

mole¹ noun *the mole on his left cheek:* **mark**, freckle, blotch, spot, blemish.

mole² noun *a well-placed mole:* **spy**, (secret) agent, undercover agent, operative, plant, infiltrator; N. Amer. informal spook.

mole³ noun *the mole protecting the harbour:* **breakwater**, groyne, dyke, pier, sea wall, causeway.

molest verb **1** *the crowd were molesting the police:* **harass**, harry, pester, beset, persecute, torment; N. Amer. informal roust. **2** *he molested a ten-year-old boy:* **(sexually) abuse**, (sexually) assault, interfere with, rape, violate; informal grope, paw.

mollify verb **1** *they mollified the protesters:* **appease**, placate, pacify, conciliate, soothe, calm (down). **2** *mollifying the fears of the public:* **allay**, assuage, alleviate, mitigate, ease, reduce, moderate, temper, tone down.
– OPPOSITES enrage.

mollycoddle verb *his parents mollycoddle him:* **pamper**, cosset, coddle, spoil, indulge, overindulge, pet, baby, nanny, nursemaid, wait on hand and foot, wrap in cotton wool.

molten adjective *molten metal:* **liquefied**, liquid, fluid, melted, flowing.

moment noun **1** *he thought for a moment:* **little while**, short time, bit, minute, instant, (split) second; informal sec, jiffy; Brit. informal tick, mo, two ticks. **2** *the moment they met:* **point (in time)**, time, hour.
■ **in a moment** very soon, in a minute, in a second, in a trice, shortly, any minute (now), in the twinkling of an eye, in (less than) no time, in no time at all; N. Amer. momentarily; informal in a jiffy, in two shakes (of a lamb's tail), before you can say Jack Robinson, in the blink of an eye; Brit. informal in a tick, in two ticks, in a mo; N. Amer. informal in a snap.

momentarily adverb **1** *he paused momentarily:* **briefly**, fleetingly, for a moment, for a second, for an instant. **2** (N. Amer.) *my husband will be here momentarily.* See IN A MOMENT at MOMENT.

momentary adjective *a momentary lapse of concentration:* **brief**, short, short-lived, fleeting, passing, transient, ephemeral.
– OPPOSITES lengthy.

momentous adjective *a momentous decision:* **important**, significant, historic, portentous, critical, crucial, life-and-death, decisive, pivotal, consequential, of consequence, far-reaching, earth-shattering.
– OPPOSITES insignificant.

momentum noun *the vehicle gained momentum as the road dipped:* **impetus**, energy, force, power, strength, thrust, speed, velocity.

monarch noun **sovereign**, ruler, Crown, crowned head, potentate; king, queen, emperor, empress, prince, princess.

monarchy noun **1** *the country is a constitutional monarchy:* **kingdom**, sovereign state, principality, empire. **2** *few questioned the justification for hereditary monarchy:* **kingship**, sovereignty, autocracy, monocracy, absolutism.

monastery noun **religious community**; friary, abbey, priory, cloister.

monastic adjective **1** *a monastic community:* **cloistered**, cloistral, claustral. **2** *a monastic existence:* **austere**, ascetic, simple, solitary, monkish, celibate, quiet, cloistered,

m

sequestered, secluded, reclusive, hermit-like, hermitic.

monetary adjective *documents with little or no monetary value:* **financial**, fiscal, pecuniary, money, cash, economic, budgetary.

money noun **1** *I haven't got enough money:* **(hard) cash**, ready money; the means, the wherewithal, funds, capital, finances, (filthy) lucre; banknotes, notes, coins, change, specie, silver, copper, currency; Brit. sterling; N. Amer. bills; N. Amer. & Austral. roll; informal dough, bread, loot, readies, shekels, moolah, the necessary; Brit. informal dosh, brass, lolly, spondulicks; N. Amer. informal dinero, bucks, mazuma; US informal greenbacks, simoleons, jack, rocks; Austral./NZ informal Oscar. **2** *she married him for his money:* **wealth**, riches, fortune, affluence, (liquid) assets, resources, means. **3** *the money here is better:* **pay**, salary, wages, remuneration.
■ **for my money** in my opinion, to my mind, in my view, as I see it, personally, in my estimation, in my judgement, if you ask me.

moneyed adjective *the Industrial Revolution created a new moneyed class:* **rich**, wealthy, affluent, well-to-do, well off, prosperous, in clover, opulent, of means, of substance; informal in the money, rolling in it, loaded, stinking/filthy rich, well heeled, made of money.
– OPPOSITES poor.

moneymaking adjective *a moneymaking scheme:* **profitable**, profit-making, remunerative, lucrative, successful, financially rewarding.
– OPPOSITES loss-making.

mongrel noun *a rough-haired mongrel:* **cross-breed**, cross, mixed breed, half-breed; tyke, cur, mutt; NZ kuri; Austral. informal mong, bitzer. adjective *a mongrel bitch:* **cross-bred**, of mixed breed, half-breed.
– OPPOSITES pedigree.

monitor noun **1** *monitors covered all entrances:* **detector**, scanner, recorder; security camera, CCTV. **2** *UN monitors:* **observer**, watchdog, overseer, supervisor. **3** *a computer monitor:* **screen**, visual display unit, VDU. verb *his movements were closely monitored:* **observe**, watch, track, keep an eye on, keep under observation, keep watch on, keep under surveillance, record, note, oversee; informal keep tabs on, keep a beady eye on.

monk noun brother, coenobite, contemplative, mendicant; friar; abbot, prior; novice, oblate, postulant; Benedictine, Black Monk, Cluniac, Carthusian, Cistercian, Dominican, White Monk.

monkey noun **1** simian, primate, ape. **2** *you little monkey!* See RASCAL.
■ **make a monkey (out) of** make someone look foolish, make a fool of, make a laughing stock of, ridicule, make fun of, poke fun at.
■ **monkey about/around** *we were*

just monkeying around upstairs: fool about/around, play about/around, clown about/around, footle about/around; informal mess about/around, horse about/around, lark (about/around); Brit. informal muck about/around.
■ **monkey with** *don't monkey with that lock:* tamper with, fiddle with, interfere with, meddle with, tinker with, play with; informal mess with; Brit. informal muck about/around with.

monocle noun **eyeglass**, glass.

monolith noun **standing stone**, menhir, sarsen (stone), megalith.

monolithic adjective **1** *a monolithic building:* **massive**, huge, vast, colossal, gigantic, immense, giant, enormous; featureless, characterless. **2** *the old monolithic Communist party:* **inflexible**, rigid, unbending, unchanging, fossilized.

monologue noun *the skilfully varied tone and pace of her 40-minute monologue:* **soliloquy**, speech, address, lecture, sermon.

monomania noun *his profound interest in the subject verges on monomania:* **obsession**, fixation, consuming passion, mania, compulsion.

monopolize verb **1** *the company has monopolized the market:* **corner**, control, take over, gain control/dominance over. **2** *he monopolized the conversation:* **dominate**, take over; informal hog. **3** *she monopolized the guest of honour:* **take up all the attention of**, keep to oneself; informal tie up.

monotonous adjective **1** *a monotonous job:* **tedious**, boring, dull, uninteresting, unexciting, wearisome, tiresome, repetitive, repetitious, unvarying, unchanging, unvaried, humdrum, routine, mechanical, mind-numbing, soul-destroying; colourless, featureless, dreary; informal deadly; Brit. informal samey; N. Amer. informal dullsville. **2** *a monotonous voice:* **toneless**, flat, uninflected, soporific.
– OPPOSITES interesting.

monotony noun **1** *the monotony of everyday life:* **tedium**, tediousness, lack of variety, dullness, boredom, repetitiveness, repetitiousness, uniformity of tone, wearisomeness, tiresomeness; lack of excitement, uneventfulness, dreariness, colourlessness, featurelessness; informal deadliness. **2** *the monotony of her voice:* **tonelessness**, flatness.

monster noun **1** *legendary sea monsters:* **fabulous creature**, mythical creature. **2** *her husband is a monster:* **brute**, fiend, beast, devil, demon, barbarian, savage, animal; informal swine, pig. **3** *the boy's a little monster:* **rascal**, imp, monkey, wretch, devil; informal horror, scamp, scallywag, tyke; Brit. informal perisher, pickle; N. Amer. informal varmint, hellion. **4** *he's a monster of a man:* **giant**, mammoth, colossus, leviathan, titan; informal jumbo.

monstrosity noun **1** *a concrete monstrosity:* **eyesore**, blot on the landscape, carbuncle, excrescence. **2** *a biological monstrosity:* **mutant**, mutation, freak (of nature), monster, abortion.

monstrous adjective **1** *a monstrous creature emerged from the blackness:* **grotesque**, hideous, ugly, ghastly, gruesome, horrible, horrific, horrifying, grisly, disgusting, repulsive, repellent, dreadful, frightening, terrifying, malformed, misshapen. **2** *a monstrous tidal wave.* See **HUGE**. **3** *such monstrous acts of violence had never been seen in the country:* **appalling**, heinous, egregious, evil, wicked, abominable, terrible, horrible, dreadful, vile, outrageous, shocking, disgraceful; unspeakable, despicable, vicious, savage, barbaric, barbarous, inhuman; Brit. informal beastly.
– OPPOSITES lovely, small.

monument noun **1** *a stone monument:* **memorial**, statue, pillar, column, obelisk, cross; cenotaph, tomb, mausoleum, shrine. **2** *a monument was placed over the grave:* **gravestone**, headstone, tombstone. **3** *the project is a monument to a past era of aviation:* **testament**, record, reminder, remembrance, memorial, commemoration.

monumental adjective **1** *they face a monumental task:* **huge**, great, enormous, gigantic, massive, colossal, mammoth, immense, tremendous, mighty, stupendous. **2** *a monumental error of judgement:* **terrible**, dreadful, awful, colossal, staggering, huge, enormous, unforgivable, egregious. **3** *one of Beethoven's most monumental piano works:* **impressive**, striking, outstanding, remarkable, magnificent, majestic, stupendous, ambitious, large-scale, grand, awe-inspiring, important, significant, distinguished, memorable, immortal.

mood noun **1** *she's in a good mood:* **frame/state of mind**, humour, temper; disposition, spirit, tenor. **2** *he's obviously in a mood:* **bad mood**, (bad) temper, sulk, pet, fit of pique; low spirits, the doldrums, the blues; informal the dumps, grump; Brit. informal paddy. **3** *the mood of the film was one of hope:* **atmosphere**, feeling, spirit, ambience, aura, character, tenor, flavour, feel, tone.
■ **in the mood** in the right frame of mind, feeling like, wanting to, inclined to, disposed to, minded to, eager to, willing to.

moody adjective *teenagers tend to get a bad name for being moody and irresponsible:* **temperamental**, emotional, volatile, capricious, changeable, mercurial; sullen, sulky, morose, glum, depressed, dejected, despondent, doleful, dour, sour, saturnine; informal blue, down in the dumps/mouth.
– OPPOSITES cheerful.

moon noun satellite.
verb **1** *stop mooning about:* **waste time**, loaf, idle, mope; Brit. informal mooch; N. Amer. informal lollygag. **2** *he's mooning over her photograph:*

mope, pine, brood, daydream, fantasize, be in a reverie.
■ **once in a blue moon** (informal) hardly ever, scarcely ever, rarely, very seldom.
■ **over the moon** (informal). See **ECSTATIC**.

moonshine noun. See **RUBBISH** noun sense 2.

moor¹ verb *a boat was moored to the quay:* **tie up**, secure, make fast, fix firmly, anchor, berth, dock.

moor² noun *a walk on the moor helped him gather his thoughts:* **upland**, moorland; grouse moor; Brit. heath, fell, wold.

moot adjective *a moot point:* **debatable**, open to discussion/question, arguable, questionable, at issue, open to doubt, disputable, controversial, contentious, disputed, unresolved, unsettled, up in the air.
verb *the idea was first mooted in the 1930s:* **raise**, bring up, broach, mention, put forward, introduce, advance, propose, suggest.

mop noun *her tousled mop of hair:* **shock**, mane, tangle, mass.
verb *a man was mopping the floor:* **wash**, clean, wipe.
■ **mop something up 1** *I mopped up the spilt coffee:* wipe up, clean up, sponge up. **2** *troops mopped up the last pockets of resistance:* finish off, deal with, dispose of, take care of, clear up, eliminate.

mope verb **1** *it's no use moping:* **brood**, sulk, be miserable, be despondent, pine, eat one's heart out, fret, grieve; informal be down in the dumps/mouth. **2** *she was moping about the house:* **languish**, moon, idle, loaf; Brit. informal mooch; N. Amer. informal lollygag.

moral adjective **1** *there are moral as well as political issues involved here:* **ethical**, social, having to do with right and wrong. **2** *a very moral man:* **virtuous**, good, righteous, upright, upstanding, high-minded, principled, honourable, honest, just, noble, incorruptible, scrupulous, respectable, decent, clean-living, law-abiding. **3** *we can at least give him our moral support:* **psychological**, emotional, mental.
– OPPOSITES dishonourable.
noun **1** *the moral of the story:* **lesson**, message, meaning, significance, signification, import, point, teaching. **2** *he has no morals:* **moral code**, code of ethics, moral standards/values, principles, standards, (sense of) morality, scruples.

morale noun *morale in the team was higher than it had been for a long time:* **confidence**, self-confidence, self-esteem, spirit(s), team spirit.

moral fibre noun *an ineffectual man with no moral fibre:* **strength of character**, fibre, fortitude, resolve, backbone, spine, mettle, firmness of purpose.

morality noun **1** *the morality of nuclear weapons:* **ethics**, rights and wrongs, ethicality. **2** *a sharp decline*

m

in morality: **virtue**, goodness, good behaviour, righteousness, rectitude, uprightness; morals, principles, honesty, integrity, propriety, honour, justice, decency. **3** *orthodox Christian morality:* **moral standards**, morals, ethics, standards/principles of behaviour, mores, standards.

moralize verb *doctors should not moralize but simply deal with the patient's medical condition:* **pontificate**, sermonize, lecture, preach; informal preachify.

morass noun **1** *the muddy morass that the flood had made of their garden:* **quagmire**, swamp, bog, marsh, mire, marshland, slough; N. Amer. moor. **2** *a morass of paperwork:* **confusion**, chaos, muddle, tangle, entanglement, imbroglio, jumble, clutter.

moratorium noun *a temporary moratorium on all nuclear testing:* **embargo**, ban, prohibition, suspension, postponement, stay, stoppage, halt, freeze, standstill, respite.

morbid adjective **1** *a morbid fascination with contemporary warfare:* **ghoulish**, macabre, unhealthy, gruesome, unwholesome; informal sick. **2** *I felt decidedly morbid:* **gloomy**, glum, melancholy, morose, dismal, sombre, doleful, despondent, dejected, sad, depressed, downcast, down, disconsolate, miserable, unhappy, downhearted, dispirited, low; informal blue, down in the dumps/mouth.
– OPPOSITES wholesome, cheerful.

mordant adjective *a mordant sense of humour:* **caustic**, trenchant, biting, cutting, acerbic, sardonic, sarcastic, scathing, acid, sharp, keen; critical, bitter, virulent, vitriolic.

more determiner *I could do with some more clothes:* **additional**, further, added, extra, increased, new, other, supplementary.
– OPPOSITES less, fewer.
adverb **1** *he was able to concentrate more on his writing:* **to a greater extent**, further, for longer, better. **2** *he was rich, and more, he was handsome:* **moreover**, furthermore, besides, what's more, in addition, also, as well, too, to boot, on top of that, into the bargain.
pronoun *we're going to need more:* **extra**, an additional amount/number, an addition, an increase.
– OPPOSITES less, fewer.
■ **more or less** approximately, roughly, nearly, almost, close to, about, of the order of, in the region of.

moreover adverb *moreover, statistics show that competition for places is growing:* **besides**, furthermore, what's more, in addition, also, as well, too, to boot, additionally, on top of that, into the bargain, more.

mores plural noun *factors that shaped the social mores of the community:* **customs**, conventions, ways, way of life, traditions, practices, habits.

morgue noun **mortuary**, funeral parlour; Brit. chapel of rest.

moribund adjective *the moribund shipbuilding industry:* **declining**, in decline, waning, dying, stagnating, stagnant, crumbling, on its last legs.
– OPPOSITES thriving.

morning noun **1** *I've got a meeting this morning:* **before noon**, before lunch(time), a.m.; Nautical & N. Amer. forenoon. **2** *morning is on its way:* **dawn**, daybreak, sunrise, first light, cockcrow; N. Amer. sunup.

moron noun. See FOOL noun sense 1.

moronic adjective. See STUPID sense 1.

morose adjective *Louis sat alone at a table, looking morose:* **sullen**, sulky, gloomy, bad-tempered, ill-tempered, dour, surly, sour, glum, moody, ill-humoured, melancholy, melancholic, doleful, miserable, depressed, dejected, despondent, downcast, Eeyorish, unhappy, in low spirits, low, down, fed up, grumpy, irritable, churlish, cantankerous, crotchety, cross, crabby, grouchy, testy, snappish, peevish, crusty; informal blue, down in the dumps/mouth.
– OPPOSITES cheerful.

morsel noun *Juliet pushed a morsel of toast into her mouth:* **mouthful**, bite, nibble, bit, soupçon, taste, spoonful, forkful, sliver, drop, dollop, spot, gobbet; titbit, bonne bouche; informal smidgen.

mortal adjective **1** *the mortal remains of the victims | all men are mortal:* **perishable**, physical, bodily, corporeal, fleshly, earthly; human, impermanent, transient, ephemeral. **2** *a mortal blow:* **deadly**, fatal, lethal, death-dealing, murderous, terminal. **3** *mortal enemies:* **irreconcilable**, deadly, sworn, bitter, out-and-out, implacable. **4** *a mortal sin:* **unpardonable**, unforgivable. **5** *living in mortal fear:* **extreme**, (very) great, terrible, awful, dreadful, intense, severe, grave, dire, unbearable.
– OPPOSITES venial.
noun *we are mere mortals:* **human (being)**, person, man/woman; earthling.

mortality noun **1** *a sense of his own mortality:* **impermanence**, transience, ephemerality, perishability; humanity; corporeality. **2** *the causes of mortality:* **death**, loss of life, dying.

mortification noun **1** *scarlet with mortification, Leonora looked away:* **embarrassment**, humiliation, chagrin, discomfiture, discomposure, shame. **2** *the mortification of the flesh:* **subduing**, suppression, subjugation, control, controlling; disciplining, chastening, punishment.

mortify verb **1** *I'd be mortified if my friends found out:* **embarrass**, humiliate, chagrin, discomfit, shame, abash, horrify, appal. **2** *he was mortified at being excluded:* **hurt**, wound, affront, offend, put out, pique, irk, annoy, vex; informal rile. **3** *mortifying the flesh:* **subdue**, suppress, subjugate, control; discipline, chasten, punish.

mortuary noun **morgue**, funeral parlour; Brit. chapel of rest.

most pronoun *most of the guests brought flowers:* **nearly all**, almost all, the greatest part/number, the majority, the bulk, the preponderance.
– OPPOSITES little, few.

mostly adverb **1** *the other passengers were mostly businessmen:* **mainly**, for the most part, on the whole, in the main, largely, by and large, to a large extent, chiefly, predominantly, principally, primarily. **2** *I mostly wear jeans:* **usually**, generally, in general, as a rule, ordinarily, normally, customarily, typically, most of the time, almost always.

moth-eaten adjective *a moth-eaten tweed jacket:* **threadbare**, worn (out), well worn, old, shabby, scruffy, tattered, ragged; informal tatty, the worse for wear; N. Amer. informal raggedy.

mother noun **1** *I will ask my mother:* **female parent**, materfamilias, matriarch; informal ma, mam, mammy, old lady, old woman; Brit. informal mum, mummy; N. Amer. informal mom, mommy. **2** *the foal's mother:* **dam**. **3** *the wish was mother of the deed:* **source**, origin, genesis, fountainhead, inspiration, stimulus.
– OPPOSITES child, father.
verb **1** *she mothered her husband:* **look after**, care for, take care of, nurse, protect, tend, raise, rear; pamper, coddle, cosset, fuss over. **2** *she mothered an illegitimate daughter:* **give birth to**, have, bear, produce; N. Amer. birth.
– OPPOSITES neglect.

motherly adjective *motherly love:* **maternal**, maternalistic, protective, caring, loving, devoted, affectionate, fond, warm, tender, gentle, kind, kindly, understanding, compassionate.

motif noun **1** *a colourful tulip motif:* **design**, pattern, decoration, figure, shape, device, emblem, ornament. **2** *a recurring motif in Pinter's work:* **theme**, idea, concept, subject, topic, leitmotif, element.

motion noun **1** *the rocking motion of the boat* | *a planet's motion around the sun:* **movement**, moving, locomotion, rise and fall, shifting; progress, passage, passing, transit, course, travel, travelling. **2** *a motion of the hand:* **gesture**, movement, signal, sign, indication; wave, nod, gesticulation. **3** *the motion failed to obtain a majority:* **proposal**, proposition, recommendation, suggestion.
verb *he motioned her to sit down:* **gesture**, signal, direct, indicate; wave, beckon, nod, gesticulate.
■ **in motion** moving, on the move, going, travelling, running, functioning, operational.
■ **set in motion** start, commence, begin, activate, initiate, launch, get under way, get

going, get off the ground; trigger off, set off, spark off, generate, cause.

motionless adjective *Rob and Graham remained motionless, not daring to look at each other:* **unmoving**, still, stationary, stock-still, immobile, static, not moving a muscle, rooted to the spot, transfixed, paralysed, frozen.
– OPPOSITES moving.

motivate verb **1** *she was primarily motivated by the desire for profit:* **prompt**, drive, move, inspire, stimulate, influence, activate, impel, push, propel, spur (on). **2** *it's the teacher's job to motivate the child:* **inspire**, stimulate, encourage, spur (on), excite, inspirit, incentivize, fire with enthusiasm.

motivation noun **1** *his motivation was financial:* **motive**, motivating force, incentive, stimulus, stimulation, inspiration, inducement, incitement, spur, reason. **2** *staff motivation:* **enthusiasm**, drive, ambition, initiative, determination, enterprise; informal get-up-and-go.

motive noun **1** *the motive for the attack:* **reason**, motivation, motivating force, rationale, grounds, cause, basis, object, purpose, intention; incentive, inducement, incitement, lure, inspiration, stimulus, stimulation, spur. **2** *religious motives in art:* **motif**, theme, idea, concept, subject, topic, leitmotif.
adjective *motive power:* **kinetic**, driving, impelling, propelling, propulsive, motor.

motley adjective *a motley collection of old clothes:* **miscellaneous**, disparate, diverse, assorted, varied, diversified, heterogeneous.
– OPPOSITES homogeneous.

mottled adjective *her mottled skin:* **blotchy**, blotched, spotted, spotty, speckled, streaked, streaky, marbled, flecked, freckled, dappled, stippled, piebald, skewbald, brindled, brindle; N. Amer. pinto; informal splotchy.

motto noun *their school motto:* **maxim**, saying, proverb, aphorism, adage, saw, axiom, apophthegm, formula, expression, phrase, dictum, precept; slogan, catchphrase; truism, cliché, platitude.

mould[1] noun **1** *the molten metal is poured into a mould:* **cast**, die, form, matrix, shape, template, pattern, frame. **2** *an actress in the traditional Hollywood mould:* **pattern**, form, shape, format, model, kind, type, style; archetype, prototype. **3** *he is a figure of heroic mould:* **character**, nature, temperament, disposition; calibre, kind, sort, variety, stamp, type.
verb **1** *a figure moulded from clay:* **shape**, form, fashion, model, work, construct, make, create, manufacture, sculpt, sculpture; forge, cast. **2** *moulding US policy:* **determine**, direct, control, guide, lead, influence, shape, form, fashion, make.

mould[2] noun *walls stained with mould:*

m

mildew, fungus, must, mouldiness, mustiness.

mould³ noun *leaf mould:* **earth**, soil, dirt, loam, humus.

moulder verb *his body still lay mouldering in some forgotten field:* **decay**, decompose, rot (away), go mouldy, go off, go bad, spoil, putrefy.

mouldy adjective *a lump of mouldy cheese:* **mildewed**, mildewy, musty, mouldering, fusty; decaying, decayed, rotting, rotten, bad, spoiled, spoilt, decomposing.

mound noun **1** *a mound of leaves:* **heap**, pile, stack, mountain; mass, accumulation, assemblage. **2** *high on the mound:* **hillock**, hill, knoll, rise, hummock, hump, embankment, bank, ridge, elevation, acclivity; Scottish brae. **3** *a burial mound:* **barrow**, tumulus; motte.
verb *mound up the rice on a serving plate:* **pile (up)**, heap (up).

mount verb **1** *he mounted the stairs:* **go up**, ascend, climb (up), scale. **2** *the committee mounted the platform:* **climb on to**, jump on to, clamber on to, get on to. **3** *they mounted their horses:* **get astride**, bestride, get on to, hop on to. **4** *the museum is mounting an exhibition:* **(put on) display**, exhibit, present, install; organize, put on, stage. **5** *the company mounted a takeover bid:* **organize**, stage, prepare, arrange, set up; launch, set in motion, initiate. **6** *their losses mounted rapidly:* **increase**, grow, rise, escalate, soar, spiral, shoot up, rocket, climb, accumulate, build up, multiply. **7** *cameras were mounted above the door:* **install**, place, fix, set, put up, put in position.
– OPPOSITES descend.
noun *a decorated photograph mount:* **setting**, backing, support, mounting, frame, stand.

mountain noun **1** *a range of mountains:* **peak**, height, mount, prominence, summit, pinnacle, alp; (**mountains**) range, massif, sierra; Scottish ben, Munro. **2** *a mountain of work:* **a great deal**, a lot; profusion, abundance, quantity, backlog; informal heap, pile, stack, slew, lots, loads, heaps, piles, tons, masses; N. Amer. informal gobs. **3** *a butter mountain:* **surplus**, surfeit, glut, oversupply.
■ **move mountains 1** *faith can move mountains:* perform miracles, work/do wonders. **2** *his fans move mountains to attend his performances:* make every effort, pull out all the stops, do one's utmost/best; informal bend/lean over backwards.

mountainous adjective **1** *a mountainous region:* **hilly**, craggy, rocky, alpine; upland, highland. **2** *mountainous waves:* **huge**, enormous, gigantic, massive, giant, colossal, immense, tremendous, mighty; informal whopping, thumping, humongous; Brit. informal whacking, ginormous.
– OPPOSITES flat, tiny.

mourn verb **1** *Isobel mourned her husband:* **grieve for**, sorrow over, lament for, weep for, wail/keen over. **2** *he mourned the loss*

of the beautiful buildings: **deplore**, bewail, bemoan, rue, regret.

mournful adjective *a mournful expression:* **sad**, sorrowful, doleful, melancholy, melancholic, woeful, grief-stricken, miserable, unhappy, heartbroken, broken-hearted, gloomy, dismal, desolate, dejected, despondent, depressed, downcast, disconsolate, woebegone, forlorn, rueful, lugubrious, joyless, cheerless.
– OPPOSITES cheerful.

mourning noun **1** *a period of mourning:* **grief**, grieving, sorrowing, lamentation, lament, keening, wailing, weeping. **2** *she was dressed in mourning:* **black (clothes)**, (widow's) weeds.

moustache noun **whiskers**, mustachios, handlebar moustache, walrus moustache, burnsides; informal tash; N. Amer. informal stash.

mousy adjective **1** *mousy hair:* **lightish brown**, brownish, brownish-grey, dun-coloured; dull, lacklustre. **2** *a small, mousy woman:* **timid**, quiet, fearful, timorous, shy, self-effacing, diffident, unassertive, unforthcoming, withdrawn, introverted, introvert.

mouth noun **1** *open your mouth:* **lips**, jaws; maw, muzzle; informal trap, chops, kisser; Brit. informal gob, cakehole; N. Amer. informal puss, bazoo. **2** *the mouth of the cave:* **entrance**, opening, entry, way in, access, ingress. **3** *the mouth of the bottle:* **opening**, rim, lip. **4** *the mouth of the river:* **outfall**, outlet, debouchment; estuary, firth. **5** (informal) *he's all mouth:* **boasting**, bragging, idle talk, bombast, braggadocio; informal hot air.
verb *he mouthed platitudes:* **utter**, speak, say; pronounce, enunciate, articulate, voice, express; say insincerely, say for form's sake.
■ **down in the mouth** (informal). See UNHAPPY sense 1.
■ **keep one's mouth shut** (informal) say nothing, keep quiet, not breathe a word, not tell a soul; informal keep mum, not let the cat out of the bag.
■ **mouth off** *he was mouthing off about his teachers:* (informal) rant, spout, declaim, sound off.

mouthful noun **1** *a mouthful of pizza:* **bite**, nibble, taste, bit, piece; spoonful, forkful. **2** *a mouthful of beer:* **draught**, sip, swallow, drop, gulp, slug; informal swig. **3** *'sesquipedalian' is a bit of a mouthful:* **tongue-twister**, long word, difficult word.

mouthpiece noun *he has no power—he's just a mouthpiece for the government:* **spokesperson**, spokesman, spokeswoman, agent, representative, propagandist, voice.

movable adjective **1** *put away all movable objects:* **portable**, transportable, transferable; mobile. **2** *movable feasts:* **variable**, changeable, alterable.
– OPPOSITES fixed.

move verb **1** *she moved to the door | don't move!* **go**, walk, proceed, progress,

advance; budge, stir, shift, change position.
2 *he moved the chair closer to the fire:*
carry, transport, transfer, shift. **3** *things
were moving too fast:* **(make) progress**,
make headway, advance, develop. **4** *he
urged the council to move quickly:* **take
action**, act, take steps, do something, take
measures; informal get moving. **5** *she's moved
to Cambridge:* **relocate**, move house, move
away/out, change address/house, leave,
go away, decamp; Brit. informal up sticks; N.
Amer. informal pull up stakes. **6** *I was deeply
moved by the story:* **affect**, touch, impress,
shake, upset, disturb, make an impression
on. **7** *she was moved to find out more about
it:* **inspire**, prompt, stimulate, motivate,
provoke, influence, rouse, induce, incite.
8 *they are not prepared to move on this issue:*
change, budge, shift one's ground, change
one's tune, change one's mind, have second
thoughts; do a U-turn, do an about-face;
Brit. do an about-turn. **9** *she moves in the
art worlds:* **circulate**, mix, socialize, keep
company, associate; informal hang out/around;
Brit. informal hang about. **10** *I move that we
adjourn:* **propose**, submit, suggest, advocate,
recommend, urge.
▸ noun **1** *his eyes followed her every move:*
movement, motion, action; gesture,
gesticulation. **2** *his recent move to London:*
relocation, change of house/address,
transfer, posting. **3** *the latest move in the war
against drugs:* **initiative**, step, action, act,
measure, manoeuvre, tactic, stratagem. **4** *it's
your move:* **turn**, go; opportunity, chance.
■ **make a move 1** *waiting for the other side
to make a move:* do something, take action,
act, take the initiative; informal get moving.
2 (Brit.) *I'd better be making a move:* leave,
take one's leave, be on one's way, get going,
depart, be off; informal push off, shove off,
split.
■ **on the move 1** *she's always on the move:*
travelling, in transit, moving, journeying, on
the road; informal on the go. **2** *the economy is
on the move:* progressing, making progress,
advancing, developing.

movement noun **1** *there was almost no
movement:* **motion**, action, activity. **2** *Rachel
made a sudden movement:* **move**, motion,
gesture, gesticulation, sign, signal. **3** *the
movement of supplies:* **transportation**, shift,
shifting, conveyance, moving, transfer.
4 *the labour movement:* **political group**,
party, faction, wing, lobby, camp. **5** *a
movement to declare war on poverty:*
campaign, crusade, drive, push. **6** *there
have been movements in the financial
markets:* **development**, change, fluctuation,
variation. **7** *the movement towards equality:*
trend, tendency, drift, swing. **8** *some
movement will be made by the end of the
month:* **progress**, progression, advance.
9 *a symphony in three movements:* **part**,
section, division. **10** *the clock's movement:*
mechanism, machinery, works, workings;
informal innards, guts.

movie noun **1** *a horror movie:* **film**, (motion)
picture, feature (film); Informal flick. **2** *let's
go to the movies:* **the cinema**, the pictures,
the silver screen; informal the flicks, the big
screen.

moving adjective **1** *moving parts | a moving
train:* **in motion**, operating, operational,
working, going, on the move, active;
movable, mobile. **2** *a moving book:* **affecting**,
touching, poignant, heart-warming, heart-
rending, emotional, disturbing; inspiring,
inspirational, stimulating, stirring. **3** *the
party's moving force:* **driving**, motivating,
dynamic, stimulating, inspirational.
– OPPOSITES fixed, stationary.

mow verb *she had mown the grass:* **cut
(down)**, trim; crop, clip.
■ **mow someone/something down** kill,
gun down, shoot down, cut down, cut
to pieces, butcher, slaughter, massacre,
annihilate, wipe out; informal blow away.

much determiner *did you get much help?* **a
lot of**, a great/good deal of, a great/large
amount of, plenty of, ample, copious,
abundant, plentiful, considerable; informal
lots of, loads of, heaps of, masses of, tons of.
– OPPOSITES little.
▸ adverb **1** *it didn't hurt much:* **greatly**, to
a great extent/degree, a great deal, a lot,
considerably, appreciably. **2** *does he come
here much?* **often**, frequently, many times,
repeatedly, regularly, habitually, routinely,
usually, normally, commonly; informal a lot.
▸ pronoun *he did so much for our team:* **a lot**,
a great/good deal, plenty; informal lots, loads,
heaps, masses.
■ **much of a muchness** (informal) very similar,
much the same, very alike, practically
identical.

muck noun **1** *I'll just clean off the muck:*
dirt, grime, filth, mud, slime, mess; informal
crud, gunk, grunge, gloop; Brit. informal gunge,
grot; N. Amer. informal guck, glop. **2** *spreading
muck on the fields:* **dung**, manure, ordure,
excrement, excreta, droppings, faeces,
sewage; N. Amer. informal cow chips, horse
apples.
■ **muck something up** (informal) make a mess
of, mess up, bungle, spoil, ruin, wreck; informal
botch, make a hash of, muff, fluff, foul up,
louse up; Brit. informal make a pig's ear of, make
a Horlicks of; N. Amer. informal goof up.
■ **muck about/around** (Brit. informal) **1** *he
was mucking about with his mates:* fool
about/around, play about/around, clown
about/around, footle about/around; informal
mess about/around, horse about/around,
lark (about/around). **2** *someone's been
mucking about with the video:* interfere,
fiddle (about/around), play about/around,
tamper, meddle, tinker; informal mess
(about/around).

mucky adjective *a pair of mucky boots:* **dirty**,
filthy, grimy, muddy, grubby, messy, soiled,
stained, smeared, slimy, sticky, bespattered;
informal cruddy, grungy, gloopy; Brit. informal

m

gungy, grotty; Austral./NZ informal scungy.
– OPPOSITES clean.

mud noun **mire**, sludge, ooze, silt, clay, dirt, soil.

muddle verb **1** *the papers have got muddled up:* **confuse**, mix up, jumble (up), disarrange, disorganize, disorder, disturb, mess up. **2** *it would only muddle you:* **bewilder**, confuse, bemuse, perplex, puzzle, baffle, nonplus, mystify.
noun **1** *the files are in a muddle:* **mess**, confusion, jumble, tangle, hotchpotch, mishmash, chaos, disorder, disarray, disorganization; N. Amer. hodgepodge. **2** *a bureaucratic muddle:* **bungle**, mix-up, misunderstanding; informal foul-up; N. Amer. informal snafu.
▪ **muddle along/through** *we're muddling along as best we can:* cope, manage, get by/along, scrape by/along, make do.

muddled adjective **1** *a muddled pile of photographs:* **jumbled**, in a jumble, in a muddle, in a mess, chaotic, in disorder, in disarray, topsy-turvy, disorganized, disordered, disorderly, mixed up, at sixes and sevens; informal higgledy-piggledy. **2** *she felt muddled:* **confused**, bewildered, bemused, perplexed, disorientated, disoriented, in a muddle, befuddled; N. Amer. informal discombobulated. **3** *muddled thinking:* **incoherent**, confused, muddle-headed, woolly.
– OPPOSITES orderly, clear.

muddy adjective **1** *muddy ground:* **waterlogged**, boggy, marshy, swampy, squelchy, squishy, mucky, slimy, spongy, wet, soft, heavy. **2** *muddy boots:* **mud-caked**, muddied, dirty, filthy, mucky, grimy, soiled. **3** *muddy water:* **murky**, cloudy, muddied, turbid; N. Amer. riled, roily. **4** *a muddy pink:* **dingy**, dirty, drab, dull, sludgy.
– OPPOSITES clean, clear.
verb **1** *don't muddy your boots:* **make muddy**, dirty, soil, spatter, bespatter. **2** *these results muddy the situation:* **make unclear**, obscure, confuse, obfuscate, blur, cloud, befog.
– OPPOSITES clarify.

muff verb (informal) *the administration muffed several of its biggest projects:* **mishandle**, mismanage, mess up, make a mess of, bungle; informal botch, make a hash of, fluff, foul up, louse up; Brit. informal make a pig's ear of, make a Horlicks of; N. Amer. informal goof up.

muffle verb **1** *everyone was muffled up in coats:* **wrap (up)**, swathe, enfold, envelop, cloak. **2** *the sound of their footsteps was muffled:* **deaden**, dull, dampen, damp down, mute, soften, quieten, tone down, mask, stifle, smother.

muffled adjective *muffled shouts:* **indistinct**, faint, muted, dull, soft, stifled, smothered.
– OPPOSITES loud.

mug noun *a china mug:* **beaker**, cup; tankard, glass, stein, flagon.
verb (informal) *he was mugged by three youths:*

assault, attack, set upon, beat up, rob; informal jump, rough up, lay into; Brit. informal duff up, do over.

muggy adjective *an unpleasantly muggy evening:* **humid**, close, sultry, sticky, oppressive, airless, stifling, suffocating, stuffy, clammy, damp, heavy, fuggy.
– OPPOSITES fresh.

mulish adjective *George could sometimes be rather mulish:* **obstinate**, stubborn, pig-headed, recalcitrant, intransigent, unyielding, inflexible, bull-headed, stiff-necked; Brit. informal bloody-minded, bolshie.

mull
▪ **mull something over** *Barney sat there for a while, mulling things over:* ponder, consider, think over/about, reflect on, contemplate, turn over in one's mind, chew over, cogitate on, give some thought to.

multicoloured adjective *multicoloured ribbons:* **kaleidoscopic**, psychedelic, colourful, multicolour, many-coloured, many-hued, rainbow, jazzy, varicoloured, variegated, harlequin, polychromatic.
– OPPOSITES monochrome.

multifarious adjective *the multifarious local and ethnic traditions that are found in the USA:* **diverse**, many, numerous, various, varied, diversified, multiple, multitudinous, multiplex, manifold, multifaceted, different, heterogeneous, miscellaneous, assorted.
– OPPOSITES homogeneous.

multiple adjective *words with multiple meanings:* **numerous**, many, various, different, diverse, several, manifold, multifarious, multitudinous.
– OPPOSITES single.

multiplicity noun *the multiplicity of species found in the rainforests:* **abundance**, scores, mass, host, array, variety; range, diversity, heterogeneity, plurality, profusion; informal loads, stacks, heaps, masses, tons.

multiply verb **1** *their difficulties seem to be multiplying:* **increase**, grow, become more numerous, accumulate, proliferate, mount up, mushroom, snowball. **2** *the rabbits have multiplied:* **breed**, reproduce, procreate.
– OPPOSITES decrease.

multitude noun **1** *a multitude of birds:* **a lot**, a great/large number, a great/large quantity, host, horde, mass, swarm, abundance, profusion; scores, quantities, droves; informal slew, lots, loads, masses, stacks, heaps, tons, dozens, hundreds, thousands, millions; N. Amer. informal gazillions. **2** *Father Peter addressed the multitude:* **crowd**, gathering, assembly, congregation, flock, throng, horde, mob; formal concourse. **3** *political power in the hands of the multitude:* **the (common) people**, the populace, the masses, the rank and file, the commonality, the commonalty, the plebeians; the hoi polloi, the mob, the proletariat, the common herd, the rabble, the proles, the plebs.

multitudinous adjective *the multitudinous*

stars: **numerous**, many, abundant, profuse, prolific, copious, multifarious, innumerable, countless, numberless, infinite.

mum¹ noun (Brit. informal) *my mum looks after me.* See **MOTHER** noun sense 1.

mum² (informal) adjective *he was keeping mum:* **silent**, quiet, mute, dumb, tight-lipped, unforthcoming, reticent.
■ **mum's the word** say nothing, keep quiet, don't breathe a word, don't tell a soul, keep it secret, keep it to yourself, keep it under your hat; informal don't let on, keep shtum, don't let the cat out of the bag.

mumble verb *the old man shuffled away, mumbling to himself:* **mutter**, murmur, speak indistinctly, talk under one's breath.

mumbo-jumbo noun *the instructions are complete mumbo-jumbo:* **nonsense**, gibberish, claptrap, rubbish, balderdash, blather, hocus-pocus; informal gobbledegook, double Dutch, argle-bargle.

munch verb *he munched his sandwich:* **chew**, champ, chomp, masticate, crunch, eat.

mundane adjective **1** *her mundane life:* **humdrum**, dull, boring, tedious, monotonous, tiresome, wearisome, unexciting, uninteresting, uneventful, unvarying, unremarkable, repetitive, repetitious, routine, ordinary, everyday, day-to-day, run-of-the-mill, commonplace, workaday; informal (plain) vanilla. **2** *the mundane world:* **earthly**, worldly, terrestrial, material, temporal, secular.
– OPPOSITES extraordinary, spiritual.

municipal adjective *land use is controlled by the municipal authorities:* **civic**, civil, metropolitan, urban, city, town, borough.
– OPPOSITES rural.

municipality noun *each municipality has its own quota of subsidy:* **borough**, town, city, district; N. Amer. precinct, township; Scottish burgh.

munificence noun *the munificence of our host:* **generosity**, bountifulness, open-handedness, magnanimity, lavishness, liberality, philanthropy, charitableness, largesse, big-heartedness, beneficence.

munificent adjective **generous**, bountiful, open-handed, magnanimous, philanthropic, princely, handsome, lavish, liberal, charitable, big-hearted, beneficent.
– OPPOSITES mean.

murder noun **1** *a brutal murder:* **killing**, homicide, assassination, liquidation, extermination, execution, slaughter, butchery, massacre; manslaughter. **2** (informal) *driving there was murder:* **hell (on earth)**, a nightmare, an ordeal, a trial, misery, torture, agony.
verb *someone tried to murder him:* **kill**, put/do to death, assassinate, execute, liquidate, eliminate, dispatch, butcher, slaughter, massacre, wipe out; informal bump off, do in, do away with, knock off, blow away, blow someone's brains out, take out,

dispose of; N. Amer. informal ice, rub out, smoke, waste.

murderer, murderess noun **killer**, assassin, serial killer, butcher, slaughterer; informal hit man, hired gun.

murderous adjective **1** *a murderous attack:* **homicidal**, brutal, violent, savage, ferocious, fierce, vicious, bloodthirsty, barbarous, barbaric; fatal, lethal, deadly, mortal, death-dealing. **2** (informal) *a murderous schedule:* **arduous**, gruelling, strenuous, punishing, onerous, exhausting, taxing, difficult, rigorous; informal killing, hellish.

murky adjective **1** *a murky winter afternoon:* **dark**, gloomy, grey, leaden, dull, dim, overcast, cloudy, clouded, sunless, dismal, dreary, bleak. **2** *murky water:* **dirty**, muddy, cloudy, turbid; N. Amer. riled, roily. **3** *her murky past:* **questionable**, suspicious, suspect, dubious, dark, mysterious, secret; informal shady.
– OPPOSITES bright, clear.

murmur noun **1** *his voice was a murmur:* **whisper**, undertone, mutter, mumble. **2** *there were murmurs in Tory ranks:* **complaint**, grumble, grouse; informal gripe, moan. **3** *the murmur of bees:* **hum**, humming, buzz, buzzing, thrum, thrumming, drone; sigh, rustle.
verb **1** *he heard them murmuring in the hall:* **mutter**, mumble, whisper, talk under one's breath, speak softly. **2** *no one murmured at the delay:* **complain**, mutter, grumble, grouse; informal gripe, moan. **3** *the wind was murmuring through the trees:* **rustle**, sigh; burble, purl.

muscle noun **1** *he had muscle but no brains:* **strength**, power, muscularity, brawn, burliness; informal beef, beefiness. **2** *financial muscle:* **influence**, power, strength, might, force, forcefulness, weight; informal clout.

muscular adjective **1** *muscular tissue:* **fibrous**, sinewy. **2** *he's very muscular:* **strong**, brawny, muscly, sinewy, powerfully built, well muscled, burly, strapping, sturdy, powerful, athletic; informal hunky, beefy.

muse¹ noun *the poet's muse:* **inspiration**, creative influence, stimulus.

muse² verb *I mused on Toby's story:* **ponder**, consider, think over/about, mull over, reflect on, contemplate, turn over in one's mind, chew over, give some thought to, cogitate on; think, be lost in contemplation/thought, daydream.

mush noun **1** *some sort of greyish mush:* **pap**, pulp, slop, paste, purée, mash; informal gloop, goo, gook; N. Amer. informal glop. **2** *romantic mush:* **sentimentality**, mawkishness; informal schmaltz, corn, slush; N. Amer. informal slop.

mushroom noun **fungus**, field mushroom, chanterelle, button mushroom, cep, champignon, shiitake, oyster mushroom.
verb *ecotourism mushroomed in the 1980s:* **proliferate**, grow/develop rapidly, burgeon, spread, increase, expand, boom, explode,

m

snowball, rocket, skyrocket; thrive, flourish.
– OPPOSITES contract.

mushy adjective *cook until the fruit is mushy:*
soft, semi-liquid, pulpy, sloppy,
spongy, squashy, squelchy, squishy; informal
gooey, gloopy; Brit. informal squidgy.
– OPPOSITES firm.

musical adjective *they burst out into*
rich, musical laughter: **tuneful**, melodic,
melodious, harmonious, sweet-sounding,
sweet, mellifluous, euphonious, euphonic.
– OPPOSITES discordant.

musician noun **player**, performer,
instrumentalist, accompanist, soloist,
virtuoso, maestro.

musing noun *his musing was interrupted*
by the sound of footsteps: **meditation**,
thinking, contemplation, deliberation,
pondering, reflection, rumination,
introspection, daydreaming, reverie,
dreaming, preoccupation, brooding.

must[1] verb *I must go:* **ought to**, should, have
(got) to, need to, be obliged to, be required
to, be compelled to.
noun (informal) *this video is a must:* **not to**
be missed, very good; necessity, essential,
requirement, requisite.

must[2] noun *a smell of must:* **mould**,
mustiness, mouldiness, mildew, fustiness.

muster verb **1** *they mustered 50,000 troops:*
assemble, mobilize, rally, raise, summon,
gather (together), mass, collect, convene,
call up, call to arms, recruit, conscript; US
draft. **2** *reporters mustered outside her house:*
congregate, assemble, gather together,
come together, collect together, convene,
mass, rally. **3** *she mustered her courage:*
summon (up), screw up, call up, rally.
noun *the colonel called a muster:* **roll-**
call, assembly, rally, meeting, gathering,
assemblage, congregation, convention;
parade, review.
■ **pass muster** be good enough, come up
to standard, come up to scratch, measure
up, be acceptable/adequate, fill/fit the bill;
informal make the grade, come/be up to snuff.

musty adjective **1** *the room smelled musty:*
mouldy, stale, fusty, damp, dank, mildewy,
smelly, stuffy, airless, unventilated; N. Amer.
informal funky. **2** *the play seemed musty:*
unoriginal, uninspired, unimaginative,
hackneyed, stale, flat, tired, banal, trite,
clichéd, old-fashioned, outdated; informal old
hat.
– OPPOSITES fresh.

mutant noun *strange-looking mutants:* **freak**
(of nature), deviant, monstrosity, monster,
mutation.

mutate verb *rhythm and blues mutated*
into rock and roll: **change**, metamorphose,
evolve; transmute, transform, convert;
humorous transmogrify.

mutation noun **1** *cells that have*
undergone mutation: **alteration**, change,
variation, modification, transformation,

metamorphosis, transmutation; humorous
transmogrification. **2** *a genetic mutation:*
mutant, freak (of nature), deviant,
monstrosity, monster.

mute adjective **1** *Yasmin remained mute:*
silent, speechless, dumb, unspeaking, tight-
lipped, taciturn; informal mum. **2** *a mute*
appeal: **wordless**, silent, dumb, unspoken,
unvoiced, unexpressed. **3** *he was deaf and*
mute: **dumb**, unable to speak.
– OPPOSITES voluble, spoken.
verb **1** *the noise was muted by the heavy*
curtains: **deaden**, muffle, dampen, soften,
quieten; stifle, smother, suppress. **2** *Bruce*
muted his criticisms: **restrain**, soften, tone
down, moderate, temper.
– OPPOSITES intensify.

muted adjective **1** *the muted hum of traffic:*
muffled, faint, indistinct, quiet, soft,
low. **2** *the landscape is painted in muted*
tones: **subdued**, pastel, delicate, subtle,
understated, restrained.

mutilate verb **1** *the bodies had been*
mutilated: **mangle**, maim, disfigure,
butcher, dismember; cripple. **2** *the carved*
screen had been mutilated: **vandalize**,
damage, deface, ruin, destroy, wreck,
violate, desecrate; N. Amer. informal trash.

mutinous adjective *mutinous troops*
seized three military bases: **rebellious**,
insubordinate, subversive, seditious,
insurgent, insurrectionary, rebel, riotous.

mutiny noun *a mutiny over pay arrears:*
insurrection, rebellion, revolt, riot,
uprising, insurgence, insubordination.
verb *thousands of soldiers mutinied:* **rise up**,
rebel, revolt, riot, disobey/defy authority,
be insubordinate.

mutter verb **1** *a group of men stood*
muttering: **talk under one's breath**,
murmur, mumble, whisper, speak in an
undertone. **2** *backbenchers muttered about*
the reshuffle: **grumble**, complain, grouse,
carp, whine; informal moan, gripe, beef,
whinge; Brit. informal chunter; N. Amer. informal
kvetch.

mutual adjective *a partnership based*
on mutual respect and understanding:
reciprocal, reciprocated, requited, returned;
common, joint, shared.

muzzle noun *the dog's velvety muzzle:* **snout**,
nose, mouth, maw.
verb *attempts to muzzle the media:* **gag**,
silence, censor, stifle, restrain, check, curb,
fetter.

muzzy adjective **1** *she felt muzzy:* **groggy**,
light-headed, faint, dizzy, befuddled,
befogged; informal dopey, woozy. **2** *a slightly*
muzzy picture: **blurred**, blurry, fuzzy,
unfocused, unclear, ill-defined, foggy, hazy.
– OPPOSITES clear.

myopic adjective **1** *a myopic patient:* **short-**
sighted, near-sighted. **2** *the government's*
myopic attitude: **unimaginative**, uncreative,

m

unadventurous, narrow-minded, small-minded, short-term.
– OPPOSITES long-sighted, far-sighted.

myriad (literary) noun *myriads of insects:* **multitude**, mass, host, horde, scores, quantities, droves; informal lots, loads, masses, stacks, tons, hundreds, thousands, millions; N. Amer. informal gazillions.
adjective *the myriad lights of the city:* **innumerable**, countless, infinite, numberless, untold, unnumbered, immeasurable, multitudinous, numerous.

mysterious adjective **1** *he vanished in mysterious circumstances:* **puzzling**, strange, peculiar, curious, funny, queer, odd, weird, bizarre, mystifying, inexplicable, baffling, perplexing, incomprehensible, unexplainable, unfathomable. **2** *he was being very mysterious:* **enigmatic**, inscrutable, secretive, reticent, evasive, furtive, surreptitious.
– OPPOSITES straightforward.

mystery noun **1** *his death remains a mystery:* **puzzle**, enigma, conundrum, riddle, secret, (unsolved) problem. **2** *her past is shrouded in mystery:* **secrecy**, obscurity, uncertainty, mystique. **3** *a murder mystery:* **thriller**, detective story/novel, murder story; informal whodunnit.

mystic, mystical adjective **1** *a mystic experience:* **spiritual**, religious, transcendental, paranormal, other-worldly, supernatural, occult, metaphysical. **2** *mystic rites:* **symbolic**, symbolical, allegorical, representational, metaphorical. **3** *a figure*
of mystical significance: **cryptic**, concealed, hidden, abstruse, arcane, esoteric, inscrutable, inexplicable, unfathomable, mysterious, secret, enigmatic.

mystify verb *I was completely mystified by his disappearance:* **bewilder**, puzzle, perplex, baffle, confuse, confound, bemuse, nonplus, throw; informal flummox, stump, bamboozle, faze, fox.

mystique noun *a certain mystique still surrounds the family:* **charisma**, glamour, romance, mystery, magic, charm, appeal, allure.

myth noun **1** *ancient Greek myths:* **(folk) tale**, (folk) story, legend, fable, saga, mythos, mythus; lore, folklore. **2** *the myths surrounding childbirth:* **misconception**, fallacy, false notion, old wives' tale, fairy story/tale, fiction; informal (tall) story, cock and bull story; kidology.

mythical adjective **1** *mythical beasts:* **legendary**, mythological, fabled, fabulous, folkloric, fairy-tale, storybook; fantastical, imaginary, imagined, fictitious. **2** *her mythical child:* **imaginary**, fictitious, make-believe, fantasy, invented, made-up, non-existent; informal pretend.

mythological adjective *the tree of life is one of the oldest of all mythological symbols:* **fabled**, fabulous, folkloric, fairy-tale, legendary, mythical, mythic, traditional; fictitious, imaginary.

mythology noun **myth(s)**, legend(s), folklore, folk tales/stories, lore, tradition.

m

Nn

nabob noun *a Wall Street nabob:* **very rich person**, tycoon, magnate, millionaire, billionaire, multimillionaire; informal fat cat.

nadir noun *it was the nadir of his career:* **the lowest point/level**, the all-time low, the bottom, rock bottom; informal the pits.
– OPPOSITES zenith.

nag verb **1** *she's constantly nagging me:* **harass**, keep on at, go on at, badger, give someone a hard time, chivvy, hound, harry, criticize, find fault with, moan at, grumble at; henpeck; informal hassle; N. Amer. informal ride; Austral. informal heavy. **2** *this has been nagging me for weeks:* **trouble**, worry, bother, plague, torment, niggle, prey on one's mind; annoy, irritate; informal bug, aggravate.
noun *she's such a nag:* **shrew**, nagger, harpy, termagant, harridan.

nagging adjective **1** *his nagging wife:* **shrewish**, complaining, grumbling, fault-finding, scolding, carping, criticizing. **2** *a nagging pain:* **persistent**, continuous, niggling, unrelenting, unremitting, unabating.

nail noun **1** *the panel is then fastened with nails:* **tack**, spike, pin, rivet; hobnail. **2** *she was biting her nails:* **fingernail**, thumbnail, toenail.
verb **1** *a board was nailed to the wall:* **fasten**, attach, fix, affix, secure, tack, hammer, pin. **2** *the pictures had nailed the lie:* **expose**, reveal, uncover, unmask, bring to light, detect, identify.
■ **hard as nails** callous, hard-hearted, heartless, unfeeling, unsympathetic, uncaring, insensitive, unsentimental, hardbitten, tough, lacking compassion.
■ **on the nail** immediately, at once, without delay, straight away, right away, promptly, directly, now, this minute; N. Amer. on the barrelhead.

naive adjective *I was very naive to begin with, but I learnt fast:* **innocent**, unsophisticated, artless, ingenuous, inexperienced, guileless, unworldly, trusting; gullible, credulous, immature, callow, raw, green; informal wet behind the ears.
– OPPOSITES worldly.

naivety noun **innocence**, ingenuousness, guilelessness, unworldliness, trustfulness; gullibility, credulousness, credulity, immaturity, callowness.

naked adjective **1** *a naked woman:* **nude**, bare, in the nude, stark naked, having nothing on, stripped, unclothed, undressed, in a state of nature; informal without a stitch on, in one's birthday suit, in the raw/buff, in the altogether, in the nuddy, mother-naked; Brit. informal starkers; N. Amer. informal buck naked. **2** *a naked flame:* **unprotected**, uncovered, exposed, unguarded. **3** *the naked branches of the trees:* **bare**, barren, denuded, stripped, uncovered. **4** *the naked truth | naked hostility:* **undisguised**, plain, unadorned, unvarnished, unqualified, stark, bald; overt, obvious, open, patent, evident, apparent, manifest, unmistakable, blatant.
– OPPOSITES clothed, covered.

nakedness noun **1** *she covered her nakedness:* **nudity**, state of undress, bareness. **2** *the nakedness of the landscape:* **bareness**, barrenness, starkness.

namby-pamby adjective *we don't want a club full of namby-pamby bleeding hearts:* **weak**, feeble, spineless, effeminate, effete, limp-wristed, ineffectual; informal wet, weedy, wimpy, sissy.

name noun **1** *her name's Gemma:* **designation**, honorific, title, tag, epithet, label; informal moniker, handle; formal denomination, appellation. **2** *the good name of the firm:* **reputation**, character, repute, standing, stature, esteem, prestige, cachet, kudos; renown, popularity, notability, distinction.
verb **1** *they named the child Phoebe:* **call**, give a name to, dub; label, style, term, title, entitle; baptize, christen. **2** *the driver was named as Jason Penter:* **identify**, specify. **3** *he has named his successor:* **choose**, select, pick, decide on, nominate, designate.

named adjective **1** *a girl named Anne:* **called**, by the name of, baptized, christened, known as; dubbed, entitled, styled, termed, labelled. **2** *the policy applies only to named individuals:* **specified**, designated, identified, cited, mentioned, singled out.

nameless adjective **1** *a nameless photographer:* **unnamed**, unidentified, anonymous, incognito, unspecified, unacknowledged, uncredited; unknown, unsung, uncelebrated. **2** *they were prone to nameless fears:* **unspeakable**, unutterable, inexpressible, indescribable; indefinable, vague, unspecified, unspecifiable.

namely adverb *he has something rare to offer, namely charisma:* **that is (to say)**, to be specific, specifically, viz., to wit.

nanny noun *the children's nanny:* **nursemaid**, au pair, childminder, childcarer; governess.
verb *stop nannying me:* **mollycoddle**, cosset, coddle, wrap in cotton wool, baby, featherbed; spoil, pamper, indulge, overindulge.

nap[1] verb *they were napping on the sofa:* **doze**, sleep (lightly), take a nap, catnap, rest, take a siesta; informal snooze, snatch forty winks, get some shut-eye; Brit. informal have a kip, get some zizz; N. Amer. informal catch some Zs.
noun *she is taking a nap:* **(light) sleep**, catnap, siesta, doze, lie-down, rest; informal snooze, forty winks, shut-eye; Brit. informal kip.
■ **catch someone napping** catch off guard, catch unawares, (take by) surprise, catch out, find unprepared; informal catch someone with their trousers/pants down; Brit. informal catch on the hop.

nap[2] noun *the nap of the velvet:* **pile**, fibres, threads, weave, surface, grain.

narcissism noun **vanity**, self-love, selfadmiration, self-absorption, self-obsession, conceit, self-centredness, self-regard, egotism, egoism.
– OPPOSITES modesty.

narcissistic adjective *he worried that he might sound narcissistic or arrogant:* **vain**, self-loving, self-admiring, self-absorbed, self-obsessed, conceited, self-centred, selfregarding, egotistic, egotistical, egoistic.

narcotic noun **soporific (drug)**, opiate, sleeping pill; painkiller, pain reliever, analgesic, anodyne, palliative, anaesthetic; tranquillizer, sedative; informal downer; Medicine stupefacient.
adjective **soporific**, sleep-inducing, opiate; painkilling, pain-relieving, analgesic, anodyne, anaesthetic, tranquillizing, sedative.

narrate verb *the story is narrated by an ageing English butler:* **tell**, relate, recount, describe, chronicle, give a report of, report; voice-over.

narration noun 1 *a narration of past events:* **account**, narrative, chronicle, description, report, relation, chronicling. 2 *his narration of the story:* **voice-over**, commentary.

narrative noun *a chronological narrative of Stark's life:* **account**, chronicle, history, description, record, report.

narrator noun 1 *the narrator of the 'Arabian Nights':* **storyteller**, teller of tales, relater, chronicler, romancer; raconteur, anecdotalist; Austral. informal magsman. 2 *the film's narrator:* **voice-over**, commentator.
– OPPOSITES listener, audience.

narrow adjective 1 *the path became narrower:* **small**, tapered, tapering, narrowing. 2 *her narrow waist:* **slender**, slim, slight, spare, attenuated, thin. 3 *crammed into a narrow space:* **confined,** cramped, tight, restricted, limited, constricted. 4 *a narrow range of products:* **limited**, restricted, circumscribed, small, inadequate,

insufficient, deficient. 5 *a narrow view of the world.* See NARROW-MINDED. 6 *nationalism in the narrowest sense of the word:* **strict**, literal, exact, precise. 7 *a narrow escape:* **by a very small margin**, close, near, by a hair's breadth; informal by a whisker.
– OPPOSITES wide, broad.
verb *the path narrowed* | *narrowing the gap between rich and poor:* **get/become/make narrower**, get/become/make smaller, taper, diminish, decrease, reduce, contract, shrink, constrict.

narrowly adverb 1 *one bullet narrowly missed him:* **(only) just**, barely, scarcely, hardly, by a hair's breadth; informal by a whisker. 2 *she looked at me narrowly:* **closely**, carefully, searchingly, attentively.

narrow-minded adjective *their own narrow-minded view of the world:* **intolerant**, illiberal, reactionary, conservative, parochial, provincial, insular, small-minded, petty, blinkered, inwardlooking, narrow, hidebound, prejudiced, bigoted; Brit. parish-pump, blimpish; N. Amer. informal jerkwater.
– OPPOSITES tolerant.

narrows plural noun **strait(s)**, sound, channel, waterway, (sea) passage.

nascent adjective *the nascent economic recovery:* **just beginning**, budding, developing, growing, embryonic, incipient, young, fledgling, evolving, emergent, dawning, burgeoning.

nastiness noun 1 *my mother tried to shut herself off from nastiness:* **unpleasantness**, disagreeableness, offensiveness, vileness, foulness. 2 *her uncharacteristic nastiness towards him:* **unkindness**, unpleasantness, unfriendliness, disagreeableness, rudeness, churlishness, spitefulness, maliciousness, meanness, ill temper, ill nature, viciousness, malevolence; informal bitchiness, cattiness.

nasty adjective 1 *a nasty smell:* **unpleasant**, disagreeable, disgusting, distasteful, awful, dreadful, horrible, terrible, vile, foul, abominable, frightful, loathsome, revolting, repulsive, odious, sickening, nauseating, repellent, repugnant, horrendous, appalling, atrocious, offensive, objectionable, obnoxious, unsavoury, unappetizing, offputting; noxious, foul-smelling, smelly, stinking, rank, fetid, malodorous, mephitic; informal ghastly, horrid, gruesome, diabolical, yucky, skanky, God-awful, gross; Brit. informal beastly, grotty, whiffy, pongy, niffy; N. Amer. informal lousy, funky; Austral. informal on the nose. 2 *the weather turned nasty:* **unpleasant**, disagreeable, foul, filthy, inclement; wet, stormy, cold, blustery. 3 *she can be really nasty to him:* **unkind**, unpleasant, unfriendly, disagreeable, rude, churlish, spiteful, malicious, mean, ill-tempered, ill-natured, vicious, malevolent, obnoxious, hateful, hurtful; informal bitchy, catty. 4 *a nasty accident* | *a nasty cut:* **serious**, dangerous,

n

bad, awful, dreadful, terrible, severe; painful, ugly. **5** *she had the nasty habit of appearing unannounced:* **annoying**, irritating, infuriating, disagreeable, unpleasant, maddening, exasperating. **6** *they wrote nasty things on the wall:* **obscene**, indecent, offensive, crude, rude, dirty, filthy, vulgar, foul, gross, disgusting, pornographic, smutty, lewd; informal sick.
– OPPOSITES nice.

nation noun **country**, (sovereign/nation) state, land, realm, kingdom, republic; fatherland, motherland; people, race.

national adjective **1** *he's active in national politics:* **state**, public, federal, governmental; civic, civil, domestic, internal. **2** *a national strike was called:* **nationwide**, countrywide, state, general, widespread.
– OPPOSITES local, international.
noun *a French national:* **citizen**, subject, native; voter.

nationalism noun *the resurgence of nationalism in Europe:* **patriotism**, patriotic sentiment, xenophobia, chauvinism, jingoism.

nationalistic adjective **patriotic**, nationalist, xenophobic, chauvinistic, jingoistic.

nationality noun **1** *in 1938 he took British nationality:* **citizenship**. **2** *all the main nationalities of Ethiopia:* **ethnic group**, ethnic minority, tribe, clan, race, nation.

nationwide adjective *a nationwide conservation scheme:* **national**, countrywide, state, general, widespread, extensive.
– OPPOSITES local.

native noun *a native of Sweden:* **inhabitant**, resident, local; citizen, national; aborigine.
– OPPOSITES foreigner.
adjective **1** *the native population:* **indigenous**, original, first, earliest, aboriginal, autochthonous. **2** *native produce | native plants:* **domestic**, home-grown, home-made, local; indigenous. **3** *a native instinct for politics:* **innate**, inherent, inborn, instinctive, intuitive, natural; hereditary, inherited, congenital, inbred, connate, connatural. **4** *her native tongue:* **mother**, vernacular.
– OPPOSITES immigrant.

nativity noun **birth**, childbirth, delivery.

natural adjective **1** *a natural occurrence:* **normal**, ordinary, everyday, usual, regular, common, commonplace, typical, routine, standard, established, customary, accustomed, habitual. **2** *natural produce:* **unprocessed**, organic, pure, wholesome, unrefined, pesticide-free, additive-free. **3** *Alex is a natural leader:* **born**, naturally gifted, untaught. **4** *his natural instincts:* **innate**, inborn, inherent, native, instinctive, intuitive; hereditary, inherited, inbred, congenital, connate, connatural. **5** *she seemed very natural:*

unaffected, spontaneous, uninhibited, relaxed, unselfconscious, genuine, open, artless, guileless, ingenuous, unpretentious, without airs. **6** *it was quite natural to think she admired him:* **reasonable**, logical, understandable, (only) to be expected, predictable.
– OPPOSITES abnormal, artificial, affected.

naturalist noun **natural historian**, life scientist, wildlife expert; biologist, botanist, zoologist, ornithologist, entomologist, ecologist, conservationist, environmentalist.

naturalistic adjective *a naturalistic drama:* **realistic**, real-life, true-to-life, lifelike, graphic, representational, photographic.
– OPPOSITES abstract.

naturalize verb **1** *he was naturalized in 1950:* **grant citizenship to**, make a citizen, give a passport to, enfranchise. **2** *coriander has now been naturalized in southern Britain:* **establish**, introduce, acclimatize, domesticate; N. Amer. acclimate.

naturally adverb **1** *he's naturally shy:* **by nature**, by character, inherently, innately, congenitally. **2** *try to act naturally:* **normally**, in a natural manner/way, unaffectedly, spontaneously, genuinely, unpretentiously; informal natural. **3** *naturally, they wanted everything kept quiet:* **of course**, as might be expected, needless to say; obviously, clearly, it goes without saying.
– OPPOSITES self-consciously.

naturalness noun *she was different— she'd lost a certain naturalness:* **unselfconsciousness**, spontaneity, spontaneousness, straightforwardness, genuineness, openness, ingenuousness, lack of sophistication, unpretentiousness.

nature noun **1** *the beauty of nature:* **the natural world**, Mother Nature, Mother Earth, the environment; the universe, the cosmos; wildlife, flora and fauna, the countryside. **2** *such crimes are, by their very nature, difficult to hide:* **essence**, inherent/basic/essential qualities, inherent/basic/essential features, character, complexion. **3** *it was not in Daisy's nature to be bitchy:* **character**, personality, disposition, temperament, make-up, psyche, constitution. **4** *they all conducted experiments of a similar nature:* **kind**, sort, type, variety, category, ilk, class, species, genre, style, cast, order, kidney, mould, stamp; N. Amer. stripe.

naughty adjective **1** *a naughty boy:* **badly behaved**, disobedient, bad, misbehaved, misbehaving, wayward, defiant, unruly, insubordinate, wilful, delinquent, undisciplined, uncontrollable, ungovernable, unbiddable, disorderly, disruptive, fractious, recalcitrant, wild, wicked, obstreperous, difficult, troublesome, awkward, contrary, perverse, incorrigible; mischievous, playful, impish, roguish, rascally; informal brattish. **2** *naughty jokes:* **indecent**, risqué, rude, racy, ribald,

bawdy, suggestive, improper, indelicate, indecorous; vulgar, dirty, filthy, smutty, crude, coarse, obscene, lewd, pornographic; informal raunchy; Brit. informal fruity, saucy; N. Amer. informal gamy; euphemistic adult.
– OPPOSITES well behaved, decent.

nausea noun *symptoms include nausea and a headache:* **sickness**, biliousness, queasiness; vomiting, retching, gagging; travel-sickness, seasickness, carsickness, airsickness.

nauseate verb **cause to feel sick**, sicken, make sick, turn someone's stomach, make someone's gorge rise; N. Amer. informal gross out.

nauseating adjective *the smell in the compartment was nauseating:* **sickening**, stomach-churning, nauseous, emetic, sickly; disgusting, revolting, offensive, loathsome, obnoxious, foul; N. Amer. vomitous; informal sick-making, gross, gut-churning.

nauseous adjective *the food made her feel nauseous:* **sick**, nauseated, queasy, bilious, green about/at the gills, ill, unwell; seasick, carsick, airsick, travel-sick; N. Amer. informal barfy.

nautical adjective *nautical charts:* **maritime**, marine, naval, seafaring; boating, sailing.

navel noun informal belly button, tummy button; Anatomy umbilicus.

navigable adjective *navigable rivers:* **passable**, negotiable, traversable; clear, open, unobstructed, unblocked.

navigate verb **1** *he navigated the yacht across the Atlantic:* **steer**, pilot, guide, direct, helm, captain; informal skipper. **2** *the upper reaches are dangerous to navigate:* **sail (across/over)**, cross, traverse, negotiate. **3** *I'll drive—you can navigate:* **map-read**, give directions.

navigation noun **1** *the navigation of the ship:* **steering**, piloting, sailing, guiding, directing, guidance. **2** *the skills of navigation:* **helmsmanship**, steersmanship, seamanship, map-reading, chart-reading.

navigator noun **helmsman**, steersman, pilot, guide; N. Amer. wheelman.

navvy noun **labourer**, manual worker, workman, worker, hand, coolie, roustabout; Austral./NZ rouseabout.

navy noun *a 600-ship navy:* **fleet**, flotilla, armada; naval task force, squadron.

nay adverb *it is difficult, nay, impossible, to understand:* **or rather**, (and) indeed, and even, in fact, actually, in truth.

near adverb **1** *her children all live near:* **close (by)**, nearby, close/near at hand, in the neighbourhood, in the vicinity, at hand, within reach, on the doorstep, a stone's throw away; informal within spitting distance. **2** *there were near perfect conditions:* **almost**, just about, nearly, practically, virtually.
preposition *a hotel near the seafront:* **close to**, close by, a short distance from, in the vicinity of, in the neighbourhood of, within reach of, a stone's throw away from; informal

within spitting distance of.
adjective **1** *the nearest house:* **close**, nearby, close/near at hand, at hand, a stone's throw away, within reach, accessible, handy, convenient; informal within spitting distance. **2** *the final judgement is near:* **imminent**, in the offing, close/near at hand, at hand, (just) round the corner, impending, looming. **3** *a near relation:* **closely related**, close, related. **4** *a near escape:* **narrow**, close, by a hair's breadth; informal by a whisker.
– OPPOSITES far, distant.
verb **1** *by dawn we were nearing Moscow:* **approach**, draw near/nearer to, get close/closer to, advance towards, close in on. **2** *the death toll is nearing 3,000:* **verge on**, border on, approach.

nearby adjective *one of the nearby villages:* **not far away/off**, close/near at hand, close (by), near, within reach, at hand, neighbouring; accessible, handy, convenient.
– OPPOSITES faraway.
adverb *her mother lives nearby:* **close (by)**, close/near at hand, near, a short distance away, in the neighbourhood, in the vicinity, at hand, within reach, on the doorstep, (just) round the corner.

nearly adverb *dinner's nearly ready:* **almost**, (just) about, more or less, practically, virtually, all but, as good as, not far off, to all intents and purposes; not quite; informal pretty much, pretty well.

near miss noun *two American bombers were involved in a near miss with a helicopter:* **close thing**, near thing, narrow escape; informal close shave.

nearness noun **1** *the town's nearness to Rome:* **closeness**, proximity, propinquity; accessibility, handiness. **2** *the nearness of death:* **imminence**, closeness, immediacy.

neat adjective **1** *the bedroom was neat and clean:* **tidy**, orderly, well ordered, in (good) order, shipshape (and Bristol fashion), in apple-pie order, spick and span, uncluttered, straight, trim. **2** *the suspect had a neat appearance:* **smart**, spruce, dapper, trim, well groomed, well turned out; N. Amer. trig; informal natty. **3** *her neat script:* **well formed**, regular, precise, elegant, well proportioned. **4** *this neat little gadget:* **compact**, well designed, handy; Brit. informal dinky. **5** *his neat footwork:* **skilful**, deft, dexterous, adroit, adept, expert; informal nifty. **6** *a neat solution:* **clever**, ingenious, inventive. **7** *neat gin:* **undiluted**, straight, unmixed; N. Amer. informal straight up. **8** (N. Amer. informal) *we had a really neat time.* See **WONDERFUL**.
– OPPOSITES untidy.

neaten verb *we neatened ourselves up for dinner:* **tidy (up)**, make neat/neater, straighten (up), smarten (up), spruce up, put in order; N. Amer. informal fix up.

neatly adverb **1** *neatly arranged papers:* **tidily**, methodically, systematically; smartly, sprucely. **2** *the point was neatly* _put:_ **cleverly**, aptly, elegantly. **3** _a neatly executed header:_ **skilfully**, deftly, adroitly, adeptly, expertly.

neatness noun **1** _the neatness of the cottage:_ **tidiness**, orderliness, trimness, spruceness; smartness. **2** _the neatness of her movements:_ **grace**, gracefulness, nimbleness, deftness, dexterity, adroitness, agility.

nebulous adjective **1** _a nebulous figure in the distance:_ **indistinct**, indefinite, unclear, vague, hazy, cloudy, fuzzy, misty, blurred, blurry, foggy; faint, shadowy, obscure, formless, amorphous. **2** _such nebulous ideas:_ **vague**, ill-defined, unclear, hazy, uncertain, indefinite, indeterminate, imprecise, unformed, muddled, confused, ambiguous. – OPPOSITES clear.

necessarily adverb _an increase in the supply of money will not necessarily have much effect on spending:_ **as a consequence**, as a result, automatically, as a matter of course, certainly, surely, definitely, incontrovertibly, undoubtedly, inevitably, unavoidably, inescapably, ineluctably, of necessity.

necessary adjective **1** _planning permission is necessary:_ **obligatory**, requisite, required, compulsory, mandatory, imperative, needed, de rigueur; essential, indispensable, vital. **2** _a necessary consequence of their actions:_ **inevitable**, unavoidable, inescapable, inexorable, ineluctable; predetermined, preordained.

necessitate verb _such a level of public expenditure would necessitate tax increases:_ **make necessary**, entail, involve, mean, require, demand, call for, be grounds for, warrant, constrain, force.

necessitous adjective _2.5 tons of dried milk was supplied to necessitous mothers:_ **needy**, poor, short of money, disadvantaged, underprivileged, in straitened circumstances, impoverished, poverty-stricken, penniless, impecunious, destitute, pauperized, indigent; Brit. on the breadline, without a penny to one's name; informal on one's uppers, hard up, without two pennies to rub together; Brit. informal in Queer Street. – OPPOSITES wealthy.

necessity noun **1** _a good book is a necessity when travelling:_ **essential**, indispensable item, requisite, prerequisite, necessary, basic, sine qua non, desideratum. **2** _political necessity forced him to resign:_ **force of circumstance**, obligation, need, call, exigency; force majeure. **3** _the necessity of growing old:_ **inevitability**, certainty, inescapability, inexorability, ineluctability. **4** _necessity made them steal:_ **poverty**, need, neediness, want, deprivation, privation, penury, destitution, indigence. ■ **of necessity** necessarily, inevitably, unavoidably, inescapably, ineluctably; as a matter of course, naturally, automatically, certainly, surely, definitely, incontrovertibly, undoubtedly.

neck
■ **neck and neck** _the six contestants are neck and neck:_ level, equal, tied, side by side; Brit. level pegging; informal even-steven(s).

necklace noun **chain**, choker, necklet; beads, pearls; pendant, locket.

necromancer noun **sorcerer**, sorceress, (black) magician, wizard, warlock, witch, enchantress, occultist, diviner; spiritualist, medium.

necromancy noun **sorcery**, (black) magic, witchcraft, witchery, wizardry, the occult, occultism, voodoo, hoodoo; divination; spiritualism.

née adjective _Jill Wyatt, née Peters:_ **born**, formerly, previously.

need verb **1** _do you need money?_ **require**, be in need of, have need of, want; be crying out for, be desperate for; demand, call for, necessitate, entail, involve; lack, be without, be short of. **2** _you needn't come:_ **have to**, be obliged to, be compelled to. **3** _she needed him so much:_ **yearn for**, pine for, long for, desire, miss.
noun **1** _there's no need to apologize:_ **necessity**, obligation, requirement, call, demand. **2** _basic human needs:_ **requirement**, essential, necessity, want, requisite, prerequisite, demand, desideratum. **3** _their need was particularly pressing:_ **neediness**, want, poverty, deprivation, privation, hardship, destitution, indigence. **4** _my hour of need:_ **difficulty**, trouble, distress; crisis, emergency, urgency, extremity. ■ **in need** needy, necessitous, deprived, disadvantaged, underprivileged, poor, impoverished, poverty-stricken, destitute, impecunious, indigent; Brit. on the breadline.

needed adjective _planning permission is needed:_ **necessary**, required, wanted, desired, lacking; essential, requisite, compulsory, obligatory, mandatory. – OPPOSITES optional.

needle noun **1** _a needle and thread:_ darner, bodkin. **2** _the virus is transmitted via needles:_ hypodermic needle; informal hype, spike. **3** _the needle on the meter:_ **indicator**, pointer, marker, arrow, hand. **4** _put the needle on the record:_ **stylus**.

needless adjective _there's no point going into needless detail:_ **unnecessary**, inessential, non-essential, unneeded, undesired, unwanted, uncalled for; gratuitous, pointless; dispensable, expendable, superfluous, redundant, excessive, supererogatory. – OPPOSITES necessary.
■ **needless to say** of course, as one would expect, not unexpectedly, it goes without saying, obviously, naturally; informal natch.

needlework noun **sewing**, stitching, embroidery, needlepoint, needlecraft, tapestry, crewel work.

needy adjective _the food went to needy_

families in the area: **poor**, deprived, disadvantaged, underprivileged, necessitous, in need, needful, hard up, in straitened circumstances, poverty-stricken, indigent, impoverished, pauperized, destitute, impecunious, penniless; Brit. on the breadline; informal on one's uppers, broke, strapped (for cash), cash-strapped, without two pennies to rub together; Brit. informal skint, stony broke, in Queer Street; N. Amer. informal stone broke.
– OPPOSITES wealthy.

ne'er-do-well noun **good-for-nothing**, layabout, loafer, idler, shirker, sluggard, slugabed, drone; informal waster, lazybones; Brit. informal skiver; N. Amer. informal bum, gold brick.

nefarious adjective *the nefarious activities of bodysnatchers:* **wicked**, evil, sinful, iniquitous, egregious, heinous, atrocious, vile, foul, abominable, odious, depraved, monstrous, fiendish, diabolical, unspeakable, despicable; villainous, criminal, corrupt, illegal, unlawful.
– OPPOSITES good.

negate verb **1** *they negated the court's ruling:* **invalidate**, nullify, neutralize, cancel; undo, reverse, annul, void, revoke, rescind, repeal, retract, countermand, overrule, overturn. **2** *he negates the political nature of education:* **deny**, dispute, contradict, controvert, refute, rebut, reject, repudiate.
– OPPOSITES validate, confirm.

negation noun **1** *negation of the findings:* **denial**, contradiction, repudiation, refutation, rebuttal; nullification, cancellation, revocation, repeal, retraction; Law disaffirmation; formal abrogation. **2** *evil is not just the negation of goodness:* **opposite**, reverse, antithesis, contrary, inverse, converse; absence, want.

negative adjective **1** *a negative reply:* **opposing**, opposed, contrary, anti-, dissenting, dissentient; saying 'no', in the negative. **2** *stop being so negative:* **pessimistic**, defeatist, gloomy, cynical, fatalistic, dismissive, antipathetic; unenthusiastic, uninterested, unresponsive. **3** *a negative effect on the economy:* **harmful**, bad, adverse, damaging, detrimental, unfavourable, disadvantageous.
– OPPOSITES positive, optimistic, favourable.
noun *he murmured a negative:* '**no'**, refusal, rejection, veto; dissension, contradiction; denial.
verb **1** *the bill was negatived by the house:* **reject**, turn down, refuse, veto, squash; informal give the thumbs down to. **2** *his arguments were negatived:* **disprove**, belie, invalidate, refute, rebut, discredit; contradict, deny, negate. **3** *they tried to negative the effect of the tax:* **neutralize**, cancel out, counteract, nullify, negate; offset, balance, counterbalance.
– OPPOSITES ratify, prove.

negativity noun *one person's negativity*

and intolerance can have a knock-on effect: **pessimism**, defeatism, gloom, cynicism, hopelessness, despair, despondency; apathy, indifference.

neglect verb **1** *she neglected the children:* **fail to look after**, leave alone, abandon. **2** *he's neglecting his work:* **pay no attention to**, let slide, not attend to, be remiss about, be lax about, leave undone, shirk. **3** *don't neglect our advice:* **disregard**, ignore, pay no attention to, take no notice of, pay no heed to, overlook; disdain, scorn, spurn. **4** *I neglected to inform her:* **fail**, omit, forget.
– OPPOSITES cherish, heed, remember.
noun **1** *the place had an air of neglect:* **disrepair**, dilapidation, deterioration, shabbiness, disuse, abandonment. **2** *her doctor was guilty of neglect:* **negligence**, dereliction of duty, remissness, carelessness, heedlessness, unconcern, laxity, slackness, irresponsibility; formal delinquency. **3** *the relative neglect of women:* **disregard**, ignoring, overlooking; inattention to, indifference to, heedlessness to.
– OPPOSITES care, attention.

neglected adjective **1** *neglected animals:* **uncared for**, abandoned; mistreated, maltreated. **2** *a neglected cottage:* **derelict**, dilapidated, tumbledown, ramshackle, untended. **3** *a neglected masterpiece of prose:* **disregarded**, forgotten, overlooked, ignored, unrecognized, unnoticed, unsung, underestimated, undervalued, unappreciated.

neglectful adjective. See NEGLIGENT.

negligent adjective *she claimed that her solicitor had been negligent:* **neglectful**, remiss, careless, lax, irresponsible, inattentive, heedless, thoughtless, unmindful, forgetful; slack, sloppy; N. Amer. derelict.
– OPPOSITES dutiful.

negligible adjective *the damage to the BMW turned out to be negligible:* **trivial**, trifling, insignificant, unimportant, minor, inconsequential; minimal, small, slight, inappreciable, infinitesimal, nugatory, petty; paltry, inadequate, insufficient, meagre, pitiful; informal minuscule, piddling, measly, poxy.
– OPPOSITES significant.

negotiable adjective **1** *the salary will be negotiable:* **open to discussion**, discussable, flexible, open to modification; unsettled, undecided. **2** *the path was negotiable on foot:* **passable**, navigable, crossable, traversable; clear, unblocked, unobstructed. **3** *negotiable cheques:* transferable; valid.

negotiate verb **1** *she refused to negotiate:* **discuss terms**, talk, consult, parley, confer, debate; compromise; mediate, intercede, arbitrate, moderate, conciliate; bargain, haggle. **2** *he negotiated a new contract:* **arrange**, broker, work out, thrash out, agree on; settle, clinch, conclude, pull off, bring off, transact; informal sort out, swing. **3** *I*

n

negotiated the obstacles: **get round**, get past, get over, clear, cross; surmount, overcome, deal with, cope with.

negotiation noun **1** the negotiations resume next week: **discussion(s)**, talks, deliberations, conference, debate, dialogue, consultation; mediation, arbitration, conciliation. **2** the negotiation of the deal: **arrangement**, brokering; settlement, conclusion, completion, transaction.

negotiator noun a team of negotiators from the UN Security Council sought to resolve the situation: **mediator**, arbitrator, arbiter, moderator, go-between, middleman, intermediary, intercessor, intervener, conciliator; representative, spokesperson, broker, bargainer.

neigh verb a horse neighed: **whinny**, bray, nicker, snicker, whicker.

neighbourhood noun **1** a quiet neighbourhood: **district**, area, locality, locale, quarter, community; part, region, zone; informal neck of the woods; Brit. informal manor; N. Amer. informal hood, nabe. **2** in the neighbourhood of Canterbury: **vicinity**, environs, purlieus, precincts, vicinage.
■ **in the neighbourhood of** the cost was believed to be in the neighbourhood of $4.5 million: approximately, about, around, roughly, in the region of, of the order of, nearly, almost, close to, just about, practically, there or thereabouts, circa; Brit. getting on for.

neighbouring adjective the owner of the neighbouring property: **adjacent**, adjoining, bordering, connecting, abutting; proximate, near, close (at hand), next-door, nearby, in the vicinity, vicinal.
– OPPOSITES remote.

neighbourly adjective he was not very neighbourly: **obliging**, helpful, friendly, kind, amiable, amicable, affable, genial, agreeable, hospitable, companionable, well disposed, civil, cordial, good-natured, nice, pleasant, generous; considerate, thoughtful, unselfish; Brit. informal decent.
– OPPOSITES unfriendly.

nemesis noun **1** this could be the bank's nemesis: **downfall**, undoing, ruin, ruination, destruction, Waterloo. **2** the nemesis that his crime deserved: **retribution**, vengeance, punishment, just deserts; fate, destiny.

neologism noun **new word**, new expression, new term, new phrase, coinage; made-up word, nonce-word.

neophyte noun **1** a neophyte of the monastery: **novice**, novitiate; postulant, catechumen. **2** cooking classes are offered to neophytes: **beginner**, learner, novice, newcomer; initiate, tyro, fledgling; trainee, apprentice, probationer; N. Amer. tenderfoot; informal rookie, newbie, newie; N. Amer. informal greenhorn.

nepotism noun the nepotism and corruption of the country's political system:

favouritism, preferential treatment, the old boy network, looking after one's own, bias, partiality, partisanship; Brit. jobs for the boys, the old school tie.
– OPPOSITES impartiality.

nerd noun I was a serious computer nerd until I discovered cars and girls: (informal) **bore**; informal dork, dweeb, geek; Brit. informal anorak, spod; N. Amer. informal Poindexter.

nerve noun **1** the nerves that transmit pain: nerve fibre, neuron, axon. **2** the match will be a test of nerve: **confidence**, assurance, cool-headedness, self-possession; courage, bravery, pluck, boldness, intrepidity, fearlessness, daring; determination, will power, spirit, backbone, fortitude, mettle, grit, stout-heartedness; informal guts, spunk; Brit. informal bottle; N. Amer. informal moxie. **3** he had the nerve to chat her up: **audacity**, cheek, effrontery, gall, temerity, presumption, boldness, brazenness, impudence, impertinence, arrogance, cockiness; informal face, front, brass neck, chutzpah; Brit. informal sauce. **4** pre-wedding nerves: **anxiety**, tension, nervousness, stress, worry, cold feet, apprehension; informal butterflies (in one's stomach), collywobbles, the jitters, the shakes; Brit. informal the (screaming) abdabs.
■ **get on someone's nerves** irritate, annoy, irk, anger, bother, vex, provoke, displease, exasperate, infuriate, gall, pique, needle, ruffle someone's feathers, try someone's patience; jar on, grate on, rankle; Brit. rub up the wrong way; informal aggravate, get to, bug, miff, peeve, rile, nettle, get up someone's nose, hack off, get someone's goat; Brit. informal nark, get on someone's wick, wind up.
■ **nerve oneself** Morag nerved herself to go on: brace oneself, steel oneself, summon one's courage, gear oneself up, prepare oneself; fortify oneself; informal psych oneself up.

nerveless adjective **1** her nerveless fingers: **inert**, lifeless; weak, powerless, feeble. **2** a nerveless lack of restraint: **confident**, self-confident, self-assured, self-possessed, cool, calm, {cool, calm, and collected}, composed, relaxed.
– OPPOSITES nervous.

nerve-racking adjective meeting him for the first time was nerve-racking to say the least: **stressful**, anxious, worrying, fraught, nail-biting, tense, difficult, trying, worrisome, daunting, frightening; informal scary, hairy.

nervous adjective **1** she comes across as a nervous woman: **highly strung**, anxious, edgy, tense, excitable, jumpy, skittish, brittle, neurotic; timid, mousy, shy, fearful; Brit. nervy. **2** he was so nervous he couldn't eat: **anxious**, worried, apprehensive, on edge, edgy, tense, stressed, agitated, uneasy, restless, worked up, keyed up, overwrought, jumpy; fearful, frightened, scared, shaky, in a cold sweat; informal with butterflies in one's stomach, jittery, twitchy, in a state,

uptight, wired, in a flap, het up; Brit. informal strung up, having kittens; N. Amer. informal spooky, squirrelly. **3** *a nervous disorder:* **neurological**, neural.
– OPPOSITES relaxed, calm.

nervous breakdown noun **(mental) collapse**, breakdown, crisis, trauma; nervous exhaustion, mental illness; informal crack-up.

nervousness noun *as he ate, she found herself chattering away to him out of nervousness:* **anxiety**, edginess, tension, agitation, stress, worry, apprehension, uneasiness, disquiet, fear, trepidation, perturbation, alarm; Brit. nerviness; informal butterflies (in one's stomach), collywobbles, the jitters, the willies, the heebie-jeebies, the shakes; Brit. informal the (screaming) abdabs.

nervy adjective. See **NERVOUS** senses 1, 2.

nest noun **1** *the birds built a nest:* **roost**, eyrie. **2** *the animals disperse rapidly from the nest:* **lair**, den, burrow, set. **3** *a cosy love nest:* **hideaway**, hideout, retreat, shelter, refuge, snuggery, den; informal hidey-hole. **4** *a nest of intrigue:* **hotbed**, den, breeding ground, cradle.

nest egg noun **(life) savings**, cache, funds, reserve.

nestle verb *he nestled up against her:* **snuggle**, cuddle, huddle, nuzzle, settle, burrow, snug down.

nestling noun **chick**, fledgling, baby bird.

net¹ noun **1** *a dress made of green net:* **netting**, meshwork, webbing, tulle, fishnet, openwork, lace, latticework. **2** *he managed to escape the net:* **trap**, snare.
verb *they netted several big criminals:* **catch**, capture, trap, entrap, snare, ensnare, bag, hook, land; informal nab, collar.

net² adjective **1** *net earnings:* **after tax**, after deductions, take-home, final; informal bottom line. **2** *the net result:* **final**, end, ultimate, closing; overall, actual, effective.
– OPPOSITES gross.
verb *she netted £50,000 from the sale:* **earn**, make, get, gain, obtain, acquire, accumulate, take home, bring in, pocket, realize, be paid; informal rake in.

nether adjective *the nether reaches of a vast, vaulted interior:* **lower**, low, bottom, bottommost, under, basal; underground.
– OPPOSITES upper.

nettle verb *a few things nettled her:* **irritate**, annoy, irk, gall, vex, anger, exasperate, infuriate, provoke; upset, displease, offend, affront, pique, get on someone's nerves, try someone's patience, ruffle someone's feathers; Brit. rub up the wrong way; N. Amer. rankle; informal peeve, aggravate, miff, rile, needle, get to, bug, get up someone's nose, hack off, get someone's goat; Brit. informal nark, get on someone's wick, wind up; N. Amer. informal tick off.

network noun **1** *a network of arteries:* **web**, lattice, net, matrix, mesh, criss-cross, grid, reticulum, reticulation. **2** *a network of lanes:* **maze**, labyrinth, warren, tangle. **3** *a network of friends:* **system**, complex, nexus, web.

neurosis noun *Max was said to be in the grip of some sort of neurosis:* **mental illness**, mental disorder, psychological disorder; psychoneurosis, psychopathy; obsession, phobia, fixation.

neurotic adjective **1** (Medicine) *neurotic patients:* **mentally ill**, mentally disturbed, unstable, unbalanced, maladjusted; psychopathic, phobic, obsessive–compulsive. **2** *a neurotic, self-obsessed woman:* **over-anxious**, oversensitive, nervous, tense, highly strung, paranoid; obsessive, fixated, hysterical, overwrought, irrational; Brit. nervy; informal twitchy.
– OPPOSITES stable, calm.

neuter adjective *I did not feel male, but rather, neuter:* **asexual**, sexless, unsexed; androgynous, epicene.
verb *have your pets neutered:* **sterilize**, castrate, spay, geld, cut, fix, desex; N. Amer. & Austral. alter; Brit. informal doctor.

neutral adjective **1** *she's neutral on this issue:* **impartial**, unbiased, unprejudiced, objective, open-minded, non-partisan, disinterested, dispassionate, detached, impersonal, unemotional, indifferent, uncommitted. **2** *Switzerland remained neutral:* **unaligned**, non-aligned, unaffiliated, unallied, uninvolved; non-combatant. **3** *a neutral topic of conversation:* **inoffensive**, bland, unobjectionable, unexceptional, anodyne, unremarkable, ordinary, commonplace; safe, harmless, innocuous. **4** *a neutral background:* **pale**, light, beige, cream, taupe, oatmeal, ecru, buff, fawn, grey; colourless, uncoloured, achromatic; indeterminate, insipid, nondescript, dull, drab.
– OPPOSITES biased, partisan, provocative, colourful.

neutralize verb *impatience at his frailty began to neutralize her fear:* **counteract**, offset, counterbalance, balance, counterpoise, countervail, compensate for, make up for; cancel out, nullify, negate, negative; equalize.

never adverb **1** *his room is never tidy:* **not ever**, at no time, not at any time, not once. **2** *she will never agree to it:* **not at all**, certainly not, not for a moment, under no circumstances, on no account; informal no way, not on your life, not in a million years; Brit. informal not on your nelly.
– OPPOSITES always, definitely.

never-ending adjective **1** *I can't stand the never-ending noise:* **incessant**, continuous, unceasing, ceaseless, constant, continual, perpetual, uninterrupted, unbroken, steady, unremitting, relentless, persistent, interminable, non-stop, endless, unending, everlasting, eternal. **2** *keeping a garden neat is one of those never-ending tasks:* **endless**,

n

countless, innumerable, untold, unlimited, limitless, boundless.

nevertheless adverb *nevertheless, it makes sense to take a few precautions:* **nonetheless**, even so, however, but, still, yet, though; in spite of that, despite that, be that as it may, for all that, that said, just the same, all the same; notwithstanding, regardless, anyway, anyhow; informal still and all.

new adjective 1 *new technology:* **recently developed**, up to date, latest, current, state-of-the-art, contemporary, advanced, recent, modern. 2 *we need new ideas:* **novel**, original, fresh, imaginative, creative, experimental; contemporary, modernist, up to date; newfangled, ultra-modern, avant-garde, futuristic; informal way out, far out. 3 *is your boat new?* **unused**, brand new, pristine, fresh, in mint condition. 4 *new neighbours moved in:* **different**, another, alternative; unfamiliar, unknown, strange; unaccustomed, untried. 5 *when one bin's full, use a new one:* **additional**, extra, supplementary, further, another, fresh. 6 *I came back a new woman:* **reinvigorated**, restored, revived, improved, refreshed, regenerated, reborn.
– OPPOSITES old, hackneyed, second-hand, present.

newborn adjective *newborn babies:* **just born**, recently born.
noun *the bacteria are fatal to newborns:* **young baby**, tiny baby, infant; Medicine neonate.

n

newcomer noun 1 *a newcomer to the village:* **(new) arrival**, immigrant, incomer, settler; stranger, outsider, foreigner, alien; N. English offcomer; informal johnny-come-lately, new kid on the block; Austral. informal blow-in. 2 *photography tips for the newcomer:* **beginner**, novice, learner; trainee, apprentice, probationer, tyro, initiate, neophyte; N. Amer. tenderfoot; informal rookie, newbie; N. Amer. informal greenhorn.

newfangled adjective *newfangled devices:* **new**, the latest, modern, ultra-modern, up to the minute, state-of-the-art, advanced, contemporary; new-fashioned; informal trendy, flash.
– OPPOSITES dated.

newly adverb *steam and ash began to erupt from a newly formed crater:* **recently**, (only) just, lately, freshly; not long ago, a short time ago, only now, of late; new-.

news noun *colleagues were stunned by the news of his death:* **report**, announcement, story, account; article, news flash, newscast, headlines, press release, communication, communiqué, bulletin; message, dispatch, statement, intelligence; disclosure, revelation, word, talk, gossip; informal scoop.

newspaper noun **paper**, journal, gazette, news-sheet; tabloid, broadsheet, quality (paper), national (paper), local (paper), daily (paper), weekly (paper); free sheet, scandal sheet; informal rag; N. Amer. informal tab.

newsworthy adjective *press releases can help to ensure that newsworthy events receive publicity:* **interesting**, topical, notable, noteworthy, important, significant, momentous, historic, remarkable, sensational.
– OPPOSITES unremarkable.

next adjective 1 *the next chapter:* **following**, succeeding, upcoming, to come. 2 *the next house in the street:* **neighbouring**, adjacent, adjoining, next-door, bordering, connected, attached; closest, nearest.
– OPPOSITES previous.
adverb *where shall we go next?* **then**, after, afterwards, after this/that, following that/this, later, subsequently.
– OPPOSITES before.
■ **next to** beside, by, alongside, by the side of, next door to, adjacent to, side by side with; close to, near, neighbouring, adjoining.

nibble verb 1 *they nibbled at mangoes:* **take small bites (from)**, pick, gnaw, peck, snack on; toy with; taste, sample; informal graze (on). 2 *the mouse nibbled his finger:* **peck**, nip, bite.
noun 1 *the fish enjoyed a nibble on the lettuce:* **bite**, gnaw, chew; taste. 2 *nuts and nibbles:* **morsel**, mouthful, bite; snack, titbit, canapé, hors d'oeuvre, bonne bouche.

nice adjective 1 *have a nice time:* **enjoyable**, pleasant, agreeable, good, satisfying, gratifying, delightful, marvellous; entertaining, amusing, diverting; informal lovely, great; N. Amer. informal neat. 2 *nice people:* **pleasant**, likeable, agreeable, personable, congenial, amiable, affable, genial, friendly, charming, delightful, engaging; sympathetic, compassionate, good. 3 *nice manners:* **polite**, courteous, civil, refined, polished, genteel, elegant. 4 *that's a rather nice distinction:* **subtle**, fine, delicate, minute, precise, strict, close; careful, meticulous, scrupulous. 5 *it's a nice day:* **fine**, pleasant, agreeable; dry, sunny, warm, mild.
– OPPOSITES unpleasant, nasty, rough.

nicety noun *there's no time for legal niceties:* **subtlety**, fine point, nuance, refinement, detail.

niche noun 1 *a niche in the wall:* **recess**, alcove, nook, cranny, hollow, bay, cavity, cubbyhole, pigeonhole. 2 *he found his niche in life:* **ideal position**, place, function, vocation, calling, métier, job.

nick noun *a slight nick in the blade:* **cut**, scratch, incision, snick, notch, chip, gouge, gash; dent, indentation.
verb *I nicked my toe:* **cut**, scratch, incise, snick, gouge, gash, score.
■ **in the nick of time** just in time, not a moment too soon, at the critical moment; N. Amer. informal under the wire.

nickname noun **sobriquet**, byname, tag, label, epithet, cognomen; pet name, diminutive, endearment; informal moniker.

nifty adjective (informal) **1** *nifty camerawork:* **skilful**, deft, agile, capable. **2** *a nifty little gadget:* **useful**, handy, practical. **3** *that's a nifty suit you're wearing:* **fashionable**, stylish, smart.
– OPPOSITES clumsy.

niggardly adjective **1** *a niggardly person:* **mean**, miserly, parsimonious, close-fisted, penny-pinching, cheese-paring, grasping, ungenerous, illiberal; informal stingy, tight, tight-fisted; N. Amer. informal cheap. **2** *niggardly rations:* **meagre**, inadequate, scanty, scant, skimpy, paltry, sparse, insufficient, deficient, short, lean, small, slender, poor, miserable, pitiful, puny; informal measly, stingy, pathetic, piddling.
– OPPOSITES generous.

niggle verb **1** *his behaviour does niggle me:* **irritate**, annoy, bother, provoke, exasperate, upset, gall, irk, rankle with; informal rile, get to, bug. **2** *he niggles on about taxes:* **complain**, fuss, carp, cavil, grumble, grouse; informal moan, nit-pick.
noun *they had some niggles about the lack of equipment:* **quibble**, trivial complaint, criticism, grumble, grouse, cavil; informal gripe, moan, beef, grouch.

night noun night-time; (hours of) darkness, dark.
– OPPOSITES day.
■ **night and day** all the time, around the clock, {morning, noon, and night}, {day in, day out}, ceaselessly, endlessly, incessantly, unceasingly, interminably, constantly, perpetually, continually, relentlessly; informal 24-7.

nightclub noun **disco**, discotheque, night spot, club, bar; N. Amer. cafe; informal niterie.

nightfall noun *we can be back in the city before nightfall:* **sunset**, sundown, dusk, twilight, evening, close of day, dark.
– OPPOSITES dawn.

nightly adjective **1** *the inhabitants were subjected to nightly raids by insurgents:* **every night**, each night, night after night. **2** *his nightly wanderings:* **nocturnal**, night-time.

nightmare noun **1** *she woke from a nightmare:* **bad dream**, night terrors. **2** *the journey was a nightmare:* **ordeal**, trial, torment, horror, hell, misery, agony, torture, murder; curse, bane.

nightmarish adjective *a nightmarish ghost story:* **unearthly**, spine-chilling, hair-raising, horrific, macabre, hideous, unspeakable, gruesome, grisly, ghastly, harrowing, disturbing; informal scary, creepy, gut-wrenching.

nihilism noun *he could not accept Bacon's nihilism:* **scepticism**, disbelief, unbelief, agnosticism, atheism; negativity, cynicism, pessimism; rejection, denial.

nihilist noun **sceptic**, disbeliever, unbeliever, agnostic, atheist; negativist, cynic, pessimist.

nil noun *they beat us three-nil:* **nothing**, none; nought, zero, 0; Tennis love; Cricket a duck; N. English nowt; informal zilch, nix, not a dicky bird; Brit. informal sweet Fanny Adams, sweet FA, not a sausage; N. Amer. informal zip, nada, a goose egg.

nimble adjective **1** *he was nimble on his feet:* **agile**, sprightly, light, spry, lively, quick, graceful, lithe, limber; skilful, deft, dexterous, adroit; informal nippy, twinkle-toed. **2** *a nimble mind:* **quick-witted**, quick, alert, lively, wide awake, observant, astute, perceptive, penetrating, discerning, shrewd, sharp; intelligent, bright, smart, clever, brilliant; informal brainy, quick on the uptake.
– OPPOSITES clumsy, dull.

nip verb **1** *the child nipped her:* **bite**, nibble, peck; pinch, tweak, squeeze, grip. **2** (Brit. informal) *I'm just nipping out:* **rush**, dash, dart, hurry, scurry, scamper; go; informal pop, whip.
noun *penguins can give a serious nip:* **bite**, peck, nibble; pinch, tweak.
■ **nip something in the bud** cut short, curtail, check, curb, thwart, frustrate, stop, halt, arrest, stifle, obstruct, block, squash, quash, subdue, crack down on, stamp out; informal put the kibosh on.
■ **nip something off** *carefully nip off older flowers:* cut, snip, trim, clip, prune, lop, dock, crop; remove, take off.

nipple noun **teat**, dug; Anatomy mamilla.

nippy adjective (informal) **1** *he's too big to be nippy:* **agile**, light-footed, nimble, light on one's feet, spry, supple, limber; informal twinkle-toed; literary lightsome. **2** *a nippy hatchback:* **fast**, quick, lively; informal zippy. **3** *it's a bit nippy in here:* **cold**, chilly, icy, bitter, raw.
– OPPOSITES lumbering, slow, warm.

nirvana noun *there are no short cuts to nirvana:* **paradise**, heaven; bliss, ecstasy, joy, peace, serenity, tranquillity; enlightenment.
– OPPOSITES hell.

nit-picking adjective (informal). See PEDANTIC.

nitty-gritty noun (informal) *now let's get down to the nitty-gritty of how the course is structured:* **basics**, essentials, essence, fundamentals, substance, quintessence, heart of the matter; nub, crux, gist, meat; informal brass tacks, nuts and bolts.

no adverb **absolutely not**, most certainly not, of course not, under no circumstances, by no means, not at all, negative, never, not really; informal nope, nah, not on your life, no way; Brit. informal no fear, not on your nelly.
– OPPOSITES yes.

nobility noun **1** *a member of the nobility:* **aristocracy**, aristocrats, peerage, peers (of the realm), lords, nobles, noblemen, noblewomen, patricians; informal aristos; Brit. informal nobs. **2** *the nobility of his deed:* **virtue**, goodness, honour, decency, integrity; magnanimity, generosity, selflessness.

noble adjective **1** *a noble family:* **aristocratic**,

n

patrician, blue-blooded, high-born, titled.
2 *a noble cause:* **righteous**, virtuous, good,
honourable, upright, decent, worthy,
moral, ethical, reputable; magnanimous,
unselfish, generous. **3** *a noble pine forest:*
magnificent, splendid, grand, stately,
imposing, dignified, proud, striking,
impressive, majestic, glorious, awesome,
monumental, statuesque, regal, imperial.
– OPPOSITES humble, dishonourable, base.
noun *Scottish nobles:* **aristocrat**, nobleman,
noblewoman, lord, lady, peer (of the realm),
peeress, patrician; informal aristo; Brit. informal
nob.

nod verb **1** *she nodded her head:* **incline**, bob,
bow, dip, wag. **2** *he nodded to me to start:*
signal, gesture, gesticulate, motion, sign,
indicate.
noun **1** *she gave a nod to the manager:* **signal**,
indication, sign, cue; gesture. **2** *a quick nod
of his head:* **inclination**, bob, bow, dip.
■ **give someone the nod 1** *the winger was
given the nod:* select, choose, pick, go for; Brit.
cap. **2** *the Lords will give the treaty the nod:*
approve, agree to, sanction, ratify, endorse,
rubber-stamp; informal OK, give something
the green light, give something the thumbs
up.
■ **nod off** *the audience began to nod off:* fall
asleep, go to sleep, doze off, drop off; informal
drift off, flake out, go out like a light; N. Amer.
informal sack out.

node noun *the intersection of two or more
such highways would become major traffic
nodes:* **junction**, intersection, interchange,
fork, confluence, convergence, crossing.

noise noun *she was dazed by the heat and the
noise:* **sound**, din, hubbub, clamour, racket,
uproar, tumult, commotion, pandemonium,
babel; informal hullabaloo; Brit. informal row.
– OPPOSITES silence.

noisy adjective **1** *a noisy crowd:* **rowdy**,
clamorous, boisterous, turbulent, rackety;
chattering, talkative, vociferous, shouting,
screaming. **2** *noisy music:* **loud**, fortissimo,
blaring, booming, deafening, thunderous,
tumultuous, clamorous, ear-splitting,
piercing, strident, cacophonous, raucous.
– OPPOSITES quiet, soft.

nomad noun *at the oasis we encountered
desert nomads:* **itinerant**, traveller, migrant,
wanderer, roamer, rover; gypsy, Bedouin;
transient, drifter, vagabond, vagrant, tramp.

nominal adjective **1** *the nominal head of the
campaign:* **in name only**, titular, formal,
official; theoretical, supposed, ostensible,
so-called. **2** *we only pay a nominal rent:*
token, symbolic; tiny, minute, minimal,
small, insignificant, trifling; Brit. peppercorn;
informal minuscule, piddling, piffling; N. Amer.
informal nickel-and-dime.
– OPPOSITES real, considerable.

nominate verb **1** *you may nominate a
candidate for leader:* **propose**, recommend,
suggest, name, put forward, present, submit.
2 *he nominated his own assistant:* **appoint**,

select, choose, elect, commission, designate,
name, delegate.

non-believer noun *I was an absolute
non-believer in spiritualism:* **unbeliever**,
disbeliever, sceptic, doubter, doubting
Thomas, cynic, nihilist; atheist, agnostic,
freethinker; infidel, pagan, heathen.

nonchalant adjective *he had tried to appear
nonchalant about the risks he was taking:*
calm, composed, unconcerned, cool, {cool,
calm, and collected}, cool as a cucumber;
indifferent, blasé, dispassionate, apathetic,
casual, insouciant; informal laid-back.
– OPPOSITES anxious.

non-combatant adjective *non-combatant
military advisers:* **non-fighting**, non-
participating, civilian; pacifist, neutral,
non-aligned.

non-committal adjective *she remained
silent, apart from a few non-committal
remarks:* **evasive**, equivocal, guarded,
circumspect, reserved; discreet,
uncommunicative, tactful, diplomatic,
vague; informal cagey.
■ **be non-committal** prevaricate, give
nothing away, dodge the issue, sidestep
the issue, hedge, fence, pussyfoot around,
beat about the bush, equivocate, temporize,
shilly-shally, vacillate, waver; Brit. hum and
haw; informal sit on the fence.

nonconformist noun *if the employees feel
industrial action is warranted they will
not tolerate nonconformists:* **dissenter**,
dissentient, protester, rebel, renegade,
schismatic; freethinker, apostate, heretic;
individualist, free spirit, maverick,
eccentric, original, deviant, misfit, dropout,
outsider; informal freak, oddball, odd fish,
weirdo; N. Amer. informal screwball, kook.

nondescript adjective *a little room
in a nondescript Victorian terraced
house:* **undistinguished**, unremarkable,
unexceptional, featureless, characterless,
unmemorable; ordinary, commonplace,
average, run-of-the-mill, mundane;
uninteresting, uninspiring, colourless,
bland; informal bog-standard; Brit. informal
common or garden.
– OPPOSITES distinctive.

none pronoun **1** *none of the fish are unusual:*
not one, not a one. **2** *none of this concerns
me:* **no part**, not a bit, not any. **3** *none can
know better than you:* **not one**, no one,
nobody, not a soul, not a single person, no
man.
– OPPOSITES all.
■ **none the ...** *we were left none the wiser:*
not at all, not a bit, not the slightest bit, in
no way, by no means any.

nonentity noun *without bargaining skills,
a president will be a nonentity in the White
House:* **nobody**, unimportant person, cipher,
non-person, nothing, small fry, lightweight,
mediocrity; informal no-hoper, non-starter.
– OPPOSITES celebrity.

non-essential adjective *killing seals for such non-essential products cannot be justified:* **unnecessary**, inessential, unessential, needless, unneeded, superfluous, uncalled for, redundant, dispensable, expendable, unimportant, extraneous.

nonetheless adverb *the rally which the government had declared illegal was, nonetheless, attended by some 6,000:* **nevertheless**, even so, however, but, still, yet, though; in spite of that, despite that, be that as it may, for all that, that said, just the same, all the same; notwithstanding, regardless, anyway, anyhow; informal still and all.

non-existent adjective *she carefully brushed a non-existent piece of lint from her skirt:* **imaginary**, imagined, unreal, fictional, fictitious, made up, invented, fanciful; fantastic, mythical; illusory, hallucinatory, chimerical, notional, shadowy, insubstantial; missing, absent.
– OPPOSITES real.

non-intervention noun *the state opted for a neutral course of non-intervention:* **laissez-faire**, non-participation, non-interference, inaction, passivity, neutrality; live and let live.

non-observance noun *appropriate sanctions for non-observance:* **infringement**, breach, violation, contravention, transgression, non-compliance, infraction; dereliction, neglect.

nonplus verb *young Lewis seemed remarkably nonplussed by the whole affair:* **surprise**, stun, dumbfound, confound, take aback, disconcert, throw (off balance); puzzle, perplex, baffle, bemuse, bewilder; informal faze, flummox, stump, bamboozle, fox; N. Amer. informal discombobulate.

nonsense noun **1** *he was talking nonsense:* **rubbish**, balderdash, gibberish, claptrap, blarney, blather, garbage; informal hogwash, rot, guff, baloney, tripe, drivel, gobbledegook, bilge, bosh, bunk, hot air, piffle, poppycock, phooey, twaddle; Brit. informal cobblers, codswallop, tosh, double Dutch; Scottish & N. English informal havers; N. Amer. informal flapdoodle, bushwa, applesauce. **2** *she stands no nonsense:* **mischief**, naughtiness, bad behaviour, misbehaviour, misconduct, misdemeanour; pranks, tricks, clowning, buffoonery, funny business; informal tomfoolery, monkey business, shenanigans, hanky-panky; Brit. informal monkey tricks, jiggery-pokery. **3** *they dismissed the concept as a nonsense:* **absurdity**, folly, stupidity, ludicrousness, inanity, foolishness, idiocy, insanity, madness.
– OPPOSITES sense, wisdom.

nonsensical adjective **1** *her nonsensical way of talking:* **meaningless**, senseless, illogical. **2** *a nonsensical generalization:* **foolish**, insane, stupid, idiotic, illogical, irrational, senseless, absurd, silly, inane, hare-brained, ridiculous, ludicrous, preposterous; informal crazy, crackpot, nutty; Brit. informal daft.
– OPPOSITES logical, sensible.

non-stop adjective *non-stop entertainment:* **continuous**, constant, continual, perpetual, incessant, unceasing, ceaseless, uninterrupted, round-the-clock; unremitting, relentless, persistent.
– OPPOSITES occasional.
adverb *we worked non-stop:* **continuously**, continually, incessantly, unceasingly, ceaselessly, all the time, constantly, perpetually, round the clock, steadily, relentlessly, persistently; informal 24-7.
– OPPOSITES occasionally.

nook noun *the bookshop's maze of nooks and crannies:* **recess**, corner, alcove, niche, bay, inglenook, cavity, cubbyhole, pigeonhole; opening, gap, aperture; hideaway, hiding place, hideout, shelter; informal hidey-hole.

noon noun *the railway operates between noon and 5 p.m. daily:* **midday**, twelve o'clock, twelve hundred hours, twelve noon, high noon, noonday.

no one pronoun *there was no one about:* **nobody**, not a soul, not anyone, not a single person, never a one, none.

norm noun **1** *norms of diplomatic behaviour:* **convention**, standard; criterion, yardstick, benchmark, touchstone, rule, formula, pattern, guide, guideline, model, exemplar. **2** *such teams are now the norm:* **standard**, usual, the rule; normal, typical, average, unexceptional, par for the course, expected.

normal adjective **1** *they issue books in the normal way:* **usual**, standard, ordinary, customary, conventional, habitual, accustomed, expected, wonted; typical, stock, common, everyday, regular, routine, established, set, fixed, traditional. **2** *they're just a normal couple:* **ordinary**, average, typical, run-of-the-mill, middle-of-the-road, common, conventional, mainstream, unremarkable, unexceptional; N. Amer. garden-variety; informal bog-standard, a dime a dozen; Brit. informal common or garden; N. Amer. informal ornery. **3** *the man was not normal:* **sane**, in one's right mind, right in the head, of sound mind, compos mentis, lucid, rational, coherent; informal all there.
– OPPOSITES unusual, insane.

normality noun *after yesterday's bomb scare, normality returned to the town centre this morning:* **normalcy**, business as usual, the daily round; routine, order, regularity.

normally adverb **1** *she wanted to walk normally:* **naturally**, conventionally, ordinarily; as usual, as normal. **2** *normally we'd keep quiet about this:* **usually**, ordinarily, as a rule, generally, in general, mostly, for the most part, by and large, mainly, most of the time, on the whole; typically, customarily, traditionally.

north adjective *the north coast of the island:* **northern**, northerly, boreal.

nose noun **1** *a punch on the nose:* snout,

n

muzzle, proboscis, trunk; informal beak, conk, snoot, schnozzle, hooter, sniffer. **2** *a nose for scandal:* **instinct**, feeling, sixth sense, intuition, insight, perception. **3** *wine with a fruity nose:* **smell**, bouquet, aroma, fragrance, perfume, scent, odour. **4** *the plane's nose dipped:* nose cone, bow, prow, front end; informal droop-snoot.
verb **1** *the dog nosed the ball:* **nuzzle**, nudge, push. **2** *she's nosing into my business:* **pry**, inquire, poke about/around, interfere (in), meddle (in); be a busybody, stick/poke one's nose in; informal be nosy (about), snoop, Austral./NZ informal stickybeak. **3** *he nosed the car into the traffic:* **ease**, inch, edge, move, manoeuvre, steer, guide.
■ **by a nose** (only) just, barely, narrowly, by a hair's breadth, by the skin of one's teeth; informal by a whisker.
■ **nose around/about/round** *the others were no doubt nosing around the wreck:* investigate, explore, ferret (about/around), rummage, search; delve into, peer into; prowl around; informal snoop about/around/round.
■ **nose something out** *he has a rare gift of nosing out little-recorded composers:* detect, find, discover, bring to light, track down, dig up, ferret out, root out, uncover, unearth, sniff out.

nosedive noun *the plane went into a nosedive:* **dive**, descent, drop, plunge, plummet, fall.
– OPPOSITES climb, rise.
verb *the device nosedived to earth:* **dive**, plunge, pitch, drop, plummet.
– OPPOSITES soar, rise.

nosegay noun *she carried a nosegay of white roses:* **posy**, bouquet, bunch, spray, sprig, buttonhole, corsage, boutonnière, tussie-mussie.

nostalgia noun *I was overcome with acute nostalgia for my days at university:* **reminiscence**, remembrance, recollection; wistfulness, regret, sentimentality.

nostalgic adjective *the smell of the sea evoked nostalgic memories of childhood holidays:* **wistful**, evocative, romantic, sentimental; regretful, dewy-eyed, maudlin.

nostrum noun **1** *they have to prove that their nostrums work:* **medicine**, quack remedy, potion, elixir, panacea, cure-all, wonder drug; informal magic bullet. **2** *they just spout right-wing nostrums:* **magic formula**, recipe for success, remedy, cure, prescription, answer.

nosy adjective (informal) *nosy neighbours:* **prying**, inquisitive, curious, busybody, spying, eavesdropping, intrusive; informal snooping, snoopy.

notability noun *the village has always enjoyed notability:* **noteworthiness**, prominence, importance, significance, eminence; fame, renown, notoriety.

notable adjective **1** *notable examples of workmanship:* **noteworthy**, remarkable,

outstanding, important, significant, momentous, memorable; marked, striking, impressive; uncommon, unusual, special, exceptional, signal. **2** *a notable author:* **prominent**, important, well known, famous, famed, noted, distinguished, great, eminent, illustrious, respected, esteemed, renowned, celebrated, acclaimed, influential, prestigious, of note.
– OPPOSITES unremarkable, unknown.
noun *movie stars and other notables:* **celebrity**, public figure, VIP, personage, notability, dignitary, worthy, luminary; star, superstar, (big) name; informal celeb, somebody, bigwig, big shot, big cheese, big fish, megastar; Brit. informal nob; N. Amer. informal kahuna, high muck-a-muck.
– OPPOSITES nonentity.

notably adverb **1** *other countries, notably the USA:* **in particular**, particularly, especially, specially; primarily, principally. **2** *these are notably short-lived birds:* **remarkably**, especially, specially, very, extremely, exceptionally, singularly, particularly, peculiarly, distinctly, significantly, unusually, extraordinarily, uncommonly, incredibly, really, decidedly, surprisingly, conspicuously; informal seriously; Brit. informal jolly, dead.

notation noun **1** *the formula is written in algebraic notation:* **symbols**, alphabet, syllabary, script; code, cipher, hieroglyphics. **2** *there were several notations in the margin:* **annotation**, jotting, comment, footnote, entry, memo, gloss, explanation; historical scholium.

notch noun **1** *a notch in the end of the arrow:* **nick**, cut, incision, score, scratch, slit, snick, slot, groove, cleft, indentation. **2** *her opinion of Nick dropped a notch:* **degree**, level, rung, point, mark, measure, grade.
verb *notch the plank where each cord wraps round it:* **nick**, cut, score, incise, carve, scratch, slit, snick, gouge, groove, furrow.
■ **notch something up** *the champion notched up four wins and five draws:* score, achieve, attain, gain, earn, make; rack up, chalk up; register, record.

note noun **1** *she made a note in her diary:* **record**, entry, item, notation, jotting, memorandum, reminder, aide-memoire; informal memo. **2** *he will take notes of the meeting:* **minutes**, records, details; report, account, commentary, transcript, proceedings, transactions; synopsis, summary, outline. **3** *notes in the margins:* **annotation**, footnote, commentary, comment; marginalia, exegesis. **4** *he dropped me a note:* **message**, communication, letter, line. **5** (Brit.) *a £20 note:* **banknote**; N. Amer. bill; US informal greenback; (**notes**) paper money. **6** *this is worthy of note:* **attention**, consideration, notice, heed, observation, regard. **7** *a composer of note:* **distinction**, importance, eminence, prestige, fame, celebrity, acclaim, renown, repute, stature,

standing, consequence, account. **8** *there was a note of hopelessness in her voice*: **tone**, intonation, inflection, sound; hint, indication, sign, element, suggestion.
verb **1** *we will note your suggestion*: **bear in mind**, be mindful of, consider, observe, heed, take notice of, pay attention to, take in. **2** *the letter noted the ministers' concern*: **mention**, refer to, touch on, indicate, point out, make known, state. **3** *note the date in your diary*: **write down**, put down, jot down, take down, inscribe, enter, mark, record, register, pencil.

notebook noun **notepad**, exercise book; register, logbook, log, diary, daybook, journal, record; Brit. jotter, pocketbook; N. Amer. scratch pad; informal memo pad.

noted adjective *the district is noted for its boutiques and restaurants*: **renowned**, well known, famous, famed, prominent, celebrated; notable, of note, important, eminent, distinguished, illustrious, acclaimed, esteemed; of distinction, of repute.
– OPPOSITES unknown.

noteworthy adjective *other noteworthy features include the carved capitals of the chancel arch*: **notable**, interesting, significant, important; remarkable, impressive, striking, outstanding, memorable, unique, special; unusual, extraordinary, singular, rare.
– OPPOSITES unexceptional.

nothing noun **1** *there's nothing I can do*: **not a thing**, not anything, nil, zero; N. English nowt; informal zilch, sweet Fanny Adams, sweet FA, nix, not a dicky bird; Brit. informal damn all, not a sausage; N. Amer. informal zip, nada. **2** *forget it—it's nothing*: **a trifling matter**, a trifle; neither here nor there; informal no big deal. **3** *he treats her as nothing*: **a nobody**, an unimportant person, a nonentity, a cipher, a non-person; Brit. small beer. **4** *the share value fell to nothing*: **zero**, nought, 0; Tennis love; Cricket a duck.
– OPPOSITES something.

 ■ **be/have nothing to do with 1** *it has nothing to do with you*: be unconnected with, be unrelated to; be irrelevant to, be inapplicable to, be inapposite to. **2** *I'll have nothing to do with him*: avoid, have no truck with, have no contact with, steer clear of, give a wide berth to.
 ■ **for nothing 1** *she hosted the show for nothing*: free (of charge), gratis, without charge, at no cost; informal for free, on the house. **2** *all this trouble for nothing*: in vain, to no avail, to no purpose, with no result, needlessly, pointlessly.
 ■ **nothing but** *he's nothing but a nuisance*: merely, only, just, solely, simply, purely, no more than.

notice noun **1** *nothing escaped his notice*: **attention**, observation, awareness, consciousness, perception; regard, consideration, scrutiny; watchfulness, vigilance, attentiveness. **2** *a notice on the wall*: **poster**, bill, handbill, advertisement, announcement, bulletin; flyer, leaflet, pamphlet; sign, card; informal ad; Brit. informal advert. **3** *times may change without notice*: **notification**, (advance) warning, announcement; information, news, communication, word. **4** *I handed in my notice*: **resignation**. **5** *the film got bad notices*: **review**, write-up, critique, criticism; Brit. informal crit.
verb *I noticed that the door was open*: **observe**, perceive, note, see, discern, detect, spot, distinguish, mark, remark; Brit. informal clock.
– OPPOSITES overlook.

 ■ **take no notice (of)** ignore, pay no attention (to), disregard, pay no heed (to), take no account (of), brush aside, shrug off, turn a blind eye (to), pass over, let go, overlook, look the other way.

noticeable adjective *there has been a noticeable shift in public opinion*: **distinct**, evident, obvious, apparent, manifest, patent, plain, clear, marked, conspicuous, unmistakable, undeniable, pronounced, prominent, striking, arresting; perceptible, discernible, detectable, observable, visible, appreciable.

noticeboard noun **pinboard**, cork board, bulletin board; hoarding.

notification noun **1** *the notification of the victim's wife*: **informing**, telling, alerting. **2** *she received notification that he was on the way*: **information**, word, advice, news, intelligence; communication, message.

notify verb **1** *we will notify you as soon as possible*: **inform**, tell, advise, apprise, let someone know, put in the picture; alert, warn. **2** *births should be notified to the registrar*: **report**, make known, announce, declare, communicate, disclose.

notion noun **1** *he had a notion that something was wrong*: **idea**, belief, conviction, opinion, view, thought, impression, perception; hypothesis, theory; (funny) feeling, (sneaking) suspicion, hunch. **2** *Claire had no notion of what he meant*: **understanding**, idea, awareness, knowledge, clue, inkling. **3** *he got a notion to return*: **impulse**, inclination, whim, desire, wish, fancy.

notional adjective *the notional dividing line between the eastern and western zones*: **hypothetical**, theoretical, speculative, conjectural, suppositional, putative, conceptual; imaginary, fanciful, unreal, illusory.
– OPPOSITES actual.

notoriety noun *the book earned him undeserved notoriety*: **infamy**, disrepute, ill repute, bad name, dishonour, discredit.

notorious adjective *the country's most notorious drug trafficker*: **infamous**, scandalous; well known, famous, famed, legendary.

n

notwithstanding preposition
*notwithstanding his workload, he is a
dedicated father:* **despite**, in spite of,
regardless of, for all.
adverb *she is bright—notwithstanding, she
is now jobless:* **nevertheless**, nonetheless,
even so, all the same, in spite of this, despite
this, however, still, yet, that said, just the
same, anyway, in any event, at any rate.
conjunction *notwithstanding that there was
no space, they played on:* **although**, even
though, though, in spite of the fact that,
despite the fact that.

nought noun *the batsman was out for nought:*
nil, zero, 0; Tennis love; Cricket a duck.

nourish verb **1** *patients must be well
nourished:* **feed**, provide for, sustain,
maintain. **2** *we nourish the talents of
children:* **encourage**, promote, foster,
nurture, cultivate, stimulate, boost, advance,
assist, help, aid, strengthen, enrich. **3** *the
hopes Ursula nourished:* **cherish**, nurture,
foster, harbour, nurse, entertain, maintain,
hold, have.

nourishing adjective *eating regular,
nourishing meals is important to keep
yourself fit and well:* **nutritious**, nutritive,
wholesome, good for one, healthy, health-
giving, healthful, beneficial, sustaining.
– OPPOSITES unhealthy.

nourishment noun *tubers from which
plants obtain nourishment:* **food**,
sustenance, nutriment, nutrition,
subsistence, provisions, provender, fare;
informal grub, nosh, chow, eats; Brit. informal
scoff; N. Amer. informal chuck.

nouveau riche plural noun *the nouveau riche
of today buy leather-covered volumes by the
metre:* **the new rich**, parvenus, arrivistes,
upstarts, social climbers, vulgarians.

novel[1] noun *curl up with a good novel:* **book**,
paperback, hardback; **story**, tale, narrative,
romance; best-seller; informal blockbuster.

novel[2] adjective *a novel way of making
money:* **new**, original, unusual, unfamiliar,
unconventional, unorthodox; different,
fresh, imaginative, innovative, innovatory,
innovational, inventive, modern, neoteric,
avant-garde, pioneering, groundbreaking,
revolutionary; rare, unique, singular,
unprecedented; experimental, untested,
untried; strange, exotic, newfangled.
– OPPOSITES traditional.

novelty noun **1** *the novelty of our
approach:* **originality**, newness, freshness,
unconventionality, unfamiliarity;
difference, imaginativeness, creativity,
innovation, modernity. **2** *we sell seasonal
novelties:* **knick-knack**, trinket, bauble, toy,
trifle, gewgaw, gimcrack, ornament; N. Amer.
kickshaw.

novice noun **1** *a five-day course for novices:*
beginner, learner, neophyte, newcomer,
initiate, tyro, fledgling; apprentice,
trainee, probationer, student, pupil; N. Amer.

tenderfoot; informal rookie, newie, newbie;
N. Amer. informal greenhorn. **2** *novices in the
convent do not wear the full nuns' habit:*
neophyte, novitiate; postulant, proselyte,
catechumen.
– OPPOSITES expert, veteran.

novitiate noun **1** *a three-year novitiate:*
probationary period, probation, trial
period, test period, apprenticeship, training
period, traineeship, training, initiation.
2 *two young novitiates:* **novice**, neophyte;
postulant, proselyte, catechumen.

now adverb **1** *I'm extremely busy now:* **at
the moment**, at present, at the present
(time/moment), at this moment in time,
currently; N. Amer. presently; Brit. informal at the
minute. **2** *television is now the main source
of news:* **nowadays**, today, these days, in
this day and age; in the present climate.
3 *you must leave now:* **at once**, straight away,
right away, right now, this minute, this
instant, immediately, instantly, directly,
without further ado, promptly, without
delay, as soon as possible; informal pronto,
a.s.a.p., straight off.
■ **as of now** from this time on, from now
on, henceforth, henceforward, from this day
forward, in future; formal hereafter.
■ **for now** for the time being, for the
moment, for the present, for the meantime.
■ **not now** later (on), sometime, one day,
some day, one of these days, sooner or
later, in due course, by and by, eventually,
ultimately.
■ **now and again** occasionally, now and
then, from time to time, sometimes, every
so often, (every) now and again, at times,
on occasion(s), (every) once in a while;
periodically, once in a blue moon.

nowadays adverb *nowadays all graduates
are computer-literate:* **these days**, today,
at the present time, in these times, in this
day and age, now, currently, at the moment,
at present, at this moment in time; in the
present climate; N. Amer. presently.

noxious adjective *noxious fumes:* **poisonous**,
toxic, deadly, harmful, dangerous,
pernicious, damaging, destructive;
unpleasant, nasty, disgusting, awful,
dreadful, horrible, terrible; vile, revolting,
foul, nauseating, appalling, offensive;
malodorous, fetid, putrid; informal ghastly,
horrid.
– OPPOSITES innocuous.

nuance noun *the expression of subtle
nuances of thought:* **fine distinction**, subtle
difference; shade, shading, gradation,
variation, degree; subtlety, nicety, overtone.

nub noun *the nub of his argument:* **crux**,
central point, main point, core, heart (of
the matter); nucleus, essence, quintessence,
kernel, marrow, meat, pith; gist, substance;
informal nitty-gritty.

nubile adjective *a nubile young girl:* **sexually
mature**, marriageable; sexually attractive,
desirable, sexy, luscious; informal beddable.

nucleus noun **1** *the nucleus of the banking world:* **core**, centre, central part, heart, nub, hub, middle, eye, focus, focal point, pivot, crux. **2** *a nucleus of union men supported him:* **small group**, caucus, cell, coterie, clique, faction.

nude adjective *a painting of a nude model:* **(stark) naked**, bare, unclothed, undressed, disrobed, stripped, unclad, in a state of nature, au naturel; informal without a stitch on, in one's birthday suit, in the raw, in the altogether, in the buff, in the nuddy; Brit. informal starkers; Scottish informal in the scud; N. Amer. informal buck naked.
– OPPOSITES clothed.

nudge verb **1** *he nudged Ben:* **poke**, elbow, dig, prod, jog, jab. **2** *the canoe nudged a bank:* **touch**, bump (against), push (against), run into. **3** *we nudged them into action:* **prompt**, encourage, stimulate, prod, galvanize. **4** *unemployment was nudging 3,000,000:* **approach**, near, come close to, be verging on, border on.
noun **1** *Maggie gave him a nudge:* **poke**, dig (in the ribs), prod, jog, jab, push. **2** *after a nudge, she remembered Lilian:* **reminder**, prompt, prompting, prod, encouragement.

nugget noun **lump**, nub, chunk, piece, hunk, wad, gobbet; N. Amer. informal gob.

nuisance noun *don't you find these long journeys a nuisance?* **annoyance**, inconvenience, bore, bother, irritation, problem, trouble, trial, burden; pest, plague, thorn in one's side/flesh; informal pain (in the neck), hassle, bind, drag, aggravation, headache; Scottish informal nyaff, skelf; N. Amer. informal nudnik; Austral./NZ informal nark.
– OPPOSITES blessing.

null adjective *their marriage was declared null:* **invalid**, null and void, void; annulled, nullified, cancelled, revoked.
– OPPOSITES valid.

nullify verb **1** *they nullified the legislation:* **annul**, render null and void, void, invalidate; repeal, reverse, rescind, revoke, cancel, abolish; countermand, do away with, terminate, quash; Law vacate. **2** *the costs would nullify any tax relief:* **cancel out**, wipe out, neutralize, negate, negative.
– OPPOSITES ratify.

numb adjective *his fingers were numb:* **without sensation**, without feeling, numbed, benumbed, desensitized, insensible, senseless, unfeeling; anaesthetized; dazed, stunned, stupefied, paralysed, immobilized, frozen.
– OPPOSITES sensitive.
verb *the cold numbed her senses:* **deaden**, benumb, desensitize, dull; anaesthetize; daze, stupefy, paralyse, immobilize, freeze.
– OPPOSITES sensitize.

number noun **1** *a whole number:* **numeral**, integer, figure, digit; character, symbol; decimal, unit; cardinal number, ordinal number. **2** *a large number of complaints:* **amount**, quantity; total, aggregate, tally; quota. **3** *the wedding of one of their number:* **group**, company, crowd, circle, party, band, crew, set; informal gang. **4** *the band performed another number:* **song**, piece (of music), tune, track; routine, sketch, dance, act.
verb **1** *visitors numbered more than two million:* **add up to**, amount to, total, come to. **2** *he numbers the fleet at a thousand:* **calculate**, count, total, compute, reckon, tally; assess; Brit. tot up. **3** *each paragraph is numbered:* **assign a number to**, mark with a number; itemize, enumerate. **4** *he numbers her among his friends:* **include**, count, reckon, deem. **5** *his days are numbered:* **limit**, restrict, fix.
■ **a number of** several, various, quite a few, sundry.
■ **without number** countless, innumerable, unlimited, endless, limitless, untold, numberless, uncountable, uncounted; numerous, many, multiple, manifold, legion.

numberless adjective *there are numberless questions to be answered:* **innumerable**, countless, unlimited, endless, limitless, untold, uncountable, uncounted; numerous, many, multiple, manifold, myriad, legion; informal more … than one can shake a stick at.

numbing adjective **1** *menthol has a numbing action:* **desensitizing**, deadening, benumbing, anaesthetic, anaesthetizing; paralysing. **2** *numbing cold:* **freezing**, raw, bitter, biting, arctic. **3** *numbing boredom:* **stupefying**, mind-numbing, stultifying; soporific.

numeral noun **number**, integer, figure, digit; character, symbol, unit.

numerous adjective *numerous studies have been published on the subject:* **(very) many**, a lot of, scores of, myriad, countless, numberless, innumerable; several, quite a few, various; plenty of, copious, a quantity of, an abundance of, a profusion of, a multitude of; frequent; informal umpteen, lots of, loads of, masses of, stacks of, heaps of, bags of, bucketloads of, tons of, oodles of, hundreds of, thousands of, millions of, more … than one can shake a stick at; Brit. informal a shedload of; N. Amer. informal gazillions of; Austral./NZ informal a swag of.
– OPPOSITES few.

nun noun **sister**, abbess, prioress, Mother Superior, Reverend Mother; novice; bride of Christ.

nuncio noun **(papal) ambassador**, legate, envoy, messenger.

nunnery noun **convent**, priory, abbey, cloister, religious community.

nuptial adjective *the nuptial festivities:* **matrimonial**, marital, marriage, wedding, conjugal, bridal; married, wedded.

nuptials plural noun *Queen Sofia arrived in Seville yesterday for her daughter's nuptials:* **wedding (ceremony)**, marriage, union.

nurse noun **1** *skilled nurses:* **carer**, caregiver;

n

informal Florence Nightingale, nursey; N. Amer. informal candy-striper. **2** *she had been his nurse in childhood:* **nanny**, nursemaid, nursery nurse, childminder, governess, au pair, childcarer, babysitter, ayah.
▸ verb **1** *they nursed smallpox patients:* **care for**, take care of, look after, tend, minister to. **2** *I nursed my sore finger:* **treat**, medicate, tend; dress, bandage, soothe; informal doctor. **3** *Rosa was nursing her baby:* **breastfeed**, suckle, feed. **4** *they nursed old grievances:* **harbour**, foster, entertain, bear, have, hold (on to), cherish, cling to, retain. **5** *our unity needs to be nursed:* **nurture**, encourage, promote, boost, assist, help, cultivate; protect, safeguard.

nurture verb **1** *she nurtured her children into adulthood:* **bring up**, care for, take care of, look after, tend, rear, raise, support, foster; parent, mother. **2** *we nurtured these plants:* **cultivate**, grow, keep, tend. **3** *he nurtured my love of art:* **encourage**, promote, stimulate, develop, foster, cultivate, boost, contribute to, assist, help, abet, strengthen, fuel.
– OPPOSITES neglect, hinder.
▸ noun **1** *we are what nature and nurture have made us:* **upbringing**, rearing, raising, childcare; training, education. **2** *the nurture of ideas:* **encouragement**, promotion, fostering, development, cultivation.
– OPPOSITES nature.

nut noun **1** *nuts in their shells:* **kernel**. **2** (informal) *some nut arrived at the office:* **maniac**, lunatic, madman, madwoman; eccentric; informal loony, nutcase, fruitcake, head case, crank, crackpot, weirdo; Brit. informal nutter, mentalist; N. Amer. informal screwball, crazy; N. Amer. & Austral./NZ informal dingbat.

nutriment noun *the egg contains sufficient nutriment for the chick up to the time of hatching:* **nourishment**, nutrients, sustenance, goodness, nutrition, food.

nutrition noun *the child was not receiving sufficient nutrition:* **nourishment**, nutriment, nutrients, sustenance, food; informal grub, chow, nosh; Brit. informal scoff.

nutritious adjective *porridge is both cheap and nutritious:* **nourishing**, good for one, full of nutrients, nutritive, nutrimental; wholesome, healthy, healthful, beneficial, sustaining.

nuts and bolts plural noun *the nuts and bolts of running an airline:* **practical details**, fundamentals, basics, practicalities, essentials, mechanics; informal nitty-gritty, ins and outs, brass tacks.

nuzzle verb **1** *the horse nuzzled at her pocket:* **nudge**, nose, prod, push. **2** *she nuzzled up to her boyfriend:* **snuggle**, cuddle, nestle, burrow, embrace, hug.

nymph noun *a nymph with winged sandals:* **sprite**, sylph, spirit.

n

Oo

oaf noun *the thoughtless actions of a few loud-mouthed oafs:* **lout**, boor, barbarian, Neanderthal, churl, bumpkin, yokel; fool, idiot, imbecile; informal cretin, ass, goon, oik, yahoo, ape, lump, clod, meathead, bonehead, lamebrain; Brit. informal muppet, clot, plonker, berk, pillock, yob, yobbo; Scottish informal nyaff, gowk; N. Amer. informal bozo, dumbhead, lummox, klutz, goofus, clunk, turkey; Austral. informal hoon, dingbat, galah, drongo.

oafish adjective *her oafish idiot of a son:* **stupid**, foolish, idiotic; loutish, awkward, gawkish, clumsy, lumbering, ape-like, cloddish, Neanderthal, uncouth, uncultured, boorish, rough, coarse, brutish, ill-mannered, unrefined; informal clodhopping, blockheaded, boneheaded, thickheaded; Brit. informal yobbish.

oasis noun **1** *an oasis near Cairo:* **watering hole**, watering place, water hole, spring. **2** *a cool oasis in a hot summer:* **refuge**, haven, retreat, sanctuary, sanctum, harbour, asylum.

oath noun **1** *an oath of allegiance:* **vow**, pledge, promise, avowal, affirmation, word (of honour), bond, guarantee. **2** *he uttered a stream of oaths:* **swear word**, profanity, expletive, four-letter word, dirty word, obscenity, vulgarity, curse, malediction; informal cuss (word).

obedient adjective *Lucinda had always been very obedient:* **compliant**, biddable, acquiescent, tractable, amenable, malleable, pliable, pliant; dutiful, good, law-abiding, deferential, respectful, duteous, well trained, well disciplined, manageable, governable, docile, tame, meek, passive, submissive, unresisting, yielding.
– OPPOSITES rebellious.

obeisance noun **1** *a gesture of obeisance:* **respect**, homage, worship, adoration, reverence, veneration, honour, submission, deference. **2** *she made a deep obeisance:* **bow**, curtsy, bob, genuflection, salaam.

obelisk noun **column**, pillar, needle, shaft, monolith, monument.

obese adjective *he ate excessively and became obese:* **fat**, overweight, corpulent, gross, stout, fleshy, heavy, portly, paunchy, well upholstered, well padded, broad in the beam, bulky, bloated, flabby; informal porky, blubbery; Brit. informal podgy.
– OPPOSITES thin.

obey verb **1** *I obeyed him without question:* **do what someone says**, carry out someone's orders; submit to, defer to, bow to, yield to. **2** *he refused to obey the order:* **carry out**, perform, act on, execute, discharge, implement, fulfil. **3** *health and safety regulations have to be obeyed:* **comply with**, adhere to, observe, abide by, act in accordance with, conform to, respect, follow, keep to, stick to; play it by the book, toe the line.
– OPPOSITES defy, ignore.

obfuscate verb *the debate all too often obfuscates the issue:* **obscure**, confuse, blur, muddle, complicate, muddy, cloud, befog; muddy the waters.
– OPPOSITES clarify.

object noun **1** *wooden objects:* **thing**, article, item, device, gadget; informal doodah, thingamajig, thingamabob, thingummy, whatsit, whatchamacallit, thingy; Brit. informal gubbins; N. Amer. informal doodad, dingus. **2** *he became the object of criticism:* **target**, butt, focus, recipient, victim. **3** *his object was to resolve the crisis:* **objective**, aim, goal, target, purpose, end (in view), plan, object of the exercise, point; ambition, design, intent, intention, idea.
verb *teachers objected to the scheme:* **protest about**, oppose, raise objections to, express disapproval of, take exception to, take issue with, take a stand against, argue against, quarrel with, condemn, draw the line at, demur at, mind, complain about, cavil at, quibble about; beg to differ; informal kick up a fuss/stink about.
– OPPOSITES approve, accept.

objection noun *the search was carried out regardless of her objections:* **protest**, protestation, demur, demurral, complaint, expostulation, grievance, cavil, quibble; opposition, argument, counter-argument, disagreement, disapproval, dissent; informal niggle.

objectionable adjective *he was one of the most objectionable people I had ever met:* **unpleasant**, disagreeable, distasteful, displeasing, off-putting, undesirable, obnoxious, offensive, nasty, horrible, horrid, disgusting, awful, terrible, dreadful, frightful, appalling, insufferable, odious, vile, foul, unsavoury, repulsive, repellent, repugnant, revolting, abhorrent, loathsome, hateful, detestable, reprehensible,

o

deplorable; informal ghastly; Brit. informal beastly.
– OPPOSITES pleasant.

objective adjective **1** *an interviewer must try to be objective:* **impartial**, unbiased, unprejudiced, non-partisan, disinterested, neutral, uninvolved, even-handed, equitable, fair, fair-minded, just, open-minded, dispassionate, detached. **2** *the world of objective knowledge:* **factual**, actual, real, empirical, verifiable.
– OPPOSITES biased, subjective.
noun *our objective is to build a profitable business:* **aim**, intention, purpose, target, goal, intent, object, object of the exercise, point, end (in view); idea, design, plan, ambition, aspiration, desire, hope.

objectively adverb *the bank will do all it can to investigate your complaint objectively:* **impartially**, without bias, without prejudice, even-handedly, dispassionately, detachedly, equitably, fairly, justly, with an open mind, without fear or favour.

objectivity noun **impartiality**, lack of bias/prejudice, fairness, fair-mindedness, neutrality, even-handedness, justice, open-mindedness, disinterest, detachment, dispassion, dispassionateness.
– OPPOSITES bias, subjectivity.

oblation noun *the priest spread his hands over the oblation:* **religious offering**, offering, sacrifice, peace offering, burnt offering, first fruits, libation.

obligate verb *the medical establishment is obligated to take action in the best interests of the public:* **oblige**, compel, commit, bind, require, constrain, force, impel, make.

obligation noun **1** *his professional obligations:* **duty**, commitment, responsibility; function, task, job, assignment, commission, burden, charge, onus, liability, accountability, requirement, debt. **2** *a sense of obligation:* **duty**, compulsion, indebtedness; duress, necessity, pressure, constraint.
■ **under an obligation** beholden, obliged, in someone's debt, indebted, obligated, owing someone a debt of gratitude, duty-bound, honour-bound.

obligatory adjective *use of seat belts in cars is now obligatory:* **compulsory**, mandatory, prescribed, required, demanded, statutory, enforced, binding, incumbent; requisite, necessary, imperative, unavoidable, inescapable, essential.
– OPPOSITES optional.

oblige verb **1** *both parties are obliged to accept the decision:* **require**, compel, bind, constrain, obligate, leave someone no option, force. **2** *I'll be happy to oblige you:* **do someone a favour**, accommodate, help, assist, serve; gratify someone's wishes, indulge, humour.

obliged adjective *if you hear from her, I'd be obliged if you'd let me know:* **thankful**, grateful, appreciative; beholden, indebted, in someone's debt.

obliging adjective *he was a cheerful, obliging sort of chap:* **helpful**, accommodating, willing, cooperative, considerate, complaisant, agreeable, amenable, generous, kind, neighbourly, hospitable, pleasant, good-natured, amiable, gracious, unselfish, civil, courteous, polite; Brit. informal decent.
– OPPOSITES unhelpful.

oblique adjective **1** *he drew an oblique line on the graph:* **slanting**, slanted, sloping, at an angle, angled, diagonal, aslant, slant, slantwise, skew, on the skew, askew, squint; N. Amer. cater-cornered. **2** *an oblique reference to what had gone before:* **indirect**, inexplicit, roundabout, circuitous, circumlocutory, implicit, implied, elliptical, evasive, backhanded. **3** *an oblique glance:* **sidelong**, sideways, furtive, covert, sly, surreptitious.
– OPPOSITES straight, direct.
noun **slash**, solidus, backslash, diagonal, virgule.

obliquely adverb **1** *the sun shone obliquely across the tower:* **diagonally**, at an angle, slantwise, sideways, sidelong, aslant. **2** *he referred obliquely to the war:* **indirectly**, in a roundabout way, not in so many words, circuitously, evasively.

obliterate verb **1** *he tried to obliterate the memory:* **erase**, eradicate, expunge, efface, wipe out, blot out, rub out, remove all traces of. **2** *a nuclear explosion that would obliterate a city:* **destroy**, wipe out, annihilate, demolish, liquidate, wipe off the face of the earth, wipe off the map; informal zap. **3** *clouds were darkening, obliterating the sun:* **hide**, obscure, blot out, block, cover, screen.

oblivion noun *they rescued him from artistic oblivion:* **obscurity**, limbo, anonymity, neglect, disregard.
– OPPOSITES fame.

oblivious adjective *she was totally oblivious to her surroundings:* **unaware**, unconscious, heedless, unmindful, insensible, unheeding, ignorant, blind, deaf, unsuspecting, unobservant; unconcerned, impervious, unaffected.
– OPPOSITES conscious.

obnoxious adjective *a thoroughly obnoxious man:* **unpleasant**, disagreeable, nasty, distasteful, offensive, objectionable, unsavoury, unpalatable, awful, terrible, dreadful, frightful, revolting, repulsive, repellent, repugnant, disgusting, odious, vile, foul, abhorrent, loathsome, nauseating, sickening, hateful, insufferable, intolerable; informal horrible, horrid, ghastly, gross, putrid, sick-making, yucky, God-awful; Brit. informal beastly.
– OPPOSITES delightful.

obscene adjective **1** *obscene literature:* **pornographic**, indecent, smutty, dirty, filthy, X-rated, adult, explicit, lewd, rude, vulgar, coarse, crude, immoral, improper, off colour; scatological, profane; informal

o

blue, porn, porno, skin. **2** *an obscene crime:* **shocking**, scandalous, vile, foul, atrocious, outrageous, heinous, odious, abhorrent, abominable, disgusting, hideous, repugnant, repulsive, revolting, repellent, loathsome, nauseating, sickening, awful, dreadful, terrible, frightful.

obscenity noun **1** *the book was banned on the grounds of obscenity:* **indecency**, immorality, impropriety, smuttiness, smut, lewdness, rudeness, vulgarity, dirt, filth, coarseness, crudity; profanity, profaneness. **2** *the men scowled and muttered obscenities:* **expletive**, swear word, oath, profanity, curse, four-letter word, dirty word, blasphemy; informal cuss, cuss word.

obscure adjective **1** *his origins and parentage remain obscure:* **unclear**, uncertain, unknown, in doubt, doubtful, dubious, mysterious, hazy, vague, indeterminate, concealed, hidden. **2** *obscure references to Proust:* **mystifying**, puzzling, perplexing, baffling, ambiguous, cryptic, enigmatic, Delphic, oracular, oblique, opaque, elliptical, unintelligible, incomprehensible, impenetrable, unfathomable; abstruse, recondite, arcane, esoteric; informal as clear as mud. **3** *an obscure Peruvian painter:* **little known**, unknown, unheard of, undistinguished, unimportant, nameless, minor; unsung, unrecognized, forgotten.
– OPPOSITES clear, plain, famous.
verb **1** *grey clouds obscured the sun:* **hide**, conceal, cover, veil, shroud, screen, mask, cloak, cast a shadow over, shadow, block, obliterate, eclipse, darken. **2** *recent events have obscured the issue:* **confuse**, complicate, obfuscate, cloud, blur, muddy; muddy the waters.
– OPPOSITES reveal, clarify.

obscurity noun **1** *the discovery rescued him from relative obscurity:* **insignificance**, inconspicuousness, unimportance, anonymity; limbo, twilight, oblivion. **2** *poems of impenetrable obscurity:* **incomprehensibility**, impenetrability, unintelligibility, opacity. **3** *the obscurities in his poems and plays:* **enigma**, puzzle, mystery, difficulty, problem.
– OPPOSITES fame, clarity.

obsequious adjective *an obsequious manservant welcomed them:* **servile**, ingratiating, sycophantic, fawning, unctuous, oily, oleaginous, grovelling, cringing, subservient, submissive, slavish; informal slimy, bootlicking, smarmy.

observable adjective *this behaviour is readily observable in all wild creatures:* **noticeable**, visible, perceptible, perceivable, detectable, distinguishable, discernible, recognizable, evident, apparent, manifest, obvious, patent, clear, distinct, plain, unmistakable.

observance noun **1** *strict observance of the rules:* **compliance**, adherence, accordance, respect, observation, fulfilment, obedience; keeping, obeying. **2** *religious observances:* **rite**, ritual, ceremony, ceremonial, celebration, practice, service, office, festival, tradition, custom, usage, formality, form.

observant adjective *lifeguards should be observant and stop risky situations before they start:* **alert**, sharp-eyed, sharp, eagle-eyed, hawk-eyed, having eyes like a hawk, keen-eyed, watchful, heedful, aware; on the lookout, on the qui vive, on guard, attentive, vigilant, having one's eyes open/peeled; informal beady-eyed, not missing a trick, on the ball.
– OPPOSITES inattentive.

observation noun **1** *detailed observation of the animal's behaviour:* **monitoring**, watching, scrutiny, examination, inspection, survey, surveillance, attention, consideration, study. **2** *his observations were concise and to the point:* **remark**, comment, statement, utterance, pronouncement, declaration; opinion, impression, thought, reflection. **3** *the observation of the law:* **observance**, compliance, adherence, respect, obedience; keeping, obeying.

observe verb **1** *she observed that all the chairs were occupied:* **notice**, see, note, perceive, discern, spot. **2** *she was alarmed to discover he had been observing her:* **watch**, look at, eye, contemplate, view, survey, regard, keep an eye on, scrutinize, keep under observation, keep watch on, keep under surveillance, monitor, keep a weather eye on; informal keep tabs on, keep a beady eye on. **3** *'You look tired,' she observed:* **remark**, comment, say, mention, declare, announce, state, pronounce. **4** *both countries agreed to observe the ceasefire:* **comply with**, abide by, keep, obey, adhere to, heed, honour, fulfil, respect, follow, consent to, acquiesce in, accept. **5** *townspeople observed the one-year anniversary of the flood:* **commemorate**, mark, keep, memorialize, remember, celebrate.

observer noun **1** *a casual observer might not have noticed:* **spectator**, onlooker, watcher, looker-on, fly on the wall, viewer, witness; informal rubberneck. **2** *industry observers expect the deal to be finalized today:* **commentator**, reporter; monitor.

obsess verb **preoccupy**, be uppermost in someone's mind, prey on someone's mind, prey on, possess, haunt, consume, plague, torment, hound, bedevil, beset, take control of, take over, have a hold on, eat up, grip.

obsessed adjective *he became obsessed by the urge to avenge his friend:* **fixated**, possessed, consumed; infatuated, besotted; informal smitten, hung up; N. Amer. informal hipped.

obsession noun *the idea grew in his mind until it became an obsession:* **fixation**, ruling/consuming passion, passion, mania, idée fixe, compulsion, preoccupation, infatuation, addiction, fetish, craze; hobby horse; phobia, complex, neurosis; informal bee in one's bonnet, hang-up, thing.

o

obsessive adjective *reckless and obsessive love:* **all-consuming**, consuming, compulsive, controlling, obsessional, fanatical, neurotic, excessive, besetting, tormenting, inescapable; informal pathological.

obsolescent adjective *industries regarded by policy makers as obsolescent:* **dying out**, on the decline, declining, waning, on the wane, disappearing, past its prime, ageing, moribund, on its last legs, out of date, outdated, old-fashioned, outmoded; informal on the way out, past it.

obsolete adjective *the phrase was obsolete after 1625:* **out of date**, outdated, outmoded, old-fashioned, démodé, passé; no longer in use, disused, fallen into disuse, superannuated, outworn, antiquated, antediluvian, anachronistic, discontinued, old, dated, archaic, ancient, fossilized, extinct, defunct, dead, bygone; informal out of the ark, prehistoric; Brit. informal past its sell-by date.
– OPPOSITES current, modern.

obstacle noun *the major obstacle to achieving that goal is money:* **barrier**, hurdle, stumbling block, obstruction, bar, block, impediment, hindrance, snag, catch, drawback, hitch, handicap, deterrent, complication, difficulty, problem, disadvantage, curb, check; informal fly in the ointment; Brit. informal spanner in the works.
– OPPOSITES advantage, aid.

obstinacy noun **stubbornness**, inflexibility, intransigence, intractability, obduracy, mulishness, pig-headedness, wilfulness, contrariness, perversity, recalcitrance, implacability; persistence, tenacity, tenaciousness, doggedness, single-mindedness, determination; Brit. informal bloody-mindedness, bolshiness.

obstinate adjective *her obstinate determination to pursue a career in radio:* **stubborn**, unyielding, inflexible, unbending, intransigent, intractable, obdurate, mulish, stubborn as a mule, pig-headed, self-willed, strong-willed, headstrong, wilful, contrary, perverse, recalcitrant, uncooperative, unmanageable, stiff-necked, uncompromising, implacable, unrelenting, immovable, unshakeable; persistent, tenacious, dogged, single-minded, adamant, determined; Brit. informal bloody-minded, bolshie; N. Amer. informal balky.
– OPPOSITES compliant.

obstreperous adjective *obstreperous customers who have had a drop too much to drink:* **unruly**, unmanageable, disorderly, undisciplined, uncontrollable, rowdy, disruptive, truculent, difficult, rebellious, mutinous, riotous, out of control, wild, turbulent, uproarious, boisterous; noisy, loud, clamorous, raucous, vociferous; Brit. informal stroppy, bolshie, rumbustious; N. Amer. informal rambunctious.
– OPPOSITES quiet, restrained.

obstruct verb **1** *ensure that air bricks and vents are not obstructed:* **block (up)**, clog (up), get in the way of, occlude, cut off, shut off, bung up, choke, dam up; barricade, bar; Brit. informal gunge up. **2** *he was charged with obstructing the traffic:* **hold up**, bring to a standstill, stop, halt, block. **3** *fears that the regime would obstruct the distribution of food:* **impede**, hinder, interfere with, hamper, block, interrupt, hold up, stand in the way of, frustrate, thwart, baulk, inhibit, hamstring, sabotage; slow down, retard, delay, stonewall, stop, halt, restrict, limit, curb, put a brake on, bridle; N. Amer. informal bork.
– OPPOSITES clear, facilitate.

obstruction noun *the issue was the major obstruction to progress:* **obstacle**, barrier, stumbling block, hurdle, bar, block, impediment, hindrance, snag, difficulty, catch, drawback, hitch, handicap, deterrent, curb, check, restriction; blockage, stoppage, congestion, bottleneck, hold-up; informal fly in the ointment; Brit. informal spanner in the works.

obstructive adjective *you're being deliberately obstructive!* **unhelpful**, uncooperative, awkward, difficult, unaccommodating, disobliging, perverse, contrary; Brit. informal bloody-minded, bolshie; N. Amer. informal balky.
– OPPOSITES helpful.

obtain verb *the newspaper obtained a copy of the letter:* **get**, acquire, come by, secure, procure, come into the possession of, pick up, be given; gain, earn, achieve, attain; informal get hold of, get/lay one's hands on, get one's mitts on, land.
– OPPOSITES lose.

obtainable adjective *frozen food is acceptable if fresh vegetable or meat are not obtainable:* **available**, to be had, in circulation, on the market, on offer, in season, at one's disposal, at hand, attainable, procurable, accessible; informal up for grabs, on tap, get-at-able.

obtrusive adjective *the proposed quarry would be very obtrusive:* **conspicuous**, prominent, noticeable, obvious, unmistakable, intrusive, out of place; informal sticking out a mile, sticking out like a sore thumb.
– OPPOSITES inconspicuous.

obtuse adjective *he wondered if the doctor was being deliberately obtuse:* **stupid**, foolish, slow-witted, slow, dull-witted, unintelligent, ignorant, simple-minded; insensitive, imperceptive, uncomprehending; informal dim, dim-witted, dense, dumb, slow on the uptake, half-witted, brain-dead, moronic, cretinous, thick, dopey, dozy, wooden-headed, boneheaded; Brit. informal divvy; Scottish & N. English informal glaikit; N. Amer. informal dumb-ass, chowderheaded.
– OPPOSITES clever.

obviate verb *the settlement obviated the need for the separate cases to be heard in court:* **preclude**, prevent, remove, get rid of, do away with, get round, rule out, eliminate, make unnecessary.

obvious adjective *it's obvious that Bob's keen on her:* **clear**, crystal clear, plain, evident, apparent, manifest, patent, conspicuous, pronounced, transparent, palpable, prominent, marked, decided, distinct, noticeable, perceptible, visible, discernible; unmistakable, indisputable, self-evident, incontrovertible, incontestable, undeniable, as plain as a pikestaff, as clear as day, staring someone in the face; overt, open, undisguised, unconcealed, frank, glaring, blatant, written all over someone; informal as plain as the nose on your face, sticking out like a sore thumb, sticking out a mile.
– OPPOSITES imperceptible.

obviously adverb *he was obviously in great pain:* **clearly**, evidently, plainly, patently, visibly, discernibly, manifestly, noticeably; unmistakably, undeniably, incontrovertibly, demonstrably, unquestionably, undoubtedly, without doubt, doubtless; of course, naturally, needless to say, it goes without saying.
– OPPOSITES perhaps.

occasion noun **1** *on a previous occasion:* **time**, instance, juncture, point; event, occurrence, affair, incident, episode, experience; situation, case, circumstance. **2** *a family occasion:* **social event**, event, affair, function, celebration, party, get-together, gathering; informal do, bash. **3** *I doubt if the occasion will arise:* **opportunity**, right moment, chance, opening, window. **4** *it's the first time I've had occasion to complain:* **reason**, cause, call, grounds, justification, need, motive.
verb *her situation occasioned a good deal of sympathy:* **cause**, give rise to, bring about, result in, lead to, prompt, elicit, call forth, produce, create, arouse, generate, engender, precipitate, provoke, stir up, inspire, spark off, trigger.
■ **on occasion**. See OCCASIONALLY.

occasional adjective *he made occasional visits:* **infrequent**, intermittent, irregular, periodic, sporadic, odd, random, uncommon, few and far between, isolated, rare; N. Amer. sometime.
– OPPOSITES regular, frequent.

occasionally adverb *he's got a flat in London now, though he still comes home occasionally:* **sometimes**, from time to time, (every) now and then, (every) now and again, at times, every so often, (every) once in a while, on occasion, periodically, at intervals, irregularly, sporadically, infrequently, intermittently, on and off, off and on.
– OPPOSITES often.

occult noun *his interest in the occult:* **the supernatural**, supernaturalism, magic, black magic, witchcraft, sorcery, necromancy, wizardry, the black arts, diabolism, devil worship, devilry, voodoo, hoodoo, white magic, mysticism; NZ makutu.
adjective *occult powers:* **supernatural**, magic, magical, mystical, mystic, psychic, preternatural, transcendental; cabbalistic, hermetic.

occupancy noun *rents paid by individuals are directly related to their occupancy of council houses:* **occupation**, tenancy, tenure, residence, residency, inhabitation, habitation, living, lease, holding, owner-occupancy.

occupant noun **1** *the occupants of the houses:* **resident**, inhabitant, owner, householder, tenant, renter, leaseholder, lessee; addressee; Brit. occupier, owner-occupier. **2** *the first occupant of the post:* **incumbent**, holder.

occupation noun **1** *his father's occupation took him abroad a lot:* **job**, profession, (line) of work, trade, employment, position, post, situation, business, career, métier, vocation, calling, craft; Austral. informal grip. **2** *her leisure occupations included horseriding:* **pastime**, activity, hobby, pursuit, interest, entertainment, recreation, amusement, divertissement. **3** *a property suitable for occupation by older people:* **residence**, residency, habitation, inhabitation, occupancy, tenancy, tenure, lease, living in. **4** *the Roman occupation of Britain:* **conquest**, capture, invasion, seizure, takeover, annexation, overrunning, subjugation, subjection, appropriation; colonization, rule, control, suzerainty.

occupational adjective *long and irregular hours are an occupational hazard in medicine:* **job-related**, work, professional, vocational, employment, business, career.

occupied adjective **1** *tasks which kept her occupied all day:* **busy**, engaged, working, at work, active; informal tied up, hard at it, on the go. **2** *all the tables were occupied:* **in use**, full, engaged, taken. **3** *only two of the flats are occupied:* **inhabited**, lived-in, tenanted, settled.
– OPPOSITES free, vacant.

occupy verb **1** *Carol occupied the basement flat:* **live in**, inhabit, be the tenant of, lodge in; move into, take up residence in; people, populate, settle; Scottish stay in. **2** *two windows occupied almost the whole of the end wall:* **take up**, fill, fill up, cover, use up. **3** *he occupies a senior post at the Treasury:* **hold**, fill, have; informal hold down. **4** *I need something to occupy my mind:* **engage**, busy, employ, distract, absorb, engross, preoccupy, hold, interest, involve, entertain, amuse, divert. **5** *the region was occupied by Soviet troops:* **capture**, seize, take possession of, conquer, invade, overrun, take over, colonize, garrison, annex, subjugate.

occur verb **1** *the accident occurred at about 3.30:* **happen**, take place, come about, transpire, materialize, arise, crop up;

N. Amer. informal **go down. 2** *the disease occurs chiefly in tropical climates:* **be found**, be present, exist, appear, prevail, present itself, manifest itself, turn up. **3** *an idea occurred to her:* **enter one's head/mind**, cross one's mind, come to mind, spring to mind, strike one, hit one, dawn on one, suggest itself.

occurrence noun **1** *vandalism used to be a rare occurrence:* **event**, incident, happening, phenomenon, affair, matter, circumstance. **2** *the occurrence of cancer increases with age:* **existence**, instance, appearance, manifestation, materialization, development; frequency, incidence, rate, prevalence.

ocean noun **the sea**; informal **the drink**; Brit. informal **the briny**.

odd adjective **1** *an odd man:* **strange**, peculiar, weird, queer, funny, bizarre, eccentric, unusual, unconventional, outlandish, quirky, zany; informal **wacky**, kooky, screwy, oddball, offbeat, off the wall. **2** *quite a few odd things had happened:* **strange**, unusual, peculiar, funny, curious, bizarre, weird, uncanny, queer, outré, unexpected, unfamiliar, abnormal, atypical, anomalous, different, out of the ordinary, out of the way, exceptional, rare, extraordinary, remarkable, puzzling, mystifying, mysterious, perplexing, baffling, unaccountable, uncommon, irregular, singular, deviant, aberrant, freakish. **3** *we have the odd drink together* | *he does odd jobs for friends:* **occasional**, casual, irregular, isolated, random, sporadic, periodic; miscellaneous, various, varied, sundry. **4** *he's wearing odd shoes:* **mismatched**, unmatched, unpaired; single, lone, solitary, extra, surplus, leftover, remaining.
– OPPOSITES normal, ordinary, regular.
■ **odd man out** outsider, exception, oddity, nonconformist, maverick, individualist, misfit, fish out of water, square peg in a round hole.

oddity noun **1** *she was regarded as a bit of an oddity:* **eccentric**, crank, misfit, maverick, nonconformist, rare bird; informal **character**, oddball, weirdo, crackpot, nut, freak; Brit. informal **nutter**; N. Amer. informal **screwball**, kook. **2** *his work remains an oddity in some respects:* **anomaly**, aberration, curiosity, rarity. **3** *the oddities of human nature:* **peculiarity**, idiosyncrasy, eccentricity, quirk, irregularity, twist.

oddment noun *oddments of material:* **scrap**, remnant, bit, piece, leftover, fragment, snippet, offcut, end, shred, tail end; Brit. informal **fag end**; (**oddments**) odds and ends, bits and pieces, bits and bobs.

odds plural noun **1** *the odds are that he is no longer alive:* **likelihood**, probability, chances, chance, balance. **2** *the odds are in our favour:* **advantage**, edge; superiority, supremacy, ascendancy.
■ **at odds 1** *he was at odds with his colleagues:* in conflict, in disagreement, on

bad terms, at cross purposes, at loggerheads, quarrelling, arguing, at daggers drawn, at each other's throats; N. Amer. **on the outs**. **2** *behaviour at odds with the interests of the company:* at variance, out of keeping, out of line, in opposition, conflicting, contrary, incompatible, inconsistent, irreconcilable.
■ **odds and ends** bits and pieces, bits and bobs, bits, pieces, stuff, paraphernalia, things, sundries, miscellanea, bric-a-brac, knick-knacks, oddments; informal **junk**; Brit. informal **odds and sods**, clobber, gubbins.

odious adjective *the odious methods they had used to suppress dissent:* **revolting**, repulsive, repellent, repugnant, disgusting, offensive, objectionable, vile, foul, abhorrent, loathsome, nauseating, sickening, hateful, detestable, execrable, abominable, monstrous, appalling, reprehensible, deplorable, insufferable, intolerable, despicable, contemptible, unspeakable, atrocious, awful, terrible, dreadful, frightful, obnoxious, unsavoury, unpalatable, unpleasant, disagreeable, nasty, distasteful; informal **ghastly, horrible, horrid, gross, God-awful**.
– OPPOSITES delightful.

odorous adjective *odorous fumes:* **smelly**, malodorous, pungent, acrid, foul-smelling, evil-smelling, stinking, reeking, fetid, rank; informal **stinky**; Brit. informal **pongy, niffy**.

odour noun **1** *an odour of sweat:* **smell**, stench, stink, reek; Brit. informal **pong**, whiff, niff, hum; N. Amer. informal **funk**. **2** *an odour of suspicion:* **atmosphere**, air, aura, quality, flavour, savour, hint, suggestion, impression, whiff.

odyssey noun **journey**, voyage, trek, travels, quest, crusade, pilgrimage, wandering, journeying.

off adjective **1** *Kate's off today:* **away**, absent, unavailable, not at work, off duty, on holiday, on leave; free, at leisure; N. Amer. **on vacation. 2** *the game's off:* **cancelled**, postponed, called off. **3** *strawberries are off:* **unavailable**, finished, sold out. **4** *the fish was a bit off:* **rotten**, bad, stale, mouldy, high, sour, rancid, turned, spoiled, putrid, putrescent. **5** (Brit. informal) *I felt decidedly off.* See OFF COLOUR sense 1. **6** (Brit. informal) *that remark was a bit off:* **unfair**, unjust, uncalled for, below the belt, unjustified, unjustifiable, unreasonable, unwarranted, unnecessary; informal **a bit much**; Brit. informal **out of order. 7** (Brit. informal) *he was really off with me:* **unfriendly**, aloof, cool, cold, distant, frosty; informal **stand-offish**.
■ **off and on** periodically, at intervals, on and off, (every) once in a while, every so often, (every) now and then/again, from time to time, occasionally, sometimes, intermittently, irregularly.

offbeat adjective (informal) *the suggestion was a little offbeat:* **unconventional**, unorthodox, unusual, eccentric, idiosyncratic, outré, strange, bizarre, weird, peculiar, odd,

freakish, outlandish, out of the ordinary, Bohemian, alternative, left-field, zany, quirky; informal wacky, freaky, way-out, off the wall, kooky, oddball.
– OPPOSITES conventional.

off colour adjective **1** (Brit.) *I'm feeling a bit off colour:* **unwell**, ill, poorly, out of sorts, indisposed, not oneself, sick, queasy, nauseous, peaky, liverish, green about the gills, run down, washed out, below par; informal under the weather, rough; Brit. informal ropy, off; Scottish informal wabbit, peely-wally; Austral./NZ informal crook. **2** *off-colour jokes:* **smutty**, dirty, rude, crude, suggestive, indecent, indelicate, risqué, racy, bawdy, naughty, blue, vulgar, ribald, broad, salacious, coarse; informal raunchy; Brit. informal fruity, saucy; euphemistic adult.
– OPPOSITES well.

offence noun **1** *he denied having committed any offence:* **crime**, illegal/unlawful act, misdemeanour, breach of the law, felony, wrongdoing, wrong, misdeed, peccadillo, sin, transgression, infringement. **2** *an offence to basic justice:* **affront**, slap in the face, insult, outrage, violation. **3** *I do not want to cause offence:* **annoyance**, anger, resentment, indignation, irritation, exasperation, wrath, displeasure, hard/bad/ill feelings, disgruntlement, pique, vexation, animosity.
■ **take offence** be offended, take exception, take something personally, feel affronted, feel resentful, take something amiss, take umbrage, get upset, get annoyed, get angry, get into a huff; Brit. informal get the hump.

offend verb **1** *I'm sorry if I offended him:* **hurt someone's feelings**, give offence to, affront, displease, upset, distress, hurt, wound; annoy, anger, exasperate, irritate, vex, pique, gall, irk, nettle, tread on someone's toes; Brit. rub up the wrong way; informal rile, rattle, peeve, needle, put someone's nose out of joint, put someone's back up. **2** *the smell of cigarette smoke offended him:* **displease**, be distasteful to, be disagreeable to, be offensive to, disgust, repel, revolt, sicken, nauseate; informal turn off; N. Amer. informal gross out. **3** *criminals who offend again and again:* **break the law**, commit a crime, do wrong, sin, transgress.

offended adjective *she was so offended she asked him to leave at once:* **affronted**, insulted, aggrieved, displeased, upset, hurt, wounded, disgruntled, put out, annoyed, angry, cross, exasperated, indignant, irritated, piqued, vexed, irked, stung, galled, nettled, resentful, in a huff, huffy, in high dudgeon; informal riled, miffed, peeved, aggravated; Brit. informal narked; N. Amer. informal sore.
– OPPOSITES pleased.

offender noun *persistent offenders:* **wrongdoer**, criminal, lawbreaker, miscreant, malefactor, felon, delinquent, culprit, guilty party, sinner, transgressor.

offensive adjective **1** *offensive remarks:* **insulting**, rude, impertinent, insolent, derogatory, disrespectful, personal, hurtful, wounding, abusive; annoying, exasperating, irritating, galling, provocative, outrageous; discourteous, uncivil, impolite. **2** *an offensive smell:* **unpleasant**, disagreeable, nasty, distasteful, displeasing, objectionable, off-putting, awful, terrible, dreadful, frightful, obnoxious, abominable, disgusting, repulsive, repellent, repugnant, revolting, abhorrent, loathsome, odious, vile, foul, sickening, nauseating; informal ghastly, horrible, horrid, gross, God-awful; Brit. informal beastly. **3** *an offensive air action:* **hostile**, attacking, aggressive, invading, combative, belligerent, on the attack.
– OPPOSITES complimentary, pleasant, defensive.
noun *a military offensive:* **attack**, assault, onslaught, drive, invasion, push, thrust, charge, sortie, sally, foray, raid, incursion, blitz, campaign.

offer verb **1** *Frank offered another suggestion:* **put forward**, proffer, give, present, come up with, suggest, recommend, propose, advance, submit, tender, render. **2** *she offered to help:* **volunteer**, volunteer one's services, be at someone's disposal, be at someone's service, step/come forward, show willing. **3** *the product is offered at a competitive price:* **put up for sale**, put on the market, sell, market, put under the hammer. **4** *he offered $200:* **bid**, tender, put in a bid of, put in an offer of. **5** *a job offering good career prospects:* **provide**, afford, supply, give, furnish, present, hold out. **6** *she offered no resistance:* **attempt**, try, give, show, express. **7** *birds were offered to the gods:* **sacrifice**, offer up, immolate.
– OPPOSITES withdraw, refuse.
noun **1** *offers of help:* **proposal**, proposition, suggestion, submission, approach, overture. **2** *the highest offer:* **bid**, tender, bidding price.
■ **on offer** on sale, up for sale, on the market; available, obtainable, to be had; N. Amer. on the block.

offering noun **1** *you may place offerings in the charity box:* **contribution**, donation, gift, present, handout, widow's mite; charity. **2** *many offerings were made to the goddess:* **sacrifice**, oblation, burnt offering, immolation, libation, first fruits.

offhand adjective *an offhand manner:* **casual**, careless, uninterested, unconcerned, indifferent, cool, nonchalant, blasé, insouciant, cavalier, glib, perfunctory, cursory, unceremonious, ungracious, dismissive, discourteous, uncivil, impolite, terse, abrupt, curt; informal off, couldn't-care-less, take-it-or-leave-it.
adverb *I can't think of a better answer offhand:* **on the spur of the moment**, without consideration, extempore, impromptu, ad lib; extemporaneously, spontaneously; informal off the cuff, off the

top of one's head, just like that.

office noun **1** *her office in Aldersgate Street:* **place of work**, place of business, workplace, workroom. **2** *the newspaper's Paris office:* **branch**, division, section, bureau, department; agency. **3** *he assumed the office of President:* **post**, position, appointment, job, occupation, role, situation, function, capacity. **4** *he was saved by the good offices of his uncle:* **assistance**, help, aid, services, intervention, intercession, mediation, agency.

officer noun *the officers of the society:* **official**, office-holder, committee member, board member; public servant, administrator, executive, functionary, bureaucrat; derogatory apparatchik.

official adjective **1** *an official inquiry:* **authorized**, approved, validated, authenticated, certified, accredited, endorsed, sanctioned, licensed, recognized, accepted, legitimate, legal, lawful, valid, bona fide, proper, ex cathedra; informal kosher. **2** *an official function:* **ceremonial**, formal, solemn, ceremonious; bureaucratic; informal stuffed-shirt.
– OPPOSITES unauthorized, informal.
noun *a union official:* **officer**, office-holder, administrator, executive, appointee, functionary; bureaucrat, mandarin; representative, agent; Brit. jack-in-office; derogatory apparatchik.

officiate verb **1** *he officiated in the first two matches:* **be in charge of**, take charge of, preside over; oversee, superintend, supervise, conduct, run. **2** *Father Buckley officiated at the wedding service:* **conduct**, perform, celebrate, solemnize.

officious adjective *the security people in the foyer were even more officious:* **self-important**, bumptious, self-assertive, pushy, overbearing, overzealous, domineering, opinionated, interfering, intrusive, meddlesome, meddling; informal bossy.
– OPPOSITES self-effacing.

offing
■ **in the offing** *important changes were in the offing:* **on the way**, coming, (close) at hand, near, imminent, in prospect, on the horizon, in the wings, just around the corner, in the air, in the wind, brewing, upcoming, forthcoming; informal on the cards.

off-key adjective **1** *an off-key rendition of 'Amazing Grace':* **out of tune**, flat, tuneless, discordant, unharmonious. **2** *the cinematic effects are distractingly off-key:* **incongruous**, inappropriate, unsuitable, out of place, out of keeping, jarring, dissonant, inharmonious.
– OPPOSITES harmonious.

offload verb **1** *the cargo was being offloaded:* **unload**, remove, empty (out), tip (out). **2** *he offloaded 5,000 of the shares:* **dispose of**, dump, jettison, get rid of, transfer, shift;

palm off, foist, fob off.

off-putting adjective **1** *an off-putting aroma:* **unpleasant**, unappealing, uninviting, unattractive, disagreeable, offensive, distasteful, unsavoury, unpalatable, unappetizing, objectionable, nasty, disgusting, repellent; informal horrid, horrible. **2** *her manner was off-putting:* **discouraging**, disheartening, demoralizing, dispiriting, daunting, disconcerting, unnerving, unsettling.

offset verb *profits and losses on each investment tend to offset each other:* **counterbalance**, balance (out), cancel (out), even out/up, counteract, countervail, neutralize, compensate for, make up for, make good, redeem.

offshoot noun **1** *the plant's offshoots:* **side shoot**, shoot, sucker, tendril, runner, scion, slip, offset, stolon; twig, branch, bough, limb. **2** *an offshoot of the growth of interest in heritage:* **outcome**, result, effect, consequence, upshot, product, by-product, spin-off, development, ramification.

offspring noun *anxious parents watched over their offspring:* **children**, sons and daughters, progeny, family, youngsters, babies, infants, brood; descendants, heirs, successors; informal kids; Brit. informal sprogs, brats; derogatory spawn.

often adverb *he often asked after you:* **frequently**, many times, many a time, on many/numerous occasions, a lot, as often as not, repeatedly, again and again; regularly, routinely, usually, habitually, commonly, generally, in many cases/instances, ordinarily; N. Amer. oftentimes.
– OPPOSITES seldom.

ogle verb *he'd been ogling her ever since she entered the room:* **leer at**, stare at, eye, make eyes at; informal eye up, give someone the glad eye, lech after, undress with one's eyes, give someone the come-on; Austral./NZ informal perv on.

ogre noun **1** *an ogre with two heads:* **monster**, giant, troll. **2** *he is not the ogre he sometimes seems to be:* **brute**, fiend, monster, beast, barbarian, savage, animal, tyrant; informal bastard, swine, pig.

ogress noun **1** *a one-eyed ogress:* **monster**, giantess. **2** *the French teacher was a real ogress:* **harridan**, tartar, termagant, gorgon, virago; informal battleaxe.

oily adjective **1** *oily substances:* **greasy**, oleaginous. **2** *oily food:* **greasy**, fatty, buttery, swimming in oil/fat. **3** *an oily man:* **unctuous**, ingratiating, smooth-talking, fulsome, flattering; obsequious, sycophantic, oleaginous; informal smarmy, slimy.

ointment noun **lotion**, cream, salve, liniment, embrocation, rub, gel, balm, emollient, unguent.

OK, okay (informal) exclamation *OK, I'll go with him:* **all right**, right, right then, right you are, very well, very good, fine; informal okey-doke(y); Brit. informal righto, righty-ho.

adjective 1 *the film was OK:* **satisfactory**, all right, acceptable, competent; adequate, tolerable, passable, reasonable, fair, decent, not bad, average, middling, moderate, unremarkable, unexceptional; informal so-so, fair-to-middling. **2** *Jo's feeling OK now:* **fine**, all right, well, in good shape, in good health, fit, healthy, as fit as a fiddle/flea. **3** *it is OK for me to come?* **permissible**, allowable, acceptable, all right, in order, permitted, fitting, suitable, appropriate.
– OPPOSITES unsatisfactory, ill.
noun *he's just given me the OK:* **authorization**, approval, seal of approval, agreement, consent, assent, permission, endorsement, ratification, sanction, approbation, confirmation, blessing, leave; informal the go-ahead, the green light, the thumbs up, say-so.
– OPPOSITES refusal.
verb *the move must be okayed by the president:* **authorize**, approve, agree to, consent to, sanction, pass, ratify, endorse, allow, give something the nod, rubber-stamp; informal give the go-ahead, give the green light, give the thumbs up.
– OPPOSITES refuse, veto.

old adjective 1 *old people:* **elderly**, aged, older, senior, advanced in years, venerable; in one's dotage, long in the tooth, grey-haired, grizzled, hoary, past one's prime, not as young as one was, ancient, decrepit, doddering, doddery, not long for this world, senescent, senile, superannuated; informal getting on, past it, over the hill, no spring chicken. **2** *old farm buildings:* **dilapidated**, broken-down, run down, tumbledown, ramshackle, decaying, crumbling, disintegrating. **3** *old clothes:* **worn**, worn out, shabby, threadbare, holey, torn, frayed, patched, tattered, moth-eaten, ragged; old-fashioned, out of date, outmoded; cast-off, hand-me-down; informal tatty. **4** *old cars:* **antique**, veteran, vintage. **5** *she's old for her years:* **mature**, wise, sensible, experienced, worldly-wise, knowledgeable. **6** *in the old days:* **bygone**, past, former, olden, of old, previous, early, earlier, earliest; medieval, ancient, classical, primeval, primordial, prehistoric. **7** *the same old phrases:* **hackneyed**, hack, banal, trite, overused, overworked, tired, worn out, stale, clichéd, platitudinous, unimaginative, stock, conventional; out of date, outdated, old-fashioned, outmoded, hoary; informal old hat, corny, played out. **8** *an old girlfriend:* **former**, previous, ex-, one-time, sometime, erstwhile.
– OPPOSITES young, new, modern.
■ **old age** declining years, advanced years, age, oldness, winter/autumn of one's life, senescence, senility, dotage.
■ **old man** senior citizen, pensioner, OAP, elder, grandfather; patriarch; informal greybeard, codger; Brit. informal buffer.
■ **old person** senior citizen, senior, (old-age) pensioner, OAP, elder, geriatric, dotard, Methuselah; N. Amer. golden ager; informal old stager, old-timer, oldie, wrinkly, crock, crumbly; N. Amer. informal oldster, woopie.
■ **old woman** senior citizen, pensioner, OAP, crone; informal old dear.

old-fashioned adjective *an old-fashioned kitchen range:* **out of date**, outdated, dated, out of fashion, outmoded, unfashionable, passé, démodé, frumpy; outworn, old, old-time, behind the times, archaic, obsolescent, obsolete, ancient, antiquated, superannuated, defunct; medieval, prehistoric, antediluvian, old-fogeyish, conservative, backward-looking, quaint, anachronistic, fusty, moth-eaten, olde worlde; informal old hat, square, not with it, out of the ark; N. Amer. informal horse-and-buggy, clunky, rinky-dink.
– OPPOSITES modern.

Olympian adjective *Kerr himself preserved an attitude of Olympian detachment:* **aloof**, distant, remote, unfriendly, uncommunicative, unforthcoming, cool; informal stand-offish.
– OPPOSITES friendly.

omen noun *a rise in imports might be an omen of recovery:* **portent**, sign, signal, token, forewarning, warning, foreshadowing, prediction, forecast, prophesy, harbinger, augury, auspice, presage; writing on the wall, indication, hint.

ominous adjective *ominous black clouds gathered on the horizon:* **threatening**, menacing, baleful, forbidding, sinister, inauspicious, unpropitious, portentous, unfavourable, unpromising; black, dark, gloomy.
– OPPOSITES promising.

omission noun 1 *the omission of recent publications from his biography:* **exclusion**, leaving out; deletion, cut, excision, elimination. **2** *the damage was not caused by any omission on behalf of the carrier:* **negligence**, neglect, neglectfulness, dereliction, forgetfulness, oversight, default, lapse, failure.

omit verb 1 *they omitted his name from the list:* **leave out**, exclude, leave off, take out, miss out, miss, drop, cut; delete, eliminate, rub out, cross out, strike out. **2** *I omitted to mention our guest lecturer:* **forget**, neglect, fail; leave undone, overlook, skip.
– OPPOSITES add, include, remember.

omnipotence noun all-powerfulness, supremacy, pre-eminence, supreme power, unlimited power; invincibility.

omnipotent adjective *an omnipotent deity:* **all-powerful**, almighty, supreme, pre-eminent; invincible, unconquerable.

omnipresent adjective *in fairy tales, evil is as omnipresent as virtue:* **ubiquitous**, all-pervasive, everywhere; rife, pervasive, prevalent.

O

omniscient adjective *the story is told by an omniscient fictional narrator:* **all-knowing**, all-wise, all-seeing.

omnivorous adjective **1** *most duck species are omnivorous:* **able to eat anything**; rare pantophagous, omnivorant. **2** *an omnivorous reader:* **undiscriminating**, indiscriminate, unselective.

on adjective *the computer's on:* **functioning**, in operation, working, in use, operating.
– OPPOSITES off.
adverb *she droned on:* **interminably**, at length, for a long time, continuously, endlessly, ceaselessly, without a pause/break.
■ **on and off**. See OFF AND ON at OFF.
■ **on and on** for a long time, for ages, for hours, at (great) length, incessantly, ceaselessly, constantly, continuously, continually, endlessly, unendingly, eternally, forever, interminably, unremittingly, relentlessly, indefatigably, without let-up, without a pause/break, without cease.

once adverb **1** *I only met him once:* **on one occasion**, one time, one single time. **2** *he did not once help:* **ever**, at any time, on any occasion, at all. **3** *they were friends once:* **formerly**, previously, in the past, at one time, at one point, once upon a time, time was when, in days/times gone by, in times past, in the (good) old days, long ago.
– OPPOSITES often, now.
conjunction *he'll be all right once she's gone:* **as soon as**, when, after.
■ **at once 1** *you must leave at once:* immediately, right away, right now, this moment/instant/second/minute, now, straight away, instantly, directly, forthwith, promptly, without delay/hesitation, without further ado; quickly, as fast as possible, as soon as possible, a.s.a.p., speedily; informal like a shot, in/like a flash, before you can say Jack Robinson. **2** *all the guests arrived at once:* at the same time, at one and the same time, (all) together, simultaneously; as a group, in unison, in concert, in chorus.
■ **once and for all** conclusively, decisively, finally, positively, definitely, definitively, irrevocably; for good, for always, forever, permanently.
■ **once in a while** occasionally, from time to time, (every) now and then/again, every so often, on occasion, at times, sometimes, off and on, at intervals, periodically, sporadically, intermittently.

oncoming adjective *he lost control on a bend and collided with an oncoming car:* **approaching**, advancing, nearing, forthcoming, on the way, imminent, impending, looming, gathering, (close) at hand, about to happen, to come.

one cardinal number **1 unit**, item. **2** *only one person came:* **a single**, a solitary, a sole, a lone. **3** *her one concern was her daughter:* **only**, single, solitary, sole. **4** *they have now become one:* **united**, a unit, unitary, amalgamated, consolidated, integrated, combined, incorporated, allied, affiliated, linked, joined, unified, in league, in partnership; wedded, married.

onerous adjective *the task proved to be more onerous than she'd expected:* **burdensome**, arduous, strenuous, difficult, hard, severe, heavy, back-breaking, oppressive, weighty, uphill, effortful, formidable, laborious, Herculean, exhausting, tiring, taxing, demanding, punishing, gruelling, exacting, wearing, wearisome, fatiguing.
– OPPOSITES easy.

oneself
■ **by oneself**. See BY.

one-sided adjective **1** *we heard a rather one-sided account from the fans:* **biased**, prejudiced, partisan, partial, preferential, discriminatory, slanted, inequitable, unfair, unjust. **2** *with Cowan and Tobel injured, it will be a one-sided game:* **unequal**, uneven, unbalanced.
– OPPOSITES impartial.

one-time adjective *a one-time county cricketer:* **former**, ex-, old, previous, sometime, erstwhile; lapsed.

ongoing adjective **1** *negotiations are ongoing:* **in progress**, under way, going on, continuing, taking place, proceeding, progressing, advancing; unfinished. **2** *an ongoing struggle:* **continuous**, continuing, uninterrupted, unbroken, non-stop, constant, ceaseless, unceasing, unending, endless, never-ending, unremitting, relentless, unfaltering.

onlooker noun *an onlooker described the scene as one of utter devastation:* **eyewitness**, witness, observer, looker-on, fly on the wall, spectator, watcher, viewer, bystander; sightseer; informal rubberneck.

only adverb **1** *there was only enough for two:* **at most**, at best, (only) just, no/not more than; barely, scarcely, hardly. **2** *he only works on one picture at a time:* **exclusively**, solely, to the exclusion of everything else. **3** *you're only saying that:* **merely**, simply, just.
adjective *their only son:* **sole**, single, one (and only), solitary, lone, unique; exclusive.

onomatopoeic adjective *'slap' is an onomatopoeic word:* **imitative**, echoic.

onset noun *treatment was administered soon after the onset of symptoms:* **start**, beginning, commencement, arrival, (first) appearance, inception, day one; outbreak.
– OPPOSITES end.

onslaught noun *the relentless onslaught on the city was taking a heavy toll:* **assault**, attack, offensive, advance, charge, onrush, rush, storming, sortie, sally, raid, descent, incursion, invasion, foray, push, thrust, drive, blitz, bombardment, barrage, salvo.

onus noun *the onus is on the plaintiff to obtain the police report:* **burden**, responsibility, liability, obligation, duty, weight, load, charge, encumbrance; cross to bear, millstone round one's neck, albatross.

ooze verb 1 *blood oozed from the wound:* **seep**, discharge, flow, exude, trickle, drip, dribble, issue, filter, percolate, escape, leak, drain, empty, bleed, sweat, well. 2 *she was positively oozing charm:* **exude**, gush, drip, pour forth, emanate, radiate.
noun *the ooze of blood:* **seepage**, seeping, discharge, flow, exudation, trickle, drip, dribble, percolation, escape, leak, leakage, drainage; secretion.

opalescent adjective *opalescent sequins reflect the light more subtly:* **iridescent**, prismatic, rainbow-like, kaleidoscopic, multicoloured, many-hued, lustrous, shimmering, glittering, sparkling, variegated, shot, moire, opaline, milky, pearly, nacreous.

opaque adjective 1 *opaque glass for bathrooms etc.* **non-transparent**, cloudy, filmy, blurred, smeared, smeary, misty, dirty, muddy, muddied, grimy. 2 *the technical jargon was opaque to her:* **obscure**, unclear, mysterious, puzzling, perplexing, baffling, mystifying, confusing, unfathomable, incomprehensible, unintelligible, impenetrable, hazy, foggy; informal as clear as mud.
– OPPOSITES transparent, clear.

open adjective 1 *the door's open:* **not shut**, not closed, unlocked, unbolted, unlatched, off the latch, unfastened, unsecured; ajar, gaping, yawning. 2 *a blue silk shirt, open at the neck:* **unfastened**, not done up, undone, unbuttoned, unzipped, loose. 3 *the main roads are open:* **clear**, passable, navigable, unblocked, unobstructed. 4 *open countryside | open spaces:* **unenclosed**, rolling, sweeping, extensive, wide (open), unfenced, exposed, unsheltered; spacious, airy, uncrowded, uncluttered; undeveloped, unbuilt-up. 5 *a map was open beside him:* **spread out**, unfolded, unfurled, unrolled, extended, stretched out. 6 *the bank wasn't open:* **trading**, working, in operation. 7 *the position is still open:* **available**, vacant, free, unfilled; informal up for grabs. 8 *the system is open to abuse:* **vulnerable**, subject, susceptible, liable, exposed, an easy target for, at risk of. 9 *she was open about her feelings:* **frank**, candid, honest, forthcoming, communicative, forthright, direct, unreserved, plain-spoken, outspoken, free-spoken, not afraid to call a spade a spade; informal upfront. 10 *open hostility:* **overt**, obvious, patent, manifest, palpable, conspicuous, plain, undisguised, unconcealed, clear, apparent, evident; blatant, flagrant, barefaced, brazen. 11 *the case is still open:* **unresolved**, undecided, unsettled, up in the air; open to debate, open for discussion, arguable, debatable, moot. 12 *an open mind:* **impartial**, unbiased, unprejudiced, objective, disinterested,

non-partisan, non-discriminatory, neutral, dispassionate, detached. 13 *I'm open to suggestions:* **receptive**, amenable, willing/ready to listen, responsive. 14 *what other options are open to us?* **available**, accessible, on hand, obtainable, on offer. 15 *an open meeting:* **public**, general, unrestricted, non-exclusive, non-restrictive.
– OPPOSITES shut.
verb 1 *she opened the front door:* **unfasten**, unlatch, unlock, unbolt, unbar; throw wide. 2 *Katherine opened the parcel:* **unwrap**, undo, untie, unseal. 3 *shall I open another bottle?* **uncork**, broach, crack (open). 4 *Adam opened the map:* **spread out**, unfold, unfurl, unroll, straighten out. 5 *he opened his heart to her:* **reveal**, uncover, expose, lay bare, bare, pour out, disclose, divulge. 6 *we're hoping to open next month:* **start trading**, open for business, set up shop, put up one's plate; N. Amer. informal hang out one's shingle. 7 *Sir Bryan opened the meeting:* **begin**, start, commence, initiate, set in motion, launch, get going, get under way, set the ball rolling, get off the ground; inaugurate; informal kick off, get the show on the road. 8 *the lounge opens on to a terrace:* **give access**, lead, be connected, communicate with.
– OPPOSITES close, shut, end.

open-air adjective *an open-air swimming pool:* **outdoor**, out-of-doors, outside, alfresco.
– OPPOSITES indoor.

opening noun 1 *an opening in the centre of the roof:* **hole**, gap, aperture, orifice, vent, crack, slit, chink; spyhole, peephole; Anatomy foramen. 2 *the opening in the wall:* **doorway**, gateway, entrance, (means of) entry, way in/out, exit. 3 *United created openings but were unable to score:* **opportunity**, chance, window (of opportunity), possibility. 4 *an opening with a stockbroker:* **vacancy**, position, job. 5 *the opening of the session:* **beginning**, start, commencement, outset; introduction, prefatory remarks, opening statement; informal kick-off. 6 *the opening of a new art gallery:* **opening ceremony**, launch, inauguration; opening/first night, premiere.

openly adverb 1 *drugs were openly on sale:* **publicly**, blatantly, flagrantly, overtly. 2 *he spoke openly of his problems:* **frankly**, candidly, explicitly, honestly, sincerely, forthrightly, bluntly, without constraint, without holding back, straight from the shoulder.
– OPPOSITES secretly.

open-minded adjective 1 *open-minded attitudes:* **unbiased**, unprejudiced, neutral, non-judgemental, non-discriminatory, objective, disinterested; tolerant, liberal, permissive, broad-minded. 2 *musicians need to be open-minded:* **receptive**, open (to suggestions), amenable, flexible, willing to change.
– OPPOSITES prejudiced, narrow-minded.

open-mouthed adjective *he stared at*

her open-mouthed: **astounded**, amazed, in amazement, surprised, stunned, bowled over, staggered, thunderstruck, aghast, stupefied, taken aback, shocked, speechless, dumbfounded, dumbstruck; informal flabbergasted; Brit. informal gobsmacked.

operate verb **1** *he can operate the machine:* **work**, make go, run, use, utilize, handle, control, manage; drive, steer, manoeuvre. **2** *the machine ceased to operate:* **function**, work, go, run, be in working/running order, be operative. **3** *the way the law operates in practice:* **take effect**, act, apply, be applied, function. **4** *Hechstetter operated the mines until 1634:* **direct**, control, manage, run, govern, administer, superintend, head (up), supervise, oversee, be in control/charge of. **5** *doctors decided to operate:* perform surgery, intervene.

operation noun **1** *the slide bars ensure smooth operation:* **functioning**, working, running, performance, action. **2** *the operation of the factory:* **management**, running, governing, administration, supervision. **3** *a heart bypass operation:* **surgery**, intervention. **4** *a military operation:* **action**, activity, exercise, undertaking, enterprise, manoeuvre, campaign. **5** *their mining operations:* **business**, enterprise, company, firm; informal outfit.

operational adjective *the two reactors became operational in 1983:* **(up and) running**, working, functioning, operative, in operation, in use, in action; in working order, workable, serviceable, functional, usable.

operative adjective **1** *the act is not operative at the moment:* **in force**, in operation, in effect, valid. **2** *the operative word:* **key**, significant, relevant, applicable, pertinent, apposite, germane, crucial, critical, pivotal.
– OPPOSITES invalid.
noun **1** *the operatives clean the machines:* **machinist**, (machine) operator, mechanic, engineer, worker, workman, (factory) hand, blue-collar worker. **2** *an operative of the CIA:* **(secret) agent**, undercover agent, spy, mole, plant, double agent; N. Amer. informal spook.

operator noun **1** *a machine operator:* **machinist**, mechanic, operative, engineer, worker. **2** *a tour operator:* **contractor**, entrepreneur, promoter, arranger, fixer. **3** (informal) *a ruthless operator:* **manipulator**, manoeuvrer, string-puller, mover and shaker, wheeler-dealer; N. Amer. informal wirepuller.

opiate noun **drug**, narcotic, sedative, tranquillizer, depressant, soporific, anaesthetic, painkiller, analgesic, anodyne; morphine, opium; informal dope.

opine verb (formal) *the minister opined that these measures were too little, too late:* **suggest**, say, declare, observe, comment, remark; think, believe, consider, maintain, imagine, reckon, guess, assume, presume,

take it, suppose; N. Amer. informal allow.

opinion noun *she did not share her husband's opinion:* **belief**, judgement, thought(s), (way of) thinking, mind, (point of) view, viewpoint, attitude, stance, position, standpoint.
■ **a matter of opinion** open to question, debatable, open to debate, a moot point.
■ **be of the opinion** believe, think, consider, maintain, reckon, estimate, feel, be convinced; N. Amer. informal allow; formal opine.
■ **in my opinion** as I see it, to my mind, (according) to my way of thinking, personally, in my estimation, if you ask me.

opinionated adjective *an arrogant and opinionated man:* **dogmatic**, of fixed views; inflexible, uncompromising, prejudiced, bigoted.

opponent noun **1** *his Republican opponent:* **rival**, adversary, opposer, the opposition, fellow contestant, (fellow) competitor, enemy, antagonist, combatant, contender, challenger. **2** *an opponent of the reforms:* **opposer**, objector, dissenter.
– OPPOSITES ally, supporter.

opportune adjective *it would seem an opportune moment to impose stricter regulation:* **auspicious**, propitious, favourable, advantageous, golden, felicitous; timely, convenient, suitable, appropriate, apt, fitting.
– OPPOSITES disadvantageous.

opportunism noun *many are saying that the early election was prompted by political opportunism:* **expediency**, pragmatism, Machiavellianism; striking while the iron is hot, making hay while the sun shines.

opportunity noun *it's an opportunity you shouldn't miss:* **(lucky) chance**, golden opportunity, favourable time/occasion/moment; time, occasion, moment, opening, option, window (of opportunity), possibility, scope, freedom; informal shot, break, look-in.

oppose verb *we oppose this move because it benefits no one:* **be against**, object to, be hostile to, be in opposition to, disagree with, dislike, disapprove of; resist, take a stand against, put up a fight against, stand up to, fight, challenge; take issue with, dispute, argue with/against, quarrel with; informal be anti.
– OPPOSITES support.

opposed adjective **1** *the population is opposed to the nuclear power plants:* **against**, (dead) set against; in opposition, averse, hostile, antagonistic, antipathetic, resistant; informal anti. **2** *their interests were opposed:* **conflicting**, contrasting, incompatible, irreconcilable, antithetical, contradictory, clashing, at variance, at odds, divergent, poles apart.
– OPPOSITES in favour of.
■ **as opposed to** in contrast with, as against, as contrasted with, rather than, instead of.

opposing adjective **1** *the two opposing points of view:* **conflicting**, contrasting, opposite, incompatible, irreconcilable, contradictory, antithetical, clashing, at variance, at odds, divergent, opposed, poles apart. **2** *opposing sides in the war:* **rival**, opposite, enemy.

opposite adjective **1** *they sat opposite each other:* **facing**, face to face with, across from; informal eyeball to eyeball with. **2** *the opposite page:* **facing**, opposing. **3** *opposite views:* **conflicting**, contrasting, incompatible, irreconcilable, antithetical, contradictory, clashing, at variance, at odds, different, differing, divergent, dissimilar, unalike, disagreeing, opposed, opposing, poles apart. **4** *opposite sides in a war:* **rival**, opposing, enemy.
– OPPOSITES same.
noun *in fact the opposite was true:* **reverse**, converse, antithesis, contrary, inverse, obverse, antipode; the other side of the coin; informal flip side.

opposition noun **1** *the proposal met with opposition:* **resistance**, hostility, antagonism, antipathy, objection, dissent, disapproval; defiance, non-compliance, obstruction. **2** *they beat the opposition—5-0:* **opponents**, opposing side, other side/team, competition, opposers, rivals, adversaries. **3** *the opposition between the public and the private domains:* **conflict**, clash, disparity, antithesis, polarity.

oppress verb **1** *the invaders oppressed the people:* **persecute**, abuse, maltreat, ill-treat, tyrannize, crush, repress, suppress, subjugate, subdue, keep down, grind down, rule with a rod of iron, ride roughshod over. **2** *the gloom oppressed her:* **depress**, make gloomy/despondent, weigh down, weigh heavily on, cast down, dampen someone's spirits, dispirit, dishearten, discourage, sadden, get down.

oppressed adjective **persecuted**, downtrodden, abused, maltreated, ill-treated, subjugated, tyrannized, repressed, subdued, crushed; disadvantaged, underprivileged.

oppression noun **persecution**, abuse, maltreatment, ill-treatment, tyranny, repression, suppression, subjection, subjugation; cruelty, brutality, injustice, hardship, suffering, misery.

oppressive adjective **1** *an oppressive dictatorship:* **harsh**, cruel, brutal, repressive, tyrannical, autocratic, dictatorial, despotic, undemocratic; ruthless, merciless, pitiless. **2** *an oppressive sense of despair:* **overwhelming**, overpowering, unbearable, unendurable, intolerable. **3** *it was grey and oppressive:* **muggy**, close, heavy, hot, humid, sticky, steamy, airless, stuffy, stifling, sultry.
– OPPOSITES lenient.

oppressor noun **persecutor**, tyrant, despot, autocrat, dictator, subjugator, tormentor.

opprobrious adjective *a couple of students shouted opprobrious remarks at him:* **abusive**, vituperative, derogatory, disparaging, denigratory, pejorative, deprecatory, insulting, offensive; scornful, contemptuous, derisive; informal bitchy.

opprobrium noun **1** *the government endured months of opprobrium:* **vilification**, abuse, vituperation, condemnation, criticism, censure, denunciation, defamation, denigration, disparagement, obloquy, derogation, slander, revilement, calumny, execration, bad press, invective; informal flak, mud-slinging, bad-mouthing; Brit. informal stick. **2** *the opprobrium of being associated with thugs:* **disgrace**, shame, dishonour, stigma, humiliation, loss of face, ignominy, disrepute, infamy, notoriety, scandal.
– OPPOSITES praise, honour.

opt verb *she opted for a cream silk shirt:* **choose**, select, pick (out), decide on, go for, settle on, plump for.

optimism noun **hopefulness**, hope, confidence, buoyancy, sanguineness, positiveness, positive attitude.

optimistic adjective **1** *she felt optimistic about the future:* **positive**, confident, hopeful, sanguine, bullish, buoyant; informal upbeat. **2** *the forecast is optimistic:* **encouraging**, promising, hopeful, reassuring, favourable, auspicious, propitious.
– OPPOSITES pessimistic.

optimum adjective *the optimum pupil-teacher ratio:* **best**, most favourable, most advantageous, ideal, perfect, prime, optimal.

option noun *the way I see it, we have two options:* **choice**, alternative, possibility, course of action.

optional adjective *registration was obligatory but voting was optional:* **voluntary**, discretionary, non-compulsory, non-mandatory.
– OPPOSITES compulsory.

opulence noun **1** *the opulence of the room:* **luxuriousness**, sumptuousness, lavishness, richness, luxury, luxuriance, splendour, magnificence, grandeur, splendidness; informal plushness. **2** *a display of opulence:* **wealth**, affluence, richness, riches, prosperity, prosperousness, money.
– OPPOSITES poverty.

opulent adjective **1** *his opulent home:* **luxurious**, sumptuous, palatial, lavishly appointed, rich, splendid, magnificent, grand, grandiose, fancy; informal plush, swanky; Brit. informal swish; N. Amer. informal swank. **2** *an opulent family:* **wealthy**, rich, affluent, well off, well-to-do, moneyed, prosperous, of substance; informal well heeled, rolling in money, loaded, stinking/filthy rich, made of money. **3** *her opulent red hair:* **copious**, abundant, profuse, prolific, plentiful, luxuriant.
– OPPOSITES spartan, poor.

opus noun *his acclaimed opus 'In Search of*

Excellence': **composition**, work (of art), oeuvre.

oracle noun *the oracle of Apollo:* **prophet**, **prophetess**, sibyl, seer, augur, prognosticator, diviner, soothsayer, fortune-teller.

oral adjective *an oral agreement:* **spoken**, verbal, unwritten, vocal, uttered, said.
– OPPOSITES written.

orate verb *he strode up and down the aisle as he orated:* **declaim**, make a speech, hold forth, speak, discourse, pontificate, preach, sermonize, sound off, spout off; informal spiel.

oration noun *his eloquent funeral oration:* **speech**, address, lecture, talk, homily, sermon, discourse, declamation; informal spiel.

orator noun **(public) speaker**, speech-maker, lecturer, declaimer, rhetorician, rhetor; informal spieler.

oratory noun *he whipped the meeting up into a frenzy with his oratory:* **rhetoric**, eloquence, grandiloquence, magniloquence, public speaking, speech-making, declamation.

orb noun *the red orb of the sun sank beneath the horizon:* **sphere**, globe, ball, circle.

orbit noun **1** *the earth's orbit around the sun:* **course**, path, circuit, track, trajectory, rotation, revolution, circle. **2** *the problem comes outside our orbit:* **sphere (of influence)**, area of activity, range, scope, ambit, compass, jurisdiction, authority, remit, domain, realm, province, territory; informal bailiwick.
▶ verb *Mercury orbits the sun:* **revolve round**, circle round, go round, travel round.

orchestrate verb **1** *the piece was orchestrated by Mozart:* **arrange**, adapt, score. **2** *he threatened to orchestrate a campaign of civil disobedience:* **organize**, arrange, plan, set up, bring about, mobilize, mount, stage, stage-manage, mastermind, coordinate, direct, engineer.

ordain verb **1** *the Church of England voted to ordain women:* **confer holy orders on**, appoint, anoint, consecrate. **2** *the path ordained by God:* **predetermine**, predestine, preordain, determine, prescribe, designate. **3** *he ordained that anyone hunting in the forest was to pay a fine:* **decree**, rule, order, command, lay down, legislate, prescribe, pronounce.

ordeal noun *both women were understandably shaken by their ordeal:* **unpleasant experience**, painful experience, trial, tribulation, nightmare, trauma, hell (on earth), trouble, difficulty, torture, torment, agony.

order noun **1** *alphabetical order:* **sequence**, arrangement, organization, disposition, system, series, succession; grouping, classification, categorization, codification, systematization. **2** *some semblance of order:* **tidiness**, neatness, orderliness, trimness. **3** *the police were needed to keep*

order: **peace**, control, law (and order), lawfulness, discipline, calm, (peace and) quiet, peacefulness, peaceableness. **4** *his sense of order:* **orderliness**, organization, method, system; symmetry, uniformity, regularity; routine. **5** *the equipment was in good order:* **condition**, state, repair, shape. **6** *I had to obey his orders:* **command**, instruction, directive, direction, decree, edict, injunction, mandate, dictate, commandment, rescript; law, rule, regulation, diktat; demand, bidding, requirement, stipulation; informal say-so; formal ordinance. **7** *the company has won the order:* **commission**, purchase order, request, requisition; booking, reservation. **8** *the lower orders of society:* **class**, level, rank, grade, degree, position, category. **9** *the established social order:* **(class) system**, hierarchy, pecking order, grading, ranking, scale. **10** *the higher orders of insects:* **taxonomic group**, class, family, species, breed; taxon. **11** *a religious order:* **community**, brotherhood, sisterhood. **12** *the Orange Order:* **organization**, association, society, fellowship, fraternity, confraternity, sodality, lodge, guild, league, union, club; sect. **13** *skills of a very high order:* **type**, kind, sort, nature, variety; quality, calibre, standard.
– OPPOSITES chaos.
▶ verb **1** *he ordered me to return:* **instruct**, command, direct, enjoin, tell, require, charge. **2** *he ordered that their assets be confiscated:* **decree**, ordain, rule, legislate, dictate, prescribe. **3** *you can order your tickets by phone:* **request**, apply for, place an order for; book, reserve. **4** *the messages are ordered chronologically:* **organize**, put in order, arrange, sort out, marshal, dispose, lay out; group, classify, categorize, catalogue, codify, systematize, systemize.
■ **in order 1** *list the dates in order:* in sequence, in alphabetical order, in numerical order, in order of priority. **2** *he found everything in order:* tidy, neat, orderly, straight, trim, shipshape (and Bristol fashion), in apple-pie order; in position, in place. **3** *I think it's in order for me to take the credit:* appropriate, fitting, suitable, acceptable, (all) right, permissible, permitted, allowable; informal okay.
■ **order someone about/around** tell someone what to do, give orders to, dictate to; lay down the law; informal boss about/around, push about/around.
■ **out of order 1** *the lift's out of order:* not working, not in working order, not functioning, broken, broken-down, out of service, out of commission, faulty, defective, inoperative; down; informal conked out, bust, (gone) kaput; N. Amer. informal on the fritz, out of whack. **2** Brit. informal *that's really out of order:* unacceptable, unfair, unjust, unjustified, uncalled for, below the belt, unreasonable, unwarranted, beyond the pale; informal not on, a bit much; Brit. informal

a bit thick, off, not cricket; Austral./NZ informal over the fence.

orderly adjective **1** *an orderly room:* **neat**, tidy, well ordered, in order, trim, in apple-pie order, spick and span. **2** *the orderly presentation of information:* **(well) organized**, efficient, methodical, systematic, meticulous, punctilious; coherent, structured, logical, well planned, well regulated, systematized. **3** *the crowd was orderly:* **well behaved**, law-abiding, disciplined, peaceful, peaceable, non-violent.
– OPPOSITES untidy, disorganized.

ordinarily adverb *he ordinarily worked outside Great Britain:* **usually**, normally, as a (general) rule, generally, in general, for the most part, mainly, mostly, most of the time, typically, habitually, commonly, routinely.

ordinary adjective **1** *the ordinary course of events:* **usual**, normal, standard, typical, common, customary, habitual, everyday, regular, routine, day-to-day. **2** *my life seemed very ordinary:* **average**, normal, run-of-the-mill, standard, typical, middle-of-the-road, conventional, unremarkable, unexceptional, workaday, undistinguished, nondescript, colourless, commonplace, humdrum, mundane, unmemorable, pedestrian, prosaic, quotidian, uninteresting, uneventful, dull, boring, bland, suburban, hackneyed; N. Amer. garden-variety; informal bog-standard, (plain) vanilla, nothing to write home about, no great shakes; Brit. informal common or garden; N. Amer. informal ornery.
– OPPOSITES unusual.
■ **out of the ordinary** unusual, exceptional, remarkable, extraordinary, unexpected, surprising, unaccustomed, unfamiliar, abnormal, atypical, different, special, exciting, memorable, noteworthy, unique, singular, outstanding; unconventional, unorthodox, strange, peculiar, odd, queer, curious, bizarre, outlandish; informal offbeat.

ordnance noun **guns**, cannon, artillery, weapons, arms; munitions.

organ noun **1** *the internal organs:* **body part**, biological structure. **2** *the official organ of the Communist Party:* **newspaper**, paper, journal, periodical, magazine, newsletter, gazette, publication, mouthpiece; informal rag.

organic adjective **1** *organic matter:* **living**, live, animate, biological, biotic. **2** *organic vegetables:* **free of chemicals**, pesticide-free, additive-free, natural. **3** *the love scenes were an organic part of the drama:* **essential**, fundamental, integral, intrinsic, vital, indispensable, inherent. **4** *a society is an organic whole:* **structured**, organized, coherent, integrated, coordinated, ordered, harmonious.

organism noun **1** *fish and other organisms:* **living thing**, being, creature, animal, plant, life form. **2** *a complex political organism:*

structure, system, organization, entity.

organization noun **1** *the organization of conferences:* **planning**, arrangement, coordination, administration, organizing, running, management. **2** *the overall organization of the book:* **structure**, arrangement, plan, pattern, order, form, format, framework, composition, constitution. **3** *his lack of organization:* **efficiency**, order, orderliness, planning. **4** *a large international organization:* **company**, firm, corporation, institution, group, consortium, conglomerate, agency, association, society; informal outfit.

organize verb **1** *our objective is to organize and disseminate information:* **(put in) order**, arrange, sort (out), assemble, marshal, put straight, group, classify, collocate, categorize, catalogue, codify, systematize, systemize; rare methodize. **2** *they organized a search party:* **make arrangements for**, arrange, coordinate, sort out, put together, fix up, set up, orchestrate, take care of, see to/about, deal with, manage, conduct, administrate, mobilize; schedule, timetable, programme.

organized adjective *a highly organized campaign:* **(well) ordered**, well run, well regulated, structured; orderly, efficient, neat, tidy, methodical; informal together.
– OPPOSITES inefficient.

orgiastic adjective *wild parties and orgiastic festivals:* **debauched**, wild, riotous, wanton, dissolute, depraved.

orgy noun **1** *a drunken orgy:* **wild party**, debauch, carousal, carouse, revel, revelry; informal binge, booze-up, bender, love-in; Brit. informal rave-up; N. Amer. informal toot. **2** *an orgy of violence:* **bout**, excess, spree, surfeit; informal binge.

orient, orientate verb **1** *there were no street names to enable her to orient herself:* **get/find one's bearings**, establish one's location. **2** *you need to orientate yourself to your new way of life:* **adapt**, adjust, familiarize, acclimatize, accustom, attune; N. Amer. acclimate. **3** *magazines oriented to the business community:* **aim**, direct, pitch, design, intend. **4** *the fires are oriented in line with the sunset:* **align**, place, position, dispose.

oriental adjective **eastern**, Far Eastern, Asian.

orientation noun **1** *the orientation of the radar station:* **positioning**, location, position, situation, placement, alignment. **2** *his orientation to his new way of life:* **adaptation**, adjustment, acclimatization. **3** *a movement that was broadly Marxist in orientation:* **attitude**, inclination. **4** *orientation courses:* **induction**, training, initiation, briefing.

orifice noun **opening**, hole, aperture, slot, slit, cleft.

origin noun **1** *the origins of life:* **beginning**,

start, commencement, origination, genesis, birth, dawning, dawn, emergence, creation, birthplace, cradle; source, basis, cause, root(s). **2** *the Latin origin of the word:* **source**, derivation, root(s), provenance, etymology; N. Amer. provenience. **3** *his Scottish origins:* **descent**, ancestry, parentage, pedigree, lineage, line (of descent), heritage, birth, extraction, family, stock, blood, bloodline.

original adjective **1** *the original inhabitants:* **indigenous**, native, aboriginal, autochthonous; first, earliest, early. **2** *original Rembrandts:* **authentic**, genuine, actual, true, bona fide; informal pukka, kosher. **3** *the film is highly original:* **innovative**, creative, imaginative, innovatory, inventive; new, novel, fresh, refreshing; unusual, unconventional, unorthodox, groundbreaking, pioneering, avant-garde, unique, distinctive.
noun **1** *a copy of the original:* **archetype**, prototype, source, master. **2** *he really is an original:* **individualist**, individual, eccentric, nonconformist, free spirit, maverick; informal character, oddball; Brit. informal one-off, odd bod; N. Amer. informal screwball, kook.

originality noun *the originality of his ideas:* **inventiveness**, ingenuity, creativeness, creativity, innovation, novelty, freshness, imagination, imaginativeness, individuality, unconventionality, uniqueness, distinctiveness.

originally adverb *the conference was originally scheduled for November:* **(at) first**, in/at the beginning, to begin with, initially, in the first place, at the outset.

originate verb **1** *the disease originates from Africa:* **arise**, have its origin, begin, start, stem, spring, emerge, emanate. **2** *Bill Levy originated the idea:* **invent**, create, initiate, devise, think up, dream up, conceive, formulate, form, develop, generate, engender, produce, mastermind, pioneer.

originator noun **inventor**, creator, architect, author, father, mother, initiator, innovator, founder, pioneer, mastermind.

ornament noun **1** *small tables covered with ornaments:* **knick-knack**, trinket, bauble, bibelot, gewgaw, gimcrack, furbelow; informal whatnot, doodah; N. Amer. informal tchotchke. **2** *the dress had no ornament at all:* **decoration**, adornment, embellishment, ornamentation, trimming, accessories.
verb *the room was highly ornamented:* **decorate**, adorn, embellish, trim, bedeck, deck (out), festoon.

ornamental adjective *ornamental plasterwork:* **decorative**, fancy, ornate, ornamented.

ornamentation noun **decoration**, adornment, embellishment, ornament, trimming, accessories.

ornate adjective **1** *an ornate mirror:* **elaborate**, decorated, embellished, adorned, ornamented, fancy, fussy, ostentatious, showy; informal flash, flashy. **2** *ornate language:* **elaborate**, flowery, florid; grandiose, pompous, pretentious, high-flown, orotund, magniloquent, grandiloquent, rhetorical, oratorical, bombastic, overwrought, overblown; informal highfalutin, purple.
– OPPOSITES plain.

orthodox adjective **1** *orthodox views:* **conventional**, mainstream, conformist, (well) established, traditional, traditionalist, prevalent, popular, conservative, unoriginal. **2** *an orthodox Hindu:* **conservative**, traditional, observant, devout, strict.
– OPPOSITES unconventional.

orthodoxy noun **1** *a pillar of orthodoxy:* **conventionality**, conventionalism, conformism, conservatism, traditionalism, conformity. **2** *Christian orthodoxies:* **doctrine**, belief, conviction, creed, dogma, credo, theory, tenet, teaching.

oscillate verb **1** *the pendulum started to oscillate:* **swing (to and fro)**, swing back and forth, sway; N. Amer. informal wigwag. **2** *he was oscillating between fear and bravery:* **waver**, swing, fluctuate, alternate, see-saw, yo-yo, sway, vacillate, hover; informal wobble.

oscillation noun **1** *the oscillation of the pendulum:* **swinging (to and fro)**, swing, swaying. **2** *his oscillation between commerce and art:* **wavering**; swinging, fluctuation, see-sawing, yo-yoing, vacillation.

ossify verb **1** *these cartilages may ossify:* **turn into bone**, become bony, harden, solidify, rigidify, petrify. **2** *ossified political institutions:* **become inflexible**, become rigid, fossilize, rigidify, stagnate.

ostensible adjective **apparent**, outward, superficial, professed, supposed, alleged, purported.
– OPPOSITES genuine.

ostensibly adverb *it is ostensibly a book about football:* **apparently**, seemingly, on the face of it, to all intents and purposes, outwardly, superficially, allegedly, supposedly, purportedly.

ostentation noun **showiness**, show, ostentatiousness, pretentiousness, vulgarity, conspicuousness, display, flamboyance, gaudiness, brashness, extravagance, ornateness, exhibitionism; informal flashiness, glitz, glitziness, ritziness.

ostentatious adjective *an ostentatious display of wealth:* **showy**, pretentious, conspicuous, flamboyant, gaudy, brash, vulgar, loud, extravagant, fancy, ornate, over-elaborate; informal flash, flashy, over the top, OTT, glitzy, ritzy; N. Amer. informal superfly.
– OPPOSITES restrained.

ostracize verb *individuals who took such*

action risked being ostracized by their fellow workers: **exclude**, shun, spurn, cold-shoulder, reject, shut out, avoid, ignore, snub, cut dead, keep at arm's length, leave out in the cold; blackball, blacklist; Brit. send to Coventry; informal freeze out; Brit. informal blank.
– OPPOSITES welcome.

other adjective **1** *these homes use other fuels:* **alternative**, different, dissimilar, disparate, distinct, separate, contrasting. **2** *are there any other questions?* **more**, further, additional, extra, added, supplementary.

otherwise adverb **1** *hurry up, otherwise we'll be late:* **or (else)**, if not. **2** *she's exhausted, but otherwise she's fine:* **in other respects**, apart from that. **3** *he could not have acted otherwise:* **in any other way**, differently.

other-worldly adjective *his face had a distant, other-wordly look:* **ethereal**, dreamy, spiritual, mystic, mystical; unearthly, unworldly, supernatural.
– OPPOSITES realistic.

ounce noun *it took every ounce of courage she possessed to board the plane:* **particle**, scrap, bit, speck, iota, whit, jot, trace, atom, shred, crumb, fragment, grain, drop, spot; informal smidgen.

oust verb *armed forces ousted the new coalition government:* **drive out**, expel, force out, throw out, remove (from office/power), eject, get rid of, depose, topple, unseat, overthrow, bring down, overturn, dismiss, dislodge, displace; informal boot out, kick out; Brit. informal turf out.

out adjective & adverb **1** *she's out at the moment:* **not here**, not at home, not in, (gone) away, elsewhere, absent. **2** *the secret was out:* **revealed**, (out) in the open, common/public knowledge, known, disclosed, divulged. **3** *the roses are out:* **in flower**, flowering, in (full) bloom, blooming, in blossom, blossoming, open. **4** *the book should be out soon:* **available**, obtainable, in the shops, published, in print. **5** *the fire was nearly out:* **extinguished**, no longer alight. **6** *smoking is out:* **forbidden**, not permitted, not allowed, proscribed, unacceptable; informal not on. **7** *he was slightly out in his calculations:* **mistaken**, inaccurate, incorrect, wrong, in error.
– OPPOSITES in.

out-and-out adjective *he really is an out-and-out chauvinist:* **utter**, downright, thoroughgoing, absolute, complete, thorough, total, unmitigated, outright, real, perfect, consummate; N. Amer. full-bore; informal deep-dyed; Brit. informal right; Austral./NZ informal fair.
– OPPOSITES partial.

outbreak noun **1** *a fresh outbreak of killings:* **eruption**, flare-up, upsurge, outburst, rash, wave, spate, flood, explosion, burst, flurry. **2** *on the outbreak of war:* **start**, beginning, commencement, onset, outset.

outburst noun *a wild outburst of applause:* **eruption**, explosion, burst, outbreak, flare-up, access, rush, flood, storm, outpouring, surge, upsurge, outflowing.

outcast noun *a social outcast:* **pariah**, persona non grata, reject, outsider.

outclass verb *he completely outclassed his rivals:* **surpass**, be superior to, be better than, outshine, overshadow, eclipse, outdo, outplay, outmanoeuvre, outstrip, get the better of, upstage; top, cap, beat, defeat, exceed; informal be a cut above, be head and shoulders above, run rings round.

outcome noun *the future of the industry could hinge on the outcome of next month's election:* **(end) result**, consequence, net result, upshot, after-effect, aftermath, conclusion, issue, end (product).

outcry noun **1** *an outcry of passion:* **shout**, exclamation, cry, yell, howl, roar, scream; informal holler. **2** *the public outcry led to the closure of the bank:* **protest(s)**, protestation(s), complaints, objections, furore, fuss, commotion, uproar, outbursts, opposition, dissent; informal hullabaloo, ballyhoo, ructions, stink.

outdated adjective *an outdated rail network:* **old-fashioned**, out of date, outmoded, out of fashion, unfashionable, dated, passé, old, behind the times, behindhand, obsolete, antiquated; informal out, old hat, square, not with it, out of the ark; N. Amer. informal horse-and-buggy, clunky.
– OPPOSITES modern.

outdistance verb **1** *the colt outdistanced the train:* **outrun**, outstrip, outpace, leave behind, get (further) ahead of; overtake, pass. **2** *the mill outdistanced all its rivals:* **surpass**, outshine, outclass, outdo, exceed, transcend, top, cap, beat, better, leave behind; informal leave standing.

outdo verb *the men tried to outdo each other in their generosity:* **surpass**, outshine, overshadow, eclipse, outclass, outmanoeuvre, get the better of, put in the shade, upstage; exceed, transcend, top, cap, beat, better, leave behind, get ahead of; informal be a cut above, be head and shoulders above, run rings round.

outdoor adjective *a popular outdoor activity:* **open air**, out-of-doors, outside, al fresco, not under cover.
– OPPOSITES indoor.

outer adjective **1** *the outer layer is a waterproof, breathable fabric:* **outside**, outermost, outward, exterior, external, surface. **2** *outer areas of the city:* **outlying**, distant, remote, faraway, furthest, peripheral; suburban.
– OPPOSITES inner.

outface verb *the Cabinet successfully outfaced the shop stewards' movement:* **stand up to**, face down, cow, overawe, intimidate.

outfit noun **1** *I need a new outfit for the wedding:* **costume**, suit, uniform, ensemble,

attire, clothes, clothing, dress, garb; informal get-up, gear, togs; Brit. informal kit, rig-out. **2** *a studio lighting outfit:* **kit**, equipment, tools, implements, tackle, apparatus, paraphernalia, things, stuff. **3** *a local manufacturing outfit:* **organization**, set-up, enterprise, company, firm, business; group, band, body, team.
▸verb *enough swords to outfit an army:* **equip**, kit out, fit out/up, rig out, supply, arm; dress, attire, clothe, deck out.

outfitter noun **clothier**, tailor, couturier, costumier, dressmaker, seamstress.

outflow noun *the seabed was forced apart by the outflow of lava:* **discharge**, outflowing, outpouring, outrush, rush, flood, deluge, issue, spurt, jet, cascade, stream, torrent, gush, outburst; flow, flux.

outgoing adjective **1** *children who are outgoing and friendly:* **extrovert**, uninhibited, unreserved, demonstrative, affectionate, warm, friendly, genial, cordial, affable, easy-going, sociable, convivial, lively, gregarious; communicative, responsive, open, forthcoming, frank. **2** *the outgoing president:* **departing**, retiring, leaving.
– OPPOSITES introverted, incoming.

outgoings plural noun *monthly outgoings exceed income:* **expenses**, expenditure, spending, outlay, payments, costs, overheads.

outgrowth noun *the eye first appears as an outgrowth from the brain:* **protuberance**, swelling, excrescence, growth, lump, bump, bulge; tumour, cancer, boil, carbuncle, pustule.

outing noun *family outings to the seaside:* **(pleasure) trip**, excursion, jaunt, expedition, day out, (mystery) tour, drive, ride, run; informal junket, spin.

outlandish adjective *he wears outlandish clothes:* **weird**, queer, far out, quirky, zany, eccentric, idiosyncratic, unconventional, unorthodox, funny, bizarre, unusual, singular, extraordinary, strange, unfamiliar, peculiar, odd, curious; informal offbeat, off the wall, way-out, wacky, freaky, kooky, kinky, oddball; N. Amer. informal in left field.
– OPPOSITES ordinary.

outlast verb *the buildings outlasted generations of occupants:* **outlive**, survive; ride out, weather, withstand.

outlaw noun *bands of outlaws:* **fugitive**, (wanted) criminal, outcast, exile, pariah; bandit, robber.
▸verb **1** *they voted to outlaw fox-hunting:* **ban**, bar, prohibit, forbid, veto, make illegal, proscribe, interdict. **2** *she feared she would be outlawed:* **banish**, exile, expel.
– OPPOSITES permit.

outlay noun *the project involved comparatively little financial outlay:* **expenditure**, expenses, spending, outgoings, cost, price, payment, investment.
– OPPOSITES profit.

outlet noun **1** *a central-heating outlet:* **vent (hole)**, way out, egress; outfall, opening, channel, conduit, duct. **2** *an outlet for farm produce:* **market**, retail outlet, marketplace, shop, store. **3** *an outlet for their energies:* **means of expression**, (means of) release, vent, avenue, channel.

outline noun **1** *the outline of the building:* **silhouette**, profile, shape, contours, form, line, delineation; diagram, sketch. **2** *an outline of expenditure for each department:* **rough idea**, thumbnail sketch, (quick) rundown, summary, synopsis, résumé, precis; essence, main points, gist, (bare) bones, draft, sketch.
▸verb **1** *the plane was outlined against the sky:* **silhouette**, define, demarcate; sketch, delineate, trace. **2** *she outlined the plan briefly:* **rough out**, sketch out, draft, give a rough idea of, summarize, precis.

outlive verb *she outlived her husband by nearly thirty years:* **live on after**, live longer than, outlast, survive.

outlook noun **1** *the two men were wholly different in outlook:* **point of view**, viewpoint, views, opinion, (way of) thinking, perspective, attitude, standpoint, stance, frame of mind. **2** *a lovely open outlook:* **view**, vista, prospect, panorama, scene, aspect. **3** *the outlook for the economy:* **prospects**, expectations, hopes, future, lookout.

outlying adjective *outlying villages:* **distant**, remote, outer, out of the way, faraway, far-flung, inaccessible, off the beaten track.

outmanoeuvre verb **1** *the English army were outmanoeuvred:* **outflank**, circumvent, bypass. **2** *he outmanoeuvred his critics:* **outwit**, outsmart, out-think, outplay, steal a march on, trick, get the better of; informal outfox, put one over on.

outmoded adjective *an outmoded Victorian building:* **out of date**, old-fashioned, out of fashion, outdated, dated, behind the times, antiquated, obsolete, passé; informal old hat, out of the ark.

out of date adjective **1** *this design is out of date:* **old-fashioned**, outmoded, out of fashion, unfashionable, frumpish, frumpy, outdated, dated, old, passé, behind the times, behindhand, obsolete, antiquated; informal out, old hat, square, not with it, out of the ark; N. Amer. informal horse-and-buggy, clunky. **2** *many of the facts are out of date:* **superseded**, obsolete, expired, lapsed, invalid, (null and) void.
– OPPOSITES fashionable, current.

out of the way adjective *he has lived in some very out-of-the-way places:* **outlying**, distant, remote, faraway, far-flung, isolated, lonely, godforsaken, inaccessible, off the beaten track.
– OPPOSITES accessible.

o

outpouring noun *outpourings of nationalist discontent:* **outburst**, eruption, explosion, effusion, welling up, gush, stream, flow, gale, flood, storm, torrent, surge, upsurge.

output noun *industrial output fell by 2.8%:* **production**, amount/quantity produced, yield, gross domestic product, out-turn; works, writings.

outrage noun **1** *widespread public outrage:* **indignation**, fury, anger, rage, disapproval, wrath, resentment. **2** *it is an outrage that I have to put up with such treatment:* **scandal**, offence, insult, injustice, disgrace. **3** *the bomb outrage:* **atrocity**, act of violence/wickedness, crime, wrong, barbarism, inhumane act.
verb *his remarks outraged his parishioners:* **enrage**, infuriate, incense, anger, scandalize, offend, give offence to, affront, shock, horrify, disgust, appal.

outrageous adjective **1** *outrageous acts of cruelty:* **shocking**, disgraceful, scandalous, atrocious, appalling, monstrous, heinous; evil, wicked, abominable, terrible, horrendous, dreadful, foul, nauseating, sickening, vile, nasty, odious, loathsome, unspeakable; Brit. informal beastly. **2** *the politician's outrageous promises:* **far-fetched**, (highly) unlikely, doubtful, dubious, questionable, implausible, unconvincing, unbelievable, incredible, preposterous, extravagant, excessive. **3** *outrageous clothes:* **eye-catching**, flamboyant, showy, gaudy, ostentatious; shameless, shocking; informal saucy, flashy.

outré adjective *the composer's more outré harmonies:* **weird**, queer, outlandish, far out, freakish, quirky, zany, eccentric, off-centre, unconventional, unorthodox, funny, bizarre, fantastic, unusual, singular, extraordinary, strange, unfamiliar, peculiar, odd, out of the way; informal way-out, wacky, freaky, kooky, oddball, off the wall; N. Amer. informal offbeat, in left field.

outright adverb **1** *he rejected the proposal outright:* **completely**, entirely, wholly, fully, totally, categorically, absolutely, utterly, flatly, unreservedly. **2** *I told her outright:* **explicitly**, directly, forthrightly, openly, frankly, candidly, honestly, sincerely, bluntly, plainly, in plain language, truthfully, to someone's face, straight from the shoulder; Brit. informal straight up. **3** *they were killed outright:* **instantly**, instantaneously, immediately, at once, straight away, then and there, on the spot. **4** *paintings have to be bought outright:* **all at once**, in one go.
adjective **1** *an outright lie:* **out-and-out**, absolute, complete, downright, utter, sheer, categorical, unqualified, unconditional. **2** *the outright winner:* **definite**, unequivocal, clear, unqualified, incontestable, unmistakable.

outrun verb *an antelope could easily outrun a lion:* **run faster than**, outstrip, outdistance,

outpace, leave behind, lose; informal leave standing.

outset noun *the project was flawed from the outset:* **start**, starting point, beginning, commencement, dawn, birth, origin, inception, opening, launch, inauguration; informal the word go.
– OPPOSITES end.

outshine verb *she was outshone by her elder sister:* **surpass**, overshadow, eclipse, outclass, put in the shade, upstage, exceed, transcend, top, cap, beat, better; informal be a cut above, be head and shoulders above, run rings round.

outside noun *the outside of the building:* **outer/external surface**, exterior, outer side/layer, case, skin, shell, covering, facade.
adjective **1** *outside lights:* **exterior**, external, outer, outdoor, out-of-doors. **2** *outside contractors:* **independent**, hired, temporary, freelance, casual, external, extramural. **3** *an outside chance:* **slight**, slender, slim, small, tiny, faint, negligible, remote, vague.
adverb *they went outside | shall we eat outside?* **outdoors**, out of doors.
– OPPOSITES inside.

outsider noun *to an outsider, the scene would have appeared normal:* **stranger**, visitor, non-member; foreigner, alien, immigrant, emigrant, émigré; incomer, newcomer, parvenu.

outsize adjective **1** *her outsize handbag:* **huge**, oversized, enormous, gigantic, very big/large, great, giant, colossal, massive, mammoth, vast, immense, tremendous, monumental, prodigious, mountainous, king-sized; informal mega, monster, whopping (great), thumping (great), humongous, jumbo, bumper; Brit. informal whacking (great), ginormous. **2** *an outsize actor:* **very large**, big, massive, fat, corpulent, stout, heavy, plump, portly, ample, bulky; informal pudgy, tubby; Brit. informal podgy.

outskirts plural noun *a house on the outskirts of the town:* **outlying districts**, edges, fringes, suburbs, suburbia; purlieus, borders, environs.

outsmart verb *buyers and sellers attempt to outsmart each other:* **outwit**, outmanoeuvre, outplay, steal a march on, trick, get the better of; informal outfox, pull a fast one on, put one over on.

outspoken adjective *an outspoken critic of the government:* **forthright**, direct, candid, frank, straightforward, honest, open, straight from the shoulder, plain-spoken; blunt, abrupt, bluff, brusque.

outspread adjective *the kestrels were soaring with outspread wings:* **fully extended**, outstretched, spread out, fanned out, unfolded, unfurled, (wide) open, opened out.

outstanding adjective **1** *an outstanding painter:* **excellent**, marvellous, magnificent, superb, fine, wonderful, superlative,

exceptional, first-class, first-rate; informal great, terrific, tremendous, super, amazing, fantastic, sensational, fabulous, ace, crack, A1, mean, awesome, out of this world; Brit. informal smashing, brilliant; N. Amer. informal neat; Austral. informal bonzer. **2** *an outstanding decorative element:* **remarkable**, extraordinary, exceptional, striking, eye-catching, arresting, impressive, distinctive, unforgettable, memorable, special, momentous, significant, notable, noteworthy; informal out of this world. **3** *how much work is still outstanding?* **to be done**, undone, unattended to, unfinished, incomplete, remaining, pending, ongoing. **4** *the firm's outstanding debts are mounting:* **unpaid**, unsettled, owing, owed, to be paid, payable, due, overdue, undischarged; N. Amer. delinquent.
– OPPOSITES unexceptional.

outstrip verb **1** *he outstripped the police cars:* **go faster than**, outrun, outdistance, outpace, leave behind, get (further) ahead of, lose; informal leave standing. **2** *demand far outstrips supply:* **surpass**, exceed, be more than, top, eclipse.

outward adjective *she put on an outward appearance of sadness:* **external**, outer, outside, exterior; surface, superficial, seeming, apparent, ostensible.
– OPPOSITES inward.

outwardly adverb *the house is outwardly no different from any of the others:* **externally**, on the surface, superficially, on the face of it, to all intents and purposes, apparently, ostensibly, seemingly.

outweigh verb *the costs outweigh the benefits:* **be greater than**, exceed, be superior to, prevail over, have the edge on/over, override, supersede, offset, cancel out, (more than) make up for, outbalance, compensate for.

outwit verb *constant vigilance is needed to outwit enemy infiltrators:* **outsmart**, outmanoeuvre, outplay, steal a march on, trick, gull, get the better of; informal outfox, pull a fast one on, put one over on.

outworn adjective *many of his doctrines are outworn today:* **out of date**, outdated, old-fashioned, out of fashion, outmoded, dated, behind the times, antiquated, obsolete, defunct, passé; informal old hat, out of the ark.
– OPPOSITES up to date.

oval adjective **egg-shaped**, ovoid, ovate, oviform, elliptical.

ovation noun *the show ended with an ovation from the audience:* **(round of) applause**, handclapping, clapping, cheering, cheers, bravos, acclaim, acclamation, tribute, standing ovation; informal (big) hand.

over preposition **1** *there will be cloud over most of the country:* **above**, on top of, higher (up) than, atop, covering. **2** *he walked over the grass:* **across**, around, throughout. **3** *he has*

three people over him: **superior to**, above, higher up than, in charge of, responsible for. **4** *over 200,000 people live in the area:* **more than**, above, in excess of, upwards of. **5** *a discussion over unemployment:* **on the subject of**, about, concerning, apropos of, with reference to, regarding, relating to, in connection with.
– OPPOSITES under.

adverb **1** *a flock of geese flew over:* **overhead**, on high, above, past, by. **2** *the relationship is over:* **at an end**, finished, concluded, terminated, ended, no more, a thing of the past. **3** *he had some money over:* **left (over)**, remaining, unused, surplus, in excess, in addition.
■ **over and above** in addition to, on top of, plus, as well as, besides, along with.
■ **over and over** repeatedly, again and again, over and over again, time and (time) again, many times over, frequently, constantly, continually, persistently, ad nauseam.

overact verb *she's a weepy actress with a strong tendency to overact:* **exaggerate**, overdo it, overplay it; informal ham it up, camp it up.

overall adjective *the overall cost:* **all-inclusive**, general, comprehensive, universal, all-embracing, gross, net, final, inclusive; wholesale, complete, across the board, global, worldwide.
adverb *overall, things have improved:* **generally (speaking)**, in general, altogether, all in all, on balance, on average, for the most part, in the main, on the whole, by and large, to a large extent.

overawe verb *Jane was often overawed by her landlady:* **intimidate**, daunt, cow, disconcert, unnerve, subdue, dismay, frighten, alarm, scare, terrify; informal psych out; N. Amer. informal buffalo.

overbalance verb *she turned round so fast that she almost overbalanced:* **fall over**, topple over, lose one's balance, tip over, keel over; push over, upend, upset.

overbearing adjective *he was at the mercy of his overbearing wife:* **domineering**, dominating, autocratic, tyrannical, despotic, oppressive, high-handed, bullying; informal bossy.

overblown adjective *an overblown piece of writing:* **overwritten**, florid, grandiose, pompous, over-elaborate, flowery, overwrought, pretentious, high-flown, turgid, grandiloquent, magniloquent, orotund; informal highfalutin.

overcast adjective *the sky was murky and overcast:* **cloudy**, clouded (over), sunless, darkened, dark, grey, black, leaden, heavy, dull, murky, dismal, dreary.
– OPPOSITES bright.

overcharge verb *clients are being overcharged:* **swindle**, charge too much, cheat, defraud, fleece, short-change; informal rip off, sting, screw, rob, diddle, do, rook;

N. Amer. informal gouge.

overcome verb **1** *we overcame the home team:* **defeat**, beat, conquer, trounce, thrash, rout, vanquish, overwhelm, overpower, get the better of, triumph over, prevail over, win over/against, outdo, outclass, worst, crush; informal drub, slaughter, clobber, hammer, lick, best, crucify, demolish, wipe the floor with, make mincemeat of, blow out of the water, take to the cleaners; Brit. informal stuff; N. Amer. informal shellac, skunk. **2** *they overcame their fear of flying:* **get the better of**, prevail over, control, get/bring under control, master, conquer, defeat, beat; get over, get a grip on, curb, subdue; informal lick, best.
adjective *they were so kind I was overcome:* **overwhelmed**, emotional, moved, affected, speechless.

overconfident adjective *her downfall came through being overconfident:* **cocksure**, cocky, smug, conceited, self-assured, brash, blustering, overbearing, presumptuous, heading for a fall, riding for a fall; informal too big for one's boots.

overcritical adjective *overcritical parents:* **fault-finding**, hypercritical, captious, carping, cavilling, quibbling, hair-splitting, over-particular; fussy, finicky, fastidious, pedantic, over-scrupulous, punctilious; informal nit-picking, pernickety.

overcrowded adjective *overcrowded trains:* **overfull**, overflowing, full to overflowing/bursting, crammed full, congested, overpopulated, overpeopled, crowded, swarming, teeming; informal bursting/bulging at the seams, full to the gunwales, jam-packed.
– OPPOSITES empty.

overdo verb **1** *she overdoes the cockney scenes:* **exaggerate**, overstate, overemphasize, overplay, go overboard with, over-dramatize; informal ham up, camp up. **2** *don't overdo the drink:* **have/use/eat/drink too much of**, overindulge in, have/use/eat/drink to excess. **3** *they overdid the beef:* **overcook**, burn, ruin.
– OPPOSITES understate.
■ **overdo it** work too hard, overwork, do too much, burn the candle at both ends, overtax oneself, drive/push oneself too hard, work/run oneself into the ground, wear oneself to a shadow, wear oneself out, bite off more than one can chew, strain oneself; informal kill oneself, knock oneself out.

overdone adjective *the flattery was overdone:* **excessive**, too much, undue, immoderate, inordinate, disproportionate, inflated, overstated, overworked, exaggerated, overemphasized, over-enthusiastic, over-effusive; informal a bit much, over the top, OTT.
– OPPOSITES understated.

overdue adjective **1** *the ship is overdue:* **late**, behind schedule, behind time, delayed, unpunctual. **2** *overdue payments:* **unpaid**, unsettled, owing, owed, payable, due, outstanding, undischarged; N. Amer. delinquent.
– OPPOSITES early, punctual.

overeat verb *most of us are inclined to overeat occasionally:* **eat too much**, be greedy, gorge (oneself), overindulge (oneself), feast, gourmandize, gluttonize; informal binge, make a pig of oneself, pig out, have eyes bigger than one's stomach; N. Amer. informal scarf out.
– OPPOSITES starve.

overemphasize verb *the importance of appropriate design methods cannot be overemphasized:* **place/lay too much emphasis on**, overstress, place/lay too much stress on, exaggerate, make too much of, overplay, overdo, over-dramatize; informal make a big thing about/of, blow up out of all proportion.
– OPPOSITES understate, play down.

overflow verb *a lot of cream had overflowed the edges of the shallow dish:* **spill over**, flow over, brim over, well over, pour forth, stream forth, flood.
noun **1** *an overflow from the tank:* **overspill**, spill, spillage, flood. **2** *to accommodate the overflow, five more offices were built:* **surplus**, excess, additional people/things, extra people/things, remainder, overspill.

overflowing adjective *the floods were caused by overflowing rivers:* **overfull**, full to overflowing/bursting, spilling over, running over, crammed full, overcrowded, overloaded; informal bursting/bulging at the seams, jam-packed.
– OPPOSITES empty.

overhang verb *the shrubs overhang the lawn:* **stick out (over)**, stand out (over), extend (over), project (over), protrude (over), jut out (over), bulge out (over), hang over.

overhaul verb *I've been overhauling the gearbox:* **service**, maintain, repair, mend, fix up, rebuild, renovate, recondition, refit, refurbish; informal do up, patch up.

overhead adverb *a burst of thunder erupted overhead:* **(up) above**, high up, (up) in the sky, on high, above/over one's head.
– OPPOSITES below.
adjective *overhead lines:* **aerial**, elevated, raised, suspended.
– OPPOSITES underground.

overheads plural noun *businesses with high overheads:* **(running) costs**, operating costs, fixed costs, expenses; Brit. oncosts.
– OPPOSITES profit.

overindulge verb **1** *we all overindulge at Christmas:* **drink/eat too much**, overeat, overdrink, be greedy, be intemperate, overindulge oneself, overdo it, drink/eat to excess, gorge (oneself), feast, gourmandize, gluttonize; informal binge, stuff oneself, go overboard, make a pig of oneself, pig oneself; N. Amer. informal scarf out. **2** *his*

O

mother had overindulged him: **spoil**, give in to, indulge, humour, pander to, pamper, mollycoddle, baby.
– OPPOSITES abstain.

overindulgence noun **intemperance**, immoderation, excess, overeating, overdrinking, gorging; informal binge.
– OPPOSITES abstinence.

overjoyed adjective *Ms Bailey was overjoyed at the birth of her daughter:* **ecstatic**, euphoric, thrilled, elated, delighted, on cloud nine/seven, in seventh heaven, jubilant, rapturous, jumping for joy, delirious, blissful, in raptures, as pleased as Punch, cock-a-hoop, as happy as a sandboy, as happy as Larry; informal over the moon, on top of the world, tickled pink; N. Amer. informal as happy as a clam; Austral. informal wrapped.
– OPPOSITES unhappy.

overlay verb *the area was overlaid with marble:* **cover**, face, surface, veneer, inlay, laminate, plaster; coat, varnish, glaze.
noun *an overlay of glass-fibre insulation:* **covering**, cover, layer, face, surface, veneer, lamination; coat, varnish, glaze, wash.

overload verb 1 *avoid overloading the ship:* **overburden**, put too much in, overcharge, weigh down. 2 *don't overload the wiring:* **strain**, overtax, overwork, overuse, swamp, oversupply, overwhelm.
noun *there was an overload of demands:* **excess**, overabundance, superabundance, profusion, glut, surfeit, surplus, superfluity; avalanche, deluge, flood.

overlook verb 1 *he overlooked the mistake:* **fail to notice**, fail to spot, miss. 2 *his work has been overlooked:* **disregard**, neglect, ignore, pay no attention/heed to, pass over, forget. 3 *she was willing to overlook his faults:* **deliberately ignore**, not take into consideration, disregard, take no notice of, make allowances for, turn a blind eye to, excuse, pardon, forgive. 4 *the breakfast room overlooks the garden:* **have a view of**, look over/across, look on to, look out on/over, give on to, command a view of.

overly adverb *she was a jealous and overly possessive woman:* **unduly**, excessively, inordinately, too; wildly, absurdly, ridiculously, outrageously, unreasonably, exorbitantly, impossibly.

overpower verb 1 *the prisoners might overpower the crew:* **gain control over**, overwhelm, prevail over, get the better of, gain mastery over, overthrow, overturn, subdue, suppress, subjugate, repress, bring someone to their knees, conquer, defeat, triumph over, worst, trounce; informal thrash, lick, best, clobber, wipe the floor with. 2 *he was overpowered by grief:* **overcome**, overwhelm, move, stir, affect, touch, stun, shake, devastate, take aback, leave speechless; informal bowl over, knock sideways; Brit. informal knock/hit for six.

overpowering adjective 1 *overpowering grief:* **overwhelming**, oppressive,

unbearable, unendurable, intolerable, shattering. 2 *an overpowering smell:* **stifling**, suffocating, strong, pungent, powerful; nauseating, offensive, acrid, fetid, mephitic. 3 *overpowering evidence:* **irrefutable**, undeniable, indisputable, incontestable, incontrovertible, compelling, conclusive.

overrate verb *it is easy to overrate what Frederick achieved:* **overestimate**, overvalue, think too much of, attach too much importance to, praise too highly.
– OPPOSITES underestimate.

overreach
■ **overreach oneself** *he waited for his opponents to overreach themselves:* try to do too much, overestimate one's ability, overdo it, overstretch oneself, wear/burn oneself out, bite off more than one can chew.

overreact verb *parents should set children a good example rather than overreact:* **react disproportionately**, act irrationally, lose one's sense of proportion, blow something up out of all proportion; Brit. informal go over the top.

override verb 1 *the court could not override her decision:* **disallow**, overrule, countermand, veto, quash, overturn, overthrow; cancel, reverse, rescind, revoke, repeal, annul, nullify, invalidate, negate, void. 2 *the government can override all opposition:* **disregard**, pay no heed to, take no account of, turn a deaf ear to, ignore, ride roughshod over. 3 *a positive attitude will override any negative thoughts:* **outweigh**, supersede, take precedence over, take priority over, offset, cancel out, (more than) make up for, outbalance, compensate for.

overriding adjective *safety was the overriding consideration:* **most important**, of greatest importance, of greatest significance, uppermost, top, first (and foremost), highest, pre-eminent, predominant, principal, primary, paramount, chief, main, major, foremost, central, key, focal, pivotal; informal number-one.

overrule verb *this ban was overruled by a federal court:* **countermand**, cancel, reverse, rescind, repeal, revoke, retract, disallow, override, veto, quash, overturn, overthrow, annul, nullify, invalidate, negate, void.

overrun verb 1 *guerrillas overran the barracks:* **invade**, storm, occupy, swarm into, surge into, inundate, overwhelm. 2 *the talks overran the deadline:* **exceed**, go beyond/over, run over.

oversee verb *it was decided to appoint a manager to oversee the building work:* **supervise**, superintend, be in charge/control of, be responsible for, look after, keep an eye on, inspect, administer, organize, manage, direct, preside over.

overseer noun **supervisor**, foreman, forewoman, team leader, controller, (line) manager, manageress, head (of department), superintendent, captain; Brit. gangmaster; informal boss, chief, governor; Brit. informal gaffer, guv'nor; N. Amer. informal straw boss; Austral. informal pannikin boss; Mining overman.

overshadow verb **1** *a massive hill overshadows the town:* **cast a shadow over**, shade, darken, conceal, obscure, screen; dominate, overlook. **2** *this feeling of tragedy overshadowed his story:* **cast gloom over**, blight, take the edge off, mar, spoil, ruin. **3** *he was overshadowed by his brilliant elder brother:* **outshine**, eclipse, surpass, exceed, be superior to, outclass, outstrip, outdo, upstage; informal be head and shoulders above.

oversight noun **1** *a stupid oversight:* **mistake**, error, omission, lapse, slip, blunder; informal slip-up, boo-boo; Brit. informal boob; N. Amer. informal goof. **2** *the omission was due to oversight:* **carelessness**, inattention, negligence, forgetfulness, laxity. **3** *school governors have oversight of the curriculum:* **supervision**, surveillance, superintendence, charge, care, administration, management.

overstate verb *he admitted that he had perhaps overstated his case:* **exaggerate**, overdo, overemphasize, overplay, dramatize, embroider, embellish; informal blow up out of all proportion.
– OPPOSITES understate.

overstatement noun **exaggeration**, overemphasis, dramatization, embroidery, embellishment, enhancement, hyperbole.

overt adjective *there was little overt opposition to parliamentary government:* **undisguised**, unconcealed, plain (to see), clear, apparent, conspicuous, obvious, noticeable, manifest, patent, open, blatant.
– OPPOSITES covert.

overtake verb **1** *a green car overtook the taxi:* **pass**, go past/by, get/pull ahead of, leave behind, outdistance, outstrip. **2** *tourism overtook coffee as the main earner of foreign currency:* **outstrip**, surpass, overshadow, eclipse, outshine, outclass; dwarf, put in the shade, exceed, top, cap. **3** *the calamity which overtook us:* **befall**, happen to, come upon, hit, strike, overwhelm, overcome, be visited on.

overthrow verb **1** *the President was overthrown:* **remove (from office/power)**, bring down, topple, depose, oust, displace, unseat. **2** *an attempt to overthrow Soviet rule:* **put an end to**, defeat, conquer.
noun **1** *the overthrow of the Shah:* **removal (from office/power)**, downfall, fall, toppling, deposition, ousting, displacement, supplanting, unseating. **2** *the overthrow of capitalism:* **ending**, defeat, displacement, fall, collapse, downfall, demise.

overtone noun *the decision may have political overtones:* **connotation**, hidden meaning, implication, association, undercurrent, undertone, echo, vibrations, hint, suggestion, insinuation, intimation, suspicion, feeling, nuance.

overture noun **1** *the overture to Don Giovanni:* **prelude**, introduction, opening, introductory movement. **2** *the overture to a long debate:* **preliminary**, prelude, introduction, lead-in, precursor, start, beginning. **3** *peace overtures:* **(opening) move**, approach, advances, feeler, signal, proposal, proposition.

overturn verb **1** *the boat overturned:* **capsize**, turn turtle, keel over, tip over, topple over, turn over; Nautical pitchpole. **2** *I overturned the stool:* **upset**, tip over, topple over, turn over, knock over, upend. **3** *the Senate may overturn this ruling:* **cancel**, reverse, rescind, repeal, revoke, retract, countermand, disallow, override, overrule, veto, quash, overthrow, annul, nullify, invalidate, negate, void.

overused adjective *overused words:* **hackneyed**, overworked, worn out, time-worn, tired, played out, clichéd, stale, trite, banal, stock, unoriginal.

overweening adjective *overweening ambition:* **overconfident**, conceited, cocksure, cocky, smug, haughty, supercilious, lofty, patronizing, arrogant, proud, vain, self-important, imperious, overbearing; informal high and mighty, uppish.
– OPPOSITES unassuming.

overweight adjective *Allen was somewhat overweight:* **fat**, obese, stout, corpulent, gross, fleshy, plump, portly, chubby, rotund, paunchy, pot-bellied, flabby, well upholstered, well padded, broad in the beam; informal porky, tubby, blubbery; Brit. informal podgy.
– OPPOSITES skinny.

overwhelm verb **1** *advancing sand dunes could overwhelm the village:* **swamp**, submerge, engulf, bury, deluge, flood, inundate. **2** *Spain overwhelmed Russia in the hockey:* **defeat (utterly/heavily)**, trounce, rout, beat (hollow), conquer, vanquish, be victorious over, triumph over, worst, overcome, overthrow, crush; informal thrash, lick, best, clobber, wipe the floor with. **3** *she was overwhelmed by a sense of tragedy:* **overcome**, move, stir, affect, touch, strike, dumbfound, shake, devastate, floor, leave speechless; informal bowl over, knock sideways; Brit. informal knock/hit for six.

overwhelming adjective **1** *an overwhelming number of players were unavailable:* **very large**, enormous, immense, inordinate, massive, huge. **2** *she had an overwhelming desire to laugh:* **very strong**, forceful, uncontrollable, irrepressible, irresistible, overpowering, compelling.

overwork verb **1** *we should not overwork:* **work too hard**, work/run oneself into the ground, wear oneself to a shadow, work one's fingers to the bone, burn the candle at both ends, overtax oneself, burn oneself out, do too much, overdo it, strain oneself,

o

overload oneself, drive/push oneself too hard; informal kill oneself, knock oneself out. **2** *my colleagues did not overwork me:* **drive (too hard)**, exploit, drive into the ground, tax, overtax, overburden, put upon, impose on.

overworked adjective **1** *overworked staff:* **stressed (out)**, stress-ridden, overtaxed, overburdened, overloaded, exhausted, worn out. **2** *an overworked phrase:* **hackneyed**, overused, worn out, tired, played out, clichéd, threadbare, stale, trite, banal, stock, unoriginal.
– OPPOSITES relaxed, original.

overwrought adjective **1** *she was too overwrought to listen:* **tense**, agitated, nervous, on edge, edgy, keyed up, worked up, highly strung, neurotic, overexcited, beside oneself, distracted, distraught, frantic, hysterical; informal in a state, in a tizzy, uptight, wound up, het up; Brit. informal strung up. **2** *the painting is overwrought:* **over-elaborate**, over-ornate, overblown, overdone, contrived, overworked, strained.
– OPPOSITES calm, understated.

owe verb *I still owe him £200:* **be in debt (to)**, be indebted (to), be in arrears (to), be under an obligation (to).

owing adjective *the rent was owing:* **unpaid**, to be paid, payable, due, overdue, undischarged, owed, outstanding, in arrears; N. Amer. delinquent.
– OPPOSITES paid.

■ **owing to** *his reading was hesitant owing to a stammer:* because of, as a result of, on account of, due to, as a consequence of, thanks to, in view of.

own adjective *he has his own reasons:*

personal, individual, particular, private, personalized, unique.
verb **1** *I own this house:* **be the owner of**, possess, be the possessor of, have in one's possession, have (to one's name). **2** *she had to own that she agreed:* **admit**, concede, grant, accept, acknowledge, agree, confess.
■ **get one's own back** (informal) have/get/take one's revenge (on), be revenged (on), hit back, get (back at), get even (with), settle accounts (with), repay, pay someone back, give someone their just deserts, retaliate (against/on), take reprisals (against), exact retribution (on), give someone a taste of their own medicine.
■ **hold one's own** stand firm, stand one's ground, keep one's end up, keep one's head above water, compete, survive, cope, get on/along.
■ **on one's own 1** *I am all on my own:* (all) alone, (all) by oneself, solitary, unaccompanied, companionless; informal by one's lonesome; Brit. informal on one's tod, on one's Jack Jones. **2** *she works well on her own:* unaided, unassisted, without help, without assistance, (all) by oneself, independently.
■ **own up** *he still couldn't own up to the lie:* confess (to), admit to, admit guilt, plead guilty, accept blame/responsibility, tell the truth (about), make a clean breast of it, tell all; informal come clean (about).

owner noun *restaurant owners:* **possessor**, holder, proprietor/proprietress, homeowner, freeholder, landlord, landlady.

ownership noun *the ownership of land:* **(right of) possession**, freehold, proprietorship, proprietary rights, title.

ox noun bull, bullock, steer; Farming beef.

Pp

pace noun **1** *he stepped back a pace:* **step**, stride. **2** *a slow, steady pace:* **gait**, stride, walk, march. **3** *he drove home at a furious pace:* **speed**, rate, velocity; informal clip, lick.
verb *she paced up and down:* **walk**, stride, tread, march, pound, patrol.

pacific adjective **1** *a pacific community:* **peace-loving**, peaceable, pacifist, non-violent, non-aggressive, non-belligerent. **2** *their pacific intentions:* **conciliatory**, peacemaking, placatory, propitiatory, appeasing, mollifying, mediatory, dovish. **3** *pacific waters:* **calm**, still, smooth, tranquil, placid, waveless, unruffled, like a millpond.
– OPPOSITES aggressive, stormy.

pacifism noun **peacemaking**, conscientious objection(s), passive resistance, peace-mongering, non-violence.

pacifist noun **peace-lover**, conscientious objector, passive resister, peacemaker, peace-monger, dove; Brit. informal conchie.
– OPPOSITES warmonger.

pacify verb *Gregory tried to think of a way of pacifying his wife.* **placate**, appease, calm (down), conciliate, propitiate, assuage, mollify, soothe.
– OPPOSITES enrage.

pack noun **1** *a pack of cigarettes:* **packet**, container, package, box, carton, parcel. **2** *a 45lb pack:* **backpack**, rucksack, knapsack, kitbag, bag, load. **3** *a pack of wolves:* **group**, herd, troop. **4** *a pack of youngsters:* **crowd**, mob, group, band, troupe, party, set, clique, gang, rabble, horde, throng, huddle, mass, assembly, gathering, host; informal crew, bunch.
verb **1** *she helped pack the hamper:* **fill (up)**, put things in, load. **2** *they packed their belongings:* **stow**, put away, store, box up. **3** *the glasses were packed in straw:* **wrap (up)**, package, parcel, swathe, swaddle, encase, enfold, envelop, bundle. **4** *Christmas shoppers packed the store:* **throng**, crowd (into), fill (to overflowing), cram, jam, squash into, squeeze into. **5** *pack the cloth against the wall:* **compress**, press, squash, squeeze, jam, tamp.
■ **pack something up** put away, tidy up/away, clear up/away.

package noun **1** *the delivery of a package:* **parcel**, packet, container, box. **2** *a complete*

package of services: **collection**, bundle, combination.
verb *goods packaged in recyclable materials:* **wrap (up)**, gift-wrap; pack (up), parcel (up), box, encase.

packaging noun **wrapping**, wrappers, packing, covering.

packed adjective *an audience of 500 in the packed conference hall:* **crowded**, full, filled (to capacity), crammed, jammed, solid, overcrowded, overfull, teeming, seething, swarming; informal jam-packed, chock-full, chock-a-block, full to the gunwales, bursting/bulging at the seams.

packet noun *a packet of cigarettes:* **pack**, carton, (cardboard) box, container, case, package.

pact noun *the guerrilla group made a peace pact with the government:* **agreement**, treaty, entente, protocol, deal, settlement, concordat; armistice, truce.

pad¹ noun **1** *a pad over the eye:* **piece of cotton wool**, dressing, pack, padding, wadding, wad. **2** *a seat pad:* **cushion**, squab. **3** *making notes on a pad:* **notebook**, notepad, writing pad, memo pad, jotter, block, sketch pad, sketchbook; N. Amer. scratch pad.
verb *a quilted jacket padded with duck feathers:* **stuff**, fill, pack, wad.
■ **pad something out** expand unnecessarily, fill out, amplify, increase, flesh out, lengthen, spin out, overdo, elaborate.

pad² verb *he padded along towards the bedroom:* **walk quietly**, tread warily, creep, tiptoe, steal, pussyfoot.

padding noun **1** *the boot has padding around the ankle:* **wadding**, cushioning, stuffing, packing, filling, lining. **2** *a concise style with no padding:* **verbiage**, verbosity, wordiness, prolixity; Brit. informal waffle.

paddle¹ noun *use the paddles to row ashore:* **oar**, scull, blade.
verb *we paddled around the bay:* **row gently**, pull, scull.

paddle² verb *children were paddling in the water:* **splash about**, wade; dabble.

paddock noun **field**, meadow, pasture; pen, pound; N. Amer. corral.

padlock verb *you should padlock ladders to something secure:* **lock (up)**, fasten, secure.

padre noun **priest**, chaplain, minister (of

p

religion), pastor, father, parson, clergyman, cleric, ecclesiastic, man of the cloth, churchman, vicar, rector, curate, preacher; informal reverend, Holy Joe, sky pilot; Austral. informal josser.

pagan noun *pagans worshipped the sun:* **heathen**, infidel, idolater, idolatress.
adjective *the pagan festival:* **heathen**, ungodly, irreligious, infidel, idolatrous.

page¹ noun *a book of 672 pages:* **folio**, sheet, side, leaf.

page² noun **1** *a page in a hotel:* **errand boy**, messenger boy; N. Amer. bellboy, bellhop. **2** *a page at a wedding:* **attendant**, pageboy, train-bearer.
verb *could you please page Mr Johnson?* **call (for)**, summon, send for.

pageant noun *the Queen attended a 1,000-horse pageant:* **parade**, procession, cavalcade, tableau (vivant); spectacle, extravaganza, show.

pageantry noun **spectacle**, display, ceremony, magnificence, pomp, splendour, grandeur, show; informal razzle-dazzle, razzmatazz.

pain noun **1** *she endured great pain:* **suffering**, agony, torture, torment, discomfort. **2** *a pain in the stomach:* **ache**, aching, soreness, throb, throbbing, sting, stinging, twinge, shooting pain, stab, pang; discomfort, irritation, tenderness. **3** *the pain of losing a loved one:* **sorrow**, grief, heartache, heartbreak, sadness, unhappiness, distress, desolation, misery, wretchedness, despair; agony, torment, torture. **4** *he took great pains to hide his feelings:* **care**, effort, bother, trouble.
verb **1** *her foot is still paining her:* **hurt**, cause pain, be painful, be sore, be tender, ache, throb, sting, twinge, cause discomfort; informal kill. **2** *the memory pains her:* **sadden**, grieve, distress, trouble, perturb, oppress, cause anguish to.
■ **be at pains** try hard, make a great effort, take (great) pains, put oneself out; strive, endeavour, try, do one's best, do one's utmost, go all out; informal bend/fall/lean over backwards.

pained adjective *she stared at Hebden with a pained expression on her face:* **upset**, hurt, wounded, injured, insulted, offended, aggrieved, displeased, disgruntled, annoyed, angered, angry, cross, indignant, irritated, resentful; informal riled, miffed, aggravated, peeved, hacked off, browned off; Brit. informal narked, cheesed off; N. Amer. informal teed off, ticked off, sore.

painful adjective **1** *a painful arm:* **sore**, hurting, tender, aching, throbbing. **2** *a painful experience:* **disagreeable**, unpleasant, nasty, bitter, distressing, upsetting, traumatic, miserable, sad, heartbreaking, agonizing, harrowing; informal gut-wrenching.

painfully adverb *the whole affair had been painfully embarrassing:* **distressingly**,

disturbingly, unendurably, unbearably, uncomfortably, unpleasantly; dreadfully; informal terribly, awfully.

painkiller noun **analgesic**, pain reliever, anodyne, anaesthetic, narcotic; palliative.

painless adjective **1** *any killing of animals should be painless:* **pain-free**. **2** *getting rid of him proved painless:* **easy**, trouble-free, effortless, simple, plain sailing; informal as easy as pie, a piece of cake, child's play, a cinch.
– OPPOSITES painful, difficult.

painstaking adjective *painstaking attention to detail:* **careful**, meticulous, thorough, assiduous, sedulous, attentive, diligent, industrious, conscientious, punctilious, scrupulous, rigorous, particular; pedantic, fussy.
– OPPOSITES slapdash.

paint noun **colouring**, colourant, tint, dye, stain, pigment, colour.
verb **1** *simply paint the ceiling:* **colour**, apply paint to, decorate, whitewash, emulsion, gloss, spray-paint, airbrush. **2** *the yobs had been painting slogans on a wall:* **daub**, smear, spray-paint, airbrush. **3** *Rembrandt painted his mother:* **portray**, picture, paint a picture of, depict, represent.

painting noun **picture**, illustration, portrayal, depiction, representation, image, artwork; oil (painting), watercolour, canvas.

pair noun *a pair of gloves:* **couple**, twosome, duo, brace, duplet, couplet, two, two of a kind, twins.
verb *a cardigan paired with a matching skirt:* **match**, put together, couple, twin.
■ **pair off/up** get together, team up, form a couple, make a twosome.

palace noun **castle**, chateau, schloss, mansion, stately home.

palatable adjective **1** *palatable meals:* **tasty**, appetizing, flavourful, flavoursome, delicious, mouth-watering, toothsome, succulent; informal scrumptious, yummy, scrummy, moreish. **2** *the truth is not always palatable:* **pleasant**, acceptable, pleasing, agreeable, to one's liking.
– OPPOSITES disagreeable.

palate noun **1** *menus to suit the tourist palate:* **(sense of) taste**, appetite, stomach. **2** *wine with a peachy palate:* **flavour**, savour, taste.

palatial adjective *a palatial five-star hotel:* **luxurious**, de luxe, magnificent, sumptuous, splendid, grand, opulent, lavish, stately, regal; fancy; Brit. upmarket; informal plush, swanky, posh, ritzy, swish.
– OPPOSITES modest.

palaver noun (informal) *what was all that palaver about?* **fuss (and bother)**, bother, commotion, trouble, rigmarole, folderol; informal song and dance, performance, to-do, carrying-on, kerfuffle, hoo-ha, hullabaloo, ballyhoo.

pale¹ noun **1** *the pales of a fence:* **stake**, post, pole, picket, upright. **2** *outside the pale of*

decency: **boundary**, confines, bounds, limits.
■ **beyond the pale** unacceptable, unseemly, improper, unsuitable, unreasonable, intolerable, disgraceful, deplorable, outrageous, scandalous, shocking; informal not on, not the done thing, out of order, out of line; Austral./NZ informal over the fence.

pale² adjective **1** *she looked pale and drawn:* **white**, pallid, pasty, wan, colourless, anaemic, bloodless, washed out, peaky, ashen, grey, whitish, whey-faced, drained, sickly, sallow, as white as a sheet, deathly pale; milky, creamy, cream, ivory, milk-white, alabaster; informal like death warmed up. **2** *pale colours:* **light**, light-coloured, pastel, muted, subtle, soft; faded, bleached, washed out. **3** *the pale light of morning:* **dim**, faint, weak, feeble. **4** *a pale imitation:* **feeble**, weak, insipid, bland, poor, inadequate; uninspired, unimaginative, lacklustre, spiritless, lifeless; informal pathetic.
– OPPOSITES dark.
verb **1** *his face paled:* **go/turn white**, grow/turn pale, blanch, lose colour. **2** *everything else pales by comparison:* **decrease in importance**, lose significance, pale into insignificance.

palisade noun **fence**, paling, barricade, stockade.

pall¹ noun *a pall of black smoke:* **cloud**, covering, cloak, veil, shroud, layer, blanket.
■ **cast a pall over** spoil, cast a shadow over, overshadow, cloud, put a damper on.

pall² verb *the high life was beginning to pall:* **become/grow tedious**, become/grow boring, lose its/their interest, lose attraction, wear off; weary, sicken, nauseate; irritate, irk.

palliative adjective *palliative medicine:* **soothing**, alleviating, sedative, calmative.
noun *antibiotics and palliatives:* **painkiller**, analgesic, pain reliever, sedative, tranquillizer, anodyne, calmative, opiate, bromide.

pallid adjective **1** *a pallid child:* **pale**, white, pasty, wan, colourless, anaemic, washed out, peaky, whey-faced, ashen, grey, whitish, drained, sickly, sallow; informal like death warmed up. **2** *pallid watercolours:* **insipid**, uninspired, colourless, uninteresting, unexciting, unimaginative, lifeless, spiritless, sterile, bland.

pallor noun *her dark hair accentuated her pallor:* **paleness**, pallidness, lack of colour, wanness, ashen hue, pastiness, peakiness, greyness, sickliness, sallowness.

palm
■ **have someone in the palm of one's hand** have control over, have influence over, have someone eating out of one's hand, have someone on a string; N. Amer. have someone in one's hip pocket.
■ **palm something off** foist, fob off, get rid of, dispose of, unload.

palmistry noun **fortune-telling**, palm-reading, clairvoyancy, chiromancy.

palpable adjective **1** *a palpable bump under the skin:* **tangible**, touchable, noticeable, detectable. **2** *his reluctance was palpable:* **perceptible**, perceivable, visible, noticeable, discernible, detectable, observable, tangible, unmistakable, transparent, self-evident; obvious, clear, plain (to see), evident, apparent, manifest, staring one in the face, written all over someone.
– OPPOSITES imperceptible.

palpitate verb *her heart began to palpitate:* **beat rapidly**, pound, throb, pulsate, pulse, thud, thump, hammer, race.

paltry adjective **1** *a paltry sum of money:* **small**, meagre, trifling, insignificant, negligible, inadequate, insufficient, derisory, pitiful, pathetic, miserable, niggardly, beggarly; informal measly, piddling, poxy. **2** *naval glory struck him as paltry:* **worthless**, petty, trivial, unimportant, insignificant, inconsequential, of little account.
– OPPOSITES considerable.

pamper verb *Trevor's big sister pampered him:* **spoil**, indulge, overindulge, cosset, mollycoddle, coddle, baby, wait on someone hand and foot.

pamphlet noun **brochure**, leaflet, booklet, circular, flyer, handbill; N. Amer. mailer, folder, dodger.

pan¹ noun **1** *a heavy pan:* **saucepan**, frying pan, wok, skillet. **2** *salt pans:* **hollow**, pit, depression, dip, crater, concavity.
verb *prospectors panned for gold:* **sift for**, search for, look for.
– OPPOSITES praise.
■ **pan out 1** *Harold's idea hadn't panned out:* succeed, be successful, work (out), turn out well. **2** *the deal panned out badly:* turn out, work out, end (up), come out, fall out, evolve.

pan² verb *the camera panned across to the building:* **swing (round)**, sweep, move, turn, circle.

panacea noun *a panacea for the country's economic problems:* **universal cure**, cure-all, cure for all ills, universal remedy, elixir, wonder drug; informal magic bullet.

panache noun *they played with panache and authority:* **flamboyance**, confidence, self-assurance, style, flair, elan, dash, verve, zest, spirit, brio, éclat, vivacity, gusto, liveliness, vitality, energy; informal pizzazz, oomph, zip, zing.

pancake noun **crêpe**, galette; blin, tortilla, tostada, chapatti, dosa, latke, blintze; N. Amer. flapjack, slapjack.

pandemic adjective *the disease is pandemic in Africa:* **widespread**, prevalent, pervasive, rife, rampant.

pandemonium noun *we heard a massive bang and then there was complete pandemonium:* **bedlam**, chaos, mayhem,

uproar, turmoil, tumult, commotion, confusion, anarchy, furore, hubbub, rumpus; informal hullabaloo.
– OPPOSITES peace.

pander
■ **pander to** *David was always there to pander to her every whim:* indulge, gratify, satisfy, cater to, give in to, accommodate, comply with.

panel noun 1 *a control panel:* **console**, instrument panel, dashboard; instruments, controls, dials. 2 *a panel of judges:* **group**, team, body, committee, board.

pang noun 1 *hunger pangs:* **(sharp) pain**, shooting pain, twinge, stab, spasm. 2 *a pang of remorse:* **qualm**, twinge, prick.

panic noun *a wave of panic:* **alarm**, anxiety, nervousness, fear, fright, trepidation, dread, terror, agitation, hysteria, consternation, perturbation, dismay, apprehension; informal flap, fluster, cold sweat, funk, tizzy; N. Amer. informal swivet.
– OPPOSITES calm.
verb 1 *there's no need to panic:* **be alarmed**, be scared, be nervous, be afraid, take fright, be agitated, be hysterical, lose one's nerve, get overwrought, get worked up; informal flap, get in a flap, lose one's cool, get into a tizzy, run around like a headless chicken, freak out, get in a stew; Brit. informal get the wind up, go into a (flat) spin, have kittens. 2 *talk of love panicked her:* **frighten**, alarm, scare, unnerve; informal throw into a tizzy, freak out; Brit. informal put the wind up.

panic-stricken adjective *the panic-stricken victims rushed out of their blazing homes:* **alarmed**, frightened, scared (stiff), terrified, terror-stricken, petrified, horrified, horror-stricken, fearful, afraid, panicky, frantic, in a frenzy, nervous, agitated, hysterical, beside oneself, worked up, overwrought; informal in a cold sweat, in a (blue) funk, in a flap, in a fluster, in a tizzy; Brit. informal in a flat spin.

panoply noun 1 *the full panoply of America's military might:* **array**, range, collection. 2 *all the panoply of religious liturgy:* **trappings**, regalia; splendour, spectacle, ceremony, ritual.

panorama noun 1 *he surveyed the panorama:* **(scenic) view**, vista, prospect, scene, scenery, landscape, seascape. 2 *a panorama of the art scene:* **overview**, survey, review, presentation, appraisal.

panoramic adjective 1 *a panoramic view:* **sweeping**, wide, extensive, scenic, commanding. 2 *a panoramic look at the 20th century:* **wide-ranging**, extensive, broad, far-reaching, comprehensive, all-embracing.

pant verb 1 *he was panting as they reached the top:* **breathe heavily**, breathe hard, puff (and blow), huff and puff, gasp, wheeze. 2 *it makes you pant for more:* **yearn for**, long for, crave, hanker after/for, ache for, hunger for, thirst for, be hungry for, be thirsty for,

wish for, desire, want; informal itch for, be dying for.
noun *breathing in shallow pants:* **gasp**, puff, wheeze, breath.

panting adjective **out of breath**, breathless, short of breath, puffed out, puffing (and blowing), huffing and puffing, gasping (for breath), wheezing, wheezy.

pantry noun **larder**, store, storeroom.

pants plural noun 1 (Brit.) **underpants**, briefs, Y-fronts, boxer shorts, boxers, long johns, (French) knickers, bikini briefs; Brit. camiknickers; N. Amer. shorts, undershorts; informal panties; Brit. informal kecks, knicks, smalls. 2 (N. Amer.). See **TROUSERS**.

pap noun 1 *tasteless pap:* **soft food**, mush, slop, pulp, purée, mash; informal goo, gloop, gook; N. Amer. informal glop. 2 *commercial pap:* **trivia**, pulp (fiction), rubbish, nonsense, froth; Brit. candyfloss; informal dreck, drivel, trash, twaddle.

paper noun 1 *the local paper ran the story:* **newspaper**, journal, gazette, periodical; tabloid, broadsheet, quality paper, daily, weekly, evening paper, Sunday paper; informal rag; N. Amer. informal tab. 2 *he has just published a paper on the topic:* **essay**, article, monograph, thesis, work, dissertation, treatise, study, report, analysis, tract, critique, exegesis, review; N. Amer. theme. 3 *personal papers:* **documents**, certificates, letters, files, deeds, records, archives, paperwork, documentation. 4 *they asked us for our papers:* **identification papers/documents**, identity card, ID, credentials.
■ **paper something over** cover up, hide, conceal, disguise, camouflage, gloss over.
■ **on paper 1** *he put his thoughts down on paper:* in writing, in black and white, in print. 2 *the combatants were evenly matched on paper:* in theory, theoretically, supposedly.

papery adjective *papery leaves:* **thin**, paper-thin, flimsy, delicate, insubstantial, light, lightweight.

par
■ **below par 1** *their performances have been below par:* substandard, inferior, not up to scratch, under par, below average, second-rate, mediocre, poor, undistinguished; informal not up to snuff; N. Amer. informal bush-league. 2 *I'm feeling below par:* slightly unwell, not (very) well, not oneself, out of sorts; ill, unwell, poorly, washed out, run down, peaky; Brit. off (colour); informal under the weather, not up to snuff, lousy, rough; Brit. informal ropy, grotty; Austral./NZ informal crook.
■ **on a par with** as good as, comparable with, in the same class/league as, equivalent to, equal to, on a level with, of the same standard as.
■ **par for the course** normal, typical, standard, usual, what one would expect.
■ **up to par** good enough, up to the mark,

satisfactory, acceptable, adequate, up to scratch; informal up to snuff.

parable noun *the parable of the prodigal son:* **allegory**, moral story/tale, fable, exemplum, apologue.

parade noun **1** *a St George's Day parade:* **procession**, march, cavalcade, motorcade, spectacle, display, pageant; review, dress parade, tattoo; Brit. march past. **2** *she walked along the parade:* **promenade**, walkway, esplanade, mall; N. Amer. boardwalk; Brit. informal prom.
verb **1** *the teams paraded through the city:* **march**, process, file, troop. **2** *she paraded up and down:* **strut**, swagger, stride. **3** *he was keen to parade his knowledge:* **display**, exhibit, make a show of, flaunt, show (off), demonstrate.

paradigm noun *the institutional arrangements of a particular society cannot serve as a paradigm for all others:* **model**, pattern, example, exemplar, standard, prototype, archetype.

paradise noun **1** *the souls in paradise:* **(the kingdom of) heaven**, the heavenly kingdom, Elysium, the Elysian Fields, Valhalla, Avalon. **2** *Adam and Eve's expulsion from Paradise:* **the Garden of Eden**, Eden. **3** *a tropical paradise:* **Utopia**, Shangri-La, heaven, idyll, nirvana. **4** *this is sheer paradise!* **bliss**, heaven, ecstasy, delight, joy, happiness, nirvana, heaven on earth.
– OPPOSITES hell.

paradox noun *the apparent paradox of simultaneous unemployment and skilled-labour shortages:* **contradiction (in terms)**, self-contradiction, inconsistency, incongruity, conflict, anomaly; enigma, puzzle, mystery, conundrum.

paradoxical adjective **contradictory**, self-contradictory, inconsistent, incongruous, anomalous; illogical, puzzling, baffling, incomprehensible, inexplicable.

paragon noun *a paragon of fortitude and cheerfulness:* **perfect example**, shining example, model, epitome, archetype, ideal, exemplar, nonpareil, embodiment, personification, quintessence, apotheosis, acme; jewel, gem, angel, treasure.

paragraph noun **1** *the concluding paragraph:* **section**, subdivision, part, subsection, division, portion, segment, passage. **2** *a paragraph in the newspaper:* **report**, article, item, piece, write-up, mention.

parallel adjective **1** *parallel lines:* **side by side**, aligned, collateral, equidistant. **2** *parallel careers:* **similar**, analogous, comparable, corresponding, like, of a kind, akin, related, equivalent, matching. **3** *a parallel universe:* **coexisting**, coexistent, concurrent; contemporaneous, simultaneous, synchronous.
– OPPOSITES divergent.
noun **1** *an exact parallel:* **counterpart**, analogue, equivalent, likeness, match,

twin, duplicate, mirror. **2** *there is an interesting parallel between these figures:* **similarity**, likeness, resemblance, analogy, correspondence, equivalence, correlation, relation, symmetry, parity.
verb **1** *his experiences parallel mine:* **resemble**, be similar to, be like, bear a resemblance to; correspond to, be analogous to, be comparable/equivalent to, equate with/to, correlate with, imitate, echo, remind one of, duplicate, mirror, follow, match. **2** *her performance has never been paralleled:* **equal**, match, rival, emulate.

paralyse verb **1** *Mrs Burrows had been paralysed by a stroke:* **disable**, cripple, immobilize, incapacitate, debilitate. **2** *Maisie was paralysed by the sight of him:* **immobilize**, transfix, become rooted to the spot, freeze, stun, render motionless. **3** *the capital was paralysed by a general strike:* **bring to a standstill**, immobilize, bring to a (grinding) halt, freeze, cripple, disable.

paralysed adjective **disabled**, crippled, handicapped, incapacitated, paralytic, powerless, immobilized, useless; Medicine paraplegic.

paralysis noun **1** *the disease can cause paralysis:* **immobility**, powerlessness, incapacity, debilitation; Medicine paraplegia. **2** *complete paralysis of the Channel ports:* **shutdown**, immobilization, stoppage.

paralytic adjective *her hands became paralytic:* **paralysed**, crippled, disabled, incapacitated, powerless, immobilized, useless.

parameter noun *they set the parameters of the debate:* **framework**, variable, limit, boundary, limitation, restriction, criterion, guideline.

paramount adjective *the safety of the staff is paramount:* **most important**, of greatest/prime importance; uppermost, supreme, chief, overriding, predominant, foremost, prime, primary, principal, highest, main, key, central, leading, major, top; informal number-one.

paranoia noun **persecution complex**, delusions, obsession, psychosis.

paranoid adjective *they probably don't mean me at all—I'm just being paranoid:* **over-suspicious**, paranoiac, suspicious, mistrustful, fearful, insecure; Brit. informal para.

parapet noun **1** *Marian leaned over the parapet:* **balustrade**, barrier, wall. **2** *the sandbags making up the parapet:* **barricade**, rampart, bulwark, bank, embankment, fortification, defence, earthwork, bastion.

paraphernalia plural noun *the paraphernalia necessary for home improvements:* **equipment**, stuff, things, apparatus, kit, implements, tools, utensils, material(s), appliances, accoutrements, appurtenances, odds and ends, bits and pieces; informal gear; Brit. informal clobber.

p

paraphrase verb *you can either quote or paraphrase literary texts:* **reword**, rephrase, put/express in other words, rewrite, gloss. noun *this paraphrase of St Paul's words:* **rewording**, rephrasing, rewriting, rewrite, rendition, rendering, gloss.

parasite noun *Sam was a parasite with no interest in anything but drink and gambling:* **hanger-on**, cadger, leech, passenger; informal bloodsucker, sponger, scrounger, freeloader; N. Amer. informal mooch; Austral./NZ informal bludger.

parcel noun **1** *a parcel of clothes:* **package**, packet; pack, bundle, box, case, bale. **2** *a parcel of land:* **plot**, piece, patch, tract; Brit. allotment; N. Amer. lot, plat.
verb **1** *she parcelled up the papers:* **pack (up)**, package, wrap (up), gift-wrap, tie up, bundle up. **2** *parcelling out commercial farmland:* **divide up**, portion out, distribute, share out, allocate, allot, apportion, hand out, dole out, dish out; informal divvy up.

parched adjective *the parched earth:* **(bone) dry**, dried up/out, arid, desiccated, dehydrated, baked, burned, scorched; withered, shrivelled.
– OPPOSITES soaking.

pardon noun **1** *pardon for your sins:* **forgiveness**, absolution, clemency, mercy, lenience, leniency. **2** *he offered them a full pardon:* **reprieve**, free pardon, amnesty, exoneration, release, acquittal, discharge.
verb **1** *I know she will pardon me:* **forgive**, absolve, have mercy on; excuse, condone, overlook. **2** *they were subsequently pardoned:* **exonerate**, acquit, amnesty; reprieve, release, free; informal let off.
– OPPOSITES blame, punish.
exclamation *Pardon?* **what (did you say)**, eh, pardon me, I beg your pardon, sorry, excuse me; informal come again.

pardonable adjective *a pardonable error:* **excusable**, forgivable, condonable, understandable, minor, venial, slight.
– OPPOSITES inexcusable.

pare verb **1** *pare the peel from the lemon:* **cut (off)**, trim (off), peel (off), strip (off), skin. **2** *domestic operations have been pared down:* **reduce**, diminish, decrease, cut (back/down), trim, slim down, prune, curtail.

parent noun **1** *her parents have divorced:* **mother, father**, birth/biological parent, progenitor; adoptive parent, foster-parent, step-parent, guardian. **2** *rhythm and blues, the parent of rock and roll:* **source**, origin, genesis, root, author, architect; precursor, forerunner, predecessor, antecedent.

parentage noun *a young woman of African parentage:* **origins**, extraction, birth, family, ancestry, lineage, heritage, pedigree, descent, blood, stock, roots.

parenthetical adjective *parenthetical remarks:* **incidental**, supplementary, in brackets, in parentheses, parenthetic; explanatory, qualifying.

parenthetically adverb **incidentally**, by the way, by the by(e), in passing, in parenthesis.

parenthood noun **childcare**, child-rearing, motherhood, fatherhood, parenting.

pariah noun *they were treated as social pariahs:* **outcast**, persona non grata, leper, undesirable, unperson.

parings plural noun **peelings**, clippings, peel, rind, cuttings, trimmings, shavings.

parish noun **1** *the parish of Poplar:* **district**, community. **2** *the vicar scandalized the parish:* **parishioners**, churchgoers, congregation, fold, flock, community.

parity noun *parity of incomes between rural workers and those in industrial occupations:* **equality**, equivalence, uniformity, consistency, correspondence, congruity, levelness, unity, coequality.

park noun **1** *we were playing in the park:* **public garden**, recreation ground, playground, play area. **2** *fifty acres of park:* **parkland**, grassland, woodland, garden(s), lawns, grounds, estate.
verb *he parked his car:* **leave**, position; stop, pull up.

parlance noun *medical parlance:* **jargon**, language, phraseology, vocabulary, terminology, talk, speech, argot, patois, cant; informal lingo, -ese, -speak.

parley noun *a peace parley:* **negotiation**, talk(s), conference, summit, discussion, powwow; informal confab.
verb *the two parties were willing to parley:* **talk**, hold talks, negotiate, discuss terms, deliberate; informal powwow.

parliament noun *the Russian parliament:* **legislature**, legislative assembly, congress, senate, (upper/lower) house, (upper/lower) chamber, diet, assembly.

parliamentary adjective *parliamentary assemblies:* **legislative**, law-making, governmental, congressional, senatorial, democratic, elected, representative.

parlour noun *a beauty parlour:* **salon**, shop, establishment, store.

parlous adjective *the parlous state of the industry:* **bad**, dire, dreadful, awful, terrible, grave, serious, desperate, precarious; sorry, poor, lamentable, hopeless; unsafe, perilous, dangerous, risky; informal dicey, hairy, chronic, woeful.

parochial adjective *parochial attitudes:* **narrow-minded**, small-minded, provincial, narrow, small-town, conservative, illiberal, intolerant; Brit. parish-pump; N. Amer. informal jerkwater.
– OPPOSITES broad-minded.

parochialism noun **narrow-mindedness**, provincialism, small-mindedness.

parody noun **1** *a parody of the gothic novel:* **satire**, burlesque, lampoon, pastiche, pasquinade, caricature, imitation, mockery;

informal spoof, take-off, send-up. **2** *a parody of the truth:* **distortion**, travesty, caricature, misrepresentation, perversion, corruption, debasement.
verb *his speciality was parodying schoolgirl fiction:* **satirize**, burlesque, lampoon, caricature, mimic, imitate, ape, copy, make fun of, travesty, take off; informal send up.

paroxysm noun *a paroxysm of rage:* **spasm**, attack, fit, burst, bout, convulsion, seizure, outburst, eruption, explosion, access.

parrot verb *they parroted slogans without appreciating their significance:* **repeat (mindlessly)**, repeat mechanically, echo.

parrot-fashion adverb *his wife had just repeated the phrase parrot-fashion:* **mechanically**, by rote, mindlessly, automatically.

parry verb **1** *Sharpe parried the blow:* **ward off**, fend off, deflect, hold off, block, counter, repel, repulse. **2** *I parried her constant questions:* **evade**, sidestep, avoid, dodge, field, fend off.

parsimonious adjective *even the parsimonious Joe paid for drinks all round:* **mean**, miserly, niggardly, close-fisted, close, penny-pinching, ungenerous, Scrooge-like; informal tight-fisted, tight, stingy, mingy; N. Amer. informal cheap.
– OPPOSITES generous.

parsimony noun **meanness**, miserliness, parsimoniousness, niggardliness, close-fistedness, closeness, penny-pinching; informal stinginess, minginess, tightness, tight-fistedness; N. Amer. cheapness.
– OPPOSITES generosity.

parson noun **vicar**, rector, clergyman, cleric, chaplain, pastor, curate, man of the cloth, ecclesiastic, minister, priest, preacher; informal reverend, padre; Austral. informal josser.

part noun **1** *the last part of the cake* | *a large part of their life:* **bit**, slice, chunk, lump, hunk, wedge, fragment, scrap, piece; portion, proportion, percentage, fraction. **2** *car parts:* **component**, bit, constituent, element, module. **3** *body parts:* **part of the body**, organ, limb, member. **4** *the third part of the book:* **section**, division, volume, chapter, act, scene, instalment. **5** *another part of the country:* **district**, neighbourhood, quarter, section, area, region. **6** *the part of Juliet:* **(theatrical) role**, character, persona. **7** *he's learning his part:* **lines**, words, script, speech; libretto, lyrics, score. **8** *he was jailed for his part in the affair:* **involvement**, role, function, hand, work, responsibility, capacity, position, participation, contribution; informal bit.
– OPPOSITES whole.
verb **1** *the curtains parted:* **separate**, divide (in two), split (in two), move apart. **2** *we parted on bad terms:* **leave**, take one's leave, say goodbye/farewell, say one's goodbyes/farewells, go one's (separate) ways, go away, depart.
– OPPOSITES join, meet.

adjective *a part payment:* **incomplete**, partial, half, semi-, limited, inadequate, insufficient, unfinished.
– OPPOSITES complete.
adverb *it is part finished:* **to a certain extent/degree**, to some extent/degree, partly, partially, in part, half, relatively, comparatively, (up) to a point, somewhat; not totally, not entirely, (very) nearly, almost, just about, all but.
– OPPOSITES completely.
■ **for the most part**. See MOST.
■ **in good part**. See GOOD.
■ **in part** to a certain extent/degree, to some extent/degree, partly, partially, slightly, in some measure, (up) to a point.
■ **on the part of** (made/done) by, carried out by, caused by, from.
■ **part with** *she had no wish to part with any of her land:* give up/away, relinquish, forgo, surrender, hand over, deliver up, dispose of.
■ **take part** participate, join in, get involved, enter, play a part/role, be a participant, contribute, have a hand, help, assist, lend a hand; informal get in on the act.
■ **take part in** participate in, engage in, join in, get involved in, share in, play a part/role in, be a participant in, contribute to, be associated with, have a hand in.
■ **take someone's part** support, give one's support to, take the side of, side with, stand by, stick up for, be supportive of, back (up), give one's backing to, be loyal to, defend, come to the defence of, champion.

partial adjective **1** *a partial recovery:* **incomplete**, limited, qualified, imperfect, fragmentary, unfinished. **2** *a very partial view of the situation:* **biased**, prejudiced, partisan, one-sided, slanted, skewed, coloured, unbalanced.
– OPPOSITES complete, unbiased.
■ **be partial to** like, love, enjoy, have a liking for, be fond of, be keen on, have a soft spot for, have a taste for, have a penchant for; informal adore, be mad about/on, have a thing about, be crazy about, be nutty about; Brit. informal be potty about; N. Amer. informal cotton to; Austral./NZ informal be shook on.

partiality noun **1** *his partiality towards their cause:* **bias**, prejudice, favouritism, favour, partisanship. **2** *her partiality for brandy:* **liking**, love, fondness, taste, soft spot, predilection, penchant, passion.

partially adverb *the plan was only partially successful:* **to a limited extent/degree**, to a certain extent/degree, partly, in part, not totally, not entirely, relatively, moderately, (up) to a point, somewhat, comparatively, slightly.

participant noun *staff are to be active participants in the decision-making process:* **participator**, contributor, party, member; entrant, competitor, player, contestant, candidate.

participate verb *400,000 people participated in the peaceful demonstration:* **take part**, engage, join, get involved, share, play a part/role, be a participant, partake, have a hand in, be associated with; cooperate, help, assist, lend a hand.

participation noun **involvement**, part, contribution, association.

particle noun **1** *minute particles of rock:* **(tiny) bit**, (tiny) piece, speck, spot, fleck; fragment, sliver, splinter. **2** *he never showed a particle of sympathy:* **iota**, jot, whit, bit, scrap, shred, crumb, drop, hint, touch, trace, suggestion, whisper, suspicion, scintilla; informal smidgen.

particular adjective **1** *a particular group of companies:* **specific**, certain, distinct, separate, discrete, definite, precise; single, individual. **2** *an issue of particular importance:* **(extra) special**, especial, exceptional, unusual, singular, uncommon, notable, noteworthy, remarkable, unique. **3** *he was particular about what he ate:* **fussy**, fastidious, finicky, meticulous, punctilious, discriminating, selective, painstaking, exacting, demanding; informal pernickety, choosy, picky; Brit. informal faddy.
– OPPOSITES general, careless.
noun *the same in every particular:* **detail**, item, point, specific, element, aspect, respect, regard, particularity, fact, feature.
■ **in particular 1** *nothing in particular:* specific, special. **2** *the poor, in particular, were hit by rising prices:* particularly, specifically, especially, specially.

particularity noun **1** *the particularity of each human being:* **individuality**, distinctiveness, uniqueness, singularity, originality. **2** *a great degree of particularity:* **detail**, precision, accuracy, thoroughness, scrupulousness, meticulousness.

particularize verb *the indictment particularized several incidents:* **specify**, detail, itemize, list, enumerate, spell out, cite, stipulate, instance.

particularly adverb **1** *the acoustics are particularly good:* **especially**, specially, very, extremely, exceptionally, singularly, peculiarly, unusually, extraordinarily, remarkably, outstandingly, amazingly, incredibly, really; informal seriously, majorly, awfully, terribly; Brit. informal jolly, dead, well. **2** *he particularly asked that I should help you:* **specifically**, explicitly, expressly, in particular, especially, specially.

parting noun **1** *an emotional parting:* **farewell**, leave-taking, goodbye, adieu, departure; valediction. **2** *they kept their parting quiet:* **separation**, break-up, split, divorce, rift, estrangement; Brit. informal bust-up. **3** *the parting of the Red Sea:* **division**, dividing, separation, separating, splitting, breaking up/apart, partition, partitioning.
adjective *a parting kiss:* **farewell**, goodbye, last, final, valedictory.

partisan noun **1** *Conservative partisans:* **supporter**, follower, adherent, devotee, champion; fanatic, fan, enthusiast, stalwart,

zealot; N. Amer. booster. **2** *the partisans opened fire from the woods:* **guerrilla**, freedom fighter, resistance fighter, underground fighter, irregular (soldier).
adjective *partisan attitudes:* **biased**, prejudiced, one-sided, discriminatory, coloured, partial, interested, sectarian, factional.
– OPPOSITES unbiased.

partisanship noun **bias**, prejudice, one-sidedness, discrimination, favour, favouritism, partiality, sectarianism, factionalism.

partition noun **1** *the partition of Palestine:* **dividing up**, partitioning, separation, division, dividing, subdivision, splitting (up), breaking up, break-up. **2** *room partitions:* **screen**, (room) divider, (dividing) wall, barrier, panel, separator.
verb **1** *the resolution partitioned Poland:* **divide (up)**, subdivide, separate, split (up), break up; share (out), parcel out. **2** *the huge hall was partitioned:* **subdivide**, divide (up); separate (off), section off, screen off.

partly adverb *the book is partly autobiographical:* **to a certain extent/degree**, to some extent/degree, in part, partially, a little, somewhat, not totally, not entirely, relatively, moderately, (up) to a point, in some measure, slightly.
– OPPOSITES completely.

partner noun **1** *business partners:* **colleague**, associate, co-worker, fellow worker, collaborator, comrade, teammate; Brit. informal oppo; Austral./NZ informal offsider. **2** *his partner in crime:* **accomplice**, confederate, accessory, collaborator, fellow conspirator, helper; informal sidekick. **3** *your relationship with your partner:* **spouse**, husband, wife, consort; lover, girlfriend, boyfriend, fiancé, fiancée, significant other, live-in lover, common-law husband/wife, man, woman, mate; informal hubby, missus, old man, old lady/woman, better half, intended, POSSLQ; Brit. informal other half.

partnership noun **1** *the close partnership between Britain and the US:* **cooperation**, association, collaboration, coalition, alliance, union, affiliation, relationship, connection. **2** *the partnership now owns twenty-two department stores:* **company**, firm, business, corporation, organization, association, consortium, syndicate.

party noun **1** *150 people attended the party:* **(social) gathering**, (social) function, get-together, celebration, reunion, festivity, jamboree, reception, at-home, soirée, social; dance, ball, ceilidh, frolic, carousal, carouse; N. Amer. fête, hoedown, shower, bake, cookout, levee; Austral./NZ corroboree; informal bash, shindig, rave, disco, do, shebang, bop, hop; Brit. informal rave-up, knees-up, beanfeast, beano, bunfight; N. Amer. informal blast, wingding, kegger; Austral./NZ informal shivoo, rage, ding, jollo, rort. **2** *a party of British tourists:* **group**, company, body,

gang, band, crowd, pack, contingent; informal bunch, crew, load. **3** *the left-wing parties:* **faction**, political party, group, grouping, cabal, junta, bloc, camp, caucus. **4** *don't mention a certain party:* **person**, individual, somebody, someone.
■ **be a party to** get involved in/with, be associated with, be a participant in.

parvenu noun **upstart**, social climber, arriviste.

pass¹ verb **1** *the traffic passing through the village:* **go**, proceed, move, progress, make one's way, travel. **2** *a car passed him:* **overtake**, go past/by, pull ahead of, overhaul, leave behind. **3** *time passed:* **elapse**, go by/past, advance, wear on, roll by, tick by. **4** *he passed the time writing letters:* **occupy**, spend, fill, use (up), employ, while away. **5** *pass me the salt:* **hand (over)**, let someone have, give, reach. **6** *he passed the ball back:* **kick**, hit, throw, lob. **7** *her estate passed to her grandson:* **be transferred**, go, be left, be bequeathed, be handed down/on, be passed on; Law devolve. **8** *his death passed almost unnoticed:* **happen**, occur, take place, come about, transpire. **9** *the storm passed:* **come to an end**, fade (away), blow over, run its course, die out, finish, end, cease. **10** *God's peace passes all human understanding:* **surpass**, exceed, transcend. **11** *he passed the exam:* **be successful in**, succeed in, gain a pass in, get through; informal sail through, scrape through. **12** *the Senate passed the bill:* **approve**, vote for, accept, ratify, adopt, agree to, authorize, endorse, legalize, enact; informal OK. **13** *she could not let that comment pass:* **go (unnoticed)**, stand, go unremarked, go undisputed. **14** *we should not pass judgement:* **declare**, pronounce, utter, express, deliver, issue. **15** *passing urine:* **discharge**, excrete, evacuate, expel, emit, release.
– OPPOSITES stop, fail, reject.
noun **1** *you must show your pass:* **permit**, warrant, authorization, licence. **2** *a cross-field pass:* **kick**, hit, throw, shot.
■ **make a pass at** make (sexual) advances to, proposition; informal come on to, make a play for; N. Amer. informal hit on, make time with, put the make on.
■ **pass away/on**. See DIE sense 1.
■ **pass as/for** *she could easily pass for someone half her age:* be mistaken for, be taken for, be accepted as.
■ **pass off 1** *the rally passed off peacefully:* take place, go off, happen, occur, be completed, turn out. **2** *when the dizziness passed off he sat up:* wear off, fade (away), pass, die down.
■ **pass someone off** *he added Natasha's name to his passport, passing her off as his daughter:* misrepresent, falsely represent; disguise.
■ **pass out** *she banged her head when she passed out:* faint, lose consciousness, black out.
■ **pass something over** *the court cannot possibly pass over these offences:* disregard, overlook, ignore, pay no attention to, let pass, gloss over, take no notice of, pay no heed to, turn a blind eye to.
■ **pass something up** *I can't pass up a bargain like this, can I?* turn down, reject, refuse, decline, give up, forgo, let pass, miss (out on); informal give something a miss.

pass² noun *a pass through the mountains:* **route**, way, road, passage, cut, gap; N. Amer. notch.

passable adjective **1** *the beer was passable:* **adequate**, all right, fairly good, acceptable, satisfactory, moderately good, not (too) bad, average, tolerable, fair; mediocre, middling, ordinary, indifferent, unremarkable, unexceptional; informal OK, so-so, nothing to write home about, no great shakes, not up to much; NZ informal half pie. **2** *the road is still passable:* **navigable**, traversable, negotiable, unblocked, unobstructed, open, clear.

passably adverb *a passably good dinner:* **quite**, rather, somewhat, fairly, reasonably, moderately, comparatively, relatively, tolerably; informal pretty.

passage noun **1** *their passage through the country:* **transit**, progress, passing, movement, motion, travelling. **2** *the passage of time:* **passing**, advance, progress, course, march. **3** *the overnight passage:* **voyage**, crossing, trip, journey. **4** *clearing a passage to the front door:* **way (through)**, route, path. **5** *a passage to the kitchen.* See PASSAGEWAY sense 1. **6** *a passage between the buildings.* See PASSAGEWAY sense 2. **7** *the nasal passages:* **duct**, orifice, opening, channel; inlet, outlet. **8** *the passage to democracy:* **transition**, development, progress, move, change, shift. **9** *a passage from 'Macbeth':* **extract**, excerpt, quotation, quote, citation, reading, piece, selection.

passageway noun **1** *secret passageways:* **corridor**, hall, passage, hallway, walkway, aisle. **2** *a narrow passageway off the main street:* **alley**, alleyway, passage, lane, path, pathway, footpath, track, thoroughfare; N. Amer. areaway.

passé adjective. See OLD-FASHIONED.

passenger noun **1** *rail passengers:* **traveller**, commuter, fare payer. **2** *we can't afford passengers:* **hanger-on**, idler, parasite; informal freeloader.

passing adjective **1** *his death was of only passing interest:* **fleeting**, transient, transitory, ephemeral, brief, short-lived, temporary, momentary. **2** *a passing glance:* **hasty**, rapid, hurried, brief, quick; cursory, superficial, casual, perfunctory.
noun **1** *the passing of time:* **passage**, course, progress, advance, march. **2** *Jack's passing:* **death**, demise, passing away/on, end, loss, quietus. **3** *the passing of the new bill:* **enactment**, ratification, approval, adoption, authorization, legalization, endorsement.
■ **in passing** incidentally, by the by/way, en passant.

p

passion noun 1 *the passion of activists:* **fervour**, ardour, enthusiasm, eagerness, zeal, zealousness, vigour, fire, fieriness, energy, fervency, animation, spirit, spiritedness, fanaticism. **2** *he worked himself up into a passion:* **(blind) rage**, fit of anger/temper, temper, towering rage, tantrum, fury, frenzy; Brit. informal paddy. **3** *hot with passion:* **love**, (sexual) desire, lust, ardour, infatuation, lasciviousness, lustfulness. **4** *his passion for football:* **enthusiasm**, love, mania, fascination, obsession, fanaticism, fixation, compulsion, appetite, addiction; informal thing. **5** *English literature is a passion with me:* **obsession**, preoccupation, craze, mania, hobby horse. **6** *the Passion of Christ:* **crucifixion**, suffering, agony, martyrdom.
– OPPOSITES apathy.

passionate adjective **1** *a passionate entreaty:* **intense**, impassioned, ardent, fervent, vehement, fiery, heated, emotional, heartfelt, eager, excited, animated, spirited, energetic, fervid, frenzied, wild, consuming, violent. **2** *McGregor is passionate about sport:* **very keen**, very enthusiastic, addicted; informal mad, crazy, hooked, nuts; N. Amer. informal nutso; Austral./NZ informal shook. **3** *a passionate kiss:* **amorous**, ardent, hot-blooded, aroused, loving, sexy, sensual, erotic, lustful; informal steamy, hot, turned on. **4** *a passionate woman:* **excitable**, emotional, fiery, volatile, mercurial, quick-tempered, highly strung, impulsive, temperamental.
– OPPOSITES apathetic.

passionless adjective *he was not as passionless as they made out:* **unemotional**, cold, cold-blooded, emotionless, frigid, cool, unfeeling, unloving, unresponsive, undemonstrative, impassive.

passive adjective **1** *a passive role:* **inactive**, non-active, non-participative, uninvolved. **2** *passive victims:* **submissive**, acquiescent, unresisting, unassertive, compliant, pliant, obedient, docile, tractable, malleable, pliable. **3** *the woman's face was passive:* **emotionless**, impassive, unemotional, unmoved, dispassionate, passionless, detached, unresponsive, undemonstrative, apathetic, phlegmatic.
– OPPOSITES active.

passport noun **1** **travel permit**, (travel) papers, visa, laissez-passer. **2** *qualifications are the passport to success:* **key**, path, way, route, avenue, door, doorway.

past adjective **1** *memories of times past:* **gone (by)**, over (and done with), no more, done, bygone, former, (of) old, olden, long-ago. **2** *the past few months:* **last**, recent, preceding. **3** *a past chairman:* **previous**, former, foregoing, erstwhile, one-time, sometime, ex-.
– OPPOSITES present, future.
noun *details about her past:* **history**, background, life (story).
preposition **1** *she walked past the cafe:* **in front of**, by. **2** *he's past retirement age:* **beyond**, in excess of.
adverb *they hurried past:* **along**, by, on.
▪ **in the past** formerly, previously, in days/years/times gone by, in former times, in the (good) old days, in days of old, in olden times, once (upon a time).

paste noun **1** *blend the ingredients to a paste:* **purée**, pulp, mush, blend. **2** *wallpaper paste:* **adhesive**, glue, gum, fixative; N. Amer. mucilage. **3** *fish paste:* **spread**, pâté.
verb *a notice was pasted on the door:* **glue**, stick, gum, fix, affix.

pastel adjective *pastel colours:* **pale**, soft, light, light-coloured, muted, subtle, subdued, soft-hued.
– OPPOSITES dark, bright.

pastiche noun **1** *a pastiche of literary models:* **mixture**, blend, medley, melange, miscellany, mixed bag, pot-pourri, mix, compound, composite, collection, assortment, conglomeration, hotchpotch, jumble, ragbag; N. Amer. hodgepodge. **2** *a pastiche of 18th-century style:* **imitation**, parody; informal take-off.

pastille noun **lozenge**, sweet, drop; tablet, pill.

pastime noun **hobby**, leisure activity/pursuit, sport, game, recreation, amusement, diversion, entertainment, interest, sideline.

past master noun *the manager was a past master at recharging faltering spirits:* **expert**, master, wizard, genius, old hand, veteran, maestro, connoisseur, authority, grandmaster; informal ace, pro, star, hotshot; Brit. informal dab hand; N. Amer. informal maven, crackerjack.

pastor noun **priest**, minister (of religion), parson, clergyman, cleric, chaplain, padre, ecclesiastic, man of the cloth, churchman, vicar, rector, curate, preacher; informal reverend; Austral. informal josser.

pastoral adjective **1** *a pastoral scene:* **rural**, country, countryside, rustic, agricultural, bucolic. **2** *his pastoral duties:* **priestly**, clerical, ecclesiastical, ministerial.
– OPPOSITES urban.

pastry noun **1** *pastries for tea:* **tart**, tartlet, pie, pasty, patty. **2** *two layers of pastry:* **crust**, piecrust, croute.

pasture noun **grazing (land)**, grassland, grass, pastureland, pasturage, ley; meadow, field; Austral./NZ run.

pasty adjective *people with pasty faces:* **pale**, pallid, wan, colourless, anaemic, ashen, white, grey, pasty-faced, washed out, sallow.

pat¹ verb *Brian patted her on the shoulder:* **tap**, slap lightly, clap, touch.
noun **1** *a pat on the cheek:* **tap**, light blow, clap, touch. **2** *a pat of butter:* **piece**, dab, lump, portion, knob, mass, gobbet, ball, curl.
▪ **pat someone on the back** congratulate, praise, take one's hat off to; commend, compliment, applaud, acclaim.

p

pat² adjective *pat answers:* **glib**, simplistic, facile, unconvincing.
adverb *his reply came rather pat:* **opportunely**, conveniently, at just/exactly the right moment, expediently, favourably, appropriately, fittingly, auspiciously, providentially, felicitously, propitiously.
■ **off pat** word-perfect, by heart, by rote, by memory, parrot-fashion.
■ **get something off pat** memorize, commit to memory, remember, learn by heart, learn (by rote).

patch noun 1 *a patch over one eye:* **cover**, eyepatch, covering, pad. 2 *a reddish patch on her wrist:* **blotch**, mark, spot, smudge, speckle, smear, stain, streak, blemish; informal splodge, splotch. 3 *a patch of ground:* **plot**, area, piece, strip, tract, parcel; bed; Brit. allotment; N. Amer. lot. 4 (Brit. informal) *they are going through a difficult patch:* **period**, time, spell, phase, stretch; Brit. informal spot.
verb *her jeans were neatly patched:* **mend**, repair, put a patch on, sew (up), stitch (up).

patchwork noun *work that was a patchwork of different styles:* **assortment**, miscellany, mixture, melange, medley, blend, mixed bag, mix, collection, selection, assemblage, combination, pot-pourri, jumble, mishmash, ragbag, hotchpotch; N. Amer. hodgepodge.

patchy adjective 1 *their teaching has been patchy:* **uneven**, bitty, varying, variable, intermittent, fitful, sporadic, erratic, irregular. 2 *patchy evidence:* **fragmentary**, inadequate, insufficient, rudimentary, limited, sketchy.
– OPPOSITES uniform, comprehensive.

patent noun *there is a patent on the chemical:* **copyright**, licence, legal protection, registered trademark.
adjective 1 *patent nonsense:* **obvious**, clear, plain, evident, manifest, self-evident, transparent, overt, conspicuous, blatant, downright, barefaced, flagrant, undisguised, unconcealed, unmistakable. 2 *patent medicines:* **proprietary**, patented, licensed, branded.

paternal adjective 1 *his face showed paternal concern:* **fatherly**, fatherlike, patriarchal; protective, solicitous, compassionate, sympathetic. 2 *his paternal grandfather:* **on one's father's side**, patrilineal.
– OPPOSITES maternal.

paternity noun *he refused to admit paternity of the child:* **fatherhood**.

path noun 1 *a path down to the beach:* **footpath**, pathway, footway, pavement, track, trail, trackway, bridleway, bridle path, lane, alley, alleyway, passage, passageway; cycle path/track; N. Amer. sidewalk, bikeway. 2 *journalists blocked his path:* **route**, way, course; direction, bearing; line; orbit, trajectory. 3 *the best path towards a settlement:* **course of action**, route, road, avenue, line, approach, tack, strategy, tactic.

pathetic adjective 1 *a pathetic groan:*

pitiful, pitiable, piteous, moving, touching, poignant, plaintive, distressing, upsetting, heartbreaking, heart-rending, harrowing, wretched, forlorn. 2 (informal) *a pathetic excuse:* **feeble**, woeful, sorry, poor, pitiful, lamentable, deplorable, contemptible, inadequate, paltry, insufficient, insubstantial, unsatisfactory.

pathfinder noun *she sees herself as a pathfinder for her daughter's generation:* **pioneer**, groundbreaker, trailblazer, trendsetter, leader, torch-bearer, pacemaker.

pathological adjective 1 *a pathological condition:* **morbid**, diseased. 2 (informal) *a pathological liar:* **compulsive**, obsessive, inveterate, habitual, persistent, chronic, hardened, confirmed.

pathos noun *the pathos of Antoine's predicament:* **poignancy**, tragedy, sadness, pitifulness, piteousness.

patience noun 1 *she tried everyone's patience:* **forbearance**, tolerance, restraint, self-restraint, stoicism; calmness, composure, equanimity, serenity, tranquillity, imperturbability, understanding, indulgence. 2 *a task requiring patience:* **perseverance**, persistence, endurance, tenacity, assiduity, application, staying power, doggedness, determination, resolve, resolution, resoluteness.

patient adjective 1 *I must ask you to be patient:* **forbearing**, uncomplaining, tolerant, resigned, stoical; calm, composed, even-tempered, imperturbable, unexcitable, accommodating, understanding, indulgent; informal unflappable, cool. 2 *a good deal of patient work:* **persevering**, persistent, tenacious, indefatigable, dogged, determined, resolved, resolute, single-minded.
noun *a doctor's patient:* **sick person**, case; invalid, convalescent, outpatient, inpatient.

patio noun **terrace**; courtyard, quadrangle, quad; N. Amer. sun deck.

patois noun *the nurse talked to me in a patois that even Italians would have had difficulty in understanding:* **vernacular**, (local) dialect, regional language; jargon, argot, cant; informal (local) lingo.

patriarch noun *the respected patriarch of the household:* **senior figure**, father, paterfamilias, leader, elder.

patrician noun *the great patricians:* **aristocrat**, grandee, noble, nobleman, noblewoman, lord, lady, peer, peeress.
adjective *patrician families:* **aristocratic**, noble, titled, blue-blooded, high-born, upper-class, landowning; informal upper-crust.

patrimony noun *constant wars and invasions have destroyed the country's cultural patrimony:* **heritage**, inheritance, birthright; legacy, bequest, endowment, bequeathal.

patriot noun *a great patriot who had died for*

p

his country: **nationalist**, loyalist; chauvinist, jingoist, flag-waver.

patriotic adjective *he felt a surge of patriotic emotion:* **nationalist**, nationalistic, loyalist, loyal; chauvinistic, jingoistic, flag-waving.
– OPPOSITES traitorous.

patriotism noun **nationalism**, allegiance/loyalty to one's country; chauvinism, jingoism, flag-waving.

patrol noun **1** *anti-poaching patrols:* **vigil**, guard, watch, monitoring, policing, beat-pounding, patrolling; reconnoitre, surveillance; informal recce. **2** *the patrol stopped a suspect:* **patrolman**, **patrolwoman**, sentinel, sentry; scout, scouting party, task force.
verb *a security guard was patrolling a housing estate:* **keep guard (on)**, guard, keep watch (on); police, pound the beat (of), make the rounds (of); stand guard (over), keep a vigil (on), defend, safeguard.

patron noun **1** *a patron of the arts:* **sponsor**, backer, financier, benefactor, benefactress, contributor, subscriber, donor; philanthropist, promoter, friend, supporter; informal angel. **2** *club patrons:* **customer**, client, frequenter, consumer, user, visitor, guest; informal regular.

patronage noun **1** *art patronage:* **sponsorship**, backing, funding, financing, promotion, assistance, support. **2** *political patronage:* **power of appointment**, favouritism, nepotism, preferential treatment. **3** *a slight note of patronage:* **condescension**, patronizing, patronization, disdain, disrespect, scorn, contempt. **4** *thank you for your patronage:* **custom**, trade, business.

patronize verb **1** *don't patronize me!* **treat condescendingly**, condescend to, look down on, talk down to, put down, treat like a child, treat with disdain. **2** *they patronized local tradesmen:* **do business with**, buy from, shop at, be a customer of, be a client of, deal with, trade with, frequent, support. **3** *he patronized a national museum:* **sponsor**, back, fund, finance, be a patron of, support, champion.

patronizing adjective *'She's a good-hearted girl,' he said in a patronizing voice:* **condescending**, disdainful, supercilious, superior, imperious, scornful, contemptuous; informal uppity, high and mighty.

patter[1] verb **1** *raindrops pattered against the window:* **go pitter-patter**, tap, drum, beat, pound, rat-a-tat, go pit-a-pat, thrum. **2** *she pattered across the floor:* **scurry**, scuttle, skip, trip.
noun *the patter of rain:* **pitter-patter**, tapping, pattering, drumming, beat, beating, pounding, rat-a-tat, pit-a-pat, clack, thrum, thrumming.

patter[2] noun **1** *this witty patter:* **prattle**, prating, blather, blither, drivel, chatter,

jabber, babble; informal yabbering, yatter. **2** *the salesmen's patter:* **(sales) pitch**, sales talk; informal line. **3** *the local patter:* **speech**, language, parlance, dialect; informal lingo.

pattern noun **1** *the pattern on the wallpaper:* **design**, decoration, motif, marking, ornament, ornamentation. **2** *working patterns:* **system**, order, arrangement, form, method, structure, scheme, plan, format, framework. **3** *this would set the pattern for a generation:* **model**, example, criterion, standard, basis, point of reference, gauge, norm, yardstick, touchstone, benchmark; blueprint, archetype, prototype.
verb *someone else is patterning my life:* **shape**, influence, model, fashion, mould, style, determine, control.

patterned adjective **decorated**, ornamented, fancy, adorned, embellished.
– OPPOSITES plain.

paucity noun *a paucity of evidence:* **scarcity**, sparseness, sparsity, dearth, shortage, poverty, insufficiency, deficiency, lack, want.
– OPPOSITES abundance.

paunch noun **pot belly**, beer belly; informal beer gut, pot.

pauper noun **poor person**, indigent, down-and-out; informal have-not.

pause noun *a pause in the conversation:* **stop**, cessation, break, halt, interruption, check, lull, respite, breathing space, discontinuation, hiatus, gap, interlude; adjournment, suspension, rest, wait, hesitation; informal let-up, breather.
verb *Hannah paused for a moment:* **stop**, cease, halt, discontinue, break off, take a break; adjourn, rest, wait, hesitate, falter, waver; informal take a breather.

pave verb *the yard was paved:* **tile**, surface, flag.
■ **pave the way for** prepare (the way) for, make preparations for, get ready for, lay the foundations for, herald, precede.

pavement noun **footpath**, walkway, footway; N. Amer. sidewalk.

paw verb **1** *their offspring were pawing each other:* **handle roughly**, pull, grab, maul, manhandle. **2** *some Casanova tried to paw her:* **fondle**, feel, maul, molest; informal grope, feel up, touch up, goose.

pawn[1] verb *he pawned his watch:* **pledge**, put in pawn, give as security, use as collateral; informal hock, put in hock.

pawn[2] noun *a pawn in the battle for the throne:* **puppet**, dupe, hostage, tool, cat's paw, instrument.

pay verb **1** *I must pay him for his work:* **reward**, reimburse, recompense, give payment to, remunerate. **2** *you must pay a few more pounds:* **spend**, expend, pay out, dish out, disburse; informal lay out, shell out, fork out, cough up; N. Amer. informal ante up, pony up. **3** *he paid his debts:* **discharge**, settle, pay off, clear, liquidate. **4** *hard work*

will pay dividends: **yield**, return, produce.
5 *he made the buses pay:* **be profitable**, make money, make a profit. **6** *it may pay you to be early:* **be advantageous to**, benefit, be of advantage to, be beneficial to. **7** *paying compliments:* **bestow**, grant, give, offer.
8 *he will pay for his mistakes:* **suffer (the consequences)**, be punished, atone, pay the penalty/price.
noun *equal pay for women:* **salary**, wages, payment; earnings, remuneration, reimbursement, income, revenue.
■ **pay someone back/out** *I'll pay you back for what you've done!* get one's revenge on, be revenged on, avenge oneself on, get back at, get even with, settle accounts with, pay someone out, exact retribution on.
■ **pay something back** *they did eventually pay me back the money:* repay, pay off, give back, return, reimburse, refund.
■ **pay for** *he had just enough money to pay for the meal:* finance, settle up for, fund; treat someone to; informal foot the bill for, shell out for, fork out for, cough up for; N. Amer. informal ante up for, pony up for.
■ **pay someone off 1** *Tim paid off the driver:* pay what one owes, discharge.
2 *paying off the police:* bribe, suborn, buy (off); informal grease someone's palm.
■ **pay something off** *you use the proceeds to pay off your loan:* pay (in full), settle, discharge, clear, liquidate.
■ **pay off** (informal) *his hard work paid off:* meet with success, be successful, be effective, get results.
■ **pay something out** *she had to pay out £300 for treatment:* spend, expend, pay, dish out, put up, part with, hand over; informal shell out, fork out/up, lay out, cough up.
■ **pay up** *he has been allowed a week to pay up:* make payment, settle up, pay (in full); informal cough up.

payable adjective *capital gains tax is payable if the shares are sold:* **due**, owed, owing, outstanding, unpaid, overdue, in arrears; N. Amer. delinquent.

payment noun **1** *there are discounts for early payment:* **remittance**, settlement, discharge, clearance, liquidation. **2** *monthly payments:* **instalment**, premium. **3** *extra payment for good performance:* **salary**, wages, pay, earnings, fee(s), remuneration, reimbursement, income.

pay-off noun (informal) **1** *the lure of enormous pay-offs:* **payment**, payout, reward; bribe, inducement, incentive; N. Amer. payola; informal kickback, sweetener, backhander; Austral. informal sling. **2** *a pay-off of £160,000:* **return (on investment)**, yield, payback, profit, gain, dividend. **3** *a dramatic pay-off:* **outcome**, denouement, culmination, conclusion, development, result.

peace noun **1** *can't a man get any peace around here?* **tranquillity**, calm, restfulness, peace and quiet, peacefulness, quiet, quietness; privacy, solitude. **2** *peace of*

mind: **serenity**, peacefulness, tranquillity, equanimity, calm, calmness, composure, ease, contentment, contentedness.
3 *there was peace in the land:* **law and order**, lawfulness, order, peacefulness, peaceableness, harmony, non-violence.
4 *a lasting peace:* **treaty**, truce, ceasefire, armistice, cessation/suspension of hostilities.
– OPPOSITES noise, war.

peaceable adjective **1** *a peaceable man:* **peace-loving**, non-violent, non-aggressive, easy-going, placid, gentle, inoffensive, good-natured, even-tempered, amiable, amicable, friendly, affable, genial, pacific, dovelike, dovish. **2** *a peaceable society:* **peaceful**, strife-free, harmonious; law-abiding, disciplined, orderly, civilized.
– OPPOSITES aggressive.

peaceful adjective **1** *everything was quiet and peaceful:* **tranquil**, calm, restful, quiet, still, relaxing, soothing, undisturbed, untroubled, private, secluded. **2** *his peaceful mood:* **serene**, calm, tranquil, composed, placid, at ease, untroubled, unworried, content. **3** *peaceful relations:* **harmonious**, at peace, peaceable, on good terms, amicable, friendly, cordial, non-violent.
– OPPOSITES noisy, agitated, hostile.

peacemaker noun **arbitrator**, arbiter, mediator, negotiator, conciliator, go-between, intermediary, pacifier, appeaser, peace-monger, pacifist, peace-lover, dove; informal peacenik.

peak noun **1** *the peaks of the mountains:* **summit**, top, crest, pinnacle, apex, crown, cap. **2** *they climbed all six peaks:* **mountain**, hill, height, mount, alp; Scottish ben, Munro.
3 *the peak of a cap:* **brim**, visor. **4** *the peak of his career:* **height**, high point/spot, pinnacle, summit, top, climax, culmination, apex, zenith, crowning point, acme, apogee, prime, heyday.
verb *Labour support has peaked:* **reach its height**, climax, reach a climax, come to a head.
adjective *storage capacity has to be adequate to meet peak loads:* **maximum**, top, greatest, highest; ultimate, best, optimum.

peaky adjective *you're looking a bit peaky:* **pale**, pasty, wan, drained, washed out, drawn, pallid, anaemic, ashen, grey, pinched, sickly, sallow; ill, unwell, poorly, indisposed, run down; Brit. off (colour); informal under the weather, rough, lousy, seedy; Brit. informal grotty, ropy.

peal noun **1** *a peal of bells:* **chime**, carillon, ring, ringing, tintinnabulation. **2** *peals of laughter:* **shriek**, shout, scream, howl, gale, fit, roar, hoot. **3** *a peal of thunder:* **rumble**, roar, boom, crash, clap, crack.
verb **1** *the bell pealed:* **ring (out)**, chime (out), clang, sound, ding, jingle. **2** *the thunder pealed:* **rumble**, roar, boom, crash, resound.

peasant noun **1** *peasants working the land:*

p

agricultural worker, small farmer, rustic, swain, villein, serf. **2** (informal) *you peasants!* See BOOR.

peccadillo noun *the sexual peccadillos of celebrities aren't necessarily news:* **misdemeanour**, petty offence, indiscretion, lapse, misdeed.

peck verb **1** *the cockerel pecked my heel:* **bite**, nip, strike, hit, tap, rap, jab. **2** *he pecked her on the cheek:* **kiss**, give someone a peck.

peculiar adjective **1** *something peculiar began to happen:* **strange**, unusual, odd, funny, curious, bizarre, weird, queer, unexpected, unfamiliar, abnormal, atypical, anomalous, out of the ordinary; exceptional, extraordinary, remarkable; puzzling, mystifying, mysterious, perplexing, baffling; suspicious, eerie, unnatural; informal fishy, creepy, spooky. **2** *peculiar behaviour:* **bizarre**, eccentric, strange, odd, weird, queer, funny, unusual, abnormal, idiosyncratic, unconventional, outlandish, quirky; informal wacky, freaky, oddball, offbeat, off the wall; N. Amer. informal wacko. **3** (informal) *I feel a bit peculiar.* See UNWELL. **4** *mannerisms peculiar to the islanders:* **characteristic of**, typical of, representative of, indicative of, suggestive of, exclusive to. **5** *their own peculiar contribution:* **distinctive**, characteristic, distinct, individual, special, unique, personal.
– OPPOSITES ordinary.

peculiarity noun **1** *a legal peculiarity:* **oddity**, anomaly, abnormality. **2** *a physical peculiarity:* **idiosyncrasy**, mannerism, quirk, foible. **3** *one of the peculiarities of the city:* **characteristic**, feature, (essential) quality, property, trait, attribute, hallmark, trademark. **4** *the peculiarity of this notion:* **strangeness**, oddness, bizarreness, weirdness, queerness, unexpectedness, unfamiliarity, anomalousness, incongruity. **5** *there is a certain peculiarity about her appearance:* **outlandishness**, bizarreness, unconventionality, idiosyncrasy, weirdness, oddness, eccentricity, unusualness, abnormality, queerness, strangeness, quirkiness; informal wackiness, freakiness.

pecuniary adjective *he was free from all pecuniary anxieties:* **financial**, monetary, money, fiscal, economic.

pedagogic adjective *they show great pedagogic skills:* **educational**, educative, pedagogical, teaching, instructional, instructive, didactic; academic, scholastic.

pedant noun *pedants insist that the 21st century started with 2001:* **dogmatist**, purist, literalist, formalist, doctrinaire, perfectionist; quibbler, hair-splitter, casuist, sophist; informal nit-picker.

pedantic adjective *a pedantic interpretation of the rules:* **over-scrupulous**, scrupulous, precise, exact, perfectionist, punctilious, meticulous, fussy, fastidious, finical, finicky; dogmatic, purist, literalist, literalistic, formalist; casuistic, sophistic; captious,

hair-splitting, quibbling; informal nit-picking, pernickety.

pedantry noun **dogmatism**, purism, literalism, formalism; over-scrupulousness, scrupulousness, perfectionism, fastidiousness, punctiliousness, meticulousness; captiousness, quibbling, hair-splitting, casuistry, sophistry; informal nit-picking.

peddle verb **1** *they are peddling water filters:* **sell (from door to door)**, hawk, tout, vend; trade (in), deal in, traffic in. **2** *peddling unorthodox views:* **advocate**, champion, preach, put forward, proclaim, propound, promote.

pedestal noun *a bust on a pedestal:* **plinth**, base, support, mounting, stand, foundation, pillar, column, pier.
■ **put someone on a pedestal** idealize, lionize, look up to, respect, hold in high regard, think highly of, admire, esteem, revere, worship.

pedestrian noun *accidents involving pedestrians:* **walker**, person on foot.
– OPPOSITES driver.
adjective *they lead such pedestrian lives:* **dull**, boring, tedious, monotonous, uneventful, unremarkable, tiresome, wearisome, uninspired, unimaginative, unexciting, uninteresting; unvarying, unvaried, repetitive, routine, commonplace, workaday; ordinary, everyday, run-of-the-mill, mundane, humdrum; informal bog-standard, (plain) vanilla; Brit. informal common or garden.
– OPPOSITES exciting.

pedigree noun *a long pedigree:* **ancestry**, descent, lineage, line (of descent), genealogy, family tree, extraction, derivation, origin(s), heritage, parentage, bloodline, background, roots.
adjective *a pedigree cat:* **pure-bred**, thoroughbred, pure-blooded.

pedlar noun **1** *pedlars of watches:* **travelling salesman**, door-to-door salesman, huckster; street trader, hawker; Brit. informal fly-pitcher. **2** *a drug pedlar:* **trafficker**, dealer; informal pusher.

peek verb **1** *they peeked from behind the curtains:* **(have a) peep**, have a peek, spy, take a sly/stealthy look, sneak a look; informal take a gander, have a squint; Brit. informal have a dekko, have/take a butcher's, take a shufti. **2** *the deer's antlers peeked out from the trees:* **appear (slowly/partly)**, show, come into view/sight, become visible, emerge, peep (out).
noun *a peek at the map:* **secret look**, sly look, stealthy look, sneaky look, peep, glance, glimpse, hurried/quick look; informal gander, squint; Brit. informal dekko, butcher's, shufti.

peel verb **1** *peel and core the fruit:* **pare**, skin, take the skin/rind off; hull, shell, husk, shuck. **2** *use a long knife to peel the veneer:* **trim (off)**, peel off, pare, strip (off), shave (off), remove. **3** *the wallpaper was*

peeling: **flake (off)**, peel off, come off in layers/strips.
noun *orange peel:* **rind**, skin, covering, zest; hull, pod, integument, shuck.

peep¹ verb **1** *I peeped through the keyhole:* **look quickly**, cast a brief look, take a secret look, sneak a look, (have a) peek, glance; informal take a gander, have a squint; Brit. informal have a dekko, have/take a butcher's, take a shufti. **2** *the moon peeped through the clouds:* **appear (slowly/partly)**, show, come into view/sight, become visible, emerge, peek, peer out.
noun *I'll just take a peep at it:* **quick look**, brief look, sneaky look, peek, glance; informal gander, squint; Brit. informal dekko, butcher's, shufti.

peep² noun **1** *I heard a quiet peep:* **cheep**, chirp, chirrup, tweet, twitter, chirr, warble. **2** *there's been not a peep out of the children:* **sound**, noise, cry, word. **3** *the painting was sold without a peep:* **complaint**, grumble, mutter, murmur, grouse, objection, protest, protestation; informal moan, gripe, grouch.
verb *the fax peeped:* **cheep**, chirp, chirrup, tweet, twitter, chirr.

peephole noun **opening**, gap, cleft, spyhole, slit, crack, chink, keyhole, squint, judas (hole).

peer¹ verb *he peered at the manuscript:* **look closely**, try to see, narrow one's eyes, screw up one's eyes, squint.

peer² noun **1** *hereditary peers:* **aristocrat**, lord, lady, peer of the realm, peeress, noble, nobleman, noblewoman, titled man/woman, patrician. **2** *his academic peers:* **equal**, coequal, fellow, confrère; contemporary.

peerage noun **aristocracy**, nobility, peers and peeresses, lords and ladies, patriciate; the House of Lords, the Lords.

peerless adjective *a peerless performance:* **incomparable**, matchless, unrivalled, inimitable, beyond compare/comparison, unparalleled, unequalled, without equal, second to none, unsurpassed, unsurpassable, nonpareil; unique, consummate, perfect, rare, transcendent, surpassing.

peeved adjective (informal) *he sounded quite peeved at the poor result:* **irritated**, annoyed, cross, angry, vexed, displeased, disgruntled, indignant, exasperated, galled, irked, put out, aggrieved, offended, affronted, piqued, nettled; informal aggravated, miffed, riled, hacked off, browned off; Brit. informal narked, cheesed off, brassed off; N. Amer. informal teed off, ticked off, sore.

peevish adjective *the remark came out sounding peevish and sensitive:* **irritable**, fractious, fretful, cross, petulant, querulous, pettish, crabby, crotchety, cantankerous, curmudgeonly, sullen, grumpy, bad-tempered, short-tempered, touchy, testy, tetchy, snappish, irascible, waspish, prickly, crusty, dyspeptic; N. English mardy; Brit. informal ratty, like a bear with a sore head; N. Amer.

informal cranky, ornery.
– OPPOSITES good-humoured.

peg noun **pin**, nail, dowel, skewer, spike, rivet, brad, screw, bolt, hook, spigot.
verb 1 *the flysheet is pegged to the ground:* **fix**, pin, attach, fasten, secure, make fast. **2** *we decided to peg our prices:* **hold down**, keep down, fix, set, hold, freeze.
■ **take someone down a peg or two** humble, humiliate, mortify, bring down, shame, embarrass, abash, put someone in their place, chasten, subdue, squash, deflate, make someone eat humble pie; informal show up, settle someone's hash, cut down to size; N. Amer. informal make someone eat crow.

pejorative adjective *'permissiveness' is used almost universally as a pejorative term:* **disparaging**, derogatory, denigratory, deprecatory, defamatory, slanderous, libellous, abusive, insulting, slighting; informal bitchy.
– OPPOSITES complimentary.

pellet noun **1** *a pellet of mud:* **little ball**, little piece. **2** *pellet wounds:* **bullet**, shot, lead shot, buckshot. **3** *rabbit pellets:* **excrement**, excreta, droppings, faeces, dung.

pell-mell adverb *men streamed pell-mell from the building:* **helter-skelter**, headlong, (at) full tilt, hotfoot, post-haste, hurriedly, hastily, recklessly, precipitately.

pelt¹ verb **1** *they pelted him with snowballs:* **bombard**, shower, attack, assail, pepper. **2** *rain was pelting down:* **pour down**, teem down, stream down, tip down, rain cats and dogs, rain hard; Brit. informal bucket down, come down in stair rods.

pelt² noun *an animal's pelt:* **skin**, hide, fleece, coat, fur.

pen¹ noun *you'll need a pen and paper:* fountain pen, ballpoint (pen), rollerball; fibre tip (pen), felt tip (pen), highlighter, marker; Brit. trademark biro.
verb *he penned a number of articles:* **write**, compose, draft, dash off; write down, jot down, set down, take down, scribble.

pen² noun *a sheep pen:* **enclosure**, fold, sheepfold, pound, compound, stockade; sty, coop; N. Amer. corral.
verb *the hostages had been penned up in a basement:* **confine**, coop (up), cage, shut in, box up/in, lock up/in, trap, imprison, incarcerate, immure.

penal adjective **1** *a penal institution:* **disciplinary**, punitive, corrective, correctional. **2** *penal rates of interest:* **exorbitant**, extortionate, excessive, outrageous, preposterous, unreasonable, inflated, sky-high.

penalize verb **1** *if you break the rules you will be penalized:* **punish**, discipline, inflict a penalty on. **2** *people with certain medical conditions would be penalized:* **handicap**, disadvantage, put at a disadvantage, cause to suffer.
– OPPOSITES reward.

p

penalty noun **1** *increased penalties for dumping oil at sea:* **punishment**, sanction, punitive action, retribution; fine, forfeit, sentence; penance. **2** *the penalties of old age:* **disadvantage**, difficulty, drawback, handicap, downside, minus; trial, tribulation, bane, affliction, burden, trouble.
– OPPOSITES reward.

penance noun *self-awareness is the necessary ingredient for penance:* **atonement**, expiation, self-punishment, self-mortification, self-abasement, amends; punishment, penalty.

penchant noun *he has a penchant for champagne:* **liking**, fondness, preference, taste, relish, appetite, partiality, soft spot, love, passion, desire, fancy, whim, weakness, inclination, bent, bias, proclivity, predilection, predisposition.

pencil noun **1** *a sharpened pencil:* lead pencil, propelling pencil. **2** *a pencil of light:* **beam**, ray, shaft, finger, gleam.
verb **1** *he pencilled his name inside the cover:* **write**, write down, jot down, scribble, note, take down. **2** *pencil a line along the top of the moulding:* **draw**, trace, sketch.

pendant noun **necklace**, locket, medallion.

pending adjective **1** *nine cases were still pending:* **unresolved**, undecided, unsettled, awaiting decision/action, undetermined, open, hanging fire, (up) in the air, ongoing, outstanding, not done, unfinished, incomplete; informal on the back burner. **2** *with a general election pending:* **imminent**, impending, about to happen, forthcoming, upcoming, on the way, coming, approaching, looming, gathering, near, nearing, close, close at hand, in the offing, to come.
preposition *they were released on bail pending an appeal:* **awaiting**, until, till, until there is/are.

pendulous adjective *this magnolia produces large, white, pendulous flowers:* **drooping**, dangling, trailing, droopy, sagging, saggy, floppy; hanging, pendent, pensile.

penetrable adjective **1** *a penetrable subsoil:* **permeable**, pervious, porous. **2** *books which are barely penetrable to anyone under 50:* **understandable**, fathomable, comprehensible, intelligible.

penetrate verb **1** *the knife penetrated his lungs:* **pierce**, puncture, make a hole in, perforate, stab, prick, gore, spike. **2** *the oil has penetrated into the stones:* **seep**, soak, percolate, filter, spread, diffuse; enter, make its way into/through, pass/move/flow into, get into; infiltrate, permeate, saturate, suffuse, drench. **3** *they penetrated enemy territory:* **infiltrate**, slip into, sneak into, insinuate oneself into. **4** *he seemed to have penetrated the mysteries of nature:* **understand**, comprehend, apprehend, fathom, grasp, perceive, discern, get to the bottom of, solve, resolve, make sense of, interpret, puzzle out, work out, unravel,

decipher, make head or tail of; informal crack, get, figure out; Brit. informal suss out. **5** *his words finally penetrated:* **register**, sink in, be understood, be comprehended, become clear, fall into place; informal click.

penetrating adjective **1** *a penetrating wind:* **piercing**, cutting, biting, stinging, keen, sharp, harsh, raw, freezing, chill, wintry, cold. **2** *a penetrating voice:* **shrill**, strident, piercing, carrying, loud, high, high-pitched, piping, ear-splitting, screechy, intrusive. **3** *a penetrating smell:* **pungent**, pervasive, strong, powerful, sharp, acrid, heady, aromatic. **4** *her penetrating gaze:* **observant**, searching, intent, alert, shrewd, perceptive, probing, piercing, sharp, keen. **5** *a penetrating analysis:* **perceptive**, insightful, keen, sharp, sharp-witted, intelligent, clever, smart, incisive, piercing, razor-edged, trenchant, astute, shrewd, clear, acute, percipient, perspicacious, discerning, sensitive, thoughtful, deep, profound.
– OPPOSITES mild, soft.

penetration noun **1** *rot that is attributable to rain penetration:* **infiltration**, entry, inflow, percolation, filtering, seepage, soaking, saturation, drenching, diffusion. **2** *remarks of great penetration:* **insight**, discernment, perception, perceptiveness, intelligence, sharp-wittedness, cleverness, incisiveness, keenness, sharpness, trenchancy, astuteness, shrewdness, acuteness, clarity, acuity, percipience, perspicacity, discrimination, sensitivity, thoughtfulness, profundity.

peninsula noun **cape**, promontory, point, head, headland, foreland, ness, horn, bill, bluff, mull.

penitence noun *the writer prays to God in penitence:* **repentance**, contrition, regret, remorse, remorsefulness, ruefulness, sorrow, sorrowfulness, pangs of conscience, self-reproach, shame, guilt, compunction.

penitent adjective **repentant**, contrite, remorseful, sorry, apologetic, regretful, conscience-stricken, rueful, ashamed, shamefaced, abject, in sackcloth and ashes.
– OPPOSITES unrepentant.

pen-name noun **pseudonym**, nom de plume, assumed name, alias, professional name.

pennant noun *pennants fly from the tower:* **flag**, standard, ensign, colour(s), banner, banderole, guidon; Brit. pendant.

penniless adjective *Van Gogh died penniless:* **destitute**, poverty-stricken, impoverished, poor, indigent, impecunious, in penury, moneyless, without a sou, necessitous, needy, on one's beam-ends; bankrupt, insolvent; Brit. on the breadline, without a penny (to one's name); informal (flat) broke, cleaned out, strapped for cash, cash-strapped, on one's uppers, without a brass farthing, bust; Brit. informal stony broke, skint; N. Amer. informal stone broke.
– OPPOSITES wealthy.

penny-pincher noun **miser**, Scrooge, niggard; informal skinflint, meanie, money-grubber, cheapskate; N. Amer. informal tightwad.
– OPPOSITES spendthrift.

penny-pinching adjective *penny-pinching governments with a utilitarian approach to the arts:* **mean**, miserly, niggardly, parsimonious, close-fisted, cheese-paring, grasping, Scrooge-like; informal stingy, mingy, tight, tight-fisted, money-grubbing.
– OPPOSITES generous.

pension noun **old-age pension**, retirement pension, regular payment, superannuation; allowance, benefit, support, welfare.

pensioner noun **retired person**, old-age pensioner, OAP, senior citizen; N. Amer. senior, retiree.

pensive adjective *a pensive mood:* **thoughtful**, reflective, contemplative, musing, meditative, introspective, ruminative, absorbed, preoccupied, deep/lost in thought, in a brown study, brooding.

pent-up adjective *a release of pent-up emotion:* **repressed**, suppressed, stifled, smothered, restrained, confined, bottled up, held in/back, kept in check, curbed, bridled.

penury noun *he couldn't face another year of penury:* **extreme poverty**, destitution, pen:1essness, impecuniousness, impoverishment, indigence, pauperism, privation, beggary.

people plural noun **1** *crowds of people:* **human beings**, persons, individuals, humans, mortals, (living) souls, personages, {men, women, and children}; informal folk, peeps. **2** *the British people:* **citizens**, subjects, electors, voters, taxpayers, residents, inhabitants, (general) public, citizenry, nation, population, populace. **3** *a man of the people:* **the common people**, the proletariat, the masses, the populace, the rank and file, the commonality, the commonalty, the third estate, the plebeians; derogatory the hoi polloi, the common herd, the great unwashed, the proles, the plebs. **4** *her people don't live far away:* **family**, parents, relatives, relations, folk, kinsmen, kin, kith and kin, kinsfolk, flesh and blood, nearest and dearest; informal folks. **5** *the peoples of Africa:* **race**, (ethnic) group, tribe, clan.
verb *the Indians who once peopled Newfoundland:* **populate**, settle (in), colonize, inhabit, live in, occupy.

pep (informal) noun *a performance full of pep:* **dynamism**, life, energy, spirit, liveliness, animation, bounce, sparkle, effervescence, verve, spiritedness, ebullience, high spirits, enthusiasm, vitality, vivacity, fire, dash, panache, elan, zest, exuberance, vigour, gusto, brio; informal feistiness, get-up-and-go, oomph, pizzazz, vim.
■ **pep something up** enliven, animate, liven up, put some/new life into, invigorate, vitalize, revitalize, vivify, ginger up,

energize, galvanize, put some spark into, stimulate, get something going, perk up, brighten up, cheer up; informal buck up.

pepper verb **1** *salt and pepper the potatoes:* **add pepper to**, season, flavour. **2** *stars peppered the desert skies:* **sprinkle**, fleck, dot, spot, stipple; cover, fill. **3** *another burst of bullets peppered the tank:* **bombard**, pelt, shower, rain down on, attack, assail, batter, strafe, rake, blitz, hit.

peppery adjective **1** *a peppery sauce:* **spicy**, spiced, peppered, hot, highly seasoned, piquant, pungent, sharp. **2** *a peppery old man:* **irritable**, cantankerous, irascible, bad-tempered, ill-tempered, grumpy, grouchy, crotchety, short-tempered, tetchy, testy, crusty, crabby, curmudgeonly, peevish, cross, fractious, pettish, prickly, waspish; informal snappish, snappy, chippy; N. Amer. informal cranky, ornery.
– OPPOSITES mild, bland, affable.

perceive verb **1** *I immediately perceived the flaws in her story:* **discern**, recognize, become aware of, see, distinguish, realize, grasp, understand, take in, make out, find, identify, hit on, comprehend, apprehend, appreciate, sense, divine; informal figure out; Brit. informal twig. **2** *he perceived a flush creeping up her neck:* **see**, discern, detect, catch sight of, spot, observe, notice. **3** *he was perceived as too negative:* **regard**, look on, view, consider, think of, judge.

perceptible adjective *a perceptible decline in public confidence:* **noticeable**, perceivable, detectable, discernible, visible, observable, recognizable, appreciable; obvious, apparent, evident, manifest, patent, clear, distinct, plain, conspicuous.

perception noun **1** *our perception of our own limitations:* **recognition**, awareness, consciousness, appreciation, realization, knowledge, grasp, understanding, comprehension, apprehension. **2** *popular perceptions of old age:* **impression**, idea, conception, notion, thought, belief, judgement, estimation. **3** *he talks with great perception:* **insight**, perceptiveness, percipience, perspicacity, understanding, sharpness, sharp-wittedness, intelligence, intuition, cleverness, incisiveness, trenchancy, astuteness, shrewdness, acuteness, acuity, discernment, sensitivity, penetration, thoughtfulness, profundity.

perceptive adjective *an extraordinarily perceptive account of their relationship:* **insightful**, discerning, sensitive, intuitive, observant; piercing, penetrating, percipient, perspicacious, penetrative, clear-sighted, far-sighted, intelligent, clever, canny, keen, sharp, sharp-witted, astute, shrewd, quick, smart, acute, discriminating; informal on the ball; N. Amer. informal heads-up.
– OPPOSITES obtuse.

perch noun *the budgerigar's perch:* **pole**, rod, branch, roost, rest, resting place.
verb **1** *three swallows perched on the*

p

telegraph wire: **roost**, sit, rest; alight, settle, land, come to rest. **2** *she perched her glasses on her nose:* **put**, place, set, rest, balance. **3** *the church is perched on a hill:* **be located**, be situated, be positioned, be sited, stand.

percipient adjective. See PERCEPTIVE.

percolate verb **1** *water percolated through the soil:* **filter**, drain, drip, ooze, seep, trickle, dribble, leak, leach. **2** *these views began to percolate through society as a whole:* **spread**, be disseminated, filter, pass; permeate, pervade. **3** *he put some coffee on to percolate:* **brew**; informal perk.

peremptory adjective *a peremptory reply:* **brusque**, imperious, high-handed, brisk, abrupt, summary, commanding, dictatorial, autocratic, overbearing, dogmatic, arrogant, overweening, lordly, magisterial, authoritarian; emphatic, firm, insistent; informal bossy.

perennial adjective *the perennial fascination with crime:* **abiding**, enduring, lasting, everlasting, perpetual, eternal, continuing, unending, unceasing, never-ending, endless, undying, ceaseless, persisting, permanent, constant, continual, unfailing, unchanging, never-changing.

perfect adjective **1** *she strove to be the perfect wife:* **ideal**, model, without fault, faultless, flawless, consummate, quintessential, exemplary, best, ultimate, copybook; unrivalled, unequalled, matchless, unparalleled, beyond compare, without equal, second to none, too good to be true, Utopian, incomparable, nonpareil, peerless, inimitable, unexcelled, unsurpassed, unsurpassable. **2** *an E-type Jaguar in perfect condition:* **flawless**, mint, as good as new, pristine, impeccable, immaculate, superb, superlative, optimum, prime, optimal, peak, excellent, faultless, as sound as a bell, unspoiled, unblemished, undamaged, spotless, unmarred; informal tip-top, A1. **3** *a perfect copy:* **exact**, precise, accurate, faithful, correct, unerring, right, true, strict; Brit. informal spot on; N. Amer. informal on the money. **4** *the perfect Christmas present for golfers everywhere:* **ideal**, just right, right, appropriate, fitting, fit, suitable, apt, made to order, tailor-made; very; Brit. informal spot on, just the job. **5** *she felt a perfect idiot:* **absolute**, complete, total, real, out-and-out, thorough, thoroughgoing, downright, utter, sheer, arrant, unmitigated, unqualified, veritable, in every respect, unalloyed; Brit. informal right; Austral./NZ informal fair.
verb *he's busy perfecting his bowling technique:* **improve**, better, polish (up), hone, refine, put the finishing/final touches to, brush up, fine-tune.

perfection noun **1** *the perfection of his technique:* **improvement**, betterment, refinement, refining, honing. **2** *for her, he was still perfection:* **the ideal**, a paragon, the ne plus ultra, the beau idéal, a nonpareil, the crème de la crème, the last word, the

ultimate; informal one in a million, the tops, the best/greatest thing since sliced bread, the bee's knees.

perfectionist noun *he's a perfectionist in all that he does:* **purist**, stickler for perfection, idealist; pedant.

perfectly adverb **1** *a perfectly cooked meal:* **superbly**, superlatively, excellently, flawlessly, faultlessly, to perfection, without fault, ideally, inimitably, incomparably, impeccably, immaculately, exquisitely, consummately; N. Amer. to a fare-thee-well; informal like a dream, to a T. **2** *I think we understand each other perfectly:* **absolutely**, utterly, completely, altogether, entirely, wholly, totally, thoroughly, fully, in every respect. **3** *you know perfectly well that is not what I meant:* **very**, quite, full; informal damn, damned; Brit. informal jolly, bloody; N. Amer. informal darned; N. English right.

perforate verb *fragments of a bullet perforated his intestines:* **pierce**, penetrate, enter, puncture, prick, bore through, riddle.

perform verb **1** *I have my duties to perform:* **carry out**, do, execute, discharge, bring about, bring off, accomplish, achieve, fulfil, complete, conduct, effect, dispatch, work, implement; informal pull off. **2** *a car which performs well at low speeds:* **function**, work, operate, run, go, respond, behave, act, acquit oneself/itself. **3** *the play has been performed in Britain:* **stage**, put on, present, mount, enact, act, produce. **4** *the band performed live in Hyde Park:* **appear**, play, be on stage.
– OPPOSITES neglect.

performance noun **1** *the evening performance:* **show**, production, showing, presentation, staging; concert, recital; Brit. house; informal gig. **2** *their performance of Mozart's Concerto in E flat:* **rendition**, rendering, interpretation, playing, acting, representation. **3** *the continual performance of a single task:* **carrying out**, execution, discharge, accomplishment, completion, fulfilment, dispatch, implementation. **4** *the performance of the processor:* **functioning**, working, operation, running, behaviour, capabilities, capability, capacity, power, potential.

performer noun **actor**, **actress**, thespian, artiste, artist, entertainer, trouper, player, musician, singer, dancer, comic, comedian, comedienne.

perfume noun **1** *a bottle of perfume:* **scent**, fragrance, eau de toilette, toilet water, eau de cologne, cologne, aftershave. **2** *the heady perfume of lilacs:* **smell**, scent, fragrance, aroma, bouquet, redolence.

perfumed adjective *perfumed soap:* **sweet-smelling**, scented, fragrant, fragranced, perfumy, aromatic.

perfunctory adjective *the guards gave a perfunctory look up and down the carriage:* **cursory**, desultory, quick, brief, hasty, hurried, rapid, fleeting, token, casual,

superficial, careless, half-hearted, sketchy, mechanical, automatic, routine, offhand, inattentive.
– OPPOSITES careful, thorough.

perhaps adverb *perhaps he'll come home tomorrow:* **maybe**, for all one knows, it could be, it may be, it's possible, possibly, conceivably; N. English happen.

peril noun *a situation fraught with peril:* **danger**, jeopardy, risk, hazard, insecurity, uncertainty, menace, threat, perilousness; pitfall, problem.

perilous adjective *a perilous journey through the mountains:* **dangerous**, fraught with danger, hazardous, risky, unsafe, treacherous; precarious, vulnerable, uncertain, insecure, exposed, at risk, in jeopardy, in danger, touch-and-go; informal dicey.
– OPPOSITES safe.

perimeter noun 1 *the perimeter of a circle:* **circumference**, outside, outer edge. 2 *the perimeter of the vast estate:* **boundary**, border, limits, bounds, confines, edge, margin, fringe(s), periphery, borderline, verge.

period noun 1 *a six-week period:* **time**, spell, interval, stretch, term, span, phase, bout, run, duration, chapter, stage; while; Brit. informal patch. 2 *the post-war period:* **era**, age, epoch, time, days, years. 3 *a double Maths period:* **lesson**, class, session. 4 *women who suffer from painful periods:* **menstruation**, menstrual flow; informal the curse, monthlies, time of the month. 5 (N. Amer.) *a comma instead of a period:* **full stop**, full point, stop, point.

periodic adjective *Michael had to make periodic visits to the hospital:* **regular**, periodical, at fixed intervals, recurrent, recurring, repeated, cyclical, cyclic, seasonal; occasional, infrequent, intermittent, sporadic, spasmodic, odd.

periodical noun *he wrote for two periodicals:* **journal**, publication, magazine, newspaper, paper, review, digest, gazette, newsletter, organ, quarterly; informal mag, book, glossy.

peripatetic adjective *his peripatetic way of life:* **nomadic**, itinerant, travelling, wandering, roving, roaming, migrant, migratory, unsettled.

peripheral adjective 1 *the city's peripheral housing estates:* **outlying**, outer, on the edge/outskirts, surrounding. 2 *mere peripheral issues:* **secondary**, subsidiary, incidental, tangential, marginal, minor, unimportant, lesser, inessential, non-essential, immaterial, ancillary.
– OPPOSITES central.

periphery noun *rambling estates on the periphery of the city:* **edge**, outer edge, margin, fringe, boundary, border, perimeter, rim, verge, borderline; outskirts, outer limits/reaches, bounds.
– OPPOSITES centre.

periphrastic adjective *the periphrastic nature of legal syntax:* **circumlocutory**, circuitous, roundabout, indirect, tautological, pleonastic, prolix, verbose, wordy, long-winded, rambling, wandering, tortuous, diffuse.

perish verb 1 *millions of soldiers perished:* **die**, lose one's life, be killed, fall, expire, meet one's death, be lost, lay down one's life, breathe one's last, pass away, go the way of all flesh, give up the ghost, go to glory, meet one's maker, go to one's last resting place, cross the great divide; informal kick the bucket, turn up one's toes, shuffle off this mortal coil, buy it, croak; Brit. informal snuff it, pop one's clogs; N. Amer. informal bite the big one, buy the farm. 2 *must these hopes perish so soon?* **come to an end**, die (away), disappear, vanish, fade, dissolve, evaporate, melt away, wither. 3 *the rubber had perished:* **go bad**, go off, spoil, rot, go mouldy, moulder, putrefy, decay, decompose.

perjure
■ **perjure oneself** lie under oath, lie, commit perjury, give false evidence/testimony.

perjury noun **lying under oath**, giving false evidence/testimony, making false statements, wilful falsehood.

perk[1] verb
■ **perk up** 1 *you seem to have perked up:* cheer up, brighten up, liven up, take heart; informal buck up. 2 *the economy has been slow to perk up:* recover, rally, improve, revive, take a turn for the better, look up, pick up, bounce back.
■ **perk someone/something up** *you could do with something to perk you up:* cheer up, liven up, brighten up, raise someone's spirits, give someone a boost/lift, revitalize, invigorate, energize, enliven, ginger up, put new life/heart into, put some spark into, rejuvenate, refresh, vitalize; informal buck up, pep up.

perk[2] noun *a job with a lot of perks:* **fringe benefit**, additional benefit, benefit, advantage, bonus, extra, plus; informal freebie; Brit. informal golden hello.

perky adjective *I felt much more perky after I put the phone down:* **cheerful**, lively, vivacious, animated, bubbly, effervescent, bouncy, spirited, high-spirited, in high spirits, cheery, merry, buoyant, ebullient, exuberant, jaunty, frisky, sprightly, spry, bright, sunny, jolly, full of the joys of spring, sparkly, pert; informal full of beans, bright-eyed and bushy-tailed, chirpy, chipper; N. Amer. informal peppy.

permanence noun *our craving for some sense of permanence in a rapidly changing world:* **stability**, durability, permanency, fixity, fixedness, changelessness, immutability, endurance, constancy, continuity, immortality, indestructibility, perpetuity, endlessness.

p

permanent adjective **1** *permanent brain damage:* **lasting**, enduring, indefinite, continuing, perpetual, everlasting, eternal, abiding, constant, irreparable, irreversible, lifelong, indissoluble, indelible, standing, perennial, unending, endless, never-ending, immutable, undying, imperishable, indestructible, ineradicable. **2** *a permanent job:* **long-term**, stable, secure, durable.
– OPPOSITES temporary.

permanently adverb **1** *the attack left her permanently disabled:* **for all time**, forever, for good, for always, for ever and ever, (for) evermore, until hell freezes over, in perpetuity, indelibly, immutably, until the end of time; N. Amer. forevermore; informal for keeps, until the cows come home, until doomsday, until kingdom come. **2** *I was permanently hungry:* **continually**, constantly, perpetually, always.

permeable adjective *permeable sandy soils:* **porous**, pervious, penetrable, absorbent, absorptive.

permeate verb **1** *the delicious smell permeated the entire flat:* **pervade**, spread through, fill, filter through, diffuse through, imbue, penetrate, pass through, percolate through, perfuse, charge, suffuse, steep, impregnate, inform. **2** *these resins are able to permeate the timber:* **soak through**, penetrate, seep through, saturate, percolate through, leach through.

permissible adjective *permissible levels of atmospheric pollution:* **permitted**, allowable, allowed, acceptable, legal, lawful, legitimate, admissible, licit, authorized, sanctioned, tolerated; informal legit, OK.
– OPPOSITES forbidden.

permission noun *you must get permission from your manager for all absences:* **authorization**, consent, leave, authority, sanction, licence, dispensation, assent, acquiescence, agreement, approval, seal of approval, approbation, endorsement, blessing, imprimatur, clearance, allowance, tolerance, sufferance, empowerment; informal the go-ahead, the thumbs up, the OK, the green light, say-so.

permissive adjective *the permissive society of the 1960s:* **liberal**, broad-minded, open-minded, free, free and easy, easy-going, live-and-let-live, latitudinarian, laissez-faire, libertarian, unprescriptive, tolerant, forbearing, indulgent, lenient; overindulgent, lax, soft.
– OPPOSITES intolerant, strict.

permit verb *I cannot permit you to leave:* **allow**, let, authorize, give someone permission, sanction, grant, give someone the right, license, empower, enable, entitle, qualify; consent to, assent to, give one's blessing to, give the nod to, acquiesce in, agree to, tolerate, countenance, admit of; legalize, legitimatize, legitimate; informal give the go-ahead to, give the thumbs up to, OK,

give the OK to, give the green light to, say the word.
– OPPOSITES ban, forbid.
noun *I need to see your permit:* **authorization**, licence, pass, ticket, warrant, document, certification; passport, visa.

permutation noun *all the possible permutations were explored:* **variation**, alteration, modification, change, shift, transformation, transmutation, mutation; humorous transmogrification.

pernicious adjective *a pernicious influence on society:* **harmful**, damaging, destructive, injurious, hurtful, detrimental, deleterious, dangerous, adverse, inimical, unhealthy, unfavourable, bad, evil, baleful, wicked, malign, malevolent, malignant, noxious, poisonous, corrupting.
– OPPOSITES beneficial.

pernickety adjective (informal) *she's very pernickety about her food:* **fussy**, difficult to please, difficult, finicky, over-fastidious, fastidious, over-particular, particular, faddish, punctilious, hair-splitting, critical, overcritical; informal nit-picking, choosy, picky; Brit. informal faddy; N. Amer. informal persnickety.
– OPPOSITES easy-going.

perpendicular adjective **1** *the perpendicular stones:* **upright**, vertical, erect, plumb, straight (up and down), on end, standing, upended. **2** *lines perpendicular to each other:* **at right angles**, at 90 degrees. **3** *the perpendicular hillside:* **steep**, sheer, precipitous, abrupt, bluff, vertiginous.
– OPPOSITES horizontal.

perpetrate verb *right-wing elements perpetrated a series of attacks and assaults:* **commit**, carry out, perform, execute, do, effect, bring about, accomplish; be guilty of, be to blame for, be responsible for, inflict, wreak; informal pull off.

perpetual adjective **1** *deep caves in perpetual darkness:* **everlasting**, never-ending, eternal, permanent, unending, endless, without end, lasting, long-lasting, constant, abiding, enduring, perennial, timeless, ageless, deathless, undying, immortal; unfailing, unchanging, never-changing, changeless, unfading. **2** *a perpetual state of fear:* **constant**, permanent, uninterrupted, continuous, unremitting, unending, unceasing, persistent, unbroken. **3** *her mother's perpetual nagging:* **interminable**, incessant, ceaseless, endless, without respite, relentless, unrelenting, persistent, continual, continuous, non-stop, never-ending, recurrent, repeated, unremitting, sustained, round-the-clock, unabating; informal eternal.
– OPPOSITES temporary, intermittent.

perpetuate verb *a monument to perpetuate the memory of those killed in the war:* **keep alive**, keep going, preserve, conserve, sustain, maintain, continue, extend, carry on, keep up, prolong; immortalize,

p

commemorate, memorialize, eternalize.

perpetuity
■ **in perpetuity** forever, permanently, for always, for good, for good and all, perpetually, (for) evermore, for ever and ever, for all time, until the end of time, until hell freezes over, eternally, for eternity, everlastingly; N. Amer. forevermore; informal for keeps, until doomsday.

perplex verb *she was perplexed by her husband's moodiness:* **puzzle**, baffle, mystify, bemuse, bewilder, confound, confuse, nonplus, disconcert, dumbfound, throw, throw/catch off balance, exercise, worry; informal flummox, be all Greek to, stump, bamboozle, floor, beat, faze, fox; N. Amer. informal discombobulate.

perplexing adjective **puzzling**, baffling, mystifying, mysterious, bewildering, confusing, disconcerting, worrying, unaccountable, difficult to understand, beyond one, paradoxical, peculiar, funny, strange, weird, odd.

perplexity noun **1** *he scratched his head in perplexity:* **confusion**, bewilderment, puzzlement, bafflement, incomprehension, mystification, bemusement; informal bamboozlement; N. Amer. informal discombobulation. **2** *the perplexities of international relations:* **complexity**, complication, intricacy, problem, difficulty, mystery, puzzle, enigma, paradox.

per se adverb *possessing a knife was not per se an unlawful act:* **in itself**, of itself, by itself, as such, intrinsically; by its very nature, in essence, by definition, essentially.

persecute verb **1** *they were persecuted for their religious beliefs:* **oppress**, abuse, victimize, ill-treat, mistreat, maltreat, tyrannize, torment, torture; martyr. **2** *she was persecuted by the press:* **harass**, hound, plague, badger, harry, intimidate, pick on, pester, bother, bedevil, bully, victimize, terrorize; N. Amer. devil; informal hassle, give someone a hard time, get on someone's back; Austral. informal heavy.

persecution noun **1** *victims of religious persecution:* **oppression**, victimization, maltreatment, ill-treatment, mistreatment, abuse, ill-usage, discrimination, tyranny; informal witch hunt. **2** *the persecution I endured at school:* **harassment**, hounding, intimidation, bullying.

perseverance noun *medicine is a field which requires dedication and perseverance:* **persistence**, tenacity, determination, staying power, indefatigability, steadfastness, purposefulness; patience, endurance, application, diligence, dedication, commitment, doggedness, assiduity, tirelessness, stamina; intransigence, obstinacy; informal stickability; N. Amer. informal stick-to-it-iveness.

persevere verb **persist**, continue, carry on, go on, keep on, keep going, struggle on,

hammer away, be persistent, be determined, see/follow something through, keep at it, press on/ahead, not take no for an answer, be tenacious, stand one's ground, stand fast/firm, hold on, go the distance, stay the course, plod on, plough on, stop at nothing, leave no stone unturned; informal soldier on, hang on, plug away, peg away, stick to one's guns, stick it out, hang in there.
– OPPOSITES give up.

persist verb **1** *Corbett persisted with his questioning.* See PERSEVERE. **2** *if dry weather persists, water the lawn thoroughly:* **continue**, hold, carry on, last, keep on, keep up, remain, linger, stay, endure.

persistence noun. See PERSEVERANCE.

persistent adjective **1** *a very persistent man:* **tenacious**, persevering, determined, resolute, purposeful, dogged, single-minded, tireless, indefatigable, patient, unflagging, untiring, insistent, importunate, relentless, unrelenting; stubborn, intransigent, obstinate, obdurate. **2** *persistent rain:* **constant**, continuous, continuing, continual, non-stop, never-ending, steady, uninterrupted, unbroken, interminable, incessant, unceasing, endless, unending, perpetual, unremitting, unrelenting, relentless, unrelieved, sustained. **3** *a persistent cough:* **chronic**, permanent, nagging, frequent; habitual.
– OPPOSITES irresolute, intermittent.

person noun **human being**, individual, man/woman, human, being, (living) soul, mortal, creature; personage, character, customer; informal type, sort, beggar, cookie; Brit. informal bod.
■ **in person** physically, in the flesh, in propria persona, personally; oneself; informal as large as life.

persona noun *his brash public persona is a facade for a very vulnerable man:* **image**, face, public face, character, personality, identity, self; front, facade, guise, exterior, role, part.

personable adjective *a personable young man:* **pleasant**, agreeable, likeable, nice, amiable, affable, charming, congenial, genial, engaging, pleasing; attractive, presentable, good-looking, nice-looking, pretty, appealing; Scottish couthy; Scottish & N. English bonny, canny.
– OPPOSITES disagreeable, unattractive.

personage noun *a succession of Hollywood personages:* **important person**, VIP, luminary, celebrity, personality, name, famous name, household name, public figure, star, leading light, dignitary, notable, notability, worthy, panjandrum; person; informal celeb, somebody, big shot, big noise; Brit. informal nob; N. Amer. informal big wheel, big kahuna.

personal adjective **1** *a highly personal style:* **distinctive**, characteristic, unique, individual, one's own, particular, peculiar, idiosyncratic, individualized, personalized.

p

2 *a personal appearance:* **in person**, in the flesh, actual, live, physical. **3** *his personal life:* **private**, intimate; confidential, secret. **4** *a personal friend:* **intimate**, close, dear, great, bosom. **5** *I have personal knowledge of the family:* **direct**, empirical, first-hand, immediate, experiential. **6** *personal remarks:* **derogatory**, disparaging, belittling, insulting, critical, rude, slighting, disrespectful, offensive, pejorative.
– OPPOSITES public, general.

personality noun **1** *her cheerful personality:* **character**, nature, disposition, temperament, make-up, persona, psyche. **2** *she had loads of personality:* **charisma**, magnetism, strength/force of personality, character, charm, presence. **3** *a famous personality:* **celebrity**, VIP, star, superstar, name, famous name, household name, big name, somebody, leading light, luminary, notable, personage, notability; informal celeb.

personalize verb *products which can be personalized to your requirements:* **customize**, individualize.

personally adverb **1** *I'd like to thank him personally:* **in person**, oneself. **2** *personally, I think it's a good idea:* **for my part**, for myself, to my way of thinking, to my mind, in my estimation, as far as I am concerned, in my view/opinion, from my point of view, from where I stand, as I see it, if you ask me, for my money, in my book; privately.
■ **take something personally** take offence, take something amiss, be offended, be upset, be affronted, take umbrage, take exception, feel insulted, feel hurt.

personification noun *he was the very personification of British pluck and diplomacy:* **embodiment**, incarnation, epitome, quintessence, essence, type, symbol, soul, model, exemplification, exemplar, image, representation.

personify verb *you personify every foreigner's image of the perfect English gentleman:* **epitomize**, embody, be the incarnation of, typify, exemplify, represent, symbolize, stand for, body forth.

personnel noun *sales personnel must dress smartly:* **staff**, employees, workforce, workers, labour force, manpower, human resources; informal liveware.

perspective noun **1** *her perspective on things had changed:* **outlook**, view, viewpoint, point of view, standpoint, position, stand, stance, angle, slant, attitude, frame of mind, frame of reference, approach, way of looking, interpretation. **2** *a perspective of the whole valley:* **view**, vista, panorama, prospect, bird's-eye view, outlook, aspect.

perspicacious adjective *his more perspicacious advisers recommended caution:* **discerning**, shrewd, perceptive, astute, penetrating, observant, percipient, sharp-witted, sharp, smart, alert, clear-sighted, far-sighted, acute, clever, canny, intelligent, insightful, wise, sage,

sensitive, intuitive, understanding, aware, discriminating; informal on the ball; N. Amer. informal heads-up.
– OPPOSITES stupid.

perspiration noun **sweat**, moisture; a lather; informal a muck sweat; Medicine hidrosis.

perspire verb *Will was perspiring heavily:* **sweat**, be dripping/pouring with sweat, glow; informal be in a muck sweat.

persuadable adjective *he was very persuadable:* **malleable**, tractable, pliable, compliant, amenable, adaptable, accommodating, cooperative, flexible, acquiescent, yielding, biddable, complaisant, like putty in one's hands, suggestible.

persuade verb **1** *he tried to persuade her to come with him:* **prevail on**, talk into, coax, convince, make, get, induce, win over, bring round, coerce, influence, sway, inveigle, entice, tempt, lure, cajole, wheedle; Law procure; informal sweet-talk, twist someone's arm. **2** *shortage of money persuaded them to abandon the scheme:* **cause**, lead, move, dispose, incline.
– OPPOSITES dissuade, deter.

persuasion noun **1** *Monica needed plenty of persuasion:* **coaxing**, persuading, coercion, inducement, convincing, blandishment, encouragement, urging, inveiglement, cajolery, enticement, wheedling; informal sweet-talking, arm-twisting. **2** *various political and religious persuasions:* **group**, grouping, sect, denomination, party, camp, side, faction, affiliation, school of thought, belief, creed, credo, faith, philosophy.

persuasive adjective *a persuasive argument:* **convincing**, cogent, compelling, potent, forceful, powerful, eloquent, impressive, influential, sound, valid, strong, effective, winning, telling; plausible, credible.
– OPPOSITES unconvincing.

pert adjective **1** *a pert little hat:* **jaunty**, neat, trim, stylish, smart, perky, rakish; informal natty; N. Amer. informal saucy. **2** *a young girl with a pert manner:* **impudent**, impertinent, cheeky, irreverent, forward, insolent, disrespectful, flippant, familiar, presumptuous, bold, as bold as brass, brazen; informal fresh, lippy, saucy; N. Amer. informal sassy.

pertain verb **1** *developments pertaining to the economy:* **concern**, relate to, be related to, be connected with, be relevant to, apply to, be pertinent to, refer to, have a bearing on, appertain to, bear on, affect, involve, touch. **2** *the stock and assets pertaining to the business:* **belong to**, be a part of, be included in. **3** *the economic situation which pertained in Britain at that time:* **exist**, be the order of the day, be the case, prevail.

pertinent adjective *she asked me a lot of very pertinent questions:* **relevant**, to the point, apposite, appropriate, suitable, fitting, fit, apt, applicable, material, germane, to the purpose, apropos.

– OPPOSITES irrelevant.

perturb verb *David's appearance perturbed his parents:* **worry**, upset, unsettle, disturb, concern, trouble, disquiet; disconcert, discomfit, unnerve, alarm, bother, distress, dismay, gnaw at, agitate, fluster, ruffle, discountenance, exercise; informal rattle.
– OPPOSITES reassure.

perturbed adjective **worried**, upset, unsettled, disturbed, concerned, troubled, anxious, ill at ease, uneasy, disquieted, fretful; disconcerted, discomposed, distressed, unnerved, alarmed, bothered, dismayed, agitated, flustered, ruffled, shaken, discountenanced; informal twitchy, rattled, fazed; N. Amer. informal discombobulated.
– OPPOSITES calm.

peruse verb *as he sipped his coffee, he perused his newspaper:* **read**, study, scrutinize, inspect, examine, wade through, look through; browse through, leaf through, scan, run one's eye over, glance through, flick through, skim through, thumb through.

pervade verb *a strong smell of floor polish pervaded the house:* **permeate**, spread through, fill, suffuse, be diffused through, imbue, penetrate, filter through, percolate through, infuse, perfuse, flow through; charge, steep, saturate, impregnate, inform.

pervasive adjective *a pervasive smell of staleness:* **prevalent**, pervading, permeating, extensive, ubiquitous, omnipresent, universal, rife, widespread, general.

perverse adjective **1** *he is being deliberately perverse:* **awkward**, contrary, difficult, unreasonable, uncooperative, unhelpful, obstructive, disobliging, recalcitrant, stubborn, obstinate, obdurate, mulish, pig-headed, bull-headed; informal cussed; Brit. informal bloody-minded, bolshie; N. Amer. informal balky. **2** *a verdict that is manifestly perverse:* **illogical**, irrational, unreasonable, wrong, wrong-headed. **3** *an evil life dedicated to perverse pleasure:* **perverted**, depraved, unnatural, abnormal, deviant, degenerate, immoral, warped, twisted, corrupt; wicked, base, evil; informal kinky, sick, pervy.
– OPPOSITES accommodating, reasonable.

perversion noun **1** *a twisted perversion of the truth:* **distortion**, misrepresentation, falsification, travesty, misinterpretation, misconstruction, twisting, corruption, subversion, misuse, misapplication, debasement. **2** *sexual perversion:* **deviance**, abnormality; depravity, degeneracy, debauchery, corruption, vice, wickedness, immorality.

perversity noun **1** *out of sheer perversity, he refused:* **contrariness**, awkwardness, recalcitrance, stubbornness, obstinacy, obduracy, mulishness, pig-headedness; informal cussedness; Brit. informal bloody-mindedness. **2** *the perversity of the decision:* **unreasonableness**, irrationality, illogicality, wrong-headedness.

pervert verb **1** *people who attempt to pervert the rules:* **distort**, corrupt, subvert, twist, bend, abuse, misapply, misuse, misrepresent, misinterpret, falsify. **2** *men can be perverted by power:* **corrupt**, lead astray, debase, warp, pollute, poison, deprave, debauch.
noun *a sexual pervert:* **deviant**, degenerate; informal perv, dirty old man, sicko.

perverted adjective *it's impossible to understand the perverted mentality of someone who could do such a thing:* **unnatural**, deviant, warped, corrupt, twisted, abnormal, unhealthy, depraved, perverse, aberrant, immoral, debauched, debased, degenerate, evil, wicked, vile, amoral, wrong, bad; informal sick, sicko, kinky, pervy.

pessimism noun **defeatism**, negativity, doom and gloom, gloominess, cynicism, fatalism; hopelessness, depression, despair, despondency, angst; informal looking on the black side.

pessimist noun *pessimists attempted to paint a picture of a nation in decline:* **defeatist**, fatalist, prophet of doom, cynic, doomsayer, doomster, Cassandra; sceptic, doubter, doubting Thomas; misery, killjoy, Job's comforter; informal doom (and gloom) merchant, wet blanket; N. Amer. informal gloomy Gus.
– OPPOSITES optimist.

pessimistic adjective *a pessimistic outlook on life:* **gloomy**, negative, defeatist, downbeat, cynical, bleak, fatalistic, dark, black, despairing, despondent, depressed, hopeless; suspicious, distrustful, doubting.
– OPPOSITES optimistic.

pest noun *that child is a real pest:* **nuisance**, annoyance, irritation, irritant, thorn in one's flesh/side, vexation, trial, the bane of one's life, menace, trouble, problem, worry, bother; informal pain (in the neck), aggravation, headache; Scottish informal skelf; N. Amer. informal nudnik; Austral./NZ informal nark.

pester verb *I've been pestered by reporters for days:* **badger**, hound, harass, plague, annoy, bother, trouble, keep after, persecute, torment, bedevil, harry, worry, beleaguer, chivvy, nag; informal hassle, bug, get on someone's back; N. English informal mither; N. Amer. informal devil.

pet¹ noun *the teacher's pet:* **favourite**, darling, the apple of one's eye; Brit. informal blue-eyed boy/girl; N. Amer. informal fair-haired boy/girl.
adjective **1** *a pet lamb:* **tame**, domesticated, domestic; Brit. house-trained; N. Amer. housebroken. **2** *his pet theory:* **favourite**, favoured, cherished, dear to one's heart; particular, special, personal.
verb **1** *the cats came to be petted:* **stroke**, caress, fondle, pat. **2** *she had always been petted by her parents:* **pamper**, spoil, mollycoddle, coddle, cosset, baby, indulge, overindulge, wrap in cotton wool. **3** *couples were petting in their cars:* **kiss and cuddle**,

p

kiss, cuddle, embrace, caress; informal canoodle, neck, smooch; Brit. informal snog; N. Amer. informal make out, get it on.
■ **pet name** affectionate name, term of endearment, endearment, nickname, diminutive, hypocoristic.

pet² noun *Mum's in a pet:* **bad mood**, mood, bad temper, temper, sulk, fit of pique, huff; Brit. informal paddy, strop.

peter
■ **peter out** *the economic recovery is in danger of petering out:* fizzle out, fade (away), die away/out, dwindle, diminish, taper off, tail off, trail away/off, wane, ebb, melt away, evaporate, disappear, come to an end, subside.

petite adjective *she was dark, petite, and sophisticated:* **small**, dainty, diminutive, slight, little, tiny, elfin, delicate, small-boned; Scottish wee; informal pint-sized.

petition noun 1 *over 1,000 people signed the petition:* **appeal**, round robin. 2 *petitions to Allah:* **entreaty**, supplication, plea, prayer, appeal, request, invocation, suit.
verb *they petitioned the king to revoke the decision:* **appeal to**, request, ask, call on, entreat, beg, implore, plead with, apply to, press, urge.

petrified adjective 1 *she looked petrified:* **terrified**, terror-stricken, horrified, scared/frightened out of one's wits, scared/frightened to death. 2 *the petrified remains of prehistoric animals:* **ossified**, fossilized, calcified.

petrify verb **terrify**, horrify, frighten, scare, scare/frighten to death, scare/frighten the living daylights out of, scare/frighten the life out of, strike terror into, put the fear of God into; paralyse, transfix; informal scare the pants off; Irish informal scare the bejesus out of.

petrol noun **fuel**, unleaded, superunleaded; N. Amer. gasoline, gas; informal juice.

petticoat noun **slip**, underskirt, half-slip, underslip, undergarment.

petty adjective 1 *petty regulations:* **trivial**, trifling, minor, small, unimportant, insignificant, inconsequential, inconsiderable, negligible, paltry, footling, pettifogging; informal piffling, piddling, fiddling. 2 *a petty form of revenge:* **small-minded**, mean, ungenerous, shabby, spiteful.
– OPPOSITES important, magnanimous.

petulant adjective *he sounded as petulant as a small child:* **peevish**, bad-tempered, querulous, pettish, fretful, cross, irritable, sulky, snappish, crotchety, touchy, tetchy, testy, fractious, grumpy, disgruntled, crabbed, crabby; informal grouchy; Brit. informal ratty; N. English informal mardy; N. Amer. informal cranky.
– OPPOSITES good-humoured.

phantom noun 1 *a phantom who haunts lonely roads:* **ghost**, apparition, spirit, spectre, wraith; informal spook. 2 *the phantoms*

of an overactive imagination: **delusion**, figment of the imagination, hallucination, illusion, chimera, vision, mirage.

phase noun 1 *the final phase of the campaign:* **stage**, period, chapter, episode, part, step, point, time, juncture. 2 *he's going through a difficult phase:* **period**, stage, time, spell; Brit. informal patch. 3 *the phases of the moon:* **aspect**, shape, form, appearance, state, condition.
■ **phase something in** introduce gradually, begin to use, ease in, roll out.
■ **phase something out** withdraw gradually, discontinue, stop using, run down, wind down.

phenomenal adjective *sales growth has been nothing short of phenomenal:* **remarkable**, exceptional, extraordinary, amazing, astonishing, astounding, sensational, stunning, incredible, unbelievable; marvellous, magnificent, wonderful, outstanding, singular, out of the ordinary, unusual, unprecedented; informal fantastic, terrific, tremendous, stupendous, awesome, out of this world.
– OPPOSITES ordinary.

phenomenon noun 1 *a rare phenomenon:* **occurrence**, event, happening, fact, situation, circumstance, experience, case, incident, episode. 2 *the band was a pop phenomenon:* **marvel**, sensation, wonder, prodigy, miracle, rarity, nonpareil.

philander verb **womanize**, have affairs, flirt; informal play around, carry on, play the field, play away, sleep around; N. Amer. informal fool around.

philanderer noun *everyone warned me he was a philanderer:* **womanizer**, Casanova, Don Juan, Lothario, flirt, ladies' man, playboy, rake, roué; informal stud, skirt-chaser, ladykiller, wolf.

philanthropic adjective *a philanthropic millionaire:* **charitable**, generous, benevolent, humanitarian, public-spirited, altruistic, magnanimous, munificent, open-handed, bountiful, liberal, generous to a fault, beneficent, caring, compassionate, unselfish, kind, kind-hearted, big-hearted.
– OPPOSITES selfish, mean.

philanthropist noun *the trust was founded by an American philanthropist:* **benefactor**, benefactress, patron, patroness, donor, contributor, sponsor, backer, helper, good Samaritan; do-gooder, Lady Bountiful; historical almsgiver.

philanthropy noun **benevolence**, generosity, humanitarianism, public-spiritedness, altruism, social conscience, charity, charitableness, brotherly love, fellow feeling, magnanimity, munificence, liberality, largesse, open-handedness, bountifulness, beneficence, unselfishness, humanity, kindness, kind-heartedness, compassion.

philistine adjective *film tastes were*

determined in the populous and philistine Midwest: **uncultured**, lowbrow, anti-intellectual, uncultivated, uncivilized, uneducated, unenlightened, commercial, materialist, bourgeois; ignorant, crass, boorish, barbarian.

philosopher noun **thinker**, theorist, theorizer, theoretician, metaphysicist, metaphysician; scholar, intellectual, sage, wise man.

philosophical adjective **1** *a philosophical question:* **theoretical**, metaphysical. **2** *a philosophical mood:* **thoughtful**, reflective, pensive, meditative, contemplative, introspective, ruminative. **3** *he was philosophical about losing the contract:* **calm**, composed, cool, collected, {cool, calm, and collected}, self-possessed, serene, tranquil, stoical, impassive, dispassionate, phlegmatic, unperturbed, imperturbable, unruffled, patient, forbearing, long-suffering, resigned, rational, realistic.

philosophize verb *he paused for a while to philosophize on racial equality:* **theorize**, speculate; pontificate, preach, sermonize, moralize.

philosophy noun **1** *the philosophy of Aristotle:* **thinking**, thought, reasoning. **2** *her political philosophy:* **beliefs**, credo, convictions, ideology, ideas, thinking, notions, theories, doctrine, tenets, principles, views, school of thought.

phlegm noun **1** **mucus**, catarrh. **2** *British phlegm and perseverance:* **calmness**, coolness, composure, equanimity, tranquillity, placidity, placidness, impassivity, stolidity, imperturbability, impassiveness, dispassionateness; informal cool, unflappability.

phlegmatic adjective *a phlegmatic attitude to every crisis:* **calm**, cool, composed, {cool, calm, and collected}, controlled, serene, tranquil, placid, impassive, stolid, imperturbable, unruffled, dispassionate, philosophical; informal unflappable.
– OPPOSITES excitable.

phobia noun **abnormal fear**, irrational fear, obsessive fear, dread, horror, terror, hatred, loathing, detestation, aversion, antipathy, revulsion; complex, neurosis; informal thing, hang-up.

phone noun **1** *she spent hours on the phone:* **telephone**, mobile (phone), cellphone; extension; Brit. informal blower; N. Amer. informal horn; Brit. rhyming slang dog and bone. **2** *give me a phone sometime:* **call**, telephone call, phone call; Brit. ring; informal buzz; Brit. informal tinkle, bell.
verb *I'll phone you later:* **telephone**, call, give someone a call; Brit. ring, ring up, give someone a ring; informal call up, give someone a buzz; Brit. informal give someone a bell/tinkle, get on the blower to; N. Amer. informal get someone on the horn.

phoney (informal) adjective *a phoney address:*

bogus, false, faux, fake, fraudulent, spurious; counterfeit, forged, feigned; pseudo, imitation, sham, man-made, mock, ersatz, synthetic, artificial; simulated, pretended, contrived, affected, insincere; informal pretend, put-on; Brit. informal cod.
– OPPOSITES authentic.
noun **1** *he's nothing but a phoney:* **impostor**, sham, fake, fraud, charlatan; informal con artist. **2** *the diamond's a phoney:* **fake**, imitation, counterfeit, forgery.

photocopy noun *he sent me a photocopy of the article:* **copy**, facsimile, duplicate; trademark Xerox, photostat, Ozalid.

photograph noun *a photograph of her father:* **picture**, photo, snap, snapshot, shot, likeness, print, slide, transparency, still, enlargement; Brit. enprint; informal tranny.
verb *she was photographed leaving the castle:* **take someone's picture/photo**, snap, shoot, film.

photographer noun **cameraman**, paparazzo, lensman; informal snapper; N. Amer. informal shutterbug.

photographic adjective **1** *a photographic record:* **pictorial**, in photographs; cinematic, filmic. **2** *a photographic memory:* **detailed**, graphic, exact, precise, accurate, vivid.

phrase noun *familiar words and phrases:* **expression**, group of words, construction, locution, term, turn of phrase; idiom, idiomatic expression; saying, tag.
verb *how could I phrase the question?* **express**, put into words, put, word, style, formulate, couch, frame, articulate, verbalize.

phraseology noun *legal phraseology:* **wording**, choice of words, phrasing, way of speaking/writing, usage, idiom, diction, parlance, words, language, vocabulary, terminology; jargon; informal lingo, -speak, -ese.

physical adjective **1** *physical pleasure:* **bodily**, corporeal, corporal, somatic; carnal, fleshly, non-spiritual. **2** *hard physical work:* **manual**, labouring, blue-collar. **3** *the physical universe:* **material**, concrete, tangible, palpable, solid, substantial, real, actual, visible.
– OPPOSITES mental, spiritual.

physician noun **doctor**, doctor of medicine, MD, medical practitioner, general practitioner, GP, clinician; specialist, consultant; informal doc, medic, medico; Brit. informal quack.

physique noun *a sturdy, muscular physique:* **body**, build, figure, frame, anatomy, shape, form, proportions; muscles, musculature; informal vital statistics, bod.

pick verb **1** *I got a job picking apples:* **harvest**, gather (in), collect, pluck. **2** *pick the time that suits you best:* **choose**, select, pick out, single out, take, opt for, plump for, elect, decide on, settle on, fix on, sift out, sort out; name, nominate. **3** *Beth picked at her food:*

p

nibble, toy with, play with, eat like a bird.
4 *he tried to pick a fight:* **provoke**, start, cause, incite, stir up, whip up, instigate, prompt, bring about.
noun **1** *take your pick:* **choice**, selection, option, decision; preference, favourite. **2** *the pick of the crop:* **best**, finest, top, choice, choicest, prime, cream, flower, prize, pearl, gem, jewel, jewel in the crown, crème de la crème, elite.
■ **pick on** *why don't you pick on somebody else?* bully, victimize, tyrannize, torment, persecute, criticize, harass, hound, taunt, tease; informal get at, have it in for, have a down on, be down on, needle.
■ **pick something out 1** *one painting was picked out for special mention:* choose, select, pick, single out, opt for, plump for, decide on, elect, settle on, fix on, sift out, sort out; name, nominate. **2** *she picked out Jessica in the crowd:* see, make out, distinguish, discern, spot, perceive, detect, notice, recognize, identify, catch sight of, glimpse.
■ **pick up** *the economy will soon pick up again:* improve, recover, be on the road to recovery, rally, make a comeback, bounce back, perk up, look up, take a turn for the better, turn the/a corner, be on the mend, make headway, make progress.
■ **pick someone/something up** lift, take up, raise, hoist, scoop up, gather up, snatch up.
■ **pick someone up 1** *I'll pick you up after lunch:* fetch, collect, call for. **2** (informal) *he picked her up in a club:* take up with; informal get off with, pull, cop off with.
■ **pick something up 1** *we picked it up at a flea market:* find, discover, come across, stumble across, happen on, chance on; acquire, obtain, come by, get, procure, purchase, buy; informal get hold of, get/lay one's hands on, get one's mitts on, bag, land. **2** *he picked up the story in the 1950s:* resume, take up, start again, recommence, continue, carry on with, go on with. **3** *she picked up a virus:* catch, contract, get, go/come down with. **4** *he told us the bits of gossip he'd picked up:* hear, hear tell, get wind of, be told, learn; glean, garner. **5** *we're picking up a distress signal:* receive, detect, get, hear.

picket noun **1** *forty pickets were arrested:* **striker**, demonstrator, protester, objector, picketer; flying picket. **2** *fences made of cedar pickets:* **stake**, post, paling; upright, stanchion, pier, piling.
verb *over 200 people picketed the factory:* **demonstrate at**, form a picket at, man the picket line at; blockade, shut off.

pickle noun **1** *a jar of pickle:* **relish**, chutney, piccalilli. **2** *steep the vegetables in pickle:* **marinade**, brine, vinegar. **3** (informal) *they got into an awful pickle:* **plight**, predicament, mess, difficulty, trouble, dire/desperate straits, problem; informal tight corner, tight spot, jam, fix, scrape, bind, hole, hot water, fine kettle of fish; Brit. informal spot of bother.

verb *fish pickled in brine:* **preserve**, souse, marinate, conserve; bottle, can, tin.

pick-me-up noun **1** *a drink that's a very good pick-me-up:* **tonic**, restorative, energizer, stimulant, refresher, reviver; informal bracer. **2** *his winning goal was a perfect pick-me-up:* **boost**, boost to the spirits, fillip, stimulant, stimulus; informal shot in the arm.

pickpocket noun **thief**, petty thief, sneak thief.

pickup noun *a pickup in the housing market:* **improvement**, recovery, revival, upturn, upswing, rally, comeback, resurgence, renewal, turn for the better.
– OPPOSITES slump.

picnic noun **1** *a picnic on the beach:* **outdoor meal**, alfresco meal; N. Amer. cookout. **2** (informal) *working for him was no picnic:* **easy task/job**, child's play, five-finger exercise, gift, walkover; informal doddle, piece of cake, money for old rope, money for jam, cinch, breeze, low-hanging fruit, kids' stuff, cakewalk, pushover; N. Amer. informal duck soup; Austral./NZ informal bludge.

pictorial adjective *a pictorial history of Gateshead:* **illustrated**, in pictures, in picture form, in photographs, photographic, graphic.

picture noun **1** *pictures in an art gallery:* **painting**, **drawing**, sketch, oil painting, watercolour, print, canvas, portrait, portrayal, illustration, artwork, depiction, likeness, representation, image, icon, miniature; fresco, mural, wall painting; informal oil. **2** *we were told not to take pictures:* **photograph**, photo, snap, snapshot, shot, print, slide, transparency, exposure, still, enlargement; Brit. enprint. **3** *a picture of the sort of person the child should be:* **concept**, idea, impression, view, (mental) image, vision, visualization, notion. **4** *the picture of health:* **personification**, embodiment, epitome, essence, quintessence, perfect example, soul, model. **5** *a picture starring Robert De Niro:* **film**, movie, feature film, motion picture; informal flick. **6** *we went to the pictures:* **the cinema**, the movies, the silver screen, the big screen; informal the flicks.
verb **1** *he was pictured with his guests:* **photograph**, take a photograph/photo of, snap, shoot, film. **2** *in the drawing they were pictured against a snowy background:* **paint**, **draw**, sketch, depict, delineate, portray, show, illustrate. **3** *Anne still pictured Richard as he had been:* **visualize**, see in one's mind's eye, conjure up a picture/image of, imagine, see, evoke.
■ **put someone in the picture** inform, fill in, explain the situation/circumstances to, bring up to date, update, brief, keep posted; informal clue in, bring up to speed.

picturesque adjective **1** *a picturesque village:* **attractive**, pretty, beautiful, lovely, scenic, charming, quaint, pleasing, delightful. **2** *a picturesque description:* **vivid**, graphic, colourful, impressive, striking.

– OPPOSITES ugly, dull.

pie noun **pastry**, tart, tartlet, quiche, pasty, patty, turnover, strudel.
■ **pie in the sky** (informal) false hope, illusion, delusion, fantasy, pipe dream, daydream, castle in the air, castle in Spain.

piebald adjective. See PIED.

piece noun **1** *a piece of cheese* | *a piece of wood:* **bit**, slice, chunk, segment, section, lump, hunk, wedge, slab, block, cake, bar, cube, stick, length; offcut, sample, fragment, sliver, splinter, wafer, chip, crumb, scrap, remnant, shred, shard, snippet; mouthful, morsel; Brit. informal wodge. **2** *the pieces of a clock:* **component**, part, bit, section, segment, constituent, element; unit, module. **3** *a piece of furniture:* **item**, article, specimen. **4** *a piece of the profit:* **share**, portion, slice, quota, part, bit, percentage, amount, quantity, ration, fraction, division; informal cut, rake-off; Brit. informal whack. **5** *pieces from his private collection:* **work (of art)**, creation, production; composition, opus. **6** *the reporter who wrote the piece:* **article**, item, story, report, essay, study, review, composition, column. **7** *the pieces on a chess board:* **token**, counter, man, disc, chip, marker.
■ **in one piece 1** *the camera was still in one piece:* unbroken, entire, whole, intact, undamaged, unharmed. **2** *I'll bring her back in one piece:* unhurt, uninjured, unscathed, safe, safe and sound.
■ **in pieces** broken, in bits, shattered, smashed, in smithereens; informal bust.
■ **go/fall to pieces** have a breakdown, break down, go out of one's mind, lose control, lose one's head, fall apart; informal crack up, lose it, come/fall apart at the seams, freak, freak out.

pièce de résistance noun *the pièce de résistance of the meal was ice cream flambé* **masterpiece**, magnum opus, chef-d'œuvre, masterwork, tour de force, showpiece, prize, jewel in the crown.

piecemeal adverb *the reforms were implemented piecemeal:* **a little at a time**, piece by piece, bit by bit, gradually, slowly, in stages, in steps, step by step, little by little, by degrees, in/by fits and starts.

pied adjective *pied horses:* **particoloured**, multicoloured, variegated, black and white, brown and white, piebald, skewbald, dappled, brindle, spotted, mottled, speckled, flecked; N. Amer. pinto.

pier noun **1** *a boat was tied to the pier:* **jetty**, quay, wharf, dock, landing, landing stage. **2** *the piers of the bridge:* **support**, cutwater, pile, piling, abutment, buttress, stanchion, prop, stay, upright, pillar, post, column.

pierce verb *the metal pierced his flesh:* **penetrate**, puncture, perforate, prick, lance; stab, spike, stick, impale, transfix, bore through, drill through.

piercing adjective **1** *a piercing shriek:* **shrill**, ear-splitting, high-pitched, penetrating, strident, loud. **2** *the piercing wind:* **bitter**, biting, cutting, penetrating, sharp, keen, stinging, raw; freezing, frigid, glacial, arctic, chill. **3** *a piercing pain:* **intense**, excruciating, agonizing, sharp, stabbing, shooting, stinging, severe, extreme, fierce, searing, racking. **4** *his piercing gaze:* **searching**, probing, penetrating, penetrative, shrewd, sharp, keen. **5** *his piercing intelligence:* **perceptive**, percipient, perspicacious, penetrating, discerning, discriminating, intelligent, quick-witted, sharp, sharp-witted, shrewd, insightful, keen, acute, astute, clever, smart, incisive, razor-edged, trenchant.

piety noun *the piety of a saint:* **devoutness**, devotion, piousness, religion, holiness, godliness, saintliness; veneration, reverence, faith, religious duty, spirituality, religious zeal, fervour; pietism, religiosity.

pig noun **1** *a herd of pigs:* **hog**, boar, sow, porker, swine, piglet; children's word piggy. **2** (informal) *he's eaten the lot, the pig:* **glutton**, guzzler; informal hog, greedy guts; Brit. informal gannet. **3** (informal) *he's been an absolute pig lately:* informal **bastard**, beast, louse, swine; Brit. informal toerag.

pigeonhole noun *journalistic pigeonholes:* **category**, categorization, class, classification, group, grouping, designation, slot.
verb **1** *they were pigeonholed as an indie guitar band:* **categorize**, compartmentalize, classify, characterize, label, brand, tag, designate. **2** *the plan was pigeonholed last year:* **postpone**, put off, put back, defer, shelve, hold over, put to one side, put on ice, mothball, put in cold storage; N. Amer. table; informal put on the back burner.

pig-headed adjective *he was an arrogant, pig-headed man:* **obstinate**, stubborn (as a mule), mulish, bull-headed, obdurate, headstrong, self-willed, wilful, perverse, contrary, recalcitrant, stiff-necked; uncooperative, inflexible, uncompromising, intractable, intransigent, unyielding; Brit. informal bloody-minded, bolshie.

pigment noun **colouring matter**, colouring, colourant, colour, tint, dye, dyestuff.

pile¹ noun **1** *a pile of stones:* **heap**, stack, mound, pyramid, mass, quantity; collection, accumulation, assemblage, store, stockpile, hoard. **2** *a huge Victorian pile:* **mansion**, stately home, manor, manor house, country house; edifice.
verb **1** *he piled up the plates:* **heap (up)**, stack (up), put on top of each other. **2** *he piled his plate with fried eggs:* **load**, heap, fill (up), lade, stack, charge, stock. **3** *his debts were piling up:* **increase**, grow, mount up, escalate, soar, spiral, leap up, shoot up, rocket, climb, accumulate, accrue, build up, multiply. **4** *we piled into the car:* **crowd**, climb, pack, squeeze, push, shove.

pile² noun *a wall supported by timber*

piles: **post**, stake, pillar, column, support, foundation, piling, abutment, pier, cutwater, buttress, stanchion, upright.

pile³ noun *a carpet with a short pile:* **nap**, fibres, threads.

pile-up noun *a pile-up on the motorway:* **crash**, multiple crash, collision, multiple collision, smash, accident, road accident; Brit. RTA (road traffic accident); N. Amer. wreck; informal smash-up; Brit. informal shunt.

pilfer verb *the gun was part of a cache pilfered from the air force:* **steal**, thieve, take, snatch, purloin, loot; informal swipe, rob, nab, rip off, lift, liberate, borrow, filch, snaffle; Brit. informal pinch, half-inch, nick, whip, knock off, nobble; N. Amer. informal heist.

pilgrim noun worshipper, devotee, believer; traveller, crusader, haji.

pilgrimage noun **religious journey**, religious expedition, hajj, crusade, mission.

pill noun *a sleeping pill:* **tablet**, capsule, caplet, pellet, lozenge, pastille.

pillage verb 1 *the abbey was pillaged:* **ransack**, rob, plunder, despoil, raid, loot; sack, devastate, lay waste, ravage, rape. 2 *columns pillaged from an ancient town:* **steal**, pilfer, thieve, take, snatch, purloin, loot; informal swipe, rob, nab, rip off, lift, liberate, borrow, filch, snaffle; Brit. informal pinch, half-inch, nick, whip, knock off, nobble; N. Amer. informal heist.
noun *the rebels were intent on pillage:* **robbery**, robbing, raiding, plunder, looting, sacking, rape, marauding.

pillar noun 1 *stone pillars:* **column**, post, support, upright, baluster, pier, pile, pilaster, stanchion, prop, newel; obelisk, monolith. 2 *a pillar of the community:* **stalwart**, mainstay, bastion, rock; leading light, worthy, backbone, support, upholder, champion.

pillory noun *offenders were put in the pillory:* **stocks**.
verb 1 *he was pilloried by the press:* **attack**, criticize, censure, condemn, denigrate, lambaste, savage, stigmatize, denounce; informal knock, slam, pan, bash, crucify, hammer; Brit. informal slate, rubbish, slag off; N. Amer. informal pummel; Austral./NZ informal bag, monster. 2 *they were pilloried at school:* **ridicule**, jeer at, sneer at, deride, mock, scorn, make fun of, poke fun at, laugh at, scoff at, tease, taunt, rag; informal kid, rib, josh, take the mickey out of; N. Amer. informal razz, pull someone's chain.

pillow noun *his head rested on the pillow:* **cushion**, bolster, pad; headrest.
verb *she pillowed her head on folded arms:* **cushion**, cradle, rest, lay, support.

pilot noun 1 *a fighter pilot:* **airman/airwoman**, flyer; captain, commander, co-pilot, wingman; informal skipper; N. Amer. informal jock. 2 *a harbour pilot:* **navigator**, helmsman, steersman, coxswain. 3 *a pilot for a TV series:* **trial**

episode; sample, experiment.
adjective *a pilot project:* **experimental**, exploratory, trial, test, sample, speculative; preliminary.
verb 1 *he piloted the jet to safety:* **navigate**, guide, manoeuvre, steer, control, direct, captain, shepherd; fly, aviate; drive; sail; informal skipper. 2 *the questionnaire has been piloted:* **test**, trial, try out; assess, investigate, examine, appraise, evaluate.

pimp noun **procurer**, procuress; brothel-keeper, madam; Brit. informal ponce.

pimple noun **spot**, pustule, bleb, boil, swelling, eruption, blackhead, carbuncle, blister; **(pimples)** acne; informal whitehead, zit; Scottish informal plook.

pin noun 1 *fasten the hem with a pin:* **tack**, safety pin, nail, staple, fastener. 2 *a broken pin in the machine:* **bolt**, peg, rivet, dowel, screw. 3 *they wore name pins:* **badge**, brooch.
verb 1 *she pinned the brooch to her dress:* **attach**, fasten, affix, fix, tack, clip; join, secure. 2 *they pinned him to the ground:* **hold**, press, hold fast, hold down; restrain, pinion, immobilize. 3 *they pinned the crime on him:* **blame for**, hold responsible for, attribute to, impute to, ascribe to; lay something at someone's door; informal stick on.
■ **pin someone/something down 1** *our troops can pin down the enemy:* confine, trap, hem in, corner, close in, shut in, hedge in, pen in, restrain, entangle, enmesh, immobilize. **2** *she tried to pin him down to a plan:* constrain, make someone commit themselves, pressure, pressurize, tie down, nail down. **3** *it evoked a memory but he couldn't pin it down:* define, put one's finger on, put into words, express, name, specify, identify, pinpoint, place.

pinch verb 1 *he pinched my arm:* **nip**, tweak, squeeze, grasp. 2 *my new shoes pinch my toes:* **hurt**, pain; squeeze, crush, cramp; be uncomfortable. 3 *I scraped and pinched to afford it:* **economize**, scrimp (and save), be sparing, be frugal, cut back, tighten one's belt, retrench, cut one's coat according to one's cloth; informal be stingy, be tight.
noun 1 *he gave her arm a pinch:* **nip**, tweak, squeeze. 2 *a pinch of salt:* **bit**, touch, dash, spot, trace, soupçon, speck, taste; informal smidgen, tad.
■ **at a pinch** if necessary, if need be, in an emergency, just possibly, with difficulty; N. Amer. in a pinch; Brit. informal at a push.
■ **feel the pinch** suffer hardship, be short of money, be poor, be impoverished.

pinched adjective *their pinched faces:* **strained**, stressed, fraught, tense, taut; tired, worn, drained, sapped; wan, peaky, pale, grey, blanched; thin, drawn, haggard, gaunt.
– OPPOSITES healthy.

pine verb 1 *I am pining away from love:* **languish**, decline, weaken, waste away, wilt, wither, fade, sicken, droop; brood, mope, moon. **2** *he was pining for his son:* **yearn**, long, ache, sigh, hunger, languish; miss, mourn, lament, grieve over, shed tears for, bemoan, rue, eat one's heart out over; informal itch.

pinion verb *he was pinioned to the ground:* **hold down**, pin down, restrain, hold fast, immobilize; tie, bind, truss (up), shackle, fetter, hobble, manacle, handcuff; informal cuff.

pink adjective **rose**, rosy, rosé, pale red, salmon, coral; flushed, blushing.

pinnacle noun **1** *pinnacles of rock:* **peak**, needle, aiguille, hoodoo, crag, tor; summit, crest, apex, tip; Geology inselberg. **2** *the pinnacles of the clock tower:* **turret**, minaret, spire, finial, shikara, mirador. **3** *the pinnacle of the sport:* **highest level**, peak, height, high point, top, apex, zenith, apogee, acme.
– OPPOSITES nadir.

pinpoint noun *a pinpoint of light:* **point**, spot, speck, dot, speckle.
adjective *pinpoint accuracy:* **precise**, strict, exact, meticulous, scrupulous, punctilious, accurate, careful.
verb *we must pinpoint the cause of the trouble:* **identify**, determine, distinguish, discover, find, locate, detect, track down, spot, diagnose, recognize, pin down, home in on, put one's finger on.

pioneer noun **1** *the pioneers of the Wild West:* **settler**, colonist, colonizer, frontiersman/woman, explorer, trailblazer. **2** *a pioneer of motoring:* **developer**, innovator, trailblazer, groundbreaker, spearhead; founder, founding father, architect, creator.
verb *he pioneered the sale of insurance:* **introduce**, develop, evolve, launch, instigate, initiate, spearhead, institute, establish, found, be the father/mother of, originate, set in motion, create; lay the groundwork, prepare the way, blaze a trail, break new ground.

pious adjective **1** *a pious family:* **religious**, devout, God-fearing, churchgoing, spiritual, prayerful, holy, godly, saintly, dedicated, reverent, dutiful, righteous. **2** *a pious platitude:* **sanctimonious**, hypocritical, insincere, self-righteous, holier-than-thou, pietistic, churchy; informal goody-goody; Brit. informal pi. **3** *a pious hope:* **forlorn**, vain, doomed, hopeless, desperate; unlikely, unrealistic.
– OPPOSITES irreligious, sincere.

pip noun **seed**, stone, pit.

pipe noun **1** *a central-heating pipe:* **tube**, conduit, hose, main, duct, line, channel, pipeline, drain; tubing, piping, siphon. **2** *he smokes a pipe:* briar (pipe), meerschaum, chibouk; hookah, narghile, hubble-bubble, bong; Brit. churchwarden; Scottish & N. English cutty. **3** *she was playing a pipe:* **whistle**, penny whistle, flute, recorder, fife; chanter. **4** *regimental pipes and drums:* **bagpipes**,

uillean pipes; pan pipes.
verb **1** *the beer is piped into barrels:* **siphon**, feed, channel, run, convey. **2** *programmes piped in from London:* **transmit**, feed, patch. **3** *he heard a tune being piped:* **play on a pipe**, tootle, whistle. **4** *a curlew piped:* **chirp**, cheep, chirrup, twitter, warble, trill, peep, sing, shrill.

pipe dream noun *the plans are likely to remain a pipe dream:* **fantasy**, false hope, illusion, delusion, daydream, chimera; castle in the air, castle in Spain; informal pie in the sky.

pipeline noun *a gas pipeline:* **pipe**, conduit, main, line, duct, tube.
■ **in the pipeline** on the way, coming, forthcoming, upcoming, imminent, about to happen, near, close, brewing, in the offing, in the wind.

piquant adjective **1** *a piquant sauce:* **spicy**, tangy, peppery, hot; tasty, flavoursome, flavourful, appetizing, savoury; pungent, sharp, tart, zesty, strong, salty. **2** *a piquant story:* **intriguing**, stimulating, interesting, fascinating, colourful, exciting, lively; spicy, provocative, racy; informal juicy.
– OPPOSITES bland, dull.

pique noun *a fit of pique:* **irritation**, annoyance, resentment, anger, displeasure, indignation, petulance, ill humour, vexation, exasperation, disgruntlement, discontent; offence, umbrage.
verb **1** *his curiosity was piqued:* **stimulate**, arouse, rouse, provoke, whet, awaken, excite, kindle, stir, galvanize. **2** *she was piqued by his neglect:* **irritate**, annoy, bother, vex, displease, upset, offend, affront, anger, exasperate, infuriate, gall, irk, nettle; informal peeve, aggravate, miff, rile, bug, needle, get someone's back up, hack off, get someone's goat; Brit. informal nark, give someone the hump; N. Amer. informal tick off, tee off.

piracy noun **1** *piracy on the high seas:* **robbery at sea**, freebooting. **2** *software piracy:* **illegal copying**, plagiarism, copyright infringement, bootlegging.

pirate noun **1** *pirates boarded the ship:* **freebooter**, marauder, raider; historical privateer. **2** *software pirates:* **copyright infringer**, plagiarist, plagiarizer.
verb *designers may pirate good ideas:* **reproduce illegally**, copy illegally, plagiarize, poach, steal, appropriate, bootleg; informal crib, lift, rip off; Brit. informal nick, pinch.

pirouette noun *she did a little pirouette:* **spin**, twirl, whirl, turn.
verb *she pirouetted before the mirror:* **spin round**, twirl, whirl, turn round, revolve, pivot.

pit[1] noun **1** *a pit in the ground:* **hole**, ditch, trench, trough, hollow, excavation, cavity, crater, pothole, shaft, mineshaft. **2** *pit closures:* **coal mine**, colliery, quarry. **3** *the pits in her skin:* **pockmark**, pock, hollow, indentation, depression, dent, dint, dimple.
verb **1** *his skin had been pitted by acne:*

mark, pockmark, scar, blemish, disfigure. **2** *raindrops pitted the bare earth:* **make holes in**, make hollows in, dent, indent, dint.
■ **pit someone/something against** *a chance to pit your wits against the world champions:* set against, match against, put in opposition to, put in competition with; compete with, contend with, vie with, wrestle with.

pit² noun *cherry pits:* **stone**, pip, seed.

pitch¹ noun **1** *the pitch was unfit for cricket:* **playing field**, field, ground, sports field; stadium, arena; Brit. park. **2** *her voice rose in pitch:* **tone**, timbre, key, modulation, frequency. **3** *the pitch of the roof:* **gradient**, slope, slant, angle, steepness, tilt, incline, inclination. **4** *her anger reached such a pitch that she screamed:* **level**, intensity, point, degree, height, extent. **5** *a pitch of the ball:* **throw**, fling, hurl, toss, lob; delivery; informal chuck, heave. **6** *his sales pitch:* **patter**, talk; informal spiel, line. **7** *street traders reserved their pitches:* **site**, place, spot, station; Scottish stance; Brit. informal patch.
verb **1** *he pitched the note into the fire:* **throw**, toss, fling, hurl, cast, lob, flip, propel, bowl; informal chuck, sling, heave, bung; N. Amer. informal peg; Austral. informal hoy; NZ informal bish. **2** *he pitched overboard:* **fall**, tumble, topple, plunge, plummet. **3** *they pitched their tents:* **put up**, set up, erect, raise. **4** *the boat pitched in the heavy seas:* **lurch**, toss (about), plunge, roll, reel, sway, rock, keel, list, wallow, labour.
■ **make a pitch for** try to obtain, try to acquire, try to get, bid for, make a bid for.
■ **pitch in** help (out), assist, lend a hand, join in, participate, contribute, do one's bit, chip in, cooperate, collaborate; Brit. informal muck in.
■ **pitch into** *he pitched into the youths with such fury that they ran off:* attack, turn on, lash out at, set upon, assault, fly at, tear into, weigh into, belabour; informal lay into, let someone have it, take a pop at; N. Amer. informal light into.

pitch² noun *cement coated with pitch:* bitumen, asphalt, tar.

pitch-black adjective *the sky was pitch-black:* **black**, dark, pitch-dark, inky, jet-black, coal-black, jet, ebony; starless, moonless.

pitcher noun *jug*, ewer, jar; N. Amer. creamer.

piteous adjective *a piteous cry:* **sad**, pitiful, pitiable, pathetic, heart-rending, heartbreaking, moving, touching; plaintive, poignant, forlorn; poor, wretched, miserable.

pitfall noun *the pitfalls of setting up an office at home:* **hazard**, danger, risk, peril, difficulty, catch, snag, stumbling block, drawback.

pith noun **1** *the pith of the argument:* **essence**, main point, fundamentals, heart, substance, nub, core, quintessence, crux, gist, meat,

kernel, marrow, burden; informal nitty-gritty. **2** *he writes with pith and exactitude:* **succinctness**, conciseness, concision, pithiness, brevity; cogency, weight, depth, force.

pithy adjective *pithy comments:* **succinct**, terse, concise, compact, short (and sweet), brief, condensed, to the point, epigrammatic, crisp, thumbnail; significant, meaningful, expressive, telling.
– OPPOSITES verbose.

pitiful adjective **1** *a child in a pitiful state:* **distressing**, sad, piteous, pitiable, pathetic, heart-rending, heartbreaking, moving, touching, tear-jerking; plaintive, poignant, forlorn; poor, sorry, wretched, abject, miserable. **2** *a pitiful £50 a month:* **paltry**, miserable, meagre, insufficient, trifling, negligible, pitiable, derisory; informal pathetic, measly, piddling, mingy; Brit. informal poxy. **3** *his performance was pitiful:* **dreadful**, awful, terrible, lamentable, hopeless, poor, bad, feeble, pitiable, woeful, inadequate, below par, deplorable, laughable; informal pathetic, useless, appalling, lousy, abysmal, dire.

pitiless adjective *a pitiless executioner:* **merciless**, unmerciful, unpitying, ruthless, cruel, heartless, remorseless, hard-hearted, cold-hearted, harsh, callous, severe, unsparing, unforgiving, unfeeling, uncaring, unsympathetic, uncharitable, brutal, inhuman, inhumane, barbaric, sadistic.
– OPPOSITES merciful.

pittance noun *the musicians were paid a pittance:* **a tiny amount**, next to nothing, very little; informal peanuts, chicken feed, slave wages; N. Amer. informal chump change.

pitted adjective **1** *his skin was pitted:* **pockmarked**, pocked, scarred, marked, blemished. **2** *the pitted lane:* **potholed**, rutted, rutty, holey, bumpy, rough, uneven.
– OPPOSITES smooth.

pity noun **1** *a voice full of pity:* **compassion**, commiseration, condolence, sympathy, fellow feeling, understanding; sorrow, regret, sadness. **2** *it's a pity he never had children:* **shame**, sad thing, bad luck, misfortune; informal crime, bummer, sin.
– OPPOSITES indifference, cruelty.
verb *they pitied me:* **feel sorry for**, feel for, sympathize with, empathize with, commiserate with, take pity on, be moved by, condole with, grieve for.
■ **take pity on** feel sorry for, relent, be compassionate towards, be sympathetic towards, have mercy on, help (out), put someone out of their misery.

pivot noun **1** *the machine turns on a pivot:* **fulcrum**, axis, axle, swivel; pin, shaft, hub, spindle, hinge, kingpin, gudgeon. **2** *the pivot of government policy:* **centre**, focus, hub, heart, nucleus, crux, keystone, cornerstone, linchpin, kingpin.
verb **1** *the panel pivots inwards:* **rotate**, turn, swivel, revolve, spin. **2** *it all pivoted on his*

response: **depend**, hinge, turn, centre, hang, rely, rest; revolve around.

pivotal adjective *Japan's pivotal role in the world economy:* **central**, crucial, vital, critical, focal, essential, key, decisive.

pixie noun **elf**, fairy, sprite, imp, brownie, puck, leprechaun.

placard noun *placards with slogans that read 'Stop the War':* **notice**, poster, sign, bill, advertisement; banner; informal ad; Brit. informal advert.

placate verb *John did his best to placate her:* **pacify**, calm, appease, mollify, soothe, win over, conciliate, propitiate, make peace with, humour; Austral./NZ square someone off.
– OPPOSITES provoke.

place noun **1** *an ideal place for dinner:* **location**, site, spot, setting, position, situation, area, region, locale; venue. **2** *foreign places:* **country**, state, area, region, town, city; locality, district. **3** *at last she had a place of her own:* **home**, house, flat, apartment; accommodation, property, pied-à-terre; rooms, quarters; informal pad, digs; Brit. informal gaff. **4** *if I were in your place, I'd agree:* **situation**, position, circumstances; informal shoes. **5** *a place was reserved for her:* **seat**, chair, space. **6** *I offered him a place in the company:* **job**, position, post, appointment, situation, office; employment. **7** *I know my place:* **status**, position, standing, rank, niche. **8** *it was not her place to sort it out:* **responsibility**, duty, job, task, role, function, concern, affair, charge; right, privilege, prerogative.
verb **1** *books were placed on the table:* **put (down)**, set (down), lay, deposit, position, plant, rest, stand, station, situate, leave; informal stick, dump, bung, park, plonk, pop; N. Amer. informal plunk. **2** *the trust you placed in me:* **put**, lay, set, invest. **3** *a survey placed the company sixth:* **rank**, order, grade, class, classify, categorize; put, set, assign. **4** *Joe couldn't quite place her:* **identify**, recognize, remember, put a name to, pin down; locate, pinpoint. **5** *we were placed with foster parents:* **accommodate**, house; allocate, assign, appoint.
■ **in place 1** *the veil was held in place by pearls:* in position, in situ. **2** *the plans are in place:* ready, set up, all set, established, arranged, in order.
■ **in place of** instead of, rather than, as a substitute for, as a replacement for, in exchange for, in lieu of; in someone's stead.
■ **out of place 1** *she never had a hair out of place:* out of position, out of order, in disarray, disarranged, in a mess, messy, topsy-turvy, muddled. **2** *he said something out of place:* inappropriate, unsuitable, unseemly, improper, untoward, out of keeping, unbecoming, wrong. **3** *she seemed out of place in a launderette:* incongruous, out of one's element, like a fish out of water; uncomfortable, uneasy.
■ **put someone in their place** humiliate,

take down a peg or two, deflate, crush, squash, humble; informal cut down to size, settle someone's hash; N. Amer. informal make someone eat crow.
■ **take place** happen, occur, come about, transpire, crop up, materialize, arise; N. Amer. informal go down.
■ **take the place of** replace, stand in for, substitute for, act for, fill in for, cover for, relieve.

placement noun **1** *the placement of the chairs:* **positioning**, placing, arrangement, position, deployment, location, disposition. **2** *teaching placements:* **job**, post, assignment, posting, position, appointment, engagement.

placid adjective **1** *she's normally very placid:* **even-tempered**, calm, tranquil, equable, equanimous, unexcitable, serene, mild, {cool, calm, and collected}, composed, self-possessed, poised, easy-going, level-headed, steady, unruffled, unperturbed, phlegmatic; informal unflappable. **2** *a placid village:* **quiet**, calm, tranquil, still, peaceful, undisturbed, restful, sleepy.
– OPPOSITES excitable, bustling.

plagiarism noun *there were accusations of plagiarism:* **copying**, infringement of copyright, piracy, theft, stealing; informal cribbing.

plagiarize verb **copy**, infringe the copyright of, pirate, steal, poach, appropriate; informal rip off, crib, borrow; Brit. informal pinch, nick.

plague noun **1** *they died of the plague:* **bubonic plague**, pneumonic plague, the Black Death; disease, sickness, epidemic. **2** *a plague of cat fleas:* **infestation**, epidemic, invasion, swarm, multitude, host. **3** *theft is the plague of restaurants:* **bane**, curse, scourge, affliction, blight.
verb **1** *he was plagued by poor health:* **afflict**, bedevil, torment, trouble, beset, dog, curse. **2** *he plagued her with questions:* **pester**, harass, badger, bother, torment, persecute, bedevil, harry, hound, trouble, irritate, nag, annoy, vex, molest; informal hassle, bug, aggravate; N. English informal mither; N. Amer. informal devil.

plain adjective **1** *it was plain that something was wrong:* **obvious**, (crystal) clear, evident, apparent, manifest, patent; discernible, perceptible, noticeable, recognizable, unmistakable, transparent; pronounced, marked, striking, conspicuous, self-evident, indisputable; as plain as a pikestaff, writ large; informal standing/sticking out like a sore thumb, standing/sticking out a mile. **2** *plain English:* **intelligible**, comprehensible, understandable, clear, coherent, uncomplicated, lucid, unambiguous, simple, straightforward, user-friendly. **3** *plain speaking:* **candid**, frank, outspoken, forthright, direct, honest, truthful, blunt, bald, explicit, unequivocal; informal upfront. **4** *a plain dress:* **simple**, ordinary, unadorned, unembellished,

p

unornamented, unostentatious, unfussy, homely, basic, modest, unsophisticated, without frills; restrained, muted; everyday, workaday. **5** *a plain girl:* **unattractive**, unprepossessing, ugly, ill-favoured, unlovely, ordinary; N. Amer. homely; informal not much to look at; Brit. informal no oil painting. **6** *it was plain bad luck:* **sheer**, pure, downright, out-and-out, unmitigated.
– OPPOSITES obscure, fancy, attractive, pretentious.
adverb *this is just plain stupid:* **downright**, utterly, absolutely, completely, totally, really, thoroughly, positively, simply, unquestionably, undeniably; informal plumb.
noun *the plains of North America:* **grassland**, flatland, lowland, pasture, meadowland, prairie, savannah, steppe; tableland, tundra, pampas, veld.

plain-spoken adjective *he was well known for being plain-spoken:* **candid**, frank, outspoken, forthright, direct, honest, truthful, open, blunt, straightforward, explicit, unequivocal, unambiguous, not afraid to call a spade a spade; informal upfront.
– OPPOSITES evasive.

plaintive adjective *a plaintive cry:* **mournful**, sad, wistful, doleful, pathetic, pitiful, piteous, melancholy, sorrowful, unhappy, wretched, woeful, forlorn, woebegone.

plan noun **1** *a plan for raising money:* **scheme**, idea, proposal, proposition, suggestion; project, programme, system, method, procedure, strategy, stratagem, formula, recipe; way, means, measure, tactic. **2** *her plan was to win a medal:* **intention**, aim, idea, intent, objective, object, goal, target, ambition. **3** *the plans for the clubhouse:* **blueprint**, drawing, diagram, sketch, layout; illustration, representation; N. Amer. plat.
verb **1** *plan your route in advance:* **organize**, arrange, work out, design, outline, map out, prepare, schedule, formulate, frame, develop, devise, concoct; plot, scheme, hatch, brew; N. Amer. slate. **2** *he plans to buy a house:* **intend**, aim, propose, mean, hope, want, wish, desire, envisage. **3** *I'm planning a new garden:* **design**, draw up, sketch out, map out; N. Amer. plat.

plane[1] noun **1** *a horizontal plane:* **flat surface**, level surface; the flat, horizontal. **2** *a higher plane of achievement:* **level**, degree, standard, stratum; position, rung, echelon.
adjective *a plane surface:* **flat**, level, horizontal, even; smooth, regular, uniform.
verb **1** *seagulls planed overhead:* **soar**, glide, float, drift, wheel. **2** *boats planed across the water:* **skim**, glide.

plane[2] noun *the plane took off:* **aircraft**, airliner, (jumbo) jet, jetliner; flying machine; Brit. aeroplane; N. Amer. airplane, ship.

planet noun **celestial body**, heavenly body, satellite, moon, earth, asteroid, planetoid.

plank noun **board**, floorboard, timber, stave.

planning noun *the planning should be every bit as enjoyable as the event itself:* **preparation(s)**, organization, arrangement, design; forethought, groundwork.

plant noun **1** *garden plants:* flower, vegetable, herb, shrub, weed; **(plants)** vegetation, greenery, flora, herbage, verdure. **2** *a CIA plant:* **spy**, informant, informer, (secret) agent, mole, infiltrator, operative; N. Amer. informal spook. **3** *the plant commenced production:* **factory**, works, foundry, mill, workshop, yard.
verb **1** *plant the seeds this autumn:* **sow**, scatter, seed; bed out, transplant. **2** *he planted his feet on the ground:* **place**, put, set, position, situate, settle; informal plonk. **3** *she planted the idea in his mind:* **instil**, implant, impress, imprint, put, place, introduce, fix, establish, lodge. **4** *letters were planted to embarrass them:* **hide**, conceal, secrete.

plaque noun *a commemorative plaque:* **plate**, tablet, panel, sign, plaquette, cartouche; Brit. brass.

plaster noun **1** *the plaster covering the bricks:* **plasterwork**, stucco, pargeting; trademark Artex. **2** *a statuette made of plaster:* **plaster of Paris**, gypsum. **3** *waterproof plasters:* **sticking plaster**, (adhesive) dressing, bandage; trademark Elastoplast, Band-Aid.
verb **1** *bread plastered with butter:* **cover thickly**, smother, spread, smear, cake, coat. **2** *his hair was plastered down with sweat:* **flatten (down)**, smooth down, slick down.

plastic adjective **1** *at high temperatures the rocks become plastic:* **malleable**, mouldable, pliable, pliant, ductile, flexible, soft, workable, bendable; informal bendy. **2** *the plastic minds of children:* **impressionable**, malleable, receptive, pliable, pliant, flexible; compliant, tractable, biddable, persuadable, susceptible, manipulable. **3** *a plastic smile:* **artificial**, false, faux, fake, superficial, pseudo, bogus, unnatural, insincere; informal phoney, pretend.
– OPPOSITES rigid, intractable, genuine.

plate noun **1** *a dinner plate:* **dish**, platter, salver, paten; historical trencher. **2** *a plate of spaghetti:* **plateful**, helping, portion, serving. **3** *steel plates:* **panel**, sheet, layer, pane, slab. **4** *a brass plate on the door:* **plaque**, sign, tablet, plaquette, cartouche; Brit. brass. **5** *the book has colour plates:* **picture**, print, illustration, photograph, photo.
verb *the roof was plated with steel:* **cover**, coat, overlay, laminate, veneer; electroplate, galvanize, gild.

plateau noun **1** *a windswept plateau:* **upland**, tableland, plain, mesa, highland. **2** *prices reached a plateau:* quiescent period; let-up, respite, lull.

platform noun **1** *he made a speech from the platform:* **stage**, dais, rostrum, podium, soapbox. **2** *the Democratic Party's platform:* **policy**, programme, party line, manifesto, plan, principles, objectives, aims.

platitude noun *a string of empty platitudes:* **cliché**, truism, commonplace, banality, old chestnut, bromide.

platitudinous adjective **hackneyed**, overworked, overused, clichéd, banal, trite, commonplace, well worn, stale, tired, unoriginal; informal corny, old hat.
– OPPOSITES original.

platonic adjective *our relationship is purely platonic:* **non-sexual**, non-physical, chaste; intellectual, friendly.
– OPPOSITES sexual.

platoon noun *a platoon of British Royal Marines:* **unit**, patrol, troop, squad, squadron, team, company, corps, outfit, detachment, contingent.

platter noun *the meat was arranged on silver platters:* **plate**, dish, salver, paten, tray.

plaudits plural noun *the network has received plaudits for its sports coverage:* **praise**, acclaim, commendation, congratulations, accolades, compliments, cheers, applause, tributes, bouquets; a pat on the back; informal a (big) hand.
– OPPOSITES criticism.

plausible adjective *a plausible explanation:* **credible**, reasonable, believable, likely, feasible, tenable, possible, conceivable, imaginable; convincing, persuasive, cogent, sound, rational, logical, thinkable.
– OPPOSITES unlikely.

play verb **1** *the children played with toys:* **amuse oneself**, entertain oneself, enjoy oneself, have fun; relax, occupy oneself, divert oneself; frolic, frisk, romp, caper; informal mess about/around, lark (about/around). **2** *I used to play football:* **take part in**, participate in, be involved in, compete in, do. **3** *Liverpool play Oxford on Sunday:* **compete against**, take on, challenge, vie with. **4** *he was to play Macbeth:* **act (the part of)**, take the role of, appear as, portray, depict, impersonate, represent, render, perform. **5** *he learned to play the flute:* **perform on**, make music on; blow, sound. **6** *the sunlight played on the water:* **dance**, flit, ripple, touch; sparkle, glint.
noun **1** *a balance between work and play:* **amusement**, entertainment, relaxation, recreation, diversion, distraction, leisure; enjoyment, pleasure, fun, games, fun and games; horseplay, merrymaking, revelry; informal living it up. **2** *a Shakespeare play:* **drama**, theatrical work; teleplay, screenplay, comedy, tragedy; production, performance, show, sketch. **3** *there was a little play in the rope:* **movement**, slack, give; room to manoeuvre, scope, latitude.
■ **play at** *like a dictator he will play at being kind and good:* **pretend to be**, pass oneself off as, masquerade as, profess to be, pose as, impersonate; fake, feign, simulate, affect; N. Amer. informal make like.
■ **play something down** *ministers sought to play down the extent of the damage:*
make light of, make little of, gloss over, de-emphasize, downplay, understate; soft-pedal, tone down, diminish, trivialize, underrate, underestimate, undervalue; disparage, belittle, scoff at, sneer at, shrug off; informal pooh-pooh.
■ **play for time** stall, temporize, delay, hold back, hang fire, procrastinate, drag one's feet.
■ **play it by ear** improvise, extemporize, ad lib; informal busk it, wing it.
■ **play on** *they play on our fears:* exploit, take advantage of, use, turn to (one's) account, profit by, capitalize on, trade on, milk, abuse.
■ **play the fool** clown about/around, fool about/around, mess about/around, lark about/around, monkey about/around, joke; informal horse about/around, act the goat; Brit. informal muck about/around.
■ **play the game** play fair, be fair, play by the rules, conform, be a good sport, toe the line.
■ **play up** (Brit. informal) **1** *the boys really did play up:* misbehave, be bad, be naughty, get up to mischief, be disobedient, cause trouble. **2** *the boiler's playing up:* malfunction, not work, be defective, be faulty; informal go on the blink, act up. **3** *his leg was playing up:* be painful, hurt, ache, be sore, cause discomfort; informal kill someone, give someone gyp.
■ **play something up** *the press has played up the problems:* emphasize, accentuate, call attention to, point up, underline, highlight, spotlight, foreground, feature, stress, accent.
■ **play up to** *he's been playing up to her the whole time:* ingratiate oneself with, curry favour with, court, fawn over, make up to, keep someone sweet, toady to, crawl to, pander to, flatter; informal soft-soap, suck up to, butter up, lick someone's boots.

playboy noun *Nigel isn't the marrying type—he's just a playboy:* **socialite**, pleasure-seeker, sybarite; ladies' man, womanizer, philanderer, rake, roué; informal ladykiller.

player noun **1** *a tournament for young players:* **participant**, contestant, competitor, contender; sportsman/woman, athlete. **2** *the players in the orchestra:* **musician**, performer, instrumentalist, soloist, virtuoso. **3** *the players of the Royal Shakespeare Company:* **actor**, actress, performer, thespian, entertainer, artist(e), trouper.

playful adjective **1** *a playful mood:* **frisky**, jolly, lively, full of fun, frolicsome, sportive, high-spirited, exuberant, perky; mischievous, impish, rascally, tricksy; informal full of beans. **2** *a playful remark:* **light-hearted**, in jest, joking, jokey, teasing, humorous, jocular, good-natured, tongue-in-cheek, facetious, frivolous, flippant, arch; informal waggish.
– OPPOSITES serious.

p

playground noun **play area**, park, playing field, recreation ground; Brit. informal rec.

playmate noun **friend**, playfellow, companion; informal chum, pal; Brit. informal mate; N. Amer. informal buddy.

plaything noun **toy**, game.

playwright noun **dramatist**, dramaturge, scriptwriter, screenwriter, writer, scenarist; tragedian.

plea noun **1** *a plea for aid:* **appeal**, entreaty, supplication, petition, request, call, suit, solicitation. **2** *her plea of a headache was unconvincing:* **claim**, explanation, defence, justification; excuse, pretext.

plead verb **1** *he pleaded with her to stay:* **beg**, implore, entreat, appeal to, supplicate, petition, request, ask, call on. **2** *she pleaded ignorance:* **claim**, use as an excuse, assert, allege, argue, state.

pleasant adjective **1** *a pleasant evening:* **enjoyable**, pleasurable, nice, agreeable, pleasing, satisfying, gratifying, good; entertaining, amusing, delightful, charming; fine, balmy; informal lovely, great. **2** *the staff are pleasant:* **friendly**, agreeable, amiable, nice, genial, cordial, likeable, amicable, good-humoured, good-natured, personable; hospitable, approachable, gracious, courteous, polite, obliging, helpful, considerate; charming, lovely, delightful, sweet, sympathetic; N. English & Scottish canny; Scottish couthy.
– OPPOSITES disagreeable.

pleasantry noun **1** *we exchanged pleasantries:* **banter**, badinage; polite remark, casual remark; N. Amer. informal josh. **2** *he laughed at his own pleasantry:* **joke**, witticism, quip, jest, gag, bon mot; informal wisecrack, crack.

please verb **1** *he'd do anything to please her:* **make happy**, give pleasure to, make someone feel good; delight, charm, amuse, entertain; satisfy, gratify, humour, oblige, content, suit; informal tickle someone pink. **2** *do as you please:* **like**, want, wish, desire, see fit, think fit, choose, will, prefer.
– OPPOSITES annoy.
adverb *please sit down:* **if you please**, if you wouldn't mind, if you would be so good; kindly, pray.

pleased adjective *Edward seemed really pleased to see me:* **happy**, glad, delighted, gratified, grateful, thankful, content, contented, satisfied; thrilled, elated, overjoyed, cock-a-hoop; informal over the moon, tickled pink, on cloud nine; Brit. informal chuffed; N. English informal made up; Austral. informal wrapped; humorous gruntled.
– OPPOSITES unhappy.

pleasing adjective **1** *a pleasing day:* **nice**, agreeable, pleasant, pleasurable, satisfying, gratifying, good, enjoyable, entertaining, amusing, delightful; informal lovely, great. **2** *her pleasing manner:* **friendly**, amiable, pleasant, agreeable, affable, nice, genial,

likeable, good-humoured, charming, engaging, delightful; informal lovely.

pleasurable adjective *a pleasurable experience:* **pleasant**, enjoyable, delightful, nice, pleasing, agreeable, gratifying; fun, entertaining, amusing, diverting; informal lovely, great.

pleasure noun **1** *she smiled with pleasure:* **happiness**, delight, joy, gladness, glee, satisfaction, gratification, contentment, enjoyment, amusement. **2** *his greatest pleasures in life:* **joy**, amusement, diversion, recreation, pastime; treat, thrill. **3** *don't mix business and pleasure:* **enjoyment**, fun, entertainment; recreation, leisure, relaxation; informal jollies. **4** *a life of pleasure:* **hedonism**, indulgence, self-indulgence, self-gratification, lotus-eating. **5** *what's your pleasure?* **wish**, desire, preference, will, inclination, choice.
■ **take pleasure in** enjoy, delight in, love, like, adore, appreciate, relish, savour, revel in, glory in; informal get a kick out of, get a thrill out of.
■ **with pleasure** gladly, willingly, happily, readily; by all means, of course.

pleat noun & verb *a curtain pleat* | *the dress is pleated at the front:* **fold**, crease, gather, tuck, crimp; pucker.

plebeian noun *plebeians and gentry lived together:* **proletarian**, commoner, working-class person, worker; peasant; informal pleb, prole.
– OPPOSITES aristocrat.
adjective **1** *people of plebeian descent:* **lower-class**, working-class, proletarian, common, peasant; mean, humble, lowly. **2** *plebeian tastes:* **uncultured**, uncultivated, unrefined, lowbrow, philistine, uneducated; coarse, uncouth, common, vulgar; informal plebby; Brit. informal non-U.
– OPPOSITES noble, refined.

plebiscite noun *a plebiscite for the approval of constitutional reforms:* **vote**, referendum, ballot, poll.

pledge noun **1** *his election pledge:* **promise**, undertaking, vow, word (of honour), commitment, assurance, oath, guarantee. **2** *he gave it as a pledge to a creditor:* **surety**, bond, security, collateral, guarantee, deposit. **3** *a pledge of my sincerity:* **token**, symbol, sign, earnest, mark, testimony, proof, evidence.
verb **1** *he pledged to root out corruption:* **promise**, vow, swear, undertake, engage, commit oneself, declare, affirm, avow. **2** *they pledged £100 million:* **promise (to give)**, donate, contribute, give, put up; Brit. covenant. **3** *his home is pledged as security against the loan:* **mortgage**, put up as collateral, guarantee, pawn.

plenary adjective **1** *the council has plenary powers:* **unconditional**, unlimited, unrestricted, unqualified, absolute, sweeping, comprehensive; plenipotentiary.

p

2 *a plenary session of the parliament:* **full**, complete, entire.

plenipotentiary noun *a plenipotentiary in Paris:* **diplomat**, dignitary, ambassador, minister, emissary, chargé d'affaires, envoy. adjective *plenipotentiary powers.* See **PLENARY** sense 1.

plentiful adjective *a plentiful supply of food:* **abundant**, copious, ample, profuse, rich, lavish, generous, bountiful, large, great, bumper, superabundant, inexhaustible, prolific; informal a gogo, galore.
– OPPOSITES scarce.

plenty noun *times of plenty:* **prosperity**, affluence, wealth, opulence, comfort, luxury; plentifulness, abundance.
pronoun *there are plenty of places:* **a lot of**, many, a great deal of, a plethora of, enough (and to spare), no lack of, sufficient, a wealth of; informal loads of, lots of, heaps of, stacks of, bucketloads of, masses of, tons of, oodles of, scads of, a slew of.

plethora noun *a plethora of newspaper opinion polls:* **excess**, abundance, superabundance, surplus, glut, superfluity, surfeit, profusion, too many, too much, enough and to spare; informal more … than one can shake a stick at.
– OPPOSITES dearth.

pliable adjective **1** *leather is pliable:* **flexible**, pliant, bendable, elastic, supple, malleable, workable, plastic, springy, ductile; informal bendy. **2** *pliable teenage minds:* **malleable**, impressionable, flexible, adaptable, pliant, compliant, biddable, tractable, yielding, amenable, susceptible, suggestible, persuadable, manipulable, receptive.
– OPPOSITES rigid, obdurate.

pliant adjective. See **PLIABLE**.

plight noun *an attempt to highlight the plight of the homeless:* **predicament**, difficult situation, dire straits, trouble, difficulty, extremity, bind; informal dilemma, tight corner, tight spot, hole, pickle, jam, fix.

plod verb **1** *Mum plodded wearily upstairs:* **trudge**, walk heavily, clump, stomp, tramp, lumber, slog; Brit. informal trog. **2** *I have to plod through the whole book:* **wade**, plough, trawl, toil, labour; informal slog.

plot noun **1** *a plot to overthrow him:* **conspiracy**, intrigue, secret plan; machinations. **2** *the plot of her novel:* **storyline**, story, scenario, action, thread. **3** *a three-acre plot:* **piece of ground**, patch, area, tract, acreage; Brit. allotment; N. Amer. lot, plat; N. Amer. & Austral./NZ homesite.
verb **1** *he plotted their downfall:* **plan**, scheme, arrange, organize, hatch, concoct, devise, dream up; informal cook up. **2** *his brother was plotting against him:* **conspire**, scheme, intrigue, collude, connive, machinate. **3** *the fifty-three sites were plotted:* **mark**, chart, map, represent, graph.

plotter noun **conspirator**, schemer, intriguer, machinator; planner.

plough verb **1** *the fields were ploughed:* **till**, furrow, harrow, cultivate, work, break up. **2** *the car ploughed into a lamp post:* **crash**, smash, career, plunge, bulldoze, hurtle, cannon, run, drive; N. Amer. informal barrel. **3** *they ploughed through deep snow:* **trudge**, plod, toil, wade; informal slog; Brit. informal trog.

ploy noun *perhaps this had been a ploy to revive her husband's fading interest:* **ruse**, tactic, move, device, stratagem, scheme, trick, gambit, plan, manoeuvre, dodge, subterfuge, wile; Brit. informal wheeze.

pluck verb **1** *he plucked a thread from his lapel:* **remove**, pick (off), pull (off/out), extract, take (off). **2** *she plucked at his T-shirt:* **pull (at)**, tug (at), clutch (at), snatch (at), grab, catch (at), tweak, jerk; informal yank. **3** *the turkeys are plucked:* **deplume**, remove the feathers from. **4** *she plucked the guitar strings:* **strum**, pick, thrum, twang; play pizzicato.
noun *the task took a lot of pluck:* **courage**, bravery, nerve, backbone, spine, daring, spirit, intrepidity, fearlessness, mettle, grit, determination, fortitude, resolve, stout-heartedness, dauntlessness, valour, heroism, audacity; informal guts, spunk, gumption; Brit. informal bottle; N. Amer. informal moxie.

plucky adjective *plucky bank staff defeated armed raiders:* **brave**, courageous, bold, daring, fearless, intrepid, spirited, game, valiant, valorous, stout-hearted, dauntless, resolute, determined, undaunted, unflinching, audacious, unafraid, doughty, mettlesome; informal gutsy, spunky.
– OPPOSITES timid.

plug noun **1** *she pulled out the plug:* **stopper**, bung, cork, seal, spigot, spile; N. Amer. stopple. **2** *a plug of tobacco:* **wad**, quid, twist, chew. **3** (informal) *a plug for his new book:* **advertisement**, promotion, commercial, recommendation, mention, good word; informal hype, push, puff, ad, boost, ballyhoo; Brit. informal advert.
verb **1** *plug the holes:* **stop (up)**, seal (up/off), close (up/off), cork, stopper, bung, block (up/off), fill (up); N. Amer. stopple. **2** (informal) *she plugged her new film:* **publicize**, promote, advertise, mention, bang the drum for, draw attention to; informal hype (up), push, puff.
■ **plug away** (informal) *he plugged away at his writing:* toil, labour, slave away, soldier on, persevere, persist, keep on, plough on; informal slog away, beaver away, peg away.

plum adjective (informal) *a plum job:* **excellent**, very good, wonderful, marvellous, choice, first-class; informal great, terrific, cushy.

plumb[1] verb *an attempt to plumb her psyche:* **explore**, probe, delve into, search, examine, investigate, fathom, penetrate, understand. adjective *a plumb drop:* **vertical**, perpendicular, straight.
■ **plumb the depths** find, experience the extremes, reach the lowest point; reach rock bottom.

p

plumb[2] verb *he plumbed in the washing machine:* **install**, put in, fit.

plume noun *ostrich plumes:* **feather**, quill.
■ **plume oneself** *he plumed himself on his latest innovation:* congratulate oneself, preen oneself, pat oneself on the back, pride oneself, boast about.

plummet verb **1** *the plane plummeted to the ground:* **plunge**, nosedive, dive, drop, fall, descend, hurtle. **2** *share prices plummeted:* **fall steeply**, plunge, tumble, drop rapidly, go down, slump; informal crash, nosedive.

plump[1] adjective *a plump child:* **chubby**, fat, stout, rotund, well padded, ample, round, chunky, portly, overweight, fleshy, paunchy, bulky, corpulent; informal tubby, roly-poly, pudgy, beefy, porky, blubbery; Brit. informal podgy, fubsy; N. Amer. informal zaftig, corn-fed.
– OPPOSITES thin.

plump[2] verb **1** *Jack plumped down on to a chair:* **flop**, **collapse**, sink, fall, drop, slump; informal plonk oneself; N. Amer. informal plank oneself. **2** *she plumped her bag on the table:* **put (down)**, set (down), place, deposit, dump, stick; informal plonk; Brit. informal bung; N. Amer. informal plunk. **3** *I plumped for a cream cake:* **choose**, decide on, go for, opt for, pick, settle on, select, take, elect.

plunder verb **1** *they plundered the countryside:* **pillage**, loot, rob, raid, ransack, despoil, strip, ravage, lay waste, devastate, sack, rape. **2** *money plundered from pension funds:* **steal**, purloin, thieve, seize, pillage; embezzle.
noun **1** *the plunder of the villages:* **looting**, pillaging, plundering, raiding, ransacking, devastation, sacking. **2** *the army took huge quantities of plunder:* **booty**, loot, stolen goods, spoils, ill-gotten gains; informal swag.

plunge verb **1** *Joy plunged into the sea:* **dive**, jump, throw oneself, launch oneself. **2** *the aircraft plunged to the ground:* **plummet**, nosedive, drop, fall, pitch, tumble, descend. **3** *the car plunged down an alley:* **charge**, hurtle, career, plough, cannon, tear; N. Amer. informal barrel. **4** *oil prices plunged:* **fall sharply**, plummet, drop, go down, tumble, slump; informal crash, nosedive. **5** *he plunged the dagger into her back:* **thrust**, jab, stab, sink, stick, ram, drive, push, shove, force. **6** *plunge the pears into water:* **immerse**, submerge, dip, dunk. **7** *the room was plunged into darkness:* **throw**, cast, pitch.
noun **1** *a plunge into the deep end:* **dive**, jump, nosedive, fall, pitch, drop, plummet, descent. **2** *a plunge in profits:* **fall**, drop, slump; informal nosedive, crash.
■ **take the plunge** commit oneself, go for it, throw caution to the wind(s), risk it; informal jump in at the deep end, go for broke.

plurality noun *a plurality of theories:* **wide variety**, diversity, range, lot, multitude, multiplicity, galaxy, wealth, profusion, abundance, plethora, host; informal load, stack, heap, mass.

plus preposition **1** *three plus three makes six:* **and**, added to. **2** *he wrote four novels plus various poems:* **as well as**, together with, along with, in addition to, and, not to mention, besides.
– OPPOSITES minus.
noun *one of the pluses of the job:* **advantage**, good point, asset, pro, (fringe) benefit, bonus, extra, attraction; informal perk.
– OPPOSITES disadvantage.

plush adjective *a plush hotel:* (informal) **luxurious**, luxury, de luxe, sumptuous, palatial, lavish, opulent, magnificent, lush, rich, expensive, fancy, grand; Brit. upmarket; informal posh, ritzy, swanky, classy; Brit. informal swish; N. Amer. informal swank.
– OPPOSITES austere.

plutocrat noun *champagne-swilling plutocrats:* **rich person**, magnate, millionaire, billionaire, multimillionaire; nouveau riche; informal fat cat, moneybags.

ply[1] verb **1** *the gondolier plied his oar:* **use**, wield, work, manipulate, handle, operate, utilize, employ. **2** *he plied a profitable trade:* **engage in**, carry on, pursue, conduct, practise. **3** *ferries ply between all lake resorts:* **go regularly**, travel, shuttle, go back and forth. **4** *she plied me with scones:* **provide**, supply, lavish, shower, regale. **5** *he plied her with questions:* **bombard**, assail, beset, pester, plague, harass, importune; informal hassle.

ply[2] noun *a three-ply tissue:* **layer**, thickness, strand, sheet, leaf.

poach verb **1** *he's been poaching salmon:* **hunt illegally**, catch illegally; steal.
2 *workers were poached by other firms:* **steal**, appropriate, purloin, take; informal nab, swipe; Brit. informal nick, pinch.

pocket noun **1** *a bag with two pockets:* **pouch**, compartment. **2** *the jewellery was beyond her pocket:* **means**, budget, resources, finances, funds, money, wherewithal; N. Amer. pocketbook. **3** *pockets of disaffection:* **(isolated) area**, patch, region, island, cluster, centre.
adjective *a pocket dictionary:* **small**, little, miniature, mini, compact, concise, abridged, potted, portable; N. Amer. vest-pocket.
verb *he pocketed $900,000 of their money:* **steal**, take, appropriate, thieve, purloin, misappropriate, embezzle; informal filch, swipe, snaffle; Brit. informal pinch, nick, whip.

pockmark noun *his face was covered with pockmarks:* **scar**, pit, pock, mark, blemish.

pod noun *pea pods:* **shell**, husk, hull, case; N. Amer. shuck.

podium noun **platform**, stage, dais, rostrum, stand, soapbox.

poem noun **verse**, rhyme, piece of poetry, song, verselet.

poet noun versifier, rhymester, rhymer, sonneteer, lyricist, lyrist; laureate; derogatory poetaster.

poetic adjective **1** *poetic compositions:*

poetical, verse, metrical, lyrical, lyric, elegiac. **2** *poetic language:* **expressive**, figurative, symbolic, flowery, artistic, elegant, fine, beautiful; sensitive, imaginative, creative.

poetry noun **poems**, verse, versification, metrical composition, rhymes, balladry.

poignancy noun **pathos**, pitifulness, piteousness, sadness, sorrow, mournfulness, wretchedness, misery, tragedy.

poignant adjective *the father of the murder victim bade a poignant farewell to his son:* **touching**, moving, sad, affecting, pitiful, piteous, pathetic, sorrowful, mournful, wretched, miserable, distressing, heart-rending, tear-jerking, plaintive, tragic.

point¹ noun **1** *the point of a needle:* **tip**, (sharp) end, extremity; prong, spike, tine, nib, barb. **2** *points of light:* **pinpoint**, dot, spot, speck, fleck. **3** *a meeting point:* **place**, position, location, site, spot, area. **4** *this point in her life:* **time**, stage, juncture, period, phase. **5** *the tension had reached such a high point:* **level**, degree, stage, pitch, extent. **6** *an important point:* **detail**, item, fact, thing, argument, consideration, factor, element; subject, issue, topic, question, matter. **7** *get to the point:* **heart of the matter**, most important part, essence, nub, keynote, core, pith, crux; meaning, significance, gist, substance, thrust, burden, relevance; informal brass tacks, nitty-gritty. **8** *what's the point of this?* **purpose**, aim, object, objective, goal, intention; use, sense, value, advantage. **9** *he had his good points:* **attribute**, characteristic, feature, trait, quality, property, aspect, side.
verb **1** *she pointed the gun at him:* **aim**, direct, level, train. **2** *the evidence pointed to his guilt:* **indicate**, suggest, evidence, signal, signify, denote, bespeak, reveal, manifest.
■ **beside the point** irrelevant, immaterial, unimportant, neither here nor there, inconsequential, incidental, out of place, unconnected, peripheral, tangential, extraneous.
■ **in point of fact** in fact, as a matter of fact, actually, in actual fact, really, in reality, as it happens, in truth.
■ **make a point of** make an effort to, go out of one's way to, put emphasis on.
■ **on the point of** (just) about to, on the verge of, on the brink of, going to, all set to.
■ **point of view** opinion, view, belief, attitude, feeling, sentiment, thoughts; position, perspective, viewpoint, standpoint, outlook.
■ **point something out** identify, show, designate, draw attention to, indicate, specify, detail, mention.
■ **point something up** emphasize, highlight, draw attention to, accentuate, underline, spotlight, foreground, put emphasis on, stress, play up, accent, bring to the fore.
■ **to the point** relevant, pertinent, apposite, germane, applicable, apropos, appropriate, apt, fitting, suitable, material.
■ **up to a point** partly, to some extent, to a certain degree, in part, somewhat, partially.

point² noun *the ship rounded the point:* **promontory**, headland, foreland, cape, peninsula, bluff, ness, horn.

point-blank adverb **1** *he fired the pistol point-blank:* **at close range**, close up, close to. **2** *she couldn't say it point-blank:* **bluntly**, directly, straight, frankly, candidly, openly, explicitly, unequivocally, unambiguously, plainly, flatly, categorically, outright.
adjective *a point-blank refusal:* **blunt**, direct, straight, straightforward, frank, candid, forthright, explicit, unequivocal, plain, clear, flat, decisive, unqualified, categorical, outright.

pointed adjective **1** *a pointed stick:* **sharp**, tapering, tapered, conical, jagged, spiky, spiked, barbed; informal pointy. **2** *a pointed remark:* **cutting**, trenchant, biting, incisive, acerbic, caustic, scathing, venomous, sarcastic; informal sarky; N. Amer. informal snarky.

pointer noun **1** *the pointer moved to 100rpm:* **indicator**, needle, arrow, hand. **2** *he used a pointer on the chart:* **stick**, rod, cane; cursor. **3** *a pointer to the outcome of the election:* **indication**, indicator, clue, hint, sign, signal, evidence, intimation, inkling, suggestion. **4** *I can give you a few pointers:* **tip**, hint, suggestion, guideline, recommendation.

pointless adjective *speculating like this is a pointless exercise:* **senseless**, futile, hopeless, fruitless, useless, needless, in vain, unavailing, aimless, idle, worthless, valueless; absurd, insane, stupid, silly, foolish.
– OPPOSITES valuable.

poise noun **1** *poise and good deportment:* **grace**, gracefulness, elegance, balance, control. **2** *in spite of the setback she retained her poise:* **composure**, equanimity, self-possession, aplomb, presence of mind, self-assurance, self-control, nerve, calm, sangfroid, dignity; informal cool, unflappability.
verb **1** *she was poised on one foot:* **balance**, hold (oneself) steady, be suspended, remain motionless, hang, hover. **2** *he was poised for action:* **prepare oneself**, ready oneself, brace oneself, gear oneself up, stand by.

poison noun **1** *a deadly poison:* **toxin**, toxicant, venom. **2** *Marianne would spread her poison:* **malice**, ill will, hate, malevolence, bitterness, spite, spitefulness, venom, acrimony, rancour; bad influence, cancer, corruption, pollution.
verb **1** *her mother poisoned her:* **give poison to**; murder. **2** *a blackmailer poisoning baby foods:* **contaminate**, put poison in, adulterate, spike, lace, doctor. **3** *the Amazon is being poisoned:* **pollute**, contaminate, taint, blight, spoil. **4** *they poisoned his mind:* **prejudice**, bias, jaundice, embitter, sour, envenom, warp, corrupt, subvert.

p

poisonous adjective **1** *a poisonous snake:* **venomous**, deadly. **2** *a poisonous chemical:* **toxic**, noxious, deadly, fatal, lethal, mortal, death-dealing. **3** *a poisonous glance:* **malicious**, malevolent, hostile, vicious, spiteful, bitter, venomous, vindictive, vitriolic, rancorous, malign, pernicious, mean, nasty; informal bitchy, catty.
– OPPOSITES harmless, non-toxic, benevolent.

poke verb **1** *she poked him in the ribs:* **prod**, jab, dig, nudge, butt, shove, jolt, stab, stick. **2** *leave the cable poking out:* **stick out**, jut out, protrude, project, extend.
noun **1** *Carrie gave him a poke:* **prod**, jab, dig, elbow, nudge. **2** *a poke in the arm:* **jab**, dig, nudge, shove, stab.
■ **poke about/around** *you've got no right to go poking about in that cupboard:* search, hunt, rummage (around), forage, grub, root about/around, scavenge, nose around, ferret (about/around); sift through, rifle through, scour, comb, probe; Brit. informal rootle (around).
■ **poke fun at** mock, make fun of, ridicule, laugh at, jeer at, sneer at, deride, scorn, scoff at, pillory, lampoon, tease, taunt, rag, chaff, jibe at; informal send up, take the mickey out of, kid, rib; Brit. informal wind up; N. Amer. informal goof on, rag on; Austral./NZ informal poke mullock at.
■ **poke one's nose into** pry into, interfere in, intrude on, butt into, meddle with; informal snoop into.

poky adjective *a poky room:* **small**, little, tiny, cramped, confined, restricted, boxy; euphemistic compact, bijou.
– OPPOSITES spacious.

polar adjective **1** *polar weather:* **Arctic**, cold, freezing, icy, glacial, chilly, gelid. **2** *two polar types of interview:* **opposite**, opposed, dichotomous, extreme, contrary, contradictory, antithetical.

polarity noun *the polarity between social and biological explanations:* **difference**, dichotomy, separation, opposition, contradiction, antithesis, antagonism.

pole[1] noun *the notice was pinned on a wooden pole:* **post**, pillar, stanchion, paling, stake, stick, support, prop, batten, bar, rail, rod, beam; staff, stave, cane, baton.

pole[2] noun *points of view at opposite poles:* **extremity**, extreme, limit, antipode.
■ **poles apart** completely different, directly opposed, antithetical, incompatible, irreconcilable, worlds apart, at opposite extremes; Brit. like chalk and cheese.

polemic noun **1** *a polemic against injustice:* **diatribe**, invective, rant, tirade, broadside, attack, harangue, condemnation, criticism, stricture, admonition, rebuke; abuse; informal blast. **2** *he is skilled in polemics:* **argumentation**, argument, debate, contention, disputation, discussion, altercation.

polemical adjective *Brunner published a*

polemical tract against Barth: **critical**, hostile, bitter, polemic, virulent, vitriolic, venomous, caustic, trenchant, cutting, acerbic, sardonic, sarcastic, scathing, sharp, incisive, devastating.

police noun the police force, police officers, policemen, policewomen, officers of the law, the forces of law and order; Brit. constabulary; informal the cops, the fuzz, (the long arm of) the law, the boys in blue; Brit. informal the (Old) Bill, coppers, bobbies, busies, the force; N. Amer. informal the heat; informal, derogatory pigs, the filth.
verb **1** *we must police the area:* **guard**, watch over, protect, defend, patrol; control, regulate. **2** *the regulations will be policed by the ministry:* **enforce**, regulate, oversee, supervise, monitor, observe, check.

police officer noun **policeman**, **policewoman**, officer (of the law); Brit. constable; N. Amer. patrolman, trooper, roundsman; informal cop; Brit. informal copper, bobby, rozzer, busy, (PC) plod; N. Amer. informal uniform; informal, derogatory pig.

policy noun *government policy:* **plans**, strategy, stratagem, approach, code, system, guidelines, theory; line, position, stance, attitude.

polish verb **1** *I polished his shoes:* **shine**, wax, buff, rub up/down; gloss, burnish; varnish, oil, glaze, lacquer, japan, shellac. **2** *polish up your essay:* **perfect**, refine, improve, hone, enhance; brush up, revise, edit, correct, rewrite, go over, touch up; informal clean up.
noun **1** *furniture polish:* **wax**, glaze, varnish; lacquer, japan, shellac. **2** *a good surface polish:* **shine**, gloss, lustre, sheen, sparkle, patina, finish. **3** *his polish made him stand out:* **sophistication**, refinement, urbanity, suaveness, elegance, style, grace, finesse, cultivation, civility, gentility, breeding, courtesy, (good) manners; informal class.

polished adjective **1** *a polished table:* **shiny**, glossy, gleaming, lustrous, glassy; waxed, buffed, burnished; varnished, glazed, lacquered, japanned, shellacked. **2** *a polished performance:* **expert**, accomplished, masterly, masterful, skilful, adept, adroit, dexterous; impeccable, flawless, perfect, consummate, exquisite, outstanding, excellent, superb, superlative, first-rate, fine; informal ace. **3** *polished manners:* **refined**, cultivated, civilized, well bred, polite, courteous, genteel, decorous, respectable, urbane, suave, sophisticated.
– OPPOSITES dull, inexpert, gauche.

polite adjective **1** *a very polite girl:* **well mannered**, civil, courteous, mannerly, respectful, deferential, well behaved, well bred, gentlemanly, ladylike, genteel, gracious, urbane; tactful, diplomatic. **2** *polite society:* **civilized**, refined, cultured, sophisticated, genteel, courtly.
– OPPOSITES rude, uncivilized.

politic adjective *I did not think it politic to express my reservations:* **wise**,

prudent, sensible, judicious, canny, sagacious, shrewd, astute; recommended, advantageous, beneficial, profitable, desirable, advisable; appropriate, suitable, fitting, apt.
– OPPOSITES unwise.

political adjective **1** *the political affairs of the nation:* **governmental**, government, constitutional, ministerial, parliamentary, diplomatic, legislative, administrative, bureaucratic; public, civic, state. **2** *he's a political man:* **politically active**, party (political); militant, factional, partisan.

politician noun **legislator**, elected official, Member of Parliament, MP, minister, statesman, stateswoman, public servant; senator, congressman/woman; informal politico, pol.

politics noun **1** *a career in politics:* **government**, affairs of state, public affairs; diplomacy. **2** *he studies politics:* **political science**, civics, statecraft. **3** *what are his politics?* **political views**, political leanings, party politics. **4** *office politics:* **power struggle**, machinations, manoeuvring, opportunism, realpolitik.

poll noun **1** *a second-round poll:* **vote**, ballot, show of hands, referendum, plebiscite; election. **2** *the poll was unduly low:* **voting figures**, vote, returns, count, tally. **3** *a poll to investigate holiday choices:* **survey**, opinion poll, straw poll, canvass, market research, census.
verb **1** *most of those who were polled supported him:* **canvass**, survey, ask, question, interview, ballot. **2** *she polled 119 votes:* **get**, gain, register, record, return.

pollute verb **1** *fish farms will pollute the lake:* **contaminate**, adulterate, taint, poison, foul, dirty, soil, infect. **2** *propaganda polluted this nation:* **corrupt**, poison, warp, pervert, deprave, defile, blight, sully.
– OPPOSITES purify.

pollution noun **1** *pollution in the rivers:* **contamination**, adulteration, impurity; dirt, filth, infection. **2** *the pollution of young minds:* **corruption**, defilement, poisoning, warping, depravation, sullying, violation.

pomp noun *the pomp and popular jubilation accompanying his arrival:* **ceremony**, ceremonial, solemnity, ritual, display, spectacle, pageantry; show, showiness, ostentation, splendour, grandeur, magnificence, majesty, stateliness, glory, opulence, brilliance, drama, resplendence, splendidness; informal razzmatazz.

pompous adjective *a pompous official who kept quoting the rules:* **self-important**, imperious, overbearing, domineering, magisterial, pontifical, sententious, grandiose, affected, pretentious, puffed up, arrogant, vain, haughty, proud, conceited, egotistic, supercilious, condescending, patronizing; informal snooty, uppity, uppish.
– OPPOSITES modest.

pond noun **pool**, waterhole, lake, tarn, reservoir, swim; Brit. stew; Scottish lochan; N. Amer. pothole; Austral./NZ tank.

ponder verb *she had plenty of time to ponder over the incident:* **think about**, contemplate, consider, review, reflect on, mull over, meditate on, muse on, deliberate about, cogitate on, dwell on, brood on, ruminate on, chew over, puzzle over, turn over in one's mind.

ponderous adjective **1** *a ponderous dance:* **clumsy**, heavy, awkward, lumbering, slow, cumbersome, ungainly, graceless, uncoordinated, blundering; informal clodhopping, clunky. **2** *his ponderous sentences:* **laboured**, laborious, awkward, clumsy, forced, stilted, unnatural, artificial; stodgy, lifeless, plodding, pedestrian, boring, dull, tedious, monotonous; over-elaborate, convoluted, windy.
– OPPOSITES light, lively.

pontificate verb *he began to pontificate about life and art:* **hold forth**, expound, declaim, preach, lay down the law, sound off, dogmatize, sermonize, moralize, lecture; informal preachify, mouth off.

pool[1] noun **1** *pools of water:* **puddle**, pond. **2** *the hotel has a pool:* **swimming pool**, baths, lido; Brit. swimming bath(s); N. Amer. natatorium.

pool[2] noun **1** *a pool of skilled labour:* **supply**, reserve(s), reservoir, fund; store, stock, accumulation, cache. **2** *a pool of money for emergencies:* **fund**, reserve, kitty, pot, bank, purse.
verb *they pooled their skills:* **combine**, amalgamate, group, join, unite, merge; fuse, conglomerate, integrate; share.

poor adjective **1** *a poor family:* **poverty-stricken**, penniless, moneyless, impoverished, necessitous, impecunious, indigent, needy, destitute, pauperized, on one's beam-ends, unable to make ends meet, without a sou; insolvent, in debt; Brit. on the breadline, without a penny (to one's name); informal (flat) broke, hard up, cleaned out, strapped, on one's uppers, without two pennies to rub together; Brit. informal skint, in Queer Street. **2** *poor workmanship:* **substandard**, below par, bad, deficient, defective, faulty, imperfect, inferior; appalling, abysmal, atrocious, awful, terrible, dreadful, unsatisfactory, second-rate, third-rate, shoddy, crude, lamentable, deplorable, inadequate, unacceptable; informal crummy, rubbishy, dire, dismal, bum, rotten, tenth-rate; Brit. informal ropy, duff, rubbish, dodgy, pants. **3** *a poor crop:* **meagre**, scanty, scant, paltry, disappointing, limited, reduced, modest, insufficient, inadequate, sparse, spare, deficient, insubstantial, skimpy, short, small, lean, slender; informal measly, stingy, pathetic, piddling. **4** *poor soil:* **unproductive**, barren, unyielding, unfruitful, uncultivatable; arid, sterile. **5** *the waters are poor in nutrients:* **deficient**,

p

lacking, wanting; short of, low on. **6** *you poor thing!* **unfortunate**, unlucky, luckless, unhappy, hapless, ill-fated, ill-starred, pitiable, pitiful, wretched.
– OPPOSITES rich, superior, good, fertile, lucky.

poorly adverb *the text is poorly written:* **badly**, deficiently, defectively, imperfectly, incompetently; appallingly, abysmally, atrociously, awfully, dreadfully; crudely, shoddily, inadequately.
adjective *she felt poorly:* **ill**, unwell, not (very) well, ailing, indisposed, out of sorts, under/below par, peaky; sick, queasy, nauseous; Brit. off colour; informal under the weather, funny, peculiar, lousy, rough; Brit. informal ropy, grotty; Scottish informal wabbit; Austral./NZ informal crook.

pop verb **1** *champagne corks popped:* **go bang**, go off; crack, snap, burst, explode. **2** *I'm just popping home:* **go**; drop in, stop by, visit; informal tootle, whip; Brit. informal nip. **3** *pop a bag over the pot:* **put**, place, slip, slide, stick, set, lay, install, position, arrange.
noun **1** *the balloons burst with a pop:* **bang**, crack, snap; explosion, report. **2** (informal) *a bottle of pop:* **fizzy drink**, soft drink, carbonated drink; N. Amer. soda; Scottish informal scoosh.
■ **pop up** *many familiar faces pop up during the twenty-six episodes:* **appear (suddenly)**, occur (suddenly), arrive, materialize, come along, happen, emerge, arise, crop up, turn up, present itself, come to light; informal show up.

pope noun **pontiff**, Bishop of Rome, Holy Father, Vicar of Christ, His Holiness.

pop music noun **pop**, popular music, chart music.

populace noun *the party misjudged the mood of the populace:* **population**, inhabitants, residents, natives; community, country, (general) public, people, nation; common people, man/woman in the street, masses, multitude, rank and file, commonality, commonalty, third estate, plebeians, proletariat; informal proles, plebs; Brit. informal Joe Public; derogatory the hoi polloi, common herd, rabble, riff-raff.

popular adjective **1** *the restaurant is very popular:* **well liked**, favoured, sought-after, in demand, desired, wanted; commercial, marketable, fashionable, in vogue, all the rage, hot; informal in, cool, big. **2** *popular science:* **non-specialist**, non-technical, amateur, lay person's, general, middle-of-the-road; accessible, simplified, plain, simple, easy, straightforward, understandable; mass-market, middlebrow, lowbrow, pop. **3** *popular opinion:* **widespread**, general, common, current, prevalent, prevailing, standard, stock; ordinary, usual, accepted, established, acknowledged, conventional, orthodox. **4** *a popular movement for independence:* **mass**, general, communal, collective, social,

collaborative, group, civil, public.
– OPPOSITES highbrow.

popularize verb **1** *tobacco was popularized by Sir Walter Raleigh:* **make popular**, make fashionable; market, publicize; informal hype. **2** *he popularized the subject:* **simplify**, make accessible, give mass-market appeal to. **3** *the report popularized the unfounded notion:* **give currency to**, spread, propagate, give credence to.

popularly adverb **1** *old age is popularly associated with illness:* **widely**, generally, universally, commonly, usually, customarily, habitually, conventionally, traditionally, as a rule. **2** *the rock was popularly known as 'Arthur's Seat':* **informally**, unofficially; by lay people. **3** *the President is popularly elected:* **democratically**, by the people.

populate verb **1** *the state is populated by 40,000 people:* **inhabit**, occupy, people; live in, reside in. **2** *an attempt to populate the island:* **settle**, colonize, people, occupy, move into, make one's home in.

population noun *measures to speed up integration of the country's immigrant population:* **inhabitants**, residents, people, citizens, citizenry, public, community, populace, society, natives, occupants.

populous adjective *the country's second most populous city:* **densely populated**, heavily populated, congested, crowded, packed, jammed, crammed, teeming, swarming, seething, crawling; informal jam-packed.
– OPPOSITES deserted.

porch noun **vestibule**, foyer, entrance (hall), entry, portico, lobby; N. Amer. ramada, stoop.

pore[1] noun *pores in the skin:* **opening**, orifice, aperture, hole, outlet, inlet, vent.

pore[2] verb *they pored over the map:* **study**, read intently, peruse, scrutinize, scan, examine, go over.

pornographic adjective *pornographic magazines:* **obscene**, indecent, crude, lewd, dirty, vulgar, smutty, filthy; erotic, titillating, arousing, suggestive, sexy, risqué; off colour, adult, X-rated, hard-core, soft-core; informal porn, porno, blue, skin.
– OPPOSITES wholesome.

pornography noun **erotica**, pornographic material, dirty books; smut, filth, vice; informal (hard/soft) porn, porno, girlie magazines, skin flicks.

porous adjective *porous rock:* **permeable**, penetrable, pervious, cellular, holey; absorbent, absorptive, spongy.
– OPPOSITES impermeable.

port[1] noun **1** *the German port of Kiel:* **seaport**, entrepôt. **2** *shells exploded down by the port:* **harbour**, dock(s), haven, marina; anchorage, moorage, harbourage, roads.

port[2] noun *push the supply pipes into the ports:* **aperture**, opening, outlet, inlet, socket, vent.

portable adjective *a portable television:* **transportable**, movable, mobile, travel; lightweight, compact, handy, convenient.

portal noun **doorway**, gateway, entrance, exit, opening; door, gate; N. Amer. entryway.

portend verb *the sound of the death-watch beetle was thought to portend the death of someone in the house:* **presage**, augur, foreshadow, foretell, prophesy; be a sign, warn, be an omen, indicate, herald, signal, bode, promise, threaten, signify, spell, denote.

portent noun **1** *a portent of things to come:* **omen**, sign, signal, token, forewarning, warning, foreshadowing, prediction, forecast, prophesy, harbinger, augury, auspice, presage; writing on the wall, indication, hint. **2** *the word carries terrifying portent:* **significance**, importance, import, consequence, meaning, weight.

portentous adjective **1** *portentous signs:* **ominous**, warning, premonitory, prognosticatory; threatening, menacing, ill-omened, foreboding, inauspicious, unfavourable. **2** *portentous dialogue:* **pompous**, bombastic, self-important, pontifical, solemn, sonorous, grandiloquent.

porter[1] noun *a porter helped with the bags:* **carrier**, bearer; N. Amer. redcap, skycap.

porter[2] noun (Brit.) *the college porter:* **doorman**, doorkeeper, commissionaire, gatekeeper.

portion noun **1** *the upper portion of the chimney:* **part**, piece, bit, section, segment. **2** *her portion of the allowance:* **share**, slice, quota, quantum, part, percentage, amount, quantity, ration, fraction, division, allocation, measure; informal cut, rake-off; Brit. informal whack. **3** *a portion of cake:* **helping**, serving, amount, quantity; plateful, bowlful; slice, piece, chunk, wedge, slab, hunk; Brit. informal wodge.
verb *she portioned out the food:* **share out**, allocate, allot, apportion; distribute, hand out, deal out, dole out, give out, dispense, mete out; informal divvy up.

portly adjective *a portly, florid-faced man:* **stout**, plump, fat, overweight, heavy, corpulent, fleshy, paunchy, pot-bellied, well padded, rotund, stocky, bulky; informal tubby, roly-poly, beefy, porky, pudgy; Brit. informal podgy; N. Amer. informal corn-fed.
– OPPOSITES slim.

portrait noun **1** *a portrait of the King:* **painting**, picture, drawing, sketch, likeness, image, study, miniature; informal oil. **2** *a vivid portrait of Italy:* **description**, portrayal, representation, depiction, impression, account; sketch, vignette, profile.

portray verb **1** *he portrays Windermere in sunny weather:* **paint**, draw, sketch, picture, depict, represent, illustrate, render. **2** *the dons portrayed by Waugh:* **describe**, depict, characterize, represent, delineate, evoke. **3** *he portrays her as a doormat:* **represent**, depict, characterize, describe, present. **4** *the actor portrays a spy:* **play**, act the part of, take the role of, represent, appear as.

portrayal noun **1** *a portrayal of a parrot:* **painting**, picture, portrait, drawing, sketch, representation, depiction, study. **2** *her portrayal of adolescence:* **description**, representation, characterization, depiction, evocation. **3** *Brando's portrayal of Corleone:* **performance as**, representation, interpretation, rendering.

pose verb **1** *pollution poses a threat to health:* **constitute**, present, create, cause, produce, be. **2** *the question posed earlier:* **raise**, ask, put, set, submit, advance, propose, suggest, moot. **3** *she posed for the artist:* **be a model**, model, sit. **4** *he posed her on the sofa:* **position**, place, put, arrange, dispose, locate, situate. **5** *fashion victims were posing at the bar:* **behave affectedly**, strike a pose, posture, attitudinize, put on airs; informal show off.
noun **1** *a sexy pose:* **posture**, position, stance, attitude, bearing. **2** *her pose of aggrieved innocence:* **pretence**, act, affectation, facade, show, front, display, masquerade, posture.
■ **pose as** pretend to be, impersonate, pass oneself off as, masquerade as, profess to be, represent oneself as.

poser[1] noun *this situation's a bit of a poser:* **difficult question**, vexed question, awkward problem, tough one, puzzle, mystery, conundrum, puzzler, enigma, riddle; informal dilemma, facer, toughie, stumper.

poser[2] noun *he's such a poser:* **exhibitionist**, poseur, poseuse, posturer; informal show-off, pseud.

poseur noun. See POSER[2].

posh adjective **1** (informal) *a posh hotel:* **smart**, stylish, fancy, high-class, fashionable, chic, luxurious, luxury, de luxe, exclusive, opulent, lavish, grand, showy; Brit. upmarket; informal classy, swanky, snazzy, plush, ritzy, flash, la-di-da; Brit. informal swish; N. Amer. informal swank, tony. **2** (Brit.) *a posh accent:* **upper-class**, aristocratic; Brit. upmarket, Home Counties; informal upper-crust, top-drawer; Brit. informal plummy, Sloaney, U.

posit verb *there are those who posit a purely biological basis for this phenomenon:* **postulate**, put forward, advance, propound, submit, hypothesize, propose, assert.

position noun **1** *the aircraft's position:* **location**, place, situation, spot, site, locality, setting, area; whereabouts, bearings, orientation. **2** *a standing position:* **posture**, stance, attitude, pose. **3** *our financial position:* **situation**, state, condition, circumstances; predicament, plight, strait(s). **4** *the two parties jockeyed for position:* **advantage**, the upper hand, the edge, the whip hand, primacy; Austral./NZ the box seat; N. Amer. informal the catbird seat. **5** *their position in society:* **status**,

place, level, rank, standing; stature, prestige, influence, reputation, importance, consequence, class. **6** *a secretarial position:* **job**, post, situation, appointment, role, occupation, employment; office, capacity, duty, function; opening, vacancy, placement. **7** *the government's position on the matter:* **viewpoint**, opinion, outlook, attitude, stand, standpoint, stance, perspective, approach, slant, thinking, policy, feelings.
▸ verb *he positioned a chair between them:* **put**, place, locate, situate, set, site, stand, station; plant, stick, install; arrange, dispose; informal plonk, park.

positive adjective **1** *a positive response:* **affirmative**, favourable, good, approving, enthusiastic, supportive, encouraging. **2** *do something positive:* **constructive**, practical, useful, productive, helpful, worthwhile, beneficial, effective. **3** *she seems a lot more positive:* **optimistic**, hopeful, confident, cheerful, sanguine, buoyant; informal upbeat. **4** *positive economic signs:* **favourable**, good, promising, encouraging, heartening, propitious, auspicious. **5** *positive proof:* **definite**, conclusive, certain, categorical, unequivocal, incontrovertible, indisputable, undeniable, unmistakable, irrefutable, reliable, concrete, tangible, clear-cut, explicit, firm, decisive, real, actual. **6** *I'm positive he's coming back:* **certain**, sure, convinced, confident, satisfied, assured; as sure as eggs is eggs.
– OPPOSITES negative, pessimistic, doubtful, unsure.

positively adverb **1** *I could not positively identify the voice:* **confidently**, definitely, emphatically, categorically, with certainty, conclusively, unquestionably, undoubtedly, indisputably, unmistakably, assuredly. **2** *he was positively livid:* **absolutely**, really, downright, thoroughly, completely, utterly, totally, extremely, fairly; informal plain.

possess verb **1** *the only hat she possessed:* **own**, have (to one's name), hold. **2** *he did not possess a sense of humour:* **have**, be blessed with, be endowed with; enjoy, boast. **3** *a supernatural force possessed him:* **take control of**, take over, control, dominate, influence; bewitch, enchant, enthral. **4** *she was possessed by a need to talk to him:* **obsess**, haunt, preoccupy, consume; eat someone up, prey on one's mind.

possessed adjective *he ran towards the door like a man possessed:* **mad**, demented, insane, crazed, berserk, out of one's mind; bewitched, enchanted, haunted, under a spell.

possession noun **1** *the estate came into their possession:* **ownership**, control, hands, keeping, care, custody, charge, hold, title, guardianship. **2** *her possession of the premises:* **occupancy**, occupation, tenure, holding, tenancy. **3** *she packed her possessions:* **belongings**, things, property, (worldly) goods, (personal) effects, assets,

chattels, movables, valuables; stuff, bits and pieces; luggage, baggage; informal gear, junk; Brit. informal clobber. **4** *colonial possessions:* **colony**, dependency, territory, holding, protectorate.
▪ **take possession of** seize, appropriate, impound, expropriate, sequestrate, sequester, confiscate; take, get, acquire, obtain, procure, possess oneself of, get hold of, get one's hands on; capture, commandeer, requisition; informal get one's mitts on.

possessive adjective **1** *he was very possessive:* **proprietorial**, overprotective, controlling, dominating, jealous, clingy. **2** *kids are possessive of their own property:* **covetous**, selfish, unwilling to share; grasping, greedy, acquisitive; N. Amer. informal grabby.

possibility noun **1** *there is a possibility that he might be alive:* **chance**, likelihood, probability, hope; risk, hazard, danger, fear. **2** *they discussed the possibility of launching a new project:* **feasibility**, practicability, chances, odds, achievability, probability. **3** *buying a smaller house is one possibility:* **option**, alternative, choice, course of action, solution. **4** *the idea has distinct possibilities:* **potential**, promise, prospects.

possible adjective **1** *it's not possible to check the figures:* **feasible**, practicable, viable, within the bounds/realms of possibility, attainable, achievable, workable; informal on, doable. **2** *a possible reason for his disappearance:* **conceivable**, plausible, imaginable, believable, likely, potential, probable, credible. **3** *a possible future leader:* **potential**, prospective, likely, probable.
– OPPOSITES unlikely.

possibly adverb **1** *possibly he took the boy with him:* **perhaps**, maybe, it is possible, for all one knows, very likely. **2** *you can't possibly refuse:* **conceivably**, under any circumstances, by any means. **3** *could you possibly help me?* **please**, kindly, be so good as to.

post¹ noun *wooden posts:* **pole**, stake, upright, shaft, prop, support, picket, strut, pillar, pale, paling, stanchion, puncheon.
▸ verb **1** *the notice posted on the wall:* **affix**, attach, fasten, display, pin (up), put up, stick (up), tack (up). **2** *the group posted a net profit:* **announce**, report, make known, publish.

post² noun (Brit.) **1** *the winners will be notified by post:* **mail**, the postal service; airmail, surface mail, registered mail; informal snail mail. **2** *did we get any post?* **letters**, correspondence, mail.
▸ verb **1** (Brit.) *post the order form today:* **send (off)**, mail, put in the post/mail, get off. **2** *post the transaction in the second column:* **record**, write in, enter, register.
▪ **keep someone posted** keep informed, keep up to date, keep in the picture, keep briefed, update, fill in; informal keep up to speed.

post³ noun **1** *there were seventy candidates*

for the post: **job**, position, appointment, situation, place; vacancy, opening; Austral. informal grip. **2** *Back to your posts!* **(assigned) position**, station, observation post.
verb 1 *he'd been posted to Berlin:* **send**, assign to a post, dispatch. **2** *armed guards were posted beside the exit:* **put on duty**, station, position, situate, locate.

poster noun *a poster advertising his latest film:* **notice**, placard, bill, sign, advertisement, affiche, playbill; Brit. fly-poster.

posterior adjective *the posterior part of the skull:* **rear**, hind, back, hinder.
– OPPOSITES anterior.
noun (humorous) *her plump posterior.* See **BOTTOM** noun sense 6.

posterity noun *their names are recorded for posterity:* **future generations**, the future.

post-haste adverb *he departed post-haste for Venice:* **as quickly as possible**, without delay, (very) quickly, speedily, without further/more ado, with all speed, promptly, immediately, at once, straight away, right away; informal pronto, straight off.

postman, postwoman noun **postal worker**; N. Amer. mailman; Brit. informal postie.

post-mortem noun **1** *the hospital carried out a post-mortem:* **autopsy**, post-mortem examination, PM, necropsy. **2** *a post-mortem of her failed relationship:* **analysis**, evaluation, assessment, appraisal, examination, review.

postpone verb *he had to postpone his scheduled trip to South Africa:* **put off/back**, delay, defer, reschedule, adjourn, shelve; N. Amer. put over, take a rain check on; informal put on ice, put on the back burner.
– OPPOSITES bring forward.

postponement noun **deferral**, deferment, delay, putting off/back, rescheduling, adjournment, shelving.

postscript noun **1** *a handwritten postscript:* **afterthought**, PS, additional remark. **2** *he added postscripts of his own:* **addendum**, supplement, appendix, codicil, afterword, addition.
– OPPOSITES preface.

postulate verb *such hypotheses have been postulated by highly reputable geologists:* **put forward**, suggest, advance, posit, hypothesize, propose; assume, presuppose, presume, take for granted.

posture noun **1** *a kneeling posture:* **position**, pose, attitude, stance. **2** *good posture:* **bearing**, carriage, stance, comportment; Brit. deportment. **3** *trade unions adopted a militant posture:* **attitude**, stance, standpoint, point of view, opinion, position, frame of mind.
verb *Keith postured, flexing his biceps:* **pose**, strike an attitude, strut.

posy noun *a posy of snowdrops and violets:* **bouquet**, bunch (of flowers), spray, nosegay, corsage; buttonhole, boutonnière.

pot noun **1** *pots and pans:* **cooking utensil**, pan, saucepan, casserole, stewpot, stockpot, dixie. **2** *earthenware pots:* **flowerpot**, planter, jardinière. **3** *Jim raked in half the pot:* **bank**, kitty, pool, purse, jackpot.

pot belly noun **paunch**, (beer) belly; informal beer gut, pot, tummy.

potency noun **1** *the potency of his words:* **forcefulness**, force, effectiveness, persuasiveness, cogency, influence, strength, authoritativeness, authority, power, powerfulness. **2** *the potency of the drugs:* **strength**, powerfulness, power, effectiveness.

potent adjective **1** *a potent political force:* **powerful**, strong, mighty, formidable, influential, dominant, forceful. **2** *a potent argument:* **forceful**, convincing, cogent, compelling, persuasive, powerful, strong. **3** *a potent drug:* **strong**, powerful, effective.
– OPPOSITES weak.

potentate noun *diplomatic missions to foreign potentates:* **ruler**, monarch, sovereign, king, queen, emperor, empress.

potential adjective *a potential source of conflict:* **possible**, likely, prospective, future, probable; latent, inherent, undeveloped.
noun *economic potential:* **possibilities**, potentiality, prospects; promise, capability, capacity.

potion noun *Dotty concocted strange potions from the herbs in her garden:* **concoction**, mixture, brew, elixir, philtre, drink, decoction; medicine, tonic.

pot-pourri noun *the book is a pot-pourri of curious animal stories:* **mixture**, assortment, collection, selection, assemblage, medley, miscellany, mix, variety, mixed bag, patchwork; ragbag, hotchpotch, mishmash, jumble, farrago; N. Amer. hodge-podge.

potter verb *we pottered down to the library:* **amble**, wander, meander, stroll, saunter, maunder; informal mosey, tootle, toddle; N. Amer. informal putter.
■ **potter about/around** do nothing much, fiddle about/around, footle about/around; informal mess about/around; Brit. informal muck about/around; N. Amer. informal putter about/around, lollygag.

pottery noun **china**, crockery, ceramics, earthenware, stoneware.

potty adjective (Brit. informal) **1** *I'm going potty.* See **CRAZY** sense 1. **2** *she's potty about you.* See **CRAZY** sense 3.

pouch noun **1** *he kept his money in a leather pouch:* **bag**, purse, sack, sac, pocket; Scottish sporran. **2** *a kangaroo's pouch:* Zoology marsupium.

pounce verb *two men pounced on him:* **jump on**, spring, leap, dive, lunge, fall on, set on, attack suddenly; informal jump, mug.
noun *a sudden pounce:* **leap**, spring, jump, dive, lunge, bound.

pound¹ verb **1** *the two men pounded him with their fists:* **beat**, strike, hit, batter,

p

thump, pummel, punch, rain blows on, belabour, hammer, thrash, set on, tear into; informal bash, clobber, wallop, beat the living daylights out of, whack, thwack, lay into, pitch into; Brit. informal slosh; N. Amer. informal light into, whale. **2** *waves pounded the seafront:* **beat against**, crash against, batter, dash against, lash, buffet. **3** *gunships pounded the capital:* **bombard**, bomb, shell, fire on. **4** *pound the cloves with salt:* **crush**, grind, pulverize, mill, mash, pulp. **5** *I heard him pounding along the gangway:* **walk/run heavily**, stomp, lumber, clomp, clump, tramp, trudge. **6** *her heart was pounding:* **throb**, thump, thud, hammer, pulse, race, go pit-a-pat.

pound² noun *ten pounds:* pound sterling, £; Brit. informal quid, smacker, nicker.

pound³ noun *a dog pound:* **enclosure**, compound, pen, yard.

pour verb **1** *blood was pouring from his nose:* **stream**, flow, run, gush, course, jet, spurt, surge, spill. **2** *Amy poured wine into his glass:* **tip**, let flow, splash, spill, decant; informal slosh, slop. **3** *it was pouring with rain:* **rain heavily/hard**, teem down, pelt down, tip down, come down in torrents/sheets, rain cats and dogs; informal be chucking it down; Brit. informal bucket down, come down in stair rods; N. Amer. informal rain pitchforks. **4** *people poured off the train:* **throng**, crowd, swarm, stream, flood, spill, surge, file.

pout verb *Crystal pouted sullenly:* **look petulant**, pull a face, look sulky.
noun *a childish pout:* **petulant expression**, sulky expression, moue.

poverty noun **1** *abject poverty:* **penury**, destitution, pauperism, pauperdom, indigence, pennilessness, impoverishment, neediness, need, hardship, impecuniousness. **2** *the poverty of choice:* **scarcity**, deficiency, dearth, shortage, paucity, insufficiency, absence, lack. **3** *the poverty of her imagination:* **inferiority**, mediocrity, poorness, sterility.
– OPPOSITES wealth, abundance.

poverty-stricken adjective *his family were poverty-stricken and starving:* **extremely poor**, impoverished, destitute, penniless, on one's beam-ends, as poor as a church mouse, in penury, impecunious, indigent, needy, in need/want; Brit. on the breadline, without a penny (to one's name); informal on one's uppers, without two pennies/farthings to rub together; Brit. informal in Queer Street.

powder noun **dust**, fine particles; talcum powder, talc.
verb **1** *she powdered her face:* **dust**, sprinkle/cover with powder. **2** *the grains are powdered:* **crush**, grind, pulverize, pound, mill.

powdered adjective *powdered milk:* dried, freeze-dried.

powdery adjective *a powdery residue:* **fine**, dry, fine-grained, powder-like, dusty, chalky, floury, sandy, crumbly, friable.

power noun **1** *the power of speech:* **ability**, capacity, capability, potential, faculty, competence. **2** *the unions wield enormous power:* **control**, authority, influence, dominance, mastery, domination, dominion, sway, weight, leverage; informal clout, teeth; N. Amer. informal drag. **3** *police have the power to stop and search:* **authority**, right, authorization, warrant, licence. **4** *a major European power:* **state**, country, nation. **5** *he hit the ball with as much power as he could:* **strength**, powerfulness, might, force, forcefulness, vigour, energy; brawn, muscle; informal punch; Brit. informal welly. **6** *the power of his arguments:* **forcefulness**, powerfulness, potency, strength, force, cogency, persuasiveness. **7** *the new engine has more power:* **driving force**, horsepower, hp, acceleration; informal oomph, grunt. **8** *generating power from waste:* **energy**, electrical power.
– OPPOSITES inability, weakness.
■ **have someone in/under one's power** have control over, have influence over, have under one's thumb, have at one's mercy, have in one's clutches, have in the palm of one's hand; N. Amer. have in one's hip pocket; informal have over a barrel.
■ **the powers that be** the authorities, the people in charge, the government.

powerful adjective **1** *powerful shoulders:* **strong**, muscular, muscly, sturdy, strapping, robust, brawny, burly, athletic, manly, well built, solid; informal beefy, hunky. **2** *a powerful drink:* **intoxicating**, hard, strong, stiff. **3** *a powerful blow:* **violent**, forceful, hard, mighty. **4** *he felt a powerful desire to kiss her:* **intense**, keen, fierce, passionate, ardent, burning, strong, irresistible, overpowering, overwhelming. **5** *a powerful nation:* **influential**, strong, important, dominant, commanding, potent, forceful, formidable. **6** *a powerful critique:* **cogent**, compelling, convincing, persuasive, forceful; dramatic, graphic, vivid, moving.
– OPPOSITES weak, gentle.

powerless adjective *we felt intimidated and powerless:* **impotent**, helpless, ineffectual, ineffective, useless, defenceless, vulnerable.

practicable adjective *it is important that all practicable steps be taken to prevent violence breaking out:* **realistic**, feasible, possible, within the bounds/realms of possibility, viable, reasonable, sensible, workable, achievable; informal doable.

practical adjective **1** *practical experience:* **empirical**, hands-on, actual, active, applied, heuristic, experiential. **2** *there are no practical alternatives:* **feasible**, practicable, realistic, viable, workable, possible, reasonable, sensible; informal doable. **3** *practical clothes:* **functional**, sensible, utilitarian, workaday. **4** *try to be more practical:* **realistic**, sensible, down-to-earth, businesslike, commonsensical, hard-

headed, no-nonsense; informal hard-nosed. **5** *a practical certainty:* **virtual**, effective, near.
– OPPOSITES theoretical.

practicality noun **1** *the practicality of the proposal:* **feasibility**, practicability, viability, workability. **2** *practicality of design:* **functionalism**, functionality, serviceability, utility. **3** *his calm practicality:* **(common) sense**, realism, pragmatism. **4** *the practicalities of army life:* **practical details**; informal nitty gritty, nuts and bolts.

practical joke noun **trick**, joke, prank, jape, hoax; informal leg-pull.

practically adverb **1** *the cinema was practically empty:* **almost**, (very) nearly, virtually, just about, all but, more or less, as good as, to all intents and purposes, verging on, bordering on; informal pretty nearly, pretty well. **2** *'You can't afford it,' he pointed out practically:* **realistically**, sensibly, reasonably.

practice noun **1** *this is common practice:* **custom**, procedure, policy, convention, tradition. **2** *it takes lots of practice | the team's final practice:* **training**, rehearsal, repetition, preparation; practice session, dummy run, run-through; informal dry run. **3** *the practice of medicine:* **profession**, career, business, work. **4** *a small legal practice:* **business**, firm, office, company; informal outfit.
■ **in practice** in reality, realistically, practically.
■ **out of practice** rusty, unpractised.
■ **put something into practice** use, make use of, put to use, utilize, apply.

practise verb **1** *he practised the songs every day:* **rehearse**, run through, go over/through, work on/at; polish, perfect. **2** *the performers were practising:* **train**, rehearse, prepare, go through one's paces. **3** *we still practise these rituals today:* **carry out**, perform, observe. **4** *she practises medicine:* **work at**, pursue a career in.

practised adjective *Sam was a practised judge of character:* **expert**, experienced, seasoned, skilled, skilful, accomplished, proficient, talented, able, adept, consummate, master, masterly; informal crack, ace, mean; N. Amer. informal crackerjack.

pragmatic adjective *my father was entirely pragmatic in his response to difficult situations:* **practical**, matter of fact, sensible, down-to-earth, commonsensical, businesslike, having both/one's feet on the ground, hard-headed, no-nonsense; informal hard-nosed.
– OPPOSITES impractical.

praise verb **1** *the police praised Pauline for her courage:* **commend**, express admiration for, applaud, pay tribute to, speak highly of, eulogize, compliment, congratulate, sing the praises of, rave about, go into raptures about, heap praise on, wax lyrical about, make much of, pat on the back, take one's hat off to, lionize, admire, hail; N. Amer. informal

ballyhoo. **2** *we praise God:* **worship**, glorify, honour, exalt, adore, pay tribute to, give thanks to, venerate, reverence.
– OPPOSITES criticize.

noun **1** *James was full of praise for the medical teams:* **approval**, acclaim, admiration, approbation, acclamation, plaudits, congratulations, commendation; tribute, accolade, compliment, a pat on the back, eulogy, panegyric. **2** *give praise to God:* **honour**, thanks, glory, worship, devotion, adoration, reverence.

praiseworthy adjective *the government's praiseworthy efforts:* **commendable**, admirable, laudable, worthy (of admiration), meritorious, estimable, exemplary.

pram noun (Brit.) pushchair; N. Amer. baby carriage, stroller.

prance verb *he was prancing around in his underpants:* **cavort**, dance, jig, trip, caper, jump, leap, spring, bound, skip, hop, frisk, romp, frolic.

prank noun *a silly student prank:* **(practical) joke**, trick, piece of mischief, escapade, stunt, caper, jape, game, hoax, antic; informal lark, leg-pull.

prattle verb *he prattled on for ages.* See CHAT verb.
noun *childish prattle.* See CHATTER noun.

pray verb **1** *let us pray:* **say one's prayers**, make one's devotions, offer a prayer/prayers. **2** *she prayed God to forgive her:* **invoke**, call on, implore, appeal to, entreat, beg, petition, supplicate.

prayer noun **1** *the priest's murmured prayers:* **invocation**, intercession, devotion. **2** *a quick prayer that she wouldn't bump into him:* **appeal**, plea, entreaty, petition, supplication, invocation; rare obsecration.

preach verb **1** *he preached to a large congregation:* **give a sermon**, sermonize, address, speak. **2** *preaching the good news of Jesus:* **proclaim**, teach, spread, propagate, expound. **3** *they preach toleration:* **advocate**, recommend, advise, urge, teach, counsel. **4** *who are you to preach at me?* **moralize**, sermonize, pontificate, lecture, harangue; informal preachify.

preacher noun **minister (of religion)**, parson, clergyman, clergywoman, member of the clergy, priest, man/woman of the cloth, man/woman of God, cleric, churchman, churchwoman, evangelist; informal reverend, padre, Holy Joe, sky pilot; N. Amer. informal preacher man; Austral. informal josser.

preaching noun **religious teaching**, message, sermons.

preamble noun *Lord Denning's preamble to the report:* **introduction**, preface, prologue; foreword, prelude, front matter; informal intro, prelims.

pre-arranged adjective *they met at pre-arranged meeting points in the city:*

p

arranged beforehand, agreed in advance, predetermined, pre-established, pre-planned.

precarious adjective *the club's precarious financial position:* **uncertain**, insecure, unpredictable, risky, parlous, hazardous, dangerous, unsafe; unsettled, unstable, unsteady, shaky; informal dicey, chancy, iffy; Brit. informal dodgy.
– OPPOSITES safe.

precaution noun *have your car serviced regularly as a precaution against mechanical breakdowns:* **safeguard**, preventative/preventive measure, safety measure, insurance; informal backstop.

precautionary adjective *keeping him in overnight was just a precautionary measure:* **preventative**, preventive, safety.

precede verb **1** *adverts preceded the film:* **go/come before**, lead (up) to, pave/prepare the way for, herald, introduce, usher in. **2** *Catherine preceded him into the studio:* **go ahead of**, go in front of, go before, go first, lead the way. **3** *he preceded the book with a poem:* **preface**, introduce, begin, open.
– OPPOSITES follow.

precedence noun *quarrels over precedence:* **priority**, rank, seniority, superiority, primacy, pre-eminence, eminence.
■ **take precedence over** take priority over, outweigh, prevail over, come before.

precedent noun *we hope to set a legal precedent:* **model**, exemplar, example, pattern, previous case, prior instance/example; paradigm, criterion, yardstick, standard.

preceding adjective *this discussion amplifies many of the issues raised in the preceding chapters:* **foregoing**, previous, prior, former, precedent, earlier, above, aforementioned, antecedent.

precept noun **1** *the precepts of Orthodox Judaism:* **principle**, rule, tenet, canon, doctrine, command, order, decree, dictate, dictum, injunction, commandment; Judaism mitzvah. **2** *precepts that her grandmother used to quote:* **maxim**, saying, adage, axiom, aphorism, apophthegm.

precinct noun **1** *a pedestrian precinct:* **area**, zone, sector. **2** *within the precincts of the City:* **bounds**, boundaries, limits, confines. **3** *the cathedral precinct:* **enclosure**, close, court.

precious adjective **1** *precious works of art:* **valuable**, costly, expensive; invaluable, priceless, beyond price. **2** *her most precious possession:* **valued**, cherished, treasured, prized, favourite, dear, dearest, beloved, darling, adored, loved, special. **3** *his precious manners:* **affected**, over-refined, pretentious; informal la-di-da; Brit. informal poncey.

precipice noun **cliff (face)**, steep cliff, rock face, sheer drop, crag, bluff, escarpment, scarp.

precipitate verb **1** *the incident precipitated a crisis:* **bring about/on**, cause, lead to, give rise to, instigate, trigger, spark, touch off, provoke, hasten, accelerate, expedite. **2** *they were precipitated down the mountain:* **hurl**, catapult, throw, plunge, launch, fling, propel.
adjective *their actions were precipitate:* **hasty**, overhasty, rash, hurried, rushed; impetuous, impulsive, spur-of-the-moment, precipitous, incautious, imprudent, injudicious, ill-advised, reckless, harum-scarum; informal previous.

precipitous adjective **1** *a precipitous drop:* **steep**, sheer, perpendicular, abrupt, sharp, vertical. **2** *his fall from power was precipitous:* **sudden**, rapid, swift, abrupt, headlong, speedy, quick, fast.

precis noun *a precis of the report:* **summary**, synopsis, résumé, abstract, outline, summarization, summation; abridgement, digest, overview, epitome; N. Amer. wrap-up.
verb *precising a passage:* **summarize**, sum up, give a summary/precis of, give the main points of; abridge, condense, shorten, synopsize, abstract, outline, abbreviate.

precise adjective **1** *precise measurements:* **exact**, accurate, correct, specific, detailed, explicit, unambiguous, definite. **2** *at that precise moment the car stopped:* **exact**, particular, very, specific. **3** *the attention to detail is very precise:* **meticulous**, careful, exact, scrupulous, punctilious, conscientious, particular, methodical, strict, rigorous.
– OPPOSITES inaccurate.

precisely adverb **1** *at 2 o'clock precisely:* **exactly**, sharp, on the dot; promptly, prompt, dead (on), on the stroke of ..., on the dot of ...; informal bang (on); Brit. informal spot on; N. Amer. informal on the button/nose. **2** *precisely the kind of man I am looking for:* **exactly**, absolutely, just, in all respects; informal to a T. **3** *fertilization can be timed precisely:* **accurately**, exactly; clearly, distinctly, strictly. **4** *'So it's all done?' 'Precisely.'* **yes**, exactly, absolutely, (that's) right, quite so, indubitably, definitely; informal you bet, I'll say.

precision noun *the deal was planned and executed with military precision:* **exactness**, exactitude, accuracy, correctness, preciseness; care, carefulness, meticulousness, scrupulousness, punctiliousness, methodicalness, rigour, rigorousness.

preclude verb *his difficulties preclude him from leading a normal life:* **prevent**, make it impossible for, rule out, stop, prohibit, debar, bar, hinder, impede, inhibit, exclude.

precocious adjective *some of the boys were extremely precocious:* **advanced for one's age**, forward, mature, gifted, talented, clever, intelligent, quick; informal smart.
– OPPOSITES backward.

preconceived adjective *some people tend to have preconceived ideas about us:* **predetermined**, prejudged; prejudiced, biased.

preconception noun *they had no preconceptions about his personality or his politics:* **preconceived idea/notion**, presupposition, assumption, presumption, prejudgement; prejudice.

precondition noun *political stability is a precondition for economic revival:* **prerequisite**, (necessary/essential) condition, requirement, necessity, essential, imperative, sine qua non; informal must.

precursor noun **1** *a three-stringed precursor of the guitar:* **forerunner**, predecessor, forefather, father, antecedent, ancestor, forebear. **2** *a precursor of disasters to come:* **harbinger**, herald, sign, indication, portent, omen.

predatory adjective **1** *predatory birds:* **predacious**, carnivorous, hunting, raptorial; of prey. **2** *a predatory gleam in his eyes:* **exploitative**, wolfish, rapacious, vulturine, vulturous.

predecessor noun **1** *the Prime Minister's predecessor:* **forerunner**, precursor, antecedent. **2** *our Victorian predecessors:* **ancestor**, forefather, forebear, antecedent.
– OPPOSITES successor, descendant.

predestined adjective *some people claim that everything is predestined:* **preordained**, ordained, predetermined, destined, fated.

predetermined adjective **1** *a predetermined budget:* **pre-arranged**, established in advance, preset, set, fixed, agreed. **2** *our predetermined fate:* **predestined**, preordained.

predicament noun *I cannot understand how you could have allowed yourself to get into such a predicament:* **difficult situation**, mess, difficulty, plight, quandary, muddle, mare's nest; informal hole, fix, jam, pickle, scrape, bind, tight spot/corner, dilemma.

predicate verb *all the social sciences are predicated on the notion that individuals are not isolated:* **base**, be dependent, found, establish, rest, ground, premise.

predict verb *it's difficult to predict what the outcome will be:* **forecast**, foretell, foresee, prophesy, anticipate, tell in advance, envision, envisage.

predictable adjective *Guido's reaction was predictable:* **foreseeable**, (only) to be expected, anticipated, foreseen, unsurprising; informal inevitable.

prediction noun *seven months later, his prediction came true:* **forecast**, prophecy, prognosis, prognostication, augury; projection, conjecture, guess.

predilection noun *her predilection for married men:* **liking**, fondness, preference, partiality, taste, penchant, weakness, soft spot, fancy, inclination, leaning, bias,

propensity, bent, proclivity, predisposition, appetite.
– OPPOSITES dislike.

predispose verb **1** *lack of exercise may predispose an individual to high blood pressure:* **make susceptible**, make liable, make prone, make vulnerable, put at risk of. **2** *attitudes which predispose people to behave badly:* **lead**, influence, sway, induce, prompt, dispose; bias, prejudice.

predisposed adjective *the audience were young and predisposed to like the film:* **inclined**, prepared, ready, of a mind, disposed, minded, willing.

predisposition noun **1** *a predisposition to heart disease:* **susceptibility**, proneness, tendency, liability, inclination, disposition, vulnerability. **2** *their political predispositions:* **preference**, predilection, inclination, leaning.

predominance noun **1** *the predominance of women carers:* **prevalence**, dominance, preponderance. **2** *Soviet military predominance:* **supremacy**, mastery, control, power, ascendancy, dominance, pre-eminence, superiority.

predominant adjective **1** *our predominant objectives:* **main**, chief, principal, most important, primary, prime, central, leading, foremost, key, paramount; informal number-one. **2** *the predominant political forces:* **controlling**, dominant, predominating, more/most powerful, pre-eminent, ascendant, superior, in the ascendancy.
– OPPOSITES subsidiary.

predominantly adverb *although predominantly a disease of older men, it is not unknown in people of his age:* **mainly**, mostly, for the most part, chiefly, principally, primarily, predominately, in the main, on the whole, largely, by and large, typically, generally, usually.

predominate verb **1** *small-scale producers predominate:* **be in the majority**, preponderate, be predominant, prevail, be most prominent. **2** *private interest predominates over the public good:* **prevail**, dominate, be dominant, carry most weight; override, outweigh.

pre-eminence noun **superiority**, supremacy, greatness, excellence, distinction, prominence, predominance, eminence, importance, prestige, stature, fame, renown, celebrity.

pre-eminent adjective *the country's pre-eminent environmentalist:* **greatest**, leading, foremost, best, finest, chief, outstanding, excellent, distinguished, prominent, eminent, important, top, famous, renowned, celebrated, illustrious, supreme; N. Amer. marquee.
– OPPOSITES undistinguished.

pre-eminently adverb *the novel is pre-eminently a realistic genre:* **primarily**, principally, above all, chiefly, mostly,

p

mainly, in particular.

pre-empt verb *his action may have pre-empted war:* **forestall**, prevent.

preen verb 1 *the robin preened its feathers:* **clean**, tidy, groom, smooth, arrange. 2 *she preened before the mirror:* **admire oneself**, primp oneself, prink oneself, groom oneself, spruce oneself up; informal titivate oneself, doll oneself up; Brit. informal tart oneself up; N. Amer. informal gussy oneself up.
■ **preen oneself** congratulate oneself, be pleased with oneself, be proud of oneself, pat oneself on the back, feel self-satisfied.

preface noun *the preface to the novel:* **introduction**, foreword, preamble, prologue, prelude; front matter; informal prelims, intro.
verb *the chapter is prefaced by a poem:* **precede**, introduce, begin, open, start.

prefatory adjective *three further prefatory remarks are necessary:* **introductory**, preliminary, opening, initial, preparatory, initiatory, precursory.
– OPPOSITES closing.

prefect noun (Brit.) **monitor**; Brit. praepostor.

prefer verb *I prefer white wine to red:* **like better**, would rather (have), would sooner (have), favour, be more partial to; choose, select, pick, opt for, go for, plump for.

preferable adjective *personal pension plans may be preferable if you change jobs frequently:* **better**, best, more desirable, more suitable, advantageous, superior, preferred, recommended.

preferably adverb *applicants should be graduates, preferably with some relevant experience:* **ideally**, if possible, for preference, from choice.

preference noun 1 *her preference for boys' games:* **liking**, partiality, predilection, proclivity, fondness, taste, inclination, leaning, bias, penchant, predisposition. 2 *my preference is rock:* **favourite**, (first) choice, selection; informal cup of tea, thing; N. Amer. informal druthers. 3 *preference will be given to applicants speaking Japanese:* **priority**, favour, precedence, preferential treatment.
■ **in preference to** rather than, instead of, in place of, sooner than.

preferential adjective *preferential interest rates may be offered to employees:* **special**, better, privileged, superior, favourable; partial, discriminatory, partisan, biased.

prefigure verb *his work prefigures that of the magic realists:* **foreshadow**, presage, be a harbinger of, herald.

pregnancy noun gestation.

pregnant adjective 1 *she is heavily pregnant:* **expecting a baby**, expectant, carrying a child; informal expecting, in the family way, preggers, with a bun in the oven; Brit. informal up the duff, in the (pudding) club, up the spout; N. Amer. informal knocked up, having swallowed a watermelon seed; Austral. informal with a joey in the pouch. 2 *a ceremony pregnant with religious significance:* **filled**, charged, heavy; full of. 3 *a pregnant pause:* **meaningful**, significant, suggestive, expressive, charged.

prehistoric adjective 1 *prehistoric times:* **primitive**, primeval, primordial, primal, ancient, early, antediluvian. 2 *the special effects look prehistoric:* **out of date**, outdated, outmoded, old-fashioned, passé, antiquated, archaic, behind the times, primitive, antediluvian; informal out of the ark; N. Amer. informal horse-and-buggy, clunky.
– OPPOSITES modern.

prejudice noun 1 *male prejudices about women:* **preconceived idea**, preconception, prejudgement. 2 *they are motivated by prejudice:* **bigotry**, bias, partisanship, partiality, intolerance, discrimination, unfairness, inequality. 3 *without prejudice to the interests of others:* **detriment**, harm, damage, injury, hurt, loss.
verb 1 *the article could prejudice the jury:* **bias**, influence, sway, predispose, make biased, make partial, colour. 2 *this could prejudice his chances of victory:* **damage**, be detrimental to, be prejudicial to, injure, harm, hurt, spoil, impair, undermine, hinder, compromise.

prejudiced adjective *his prejudiced views:* **biased**, bigoted, discriminatory, partisan, intolerant, narrow-minded, unfair, unjust, inequitable, coloured.
– OPPOSITES impartial.

prejudicial adjective *disclosure of the information would be prejudicial to the interests of the company:* **detrimental**, damaging, injurious, harmful, disadvantageous, hurtful, deleterious.
– OPPOSITES beneficial.

preliminary adjective *the discussions are still at a preliminary stage:* **preparatory**, introductory, initial, opening, prefatory, precursory; early, exploratory.
– OPPOSITES final.
noun 1 *he began without any preliminaries:* **introduction**, preamble, opening/prefatory remarks, formalities. 2 *a preliminary to the resumption of war:* **prelude**, preparation, preparatory measure, preliminary action.
■ **preliminary to** in preparation for, before, in advance of, prior to, preparatory to.

prelude noun 1 *a ceasefire was a prelude to peace negotiations:* **preliminary**, overture, opening, preparation, introduction, start, commencement, beginning, lead-in, precursor. 2 *an orchestral prelude:* **overture**, introductory movement, introduction, opening. 3 *the passage forms a prelude to Part III:* **introduction**, preface, prologue, foreword, preamble; informal intro.

premature adjective 1 *his premature death:* **untimely**, (too) early, unseasonable, before time. 2 *a premature baby:* **preterm**; informal prem. 3 *such a step would be premature:* **rash**, overhasty, hasty, precipitate,

p

impulsive, impetuous; informal previous.
– OPPOSITES overdue.

prematurely adverb **1** *Sam was born prematurely:* **too soon**, too early, ahead of time; preterm. **2** *don't act prematurely:* **rashly**, over-hastily, hastily, precipitately, precipitously.

premeditated adjective *premeditated murder:* **planned**, intentional, deliberate, pre-planned, calculated, cold-blooded, conscious, pre-arranged.
– OPPOSITES spontaneous.

premeditation noun **(advance) planning**, forethought, pre-planning, (criminal) intent; Law malice aforethought.

premier adjective *a premier chef:* **leading**, foremost, chief, principal, head, top-ranking, top, prime, primary, first, highest, pre-eminent, senior, outstanding, master; N. Amer. ranking; informal top-notch.
noun *the Italian premier:* **head of government**, prime minister, PM, president, chancellor.

premiere noun *the new musical is having its world premiere at the Haymarket Theatre tonight:* **first performance**, first night, opening night.

premise noun *the premise that human life consists of a series of choices:* **proposition**, assumption, hypothesis, thesis, presupposition, postulation, postulate, supposition, presumption, surmise, conjecture, speculation, assertion, belief.

premises plural noun *the company had moved to new premises in Gloucester:* **building(s)**, property, site, office.

premium noun **1** *monthly premiums of £30:* **(regular) payment**, instalment. **2** *you must pay a premium for organic fruit:* **surcharge**, additional payment, extra amount. **3** *a foreign service premium:* **bonus**, extra; incentive, inducement; informal perk.
■ **at a premium** scarce, in great demand, hard to come by, in short supply, thin on the ground.
■ **put/place a premium on 1** *I place a high premium on our relationship:* value greatly, attach great/special importance to, set great store by, put a high value on. **2** *the high price of oil put a premium on the coal industry:* make valuable, make invaluable, make important.

premonition noun *he had a premonition of imminent disaster:* **foreboding**, presentiment, intuition, (funny) feeling, hunch, suspicion, feeling in one's bones; misgiving, apprehension, fear.

preoccupation noun **1** *an air of preoccupation:* **pensiveness**, concentration, engrossment, absorption, self-absorption, musing, thinking, deep thought, brown study, brooding; abstraction, absent-mindedness, distraction, forgetfulness, inattentiveness, wool-gathering,

daydreaming. **2** *their main preoccupation was feeding their family:* **obsession**, concern; passion, enthusiasm, hobby horse.

preoccupied adjective **1** *officials preoccupied with their careers:* **obsessed**, concerned, absorbed, engrossed, intent, involved, wrapped up. **2** *she looked preoccupied:* **lost/deep in thought**, in a brown study, pensive, absent-minded, distracted, abstracted.

preoccupy verb **engross**, concern, absorb, take up someone's attention, distract, obsess, occupy, prey on someone's mind.

preordain verb *he believes that everything we do is preordained:* **predestine**, destine, foreordain, ordain, fate, predetermine, determine.

preparation noun **1** *the preparation of contingency plans:* **devising**, putting together, drawing up, construction, composition, production, getting ready, development. **2** *preparations for the party:* **arrangements**, planning, plans, preparatory measures. **3** *preparation for exams:* **instruction**, teaching, coaching, training, tutoring, drilling, priming. **4** *a preparation that kills off mites:* **mixture**, compound, concoction, solution, tincture, medicine, potion, cream, ointment, lotion.

preparatory adjective *preparatory work:* **preliminary**, initial, introductory, prefatory, opening, preparative, precursory.
■ **preparatory to** in preparation for, before, prior to, preliminary to.

prepare verb **1** *I want you to prepare a report:* **make/get ready**, put together, draw up, produce, arrange, assemble, construct, compose, formulate. **2** *the meal was easy to prepare:* **cook**, make, get, put together, concoct; informal fix, rustle up; Brit. informal knock up. **3** *preparing for war:* **get ready**, make preparations, arrange things, make provision, get everything set. **4** *athletes preparing for the Olympics:* **train**, get into shape, practise, get ready. **5** *I must prepare for my exams:* **study**, revise; Brit. informal swot. **6** *this course prepares students for their exams:* **instruct**, coach, train, tutor, drill, prime. **7** *prepare yourself for a shock:* **brace**, make ready, tense, steel, steady.

prepared adjective **1** *he needs to be well prepared:* **ready**, (all) set, equipped, primed; waiting, on hand, poised, in position. **2** *I'm not prepared to cut the price:* **willing**, ready, disposed, predisposed, (favourably) inclined, of a mind, minded.

preponderance noun **1** *the preponderance of women among older people:* **prevalence**, predominance, dominance. **2** *the preponderance of the evidence:* **bulk**, majority, greater quantity, larger part, best/better part, most; almost all. **3** *the preponderance of the trade unions:* **predominance**, dominance, ascendancy, supremacy, power.

p

preponderant adjective *the Western states remained militarily preponderant in the region:* **dominant**, predominant, preeminent, in control, more/most powerful, superior, supreme, ascendant, in the ascendancy.

prepossessing adjective *he was not a prepossessing sight:* **attractive**, beautiful, pretty, handsome, good-looking, fetching, charming, delightful, enchanting, captivating.
– OPPOSITES ugly.

preposterous adjective *a preposterous suggestion:* **absurd**, ridiculous, foolish, stupid, ludicrous, farcical, laughable, comical, risible, nonsensical, senseless, insane, outrageous, monstrous, informal crazy.
– OPPOSITES sensible.

prerequisite noun *training is a prerequisite for competence:* **(necessary) condition**, precondition, essential, requirement, requisite, necessity, sine qua non; informal must.
adjective *the prerequisite qualifications:* **necessary**, required, called for, essential, requisite, obligatory, compulsory.
– OPPOSITES unnecessary.

prerogative noun *in some countries, higher education is predominantly the prerogative of the rich:* **entitlement**, right, privilege, advantage, due, birthright.

presage verb *the owl's hooting presages death:* **portend**, augur, foreshadow, foretell, prophesy, be an omen of, herald, be a sign of, be the harbinger of, warn of, be a presage of, signal, bode, promise, threaten.
noun *a sombre presage of his final illness:* **omen**, sign, indication, portent, warning, forewarning, harbinger, augury, prophecy, foretoken.

prescience noun *with the uncanny prescience of children, they had divined that he was a fake:* **far-sightedness**, foresight, foreknowledge; psychic powers, clairvoyance; prediction, prognostication, divination, prophesy, augury; insight, intuition, perception, percipience.

prescient adjective **prophetic**, predictive, visionary; psychic, clairvoyant; far-sighted, prognostic, divinatory; insightful, intuitive, perceptive, percipient.

prescribe verb **1** *the doctor prescribed antibiotics:* **write a prescription for**, authorize. **2** *traditional values prescribe a life of domesticity:* **advise**, recommend, advocate, suggest, endorse, champion, promote. **3** *rules prescribing your duty:* **stipulate**, lay down, dictate, specify, determine, establish, fix.

prescription noun **1** *the doctor wrote a prescription:* **instruction**, authorization; informal script. **2** *he fetched the prescription from the chemist:* **medicine**, drug, medication. **3** *a painless prescription for improvement:* **method**, measure;

recommendation, suggestion, recipe, formula.

prescriptive adjective *guidelines must avoid being too prescriptive:* **dictatorial**, narrow, rigid, authoritarian, arbitrary, repressive, dogmatic.

presence noun **1** *the presence of a train was indicated electrically:* **existence**, being there. **2** *I requested the presence of an adjudicator:* **attendance**, appearance; company, companionship. **3** *a woman of great presence:* **aura**, charisma, (strength/force of) personality; poise, self-assurance, self-confidence. **4** *she felt a presence in the castle:* **ghost**, spirit, spectre, phantom, apparition, supernatural being; informal spook.
– OPPOSITES absence.
■ **presence of mind** composure, equanimity, self-possession, level-headedness, self-assurance, calmness, sangfroid, imperturbability; alertness, quick-wittedness; informal cool, unflappability.

present[1] adjective **1** *a doctor must be present at the ringside:* **in attendance**, here, there, near, nearby, (close/near) at hand, available. **2** *organic compounds are present in the waste:* **in existence**, existing, existent. **3** *the present economic climate:* **current**, present-day, existing.
– OPPOSITES absent.
noun *forget the past and think about the present:* **now**, today, the present time/moment, the here and now.
– OPPOSITES past, future.
■ **at present** at the moment, just now, right now, at the present time, currently, at this moment in time.
■ **for the present** for the time being, for now, for the moment, for a while, temporarily, pro tem.
■ **the present day** modern times, nowadays.

present[2] verb **1** *Eddy presented a cheque to the winner:* **hand over/out**, give (out), confer, bestow, award, grant, accord. **2** *the committee presented its report:* **submit**, set forth, put forward, proffer, offer, tender, table. **3** *may I present my wife?* **introduce**, make known, acquaint someone with. **4** *I called to present my warmest compliments:* **offer**, give, express. **5** *they presented their new product last month:* **demonstrate**, show, put on show/display, exhibit, display, launch, unveil. **6** *presenting good quality opera:* **stage**, put on, produce, perform. **7** *she presents a TV show:* **host**, introduce, compère, be the presenter of; N. Amer. informal emcee. **8** *the authorities present him as a common criminal:* **represent**, describe, portray, depict.
■ **present oneself 1** *he presented himself at ten o'clock:* be present, make an appearance, appear, turn up, arrive. **2** *an opportunity that presented itself:* occur, arise, happen, come about/up, appear, crop up, turn up.

present[3] noun *a birthday present:* **gift**, donation, offering, contribution; informal prezzie, freebie.

presentable adjective **1** *I'm making the place look presentable:* **tidy**, neat, straight, clean, spick and span, in good order, shipshape (and Bristol fashion). **2** *make yourself presentable:* **smartly dressed**, tidily dressed, tidy, well groomed, trim, spruce; informal natty. **3** *he has directed some presentable videos:* **fairly good**, passable, all right, satisfactory, moderately good, not (too) bad, average, fair; informal OK.

presentation noun **1** *the presentation of his certificate:* **awarding**, presenting, giving, handing over/out, bestowal, granting, award. **2** *the presentation of food:* **appearance**, arrangement, packaging, disposition, display, layout. **3** *her presentation to the Queen:* **introduction**, making known. **4** *the presentation of new proposals:* **submission**, proffering, offering, tendering, advancing, proposal, suggestion, mooting, tabling. **5** *a sales presentation:* **demonstration**, talk, lecture, address, speech, show, exhibition, display, introduction, launch, launching, unveiling. **6** *a presentation of his latest play:* **staging**, production, performance, mounting, showing.

presentiment noun *I understood that you had some sort of presentiment of disaster:* **premonition**, foreboding, intuition, (funny) feeling, hunch, feeling in one's bones, sixth sense.

presently adverb **1** *I shall see you presently:* **soon**, shortly, directly, quite soon, in a short time, in a little while, at any moment/minute/second, in next to no time, before long; N. Amer. momentarily; informal pretty soon, any moment now, in a jiffy, before you can say Jack Robinson, in two shakes of a lamb's tail; Brit. informal in a mo. **2** *he is presently abroad:* **at present**, currently, at the/this moment, at the present moment/time, now, nowadays, these days; Brit. informal at the minute.

preservation noun **1** *wood preservation:* **conservation**, protection, care. **2** *the preservation of the status quo:* **continuation**, conservation, maintenance, upholding, sustaining, perpetuation. **3** *the preservation of food:* **conserving**, bottling, canning, freezing, drying; curing, smoking, pickling.

preserve verb **1** *oil helps preserve wood:* **conserve**, protect, maintain, care for, look after. **2** *they wish to preserve the status quo:* **continue (with)**, conserve, keep going, maintain, uphold, sustain, perpetuate. **3** *preserving him from harassment:* **guard**, protect, keep, defend, safeguard, shelter, shield. **4** *spices enable us to preserve food:* **conserve**, bottle, can, freeze, dry; cure, smoke, pickle.
noun **1** *strawberry preserve:* **jam**, jelly, marmalade, conserve. **2** *the preserve of an*

educated middle class: **domain**, area, field, sphere, orbit, realm, province, territory; informal turf, bailiwick. **3** *a game preserve:* **sanctuary**, (game) reserve, reservation.

preside verb *the chairman presides at the meeting:* **chair**, be chairman/ chairwoman/chairperson, officiate (at), conduct, lead.
■ **preside over** be in charge of, be responsible for, be at the head/helm of, head, be head of, manage, administer, be in control of, control, direct, lead, govern, rule, command, supervise, oversee; informal head up, be boss of, be in the driving/driver's seat, be in the saddle.

president noun **1** *the president of the society:* **head**, chief, director, leader, governor, principal, master; N. Amer. informal prexy. **2** *the president of the company:* **chairman**, chairwoman; managing director, MD, chief executive (officer), CEO.

press verb **1** *press the paper down firmly:* **push (down)**, press down, depress, hold down, force, thrust, squeeze, compress. **2** *his shirt was pressed:* **smooth (out)**, iron, remove creases from. **3** *we pressed the grapes:* **crush**, squeeze, mash, pulp, pound, pulverize, macerate. **4** *she pressed the child to her bosom:* **clasp**, hold close, hug, cuddle, squeeze, clutch, grasp, embrace. **5** *Winnie pressed his hand:* **squeeze**, grip, clutch. **6** *the crowd pressed round:* **cluster**, gather, converge, congregate, flock, swarm, throng, crowd. **7** *the government pressed its claim:* **plead**, urge, advance insistently, present, submit, put forward. **8** *they pressed him to agree:* **urge**, put pressure on, pressurize, force, push, coerce, dragoon, steamroller, browbeat; informal lean on, put the screws on, twist someone's arm, railroad, bulldoze. **9** *they pressed for a ban on the ivory trade:* **call**, ask, clamour, push, campaign, demand.
noun **1** *a private press:* **publishing house**, printing company; printing press. **2** *the freedom of the press:* **the media**, the newspapers, the papers, the news media, the fourth estate; journalists, reporters, newspapermen, newsmen, newspaper women, pressmen, presswomen; informal journos, news hounds; N. Amer. informal newsies. **3** *the company had some bad press:* **(press) reports**, press coverage, press articles, press reviews.
■ **be pressed for** have too little, be short of, have insufficient, lack, be lacking (in), be deficient in, need, be/stand in need of; informal be strapped for.
■ **press on** *the team regrouped and pressed on:* **proceed**, keep going, continue, carry on, make progress, make headway, press ahead, forge on/ahead, push on, keep on, struggle on, persevere, keep at it, stay with it, plod on, plough on; informal soldier on, plug away, peg away, stick at it.

pressing adjective **1** *a pressing problem:*

urgent, critical, crucial, acute, desperate, serious, grave, life-and-death. **2** *a pressing engagement:* **important**, high-priority, critical, crucial, compelling, inescapable.

pressure noun **1** *a confined gas exerts a constant pressure:* **physical force**, load, stress, thrust; compression, weight. **2** *they put pressure on us to borrow money:* **coercion**, force, compulsion, constraint, duress; pestering, harassment, nagging, badgering, intimidation, arm-twisting, pressurization, persuasion. **3** *she had a lot of pressure from work:* **strain**, stress, tension, trouble, difficulty; informal hassle.
verb *they pressured him into resigning.* See **PRESSURIZE**.

pressurize verb *he tried to pressurize Buffy into selling:* **coerce**, pressure, put pressure on, press, push, persuade, force, bulldoze, hound, harass, nag, harry, badger, goad, pester, browbeat, bully, bludgeon, intimidate, dragoon, twist someone's arm; informal railroad, lean on; N. Amer. informal hustle.

prestige noun *he experienced a tremendous increase in prestige following his victory:* **status**, standing, stature, prestigiousness, reputation, repute, regard, fame, note, renown, honour, esteem, celebrity, importance, prominence, influence, eminence; kudos, cachet; informal clout.

prestigious adjective **1** *prestigious journals:* **reputable**, distinguished, respected, esteemed, eminent, august, highly regarded, well thought of, acclaimed, authoritative, celebrated, illustrious, leading, renowned. **2** *a prestigious job:* **impressive**, important, prominent, high-ranking, influential, powerful, glamorous; well paid, expensive; Brit. upmarket.
–OPPOSITES obscure, minor.

presumably adverb *presumably he'll get the job:* **I presume**, I expect, I assume, I take it, I suppose, I imagine, I dare say, I guess, in all probability, probably, in all likelihood, as likely as not, doubtless, undoubtedly, no doubt.

presume verb **1** *I presumed that it had once been an attic:* **assume**, suppose, dare say, imagine, take it, expect, believe, think, surmise, guess, judge, conjecture, speculate, postulate, presuppose. **2** *let me presume to give you some advice:* **venture**, dare, have the audacity/effrontery, be so bold as, take the liberty of.
■ **presume on** *he was wary of presuming on their friendship:* take (unfair) advantage of, exploit, take liberties with; count on, bank on, place reliance on.

presumption noun **1** *this presumption may be easily rebutted:* **assumption**, supposition, presupposition, belief, guess, judgement, surmise, conjecture, speculation, hypothesis, postulation, inference, deduction, conclusion. **2** *he apologized for his presumption:* **brazenness**, audacity, boldness, audaciousness,

temerity, arrogance, presumptuousness, forwardness; cockiness, insolence, impudence, bumptiousness, impertinence, effrontery, cheek, cheekiness; rudeness, impoliteness, disrespect, familiarity; informal nerve, brass neck, chutzpah; N. Amer. informal sass, sassiness.

presumptive adjective **1** *a presumptive diagnosis:* **conjectural**, speculative, tentative; theoretical, unproven, unconfirmed. **2** *the heir presumptive:* **probable**, likely, prospective, assumed, supposed, expected.

presumptuous adjective *it's rather presumptuous to judge my character on such short acquaintance:* **brazen**, overconfident, arrogant, bold, audacious, forward, familiar, impertinent, insolent, impudent, cocky; cheeky, rude, impolite, uncivil, bumptious; N. Amer. informal sassy.

presuppose verb **1** *this presupposes the existence of a policy-making group:* **require**, necessitate, imply, entail, mean, involve, assume. **2** *I had presupposed that theme parks make people happy:* **presume**, assume, take it for granted, take it as read, suppose, surmise, think, accept, consider.

presupposition noun **presumption**, assumption, preconception, supposition, hypothesis, surmise, thesis, theory, premise, belief, postulation.

pretence noun **1** *cease this pretence:* **make-believe**, putting on an act, acting, dissembling, shamming, faking, feigning, simulation, dissimulation, play-acting, posturing; deception, deceit, deceitfulness, fraud, fraudulence, duplicity, subterfuge, trickery, dishonesty, hypocrisy, falsity, lying, mendacity; informal kidology. **2** *he made a pretence of being unconcerned:* **(false) show**, semblance, affectation, (false) appearance, outward appearance, impression, (false) front, guise, facade, display. **3** *she had dropped any pretence to faith:* **claim**, profession. **4** *he was absolutely without pretence:* **pretentiousness**, display, ostentation, affectation, showiness, posturing, humbug.
–OPPOSITES honesty.

pretend verb **1** *they just pretend to listen:* **make as if**, profess, affect; dissimulate, dissemble, put it on, put on a false front, go through the motions, sham, fake it. **2** *I'll pretend to be the dragon:* **put on an act**, make believe, play at, act, play-act, impersonate. **3** *it was useless to pretend innocence:* **feign**, sham, fake, simulate, put on, counterfeit, affect. **4** *he cannot pretend to sophistication:* **claim**, lay claim to, purport to have, profess to have.

pretended adjective *her eyes widened in pretended astonishment:* **fake**, faked, affected, assumed, professed, spurious, mock, imitation, simulated, make-believe, pseudo, sham, false, bogus; informal pretend, phoney.

pretender noun *a pretender to the throne:* **claimant**, aspirant.

pretension noun 1 *the author has no pretension to exhaustive coverage:* **aspiration**, claim, assertion, pretence, profession. 2 *she spoke without pretension:* **pretentiousness**, affectation, affectedness, ostentation, ostentatiousness, artificiality, airs, posing, posturing, show, flashiness; pomposity, pompousness, grandiosity, grandiloquence, magniloquence.

pretentious adjective *Clytemnestra is a pretentious name for a dog:* **affected**, ostentatious, showy, overambitious, pompous, artificial, inflated, overblown, high-sounding, flowery, grandiose, elaborate, extravagant, flamboyant, ornate, grandiloquent, magniloquent; N. Amer. sophomoric; informal flashy, highfalutin, la-di-da, pseudo; Brit. informal poncey.

pretext noun *he called at her home on the pretext of enquiring after Mr Bradshaw:* **(false) excuse**, ostensible reason, alleged reason; guise, ploy, pretence, ruse.

prettify verb *the landscape had been tamed and weakened by man's attempts to prettify nature:* **beautify**, make attractive, make pretty, titivate, adorn, ornament, decorate, smarten (up); informal doll up, do up, give something a facelift; Brit. informal tart up.

pretty adjective *a pretty child:* **attractive**, lovely, good-looking, nice-looking, personable, fetching, prepossessing, appealing, charming, delightful, cute, as pretty as a picture; Scottish & N. English bonny; informal easy on the eye.
– OPPOSITES plain, ugly.
adverb *a pretty large sum:* **quite**, rather, somewhat, fairly, reasonably, comparatively, relatively.
verb *she's prettying herself:* **beautify**, make attractive, make pretty, prettify, titivate, adorn, ornament, smarten; informal do oneself up; Brit. informal tart.oneself up.

prevail verb 1 *common sense will prevail:* **win (out/through)**, triumph, be victorious, carry the day, come out on top, succeed, prove superior, conquer, overcome; rule, reign. 2 *the conditions that prevailed in the 1950s:* **exist**, be in existence, be present, be the case, occur, be prevalent, be current, be the order of the day, be customary, be common, be widespread, be in force/effect.
■ **prevail on/upon** *Jane had prevailed on Dorothy to come:* **persuade**, induce, talk someone into, coax, convince, make, get, press someone into, argue someone into, urge, pressure someone into, pressurize someone into, coerce; informal sweet-talk, soft-soap.

prevailing adjective *a research project examined prevailing attitudes in the classroom:* **current**, existing, prevalent, usual, common, general, widespread.

prevalence noun *the prevalence of smoking*

among teenagers: **commonness**, currency, widespread presence, generality, popularity, pervasiveness, universality, extensiveness; rampancy, rifeness.

prevalent adjective **widespread**, prevailing, frequent, usual, common, current, popular, general, universal; endemic, rampant, rife.
– OPPOSITES rare.

prevaricate verb *he seemed to prevaricate when journalists asked pointed questions about his involvement:* **be evasive**, beat about the bush, hedge, fence, shilly-shally, dodge (the issue), sidestep (the issue), equivocate; temporize, stall (for time); Brit. hum and haw.

prevent verb *action must be taken to prevent further accidents:* **stop**, put a stop to, avert, nip in the bud, fend off, stave off, ward off; hinder, impede, hamper, obstruct, baulk, foil, thwart, forestall, counteract, inhibit, curb, restrain, preclude, pre-empt, save, help; disallow, prohibit, forbid, proscribe, exclude, debar, bar.
– OPPOSITES allow.

preventive adjective 1 *preventive maintenance:* **pre-emptive**, deterrent, precautionary, protective. 2 *preventive medicine:* **prophylactic**, disease-preventing.
noun 1 *a preventive against crime:* **precautionary measure**, deterrent, safeguard, security, protection, defence. 2 *disease preventives:* **prophylactic (device)**, prophylactic medicine, preventive drug.

previous adjective 1 *the previous five years | her previous boyfriend:* **foregoing**, preceding, antecedent; old, earlier, prior, former, ex-, past, last, sometime, one-time, erstwhile. 2 (informal) *I was a bit previous:* **overhasty**, hasty, premature, precipitate, impetuous; informal ahead of oneself.
– OPPOSITES next.
■ **previous to** before, prior to, until, (leading) up to, earlier than, preceding.

previously adverb *museums and art galleries which had previously been open to the public:* **formerly**, earlier (on), before, hitherto, once, at one time, in the past, in days/times gone by, in bygone days, in times past, in former times; in advance, already, beforehand.

prey noun 1 *the lions killed their prey:* **quarry**, kill. 2 *she was easy prey:* **victim**, target, dupe, gull; informal sucker, soft touch, pushover; N. Amer. informal patsy, sap, schlemiel; Austral./NZ informal dill.
– OPPOSITES predator.
■ **prey on** 1 *hoverfly larvae prey on aphids:* **hunt**, catch; eat, feed on, live on/off. 2 *they prey on the elderly:* **exploit**, victimize, pick on, take advantage of; trick, swindle, cheat, hoodwink, fleece; informal con. 3 *the problem preyed on his mind:* **oppress**, weigh (heavily) on, lie heavy on, gnaw at; trouble, worry, beset, disturb, distress, haunt, nag, torment, plague, obsess.

price noun 1 *the purchase price:* **cost**, asking

p

price, charge, fee, fare, levy, amount, sum; outlay, expense, expenditure; valuation, quotation, estimate; informal, humorous damage. **2** *spinsterhood was the price of her career:* **consequence**, result, cost, penalty, sacrifice; downside, snag, drawback, disadvantage, minus. **3** *he had a price on his head:* **reward**, bounty, premium.
verb *a ticket is priced at £5.00:* **fix/set the price of**, cost, value, rate; estimate.
■ **at a price** at a high price/cost, at considerable cost, for a great deal of money. ■ **at any price** whatever the price, at whatever cost, no matter (what) the cost.
■ **beyond price**. See PRICELESS sense 1.

priceless adjective **1** *priceless works of art:* **of incalculable value/worth**, of immeasurable value/worth, invaluable, beyond price; irreplaceable, incomparable, unparalleled. **2** (informal) *that's priceless!* See HILARIOUS sense 1.
– OPPOSITES worthless, cheap.

pricey adjective (informal). See EXPENSIVE.

prick verb **1** *prick the potatoes with a fork:* **pierce**, puncture, make/put a hole in, stab, perforate, nick, jab. **2** *his eyes began to prick:* **sting**, smart, burn, prickle. **3** *his conscience pricked him:* **trouble**, worry, distress, perturb, disturb, cause someone anguish, afflict, torment, plague, prey on, gnaw at. **4** *ambition pricked him on to greater effort:* **goad**, prod, incite, provoke, urge, spur, stimulate, encourage, inspire, motivate, push, propel, impel. **5** *the horse pricked up its ears:* **raise**, erect.
noun **1** *a prick in the leg:* **jab**, sting, pinprick, stab. **2** *the prick of tears behind her eyelids:* **sting**, stinging, smart, smarting, burning. **3** *the prick of conscience:* **pang**, twinge, stab.
■ **prick up one's ears** listen carefully, pay attention, become attentive, begin to take notice, attend; informal be all ears.

prickle noun **1** *the cactus is covered with prickles:* **thorn**, needle, barb, spike, point, spine. **2** *Willie felt a cold prickle of fear:* **tingle**, tingling (sensation), prickling sensation, chill, thrill.
verb *its tiny spikes prickled his skin:* **sting**, prick.

prickly adjective **1** *a prickly hedgehog:* **spiky**, spiked, thorny, barbed, spiny; briary, brambly; rough, scratchy. **2** *my skin feels prickly:* **tingly**, tingling, prickling. **3** *a prickly character.* See IRRITABLE. **4** *the prickly question of the refugees:* **problematic**, awkward, ticklish, tricky, delicate, sensitive, difficult, knotty, thorny, irksome, tough, troublesome, bothersome, vexatious.

pride noun **1** *their triumphs were a source of pride:* **self-esteem**, dignity, honour, self-respect, self-worth, self-regard, pride in oneself. **2** *take pride in a good job well done:* **pleasure**, joy, delight, gratification, fulfilment, satisfaction, sense of achievement. **3** *he refused her offer out of pride:* **arrogance**, vanity, self-

importance, hubris, conceit, conceitedness, self-love, self-adulation, self-admiration, narcissism, egotism, superciliousness, haughtiness, snobbery, snobbishness; informal big-headedness. **4** *the bull is the pride of the herd:* **best**, finest, top, cream, pick, choice, prize, glory, the jewel in the crown. **5** *the vegetable garden was the pride of the gardener:* **source of satisfaction**, pride and joy, treasured possession, joy, delight.
– OPPOSITES shame, humility.
■ **pride oneself on** *she prided herself on her sincerity:* be proud of, be proud of oneself for, take pride in, take satisfaction in, congratulate oneself on, pat oneself on the back for.

priest noun **clergyman, clergywoman**, minister (of religion), cleric, ecclesiastic, pastor, vicar, rector, parson, churchman, churchwoman, man/woman of the cloth, man/woman of God, father, curate, chaplain, curé, evangelist, preacher; Scottish kirkman; N. Amer. dominie; informal reverend, padre, Holy Joe, sky pilot; Austral. informal josser.

priestly adjective *performing priestly duties:* **clerical**, pastoral, priestlike, ecclesiastical, sacerdotal, hieratic, rectorial.

prig noun *she was religious but not a prig:* **prude**, puritan, killjoy, Mrs Grundy; informal goody-goody, holy Joe; N. Amer. informal bluenose.

priggish adjective *a priggish old woman:* **self-righteous**, holier-than-thou, sanctimonious, moralistic, prudish, puritanical, prim, strait-laced, stuffy, prissy, narrow-minded; informal goody-goody, starchy.
– OPPOSITES broad-minded.

prim adjective *a prim, fastidious woman:* **demure**, (prim and) proper, formal, stuffy, strait-laced, prudish; prissy, mimsy, priggish, puritanical; Brit. po-faced; informal starchy.

primacy noun *the primacy of industry over agriculture:* **greater importance**, priority, precedence, pre-eminence, superiority, supremacy, ascendancy, dominance, dominion, leadership.

prima donna noun **1** *Angelica's solo is provided to give the prima donna another short aria:* **leading soprano**, leading lady, diva, (opera) star, principal singer. **2** *you were a decent sort, a team player—very different from these prima donna types.* See TEMPERAMENTAL.

primal adjective **1** *primal masculine instincts:* **basic**, fundamental, essential, elemental, vital, central, intrinsic, inherent. **2** *the primal source of living things:* **original**, initial, earliest, first, primitive, primeval.

primarily adverb **1** *the bishop was primarily a leader of the local community:* **first (and foremost)**, firstly, essentially, in essence, fundamentally, principally, predominantly, basically. **2** *such work is undertaken primarily for large institutions:* **mostly**, for the most part, chiefly, mainly, in the main, on the whole, largely, to a large extent, especially, generally, usually, typically, commonly, as a rule.

primary adjective **1** *our primary role:* **main**, chief, key, prime, central, principal, foremost, first, most important, predominant, paramount; informal number-one. **2** *the primary cause:* **original**, earliest, initial, first; essential, fundamental, basic.
– OPPOSITES secondary.

prime[1] adjective **1** *his prime reason for leaving:* **main**, chief, key, prime, primary, central, principal, foremost, first, most important, paramount, major; informal number-one. **2** *the prime cause of flooding:* **fundamental**, basic, essential, primary, central. **3** *prime agricultural land:* **top-quality**, top, best, first-class, first-rate, grade A, superior, supreme, choice, select, finest; excellent, superb, fine; informal tip-top, A1, top-notch. **4** *a prime example:* **archetypal**, prototypical, typical, classic, excellent, characteristic, quintessential.
– OPPOSITES secondary, inferior.
noun *he is in his prime:* **heyday**, best days/years, prime of one's life; youth, salad days; peak, pinnacle, high point/spot, zenith.

prime[2] verb **1** *he primed the gun:* **prepare**, load, get ready. **2** *Lucy had primed him carefully:* **brief**, fill in, prepare, put in the picture, inform, advise, instruct, coach, drill; informal clue in, give someone the low-down.

prime minister noun **premier**, first minister, head of the government.

primeval adjective **1** *primeval forest:* **ancient**, earliest, first, prehistoric, antediluvian, primordial; pristine, original, virgin. **2** *primeval fears:* **instinctive**, primitive, basic, primal, primordial, intuitive, inborn, innate, inherent.

primitive adjective **1** *primitive times:* **ancient**, earliest, first, prehistoric, antediluvian, primordial, primeval, primal. **2** *primitive peoples:* **uncivilized**, barbarian, barbaric, barbarous, savage, ignorant, uncultivated. **3** *primitive tools:* **crude**, simple, rough (and ready), basic, rudimentary, unrefined, unsophisticated, rude, makeshift. **4** *primitive art:* **simple**, natural, unsophisticated, unaffected, undeveloped, unpretentious.
– OPPOSITES sophisticated, civilized.

primordial adjective **1** *the primordial oceans:* **ancient**, earliest, first, prehistoric, antediluvian, primeval. **2** *their primordial desires:* **instinctive**, primitive, basic, primal, primeval, intuitive, inborn, innate, inherent.

primp verb *Fran primped her hair:* **groom**, tidy, arrange, brush, comb; smarten (up), spruce up; informal titivate, doll up; Brit. informal tart up; N. Amer. informal gussy up.

prince noun **ruler**, sovereign, monarch, king, princeling; crown prince; emir, sheikh, sultan, maharaja, raja.

princely adjective **1** *princely buildings.* See SPLENDID sense 1. **2** *a princely sum.* See HANDSOME sense 3.

principal adjective *the principal cause of poor air quality:* **main**, chief, primary, leading, foremost, first, most important, predominant, dominant, (most) prominent; key, crucial, vital, essential, basic, prime, central, focal; premier, paramount, major, overriding, cardinal, pre-eminent, uppermost, highest, top, topmost; informal number-one.
– OPPOSITES minor.
noun **1** *the principal of the firm:* **chief**, chief executive (officer), CEO, chairman, chairwoman, managing director, MD, president, director, manager, head; informal boss; Brit. informal gaffer, governor. **2** *the school's principal:* **head (teacher)**, headmaster, headmistress; dean, rector, chancellor, vice-chancellor, president, provost; N. Amer. informal prexy. **3** *a principal in a soap opera:* **leading actor/actress**, leading player/performer, leading role, lead, star. **4** *repayment of the principal:* **capital (sum)**, debt, loan.

principally adverb *the decline is principally due to overfishing:* **mainly**, mostly, chiefly, for the most part, in the main, on the whole, largely, to a large extent, predominantly, basically, primarily.

principle noun **1** *elementary principles:* **truth**, proposition, concept, idea, theory, assumption, fundamental, essential. **2** *the principle of laissez-faire:* **doctrine**, belief, creed, credo, (golden) rule, criterion, tenet, code, ethic, dictum, canon, law. **3** *a woman of principle | sticking to one's principles:* **morals**, morality, (code of) ethics, beliefs, ideals, standards; integrity, uprightness, righteousness, virtue, probity, (sense of) honour, decency, conscience, scruples.
■ **in principle 1** *there is no reason, in principle, why we couldn't work together:* **in theory**, theoretically, on paper. **2** *he has accepted the idea in principle:* **in general**, in essence, on the whole, in the main.

principled adjective *she took a principled feminist stance:* **moral**, ethical, virtuous, righteous, upright, upstanding, high-minded, honourable, honest, incorruptible.

print verb **1** *four newspapers are printed in the town:* **set in print**, send to press, run off, reprint. **2** *patterns were printed on the cloth:* **imprint**, impress, stamp, mark. **3** *they printed 30,000 copies:* **publish**, issue, release, circulate. **4** *the incident is printed on her memory:* **register**, record, impress, imprint, engrave, etch, stamp, mark.
noun **1** *small print:* **type**, printing, letters, lettering, characters, type size, typeface, font. **2** *prints of his left hand:* **impression**, fingerprint, footprint. **3** *sporting prints:* **picture**, design, engraving, etching, lithograph, linocut, woodcut. **4** *prints and negatives:* **photograph**, photo, snap,

p

snapshot, picture, still; Brit. enprint.
5 *soft floral prints*: **printed cloth/fabric**, patterned cloth/fabric, chintz.
■ **in print** published, printed, available in bookshops.
■ **out of print** no longer available, unavailable, unobtainable.

prior adjective *by prior arrangement*: **earlier**, previous, preceding, foregoing, antecedent, advance.
– OPPOSITES subsequent.
■ **prior to** before, until, till, up to, previous to, earlier than, preceding, leading up to.

priority noun **1** *safety is our priority*: **prime concern**, most important consideration, primary issue. **2** *giving priority to primary education*: **precedence**, greater importance, preference, pre-eminence, predominance, primacy, first place. **3** *traffic on the roundabout has priority*: **right of way**.

priory noun *religious house*, abbey, cloister; monastery, friary; convent, nunnery.

prise verb **1** *I prised the lid off*: **lever**, jemmy; wrench, wrest, twist; N. Amer. pry, jimmy. **2** *he had to prise information from them*: **wring**, wrest, worm out, winkle out, screw, squeeze, extract.

prison noun **jail**, lock-up, penal institution, detention centre; Brit. young offender institution; N. Amer. jailhouse, penitentiary, correctional facility; informal clink, slammer, stir, jug, brig; Brit. informal nick; N. Amer. informal can, pen, cooler, pokey, slam; (**be in prison**) informal be inside, be behind bars, do time; Brit. informal do bird, do porridge.

prisoner noun **1** *a prisoner serving a life sentence*: **convict**, detainee, inmate; informal jailbird, con; Brit. informal (old) lag; N. Amer. informal yardbird. **2** *the army took many prisoners*: **prisoner of war**, POW, internee, captive.

prissy adjective *he hated it when she swore, but he didn't like to sound prissy*: **prudish**, priggish, prim, prim and proper, strait-laced, Victorian, old-maidish, schoolmistressy, schoolmarmish; Brit. po-faced; informal starchy.
– OPPOSITES broad-minded.

pristine adjective *a pristine white handkerchief*: **immaculate**, perfect, in mint condition, as new, unspoilt, spotless, flawless, clean, fresh, new, virgin, pure, unused.
– OPPOSITES dirty, spoilt.

privacy noun *a walled garden ensures complete privacy*: **seclusion**, solitude, isolation, freedom from disturbance, freedom from interference.

private adjective **1** *his private plane*: **personal**, own, individual, special, exclusive, privately owned. **2** *private talks*: **confidential**, secret, classified, unofficial, off the record, closet, in camera; backstage, privileged, one-on-one, tête-à-tête. **3** *private thoughts*: **intimate**, personal, secret; innermost, undisclosed, unspoken,

unvoiced. **4** *a very private man*: **reserved**, introvert, introverted, self-contained, reticent, discreet, uncommunicative, unforthcoming, retiring, unsociable, withdrawn, solitary, reclusive, hermitic. **5** *they found a private place in which to talk*: **secluded**, solitary, undisturbed, concealed, hidden, remote, isolated, out of the way, sequestered. **6** *the Queen attended in a private capacity*: **unofficial**, personal. **7** *private industry*: **independent**, non-state; privatized, denationalized; commercial, private-enterprise.
– OPPOSITES public, open, extrovert, busy, crowded, official, state, nationalized.
noun *a private in the army*: **private soldier**, common soldier; trooper; Brit. sapper, gunner, ranker; US GI; Brit. informal Tommy, squaddie.
■ **in private** in secret, secretly, privately, behind closed doors, in camera, à huis clos; in confidence, confidentially, between ourselves, entre nous, off the record.

private detective noun **private investigator**; Brit. enquiry agent; informal private eye, PI, sleuth, snoop; N. Amer. informal shamus, gumshoe.

privately adverb **1** *we must talk privately*: **in secret**, secretly, in private, behind closed doors, in camera, à huis clos; in confidence, confidentially, between ourselves, entre nous, off the record. **2** *privately, I am glad*: **secretly**, inwardly, deep down, personally, unofficially. **3** *he lived very privately*: **out of the public eye**, out of public view, in seclusion, in solitude, alone.
– OPPOSITES publicly.

privation noun *years of rationing and privation*: **deprivation**, hardship, destitution, impoverishment, want, need, neediness, austerity.
– OPPOSITES plenty, luxury.

privilege noun **1** *senior pupils have certain privileges*: **advantage**, benefit; prerogative, entitlement, right; concession, freedom, liberty. **2** *it was a privilege to meet her*: **honour**, pleasure. **3** *parliamentary privilege*: **immunity**, exemption, dispensation.

privileged adjective **1** *a privileged background*: **wealthy**, rich, affluent, prosperous; **lucky**, fortunate, elite, favoured; (socially) advantaged. **2** *privileged information*: **confidential**, private, secret, restricted, classified, not for publication, off the record, inside; informal hush-hush. **3** *MPs are privileged*: **immune (from prosecution)**, protected, exempt, excepted.
– OPPOSITES underprivileged, disadvantaged, public, liable.

privy adjective *he was not privy to the discussions*: **in the know about**, acquainted with, in on, informed of, advised of, apprised of; informal genned up on, clued up on, wise to.
noun *he went out to the privy*. See **TOILET** sense 1.

prize noun **1** *an art prize*: **award**, reward,

premium, purse; trophy, medal; honour, accolade, crown, laurels, palm. **2** *the prizes of war:* **spoils**, booty, plunder, loot, pickings.
adjective **1** *a prize bull:* **champion**, award-winning, prize-winning, winning, top, best. **2** *a prize example:* **outstanding**, excellent, superlative, superb, supreme, very good, prime, fine, magnificent, marvellous, wonderful; informal great, terrific, tremendous, fantastic. **3** *a prize idiot:* **utter**, complete, total, absolute, real, perfect, positive, veritable; Brit. informal right, bloody; Austral./NZ informal fair.
– OPPOSITES second-rate.
verb *many collectors prize his work:* **value**, set great store by, rate highly, attach great importance to, esteem, hold in high regard, think highly of, treasure, cherish.

prized adjective *his prized collection of soccer memorabilia:* **treasured**, precious, cherished, much loved, beloved, valued, esteemed, highly regarded.

prizewinner noun **champion**, winner, gold medallist, victor; informal champ, number one.

probability noun **1** *the probability of winning:* **likelihood**, prospect, expectation, chance, chances, odds. **2** *relegation is a distinct probability:* **probable event**, prospect, possibility, good/fair/reasonable bet.

probable adjective *it is probable that the economic situation will deteriorate further:* **likely**, most likely, odds-on, expected, anticipated, predictable, foreseeable, ten to one; informal on the cards, a good/fair/reasonable bet.
– OPPOSITES unlikely.

probably adverb *I knew I would probably never see her again:* **in all likelihood**, in all probability, as like(ly) as not, (very/most) likely, ten to one, the chances are, doubtless, no doubt.

probation noun *clerks were only paid a proper salary after the first three years of probation:* **trial period**, test period, experimental period, trial.

probe noun *a probe into an air crash:* **investigation**, enquiry, examination, inquest, exploration, study, analysis.
verb **1** *hands probed his body:* **examine**, feel, feel around, explore, prod, poke, check. **2** *police probed the tragedy:* **investigate**, enquire into, look into, study, examine, scrutinize, go into, carry out an inquest into.

probity noun *the chancellor exuded confidence and fiscal probity:* **integrity**, honesty, uprightness, decency, morality, rectitude, goodness, virtue, right-mindedness, trustworthiness, truthfulness, honour.
– OPPOSITES untrustworthiness.

problem noun **1** *they ran into a problem:* **difficulty**, trouble, worry, complication, difficult situation; snag, hitch, drawback, stumbling block, obstacle, hurdle, hiccup,

setback, catch; predicament, plight; misfortune, mishap, misadventure; informal dilemma, headache, prob, facer. **2** *I don't want to be a problem:* **nuisance**, bother, pest, irritant, thorn in one's side/flesh, vexation; informal drag, pain, pain in the neck. **3** *arithmetical problems:* **puzzle**, question, poser, enigma, riddle, conundrum; informal teaser, brain-teaser.
adjective *a problem child:* **troublesome**, difficult, unmanageable, unruly, disobedient, uncontrollable, recalcitrant, delinquent.
– OPPOSITES well behaved, manageable.

problematic adjective *the piece is among the most problematic of all his major works:* **difficult**, hard, taxing, troublesome, tricky, awkward, controversial, ticklish, complicated, complex, knotty, thorny, prickly, vexed; informal sticky; Brit. informal dodgy.
– OPPOSITES easy, simple, straightforward.

procedure noun *the council agreed a procedure for dealing with future breaches of the law:* **course of action**, line of action, policy, series of steps, method, system, strategy, way, approach, formula, mechanism, methodology, MO (modus operandi), technique; routine, drill, practice.

proceed verb **1** *she was uncertain how to proceed:* **begin**, make a start, get going, move, set something in motion; **take action**, act, go on, go ahead, make progress, make headway. **2** *he proceeded down the road:* **go**, make one's way, advance, move, progress, carry on, press on, push on. **3** *we should proceed with the talks:* **go ahead**, carry on, go on, continue, keep on, get on, get ahead; pursue, prosecute. **4** *there is not enough evidence to proceed against him:* **take someone to court**, start/take proceedings against, start an action against, sue. **5** *all power proceeds from God:* **originate**, spring, stem, come, derive, arise, issue, flow, emanate.
– OPPOSITES stop.

proceedings plural noun **1** *the evening's proceedings:* **events**, activities, happenings, goings-on, doings. **2** *the proceedings of the meeting:* **report**, transactions, minutes, account, record(s); annals, archives. **3** *legal proceedings:* **legal action**, court/judicial proceedings, litigation; lawsuit, case, prosecution.

proceeds plural noun *all proceeds from the event will go to Animal Welfare:* **profits**, earnings, receipts, returns, takings, income, revenue; N. Amer. take.

process noun **1** *investigation is a long process:* **procedure**, operation, action, activity, exercise, affair, business, job, task, undertaking. **2** *a new canning process:* **method**, system, technique, means, practice, way, approach, methodology.
verb *applications are processed rapidly:* **deal with**, attend to, see to, sort out, handle, take

p

care of, action.
■ **in the process of** in the middle of, in the course of, in the midst of, in the throes of, busy with, occupied in/with, taken up with/by, involved in.

procession noun **1** *a procession through the town:* **parade**, march, march past, cavalcade, motorcade, cortège; column, file, train. **2** *a procession of dance routines:* **series**, succession, stream, string, sequence, run.

proclaim verb **1** *messengers proclaimed the good news:* **declare**, announce, pronounce, state, make known, give out, advertise, publish, broadcast, promulgate, trumpet, blazon. **2** *the men proclaimed their innocence:* **assert**, declare, profess, maintain, protest. **3** *he proclaimed himself president.* **declare**, pronounce, announce.

proclamation noun *the shooting resulted in the proclamation of a state of emergency:* **declaration**, announcement, pronouncement, statement, notification, publication, broadcast, promulgation, blazoning; assertion, profession, protestation; **decree**, order, edict, ruling.

proclivity noun *his sexual proclivities are none of your business:* **inclination**, tendency, leaning, disposition, proneness, propensity, bent, bias, penchant, predisposition; predilection, partiality, liking, preference, taste, fondness, weakness.

procrastinate verb *fear of failure is often the reason why people procrastinate:* **delay**, put off doing something, postpone action, defer action, be dilatory, use delaying tactics, stall, temporize, drag one's feet/heels, take one's time, play for time, play a waiting game.

procreate verb *the biological imperative to procreate:* **produce offspring**, reproduce, multiply, propagate, breed.

procure verb **1** *he managed to procure a coat:* **obtain**, acquire, get, find, come by, secure, pick up; buy, purchase; informal get hold of, get one's hands on. **2** *the police found that he was procuring:* **pimp**; Brit. informal ponce.

prod verb **1** *Cassie prodded him in the chest:* **poke**, jab, dig, elbow, butt, stab. **2** *they hoped to prod the government into action:* **spur**, stimulate, stir, rouse, prompt, drive, galvanize; persuade, urge, chivvy; incite, goad, egg on, provoke.
noun **1** *a prod in the ribs:* **poke**, jab, dig, elbow, butt, thrust. **2** *they need a prod to get them to act:* **stimulus**, push, prompt, reminder, spur; incitement, goad.

prodigal adjective **1** *prodigal habits die hard:* **wasteful**, extravagant, spendthrift, profligate, improvident, imprudent. **2** *a composer who is prodigal with his talents:* **generous**, lavish, liberal, unstinting, unsparing.
– OPPOSITES thrifty, mean.

prodigious adjective *his prodigious talent:* **enormous**, huge, colossal, immense, vast, great, massive, gigantic, mammoth, tremendous, inordinate, monumental; amazing, astonishing, astounding, staggering, stunning, remarkable, phenomenal, terrific, miraculous, impressive, striking, startling, sensational, spectacular, extraordinary, exceptional, breathtaking, incredible; informal humongous, stupendous, fantastic, fabulous, mega, awesome; Brit. informal ginormous.
– OPPOSITES small, unexceptional.

prodigy noun **1** *a seven-year-old prodigy:* **genius**, mastermind, virtuoso, wunderkind, wonder child; informal whizz-kid, whizz, wizard. **2** *Germany seemed a prodigy of industrial discipline:* **model**, classic example, paragon, paradigm, epitome, exemplar, archetype.

produce verb **1** *the company produces furniture:* **manufacture**, make, construct, build, fabricate, put together, assemble, turn out, create; mass-produce; informal churn out. **2** *the vineyards produce excellent wines:* **yield**, grow, give, supply, provide, furnish, bear, bring forth. **3** *she produced ten puppies:* **give birth to**, bear, deliver, bring forth, bring into the world. **4** *he produced five novels:* **create**, originate, fashion, turn out; compose, write, pen; paint. **5** *she produced an ID card:* **pull out**, extract, fish out; present, offer, proffer, show. **6** *no evidence was produced:* **present**, offer, provide, furnish, advance, put forward, bring forward, come up with. **7** *that will produce a reaction:* **give rise to**, bring about, cause, occasion, generate, engender, lead to, result in, effect, induce, set off; provoke, precipitate, breed, spark off, trigger. **8** *James produced the play:* **stage**, put on, mount, present.
noun *fresh produce:* **food**, foodstuff(s), products; harvest, crops, fruit, vegetables, greens; Brit. greengrocery.

producer noun **1** *a car producer:* **manufacturer**, maker, builder, constructor, fabricator. **2** *coffee producers:* **grower**, farmer. **3** *the producer of the show:* **impresario**, manager, administrator, promoter, regisseur.

product noun **1** *a household product:* **artefact**, commodity, manufactured article; creation, invention; (**products**) goods, wares, merchandise, produce. **2** *his skill is a product of experience:* **result**, consequence, outcome, effect, upshot, fruit, by-product, spin-off.

production noun **1** *the production of cars:* **manufacture**, making, construction, building, fabrication, assembly, creation; mass production. **2** *the production of literary works:* **creation**, origination, fashioning; composition, writing. **3** *agricultural production:* **output**, yield; productivity. **4** *admission only on production of a ticket:* **presentation**, proffering, showing. **5** *a theatre production:* **performance**, staging, presentation, show, piece, play.

productive adjective **1** *a productive artist:* **prolific**, inventive, creative; energetic. **2** *productive talks:* **useful**, constructive, profitable, fruitful, gainful, valuable, effective, worthwhile, helpful. **3** *productive land:* **fertile**, fruitful, rich, fecund.
– OPPOSITES sterile, barren.

productivity noun **1** *workers have boosted productivity:* **efficiency**, work rate; output, yield, production. **2** *the productivity of the soil:* **fruitfulness**, fertility, richness, fecundity.
– OPPOSITES sterility, barrenness.

profane adjective **1** *subjects both sacred and profane:* **secular**, lay, non-religious, temporal. **2** *a profane man:* **irreverent**, irreligious, ungodly, godless, unbelieving, impious, disrespectful, sacrilegious. **3** *profane language:* **obscene**, blasphemous, indecent, foul, vulgar, crude, filthy, dirty, smutty, coarse, rude, offensive, indecorous.
– OPPOSITES religious, sacred, reverent, decorous.
verb *invaders profaned our temples:* **desecrate**, violate, defile, treat sacrilegiously.

profanity noun **1** *he hissed a profanity | an outburst of profanity:* **oath**, swear word, expletive, curse, obscenity, four-letter word, dirty word; blasphemy, swearing, foul language, bad language, cursing; informal cuss, cuss word; formal imprecation. **2** *some traditional festivals were tainted with profanity:* **sacrilege**, blasphemy, irreligion, ungodliness, impiety, irreverence, disrespect.

profess verb **1** *he professed his love:* **declare**, announce, proclaim, assert, state, affirm, avow, maintain, protest. **2** *she professed to loathe publicity:* **claim**, pretend, purport, affect; make out; informal let on. **3** *the Emperor professed Christianity:* **affirm one's faith in**, affirm one's allegiance to, avow, confess.

professed adjective **1** *his professed ambition:* **claimed**, supposed, ostensible, self-styled, apparent, pretended, purported. **2** *a professed Christian:* **declared**, self-acknowledged, self-confessed, confessed, sworn, avowed, confirmed.

profession noun **1** *his chosen profession of teaching:* **career**, occupation, calling, vocation, métier, line (of work), walk of life, job, business, trade, craft; informal racket. **2** *a profession of allegiance:* **declaration**, affirmation, statement, announcement, proclamation, assertion, avowal, vow, claim, protestation.

professional adjective **1** *people in professional occupations:* **white-collar**, non-manual. **2** *a professional cricketer:* **paid**, salaried. **3** *a thoroughly professional performance:* **expert**, accomplished, skilful, masterly, masterful, fine, polished, skilled, proficient, competent, able, experienced, practised, trained, seasoned, businesslike, deft; informal ace, crack, top-notch. **4** *not a*

professional way to behave: **appropriate**, fitting, proper, honourable, ethical, correct, comme il faut.
– OPPOSITES manual, amateur, amateurish, inappropriate, unethical.
noun **1** *affluent young professionals:* **white-collar worker**, office worker. **2** *his first season as a professional:* **paid player**, salaried player, professional player; informal pro. **3** *she was a real professional on stage:* **expert**, virtuoso, old hand, master, maestro, past master; informal pro, ace, wizard, whizz, hotshot; Brit. informal dab hand; N. Amer. informal maven, crackerjack.
– OPPOSITES manual worker, amateur.

professor noun *a professor of French at Oxford University:* **holder of a chair**, head of faculty, head of department; N. Amer. full professor; informal prof.

proffer verb *Coleman proffered his resignation:* **offer**, tender, submit, extend, volunteer, suggest, propose, put forward; hold out.
– OPPOSITES refuse, withdraw.

proficiency noun **skill**, expertise, experience, accomplishment, competence, mastery, prowess, professionalism, deftness, adroitness, dexterity, finesse, ability, facility; informal know-how.
– OPPOSITES incompetence.

proficient adjective *a proficient horsewoman:* **skilled**, skilful, expert, experienced, accomplished, competent, masterly, adept, adroit, deft, dexterous, able, professional, consummate, complete, master; informal crack, ace, mean.
– OPPOSITES incompetent.

profile noun **1** *his handsome profile:* **side view**, outline, silhouette, contour, shape, form, figure, lines. **2** *she wrote a profile of the organization:* **description**, account, study, portrait, portrayal, depiction, rundown, sketch, outline.
verb *he was profiled in the Irish Times:* **describe**, write about, give an account of, portray, depict, sketch, outline.
■ **keep a low profile** lie low, keep quiet, keep out of the public eye, avoid publicity, keep out of sight.

profit noun **1** *the firm made a profit:* **(financial) gain**, return(s), yield, proceeds, earnings, winnings, surplus, excess; informal pay dirt, bottom line; Brit. informal bunce. **2** *there was little profit in going on:* **advantage**, benefit, value, use, good, avail; informal mileage.
– OPPOSITES loss, disadvantage.
verb **1** *the company will not profit from the disposal:* **make money**, make a profit; informal rake it in, clean up, make a packet, make a killing, make a bundle; N. Amer. informal make big bucks, make a fast/quick buck. **2** *how will that profit us?:* **benefit**, be beneficial to, be of benefit to, be advantageous to, be of advantage to, be of use to, be of value to, do

someone good, help, be of service to, serve, assist, aid.
– OPPOSITES lose, disadvantage.
■ **profit by/from** *loopholes in the law allowed landlords to profit from the situation:* benefit from, take advantage of, derive benefit from, capitalize on, make the most of, turn to one's advantage, put to good use, do well out of, exploit, gain from; informal cash in on.

profitable adjective **1** *a profitable company:* **moneymaking**, profit-making, commercial, successful, money-spinning, solvent, in the black, gainful, remunerative, financially rewarding, paying, lucrative, bankable. **2** *profitable study:* **beneficial**, useful, advantageous, valuable, productive, worthwhile; rewarding, fruitful, illuminating, informative, well spent.
– OPPOSITES loss-making, fruitless, useless.

profiteer verb *a shopkeeper was charged with profiteering:* **overcharge**, racketeer; cheat someone, fleece someone; informal rip someone off, rob someone.
noun *he was a war profiteer:* **racketeer**, exploiter, black marketeer; informal bloodsucker.

profligate adjective **1** *profligate local authorities:* **wasteful**, extravagant, spendthrift, improvident, prodigal. **2** *a profligate lifestyle:* **dissolute**, degenerate, dissipated, debauched, corrupt, depraved; **promiscuous**, loose, wanton, licentious, libertine, decadent, abandoned, fast; **sybaritic**, voluptuary.
– OPPOSITES thrifty, frugal, moral, upright.
noun *he was an out-and-out profligate:* **libertine**, debauchee, degenerate, dissolute, roué, rake, loose-liver; sybarite, voluptuary.

profound adjective **1** *profound relief:* **heartfelt**, intense, keen, great, extreme, acute, severe, sincere, earnest, deep, deep-seated, overpowering, overwhelming, fervent, ardent. **2** *profound silence:* **complete**, utter, total, absolute. **3** *a profound change:* **far-reaching**, radical, extensive, sweeping, exhaustive, thoroughgoing. **4** *a profound analysis:* **wise**, learned, clever, intelligent, scholarly, sage, erudite, discerning, penetrating, perceptive, astute, thoughtful, insightful, percipient. **5** *profound truths:* **complex**, abstract, deep, weighty, difficult, abstruse, recondite, esoteric.
– OPPOSITES superficial, mild, slight, simple.

profuse adjective **1** *he offered profuse apologies:* **copious**, prolific, abundant, liberal, unstinting, fulsome, effusive, extravagant, lavish, gushing; informal over the top, gushy. **2** *among the profuse blooms in the garden:* **luxuriant**, plentiful, copious, abundant, lush, rich, exuberant, riotous, teeming, rank, rampant; informal jungly.
– OPPOSITES meagre, sparse.

profusion noun *a profusion of shrubs and flowers:* **abundance**, mass, host, cornucopia,

riot, plethora, superabundance; informal sea, wealth.

progenitor noun **1** *the progenitor of an illustrious family:* **ancestor**, forefather, forebear, parent, primogenitor. **2** *the progenitor of modern jazz:* **originator**, creator, founder, architect, inventor, pioneer.

progeny noun *physical characteristics are passed on from parents to their progeny:* **offspring**, young, babies, children, sons and daughters, family, brood; **descendants**, heirs, scions.

prognosis noun *it is very difficult to make an accurate prognosis:* **forecast**, prediction, prognostication, prophecy, divination, augury.

programme noun **1** *our programme for the day:* **schedule**, agenda, calendar, timetable; order of events, line-up. **2** *the government's reform programme:* **scheme**, plan of action, series of measures, strategy. **3** *a television programme:* **broadcast**, production, show, presentation, transmission, performance, telecast; informal prog. **4** *a programme of study:* **course**, syllabus, curriculum. **5** *my collection of theatre programmes:* **guide**, list of performers; N. Amer. playbill.
verb *they programmed the day well:* **arrange**, organize, schedule, plan, map out, timetable, line up; N. Amer. slate.

progress noun **1** *boulders made progress difficult:* **forward movement**, advance, going, progression, headway, passage. **2** *scientific progress seems to accelerate all the time:* **development**, advance, advancement, headway, step(s) forward; improvement, betterment, growth.
– OPPOSITES relapse.
verb **1** *they progressed slowly down the road:* **go**, make one's way, move, move forward, go forward, proceed, advance, go on, continue, make headway, work one's way. **2** *the school has progressed rapidly:* **develop**, make progress, advance, make headway, take steps forward, move on, get on, gain ground; improve, get better, come on, come along, make strides; thrive, prosper, blossom, flourish; informal be getting there.
– OPPOSITES relapse.
■ **in progress** under way, going on, ongoing, happening, occurring, taking place, proceeding, continuing; unfinished, on the stocks; N. Amer. in the works.

progression noun *progression to the next stage depends on the test results:* **progress**, advancement, movement, passage, march; development, evolution, growth.

progressive adjective **1** *there has been progressive deterioration:* **continuing**, continuous, increasing, growing, developing, ongoing, accelerating, escalating; gradual, step-by-step, cumulative. **2** *he has very progressive views:* **modern**, liberal, advanced, forward-

thinking, enlightened, enterprising, innovative, pioneering, dynamic, bold, avant-garde, reforming, reformist, radical; informal go-ahead.
– OPPOSITES conservative, reactionary.
noun *he is very much a progressive:* **innovator**, reformer, reformist, liberal, libertarian.

prohibit verb 1 *state law prohibits gambling:* **forbid**, ban, bar, interdict, proscribe, make illegal, embargo, outlaw, disallow, veto. 2 *a cash shortage prohibited the visit:* **prevent**, stop, rule out, preclude, make impossible.
– OPPOSITES allow.

prohibited adjective *smoking is prohibited in many public places:* **illegal**, illicit, against the law, verboten; Islam haram; informal not on, out, no go.
– OPPOSITES permitted.

prohibition noun 1 *the prohibition of cannabis:* **banning**, forbidding, prohibiting, barring, debarment, vetoing, proscription, interdiction, outlawing. 2 *a prohibition was imposed:* **ban**, bar, interdict, veto, embargo, injunction, moratorium.

prohibitive adjective *the cost of the project was simply prohibitive:* **excessively high**, sky-high, over-inflated; out of the question, beyond one's means; extortionate, unreasonable, exorbitant; informal steep, criminal.

project noun 1 *an engineering project:* **scheme**, plan, programme, enterprise, undertaking, venture; proposal, idea, concept. 2 *I've got a history project to hand in next week:* **assignment**, piece of work, piece of research, task.
verb 1 *profits are projected to rise:* **forecast**, predict, expect, estimate, calculate, reckon. 2 *his projected book:* **intend**, plan, propose, devise, design, outline. 3 *balconies projected over the lake:* **stick out**, jut (out), protrude, extend, stand out, bulge out, poke out, thrust out, cantilever. 4 *seeds are projected from the tree:* **propel**, discharge, launch, throw, cast, fling, hurl, shoot. 5 *the sun projected his shadow on the wall:* **cast**, throw, send, shed, shine. 6 *she tried to project a calm image:* **convey**, put across, put over, communicate, present, promote.

projectile noun **missile**.

projecting adjective *she had projecting teeth:* **sticking out**, protuberant, protruding, prominent, jutting, overhanging, proud, bulging; informal sticky-out.
– OPPOSITES sunken, flush.

projection noun 1 *a sales projection:* **forecast**, prediction, prognosis, expectation, estimate. 2 *tiny projections on the cliff face:* **protuberance**, protrusion, sticking-out bit, prominence, eminence, outcrop, outgrowth, jut, jag, snag; overhang, ledge, shelf; informal sticky-out bit.

proletarian adjective *a proletarian*

background: **working-class**, plebeian, cloth-cap, common.
– OPPOSITES aristocratic.
noun *disaffected proletarians:* **working-class person**, worker, plebeian, commoner, man/woman/person in the street; derogatory prole.
– OPPOSITES aristocrat.

proletariat noun **the workers**, working-class people, wage-earners, the labouring classes, the common people, the lower classes, the masses, the commonalty, the rank and file, the third estate, the plebeians; derogatory the hoi polloi, the plebs, the proles, the great unwashed, the mob, the rabble.
– OPPOSITES aristocracy.

proliferate verb *the debate continued, and articles in the media proliferated:* **increase rapidly**, grow rapidly, multiply, rocket, mushroom, snowball, burgeon, run riot.
– OPPOSITES decrease, dwindle.

prolific adjective 1 *a prolific crop of tomatoes:* **plentiful**, abundant, bountiful, profuse, copious, luxuriant, rich, lush; fruitful, fecund. 2 *Haydn was a prolific composer:* **productive**, creative, inventive, fertile.

prolix adjective *his prolix speeches could often be tiresome:* **long-winded**, verbose, wordy, pleonastic, discursive, rambling, long-drawn-out, overlong, lengthy, protracted, interminable; informal windy; Brit. informal waffly.

prologue noun *the prologue to his book:* **introduction**, foreword, preface, preamble, prelude; informal intro.
– OPPOSITES epilogue.

prolong verb *unwilling to prolong the conversation, Kate said her goodbyes:* **lengthen**, extend, draw out, drag out, protract, spin out, stretch out, string out, elongate; carry on, continue, keep up, perpetuate.
– OPPOSITES shorten.

promenade noun 1 *the tree-lined promenade:* **esplanade**, front, seafront, parade, walk, boulevard, avenue; N. Amer. boardwalk; Brit. informal prom. 2 *our nightly promenade:* **walk**, stroll, turn, amble, airing.
verb *we promenaded in the park:* **walk**, stroll, saunter, wander, amble, stretch one's legs, take a turn.

prominence noun 1 *his rise to prominence:* **fame**, celebrity, eminence, pre-eminence, importance, distinction, greatness, note, notability, prestige, stature, standing, position, rank. 2 *the press gave prominence to the reports:* **good coverage**, importance, precedence, weight, a high profile, top billing. 3 *a rocky prominence:* **hillock**, hill, hummock, mound; outcrop, crag, spur, rise; ridge, arête; peak, pinnacle; promontory, cliff, headland.

prominent adjective 1 *a prominent surgeon:* **important**, well known, leading, eminent, distinguished, notable, noteworthy, noted,

p

illustrious, celebrated, famous, renowned, acclaimed, famed, influential; N. Amer. major-league. **2** *prominent cheekbones:* **protuberant**, protruding, projecting, jutting (out), standing out, sticking out, proud, bulging, bulbous. **3** *a prominent feature of the landscape:* **conspicuous**, noticeable, easily seen, obvious, unmistakable, eye-catching, pronounced, salient, striking, dominant; obtrusive.
– OPPOSITES unimportant, unknown, inconspicuous.

promiscuity noun **licentiousness**, wantonness, immorality; informal sleeping around, sluttishness, whorishness.
– OPPOSITES chastity, virtue.

promiscuous adjective **1** *a promiscuous woman:* **licentious**, sexually indiscriminate, wanton, immoral, of easy virtue, fast; informal easy, swinging, sluttish, whorish; N. Amer. informal roundheeled; Brit. informal slaggy. **2** *promiscuous reading:* **indiscriminate**, undiscriminating, unselective, random, haphazard, irresponsible, unthinking, unconsidered.
– OPPOSITES chaste, virtuous, selective.

promise noun **1** *you broke your promise:* **word (of honour)**, assurance, pledge, vow, guarantee, oath, bond, undertaking, agreement, commitment, contract, covenant. **2** *he shows promise:* **potential**, ability, aptitude, capability, capacity. **3** *dawn came with a promise of fine weather:* **indication**, hint, suggestion, sign.
verb **1** *she promised to go:* **give one's word**, swear, pledge, vow, undertake, guarantee, contract, engage, give an assurance, commit oneself, bind oneself, swear/take an oath, covenant. **2** *the skies promised sunshine:* **indicate**, lead one to expect, point to, denote, signify, be a sign of, be evidence of, give hope of, bespeak, presage, augur, herald, bode, portend.

promising adjective **1** *he made a promising start:* **good**, encouraging, favourable, hopeful, full of promise, auspicious, propitious, bright, rosy, heartening, reassuring. **2** *a promising actor:* **with potential**, budding, up-and-coming, rising, coming, in the making.
– OPPOSITES unfavourable, hopeless.

promontory noun **headland**, point, cape, head, foreland, horn, bill, ness, naze, peninsula; Scottish mull.

promote verb **1** *she's been promoted at work:* **upgrade**, give promotion to, elevate, advance, move up. **2** *an organization promoting justice:* **encourage**, further, advance, assist, aid, help, contribute to, foster, nurture, develop, boost, stimulate, forward, work for. **3** *she is promoting her new film:* **advertise**, publicize, give publicity to, beat/bang the drum for, market, merchandise; informal push, plug, hype, puff, boost; N. Amer. informal ballyhoo, flack.
– OPPOSITES demote, obstruct, play down.

promoter noun *promoters of alternative tourism point to its contribution to economic growth:* **advocate**, champion, supporter, backer, proponent, protagonist, campaigner; N. Amer. booster.

promotion noun **1** *her promotion at work means a pay increase:* **upgrading**, preferment, elevation, advancement, step up (the ladder). **2** *the charity works for the promotion of justice:* **encouragement**, furtherance, furthering, advancement, assistance, aid, help, contribution to, fostering, boosting, stimulation; N. Amer. boosterism. **3** *the promotion of her new film:* **advertising**, publicizing, marketing; publicity, campaign, propaganda; informal hard sell, plug, hype, puff; N. Amer. informal ballyhoo.
– OPPOSITES demotion, obstruction, playing down.

prompt verb **1** *curiosity prompted him to look:* **induce**, make, move, motivate, lead, dispose, persuade, incline, encourage, stimulate, prod, impel, spur on, inspire. **2** *the statement prompted a hostile reaction:* **give rise to**, bring about, cause, occasion, result in, lead to, elicit, produce, bring on, engender, induce, precipitate, trigger, spark off, provoke. **3** *the actors needed prompting:* **remind**, cue, feed, help out; jog someone's memory.
– OPPOSITES deter.
adjective *a prompt reply:* **quick**, swift, rapid, speedy, fast, direct, immediate, instant, expeditious, early, punctual, in good time, on time, timely.
– OPPOSITES slow, late.
adverb *he set off at 3.30 prompt:* **exactly**, precisely, sharp, on the dot, dead, punctually, on the nail; informal bang on; N. Amer. informal on the button, on the nose.
noun *he stopped, and Julia supplied a prompt:* **reminder**, cue, feed.

promptly adverb **1** *William arrived promptly at 7.30:* **punctually**, on time; informal on the dot, bang on; Brit. informal spot on; N. Amer. informal on the button, on the nose. **2** *I expect the matter to be dealt with promptly:* **without delay**, straight away, right away, at once, immediately, now, as soon as possible; quickly, swiftly, rapidly, speedily, fast, expeditiously; N. Amer. momentarily; informal pronto, a.s.a.p., p.d.q. (pretty damn quick).
– OPPOSITES late, slowly.

promulgate verb **1** *they promulgated their own views:* **make known**, make public, publicize, spread, communicate, propagate, disseminate, broadcast, promote, preach. **2** *the law was promulgated in 1942:* **put into effect**, enact, implement, enforce.

prone adjective **1** *softwood is prone to rotting | prone to error:* **susceptible**, vulnerable, subject, open, liable, given, predisposed, likely, disposed, inclined, apt; at risk of. **2** *his prone body:* **(lying) face down**, face downwards, on one's stomach/front; lying

flat/down, horizontal, prostrate.
– OPPOSITES resistant, immune, upright.

prong noun **tine**, spike, point, tip, projection.

pronounce verb **1** *his name is difficult to pronounce:* **say**, enunciate, articulate, utter, voice, sound, vocalize, get one's tongue round. **2** *the doctor pronounced that I had a virus:* **announce**, proclaim, declare, affirm, assert; judge, rule, decree.

pronounced adjective *a strong voice with a pronounced German accent:* **noticeable**, marked, strong, conspicuous, striking, distinct, prominent, unmistakable, obvious, recognizable, identifiable.
– OPPOSITES slight.

pronouncement noun *his public pronouncements were brilliantly timed and phrased:* **announcement**, proclamation, declaration, assertion; judgement, ruling, decree.

pronunciation noun *her Merseyside pronunciation:* **accent**, manner of speaking, speech, diction, delivery, elocution, intonation; articulation, enunciation, voicing, vocalization.

proof noun **1** *proof of ownership:* **evidence**, verification, corroboration, authentication, confirmation, certification, documentation, validation, attestation, substantiation. **2** *the proofs of a book:* **page proof**, galley proof, galley, pull, slip; revise.
adjective *no system is proof against theft:* **resistant**, immune, unaffected, invulnerable, impenetrable, impervious, repellent.

prop noun **1** *the roof is held up by props:* **pole**, post, support, upright, brace, buttress, stay, strut, stanchion, shore, pier, pillar, pile, piling, bolster, truss, column. **2** *a prop for the economy:* **mainstay**, pillar, anchor, backbone, support, foundation, cornerstone.
verb **1** *he propped his bike against the wall:* **lean**, rest, stand, balance, steady. **2** *this post is propping the wall up:* **hold up**, shore up, bolster up, buttress, support, brace, underpin. **3** *they prop up loss-making industries:* **subsidize**, underwrite, fund, finance.

propaganda noun *political propaganda:* **information**, promotion, advertising, publicity; agitprop, disinformation, counter-information, the big lie; informal info, hype, plugging.

propagandist noun *an enthusiastic propagandist for the government's reforms:* **promoter**, champion, supporter, proponent, advocate, campaigner, crusader, publicist, evangelist, apostle; informal plugger.

propagate verb **1** *an easy plant to propagate:* **breed**, grow, cultivate. **2** *these shrubs propagate easily:* **reproduce**, multiply, proliferate, increase, spread, self-seed, self-sow. **3** *they propagated socialist ideas:* **spread**, disseminate, communicate, make known, promulgate, circulate, broadcast,

publicize, proclaim, preach, promote.

propel verb **1** *a boat propelled by oars:* **move**, power, push, drive. **2** *he propelled the ball into the air:* **throw**, thrust, toss, fling, hurl, launch, pitch, project, send, shoot. **3** *confusion propelled her into action:* **spur**, drive, prompt, precipitate, catapult, motivate, force, impel.

propeller noun **rotor**, screw, airscrew; informal prop.

propensity noun *her propensity to jump to conclusions:* **tendency**, inclination, predisposition, proneness, proclivity, readiness, liability, disposition, leaning, weakness.

proper adjective **1** *he's not a proper scientist:* **real**, genuine, actual, true, bona fide; informal kosher. **2** *the proper channels:* **right**, correct, accepted, orthodox, conventional, established, official, formal, regular, acceptable, appropriate. **3** *they were terribly proper:* **respectable**, decorous, seemly, decent, refined, ladylike, gentlemanly, genteel; formal, conventional, correct, comme il faut, done, orthodox, polite, punctilious.
– OPPOSITES fake, inappropriate, wrong, unconventional.

property noun **1** *lost property:* **possessions**, belongings, things, effects, stuff, chattels, movables; resources, assets, valuables, fortune, capital, riches, wealth; informal gear. **2** *private property:* **building(s)**, premises, house(s), land, estates; N. Amer. real estate. **3** *garlic is known for its healing properties:* **quality**, attribute, characteristic, feature, power, trait, mark, hallmark.

prophecy noun **1** *her prophecy is coming true:* **prediction**, forecast, prognostication, prognosis, divination, augury. **2** *the gift of prophecy:* **foretelling the future**, fortune-telling, crystal-gazing, prediction, second sight, prognostication, divination, augury, soothsaying.

prophesy verb *many commentators prophesied disaster:* **predict**, foretell, forecast, foresee, forewarn of, prognosticate.

prophet, prophetess noun **seer**, soothsayer, fortune-teller, clairvoyant, diviner; oracle, augur, sibyl.
■ **prophet of doom** pessimist, doom-monger, doomsayer, doomster, Cassandra, Jeremiah; informal doom (and gloom) merchant.

prophetic adjective *his words proved prophetic—in less than a week he was dead:* **prescient**, predictive, far-seeing, prognostic, divinatory, sibylline, apocalyptic.

prophylactic adjective *prophylactic measures:* **preventive**, preventative, precautionary, protective, inhibitory.
noun *a prophylactic against malaria:* **preventive measure**, precaution,

p

safeguard, safety measure; preventive medicine.

prophylaxis noun *the use of HRT as a prophylaxis against osteoporosis:* **preventive treatment**, prevention, protection, precaution.

propitiate verb *George's attempts to propitiate his father did not work:* **appease**, placate, mollify, pacify, make peace with, conciliate, make amends to, soothe, calm.
– OPPOSITES provoke.

propitious adjective *the timing for such a meeting seemed propitious:* **favourable**, auspicious, promising, providential, advantageous, optimistic, bright, rosy, heaven-sent, hopeful; opportune, timely.
– OPPOSITES inauspicious, unfortunate.

proponent noun *a strong proponent of the free market and liberal trade policies:* **advocate**, champion, supporter, backer, promoter, protagonist, campaigner; N. Amer. booster.

proportion noun **1** *a small proportion of the land:* **part**, portion, amount, quantity, bit, piece, percentage, fraction, section, segment, share. **2** *the proportion of water to alcohol:* **ratio**, distribution, relative amount/number; relationship. **3** *the drawing is out of proportion:* **balance**, symmetry, harmony, correspondence, correlation, agreement. **4** *men of huge proportions:* **size**, dimensions, magnitude, measurements; mass, volume, bulk; expanse, extent, width, breadth.

proportional adjective *an increase in working hours unaccompanied by a proportional increase in wages:* **corresponding**, proportionate, comparable, in proportion, pro rata, commensurate, equivalent, consistent, relative, analogous.
– OPPOSITES disproportionate.

proposal noun **1** *the proposal was rejected:* **scheme**, plan, idea, project, programme, manifesto, motion, proposition, suggestion, submission. **2** *the proposal of a new constitution:* **putting forward**, proposing, suggesting, submitting.
– OPPOSITES withdrawal.

propose verb **1** *he proposed a solution:* **put forward**, suggest, submit, advance, offer, present, move, come up with, lodge, table, nominate. **2** *do you propose to go?* **intend**, mean, plan, have in mind/view, resolve, aim, purpose, think of, aspire, want. **3** *you've proposed to her!* **offer marriage**, make an offer of marriage, ask someone to marry you; informal pop the question.
– OPPOSITES withdraw.

proposition noun **1** *the analysis derives from one proposition:* **theory**, hypothesis, thesis, argument, premiss, theorem, concept, idea, statement. **2** *a business proposition:* **proposal**, scheme, plan, project, idea, programme, bid. **3** *doing it for real is a very different proposition:* **task**, job, undertaking,

venture, activity, affair, problem.
verb *he never dared proposition her:* **propose sex with**, make sexual advances to, make an indecent proposal to, make an improper suggestion to; informal give someone the come-on.

propound verb *the theory of relativity was first propounded by Albert Einstein:* **put forward**, advance, offer, proffer, present, set forth, submit, tender, suggest, introduce, postulate, propose, pose, posit; advocate, promote, peddle, spread.

proprietor, proprietress noun **owner**, possessor, holder, master/mistress; landowner, landlord/landlady; innkeeper, hotel-keeper, hotelier, shopkeeper; Brit. publican.

propriety noun **1** *he behaves with the utmost propriety:* **decorum**, respectability, decency, correctness, protocol, appropriateness, suitability, good manners, courtesy, politeness, rectitude, morality, civility, modesty, demureness; sobriety, refinement, discretion. **2** *he was careful to preserve the proprieties in public:* **etiquette**, convention(s), social grace(s), niceties, one's Ps and Qs, protocol, standards, civilities, formalities, accepted behaviour, good form, the done thing, the thing to do, punctilio.
– OPPOSITES indecorum.

propulsion noun *these seabirds use their wings for propulsion under water:* **thrust**, motive force, impetus, impulse, drive, driving force, actuation, push, pressure, power.

prosaic adjective *Bloomwater's present owner was a more prosaic figure:* **ordinary**, everyday, commonplace, conventional, straightforward, routine, run-of-the-mill, workaday; **unimaginative**, uninspired, uninspiring, matter-of-fact, dull, dry, dreary, tedious, boring, humdrum, mundane, pedestrian, tame, plodding; bland, insipid, banal, trite, literal, factual, unpoetic, unemotional, unsentimental.
– OPPOSITES interesting, imaginative, inspired.

proscribe verb **1** *gambling was proscribed:* **forbid**, prohibit, ban, bar, interdict, make illegal, embargo, outlaw, disallow, veto. **2** *the book was proscribed by the Church:* **condemn**, denounce, attack, criticize, censure, damn, reject.
– OPPOSITES allow, authorize, accept.

proscription noun **1** *the proscription of alcohol:* **banning**, forbidding, prohibition, prohibiting, barring, debarment, vetoing, interdiction, outlawing. **2** *a proscription was imposed:* **ban**, prohibition, bar, interdict, veto, embargo, moratorium. **3** *the proscription of his recordings:* **condemnation**, denunciation, attacking, criticism, censuring, damning, rejection.
– OPPOSITES allowing, authorization, acceptance.

prosecute verb **1** *we always prosecute*

shoplifters: **take to court**, bring/institute legal proceedings against, bring an action against, take legal action against, sue, try, bring to trial, put on trial, put in the dock, bring a suit against, indict, arraign; N. Amer. impeach; informal have the law on. **2** *they helped him prosecute the war:* **pursue**, fight, wage, carry on, conduct, direct, engage in, proceed with, continue (with), keep on with.
– OPPOSITES defend, let off, give up.

proselyte noun **convert**, new believer, catechumen.

proselytize verb **1** *I'm not here to proselytize:* **evangelize**, convert, save, redeem, win over, preach (to), recruit, act as a missionary. **2** *he wanted to proselytize his ideas:* **promote**, advocate, champion, advance, further, spread, proclaim, peddle, preach, endorse, urge, recommend, boost.

prospect noun **1** *there is little prospect of success:* **likelihood**, hope, expectation, anticipation, (good/poor) chance, odds, probability, possibility, promise, lookout; fear, danger. **2** *unemployed people who want to improve their job prospects:* **possibilities**, potential, promise, expectations, outlook. **3** *a daunting prospect:* **vision**, thought, idea; task, undertaking. **4** *Jimmy is an exciting prospect:* **candidate**, possibility; informal catch. **5** *there is a pleasant prospect from the lounge:* **view**, vista, outlook, perspective, panorama, aspect, scene; picture, spectacle, sight.
verb *they are prospecting for oil:* **search**, look, explore, survey, scout, hunt, reconnoitre, examine, inspect.
■ **in prospect** expected, likely, coming soon, on the way, to come, at hand, near, imminent, in the offing, in store, on the horizon, just around the corner, in the air, in the wind, brewing, looming; informal on the cards.

prospective adjective *the prospective buyer should always endeavour to negotiate:* **potential**, possible, probable, likely, future, eventual, -to-be, soon-to-be, in the making; intending, aspiring, would-be; forthcoming, approaching, coming, imminent.

prospectus noun *this format is ideal for a school or company prospectus:* **brochure**, pamphlet, description, particulars, announcement, advertisement; syllabus, curriculum, catalogue, programme, list, scheme, schedule.

prosper verb *the European personal computer market continued to prosper:* **flourish**, thrive, do well, bloom, blossom, burgeon, progress, do all right for oneself, get ahead, get on (in the world), be successful; informal go places.
– OPPOSITES fail, flounder.

prosperity noun *Britain's prosperity depends on its exports:* **success**, profitability, affluence, wealth, opulence, luxury, the good life, milk and honey, (good) fortune, ease, plenty, comfort, security, well-being.

– OPPOSITES hardship, failure.

prosperous adjective *a prosperous family shipping firm:* **thriving**, flourishing, successful, strong, vigorous, profitable, lucrative, expanding, booming, burgeoning; **affluent**, wealthy, rich, moneyed, well off, well-to-do, opulent, substantial, in clover; informal on a roll, on the up and up, in the money.
– OPPOSITES ailing, poor.

prostitute noun **whore**, sex worker, call girl; rent boy; informal tart, pro, moll, working girl, member of the oldest profession; Brit. informal tom, woman on the game, renter; N. Amer. informal hooker, hustler, chippy; black English ho.
verb *they prostituted their art:* **betray**, sacrifice, sell, sell out, debase, degrade, demean, devalue, cheapen, lower, shame, misuse, pervert; abandon one's principles, be untrue to oneself.

prostitution noun **whoring**, the sex industry, streetwalking, Mrs Warren's profession, sex tourism; informal the oldest profession, the trade; rough trade; Brit. informal the game; N. Amer. informal hooking, hustling.

prostrate adjective **1** *the prostrate figure on the ground:* **prone**, lying flat, lying down, stretched out, spreadeagled, sprawling, horizontal, recumbent; rare procumbent. **2** *his wife was prostrate with shock:* **overwhelmed**, overcome, overpowered, brought to one's knees, stunned, dazed; speechless, helpless; informal knocked/hit for six. **3** *the fever left me prostrate:* **worn out**, exhausted, fatigued, tired out, sapped, dog-tired, spent, drained, debilitated, enervated, laid low; informal all in, done in, dead, dead beat, dead on one's feet, ready to drop, fagged out, bushed, frazzled, worn to a frazzle; Brit. informal whacked, knackered; N. Amer. informal pooped.
– OPPOSITES upright, fresh.
verb *she was prostrated by the tragedy:* **overwhelm**, overcome, overpower, bring to one's knees, devastate, debilitate, weaken, enfeeble, enervate, lay low, wear out, exhaust, tire out, drain, sap, wash out, take it out of; informal knacker, frazzle, do in; N. Amer. informal poop.
■ **prostrate oneself** throw oneself flat/down, lie down, stretch oneself out, throw oneself at someone's feet.

prostration noun **collapse**, weakness, debility, lassitude, exhaustion, fatigue, tiredness, enervation, emotional exhaustion.

protagonist noun **1** *the protagonist in the plot:* **central character**, principal, hero/heroine, leading man/lady, title role, lead. **2** *a protagonist of deregulation:* **champion**, advocate, upholder, supporter, backer, promoter, proponent, exponent, campaigner, fighter, crusader, apostle, apologist; N. Amer. booster.
– OPPOSITES opponent.

protect verb *he tried to protect Kelly from the attack:* **keep safe**, keep from harm, save,

p

safeguard, preserve, defend, shield, cushion, insulate, hedge, shelter, screen, secure, fortify, guard, watch over, look after, take care of, keep; inoculate.
– OPPOSITES expose, neglect, attack, harm.

protection noun 1 *protection against frost:* **defence**, security, shielding, preservation, conservation, safe keeping, safeguarding, safety, sanctuary, shelter, refuge, lee, immunity, insurance, indemnity. 2 *under the protection of the Church:* **safe keeping**, care, charge, keeping, protectorship, guidance, aegis, auspices, umbrella, guardianship, support, patronage, championship, providence. 3 *a strip of woodland provides good protection against noise:* **barrier**, buffer, shield, screen, hedge, cushion, preventative, armour, refuge, bulwark.

protective adjective 1 *protective clothing:* **preservative**, protecting, safeguarding, shielding, defensive, safety, precautionary, preventive, preventative. 2 *he felt protective towards the girl:* **solicitous**, caring, warm, paternal/maternal, fatherly/motherly, gallant, chivalrous; overprotective, possessive, jealous.

protector noun 1 *a protector of the environment:* **defender**, preserver, guardian, guard, champion, watchdog, ombudsman, knight in shining armour, guardian angel, patron, chaperon, escort, keeper, custodian, bodyguard, minder; informal hired gun. 2 *ear protectors:* **guard**, shield, buffer, cushion, pad, screen.

protégé, protégée noun *Ruskin submitted his protégé's name for election:* **pupil**, student, trainee, apprentice; disciple, follower; discovery, find, ward.

protest noun 1 *he resigned as a protest:* **objection**, complaint, exception, disapproval, challenge, dissent, demurral, remonstration, fuss, outcry. 2 *women staged a protest:* **demonstration**, (protest) march, rally; sit-in, occupation; work-to-rule, industrial action, stoppage, strike, walkout, mutiny, picket, boycott; informal demo.
– OPPOSITES support, approval.
verb 1 *residents protested at the plans:* **express opposition**, object, dissent, take issue, make/take a stand, put up a fight, kick, take exception, complain, express disapproval, disagree, demur, remonstrate, make a fuss, cry out, speak out, rail, inveigh, fulminate; informal kick up a fuss/stink. 2 *people protested outside the cathedral:* **demonstrate**, march, hold a rally, sit in, occupy somewhere; work to rule, take industrial action, stop work, down tools, strike, go on strike, walk out, mutiny, picket somewhere; boycott something. 3 *he protested his innocence:* **insist on**, maintain, assert, affirm, announce, proclaim, declare, profess, contend, argue, claim, vow, swear (to), stress.
– OPPOSITES acquiesce, support, deny.

protestation noun 1 *his protestations of*

innocence: **declaration**, announcement, profession, assertion, insistence, claim, affirmation, assurance, oath, vow. 2 *we helped him despite his protestations:* **objection**, protest, exception, complaint, disapproval, opposition, challenge, dissent, demurral, remonstration, fuss, outcry; informal stink.
– OPPOSITES denial, acquiescence, support.

protester noun 1 *the council lost protesters' letters:* **objector**, opposer, opponent, complainant, complainer, dissenter, dissident, nonconformist. 2 *the protesters were moved on:* **demonstrator**, protest marcher; striker, mutineer, picket.

protocol noun 1 *a stickler for protocol:* **etiquette**, conventions, formalities, customs, rules of conduct, procedure, ritual, accepted behaviour, propriety, proprieties, one's Ps and Qs, decorum, good form, the done thing, the thing to do, punctilio. 2 *the two countries signed a protocol:* **agreement**, treaty, entente, concordat, convention, deal, pact, contract, compact.

prototype noun 1 *a prototype of the weapon:* **original**, first example/model, master, mould, template, framework, mock-up, pattern, sample; **design**, guide, blueprint. 2 *the prototype of an ideal wife:* **typical example**, paradigm, archetype, exemplar.

protract verb *the Opposition will try to protract the discussion:* **prolong**, lengthen, extend, draw out, drag out, spin out, stretch out, string out, elongate; carry on, continue, keep up, perpetuate; filibuster.
– OPPOSITES curtail, shorten.

protracted adjective **prolonged**, long-lasting, extended, long-drawn-out, spun out, dragged out, strung out, lengthy, long.
– OPPOSITES short.

protrude verb *a handle protrudes from the motor housing:* **stick out**, jut (out), project, extend, stand out, bulge out, poke out, thrust out, cantilever.

protruding adjective **sticking out**, protuberant, projecting, prominent, jutting, overhanging, proud, bulging; informal sticky-out.
– OPPOSITES sunken, flush.

protrusion noun 1 *the neck vertebrae have short vertical protrusions:* **bump**, lump, knob; protuberance, projection, sticking-out bit, prominence, swelling, eminence, outcrop, outgrowth, jut, jag, snag; ledge, shelf, ridge; informal sticky-out bit. 2 *protrusion of the lips:* **sticking out**, jutting, projection, obtrusion, prominence; swelling, bulging.

protuberance noun *a protuberance on the fuselage can cause drag:* **bump**, lump, knob, projection, protrusion, sticking-out bit, prominence, swelling, eminence, outcrop, outgrowth, jut, jag, snag; ledge, shelf, ridge; informal sticky-out bit.

protuberant adjective **sticking out**,

protruding, projecting, prominent, jutting, overhanging, proud, bulging; informal sticky out.
– OPPOSITES sunken, flush.

proud adjective **1** *the proud parents beamed:* **pleased**, glad, happy, delighted, joyful, overjoyed, thrilled, satisfied, gratified, content. **2** *this is a proud day for the school:* **pleasing**, gratifying, satisfying, cheering, heart-warming; happy, good, glorious, memorable, notable, red-letter. **3** *the family were poor but proud:* **self-respecting**, dignified, noble, worthy; independent. **4** *I'm not too proud to admit I'm wrong:* **arrogant**, conceited, vain, self-important, full of oneself, puffed up, jumped-up, smug, complacent, disdainful, condescending, scornful, supercilious, snobbish, imperious, pompous, overbearing, bumptious, haughty; informal big-headed, swollen-headed, too big for one's boots, high and mighty, stuck-up, uppity, snooty, highfalutin; Brit. informal toffee-nosed. **5** *the proud ships:* **magnificent**, splendid, resplendent, grand, noble, stately, imposing, dignified, striking, impressive, majestic, glorious, awe-inspiring, awesome, monumental. **6** *the switch is proud of the wall:* **projecting**, sticking out/up, jutting (out), protruding, prominent, raised, convex, elevated.
– OPPOSITES ashamed, shameful, humble, modest, unimpressive, concave, flush.

prove verb **1** *that proves I'm right:* **show (to be true)**, demonstrate (the truth of), show beyond doubt, manifest, produce proof/evidence; witness to, give substance to, determine, substantiate, corroborate, verify, ratify, validate, authenticate, document, bear out, confirm. **2** *the rumour proved to be correct:* **turn out**, be found, happen.
– OPPOSITES disprove.
■ **prove oneself** demonstrate one's abilities/qualities, show one's (true) mettle, show what one is made of.

provenance noun *the police were suspicious about the provenance of the paintings:* **origin**, source, place of origin; birthplace, fount, roots, pedigree, derivation, root, etymology; N. Amer. provenience.

proverb noun **saying**, adage, saw, maxim, axiom, motto, bon mot, aphorism, apophthegm, epigram, gnome, dictum, precept; words of wisdom.

proverbial adjective *the pirate's greed was as proverbial as his cowardice:* **well known**, famous, famed, renowned, traditional, time-honoured, legendary; notorious, infamous.

provide verb **1** *the Foundation will provide funds:* **supply**, give, issue, furnish, come up with, dispense, bestow, impart, produce, yield, bring forth, bear, deliver, donate, contribute, pledge, advance, spare, part with, allocate, distribute, allot, put up; informal fork out, lay out; N. Amer. informal ante up, pony up. **2** *he was provided with enough*

tools: **equip**, furnish, issue, supply, outfit; fit out, rig out, kit out, arm, provision; informal fix up. **3** *he had to provide for his family:* **feed**, nurture, nourish; **support**, maintain, keep, sustain, provide sustenance for, fend for, finance, endow. **4** *the test may provide the answer:* **make available**, present, offer, afford, give, add, bring, yield, impart. **5** *we have provided for further restructuring:* **prepare**, allow, make provision, be prepared, arrange, get ready, plan, cater. **6** *the banks have to provide against bad debts:* **take precautions**, take steps/measures, guard, forearm oneself; make provision for. **7** *the Act provides that factories must be kept clean:* **stipulate**, lay down, make it a condition, require, order, ordain, demand, prescribe, state, specify.
– OPPOSITES refuse, withhold, deprive, neglect.

provided conjunction *the clove pink needs no special cultivation, provided it has well-drained soil:* **if**, on condition that, providing (that), provided that, presuming (that), assuming (that), on the assumption that, as long as, given (that), with the provision/proviso that, with/on the understanding that, contingent on.

providence noun **1** *a life mapped out by providence:* **fate**, destiny, nemesis, kismet, God's will, divine intervention, predestination, predetermination, the stars; one's lot (in life). **2** *he had a streak of providence:* **prudence**, foresight, forethought, far-sightedness, judiciousness, shrewdness, circumspection, wisdom, sagacity, common sense; careful budgeting, thrift, economy.

provident adjective *we have to be vaguely provident, but no real sacrifices are demanded:* **prudent**, far-sighted, judicious, shrewd, circumspect, forearmed, wise, sagacious, sensible; thrifty, economical.
– OPPOSITES improvident.

providential adjective *the battle was won with the aid of a providential wind:* **opportune**, advantageous, favourable, auspicious, propitious, heaven-sent, welcome, golden, lucky, happy, fortunate, felicitous, timely, well timed, seasonable, convenient, expedient.
– OPPOSITES inopportune.

provider noun *the state is still the main provider of welfare:* **supplier**, donor, giver, contributor, source.

providing conjunction. See **PROVIDED**.

province noun **1** *a province of the Ottoman Empire:* **territory**, region, state, department, canton, area, district, sector, zone, division. **2** *people in the provinces:* **non-metropolitan areas/counties**, the rest of the country, middle England/America, rural areas/districts, the countryside, the backwoods, the wilds; informal the sticks, the middle of nowhere; N. Amer. informal the boondocks. **3** *that's outside my province:*

p

responsibility, area of activity, area of interest, knowledge, department, sphere, world, realm, field, domain, territory, orbit, preserve, line of country; business, affair, concern; speciality, forte; jurisdiction, authority; informal pigeon, bailiwick, turf.

provincial adjective **1** *the provincial government:* **regional**, state, territorial, district, local; sectoral, zonal, cantonal, county. **2** *provincial areas:* **non-metropolitan**, small-town, non-urban, outlying, rural, country, rustic, backwoods, backwater; informal one-horse; N. Amer. informal hick, freshwater. **3** *they're so dull and provincial:* **unsophisticated**, narrow-minded, parochial, small-town, suburban, insular, parish-pump, inward-looking, conservative; small-minded, blinkered, bigoted, prejudiced; N. Amer. informal jerkwater, corn-fed.
– OPPOSITES national, metropolitan, cosmopolitan, sophisticated, broad-minded.
noun *they were dismissed as provincials:* **(country) bumpkin**, country cousin, rustic, yokel, village idiot, peasant; Irish informal culchie; N. Amer. informal hayseed, hick, rube, hillbilly.
– OPPOSITES sophisticate.

provision noun **1** *the provision of weapons to guerrillas:* **supplying**, supply, providing, giving, presentation, donation; equipping, furnishing. **2** *there has been limited provision for gifted children:* **facilities**, services, amenities, resource(s), arrangements; means, funds, benefits, assistance, allowance(s). **3** *provisions for the trip:* **supplies**, food and drink, stores, groceries, foodstuff(s), provender, rations; informal grub, eats, nosh; N. Amer. informal chuck. **4** *he made no provision for the future:* **preparations**, plans, arrangements, pre-arrangement, precautions, contingency. **5** *the provisions of the Act:* **term**, clause, requirement, specification, stipulation; proviso, condition, qualification, restriction, limitation.

provisional adjective *a provisional government:* **interim**, temporary, pro tem; transitional, changeover, stopgap, short-term, fill-in, acting, caretaker, TBC (to be confirmed), subject to confirmation; pencilled in, working, tentative, contingent.
– OPPOSITES permanent, definite.

provisionally adverb *he was appointed provisionally for one year:* **temporarily**, short-term, pro tem, for the interim, for the present, for the time being, for now, for the nonce; subject to confirmation, in an acting capacity, conditionally, tentatively.

proviso noun *he let his house out for one year, with the proviso that his own staff should remain to run it:* **condition**, stipulation, provision, clause, rider, qualification, restriction, caveat.

provocation noun **1** *he remained calm despite severe provocation:* **goading**, prodding, egging on, incitement, pressure; annoyance, irritation, nettling; harassment, plaguing, molestation; teasing, taunting, torment; affront, insults; informal hassle, aggravation. **2** *without provocation, Jones punched Mr Cartwright:* **justification**, excuse, pretext, occasion, call, motivation, motive, cause, grounds, reason, need.

provocative adjective **1** *provocative remarks:* **annoying**, irritating, exasperating, infuriating, maddening, vexing, galling; insulting, offensive, inflammatory, incendiary, controversial; informal aggravating, in-your-face. **2** *a provocative pose:* **sexy**, sexually arousing, sexually exciting, alluring, seductive, suggestive, inviting, tantalizing, titillating; indecent, pornographic, indelicate, immodest, shameless; erotic, sensuous, slinky, coquettish, amorous, flirtatious; informal tarty, come-hither.
– OPPOSITES soothing, calming, modest, decorous.

provoke verb **1** *the plan has provoked outrage:* **arouse**, produce, evoke, cause, give rise to, occasion, call forth, elicit, induce, excite, spark off, touch off, kindle, generate, engender, instigate, result in, lead to, bring on, precipitate, prompt, trigger. **2** *he was provoked into replying:* **goad**, spur, prick, sting, prod, egg on, incite, rouse, stir, move, stimulate, motivate, excite, inflame, work/fire up, impel. **3** *he wouldn't be provoked:* **annoy**, anger, incense, enrage, irritate, infuriate, exasperate, madden, nettle, get/take a rise out of, ruffle, ruffle someone's feathers, make someone's hackles rise; harass, harry, plague, molest; tease, taunt, torment; Brit. rub up the wrong way; informal peeve, aggravate, hassle, miff, rile, needle, get, bug, hack off, make someone's blood boil, get under someone's skin, get in someone's hair, get/put someone's back up, get up someone's nose, get someone's goat, get across someone; Brit. informal wind up, nark; N. Amer. informal rankle, ride, gravel.
– OPPOSITES allay, deter, pacify, appease.

prow noun *the prow of a ship:* **bow(s)**, stem, front, nose, head, cutwater; Brit. humorous sharp end.

prowess noun **1** *his prowess as a winemaker:* **skill**, expertise, mastery, facility, ability, capability, capacity, savoir faire, talent, genius, adeptness, aptitude, dexterity, deftness, competence, accomplishment, proficiency, finesse; informal know-how. **2** *the knights' prowess in battle:* **courage**, bravery, gallantry, valour, heroism, intrepidity, nerve, pluck, pluckiness, boldness, daring, audacity, fearlessness; informal bottle, guts, spunk; N. Amer. informal moxie, sand.
– OPPOSITES inability, ineptitude, cowardice.

prowl verb *youths have been prowling around the back of the flats:* **move stealthily**, slink, skulk, steal, nose, pussyfoot, sneak, stalk, creep; informal snoop.

p

proximity noun *their minds were concentrated by the proximity of the enemy:* **closeness**, nearness, propinquity; accessibility, handiness.

proxy noun *any member is entitled to appoint another person as his proxy to attend and vote instead of him:* **deputy**, representative, substitute, delegate, agent, surrogate, stand-in, attorney, go-between.

prude noun *he's very correct but no prude:* **puritan**, prig, killjoy, moralist, pietist; informal goody-goody; N. Amer. informal bluenose.

prudence noun **1** *you have gone beyond the bounds of prudence:* **wisdom**, judgement, good judgement, common sense, sense, sagacity, shrewdness, advisability. **2** *financial prudence:* **caution**, care, providence, far-sightedness, foresight, forethought, shrewdness, circumspection; thrift, economy.
– OPPOSITES folly, recklessness, extravagance.

prudent adjective **1** *it is prudent to obtain consent:* **wise**, well judged, sensible, politic, judicious, sagacious, sage, shrewd, advisable, well advised. **2** *a prudent approach to borrowing:* **cautious**, careful, provident, far-sighted, judicious, shrewd, circumspect; thrifty, economical.
– OPPOSITES unwise, reckless, extravagant.

prudish adjective *his grandmother was a rather prudish woman:* **puritanical**, priggish, prim, prim and proper, moralistic, pietistic, sententious, censorious, strait-laced, Victorian, old-maidish, stuffy; informal goody-goody.
– OPPOSITES permissive.

prune verb **1** *I pruned the roses:* **cut back**, trim, thin, pinch back, clip, shear, pollard, top, dock. **2** *prune lateral shoots of wisteria:* **cut off**, lop (off), chop off, clip, snip (off), nip off, dock. **3** *staff numbers have been pruned:* **reduce**, cut (back/down), pare (down), slim down, make reductions in, make cutbacks in, trim, decrease, diminish, downsize, axe, shrink; informal slash.
– OPPOSITES increase.

prurient adjective *she'd been the subject of much prurient curiosity:* **salacious**, licentious, voyeuristic, lascivious, lecherous, lustful, lewd, libidinous, lubricious.

pry verb *I didn't mean to pry:* **enquire impertinently**, be inquisitive, be curious, poke about/around, ferret (about/around), spy, be a busybody; eavesdrop, listen in, tap someone's phone, intrude; informal stick/poke one's nose in/into, be nosy, nose, snoop; Austral./NZ informal stickybeak.
– OPPOSITES mind one's own business.

psalm noun **sacred song**, religious song, hymn, song of praise; chant, plainsong; (**psalms**) psalmody, psalter.

pseud noun *what a pseud to tell her she had a Pre-Raphaelite face:* **poser**, poseur,

pretentious person, sham, fraud; informal show-off, phoney.

pseudo adjective *a pseudo science:* **bogus**, sham, phoney, artificial, mock, ersatz, quasi-, fake, false, faux, spurious, deceptive, misleading, assumed, contrived, affected, insincere; informal pretend, put-on; Brit. informal cod.
– OPPOSITES genuine.

pseudonym noun *Hanbury wrote a novel under the pseudonym of James Aston:* **pen-name**, nom de plume, assumed name, false name, alias, professional name, sobriquet, stage name, nom de guerre.

psych (informal)
■ **psych someone out** *guys try to lift heavy weights in a mistaken attempt to psych the others out:* **intimidate**, daunt, browbeat, bully, cow, tyrannize, scare, terrorize, frighten, dishearten, unnerve, subdue; informal bulldoze; N. Amer. informal buffalo.
■ **psych oneself up** *we had to psych ourselves up for the race:* **nerve oneself**, steel oneself, brace oneself, summon one's courage, prepare oneself, gear oneself up, urge oneself on, gird (up) one's loins.

psyche noun *Laura saw clearly the effect of beautiful surroundings on the psyche:* **soul**, spirit, (inner) self, ego, true being, inner man/woman, persona, subconscious, mind, intellect.
– OPPOSITES body.

psychiatrist noun **psychotherapist**, psychoanalyst; informal shrink, head doctor; Brit. humorous trick cyclist.

psychic adjective **1** *psychic powers:* **supernatural**, paranormal, other-worldly, supernormal, preternatural, metaphysical, extrasensory, magic, magical, mystical, mystic, occult. **2** *I'm not psychic:* **clairvoyant**, telepathic, having second sight, having a sixth sense. **3** *the children's psychic development:* **emotional**, spiritual, inner; cognitive, psychological, intellectual, mental, psychiatric, psychogenic.
– OPPOSITES normal, physical.
noun *she is a psychic:* **clairvoyant**, fortune-teller, crystal-gazer, seer; medium, spiritualist; telepathist, telepath, mind-reader, palmist, palm-reader.

psychological adjective **1** *his psychological state:* **mental**, emotional, intellectual, inner, cerebral, brain, rational, cognitive. **2** *her pain was psychological:* **(all) in the mind**, psychosomatic, emotional, irrational, subjective, subconscious, unconscious.
– OPPOSITES physical.

psychology noun *the psychology of the road user:* **mindset**, mind, mental processes, thought processes, way of thinking, cast of mind, mentality, persona, psyche, (mental) attitude(s), make-up, character; informal what makes someone tick.

psychopath noun *Rick was a dangerous psychopath who might kill again:* **madman**,

madwoman, maniac, lunatic, psychotic, sociopath; informal loony, fruitcake, nutcase, nut, psycho, schizo, head case, headbanger, sicko; Brit. informal nutter, mentalist; N. Amer. informal screwball, crazy, kook, meshuggener.

psychopathic adjective. See MAD sense 1.

psychosomatic adjective *psychosomatic illness:* **(all) in the mind**, psychological, irrational, stress-related, stress-induced, subjective, subconscious, unconscious.

psychotic adjective. See MAD sense 1.

pub noun (Brit.) **bar**, inn, tavern, hostelry, wine bar, taproom, roadhouse; Brit. public house; Austral./NZ hotel; informal watering hole; Brit. informal local, boozer.

puberty noun *the onset of puberty may occur as early as eleven or twelve:* **adolescence**, pubescence, sexual maturity, growing up; youth, young adulthood, teenage years, teens.

public adjective **1** *public affairs:* **state**, national, federal, government; constitutional, civic, civil, official, social, municipal, community, communal, local; nationalized. **2** *there is great public demand for information on food:* **popular**, general, common, communal, collective, shared, joint, universal, widespread. **3** *a public figure:* **prominent**, well known, important, leading, eminent, distinguished, notable, noteworthy, noted, celebrated, household, famous, famed, influential; N. Amer. major-league. **4** *public places:* **open (to the public)**, communal, accessible to all, available, free, unrestricted, community. **5** *the news became public:* **known**, published, publicized, in circulation, exposed, overt, plain, obvious.
– OPPOSITES private, obscure, unknown, restricted, secret.
noun **1** *the British public:* **people**, citizens, subjects, general public, electors, electorate, voters, taxpayers, residents, inhabitants, citizenry, population, populace, community, society, country, nation, world; everyone. **2** *his adoring public:* **audience**, spectators, followers, following, fans, devotees, aficionados, admirers; patrons, clientele, market, consumers, buyers, customers, readers.
■ **in public** publicly, in full view of people, openly, in the open, for all to see, undisguisedly, blatantly, flagrantly, brazenly, with no attempt at concealment, overtly.

publication noun **1** *the author of this publication:* **book**, volume, title, work, tome, opus; newspaper, paper, magazine, periodical, newsletter, bulletin, journal, report; organ, booklet, brochure, catalogue; daily, weekly, monthly, quarterly, annual; informal rag, mag, 'zine. **2** *the publication of her new book:* **issuing**, announcement, publishing, printing, notification, reporting, declaration, communication, proclamation, broadcasting, publicizing, advertising, distribution, spreading, dissemination,

promulgation, issuance, appearance.

publicity noun **1** *the blaze of publicity:* **public attention**, public interest, public notice, media attention/interest, exposure, glare, limelight. **2** *publicity should boost sales:* **promotion**, advertising, propaganda; boost, push; informal hype, ballyhoo, puff, puffery, build-up, razzmatazz; plug.

publicize verb **1** *I never publicize the fact:* **make known**, make public, publish, announce, report, post, communicate, broadcast, issue, put out, distribute, spread, promulgate, disseminate, circulate, air; disclose, reveal, divulge, leak. **2** *he just wants to publicize his book:* **advertise**, promote, build up, talk up, push, beat the drum for, boost; informal hype, plug, puff (up).
– OPPOSITES conceal, suppress.

public-spirited adjective *the debris was left for public-spirited citizens to remove:* **community-minded**, socially concerned, philanthropic, charitable; **altruistic**, humanitarian, generous, unselfish.

publish verb **1** *we publish novels:* **issue**, bring out, produce, print. **2** *he ought to publish his views:* **make known**, make public, publicize, announce, report, post, communicate, broadcast, issue, put out, distribute, spread, promulgate, disseminate, circulate, air; disclose, reveal, divulge, leak.

pucker verb *she puckered her forehead:* **wrinkle**, crinkle, crease, furrow, crumple, rumple, ruck up, scrunch up, corrugate, ruffle, screw up, shrivel; cockle.
noun *a pucker in the sewing:* **wrinkle**, crinkle, crumple, corrugation, furrow, line, fold.

puckish adjective *he had a very puckish sense of humour:* **mischievous**, naughty, impish, roguish, playful, arch, prankish; informal waggish.

pudding noun **dessert**, sweet, second course, last course; Brit. informal afters, pud.

puddle noun *puddles of water:* **pool**, spill, splash.

puerile adjective *a puerile argument:* **childish**, immature, infantile, juvenile, babyish; silly, inane, fatuous, jejune, asinine, foolish, petty.
– OPPOSITES mature, sensible.

puff noun **1** *a puff of wind:* **gust**, blast, flurry, rush, draught, waft, breeze, breath. **2** *he took a puff at his cigar:* **pull**; informal drag.
verb **1** *he walked fast, puffing a little:* **breathe heavily**, pant, blow; gasp, fight for breath. **2** *she puffed at her cigarette:* **smoke**, draw on, drag on, suck at/on.
■ **puff out/up** *if she went for a walk her ankles puffed up:* **bulge**, swell (out), stick out, distend, tumefy, balloon (up/out), expand, inflate, enlarge.
■ **puff something out/up** *he puffed out his cheeks:* distend, expand, dilate, inflate, blow up, pump up, enlarge, bloat.

puffed adjective *I'll be too puffed to dance properly:* **out of breath**, breathless, short of breath; panting, puffing, gasping, wheezing, wheezy, winded; informal out of puff.

puffed-up adjective *he was just another puffed-up tinpot dictator:* **self-important**, conceited, arrogant, bumptious, pompous, overbearing; affected, stiff, vain, proud; informal snooty, uppity, uppish.

puffy adjective *her eyes were puffy from crying:* **swollen**, puffed up, distended, enlarged, inflated, dilated, bloated, engorged, bulging.

pugnacious adjective *the bouncer that night was a pugnacious 42-year-old from East London:* **combative**, aggressive, antagonistic, belligerent, bellicose, warlike, quarrelsome, argumentative, contentious, disputatious, hostile, threatening, truculent; fiery, hot-tempered.
– OPPOSITES peaceable.

pull verb **1** *he pulled the box towards him:* **tug**, haul, drag, draw, tow, heave, lug, jerk, wrench; informal yank. **2** *he pulled the bad tooth out:* **extract**, take out, remove. **3** *she pulled a muscle:* **strain**, sprain, wrench, turn, rick, tear; damage. **4** *race day pulled big crowds:* **attract**, draw, bring in, pull in, lure, seduce, entice, tempt, beckon, interest, fascinate.
– OPPOSITES push, repel.
noun **1** *give the chain a pull:* **tug**, jerk, heave; informal yank. **2** *she took a pull on her beer:* **gulp**, draught, drink, swallow, mouthful, slug; informal swill, swig. **3** *he took a long pull on a cigarette:* **puff**; informal drag. **4** *she felt the pull of the sea:* **attraction**, draw, lure, allurement, enticement, magnetism, temptation, fascination, appeal. **5** *he has a lot of pull in finance:* **influence**, sway, power, authority, say, prestige, standing, weight, leverage, muscle, teeth; informal clout.
■ **pull something apart** dismantle, disassemble, take/pull to pieces, take/pull to bits, take apart, strip down; demolish, destroy, break up.
■ **pull back** *the army was forced to pull back:* withdraw, retreat, fall back, back off; pull out, retire, disengage; flee, turn tail.
■ **pull something down** *several old buildings were pulled down:* demolish, knock down, tear down, dismantle, raze (to the ground), level, flatten, bulldoze, destroy.
■ **pull in** *a police car pulled in behind:* stop, halt, come to a halt, pull over, pull up, draw up, brake, park.
■ **pull someone/something in 1** *they pulled in big audiences.* See PULL verb sense 4. **2** (informal) *the police pulled him in:* arrest, apprehend, detain, take into custody, seize, capture, catch; informal collar, nab, nick, pinch, run in, bust, feel someone's collar.
■ **pull someone's leg** tease, fool, play a trick on, rag, pull the wool over someone's eyes; informal kid, rib, lead up the garden path, take for a ride; Brit. informal wind up, have on.
■ **pull something off** *they pulled off a daring crime:* achieve, fulfil, succeed in,

accomplish, bring off, carry off, perform, discharge, complete, clinch, fix, effect, engineer.
■ **pull out** *one of their star players has pulled out with stomach trouble:* withdraw, resign, leave, retire, step down, bow out, back out, give up; informal quit.
■ **pull through** *she has serious injuries, but we are all praying for her to pull through:* get better, get well again, improve, recover, rally, come through, recuperate.
■ **pull something to pieces 1** *don't pull my radio to pieces.* See PULL SOMETHING APART. **2** *they pulled the plan to pieces:* criticize, attack, censure, condemn, find fault with, pillory, maul, savage; informal knock, slam, pan, bash, crucify, lay into, roast; Brit. informal slate, rubbish, slag off.
■ **pull oneself together** regain one's composure, recover, get a grip on oneself, get over it; informal snap out of it, get one's act together, buck up.
■ **pull up.** See PULL IN.
■ **pull someone up** *he grinned unabashedly when his mother pulled me up:* reprimand, rebuke, scold, chide, chastise, upbraid, berate, reprove, reproach, censure, take to task, admonish, lecture, read someone the Riot Act, haul over the coals; informal tell off, bawl out, dress down, give someone hell, give someone an earful; Brit. informal tick off, carpet, give someone a rollicking; N. Amer. informal chew out; Austral. informal monster.

pulp noun **1** *he kneaded it into a pulp:* **mush**, mash, paste, purée, pomace, pap, slop, slush, mulch; informal gloop, goo; N. Amer. informal glop. **2** *the sweet pulp on cocoa seeds:* **flesh**, marrow, meat.
verb *pulp the gooseberries:* **mash**, purée, cream, crush, press, liquidize, liquefy, sieve, squash, pound, macerate, grind, mince.
adjective *pulp fiction:* **trashy**, cheap, sensational, lurid, tasteless; informal tacky, rubbishy.

pulpit noun **stand**, lectern, platform, podium, stage, dais, rostrum.

pulsate verb *the flesh of the clam pulsates gently as water is pumped through it:* **palpitate**, pulse, throb, pump, undulate, surge, heave, rise and fall; beat, thump, drum, thrum; flutter, quiver.

pulse[1] noun **1** *the pulse in her neck:* **heartbeat**, pulsation, pulsing, throbbing, pounding. **2** *the pulse of the music:* **rhythm**, beat, tempo, cadence, pounding, thudding, drumming. **3** *pulses of ultrasound:* **burst**, blast, spurt, impulse, surge.
verb *music pulsed through the building:* **throb**, pulsate, vibrate, beat, pound, thud, thump, drum, thrum, reverberate, echo.

pulse[2] noun *eat plenty of pulses:* **legume**, pea, bean, lentil.

pulverize verb *the seeds are pulverized into flour:* **grind**, crush, pound, powder, mill, crunch, squash, press, pulp, mash, sieve, mince, macerate.

pummel verb *he felt like a boxer who had been pummelled mercilessly:* **batter**, pound, belabour, drub, beat; punch, strike, hit, thump, thrash; informal clobber, wallop, bash, whack, beat the living daylights out of, give someone a (good) hiding, belt, biff, lay into, lam; Brit. informal slosh; N. Amer. informal bust, slug; Austral./NZ informal quilt.

pump verb **1** *I pumped air out of the tube:* **force**, drive, push; suck, draw, tap, siphon, withdraw, expel, extract, bleed, drain. **2** *she pumped up the tyre:* **inflate**, aerate, blow up, fill up; swell, enlarge, distend, expand, dilate, puff up. **3** *blood was pumping from his leg:* **spurt**, spout, squirt, jet, surge, spew, gush, stream, flow, pour, spill, well, cascade, run, course.

pun noun **play on words**, wordplay, double entendre, innuendo, witticism, quip, bon mot.

punch¹ verb *Jim punched him in the face:* **hit**, strike, thump, jab, smash, welt, cuff, clip; batter, buffet, pound, pummel; informal sock, slug, biff, bop, wallop, clobber, bash, whack, thwack, clout, lam, whomp; Brit. informal stick one on, dot, slosh; N. Amer. informal boff, bust; Austral./NZ informal quilt.
noun **1** *a punch on the nose:* **blow**, hit, knock, thump, box, jab, clip, welt; uppercut, hook; informal sock, slug, biff, bop, wallop, bash, whack, clout, belt; N. Amer. informal boff, bust. **2** *the album is full of punch:* **vigour**, liveliness, vitality, drive, strength, zest, verve, enthusiasm; impact, bite, kick; informal oomph, zing.

punch² verb *he punched her ticket:* **make a hole in**, perforate, puncture, pierce, prick, hole, spike, skewer.

punchy adjective *punchy dialogue:* **forceful**, incisive, strong, powerful, vigorous, dynamic, effective, impressive, telling, compelling; dramatic, passionate, graphic, vivid, potent, authoritative, aggressive; informal in-your-face.
– OPPOSITES ineffectual.

punctilious adjective *his punctilious implementation of orders impressed the king:* **meticulous**, conscientious, diligent, scrupulous, careful, painstaking, rigorous, perfectionist, methodical, particular, strict; fussy, fastidious, finicky, pedantic; informal nit-picking, pernickety; N. Amer. informal persnickety.
– OPPOSITES careless.

punctual adjective *Mrs Marsh liked her guests to be punctual:* **on time**, prompt, on schedule, in (good) time; informal on the dot.
– OPPOSITES late.

punctuate verb **1** *how to punctuate direct speech:* **add punctuation to**, put punctuation marks in, dot, apostrophize. **2** *slides punctuated the talk:* **break up**, interrupt, intersperse, pepper, sprinkle, scatter.

puncture noun **1** *the tyre developed a*

puncture: **hole**, perforation, rupture; cut, slit; leak. **2** *my car has a puncture:* **flat tyre**; informal flat.
verb **1** *he punctured her balloon:* **pierce**, rupture, perforate, make a hole in stab, cut, slit, prick, spike, stick, lance; deflate. **2** *the earlier mood of optimism was punctured:* **put an end to**, cut short, deflate, reduce.

pundit noun *a leading pundit predicts a further interest-rate cut this year:* **expert**, authority, specialist, doyen(ne), master, guru, sage, savant; informal buff, whizz.

pungent adjective **1** *a pungent marinade:* **strong**, powerful, pervasive, penetrating; sharp, acid, sour, biting, bitter, tart, vinegary, tangy; highly flavoured, aromatic, spicy, piquant, peppery, hot. **2** *pungent remarks:* **caustic**, biting, trenchant, cutting, acerbic, sardonic, sarcastic, scathing, acrimonious, barbed, sharp, tart, incisive, bitter, venomous, waspish.
– OPPOSITES bland, mild.

punish verb **1** *they punished their children:* **discipline**, bring someone to book, teach someone a lesson; tan someone's hide; informal murder, wallop, come down on (like a ton of bricks), have someone's guts for garters; Brit. informal give someone what for. **2** *higher charges would punish the poor:* **penalize**, unfairly disadvantage, handicap, hurt, wrong, ill-use, maltreat. **3** *the strikers punished the defence's mistakes:* **exploit**, take advantage of, turn to account, profit from, capitalize on, cash in on; informal walk all over.

punishable adjective *money-laundering is a punishable offence:* **illegal**, unlawful, illegitimate, criminal, felonious, actionable, indictable, penal; blameworthy, dishonest, fraudulent, unauthorized, outlawed, banned, forbidden, prohibited, interdicted, proscribed.

punishing adjective *a punishing schedule:* **arduous**, demanding, taxing, onerous, burdensome, strenuous, rigorous, stressful, trying; hard, difficult, tough, exhausting, tiring, gruelling, crippling, relentless; informal killing.
– OPPOSITES easy.

punishment noun **1** *the punishment of the guilty:* **penalizing**, punishing, disciplining; retribution. **2** *the teacher imposed punishments:* **penalty**, penance, sanction, sentence, one's just deserts; discipline, correction, vengeance, justice, judgement; informal comeuppance. **3** *both boxers took punishment:* **a battering**, a thrashing, a beating, a drubbing; informal a hiding. **4** *ovens take continual punishment:* **maltreatment**, mistreatment, abuse, ill-use, manhandling; damage, harm.

punitive adjective **1** *punitive measures:* **penal**, disciplinary, corrective, correctional, retributive. **2** *punitive taxes:* **harsh**, severe, stiff, stringent, burdensome, demanding, crushing, crippling; high,

p

sky-high, inflated, exorbitant, extortionate, excessive, inordinate, unreasonable; Brit. swingeing.

puny adjective **1** *he grew up puny:* **undersized**, undernourished, underfed, stunted, slight, small, little; weak, feeble, sickly, delicate, frail, fragile; informal weedy, pint-sized. **2** *puny efforts to save their homes:* **pitiful**, pitiable, inadequate, insufficient, derisory, miserable, sorry, meagre, paltry, trifling, inconsequential; informal pathetic, measly, piddling.
– OPPOSITES sturdy, substantial.

pupil noun **1** *former pupils of the school:* **student**, scholar; schoolchild, schoolboy, schoolgirl. **2** *the guru's pupils:* **disciple**, follower, student, protégé, apprentice, trainee, novice.

puppet noun **1** *a show with puppets:* **marionette**; glove puppet, hand puppet, finger puppet. **2** *a puppet of the government:* **pawn**, tool, instrument, cat's paw, poodle, creature, dupe; mouthpiece, minion, stooge.

purchase verb *we purchased the software:* **buy**, pay for, acquire, obtain, pick up, snap up, take, procure; invest in; informal get hold of, score.
– OPPOSITES sell.
noun **1** *he's happy with his purchase:* **acquisition**, buy, investment, order, bargain; shopping, goods. **2** *he could get no purchase on the wall:* **grip**, grasp, hold, foothold, toehold, anchorage, attachment, support; resistance, friction, leverage.
– OPPOSITES sale.

purchaser noun **buyer**, shopper, customer, consumer, patron; Law vendee.

pure adjective **1** *pure gold:* **unadulterated**, uncontaminated, unmixed, undiluted, unalloyed, unblended; sterling, solid, refined, 100%; clarified, clear, filtered, flawless, perfect, genuine, real. **2** *the air is so pure:* **clean**, clear, fresh, sparkling, unpolluted, uncontaminated, untainted; wholesome, natural, healthy; sanitary, uninfected, disinfected, germ-free, sterile, sterilized, aseptic. **3** *pure in body and mind:* **virtuous**, moral, ethical, good, righteous, saintly, honourable, reputable, wholesome, clean, honest, upright, upstanding, exemplary, irreproachable; chaste, virginal, maidenly; decent, worthy, noble, blameless, guiltless, spotless, unsullied, uncorrupted, undefiled; informal squeaky clean. **4** *pure maths:* **theoretical**, abstract, conceptual, academic, hypothetical, speculative, conjectural. **5** *three hours of pure magic:* **sheer**, utter, absolute, out-and-out, complete, total, perfect, unmitigated.
– OPPOSITES adulterated, polluted, immoral, practical.

purely adverb *he seemed to regard the exchange purely as a joke:* **entirely**, completely, absolutely, wholly, exclusively, solely, only, just, merely.

purgative adjective *purgative medicine:*

laxative, evacuant, aperient.
noun *orris root is a purgative:* **laxative**, evacuant, aperient, enema.

purgatory noun *the pre-med year was a necessary term of purgatory:* **torment**, torture, misery, suffering, affliction, anguish, agony, woe, hell; an ordeal, a nightmare.
– OPPOSITES paradise.

purge verb **1** *he purged them of their doubt:* **cleanse**, clear, purify, wash, shrive, absolve; rare lustrate. **2** *lawbreakers were purged from the army:* **remove**, get rid of, expel, eject, exclude, dismiss, sack, oust, eradicate, clear out, weed out.
noun *the purge of dissidents:* **removal**, expulsion, ejection, exclusion, eviction, dismissal, sacking, ousting, eradication.

purify verb **1** *trees help to purify the air:* **clean**, cleanse, refine, decontaminate; filter, clarify, clear, freshen, deodorize; sanitize, disinfect, sterilize. **2** *they purify themselves before the ceremony:* **purge**, cleanse, unburden, deliver; redeem, shrive, exorcize, sanctify; rare lustrate.

purist noun *the purist will point out that every aircraft accident results from human error of some kind:* **pedant**, perfectionist, formalist, literalist, stickler, traditionalist, doctrinaire, quibbler, dogmatist; informal nit-picker.

puritan noun *today's puritans impede frank talk about sexuality:* **moralist**, pietist, prude, prig, killjoy; ascetic; informal goody-goody, Holy Joe; N. Amer. informal bluenose.

puritanical adjective **moralistic**, puritan, pietistic, strait-laced, stuffy, prudish, prim, priggish; narrow-minded, sententious, censorious; austere, severe, ascetic, abstemious; informal goody-goody, starchy.
– OPPOSITES permissive.

purity noun **1** *the purity of our tap water:* **cleanness**, clearness, clarity, freshness; sterility. **2** *they sought purity in a foul world:* **virtue**, morality, goodness, righteousness, saintliness, piety, honour, honesty, integrity, decency, ethicality, impeccability; innocence, chastity.

purport verb *this work purports to be authoritative:* **claim**, profess, pretend; appear, seem; be ostensibly, pose as, impersonate, masquerade as, pass for.
noun *the purport of his remarks:* **gist**, substance, drift, implication, intention, meaning, significance, sense, essence, thrust, message.

purpose noun **1** *the purpose of his visit:* **motive**, motivation, grounds, cause, occasion, reason, point, basis, justification. **2** *their purpose was to subvert the economy:* **intention**, aim, object, objective, goal, end, plan, scheme, target; ambition, aspiration. **3** *I cannot see any purpose in it:* **advantage**, benefit, good, use, value, merit, worth, profit; informal mileage, percentage. **4** *the* *original purpose of the porch:* **function**, role, use. **5** *they started the game with purpose:* **determination**, resolution, resolve, steadfastness, backbone, drive, push, enthusiasm, ambition, motivation, commitment, conviction, dedication; informal get-up-and-go.

■ **on purpose** deliberately, intentionally, purposely, by design, wilfully, knowingly, consciously, of one's own volition; expressly, specifically, especially, specially.

purposeful adjective *the purposeful stride of a great barrister:* **determined**, resolute, steadfast, single-minded; enthusiastic, motivated, committed, dedicated, persistent, dogged, unfaltering, unshakeable.
– OPPOSITES aimless.

purposely adverb. See **ON PURPOSE** at **PURPOSE**.

purse noun **1** *the money fell out of her purse:* **wallet**, money bag; N. Amer. change purse, billfold. **2** (N. Amer.) *a woman's purse.* See **HANDBAG**. **3** *the public purse:* **fund(s)**, kitty, coffers, pool, bank, treasury, exchequer; money, finances, wealth, reserves, cash, capital, assets. **4** *the fight will net him a $75,000 purse:* **prize**, reward, award; winnings, stake(s).
verb *he pursed his lips:* **press together**, compress, tighten, pucker, pout.

pursue verb **1** *I pursued him down the garden:* **follow**, run after, chase; hunt, stalk, track, trail, shadow, hound, course; informal tail. **2** *pursue the goal of political union:* **strive for**, work towards, seek, search for, aim at/for, aspire to. **3** *he had been pursuing her for weeks:* **woo**, pay court to, chase, run after; informal make up to. **4** *she pursued a political career:* **engage in**, be occupied in, practise, follow, prosecute, conduct, ply, take up, undertake, carry on. **5** *we will not pursue the matter:* **investigate**, research, inquire into, look into, examine, scrutinize, analyse, delve into, probe.
– OPPOSITES avoid, shun.

pursuit noun **1** *the pursuit of profit:* **striving towards**, quest after/for, search for; aim, goal, objective, dream. **2** *a worthwhile pursuit:* **activity**, hobby, pastime, diversion, recreation, relaxation, divertissement, amusement; occupation, trade, vocation, business, work, job, employment.

purveyor noun *a local purveyor of gourmet sandwiches:* **seller**, vendor, retailer, supplier, stockist, trader, pedlar, hawker; Brit. tout.

pus noun **suppuration**, matter; discharge, secretion.

push verb **1** *she tried to push him away:* **shove**, thrust, propel; send, drive, force, prod, poke, nudge, elbow, shoulder; sweep, bundle, hustle, manhandle. **2** *she pushed her way into the flat:* **force**, shove, thrust, squeeze, jostle, elbow, shoulder, bundle, hustle; work, inch. **3** *he pushed the panic button:* **press**, depress, bear down on, hold

down, squeeze; operate, activate. **4** *don't push her to join in:* **urge**, press, pressure, pressurize, force, impel, coerce, nag; prevail on, browbeat into; informal lean on, twist someone's arm, bulldoze. **5** *they push their own products:* **advertise**, publicize, promote, bang the drum for; sell, market, merchandise; informal plug, hype (up), puff, flog; N. Amer. informal ballyhoo.
– OPPOSITES pull.

noun **1** *I felt a push in the back:* **shove**, thrust, nudge, ram, bump, jolt, butt, prod, poke. **2** *the enemy's eastward push:* **advance**, drive, thrust, charge, attack, assault, onslaught, onrush, offensive, sortie, sally, incursion.

■ **push someone around** bully, domineer, ride roughshod over, trample on, bulldoze, browbeat, tyrannize, intimidate, threaten, victimize, pick on; informal lean on, boss about/around.

■ **push for** *the trade unions will be likely to push for wage increases:* demand, call for, request, press for, campaign for, lobby for, speak up for; urge, promote, advocate, champion, espouse.

■ **push on** *I decided to push on towards the coast:* press on, continue one's journey, carry on, advance, proceed, go on, progress, make headway, forge ahead.

pushover noun **1** *the teacher was a pushover:* **weakling**, feeble opponent, man of straw; informal soft touch, easy touch, easy meat. **2** *this course is no pushover:* **easy task**, walkover, five-finger exercise, gift; child's play; informal doddle, piece of cake, picnic, money for old rope, cinch, breeze, low-hanging fruit; Brit. informal doss; N. Amer. informal duck soup, snap; Austral./NZ informal bludge.

pushy adjective *behind every successful child there is a pushy parent:* **assertive**, self-assertive, overbearing, domineering, aggressive, forceful, forward, bold, bumptious, officious; thrusting, ambitious, overconfident, cocky; informal bossy.
– OPPOSITES submissive.

pusillanimous adjective *the President's increasingly pusillanimous stance on social issues:* **timid**, timorous, cowardly, fearful, faint-hearted, lily-livered, spineless, craven, shrinking; informal chicken, gutless, wimpy, wimpish, sissy, yellow, yellow-bellied.
– OPPOSITES brave.

pussyfoot verb *you can't pussyfoot around with this:* **equivocate**, tergiversate, be evasive, be non-committal, sidestep the issue, prevaricate, quibble, hedge, beat about the bush; Brit. hum and haw; informal duck the question, sit on the fence, shilly-shally.

pustule noun **pimple**, spot, bleb, boil, swelling, eruption, carbuncle, blister, abscess; informal whitehead, zit; Scottish informal plook.

put verb **1** *she put the parcel on a chair:* **place**, set (down), lay (down), deposit, position, settle; leave, plant; informal stick, dump, bung, park, plonk, pop; N. Amer. informal plunk. **2** *he didn't want to be put in a category:* **assign to**, consign to, allocate to, place in. **3** *don't put the blame on me:* lay, pin, place, fix; attribute to, impute to, assign to, allocate to, ascribe to. **4** *the proposals were put to the committee:* **submit**, present, tender, offer, proffer, advance, suggest, propose. **5** *she put it bluntly:* **express**, word, phrase, frame, formulate, render, convey, couch; state, say, utter.

■ **put about** *the ship put about:* turn round, come about, change course.

■ **put something about** *the rumour had been put about:* spread, circulate, make public, disseminate, broadcast, publicize, pass on, propagate, bandy about.

■ **put something across/over** *the party needs to put across its message more effectively:* communicate, convey, get across/over, explain, make clear, spell out, clarify; get through to someone.

■ **put something aside 1** *we've got a bit put aside in the bank:* save, put by, set aside, deposit, reserve, store, stockpile, hoard, stow, cache; informal salt away, squirrel away, stash away. **2** *they put aside their differences:* disregard, set aside, ignore, forget, discount, bury.

■ **put something away 1** *I put away some money.* See **PUT SOMETHING ASIDE** sense 1. **2** *she never puts her things away:* replace, put back, tidy away, tidy up, clear away.

■ **put something back 1** *he put the books back:* replace, return, restore, put away, tidy away. **2** *they put back the film's release date.* See **PUT SOMETHING OFF**.

■ **put someone down 1** (informal) *he often puts me down:* criticize, belittle, disparage, deprecate, denigrate, slight, humiliate, shame, crush, squash, deflate; informal show up, cut down to size. **2** *I put him down as shy:* consider to be, judge to be, reckon to be, take to be; regard, have down, take for.

■ **put something down 1** *he put his ideas down on paper:* write down, note down, jot down, take down, set down; list, record, register, log. **2** *they put down the rebellion:* suppress, check, crush, quash, squash, quell, overthrow, stamp out, repress, subdue. **3** *the horse had to be put down:* destroy, put to sleep, put out of its misery, put to death, kill. **4** *put it down to the heat:* attribute, ascribe, chalk up, impute; blame on.

■ **put something forward**. See **PUT** sense 4.

■ **put in for** *some people put in for voluntary redundancy:* apply for, put in an application for, try for; request, seek, ask for.

■ **put someone off** *the smell put Lisa off:* deter, discourage, dissuade, daunt, unnerve, intimidate, scare off, repel, repulse; distract, disturb, divert, sidetrack; informal turn off.

■ **put something off** *it's very easy to put off difficult decisions:* postpone, defer, delay, put back, adjourn, hold over, reschedule, shelve, table; informal put on ice, put on the back burner.

■ **put it on** *he laughed but Olivia thought he was putting it on:* pretend, play-act, make believe, fake it, go through the motions.

■ **put something on 1** *she put on jeans:* dress in, don, pull on, throw on, slip into, change into; informal doll oneself up in. **2** *I put the light on:* switch on, turn on, activate. **3** *they put on an extra train:* provide, lay on, supply, make available. **4** *the museum put on an exhibition:* organize, stage, mount, present, produce. **5** *she put on an American accent:* feign, fake, simulate, affect, assume.

■ **put one over on** (informal). See **HOODWINK**.

■ **put someone out 1** *Maria was put out by the slur:* annoy, anger, irritate, offend, affront, displease, irk, vex, pique, nettle, gall, upset; informal rile, miff, peeve; Brit. informal nark. **2** *I don't want to put you out:* inconvenience, trouble, bother, impose on, disoblige; informal put someone on the spot.

■ **put something out 1** *firemen put out the blaze:* extinguish, quench, douse, smother; blow out, snuff out. **2** *he put out a press release:* issue, publish, release, bring out, circulate, publicize, post.

■ **put someone up 1** *we can put him up for a few days:* accommodate, house, take in, lodge, quarter, billet; give someone a roof over their head. **2** *they put up a candidate:* nominate, propose, put forward, recommend.

■ **put something up 1** *the building was put up 100 years ago:* build, construct, erect, raise. **2** *she put up a poster:* display, pin up, stick up, hang up, post. **3** *we put up alternative schemes:* propose, put forward, present, submit, suggest, tender. **4** *the chancellor put up taxes:* increase, raise; informal jack up, hike, bump up. **5** *he put up most of the funding:* provide, supply, furnish, give, contribute, donate, pledge, pay; informal fork out, cough up, shell out; N. Amer. informal ante up, pony up.

■ **put upon** (informal) *his eagerness to please ensured that he was put upon:* take advantage of, impose on, exploit, use, misuse; informal walk all over.

■ **put someone up to something** (informal) *Who else would play a trick like that on me? I expect Rose put him up to it:* persuade to, encourage to, urge to, egg on to, incite to, goad into.

■ **put up with** *Harriet told him she was not prepared to put up with such behaviour:* tolerate, take, stand (for), accept, stomach, swallow, endure, bear, support, take something lying down; informal abide, lump it; Brit. informal stick, be doing with.

putative adjective *the putative father of her child:* **supposed**, assumed, presumed; accepted, recognized; commonly regarded, presumptive, alleged, reputed, reported, rumoured.

put-down noun (informal) *he was still smarting from the put-down:* **snub**, slight, affront, rebuff, sneer, disparagement, humiliation, barb, jibe, criticism; informal dig.

p

putrefy verb *the sickly smell of putrefying flesh:* **decay**, rot, decompose, go bad, go off, spoil, fester, perish, deteriorate; moulder.

putrid adjective *putrid meat:* **decomposing**, decaying, rotting, rotten, bad, off, putrefied, putrescent, rancid, mouldy; foul, fetid, rank.

puzzle verb **1** *her decision puzzled me:* **perplex**, confuse, bewilder, bemuse, baffle, mystify, confound, nonplus; informal flummox, faze, stump, beat; N. Amer. informal discombobulate. **2** *she puzzled over the problem:* **think hard about**, mull over, muse over, ponder, contemplate, meditate on, consider, deliberate on, chew over, wonder about. **3** *she tried to puzzle out what he meant:* **work out**, understand, comprehend, sort out, reason out, solve, make sense of, make head or tail of, unravel, decipher; informal figure out, suss out.
noun *the poem has always been a puzzle:* **enigma**, mystery, paradox, conundrum, poser, riddle, problem; informal stumper.

puzzled adjective *Fiona looked puzzled:* **perplexed**, confused, bewildered, bemused, baffled, mystified, confounded, nonplussed, at a loss, at sea; informal flummoxed, stumped, fazed, clueless; N. Amer. informal discombobulated.

puzzling adjective *his explanation was rather puzzling:* **baffling**, perplexing, bewildering, confusing, complicated, unclear, mysterious, enigmatic, ambiguous, obscure, abstruse, unfathomable, incomprehensible, impenetrable, cryptic.
– OPPOSITES clear.

pygmy noun **1** *a Congo pygmy:* **very small person**, person of restricted growth, midget, dwarf, homunculus, manikin; Lilliputian; informal shrimp. **2** *an intellectual pygmy:* **lightweight**, mediocrity, nonentity, nobody, cipher; small fry; informal pipsqueak, no-hoper; Brit. informal squit; N. Amer. informal picayune.
– OPPOSITES giant.

pyromaniac noun **arsonist**, incendiary; Brit. fire-raiser; informal firebug, pyro; N. Amer. informal torch.

Qq

quack noun *the man is a quack selling fake medicines:* **swindler**, charlatan, trickster, fraud, fraudster, impostor, hoaxer; informal con man; N. Amer. informal **grifter**; Austral. informal shicer.

quadrangle noun **courtyard**, quad, court, cloister, precinct; square, plaza, piazza.

quaff verb **drink**, swallow, gulp (down), guzzle, slurp, down, drain, empty; imbibe, partake of, consume, sup, sip; informal sink, glug, swig, swill, slug, knock back, toss off; Brit. informal get outside (of), shift, murder, neck; N. Amer. informal **chug**, snarf (down).

quagmire noun **swamp**, morass, bog, marsh, mire.

quail verb **cower**, cringe, flinch, shrink, recoil, shy (away), pull back; shiver, tremble, shake, quake, blench, blanch.

quaint adjective **1** *narrow streets lead down to a quaint bridge:* **picturesque**, charming, sweet, attractive, old-fashioned; Brit. twee; N. Amer. cunning. **2** *Polybius comments on the quaint customs of the Romans:* **unusual**, curious, eccentric, quirky, bizarre, whimsical, unconventional; informal offbeat.
– OPPOSITES ugly, ordinary.

quake verb **1** *the ground quaked as they walked on it:* **shake**, tremble, quiver, shudder, sway, rock, wobble, move, heave, convulse. **2** *we quaked whenever we saw soldiers:* **tremble**, shake, quiver, shiver; blench, blanch, flinch, shrink, recoil, cower, cringe.

qualification noun **1** *I have a professional teaching qualification:* **certificate**, diploma, degree, licence, document, warrant. **2** *I can't accept it without some qualification:* **modification**, reservation; alteration, amendment, revision, moderation, mitigation; condition, proviso, caveat.

qualified adjective **certified**, certificated, chartered, licensed, professional; trained, fit, competent, accomplished, proficient, skilled, experienced, expert.

qualify verb **1** *do you qualify for free travel?* **be eligible**, meet the requirements; be entitled to, be allowed. **2** *many of the new arrivals qualify as refugees:* **count**, be considered, be designated, be eligible. **3** *she qualified as a solicitor last year:* **be certified**, be licensed; pass, graduate, make the grade, succeed, pass muster. **4** *the course qualified them to teach children:*

authorize, empower, allow, permit, license. **5** *the authors later qualified their findings:* **modify**, limit, restrict; moderate, temper, modulate, mitigate.

quality noun **1** *the system compresses TV signals while retaining their quality:* **standard**, grade, class, calibre, condition, character, nature, form, rank, value, level. **2** *work of such quality remains a rarity:* **excellence**, superiority, merit, worth, value, virtue, calibre, eminence, distinction, incomparability; talent, skill, virtuosity, craftsmanship. **3** *she has many good qualities:* **feature**, trait, attribute, characteristic, point, aspect, facet, side, property.

qualm noun *I have no qualms about going to Japan:* **misgiving**, doubt, reservation, second thought, worry, concern, anxiety; (**qualms**) hesitation, demur, reluctance, apprehension, trepidation, unease; scruples, compunction.

quandary noun *they are still in a quandary over whether to ditch the idea:* **predicament**, plight, difficult situation; trouble, muddle, mess, confusion, difficulty; informal dilemma, sticky situation, pickle, hole, stew, fix, bind, jam.

quantity noun **1** *the quantity of food collected was very impressive:* **amount**, total, aggregate, sum, quota, mass, weight, volume, bulk; proportion, portion, part. **2** *police divers recovered a quantity of ammunition:* **amount**, lot, great deal, good deal, an abundance, a wealth, a profusion, plenty; informal piles, oodles, tons, lots, loads, heaps, masses, stacks, bags; Brit. informal shedloads.

quarrel noun *they had a quarrel about money:* **argument**, disagreement, squabble, fight, dispute, wrangle, clash, altercation, feud, contretemps, disputation, falling-out, shouting match; informal tiff, slanging match, run-in; Brit. informal barney, row, bust-up.
verb *I should be sorry to quarrel over it:* **argue**, fight, disagree, fall out; differ, be at odds; bicker, squabble, cross swords, lock horns, be at each other's throats; Brit. informal row.

■ **quarrel with** *you can't quarrel with the verdict:* **fault**, criticize, object to, oppose, take exception to; attack, take issue with, impugn, contradict, dispute, controvert; informal knock; formal gainsay.

q

quarrelsome adjective **argumentative**, confrontational, captious, pugnacious, combative, antagonistic, bellicose, belligerent, cantankerous; Brit. informal stroppy; N. Amer. informal scrappy.
– OPPOSITES peaceable.

quarry noun **prey**, victim; object, goal, target; kill, game.

quarter noun **1** *the Latin quarter of Paris:* **district**, area, region, part, side, neighbourhood, precinct, locality, sector, zone; ghetto, community, enclave. **2** *the servants' quarters:* **accommodation**, lodgings, rooms, chambers; home, residence; informal pad, digs; formal abode, domicile. **3** *the riot squads gave no quarter:* **mercy**, leniency, clemency, lenity, compassion, pity, charity, sympathy, tolerance.
verb *they were quartered in a huge villa:* **accommodate**, house, board, lodge, put up, take in, install, shelter; Military billet.

quash verb **1** *the appeal judge may quash the sentence:* **cancel**, reverse, rescind, repeal, revoke, retract, countermand, withdraw, overturn, overrule, veto, annul, nullify, invalidate, negate, void. **2** *we want to quash these rumours once and for all:* **put an end to**, stamp out, crush, check, curb, nip in the bud, squash, quell, subdue, suppress, extinguish, stifle.
– OPPOSITES validate.

quasi- combining form **1** *a quasi-scientific body studying cosmic rays:* **supposedly**, allegedly, ostensibly, outwardly, superficially, purportedly, nominally; pseudo-. **2** *a quasi-autonomous organization:* **partly**, partially, part, to a certain extent, to some extent, half, relatively, comparatively, (up) to a point.

quaver verb *his voice quavered with emotion:* **tremble**, waver, quiver, shake, vibrate, oscillate, fluctuate, falter.

quay noun **wharf**, pier, jetty, landing stage, berth; marina, dock, harbour.

queasy adjective *he still felt queasy and was grateful for the fresh air:* **nauseous**, nauseated, bilious, sick; ill, unwell, poorly, green about the gills; Brit. off colour.

queen noun **1** *the Queen was crowned:* **monarch**, sovereign, ruler, head of state; Her Majesty. **2** (informal) *the queen of soul music:* **doyenne**, star, superstar, leading light, big name, queen bee, prima donna, idol, heroine, favourite, darling, goddess.

queer adjective *it seemed queer to see him here:* **odd**, strange, unusual, funny, peculiar, curious, bizarre, weird, uncanny, freakish, eerie, unnatural; unconventional, unorthodox, unexpected, unfamiliar, abnormal, anomalous, atypical, untypical, out of the ordinary, incongruous, irregular; puzzling, perplexing, baffling, unaccountable; informal fishy, creepy, spooky, freaky; Brit. informal rum.
– OPPOSITES normal.
verb *he inadvertently queered the whole*

deal: **spoil**, ruin, wreck, destroy, scotch, disrupt, undo, thwart, foil, blight, cripple, undermine; informal botch, blow, put the kibosh on; Brit. informal scupper.

quell verb **1** *troops were called in to quell the unrest:* **put an end/stop to**, end, crush, put down, check, crack down on, curb, nip in the bud, squash, quash, suppress, overcome. **2** *he managed to quell his initial misgivings:* **calm**, soothe, settle, quieten, quiet, silence, allay, assuage, mitigate, moderate.

quench verb *they quenched their thirst with spring water:* **satisfy**, slake, sate, satiate, gratify, relieve, assuage.

querulous adjective *the old man complained in a querulous voice:* **petulant**, peevish, pettish, complaining, fractious, fretful, irritable, testy, tetchy, cross, snappish, crabby, crotchety, cantankerous, miserable, moody, grumpy, bad-tempered, sullen, sulky, sour, churlish; informal snappy, grouchy, whingy; Brit. informal ratty, cranky; N. English informal mardy; N. Amer. informal soreheaded.

query noun **1** *we are happy to answer any queries:* **question**, enquiry. **2** *there was a query as to who owned the hotel:* **doubt**, uncertainty, question (mark), reservation; scepticism.
verb **1** *'Why do that?' queried Isobel:* **ask**, enquire, question. **2** *folk may query his credentials:* **question**, call into question, challenge, dispute, cast aspersions on, doubt, have suspicions/reservations about.

quest noun *nothing will stop their quest for her killer:* **search**, hunt.
■ **in quest of** in search of, in pursuit of, seeking, looking for, on the lookout for, after.

question noun **1** *please answer my question:* **enquiry**, query. **2** *there is no question that he is ill:* **doubt**, dispute, argument, debate, uncertainty, dubiousness, reservation. **3** *he wrote essays on the political questions of the day:* **issue**, matter, business, problem, concern, topic, theme, case; debate, argument, dispute, controversy.
– OPPOSITES answer, certainty.
verb **1** *the magistrate may question the suspect:* **interrogate**, cross-examine, cross-question, quiz; interview, debrief, examine, give someone the third degree; informal grill, pump. **2** *she questioned his motives:* **query**, call into question, challenge, dispute, cast aspersions on, doubt, suspect, have suspicions/reservations about.
■ **beyond question 1** *her loyalty is beyond question:* undoubted, beyond doubt, certain, indubitable, indisputable, incontrovertible, unquestionable, undeniable, clear, patent, manifest. **2** *the results demonstrated this beyond question:* indisputably, irrefutably, incontestably, incontrovertibly, unquestionably, undeniably, undoubtedly, beyond doubt, without doubt, clearly, patently, obviously.

■ **in question** *the aircraft in question were seen flying over Hamburg:* at issue, under discussion, under consideration, on the agenda.

■ **out of the question** *going back to the station was clearly out of the question:* impossible, impracticable, unfeasible, unworkable, inconceivable, unimaginable, unrealizable, unsuitable; informal not on.

questionable adjective **1** *his jokes are of questionable taste:* **doubtful**, contentious, controversial, dubious, uncertain, debatable, arguable; unverified, unprovable, unresolved, unconvincing, implausible, improbable; borderline, marginal, moot; informal iffy; Brit. informal dodgy. **2** *some of his questionable financial dealings have been investigated:* **suspicious**, suspect, dubious, irregular, odd, strange, murky, dark, unsavoury, disreputable; informal funny, fishy, shady, iffy; Brit. informal dodgy.
– OPPOSITES indisputable, honest.

queue noun **1** *there was a queue of people waiting for the bus:* **line**, row, column, file, chain, string; procession; waiting list; N. Amer. wait list; Brit. informal crocodile. **2** *he was in a taxi, stuck in a queue along Knightsbridge:* **(traffic) jam**, tailback, gridlock; N. Amer. backup; informal snarl-up.
verb *we queued for ice creams:* **line up**, form a queue, queue up, wait in line, form a line.

quibble noun *I have just one quibble:* **criticism**, objection, complaint, protest, argument, exception, grumble, grouse, cavil; informal niggle, moan, gripe, beef.
verb *no one quibbled with the title:* **object to**, find fault with, complain about, cavil at; split hairs, chop logic; criticize, query; informal nit-pick.

quick adjective **1** *John was generally a quick worker:* **fast**, swift, rapid, speedy, high-speed, expeditious, brisk, smart; lightning, whirlwind, fast-track, whistle-stop, breakneck; informal nippy, zippy.
2 *she took a quick look behind her:* **hasty**, hurried, cursory, perfunctory, desultory; superficial, summary; brief, short, fleeting, transient, transitory, short-lived, lightning, momentary. **3** *we are hoping for a quick end to the recession:* **sudden**, instantaneous, immediate, instant, abrupt, precipitate. **4** *she isn't as quick as the others:* **intelligent**, bright, clever, astute, quick-witted, sharp-witted, smart; observant, alert, sharp, perceptive; informal on the ball, quick on the uptake.
– OPPOSITES slow, long.

quicken verb **1** *she unconsciously quickened her pace:* **speed up**, accelerate, step up; informal gee up. **2** *the film quickened his interest in nature:* **stimulate**, excite, arouse, rouse, stir up, activate, galvanize, whet, inspire, kindle; invigorate, revive, revitalize.

quickly adverb **1** *he walked quickly down the road:* **fast**, swiftly, briskly, rapidly, speedily, at the double, post-haste, hotfoot;

informal double quick, p.d.q. (pretty damn quick); N. Amer. informal lickety-split. **2** *you'd better leave quickly:* **immediately**, directly, at once, now, straight away, right away, instantly, forthwith, without delay, without further ado; soon, promptly, early; N. Amer. momentarily; informal like a shot, a.s.a.p. (as soon as possible), pronto, before you can say Jack Robinson, straight off. **3** *he calmed the animal and quickly inspected it:* **briefly**, fleetingly, briskly; hastily, hurriedly, cursorily, perfunctorily, superficially, desultorily.

quick-witted adjective **intelligent**, bright, clever, gifted, able, astute, quick, smart, sharp-witted; observant, alert, sharp, perceptive; informal brainy, on the ball, quick on the uptake.
– OPPOSITES slow.

quiet adjective **1** *the whole pub went quiet:* **silent**, still, hushed, noiseless, soundless; mute, dumb, speechless. **2** *she spoke in a quiet voice:* **soft**, low, muted, muffled, faint, indistinct, inaudible, hushed, whispered. **3** *a quiet village outside Perth:* **peaceful**, sleepy, tranquil, calm, still, restful, undisturbed, untroubled; unfrequented. **4** *can I have a quiet word?* **private**, confidential, secret, discreet, unofficial, off the record. **5** *you can't keep it quiet for long:* **secret**, confidential, classified, unrevealed, undisclosed, unknown, under wraps; informal hush-hush, mum.
– OPPOSITES loud, busy, public.
noun *after London, we longed for the quiet of the countryside:* **peacefulness**, peace, restfulness, calm, tranquillity, serenity; silence, quietness, stillness, still, hush.

quieten verb **1** *the teacher had to stop to quieten the children down:* **silence**, hush, shush, quiet; informal shut up. **2** *her travelling companions had quietened:* **fall silent**, stop talking, break off, shush; informal shut up, clam up, pipe down, shut one's mouth.

quietly adverb **1** *she quietly entered the room:* **silently**, in silence, noiselessly, soundlessly, inaudibly; mutely, dumbly. **2** *he spoke quietly so as not to disturb anyone:* **softly**, in a low voice, in a whisper, in a murmur, under one's breath, sotto voce, gently, faintly, weakly, feebly. **3** *some bonds were sold quietly to club members:* **discreetly**, privately, confidentially, secretly, unofficially, off the record. **4** *she is quietly confident:* **calmly**, patiently, placidly, serenely.

quilt noun **duvet**, cover(s); Brit. eiderdown; N. Amer. comforter, puff; Austral. trademark Doona.

quintessence noun **perfect example**, exemplar, prototype, stereotype, picture, epitome, embodiment, idea.

quintessential adjective **typical**, prototypical, stereotypical, archetypal, classic, model, standard, stock, representative, conventional; ideal, consummate, exemplary, best, ultimate.

q

quip noun *the quip failed to provoke a smile:* **joke**, remark, witticism, jest, pun, pleasantry, bon mot; informal one-liner, gag, crack, wisecrack, funny.
verb *'Enjoy your trip?' he quipped:* **joke**, jest, pun; informal wisecrack.

quirk noun **1** *they all know his quirks and mannerisms:* **idiosyncrasy**, peculiarity, oddity, eccentricity, foible, whim, vagary, caprice, habit, characteristic, trait, fad; informal hang-up. **2** *we met by a quirk of fate:* **chance**, fluke, freak, anomaly, twist.

quirky adjective **eccentric**, idiosyncratic, unconventional, unorthodox, unusual, strange, bizarre, peculiar, odd, outlandish, zany; informal wacky, freaky, way-out, far out, kooky, offbeat.
– OPPOSITES conventional.

quit verb **1** *he quit the office at 12.30:* **leave**, vacate, exit, depart from, withdraw from; abandon, desert. **2** (informal) *he's decided to quit his job:* **resign from**, leave, give up, stand down from, relinquish, vacate, walk out on, retire from; informal chuck, pack in.

quite adverb **1** *two quite different types of rubber:* **completely**, entirely, totally, wholly, absolutely, utterly, thoroughly, altogether. **2** *red hair is quite common:* **fairly**, rather, somewhat, slightly, relatively, comparatively, moderately, reasonably, to a certain extent; informal pretty, kind of, sort of.

quiver verb *I quivered with terror:* **tremble**, shake, shiver, quaver, quake, shudder.
noun *there was a quiver in her voice:* **tremor**, tremble, shake, quaver, flutter, fluctuation, waver.

quixotic adjective *the new building is a vast, exciting, and perhaps quixotic project:* **idealistic**, romantic, visionary, Utopian, extravagant, starry-eyed, unrealistic, unworldly; impracticable, unworkable, impossible.

quiz noun **1** *a music quiz:* **competition**, test. **2** (informal) *jockey faces quiz over bribes:* **interrogation**, questioning, interview, examination, the third degree; informal grilling.
verb *a man was being quizzed by police:* **question**, interrogate, cross-examine, cross-question, interview, sound out, give someone the third degree; informal grill, pump.

quizzical adjective *he gave me a quizzical look:* **enquiring**, questioning, curious, amused, mocking, teasing.

quota noun **allocation**, share, allowance, limit, ration, portion, dispensation, slice (of the cake); percentage, commission; proportion, fraction, bit, amount, quantity; informal cut, rake-off; Brit. informal whack.

quotation noun **1** *a quotation from Dryden:* **citation**, quote, excerpt, extract, passage, line, paragraph, verse, phrase; reference, allusion; N. Amer. cite. **2** *we will send you a quotation for the building work:* **estimate**, quote, price, tender, bid, costing, charge, figure.

quote verb **1** *he quoted a sentence from the book:* **recite**, repeat, reproduce; take, extract. **2** *she quoted one case in which a girl died:* **cite**, mention, refer to, name, instance, specify, identify; relate, recount; allude to, point out, present, offer, advance.
noun. See QUOTATION.

q

Rr

rabbit noun Brit. coney; informal bunny.

rabble noun 1 *a rabble of noisy, angry youths:* **mob**, crowd, throng, gang, swarm, horde, pack, mass, group. 2 *democracy was taken to mean rule by the rabble:* **the common people**, the masses, the populace, the multitude, the rank and file, the mob, the proletariat, the peasantry, the hoi polloi, the lower classes, the riff-raff; informal the proles, the plebs.
– OPPOSITES nobility.

rabble-rouser noun *he was nothing more than a Communist rabble-rouser:* **agitator**, troublemaker, instigator, firebrand, revolutionary, demagogue.

rabid adjective *a rabid anti-royalist:* **extreme**, fanatical, maniacal, passionate, fervent, diehard, uncompromising; informal gung-ho, raving.
– OPPOSITES moderate.

race¹ noun 1 *Dave won the race and Andy came second:* **contest**, competition, event, fixture, heat, trial(s). 2 *the race for naval domination accelerated:* **competition**, rivalry, contention, scrabble; quest.
verb 1 *he will race in the final:* **compete**, contend; run, take part. 2 *Claire raced after him:* **hurry**, dash, rush, run, sprint, bolt, dart, gallop, career, charge, shoot, hurtle, hare, fly, speed, scurry; informal tear, belt, pelt, scoot, hotfoot it, leg it; Brit. informal bomb; N. Amer. informal hightail it. 3 *she tried to calm herself, but her heart was racing:* **pound**, beat, throb, thud, thump, hammer, palpitate, flutter, pitter-patter, quiver, pump.

race² noun 1 *pupils of many different races:* **ethnic group**, racial type, (ethnic) origin. 2 *we Scots were a bloodthirsty race:* **people**, nation; informal bunch, lot.

racial adjective **ethnic**, ethnological, race-related; cultural, national, tribal.

racism noun **(racial) discrimination**, (racial) prejudice, xenophobia, racialism, chauvinism, bigotry; anti-Semitism.

racist noun *he was exposed as a racist:* **(racial) bigot**, racialist, xenophobe, chauvinist; anti-Semite.
adjective *a racist society:* **(racially) discriminatory**, racialist, prejudiced, bigoted; anti-Semitic.

rack noun *we put the cake on a wire rack to cool:* **frame**, framework, stand, holder, trestle, support, shelf.
verb *she was racked with guilt:* **torment**, afflict, torture; plague, bedevil, persecute, trouble, worry.

racket noun *the engine makes the most incredible racket:* **noise**, din, hubbub, clamour, uproar, tumult, commotion, rumpus, pandemonium, babel; informal hullabaloo; Brit. informal row.

raconteur noun **storyteller**, narrator, anecdotalist, conversationalist; Austral. informal magsman.

racy adjective *the show included a rather racy striptease revue:* **risqué**, suggestive, naughty, sexy, spicy, ribald; indecorous, indecent, immodest, off colour, dirty, rude, smutty, crude, salacious; N. Amer. gamy; informal raunchy, blue; Brit. informal saucy; euphemistic adult.
– OPPOSITES prim.

radiance noun *the bronze plate caught the sun and flashed its radiance across her face:* **light**, brightness, brilliance, luminosity, beams, rays, illumination, blaze, glow, gleam, lustre, glare; luminescence, incandescence.

radiant adjective 1 *we lay beneath the radiant moon:* **shining**, bright, brilliant, gleaming, glowing, ablaze, luminous, luminescent, lustrous, incandescent, dazzling. 2 *she looked flushed and radiant:* **joyful**, elated, thrilled, overjoyed, jubilant, rapturous, ecstatic, euphoric, in seventh heaven, on cloud nine, delighted; informal on top of the world, over the moon; Austral. informal wrapped.
– OPPOSITES dark, gloomy.

radiate verb 1 *the hot stars radiate energy:* **emit**, give off, give out, discharge, diffuse; shed, cast. 2 *a faint light radiated from the hall:* **shine**, beam, emanate. 3 *four spokes radiate from the hub:* **fan out**, spread out, branch out/off, extend, issue.

radical adjective 1 *radical reform is long overdue:* **thoroughgoing**, thorough, complete, total, comprehensive, exhaustive, sweeping, far-reaching, wide-ranging, extensive, profound, major, stringent, rigorous. 2 *there are radical differences between the two theories:* **fundamental**, basic, essential; structural, deep-seated, intrinsic, organic, profound. 3 *he became involved in a radical political movement:* **revolutionary**; extreme, extremist, fanatical, militant.

r

– OPPOSITES superficial, minor, conservative.
noun *the arrested man was a left-wing radical:*
revolutionary; militant, zealot, extremist,
fanatic, diehard.
– OPPOSITES conservative.

raffish adjective *his cosmopolitan, raffish*
air was beginning to annoy me: **rakish**,
unconventional, bohemian; devil-may-care,
casual.
– OPPOSITES conventional.

raffle noun **lottery**, (prize) draw,
sweepstake, sweep, tombola; N. Amer. lotto.

rag noun **1** *he wiped his hands on an oily rag:*
cloth, duster; N. Amer. informal schmatte. **2** *a*
man dressed in rags: **tatters**, old clothes;
cast-offs, hand-me-downs.

ragbag noun *a ragbag of products of all*
shapes and sizes: **jumble**, hotchpotch,
mishmash, mess, hash; assortment, mixture,
miscellany, medley, mixed bag, melange,
variety, diversity, pot-pourri; N. Amer.
hodgepodge.

rage noun **1** *his rage is due to frustration:*
fury, anger, wrath, outrage, indignation,
temper, spleen, resentment, pique,
annoyance, vexation, displeasure; tantrum,
frenzy; literary ire, choler. **2** *the current*
rage for DIY: **craze**, passion, fashion,
taste, trend, vogue, fad, enthusiasm,
obsession, compulsion, fixation, fetish,
mania, preoccupation; informal thing.
verb **1** *she raged silently all the way back to*
the cottage: **seethe**, be beside oneself, rant
and rave, storm, fume, spit; informal foam at
the mouth, have a fit. **2** *he raged against*
the reforms: **protest about**, complain about,
oppose, denounce; fulminate, storm, rail;
informal kick up a stink about. **3** *a storm was*
raging outside: **blow**, howl; thunder.

ragged adjective **1** *a pair of ragged jeans:*
tattered, in tatters, torn, ripped, holey,
in holes, moth-eaten, frayed, worn (out),
falling to pieces, threadbare, scruffy,
shabby; informal tatty. **2** *a ragged child*
ran through the garden: **shabby**, scruffy,
down at heel, unkempt, dressed in rags.
3 *a ragged coastline stretched off into the*
distance: **jagged**, craggy, rugged, uneven,
rough, irregular; serrated, indented; technical
crenulated.
– OPPOSITES smart.

raging adjective **1** *a raging mob howled*
for vengeance: **angry**, furious, enraged,
incensed, infuriated, irate, fuming, seething,
ranting; informal livid, wild; literary wrathful.
2 *we fought the raging seas in vain:* **stormy**,
violent, wild, turbulent, tempestuous.

raid noun **1** *the raid on Dieppe:* **attack**,
assault, blitz, incursion, sortie; onslaught,
charge, offensive, invasion, blitzkrieg.
2 *clothing was stolen during a raid on the*
shop: **robbery**, burglary, hold-up, break-in,
ram raid; informal smash-and-grab, stick-up;
Brit. informal blag; N. Amer. informal heist. **3** *police*
found stolen ammunition during a raid on

the flat: **swoop**, search; N. Amer. informal bust,
takedown.
verb **1** *they raided enemy ships in the harbour:*
attack, assault, set upon, swoop on, blitz,
assail, storm, rush. **2** *armed men raided the*
store: **rob**, hold up, break into; plunder,
steal from, pillage, loot, ransack, sack; informal
stick up. **3** *their homes were raided by police:*
search, swoop on; N. Amer. informal bust.

raider noun **robber**, burglar, thief,
housebreaker, plunderer, pillager, looter,
marauder; attacker, assailant, invader.

rail verb *he rails against injustice and*
oppression: **protest**, fulminate, inveigh,
rage, speak out, make a stand; expostulate
about, criticize, denounce, condemn.

railing noun **fence**, fencing, rail(s), paling,
palisade, balustrade, banister, hurdle.

rain noun *the rain had stopped:* **rainfall**,
precipitation, raindrops, wet weather;
drizzle, mizzle, shower, rainstorm,
cloudburst, torrent, downpour, deluge,
storm.
verb **1** *it rained heavily during the night:* **pour**
(down), pelt down, tip down, teem down,
beat down, lash down, sheet down, rain
cats and dogs; fall, drizzle, spit; informal be
chucking it down; Brit. informal bucket down.
2 *bombs rained on the city:* **fall**, hail, drop,
shower.

rainy adjective **wet**, showery, drizzly, damp,
inclement.

raise verb **1** *he raised a hand in greeting:* **lift**
(up), hold aloft, elevate, uplift, upraise,
upthrust; hoist, haul up, hitch up; Brit. informal
hoick up. **2** *he raised himself in the bed:* **sit**
up, stand up. **3** *there was no alternative*
but to raise prices: **increase**, put up, push
up, up, escalate, inflate; informal hike (up),
jack up, bump up. **4** *he raised his voice*
slightly: **amplify**, louden, magnify. **5** *they*
were able to raise public awareness of the
issues involved: **boost**, intensify, increase,
heighten, augment. **6** *the temple was raised*
in 900 BC: **build**, construct, erect, assemble,
put up. **7** *how will you raise the money?*
get, obtain, acquire; accumulate, amass,
collect, fetch, net, make. **8** *the region raised*
an army to fight for the government: **recruit**,
enlist, sign up, conscript, call up, mobilize,
rally, assemble; US draft. **9** *a tax raised*
on imports: **levy**, impose, exact, demand,
charge. **10** *he raised several objections to*
the scheme: **bring up**, air; present, table,
propose, submit, advance, suggest, moot, put
forward. **11** *most parents raise their children*
successfully: **bring up**, rear, nurture, look
after, care for, provide for, mother, parent,
tend, cherish; educate, train. **12** *he raised*
cattle in Nebraska: **breed**, rear, keep, tend;
grow, farm, cultivate, produce.
– OPPOSITES lower, reduce, demolish.
noun *the workers wanted a raise:* **pay rise**,
pay increase, increment.

raised adjective *the plate bears an inscription*
in raised letters: **embossed**, relief, die-

stamped; convex, bumpy.

rake verb **1** *he raked the leaves into a pile:* **scrape**, collect, gather. **2** *she raked the gravel:* **smooth (out)**, level, even out, flatten, comb. **3** *the cat raked his arm with its claws:* **scratch**, lacerate, scrape, rasp, graze, grate; Medicine excoriate. **4** *she raked a hand through her hair:* **drag**, pull, scrape, tug, comb. **5** *machine-gun fire raked the streets:* **sweep**, pepper, strafe.

rakish adjective *his moustache gave him a slightly rakish look:* **dashing**, debonair, stylish, jaunty, devil-may-care; raffish, disreputable.

rally verb **1** *the French troops rallied and held their ground:* **regroup**, reassemble, re-form. **2** *ministers rallied to denounce the rumours:* **get together**, band together, assemble, join forces, unite, ally, collaborate, cooperate, pull together. **3** *share prices rallied in the afternoon:* **recover**, improve, get better, pick up, revive, bounce back, perk up, look up, turn a corner.
– OPPOSITES disperse, disband, slump.
noun **1** *there was a rally in support of the strike:* **(mass) meeting**, gathering, assembly; demonstration, (protest) march; informal demo. **2** *investors are hoping for a rally in oil prices:* **recovery**, upturn, improvement, comeback, resurgence.
– OPPOSITES slump.

ram verb **1** *he rammed his sword back into its sheath:* **force**, thrust, plunge, push, sink, dig, stick, cram, jam, stuff, pack. **2** *a stolen van rammed the police car:* **hit**, strike, crash into, collide with, impact, run into, smash into, bump (into), butt.

ramble verb **1** *we rambled around the Cornwall countryside:* **walk**, hike, tramp, trek, backpack; wander, stroll, saunter, amble, roam, range, rove, traipse; Scottish & Irish stravaig; informal mosey, tootle; Brit. informal pootle; formal perambulate. **2** *she does ramble on about environmental issues:* **chatter**, babble, prattle, prate, blather, gabble, jabber, twitter, rattle; informal jaw, gas, gab, yak, yabber; Brit. informal witter, chunter, natter, waffle, rabbit.
noun *we were looking forward to a leisurely ramble in the hills:* **walk**, hike, trek; wander, stroll, saunter, amble, roam, traipse, jaunt, promenade; informal mosey, tootle; Brit. informal pootle.

rambler noun **walker**, hiker, backpacker, wanderer, rover; literary wayfarer.

rambling adjective **1** *a long, rambling speech:* **long-winded**, verbose, wordy, prolix; digressive, roundabout, circuitous, circumlocutory; disconnected, disjointed, incoherent. **2** *we walked through a maze of narrow, rambling streets:* **winding**, twisting, twisty, labyrinthine; sprawling.
– OPPOSITES concise.

ramification noun *the political ramifications of closing the factory would be*

immense: **consequence**, result, aftermath, outcome, effect, upshot; implication; by-product.

ramp noun **slope**, bank, incline, gradient, tilt; rise, ascent, acclivity; drop, descent, declivity.

rampage verb *angry mobs rampaged through the streets:* **riot**, run riot, go on the rampage, run amok, go berserk; storm, charge, tear.
■ **go on the rampage** riot, rampage, go berserk, run amok; N. Amer. informal go postal.

rampant adjective **1** *the rampant inflation of the mid 70s:* **uncontrolled**, unrestrained, unchecked, unbridled, widespread; out of control, rife. **2** *Oriental women were often a symbol of rampant sexuality:* **intense**, strong, violent, forceful, passionate; unbridled; fanatical. **3** *the house was obscured by a sea of rampant vegetation:* **luxuriant**, lush, rich, riotous, profuse, vigorous.
– OPPOSITES controlled, mild.

rampart noun **wall**, embankment, earthwork, parapet, battlement, bulwark.

ramshackle adjective *he lived up the hill in a ramshackle old cottage:* **tumbledown**, dilapidated, derelict, decrepit, neglected, run down, gone to rack and ruin, crumbling, decaying; rickety, shaky, unsound; N. Amer. informal shacky.
– OPPOSITES sound.

rancid adjective **sour**, stale, turned, rank, putrid, foul, rotten, bad, off; gamy, high, fetid, stinking, malodorous, foul-smelling; literary noisome.
– OPPOSITES fresh.

rancorous adjective **bitter**, spiteful, hateful, resentful, acrimonious, malicious, malevolent, hostile, venomous, vindictive, baleful, vitriolic, vengeful, pernicious, mean, nasty; informal bitchy, catty.
– OPPOSITES amicable.

rancour noun *there was an atmosphere of rancour and distrust:* **bitterness**, spite, hate, hatred, resentment, malice, ill will, malevolence, animosity, antipathy, enmity, hostility, acrimony, venom, vitriol.

random adjective *drivers were subjected to random spot checks:* **arbitrary**, unplanned, undirected, casual, indiscriminate, non-specific, haphazard, stray, erratic; chance, accidental.
– OPPOSITES systematic.
■ **at random** unsystematically, arbitrarily, randomly, unmethodically, haphazardly.

range noun **1** *the T 72 has the longest range and the most accurate cannons of any tank:* **span**, scope, compass, sweep, extent, area, field, orbit, ambit, horizon, latitude. **2** *we flew over a range of mountains:* **row**, chain, sierra, ridge, massif; line, string, series. **3** *we have introduced a new range of quality foods:* **assortment**, variety, diversity, mixture, collection, array, selection, choice. **4** *she put the dish into the range:* **stove**, cooker;

r

trademark Aga. **5** *cows grazed on the open range:* **pasture**, pastureland, grass, grassland, grazing land, prairie, veld; Scottish shieling.
verb **1** *charges range from 1% to 5%:* **vary**, fluctuate, differ; extend, stretch, reach, cover, go, run. **2** *on the stalls are ranged all sorts of fresh foods:* **arrange**, line up, order, position, dispose, set out, array.
3 *herdsmen ranged over the steppes:* **roam**, rove, traverse, travel, journey, wander, drift, ramble, meander, stroll, traipse, walk, hike, trek.

rangy adjective **long-legged**, long-limbed, leggy, tall; slender, slim, lean, thin, gangling, gangly, lanky, spindly, skinny, spare.
– OPPOSITES squat.

rank[1] noun **1** *he was elevated to ministerial rank:* **position**, level, grade; class, status, standing; dated station. **2** *the first rank of riflemen was instructed to fire:* **row**, line, file, column, string, train, procession.
verb **1** *the plant is ranked as endangered:* **classify**, class, categorize, rate, grade, bracket, group, pigeonhole, designate; catalogue, file, list. **2** *he ranked below the others:* **have a rank**, be graded, have a status, be classed, be classified, be categorized; belong. **3** *rows of tulips were ranked like guardsmen:* **line up**, align, order, arrange, dispose, set out, array, range.

rank[2] adjective **1** *rank vegetation covered the clearing:* **abundant**, lush, luxuriant, dense, profuse, vigorous, overgrown. **2** *sheep were everywhere, and there was a rank smell from underfoot:* **offensive**, unpleasant, nasty, revolting, sickening, obnoxious, noxious; foul, fetid, smelly, stinking, reeking, high, off, rancid, putrid, malodorous; Brit. informal niffy, pongy, whiffy, humming; literary noisome. **3** *this failure was down to rank stupidity:* **downright**, utter, outright, out-and-out, absolute, complete, sheer, arrant, thoroughgoing, unqualified, unmitigated, positive, perfect, patent, pure, total.
– OPPOSITES sparse, pleasant.

rankle verb *his wife's early morning lethargy never failed to rankle with him:* **cause resentment**, annoy, upset, anger, irritate, offend, affront, displease, provoke, irk, vex, pique, nettle, gall; informal rile, miff, peeve, aggravate, hack off; Brit. informal nark; N. Amer. informal tick off.

ransack verb **plunder**, pillage, raid, rob, loot, sack, strip, despoil; ravage, devastate, turn upside down; scour, rifle, comb, search.

ransom noun *they demanded a huge ransom:* **pay-off**, payment, sum, price.
verb *the girl was ransomed for £4 million:* **release**, free, deliver, liberate, rescue.

rant verb *she ranted on about the unfairness of it all:* **hold forth**, go on, fulminate, sound off, spout, pontificate, bluster, declaim; shout, yell, bellow; informal mouth off.
noun *he went into a rant about the decline in morality:* **tirade**, diatribe, broadside, polemic.

rap verb **1** *she rapped his fingers with a ruler:* **hit**, strike; informal whack, thwack, bash, wallop; literary smite. **2** *I rapped on the door:* **knock**, tap, bang, hammer, pound.
noun **1** *she received a rap on the knuckles:* **blow**, knock, bang, crack; informal whack, thwack, bash, wallop. **2** *there was a rap at the door:* **knock**, tap, rat-tat, bang, hammering, pounding.

rapacious adjective *the view of American finance as a casino full of rapacious capitalists:* **grasping**, greedy, avaricious, acquisitive, covetous; mercenary, materialistic; insatiable, predatory; informal money-grubbing; N. Amer. informal grabby.
– OPPOSITES generous.

rape noun **1** *he was charged with rape:* **sexual assault**, sexual abuse. **2** *the rape of the rainforests:* **destruction**, violation, ravaging, pillaging, plundering, desecration, defilement, sacking, sack.
verb **1** *he raped her at knifepoint:* **sexually assault**, sexually abuse, violate, force oneself on; literary ravish. **2** *they have raped our country:* **ravage**, violate, desecrate, defile, plunder, pillage, despoil; lay waste, ransack, sack.

rapid adjective **quick**, fast, swift, speedy, expeditious, express, brisk; lightning, meteoric, whirlwind; sudden, instantaneous, instant, immediate; hurried, hasty, precipitate; informal p.d.q. (pretty damn quick); literary fleet.
– OPPOSITES slow.

rapidly adverb **quickly**, fast, swiftly, speedily, at the speed of light, post-haste, hotfoot, at full tilt, briskly; hurriedly, hastily, in haste, in a rush, precipitately; informal like a shot, double quick, p.d.q. (pretty damn quick), in a flash, hell for leather, at the double, like a bat out of hell, like (greased) lightning, like mad, like the wind; Brit. informal like the clappers, at a rate of knots, like billy-o; N. Amer. informal lickety-split; literary apace.
– OPPOSITES slowly.

rapport noun *he had a real rapport with his team:* **affinity**, close relationship, (mutual) understanding, bond, empathy, sympathy, accord.

rapt adjective *they watched in rapt attention:* **fascinated**, enthralled, spellbound, captivated, riveted, gripped, mesmerized, enchanted, entranced, bewitched; transported, enraptured, thrilled, ecstatic.
– OPPOSITES inattentive.

rapture noun *she gazed at him in rapture:* **ecstasy**, bliss, exaltation, euphoria, elation, joy, enchantment, delight, happiness, pleasure.
■ **go into raptures** enthuse, rhapsodize, rave, gush, wax lyrical; praise something to the skies.

rapturous adjective *he was given a rapturous reception by the flag-waving crowds:* **ecstatic**, joyful, elated, euphoric, enraptured, blissful, happy; enthusiastic, delighted, thrilled, overjoyed, rapt.

rare adjective **1** *they treasured their rare moments of privacy:* **infrequent**, scarce, sparse, few and far between, thin on the ground, like gold dust; occasional, limited, odd, isolated, unaccustomed, unwonted; Brit. out of the common. **2** *he collects rare stamps:* **unusual**, recherché, uncommon, unfamiliar, atypical, singular. **3** *he is a man of rare talent:* **exceptional**, outstanding, unparalleled, peerless, matchless, unique, unrivalled, inimitable, beyond compare, without equal, second to none, unsurpassed; consummate, superior, superlative, first-class; informal A1, top-notch.
– OPPOSITES common, commonplace.

rarefied adjective *this rarefied musical world is closed to all but the most sensitive of artists:* **esoteric**, exclusive, select; elevated, lofty.

rarely adverb **seldom**, infrequently, hardly (ever), scarcely, not often; once in a while, now and then, occasionally; informal once in a blue moon.
– OPPOSITES often.

raring adjective *the mission crew are raring to go:* **eager**, keen, enthusiastic; impatient, longing, desperate; ready; informal dying, itching, gagging.

rarity noun **1** *the rarity of earthquakes in the UK has made many people complacent:* **infrequency**, rareness, unusualness, uncommonness, scarcity, scarceness. **2** *this book is something of a rarity:* **collector's item**, rare bird, rara avis; wonder, one of a kind; curiosity, oddity; Brit. informal one-off.

rascal noun **scallywag**, imp, monkey, mischief-maker, wretch; informal scamp, tyke, horror, monster; Brit. informal perisher; N. Amer. informal varmint; archaic rapscallion.

rash[1] noun **1** *next day, he broke out in a rash:* **spots**, breakout, eruption; hives; Medicine erythema, exanthema, urticaria. **2** *the incident provoked a rash of articles in the press:* **series**, succession, spate, wave, flood, deluge, torrent; outbreak, epidemic, flurry.

rash[2] adjective *this was a rash decision that he will live to regret:* **reckless**, impulsive, impetuous, hasty, foolhardy, incautious, precipitate; careless, heedless, thoughtless, imprudent, foolish.
– OPPOSITES prudent.

rasp verb *'Help!' he rasped:* **croak**, squawk, caw, say hoarsely.

rasping adjective **harsh**, grating, jarring; raspy, scratchy, hoarse, rough, gravelly, croaky, gruff, husky, throaty, guttural.

rate noun **1** *a fixed rate of interest:* **percentage**, ratio, proportion; scale, standard. **2** *an hourly rate of £30:* **charge**, price, cost, tariff, fare, levy, toll; fee, remuneration, payment, wage, allowance. **3** *the rate of change has increased:* **speed**, pace, tempo, velocity, momentum.
verb **1** *they were asked to rate their ability*

at various driving manoeuvres: **assess**, evaluate, appraise, judge, weigh up, estimate, calculate, gauge, measure; grade, rank, classify, categorize. **2** *the scheme was rated as no more than moderately effective:* **consider**, judge, reckon, think, hold, deem, find; regard as, look on as, count as. **3** *he rated only a brief mention in the report:* **merit**, deserve, warrant, be worthy of, be deserving of.

rather adverb **1** *it's rather complicated to explain:* **quite**, a bit, a little, fairly, slightly, somewhat, relatively, to some degree, comparatively; informal pretty, sort of, kind of. **2** *her true feelings—or rather, lack of feelings:* **more precisely**, to be precise, to be exact, strictly speaking. **3** *she seemed sad rather than angry:* **more**; as opposed to, instead of. **4** *it was not impulsive, but rather a considered decision:* **on the contrary**, instead.

ratify verb **confirm**, approve, sanction, endorse, agree to, accept, uphold, authorize, formalize, validate, recognize; sign.
– OPPOSITES reject.

rating noun *the hotel's four-star rating is well deserved:* **grade**, grading, classification, ranking, rank, category, designation; assessment, evaluation, appraisal; mark, score.

ratio noun **proportion**, comparative number, correlation, relationship, correspondence; percentage, fraction, quotient.

ration noun **1** *she allowed herself a daily ration of chocolate:* **allowance**, allocation, quota, share, portion, helping; amount, quantity, measure, proportion, percentage. **2** *the garrison ran out of rations:* **supplies**, provisions, food, foodstuff, provender; stores; informal grub, eats; N. Amer. informal chuck; formal comestibles; dated victuals.
verb *after the war, fuel supplies were still rationed:* **control**, limit, restrict; conserve.

rational adjective **1** *a rational approach to the problem:* **logical**, reasoned, sensible, reasonable, cogent, intelligent, judicious, shrewd, common-sense, sound, prudent; down-to-earth, practical, pragmatic. **2** *she was not rational at the time of signing the agreement:* **sane**, compos mentis, in one's right mind, of sound mind; normal, balanced, lucid, coherent; informal all there. **3** *we like to think that man is a rational being:* **intelligent**, thinking, reasoning; cerebral, logical, analytical.
– OPPOSITES illogical, insane.

rationale noun **reason(s)**, reasoning, thinking, logic, grounds, sense; principle, theory, argument, case; motive, motivation, explanation, justification, excuse; the whys and wherefores.

rationalize verb **1** *he tried to rationalize his behaviour:* **justify**, explain (away), account for, defend, vindicate, excuse. **2** *they embarked on an attempt to rationalize the industry:* **streamline**, reorganize,

r

modernize, update; trim, hone, simplify, downsize, prune.

rattle verb **1** *hailstones rattled against the window:* **clatter**, patter; clink, clunk. **2** *he rattled some coins:* **jingle**, jangle, clink, tinkle. **3** *the bus rattled along:* **jolt**, bump, bounce, jounce, shake, judder. **4** *the government were clearly rattled by the strike:* **unnerve**, disconcert, disturb, fluster, shake, perturb, discompose, discomfit, ruffle, throw; informal faze.
noun *I heard the rattle of bottles as he stacked the crates:* **clatter**, clank, clink, clang; jingle, jangle.
■ **rattle something off** *she rattled off the names of the films he had directed:* reel off, recite, list, fire off, run through, enumerate.
■ **rattle on/away** *she found herself rattling on about the meaning of life:* prattle, babble, chatter, gabble, prate, go on, jabber, gibber, blether, ramble; informal gab, yak, yap; Brit. informal witter, rabbit, chunter, waffle.

raucous adjective **1** *outbursts of raucous laughter drifted across the fields:* **harsh**, strident, screeching, piercing, shrill, grating, discordant, dissonant; noisy, loud, cacophonous. **2** *she found herself on a raucous hen night:* **rowdy**, noisy, boisterous, roisterous, wild.
– OPPOSITES soft, quiet.

raunchy adjective (informal). See **SEXY** sense 2.

ravage verb *their land had been ravaged by famine and plague:* **lay waste**, devastate, ruin, destroy, wreak havoc on, leave desolate; pillage, plunder, despoil, ransack, sack, loot.

rave verb **1** *the old man was raving about Armageddon:* **talk wildly**, babble, jabber, gibber, go on. **2** *he raved about her talent and predicted she'd win:* **praise**, go into raptures about/over, wax lyrical about, sing the praises of, rhapsodize over, enthuse about/over, acclaim, eulogize, extol; N. Amer. informal ballyhoo; formal laud.
– OPPOSITES criticize.

raven adjective *raven hair:* **black**, jet-black, ebony; literary sable.

ravenous adjective **1** *by dinner time I'm absolutely ravenous:* **starving**, famished. **2** *nothing would satisfy her ravenous appetite:* **voracious**, insatiable; greedy, gluttonous.

ravine noun **gorge**, canyon, gully, defile, couloir; chasm, abyss, gulf; S. English chine; N. English clough, gill, thrutch; N. Amer. gulch, coulee.

raving adjective **1** *she's raving mad.* See **MAD** sense 1. **2** *a raving beauty:* **very great**, remarkable, extraordinary, singular, striking, outstanding, stunning.

ravings plural noun *he dismissed her words as the ravings of a hysterical woman:* **gibberish**, rambling, babbling, wild/incoherent talk.

ravishing adjective **beautiful**, gorgeous,

stunning, wonderful, lovely, striking, magnificent, dazzling, radiant, delightful, charming, enchanting; informal amazing, sensational, fantastic, fabulous, terrific; Brit. informal smashing; N. Amer. informal bodacious.
– OPPOSITES hideous.

raw adjective **1** *a piece of raw carrot:* **uncooked**, fresh. **2** *the cost of raw materials is likely to rise:* **unprocessed**, untreated, unrefined, crude, natural. **3** *a bunch of raw recruits:* **inexperienced**, new, untrained, untried, untested; callow, immature, green, naive; informal wet behind the ears. **4** *his skin is raw in places:* **sore**, red, painful, tender; abraded, chafed; Medicine excoriated. **5** *it was a raw morning with a bitter east wind:* **bleak**, cold, chilly, freezing, icy, icy-cold, wintry, bitter; informal nippy; Brit. informal parky. **6** *the raw emotions depicted in such stories are hard to deal with:* **strong**, intense, passionate, fervent, powerful, violent; undisguised, unconcealed, unrestrained, uninhibited, naked. **7** *the show contained raw, contemporary images of Latin America:* **realistic**, unembellished, unvarnished, brutal, harsh.
– OPPOSITES cooked, processed.

ray noun *rays of light shone through the trees:* **beam**, shaft, streak, stream.

raze verb **destroy**, demolish, tear down, pull down, knock down, level, flatten, bulldoze, wipe out, lay waste.

re preposition **about**, concerning, regarding, with regard to, relating to, apropos (of), on the subject of, in respect of, with reference to, in connection with.

reach verb **1** *Travis reached out a hand:* **stretch out**, hold out, extend, outstretch, thrust out, stick out. **2** *reach me that book:* **pass**, hand, give, let someone have. **3** *soon she reached Helen's house:* **arrive at**, get to, come to; end up at. **4** *the temperature reached 94 degrees:* **attain**, get to; rise to, climb to; fall to, sink to, drop to; informal hit. **5** *the two leaders failed to reach an agreement:* **achieve**, work out, draw up, put together, negotiate, thrash out, hammer out. **6** *I have been trying to reach you all day:* **get in touch with**, contact, get through to, get, speak to; informal get hold of. **7** *our central concern is to reach more people:* **influence**, sway, get (through) to, make an impression on, have an impact on.
noun **1** *Bobby moved out of her reach:* **grasp**, range. **2** *set yourself small goals that are within your reach:* **capabilities**, capacity. **3** *they may be beyond the reach of the law by now:* **jurisdiction**, authority, influence; scope, range, compass, ambit.

react verb **1** *how would he react if she told him the truth?* **behave**, act, take it, conduct oneself; respond, reply, answer. **2** *perhaps it's no wonder he reacted against the new regulations:* **rebel against**, oppose, rise up against.

reaction noun **1** *his reaction had bewildered*

her: **response**, answer, reply, rejoinder, retort, riposte; informal **comeback**. **2** *a reaction against modernism is inevitable:* **backlash**, swing. **3** *the forces of reaction:* **conservatism**, the right (wing), the extreme right.

reactionary adjective *government policy became increasingly reactionary:* **right-wing**, conservative, rightist, traditionalist, conventional, unprogressive.
– OPPOSITES progressive.
noun *he was later to become an extreme reactionary:* **right-winger**, (arch-) conservative, rightist, traditionalist.
– OPPOSITES radical.

read verb **1** *he was reading the newspaper:* **peruse**, study, scrutinize, look through; pore over, be absorbed in; run one's eye over, cast an eye over, leaf through, scan, flick through, skim through, thumb through. **2** *he read her a passage from the letter:* **read out/aloud**, recite, declaim. **3** *I can't read my own writing:* **decipher**, make out, make sense of, interpret, understand. **4** *his remark could be read as a criticism:* **interpret**, take (to mean), construe, see, understand. **5** *the dial read 70 mph:* **indicate**, register, record, display, show. **6** *he read modern history at university:* **study**, take; informal do; N. Amer. & Austral./NZ major in.
noun *here, have a read of this:* **perusal**, study, scan; look (at), browse (through), leaf (through), flick (through), skim (through).
■ **read something into something** *officials cautioned against reading too much into the statistics:* infer from, interpolate from, assume from, attribute to; read between the lines.
■ **read up on** *Chris had read up on this well in advance:* study; informal bone up on; Brit. informal mug up on, swot.

readable adjective **1** *the inscription is still perfectly readable:* **legible**, easy to read, decipherable, clear, intelligible, comprehensible. **2** *her novels are immensely readable:* **enjoyable**, entertaining, interesting, absorbing, gripping, enthralling, engrossing, stimulating; informal unputdownable.
– OPPOSITES illegible.

readily adverb **1** *Durkin readily offered to drive him to the station:* **willingly**, without hesitation, unhesitatingly, ungrudgingly, gladly, happily, eagerly, promptly. **2** *the island is readily accessible:* **easily**, with ease, without difficulty.
– OPPOSITES reluctantly.

readiness noun **1** *he questioned their readiness to accept new technology:* **willingness**, enthusiasm, eagerness, keenness; promptness, quickness, alacrity. **2** *we need to maintain our forces in a state of readiness:* **preparedness**, preparation. **3** *I was surprised at the readiness of his reply:* **promptness**, quickness, rapidity, swiftness, speed, speediness.

reading noun **1** *a cursory reading of the financial pages shows this to be the case:* **perusal**, study, scan, scanning; browse (through), look (through), glance (through), leaf (through), flick (through), skim (through). **2** *there were a series of readings from the Bible:* **passage**, lesson; section, piece; recital, recitation. **3** *my reading of the situation is quite different:* **interpretation**, construal, understanding, explanation, analysis. **4** *a man came to take a meter reading:* **record**, figure, indication, measurement.

ready adjective **1** *are you ready?* **prepared**, (all) set, organized, primed; informal fit, psyched up, geared up, revved up. **2** *everything is ready:* **completed**, finished, prepared, organized, done, arranged, fixed, in readiness. **3** *he's always ready to help:* **willing**, prepared, pleased, inclined, disposed, predisposed; eager, keen, happy, glad; informal game. **4** *she looked ready to collapse:* **about to**, on the point of, on the verge of, close to, liable to, likely to. **5** *we always kept a ready supply of food:* **(easily) available**, accessible; handy, close/near at hand, to/on hand, convenient, within reach, at the ready, near, at one's fingertips. **6** *he is blessed with great charm and a ready wit:* **prompt**, quick, swift, speedy, fast, immediate, unhesitating.
verb *he needed time to ready himself:* **prepare**, get/make ready, organize, gear oneself up; informal psych oneself up.
■ **at the ready** *a group of parents stood, camcorders at the ready:* in position, poised, ready for use/action, waiting; N. Amer. on deck.
■ **make ready** *the crew were busy making ready for our departure:* prepare, make preparations, get everything ready, gear up for.

ready-made adjective **1** *I dislike ready-made clothing:* **ready-to-wear**; Brit. off the peg; N. Amer. off the rack. **2** *ready-made meals used to be stodgy and bland:* **pre-cooked**, oven-ready, convenience.
– OPPOSITES tailor-made.

real adjective **1** *is she a fictional character or a real person?* **actual**, non-fictional, factual; historical; material, physical, tangible, concrete, palpable. **2** *do you think it's real gold?* **genuine**, authentic, bona fide; informal pukka, kosher. **3** *that's not my real name:* **true**, actual. **4** *there were tears of real grief in his eyes:* **sincere**, genuine, true, unfeigned, heartfelt, unaffected. **5** *he was a real man:* **proper**, true; authentic; informal regular. **6** *you're a real idiot:* **complete**, utter, thorough, absolute, total, prize, perfect; Brit. informal right, proper; Austral./NZ informal fair.
– OPPOSITES imaginary, imitation.
adverb (N. Amer. informal) *that's real good of you.* See **VERY** adverb.

realism noun **1** *his optimism was tinged with realism:* **pragmatism**, practicality, common sense, level-headedness. **2** *both stories portrayed frontier life with a degree of realism:* **authenticity**, fidelity, verisimilitude, truthfulness, faithfulness, accuracy; naturalism.

realistic adjective **1** *you've got to be realistic and accept what has happened:* **practical**, pragmatic, matter-of-fact, down-to-earth, sensible, commonsensical; rational, reasonable, level-headed, clear-sighted, businesslike; informal having both/one's feet on the ground, hard-nosed, no-nonsense. **2** *a regional settlement remains a realistic aim:* **achievable**, attainable, feasible, practicable, viable, reasonable, sensible, workable; informal doable. **3** *a realistic portrayal of war:* **true (to life)**, lifelike, truthful, faithful, real-life, naturalistic, graphic, authentic.
– OPPOSITES idealistic, impracticable.

reality noun **1** *he is incapable of distinguishing fantasy from reality:* **the real world**, real life, actuality; truth; physical existence. **2** *the harsh realities of life:* **fact**, actuality, truth. **3** *the reality of Marryat's account remains unquestioned:* **verisimilitude**, authenticity, realism, fidelity, faithfulness.
– OPPOSITES fantasy.

■ **in reality** *she sounded sympathetic but in reality she was furious:* in (actual) fact, in point of fact, as a matter of fact, really, in truth; in practice.

realization noun **1** *there was a growing realization of the danger:* **awareness**, understanding, comprehension, consciousness, appreciation, recognition, discernment; formal cognizance. **2** *the realization of our dreams was a thrilling experience for all concerned:* **fulfilment**, achievement, accomplishment, attainment.

realize verb **1** *he suddenly realized what she meant:* **register**, perceive, discern, be/become aware of (the fact that), be/become conscious of (the fact that), notice; understand, grasp, comprehend, see, recognize, work out, fathom (out), apprehend; informal latch on to, cotton on to, tumble to, savvy, figure out, get (the message); Brit. informal twig, suss; formal be/become cognizant of. **2** *they realized their dream by restoring the castle:* **fulfil**, achieve, accomplish, make a reality, make happen, bring to fruition, bring about/off, carry out/through; formal effectuate.

really adverb **1** *he is really very wealthy:* **in (actual) fact**, actually, in reality, in point of fact, as a matter of fact, in truth, to tell the truth. **2** *he really likes her:* **genuinely**, truly, honestly; undoubtedly, without a doubt, indubitably, certainly, assuredly, unquestionably; archaic verily. **3** *they were really kind to me:* **very**, extremely, thoroughly, decidedly, dreadfully, exceptionally, exceedingly, immensely, tremendously, uncommonly, remarkably, eminently, extraordinarily,

most, downright; Scottish unco; N. Amer. quite; informal awfully, terribly, terrifically, fearfully, right, devilishly, ultra, too ... for words, seriously, majorly; Brit. informal jolly, ever so, dead, well, fair; N. Amer. informal real, mighty, awful, plumb, powerful, way; informal, dated devilish, frightfully; archaic exceeding. exclamation *'They've split up.' 'Really?'* **is that so**, is that a fact, well I never (did); informal {well, knock/blow me down with a feather}; Brit. informal {well, I'll be blowed}.

realm noun **1** *his prime concern was to promote peace in the realm:* **kingdom**, country, land, dominion, nation. **2** *the realm of academic research is new to me:* **domain**, sphere, area, field, world, province, territory, arena.

reap verb *the company is reaping the benefits of these investments:* **receive**, obtain, get, acquire, secure, realize, enjoy.

rear[1] verb **1** *I was born and reared in Newcastle:* **bring up**, care for, look after, nurture, parent; educate; N. Amer. raise. **2** *he reared cattle and sheep:* **breed**, raise, keep; grow, cultivate. **3** *Harry stiffened and reared his head:* **raise**, lift (up), hold up, uplift. **4** *Creagan Hill reared up before them:* **rise (up)**, tower, soar, loom.

rear[2] noun **1** *the door at the rear of the building was unlocked:* **back (part)**, hind part, back end; Nautical stern. **2** *get to the rear of the queue:* **(tail) end**, rear end, back end, tail; N. Amer. tag end. **3** *he slapped her on the rear.* See BOTTOM noun sense 6.
– OPPOSITES front.
adjective *the rear bumper was dented:* **back**, end, rearmost; hind, hinder, hindmost; technical posterior.

rearrange verb **1** *the furniture has been rearranged to make more room:* **reposition**, move round, change round, arrange differently. **2** *Tony had rearranged his work schedule:* **reorganize**, alter, adjust, change (round), reschedule; informal jigger.

reason noun **1** *the main reason for his decision was lack of funds:* **cause**, ground(s), basis, rationale; motive, motivation, purpose, point, aim, intention, objective, goal; explanation, justification, argument, defence, vindication, excuse, pretext. **2** *now voices are railing against reason and science:* **rationality**, logic, logical thought, reasoning, cognition; formal ratiocination. **3** *he felt he was losing his reason:* **sanity**, mind, mental faculties; senses, wits; informal marbles. **4** *he continues, against reason, to love her:* **good sense**, good judgement, common sense, wisdom, sagacity, reasonableness.
verb **1** *a young child is unable to reason:* **think rationally**, think logically, use one's head/brain, think things through. **2** *Scott reasoned that Annabel might be ill:* **calculate**, come to the conclusion, conclude, reckon, think, judge, deduce, infer, surmise; informal figure. **3** *her husband tried to reason*

with her: **talk round**, bring round, win round, persuade, prevail on, convince, make someone see the light.
■ **with (good) reason** *he was anxious, with good reason, about his political survival:* justifiably, justly, legitimately, (quite) rightly, (not un)reasonably.

reasonable adjective **1** *he's a reasonable man | it seemed a reasonable explanation:* **sensible**, rational, logical, fair, fair-minded, just, equitable; intelligent, wise, level-headed, practical, realistic; sound, (well) reasoned, valid, commonsensical; tenable, plausible, credible, believable. **2** *you must take all reasonable precautions to ensure his safety:* **within reason**, practicable, sensible; appropriate; suitable. **3** *most hire cars are in reasonable condition:* **fairly good**, acceptable, satisfactory, average, adequate, fair, all right, tolerable, passable; informal OK. **4** *good hot food at reasonable prices:* **inexpensive**, moderate, low, cheap, budget, bargain; competitive.

reasoned adjective *we succeeded through reasoned argument:* **logical**, rational, well thought out, clear, lucid, coherent, cogent, well expressed, well presented, considered, sensible.

reasoning noun *what was the reasoning behind the decision?* **thinking**, reason, (train of) thought, thought process, logic, analysis, interpretation, explanation, rationalization; reasons, rationale, arguments.

reassure verb **put/set someone's mind at rest**, put someone at ease, encourage, inspirit, hearten, buoy up, cheer up; comfort, soothe.
– OPPOSITES alarm.

rebate noun **(partial) refund**, repayment; discount, deduction, reduction, decrease.

rebel noun **1** *the rebels took control of the capital:* **revolutionary**, insurgent, revolutionist, mutineer, insurrectionist, guerrilla, terrorist, freedom fighter. **2** *the modern concept of the artist as a rebel:* **nonconformist**, dissenter, dissident, iconoclast, maverick.
verb **1** *the citizens rebelled against this new law:* **revolt**, mutiny, riot, rise up, take up arms, stage/mount a rebellion, be insubordinate. **2** *his stomach rebelled at the thought of food:* **recoil**, show/feel repugnance. **3** *most teenagers rebel against their parents:* **defy**, disobey, refuse to obey, kick against, challenge, oppose, resist.
– OPPOSITES obey.
adjective **1** *rebel troops were executed on the spot:* **insurgent**, revolutionary, mutinous, rebellious, insurrectionary. **2** *the rebel MPs have given the government a rough ride:* **rebellious**, defiant, disobedient, insubordinate, subversive, resistant, recalcitrant; nonconformist, maverick, iconoclastic.
– OPPOSITES compliant.

rebellion noun **1** *troops were sent in*

to suppress the rebellion: **uprising**, revolt, insurrection, mutiny, revolution, insurgence, insurgency; rioting, riot, disorder, unrest. **2** *he resigned as an act of rebellion:* **defiance**, disobedience, rebelliousness, insubordination, subversion, subversiveness, resistance.

rebellious adjective **1** *rebellious troops went on the rampage:* **rebel**, insurgent, mutinous, mutinying, insurrectionary. **2** *a rebellious adolescent:* **defiant**, disobedient, insubordinate, unruly, mutinous, wayward, obstreperous, recalcitrant, intractable; Brit. informal bolshie; formal refractory.

rebirth noun **revival**, renaissance, resurrection, reawakening, renewal, regeneration; revitalization, rejuvenation; formal renascence.

rebound verb **1** *the ball rebounded off the wall:* **bounce (back)**, spring back, ricochet, boomerang; N. Amer. carom. **2** *later, sterling rebounded and closed half a cent higher:* **recover**, rally, pick up, make a recovery. **3** *Thomas's tactics rebounded on him:* **backfire**, boomerang, have unwelcome repercussions; archaic redound on.

rebuff verb *his offer was immediately rebuffed:* **reject**, turn down, spurn, refuse, decline, repudiate; snub, slight, repulse, repel, dismiss, brush off, give someone the cold shoulder; informal give someone the brush-off; N. Amer. informal give someone the bum's rush.
– OPPOSITES accept.
noun *the rebuff did little to dampen his ardour:* **rejection**, snub, slight, repulse; refusal, spurning, cold-shouldering, discouragement; informal brush-off, kick in the teeth, slap in the face.

rebuild verb **reconstruct**, renovate, restore, remodel, remake, reassemble.
– OPPOSITES demolish.

rebuke verb *she never rebuked him in front of others:* **reprimand**, reproach, scold, admonish, reprove, chastise, upbraid, berate, take to task, criticize, censure; informal tell off, give someone a telling-off, give someone a talking-to, give someone a dressing-down, give someone an earful; Brit. informal tick off; N. Amer. informal chew out, ream out; Austral. informal monster; formal castigate.
– OPPOSITES praise.
noun *Damian was silenced by the rebuke:* **reprimand**, reproach, reproof, scolding, admonishment, admonition, reproval, upbraiding; informal telling-off, dressing-down; Brit. informal ticking-off; formal castigation.
– OPPOSITES compliment.

rebut verb **refute**, deny, disprove; invalidate, negate, contradict, controvert, counter, discredit, give the lie to, explode; informal shoot full of holes; formal confute.
– OPPOSITES confirm.

rebuttal noun **refutation**, denial,

countering, invalidation, negation, contradiction.

recalcitrant adjective **uncooperative**, intractable, insubordinate, defiant, rebellious, wilful, wayward, headstrong, self-willed, contrary, perverse, difficult, awkward; Brit. informal bloody-minded, bolshie, stroppy; formal refractory; archaic contumacious.
– OPPOSITES amenable.

recall verb **1** *he recalled his student days with affection:* **remember**, recollect, call to mind; think back on/to, look back on, reminisce about. **2** *the French ambassador was recalled:* **summon back**, order back, call back.
– OPPOSITES forget.
noun **1** *the recall of the ambassador created a stir:* **summoning back**, ordering back, calling back. **2** *people can improve their recall of dreams with practice:* **recollection**, remembrance, memory.

recant verb **1** *he was forced to recant his political beliefs:* **renounce**, disavow, deny, repudiate, renege on; formal forswear, abjure. **2** *charged with heresy, he refused to recant:* **change one's mind;** backtrack.

recapitulate verb *allow me to recapitulate some of the main points of the argument:* **summarize**, sum up; restate, repeat, reiterate, go over, review; informal recap.

recede verb **1** *the flood waters receded:* **retreat**, go back/down, move back/away, withdraw, ebb, subside, abate. **2** *the lights receded into the distance:* **disappear**, fade, be lost (to view). **3** *fears of widespread violence have receded:* **diminish**, lessen, decrease, dwindle, fade, abate, subside, ebb, wane.
– OPPOSITES advance, grow.

receipt noun **1** *the receipt of his letter threw Clara into ecstasy:* **receiving**, getting, obtaining, gaining; arrival, delivery. **2** *always make sure you get a receipt:* **proof of purchase**, ticket. **3** *receipts from council house sales:* **proceeds**, takings, money/payment received, income, revenue, earnings; profits, (financial) return(s); N. Amer. take.

receive verb **1** *Tony received an award | they received £650 in damages:* **be given**, be presented with, be awarded, collect; get, obtain, gain, acquire; win, be paid, earn, gross, net. **2** *she received a letter from the council threatening court action:* **be sent**, be in receipt of, accept (delivery of). **3** *Alec received the news on Monday:* **be told of**, be informed of, be notified of, hear, discover, find out (about), learn; informal get wind of. **4** *she received a serious injury:* **experience**, sustain, undergo, meet with; suffer, get. **5** *the couple looked radiant as they received their guests:* **greet**, welcome, meet, say hello to. **6** *she's not receiving visitors at the moment:* **entertain**, be at home to, take.
– OPPOSITES give, send.

receiver noun **1** *the sender, or the receiver, can fill in the amount as appropriate:*

recipient, beneficiary. **2** *he picked up the receiver and waited:* **handset**, earpiece.
– OPPOSITES donor.

recent adjective **1** *recent research has failed to support this claim:* **new**, the latest, current, fresh, modern, contemporary, up to date, up to the minute. **2** *his recent visit was a huge success:* **not long past**, occurring recently, just gone.
– OPPOSITES old.

recently adverb **not long ago**, a short time ago, in the past few days/weeks/months, a little while back; lately, latterly, just now.

receptacle noun **container**, holder, repository; box, tin, bin, can, canister, case, pot, bag.

reception noun **1** *the reception of foreign diplomats was his wife's responsibility:* **greeting**, welcoming, entertaining, meeting. **2** *they met with a chilly reception from my mother:* **response**, reaction, treatment. **3** *there was a small reception after the preview:* **party**, function, soirée; N. Amer. levee; informal do, bash; Brit. informal rave-up, knees-up, beanfeast, bunfight, beano.

receptive adjective *a smile will certainly make people far more receptive to you:* **open-minded**, responsive, amenable, well disposed, flexible, approachable, accessible.
– OPPOSITES unresponsive.

recess noun **1** *the two recesses had been fitted with bookshelves:* **alcove**, bay, niche, nook, corner, hollow, oriel. **2** *he disappeared into the recesses of Broadcasting House:* **heart**, depths, bowels. **3** *the Christmas recess begins on Thursday:* **adjournment**, break, interlude, interval, rest; holiday, vacation; informal breather.
verb *let's recess for lunch:* **adjourn**, take a recess, stop, (take a) break; informal take five.

recession noun **(economic) decline**, downturn, depression, slump, slowdown.
– OPPOSITES boom.

recherché adjective *most of the titles are recherché and long out of stock:* **obscure**, rare, esoteric, abstruse, arcane, recondite, exotic, strange, unusual, unfamiliar.

recipe noun **1** *a quick and tasty recipe:* **cooking instructions**, formula; dish, offering, preparation. **2** *low taxes are not always a recipe for success:* **means**, prescription, formula, blueprint.

recipient noun **receiver**, beneficiary, legatee, donee.
– OPPOSITES donor.

reciprocal adjective *reciprocal care between neighbours grows where trust is high:* **mutual**, common, shared, joint, corresponding, complementary.

reciprocate verb **1** *I was happy to reciprocate:* **do the same (in return)**, return the favour. **2** *her love for him was not reciprocated:* **requite**, return, give back.

recital noun **1** *he gave his first piano recital at the age of 16:* **concert**, (musical) performance, solo (performance); informal gig. **2** *her recital of Adam's failures:* **enumeration**, list, litany, catalogue, listing, detailing; account, report, description, recapitulation, recounting. **3** *a recital of the Lord's Prayer.* See **RECITATION** sense 1.

recitation noun **1** *the recitation of his poem was greeted with wild applause:* **recital**, saying aloud, declamation, rendering, rendition, delivery, performance. **2** *do not respond to a question with a recitation of your life story:* **account**, description, narration, narrative, story. **3** *songs and recitations:* **reading**, passage; poem, verse, monologue.

recite verb **1** *he began to recite verses of the Koran:* **repeat (from memory)**, say aloud, declaim, quote, deliver, render. **2** *Sir John recited the facts they knew:* **enumerate**, list, detail, reel off; recount, relate, describe, narrate, give an account of, recapitulate, repeat.

reckless adjective **rash**, careless, thoughtless, heedless, unheeding, hasty, overhasty, precipitate, precipitous, impetuous, impulsive, daredevil, devil-may-care; irresponsible, foolhardy, over-adventurous, audacious; ill-advised, injudicious, madcap, imprudent, unwise, ill-considered; literary temerarious.
– OPPOSITES careful.

reckon verb **1** *the cost was reckoned at £6,000:* **calculate**, compute, work out, put a figure on, figure; count (up), add up, total; Brit. tot up. **2** *Anselm reckoned Hugh among his friends:* **include**, count, consider to be, regard as, look on as. **3** (informal) *I reckon I can manage that:* **believe**, think, be of the opinion/view, be convinced, dare say, imagine, guess, suppose, consider; informal figure. **4** *category A prisoners are reckoned the most dangerous:* **regard as**, consider, judge, hold to be, think of as; deem, rate, gauge, count. **5** *when I spend that much I reckon to get good value for money:* **expect**, anticipate, hope to, be looking to; count on, rely on, depend on, bank on; N. Amer. informal figure on.
■ **reckon with 1** *it's her mother you'll have to reckon with:* deal with, contend with, face (up to). **2** *they hadn't reckoned with her burning ambition:* take into account, take into consideration, bargain for/on, anticipate, foresee, be prepared for, consider; formal take cognizance of.
■ **reckon without** *unfortunately, he had reckoned without the police sniffer dogs:* overlook, fail to take account of, disregard, forget about.

reckoning noun **1** *by my reckoning, this comes to £2 million:* **calculation**, estimation, computation, working out, summation, addition. **2** *a refusal by Sasha cost them 20 points and sent them out of the reckoning:* **competition**, running.
■ **day of reckoning** *the idea of training*

hard was soon shelved, and the day of reckoning drew nearer: judgement day, day of retribution, doomsday; informal crunch.

reclaim verb **1** *travelling expenses can be reclaimed:* **get back**, claim back, recover, regain, retrieve, recoup. **2** *the fuel rods are reprocessed to reclaim the uranium:* **recover**, save, rescue, recycle, reuse, reprocess.

recline verb **lie (down/back)**, lean back; be recumbent; relax, repose, loll, lounge, sprawl, stretch out; literary couch.

reclusive adjective **solitary**, secluded, isolated, hermit-like, cloistered.
– OPPOSITES gregarious.

recognition noun **1** *there was no sign of recognition on his face:* **identification**, recollection, remembrance. **2** *his recognition of his lack of experience is very refreshing:* **acknowledgement**, acceptance, admission; realization, awareness, consciousness, knowledge, appreciation; formal cognizance. **3** *we have sought official recognition on several occasions:* **approval**, certification, accreditation, endorsement, validation. **4** *you deserve recognition for the tremendous job you are doing:* **appreciation**, gratitude, thanks, congratulations, credit, commendation, acclaim, acknowledgement.

recognizable adjective **identifiable**, noticeable, perceptible, discernible, detectable, distinguishable, observable, perceivable; distinct, unmistakable, clear.
– OPPOSITES imperceptible.

recognize verb **1** *Hannah recognized him at once:* **identify**, place, know, put a name to; remember, recall, recollect; know by sight; Scottish & N. English ken. **2** *though they never liked him, they recognized Alan's ability:* **acknowledge**, accept, admit; realize, be aware of, be conscious of, perceive, discern, appreciate; formal be cognizant of. **3** *many therapists are recognized by the BPS:* **approve**, certify, accredit, endorse, sanction, validate. **4** *the Trust has finally recognized their hard work:* **pay tribute to**, show appreciation of, appreciate, be grateful for, acclaim, commend.

recoil verb **1** *as he leaned towards her, she instinctively recoiled:* **draw back**, jump back, pull back; flinch, shy away, shrink (back), blench. **2** *he pictured them in his mind and recoiled from the thought:* **feel revulsion** at, feel disgust at, be unable to stomach, shrink from, baulk at. **3** *his rifle recoiled violently:* **kick (back)**, jump, jerk, spring (back). **4** *his attempts to discredit them will eventually recoil on him:* **have an adverse effect on**, rebound on, affect, backfire.
noun *the recoil of the gun:* **kickback**, kick, jump.

recollect verb **remember**, recall, call to mind, think of; think back to, look back on, reminisce about.
– OPPOSITES forget.

recollection noun **memory**, remembrance,

impression, reminiscence.

recommend verb **1** *his former employer recommended him for the post:* **advocate**, endorse, commend, suggest, put forward, propose, nominate, put up; speak well of, put in a good word for, vouch for; informal plug. **2** *the committee recommended a cautious approach:* **advise**, counsel, urge, exhort, enjoin, prescribe, argue for, back, support; suggest, advocate, propose.

recommendation noun **1** *the government accepted the advisory group's recommendations:* **advice**, counsel, guidance, direction, enjoinder; suggestion, proposal. **2** *a personal recommendation is best when looking for an agent:* **commendation**, endorsement, good word, testimonial; suggestion, tip; informal plug.

recompense verb **1** *offenders should recompense their victims:* **compensate**, indemnify, repay, reimburse, make reparation to, make amends to. **2** *she wanted to recompense him in some way:* **reward**, pay back.
noun *damages were paid in recompense:* **compensation**, reparation, restitution, indemnification, indemnity; reimbursement, repayment, redress.

reconcile verb **1** *the news of his death reconciled us:* **reunite**, bring (back) together (again), restore friendly relations between, mollify; formal conciliate. **2** *he is trying to reconcile his religious beliefs with his career:* **fit**, harmonize, square, make congruent, balance, combine. **3** *they had to reconcile themselves to drastic losses:* **(come to) accept**, resign oneself to, come to terms with, learn to live with, get used to, make the best of.
– OPPOSITES estrange.

reconciliation noun **1** *the reconciliation of the disputants was a long way off:* **reuniting**, reunion, bringing together (again), conciliation, reconcilement. **2** *they are hoping for a reconciliation of their differences:* **resolution**, settlement, settling, resolving, mending, remedying. **3** *there was little hope of reconciliation:* **restoration of harmony**, agreement, compromise, understanding, peace; formal concord. **4** *the reconciliation of theory with practice can be problematic:* **harmonizing**, harmonization, squaring, balancing.

recondite adjective *such recondite topics as Elizabethan Classicists, and early translations of Homer:* **obscure**, abstruse, arcane, esoteric, recherché, profound, difficult, complex, complicated, involved; incomprehensible, unfathomable, impenetrable, cryptic, opaque.

recondition verb **overhaul**, rebuild, renovate, restore, repair, reconstruct, remodel, refurbish; informal do up, revamp.

reconnaissance noun **(preliminary) survey**, exploration, observation, investigation, examination, inspection; patrol, search; reconnoitring, scouting (out); informal recce; N. Amer. informal recon.

reconnoitre verb **survey**, explore, scout (out); investigate, examine, scrutinize, inspect, observe, take a look at; patrol; informal recce, make a recce of, check out; N. Amer. informal recon.

reconsider verb **rethink**, review, revise, re-examine, re-evaluate, reassess, reappraise; change, alter, modify; have second thoughts, change one's mind.

reconsideration noun **review**, rethink, re-examination, reassessment, re-evaluation, reappraisal.

reconstruct verb **1** *the building had to be substantially reconstructed:* **rebuild**, restore, renovate, recreate, remake, reassemble, remodel, refashion, revamp, recondition, refurbish. **2** *reconstructing the events of that day has proved hard:* **recreate**, build up a picture/impression of, piece together, re-enact.

record noun **1** *written records of the past:* **account(s)**, document(s), documentation, data, file(s), dossier(s), evidence, report(s); annal(s), archive(s), chronicle(s); minutes, transactions, proceedings, transcript(s); certificate(s), deed(s), register, log, logbook. **2** *I enjoy listening to records:* **album**, vinyl; dated LP, EP, single, forty-five, seventy-eight. **3** *he would have gone to prison had it not been for his previous good record:* **history**, track record, reputation. **4** *he's got a record as long as my arm:* **criminal record**, police record; previous; Brit. informal form; N. Amer. informal rap sheet. **5** *it was a great run, and a new British record:* **best performance**; personal best, fastest time; world record. **6** *this will be a lasting record of what they have achieved:* **reminder**, memorial, souvenir, memento, remembrance, testament.
adjective *the company has announced record profits:* **record-breaking**, best ever, worst ever, unsurpassed, unparalleled, unequalled, second to none.
verb **1** *the doctor recorded her blood pressure:* **write down**, take down, note, make a note of, jot down; document, put on record, enter, minute, register, log; list, catalogue. **2** *the team recorded their fourth away win:* **achieve**, accomplish, chalk up, notch up; informal clock up. **3** *the recital was recorded live:* **make a record/recording of**, tape, tape-record; video-record, videotape, video.
■ **off the record 1** *his comments were strictly off the record:* **unofficial**, confidential, in (strict) confidence, not to be made public. **2** *they admitted, off the record, that they had made a mistake:* **unofficially**, privately, in (strict) confidence, confidentially, between ourselves.

recorder noun **tape recorder**, cassette recorder; video (recorder), VCR, videotape recorder.

recount verb **tell**, relate, narrate, give an account of, describe, report, outline, delineate, relay, convey, communicate, impart.

recoup verb **get back**, regain, recover, win back, retrieve, redeem, recuperate.

recourse noun *surgery may be the only recourse:* **option**, possibility, alternative, resort, way out, hope, remedy, choice, expedient.
■ **have recourse to** *all three countries had recourse to the IMF for loans:* resort to, make use of, avail oneself of, turn to, call on, look to, fall back on.

recover verb **1** *he's recovering from a heart attack:* **recuperate**, get better, convalesce, regain one's strength, get stronger, get back on one's feet; be on the mend, pick up, rally, respond to treatment, improve, heal, pull through, bounce back. **2** *later, shares recovered:* **rally**, improve, pick up, make a recovery, rebound, bounce back. **3** *the stolen material has been recovered:* **retrieve**, regain (possession of), get back, recoup, reclaim, repossess, redeem, recuperate, find (again), track down. **4** *we saw gold coins recovered from a wreck:* **salvage**, save, rescue, retrieve.
– OPPOSITES deteriorate.

recovery noun **1** *her recovery may be slow, even with physiotherapy:* **recuperation**, convalescence. **2** *the economy was showing signs of recovery:* **improvement**, rallying, picking up, upturn, upswing. **3** *the recovery of the stolen goods was a high priority:* **retrieval**, regaining, repossession, getting back, reclamation, recouping, redemption.
– OPPOSITES relapse, deterioration.

recreation noun **1** *cycling is a popular form of recreation:* **pleasure**, leisure, relaxation, fun, enjoyment, entertainment, amusement; play, sport; informal R & R; N. Amer. informal rec. **2** *his favourite recreations were skating and fishing:* **pastime**, hobby, leisure activity.
– OPPOSITES work.

recrimination noun **accusation(s)**, counter-accusation(s), countercharge(s), counter-attack(s), retaliation(s).

recruit verb **1** *more soldiers were recruited:* **enlist**, call up, conscript; US draft, muster in. **2** *the company is currently recruiting staff:* **hire**, employ, take on; enrol, sign up, engage.
– OPPOSITES disband, dismiss.
noun **1** *hundreds of new recruits were enlisted:* **conscript**; US draftee; Brit. informal sprog; N. Amer. informal yardbird. **2** *the profession continues to attract top-quality recruits:* **trainee**, newcomer, initiate, beginner, novice; N. Amer. tenderfoot, hire; informal rookie, newbie; N. Amer. informal greenhorn.

rectify verb *mistakes made now cannot be rectified later:* **correct**, (put) right, put to rights, sort out, deal with, amend, remedy, repair, fix, make good, resolve, settle; informal patch up.

rectitude noun *no one dared challenge the rectitude of the chief constable:*

righteousness, goodness, virtue, morality, honour, honourableness, integrity, principle, probity, honesty, trustworthiness, uprightness, decency, good character.

recumbent adjective *he stepped over a recumbent body:* **lying**, flat, horizontal, stretched out, sprawled (out), reclining, prone, prostrate, supine; lying down.
– OPPOSITES upright.

recuperate verb *after the operation, he went to France to recuperate:* **get better**, recover, convalesce, get well, regain one's strength/health, get over something.

recur verb **happen again**, reoccur, occur again, repeat (itself); come back (again), return, reappear, appear again.

recurrent adjective **repeated**, recurring, repetitive, periodic, cyclical, seasonal, perennial, regular, frequent; intermittent, sporadic, spasmodic.

recycle verb **reuse**, reprocess, reclaim, recover; salvage, save.

red adjective **1** *a red dress:* **scarlet**, vermilion, ruby, cherry, cerise, cardinal, carmine, wine, blood-red; coral, cochineal, rose; brick-red, maroon, rusty, rufous; reddish. **2** *he was red in the face:* **flushed**, reddish, pink, pinkish, florid, rubicund; ruddy, rosy, glowing; burning, feverish; literary rubescent. **3** *his eyes were red:* **bloodshot**, swollen, sore. **4** *she had long red hair:* reddish, auburn, Titian, chestnut, carroty, ginger.
■ **in the red** overdrawn, in debt, in debit, in deficit, in arrears.

red-blooded adjective **manly**, masculine, virile, macho.

redden verb **go/turn red**, blush, flush, colour (up), burn.

redeem verb **1** *one feature alone redeems the book:* **save**, compensate for, vindicate. **2** *he fell in the first race, but fully redeemed himself next time:* **vindicate**, free from blame, absolve. **3** *Billy finally redeemed his drums from the pawnbrokers:* **retrieve**, regain, recover, get back, reclaim, repossess; buy back. **4** *this voucher can be redeemed at any branch:* **exchange**, cash in, convert, trade in.

redemption noun **1** *cash must be made available for the redemption of their possessions:* **retrieval**, recovery, reclamation, repossession, return. **2** *the redemption of credit vouchers is optional:* **exchange**, cashing in, conversion. **3** *the redemption of the mortgage:* **paying off/back**, discharge, clearing, honouring.

redolent adjective **1** *the old church is redolent of everything English:* **evocative**, suggestive, reminiscent. **2** (literary) *the air was redolent of incense:* **smelling of**, scented with, fragrant with, perfumed with.

redoubtable adjective *the redoubtable Miss Fortescue chaired as usual:* **formidable**, awe-inspiring, fearsome, daunting; impressive, commanding, indomitable, invincible,

r

doughty, mighty.

redress verb **1** *people no longer take to the streets to redress social wrongs:* **rectify**, correct, right, put right, compensate for, amend, remedy, make good, resolve, settle. **2** *we aim to redress the balance as soon as possible:* **even up**, regulate, equalize.
noun *your best hope of redress is through the courts:* **compensation**, reparation, restitution, recompense, repayment, indemnity, indemnification, retribution, satisfaction; justice.

reduce verb **1** *the aim is to reduce pollution:* **lessen**, make smaller, lower, bring down, decrease, diminish, minimize; shrink, narrow, contract, shorten; axe, cut (back/down), trim, slim (down), prune, rationalize; informal chop. **2** *he reduced her to tears:* **bring to**, bring to the point of, drive to. **3** *bread has been reduced:* **make cheaper**, lower the price of, cut (in price), mark down, discount, put on sale; informal slash, knock down.
– OPPOSITES increase, put up.
■ **reduced circumstances** *as time passed, his reduced circumstances became more and more evident:* poverty, ruin, bankruptcy; indigence, penury, destitution; need.

reduction noun **1** *a reduction in pollution levels:* **lessening**, lowering, decrease, diminution. **2** *the closure has led to a reduction in staff:* **cut**, cutback, scaling down, trimming, pruning, axing, chopping, streamlining, downsizing, rationalization. **3** *there has been a reduction in inflationary pressure:* **easing**, lightening, moderation, alleviation. **4** *he suffered a reduction in status:* **demotion**, downgrading, lowering. **5** *there have been substantial reductions:* **discount**, markdown, deduction, (price) cut, concession.

redundancy noun **sacking**, dismissal, lay-off, discharge; unemployment; cutback, downsizing.

redundant adjective **1** *many country churches are sadly redundant:* **unnecessary**, not required, unneeded, uncalled for, surplus (to requirements), superfluous. **2** *2,000 workers were now redundant:* **sacked**, dismissed, laid off, discharged; unemployed, jobless, out of work.
– OPPOSITES employed.

reef noun **shoal**, bar, sandbar, sandbank, spit; Scottish skerry.

reek verb *the whole place reeked:* **stink**, smell; Brit. informal niff, pong, whiff.
noun *the reek of cattle dung:* **stink**, smell, stench, malodour; Brit. informal niff, pong, whiff; literary miasma.

reel verb **1** *he reeled as the ship began to roll:* **stagger**, lurch, sway, rock, stumble, totter, wobble, falter. **2** *we were still reeling from the share crisis:* **be shaken**, be stunned, be in shock, be shocked, be taken aback, be staggered, be aghast, be upset.

■ **reel something off** *Theresa reeled off her ailments like a shopping list:* recite, rattle off, list, run through, enumerate, detail, itemize.

refer verb **1** *he referred indirectly to various errors in the article:* **mention**, make reference to, allude to, touch on, speak of/about, talk of/about, write about, comment on, deal with, point out, call attention to. **2** *the matter has now been referred to my solicitor:* **pass**, hand on/over, send on, transfer, remit, entrust, assign. **3** *these figures refer only to 2001:* **apply to**, be relevant to, concern, relate to, be connected with, pertain to, appertain to, be pertinent to, have a bearing on, cover. **4** *the name refers to a Saxon village:* **denote**, describe, indicate, mean, signify, designate. **5** *the constable referred to his notes:* **consult**, turn to, look at, have recourse to, glance at, check.

referee noun **1** *the referee blew his whistle again:* **umpire**, judge; informal ref. **2** *include the names of two referees with your application:* **supporter**, character witness, advocate.
verb **1** *he refereed the game for the last time:* **umpire**, judge. **2** *they asked him to referee in the dispute:* **arbitrate**, mediate; adjudicate.

reference noun **1** *his journal contains many references to railways:* **mention of**, allusion to, comment on, remark about. **2** *references are given in the bibliography:* **source**, citation, authority, credit; data. **3** *it can only be resolved by reference to a higher court:* **referral**, transfer, remission. **4** *he received a glowing reference:* **testimonial**, character reference, recommendation.
■ **with reference to** apropos, with regard to, regarding, with respect to, on the subject of, re; in relation to, relating to, in connection with.

referendum noun **vote**, plebiscite, ballot, poll.

refine verb **1** *we lose fibre by refining our cereal foods:* **purify**, process, treat; homogenize. **2** *this is helping students to refine their language skills:* **improve**, perfect, polish (up), hone, fine-tune; informal tweak.

refined adjective **1** *we don't need highly refined sugar:* **purified**, processed, treated. **2** *she was very refined, a real lady:* **cultivated**, cultured, polished, stylish, elegant, sophisticated, urbane; polite, gracious, well mannered, well bred, gentlemanly, ladylike, genteel. **3** *a person of refined taste such as yourself:* **discriminating**, discerning, fastidious, exquisite, impeccable, fine.
– OPPOSITES crude, coarse.

refinement noun **1** *the refinement of sugar:* **purification**, refining, processing, treatment, treating. **2** *he feels his writing needs endless refinement:* **improvement**, polishing, honing, fine-tuning, touching

r

up, finishing off, revision, editing. **3** *she was a woman of great refinement:* **style**, elegance, finesse, polish, sophistication, urbanity; politeness, grace, graciousness, good manners, good breeding, gentility; cultivation, taste, discrimination.

reflect verb **1** *the snow reflected the light:* **send back**, throw back, cast back. **2** *their expressions reflected their feelings:* **indicate**, show, display, demonstrate, be evidence of, register, reveal, betray, disclose; express, communicate; formal evince. **3** *he reflected on his responsibilities:* **think about**, give thought to, consider, give consideration to, review, mull over, contemplate, cogitate about/on, meditate on, muse on, brood on/over, turn over in one's mind; archaic pore on.

■ **reflect badly on** *the incident reflected badly on the government:* discredit, disgrace, shame, put in a bad light, damage, tarnish the reputation of, give a bad name to, bring into disrepute.

reflection noun **1** *she looked at her reflection in the mirror:* **image**, likeness. **2** *your hands are a reflection of your well-being:* **indication**, display, demonstration, manifestation; expression, evidence. **3** *the results of the survey are no reflection on the business as a whole:* **slur**, aspersion, imputation, reproach, shame, criticism. **4** *after some reflection, he turned the offer down:* **thought**, thinking, consideration, contemplation, deliberation, pondering, meditation, musing, rumination; formal cogitation. **5** *write down your reflections on the subject:* **opinion**, thought, view, belief, feeling, idea, impression, conclusion, assessment; comment, observation, remark.

reflex adjective *sneezing is a reflex action:* **instinctive**, automatic, involuntary, reflexive, impulsive, intuitive, spontaneous, unconscious, unconditioned, untaught, unlearned.
– OPPOSITES conscious.

reform verb **1** *a comprehensive plan to reform the health-care system:* **improve**, (make) better, ameliorate, refine; alter, make alterations to, change, adjust, adapt, amend, revise, reshape, refashion, redesign, restyle, revamp, rebuild, reconstruct, remodel, reorganize. **2** *after his marriage he reformed completely:* **mend one's ways**, change for the better, turn over a new leaf, improve.
noun *reform of the prison system is a high priority:* **improvement**, amelioration, refinement; alteration, change, adaptation, amendment, revision, reshaping, refashioning, redesigning, restyling, revamp, revamping, renovation, rebuilding, reconstruction, remodelling, reorganizing, reorganization.

refrain verb **abstain**, desist, hold back, stop oneself, forbear, avoid, eschew, shun, renounce; informal swear off; formal forswear.

refresh verb **1** *I'm sure the cool air will refresh me:* **reinvigorate**, revitalize, revive, restore, fortify, enliven, perk up, stimulate, freshen, energize, exhilarate, reanimate, wake up, revivify, inspirit; blow away the cobwebs; informal buck up, pep up. **2** *let me refresh your memory:* **jog**, stimulate, prompt, prod. **3** (N. Amer.) *I refreshed his glass:* **refill**, top up, replenish, recharge; (N. Amer.) freshen.
– OPPOSITES weary.

refreshing adjective **1** *enjoy a refreshing drink in our juice bar:* **invigorating**, revitalizing, reviving, restoring, bracing, fortifying, enlivening, inspiriting, stimulating, energizing, exhilarating. **2** *this is a refreshing change of direction:* **welcome**, stimulating, fresh, imaginative, innovative, innovatory.

refreshment noun **1** *refreshments were available in the interval:* **food and drink**, sustenance, provender; snacks, titbits, eatables; informal nibbles, eats, grub, nosh; formal comestibles; literary viands; dated victuals. **2** *we are in need of spiritual refreshment:* **invigoration**, revival, stimulation, reanimation, revivification, rejuvenation, regeneration, renewal.

refrigerate verb **keep cold**, cool (down), chill.
– OPPOSITES heat.

refuge noun **1** *homeless people are seeking refuge in subway stations:* **shelter**, protection, safety, security, asylum, sanctuary. **2** *she founded a refuge for mountain gorillas:* **sanctuary**, shelter, place of safety, (safe) haven; retreat, bolt-hole, hiding place, hideaway, hideout.

refugee noun **displaced person**, DP, fugitive, asylum seeker, exile, émigré, stateless person; migrant; Austral. informal reffo.

refund verb **1** *we will refund your money if you're not satisfied:* **repay**, give back, return, pay back. **2** *they refunded the subscribers:* **reimburse**, compensate, recompense, remunerate, indemnify.
noun *I loudly demanded a full refund:* **repayment**, reimbursement, rebate.

refurbish verb **renovate**, recondition, rehabilitate, revamp, overhaul, restore, renew, redevelop, rebuild, reconstruct; redecorate, spruce up, upgrade, refit; N. Amer. bring up to code; informal do up; N. Amer. informal rehab.

refusal noun **1** *we had one refusal to our invitation:* **non-acceptance**, no, dissent, demurral, negation, turndown; regrets. **2** *you can have first refusal:* **option**, choice, opportunity to purchase. **3** *the refusal of planning permission was a disappointment:* **withholding**, denial, turndown.

refuse[1] verb **1** *he refused their invitation:* **decline**, turn down, say no to; reject, spurn, rebuff, dismiss; send one's regrets; informal pass up. **2** *the Council refused planning permission:* **withhold**, not grant, deny.

r

– OPPOSITES accept, grant.

refuse[2] noun *piles of refuse lay in the streets:* **rubbish**, waste, debris, litter, detritus, dross; dregs, leftovers; N. Amer. garbage, trash; Austral./NZ mullock; informal dreck, junk.

refute verb **1** *there have been numerous attempts to refute Einstein's theory:* **disprove**, prove wrong/false, controvert, rebut, give the lie to, explode, debunk, discredit, invalidate; informal shoot full of holes; formal confute. **2** *she refuted the allegation:* **deny**, reject, repudiate, rebut; contradict; formal gainsay.

regain verb **recover**, get back, win back, recoup, retrieve, reclaim, repossess; take back, retake, recapture, reconquer.

regal adjective **1** *a regal feast was laid before him.* See **SPLENDID** sense 1. **2** *his regal forebears:* **royal**, kingly, queenly, princely.

regale verb **1** *they were regaled with refreshments wherever they went:* **entertain**, wine and dine, fête, feast, serve, feed. **2** *he regaled her with colourful stories:* **entertain**, amuse, divert, delight, fascinate, captivate.

regard verb **1** *we regard these results as very encouraging:* **consider**, look on, view, see, think of, judge, deem, estimate, assess, reckon, adjudge, rate, gauge. **2** *he regarded her coldly:* **look at**, contemplate, eye, gaze at, stare at; watch, observe, view, study, scrutinize; literary behold.
noun **1** *he has no regard for human life:* **consideration**, care, concern, thought, notice, heed, attention. **2** *doctors are held in high regard:* **esteem**, respect, acclaim, admiration, approval, approbation, estimation. **3** *Jamie sends his regards:* **best wishes**, greetings, kind/kindest regards, felicitations, salutations, respects, compliments, best, love. **4** *in this regard I'm afraid I disagree with you:* **respect**, aspect, point, item, particular, detail, specific; matter, issue, topic, question.
■ **with regard to.** See **REGARDING**.

regarding preposition **concerning**, as regards, with/in regard to, with respect to, with reference to, relating to, respecting, re, apropos, apropos of, on the subject of, in connection with, vis-à-vis.

regardless adverb *he decided to go, regardless:* **anyway**, anyhow, in any case, nevertheless, nonetheless, despite everything, in spite of everything, even so, all the same, in any event, come what may; informal irregardless.
■ **regardless of** irrespective of, without regard to, without reference to, disregarding, without consideration of, discounting, ignoring, notwithstanding, no matter.

regenerate verb **revive**, revitalize, renew, restore, breathe new life into, revivify, rejuvenate, reanimate, resuscitate; informal give a shot in the arm to.

regime noun **1** *the former Communist regime:*

government, authorities, rule, authority, control, command, administration, leadership; system, establishment. **2** *there is a very favourable tax regime here:* **system**, arrangement, scheme; order, pattern, method, procedure, routine, course, plan, programme.

regiment noun *the regiment was fighting in France:* **unit**, outfit, force, corps, division, brigade, battalion, squadron, company, platoon.
verb *their life is strictly regimented:* **organize**, order, systematize, control, regulate, manage, discipline.

regimented adjective **strictly regulated**, organized, disciplined, controlled, ordered, systematic, orderly; rigid, inflexible.

region noun *he lived in the western region of the country:* **district**, province, territory, division, area, section, sector, zone, belt, part, quarter; informal parts.
■ **in the region of.** See **APPROXIMATELY**.

regional adjective **1** *there is considerable regional variation:* **geographical**, territorial; from region to region. **2** *we want a regional parliament:* **local**, localized, provincial, district, parochial.
– OPPOSITES national.

register noun **1** *are you on the register of electors?:* **list**, listing, roll, roster, index, directory, catalogue, inventory. **2** *we checked the parish register:* **record**, chronicle, log, logbook, ledger, archive; annals, files. **3** *he uses the lower register of the piano:* **range**, reaches; notes, octaves.
verb **1** *I wish to register a complaint:* **record**, put on record, enter, file, lodge, write down, put in writing, submit, report, note, minute, log. **2** *it is not too late to register:* **enrol**, put one's name down, enlist, sign on/up, apply. **3** *the dial registered a speed of 100 mph:* **indicate**, read, record, show, display. **4** *her face registered anger:* **display**, show, express, exhibit, betray, evidence, reveal, manifest, demonstrate, bespeak; formal evince. **5** *the content of her statement simply did not register:* **make an impression**, get through, sink in, penetrate, have an effect, strike home.

regress verb **revert**, retrogress, relapse, lapse, backslide, slip back; deteriorate, decline, worsen, degenerate, get worse; informal go downhill.
– OPPOSITES progress.

regret verb **1** *they came to regret their decision:* **be sorry about**, rue, repent (of). **2** *this is a poem regretting the passing of his youth:* **mourn**, grieve for/over, lament, sorrow for, deplore.
– OPPOSITES welcome.
noun **1** *both players later expressed regret:* **remorse**, sorrow, contrition, contriteness, repentance, penitence, guilt, compunction, remorsefulness, ruefulness. **2** *please give your grandmother my regrets:* **apology**, apologies; refusal. **3** *they left the area*

with genuine regret: **sadness**, sorrow, disappointment, unhappiness, grief.
– OPPOSITES satisfaction.

regretful adjective **sorry**, remorseful, contrite, repentant, rueful, penitent, conscience-stricken, apologetic, guilt-ridden, ashamed, shamefaced.
– OPPOSITES unrepentant.

regrettable adjective **undesirable**, unfortunate, unwelcome, sorry, woeful, disappointing; deplorable, lamentable, shameful, disgraceful.

regular adjective **1** *plant them at regular intervals in a light soil:* **uniform**, even, consistent, constant, unchanging, unvarying, fixed. **2** *the device provides a regular beat:* **rhythmic**, steady, even, uniform, constant, unchanging, unvarying. **3** *the proposal is the subject of regular protests:* **frequent**, repeated, continual, recurrent, periodic, constant, perpetual, numerous. **4** *these are regular methods of business:* **established**, conventional, orthodox, proper, official, approved, bona fide, standard, usual, traditional, tried and tested. **5** *we have a regular procedure for recording attendance:* **methodical**, systematic, structured, well ordered, well organized, orderly, efficient. **6** *his regular route to work took him past the church:* **usual**, normal, customary, habitual, routine, typical, accustomed, established.
– OPPOSITES erratic, occasional.

regulate verb **1** *the flow of the river has been regulated:* **control**, adjust, manage. **2** *we have introduced a new act regulating businesses:* **supervise**, police, monitor, check (up on), be responsible for; control, manage, direct, guide, govern.

regulation noun **1** *we are hampered by EU regulations:* **rule**, ruling, order, directive, act, law, by-law, statute, edict, canon, pronouncement, dictate, dictum, decree, fiat, command, precept. **2** *the regulation of blood sugar is essential:* **adjustment**, control, management, balancing. **3** *the government is committed to the regulation of financial services:* **supervision**, policing, superintendence, monitoring, inspection; control, management.
adjective *regulation dress went by the board in such circumstances:* **official**, prescribed, set, fixed, mandatory, compulsory, obligatory.
– OPPOSITES unofficial.

regurgitate verb **1** *a cow or other ruminant continually regurgitates food:* **vomit**, disgorge, bring up. **2** *he could regurgitate facts for the exams:* **repeat**, say again, restate, reiterate, recite, parrot; informal trot out.

rehabilitate verb **1** *efforts to rehabilitate patients have proved unsuccessful:* **restore**, reintegrate, readapt; N. Amer. informal rehab. **2** *former dissidents were gradually rehabilitated:* **reinstate**, restore, bring back; pardon, absolve, exonerate, forgive;

formal exculpate. **3** *we are committed to rehabilitating vacant housing:* **recondition**, restore, renovate, refurbish, revamp, overhaul, redevelop, rebuild, reconstruct; redecorate, spruce up; upgrade, refit, modernize; informal do up; N. Amer. informal rehab.

rehearsal noun **practice (session)**, trial, read-through, run-through; informal dry run.

rehearse verb **1** *I rehearsed the role ceaselessly:* **prepare**, practise, read through, run through/over, go over. **2** *he was still rehearsing with the rest of the band:* **practise**, play. **3** *he rehearsed the Vienna Philharmonic in a work by Mozart:* **train**, drill, prepare, coach, put someone through their paces. **4** *the document rehearsed all the arguments in favour of the award:* **enumerate**, list, itemize, detail, spell out, catalogue, recite, rattle off; restate, repeat, reiterate, recapitulate, go over, run through; informal recap.

reign verb **1** *Robert II reigned for nineteen years:* **be king/queen**, be monarch, be sovereign, sit on the throne, rule. **2** *for a few moments, chaos reigned:* **prevail**, exist, be present, be the case, occur, be prevalent, be current, be rife, be rampant, be the order of the day, be in force, be in effect; formal obtain.
noun **1** *the later years of Henry's reign were far from happy:* **rule**, sovereignty, monarchy. **2** *his reign as manager was at an end:* **time**, period, incumbency, managership, leadership.

reigning adjective **1** *the reigning monarch:* **ruling**; on the throne. **2** *he is the reigning world champion:* **incumbent**, current.

reimburse verb **1** *they will reimburse your travel costs:* **repay**, refund, return, pay back. **2** *don't worry, we'll reimburse you in full:* **compensate**, recompense, repay.

rein verb *they reined back costs:* **restrain**, check, curb, constrain, hold back/in, keep under control, regulate, restrict, control, curtail, limit.
■ **free rein** *you'd be given free rein to run the show how you wanted it:* freedom, a free hand, leeway, latitude, flexibility, liberty, independence, free play, licence, room to manoeuvre, carte blanche.
■ **keep a tight rein on** *Labour said it would keep a tight rein on spending:* exercise strict control over, regulate, discipline, regiment, keep in line.

reincarnation noun **rebirth**, transmigration of the soul, metempsychosis.

reinforce verb **1** *hundreds of volunteers reinforced the dam:* **strengthen**, fortify, bolster up, shore up, buttress, prop up, underpin, brace, support. **2** *we are reinforcing links between colleges and companies:* **strengthen**, fortify, support; cement, boost, promote, encourage, deepen, enrich, enhance, intensify, improve. **3** *the need to reinforce NATO troops on the ground:*

r

augment, increase, add to, supplement, boost, top up.

reinforcement noun **1** *the reinforcement of our defences is a high priority:* **strengthening**, fortification, bolstering, shoring up, buttressing, bracing. **2** *there is a need for reinforcement of the task force:* **augmentation**, increase, supplementing, boosting, topping up. **3** *they returned later with reinforcements:* **additional troops**, more/extra troops, auxiliaries, reserves; support, backup, help.

reinstate verb **restore**, return to power, put back, bring back, reinstitute, reinstall.

reiterate verb **repeat**, say again, restate, recapitulate, go over (and over), rehearse.

reject verb **1** *the miners rejected the government's offer:* **turn down**, refuse, decline, say no to, spurn; informal give the thumbs down to. **2** *she had been in love with Jamie, but he had rejected her:* **rebuff**, spurn, shun, snub, repudiate, cast off/aside, discard, abandon, desert, turn one's back on, have nothing (more) to do with, wash one's hands of; informal give someone the brush-off; literary forsake.
– OPPOSITES accept.
noun *I got it cheap—it's only a reject:* **discard**, second.

rejection noun **1** *the chairman is expected to issue a rejection of the offer:* **refusal**, declining, turning down, dismissal, spurning. **2** *it took a while to get over Madeleine's rejection of him:* **repudiation**, rebuff, spurning, abandonment, desertion; informal brush-off.

rejoice verb **1** *they rejoiced when they discovered a complete dinosaur skeleton:* **be joyful**, be happy, be pleased, be glad, be delighted, be elated, be ecstatic, be euphoric, be overjoyed, be as pleased as Punch, be cock-a-hoop, be jubilant, be in raptures, be beside oneself with joy, be delirious, be thrilled, be on cloud nine, be in seventh heaven; celebrate, make merry; informal be over the moon, be on top of the world; Austral. informal be wrapped. **2** *he rejoiced in their success:* **take delight**, find/take pleasure, feel satisfaction, find joy, enjoy, revel in, glory in, delight in, relish, savour.
– OPPOSITES mourn.

rejoicing noun **happiness**, pleasure, joy, gladness, delight, elation, jubilation, exuberance, exultation, celebration, revelry, merrymaking.

rejoin verb *the path rejoins the main road further on:* **return to**, be reunited with, join again, regain.

rejoinder noun *a smart rejoinder usually occurs to me on the bus later:* **answer**, reply, response, retort, riposte, counter; informal comeback.

rejuvenate verb *the leadership change was an attempt to rejuvenate the party:* **revive**, revitalize, regenerate, breathe new life into, reanimate, resuscitate, refresh, reawaken, put new life into; informal give a shot in the arm to, pep up, buck up.

relapse verb **1** *most patients get well, but a few relapse:* **get ill/worse again**, have/suffer a relapse, deteriorate, degenerate, take a turn for the worse. **2** *she relapsed into silence:* **revert**, lapse; slip back.
– OPPOSITES improve.
noun **1** *only one patient suffered a relapse:* **deterioration**, turn for the worse. **2** *nobody could foresee his relapse into alcoholism:* **decline**, lapse, deterioration, degeneration, reversion, regression, retrogression, fall, descent, slide.

relate verb **1** *he related many other such stories over the years:* **tell**, recount, narrate, report, chronicle, outline, delineate, retail, recite, repeat, communicate, impart. **2** *mortality is related to unemployment levels:* **connect (with)**, associate (with), link (with), correlate (with), ally (with), couple (with). **3** *the charges relate to offences committed in August:* **apply**, be relevant, concern, pertain to, be pertinent to, have a bearing on, appertain to, involve. **4** *she cannot relate to her stepfather:* **get on (well)**, have a rapport, feel sympathy, feel for, identify with, empathize with, understand; informal hit it off with.

related adjective **1** *a mixture of several related ideas:* **connected**, interconnected, associated, linked, coupled, allied, affiliated, concomitant, corresponding, analogous, kindred, parallel, comparable, homologous, equivalent. **2** *are you two related?* **of the same family**, kin; consanguineous.
– OPPOSITES unconnected.

relation noun **1** *he understood the relation between church and state:* **connection**, relationship, association, link, correlation, correspondence, parallel, alliance, bond, interrelation, interconnection. **2** *this information had no relation to national security:* **relevance**, applicability, reference, pertinence, bearing. **3** *are you a relation of his?* **relative**, member of the family, kinsman, kinswoman; **(relations)** family, (kith and) kin, kindred. **4** *he sought to improve relations with India:* **dealings**, communication, relationship, connections, contact, interaction. **5** *sexual relations.* See SEX sense 1.

relationship noun **1** *the relationship between diet and diabetes is well established:* **connection**, relation, association, link, correlation, correspondence, parallel, alliance, bond, interrelation, interconnection. **2** *we have evidence of their relationship with a common ancestor:* **family ties/connections**, blood relationship, kinship, affinity. **3** *he reacted badly to the end of their relationship:* **romance**, (love) affair, love, liaison.

relative adjective **1** *do not underestimate the relative importance of each factor:*

comparative, respective, comparable, correlative, parallel, corresponding. **2** *the food required is relative to body weight:* **proportionate**, proportional, in proportion, commensurate, corresponding. **3** *Semtex could be smuggled with relative ease:* **moderate**, reasonable, a fair degree of, considerable, comparative.
noun *he's a relative of mine:* **relation**, member of someone's/the family, kinsman, kinswoman; **(relatives)** family, (kith and) kin, kindred, kinsfolk.

relatively adverb **comparatively**, by comparison; quite, fairly, reasonably, rather, somewhat, to a certain extent/degree, tolerably; informal pretty, kind of, sort of.

relax verb **1** *yoga is helpful in learning to relax:* **unwind**, loosen up, ease up/off, slow down, de-stress, unbend, rest, put one's feet up, take it easy; informal unbutton; N. Amer. informal hang loose, chill out. **2** *a walk will relax you:* **calm (down)**, unwind, loosen up, soothe, pacify, compose. **3** *he relaxed his grip on the mug:* **loosen**, loose, slacken, unclench, weaken, lessen. **4** *she felt her muscles relax:* **become less tense**, loosen, slacken, unknot. **5** *the ministry relaxed some of the restrictions:* **moderate**, modify, temper, ease (up on), loosen, lighten, dilute, weaken, reduce, decrease; informal let up on.
– OPPOSITES tense, tighten.

relaxation noun **1** *I was in a state of relaxation:* **(mental) repose**, calm, tranquillity, peacefulness. **2** *I just play for relaxation nowadays:* **recreation**, enjoyment, amusement, entertainment, fun, pleasure, leisure; informal R & R. **3** *skills for coping with anxiety include muscle relaxation:* **loosening**, slackening, loosing. **4** *relaxation of censorship rules:* **moderation**, easing, loosening, lightening, alleviation, mitigation, dilution, weakening, reduction; informal letting up.

relay noun *we heard a live relay of the performance:* **broadcast**, transmission, showing.
verb *it is not helpful relaying messages through a third party:* **pass on**, hand on, transfer, repeat, communicate, send, transmit, disseminate, spread, circulate.

release verb **1** *all political prisoners were released:* **(set) free**, let go/out, allow to leave, liberate, set at liberty. **2** *Burke released the animal into the garden:* **untie**, undo, loose, let go, unleash. **3** *this policy change released staff for other duties:* **make available**, free (up), supply, furnish, provide. **4** *she released Stephen from his promise:* **excuse**, exempt, discharge, deliver, absolve; informal let off. **5** *police released the news yesterday:* **make public**, make known, issue, break, announce, declare, report, reveal, divulge, disclose, publish, broadcast, circulate, communicate, disseminate. **6** *the film has been released on video:* **launch**, put out, put on sale, bring out, make available.

– OPPOSITES imprison, tie up.
noun **1** *the government ordered the release of 100 political prisoners:* **freeing**, liberation, deliverance; freedom, liberty. **2** *the release of the news is subject to approval:* **issuing**, announcement, declaration, reporting, revealing, divulging, disclosure, publication, communication, dissemination. **3** *the group's last release was a best seller:* CD, album, single, record; video, film; book.

relegate verb *we've been relegated to the Second Division:* **downgrade**, lower (in rank/status), put down, move down; demote, degrade.
– OPPOSITES upgrade.

relent verb *the government finally relented:* **change one's mind**, do a U-turn, back-pedal, back down, give way/in, capitulate, concede; Brit. do an about-turn; formal accede.

relentless adjective **1** *their relentless pursuit of quality has paid dividends:* **persistent**, continuing, constant, continual, continuous, non-stop, never-ending, interminable, incessant, unceasing, endless, unending, unremitting, unrelenting, unrelieved; unfaltering, unflagging, untiring, unwavering, dogged, single-minded, tireless, indefatigable. **2** *he proved to be a relentless taskmaster:* **harsh**, grim, cruel, severe, strict, remorseless, merciless, pitiless, ruthless, unmerciful, heartless, hard-hearted, unforgiving; inflexible, unbending, uncompromising, unyielding.

relevant adjective **pertinent**, applicable, apposite, material, to the point, germane; connected, related, linked.

reliable adjective **1** *there is an absence of reliable evidence:* **dependable**, good, well founded, authentic, valid, genuine, sound, true. **2** *Jim proved a reliable friend:* **trustworthy**, dependable, good, true, faithful, devoted, steadfast, staunch, constant, loyal, trusty, dedicated, unfailing; truthful, honest. **3** *the new bikes have more reliable brakes:* **dependable**, safe. **4** *it's a reliable firm, one we've used before:* **reputable**, dependable, trustworthy, honest, responsible, established, proven.
– OPPOSITES untrustworthy.

reliance noun **1** *a personal pension reduces reliance on the state:* **dependence**, dependency. **2** *he displayed a lack of reliance on his own judgement:* **trust**, confidence, faith, belief, conviction.

relic noun *the farmer uncovered a Viking relic:* **artefact**, antiquity, antique.

relief noun **1** *it was such a relief to share my worries:* **reassurance**, consolation, comfort, solace. **2** *I used opium for the relief of pain:* **alleviation,**, relieving, assuagement, palliation, allaying, soothing, easing, lessening, reduction. **3** *all she needed was a little light relief:* **respite**, amusement, diversion, entertainment, jollity, jollification, recreation.
– OPPOSITES intensification.

r

relieve verb **1** *this simple device helps relieve pain:* **alleviate**, mitigate, assuage, ease, dull, reduce, lessen, diminish. **2** *study was a way of relieving the boredom:* **counteract**, reduce, alleviate, mitigate; interrupt, vary, stop, dispel, prevent. **3** *there was no shortage of helpers to relieve us:* **replace**, take over from, stand in for, fill in for, substitute for, deputize for, cover for. **4** *this relieves the teacher of a heavy load:* **(set) free**, release, exempt, excuse, absolve, let off, discharge.
– OPPOSITES aggravate.

relieved adjective **glad**, thankful, grateful, pleased, happy, reassured.
– OPPOSITES worried.

religion noun **faith**, belief, worship, creed; sect, cult, church, faith community, denomination.

religious adjective **1** *I am not a religious person:* **devout**, pious, reverent, godly, God-fearing, churchgoing; practising, committed. **2** *she would not compromise her religious beliefs:* **spiritual**, theological, scriptural, doctrinal, ecclesiastical, church, churchly, holy, divine, sacred. **3** *pay religious attention to detail:* **scrupulous**, conscientious, meticulous, sedulous, punctilious, strict, rigorous, close.
– OPPOSITES atheistic, secular.

relinquish verb **1** *he relinquished control of the company:* **renounce**, give up/away, hand over, let go of. **2** *he offered to relinquish his post:* **leave**, resign from, stand down from, bow out of, give up; informal quit, chuck. **3** *she relinquished her grip:* **let go**, release, loose, loosen, relax.
– OPPOSITES retain, continue.

relish noun **1** *he dug into his food with relish:* **enjoyment**, gusto, delight, pleasure, glee, rapture, satisfaction, contentment, appreciation, enthusiasm, appetite; humorous delectation. **2** *the sauce may be served as a hot relish:* **condiment**, sauce, dressing, flavouring, seasoning, dip.
– OPPOSITES dislike.
verb *he was relishing his moment of glory:* **enjoy**, delight in, love, adore, take pleasure in, rejoice in, appreciate, savour, revel in, luxuriate in, glory in.

reluctance noun **unwillingness**, disinclination; hesitation, wavering; doubts, second thoughts, misgivings.

reluctant adjective **1** *her parents were reluctant to buy her a cat:* **unwilling**, disinclined, unenthusiastic, resistant, resisting, opposed; hesitant. **2** *Hilary gave a reluctant smile:* **shy**, bashful, coy, diffident, reserved, timid, timorous. **3** *he was reluctant to leave the house in the dark:* **loath**, unwilling, disinclined, indisposed.
– OPPOSITES willing, eager.

rely verb **1** *we can rely on his discretion:* **depend**, count, bank, reckon; be confident of, be sure of, believe in, have faith in, trust in; informal swear by; N. Amer. informal figure on.

2 *law centres have had to rely on government funding:* **be dependent**, depend.

remain verb **1** *until something is done, the problem will remain:* **continue**, endure, last, abide, carry on, persist, stay (around), prevail, survive, live on. **2** *he remained in hospital for a month:* **stay (behind/put)**, wait (around), be left, hang on; informal hang around/round; Brit. informal hang about. **3** *union leaders remain sceptical:* **continue to be**, stay, keep, persist in being, carry on being. **4** *we should leave them alone for the few minutes that remain:* **be left (over)**, be still available, be unused.

remainder noun **residue**, balance, remaining part/number, rest, others, those left, remnant(s), surplus, extra, excess, overflow.

remaining adjective **1** *the jobs of the remaining workers are safe:* **residual**, surviving, left (over); extra, surplus, spare, superfluous, excess. **2** *he settled his remaining debts:* **unsettled**, outstanding, unfinished, incomplete, unattended to. **3** *my only remaining memories of my first five years:* **surviving**, lasting, enduring, continuing, persisting, abiding.

remains plural noun **1** *she downed the remains of her drink:* **remainder**, residue, remaining part/number, rest, remnant(s). **2** *the Roman remains include baths and an arch:* **antiquities**, relics. **3** *the saint's remains are housed in the cathedral:* **corpse**, (dead) body, carcass; bones, skeleton; Medicine cadaver.

remark verb **1** *'You're quiet,' he remarked:* **comment**, say, observe, mention, reflect, state, declare, announce, pronounce, assert. **2** *many critics remarked on the rapport between the two stars:* **comment**, mention, refer to, speak of, pass comment on.
noun *his remarks have been misinterpreted:* **comment**, statement, utterance, observation, declaration, pronouncement.

remarkable adjective **extraordinary**, exceptional, amazing, astonishing, astounding, marvellous, wonderful, sensational, stunning, incredible, unbelievable, phenomenal, outstanding, momentous; out of the ordinary, unusual, uncommon, surprising; informal fantastic, terrific, tremendous, stupendous, awesome; literary wondrous.
– OPPOSITES ordinary.

remedy noun **1** *we provide traditional herbal remedies:* **treatment**, cure, medicine, medication, medicament. **2** *marriage is seen as a remedy for all kinds of problems:* **solution**, answer, cure, antidote, curative, nostrum, panacea, cure-all; informal magic bullet.
verb **1** *little has been done to remedy the situation:* **put/set right**, put/set to rights, right, rectify, solve, sort out, straighten out, resolve, correct, repair, mend, make good. **2** *anaemia can be remedied by iron tablets:*

cure, treat, heal, make better; relieve, ease, alleviate, palliate.

remember verb **1** *I remembered happier times*: **recall**, call to mind, recollect, think of; reminisce about, look back on. **2** *can you remember all that, or shall I write it down?* **memorize**, commit to memory, retain; learn off by heart. **3** *you must remember she's only five*: **bear/keep in mind**, not forget; take into account, take into consideration. **4** *remember to feed the cat*: **be sure**, be certain; mind that you, make sure that you. **5** *remember me to Alice*: **send one's best wishes to**, send one's regards to, give one's love to, say hello to. **6** *the nation remembered those who gave their lives*: **commemorate**, pay tribute to, honour, salute, pay homage to.
– OPPOSITES forget.

remembrance noun **1** *his face took on an expression of remembrance*: **recollection**, reminiscence; remembering, recalling, recollecting, reminiscing. **2** *we sold poppies in remembrance of those who died*: **commemoration**, memory, recognition.

remind verb **1** *I left a note to remind him*: **jog someone's memory**, help someone remember, prompt. **2** *the song reminded me of my sister*: **make one think of**, cause one to remember, put one in mind of, bring/call to mind, evoke.

reminder noun **prompt**, aide-memoire; mnemonic.

reminisce verb **remember**, cast one's mind back to, look back on, be nostalgic about, recall, recollect, reflect on, call to mind.

reminiscences plural noun **memories**, recollections, reflections, remembrances.

reminiscent adjective *a sophisticated style reminiscent of Italian art*: **similar to**, comparable with, evocative of, suggestive of, redolent of.

remiss adjective *I can see that I have been very remiss*: **negligent**, neglectful, irresponsible, careless, thoughtless, heedless, lax, slack, slipshod, lackadaisical; N. Amer. derelict; informal **sloppy**.
– OPPOSITES careful.

remission noun **1** *we demanded the remission of all parking fees*: **cancellation**, setting aside, suspension, revocation. **2** *the cancer is in remission*: **respite**, abeyance. **3** *the wind howled without remission*: **respite**, lessening, abatement, easing, decrease, reduction, diminution, dying down, slackening, lull; informal **let-up**. **4** *the remission of sins*: **forgiveness**, pardoning, absolution, exoneration; formal exculpation.

remit verb **1** *the fines imposed on him were remitted*: **cancel**, set aside, suspend, revoke. **2** *they refused to remit the customs duties to the authorities*: **send**, dispatch, forward, hand over; pay.
noun *that decision is outside his remit*: **area (of responsibility)**, sphere, orbit, scope,

ambit, province; brief, instructions, orders; informal bailiwick.

remittance noun **1** *send the form with your remittance*: **payment**, money, fee; cheque; formal monies. **2** *he receives a monthly remittance*: **allowance**, sum of money.

remnant noun **1** *we cleared up the remnants of the picnic*: **remains**, remainder, leftovers, residue, rest. **2** *she made a rag doll from remnants of cloth*: **scrap**, piece, bit, fragment, shred, offcut, oddment.

remonstrate verb **1** *'I'm not a child!' he remonstrated*: **protest**, complain, expostulate; argue with, take issue with. **2** *the outraged deputies remonstrated against this proposal*: **object strongly to**, protest against, argue against, oppose strongly, make a fuss about, challenge; deplore, condemn, denounce, criticize; informal kick up a fuss/stink about.

remorse noun **contrition**, regret, repentance, penitence, guilt, compunction, remorsefulness, ruefulness, contriteness; pangs of conscience.

remorseful adjective **sorry**, full of regret, regretful, contrite, repentant, penitent, guilt-ridden, conscience-stricken, guilty, chastened.
– OPPOSITES unrepentant.

remorseless adjective **1** *this law left an unhappy debtor to the mercy of a remorseless creditor*: **heartless**, pitiless, merciless, ruthless, callous, cruel, hard-hearted, inhumane, unmerciful, unforgiving, unfeeling. **2** *the remorseless Soviet military build-up continued*: **relentless**, unrelenting, unremitting, unabating, inexorable, unstoppable.
– OPPOSITES compassionate.

remote adjective **1** *many doctors practise in areas that are remote from hospitals*: **far away**, distant, far (off), far removed. **2** *a remote mountain village*: **isolated**, out of the way, off the beaten track, secluded, lonely, in the back of beyond, godforsaken, inaccessible; N. Amer. in the backwoods, lonesome; Austral./NZ in the backblocks, in the booay; informal in the sticks, in the middle of nowhere; N. Amer. informal in the tall timbers; Austral./NZ informal beyond the black stump. **3** *it is still only a remote possibility*: **unlikely**, improbable, implausible, doubtful, dubious; faint, slight, slim, small, slender. **4** *she seems very remote*: **aloof**, distant, detached, withdrawn, reserved, uncommunicative, unforthcoming, unapproachable, unresponsive, unfriendly, unsociable; informal stand-offish.
– OPPOSITES close, central.

removal noun **1** *the lieutenant ordered the removal of all heavy artillery*: **taking away**, moving, withdrawal. **2** *opposition parties demanded his removal from office*: **dismissal**, ejection, expulsion, ousting, displacement, deposition; N. Amer. ouster; informal sacking, firing. **3** *the*

r

removal of customs barriers within the EU: **withdrawal**, elimination, taking away. **4** the removal of any errors is a high priority: **deletion**, elimination, erasing, effacing, obliteration.
– OPPOSITES installation.

remove verb **1** switch off the power and remove the plug: **detach**, unfasten; pull out, take out, disconnect, extract. **2** she took the box and removed the lid: **take off**, undo, unfasten, lift (off). **3** he removed a note from his wallet: **take out**, produce, bring out, get out, pull out, withdraw. **4** police removed several boxes of documents: **take away**, carry away, move, transport; confiscate; informal cart off. **5** in the bathroom Sheila removed the mud: **clean off**, wash off/away, wipe off/away, rinse off. **6** Henry removed his coat: **take off**, pull off, slip out of; Brit. informal peel off. **7** he was removed from his post as head of security: **dismiss**, discharge, get rid of, dislodge, displace, expel, oust, depose; informal sack, fire, kick out, boot out; Brit. informal turf out. **8** in the spring, tax relief on premiums was removed: **withdraw**, abolish, eliminate, get rid of, do away with, stop, cut, axe. **9** Gabriel removed two words from the title: **delete**, erase, rub out, cross out, strike out, score out.
– OPPOSITES attach, insert, replace.

remunerate verb **pay**, reward, reimburse, recompense.

remuneration noun it's a demanding job which deserves adequate remuneration: **payment**, pay, salary, wages; earnings, fee(s), reward, recompense, reimbursement; formal emolument(s).

remunerative adjective **lucrative**, well paid, financially rewarding; profitable.

renaissance noun Auerbach has spearheaded a renaissance in British figurative art: **revival**, renewal, resurrection, reawakening, re-emergence, rebirth, reappearance, resurgence, regeneration; formal renascence.

rend verb a crisis which threatened to rend the alliance apart: **tear/rip apart**, tear/rip in two, split, rupture, sever; literary tear/rip asunder, sunder.

render verb **1** her fury rendered her speechless: **make**, cause to be/become, leave. **2** I am in the process of rendering assistance: **give**, provide, supply, furnish, contribute; offer, proffer. **3** the relevant invoices have since been rendered by the accountants: **send in**, present, submit. **4** her paintings are rendered in wonderfully vivid colours: **paint**, draw, depict, portray, represent, execute. **5** the film's Jewish characters are vividly rendered: **act**, perform, play, depict, interpret. **6** the phrase was almost impossible to render into English: **translate**, put, express, rephrase, reword.

rendezvous noun Edward was late for their rendezvous: **meeting**, appointment, assignation; informal date; literary tryst.

verb the bar where they had agreed to rendezvous: **meet**, come together, gather, assemble.

rendition noun **1** our stirring rendition of Beethoven's Fifth: **performance**, rendering, interpretation, presentation, execution, delivery. **2** the artist's rendition of Adam and Eve is revolutionary: **depiction**, portrayal, representation. **3** an interpreter's rendition of the message: **translation**, interpretation, version.

renegade noun he was denounced as a renegade: **traitor**, defector, deserter, turncoat, rebel, mutineer.
adjective 350 troops led by a renegade colonel: **treacherous**, traitorous, disloyal, treasonous, rebel, mutinous.
– OPPOSITES loyal.

renege verb he has reneged on his promise to keep taxes down: **default on**, fail to honour, go back on, break, back out of, withdraw from, retreat from, welsh on, backtrack on; break one's word/promise.
– OPPOSITES honour.

renew verb **1** I renewed my search: **resume**, return to, take up again, start again, restart, recommence; continue (with), carry on (with). **2** they renewed their vows at a cathedral service: **reaffirm**, reassert; repeat, reiterate, restate. **3** she needed something to renew her interest in life: **revive**, regenerate, revitalize, reinvigorate, restore, resuscitate, breathe new life into. **4** the hotel was completely renewed in 1990: **renovate**, restore, refurbish, modernize, overhaul, redevelop, rebuild, reconstruct, remodel; N. Amer. bring something up to code; informal do up; N. Amer. informal rehab. **5** they renewed Jackie's contract after three months: **extend**, prolong.

renewal noun **1** the renewal of our friendship has meant a lot to me: **resumption**, recommencement, re-establishment; continuation. **2** we need a source of spiritual renewal: **regeneration**, revival, reinvigoration, revitalization. **3** the comprehensive scheme of urban renewal: **renovation**, restoration, modernization, reconditioning, overhauling, redevelopment, rebuilding, reconstruction.

renounce verb **1** Edward renounced his claim to the throne: **give up**, relinquish, abandon, abdicate, surrender, waive, forgo. **2** Hungary renounced the agreement on environmental grounds: **reject**, refuse to abide by, repudiate. **3** she renounced her entire family: **repudiate**, deny, reject, abandon, wash one's hands of, turn one's back on, disown, spurn, shun; literary forsake.
– OPPOSITES assert, accept.

renovate verb **modernize**, restore, refurbish, revamp, recondition, rehabilitate, overhaul, redevelop; update, upgrade, refit; N. Amer. bring something up to code; informal do up; N. Amer. informal rehab.

renown noun **fame**, distinction, eminence,

pre-eminence, prominence, repute, reputation, prestige, acclaim, celebrity, notability.

renowned adjective *Satyajit Ray, the renowned Indian film-maker:* **famous**, celebrated, famed, eminent, distinguished, acclaimed, illustrious, pre-eminent, prominent, great, esteemed, of note, well known.
– OPPOSITES unknown.

rent¹ noun *I can't afford to pay the rent:* **charges**, rental.
verb **1** *she rented a car:* **hire**, lease, charter. **2** *if you don't want to sell it, why don't you rent it out?* **let (out)**, lease (out), hire (out); sublet, sublease.

rent² noun *his knee poked through the rent in his trousers:* **rip**, tear, split, hole, slash, slit.

renunciation noun **1** *Henry's renunciation of his throne:* **relinquishment**, giving up, abandonment, abdication, surrender, waiving, foregoing. **2** *his renunciation of luxury made him feel very holy:* **abstention**, refraining, going without, giving up, eschewal **3** *their renunciation of terrorism has to be genuine:* **repudiation**, rejection, abandonment.

reorganize verb **restructure**, change, alter, adjust, transform, shake up, rationalize, rearrange, reshape, overhaul.

repair¹ verb **1** *the car was taken to a garage to be repaired:* **mend**, fix (up), put/set right, restore (to working order), overhaul, service; informal patch up. **2** *they repaired the costumes in a few minutes:* **mend**, darn; informal patch up. **3** *the government is now repairing relations with other countries:* **put/set right**, mend, fix, straighten out, improve; informal patch up. **4** *she sought to repair the wrong she had done:* **rectify**, make good, (put) right, correct, make up for, make amends for, make reparation for.
noun **1** *the building is in need of repair:* **restoration**, fixing (up), mending, renovation, refurbishment. **2** *a virtually invisible repair:* **mend**, darn. **3** *all the tools are in good repair:* **condition**, working order, state, shape, fettle; Brit. informal nick.

repair² verb (formal) *relax in the stylish bar before repairing to the dining room:* **go to**, head for, adjourn to, wend one's way to, make one's way to, move to, withdraw; literary betake oneself to.

reparation noun *ways in which offenders may make reparation to their victims:* **amends**, restitution, redress, compensation, recompense, repayment, atonement.

repartee noun **banter**, badinage, bantering, raillery, witticism(s), ripostes, sallies, quips, joking, jesting, chaff, chaffing; formal persiflage.

repast noun (formal) **meal**, feast, banquet; informal spread, feed, bite (to eat); Brit. informal nosh-up.

repay verb **1** *I'm making an effort to*

repay customers who have been cheated: **reimburse**, refund, pay back/off, recompense, compensate, indemnify. **2** *the grants have to be repaid in full:* **pay back**, return, refund, reimburse. **3** *Walsh intends to repay them for the gamble they took when giving him the job last summer:* **reward**, recompense, pay back.

repayment noun *the repayment of tax:* **refund**, reimbursement, paying back.

repeal verb *the Act was repealed in 1990:* **revoke**, rescind, cancel, reverse, annul, nullify, declare null and void, quash, abolish.
– OPPOSITES enact.
noun *the repeal of the law has proved controversial:* **revocation**, rescinding, cancellation, reversal, annulment, nullification, quashing, abolition.

repeat verb **1** *she repeated her story in a flat voice:* **say again**, restate, reiterate, go/run through again, recapitulate; informal recap. **2** *children can remember and repeat large chunks of text:* **recite**, quote, parrot, regurgitate; informal trot out. **3** *Steele was invited to repeat his work in a laboratory:* **do again**, redo, replicate, duplicate. **4** *the episodes were repeated on Thursday nights:* **show again**, rerun, reshow.
noun **1** *the final was a repeat of the previous year's fixture:* **repetition**, duplication, replication, duplicate. **2** *repeats of his TV show are shown constantly:* **rerun**.

repeated adjective **recurrent**, frequent, persistent, continual, incessant, constant; regular, periodic, numerous.
– OPPOSITES occasional.

repeatedly adverb **frequently**, often, again and again, over and over (again), time and (time) again, many times, many a time; persistently, recurrently, constantly, continually, regularly; N. Amer. oftentimes; informal 24-7.

repel verb **1** *the rebels were repelled by army units:* **fight off**, repulse, drive back/away, force back, beat back, push back; hold off, ward off, keep at bay; Brit. see off. **2** *the plastic coating will repel water:* **be impervious to**, be impermeable to, keep out, resist. **3** *the thought of kissing him repelled me:* **revolt**, disgust, repulse, sicken, nauseate, turn someone's stomach, be repulsive, be distasteful, be repugnant; informal turn off; N. Amer. informal gross out.

repellent adjective **1** *critics found the film repellent:* **revolting**, repulsive, disgusting, repugnant, sickening, nauseating, stomach-turning, nauseous, vile, nasty, foul, horrible, awful, dreadful, terrible, obnoxious, loathsome, offensive, objectionable, abhorrent, odious, hateful, execrable; N. Amer. vomitous; informal ghastly, horrid, gross, yucky, icky; literary noisome. **2** *a water-repellent coating:* **impermeable**, impervious; -proof, -resistant.
– OPPOSITES delightful.

repent verb **feel remorse**, regret, be sorry,

be ashamed.

repentance noun **remorse**, contrition, contriteness, penitence, regret, ruefulness, remorsefulness, shame, guilt.

repentant adjective **penitent**, contrite, regretful, rueful, remorseful, apologetic, chastened, ashamed, shamefaced.
– OPPOSITES impenitent.

repercussion noun **consequence**, result, effect, outcome; reverberation, backlash, aftermath, fallout.

repertoire noun **collection**, stock, range, repertory, reserve, store, repository, supply.

repetition noun **1** *the statistics have already been quoted and they bear repetition:* **reiteration**, repeating, restatement, retelling. **2** *the repetition of words you have just heard:* **repeating**, echoing, parroting. **3** *she didn't want a repetition of the scene in the kitchen:* **recurrence**, reoccurrence, rerun, repeat. **4** *there is some repetition, but not enough to detract from the book's message:* **repetitiousness**, repetitiveness, redundancy, tautology.

repetitious adjective *repetitious work.* See REPETITIVE.

repetitive adjective **monotonous**, tedious, boring, humdrum, mundane, dreary, tiresome; unvaried, unchanging, unvarying, recurrent, recurring, repeated, repetitious, routine, mechanical.

rephrase verb **reword**, put in other words, express differently, paraphrase.

replace verb **1** *Adam replaced the receiver:* **put back**, return, restore. **2** *a new chairman came in to replace him:* **take the place of**, succeed, take over from, supersede; stand in for, substitute for, deputize for, cover for, relieve; informal step into someone's shoes/boots. **3** *she replaced the spoon with a fork:* **substitute**, exchange, change, swap.
– OPPOSITES remove.

replacement noun **1** *the teacher was ill and we had to find a replacement:* **successor**; substitute, stand-in, locum, relief, cover. **2** *the wiring was in need of replacement:* **renewal**, replacing.

replenish verb **1** *she replenished their glasses:* **refill**, top up, fill up, recharge; N. Amer. freshen. **2** *their supplies were replenished by a new airlift:* **stock up**, restock, restore, replace.
– OPPOSITES empty, exhaust.

replete adjective **1** *the guests, replete with this sumptuous dinner, lingered over coffee:* **well fed**, sated, satiated, full (up); glutted, gorged; informal stuffed. **2** *a sumptuous environment replete with priceless antiques:* **filled**, full, well stocked, well supplied, crammed, packed, jammed, teeming, overflowing, bursting; informal jam-packed, chock-a-block.

replica noun **copy**, model, duplicate, reproduction; dummy, imitation, facsimile.

replicate verb **copy**, reproduce, duplicate,

recreate, repeat; clone.

reply verb *Rachel didn't bother to reply:* **answer**, respond, rejoin, retort, riposte, come back, write back.
noun *he waited for a reply:* **answer**, response, rejoinder, retort, riposte; informal comeback.

report verb **1** *the government reported a fall in inflation:* **announce**, describe, detail, outline, communicate, divulge, disclose, reveal, make public, publish, broadcast, proclaim, publicize. **2** *I reported him to the police:* **inform on**; informal shop, tell on, squeal on, rat on, peach on; Brit. informal grass on. **3** *Juliet reported for duty:* **present oneself**, arrive, turn up, clock in, sign in; Brit. clock on; N. Amer. punch in; informal show up.
noun **1** *I've asked for a full report on the meeting:* **account**, review, record, description, statement; transactions, proceedings, transcripts, minutes. **2** *the police received reports of drug dealing:* **news**, information, word, intelligence. **3** *I followed his progress through the newspaper reports:* **story**, account, article, piece, item, column, feature, bulletin, dispatch. **4** (Brit.) *his last school report had been good:* **assessment**, evaluation, appraisal; N. Amer. report card. **5** *reports of his imminent resignation circulated:* **rumour**, whisper; informal buzz. **6** *they heard the report of a gun:* **bang**, blast, crack, shot, gunshot, explosion, boom.

reporter noun **journalist**, correspondent, newspaperman, newspaperwoman, newsman, newswoman, columnist, blogger; Brit. pressman; N. Amer. legman, wireman; Austral. roundsman; informal news hound, hack, stringer, journo; N. Amer. informal newsy.

repose noun *in repose, her face still showed signs of strain:* **rest**, relaxation, inactivity; sleep, slumber.
verb **1** *the diamond reposed on a bed of velvet:* **lie**, rest, be placed, be situated. **2** *the beds on which we reposed:* **lie (down)**, recline, rest, sleep.

repository noun **store**, storehouse, depository; reservoir, bank, cache, treasury, fund, mine.

reprehensible adjective **deplorable**, disgraceful, discreditable, despicable, blameworthy, culpable, wrong, bad, shameful, dishonourable, objectionable, opprobrious, repugnant, inexcusable, unforgivable, indefensible, unjustifiable; criminal, sinful, scandalous, iniquitous; formal exceptionable.
– OPPOSITES praiseworthy.

represent verb **1** *many of Dickens' characters represent a single quality:* **symbolize**, stand for, personify, epitomize, typify, embody, illustrate. **2** *the initials which represent her qualifications:* **stand for**, designate, denote; literary betoken. **3** *the goddess Hathor is represented as a woman with cow's horns:* **depict**, portray, render, picture, delineate, show, illustrate. **4** *ageing represents a threat to one's independence:*

constitute, be, amount to. **5** *his solicitor represented him in court:* **appear for**, act for, speak on behalf of.

representation noun **1** *Rossetti's representation of women is weak:* **portrayal**, depiction, delineation, presentation, renuition. **2** *representations of the human form:* **likeness**, painting, drawing, picture, illustration, sketch, image, model, figure, figurine, statue, statuette.

representative adjective **1** *here is a representative sample:* **typical**, characteristic, illustrative. **2** *a system of representative government:* **elected**, elective, democratic, popular.
– OPPOSITES atypical, totalitarian.
noun **1** *a representative of the Royal Society:* **spokesperson**, spokesman, spokeswoman, agent, official, mouthpiece. **2** *a sales representative:* **(commercial) traveller**, (travelling) salesman, saleswoman, agent; informal rep; N. Amer. informal drummer. **3** *the Cambodian representative at the UN:* **delegate**, commissioner, ambassador, attaché, envoy, emissary, chargé d'affaires, deputy. **4** *our representatives in parliament:* **Member (of Parliament)**, MP; councillor; N. Amer. Member of Congress, congressman, congresswoman, senator. **5** *he acted as his father's representative:* **deputy**, substitute, stand-in, proxy.

repress verb **1** *the rebellion was successfully repressed:* **suppress**, quell, quash, subdue, put down, crush, extinguish, stamp out, defeat, conquer, rout, overwhelm, contain. **2** *the ruling class repressed and exploited the workers:* **oppress**, subjugate, keep down, rule with a rod of iron, intimidate, tyrannize, crush. **3** *in childhood, these emotions may well be repressed:* **restrain**, hold back/in, keep back, suppress, keep in check, control, keep under control, curb, stifle, bottle up; informal button up, keep the lid on.

repressed adjective **1** *a repressed country:* **oppressed**, subjugated, subdued, tyrannized. **2** *repressed feelings:* **restrained**, suppressed, held back/in, kept in check, stifled, pent up, bottled up. **3** *he is a reclusive, emotionally repressed man:* **inhibited**, frustrated, restrained; informal uptight, hung up.
– OPPOSITES democratic, uninhibited.

repression noun **1** *the brutal repression of peaceful protests:* **suppression**, quashing, subduing, crushing, stamping out. **2** *20 years of political repression:* **oppression**, subjugation, suppression, tyranny, despotism, authoritarianism. **3** *the repression of sexual urges:* **restraint**, restraining, holding back, keeping back, suppression, keeping in check, control, stifling, bottling up.

repressive adjective **oppressive**, authoritarian, despotic, tyrannical, dictatorial, autocratic, totalitarian, undemocratic.

reprieve verb **1** *she was sentenced to death, then reprieved:* **pardon**, spare, grant an amnesty to, amnesty; informal let off (the hook). **2** *the project has been reprieved:* **save**, rescue.
noun *he was saved by a last-minute reprieve:* **stay of execution**, remission, pardon, amnesty; US Law continuance; informal let-off.

reprimand verb *he was publicly reprimanded for his behaviour:* **rebuke**, admonish, chastise, chide, upbraid, reprove, reproach, scold, berate, take to task, lambaste, haul over the coals, criticize, censure; informal tell off, give someone a telling-off, give someone a talking-to, dress down, give someone a dressing-down, give someone an earful, give someone a roasting, bawl out, blast; Brit. informal tick off, carpet, tear off a strip, give someone what for, give someone a wigging, give someone a rocket, give someone a rollicking; N. Amer. informal chew out, ream out; Austral. informal monster; formal castigate.
– OPPOSITES praise.
noun *they received a severe reprimand:* **rebuke**, reproof, admonishment, admonition, reproach, reproval, scolding, upbraiding, censure; informal telling-off, dressing-down, earful, roasting, tongue-lashing; Brit. informal ticking-off, carpeting, wigging, rocket, rollicking.
– OPPOSITES commendation.

reprisal noun **retaliation**, counter-attack, comeback; revenge, vengeance, retribution.

reproach verb *Albert reproached him for being late.* See REPRIMAND verb.
noun *an expression of reproach.* See REPRIMAND noun.
■ **beyond/above reproach** *her public image had to be beyond reproach:* **perfect**, blameless, above suspicion, without fault, faultless, flawless, irreproachable, exemplary, impeccable, immaculate, unblemished, spotless, untarnished, stainless, unsullied, whiter than white; informal squeaky clean.

reproachful adjective **disapproving**, reproving, critical, censorious, disparaging, withering, accusatory, admonitory.
– OPPOSITES approving.

reprobate noun *even a hardened reprobate like myself has standards:* **rogue**, rascal, scoundrel, miscreant, good-for-nothing, villain, wretch, rake, degenerate; informal, dated rotter; dated cad; archaic blackguard.

reproduce verb **1** *each artwork is reproduced in full colour:* **copy**, duplicate, replicate; photocopy, xerox, photostat, print. **2** *this work has not been reproduced in other laboratories:* **repeat**, replicate, recreate, redo; simulate, imitate, emulate, mirror, mimic. **3** *some animals reproduce prolifically:* **breed**, produce offspring, procreate, propagate, multiply.

reproduction noun **1** *the reproduction of copyrighted material:* **copying**, duplication,

r

duplicating; photocopying, xeroxing, photostatting, reprinting. **2** *this is a reproduction of the original:* **print**, copy, reprint, duplicate, facsimile, carbon copy, photocopy; trademark Xerox. **3** *the means of reproduction varies from species to species:* **breeding**, procreation, multiplying, propagation.

reproductive adjective **generative**, procreative, propagative; sexual, genital.

reproof noun **rebuke**, reprimand, reproach, admonishment, admonition; disapproval, censure, criticism, condemnation; informal telling-off, dressing down; Brit. informal ticking-off.

reptilian adjective **reptile**, saurian; cold-blooded.

repudiate verb **1** *in 1924 she repudiated communism:* **reject**, renounce, abandon, give up, turn one's back on, disown, cast off, lay aside; formal forswear. **2** *Cranham repudiated the allegations:* **deny**, refute, contradict, controvert, rebut, dispute, dismiss, brush aside; formal gainsay. **3** *Egypt repudiated the treaty:* **cancel**, revoke, rescind, reverse, overrule, overturn, invalidate, nullify; disregard, flout, renege on; formal abrogate.
– OPPOSITES embrace, confirm.

repudiation noun **1** *he sees repudiation of art as starving the soul of nourishment:* **rejection**, renunciation, abandonment, giving up. **2** *this was a direct repudiation of the Chancellor's statement:* **denial**, refutation, rebuttal, rejection. **3** *they would oppose the Nantucket Treaty, and demand its repudiation in Congress:* **cancellation**, revocation, rescindment, reversal, invalidation, nullification.

repugnance noun **revulsion**, disgust, abhorrence, repulsion, loathing, hatred, detestation, aversion, distaste, antipathy; archaic disrelish.

repugnant adjective **abhorrent**, revolting, repulsive, repellent, disgusting, offensive, objectionable, vile, foul, nasty, loathsome, sickening, nauseating, hateful, detestable, execrable, abominable, monstrous, appalling, insufferable, intolerable, unacceptable, contemptible, unsavoury, unpalatable; informal ghastly, gross, horrible, horrid; literary noisome.
– OPPOSITES pleasant.

repulse verb **1** *the rebels were once again repulsed:* **repel**, drive back/away, fight back/off, put to flight, force back, beat off/back; ward off, hold off; Brit. see off. **2** *she tried to show him affection, but was repulsed:* **rebuff**, reject, spurn, snub, cold-shoulder; informal give someone the brush-off, freeze out; Brit. informal knock back. **3** *his bid for the company was repulsed:* **reject**, turn down, refuse, decline. **4** *the brutality of the film repulsed her:* **revolt**, disgust, repel, sicken, nauseate, turn someone's stomach, be repugnant to; informal turn off; N. Amer. informal gross out.

noun **1** *the repulse of the attack afforded some breathing space:* **repelling**, driving back; warding off, holding off. **2** *he was mortified by this repulse:* **rebuff**, rejection, snub, slight; informal brush-off, knock-back.

repulsion noun **disgust**, revulsion, abhorrence, repugnance, nausea, horror, aversion, abomination, distaste; archaic disrelish.

repulsive adjective **revolting**, disgusting, abhorrent, repellent, repugnant, offensive, objectionable, vile, foul, nasty, loathsome, sickening, nauseating, hateful, detestable, execrable, abominable, monstrous, noxious, horrendous, awful, terrible, dreadful, frightful, obnoxious, unsavoury, unpleasant, disagreeable, distasteful; ugly, hideous, grotesque; informal ghastly, horrible, horrid, gross; literary noisome.
– OPPOSITES attractive.

reputable adjective **well thought of**, highly regarded, (well) respected, respectable, of (good) repute, prestigious, established; reliable, dependable, trustworthy.
– OPPOSITES disreputable.

reputation noun **(good) name**, character, repute, standing, stature, status, position, renown, esteem, prestige; N. Amer. informal rep, rap.

repute noun **1** *a woman of ill repute:* **reputation**, name, character. **2** *a firm of international repute:* **fame**, renown, distinction, high standing, stature, prestige.

reputed adjective **1** *they are reputed to be very rich:* **thought**, said, reported, rumoured, believed, held, considered, regarded, deemed, alleged. **2** *his reputed father died in obscurity:* **supposed**, putative, apparent. **3** *he rose to become a reputed naturalist:* **well thought of**, (well) respected, highly regarded.

reputedly adverb **supposedly**, by all accounts, so I'm told, so people say, allegedly.

request noun **1** *we received several requests for assistance:* **appeal**, entreaty, plea, petition, application, demand, call. **2** *Charlotte spoke with him at Ursula's request:* **bidding**, entreaty, demand, insistence. **3** *indicate your requests on the booking form:* **requirement**, wish, desire; choice.
verb **1** *the government requested military aid:* **ask for**, appeal for, call for, seek, solicit, plead for, apply for, demand. **2** *I requested him to help:* **call on**, beg, entreat, implore; literary beseech.

require verb **1** *the child required hospital treatment:* **need**, be in need of. **2** *it was a situation requiring patience:* **necessitate**, demand, call for, involve, entail. **3** *unquestioning obedience is required:* **demand**, insist on, call for, ask for, expect. **4** *she was required to pay costs:* **order**, instruct, command, enjoin, oblige, compel, force. **5** *do you require anything else?* **want**, wish for, desire, lack, be short of.

required adjective **1** *this book is required reading:* **essential**, vital, indispensable, necessary, compulsory, obligatory, mandatory, prescribed. **2** *cut it to the required length:* **desired**, preferred, chosen; correct, proper, right.
– OPPOSITES optional.

requirement noun **need**, wish, demand, want, necessity, essential, prerequisite, stipulation.

requisite adjective *he lacks the requisite skills:* **necessary**, required, prerequisite, essential, vital.
– OPPOSITES optional.
noun **1** *toilet requisites will be supplied:* **requirement**, need, necessity, essential. **2** *a university degree has become a requisite for a successful career:* **necessity**, essential (requirement), prerequisite, precondition, sine qua non; informal **must**.

requisition noun **1** *the department has placed requisitions for extra staff:* **order**, request, call, application, claim, demand. **2** *the illegal requisition of cultural treasures:* **appropriation**, commandeering, seizure, confiscation, expropriation.
verb *the house was requisitioned by the army:* **commandeer**, appropriate, take over, take possession of, occupy, seize, confiscate, expropriate.

rescind verb *the Ombudsman cannot rescind planning permission:* **revoke**, repeal, cancel, reverse, overturn, overrule, annul, nullify, void, invalidate, quash, abolish.
– OPPOSITES enforce.

rescue verb **1** *an attempt to rescue the hostages:* **save**, come to the aid of; (set) free, release, liberate. **2** *Boyd bent hastily to rescue his papers:* **retrieve**, recover, salvage, get back.
noun *the rescue of 10 crewmen:* **saving**, rescuing; release, freeing, liberation, deliverance, redemption.
■ **come to someone's rescue** help, assist, lend a (helping) hand to, bail out; informal save someone's bacon, save someone's neck, save someone's skin.

research noun **1** *we oppose the use of animals in medical research:* **investigation**, experimentation, testing, analysis, fact-finding, examination, scrutiny, scrutinization. **2** *he could no longer afford to continue his researches:* **experiments**, experimentation, tests, inquiries, studies.
verb **1** *the phenomenon has been widely researched:* **investigate**, study, inquire into, look into, probe, explore, analyse, examine, scrutinize, review. **2** *I researched all the available material:* **study**, read (up on), sift through; informal check out.

resemblance noun **similarity**, likeness, similitude, correspondence, congruity, congruence, coincidence, conformity, agreement, equivalence, comparability,

parallelism, uniformity, sameness.

resemble verb **look like**, be similar to, be like, bear a resemblance to, remind one of, take after, favour, have the look of; approximate to, smack of, have (all) the hallmarks of, correspond to.

resent verb *she resented all the attention that her sister got:* **begrudge**, feel aggrieved at/about, feel bitter about, grudge, be annoyed at/about, be resentful of, dislike, take exception to, object to, take amiss, take offence at, take umbrage at, bear/harbour a grudge about.
– OPPOSITES welcome.

resentful adjective **aggrieved**, indignant, irritated, piqued, put out, in high dudgeon, dissatisfied, disgruntled, discontented, offended, bitter, jaundiced; envious, jealous; informal miffed, peeved; Brit. informal narked; N. Amer. informal sore.

resentment noun **bitterness**, indignation, irritation, pique, dissatisfaction, disgruntlement, discontentment, discontent, resentfulness, bad feelings, hard feelings, ill will, acrimony, rancour, animosity, jaundice; envy, jealousy.

reservation noun **1** *the government expressed grave reservations about the proposals:* **doubt**, qualm, scruple; misgivings, scepticism, unease, hesitation, objection. **2** *groups should make reservations well in advance:* **(advance) booking**. **3** *the reservation of the room has been confirmed:* **booking**, ordering, securing. **4** *the Yanomami Indian reservation:* **reserve**, enclave, sanctuary, territory, homeland.
■ **without reservation** wholeheartedly, unreservedly, without qualification, fully, completely, totally, entirely, wholly, unconditionally.

reserve verb **1** *ask your newsagent to reserve you a copy:* **put to one side**, put aside, set aside, keep (back), save, hold back, keep in reserve, earmark. **2** *he reserved a table for three:* **book**, make a reservation for, order, secure. **3** *the management reserves the right to alter the programme:* **retain**, keep, hold. **4** *reserve your judgement until you know him better:* **defer**, postpone, put off, delay, withhold.
noun **1** *Harriet has used some of her precious reserves of petrol for the journey:* **stock**, store, supply, stockpile, pool, hoard, cache. **2** *a nature reserve:* **national park**, sanctuary, preserve, conservation area. **3** *Carrie found it hard to penetrate his natural reserve:* **reticence**, detachment, distance, remoteness, coolness, aloofness, constraint, formality; shyness, diffidence, timidity, taciturnity, inhibition.
adjective *a reserve goalkeeper:* **substitute**, stand-in, relief, replacement, fallback, spare, extra.
■ **in reserve** available, to/on hand, ready, in readiness, set aside, at one's disposal.

reserved adjective **1** *Sewell is rather reserved:*

r

reticent, quiet, private, uncommunicative, unforthcoming, undemonstrative, unsociable, formal, constrained, cool, aloof, detached, distant, remote, unapproachable, unfriendly, withdrawn, secretive, silent, taciturn; shy, retiring, diffident, timid, self-effacing, inhibited, introverted. **2** *the corner table is reserved, I'm afraid:* **booked**, taken, spoken for, pre-arranged.
– OPPOSITES outgoing.

reservoir noun **1** *we went sailing on the reservoir:* lake; water supply; Scottish loch. **2** *the toner reservoir is in a detachable cartridge:* **receptacle**, container, holder, repository, tank.

reshuffle verb *the prime minister reshuffled his cabinet:* **reorganize**, restructure, rearrange, change (around), shake up, shuffle.
noun *a management reshuffle:* **reorganization**, restructuring, change, rearrangement; informal shake-up.

reside verb **1** *most students reside in flats:* **live in**, occupy, inhabit, stay in, lodge in; formal dwell in. **2** *the paintings reside in an air-conditioned vault:* **be situated**, be found, be located, lie. **3** *executive power resides in the president:* **be vested in**, be bestowed on, be conferred on, be in the hands of.

residence noun *her private residence:* **home**, house, place of residence, address; quarters, lodgings; informal pad; formal dwelling (place), domicile, abode.

resident noun **1** *the residents of New York City:* **inhabitant**, local, citizen, native; householder, homeowner, occupier, tenant; formal denizen. **2** (Brit.) *the bar is open to residents only:* **guest**, lodger.
adjective **1** *he is currently resident in the UK:* **living**, residing; formal dwelling. **2** *we have a resident nanny:* **live-in**, living in. **3** *the resident registrar in obstetrics:* **permanent**, incumbent.

residential adjective **suburban**, commuter, dormitory.

residual adjective **1** *residual heat is used to dry the dishes:* **remaining**, leftover, unused, unconsumed. **2** *she still feels some residual affection for her husband:* **lingering**, enduring, abiding, surviving, vestigial.

residue noun **remainder**, remaining part, rest, remnant(s); surplus, extra, excess; remains, leftovers.

resign verb **1** *the senior manager resigned after the losses were announced:* **leave**, hand in one's notice, give notice, stand down, step down; informal quit. **2** *19 MPs resigned their seats:* **give up**, leave, vacate, stand down from; informal quit. **3** *we resigned ourselves to a long wait:* **reconcile oneself to**, become resigned to, come to terms with.

resignation noun **1** *his resignation from his government post:* **departure**, leaving, standing down, stepping down;

informal quitting. **2** *she handed in her resignation:* **notice**. **3** *he accepted his fate with resignation:* **patience**, forbearance, stoicism, fortitude, fatalism, acceptance, acquiescence, compliance, passivity.

resigned adjective **patient**, long-suffering, uncomplaining, forbearing, stoical, philosophical, fatalistic, acquiescent, compliant, passive.

resilient adjective **1** *a resilient underlay prolongs the life of your carpet:* **flexible**, pliable, supple; durable, hard-wearing, stout, strong, sturdy, tough. **2** *he was still young and resilient:* **strong**, tough, hardy, buoyant, irrepressible.

resist verb **1** *the vine is able to resist cold winters:* **withstand**, combat, weather, endure, be resistant to, keep out. **2** *they resisted his attempts to change things:* **oppose**, fight, object to, defy, set one's face against; obstruct, impede, hinder, block, thwart, frustrate. **3** *I resisted the urge to say anything:* **refrain from**, abstain from, forbear from, desist from, not give in to, restrain oneself from, stop oneself from. **4** *she tried to resist him:* **struggle with/against**, fight (against), stand up to, withstand, hold off; fend off, ward off.
– OPPOSITES welcome, submit.
■ **cannot resist** *he is a man who cannot resist a challenge:* love, adore, relish, have a weakness for, be very keen on, like, delight in, enjoy, take great pleasure in; informal be mad about, get a kick/thrill out of.

resistance noun **1** *resistance to change:* **opposition**, hostility, refusal to accept. **2** *James put up a spirited resistance:* **opposition**, fight, stand, struggle. **3** *he joined the French resistance:* **resistance movement**, freedom fighters, underground, partisans, insurgents.

resistant adjective **1** *the membrane is resistant to water:* **impervious**, unsusceptible, immune, invulnerable. **2** *she is very resistant to change:* **opposed**, averse, hostile, inimical, against; informal anti.

resolute adjective **determined**, purposeful, resolved, adamant, single-minded, firm, unswerving, unwavering, steadfast, staunch, stalwart, unfaltering, unhesitating, persistent, indefatigable, tenacious, strong-willed, unshakeable; stubborn, dogged, obstinate, obdurate, inflexible, intransigent, implacable, unyielding, unrelenting.
– OPPOSITES half-hearted.

resolution noun **1** *despite her resolution not to smoke, she felt tempted:* **intention**, resolve, decision, intent, aim, plan; commitment, pledge, promise. **2** *the committee passed the resolution unanimously:* **motion**, proposal, proposition; N. Amer. resolve. **3** *she handled the work with resolution:* **determination**, purpose, purposefulness, resolve, resoluteness, single-mindedness, firmness (of purpose); steadfastness, staunchness, perseverance, persistence, indefatigability, tenacity, tenaciousness, staying power, dedication, commitment. **4** *a satisfactory resolution of the problem:* **solution**, answer, end, ending, settlement, conclusion.

resolve verb **1** *this matter cannot be resolved overnight:* **settle**, sort out, solve, find a solution to, fix, straighten out, deal with, put right, put to rights, rectify; informal hammer out, thrash out, figure out. **2** *Charity resolved not to wait any longer:* **determine**, decide, make up one's mind, take a decision. **3** *the committee resolved that the project should proceed:* **vote**, pass a resolution, rule, decide formally, agree.
noun *their intimidation merely strengthened his resolve.* See **RESOLUTION** sense 3.

resolved adjective **determined**, hell-bent, intent, set.

resonant adjective **1** *a resonant voice with a Welsh lilt:* **deep**, low, sonorous, full, vibrant, rich, clear, ringing; loud, booming, thunderous. **2** *valleys resonant with the sound of church bells:* **reverberating**, reverberant, resounding, echoing, filled. **3** *that most resonant of words—home:* **evocative**, suggestive, expressive, redolent.

resort noun **1** *they could settle the matter without resort to legal proceedings:* **recourse to**, turning to, use of. **2** *strike action is our last resort:* **expedient**, measure, step, recourse, alternative, option, choice, possibility, hope.
■ **in the last resort** *that belief, in the last resort, is what separates modern from medieval man:* ultimately, in the end, at the end of the day, in the long run, when all is said and done.
■ **resort to** *I don't have to resort to such underhand tricks:* have recourse to, fall back on, turn to, make use of, use, employ, avail oneself of; stoop to, descend to, sink to.

resound verb **1** *the explosion resounded round the silent street:* **echo**, reverberate, ring out, boom, thunder, rumble. **2** *a large building resounding with the clang of hammers:* **reverberate**, echo, resonate, ring.

resounding adjective **1** *a resounding bass voice:* **reverberant**, reverberating, resonant, resonating, echoing, ringing, sonorous, deep, rich, clear; loud, booming. **2** *the show was a resounding success:* **enormous**, huge, very great, tremendous, terrific, colossal; emphatic, decisive, conclusive, outstanding, remarkable, phenomenal.

resource noun **1** *use your resources efficiently:* **assets**, funds, wealth, money, capital; staff; supplies, materials, store(s), stock(s), reserve(s). **2** *your tutor is there as a resource:* **facility**, amenity, aid, help, support.

resourceful adjective **ingenious**, enterprising, inventive, creative; clever, talented, able, capable.

respect noun **1** *the respect due to a great artist:* **esteem**, regard, high opinion, admiration, reverence, deference, honour. **2** *he spoke to her with respect:* **due regard**, politeness, courtesy, civility, deference. **3** *it was normal to pay one's respects to the local military leader:* **(kind) regards**, compliments, greetings, best/good wishes, felicitations, salutations. **4** *the report was accurate in every respect:* **aspect**, regard, facet, feature, way, sense, particular, point, detail.
– OPPOSITES contempt.
verb **1** *he is highly respected for his achievements:* **esteem**, admire, think highly of, have a high opinion of, hold in high regard, hold in (high) esteem, look up to, revere, reverence, honour. **2** *they respected our privacy:* **show consideration for**, have regard for, observe, be mindful of, be heedful of. **3** *her father respected her wishes:* **abide by**, comply with, follow, adhere to, conform to, act in accordance with, defer to, obey, observe, keep (to).
– OPPOSITES despise, disobey.
■ **with respect to/in respect of** concerning, regarding, in/with regard to, with reference to, respecting, re, about, apropos, on the subject of, in connection with, vis-à-vis.

respectable adjective **1** *she came from a respectable middle-class background:* **reputable**, upright, honest, honourable, trustworthy, decent, good, well bred, clean-living. **2** *he earns a respectable salary:* **fairly good**, decent, fair, reasonable, moderately good; substantial, considerable, sizeable.
– OPPOSITES disreputable, paltry.

respectful adjective **deferential**, reverent, reverential, dutiful; polite, well mannered, civil, courteous, gracious.
– OPPOSITES rude.

respective adjective *the girls had gone back to their respective schools:* **separate**, personal, own, particular, individual, specific, special, appropriate, different, various.

respite noun **1** *the thought of a brief respite was tempting:* **rest**, break, breathing space, interval, intermission, interlude, recess, lull, pause, time out; relief, relaxation, repose; informal breather, let-up. **2** *granting them respite from debts allowed them to serve in the army:* **postponement**, deferment, delay, reprieve.

resplendent adjective **splendid**, magnificent, brilliant, dazzling, glittering, gorgeous, impressive, imposing, spectacular, striking, stunning, majestic; informal splendiferous.

respond verb **1** *they do not respond to questions:* **answer**, reply. **2** *'No,' she responded:* **reply**, answer, say, retort, riposte, counter. **3** *the police were slow to respond:* **react**, make a response, reciprocate, retaliate.

r

response noun **1** *his response to the question:* **answer**, reply, retort, riposte; informal comeback. **2** *the move drew an angry response from the opposition benches:* **reaction**, reply, retaliation; informal comeback.
– OPPOSITES question.

responsibility noun **1** *it was his responsibility to find witnesses:* **duty**, task, function, job, role, business; Brit. informal pigeon. **2** *the organization denied responsibility for the bomb attack:* **blame**, fault, guilt, culpability, liability. **3** *teenagers need to have a sense of responsibility:* **trustworthiness**, (common) sense, maturity, reliability, dependability. **4** *he has shown an aptitude for managerial responsibility:* **authority**, control, power, leadership.

responsible adjective **1** *who is responsible for prisons?* **in charge of**, in control of, at the helm of, accountable for, liable for. **2** *I am responsible for the mistake:* **accountable**, answerable, to blame, guilty, culpable, blameworthy, at fault, in the wrong. **3** *a responsible job:* **important**, powerful. **4** *he is responsible to the president:* **answerable**, accountable. **5** *he is a responsible tenant:* **trustworthy**, sensible, mature, reliable, dependable.

responsive adjective **quick to react**, reactive, receptive, open to suggestions, amenable, flexible, forthcoming.

rest¹ verb **1** *he needed to rest:* **relax**, take a rest, ease up/off, let up, slow down, have/take a break, unbend, unwind, recharge one's batteries, be at leisure, take it easy, put one's feet up; lie down, go to bed, have/take a nap, catnap, doze, sleep; informal take five, have/take a breather, snatch forty winks, get some shut-eye; Brit. informal have a kip; N. Amer. informal chill out, catch some Zs. **2** *his hands rested on the rail:* **lie**, be laid, repose, be placed, be positioned, be supported by. **3** *she rested her basket on the ground:* **support**, prop (up), lean, lay, set, stand, position, place, put.
noun **1** *you need to get some rest:* **repose**, relaxation, leisure, respite, time off, breathing space; sleep, nap, doze; informal shut-eye, snooze, lie-down, forty winks; Brit. informal kip. **2** *I was in need of a short rest from work:* **holiday**, vacation, break, breathing space, interval, interlude, intermission, time off/out; informal breather. **3** *she took the poker from its rest:* **stand**, base, holder, support, rack, frame, shelf.

rest² noun *the rest of the board are appointees:* **remainder**, residue, balance, remaining part/number/quantity, others, those left, remains, remnant(s), surplus, excess.

restaurant noun **eating place**, bistro, cafe, cafeteria, self-service, carvery, brasserie; N. Amer. diner; informal eatery.

restful adjective **relaxed**, relaxing, quiet, calm, calming, tranquil, soothing, peaceful, placid, reposeful, leisurely, undisturbed, untroubled.
– OPPOSITES exciting.

restitution noun **1** *claims for the restitution of the land seized by the occupying power:* **return**, restoration, handing back, surrender. **2** *he was ordered to pay $50,000 in restitution for the damage caused:* **compensation**, recompense, reparation, damages, indemnification, indemnity, reimbursement, repayment, remuneration, redress.

restive adjective **1** *Edward will be getting restive without any supper.* See RESTLESS sense 1. **2** *the militants are becoming increasingly restive:* **unruly**, disorderly, uncontrollable, unmanageable, wilful, recalcitrant, insubordinate; Brit. informal bolshie; formal refractory.

restless adjective **1** *Maria was restless:* **uneasy**, ill at ease, restive, fidgety, edgy, on edge, tense, worked up, nervous, agitated, anxious, on tenterhooks, keyed up; Brit. nervy; informal jumpy, jittery, twitchy, uptight, like a cat on a hot tin roof; Brit. informal like a cat on hot bricks. **2** *he had spent a restless night:* **sleepless**, wakeful; fitful, broken, disturbed, troubled, unsettled.

restlessness noun **unease**, restiveness, edginess, tenseness, nervousness, agitation, anxiety, fretfulness, apprehension, disquiet; informal jitteriness.

restoration noun **1** *the opposition demanded the restoration of democracy:* **reinstatement**, reinstitution, re-establishment, reimposition, return. **2** *the restoration of derelict housing:* **repair**, repairing, fixing, mending, refurbishment, reconditioning, rehabilitation, rebuilding, reconstruction, overhaul, redevelopment, renovation; N. Amer. informal rehab.

restore verb **1** *his aim was to restore democracy:* **reinstate**, bring back, reinstitute, reimpose, reinstall, re-establish. **2** *he restored the bicycle to its rightful owner:* **return**, give back, hand back. **3** *the building has been carefully restored:* **repair**, fix, mend, refurbish, recondition, rehabilitate, rebuild, reconstruct, remodel, overhaul, redevelop, renovate; informal do up; N. Amer. informal rehab.
– OPPOSITES abolish.

restrain verb **1** *Charles restrained his anger:* **control**, keep under control, check, hold/keep in check, curb, suppress, repress, contain, dampen, subdue, smother, choke back, stifle, bottle up, rein back/in; informal keep the lid on. **2** *she could barely restrain herself from swearing:* **prevent**, stop, keep, hold back. **3** *the policeman had used his truncheon to restrain a man he had arrested:* **control**, hold (down/back), keep under control, secure.

restrained adjective **1** *Julie was quite restrained:* **self-controlled**, self-restrained, sober, steady, unemotional, undemonstrative. **2** *the restrained elegance of the new floral wallpapers:* **muted**, soft, discreet, subtle, quiet, unobtrusive, understated, tasteful.

restraint noun **1** *he acts as a restraint on their impulsiveness:* **constraint**, check, control, restriction, limitation, curtailment; rein, bridle, brake, damper, impediment, obstacle. **2** *the customary restraint of the police:* **self-control**, self-restraint, self-discipline, control, moderation, prudence, judiciousness. **3** *the room has been decorated with commendable restraint:* **subtlety**, understatedness, taste, tastefulness, discretion, discrimination. **4** *a child restraint:* **belt**, harness, strap.

restrict verb **1** *a busy working life restricted his leisure activities:* **limit**, regulate, control, moderate, cut down. **2** *the cuff supports the ankle without restricting movement:* **hinder**, interfere with, impede, hamper, obstruct, block, check, curb. **3** *he restricted himself to a 15-minute speech:* **confine**, limit.

restricted adjective **1** *the result of cramming so much into a restricted space:* **cramped**, confined, constricted, small, narrow, tight. **2** *people on a restricted calorie intake:* **limited**, controlled, regulated, reduced. **3** *she parked in a restricted zone:* **out of bounds**, off limits, private. **4** *restricted information:* **(top) secret**, classified; informal hush-hush.
– OPPOSITES unlimited.

restriction noun **1** *there is no restriction on the number of places:* **limitation**, limit, constraint, control, check, curb. **2** *the restriction of personal freedom:* **reduction**, limitation, diminution, curtailment. **3** *restriction of movement:* **hindrance**, impediment, slowing, reduction, limitation.

result noun **1** *stress is the result of overwork:* **consequence**, outcome, upshot, sequel, effect, reaction, repercussion, ramification, conclusion, culmination. **2** *what is your result?* **answer**, solution; sum, total, product. **3** *exam results:* **mark**, score, grade. **4** *the result of the trial:* **verdict**, decision, outcome, conclusion, judgement, findings, ruling.
– OPPOSITES cause.
verb **1** *differences between species could result from their habitat:* **follow**, ensue, develop, stem, spring, arise, derive, evolve, proceed; occur, happen, take place, come about; be caused by, be brought about by, be produced by. **2** *the shooting resulted in five deaths:* **end in**, culminate in, finish in, terminate in, lead to, prompt, precipitate, trigger; cause, bring about, occasion, effect, give rise to, produce, engender, generate.

resume verb **1** *the government agreed to resume negotiations:* **restart**, recommence, begin again, start again, reopen, renew, return to, continue with, carry on with. **2** *the priest resumed his kneeling posture:* **return to**, come back to, take up again, reoccupy.

– OPPOSITES suspend, abandon.

résumé noun **summary**, precis, synopsis, abstract, outline, summarization, summation, epitome; abridgement, digest, condensation, abbreviation, overview, review.

resumption noun **1** **restart**, restarting, recommencement, reopening. **2** **continuation**, carrying on, renewal, return to.

resurgence noun *there has been a resurgence of interest in the scheme:* **renewal**, revival, recovery, comeback, reawakening, resurrection, reappearance, re-emergence, regeneration.

resurrect verb *it gives him a chance to resurrect his career:* **revive**, restore, regenerate, revitalize, breathe new life into, reinvigorate, resuscitate, rejuvenate, stimulate, re-establish, relaunch.

resuscitate verb **1** *medics tried to resuscitate him:* **bring round**, revive; give artificial respiration to, give the kiss of life to. **2** *measures to resuscitate the economy:* **revive**, resurrect, restore, regenerate, revitalize, breathe new life into, reinvigorate, rejuvenate, stimulate.

retain verb **1** *the government retained a share in the privatized industries:* **keep (possession of)**, keep hold of, hold on to, hang on to. **2** *existing footpaths are to be retained:* **maintain**, keep, preserve, conserve. **3** *some students retain facts easily:* **remember**, memorize, hold on to.
– OPPOSITES give up, abolish.

retaliate verb *if you retaliate when provoked, you'll just get hurt worse:* **fight back**, hit back, respond, react, reply, reciprocate, counter-attack, give someone a taste of their own medicine; get even, pay someone back; informal get one's own back.

retaliation noun **revenge**, vengeance, reprisal, retribution, requital, recrimination, repayment; response, reaction, reply, counter-attack.

retard verb *the worst thing governments can do is retard this process:* **delay**, slow down/up, hold back/up, set back, postpone, put back, detain, decelerate; hinder, hamper, obstruct, inhibit, impede, check, restrain, restrict.
– OPPOSITES accelerate.

retch verb **1** *the sour taste made her retch:* **gag**, heave; informal keck. **2** *he retched all over the table.* See VOMIT verb sense 1.

reticence noun **reserve**, restraint, diffidence, shyness; unresponsiveness, quietness, taciturnity, secretiveness.

reticent adjective *Smith was extremely reticent about his personal affairs:* **reserved**, withdrawn, introverted, inhibited, diffident, shy; uncommunicative, unforthcoming, unresponsive, tight-lipped, quiet, taciturn, silent, guarded, secretive.
– OPPOSITES expansive.

r

retinue noun **entourage**, escort, company, court, staff, personnel, household, train, suite, following, bodyguard; aides, attendants, servants, retainers, groupies.

retire verb **1** *he retired two years ago:* **give up work**, stop working, stop work. **2** *Gillian retired to her office:* **withdraw**, go away, take oneself off, decamp, shut oneself away; formal repair. **3** *every effort was made to persuade his forces to retire:* **retreat**, withdraw, pull back, fall back, disengage, back off, give ground. **4** *everyone retired early that night:* **go to bed**, call it a day, go to sleep; informal turn in, hit the hay/sack.

retired adjective *a retired schoolteacher:* **former**, ex-, past, in retirement, elderly; **(the retired)** (old-age) pensioners, OAPs, senior citizens; N. Amer. seniors, retirees.

retiring adjective **1** *the retiring president:* **departing**, outgoing. **2** *he was such a quiet, retiring man:* **shy**, diffident, self-effacing, unassuming, unassertive, reserved, reticent, quiet, timid, modest; private, withdrawn, reclusive, unsociable.
– OPPOSITES incoming, outgoing.

retort verb *'Oh, sure,' she retorted:* **answer**, reply, respond, say, return, counter, riposte, retaliate, snap back.
noun *a sarcastic retort:* **answer**, reply, response, return, counter, rejoinder, riposte, retaliation; informal comeback.

retract verb **1** *the sea otter can retract its claws:* **pull in/back**, draw in. **2** *he soon retracted his allegation:* **take back**, withdraw, recant, disavow, repudiate, renounce, reverse, revoke, rescind, go back on, backtrack on.

retreat verb **1** *the American army was forced to retreat:* **withdraw**, retire, draw back, pull back/out, fall back, give way, give ground. **2** *the government had to retreat over the plan:* **change one's mind**, change one's plans; back down, climb down, do a U-turn, backtrack, back-pedal, give in, concede defeat; Brit. do an about-turn.
– OPPOSITES advance.
noun **1** *a counteroffensive caused the retreat of the imperial army:* **withdrawal**, pulling back. **2** *Democrats welcomed the President's retreat on the tax issue:* **climbdown**, about-face, U-turn; Brit. about-turn. **3** *she invited us to her retreat in rural Sweden:* **refuge**, haven, sanctuary; hideaway, hideout, hiding place; informal hidey-hole.

retrench verb **1** *not all the directors wanted to retrench:* **economize**, cut back, make cutbacks, make savings, make economies, tighten one's belt. **2** *welfare services will have to be retrenched:* **reduce**, cut (back/down), pare (down), slim down, trim, prune, streamline, rationalize; informal slash.
– OPPOSITES splash out, expand.

retribution noun *the assassins were cornered, awaiting inevitable retribution:* **punishment**, penalty, one's just deserts; revenge, reprisal, requital, retaliation, vengeance, an eye for an eye (and a tooth for a tooth), tit for tat; redress, reparation, restitution, recompense, repayment, atonement, amends.

retrieve verb **1** *I retrieved our football from their garden:* **get back**, bring back, recover, recoup, reclaim, repossess, redeem. **2** *they were working hard to retrieve the situation:* **put/set right**, rectify, remedy, restore, sort out, straighten out, resolve.

retrograde adjective **1** *the closure of the factory is a retrograde step:* **for the worse**, regressive, negative, downhill, unwelcome, backward. **2** *the retrograde motion of the planets:* **backward(s)**, reverse, rearward.
– OPPOSITES positive.

retrospect
■ **in retrospect** looking back, on reflection, in/with hindsight.

retrospective adjective *the Government introduced retrospective legislation to change the rules:* **backdated**, retroactive, ex post facto.

return verb **1** *he returned to London:* **go back**, come back, arrive back, go home, come home. **2** *the symptoms returned after a few days:* **recur**, reoccur, repeat (itself); reappear. **3** *he returned the money he had been given:* **give back**, hand back; pay back, repay. **4** *Peter returned the book to the shelf:* **restore**, put back, replace, reinstall. **5** *he just managed to return the volley:* **hit back**, throw back, get back. **6** *she returned his kiss:* **reciprocate**, give in return, repay, give back. **7** *'Later,' returned Isabel coldly:* **answer**, reply, respond, counter, retort. **8** *the jury returned a unanimous verdict:* **deliver**, bring in, hand down. **9** *the club returned a small profit:* **yield**, earn, realize, net, gross, clear. **10** *the Labour candidate was returned with a reduced majority:* **elect**, vote in, choose, select.
– OPPOSITES depart, disappear, keep.
noun **1** *failing health forced his return to Paris:* **homecoming**, retreat, withdrawal. **2** *the fund is a buffer against the return of hard times:* **recurrence**, reoccurrence, repeat, repetition, reappearance, revival, resurrection, re-emergence, resurgence. **3** *I requested the return of my books:* **giving back**, handing back, replacement, restoration, reinstatement, restitution. **4** *I bought two returns to London:* N. Amer. round trip ticket/fare. **5** *the company hoped for a quick return on its investments:* **yield**, profit, gain, revenue, interest, dividend; Brit. informal bunce.
– OPPOSITES departure, disappearance, single.
■ **in return for** in exchange for, as a reward for, as compensation for, for.

revamp verb *they are planning to revamp the kitchen:* **renovate**, redecorate, refurbish, recondition, rehabilitate, overhaul, make over; upgrade, refit, re-equip; remodel, refashion, redesign, restyle; informal do up,

give something a facelift; Brit. informal tart up;
N. Amer. informal rehab.

reveal verb **1** *the police can't reveal his
whereabouts:* **divulge**, disclose, tell, let
slip/drop, give away/out, blurt (out),
release, leak; make known, make public,
broadcast, publicize, circulate, disseminate;
informal let on. **2** *he let the garage door slide
up to reveal his new car:* **show**, display,
exhibit, disclose, uncover. **3** *the data reveals
a good deal of information about Norman
household life:* **bring to light**, uncover, lay
bare, unearth, unveil.
– OPPOSITES hide.

revel verb *he revelled in the applause which
greeted his appearance:* **enjoy**, delight in,
love, like, adore, be pleased by, take pleasure
in, appreciate, relish, lap up, savour; informal
get a kick out of.
noun *there are a few spots in town for
late-night revels:* **celebration**, festivity,
jollification, merrymaking, carousal, spree;
party, jamboree; informal rave, shindig, bash;
Brit. informal rave-up, knees-up; N. Amer. informal
wingding, blast; Austral. informal rage, ding,
jollo.

revelation noun **1** *Washington has been
rocked by further revelations about his
personal life:* **disclosure**, announcement,
report; admission, confession. **2** *the
plot hinges on the revelation of a secret:*
divulging, divulgence, disclosure,
disclosing, letting slip/drop, giving
away/out, leaking, leak, betrayal, unveiling,
making known, making public, broadcasting,
publicizing, dissemination, reporting,
report, declaring, declaration.

reveller noun **merrymaker**, partygoer,
carouser, roisterer.

revelry noun **celebration(s)**, parties,
revels, festivity, festivities, jollification,
merrymaking, carousing, carousal,
roistering; informal partying.

revenge noun **1** *she is seeking revenge for
the murder of her husband:* **vengeance**,
retribution, retaliation, reprisal, requital,
recrimination, an eye for an eye (and a tooth
for a tooth), redress, satisfaction. **2** *they
were so filled with revenge that they shot his
father:* **vengefulness**, vindictiveness, vitriol,
spite, spitefulness, malice, maliciousness,
malevolence, ill will, animosity, hate,
hatred, rancour, bitterness.
verb **1** *he was determined to revenge his
brother's murder:* **avenge**, take/exact
revenge for, exact retribution for, get/obtain
redress for. **2** *I'll be revenged on the whole
pack of you:* **take revenge on**, get one's
revenge on, avenge oneself on, take
vengeance on, get even with, settle a/the
score with, pay back, take reprisals against;
informal get one's own back on.

revenue noun **income**, takings, receipts,
proceeds, earnings; profit(s); Brit. informal
bunce.
– OPPOSITES expenditure.

reverberate verb *the shot reverberated
around the valley:* **resound**, echo, re-echo,
resonate, ring, boom, rumble.

reverberation noun **resonance**, echo,
echoing, resounding, ringing, booming,
rumbling.

revere verb *children revered their teachers in
those days:* **respect**, admire, think highly of,
have a high opinion of, esteem, hold in high
esteem/regard, look up to.
– OPPOSITES despise.

reverence noun *reverence for the
countryside runs deep here:* **esteem**,
regard, respect, admiration, appreciation,
estimation, favour.
– OPPOSITES scorn.

reverent adjective **respectful**, reverential,
admiring, devoted, devout, dutiful, awed,
deferential.

reverie noun **daydream**, daydreaming,
trance, musing; inattention, inattentiveness,
wool-gathering, preoccupation, absorption,
abstraction, lack of concentration.

reversal noun **1** *there was to be no reversal
on this issue:* **turnaround**, turnabout,
about-face, volte-face, change of heart, U-
turn, backtracking; Brit. about-turn. **2** *there
will have to be a reversal of roles:* **swap**,
exchange, change, swapping, interchange.
3 *the reversal of the decision followed intense
public criticism:* **alteration**, changing;
countermanding, undoing, overturning,
overthrow, disallowing, overriding,
overruling, veto, vetoing, revocation,
repeal, rescinding, annulment, nullification,
voiding, invalidation. **4** *a late penalty was
the only reversal they suffered:* **setback**,
reverse, upset, failure, misfortune, mishap,
disaster, blow, disappointment, adversity,
hardship, affliction, vicissitude, defeat; bad
luck.

reverse verb **1** *the car reversed into a lamp
post:* **back**, drive back/backwards, move
back/backwards. **2** *reverse the bottle in the
ice bucket:* **turn upside down**, turn over,
upend, upturn, invert. **3** *I reversed my jacket:*
turn inside out. **4** *it may be a good idea
if you reverse your roles:* **swap (round)**,
change (round), exchange, interchange,
switch (round). **5** *the umpire reversed
the decision:* **alter**, change; overturn,
overthrow, disallow, override, overrule,
veto, revoke, repeal, rescind, annul, nullify,
void, invalidate; Brit. do an about-turn on.
adjective *here are the results in reverse
order:* **backward(s)**, reversed, inverted,
transposed.
noun **1** *the reverse is the case:* **opposite**,
contrary, converse, inverse, obverse,
antithesis. **2** *the deadlines are listed on the
reverse of the page:* **other side**, reverse side,
back, underside, wrong side.

revert verb **1** *life will soon revert to normal:*
return, go back, change back, default;
fall back, regress, relapse. **2** *the property*

r

reverted to the landlord: **be returned.**

review noun **1** *the Council undertook a spending review:* **analysis**, evaluation, assessment, appraisal, examination, investigation, inquiry, probe, inspection, study. **2** *the rent is due for review:* **reconsideration**, reassessment, re-evaluation, reappraisal; change, alteration, modification, revision. **3** *he began to write book reviews:* **criticism**, critique, assessment, evaluation, commentary; Brit. informal crit. **4** *their annual review of the local economy:* **survey**, report, study, account, description, statement, overview.
verb **1** *first, I reviewed the evidence:* **survey**, study, research, consider, analyse, examine, scrutinize, explore, look into, probe, investigate, inspect, assess, appraise; informal size up. **2** *the referee reviewed his decision:* **reconsider**, re-examine, reassess, re-evaluate, reappraise, rethink; change, alter, modify, revise. **3** *once in bed, he reviewed the day:* **remember**, recall, reflect on, think through, go over in one's mind, look back on. **4** *she reviewed the play for a local paper:* **comment on**, evaluate, assess, appraise, judge, critique, criticize.

reviewer noun **critic**, **commentator**, judge, observer, pundit, analyst.

revile verb *he was arrested and reviled as a traitor:* **criticize**, censure, condemn, attack, inveigh against, rail against, lambaste, denounce; slander, libel, malign, vilify, besmirch, abuse; informal knock, slam, pan, crucify, roast, bad-mouth; Brit. informal slate, rubbish, slag off; N. Amer. informal pummel; Austral./NZ informal bag, monster; formal excoriate.
– OPPOSITES praise.

revise verb **1** *she eventually revised her opinion:* **reconsider**, review, re-examine, reassess, re-evaluate, reappraise, rethink; change, alter, modify. **2** *the editor has completely revised the text:* **amend**, emend, correct, alter, change, edit, rewrite, redraft, rephrase, rework. **3** (Brit.) *you need to revise all your lecture notes:* **go over**, reread, memorize, cram; informal bone up on; Brit. informal swot up (on).

revision noun **1** *the conference called for a revision of the Prayer Book:* **emendation**, correction, alteration, adaptation, editing, rewriting, redrafting. **2** *the report called for a major revision of the exam system:* **reconsideration**, review, re-examination, reassessment, re-evaluation, reappraisal, rethink; change, alteration, modification. **3** (Brit.) *he was doing some last-minute revision:* **rereading**, memorizing, cramming; Brit. informal swotting.

revitalize verb **reinvigorate**, re-energize, boost, regenerate, revive, revivify, rejuvenate, reanimate, resuscitate, refresh, stimulate, breathe new life into; informal give a shot in the arm to, pep up, buck up.

revival noun **1** *a revival in the economy:*

improvement, rallying, change for the better, upturn, upswing, resurgence. **2** *there is widespread interest in the revival of traditional crafts:* **comeback**, re-establishment, reintroduction, restoration, reappearance, resurrection, regeneration, rejuvenation.
– OPPOSITES downturn, disappearance.

revive verb **1** *attempts to revive her failed:* **resuscitate**, bring round, bring back. **2** *the man soon revived:* **regain consciousness**, come round, wake up. **3** *a cup of tea revived her:* **reinvigorate**, revitalize, refresh, energize, reanimate, resuscitate, revivify, rejuvenate, regenerate, enliven, stimulate. **4** *we are reviving old traditions:* **reintroduce**, re-establish, restore, resurrect, bring back, regenerate, resuscitate.

revoke verb *the Board has the power to revoke the bank's licence:* **cancel**, repeal, rescind, reverse, annul, nullify, void, invalidate, countermand, retract, withdraw, overrule, override.

revolt verb **1** *the people revolted against colonial rule:* **rebel**, rise (up), take to the streets, riot, mutiny. **2** *the smell of the meat revolted him:* **disgust**, sicken, nauseate, make someone sick, turn someone's stomach, be repugnant to, be repulsive to, put off, be offensive to; informal turn off; N. Amer. informal gross out.
noun *there was an armed revolt:* **rebellion**, revolution, insurrection, mutiny, uprising, riot; rioting, insurgence, seizure of power, coup (d'état).

revolting adjective **disgusting**, sickening, nauseating, stomach-turning, stomach-churning, repulsive, repellent, repugnant, appalling, abominable, hideous, horrible, awful, dreadful, terrible, obnoxious, vile, nasty, foul, loathsome, offensive, objectionable, off-putting, distasteful, disagreeable; N. Amer. vomitous; informal ghastly, putrid, horrid, gross, gut-churning, yucky, skanky, icky; literary noisome.
– OPPOSITES attractive, pleasant.

revolution noun **1** *the French Revolution:* **rebellion**, revolt, insurrection, mutiny, uprising, riot, rioting, insurgence, coup (d'état). **2** *a revolution in printing techniques:* **dramatic/profound change**, alteration, sea change, metamorphosis, transformation, innovation, reorganization, restructuring; informal shake-up; N. Amer. informal shakedown. **3** *one revolution of the wheel takes 15 seconds:* **(single) turn**, rotation, circle, spin; circuit, lap.

revolutionary adjective **1** *revolutionary troops loyal to Aristide:* **rebellious**, rebel, insurgent, rioting, mutinous, renegade, insurrectionary, insurrectionist, seditious, subversive; extremist. **2** *a society undergoing revolutionary change:* **thoroughgoing**, thorough, complete, total, absolute, utter, comprehensive, sweeping, far-reaching, extensive, profound. **3** *a revolutionary kind*

r

of wheelchair: **new**, novel, original, unusual, unconventional, unorthodox, innovative, innovatory, radical, pioneering.
noun *the political revolutionaries hung on to power:* **rebel**, insurgent, mutineer, insurrectionist, agitator, subversive.

revolutionize verb **transform**, (dramatically) alter, shake up, turn upside down, restructure, reorganize, transmute, metamorphose; humorous transmogrify.

revolve verb **1** *overhead, a fan revolved slowly:* **go round**, turn round, rotate, spin. **2** *the moon revolves around the earth:* **circle**, travel, orbit. **3** *his life revolves around cars:* **be concerned with**, be preoccupied with, focus on, centre around.

revulsion noun **disgust**, repulsion, abhorrence, repugnance, nausea, horror, aversion, abomination, distaste.
– OPPOSITES delight.

reward noun *a reward for its safe return:* **recompense**, prize, award, honour, decoration, bonus, premium, bounty, present, gift, payment; informal pay-off, perk; formal perquisite.
verb *they were well rewarded:* **recompense**, pay, remunerate, make something worth someone's while; give an award to.
– OPPOSITES punish.

rewarding adjective **satisfying**, gratifying, pleasing, fulfilling, enriching, edifying, beneficial, illuminating, worthwhile, productive, fruitful.

reword verb **rewrite**, rephrase, recast, express differently, redraft, revise; paraphrase.

rewrite verb **revise**, recast, reword, rephrase, redraft.

rhetoric noun **1** *he excelled in rhetoric:* **oratory**, eloquence, command of language, way with words, speech-making. **2** *the approach was strong on rhetoric but weak on detail:* **bombast**, words, talk, grandiloquence, magniloquence, pomposity, wordiness, verbosity; informal hot air.

rhetorical adjective *a series of expressions used for rhetorical effect:* **stylistic**, oratorical, linguistic, verbal.

rhyme noun **poem**, piece of poetry, verse; (**rhymes**) poetry, doggerel.

rhythm noun **1** *the rhythm of the music:* **beat**, cadence, tempo, time, pulse, throb, swing. **2** *poetic features such as rhythm:* **metre**, measure, stress, accent, cadence. **3** *the rhythm of daily life:* **pattern**, (ebb and) flow, tempo.

rhythmic adjective **rhythmical**, steady, measured, throbbing, beating, pulsating, regular, even.

ribald adjective. See CRUDE sense 3.

rich adjective **1** *rich people pay higher rates of tax:* **wealthy**, affluent, moneyed, well off, well-to-do, prosperous, opulent; informal rolling in money/it, in the money, loaded, stinking rich, filthy rich, well heeled, made of money. **2** *rich furnishings and tapestries:* **sumptuous**, opulent, luxurious, luxury, de luxe, lavish, gorgeous, splendid, magnificent, costly, expensive, fancy; informal posh, plush, ritzy, swanky, classy; Brit. informal swish; N. Amer. informal swank. **3** *a garden rich in spring flowers:* **abounding**, well provided, well stocked, crammed, packed, teeming, bursting; informal jam-packed, chock-a-block, chock-full; Austral./NZ informal chocker. **4** *the town offers a rich supply of restaurants:* **plentiful**, abundant, copious, ample, profuse, lavish, liberal, generous, bountiful. **5** *blackcurrant bushes require a rich soil:* **fertile**, productive, fecund, fruitful. **6** *mussels do not need a rich sauce:* **creamy**, fatty, heavy. **7** *the rich colours of autumn:* **strong**, deep, full, intense, vivid, brilliant. **8** *her rich contralto voice:* **sonorous**, full, resonant, deep, clear, mellow, mellifluous.
– OPPOSITES poor, light.

riches plural noun **money**, wealth, funds, (hard) cash, (filthy) lucre, wherewithal, means, (liquid) assets, capital, resources, reserves; opulence, affluence, prosperity; informal dough, bread, loot, readies, moolah, the necessary; Brit. informal dosh, brass, lolly, spondulicks; N. Amer. informal bucks, mazuma, dinero; US informal greenbacks, simoleons, jack, rocks; Austral./NZ informal Oscar.

richly adverb **1** *he gazed round the richly furnished chamber:* **sumptuously**, opulently, luxuriously, lavishly, gorgeously, splendidly, magnificently; informal poshly, plushly, ritzily, swankily, classily; Brit. informal swishly. **2** *the joy she so richly deserves:* **fully**, thoroughly, well, completely, wholly, totally, entirely, absolutely, amply, utterly.
– OPPOSITES meanly.

rickety adjective **shaky**, unsteady, unsound, unsafe, tumbledown, broken-down, dilapidated, ramshackle; informal shambly; N. Amer. informal shacky.

rid verb *we are ridding the building of asbestos:* **clear**, free, purge, rout, strip.
■ **get rid of 1** *we must get rid of some stuff:* **dispose of**, throw away/out, clear out, discard, scrap, dump, bin, jettison; informal chuck (away), ditch, junk, get shut of; Brit. informal get shot of. **2** *the cats soon got rid of the rats:* **destroy**, exterminate, eliminate, annihilate, obliterate, wipe out, kill.

riddle[1] noun *they hope for an answer to this riddle:* **puzzle**, conundrum, problem, question, poser, enigma, mystery.

riddle[2] verb **1** *his car was riddled by gunfire:* **perforate**, hole, pierce, puncture, pepper. **2** *he was riddled with cancer:* **permeate**, suffuse, fill, pervade, imbue, saturate, overrun, beset.

ride verb **1** *she can ride a horse:* **sit on**, mount, bestride; manage, handle, control, use, operate, work. **2** *they ride round the town on motor bikes:* **travel**, move, proceed, make

r

one's way; drive, cycle; roar, speed, hurtle; trot, canter, gallop.
noun *he took us out for a ride:* **trip**, journey, drive, run, excursion, outing, jaunt; lift; informal spin.

ridicule noun *he was subjected to ridicule by his colleagues:* **mockery**, derision, laughter, scorn, scoffing, contempt, jeering, sneering, sneers, jibes, jibing, teasing, taunts, taunting, sarcasm, satire; informal kidding, ribbing, joshing; N. Amer. informal goofing, razzing; Austral./NZ informal chiacking.
– OPPOSITES respect.
verb *his theory was ridiculed:* **deride**, mock, laugh at, heap scorn on, jeer at, jibe at, sneer at, treat with contempt, scorn, make fun of, poke fun at, scoff at, satirize, lampoon, caricature, parody, tease, taunt; informal kid, rib, josh, take the mickey out of; N. Amer. informal goof on, rag on, razz, pull someone's chain; Austral./NZ informal chiack, poke mullock at, sling off at.

ridiculous adjective **1** *the car looked ridiculous:* **laughable**, absurd, comical, funny, hilarious, risible, farcical, silly, ludicrous. **2** *it was a ridiculous suggestion:* **stupid**, silly, foolish, foolhardy, inane, fatuous, childish, puerile, half-baked, hare-brained, ill-thought-out, crackpot, idiotic. **3** *this is a ridiculous exaggeration:* **absurd**, preposterous, ludicrous, laughable, risible, nonsensical, senseless, outrageous.
– OPPOSITES sensible.

rife adjective **1** *violence is rife in our cities:* **widespread**, general, common, universal, extensive, ubiquitous, omnipresent, endemic, inescapable, insidious, prevalent. **2** *the village was rife with gossip:* **overflowing**, bursting, alive, teeming, abounding.
– OPPOSITES unknown.

riff-raff noun **rabble**, scum, the lowest of the low, undesirables; informal peasants, plebs, proles.
– OPPOSITES elite.

rifle verb **1** *she rifled through her wardrobe:* **rummage**, search, hunt, forage. **2** *he kept her talking while his accomplice rifled her home:* **burgle**, rob, loot, raid, plunder, ransack.

rift noun **1** *a deep rift in the Arctic ice:* **crack**, fault, flaw, split, break, breach, fissure, fracture, cleft, crevice, cavity, opening. **2** *the rift between them:* **breach**, division, split, gap, gulf; quarrel, squabble, disagreement, falling-out, row, argument, dispute, conflict, feud; estrangement; informal spat, scrap; Brit. informal bust-up.

rig[1] verb **1** *the boats were rigged with a single sail:* **equip**, kit out, fit out, supply, furnish, provide, arm. **2** *I rigged myself out in black:* **dress**, clothe, attire, robe, garb, array, deck out, drape, accoutre, outfit, get up, trick out/up; informal doll up. **3** *he will rig up a shelter:* **set up**, erect, assemble; throw together, cobble together, put together, get

together, whip up, improvise, contrive; Brit. informal knock up.
noun *he owned a CB radio rig:* **apparatus**, appliance, machine, device, instrument, contraption, system; tackle, gear, kit, outfit.

rig[2] verb *they rigged the election:* **manipulate**, engineer, distort, misrepresent, tamper with, doctor; informal fix; Brit. informal fiddle.

right adjective **1** *it wouldn't be right to do that:* **just**, fair, proper, good, upright, righteous, virtuous, moral, ethical, honourable, honest; lawful, legal. **2** *the right answer:* **correct**, accurate, exact, precise; proper, valid, conventional, established, official, formal; Brit. informal spot on. **3** *the right person for the job:* **suitable**, appropriate, fitting, correct, proper, desirable, preferable, ideal. **4** *you've come at the right time:* **opportune**, advantageous, favourable, propitious, good, lucky, happy, fortunate, providential, felicitous; timely, seasonable, convenient, expedient, suitable, appropriate. **5** *he's not right in the head:* **sane**, lucid, rational, balanced, compos mentis; informal all there. **6** *he doesn't look right:* **healthy**, well, fit, normal, up to par; informal up to scratch. **7** *my right hand:* **dextral**. **8** (informal) *it's a right mess:* **absolute**, complete, total, real, thorough, perfect, utter, sheer, unmitigated, veritable.
– OPPOSITES wrong, insane, unhealthy.
adverb 1 *she was right at the limit of her patience:* **completely**, fully, totally, absolutely, utterly, thoroughly, quite. **2** *the hotel is right in the middle of the village:* **exactly**, precisely, directly, immediately, just, squarely, dead; informal (slap) bang, smack, plumb; N. Amer. informal smack dab. **3** *keep going right on till you come to the lights:* **straight**, directly, all the way. **4** (informal) *he'll be right down:* **straight**, immediately, instantly, at once, straight away, now, right now, this minute, directly, forthwith, without further ado, promptly, quickly, a.s.a.p., as soon as possible; N. Amer. in short order; informal straight off, p.d.q. (pretty damn quick), pronto; N. Amer. informal lickety-split. **5** *I think I heard right:* **correctly**, accurately, properly, precisely, aright, rightly, perfectly. **6** *make sure you're treated right:* **well**, properly, justly, fairly, equitably, impartially, honourably, lawfully, legally. **7** *things will turn out right:* **well**, for the best, favourably, happily, advantageously, profitably, providentially, luckily, conveniently.
– OPPOSITES wrong, badly.
noun 1 *the difference between right and wrong:* **goodness**, righteousness, virtue, integrity, rectitude, propriety, morality, truth, honesty, honour, justice, fairness, equity; lawfulness, legality. **2** *you have the right to say no:* **entitlement**, prerogative, privilege, advantage, birthright, liberty, authority, power, licence, permission, dispensation, leave, sanction.
– OPPOSITES wrong.

verb *we must do what we can to right the situation:* **remedy**, put right, rectify, retrieve, fix, resolve, sort out, settle, square; straighten out, correct, repair, mend, redress, make good, ameliorate, better.
■ **by rights** *by rights, these young people should be going to college:* properly, correctly, technically, in fairness; legally.
■ **in the right** justified, vindicated, right.
■ **put something to rights.** See RIGHT verb.
■ **right away** at once, straight away, (right) now, this (very) minute, this instant, immediately, instantly, directly, forthwith, without further ado, promptly, quickly, without delay, a.s.a.p., as soon as possible; N. Amer. in short order; informal straight off, p.d.q. (pretty damn quick), pronto; N. Amer. informal lickety-split.
■ **within one's rights** *she was within her rights to refuse:* entitled, permitted, allowed, at liberty, empowered, authorized, qualified, licensed, justified.

righteous adjective **1** *rules for righteous living:* **good**, virtuous, upright, upstanding, decent; ethical, principled, moral, high-minded, law-abiding, honest, honourable, blameless, irreproachable, noble; saintly, angelic, godly, pure. **2** *a look of righteous anger came over his face:* **justifiable**, justified, legitimate, defensible, supportable, rightful; admissible, allowable, understandable, excusable, acceptable, reasonable.
– OPPOSITES sinful, unjustifiable.

rightful adjective **1** *I intend to return the car to its rightful owner:* **legal**, lawful, real, true, proper, correct, recognized, genuine, acknowledged, approved, licensed, valid, bona fide, de jure. **2** *women have been denied their rightful place in society:* **deserved**, merited, due, just, right, fair, proper, fitting, appropriate, suitable.

right-wing adjective **conservative**, rightist, ultra-conservative, blimpish, diehard; reactionary, traditionalist, conventional, unprogressive; fascistic, fascist, neo-fascist; neoconservative; Nazi, neo-Nazi.
– OPPOSITES left-wing.

rigid adjective **1** *sandwiches are best kept in a rigid container:* **stiff**, hard, firm, inflexible, unbending, unyielding, inelastic. **2** *we established a rigid feeding routine for the dogs:* **fixed**, set, firm, inflexible, unalterable, unchangeable, immutable, unvarying, invariable, hard and fast, cast-iron. **3** *poorer nations warned against a rigid approach to funding:* **strict**, severe, stern, stringent, rigorous, inflexible, uncompromising, intransigent.
– OPPOSITES flexible, lenient.

rigmarole noun **fuss**, bother, trouble, ado, pother; NZ bobsy-die; informal palaver, song and dance, performance, to-do, pantomime, hassle; Brit. informal carry-on.

rigorous adjective **1** *rigorous attention to detail:* **meticulous**, conscientious,

punctilious, careful, diligent, attentive, scrupulous, painstaking, exact, precise, accurate, thorough, particular, strict, demanding, exacting. **2** *the rigorous enforcement of school rules:* **strict**, severe, stern, stringent, tough, harsh, rigid, relentless, unsparing, inflexible, draconian, intransigent, uncompromising, exacting.
– OPPOSITES slapdash, lax.

rigour noun **1** *the mine operated under conditions of some rigour:* **strictness**, severity, stringency, toughness, harshness, rigidity, inflexibility, intransigence. **2** *a speech noted for its intellectual rigour:* **meticulousness**, thoroughness, carefulness, diligence, scrupulousness, exactness, exactitude, precision, accuracy, correctness, strictness. **3** *she could not face the rigours of the journey:* **hardship**, harshness, severity, adversity; ordeal, misery, trial; discomfort, inconvenience, privation.

rim noun **1** *the rim of her cup:* **brim**, edge, lip. **2** *the rim of the crater:* **edge**, border, side, margin, brink, fringe, boundary, perimeter, limits, periphery.

rind noun *orange rind:* **skin**, peel, zest.

ring[1] noun **1** *there's a ring round the moon:* **circle**, band, halo, disc. **2** *she wore a ring:* wedding ring, engagement ring, signet ring, band. **3** *the crowd went wild as he stepped into the ring:* **arena**, enclosure, field, ground; amphitheatre, stadium. **4** *a ring of onlookers formed around them:* **circle**, group, knot, cluster, bunch, band, throng, crowd, flock, pack. **5** *a spy ring existed right under their noses:* **gang**, syndicate, cartel, mob, circle, organization, association, society, alliance, league, coterie, racket.
verb *police ringed the building:* **surround**, circle, encircle, encompass, girdle, enclose, hem in, confine, seal off.

ring[2] verb **1** *church bells rang all day:* **toll**, sound, peal, chime, clang, bong, ding, jingle, tinkle. **2** *the room rang with laughter:* **resound**, reverberate, resonate, echo. **3** *I'll ring you tomorrow:* **telephone**, phone (up), call (up); reach, dial; informal give someone a buzz; Brit. informal give someone a bell, give someone a tinkle, get on the blower to; N. Amer. informal get someone on the horn.
noun **1** *there was the ring of a bell from the gate:* **chime**, toll, peal, clang, clink, ding, jingle, tinkle, tintinnabulation, sound. **2** *I'll give Chris a ring tomorrow:* **call**, telephone call, phone call; informal buzz; Brit. informal bell, tinkle.

rinse verb **wash (out)**, clean, cleanse, bathe; dip, drench, splash, swill, sluice, hose down.

riot noun **1** *there were riots in the capital:* **uproar**, commotion, upheaval, disturbance, furore, tumult, melee, scuffle, fracas, fray, brawl, free-for-all; violence, fighting, vandalism, mayhem, turmoil, lawlessness, anarchy; N. Amer. informal wilding. **2** *the garden was a riot of colour:* **mass**, sea; splash, show, exhibition, display.

r

verb *the miners rioted and attacked the local party HQ:* **(go on the) rampage**, run riot, fight in the streets, run wild, run amok, go berserk.

■ **run riot 1** *the children can run riot in the family rooms:* (go on the) rampage, riot, run amok, go berserk, go out of control; informal raise hell. **2** *the vegetation has run riot:* grow profusely, spread uncontrolled, grow rapidly, spread like wildfire; burgeon, multiply, rocket.

riotous adjective **1** *the demonstration turned riotous:* **unruly**, rowdy, disorderly, uncontrollable, unmanageable, undisciplined, uproarious, tumultuous; violent, wild, ugly, lawless, anarchic. **2** *a riotous party:* **boisterous**, lively, loud, noisy, unrestrained, uninhibited, uproarious, unruly, rollicking; Brit. informal rumbustious; N. Amer. informal rambunctious.
– OPPOSITES peaceable.

rip verb **1** *he ripped the posters down:* **tear**, wrench, wrest, pull, snatch, tug, prise, heave, drag, peel, pluck; informal yank. **2** *she ripped Leo's note into pieces:* **tear**, hack, slash, cut.
noun *there's a rip in my sleeve:* **tear**, slit, split, rent, laceration, cut, gash, slash.

ripe adjective **1** *a nice ripe tomato:* **mature**, ripened, full-grown, ready to eat; luscious, juicy, tender, sweet, succulent. **2** *the dock is ripe for development:* **ready**, fit, suitable, right. **3** *the time is ripe for his return:* **right**, opportune, advantageous, favourable, auspicious, propitious, promising, good, fortunate, benign, providential, felicitous, seasonable; convenient, suitable, appropriate, apt, fitting.
– OPPOSITES unsuitable, young.

ripen verb grow, mature, mellow.

riposte noun *his mother forestalled his indignant riposte by replacing the receiver:* **retort**, counter, rejoinder, sally, return, answer, reply, response; informal comeback.
verb *'Heaven help you,' riposted Sally:* **retort**, counter, rejoin, return, retaliate, answer, reply, respond, come back.

ripple noun *he blew ripples in his coffee:* **wavelet**, wave, undulation, ridge, ruffle.
verb *a breeze rippled the lake:* ruffle, wrinkle.

rise verb **1** *the sun rose across the bay:* **move up/upwards**, come up, make one's/its way up, arise, ascend, climb, mount, soar. **2** *the mountains rose above us:* **loom**, tower, soar, rise up, rear (up). **3** *prices rose by a third:* **go up**, increase, soar, shoot up, surge, leap, jump, rocket, escalate, spiral. **4** *living standards have risen:* **improve**, get better, advance, go up, soar, shoot up. **5** *his voice rose in anger:* **get louder**, grow, increase, swell, intensify. **6** *he rose from his chair:* **stand up**, get to one's feet, get up, jump up, leap up; formal arise. **7** *he rises at dawn:* **get up**, get out of bed, rouse oneself, stir, bestir oneself, be up and about; informal rise and shine, shake a leg, surface; formal arise. **8** *the court rose at midday:* **adjourn**, recess, be

suspended, pause, take a break; informal knock off, take five. **9** *he rose through the ranks to become managing director:* **progress**, climb, advance, get on, work one's way, be promoted. **10** *the dough started to rise:* **swell**, expand, enlarge, puff up. **11** *the ground rose gently:* **slope upwards**, go uphill, incline, climb.
– OPPOSITES fall, descend, drop, sit, retire, resume, shelve.
noun **1** *a price rise:* **increase**, hike, leap, upsurge, upswing, climb, escalation. **2** *he got a rise of 11%:* **raise**, pay increase, wage increase; hike, increment. **3** *a rise in standards:* **improvement**, upturn, leap. **4** *they were alarmed by Hitler's rise to power:* **progress**, climb, promotion, elevation. **5** *we walked up the rise:* **slope**, incline, acclivity, hillock, hill; formal eminence.

risible adjective **laughable**, ridiculous, absurd, comical, amusing, funny, hilarious, farcical, silly, ludicrous, hysterical.

risk noun **1** *there is a certain amount of risk involved:* **chance**, uncertainty, unpredictability, precariousness, instability, insecurity, perilousness, riskiness. **2** *the risk of fire:* **possibility**, chance, probability, likelihood, danger, peril, threat, menace, fear, prospect.
– OPPOSITES safety, impossibility.
verb **1** *he risked his life to save them:* **endanger**, imperil, jeopardize, gamble (with), chance; put on the line, put in jeopardy. **2** *in a tweed coat you risk getting cold and wet:* **be in danger of**, run the risk of, stand a chance of.
■ **at risk** in danger, in peril, in jeopardy, under threat.

risky adjective *you may not get insurance cover for such a risky undertaking:* **dangerous**, hazardous, perilous, fraught with danger, unsafe, insecure, precarious, touch-and-go, treacherous; uncertain, unpredictable; informal chancy, dicey, hairy; N. Amer. informal gnarly.

risqué adjective *less of the risqué jokes, please:* **ribald**, rude, bawdy, racy, earthy, indecent, suggestive, improper, naughty, locker-room; vulgar, dirty, smutty, crude, coarse, obscene, lewd, X-rated; informal blue, raunchy; Brit. informal fruity, off colour, saucy; N. Amer. informal gamy.

rite noun *a strange religious rite:* **ceremony**, ritual, ceremonial; service, sacrament, liturgy, worship, office; act, practice, custom, tradition, convention, institution, procedure.

ritual noun *the official thanksgiving was an elaborate civic ritual:* **ceremony**, rite, ceremonial, observance; service, sacrament, liturgy, worship; act, practice, custom, tradition, convention, formality, procedure, protocol.
adjective *the ritual burial was to ward off evil spirits:* **ceremonial**, ritualistic, prescribed, set, formal; sacramental,

liturgical; traditional, conventional.

rival noun **1** *I was his chief rival for the nomination:* **opponent**, challenger, competitor, contender; adversary, antagonist, enemy; literary foe. **2** *in terms of versatility, the tool has no rival:* **equal**, match, peer, equivalent, counterpart, like.
– OPPOSITES ally.
verb *few countries can rival Slovakia for scenery:* **match**, compare with, compete with, vie with, equal, be in the same league as, be on a par with, touch, challenge; informal hold a candle to.
adjective *the rival candidates were due to attend the meeting:* **competing**, opposing, contending.

rivalry noun **competitiveness**, competition, contention; opposition, conflict, feuding, antagonism, friction, enmity.

riven adjective *a country riven by civil war:* **torn apart**, split, rent, severed; literary cleft, torn asunder.

river noun **1 watercourse**, waterway, tributary, stream, rivulet, brook, inlet, rill, runnel; Scottish & N. English burn; N. English beck; S. English bourn; N. Amer. & Austral./NZ creek; Austral. billabong. **2** *a river of molten lava:* **stream**, torrent, flood, deluge, cascade.

riveted adjective **1** *she stood riveted to the spot:* **fixed**, rooted, frozen, glued. **2** *he was riveted by the newsreels:* **fascinated**, engrossed, gripped, captivated, enthralled, spellbound, mesmerized, transfixed.
– OPPOSITES bored.

riveting adjective **fascinating**, gripping, engrossing, interesting, intriguing, absorbing, captivating, enthralling, compelling, spellbinding, mesmerizing; informal unputdownable.
– OPPOSITES boring.

road noun **1** *the roads were crowded with traffic:* **street**, thoroughfare, roadway, carriageway, avenue, bypass, ring road, trunk road, byroad; lane, crescent, drive, parade, row; Brit. dual carriageway, clearway, motorway; N. Amer. highway, freeway, parkway, throughway, expressway; US turnpike, interstate. **2** *the road to economic recovery:* **way**, path, route, course.
■ **on the road** on tour, touring, travelling.

roam verb *they roamed far and wide in search of their ideal spot:* **wander**, rove, ramble, drift, walk, traipse; range, travel, tramp, traverse, trek; Scottish & Irish stravaig; informal cruise, mosey; formal perambulate.

roar noun **1** *the roars of the crowd increased in intensity:* **shout**, bellow, yell, cry, howl; clamour; informal holler. **2** *the roar of the sea:* **boom**, crash, rumble, thundering. **3** *his claims were greeted with roars of laughter:* **guffaw**, howl, hoot, shriek, gale, peal.
verb **1** *'Get out!' roared Angus:* **bellow**, yell, shout, bawl, howl; informal holler. **2** *thunder roared overhead:* **boom**, rumble, crash, roll, thunder. **3** *the movie left them roaring with laughter:* **guffaw**, laugh, hoot; informal split one's sides, be rolling in the aisles, be doubled up, crack up, be in stitches; Brit. informal crease up, fall about. **4** *a motorbike roared past:* **speed**, zoom, whizz, flash; informal belt, tear, zip; Brit. informal bomb.

roaring adjective *a roaring fire:* **blazing**, burning, flaming.

roast verb **cook**, bake, grill; N. Amer. broil.

roasting (informal) adjective *a roasting day in London:* **hot**, sweltering, scorching, blistering, searing, torrid; informal boiling (hot), baking (hot).
noun *the boss gave him a roasting.* See LECTURE noun sense 2.

rob verb **1** *the gang robbed the local bank:* **burgle**, steal from, hold up, break into; raid, loot, plunder, pillage; N. Amer. burglarize; informal do, turn over, knock off, stick up. **2** *he robbed an old woman:* **steal from**; informal mug, jump; N. Amer. informal clip. **3** *he was robbed of his savings:* **cheat**, swindle, defraud; informal do out of, con out of; N. Amer. informal stiff. **4** *defeat robbed him of his title:* **deprive**, strip, divest; deny.

robber noun **burglar**, thief, housebreaker, mugger, shoplifter; raider, looter; bandit; informal crook; literary brigand.

robbery noun **burglary**, theft, thievery, stealing, breaking and entering, housebreaking, larceny, shoplifting; hold-up, break-in, raid; informal mugging, smash-and-grab, stick-up; Brit. informal blag; N. Amer. informal heist.

robe noun **1** *the woman wore a black robe:* **cloak**, kaftan, djellaba, wrap, mantle, cape; N. Amer. wrapper. **2** (**robes**) *coronation robes:* **garb**, regalia, costume, finery; garments, clothes; formal apparel; archaic raiment, vestments. **3** *she had on a short towelling robe:* **dressing gown**, bathrobe, housecoat; N. Amer. wrapper.

robot noun **automaton**, android, golem, cyborg; informal bot, droid.

robust adjective **1** *a large, robust man:* **strong**, vigorous, sturdy, tough, powerful, solid, muscular, rugged, hardy, strapping, brawny, burly, husky; healthy, (fighting) fit, hale and hearty, lusty, in fine fettle; informal beefy, hunky. **2** *these knives are very robust:* **durable**, resilient, tough, hard-wearing, long-lasting, sturdy, strong. **3** *Libby took her usual robust view of things:* **down-to-earth**, practical, realistic, pragmatic, common-sense, commonsensical, matter-of-fact, businesslike, sensible, unromantic, unsentimental; informal no-nonsense.
– OPPOSITES frail, fragile, romantic.

rock[1] verb **1** *the ship rocked on the water:* **move to and fro**, move back and forth, sway, see-saw; roll, pitch, plunge, toss, lurch, reel, list; wobble, oscillate. **2** *the building began to rock:* **shake**, vibrate, quake, tremble. **3** *Wall Street was rocked by the news:* **stun**, shock, stagger, astonish, startle, surprise, shake

r

(up), take aback, throw, unnerve, rattle, disconcert.

rock² noun **1** *a gully strewn with rocks:* **boulder**, stone, pebble; Austral. informal goolie. **2** *a castle built on a rock:* **crag**, cliff, outcrop. **3** *he was the rock on which they relied:* **foundation**, cornerstone, support, prop, mainstay; tower of strength, bulwark, anchor.
■ **on the rocks** (informal) **1** *her marriage is on the rocks:* in difficulty, in trouble, breaking up, over; in tatters, in ruins, ruined. **2** *a Scotch on the rocks:* with ice, on ice.

rocket noun *guerrillas fired rockets at the capital:* **missile**, projectile.
verb **1** *prices have rocketed:* **shoot up**, soar, increase, rise, escalate, spiral; informal go through the roof. **2** *they rocketed into the alley:* **speed**, zoom, shoot, whizz, tear, career; Brit. informal bomb; N. Amer. informal barrel, hightail it.
– OPPOSITES plummet.

rocky¹ adjective *a rocky path:* **stony**, pebbly, shingly; rough, bumpy; craggy, mountainous.

rocky² adjective *the couple had a rocky marriage:* **difficult**, problematic, precarious, unstable, unreliable, undependable; informal iffy, up and down.
– OPPOSITES stable.

rococo adjective *the hall has a rococo interior:* **ornate**, fancy, elaborate, extravagant, baroque; fussy, busy, ostentatious, showy; flowery, florid, flamboyant, high-flown, magniloquent, orotund, bombastic, overwrought, overblown, inflated; informal highfalutin.
– OPPOSITES plain.

rod noun *an iron rod:* **bar**, stick, pole, baton, staff; shaft, strut, rail, spoke.

rogue noun **1** *he's a rogue without ethics or scruples:* **scoundrel**, villain, good-for-nothing, ne'er-do-well, wretch; informal rat, louse, crook; informal, dated rotter. **2** *your boy's a little rogue:* **rascal**, imp, devil, monkey; informal scamp, scallywag, monster, horror, terror, tyke; Brit. informal perisher; N. Amer. informal hellion.

roguish adjective **1** *a roguish and untrustworthy character:* **unprincipled**, dishonest, deceitful, unscrupulous, untrustworthy; wicked, villainous; informal shady, rascally. **2** *he gave me a roguish grin:* **mischievous**, playful, teasing, cheeky, naughty, wicked, impish, devilish, arch; informal waggish.

roister verb *the mansions in which the nobility had once roistered:* **enjoy oneself**, celebrate, revel, carouse, frolic, romp, have fun, make merry, rollick; informal party, live it up, whoop it up, have a ball, make whoopee.

role noun **1** *I had a small role in the film:* **part**, character. **2** *his role as president of the society:* **capacity**, position, job, post, office,

duty, responsibility, mantle, place; function, part.

roll verb **1** *the bottle rolled off the table:* **bowl**, spin, rotate. **2** *waiters rolled in the trolleys:* **wheel**, push, trundle. **3** *we rolled past endless fields:* **travel**, go, move, pass, cruise, sweep. **4** *the months rolled by:* **pass**, go, slip, fly; elapse, wear on, march on. **5** *tears rolled down her cheeks:* **flow**, run, course, stream, pour, spill, trickle. **6** *the mist rolled in:* **billow**, undulate, tumble. **7** *he rolled his handkerchief into a ball:* **wind**, coil, fold, curl; twist. **8** *roll out the pastry:* **flatten**, level; even out. **9** *the ship began to roll:* **lurch**, toss, rock, pitch, plunge, sway, reel, list, keel. **10** *thunder rolled overhead:* **rumble**, reverberate, echo, resound, boom, roar, grumble.
noun **1** *a roll of wrapping paper:* **cylinder**, tube, scroll. **2** *a roll of film:* **reel**, spool. **3** *a roll of notes:* **wad**, bundle. **4** *a roll of the dice:* **throw**, toss, turn, spin. **5** *crusty rolls:* **bun**, bagel; Brit. bap, muffin; N. English barm; N. Amer. hoagie. **6** *the parish has 100 on its electoral roll:* **list**, register, directory, record, file, index, catalogue, inventory; census.
■ **roll in** (informal) **1** *money has been rolling in:* pour in, flood in, flow in. **2** *he rolled in at nine o'clock:* arrive, turn up, appear, show one's face; informal show up, roll up, blow in.
■ **roll something out** *Pure Software Inc has rolled out version 2 of its new error detection tool:* introduce, unveil, reveal, bring in/out, release.
■ **roll up** (informal). See ROLL IN sense 2.

rollicking adjective *stuff about pirates and fairies, all rolled into a rollicking family film called Hook:* **lively**, boisterous, exuberant, spirited; riotous, noisy, wild, rowdy, roisterous; Brit. informal rumbustious; N. Amer. informal rambunctious.

romance noun **1** *despite the age gap, their romance blossomed:* **love**, passion, ardour, adoration, devotion; affection, fondness, attachment. **2** *a best-selling author of historical romances:* **love story**, novel; romantic fiction; informal tear-jerker, bodice ripper. **3** *the romance of the Far East:* **mystery**, glamour, excitement, exoticism, mystique; appeal, allure, charm.

romantic adjective **1** *he's very handsome, and so romantic:* **loving**, amorous, passionate, tender, affectionate; informal lovey-dovey. **2** *the DJ kept all the romantic records for the end of the night:* **sentimental**, hearts-and-flowers; mawkish, sickly, saccharine, syrupy; informal slushy, mushy, sloppy, schmaltzy, gooey, treacly, cheesy, corny; Brit. informal soppy; N. Amer. informal cornball, sappy. **3** *a beautiful cottage in a romantic setting:* **idyllic**, picturesque, fairy-tale; beautiful, lovely, charming, pretty. **4** *romantic notions of rural communities:* **idealistic**, idealized, unrealistic, fanciful, impractical; head-in-the-clouds, starry-eyed, optimistic, hopeful, visionary, utopian, fairy-tale.

r

– OPPOSITES unsentimental, realistic.
noun *he's an incurable romantic:* **idealist**,
sentimentalist, romanticist; dreamer,
visionary, utopian; N. Amer. fantast.
– OPPOSITES realist.

Romeo noun **ladies' man**, Don Juan,
Casanova, Lothario, womanizer, playboy,
lover, seducer, philanderer, flirt; gigolo;
informal ladykiller, stud.

romp verb **1** *two fox cubs romped playfully
on the bank:* **play**, frolic, frisk, gambol, skip,
prance, caper, cavort, rollick. **2** *South Africa
romped to a six-wicket win over India:* **sail**,
coast, sweep; win hands down, run away
with it; informal win by a mile, walk it.

room noun **1** *there isn't much room in here:*
space; headroom, legroom; area, expanse,
extent; informal elbow room. **2** *there's always
room for improvement:* **scope**, capacity,
leeway, latitude, freedom; opportunity,
chance.
verb *he roomed there in September:* **lodge**,
board, live, stay; be quartered, be housed;
formal dwell, reside.

roomy adjective **spacious**, capacious,
sizeable, generous, big, large, extensive;
voluminous, ample; formal commodious.
– OPPOSITES cramped.

root noun **1** *the fungus attacks the plant's
roots:* rootstock, tuber, rootlet; Botany
rhizome, radicle. **2** *the root of the problem:*
source, origin, germ, beginnings, genesis;
cause, reason, basis, foundation, bottom,
seat; core, heart, nub, essence. **3** *by going
commercial, he has rejected his roots:*
origins, beginnings, family, ancestors,
predecessors, heritage; birthplace,
homeland.
verb **1** *has the shoot rooted?* **take (root)**, grow
(roots), establish. **2** *he rooted around in the
cupboard:* **rummage**, hunt, search, rifle,
delve, forage, dig, nose, poke; Brit. informal
rootle.
■ **root and branch 1** *the firm should be
eradicated, root and branch:* completely,
entirely, wholly, totally, thoroughly. **2** *a
root-and-branch reform:* complete, total,
thorough, radical.
■ **root something out** *we are determined
to root out corruption:* eradicate, eliminate,
weed out, destroy, wipe out, stamp out,
extirpate, abolish, end, put a stop to.
■ **take root 1** *leave the plants to take root:*
germinate, sprout, establish, strike, take.
2 *Christianity took root in Persia:* become
established, take hold; develop, thrive,
flourish.

rooted adjective **1** *such views are rooted
in Indian culture:* **embedded**, fixed,
established, entrenched, ingrained.
2 *Neil was rooted to the spot:* **frozen**,
riveted, paralysed, glued, fixed; stock-still,
motionless, unmoving.

rootless adjective *it's so hard being rootless
in a foreign country:* **itinerant**, unsettled,
drifting, roving, footloose; homeless, of no

fixed abode.

rope noun **cord**, cable, line, hawser; string.
verb *his feet were roped together:* **tie**, bind,
lash, truss; secure, moor, fasten, attach;
hitch, tether, lasso.
■ **rope someone in/into** persuade to/into,
talk into, inveigle into; enlist, engage.

roster noun **schedule**, list, listing, register,
agenda, calendar, table; Brit. rota.

rostrum noun **dais**, platform, podium, stage;
soapbox.

rosy adjective **1** *a rosy complexion:* **pink**,
pinkish, reddish; glowing, healthy, fresh,
radiant, blooming; blushing, flushed; ruddy,
high-coloured, florid. **2** *his future looks rosy:*
promising, optimistic, auspicious, hopeful,
encouraging, favourable, bright, golden;
informal upbeat.
– OPPOSITES pale, bleak.

rot verb **1** *the floorboards rotted away:* **decay**,
decompose, become rotten; disintegrate,
crumble, perish. **2** *the meat began to rot:* **go
bad**, go off, spoil; moulder, putrefy, fester.
3 *poor neighbourhoods have been left to rot:*
deteriorate, degenerate, decline, decay, go
to rack and ruin, go to seed, go downhill;
informal go to pot, go to the dogs.
– OPPOSITES improve.
noun **1** *the leaves turned black with rot:*
decay, decomposition, mould, mildew,
blight, canker; putrefaction, putrescence.
2 *traditionalists said the rot had set in:*
deterioration, decline; corruption, cancer,
canker.
– OPPOSITES sense.

rota noun (Brit.). See ROSTER.

rotary adjective **rotating**, rotatory,
rotational, revolving, turning, spinning,
gyrating.

rotate verb **1** *the wheels rotate continuously
to provide power:* **revolve**, go round, turn
(round), spin, gyrate, whirl, twirl, swivel,
circle, pivot. **2** *many nurses rotate jobs:*
alternate, take turns, change, switch,
interchange, exchange, swap; move around.

rotation noun **1** *the rotation of the wheels:*
revolving, turning, spinning, gyration,
circling. **2** *a rotation of the Earth:* **turn**,
revolution, orbit, spin. **3** *each member is
chair for six months in rotation:* **sequence**,
succession; alternation, cycle.

rote
■ **by rote** *they were able to recite Newton's
laws by rote:* mechanically, automatically,
parrot-fashion, unthinkingly, mindlessly;
from memory, by heart.

rotten adjective **1** *the smell of rotten meat:*
decaying, rotting, bad, off, decomposing,
putrid, putrescent, perished, mouldy,
mouldering, mildewy, rancid, festering,
fetid; addled; maggoty, wormy, flyblown.
2 *rotten teeth:* **decaying**, decayed, carious,
black; disintegrating, crumbling. **3** *he's
rotten to the core:* **corrupt**, unprincipled,
dishonest, dishonourable, unscrupulous,

r

untrustworthy, immoral; villainous, bad, wicked, evil, iniquitous, venal; informal crooked, warped; Brit. informal bent. **4** (informal) *it was a rotten thing to do:* **nasty**, unkind, unpleasant, vile, contemptible, despicable, shabby; spiteful, mean, malicious, hateful, hurtful; unfair, uncalled for; informal dirty, low-down; Brit. informal out of order. **5** (informal) *he was a rotten singer:* **bad**, poor, dreadful, awful, terrible, frightful, atrocious, hopeless; informal crummy, pathetic, useless, lousy, appalling, abysmal, dire; informal duff, rubbish, pants. **6** (informal) *I feel rotten about it:* **guilty**, remorseful, ashamed, shamefaced, chastened, contrite, sorry, regretful, repentant, penitent. **7** (informal) *I felt rotten with that cold.* See ILL adjective sense 1.
– OPPOSITES fresh, honourable, kind, good, well.

rotund adjective **1** *he was a small, rotund man:* **plump**, chubby, fat, stout, portly, dumpy, round, chunky, overweight, heavy, paunchy, ample; flabby, fleshy, bulky, corpulent, obese; informal tubby, roly-poly, pudgy, beefy, porky, blubbery; Brit. informal podgy; N. Amer. informal zaftig, corn-fed. **2** *huge stoves bearing rotund cauldrons blazed away:* **round**, bulbous, spherical.
– OPPOSITES thin.

rough adjective **1** *she stumbled on the rough ground:* **uneven**, irregular, bumpy, lumpy, knobbly, stony, rocky, rugged, rutted, pitted, rutty. **2** *the terrier's coat is rough and thick:* **coarse**, bristly, scratchy, prickly; shaggy, hairy, bushy. **3** *the cream brings relief to rough skin:* **dry**, leathery, weather-beaten; chapped, calloused, scaly, scabrous. **4** *his voice was rough and angry:* **gruff**, hoarse, harsh, rasping, raspy, husky, throaty, gravelly, guttural. **5** *a bottle of rough red wine:* **sharp**, sour, acidic, acid, vinegary. **6** *he gets pretty rough when he's drunk:* **violent**, brutal, vicious; **aggressive**, belligerent, pugnacious, thuggish; boisterous, rowdy, disorderly, unruly, riotous. **7** *a machine that can take rough handling:* **careless**, clumsy, inept, unskilful. **8** *Sophie disliked his rough manners:* **boorish**, loutish, oafish, brutish, coarse, crude, uncouth, vulgar, unrefined, unladylike, ungentlemanly, uncultured, uncivil, ungracious, rude. **9** *we were tossed about for days on rough seas:* **turbulent**, stormy, tempestuous, violent, heavy, heaving, choppy. **10** (informal) *I've had a rough time recently:* **difficult**, hard, tough, bad, unpleasant; demanding, arduous. **11** (informal) *you were a bit rough on her:* **harsh**, hard, tough, stern, severe, unfair, unjust; insensitive, nasty, cruel, unkind, unsympathetic, brutal, heartless, merciless. **12** (informal) *I'm feeling really rough.* See ILL adjective sense 1. **13** *she produced a rough draft:* **preliminary**, hasty, quick, sketchy, cursory, basic, crude, rudimentary, raw, unpolished; incomplete, unfinished. **14** *a rough estimate:*

approximate, inexact, imprecise, vague, estimated, hazy; N. Amer. informal ballpark. **15** *the accommodation is rather rough:* **plain**, basic, simple, rough and ready, rude, crude, primitive, spartan.
– OPPOSITES smooth, sleek, soft, dulcet, sweet, gentle, careful, refined, calm, easy, kind, well, exact, luxurious.

■ **rough something out** *by the end of the morning the whole figure had been roughed out:* draft, sketch out, outline, block out, mock up.

■ **rough someone up** (informal) *since then I had been roughed up, shot at, and nearly drowned:* beat up, attack, assault, knock about/around, batter, manhandle; informal do over, beat the living daylights out of; Brit. informal duff up.

rough and ready adjective **basic**, simple, crude, unrefined, unsophisticated; makeshift, provisional, stopgap, improvised, extempory, ad hoc; hurried, sketchy.

roughly adverb **1** *he shoved her roughly away:* **violently**, forcefully, forcibly, abruptly, unceremoniously. **2** *they treated him roughly:* **harshly**, unkindly, unsympathetically; brutally, savagely, mercilessly, cruelly, heartlessly. **3** *a deal worth roughly £2.4 million:* **approximately**, (round) about, around, circa, in the region of, of the order of, or so, or thereabouts, more or less, give or take; nearly, close to, approaching; Brit. getting on for.

round adjective **1** *a small round window:* **circular**, disc-shaped; spherical, globular, globe-shaped; cylindrical; bulbous, rounded, rotund; technical annular. **2** *a short, round man:* **plump**, chubby, fat, stout, rotund, portly, dumpy, chunky, overweight, pot-bellied, paunchy; corpulent, fleshy, bulky, obese; informal tubby, roly-poly, pudgy, beefy, porky, blubbery; Brit. informal podgy; N. Amer. informal zaftig, corn-fed. **3** *a round dozen:* **complete**, entire, whole, full.
– OPPOSITES thin, reedy.

noun **1** *mould the dough into rounds:* **ball**, sphere, globe, orb, circle, disc, ring, hoop. **2** *a policeman on his rounds:* **circuit**, beat, route, tour. **3** *the first round of the contest:* **stage**, level; heat, game, bout, contest. **4** *an endless round of late-night parties:* **succession**, sequence, series, cycle. **5** *the gun fires thirty rounds a second:* **bullet**, cartridge, shell, shot.

preposition & adverb **1** *the maze of alleys round the station:* **around**, about, encircling; near, in the vicinity of. **2** *casinos dotted round the south of France:* **throughout**, all over, here and there in.

verb *the ship rounded the Cape of Good Hope:* **go round**, travel round, skirt.

■ **round about** *he earns round about £40,000 a year:* approximately, about, around, circa, roughly, of the order of, something like, more or less, as near as dammit, close to, practically; or so, or thereabouts, give or take a few; not far off, nearly, almost, approaching; Brit. getting on for.

■ **round the clock 1** *I've got a team working round the clock:* day and night, night and day, all the time, {morning, noon, and night}, continuously, non-stop, steadily, unremittingly; informal 24-7. **2** *round-the-clock supervision:* continuous, constant, non-stop, continual, uninterrupted.

■ **round something off** *the party rounded off a successful year:* complete, finish off, crown, cap, top; conclude, close, end.

■ **round on someone** *Guido rounded on Rosie, as though she were to blame:* turn on, attack, snap at, weigh into, let fly at, lash out at, hit out at; informal bite someone's head off, jump down someone's throat, lay into, tear into; Brit. informal have a go at; N. Amer. informal light into.

■ **round someone/something up** gather together, herd together, muster, marshal, rally, assemble, collect, group; N. Amer. corral.

roundabout adjective **1** *the bus took a very roundabout route:* **circuitous**, indirect, meandering, serpentine, tortuous. **2** *I asked in a roundabout sort of way:* **indirect**, oblique, circuitous, circumlocutory, periphrastic, digressive, long-winded; evasive.
– OPPOSITES direct.
noun (Brit.) **1** *go straight on at the roundabout:* N. Amer. rotary, traffic circle. **2** *a roundabout with wooden horses:* **merry-go-round**, carousel.

roundly adverb **1** *the 13 per cent pay increase was roundly condemned:* **vehemently**, emphatically, fiercely, forcefully, severely; plainly, frankly, candidly. **2** *she was roundly defeated by two votes to one:* **utterly**, completely, thoroughly, decisively, conclusively, heavily, soundly.

round-up noun *the Monday sports round-up:* **summary**, synopsis, overview, review, outline, digest, precis; N. Amer. wrap-up; informal recap.

rouse verb **1** *he roused Ralph at dawn:* **wake (up)**, awaken, arouse; Brit. informal knock up; formal waken. **2** *she roused and looked around:* **wake up**, awake, awaken, come to, get up, rise, bestir oneself; formal arise. **3** *he roused the crowd with a stirring speech:* **stir up**, excite, galvanize, electrify, stimulate, inspire, inspirit, move, inflame, agitate, goad, provoke; incite, spur on; N. Amer. light a fire under. **4** *he's got a nasty temper when he's roused:* **provoke**, annoy, anger, infuriate, madden, incense, vex, irk; informal aggravate. **5** *her disappearance roused my suspicions:* **arouse**, awaken, prompt, provoke, stimulate, pique, trigger, spark off, touch off, kindle, elicit.
– OPPOSITES calm, pacify, allay.

rousing adjective *there was rousing singing from the congregation:* **stirring**,

inspiring, exciting, stimulating, moving, electrifying, invigorating, energizing, exhilarating; enthusiastic, vigorous, spirited; inflammatory.

rout noun **1** *the army's offensive turned into an ignominious rout:* **retreat**, flight. **2** *Newcastle scored 13 tries in the 76–4 rout:* **defeat**, trouncing, annihilation; debacle, fiasco; informal licking, hammering, thrashing, pasting, drubbing, massacre.
– OPPOSITES victory.
verb **1** *his army was routed at the Battle of Milvian Bridge:* **put to flight**, drive off, scatter; defeat, beat, conquer, vanquish, crush, overpower. **2** *the German routed the defending champion:* **beat hollow**, trounce, defeat, get the better of; informal lick, hammer, clobber, thrash, paste, demolish, annihilate, drub, cane, wipe the floor with, walk all over, make mincemeat of, massacre, slaughter; Brit. informal stuff; N. Amer. informal cream, shellac, skunk.
– OPPOSITES lose.

route noun *I know a different route to the shops:* **way**, course, road, path, direction; passage, journey.
verb *enquiries are routed to the relevant desk:* **direct**, send, convey, dispatch, forward.

routine noun **1** *his morning routine never varied:* **procedure**, practice, pattern, drill, regime, regimen; programme, schedule, plan; formula, method, system; customs, habits. **2** *his stand-up routine is hilarious:* **act**, performance, number, turn, piece; informal spiel, patter.
adjective **1** *a routine health check:* **standard**, regular, customary, normal, usual, ordinary, typical; everyday, common, commonplace, conventional, habitual. **2** *a routine action movie:* **boring**, tedious, tiresome, wearisome, monotonous, humdrum, run-of-the-mill, prosaic, dreary, pedestrian; predictable, hackneyed, stock, unimaginative, unoriginal, banal, trite.
– OPPOSITES unusual.

rove verb **wander**, roam, ramble, drift, meander; range, travel; Scottish stravaig.

row¹ noun **1** *rows of small children stood in the corridor:* **line**, column, file, queue; procession, chain, string, succession; informal crocodile. **2** *the middle row of seats was empty:* **tier**, line, rank, bank.

■ **in a row** *three days in a row:* consecutively, in succession; running, straight; informal on the trot.

row² (Brit. informal) noun **1** *have you two had a row?* **argument**, quarrel, squabble, fight, contretemps, falling-out, disagreement, dispute, clash, altercation, shouting match; informal tiff, set-to, run-in, slanging match, spat; Brit. informal barney, bust-up. **2** *I could hardly hear over the row the crowd was making:* **din**, noise, racket, clamour, uproar, tumult, hubbub, commotion, brouhaha, rumpus, pandemonium, babel; informal hullabaloo.

r

verb *they rowed about money:* **argue**, quarrel, squabble, bicker, fight, fall out, disagree, have words, dispute, wrangle, cross swords, lock horns, be at loggerheads; informal scrap.

rowdy adjective *gangs of rowdy youths:* **unruly**, disorderly, obstreperous, riotous, undisciplined, uncontrollable, ungovernable, disruptive, out of control, rough, wild, lawless; boisterous, uproarious, noisy, loud; Brit. informal rumbustious; N. Amer. informal rambunctious.
– OPPOSITES peaceful.
noun *the pub filled up with rowdies:* **ruffian**, troublemaker, lout, hooligan, thug, hoodlum; Brit. tearaway; informal tough, bruiser, yahoo; Brit. informal rough, yob, yobbo.

royal adjective **regal**, kingly, queenly, princely; sovereign, monarchical.

rub verb **1** *Polly rubbed her arm:* **massage**, knead; stroke, pat. **2** *he rubbed sun lotion on her back:* **apply**, smear, spread, work in, massage. **3** *my shoes rub painfully:* **chafe**, pinch; hurt, be painful.
noun **1** *she gave his back a rub:* **massage**, rub-down. **2** *I gave my shoes a rub:* **polish**, wipe, clean.
■ **rub along** (Brit. informal) *neither of them understood how they had managed to rub along; yet they had:* **manage**, cope, get by, make do, muddle along/through; informal make out.
■ **rub it in** (informal) *to rub it in he then scored from a free kick:* **emphasize**, stress, underline, highlight; go on, harp on; informal rub someone's nose in it.
■ **rub off on** *my father had a dislike for science which rubbed off on me:* be transferred to, be passed on to, be transmitted to, be communicated to; affect, influence.
■ **rub something out** erase, delete, remove, efface, obliterate, expunge.
■ **rub someone up the wrong way** (Brit.). See ANNOY.

rubbish noun **1** *throw away that rubbish:* **refuse**, waste, litter, debris, detritus, scrap, dross; flotsam and jetsam, lumber; sweepings, scraps, dregs; N. Amer. garbage, trash; informal junk. **2** *she's talking rubbish:* **nonsense**, balderdash, gibberish, claptrap, blarney, moonshine, garbage; informal hogwash, baloney, tripe, drivel, bilge, bunk, piffle, poppycock, phooey, twaddle, gobbledegook; Brit. informal codswallop, cobblers, tosh, cack; Scottish & N. English informal havers; N. Amer. informal bushwa, applesauce.
verb (Brit. informal) *they often rubbish the trade unions.* See CRITICIZE.
adjective (Brit. informal) *a rubbish team.* See HOPELESS sense 3.

rubbishy adjective (informal) *an old piece of rubbishy meat:* **worthless**, substandard, trashy, inferior, second-rate, third-rate, poor-quality, cheap, shoddy; bad, poor, dreadful, awful, terrible; informal crummy, appalling, lousy, dire, tacky; Brit. informal duff,

chronic, rubbish, pants.

rubble noun **debris**, remains, ruins, wreckage.

ruction noun (informal) **1** *what is this ruction going on outside?* **disturbance**, noise, racket, din, commotion, fuss, uproar, furore, hue and cry, rumpus, fracas. **2** (**ructions**) (Brit.) *if Mrs Salt catches her there'll be ructions:* trouble, hell to pay; informal a to-do, a hullabaloo, a hoo-ha, a stink, a kerfuffle; Brit. informal a row, a carry-on.

ruddy adjective *a ruddy complexion:* **rosy**, red, pink, roseate, rubicund; healthy, glowing, fresh; flushed, blushing; florid, high-coloured.
– OPPOSITES pale.

rude adjective **1** *a rude, arrogant young man:* **ill-mannered**, bad-mannered, impolite, discourteous, uncivil; impertinent, insolent, impudent, disrespectful, cheeky; churlish, curt, brusque, brash, offhand, short, sharp; offensive, insulting, derogatory, disparaging, abusive; tactless, undiplomatic, uncomplimentary. **2** *rude jokes:* **vulgar**, coarse, smutty, dirty, filthy, crude, lewd, obscene, off colour, offensive, indelicate, tasteless; risqué, naughty, ribald, bawdy, racy; informal blue; Brit. informal near the knuckle; N. Amer. informal gamy; euphemistic adult.
– OPPOSITES polite, clean.

rudimentary adjective **1** *this can be done by anyone with rudimentary carpentry skills:* **basic**, elementary, primary, fundamental, essential. **2** *the equipment in the workshop was rudimentary:* **primitive**, crude, simple, unsophisticated, rough (and ready), makeshift.
– OPPOSITES advanced, sophisticated.

rudiments plural noun *the rudiments of artistic knowledge:* **basics**, fundamentals, essentials, first principles, foundation; informal nuts and bolts, ABC.

rue verb *she might live to rue this impetuous decision:* **regret**, repent of; deplore, lament, bemoan, bewail.

rueful adjective *she gave a rueful grin:* **regretful**, apologetic, sorry, remorseful, shamefaced, sheepish, hangdog, contrite, repentant, penitent, conscience-stricken, self-reproachful; sorrowful, sad.

ruffian noun **thug**, lout, hooligan, hoodlum, vandal, delinquent, rowdy, scoundrel, villain, rogue, bully boy, brute; informal tough, bruiser, heavy, yahoo; Brit. informal rough, yob, yobbo; N. Amer. informal goon.

ruffle verb **1** *he ruffled her hair:* **disarrange**, tousle, dishevel, rumple, riffle, disorder, mess up, tangle; N. Amer. informal muss up. **2** *the wind ruffled the water:* **ripple**, riffle. **3** *don't let him ruffle you:* **annoy**, irritate, vex, nettle, anger, exasperate; disconcert, unnerve, fluster, agitate, harass, upset, disturb, discomfit, put off, perturb, unsettle, bother, worry, trouble; informal rattle, faze, throw, get to, rile, needle, aggravate, bug,

r

peeve; Brit. informal wind up, nark.
– OPPOSITES smooth, soothe.
noun *a shirt with ruffles:* **frill**, flounce, ruff, ruche.

rug noun **1** *they sat on the rug:* **mat**, carpet; hearthrug; N. Amer. floorcloth. **2** *he was wrapped in a tartan rug:* **blanket**, coverlet, throw, wrap; N. Amer. lap robe.

rugged adjective **1** *the rugged coast path meanders among tall cliffs:* **rough**, uneven, bumpy, rocky, stony, pitted, jagged, craggy. **2** *a rugged off-road vehicle:* **robust**, durable, sturdy, strong, tough, resilient. **3** *up on the scaffold were two rugged manly types:* **well built**, burly, strong, muscular, muscly, brawny, strapping, husky, hulking; tough, hardy, robust, sturdy, lusty, solid; informal hunky, beefy. **4** *a frown crossed his rugged features:* **strong**, craggy, rough-hewn; manly, masculine; irregular, weathered.
– OPPOSITES smooth, flimsy, weedy, delicate.

ruin noun **1** *the buildings may now be saved from ruin:* **disintegration**, decay, disrepair, dilapidation, ruination; destruction, demolition, wreckage. **2** *the ruins of a church:* **remains**, remnants, fragments, relics; rubble, debris, wreckage. **3** *this spells electoral ruin for Labour:* **downfall**, collapse, defeat, undoing, failure, breakdown, ruination; Waterloo. **4** *many shopkeepers are facing ruin:* **bankruptcy**, insolvency, penury, poverty, destitution, impoverishment, indigence; failure.
– OPPOSITES preservation, triumph, wealth.
verb **1** *don't let her ruin my plans:* **wreck**, destroy, spoil, mar, blight, shatter, dash, torpedo, scotch, mess up; sabotage; informal screw up, foul up, put the kibosh on, do for, nix, queer; Brit. informal scupper. **2** *the bank's collapse ruined them all:* **bankrupt**, make insolvent, impoverish, pauperize, wipe out, break, cripple; bring someone to their knees. **3** *a country ruined by civil war:* **destroy**, devastate, lay waste, ravage; raze, demolish, wreck, wipe out, flatten.
– OPPOSITES save, rebuild.
■ **in ruins 1** *the abbey is in ruins:* derelict, ruined, in disrepair, falling to pieces, dilapidated, tumbledown, ramshackle, decrepit, decaying, ruinous. **2** *his career is in ruins:* destroyed, ruined, in pieces, in ashes; over, finished; informal in tatters, on the rocks, done for.

ruined adjective derelict, in ruins, dilapidated, ruinous, tumbledown, ramshackle, decrepit, falling to pieces, crumbling, decaying, disintegrating.

ruinous adjective **1** *the spectre of a ruinous trade war loomed:* **disastrous**, devastating, catastrophic, calamitous, crippling, crushing, damaging, destructive, harmful; costly. **2** *ruinous interest rates:* **extortionate**, exorbitant, excessive, sky-high, outrageous, inflated; Brit. over the odds; informal criminal, steep.

rule noun **1** *health and safety rules:*

regulation, ruling, directive, order, act, law, statute, edict, canon, mandate, command, dictate, decree, fiat, injunction, commandment, stipulation, requirement, guideline, direction; formal ordinance. **2** *the general rule is that problems are referred to the committee:* **procedure**, practice, protocol, convention, norm, routine, custom, habit; formal praxis. **3** *Punjab came under British rule:* **control**, jurisdiction, command, power, dominion; government, administration, sovereignty, leadership, supremacy, authority; raj.
verb **1** *El Salvador was ruled by Spain:* **govern**, preside over, control, lead, dominate, run, head, administer, manage. **2** *Mary ruled for six years:* **be in power**, be in control, be in command, be in charge, govern; reign, be monarch, be sovereign. **3** *the judge ruled that the men be set free:* **decree**, order, pronounce, judge, adjudge, ordain; decide, find, determine, resolve, settle. **4** *on the streets, chaos ruled:* **prevail**, predominate, be the order of the day, reign supreme; formal obtain.
■ **as a rule** usually, generally, in general, normally, ordinarily, customarily, for the most part, on the whole, by and large, in the main, mainly, mostly, commonly, typically.
■ **rule something out** exclude, eliminate, disregard; preclude, prohibit, prevent, disallow.

ruler noun **leader**, sovereign, monarch, potentate, king, queen, emperor, empress, prince, princess; crowned head, head of state, president, premier, governor; overlord, chief, chieftain, lord; dictator, autocrat.
– OPPOSITES subject.

ruling noun *the judge's ruling was severely criticized:* **judgement**, decision, adjudication, finding, verdict; pronouncement, resolution, decree, injunction.
adjective **1** *Japan's ruling party:* **governing**, controlling, commanding, supreme, leading, dominant. **2** *football was their ruling passion:* **main**, chief, principal, major, prime, dominating, foremost; predominant, central, focal; informal number-one.

rumble verb **boom**, thunder, roll, roar, resound, reverberate, echo, grumble.

ruminate verb *we ruminated on the meaning of life:* **think about**, contemplate, consider, meditate on, muse on, mull over, ponder on/over, deliberate about/on, chew over, puzzle over; formal cogitate about.

rummage verb *she rummaged around in her bag for her keys:* **search**, hunt, root about/around, ferret about/around, fish about/around, poke around in, dig, delve, go through, explore, sift through, rifle through.

rumour noun **gossip**, hearsay, talk, tittle-tattle, speculation, word; (**rumours**) reports, stories, whispers; informal the grapevine, the word on the street, the buzz;

N. Amer. informal scuttlebutt.

rump noun **1** *he removed his hand from Shirley's rump:* **rear (end)**, backside, seat; buttocks, cheeks; Brit. bottom; informal behind, BTM, sit-upon, derrière; Brit. informal bum, botty, jacksie; N. Amer. informal butt, fanny, tush, tail, buns, booty, heinie; humorous fundament, posterior, stern; Anatomy nates. **2** *the rump of the army:* **remainder**, rest, remnant, remains.

rumple verb **1** *the sheet was rumpled:* **crumple**, crease, wrinkle, crinkle, ruck (up), scrunch up. **2** *Ian rumpled her hair:* **ruffle**, disarrange, tousle, dishevel, riffle; mess up; N. Amer. informal muss up.
– OPPOSITES smooth.

rumpus noun **disturbance**, commotion, uproar, furore, brouhaha, hue and cry, ruckus; fracas, melee, tumult, noise, racket, din; informal to-do, hullabaloo, hoo-ha, kerfuffle, ballyhoo; Brit. informal row, carry-on; Scottish informal stooshie.

run verb **1** *she ran across the road:* **sprint**, race, dart, rush, dash, hasten, hurry, scurry, scamper, hare, bolt, fly, gallop, career, charge, shoot, hurtle, speed, zoom, go like lightning, go hell for leather, go like the wind; jog, trot; informal tear, pelt, scoot, hotfoot it, leg it, belt, zip, whip; Brit. informal bomb; N. Amer. informal hightail it, barrel. **2** *the robbers turned and ran:* **flee**, run away, run off, run for it, take flight, make off, take off, take to one's heels, make a break for it, bolt, make one's getaway, escape; informal beat it, clear off/out, vamoose, skedaddle, split, leg it, scram; Brit. informal do a runner, scarper, do a bunk; N. Amer. informal light out, take a powder, skidoo; Austral. informal shoot through. **3** *he ran in the marathon:* **compete**, take part, participate. **4** *a shiver ran down my spine:* **go**, pass, slide, move, travel. **5** *he ran his eye down the list:* **cast**, pass, skim, flick. **6** *the road runs the length of the valley:* **extend**, stretch, reach, continue. **7** *rainwater ran from the eaves:* **flow**, pour, stream, gush, flood, cascade, roll, course, spill, trickle, drip, dribble, leak. **8** *a bus runs to Sorrento three times a day:* **travel**, shuttle, go. **9** *I'll run you home:* **drive**, take, bring, ferry, chauffeur, give someone a lift. **10** *he runs a transport company:* **be in charge of**, manage, direct, control, head, govern, supervise, superintend, oversee; operate, conduct, own. **11** *it's expensive to run a car:* **maintain**, keep, own, have; drive. **12** *they ran some tests:* **carry out**, do, perform, execute. **13** *he left the engine running:* **operate**, function, work, go; tick over, idle. **14** *the lease runs for twenty years:* **be valid**, last, be in effect, be operative, continue, be effective. **15** *the show ran for two years:* **continue**, be on; be performed, be screened, be shown. **16** *he ran for president in 1984:* **stand for**, be a candidate for, be a contender for. **17** *the paper ran the story on Friday:* **publish**, print, feature, carry, put out, release, issue. **18** *they*

were run out of town: **chase**, drive, hound.
noun **1** *his early morning run along the river bank:* **sprint**, jog, dash, gallop, trot. **2** *she volunteered to do the school run:* **route**, journey; circuit, round, beat. **3** *we went for a run in the car:* **drive**, ride, turn; trip, excursion, outing, jaunt, airing; informal spin, tootle; Scottish informal hurl. **4** *an unbeaten run of victories:* **series**, succession, sequence, string, chain, streak, spell, stretch, spate. **5** *against the run of play, he scored again:* **trend**, tendency, course, direction, movement, drift, tide. **6** *the wire mesh of a chicken run:* **enclosure**, pen, coop. **7** *she had a run in her tights:* **ladder**, rip, tear, snag, hole.

■ **in the long run** eventually, in the end, ultimately, when all is said and done, in the fullness of time; Brit. informal at the end of the day.
■ **on the run** on the loose, at large, loose; running away, fleeing; informal AWOL; N. Amer. informal on the lam.
■ **run across** *we ran across David while we were in LA:* meet (by chance), come across, run into, chance on, stumble on, happen on; informal bump into.
■ **run along** (informal) *run along now, can't you see I'm busy?* go away, be off with you, shoo; informal scram, buzz off, skedaddle, scat, beat it, get lost, shove off, clear off; Brit. informal hop it.
■ **run away 1** *her attacker ran away.* See RUN verb sense 2. **2** *she ran away with the championship:* win easily, win hands down; informal win by a mile, walk it, romp home.
■ **run someone down 1** *he was run down by joyriders:* run over, knock down/over; hit, strike. **2** *she ran him down in front of other people:* criticize, denigrate, belittle, disparage, deprecate, find fault with; informal put down, knock, bad-mouth; Brit. informal rubbish, slag off; formal derogate.
■ **run something down 1** *she finally ran a copy of the book down:* find, discover, locate, track down, trace, unearth. **2** *employers ran down their workforces gradually:* reduce, cut back on, downsize, decrease, trim; phase out, wind down/up.
■ **run someone in** (informal). See ARREST verb sense 1.
■ **run into 1** *a car ran into his van:* collide with, hit, strike, crash into, smash into, plough into, ram, impact. **2** *I ran into Hugo the other day:* meet (by chance), run across, chance on, stumble on, happen on; informal bump into. **3** *we ran into a problem:* experience, encounter, meet with, be faced with, be confronted with. **4** *his debts run into six figures:* reach, extend to, be as much as.
■ **run off 1** *the youths ran off.* See RUN verb sense 2. **2** (informal) *he ran off with her money.* See STEAL verb sense 1.
■ **run something off 1** *would you run off that list for me?* copy, photocopy, xerox, duplicate, print, produce, do. **2** *run off some*

of the excess water: drain, bleed, draw off, pump out.

■ **run on 1** *the call ran on for hours:* continue, go on, carry on, last, keep going, stretch. **2** *your mother does run on:* talk incessantly, talk a lot, go on, chatter on, ramble on; informal yak, gab, yabber; Brit. informal rabbit on, witter on, chunter on, talk the hind leg off a donkey; N. Amer. informal run off at the mouth.

■ **run out 1** *food supplies were running out:* be used up, dry up, be exhausted, be finished, peter out. **2** *they soon ran out of cash:* be out of; use up, consume, eat up; informal be fresh out of, be cleaned out of. **3** *her contract ran out in June:* expire, end, terminate, finish; lapse.

■ **run out on someone** (informal). See ABANDON verb sense 3.

■ **run over 1** *the bathwater's running over:* overflow, spill over. **2** *he quickly ran over the story:* recapitulate, repeat, run through, go over, reiterate, review; look over, read through; informal recap on.

■ **run someone over**. See RUN SOMEONE DOWN sense 1.

■ **run through 1** *the attitude that runs through his writing:* pervade, permeate, suffuse, imbue, inform. **2** *he ran through his notes*. See RUN OVER sense 3. **3** *let's run through scene three:* rehearse, practise, go over, repeat; N. Amer. run down; informal recap on.

■ **run someone through** *Campbell threatened to run him through with his sword:* stab, pierce, transfix, impale.

■ **run to 1** *the bill ran to £22,000:* amount to, add up to, total, come to, equal, reach, be as much as. **2** *sorry, but we can't run to champagne:* afford, stretch to, manage.

runaway noun *a teenage runaway:* **fugitive**, escapee; refugee; truant; absconder, deserter.
adjective **1** *a runaway horse:* **out of control**, escaped, loose, on the loose. **2** *a runaway victory:* **easy**, effortless; informal as easy as pie. **3** *runaway inflation:* **rampant**, out of control, unchecked, unbridled.

rundown noun *can you give me a quick rundown of the findings?* **summary**, synopsis, precis, run-through, review, overview, briefing, sketch, outline; informal low-down, recap.

run down adjective **1** *a run-down area of London:* **dilapidated**, tumbledown, ramshackle, derelict, ruinous, in ruins, crumbling; neglected, uncared-for, depressed, seedy, shabby, slummy, squalid; Brit. informal grotty. **2** *she was feeling rather run down:* **unwell**, ill, poorly, unhealthy, peaky; tired, drained, exhausted, fatigued, worn out, below par, washed out; Brit. off colour; informal under the weather; Brit. informal off, ropy, knackered; Scottish informal wabbit; Austral./NZ informal crook; dated seedy.
– OPPOSITES well maintained, salubrious,

healthy.

runner noun **1** *the runners were limbering up:* **athlete**, sprinter, hurdler, racer, jogger. **2** *a runner from the strawberry plant:* **shoot**, offshoot, sprout, tendril; Botany stolon. **3** *the bookmaker employed three runners:* **messenger**, courier, errand boy; informal gofer.

running noun **1** *his running was particularly fast:* **sprinting**, sprint, racing, jogging, jog. **2** *the running of the school:* **administration**, management, organization, coordination, orchestration, handling, direction, control, regulation, supervision. **3** *the smooth running of her department:* **operation**, working, function, performance.
adjective **1** *I heard the sound of running water:* **flowing**, gushing, rushing, moving. **2** *a running argument:* **ongoing**, sustained, continuous, incessant, ceaseless, constant, perpetual; recurrent, recurring. **3** *she was late two days running:* **in succession**, in a row, in sequence, consecutively; straight, together; informal on the trot.

■ **in the running** *he's in the running for a prize:* likely to get, a candidate for, in line for, on the shortlist for, up for.

runny adjective **liquefied**, liquid, fluid, melted, molten; watery, thin.
– OPPOSITES solid.

run-of-the-mill adjective **ordinary**, average, middle-of-the-road, commonplace, humdrum, mundane, standard, nondescript, characterless, conventional; unremarkable, unexceptional, uninteresting, dull, boring, routine, bland, lacklustre; N. Amer. garden-variety; informal bog-standard, nothing to write home about, nothing special, a dime a dozen; Brit. informal common or garden.
– OPPOSITES exceptional.

rupture noun **1** *a recent series of pipeline ruptures:* **break**, fracture, crack, burst, split, fissure. **2** *the rupture was due to personal differences:* **rift**, estrangement, falling-out, break-up, breach, split, separation, parting, division, schism; informal bust-up.
verb **1** *the reactor core might rupture:* **break**, fracture, crack, breach, burst, split; informal bust. **2** *the problem ruptured their relationships:* **sever**, break off, breach, disrupt.

rural adjective **country**, countryside, bucolic, rustic, pastoral; agricultural, agrarian; literary sylvan.
– OPPOSITES urban.

ruse noun **ploy**, stratagem, tactic, scheme, trick, gambit, cunning plan, dodge, subterfuge, machination, wile; Brit. informal wheeze.

rush verb **1** *she rushed home:* **hurry**, dash, run, race, sprint, bolt, dart, gallop, career, charge, shoot, hurtle, hare, fly, speed, zoom, scurry, scuttle, scamper, hasten; informal tear, belt, pelt, scoot, zip, whip, hotfoot it, leg it; Brit. informal bomb; N. Amer. informal hightail it. **2** *water rushed along the gutters:* **flow**, pour,

gush, surge, stream, cascade, run, course.
3 *the tax bill was rushed through parliament:*
push, hurry, hasten, speed, hustle, press,
force. **4** *demonstrators rushed the cordon of
troops:* **attack**, charge, run at, assail, storm.
noun **1** *Tim made a rush for the exit:* **dash**,
run, sprint, dart, bolt, charge, scramble,
break. **2** *I wanted to beat the lunchtime rush:*
congestion, hustle and bustle, commotion,
hubbub, hurly-burly, stir. **3** *there was a last-
minute rush for flights:* **demand**, clamour,
call, request; run on. **4** *he was in no rush to
leave:* **hurry**, haste, urgency. **5** *I experienced
a rush of adrenalin:* **surge**, flow, flood, spurt,
stream; dart, thrill, flash. **6** *a rush of cold
night air:* **gust**, draught, flurry. **7** *I made
a sudden rush at him:* **charge**, onslaught,
attack, assault, onrush.
adjective *a rush job:* **urgent**, high-priority,
emergency; hurried, hasty, fast, quick, swift;
N. Amer. informal hurry-up.

rushed adjective **1** *a rushed divorce:* **hasty**,
fast, speedy, quick, swift, rapid, hurried.
2 *he was too rushed to enjoy his stay:* **pushed
for time**, pressed for time, busy, in a hurry,
run off one's feet.
– OPPOSITES leisurely.

rust verb **corrode**, oxidize, become rusty,
tarnish.

rustic adjective **1** *a rustic setting:* **rural**,
country, countryside, countrified, pastoral,
bucolic; agricultural, agrarian; literary sylvan.

2 *rustic wooden tables:* **plain**, simple,
homely, unsophisticated; rough, rude,
crude.
– OPPOSITES urban, ornate.

rustle verb **1** *her dress rustled as she moved:*
swish, whoosh, whisper, sigh. **2** *he was
making a lot of money rustling cattle:* **steal**,
thieve, take; abduct, kidnap.
noun *the rustle of the leaves:* **swish**, whisper,
rustling; literary susurration.
■ **rustle something up** (informal) prepare,
throw/put together, make, assemble; informal
fix; Brit. informal knock up.

rusty adjective **1** *rusty wire:* **rusted**, rust-
covered, corroded, oxidized; tarnished,
discoloured. **2** *his hair was a rusty colour:*
reddish-brown, chestnut, auburn, tawny,
russet, coppery, copper, Titian, red. **3** *my
French is a little rusty:* **out of practice**, below
par; unpractised, deficient, impaired, weak.

rut noun **furrow**, groove, trough, ditch,
hollow, pothole, crater.

ruthless adjective *a ruthless killer:* **merciless**,
pitiless, cruel, heartless, hard-hearted,
cold-hearted, cold-blooded, harsh, callous,
unmerciful, unforgiving, uncaring,
unsympathetic, uncharitable; remorseless,
unbending, inflexible, implacable; brutal,
inhuman, inhumane, barbarous, barbaric,
savage, sadistic, vicious.
– OPPOSITES merciful.

r

Ss

sable adjective *a sable curtain starred with gold:* **black**, jet-black, pitch-black, ebony, raven, sooty, dusky, inky, coal-black.

sabotage noun *the fire may have been an act of sabotage:* **vandalism**, wrecking, destruction, impairment, incapacitation, damage; subversion, obstruction, disruption, spoiling, undermining; Brit. informal a spanner in the works.
verb *a guerrilla group sabotaged the national electricity grid:* **vandalize**, wreck, damage, destroy, cripple, impair, incapacitate; obstruct, disrupt, spoil, ruin, undermine, threaten, subvert.

sac noun **bag**, pouch; Medicine blister, cyst.

saccharine adjective *saccharine love songs:* **sentimental**, sickly, mawkish, cloying, sugary, sickening, nauseating; informal mushy, slushy, schmaltzy, weepy, gooey, drippy, cheesy, corny, toe-curling; Brit. informal soppy, twee; N. Amer. informal cornball, sappy.

sack¹ noun **1** *a sack of flour:* **bag**, pouch, pocket, pack. **2** (informal) *work hard or you'll get the sack:* **dismissal**, discharge, redundancy; informal the boot, the bullet, the axe, the heave-ho, one's marching orders, the elbow, the push; Brit. informal one's cards.
verb (informal) *she was sacked for stealing:* **dismiss**, discharge, lay off, make redundant, let go, throw out; informal fire, kick out, boot out, give someone the bullet, give someone the sack, give someone their marching orders, show someone the door, send packing; Brit. informal give someone their cards.

sack² verb *raiders sacked the town:* **ravage**, lay waste, devastate, raid, ransack, strip, plunder, despoil, pillage, loot, rob.

sackcloth noun **hessian**, sacking, hopsack, burlap; N. Amer. gunny.
■ **wearing sackcloth and ashes** penitent, contrite, regretful, sorrowful, rueful, remorseful, apologetic, ashamed, guilt-ridden, chastened, shamefaced, self-reproachful, guilty.

sacred adjective **1** *the priest entered the sacred place:* **holy**, hallowed, blessed, consecrated, sanctified, venerated, revered. **2** *sacred music:* **religious**, spiritual, devotional, church, ecclesiastical. **3** *the hill is sacred to the tribe:* **sacrosanct**, inviolable, inviolate, invulnerable, untouchable, protected, defended, secure.

– OPPOSITES secular, profane.

sacrifice noun **1** *the sacrifice of animals:* **ritual slaughter**, offering, oblation, immolation. **2** *the calf was a sacrifice:* **(votive) offering**, burnt offering, gift, oblation. **3** *the sacrifice of sovereignty:* **surrender**, giving up, abandonment, renunciation, forfeiture, relinquishment, resignation, abdication.
verb **1** *two goats were sacrificed:* **offer up**, immolate, slaughter. **2** *he sacrificed his principles:* **give up**, abandon, surrender, forgo, renounce, forfeit, relinquish, resign, abdicate; betray.

sacrificial adjective *the altar may have been used for sacrificial offerings:* **votive**, oblatory, oblational; expiatory, propitiatory.

sacrilege noun *the sacrilege of committing a murder on holy ground:* **desecration**, profanity, profanation, blasphemy, impiety, irreligion, unholiness, irreverence, disrespect.

– OPPOSITES piety.

sacrilegious adjective *he condemned the book as a vicious, sacrilegious attack on their faith:* **profane**, blasphemous, impious, sinful, irreverent, irreligious, unholy, disrespectful.

sacrosanct adjective *the individual's right to work has been upheld as sacrosanct:* **sacred**, hallowed, respected, inviolable, inviolate, unimpeachable, invulnerable, untouchable, inalienable; protected, defended, secure, safe.

sad adjective **1** *we felt sad when we left:* **unhappy**, sorrowful, dejected, depressed, downcast, miserable, down, despondent, despairing, disconsolate, desolate, wretched, glum, gloomy, doleful, dismal, melancholy, mournful, woebegone, forlorn, crestfallen, heartbroken, inconsolable; informal blue, down in the mouth, down in the dumps. **2** *they knew her sad story:* **tragic**, unhappy, unfortunate, awful, miserable, wretched, sorry, pitiful, pathetic, traumatic, heartbreaking, heart-rending, harrowing. **3** *a sad state of affairs:* **unfortunate**, regrettable, sorry, deplorable, lamentable, pitiful, shameful, disgraceful.

– OPPOSITES happy, cheerful, fortunate.

sadden verb *I was saddened by the number of casualties:* **depress**, dispirit, deject, dishearten, grieve, desolate, discourage,

s

upset, get down, bring down, break someone's heart.

saddle verb *they were saddled with the children:* **burden**, encumber, lumber, hamper; land, charge; impose something on, thrust something on, fob something off on to.

sadism noun **callousness**, Schadenfreude, barbarity, brutality, cruelty, cold-bloodedness, inhumanity, ruthlessness, heartlessness; perversion.

sadistic adjective *a sadistic killer:* **callous**, barbarous, vicious, brutal, cruel, fiendish, cold-blooded, inhuman, ruthless, heartless; perverted.

sadness noun *there will be great sadness at this news:* **unhappiness**, sorrow, dejection, depression, misery, despondency, despair, desolation, wretchedness, gloom, gloominess, dolefulness, melancholy, mournfulness, woe, heartache, grief.

safe adjective **1** *the jewels are safe in the bank:* **secure**, protected, shielded, sheltered, guarded, out of harm's way. **2** *the lost children are all safe:* **unharmed**, unhurt, uninjured, unscathed, all right, well, in one piece, out of danger; informal OK. **3** *a safe place to hide:* **secure**, sound, impregnable, unassailable, invulnerable. **4** *a safe driver:* **cautious**, circumspect, prudent, attentive; unadventurous, conservative, unenterprising. **5** *the drug is safe:* **harmless**, innocuous, benign, non-toxic, non-poisonous; wholesome.
– OPPOSITES insecure, dangerous, reckless, harmful.
noun *I keep the ring in a safe:* **strongbox**, safety-deposit box, safe-deposit box, coffer, casket; strongroom, vault.

safeguard noun *a safeguard against crises:* **protection**, defence, guard, screen, buffer, preventive, precaution, provision, security; surety, cover, insurance, indemnity.
verb *the contract will safeguard 1000 jobs:* **protect**, preserve, conserve, save, secure, shield, guard, keep safe.
– OPPOSITES jeopardize.

safety noun **1** *the safety of the residents:* **welfare**, well-being, protection, security. **2** *the safety of ferries:* **security**, soundness, dependability, reliability. **3** *we reached the safety of the shore:* **shelter**, sanctuary, refuge.

sag verb **1** *he sagged back in his chair:* **sink**, slump, loll, flop, crumple. **2** *the floors all sag:* **dip**, droop, bulge, bag. **3** *production has sagged:* **decline**, fall (off), drop, decrease, diminish, slump, plummet; informal nosedive.

saga noun **1** *Celtic tribal sagas:* **epic**, chronicle, legend, folk tale, romance, history, narrative, adventure, myth, fairy story. **2** *the saga of how they met:* **long story**, rigmarole; chain of events; informal spiel.

sagacious adjective *they were sagacious enough to avoid any outright confrontation:*

wise, clever, intelligent, knowledgeable, sensible, sage; discerning, judicious, canny, perceptive, astute, shrewd, prudent, thoughtful, insightful, perspicacious; informal streetwise.
– OPPOSITES foolish.

sage noun *the Chinese sage Confucius:* **wise man/woman**, learned person, philosopher, thinker, scholar, savant; authority, expert, guru.
adjective *some very sage comments.* See SAGACIOUS.

sail noun *the ship's sails:* **canvas**.
verb **1** *we sailed across the Atlantic:* **voyage**, travel by water, steam, navigate, cruise. **2** *you can learn to sail here:* **yacht**, boat, go sailing; crew, helm. **3** *we sail tonight:* **set sail**, put to sea, leave port, hoist sail, weigh anchor, shove off. **4** *he is sailing the ship:* **steer**, pilot, navigate, con, helm, captain; informal skipper. **5** *clouds were sailing past:* **glide**, drift, float, flow, sweep, skim, coast, flit.
■ **sail through** *she sailed through her GCSEs:* succeed easily at, pass easily, romp through, walk through.

sailor noun **seaman**, seafarer, mariner; boatman, yachtsman, yachtswoman; hand; informal (old) salt, sea dog, bluejacket; Brit. informal matelot.

saintly adjective *he was a saintly but somewhat ineffective archbishop:* **holy**, godly, pious, religious, devout, spiritual, prayerful; virtuous, righteous, good, moral, innocent, sinless, guiltless, irreproachable, spotless, uncorrupted, pure, angelic.
– OPPOSITES ungodly.

sake noun **1** *this is simplified for the sake of clarity:* **purpose**, reason, aim, end, objective, object, goal, motive. **2** *she had to be brave for her daughter's sake:* **benefit**, advantage, good, well-being, welfare, interest, profit.

salacious adjective **1** *salacious writing:* **pornographic**, obscene, indecent, crude, lewd, vulgar, dirty, filthy; erotic, titillating, arousing, suggestive, sexy, risqué, ribald, smutty, bawdy; X-rated; informal porn, porno, blue; euphemistic adult. **2** *salacious women:* **lustful**, lecherous, licentious, lascivious, libidinous, prurient, lewd; debauched, wanton, loose, fast, impure, unchaste, degenerate, sinful, depraved, promiscuous; informal randy, horny, raunchy, pervy.

salary noun *his annual salary was £35,000:* **pay**, wages, earnings, payment, remuneration, fee(s), stipend, income.

sale noun **1** *the sale of firearms:* **selling**, vending; dealing, trading. **2** *they make a sale every minute:* **deal**, transaction, bargain.
– OPPOSITES purchase.
■ **for sale** on the market, on sale, on offer, available, purchasable, obtainable.

salesperson noun **sales assistant**, salesman, saleswoman, shop assistant, seller, agent; shopkeeper, trader, merchant, dealer,

S

pedlar, hawker; N. Amer. clerk; informal counter-jumper, rep.

salient adjective *the salient points stuck out clearly in her mind:* **important**, main, principal, major, chief, primary; notable, noteworthy, outstanding, conspicuous, striking, noticeable, obvious, remarkable, prominent, predominant, dominant; key, crucial, vital, essential, pivotal, prime, central, paramount.
– OPPOSITES minor.

saliva noun spit, spittle, dribble, drool, slaver, slobber, sputum.

sallow adjective *his cheeks were sunken and sallow:* **yellowish**, jaundiced, pallid, wan, pale, anaemic, bloodless, pasty; unhealthy, sickly, washed out, peaky; informal like death warmed up.

sally noun 1 *the garrison made a sally against us:* **sortie**, charge, foray, thrust, drive, offensive, attack, assault, raid, incursion, invasion, onset, onslaught. 2 *a fruitless sally into Wales:* **expedition**, excursion, trip, outing, jaunt, visit. 3 *he was delighted with his sally:* **witticism**, smart remark, quip, barb, pleasantry; joke, pun, jest, bon mot; retort, riposte, counter, rejoinder; informal gag, wisecrack, comeback.

salon noun 1 *a hairdressing salon:* **shop**, parlour, establishment, premises; boutique, store. 2 *the chateau's mirrored salon:* **reception room**, drawing room, sitting room, living room, lounge.

salt adjective *salt water:* **salty**, salted, saline, briny, brackish.
■ **with a pinch of salt** with reservations, with misgivings, sceptically, cynically, doubtfully, doubtingly, suspiciously, quizzically, incredulously.

salty adjective 1 *salty water:* **salt**, salted, saline, briny, brackish. 2 *a salty sense of humour:* **earthy**, colourful, spicy, racy, naughty, vulgar, rude; piquant, biting.

salubrious adjective 1 *I found the climate salubrious:* **healthy**, health-giving, healthful, beneficial, wholesome. 2 *a salubrious area of London:* **pleasant**, agreeable, nice, select, high-class; Brit. upmarket; informal posh, swanky, classy; Brit. informal swish; N. Amer. informal swank.
– OPPOSITES unhealthy, unpleasant.

salutary adjective *a salutary lesson on the fragility of nature:* **beneficial**, advantageous, good, profitable, productive, helpful, useful, valuable, worthwhile; timely.
– OPPOSITES unwelcome.

salutation noun *her early morning salutation was delivered with chilly sangfroid:* **greeting**, salute, address, welcome.

salute noun 1 *he gave the Brigadier a salute:* **greeting**, salutation, gesture of respect, obeisance, acknowledgement, welcome, address. 2 *a salute to British courage:* **tribute**, testimonial, homage, toast, honour, eulogy; celebration of, acknowledgement of.
verb 1 *he saluted the ambassadors:* **greet**, address, hail, welcome, acknowledge, toast; make obeisance to. 2 *we salute a great photographer:* **pay tribute to**, pay homage to, honour, celebrate, acknowledge, take one's hat off to.

salvage verb 1 *an attempt to salvage the vessel:* **rescue**, save, recover, retrieve, raise, reclaim. 2 *he salvaged a precious point for his club:* **retain**, preserve, conserve; regain, recoup, redeem, snatch.
noun *the salvage is taking place off the coast:* **rescue**, recovery, reclamation.

salvation noun 1 *salvation by way of repentance:* **redemption**, deliverance, reclamation. 2 *that conviction was her salvation:* **lifeline**, preservation; means of escape, help.
– OPPOSITES damnation.

salve noun *lip salve:* **ointment**, cream, balm, unguent, emollient; embrocation, liniment.
verb *she did it to salve her conscience:* **soothe**, assuage, ease, allay, lighten, alleviate, comfort, mollify.

salver noun *he offered her caviar from a silver salver:* **platter**, plate, dish, paten, tray.

same adjective 1 *we stayed at the same hotel:* **identical**, selfsame, very same, one and the same. 2 *they had the same symptoms:* **matching**, identical, alike, duplicate, carbon-copy, twin; indistinguishable, interchangeable, corresponding, equivalent, parallel, like, comparable, similar, congruent, concordant, consonant. 3 *it happened that same month:* **selfsame**; aforesaid, aforementioned. 4 *they provide the same menu worldwide:* **unchanging**, unvarying, unvaried, invariable, consistent, uniform, regular.
– OPPOSITES another, different, dissimilar, varying.
noun *Louise said the same:* **the same thing**, the aforementioned, the aforesaid, the above-mentioned.
■ **all the same 1** *I was frightened all the same:* in spite of everything, despite that, nevertheless, nonetheless, even so, however, but, still, yet, though, be that as it may, just the same, at the same time, in any event, notwithstanding, regardless, anyway, anyhow; informal still and all. 2 *it's all the same to me:* immaterial, of no importance, of no consequence, inconsequential, unimportant, of little account, irrelevant, insignificant, trivial, petty.

sample noun 1 *a sample of the fabric:* **specimen**, example, bit, snippet, swatch, exemplification, representative piece; prototype, test piece, dummy, pilot, trial, taste, taster, tester. 2 *a sample of 10,000 people nationwide:* **cross section**, variety, sampling, test.
verb *we sampled the culinary offerings:* **try (out)**, taste, test, put to the test, experiment

S

with; appraise, evaluate; informal check out.
adjective **1** *the sample group is small:*
representative, illustrative, selected,
specimen, test, trial, typical. **2** *a sample copy
can be obtained:* **specimen**, test, trial, pilot,
dummy.

sanatorium noun **infirmary**, clinic,
hospital, medical centre, hospice; sickbay,
sickroom; N. Amer. sanitarium; informal san.

sanctify verb **1** *he came to sanctify the site:*
consecrate, bless, make holy, hallow, make
sacred, dedicate to God. **2** *they sanctified
themselves:* **purify**, cleanse, free from sin,
absolve, unburden, redeem; rare lustrate.
3 *we must not sanctify this outrage:* **approve**,
sanction, condone, vindicate, endorse,
support, back, permit, allow, authorize,
legitimize, legitimatize.

sanctimonious adjective *one tries to set a bit
of an example, if that's not too sanctimonious:*
self-righteous, holier-than-thou, pious,
pietistic, churchy, moralizing, smug,
superior, priggish, hypocritical, insincere;
informal goody-goody, pi.

sanction noun **1** *trade sanctions:* **penalty**,
punishment, deterrent; punitive action,
discipline, penalization, restriction;
embargo, ban, prohibition, boycott.
2 *the scheme has the sanction of the
court:* **authorization**, consent, leave,
permission, authority, warrant, licence,
dispensation, assent, acquiescence,
agreement, approval, approbation,
endorsement, accreditation, ratification,
validation, blessing, imprimatur; informal the
go-ahead, the thumbs up, the OK, the green
light.
– OPPOSITES reward, prohibition.
verb **1** *the rally was sanctioned by the
government:* **authorize**, permit, allow,
warrant, accredit, license, endorse, approve,
accept, back, support; informal OK. **2** *the
penalties available to sanction crime:*
punish, discipline someone for.
– OPPOSITES prohibit.

sanctity noun **1** *the sanctity of St Francis:*
holiness, godliness, blessedness, saintliness,
spirituality, piety, piousness, devoutness,
righteousness, goodness, virtue, purity;
formal sanctitude. **2** *the sanctity of the
family meal:* **sacrosanctity**, inviolability,
importance, paramountcy.

sanctuary noun **1** *the sanctuary at
Delphi:* **holy place**, temple; shrine, altar;
sanctum, sacrarium, holy of holies, sanctum
sanctorum. **2** *the island is our sanctuary:*
refuge, haven, harbour, port in a storm,
oasis, shelter, retreat, bolt-hole, hideaway,
fastness. **3** *he was given sanctuary in
the embassy:* **safety**, protection, shelter,
immunity, asylum. **4** *a bird sanctuary:*
reserve, park, reservation, preserve.

sanctum noun **1** *the sanctum in the temple:*
holy place, shrine, sanctuary, holy of holies,
sanctum sanctorum. **2** *a private sanctum for*

the bar's regulars: **refuge**, retreat, bolt-hole,
hideout, hideaway, den.

sand noun *she ran across the sand:* **beach**,
sands, shore, seashore; (sand) dunes.

sane adjective **1** *the accused is presumed to be
sane:* **of sound mind**, in one's right mind,
compos mentis, lucid, rational, balanced,
stable, normal; informal all there. **2** *it isn't sane
to use nuclear weapons:* **sensible**, practical,
advisable, responsible, realistic, prudent,
wise, reasonable, rational, level-headed,
commonsensical, judicious, politic.
– OPPOSITES mad, foolish.

sangfroid noun *he recovered his usual
sangfroid:* **composure**, equanimity,
self-possession, equilibrium, aplomb,
poise, self-assurance, self-control, nerve,
calm, presence of mind; informal cool,
unflappability.

sanguine adjective *he is sanguine about the
advance of technology:* **optimistic**, bullish,
hopeful, buoyant, positive, confident,
cheerful, cheery; informal upbeat.
– OPPOSITES gloomy.

sanitary adjective *improvements in health are
also the result of more sanitary conditions:*
hygienic, clean, antiseptic, aseptic, sterile,
uninfected, disinfected, unpolluted,
uncontaminated; salubrious, healthy,
wholesome.

sanitize verb **1** *the best way to sanitize a
bottle:* **sterilize**, disinfect, clean, cleanse,
purify, fumigate, decontaminate. **2** *the
diaries have not been sanitized:* **make
presentable**, make acceptable, make
palatable, clean up; expurgate, bowdlerize,
censor.

sanity noun **1** *she was losing her sanity:*
mental health, faculties, reason, rationality,
saneness, stability, lucidity; sense, wits,
mind. **2** *sanity has prevailed:* **(common)
sense**, wisdom, prudence, judiciousness,
rationality, soundness, sensibleness.

sap noun **1** *sap from the roots of trees:*
juice, secretion, fluid, liquid. **2** *they're
full of youthful sap:* **vigour**, energy, drive,
dynamism, life, spirit, liveliness, sparkle,
verve, ebullience, enthusiasm, gusto,
vitality, vivacity, fire, zest, zeal, exuberance;
informal get-up-and-go, oomph, vim.
verb *they sapped the will of the troops:* **erode**,
wear away/down, deplete, reduce, lessen,
attenuate, undermine, exhaust, drain, bleed.

sarcasm noun **derision**, mockery, ridicule,
scorn, sneering, scoffing; irony.

sarcastic adjective *I've had enough of
your sarcastic comments:* **sardonic**,
ironic, ironical; derisive, snide, scornful,
contemptuous, mocking, sneering, jeering;
caustic, scathing, trenchant, cutting, sharp,
acerbic; Brit. informal sarky; N. Amer. informal
snarky.

sardonic adjective *his sardonic wit:* **mocking**,
satirical, sarcastic, ironical, ironic; cynical,
scornful, contemptuous, derisive, derisory,

sneering, jeering; scathing, caustic, trenchant, cutting, sharp, acerbic; Brit. informal sarky.

sash noun **belt**, cummerbund, waistband, girdle, obi.

Satan noun. See DEVIL sense 1.

satanic adjective *satanic atrocities:* **diabolical**, fiendish, devilish, demonic, demoniacal, ungodly, hellish, infernal, wicked, evil, sinful, iniquitous, nefarious, vile, foul, abominable, unspeakable, loathsome, monstrous, heinous, hideous, horrible, horrifying, shocking, appalling, dreadful, awful, terrible, ghastly, abhorrent, despicable, damnable.

sate verb. See SATIATE.

satellite noun **1** *the European Space Agency's ERS-1 satellite:* **space station**, space capsule, spacecraft; sputnik. **2** *Bulgaria was then a Russian satellite:* **dependency**, colony, protectorate, possession, holding. ▶ adjective *a satellite state:* **dependent**, subordinate, subsidiary; puppet.

satiate verb *he leaned back against the cushions, satiated by the Christmas fare:* **fill**, satisfy, sate; slake, quench; gorge, stuff, surfeit, glut, cloy, sicken, nauseate.

satiny adjective *the satiny, honey-coloured wood:* **smooth**, shiny, glossy, shining, gleaming, lustrous, sleek, silky.

satire noun **1** *a satire on American politics:* **parody**, burlesque, caricature, lampoon, skit, pasquinade; informal spoof, take-off, send-up. **2** *he has become the subject of satire:* **mockery**, ridicule, derision, scorn, caricature; irony, sarcasm.

satirical adjective *a collection of satirical essays on English social life:* **mocking**, ironic, ironical, satiric, sarcastic, sardonic; caustic, trenchant, mordant, biting, cutting, stinging, acerbic; critical, irreverent, disparaging, disrespectful.

satirize verb **mock**, ridicule, deride, make fun of, poke fun at, parody, lampoon, burlesque, caricature, take off; criticize; informal send up, take the mickey out of.

satisfaction noun **1** *he derived great satisfaction from his work:* **contentment**, content, pleasure, gratification, fulfilment, enjoyment, happiness, pride; self-satisfaction, smugness, complacency. **2** *the satisfaction of consumer needs:* **fulfilment**, gratification; appeasement, assuaging. **3** *investors turned to the courts for satisfaction:* **compensation**, recompense, redress, reparation, restitution, repayment, payment, settlement, reimbursement, indemnification, indemnity.

satisfactory adjective *the brakes are satisfactory, if not particularly powerful:* **adequate**, all right, acceptable, good enough, sufficient, reasonable, quite good, competent, fair, decent, average, passable; fine, in order, up to scratch, up to the mark, up to standard, up to par; informal OK, so-so.

– OPPOSITES inadequate, poor.

satisfied adjective **1** *a satisfied smile:* **pleased**, well pleased, content, contented, happy, proud, triumphant; smug, self-satisfied, pleased with oneself, complacent; Brit. informal like the cat that's got the cream. **2** *the pleasure of satisfied desire:* **fulfilled**, gratified. **3** *I am satisfied that she is happy with the decision:* **convinced**, certain, sure, positive, persuaded, easy in one's mind.

– OPPOSITES discontented, unhappy.

satisfy verb **1** *a last chance to satisfy his hunger for romance:* **fulfil**, gratify, meet, fill; indulge, cater to, pander to; appease, assuage; quench, slake, satiate, sate, take the edge off. **2** *she satisfied herself that it had been an accident:* **convince**, persuade, assure; reassure, put someone's mind at rest. **3** *products which satisfy the EU's criteria:* **comply with**, meet, fulfil, answer, conform to; measure up to, come up to; suffice, be good enough, fit/fill the bill. **4** *there was insufficient collateral to satisfy the loan:* **repay**, pay (off), settle, make good, discharge, square, liquidate, clear.

– OPPOSITES frustrate.

satisfying adjective *it's hard work but very satisfying:* **fulfilling**, rewarding, gratifying, pleasing, enjoyable, pleasurable, to one's liking.

saturate verb **1** *heavy rain saturated the ground:* **soak**, drench, waterlog, wet through; souse, steep, douse. **2** *the air was saturated with the stench of joss sticks:* **permeate**, suffuse, imbue, pervade, charge, infuse, fill. **3** *the company has saturated the market:* **flood**, glut, oversupply, overfill, overload.

saturated adjective **1** *his trousers were saturated:* **soaked**, soaking (wet), wet through, sopping (wet), sodden, dripping, wringing wet, drenched; soaked to the skin, like a drowned rat. **2** *the saturated ground:* **waterlogged**, soggy, squelchy, heavy, muddy, boggy.

– OPPOSITES dry.

saturnine adjective **1** *a saturnine temperament:* **gloomy**, sombre, melancholy, moody, lugubrious, dour, glum, morose, unsmiling, humourless. **2** *his saturnine good looks:* **swarthy**, dark, dark-skinned, dark-complexioned; mysterious, mercurial, moody.

– OPPOSITES cheerful.

sauce noun *a piquant sauce:* **relish**, condiment, ketchup; dip, dressing; jus, coulis.

saucepan noun **pan**, pot, casserole, skillet, stockpot, stewpot; billy, billycan.

saucy adjective (informal) **1** (Brit.) *saucy postcards:* **suggestive**, titillating, risqué, rude, bawdy, racy, ribald, spicy; informal raunchy, smutty, nudge-nudge; Brit. informal fruity; N. Amer. informal gamy. **2** *you saucy little minx!* **cheeky**, impudent, impertinent, irreverent, forward,

disrespectful, bold, as bold as brass, brazen; informal fresh, lippy, mouthy; N. Amer. informal sassy. **3** (N. Amer.) *the cap sat at a saucy angle on her black hair:* **jaunty**, rakish, sporty, raffish.
– OPPOSITES demure, polite.

saunter verb *they sauntered back to the car:* **stroll**, amble, wander, meander, drift, walk; stretch one's legs, take the air; informal mosey, tootle; Brit. pootle.

savage adjective **1** *savage dogs:* **ferocious**, fierce; wild, untamed, undomesticated, feral. **2** *a savage assault:* **vicious**, brutal, cruel, sadistic, ferocious, fierce, violent, bloody, murderous, homicidal, bloodthirsty. **3** *a savage attack on European free-trade policy:* **fierce**, blistering, scathing, searing, stinging, devastating, mordant, trenchant, caustic, cutting, biting, withering, virulent, vitriolic. **4** *a savage race:* **primitive**, uncivilized, unenlightened, non-literate, in a state of nature. **5** *a savage landscape:* **rugged**, rough, wild, inhospitable, uninhabitable. **6** *a savage blow for the town:* **severe**, crushing, devastating, crippling, terrible, awful, dreadful, dire, catastrophic, calamitous, ruinous.
– OPPOSITES tame, mild, civilized.
noun **1** *she'd expected mud huts and savages:* **barbarian**, wild man, wild woman, primitive. **2** *she described her son's assailants as savages:* **brute**, beast, monster, barbarian, sadist, animal.
verb **1** *he was savaged by a dog:* **maul**, attack, tear to pieces, lacerate, claw, bite. **2** *critics savaged the film:* **criticize severely**, attack, lambaste, condemn, denounce, pillory, revile; informal pan, tear to pieces, hammer, slam, do a hatchet job on, crucify; Brit. informal slate, rubbish; N. Amer. informal trash; Austral./NZ informal bag, monster.

savant noun *Sir Isaiah Berlin, the Oxford savant:* **intellectual**, scholar, sage, philosopher, thinker, wise/learned person; guru, master, pandit.
– OPPOSITES ignoramus.

save verb **1** *the captain was saved by his crew:* **rescue**, come to someone's rescue, save someone's life; set free, free, liberate, deliver, extricate; bail out; informal save someone's bacon/neck/skin. **2** *the farmhouse has been saved from demolition:* **preserve**, keep safe, keep, protect, safeguard; salvage, retrieve, reclaim, rescue. **3** *start saving old newspapers for wrapping china:* **put aside**, set aside, put by, put to one side, save up, keep, retain, reserve, conserve, stockpile, store, hoard, save for a rainy day; informal salt away, squirrel away, stash away, hang on to. **4** *asking me first would have saved a lot of trouble:* **prevent**, obviate, forestall, spare; stop; avoid, avert.

saving noun **1** *a considerable saving in development costs:* **reduction**, cut, decrease, economy. **2** *I'll have to use some of my savings:* **nest egg**, money put by for a rainy

day, life savings; capital, assets, funds, resources, reserves.

saving grace noun *the bungalow's only saving grace was a room with spectacular views of the sea:* **redeeming feature**, good point, thing in its/one's favour, advantage, asset, selling point.

saviour noun *the country's saviour:* **rescuer**, liberator, deliverer, emancipator; champion, knight in shining armour, friend in need, good Samaritan.

savoir faire noun *he had been faced with a situation that even his charm and savoir faire had been unable to resolve:* **social skill**, social grace(s), urbanity, suavity, finesse, sophistication, poise, aplomb, adroitness, polish, style, smoothness, tact, tactfulness, diplomacy, discretion, delicacy, sensitivity; informal savvy.
– OPPOSITES gaucheness.

savour verb **1** *she wanted to savour every moment:* **relish**, enjoy (to the full), appreciate, delight in, revel in, smack one's lips over, luxuriate in, bask in. **2** *such a declaration savoured of immodesty:* **suggest**, smack of, have the hallmarks of, seem like, have the air of, show signs of.
noun **1** *the subtle savour of wood smoke:* **smell**, aroma, fragrance, scent, perfume, bouquet; taste, flavour, tang, smack. **2** *a savour of bitterness seasoned my feelings for him:* **trace**, hint, suggestion, touch, smack. **3** *her usual diversions had lost their savour:* **piquancy**, interest, attraction, flavour, spice, zest, excitement, enjoyment; informal zing.

savoury adjective **1** *sweet or savoury dishes:* **salty**, spicy, piquant, tangy. **2** *a rich, savoury aroma:* **appetizing**, mouthwatering, delicious, delectable, luscious, tasty, flavoursome, flavourful, palatable, toothsome; informal scrumptious, finger-licking, yummy, scrummy, moreish. **3** *one of the less savoury aspects of the affair:* **acceptable**, pleasant, respectable, wholesome, honourable, proper, seemly.
– OPPOSITES sweet, unappetizing.
noun *cocktail savouries:* **canapé**, hors d'oeuvre, appetizer, titbit.

savvy (informal) noun *his political savvy.* See ACUMEN.
adjective *a savvy investor.* See SHREWD.

saw noun *spare me the old saw about eggs and omelettes:* **saying**, maxim, proverb, aphorism, axiom, adage, apophthegm, epigram, gnome.

say verb **1** *she felt her stomach flutter as he said her name:* **speak**, utter, voice, pronounce, give voice to, vocalize. **2** *'I must go,' she said:* **declare**, state, announce, remark, observe, mention, comment, note, add; reply, respond, answer, rejoin; informal come out with. **3** *Newall says he's innocent:* **claim**, maintain, assert, hold, insist, contend; allege, profess; formal opine, aver. **4** *I can't conjure up the words to say how I feel:* **express**, put into words,

s

phrase, articulate, communicate, make known, put/get across, convey, verbalize; reveal, divulge, impart, disclose; imply, suggest. **5** *they sang hymns and said a prayer:* **recite**, repeat, utter, deliver, perform, declaim, orate. **6** *the dial of her watch said 1.20:* **indicate**, show, read. **7** *I'd say it's about five miles:* **estimate**, judge, guess, hazard a guess, predict, speculate, surmise, conjecture, venture; informal reckon. **8** *let's say you'd just won a million pounds:* **suppose**, assume, imagine, presume, hypothesize, postulate, posit.
noun **1** *everyone is entitled to their say:* **chance to speak**, turn to speak, opinion, view, voice; informal twopence worth, twopenn'orth. **2** *don't I have any say in the matter?* **influence**, sway, weight, voice, input, share, part.
■ **that is to say** in other words, to put it another way; i.e., that is, to wit, viz., namely.
■ **to say the least** to put it mildly, putting it mildly, without any exaggeration, at the very least.

saying noun *you know the old saying about all work and no play?* **proverb**, maxim, aphorism, axiom, adage, saw, tag, motto, apophthegm, epigram, dictum, gnome; expression, phrase, formula; slogan, catchphrase; platitude, cliché, commonplace, truism.
■ **it goes without saying** of course, naturally, needless to say, it's taken for granted, it's understood/assumed, it's taken as read, it's an accepted fact; obviously, self-evidently, manifestly; informal natch.

scalding adjective *a jet of scalding water:* **extremely hot**, burning, blistering, searing, red-hot; piping hot; informal boiling (hot), sizzling.

scale[1] noun **1** *the reptile's scales:* **plate**. **2** *scales on the skin:* **flake**; (**scales**) scurf, dandruff. **3** *scale in kettles:* **limescale**, deposit, encrustation; Brit. fur.

scale[2] noun **1** *opposite ends of the social scale:* **hierarchy**, ladder, ranking, pecking order, order, spectrum; succession, sequence, series. **2** *the scale of the map:* **ratio**, proportion, relative size. **3** *no one foresaw the scale of the disaster:* **extent**, size, scope, magnitude, dimensions, range, breadth, compass, degree, reach.
verb *thieves scaled an 8ft high fence:* **climb**, ascend, clamber up, shin (up), scramble up, mount; N. Amer. shinny (up).
■ **scale something down** *manufacturing capacity has been scaled down:* **reduce**, cut down, cut back, cut, decrease, lessen, lower, trim, slim down, prune.
■ **scale something up** *the departments intend to scale up their activities:* **increase**, expand, augment, build up, add to; step up, boost, escalate.

scaly adjective *scaly patches of dead skin:* **dry**, flaky, flaking, scurfy, rough, scabrous, mangy, scabious.

scamper verb *his dogs scampered around the yard:* **scurry**, scuttle, dart, run, rush, race, dash, hurry, hasten; informal scoot.

scan verb **1** *Adam scanned the horizon:* **scrutinize**, examine, study, inspect, survey, search, scour, sweep, rake; look at, stare at, gaze at, eye, watch; informal check out; N. Amer. informal scope. **2** *I scanned the papers:* **glance through**, look through, have a look at, run/cast one's eye over, skim through, flick through, flip through, leaf through, thumb through.
noun **1** *a careful scan of the terrain:* **inspection**, scrutiny, examination, survey. **2** *a quick scan through the report:* **glance**, look, flick, browse. **3** *a brain scan:* **examination**, screening.

scandal noun **1** *revelation of the sex scandal forced him to resign:* **wrongdoing**, impropriety, misconduct, immoral behaviour, unethical behaviour; offence, transgression, crime, sin; skeleton in the closet; informal -gate. **2** *it's a scandal that the disease is not adequately treated:* **disgrace**, outrage, injustice; (crying) shame. **3** *there is no scandal attached to her name:* **malicious gossip**, malicious rumour(s), slander, libel, calumny, defamation, aspersions, muckraking; informal dirt.

scandalize verb *Henry is said to have been scandalized by William's conduct:* **shock**, appal, outrage, horrify, disgust; offend, affront, insult, cause raised eyebrows.
– OPPOSITES impress.

scandalous adjective **1** *a scandalous waste of taxpayers' money:* **disgraceful**, shocking, outrageous, monstrous, criminal, wicked, shameful, appalling, deplorable, reprehensible, inexcusable, intolerable, insupportable, unforgivable, unpardonable. **2** *a series of scandalous liaisons:* **discreditable**, disreputable, dishonourable, improper, unseemly, sordid. **3** *scandalous rumours:* **scurrilous**, malicious, slanderous, libellous, defamatory.

scant adjective *he paid scant attention to these wider issues:* **little**, little or no, minimal, limited, negligible, meagre; insufficient, inadequate, deficient.
– OPPOSITES abundant, ample.

scanty adjective **1** *their scanty wages:* **meagre**, scant, minimal, limited, modest, restricted, sparse; tiny, small, paltry, negligible, insufficient, inadequate, deficient; scarce, in short supply, thin on the ground, few and far between; informal measly, piddling, mingy, pathetic. **2** *her scanty nightdress:* **skimpy**, revealing, short, brief; low, low-cut; indecent.
– OPPOSITES ample, plentiful.

scapegoat noun *he has been made a scapegoat for pointing out the risks:* **whipping boy**, Aunt Sally; informal fall guy; N. Amer. informal patsy.

scar noun **1** *the scar on his left cheek:* **cicatrix**, mark, blemish, disfigurement, discoloration;

S

pockmark, pock, pit; lesion, stigma. **2** *deep psychological scars:* **trauma**, damage, injury. **verb 1** *he's likely to be scarred for life:* **disfigure**, mark, blemish; pockmark, pit. **2** *a landscape which has been scarred by strip-mining:* **damage**, spoil, mar, deface, injure. **3** *she was profoundly scarred by the incident:* **traumatize**, damage, injure; distress, disturb, upset.

scarce adjective **1** *food was scarce:* **in short supply**, scant, scanty, meagre, sparse, hard to find, hard to come by, insufficient, deficient, inadequate; at a premium, like gold dust; paltry, negligible; informal not to be had for love nor money. **2** *birds that prefer dense forest are becoming scarcer:* **rare**, few and far between, thin on the ground; uncommon, unusual; Brit. out of the common.
– OPPOSITES plentiful.

scarcely adverb **1** *she could scarcely hear what he was saying:* **hardly**, barely, only just; almost not. **2** *I scarcely ever see him:* **rarely**, seldom, infrequently, not often, hardly ever, every once in a while; informal once in a blue moon. **3** *this could scarcely be accidental:* **surely not**, not, hardly, certainly not, not at all, on no account, under no circumstances, by no means; N. Amer. noway.
– OPPOSITES often.

scarcity noun *the scarcity of affordable housing:* **shortage**, dearth, lack, undersupply, insufficiency, paucity, scantness, meagreness, sparseness, poverty; deficiency, inadequacy; unavailability, absence.

scare verb *stop it, you're scaring me:* **frighten**, startle, alarm, terrify, petrify, unnerve, intimidate, terrorize, cow; strike terror into, put the fear of God into, chill someone to the bone/marrow, make someone's blood run cold; informal frighten/scare the living daylights out of, scare stiff, frighten/scare someone out of their wits, scare witless, frighten/scare to death, scare the pants off, make someone's hair stand on end, throw into a blue funk, make someone jump out of their skin; Brit. informal put the wind up, make someone's hair curl; N. Amer. informal spook. **noun** *you gave me a scare—how did you get here?* **fright**, shock, start, turn, jump.

scared adjective *it was growing dark and she began to feel scared:* **frightened**, afraid, fearful, nervous, panicky; terrified, petrified, horrified, panic-stricken, scared stiff, frightened/scared out of one's wits, scared witless, frightened/scared to death; Scottish feart; informal in a cold sweat, in a (blue) funk; Brit. informal funky, windy; N. Amer. informal spooked.

scaremonger noun **alarmist**, prophet of doom, Cassandra, voice of doom, doommonger; informal doom (and gloom) merchant.

scarf noun **muffler**, headscarf, headsquare, square; mantilla, stole, tippet; N. Amer. babushka.

scarper verb (Brit. informal). See RUN verb sense 2.

scary adjective (informal) *a scary movie:* **frightening**, alarming, terrifying, hair-raising, spine-chilling, blood-curdling, horrifying, nerve-racking, unnerving; eerie, sinister; informal creepy, spine-tingling, spooky, hairy.

scathing adjective *he launched a scathing attack on the government:* **withering**, blistering, searing, devastating, fierce, ferocious, savage, severe, stinging, biting, cutting, mordant, trenchant, virulent, caustic, vitriolic, scornful, sharp, bitter, harsh, unsparing.
– OPPOSITES mild.

scatter verb **1** *scatter the seeds as evenly as possible:* **throw**, strew, toss, fling; sprinkle, spread, distribute, sow, broadcast, disseminate. **2** *the crowd scattered | onlookers were scattered in all directions:* **disperse**, break up, disband, separate, go separate ways, dissolve; drive, send, put to flight, chase. **3** *the sky was scattered with stars:* **fleck**, stud, dot, cover, sprinkle, stipple, spot, pepper.
– OPPOSITES gather, assemble.

scatterbrained adjective *a scatterbrained young woman:* **absent-minded**, forgetful, disorganized; dreamy, wool-gathering, with one's head in the clouds, feather-brained, giddy; informal scatty, with a mind/memory like a sieve, dizzy, dippy.

scavenge verb *pigs and poultry scavenged for food around the farm:* **search**, hunt, look, forage, rummage, root about/around, grub about/around.

scenario noun **1** *Walt wrote scenarios for a major Hollywood studio:* **plot**, outline, storyline, framework; screenplay, script; formal diegesis. **2** *every possible scenario must be explored:* **sequence of events**, course of events, chain of events, situation. **3** *this film has a more contemporary scenario:* **setting**, background, context, scene, milieu.

scene noun **1** *the scene of the accident:* **location**, site, place, position, point, spot; locale, whereabouts. **2** *the scene is London, in the late 1890s:* **background**, setting, context, milieu, backdrop, mise en scène. **3** *terrible scenes of violence:* **incident**, event, episode, happening. **4** *an impressive mountain scene:* **view**, vista, outlook, panorama, sight; landscape, scenery. **5** *she made an embarrassing scene:* **fuss**, exhibition of oneself, performance, tantrum, commotion, disturbance, row, upset, furore, brouhaha; informal to-do; Brit. informal carry-on. **6** *the political scene:* **arena**, stage, sphere, world, milieu, realm, domain; area of interest, field, province, preserve. **7** *a scene from a Laurel and Hardy film:* **clip**, section, segment, part, sequence.
■ **behind the scenes** secretly, in secret, privately, in private, behind closed doors, surreptitiously; informal on the quiet, on the q.t.

scenery noun **1** *the beautiful scenery of west*

Wales: **landscape**, countryside, country, terrain, topography, setting, surroundings, environment; view, vista, panorama. **2** *we all helped with the scenery and costumes:* **stage set**, set, mise en scène, flats, backdrop, drop curtain; Brit. backcloth.

scenic adjective *the most scenic route from Florence to Siena:* **picturesque**, pretty, pleasing, attractive, lovely, beautiful, charming, pretty as a picture, easy on the eye; impressive, striking, spectacular, breathtaking; panoramic.

scent noun **1** *the scent of freshly cut hay:* **smell**, fragrance, aroma, perfume, redolence, savour, odour; bouquet, nose. **2** *a bottle of scent:* **perfume**, fragrance, toilet water, eau de toilette, cologne; eau de cologne. **3** *the hounds picked up the scent of a hare:* **spoor**, trail, track; Hunting foil, wind.
▶verb **1** *a shark can scent blood from over half a kilometre away:* **smell**, detect the smell of, get a whiff of. **2** *Rose looked at him, scenting a threat:* **sense**, become aware of, detect, discern, recognize, get wind of.

scented adjective *scented soap:* **perfumed**, fragranced, perfumy; sweet-smelling, fragrant, aromatic.

sceptic noun **1** *sceptics said the marriage wouldn't last:* **cynic**, doubter; pessimist, prophet of doom. **2** *sceptics who have found faith:* **agnostic**, atheist, unbeliever, non-believer, disbeliever, doubting Thomas.

sceptical adjective *they were sceptical about the Treasury's forecast of inflation dropping:* **dubious**, doubtful, taking something with a pinch of salt, doubting; cynical, distrustful, mistrustful, suspicious, disbelieving, unconvinced, incredulous, scoffing; pessimistic, defeatist.
– OPPOSITES certain, convinced.

scepticism noun **1** *his ideas were met with scepticism:* **doubt**, doubtfulness, a pinch of salt; disbelief, cynicism, distrust, mistrust, suspicion, incredulity; pessimism, defeatism. **2** *he passed from scepticism to religious belief:* **agnosticism**, doubt; atheism, unbelief, non-belief.

schedule noun **1** *we need to draw up a production schedule:* **plan**, programme, timetable, scheme. **2** *I have a very busy schedule:* **timetable**, agenda, diary, calendar; itinerary.
▶verb *another meeting was scheduled for April 20:* **arrange**, organize, plan, programme, timetable, set up, line up; N. Amer. slate.
■ **behind schedule** late, running late, overdue, behind time, behind, behindhand.

scheme noun **1** *adventurous fund-raising schemes:* **plan**, project, plan of action, programme, strategy, stratagem, tactic, game plan, course/line of action; system, procedure, design, formula, recipe; Brit. informal wheeze. **2** *police uncovered a scheme to steal the paintings:* **plot**, intrigue, conspiracy; ruse, ploy, stratagem, manoeuvre, subterfuge; machinations;

informal game, racket. **3** *the sonnet's rhyme scheme:* **arrangement**, system, organization, configuration, pattern, format.
▶verb *he schemed to bring about the collapse of the government:* **plot**, hatch a plot, conspire, intrigue, connive, manoeuvre, plan.

scheming adjective *they had mean, scheming little minds:* **cunning**, crafty, calculating, devious, designing, conniving, wily, sly, tricky, artful, guileful, slippery, slick, manipulative, Machiavellian, unscrupulous, disingenuous; duplicitous, deceitful, underhand, treacherous.
– OPPOSITES ingenuous, honest.

schism noun *the widening schism between church leaders and politicians:* **division**, split, rift, breach, rupture, break, separation, severance; chasm, gulf; discord, disagreement, dissension.

schismatic adjective **separatist**, heterodox, dissident, dissentient, dissenting, heretical; breakaway, splinter.
– OPPOSITES orthodox.

scholar noun *a leading biblical scholar:* **academic**, intellectual, learned person, man/woman of letters, mind, intellect, savant, polymath, highbrow, bluestocking; authority, expert; informal egghead; N. Amer. informal pointy-head.

scholarly adjective **1** *an earnest, scholarly man:* **learned**, erudite, academic, well read, widely read, intellectual, literary, lettered, educated, knowledgeable, highbrow; studious, bookish, donnish, bluestocking, cerebral; N. Amer. informal pointy-headed. **2** *a scholarly career:* **academic**, scholastic, pedagogic.
– OPPOSITES uneducated, illiterate.

scholarship noun **1** *a centre of medieval scholarship:* **learning**, book learning, knowledge, erudition, education, letters, culture, academic study, academic achievement. **2** *a scholarship of £200 per term:* **grant**, award, endowment, payment; Brit. bursary, exhibition.

scholastic adjective *scholastic achievements:* **academic**, educational, school, scholarly.

school noun **1** *their children went to the village school:* **educational institution**; academy, college; seminary; alma mater. **2** *the university's School of English:* **department**, faculty, division. **3** *the Barbizon School:* **group**, set, circle; followers, following, disciples, apostles, admirers, devotees, votaries; proponents, adherents. **4** *the school of linguistics associated with his ideas:* **way of thinking**, school of thought, persuasion, creed, credo, doctrine, belief, faith, opinion, point of view; approach, method, style.
▶verb **1** *he was born in Paris and schooled in Lyon:* **educate**, teach, instruct. **2** *he schooled her in horsemanship:* **train**, teach, tutor, coach, instruct, drill, discipline, direct, guide, prepare, groom; prime, verse.

S

schooling noun **1** *his parents paid for his schooling:* **education**, teaching, tuition, instruction, tutoring, tutelage; lessons; (book) learning. **2** *the schooling of horses:* **training**, coaching, instruction, drill, drilling, discipline, disciplining.

schoolteacher noun **teacher**, schoolmaster, schoolmistress, tutor, educationist; Brit. master, mistress; N. Amer. informal schoolmarm; Austral./NZ informal chalkie, schoolie.

science noun **1** *a science teacher:* physics, chemistry, biology; physical sciences, life sciences. **2** *the science of criminology:* **branch of knowledge**, body of knowledge/information, area of study, discipline, field.

scientific adjective **1** *scientific research:* technological, technical; research-based, knowledge-based, empirical. **2** *you need to approach it in a more scientific way:* **systematic**, methodical, organized, well organized, ordered, orderly, meticulous, rigorous; exact, precise, accurate, mathematical; analytical, rational.

scintilla noun *there is not a scintilla of truth in it:* **particle**, iota, jot, whit, atom, speck, bit, trace, ounce, shred, crumb, fragment, grain, drop, spot, mite, modicum, hint, touch, suggestion, whisper, suspicion; informal smidgen, tad.

scintillate verb **sparkle**, shine, gleam, glitter, flash, shimmer, twinkle, glint, glisten, wink.

scintillating adjective **1** *a scintillating diamond necklace:* **sparkling**, shining, bright, brilliant, gleaming, glittering, twinkling, shimmering. **2** *a scintillating second-half performance:* **brilliant**, dazzling, exciting, exhilarating, stimulating; sparkling, lively, vivacious, vibrant, animated, ebullient, effervescent; witty, clever.
– OPPOSITES dull, boring.

scion noun **1** *a scion of the tree:* **cutting**, graft, slip; shoot, offshoot, twig. **2** *the scion of an aristocratic family:* **descendant**; heir, successor; child, offspring.

scoff verb *they scoffed at her article:* **mock**, deride, ridicule, sneer at, jeer at, jibe at, taunt, make fun of, poke fun at, laugh at, scorn, laugh to scorn, dismiss, make light of, belittle; informal pooh-pooh.

scold verb *Mum took Anna away, scolding her for her bad behaviour:* **rebuke**, reprimand, reproach, reprove, admonish, remonstrate with, chastise, chide, upbraid, berate, take to task, read someone the Riot Act, give someone a piece of one's mind, haul over the coals; informal tell off, dress down, give someone an earful, give someone a roasting, rap over the knuckles, let someone have it, bawl out, give someone hell; Brit. informal tick off, have a go at, carpet, tear someone off a strip, give someone what for, give someone some stick, give someone a

rollicking/rocket/row; N. Amer. informal chew out, ream out; Austral. informal monster.
– OPPOSITES praise.

scoop noun **1** *a measuring scoop:* **spoon**, ladle, dipper; bailer. **2** *a scoop of vanilla ice cream:* **spoonful**, ladleful, portion, lump, ball; informal dollop. **3** (informal) *reporters competed for scoops:* **exclusive (story)**, inside story, exposé, revelation.
verb **1** *a hole was scooped out in the floor:* **hollow out**, gouge out, dig, excavate, cut out. **2** *cut the tomatoes in half and scoop out the flesh:* **remove**, take out, spoon out, scrape out. **3** *she scooped up armfuls of clothes:* **pick up**, gather up, lift, take up; snatch up, grab.

scoot verb (informal). See DASH verb sense 1.

scope noun **1** *the scope of the investigation:* **extent**, range, breadth, width, reach, sweep, purview, span, horizon; area, sphere, field, realm, compass, orbit, ambit, terms/field of reference, jurisdiction, remit; confine, limit; gamut. **2** *the scope for change is limited by political realities:* **opportunity**, freedom, latitude, leeway, capacity, liberty, room (to manoeuvre), elbow room; possibility, chance.

scorch verb **1** *the buildings were scorched by the fire:* **burn**, sear, singe, char, blacken, discolour. **2** *grass scorched by the sun:* **dry up**, desiccate, parch, wither, shrivel; burn, bake.

scorching adjective **1** *the scorching July sun:* **extremely hot**, red-hot, blazing, flaming, fiery, burning, blistering, searing, sweltering, torrid; N. Amer. broiling; informal boiling (hot), baking (hot), sizzling. **2** *scorching criticism:* **fierce**, savage, scathing, withering, blistering, searing, devastating, stringent, severe, harsh, stinging, biting, mordant, trenchant, caustic, virulent, vitriolic.
– OPPOSITES freezing, mild.

score noun **1** *the final score was 4–3:* **result**, outcome; total, sum total, tally, count. **2** *an IQ score of 161:* **rating**, grade, mark, percentage. **3** *I've got a score to settle with you:* **grievance**, bone to pick, axe to grind, grudge, complaint; dispute, bone of contention. **4** *scores of complaints:* **a great many**, a lot, a great/good deal, large quantities, plenty; informal lots, umpteen, a slew, loads, masses, stacks, scads, heaps, piles, bags, tons, oodles, dozens, hundreds, thousands, millions, billions; Brit. informal shedloads; N. Amer. informal a bunch, gazillions; Austral./NZ informal a swag.
verb **1** *he's already scored 13 goals this season:* **get**, gain, chalk up, achieve, make; record, rack up, notch up; informal bag, knock up. **2** *the piece was scored for flute, violin, and continuo:* **orchestrate**, arrange, set, adapt; write, compose. **3** *score the wood in criss-cross patterns:* **scratch**, cut, notch, incise, scrape, nick, snick, chip, gouge; mark.
■ **score points off** get the better of, gain

s

the advantage over, outdo, worst, have the edge over; have the last laugh on, make a fool of, humiliate; informal get/be one up on, get one over on, best.

■ **score something out/through** *she scored out the last word:* cross out, strike out, put a line through, ink out, blue-pencil, scratch out; delete, obliterate, expunge.

scorn noun *he was unable to hide the scorn in his voice:* **contempt**, derision, contemptuousness, disdain, derisiveness, mockery, sneering.
– OPPOSITES admiration, respect.
verb **1** *critics scorned the painting:* **deride**, hold in contempt, treat with contempt, pour/heap scorn on, look down on, look down one's nose at, disdain, curl one's lip at, mock, scoff at, sneer at, jeer at, laugh at, laugh out of court; disparage, slight; dismiss, cock a snook at, spit in the eye/face of, thumb one's nose at; informal turn one's nose up at. **2** *'I am a woman scorned,' she thought:* **spurn**, rebuff, reject, ignore, shun, snub. **3** *she would have scorned to stoop to such tactics:* **refuse to**, refrain from, not lower oneself to; be above, consider it beneath one.
– OPPOSITES admire, respect.

scornful adjective *Isabel ignored his scornful remarks:* **contemptuous**, derisive, withering, mocking, scoffing, sneering, jeering, scathing, snide, disparaging, supercilious, disdainful, superior.
– OPPOSITES admiring, respectful.

scotch verb *their plans were scotched by the Pentagon:* **put an end to**, put a stop to, nip in the bud, put the lid on; ruin, wreck, destroy, smash, shatter, demolish, queer; frustrate, thwart; informal put paid to, put the kibosh on; Brit. informal scupper.

scot-free adverb *the real criminals behind the racket are getting away scot-free:* **unpunished**, without punishment; unscathed, unhurt, unharmed, without a scratch.

Scotland noun Caledonia; Brit. north of the border; informal the land of cakes.

scoundrel noun *the lying scoundrel admitted that he was married to another woman:* **rogue**, rascal, miscreant, good-for-nothing, reprobate; cheat, swindler, fraudster, trickster, charlatan; informal villain, bastard, beast, son of a bitch, SOB, rat, louse, swine, dog, skunk, heel, snake (in the grass), wretch, scumbag; Irish informal sleeveen, spalpeen; N. Amer. informal rat fink.

scour¹ verb *she scoured the cooker and cleaned out the cupboards:* **scrub**, rub, clean, wash, cleanse, wipe; polish, buff (up), shine, burnish; abrade.

scour² verb *Christine scoured the shops for a gift:* **search**, comb, hunt through, rummage through, go through with a fine-tooth comb, root through, rake through, leave no stone unturned, look high and low in; ransack, turn upside-down; Austral./NZ informal fossick through.

scourge noun *inflation was the scourge of the mid-1970s:* **affliction**, bane, curse, plague, menace, evil, misfortune, burden, cross to bear; blight, cancer, canker.
– OPPOSITES blessing, godsend.
verb *a disease which scourged the English for centuries:* **afflict**, plague, torment, torture, curse, oppress, burden, bedevil, beset.

scout noun **1** *scouts reported that the enemy were massing ahead:* **lookout**, outrider, advance guard, vanguard; spy. **2** *a lengthy scout round the area:* **reconnaissance**, reconnoitre; exploration, search, expedition; informal recce; Brit. informal shufti; N. Amer. informal recon. **3** *a record company scout:* **talent spotter**, talent scout; N. Amer. informal bird dog.
verb **1** *I scouted around for some logs:* **search**, look, hunt, ferret about/around, root about/around. **2** *a night patrol was sent to scout out the area:* **reconnoitre**, explore, make a reconnaissance of, inspect, investigate, spy out, survey; examine, scan, study, observe; informal make a recce of, check out, case; Brit. informal take a shufti round; N. Amer. informal recon.

scowl verb *she scowled at him defiantly:* **glower**, frown, glare, grimace, lour, look daggers at, give someone a black look; make a face, pull a face, turn the corners of one's mouth down, pout; informal give someone a dirty look.
– OPPOSITES smile, grin.

scraggy adjective *a scraggy mongrel:* **scrawny**, thin, as thin as a rake, skinny, skin-and-bones, gaunt, bony, angular, gawky, raw-boned.
– OPPOSITES fat.

scramble verb **1** *we scrambled over the boulders:* **clamber**, climb, crawl, claw one's way, scrabble, grope one's way, struggle; N. Amer. shinny. **2** *small children scrambled for the scattered coins:* **jostle**, scuffle, tussle, struggle, strive, compete, contend, vie, jockey. **3** *scramble the letters and pick seven:* **mix up**, jumble (up), disarrange, disorganize, disorder, muddle, confuse, disturb, mess up.
noun **1** *a short scramble over the rocks:* **clamber**, climb, trek. **2** *I lost Tommy in the scramble for a seat:* **tussle**, jostle, scrimmage, scuffle, struggle, free-for-all, competition, contention, vying, jockeying; muddle, confusion, melee.

scrap noun **1** *a scrap of paper:* **fragment**, piece, bit, snippet, shred; offcut, oddment, remnant. **2** *there wasn't a scrap of evidence:* **bit**, speck, iota, particle, ounce, whit, jot, atom, shred, scintilla, tittle, jot or tittle; informal smidgen, tad. **3** *he slept rough and lived on scraps:* **leftovers**, leavings, crumbs, scrapings, remains, remnants, residue, odds and ends, bits and pieces. **4** *the whole thing was made from bits of scrap:* **waste**, rubbish,

S

refuse, litter, debris, detritus; flotsam and jetsam; N. Amer. garbage, trash; informal junk.

verb 1 *old cars which are due to be scrapped:* **throw away**, throw out, dispose of, get rid of, toss out, throw on the scrap heap, discard, remove, dispense with, lose, bin; decommission, recycle, break up, demolish; informal chuck (away/out), ditch, dump, junk, get shut of; Brit. informal get shot of; N. Amer. informal trash. **2** *campaigners called for the plans to be scrapped:* **abandon**, drop, abolish, withdraw, throw out, do away with, put an end to, cancel, axe, jettison; informal ditch, dump, junk.
– OPPOSITES keep, preserve.

scrape verb **1** *we scraped all the paint off the windows:* **abrade**, grate, sand, sandpaper, scour, scratch, rub, file, rasp. **2** *their boots scraped along the floor:* **grate**, creak, rasp, grind, scratch. **3** *she scraped her hair back behind her ears:* **rake**, drag, pull, tug, draw. **4** *Ellen had scraped her shins on the wall:* **graze**, scratch, abrade, scuff, rasp, skin, rub raw, cut, lacerate, bark, chafe.
noun 1 *the scrape of her key in the lock:* **grating**, creaking, grinding, rasp, rasping, scratch, scratching. **2** *there was a long scrape on his shin:* **graze**, scratch, abrasion, cut, laceration, wound. **3** (informal) *he's always getting into scrapes:* **predicament**, plight, tight corner/spot, ticklish/tricky situation, problem, crisis, mess, muddle; informal jam, fix, stew, bind, hole, hot water, a pretty/fine kettle of fish; Brit. informal spot of bother.
■ **scrape by** *students have to scrape by on an inadequate grant:* manage, cope, survive, muddle through/along, make ends meet, get by/along, make do, keep the wolf from the door, keep one's head above water, eke out a living; informal make out.

scrappy adjective *the match was a scrappy affair:* **disorganized**, untidy, disjointed, unsystematic, uneven, bitty, sketchy; piecemeal; fragmentary, incomplete, unfinished.

scratch verb **1** *the paintwork was scratched:* **score**, abrade, scrape, scuff. **2** *thorns scratched her skin:* **graze**, scrape, abrade, skin, rub raw, cut, lacerate, bark, chafe; wound. **3** *many names had been scratched out:* **cross out**, strike out, score out, delete, erase, remove, eliminate, expunge, obliterate. **4** *she was forced to scratch from the race:* **withdraw**, pull out of, back out of, bow out of, stand down.
noun 1 *he had two scratches on his cheek:* **graze**, scrape, abrasion, cut, laceration, wound. **2** *a scratch on the paintwork:* **score**, mark, line, scrape.
■ **up to scratch** good enough, up to the mark, up to standard, up to par, satisfactory, acceptable, adequate, passable, sufficient, all right; informal OK, up to snuff.

scrawl verb *he scrawled his name at the bottom of the page:* **scribble**, write hurriedly, write untidily, dash off.

noun *pages of handwritten scrawl:* **scribble**, squiggle(s), hieroglyphics; rare cacography.

scrawny adjective *he was small and scrawny:* **skinny**, thin, as thin as a rake, skin-and-bones, gaunt, bony, angular, gawky, scraggy.
– OPPOSITES fat.

scream verb *he screamed in pain:* **shriek**, screech, yell, howl, shout, bellow, bawl, cry out, call out, yelp, squeal, wail, squawk; informal holler.
noun 1 *a scream of pain:* **shriek**, screech, yell, howl, shout, bellow, bawl, cry, yelp, squeal, wail, squawk; informal holler, hoot; the whole thing's a scream: **laugh**, informal gas, giggle, riot, bundle of fun/laughs. **3** (informal) *he's an absolute scream:* **wit**, hoot, comedian, comic, entertainer, joker, clown, character; informal gas, giggle, riot.

screech verb. See SCREAM verb.

screen noun **1** *he dressed hurriedly behind the screen:* **partition**, (room) divider; windbreak. **2** *a computer with a 19-inch screen:* **display**, monitor, visual display unit, VDU; cathode-ray tube, CRT. **3** *every window has a screen because of mosquitoes:* **mesh**, net, netting. **4** *the hedge acts as a screen against the wind:* **buffer**, protection, shield, shelter, guard.
verb 1 *the end of the hall had been screened off:* **partition off**, divide off, separate off, curtain off. **2** *the cottage was screened by the trees:* **conceal**, hide, veil; shield, shelter, shade, protect, guard, safeguard. **3** *the prospective candidates will have to be screened:* **vet**, check, check up on, investigate; informal check out. **4** *all donated blood is screened for the virus:* **check**, test, examine, investigate. **5** *the programme is screened on Thursday evenings:* **show**, broadcast, transmit, televise, put out, put on the air.

screw noun **1** *stainless steel screws:* **bolt**, fastener; nail, pin, tack, spike, rivet, brad. **2** *the handle needs a couple of screws to tighten it:* **turn**, twist, wrench. **3** *the ship's twin screws:* **propeller**, rotor.
verb 1 *he screwed the lid back on the jar:* **tighten**, turn, twist, wind. **2** *the bracket was screwed in place:* **fasten**, secure, fix, attach.
■ **screw something up 1** *Christina screwed up her face in disgust:* wrinkle (up), pucker, crumple, crease, furrow, contort, distort, twist, purse. **2** (informal) *they'll screw up the whole economy:* wreck, ruin, destroy, wreak havoc on, damage, spoil, mar; dash, shatter, scotch, make a mess of, mess up; informal louse up, foul up, put the kibosh on, banjax, do for, nix, queer; Brit. informal scupper, cock up.

scribble verb *he scribbled a few lines on a piece of paper:* **scrawl**, write hurriedly, write untidily, scratch, dash off, jot (down); doodle.
noun *a page of scribble:* **scrawl**, squiggle(s), jottings; doodle, doodlings; rare cacography.

scrimp verb *she scrimped for six months to buy a pair of evening gloves:* **economize**, skimp, scrimp and save, save; be thrifty, be frugal, tighten one's belt, cut back, husband one's resources, draw in one's horns, watch one's pennies; N. Amer. pinch the pennies.

script noun **1** *her neat, tidy script:* **handwriting**, writing, hand, pen, penmanship, calligraphy. **2** *the script of the play:* **text**, screenplay; libretto; score; lines, dialogue, words.

Scrooge noun **miser**, penny-pincher, pinchpenny, niggard; informal skinflint, meanie, money-grubber, cheapskate; N. Amer. informal tightwad.
– OPPOSITES spendthrift.

scrounge verb *they were always scrounging food from the tourists:* **beg**, borrow; informal cadge, sponge, bum, touch someone for; Brit. informal scab; N. Amer. informal mooch; Austral./NZ informal bludge.

scrounger noun **beggar**, borrower, parasite, cadger; informal sponger, freeloader; N. Amer. informal mooch, moocher, schnorrer; Austral./NZ informal bludger.

scrub¹ verb *he scrubbed the kitchen floor:* **scour**, rub; clean, cleanse, wash, wipe.

scrub² noun *there the buildings ended and the scrub began:* **brush**, brushwood, scrubland, undergrowth.

scruffy adjective *he wore scruffy jeans:* **shabby**, worn, down at heel, ragged, tattered, mangy, dirty; untidy, unkempt, bedraggled, messy, dishevelled, ill-groomed; informal tatty, the worse for wear; N. Amer. informal raggedy.
– OPPOSITES smart, tidy.

scrumptious adjective (informal) *a piece of scrumptious gateau:* **delicious**, delectable, mouth-watering, tasty, appetizing, rich, savoury, flavoursome, flavourful, toothsome; succulent, luscious; informal scrummy, yummy; Brit. informal moreish; N. Amer. informal finger-licking, nummy.
– OPPOSITES unpalatable.

scrunch verb *Flora scrunched the handkerchief into a ball:* **crumple**, crunch, crush, rumple, screw up, squash, squeeze, compress; informal squidge.

scruples plural noun *he had no scruples about eavesdropping:* **qualms**, compunction, pangs/twinges of conscience, hesitation, reservations, second thoughts, doubt(s), misgivings, uneasiness, reluctance.

scrupulous adjective **1** *scrupulous attention to detail:* **careful**, meticulous, painstaking, thorough, assiduous, sedulous, attentive, conscientious, punctilious, searching, close, minute, rigorous, particular, strict. **2** *a scrupulous man:* **honest**, honourable, upright, upstanding, high-minded, right-minded, moral, ethical, good, virtuous, principled, incorruptible.
– OPPOSITES careless, dishonest.

scrutinize verb *Basil scrutinized the painting:* **examine**, inspect, survey, study, look at, peruse; investigate, explore, probe, inquire into, go into, check.

scrutiny noun *Frick continued his scrutiny of the room:* **examination**, inspection, survey, study, perusal; investigation, exploration, probe, inquiry; informal going-over.

scud verb *a few dark clouds scudded across the sky:* **speed**, race, rush, sail, shoot, sweep, skim, whip, whizz, flash, fly, scurry, flit, scutter.

scuff verb *the girl scuffed the toe of her shoe in the gravel:* **scrape**, scratch, rub, abrade; mark.

scuffle noun *there was a scuffle outside the pub:* **fight**, struggle, tussle, brawl, fracas, free-for-all, rough and tumble, scrimmage; informal scrap, dust-up, punch-up, set-to, shindy; N. Amer. informal rough house.
verb *demonstrators scuffled with police:* **fight**, struggle, tussle, exchange blows, come to blows, brawl, clash; informal scrap.

sculpt verb *the Minoans were adept at sculpting human figures from ivory:* **carve**, model, chisel, sculpture, fashion, form, shape, cast, cut, hew.

sculpture noun *a bronze sculpture:* **model**, carving, statue, statuette, figure, figurine, effigy, bust, head, likeness.
verb *the choir stalls were carefully sculptured.* See SCULPT.

scum noun **1** *the water was covered with a thick green scum:* **film**, layer, covering, froth; filth, dross, dirt. **2** (informal) *drug dealers are scum:* **despicable people**, the lowest of the low, the dregs of society, vermin, riff-raff; informal the scum of the earth, dirt.

scupper (Brit.) verb **1** *the captain decided to scupper the ship:* **sink**, scuttle, submerge, send to the bottom. **2** (informal) *he denied trying to scupper the agreement:* **ruin**, wreck, destroy, sabotage, torpedo, spoil, mess up; informal screw up, foul up, put the kibosh on, banjax, do for.

scurrilous adjective *a scurrilous attack on her character:* **defamatory**, slanderous, libellous, scandalous, insulting, offensive, gross; abusive, vituperative, malicious; informal bitchy.

scurry verb *pedestrians scurried for cover:* **hurry**, hasten, run, rush, dash; scamper, scuttle, scramble; Brit. scutter; informal scoot, beetle.
– OPPOSITES amble.
noun *there was a scurry to get out:* **rush**, race, dash, run, hurry; scramble, bustle.

scuttle verb. See SCURRY verb.

sea noun **1** *the sea sparkled in the sun:* **(the) ocean**, the waves; informal the drink; Brit. informal the briny. **2** *the boat overturned in the heavy seas:* **waves**, swell, breakers, rollers, combers; informal boomers. **3** *a sea of roofs and turrets:* **expanse**, stretch, area, tract, sweep, blanket, sheet, carpet, mass; multitude, host, profusion, abundance, plethora.
– OPPOSITES land.

S

adjective *sea creatures:* **marine**, ocean, oceanic; saltwater, seawater; ocean-going, seagoing, seafaring; maritime, naval, nautical.

■ **at sea** confused, perplexed, puzzled, baffled, mystified, bemused, bewildered, nonplussed, disconcerted, disoriented, dumbfounded, at a loss, at sixes and sevens; informal flummoxed, bamboozled, fazed; N. Amer. informal discombobulated.

seafaring adjective *an ancient seafaring people:* **maritime**, nautical, naval, seagoing, sea.

seal noun **1** *the seal round the bath:* **sealant**, sealer, adhesive. **2** *the king put his seal on the letter:* **emblem**, symbol, insignia, device, badge, crest, coat of arms, mark, monogram, stamp. **3** *the Minister gave his seal of approval to the project:* **ratification**, approval, blessing, consent, agreement, permission, sanction, endorsement, clearance.
verb **1** *she quietly sealed the door behind her:* **fasten**, secure, shut, close, lock, bolt. **2** *seal each bottle while it is hot:* **stop up**, seal up, make airtight/watertight, cork, stopper, plug. **3** *police sealed off the High Street:* **close off**, shut off, cordon off, fence off, isolate. **4** *he held out his hand to seal the bargain:* **clinch**, secure, settle, conclude, complete, establish, set the seal on, confirm, guarantee; informal sew up.

seam noun **1** *the seam on her sleeve was coming undone:* **join**, stitching. **2** *a seam of coal:* **layer**, stratum, vein, lode.

seaman noun **sailor**, seafarer, mariner, boatman, hand; informal (old) salt, sea dog, bluejacket; Brit. informal matelot.
– OPPOSITES landlubber.

seamy adjective *he seemed very knowledgeable about the seamy side of life:* **sordid**, disreputable, seedy, sleazy, squalid, insalubrious, unwholesome, unsavoury, rough, unpleasant.
– OPPOSITES salubrious.

sear verb **1** *the heat of the blast seared his face:* **scorch**, burn, singe, char. **2** *sear the meat before adding the other ingredients:* **flash-fry**, seal, brown. **3** *his betrayal had seared her terribly:* **hurt**, wound, pain, cut to the quick, sting; distress, grieve, upset, trouble, harrow, torment, torture.

search verb **1** *I searched for the key in my handbag:* **hunt**, look, seek, forage, fish about/around, look high and low, cast about/around, ferret about/around, root about/around, rummage about/around; Brit. informal rootle about/around. **2** *he searched the house thoroughly:* **look through**, hunt through, explore, scour, rifle through, go through, sift through, comb, go through with a fine-tooth comb; turn upside down, turn inside out, leave no stone unturned in; Austral./NZ informal fossick through. **3** *the guards searched him for weapons:* **examine**, inspect, check, frisk.

noun *we continued our search for a hotel:* **hunt**, look, quest; pursuit.
■ **in search of** searching for, hunting for, seeking, looking for, on the lookout for, in pursuit of.

searching adjective *searching questions:* **penetrating**, piercing, probing, penetrative, keen, shrewd, sharp, intent.

searing adjective **1** *the searing heat:* **scorching**, blistering, sweltering, blazing (hot), burning, fiery, torrid; informal boiling (hot), baking (hot), sizzling, roasting. **2** *searing pain:* **intense**, excruciating, agonizing, sharp, stabbing, shooting, stinging, severe, extreme, racking. **3** *a searing attack:* **fierce**, savage, blistering, scathing, stinging, devastating, mordant, trenchant, caustic, cutting, biting, withering.

seaside noun *a day out at the seaside:* **coast**, shore, seashore, waterside; beach, sand, sands.

season noun *the rainy season:* **period**, time, time of year, spell, term.
verb **1** *season the casserole to taste:* **flavour**, add flavouring to, add salt/pepper to, spice. **2** *his albums include standard numbers seasoned with a few of his own tunes:* **enliven**, leaven, spice (up), liven up; informal pep up.
■ **in season** available, obtainable, to be had, on offer, on the market; plentiful, abundant.

seasonable adjective *seasonable weather:* **usual**, expected, predictable, normal for the time of year.

seasoned adjective *seasoned travellers:* **experienced**, practised, well versed, knowledgeable, established, habituated, veteran, hardened, battle-scarred.
– OPPOSITES inexperienced.

seasoning noun **flavouring**, salt and pepper, herbs, spices, condiments.

seat noun **1** *a wooden seat:* **chair**, bench, stool, settle, stall; (**seats**) seating, room; Brit. informal pew. **2** *the seat of government:* **headquarters**, base, centre, nerve centre, hub, heart; location, site, whereabouts, place. **3** *the family's country seat:* **residence**, ancestral home, mansion, stately home.
verb **1** *they seated themselves round the table:* **position**, put, place; ensconce, install, settle; informal plonk, park. **2** *the hall seats 500:* **have room for**, contain, take, sit, hold, accommodate.

seating noun *the theatre has seating for 600:* **seats**, room, places, chairs, accommodation.

secede verb *the Kingdom of Belgium seceded from the Netherlands in 1830:* **withdraw from**, break away from, break with, separate (oneself) from, leave, split with, split off from, disaffiliate from, resign from, pull out of; informal quit.
– OPPOSITES join.

secluded adjective *the house overlooks a quiet, secluded garden:* **sheltered**,

private, concealed, hidden, unfrequented, sequestered, tucked away.
– OPPOSITES busy.

seclusion noun *he spends much of his time in seclusion at his mountain cottage:* **isolation**, solitude, retreat, privacy, retirement, withdrawal, purdah, concealment, hiding, secrecy.

second¹ adjective **1** *the second day of the trial:* **next**, following, subsequent, succeeding. **2** *he keeps a second pair of glasses in his office:* **additional**, extra, alternative, another, spare, backup, relief, fallback; N. Amer. alternate. **3** *he dropped down to captain the second team:* **secondary**, lower, subordinate, subsidiary, lesser, inferior. **4** *the conflict could turn into a second Vietnam:* **another**, new; repeat of, copy of, carbon copy of.
– OPPOSITES first.
noun *Eva had been working as his second:* **assistant**, attendant, helper, aide, supporter, auxiliary, right-hand man/woman, girl/man Friday, second in command, number two, deputy, understudy, subordinate; informal sidekick.
verb *George Beale seconded the motion:* **formally support**, give one's support to, vote for, back, approve, endorse.
■ **second to none** incomparable, matchless, unrivalled, inimitable, beyond compare/comparison, unparalleled, without parallel, unequalled, without equal, in a class of its own, peerless, unsurpassed, unsurpassable, nonpareil, unique; perfect, consummate, transcendent, surpassing, superlative, supreme; formal unexampled.

second² noun *I'll only be gone for a second:* **moment**, bit, little while, short time, instant, split second; informal sec, jiffy; Brit. informal mo, tick, two ticks.
■ **in a second** very soon, in a minute, in a moment, in a trice, shortly, any minute (now), in the twinkling of an eye, in (less than) no time, in no time at all; N. Amer. momentarily; informal in a jiffy, in two shakes (of a lamb's tail), before you can say Jack Robinson, in the blink of an eye; Brit. informal in a tick, in two ticks, in a mo; N. Amer. informal in a snap.

second³ verb *he was seconded to their Welsh office:* **assign temporarily**, lend; transfer, move, shift, relocate, assign, reassign, send.

secondary adjective **1** *a secondary issue:* **less important**, subordinate, lesser, minor, peripheral, incidental, ancillary, subsidiary, non-essential, inessential, of little account, unimportant. **2** *secondary infections:* **accompanying**, attendant, concomitant, consequential, resulting, resultant.
– OPPOSITES primary, main.

second-class adjective *we were treated like second-class citizens:* **second-rate**, second-best, inferior, lesser, unimportant.

second-hand adjective **1** *second-hand clothes:* **used**, old, worn, pre-owned,

handed-down, hand-me-down, cast-off; Brit. Informal reach-me-down. **2** *second-hand information:* **indirect**, derivative; vicarious.
– OPPOSITES new, direct.
adverb *I was discounting anything I heard second-hand:* **indirectly**, at second-hand, on the bush telegraph; informal on the grapevine.
– OPPOSITES directly.

secondly adverb *firstly it is wrong and secondly it is difficult to implement:* **furthermore**, also, moreover; second, in the second place, next; secondarily.

second-rate adjective *he replied tetchily that he never made second-rate films:* **inferior**, substandard, low-quality, below par, bad, poor, deficient, defective, faulty, imperfect, shoddy, inadequate, insufficient, unacceptable; Brit. informal ropy, duff, rubbish.
– OPPOSITES first-rate, excellent.

secrecy noun **1** *the secrecy of the material:* **confidentiality**, classified nature. **2** *a government which thrived on secrecy:* **secretiveness**, covertness, furtiveness, surreptitiousness, stealth, stealthiness.

secret adjective **1** *a secret plan:* **confidential**, top secret, classified, undisclosed, unknown, private, under wraps; informal hush-hush. **2** *a secret drawer in the table:* **hidden**, concealed, disguised; invisible. **3** *a secret operation to infiltrate terrorist groups:* **clandestine**, covert, undercover, underground, surreptitious, stealthy, furtive, cloak-and-dagger, hole and corner, closet; informal hush-hush. **4** *a secret message | a secret code:* **cryptic**, encoded, coded; mysterious, abstruse, recondite, arcane, esoteric, cabbalistic. **5** *a secret place:* **secluded**, private, concealed, hidden, unfrequented, out of the way, tucked away. **6** *a very secret person.* See **SECRETIVE**.
– OPPOSITES public, open.
noun **1** *he just can't keep a secret:* **confidential matter**, confidence, private affair; skeleton in the cupboard. **2** *the secrets of the universe:* **mystery**, enigma, paradox, puzzle, conundrum, poser, riddle. **3** *the secret of their success:* **recipe**, (magic) formula, blueprint, key, answer, solution.
■ **in secret** secretly, in private, privately, behind closed doors, behind the scenes, in camera, under cover, under the counter, discreetly, behind someone's back, furtively, stealthily, on the sly, on the quiet, conspiratorially, covertly, clandestinely, on the side; informal on the q.t..

secret agent noun **spy**, double agent, counterspy, undercover agent, operative, plant, mole; N. Amer. informal spook.

secretary noun **assistant**, personal assistant, PA, administrator, amanuensis, girl/man Friday.

secrete¹ verb *a substance secreted by the prostate gland:* **produce**, discharge, emit, excrete, release, send out.
– OPPOSITES absorb.

secrete² verb *we secreted ourselves in the*

S

bushes: **conceal**, hide, cover up, veil, shroud, screen, stow away; bury, cache; informal stash away.
– OPPOSITES reveal.

secretive adjective *a secretive person:* **uncommunicative**, secret, unforthcoming, playing one's cards close to one's chest, reticent, reserved, silent, non-communicative, quiet, tight-lipped, close-mouthed, taciturn.
– OPPOSITES open, communicative.

secretly adverb 1 *they met secretly for a year:* **in secret**, in private, privately, behind closed doors, in camera, behind the scenes, under cover, under the counter, behind someone's back, furtively, stealthily, on the sly, on the quiet, conspiratorially, covertly, clandestinely, on the side; informal on the q.t.. 2 *he was secretly jealous of Bartholomew:* **privately**, in one's heart (of hearts), deep down.

sect noun *he joined a rather weird religious sect:* **(religious) cult**, religious group, faith community, denomination, persuasion, religious order; splinter group, faction.

sectarian adjective *the party should offer voters a real alternative to sectarian politics:* **factional**, separatist, partisan, parti pris; doctrinaire, dogmatic, extreme, fanatical, rigid, inflexible, bigoted, hidebound, narrow-minded.
– OPPOSITES tolerant, liberal.

section noun 1 *the separate sections of a train:* **part**, piece, bit, segment, component, division, portion, element, unit, constituent. 2 *the last section of the questionnaire:* **subdivision**, part, subsection, division, portion, bit, chapter, passage, clause. 3 *the reference section of the library:* **department**, area, part, division.

sector noun 1 *every sector of the industry is affected:* **part**, branch, arm, division, area, department, field, sphere. 2 *the north-eastern sector of the town:* **district**, quarter, part, section, zone, region, area, belt.

secular adjective *secular music:* **non-religious**, lay, temporal, worldly, earthly, profane.
– OPPOSITES holy, religious.

secure adjective 1 *check to ensure that all bolts are secure:* **fastened**, fixed, secured, done up; closed, shut, locked. 2 *an environment in which children can feel secure:* **safe**, protected from harm/danger, out of from danger, sheltered, safe and sound, out of harm's way, in a safe place, in safe hands, invulnerable; at ease, unworried, relaxed, happy, confident. 3 *a secure future:* **certain**, assured, reliable, dependable, settled, fixed.
– OPPOSITES loose, vulnerable, uncertain.
verb 1 *pins secure the handle to the main body:* **fix**, attach, fasten, affix, connect, couple. 2 *the doors had not been properly secured:* **fasten**, close, shut, lock, bolt, chain, seal. 3 *he leapt out to secure the boat:* **tie up**,

moor, make fast; anchor. 4 *they sought to secure the country against attack:* **protect**, make safe, fortify, strengthen. 5 *a written constitution would secure the rights of the individual:* **assure**, ensure, guarantee, protect, confirm, establish. 6 *the division secured a major contract:* **obtain**, acquire, gain, get, get possession of; informal get hold of, land.

security noun 1 *the security of the nation's citizens:* **safety**, freedom from danger, protection, invulnerability. 2 *he could give her the security she needed:* **peace of mind**, feeling of safety, stability, certainty, happiness, confidence. 3 *security at the court was tight:* **safety measures**, safeguards, surveillance, defence, protection. 4 *additional security for your loan may be required:* **guarantee**, collateral, surety, pledge, bond.
– OPPOSITES vulnerability, danger.

sedate[1] verb *the patient had to be sedated:* **tranquillize**, put under sedation, drug.

sedate[2] adjective 1 *a sedate pace:* **slow**, steady, dignified, unhurried, relaxed, measured, leisurely, slow-moving, easy, easy-going, gentle. 2 *he had lived a sedate and straightforward life:* **calm**, placid, tranquil, quiet, uneventful; boring, dull.
– OPPOSITES exciting, fast.

sedative adjective *sedative drugs:* **tranquillizing**, calming, calmative, relaxing, soporific; depressant.
noun *the doctor gave him a sedative:* **tranquillizer**, calmative, sleeping pill, narcotic, opiate; depressant; informal trank, sleeper, downer.

sedentary adjective *a sedentary job:* **sitting**, seated, desk-bound; inactive.
– OPPOSITES active.

sediment noun *there is a thick layer of sediment on the bottom:* **dregs**, lees, precipitate, deposit, grounds, settlings, residue, remains; silt, alluvium.

sedition noun **rabble-rousing**, incitement to rebel, subversion, troublemaking, provocation; rebellion, insurrection, mutiny, insurgence, civil disorder.

seditious adjective *a seditious speech:* **rabble-rousing**, provocative, inflammatory, subversive, troublemaking; rebellious, insurrectionist, mutinous, insurgent.

seduce verb 1 *he took her to his hotel room and tried to seduce her:* **persuade to have sex**; euphemistic have one's (wicked) way with, take advantage of. 2 *a firm which had seduced customers into buying worthless products:* **attract**, allure, lure, tempt, entice, beguile, inveigle, manoeuvre.

seducer noun *the man was an accomplished seducer:* **womanizer**, philanderer, Romeo, Don Juan, Lothario, Casanova, playboy, ladies' man; informal ladykiller, wolf, skirt-chaser.

S

seductive adjective *she appears in the guise of a seductive temptress:* **sexy**, alluring, tempting, exciting, provocative, sultry, slinky; coquettish, flirtatious; informal vampish, come-hither, come-to-bed.

seductress noun **temptress**, siren, femme fatale, Mata Hari; flirt, coquette; informal vamp.

sedulous adjective *he picked a spine from his leg with sedulous care:* **diligent**, careful, meticulous, thorough, assiduous, attentive, industrious, conscientious, ultra-careful, punctilious, scrupulous, painstaking, minute, rigorous, particular.

see¹ verb **1** *he saw her running across the road:* **discern**, spot, notice, catch sight of, glimpse, catch/get a glimpse of, make out, pick out, spy, distinguish, detect, perceive, note; informal clap/lay/set eyes on, clock. **2** *I saw a documentary about it last week:* **watch**, look at, view; catch. **3** *would you like to see over the house?* **inspect**, view, look round, tour, survey, examine, scrutinize; informal give something a/the once-over. **4** *I finally saw what she meant:* **understand**, grasp, comprehend, follow, take in, realize, appreciate, recognize, work out, get the drift of, perceive, fathom (out); informal get, latch on to, cotton on to, catch on to, tumble to, savvy, figure out, get a fix on; Brit. informal twig, suss (out). **5** *I must go and see what Victor is up to:* **find out**, discover, learn, ascertain, determine, establish. **6** *see that no harm comes to him:* **ensure**, make sure/certain, see to it, take care, mind. **7** *I see trouble ahead:* **foresee**, predict, forecast, prophesy, anticipate, envisage, picture, visualize. **8** *about a year later, I saw him in town:* **encounter**, meet, run into/across, come across, stumble on/across, happen on, chance on; informal bump into. **9** *they see each other from time to time:* **meet**, meet up with, get together with, socialize with. **10** *you'd better see a doctor:* **consult**, confer with, talk to, speak to, have recourse to, call on, call in, turn to, ask. **11** *he's seeing someone else now:* **go out with**, date, take out, be involved with; informal go steady with. **12** *he saw her to her car:* **escort**, accompany, show, walk, conduct, lead, take, usher, attend.
▪ **see about** *I'll go and see about fixing a meal:* arrange, see to, deal with, take care of, look after, attend to, sort out.
▪ **see through** *I saw through him from the start:* understand, get/have the measure of, read like a book; informal be wise to, have someone's number, know someone's (little) game.
▪ **see someone through** *it was Francine's devotion which saw him through:* sustain, encourage, buoy up, keep going, support, be a tower of strength to, comfort, help (out), stand by, stick by.
▪ **see something through** *I want to see the job through:* persevere with, persist with, continue (with), carry on with, keep at, follow through, stay with; informal stick at, stick it out, hang in there.
▪ **see to** *I'll see to Dad's tea:* attend to, deal with, see about, take care of, look after, sort out, fix, organize, arrange.

see² noun *a bishop's see:* **diocese**, bishopric.

seed noun **1** *sow the seeds in trays or pots:* pip, stone, kernel; ovule. **2** *each war contains within it the seeds of a fresh war:* **genesis**, source, origin, root, starting point, germ, beginnings, potential (for); cause, reason, motivation, motive, grounds.
▪ **go/run to seed** deteriorate, degenerate, decline, decay, fall into decay, go to rack and ruin, go downhill, moulder, rot; informal go to pot, go to the dogs, go down the toilet.

seedy adjective **1** *the seedy world of prostitution:* **sordid**, disreputable, seamy, sleazy, squalid, unwholesome, unsavoury. **2** *a seedy block of flats:* **dilapidated**, tumbledown, ramshackle, falling to pieces, decrepit, gone to rack and ruin, run down, down at heel, shabby, dingy, slummy, insalubrious, squalid; informal crummy; Brit. informal grotty.
– OPPOSITES high-class.

seek verb **1** *they sought shelter from the winter snows:* **search for**, try to find, look for, be on the lookout for, be after, hunt for, be in quest of. **2** *the company is seeking a judicial review of the decision:* **try to obtain**, work towards, be intent on, aim at/for. **3** *he sought help from the police:* **ask for**, request, solicit, call for, entreat, beg for, petition for, appeal for, apply for, put in for. **4** *we constantly seek to improve the service:* **try**, attempt, endeavour, strive, work, do one's best.

seem verb *she seemed annoyed at this:* **appear (to be)**, have the appearance/air of being, give the impression of being, look, look as though one is, look like, show signs of, look to be; come across as, strike someone as, sound.

seeming adjective *there is a seeming contradiction here:* **apparent**, ostensible, supposed, outward, surface, superficial; pretended, feigned.
– OPPOSITES actual, genuine.

seemingly adverb **apparently**, on the face of it, to all appearances, as far as one can see/tell, on the surface, to all intents and purposes, outwardly, superficially, supposedly.

seemly adjective *it was not thought seemly to look in a mirror in those days:* **decorous**, proper, decent, becoming, fitting, suitable, appropriate, apt, apposite, meet, in good taste, genteel, polite, the done thing, right, correct, acceptable, comme il faut.
– OPPOSITES unseemly, unbecoming.

seep verb *oil continued to seep out of the sunken vessel:* **ooze**, trickle, exude, drip, dribble, flow, issue, escape, leak, drain, bleed, filter, percolate, soak.

S

seer noun *a seer had foretold that the earl would assume the throne:* **soothsayer**, oracle, prophet(ess), augur, prognosticator, diviner, fortune-teller, crystal-gazer, clairvoyant, psychic; Scottish spaewife.

see-saw verb *the market see-sawed as rumours spread:* **fluctuate**, swing, go up and down, rise and fall, oscillate, alternate, yo-yo, vary.

seethe verb **1** *the brew seethed:* **boil**, bubble, simmer, foam, froth, fizz, effervesce. **2** *the water seethed with fish:* **teem**, swarm, boil, swirl, churn, surge. **3** *I seethed at the injustice of it all:* **be angry**, be furious, be enraged, be incensed, be beside oneself, boil, simmer, rage, rant, rave, storm, fume, smoulder; informal be livid, be wild, foam at the mouth, be steamed up, be hot under the collar; Brit. informal do one's nut, throw a wobbly.

see-through adjective *a dress with see-through sleeves:* **transparent**, translucent, clear, limpid, pellucid; thin, lightweight, flimsy, sheer, diaphanous, filmy, gossamer, chiffony, gauzy.
– OPPOSITES opaque.

segment noun **1** *orange segments:* **piece**, bit, section, part, chunk, portion, division, slice; fragment, wedge, lump, tranche. **2** *all segments of society:* **part**, section, sector, division, portion, constituent, element, unit, compartment; branch, wing.
verb *they plan to segment their market share:* **divide (up)**, subdivide, separate, split, cut up, carve up, slice up, break up; segregate, divorce, partition, section.
– OPPOSITES amalgamate.

segregate verb *he campaigns for routes which segregate cycles from motor vehicles:* **separate**, set apart, keep apart, isolate, quarantine, closet; partition, divide, detach, disconnect, sever, dissociate.
– OPPOSITES amalgamate.

seize verb **1** *she seized the microphone:* **grab**, grasp, snatch, take hold of, get one's hands on; grip, clutch; Brit. informal nab. **2** *rebels seized the air base:* **capture**, take, overrun, occupy, conquer, take over. **3** *the drugs were seized by customs:* **confiscate**, impound, commandeer, requisition, appropriate, expropriate, take away. **4** *terrorists seized his wife:* **kidnap**, abduct, take captive, take prisoner, take hostage, hold to ransom; informal snatch.
– OPPOSITES relinquish, release.

■ **seize on** *they seized on the opportunity:* take advantage of, exploit, grasp with both hands, leap at, jump at, pounce on.

seizure noun **1** *Napoleon's seizure of Spain:* **capture**, takeover, annexation, invasion, occupation, colonization. **2** *the seizure of defaulters' property:* **confiscation**, appropriation, expropriation, sequestration. **3** *the seizure of UN staff by rebels:* **kidnapping**, kidnap, abduction. **4** *the baby suffered a seizure:* **convulsion**, fit, spasm, paroxysm.

seldom adverb *he was seldom absent:* **rarely**, infrequently, hardly (ever), scarcely (ever), almost never; now and then, occasionally, sporadically; informal once in a blue moon.
– OPPOSITES often.

select verb *select the correct tool for the job:* **choose**, pick (out), single out, sort out, take; opt for, decide on, settle on, determine, nominate, appoint, elect.
adjective **1** *a select group of SAS members:* **choice**, hand-picked, prime, first-rate, first-class, superior, finest, best, top-class, supreme, superb, excellent; informal A1, top-notch. **2** *a select clientele:* **exclusive**, elite, favoured, privileged; wealthy; informal posh.
– OPPOSITES inferior.

selection noun **1** *Jim made his selection of toys:* **choice**, pick; option, preference. **2** *we offer a wide selection of dishes:* **range**, array, diversity, variety, assortment, mixture. **3** *a selection of his poems:* **anthology**, assortment, collection, assemblage; miscellany, medley, pot-pourri.

selective adjective *he is very selective in his reading:* **discerning**, discriminating, discriminatory, critical, exacting, demanding, particular; fussy, fastidious, faddish; informal choosy, pernickety, picky; Brit. informal faddy.

self noun *these whispers come from our inner self:* **ego**, I, oneself, persona, person, identity, character, personality, psyche, soul, spirit, mind, inner self.
– OPPOSITES other.

self-assembly noun *kits for self-assembly:* **do-it-yourself**, DIY.
adjective *self-assembly furniture:* **flat-pack**, kit, self-build, do-it-yourself, DIY.

self-assurance noun **self-confidence**, confidence, assertiveness, self-reliance, self-possession, composure, presence of mind, aplomb.
– OPPOSITES diffidence.

self-assured adjective *a stubborn and self-assured lady:* **self-confident**, confident, assertive, assured, authoritative, commanding, self-reliant, self-possessed, poised.

self-centred adjective *your father's too self-centred to care what you do:* **egocentric**, egotistic, egotistical, egomaniacal, self-absorbed, self-obsessed, self-seeking, self-interested, self-serving; narcissistic, vain; inconsiderate, thoughtless; informal looking after number one.

self-confidence noun *she took care to build up his self-confidence by involving him in the planning:* **morale**, confidence, self-assurance, assurance, assertiveness, self-reliance, self-possession, composure.

self-conscious adjective *he gave me a self-conscious grin:* **embarrassed**, uncomfortable, uneasy, nervous; unnatural, inhibited, gauche, awkward; modest, shy, diffident, bashful, retiring, shrinking.

– OPPOSITES confident.

self-contained adjective **1** *each train was a self-contained unit:* **complete**, independent, separate, free-standing, enclosed. **2** *a very self-contained child:* **independent**, self-sufficient, self-reliant; introverted, quiet, private, aloof, insular, reserved, reticent, secretive.

self-control noun *he had recovered his self-control:* **self-discipline**, restraint, self-possession, will power, composure, coolness; moderation, temperance, abstemiousness; informal cool.

self-denial noun *a farm built up over the years by hard work and self-denial:* **self-sacrifice**, selflessness, unselfishness; self-discipline, asceticism, self-deprivation, abstemiousness, abstinence, abstention; moderation, temperance.
– OPPOSITES self-indulgence.

self-discipline noun *his observance of his diet was a show of tremendous self-discipline:* **self-control**; restraint, self-restraint; will power, purposefulness, strong-mindedness, resolve, moral fibre; doggedness, persistence, determination, grit.

self-employed adjective *a self-employed painter and decorator:* **freelance**, independent, casual; consultant, consulting; temporary, jobbing, visiting, outside, external, extramural, peripatetic.

self-esteem noun *assertiveness training for those with low self-esteem:* **self-respect**, pride, dignity, self-regard, faith in oneself; morale, self-confidence, confidence, self-assurance.

self-evident adjective *the reason for this is self-evident:* **obvious**, clear, plain, evident, apparent, manifest, patent; distinct, transparent, overt, conspicuous, palpable, unmistakable, undeniable.
– OPPOSITES unclear.

self-explanatory adjective *this paragraph is largely self-explanatory:* **easily understood**, comprehensible, intelligible, straightforward, unambiguous, accessible, crystal clear, user-friendly, simple, self-evident, obvious.
– OPPOSITES impenetrable.

self-governing adjective *Singapore became a self-governing state in 1959:* **independent**, sovereign, autonomous, free; self-legislating, self-determining.
– OPPOSITES dependent.

self-important adjective *he was given the nickname Colonel because he was so self-important:* **conceited**, arrogant, bumptious, full of oneself, puffed up, swollen-headed, pompous, overbearing, opinionated, cocky, presumptuous, sententious, vain, overweening, proud, egotistical; informal snooty, uppity, uppish.
– OPPOSITES humble.

self-indulgent adjective *a self-indulgent*

extra hour of sleep: **hedonistic**, pleasure-seeking, sybaritic, indulgent, luxurious, lotus-eating, epicurean; intemperate, immoderate, overindulgent, excessive, extravagant, licentious, dissolute, decadent.
– OPPOSITES abstemious.

self-interest noun *laissez-faire is an economic system based on individualism and self-interest:* **self-seeking**, self-serving, self-obsession, self-absorption, self-regard, egocentrism, egotism, egomania, selfishness; informal looking after number one.
– OPPOSITES altruism.

self-interested adjective **self-seeking**, self-serving, self-obsessed, self-absorbed, wrapped up in oneself, egocentric, egotistic, egotistical, egomaniacal, selfish.

selfish adjective *he is just selfish by nature:* **egocentric**, egotistic, egotistical, egomaniacal, self-centred, self-absorbed, self-obsessed, self-seeking, self-serving, wrapped up in oneself; inconsiderate, thoughtless, unthinking, uncaring, uncharitable; mean, miserly, grasping, greedy, mercenary, acquisitive, opportunistic; informal looking after number one.
– OPPOSITES altruistic.

selfless adjective *an act of selfless devotion:* **unselfish**, altruistic, self-sacrificing, self-denying; considerate, compassionate, kind, noble, generous, magnanimous, ungrudging, charitable, benevolent, open-handed.
– OPPOSITES inconsiderate.

self-possessed adjective *a woman who has been shy or awkward can become quite self-possessed as she cares for her new baby:* **assured**, self-assured, calm, cool, composed, at ease, unperturbed, unruffled, confident, self-confident, poised, imperturbable; informal together, unfazed, unflappable.
– OPPOSITES unsure.

self-possession noun **composure**, assurance, self-assurance, self-control, imperturbability, impassivity, equanimity, nonchalance, confidence, self-confidence, poise, aplomb, presence of mind, nerve, sangfroid; informal cool.

self-reliant adjective *ineligible for social security, they have to be entirely self-reliant:* **self-sufficient**, self-supporting, self-sustaining, able to stand on one's own two feet; independent, autarkic.

self-respect noun *she lost her self-respect when her husband was attracted to her colleague:* **self-esteem**, self-regard, amour propre, faith in oneself, pride, dignity, morale, self-confidence.

self-restraint noun *with great self-restraint, he did not grab the rod from his friend's hand:* **self-control**, restraint, self-discipline, self-possession, will power, moderation, temperance, abstemiousness, abstention.
– OPPOSITES self-indulgence.

s

self-righteous adjective *you're too self-righteous to see your own frailties:* **sanctimonious**, holier-than-thou, self-satisfied, smug, priggish, complacent, pious, moralizing, superior, hypocritical; informal goody-goody.
– OPPOSITES humble.

self-sacrifice noun *self-sacrifice involved giving up her fine mansion and living in cheap lodgings:* **self-denial**, selflessness, unselfishness; self-discipline, abstinence, asceticism, abnegation, self-deprivation, moderation, austerity, temperance, abstention.

self-satisfied adjective *a self-satisfied smile:* **complacent**, self-congratulatory, smug, superior, puffed up, pleased with oneself; informal goody-goody, I'm-all-right-Jack; Brit. informal like the cat that's got the cream.

self-seeking adjective *the self-seeking aggrandizement of Party bosses:* **self-interested**, self-serving, selfish; egocentric, egotistic, egotistical, self-obsessed, self-absorbed; inconsiderate, thoughtless, unthinking; informal looking after number one.
– OPPOSITES altruistic.

self-styled adjective *self-styled experts:* **would-be**, so-called, self-appointed, self-titled, professed, self-confessed, soi-disant.

self-sufficient adjective *the economy became nearly self-sufficient in many foodstuffs:* **self-supporting**, self-reliant, self-sustaining, able to stand on one's own two feet; independent, autarkic.

sell verb **1** *they are selling their house:* **put up for sale**, offer for sale, put on sale, dispose of, vend, auction (off); trade, barter. **2** *he sells cakes:* **trade in**, deal in, traffic in, stock, carry, offer for sale, peddle, hawk, retail, market. **3** *the book should sell well:* **go**, be bought, be purchased; move, be in demand. **4** *it sells for £79.95:* **cost**, be priced at, retail at, go for, be. **5** *he still has to sell the deal to Congress:* **promote**; persuade someone to accept, talk someone into, bring someone round to, win someone over to, win approval for.
– OPPOSITES buy.

▪ **sell out 1** *we've sold out of petrol:* have none left, be out of stock, have run out; informal be fresh out, be cleaned out. **2** *the edition sold out quickly:* be bought up, be depleted, be exhausted. **3** *they say the band has sold out:* abandon one's principles, prostitute oneself, sell one's soul, betray one's ideals, be untrue to oneself; debase oneself, degrade oneself, demean oneself.

▪ **sell someone out** *you sold me out to the cops, didn't you?* betray, inform on; be disloyal to, be unfaithful to, double-cross, break faith with, stab in the back; informal tell on, sell down the river, blow the whistle on, squeal on, stitch up, peach on, do the dirty on; Brit. informal grass on, shop; N. Amer. informal finger.

▪ **sell someone short** undervalue, underrate, underestimate, disparage, deprecate, belittle.

seller noun *sellers of fruit and vegetables:* **vendor**, retailer, purveyor, supplier, stockist, trader, merchant, dealer; shopkeeper, salesperson, salesman, saleswoman, sales assistant, shop assistant, travelling salesperson, pedlar, hawker; auctioneer; N. Amer. clerk; informal counter-jumper.

semblance noun *there remained at least a semblance of discipline:* (**outward**) **appearance**, air, show, facade, front, veneer, guise, pretence.

seminal adjective *her paper is still considered a seminal work on the subject:* **influential**, formative, groundbreaking, pioneering, original, innovative; major, important.

seminar noun **1** *a seminar for education officials:* **conference**, symposium, meeting, convention, forum, summit, discussion, consultation. **2** *teaching in the form of seminars:* **study group**, workshop, tutorial, class, lesson.

seminary noun **theological college**, rabbinical college, Talmudical college; academy, training college, training institute, school.

send verb **1** *they sent a message to HQ:* **dispatch**, post, mail, address, consign, direct, forward; transmit, convey, communicate; telephone, phone, broadcast, radio, fax, email. **2** *we sent for a doctor:* **call**, summon, contact; ask for, request, order. **3** *the pump sent out a jet of petrol:* **propel**, project, eject, deliver, discharge, spout, fire, shoot, release; throw, let fly; informal chuck. **4** *the barrels send off nasty fumes:* **emit**, give off, discharge, exude, send out, release, leak. **5** *it's enough to send one mad:* **make**, drive, turn.
– OPPOSITES receive.

▪ **send someone down 1** (Brit.) *she was sent down from Cambridge:* expel, exclude; Brit. rusticate. **2** (informal) *he was sent down for life:* send to prison, imprison, jail, incarcerate, lock up, confine, detain, intern; informal put away; Brit. informal bang up.

▪ **send someone off** (Sport) order off, dismiss; show someone the red card; informal red-card, send for an early bath, sin-bin.

send-off noun *she was given a rousing send-off at her retirement party:* **farewell**, goodbye, adieu, leave-taking, valediction; funeral.
– OPPOSITES welcome.

senile adjective *she couldn't cope with her senile husband:* **doddering**, doddery, decrepit, senescent, declining, infirm, feeble; aged, long in the tooth, in one's dotage; mentally confused, having Alzheimer's (disease), having senile dementia; informal past it, gaga.

senior adjective **1** *senior school pupils:* **older**,

elder. **2** *a senior officer:* **superior**, higher-ranking, high-ranking, more important; top, chief; N. Amer. ranking. **3** *Albert Stone Senior:* **the Elder**; Brit. major; N. Amer. I.
– OPPOSITES junior, subordinate.

senior citizen noun **retired person**, (old-age) pensioner, OAP; old person, elderly person, geriatric, dotard, Methuselah; N. Amer. senior, retiree, golden ager; informal old stager, old-timer, oldie, oldster, wrinkly, crumbly; Brit. informal buffer.

seniority noun *the Chief Clerk was next in seniority:* **rank**, superiority, standing, primacy, precedence, priority; age.

sensation noun **1** *a sensation of light:* **feeling**, sense, awareness, consciousness, perception, impression. **2** *I caused a sensation by donating £1m:* **commotion**, stir, uproar, furore, scandal, impact; interest, excitement; informal splash, to-do, hullabaloo. **3** *the new cars were a sensation:* **triumph**, success, sell-out; talking point; informal smash (hit), hit, winner, crowd-puller, wow, knockout.

sensational adjective **1** *a sensational murder trial:* **shocking**, scandalous, appalling; amazing, startling, astonishing, staggering; stirring, exciting, thrilling, electrifying; fascinating, interesting, noteworthy, significant, remarkable, momentous, historic, newsworthy. **2** *sensational stories:* **over-dramatized**, dramatic, melodramatic, exaggerated, sensationalist, sensationalistic; graphic, explicit, lurid; informal shock-horror, juicy. **3** (informal) *she looked sensational:* **gorgeous**, stunning, wonderful, exquisite, lovely, radiant, delightful, charming, enchanting, captivating; striking, spectacular, remarkable, outstanding, arresting, eye-catching; marvellous, superb, excellent, fine, first-class; informal great, terrific, tremendous, super, fantastic, fabulous, fab, heavenly, divine, knockout, delectable, scrumptious, awesome, magic, wicked, out of this world; Brit. informal smashing, brilliant.
– OPPOSITES dull, understated, unremarkable.

sense noun **1** *the sense of touch:* **sensory faculty**, feeling, sensation, perception; sight, hearing, touch, taste, smell. **2** *a sense of guilt:* **feeling**, awareness, sensation, consciousness, recognition. **3** *a sense of humour:* **appreciation**, awareness, understanding, comprehension, discernment. **4** *she had the sense to press the panic button:* **wisdom**, common sense, sagacity, discernment, perception; wit, intelligence, cleverness, shrewdness, judgement, reason, logic, brain(s); informal gumption, nous, horse sense, savvy; Brit. informal loaf, common; N. Amer. informal smarts. **5** *I can't see the sense in this:* **purpose**, point, reason, object, motive; use, value, advantage, benefit. **6** *the different senses of 'well':* **meaning**, definition,

import, signification, significance, purport, implication, nuance; drift, gist, thrust, tenor, message.
– OPPOSITES stupidity.
verb *she sensed their hostility:* **discern**, feel, observe, notice, recognize, pick up, be aware of, distinguish, make out, identify; comprehend, apprehend, see, appreciate, realize; suspect, have a funny feeling about, have a hunch, divine, intuit; informal catch on to; Brit. informal twig.

senseless adjective **1** *they found him senseless on the floor:* **unconscious**, stunned, insensible, insensate, comatose, knocked out, out cold, out for the count; numb; informal KO'd, dead to the world; Brit. informal spark out. **2** *a senseless waste:* **pointless**, futile, useless, needless, unavailing, in vain, purposeless, meaningless, unprofitable; absurd, foolish, insane, stupid, idiotic, ridiculous, ludicrous, mindless, illogical.
– OPPOSITES conscious, wise.

sensibility noun **1** *study leads to the growth of sensibility:* **sensitivity**, finer feelings, delicacy, taste, discrimination, discernment; understanding, insight, empathy, appreciation; feeling, intuition, responsiveness, receptiveness, perceptiveness, awareness. **2** *the wording might offend their sensibilities:* **(finer) feelings**, emotions, sensitivities, moral sense.

sensible adjective *isn't this the sensible thing to do?* **practical**, realistic, responsible, reasonable, commonsensical, rational, logical, sound, balanced, sober, no-nonsense, pragmatic, level-headed, thoughtful, down-to-earth, wise, prudent, judicious, sagacious, shrewd.
– OPPOSITES foolish.

sensitive adjective **1** *she's sensitive to changes in temperature:* **responsive to**, reactive to, sentient of, sensitized to; aware of, conscious of, alive to; susceptible to, affected by, vulnerable to; attuned to. **2** *sensitive skin:* **delicate**, fragile; tender, sore, raw. **3** *the matter needs sensitive handling:* **tactful**, careful, thoughtful, diplomatic, delicate, subtle, kid-glove; sympathetic, compassionate, understanding, intuitive, responsive, insightful. **4** *he's sensitive about his bald patch:* **touchy**, oversensitive, hypersensitive, easily offended, easily upset, easily hurt, thin-skinned, defensive; paranoid, neurotic; informal twitchy, uptight. **5** *a sensitive issue:* **difficult**, delicate, tricky, awkward, problematic, ticklish, precarious, controversial, emotive; informal sticky.
– OPPOSITES impervious, resilient, clumsy, thick-skinned, uncontroversial.

sensitivity noun **1** *the sensitivity of the skin:* **responsiveness**, sensitiveness, reactivity; susceptibility, vulnerability. **2** *the job calls for sensitivity:* **consideration**, care, thoughtfulness, tact, diplomacy, delicacy,

S

subtlety, finer feelings; understanding, empathy, sensibility, feeling, intuition, responsiveness, receptiveness; perception, discernment, insight; savoir faire. **3** *her sensitivity on the subject of boyfriends:* **touchiness**, oversensitivity, hypersensitivity, defensiveness. **4** *the sensitivity of the issue:* **delicacy**, trickiness, awkwardness, ticklishness.

sensual adjective **1** *sensual pleasure:* **physical**, carnal, bodily, fleshly, animal; hedonistic, epicurean, sybaritic, voluptuary. **2** *a beautiful, sensual woman:* **sexually attractive**, sexy, voluptuous, sultry, seductive, passionate; sexually arousing, erotic, sexual.
– OPPOSITES spiritual, passionless.

sensuality noun *her heavy eyelids gave her face an air of sleepy sensuality:* **sexiness**, sexual attractiveness, sultriness, seductiveness; sexuality, eroticism; physicality, carnality.

sensuous adjective **1** *big sensuous canvases:* **aesthetically pleasing**, gratifying, rich, sumptuous, luxurious; sensory, sensorial. **2** *sensuous lips:* **sexually attractive**, sexy, seductive, voluptuous, luscious, lush.

sentence noun *her husband is serving a three-year sentence for fraud:* **prison term**, prison sentence; punishment; informal time, stretch, stint; Brit. informal porridge, bird.
verb *they were sentenced to death:* **condemn**, doom; convict, punish.

sententious adjective *his sententious remarks were unbearable:* **moralistic**, moralizing, sanctimonious, self-righteous, pietistic, pious, priggish, judgemental; pompous, pontifical, self-important; informal preachifying, preachy; Brit. informal pi.

sentient adjective *sentient creatures:* **(capable of) feeling**, living, live; conscious, aware, responsive, reactive.

sentiment noun **1** *the comments echo my own sentiments:* **view**, feeling, attitude, thought, opinion, belief. **2** *there's no room for sentiment in sport:* **sentimentality**, sentimentalism, mawkishness, emotionalism; emotion, sensibility, soft-heartedness, tender-heartedness; informal schmaltz, mush, slushiness, corniness, cheese; Brit. informal soppiness; N. Amer. informal sappiness.

sentimental adjective **1** *she kept the vase for sentimental reasons:* **nostalgic**, tender, emotional, affectionate. **2** *the film is too sentimental:* **mawkish**, over-emotional, cloying, sickly, saccharine, sugary; romantic, hearts-and-flowers, touching; Brit. twee; informal slushy, mushy, weepy, tear-jerking, schmaltzy, lovey-dovey, gooey, drippy, cheesy, corny; Brit. informal soppy; N. Amer. informal cornball, sappy, hokey. **3** *she is sentimental about animals:* **soft-hearted**, tender-hearted, soft; informal soppy.
– OPPOSITES practical, gritty.

sentry noun **guard**, sentinel, lookout, watch, watchman, patrol.

separable adjective *body and soul are not separable:* **divisible**, distinct, independent, distinguishable; detachable, removable.

separate adjective **1** *his personal life was separate from his job:* **unconnected**, unrelated, different, distinct, discrete; detached, divorced, disconnected, independent, autonomous. **2** *the infirmary was separate from the school:* **set apart**, detached, disjoined; fenced off, cut off, segregated, isolated; free-standing, self-contained.
– OPPOSITES linked, attached.
verb **1** *they separated two rioting mobs:* **split (up)**, break up, part, pull apart, divide. **2** *the connectors can be separated:* **disconnect**, detach, disengage, uncouple, unyoke, disunite, disjoin; split, divide, sever; disentangle. **3** *the wall that separated the two estates:* **partition**, divide, come between, keep apart; bisect, intersect. **4** *the south aisle was separated off:* **isolate**, partition off, section off; close off, shut off, cordon off, fence off, screen off. **5** *they separated at the airport:* **part (company)**, go their separate ways, split up; say goodbye; disperse, disband, scatter. **6** *the road separated:* **fork**, divide, branch, bifurcate, diverge. **7** *her parents separated:* **split up**, break up, part, be estranged, divorce. **8** *separate fact from fiction:* **isolate**, set apart, segregate; distinguish, differentiate, dissociate; sort out, sift out, filter out, remove, weed out. **9** *those who separate themselves from society:* **break away from**, break with, secede from, withdraw from, leave, quit, dissociate oneself from, delink from, resign from, drop out of, repudiate, reject.
– OPPOSITES unite, join, link, meet, merge, marry.

separately adverb *I'll have to interview you all separately:* **individually**, one by one, one at a time, singly, severally; apart, independently, alone, by oneself, on one's own.

separation noun **1** *the separation of the two companies:* **disconnection**, detachment, severance, dissociation, disunion, disaffiliation, segregation, partition. **2** *her parents' separation:* **break-up**, split, parting (of the ways), estrangement, rift, rupture, breach; divorce; Brit. informal bust-up. **3** *the separation between art and life:* **distinction**, difference, differentiation, division, dividing line; gulf, gap, chasm.

septic adjective *a septic finger:* **infected**, festering, suppurating, pus-filled, putrid, putrefying, poisoned, diseased.

sepulchral adjective *a speech delivered in sepulchral tones:* **gloomy**, lugubrious, sombre, melancholy, melancholic, sad, sorrowful, mournful, doleful, dismal.
– OPPOSITES cheerful.

sepulchre noun **tomb**, vault, burial chamber, mausoleum, crypt, undercroft, catacomb; grave.

sequel noun **1** *the film inspired a sequel:* **follow-up**, continuation. **2** *the sequel was an armed uprising:* **consequence**, result, upshot, outcome, development, issue, postscript; effect, after-effect, aftermath; informal pay-off.

sequence noun **1** *the sequence of events:* **succession**, order, course, series, chain, train, string, progression, chronology; pattern, flow. **2** *a sequence from his film:* **excerpt**, clip, extract, episode, section.

sequester verb **1** *he sequestered himself from the world:* **isolate oneself**, hide away, shut oneself away, seclude oneself, cut oneself off, segregate oneself; closet oneself, withdraw, retire. **2** *the government sequestered his property.* See SEQUESTRATE.

sequestrate verb *in November 1956 the property was sequestrated by the Egyptian authorities:* **confiscate**, seize, take, sequester, appropriate, expropriate, impound, commandeer.

seraphic adjective *he listened with an expression of seraphic contentment on his face:* **blissful**, beatific, sublime, rapturous, ecstatic, joyful, rapt; serene, ethereal; cherubic, saintly, angelic.

serendipitous adjective *their diligent efforts were coupled with the joys of serendipitous discovery:* **chance**, accidental, coincidental; lucky, fluky, fortuitous; unexpected, unforeseen.

serendipity noun **(happy) chance**, (happy) accident, fluke; luck, good luck, good fortune, fortuity, providence; happy coincidence.

serene adjective **1** *on the surface she seemed serene:* **calm**, composed, tranquil, peaceful, untroubled, relaxed, at ease, unperturbed, unruffled, unworried; placid, equable; N. Amer. centered; informal together, unflappable. **2** *serene valleys:* **peaceful**, tranquil, quiet, still, restful, relaxing, undisturbed.
– OPPOSITES agitated, turbulent.

series noun **1** *a series of lectures:* **succession**, sequence, string, chain, run, round; spate, wave, rash; set, course, cycle; row, line; formal concatenation. **2** *a new drama series:* **serial**, programme; soap opera; informal soap.

serious adjective **1** *a serious expression:* **solemn**, earnest, grave, sombre, sober, unsmiling, poker-faced, stern, grim, dour, humourless, stony-faced; thoughtful, preoccupied, pensive. **2** *serious decisions:* **important**, significant, consequential, momentous, weighty, far-reaching, major, grave; urgent, pressing, crucial, critical, vital, life-and-death, high-priority. **3** *give serious consideration to this:* **careful**, detailed, in-depth, deep, profound, meaningful. **4** *a serious play:* **intellectual**, highbrow, heavyweight, deep, profound, literary, learned, scholarly; informal heavy. **5** *serious injuries:* **severe**, grave, bad, critical, acute, terrible, dire, dangerous, perilous, parlous. **6** *we're serious about equality:* **in earnest**, earnest, sincere, wholehearted, genuine; committed, resolute, determined.
– OPPOSITES light-hearted, trivial, superficial, lowbrow, minor, half-hearted.

seriously adverb **1** *Faye nodded seriously:* **solemnly**, earnestly, gravely, soberly, sombrely, sternly, grimly, dourly, humourlessly; pensively, thoughtfully. **2** *she was seriously injured:* **severely**, gravely, badly, critically, acutely, dangerously. **3** *do you seriously expect me to come?* **really**, actually, honestly. **4** *seriously, I'm very pleased:* **joking aside**, to be serious, honestly, truthfully, truly, I mean it; informal Scout's honour; Brit. informal straight up. **5** (informal) *'I've resigned.' 'Seriously?'* **really**, is that so, is that a fact, you're joking, well I never, go on, you don't say; informal you're kidding; Brit. informal {well, I'll be blowed}.

sermon noun **1** *he preached a sermon:* **homily**, address, speech, talk, discourse, oration; lesson. **2** *the headmaster gave them a lengthy sermon:* **lecture**, tirade, harangue, diatribe; speech, disquisition, monologue; reprimand, reproach, reproof, admonishment, admonition, reproval, remonstration, criticism; informal telling-off, talking-to, dressing-down, earful; Brit. informal ticking-off, row, rocket, rollicking

serpentine adjective **1** *a serpentine path:* **winding**, windy, zigzag, twisty, twisting and turning, meandering, sinuous, snaky, tortuous. **2** *serpentine election rules:* **complicated**, complex, intricate, involved, tortuous, convoluted, elaborate, knotty, confusing, bewildering, baffling, impenetrable.
– OPPOSITES straight, simple.

serrated adjective *a ten-inch hunting knife with a serrated blade:* **jagged**, sawtoothed, sawtooth, zigzag, notched, indented, toothed, denticulated.
– OPPOSITES smooth.

serried adjective *the serried mass of dark conifers:* **close together**, packed together, close-set, dense, tight, compact.

servant noun **1** *servants were cleaning the hall:* **attendant**, retainer; domestic (worker), (hired) help, cleaner; lackey, flunkey, minion; maid, housemaid, footman, page (boy), valet, butler, batman, manservant; housekeeper, steward; drudge, menial, slave; Brit. informal Mrs Mop, daily (woman), skivvy, scout. **2** *a servant of the Labour Party:* **helper**, supporter, follower.

serve verb **1** *they served their masters faithfully:* **work for**, be in the service of, be employed by; obey. **2** *this job serves the community:* **be of service to**, be of use to, help, assist, aid, make a contribution to, do one's bit for, do something for, benefit. **3** *she served on the committee for years:* **be**

S

a member of, work on, be on, sit on, have a place on. **4** *he served his apprenticeship in Scotland:* **carry out**, perform, do, fulfil, complete, discharge; spend. **5** *serve the soup hot:* **dish up/out**, give out, distribute; present, provide, supply; eat. **6** *she served another customer:* **attend to**, deal with, see to; **assist**, help, look after. **7** *they served him with a writ:* **present**, deliver, give, hand over. **8** *a saucer serving as an ashtray:* **act as**, function as, do the work of, be a substitute for. **9** *official forms will serve in most cases:* **suffice**, be adequate, be good enough, fit/fill the bill, do, answer, be useful, meet requirements, suit.

service noun **1** *your conditions of service:* **work**, employment, employ, labour. **2** *he has done us a service:* **favour**, kindness, good turn, helping hand; (**services**) **assistance**, help, aid, offices, ministrations. **3** *the food and service were excellent:* **waiting**, waitressing, serving, attention, attendance. **4** *products which give reliable service:* **use**, usage; functioning. **5** *he took his car in for a service:* **overhaul**, maintenance check, servicing. **6** *a marriage service:* **ceremony**, ritual, rite, observance; liturgy, sacrament; formal ordinance. **7** *a range of local services:* **amenity**, facility, resource, utility. **8** *soldiers leaving the services:* **(armed) forces**, armed services, military; army, navy, air force.
verb *the appliances are serviced regularly:* **overhaul**, check, go over, maintain; repair, mend, recondition.
■ **be of service** help, assist, benefit, be of assistance, be beneficial, serve, be useful, be of use, be valuable; do someone a good turn.
■ **out of service** out of order, broken, broken-down, out of commission, unserviceable, faulty, defective, inoperative, in disrepair; down; informal conked out, bust, kaput, on the blink, acting up, shot; Brit. informal knackered.

serviceable adjective **1** *a serviceable heating system:* **in working order**, working, functioning, functional, operational, operative; usable, workable, viable. **2** *serviceable lace-up shoes:* **functional**, utilitarian, sensible, practical; **hard-wearing**, durable, tough, robust.
– OPPOSITES unusable, impractical.

servile adjective *his attitude towards Mandeville can only be described as servile:* **obsequious**, sycophantic, deferential, subservient, fawning, ingratiating, unctuous, grovelling, toadyish, slavish, humble, self-abasing; informal slimy, bootlicking, smarmy, sucky; N. Amer. informal apple-polishing.
– OPPOSITES assertive.

serving noun *a large serving of spaghetti:* **portion**, helping, plateful, plate, bowlful; amount, quantity, ration.

servitude noun *slaves were bought and sold and kept in servitude:* **slavery**, enslavement, bondage, subjugation, subjection, domination.
– OPPOSITES liberty.

session noun **1** *a special session of the committee:* **meeting**, sitting, assembly, conclave, plenary; hearing; conference, discussion, forum, symposium; Scottish sederunt, diet; N. Amer. & NZ caucus. **2** *training sessions:* **period**, time, spell, stretch, bout. **3** *the next college session begins in August:* **academic year**, school year; term, semester; N. Amer. trimester.

set¹ verb **1** *Beth set the bag on the table:* **put (down)**, place, lay, deposit, position, settle, leave, stand, plant, posit; informal stick, dump, bung, park, plonk, pop; N. Amer. informal plunk. **2** *the cottage is set on a hill:* **be situated**, be located, lie, stand, be sited, be perched. **3** *the fence is set in concrete:* **fix**, embed, insert; mount. **4** *a ring set with precious stones:* **adorn**, ornament, decorate, embellish. **5** *I'll go and set the table:* **lay**, prepare, arrange. **6** *we set them some easy tasks:* **assign**, allocate, give, allot, prescribe. **7** *just set your mind to it:* **apply**, address, direct, aim, turn, focus, concentrate. **8** *they set a date for the election:* **decide on**, select, choose, arrange, schedule; fix (on), settle on, determine, designate, name, appoint, specify, stipulate. **9** *he set his horse towards her:* **direct**, steer, orientate, point, aim, train. **10** *his jump set a national record:* **establish**, create, institute. **11** *he set his watch:* **adjust**, regulate, synchronize; calibrate; put right, correct; programme, activate, turn on. **12** *the adhesive will set in an hour:* **solidify**, harden, stiffen, thicken, gel, gelatinize; cake, congeal, coagulate, clot; freeze, crystallize. **13** *the sun was setting:* **go down**, sink, dip; vanish, disappear.
– OPPOSITES melt, rise.
■ **set about 1** *Mike set about raising £5000:* **begin**, start, commence, go about, get to work on, get down to, embark on, tackle, address oneself to, undertake. **2** *the youths set about him:* **attack**, assail, assault, hit, strike, beat, thrash, pummel, wallop, tear into, set upon, fall on; informal lay into, lace into, pitch into, let someone have it, do over, work over, rough up, knock about/around; Brit. informal duff up, have a go at; N. Amer. informal beat up on.
■ **set someone against someone else** alienate from, estrange from; drive a wedge between, sow dissension, set at odds.
■ **set someone apart** *his ability and self-effacing modesty have set him apart:* distinguish, differentiate, mark out, single out, separate, demarcate.
■ **set something apart** *one pew was set apart from the rest:* isolate, separate, segregate, put to one side.
■ **set something aside 1** *set aside some money each month:* save, put by, put aside, put away, lay by, keep, reserve; store, stockpile, hoard, stow away, cache, withhold; informal salt away, squirrel away,

S

stash away. **2** *he set aside his cup:* put down, cast aside, discard, abandon, dispense with. **3** *set aside your differences:* disregard, put aside, ignore, forget, discount, shrug off, bury. **4** *the Appeal Court set aside the decision:* overrule, overturn, reverse, revoke, countermand, nullify, annul, cancel, quash, dismiss, reject, repudiate.

■ **set someone back** (informal). See **COST** verb sense 1.

■ **set someone/something back** *the growth of American trade unionism was set back by economic depression:* delay, hold up, hold back, slow down/up, retard, check, decelerate; hinder, impede, obstruct, hamper, inhibit, frustrate, thwart.

■ **set something down 1** *he set down his thoughts:* write down, put in writing, jot down, note down, make a note of; record, register, log. **2** *we set down a code of practice:* formulate, draw up, establish, frame; lay down, determine, fix, stipulate, specify, prescribe, impose, ordain.

■ **set something forth** *the policy paper of March 2 sets forth the core of Labour's programme:* present, describe, set out, detail, delineate, explain, expound; state, declare, announce; submit, offer, put forward, advance, propose, propound.

■ **set someone free** release, free, let go, turn loose, let out, liberate, deliver, emancipate.

■ **set in** *bad weather set in:* begin, start, arrive, come, develop.

■ **set off** *on the appointed day, we set off for Heathrow:* set out, start out, sally forth, leave, depart, embark, set sail; informal hit the road.

■ **set something off 1** *the bomb was set off:* detonate, explode, blow up, touch off, trigger; ignite. **2** *it set off a wave of protest:* give rise to, cause, lead to, set in motion, occasion, bring about, initiate, precipitate, prompt, trigger (off), spark (off), touch off, provoke, incite. **3** *the blue dress set off her auburn hair:* enhance, bring out, emphasize, show off, throw into relief; complement.

■ **set on/upon** *he and his friends were set on by a gang:* attack, assail, assault, hit, strike, beat, thrash, pummel, wallop, set about, fall on; informal lay into, lace into, let someone have it, get stuck into, work over, rough up, knock about/around; Brit. informal duff up, have a go at; N. Amer. informal beat up on, light into.

■ **set one's heart on** want desperately, wish for, desire, long for, yearn for, hanker after, ache for, hunger for, thirst for, burn for; informal be itching for, be dying for.

■ **set out 1** *he set out early.* See **SET OFF**. **2** *you've done what you set out to achieve:* aim, intend, mean, seek; hope, aspire, want.

■ **set something out 1** *the gifts were set out on tables:* arrange, lay out, put out, array, dispose, display, exhibit. **2** *they set out some guidelines:* present, set forth, detail; state,

declare, announce; submit, put forward, advance, propose, propound.

■ **set someone up 1** *his father set him up in business:* establish, finance, fund, back, subsidize. **2** (informal) *she set him up for Newley's murder:* falsely incriminate, frame, entrap; Brit. informal fit up.

■ **set something up 1** *a monument to her memory was set up:* erect, put up, construct, build, raise, elevate. **2** *she set up her own business:* establish, start, begin, initiate, institute, put in place, found, create. **3** *set up a meeting:* arrange, organize, fix (up), schedule, timetable, line up.

set² noun **1** *a set of colour postcards:* **group**, collection, series; assortment, selection, compendium, batch, number; arrangement, array. **2** *the literary set:* **clique**, coterie, circle, crowd, group, crew, band, company, ring, camp, fraternity, school, faction, league; informal gang, bunch. **3** *a chemistry set:* **kit**, apparatus, equipment, outfit. **4** *a set of cutlery:* **canteen**, box, case. **5** *a set of china:* **service**. **6** *he's in the bottom set at school:* **class**, form, group; stream, band. **7** *the set of his shoulders:* **posture**, cast, attitude; bearing, carriage. **8** *a stage set:* **scenery**, setting, backdrop, flats; mise en scène.

set³ adjective **1** *a set routine:* **fixed**, established, predetermined, hard and fast, pre-arranged, prescribed, specified, defined; unvarying, unchanging, invariable, unvaried, rigid, inflexible, cast-iron, strict, settled, predictable; routine, standard, customary, regular, usual, habitual, accustomed, wonted. **2** *she had set ideas:* **inflexible**, rigid, fixed, firm, deep-rooted, deep-seated, ingrained, entrenched. **3** *he had a set speech for such occasions:* **stock**, standard, routine, rehearsed, well worn, formulaic, conventional. **4** *I was all set for the evening:* **ready**, prepared, organized, equipped, primed; informal geared up, psyched up. **5** *he's set on marrying her:* **determined to**, intent on, bent on, hell-bent on, resolute about, insistent about. **6** *you were dead set against the idea:* **opposed to**, averse to, hostile to, resistant to, antipathetic to, unsympathetic to; informal anti.
– OPPOSITES variable, flexible, original, unprepared, uncertain.

setback noun *Alexander was faced with one setback after another:* **problem**, difficulty, hitch, complication, upset, disappointment, misfortune, mishap, reversal; blow, stumbling block, hindrance, impediment, obstruction; delay, hold-up; informal glitch, hiccup.
– OPPOSITES breakthrough.

settee noun **sofa**, couch, divan, chaise longue, chesterfield; Brit. put-you-up; N. Amer. davenport, day bed.

setting noun **1** *a rural setting:* **surroundings**, position, situation, environment, background, backdrop, milieu, environs, habitat; spot, place, location, locale, site, scene; area, region, district. **2** *a garnet in a gold setting:* **mount**, fixture, surround.

settle verb **1** *they settled the dispute:* **resolve**, sort out, solve, clear up, end, fix, work out, iron out, straighten out, set right, rectify, remedy, reconcile; informal patch up. **2** *she settled their affairs:* **put in order**, sort out, tidy up, arrange, organize, order, clear up. **3** *they settled on a date for the wedding:* **decide on**, set, fix, agree on, name, establish, arrange, appoint, designate, assign; choose, select, pick. **4** *she went down to the lobby to settle her bill:* **pay**, settle up, square, clear, defray. **5** *they settled for a 4.2% pay rise:* **accept**, agree to, assent to. **6** *he settled in London:* **make one's home**, set up home, take up residence, put down roots, establish oneself; live, move to, emigrate to. **7** *immigrants settled much of Australia:* **colonize**, occupy, inhabit, people, populate. **8** *Catherine settled down to her work:* **apply oneself to**, get down to, set about, attack; concentrate on, focus on, devote oneself to. **9** *the class wouldn't settle down:* **calm down**, quieten down, be quiet, be still; informal shut up. **10** *a brandy will settle your nerves:* **calm**, quieten, quiet, soothe, pacify, quell; sedate, tranquillize. **11** *he settled into an armchair:* **sit down**, seat oneself, install oneself, ensconce oneself, plant oneself; informal park oneself, plonk oneself. **12** *a butterfly settled on the flower:* **land**, come to rest, alight, descend, perch. **13** *sediment settles at the bottom:* **sink**, subside, fall, gravitate.
– OPPOSITES agitate, rise.

settlement noun **1** *a pay settlement:* **agreement**, deal, arrangement, resolution, bargain, understanding, pact. **2** *the settlement of the dispute:* **resolution**, settling, solution, reconciliation. **3** *a frontier settlement:* **community**, colony, outpost, encampment, post; village, commune. **4** *the settlement of the area:* **colonization**, settling, populating. **5** *the settlement of their debts:* **payment**, discharge, defrayal, liquidation, clearance.

settler noun **colonist**, colonizer, frontiersman, frontierswoman, pioneer; immigrant, newcomer, incomer; N. Amer. historical homesteader.
– OPPOSITES native.

sever verb **1** *the head was severed from the body:* **cut off**, chop off, detach, disconnect, dissever, separate, part, amputate, dock. **2** *a knife had severed the artery:* **cut (through)**, rupture, split, pierce. **3** *they severed diplomatic relations:* **break off**, discontinue, suspend, end, terminate, cease, dissolve.
– OPPOSITES join, maintain.

several adjective **1** *several people:* **some**, a number of, a few; various, assorted, sundry, diverse. **2** *they sorted out their several responsibilities:* **respective**, individual,

own, particular, specific; separate, different, disparate, distinct; various.

severe adjective **1** *severe injuries:* **acute**, very bad, serious, grave, critical, dreadful, terrible, awful; dangerous, parlous, life-threatening. **2** *severe storms:* **fierce**, violent, strong, powerful, intense; tempestuous, turbulent. **3** *a severe winter:* **harsh**, bitter, cold, bleak, freezing, icy, arctic, extreme. **4** *a severe headache:* **excruciating**, agonizing, intense, dreadful, awful, terrible, unbearable, intolerable; informal splitting, pounding. **5** *a severe test of their stamina:* **difficult**, demanding, tough, arduous, formidable, exacting, rigorous, punishing, onerous, gruelling. **6** *severe criticism:* **harsh**, scathing, sharp, strong, fierce, savage, scorching, devastating, trenchant, caustic, biting, withering. **7** *severe tax penalties:* **extortionate**, excessive, unreasonable, inordinate, outrageous, sky-high, harsh, stiff; punitive; Brit. swingeing. **8** *they received severe treatment:* **harsh**, stern, hard, inflexible, uncompromising, unrelenting, merciless, pitiless, ruthless, draconian, oppressive, repressive, punitive; brutal, cruel, savage. **9** *his severe expression:* **stern**, dour, grim, forbidding, disapproving, unsmiling, unfriendly, sombre, grave, serious, stony, steely; cold, frosty. **10** *a severe style of architecture:* **plain**, simple, austere, unadorned, unembellished, unornamented, stark, spartan, ascetic; clinical, uncluttered.
– OPPOSITES minor, gentle, mild, easy, lenient, friendly, ornate.

severely adverb **1** *he was severely injured:* **badly**, seriously, critically; fatally; formal grievously. **2** *she was severely criticized:* **sharply**, roundly, soundly, fiercely, savagely. **3** *murderers should be treated more severely:* **harshly**, strictly, sternly, rigorously, mercilessly, pitilessly, roughly, sharply; with a rod of iron; brutally, cruelly, savagely. **4** *she looked severely at Harriet:* **sternly**, grimly, dourly, disapprovingly; coldly, frostily. **5** *she dressed severely in black:* **plainly**, simply, austerely, starkly.

sew verb *she sewed the seams of the tunic:* **stitch**, tack, baste, seam, hem; embroider.
■ **sew something up** *the tear was sewn up:* darn, mend, repair, patch.

sewing noun **stitching**, needlework, needlecraft, fancy-work.

sex noun **1** *they talked about sex:* **sexual intercourse**, intercourse, lovemaking, making love, sex act, (sexual) relations; mating, copulation; informal nooky; Brit. informal bonking, rumpy pumpy, how's your father. **2** *teach your children about sex:* **the facts of life**, reproduction; informal the birds and the bees. **3** *adults of both sexes:* **gender**.
■ **have sex** have sexual intercourse, make love, sleep with, go to bed; mate, copulate; seduce, rape; informal do it, go all the way, know in the biblical sense; Brit. informal bonk;

N. Amer. informal get it on; euphemistic be intimate.

sex appeal noun *she just oozes sex appeal:* **sexiness**, seductiveness, sexual attractiveness, desirability, sensuality, sexuality; informal it, SA.

sexism noun *he admitted that the company had been accused of sexism:* **sexual discrimination**, chauvinism, prejudice, bias.

sexual adjective **1** *the sexual organs:* **reproductive**, genital, sex, procreative. **2** *sexual activity:* **carnal**, erotic. **3** *she's so sexual.* See SEXY sense 1.

sexual intercourse noun. See SEX sense 1.

sexuality noun **1** *she had a powerful sexuality:* **sensuality**, sexiness, seductiveness, desirability, eroticism, physicality; sexual appetite, passion, desire, lust. **2** *I'm open about my sexuality:* **sexual orientation**, sexual preference, leaning, persuasion; heterosexuality, homosexuality, lesbianism, bisexuality. **3** *sexuality within holy matrimony:* **sexual activity**, sexual relations, sexual intercourse, sex, procreation.

sexy adjective **1** *she's so sexy:* **sexually attractive**, seductive, desirable, alluring, sensual, sultry, slinky, provocative, tempting, tantalizing; nubile, luscious, lush; informal fanciable, beddable; Brit. informal fit; N. Amer. informal foxy, cute; Austral. informal spunky. **2** *sexy videos:* **erotic**, sexually explicit, arousing, exciting, stimulating, hot, titillating, racy, naughty, risqué, adult, X-rated; rude, pornographic, crude, lewd; informal raunchy, steamy, porno, blue, skin. **3** *they weren't feeling sexy:* **(sexually) aroused**, sexually excited, amorous, lustful, passionate; informal horny, hot, turned on, sexed up; Brit. informal randy. **4** (informal) *a sexy sales promotion:* **exciting**, stimulating, interesting, appealing, intriguing.

shabby adjective **1** *a shabby little bar:* **run down**, down at heel, scruffy, dilapidated, ramshackle, tumbledown; seedy, slummy, insalubrious, squalid, sordid; informal crummy, scuzzy, shambly; Brit. informal grotty; N. Amer. informal shacky. **2** *a shabby grey coat:* **scruffy**, old, worn out, threadbare, ragged, frayed, tattered, battered, faded, moth-eaten, mangy; informal tatty, ratty, the worse for wear; N. Amer. informal raggedy. **3** *her shabby treatment of Ben:* **contemptible**, despicable, dishonourable, discreditable, mean, low, dirty, hateful, shameful, sorry, ignoble, unfair, unworthy, unkind, shoddy, nasty; informal rotten, low-down; Brit. informal beastly.
– OPPOSITES smart, honourable.

shack noun **hut**, shanty, cabin, lean-to, shed; hovel; Scottish bothy, shieling.

shackle verb **1** *he was shackled to the wall:* **chain**, fetter, manacle; secure, tie (up), bind, tether, hobble; put in chains, clap in irons, handcuff. **2** *journalists were shackled by a new law:* **restrain**, restrict, limit, constrain, handicap, hamstring, hamper, hinder, impede, obstruct, inhibit, check, curb.

shackles plural noun **1** *the men filed through their shackles:* **chains**, fetters, irons, leg irons, manacles, handcuffs; bonds; informal cuffs, bracelets. **2** *the shackles of bureaucracy:* **restrictions**, restraints, constraints, impediments, hindrances, obstacles, barriers, obstructions, checks, curbs.

shade noun **1** *they sat in the shade:* **shadow(s)**, shadiness, shelter, cover; cool. **2** *shades of blue:* **colour**, hue, tone, tint, tinge. **3** *shades of meaning:* **nuance**, gradation, degree, difference, variation, variety; nicety, subtlety; undertone, overtone. **4** *her skirt was a shade too short:* **little**, bit, trace, touch, modicum, tinge; slightly, rather, somewhat; informal tad, smidgen. **5** *the window shade:* **blind**, curtain, screen, cover, covering; awning, canopy.
– OPPOSITES light.
verb **1** *vines shaded the garden:* **cast a shadow over**, shadow, shelter, cover, screen; darken. **2** *she shaded in the picture:* **darken**, colour in, pencil in, block in, fill in; cross-hatch. **3** *the sky shaded from turquoise to blue:* **change**, transmute, turn, go; merge, blend.
■ **put someone/something in the shade** surpass, outshine, outclass, overshadow, eclipse, transcend, cap, top, outstrip, outdo, put to shame, beat, outperform, upstage; informal run rings around, be a cut above, leave standing.
■ **shades of** echoes of, a reminder of, memories of, suggestions of, hints of.

shadow noun **1** *he saw her shadow in the doorway:* **silhouette**, outline, shape, contour, profile. **2** *he emerged from the shadows:* **shade**, darkness, twilight; gloom, murkiness. **3** *she knew without any shadow of doubt:* **trace**, scrap, shred, crumb, iota, scintilla, jot, whit, grain; informal smidgen, smidge, tad. **4** *a shadow of a smile:* **trace**, hint, suggestion, suspicion, ghost, glimmer. **5** *he's a shadow of his former self:* **inferior version**, poor imitation, apology, travesty; remnant.
verb *he is shadowing a poacher:* **follow**, trail, track, stalk, pursue, hunt; informal tail, keep tabs on.

shadowy adjective **1** *a shadowy corridor:* **dark**, dim, gloomy, murky, crepuscular, shady, shaded. **2** *a shadowy figure:* **indistinct**, hazy, indefinite, vague, nebulous, ill-defined, faint, blurred, blurry, unclear, indistinguishable, unrecognizable; ghostly, spectral, wraithlike.
– OPPOSITES bright, clear.

shady adjective **1** *a shady garden:* **shaded**, shadowy, dim, dark; sheltered, screened, shrouded; leafy. **2** (informal) *shady deals:* **suspicious**, suspect, questionable, dubious, doubtful, disreputable, untrustworthy,

S

dishonest, dishonourable, devious, underhand, unscrupulous, irregular, unethical; N. Amer. snide; informal fishy, murky; Brit. informal dodgy; Austral./NZ informal shonky.
– OPPOSITES bright, honest.

shaft noun 1 *the shaft of a golf club:* **pole**, shank, stick, rod, staff; handle, hilt, stem. 2 *shafts of sunlight:* **ray**, beam, gleam, streak, finger. 3 *a ventilation shaft:* **mineshaft**, tunnel, passage, pit, adit, downcast, upcast; borehole, bore; duct, well, flue, vent.

shaggy adjective *his shaggy beard:* **hairy**, bushy, thick, woolly; tangled, tousled, unkempt, dishevelled, untidy, matted.
– OPPOSITES sleek.

shake verb 1 *the whole building shook:* **vibrate**, tremble, quiver, quake, shiver, shudder, judder, jiggle, wobble, rock, sway; convulse. 2 *she shook the bottle:* **jiggle**, joggle, agitate; informal waggle. 3 *he shook his stick at them:* **brandish**, wave, flourish, swing, wield; informal waggle. 4 *the look in his eyes really shook her:* **upset**, distress, disturb, unsettle, disconcert, discompose, disquiet, unnerve, trouble, throw off balance, agitate, fluster; shock, alarm, frighten, scare, worry; informal rattle. 5 *this will shake their confidence:* **weaken**, undermine, damage, impair, harm; reduce, diminish, decrease.
– OPPOSITES soothe, strengthen.
noun 1 *he gave his coat a shake:* **jiggle**, joggle; informal waggle. 2 *a shake of his fist:* **flourish**, brandish, wave. 3 *it gives me the shakes:* **tremors**, delirium tremens; informal DTs, jitters, willies, heebie-jeebies, yips; Austral. informal Joe Blakes.

■ **shake someone off** *Manville thought he had shaken off his pursuer:* get away from, escape, elude, dodge, lose, leave behind, get rid of, give someone the slip, throw off the scent; Brit. informal get shot of.

■ **shake something off** *he has shaken off his back trouble:* recover from, get over; get rid of, free oneself from; Brit. informal get shot of; N. Amer. informal shuck off.

■ **shake someone/something up** 1 *the accident shook him up.* See SHAKE verb sense 4. 2 *plans to shake up the legal profession:* reorganize, restructure, revolutionize, alter, change, transform, reform, overhaul.

shaky adjective 1 *shaky legs:* **trembling**, shaking, tremulous, quivering, quivery, unsteady, wobbly, weak; tottering, tottery, teetering, doddery; informal trembly. 2 *I feel a bit shaky:* **faint**, dizzy, light-headed, giddy; weak, wobbly, quivery, groggy, muzzy; informal trembly, woozy. 3 *a shaky table:* **unsteady**, unstable, wobbly, precarious, rocky, rickety, ramshackle; Brit. informal wonky. 4 *the evidence is shaky:* **unreliable**, untrustworthy, questionable, dubious, doubtful, tenuous, suspect, flimsy, weak, unsound, unsupported, unsubstantiated, unfounded; informal iffy; Brit. informal dodgy.
– OPPOSITES steady, stable, sound.

shallow adjective *a shallow analysis*

of contemporary society: **superficial**, facile, simplistic, oversimplified; flimsy, insubstantial, lightweight, empty, trivial, trifling; surface, skin-deep; frivolous, foolish, silly.
– OPPOSITES profound.

sham noun 1 *his tenderness had been a sham:* **pretence**, fake, act, fiction, simulation, fraud, feint, lie, counterfeit; humbug. 2 *the doctor was a sham:* **charlatan**, fake, fraud, impostor, pretender; quack, mountebank; informal phoney.
adjective *sham togetherness:* **fake**, pretended, feigned, simulated, false, faux, artificial, bogus, insincere, contrived, affected, make-believe, fictitious; imitation, mock, counterfeit, fraudulent; informal pretend, put-on, phoney, pseudo; Brit. informal cod.
– OPPOSITES genuine.
verb 1 *she shams indifference:* **feign**, fake, pretend, put on, simulate, affect. 2 *was he ill or just shamming?* **pretend**, fake, dissemble; malinger; informal put it on; Brit. informal swing the lead.

shamble verb *he shambled off down the corridor:* **shuffle**, drag one's feet, lumber, totter, dodder; hobble, limp.

shambles plural noun 1 *we have to sort out this shambles:* **chaos**, mess, muddle, confusion, disorder, havoc, mare's nest; Brit. informal dog's dinner/breakfast. 2 *the room was a shambles:* **mess**, pigsty; informal disaster area; Brit. informal tip.

shambolic adjective (Brit. informal). See CHAOTIC.

shame noun 1 *her face was scarlet with shame:* **humiliation**, mortification, chagrin, ignominy, embarrassment, indignity, abashment, discomfort. 2 *I felt shame at telling a lie:* **guilt**, remorse, contrition, compunction. 3 *he brought shame on the family:* **disgrace**, dishonour, discredit, degradation, ignominy, disrepute, infamy, scandal, opprobrium, contempt. 4 *it's a shame she never married:* **pity**, misfortune, sad thing; bad luck; informal bummer, crime, sin.
– OPPOSITES pride, honour.
verb 1 *you shamed your family's name:* **disgrace**, dishonour, discredit, degrade, debase; stigmatize, taint, sully, tarnish, besmirch, blacken, drag through the mud. 2 *he was shamed in public:* **humiliate**, mortify, chagrin, embarrass, abash, chasten, humble, take down a peg or two, cut down to size; informal show up; N. Amer. informal make someone eat crow.
– OPPOSITES honour.

■ **put someone/something to shame** outshine, outclass, eclipse, surpass, excel, outstrip, outdo, put in the shade, upstage; informal run rings around, leave standing; Brit. informal knock spots off.

shamefaced adjective *Giles looked shamefaced:* **ashamed**, abashed, sheepish, guilty, conscience-stricken, guilt-ridden, contrite, sorry, remorseful, repentant,

S

penitent, regretful, rueful, apologetic; embarrassed, mortified, red-faced, chagrined, humiliated; informal with one's tail between one's legs.
– OPPOSITES unrepentant.

shameful adjective **1** *shameful behaviour:* **disgraceful**, deplorable, despicable, contemptible, dishonourable, discreditable, reprehensible, low, unworthy, ignoble, shabby; shocking, scandalous, outrageous, abominable, atrocious, appalling, vile, odious, heinous, egregious, loathsome, bad; inexcusable, unforgivable; informal low-down, hateful. **2** *a shameful secret:* **embarrassing**, mortifying, humiliating, degrading, ignominious.
– OPPOSITES admirable.

shameless adjective *his shameless hypocrisy:* **flagrant**, blatant, barefaced, overt, brazen, brash, audacious, outrageous, undisguised, unconcealed, transparent; immodest, indecorous; unabashed, unashamed, unblushing, unrepentant.
– OPPOSITES modest.

shanty noun **shack**, hut, cabin, lean-to, shed; hovel; Scottish bothy, shieling.

shape noun **1** *the shape of the dining table:* **form**, appearance, configuration, formation, structure; figure, build, physique, body; contours, lines, outline, silhouette, profile. **2** *a spirit in the shape of a fox:* **guise**, likeness, semblance, form, appearance, image. **3** *you're in pretty good shape:* **condition**, health, trim, fettle, order; Brit. informal nick.
verb **1** *the metal is shaped into tools:* **form**, fashion, make, mould, model, cast; sculpt, sculpture, carve, cut, whittle. **2** *attitudes were shaped by his report:* **determine**, form, fashion, mould, define, develop; influence, affect.
■ **shape up 1** *her work is shaping up nicely:* improve, get better, progress, show promise; develop, take shape, come on, come along. **2** *a regime to help you shape up:* get fit, get into shape, tone up; slim, lose weight.
■ **take shape** become clear, become definite, become tangible, crystallize, come together, fall into place.

shapeless adjective **1** *shapeless lumps:* **formless**, amorphous, unformed, indefinite. **2** *a shapeless dress:* **baggy**, saggy, ill-fitting, sack-like, oversized, unshapely, formless.

shapely adjective *Katherine's shapely figure was swathed in blue silk:* **well proportioned**, clean-limbed, curvaceous, voluptuous, full-figured, Junoesque; attractive, sexy; informal curvy.

shard noun *shards of glass:* **fragment**, sliver, splinter, shiver, chip, piece, bit, particle.

share noun *her share of the profits:* **portion**, part, division, quota, quantum, allowance, ration, allocation, measure, due; percentage, commission, dividend; helping, serving; informal cut, slice, rake-off; Brit. informal whack, divvy.
verb **1** *we share the bills:* **split**, divide, go halves on; informal go fifty-fifty, go Dutch. **2** *they shared out the peanuts:* **apportion**, divide up, allocate, portion out, ration out, parcel out, measure out; carve up; Brit. informal divvy up. **3** *we all share in the learning process:* **participate in**, take part in, play a part in, be involved in, contribute to, have a hand in, partake in.

sharp adjective **1** *a sharp knife:* **keen**, razor-edged; sharpened, honed. **2** *a sharp pain:* **excruciating**, agonizing, intense, stabbing, shooting, severe, acute, keen, fierce, searing; exquisite. **3** *a sharp taste:* **tangy**, piquant, strong; **acidic**, acid, sour, tart, pungent, acrid, bitter, acidulous. **4** *a sharp cry of pain:* **loud**, piercing, shrill, high-pitched, penetrating, harsh, strident, ear-splitting, deafening. **5** *a sharp wind:* **cold**, chilly, chill, brisk, keen, penetrating, biting, icy, bitter, freezing, raw; informal nippy; Brit. informal parky. **6** *sharp words:* **harsh**, bitter, cutting, scathing, caustic, barbed, trenchant, acrimonious, acerbic, sarcastic, sardonic, spiteful, venomous, malicious, vitriolic, vicious, hurtful, nasty, cruel, abrasive; informal bitchy, catty. **7** *a sharp sense of loss:* **intense**, acute, keen, strong, bitter, fierce, heartfelt, overwhelming. **8** *her nose is sharp:* **pointed**, tapering, tapered; spiky; informal pointy. **9** *the lens brings it into sharp focus:* **distinct**, clear, crisp; stark, obvious, marked, definite, pronounced. **10** *a sharp increase:* **sudden**, abrupt, rapid; steep, precipitous. **11** *a sharp corner:* **hairpin**, tight. **12** *the edge of the gully had a very sharp drop:* **steep**, sheer, abrupt, precipitous, vertical. **13** *sharp eyes:* **keen**, perceptive, observant, acute, beady, hawklike. **14** *she was sharp and witty:* **perceptive**, percipient, perspicacious, incisive, sensitive, keen, acute, quick-witted, clever, shrewd, canny, astute, intelligent, intuitive, bright, alert, smart, quick off the mark, insightful, knowing; informal on the ball, quick on the uptake, savvy; Brit. informal suss; Scottish & N. English informal pawky; N. Amer. informal heads-up.
– OPPOSITES blunt, mild, sweet, soft, kind, rounded, indistinct, gradual, slow, weak, stupid, naive.
adverb **1** *nine o'clock sharp:* **precisely**, exactly, on the dot; promptly, prompt, punctually, dead on; informal on the nose; N. Amer. informal on the button. **2** *the recession pulled people up sharp:* **abruptly**, suddenly, sharply, unexpectedly.
– OPPOSITES roughly.

sharpen verb **1** *sharpen the carving knife:* **hone**, whet, strop, grind, file. **2** *the players are sharpening up their skills:* **improve**, brush up, polish up, better, enhance; hone, fine-tune, perfect.

sharp-eyed adjective *a sharp-eyed witness contacted the police with details of a car spotted nearby:* **observant**, perceptive, eagle-eyed, hawk-eyed, keen-eyed, gimlet-

S

eyed; watchful, vigilant, alert, on the lookout; informal beady-eyed.

shatter verb 1 *the glasses shattered:* **smash**, break, splinter, crack, fracture, fragment, disintegrate, shiver; informal bust. 2 *the announcement shattered their hopes:* **destroy**, wreck, ruin, dash, crush, devastate, demolish, torpedo, scotch; informal put the kibosh on, banjax, do for, put paid to; Brit. informal scupper. 3 *we were shattered by the news:* **devastate**, shock, stun, daze, traumatize, crush, distress; informal knock sideways; Brit. informal knock for six.

shave verb 1 *he shaved his beard:* **cut off**, snip off; crop, trim, barber. 2 *shave off excess wood:* **plane**, pare, whittle, scrape. 3 *shave Parmesan over the top:* **grate**, shred. 4 *he shaved the MP's majority to 2,000:* **reduce**, cut, lessen, decrease, pare down, shrink, slim down. 5 *his shot shaved the post:* **graze**, brush, touch, glance off, kiss.

sheaf noun *a sheaf of papers:* **bundle**, bunch, stack, pile, heap, mass; Brit. informal wodge.

sheath noun 1 *put the sword in its sheath:* **scabbard**, case. 2 *the wire has a plastic sheath:* **covering**, cover, case, casing, envelope, sleeve, wrapper, capsule.

shed¹ noun *the rabbit lives in the shed:* **hut**, lean-to, outhouse, outbuilding; shack; potting shed, woodshed; Brit. lock-up.

shed² verb 1 *the trees shed their leaves:* **drop**, scatter, spill. 2 *the caterpillar shed its skin:* **slough off**, cast off, moult. 3 *we shed our jackets:* **take off**, remove, shrug off, discard, doff, climb out of, slip out of, divest oneself of; Brit. informal peel off. 4 *much blood has been shed:* **spill**, discharge. 5 *the firm is to shed ten workers:* **make redundant**, dismiss, let go, discharge, get rid of, discard; informal sack, fire, give someone their marching orders, send packing, give someone the push, boot out. 6 *they must shed their illusions:* **discard**, get rid of, dispose of, do away with, drop, abandon, jettison, scrap, cast aside, dump, reject, repudiate; informal ditch, junk, get shut of; Brit. informal get shot of. 7 *the moon shed a watery light:* **cast**, radiate, diffuse, disperse, give out.
– OPPOSITES don, hire, keep.
■ **shed tears** weep, cry, sob; lament, grieve, mourn; Scottish greet; informal blub, blubber, boohoo.

sheen noun *her hair, once so dark and lustrous, had lost its sheen:* **shine**, lustre, gloss, patina, shininess, burnish, polish, shimmer, brilliance, radiance.

sheep noun ram, ewe, lamb, wether, bellwether, tup; Austral. informal jumbuck, woolly.

sheepish adjective *Sam looked sheepish and apologetic:* **embarrassed**, uncomfortable, hangdog, self-conscious; shamefaced, ashamed, abashed, mortified, chastened, remorseful, contrite, apologetic, rueful, regretful, penitent, repentant.

sheer¹ adjective 1 *the sheer audacity of the plan:* **utter**, complete, absolute, total, pure, downright, out-and-out, arrant, thorough, thoroughgoing, patent, veritable, unmitigated, plain; Austral./NZ informal fair. 2 *a sheer drop:* **precipitous**, steep, vertical, perpendicular, abrupt, bluff, sharp. 3 *a sheer dress:* **diaphanous**, gauzy, filmy, floaty, gossamer, thin, translucent, transparent, see-through, insubstantial.
– OPPOSITES gradual, thick.

sheer² verb 1 *the boat sheered off along the coast:* **swerve**, veer, slew, skew, swing, change course. 2 *her mind sheered away from his image:* **turn away**, flinch, recoil, shy away; avoid.

sheet noun 1 *she changed the sheets:* **bed linen**, linen, bedclothes. 2 *a sheet of ice:* **layer**, stratum, covering, blanket, coating, coat, film, skin. 3 *a sheet of glass:* **pane**, panel, piece, plate; slab. 4 *she put a fresh sheet of paper in the printer:* **piece**, leaf, page, folio. 5 *a sheet of ice:* **expanse**, area, stretch, sweep.

shelf noun 1 *the plant on the shelf:* **ledge**, sill, bracket, rack; mantelpiece; shelving. 2 *the waters above the shelf:* **sandbank**, sandbar, bank, bar, reef, shoal.
■ **on the shelf** unmarried, single, unattached; lonely, unloved, neglected.

shell noun 1 *a crab shell:* **carapace**, exterior; armour. 2 *peanut shells:* **pod**, husk, hull, casing, case, covering, integument; N. Amer. shuck. 3 *shells passing overhead:* **projectile**, bomb, explosive; grenade; bullet, cartridge. 4 *the metal shell of the car:* **framework**, frame, chassis, skeleton; hull, exterior.
verb 1 *they were shelling peas:* **hull**, pod, husk; N. Amer. shuck. 2 *rebel artillery shelled the city:* **bombard**, fire on, shoot at, attack, bomb, blitz, strafe.

shellfish noun crustacean, bivalve, mollusc.

shelter noun 1 *the trees provide shelter for animals:* **protection**, cover, screening, shade; safety, security, refuge, sanctuary, asylum. 2 *a shelter for abandoned cats:* **sanctuary**, refuge, home, haven, safe house; harbour, port in a storm.
– OPPOSITES exposure.
verb 1 *the hut sheltered him from the wind:* **protect**, shield, screen, cover, shade, save, safeguard, preserve, defend, cushion, guard, insulate. 2 *the anchorage where the convoy sheltered:* **take shelter**, take refuge, seek sanctuary, take cover; informal hole up.
– OPPOSITES expose.

sheltered adjective 1 *a sheltered stretch of water:* **protected**, screened, shielded, covered; shady; cosy. 2 *she led a sheltered life:* **secluded**, cloistered, isolated, protected, withdrawn, sequestered, reclusive; privileged, secure, safe, quiet.

shelve verb *plans to reopen the school have been shelved:* **postpone**, put off, delay, defer, put back, reschedule, hold over/off, put to

S

one side, suspend, stay, keep in abeyance, mothball; abandon, drop, give up, stop, cancel, jettison, axe; N. Amer. put over, table, take a rain check on; informal put on ice, put on the back burner, ditch, dump, junk.
– OPPOSITES execute.

shepherd verb *we shepherded them away:* **usher**, steer, herd, lead, take, escort, guide, conduct, marshal, walk; show, see, chaperone.

shield noun *a shield against dirt:* **protection**, guard, defence, cover, screen, security, shelter, safeguard, protector.
verb *he shielded his eyes:* **protect**, cover, screen, shade; save, safeguard, preserve, defend, secure, guard; cushion, insulate.
– OPPOSITES expose.

shift verb **1** *he shifted some chairs:* **move**, carry, transfer, transport, convey, lug, haul, fetch, switch, relocate, reposition, rearrange; informal cart. **2** *she shifted her position:* **change**, alter, adjust, vary; modify, revise, reverse, retract; do a U-turn. **3** *the cargo has shifted:* **move**, slide, slip, be displaced. **4** *the wind shifted:* **veer**, alter, change, turn, swing round. **5** (Brit.) *this brush really shifts the dirt:* **get rid of**, remove, get off, budge, lift, expunge.
– OPPOSITES keep.
noun **1** *the southward shift of people:* **movement**, move, transference, transport, transposition, relocation. **2** *a shift in public opinion:* **change**, alteration, adjustment, amendment, variation, modification, revision, reversal, retraction, U-turn; Brit. about-turn. **3** *they worked three shifts:* **stint**, stretch, spell of work. **4** *the night shift went home:* **workers**, crew, gang, team, squad, patrol.
■ **shift for oneself** *the least and the most able were left to shift for themselves:* cope, manage, survive, make it, fend for oneself, take care of oneself, make do, get by/along, scrape by/along, muddle through; stand on one's own two feet; informal make out.

shiftless adjective *he thought the whole family shiftless and dishonest:* **lazy**, idle, indolent, slothful, lethargic, lackadaisical; spiritless, apathetic, feckless, good-for-nothing, worthless; unambitious, unenterprising.

shifty adjective (informal) *he had a shifty look about him:* **devious**, evasive, slippery, duplicitous, false, deceitful, underhand, untrustworthy, dishonest, shady, wily, crafty, tricky, sneaky, treacherous, artful, sly, scheming; N. Amer. snide; Brit. informal dodgy; Austral./NZ informal shonky.
– OPPOSITES honest.

shilly-shally verb *the government shilly-shallied about the matter:* **dither**, be indecisive, be irresolute, vacillate, waver, hesitate, blow hot and cold, falter, drag one's feet; Brit. haver, hum and haw; Scottish swither; informal dilly-dally.

shimmer verb *the lake shimmered:* **glint**,

glisten, twinkle, sparkle, flash, scintillate, gleam, glow, glimmer, glitter, wink.
noun *the shimmer of lights from the traffic:* **glint**, twinkle, sparkle, flash, gleam, glow, glimmer, lustre, glitter.

shin verb *he shinned up a tree:* **climb**, clamber, scramble, swarm, shoot, go; mount, ascend, scale; descend; N. Amer. shinny.

shine verb **1** *the sun shone:* **emit light**, beam, radiate, gleam, glow, glint, glimmer, sparkle, twinkle, glitter, glisten, shimmer, flash, flare, glare, fluoresce, luminesce. **2** *she shone his shoes:* **polish**, burnish, buff, wax, gloss, rub up. **3** *they shone at university:* **excel**, be outstanding, be brilliant, be successful, stand out.
noun **1** *the shine of the moon on her face:* **light**, brightness, gleam, glow, glint, glimmer, sparkle, twinkle, glitter, glisten, shimmer, beam, glare, radiance, illumination, luminescence, luminosity, incandescence. **2** *linseed oil restores the shine:* **polish**, burnish, gleam, gloss, lustre, sheen, patina.

shining adjective **1** *a shining expanse of water:* **gleaming**, bright, brilliant, illuminated, lustrous, glowing, glinting, sparkling, twinkling, glittering, glistening, shimmering, dazzling, luminous, luminescent, incandescent. **2** *a shining face:* **glowing**, beaming, radiant, happy. **3** *shining chromium tubes:* **shiny**, bright, polished, gleaming, glossy, glassy, sheeny, lustrous.
■ **a shining example** *a shining example of British enterprise:* paragon, model, epitome, archetype, ideal, exemplar, nonpareil, paradigm, quintessence, the crème de la crème, the beau idéal, acme, jewel, flower, treasure; informal one in a million, the bee's knees.

shiny adjective *a shiny red mackintosh:* **glossy**, glassy, bright, polished, gleaming, satiny, sheeny, lustrous.
– OPPOSITES matt.

ship noun **boat**, vessel, craft.

shirk verb **1** *she didn't shirk any task:* **evade**, dodge, avoid, get out of, sidestep, shrink from, shun, slide out of, skip, miss; neglect; informal duck (out of), cop out of; Brit. informal skive off; N. Amer. informal cut; Austral./NZ informal duck-shove. **2** *no one shirked:* **avoid one's duty**, be remiss, be negligent, play truant; Brit. informal skive (off), swing the lead, scrimshank, slack off; N. Amer. informal goof off, play hookey.

shirker noun **dodger**, truant, absentee, layabout, loafer, idler; informal slacker; Brit. informal skiver.

shiver¹ verb *she was shivering with fear:* **tremble**, quiver, shake, shudder, quaver, quake.
noun *she gave a shiver as the door opened:* **tremble**, quiver, shake, shudder, quaver, quake, tremor, twitch.

shiver² noun *a shiver of glass:* **splinter**, sliver,

S

shard, fragment, chip, shaving, smithereen, particle, bit, piece.

shivery adjective **trembling**, trembly, quivery, shaky, shuddering, shuddery, quavery, quaking; cold, chilly.

shoal noun *three ships ran aground on the shoal:* **sandbank**, bank, mudbank, bar, sandbar, tombolo, shelf, cay.

shock[1] noun **1** *the news came as a shock:* **blow**, upset, disturbance; surprise, revelation, a bolt from the blue, thunderbolt, bombshell, rude awakening, eye-opener; informal whammy. **2** *you gave me a shock:* **fright**, scare, jolt, start; informal turn. **3** *she was suffering from shock:* **trauma**, traumatism, prostration; collapse, breakdown. **4** *the first shock of the earthquake:* **vibration**, reverberation, shake, jolt, jar, jerk; impact, blow.
verb *the murder shocked the nation:* **appal**, horrify, outrage, revolt, disgust, nauseate, sicken; traumatize, distress, upset, disturb, disquiet, unsettle; stun, rock, stagger, astound, astonish, amaze, startle, surprise, dumbfound, shake, take aback, throw, unnerve.

shock[2] noun *a shock of red hair:* **mass**, mane, mop, thatch, head, crop, bush, frizz, tangle, cascade, halo.

shocking adjective *it was the next day before they heard the shocking news:* **appalling**, horrifying, horrific, dreadful, awful, frightful, terrible; scandalous, outrageous, disgraceful, vile, abominable, abhorrent, atrocious; odious, repugnant, disgusting, nauseating, sickening, loathsome; distressing, upsetting, disturbing, disquieting, unsettling; staggering, amazing, astonishing, startling, surprising.

shoddy adjective **1** *shoddy goods:* **poor-quality**, inferior, second-rate, third-rate, cheap, cheapjack, trashy, jerry-built; informal tacky, rubbishy, junky; Brit. informal duff, rubbish. **2** *shoddy workmanship:* **careless**, slapdash, sloppy, slipshod, scrappy, crude; negligent, cursory.
– OPPOSITES quality, careful.

shoemaker noun **cobbler**, bootmaker, clogger; Scottish & N. English souter.

shoot verb **1** *they shot him in the street:* **gun down**, mow down, hit, wound, injure; put a bullet in, pick off, bag, fell, kill; informal pot, blast, pump full of lead, plug. **2** *they shot at the enemy:* **fire**, open fire, aim, snipe, let fly; bombard, shell. **3** *faster than a gun can shoot bullets:* **discharge**, fire, launch, loose off, let fly, emit. **4** *a car shot past:* **race**, speed, flash, dash, dart, rush, hurtle, streak, whizz, go like lightning, go hell for leather, zoom, charge; career, sweep, fly, wing; informal belt, scoot, scorch, tear, zip, whip, step on it, burn rubber; Brit. informal bomb, bucket, shift; N. Amer. informal clip, hightail it, barrel. **5** *the plant failed to shoot:* **sprout**, bud, burgeon, germinate. **6** *the film was shot*

in Tunisia: **film**, photograph, take, snap, capture, record; televise, video.
noun *nip off the new shoots:* **sprout**, bud, offshoot, scion, sucker, spear, runner, tendril, sprig.

shop noun **1** *a shop selling clothes:* **store**, (retail) outlet, boutique, cash and carry, emporium, department store, supermarket, hypermarket, superstore, chain store, concession, market, mart, trading post; N. Amer. minimart. **2** *he works in the machine shop:* **workshop**, workroom, plant, factory, works, industrial unit, mill, foundry, yard.
verb *he was shopping for spices:* **go to the shops**; buy, purchase, get, acquire, obtain, pick up, snap up, procure, stock up on; humorous indulge in retail therapy.

shopkeeper noun **shop-owner**, shop manager, vendor, retailer, dealer, seller, trader, wholesaler, salesperson, tradesman, distributor; N. Amer. storekeeper.

shopper noun **buyer**, purchaser, customer, consumer, client, patron.

shopping centre noun **shopping precinct**, (shopping) mall, (shopping) arcade, galleria, parade; marketplace, mart; N. Amer. plaza.

shore[1] noun *he swam out from the shore:* **seashore**, beach, foreshore, sand(s), shoreline, waterside, front, coast, seaboard.

shore[2] verb *we had to shore up the building:* **prop up**, hold up, bolster, support, brace, buttress, strengthen, fortify, reinforce, underpin.

short adjective **1** *a short piece of string:* **small**, little, tiny; informal teeny. **2** *short people:* **small**, little, petite, tiny, diminutive, stubby, elfin, dwarfish, midget, pygmy, Lilliputian, minuscule, miniature; Scottish wee; informal pint-sized, teeny, knee-high to a grasshopper. **3** *a short report:* **concise**, brief, succinct, compact, summary, economical, crisp, pithy, epigrammatic, laconic, thumbnail, abridged, abbreviated, condensed, synoptic, summarized, contracted, truncated. **4** *a short time:* **brief**, momentary, temporary, short-lived, impermanent, cursory, fleeting, passing, fugitive, lightning, transitory, transient, ephemeral, quick. **5** *money is a bit short:* **scarce**, in short supply, scant, meagre, sparse, insufficient, deficient, inadequate, lacking, wanting. **6** *he was rather short with her:* **curt**, sharp, abrupt, blunt, brusque, terse, offhand, gruff, surly, testy, rude, uncivil; informal snappy.
– OPPOSITES long, tall, plentiful, courteous.
adverb *she stopped short:* **abruptly**, suddenly, sharply, all of a sudden, all at once, unexpectedly, without warning, out of the blue.
■ **in short** briefly, in a word, in a nutshell, in precis, in essence, to come to the point; in conclusion, in summary, to sum up.
■ **short of 1** *we are short of nurses:* deficient in, lacking, wanting, in need of, low on, short on, missing; informal strapped for, pushed for,

minus. **2** *short of searching everyone, there is nothing we can do:* apart from, other than, aside from, besides, except (for), excepting, without, excluding, not counting, save (for).

shortage noun *the shortage of people with adequate training:* **scarcity**, sparseness, sparsity, dearth, paucity, poverty, insufficiency, deficiency, inadequacy, famine, lack, want, deficit, shortfall, rarity.
– OPPOSITES abundance.

shortcoming noun *he was fully aware of his own shortcomings:* **defect**, fault, flaw, imperfection, deficiency, limitation, failing, drawback, weakness, weak point, foible, frailty, vice.
– OPPOSITES strength.

shorten verb *you can shorten your essay without losing its balance:* **make shorter**, abbreviate, abridge, condense, precis, synopsize, contract, compress, reduce, shrink, diminish, cut (down), dock, trim, crop, pare down, prune, curtail, truncate.
– OPPOSITES extend.

short-lived adjective *this was a short-lived setback:* **brief**, short, momentary, temporary, impermanent, cursory, fleeting, passing, fugitive, lightning, transitory, transient, ephemeral, quick.

shortly adverb **1** *she will be with you shortly:* **soon**, presently, in a little while, at any moment, in a minute, in next to no time, before long, by and by; N. Amer. momentarily; informal anon, any time now, pretty soon, before one can say Jack Robinson, in a jiffy; Brit. informal in a mo, sharpish. **2** *'I know,' he replied shortly:* **curtly**, sharply, abruptly, bluntly, brusquely, tersely, gruffly, snappily, testily, rudely.

short-sighted adjective **1** *I'm a little short-sighted:* **myopic**, near-sighted; informal as blind as a bat. **2** *short-sighted critics:* **narrow-minded**, unimaginative, improvident, small-minded, insular, parochial, provincial.
– OPPOSITES long-sighted, imaginative.

short-staffed adjective *we're rather short-staffed around Christmas:* **understaffed**, short-handed, undermanned, below strength.

short-tempered adjective *she was short-tempered with him:* **irritable**, irascible, hot-tempered, quick-tempered, snappish, fiery, touchy, volatile; cross, crabby, crotchety, cantankerous, grumpy, ill-tempered, bad-tempered, testy, tetchy, prickly, choleric; informal snappy, chippy, grouchy, cranky, on a short fuse; Brit. informal narky, ratty, eggy, like a bear with a sore head; N. Amer. informal soreheaded.
– OPPOSITES placid.

shot[1] noun **1** *a shot rang out:* report of a gun, crack, bang, blast; (**shots**) gunfire. **2** *the cannon have run out of shot:* **bullets**, cannonballs, pellets, ammunition. **3** *a winning shot:* **stroke**, hit, strike; kick, throw,

pitch, lob. **4** *Mike was an excellent shot:* **marksman**, markswoman, shooter. **5** *a shot of us on holiday:* **photograph**, photo, snap, snapshot, picture, print, slide, still; Brit. enprint. **6** *tetanus shots:* **injection**, inoculation, immunization, vaccination, booster; informal jab.
■ **a shot in the dark** (wild) guess, surmise, supposition, conjecture, speculation.
■ **like a shot** (informal) without hesitation, unhesitatingly, eagerly, enthusiastically; immediately, at once, right away/now, straight away, instantly, instantaneously, without delay; informal in/like a flash, before one can say Jack Robinson.

shot[2] adjective *shot silk:* **variegated**, mottled; multicoloured, varicoloured; iridescent, opalescent.

shoulder verb **1** *Britain shouldered the primary responsibility:* **take on (oneself)**, undertake, accept, assume; bear, carry. **2** *another lad shouldered him aside:* **push**, shove, thrust, jostle, force, bulldoze, bundle.
■ **give someone the cold shoulder** snub, shun, cold-shoulder, ignore, cut (dead), rebuff, spurn, ostracize; informal give someone the brush-off, freeze out; Brit. informal give someone send to Coventry; N. Amer. informal give someone the brush.
■ **put one's shoulder to the wheel** get (down) to work, apply oneself, set to work, buckle down, roll up one's sleeves; work hard, be diligent, be industrious, exert oneself.
■ **shoulder to shoulder 1** *the regiment lined up shoulder to shoulder:* side by side, abreast, alongside (each other). **2** *he fought shoulder to shoulder with the others:* united, (working) together, jointly, in partnership, in collaboration, in cooperation, side by side, in alliance.

shout verb *'Help,' he shouted:* **yell**, cry (out), call (out), roar, howl, bellow, bawl, call at the top of one's voice, clamour, shriek, scream; raise one's voice, vociferate; informal holler.
– OPPOSITES whisper.
noun *a shout of pain:* **yell**, cry, call, roar, howl, bellow, bawl, clamour, vociferation, shriek, scream; informal holler.

shove verb **1** *she shoved him back into the chair:* **push**, thrust, propel, drive, force, ram, knock, elbow, shoulder; jostle, bundle, hustle, manhandle. **2** *she shoved past him:* **push (one's way)**, force one's way, barge (one's way), elbow (one's way), shoulder one's way.
noun *a hefty shove:* **push**, thrust, bump, jolt.

shovel noun *a pick and shovel:* **spade**; Austral./NZ banjo.
verb *shovelling snow:* **scoop (up)**, dig, excavate.

show verb **1** *the stitches do not show:* **be visible**, be seen, be in view, be obvious. **2** *he wouldn't show the picture:* **display**, exhibit, put on show/display, put on view, parade, uncover, reveal. **3** *Frank showed*

his frustration: **manifest**, exhibit, reveal, convey, communicate, make known; express, proclaim, make plain, make obvious, disclose, betray. **4** *I'll show you how to make a daisy chain:* **demonstrate**, explain, describe, illustrate; teach, instruct, give instructions. **5** *recent events show this to be true:* **prove**, demonstrate, confirm, show beyond doubt; substantiate, corroborate, verify, establish, attest, certify, testify, bear out. **6** *a young woman showed them to their seats:* **escort**, accompany, take, conduct, lead, usher, guide, direct, steer, shepherd.
– OPPOSITES conceal.
noun **1** *a spectacular show of bluebells:* **display**, array, exhibition, presentation, exposition, spectacle. **2** *the motor show:* **exhibition**, exposition, fair, extravaganza, spectacle; N. Amer. exhibit. **3** *they took in a show:* **(theatrical) performance**, musical, play. **4** *she's only doing it for show:* **appearance**, display, impression, ostentation, image. **5** *Drew made a show of looking busy:* **pretence**, outward appearance, (false) front, guise, semblance, pose, parade. **6** (informal) *I don't run the show:* **undertaking**, affair, operation, proceedings, enterprise, business, venture.
■ **show off** (informal) *he was showing off, trying to make a really big impression:* behave affectedly, put on airs, put on an act, swagger around, swank, strut, strike an attitude, posture; draw attention to oneself; N. Amer. informal cop an attitude.
■ **show something off** *the easel was commonly used to show off a painting:* display, show to advantage, exhibit, demonstrate, parade, draw attention to, flaunt.
■ **show up** *cancers show up on X-rays:* be visible, be obvious, be seen, be revealed.
■ **show someone/something up 1** *the sun showed up the shabbiness of the room:* expose, reveal, make visible, make obvious, highlight. **2** (informal) *they showed him up in front of his friends.* See HUMILIATE.

showdown noun *the government was contemplating a future showdown with the miners:* **confrontation**, clash, face-off.

shower noun **1** *a shower of rain:* **(light) fall**, drizzle, sprinkling, mizzle. **2** *a shower of arrows:* **volley**, hail, salvo, bombardment, barrage, fusillade, cannonade. **3** *a shower of awards:* **avalanche**, deluge, flood, spate, flurry; profusion, abundance, plethora.
verb **1** *confetti showered down on us:* **rain**, fall, hail. **2** *she showered them with gifts:* **deluge**, flood, inundate, swamp, engulf; overwhelm, overload, snow under. **3** *showering honours on his cronies:* **lavish**, heap, bestow freely.

showing noun **1** *another showing of the series:* **presentation**, broadcast, airing, televising. **2** *the party's present showing:* **performance**, (track) record, results, success, achievement.

showman noun **1** *a travelling showman:* **impresario**, stage manager; ringmaster, host, compère, master of ceremonies, MC; presenter; N. Amer. informal emcee. **2** *he is a great showman:* **entertainer**, performer, virtuoso.

show-off noun (informal) *he was a show-off with a big, flashy car:* **exhibitionist**, extrovert, poser, poseur, peacock, swaggerer, self-publicist; informal pseud.

showy adjective *showy costume jewellery:* **ostentatious**, conspicuous, pretentious, flamboyant, gaudy, garish, brash, vulgar, loud, extravagant, fancy, ornate, over-elaborate, kitsch; informal flash, flashy, glitzy, ritzy, swanky; N. Amer. informal superfly.
– OPPOSITES restrained.

shred noun **1** *her dress was torn to shreds:* **tatter**, scrap, strip, ribbon, rag, fragment, sliver, (tiny) bit/piece. **2** *not a shred of evidence:* **scrap**, bit, speck, iota, particle, ounce, whit, jot, crumb, morsel, fragment, grain, drop, trace, scintilla, spot; informal smidgen.
verb *shredding vegetables:* **chop finely**, cut up, tear up, grate, mince, macerate, grind.

shrew noun *Matilda has the reputation of being a shrew:* **virago**, dragon, termagant, fishwife, witch, tartar, hag; informal battleaxe, old bag, old bat.

shrewd adjective *a shrewd businessman:* **astute**, sharp-witted, sharp, smart, acute, intelligent, clever, canny, perceptive, perspicacious, sagacious, wise; informal on the ball, savvy; N. Amer. informal heads-up.
– OPPOSITES stupid.

shrewdness noun **astuteness**, sharp-wittedness, acuteness, acumen, acuity, intelligence, cleverness, smartness, wit, canniness, common sense, discernment, insight, understanding, perception, perceptiveness, perspicacity, perspicaciousness, discrimination, sagacity, sageness; informal nous, horse sense, savvy.

shriek verb *she shrieked with laughter:* **scream**, screech, squeal, squawk, roar, howl, shout, yelp; informal holler.
noun *a shriek of laughter:* **scream**, screech, squeal, squawk, roar, howl, shout, yelp; informal holler.

shrill adjective *a shrill scream rent the air:* **high-pitched**, piercing, high, sharp, ear-piercing, ear-splitting, penetrating, screeching, shrieking, screechy.

shrine noun **1** *the shrine of St James:* **holy place**, temple, church, chapel, tabernacle, sanctuary, sanctum. **2** *a shrine to the Beatles:* **memorial**, monument.

shrink verb **1** *the number of competitors shrank:* **get smaller**, become/grow smaller, contract, diminish, lessen, reduce, decrease, dwindle, decline, fall off, drop off. **2** *he shrank back against the wall:* **draw back**, recoil, back away, retreat, withdraw, cringe, cower, quail. **3** *he doesn't shrink from naming*

names: **recoil**, shy away, demur, flinch, have scruples, have misgivings, have qualms, be loath, be reluctant, be unwilling, be averse, fight shy of, be hesitant, be afraid, hesitate, baulk at.
– OPPOSITES expand, increase.

shrivel verb *full sun is likely to shrivel the leaves:* **wither**, shrink; wilt; dry up, desiccate, dehydrate, parch, frazzle.

shroud noun **1** *the Turin Shroud:* **winding sheet**; historical cerements. **2** *a shroud of mist | a shroud of secrecy:* **covering**, cover, cloak, mantle, blanket, layer, cloud, veil.
verb *a mist shrouded the jetties:* **cover**, envelop, veil, cloak, blanket, screen, conceal, hide, mask, obscure.

shrub noun **bush**, woody plant.

shrug
■ **shrug something off** *he shrugged off suggestions that he was keen to quit politics:* disregard, dismiss, take no notice of, ignore, pay no heed to, play down, make light of.

shudder verb *she shuddered at the thought:* **shake**, shiver, tremble, quiver, vibrate, palpitate.
noun *a shudder racked his body:* **shake**, shiver, tremor, tremble, trembling, quiver, quivering, vibration, palpitation.

shuffle verb **1** *they shuffled along the passage:* **shamble**, drag one's feet, totter, dodder. **2** *she shuffled her feet:* **scrape**, drag, scuffle, scuff. **3** *he shuffled the cards:* **mix (up)**, mingle, rearrange, jumble.

shun verb *he was shunned in public by his former colleagues:* **avoid**, evade, eschew, steer clear of, shy away from, fight shy of, keep one's distance from, give a wide berth to, have nothing to do with; snub, give someone the cold shoulder, cold-shoulder, ignore, cut (dead), look right through; reject, rebuff, spurn, ostracize; informal give someone the brush-off, freeze out, stiff-arm; Brit. informal send to Coventry; N. Amer. informal give someone the bum's rush, give someone the brush.
– OPPOSITES welcome.

shut verb *please shut the door:* **close**, pull/push to, slam, fasten; put the lid on, bar, lock, secure.
– OPPOSITES open, unlock.
■ **shut down** *the factory has shut down:* cease activity, close (down), cease operating, cease trading, be shut (down); informal fold.
■ **shut someone/something in** *she pushed the dogs into the room and shut them in:* confine, enclose, impound, shut up, pen (in/up), fence in, immure, lock up/in, cage, imprison, intern, incarcerate; N. Amer. corral.
■ **shut someone/something out 1** *he shut me out of the house:* lock out, keep out, refuse entrance to. **2** *she shut out the memories:* block, suppress. **3** *the bamboo shut out the light:* keep out, block out, screen, veil.
■ **shut up** (informal) be quiet, keep quiet, hold one's tongue, keep one's lips sealed; stop

talking, quieten (down); informal keep mum, button it, cut the cackle, shut it, shut your face/mouth/trap, belt up, put a sock in it, give it a rest; Brit. informal shut your gob; N. Amer. informal save it.
■ **shut someone/something up 1** *I haven't shut the hens up yet.* See SHUT SOMEONE/SOMETHING IN. **2** (informal) *that should shut them up:* quieten (down), silence, hush, shush, quiet, gag, muzzle.

shuttle verb *minibuses shuttle between the centre and the car park:* **ply**, run, commute, go/travel back and forth, go/travel to and fro; ferry.

shy adjective *I was painfully shy:* **bashful**, diffident, timid, sheepish, reserved, reticent, introverted, retiring, self-effacing, withdrawn, timorous, mousy, nervous, insecure, unconfident, inhibited, repressed, self-conscious, embarrassed.
– OPPOSITES confident.
■ **shy away from** *don't shy away from saying what you think:* flinch, demur, recoil, hang back, have scruples, have misgivings, have qualms, be chary, be diffident, be bashful, fight shy, be coy; be loath, be reluctant, be unwilling, be disinclined, be hesitant, hesitate, baulk at; informal boggle at.

shyness noun **bashfulness**, diffidence, sheepishness, reserve, reservedness, introversion, reticence, timidity, timidness, timorousness, mousiness, lack of confidence, inhibitedness, self-consciousness, embarrassment, coyness, demureness.

sibling noun brother, sister; Zoology sib.

sick adjective **1** *the children are sick:* **ill**, unwell, poorly, ailing, indisposed, not oneself; Brit. off colour; informal laid up, under the weather; Austral./NZ informal crook. **2** *he was feeling sick:* **nauseous**, nauseated, queasy, bilious, green about the gills; seasick, carsick, airsick, travel-sick; informal about to throw up. **3** *I'm sick of this music:* **fed up**, bored, tired, weary. **4** (informal) *a sick joke:* **macabre**, black, ghoulish, morbid, perverted, gruesome, sadistic, cruel.
– OPPOSITES well.
■ **be sick** (Brit.) vomit, throw up, retch, heave, gag; informal chunder, chuck up, hurl, spew, keck; Brit. informal honk; N. Amer. informal spit up, barf, upchuck, toss one's cookies.

sicken verb **1** *the stench sickened him:* **cause to feel sick/nauseous**, make sick, turn someone's stomach, revolt, disgust; informal make someone want to throw up; N. Amer. informal gross out. **2** *she sickened and died:* **become ill**, fall ill, be taken ill/sick, catch something. **3** *I'm sickening for something:* **become ill with**, fall ill with, be taken ill with, show symptoms of, develop, come down with; Brit. go down with; N. Amer. informal take sick with.
– OPPOSITES recover.

sickening adjective *there were some sickening photographs of the dead boys:*

S

nauseating, stomach-turning, stomach-churning, repulsive, revolting, disgusting, repellent, repugnant, appalling, obnoxious, nauseous, vile, nasty, foul, loathsome, offensive, objectionable, off-putting, distasteful, obscene, gruesome, grisly; N. Amer. vomitous; informal gross.

sickly adjective **1** *a sickly child:* **unhealthy**, in poor health, delicate, frail, weak. **2** *sickly faces:* **pale**, wan, pasty, sallow, pallid, ashen, anaemic. **3** *a sickly green:* **insipid**, pale, light, light-coloured, washed out, faded. **4** *sickly love songs:* **sentimental**, mawkish, cloying, sugary, syrupy, saccharine; informal mushy, slushy, schmaltzy, weepy, lovey-dovey, corny; Brit. informal soppy; N. Amer. informal cornball, sappy, hokey, three-hankie.
– OPPOSITES healthy.

sickness noun **1** *she was absent through sickness:* **illness**, disease, ailment, complaint, infection, malady, infirmity, indisposition; informal bug, virus; Brit. informal lurgy; Austral. informal wog. **2** *a wave of sickness:* **nausea**, biliousness, queasiness. **3** *he suffered sickness and diarrhoea:* **vomiting**, retching, gagging; travel-sickness, seasickness, carsickness, airsickness, motion sickness; informal throwing up, puking.

side noun **1** *the side of the road:* **edge**, border, verge, boundary, margin, fringe(s), flank, bank, perimeter, extremity, periphery, (outer) limit, limits, bounds. **2** *the wrong side of the road:* **half**, part; carriageway, lane. **3** *the east side of the city:* **district**, quarter, area, region, part, neighbourhood, sector, section, zone, ward. **4** *one side of the paper:* **surface**, face, plane. **5** *his side of the argument:* **point of view**, viewpoint, perspective, opinion, way of thinking, standpoint, position, outlook, slant, angle. **6** *the losing side in the war:* **faction**, camp, bloc, party, wing. **7** *the players in their side:* **team**, squad, line-up. **8** (Brit. informal) *there's absolutely no side about her.* See **AFFECTATION** sense 1.
– OPPOSITES centre, end.
adjective **1** *elaborate side pieces:* **lateral**, wing, flanking. **2** *a side issue:* **subordinate**, lesser, lower-level, secondary, minor, peripheral, incidental, ancillary, subsidiary, of little account, extraneous.
– OPPOSITES front, central.
verb *siding with the underdog.* See **TAKE SOMEONE'S SIDE**.
■ **side by side 1** *they cycled along side by side:* **alongside** (each other), beside each other, abreast, shoulder to shoulder, close together. **2** *most transactions proceed side by side:* at (one and) the same time, simultaneously, contemporaneously.
■ **take someone's side** support, take someone's part, side with, be on someone's side, stand by, back, give someone one's backing, be loyal to, defend, champion, ally (oneself) with, sympathize with, favour.

sideline noun *he founded the company as a*

sideline: **secondary occupation**, second job; hobby, leisure activity/pursuit, recreation.
■ **on the sidelines** without taking part, without getting involved.

sidelong adjective *a sidelong glance:* **indirect**, oblique, sideways, sideward; surreptitious, furtive, covert, sly.
– OPPOSITES overt.
adverb *he looked sidelong at her:* **indirectly**, obliquely, sideways, out of the corner of one's eye; surreptitiously, furtively, covertly, slyly.

sidestep verb *he neatly sidestepped the questions about crime:* **avoid**, evade, dodge, circumvent, skirt round, bypass; informal duck.

sidetrack verb *he allows himself to be constantly sidetracked by minor problems:* **distract**, divert, deflect, draw away.

sideways adverb **1** *I slid off sideways:* **to the side**, laterally. **2** *the expansion slots are mounted sideways:* **edgewise**, sidewards, side first, edgeways, end on. **3** *he looked sideways at her.* See **SIDELONG** adverb.
adjective **1** *sideways force:* **lateral**, sideward, on the side, side to side. **2** *a sideways look.* See **SIDELONG** adjective.

sidle verb *she sidled into the room apologetically:* **creep**, sneak, slink, slip, slide, steal, edge, inch, move furtively.

siege noun **blockade**, encirclement.
– OPPOSITES relief.

siesta noun *after lunch they would take a siesta:* **afternoon sleep**, nap, catnap, doze, rest; informal snooze, lie-down, forty winks, a bit of shut-eye; Brit. informal kip.

sieve noun *use a sieve to strain the mixture:* **strainer**, sifter, filter, riddle, screen.
verb **1** *sieve the mixture into a bowl:* **strain**, sift, screen, filter, riddle. **2** *the coins were sieved from the ash:* **separate out**, filter out, sift, sort out, divide, segregate, extract.

sift verb **1** *sift the flour into a large bowl:* **sieve**, strain, screen, filter, riddle. **2** *we sift out unsuitable applications:* **separate out**, filter out, sort out, put to one side, weed out, get rid of, remove. **3** *investigators are sifting through the wreckage:* **search through**, look through, examine, inspect, scrutinize, pore over, investigate, analyse, dissect, review.

sigh verb **1** *she sighed with relief:* **breathe out**, exhale; groan, moan. **2** *the wind sighed in the trees:* **rustle**, whisper, murmur, sough. **3** *he sighed for days gone by:* **yearn**, long, pine, ache, grieve, cry for/over, weep for/over, rue, miss, mourn, lament, hanker for/after.

sight noun **1** *she has excellent sight:* **eyesight**, vision, eyes, faculty of sight, visual perception. **2** *her first sight of it:* **view**, glimpse, glance, look. **3** *within sight of the enemy:* **range of vision**, field of vision, view. **4** *historic sights:* **landmark**, place of interest, monument, spectacle, view, marvel, wonder. **5** (informal) *I must look a sight:*

eyesore, spectacle, mess; informal fright.
verb *one of the helicopters sighted wreckage:*
glimpse, catch/get a glimpse of, catch sight
of, see, spot, spy, notice, observe.
■ **catch sight of** glimpse, catch/get a
glimpse of, see, spot, spy, make out, pick
out, sight, have sight of.
■ **set one's sights on** aspire to, aim at/for,
try for, strive for/towards, work towards.

sightseer noun **1** *sightseers to the city:*
tourist, visitor, tripper, holidaymaker;
Brit. informal grockle. **2** *gawping sightseers:*
busybody, gawker; informal rubberneck; Brit.
informal gawper.

sign noun **1** *a sign of affection:* **indication**,
signal, symptom, pointer, suggestion,
intimation, mark, manifestation,
demonstration, token, evidence. **2** *a sign
of things to come:* **portent**, omen, warning,
forewarning, augury, presage; promise,
threat. **3** *at his sign the soldiers followed:*
gesture, signal, wave, gesticulation, cue,
nod. **4** *signs saying 'keep out':* **notice**,
signpost, signboard, warning sign, road
sign, traffic sign. **5** *the dancers were daubed
with signs:* **symbol**, mark, cipher, letter,
character, figure, hieroglyph, ideogram,
rune, emblem, device, logo.
verb **1** *he signed the letter:* **autograph**,
endorse, initial, countersign. **2** *the
government signed the agreement:* **endorse**,
validate, certify, authenticate, sanction,
authorize; agree to, approve, ratify, adopt,
give one's approval to; informal give something
the go-ahead, give something the green
light, give something the thumbs up. **3** *he
signed his name:* **write**, inscribe, pen. **4** *we
have signed a new player:* **recruit**, hire,
engage, employ, take on, appoint, sign
on/up, enlist. **5** *she signed to Susan to leave:*
gesture, signal, give a sign to, motion; wave,
beckon, nod.
■ **sign on/up** *he signed on for a career in the
Air Force:* enlist, take a job, join (up), enrol,
register, volunteer.
■ **sign someone on/up.** See SIGN verb sense
4.
■ **sign something over** *they have signed
over ownership of the animals to the RSPCA:*
transfer, make over, hand over, bequeath,
pass on, transmit, cede.

signal¹ noun **1** *a signal to stop:* **gesture**,
sign, wave, gesticulation, cue, indication,
warning, motion. **2** *a clear signal that the
company is in trouble:* **indication**, sign,
symptom, hint, pointer, intimation, clue,
demonstration, evidence, proof. **3** *the
encroaching dark is a signal for people to
emerge:* **cue**, prompt, impetus, stimulus;
informal go-ahead.
verb **1** *the driver signalled to her to cross:*
gesture, sign, give a sign to, direct,
motion; wave, beckon, nod. **2** *they signalled
displeasure by refusing to cooperate:*
indicate, show, express, communicate,
proclaim, declare. **3** *his death signals the*

end of an era: **mark**, signify, mean, be a sign
of, be evidence of, herald.

signal² adjective *although a signal failure,
the campaign produced one benefit:*
notable, noteworthy, remarkable,
striking, glaring, significant, momentous,
memorable, unforgettable, obvious, special,
extraordinary, exceptional, conspicuous.

significance noun **1** *a matter of considerable
significance:* **importance**, import,
consequence, seriousness, gravity, weight,
magnitude, momentousness; formal moment.
2 *the significance of his remarks:* **meaning**,
sense, signification, import, thrust, drift,
gist, implication, message, essence,
substance, point.

significant adjective **1** *a significant increase:*
notable, noteworthy, worthy of attention,
remarkable, important, of importance, of
consequence; serious, crucial, weighty,
momentous, uncommon, unusual, rare,
extraordinary, exceptional, special. **2** *a
significant look:* **meaningful**, expressive,
eloquent, suggestive, knowing, telling.

significantly adverb **1** *significantly better:*
notably, remarkably, outstandingly,
importantly, crucially, materially,
appreciably, markedly, considerably,
obviously, conspicuously, strikingly,
signally. **2** *he paused significantly:*
meaningfully, expressively, eloquently,
revealingly, suggestively, knowingly.

signify verb **1** *this signified a fundamental
change:* **be evidence of**, be a sign of,
mark, signal, mean, spell, be symptomatic
of, herald, indicate. **2** *the egg signifies
life:* **mean**, denote, designate, represent,
symbolize, stand for. **3** *signify your
agreement by signing below:* **express**,
indicate, show, proclaim, declare. **4** *the
locked door doesn't signify:* **mean anything**,
be of importance, be important, be
significant, be of significance, be of account,
count, matter, be relevant.

silence noun **1** *the silence of the night:*
quietness, quiet, quietude, still, stillness,
hush, tranquillity, noiselessness,
soundlessness, peacefulness, peace
(and quiet). **2** *she was reduced to
silence:* **speechlessness**, wordlessness,
dumbness, muteness, taciturnity.
3 *the politicians kept their silence:*
secretiveness, secrecy, reticence,
taciturnity, uncommunicativeness.
– OPPOSITES sound.
verb **1** *he silenced her with a kiss:* **quieten**,
quiet, hush, shush; gag, muzzle, censor.
2 *silencing outside noises:* **muffle**, deaden,
soften, mute, smother, dampen, damp down,
mask, suppress, reduce. **3** *this would silence
their complaints:* **stop**, put an end to, put a
stop to.

silent adjective **1** *the night was silent:*
completely quiet, still, hushed, inaudible,
noiseless, soundless. **2** *the right to remain
silent:* **speechless**, quiet, unspeaking,

S

dumb, mute, taciturn, uncommunicative, tight-lipped; informal mum. **3** *silent thanks:* **unspoken**, wordless, unsaid, unexpressed, unvoiced, tacit, implicit, understood.
– OPPOSITES audible, noisy.

silently adverb **1** *Nancy crept silently up the stairs:* **quietly**, inaudibly, noiselessly, soundlessly, in silence. **2** *they drove on silently:* **without a word**, saying nothing, in silence. **3** *I silently said goodbye:* **without words**, wordlessly, in one's head, tacitly, implicitly.
– OPPOSITES audibly, out loud.

silhouette noun *the silhouette of the dome:* **outline**, contour(s), profile, form, shape, figure, shadow.
verb *the castle was silhouetted against the sky:* **outline**, delineate, define; stand out.

silky adjective *she had long, silky hair:* **smooth**, soft, sleek, fine, glossy, satiny, silken.

silly adjective **1** *don't be so silly:* **foolish**, stupid, unintelligent, idiotic, brainless, mindless, witless, imbecilic, doltish; imprudent, thoughtless, rash, reckless, foolhardy, irresponsible; mad, scatterbrained, feather-brained; frivolous, giddy, inane, immature, childish, puerile, empty-headed; informal crazy, dotty, scatty, loopy, screwy, thick, thickheaded, birdbrained, pea-brained, dopey, dim, dim-witted, half-witted, dippy, blockheaded, boneheaded, lamebrained; Brit. informal daft, divvy; N. Amer. informal chowderheaded. **2** *that was a silly thing to do:* **unwise**, imprudent, thoughtless, foolish, stupid, idiotic, senseless, mindless; rash, reckless, foolhardy, irresponsible, injudicious, misguided, irrational; informal crazy; Brit. informal daft. **3** *he would brood about silly things:* **trivial**, trifling, frivolous, footling, petty, small, insignificant, unimportant; informal piffling, piddling; N. Amer. informal small-bore. **4** *he drank himself silly:* **senseless**, insensible, unconscious, stupid, into a stupor, into senselessness, stupefied.
– OPPOSITES sensible.

silt noun *the flooding brought more silt:* **sediment**, deposit, alluvium, mud.
verb *the harbour had silted up:* **become blocked**, become clogged, fill up (with silt).

silver noun **1** *freshly polished silver:* **silverware**, (silver) plate; cutlery, {knives, forks, and spoons}. **2** *a handful of silver:* **coins**, coinage, specie; (small) change, loose change. **3** *she won three silvers:* **silver medal**, second prize.
adjective **1** *silver hair:* **grey**, greyish, white. **2** *the silver water:* **silvery**, shining, lustrous, gleaming.

similar adjective **1** *you two are very similar:* **alike**, (much) the same, indistinguishable, almost identical, homogeneous; informal much of a muchness. **2** *northern India and similar areas:* **comparable**, like, corresponding, homogeneous, equivalent, analogous.

3 *other parts were similar to Wales:* **like**, much the same as, comparable to.
– OPPOSITES different, unlike.
▪ **be similar to** resemble, look like, have the appearance of.

similarity noun *the similarity between him and his daughter was startling:* **resemblance**, likeness, sameness, similitude, comparability, correspondence, parallel, equivalence, homogeneity, indistinguishability, uniformity.

similarly adverb *The diaries of politicians tend to be self-justificatory. Similarly, autobiographies may be idealized.* **likewise**, in similar fashion, in like manner, comparably, correspondingly, uniformly, indistinguishably, analogously, homogeneously, equivalently, in the same way, the same, identically.

similitude noun. See SIMILARITY.

simmer verb **1** *the soup was simmering on the stove:* **boil gently**, cook gently, bubble. **2** *she was simmering with resentment:* **be furious**, be enraged, be angry, be incensed, be infuriated, seethe, fume, smoulder; informal be steamed up, be hot under the collar.
▪ **simmer down** *he stormed out of the theatre in a rage, but soon simmered down:* become less angry, cool off/down, be placated, control oneself, become calmer, calm down, become quieter, quieten down.

simper verb *she simpered, looking pleased with herself:* **smile affectedly**, smile coquettishly, look coy.

simple adjective **1** *it's really pretty simple:* **straightforward**, easy, uncomplicated, uninvolved, effortless, painless, undemanding, elementary, child's play; informal as easy as falling off a log, as easy as pie, as easy as ABC, a piece of cake, a cinch, no sweat, a doddle, a pushover, money for old rope, kids' stuff, a breeze, low-hanging fruit; Brit. informal easy-peasy, a doss; N. Amer. informal duck soup, a snap; Austral./NZ informal a bludge, a snack. **2** *simple language:* **clear**, plain, straightforward, intelligible, comprehensible, uncomplicated, in words of one syllable, accessible; informal user-friendly. **3** *a simple white blouse:* **plain**, unadorned, undecorated, unembellished, unornamented, unelaborate, basic, unsophisticated, no-frills; classic, understated, uncluttered, restrained. **4** *the simple truth:* **candid**, frank, honest, sincere, plain, absolute, unqualified, bald, stark, unadorned, unvarnished, unembellished. **5** *simple country people:* **unpretentious**, unsophisticated, ordinary, unaffected, unassuming, natural, honest-to-goodness; N. Amer. cracker-barrel. **6** *he's a bit simple:* **having learning difficulties**, having special (educational) needs; of low intelligence, simple-minded, unintelligent, backward, (mentally) retarded. **7** *simple chemical substances:* **non-compound**, non-complex,

uncombined, unblended, unalloyed, pure, single.
– OPPOSITES difficult, complex, fancy, compound.

simpleton noun. See FOOL noun sense 1.

simplicity noun 1 *the simplicity of the recipes:* **straightforwardness**, ease, easiness, simpleness, effortlessness. 2 *the simplicity of the language:* **clarity**, clearness, plainness, simpleness, intelligibility, comprehensibility, understandability, straightforwardness, accessibility. 3 *the building's simplicity:* **plainness**, lack/absence of adornment, lack/absence of decoration, austerity, spareness, clean lines. 4 *the simplicity of their lifestyle:* **unpretentiousness**, ordinariness, lack of sophistication, lack of affectation, naturalness.

simplify verb *the government intends to simplify the existing legislation:* **make simple/simpler**, make easy/easier to understand, make plainer, clarify, make more comprehensible/intelligible; paraphrase, put in words of one syllable.
– OPPOSITES complicate.

simplistic adjective *the proposed solutions are far too simplistic:* **facile**, superficial, oversimple, oversimplified; shallow, jejune, naive; N. Amer. informal dime-store.

simply adverb 1 *he spoke simply and forcefully:* **straightforwardly**, directly, clearly, plainly, intelligibly, lucidly, unambiguously. 2 *she was dressed simply:* **plainly**, without adornment, without decoration, without ornament/ornamentation, soberly, unfussily, unelaborately, classically. 3 *they lived simply:* **unpretentiously**, modestly, quietly. 4 *they are welcomed simply because they have plenty of money:* **merely**, just, purely, solely, only. 5 *Mrs Marks was simply livid:* **utterly**, absolutely, completely, positively, really; informal plain. 6 *it's simply the best thing ever written:* **without doubt**, unquestionably, undeniably, incontrovertibly, certainly, categorically.

simulate verb 1 *they simulated pleasure:* **feign**, pretend, fake, sham, affect, put on, give the appearance of. 2 *simulating conditions in space:* **imitate**, reproduce, replicate, duplicate, mimic.

simulated adjective 1 *simulated fear:* **feigned**, fake, mock, affected, sham, insincere, false, faux, bogus; informal pretend, put-on, phoney. 2 *simulated leather:* **artificial**, imitation, fake, mock, synthetic, man-made, ersatz.
– OPPOSITES real.

simultaneous adjective *officers carried out simultaneous raids on homes across the city:* **concurrent**, happening at the same time, contemporaneous, concomitant, coinciding, coincident, synchronous, synchronized.

simultaneously adverb *Alison and Frank*

spoke simultaneously: **at (one and) the same time**, at the same instant/moment, at once, concurrently, concomitantly; (all) together, in unison, in concert, in chorus.

sin noun 1 *a sin in the eyes of God:* **immoral act**, wrong, wrongdoing, act of evil/wickedness, transgression, crime, offence, misdeed, misdemeanour. 2 *the human capacity for sin:* **wickedness**, wrongdoing, wrong, evil, evil-doing, sinfulness, immorality, iniquity, vice, crime. 3 (informal) *wasting money—it's a sin:* **scandal**, crime, disgrace, outrage.
– OPPOSITES virtue.
verb *I have sinned:* **commit a sin**, commit an offence, transgress, do wrong, commit a crime, break the law, misbehave, go astray.

sincere adjective 1 *our sincere gratitude:* **heartfelt**, wholehearted, profound, deep; genuine, real, unfeigned, unaffected, true, honest, bona fide. 2 *a sincere person:* **honest**, genuine, truthful, unhypocritical, straightforward, direct, frank, candid; informal straight, upfront, on the level; N. Amer. informal on the up and up.

sincerely adverb *I sincerely hope that this scheme will succeed:* **genuinely**, honestly, really, truly, truthfully, wholeheartedly, earnestly, fervently.

sincerity noun **honesty**, genuineness, truthfulness, integrity, probity, trustworthiness; straightforwardness, openness, candour, candidness.

sinewy adjective *he was tall, blonde and sinewy:* **muscular**, muscly, brawny, powerfully built, burly, strapping, sturdy, rugged, strong, powerful, athletic, muscle-bound; informal hunky, beefy.
– OPPOSITES puny.

sinful adjective 1 *sinful conduct:* **immoral**, wicked, (morally) wrong, wrongful, evil, bad, iniquitous, corrupt, criminal, nefarious, depraved, degenerate; rare peccable. 2 *a sinful waste of money:* **reprehensible**, scandalous, disgraceful, deplorable, shameful, criminal.
– OPPOSITES virtuous.

sinfulness noun **immorality**, wickedness, sin, wrongdoing, evil, evil-doing, iniquitousness, corruption, depravity, degeneracy, vice.
– OPPOSITES virtue.

sing verb 1 *Miguelito began to sing:* **croon**, carol, trill, troll, chant, intone, chorus. 2 *the birds were singing:* **warble**, trill, chirp, chirrup, cheep, peep. 3 *he sang out a greeting:* **call (out)**, cry (out), shout, yell; informal holler.

singe verb *the fire singed my sleeve:* **scorch**, burn, sear, char.

singer noun **vocalist**, soloist, songster, songstress, cantor.

single adjective 1 *a single red rose:* **one (only)**, sole, lone, solitary, by itself/oneself, unaccompanied, alone. 2 *she wrote down*

S

every single word: **individual**, separate, distinct, particular. **3** *is she single?* **unmarried**, unwed, unwedded, unattached, free, a bachelor, a spinster.
– OPPOSITES double, married.
■ **single someone/something out** *the prime minister singled him out for promotion:* select, pick out, choose, decide on; target, earmark, mark out, separate out, set apart.

single-handed adverb *he's been running the place single-handed:* **by oneself**, alone, on one's own, solo, unaided, unassisted, without help.

single-minded adjective *I've never met anyone so ambitious and single-minded:* **determined**, committed, unswerving, unwavering, resolute, purposeful, devoted, dedicated, uncompromising, tireless, tenacious, persistent, indefatigable, dogged.
– OPPOSITES half-hearted.

singly adverb *we should interview people singly and discreetly:* **one by one**, one at a time, one after the other, individually, separately, by oneself, on one's own.
– OPPOSITES together.

singular adjective **1** *the gallery's singular capacity to attract sponsors:* **remarkable**, extraordinary, exceptional, outstanding, signal, notable, noteworthy; rare, unique, unparalleled, unprecedented, amazing, astonishing, phenomenal, astounding; informal fantastic, terrific. **2** *why was Betty behaving in so singular a fashion?* **strange**, unusual, odd, peculiar, funny, curious, extraordinary, bizarre, eccentric, weird, queer, unexpected, unfamiliar, abnormal, atypical, unconventional, out of the ordinary, untypical, puzzling, mysterious, perplexing, baffling, unaccountable.

singularity noun **1** *the singularity of their concerns:* **uniqueness**, distinctiveness. **2** *his singularities:* **idiosyncrasy**, quirk, foible, peculiarity, oddity, eccentricity.

singularly adverb. See EXTREMELY.

sinister adjective **1** *there was a sinister undertone in his words:* **menacing**, threatening, ominous, forbidding, baleful, frightening, alarming, disturbing, disquieting, dark, black. **2** *a sinister motive:* **evil**, wicked, criminal, corrupt, nefarious, villainous, base, vile, malevolent, malicious; informal shady.
– OPPOSITES innocent.

sink verb **1** *the coffin sank below the waves:* **become submerged**, be engulfed, go down, drop, fall, descend. **2** *the cruise liner sank yesterday:* **founder**, go under, submerge. **3** *they sank their ships:* **scuttle**, send to the bottom; Brit. informal scupper. **4** *the announcement sank hopes of a recovery:* **destroy**, ruin, wreck, put an end to, demolish, smash, shatter, dash; informal put the kibosh on, put paid to; Brit. informal scupper. **5** *they agreed to sink their differences:* **ignore**,

overlook, disregard, forget, put aside, set aside, bury. **6** *I sank myself in student life:* **immerse**, plunge, lose, bury. **7** *the plane sank towards the airstrip:* **descend**, drop, go down/downwards. **8** *the sun was sinking:* **set**, go down/downwards. **9** *Loretta sank into an armchair:* **lower oneself**, flop, collapse, drop down, slump; informal plonk oneself. **10** *her voice sank to a whisper:* **fall**, drop, become/get quieter, become/get softer. **11** *she would never sink to your level:* **stoop**, lower oneself, descend. **12** *sink the pots into the ground:* **embed**, insert, drive, plant. **13** *sinking a gold mine:* **dig**, excavate, bore, drill. **14** *they sank their life savings in the company:* **invest**, venture, risk.
– OPPOSITES float, rise.
noun *he washed himself at the sink:* **basin**, washbasin, handbasin.
■ **sink in** *Peter read the letter twice before its meaning sank in:* register, be understood, be comprehended, be grasped, get through.

sinless adjective *she was asleep, looking as careless and sinless as a child:* **innocent**, pure, virtuous, as pure as the driven snow, uncorrupted, faultless, blameless, guiltless, immaculate.
– OPPOSITES wicked.

sinner noun **wrongdoer**, evil-doer, transgressor, miscreant, offender, criminal.

sinuous adjective **1** *a sinuous river:* **winding**, windy, serpentine, curving, twisting, meandering, snaking, zigzag, curling, coiling. **2** *sinuous grace:* **lithe**, supple, agile, graceful, loose-limbed, limber, lissom.

sip verb *Amanda sipped her coffee:* **drink slowly**.
noun *a sip of whisky:* **mouthful**, swallow, drink, drop, dram, nip; informal swig.

siren noun **1** *an air-raid siren:* **alarm**, warning bell, danger signal. **2** *the siren's allure:* **seductress**, temptress, femme fatale; flirt, coquette; informal mantrap, vamp.

sissy (informal) noun *he's a real sissy.* See DRIP noun sense 2.
adjective *don't be so sissy:* **cowardly**, weak, feeble, spineless, effeminate, effete, unmanly; informal wet, weedy, wimpish, wimpy.

sister noun **1** *I have two sisters:* **female sibling**. **2** *our European sisters:* **comrade**, partner, colleague. **3** *the sisters in the convent:* **nun**, novice, abbess, prioress.

sit verb **1** *you'd better sit down:* **take a seat**, seat oneself, be seated, perch, ensconce oneself, plump oneself, flop; informal take the load/weight off one's feet, plonk oneself; Brit. informal take a pew. **2** *she sat the package on the table:* **put (down)**, place, set (down), lay, deposit, rest, stand; informal stick, bung, dump, park, plonk. **3** *she sat for Picasso:* **pose**, model. **4** *a hotel sitting on the bank of the River Dee:* **be situated**, be located, be sited, stand. **5** *the committee sits on*

Saturday: **be in session**, meet, be convened.
6 *women jurists sit on the tribunal.* **serve on**,
have a seat on, be a member of.
– OPPOSITES stand.
■ **sit back** *sit back and enjoy the music:* relax,
unwind, lie back; informal let it all hang out,
veg out; N. Amer. informal hang loose, chill out.
■ **sit in for** *the group sat in for the house
band:* stand in for, fill in for, cover for,
substitute for, deputize for; informal sub for.
■ **sit in on** *I sat in on a training session
for therapists:* attend, be present at, be an
observer at, observe; N. Amer. audit.
■ **sit tight** (informal) **1** *just sit tight:* stay put,
wait there, remain in one's place. **2** *we're
advising our clients to sit tight:* take no
action, wait, hold back, bide one's time;
informal hold one's horses.

site noun *the site of the battle:* **location**, place,
position, situation, locality, whereabouts.
verb *bins sited at police stations:* **place**, put,
position, situate, locate.

sitting noun *all-night sittings:* **session**,
meeting, assembly; hearing.
adjective *a sitting position:* **sedentary**, seated.
– OPPOSITES standing.

sitting room noun **living room**, lounge,
front room, drawing room, reception room,
family room.

situate verb *hypermarkets are usually
situated on the outskirts of towns:* **locate**,
site, position, place, station, build.

situation noun **1** *their financial situation:*
circumstances, (state of) affairs, state,
condition. **2** *I'll fill you in on the situation:*
the facts, how things stand, the lie of the
land, what's going on; Brit. the state of play;
N. Amer. the lay of the land; informal the score.
3 *the hotel's pleasant situation:* **location**,
position, spot, site, setting, environment.
4 *he was offered a situation in America:* **job**,
post, position, appointment; employment.

size noun *the room was of medium size:*
dimensions, measurements, proportions,
magnitude, largeness, bigness, area,
expanse; breadth, width, length, height,
depth; immensity, hugeness, vastness.
verb *the drills are sized in millimetres:* **sort**,
categorize, classify.

sizeable adjective *sizeable sums of money:*
fairly large, substantial, considerable,
respectable, significant, largish, biggish,
goodly.
– OPPOSITES small.

sizzle verb *slabs of bacon sizzled in the pan:*
crackle, frizzle, sputter, spit.

skeletal adjective **1** *a skeletal man:*
emaciated, very thin, as thin as a rake,
cadaverous, skin-and-bones, skinny, bony,
gaunt; informal anorexic. **2** *a skeletal account:*
lacking in detail, incomplete, outline,
fragmentary, sketchy; thumbnail.
– OPPOSITES fat, detailed.

skeleton noun **1** *the human skeleton:* **bones**.

2 *she was no more than a skeleton:* **skin
and bone**; informal bag of bones. **3** *a concrete
skeleton:* **framework**, frame, shell. **4** *the
skeleton of a report:* **outline**, (rough) draft,
abstract, (bare) bones.
adjective *a skeleton staff:* **minimum**,
minimal, basic; essential.

sketch noun **1** *a sketch of the proposed design:*
(preliminary) drawing, outline; diagram,
design, plan; informal rough. **2** *she gave a
rough sketch of what had happened:* **outline**,
brief description, rundown, main points,
thumbnail sketch, (bare) bones; summary,
synopsis, summarization, precis, résumé;
N. Amer. wrap-up. **3** *a biographical sketch:*
description, portrait, profile, portrayal,
depiction. **4** *a hilarious sketch:* **skit**, scene,
piece, act, item, routine.
verb **1** *he sketched the garden:* **draw**, make a
drawing of, draw a picture of, pencil, rough
out, outline. **2** *the company sketched out its
plans:* **describe**, outline, give a brief idea of,
rough out; summarize, precis.

sketchily adverb *the idea is only sketchily
outlined in the prologue:* **perfunctorily**,
cursorily, incompletely, patchily, vaguely,
imprecisely; hastily, hurriedly.

sketchy adjective *he has only provided sketchy
details:* **incomplete**, patchy, fragmentary,
cursory, perfunctory, scanty, vague,
imprecise; hurried, hasty.
– OPPOSITES detailed.

skilful adjective *he was also a skilful
diplomat:* **expert**, accomplished, skilled,
masterly, master, virtuoso, consummate,
proficient, talented, gifted, adept, adroit,
deft, dexterous, able, good, competent,
capable, brilliant, handy; informal mean,
wicked, crack, ace, wizard; N. Amer. informal
crackerjack.

skill noun **1** *his skill as a politician:* **expertise**,
skilfulness, expertness, adeptness,
adroitness, deftness, dexterity, ability,
prowess, mastery, competence, capability,
aptitude, artistry, virtuosity, talent.
2 *bringing up a family gives you many skills:*
accomplishment, strength, gift.
– OPPOSITES incompetence.

skilled adjective *skilled engineers:*
experienced, trained, qualified, proficient,
practised, accomplished, expert, skilful,
talented, gifted, adept, adroit, deft,
dexterous, able, good, competent; informal
crack; N. Amer. informal crackerjack.
– OPPOSITES inexperienced.

skim verb **1** *skim off the scum:* **remove**, cream
off, scoop off. **2** *the boat skimmed over the
water:* **glide**, move lightly, slide, sail, skate,
float. **3** *he skimmed the pebble across the
water:* **throw**, toss, cast, pitch; bounce. **4** *she
skimmed through the newspaper:* **glance**,
flick, flip, leaf, thumb, read quickly, scan,
run one's eye over. **5** *Hannah skimmed over
this part of the story:* **mention briefly**, pass
over quickly, skate over, gloss over.
– OPPOSITES elaborate on.

S

skimp verb **1** *don't skimp on the quantity:* **stint on**, scrimp on, economize on, cut back on, be sparing, be frugal, be mean, be parsimonious, cut corners; informal be stingy, be mingy, be tight. **2** *the process cannot be skimped:* **do hastily**, do carelessly.

skimpy adjective **1** *a skimpy black dress:* **revealing**, short, low, low-cut; flimsy, thin, see-through, indecent. **2** *my information is rather skimpy:* **meagre**, scanty, sketchy, limited, paltry, deficient, sparse.

skin noun **1** *these chemicals could damage the skin:* **epidermis**, dermis, derma. **2** *Mary's fair skin:* **complexion**, colouring, skin colour/tone, pigmentation. **3** *leopard skins:* **hide**, pelt, fleece. **4** *a banana skin:* **peel**, rind, integument. **5** *milk with a skin on it:* **film**, layer, membrane. **6** *the plane's skin was damaged:* **casing**, exterior.
verb **1** *skin the tomatoes:* **peel**, pare, hull. **2** *he skinned his knee:* **graze**, scrape, abrade, bark, rub something raw, chafe; Medicine excoriate.
■ **by the skin of one's teeth** (only) just, narrowly, by a hair's breadth, by a very small margin; informal by a whisker.

skin-deep adjective *their left-wing attitudes were only skin-deep:* **superficial**, (on the) surface, external, outward, shallow.

skinny adjective. See THIN adjective sense 3.

skip verb **1** *skipping down the path:* **caper**, prance, trip, dance, bound, bounce, gambol, frisk, romp, cavort. **2** *we skipped the boring stuff:* **omit**, leave out, miss out, dispense with, pass over, skim over, disregard; informal give something a miss. **3** *I skipped school:* **play truant from**, miss; N. Amer. cut; Brit. informal skive off; N. Amer. informal play hookey from; Austral./NZ informal play the wag from. **4** *I skipped through the magazine:* **have a quick look at**, flick through, flip through, leaf through.

skirmish noun **1** *the unit was caught up in a skirmish:* **fight**, battle, clash, conflict, encounter, engagement, fray, combat. **2** *there was a skirmish over the budget:* **argument**, quarrel, squabble, contretemps, disagreement, difference of opinion, falling-out, dispute, clash, altercation; informal tiff, spat; Brit. informal row, barney, ding-dong.
verb *they skirmished with enemy soldiers:* **fight**, (do) battle with, engage with, close with, combat, clash with.

skirt verb **1** *he skirted the city:* **go round**, walk round, circle. **2** *the fields that skirt the highway:* **border**, edge, flank, line, lie alongside. **3** *he carefully skirted round the subject:* **avoid**, evade, sidestep, dodge, pass over, gloss over; informal duck; Austral./NZ informal duck-shove.

skit noun *an old vaudeville skit:* **comedy sketch**, comedy act, parody, pastiche, burlesque, satire, pasquinade; informal spoof, take-off, send-up.

skittish adjective **1** *she grew increasingly skittish:* **playful**, lively, high-spirited, sportive, frisky. **2** *his horse was skittish:* **restive**, excitable, nervous, skittery, jumpy, highly strung.

skulduggery noun *there is no evidence to support any allegations of skulduggery:* **trickery**, fraudulence, sharp practice, underhandedness, chicanery; informal shenanigans, funny business, monkey business; Brit. informal monkey tricks, jiggery-pokery; N. Amer. informal monkeyshines.

skulk verb *he spent most of his time skulking about in the corridors:* **lurk**, loiter, hide; creep, sneak, slink, prowl, pussyfoot.

slab noun *slabs of concrete:* **piece**, block, hunk, chunk, lump; cake, tablet, brick.

slack adjective **1** *the rope went slack:* **loose**, limp, hanging, flexible. **2** *slack skin:* **flaccid**, flabby, loose, sagging, saggy. **3** *business is slack:* **sluggish**, slow, quiet, slow-moving, flat, depressed, stagnant. **4** *slack accounting procedures:* **lax**, negligent, remiss, careless, slapdash, slipshod, lackadaisical, inefficient, casual; informal sloppy, slap-happy.
– OPPOSITES tight, taut.
noun **1** *the rope had some slack in it:* **looseness**, play, give. **2** *foreign demand will help pick up the slack:* **surplus**, excess, residue, spare capacity. **3** *a little slack in the daily routine:* **lull**, pause, respite, break, hiatus, breathing space; informal let-up, breather.
verb **1** *the horse slacked his pace:* **reduce**, lessen, slacken, slow. **2** (Brit. informal) *no slacking!* **idle**, shirk, be lazy, be indolent, waste time, lounge about; Brit. informal skive; N. Amer. informal goof off.
■ **slack off 1** *the rain has slacked off:* **decrease**, subside, let up, ease off, abate, diminish, die down, fall off. **2** *slack off a bit!* relax, take things easy, let up, ease up/off, loosen up, slow down; N. Amer. informal hang loose, chill out.
■ **slack up** *the horse slacked up:* **slow (down)**, decelerate, reduce speed.

slacken verb **1** *he slackened his grip:* **loosen**, release, relax, loose, lessen, weaken. **2** *he slackened his pace:* **slow (down)**, become/get/make slower, decelerate, slack (up). **3** *the rain is slackening:* **decrease**, lessen, subside, ease up/off, let up, abate, slack off, diminish, die down, fall off.
– OPPOSITES tighten.

slacker noun (informal). See LAYABOUT.

slake verb *slake your thirst with a citron pressé:* **quench**, satisfy, sate, satiate, relieve, assuage.

slam verb **1** *he slammed the door behind him:* **bang**, shut/close with a bang, shut/close noisily, shut/close with force. **2** *the car slammed into a lamp post:* **crash into**, smash into, collide with, hit, strike, ram, plough into, run into, bump into; N. Amer. impact.

slander noun *he could sue us for slander:* **defamation (of character)**, character assassination, calumny, libel;

scandalmongering, malicious gossip, disparagement, denigration, aspersions, vilification, traducement, obloquy; lie, slur, smear, false accusation; informal mud-slinging, bad-mouthing.
verb *they were accused of slandering the minister:* **defame (someone's character)**, blacken someone's name, tell lies about, speak ill/evil of, sully someone's reputation, libel, smear, cast aspersions on, spread scandal about, besmirch, tarnish, taint; malign, traduce, vilify, disparage, denigrate, run down; N. Amer. slur.

slanderous adjective *you have no right to make such slanderous accusations:* **defamatory**, denigratory, disparaging, libellous, pejorative, false, misrepresentative, scurrilous, scandalous, malicious, abusive, insulting; informal mud-slinging.
– OPPOSITES complimentary.

slang noun **informal language**, colloquialisms, patois, argot, cant.

slant verb **1** *the floor was slanting:* **slope**, tilt, incline, be at an angle, tip, cant, lean, dip, pitch, shelve, list, bank. **2** *their findings were slanted in our favour:* **bias**, distort, twist, skew, weight, give a bias to.
noun 1 *the slant of the roof:* **slope**, incline, tilt, gradient, pitch, angle, cant, camber, inclination. **2** *a feminist slant:* **point of view**, viewpoint, standpoint, stance, angle, perspective, approach, view, attitude, position; bias, leaning.

slanting adjective *the slanting angle of the deck:* **oblique**, sloping, at an angle, on an incline, inclined, tilting, tilted, slanted, aslant, diagonal, canted, cambered.

slap verb **1** *he slapped her hard:* **hit**, strike, smack, clout, cuff, thump, punch, spank; informal whack, thwack, wallop, biff, bash; Brit. informal slosh; N. Amer. informal boff, slug, bust; Austral./NZ informal dong, quilt. **2** *he slapped down a £10 note:* **fling**, throw, toss, slam, bang; informal plonk. **3** *slap on a coat of paint:* **daub**, plaster, spread.
noun *a slap across the cheek:* **smack**, blow, thump, cuff, clout, punch, spank; informal whack, thwack, wallop, clip, biff, bash.
■ **a slap in the face** rebuff, rejection, snub, insult, put-down, humiliation.
■ **a slap on the back** congratulations, commendation, approbation, approval, accolades, compliments, tributes, a pat on the back, praise, acclaim, acclamation.
■ **a slap on the wrist** reprimand, rebuke, reproof, scolding, admonishment; informal telling-off, rap over the knuckles, dressing-down; Brit. informal ticking-off, wigging; Austral./NZ informal serve.

slapdash adjective *he gave a slapdash performance:* **careless**, slipshod, hurried, haphazard, unsystematic, untidy, messy, hit-or-miss, negligent, neglectful, lax; informal sloppy, slap-happy; Brit. informal shambolic.
– OPPOSITES meticulous.

slash verb *her tyres had been slashed:* **cut (open)**, gash, slit, split open, lacerate, knife, make an incision in.
noun 1 *a slash across his temple:* **cut**, gash, laceration, slit, incision; wound. **2** *sentence breaks are indicated by slashes:* **solidus**, oblique, backslash.

slatternly adjective *a slatternly girl wearing cardigans and a thick scarf:* **slovenly**, untidy, messy, scruffy, unkempt, ill-groomed, dishevelled, frowzy; N. Amer. informal raggedy.

slaughter verb **1** *the animals were slaughtered:* **kill**, butcher. **2** *innocent civilians are being slaughtered:* **massacre**, murder, butcher, kill (off), annihilate, exterminate, liquidate, eliminate, destroy, decimate, wipe out, put to death.
noun 1 *the slaughter of 20 demonstrators:* **massacre**, murdering, (mass) murder, mass killing, mass execution, annihilation, extermination, liquidation, decimation, carnage, butchery, genocide. **2** *a scene of slaughter:* **carnage**, bloodshed, bloodletting, bloodbath.

slaughterhouse noun **abattoir**; Brit. butchery.

slave noun **1** *the work was done by slaves:* **serf**, vassal, thrall. **2** *Anna was his willing slave:* **drudge**, servant, man/maid of all work, lackey; informal gofer; Brit. informal skivvy, dogsbody, poodle.
– OPPOSITES freeman, master.
verb *slaving away for a pittance:* **toil**, labour, grind, sweat, work one's fingers to the bone, work like a Trojan/dog; informal work one's socks off, kill oneself, sweat blood, slog away; Brit. informal graft; Austral./NZ informal bullock.

slaver verb *the Labrador was slavering at the mouth:* **drool**, slobber, dribble, salivate.

slavery noun **1** *thousands were sold into slavery:* **bondage**, enslavement, servitude, thraldom, thrall, serfdom, vassalage. **2** *this work is sheer slavery:* **drudgery**, toil, (hard) slog, hard labour, grind.
– OPPOSITES freedom.

slavish adjective **1** *slavish lackeys of the government:* **servile**, subservient, fawning, obsequious, sycophantic, toadying, unctuous; informal bootlicking, forelock-tugging; N. Amer. informal apple-polishing. **2** *slavish copying:* **unoriginal**, uninspired, unimaginative, uninventive, imitative.

sleazy adjective **1** *sleazy arms dealers:* **corrupt**, immoral, unsavoury, disreputable; informal shady, sleazoid. **2** *a sleazy bar:* **squalid**, seedy, seamy, sordid, insalubrious, mean, cheap, low-class, run down; informal scruffy, scuzzy, crummy, skanky; Brit. informal grotty.
– OPPOSITES reputable, upmarket.

sledge noun **toboggan**, bobsleigh, sleigh; N. Amer. sled.

sleek adjective **1** *his sleek dark hair:* **smooth**, glossy, shiny, shining, lustrous, silken, silky.

S

2 *the car's sleek lines:* **streamlined**, trim, elegant, graceful. **3** *sleek young men in city suits:* **well groomed**, stylish, wealthy-looking.

sleep noun *go and have a sleep:* **nap**, doze, siesta, catnap, beauty sleep; informal snooze, forty winks, a bit of shut-eye; Brit. informal kip, zizz.

verb *she slept for about an hour:* **be asleep**, doze, take a siesta, take a nap, catnap, sleep like a log/top; informal snooze, snatch forty winks, get some shut-eye; Brit. informal (have a) kip, get one's head down, (get some) zizz; N. Amer. informal catch some Zs; humorous be in the land of Nod.
– OPPOSITES wake up.
■ **go to sleep** fall asleep, get to sleep; informal drop off, nod off, drift off, crash out, flake out; N. Amer. informal sack out, zone out.
■ **put something to sleep** put down, destroy.

sleepiness noun **drowsiness**, tiredness, somnolence, languor, languidness, doziness; lethargy, sluggishness, lassitude, enervation.

sleepless adjective *she spent a sleepless night agonizing over what had happened:* **wakeful**, restless, without sleep, insomniac; (wide) awake, unsleeping, tossing and turning.

sleeplessness noun **insomnia**, wakefulness.

sleepwalker noun **somnambulist**.

sleepy adjective **1** *she felt very sleepy:* **drowsy**, tired, somnolent, languid, languorous, heavy-eyed, asleep on one's feet; lethargic, sluggish, enervated, torpid; informal dopey. **2** *the sleepy heat of the afternoon:* **soporific**, sleep-inducing, somnolent. **3** *a sleepy little village:* **quiet**, peaceful, tranquil, placid, slow-moving; dull, boring.
– OPPOSITES awake, alert.

sleight of hand noun **1** *impressive sleight of hand:* **dexterity**, adroitness, deftness, skill. **2** *financial sleight of hand:* **deception**, deceit, dissimulation, chicanery, trickery, sharp practice.

slender adjective **1** *her tall slender figure:* **slim**, lean, willowy, sylphlike, svelte, lissom, graceful; slight, slightly built, thin, skinny. **2** *slender evidence:* **meagre**, limited, slight, scanty, scant, sparse, paltry, insubstantial, insufficient, deficient, negligible. **3** *the chances seemed slender:* **faint**, remote, flimsy, tenuous, fragile, slim; unlikely, improbable.
– OPPOSITES plump.

slice noun **1** *a slice of fruitcake:* **piece**, portion, slab, rasher, sliver, wafer, shaving. **2** *a huge slice of public spending:* **share**, part, portion, tranche, piece, proportion, allocation, percentage.
verb **1** *slice the cheese thinly:* **cut (up)**, carve. **2** *one man had his ear sliced off:* **cut off**, sever, chop off, shear off.

slick adjective **1** *a slick advertising campaign:* **efficient**, smooth, smooth-running, polished, well organized, well run, streamlined. **2** *his slick use of words:* **glib**, smooth, fluent, plausible. **3** *a slick salesman:* **suave**, urbane, polished, assured, self-assured, smooth-talking, glib; informal smarmy. **4** *her slick brown hair:* **shiny**, glossy, shining, sleek, smooth, oiled. **5** *the pavements were slick with rain:* **slippery**, slithery, wet, greasy; informal slippy.
verb *his hair was slicked down:* **smooth**, sleek, grease, oil, gel; informal smarm.

slide verb **1** *the glass slid across the table:* **glide**, move smoothly, slip, slither, skim, skate; skid, slew. **2** *tears slid down her cheeks:* **trickle**, run, flow, pour, stream. **3** *four men slid out of the shadows:* **creep**, steal, slink, slip, tiptoe, sidle. **4** *the country is sliding into recession:* **sink**, fall, drop, descend; decline, degenerate.
noun **1** *the current slide in house prices:* **fall**, decline, drop, slump, downturn, downswing. **2** *a slide show:* **transparency**, diapositive.
– OPPOSITES rise.
■ **let something slide** neglect, pay little/no attention to, not attend to, be remiss about, let something go downhill.

slight adjective **1** *the chance of success is slight:* **small**, modest, tiny, minute, inappreciable, negligible, insignificant, minimal, remote, slim, faint; informal minuscule. **2** *the book is a slight work:* **minor**, inconsequential, trivial, unimportant, lightweight, superficial, shallow. **3** *Elizabeth's slight figure:* **slim**, slender, petite, diminutive, small, delicate, dainty.
– OPPOSITES considerable.
verb *he had been slighted:* **insult**, snub, rebuff, repulse, spurn, treat disrespectfully, give someone the cold shoulder, cut (dead); scorn; informal give someone the brush-off, freeze out, stiff-arm.
– OPPOSITES respect.
noun *an unintended slight:* **insult**, affront, snub, rebuff; informal put-down, dig.
– OPPOSITES compliment.

slighting adjective *slighting references to foreigners:* **insulting**, disparaging, derogatory, disrespectful, denigratory, pejorative, abusive, offensive, defamatory, slanderous, scurrilous; disdainful, scornful, contemptuous.

slightly adverb *she felt slightly ill at ease:* **a little**, a bit, somewhat, rather, moderately, to a certain extent, faintly, vaguely, a shade.
– OPPOSITES very.

slim adjective **1** *she was tall and slim:* **slender**, lean, thin, willowy, sylphlike, svelte, lissom, trim, slight, slightly built. **2** *a slim silver bracelet:* **narrow**, slender, slimline. **3** *a slim chance of escape:* **slight**, small, slender, faint, poor, remote, unlikely, improbable.
– OPPOSITES plump.
verb **1** *I'm trying to slim:* **lose weight**, get

thinner, lose some pounds/inches, get into shape; N. Amer. slenderize. **2** *the number of staff had been slimmed down:* **reduce**, cut (down/back), scale down, decrease, diminish, pare down.

slime noun *the steps were covered in green and black slime:* **ooze**, sludge, muck, mud, mire; informal goo, gunk, gook, gloop; Brit. informal gunge; N. Amer. informal guck, glop.

slimy adjective **1** *the floor was slimy:* **slippery**, slithery, greasy, muddy, mucky, sludgy, wet, sticky; informal slippy, gunky, gooey, gloopy. **2** (informal) *her slimy press agent.* See OBSEQUIOUS.

sling noun **1** *she had her arm in a sling:* **(support) bandage**, support, strap. **2** *armed only with a sling:* **catapult**, slingshot; Austral./NZ shanghai.
verb *a hammock was slung between two trees:* **hang**, suspend, string, swing.

slink verb *she slunk past the open door of the living room:* **creep**, sneak, steal, slip, slide, sidle, tiptoe, pussyfoot.

slinky adjective (informal) **1** *a slinky black dress:* **tight-fitting**, close-fitting, figure-hugging, sexy. **2** *her slinky elegance:* **sinuous**, willowy, graceful, sleek.

slip¹ verb **1** *she slipped on the ice:* **slide**, skid, slither, glide; fall (over), lose one's balance, tumble. **2** *the envelope slipped through Luke's fingers:* **fall**, drop, slide. **3** *we slipped out by a back door:* **creep**, steal, sneak, slide, sidle, slope, slink, tiptoe. **4** *standards have slipped:* **decline**, deteriorate, degenerate, worsen, get worse, fall (off), drop; informal go downhill, go to the dogs, go to pot. **5** *the bank's shares slipped 1.5p:* **drop**, go down, sink, slump, decrease, depreciate. **6** *the hours slipped by:* **pass**, elapse, go by/past, roll by/past, fly by/past, tick by/past. **7** *she slipped the map into her pocket:* **put**, tuck, shove; informal pop, stick, stuff. **8** *Sarah slipped into a black skirt:* **put on**, pull on, don, dress/clothe oneself in; change into. **9** *she slipped out of her clothes:* **take off**, remove, pull off, doff; Brit. informal peel off. **10** *he slipped the knot of his tie:* **untie**, unfasten, undo.
noun **1** *a single slip could send them plummeting downwards:* **false step**, misstep, slide, skid, fall, tumble. **2** *a careless slip:* **mistake**, error, blunder, gaffe, slip of the tongue/pen; oversight, omission, lapse, inaccuracy; informal slip-up, boo-boo, howler; Brit. informal boob, clanger, bloomer; N. Amer. informal goof, blooper, bloop. **3** *a silk slip:* **underskirt**, petticoat, underslip.
■ **let something slip** reveal, disclose, divulge, let out, give away, blurt out; give the game away; informal let on, blab, let the cat out of the bag, spill the beans; Brit. informal blow the gaff.
■ **slip away 1** *they managed to slip away:* escape, get away, break free; informal fly the coop; Brit. informal do a bunk, do a runner;

N. Amer. informal take a powder. **2** *she slipped away in her sleep.* See DIE sense 1.
■ **slip up** (informal) *we can't afford to slip up like that again:* make a mistake, (make a) blunder, get something wrong, make an error, err; informal make a bloomer, make a boo-boo; Brit. informal boob, drop a clanger; N. Amer. informal goof up.

slip² noun **1** *a slip of paper:* **piece of paper**, scrap of paper, sheet, note; chit; informal stickie. **2** *they took slips from rare plants:* **cutting**, graft; scion, shoot, offshoot.
■ **a slip of a …** *a slip of a girl:* small, slender, slim, slight, slightly built, petite, little, tiny, diminutive; informal pint-sized.

slipper noun **1** *he pulled on his slippers:* carpet slipper, bedroom slipper, house shoe; N. Amer. slipperette. **2** *satin slippers:* pump, mule.

slippery adjective **1** *the roads are slippery:* **slithery**, greasy, oily, icy, glassy, smooth, slimy, wet; informal slippy. **2** *a slippery customer:* **evasive**, unreliable, unpredictable; devious, crafty, cunning, wily, tricky, artful, slick, sly, sneaky, scheming, untrustworthy, deceitful, duplicitous, dishonest, treacherous, two-faced; N. Amer. snide; informal shady, shifty; Brit. informal dodgy; Austral./NZ informal shonky.

slipshod adjective *he'd caused many problems with his slipshod management:* **careless**, lackadaisical, slapdash, disorganized, haphazard, hit-or-miss, untidy, messy, unsystematic, unmethodical, casual, negligent, neglectful, remiss, lax, slack; informal sloppy, slap-happy.
– OPPOSITES meticulous.

slit noun **1** *three diagonal slits:* **cut**, incision, split, slash, gash, laceration. **2** *a slit in the curtains:* **opening**, gap, chink, crack, aperture, slot.
verb *he threatened to slit her throat:* **cut**, slash, split open, slice open, gash, lacerate, make an incision in.

slither verb *a snake slithered silently across the grass:* **slide**, slip, glide, wriggle, crawl; skid.

sliver noun *slivers of glass:* **splinter**, shard, shiver, chip, flake, shred, scrap, slither, shaving, paring, piece, fragment.

slob noun (informal) *her no-good slob of a husband:* **layabout**, good-for-nothing, sluggard, laggard; informal slacker, couch potato.

slobber verb *Fido tended to slobber:* **drool**, slaver, dribble, salivate.

slog verb **1** *they were all slogging away:* **work hard**, toil, labour, work one's fingers to the bone, work like a Trojan/dog, exert oneself, grind, slave, grub, plough, plod, peg; informal beaver, plug, work one's guts out, work one's socks off, sweat blood; Brit. informal graft; Austral./NZ informal bullock. **2** *they slogged around the streets:* **trudge**, tramp, traipse, toil, plod, plot, trek, footslog, drag oneself.
– OPPOSITES relax.

S

noun **1** *10 months' hard slog:* **hard work**, toil, toiling, labour, effort, exertion, grind, drudgery; informal sweat; Brit. informal graft; Austral./NZ informal (hard) yakka. **2** *a steady uphill slog:* **trudge**, tramp, traipse, plod, trek, footslog.
– OPPOSITES leisure.

slogan noun *well-known advertising slogans:* **catchphrase**, catchline, jingle; N. Amer. informal tag line.

slop verb *water slopped over the edge:* **spill**, flow, overflow, run, slosh, splash.

slope noun **1** *the slope of the roof:* **gradient**, incline, angle, slant, inclination, pitch, decline, ascent, declivity, acclivity, rise, fall, tilt, tip, downslope, upslope; N. Amer. grade, downgrade, upgrade. **2** *a grassy slope:* **hill**, hillside, hillock, bank, escarpment, scarp. **3** *the ski slopes:* **piste**, run, nursery slope, dry slope; N. Amer. trail.
verb *the garden sloped down to a stream:* **slant**, incline, tilt; drop away, fall away, decline, descend, shelve, lean; rise, ascend, climb.

sloping adjective *a sloping floor:* **at a slant**, on the slant, at an angle, slanting, slanted, leaning, inclining, inclined, angled, cambered, canted, tilting, tilted, dipping, declivitous, acclivitous.
– OPPOSITES level.

sloppy adjective **1** *sloppy chicken curry:* **runny**, watery, thin, liquid, semi-liquid, mushy; informal gloopy. **2** *United's defending was sloppy:* **careless**, slapdash, slipshod, lackadaisical, haphazard, lax, slack, slovenly; informal slap-happy; Brit. informal shambolic. **3** *sloppy T-shirts:* **baggy**, loose-fitting, loose, generously cut; shapeless, sack-like, oversized. **4** *he wrote really sloppy letters:* **sentimental**, mawkish, cloying, saccharine, sugary, syrupy; romantic, hearts-and-flowers; informal slushy, schmaltzy, lovey-dovey; Brit. informal soppy; N. Amer. informal cornball, sappy, hokey, three-hankie.

slosh verb **1** *beer sloshed over the side of the glass:* **spill**, slop, splash, flow, overflow. **2** *workers sloshed round in boots:* **splash**, swash, squelch, wade; informal splosh. **3** *she sloshed more wine into her glass:* **pour**, slop, splash.

slot noun **1** *he slid a coin into the slot:* **aperture**, slit, crack, hole, opening. **2** *a mid-morning slot:* **spot**, time, period, niche, space; informal window.
verb *he slotted a cassette into the machine:* **insert**, put, place, slide, slip.

sloth noun **laziness**, idleness, indolence, slothfulness, inactivity, inertia, sluggishness, shiftlessness, apathy, accidie, listlessness, lassitude, lethargy, languor, torpidity.
– OPPOSITES industriousness.

slothful adjective *fatigue made him slothful:*

lazy, idle, indolent, work-shy, inactive, sluggish, apathetic, lethargic, listless, languid, torpid; informal bone idle.

slouch verb *Nick slouched back in his chair:* **slump**, hunch; loll, droop.

slovenly adjective **1** *his slovenly appearance:* **scruffy**, untidy, messy, unkempt, ill-groomed, slatternly, dishevelled, bedraggled, tousled, rumpled, frowzy; informal slobbish, slobby; N. Amer. informal raggedy, raunchy. **2** *his work is slovenly:* **careless**, slapdash, slipshod, haphazard, hit-or-miss, untidy, messy, negligent, lax, lackadaisical, slack; informal sloppy, slap-happy.
– OPPOSITES tidy, careful.

slow adjective **1** *their slow walk home:* **unhurried**, leisurely, steady, sedate, slow-moving, plodding, dawdling, sluggish, sluggardly. **2** *a slow process:* **long-drawn-out**, time-consuming, lengthy, protracted, prolonged, gradual. **3** *he can be so slow:* **obtuse**, stupid, unperceptive, insensitive, bovine, stolid, slow-witted, dull-witted, unintelligent, doltish, witless; informal dense, dim, dim-witted, thick, slow on the uptake, dumb, dopey, boneheaded; Brit. informal dozy; N. Amer. informal chowderheaded. **4** *they were slow to voice their opinions:* **reluctant**, unwilling, disinclined, loath, hesitant, afraid, chary, shy. **5** *the slow season:* **sluggish**, slack, quiet, inactive, flat, depressed, stagnant, dead. **6** *a slow narrative:* **dull**, boring, uninteresting, unexciting, uneventful, tedious, tiresome, wearisome, monotonous, dreary, lacklustre.
– OPPOSITES fast.
verb **1** *the traffic forced him to slow down:* **reduce speed**, go slower, decelerate, brake. **2** *you need to slow down:* **take it easy**, ease up/off, take a break, slack off, let up; N. Amer. informal chill out, hang loose. **3** *this would slow down economic growth:* **hold back/up**, delay, retard, set back; restrict, check, curb, inhibit, impede, obstruct, hinder, hamper.
– OPPOSITES accelerate.

slowly adverb **1** *Rose walked off slowly:* **at a slow pace**, without hurrying, unhurriedly, steadily, at a leisurely pace, at a snail's pace. **2** *her health is improving slowly:* **gradually**, bit by bit, little by little, slowly but surely, step by step.
– OPPOSITES quickly.

sludge noun **mud**, muck, mire, ooze, silt, alluvium; informal gunk, crud, gloop, gook, goo; Brit. informal gunge, grot; N. Amer. informal guck, glop.

sluggish adjective **1** *Alex felt tired and sluggish:* **lethargic**, listless, lacking in energy, lifeless, inert, inactive, slow, torpid, languid, apathetic, weary, tired, fatigued, sleepy, drowsy, enervated; lazy, idle, indolent, slothful; N. Amer. logy; informal dozy, dopey. **2** *the economy is sluggish:* **inactive**, quiet, slow, slack, flat, depressed, stagnant.
– OPPOSITES vigorous.

sluice verb 1 *crews sluiced down the decks:* **wash (down)**, rinse, clean, cleanse. 2 *the water sluiced out:* **pour**, flow, run, gush, stream, course, flood, surge, spill.

slum noun **hovel**; (**slums**) ghetto, shanty town.

slummy adjective *a slummy area of town:* **seedy**, insalubrious, squalid, sleazy, run down, down at heel, shabby, dilapidated; informal scruffy, skanky; Brit. informal grotty; N. Amer. informal shacky.
– OPPOSITES upmarket.

slump verb 1 *he slumped into a chair:* **sit heavily**, flop, flump, collapse, sink, fall; informal plonk oneself. 2 *house prices slumped:* **fall steeply**, plummet, tumble, drop, go down; informal crash, nosedive. 3 *reading standards have slumped:* **decline**, deteriorate, degenerate, worsen, slip; informal go downhill.
noun 1 *a slump in profits:* **steep fall**, drop, tumble, downturn, downswing, slide, decline, decrease; informal nosedive. 2 *an economic slump:* **recession**, economic decline, depression, slowdown, stagnation.
– OPPOSITES rise, boom.

slur verb *she was slurring her words:* **mumble**, speak unclearly, garble.
noun *a gross slur:* **insult**, slight, slander, slanderous statement, aspersion, smear, allegation.

slush noun *he wiped the slush off his shoes:* **melting snow**, wet snow, mush, sludge.

slut noun **promiscuous woman**, prostitute, whore; informal tart, floozie, pro; Brit. informal scrubber, slag, slapper; N. Amer. informal tramp, hooker, hustler, roundheel.

sly adjective 1 *she's rather sly:* **cunning**, crafty, clever, wily, artful, guileful, tricky, scheming, devious, deceitful, duplicitous, dishonest, underhand, sneaky. 2 *a sly grin:* **roguish**, mischievous, impish, playful, wicked, arch, knowing. 3 *she took a sly sip of water:* **surreptitious**, furtive, stealthy, covert.
■ **on the sly** in secret, secretly, furtively, surreptitiously, covertly, clandestinely, on the quiet, behind someone's back.

smack¹ noun 1 *she gave him a smack:* **slap**, clout, cuff, blow, spank, rap, swat, crack, thump, punch; informal whack, thwack, clip, biff, wallop, swipe, bop, belt, bash, sock. 2 *the parcel landed with a smack:* **bang**, crash, crack, thud, thump.
verb 1 *he tried to smack her:* **slap**, hit, strike, spank, cuff, clout, thump, punch, swat; box someone's ears; informal whack, clip, wallop, biff, swipe, bop, belt, bash, sock; Scottish & N. English informal skelp; N. Amer. informal boff, slug, bust. 2 *the waiter smacked a plate down:* **bang**, slam, crash, thump; sling, fling; informal plonk; N. Amer. informal plunk.

smack² noun 1 *the beer has a smack of hops:* **taste**, flavour, savour. 2 *a smack of bitterness in his words:* **trace**, tinge, touch, suggestion, hint, overtone, suspicion, whisper.
■ **smack of 1** *the tea smacked of tannin:* **taste of**, have the flavour of. 2 *the plan smacked of self-promotion:* **suggest**, hint at, have overtones of, give the impression of, have the stamp of; smell of, reek of.

small adjective 1 *a small flat:* **little**, compact, bijou, tiny, miniature, mini; minute, microscopic, minuscule; toy, baby; poky, cramped, boxy; Scottish wee; informal tiddly, teeny, teensy, itsy-bitsy, itty-bitty, pocket-sized, half-pint, dinky, ickle; Brit. informal titchy; N. Amer. informal little-bitty. 2 *a very small man:* **short**, little, petite, diminutive, elfin, tiny, puny, undersized, stunted, dwarfish, midget, pygmy, Lilliputian; Scottish wee; informal teeny, pint-sized. 3 *a few small changes:* **slight**, minor, unimportant, trifling, trivial, insignificant, inconsequential, negligible, nugatory, infinitesimal; informal minuscule, piffling, piddling. 4 *small helpings:* **inadequate**, meagre, insufficient, ungenerous; informal measly, stingy, mingy, pathetic. 5 *they made him feel small:* **foolish**, stupid, insignificant, unimportant; embarrassed, humiliated, uncomfortable, mortified, ashamed; crushed. 6 *a small farmer:* **small-scale**, small-time; modest, unpretentious, humble.
– OPPOSITES big, tall, major, ample, substantial.

small-minded adjective *a bunch of small-minded bigots:* **narrow-minded**, petty, mean-spirited, uncharitable; close-minded, short-sighted, myopic, blinkered, inward-looking, unimaginative, parochial, provincial, insular, small-town; intolerant, illiberal, conservative, hidebound, dyed-in-the-wool, set in one's ways, inflexible; prejudiced, bigoted; Brit. parish-pump, blimpish.
– OPPOSITES tolerant.

small-time adjective *small-time crooks:* **minor**, small-scale; petty, unimportant, insignificant, inconsequential; N. Amer. minor-league; informal penny-ante, piddling; N. Amer. informal two-bit, bush-league, picayune.
– OPPOSITES major.

smarmy adjective (informal) *he's too smarmy:* **unctuous**, ingratiating, slick, oily, greasy, obsequious, sycophantic, fawning; informal slimy, sucky.

smart adjective 1 *you look very smart:* **well dressed**, stylish, chic, fashionable, modish, elegant, neat, spruce, trim, dapper, besuited; N. Amer. trig; informal snazzy, natty, sharp, cool; N. Amer. informal sassy, spiffy, fly, kicky. 2 *a smart restaurant:* **fashionable**, stylish, high-class, exclusive, chic, fancy; Brit. upmarket; N. Amer. high-toned; informal trendy, posh, ritzy, plush, classy, swanky, glitzy; Brit. informal swish; N. Amer. informal swank. 3 *a smart pace:* **brisk**, quick, fast, rapid, swift, lively, spanking, energetic, vigorous; informal snappy,

S

cracking. **4** *a smart blow on the snout:* **sharp**, severe, forceful, violent.
– OPPOSITES untidy, downmarket, stupid, slow, gentle.
verb **1** *her eyes were smarting:* **sting**, burn, tingle, prickle; hurt, ache. **2** *she smarted at the accusations:* **feel annoyed**, feel upset, take offence, feel aggrieved, feel indignant, be put out, feel hurt.
■ **look smart** (Brit.) be quick, hurry up, speed up; informal make it snappy, get cracking, get moving, step on it; Brit. informal get one's skates on, stir one's stumps; N. Amer. informal get a wiggle on.

smarten verb *the cottages had been smartened up:* **spruce up**, clean up, tidy up, neaten, tidy; groom, freshen, preen, primp, beautify; redecorate, refurbish, modernize; informal do up, titivate, doll up; Brit. informal tart up, posh up; N. Amer. informal gussy up.

smash verb **1** *he smashed a window:* **break**, shatter, splinter, crack, shiver; informal bust. **2** *she's smashed the car:* **crash**, wreck; Brit. write off; Brit. informal prang; N. Amer. informal total. **3** *they smashed into a wall:* **crash into**, collide with, hit, strike, ram, smack into, slam into, plough into, run into, bump into; N. Amer. impact. **4** *Don smashed him over the head:* **hit**, strike, thump, punch, smack; informal whack, bash, biff, bop, clout, wallop, crown; Brit. informal slosh, dot; N. Amer. informal slug. **5** *he smashed their hopes of glory:* **destroy**, wreck, ruin; shatter, dash, crush, devastate, demolish, overturn, scotch; informal put the kibosh on, do for, put paid to, queer; Brit. informal scupper.
noun **1** *the smash of glass:* **breaking**, shattering, crash. **2** *a motorway smash:* **crash**, collision, accident, bump; Brit. RTA; N. Amer. wreck; informal pile-up, smash-up; Brit. informal prang, shunt. **3** (informal) *a box-office smash:* **success**, sensation, sell-out, triumph; informal (smash) hit, winner, crowd-puller, knockout, wow, biggie.

smashing adjective (Brit. informal). See MARVELLOUS sense 2.

smattering noun *Edward had only a smattering of Welsh:* **bit**, little, modicum, touch, soupçon; nodding acquaintance; rudiments, basics; informal smidgen, smidge, tad.

smear verb **1** *the table was smeared with grease:* **streak**, smudge, mark, soil, dirty; informal splotch, splodge. **2** *smear the meat with olive oil:* **cover**, coat, grease. **3** *she smeared sunblock on her skin:* **spread**, rub, daub, slap, slather, smother, plaster, cream, slick; apply. **4** *they are trying to smear our reputation:* **sully**, tarnish, blacken, drag through the mud, taint, damage, defame, discredit, malign, slander, libel; N. Amer. slur; informal do a hatchet job on.
noun **1** *smears of blood:* **streak**, smudge, daub, dab, spot, patch, blotch, mark; informal splotch, splodge. **2** *press smears about his closest aides:* **false accusation**, lie, untruth,

slur, slander, libel, defamation, calumny.

smell noun *the smell of the kitchen:* **odour**, aroma, fragrance, scent, perfume, redolence; bouquet, nose; stench, stink, reek; Brit. informal pong, niff, whiff, hum; Scottish informal guff; N. Amer. informal funk.
verb **1** *he smelled her perfume:* **scent**, get a sniff of, detect. **2** *the dogs smelled each other:* **sniff**, nose. **3** *the cellar smells:* **stink**, reek, have a bad smell; Brit. informal pong, hum, niff, whiff. **4** *it smells like a hoax to me:* **smack of**, have the hallmarks of, seem like, have the air of, suggest.

smelly adjective *smelly fish:* **foul-smelling**, stinking, reeking, fetid, malodorous, pungent, rank, noxious; off, gamy, high; musty, fusty; informal stinky; Brit. informal pongy, whiffy, humming; N. Amer. informal funky.

smile verb *he smiled at her:* **beam**, grin (from ear to ear), dimple, twinkle; smirk, simper; leer.
– OPPOSITES frown.
noun *the smile on her face:* **beam**, grin, twinkle; smirk, simper; leer.

smirk verb *she turned and smirked at Ed:* **smile smugly**, simper, snigger; leer.

smitten adjective **1** *he was smitten with cholera:* **struck down**, laid low, suffering, affected, afflicted, plagued, stricken. **2** *Jane's smitten with you:* **infatuated**, besotted, in love, obsessed, head over heels; enamoured of, attracted to, taken with; captivated, enchanted, under someone's spell; informal bowled over, swept off one's feet, crazy about, mad about, keen on, gone on, sweet on; Brit. informal potty about.

smog noun fog, haze; fumes, smoke, pollution; Brit. informal pea-souper.

smoke verb **1** *the fire was smoking:* **smoulder**, emit smoke. **2** *he smoked his cigarette:* **puff on**, draw on, pull on; inhale; light; informal drag on. **3** *they smoke their salmon:* **cure**, preserve, dry.
noun *the smoke from the bonfire:* **fumes**, exhaust, gas, vapour; smog.

smoky adjective **1** *the smoky atmosphere:* **smoke-filled**, sooty, smoggy, hazy, foggy, murky, thick; Brit. informal fuggy. **2** *her smoky eyes:* **grey**, sooty, dark, black.

smooth adjective **1** *the smooth flat rocks:* **even**, level, flat, plane; unwrinkled, featureless; glassy, glossy, silky, polished. **2** *his face was smooth:* **clean-shaven**, hairless. **3** *a smooth sauce:* **creamy**, velvety, blended. **4** *a smooth sea:* **calm**, still, tranquil, undisturbed, unruffled, even, flat, waveless, like a millpond. **5** *the smooth running of the equipment:* **steady**, regular, uninterrupted, unbroken, fluid, fluent; straightforward, easy, effortless, trouble-free. **6** *a smooth wine:* **mellow**, mild, agreeable, pleasant. **7** *the smooth tone of the clarinet:* **dulcet**, soft, soothing, mellow, sweet, silvery, honeyed, mellifluous, melodious, lilting, lyrical, harmonious. **8** *a smooth, confident*

man: **suave**, urbane, sophisticated, polished, debonair; courteous, gracious, glib, slick, ingratiating, unctuous; informal smarmy.
– OPPOSITES uneven, rough, hairy, lumpy, irregular, raucous, gauche.
verb 1 *she smoothed the soil:* **flatten**, level (out/off), even out/off; press, roll, steamroll, iron, plane. **2** *a plan to smooth the way for the agreement:* **ease**, facilitate, clear the way for, pave the way for, expedite, assist, aid, help, oil the wheels of, lubricate.

smoothly adverb **1** *her hair was combed smoothly back:* **evenly**, level, flat, flush. **2** *the door closed smoothly:* **fluidly**, fluently, steadily, frictionlessly, easily; quietly. **3** *the plan had gone smoothly:* **without a hitch**, like clockwork, without difficulty, easily, effortlessly, according to plan, satisfactorily, very well; informal like a dream, swimmingly.

smother verb **1** *she tried to smother her baby:* **suffocate**, asphyxiate, stifle, choke. **2** *we smothered the flames:* **extinguish**, put out, snuff out, dampen, douse, stamp out, choke. **3** *we smothered ourselves with suncream:* **smear**, daub, spread, cover. **4** *their granny always smothers them:* **overwhelm**, inundate, envelop, cocoon; Brit. wrap someone in cotton wool. **5** *she smothered a sigh:* **stifle**, muffle, strangle, repress, suppress, hold back, fight back, bite back, swallow, contain, bottle up, conceal, hide; bite one's lip; informal keep a/the lid on.

smoulder verb **1** *the bonfire still smouldered:* **smoke**, glow, burn. **2** *she was smouldering with resentment:* **seethe**, boil, fume, burn, simmer, be boiling over, be beside oneself; informal be livid.

smudge noun *a smudge of blood:* **streak**, smear, mark, stain, blotch, stripe, blob, dab; informal splotch, splodge.
verb 1 *her face was smudged with dust:* **streak**, mark, dirty, soil, blotch, blacken, smear, blot, daub, stain; informal splotch, splodge. **2** *she smudged her make-up:* **smear**, streak, mess up.

smug adjective *he was feeling smug after his win:* **self-satisfied**, self-congratulatory, complacent, superior, pleased with oneself, self-approving; Brit. informal like the cat that got the cream, I'm-all-right-Jack.

smuggle verb *they smuggled drugs into Britain:* **import/export illegally**, traffic in, run.

smuggler noun **contrabandist**, runner, courier; informal mule, moonshiner.

smutty adjective *smutty jokes:* **vulgar**, rude, crude, dirty, filthy, salacious, coarse, obscene, lewd, pornographic, X-rated; risqué, racy, earthy, bawdy, suggestive, naughty, ribald, off colour; informal blue, raunchy; Brit. informal near the knuckle, saucy; N. Amer. informal gamy; euphemistic adult.

snack noun *she made herself a snack:* **light meal**, sandwich, treat, refreshments, nibbles, titbit(s); informal bite (to eat); Brit. informal clevenses.
verb *don't snack on sugary foods:* **eat between meals**, nibble, munch; informal graze.

snag noun **1** *the snag is that this might affect inflation:* **complication**, difficulty, catch, hitch, obstacle, stumbling block, pitfall, problem, impediment, hindrance, inconvenience, setback, hurdle, disadvantage, downside, drawback. **2** *smooth rails with no snags:* **sharp projection**, jag; thorn, spur. **3** *a snag in her tights:* **tear**, rip, hole, gash, slash; ladder, run.
verb 1 *she snagged her tights:* **tear**, rip, ladder. **2** *the zip snagged on the fabric:* **catch**, get caught, hook.

snake noun *the snake shed its skin:* literary serpent; Zoology ophidian; Austral./NZ rhyming slang Joe Blake.
verb *the road snakes inland:* **twist**, wind, meander, zigzag, curve.
■ **snake in the grass** traitor, turncoat, betrayer, informer, back-stabber, double-crosser, quisling, Judas; fraudster, trickster, charlatan; informal two-timer, rat.

snap verb **1** *the ruler snapped:* **break**, fracture, splinter, come apart, split, crack; informal bust. **2** *she snapped after years of violence:* **flare up**, lose one's self-control, freak out, go to pieces, get worked up; informal crack up, lose one's cool, blow one's top, fly off the handle; Brit. informal throw a wobbly. **3** *a dog was snapping at his heels:* **bite**; gnash its teeth. **4** *'Shut up!' Anna snapped:* **say roughly**, say brusquely, say abruptly, say angrily, bark, snarl, growl; retort, rejoin, retaliate; round on someone; informal jump down someone's throat. **5** *photographers snapped the royals:* **photograph**, picture, take, shoot, film, capture.
noun 1 *she closed her purse with a snap:* **click**, crack, pop. **2** *a cold snap:* **period**, spell, time, interval, stretch; Brit. informal patch.
■ **snap out of it** (informal) recover, get a grip, pull oneself together, get over it, get better, cheer up, perk up; informal buck up.
■ **snap something up** *people are snapping up bargains all over the place:* buy eagerly, accept eagerly, jump at, take advantage of, grab, seize (on), grasp with both hands, pounce on.

snappy adjective (informal) **1** *why is he so snappy this morning?* **irritable**, irascible, short-tempered, hot-tempered, quick-tempered, snappish, fiery, touchy, volatile; cross, crabby, crotchety, cantankerous, grumpy, bad-tempered, testy, tetchy; informal chippy, grouchy, cranky, on a short fuse; Brit. informal narky, ratty, eggy, like a bear with a sore head; N. Amer. informal soreheaded. **2** *a snappy catchphrase:* **concise**, succinct, memorable, catchy, neat, clever, crisp, pithy, witty, incisive, brief, short. **3** *a snappy dresser:* **smart**, fashionable, stylish, chic, modish, elegant, neat, spruce, trim, dapper; informal

S

snazzy, natty, sharp, nifty, cool; N. Amer. informal sassy, spiffy, fly.
– OPPOSITES peaceable, long-winded, slovenly.
■ **make it snappy** hurry (up), be quick (about it), get a move on, look lively, speed up; informal get cracking, step on it, move it, buck up, shake a leg; Brit. informal get your skates on; N. Amer. informal get a wiggle on.

snare noun **1** *the hare was caught in a snare:* **trap**, gin, net, noose. **2** *avoid the snares of the new law:* **pitfall**, trap, catch, danger, hazard, peril; web, mesh.
verb **1** *game birds were snared:* **trap**, catch, net, bag, ensnare, entrap. **2** *he managed to snare an heiress:* **ensnare**, catch, get hold of, bag, hook, land.

snarl[1] verb **1** *the wolves are snarling:* **growl**, gnash one's teeth. **2** *'Shut it!' he snarled:* **say roughly**, say brusquely, say nastily, bark, snap, growl; informal jump down someone's throat.

snarl[2] verb **1** *the rope got snarled up in a bush:* **tangle**, entangle, entwine, enmesh, ravel, knot, foul. **2** *this case has snarled up the court process:* **complicate**, confuse, muddle, jumble; informal mess up.

snatch verb **1** *she snatched the sandwich:* **grab**, seize, take hold of, get one's hands on, take, pluck; grasp at, clutch at. **2** *(informal) someone snatched my bag.* See **STEAL** verb sense 1. **3** *(informal) she snatched the newborn from the hospital.* See **ABDUCT**. **4** *he snatched victory in the last minute:* **seize**, pluck, wrest, achieve, secure, obtain; scrape.
noun **1** *brief snatches of sleep:* **period**, spell, time, fit, bout, interval, stretch. **2** *a snatch of conversation:* **fragment**, snippet, bit, scrap, part, extract, excerpt, portion.

sneak verb **1** *I sneaked out:* **creep**, slink, steal, slip, slide, sidle, edge, move furtively, tiptoe, pussyfoot, pad, prowl. **2** *she sneaked a camera in:* **bring/take surreptitiously**, bring/take secretly, bring/take illicitly, smuggle, spirit, slip. **3** *he sneaked a doughnut:* **take furtively**, take surreptitiously; steal; informal snatch.
noun *(Brit. informal) Ethel was the class sneak:* **informer**, traitor; informal snitch, squealer, rat, whistle-blower; Brit. informal grass; Scottish informal clype; N. Amer. informal fink; Austral./NZ informal dobber.
adjective *a sneak preview:* **furtive**, secret, stealthy, sly, surreptitious, clandestine, covert; private, quick.

sneaking adjective **1** *she had a sneaking admiration for him:* **secret**, private, hidden, concealed, unvoiced, undisclosed, undeclared, unavowed. **2** *a sneaking feeling:* **niggling**, nagging, lurking, insidious, lingering, gnawing, persistent.

sneaky adjective *it was a sneaky trick and I fell for it:* **sly**, crafty, cunning, wily, artful, scheming, devious, guileful, deceitful, duplicitous, underhand, unscrupulous; furtive, secretive, secret, stealthy,

surreptitious, clandestine, covert; informal foxy, shifty, dirty.
– OPPOSITES honest.

sneer noun **1** *she had a sneer on her face:* **smirk**, curl of the lip, disparaging smile, contemptuous smile, cruel smile. **2** *the sneers of others:* **jibe**, barb, jeer, taunt, insult, slight, affront, slur; informal dig.
verb **1** *he looked at me and sneered:* **smirk**, curl one's lip, smile disparagingly, smile contemptuously, smile cruelly. **2** *it is easy to sneer at them:* **scoff at**, scorn, disdain, mock, jeer at, hold in contempt, ridicule, deride, insult, slight; N. Amer. slur.

snicker verb *they all snickered at her:* **snigger**, titter, giggle, chortle, simper.
noun *he could not suppress a snicker:* **snigger**, titter, giggle, chortle, simper.

snide adjective *I'm fed up with your snide remarks:* **disparaging**, derogatory, deprecating, denigratory, insulting, contemptuous; mocking, taunting, sneering, scornful, derisive, sarcastic, spiteful, nasty, mean; Brit. informal sarky.

sniff verb **1** *she sniffed and blew her nose:* **inhale**, breathe in; snuffle. **2** *Tom sniffed the fruit:* **smell**, scent, get a whiff of.
noun **1** *she gave a loud sniff:* **snuffle**, inhalation. **2** *a sniff of fresh air:* **smell**, scent, whiff; lungful.
■ **sniff at** scorn, disdain, hold in contempt, look down one's nose at, treat as inferior, look down on, sneer at, scoff at; informal turn one's nose up at.

snigger verb *they snigger at him behind his back:* **snicker**, titter, giggle, chortle, laugh; sneer, smirk.
noun *the joke got hardly a snigger:* **snicker**, titter, giggle, chortle, laugh; sneer, smirk.

snip verb **1** *an usher snipped our tickets:* **cut**, clip, snick, slit, nick, notch. **2** *snip off the faded flowers:* **cut off**, trim (off), clip, prune, chop off, lop (off), dock, crop, sever, detach, remove, take off.
noun **1** *make snips along the edge:* **cut**, slit, snick, nick, notch, incision. **2** *snips of wallpaper:* **scrap**, snippet, cutting, shred, remnant, fragment, sliver, bit, piece.

snippet noun *snippets of information:* **piece**, bit, scrap, fragment, particle, shred; excerpt, extract.

snivel verb **1** *he slumped in a chair, snivelling:* **sniffle**, snuffle, whimper, whine, weep, cry; Scottish greet; informal blub, blubber, boohoo; Brit. informal grizzle. **2** *don't snivel about what you get:* **complain**, mutter, grumble, grouse, groan, carp, bleat, whine; informal gripe, moan, grouch, beef, bellyache, whinge, sound off; Brit. informal create; N. Amer. informal kvetch.

snobbery noun *there was a complete lack of snobbery about staff mingling with guests:* **affectation**, pretension, pretentiousness, arrogance, haughtiness, airs and graces, elitism; disdain, condescension, superciliousness; informal snootiness, uppitiness; Brit. informal side.

snobbish adjective *the writer takes a rather snobbish tone:* **elitist**, snobby, superior, supercilious; arrogant, haughty, disdainful, condescending; pretentious, affected; informal snooty, uppity, high and mighty, la-di-da, stuck-up, hoity-toity, snotty; Brit. informal toffee-nosed.

snoop (informal) verb **1** *don't snoop into our affairs:* **pry**, inquire, be inquisitive, be curious, poke about/around, be a busybody, poke one's nose into; interfere (in/with), meddle (in/with), intrude (on); informal be nosy; Austral./NZ informal stickybeak. **2** *they snooped around the building:* **investigate**, explore, search, nose, have a good look; prowl around.
noun **1** *he went for a snoop around:* **search**, nose, look, prowl, ferret, poke, investigation. **2** *your email records could be available to criminals and snoops.* See **SNOOPER**.

snooper noun **meddler**, busybody, eavesdropper; investigator, detective; informal nosy parker, Paul Pry, snoop, private eye, PI, sleuth; N. Amer. informal gumshoe; Austral./NZ informal stickybeak.

snooty adjective (informal) *snooty neighbours:* **arrogant**, proud, haughty, conceited, aloof, superior, self-important, disdainful, supercilious, snobbish, snobby, patronizing, condescending; informal uppity, high and mighty, la-di-da, stuck-up, hoity-toity; Brit. informal toffee-nosed.
– OPPOSITES modest.

snooze (informal) noun *a good place for a snooze:* **nap**, doze, sleep, rest, siesta, catnap; informal forty winks; Brit. informal kip; literary slumber.
verb *she gently snoozed:* **nap**, doze, sleep, rest, take a siesta, catnap; informal snatch forty winks, get some shut-eye; Brit. informal kip, get one's head down; N. Amer. informal catch some Zs; literary slumber.

snout noun **muzzle**, nose, proboscis, trunk; Scottish & N. English neb.

snub verb *they snubbed their hosts:* **rebuff**, spurn, repulse, cold-shoulder, brush off, give the cold shoulder to, keep at arm's length; cut (dead), ignore; insult, slight, affront, humiliate; informal freeze out, knock back; N. Amer. informal stiff.
noun *a very public snub:* **rebuff**, repulse, slap in the face; humiliation, insult, slight, affront; informal brush-off, put-down.

snuff verb *a breeze snuffed out the candle:* **extinguish**, put out, douse, smother, choke, blow out, quench, stub out.

snug adjective **1** *our tents were snug:* **cosy**, comfortable, warm, homely, welcoming, restful, reassuring, intimate, sheltered, secure; informal comfy. **2** *a snug dress:* **tight**, skintight, close-fitting, figure-hugging, slinky.
– OPPOSITES bleak, loose.

snuggle verb *I snuggled down in my sleeping*

bag: **nestle**, curl up, huddle (up), cuddle up, nuzzle, settle; N. Amer. snug down.

soak verb **1** *soak the beans in water:* **immerse**, steep, submerge, submerse, dip, dunk, bathe, douse, marinate, souse. **2** *we got soaked outside:* **drench**, wet through, saturate, waterlog, deluge, inundate, submerge, drown, swamp. **3** *the sweat soaked through his clothes:* **permeate**, penetrate, percolate, seep into, spread through, infuse, impregnate. **4** *use towels to soak up the water:* **absorb**, suck up, blot (up), mop (up), sponge up, sop up.

soaking adjective *get your jacket off, it's soaking:* **drenched**, wet (through), soaked (through), sodden, soggy, waterlogged, saturated, sopping wet, dripping wet, wringing wet.
– OPPOSITES parched.

soar verb **1** *the bird soared into the air:* **fly**, wing, ascend, climb, rise; take off, take flight. **2** *the gulls soared on the winds:* **glide**, plane, float, drift, wheel, hover. **3** *the cost of living soared:* **increase**, escalate, shoot up, rise, spiral; informal go through the roof, skyrocket.
– OPPOSITES plummet.

sob verb *he broke down and sobbed like a child:* **weep**, cry, shed tears, snivel, whimper; howl, bawl; Scottish greet; informal blub, blubber, boohoo; Brit. informal grizzle.

sober adjective **1** *the driver was clearly sober:* **not drunk**, clear-headed; teetotal, abstinent, abstemious, dry; informal on the wagon. **2** *a sober view of life:* **serious**, solemn, sensible, thoughtful, grave, sombre, staid, level-headed, businesslike, down-to-earth, commonsensical, pragmatic, conservative; unemotional, dispassionate, objective, matter-of-fact, no-nonsense, rational, logical, straightforward; Scottish douce. **3** *a sober suit:* **sombre**, subdued, severe; conventional, traditional, quiet, drab, plain.
– OPPOSITES drunk, frivolous, sensational, flamboyant.
verb **1** *I ought to sober up:* **become sober**; informal dry out. **2** *his expression sobered her:* **make serious**, subdue, calm down, quieten, steady; bring down to earth, make someone stop and think, give someone pause for thought.

sobriety noun **1** *she noted his sobriety:* **soberness**, clear-headedness; abstinence, teetotalism, non-indulgence, abstemiousness, temperance. **2** *the mayor is a model of sobriety:* **seriousness**, solemnity, gravity, dignity, level-headedness, common sense, pragmatism, practicality, self-control, self-restraint, conservatism.

so-called adjective *she could trust him more than any of her so-called friends:* **supposed**, alleged, presumed, ostensible, reputed; nominal, titular, self-styled, professed, would-be, self-appointed, soi-disant.

sociable adjective *being a sociable person,*

Eva loved entertaining: **friendly**, affable, companionable, gregarious, convivial, clubbable, amicable, cordial, warm, genial; communicative, responsive, forthcoming, open, outgoing, extrovert, hail-fellow-well-met, approachable; informal chummy, clubby; Brit. informal matey.
– OPPOSITES unfriendly.

social adjective **1** *a major social problem:* **communal**, community, collective, group, general, popular, civil, public, societal. **2** *a social club:* **recreational**, leisure, entertainment, amusement. **3** *a uniquely social animal:* **gregarious**, interactional; organized.
– OPPOSITES individual.
noun *the club has a social once a month:* **party**, gathering, function, get-together; celebration, reunion, jamboree; informal bash, shindig, do; Brit. informal rave-up, knees-up, beano, bunfight, jolly.

socialism noun **leftism**, Fabianism, labourism, welfarism; radicalism, progressivism, social democracy; communism, Marxism, Leninism, Maoism; historical Bolshevism.

socialist adjective *the socialist movement:* **left-wing**, leftist, Labour, Labourite, labourist, Fabian, progressive, reform; radical, revolutionary, militant, red; communist, Marxist, Leninist, Maoist; informal, derogatory lefty, Bolshie, Commie.
– OPPOSITES conservative.
noun *a well-known socialist:* **left-winger**, leftist, Fabian, Labourite, labourist, progressive, progressivist, reformer; radical, revolutionary, militant, red; communist, Marxist, Leninist, Maoist; informal, derogatory lefty, Bolshie, Commie.
– OPPOSITES conservative.

socialize verb *guests can socialize in a real holiday atmosphere:* **interact**, converse, be sociable, mix, mingle, get together, meet, fraternize, consort; entertain, go out; informal hobnob.

society noun **1** *a danger to society:* **the community**, the (general) public, the people, the population; civilization, humankind, mankind, humanity. **2** *an industrial society:* **culture**, community, civilization, nation, population. **3** *Lady Angela will help you enter society:* **high society**, polite society, the upper classes, the elite, the A-list, the county set, the smart set, the beautiful people, the beau monde, the haut monde; informal the upper crust, the top drawer. **4** *a local history society:* **association**, club, group, circle, fellowship, guild, lodge, fraternity, brotherhood, sisterhood, sorority, league, union, alliance. **5** *she shunned the society of others:* **company**, companionship, fellowship, friendship, comradeship, camaraderie.

sodden adjective **1** *his clothes were sodden:* **soaking**, soaked (through), wet (through), saturated, drenched, sopping wet, wringing

wet. **2** *sodden fields:* **waterlogged**, soggy, saturated, boggy, swampy, miry, marshy; heavy, squelchy, soft.
– OPPOSITES arid.

sofa noun **settee**, couch, divan, chaise longue, chesterfield; Brit. put-you-up; N. Amer. davenport, day bed.

soft adjective **1** *soft fruit:* **mushy**, squashy, pulpy, pappy, slushy, squelchy, squishy, doughy; informal gooey; Brit. informal squidgy. **2** *soft ground:* **swampy**, marshy, boggy, miry, oozy; heavy, squelchy. **3** *a soft cushion:* **squashy**, spongy, compressible, supple, springy, pliable, pliant, resilient, malleable. **4** *soft fabric:* **velvety**, smooth, fleecy, downy, furry, silky, silken, satiny. **5** *soft light:* **dim**, low, faint, subdued, muted, mellow. **6** *soft colours:* **pale**, pastel, muted, understated, restrained, subdued, subtle. **7** *soft voices:* **quiet**, low, faint, muted, subdued, muffled, hushed, whispered, stifled, murmured, gentle, dulcet; indistinct, inaudible. **8** *she's too soft with her pupils:* **lenient**, easy-going, tolerant, forgiving, forbearing, indulgent, clement, permissive, liberal, lax. **9** (informal) *he's soft in the head:* **foolish**, stupid, simple, brainless, mindless; mad, scatterbrained, feather-brained; slow, weak, feeble; informal dopey, dippy, dotty, scatty, loopy; Brit. informal daft; Scottish & N. English informal glaikit.
– OPPOSITES hard, firm, rough, harsh, lurid, strident, strict, sensible.

soften verb *he tried to soften the blow of new taxes:* **alleviate**, ease, relieve, soothe, take the edge off, assuage, cushion, moderate, mitigate, palliate, diminish, blunt, deaden.
■ **soften someone up** *he would soften up potential buyers in the pub before a sale:* **charm**, win over, persuade, influence, weaken, disarm, sweeten, butter up, soft-soap.

soft-hearted adjective *you ought to have turned her away, but you were always soft-hearted:* **kind**, kindly, tender-hearted, tender, gentle, sympathetic, compassionate, humane; generous, indulgent, lenient, merciful, benevolent.

softly-softly adjective *we tried a softly-softly approach:* **cautious**, circumspect, discreet, gentle, patient, tactful, diplomatic.

soggy adjective *the thick, soggy mass of fallen leaves:* **mushy**, squashy, pulpy, slushy, squelchy, squishy; swampy, marshy, boggy, miry; soaking, soaked through, wet, saturated, drenched; Brit. informal squidgy.

soil^1 noun **1** *acid soil:* **earth**, loam, dirt, clay, sod, turf; ground. **2** *British soil:* **territory**, land, domain, dominion, region, country.

soil^2 verb **1** *he soiled his tie:* **dirty**, stain, splash, spot, spatter, splatter, smear, smudge, sully, soil, foul; informal muck up. **2** *our reputation is being soiled:* **dishonour**, damage, sully, stain, blacken, tarnish, taint, blemish, defile, blot, smear, drag through the mud.

s

solace noun *they found solace in each other:* **comfort**, consolation, cheer, support, relief.

soldier noun **fighter**, trooper, serviceman, servicewoman; warrior; US GI; Brit. informal squaddie.

■ **soldier on** (informal). See **PERSEVERE**.

sole adjective *my sole aim was to contribute to the national team:* **only**, one (and only), single, solitary, lone, unique, exclusive.

solely adverb *people are appointed solely on the basis of merit:* **only**, simply, just, merely, uniquely, exclusively, entirely, wholly; alone.

solemn adjective **1** *a solemn occasion:* **dignified**, ceremonious, ceremonial, stately, formal, courtly, majestic; imposing, awe-inspiring, splendid, magnificent, grand. **2** *he looked very solemn:* **serious**, grave, sober, sombre, unsmiling, stern, grim, dour, humourless; pensive, meditative. **3** *a solemn promise:* **sincere**, earnest, honest, genuine, firm, heartfelt, wholehearted, sworn.
– OPPOSITES frivolous, light-hearted, insincere.

solemnize verb *the wedding was solemnized in the Dutch Reformed Church:* **perform**, celebrate; formalize, officiate at.

solicit verb **1** *Phil tried to solicit her help:* **ask for**, request, seek, apply for, put in for, call for, press for, beg, plead for. **2** *they are solicited for their opinions:* **ask**, beg, implore, plead with, entreat, appeal to, lobby, petition, importune, supplicate, call on, press. **3** *the girls gathered to solicit:* **work as a prostitute**, make sexual advances, tout (for business); N. Amer. informal hustle.

solicitor noun (Brit.) **lawyer**, legal representative, legal practitioner, notary (public), advocate, attorney; Brit. articled clerk; Scottish law agent; informal brief.

solicitous adjective *she was always solicitous about the welfare of her students:* **concerned**, caring, considerate, attentive, mindful, thoughtful, interested; anxious, worried.

solid adjective **1** *the ice cream was solid:* **hard**, rock-hard, rigid, firm, solidified, set, frozen, concrete. **2** *solid gold:* **pure**, 24-carat, unalloyed, unadulterated, genuine. **3** *a solid line:* **continuous**, uninterrupted, unbroken, non-stop, undivided. **4** *solid houses:* **well built**, sound, substantial, strong, sturdy, durable. **5** *a solid argument:* **well founded**, valid, sound, reasonable, logical, authoritative, convincing, cogent, plausible, credible, reliable. **6** *a solid friendship:* **dependable**, reliable, firm, unshakeable, trustworthy, stable, steadfast, staunch, constant. **7** *the company is very solid:* **financially sound**, secure, creditworthy, profit-making, solvent, in credit, in the black. **8** *solid support from their colleagues:* **unanimous**, united, consistent, undivided.
– OPPOSITES liquid, alloyed, broken, flimsy, untenable, unreliable.

solidarity noun *there was a great feeling of solidarity between us all:* **unanimity**, unity, like-mindedness, agreement, accord, harmony, consensus, concurrence, cooperation, cohesion.

solidify verb *these droplets of liquefied rock solidify rapidly:* **harden**, set, freeze, thicken, stiffen, congeal, cake, dry, bake; ossify, fossilize, petrify.
– OPPOSITES liquefy.

soliloquy noun *Viola ends the scene with a soliloquy:* **monologue**, speech, address, lecture, oration, sermon, homily, aside.

solitary adjective **1** *a solitary life:* **lonely**, companionless, unaccompanied, by oneself, on one's own, alone, friendless; antisocial, unsociable, withdrawn, reclusive, cloistered, hermitic; N. Amer. lonesome. **2** *solitary farmsteads:* **isolated**, remote, lonely, out of the way, in the back of beyond, outlying, off the beaten track, godforsaken, obscure, inaccessible, cut-off; secluded, private, sequestered, desolate; N. Amer. in the backwoods; Austral./NZ in the backblocks; informal in the sticks, in the middle of nowhere; N. Amer. informal in the boondocks; Austral./NZ informal beyond the black stump. **3** *a solitary piece of evidence:* **single**, lone, sole, unique; only, one, individual; odd.
– OPPOSITES sociable, accessible.

solitude noun *she savoured her solitude:* **loneliness**, solitariness, isolation, seclusion, sequestration, withdrawal, privacy, peace.

solo adjective *a solo flight:* **unaccompanied**, single-handed, companionless, unescorted, unattended, unchaperoned, independent, solitary; alone, on one's own, by oneself.
– OPPOSITES accompanied.
adverb *she sailed solo:* **unaccompanied**, alone, on one's own, single-handed(ly), by oneself, unescorted, unattended, unchaperoned, unaided, independently.
– OPPOSITES accompanied.

solution noun **1** *an easy solution to the problem:* **answer**, result, resolution, way out, panacea; key, formula, explanation, interpretation. **2** *a solution of ammonia in water:* **mixture**, mix, blend, compound, suspension, tincture, infusion, emulsion.

solve verb *that doesn't solve our immediate problem:* **resolve**, answer, work out, find a solution to, find the key to, puzzle out, fathom, decipher, decode, clear up, straighten out, get to the bottom of, unravel, piece together, explain; informal figure out, crack; Brit. informal suss out.

solvent adjective *interest rate rises have very severe effects on normally solvent companies:* **financially sound**, debt-free, in the black, in credit, creditworthy, solid, secure, profit-making.

sombre adjective **1** *sombre clothes:* **dark**, drab, dull, dingy; restrained, subdued, sober, funereal. **2** *a sombre expression:* **solemn**, earnest, serious, grave, sober, unsmiling,

S

stern, grim, dour, humourless; gloomy, depressed, sad, melancholy, dismal, doleful, mournful, lugubrious. – OPPOSITES bright, cheerful.

somehow adverb *I knew that I had to be involved somehow:* **by some means**, by any means, in some way, one way or another, no matter how, by fair means or foul, by hook or by crook, come what may.

sometime adverb **1** *I'll visit sometime:* **some day**, one day, one of these (fine) days, at a future date, sooner or later, by and by, in due course, in the fullness of time, in the long run. **2** *it happened sometime on Sunday:* **at some time**, at some point; during, in the course of. – OPPOSITES never.
adjective *the sometime editor of the paper:* **former**, past, previous, prior, foregoing, late, erstwhile, one-time, ex-.

sometimes adverb *sometimes I want to do things on my own:* **occasionally**, from time to time, now and then, every so often, once in a while, on occasion, at times, off and on, at intervals, periodically, sporadically, spasmodically, intermittently.

somewhat adverb **1** *matters have improved somewhat:* **a little**, a bit, to some extent, (up) to a point, in some measure, rather, quite; N. Amer. informal some; informal kind of, sort of. **2** *a somewhat thicker book:* **slightly**, relatively, comparatively, moderately, fairly, rather, quite, marginally. – OPPOSITES greatly.

somnolent adjective **1** *he felt somnolent after lunch:* **sleepy**, drowsy, tired, languid, dozy, groggy, lethargic, sluggish, enervated, torpid; informal snoozy, dopey, yawny; literary slumberous. **2** *a somnolent village:* **quiet**, restful, tranquil, calm, peaceful, relaxing, soothing, undisturbed, untroubled.

son noun **male child**, boy, heir; descendant, offspring; informal lad.

song noun **1** *a beautiful song:* **air**, strain, ditty, melody, tune, number, track. **2** *the song of the birds:* **call(s)**, chirping, cheeping, peeping, chirruping, warble(s), warbling, trilling, twitter, birdsong.
■ **song and dance** (informal). See FUSS noun sense 1.

songster, songstress noun **singer**, vocalist, soloist, crooner, chorister, choirboy, choirgirl; alto, bass, baritone, contralto, tenor, soprano; balladeer; informal warbler, popster, soulster, folkie.

sonorous adjective **1** *a sonorous voice:* **resonant**, rich, full, round, booming, deep, clear, mellow, orotund, fruity, strong, resounding, reverberant. **2** *sonorous words of condemnation:* **impressive**, imposing, grandiloquent, magniloquent, high-flown, lofty, orotund, bombastic, grandiose, pompous, pretentious, overblown, turgid; oratorical, rhetorical; informal highfalutin.

soon adverb **1** *we'll be there soon:* **shortly**, presently, in the near future, before long, in a little while, in a minute, in a moment, in an instant, in the twinkling of an eye, in no time, before you know it, any minute (now), any day (now), by and by; informal pronto, in a jiffy, before you can say Jack Robinson, anon; Brit. informal sharpish, in a tick, in two ticks. **2** *how soon can you get here?* **early**, quickly, promptly, speedily, punctually.

sooner adverb **1** *he should have done it sooner:* **earlier**, before, beforehand, in advance, ahead of time; already. **2** *I would sooner stay:* **rather**, preferably, by preference, by choice, more willingly, more readily.

soothe verb **1** *Rachel tried to soothe him:* **calm (down)**, pacify, comfort, hush, quiet, subdue, settle (down), lull, tranquillize; appease, conciliate, mollify; Brit. quieten (down). **2** *an anaesthetic to soothe the pain:* **alleviate**, ease, relieve, take the edge off, assuage, allay, lessen, palliate, diminish, decrease, dull, blunt, deaden. – OPPOSITES agitate, aggravate.

soothing adjective **1** *soothing music:* **relaxing**, restful, calm, calming, tranquil, peaceful, reposeful, tranquillizing, soporific. **2** *soothing ointment:* **palliative**, mild, calmative.

sophisticated adjective **1** *sophisticated techniques:* **advanced**, modern, state of the art, the latest, new, up to the minute; innovatory, trailblazing, revolutionary, futuristic, avant-garde; complex, complicated, intricate. **2** *a sophisticated woman:* **worldly**, worldly-wise, experienced, enlightened, cosmopolitan, knowledgeable; urbane, cultured, cultivated, civilized, polished, refined; elegant, stylish; informal cool. – OPPOSITES crude, naive.

sophistication noun **worldliness**, experience; urbanity, culture, civilization, polish, refinement; elegance, style, poise, finesse, savoir faire; informal cool.

soporific adjective *soporific drugs:* **sleep-inducing**, sedative, somnolent, calmative, tranquillizing, narcotic, opiate; drowsy, sleepy, somniferous; Medicine hypnotic. – OPPOSITES invigorating.
noun *she was given a soporific:* **sleeping pill**, sedative, calmative, tranquillizer, narcotic, opiate; Medicine hypnotic. – OPPOSITES stimulant.

sorcerer, sorceress noun **wizard**, witch, magician, warlock, enchanter, enchantress, magus; shaman, witch doctor.

sorcery noun **(black) magic**, the black arts, witchcraft, wizardry, enchantment, spells, incantation, witching, witchery, thaumaturgy; shamanism; Irish pishogue.

sordid adjective **1** *a sordid love affair:* **sleazy**, seedy, seamy, unsavoury, tawdry, cheap, debased, degenerate, dishonourable, disreputable, discreditable, contemptible, ignominious, shameful, wretched,

abhorrent. **2** *a sordid little street:* **squalid**, slummy, dirty, filthy, mucky, grimy, shabby, messy, soiled, scummy, unclean; informal cruddy, grungy, crummy, scuzzy; Brit. informal grotty.
– OPPOSITES respectable, immaculate.

sore adjective **1** *a sore leg:* **painful**, hurting, hurt, aching, throbbing, smarting, stinging, agonizing, excruciating; inflamed, sensitive, tender, raw, bruised, wounded, injured. **2** *we are in sore need of you:* **dire**, urgent, pressing, desperate, parlous, critical, crucial, acute, grave, serious, drastic, extreme, life-and-death, great, terrible.
noun *a sore on his leg:* **inflammation**, swelling, lesion; wound, scrape, abrasion, cut, laceration, graze, contusion, bruise; ulcer, boil, abscess, carbuncle.

sorrow noun **1** *he felt sorrow at her death:* **sadness**, unhappiness, misery, despondency, regret, depression, despair, desolation, dejection, wretchedness, gloom, dolefulness, melancholy, woe, heartache, grief. **2** *the sorrows of life:* **trouble**, difficulty, problem, adversity, misery, woe, affliction, trial, tribulation, misfortune, setback, reverse, blow, failure, tragedy.
– OPPOSITES joy.

sorrowful adjective **1** *sorrowful eyes:* **sad**, unhappy, dejected, regretful, downcast, miserable, downhearted, despondent, despairing, disconsolate, desolate, glum, gloomy, doleful, dismal, melancholy, mournful, woeful, woebegone, forlorn, crestfallen, heartbroken; informal blue, down in the mouth, down in the dumps. **2** *sorrowful news:* **tragic**, sad, unhappy, awful, miserable, sorry, pitiful; traumatic, upsetting, depressing, distressing, dispiriting, heartbreaking, harrowing.

sorry adjective **1** *I was sorry to hear about his accident:* **sad**, unhappy, sorrowful, distressed, upset, downcast, downhearted, disheartened, despondent; heartbroken, inconsolable, grief-stricken. **2** *he felt sorry for her:* **full of pity**, sympathetic, compassionate, moved, consoling, empathetic, concerned. **3** *I'm sorry if I was brusque:* **regretful**, remorseful, contrite, repentant, rueful, penitent, apologetic, abject, guilty, self-reproachful, ashamed, sheepish, shamefaced. **4** *he looks a sorry sight:* **pitiful**, pitiable, heart-rending, distressing; unfortunate, unhappy, wretched, unlucky, shameful, regrettable, awful.
– OPPOSITES glad, unsympathetic, unrepentant.

sort noun *what sort of book is it?* **type**, kind, nature, manner, variety, class, category, style; calibre, quality, form, group, set, bracket, genre, species, family, order, generation, vintage, make, model, brand, stamp, ilk, kidney, cast, grain, mould; N. Amer. stripe.
verb **1** *they sorted things of similar size:*

classify, class, categorize, catalogue, grade, group; organize, arrange, order, marshal, assemble, systematize, systemize, pigeonhole. **2** *the problem was soon sorted:* **resolve**, settle, solve, fix, work out, straighten out, deal with, put right, set right, rectify, iron out; answer, explain, fathom, unravel, clear up; informal sew up, hammer out, thrash out, patch up, figure out.
■ **sort of** (informal) **1** *you look sort of familiar:* slightly, faintly, remotely, vaguely; somewhat, moderately, quite, rather, fairly, reasonably, relatively; informal pretty, kind of. **2** *he sort of pirouetted:* as it were, kind of, somehow.
■ **sort something out 1** *she sorted out the clothes.* See SORT verb sense 1. **2** *they must sort out their problems.* See SORT verb sense 2.

sortie noun **1** *the garrison mounted a sortie against their besiegers:* **foray**, sally, charge, offensive, attack, assault, onset, onslaught, thrust, drive. **2** *a bomber sortie:* **raid**, flight, mission, operation.

soul noun **1** *seeing the soul through the eyes:* **spirit**, psyche, (inner) self, inner being, life force, vital force; individuality, make-up, subconscious, anima; Philosophy pneuma; Hinduism atman. **2** *he is the soul of discretion:* **embodiment**, personification, incarnation, epitome, quintessence, essence; model, exemplification, exemplar, image, manifestation. **3** *there was not a soul in sight:* **person**, human being, individual, man, woman, mortal, creature. **4** *their music lacked soul:* **inspiration**, feeling, emotion, passion, animation, intensity, fervour, ardour, enthusiasm, warmth, energy, vitality, spirit.

soulful adjective *she gave him a soulful glance:* **emotional**, deep, profound, fervent, heartfelt, sincere, passionate; meaningful, significant, eloquent, expressive; moving, stirring; sad, mournful, doleful.

soulless adjective **1** *a soulless room:* **characterless**, featureless, bland, dull, colourless, lacklustre, dreary, drab, uninspiring, undistinguished, anaemic, insipid. **2** *it was soulless work:* **boring**, dull, tedious, dreary, humdrum, tiresome, wearisome, uninteresting, uninspiring, unexciting, soul-destroying, mind-numbing, dry; monotonous, repetitive.
– OPPOSITES exciting.

sound¹ noun **1** *the sound of the car:* **noise**, note; din, racket, row, hubbub; resonance, reverberation. **2** *she did not make a sound:* **utterance**, cry, word, noise, peep; informal cheep. **3** *the sound of the flute:* **music**, tone, notes. **4** *I don't like the sound of that:* **idea**, thought, concept, prospect, description.
– OPPOSITES silence.

verb **1** *the buzzer sounded:* **make a noise**, resonate, resound, reverberate, go off, blare; ring, chime, peal. **2** *drivers must sound their horns:* **blow**, blast, toot, blare; operate, set off; ring. **3** *do you sound the 'h'?* **pronounce**,

S

verbalize, voice, enunciate, articulate, vocalize, say. **4** *she sounded a warning:* **utter**, voice, deliver, express, speak, announce, pronounce. **5** *it sounds a crazy idea:* **appear**, look (like), seem, strike someone as being, give every indication of being.

sound² adjective **1** *your heart is sound:* **healthy**, in good condition, in good shape, fit, hale and hearty, in fine fettle; undamaged, unimpaired. **2** *a sound building:* **well built**, solid, substantial, strong, sturdy, durable, stable, intact, unimpaired. **3** *sound advice:* **well founded**, valid, reasonable, logical, weighty, authoritative, reliable. **4** *a sound judge of character:* **reliable**, dependable, trustworthy, fair; good, sensible, wise, judicious, sagacious, shrewd, perceptive. **5** *financially sound:* **solvent**, debt-free, in the black, in credit, creditworthy, secure. **6** *a sound sleep:* **deep**, undisturbed, uninterrupted, untroubled, peaceful. **7** *a sound thrashing:* **thorough**, proper, real, complete, unqualified, out-and-out, thoroughgoing, severe; informal right (royal).
– OPPOSITES unhealthy, unsafe, unreliable, insolvent, light.

sound³ verb *sound the depth of the river:* **measure**, gauge, determine, test, investigate, survey, plumb, fathom, probe.
■ **sound someone/something out** *officials arrived to sound out public opinion:* investigate, test, check, examine, probe, research, look into; canvass, survey, poll, question, interview, sample; informal pump.

sound⁴ noun *an oil spill in Prince William Sound:* **channel**, (sea) passage, strait(s), narrows, waterway; inlet, arm (of the sea), fjord, creek, bay; estuary, firth.

soup noun **broth**, potage, consommé, bouillon, chowder, bisque.

sour adjective **1** *sour wine:* **acid**, acidic, acidy, acidulated, tart, bitter, sharp, vinegary, pungent; N. Amer. acerb. **2** *sour milk:* **bad**, off, turned, curdled, rancid, high, rank, foul, fetid. **3** *a sour old man:* **embittered**, resentful, rancorous, jaundiced, bitter; nasty, spiteful, irritable, peevish, fractious, cross, crabby, crotchety, cantankerous, querulous, grumpy, bad-tempered, ill-humoured, sullen, surly, churlish; informal snappy, grouchy; Brit. informal ratty, stroppy, shirty; N. Amer. informal cranky, soreheaded.
– OPPOSITES sweet, fresh, amiable.
verb **1** *the war had soured him:* **embitter**, disillusion, disenchant, poison, alienate; dissatisfy, frustrate. **2** *the dispute soured relations:* **spoil**, mar, damage, harm, impair, wreck, upset, poison, blight, tarnish.
– OPPOSITES improve.

source noun **1** *the source of the river:* **spring**, origin, (well) head, headspring, headwater(s). **2** *the source of the rumour:* **origin**, birthplace, spring, fountainhead, fount, starting point; history, genesis, start, derivation, root, beginning, genesis, start,

rise; author, originator, initiator, inventor; N. Amer. provenience. **3** *a historian uses primary and secondary sources:* **reference**, authority, informant; document.

souse verb *a crunchy bruschetta soused in green olive oil:* **drench**, douse, soak, steep, saturate, plunge, immerse, submerge, dip, sink, dunk.

soused adjective *a soused herring:* **pickled**, marinated, soaked, steeped.

south adjective *the south coast of England:* **southern**, southerly, meridional, austral.

souvenir noun *the recording provides a souvenir of a great production:* **memento**, keepsake, reminder, remembrance, token, memorial, trophy, relic.

sovereign noun **ruler**, monarch, crowned head, head of state, potentate, suzerain, overlord, dynast, leader; king, queen, emperor, empress, prince, princess, tsar, royal duke, regent, mogul, emir, sheikh, sultan, maharaja, raja.
adjective **1** *they have sovereign control of their territory:* **supreme**, absolute, unlimited, unrestricted, boundless, ultimate, total, unconditional, full; principal, chief, dominant, predominant, ruling; royal, regal, monarchical. **2** *a sovereign state:* **independent**, autonomous, self-governing, self-determining; non-aligned, free.

sovereignty noun **1** *their sovereignty over the islands:* **jurisdiction**, rule, supremacy, dominion, power, ascendancy, suzerainty, hegemony, domination, authority, control, influence. **2** *full sovereignty was achieved in 1955:* **autonomy**, independence, self-government, self-rule, home rule, self-determination, freedom.

sow verb **1** *sow the seeds in rows:* **plant**, scatter, spread, broadcast, disperse, strew, disseminate, distribute; drill, dibble, seed. **2** *the new policy has sown confusion:* **cause**, bring about, occasion, create, lead to, produce, engender, generate, prompt, initiate, precipitate, trigger, provoke; culminate in, entail, necessitate; foster.

space noun **1** *there was not enough space:* **room**, capacity, area, volume, expanse, extent, scope, latitude, margin, leeway, play, clearance. **2** *green spaces in London:* **area**, expanse, stretch, sweep, tract. **3** *the space between the timbers:* **gap**, interval, opening, aperture, cavity, cranny, fissure, crack, interstice, lacuna. **4** *write your name in the appropriate space:* **blank**, gap, box. **5** *a space of seven years:* **period**, span, time, duration, stretch, course, interval. **6** *the first woman in space:* **outer space**, deep space; the universe, the galaxy, the solar system; infinity.
verb *the chairs were spaced widely:* **position**, arrange, range, array, dispose, lay out, locate, situate, set, stand.

spaceman, spacewoman noun **astronaut**, cosmonaut, taikonaut, space

traveller, space cadet; N. Amer. informal
jock.

spacious adjective *a spacious house:* **roomy**,
capacious, palatial, airy, sizeable, generous,
large, big, vast, immense; extensive,
expansive, sweeping, rolling, rambling,
open.
– OPPOSITES cramped.

spadework noun *the politicians coming
along have benefited from the spadework
done for them:* **groundwork**, preliminary
work, preliminaries, preparatory measures,
preparations, planning, foundations; hard
work, donkey work, labour, drudgery, toil;
informal grind; Brit. informal graft.

span noun **1** *a six-foot wing span:* **extent**,
length, width, reach, stretch, spread,
distance, range. **2** *the span of one working
day:* **period**, space, time, duration, course,
interval.
verb **1** *an arch spanned the stream:* **bridge**,
cross, traverse, pass over. **2** *his career
spanned twenty years:* **last**, cover, extend,
spread over, comprise.

spank verb *she was spanked for spilling ink
on the carpet:* **smack**, slap, hit, cuff; informal
wallop, belt, whack, give someone a hiding;
Scottish & N. English skelp.

spar verb *the sight of husband and wife
sparring in public:* **quarrel**, argue, fight,
disagree, differ, be at odds, be at variance,
fall out, dispute, squabble, wrangle, bandy
words, cross swords, lock horns, be at
loggerheads; informal scrap, argufy, spat; Brit.
informal row.

spare adjective **1** *a spare set of keys:* **extra**,
supplementary, additional, second, other,
alternative; emergency, reserve, backup,
relief, fallback, substitute; fresh; N. Amer.
alternate. **2** *they sold off the spare land:*
surplus, superfluous, excessive; redundant,
unnecessary, inessential, unessential,
unneeded, uncalled for, dispensable,
disposable, expendable, unwanted; informal
going begging. **3** *your spare time:* **free**,
leisure, own.
verb **1** *he could not spare any money:* **afford**,
do without, manage without, dispense with,
part with, give, provide. **2** *they were spared
by their captors:* **pardon**, let off, forgive,
reprieve, release, free; leave uninjured,
leave unhurt; be merciful to, show mercy
to, have mercy on, be lenient to, have pity
on.
■ **to spare** left (over), remaining, unused,
unneeded, not required, still available,
surplus (to requirements), superfluous,
extra; informal going begging.

sparing adjective *he was more sparing with
his admiration than with his criticism:*
thrifty, economical, frugal, canny, careful,
prudent, cautious; mean, miserly, niggardly,
parsimonious, close-fisted, penny-pinching,
cheese-paring, ungenerous, close, grasping;
informal stingy, tight-fisted, tight, mingy,
money-grubbing; N. Amer. informal cheap.

– OPPOSITES lavish.

spark noun **1** *a spark of light:* **flash**, glint,
twinkle, flicker, flare, pinprick. **2** *not a
spark of truth in the story:* **particle**, iota,
jot, whit, glimmer, atom, bit, trace, vestige,
ounce, shred, crumb, grain, mite, hint,
touch, suggestion, whisper, scintilla; informal
smidgen, tad.
verb *the trial sparked a furious row:* **cause**,
give rise to, lead to, occasion, bring about,
start, initiate, precipitate, prompt, trigger
(off), provoke, stimulate, stir up.

sparkle verb **1** *her earrings sparkled:* **glitter**,
glint, glisten, twinkle, flash, blink, wink,
shimmer, shine, gleam. **2** *she sparkled as the
hostess:* **be lively**, be vivacious, be animated,
be ebullient, be exuberant, be bubbly, be
effervescent, be witty, be full of life.
noun *the sparkle of the pool:* **glitter**, glint,
twinkle, flicker, shimmer, flash, shine,
gleam.

sparkling adjective **1** *sparkling wine:*
effervescent, fizzy, carbonated, aerated,
gassy, bubbly, frothy; mousseux, spumante.
2 *a sparkling performance:* **brilliant**,
dazzling, scintillating, exciting, exhilarating,
stimulating, invigorating; vivacious, lively,
vibrant, animated.
– OPPOSITES still, dull.

sparse adjective *areas of sparse population:*
scant, scanty, scattered, scarce, infrequent,
few and far between; meagre, paltry,
skimpy, limited, in short supply.
– OPPOSITES abundant.

spartan adjective *a spartan life:* **austere**,
harsh, hard, frugal, stringent, rigorous,
strict, stern, severe; ascetic, abstemious;
bleak, joyless, grim, bare, stark, plain.
– OPPOSITES luxurious.

spasm noun **1** *a muscle spasm:* **contraction**,
convulsion, cramp; twitch, jerk, tic, shudder,
shiver, tremor. **2** *a spasm of coughing:* **fit**,
paroxysm, attack, burst, bout, seizure,
outburst, outbreak, access; informal splurt.

spasmodic adjective *spasmodic fighting
continued:* **intermittent**, fitful, irregular,
sporadic, erratic, occasional, infrequent,
scattered, patchy, isolated, periodic,
periodical, on and off.

spate noun *a spate of burglaries:* **series**,
succession, run, cluster, string, rash,
epidemic, outbreak, wave, flurry, rush,
flood, deluge, torrent.

spatter verb *specks of blood spattered his
face:* **splash**, bespatter, splatter, spray,
sprinkle, shower, speck, speckle, fleck,
mottle, blotch, mark, cover; informal splotch;
Brit. informal splodge.

spawn verb *he wrote in a dry style that
spawned hundreds of imitations:* **give rise to**,
bring about, occasion, generate, engender,
originate; lead to, result in, effect, induce,
initiate, start, set off, precipitate, trigger;
breed, bear.

speak verb **1** *she refused to speak about it:*

S

talk, say anything/something; utter, state, declare, tell, voice, express, pronounce, articulate, enunciate, vocalize, verbalize. **2** *we spoke the other day:* **converse**, have a conversation, talk, communicate, chat, pass the time of day, have a word, gossip; informal have a confab, chew the fat; Brit. informal natter; N. Amer. informal shoot the breeze. **3** *the Minister spoke for two hours:* **give a speech**, talk, lecture, hold forth, discourse, expound, expatiate, orate, sermonize, pontificate; informal spout, spiel, speechify, jaw, sound off. **4** *he was spoken of as a promising student:* **mention**, talk about, discuss, refer to, remark on, allude to. **5** *his expression spoke disbelief:* **indicate**, show, display, register, reveal, betray, exhibit, manifest, express, convey, impart, bespeak, communicate, evidence; suggest, denote, reflect; formal evince.

■ **speak for 1** *she speaks for the Liberal Democrats:* represent, act for, appear for, express the views of, be spokesperson for. **2** *I spoke for the motion:* advocate, champion, uphold, defend, support, promote, recommend, back, endorse, sponsor, espouse.

■ **speak out** *women have been speaking out on this issue for some time:* speak publicly, speak openly, speak frankly, speak one's mind, sound off, stand up and be counted.

■ **speak up** *you'll have to speak up to be heard:* speak loudly, speak clearly, raise one's voice; shout, yell, bellow; informal break holler.

speaker noun **speech-maker**, lecturer, talker, speechifier, orator, declaimer, rhetorician; spokesperson, spokesman/woman, mouthpiece; reader, lector, commentator, broadcaster, narrator; informal tub-thumper, spieler.

spear noun **javelin**, lance, assegai, harpoon, bayonet; gaff, leister.

spearhead noun *the spearhead of the struggle against Fascism:* **leader(s)**, driving force; forefront, front runner(s), front line, vanguard, van, cutting edge.
verb *she spearheaded the campaign:* **lead**, head, front; lead the way, be in the van, be in the vanguard.

special adjective **1** *a very special person:* **exceptional**, unusual, singular, uncommon, notable, noteworthy, remarkable, outstanding, unique. **2** *our town's special character:* **distinctive**, distinct, individual, particular, specific, peculiar. **3** *a special occasion:* **momentous**, significant, memorable, signal, important, historic, festive, gala, red-letter. **4** *a special tool for cutting tiles:* **specific**, particular, purpose-built, tailor-made, custom-built.
– OPPOSITES ordinary, general.

specialist noun *a specialist in electronics:* **expert**, authority, pundit, professional; connoisseur; master, maestro, adept, virtuoso; informal pro, buff, ace, whizz,

hotshot; Brit. informal **dab hand**; N. Amer. informal maven.
– OPPOSITES amateur.

speciality noun **1** *his speciality was watercolours:* **forte**, strong point, strength, métier, strong suit, talent, skill, bent, gift; informal bag, thing, cup of tea. **2** *a speciality of the region:* **delicacy**, specialty, fine food/product, traditional food/product.

species noun *there are several species of spadefoot toad:* **type**, kind, sort; genus, family, order, breed, strain, variety, class, classification, category, set, bracket; style, manner, form, genre; generation, vintage.

specific adjective **1** *I use this place for a specific purpose:* **particular**, specified, fixed, set, determined, distinct, definite; single, individual, peculiar, discrete, express, precise. **2** *I gave specific instructions:* **detailed**, explicit, express, clear-cut, unequivocal, precise, exact, meticulous, strict, definite.
– OPPOSITES general, vague.

specification noun **1** *clear specification of objectives:* **statement**, identification, definition, description, setting out, framing, designation, detailing, enumeration; stipulation, prescription. **2** *a shelter built to their specifications:* **instructions**, guidelines, parameters, stipulations, requirements, conditions, provisions, restrictions, order; description, details.

specify verb *the manufacturer would not specify the sums involved:* **state**, name, identify, define, describe, set out, frame, itemize, detail, list, spell out, enumerate, particularize, cite, instance; stipulate, prescribe.

specimen noun *he was asked for a specimen of his handwriting:* **sample**, example, instance, illustration, demonstration, exemplification; bit, snippet; model, prototype, pattern, dummy, pilot, trial, taster, tester.

specious adjective *a specious argument:* **misleading**, deceptive, false, fallacious, unsound, casuistic, sophistic; plausible.

speck noun **1** *a mere speck in the distance:* **dot**, pinprick, spot, fleck, speckle. **2** *a speck of dust:* **particle**, grain, atom, molecule; bit, trace.

speckled adjective *a large speckled brown egg:* **flecked**, speckly, specked, freckled, freckly, spotted, spotty, dotted, mottled, dappled.

spectacle noun **1** *a spectacle fit for a monarch:* **display**, show, pageant, parade, performance, exhibition, extravaganza, spectacular. **2** *they were rather an odd spectacle:* **sight**, vision, scene, prospect, vista, picture. **3** *don't make a spectacle of yourself:* **exhibition**, laughing stock, fool, curiosity.

spectacles plural noun **glasses**, eyewear; N. Amer. eyeglasses; informal specs.

spectacular adjective **1** *a spectacular*

S

victory: **impressive**, magnificent, splendid, dazzling, sensational, dramatic, remarkable, outstanding, memorable, unforgettable. **2** *a spectacular view:* **striking**, picturesque, eye-catching, breathtaking, arresting, glorious; informal out of this world.
– OPPOSITES unimpressive, dull.
noun *a spectacular put on for the tourists.* See SPECTACLE sense 1.

spectator noun *the game attracted about 40,000 spectators:* **watcher**, viewer, observer, onlooker, bystander, witness; commentator, reporter, blogger, monitor.
– OPPOSITES participant.

spectral adjective **ghostly**, phantom, wraithlike, shadowy, incorporeal, insubstantial, disembodied, unearthly, other-worldly; informal spooky.

spectre noun **1** *the spectres in the crypt:* **ghost**, phantom, apparition, spirit, wraith, shadow, presence; informal spook. **2** *the looming spectre of war:* **threat**, menace, shadow, cloud; prospect; danger, peril, fear, dread.

spectrum noun *a broad spectrum of opinion:* **range**, gamut, sweep, scope, span; compass, orbit, ambit.

speculate verb **1** *they speculated about my private life:* **conjecture**, theorize, hypothesize, guess, surmise; think, wonder, muse. **2** *investors speculate on the stock market:* **gamble**, take a risk, venture, wager; invest, play the market; Brit. informal have a flutter, punt.

speculative adjective **1** *any discussion is largely speculative:* **conjectural**, suppositional, theoretical, hypothetical, putative, academic, notional, abstract; tentative, unproven, unfounded, groundless, unsubstantiated. **2** *a speculative investment:* **risky**, hazardous, unsafe, uncertain, unpredictable; informal chancy, dicey, iffy; Brit. informal dodgy.

speech noun **1** *he doesn't have the power of speech:* **speaking**, talking, verbal expression, verbal communication. **2** *her speech was slurred:* **diction**, elocution, articulation, enunciation, pronunciation; utterance, words. **3** *an after-dinner speech:* **talk**, address, lecture, discourse, oration, disquisition, peroration, deliverance, presentation; sermon, homily; monologue, soliloquy; informal spiel. **4** *Spanish popular speech:* **language**, tongue, parlance, idiom, dialect, vernacular, patois; informal lingo, patter, -speak, -ese.

speechless adjective *she was momentarily speechless:* **lost for words**, dumbstruck, bereft of speech, tongue-tied, inarticulate, mute, dumb, voiceless, silent.
– OPPOSITES verbose.

speed noun **1** *the speed of their progress:* **rate**, pace, tempo, momentum. **2** *the speed with which they responded:* **rapidity**, swiftness, speediness, quickness, dispatch, promptness, immediacy, briskness, sharpness, haste, hurry, precipitateness; acceleration, velocity; informal lick, clip.
verb 1 *I sped home:* **hurry**, rush, dash, run, race, sprint, bolt, dart, gallop, career, charge, shoot, hurtle, hare, fly, zoom, scurry, scuttle, scamper, hasten; informal tear, belt, pelt, scoot, zip, whip, hotfoot it, leg it; Brit. informal bomb; N. Amer. informal hightail it. **2** *a holiday will speed his recovery:* **hasten**, expedite, speed up, accelerate, advance, further, promote, boost, stimulate, aid, assist, facilitate.
– OPPOSITES slow, hinder.
■ **speed up** *Smith shouted at them to speed up:* hurry up, accelerate, go faster, get a move on, put a spurt on, pick up speed, gather speed; informal get cracking, get moving, step on it, shake a leg; Brit. informal get one's skates on; N. Amer. informal get a wiggle on.

speedily adverb *you should ensure that complaints are handled speedily:* **rapidly**, swiftly, quickly, fast, post-haste, at the speed of light, at full tilt; promptly, immediately, briskly; hastily, hurriedly, precipitately; informal p.d.q. (pretty damn quick), double quick, hell for leather, at the double, like the wind, like (greased) lightning; Brit. informal like the clappers, like billy-o; N. Amer. informal lickety-split.

speedy adjective **1** *a speedy reply:* **rapid**, swift, quick, fast; prompt, immediate, expeditious, express, brisk, sharp; whirlwind, lightning, meteoric; hasty, hurried, precipitate, breakneck, rushed; informal p.d.q. (pretty damn quick), snappy, quickie. **2** *a speedy hatchback:* **fast**, high-speed; informal nippy, zippy.
– OPPOSITES slow.

spell¹ verb *the drought spelled disaster for them:* **signal**, signify, mean, amount to, add up to, constitute; portend, augur, herald, bode, promise; involve.
■ **spell something out** *Chapman spelled out his aims for the club:* explain, make clear, make plain, elucidate, clarify; specify, itemize, detail, enumerate, list, expound, particularize, catalogue.

spell² noun **1** *the witch recited a spell:* **incantation**, charm, conjuration, formula; (**spells**) magic, sorcery, witchcraft; N. Amer. hex. **2** *she surrendered to his spell:* **influence**, (animal) magnetism, charisma, allure, lure, charm, attraction, enticement; magic, romance, mystique.
■ **cast a spell on** bewitch, enchant, entrance; curse, jinx, witch; N. Amer. hex.

spell³ noun **1** *a spell of dry weather:* **period**, time, interval, season, stretch, run, course, streak; Brit. informal patch. **2** *a spell of dizziness:* **bout**, fit, attack.

spellbinding adjective *a spellbinding tale of her life in the Far East:* **fascinating**, enthralling, entrancing, bewitching,

captivating, riveting, engrossing, gripping, absorbing, compelling, compulsive, mesmerizing, hypnotic.
– OPPOSITES boring.

spellbound adjective *the audience was spellbound:* **enthralled**, fascinated, rapt, riveted, transfixed, gripped, captivated, bewitched, enchanted, mesmerized, hypnotized; informal hooked.

spend verb 1 *she spent £185 on shoes:* **pay out**, dish out, expend, disburse; squander, waste, fritter away; lavish; informal fork out, lay out, shell out, cough up, blow, splash out, splurge; Brit. informal stump up, blue; N. Amer. informal pony up. 2 *the morning was spent gardening:* **pass**, occupy, fill, take up, while away. 3 *I've spent hours on this essay:* **put in**, devote; waste. 4 *the storm had spent its force:* **use up**, consume, exhaust, deplete, drain.

spendthrift noun *he is such a spendthrift:* **profligate**, prodigal, squanderer, waster; informal big spender.
– OPPOSITES miser.
adjective *his spendthrift father:* **profligate**, improvident, thriftless, wasteful, extravagant, prodigal.
– OPPOSITES frugal.

spent adjective 1 *a spent force:* **used up**, consumed, exhausted, finished, depleted, drained; informal burnt out. 2 *that's enough—I'm spent:* **exhausted**, tired (out), weary, worn out, dog-tired, on one's last legs, drained, fatigued, ready to drop; informal done in, all in, dead on one's feet, dead beat, bushed, wiped out, frazzled; Brit. informal knackered, whacked; N. Amer. informal pooped, tuckered out.

spew verb *factories spewed out yellow smoke:* **emit**, discharge, eject, expel, belch out, pour out, spout, gush, spurt, disgorge.

sphere noun 1 *a glass sphere:* **globe**, ball, orb, spheroid, globule, round; bubble. 2 *our sphere of influence:* **area**, field, compass, orbit; range, scope, extent. 3 *the sphere of foreign affairs:* **domain**, realm, province, field, area, territory, arena, department.

spherical adjective *a spherical Japanese lantern:* **round**, globular, globose, globoid, globe-shaped, spheroidal, spheric.

spice noun 1 *the spices in curry powder:* **seasoning**, flavouring, condiment. 2 *the risk added spice to their affair:* **excitement**, interest, colour, piquancy, zest; an edge; informal a kick.
■ **spice something up** *spice up your life with this new seductive fragrance:* **enliven**, make more exciting, vitalize, perk up, put some life into, ginger up, galvanize, electrify, boost; informal pep up, jazz up, buck up.

spick and span adjective *the whole place was spick and span:* **neat**, tidy, orderly, well kept, shipshape (and Bristol fashion), in apple-pie order; immaculate, uncluttered, trim, spruce; spotless.
– OPPOSITES untidy.

spicy adjective 1 *a spicy casserole:* **piquant**, tangy, peppery, hot, picante; spiced, seasoned; tasty, flavoursome, zesty, strong, pungent. 2 *spicy stories:* **entertaining**, colourful, lively, spirited, exciting, piquant, zesty; risqué, racy, scandalous, ribald, titillating, bawdy, naughty, salacious, dirty, smutty; informal raunchy, juicy; Brit. informal saucy, fruity; N. Amer. informal gamy.
– OPPOSITES bland, boring.

spiel noun (informal) *he went into his long spiel about recycling:* **speech**, patter, (sales) pitch, talk; monologue; rigmarole, story, saga.

spike noun 1 *a metal spike:* **prong**, barb, point; skewer, stake, spit; tine, pin; spur. 2 *the spikes of a cactus:* **thorn**, spine, prickle, bristle; Zoology spicule.
verb 1 *she spiked an oyster:* **impale**, spear, skewer; pierce, penetrate, perforate, stab, stick, transfix. 2 (informal) *his drink was spiked with drugs:* **adulterate**, contaminate, drug, lace; informal dope, doctor, cut.

spill verb 1 *Kevin spilled his drink:* **knock over**, tip over, upset, overturn. 2 *the bath water spilled on to the floor:* **overflow**, flow, pour, run, slop, slosh, splash; leak, escape. 3 *students spilled out of the building:* **stream**, pour, surge, swarm, flood, throng, crowd. 4 *the horse spilled his rider:* **unseat**, throw, dislodge, unhorse.
noun 1 *an oil spill:* **spillage**, leak, leakage, overflow, flood. 2 *he took a spill in the opening race:* **fall**, tumble; informal header, cropper, nosedive.

spin verb 1 *the bike wheels are spinning:* **revolve**, rotate, turn, go round, whirl, gyrate, circle. 2 *she spun round to face him:* **whirl**, wheel, twirl, turn, swing, twist, swivel, pirouette, pivot. 3 *her head was spinning:* **reel**, whirl, go round, swim. 4 *she spun me a yarn:* **tell**, recount, relate, narrate; weave, concoct, invent, fabricate, make up.
noun 1 *a spin of the wheel:* **rotation**, revolution, turn, whirl, twirl, gyration. 2 *a positive spin on the campaign:* **slant**, angle, twist, bias. 3 *he took Lily for a spin in the car:* **trip**, jaunt, outing, excursion, journey; drive, ride, run, turn, airing; informal tootle; Scottish informal hurl.
■ **spin something out** *the longer you can spin out the negotiations the better:* **prolong**, protract, draw out, drag out, string out, extend, carry on, continue; fill out, pad out.

spindle noun **rod**, axle, pivot, pin, capstan; axis.

spindly adjective 1 *he was pale and spindly:* **lanky**, thin, skinny, lean, spare, gangling, gangly, scrawny, bony, rangy, angular. 2 *spindly chairs:* **rickety**, flimsy, wobbly, shaky.
– OPPOSITES stocky.

spine noun 1 *he injured his spine:* **backbone**, spinal column, vertebral column; back.

2 *the spine of his philosophy:* **core**, centre, cornerstone, foundation, basis. **3** *the spines of a hedgehog:* **needle**, quill, bristle, barb, spike, prickle; thorn.

spine-chilling adjective *a spine-chilling ghost story:* **terrifying**, blood-curdling, petrifying, hair-raising, frightening, scaring, chilling, horrifying, fearsome; eerie, sinister, ghostly; Scottish eldritch; informal scary, creepy, spooky.
– OPPOSITES comforting, reassuring.

spineless adjective *a spineless coward:* **weak**, weak-willed, weak-kneed, feeble, soft, ineffectual, irresolute, indecisive; **cowardly**, timid, timorous, fearful, faint-hearted, pusillanimous, craven, unmanly, namby-pamby, lily-livered, chicken-hearted; informal wimpish, wimpy, sissy, chicken, yellow, yellow-bellied, gutless; Brit. informal wet.
– OPPOSITES bold, brave, strong-willed.

spiny adjective *spiny clumps of blackthorn:* **prickly**, spiky, thorny, bristly, bristled, spiked, barbed, scratchy, sharp.

spiral adjective *a spiral column of smoke:* **coiled**, helical, corkscrew, curling, winding, twisting, whorled.
noun *a spiral of smoke:* **coil**, helix, corkscrew, curl, twist, gyre, whorl, scroll.
verb **1** *smoke spiralled up:* **coil**, wind, swirl, twist, wreathe, snake, gyrate. **2** *prices spiralled:* **soar**, shoot up, rocket, increase rapidly, rise rapidly, escalate, climb; informal skyrocket, go through the roof. **3** *the economy is spiralling downward:* **deteriorate**, decline, degenerate, worsen, get worse; informal go downhill, take a nosedive, go to pot, go to the dogs, hit the skids, go down the tubes.
– OPPOSITES fall, improve.

spire noun **steeple**, flèche.

spirit noun **1** *harmony between body and spirit:* **soul**, psyche, (inner) self, inner being, inner man/woman, mind, ego, id. **2** *a spirit haunts the island:* **ghost**, phantom, spectre, apparition, wraith, presence; informal spook. **3** *that's the spirit:* **attitude**, frame of mind, way of thinking, point of view, outlook, thoughts, ideas. **4** *she was in good spirits when I left:* **mood**, frame of mind, state of mind, emotional state, humour, temper. **5** *team spirit:* **morale**, esprit de corps. **6** *the spirit of the age:* **ethos**, prevailing tendency, motivating force, essence, quintessence; atmosphere, mood, feeling, climate; attitudes, beliefs, principles, standards, ethics. **7** *his spirit never failed him:* **courage**, bravery, pluck, valour, strength of character, fortitude, backbone, mettle, stout-heartedness, determination, resolution, resolve, fight, grit; informal guts, spunk; Brit. informal bottle; N. Amer. informal sand, moxie. **8** *they played with great spirit:* **enthusiasm**, eagerness, keenness, liveliness, vivacity, vivaciousness, animation, energy, verve, vigour, dynamism,

zest, dash, elan, panache, sparkle, exuberance, gusto, brio, pep, fervour, zeal, fire, passion; informal get-up-and-go. **9** *the spirit of the law:* **real/true meaning**, true intention, essence, substance. **10** *he drinks spirits:* **strong liquor/drink**; informal hard stuff, firewater, hooch; Brit. informal short.
– OPPOSITES body, flesh.
■ **spirit someone/something away** *the girl was spirited away before we got anywhere near her:* **whisk away/off**, vanish with, make off with, make someone/something disappear, run away with, abscond with, carry off, steal someone/something away, abduct, kidnap, snatch, seize.

spirited adjective *an attractive and spirited young woman:* **lively**, vivacious, vibrant, full of life, vital, animated, high-spirited, sparkling, sprightly, energetic, active, vigorous, dynamic, dashing, enthusiastic, passionate; determined, resolute, purposeful; informal feisty, spunky, have-a-go, gutsy; N. Amer. informal peppy.
– OPPOSITES timid, apathetic, lifeless.

spiritless adjective *Lilian was a pallid, spiritless woman:* **apathetic**, passive, unenthusiastic, lifeless, listless, weak, feeble, spineless, languid, bloodless, insipid, characterless, submissive, meek, irresolute, indecisive; lacklustre, flat, colourless, passionless, uninspired, wooden, dry, anaemic, vapid, dull, boring, wishy-washy.
– OPPOSITES spirited, lively.

spiritual adjective **1** *your spiritual self:* **non-material**, incorporeal, intangible; inner, mental, psychological; transcendent, ethereal, other-worldly, mystic, mystical, metaphysical. **2** *spiritual writings:* **religious**, sacred, divine, holy, non-secular, church, ecclesiastical, devotional.
– OPPOSITES physical, secular.

spit[1] verb **1** *Cranston coughed and spat:* **expectorate**, hawk; Brit. informal gob. **2** *'Go to hell,' she spat:* **snap**, say angrily, hiss. **3** *the fat began to spit:* **sizzle**, hiss; crackle, sputter. **4** (Brit.) *it began to spit:* **rain lightly**, drizzle, spot; N. English mizzle; N. Amer. sprinkle.
noun *spit dribbled from his mouth:* **spittle**, saliva, sputum, slobber, dribble; Brit. informal gob.

spit[2] noun *chicken cooked on a spit:* **skewer**, brochette, rotisserie.

spite noun *he said it out of spite:* **malice**, malevolence, ill will, vindictiveness, vengefulness, revenge, malignity, evil intentions, animus, enmity; informal bitchiness, cattiness.
– OPPOSITES benevolence.
verb *he did it to spite me:* **upset**, hurt, make miserable, grieve, distress, wound, pain, torment, injure.
– OPPOSITES please.
■ **in spite of** despite, notwithstanding, regardless of, for all; undeterred by, in

S

defiance of, in the face of; even though, although.

spiteful adjective *the other girls made spiteful remarks about Paula:* **malicious**, malevolent, evil-intentioned, vindictive, vengeful, malign, mean, nasty, hurtful, mischievous, wounding, cruel, unkind; informal bitchy, catty.
– OPPOSITES benevolent.

splash verb 1 *splash your face with cool water:* **sprinkle**, spray, shower, splatter, slosh, slop, squirt; daub; wet. 2 *his boots were splashed with mud:* **spatter**, bespatter, splatter, speck, speckle, blotch, smear, stain, mark; Scottish & Irish slabber; informal splotch, splodge. 3 *waves splashed on the beach:* **swash**, wash, break, lap; dash, beat, lash, batter, crash, buffet. 4 *children splashed in the water:* **paddle**, wade, slosh; wallow; informal splosh. 5 *the story was splashed across the front pages:* **blazon**, display, spread, plaster, trumpet, publicize; informal splatter.
noun 1 *a splash of fat on his shirt:* **spot**, blob, dab, daub, smudge, smear, speck, fleck; mark, stain; informal splotch, splodge. 2 *a splash of lemonade:* **drop**, dash, bit, spot, soupçon, dribble, driblet; Scottish informal scoosh. 3 *a splash of colour:* **patch**, burst, streak.
■ **make a splash** (informal) cause a sensation, cause a stir, attract attention, draw attention to oneself/itself, get noticed, make an impression, make an impact.
■ **splash out** *she splashed out on a Mercedes:* (Brit. informal) be extravagant, go on a spending spree, spare no expense, spend lavishly; informal lash out, splurge; Brit. informal push the boat out.

spleen noun *he vented his spleen on me:* **bad temper**, bad mood, ill temper, ill humour, anger, wrath, vexation, annoyance, irritation, displeasure, dissatisfaction, resentment, rancour; spite, ill feeling, malice, maliciousness, bitterness, animosity, antipathy, hostility, malevolence, venom, gall, malignance, malignity, acrimony, bile, hatred, hate.
– OPPOSITES good humour.

splendid adjective 1 *splendid costumes:* **magnificent**, sumptuous, grand, impressive, imposing, superb, spectacular, resplendent, opulent, luxurious, de luxe, rich, fine, costly, expensive, lavish, ornate, gorgeous, glorious, dazzling, elegant, handsome, beautiful; stately, majestic, princely, noble, proud, palatial; informal plush, posh, swanky, ritzy, splendiferous; Brit. informal swish; N. Amer. informal swank. 2 *we had a splendid holiday:* **excellent**, wonderful, marvellous, superb, glorious, sublime, lovely, delightful, first-class, first-rate; informal super, great, amazing, fantastic, terrific, tremendous, phenomenal, sensational, heavenly, gorgeous, dreamy, grand, fabulous, fab, awesome, magic, ace, cool, mean, bad, wicked, mega, crucial, far out, A1, sound, out of this world; Brit. informal

smashing, brilliant, brill; N. Amer. informal dandy, neat; Austral./NZ informal beaut, bonzer.
– OPPOSITES modest, awful.

splendour noun *a wedding long remembered for its splendour:* **magnificence**, sumptuousness, grandeur, impressiveness, resplendence, opulence, luxury, richness, fineness, lavishness, ornateness, glory, beauty, elegance; majesty, stateliness; informal ritziness, splendiferousness.
– OPPOSITES ordinariness, simplicity, modesty.

splice verb *the ropes are spliced together:* **interweave**, braid, plait, entwine, intertwine, interlace, knit, mesh; Nautical marry.

splinter noun *a splinter of wood:* **sliver**, shiver, chip, shard; fragment, piece, bit, shred; Scottish skelf; (**splinters**) matchwood, flinders.
verb *the windscreen splintered:* **shatter**, break into tiny pieces, smash, smash into smithereens, fracture, split, crack, disintegrate, crumble.

split verb 1 *the axe split the wood:* **break**, chop, cut, hew, lop, cleave; snap, crack. 2 *the ice cracked and split:* **break apart**, fracture, rupture, fissure, snap, come apart, splinter. 3 *her dress was split:* **tear**, rip, slash, slit. 4 *the issue could split the Party:* **divide**, disunite, separate, sever; bisect, partition. 5 *they split the money between them:* **share (out)**, divide (up), apportion, allocate, allot, distribute, dole out, parcel out, measure out; carve up, slice up; informal divvy up. 6 *the path split:* **fork**, divide, bifurcate, diverge, branch. 7 *they split up last year:* **break up**, separate, part, part company, become estranged; divorce, get divorced; Brit. informal bust up.
– OPPOSITES mend, join, unite, pool, converge, get together, marry.
noun 1 *a split in the rock face:* **crack**, fissure, cleft, crevice, break, fracture, breach. 2 *a split in the curtain:* **rip**, tear, cut, rent, slash, slit. 3 *a split in the Party:* **division**, rift, breach, schism, rupture, partition, separation, severance, scission, break-up. 4 *the acrimonious split with his wife:* **break-up**, split-up, separation, parting, estrangement, rift; divorce; Brit. informal bust-up.
– OPPOSITES marriage.
■ **split hairs** quibble, cavil, carp, niggle, chop logic; informal nit-pick.

spoil verb 1 *too much sun spoils the complexion:* **mar**, damage, impair, blemish, disfigure, blight, flaw, deface, scar, injure, harm; ruin, destroy, wreck; be a blot on the landscape; rare disfeature. 2 *rain spoiled my plans:* **ruin**, wreck, destroy, upset, undo, mess up, make a mess of, dash, sabotage, scotch, torpedo; informal foul up, louse up, muck up, screw up, put the kibosh on, banjax, do for; Brit. informal cock up, scupper, throw a spanner in the works of. 3 *his sisters*

spoil *him*: **overindulge**, pamper, indulge, mollycoddle, cosset, coddle, baby, wait on hand and foot, kill with kindness; nanny.
4 *stockpiled food may spoil*: **go bad**, go off, go rancid, turn, go sour, go mouldy, go rotten, rot, perish.
– OPPOSITES improve, enhance, further, help, neglect, be strict with, keep.
■ **spoiling for** *Cooper was spoiling for a fight*: eager for, itching for, looking for, keen to have, after, bent on, longing for.

spoils plural noun **1** *the spoils of war*: **booty**, loot, stolen goods, plunder, ill-gotten gains, haul, pickings; informal swag, boodle. **2** *the spoils of office*: **benefits**, advantages, perks, prize.

spoilsport noun *don't be such a spoilsport!* **killjoy**, dog in the manger, misery, damper; informal wet blanket, party-pooper.

spoken adjective *spoken communication*: **verbal**, oral, vocal, viva voce, uttered, said, stated; unwritten; by word of mouth.
– OPPOSITES non-verbal, written.
■ **spoken for 1** *the money is spoken for*: reserved, set aside, claimed, owned, booked. **2** *Claudine is spoken for*: attached, going out with someone, in a relationship; informal going steady.

spokesman, spokeswoman noun **spokesperson**, representative, agent, mouthpiece, voice, official; informal spin doctor.

sponge verb **1** *I'll sponge your face*: **wash**, clean, wipe, swab; mop, rinse, sluice, swill. **2** (informal) *he lived by sponging off others*: **scrounge**, be a parasite, beg; live off; informal freeload, cadge, bum; N. Amer. informal mooch; Austral./NZ bludge.

spongy adjective *the material has a spongy texture*: **soft**, squashy, cushioned, cushiony, compressible, yielding; springy, resilient, elastic; porous, absorbent, permeable; Brit. informal squidgy.
– OPPOSITES hard, solid.

sponsor noun *the money came from sponsors*: **backer**, patron, promoter, benefactor, benefactress, supporter, contributor, subscriber, friend, guarantor, underwriter; informal angel.
verb *a bank sponsored the event*: **finance**, put up the money for, fund, subsidize, back, promote, support, contribute to, be a patron of, guarantee, underwrite; informal foot the bill for, pick up the tab for; N. Amer. informal bankroll.

sponsorship noun **backing**, support, promotion, patronage, subsidy, funding, financing, aid, financial assistance.

spontaneous adjective **1** *a spontaneous display of affection*: **unplanned**, unpremeditated, unrehearsed, impulsive, impetuous, unstudied, impromptu, spur-of-the-moment, extempore, extemporaneous; unforced, voluntary, unconstrained, unprompted, unbidden, unsolicited; informal off-the-cuff. **2** *a spontaneous reaction to danger*: **reflex**, automatic, mechanical, natural, knee-jerk, involuntary, unthinking, unconscious, instinctive, instinctual; informal gut. **3** *a spontaneous kind of person*: **natural**, uninhibited, relaxed, unselfconscious, unaffected, open, genuine, easy, free and easy; impulsive, impetuous.
– OPPOSITES planned, calculated, conscious, voluntary, inhibited.

spontaneously adverb **1** *they applauded spontaneously*: **without being asked**, of one's own accord, voluntarily, on impulse, impulsively, on the spur of the moment, extempore, extemporaneously; informal off the cuff. **2** *he reacted spontaneously*: **without thinking**, automatically, mechanically, unthinkingly, involuntarily, instinctively, naturally, by oneself/itself.

sporadic adjective *we braved the sporadic showers*: **occasional**, infrequent, irregular, periodic, scattered, patchy, isolated, odd; intermittent, spasmodic, fitful, desultory, erratic, unpredictable.
– OPPOSITES frequent, steady, continuous.

sport noun *we did a lot of sport*: **(competitive) game(s)**, physical recreation, physical activity, physical exercise; pastime.
verb *he sported a beard*: **wear**, have on, dress in; **display**, exhibit, show off, flourish, parade, flaunt.

sporting adjective *it was jolly sporting of you to let me have first go*: **sportsmanlike**, generous, gentlemanly, considerate; fair, just, honourable; Brit. informal decent.
– OPPOSITES dirty, unfair.

sporty adjective (informal) **1** *he's quite a sporty type*: **athletic**, fit, active, energetic. **2** *a sporty outfit*: **stylish**, smart, jaunty; **casual**, informal; informal trendy, cool, snazzy; N. Amer. informal sassy. **3** *a sporty car*: **fast**, speedy; informal nippy, zippy.
– OPPOSITES unfit, lazy, formal, sloppy, slow.

spot noun **1** *a grease spot on the wall*: **mark**, patch, dot, fleck, smudge, smear, stain, blotch, blot, splash; informal splotch, splodge. **2** *a spot on his nose*: **pimple**, pustule, blackhead, boil, swelling, eruption, wen; **(spots)** acne; informal zit, whitehead; Scottish informal plook. **3** *a secluded spot*: **place**, location, site, position, point, situation, scene, setting, locale, locality, area, neighbourhood, region; venue. **4** *social policy has a regular spot on the agenda*: **position**, place, slot, space. **5** *would you like a spot of lunch?* **bit**, little, some, small amount, morsel, bite, mouthful; drop, splash; informal smidgen, tad.
verb **1** *she spotted him in his car*: **notice**, see, observe, note, discern, detect, perceive, make out, recognize, identify, locate; catch sight of, glimpse; Brit. informal clock. **2** *her clothes were spotted with grease*: **stain**, mark, fleck, speckle, smudge, streak, splash, spatter; informal splotch, splodge.
■ **on the spot** immediately, at once, straight

away, right away, without delay, without hesitation, that instant, directly, there and then, then and there, forthwith, instantly, summarily; N. Amer. in short order.

spotless adjective **1** *the kitchen was spotless:* **perfectly clean**, ultra-clean, pristine, immaculate, shining, shiny, gleaming, spick and span. **2** *a spotless reputation:* **unblemished**, unsullied, untarnished, untainted, unstained, pure, whiter than white, innocent, impeccable, blameless, irreproachable, above reproach; informal squeaky clean.
– OPPOSITES dirty, tarnished, impure.

spotlight noun *she was constantly in the spotlight:* **public eye**, glare of publicity, limelight; focus of public/media attention.
verb *this article spotlights the problem:* **focus attention on**, highlight, point up, draw/call attention to, give prominence to, throw into relief, turn the spotlight on, bring to the fore.

spotted adjective **1** *the spotted leaves:* **mottled**, dappled, speckled, flecked, freckled, freckly, dotted, stippled, brindle(d); informal splotchy. **2** *a black-and-white spotted dress:* **polka-dot**, spotty, dotted.
– OPPOSITES plain.

spotty adjective **1** *a spotty dog:* **spotted**, mottled, speckled, speckly, flecked, specked, stippled; informal splodgy, splotchy. **2** *a spotty dress:* **polka-dot**, spotted, dotted. **3** (Brit.) *his spotty face:* **pimply**, pimpled, acned; Scottish informal plooky.

spouse noun **partner**, mate, consort; informal better half; Brit. informal other half. See also HUSBAND noun, WIFE.

spout verb **1** *lava was spouting from the crater:* **spurt**, gush, spew, erupt, shoot, squirt, spray; disgorge, discharge, emit, belch forth. **2** *he spouts on foreign affairs:* **hold forth**, sound off, go on, talk at length, expatiate; informal mouth off, speechify, spiel.
noun *a can with a spout:* **nozzle**, lip, rose.

sprawl verb **1** *he sprawled on a sofa:* **stretch out**, lounge, loll, lie, recline, drape oneself, slump, flop, slouch. **2** *the town sprawled ahead of them:* **spread**, stretch, extend, be strung out, be scattered, straggle, spill.

spray[1] noun **1** *a spray of water:* **shower**, sprinkling, sprinkle, jet, mist, drizzle; spume, spindrift; foam, froth. **2** *a perfume spray:* **atomizer**, vaporizer, aerosol, sprinkler; nebulizer.
verb **1** *water was sprayed around:* **sprinkle**, shower, spatter; scatter, disperse, diffuse; mist; douche. **2** *water sprayed into the air:* **spout**, jet, gush, spurt, shoot, squirt.

spray[2] noun **1** *a spray of holly:* **sprig**, twig. **2** *a spray of flowers:* **bouquet**, bunch, posy, nosegay; corsage, buttonhole, boutonnière.

spread verb **1** *he spread the map out:* **lay out**, open out, unfurl, unroll, roll out; straighten out, fan out; stretch out, extend. **2** *the*

landscape spread out below: **extend**, stretch, open out, be displayed, be exhibited, be on show; sprawl. **3** *papers were spread all over his desk:* **scatter**, strew, disperse, distribute. **4** *he's been spreading rumours:* **disseminate**, circulate, pass on, put about, communicate, diffuse, make public, make known, purvey, broadcast, publicize, propagate, promulgate; repeat. **5** *she spread cold cream on her face:* **smear**, daub, plaster, slather, lather, apply, put; smooth, rub. **6** *he spread the toast with butter:* **cover**, coat, layer, daub, smother; butter.
– OPPOSITES fold up, suppress.
noun **1** *the spread of learning:* **expansion**, proliferation, extension, growth, buildout; dissemination, diffusion, transmission, propagation. **2** *a spread of six feet:* **span**, width, extent, stretch, reach. **3** *the immense spread of the heavens:* **expanse**, area, sweep, stretch. **4** *a wide spread of subjects:* **range**, span, spectrum, sweep; variety.

spree noun **1** *a shopping spree:* **unrestrained bout**, orgy; informal binge, splurge; humorous retail therapy. **2** *a drinking spree:* **drinking bout**, debauch; informal binge, bender, session, booze-up, blind; Scottish informal skite; N. Amer. informal jag, toot.

sprig noun *a sprig of lilac:* **small stem**, spray, twig.

sprightly adjective *she was quite sprightly for her age:* **spry**, lively, agile, nimble, energetic, active, full of energy, vigorous, spirited, animated, vivacious, frisky; informal full of vim and vigour; N. English informal wick.
– OPPOSITES doddery, lethargic.

spring verb **1** *the cat sprang off her lap:* **leap**, jump, bound, vault, hop. **2** *the branch sprang back:* **fly**, whip, flick, whisk, kick, bounce. **3** *all art springs from feelings:* **originate**, derive, arise, stem, emanate, proceed, issue, evolve, come. **4** *fifty men sprang from nowhere:* **appear suddenly**, appear unexpectedly, materialize, pop up, shoot up, sprout, develop quickly; proliferate, mushroom. **5** *he sprang the truth on me:* **announce suddenly/unexpectedly**, reveal suddenly/unexpectedly, surprise someone with.
noun **1** *with a sudden spring he leapt on to the table:* **leap**, jump, bound, vault, hop; pounce. **2** *the mattress has lost its spring:* **springiness**, bounciness, bounce, resilience, elasticity, flexibility, stretch, stretchiness, give. **3** *there was a spring in his step:* **buoyancy**, bounce, energy, liveliness, jauntiness, sprightliness, confidence. **4** *a mineral spring:* **well head**, source, spa, geyser.

springy adjective *the turf was springy beneath her feet:* **elastic**, stretchy, stretchable, tensile; flexible, pliant, pliable, whippy; bouncy, resilient, spongy.
– OPPOSITES rigid, squashy.

sprinkle verb **1** *he sprinkled water over the towel:* **splash**, trickle, spray, shower; spatter.

2 *sprinkle sesame seeds over the top:* **scatter**, strew; drizzle. **3** *sprinkle the cake with icing sugar:* **dredge**, dust. **4** *the sky was sprinkled with stars:* **dot**, stipple, stud, fleck, speckle, spot, pepper; scatter, cover.

sprinkling noun **1** *a sprinkling of nutmeg:* **scattering**, sprinkle, scatter, dusting; pinch, dash. **2** *mainly women, but a sprinkling of men:* **few**, one or two, couple, handful, small number, trickle, scattering.

sprint verb *she sprinted across the square:* **run**, race, dart, rush, dash, hasten, hurry, scurry, scamper, hare, bolt, fly, gallop, career, charge, shoot, hurtle, speed, zoom, go like lightning, go hell for leather, go like the wind; jog, trot; informal tear, pelt, scoot, hotfoot it, leg it, belt, zip, whip; Brit. informal bomb; N. Amer. informal hightail it, barrel.
– OPPOSITES walk.

sprite noun **fairy**, elf, pixie, imp, brownie, puck, peri, kelpie, leprechaun; nymph, nixie, sylph, naiad.

sprout verb **1** *the weeds begin to sprout:* **germinate**, put/send out shoots, bud, burgeon. **2** *he had sprouted a beard:* **grow**, develop, put/send out. **3** *parsley sprouted from the pot:* **spring up**, shoot up, come up, grow, burgeon, develop, appear.

spruce adjective *the Captain looked very spruce:* **neat**, well groomed, well turned out, well dressed, smart, trim, dapper, elegant, chic; informal natty, snazzy; N. Amer. informal spiffy, trig.
– OPPOSITES untidy.
verb **1** *the cottage had been spruced up:* **smarten**, tidy, neaten, put in order, clean; informal do up; Brit. informal tart up, posh up; N. Amer. informal gussy up. **2** *Sarah had spruced herself up:* **groom**, tidy, smarten, preen, primp, prink; N. Amer. trig; informal titivate, doll up; Brit. informal tart up.

spry adjective *he's remarkably spry for a man of his age:* **sprightly**, lively, agile, nimble, energetic, active, full of energy, vigorous, spirited, animated, vivacious, frisky; informal full of vim and vigour; N. English informal wick.
– OPPOSITES doddery, lethargic.

spume noun *the spume of the white-capped waves:* **foam**, froth, surf, spindrift, bubbles.

spur noun **1** *competition can be a spur:* **stimulus**, incentive, encouragement, inducement, fillip, impetus, prod, motivation, inspiration; informal kick up the backside, shot in the arm. **2** *a spur of bone:* **projection**, spike, point.
– OPPOSITES disincentive, discouragement.
verb *the thought spurred him into action:* **stimulate**, encourage, prompt, propel, prod, induce, impel, motivate, move, galvanize, inspire, incentivize, urge, drive, egg on, stir; incite, goad, provoke, prick, sting; N. Amer. light a fire under.
– OPPOSITES discourage.
■ **on the spur of the moment** impulsively, on impulse, impetuously, without thinking, without premeditation, unpremeditatedly,

impromptu, extempore, spontaneously; informal off the cuff.

spurious adjective *it was possible to arrange retirements on spurious medical grounds:* **bogus**, fake, false, counterfeit, forged, fraudulent, sham, artificial, imitation, simulated, feigned, deceptive, misleading; informal phoney, pretend; Brit. informal cod.
– OPPOSITES genuine.

spurn verb *he spurned the offer of a drink:* **reject**, rebuff, scorn, turn down, treat with contempt, disdain, look down one's nose at, despise; snub, slight, jilt, dismiss, brush off, turn one's back on; give someone the cold shoulder, cold-shoulder; informal turn one's nose up at, give someone the brush-off, kick in the teeth; Brit. informal knock back; N. Amer. informal give someone the bum's rush.
– OPPOSITES welcome, accept.

spurt verb *water spurted from the tap:* **squirt**, shoot, jet, erupt, gush, pour, stream, pump, surge, spew, course, well, spring, burst; disgorge, discharge, emit, belch forth, expel, eject; Brit. informal sloosh.
noun **1** *a spurt of water:* **squirt**, jet, spout, gush, stream, rush, surge, flood, cascade, torrent. **2** *a spurt of courage:* **burst**, fit, bout, rush, spate, surge, attack, outburst, blaze. **3** *Daisy put on a spurt:* **burst of speed**, turn of speed, sprint, rush, burst of energy.

spy noun *a foreign spy:* **secret agent**, intelligence agent, double agent, counterspy, mole, plant, scout; informal snooper; N. Amer. informal spook.
verb **1** *he spied for the West:* **be a spy**, gather intelligence, work for the secret service; informal snoop. **2** *investigators spied on them:* **observe furtively**, keep under surveillance/observation, watch, keep a watch on, keep an eye on. **3** *she spied a coffee shop:* **notice**, observe, see, spot, sight, catch sight of, glimpse, make out, discern, detect; informal clap/lay/set eyes on.

spying noun **espionage**, intelligence gathering, surveillance, infiltration, undercover work, cloak-and-dagger activities.

squabble noun *there was a squabble over which way they should go:* **quarrel**, disagreement, row, argument, contretemps, falling-out, dispute, clash, altercation, shouting match, exchange, war of words; informal tiff, set-to, run-in, slanging match, shindig, shindy, stand-up, spat, scrap, dust-up; Brit. informal barney, ding-dong; N. Amer. informal rhubarb.
verb *the boys were squabbling over a ball:* **quarrel**, row, argue, bicker, fall out, disagree, have words, dispute, spar, cross swords, lock horns, be at loggerheads; informal scrap, argufy.

squad noun **1** *an assassination squad:* **team**, crew, gang, band, cell, body, mob, outfit, force. **2** *a firing squad:* **detachment**, detail, unit, platoon, battery, troop, patrol, squadron, cadre, commando.

S

squalid adjective **1** *a squalid prison:* **dirty**, filthy, grubby, grimy, mucky, slummy, foul, vile, poor, sorry, wretched, miserable, mean, seedy, shabby, sordid, insalubrious; **neglected**, uncared-for, broken-down, run down, down at heel, depressed, dilapidated, ramshackle, tumbledown, gone to rack and ruin, crumbling, decaying; informal scruffy, crummy, shambly, ratty; Brit. informal grotty; N. Amer. informal shacky. **2** *a squalid deal with the opposition:* **improper**, sordid, unseemly, unsavoury, sleazy, seedy, seamy, shoddy, cheap, base, low, corrupt, dishonest, dishonourable, disreputable, despicable, discreditable, disgraceful, contemptible, shameful.
– OPPOSITES clean, pleasant, smart, upmarket, proper, decent.

squall noun *squalls of driving rain:* **gust**, storm, blast, flurry, shower, gale, blow, rush.

squally adjective *squally showers of rain:* **stormy**, gusty, gusting, blustery, blustering, windy, blowy; wild, tempestuous, rough.
– OPPOSITES steady, calm.

squalor noun *they lived in squalor:* **dirt**, filth, grubbiness, grime, muck, foulness, vileness, poverty, wretchedness, meanness, seediness, shabbiness, sordidness, sleaziness, insalubrity; **neglect**, decay, dilapidation; informal scruffiness, crumminess, grunge, rattiness; Brit. informal grottiness.
– OPPOSITES cleanliness, pleasantness, smartness.

squander verb *£100 million of taxpayers' money has been squandered on administering the tax:* **waste**, misspend, misuse, throw away, fritter away, spend recklessly, lavish, spend unwisely, spend like water; informal blow, go through, splurge, pour down the drain; Brit. informal blue.
– OPPOSITES manage, make good use of, save.

square noun *a shop in the square:* market square, marketplace, plaza, piazza.
adjective **1** *a square table:* **quadrilateral**, rectangular, oblong, right-angled, at right angles, perpendicular; straight, level, parallel, horizontal, upright, vertical, true, plane. **2** *the sides were square at half-time:* **level**, even, drawn, equal, tied; neck and neck, level pegging, nip and tuck, side by side, evenly matched; informal even-steven(s). **3** *I'm going to be square with you:* **fair**, honest, just, equitable, straight, true, upright, above board, ethical, decent, proper; informal on the level.
– OPPOSITES crooked, uneven, underhand.
verb **1** *the theory does not square with the data:* **agree**, tally, be in agreement, be consistent, match up, correspond, fit, coincide, accord, conform, be compatible. **2** *his goal squared the match 1–1:* **level**, even, make equal. **3** *would you square up the bill?* **pay**, settle, discharge, clear, meet. **4** (informal) *they tried to square the press:* **bribe**, buy off, buy, corrupt, suborn; informal grease

someone's palm, give a backhander to. **5** *Tom squared things with his boss:* **resolve**, sort out, settle, clear up, work out, iron out, smooth over, straighten out, deal with, put right, set right, put to rights, rectify, remedy; informal patch up.

squash verb **1** *the fruit got squashed:* **crush**, squeeze, flatten, compress, press, smash, distort, pound, trample, stamp on; pulp, mash, cream, liquidize, beat, pulverize. **2** *she squashed her clothes inside the bag:* **force**, ram, thrust, push, cram, jam, stuff, pack, compress, squeeze, wedge, press. **3** *the proposal was immediately squashed:* **reject**, block, cancel, scotch, frustrate, thwart, suppress, put a stop to, nip in the bud, put the lid on; informal put paid to, put the kibosh on, stymie; Brit. informal dish, scupper.

squashy adjective **1** *a squashy pillow:* **springy**, resilient, spongy, soft, pliant, pliable, yielding, elastic, cushiony, compressible. **2** *squashy pears:* **mushy**, pulpy, pappy, slushy, squelchy, squishy, oozy, doughy, soft; Brit. informal squidgy.
– OPPOSITES firm, hard.

squat verb *I was squatting on the floor:* **crouch (down)**, hunker (down), sit on one's haunches, sit on one's heels.
adjective *he was muscular and squat:* **stocky**, thickset, dumpy, stubby, stumpy, short, small; Brit. informal fubsy.

squawk verb & noun *a pheasant squawked | the gull gave a squawk:* **screech**, squeal, shriek, scream, croak, crow, caw, cluck, cackle, hoot, cry, call.

squeak noun & verb **1** *the vole's dying squeak | the rat squeaked:* **peep**, cheep, pipe, piping, squeal, tweet, yelp, whimper. **2** *the squeak of the hinge | the hinges of the gate squeaked:* **screech**, creak, scrape, grate, rasp, jar, groan.

squeal noun *the harsh squeal of a fox:* **screech**, scream, shriek, squawk.
verb **1** *a dog squealed:* **screech**, scream, shriek, squawk. **2** *the bookies only squealed because we beat them:* **complain**, protest, object, grouse, grumble, whine, wail, carp, squawk; informal kick up a fuss, kick up a stink, gripe, grouch, bellyache, moan, bitch, beef, whinge; N. English informal mither.

squeamish adjective **1** *I'm too squeamish to gut fish:* **easily nauseated**, nervous; (**be squeamish about**) **be put off by**, cannot stand the sight of, ... makes one feel sick. **2** *less squeamish nations will sell them arms:* **scrupulous**, principled, fastidious, particular, punctilious, honourable, upright, upstanding, high-minded, righteous, right-minded, moral, ethical.

squeeze verb **1** *I squeezed the bottle:* **compress**, press, crush, squash, pinch, nip, grasp, grip, clutch, flatten. **2** *squeeze the juice from both oranges:* **extract**, press, force, express. **3** *Sally squeezed her feet into the sandals:* **force**, thrust, cram, ram, jam, stuff, pack, wedge, press, squash. **4** *we all squeezed*

into Steve's van: **crowd**, crush, cram, pack, jam, squash, wedge oneself, shove, push, force one's way. **5** *he would squeeze more money out of Bill:* **extort**, force, extract, wrest, wring, milk; informal bleed someone of something.
noun **1** *he gave her hand a squeeze:* **press**, pinch, nip; grasp, grip, clutch, hug, clasp; compression. **2** *it was a tight squeeze in the tiny hall:* **crush**, jam, squash, press, huddle; congestion. **3** *a squeeze of lemon juice:* **few drops**, dash, splash, dribble, trickle, spot, hint, touch.

squint verb **1** *the sun made them squint:* **screw up one's eyes**, narrow one's eyes, peer, blink. **2** *he has squinted from birth:* **be cross-eyed**, have a squint, suffer from strabismus; Scottish be skelly; Brit. informal be boss-eyed.
noun *does he have a squint?* **cross-eyes**, strabismus; Brit. informal boss-eye.

squire noun *the squire of the village:* **landowner**, landholder, landlord, lord of the manor, country gentleman.

squirm verb **1** *I tried to squirm away:* **wriggle**, wiggle, writhe, twist, slide, slither, turn, shift, fidget, jiggle, twitch, thresh, flounder, flail, toss and turn. **2** *he squirmed as everyone laughed:* **wince**, shudder, feel embarrassed, feel ashamed.

squirrel
■ **squirrel something away** *try to squirrel a little cash away for a rainy day:* save, put aside, put by, lay by, set aside, lay aside, keep in reserve, stockpile, accumulate, stock up with/on, hoard; informal salt away, stash away.

squirt verb **1** *a jet of ink squirted out of the tube:* **spurt**, shoot, spray, fountain, jet, erupt; gush, rush, pump, surge, stream, spew, well, spring, burst, issue, emanate; emit, belch forth, expel, eject; Brit. informal sloosh. **2** *she squirted me with scent:* **splash**, wet, spray, shower, spatter, splatter, sprinkle; Scottish & Irish slabber.
noun *a squirt of water:* **spurt**, jet, spray, fountain, gush, stream, surge.

stab verb **1** *he stabbed him in the stomach:* **knife**, run through, skewer, spear, bayonet, gore, spike, stick, impale, transfix, pierce, prick, puncture. **2** *she stabbed at the earth with a fork:* **lunge**, thrust, jab, poke, prod, dig.
noun **1** *a stab in the leg:* **knife wound**, puncture, incision, prick, cut, perforation. **2** *they made stabs into the air:* **lunge**, thrust, jab, poke, prod, dig, punch. **3** *a stab of pain:* **twinge**, pang, throb, spasm, cramp, dart, blaze, prick, flash, thrill.
■ **stab someone in the back** betray, be disloyal to, be unfaithful to, desert, break one's promise to, double-cross, break faith with, sell out, play false, inform on/against; informal tell on, sell down the river, squeal on, stitch up, peach on, do the dirty on; Brit. informal grass on, shop; N. Amer. informal rat out,

finger, drop a/the dime on; Austral. informal pimp on, pool, put someone's pot on.

stability noun **1** *the stability of play equipment:* **firmness**, solidity, steadiness, strength, security, safety. **2** *his mental stability:* **balance of mind**, mental health, sanity, normality, soundness, rationality, reason, sense. **3** *the stability of their relationship:* **steadiness**, firmness, solidity, strength, durability, lasting nature, enduring nature, permanence, changelessness, invariability, immutability, indestructibility, reliability, dependability.

stable adjective **1** *a stable tent:* **firm**, solid, steady, secure, fixed, fast, safe, moored, anchored, stuck down, immovable. **2** *a stable person:* **well balanced**, of sound mind, compos mentis, sane, normal, right in the head, rational, steady, reasonable, sensible, sober, down-to-earth, matter-of-fact, having both one's feet on the ground; informal all there. **3** *a stable relationship:* **secure**, solid, strong, steady, firm, sure, steadfast, unwavering, unvarying, unfaltering, unfluctuating; established, abiding, durable, enduring, lasting, permanent, reliable, dependable.
– OPPOSITES loose, wobbly, unbalanced, rocky, changeable.

stack noun **1** *a stack of boxes:* **heap**, pile, mound, mountain, pyramid, tower. **2** *a stack of hay:* **haystack**, rick, hayrick, stook, mow, shock. **3** **chimney**, smokestack, funnel, exhaust pipe.
– OPPOSITES few, little.
verb **1** *Leo was stacking plates:* **heap (up)**, pile (up), make a heap/pile/stack of; assemble, put together, collect, hoard, store, stockpile. **2** *they stacked the shelves:* **load**, fill (up), lade, pack, charge, stuff, cram; stock.
– OPPOSITES distribute, empty.

stadium noun **arena**, field, ground, pitch; bowl, amphitheatre, coliseum, ring, dome, manège; track, course, racetrack, racecourse, speedway, velodrome; (in ancient Rome) circus.

staff noun **1** *there is a reluctance to take on new staff:* **employees**, workers, workforce, personnel, human resources, manpower, labour; informal liveware. **2** *he carried a wooden staff:* **stick**, stave, pole, crook. **3** *a staff of office:* **rod**, tipstaff, cane, mace, wand, sceptre, crozier, verge.
verb *the centre is staffed by teachers:* **man**, people, crew, work, operate, occupy.

stage noun **1** *this stage of the development:* **phase**, period, juncture, step, point, time, moment, instant, level. **2** *the last stage of the race:* **part**, section, portion, stretch, leg, lap, circuit. **3** *a theatre stage:* **platform**, dais, stand, grandstand, staging, apron, rostrum, podium. **4** *she has written for the stage:* **theatre**, drama, dramatics, dramatic art, thespianism; informal the boards. **5** *the political stage:* **scene**, setting; context, frame, sphere, field, realm, arena, backdrop; affairs.
verb **1** *they staged two plays:* **put on**, put

S

before the public, present, produce, mount, direct; perform, act, give. **2** *workers staged a protest:* **organize**, arrange, coordinate, lay on, put together, get together, set up; orchestrate, choreograph, mastermind, engineer; take part in, participate in, join in.

stagger verb **1** *he staggered to the door:* **lurch**, walk unsteadily, reel, sway, teeter, totter, stumble, wobble. **2** *I was absolutely staggered:* **amaze**, astound, astonish, surprise, startle, stun, confound, dumbfound, stupefy, daze, nonplus, take aback, leave open-mouthed, leave aghast; informal flabbergast, bowl over; Brit. informal knock for six. **3** *meetings are staggered throughout the day:* **spread (out)**, space (out), time at intervals, overlap. **4** *stagger the screws at each joint:* **alternate**, step, arrange in a zigzag.

stagnant adjective **1** *stagnant water:* **still**, motionless, static, stationary, standing, dead, slack; **foul**, stale, putrid, smelly. **2** *a stagnant economy:* **inactive**, sluggish, slow-moving, lethargic, static, flat, depressed, declining, moribund, dying, dead, dormant.
– OPPOSITES flowing, fresh, active, vibrant.

stagnate verb **1** *obstructions allow water to stagnate:* **stop flowing**, become stagnant, become trapped; stand; become foul, become stale; fester, putrefy. **2** *exports stagnated:* **languish**, decline, deteriorate, fall, become stagnant, do nothing, stand still, be sluggish.
– OPPOSITES flow, rise, boom.

staid adjective *staid old ladies:* **sedate**, respectable, quiet, serious, serious-minded, steady, conventional, traditional, unadventurous, unenterprising, set in one's ways, sober, proper, decorous, formal, stuffy, stiff; informal starchy, stick-in-the-mud.
– OPPOSITES frivolous, daring, informal.

stain verb **1** *her clothing was stained with blood:* **discolour**, blemish, soil, mark, muddy, spot, spatter, splatter, smear, splash, smudge, blotch, blacken. **2** *the report stained his reputation:* **damage**, injure, harm, sully, blacken, tarnish, taint, smear, bring discredit to, dishonour, drag through the mud. **3** *the wood was stained:* **colour**, tint, dye, tinge, pigment, colour-wash.
noun **1** *a mud stain:* **mark**, spot, spatter, splatter, blotch, smudge, smear. **2** *a stain on his character:* **blemish**, injury, taint, blot, smear, discredit, dishonour; damage. **3** *dark wood stain:* **tint**, colour, dye, tinge, pigment, colourant, colour wash.

stake[1] noun *a stake in the ground:* **post**, pole, stick, spike, upright, support, prop, strut, pale, paling, picket, pile, piling, cane.
verb **1** *the plants have to be staked:* **prop up**, tie up, tether, support, hold up, brace, truss. **2** *he staked his claim:* **assert**, declare, proclaim, state, make, lay, put in.
■ **stake something out 1** *builders staked out the plot:* mark off/out, demarcate,

measure out, delimit, fence off, section off, close off, shut off, cordon off. **2** (informal) *the police staked out his flat:* observe, watch, keep an eye on, keep under observation, keep watch on, monitor, keep under surveillance, surveil; informal keep tabs on, keep a tab on, case.

stake[2] noun **1** *playing dice for high stakes:* **bet**, wager, ante. **2** *they are racing for record stakes:* **prize money**, purse, pot, winnings. **3** *low down in the popularity stakes:* **competition**, contest, battle, challenge, rivalry, race, running, struggle, scramble. **4** *a 40% stake in the business:* **share**, interest, ownership, involvement.
verb *he staked all his week's pay:* **bet**, wager, lay, put on, gamble, chance, venture, risk, hazard.

stale adjective **1** *stale food:* **old**, past its best, past its sell-by date; off, dry, hard, musty, rancid. **2** *stale air:* **stuffy**, close, musty, fusty, stagnant, frowzy; Brit. frowsty, fuggy. **3** *stale beer:* **flat**, turned, spoiled, off, insipid, tasteless. **4** *stale jokes:* **hackneyed**, tired, worn out, overworked, threadbare, warmed-up, banal, trite, clichéd, platitudinous, unoriginal, unimaginative, uninspired, flat, out of date, outdated, outmoded, passé, archaic, obsolete; N. Amer. warmed-over; informal old hat, corny, out of the ark, played out.
– OPPOSITES fresh, original.

stalemate noun *the talks had reached a stalemate:* **deadlock**, impasse, stand-off; draw, tie, dead heat.

stalk[1] noun *the stalk of a plant:* **stem**, shoot, trunk, stock, cane, bine, bent, haulm, straw, reed.

stalk[2] verb **1** *a stoat was stalking a rabbit:* **creep up on**, trail, follow, shadow, track down, go after, be after, course, hunt; informal tail. **2** *she stalked out:* **strut**, stride, march, flounce, storm, stomp, sweep.

stall noun **1** *a market stall:* **stand**, table, counter, booth, kiosk. **2** *stalls for larger animals:* **pen**, coop, sty, corral, enclosure, compartment. **3** (Brit.) *theatre stalls:* N. Amer. orchestra, parterre.
verb **1** *the Government has stalled the project:* **obstruct**, impede, interfere with, hinder, hamper, block, interrupt, hold up, hold back, thwart, baulk, sabotage, delay, stonewall, check, stop, halt, derail, put a brake on; informal stymie; N. Amer. informal bork. **2** *quit stalling:* **use delaying tactics**, play for time, temporize, gain time, procrastinate, hedge, beat about the bush, drag one's feet, delay, filibuster, stonewall. **3** *stall him for a bit:* **delay**, divert, distract; **hold off**, stave off, fend off, keep off, ward off, keep at bay.

stalwart adjective *a stalwart supporter of the cause:* **staunch**, loyal, faithful, committed, devoted, dedicated, dependable, reliable, steady, constant, trusty, hard-working, steadfast, redoubtable, unwavering.
– OPPOSITES disloyal, unfaithful, unreliable.

S

stamina noun *their secret is stamina rather than speed:* **endurance**, staying power, tirelessness, fortitude, strength, energy, toughness, determination, tenacity, perseverance, grit.

stammer verb *he began to stammer:* **stutter**, stumble over one's words, hesitate, falter, pause, halt, splutter.
noun *he had a stammer:* **stutter**, speech impediment, speech defect.

stamp verb **1** *he stamped on my toe:* **trample**, step, tread, tramp; **crush**, squash, flatten. **2** *John stamped off, muttering:* **stomp**, stump, clomp, clump. **3** *the name is stamped on the cover:* **imprint**, print, impress, punch, inscribe, emboss, brand, frank. **4** *his face was stamped on Martha's memory:* **fix**, inscribe, etch, carve, imprint, impress. **5** *his style stamps him as a player to watch:* **identify**, characterize, brand, distinguish, classify, mark out, set apart, single out.
noun **1** *the stamp of authority:* **mark**, hallmark, indication, sign, seal, sure sign, telltale sign, quality, smack, smell, savour, air. **2** *he was of a very different stamp:* **type**, kind, sort, variety, class, category, classification, style, description, condition, calibre, status, quality, nature, ilk, kidney, cast, grain, mould; N. Amer. stripe.
■ **stamp something out** *urgent action is required to stamp out corruption:* put an end/stop to, end, stop, crush, put down, crack down on, curb, nip in the bud, scotch, squash, quash, quell, subdue, suppress, extinguish, stifle, abolish, get rid of, eliminate, eradicate, beat, overcome, defeat, destroy, wipe out; informal put the kibosh on.

stampede noun *the noise caused a stampede:* **charge**, panic, rush, flight, rout.
verb *the sheep stampeded:* **bolt**, charge, flee, take flight; race, rush, career, sweep, run.

stance noun **1** *a natural golfer's stance:* **posture**, body position, pose, attitude. **2** *a liberal stance:* **attitude**, stand, point of view, viewpoint, opinion, way of thinking, outlook, standpoint, position, angle, perspective, approach, line, policy.

stand verb **1** *Lionel stood in the doorway:* **be on one's feet**, be upright, be erect, be vertical. **2** *the men stood up:* **rise**, get/rise to one's feet, get up, straighten up, pick oneself up, find one's feet, be upstanding. **3** *today a house stands on the site:* **be**, be situated, be located, be positioned, be sited, have been built. **4** *he stood the book on the shelf:* **put**, set, set up, erect, upend, place, position, locate, prop, lean, stick, install, arrange; informal park. **5** *my decision stands:* **remain in force**, remain valid/effective/operative, remain in operation, hold, hold good, apply, be the case, exist. **6** *his heart could not stand the strain:* **withstand**, endure, bear, put up with, take, cope with, handle, sustain, resist, stand up to. **7** (informal) *I won't stand cheek:* **endure**, tolerate, bear, put up with, take, abide, support, countenance; Scottish thole;

informal swallow, stomach; Brit. informal stick, wear.
– OPPOSITES sit, lie, sit down, lie down.
noun **1** *the party's stand on immigration:* **attitude**, stance, point of view, viewpoint, opinion, way of thinking, outlook, standpoint, position, approach, thinking, policy, line. **2** *a stand against tyranny:* **opposition**, resistance, objection, hostility, animosity. **3** *a large mirror on a stand:* **base**, support, mounting, platform, rest, plinth, bottom; tripod, rack, trivet. **4** *a beer stand:* **stall**, counter, booth, kiosk, tent.
■ **stand by** wait, be prepared, be in (a state of) readiness, be ready for action, be on full alert, wait in the wings.
■ **stand by someone/something 1** *she stood by her husband:* remain/be loyal to, stick with/by, remain/be true to, stand up for, support, back up, defend, stick up for. **2** *the government must stand by its pledges:* abide by, keep (to), adhere to, hold to, stick to, observe, comply with.
■ **stand for 1** *V stands for volts:* mean, be an abbreviation of, represent, signify, denote, indicate, symbolize. **2** *we stand for animal welfare:* advocate, champion, uphold, defend, stand up for, support, back, endorse, be in favour of, promote, recommend, urge.
■ **stand in** deputize, act, act as deputy, substitute, fill in, sit in, do duty, take over, act as locum, be a proxy, cover, hold the fort, step into the breach; replace, relieve, take over from; informal sub, fill someone's shoes, step into someone's shoes; N. Amer. pinch-hit.
■ **stand out 1** *his veins stood out:* project, stick out, bulge (out), be proud, jut (out). **2** *she stood out in the crowd:* be noticeable, be visible, be obvious, be conspicuous, stick out, be striking, be distinctive, be prominent, attract attention, catch the eye, leap out, show up; informal stick/stand out a mile, stick/stand out like a sore thumb.
■ **stand up** *he has no proof that would stand up in court:* remain/be valid, be sound, be plausible, hold water, hold up, stand questioning, survive investigation, bear examination, be verifiable.
■ **stand someone up** *she threw eggs over his car after he stood her up:* fail to keep a date with, fail to meet, fail to keep an appointment with, jilt.
■ **stand up for someone/something** *we should stand up for democracy:* support, defend, back, back up, stick up for, champion, promote, uphold, take someone's part, take the side of, side with.
■ **stand up to someone/something 1** *she stood up to her parents:* defy, confront, challenge, resist, take on, put up a fight against, argue with, take a stand against. **2** *the old house has stood up to the war:* withstand, survive, come through (unscathed), outlast, outlive, weather, ride out, ward off.

standard noun **1** *the standard of her work:* **quality**, level, grade, calibre, merit,

S

excellence. **2** *a safety standard:* **guideline**, norm, yardstick, benchmark, measure, criterion, guide, touchstone, model, pattern, example, exemplar. **3** *a standard to live by:* **principle**, ideal; (**standards**) code of behaviour, code of honour, morals, scruples, ethics. **4** *the regiment's standard:* **flag**, banner, pennant, ensign, colour(s), banderole, guidon; Brit. pendant.
▸adjective **1** *the standard way of doing it:* **normal**, usual, typical, stock, common, ordinary, customary, conventional, wonted, established, settled, set, fixed, traditional, prevailing. **2** *the standard work on the subject:* **definitive**, established, classic, recognized, accepted, authoritative, most reliable, exhaustive.
– OPPOSITES unusual, special.

standardize verb *they attempted to standardize the names of the plants they were growing:* **systematize**, make consistent, make uniform, make comparable, regulate, normalize, bring into line, equalize, homogenize, regiment.

stand-in noun *a stand-in for the minister:* **substitute**, replacement, deputy, surrogate, proxy, understudy, locum, supply, fill-in, cover, relief, stopgap; informal temp; N. Amer. informal pinch-hitter.
▸adjective *a stand-in goalkeeper:* **substitute**, replacement, deputy, fill-in, stopgap, supply, surrogate, relief, acting, temporary, provisional, caretaker; N. Amer. informal pinch-hitting.

standing noun **1** *his standing in the community:* **status**, rank, ranking, position; reputation, estimation, stature. **2** *a person of some standing:* **seniority**, rank, eminence, prominence, prestige, repute, stature, esteem, importance, account, consequence, influence, distinction; informal clout. **3** *a squabble of long standing:* **duration**, existence, continuance, endurance, life.
▸adjective **1** *standing stones:* **upright**, erect, vertical, plumb, upended, on end, perpendicular; on one's feet; not yet reaped; Heraldry rampant. **2** *standing water:* **stagnant**, still, motionless, static, stationary, dead, slack. **3** *a standing invitation:* **permanent**, perpetual, everlasting, continuing, abiding, indefinite, open-ended; regular, repeated.
– OPPOSITES flat, lying down, seated, flowing, temporary, occasional.

stand-off noun *the 16-day-old stand-off was no closer to being resolved:* **deadlock**, stalemate, impasse; draw, tie, dead heat; suspension of hostilities, lull.

stand-offish adjective (informal) *she is very stand-offish with strangers:* **aloof**, distant, remote, detached, withdrawn, reserved, uncommunicative, unforthcoming, unapproachable, unresponsive, unfriendly, unsociable, introspective, introverted.
– OPPOSITES friendly, approachable, sociable.

standpoint noun *she writes on religion from the standpoint of a believer:* **point of view**, viewpoint, vantage point, attitude, stance, view, opinion, position, way of thinking, outlook, perspective.

standstill noun *the traffic came to a standstill:* **halt**, stop, dead stop, stand.

staple adjective *rice was the staple crop grown in most villages:* **main**, principal, chief, major, primary, leading, foremost, first, most important, predominant, dominant, (most) prominent, basic, standard, prime, premier; informal number-one.

star noun **1** *the sky was full of stars:* **celestial body**, heavenly body, sun; asteroid, planet. **2** *the stars of the film:* **principal**, leading lady/man, lead, female/male lead, hero, heroine. **3** *a star of the world of chess:* **celebrity**, superstar, big name, famous name, household name, someone, somebody, lion, leading light, VIP, personality, personage, luminary; informal celeb, big shot, big noise, megastar.
– OPPOSITES nobody.
▸adjective **1** *a star pupil:* **brilliant**, talented, gifted, able, exceptional, outstanding, bright, clever, masterly, consummate, precocious, prodigious. **2** *the star attraction:* **top**, leading, best, greatest, foremost, major, pre-eminent, champion.
– OPPOSITES poor, minor.

starchy adjective (informal). See STAID.

stare verb *he stared at her in amazement:* **gaze**, gape, goggle, glare, ogle, peer; informal gawk, rubberneck; Brit. informal gawp.

stark adjective **1** *a stark silhouette:* **sharp**, sharply defined, well focused, crisp, distinct, obvious, evident, clear, clear-cut, graphic, striking. **2** *a stark landscape:* **desolate**, bare, barren, arid, vacant, empty, forsaken, godforsaken, bleak, sombre, depressing, cheerless, joyless. **3** *a stark room:* **austere**, severe, bleak, plain, simple, bare, unadorned, unembellished, undecorated. **4** *stark terror:* **sheer**, utter, complete, absolute, total, pure, downright, out-and-out, outright; rank, thorough, consummate, unqualified, unmitigated, unalloyed. **5** *the stark facts:* **blunt**, bald, bare, simple, basic, plain, unvarnished, harsh, grim.
– OPPOSITES fuzzy, indistinct, pleasant, ornate, disguised.
▸adverb *stark naked:* **completely**, totally, utterly, absolutely, downright, dead, entirely, wholly, fully, quite, altogether, thoroughly, truly.

start verb **1** *the meeting starts at 7.45:* **begin**, commence, get under way, go ahead, get going; informal kick off. **2** *this was how her illness had started:* **come into being**, begin, commence, be born, come into existence, appear, arrive, come forth, emerge, erupt, burst out, arise, originate, develop. **3** *she started her own charity:* **establish**, set up, found, create, bring into being, institute, initiate, inaugurate, introduce, open, launch, float, kick-start, get something off

the ground, pioneer, organize, mastermind; informal kick something off. **4** *we had better start on the work:* **make a start**, begin, commence, take the first step, make the first move, get going, go ahead, set things moving, start/get/set the ball rolling, buckle to/down, turn to; informal get moving, get cracking, get stuck in, get down to it, get to it, get down to business, get one's finger out, get the show on the road, take the plunge, kick off, get off one's backside, fire away; Brit. informal get weaving. **5** *he started across the field:* **set off**, set out, start out, set forth, begin one's journey, get on the road, depart, leave, get under way, make a start, sally forth, embark, sail; informal hit the road. **6** *you can start the machine:* **activate**, set in motion, switch on, start up, turn on, fire up, boot up; energize, actuate, set off, start off, set something going/moving. **7** *the machine started:* **begin working**, start up, get going, spring into life. **8** *'Oh my!' she said, starting:* **flinch**, jerk, jump, twitch, recoil, shy, shrink, blench, wince.
– OPPOSITES finish, stop, clear up, wind up, hang about, give up, arrive, stay, close down.
▸ **noun 1** *the start of the event:* **beginning**, commencement, inception. **2** *the start of her illness:* **onset**, commencement, emergence, (first) appearance, arrival, eruption, dawn, birth. **3** *a quarter of an hour's start:* **lead**, head start, advantage. **4** *a start in life:* **advantageous beginning**, flying start, helping hand, lift, assistance, support, encouragement, boost, kick-start; informal break, leg up. **5** *she awoke with a start:* **jerk**, twitch, flinch, wince, spasm, convulsion, jump.
– OPPOSITES end, finish, handicap.

startle verb *a sudden sound in the doorway startled her:* **surprise**, frighten, scare, alarm, give someone a shock/fright/jolt, make someone jump; **perturb**, unsettle, agitate, disturb, disconcert, disquiet; informal give someone a turn, make someone jump out of their skin.
– OPPOSITES put at ease.

startling adjective *startling news awaited him at Naples:* **surprising**, astonishing, amazing, unexpected, unforeseen, staggering, shocking, stunning; extraordinary, remarkable, dramatic; disturbing, unsettling, perturbing, disconcerting, disquieting; frightening, alarming, scary.
– OPPOSITES predictable, ordinary.

starvation noun *the country's people face starvation as a result of the civil war:* **extreme hunger**, lack of food, famine, undernourishment, malnourishment, fasting; deprivation of food; death from lack of food.

starving adjective *she devotes her energies to helping starving children:* **dying of hunger**, deprived of food, undernourished,

malnourished, starved, half-starved; very hungry, ravenous, famished, empty, hollow; fasting.
– OPPOSITES full.

stash (informal) verb *he stashed his things away:* **store**, stow, pack, load, cache, hide, conceal, secrete; hoard, save, stockpile; informal salt away, squirrel away.
▸ **noun** *a stash of money:* **cache**, hoard, stock, stockpile, store, supply, accumulation, collection, reserve.

state[1] noun **1** *the state of the economy:* **condition**, shape, situation, circumstances, position; predicament, plight. **2** (informal) *don't get into a state:* **fluster**, frenzy, fever, fret, panic, state of agitation/anxiety; informal flap, tizzy, tiz-woz, dither, stew, sweat; N. Amer. informal twit. **3** *an autonomous state:* **country**, nation, land, sovereign state, nation state, kingdom, realm, power, republic, confederation, federation. **4** *the country is divided into thirty-two states:* **province**, federal state, region, territory, canton, department, county, district; Brit. shire. **5** *the power of the state:* **government**, parliament, administration, regime, authorities.
▸ **adjective** *a state visit to China:* **ceremonial**, official, formal, governmental, national, public.
– OPPOSITES unofficial, private, informal.

state[2] verb *I stated my views:* **express**, voice, utter, put into words, declare, affirm, assert, announce, make known, put across/over, communicate, air, reveal, disclose, divulge, proclaim, present, expound; set out, set down; informal come out with.

stated adjective *routine health checks at stated intervals:* **specified**, fixed, settled, set, agreed, declared, designated, laid down.
– OPPOSITES undefined, irregular, tacit.

stately adjective *a stately procession:* **dignified**, majestic, ceremonious, courtly, imposing, impressive, solemn, awe-inspiring, regal, elegant, grand, glorious, splendid, magnificent, resplendent; slow-moving, measured, deliberate.

statement noun *do you agree with this statement?* **declaration**, expression of views/facts, affirmation, assertion, announcement, utterance, communication, proclamation, presentation, expounding; account, testimony, evidence, report, bulletin, communiqué.

state-of-the-art adjective *the studio boasted the finest state-of-the-art recording equipment:* **modern**, ultra-modern, the latest, new, the newest, up to the minute; advanced, highly developed, innovatory, trailblazing, revolutionary; sophisticated.

statesman, stateswoman noun senior **politician**, respected political figure, elder statesman, political leader, national leader.

static adjective **1** *static prices:* **unchanged**, fixed, stable, steady, unchanging, changeless, unvarying, invariable, constant,

S

consistent. **2** *a static display:* **stationary**, motionless, immobile, unmoving, still, stock-still, at a standstill, at rest, not moving a muscle, like a statue, rooted to the spot, frozen, inactive, inert, lifeless, inanimate.
– OPPOSITES variable, mobile, active, dynamic.

station noun **1** *a railway station:* **stopping place**, stop, halt, stage; terminus, terminal, depot. **2** *a research station:* **establishment**, base, camp, post, depot; mission; site, facility, installation, yard. **3** *a police station:* **office**, depot, base, headquarters; N. Amer. precinct, station house; informal cop shop; Brit. informal nick. **4** *a radio station:* **channel**, broadcasting organization; wavelength. **5** (Austral./NZ) *a sheep station:* **ranch**, range; farm. **6** *the lookout resumed his station:* **post**, position, place.
verb *the regiment was stationed at Woolwich:* **put on duty**, post, position, place; establish, install; deploy, base, garrison.

stationary adjective **1** *a stationary car:* **static**, parked, stopped, motionless, immobile, unmoving, still, stock-still, at a standstill, at rest; not moving a muscle, like a statue, rooted to the spot, frozen, inactive, inert, lifeless, inanimate. **2** *a stationary population:* **unchanging**, unvarying, invariable, constant, consistent, unchanged, changeless, fixed, stable, steady.
– OPPOSITES moving, shifting.

statue noun **sculpture**, figure, effigy, statuette, figurine, idol; carving, bronze, graven image, model; bust, head.

statuesque adjective *the headmistress was statuesque:* **tall and dignified**, imposing, striking, stately, majestic, noble, magnificent, splendid, impressive, regal.

stature noun **1** *she was small in stature:* **height**, tallness; size, build. **2** *an architect of international stature:* **reputation**, repute, standing, status, position, prestige, distinction, eminence, pre-eminence, prominence, importance, influence, note, fame, celebrity, renown, acclaim.

status noun **1** *the status of women:* **standing**, rank, ranking, position, social position, level, place, estimation. **2** *wealth and status:* **prestige**, kudos, cachet, standing, stature, regard, fame, note, renown, honour, esteem, image, importance, prominence, consequence, distinction, influence, authority, eminence.

statute noun *statutes dealing with non-fatal offences:* **law**, regulation, enactment, act, bill, decree, edict, rule, ruling, resolution, dictum, command, order, directive, pronouncement, proclamation, dictate, diktat, fiat, by-law.

staunch[1] adjective *a staunch supporter:* **stalwart**, loyal, faithful, committed, devoted, dedicated, dependable, reliable, steady, constant, trusty, hard-working, steadfast, redoubtable, unwavering.
– OPPOSITES disloyal, unfaithful, unreliable.

staunch[2] verb *she tried to staunch the flow of blood:* **stem**, stop, halt, check, hold back, restrain, restrict, control, contain, curb; block, dam; slow, lessen, reduce, diminish; N. Amer. stanch.

stave
■ **stave something in** *the door was staved in:* break in, smash in, put a hole in, push in, kick in, cave in.
■ **stave something off** *the government is introducing emergency measures to stave off a crisis:* avert, prevent, avoid, counter, preclude, forestall, nip in the bud; ward off, fend off, head off, keep off, keep at bay.

stay[1] verb **1** *he stayed where he was:* **remain (behind)**, stay behind, stay put; wait, linger, stick, be left, hold on, hang on, lodge; informal hang around/round; Brit. informal hang about. **2** *they won't stay hidden:* **continue (to be)**, remain, keep, persist in being, carry on being, go on being. **3** *our aunt is staying with us:* **visit**, spend time, put up, stop (off/over); holiday; lodge, room, board, have rooms, be housed, be accommodated, be quartered, be billeted; N. Amer. vacation.
– OPPOSITES leave.
noun **1** *a stay at a hotel:* **visit**, stop, stop-off, stopover, break, holiday; N. Amer. vacation. **2** *a stay of judgement:* **postponement**, putting off, delay, deferment, deferral, putting back; adjournment, suspension, prorogation; N. Amer. tabling.

stay[2] noun *the stays holding up the aerial:* **strut**, wire, brace, tether, guy, prop, rod, support, truss.
verb *her masts were well stayed:* **brace**, tether, strut, wire, guy, prop, support, truss.

steadfast adjective **1** *a steadfast friend:* **loyal**, faithful, committed, devoted, dedicated, dependable, reliable, steady, true, constant, staunch, trusty. **2** *a steadfast policy:* **firm**, determined, resolute, relentless, implacable, single-minded; unchanging, unwavering, unhesitating, unfaltering, unswerving, unyielding, unflinching, uncompromising.
– OPPOSITES disloyal, irresolute.

steady adjective **1** *the ladder must be steady:* **stable**, firm, fixed, secure, fast, safe, immovable, unshakeable, dependable; anchored, moored, jammed, rooted, braced. **2** *keep the camera steady:* **motionless**, still, unshaking, static, stationary, unmoving. **3** *a steady gaze:* **fixed**, intent, unwavering, unfaltering. **4** *a steady young man:* **sensible**, level-headed, rational, settled, mature, down-to-earth, full of common sense, reliable, dependable, sound, sober, serious-minded, responsible, serious. **5** *a steady income:* **constant**, unchanging, regular, consistent, invariable; continuous, continual, unceasing, ceaseless, perpetual, unremitting, unwavering, unfaltering, unending, endless, round-the-clock, all-year-round. **6** *a steady boyfriend:* **regular**, usual, established, settled, firm, devoted, faithful.

– OPPOSITES unstable, loose, shaky, darting, flighty, immature, fluctuating, sporadic, occasional.

verb 1 *he steadied the rifle:* **stabilize**, hold steady; brace, support; balance, poise; secure, fix, make fast. **2** *she needed a moment to steady her nerves:* **calm**, soothe, quieten, compose, settle; subdue, quell, control, get a grip on.

steal verb 1 *the raiders stole a fax machine:* **purloin**, thieve, take, take for oneself, help oneself to, loot, pilfer, run off with, carry off, shoplift; embezzle, misappropriate; have one's fingers/hand in the till; informal walk off with, rob, swipe, nab, rip off, lift, liberate, borrow, filch, snaffle, snitch; Brit. informal nick, pinch, half-inch, whip, knock off, nobble; N. Amer. informal heist. **2** *his work was stolen by his tutor:* **plagiarize**, copy, pass off as one's own, pirate, poach, borrow; informal rip off, lift, pinch, nick, crib. **3** *he stole a kiss:* **snatch**, sneak, get stealthily/surreptitiously. **4** *he stole out of the room:* **creep**, sneak, slink, slip, slide, glide, tiptoe, sidle, slope, edge.

stealing noun *he was convicted of stealing:* **theft**, thieving, thievery, robbery, larceny, burglary, shoplifting, pilfering, pilferage, looting, misappropriation; embezzlement.

stealth noun furtiveness, secretiveness, secrecy, surreptitiousness, sneakiness, slyness.
– OPPOSITES openness.

stealthy adjective *stealthy footsteps:* **furtive**, secretive, secret, surreptitious, sneaking, sly, clandestine, covert, conspiratorial.
– OPPOSITES open.

steam noun 1 *steam from the kettle:* **water vapour**, condensation, mist, haze, fog, moisture. **2** *he ran out of steam:* **energy**, vigour, vitality, stamina, enthusiasm; **momentum**, impetus, force, strength, thrust, impulse, push, drive; speed, pace.
■ **let off steam** (informal) give vent to one's feelings, speak one's mind, speak out, sound off, lose one's inhibitions, let oneself go; use up surplus energy.
■ **steam up** mist (up/over), fog (up), become misty/misted.

steamy adjective 1 *the steamy jungle:* **humid**, muggy, sticky, dripping, moist, damp, clammy, sultry, sweaty, steaming. **2** (informal) *a steamy love scene.* See EROTIC. **3** (informal) *they had a steamy affair:* **passionate**, torrid, amorous, ardent, lustful; informal sizzling, hot, red-hot.

steel
■ **steel oneself** *his team were steeling themselves for disappointment:* **brace oneself**, nerve oneself, summon (up) one's courage, screw up one's courage, gear oneself up, prepare oneself, get in the right frame of mind; fortify oneself, harden oneself; informal psych oneself up.

steely adjective 1 *steely light:* **blue-grey**, grey, steel-coloured, steel-grey, iron-grey. **2** *steely muscles:* **hard**, firm, toned,

rigid, stiff, tense, tensed, taut. **3** *steely eyes:* **cruel**, unfeeling, merciless, ruthless, pitiless, heartless, hard-hearted, hard, stony, cold-blooded, cold-hearted, harsh, callous, severe, unrelenting, unpitying, unforgiving, uncaring, unsympathetic. **4** *steely determination:* **resolute**, firm, steadfast, dogged, single-minded; bitter, burning, ferocious, fanatical; ruthless, iron, grim, gritty; unquenchable, unflinching, unswerving, unfaltering, untiring, unwavering.
– OPPOSITES flabby, kind, half-hearted.

steep¹ adjective 1 *steep cliffs:* **precipitous**, sheer, abrupt, sharp, perpendicular, vertical, bluff, vertiginous. **2** *a steep increase:* **sharp**, sudden, precipitate, precipitous, rapid.
– OPPOSITES gentle, gradual, reasonable.

steep² verb 1 *the ham is then steeped in brine:* **marinade**, marinate, soak, souse, macerate; pickle. **2** *winding sheets were steeped in mercury sulphate:* **soak**, saturate, immerse, wet through, drench. **3** *a city steeped in history:* **imbue with**, fill with, permeate with, pervade with, suffuse with, infuse with, soak in.

steeple noun spire, tower; bell tower, belfry, campanile; minaret.

steer verb 1 *he steered the boat:* **guide**, direct, manoeuvre, drive, pilot, navigate. **2** *Luke steered her down the path:* **guide**, conduct, direct, lead, take, usher, shepherd, marshal, herd.
■ **steer clear of** keep away from, keep one's distance from, keep at arm's length, give a wide berth to, avoid, avoid dealing with, have nothing to do with, shun, eschew.

stem¹ noun *a plant stem:* **stalk**, shoot, trunk, stock, cane, bine.
■ **stem from** *her depression stems from domestic difficulties:* have its origins in, arise from, originate from, spring from, derive from, come from, emanate from, flow from, proceed from; be caused by, be brought on/about by, be produced by.

stem² verb *he stemmed the flow of blood:* **staunch**, stop, halt, check, hold back, restrict, control, contain, curb; block, dam; slow, lessen, reduce, diminish; N. Amer. stanch.

stench noun *the stench made me feel sick:* **stink**, reek; Brit. informal niff, pong, whiff, hum; Scottish informal guff; N. Amer. informal funk.

step noun 1 *Frank took a step forward:* **pace**, stride. **2** *she heard a step on the stairs:* **footstep**, footfall, tread. **3** *she left the room with a springy step:* **gait**, walk, tread. **4** *it is only a step to the river:* **short distance**, stone's throw, spitting distance; informal {a hop, skip, and jump}. **5** *the top step:* **stair**, tread; (**steps**) stairs, staircase, stairway. **6** *each step of the ladder:* **rung**, tread. **7** *resigning is a very serious step:* **course of action**, measure, move, act, action, initiative, manoeuvre, operation.

S

8 *a significant step towards a ceasefire:*
advance, development, move, movement;
breakthrough. **9** *the first step on the
managerial ladder:* **stage**, level, grade, rank,
degree; notch.
verb **1** *she stepped forward:* **walk**, move,
tread, pace, stride. **2** *the bull had stepped
on his hat:* **tread**, stamp, trample; squash,
crush, flatten.
■ **in step** *he is in step with mainstream
thinking:* in accord, in harmony, in
agreement, in tune, in line, in keeping, in
conformity.
■ **mind/watch one's step** be careful,
take care, step/tread carefully, exercise
care/caution, mind how one goes, look out,
watch out, be wary, be on one's guard, be on
the qui vive.
■ **out of step** *the paper was often out of step
with public opinion:* at odds, at variance, in
disagreement, out of tune, out of line, not
in keeping, out of harmony.
■ **step by step** one step at a time, bit by
bit, gradually, in stages, by degrees, slowly,
steadily.
■ **step down** *he was forced to step down:*
resign, stand down, give up one's post/job,
bow out, abdicate; informal quit.
■ **step in 1** *nobody stepped in to save the
bank:* intervene, intercede, involve oneself,
become/get involved, take a hand. **2** *I
stepped in for a sick colleague:* stand in, sit in,
fill in, cover, substitute, take over; replace,
take someone's place; informal sub.
■ **step something up 1** *the army stepped up
its offensive:* increase, intensify, strengthen,
augment, escalate; informal up, crank up. **2** *I
stepped up my pace:* speed up, increase,
accelerate, quicken, hasten.

stereotype noun *the stereotype of the
rancher:* **standard/conventional image**,
received idea, cliché, hackneyed idea,
formula.
verb *women are often stereotyped
as scheming:* **typecast**, pigeonhole,
conventionalize, categorize, label,
tag.

stereotyped adjective *stereotyped images
of village life:* **stock**, conventional,
stereotypical, standard, formulaic,
predictable; hackneyed, clichéd, cliché-
ridden, banal, trite, unoriginal, typecast;
informal corny, old hat.
– OPPOSITES unconventional, original.

sterile adjective **1** *mules are sterile:* **infertile**,
unable to reproduce/conceive, unable
to have children/young. **2** *sterile desert:*
unproductive, infertile, unfruitful,
uncultivatable, barren. **3** *a sterile debate:*
pointless, unproductive, unfruitful,
unrewarding, useless, unprofitable,
profitless, futile, vain, idle. **4** *sterile
academicism:* **unimaginative**, uninspired,
uninspiring, unoriginal, stale, lifeless,
musty. **5** *sterile conditions:* **aseptic**,
sterilized, germ-free, antiseptic, disinfected;

uncontaminated, unpolluted, pure, clean;
sanitary, hygienic.
– OPPOSITES fertile, productive, creative,
original, septic.

sterilize verb **1** *the scalpel was sterilized:*
disinfect, fumigate, decontaminate,
sanitize; pasteurize; clean, cleanse, purify.
2 *over 6.5 million people were sterilized:*
make unable to have children, make
infertile, hysterectomize, vasectomize.
3 *stray pets are usually sterilized:* **neuter**,
castrate, spay, geld, cut, fix, desex; N. Amer. &
Austral. alter; Brit. informal doctor.
– OPPOSITES contaminate.

sterling adjective (Brit.) *the organization does
sterling work for youngsters:* **excellent**, first-
rate, first-class, exceptional, outstanding,
splendid, superlative, praiseworthy,
laudable, commendable, admirable,
valuable, worthy, deserving.
– OPPOSITES poor, unexceptional.

stern[1] adjective **1** *a stern expression:* **serious**,
unsmiling, frowning, severe, forbidding,
grim, unfriendly, austere, dour, stony,
flinty, steely, unrelenting, unforgiving,
unbending, unsympathetic, disapproving.
2 *stern measures:* **strict**, severe, stringent,
harsh, drastic, hard, tough, extreme, rigid,
ruthless, rigorous, exacting, demanding,
uncompromising, unsparing, inflexible,
authoritarian, draconian.
– OPPOSITES genial, friendly, lenient, lax.

stern[2] noun *the stern of the ship:* **rear (end)**,
back, after end, poop, transom, tail.
– OPPOSITES bow.

stew noun *a beef stew:* **casserole**, hotpot,
ragout, goulash, carbonnade, daube,
grillade; N. Amer. burgoo.
verb *stew the meat for an hour:* **braise**,
casserole, simmer, boil; jug.

steward noun **1** *an air steward:* **flight
attendant**, cabin attendant; stewardess,
air hostess; N. Amer. informal stew. **2** *the race
stewards:* **official**, marshal, organizer. **3** *the
steward of the estate:* **(estate) manager**,
agent, overseer, custodian, caretaker; Brit.
land agent, bailiff; Scottish factor.

stick[1] noun **1** *a fire made of sticks:* **piece of
wood**, twig, small branch. **2** *he walks with a
stick:* **walking stick**, cane, staff, alpenstock,
crook, crutch. **3** *the plants need supporting
on sticks:* **cane**, pole, post, stake, upright.
4 *he beat me with a stick:* **club**, cudgel,
bludgeon, shillelagh; truncheon, baton;
cane, birch, switch, rod; Brit. informal cosh.
– OPPOSITES praise, commendation.
■ **the sticks** (informal) the country, the
countryside, rural areas, the provinces;
the backwoods, the back of beyond, the
wilds, the hinterland, a backwater; N. Amer.
the backcountry, the backland; Austral./NZ
the backblocks, the booay; S. African the
backveld, the platteland; informal the middle
of nowhere; N. Amer. informal the boondocks,
the boonies; Austral./NZ informal Woop Woop,
beyond the black stump.

stick² verb **1** *he stuck his fork into the sausage:* **thrust**, push, insert, jab, poke, dig, plunge. **2** *the bristles stuck into his skin:* **pierce**, penetrate, puncture, prick, stab. **3** *the cup stuck to its saucer:* **adhere**, cling, be fixed, be glued. **4** *stick the stamp there:* **affix**, attach, fasten, fix; paste, glue, gum, tape, Sellotape, pin, tack. **5** *the wheels stuck fast:* **become trapped**, become jammed, jam, catch, become wedged, become lodged, become fixed, become embedded. **6** *that sticks in his mind:* **remain**, stay, linger, dwell, persist, continue, last, endure. **7** *the charges won't stick:* **be upheld**, hold, be believed; informal hold water.

■ **stick at** *if you wish to learn a language, you must stick at it:* **persevere with**, persist with, keep at, work at, continue with, carry on with, not give up with, hammer away at, stay with; go the distance, stay the course; informal soldier on with, hang in there.

■ **stick by** *whatever happens I'll stick by him:* **be loyal to**, be faithful to, be true to, stand by, keep faith with, keep one's promise to.

■ **stick it out** *I decided to stick it out for another couple of months:* **put up with it**, grin and bear it, keep at it, keep going, stay with it, see it through; persevere, persist, carry on, struggle on; informal hang in there, soldier on, tough it out.

■ **stick out 1** *his front teeth stuck out:* **protrude**, jut (out), project, stand out, extend, poke out; bulge, overhang. **2** *they stuck out in their strange clothes:* **be noticeable**, be visible, be obvious, be conspicuous, stand out, be obtrusive, be prominent, attract attention, catch the eye, leap out, show up; informal stick/stand out a mile, stick/stand out like a sore thumb.

■ **stick to** *he stuck to his promise:* **abide by**, keep, adhere to, hold to, comply with, fulfil, make good, stand by.

■ **stick up for** *I don't know anyone else who would stick up for me the way you do:* **support**, take someone's side, side with, be on the side of, stand by, stand up for, take someone's part, defend, come to the defence of, champion, speak up for, fight for.

stick-in-the-mud noun *he was an old stick-in-the-mud:* (informal) **(old) fogey**, conservative, fossil, troglodyte; Brit. museum piece; informal fuddy-duddy, square, stuffed shirt.

sticky adjective **1** *sticky tape:* **(self-)adhesive**, gummed. **2** *sticky clay:* **glutinous**, viscous, viscid, ropy; gluey, tacky, gummy, treacly, syrupy; Brit. claggy; informal gooey, gloopy, icky; Brit. informal gungy; N. Amer. informal gloppy. **3** *sticky weather:* **humid**, muggy, close, sultry, steamy, sweaty. **4** *a sticky situation:* **awkward**, difficult, tricky, ticklish, problematic, delicate, touch-and-go, embarrassing, sensitive, uncomfortable; informal hairy.

– OPPOSITES dry, fresh, cool, easy.

stiff adjective **1** *stiff cardboard:* **rigid**, hard, firm, inelastic, inflexible. **2** *a stiff paste:* **semi-solid**, viscous, viscid, thick, stiffened, firm. **3** *I'm stiff all over:* **aching**, achy, painful; arthritic, rheumatic; informal creaky, rheumaticky, rusty. **4** *a rather stiff manner:* **formal**, reserved, unfriendly, chilly, cold, frigid, icy, austere, wooden, forced, strained, stilted; informal starchy, uptight, stand-offish. **5** *a stiff fine:* **harsh**, severe, heavy, crippling, punishing, stringent, drastic, draconian; Brit. swingeing. **6** *stiff resistance:* **vigorous**, determined, full of determination, strong, spirited, resolute, tenacious, steely, four-square, unflagging, unyielding, dogged, stubborn, obdurate; N. Amer. rock-ribbed. **7** *a stiff climb:* **difficult**, hard, arduous, tough, strenuous, laborious, uphill, exacting, tiring, demanding, formidable, challenging, punishing, gruelling; informal killing, hellish; Brit. informal knackering. **8** *a stiff breeze:* **strong**, fresh, brisk. **9** *a stiff drink:* **strong**, potent, alcoholic.

– OPPOSITES flexible, runny, supple, relaxed, lenient, half-hearted, easy, gentle, weak.

stiffen verb **1** *stir until the mixture stiffens:* **become stiff**, thicken; set, become solid, solidify, harden, gel, congeal, coagulate, clot. **2** *she stiffened her muscles | without exercise, joints will stiffen:* **make/become stiff**, tense (up), tighten, tauten. **3** *intimidation stiffened their resolve:* **strengthen**, harden, toughen, fortify, reinforce, give a boost to.

– OPPOSITES soften, liquefy, relax, weaken.

stifle verb **1** *she stifled him with a bolster:* **suffocate**, choke, asphyxiate, smother. **2** *Eleanor stifled a giggle:* **suppress**, smother, restrain, fight back, choke back, gulp back, check, swallow, curb, silence. **3** *cartels stifle competition:* **constrain**, hinder, hamper, impede, hold back, curb, check, restrain, prevent, inhibit, suppress.

– OPPOSITES let out, encourage.

stifling adjective *in summer, Venice is often stifling:* **airless**, suffocating, oppressive; very hot, sweltering; humid, close, muggy; informal boiling.

– OPPOSITES fresh.

stigma noun *the stigma of bankruptcy:* **shame**, disgrace, dishonour, ignominy, opprobrium, humiliation.

– OPPOSITES honour, credit.

stigmatize verb *the institution was stigmatized as a last resort for the destitute:* **condemn**, denounce; brand, label, mark out; disparage, vilify, pillory, pour scorn on, defame.

still adjective **1** *Polly lay still:* **motionless**, unmoving, not moving a muscle, stock-still, immobile, like a statue, as if turned to stone, rooted to the spot, transfixed, static, stationary. **2** *a still night:* **quiet**, silent, hushed, soundless, noiseless, undisturbed; **calm**, peaceful, serene, windless. **3** *the lake was still:* **calm**, flat, even, smooth, placid, tranquil, pacific, waveless, glassy, like a millpond, unruffled.

S

– OPPOSITES moving, active, noisy, rough.
noun *the still of the night:* **quietness**, quiet, quietude, silence, stillness, hush, soundlessness; calm, tranquillity, peace, serenity.
– OPPOSITES noise.
adverb 1 *he's still here:* **up to this time**, up to the present time, until now, even now, yet. 2 *He's crazy. Still, he's harmless:* **nevertheless**, nonetheless, all the same, just the same, anyway, anyhow, even so, yet, but, however, notwithstanding, despite that, in spite of that, for all that, be that as it may, in any event, at any rate; informal still and all.
verb 1 *he stilled the crowd:* **quieten**, quiet, silence, hush; calm, settle, pacify, soothe, lull, allay, subdue. 2 *the wind stilled:* **abate**, die down, lessen, subside, ease up/off, let up, moderate, slacken, weaken.
– OPPOSITES stir up, get stronger, get up.

stilted adjective *stilted conversation:* **strained**, forced, contrived, constrained, laboured, stiff, self-conscious, awkward, unnatural, wooden.
– OPPOSITES natural, spontaneous.

stimulant noun 1 *caffeine is a stimulant:* **tonic**, restorative; antidepressant; informal pep pill, upper, pick-me-up, bracer. 2 *a stimulant to discussion:* **stimulus**, incentive, encouragement, impetus, inducement, fillip, boost, spur, prompt; informal shot in the arm.
– OPPOSITES sedative, deterrent.

stimulate verb *I want to stimulate their imaginations:* **encourage**, act as a stimulus/incentive/impetus/fillip/spur to, prompt, prod, move, motivate, trigger, spark, spur on, galvanize, activate, kindle, fire, fire with enthusiasm, fuel, whet, nourish; inspire, incentivize, inspirit, rouse, excite, animate, electrify; N. Amer. light a fire under, spirit someone up.
– OPPOSITES discourage.

stimulating adjective 1 *plant extracts which have a stimulating effect on the circulation:* **restorative**, tonic, invigorating, bracing, energizing, reviving, refreshing, revitalizing. 2 *a stimulating lecture:* **thought-provoking**, interesting, fascinating, inspiring, inspirational, lively, sparkling, exciting, stirring, rousing, intriguing, giving one food for thought, refreshing; provocative, challenging.
– OPPOSITES sedative, uninspiring.

stimulus noun *cheap energy provided a major stimulus to economic development in western Europe:* **spur**, stimulant, encouragement, impetus, boost, prompt, prod, incentive, inducement, inspiration, fillip; motivation, impulse; informal shot in the arm.
– OPPOSITES deterrent.

sting noun 1 *a bee sting:* **prick**, wound, injury, puncture. 2 *this cream will take the sting away:* **smart**, pricking; pain, soreness, hurt, irritation. 3 *the sting of his betrayal:* **heartache**, heartbreak, agony, torture, torment, hurt, pain, anguish. 4 *there was*

a sting in her words: **sharpness**, severity, bite, edge, pointedness, asperity; sarcasm, acrimony, malice, spite, venom.
verb 1 *she was stung by a scorpion:* **prick**, wound; poison. 2 *the smoke made her eyes sting:* **smart**, burn, hurt, be irritated, be sore. 3 *the criticism stung her:* **upset**, wound, cut to the quick, sear, grieve, hurt, pain, torment, mortify. 4 *he was stung into action:* **provoke**, goad, incite, spur, prick, prod, rouse, drive, galvanize.
– OPPOSITES deter.

stink verb 1 *his clothes stank of sweat:* **reek**, smell (foul/bad/disgusting), stink/smell to high heaven. 2 (informal) *the values of our society stink:* **be very unpleasant**, be abhorrent, be despicable, be contemptible, be disgusting, be vile, be foul; N. Amer. informal suck. 3 (informal) *the whole affair stinks of a set-up:* **smack**, reek, give the impression, have all the hallmarks; strongly suggest.
noun *the stink of sweat:* **stench**, reek, foul/bad smell, malodour; Brit. informal pong, niff, hum; Scottish informal guff; N. Amer. informal funk.

stinking adjective 1 *stinking rubbish:* **foul-smelling**, smelly, reeking, fetid, malodorous, rank, putrid, noxious; informal stinky, reeky; Brit. informal niffing, niffy, pongy, whiffy, humming; N. Amer. informal funky. 2 (informal) *a stinking cold:* **dreadful**, awful, terrible, frightful, ghastly, nasty, foul, vile; Brit. informal rotten, shocking.
– OPPOSITES sweet-smelling, slight.

stint verb *we saved by stinting on food:* **skimp**, scrimp, be economical, economize, be sparing, hold back, be frugal; be mean, be parsimonious; limit, restrict; informal be stingy, be mingy, be tight.
noun *a two-week stint in the office:* **spell**, stretch, turn, session, term, shift, tour of duty.

stipulate verb *he stipulated certain conditions before their marriage:* **specify**, set down, set out, lay down; demand, require, insist on, make a condition of, prescribe, impose.

stipulation noun *the only stipulation was that Edwards should retain his job as chairman for three years:* **condition**, precondition, proviso, provision, prerequisite, specification; demand, requirement; rider, caveat, qualification.

stir verb 1 *stir the mixture well:* **mix**, blend, agitate; beat, whip, whisk, fold in; N. Amer. muddle. 2 *Travis stirred in his sleep:* **move slightly**, change one's position, shift. 3 *a breeze stirred the leaves:* **disturb**, rustle, shake, move, flutter, agitate. 4 *he finally stirred at ten o'clock:* **get up**, get out of bed, rouse oneself, rise; **wake (up)**, awaken; informal rise and shine, surface, show signs of life. 5 *I never stirred from here:* **move**, budge, make a move, shift, go away; leave. 6 *symbolism can stir the imagination:* **arouse**, rouse, fire, kindle,

inspire, stimulate, excite, awaken, quicken.
7 *the war stirred him to action:* **spur**, drive,
rouse, prompt, propel, prod, motivate,
encourage; urge, impel; provoke, goad, prick,
sting, incite; N. Amer. light a fire under.
– OPPOSITES go to bed, go to sleep, stay,
stultify.
noun *the news caused a stir:* **commotion**,
disturbance, fuss, excitement, turmoil,
sensation; informal to-do, hoo-ha, hullabaloo,
flap, splash.
■ **stir something up** *his remarks stirred
up a furore:* whip up, work up, foment, fan
the flames of, trigger, spark off, precipitate,
excite, provoke, incite.

stirring adjective *stirring accounts of
our heroic history:* **exciting**, thrilling,
rousing, stimulating, moving, inspiring,
inspirational, passionate, impassioned,
emotional, heady.
– OPPOSITES boring, pedestrian.

stitch noun *he was panting and had a stitch:*
sharp pain, stabbing pain, shooting pain,
stab of pain, pang, twinge, spasm.
verb *the seams are stitched by hand:* **sew**,
baste, tack; seam, hem; darn.
■ **stitch someone up** (Brit. informal) *he was
stitched up by outsiders:* falsely incriminate,
get someone into trouble; informal frame, set
up; Brit. informal fit someone up, drop someone
in it.

stock noun **1** *the shop carries little stock:*
merchandise, goods, wares, items/articles
for sale, inventory. **2** *a stock of fuel:* **store**,
supply, stockpile, reserve, hoard, cache,
bank, accumulation, quantity, collection.
3 *farm stock:* **animals**, livestock, beasts;
flocks, herds. **4** *blue-chip stocks:* **shares**,
securities, equities, bonds. **5** *his mother
was of French stock:* **descent**, ancestry,
origin(s), parentage, pedigree, lineage, line
(of descent), heritage, birth, extraction,
family, blood, bloodline. **6** *chicken stock:*
bouillon, broth. **7** *the stock of a weapon:*
handle, butt, haft, grip, shaft, shank.
adjective 1 *a stock size:* **standard**, regular,
normal, established, set; common,
readily/widely available; staple. **2** *the
stock response:* **usual**, routine, predictable,
set, standard, staple, customary, familiar,
conventional, traditional, stereotyped,
clichéd, hackneyed, unoriginal, formulaic.
– OPPOSITES non-standard, original, unusual.
verb 1 *we do not stock GM food:* **sell**, carry,
keep (in stock), offer, have (for sale), retail,
supply. **2** *the fridge was well stocked with
milk:* **supply**, provide, furnish, provision,
equip, fill, load.
■ **in stock** for/on sale, (immediately)
available, on the shelf.
■ **stock up on/with** *you'd better stock up
with fuel:* amass supplies of, stockpile,
hoard, cache, lay in, buy up/in, put away/by,
put/set aside, collect, accumulate, save;
informal squirrel away, salt away, stash away.
■ **take stock of** review, assess, weigh up,

appraise, evaluate; informal size up.

stockings plural noun **nylons**, stay-ups;
tights; hosiery, hose; N. Amer. pantyhose.

stockpile noun *a stockpile of weapons:* **stock**,
store, supply, accumulation, collection,
reserve, hoard, cache; informal stash.
verb *food had been stockpiled:* **store up**,
amass, accumulate, store (up), stock up
on, hoard, cache, collect, lay in, put away,
put/set aside, put by, put away for a rainy
day, stow away, save; informal salt away, stash
away.

stocky adjective *a short, stocky man:* **thickset**,
sturdy, heavily built, chunky, burly,
strapping, brawny, solid, heavy, hefty, beefy.
– OPPOSITES slender, skinny.

stodgy adjective **1** *a stodgy pudding:* **solid**,
substantial, filling, hearty, heavy, starchy,
indigestible. **2** *stodgy writing:* **boring**, dull,
uninteresting, dreary, turgid, tedious, dry,
heavy going, unimaginative, uninspired,
unexciting, unoriginal, monotonous,
humdrum, prosaic, staid; informal deadly,
square.
– OPPOSITES light, interesting, lively.

stoical adjective *my mother was more stoical
and scorned such self-pity:* **long-suffering**,
uncomplaining, patient, forbearing,
accepting, tolerant, resigned, phlegmatic,
philosophical.
– OPPOSITES complaining, intolerant.

stoicism noun **patience**, forbearance,
resignation, fortitude, endurance,
acceptance, tolerance, philosophicalness,
phlegm.
– OPPOSITES intolerance.

stoke verb *Dad returned to his chair while
I stoked the fire:* **add fuel to**, mend, keep
burning, tend.

stolid adjective *a stolid, slow-speaking man:*
impassive, phlegmatic, unemotional, cool,
calm, placid, unexcitable; dependable;
unimaginative, dull.
– OPPOSITES emotional, lively, imaginative.

stomach noun **1** *a stomach pain:* **abdomen**,
belly, gut, middle; informal tummy, tum,
breadbasket, insides. **2** *his fat stomach:*
paunch, pot belly, beer belly, girth; informal
beer gut, pot, tummy, spare tyre, middle-
aged spread; N. Amer. informal bay window.
3 *he had no stomach for it:* **appetite**, taste,
hunger, thirst; inclination, desire, relish,
fancy.
verb 1 *I can't stomach butter:* **digest**, keep
down, manage to eat/consume, tolerate,
take. **2** *they couldn't stomach the sight of it:*
tolerate, put up with, take, stand, endure,
bear; Scottish thole; informal hack, abide; Brit.
informal stick.

stomach ache noun **indigestion**, dyspepsia,
colic, gripe; informal bellyache, tummy ache,
gut ache, collywobbles.

stone noun **1** *someone threw a stone at me:*
rock, pebble, boulder. **2** *a commemorative
stone:* **tablet**, monument, monolith, obelisk;

S

gravestone, headstone, tombstone. **3** *paving stones:* **slab**, flagstone, flag, sett. **4** *a precious stone:* **gem**, gemstone, jewel, semi-precious stone, brilliant; informal rock, sparkler. **5** *a peach stone:* **kernel**, seed, pip, pit.

stony adjective **1** *a stony path:* **rocky**, pebbly, gravelly, shingly; rough, hard. **2** *a stony stare:* **unfriendly**, hostile, cold, chilly, frosty, icy; hard, flinty, steely, stern, severe; fixed, expressionless, blank, poker-faced, deadpan; unfeeling, uncaring, unsympathetic, indifferent, cold-hearted, callous, heartless, hard-hearted, stony-hearted, merciless, pitiless.
– OPPOSITES smooth, friendly, sympathetic.

stooge noun **1** *a government stooge:* **underling**, minion, lackey, subordinate; henchman; **puppet**, pawn, cat's paw; informal sidekick; Brit. informal dogsbody, poodle. **2** *a comedian's stooge:* **butt**, foil, straight man.

stoop verb **1** *she stooped to pick up the pen:* **bend (over/down)**, lean over/down, crouch (down). **2** *he stooped his head:* **lower**, bend, incline, bow, duck. **3** *he stoops when he walks:* **hunch one's shoulders**, walk with a stoop, be round-shouldered. **4** *Davis would stoop to crime:* **lower oneself**, sink, descend, resort; go as far as, sink as low as.
noun *a man with a stoop:* **hunch**, round shoulders; curvature of the spine; Medicine kyphosis.

stop verb **1** *we can't stop the decline:* **put an end/stop/halt to**, bring to an end/stop/halt/close/standstill, end, halt; finish, terminate, wind up, discontinue, cut short, interrupt, nip in the bud; deactivate, shut down. **2** *he stopped running:* **cease**, discontinue, desist from, break off; give up, abandon, abstain from, cut out; informal quit, leave off, knock off, pack in, lay off, give over; Brit. informal jack in. **3** *the car stopped:* **pull up**, draw up, come to a stop/halt, come to rest, pull in, pull over; park. **4** *the music stopped:* **come to an end/stop/standstill**, cease, end, finish, draw to a close, be over, conclude, terminate; pause, break off; peter out, fade away. **5** *divers stopped the flow of oil:* **stem**, staunch, hold back, check, curb, block, dam; N. Amer. stanch. **6** *the police stopped her leaving:* **prevent**, hinder, obstruct, impede, block, bar, preclude; dissuade from.
– OPPOSITES start, begin, continue, allow, encourage, expedite, pay, open.
noun **1** *all business came to a stop:* **halt**, end, finish, close, standstill; cessation, conclusion, stoppage, discontinuation. **2** *a brief stop in the town:* **break**, stopover, stop-off, stay, visit. **3** *the next stop is Oxford Street:* **stopping place**, halt, station, stage. **4** *a full stop:* **(full) point**; N. Amer. period.
– OPPOSITES start, beginning, continuation.
■ **put a stop to**. See **STOP** verb senses 1, 7.
■ **stop off/over** *we decided to stop over in Paris:* break one's journey, take a break, pause; stay, remain, put up, lodge, rest.

stopgap noun *that old plane was merely a stopgap:* **temporary solution**, expedient, makeshift; substitute, stand-in.
adjective *a stopgap measure:* **temporary**, provisional, interim, pro tem, short-term, working, makeshift, emergency; caretaker, acting, stand-in, fill-in.
– OPPOSITES permanent.

stopover noun *a brief stopover in the United Kingdom en route to the US:* **break**, stop, stop-off, visit, stay.

stoppage noun **1** *the stoppage of production:* **discontinuation**, stopping, halting, cessation, termination, end, finish; interruption, suspension, breaking off. **2** *a stoppage of the blood supply:* **obstruction**, blocking, blockage, block.
– OPPOSITES start, continuation.

stopper noun *a cologne bottle with a cork and chrome stopper:* **bung**, plug, cork, spigot, spile, seal; N. Amer. stopple.

store noun **1** *a store of food:* **stock**, supply, stockpile, hoard, cache, reserve, bank, pool. **2** *a grain store:* **storeroom**, storehouse, repository, depository, stockroom, depot, warehouse, magazine; informal lock-up. **3** *ship's stores:* **supplies**, provisions, stocks, necessities; food, rations, provender; materials, equipment, hardware. **4** *a DIY store:* **shop**, (retail) outlet, boutique, department store, chain store, emporium; supermarket, hypermarket, superstore, megastore.
verb *rabbits don't store food:* **keep**, keep in reserve, stockpile, lay in, put/set aside, put away/by, put away for a rainy day, save, collect, accumulate, hoard, cache; informal squirrel away, salt away, stash away.
– OPPOSITES use, discard.
■ **set (great) store by** value, attach great importance to, put a high value on, put a premium on; think highly of, hold in (high) regard, have a high opinion of; informal rate.

storehouse noun **warehouse**, depository, repository, store, storeroom, depot.

storey noun *a small flat on the second storey:* **floor**, level, deck.

storm noun **1** *the severe storms that battered Orkney:* **tempest**, squall; gale, hurricane, tornado, cyclone, typhoon; thunderstorm, rainstorm, monsoon, hailstorm, snowstorm, blizzard; N. Amer. williwaw, windstorm. **2** *a storm of bullets:* **volley**, salvo, fusillade, barrage, cannonade; shower, spray, hail, rain. **3** *there was a storm over his remarks:* **uproar**, outcry, fuss, furore, brouhaha, rumpus, trouble, hue and cry, controversy; informal to-do, hoo-ha, hullabaloo, ballyhoo, ructions, stink; Brit. informal row. **4** *a storm of protest:* **outburst**, outbreak, explosion, eruption, outpouring, surge, blaze, flare-up, wave.
verb **1** *she stormed out:* **stride angrily**, stomp, march, stalk, flounce, stamp, fling. **2** *his mother stormed at him:* **rant**, rave, shout,

bellow, roar, thunder, rage. **3** *police stormed the building:* **attack**, charge, rush, assail, descend on, swoop on.

stormy adjective **1** *stormy weather:* **blustery**, squally, windy, gusty, blowy; rainy, thundery; wild, tempestuous, turbulent, violent, rough, foul. **2** *a stormy debate:* **angry**, heated, fiery, fierce, furious, passionate, lively.
– OPPOSITES calm, fine, peaceful.

story noun **1** *an adventure story:* **tale**, narrative, account, anecdote; informal yarn, spiel. **2** *the novel has a good story:* **plot**, storyline, scenario. **3** *the story appeared in the papers:* **news item**, news report, article, feature, piece. **4** *there have been a lot of stories going round:* **rumour**, piece of gossip, whisper; speculation; Austral./NZ informal furphy. **5** *Harper changed his story:* **testimony**, statement, report, account, version. **6** *Ellie never told stories.* See FALSEHOOD sense 1.

storyteller noun **narrator**, teller of tales, raconteur, raconteuse, fabulist, anecdotalist; Austral. informal magsman.

stout adjective **1** *a short stout man:* **fat**, plump, portly, rotund, dumpy, chunky, corpulent; stocky, burly, bulky, hefty, solidly built, thickset; informal tubby, pudgy; Brit. informal podgy, fubsy; N. Amer. informal zaftig, corn-fed. **2** *stout leather shoes:* **strong**, sturdy, solid, substantial, robust, tough, durable, hard-wearing. **3** *stout resistance:* **determined**, vigorous, forceful, spirited; staunch, steadfast, stalwart, firm, resolute, unyielding, dogged; brave, bold, courageous, valiant, valorous, gallant, fearless, doughty, intrepid; informal gutsy, spunky.
– OPPOSITES thin, flimsy, feeble.

stout-hearted adjective *a stout-hearted man who was not easily deterred:* **brave**, determined, courageous, bold, plucky, spirited, valiant, valorous, gallant, fearless, doughty, intrepid, stalwart; informal gutsy, spunky.

stove noun **oven**, range, cooker.

stow verb *Barney stowed her luggage in the boot:* **pack**, load, store, place, put (away), deposit, stash.
– OPPOSITES unload.
■ **stow away** *he stowed away on a ship bound for South Africa:* **hide**, conceal oneself, travel secretly.

straddle verb **1** *she straddled the motorbike:* **sit/stand astride**, bestride, mount, get on. **2** *a mountain range straddling the border:* **lie on both sides of**, extend across, span.

strafe verb *military aircraft strafed the village:* **bomb**, shell, bombard, fire on, machine-gun, rake with gunfire.

straggle verb *a few of the men were straggling some half a mile behind the rest:* **trail**, lag, dawdle, walk slowly; fall behind, bring up the rear.

straggly adjective *a thin woman with straggly hair:* **untidy**, messy, unkempt, straggling, dishevelled.

straight adjective **1** *a long, straight road:* **unswerving**, undeviating, linear, as straight as an arrow, uncurving, unbending. **2** *that picture isn't straight:* **level**, even, in line, aligned, square; vertical, upright, perpendicular; horizontal. **3** *we must get the place straight:* **in order**, (neat and) tidy, neat, shipshape (and Bristol fashion), orderly, spick and span, organized, arranged, sorted out, straightened out. **4** *a straight answer:* **honest**, direct, frank, candid, truthful, sincere, forthright, straightforward, plain-spoken, blunt, straight from the shoulder, unequivocal, unambiguous; informal upfront. **5** *straight thinking:* **logical**, rational, clear, lucid, sound, coherent. **6** *three straight wins:* **successive**, in succession, consecutive, in a row, running; informal on the trot. **7** *straight brandy:* **undiluted**, neat, pure; N. Amer. informal straight up.
– OPPOSITES winding, crooked, untidy, evasive.
adverb **1** *he looked me straight in the eyes:* **right**, directly, squarely, full; informal smack, (slap) bang; N. Amer. informal spang, smack dab. **2** *she drove straight home:* **directly**, right, by a direct route. **3** *I'll call you straight back:* **right away**, straight away, immediately, directly, at once. **4** *I told her straight:* **frankly**, directly, candidly, honestly, forthrightly, plainly, point-blank, bluntly, flatly, straight from the shoulder, without beating about the bush, without mincing words, unequivocally, unambiguously, in plain English, to someone's face; Brit. informal straight up. **5** *he can't think straight:* **logically**, rationally, clearly, lucidly, coherently, cogently.
■ **go straight** reform, mend one's ways, turn over a new leaf, get back on the straight and narrow.
■ **straight away** at once, right away, (right) now, this/that (very) minute, this/that instant, immediately, instantly, directly, forthwith, without further/more ado, promptly, quickly, without delay, then and there, here and now, a.s.a.p., as soon as possible, as quickly as possible; N. Amer. in short order; informal straight off, in double quick time, p.d.q., pretty damn quick, pronto, before you can say Jack Robinson; N. Amer. informal lickety-split.
■ **straight from the shoulder.** See STRAIGHT adverb sense 4.

straighten verb **1** *Rory straightened his tie:* **make straight**, adjust, arrange, rearrange, (make) tidy, spruce up. **2** *we must straighten things out with Viola:* **put/set right**, sort out, clear up, settle, resolve, put in order, regularize, rectify, remedy; informal patch up. **3** *he straightened up:* **stand up (straight)**, stand upright.

S

straightforward adjective **1** *the process was remarkably straightforward:* **uncomplicated**, simple, easy, effortless, painless, undemanding, plain sailing, child's play; informal as easy as falling off a log, as easy as pie, a piece of cake, a cinch, a snip, a doddle, a breeze, a cakewalk; Brit. informal easy-peasy, a doss; N. Amer. informal duck soup, a snap; Austral./NZ informal a bludge, a snack. **2** *a straightforward man:* **honest**, frank, candid, open, truthful, sincere, on the level; forthright, plain-speaking, direct, unambiguous; informal upfront; N. Amer. informal on the up and up.
– OPPOSITES complicated.

strain[1] verb **1** *take care that you don't strain yourself:* **overtax**, overwork, overextend, overreach, drive too far, overdo it; exhaust, wear out; informal knacker, knock oneself out. **2** *you have strained a muscle:* **injure**, damage, pull, wrench, twist, sprain. **3** *we strained to haul the guns up the slope:* **struggle**, labour, toil, make every effort, try very hard, break one's back, push/drive oneself to the limit; informal pull out all the stops, go all out, bust a gut; Austral. informal go for the doctor. **4** *the flood of refugees is straining the relief services:* **make excessive demands on**, overtax, be too much for, test, tax, put a strain on. **5** *the bear strained at the chain:* **pull**, tug, heave, haul, jerk; informal yank. **6** *strain the mixture:* **sieve**, sift, filter, screen, riddle.
noun **1** *the rope snapped under the strain:* **tension**, tightness, tautness. **2** *muscle strain:* **injury**, sprain, wrench, twist. **3** *the strain of her job:* **pressure**, demands, burdens, stress; informal hassle. **4** *Melissa was showing signs of strain:* **stress**, (nervous) tension; exhaustion, fatigue, pressure of work, overwork. **5** *the strains of Brahms's lullaby:* **sound**, music; melody, tune.

strain[2] noun **1** *a different strain of flu:* **variety**, kind, type, sort; breed, genus. **2** *Hawthorne was of Puritan strain:* **descent**, ancestry, origin(s), parentage, lineage, extraction, family, roots. **3** *there was a strain of insanity in the family:* **tendency**, susceptibility, propensity, proneness; trait, disposition. **4** *they have injected a strain of solemnity into the film:* **element**, strand, vein, note, trace, touch, suggestion, hint.

strained adjective **1** *relations between them were strained:* **awkward**, tense, uneasy, uncomfortable, edgy, difficult, troubled. **2** *Jean's strained face:* **drawn**, careworn, worn, pinched, tired, exhausted, drained, haggard. **3** *a strained smile:* **forced**, constrained, unnatural; artificial, insincere, false, affected, put-on.
– OPPOSITES friendly.

strainer noun sieve, colander, filter, sifter, riddle, screen.

strait noun **1** *a strait about six miles wide:* **channel**, sound, inlet, stretch of water. **2** *the company is in desperate straits:* a **bad/difficult situation**, difficulty, trouble, crisis, a mess, a predicament, a plight; informal hot/deep water, a jam, a hole, a bind, a fix, a scrape.

straitened adjective *he died in 1886, leaving the family in straitened circumstances:* **impoverished**, poverty-stricken, poor, destitute, penniless, on one's beam-ends, as poor as a church mouse, in penury, impecunious, unable to make ends meet, in reduced circumstances; Brit. on the breadline; informal (flat) broke, strapped for cash, cash-strapped, on one's uppers; Brit. informal stony broke, skint, in Queer Street; N. Amer. informal stone broke.

strait-laced adjective *his strait-laced parents were horrified:* **prim (and proper)**, prudish, puritanical, prissy, mimsy, niminy-piminy; conservative, old-fashioned, stuffy, staid, narrow-minded; informal starchy, square, fuddy-duddy.
– OPPOSITES broad-minded.

strand noun **1** *strands of wool:* **thread**, filament, fibre; length, ply. **2** *the various strands of the ecological movement:* **element**, component, factor, ingredient, aspect, feature, strain.

stranded adjective **1** *a stranded ship:* **beached**, grounded, run aground, high and dry; shipwrecked, wrecked, marooned. **2** *she was stranded in a strange city:* **helpless**, without resources, in difficulties; in the lurch, abandoned, deserted.

strange adjective **1** *strange things have been happening:* **unusual**, odd, curious, peculiar, funny, bizarre, weird, uncanny, queer, unexpected, unfamiliar, atypical, anomalous, out of the ordinary, extraordinary, puzzling, mystifying, mysterious, perplexing, baffling, unaccountable, inexplicable, singular, freakish; suspicious, questionable; eerie, unnatural; informal fishy, creepy, spooky. **2** *strange clothes:* **weird**, eccentric, odd, peculiar, funny, bizarre, unusual; unconventional, outlandish, freakish, quirky, zany; informal wacky, way out, freaky, kooky, offbeat, off the wall; N. Amer. informal screwy, wacko. **3** *when children visit a strange house, they are often a little shy:* **unfamiliar**, unknown, new. **4** *Jean was feeling strange:* **ill**, unwell, poorly, peaky; Brit. off colour; informal under the weather, funny, peculiar, lousy; Brit. informal off, ropy, grotty; Austral./NZ informal crook.
– OPPOSITES ordinary, familiar.

strangeness noun *the strangeness of Eliot's behaviour:* **oddity**, eccentricity, peculiarity, curiousness, bizarreness, weirdness, queerness, unusualness, abnormality, unaccountability, inexplicability, incongruousness, outlandishness, singularity.

stranger noun *he was a stranger in the town:* **newcomer**, new arrival, visitor, outsider; Austral. informal blow-in.

■ **a stranger to** *Harker was a stranger to self-doubt*: unaccustomed to, unfamiliar with, unused to, new to, fresh to, inexperienced in.

strangle verb **1** *the victim was strangled with a scarf*: **throttle**, choke, garrotte; informal strangulate. **2** *she strangled a sob*: **suppress**, smother, stifle, repress, restrain, fight back, choke back. **3** *bureaucracy is strangling commercial activity*: **hamper**, hinder, impede, restrict, inhibit, curb, check, constrain, squash, crush, suppress, repress.

strap noun *thick leather straps*: **thong**, tie, band, belt.
verb **1** *a bag was strapped to the bicycle*: **fasten**, secure, tie, bind, make fast, lash, truss. **2** *his knee was strapped up*: **bandage**, bind. **3** *his father strapped him*. See LASH verb sense 1.

strapping adjective *they had three strapping sons*: **big**, strong, well built, brawny, burly, broad-shouldered, muscular, rugged; informal hunky, beefy.
– OPPOSITES weedy.

stratagem noun *he deployed various cunning stratagems*: **plan**, scheme, tactic, manoeuvre, ploy, device, trick, ruse, plot, machination, dodge; subterfuge, artifice; Brit. informal wheeze; Austral. informal lurk.

strategic adjective *strategic planning is the responsibility of top management*: **planned**, calculated, tactical, politic, judicious, prudent, shrewd.

strategy noun **1** *the government's economic strategy*: **master plan**, grand design, game plan, plan (of action), policy, programme; tactics. **2** *military strategy*: **the art of war**, (military) tactics.

stratum noun **1** *a stratum of flint*: **layer**, vein, seam, lode, bed. **2** *this stratum of society*: **level**, class, echelon, rank, grade, group, set; caste.

stray verb **1** *the gazelle had strayed from the herd*: **wander off**, go astray, get separated, get lost. **2** *we strayed from our original topic*: **digress**, deviate, wander, get sidetracked, go off at a tangent; get off the subject.
adjective **1** *a stray dog*: **homeless**, lost, strayed, gone astray, abandoned. **2** *a stray bullet*: **random**, chance, freak, unexpected, isolated, lone, single.
noun *wardens who deal with strays*: **homeless animal**, stray dog/cat, waif.

streak noun **1** *a streak of orange light*: **band**, line, strip, stripe, vein, slash, ray. **2** *green streaks on her legs*: **mark**, smear, smudge, stain, blotch; informal splotch. **3** *a streak of self-destructiveness*: **element**, vein, touch, strain; trait, characteristic. **4** *a winning streak*: **period**, spell, stretch, run; Brit. informal patch.
verb **1** *the sky was streaked with red*: **stripe**, band, fleck. **2** *overalls streaked with paint*: **mark**, daub, smear; informal splotch.

streaky adjective *a songbird with streaky brown plumage*: **striped**, stripy, streaked, banded, veined, brindled.

stream noun **1** *a mountain stream*: **brook**, rivulet, rill, runnel, streamlet, freshet; tributary; Scottish & N. English burn; N. English beck; S. English bourn; N. Amer. & Austral./NZ creek; Austral. billabong. **2** *a stream of boiling water*: **jet**, flow, rush, gush, surge, torrent, flood, cascade, outpouring, outflow. **3** *a steady stream of visitors*: **succession**, series, string.
verb **1** *tears were streaming down her face*: **flow**, pour, course, run, gush, surge, flood, cascade, spill. **2** *children streamed out of the classrooms*: **pour**, surge, flood, swarm, pile, crowd. **3** *a flag streamed from the mast*: **flutter**, float, flap, fly, blow, waft, wave.

streamer noun **pennant**, pennon, flag, banderole, banner.

streamlined adjective **1** *a new generation of streamlined aluminium trams*: **aerodynamic**, smooth, sleek, elegant. **2** *a streamlined organization*: **efficient**, smooth-running, well run, slick; time-saving, labour-saving.

street noun *Amsterdam's narrow cobbled streets*: **road**, thoroughfare, avenue, drive, boulevard, parade; side street/road, lane; N. Amer. highway.
■ **the man/woman in the street** an ordinary person, Mr/Mrs Average; Brit. informal Joe Bloggs, Joe Public, the man on the Clapham omnibus; N. Amer. informal John Doe, Joe Sixpack.
■ **on the streets** homeless, sleeping rough, down and out.

strength noun **1** *a man of enormous physical strength*: **power**, brawn, muscle, muscularity, burliness, sturdiness, robustness, toughness, hardiness; vigour, force, might; informal beef. **2** *Oliver began to regain his strength*: **health**, fitness, vigour, stamina. **3** *her great inner strength*: **fortitude**, resilience, spirit, backbone, strength of character; courage, bravery, pluck, pluckiness, courageousness, grit; informal guts, spunk. **4** *the strength of the retaining wall*: **robustness**, sturdiness, firmness, toughness, soundness, solidity, durability. **5** *Europe's military strength*: **power**, influence, dominance, ascendancy, supremacy; informal clout. **6** *the strength of feeling against the president*: **intensity**, vehemence, force, forcefulness, depth, ardour, fervour. **7** *the strength of their argument*: **cogency**, forcefulness, force, weight, power, potency, persuasiveness, soundness, validity. **8** *what are your strengths?* **strong point**, advantage, asset, forte, aptitude, talent, skill; speciality.
– OPPOSITES weakness.
■ **on the strength of** because of, by virtue of, on the basis of.

strengthen verb **1** *calcium strengthens growing bones*: **make strong/stronger**, build up, give strength to. **2** *engineers strengthened the walls*: **reinforce**, make

S

stronger, buttress, shore up, underpin.
3 *strengthened glass:* **toughen**, temper,
anneal. **4** *the wind had strengthened:* **become**
strong/stronger, gain strength, intensify,
pick up. **5** *his insistence strengthened*
her determination: **fortify**, bolster, make
stronger, boost, reinforce, harden, stiffen,
toughen, fuel. **6** *they strengthened their*
efforts: **step up**, increase, escalate; informal
up, crank up, beef up. **7** *the argument is*
strengthened by this evidence: **reinforce**,
lend more weight to; support, back up,
confirm, bear out, corroborate.
– OPPOSITES weaken.

strenuous adjective **1** *a strenuous climb:*
arduous, difficult, hard, tough, taxing,
demanding, exacting, exhausting, tiring,
gruelling, back-breaking; informal killing;
Brit. informal knackering. **2** *strenuous efforts:*
vigorous, energetic, zealous, forceful,
strong, spirited, intense, determined,
resolute, tenacious, tireless, indefatigable,
dogged.
– OPPOSITES easy, half-hearted.

stress noun **1** *he's under a lot of stress:* **strain**,
pressure, (nervous) tension, worry, anxiety,
trouble, difficulty; informal hassle. **2** *laying*
greater stress on education: **emphasis**,
importance, weight. **3** *the stress falls*
on the first syllable: **emphasis**, accent,
accentuation; beat; Prosody ictus. **4** *the stress*
is uniform across the bar: **pressure**, tension,
strain.
verb **1** *they stressed the need for reform:*
emphasize, draw attention to, underline,
underscore, point up, place emphasis on, lay
stress on, highlight, accentuate, press home.
2 *the last syllable is stressed:* **emphasize**,
place the accent on. **3** *all the staff were*
stressed: **overstretch**, overtax, push to the
limit, pressurize, pressure, make tense,
worry, harass; informal hassle.
– OPPOSITES play down.

stressful adjective *he had had a particularly*
stressful day: **demanding**, trying, taxing,
difficult, hard, tough; fraught, traumatic,
pressured, tense, frustrating.
– OPPOSITES relaxing.

stretch verb **1** *this material stretches:* **be**
elastic, be stretchy, be tensile. **2** *he stretched*
the elastic: **pull (out)**, draw out, extend,
lengthen, elongate, expand. **3** *stretch your*
weekend into a vacation: **prolong**, lengthen,
make longer, extend, spin out. **4** *my budget*
won't stretch to a new car: **be sufficient**
for, be enough for, cover; afford, have
the money for. **5** *the court case stretched*
their finances: **put a strain on**, overtax,
overextend, drain, sap. **6** *stretching the truth:*
bend, strain, distort, exaggerate, embellish.
7 *she stretched out her hand to him:* **reach**
out, hold out, extend, outstretch, proffer.
8 *he stretched his arms:* **extend**, straighten
(out). **9** *she stretched out on the sofa:* **lie**
down, recline, lean back, be recumbent,
sprawl, lounge, loll. **10** *the desert stretches*

for miles: **extend**, spread, continue.
– OPPOSITES shorten.
noun **1** *magnificent stretches of forest:*
expanse, area, tract, belt, sweep, extent.
2 *a four-hour stretch:* **period**, time, spell,
run, stint, session, shift.
adjective *stretch fabrics:* **stretchy**,
stretchable, elastic.

strew verb *his room was strewn with books*
and papers: **scatter**, spread, disperse, litter,
toss.

stricken adjective *Raymond was stricken with*
grief: **troubled**, (deeply) affected, afflicted,
struck, hit.

strict adjective **1** *a strict interpretation of*
the law: **precise**, exact, literal, faithful,
accurate, careful, meticulous, rigorous.
2 *strict controls on spending:* **stringent**,
rigorous, severe, harsh, hard, rigid, tough.
3 *strict parents:* **stern**, severe, harsh,
uncompromising, authoritarian, firm,
austere. **4** *this will be treated in strict*
confidence: **absolute**, utter, complete, total.
5 *a strict Roman Catholic:* **orthodox**, devout,
conscientious.
– OPPOSITES loose, liberal.

strictness noun **1** *the strictness of the laws:*
severity, harshness, rigidity, rigidness,
stringency, rigorousness, sternness.
2 *the provision has been interpreted with*
strictness: **precision**, preciseness, accuracy,
exactness, faithfulness; meticulousness,
scrupulousness.
– OPPOSITES imprecision.

stricture noun **1** *the strictures on Victorian*
women: **constraint**, restriction, limitation,
restraint, curb, impediment, barrier,
obstacle. **2** *the constant strictures of the*
nuns: **criticism**, censure, condemnation,
reproof, reproach, admonishment.
– OPPOSITES freedom, praise.

stride verb *she came striding down the path:*
march, pace, step.
noun *long swinging strides:* **(long/large) step**,
pace.
■ **take something in one's stride** deal with
easily, cope with easily, not bat an eyelid.

strident adjective *a strident voice interrupted*
the consultation: **harsh**, raucous, rough,
grating, rasping, jarring, loud, shrill,
screeching, piercing, ear-piercing.
– OPPOSITES soft.

strife noun *the history of the Empire is*
full of strife: **conflict**, friction, discord,
disagreement, dissension, dispute,
argument, quarrelling, wrangling, bickering,
controversy; ill/bad feeling, falling-out, bad
blood, hostility, animosity.
– OPPOSITES peace.

strike verb **1** *the teacher struck Mary:* **hit**,
slap, smack, beat, thrash, spank, thump,
punch, cuff; cane, lash, whip, club; Austral./NZ
informal quilt; informal clout, wallop, belt,
whack, thwack, bash, clobber, bop, biff. **2** *he*
struck the gong: **bang**, beat, hit; informal bash,

wallop. **3** *the car struck a tree:* **crash into**, collide with, hit, run into, bump into, smash into; N. Amer. impact. **4** *Jennifer struck the ball:* **hit**, drive, propel; informal clout, wallop, swipe. **5** *he struck a match:* **ignite**, light. **6** *she was asleep when the killer struck:* **attack**, set upon someone, fall on someone, assault someone. **7** *the disease is striking 3,000 people a year:* **affect**, afflict, attack, hit. **8** *striking a balance:* **achieve**, reach, arrive at, find, attain, establish. **9** *we have struck a bargain:* **agree (on)**, come to an agreement on, settle on; informal clinch. **10** *he struck a heroic pose:* **assume**, adopt, take on/up, affect; N. Amer. informal cop. **11** *they have struck oil:* **discover**, find, come upon. **12** *a thought struck her:* **occur to**, come to (mind), dawn on one, hit, spring to mind, enter one's head. **13** *you strike me as intelligent:* **seem to**, appear to, give the impression to. **14** *train drivers are striking:* **take industrial action**, go on strike, down tools, walk out.
noun **1** *a 48-hour strike:* **industrial action**, walkout. **2** *a military strike:* **(air) attack**, assault, bombing.
■ **strike something out** delete, cross out, erase, rub out.
■ **strike something up 1** *the band struck up another tune:* begin to play, start playing. **2** *we struck up a friendship:* begin, start, commence, embark on, establish.

striking adjective **1** *Lizzie bears a striking resemblance to her sister:* **noticeable**, obvious, conspicuous, evident, marked, notable, unmistakable, strong; remarkable, extraordinary, incredible, amazing, astounding, astonishing, staggering. **2** *Kenya's striking landscape:* **impressive**, imposing, grand, splendid, magnificent, spectacular, breathtaking, superb, marvellous, wonderful, stunning, staggering, sensational, dramatic. **3** *she has striking good looks:* **stunning**, attractive, good-looking, beautiful, glamorous, gorgeous, prepossessing, ravishing, handsome, pretty; informal knockout.
– OPPOSITES unremarkable.

string noun **1** *a ball of string:* **twine**, cord, yarn, thread, strand. **2** *they lease their pubs to a string of brewers:* **chain**, group, firm, company. **3** *a string of convictions:* **series**, succession, chain, sequence, run, streak. **4** *a string of wagons:* **queue**, procession, line, file, column, convoy, train, cavalcade. **5** *a string of pearls:* **strand**, rope, necklace. **6** *a guaranteed loan with no strings:* **conditions**, qualifications, provisions, provisos, caveats, stipulations, riders, prerequisites, limitations, limits, constraints, restrictions; informal catches.
verb **1** *lights were strung across the promenade:* **hang**, suspend, sling, stretch, run; thread, loop, festoon. **2** *beads strung on a silver chain:* **thread**, loop, link.
■ **string along** *with my name I could always string along with the Irish gang:* go along, come too, accompany, join (up with).

■ **string someone along** (informal) *she had no plans to marry him—she was just stringing him along:* mislead, deceive, take advantage of, dupe, hoax, fool, make a fool of, play with, toy with, dally with, trifle with; informal lead up the garden path, take for a ride.
■ **string something out 1** *stringing out a story:* spin out, drag out, lengthen. **2** *there are airfields strung out along the Gulf:* spread out, space out, distribute, scatter.

stringent adjective *the safety regulations are very stringent:* **strict**, firm, rigid, rigorous, severe, harsh, tough, tight, exacting, demanding, inflexible, hard and fast.

stringy adjective **1** *stringy hair:* **straggly**, lank, thin. **2** *he had the thin, stringy look of a rider:* **lanky**, gangling, gangly, rangy, wiry, bony, skinny, scrawny, thin, spare, gaunt. **3** *stringy meat:* **fibrous**, gristly, sinewy, chewy, tough, leathery.

strip[1] verb **1** *he stripped and got into bed:* **undress**, strip off, take one's clothes off, unclothe, disrobe, strip naked. **2** *stripping off paint:* **peel**, remove, take off, scrape, rub, clean. **3** *they stripped him of his doctorate:* **take away from**, dispossess, deprive, confiscate, divest, relieve. **4** *they stripped down my engine:* **dismantle**, disassemble, take to bits/pieces, take apart. **5** *the house had been stripped:* **empty**, clear, clean out, plunder, rob, burgle, loot, pillage, ransack, despoil, sack.
– OPPOSITES dress.
noun *the team's new strip:* **outfit**, clothes, clothing, garments, dress, garb; Brit. kit; informal gear, get-up; Brit. informal rig-out.

strip[2] noun *a strip of paper:* **(narrow) piece**, bit, band, belt, ribbon, slip, shred.

stripe noun *green tracksuit bottoms with a yellow stripe on the side:* **line**, band, strip, belt, bar, streak, vein, flash, blaze.

stripy adjective *a stripy T-shirt:* **striped**, barred, lined, banded; streaky, variegated.

strive verb **1** *I shall strive to be virtuous:* **try (hard)**, attempt, endeavour, aim, venture, make an effort, exert oneself, do one's best, do all one can, do one's utmost, labour, work; informal go all out, give it one's best shot, pull out all the stops. **2** *scholars must strive against bias:* **struggle**, fight, battle, combat; campaign, crusade.

stroke noun **1** *five strokes of the axe:* **blow**, hit, thump, punch, slap, smack, cuff, knock; informal wallop, clout, whack, thwack, bash, biff, swipe. **2** *cricket strokes:* **shot**, hit, strike. **3** *finish the sawcut with slow, gentle strokes:* **movement**, action, motion. **4** *broad brush strokes:* **mark**, line. **5** *a stroke of genius:* **feat**, accomplishment, achievement, master stroke. **6** *the budget was full of bold strokes:* **detail**, touch, point. **7** *he suffered a stroke:* **thrombosis**, seizure.
verb *she stroked the cat:* **caress**, fondle, pat, pet, touch, rub, massage, soothe.

stroll verb *they strolled along the river:*

S

saunter, amble, wander, meander, ramble, promenade, walk, go for a walk, stretch one's legs, get some air; informal mosey.
noun *a stroll in the park:* **saunter**, amble, wander, walk, turn, promenade; informal mosey.

strong adjective **1** *a strong lad:* **powerful**, muscular, brawny, powerfully built, strapping, sturdy, burly, meaty, robust, athletic, tough, rugged, lusty, strong as an ox/horse; informal beefy, hunky, husky. **2** *she hasn't been strong since father's death:* **well**, healthy, in good health, (fighting) fit, robust, vigorous, blooming, thriving, hale and hearty, in fine fettle; informal in the pink. **3** *a lady of strong character:* **forceful**, determined, spirited, self-assertive, tough, tenacious, formidable, redoubtable, strong-minded; informal gutsy, feisty. **4** *a strong fortress:* **secure**, well built, indestructible, well fortified, well protected, impregnable, solid. **5** *strong cotton bags:* **durable**, hard-wearing, heavy-duty, tough, sturdy, well made, long-lasting. **6** *the current is very strong:* **forceful**, powerful, vigorous, fierce, intense. **7** *a strong interest in literature:* **keen**, eager, passionate, fervent. **8** *strong feelings:* **intense**, forceful, passionate, ardent, fervent, fervid, deep-seated. **9** *a strong supporter of the women's movement:* **keen**, eager, enthusiastic, dedicated, staunch, loyal, steadfast. **10** *strong arguments:* **compelling**, cogent, forceful, powerful, potent, weighty, convincing, sound, valid, well founded, persuasive, influential. **11** *a need for strong action:* **firm**, forceful, drastic, extreme. **12** *she bore a very strong resemblance to Vera:* **marked**, noticeable, pronounced, distinct, definite, unmistakable, notable. **13** *a strong voice:* **loud**, powerful, forceful, resonant, sonorous, rich, deep, booming. **14** *strong language:* **bad**, foul, obscene, profane. **15** *a strong blue colour:* **intense**, deep, rich, bright, brilliant, vivid. **16** *strong lights:* **bright**, brilliant, dazzling, glaring. **17** *strong black coffee:* **concentrated**, undiluted. **18** *strong cheese:* **highly flavoured**, flavourful, flavoursome; piquant, tangy, spicy.
– OPPOSITES weak, gentle, mild.

strong-arm adjective *strong-arm tactics were deployed by both sides:* **aggressive**, forceful, bullying, coercive, threatening, intimidatory; informal bully-boy.

strongbox noun **safe**, safe-deposit box, cash/money box.

stronghold noun **1** *the enemy stronghold:* **fortress**, fort, castle, citadel, garrison. **2** *a Tory stronghold:* **bastion**, centre, hotbed.

strong-minded adjective *a strong-minded social reformer:* **determined**, firm, resolute, purposeful, strong-willed, uncompromising, unbending, forceful, persistent, tenacious, dogged; informal gutsy, spunky.

strong-willed adjective *he was strong-willed*

and independent: **determined**, resolute, stubborn, obstinate, wilful, headstrong, strong-minded, self-willed, unbending, unyielding, intransigent, intractable, obdurate, recalcitrant.

stroppy adjective (Brit. informal). See **BAD-TEMPERED**.

structure noun **1** *a vast Gothic structure:* **building**, edifice, construction, erection, pile. **2** *the structure of local government:* **construction**, form, formation, shape, composition, anatomy, make-up; constitution; organization, system, arrangement, design, framework, configuration.
verb *the programme is structured around periods of residential study:* **arrange**, organize, design, shape, construct, build, put together.

struggle verb **1** *they struggled to do better:* **strive**, try hard, endeavour, make every effort, do one's best/utmost, bend over backwards, put oneself out; informal go all out, give it one's best shot; formal essay. **2** *James struggled with the raiders:* **fight**, grapple, wrestle, scuffle, brawl, spar; informal scrap. **3** *the teams struggled to be first:* **compete**, contend, vie, fight, battle, jockey. **4** *she struggled over the dunes:* **scramble**, flounder, stumble, fight/battle one's way, labour.
noun **1** *the struggle for justice:* **endeavour**, striving, effort, exertion, labour; campaign, battle, crusade, drive, push. **2** *they were arrested without a struggle:* **fight**, scuffle, brawl, tussle, wrestling bout, skirmish, fracas, melee; breach of the peace; informal scrap, dust-up, punch-up; Brit. informal bust-up, ding-dong. **3** *many perished in the struggle:* **conflict**, fight, battle, confrontation, clash, skirmish; hostilities, fighting, war, warfare, campaign. **4** *a struggle within the leadership:* **contest**, competition, fight, clash; rivalry, friction, feuding, conflict. **5** *life has been a struggle for me:* **effort**, trial, trouble, stress, strain, battle; informal grind, hassle.

strut verb *he strutted around his vast office:* **swagger**, swank, parade, stride, sweep; N. Amer. informal sashay.

stub noun **1** *a cigarette stub:* **butt**, (tail) end; informal dog-end. **2** *a ticket stub:* **counterfoil**, ticket slip, tab. **3** *a stub of pencil:* **stump**, remnant, (tail) end.

stubble noun **1** *a field of stubble:* **stalks**, straw. **2** *a weather-beaten face covered in grey stubble:* **bristles**, whiskers, facial hair; informal five o'clock shadow.

stubbly adjective *his stubbly chin:* **bristly**, unshaven, whiskered; prickly, rough, coarse, scratchy.

stubborn adjective **1** *you're too stubborn to admit it:* **obstinate**, stubborn as a mule, headstrong, wilful, strong-willed, pig-headed, obdurate, difficult, contrary, perverse, recalcitrant, inflexible, iron-willed, uncompromising, unbending;

S

informal stiff-necked; Brit. informal bolshie, bloody-minded; N. Amer. informal balky; formal pertinacious, refractory. **2** *stubborn stains:* **indelible**, permanent, persistent, tenacious, resistant.
– OPPOSITES compliant.

stubby adjective *a small stubby man with glasses:* **dumpy**, stocky, chunky, chubby, squat; short, stumpy, dwarfish.
– OPPOSITES slender, tall.

stuck adjective **1** *a message was stuck to his screen:* **fixed**, fastened, attached, glued, pinned. **2** *the gate was stuck:* **immovable**, stuck fast, jammed. **3** *if you get stuck, leave a blank:* **baffled**, beaten, at a loss, at one's wits' end; informal stumped, bogged down, flummoxed, fazed, bamboozled.
■ **get stuck into** (informal) *Walsh got stuck into the project:* get down to, make a start on, commence, embark on, get to work at, tackle, throw oneself into.
■ **stuck with** *he was stuck with her for two months:* lumbered with, left with, made responsible for.

stuck-up adjective (informal). See CONCEITED.

studded adjective *a gold cigarette box studded with jewels:* **dotted**, scattered, sprinkled, covered, spangled.

student noun **1** *a university student:* **undergraduate**, postgraduate, scholar; freshman, freshwoman, finalist; N. Amer. sophomore; Brit. informal fresher. **2** *a former student of the school:* **pupil**, schoolchild, schoolboy, schoolgirl, scholar. **3** *a nursing student:* **trainee**, apprentice, probationer, recruit, novice; informal rookie.

studied adjective *the words were said with studied politeness:* **deliberate**, careful, considered, conscious, calculated, intentional; affected, forced, strained, artificial.

studio noun **workshop**, workroom, atelier.

studious adjective **1** *a studious nature:* **scholarly**, academic, bookish, intellectual, erudite, learned, donnish. **2** *he gave studious attention to the question:* **diligent**, careful, attentive, assiduous, painstaking, thorough, meticulous. **3** *his studious absence from public view:* **deliberate**, wilful, conscious, intentional.

study noun **1** *two years of study:* **learning**, education, schooling, academic work, scholarship, tuition, research; informal swotting, cramming. **2** *a study of global warming:* **investigation**, enquiry, research, examination, analysis, review, survey. **3** *Father was in his study:* **office**, workroom, studio. **4** *a critical study:* **essay**, article, work, review, paper, dissertation, disquisition.
verb **1** *Anne studied hard:* **work**, revise; informal swot, cram, mug up. **2** *he studied electronics:* **learn**, read, be taught. **3** *Thomas was studying child development:* **investigate**, inquire into, research, look into, examine, analyse, explore, review, appraise, conduct

a survey of. **4** *she studied her friend thoughtfully:* **scrutinize**, examine, inspect, consider, regard, look at, eye, observe, watch, survey; informal check out; N. Amer. informal eyeball.
■ **in a brown study** lost in thought, in a reverie, musing, ruminating, cogitating, dreaming, daydreaming; informal miles away.

stuff noun **1** *suede is tough stuff:* **material**, fabric, cloth, textile; matter, substance. **2** *first-aid stuff:* **items**, articles, objects, goods; informal things, bits and pieces, odds and ends. **3** *all my stuff is in the suitcase:* **belongings**, (personal) possessions, effects, goods (and chattels), paraphernalia; informal gear, things, kit; Brit. informal clobber, gubbins. **4** *he knows his stuff:* **facts**, information, data, subject; informal onions.
verb **1** *feathers were used to stuff the pillows:* **fill**, pack, pad, upholster. **2** *Robyn stuffed her clothes into a bag:* **shove**, thrust, push, ram, cram, squeeze, force, jam, pack, pile, stick. **3** *my nose was stuffed up:* **block**, bung, congest, obstruct.
■ **stuff and nonsense** (Brit. informal). See NONSENSE sense 1.

stuffing noun **1** *the stuffing is coming out of the armchair:* **padding**, wadding, filling, upholstery, packing, filler. **2** *sage and onion stuffing:* **filling**, forcemeat; N. Amer. dressing.

stuffy adjective **1** *a stuffy atmosphere:* **airless**, close, musty, stale; Brit. frowsty; Brit. informal fuggy. **2** *a stuffy young man:* **staid**, sedate, sober, prim, priggish, strait-laced, conformist, conservative, old-fashioned; informal square, straight, starchy, fuddy-duddy. **3** *a stuffy nose:* **blocked**, stuffed up, bunged up.
– OPPOSITES airy, clear.

stultify verb **1** *the free market was stultified by the welfare state:* **hamper**, impede, thwart, frustrate, foil, suppress, smother. **2** *he stultifies her with too much gentleness:* **bore**, make bored, dull, numb, benumb, stupefy.

stumble verb **1** *he stumbled and fell heavily:* **trip (over/up)**, lose one's balance, lose/miss one's footing, slip. **2** *he stumbled back home:* **stagger**, totter, teeter, dodder, blunder, hobble, move clumsily. **3** *he stumbled through his speech:* **stammer**, stutter, hesitate, falter, speak haltingly; informal fluff one's lines.
■ **stumble across/on** *scientists stumbled across the vaccine by chance:* come across/upon, chance on, happen on, light on; discover, find, unearth, uncover; informal dig up.

stumbling block noun *the language problem is a fundamental stumbling block:* **obstacle**, hurdle, barrier, bar, hindrance, impediment, handicap, disadvantage; snag, hitch, catch, drawback, difficulty, problem, weakness, defect, pitfall; informal fly in the ointment, hiccup.

stump verb **1** (informal) *they were stumped*

S

by the question: **baffle**, perplex, puzzle, confound, nonplus, defeat, put at a loss; informal flummox, fox, throw, floor. **2** *she stumped along the landing:* **stomp**, stamp, clomp, clump, lumber, thump, thud.
■ **stump something up** (Brit. informal) pay (up), dish out, contribute; informal fork out, shell out, lay out, cough up, chip in; N. Amer. informal ante up, pony up.

stumpy adjective *a stumpy little man:* **short**, stubby, squat, stocky, chunky.
– OPPOSITES long, thin.

stun verb **1** *a glancing blow stunned Gary:* **daze**, stupefy, knock unconscious, knock out, lay out. **2** *she was stunned by the news:* **astound**, amaze, astonish, dumbfound, stupefy, stagger, shock, take aback; informal flabbergast, knock sideways, bowl over; Brit. informal knock for six.

stunning adjective **1** *a stunning win:* **remarkable**, extraordinary, staggering, incredible, outstanding, amazing, astonishing, marvellous, phenomenal, splendid; informal fabulous, fantastic, tremendous. **2** *she was looking stunning.* See BEAUTIFUL.
– OPPOSITES ordinary.

stunt¹ verb *a disease that stunts growth:* **inhibit**, impede, hamper, hinder, restrict, retard, slow, curb, check.
– OPPOSITES encourage.

stunt² noun *acrobatic stunts:* **feat**, exploit, trick.

stunted adjective *a clump of stunted trees:* **small**, undersize(d), diminutive.

stupefaction noun **1** *alcoholic stupefaction:* **oblivion**, obliviousness, unconsciousness, insensibility, stupor, daze. **2** *Don shook his head in stupefaction:* **bewilderment**, confusion, perplexity, wonder, amazement, astonishment.

stupefy verb **1** *the blow had stupefied her:* **stun**, daze, knock unconscious, knock out, lay out. **2** *they were stupefied:* **drug**, sedate, tranquillize, intoxicate, inebriate; informal dope. **3** *the amount stupefied us:* **shock**, stun, astound, dumbfound, overwhelm, stagger, amaze, astonish, take aback, take someone's breath away; informal flabbergast, knock sideways, bowl over, floor; Brit. informal knock for six.

stupendous adjective **1** *stupendous achievements:* **amazing**, astounding, astonishing, extraordinary, remarkable, phenomenal, staggering, breathtaking; informal fantastic, mind-boggling, awesome. **2** *a building of stupendous size:* **colossal**, immense, vast, gigantic, massive, mammoth, huge, enormous.
– OPPOSITES ordinary.

stupid adjective **1** *they're rather stupid:* **unintelligent**, ignorant, dense, foolish, dull-witted, slow, simple-minded, vacuous, vapid, idiotic, imbecilic, imbecile, obtuse, doltish; informal thick (as two short planks), dim, dumb, dopey, dozy, moronic, cretinous, pea-brained, half-witted, soft in the head, boneheaded, thickheaded, wooden-headed, muttonheaded; Brit. informal barmy, daft, not the full shilling. **2** *a stupid mistake:* **foolish**, silly, unintelligent, idiotic, scatterbrained, nonsensical, senseless, unthinking, ill-advised, ill-considered, unwise, injudicious; inane, absurd, ludicrous, ridiculous, laughable, risible, fatuous, asinine, mad, insane, lunatic; informal crazy, dopey, cracked, half-baked, cockeyed, hare-brained, nutty, dotty, batty, gormless, cuckoo, loony, loopy, off one's head, off one's trolley; Brit. informal potty. **3** *he drank himself stupid:* **into a stupor**, into a daze, into oblivion; stupefied, dazed, unconscious.
– OPPOSITES intelligent, sensible.

stupidity noun **1** *he cursed their stupidity:* **lack of intelligence**, foolishness, denseness, brainlessness, ignorance, dull-wittedness, slow-wittedness, doltishness, slowness; informal thickness, dimness, dopiness, doziness. **2** *she blushed at her stupidity:* **foolishness**, folly, silliness, idiocy, brainlessness, senselessness, injudiciousness, ineptitude, inaneness, inanity, absurdity, ludicrousness, ridiculousness, fatuousness, madness, insanity, lunacy; informal craziness; Brit. informal daftness.

stupor noun *they left him slumped in a drunken stupor:* **daze**, state of unconsciousness, torpor, insensibility, oblivion.

sturdy adjective **1** *a sturdy lad:* **strapping**, well built, muscular, athletic, strong, hefty, brawny, powerful, solid, burly, rugged, robust, tough, hardy, lusty; informal husky, beefy, meaty. **2** *sturdy boots:* **robust**, strong, strongly made, well built, solid, stout, tough, resilient, durable, long-lasting, hard-wearing. **3** *sturdy resistance:* **vigorous**, strong, stalwart, firm, determined, resolute, staunch, steadfast.
– OPPOSITES weak.

stutter verb *he stuttered over a word:* **stammer**, stumble, falter.
noun *a bad stutter:* **stammer**, speech impediment, speech defect.

style noun **1** *differing styles of management:* **manner**, way, technique, method, methodology, approach, system, mode, form, modus operandi; informal MO. **2** *a non-directive style of counselling:* **type**, kind, variety, sort, genre, school, brand, pattern, model. **3** *wearing clothes with style:* **flair**, stylishness, elegance, grace, gracefulness, poise, polish, suaveness, sophistication, urbanity, chic, dash, panache, elan; informal class, pizzazz. **4** *Laura travelled in style:* **comfort**, luxury, elegance, opulence, lavishness. **5** *modern styles:* **fashion**, trend, vogue, mode.
verb **1** *sportswear styled by Karl:* **design**, fashion, tailor. **2** *men who were styled*

'knight': **call**, name, title, entitle, dub, designate, term, label, tag, nickname.

stylish adjective *a stylish gown:* **fashionable**, modish, voguish, modern, up to date; smart, sophisticated, elegant, chic, dapper, dashing; informal trendy, natty, classy, nifty, ritzy, snazzy; N. Amer. informal fly, kicky, tony, spiffy.
– OPPOSITES unfashionable.

stymie verb (informal). See HAMPER².

suave adjective *a suave middle-aged man:* **charming**, sophisticated, debonair, urbane, polished, refined, poised, self-possessed, dignified, civilized, gentlemanly, gallant; smooth, polite, well mannered, civil, courteous, affable, tactful, diplomatic.
– OPPOSITES unsophisticated.

subconscious adjective *subconscious desires:* **unconscious**, latent, suppressed, repressed, subliminal, dormant, underlying, innermost; informal bottled up.
noun *the creative powers of the subconscious:* **(unconscious) mind**, imagination, inner(most) self, psyche.

subdue verb 1 *he subdued all his enemies:* **conquer**, defeat, vanquish, overcome, overwhelm, crush, quash, beat, trounce, subjugate, suppress, bring someone to their knees; informal lick, thrash, hammer. 2 *she could not subdue her longing:* **curb**, restrain, hold back, constrain, contain, repress, suppress, stifle, smother, keep in check, rein in, control, master, quell; informal keep a/the lid on.

subdued adjective 1 *Lewis's subdued air:* **sombre**, low-spirited, downcast, sad, dejected, depressed, gloomy, despondent, dispirited, disheartened, forlorn, woebegone; withdrawn, preoccupied; informal down in the mouth, down in the dumps, in the doldrums. 2 *subdued voices:* **hushed**, muted, quiet, low, soft, faint, muffled, indistinct. 3 *subdued light:* **dim**, muted, softened, soft, lowered, subtle.
– OPPOSITES cheerful, bright.

subject noun 1 *the subject of this chapter:* **theme**, subject matter, topic, issue, question, concern, point; substance, essence, gist. 2 *popular university subjects:* **branch of study**, discipline, field. 3 *six subjects did the trials:* **participant**, volunteer; informal guinea pig. 4 *British subjects:* **citizen**, national; taxpayer, voter. 5 *a loyal subject:* **liege**, liegeman, vassal, henchman, follower.
verb *they were subjected to violence:* **put through**, treat with, expose to.
■ **subject to** 1 *it is subject to budgetary approval:* conditional on, contingent on, dependent on. 2 *horses are subject to coughs:* susceptible to, liable to, prone to, vulnerable to, predisposed to, at risk of. 3 *we are all subject to the law:* bound by, constrained by, accountable to.

subjection noun *the subjection of aboriginal peoples:* **subjugation**, domination,

oppression, mastery, repression, suppression.

subjective adjective *standards can be judged on quantitative data rather than on subjective opinion:* **personal**, individual, emotional, instinctive, intuitive.
– OPPOSITES objective.

subjugate verb *Norman leaders had subjugated most of Ireland's Gaelic population:* **conquer**, vanquish, defeat, crush, quash, bring someone to their knees, enslave, subdue, suppress.
– OPPOSITES liberate.

sublime adjective 1 *sublime music:* **exalted**, elevated, noble, lofty, awe-inspiring, majestic, magnificent, glorious, superb, wonderful, marvellous, splendid; informal fantastic, fabulous, terrific, heavenly, divine, out of this world. 2 *the sublime confidence of youth:* **supreme**, total, complete, utter, consummate.

subliminal adjective *subliminal messages:* **subconscious**; hidden, concealed.
– OPPOSITES explicit.

submerge verb 1 *the U-boat submerged:* **go under water**, dive, sink. 2 *submerge the bowl in water:* **immerse**, plunge, sink. 3 *the farmland was submerged:* **flood**, inundate, deluge, swamp. 4 *she was submerged in work:* **overwhelm**, inundate, deluge, swamp, bury, engulf, snow under.
– OPPOSITES surface.

submission noun 1 *submission to authority:* **yielding**, capitulation, acceptance, consent, compliance. 2 *Tim raised his hands in submission:* **surrender**, capitulation, resignation, defeat. 3 *he wanted her total submission:* **compliance**, submissiveness, acquiescence, passivity, obedience, docility, deference, subservience, servility, subjection. 4 *a report for submission to the Board:* **presentation**, presenting, proffering, tendering, proposal, proposing. 5 *the plan was put forward by Stirling in his original submission:* **proposal**, suggestion, proposition, recommendation. 6 *the judge rejected their submission:* **argument**, assertion, contention, statement, claim, allegation.
– OPPOSITES defiance, resistance.

submissive adjective *Mary was far from being a timidly submissive woman:* **compliant**, yielding, acquiescent, unassertive, passive, meek, biddable, dutiful, docile, pliant; informal under someone's thumb.

submit verb 1 *she submitted under duress:* **give in/way**, yield, back down, cave in, capitulate; surrender, knuckle under. 2 *he refused to submit to their authority:* **be governed by**, abide by, be regulated by, comply with, accept, adhere to, be subject to, agree to, consent to, conform to. 3 *we submitted an unopposed bid:* **put forward**, present, offer, proffer, tender,

S

propose, suggest; put in, send in, register.
4 *they submitted that the judgement was inappropriate:* **contend**, assert, argue, state, claim, posit, postulate.
– OPPOSITES resist, withdraw.

subnormal adjective *subnormal trade activity:* **below average**, below normal, low, poor.

subordinate adjective **1** *subordinate staff:* **lower-ranking**, junior, lower, supporting. **2** *a subordinate rule:* **secondary**, lesser, minor, subsidiary, subservient, ancillary, auxiliary, peripheral, marginal; supplementary, accessory.
– OPPOSITES senior.
noun *the manager and his subordinates:* **junior**, assistant, second (in command), number two, right-hand man/woman, deputy, aide, underling, minion; informal sidekick.
– OPPOSITES superior.

subordination noun *she could not tolerate a life of subordination:* **inferiority**, subjection, subservience, submission, servitude.

subscribe verb **1** *we subscribe to 'Private Eye':* **pay a subscription**, take, buy regularly. **2** *millions subscribe to the NSPCC:* **donate**, make a donation, make a subscription, give (money), contribute towards. **3** *I can't subscribe to that theory:* **agree with**, accept, believe in, endorse, back, support, champion; formal accede to.

subscriber noun **(regular) reader**, member, patron, supporter, backer, contributor.

subscription noun **1** *the club's subscription:* **membership fee**, dues, annual payment, charge. **2** *the school was built by public subscription:* **donation**, contribution, gift, grant.

subsequent adjective *the subsequent months:* **following**, ensuing, succeeding, later, future, coming, to come, next.
– OPPOSITES previous.
■ **subsequent to** following, after, at the close/end of.

subsequently adverb *he made a bid for the remaining shares and subsequently acquired them:* **later (on)**, at a later date, afterwards, in due course, following this/that, eventually; informal after a bit.

subservient adjective **1** *subservient women:* **submissive**, deferential, compliant, obedient, dutiful, biddable, docile, passive, unassertive, subdued, downtrodden; informal under someone's thumb. **2** *individual rights are subservient to the interests of the state:* **subordinate**, secondary, subsidiary, peripheral, ancillary, auxiliary, less important.
– OPPOSITES independent.

subside verb **1** *wait until the storm subsides:* **abate**, let up, quieten down, calm, slacken (off), ease (up), relent, die down, recede, lessen, soften, diminish, decline, dwindle, weaken, fade, wane, ebb. **2** *the flood has subsided:* **recede**, ebb, fall, go down, get lower, abate. **3** *the volcano is gradually subsiding:* **sink**, settle, cave in, collapse, crumple, give way. **4** *Sarah subsided into a chair:* **slump**, flop, sink, collapse; informal flump, plonk oneself.
– OPPOSITES intensify, rise.

subsidiary adjective *a subsidiary company:* **subordinate**, secondary, ancillary, auxiliary, subservient, supplementary, peripheral.
– OPPOSITES principal.
noun *two major subsidiaries:* **subordinate company**, branch, division, subdivision, derivative, offshoot.

subsidize verb *they were unwilling to subsidize the poorer southern republics:* **give money to**, pay a subsidy to, contribute to, invest in, sponsor, support, fund, finance, underwrite; informal shell out for, fork out for, cough up for; N. Amer. informal bankroll.

subsidy noun *the theatre receives a subsidy of 1.7 million pounds a year:* **grant**, allowance, endowment, contribution, donation, bursary, handout; backing, support, sponsorship, finance, funding.

subsist verb *he subsists on his pension:* **survive**, live, stay alive, exist, eke out an existence; support oneself, manage, get along/by, make (both) ends meet.

subsistence noun **1** *they depend on fish for subsistence:* **survival**, existence, living, life, sustenance, nourishment. **2** *the money needed for his subsistence:* **maintenance**, keep, upkeep, livelihood, board (and lodging), nourishment, food.

substance noun **1** *an organic substance:* **material**, matter, stuff. **2** *ghostly figures with no substance:* **solidity**, body, corporeality; density, mass, weight, shape, structure. **3** *none of the objections has any substance:* **meaningfulness**, significance, importance, import, validity, foundation; formal moment. **4** *the substance of the tale is very thin:* **content**, subject matter, theme, message, essence.

substandard adjective *children were being educated in substandard buildings:* **inferior**, second-rate, low-quality, poor, below par, imperfect, faulty, defective, shoddy, shabby, unsound, unsatisfactory; informal tenth-rate, crummy, lousy; Brit. informal duff, ropy, rubbish, chronic, pants.
– OPPOSITES outstanding.

substantial adjective **1** *substantial beings:* **real**, true, actual; physical, solid, material, concrete, corporeal. **2** *substantial progress had been made:* **considerable**, real, significant, important, notable, major, valuable, useful. **3** *substantial damages:* **sizeable**, considerable, significant, large, ample, appreciable, goodly. **4** *substantial Victorian villas:* **sturdy**, solid, stout, strong, well built, durable, long-lasting, hard-wearing. **5** *substantial country gentlemen:* **hefty**, stout, sturdy, large, solid, bulky,

S

burly, well built, portly. **6** *substantial agreement:* **fundamental**, essential, basic.
– OPPOSITES negligible, flimsy, puny.

substantially adverb **1** *the cost has fallen substantially:* **considerably**, significantly, to a great/large extent, greatly, markedly, appreciably. **2** *the draft was substantially accepted:* **largely**, for the most part, by and large, on the whole, in the main, mainly, in essence, basically, fundamentally, to all intents and purposes.
– OPPOSITES slightly.

substantiate verb *none of the allegations were ever substantiated:* **prove**, show to be true, give substance to, support, uphold, bear out, justify, vindicate, validate, corroborate, verify, authenticate, confirm, endorse, give credence to.
– OPPOSITES disprove.

substitute noun *substitutes for permanent employees:* **replacement**, deputy, relief, proxy, reserve, surrogate, cover, stand-in, locum (tenens), understudy; informal sub.
adjective *a substitute teacher:* **acting**, replacement, deputy, relief, reserve, surrogate, stand-in, temporary, caretaker, interim, provisional.
– OPPOSITES permanent, original.
verb **1** *curd cheese can be substituted for yogurt:* **exchange**, replace with, use instead of, use as an alternative to, use in place of, swap. **2** *the Senate was empowered to substitute for the President:* **deputize**, act as deputy, act as a substitute, stand in, cover; replace, relieve, take over from; informal sub, fill someone's boots/shoes.

substitution noun *the substitution of a steam locomotive for horsepower:* **exchange**, change; replacement, replacing, swapping, switching.

subterfuge noun **1** *the use of subterfuge by journalists:* **trickery**, intrigue, deviousness, deceit, deception, dishonesty, cheating, duplicity, guile, cunning, craftiness, chicanery, pretence, fraud, fraudulence; informal kidology. **2** *a disreputable subterfuge:* **trick**, hoax, ruse, wile, ploy, stratagem, artifice, dodge, bluff, pretence, deception, fraud, blind, smokescreen; informal con, scam.
– OPPOSITES honesty.

subtle adjective **1** *subtle colours:* **understated**, muted, subdued; delicate, faint, pale, soft, indistinct. **2** *subtle distinctions:* **fine**, fine-drawn, nice, overnice, hair-splitting. **3** *a subtle mind:* **astute**, keen, quick, fine, acute, sharp, shrewd, perceptive, discerning, discriminating, penetrating, sagacious, wise, clever, intelligent. **4** *a subtle plan:* **ingenious**, clever, cunning, crafty, wily, artful, devious.
– OPPOSITES garish, broad, stupid.

subtlety noun **1** *the subtlety of the flavour:* **delicacy**, delicateness, subtleness; understatedness, mutedness, softness. **2** *classification is fraught with subtlety:* **fineness**, subtleness, niceness, nicety,

nuance. **3** *the subtlety of the human mind:* **astuteness**, keenness, acuteness, sharpness, canniness, shrewdness, perceptiveness, discernment, discrimination, percipience, perspicacity, wisdom, cleverness, intelligence. **4** *the subtlety of their tactics:* **ingenuity**, cleverness, skilfulness, adroitness, cunning, guile, craftiness, wiliness, artfulness, deviousness.

subtract verb *the value of their child benefit is subtracted from their total welfare payments:* **take away/off**, deduct, debit, dock; informal knock off, minus.
– OPPOSITES add.

suburb noun *a densely populated suburb of Amsterdam:* **residential area**, dormitory area, commuter belt; suburbia.

suburban adjective **1** *a suburban area:* **residential**, commuter, dormitory. **2** *her drab suburban existence:* **dull**, boring, uninteresting, conventional, ordinary, commonplace, unremarkable, unexceptional; provincial, unsophisticated, parochial, bourgeois, middle-class.

subversive adjective *subversive activities:* **disruptive**, troublemaking, inflammatory, insurrectionary; seditious, revolutionary, rebellious, rebel, renegade, dissident.
noun *a dangerous subversive:* **troublemaker**, dissident, agitator, revolutionary, renegade, rebel.
– OPPOSITES conformist.

subvert verb **1** *a plot to subvert the state:* **destabilize**, unsettle, overthrow, overturn; bring down, topple, depose, oust; disrupt, wreak havoc on, sabotage, ruin, undermine, weaken, damage. **2** *attempts to subvert Soviet youth:* **corrupt**, pervert, deprave, contaminate, poison, embitter.

subway noun **1** *he walked through the subway:* **underpass**, (pedestrian) tunnel. **2** *Tokyo's subway:* **underground (railway)**, metro; Brit. informal tube.

succeed verb **1** *Darwin succeeded where others had failed:* **triumph**, achieve success, be successful, do well, flourish, thrive; informal make it, make the grade, make a name for oneself. **2** *the plan succeeded:* **be successful**, turn out well, work (out), be effective; informal come off, pay off. **3** *Rosebery succeeded Gladstone as Prime Minister:* **replace**, take the place of, take over from, follow, supersede; informal step into someone's shoes. **4** *he succeeded to the throne:* **inherit**, assume, acquire, attain; formal accede to.
– OPPOSITES fail, precede.

succeeding adjective *strands of DNA are reproduced through succeeding generations:* **subsequent**, successive, following, ensuing, later, future, coming.

success noun **1** *the success of the scheme:* **favourable outcome**, successfulness, successful result, triumph. **2** *the trappings of success:* **prosperity**, prosperousness,

S

affluence, wealth, riches, opulence. **3** *a West End success:* **triumph**, best-seller, box-office success, sell-out; informal (smash) hit, winner. **4** *her performance made her an overnight success:* **star**, superstar, celebrity, big name, household name; informal celeb, megastar.
– OPPOSITES failure.

successful adjective **1** *a successful campaign:* **victorious**, triumphant; fortunate, lucky. **2** *a successful designer:* **prosperous**, affluent, wealthy, rich; doing well, famous, eminent, top; informal on the up and up. **3** *successful companies:* **flourishing**, thriving, booming, buoyant, doing well, profitable, moneymaking, lucrative; informal on the up and up.

succession noun **1** *a succession of exciting events:* **sequence**, series, progression, chain, cycle, round, string, train, line, run, flow, stream. **2** *his succession to the throne:* **accession**, elevation, assumption.
■ **in succession** one after the other, in a row, consecutively, successively, in sequence; running; informal on the trot.

successive adjective *the team have made a great start with three successive wins:* **consecutive**, in a row, straight, sequential, in succession, running; informal on the trot.

successor noun *Mary was the rightful successor to the English throne:* **heir (apparent)**, inheritor, next-in-line.
– OPPOSITES predecessor.

succinct adjective *use short, succinct sentences:* **concise**, short (and sweet), brief, compact, condensed, crisp, laconic, terse, to the point, pithy, epigrammatic, synoptic, gnomic.
– OPPOSITES verbose.

succour noun *providing succour in times of need:* **aid**, help, a helping hand, assistance; comfort, ease, relief, support.
verb *the prisoners were succoured:* **help**, aid, bring aid to, give/render assistance to, assist, lend a (helping) hand to; minister to, care for, comfort, bring relief to, support, take care of, look after, attend to.

succulent adjective *a succulent fillet of beef:* **juicy**, moist, luscious, soft, tender; choice, mouth-watering, appetizing, flavoursome, tasty, delicious; informal scrumptious, scrummy.
– OPPOSITES dry.

succumb verb **1** *she succumbed to temptation:* **yield**, give in/way, submit, surrender, capitulate, cave in. **2** *he succumbed to the disease:* **die from/of**; catch, develop, contract, fall ill with; informal come/go down with.
– OPPOSITES resist.

suck verb **1** *they sucked orange juice through straws:* **sip**, sup, siphon, slurp, draw, drink. **2** *Fran sucked in a deep breath:* **draw**, pull, breathe, gasp; inhale, inspire. **3** *they got sucked into petty crime:* **implicate in**, involve in, draw into; informal mix up in.

4 (N. Amer. informal) *the weather sucks:* **be very bad**, be awful, be terrible, be dreadful, be horrible; informal stink.

suckle verb *they employed a wet nurse to suckle their babies:* **breastfeed**, feed, nurse.

sudden adjective *a sudden downpour took us by surprise:* **unexpected**, unforeseen, unanticipated, unlooked-for; immediate, instantaneous, instant, precipitous, precipitate, abrupt, rapid, swift, quick.

suddenly adverb *she suddenly began to laugh:* **immediately**, instantaneously, instantly, straight away, all of a sudden, all at once, promptly, abruptly, swiftly; unexpectedly, without warning, without notice, out of the blue; informal straight off, in a flash, like a shot.
– OPPOSITES gradually.

suds plural noun **lather**, foam, froth, bubbles, soap.

sue verb **1** *he sued for negligence:* **take legal action**, take to court, bring an action/suit, proceed against; informal have the law on. **2** *suing for peace:* **appeal**, petition, ask, solicit, request, seek.

suffer verb **1** *I hate to see him suffer:* **hurt**, ache, be in pain, feel pain; be in distress, be upset, be miserable. **2** *he suffers from asthma:* **be afflicted by**, be affected by, be troubled with, have. **3** *England suffered a humiliating defeat:* **undergo**, experience, be subjected to, receive, endure, face. **4** *the school's reputation has suffered:* **be impaired**, be damaged, deteriorate, decline.

suffering noun *the war caused widespread civilian suffering:* **hardship**, distress, misery, wretchedness, adversity, tribulation; pain, agony, anguish, trauma, torment, torture, hurt, affliction, sadness, unhappiness, sorrow, grief, woe, angst, heartache, heartbreak, stress.

suffice verb *the wages only suffice for necessities:* **be enough**, be sufficient, be adequate, do, serve, meet requirements, satisfy demands, answer/meet one's needs, answer/serve the purpose; informal fit/fill the bill, hit the spot.

sufficient adjective & determiner *they had secured sufficient evidence to justify a charge:* **enough**, adequate, plenty of, ample.
– OPPOSITES inadequate.

suffocate verb **1** *she suffocated her victim:* **smother**, asphyxiate, stifle; choke, strangle. **2** *she was suffocating in the heat:* **be breathless**, be short of air, struggle for air; be too hot, swelter; informal roast, bake, boil.

suffrage noun *the congress is elected for five years by universal adult suffrage:* **franchise**, right to vote, the vote, enfranchisement, ballot.

suffuse verb *a feeling of relief suffused her:* **permeate**, spread over, spread throughout, cover, bathe, pervade, wash, saturate, imbue.

sugary adjective **1** *sugary snacks:* **sweet**, sugared, sickly. **2** *sugary romance:*

sentimental, mawkish, cloying, sickly (sweet), saccharine, syrupy; informal soppy, schmaltzy, slushy, mushy, sloppy, cutesy, corny.
– OPPOSITES sour.

suggest verb 1 *Ruth suggested a holiday:* **propose**, put forward, recommend, advocate; advise, urge, encourage, counsel. 2 *evidence suggests that teenagers are responsive to price increases:* **indicate**, lead to the belief, argue, demonstrate, show; formal evince. 3 *sources suggest that the Prime Minister will change his cabinet:* **hint**, insinuate, imply, intimate, indicate. 4 *the seduction scenes suggest his guilt and her loneliness:* **convey**, express, impart, imply, intimate, smack of, evoke, conjure up.

suggestion noun 1 *some suggestions for tackling this problem:* **proposal**, proposition, motion, submission, recommendation; advice, counsel, hint, tip, clue, idea. 2 *the suggestion of a smirk:* **hint**, trace, touch, suspicion, dash, soupçon; ghost, semblance, shadow, glimmer, impression, whisper. 3 *there is no suggestion that he was party to a conspiracy:* **insinuation**, hint, implication, intimation, innuendo, imputation.

suggestive adjective 1 *suggestive remarks:* **indecent**, indelicate, improper, unseemly, sexual, sexy, smutty, dirty, ribald, bawdy, racy, risqué, lewd, vulgar, coarse, salacious. 2 *an odour suggestive of a brewery:* **redolent**, evocative, reminiscent; characteristic, indicative, typical.

suicide noun *she committed suicide:* **self-destruction**, taking one's own life, self-murder; informal topping oneself.

suit noun 1 *a pinstriped suit:* **outfit**, set of clothes, ensemble. 2 *a medical malpractice suit:* **legal action**, lawsuit, (court) case, action, (legal/judicial) proceedings, litigation. 3 *they spurned his suit:* **entreaty**, request, plea, appeal, petition, supplication, application.
verb 1 *blue really suits you:* **look good on**, enhance the appearance of, become, flatter. 2 *savings schemes to suit all pockets:* **be convenient for**, be acceptable to, be suitable for, meet the requirements of; informal fit the bill. 3 *recipes ideally suited to students:* **tailor**, fashion, adjust, adapt, modify, fit, gear, design.

suitable adjective 1 *suitable employment opportunities:* **acceptable**, satisfactory, fitting; informal right up someone's street. 2 *a drama suitable for all ages:* **appropriate**, fitting, fit, acceptable, right. 3 *music suitable for a lively dinner party:* **appropriate**, suited, befitting, in keeping with; informal cut out for. 4 *they treated him with suitable respect:* **proper**, seemly, decent, appropriate, fitting, befitting, correct, due. 5 *suitable candidates:* **well qualified**, well suited, appropriate, fitting.
– OPPOSITES inappropriate.

suitcase noun **travelling bag**, travel bag,

case, valise, overnight case, portmanteau, vanity case; (**suitcases**) luggage, baggage.

suite noun 1 *a penthouse suite:* **apartment**, flat, (set of) rooms. 2 *the Queen and her suite:* **retinue**, entourage, train, escort, royal household, court; attendants, retainers, servants.

suitor noun *she decided to marry her suitor:* **admirer**, wooer, boyfriend, sweetheart, lover.

sulk verb *Dad was sulking over the loss of the money:* **mope**, brood, be sullen, have a long face, be in a bad mood, be in a huff, be grumpy, be moody; informal be down in the dumps.
noun *he sank into a deep sulk:* **(bad) mood**, fit of ill humour, fit of pique, pet, huff, (bad) temper, the sulks, the blues; informal grump.

sulky adjective *disappointment was making her sulky:* **sullen**, surly, moping, pouting, moody, sour, piqued, petulant, disgruntled, ill-humoured, in a bad mood, having a fit of the sulks, out of humour, fed up, put out; bad-tempered, grumpy, huffy, glum, gloomy, morose; informal grouchy.
– OPPOSITES cheerful.

sullen adjective *a bunch of sullen, spoilt brats:* **surly**, sulky, pouting, sour, morose, resentful, glum, moody, gloomy, grumpy, bad-tempered, ill-tempered; unresponsive, uncommunicative, uncivil, unfriendly.
– OPPOSITES cheerful.

sully verb *they were outraged that anyone should sully their good name:* **taint**, defile, soil, tarnish, stain, blemish, pollute, spoil, mar.

sultry adjective 1 *a sultry day:* **humid**, close, airless, stifling, oppressive, muggy, sticky, sweltering, tropical, heavy; hot; informal boiling, roasting. 2 *a sultry film star:* **passionate**, attractive, sensual, sexy, voluptuous, erotic, seductive.
– OPPOSITES refreshing.

sum noun 1 *a large sum of money:* **amount**, quantity, volume. 2 *just a small sum:* **amount of money**, price, charge, fee, cost. 3 *the sum of two numbers:* **total**, grand total, sum total, tally, aggregate, summation. 4 *the sum of his wisdom:* **entirety**, totality, total, whole, aggregate, summation, beginning and end. 5 *we did sums at school:* **problem**, calculation; (**sums**) arithmetic, mathematics, computation; Brit. informal maths; N. Amer. informal math.
– OPPOSITES difference.

■ **sum up** *he was summing up on day two of a historic test case:* summarize the evidence, review the evidence, give a summing-up.

■ **sum someone/something up** 1 *one reviewer summed it up as 'compelling':* evaluate, assess, appraise, rate, weigh up, gauge, judge, deem, adjudge, estimate, form an opinion of. 2 *he summed up his reasons:* summarize, make/give a summary of, precis, outline, give an outline of, recapitulate, review; informal recap.

S

summarily adverb *he was accused of conspiracy and summarily executed:* **immediately**, instantly, right away, straight away, at once, on the spot, promptly; speedily, swiftly, rapidly, without delay; arbitrarily, without formality, peremptorily, without due process.

summarize verb *he summarized these ideas in a single phrase:* **sum up**, abridge, condense, encapsulate, outline, give an outline of, put in a nutshell, recapitulate, give/make a summary of, give a synopsis of, precis, give a résumé of, give the gist of; informal recap.

summary noun *a summary of the findings:* **synopsis**, precis, résumé, abstract, digest, encapsulation, abbreviated version; outline, sketch, rundown, review, summing-up, overview, recapitulation, epitome, conspectus; informal recap.
adjective **1** *a summary financial statement:* **abridged**, abbreviated, shortened, condensed, concise, succinct, short, brief, pithy; formal compendious.
2 *summary execution:* **immediate**, instant, instantaneous, on-the-spot; speedy, swift, rapid, without delay, sudden; arbitrary, without formality, peremptory.

summer house noun **gazebo**, pavilion, belvedere.

summit noun **1** *the summit of Mont Blanc:* **(mountain) top**, peak, crest, crown, apex, tip, cap, hilltop. **2** *the summits of world literature:* **acme**, peak, height, pinnacle, zenith, climax, high point/spot, highlight, crowning glory, best, finest, nonpareil. **3** *the next superpower summit:* **meeting**, negotiation, conference, talk(s), discussion.
– OPPOSITES base, nadir.

summon verb **1** *he was summoned to the Embassy:* **send for**, call for, request the presence of; ask, invite. **2** *they were summoned as witnesses:* **serve with a summons**, summons, subpoena, cite, serve with a citation. **3** *the chair summoned a meeting:* **convene**, assemble, order, call, announce. **4** *he summoned the courage to move closer:* **muster**, gather, collect, rally, screw up. **5** *summoning up their memories of home:* **call to mind**, call up/forth, conjure up, evoke, recall, revive, arouse, kindle, awaken, spark (off). **6** *they summoned spirits of the dead:* **conjure up**, call up, invoke.

summons noun **1** *the court issued a summons:* **writ**, subpoena, warrant, court order; Law citation. **2** *a summons to go to the boss's office:* **order**, directive, command, instruction, demand, decree, injunction, edict, call, request.
verb *he was summonsed to appear in court:* **subpoena**, summon, cite, serve with a citation.

sumptuous adjective *a sumptuous palace:* **lavish**, luxurious, opulent, magnificent, resplendent, gorgeous, splendid, grand,
lavishly appointed, palatial, rich; informal plush, ritzy; Brit. informal swish.
– OPPOSITES plain.

sun noun *she could feel the sun on her face:* **sunshine**, sunlight, daylight, light, warmth; beams, rays.
■ **sun oneself.** See SUNBATHE.

sunbathe verb *she lay sunbathing on the hot sand:* **sun oneself**, bask, get a tan, tan oneself; informal catch some rays.

sunburnt adjective **1** *his sunburnt shoulders:* **burnt**, sunburned, red, scarlet. **2** *a handsome sunburnt face:* **tanned**, suntanned, brown, bronzed, bronze.
– OPPOSITES pale.

Sunday noun **the Sabbath**.

sundry adjective *radiators and sundry other items were sent out to various workshops:* **various**, varied, miscellaneous, assorted, mixed, diverse, diversified; several, numerous, many, manifold, multifarious, multitudinous.

sunken adjective **1** *sunken eyes:* **hollowed**, hollow, depressed, deep-set, concave, indented. **2** *a sunken garden:* **below ground level**, at a lower level, lowered.

sunless adjective **1** *a cold sunless day:* **dark**, overcast, cloudy, grey, gloomy, dismal, murky, dull. **2** *the sunless side of the house:* **shady**, shadowy, dark, gloomy.

sunlight noun **daylight**, sun, sunshine, sun's rays, (natural) light.

sunny adjective **1** *a sunny day:* **bright**, sunshiny, sunlit, clear, fine, cloudless, without a cloud in the sky. **2** *a sunny disposition:* **cheerful**, cheery, happy, light-hearted, bright, merry, joyful, bubbly, blithe, jolly, jovial, animated, buoyant, ebullient, upbeat, vivacious. **3** *look on the sunny side:* **optimistic**, rosy, bright, hopeful, auspicious, favourable.
– OPPOSITES dull, miserable.

sunrise noun *the infantry advanced at sunrise:* **(crack of) dawn**, daybreak, break of day, first light, (early) morning, cockcrow; N. Amer. sunup.

sunset noun *strolling along the beach at sunset:* **nightfall**, close of day, twilight, dusk, evening; N. Amer. sundown.

sunshine noun *relaxing in the sunshine:* **sunlight**, sun, sun's rays, daylight, (natural) light.

super adjective (informal) *win a super day out at York:* **excellent**, superb, superlative, first-class, outstanding, marvellous, magnificent, wonderful, splendid, glorious; informal great, fantastic, fabulous, terrific, ace, divine, A1, wicked, cool; Brit. informal smashing, brilliant, brill.
– OPPOSITES rotten.

superannuated adjective **1** *a superannuated civil servant:* **pensioned (off)**, retired; elderly, old. **2** *superannuated computing equipment:* **old**, old-fashioned, antiquated, out of date, outmoded, broken-down, obsolete, disused, defunct; informal clapped out.

superb adjective **1** *he scored a superb goal:* **excellent**, superlative, first-rate, first-class, outstanding, remarkable, marvellous, magnificent, wonderful, splendid, admirable, noteworthy, impressive, fine, exquisite, exceptional, glorious; informal great, fantastic, fabulous, terrific, super, awesome, ace, cool, A1; Brit. informal brilliant, brill, smashing. **2** *a superb diamond necklace:* **magnificent**, majestic, splendid, grand, impressive, imposing, awe-inspiring, breathtaking; gorgeous.
– OPPOSITES poor, inferior.

supercilious adjective *a supercilious young minister:* **arrogant**, haughty, conceited, disdainful, overbearing, pompous, condescending, superior, patronizing, imperious, proud, snobbish, snobby, smug, scornful, sneering; informal hoity-toity, high and mighty, uppity, snooty, stuck-up, snotty, jumped up, too big for one's boots.

superficial adjective **1** *superficial burns:* **surface**, exterior, external, outer, outside, slight. **2** *a superficial friendship:* **shallow**, surface, skin-deep, artificial; empty, hollow, meaningless. **3** *a superficial investigation:* **cursory**, perfunctory, casual, sketchy, desultory, token, slapdash, offhand, rushed, hasty, hurried. **4** *its spines gave it a superficial resemblance to a hedgehog:* **apparent**, seeming, outward, ostensible, cosmetic, slight. **5** *a superficial biography:* **trivial**, lightweight. **6** *a superficial person:* **facile**, shallow, flippant, empty-headed, trivial, frivolous, silly, inane.
– OPPOSITES deep, thorough.

superficially adverb *some reptiles and amphibians are superficially very alike:* **apparently**, seemingly, ostensibly, outwardly, on the surface, on the face of it, to all intents and purposes, at first glance, to the casual eye.

superfluity noun **surplus**, excess, overabundance, glut, surfeit, profusion, plethora.
– OPPOSITES shortage.

superfluous adjective **1** *superfluous material:* **surplus (to requirements)**, redundant, unneeded, excess, extra, (to) spare, remaining, unused, left over, in excess, waste. **2** *words seemed superfluous:* **unnecessary**, unneeded, redundant, uncalled for, unwarranted.
– OPPOSITES necessary.

superhuman adjective **1** *a superhuman effort:* **extraordinary**, phenomenal, prodigious, stupendous, exceptional, immense, heroic. **2** *superhuman power:* **divine**, holy, heavenly. **3** *superhuman beings:* **supernatural**, preternatural, paranormal, other-worldly, unearthly.
– OPPOSITES mundane.

superintend verb *he was expected to*

superintend a grand banquet: **supervise**, oversee, be in charge of, be in control of, preside over, direct, administer, manage, run, be responsible for.

superintendent noun **1** *the superintendent of the museum:* **manager**, director, administrator, supervisor, overseer, controller, chief, head, governor; informal boss. **2** (N. Amer.) *the building's superintendent:* **caretaker**, janitor, warden, porter.

superior adjective **1** *a superior officer:* **higher-ranking**, higher-level, senior, higher, higher-up. **2** *the superior candidate:* **better**, more expert, more skilful; worthier, fitter, preferred. **3** *superior workmanship:* **finer**, better, higher-grade, of higher quality, greater; accomplished, expert. **4** *superior chocolate:* **good-quality**, high-quality, first-class, first-rate, top-quality; choice, select, exclusive, prime, prize, fine, excellent, best, choicest, finest. **5** *a superior hotel:* **high-class**, upper-class, select, exclusive; Brit. upmarket; informal classy, posh. **6** *Jake regarded her with superior amusement:* **condescending**, supercilious, patronizing, haughty, disdainful, pompous, snobbish; informal high and mighty, hoity-toity, snooty, stuck-up.
– OPPOSITES junior, inferior.
noun *my immediate superior:* **manager**, chief, supervisor, senior, controller, foreman; informal boss.
– OPPOSITES subordinate.

superiority noun *the military superiority of the government forces:* **supremacy**, advantage, lead, dominance, primacy, ascendancy, eminence.
– OPPOSITES inferiority.

superlative adjective *he is without doubt a superlative photographer:* **excellent**, magnificent, wonderful, marvellous, supreme, consummate, outstanding, remarkable, fine, choice, first-rate, first-class, premier, prime, unsurpassed, unequalled, unparalleled, unrivalled, pre-eminent; informal crack, ace, wicked; Brit. informal brilliant.
– OPPOSITES mediocre.

supernatural adjective **1** *supernatural powers:* **paranormal**, psychic, magic, magical, occult, mystic, mystical, superhuman, supernormal. **2** *a supernatural being:* **ghostly**, phantom, spectral, other-worldly, unearthly, unnatural.

supersede verb *I found myself superseded by much younger men:* **replace**, take the place of, take over from, succeed; supplant, displace, oust, overthrow, remove, unseat; informal fill someone's shoes/boots.

superstition noun **1** *the old superstitions held by sailors:* **myth**, belief, old wives' tale; legend, story. **2** *medicine was riddled with superstition:* **unfounded belief**, credulity, fallacy, delusion, illusion; magic, sorcery.

superstitious adjective **1** *superstitious beliefs:* **mythical**, irrational, illusory,

S

groundless, unfounded; traditional. **2** *he's incredibly superstitious:* **credulous**, naive, gullible.
– OPPOSITES factual, sceptical.

supervise verb **1** *he had to supervise the loading:* **superintend**, oversee, be in charge of, preside over, direct, manage, run, look after, be responsible for, govern, organize, handle. **2** *you may need to supervise the patient:* **watch**, oversee, keep an eye on, observe, monitor, mind.

supervision noun **1** *the supervision of the banking system:* **administration**, management, control, charge; superintendence, regulation, government, governance. **2** *keep your children under supervision:* **observation**, guidance, custody, charge, safe keeping, care, guardianship; control.

supervisor noun *she exchanged a few words with the shift supervisor:* **manager**, director, overseer, controller, superintendent, governor, chief, head; steward, foreman; Brit. ganger, gangmaster; informal boss; Brit. informal gaffer.

supine adjective **1** *she lay supine on the sand:* **flat on one's back**, face upwards, flat, horizontal, recumbent, stretched out. **2** *the government was supine in the face of racial injustice:* **weak**, spineless, yielding, effete; docile, acquiescent, pliant, submissive, passive, inert, spiritless.
– OPPOSITES prostrate, strong.

supper noun **dinner**, evening meal, main meal; snack, bite to eat; Brit. tea.

supplant verb **1** *motorways supplanted the network of A-roads:* **replace**, supersede, displace, take over from, substitute for, override. **2** *the man he supplanted as Prime Minister:* **oust**, usurp, overthrow, remove, topple, unseat, depose, dethrone; succeed, come after; informal fill someone's shoes/boots.

supple adjective **1** *her supple body:* **lithe**, limber, lissom(e), willowy, flexible, loose-limbed, agile, acrobatic, nimble, double-jointed. **2** *supple leather:* **pliant**, pliable, flexible, soft, bendable, workable, malleable, stretchy, elastic, springy, yielding, rubbery.
– OPPOSITES stiff, rigid.

supplement noun **1** *a supplement to the essay:* **appendix**, addendum, end matter, tailpiece, codicil, postscript, addition, coda. **2** *a special supplement with today's paper:* **pull-out**, insert, extra section. **3** *a single room supplement:* **surcharge**, addition, increase.
verb *they supplemented their incomes by spinning:* **augment**, increase, add to, boost, swell, amplify, enlarge, top up.

supplementary adjective **1** *supplementary income:* **additional**, supplemental, extra, more, further; add-on, subsidiary, auxiliary, ancillary. **2** *a supplementary*

index: **appended**, attached, added, extra, accompanying.

suppliant noun *they were not mere suppliants:* **petitioner**, supplicant, pleader, beggar, applicant.
adjective *those around her were suppliant:* **pleading**, begging, imploring, entreating, supplicating; on bended knee.

supply verb **1** *they supplied money to rebels:* **give**, contribute, provide, furnish, donate, bestow, grant, endow, impart; dispense, disburse, allocate, assign; informal fork out, shell out. **2** *the lake supplies the city with water:* **provide**, furnish, endow, serve, confer; equip, arm. **3** *windmills supply their power needs:* **satisfy**, meet, fulfil, cater for.
noun **1** *a limited supply of food:* **stock**, store, reserve, reservoir, stockpile, hoard, cache; storehouse, repository; fund, mine, bank. **2** *the supply of alcoholic liquor:* **provision**, dissemination, distribution, serving. **3** *go to a supermarket for supplies:* **provisions**, stores, stocks, rations, food, foodstuffs, eatables, produce, necessities; informal eats; formal comestibles.
adjective *a supply teacher:* **substitute**, stand-in, fill-in, locum, temporary, stopgap.

support verb **1** *a roof supported by pillars:* **hold up**, bear, carry, prop up, keep up, brace, shore up, underpin, buttress, reinforce. **2** *he struggled to support his family:* **provide for**, maintain, sustain, keep, take care of, look after. **3** *she supported him to the end:* **comfort**, encourage, sustain, buoy up, hearten, fortify, console, solace, reassure; informal buck up. **4** *evidence to support the argument:* **substantiate**, back up, bear out, corroborate, confirm, attest to, verify, prove, validate, authenticate, endorse, ratify. **5** *the money supports charitable projects:* **help**, aid, assist; contribute to, back, subsidize, fund, finance; N. Amer. informal bankroll. **6** *an independent candidate supported by locals:* **back**, champion, help, assist, aid, abet, favour, encourage; vote for, stand behind, defend; sponsor, second, promote, endorse, sanction; informal throw one's weight behind. **7** *they support human rights:* **advocate**, promote, champion, back, espouse, be in favour of, recommend, defend, subscribe to. **8** *I could not support the grief:* **endure**, bear, tolerate, stand, put up with, abide, stomach, sustain.
– OPPOSITES neglect, contradict, oppose.
noun **1** *bridge supports:* **pillar**, post, prop, upright, crutch, plinth, brace, buttress; base, substructure, foundation, underpinning. **2** *I was lucky to have their support:* **encouragement**, friendship, strength, consolation, solace, succour, relief. **3** *he was a great support:* **comfort**, help, assistance, tower of strength, prop, mainstay. **4** *support for community services:* **contributions**, backing, donations, money, subsidy, funding, funds, finance, capital. **5** *they voiced their support for him:* **backing**, help,

S

assistance, aid, endorsement, approval; votes, patronage. **6** *a surge in support for decentralization:* **advocacy**, backing, promotion, championship, espousal, defence, recommendation.

supporter noun **1** *supporters of gun control:* **advocate**, backer, adherent, promoter, champion, defender, upholder, crusader, proponent, campaigner, apologist. **2** *Labour supporters:* **backer**, helper, adherent, follower, ally, voter, disciple; member. **3** *the charity relies on its supporters:* **contributor**, donor, benefactor, sponsor, backer, patron, subscriber, well-wisher. **4** *the team's supporters:* **fan**, follower, enthusiast, devotee, admirer; informal buff, addict.

supportive adjective **1** *a supportive teacher:* **encouraging**, caring, sympathetic, reassuring, understanding, concerned, helpful, kind, kindly. **2** *we are supportive of the proposal:* **in favour of**, favourable to, pro, on the side of, sympathetic to, well disposed to, receptive to.

suppose verb **1** *I suppose he's used to this:* **assume**, presume, expect, dare say, take it (as read); believe, think, fancy, suspect, sense, trust; guess, surmise, reckon, conjecture, deduce, infer, gather. **2** *suppose you had a spacecraft:* **assume**, imagine, (let's) say; hypothesize, theorize, speculate. **3** *the theory supposes rational players:* **require**, presuppose, imply, assume; call for, need.

supposed adjective **1** *the supposed phenomena:* **apparent**, ostensible, seeming, alleged, putative, reputed, rumoured, claimed, purported; professed, declared, assumed, presumed. **2** *I'm supposed to meet him at 8.30:* **meant**, intended, expected; required, obliged.

supposition noun *there is a widespread supposition that there is nothing of any value in these techniques:* **belief**, surmise, idea, notion, suspicion, conjecture, speculation, inference, theory, hypothesis, postulation, guess, feeling, hunch, assumption, presumption.

suppress verb **1** *they could suppress the rebellion:* **subdue**, repress, crush, quell, quash, squash, stamp out; defeat, conquer, overpower, put down, crack down on; end, stop, terminate, halt. **2** *she suppressed her irritation:* **conceal**, restrain, stifle, smother, bottle up, hold back, control, check, curb, contain, bridle, inhibit, keep a rein on, put a lid on. **3** *the report was suppressed:* **censor**, keep secret, conceal, hide, hush up, gag, withhold, cover up, stifle; ban, proscribe, outlaw; sweep under the carpet.
– OPPOSITES incite, reveal.

supremacy noun *they asserted the supremacy of the people over parliament:* **ascendancy**, predominance, primacy, dominion, hegemony, authority, mastery, control, power, rule, sovereignty, influence;

dominance, superiority, advantage, the upper hand, the whip hand, the edge; distinction, greatness.

supreme adjective **1** *the supreme commander:* **highest ranking**, chief, head, top, foremost, principal, superior, premier, first, prime; greatest, dominant, predominant, pre-eminent. **2** *a supreme achievement:* **extraordinary**, remarkable, incredible, phenomenal, rare, exceptional, outstanding, great, incomparable, unparalleled, peerless. **3** *the supreme sacrifice:* **ultimate**, final, last; utmost, extreme, greatest, highest.
– OPPOSITES subordinate, insignificant.

sure adjective **1** *I am sure that they didn't think you rude:* **certain**, positive, convinced, confident, definite, assured, satisfied, persuaded; unhesitating, unwavering, unshakeable. **2** *someone was sure to be blamed:* **bound**, likely, destined, fated. **3** *a sure winner with the children:* **guaranteed**, unfailing, infallible, unerring, assured, certain, inevitable, as sure as eggs is eggs; informal sure-fire. **4** *he entered in the sure knowledge that he would win:* **unquestionable**, indisputable, irrefutable, incontrovertible, undeniable, indubitable, undoubted, absolute, categorical, true, certain; obvious, evident, plain, clear, conclusive, definite. **5** *a sure sign that he's worried:* **reliable**, dependable, trustworthy, unfailing, infallible, certain, unambiguous, true, foolproof, established, effective; informal sure-fire; formal efficacious. **6** *the sure hand of the soloist:* **firm**, steady, stable, secure, confident, steadfast, unfaltering, unwavering.
– OPPOSITES uncertain, unlikely.
exclamation *'Can I come too?' 'Sure.'* **yes**, all right, of course, indeed, certainly, absolutely, agreed; informal OK, yeah, yep, uh-huh, you bet, I'll say, sure thing.
■ **be sure to** *be sure to send your press releases to the news desk:* **remember to**, don't forget to, see that you, mind that you, take care to, be certain to.
■ **make sure** **check**, confirm, make certain, ensure, assure; verify, corroborate, substantiate.

surely adverb **1** *surely you remembered? it must be the case that,* assuredly, without question. **2** *I will surely die:* **certainly**, for sure, definitely, undoubtedly, without doubt, doubtless, indubitably, unquestionably, without fail, inevitably. **3** *slowly but surely manipulating the public:* **firmly**, steadily, confidently, assuredly, unhesitatingly, unfalteringly, unswervingly, determinedly, doggedly.

surface noun *the surface of the door:* **outside**, exterior; top, side; finish, veneer.
– OPPOSITES inside, interior.
adjective *surface appearances:* **superficial**, external, exterior, outward, ostensible, apparent, cosmetic, skin deep.
– OPPOSITES underlying.

S

verb **1** *a submarine surfaced:* **come to the surface**, come up, rise. **2** *the idea first surfaced in the sixties:* **emerge**, arise, appear, come to light, crop up, materialize, spring up.
– OPPOSITES dive.

■ **on the surface** at first glance, to the casual eye, outwardly, to all appearances, apparently, ostensibly, superficially, externally.

surfeit noun *a surfeit of apples:* **excess**, surplus, abundance, oversupply, superabundance, superfluity, glut, avalanche, deluge; overdose; too much; informal bellyful.
– OPPOSITES lack.

surge noun **1** *a surge of water:* **gush**, rush, outpouring, stream, flow. **2** *a surge in oil production:* **increase**, rise, growth, upswing, upsurge, escalation, leap. **3** *a sudden surge of anger:* **rush**, storm, torrent, blaze, outburst, eruption. **4** *the surge of sea:* **swell**, heaving, rolling, roll, swirling; tide.
verb **1** *the water surged into people's homes:* **gush**, rush, stream, flow, burst, pour, cascade, spill, overflow, sweep, roll. **2** *the Dow Jones index surged 47.63 points:* **increase**, rise, grow, escalate, leap. **3** *the sea surged:* **swell**, heave, rise, roll.

surly adjective *a surly shop assistant:* **sullen**, sulky, moody, sour, unfriendly, unpleasant, scowling, unsmiling; bad-tempered, grumpy, crotchety, prickly, cantankerous, irascible, testy, short-tempered; abrupt, brusque, curt, gruff, churlish, ill-humoured, crabby, uncivil; informal grouchy.
– OPPOSITES pleasant.

surmise verb *she surmised that he was keen to leave:* **guess**, conjecture, suspect, deduce, infer, conclude, theorize, speculate, divine; assume, presume, suppose, understand, gather, feel, sense, think, believe, imagine, fancy, reckon.

surmount verb **1** *his reputation surmounts language barriers:* **overcome**, conquer, prevail over, triumph over, beat, vanquish; clear, cross, pass over; resist, endure. **2** *they surmounted the ridge:* **climb over**, top, ascend, scale, mount. **3** *the dome is surmounted by a statue:* **cap**, top, crown, finish.
– OPPOSITES descend.

surname noun **family name**, last name; patronymic.

surpass verb *radio far surpasses the press as a source of news:* **excel**, exceed, transcend; outdo, outshine, outstrip, outclass, overshadow, eclipse; improve on, top, trump, cap, beat, better, outperform.

surplus noun *a surplus of grain:* **excess**, surfeit, superabundance, superfluity, oversupply, glut, profusion, plethora; remainder, residue, remains, leftovers.
– OPPOSITES dearth.
adjective *surplus adhesive:* **excess**, leftover, unused, remaining, extra, additional,

spare; superfluous, redundant, unwanted, unneeded, dispensable, expendable.
– OPPOSITES insufficient.

surprise noun **1** *Kate looked at me in surprise:* **astonishment**, amazement, wonder, incredulity, bewilderment, stupefaction, disbelief. **2** *the test came as a big surprise:* **shock**, bolt from the blue, bombshell, revelation, rude awakening, eye-opener; informal turn up for the books, shocker.
verb **1** *I was so surprised that I dropped it:* **astonish**, amaze, startle, astound, stun, stagger, shock; leave open-mouthed, take someone's breath away, dumbfound, daze, take aback, shake up; informal bowl over, floor, flabbergast; Brit. informal knock for six. **2** *she surprised a burglar:* **catch unawares**, catch off guard, catch red-handed, catch in the act, catch out; Brit. informal catch on the hop.

surprised adjective *he was surprised at the news:* **astonished**, amazed, astounded, startled, stunned, staggered, nonplussed, shocked, taken aback, stupefied, dumbfounded, dumbstruck, speechless, thunderstruck, confounded, shaken up; informal bowled over, flabbergasted, floored, flummoxed.

surprising adjective *he moves with surprising speed:* **unexpected**, unforeseen, unpredictable; astonishing, amazing, startling, astounding, staggering, incredible, extraordinary, breathtaking, remarkable; informal mind-blowing.

surrender verb **1** *the army surrendered:* **capitulate**, give in, give (oneself) up, give way, yield, concede (defeat), submit, climb down, back down, cave in, relent, crumble; lay down one's arms, raise the white flag, throw in the towel/sponge. **2** *they surrendered power to the government:* **give up**, relinquish, renounce, forgo, forswear; cede, abdicate, waive, forfeit, sacrifice; hand over, turn over, yield, resign, transfer, grant. **3** *surrender all hope of changing things:* **abandon**, give up, cast aside.
– OPPOSITES resist, seize.
noun **1** *the surrender of the hijackers:* **capitulation**, submission, yielding, succumbing, acquiescence; fall, defeat. **2** *a surrender of power to the shop floor:* **relinquishment**, renunciation, cession, abdication, resignation, transfer.

surreptitious adjective *Rory tried to sneak a surreptitious glance at Adam's wristwatch:* **secret**, secretive, stealthy, clandestine, sneaky, sly, furtive; concealed, hidden, undercover, covert, veiled, cloak-and-dagger.
– OPPOSITES blatant.

surrogate noun *some argue that modern commerce is a surrogate for warfare:* **substitute**, proxy, replacement; deputy, representative, stand-in, standby, stopgap, relief, understudy.

surround verb *we were surrounded by cops:* **encircle**, enclose, encompass, ring; fence in,

s

hem in, confine, bound, circumscribe, cut off; besiege, trap.
noun *a fireplace with a wood surround:* **border**, edging, edge, perimeter, boundary, margin, skirting, fringe.

surrounding adjective *the surrounding countryside:* **neighbouring**, nearby, near, neighbourhood, local; adjoining, adjacent, bordering, abutting; encircling, encompassing.

surroundings plural noun *a family-run hotel in exotic surroundings:* **environment**, setting, milieu, background, backdrop; conditions, circumstances, situation, context; vicinity, locality, habitat.

surveillance noun *leading members of the party were to be kept under surveillance:* **observation**, scrutiny, watch, view, inspection, supervision; spying, espionage, infiltration, reconnaissance; informal bugging, wiretapping, recon.

survey verb 1 *he surveyed his work:* **look at**, look over, observe, view, contemplate, regard, gaze at, stare at, eye; scrutinize, examine, inspect, scan, study, consider, review, take stock of; informal size up. **2** *they surveyed 4000 drug users:* **interview**, question, canvass, poll, cross-examine, investigate, research, study, probe, sample. **3** *he was asked to survey the house:* **appraise**, assess, prospect; make a survey of, value.
noun 1 *a survey of the current literature:* **study**, review, consideration, overview; scrutiny, examination, inspection, appraisal. **2** *a survey of sexual behaviour:* **poll**, review, investigation, inquiry, study, probe, questionnaire, census, research. **3** *a thorough survey of the property:* **appraisal**, assessment, valuation, estimate, estimation.

survive verb 1 *he survived by escaping through a hole:* **remain alive**, live, sustain oneself, pull through, get through, hold on/out, make it, keep body and soul together. **2** *the theatre must survive:* **continue**, remain, persist, endure, live on, persevere, abide, go on, carry on, be extant, exist. **3** *he was survived by his sons:* **outlive**, outlast; live longer than.

susceptible adjective 1 *susceptible children:* **impressionable**, credulous, gullible, innocent, ingenuous, naive, easily led; defenceless, vulnerable; persuadable, tractable; sensitive, responsive, thin-skinned. **2** *people susceptible to blackmail:* **open to**, receptive to, vulnerable to; an easy target for. **3** *he is susceptible to ulcers:* **liable to**, prone to, subject to, inclined to, predisposed to, disposed to, given to, at risk of. **4** *the database will be susceptible of exploitation:* **open to**, capable of, admitting of, receptive of, responsive to.
– OPPOSITES sceptical, immune, resistant.

suspect verb 1 *I suspected she'd made a mistake:* **have a suspicion**, have a feeling, feel, (be inclined to) think, fancy, reckon, guess, surmise, conjecture, conclude, have

a hunch; suppose, presume, deduce; fear. **2** *he had no reason to suspect my honesty:* **doubt**, distrust, mistrust, have misgivings about, be sceptical about, have qualms about, be suspicious of, be wary of, harbour reservations about; informal smell a rat.
noun *a murder suspect:* **suspected person**, accused, defendant.
adjective *a suspect package:* **suspicious**, dubious, doubtful, untrustworthy; odd, queer; informal fishy, funny, shady; Brit. informal dodgy.

suspend verb 1 *the court case was suspended:* **adjourn**, interrupt, break off, postpone, delay, defer, shelve, put off, intermit, prorogue, hold over, hold in abeyance; cut short, discontinue, dissolve, disband, terminate;
N. Amer. table; informal put on ice, put on the back burner, mothball; N. Amer. informal take a rain check on. **2** *he was suspended from his duties:* **exclude**, debar, remove, eliminate, expel, eject. **3** *lights were suspended from the ceiling:* **hang**, sling, string; swing, dangle.

suspense noun *I can't bear the suspense:* **tension**, uncertainty, doubt, anticipation, expectation, expectancy, excitement, anxiety, apprehension, strain.
■ **in suspense** eagerly, agog, with bated breath, on tenterhooks; on edge, anxious, edgy, jumpy, keyed up, uneasy; informal uptight, jittery.

suspension noun 1 *the suspension of army operations:* **adjournment**, interruption, postponement, delay, deferral, deferment, stay, prorogation; armistice; cessation, end, halt, stoppage, dissolution, disbandment, termination. **2** *his suspension from school:* **exclusion**, debarment, removal, elimination, expulsion, ejection; Brit. rustication.

suspicion noun 1 *she had a suspicion that he didn't like her:* **intuition**, feeling, impression, inkling, hunch, fancy, notion, supposition, belief, idea, theory; presentiment, premonition; informal gut feeling, sixth sense. **2** *I confronted him with my suspicions:* **misgiving**, doubt, qualm, reservation, hesitation, question; scepticism, uncertainty, distrust, mistrust. **3** *wine with a suspicion of soda:* **trace**, touch, suggestion, hint, soupçon, tinge, shade, whiff, bit, drop, dash, taste, jot, mite.

suspicious adjective 1 *she gave him a suspicious look:* **doubtful**, unsure, dubious, wary, chary, sceptical, distrustful, mistrustful, disbelieving, cynical. **2** *a highly suspicious character:* **disreputable**, unsavoury, dubious, suspect, dishonest-looking, funny-looking, slippery; informal shifty, shady; Brit. informal dodgy. **3** *she disappeared in suspicious circumstances:* **questionable**, odd, strange, dubious, irregular, queer, funny, doubtful, mysterious, murky; informal fishy; Brit. informal dodgy.
– OPPOSITES trusting, honest, innocent.

S

sustain verb **1** *the balcony might not sustain the weight:* **bear**, support, carry, stand, keep up, prop up, shore up, underpin. **2** *her memories sustained her:* **comfort**, help, assist, encourage, succour, support, give strength to, buoy up, carry, cheer up, hearten; informal buck up. **3** *they were unable to sustain a coalition:* **continue**, carry on, keep up, keep alive, maintain, preserve, conserve, perpetuate, retain. **4** *she had bread and cheese to sustain her:* **nourish**, feed, nurture; maintain, preserve, keep alive, keep going, provide for. **5** *she sustained slight injuries:* **undergo**, experience, suffer, endure. **6** *the allegation was not sustained:* **uphold**, validate, ratify, vindicate, confirm, endorse; verify, corroborate, substantiate, bear out, prove, authenticate, back up, evidence, justify.

sustained adjective *a sustained attack:* **continuous**, ongoing, steady, continual, constant, prolonged, persistent, non-stop, perpetual, unabating, relentless, unrelieved, unbroken, never-ending, incessant, unceasing, ceaseless, round the clock.
– OPPOSITES sporadic.

sustenance noun **1** *the creature needs sustenance:* **nourishment**, food, nutriment, nutrition, provisions, provender, rations; informal grub, chow; Brit. informal scoff. **2** *the sustenance of his family:* **support**, maintenance, keep, living, livelihood, subsistence, income.

swagger verb *we swaggered into the arena:* **strut**, parade, stride; walk confidently; informal sashay.
noun **1** *a slight swagger in his stride:* **strut**; confidence, arrogance, ostentation. **2** *he was full of swagger:* **bluster**, braggadocio, bumptiousness, vainglory; informal swank.

swallow verb **1** *she couldn't swallow anything:* **eat**, gulp down, consume, devour, put away; ingest, assimilate; drink, guzzle, quaff, imbibe, sup, slug; informal polish off, swig, swill, down; Brit. informal scoff. **2** *I can't swallow any more of your insults:* **tolerate**, endure, stand, put up with, bear, abide, countenance, stomach, take, accept; informal hack; Brit. informal stick; formal brook. **3** *he swallowed my story:* **believe**, credit, accept, trust; informal fall for, buy, go for, {swallow something, hook, line, and sinker}. **4** *she swallowed her pride:* **restrain**, repress, suppress, hold back, fight back; overcome, check, control, curb, rein in; silence, muffle, stifle, smother, hide, bottle up; informal keep a/the lid on.
■ **swallow someone/something up 1** *the darkness swallowed them up:* engulf, swamp, devour, overwhelm, overcome. **2** *the colleges were swallowed up by universities:* take over, engulf, absorb, assimilate, incorporate.

swamp noun *his horse got stuck in a swamp:* **marsh**, bog, quagmire, mire, morass, fen; quicksand; N. Amer. bayou.

verb **1** *the rain was swamping the dry roads:* **flood**, inundate, deluge, immerse; soak, drench, saturate. **2** *he was swamped by media attention:* **overwhelm**, inundate, flood, deluge, engulf, snow under, overload, overpower, weigh down, besiege, beset.

swampy adjective *the swampy ground:* **marshy**, boggy, fenny, miry; soft, soggy, muddy, spongy, heavy, squelchy, waterlogged, sodden, wet.

swap verb **1** *I swapped some toys for a set of dice:* **exchange**, trade, barter, interchange, bargain; switch, change, replace. **2** *we swapped jokes:* **bandy**, exchange, trade, reciprocate.
noun *a job swap:* **exchange**, interchange, trade, switch, trade-off, substitution.

swarm noun **1** *a swarm of bees:* **hive**, flock, collection. **2** *a swarm of gendarmes:* **crowd**, multitude, horde, host, mob, gang, throng, mass, army, troop, herd, pack.
verb *reporters were swarming all over the place:* **flock**, crowd, throng, surge, stream.
■ **be swarming with** *the field was swarming with sightseers:* be crowded with, be thronged with, be overrun with, be full of, abound in, be teeming with, bristle with, be alive with, be crawling with, be infested with, overflow with, be prolific in, be abundant in; informal be thick with.

swarthy adjective *the tanned, swarthy skin of his face:* **dark-skinned**, olive-skinned, dusky, tanned.
– OPPOSITES pale.

swathe verb *his hands were swathed in bandages:* **wrap**, envelop, bind, swaddle, bandage, cover, shroud, drape, wind, enfold, sheathe.

sway verb **1** *the curtains swayed in the breeze:* **swing**, shake, oscillate, undulate, move to and fro, move back and forth. **2** *she swayed on her feet:* **stagger**, wobble, rock, lurch, reel, roll, list, stumble, pitch. **3** *we are swayed by the media:* **influence**, affect, bias, persuade, talk round, win over; manipulate, bend, mould. **4** *you must not be swayed by emotion:* **rule**, govern, dominate, control, guide.
noun **1** *the sway of her hips:* **swing**, roll, shake, oscillation, undulation. **2** *a province under the sway of the Franks:* **jurisdiction**, rule, government, sovereignty, dominion, control, command, power, authority, ascendancy, domination, mastery.
■ **hold sway** hold power, wield power, exercise power, rule, be in control, predominate; have the upper hand, have the edge, have the whip hand; informal run the show, be in the driving seat, be in the saddle.

swear verb **1** *they swore to marry each other:* **promise**, vow, pledge, give one's word, take an oath, undertake, guarantee. **2** *she swore she would never go back:* **insist**, avow, pronounce, declare, proclaim, assert, profess, maintain, contend, emphasize, stress. **3** *Kate spilled wine and swore:* **curse**, blaspheme, utter profanities, utter oaths, use bad language, take the Lord's name in vain; informal cuss, eff and blind.

■ **swear by** (informal) *Iris swears by her yoga:* express confidence in, have faith in, trust, believe in; set store by, value; informal rate.

swearing noun *sixty per cent thought there was too much swearing on TV:* **bad language**, strong language, cursing, blaspheming, blasphemy; profanities, obscenities, curses, oaths, expletives, swear words; informal cussing, effing and blinding, four-letter words; formal imprecation.

sweat noun **1** *he was drenched with sweat:* **perspiration**, moisture, dampness, wetness. **2** (informal) *he got into such a sweat about that girl:* **fluster**, panic, frenzy, fever, pother; informal state, flap, tizzy, dither, stew, lather; N. Amer. informal twit.
verb **1** *she was sweating heavily:* **perspire**, swelter, glow; be damp, be wet; secrete. **2** *I've sweated over this for six months:* **work (hard)**, work like a Trojan, labour, toil, slog, slave, work one's fingers to the bone; informal graft, plug away.

sweaty adjective *his sweaty palms:* **perspiring**, sweating, clammy, sticky, glowing; moist, damp.

sweep verb **1** *she swept the floor:* **brush**, clean, scrub, wipe, mop, dust, scour; informal do. **2** *I swept the crumbs off:* **remove**, brush, clean, clear, whisk. **3** *he was swept out to sea:* **carry**, pull, drag, tow. **4** *riots swept the country:* **engulf**, overwhelm, flood. **5** *he swept down the stairs:* **glide**, sail, breeze, drift, flit, flounce; stride, stroll, swagger. **6** *a limousine swept past:* **glide**, sail, rush, race, streak, speed, fly, zoom, whizz, hurtle; informal tear, whip. **7** *police swept the conference room:* **search**, probe, check, explore, go through, scour, comb.
noun **1** *a great sweep of his hand:* **gesture**, stroke, wave, movement. **2** *a security sweep:* **search**, hunt, exploration, probe. **3** *a long sweep of golden sand:* **expanse**, tract, stretch, extent, plain. **4** *the broad sweep of our interests:* **range**, span, scope, compass, reach, spread, ambit, remit, gamut, spectrum, extent.

■ **sweep something aside** *he swept aside the criticism:* disregard, ignore, take no notice of, dismiss, shrug off, forget about, brush aside.

■ **sweep something under the carpet** hide, conceal, suppress, hush up, keep quiet about, censor, gag, withhold, cover up, stifle.

sweeping adjective **1** *sweeping changes:* **extensive**, wide-ranging, global, broad, comprehensive, all-inclusive, all-embracing, far-reaching, across the board; thorough, radical; informal wall-to-wall. **2** *a sweeping victory:* **overwhelming**, decisive, thorough, complete, total, absolute, out-and-out, unqualified. **3** *sweeping statements:* **wholesale**, blanket, generalized, all-inclusive, unqualified, indiscriminate, universal, oversimplified, imprecise. **4** *sweeping banks of heather:* **broad**, extensive, expansive, vast, spacious, boundless, panoramic.
– OPPOSITES limited, narrow, focused, small.

sweet adjective **1** *sweet biscuits:* **sugary**, sweetened, saccharine; sugared, honeyed, candied, glacé; sickly, cloying. **2** *the sweet scent of roses:* **fragrant**, aromatic, perfumed. **3** *her sweet voice:* **dulcet**, melodious, lyrical, mellifluous, musical, tuneful, soft, harmonious, silvery, honeyed, mellow, rich, golden. **4** *life was still sweet:* **pleasant**, pleasing, agreeable, delightful, nice, satisfying, gratifying, good, acceptable, fine; informal lovely, great. **5** *she has a sweet nature:* **likeable**, appealing, engaging, amiable, pleasant, agreeable, genial, friendly, nice, kind, thoughtful, considerate; charming, enchanting, captivating, delightful, lovely. **6** *she looks quite sweet:* **cute**, lovable, adorable, endearing, charming, attractive, dear. **7** *my sweet Lydia:* **dear**, dearest, darling, beloved, loved, cherished, precious, treasured.
– OPPOSITES sour, savoury, harsh, disagreeable.
noun **1** *sweets for the children:* **confectionery**, chocolate, bonbon, fondant, toffee; N. Amer. candy; informal sweetie. **2** *a delicious sweet for the guests:* **dessert**, pudding, second course, last course; Brit. informal afters, pud. **3** *happy birthday, my sweet!* **dear**, darling, dearest, love, sweetheart, beloved, honey, pet, treasure, angel.

sweeten verb **1** *sweeten the milk with honey:* **make sweet**, add sugar to, sugar, sugar-coat. **2** *he chewed gum to sweeten his breath:* **freshen**, refresh, purify, deodorize, perfume. **3** *try to sweeten the bad news:* **soften**, ease, alleviate, mitigate, temper, cushion; embellish, embroider. **4** (informal) *a bigger dividend to sweeten shareholders:* **mollify**, placate, soothe, soften up, pacify, appease, win over.

sweetheart noun **1** *you look lovely, sweetheart:* **darling**, dear, dearest, love, beloved, sweet; informal honey, sweetie, sugar, baby, babe, poppet. **2** *my high-school sweetheart:* **lover**, love, girlfriend, boyfriend, beloved, significant other, lady love, loved one, suitor, admirer; informal steady, flame.

swell verb **1** *her lip swelled up:* **expand**, bulge, distend, inflate, dilate, bloat, puff up, balloon, fatten, fill out, tumefy; rare intumesce. **2** *the population swelled:* **grow**, enlarge, increase, expand, rise, escalate, multiply, proliferate, snowball, mushroom. **3** *she swelled with pride:* **be filled**, be bursting, brim, overflow. **4** *the graduate scheme swelled entry numbers:* **increase**, enlarge, augment, boost, top up, step up, multiply. **5** *the music swelled to fill the house:*

S

grow loud, grow louder, amplify, intensify, heighten.
– OPPOSITES shrink, decrease, quieten.
noun **1** *a brief swell in the volume:* **increase**, rise, escalation, surge, boost. **2** *a heavy swell on the sea:* **surge**, wave, undulation, roll.
– OPPOSITES decrease, dip.

swelling noun *he had a great swelling under his eye:* **bump**, lump, bulge, protuberance, enlargement, distension, prominence, protrusion, node, nodule, tumescence; boil, blister, bunion, carbuncle.

sweltering adjective *a sweltering afternoon:* **hot**, stifling, humid, sultry, sticky, muggy, close, stuffy; tropical, torrid, searing, blistering; informal boiling (hot), baking, roasting, sizzling.
– OPPOSITES freezing.

swerve verb *a car swerved into her path:* **veer**, deviate, skew, diverge, sheer, weave, zigzag, change direction.
noun *the bowler regulated his swerve:* **curve**, curl, deviation, twist; N. Amer. English.

swift adjective **1** *a swift decision:* **prompt**, rapid, sudden, immediate, instant, instantaneous; abrupt, hasty, hurried, precipitate, headlong. **2** *swift runners:* **fast**, rapid, quick, speedy, high-speed, brisk, lively; express, breakneck; fleet-footed; informal nippy, supersonic.
– OPPOSITES slow, leisurely.

swill verb *he swilled out a glass:* **wash**, rinse, sluice, clean, flush.
noun *swill for the pigs:* **pigswill**, mash, slops, scraps, refuse, scourings, leftovers.

swim verb **1** *they swam in the pool:* **bathe**, take a dip, splash around; float, tread water. **2** *his food was swimming in gravy:* **be saturated in**, be drenched in, be soaked in, be steeped in, be immersed in, be covered in, be full of.

swimmingly adverb *everything was going swimmingly:* **well**, smoothly, easily, effortlessly, like clockwork, without a hitch, as planned, to plan; informal like a dream, like magic.

swimming pool noun **pool**, baths, lido, piscina; Brit. swimming bath(s); N. Amer. natatorium.

swimsuit noun **bathing suit**, bathing dress, (swimming) trunks, bikini; swimwear; Brit. bathing costume, swimming costume; informal cossie; Austral./NZ informal bathers.

swindle verb *I was swindled out of my money:* **defraud**, cheat, trick, dupe, deceive, fool, hoax, hoodwink, bamboozle; informal fleece, do, con, sting, diddle, swizzle, rip off, take for a ride, pull a fast one on, put one over on, take to the cleaners, gull; N. Amer. informal stiff, euchre.
noun *an insurance swindle:* **fraud**, trick, deception, deceit, cheat, sham, artifice, ruse, dodge, racket, wile; sharp practice; informal con, fiddle, diddle, rip-off, flimflam, swizzle, swizz; N. Amer. informal bunco.

swindler noun **fraudster**, fraud, (confidence) trickster, cheat, rogue, mountebank, charlatan, impostor, hoaxer; informal con man, con artist, shark, sharp, hustler, phoney, crook.

swing verb **1** *the sign swung in the wind:* **sway**, oscillate, move back and forth, move to and fro, wave, wag, rock, flutter, flap. **2** *Helen swung the bottle:* **brandish**, wave, flourish, wield, shake, wag, twirl. **3** *this road swings off to the north:* **curve**, bend, veer, turn, bear, wind, twist, deviate, slew, skew, drift, head. **4** *the balance swung from one party to the other:* **change**, fluctuate, shift, alter, oscillate, waver, alternate, see-saw, yo-yo, vary. **5** (informal) *their persistence finally swung it for him:* **accomplish**, achieve, obtain, acquire, get, secure, net, win, attain, bag, hook; informal wangle, land, fix (up).
noun **1** *a swing of the pendulum:* **oscillation**, sway, wave. **2** *the swing to the Conservatives:* **change**, move; turnaround, turnabout, reversal, about turn, about face, volte face, change of heart, U-turn, sea change. **3** *a swing towards plain food:* **trend**, tendency, drift, movement. **4** *a mood swing:* **fluctuation**, change, shift, variation, oscillation.

swingeing adjective (Brit.) *swingeing cuts in public expenditure:* **severe**, extreme, serious, substantial, drastic, harsh, punishing, excessive, heavy.
– OPPOSITES minor.

swipe (informal) verb *he swiped at her head:* **swing**, lash out; strike, hit, slap, cuff; informal belt, wallop, sock, biff, clout.
noun *she took a swipe at his face:* **swing**, stroke, strike, hit, slap, cuff, clip; informal belt, wallop.

swirl verb *the snow swirled around them:* **whirl**, eddy, billow, spiral, circulate, revolve, spin, twist; flow, stream, surge, seethe.

switch noun **1** *the switch on top of the telephone:* **button**, lever, control, dial. **2** *a switch from direct to indirect taxation:* **change**, move, shift, transition, transformation; reversal, turnaround, U-turn, changeover, transfer, conversion; substitution, exchange. **3** *a switch of willow:* **branch**, twig, stick, rod.
verb **1** *he switched sides:* **change**, shift; reverse; informal chop and change. **2** *he managed to switch envelopes:* **exchange**, swap, interchange, trade, substitute, replace, rotate.
■ **switch something on** *he switched the kettle on:* turn on, power up, put on, activate, start, set going, set in motion, operate, initiate, actuate, initialize, energize, boot up, spin up.
■ **switch something off** *she switched the TV off:* turn off, shut off, power down, stop, cut, halt, deactivate, spin down.

swivel verb *she swivelled round in her seat:* **turn**, rotate, revolve, pivot, swing; spin,

s

twirl, whirl, wheel, gyrate, pirouette.

swollen adjective *swollen glands:* **distended**, expanded, enlarged, bulging, inflated, dilated, bloated, puffed up, puffy, tumescent; inflamed.

swoop verb **1** *pigeons swooped down after the grain:* **dive**, descend, sweep, pounce, plunge, pitch, nosedive; rush, dart, speed, zoom. **2** *police swooped on the flat:* **raid**, search; pounce on, attack, assault, assail, charge; N. Amer. informal bust.
noun *an early morning swoop by police:* **raid**; attack, assault; N. Amer. informal bust, takedown.

sword noun *a ceremonial sword:* **blade**, foil, épée, cutlass, rapier, sabre, scimitar.
■ **cross swords** quarrel, disagree, dispute, wrangle, bicker, be at odds, be at loggerheads, lock horns; fight, contend; informal scrap.

sybaritic adjective *the brothers' opulent and sybaritic lifestyle:* **luxurious**, extravagant, lavish, self-indulgent, pleasure-seeking, sensual, voluptuous, hedonistic, epicurean, lotus-eating, libertine, debauched, decadent.
– OPPOSITES ascetic.

sycophant noun *he was surrounded by flatterers and sycophants:* **toady**, creep, crawler, fawner, flatterer, truckler, groveller, doormat, lickspittle, kowtower, Uriah Heep; informal bootlicker, yes-man.

sycophantic adjective **obsequious**, servile, subservient, deferential, grovelling, toadying, fawning, flattering, ingratiating, cringing, unctuous, slavish; informal smarmy, bootlicking.

syllabus noun *the A-level chemistry syllabus:* **curriculum**, course (of study), programme of study, course outline; timetable, schedule.

symbol noun **1** *the lotus is the symbol of purity:* **emblem**, token, sign, representation, figure, image; metaphor, allegory. **2** *the chemical symbol for helium:* **sign**, character, mark, letter, ideogram. **3** *the Red Cross symbol:* **logo**, emblem, badge, stamp, trademark, crest, insignia, coat of arms, seal, device, monogram, hallmark, flag, motif.

symbolic adjective **1** *the Colosseum is symbolic of the Roman Empire:* **emblematic**, representative, typical, characteristic, symptomatic. **2** *symbolic language:* **figurative**, representative, illustrative, emblematic, metaphorical, allegorical, parabolic, allusive, suggestive; meaningful, significant.
– OPPOSITES literal.

symbolize verb *the wheel symbolizes the power of peaceful change:* **represent**, stand for, be a sign of, exemplify; denote, signify, mean, indicate, convey, express, imply, suggest, allude to; embody, epitomize, encapsulate, personify, typify.

symmetrical adjective **regular**, uniform, consistent; evenly shaped, aligned, equal; mirror-image; balanced, proportional, even.

symmetry noun *the garden is neat, laid out with perfect symmetry:* **regularity**, evenness, uniformity, consistency, conformity, correspondence, equality; balance, proportions; formal concord.

sympathetic adjective **1** *a sympathetic listener:* **compassionate**, caring, concerned, solicitous, empathetic, understanding, sensitive; commiserative, pitying, consoling, comforting, supportive, encouraging; considerate, kind, tender-hearted. **2** *the most sympathetic character in the book:* **likeable**, pleasant, agreeable, congenial, friendly, genial. **3** *I was sympathetic to his cause:* **in favour of**, in sympathy with, pro, on the side of, supportive of, encouraging of; well disposed to, favourably disposed to, receptive to.
– OPPOSITES unfeeling, opposed.

sympathize verb **1** *he sympathized with his wife:* **pity**, feel sorry for, show compassion for, commiserate, offer condolences to, feel for, show concern, show interest; console, comfort, solace, soothe, support, encourage; empathize with, identify with, understand, relate to. **2** *they sympathize with the critique:* **agree with**, support, be in favour of, go along with, favour, approve of, back, side with.

sympathizer noun *a Nazi sympathizer:* **supporter**, backer, well-wisher, advocate, ally, partisan; collaborator, fraternizer, conspirator, quisling.

sympathy noun **1** *he shows sympathy for the poor:* **compassion**, caring, concern, solicitude, empathy; commiseration, pity, condolence, comfort, solace, support, encouragement; consideration, kindness. **2** *they might publicize John's case out of sympathy with a fellow journalist:* **rapport**, fellow feeling, affinity, empathy, harmony, accord, compatibility; fellowship, camaraderie. **3** *their sympathy with the Republicans:* **agreement**, favour, approval, approbation, support, encouragement, partiality; association, alignment, affiliation.
– OPPOSITES indifference, hostility.

symptom noun **1** *the symptoms of the disease:* **manifestation**, indication, indicator, sign, mark, feature, trait. **2** *a symptom of the country's present turmoil:* **expression**, sign, indication, mark, token, manifestation; portent, warning, clue, hint; testimony, evidence, proof.

symptomatic adjective *such incidents were symptomatic of tensions within the socialist movement:* **indicative**, characteristic, suggestive, typical, representative, symbolic.

synopsis noun *a basic synopsis of the play:* **summary**, summarization, precis, abstract, outline, digest, rundown, round-up, abridgement.

synthesis noun *the painting is a synthesis of*

S

elements from a variety of different types of art: **combination**, union, amalgam, blend, mixture, compound, fusion, composite, alloy; unification, amalgamation, marrying.

synthetic adjective synthetic leather: **artificial**, fake, false, faux, imitation, mock, simulated, ersatz, substitute; pseudo, so-called; man-made, manufactured, fabricated; informal phoney, pretend.
- OPPOSITES natural.

syrupy adjective syrupy medicine: **oversweet**, sweet, sugary, treacly, honeyed, saccharine; thick, sticky, gluey, viscid, glutinous; informal gooey.

system noun 1 a system of canals: **structure**, organization, arrangement, complex, network; informal set-up. 2 a system for regulating sales: **method**, methodology, technique, process, procedure, approach, practice; means, way, mode, framework, modus operandi; scheme, plan, policy, programme, regimen, formula, routine. 3 there was no system in his work: **order**, method, orderliness, systematization, planning, logic, routine. 4 youngsters have no faith in the system: **the establishment**, the administration, the authorities, the powers that be; bureaucracy, officialdom; the status quo.

systematic adjective these interviews were conducted in a systematic way: **structured**, methodical, organized, orderly, planned, systematized, regular, routine, standardized, standard; logical, coherent, consistent; efficient, businesslike, practical.
- OPPOSITES disorganized.

Tt

tab noun tag, label, flap.

table noun 1 *put the plates on the table:* **bench**, buffet, stand, counter, work surface, worktop; desk, bar. 2 *the report has numerous tables:* **chart**, diagram, figure, graph, plan; list, tabulation, index.
verb *she tabled a question in parliament:* **submit**, put forward, propose, suggest, move, lodge, file, introduce, air, moot.

tableau noun *the girl fixed her eyes upon the central figure in the tableau before her:* **scene**, arrangement, grouping, group; picture, spectacle, image, vignette.

tablet noun 1 *a carved stone tablet:* **slab**, stone, panel, plaque, plate, sign. 2 *a headache tablet:* **pill**, capsule, lozenge, pastille; informal tab. 3 *a tablet of soap:* **bar**, cake, slab, brick, block, chunk, piece.

taboo noun *the taboo against working on the sabbath:* **prohibition**, proscription, veto, interdict, ban, restriction.
adjective *gambling was taboo in our house:* **forbidden**, prohibited, banned, proscribed, outlawed, illegal, illicit, unlawful; unmentionable; rude, impolite; Islam haram; NZ tapu; informal no go.
– OPPOSITES acceptable.

tabulate verb **chart**, arrange, order, organize, systematize, catalogue, list, index, classify, class, codify; compile, group, log, grade, rate.

tacit adjective *the deal relies on this tacit agreement:* **implicit**, understood, implied, inferred, hinted, suggested; unspoken, unstated, unsaid, unexpressed, unvoiced; taken for granted, taken as read.
– OPPOSITES explicit.

taciturn adjective *Mark was a shy, taciturn man:* **untalkative**, uncommunicative, reticent, unforthcoming, quiet, secretive, tight-lipped, close-mouthed; silent, mute, dumb, inarticulate; reserved, withdrawn.
– OPPOSITES talkative.

tack noun 1 *tacks held the carpet down:* **pin**, drawing pin, nail, staple, rivet, stud. 2 *he changed tack and tried a different approach:* **approach**, way, method; policy, procedure, technique, tactic, plan, strategy, stratagem; path, line, angle, direction, course.
verb 1 *there was a photo tacked to the wall:* **pin**, nail, staple, fix, fasten, attach, secure, affix. 2 *the dress was roughly tacked together:* **stitch**, sew, bind. 3 *poems tacked on at the*

end of the book: **add**, append, join, tag.

tackle noun 1 *he's brought his fishing tackle:* **equipment**, gear, apparatus, kit, hardware; implements, instruments, accoutrements, paraphernalia, trappings, appurtenances; informal things, stuff, clobber, bits and pieces. 2 *they attached lifting tackle and hauled it on deck:* **gear**; pulleys, hoist, crane, winch. 3 *a hard tackle by the scrum half:* **interception**, challenge, block, attack.
verb 1 *we must tackle environmental problems now:* **get to grips with**, address, get to work on, set one's hand to, approach, take on, attend to, see to, try to sort out; deal with, take care of, handle, manage; informal get stuck into, have a crack at, have a go at. 2 *I tackled Nina about it and she admitted it:* **confront**, speak to, interview, question, cross-examine; accost, waylay; remonstrate with. 3 *he was stabbed as he tackled a masked intruder:* **confront**, face up to, take on, contend with, challenge; seize, grab, grapple with, intercept, stop; bring down, floor, fell; informal have a go at. 4 *the winger got tackled:* **intercept**, challenge, block, stop, attack.

tacky[1] adjective *the paint was still tacky:* **sticky**, wet, gluey, gummy, adhesive, viscous, viscid, treacly; informal gooey.
– OPPOSITES dry, set.

tacky[2] adjective *a tacky game show:* **tawdry**, tasteless, kitsch, vulgar, crude, garish, gaudy, showy, trashy, cheap, cheesy, second-rate; Brit. informal naff.
– OPPOSITES tasteful.

tact noun **diplomacy**, tactfulness, sensitivity, understanding, thoughtfulness, consideration, delicacy, discretion, prudence, judiciousness, subtlety, savoir faire.

tactful adjective **diplomatic**, discreet, considerate, sensitive, understanding, thoughtful, delicate, judicious, politic, perceptive, subtle; courteous, polite, decorous, respectful.
– OPPOSITES tactless.

tactic noun 1 *they resorted to tactics such as returning reports for further clarification:* **scheme**, stratagem, plan, manoeuvre; method, expedient, gambit, move, approach, tack; device, trick, ploy, dodge, ruse, machination, contrivance; informal wangle. 2 *the use of highly trained riot police and*

t

aggressive new tactics: **policy**, method; generalship, organization, planning, direction, orchestration.

tactical adjective **calculated**, planned, strategic; prudent, politic, diplomatic, judicious, shrewd, cunning, artful.

tactless adjective **insensitive**, inconsiderate, thoughtless, indelicate, undiplomatic, unsubtle, clumsy, heavy-handed, graceless, awkward, inept, gauche; blunt, frank, outspoken, abrupt, gruff, rough; imprudent, injudicious, unwise; rude, impolite, discourteous, crass, tasteless.
– OPPOSITES tactful.

tag noun 1 I looked for a price tag: **label**, ticket, badge, mark, marker, tab, sticker, docket, stub, counterfoil, flag. 2 he gained a 'bad boy' tag: **designation**, label, description, characterization, identity; nickname, name, epithet, title, sobriquet; informal handle, moniker.
verb 1 bottles tagged with coloured stickers: **label**, mark, ticket, identify, flag, indicate. 2 he was tagging along behind her: **follow**, trail; come after, go after, shadow, dog; accompany, attend, escort; informal tail.

tail noun 1 the dog's tail began to wag: **brush**, scut; tailpiece, tail feathers; hindquarters. 2 the tail of the queue: **rear**, end, back, extremity; bottom; Brit. informal fag end.
– OPPOSITES head, front, start.
verb (informal) the paparazzi tailed them all over London: **follow**, shadow, stalk, trail, track, hunt, hound, dog, pursue, chase.
■ **tail off/away** the old lady's voice tailed off: fade, wane, ebb, dwindle, decrease, lessen, diminish, decline, subside, abate, drop off, peter out, taper off; let up, ease off, die away, die down, come to an end.

tailback noun **traffic jam**, queue, line; congestion.

tailor noun **outfitter**, dressmaker, couturier, (fashion) designer; clothier, costumier, seamstress.
verb services can be tailored to customer requirements: **customize**, adapt, adjust, modify, change, convert, alter, attune, mould, gear, fit, cut, shape, tune.

taint noun nowhere is free from the taint of corruption: **trace**, touch, suggestion, hint, tinge; stain, blot, blemish, stigma.
verb 1 the wilderness is tainted by pollution: **contaminate**, pollute, adulterate, infect, blight, spoil, soil, ruin, destroy. 2 fraudulent firms taint the reputation of our business: **tarnish**, sully, blacken, stain, blot, blemish, stigmatize, mar, corrupt, defile, soil, muddy, damage, harm, hurt; drag through the mud; literary besmirch.
– OPPOSITES clean, improve.

take verb 1 Anna smiled as she took his hand: **lay hold of**, get hold of; grasp, grip, clasp, clutch, grab. 2 he took an envelope from his pocket: **remove**, pull, draw, withdraw, extract, fish, produce. 3 the following passage

is taken from my book: **extract**, quote, cite, excerpt, derive, abstract, copy, cull. 4 she took a little wine with her dinner: **drink**, have, imbibe; consume, swallow, sink, eat, ingest. 5 many thousands of prisoners were taken: **capture**, seize, catch, arrest, apprehend, take into custody; carry off, abduct. 6 someone's taken my car: **steal**, remove, appropriate, make off with, pilfer, purloin; informal filch, swipe, snaffle; Brit. informal pinch, nick. 7 take four from the total: **subtract**, deduct, remove; discount; informal knock off, minus. 8 all the seats had been taken: **occupy**, use, utilize, fill, hold; reserve, engage; informal bag. 9 I have taken a room in a nearby house: **rent**, lease, hire, charter; reserve, book, engage. 10 in the end, I took the job: **accept**, undertake. 11 he takes 'The Observer': **subscribe to**, buy, read. 12 a nurse took his temperature: **ascertain**, determine, establish, measure, find out, discover; calculate, compute, evaluate, rate, assess, gauge. 13 he started to take notes: **write**, make, note (down), jot (down); scribble, scrawl. 14 I took the equipment back to London: **bring**, carry, bear, transport, convey, move, transfer, shift, ferry; informal cart, tote. 15 the priest took her home: **escort**, accompany, help, assist, show, lead, guide, see, usher, convey. 16 he took the train as far as Acton: **travel on/by**, journey on, go on/by; use. 17 the town takes its name from the lake: **derive**, get, obtain, come by, acquire, pick up. 18 she took the prize for best individual speaker: **receive**, obtain, gain, get, acquire, collect, accept, be awarded; secure, come by, win, earn, pick up, carry off; informal land, bag, net, scoop. 19 I took the chance to postpone the ceremony: **act on**, take advantage of, capitalize on, use, exploit, make the most of, leap at, jump at, pounce on, seize, grasp, grab, accept. 20 he took great pleasure in helping people: **derive**, draw, acquire, obtain, get, gain, extract, procure; experience, feel. 21 Liz took the news badly: **receive**, respond to, react to, meet, greet; deal with, cope with. 22 do you take me for a fool? **regard as**, consider to be, view as, see as, believe to be, reckon to be, imagine to be, assume to be. 23 I take it that you are hungry: **assume**, presume, suppose, imagine, expect, reckon, gather, dare say, trust, surmise, deduce, guess, conjecture, fancy, suspect. 24 I take your point: **accept**, appreciate, acknowledge, sympathize with, agree with; understand, grasp, get, comprehend, apprehend, see, follow . 25 Shirley was rather taken with him: **captivate**, enchant, charm, delight, attract, beguile, enthral, entrance, infatuate, dazzle; amuse, divert, entertain; informal tickle someone's fancy. 26 I can't take much more of this: **endure**, bear, tolerate, stand, put up with, abide, stomach, accept, allow, countenance, support, shoulder; formal brook. 27 all applicants must take an aptitude test: **carry out**, do, complete, conduct, perform; execute, discharge, accomplish, fulfil. 28 I took *English and French*: **study**, learn, have lessons in; take up, pursue; Brit. read; informal do. **29** *the journey took six hours*: **last**, continue for, go on for, carry on for; require, call for, need, necessitate, entail, involve. **30** *the dye did not take*: **be effective**, take effect, hold, root, be productive, be effectual, be useful; work, operate, succeed, function; formal be efficacious.

– OPPOSITES give, free, add, refuse, miss.

noun 1 *he is determined to increase the state's tax take*: **revenue**, income, gain, profit; takings, proceeds, returns, receipts, winnings, pickings, earnings, spoils; purse; Brit. informal bunce. **2** *we need someone with a clapperboard for the start of each take*: **scene**, sequence; version, attempt. **3** *her wry take on gender issues*: **view of**, reading of, version of, interpretation of, understanding of, account of, analysis of.

■ **take after** *Jenny takes after her mother*: resemble, look like; remind one of, make one think of; informal be the spitting image of.

■ **take against** *Bernard soon took against the idea*: take a dislike to, view with disfavour, look askance at.

■ **take something apart** *we took the washing machine apart*: dismantle, take to pieces, disassemble, strip down; tear/pull apart, demolish, destroy, wreck.

■ **take someone back** *the song took me back to my time in Vienna*: evoke, remind one of, conjure up, summon up; echo, suggest.

■ **take something back 1** *I take back every word*: retract, withdraw, renounce, disclaim, unsay, disavow, recant. **2** *I must take the keys back to Marjorie*: return, bring back, give back, restore.

■ **take something down** *the policeman took down her particulars*: write down, note down, jot down, set down, record, register, document, minute.

■ **take someone in 1** *Mrs Smith took in paying guests*: accommodate, board, house, feed, put up, admit, receive; harbour. **2** *you were taken in by a cruel hoax*: deceive, delude, hoodwink, mislead, trick, dupe, fool, cheat, defraud, swindle, outwit, gull, hoax, bamboozle; informal con, put one over on.

■ **take something in 1** *at first she could hardly take in the news*: comprehend, understand, grasp, follow, absorb; informal get. **2** *this route takes in some superb scenery*: include, encompass, embrace, contain, cover, incorporate, hold.

■ **take someone in hand** *someone has to take him in hand*: control, be in charge of, dominate, master; reform, improve, correct, change, rehabilitate.

■ **take something in hand** *the time has come to take matters in hand*: deal with, apply oneself to, get to grips with, set one's hand to, grapple with, take on, attend to, see to, sort out, take care of, handle, manage; informal get stuck into.

■ **take it out of someone** *I had no idea how much walking would take it out of me*: exhaust, drain, enervate, tire, fatigue, wear out, weary, debilitate; informal knacker, poop.

■ **take off 1** *the horse took off at great speed*: run away/off, flee, abscond, take flight, decamp, leave, go, depart, make off, bolt, take to one's heels, escape; informal split, clear off, skedaddle, vamoose. **2** *the plane finally took off*: become airborne, take to the air, take wing; lift off, blast off. **3** *the idea really took off*: succeed, do well, become popular, catch on, prosper, flourish, thrive, boom.

■ **take someone off** *when he took off the prime minister he made everyone laugh*: mimic, impersonate, imitate, ape, parody, mock, caricature, satirize, burlesque, lampoon, ridicule; informal spoof, send up.

■ **take oneself off** *I took myself off to the office*: withdraw, retire, leave, exit, depart, go away, quit; informal clear off.

■ **take someone on 1** *there was no real challenger to take him on*: compete against, oppose, challenge, confront, face, fight, vie with, contend with, stand up to. **2** *we took on extra staff for the summer*: engage, hire, employ, enrol, enlist, sign up; informal take on board.

■ **take something on 1** *he was forced to take on more responsibility*: undertake, accept, assume, shoulder, carry, bear. **2** *the study took on a political dimension*: acquire, assume, come to have.

■ **take someone out** *he asked if he could take her out*: go out with, escort, partner, accompany, go with; romance, woo; informal date, see.

■ **take something over** *she took over the paper in 1989*: assume control of, take charge of, take command of.

■ **take one's time** go slowly, dally, dawdle, delay, linger, drag one's feet, waste time, kill time; informal dilly-dally.

■ **take to 1** *he took to keeping his money in a sock*: make a habit of, resort to, turn to, have recourse to; start, commence. **2** *Ruth took to him instantly*: like, get on with, be friendly towards; informal take a shine to. **3** *the new dog has really taken to racing*: become good at, develop an ability for; like, enjoy.

■ **take something up 1** *when he retired he took up painting*: start, begin; informal get into. **2** *the meetings took up all her time*: consume, fill, absorb, use, occupy; waste, squander. **3** *her cousin took up the story*: resume, recommence, restart, carry on, continue, pick up, return to. **4** *he took up their offer of a job*: accept, say yes to, agree to, adopt; formal accede to. **5** *take the skirt up an inch or so*: shorten, turn up; raise, lift.

■ **take up with** *she took up with a middle-aged artist*: become friends with, go around with, fall in with, string along with, get involved with, start seeing; informal knock around with, hang out/around with.

take-off **noun 1** *the plane crashed on take-off*: **departure**, lift-off, launch, blast-off. **2** (informal) *a take-off of a talent show*: **parody**, pastiche, mockery, caricature,

t

satire, lampoon, mimicry, imitation, impersonation, impression; informal send-up, spoof.
– OPPOSITES touchdown.

takeover noun **buyout**, merger, amalgamation; purchase, acquisition.

takings plural noun **proceeds**, returns, receipts, earnings, winnings, pickings, spoils; profit, gain, income, revenue; gate, purse.

tale noun *a grim tale of witches and black magic:* **story**, narrative, anecdote, report, account, history; legend, fable, myth, parable, allegory, saga; informal yarn.

talent noun *you don't often find someone with a talent for this sort of work:* **flair**, aptitude, facility, gift, knack, technique, touch, bent, ability, expertise, capacity, faculty; strength, forte, genius, brilliance; dexterity, skill, artistry.

talented adjective *he is very talented at music:* **gifted**, skilful, skilled, accomplished, brilliant, expert, consummate, masterly, adroit, dexterous, able, competent, capable, apt, deft, adept, proficient; informal crack, ace.
– OPPOSITES inept.

talisman noun **(lucky) charm**, fetish, amulet, mascot, totem.

talk verb **1** *I was talking to a friend from Glasgow:* **speak**, chat, chatter, gossip, prattle, babble, rattle on, blather; informal yak, gab, jaw, chew the fat; Brit. informal natter, rabbit, witter, chunter; N. Amer. informal rap; Austral./NZ informal mag. **2** *they were able to talk in peace:* **converse**, communicate, speak, confer, consult; negotiate, parley; informal have a confab, chew the fat/rag, rap. **3** *thankfully, I was able to talk in English:* **speak (in)**, talk in, communicate in, converse in, express oneself in; use. **4** *nothing they did would make her talk:* **confess**, speak out/up, reveal all, tell tales, give the game away, open one's mouth; informal come clean, blab, squeal, let the cat out of the bag, spill the beans, grass. **5** *we'd better go or people will talk:* **gossip**, pass comment, make remarks; criticize.
noun **1** *he was bored with all this talk:* **chatter**, gossip, prattle, jabbering, babbling, gabbling; informal yakking, gabbing; Brit. informal nattering, rabbiting. **2** *she needed to have a talk with Vivian:* **conversation**, chat, discussion, tête-à-tête, heart-to-heart, dialogue, powwow, consultation, conference, meeting; informal confab, jaw, chit-chat, gossip; formal colloquy. **3** *the peace talks were held in Rome:* **negotiations**, discussions; conference, summit, meeting, consultation, dialogue, symposium, seminar, conclave; mediation, arbitration; informal powwow. **4** *she gave a talk on her travels in Ghana:* **lecture**, speech, address, discourse, oration, presentation, report, sermon; informal spiel. **5** *there was talk of a takeover:* **gossip**, rumour, hearsay, tittle-tattle; news, report. **6** *I was getting a bit bored with hearing nothing but baby talk:* **speech**, language,

words; informal lingo.
■ **talk back** *he was always talking back to Dad:* answer back, be impertinent, be cheeky, be rude; contradict, argue with, disagree with.
■ **talk something down** *people constantly talk down the coal industry:* denigrate, deprecate, disparage, belittle, diminish, criticize; informal knock, put down.
■ **talk down to** *students on the course were talked down to as though they were children:* condescend to, patronize, look down one's nose at, put down.
■ **talk someone into something** *he talked her into parting with her art collection:* persuade into, argue into, cajole into, coax into, bring round to, inveigle into, wheedle into, sweet-talk into, prevail on someone to; informal hustle, fast-talk.
■ **talk of something** *he even talked of suicide:* mention, refer to, speak about, discuss, allude to.

talkative adjective **chatty**, loquacious, garrulous, voluble, conversational, communicative; gossipy; long-winded, wordy, verbose; informal gabby, mouthy.
– OPPOSITES taciturn.

talker noun **conversationalist**, speaker, communicator, orator, raconteur; chatterbox, gossip.

tall adjective **1** *he was a very tall man:* **big**, large, huge, towering, colossal, gigantic, giant, monstrous; leggy. **2** *we were hemmed in by tall buildings:* **high**, big, lofty, towering, elevated; multi-storey. **3** *she's five feet tall:* **in height**, high, from head to toe; from top to bottom.
– OPPOSITES short, low, wide, credible.

tally noun **1** *he keeps a tally of the score:* **running total**, count, record, reckoning, register, account, roll; census, poll. **2** *his tally of 1,816 wickets is still a county record:* **total**, score, count, sum.
verb **1** *these statistics tally with government figures:* **correspond**, agree, accord, concur, coincide, match, fit, be consistent, conform, equate, harmonize, be in tune, dovetail, correlate, parallel; informal square; N. Amer. informal jibe. **2** *the votes were tallied using an abacus:* **count**, calculate, add up, total, compute; figure out, work out, reckon, measure, quantify; Brit. tot up.
– OPPOSITES disagree.

tame adjective **1** *there are tame kangaroos in many wild-life parks:* **domesticated**, domestic, docile, tamed, broken, trained; gentle, mild; pet; Brit. house-trained; N. Amer. housebroken. **2** *the concert was a pretty tame affair:* **unexciting**, uninteresting, uninspiring, dull, bland, flat, insipid, spiritless, pedestrian, colourless, run-of-the-mill, mediocre, ordinary, humdrum, boring; harmless, safe, inoffensive.
– OPPOSITES wild, uncooperative, exciting.
verb *wild parrots can be tamed:* **domesticate**, break, train, master, subdue.

t

tamper verb *she saw them tampering with her car:* **interfere**, monkey around, meddle, tinker, fiddle, fool around, play around; doctor, alter, change, adjust, damage, deface, vandalize; informal mess about/around; Brit. informal muck about/around.

tan adjective *he wore a tan waistcoat:* **yellowish-brown**, light brown, pale brown, tawny.
verb *use a sunscreen to help you tan:* **become suntanned**, get a suntan, (go) brown, bronze.

tang noun **flavour**, taste, savour; sharpness, zest, bite, edge, smack, piquancy, spice; smell, odour, aroma, fragrance, perfume, redolence; informal kick, pep.

tangible adjective **1** *we offer a tangible product rather than a service:* **actual**, palpable, material, physical, real, substantial, corporeal, solid, concrete. **2** *organizations want to see some tangible benefit from the scheme:* **visible**, noticeable actual, definite, clear, clear-cut, distinct, manifest, evident, unmistakable, perceptible, discernible.
– OPPOSITES abstract.

tangle verb **1** *the wool got tangled:* **entangle**, snarl, catch, entwine, twist, ravel, knot, enmesh, coil, mat, jumble, muddle. **2** *he tangled with his old rival:* **come into conflict**, dispute, argue, quarrel, fight, wrangle, squabble, contend, cross swords, lock horns.
noun **1** *all I could see was a tangle of branches:* **snarl**, mass, knot, mesh, mishmash. **2** *the defence got into an awful tangle:* **muddle**, jumble, mix-up, confusion, shambles.

tangled adjective **1** *her tangled hair took hours to sort out:* **knotted**, knotty, ravelled, entangled, snarled (up), twisted, matted, tangly, messy; tousled, unkempt, ratty; informal mussed up. **2** *a tangled bureaucratic mess:* **confused**, jumbled, mixed up, messy, chaotic, complicated, involved, complex, intricate, knotty, tortuous.
– OPPOSITES simple.

tangy adjective **zesty**, sharp, acid, acidic, tart, sour, bitter, piquant, spicy, tasty, flavoursome, pungent.
– OPPOSITES bland.

tank noun **1** *we have no hot water tank:* **container**, receptacle, vat, cistern, repository, reservoir, basin. **2** *a tank full of fish:* **aquarium**, bowl. **3** *the army's use of tanks:* **armoured vehicle**; armour.

tantalize verb **tease**, torment, torture, bait; tempt, entice, lure, allure, beguile; excite, fascinate, titillate, intrigue.

tantamount adjective *this behaviour is tantamount to mutiny:* **equivalent to**, equal to, as good as, more or less, much the same as, comparable to, on a par with, commensurate with.

tantrum noun **fit (of temper/rage)**, outburst, pet, paroxysm, frenzy, (bad) mood, huff, scene; informal paddy, wax, wobbly; N. Amer. informal hissy fit.

tap¹ noun **1** *she turned the tap on:* **valve**, stopcock, cock, spout; N. Amer. faucet, spigot. **2** *the Act gave the Home Secretary the power to authorize phone taps:* **surveillance**, monitoring, intercept; bug.
verb **1** *their telephones were tapped:* **bug**, monitor. **2** *the resources were to be tapped for our benefit:* **draw on**, exploit, milk, mine, use, utilize, turn to account.
∎ **on tap 1** *beers on tap:* on draught, cask-conditioned, real-ale, from the barrel/cask/keg. **2** (informal) *trained staff are on tap at all times:* on hand, at hand, available, ready, handy, accessible, standing by.

tap² verb **1** *she tapped on the door:* **knock**, rap, strike, beat, drum. **2** *Dad tapped me on the knee:* **pat**, hit, strike, slap, jab, poke, dig.
noun **1** *there was a sharp tap at the door:* **knock**, rap. **2** *Jack was startled by a tap on the shoulder:* **pat**, blow, slap, jab, poke, dig.

tape noun **1** *she produced a package tied with tape:* **binding**, ribbon, string, braid. **2** *secure the bandage with tape:* **adhesive tape**, sticky tape, masking tape; trademark Sellotape. **3** *they listened to tapes:* **(audio) cassette**, (tape) recording, audio tape; reel, spool; video.
verb **1** *a card was taped to the lid of the box:* **bind**, stick, fix, fasten, secure, attach. **2** *police taped his confession:* **record**, tape-record; video.

taper verb **1** *the leaves taper at the tip:* **narrow**, thin (out), come to a point, attenuate. **2** *the meetings soon tapered off:* **decrease**, lessen, dwindle, diminish, reduce, decline, die down, peter out, wane, ebb, slacken (off), fall off, let up, thin out.
– OPPOSITES thicken, increase.

target noun **1** *the targets are positioned at a range of 200 yards:* **mark**, bullseye, goal. **2** *eagles can spot their targets from half a mile:* **prey**, quarry, kill. **3** *they exceeded their profit target last year:* **objective**, goal, aim, end; plan, intention, intent, design, aspiration, ambition, ideal, desire, wish. **4** *she was the target for a wave of abuse from the press:* **victim**, butt, recipient, focus, object, subject.
verb **1** *he was targeted by a gunman:* **pick out**, single out, earmark, fix on; attack, aim at. **2** *the product is targeted at a very specific market:* **aim**, direct, level, intend, focus.
∎ **on target 1** *the striker was bang on target:* accurate, precise, unerring, sure, on the mark; Brit. informal spot on. **2** *the project was on target:* on schedule, on track, on course, on time.

tariff noun **tax**, duty, toll, excise, levy, charge, rate, fee; price list.

tarnish verb **1** *gold does not tarnish easily:* **discolour**, rust, oxidize, corrode, stain, dull, blacken. **2** *he felt that this behaviour tarnished his reputation:* **sully**, blacken, stain, blemish, blot, taint, soil,

t

ruin, disgrace, mar, damage, harm, hurt, undermine; literary besmirch.
– OPPOSITES polish, enhance.
noun *this will not overcome the tarnish on his reputation:* **smear**, stain, blemish, blot, taint, stigma.

tart[1] noun *a jam tart:* **pastry**, flan, tartlet, quiche, pie.

tart[2] verb (informal) **1** *she tarted herself up for the evening:* **dress up**, make up, smarten up, preen oneself, beautify oneself, groom oneself; informal doll oneself up, titivate oneself. **2** *we must tart this place up a bit:* **decorate**, renovate, refurbish, redecorate; smarten up; informal do up, fix up.

tart[3] adjective **1** *choose an apple that is quite tart:* **sour**, sharp, acid, acidic, zesty, tangy, piquant; lemony, acetic. **2** *she regretted her rather tart reply:* **acerbic**, sharp, biting, cutting, astringent, caustic, trenchant, incisive, barbed, scathing, sarcastic.
– OPPOSITES sweet, kind.

task noun *she has set herself a daunting task:* **job**, duty, chore, charge, assignment, detail, mission, engagement, occupation, undertaking, exercise, business, responsibility, burden, endeavour, enterprise, venture.
■ **take someone to task** *he took some experts to task for their optimistic predictions:* **rebuke**, reprimand, reprove, reproach, remonstrate with, upbraid, scold, berate, lecture, censure, criticize, admonish, chide, chasten, arraign; informal tell off, bawl out, give someone a dressing-down; Brit. informal tick off; formal castigate.

taste noun **1** *a cheese with a distinctive sharp taste:* **flavour**, savour, relish, tang, smack. **2** *would you care for a taste of brandy?* **mouthful**, drop, bit, sip, nip, swallow, touch, soupçon, dash, modicum. **3** *honey is too sweet for my taste:* **palate**, taste buds, appetite, stomach. **4** *a millionaire with a taste for adventure:* **liking**, love, fondness, fancy, desire, preference, penchant, predilection, inclination, partiality; hankering, appetite, hunger, thirst, relish. **5** *this was my first taste of prison:* **experience**, impression; exposure to, contact with, involvement with. **6** *the house was furnished with immense taste:* **judgement**, discrimination, discernment, tastefulness, refinement, finesse, elegance, grace, style. **7** *the photo was rejected on grounds of taste:* **decorum**, propriety, etiquette, politeness, delicacy, nicety, sensitivity, discretion, tastefulness.
– OPPOSITES dislike.
verb **1** *Adam tasted the wine:* **sample**, test, try; sip. **2** *he could taste blood:* **perceive**, discern, make out, detect, distinguish. **3** *a beer that tasted of cashews:* **have a flavour**, savour, smack, be reminiscent; suggest. **4** *it'll be good to taste real coffee again:* **consume**, drink, partake of, have, enjoy; eat, devour. **5** *he tasted defeat for the first time:* **experience**, encounter, come face to

face with, come up against, undergo; know.

tasteful adjective **1** *the decor is simple and tasteful:* **aesthetically pleasing**, in good taste, refined, cultured, elegant, stylish, smart, chic, attractive, exquisite. **2** *this video is erotic but tasteful:* **decorous**, proper, seemly, respectable, appropriate, modest.
– OPPOSITES tasteless, improper.

tasteless adjective **1** *the vegetables are tasteless:* **flavourless**, bland, insipid, unappetizing, savourless, watery, weak. **2** *there was tasteless leather panelling everywhere:* **vulgar**, crude, tawdry, garish, gaudy, loud, trashy, showy, ostentatious, cheap, inelegant; informal flash, flashy, tacky, kitsch; Brit. informal naff. **3** *this was a tasteless remark:* **crude**, vulgar, indelicate, uncouth, crass, tactless, undiplomatic, indiscreet, inappropriate, offensive.
– OPPOSITES tasty, tasteful, seemly.

tasty adjective **delicious**, palatable, luscious, mouth-watering, delectable, toothsome, flavoursome, flavourful; appetizing, tempting; informal yummy, scrummy, scrumptious, finger-licking, moreish.
– OPPOSITES bland.

tatters plural noun *the satin had frayed to tatters:* **rags**, scraps, shreds, bits, pieces, ribbons.
■ **in tatters 1** *his clothes were in tatters:* **ragged**, tattered, torn, ripped, frayed, in pieces, worn out, moth-eaten, falling to pieces, threadbare. **2** *her marriage is in tatters:* **in ruins**, on the rocks, destroyed, finished, devastated.

taunt noun *he ignored the taunts of his classmates:* **jeer**, jibe, sneer, insult, barb, catcall; (**taunts**) teasing, provocation, goading, derision, mockery; informal dig, put-down.
verb *she taunted him about his job:* **jeer at**, sneer at, scoff at, poke fun at, make fun of, get at, insult, tease, chaff, torment, goad, ridicule, deride, mock, heckle; N. Amer. ride; informal rib, needle, rag, guy.

taut adjective **1** *the rope was pulled taut:* **tight**, rigid. **2** *his muscles remained taut:* **flexed**, tense, hard, solid, firm, rigid, stiff.
– OPPOSITES slack, relaxed.

tavern noun **bar**, inn, hostelry, taphouse; Brit. pub, public house; informal watering hole; Brit. informal local, boozer; dated alehouse.

tawdry adjective **gaudy**, flashy, showy, garish, loud; tasteless, vulgar, trashy, junky, cheap (and nasty), cheapjack, shoddy, shabby, gimcrack; informal rubbishy, tacky, kitsch.
– OPPOSITES tasteful.

tax noun **duty**, excise, customs, dues; levy, tariff, toll, charge, fee.
– OPPOSITES rebate.
verb **1** *they tax foreign companies more harshly:* **charge (duty on)**. **2** *his constant whining taxed her patience:* **strain**, stretch,

try; wear out, exhaust, sap, drain, weary, weaken.

taxing adjective **demanding**, exacting, challenging, burdensome, arduous, onerous, difficult, hard, tough, laborious, back-breaking, strenuous, rigorous, punishing; tiring, exhausting, wearing, stressful; informal murderous.
– OPPOSITES easy.

teach verb **1** *she teaches small children:* **educate**, instruct, school, tutor, coach, train; verse, indoctrinate; drill, discipline. **2** *I taught English:* **give lessons in**, lecture in, be a teacher of. **3** *teach your teenager how to negotiate:* **train**, show, guide, instruct, demonstrate.

teacher noun **educator**, tutor, instructor, master, mistress, schoolmarm, governess; coach, trainer; lecturer, professor, don; guide, mentor, guru, counsellor; Austral./NZ informal chalkie, schoolie; formal pedagogue.

team noun **1** *the company's new sales team | the cricket team:* **group**, squad, company, party, crew, troupe, band, side, line-up; informal bunch, gang, posse. **2** *a team of horses:* **pair**, yoke, duo, set.
verb **1** *the horses are teamed in pairs:* **harness**, yoke, hitch, couple. **2** *team a T-shirt with matching shorts:* **match**, coordinate, complement, pair up.
■ **team up** *she teamed up with another artist for an exhibition:* join (forces), collaborate, get together, work together; unite, combine, cooperate, link, associate, club together.

tear¹ verb **1** *I tore the letter into pieces:* **rip up**, pull to pieces, shred. **2** *his flesh was torn:* **lacerate**, cut (open), gash, slash, scratch, hack, pierce, stab; injure, wound. **3** *the traumas tore her family apart:* **split**, break; divide, sever, disunite, rupture; literary rend, sunder. **4** *Gina tore the book from his hands:* **snatch**, grab, seize, rip, wrench, wrest, pull, pluck; informal yank. **5** (informal) *Jack tore down the street:* **sprint**, race, run, dart, rush, dash, hasten, hurry, hare, bolt, fly, career, charge, shoot, hurtle, speed, whizz, zoom, go like lightning, go like the wind; informal pelt, scoot, hotfoot it, leg it, belt, zip, whip; Brit. informal go like the clappers, bomb, bucket; N. Amer. informal hightail it.
– OPPOSITES unite.
noun *there was a tear in her dress:* **rip**, hole, split, slash, slit; ladder, snag.
■ **tear something down** demolish, knock down, raze (to the ground), flatten, level, bulldoze; dismantle, disassemble.

tear² noun *tears in her eyes:* **teardrop**.
■ **in tears** crying, weeping, sobbing, wailing, howling, bawling, whimpering; tearful, upset; informal weepy, teary, blubbing, blubbering.

tearaway noun **hooligan**, hoodlum, ruffian, lout, rowdy, roughneck; Austral. larrikin; Brit. informal yob, yobbo; Austral./NZ informal roughie.

tearful adjective **1** *Georgina was tearful:* **close to tears**, emotional, upset, distressed, sad, unhappy; in tears, crying, weeping, sobbing, snivelling; informal weepy, teary; formal lachrymose. **2** *it was a tearful farewell:* **emotional**, upsetting, distressing, sad, heartbreaking, sorrowful; poignant, moving, touching, tear-jerking.
– OPPOSITES cheerful.

tease verb *the girl teased me for being so vain:* **make fun of**, poke fun at, laugh at; taunt, bait, goad, pick on; deride, mock, ridicule; informal take the mickey out of, rag, send up, rib, josh, have on, pull someone's leg; Brit. informal wind up; N. Amer. informal pull someone's chain, razz; Austral./NZ informal poke mullock at.

technical adjective **1** *an important technical achievement:* **practical**, scientific, technological, high-tech. **2** *this might seem very technical, but it isn't:* **specialist**, specialized, scientific; complex, complicated, esoteric. **3** *a technical fault:* **mechanical**; operational.

technique noun **1** *there are different techniques for solving the problem:* **method**, approach, procedure, system, modus operandi, MO, way; means, strategy, tack, tactic, line; routine, practice. **2** *I was impressed with his technique:* **skill**, ability, proficiency, expertise, mastery, talent, genius, artistry, craftsmanship; aptitude, adroitness, deftness, dexterity, facility, competence; informal know-how.

tedious adjective *another tedious lecture to go to:* **boring**, dull, monotonous, repetitive, unvaried, uneventful; characterless, colourless, lifeless, insipid, uninteresting, unexciting, uninspiring, flat, bland, dry, stale, tired, lacklustre, stodgy, dreary, humdrum, mundane; mind-numbing, soul-destroying, wearisome, tiring, tiresome, irksome, trying, frustrating; informal deadly, not up to much; Brit. informal samey; N. Amer. informal dullsville.
– OPPOSITES exciting.

tedium noun **monotony**, boredom, ennui, uniformity, routine, dreariness, dryness, banality, insipidity.
– OPPOSITES variety.

teem¹ verb *the pond was teeming with fish:* **be full of**, be filled with, be alive with, be brimming with, abound in, be swarming with; be packed with, be crawling with, be overrun with, bristle with, seethe with, be thick with; informal be jam-packed with, be chock-a-block with, be chock-full with.

teem² verb *the rain was teeming down:* **pour**, pelt, tip, beat, lash, sheet; come down in torrents, rain cats and dogs; informal be chucking it down; Brit. informal bucket down.

teenage adjective **adolescent**, teenaged, youthful, young, juvenile; informal teen.

teenager noun **adolescent**, youth, young person, minor, juvenile; informal teen, teeny-bopper.

teeny adjective (informal). See TINY.

t

teeter verb 1 *Daisy teetered towards them:* **totter**, wobble, toddle, sway, stagger, stumble, reel, lurch, pitch. 2 *the situation teetered between tragedy and farce:* **see-saw**, veer, fluctuate, oscillate, swing, alternate, waver.

teetotal adjective **abstinent**, abstemious; sober, dry; informal on the wagon.
– OPPOSITES alcoholic.

telepathic adjective **psychic**, clairvoyant.

telepathy noun **mind-reading**, thought transference; extrasensory perception, ESP; clairvoyance, sixth sense; psychometry.

telephone noun *Sophie picked up the telephone:* **phone**, handset, receiver; informal blower; N. Amer. informal horn.
verb *he telephoned me last night:* **phone**, call, dial; get, reach; Brit. ring (up); informal call up, give someone a buzz, get on the blower to; give someone a bell, give someone a tinkle; N. Amer. informal get someone on the horn.

televise verb **broadcast**, screen, air, telecast; transmit, relay.

television noun **TV**; informal the small screen; Brit. informal telly, the box; N. Amer. informal the tube.

tell verb 1 *why didn't you tell me before?* **inform**, notify, apprise, let know, make aware, acquaint with, advise, put in the picture, brief, fill in; alert, warn; informal clue in/up. 2 *she told the story slowly:* **relate**, recount, narrate, unfold, report, recite, describe, sketch, weave, spin; utter, voice, state, declare, communicate, impart, divulge. 3 *she told him to leave:* **instruct**, order, command, direct, charge, enjoin, call on, require. 4 *I tell you, I did nothing wrong:* **assure**, promise, give one's word, swear, guarantee. 5 *the figures tell a different story:* **reveal**, show, indicate, be evidence of, disclose, convey, signify. 6 *promise you won't tell?* **give the game away**, talk, tell tales, tattle; informal spill the beans, let the cat out of the bag, blab; Brit. informal blow the gaff. 7 *she was bound to tell on him:* **inform on**, tell tales on, give away, denounce, sell out; informal split on, blow the whistle on, rat on, peach on, squeal on; Brit. informal grass on, sneak on, shop; N. Amer. informal finger; Austral./NZ informal dob on. 8 *it was hard to tell what he said:* **ascertain**, determine, work out, make out, deduce, discern, perceive, see, identify, recognize, understand, comprehend; informal figure out; Brit. informal suss out. 9 *he couldn't tell one from the other:* **distinguish**, differentiate, discriminate. 10 *the strain began to tell on him:* **take its toll**, leave its mark; affect.
■ **tell someone off** (informal). See REPRIMAND verb.

teller noun 1 *the cheque is handed to the teller, accompanied by a deposit slip:* **cashier**, clerk. 2 *such tales held more truth than their tellers realized:* **narrator**; raconteur storyteller, anecdotalist.

telling adjective *this is a telling critique of the military mind:* **revealing**, significant, weighty, important, meaningful, influential, striking, potent, powerful, compelling.
– OPPOSITES insignificant.

telling-off noun (informal). See REPRIMAND noun.

telltale adjective *I noticed the telltale blush on her face:* **revealing**, revelatory, suggestive, meaningful, significant, meaning; informal giveaway.
noun *'Sue did it,' said Nigel the telltale:* **informer**, whistle-blower, N. Amer. tattletale; informal snitch, squealer; Brit. informal sneak; Scottish informal clype.

temerity noun *a customs officer once had the temerity to stop her and search her baggage:* **audacity**, nerve, effrontery, impudence, impertinence, cheek, gall, presumption; daring; informal face, front, (brass) neck, chutzpah.

temper noun 1 *he walked out in a temper:* **(fit of) rage**, fury, fit of pique, tantrum, (bad) mood, pet, sulk, huff; Brit. informal strop, paddy; N. Amer. informal hissy fit. 2 *this was an uncharacteristic display of temper:* **anger**, fury, rage, annoyance, vexation, irritation, irritability, ill humour, spleen, pique, petulance, testiness, tetchiness, crabbiness; Brit. informal stroppiness; literary ire. 3 *she struggled to keep her temper:* **composure**, equanimity, self-control, self-possession, sangfroid, calm, good humour; informal cool.
verb 1 *the steel is tempered by heat treatment:* **harden**, strengthen, toughen, fortify, anneal. 2 *their idealism is tempered with realism:* **moderate**, modify, modulate, mitigate, alleviate, reduce, weaken, lighten, soften.
■ **lose one's temper** get angry, fly into a rage, erupt, lose control, go berserk, breathe fire, flare up, boil over; informal go mad, go crazy, go bananas, have a fit, see red, fly off the handle, blow one's top, do one's nut, hit the roof, go off the deep end, go ape, flip, lose one's rag, freak out; Brit. informal go spare, go crackers, throw a wobbly.

temperament noun **disposition**, nature, character, personality, make-up, constitution, mind, spirit; stamp, mettle, mould; mood, frame of mind, attitude, outlook, humour.

temperamental adjective 1 *a temperamental chef:* **volatile**, excitable, emotional, mercurial, capricious, erratic, unpredictable, changeable, inconsistent; hot-headed, fiery, quick-tempered, irritable, irascible, impatient; touchy, moody, sensitive, oversensitive, highly strung, neurotic, melodramatic. 2 *he had a temperamental dislike of conflict:* **inherent**, innate, natural, inborn, constitutional, deep-rooted, ingrained, congenital.
– OPPOSITES placid.

temperance noun **teetotalism**, abstinence, abstention, sobriety, self-restraint; prohibition.
– OPPOSITES alcoholism.

temperate adjective **1** *I prefer more temperate climates:* **mild**, clement, benign, gentle, balmy. **2** *he was temperate in his consumption:* **self-restrained**, restrained, moderate, self-controlled, disciplined; abstemious, self-denying, austere, ascetic; teetotal, abstinent.
– OPPOSITES extreme.

tempest noun **storm**, gale, hurricane; tornado, whirlwind, cyclone, typhoon.

tempestuous adjective **1** *the fleet sailed along the coast of England and across the tempestuous Irish Sea:* **stormy**, blustery, squally, wild, turbulent, windy, gusty, blowy, rainy; foul, nasty, inclement. **2** *the story centres on the tempestuous relationship between a father and his three daughters:* **turbulent**, stormy, tumultuous, wild, lively, heated, explosive, feverish, frenetic, frenzied. **3** *the outspoken and tempestuous Galileo:* **emotional**, passionate, impassioned, fiery, intense; temperamental, volatile, excitable, mercurial, capricious, unpredictable, quick-tempered.
– OPPOSITES calm, peaceful, placid.

temple noun **house of God**, shrine, sanctuary; church, cathedral, mosque, synagogue, gurdwara, mandir, pagoda.

tempo noun **1** *the tempo of the music quickened:* **cadence**, speed, rhythm, beat, time, pulse; measure, metre. **2** *the frantic tempo of life in Western society:* **pace**, rate, speed, velocity.

temporal adjective *his intellectual achievements and the temporal power he has secured:* **secular**, non-spiritual, worldly, profane, material, mundane, earthly, terrestrial; non-religious, lay.
– OPPOSITES spiritual.

temporarily adverb **1** *the girl was temporarily placed with a foster-family:* **for the time being**, for the moment, for now, for the present, in the interim, in/for the meantime, in the meanwhile; provisionally, pro tem; informal for the minute. **2** *he was temporarily blinded by the light:* **briefly**, for a short time, momentarily, fleetingly.
– OPPOSITES permanently.

temporary adjective **1** *we were living in temporary accommodation:* **short-term**, interim, makeshift, stopgap. **2** *the temporary captain:* **acting**, provisional, stand-in, caretaker. **3** *a temporary loss of self-control:* **brief**, short-lived, momentary, fleeting, passing.
– OPPOSITES permanent, lasting.

tempt verb **1** *the manager tried to tempt him to stay:* **entice**, persuade, convince, inveigle, induce, cajole, coax, woo; informal sweet-talk. **2** *more customers are being tempted by credit:* **allure**, attract, appeal to, whet the appetite of; lure, seduce, beguile, tantalize, draw.
– OPPOSITES discourage, deter.

temptation noun **1** *Mary resisted the temptation to answer back:* **desire**, urge, itch, impulse, inclination. **2** *the temptations of London:* **lure**, allurement, enticement, seduction, attraction, draw, pull; siren song.

tempting adjective **enticing**, alluring, attractive, appealing, inviting, captivating, seductive, beguiling, tantalizing; irresistible.
– OPPOSITES off-putting, uninviting.

ten cardinal number **decade**.

tenable adjective *ideas that, 150 years later, are no longer tenable:* **defensible**, justifiable, supportable, sustainable, arguable, able to hold water, reasonable, rational, sound, viable, plausible, credible.
– OPPOSITES indefensible.

tenacious adjective *you're tenacious and you get at the truth:* **persevering**, persistent, determined, dogged, strong-willed, tireless, indefatigable, resolute, patient, purposeful, unflagging, staunch, steadfast, untiring, unwavering, unswerving, unshakeable, unyielding, insistent; N. Amer. rock-ribbed.
– OPPOSITES irresolute.

tenacity noun **persistence**, determination, perseverance, doggedness, strength of purpose, bulldog spirit, tirelessness, indefatigability, resolution, resoluteness, resolve, firmness, patience, purposefulness, staunchness, steadfastness, staying power, application.

tenancy noun **occupancy**, occupation, period of occupancy/occupation, residence, habitation, holding, possession; tenure, lease, rental, leasehold.

tenant noun **occupant**, resident, inhabitant; leaseholder, lessee, renter; Brit. occupier, sitting tenant.
– OPPOSITES owner, freeholder.

tend¹ verb **1** *I tend to get very involved in my work:* **be inclined**, be apt, be disposed, be prone, be liable, have a tendency, have a propensity. **2** *younger voters tended towards the left:* **incline**, lean, gravitate, move; prefer, favour; N. Amer. trend.

tend² verb *alone again, she tended her garden:* **look after**, take care of, care for, minister to, attend to, see to, wait on; watch over, keep an eye on, mind, protect, watch, guard; nurse, nurture, cherish.
– OPPOSITES neglect.

tendency noun **1** *his tendency to take the law into his own hands:* **propensity**, proclivity, proneness, aptness, likelihood, inclination, disposition, predisposition, bent, leaning, penchant, predilection, susceptibility, liability; readiness; habit. **2** *this tendency towards cohabitation:* **trend**, movement, drift, swing, gravitation, direction, course, bias.

tender¹ adjective **1** *he is a gentle, tender man:* **caring**, kind, kindly, kind-hearted,

t

soft-hearted, tender-hearted, compassionate, gentle, mild, benevolent, generous, giving, humane. **2** *he planted a tender kiss on her forehead:* **affectionate**, fond, loving, emotional, warm, gentle, soft; informal lovey-dovey. **3** *enjoy an album of tender love songs:* **romantic**, sentimental, emotional, emotive, touching, moving, poignant; Brit. informal soppy. **4** *simmer until the meat is tender:* **soft**; succulent, juicy; tenderized. **5** *these tender young plants need lots of care:* **delicate**, easily damaged, fragile. **6** *her ankle was swollen and tender:* **sore**, painful, sensitive, inflamed, raw, red, chafed, bruised; hurting, aching, throbbing, smarting. **7** *the tender age of fifteen:* **young**, youthful; impressionable, inexperienced, immature, unsophisticated, unseasoned, juvenile, callow, green, raw; informal wet behind the ears.
– OPPOSITES hard-hearted, callous, tough.

tender² verb **1** *she tendered her resignation:* **offer**, proffer, present, put forward, propose, suggest, advance, submit, extend, give, render; hand in. **2** *two firms of interior decorators tendered for the work:* **put in a bid**, bid, quote, give an estimate.
noun *six contractors were invited to submit tenders:* **bid**, offer, quotation, quote, estimate, price; proposal, submission.

tenderness noun **1** *I felt an enormous tenderness for her:* **affection**, fondness, love, devotion, emotion, sentiment. **2** *with unexpected tenderness, he told her what had happened:* **kindness**, kindliness, kind-heartedness, tender-heartedness, compassion, care, concern, sympathy, gentleness, benevolence, generosity.
3 *abdominal tenderness:* **soreness**, pain, inflammation, bruising; ache, aching, smarting, throbbing.

tenet noun *Hitler's values negated the basic tenets of civilization:* **principle**, belief, doctrine, precept, creed, credo, article of faith, dogma, canon; theory, thesis, conviction, idea, view, opinion, position, hypothesis, postulation; (**tenets**) ideology, code of belief, teaching(s).

tenor noun **1** *White House officials played down the revolutionary tenor of the President's comments:* **sense**, meaning, theme, drift, thread, import, purport, intent, intention, thrust, significance, message; gist, essence, substance, spirit. **2** *it was clear from the whole tenor of the case that the tribunal was not satisfied:* **course**, direction, movement, drift, current, trend.

tense adjective **1** *she rubbed the tense muscles of his neck:* **taut**, tight, rigid, stretched, strained, stiff. **2** *Loretta was feeling tense and irritable:* **anxious**, nervous, on edge, edgy, strained, stressed, under pressure, agitated, ill at ease, uneasy, restless, worked up, keyed up, overwrought, jumpy, on tenterhooks, with one's stomach in knots, worried, apprehensive, panicky; Brit. nervy;

informal a bundle of nerves, jittery, twitchy, uptight, stressed out; N. Amer. informal spooky, squirrelly. **3** *it was a tense moment for everyone:* **nerve-racking**, stressful, anxious, worrying, fraught, charged, strained, nail-biting, difficult, uneasy, uncomfortable; exciting.
– OPPOSITES slack, calm.
verb *Hebden tensed his muscles:* **tighten**, tauten, tense up, contract, brace, stiffen; screw up, knot, strain, stretch; N. Amer. squinch up.
– OPPOSITES relax.

tension noun **1** *I adjusted the tension of the rope:* **tightness**, tautness, rigidity; pull, traction. **2** *the tension was unbearable:* **strain**, stress, anxiety, pressure; suspense, uncertainty, anticipation, excitement; informal butterflies (in one's stomach), collywobbles. **3** *months of tension between the military and the government:* **strained relations**, strain; ill feeling, friction, antagonism, antipathy, hostility, enmity.

tentative adjective **1** *tentative arrangements | a tentative conclusion:* **provisional**, unconfirmed, pencilled in, preliminary, to be confirmed, TBC, subject to confirmation; speculative, conjectural, untried, unproven, exploratory, experimental, trial, test, pilot. **2** *he took a few tentative steps:* **hesitant**, uncertain, cautious, timid, hesitating, faltering, shaky, unsteady, halting; wavering, unsure.
– OPPOSITES definite, confident.

tenterhooks
■ **on tenterhooks** *she had been on tenterhooks all night, waiting for Joe to return:* **in suspense**, waiting with bated breath; anxious, nervous, nervy, apprehensive, worried, worried sick, on edge, edgy, tense, strained, stressed, agitated, restless, worked up, keyed up, jumpy, with one's stomach in knots, with one's heart in one's mouth, like a cat on a hot tin roof; informal with butterflies in one's stomach, jittery, twitchy, in a state, uptight; N. Amer. informal spooky, squirrelly.

tenuous adjective *the tenuous link between interest rates and investment:* **slight**, insubstantial, flimsy, weak, doubtful, dubious, questionable, suspect; vague, nebulous, hazy.
– OPPOSITES convincing, strong.

tenure noun **1** *residents should at least have security of tenure:* **tenancy**, occupancy, occupation, residence; possession, ownership. **2** *his tenure as Secretary of State for Industry:* **incumbency**, term (of office), period (of/in office), time (in office).

tepid adjective **1** *tepid water:* **lukewarm**, warmish, slightly warm; at room temperature. **2** *his speech received a tepid response:* **unenthusiastic**, apathetic, half-hearted, indifferent, cool, lukewarm, uninterested; informal unenthused.
– OPPOSITES hot, cold, enthusiastic.

term noun **1** *a dictionary of scientific and technical terms:* **word**, expression, phrase, turn of phrase, idiom; name, title, designation, label. **2** *a protest in the strongest possible terms:* **language**, phraseology, terminology; words, phrases, expressions. **3** *the terms of the contract:* **conditions**, stipulations, specifications, provisions, provisos; restrictions, qualifications; particulars, details, points. **4** *a policy offering more favourable terms:* **rates**, prices, charges, costs, fees; tariff. **5** *the President is elected for a four-year term:* **period**, time, spell, stint, duration; stretch, run; period of office, incumbency. **6** *the summer term:* **session**; N. Amer. semester, trimester, quarter.
verb *he has been termed the father of modern theology:* **call**, name, entitle, title, style, designate, describe as, dub, label, tag; nickname.
■ **come to terms with** *she eventually came to terms with her situation:* accept, come to accept, reconcile oneself to, learn to live with, become resigned to, make the best of; face up to.

terminal adjective **1** *a terminal illness:* **incurable**, untreatable, inoperable; fatal, mortal, deadly. **2** *terminal patients:* **dying**, near death; incurable. **3** *a terminal bonus may be payable when a policy matures:* **final**, last, concluding, closing, end.
noun **1** *a railway terminal:* **station**, last stop, end of the line; depot; Brit. terminus. **2** *a computer terminal:* **workstation**, VDU, visual display unit, monitor.

terminate verb **1** *the bosses decided to terminate his contract on December 31:* **end**, bring to a close/conclusion, close, conclude, finish, stop, put an end to, wind up, discontinue, cease, abort, axe; informal pull the plug on. **2** *the train will terminate in Stratford:* **end its journey**, finish up, stop. **3** *the consultant assumed I would terminate the pregnancy:* **abort**, end.
– OPPOSITES begin, start, continue.

termination noun **1** *the termination of a contract:* **ending**, end, closing, close, conclusion, finish, stopping, winding up, discontinuance, discontinuation; cancellation, dissolution; informal wind-up. **2** *she had a termination:* **abortion**.
– OPPOSITES start, beginning.

terminology noun **phraseology**, terms, expressions, words, language, parlance, vocabulary, nomenclature; usage, idiom; jargon, cant, argot; informal lingo, -speak, -ese.

terminus noun (Brit.) **station**, last stop, end of the line, terminal; depot, garage.

terrain noun **land**, ground, territory; topography, landscape, countryside, country.

terrestrial adjective **earthly**, worldly, mundane, earthbound.

terrible adjective **1** *a terrible crime* | *terrible injuries:* **dreadful**, awful, appalling, horrific, horrifying, horrible, horrendous, atrocious, abominable, abhorrent, frightful, shocking, hideous, ghastly, grim, dire, unspeakable, gruesome, monstrous, sickening, heinous, vile; serious, grave, acute; formal grievous. **2** *there was a terrible smell in the room:* **nasty**, disgusting, awful, dreadful, ghastly, horrid, horrible, vile, foul, abominable, frightful, loathsome, revolting, repulsive, odious, nauseating, repellent, horrendous, hideous, appalling; informal gruesome, putrid, yucky, sick-making, God-awful, gross; Brit. informal beastly. **3** *he was in terrible pain:* **severe**, extreme, intense, excruciating, agonizing, unbearable, intolerable, unendurable. **4** *that's a terrible thing to say:* **unkind**, nasty, unpleasant, foul, obnoxious, vile, contemptible, despicable, wretched, shabby; spiteful, mean, malicious, poisonous, mean-spirited, cruel, hateful, hurtful; unfair, uncharitable, uncalled for, below the belt, unwarranted; Brit. informal beastly. **5** *the film was terrible:* **(really) bad**, dreadful, awful, frightful, atrocious, hopeless, poor; informal pathetic, pitiful, useless, lousy, appalling, abysmal, dire; Brit. informal duff, chronic, poxy, rubbish, pants. **6** (informal) *the place was in a terrible mess* | *you're a terrible flirt:* **real**, proper, awful, dreadful, frightful, shocking; informal impossible, fearful; Brit. informal right; incorrigible, outrageous. **7** *I feel terrible—I've been in bed all day:* **ill**, poorly, sick, queasy, nauseous, nauseated; faint, dizzy; informal rough, lousy, awful, dreadful; Brit. informal grotty, ropy. **8** *he still feels terrible about what he did to John:* **guilty**, conscience-stricken, remorseful, guilt-ridden, ashamed, chastened, contrite, sorry.
– OPPOSITES minor, slight, pleasant, wonderful.

terribly adverb **1** (informal) *she's terribly upset:* **very**, extremely, really, terrifically, tremendously, immensely, thoroughly, dreadfully, exceptionally, remarkably, extraordinarily, exceedingly; N. English right; informal awfully, seriously, majorly; Brit. informal jolly, ever so, dead, well; N. Amer. informal real, mighty, awful; informal, dated frightfully. **2** *he played terribly:* **very badly**, atrociously, awfully, dreadfully, appallingly, execrably; informal abysmally, pitifully, diabolically. **3** (informal) *I shall miss you terribly:* **very much**, greatly, a great deal, a lot, lots; informal loads.

terrific adjective **1** *there was a terrific bang:* **tremendous**, huge, massive, gigantic, colossal, mighty, great, prodigious, formidable; intense, extreme, extraordinary; informal mega, whopping great, humongous; Brit. informal whacking great, ginormous. **2** (informal) *a terrific game of top-quality football* | *you look terrific:* **marvellous**, wonderful, sensational, outstanding, superb, excellent, first-rate, first-class, dazzling, out of this world, breathtaking;

t

informal great, fantastic, fabulous, fab, mega, super, ace, magic, cracking, cool, wicked, awesome; Brit. informal brilliant, brill, smashing; Austral./NZ informal bonzer.

terrified adjective **petrified**, frightened, scared, scared/frightened to death, scared stiff, scared/frightened out of one's wits, scared witless, horrified, with one's heart in one's mouth, shaking in one's shoes.

terrify verb **petrify**, horrify, frighten, scare, scare/frighten to death, scare/frighten the living daylights out of, scare/frighten the life out of, scare/frighten someone out of their wits, scare witless, strike terror into, put the fear of God into; informal scare the pants off; Irish informal scare the bejesus out of.

territory noun **1** *a tiny British territory on the outskirts of Polynesia:* **area**, region, enclave; country, state, land, dependency, colony, dominion, protectorate, fief, possession, holding. **2** *the AWB were involved in guerrilla training on South African territory:* **terrain**, land, ground, countryside.

terror noun **1** *she screamed in terror:* **fear**, dread, horror, fear and trembling, fright, alarm, panic, shock. **2** *the terrors of her own mind:* **demon**, fiend, devil, monster; horror, nightmare. **3** (informal) *he turned out to be a right little terror:* **rascal**, devil, imp, monkey, horror; scallywag, mischief-maker; informal scamp; Brit. informal perisher; N. Amer. informal varmint.

terrorist noun guerrilla, paramilitary, hijacker, revolutionary, radical, freedom fighter; bomber, gunman.

terrorize verb **persecute**, victimize, torment, tyrannize, intimidate, menace, threaten, bully, browbeat; scare, frighten, terrify, petrify.

terse adjective *he issued a terse warning:* **brief**, short, to the point, concise, succinct, crisp, pithy, incisive, short and sweet, laconic, elliptical; brusque, abrupt, curt, clipped, blunt.
– OPPOSITES long-winded, polite.

test noun **1** *a series of scientific tests:* **trial**, experiment, pilot, try-out; check, examination, assessment, evaluation, appraisal, investigation, inspection, analysis, scrutiny, study, probe, exploration; screening. **2** *candidates may be required to take a test:* **exam**, examination; N. Amer. quiz. **3** *the test of a good sparkling wine is how long the bubbles last:* **criterion**, proof, indication, yardstick, touchstone, standard, measure, litmus test, acid test.
verb **1** *a small-scale prototype was tested:* **try out**, trial, put to the test, put through its paces, experiment on/with, pilot; check, examine, assess, evaluate, appraise, probe, explore; sample; screen. **2** *such behaviour would test any marriage:* **put a strain on**, strain, tax, try; stretch, challenge.

testament noun *an achievement which is a*

testament to his professionalism: **testimony**, witness, evidence, proof, attestation; demonstration, indication, exemplification; monument, tribute.

testify verb **1** *you may be required to testify in court:* **give evidence**, be a witness, appear. **2** *he testified that he had been threatened by a fellow officer:* **attest**, swear, state on oath, state, declare, assert, affirm; allege, submit, claim. **3** *the exhibits testify to the talents of the local sculptors:* **be evidence/proof of**, attest to, confirm, prove, bear out; show, demonstrate, bear witness to, indicate, reveal, bespeak.

testimonial noun **reference**, recommendation, commendation.

testimony noun **1** *Smith was in court to hear her testimony:* **evidence**, (sworn) statement, attestation, affidavit; declaration, assertion, affirmation; allegation, submission, claim; Law deposition. **2** *the work is a testimony to his professional commitment:* **testament**, proof, evidence, attestation, witness; confirmation; demonstration, indication.

testing adjective *it was a testing time for the organization:* **difficult**, challenging, tough, hard, demanding, taxing, stressful.
– OPPOSITES easy.

testy adjective. See TETCHY.

tetchy adjective **irritable**, cantankerous, irascible, bad-tempered, grumpy, grouchy, crotchety, crabby, testy, ill-tempered, ill-humoured, peevish, cross, fractious, pettish, crabbed, prickly, waspish; informal snappish, snappy, chippy; Brit. informal shirty, stroppy, narky, ratty; N. Amer. informal cranky, ornery.
– OPPOSITES good-humoured.

tête-à-tête noun **conversation**, chat, talk, heart-to-heart, one-on-one, one-to-one; informal confab, chinwag; Brit. informal natter; formal confabulation.

tether verb *the horse had been tethered to a post:* **tie (up)**, hitch, rope, chain; fasten, secure.
– OPPOSITES unleash.

text noun **1** *the pictures are clear and relate well to the text:* **words**, copy; content, body. **2** *a list of recommended texts:* **book**, textbook, publication, work; journal, periodical; set book/text. **3** *a text from the First Book of Samuel:* **passage**, extract, quotation, verse, line; reading.

textiles plural noun **fabrics**, cloths, materials.

texture noun **feel**, touch; appearance, finish, surface, grain; quality, consistency; weave, nap.

thank verb **express (one's) gratitude to**, express/offer/extend one's thanks to, say thank you to, show one's appreciation to.

thankful adjective **grateful**, filled with gratitude, relieved, pleased, glad.

thankless adjective *a thankless task:* **unenviable**, difficult, unpleasant, unrewarding; unappreciated, unrecognized,

thanks plural noun *they expressed their thanks and wished her well:* **gratitude**, appreciation; acknowledgement, recognition, credit.
exclamation *thanks for being so helpful:* **thank you**, many thanks, thanks very much, thanks a lot, thank you kindly, much obliged, much appreciated, bless you; informal cheers, thanks a million; Brit. informal ta.
■ **thanks to** *Scully survives, thanks to a bullet-proof vest:* as a result of, owing to, due to, because of, through, as a consequence of, on account of, by virtue of, by dint of.

thaw verb **melt**, unfreeze, soften, liquefy, dissolve; defrost; N. Amer. unthaw.
– OPPOSITES freeze.

theatre noun **1** *there's a good play on at the local theatre:* **playhouse**, auditorium, amphitheatre. **2** *what made you go into the theatre?* **acting**, performing, the stage; drama, the dramatic arts, dramaturgy; show business; informal the boards, show biz. **3** *the lecture theatre was packed:* **hall**, room, auditorium. **4** *they had 200,000 personnel in the theatre of war by December:* **scene**, arena, field, sphere.

theatrical adjective **1** *a theatrical career:* **stage**, dramatic, thespian, dramaturgical; show-business; informal showbiz. **2** *Henry looked over his shoulder with theatrical caution:* **exaggerated**, ostentatious, actressy, stagy, showy, melodramatic, overacted, overdone, histrionic, affected, mannered; informal hammy, ham, camp.

theft noun **robbery**, stealing, thieving, larceny, thievery, shoplifting, burglary, misappropriation, embezzlement; raid, hold-up; informal smash-and-grab; N. Amer. informal heist, stick-up.

theme noun **1** *the theme of her speech:* **subject**, topic, subject matter, matter, thesis, argument, text, thrust; thread, motif, keynote. **2** *the first violin takes up the theme:* **melody**, tune, air; motif, leitmotif.

then adverb **1** *I was living in Cairo then:* **at that time**, in those days; at that point (in time), at that moment, on that occasion. **2** *she won the first and then the second game:* **next**, after that, afterwards, subsequently. **3** *there's the money I'm owed, and then there's another problem:* **in addition**, also, besides, as well, additionally, on top of that, over and above that, moreover, furthermore, what's more, to boot; too.

theoretical adjective **1** *theoretical debate without supporting evidence is unscientific:* **conceptual**, intellectual, abstract, academic; speculative. **2** *netball involves physical contact, and therefore a theoretical risk:* **hypothetical**, notional, assumed, presumed, untested, unproven, unsubstantiated.
– OPPOSITES practical, real.

theorize verb **speculate**, conjecture, hypothesize, postulate, propose, posit, suppose.

theory noun **1** *I reckon that confirms my theory:* **hypothesis**, thesis, conjecture, supposition, speculation, postulation, postulate, proposition, premise, assumption, presupposition; opinion, view, belief, contention. **2** *modern economic theory | the theory of relativity:* **principles**, ideas, concepts; philosophy, ideology, science.
■ **in theory** *in theory this method is ideal:* in principle, on paper, in the abstract, all things being equal, in an ideal world; hypothetically.

therapeutic adjective **1** *the therapeutic effects of acupuncture:* **healing**, curative, remedial, medicinal, restorative, health-giving, reparative, corrective, beneficial, positive, good, salutary. **2** *he liked housework—it was therapeutic and helped relieve the stress:* **calming**, relaxing, restful, soothing; helpful, beneficial.
– OPPOSITES harmful, stressful.

therapist noun **psychologist**, psychotherapist, analyst, psychoanalyst, psychiatrist; informal shrink; Brit. humorous trick cyclist.

therapy noun **1** *a wide range of complementary therapies:* **treatment**, remedy, cure. **2** *he's currently in therapy:* **psychotherapy**, psychoanalysis, analysis.

thereabouts adverb **1** *the land thereabouts was all owned by the Vachel family:* **near there**, around there. **2** *they sold it for five million or thereabouts:* **approximately**, or so, give or take a bit, not far off; Brit. getting on for; N. Amer. informal in the ballpark of.

thereafter adverb **after that**, following that, afterwards, subsequently, then, next.
– OPPOSITES hitherto.

therefore adverb **consequently**, so, as a result, hence, thus, accordingly, for that reason, ergo.

thesis noun **1** *the central thesis of his lecture:* **theory**, contention, argument, line of argument, proposal, proposition, premise, assumption, hypothesis, postulation, supposition. **2** *he's researching his thesis at the moment:* **dissertation**, essay, paper, treatise, disquisition, composition, monograph, study; N. Amer. theme.

thick adjective **1** *the walls are five feet thick:* **in extent/diameter**, across, wide, broad, deep. **2** *his short, thick legs:* **stocky**, sturdy, chunky, hefty, thickset, beefy, meaty, big, solid; fat, stout, plump. **3** *a thick Aran sweater:* **chunky**, bulky, heavy, cable-knit; woollen, woolly. **4** *the thick summer vegetation:* **plentiful**, abundant, profuse, luxuriant, bushy, rich, riotous; rank, rampant; dense, close-packed, impenetrable, impassable. **5** *he smeared a thick paste over the wall:* **semi-solid**, firm, stiff, stiffened, heavy; clotted, coagulated, viscous, gelatinous; concentrated. **6** *a*

t

motorway pile-up in thick fog: **dense**, heavy, opaque, impenetrable, soupy, murky. **7** (informal) *he's a bit thick.* See **STUPID** sense 1. **8** *Guy's voice was thick with desire:* **husky**, hoarse, throaty, guttural, gravelly, rough. **9** *he spoke in a thick Scottish accent:* **obvious**, pronounced, marked, broad, strong, rich, decided, distinct.
– OPPOSITES thin, slender.
noun *he found himself in the thick of the crisis:* **midst**, centre, hub, middle, core, heart.

thicken verb **become thick/thicker**, stiffen, condense; solidify, set, gel, congeal, clot, coagulate, cake.

thicket noun **copse**, coppice, grove, brake, covert, clump; wood; Brit. spinney.

thickness noun **1** *the gateway is several feet in thickness:* **width**, breadth, depth, diameter. **2** *several thicknesses of limestone:* **layer**, stratum, seam, vein; sheet.

thickset adjective *a thickset man with a florid complexion:* **stocky**, sturdy, heavily built, well built, chunky, burly, strapping, brawny, solid, heavy, hefty, beefy, meaty.
– OPPOSITES slight.

thick-skinned adjective **insensitive**, unfeeling, tough, impervious, hardened, case-hardened; informal hard-boiled.
– OPPOSITES sensitive.

thief noun **robber**, burglar, housebreaker, cat burglar, shoplifter, pickpocket, sneak thief, mugger; embezzler, swindler; criminal, villain; kleptomaniac; informal crook.

thieve verb **steal**, take, purloin, help oneself to, snatch, pilfer; embezzle, misappropriate; have one's fingers/hand in the till; informal rob, swipe, nab, rip off, lift, liberate, filch, snaffle; Brit. informal nick, pinch, half-inch, whip, knock off, nobble; N. Amer. informal heist.

thieving noun **theft**, stealing, thievery, robbery, larceny, pilfering; burglary, shoplifting, embezzlement.

thin adjective **1** *a thin white line was painted on the wall:* **narrow**, fine, attenuated. **2** *she was wearing a thin cotton nightdress:* **lightweight**, light, fine, delicate, floaty, flimsy, diaphanous, gossamer, insubstantial; sheer, gauzy, filmy, transparent, see-through. **3** *a tall, thin woman dressed all in black:* **slim**, lean, slender, rangy, willowy, svelte, sylphlike, spare, slight; **skinny**, underweight, scrawny, scraggy, bony, angular, raw-boned, hollow-cheeked, gaunt, as thin as a rake, stick-like, skin-and-bones, emaciated, skeletal, wasted, pinched, undernourished, underfed; lanky, spindly, gangly, gangling, weedy; informal anorexic, like a bag of bones. **4** *he ran a hand over his thin grey hair:* **sparse**, scanty, wispy, thinning. **5** *I was offered a bowl of thin soup:* **watery**, weak, dilute, diluted; runny, sloppy. **6** *her thin voice trailed off:* **weak**, faint, feeble, small, soft; reedy, high-pitched. **7** *the plot of the movie is very thin:*

insubstantial, flimsy, slight, feeble, lame, poor, weak, tenuous, inadequate.
– OPPOSITES thick, broad, fat, abundant.
verb **1** *the paint must be thinned before use:* **dilute**, water down, weaken. **2** *the crowds were beginning to thin out:* **disperse**, dissipate, scatter; become less dense/numerous, decrease, diminish, dwindle.

thing noun **1** *the room was full of strange things:* **object**, article, item, artefact, commodity; device, gadget, instrument, utensil, tool, implement; entity, body; informal doodah, whatsit, whatchamacallit, thingummy, thingy, thingamabob, thingamajig; Brit. informal gubbins; N. Amer. informal doodad, dingus. **2** *I'll come back tomorrow to collect my things:* **belongings**, possessions, stuff, property, worldly goods, (personal) effects, paraphernalia, bits and pieces, bits and bobs; luggage, baggage, bags; informal gear, junk; Brit. informal clobber. **3** *he went to get his gardening things:* **equipment**, apparatus, gear, kit, tackle, stuff; implements, tools, utensils, paraphernalia; accoutrements. **4** *I've got several things to do today:* **activity**, act, action, deed, undertaking, exploit, feat; task, job, chore. **5** *I've got other things on my mind just now:* **thought**, notion, idea; concern, matter, worry, preoccupation. **6** *I keep remembering things he said:* **remark**, statement, comment, observation, declaration, pronouncement. **7** *quite a few odd things happened:* **incident**, episode, event, happening, occurrence, phenomenon. **8** *how are things with you?* **matters**, affairs, circumstances, conditions, relations; state of affairs, situation, life. **9** *one of the things I like about you is your optimism:* **characteristic**, quality, attribute, property, trait, feature, point, aspect, facet. **10** *there's another thing you should know:* **fact**, piece of information, point, detail, particular, factor. **11** *the thing is, I'm not sure if it's what I want:* **fact**, point, issue, problem. **12** *you lucky thing!* **person**, soul, creature, wretch; informal devil, beggar, bastard. **13** *Dora developed a thing about noise:* **phobia**, fear, dislike, aversion; obsession, fixation; complex, neurosis; informal hang-up, bee in one's bonnet. **14** *she had a thing about men who wore glasses:* **penchant**, preference, taste, inclination, partiality, predilection, soft spot, weakness, fancy, fondness, liking, love; fetish, obsession, fixation. **15** *books aren't really my thing:* **what one likes**, what interests one; informal one's cup of tea, one's bag, what turns one on. **16** *it's the latest thing:* **fashion**, trend.

think verb **1** *I think he's gone home:* **believe**, be of the opinion, be of the view, be under the impression; expect, imagine, anticipate; surmise, suppose, guess, fancy; conclude, determine, reason; informal reckon, figure. **2** *his family was thought to be enormously* rich: **deem**, judge, hold, reckon, consider, presume, estimate; regard as, view as. **3** *Jack thought for a moment:* **ponder**, reflect, deliberate, consider, meditate, contemplate, muse, ruminate, be lost in thought, brood; concentrate, rack one's brains; informal put on one's thinking cap, sleep on it; formal cogitate. **4** *she thought of all the visits she had made to her father:* **recall**, remember, recollect, call to mind, think back to. **5** *she forced herself to think of how he must be feeling:* **imagine**, picture, visualize, envisage; dream about, fantasize about.

■ **think better of** *Lisa was about to say no, but then thought better of it:* have second thoughts about, think twice about, think again about, change one's mind about; reconsider, decide against; informal get cold feet about.

■ **think something over** *she went home to think over his offer:* consider, contemplate, deliberate about, weigh up, consider the pros and cons of, mull over, ponder, reflect on, muse on, ruminate on.

■ **think something up** *the idea was thought up by one of my students:* devise, dream up, come up with, invent, create, concoct, make up; hit on.

thinker noun **theorist**, philosopher, scholar, savant, sage, intellectual.

thinking adjective *every thinking person acknowledges that we're in a mess:* **intelligent**, sensible, reasonable, rational; logical, analytical; thoughtful, reflective, meditative, contemplative, pensive, philosophical.
– OPPOSITES stupid, irrational.
noun *what was the thinking behind the campaign?* **reasoning**, idea(s), theory, thoughts, line of thought, philosophy, beliefs; opinion(s), view(s), position, judgement, assessment, evaluation.

third-rate adjective **substandard**, bad, inferior, poor, poor-quality, low-grade, inadequate, unsatisfactory, unacceptable; appalling, abysmal, atrocious, awful, terrible, dreadful, execrable, frightful, miserable, wretched, pitiful; jerry-built, shoddy, tinny, trashy; N. Amer. cheapjack; informal lousy, diabolical, rotten, dire, bum, crummy, rubbishy; Brit. informal ropy, duff, pants.
– OPPOSITES excellent.

thirst noun **1** *I need a drink—I'm dying of thirst:* **thirstiness**, dryness; dehydration. **2** *his thirst for knowledge:* **craving**, desire, longing, yearning, hunger, hankering, keenness, eagerness, lust, appetite; informal yen, itch.
verb *she thirsted for power:* **crave**, want, covet, desire, hunger for, lust after, hanker after, have one's heart set on; wish, long.

thirsty adjective **longing for a drink**, dry, dehydrated; informal parched, gasping; Brit. informal spitting feathers; Austral./NZ informal spitting chips.

thorn noun **prickle**, spike, barb, spine.

thorny adjective **1** *dense thorny undergrowth:* **prickly**, spiky, barbed, spiny, sharp. **2** *the thorny subject of confidentiality:* **problematic**, tricky, ticklish, delicate, controversial, awkward, difficult, knotty, tough, taxing, trying, troublesome; complicated, complex, involved, intricate; vexed; informal sticky.

thorough adjective **1** *a thorough investigation was called for:* **rigorous**, in-depth, exhaustive, thoroughgoing, minute, detailed, close, meticulous, methodical, careful, complete, comprehensive, full, extensive, widespread, sweeping. **2** *he is slow but thorough:* **meticulous**, scrupulous, assiduous, conscientious, painstaking, punctilious, methodical, careful, diligent. **3** *the child is being a thorough nuisance:* **utter**, downright, thoroughgoing, absolute, complete, total, out-and-out, real, perfect, proper, sheer, unqualified, unmitigated; Brit. informal right; Austral./NZ informal fair.
– OPPOSITES superficial, cursory.

thoroughbred adjective **pure-bred**, pedigree, pure, pure-blooded.

thoroughfare noun **1** *the park is being used as a thoroughfare:* **through road**, access route. **2** *the teeming thoroughfares of central London:* **street**, road, roadway, avenue, boulevard, main road, high road, A road, B road; N. Amer. highway, freeway, throughway.

thoroughly adverb **1** *we will investigate all complaints thoroughly:* **rigorously**, in depth, exhaustively, from top to bottom, minutely, closely, in detail, meticulously, scrupulously, assiduously, conscientiously, painstakingly, methodically, carefully, comprehensively, fully. **2** *she is thoroughly spoilt:* **utterly**, downright, absolutely, completely, totally, entirely, really, perfectly, positively, in every respect, through and through; informal plain, clean.

though conjunction *though she smiled bravely, she looked pale and tired:* **although**, even though/if, in spite of the fact that, notwithstanding (the fact) that, for all that.
adverb *You can't always do that. You can try, though.* **nevertheless**, nonetheless, even so, however, be that as it may, for all that, despite that, having said that.

thought noun **1** *what are your thoughts on the matter?* **idea**, notion, opinion, view, impression, feeling, theory; judgement, assessment, conclusion. **2** *he gave up any thought of taking a degree:* **hope**, aspiration, ambition, dream; intention, idea. **3** *it only took a moment's thought:* **thinking**, contemplation, musing, pondering, consideration, reflection, introspection, deliberation, rumination, meditation, brooding, reverie, concentration. **4** *have you no thought for others?* **compassion**, sympathy, care, concern, regard, solicitude, empathy; consideration, understanding, sensitivity.

t

thoughtful adjective **1** *Albert paused, looking thoughtful:* **pensive**, reflective, contemplative, meditative, introspective, philosophical, ruminative, absorbed, engrossed, rapt, preoccupied, deep/lost in thought. **2** *how very thoughtful of you!* **considerate**, caring, attentive, understanding, sympathetic, solicitous, concerned, helpful, friendly, obliging, accommodating, neighbourly, unselfish, kind, compassionate, charitable.
– OPPOSITES vacant, inconsiderate.

thoughtless adjective *I'm so sorry—how thoughtless of me:* **inconsiderate**, uncaring, insensitive, unkind, tactless, undiplomatic, indiscreet, careless.
– OPPOSITES considerate.

thousand cardinal number informal K, thou.

thrash verb **1** *she thrashed him across the head and shoulders:* **hit**, beat, strike, batter, thump, hammer, pound, rain blows on; assault, attack; cudgel, club, birch; informal wallop, belt, bash, whack, thwack, clout, clobber, slug, tan, biff, bop, sock, beat the living daylights out of, give someone a good hiding. **2** (informal) *Newcastle were thrashed 8–1.* See TROUNCE. **3** *he was thrashing around in pain:* **flail**, writhe, thresh, jerk, toss, twist, twitch.
■ **thrash something out 1** *it's better if we can thrash out our difficulties first:* **resolve**, settle, sort out, straighten out, iron out, clear up; talk through, discuss, debate, air, ventilate. **2** *they tried to thrash out an agreement:* **work out**, negotiate, agree on, bring about, hammer out, produce, effect.

thread noun *a needle and thread:* **cotton**, yarn, filament, fibre.
verb **1** *he threaded the rope through a pulley:* **pass**, string, work, ease, push, poke. **2** *she threaded her way through the tables:* **weave one's way**, inch one's way, wind one's way, squeeze one's way, make one's way.

threadbare adjective *we have just replaced that threadbare stair carpet:* **worn**, well worn, old, thin, worn out, holey, moth-eaten, mangy, ragged, frayed, tattered, battered; decrepit, shabby, scruffy, unkempt; having seen better days, falling apart at the seams, falling to pieces; informal tatty, ratty; N. Amer. informal raggedy.

threat noun **1** *Maggie ignored his threats:* **threatening remark**, warning, ultimatum. **2** *the tower poses a possible threat to aircraft:* **danger**, peril, hazard, menace, risk. **3** *the company faces the threat of liquidation proceedings:* **possibility**, chance, probability, likelihood, risk.

threaten verb **1** *how dare you threaten me!* **menace**, intimidate, browbeat, bully, terrorize. **2** *these events could threaten the stability of Europe:* **endanger**, be a danger/threat to, jeopardize, imperil, put at risk, put in jeopardy.

threatening adjective **1** *a threatening letter:* **menacing**, intimidating, bullying, frightening, hostile. **2** *banks of threatening clouds:* **ominous**, sinister, menacing, dark, black, thunderous.

three cardinal number **trio**, threesome, triple, triad, trinity, troika, triumvirate, trilogy, triptych, trefoil, three-piece, triplets.

threesome noun **trio**, triumvirate, triad, trinity, troika; triplets.

threshold noun **1** *he paused on the threshold of the church:* **doorstep**, doorway, entrance, entry, door, gate, gateway, portal. **2** *we are on the threshold of a new era:* **start**, beginning, brink, verge, dawn, opening, debut; informal kick-off. **3** *the human threshold of pain:* **limit**, minimum.

thrift noun **frugality**, economy, economizing, thriftiness, providence, prudence, good management/husbandry, saving, scrimping and saving, abstemiousness, parsimony, penny-pinching.
– OPPOSITES extravagance.

thrifty adjective **frugal**, economical, sparing, careful, provident, prudent, abstemious, parsimonious, penny-pinching; N. Amer. forehanded.
– OPPOSITES extravagant.

thrill noun **1** *the thrill of jumping out of an aeroplane:* **excitement**, feeling, sensation; stimulation, pleasure, tingle; fun, enjoyment, amusement, delight, joy; informal buzz, kick; N. Amer. informal charge. **2** *a thrill of excitement ran through her:* **wave**, rush, surge, flash, blaze, stab, dart, throb, tremor, quiver, flutter, shudder.
verb **1** *his romantic words thrilled her:* **excite**, stimulate, arouse, inspire, delight, exhilarate, intoxicate, stir, electrify, galvanize, move, fire (with enthusiasm), fire someone's imagination; informal give someone a buzz, give someone a kick; N. Amer. informal give someone a charge. **2** *he thrilled at the sound of her voice:* **be/feel excited**, tingle; informal get a buzz out of, get a kick out of; N. Amer. informal get a charge out of.
– OPPOSITES bore.

thrilling adjective **exciting**, stirring, action-packed, rip-roaring, gripping, riveting, fascinating, dramatic, hair-raising; rousing, stimulating, moving, inspirational, inspiring, electrifying, heady, soul-stirring.
– OPPOSITES boring.

thrive verb *a plant that thrives in sandy soil:* **flourish**, prosper, burgeon, bloom, blossom, do well, advance, progress in/by leaps and bounds, succeed, boom.
– OPPOSITES decline, wither.

thriving adjective *a thriving market town:* **flourishing**, prosperous, prospering, growing, developing, burgeoning, blooming, healthy, successful, booming, profitable, expanding; informal going strong.
– OPPOSITES moribund.

throat noun **gullet**, oesophagus; windpipe, trachea; maw; archaic gorge.

throaty adjective **gravelly**, husky, rough, guttural, deep, thick, gruff, growly, growling, hoarse, croaky, croaking; rasping. – OPPOSITES high-pitched.

throb verb *her arms and legs throbbed with tiredness:* **pulsate**, beat, pulse, palpitate, pound, thud, thump, drum, thrum, vibrate, go pit-a-pat, quiver.
noun *the throb of the ship's engines:* **pulsation**, beat, pulse, palpitation, pounding, thudding, thumping, drumming, thrumming, pit-a-pat.

throes plural noun *meanwhile, the death throes of the Labour government were beginning:* **agony**, pain, pangs, suffering, torture; literary travail.
■ **in the throes of** *we are in the throes of an anguished debate between the environmental unit and the energy department:* in the middle of, in the midst of, busy with, occupied with, taken up with/by, involved in; struggling with, wrestling with, grappling with, dealing with.

thrombosis noun **(blood) clot**, embolism, embolus, thrombus, infarction.

throng noun *throngs of people blocked her way:* **crowd**, horde, mass, multitude, host, army, herd, flock, drove, swarm, sea, troupe, pack, crush; company, gathering, assembly, assemblage, congregation; informal gaggle, bunch, gang.
verb **1** *the pavements were thronged with tourists:* **fill**, crowd, pack, cram, jam. **2** *visitors thronged round him:* **crowd**, cluster, mill, swarm, congregate, gather.

throttle verb **choke**, strangle, garrotte.

through preposition **1** *we drove through the tunnel:* **into and out of**, to the other/far side of, from one side to the other of. **2** *he got the job through an advertisement:* **by means of**, by way of, by dint of, via, using, thanks to, by virtue of, as a result of, as a consequence of, on account of, owing to, because of. **3** *he worked through the night:* **throughout**, all through, for the duration of, until/to the end of.
adverb *as soon as we opened the gate they came streaming through:* **from one side to the other**, from one end to another.
adjective *a through train:* **direct**, non-stop.
■ **through and through** *he was obviously a city kid through and through:* in every respect, to the core; thoroughly, utterly, absolutely, completely, totally, wholly, fully, entirely, unconditionally, unreservedly, altogether, out-and-out.

throughout preposition **1** *the dispute had repercussions throughout Europe:* **all over**, in every part of, everywhere in, all/right through, all round. **2** *Rose had generally been very fit throughout her life:* **all through**, all, for the duration of, for the whole of.

throw verb **1** *she threw the ball back:* **hurl**, toss, fling, pitch, cast, lob, launch, catapult, project, propel; bowl; informal chuck, heave, sling, bung; N. Amer. informal peg; Austral. informal hoy, NZ informal bish. **2** *he threw the door open:* **push**, thrust, fling, bang. **3** *a chandelier threw its light over the walls:* **cast**, send, give off, emit, radiate, project. **4** *he threw another punch:* **deliver**, give, land. **5** *she threw a withering glance at him:* **direct**, cast, send, dart, shoot. **6** *his question threw me:* **disconcert**, unnerve, fluster, ruffle, agitate, discomfit, put off, throw off balance, discountenance, unsettle, confuse; informal rattle, faze; N. Amer. informal discombobulate. **7** *he threw a farewell party for them:* **give**, host, hold, have, provide, put on, lay on, arrange, organize.
noun *we were allowed two throws each:* **lob**, pitch; go; bowl, ball.
■ **throw something away 1** *she hated throwing old clothes away:* discard, throw out, dispose of, get rid of, do away with, toss out, scrap, throw on the scrap heap, clear out, dump, jettison; informal chuck (away/out), ditch, bin, junk, get shut of; Brit. informal get shot of. **2** *Cambridge threw away a 15–0 lead:* squander, waste, fritter away, fail to exploit, lose, let slip; informal blow, throw something down the drain.
■ **throw something off** *Zimbabwe was concerned to throw off its colonial past:* shake off, get away from, escape, get rid of, dodge, lose, leave behind.
■ **throw someone out 1** *Jim was thrown out after climbing onto the stage:* expel, eject, evict, show someone the door; banish, deport, exile; informal boot out, kick out, give someone the boot; Brit. informal turf out. **2** *the government was thrown out after only eight months:* remove, get rid of, depose, topple, unseat, overthrow, bring down, overturn, dislodge, displace, supplant; informal boot out, kick out, give someone the boot; Brit. informal turf out.
■ **throw something out 1** *throw out food that's past its sell-by date.* See THROW SOMETHING AWAY sense 1. **2** *his case was thrown out by the magistrate:* reject, dismiss, turn down, refuse, disallow, veto. **3** *a light bulb throws out a lot of heat:* radiate, emit, give off, send out, diffuse.
■ **throw up** (informal). See VOMIT verb sense 1.

throwaway adjective **1** *they serve meals on throwaway plates rather than have a dishwasher:* **disposable**, non-returnable; single-use. **2** *we are a throwaway society:* **consumer(ist)**; wasteful. **3** *a series of throwaway remarks:* **casual**, passing, careless, unthinking, unconsidered, offhand.

thrust verb **1** *she thrust her hands into her pockets:* **shove**, push, force, plunge, stick, drive, propel, ram, poke. **2** *fame had been thrust on him:* **force**, foist, impose, inflict. **3** *he thrust his way past her:* **push**, shove, force, elbow, shoulder, barge.
noun **1** *he gave the gate a hard thrust:* **shove**, push, poke. **2** *a sudden armoured thrust*

t

by the Third Army: **advance**, push, drive, attack, assault, onslaught, offensive, charge, sortie, foray, raid, sally, invasion, incursion. **3** only one engine is producing thrust: **force**, propulsion, power, impetus, momentum. **4** they failed to grasp the thrust of the speech: **gist**, substance, drift, meaning, significance, signification, sense, theme, message, import, tenor.

thrusting adjective a thrusting young politician: **ambitious**, pushy, forceful, aggressive, assertive, self-assertive, full of oneself, determined, power-hungry.
– OPPOSITES meek.

thud noun & verb **thump**, clunk, clonk, crash, smack, bang; stomp, stamp, clump, clomp; informal wham.

thug noun **ruffian**, lout, hooligan, bully boy, vandal, hoodlum, gangster, villain, criminal; informal tough, bruiser, heavy, hired gun; Brit. informal rough; N. Amer. informal hood, goon.

thumb noun technical pollex.
verb **1** he thumbed through his notebook: **leaf**, flick, flip, riffle, skim, browse, look. **2** his dictionaries were thumbed and ink-stained: **soil**, mark, make dog-eared. **3** he was thumbing his way across France: **hitch-hike**; informal hitch, hitch/thumb a lift.

thumbnail adjective a thumbnail sketch of the political climate at the time: **concise**, short, brief, succinct, to the point, compact, crisp, short and sweet, quick, rapid; potted.

thump verb **1** the two men kicked and thumped him: **hit**, strike, smack, cuff, punch, belabour, pound, pummel, box someone's ears; informal whack, wallop, bash, biff, bop, lam, clout, clobber, sock, swipe, crown, belt, lay into, let someone have it; Brit. informal stick one on, slosh; N. Amer. informal slug, boff. **2** her heart thumped with fright: **throb**, pound, thud, hammer, pulsate, pulse, pump, palpitate, race, beat.
noun **1** a well-aimed thump on the jaw: **blow**, punch, box, cuff, smack; informal whack, thwack, wallop, bash, belt, biff, clout, swipe; Brit. informal slosh; N. Amer. informal boff, slug. **2** she put the box down with a thump: **thud**, clunk, clonk, crash, smack, bang.

thumping adjective **1** he could hear nothing above the thumping noise of his own heart: **thudding**, pounding, throbbing, pulsating, banging, hammering, drumming. **2** (informal) a thumping 64 per cent majority | a thumping victory: **enormous**, huge, massive, vast, tremendous, substantial, prodigious, gigantic, giant, terrific, fantastic, colossal, immense, mammoth, monumental, stupendous; emphatic, decisive, conclusive, striking, impressive, outstanding, remarkable, extraordinary, resounding, phenomenal; informal whopping, thundering; Brit. informal whacking.
adverb (informal) a thumping good read. See VERY adverb.

thunder noun **1** thunder and lightning: **thunderclap**. **2** the ceaseless thunder of the traffic: **rumble**, rumbling, boom, booming, roar, roaring, pounding, thud, thudding, crash, crashing.
verb **1** below me the surf thrashed and thundered: **rumble**, boom, roar, pound, thud, thump, bang; resound, reverberate, beat. **2** 'Answer me!' he thundered: **roar**, bellow, bark, yell, shout, bawl; informal holler.

thunderous adjective the applause was thunderous: **deafening**, tumultuous, booming, roaring, resounding, reverberant, ringing, loud, ear-splitting, noisy.

thunderstruck adjective **astonished**, amazed, astounded, staggered, surprised, startled, stunned, shocked, aghast, taken aback, dumbfounded, dumbstruck, stupefied, dazed, speechless; informal flabbergasted; Brit. informal gobsmacked, knocked for six.

thus adverb the studio handled production, thus cutting its costs: **thereby**, so, consequently, ergo, accordingly, hence, as a result.
■ **thus far** Stephen has shown himself very capable thus far: so far, (up) until now, up to now, up to this point, hitherto.

thwart verb a fund was set up to thwart the plans of their former manager: **foil**, frustrate, stand in the way of, forestall, derail, dash; stop, check, block, prevent, defeat, impede, obstruct, snooker, hinder, hamper; informal put paid to, put the kibosh on, do for, stymie; Brit. informal scupper.
– OPPOSITES facilitate.

tic noun **twitch**, spasm, jerk, tremor.

tick noun **1** put a tick against the item of your choice: **mark**, stroke; N. Amer. check, check mark. **2** the tick of his watch: **ticking**, tick-tock, click, clicking, tap, tapping.
verb **1** tick the appropriate box: **put a tick in/against**, mark, check off, indicate; N. Amer. check. **2** I could hear the clock ticking: click; tap.

ticket noun **1** can I see your ticket? **pass**, authorization, permit; token, coupon, voucher. **2** a price ticket: **label**, tag, sticker, tab, marker, docket.

tickle verb the idea tickled Lewis: **amuse**, entertain, divert, please, delight.

ticklish adjective **1** privacy is a ticklish business where close neighbours are concerned: **difficult**, problematic, tricky, delicate, sensitive, awkward, prickly, thorny, tough; vexed; informal sticky. **2** a metal curry comb is kind to even a ticklish horse: **sensitive**, delicate, soft, tender.

tide noun **1** ships come up the river with the tide: **tidal flow**, ebb and flow, current. **2** the whole tide of history seemed to be quickening: **course**, movement, direction, trend, current, drift, run, turn, tendency, tenor.
■ **tide someone over** she needed a small loan to tide her over: sustain, keep someone going, keep someone's head above water, see someone through; keep the wolf from

the door; help out.

tidings plural noun (literary) *I'm sorry to be the bearer of such bad tidings:* **news**, information, intelligence, word, reports, notification, communication; informal info, the low down.

tidy adjective 1 *a tidy room:* **neat**, as neat as a new pin, orderly, well ordered, in (good) order, well kept, shipshape (and Bristol fashion), in apple-pie order, immaculate, spick and span, uncluttered, straight, trim, spruce. 2 *he's a very tidy person:* **neat**, trim, spruce, dapper, well groomed, well turned out; (well) organized, meticulous; fastidious; informal natty. 3 (informal) *a tidy sum:* **large**, sizeable, considerable, substantial, generous, significant, appreciable, handsome, respectable, decent, goodly; informal not to be sneezed at.
– OPPOSITES messy.
verb 1 *I'd better tidy up the living room:* **put in order**, clear up, sort out, straighten (up), clean up, spruce up. 2 *she tidied herself up in the bathroom:* **groom oneself**, spruce oneself up, freshen oneself up, smarten oneself up; informal titivate oneself.

tie verb 1 *they tied Max to a chair:* **bind**, tether, hitch, strap, truss, fetter, rope, chain, make fast, moor, lash, attach, fasten, fix, secure, join, connect, link, couple. 2 *he bent to tie his shoelaces:* **do up**, lace, fasten, knot. 3 *women can feel tied by childcare responsibilities:* **restrict**, restrain, limit, tie down, constrain, trammel, confine, cramp, hamper, handicap, hamstring, encumber, shackle, inhibit. 4 *a pay deal tied to a productivity agreement:* **link**, connect, couple, relate, join, marry; make conditional on, bind up with. 5 *they tied for second place:* **draw**, be equal, be even, be neck and neck.
noun 1 *he tightened the ties of his robe:* **lace**, string, cord, fastening, fastener. 2 *a collar and tie:* **necktie**, bow tie, string tie; Brit. bootlace tie. 3 *it is important that we maintain our family ties:* **bond**, connection, link, relationship, attachment, affiliation, allegiance, friendship. 4 *there was a tie for first place:* **draw**, dead heat, deadlock. 5 (Brit.) *Turkey's World Cup tie against Holland:* **match**, game, contest, fixture, event.
■ **tie someone down** *she was afraid of being tied down.* See TIE verb sense 3.
■ **tie in (with)** 1 *the venue has been selected to tie in with preparations for the British Open:* fit in, harmonize, dovetail; take advantage of, exploit. 2 *does it all tie in when you look at the original requirements?* be consistent, tally, agree, accord, concur, be in tune, correspond, match; informal square; N. Amer. informal jibe.
■ **tie someone/something up** 1 *robbers tied her up and ransacked her home:* bind, truss (up), chain (up), handcuff. 2 *he is tied up in meetings all morning:* occupy, engage, keep busy. 3 *they were anxious to tie up the contract:* finalize, conclude, complete,

finish off, seal, set the seal on, settle, secure, clinch; informal wrap up.

tie-in noun **connection**, link, association, correlation, tie-up, interrelation, relationship, relation, interconnection.

tier noun 1 *I saw two tiers of empty seats:* **row**, rank, bank, line; layer, level. 2 *the most senior tier of management:* **grade**, echelon, layer, level, stratum.

tight adjective 1 *he took a tight grip on her arm:* **firm**, fast, secure, fixed, clenched. 2 *the rope was pulled tight:* **taut**, rigid, stiff, tense, stretched, strained. 3 *tight jeans:* **tight-fitting**, close-fitting, narrow, figure-hugging, skintight; informal spray-on. 4 *the stuffing is a tight mass of fibres:* **compact**, compacted, compressed, dense, solid. 5 *it was certainly a tight space:* **small**, tiny, narrow, limited, restricted, confined, cramped, constricted, uncomfortable. 6 *tight limits on the use of pesticides:* **strict**, rigorous, stringent, tough, rigid, firm, uncompromising. 7 *he's in a tight spot:* **difficult**, tricky, delicate, awkward, problematic, worrying, precarious; informal sticky; Brit. informal dodgy. 8 *a nice tight piece of writing:* **succinct**, concise, pithy, incisive, crisp, condensed, to the point. 9 *it's going to be a tight race:* **close**, even, evenly matched, well matched; hard-fought, neck and neck. 10 *money is a bit tight just now:* **limited**, restricted, in short supply, scarce, depleted, diminished, low, inadequate, insufficient.
– OPPOSITES slack, loose.

tighten verb 1 *I tightened the screws:* **make tighter**, make fast, screw up. 2 *he tightened his grip:* **strengthen**, make stronger, harden. 3 *she tightened the rope:* **tauten**, make/draw taut, make/draw tight, stretch, strain, stiffen, tense. 4 *he tightened his lips:* **narrow**, constrict, contract, compress, screw up, pucker, purse; N. Amer. squinch. 5 *security in the area has been tightened:* **increase**, make stricter, toughen up, heighten, scale up; informal beef up .
– OPPOSITES loosen, slacken, relax.

tight-fisted adjective **mean**, miserly, parsimonious, niggardly, close-fisted, penny-pinching, cheese-paring, Scrooge-like, close; informal stingy, tight; N. Amer. informal cheap.
– OPPOSITES generous.

tight-lipped adjective **reticent**, uncommunicative, unforthcoming, close-mouthed, silent, taciturn; informal mum.
– OPPOSITES forthcoming.

till¹ preposition & conjunction *he stayed till 7 | I'll stay here till you get back.* See UNTIL senses 1, 2.

till² noun *she counted the money in the till:* **cash register**, cash box, cash drawer, strongbox; checkout, cash desk.

tilt verb *the ground seemed to tilt:* **slope**, tip, lean, list, bank, slant, incline, pitch, cant, careen, angle.

t

noun *we found a tilt of some 45°:* **slope**, list, camber, gradient, bank, slant, incline, pitch, cant, bevel, angle.

■ **(at) full tilt** *they charged full tilt down the side of the hill:* (at) full speed, (at) full pelt, as fast as one's legs can carry one, at a gallop, helter-skelter, headlong, pell-mell, at breakneck speed; informal hell for leather, at the double, a mile a minute, like the wind, like a bat out of hell, like a scalded cat, like (greased) lightning; Brit. informal like the clappers, at a rate of knots, like billy-o; N. Amer. informal lickety-split; literary apace.

timber noun **1** *the houses were built of timber:* **wood**; N. Amer. lumber. **2** *we burned the timbers of wrecked ships:* **beam**, spar, plank, batten, lath, board, joist, rafter.

timbre noun **tone**, sound, quality, voice, colour, tonality, resonance.

time noun **1** *what time is it?* **hour**. **2** *late at night was the best time to leave:* **moment**, point (in time), occasion, hour, minute, second, instant, juncture, stage. **3** *he worked there for a time:* **while**, spell, stretch, stint, span, season, interval, period, length of time, duration, run, space, phase, stage, term; Brit. informal patch. **4** *the time of the dinosaurs:* **era**, age, epoch, period, years, days; generation, date. **5** *I've known a lot of women in my time:* **lifetime**, life, life span, days, time on earth, existence, threescore years and ten. **6** *he had been a professional actor in his time:* **heyday**, day, prime. **7** *times are hard at the moment:* **conditions**, circumstances, life, state of affairs, things; the situation, the living. **8** *tunes in waltz time:* **rhythm**, tempo, beat; metre, measure, cadence, pattern.

verb *the meeting was timed for three o'clock:* **schedule**, set, set up, arrange, organize, fix, fix up, book, line up, slot in, pre-arrange, timetable, plan; N. Amer. slate.

■ **ahead of time** *the bridge was ready ahead of time:* early, in good time, with time to spare, in advance.

■ **ahead of one's/its time** *Tacoma is ahead of its time in its attempts to help drug addicts:* revolutionary, avant-garde, futuristic, innovatory, innovative, trailblazing, pioneering, groundbreaking, advanced.

■ **all the time** *he works all the time:* constantly, the entire/whole time, around the clock, day and night, night and day, {morning, noon, and night}, {day in, day out}, at all times, always, without a break, ceaselessly, endlessly, incessantly, perpetually, permanently, interminably, continuously, continually, eternally, unremittingly, remorselessly, relentlessly; N. Amer. without surcease; informal 24-7.

■ **at one time** *she was a nurse at one time:* formerly, previously, once, in the past, at one point, once upon a time, time was when, in days/times gone by, in times past, in the (good) old days, long ago.

■ **at the same time 1** *they arrived at the same time:* simultaneously, at the same

instant/moment, (both/all) together, as a group, at once, at one and the same time; in unison, in concert, en masse, as one. **2** *I can't really explain it, but at the same time I'm not convinced:* nonetheless, even so, however, but, still, yet, though; in spite of that, despite that, be that as it may, for all that, that said; notwithstanding, regardless, anyway, anyhow; informal still and all.

■ **at times** *at times she is very cruel:* occasionally, sometimes, from time to time, now and then, every so often, once in a while, on occasion, off and on, at intervals, periodically, sporadically.

■ **behind the times** *the children considered dad to be behind the times:* old-fashioned, out of date, outmoded, outdated, dated, old, passé; informal square, not with it, out of the ark; N. Amer. informal horse-and-buggy, clunky.

■ **for the time being** for now, for the moment, for the present, in the interim, for the nonce, in/for the meantime, for a short time, briefly; temporarily, provisionally, pro tem; informal for the minute.

■ **from time to time** occasionally, sometimes, now and then, every so often, once in a while, on occasion, off and on, at intervals, periodically, sporadically.

■ **in good time** *we'll be there in good time:* punctually, on time, early, with time to spare, ahead of time/schedule.

■ **in time 1** *I came back in time for the party:* early enough, in good time, punctually, on time, not too late, with time to spare, on schedule. **2** *in time, she forgot about him:* eventually, in the end, in due course, by and by, finally; one day, some day, sometime, sooner or later.

■ **many a time** *many a time they went to bed hungry:* frequently, regularly, often, very often, all the time, habitually, customarily, routinely; again and again, time and again, over and over again, repeatedly, recurrently, continually; N. Amer. oftentimes.

■ **on time** *the train arrived on time:* punctually, in good time, to/on schedule, when expected; informal on the dot, bang on time.

■ **time after time** *the camera produces excellent results time after time:* repeatedly, frequently, often, again and again, over and over (again), time and (time) again, many times, many a time; persistently, recurrently, constantly, continually; N. Amer. oftentimes.

time-honoured adjective *the barley is turned by hand in the time-honoured fashion:* **traditional**, established, long-established, long-standing, long-lived, age-old, enduring, lasting, tried and tested.

timeless adjective *this pretty wall clock has timeless good looks:* **lasting**, enduring, classic, ageless, permanent, perennial, abiding, unfailing, unchanging, unvarying, never-changing, changeless, unfading, unending, undying, deathless, immortal, eternal, everlasting, immutable.

– OPPOSITES ephemeral.

timely adjective *a timely warning:* **opportune**, well timed, at the right time, convenient, appropriate, expedient, seasonable, felicitous.
– OPPOSITES ill-timed.

timetable noun *a bus timetable | I have a very full timetable:* **schedule**, programme, agenda, calendar; list, itinerary.
verb *German lessons were timetabled on Wednesday:* **schedule**, set, arrange, organize, fix, time, line up; N. Amer. slate.

time-worn adjective *a time-worn aphorism:* **hackneyed**, trite, banal, platitudinous, clichéd, stock, conventional, unoriginal, overused, overworked, tired, stale; informal old hat.
– OPPOSITES new, fresh.

timid adjective **easily frightened**, fearful, afraid, faint-hearted, timorous, nervous, scared, frightened, cowardly, pusillanimous, lily-livered, spineless, shy, diffident, self-effacing; informal wimpish, wimpy, chicken, gutless.
– OPPOSITES bold.

tincture noun *tincture of iodine:* **solution**, suspension, infusion, elixir.

tinge verb **1** *a mass of white blossom tinged with pink:* **tint**, colour, stain, shade. **2** *his optimism is tinged with realism:* **influence**, affect, touch, flavour, colour, qualify.
noun **1** *the light had a blue tinge to it:* **tint**, colour, shade, tone, hue. **2** *a tinge of cynicism:* **trace**, note, touch, suggestion, hint, bit, scintilla, savour, flavour, element, streak, vein, suspicion, soupçon.

tingle verb *her flesh still tingled from the shock:* **prickle**, sting; tremble, quiver, shiver.
noun *she felt a tingle of anticipation:* **prickle**, tingling, pricking, sting, stinging; tremor, thrill, quiver, shiver; goose pimples; N. Amer. goosebumps.

tinker verb *a workman was tinkering with the engine:* **fiddle with**, adjust, play about with; informal rearrange the deckchairs on the Titanic; Brit. informal muck about with.

tinkle verb *the bell tinkled:* **ring**, jingle, jangle, chime, peal, ding, ping.
noun **1** *the tinkle of the doorbell:* **ring**, chime, peal, ding, ping, jingle, jangle. **2** (Brit. informal) *I'll give them a tinkle:* **(telephone) call**, phone, call; informal buzz; Brit. informal ring, bell.

tinny adjective **1** *tinny music played in the background:* **jangly**, jangling, jingling, jingly. **2** *a tinny little car:* **cheap**, gimcrack, shoddy, jerry-built; informal tacky, tatty, rubbishy.

tint noun *the sky was taking on an apricot tint:* **shade**, colour, tone, hue, tinge, cast, tincture, flush, blush.

tiny adjective **minute**, minuscule, microscopic, very small, little, mini, diminutive, miniature, scaled down, baby, toy, dwarf, pygmy, Lilliputian; Scottish wee; informal teeny, teeny-weeny, teensy, teensy-weensy, itsy-bitsy, tiddly, pint-sized; Brit. informal titchy; N. Amer. informal little-bitty.
– OPPOSITES huge.

tip¹ noun **1** *the tip of the spear was still sharp:* **point**, end, extremity, head, spike, prong, tine, nib. **2** *the sticks have steel tips fitted to protect them:* **cap**, cover, ferrule.

tip² verb **1** *the boat tipped over:* **overturn**, turn over, topple (over), fall (over); keel over, capsize, turn turtle. **2** *a whale could tip over a small boat:* **upset**, overturn, topple over, turn over, knock over, push over, upend, capsize. **3** *the car tipped to one side:* **lean**, tilt, list, slope, bank, slant, incline, pitch. **4** *she tipped the water into the trough:* **pour**, empty, drain, unload, dump; decant.
noun (Brit.) *rubbish must be taken to the tip:* **dump**, rubbish dump; Canadian nuisance grounds.

tip³ noun **1** *he left the waiter a generous tip:* **gratuity**; present, gift, reward. **2** *lots of useful tips to help you make the right choice:* **piece of advice**, suggestion, pointer, recommendation; clue, hint.

tip-off noun (informal) *the police were acting on an anonymous tip-off:* **piece of information**, warning, lead, forewarning; hint, clue; advice, information, notification.

tipsy adjective **merry**, mellow, slightly drunk; Brit. informal tiddly, squiffy.
– OPPOSITES sober.

tirade noun *TV bosses have scrapped a tribute to the footballer because of his drunken tirade:* **diatribe**, harangue, rant, onslaught, attack, polemic, denunciation, broadside, fulmination, condemnation, censure, criticism, tongue-lashing.

tire verb **1** *the ascent grew steeper and he began to tire:* **get tired**, weaken, grow weak, flag, droop. **2** *the journey had tired him:* **fatigue**, tire out, exhaust, wear out, drain, weary, wash out, overtire, enervate; informal knock out, take it out of, do in; Brit. informal knacker. **3** *they soon tired of his difficult behaviour:* **weary**, get tired, get fed up, get sick, get bored; informal have had something up to here.

tired adjective **1** *you're just tired from travelling:* **exhausted**, worn out, weary, fatigued, dog-tired, bone-tired, ready to drop, drained, enervated, jaded; informal done in, all in, dead beat, shattered, bushed, knocked out, wiped out, bushwhacked; Brit. informal knackered, whacked (out), jiggered; N. Amer. informal pooped, tuckered out; Austral./NZ informal stonkered. **2** *are you tired of having him here yet?* **fed up with**, weary of, bored with/by, sick (and tired) of; informal up to here with. **3** *a series of tired jokes about Germany:* **hackneyed**, overused, overworked, worn out, stale, clichéd, hoary, stock, stereotyped, predictable, unimaginative, unoriginal, uninspired, dull, boring, routine; informal old hat, corny, played out.
– OPPOSITES energetic, lively, fresh.

t

tiredness noun **fatigue**, weariness, exhaustion, enervation, inertia; sleepiness, drowsiness, somnolence.
– OPPOSITES energy.

tireless adjective **vigorous**, energetic, industrious, determined, enthusiastic, keen, zealous, spirited, dynamic, tenacious, persevering, stout, untiring, unwearying, indefatigable, unflagging.
– OPPOSITES lazy.

tiresome adjective *another of his tiresome complaints:* **boring**, dull, tedious, wearisome, wearing, uninteresting, uneventful, humdrum; annoying, irritating, trying, irksome, vexatious, troublesome; informal aggravating, pesky.
– OPPOSITES interesting, pleasant.

tiring adjective **exhausting**, wearying, taxing, fatiguing, wearing, enervating, draining; hard, heavy, arduous, strenuous, onerous, uphill, demanding, gruelling; informal killing, murderous; Brit. informal knackering.

tissue noun **1** *the X-rays were able to penetrate living tissue:* **matter**, material, substance; flesh. **2** *a box of tissues:* **paper handkerchief**, paper towel; trademark Kleenex.

titanic adjective **huge**, great, enormous, gigantic, massive, colossal, monumental, mammoth, immense, tremendous, terrific, mighty, stupendous, prodigious, gargantuan, Herculean; informal humongous, whopping, thumping, mega; Brit. informal whacking, ginormous.

titbit noun **1** *a plate of tasty titbits:* **delicacy**, tasty morsel, dainty, treat; snack, nibble, savoury, appetizer; informal goody; N. Amer. tidbit. **2** *a fascinating titbit:* **piece of gossip**, bit of scandal, piece of information.

titillate verb **arouse**, excite, tantalize, stimulate, stir, thrill, interest, attract, fascinate; informal turn on.
– OPPOSITES bore.

titillating adjective **arousing**, exciting, stimulating, sexy, thrilling, provocative, tantalizing, interesting, fascinating; suggestive, salacious, lurid; Brit. informal saucy.
– OPPOSITES boring.

titivate verb (informal) *she titivated herself in front of the hall mirror:* **groom**, smarten (up), spruce up, freshen up, preen, primp, prink; tidy, arrange; informal doll up, tart up; N. Amer. informal gussy up.

title noun **1** *I forgot the title of the book:* **name**. **2** *the company publishes 400 titles a year:* **publication**, work, book, newspaper, paper, magazine, periodical. **3** *the title of Duke of Marlborough:* **designation**, name, form of address; epithet; rank, office, position; informal moniker, handle; formal denomination. **4** *an Olympic title:* **championship**, crown, first place; medal, gold.
verb *a policy paper titled 'Law and Order':* **call**, entitle, name, dub, designate, style, term.

titter verb & noun **giggle**, snigger, snicker, tee-hee, chuckle, laugh; informal chortle.

tittle-tattle noun *she would never listen to tittle-tattle:* **gossip**, rumour(s), idle talk, hearsay, whispers; scandal; informal dirt; Brit. informal goss; N. Amer. informal scuttlebutt.

titular adjective *the titular head of a university:* **nominal**, in title/name only, ceremonial; token, puppet.

toady noun *a conniving little toady:* **sycophant**, flatterer, creep, crawler, lickspittle; informal bootlicker, yes-man.
verb *she imagined him toadying to his rich clients:* **grovel to**, ingratiate oneself with, kowtow to, pander to, crawl to, bow and scrape to, dance attendance on, curry favour with, make up to, fawn on/over; informal suck up to, lick someone's boots, butter up.

toast noun **1** *he raised his glass in a toast:* **tribute**, salute, salutation. **2** *he was the toast of the West End:* **darling**, favourite, pet, heroine, hero; talk; Brit. informal blue-eyed boy/girl; N. Amer. informal fair-haired boy/girl.
verb **1** *she toasted her hands in front of the fire:* **warm (up)**, heat, heat (up). **2** *we toasted the couple with champagne:* **drink (to)**, drink the health of, drink to, salute, honour, pay tribute to.

today adverb **1** *the work must be finished today:* **this (very) day**, this morning, this afternoon, this evening. **2** *the complex tasks demanded of computers today:* **nowadays**, now, these days, in these times, in this day and age, currently, at the moment, at present, at this moment in time; in the present climate; N. Amer. presently.

toddle verb *the child toddled towards him:* **totter**, teeter, wobble, falter, stumble.

together adverb **1** *they are good friends and work together:* **with each other**, in conjunction, jointly, in cooperation, in collaboration, in partnership, in combination, in league, side by side, hand in hand, shoulder to shoulder, cheek by jowl; in collusion, hand in glove. **2** *they both spoke together:* **simultaneously**, at the same time, at once, all together, as a group, in unison, in concert, in chorus, as one, with one voice.
– OPPOSITES separately.

toil verb **1** *she rolled up her sleeves and toiled all night:* **work (hard)**, labour, slave (away), grind away, strive, work one's fingers to the bone, work like a Trojan/slave, keep one's nose to the grindstone; informal slog away, plug away, peg away, beaver away, work one's guts out, work one's socks off, sweat blood; Brit. informal graft. **2** *she began to toil up the cliff path:* **struggle**, trudge, tramp, traipse, slog, plod, trek, footslog, drag oneself; N. Amer. informal schlep.
– OPPOSITES rest, relax.
noun *all he knew was a life of toil:* **hard work**, labour, exertion, slaving, drudgery, effort, industry, {blood, sweat, and tears}; informal slog, elbow grease; Brit. informal graft.

toilet noun **1** *he had to go to the toilet:* **lavatory**, WC, water closet, (public) convenience, cloakroom, powder room, urinal, privy, latrine, jakes; N. Amer. washroom, bathroom, rest room, men's/ladies' room, commode, comfort station; Nautical heads; informal little girls'/boys' room, smallest room; Brit. informal loo, bog, the Ladies, the Gents, khazi, lav; N. Amer. informal can, john; Austral./NZ informal dunny. **2** *she had always taken a long time over her toilet:* **washing**, bathing, showering; grooming, dressing, make-up; formal or humorous ablutions.

token noun **1** *please accept this as a token of our appreciation:* **symbol**, sign, emblem, badge, representation, indication, mark, manifestation, expression, pledge, demonstration, recognition; evidence, proof. **2** *a book token:* **voucher**, coupon. **3** *I need a car-wash token:* **counter**, disc, chip, piece, man.
adjective **1** *a one-day token strike:* **symbolic**, emblematic, indicative. **2** *the practice now meets only token resistance:* **perfunctory**, slight, nominal, minimal, minor, mild, superficial, inconsequential.

tolerable adjective **1** *we try to make life more tolerable for them:* **bearable**, endurable, supportable, acceptable. **2** *he had a tolerable voice:* **fairly good**, passable, adequate, all right, acceptable, satisfactory, not (too) bad, average, fair; informal OK, so-so.
– OPPOSITES unacceptable.

tolerance noun **1** *an attitude of tolerance towards other people:* **acceptance**, toleration; open-mindedness, broad-mindedness, forbearance, liberalism; patience, charity, indulgence, understanding. **2** *the plant's tolerance of pollution:* **endurance**, resilience; resistance. **3** *a 1% maximum tolerance in measurement:* **deviation**, variation, play; inaccuracy, imprecision.

tolerant adjective **open-minded**, forbearing, broad-minded, liberal, unprejudiced, unbiased; patient, long-suffering, understanding, charitable, lenient, indulgent, permissive, free and easy, easy-going, lax.
– OPPOSITES intolerant.

tolerate verb **1** *a regime that is unwilling to tolerate dissent:* **allow**, permit, condone, accept, swallow, countenance; formal brook. **2** *he couldn't tolerate her moods any longer:* **endure**, put up with, bear, take, stand, support, stomach; informal hack, abide; Brit. informal stick, wear, be doing with.

toleration noun **acceptance**, tolerance, endurance; forbearance, liberality, open-mindedness, broad-mindedness, liberalism; patience, charity, indulgence, understanding.

toll[1] noun **1** *a motorway toll:* **charge**, fee, payment, levy, tariff, tax. **2** *the toll of dead and injured:* **number**, count, tally, total, sum

total, grand total, sum; record, list, listing.

toll[2] verb *I heard the bell toll:* **ring (out)**, chime, strike, peal; sound, clang, resound, reverberate.

tomb noun **burial chamber**, sepulchre, mausoleum, vault, crypt, catacomb; last/final resting place, grave, barrow, burial mound; historical charnel house.

tombstone noun **gravestone**, headstone, stone; memorial, monument.

tome noun *every 10 years he publishes a weighty tome about British social life:* **volume**, book, work, opus, publication, title.

tomfoolery noun **silliness**, fooling around, clowning, capers, antics, pranks, tricks, buffoonery, skylarking, nonsense, horseplay, mischief, foolishness, foolery; informal larks, shenanigans.

tone noun **1** *the warm tone of the tuba:* **timbre**, sound, sound quality, voice, colour. **2** *his friendly tone:* **intonation**, tone of voice, voice. **3** *the somewhat impatient tone of his letter:* **mood**, air, feel, flavour, note, attitude, character, temper; tenor, vein, drift, gist. **4** *all I got was a dialling tone:* **note**, signal, beep, bleep. **5** *light tones of primrose, lavender, and rose:* **shade**, colour, hue, tint, tinge.
verb *the caramel shirt toned well with her cream skirt:* **harmonize**, go, blend, coordinate, team; match, suit, complement.
■ **tone something down 1** *the colour needs to be toned down a bit:* soften, lighten, mute, subdue. **2** *the papers refused to tone down their criticism:* moderate, modify, modulate, mitigate, temper, dampen, soften, subdue.

tongue noun **1** *he spoke in a foreign tongue:* **language**, mother tongue, native tongue; informal lingo. **2** *her sharp tongue:* **way/manner of speaking**, speech, parlance.

tongue-tied adjective **lost for words**, speechless, struck dumb, dumbstruck; mute, dumb, silent.
– OPPOSITES loquacious.

tonic noun **1** *ginseng can be used as a natural tonic:* **stimulant**, restorative, refresher; informal pick-me-up, bracer; Medicine analeptic. **2** *we found the change of scene a real tonic:* **stimulant**, boost, fillip; informal shot in the arm, pick-me-up.

too adverb **1** *invasion would be too risky:* **excessively**, overly, over, unduly, immoderately, inordinately, unreasonably, extremely, very. **2** *he was unhappy, too, you know:* **also**, as well, in addition, additionally, into the bargain, besides, furthermore, moreover, on top of that, to boot.

tool noun *garden tools:* **implement**, utensil, instrument, device, apparatus, gadget, appliance, machine, contrivance, contraption; informal gizmo.
verb *the red leather cover is tooled in gold:* **ornament**, embellish, decorate, work, cut, chase.

tooth noun **fang**, tusk; molar, incisor; informal gnasher.

top noun **1** *we got to the top of the cliff:* **summit**, peak, pinnacle, crest, crown, brow, head, tip, apex, vertex. **2** *the top of the table:* **upper part**, upper surface, upper layer. **3** *remove the carrots' green tops:* **leaves**, shoots, stem, stalk. **4** *the top of the coffee jar:* **lid**, cap, cover, stopper, cork. **5** *by 1981 he was at the top of his profession:* **high point**, height, peak, pinnacle, zenith, acme, culmination, climax, crowning point; prime.
– OPPOSITES bottom, base.
adjective **1** *the top floor:* **highest**, topmost, uppermost, upmost. **2** *the world's top scientists:* **foremost**, leading, principal, pre-eminent, greatest, best, finest, elite; informal top-notch. **3** *a top Paris hotel:* **prime**, excellent, superb, superior, choice, select, top-quality, first-rate, first-class, grade A, best, finest, premier, superlative, second to none; informal top-notch. **4** *they are travelling at top speed:* **maximum**, maximal, greatest, utmost.
– OPPOSITES bottom, lowest, minimum.
verb **1** *sales are expected to top £1.3 billion:* **exceed**, surpass, go beyond, better, beat, outstrip, outdo, outshine, eclipse, go one better than. **2** *their debut CD is currently topping the charts:* **lead**, be at the top of. **3** *they topped the rise of a mist-shrouded valley:* **reach the top of**, crest, climb, scale, ascend, mount. **4** *chocolate mousse topped with cream:* **cover**, cap, coat, smother; finish, garnish.
■ **over the top** (informal) excessive, immoderate, inordinate, extreme, exaggerated, extravagant, overblown, too much, unreasonable, disproportionate, undue, unwarranted, uncalled for, unnecessary, going too far; informal a bit much, OTT.
■ **top something up** fill, refill, refresh, freshen, replenish, recharge, resupply; supplement, add to, augment.

topic noun **subject**, subject matter, theme, issue, matter, point, question, concern, argument, thesis, text, keynote.

topical adjective **current**, up to date, up to the minute, contemporary, recent, relevant; newsworthy, in the news.
– OPPOSITES out of date.

topmost adjective **1** *the tree's topmost branches:* **highest**, top, uppermost, upmost. **2** *the topmost authority on the subject:* **foremost**, leading, principal, premier, prime, top, greatest, best, supreme, pre-eminent, outstanding, most important, main, chief; N. Amer. ranking; informal number-one.

topple verb **1** *she toppled over:* **fall**, tumble, overbalance, overturn, tip, keel; lose one's balance. **2** *protesters toppled a huge statue:* **knock over**, upset, push over, tip over, upend. **3** *a plot to topple the government:* **overthrow**, oust, unseat, overturn, bring down, defeat, get rid of, dislodge, eject.

topsy-turvy adjective **1** *there is one constant in a topsy-turvy world:* **upside-down**, muddled, chaotic, mad, crazy, messed-up. **2** *everything in the flat was topsy-turvy:* **in disarray**, in a mess, in a muddle, in disorder, disordered, in chaos, disorganized, awry, upside down, at sixes and sevens; informal every which way, higgledy-piggledy.
– OPPOSITES neat.

torch noun *an electric torch:* **lamp**, light, flashlight.
verb (informal) *one of the shops had been torched:* **burn**, set fire to, set on fire, set light to, set alight, incinerate.

torment noun *months of mental and emotional torment:* **agony**, suffering, torture, pain, anguish, misery, distress, affliction, trauma, wretchedness; hell, purgatory.
verb **1** *she was tormented by shame:* **torture**, afflict, rack, harrow, plague, haunt, distress, agonize. **2** *she began to torment the two younger boys:* **tease**, taunt, bait, harass, provoke, goad, plague, bother, trouble, persecute; informal needle.

torn adjective **1** *a torn shirt:* **ripped**, rent, cut, slit; ragged, tattered, in tatters, in ribbons. **2** *she was torn between the two options:* **wavering**, vacillating, irresolute, dithering, uncertain, unsure, undecided, in two minds.

tornado noun **whirlwind**, cyclone, typhoon, storm, hurricane; N. Amer. informal twister.

torpor noun *my opportunity to escape from the torpor into which I had sunk:* **lethargy**, sluggishness, inertia, inactivity, lifelessness, listlessness, languor, lassitude, laziness, idleness, indolence, sloth, accidie, passivity, somnolence, weariness, sleepiness.

torrent noun **1** *a torrent of water:* **flood**, deluge, inundation, spate, cascade, rush, stream, current, flow, tide. **2** *a torrent of abuse:* **outburst**, outpouring, stream, flood, volley, barrage, tide, spate.
– OPPOSITES trickle.

torrential adjective *torrential rain caused the game to be stopped:* **copious**, heavy, teeming, severe, relentless, violent.

torrid adjective **1** *I was panting like a dog in the torrid heat and thin air:* **hot**, dry, scorching, searing, blazing, blistering, sweltering, burning; informal boiling (hot), baking (hot), sizzling. **2** *a torrid affair:* **passionate**, ardent, lustful, amorous; informal steamy, sizzling, hot.
– OPPOSITES cold.

tortuous adjective **1** *a tortuous route up the mountain:* **twisting**, twisty, twisting and turning, winding, windy, zigzag, sinuous, snaky, meandering, serpentine. **2** *a tortuous argument:* **convoluted**, complicated, complex, labyrinthine, involved, confusing, hard to follow.
– OPPOSITES straight, straightforward.

torture noun **1** *the torture of political*

prisoners: **abuse**; ill-treatment, maltreatment, persecution. **2** *the sheer torture of waiting for the results*: **torment**, agony, suffering, anguish, misery, distress, trauma; hell, purgatory.
verb **1** *the security forces routinely tortured suspects*: **abuse**, ill-treat, mistreat, maltreat, persecute; informal work over. **2** *he was tortured by grief*: **torment**, rack, afflict, harrow, plague, agonize, crucify.

toss verb **1** *he tossed his tools into the boot*: **throw**, hurl, fling, sling, cast, pitch, lob, propel, project, launch; informal heave, chuck. **2** *he tossed a coin and it landed heads up*: **flip**, flick, spin. **3** *the ship tossed about on the waves*: **pitch**, lurch, rock, roll, plunge, reel, list, keel, sway, wallow, make heavy weather. **4** *toss the salad ingredients together*: **shake**, stir, turn, mix, combine.

tot[1] noun **1** *the wee tot looks just like her mum*: **infant**, baby, toddler, tiny tot, child, little one, mite; Scottish bairn, wean. **2** *a tot of rum*: **dram**, drink, nip, drop, slug; informal shot, finger, snifter.

tot[2] verb **1** *he totted up some figures*: **add**, total, count, calculate, compute, reckon, tally. **2** *we've totted up 89 victories*: **accumulate**, build up, amass, accrue, notch up.

total adjective **1** *the total cost of the funeral*: **entire**, complete, whole, full, comprehensive, combined, aggregate, gross, overall. **2** *it was a total disaster*: **complete**, utter, absolute, thorough, perfect, downright, out-and-out, outright, thoroughgoing, all-out, sheer, positive, prize, rank, unmitigated, unqualified; Brit. informal right, proper.
– OPPOSITES partial.
noun *a total of £160,000*: **sum**, sum total, grand total, aggregate; whole, entirety, totality.
verb **1** *the prize money totalled £33,050*: **add up to**, amount to, come to, run to, make, work out as. **2** *he totalled up his score*: **add (up)**, count, reckon, tot up, compute, work out.

totalitarian adjective **autocratic**, undemocratic, one-party, dictatorial, tyrannical, despotic, fascistic, oppressive, repressive, illiberal; authoritarian, absolute, absolutist, fundamentalist.
– OPPOSITES democratic.

totality noun **entirety**, whole, total, aggregate, sum, sum total; all, everything.

totally adverb **completely**, entirely, wholly, thoroughly, fully, utterly, absolutely, perfectly, unreservedly, unconditionally, quite, altogether, downright; in every way, in every respect, one hundred per cent, every inch, to the hilt; informal dead, deadly.
– OPPOSITES partly.

totter verb *he tottered off down the road*: **teeter**, stagger, wobble, stumble, shuffle, shamble, toddle; reel, sway, roll, lurch.

touch verb **1** *his shoes were touching the end of the bed*: **be in contact with**, come into contact with, meet, join, connect with, converge with, be contiguous with, be against. **2** *he touched her cheek*: **press lightly**, tap, pat; feel, stroke, fondle, caress, pet; brush, graze. **3** *sales touched twenty grand last year*: **reach**, attain, come to, make; rise to, soar to; informal hit. **4** *nobody can touch him when he's on form*: **compare with**, be on a par with, equal, match, be a match for, be in the same class/league as, parallel, rival, come close to, measure up to; better, beat; informal hold a candle to. **5** *you're not supposed to touch the things in the exhibition*: **handle**, hold, pick up, feel, move; meddle with, play (about) with, fiddle with, interfere with, tamper with, disturb; use, make use of. **6** *state companies which have been touched by privatization*: **affect**, have an effect/impact on, make a difference to. **7** *Lisa felt touched by her kindness*: **affect**, move, tug at someone's heartstrings; leave an impression on, have an effect on.
noun **1** *he could feel the hairs rising on his arms at her touch*: **feel**, caress, grip, embrace; hand(s), finger(s); contact. **2** *he has lost none of his political touch*: **skill**, skilfulness, expertise, dexterity, deftness, adroitness, adeptness, ability, talent, flair, facility, proficiency, knack, technique, approach, style. **3** *there was a touch of bitterness in her voice* | *add a touch of vinegar*: **trace**, bit, suggestion, suspicion, hint, scintilla, tinge, overtone, undertone; dash, taste, spot, drop, dab, pinch, speck, soupçon. **4** *the gas lights are a nice touch*: **detail**, feature, point; addition, accessory. **5** *have you been in touch with him?* **contact**, communication, correspondence; connection, association.
■ **touch and go** *I reduced the odds, but it was still touch and go*: **uncertain**, close; precarious, risky, hazardous, dangerous, critical, hanging by a thread.
■ **touch down** *his plane touched down at Nice airport*: **land**, alight, come down, put down, arrive.
■ **touch something off** *the plan touched off a major political storm*: **cause**, spark off, trigger (off), start, set in motion, ignite, stir up, provoke, give rise to, lead to, generate.
■ **touch on/upon 1** *many television programmes have touched on the subject*: **refer to**, mention, comment on, remark on, bring up, raise, broach, allude to; cover, deal with. **2** *a self-confident manner touching on the arrogant*: **come close to**, verge on, border on, approach.
■ **touch someone up** (Brit. informal) **fondle**, molest, feel up; informal grope, paw, maul, goose; N. Amer. informal cop a feel.
■ **touch something up 1** *these paints are handy for touching up small areas*: **repaint**, retouch, patch up, fix up; renovate, refurbish, revamp; informal do up. **2** *touch up your CV and improve your interview skills*: **improve**, enhance, make better, refine;

t

informal **tweak**.

touching adjective **moving**, affecting, heart-warming, emotional, emotive, tender, sentimental; poignant, sad, tear-jerking.

touchstone noun *for nationalists, the touchstone is their degree of independence from the US:* **criterion**, standard, yardstick, benchmark, barometer, litmus test; measure, point of reference, norm, gauge, test, guide, exemplar, model, pattern.

touchy adjective **1** *she can be so touchy:* **sensitive**, oversensitive, hypersensitive, easily offended, thin-skinned, highly strung, tense; irritable, tetchy, testy, crotchety, peevish, querulous, bad-tempered, petulant, pettish; informal snappy, ratty; N. Amer. informal cranky. **2** *a touchy subject:* **delicate**, sensitive, tricky, ticklish, embarrassing, awkward, difficult; contentious, controversial.
– OPPOSITES affable.

tough adjective **1** *I donned a pair of tough leather gloves:* **durable**, strong, resilient, sturdy, rugged, solid, stout, hard-wearing, long-lasting, heavy-duty, well built, made to last. **2** *the steak was rather tough:* **chewy**, leathery, gristly, stringy, fibrous. **3** *he'll survive—he's pretty tough:* **robust**, resilient, strong, hardy, rugged, fit; informal hard. **4** *tough sentencing for persistent offenders:* **strict**, stern, severe, stringent, rigorous, hard, firm, hard-hitting, uncompromising; unsentimental, unsympathetic. **5** *the training was pretty tough:* **hard**, difficult, demanding, exacting, strenuous, gruelling, arduous, heavy (going), taxing, tiring, exhausting, punishing, laborious, stressful. **6** *these are tough questions for American policy-makers:* **difficult**, hard, knotty, thorny, tricky.
– OPPOSITES soft, weak, easy.
noun *a gang of toughs:* **ruffian**, thug, hoodlum, hooligan, bully boy; Brit. rough; informal roughneck, heavy, bruiser; Brit. informal yob, yobbo.

toughen verb **1** *the process toughens the wood fibres:* **strengthen**, fortify, reinforce, harden, temper, anneal. **2** *measures to toughen prison discipline:* **stiffen**, tighten up; increase, step up; informal beef up.

tour noun **1** *a three-day walking tour:* **trip**, excursion, journey, expedition, jaunt, outing; trek, safari. **2** *we had a tour of the factory:* **visit**, inspection, guided tour, walkabout. **3** *his tour of duty in Ulster:* **stint**, stretch, spell, turn, assignment, period.
verb **1** *this hotel is well placed for touring Somerset:* **travel round**, explore, visit, holiday in; informal do. **2** *the prince toured a local factory:* **visit**, go round, walk round, inspect.

tourist noun **holidaymaker**, traveller, sightseer, visitor, backpacker, globetrotter, day tripper, tripper; N. Amer. vacationer, vacationist, out-of-towner.
– OPPOSITES local.

tournament noun **competition**, contest, championship, meeting, meet, event, match, fixture.

tousled adjective *she ran a hand through her tousled hair:* **untidy**, dishevelled, wind-blown, messy, disordered, disarranged, messed up, rumpled, uncombed, ungroomed, tangled, wild, unkempt; informal mussed up.
– OPPOSITES neat, tidy.

tout verb **1** *in the street, merchants were touting their wares:* **peddle**, sell, hawk, offer for sale; informal flog. **2** *minicab drivers were touting for business:* **solicit**, seek, drum up, look; ask, petition, appeal, canvas. **3** *he's being touted as the next Scotland manager:* **recommend**, speak of, talk of; predict; Brit. tip.

tow verb *the car was towed back to the garage:* **pull**, haul, drag, draw, tug, lug.
■ **in tow** *he arrived with his new girlfriend in tow:* in attendance, by one's side, in one's charge; accompanying, following.

towards preposition **1** *they were driving towards her flat:* **in the direction of**, to; on the way to, on the road to, en route for. **2** *towards evening dark clouds gathered:* **just before**, shortly before, near, nearing, around, approaching, close to, coming to, getting on for. **3** *her attitude towards politics:* **with regard to**, as regards, regarding, in/with regard to, respecting, in relation to, concerning, about, apropos. **4** *a grant towards the cost of new buses:* **as a contribution to**, for, to help with.

tower noun **platform**, derrick, crane, mast, block; **steeple**, spire; minaret; belfry, campanile; gazebo.
verb *snow-capped peaks towered over the valley:* **soar**, rise, rear, loom; overshadow, overhang, dominate.

towering adjective **1** *the uplands were pierced by towering crags and cliffs:* **high**, tall, lofty, soaring, multi-storey; giant, gigantic, enormous, huge, massive; informal ginormous. **2** *he was a towering intellect:* **outstanding**, pre-eminent, leading, foremost, finest, top, surpassing, supreme, great, incomparable, unrivalled, unsurpassed, peerless. **3** *he was in a towering rage:* **terrible**, intense, overpowering, mighty, violent, vehement, passionate; incandescent, burning.

town noun **built-up area**, conurbation, municipality; city, metropolis, megalopolis; Brit. borough; Scottish burgh; N. Amer. burg.
– OPPOSITES country.

toxic adjective **poisonous**, virulent, noxious, dangerous, harmful, injurious, pernicious.
– OPPOSITES harmless.

toy noun **1** *he always gets loads of toys for Christmas:* **plaything**, game. **2** *an executive toy:* **gadget**, device; trinket, knick-knack; informal gizmo.
adjective *he brandished a toy gun:* **model**,

imitation, replica; miniature.

■ **toy with 1** *I was toying with the idea of writing a book:* think about, consider, flirt with, entertain the possibility of; informal kick around. **2** *Adam toyed with his glasses:* fiddle with, play with, fidget with, twiddle; finger. **3** *she toyed with her food:* nibble, pick at, peck at, move around the plate.

trace verb **1** *police hope to trace the owner of the jewellery:* **track down**, find, discover, detect, unearth, turn up, hunt down, ferret out, run to ground. **2** *she traced a pattern in the sand with her toe:* **draw**, write, outline, mark. **3** *the analysis traces the history of such beliefs:* **outline**, map out, sketch out, delineate, depict, show, indicate.
noun **1** *no trace had been found of the missing plane:* **vestige**, sign, mark, indication, evidence, clue; remains, remnant, relic, survival. **2** *a trace of bitterness crept into her voice:* **bit**, touch, hint, suggestion, suspicion, shadow, whiff; drop, dash, tinge, speck, shred; informal smidgen, tad. **3** *the ground was hard and they left no traces:* **trail**, tracks, marks, prints, footprints; spoor.

track noun **1** *we followed a gravel track:* **path**, pathway, footpath, lane, trail, route, way, course. **2** *the final lap of the track:* **course**, racecourse, racetrack; velodrome; Brit. circuit. **3** *he found the tracks of a grey fox:* **traces**, marks, prints, footprints, trail, spoor. **4** *commuters had to walk along the tracks:* **rail**, line, railway line. **5** *the album's title track:* **song**, recording, number, piece.
verb *he tracked a bear for 40 km:* **follow**, trail, trace, pursue, shadow, stalk, keep an eye on, keep in sight; informal tail.
■ **keep track of** *an online diary that allows you to keep track of your appointments:* monitor, follow, keep up with, keep an eye on; keep in touch with, keep up to date with; informal keep tabs on.
■ **track someone/something down** *it took seven years to track down the wreck of the ship:* discover, find, detect, hunt down/out, unearth, uncover, turn up, dig up, ferret out, bring to light, run to earth, run to ground.

tract noun *the chiefs owned large tracts of land:* **area**, region, expanse, sweep, stretch, extent, belt, swathe, zone.

tractable adjective *children are not as tractable as they used to be:* **malleable**, manageable, amenable, pliable, governable, yielding, complaisant, compliant, persuadable, accommodating, docile, biddable, obedient, submissive, meek.
– OPPOSITES recalcitrant.

traction noun **grip**, purchase, friction, adhesion.

trade noun **1** *the illicit trade in stolen cattle:* **commerce**, buying and selling, dealing, traffic, trafficking, business, marketing, merchandising; dealings, transactions. **2** *the glazier's trade:* **craft**, occupation, job, career, profession, business, line (of work), métier, vocation, calling, walk of life, field; work, employment.
verb **1** *he made his fortune trading in beaver pelts:* **deal**, buy and sell, traffic, market, merchandise, peddle; informal hawk, flog. **2** *the business is trading at a loss:* **operate**, run, do business. **3** *I traded the old machine for a newer model:* **swap**, exchange, switch; barter.
■ **trade on** *he trades on his friendship with powerful people:* exploit, take advantage of, capitalize on, profit from, use, make use of; milk; informal cash in on.

trademark noun **1** *the company's trademark:* **logo**, emblem, sign, mark, stamp, symbol, device, badge, crest, monogram, colophon; trade name, brand name, proprietary name. **2** *it had all the trademarks of a Mafia hit:* **characteristic**, hallmark, telltale sign, sign, trait, quality, attribute, feature.

trader noun **dealer**, merchant, buyer, seller, buyer and seller, marketeer, merchandiser, broker, agent; distributor, vendor, purveyor, supplier, trafficker; shopkeeper, retailer, wholesaler.

tradesman, tradeswoman noun
1 *tradesmen standing nonchalantly outside their stores:* **shopkeeper**, retailer, vendor, wholesaler; N. Amer. storekeeper. **2** *a qualified tradesman:* **craftsman**, workman, artisan.

tradition noun *an age-old tradition in our society:* **custom**, practice, convention, ritual, observance, way, unwritten law, usage, habit, institution.

traditional adjective *traditional Christmas fare:* **long-established**, customary, time-honoured, established, classic, wonted, accustomed, standard, regular, normal, conventional, usual, orthodox, habitual, set, fixed, routine, ritual; old, age-old.

traffic noun **1** *the bridge is not open to traffic:* **vehicles**, cars, lorries, trucks. **2** *they might be stuck in traffic:* **traffic jam(s)**, congestion, gridlock, tailbacks, hold-ups, queues; informal snarl-ups. **3** *the increased use of railways for goods traffic:* **transport**, transportation, freight, shipping. **4** *the illegal traffic in stolen art:* **trade**, trading, trafficking, dealing, commerce, business, buying and selling; smuggling, black market; dealings, transactions.
verb *he confessed to trafficking in gold and ivory:* **trade**, deal, do business, buy and sell; smuggle; informal run.

tragedy noun **disaster**, calamity, catastrophe, cataclysm; misfortune, vicissitude, trial, tribulation, affliction, adversity.

tragic adjective **1** *a tragic accident:* **disastrous**, calamitous, catastrophic, cataclysmic, devastating, terrible, dreadful, awful, appalling, horrendous; fatal, deadly, mortal, lethal. **2** *a tragic tale:* **sad**, unhappy, pathetic, moving, distressing, painful, harrowing, heart-rending, wretched, sorry; melancholy, doleful, mournful; informal gut-wrenching. **3** *a tragic waste of talent:*

t

dreadful, terrible, awful, deplorable, lamentable, regrettable; formal grievous.
– OPPOSITES fortunate, happy.

trail noun **1** *he left a trail of clues | a trail of devastation:* **series**, string, chain, succession, sequence; aftermath. **2** *hungry wolves on the trail of their injured prey:* **track**, spoor, path, scent; traces, marks, signs, prints, footprints. **3** *the plane's vapour trail:* **wake**, tail, stream. **4** *a trail of ants:* **line**, column, train, file, procession, string, chain, convoy; queue. **5** *country parks with nature trails:* **path**, pathway, way, footpath, track, course, route.
verb **1** *her robe trailed along the ground:* **drag**, sweep, be drawn; dangle, hang (down), droop. **2** *the roses grew wild, their stems trailing over the banks:* **hang**, droop, fall, spill, cascade. **3** *Sharpe suspected that they were trailing him:* **follow**, pursue, track, shadow, stalk; informal tail. **4** *the defending champions were trailing 10–5 at half time:* **lose**, be down, be behind, lag behind. **5** *I hate trailing round the shops:* **trudge**, plod, drag oneself, traipse, trek; N. Amer. informal schlep. **6** *her voice trailed off:* **fade**, tail off/away, grow faint, die away, dwindle, subside, peter out, fizzle out.

train verb **1** *an engineer trained in remote-sensing techniques:* **instruct**, teach, coach, tutor, school, educate, prime, drill, ground; inculcate, indoctrinate. **2** *she's training to be a hairdresser:* **study**, learn, prepare. **3** *with the Olympics in mind, athletes are training hard:* **exercise**, work out, get into shape, practise. **4** *she trained the gun on his chest:* **aim**, point, direct, level, focus; take aim, zero in on.
noun **1** *we saw a train of elephants:* **procession**, line, file, column, convoy, cavalcade, caravan, queue, string. **2** *a minister and his train of attendants:* **retinue**, entourage, cortège, following, staff, household, court; attendants, retainers, followers, bodyguards, groupies. **3** *a bizarre train of events:* **chain**, string, series, sequence, succession, set, course, cycle, concatenation.

trainer noun **coach**, instructor, teacher, tutor; handler.

training noun **1** *in-house training for staff:* **instruction**, teaching, coaching, tuition, tutoring, schooling, education; indoctrination, inculcation. **2** *four months' hard training before the match:* **exercise**, exercises, working out; practice, preparation.

traipse verb *I haven't time to go traipsing round art galleries:* **trudge**, trek, tramp, trail, plod, drag oneself, slog; Brit. informal trog; N. Amer. informal schlep.

trait noun **characteristic**, attribute, feature, (essential) quality, property; habit, custom, mannerism, idiosyncrasy, peculiarity, quirk, oddity, foible.

traitor noun *he was tried in a military court as a traitor:* **betrayer**, back-stabber, double-crosser, double-dealer, renegade, Judas, quisling, fifth columnist; turncoat, defector, deserter; collaborator, informer, double agent; informal snake in the grass, two-timer.

traitorous adjective **treacherous**, disloyal, treasonous, back-stabbing; double-crossing, double-dealing, faithless, unfaithful, two-faced, false-hearted, duplicitous, deceitful, false; informal two-timing; literary perfidious.
– OPPOSITES loyal.

trajectory noun **course**, path, route, track, line, orbit.

tramp verb **1** *men were tramping through the shrubbery:* **trudge**, plod, stamp, trample, lumber, clump, clomp, stump, stomp; informal traipse, galumph. **2** *he spent ten days tramping through the jungle:* **trek**, slog, trudge, drag oneself, walk, hike, march, traipse; N. Amer. informal schlep.
noun **1** *a dirty old tramp:* **vagrant**, vagabond, homeless person, down-and-out; traveller, drifter; beggar, mendicant; N. Amer. hobo; Austral./NZ bagman; informal bag lady; N. Amer. informal bum. **2** *the regular tramp of the sentry's boots:* **footstep**, step, footfall, tread, stamp, stomp. **3** *we went for a tramp round Norwich:* **trek**, slog, trudge, hike, march, walk; N. Amer. informal schlep.

trample verb **tread**, tramp, stamp, stomp, walk over; squash, crush, flatten.

trance noun **daze**, stupor, dream, fugue; Scottish dwam.

tranquil adjective **1** *a wonderfully tranquil village:* **peaceful**, calm, restful, quiet, still, relaxing, undisturbed. **2** *Martha smiled, perfectly tranquil:* **calm**, serene, relaxed, unruffled, unperturbed, unflustered, untroubled, composed, {cool, calm, and collected}.
– OPPOSITES busy, excitable.

tranquillity noun **1** *the tranquillity of the Norfolk countryside:* **peace**, peacefulness, restfulness, repose, calm, calmness, quiet, quietness, stillness. **2** *the incident jolted her out of her tranquillity:* **composure**, calmness, serenity.

tranquillize verb **sedate**, put under sedation, drug.

tranquillizer noun **sedative**, barbiturate, sleeping pill, narcotic, opiate; informal trank, downer.
– OPPOSITES stimulant.

transact verb **conduct**, carry out, negotiate, do, perform, execute, take care of; settle, conclude, finish, clinch, accomplish.

transaction noun **1** *property transactions:* **deal**, undertaking, arrangement, bargain, negotiation, agreement, settlement; proceedings. **2** *the transactions of the Historical Society:* **proceedings**, report, record(s), minutes, account; archives. **3** *the transaction of government business:* **conduct**, carrying out, negotiation, performance, execution.

transcend verb **1** *an issue that transcended*

party politics: **go beyond**, rise above, cut across. **2** *his military exploits far transcended those of his predecessors:* **surpass**, exceed, beat, top, cap, outdo, outclass, outstrip, leave behind, outshine, eclipse, overshadow, put in the shade, upstage.

transcribe verb **1** *each interview was taped and transcribed:* **write out**, copy out, put on paper. **2** *a person who can take and transcribe shorthand:* **transliterate**, interpret, translate.

transcript noun **text**, transliteration, written/printed record.

transfer verb **1** *the hostages were transferred to a safe house:* **move**, convey, take, bring, shift, remove, carry, transport; transplant, relocate, resettle. **2** *the property was transferred to his wife:* **hand over**, pass on, make over, turn over, sign over, consign, devolve, assign, delegate.
noun *he died shortly after his transfer to hospital:* **move**, conveyance, transferral, transference, relocation, removal, transplantation.

transfigure verb **transform**, transmute, change, alter, metamorphose; humorous transmogrify.

transfix verb **1** *he was transfixed by the images on the screen:* **mesmerize**, hypnotize, spellbind, bewitch, captivate, entrance, enthral, fascinate, enrapture, grip, rivet; root to the spot, paralyse. **2** *a field mouse is transfixed by the owl's curved talons:* **impale**, stab, spear, pierce, spike, skewer, gore, stick, run through.

transform verb **change**, alter, convert, metamorphose, transfigure, transmute; revolutionize, overhaul; remodel, reshape, remould, redo, reconstruct, rebuild, reorganize, rearrange, rework, renew, revamp, remake; humorous transmogrify.

transformation noun **change**, alteration, conversion, metamorphosis, transfiguration, transmutation, sea change; revolution, overhaul; remodelling, reshaping, remoulding, redoing, reconstruction, rebuilding, reorganization, rearrangement, reworking, renewal, revamp, remaking; humorous transmogrification.

transgress verb **1** *if they transgress, the punishment is harsh:* **misbehave**, behave badly, break the law, err, fall from grace, stray from the straight and narrow, sin, do wrong, go astray. **2** *she had transgressed an unwritten social law:* **infringe**, breach, contravene, disobey, defy, violate, break, flout.

transgression noun *this was a punishment for past transgressions:* **offence**, crime, sin, wrong, wrongdoing, misdemeanour, misdeed, lawbreaking; error, lapse, fault.

transgressor noun **wrongdoer**, offender, miscreant, lawbreaker, criminal, villain, felon, malefactor, guilty party, culprit; sinner, evil-doer.

transient adjective *these transient joys will fade all too soon:* **transitory**, temporary, short-lived, short-term, ephemeral, impermanent, brief, short, momentary, fleeting, passing, fugitive, {here today, gone tomorrow}; literary evanescent.
– OPPOSITES permanent.

transit noun *the transit of goods between states:* **transport**, transportation, movement, conveyance, shipment, haulage, carriage, transfer.
■ **in transit** en route, on the journey, on the way, along/on the road, during transport.

transition noun **change**, passage, move, transformation, conversion, metamorphosis, alteration, changeover, shift, switch, jump, leap, progression, progress, development, evolution.

transitional adjective **1** *we are in a transitional period:* **intermediate**, interim, changeover; changing, fluid, unsettled. **2** *the transitional government:* **interim**, temporary, provisional, pro tem, acting, caretaker.

transitory adjective **transient**, temporary, brief, short, short-lived, short-term, impermanent, ephemeral, momentary, fleeting, passing, fugitive, {here today, gone tomorrow}; literary evanescent.
– OPPOSITES permanent.

translate verb **1** *the German original had been translated into English:* **render**, put, express, convert, change; transcribe, transliterate; paraphrase, reword, rephrase; decipher, decode, gloss. **2** *interesting ideas cannot always be translated into effective movies:* **change**, transform, alter, adapt, turn, transmute; humorous transmogrify.

translation noun **1** *the translation of the Bible into English:* **rendition**, rendering, conversion; transcription, transliteration. **2** *the translation of these policies into practice:* **conversion**, change, transformation, alteration, adaptation, transmutation.

translucent adjective **semi-transparent**, pellucid, limpid, clear; diaphanous, gossamer, sheer.
– OPPOSITES opaque.

transmission noun **1** *the transmission of knowledge and culture to the next generation:* **transference**, transferral, communication, conveyance; dissemination, spreading, circulation. **2** *the transmission of the film was delayed:* **broadcasting**, relaying, airing, televising. **3** *a live transmission from Berlin:* **broadcast**, programme, show.

transmit verb **1** *the use of computers to transmit information:* **transfer**, pass on, hand on, communicate, convey, impart, channel, carry, relay, dispatch; disseminate, spread, circulate. **2** *the programme will be transmitted on Sunday:* **broadcast**, relay, send out, air, televise.

transmute verb *the pain and grief*

t

that motivate can be transmuted into
pleasure: **change**, alter, adapt, transform,
convert, metamorphose, translate; humorous
transmogrify.

transparency noun 1 the transparency of
the glass: **translucency**, limpidity, clearness,
clarity. 2 colour transparencies: **slide**,
diapositive.

transparent adjective 1 transparent blue
water: **clear**, crystal clear, see-through,
translucent, pellucid, limpid, glassy. 2 fine
transparent fabrics: **see-through**, sheer,
filmy, gauzy, diaphanous. 3 the symbolism
of this myth is transparent: **obvious**,
unambiguous, unequivocal, clear, crystal
clear, plain, (as) plain as the nose on your
face, apparent, unmistakable, manifest,
conspicuous, patent, palpable, indisputable,
evident, self-evident.
– OPPOSITES opaque, obscure.

transpire verb 1 it transpired that her family
had moved away: **become known**, emerge,
come to light, be revealed, turn out, come
out, be discovered, prove to be the case. 2 I'm
going to find out exactly what transpired:
happen, occur, take place, arise, come about,
turn up, chance, befall.

transplant verb 1 it was proposed to
transplant the club to the vacant site:
transfer, move, remove, shift, relocate,
take. 2 the seedlings should be transplanted
into larger pots: **replant**, repot, relocate.
3 kidneys must be transplanted within 48
hours of removal: **transfer**, implant.

transport verb 1 the concrete blocks were
transported by lorry: **convey**, carry, take,
transfer, move, shift, send, deliver, truck,
ship, ferry; informal cart. 2 she was completely
transported by the excitement: **thrill**, delight,
carry away, enrapture, entrance, enchant,
enthral, electrify, captivate, bewitch,
fascinate, spellbind, charm.
noun 1 alternative forms of transport:
conveyance, transportation; vehicle. 2 the
transport of crude oil: **transportation**,
conveyance, carriage, shipment, shipping,
haulage; transit.

transpose verb 1 the blue and black plates
were transposed: **interchange**, exchange,
switch, swap (round), reverse, invert. 2 the
themes are transposed from the sphere of
love to that of work: **transfer**, shift, relocate,
transplant, move, displace.

transverse adjective **crosswise**, crossways,
cross, horizontal, diagonal, oblique.

trap noun 1 an animal caught in a trap: **snare**,
net, gin; N. Amer. deadfall. 2 the question was
set as a trap: **trick**, ploy, ruse, deception,
subterfuge; booby trap; informal set-up.
verb 1 police trapped the two men, who
admitted blackmail: **snare**, entrap, ensnare,
lay a trap for; capture, catch, corner. 2 a rat
was trapped in the barn: **confine**, cut off,
corner, shut in, pen in, hem in; imprison,
hold captive. 3 I hoped to trap him into
an admission: **trick**, dupe, deceive, lure,

inveigle, beguile, fool, hoodwink; catch out,
trip up.

trappings plural noun the spectacular
ritual and trappings of the monarchy:
accessories, accoutrements, appurtenances,
accompaniments, ornamentation,
adornment, decoration; regalia, panoply,
paraphernalia, apparatus, finery, equipment,
gear, effects, things.

trash noun 1 (N. Amer.) the subway entrance
was blocked with trash: **rubbish**, refuse,
waste, litter, junk, detritus; N. Amer. garbage.
2 (informal) if they read at all, they read
this trash: **rubbish**, nonsense, trivia, pulp
(fiction), pap; N. Amer. garbage; informal drivel,
dreck.
verb (N. Amer. informal) the apartment had
been totally trashed: **wreck**, ruin, destroy,
devastate; vandalize; informal total.

trauma noun 1 the trauma of divorce took its
toll: **shock**, upheaval, distress, stress, strain,
pain, anguish, suffering, upset, agony,
misery, sorrow, grief, heartache, heartbreak,
torture; ordeal, trial, tribulation, trouble,
worry, anxiety; nightmare. 2 the gallstone
can be extracted without severe trauma to
the liver: **injury**, damage, wounding; cut,
laceration, lesion, abrasion, contusion.

traumatic adjective **disturbing**, shocking,
distressing, upsetting, heartbreaking,
painful, agonizing, hurtful, stressful,
damaging, injurious, harmful, awful,
terrible, devastating, harrowing; informal
gut-wrenching.

travel verb 1 he spent much of his time
travelling abroad: **journey**, tour, take a trip,
voyage, go sightseeing, globetrot, backpack;
informal gallivant. 2 we travelled the length
and breadth of the island: **journey through**,
cross, traverse, cover; roam, rove, range,
trek. 3 light travels faster than sound: **move**,
be transmitted.
noun he amassed great wealth during
his travels: **journeys**, expeditions, trips,
tours, excursions, voyages, explorations,
wanderings; travelling, touring, sightseeing,
backpacking, globetrotting; informal
gallivanting.

traveller noun 1 thousands of travellers were
left stranded: **tourist**, tripper, holidaymaker,
sightseer, visitor, globetrotter, backpacker;
pilgrim; passenger, commuter; N. Amer.
vacationer, vacationist. 2 a travellers' site:
gypsy, Romany; nomad, migrant, wanderer,
itinerant, drifter; tramp, vagrant; dialect
didicoi.

travelling adjective 1 the travelling
population: **nomadic**, itinerant, peripatetic,
wandering, migrant, vagrant, of no fixed
address/abode; gypsy, Romany. 2 a little
travelling clock: **portable**, lightweight,
compact, miniature.

traverse verb 1 he traversed the deserts
of Persia: **travel over/across**, cross,
journey over/across, pass over; cover; ply;
wander, roam, range. 2 a ditch traversed

by a wooden bridge: **cross**, bridge, span; extend/lie/stretch across.

travesty noun *this is a travesty of justice:* **misrepresentation**, distortion, perversion, corruption, poor substitute, mockery, parody, caricature; farce, charade, pantomime, sham; informal apology for, excuse for.

treacherous adjective **1** *two treacherous Scottish lords betrayed Wallace's whereabouts:* **traitorous**, disloyal, faithless, unfaithful, duplicitous, deceitful, false, back-stabbing, double-crossing, double-dealing, two-faced, untrustworthy, unreliable; informal two-timing; literary perfidious. **2** *treacherous driving conditions:* **dangerous**, hazardous, perilous, unsafe, precarious, risky; informal dicey, hairy.
– OPPOSITES loyal, faithful, reliable, safe.

treachery noun **betrayal**, disloyalty, faithlessness, unfaithfulness, infidelity, breach of trust, duplicity, deceit, deception, stab in the back, back-stabbing, double-dealing, untrustworthiness; treason; informal two-timing; literary perfidy.

tread verb **1** *he trod purposefully down the hall:* **walk**, step, stride, pace, go; march, tramp, plod, stomp, trudge. **2** *the snow had been trodden down by the horses:* **crush**, flatten, press, squash; trample, tramp, stamp; compact.
noun *we heard his heavy tread on the stairs:* **step**, footstep, footfall, tramp.

treason noun **treachery**; disloyalty, betrayal, faithlessness; sedition, subversion, mutiny, rebellion; literary perfidy.
– OPPOSITES allegiance, loyalty.

treasonable adjective **traitorous**, treacherous, disloyal; seditious, subversive, mutinous, rebellious; literary perfidious.
– OPPOSITES loyal.

treasure noun **1** *they uncovered a casket of treasure:* **riches**, valuables, jewels, gems, gold, money, cash; wealth, fortune; Brit. treasure trove. **2** *art treasures:* **valuable**, work of art, masterpiece. **3** (informal) *she's a real treasure:* **gem**, angel; find, prize; informal star, one of a kind, one in a million.
verb *I treasure the photographs I took of Jack:* **cherish**, hold dear, prize, value (greatly); adore, dote on, love dearly, be devoted to, worship.

treasury noun **1** *she transferred billions from the national treasury to her own account:* **exchequer**, purse; bank, coffers. **2** *the area is a treasury of early fossils:* **rich source**, repository, storehouse, treasure house; fund, mine, bank.

treat verb **1** *Charlotte treated him very badly:* **behave towards**, act towards, use; deal with, handle. **2** *police are treating the fire as arson:* **regard**, consider, view, look on; put down as. **3** *the book treats its subject with great insight:* **deal with**, tackle, handle, discuss, explore, investigate;

consider, study, analyse. **4** *she was treated at Addenbrooke's Hospital:* **care for**, nurse, tend, attend to. **5** *the plants may prove useful in treating cancer:* **cure**, heal, remedy, deal with, manage. **6** *he treated her to a slap-up lunch:* **stand**; take out for, buy, give; pay for; entertain, wine and dine; informal foot the bill for. **7** *delegates were treated to authentic Indonesian dance performances:* **regale with**, entertain with/by, fête with, amuse with, divert with.
noun **1** *I bought you some chocolate as a treat:* **present**, gift, delicacy, luxury, indulgence, extravagance. **2** *it was a real treat to see them:* **pleasure**, delight, thrill, joy.

treatise noun *his famous treatise on medical ethics:* **disquisition**, essay, paper, work, exposition, discourse, dissertation, thesis, monograph, study, critique.

treatment noun **1** *the company's appalling treatment of its workers:* **behaviour towards**, conduct towards; handling of, dealings with. **2** *she's responding well to treatment:* **(medical) care**, therapy, nursing; medication, drugs. **3** *her treatment of the topic:* **discussion**, handling, investigation, exploration, consideration, study, analysis, critique.

treaty noun **agreement**, settlement, pact, deal, entente, concordat, accord, protocol, compact, convention, contract, covenant, bargain, pledge.

trek noun *a three-day trek across the desert:* **journey**, trip, expedition, safari, odyssey; hike, march, slog, footslog, tramp, walk; long haul.
verb *we trekked through the jungle for weeks:* **hike**, tramp, march, slog, footslog, trudge, traipse, walk; travel, journey.

trellis noun **lattice**, framework; network, mesh, tracery; grille, grid, grating; latticework, trelliswork; technical reticulation.

tremble verb **1** *Joe's hands were trembling:* **shake**, quiver, twitch; quaver, waver. **2** *the entire building trembled:* **shake**, shudder, judder, wobble, rock, vibrate, move, sway, totter, teeter. **3** *she trembled at the thought of what he had in store for her:* **be afraid**, be frightened, be apprehensive, worry, shake (in one's shoes); quail, shrink, blench.
noun *I noticed the slight tremble in her hands:* **tremor**, shake, shakiness, trembling, quiver, twitch.
– OPPOSITES steadiness.

tremendous adjective **1** *tremendous sums of money:* **huge**, enormous, immense, colossal, massive, prodigious, stupendous, monumental, mammoth, vast, gigantic, giant, mighty, epic, titanic, towering, king-size(d), gargantuan; substantial, considerable; informal whopping, thumping, astronomical, humongous; Brit. informal whacking, ginormous. **2** *there was a tremendous explosion:* **loud**, deafening, ear-splitting, booming, thundering, thunderous, resounding. **3** (informal) *I've seen him play*

t

and he's tremendous: **excellent**, splendid, wonderful, marvellous, magnificent, superb, glorious, sublime, lovely, delightful, too good to be true; informal super, great, amazing, fantastic, terrific, sensational, heavenly, divine, gorgeous, grand, fabulous, fab, awesome, magic, ace, wicked, mind-blowing, far out, out of this world; Brit. informal smashing, brilliant, brill; N. Amer. informal boss; Austral./NZ informal beaut, bonzer.
– OPPOSITES tiny, small, poor.

tremor noun **1** *the sudden tremor of her hands:* **trembling**, shaking, shakiness, tremble, shake, quivering, quiver, twitching, twitch, tic. **2** *a tremor of fear ran through her:* **frisson**, shiver, spasm, thrill, tingle, stab; wave, surge, rush, ripple. **3** *the epicentre of the tremor:* **earthquake**, earth tremor, shock; informal quake; N. Amer. informal temblor.

tremulous adjective **1** *he addressed the crowd in a tremulous voice:* **shaky**, trembling, shaking, unsteady, quavering, quivering, quaking, weak. **2** *he gave a tremulous smile:* **timid**, diffident, shy, hesitant, uncertain, nervous, fearful, frightened, scared, anxious, apprehensive; informal trepidatious.
– OPPOSITES steady, confident.

trench noun **ditch**, channel, trough, excavation, furrow, rut, conduit, cut, drain, waterway, watercourse, moat.

trenchant adjective *he made trenchant criticisms of her leadership style:* **incisive**, penetrating, sharp, keen, acute, shrewd, rapier-like, piercing; vigorous, forceful, strong, telling, emphatic, forthright; cutting, biting.
– OPPOSITES vague.

trend noun **1** *an upward trend in unemployment:* **tendency**, movement, drift, swing, shift, course, current, direction, inclination, leaning. **2** *the latest trend in dance music:* **fashion**, vogue, style, mode, craze, mania, rage; informal fad, thing.

trendy adjective (informal) **fashionable**, in vogue, popular, (bang) up to date, up to the minute, modern, all the rage, modish, à la mode, trendsetting; stylish, chic, designer; informal cool, funky, in, hot, big, hip, happening, sharp, groovy, snazzy, with it; N. Amer. informal tony, kicky.
– OPPOSITES unfashionable.

trepidation noun **fear**, apprehension, dread, fearfulness, agitation, anxiety, worry, nervousness, tension, misgivings, unease, uneasiness, foreboding, disquiet, dismay, consternation, alarm, panic; informal butterflies, jitteriness, the jitters, a cold sweat, the heebie-jeebies, the willies, the shakes, collywobbles, cold feet; Brit. informal the (screaming) abdabs.
– OPPOSITES equanimity, composure.

trespass verb *there is no excuse for trespassing on railway property:* **enter without permission**, encroach on, invade; squat.

noun *his alleged trespass on council land:* **unlawful entry**, intrusion, encroachment, invasion.

trespasser noun **intruder**, interloper, unwelcome visitor; squatter.

tresses plural noun **hair**, head of hair, mane, mop (of hair), shock of hair; locks, curls, ringlets, dreadlocks, corn rows.

trial noun **1** *the trial is expected to last several weeks:* **(court) case**, lawsuit, suit, hearing, inquiry, tribunal, litigation, (legal/judicial) proceedings, (legal) action; court martial; appeal, retrial. **2** *the drug is undergoing clinical trials:* **test**, try-out, experiment, pilot study; examination, check, assessment, evaluation, appraisal, trial/test run, dummy run; informal dry run. **3** *she could be a bit of a trial at times:* **nuisance**, pest, bother, irritant, problem, inconvenience, plague, thorn in one's flesh, the bane of one's life, one's cross to bear; informal pain, pain in the neck/backside, headache, drag, nightmare; Scottish informal skelf; N. Amer. informal pain in the butt, nudnik, burr under/in someone's saddle.
adjective *a three-month trial period:* **test**, experimental, pilot, exploratory, probationary, provisional.
verb *the electronic cash card has been trialled by several banks:* **test**, try out, put to the test, put through its paces; pilot.

tribe noun **(ethnic) group**, people, nation; family, dynasty, house; clan.

tribulation noun **1** *the tribulations of her personal life:* **trouble**, difficulty, problem, worry, anxiety, burden, ordeal, trial, adversity, hardship, tragedy, trauma, affliction; setback, blow; informal hassle. **2** *his time of tribulation was just beginning:* **suffering**, distress, trouble, misery, wretchedness, unhappiness, sadness, heartache, woe, grief, pain, anguish, agony.

tribunal noun **1** *he was summoned to a rent tribunal:* **board**, panel, committee. **2** *an international war-crimes tribunal:* **court**, court of justice, law court, law court; court of inquiry; N. Amer. forum.

tribute noun **1** *tributes flooded in from friends and colleagues:* **accolade**, praise, commendation, salute, testimonial, homage, eulogy, paean; congratulations, compliments, plaudits; formal encomium. **2** *it is a tribute to his determination that he ever played again:* **testimony**, indication, manifestation, evidence, proof, attestation.
– OPPOSITES criticism, condemnation.
■ **pay tribute to** praise, sing the praises of, speak highly of, commend, acclaim, take one's hat off to, applaud, salute, honour, show appreciation of, recognize, acknowledge, pay homage to, extol; formal laud.

trick noun **1** *he's capable of any mean trick:* **stratagem**, ploy, ruse, scheme, device, manoeuvre, contrivance, machination,

artifice, wile, dodge; deceit, deception, trickery, subterfuge, chicanery, sharp practice; swindle, hoax, fraud, confidence trick; informal con (trick), set-up, game, scam, sting; Brit. informal wheeze; N. Amer. informal bunco. **2** *I think he's playing a trick on us:* **(practical) joke**, prank, jape; informal leg-pull, spoof, put-on. **3** *he entertained the kids with conjuring tricks:* **feat**, stunt; (**tricks**) **sleight of hand**, legerdemain, prestidigitation; magic. **4** *it was probably a trick of the light:* **illusion**, optical illusion, figment of the imagination; mirage; hallucination. **5** *the tricks of the trade:* **knack**, art, skill, technique; secret.
verb *many people have been tricked by villains with false identity cards:* **deceive**, delude, hoodwink, mislead, take in, dupe, fool, double-cross, cheat, defraud, swindle, catch out, gull, hoax, bamboozle; informal con, diddle, put one over on, pull a fast one on, pull the wool over someone's eyes, take for a ride, lead up the garden path, shaft, do; N. Amer. informal sucker, snooker, gold-brick; Austral. informal pull a swifty on.
■ **trick someone/something out** *she was tricked out in a red sash and a necklace of silver dollars:* **dress (up)**, attire, array, rig out, garb, get up; adorn, decorate, deck (out), bedeck, embellish, ornament, festoon.

trickery noun **deception**, deceit, dishonesty, cheating, duplicity, double-dealing, sleight of hand, guile, craftiness, deviousness, subterfuge, skulduggery, chicanery, fraud, fraudulence, swindling, sharp practice; informal monkey business, funny business, jiggery-pokery, kidology.
– OPPOSITES honesty.

trickle verb *blood was trickling from two cuts in his lip:* **drip**, dribble, ooze, leak, seep, spill.
– OPPOSITES pour, gush.
noun *trickles of water ran down his arm:* **dribble**, drip, thin stream, rivulet.

trickster noun **swindler**, cheat, fraud, fraudster; charlatan, impostor, sham, hoaxer; rogue, villain, scoundrel; informal con man/artist; N. Amer. informal grifter, bunco artist; Austral. informal illywhacker, magsman.

tricky adjective **1** *this is a tricky situation for him:* **difficult**, awkward, problematic, delicate, ticklish, sensitive, embarrassing, touchy; risky, uncertain, precarious; thorny, knotty; informal sticky, dicey; N. Amer. informal gnarly. **2** *he was a tricky and unscrupulous politician:* **cunning**, crafty, wily, guileful, artful, devious, sly, scheming, calculating, designing, sharp, shrewd, astute, canny; duplicitous, dishonest, deceitful.
– OPPOSITES straightforward, honest.

tried and trusted adjective **reliable**, dependable, trustworthy, trusted, certain, sure; proven, proved, tested, tried and tested, established, fail-safe; reputable.

trifle noun **1** *we needn't bother the headmaster over such a trifle:* triviality, bagatelle,

inessential, nothing; technicality; (**trifles**) trivia, minutiae. **2** *he bought it for a trifle:* **next to nothing**, very small amount; informal peanuts; N. Amer. informal chump change.
■ **a trifle** *he looked a trifle apprehensive:* a little, a bit, somewhat, a touch, a spot, a mite, a whit; informal a tad.
■ **trifle with** *men who trifle with women's affections:* play with, toy with, dally with, play fast and loose with; informal mess about with.

trifling adjective **trivial**, unimportant, insignificant, inconsequential, petty, minor, of little/no account, of little/no consequence, footling, incidental; silly, small, tiny, inconsiderable, nominal, negligible; informal piffling, piddling, fiddling.
– OPPOSITES important.

trigger verb **1** *the incident triggered an acrimonious debate:* **precipitate**, prompt, trigger off, set off, spark (off), touch off, provoke, stir up; cause, give rise to, lead to, set in motion, occasion, bring about, generate, engender, begin, start, initiate. **2** *burglars had triggered the alarm:* **activate**, set off, set going, trip.

trill verb **warble**, sing, chirp, chirrup, tweet, twitter, cheep, peep.

trim verb **1** *his hair had been washed and trimmed:* **cut**, barber, crop, shorten, clip, snip, shear; style, neaten, shape, tidy up. **2** *trim off the lower leaves using a sharp knife:* **cut off**, remove, take off, chop off, lop off; prune, pollard. **3** *production costs need to be trimmed:* **reduce**, decrease, cut down, cut back, scale down, prune, slim down, pare down, dock. **4** *the story was severely trimmed for the film version:* **shorten**, abridge, condense, abbreviate, telescope, truncate. **5** *a pair of black leather gloves trimmed with fake fur:* **decorate**, adorn, ornament, embellish; edge, pipe, border, hem, fringe.
noun **1** *white curtains with a blue trim:* **edging**, trimming, ornamentation, adornment, embellishment; border, piping, hem, fringe, frill. **2** *hair in desperate need of a trim:* **haircut**, cut, clip, snip; pruning; tidy-up.
adjective **1** *a cropped, fitted jacket looks nice and trim with a long-line skirt:* **smart**, stylish, chic, spruce, dapper, elegant, crisp; N. Amer. trig; informal natty, sharp; N. Amer. informal spiffy. **2** *he always kept his garden trim:* **neat**, tidy, neat and tidy, orderly, in (good) order, well kept, well maintained, shipshape (and Bristol fashion), in apple-pie order, immaculate, spick and span. **3** *her trim figure appeared in the doorway:* **slim**, slender, lean, clean-limbed, sleek, willowy, lissom, sylphlike, svelte; streamlined.
– OPPOSITES untidy, messy.
■ **in trim** *she keeps herself in trim with regular exercise:* fit, in good health; slim, in shape.

trimming noun **1** *a black party dress*

t

with lace trimming: **decoration**, trim, ornamentation, adornment, embroidery; border, edging, piping, fringes, frills. **2** *roast turkey with all the trimmings:* **accompaniments**, extras, frills, accessories, accoutrements, trappings, paraphernalia; garnishing, garnish. **3** *I've swept up all the hedge trimmings:* **cuttings**, clippings, parings, shavings.

trinket noun **knick-knack**, bauble, ornament, curio, trifle, toy, novelty, gimcrack; N. Amer. kickshaw; N. Amer. informal tchotchke.

trio noun **threesome**, three, triumvirate, triad, troika, trinity; trilogy, triptych; triplets.

trip verb **1** *he tripped on the loose stones:* **stumble**, lose one's footing, slip, lose one's balance, fall (down), tumble, topple. **2** *the question was intended to trip him up:* **catch out**, trick, outwit, outsmart; throw off balance, disconcert, unsettle, discountenance, discomfit; informal throw, wrong-foot; Brit. informal catch on the hop. **3** *they tripped up the terrace steps:* **skip**, run, dance, prance, bound, spring, scamper. **4** *Hoffman had tripped the alarm:* **set off**, activate, trigger; turn on, switch on, throw. noun **1** *we went on a trip to Paris:* **excursion**, outing, jaunt; **holiday**, visit, tour, journey, expedition, voyage; drive, run, day out, day trip; informal spin. **2** *trips and falls cause nearly half such accidents:* **stumble**, slip; fall, tumble, spill.

triple adjective **1** *a triple alliance:* **three-way**, tripartite; threefold. **2** *they paid him triple the going rate:* **three times**, treble.

trite adjective *this observation struck me as both trite and irrelevant:* **banal**, hackneyed, clichéd, platitudinous, vapid, commonplace, conventional, stereotyped, overused, overdone, overworked, stale, worn out, time-worn, tired, hoary, hack, unimaginative, unoriginal, uninteresting, dull; informal old hat, corny, played out; N. Amer. informal cornball.
– OPPOSITES original, imaginative.

triumph noun **1** *the garden was built to celebrate Napoleon's many triumphs:* **victory**, win, conquest, success; achievement. **2** *his eyes shone with triumph:* **jubilation**, exultation, elation, delight, joy, happiness, glee, pride, satisfaction. **3** *the bridge is a triumph of Victorian engineering:* **tour de force**, masterpiece, coup, wonder, sensation.
– OPPOSITES defeat, disappointment.
verb **1** *he triumphed in the British Grand Prix:* **win**, succeed, come first, be victorious, carry the day, carry all before one, prevail, take the honours, come out on top. **2** *they had no chance of triumphing over the Nationalists:* **defeat**, beat, conquer, overcome, overpower, overwhelm, get the better of; prevail against, subdue, subjugate; informal lick, best.
– OPPOSITES lose.

triumphant adjective **1** *the triumphant*

British team: **victorious**, successful, winning, conquering; undefeated, unbeaten. **2** *she looked up, a triumphant expression on her face:* **jubilant**, exultant, elated, rejoicing, joyful, joyous, delighted, gleeful, proud; gloating.
– OPPOSITES unsuccessful, despondent.

trivia plural noun **(petty) details**, minutiae, niceties, technicalities, trivialities, trifles, non-essentials.

trivial adjective **1** *your problems are trivial in comparison with Peter's:* **unimportant**, insignificant, inconsequential, minor, of no account, of no consequence, of no importance; incidental, inessential, non-essential, petty, trifling, footling, small, slight, little, inconsiderable, negligible, paltry; informal piddling, piffling, fiddling. **2** *I used to be quite a trivial person:* **frivolous**, superficial, shallow, unthinking, empty-headed, feather-brained, lightweight, foolish, silly.
– OPPOSITES important, significant, serious.

triviality noun **1** *the triviality of the subject matter annoyed me:* **unimportance**, insignificance, inconsequentiality, pettiness. **2** *he need not concern himself with such trivialities:* **(minor) detail**, trifle, non-essential, nothing; technicality; (**trivialities**) trivia, minutiae.

trivialize verb **minimize**, play down, underestimate, underplay, make light of, treat lightly, dismiss; informal pooh-pooh.

troop noun **1** *a troop of tourists tramped along behind a tiny guide:* **group**, party, band, gang, bevy, body, company, troupe, crowd, throng, horde, pack, drove, flock, swarm, multitude, host, army; informal bunch, gaggle, crew, posse. **2** *British troops were stationed here:* **soldiers**, (armed) forces, servicemen/women; the services, the army, the military, soldiery.
verb **1** *we trooped out of the hall:* **walk**, march, file; flock, crowd, throng, stream, swarm, surge, spill. **2** *Caroline and I trooped wearily home:* **trudge**, plod, traipse, trail, drag oneself, tramp; N. Amer. informal schlep.

trophy noun **cup**, medal; prize, award.

tropical adjective **(very) hot**, sweltering, humid, sultry, steamy, sticky, oppressive, stifling, suffocating, heavy; informal boiling.
– OPPOSITES cold, arctic.

trot verb *Doyle trotted across the patio:* **run**, jog; scuttle, scurry, bustle, scamper.
■ **on the trot** (Brit. informal) *they lost seven matches on the trot:* in succession, one after the other, in a row, consecutively, successively; running, straight.
■ **trot something out** (informal) *he trotted out the official Downing Street line:* recite, repeat, regurgitate, churn out; come out with, produce.

trouble noun **1** *you've caused enough trouble already:* **problems**, difficulty, bother, inconvenience, worry, anxiety,

distress, stress, agitation, harassment, unpleasantness; Informal hassle. **2** *she poured out all her troubles:* **problem**, misfortune, difficulty, trial, tribulation, trauma, burden, pain, woe, grief, heartache, misery, affliction, suffering. **3** *he's gone to a lot of trouble to help you:* **bother**, inconvenience, fuss, effort, exertion, work, labour; pains, care, attention, thought. **4** *I wouldn't want to be a trouble to her:* **nuisance**, bother, inconvenience, irritation, irritant, problem, trial, pest, thorn in someone's flesh/side; informal headache, pain, pain in the neck/backside, drag; N. Amer. informal pain in the butt, nudnik. **5** *you're too gullible, that's your trouble:* **problem**, difficulty; weakness, weak point, failing, fault, imperfection, defect, blemish. **6** *he had a history of heart trouble:* **disease**, illness, sickness, ailments, complaints, problems; disorder, disability. **7** *the crash was due to engine trouble:* **malfunction**, failure, breakdown. **8** *a match marred by serious crowd trouble:* **disturbance**, disorder, unrest, fighting, ructions, fracas.
verb **1** *this matter had been troubling her for some time:* **worry**, bother, concern, disturb, upset, agitate, distress, perturb, annoy, irritate, vex, irk, nag, niggle, prey on someone's mind, weigh down, burden; informal bug. **2** *he was troubled by bouts of ill health:* **afflict**, burden; suffer from, be cursed with. **3** *I'm sorry to trouble you:* **inconvenience**, bother, impose on, disturb, put out, disoblige; informal hassle.
■ **in trouble** in difficulty, in difficulties, in a mess, in a bad way, in a predicament; informal in a tight corner/spot, in a fix, in a hole, in hot water, in a pickle, in the soup, up against it; Brit. informal up a gum tree.

troubled adjective **1** *Joanna looked troubled:* **anxious**, worried, concerned, perturbed, disturbed, bothered, ill at ease, uneasy, unsettled, agitated; distressed, upset, dismayed. **2** *we live in troubled times:* **difficult**, challenging, problematic, interesting, unsettled, hard, tough, stressful, dark.

troublemaker noun **mischief-maker**, rabble-rouser, firebrand, agitator, agent provocateur, ringleader, incendiary; demagogue; scandalmonger, gossipmonger, meddler; informal stirrer.

troublesome adjective **1** *this is indeed a troublesome problem:* **annoying**, irritating, exasperating, maddening, infuriating, irksome, vexatious, vexing, bothersome, tiresome, worrying, worrisome, disturbing, upsetting, niggling, nagging; difficult, awkward, problematic, taxing; informal aggravating; N. Amer. informal pesky. **2** *she really is a troublesome child:* **difficult**, awkward, trying, demanding, uncooperative, rebellious, unmanageable, unruly, obstreperous, disruptive, badly behaved, disobedient, naughty, recalcitrant.

– OPPOSITES simple, cooperative.

trough noun **1** *a large feeding trough:* **manger**, feedbox, feeder, crib. **2** *we dug a thirty-yard trough:* **channel**, conduit, trench, ditch, gully, drain, culvert, flume, gutter.

trounce verb **defeat (utterly)**, beat hollow, rout, crush, overwhelm; informal hammer, clobber, thrash, drub, pulverize, massacre, crucify, demolish, destroy, annihilate, wipe the floor with, make mincemeat of, murder; Brit. informal stuff; N. Amer. informal shellac, cream, skunk.

troupe noun **group**, company, band, ensemble, set; cast.

trousers plural noun **slacks**, jeans; N. Amer. pants; Brit. informal trews, strides, kecks, breeches; Austral. informal daks.

truant
■ **play truant** stay away from school, truant; Brit. informal skive (off), bunk off; Irish informal mitch (off); N. Amer. informal play hookey, goof off; Austral./NZ informal play the wag.

truce noun **ceasefire**, armistice, suspension of hostilities, peace; respite, lull; informal let-up.

truck[1] noun *a heavily laden truck:* **lorry**, wagon, heavy goods vehicle, juggernaut; van, pickup (truck); Brit. HGV; dated pantechnicon.

truck[2] noun *we are to have no truck with him:* **dealings**, association, contact, communication, connection, relations; business, trade.

truculent adjective *she grumbled about truculent security guards:* **defiant**, aggressive, antagonistic, belligerent, pugnacious, confrontational, obstreperous, argumentative, quarrelsome, uncooperative; Brit. informal stroppy, bolshie.
– OPPOSITES cooperative, amiable.

trudge verb **plod**, tramp, drag oneself, plough, slog, toil, trek; informal traipse; N. Amer. informal schlep.

true adjective **1** *you'll see that what I say is true:* **correct**, accurate, right, verifiable, in accordance with the facts, the case, so; faithful, literal, factual, unvarnished. **2** *people are still willing to pay for true craftsmanship:* **genuine**, authentic, real, actual, bona fide, proper; informal honest-to-goodness, kosher, pukka, legit, the real McCoy; Austral./NZ informal dinkum. **3** *who is the true owner of the goods?* **rightful**, legitimate, legal, lawful, authorized, bona fide. **4** *there is a need for true repentance:* **sincere**, genuine, real, unfeigned, heartfelt, from the heart. **5** *he is a true friend:* **loyal**, faithful, constant, devoted, staunch, steadfast, unswerving, unwavering; trustworthy, trusty, reliable, dependable. **6** *a true reflection of life in the 50s:* **accurate**, true to life, faithful, telling it like it is, realistic, close, authentic, lifelike.
– OPPOSITES untrue, false, disloyal, inaccurate.

true-blue adjective *they are true-blue*

supporters of the club: **staunch**, loyal, faithful, stalwart, committed, card-carrying, confirmed, dyed-in-the-wool, devoted, dedicated, firm, steadfast, unswerving, unwavering, unfaltering.
– OPPOSITES fickle.

truism noun **platitude**, commonplace, cliché, stock phrase, banality, old chestnut.

truly adverb **1** *tell me truly what you want:* **truthfully**, honestly, frankly, candidly, openly, to someone's face, laying one's cards on the table; informal pulling no punches. **2** *I'm truly grateful to them:* **sincerely**, genuinely, really, indeed, from the bottom of one's heart, heartily, profoundly; very, extremely, dreadfully, immensely, tremendously, incredibly, most; informal awfully, terribly, terrifically, fearfully; Brit. informal jolly, ever so. **3** *a truly dreadful song:* **really**, absolutely, simply, utterly, totally, perfectly, thoroughly, positively, completely. **4** *this is truly a miracle:* **without (a) doubt**, unquestionably, undoubtedly, certainly, surely, definitely, beyond doubt/question, indubitably, undeniably, beyond the shadow of a doubt; in truth, really, in reality, actually, in fact. **5** *the streaming system does not truly reflect children's ability:* **accurately**, correctly, exactly, precisely, faithfully.

trump verb *by wearing the simplest of dresses, she had trumped them all:* **outshine**, outclass, upstage, put in the shade, eclipse, surpass, outdo, outperform; beat, better, top, cap; informal leave standing; Brit. informal knock spots off.

trumped up adjective *the men were arrested on trumped-up charges of espionage:* **bogus**, spurious, specious, false, fabricated, invented, manufactured, contrived, made-up, fake; informal phoney.
– OPPOSITES genuine.

trumpet verb **1** *'Come on!' he trumpeted:* **shout**, bellow, roar, yell, cry out, call out; informal holler. **2** *companies trumpeted their enthusiasm for the multimedia revolution:* **proclaim**, announce, declare, shout from the rooftops.
■ **blow one's own trumpet** boast, brag, sing one's own praises, show off, swank, congratulate oneself; N. Amer. informal blow/toot one's own horn; Austral./NZ informal skite.

truncate verb **shorten**, cut, cut short, curtail, bring to an untimely end; abbreviate, condense, reduce.
– OPPOSITES lengthen, extend.

truncheon noun (Brit.) **baton**, club, cudgel, bludgeon; stick, staff; Brit. life preserver; N. Amer. billy, blackjack, nightstick; Brit. informal cosh.

trunk noun **1** *she leaned against the trunk of a tree:* **stem**, bole, stock. **2** *he revealed his powerful trunk:* **torso**, body. **3** *an elephant's trunk:* **proboscis**, nose, snout. **4** *the stuff was kept in an enormous tin trunk:* **chest**, box, crate, coffer; case. **5** (N. Amer.) *the trunk of his car was open:* **luggage compartment**; Brit. boot.

truss noun *the bridge is supported by three steel trusses:* **support**, buttress, joist, brace, prop, strut, stay, stanchion, pier.
verb *they trussed us up with ropes and chains:* **tie up**, bind, chain up; pinion, tether, secure.

trust noun **1** *good relationships are built on trust:* **confidence**, belief, faith, certainty, assurance, conviction; reliance. **2** *as manager, you occupy a position of trust:* **responsibility**. **3** *the money is to be held in trust for his son:* **safe keeping**, keeping, protection, charge, care, custody; trusteeship, guardianship.
– OPPOSITES distrust, mistrust, doubt.
verb **1** *I should never have trusted her:* **put one's trust in**, have faith in, have (every) confidence in, believe in, pin one's hopes/faith on. **2** *he can be trusted to carry out an impartial investigation:* **rely on**, depend on, bank on, count on, be sure of. **3** *I trust we shall meet again:* **hope**, expect, take it, assume, presume. **4** *they don't like to trust their money to anyone outside the family:* **entrust**, consign, commit, give, hand over, turn over, assign.
– OPPOSITES distrust, mistrust, doubt.

trustee noun **administrator**, agent; custodian, keeper, steward, depositary; executor, executrix.

trusting adjective *I would have written up a formal contract—you're too trusting:* **trustful**, unsuspecting, unquestioning, unguarded, unwary; naive, innocent, childlike, ingenuous, wide-eyed, credulous, gullible.
– OPPOSITES distrustful, suspicious.

trustworthy adjective *leave a spare key with a trustworthy neighbour:* **reliable**, dependable, honest, honourable, upright, principled, true, truthful, as good as one's word, ethical, virtuous, incorruptible, unimpeachable, above suspicion; responsible; safe, sound, reputable; informal on the level; N. Amer. informal straight-up.
– OPPOSITES unreliable.

trusty adjective *Lewis races around, long locks flowing and trusty musket in tow:* **reliable**, dependable, trustworthy, unfailing, trusted; loyal, faithful, true, staunch, steadfast, constant.
– OPPOSITES unreliable.

truth noun **1** *he doubted the truth of her statement:* **veracity**, truthfulness, verity, sincerity, candour, honesty; accuracy, correctness, validity, factuality, authenticity. **2** *it's the truth, I swear it:* **what happened**, the case, so; gospel (truth), the honest truth. **3** *truth is stranger than fiction:* **fact(s)**, reality, real life, actuality. **4** *these ideas are accepted as scientific truths:* **fact**, verity, certainty; law, principle.
– OPPOSITES lies, fiction, falsehood.

■ **in truth** *in truth Gouzenko's knowledge was extremely limited, but no one appreciated that:* in (actual) fact, in point of fact, in reality, really, actually, to tell the truth, if truth be told.

truthful adjective **1** *I want a truthful answer:* **honest**, sincere, trustworthy, genuine; candid, frank, open, forthright, straight; informal upfront, on the level; N. Amer. informal on the up and up. **2** *a truthful account of what happened:* **true**, accurate, correct, factual, faithful, reliable; unvarnished, unembellished.
– OPPOSITES deceitful, untrue.

try verb **1** *I will try to help him:* **attempt**, endeavour, make an effort, exert oneself, strive, do one's best, do one's utmost, move heaven and earth; informal have a go, give it one's best shot, bend over backwards, bust a gut, do one's damnedest, pull out all the stops, go all out, knock oneself out. **2** *try it and see what you think:* **test**, put to the test, sample, taste, inspect, investigate, examine, appraise, evaluate, assess; informal check out, give something a go/whirl. **3** *Mary tried everyone's patience:* **tax**, strain, test, stretch, sap, drain, exhaust, wear out. **4** *the case is to be tried by a jury:* **adjudicate**, consider, hear, examine.
noun *I'll have one last try:* **attempt**, effort, endeavour; informal go, shot, crack, stab, bash, whack.
■ **try something out** test, trial, experiment with; pilot; put through its paces; assess, evaluate.

trying adjective **1** *it's been a very trying day:* **stressful**, taxing, demanding, difficult, tough, hard, pressured, frustrating, fraught; arduous, gruelling, tiring, exhausting; informal hellish. **2** *Steve was very trying at the best of times:* **annoying**, irritating, exasperating, maddening, infuriating; tiresome, irksome, troublesome, bothersome; informal aggravating.
– OPPOSITES easy, accommodating.

tub noun **1** *a large wooden tub:* **container**, butt, barrel, cask, drum, keg. **2** *a tub of yogurt:* **pot**, carton. **3** *I was enjoying a soak in the tub:* **bath**, bathtub; hot tub.

tubby adjective (informal) **chubby**, plump, stout, dumpy, chunky, portly, rotund, round, fat, overweight, fleshy, paunchy, pot-bellied, corpulent; informal pudgy, beefy, porky, roly-poly, blubbery; Brit. informal podgy; N. Amer. informal corn-fed.
– OPPOSITES skinny.

tuck verb **1** *he tucked his shirt into his trousers:* **push**, insert, slip; thrust, stuff, stick, cram; informal pop. **2** *he tucked the knife behind his seat:* **hide**, conceal, secrete; store, stow; informal stash.
noun *she wore a red dress with tucks all along the bodice:* **pleat**, gather, fold, ruffle.
■ **tuck someone in/up** *he carried her back to bed and tucked her in:* make comfortable, settle down, cover up; put to bed.

■ **tuck in/into** (informal) *I tucked into the bacon and eggs:* eat heartily, devour, consume, gobble up, wolf down; informal get stuck into, dispose of, polish off, get outside of, put away, scoff (down); Brit. informal shift; N. Amer. informal scarf (down/up), snarf (down/up).

tuft noun **1** *spiky tufts of grass grew on the forecourt:* **clump**, bunch, knot, cluster, tussock. **2** *she tugged at a tuft of hair:* **lock**, wisp; crest, topknot, plume.

tug verb **1** *Ben tugged at her sleeve:* **pull**, pluck, tweak, twitch, jerk, wrench; catch hold of; informal yank. **2** *she tugged him towards the door:* **drag**, pull, lug, draw, haul, heave, tow, trail.
noun *one good tug would loosen all that earth:* **pull**, jerk, wrench, heave; informal yank.

tuition noun **instruction**, teaching, coaching, tutoring, tutelage, lessons, education, schooling; training, drill, preparation, guidance.

tumble verb **1** *he tumbled over:* **fall (over/down)**, topple over, lose one's balance, keel over, go headlong, go head over heels, trip (up), stumble; informal come a cropper. **2** *a brook tumbled over the rocks:* **cascade**, fall, flow, pour, spill, stream. **3** *oil prices tumbled:* **plummet**, plunge, fall, dive, nosedive, drop, slump, slide, decrease, decline; informal crash.
– OPPOSITES rise.
noun **1** *I took a tumble in the nettles:* **fall**, trip, spill; informal nosedive, header. **2** *a tumble in share prices:* **drop**, fall, plunge, dive, nosedive, slump, decline, collapse; informal crash.
– OPPOSITES rise.

tumbledown adjective **dilapidated**, ramshackle, decrepit, neglected, run down, gone to rack and ruin, falling to pieces, decaying, derelict, crumbling; rickety, shaky; N. Amer. informal shacky.

tumbler noun **(drinking) glass**, beaker.

tummy noun (informal) **stomach**, abdomen, belly, gut, middle; informal tum, insides; Austral. informal bingy.

tumour noun **(cancerous) growth**, malignant growth, cancer, malignancy; lump, growth, swelling; Medicine carcinoma, sarcoma.

tumult noun **1** *she added her voice to the tumult:* **clamour**, din, noise, racket, uproar, commotion, ruckus, rumpus, hubbub, pandemonium, babel, bedlam, brouhaha, furore, fracas, melee, frenzy; Scottish & N. English stramash; informal hullabaloo; Brit. informal row. **2** *we have endured years of political tumult:* **turmoil**, confusion, disorder, unrest, chaos, turbulence, mayhem, havoc, upheaval, ferment, agitation, trouble.
– OPPOSITES tranquillity.

tumultuous adjective **1** *he arrived to tumultuous applause:* **loud**, deafening, thunderous, uproarious, noisy, clamorous,

vociferous. **2** *a tumultuous crowd had gathered:* **disorderly**, unruly, rowdy, turbulent, boisterous, excited, agitated, restless, wild, riotous, frenzied; Brit. informal rumbustious.
– OPPOSITES soft, orderly.

tune noun *she hummed a cheerful tune:* **melody**, air, strain, theme; song, jingle, ditty.
verb **1** *they tuned their guitars:* **adjust**, harmonize; fiddle with. **2** *a body clock tuned to the tides:* **attune**, adapt, adjust; regulate, modulate.
■ **change one's tune** *by the following week, she had changed her tune:* change one's mind, do a U-turn, have a change of heart; Brit. do an about-turn.

tuneful adjective **melodious**, melodic, musical, mellifluous, dulcet, euphonious, harmonious, lyrical, lilting, sweet.
– OPPOSITES discordant.

tuneless adjective **discordant**, unmelodious, dissonant, harsh, cacophonous.
– OPPOSITES melodious.

tunnel noun *we built a tunnel under the hill:* **passage**, underpass, subway; shaft; burrow, hole.
verb *he tunnelled under the fence:* **dig**, burrow, mine, bore, drill.

turbid adjective *the turbid waters of the Mississippi:* **murky**, opaque, cloudy, muddy, thick; N. Amer. roily.
– OPPOSITES limpid.

turbulent adjective **1** *the country's turbulent past has not been forgotten:* **tempestuous**, stormy, unstable, unsettled, tumultuous, chaotic; violent, anarchic, lawless. **2** *we found ourselves adrift on the turbulent southern seas:* **rough**, stormy, tempestuous, storm-tossed, heavy, violent, wild, seething, choppy, agitated, boisterous.
– OPPOSITES peaceful, calm.

turf noun **1** *they walked across the turf:* **grass**, lawn, sod. **2** (informal) *he was keen to protect his turf:* **territory**, domain, province, preserve, sphere of influence; stamping ground; informal bailiwick; Brit. informal patch, manor.
verb *the lawns have been turfed:* **grass (over)**.
■ **turf someone/something out** (informal). See EJECT sense 3.

turgid adjective *his turgid prose sent me to sleep:* **bombastic**, pompous, overblown, inflated, high-flown, affected, pretentious, grandiose, florid, ornate, magniloquent, grandiloquent, orotund; informal highfalutin.
– OPPOSITES simple.

turmoil noun **confusion**, upheaval, turbulence, tumult, disorder, disturbance, agitation, ferment, unrest, trouble, disruption, chaos, mayhem; uncertainty; N. Amer. informal tohubohu.
– OPPOSITES peace.
■ **in turmoil** *as he spoke, his mind was in turmoil:* confused, in a whirl, at sixes and

sevens; reeling, disorientated; informal all over the place.

turn verb **1** *the wheels were still turning:* **go round**, revolve, rotate, spin, roll, circle, wheel, whirl, gyrate, swivel, pivot. **2** *I turned and headed back:* **change direction**, change course, make a U-turn, turn about/round, wheel round. **3** *the car turned the corner:* **go round**, round, negotiate, take. **4** *the path turned to right and left:* **bend**, curve, wind, twist, meander, snake, zigzag. **5** *he turned his pistol on Liam:* **aim at**, point at, level at, direct at, train on; focus on. **6** *their honeymoon turned into a nightmare:* **become**, develop into, turn out to be; be transformed into, metamorphose into. **7** *Emma turned red:* **become**, go, grow, get. **8** *he turned the house into flats:* **convert**, change, transform, make; adapt, modify, rebuild, reconstruct. **9** *in later life, he turned to politics:* **take up**, become/get involved in, go in for, enter, undertake; informal get into. **10** *we can now turn to another topic:* **move on to**, go on to, consider, attend to, address; take up. **11** *the chair legs were turned on a lathe:* **fashion**, make, shape, form.
noun **1** *a turn of the wheel sent us skidding across the road:* **rotation**, revolution, spin, whirl, gyration, swivel. **2** *the vehicle slowed and made a turn to the left:* **change of direction**, move, lurch. **3** *we're approaching the turn:* **bend**, corner; turning, junction, crossroads; N. Amer. turnout; Brit. hairpin bend. **4** *you'll get your turn in a minute:* **opportunity**, chance, say; stint, time; try; informal go, shot, stab, crack. **5** *a highly entertaining comic turn:* **act**, routine, performance, number, piece. **6** *you gave me quite a turn!* **shock**, start, surprise, jolt; fright, scare. **7** *she did me some good turns:* **service**, deed, act; favour, kindness; disservice, wrong.
■ **in turn** *let's deal with these points in turn:* one after the other, one by one, one at a time, in succession, successively, sequentially.
■ **turn of events** *she was utterly unprepared for this turn of events:* development, incident, occurrence, happening, circumstance.
■ **turn against someone** *people had turned against him after the court case:* become hostile to, take a dislike to.
■ **turn someone away** *reporters were turned away from the college:* send away, reject, rebuff, repel, cold-shoulder; informal send packing.
■ **turn back** *they turned back before reaching the church:* retrace one's steps, go back, return; retreat.
■ **turn someone/something down 1** *his novel was turned down by every major publisher:* reject, spurn, rebuff, refuse, decline; Brit. informal knock back. **2** *Pete turned the sound down:* reduce, lower, decrease, lessen; muffle, mute.
■ **turn in** (informal) *I think I'll turn in:* go to

bed, retire, call it a day; informal hit the hay, hit the sack.

■ **turn someone in** *she turned her husband in to the police:* betray, inform on, denounce, sell out, stab someone in the back; informal split on, blow the whistle on, rat on, peach on, squeal on; Brit. informal grass on, shop; N. Amer. informal finger; Austral./NZ informal dob on.

■ **turn of mind** *the book is for those of a less scientific turn of mind:* disposition, inclination, tendency, propensity, bias, bent.

■ **turn off** *they turned off the road and stopped:* leave, branch off; informal take a left/right; N. Amer. informal hang a left/right.

■ **turn something off** *she turned off the light:* switch off, shut off, power down, put off, extinguish, deactivate; informal kill, cut.

■ **turn on** *the decision turned on the meaning of the word 'reasonable':* depend on, rest on, hinge on, be contingent on, be decided by.

■ **turn someone on** (informal). See AROUSE sense 3.

■ **turn something on** *she turned on the TV:* switch on, power up, put on, start up, boot up, activate, trip.

■ **turn on someone** *he turned on her with cold savagery:* attack, set on, fall on, let fly at, lash out at, hit out at, round on; informal lay into, tear into, let someone have it, bite someone's head off, jump down someone's throat; Brit. informal have a go at; N. Amer. informal light into.

■ **turn out 1** *a huge crowd turned out to meet us:* come, be present, attend, appear, turn up, arrive; assemble, gather; informal show up. **2** *it turned out that she had been abroad:* transpire, emerge, come to light, become apparent. **3** *things didn't turn out as I'd intended:* happen, occur, come about; develop, work out, come out, end up; informal pan out; formal eventuate.

■ **turn someone out** *her father turned her out when she got pregnant:* throw out, eject, evict, expel, oust, drum out, banish; informal kick out, send packing, boot out, show someone the door, turf out.

■ **turn something out 1** *turn out the light.* See TURN SOMETHING OFF. **2** *they turn out a million engines a year:* produce, make, manufacture, fabricate, put out, churn out. **3** *she turned out the cupboards:* clear out, clean out, empty (out).

■ **turn over** *the little dinghy turned over in the wind:* overturn, upturn, capsize, keel over, turn turtle, be upended.

■ **turn something over 1** *I turned over a few pages and then noticed the picture:* flip over, flick through, leaf through. **2** *she turned the proposal over in her mind:* think about/over, consider, weigh up, ponder, contemplate, reflect on, chew over, mull over, muse on, ruminate on. **3** *he turned over the business to his brother:* transfer, hand over, pass on, consign, commit.

■ **turn of phrase** *he is famed for his non-committal turns of phrase:* expression,

idiom, phrase, term, word.

■ **turn to someone/something 1** *they turned to social services for advice:* seek help from, have recourse to, approach, apply to, appeal to. **2** *he turned to drink:* take to, resort to.

■ **turn up 1** *the missing documents turned up:* be found, be discovered, be located, reappear. **2** *the plane finally turned up:* arrive, appear, present oneself; informal show (up), show one's face. **3** *I'm sure something better will turn up:* present itself, occur, happen, crop up.

■ **turn something up 1** *she turned up the volume:* increase, raise, amplify, intensify. **2** *they turned up lots of information:* discover, uncover, unearth, find, dig up, ferret out, root out, expose. **3** *I turned up the hem:* take up, raise; shorten.

turncoat noun traitor, renegade, defector, deserter, Judas; fifth columnist, quisling; informal rat.

turning noun **turn-off**, turn, side road, exit; N. Amer. turnout.

turning point noun **watershed**, critical moment, decisive moment, moment of truth, crossroads, crisis.

turnout noun *the lecture attracted a good turnout:* **attendance**, audience, house; crowd, gathering, throng, assembly, assemblage, congregation.

turnover noun **1** *we have an annual turnover of £2.25 million:* **(gross) revenue**, income, yield; sales. **2** *DDI has a high turnover of staff:* **change**, movement, throughput.

tussle noun *his glasses were smashed in the tussle:* **scuffle**, fight, struggle, skirmish, brawl, scrum, rough and tumble, free-for-all, fracas, fray, rumpus, melee; Irish, N. Amer., & Austral. donnybrook; informal scrap, dust-up, punch-up, spat, ruck; Brit. informal ding-dong, bust-up; Scottish informal rammy.
verb *demonstrators tussled with police:* **scuffle**, fight, struggle, brawl, grapple, wrestle, clash; informal scrap; N. Amer. informal rough-house.

tutor noun *he was a history tutor:* **teacher**, instructor, educator, lecturer, trainer, mentor; formal pedagogue.
verb *he was tutored at home:* **teach**, instruct, educate, school, coach, train, drill.

tutorial noun **lesson**, class, seminar.

tweak verb **1** *he tweaked the boy's ear:* **pull**, jerk, tug, twist, twitch, pinch, squeeze. **2** (informal) *the programme can be tweaked to suit your needs:* **adjust**, modify, alter, change, adapt; refine.
noun **1** *he gave her hair a tweak:* **pull**, jerk, tug, twist, pinch, twitch, squeeze. **2** (informal) *a few minor tweaks were required:* **adjustment**, modification, alteration, change; refinement.

twee adjective (Brit.) **1** *I love all those twee little shops:* **quaint**, sweet, dainty, pretty; informal cute. **2** *the lyrics are too twee in places:*

t

sentimental, over-sentimental, mawkish, sickly; Brit. informal soppy.

twelve cardinal number **dozen**, zodiac.

twenty cardinal number **score**.

twiddle verb *she twiddled the dials impatiently:* **turn**, twist, swivel, twirl; adjust, move, jiggle; fiddle with, play with.
■ **twiddle one's thumbs** be idle, kick one's heels, kill time, waste time; informal hang around/round; Brit. informal hang about.

twig[1] noun *leafy twigs:* **stick**, sprig, shoot, stem.

twig[2] verb (Brit. informal) *she finally twigged what I was on about:* **realize**, understand, grasp, comprehend, take in, fathom, see, recognize; informal latch on to, cotton on to, tumble to, get, get wise to, figure out; Brit. informal suss.

twilight noun **1** *we arrived at twilight:* **dusk**, sunset, sundown, nightfall, evening, close of day. **2** *the tower was scarcely visible in the twilight:* **half-light**, semi-darkness, gloom.
– OPPOSITES dawn.
adjective *he inhabited a sinister twilight world of treason and murder:* **shadowy**, dark, shady, obscure, hidden; sinister.

twin adjective **1** *he regarded the twin towers of the stadium:* **matching**, identical, matched, paired. **2** *the twin aims of conservation and recreation:* **twofold**, double, dual; related, linked, connected; corresponding, parallel, complementary, equivalent.

twine noun *a ball of twine:* **string**, cord, thread, yarn.
verb **1** *she twined her arms around him:* **wind**, entwine, wrap, wreathe. **2** *convolvulus twined around the tree:* **entwine itself**, coil, loop, twist, spiral, curl. **3** *a flower was twined in her hair:* **weave**, interlace, intertwine, braid, twist.

twinge noun **1** *she experienced twinges in her stomach:* **pain**, spasm, ache, throb; cramp, stitch. **2** *I felt a twinge of guilt:* **pang**, prick; qualm, scruple.

twinkle verb *the lights of the city twinkled:* **glitter**, sparkle, shine, glimmer, shimmer, glint, gleam, glisten, flicker, flash, wink.
noun *the twinkle of the lights:* **glitter**, sparkle, glimmer, shimmer, glint, gleam, flicker, flash, wink.

twinkling adjective **sparkling**, glistening, glittering, glimmering, glinting, gleaming, flickering, winking, shining, scintillating.

twirl verb **1** *she twirled her parasol:* **spin**, whirl, turn, gyrate, pivot, swivel, twist, revolve, rotate. **2** *she twirled her hair round her fingers:* **wind**, twist, coil, curl, wrap.
noun *she did a quick twirl:* **pirouette**, spin, whirl, turn, twist, rotation, revolution, gyration.

twist verb **1** *the impact twisted the chassis of the car:* **crumple**, crush, buckle, mangle, warp, deform, distort. **2** *her face twisted with rage:* **contort**, screw up. **3** *Ma anxiously twisted a handkerchief:* **wring**, squeeze. **4** *he*

twisted round in his seat: **turn (round)**, swivel (round), spin (round), pivot, rotate, revolve. **5** *she twisted out of his grasp:* **wriggle**, squirm, worm, wiggle. **6** *I've twisted my ankle:* **sprain**, wrench, turn, rick, crick. **7** *you are twisting my words:* **distort**, misrepresent, change, alter, pervert, warp, skew, misinterpret, misconstrue, spin. **8** *he twisted the radio knob:* **twiddle**, adjust, turn, rotate, swivel, spin. **9** *she twisted her hair round her finger:* **wind**, twirl, coil, curl, wrap. **10** *the wires were twisted together:* **intertwine**, twine, interlace, weave, plait, braid, coil, wind. **11** *the road twisted and turned:* **wind**, bend, curve, turn, meander, weave, zigzag, swerve, snake.
noun **1** *her voice faded with the twist of a dial:* **turn**, twirl, spin. **2** *long twists of black hair stuck out from under her hat:* **ringlet**, curl, corkscrew, coil; lock, hank. **3** *the twists in the road made me sick:* **bend**, curve, turn, zigzag, kink, dog-leg; Brit. hairpin bend. **4** *the twists of the plot are quite baffling:* **convolution**, complication, complexity, intricacy; surprise, revelation. **5** *a new twist on an old theme:* **interpretation**, slant, outlook, angle, approach, treatment; variation, take.
■ **twist someone's arm** (informal) pressurize, coerce, force; persuade; informal lean on, bulldoze, railroad, put the screws on.

twisted adjective **1** *a mass of twisted metal:* **crumpled**, bent, crushed, buckled, warped, misshapen, distorted, deformed. **2** *he gave me a twisted smile:* **crooked**, lopsided; contorted, wry. **3** *his twisted mind:* **perverted**, warped, deviant, depraved, corrupt, abnormal, unhealthy, aberrant, distorted, corrupted, debauched, debased; informal sick, kinky, pervy.

twisty adjective **winding**, windy, twisting, bendy, zigzag, meandering, curving, sinuous, snaky.
– OPPOSITES straight.

twitch verb **1** *he twitched and then lay still:* **jerk**, convulse, have a spasm, quiver, tremble, shiver, shudder. **2** *he twitched the note out of my hand:* **snatch**, tweak, pluck, pull, tug; informal yank.
noun **1** *a twitch of her lips was all I could make out:* **spasm**, convulsion, quiver, tremor, shiver, shudder; tic. **2** *he felt a twitch of annoyance:* **pang**, twinge, dart, stab, prick.

twitter verb *sparrows twittered under the eaves:* **chirp**, chirrup, cheep, tweet, peep, chatter, trill, warble, sing.
noun *I heard a bird's twitter:* **chirp**, chirrup, cheep, tweet, peep, trill, warble, song.

two cardinal number **pair**, duo, duet, double, dyad, duplet, tandem; archaic twain.

two-faced adjective **deceitful**, insincere, double-dealing, hypocritical, back-stabbing, false, untrustworthy, duplicitous, deceiving, dissembling, dishonest; disloyal, treacherous, faithless; literary perfidious.
– OPPOSITES sincere.

t

twosome noun **couple**, pair, duo.

tycoon noun **magnate**, mogul, businessman, captain of industry, industrialist, financier, entrepreneur; millionaire, multimillionaire; informal big shot, bigwig, honcho; Brit. informal supremo; N. Amer. informal big wheel, kahuna; derogatory fat cat.

type noun **1** *a curate of the old-fashioned type:* **kind**, sort, variety, class, category, set, genre, species, order, breed, race; style, nature, manner, rank; generation, vintage, school; stamp, ilk, cast, grain, mould; N. Amer. stripe. **2** (informal) *I hate all these sporty types:* **person**, individual, character, sort; Brit. informal bod. **3** *the headings are in italic type:* **print**, typeface, face, characters, lettering, letters; font; Brit. fount.

typhoon noun **cyclone**, tropical storm, storm, tornado, hurricane, whirlwind; N. Amer. informal twister.

typical adjective **1** *a typical example of art deco:* **representative**, classic, quintessential, archetypal, model, prototypical, stereotypical. **2** *it was a fairly typical day:* **normal**, average, ordinary, standard, regular, routine, run-of-the-mill, conventional, unremarkable, unexceptional; informal bog-standard. **3** *it's typical of him to forget:* **characteristic**, in keeping, usual, normal, par for the course, predictable, true to form; customary, habitual.
– OPPOSITES unusual, exceptional, uncharacteristic.

typify verb *he typified a new breed of civil servant:* **epitomize**, exemplify, characterize, be representative of; personify, embody.

tyrannical adjective *the word 'cult' implies a deranged, tyrannical leader:* **dictatorial**, despotic, autocratic, oppressive, repressive, totalitarian, undemocratic, illiberal; authoritarian, high-handed, imperious, harsh, strict, iron-handed, severe, cruel, brutal, ruthless.
– OPPOSITES liberal.

tyrannize verb *as a little boy he was tyrannized by his mother:* **dominate**, dictate to, browbeat, intimidate, bully, lord it over; persecute, victimize, torment; oppress, rule with a rod of iron, repress, crush, subjugate.

tyranny noun **despotism**, absolute power, autocracy, dictatorship, totalitarianism, fascism; oppression, repression, subjugation, enslavement; authoritarianism, bullying, severity, cruelty, brutality, ruthlessness.

tyrant noun *an evil tyrant who has imprisoned all who oppose his regime:* **dictator**, despot, autocrat, authoritarian, oppressor; slave-driver, martinet, bully.

tyro noun *he first entered parliament in 1977 as a 34-year-old political tyro:* **novice**, beginner, learner, neophyte, newcomer, initiate, fledgling; apprentice, trainee, probationer; N. Amer. tenderfoot; informal rookie, newie, newbie; N. Amer. informal greenhorn.
– OPPOSITES veteran.

t

Uu

ubiquitous adjective *tracking stray dogs may soon be easier thanks to the ubiquitous microchip:* **omnipresent**, ever-present, everywhere, all over the place, all-pervasive; universal, worldwide, global; rife, prevalent, far-reaching, inescapable.
– OPPOSITES rare.

UFO noun flying saucer, foo fighter.

ugly adjective **1** *an old man with a horribly ugly face:* **unattractive**, ill-favoured, hideous, plain, unlovely, unprepossessing, unsightly, horrible, frightful, awful, ghastly, unpleasant, vile, revolting, repellent, repugnant; grotesque, monstrous, reptilian, misshapen, deformed, disfigured; N. Amer. homely; informal not much to look at; Brit. informal no oil painting. **2** *things got pretty ugly:* **unpleasant**, nasty, disagreeable, alarming, tense, charged, serious, grave; dangerous, perilous, threatening, menacing, hostile, ominous, sinister. **3** *an ugly rumour:* **horrible**, despicable, reprehensible, nasty, appalling, objectionable, offensive, obnoxious, vile, dishonourable, rotten, vicious, spiteful.
– OPPOSITES beautiful, pleasant.

ulcer noun *most leg ulcers will heal spontaneously:* **sore**, ulceration, abscess, boil, carbuncle, blister, gumboil, wen.

ulterior adjective *could there be an ulterior motive behind his request?* **underlying**, undisclosed, undivulged, concealed, hidden, covert, secret, personal, private, selfish.
– OPPOSITES overt.

ultimate adjective **1** *the decline and ultimate collapse of the Empire:* **eventual**, final, concluding, terminal, end; resulting, ensuing, consequent, subsequent. **2** *ultimate truths about civilization:* **fundamental**, basic, primary, elementary, elemental, absolute, central, key, crucial, essential, pivotal. **3** *the ultimate gift for cat lovers:* **best**, ideal, greatest, supreme, paramount, superlative, highest, utmost, optimum, quintessential.
noun *a studio apartment offering the ultimate in luxury living:* **utmost**, optimum, last word, height, epitome, peak, pinnacle, acme, zenith, nonpareil, dernier cri, ne plus ultra; informal the bee's knees, the cat's pyjamas/whiskers.

ultimately adverb **1** *the cost will ultimately fall on us:* **eventually**, in the end, in the

long run, at length, finally, sooner or later, in time, in the fullness of time, when all is said and done, one day, some day, sometime; informal when push comes to shove; Brit. informal at the end of the day. **2** *two ultimately contradictory reasons:* **fundamentally**, basically, primarily, essentially, at heart, deep down.

ultra- combining form *an ultra-conservative view:* **extremely**, exceedingly, excessively, immensely, especially, exceptionally; N. English right; informal mega, mucho, majorly, oh-so; Brit. informal dead, ever so, well; N. Amer. informal real.

umbrage noun
■ **take umbrage** *she took umbrage at his remarks:* take offence, take exception, be aggrieved, be affronted, be annoyed, be angry, be indignant, be put out, be insulted, be hurt, be piqued, be resentful, be disgruntled, go into a huff; informal be miffed, have one's nose put out of joint; Brit. informal get the hump.

umbrella noun **1** *they huddled under the umbrella:* parasol, sunshade; Brit. informal brolly. **2** *the groups worked under the umbrella of the Liberal Party:* **aegis**, auspices, patronage, protection, guardianship, support, backing, agency, guidance, care, charge, responsibility, cover.

umpire noun *the umpire reversed his decision:* **referee**, linesman, adjudicator, arbitrator, judge, moderator; informal ref; N. Amer. informal ump.
verb *he umpired a boat race:* **referee**, adjudicate, arbitrate, judge, moderate, oversee; Cricket stand; informal ref.

unabashed adjective *she watched the meeting with unabashed interest:* **unashamed**, shameless, unembarrassed, brazen, audacious, barefaced, blatant, flagrant, bold, cocky, unrepentant, undaunted, unconcerned, fearless.
– OPPOSITES sheepish.

unable adjective *she was unable to conceal her surprise:* **powerless**, impotent, at a loss, inadequate, incompetent, unfit, unqualified, incapable.

unabridged adjective *each story is unabridged and wholly authentic:* **complete**, entire, whole, intact, uncut, unshortened, unexpurgated.

unacceptable adjective *four boys have*

been suspended for unacceptable behaviour: **intolerable**, insufferable, unsatisfactory, inadmissible, inappropriate, unsuitable, undesirable, unreasonable, insupportable; offensive, obnoxious, disagreeable, disgraceful, deplorable, beyond the pale, bad; informal not on, a bit much, too much, out of order; Brit. informal a bit thick, a bit off, not cricket.
– OPPOSITES satisfactory.

unaccompanied adjective *our parents would not let us go out unaccompanied in the evenings:* **alone**, on one's own, by oneself, solo, lone, solitary, single-handed; unescorted, unattended, unchaperoned; informal by one's lonesome; Brit. informal on one's tod, on one's Jack Jones; Austral./NZ informal on one's Pat Malone.

unaccomplished adjective *an unaccomplished poet:* **inexpert**, unskilful, unskilled, amateur, amateurish, unqualified, untrained; incompetent, maladroit.
– OPPOSITES skilful.

unaccountable adjective **1** *for some unaccountable reason, the horses drawing the cart stopped short:* **inexplicable**, insoluble, incomprehensible, unfathomable, impenetrable, puzzling, perplexing, baffling, bewildering, mystifying, mysterious, inscrutable, peculiar, strange, queer, odd, obscure; informal weird, freaky; Brit. informal rum. **2** *the Council is unaccountable to anyone:* **unanswerable**, not liable; free, exempt, immune; unsupervised.

unaccustomed adjective **1** *she was unaccustomed to being bossed about:* **unused**, new, fresh; unfamiliar with, inexperienced in, unconversant with, unacquainted with. **2** *he showed unaccustomed emotion:* **unusual**, unfamiliar, uncommon, unwonted, exceptional, extraordinary, rare, surprising, abnormal, atypical.
– OPPOSITES habitual.

unacquainted adjective *I regret that I am unacquainted with the place:* **unfamiliar**, unaccustomed, unused; inexperienced, ignorant, uninformed, unenlightened, unconversant; informal in the dark.
– OPPOSITES familiar.

unadorned adjective *they preferred sparse and unadorned church interiors:* **unembellished**, unornamented, undecorated, unfussy, no-nonsense, no-frills; plain, basic, restrained; bare, bald, austere, stark, spartan, clinical.
– OPPOSITES ornate.

unadventurous adjective *he led a leisurely, unadventurous life:* **cautious**, careful, circumspect, wary, hesitant, timid, conservative, conventional, unenterprising, unexciting, unimaginative; boring, strait-laced, stuffy, narrow-minded; informal square, straight, stick-in-the-mud.
– OPPOSITES enterprising.

unaffected adjective **1** *they are unaffected by the cabinet reshuffle:* **unchanged**, unaltered,

uninfluenced; untouched, unmoved, unresponsive to; proof against, impervious to, immune to. **2** *his manner was unaffected:* **unassuming**, unpretentious, down-to-earth, natural, easy, uninhibited, open, artless, guileless, ingenuous, unsophisticated. **3** *she was welcomed with unaffected warmth:* **genuine**, real, sincere, honest, earnest, wholehearted, heartfelt, true, bona fide, frank, open; informal upfront.
– OPPOSITES influenced, pretentious, false, feigned.

unafraid adjective *these companies are unafraid of risks:* **undaunted**, unabashed, fearless, brave, courageous, plucky, intrepid, stout-hearted, bold, daring, confident, audacious, mettlesome, unshrinking; informal gutsy, spunky.
– OPPOSITES timid.

unanimous adjective **1** *doctors were unanimous about the effects:* **united**, in agreement, in accord, of one mind, in harmony, concordant, undivided. **2** *a unanimous vote:* **uniform**, consistent, united, concerted, congruent.
– OPPOSITES divided.

unanswerable adjective **1** *an unanswerable case for investment:* **irrefutable**, indisputable, undeniable, incontestable, incontrovertible; conclusive, absolute, positive. **2** *it was no use pondering on unanswerable questions:* **insoluble**, unsolvable, insolvable, inexplicable, unexplainable.
– OPPOSITES weak, obvious.

unanswered adjective *there were a number of unanswered questions:* **unresolved**, undecided, unsettled, undetermined; pending, open to question, up in the air, doubtful, disputed.

unappetizing adjective *an unappetizing leg of chicken in breadcrumbs:* **unpalatable**, uninviting, unappealing, unpleasant, off-putting, disagreeable, distasteful, unsavoury, insipid, tasteless, flavourless, dull; inedible, uneatable, revolting; informal yucky, gross.
– OPPOSITES tempting.

unapproachable adjective
1 *unapproachable islands:* **inaccessible**, unreachable, remote, out of the way, isolated, far-flung; informal off the beaten track, in the middle of nowhere, in the sticks, unget-at-able. **2** *her boss appeared unapproachable:* **aloof**, distant, remote, detached, reserved, withdrawn, uncommunicative, guarded, undemonstrative, unresponsive, unforthcoming, unfriendly, unsympathetic, unsociable; cool, cold, frosty, stiff, formal; informal stand-offish.
– OPPOSITES accessible, friendly.

unarmed adjective *troops fired into a crowd of unarmed civilians:* **defenceless**, weaponless; unprotected, undefended, unguarded, unshielded, vulnerable,

u

exposed, assailable, pregnable.

unassailable adjective **1** *an unassailable fortress:* **impregnable**, invulnerable, impenetrable, inviolable, invincible, unconquerable; secure, safe, strong, indestructible. **2** *his logic was unassailable:* **indisputable**, undeniable, unquestionable, incontestable, incontrovertible, irrefutable, indubitable, watertight, sound, good, sure, manifest, patent, obvious.
– OPPOSITES defenceless.

unassertive adjective *she seemed unassertive and lacking confidence:* **passive**, retiring, unforthcoming, submissive, unassuming, self-effacing, modest, humble, meek, unconfident, diffident, shy, timid, insecure; informal mousy.
– OPPOSITES bold.

unassuming adjective *a quiet, unassuming man:* **modest**, self-effacing, humble, meek, reserved, diffident; unobtrusive, unostentatious, unpretentious, unaffected, natural, artless, ingenuous.

unattached adjective **1** *they were both unattached:* **single**, unmarried, unwed, partnerless, uncommitted, available, footloose and fancy free, on one's own; on the shelf, unloved. **2** *we are unattached to any organization:* **unaffiliated**, unallied, autonomous, independent, non-aligned, self-governing, neutral, separate, unconnected, detached.
– OPPOSITES married.

unattended adjective **1** *his cries went unattended:* **ignored**, disregarded, neglected, passed over. **2** *an unattended vehicle:* **unguarded**, unwatched, alone, solitary; abandoned. **3** *she had to walk there unattended:* **unaccompanied**, unescorted, partnerless, unchaperoned, alone, on one's own, by oneself, solo; informal by one's lonesome; Brit. informal on one's tod, on one's Jack Jones; Austral./NZ informal on one's Pat Malone.

unattractive adjective *an unattractive little town:* **ugly**, plain, ill-favoured, unappealing, unsightly, unlovely, unprepossessing, displeasing; hideous, monstrous, grotesque; N. Amer. homely; informal not much to look at, as ugly as sin; Brit. informal no oil painting.
– OPPOSITES beautiful.

unauthorized adjective *they issued a ban on all unauthorized rallies:* **unofficial**, unsanctioned, unaccredited, unlicensed, unwarranted, unapproved; disallowed, prohibited, banned, barred, forbidden, outlawed, illegal, illegitimate, illicit, proscribed.
– OPPOSITES official.

unavailing adjective *persistent calls for justice were unavailing:* **ineffective**, ineffectual, inefficacious, vain, futile, useless, unsuccessful, fruitless, profitless, unprofitable, to no avail, abortive.
– OPPOSITES effective.

unavoidable adjective *workers have been told that redundancies are unavoidable:* **inescapable**, inevitable, inexorable, assured, certain, predestined, predetermined, ineluctable; necessary, compulsory, required, obligatory, mandatory.

unaware adjective *the President was unaware of what was going on:* **ignorant**, unknowing, unconscious, heedless, unmindful, oblivious, unsuspecting, uninformed, unenlightened, unwitting, innocent; inattentive, unobservant, unperceptive, blind, deaf; informal in the dark.
– OPPOSITES conscious.

unawares adverb **1** *brigands caught them unawares:* **by surprise**, unexpectedly, without warning, suddenly, abruptly, unprepared, off-guard; informal with one's trousers down, napping; Brit. informal on the hop. **2** *the roach approached the pike unawares:* **unknowingly**, unwittingly, unconsciously; unintentionally, inadvertently, accidentally, by mistake.
– OPPOSITES prepared, knowingly.

unbalanced adjective **1** *he is unbalanced and dangerous:* **unstable**, mentally ill, deranged, demented, disturbed, unhinged, insane, mad, out of one's mind, non compos mentis; informal crazy, loopy, loony, nuts, nutty, cracked, screwy, batty, dotty, cuckoo, bonkers, mental, off one's head, round the bend/twist; Brit. informal barmy, potty, crackers, barking, off one's rocker; N. Amer. informal nutso, squirrelly. **2** *a most unbalanced article:* **biased**, prejudiced, one-sided, partisan, inequitable, unjust, unfair, parti pris.
– OPPOSITES sane, unbiased.

unbearable adjective *the frustration is almost unbearable:* **intolerable**, insufferable, insupportable, unendurable, unacceptable, unmanageable, more than flesh and blood can stand, overpowering; informal too much.
– OPPOSITES tolerable.

unbeatable adjective *she has been in unbeatable form since her World Championship triumph:* **invincible**, unstoppable, unassailable, indomitable, unconquerable, unsurpassable, matchless, peerless; supreme.

unbeaten adjective *Edinburgh are the only unbeaten team in the division:* **undefeated**, unconquered, unsurpassed, unequalled, unrivalled; triumphant, victorious, supreme, matchless, second to none.

unbecoming adjective **1** *a stout lady in an unbecoming sundress:* **unflattering**, unattractive, unsightly, plain, ugly, hideous; unsuitable. **2** *conduct unbecoming to the Senate:* **inappropriate**, unfitting, unbefitting, unsuitable, unsuited, inapt, out of keeping, untoward, incorrect, unacceptable; unworthy, improper, unseemly, undignified.
– OPPOSITES flattering, appropriate.

unbelief noun *a symptom of unbelief was an inability to pray:* **atheism**, non-belief, agnosticism, apostasy, irreligion, godlessness, nihilism; scepticism, cynicism, disbelief, doubt.
– OPPOSITES faith.

unbelievable adjective *your audacity is simply unbelievable:* **incredible**, beyond belief, inconceivable, unthinkable, unimaginable; unconvincing, far-fetched, implausible, improbable; informal hard to swallow.
– OPPOSITES credible.

unbend verb **1** *I couldn't unbend my knees:* **straighten (out)**, extend, flex, uncurl. **2** *if you'd only unbend a little:* **relax**, unwind, de-stress, loosen up, let oneself go; informal let one's hair down, let it all hang out, hang loose.

unbending adjective **1** *an unbending and somewhat formal man:* **aloof**, formal, stiff, reserved, remote, distant, forbidding, cool, unfeeling, unemotional, unfriendly, austere; informal uptight, stand-offish. **2** *unbending attitudes:* **uncompromising**, inflexible, unyielding, hard-line, tough, strict, firm, resolute, determined, unrelenting, relentless, inexorable, intransigent, immovable.

unbiased adjective *unbiased professional advice:* **impartial**, unprejudiced, neutral, non-partisan, disinterested, detached, dispassionate, objective, open-minded, equitable, even-handed, fair.
– OPPOSITES prejudiced.

unbidden adjective **1** *an unbidden guest:* **uninvited**, unasked, unsolicited; unwanted, unwelcome. **2** *unbidden excitement grew deep inside her:* **spontaneous**, unprompted, voluntary, unforced, unplanned, unpremeditated; informal off-the-cuff.

unblemished adjective *he had an unblemished record as a law-abiding citizen:* **impeccable**, flawless, faultless, perfect, pure, whiter than white, clean, spotless, unsullied, unspoilt, undefiled, untouched, untarnished, unpolluted; incorrupt, guiltless, sinless, innocent, blameless; informal squeaky clean.
– OPPOSITES flawed.

unborn adjective **1** *your unborn child:* **embryonic**, fetal, in utero; expected. **2** *the unborn generations:* **future**, coming, forthcoming, subsequent.

unbounded adjective *I retained my unbounded enthusiasm for work:* **unlimited**, boundless, limitless, illimitable, unrestrained, unrestricted, unconstrained, uncontrolled, unchecked, unbridled; untold, immeasurable, endless, unending, interminable, everlasting, infinite, inexhaustible.
– OPPOSITES limited.

unbreakable adjective *a new type of*

unbreakable plastic bottle: **shatterproof**, indestructible, imperishable, durable, long-lasting; toughened, sturdy, stout, resistant, hard-wearing, heavy-duty.
– OPPOSITES fragile.

unbridled adjective *she strikes the ball with an unbridled enthusiasm:* **unrestrained**, unconstrained, uncontrolled, uninhibited, unrestricted, unchecked, uncurbed, rampant, runaway, irrepressible, unstoppable, intemperate, immoderate.
– OPPOSITES restrained.

unbroken adjective **1** *the last unbroken window:* **undamaged**, unimpaired, unharmed, unscathed, untouched, sound, intact, whole, perfect. **2** *an unbroken horse:* **untamed**, undomesticated, wild, feral. **3** *an unbroken chain of victories:* **uninterrupted**, continuous, endless, constant, unremitting, ongoing. **4** *his record is still unbroken:* **unbeaten**, undefeated, unsurpassed, unrivalled, unmatched, supreme.

unburden verb *she had a sudden wish to unburden herself:* **open one's heart**, confess, tell all; informal come clean.

uncalled
 ■ **uncalled for** *I'm ignoring that uncalled-for remark:* **gratuitous**, unnecessary, needless, inessential; undeserved, unmerited, unwarranted, unjustified, unreasonable, unfair, inappropriate, pointless; unasked, unsolicited, unrequested, unprompted, unprovoked, unwelcome.

uncanny adjective **1** *the silence was uncanny:* **eerie**, unnatural, unearthly, other-worldly, ghostly, strange, abnormal, weird, bizarre, freakish; Scottish eldritch; informal creepy, spooky, freaky. **2** *there was an uncanny resemblance between the two pictures:* **striking**, remarkable, extraordinary, exceptional, incredible, noteworthy, notable, arresting.

unceasing adjective *the unceasing efforts of the staff:* **incessant**, ceaseless, constant, continual, unabating, interminable, endless, unending, never-ending, everlasting, eternal, perpetual, continuous, non-stop, uninterrupted, unbroken, unremitting, persistent, relentless, unrelenting, unrelieved, sustained.

unceremonious adjective **1** *an unceremonious dismissal:* **abrupt**, sudden, hasty, hurried, summary, perfunctory, undignified; rude, impolite, discourteous, offhand. **2** *an unceremonious man:* **informal**, casual, relaxed, easy-going, familiar, natural, open; informal laid-back.
– OPPOSITES formal.

uncertain adjective **1** *the effects are uncertain:* **unknown**, debatable, open to question, in doubt, undetermined, unsure, in the balance, up in the air; unpredictable, unforeseeable, incalculable; risky, chancy; informal iffy. **2** *uncertain weather:* **changeable**, variable, changeful, irregular, unpredictable, unreliable,

u

unsettled, erratic, fluctuating. **3** *Ed was uncertain about the decision:* **unsure**, doubtful, dubious, undecided, irresolute, hesitant, blowing hot and cold, vacillating, vague, unclear, ambivalent, in two minds. **4** *an uncertain smile:* **hesitant**, tentative, faltering, unsure, unconfident.
– OPPOSITES predictable, sure, confident.

unchangeable adjective *many people think of personality characteristics as virtually unchangeable:* **unalterable**, immutable, invariable, changeless, fixed, hard and fast, cast-iron, set in stone, established, permanent, enduring, abiding, lasting, indestructible, ineradicable, irreversible.
– OPPOSITES variable.

unchanging adjective *the unchanging passivity of her face enraged him:* **consistent**, constant, regular, unvarying, predictable, stable, steady, fixed, permanent, perpetual, eternal; sustained, lasting, persistent.

uncharitable adjective *I regretted all the uncharitable things I had thought or said:* **mean**, mean-spirited, unkind, selfish, self-centred, inconsiderate, thoughtless, insensitive, unfriendly, unsympathetic, uncaring, ungenerous, ungracious, unfair.

uncharted adjective *we ran Borneo's uncharted rapids in canoes:* **unexplored**, undiscovered, unmapped, untravelled, unfamiliar, unplumbed, unknown.

uncivil adjective *he'd been short and uncivil with her:* **impolite**, rude, discourteous, disrespectful, unmannerly, bad-mannered, impertinent, impudent, ungracious; brusque, sharp, curt, offhand, gruff, churlish; informal off, fresh.
– OPPOSITES polite.

uncivilized adjective *uncivilized behaviour:* **uncouth**, coarse, rough, boorish, vulgar, philistine, uneducated, uncultured, uncultivated, benighted, unsophisticated, unpolished; ill-bred, ill-mannered, thuggish, loutish; barbarian, primitive, savage, brutish.

unclean adjective **1** *unclean premises:* **dirty**, filthy, grubby, grimy, mucky, foul, impure, tainted, soiled, unwashed; polluted, contaminated, infected, insanitary, unhygienic, unhealthy, germy, disease-ridden; informal yucky, cruddy; Brit. informal grotty, gungy. **2** *sex was considered unclean:* **sinful**, immoral, bad, wicked, evil, corrupt, impure, unwholesome, sordid, disgusting, debased, degenerate, depraved. **3** *pork is an unclean meat for Muslims:* **impure**; forbidden, taboo.
– OPPOSITES pure, halal, kosher.

unclear adjective *it was unclear how much fluid had leaked out:* **uncertain**, unsure, unsettled, up in the air, debatable, open to question, in doubt, doubtful; ambiguous, equivocal, indefinite, vague, mysterious, obscure, hazy, foggy, nebulous; informal iffy.
– OPPOSITES evident.

unclothed adjective *she felt awkwardly unclothed in her skimpy bikini:* **naked**, bare, nude, stripped, undressed, in a state of nature; informal in one's birthday suit, in the buff, in the raw, in the altogether, in the nuddy; Brit. informal starkers; Scottish informal in the scud; N. Amer. informal buck naked.
– OPPOSITES dressed.

uncomfortable adjective **1** *an uncomfortable chair:* **painful**, disagreeable, intolerable, unbearable, confining, cramped. **2** *I felt uncomfortable in her presence:* **uneasy**, awkward, nervous, tense, strained, edgy, restless, embarrassed, troubled, worried, anxious, unquiet, fraught; informal rattled, twitchy; N. Amer. informal discombobulated, antsy.
– OPPOSITES relaxed.

uncommitted adjective **1** *politicians were scrambling to woo uncommitted voters:* **floating**, undecided, non-partisan, unaffiliated, neutral, impartial, independent, undeclared, uncertain; informal sitting on the fence. **2** *a book about the uncommitted male:* **unmarried**, unattached, unwed, partnerless; footloose and fancy free, available, single, lone.
– OPPOSITES aligned, attached.

uncommon adjective **1** *an uncommon plant:* **unusual**, abnormal, rare, atypical, unconventional, unfamiliar, strange, odd, curious, extraordinary, outlandish, novel, singular, peculiar, queer, bizarre; alien; informal weird, oddball, offbeat. **2** *abductions are uncommon:* **rare**, scarce, few and far between, exceptional, abnormal, isolated, infrequent, irregular; Brit. out of the common. **3** *she displays an uncommon capacity for hard work:* **remarkable**, extraordinary, exceptional, singular, particular, marked, outstanding, noteworthy, significant, especial, special, signal, superior, unique, unparalleled, prodigious; informal mind-boggling.

uncommonly adverb *he is an uncommonly good talker:* **unusually**, remarkably, extraordinarily, exceptionally, singularly, particularly, especially, decidedly, notably, eminently, extremely, very; N. English right; informal awfully, terribly, seriously; Brit. informal jolly, dead.

uncommunicative adjective *he had always been quiet and uncommunicative:* **taciturn**, quiet, unforthcoming, reserved, reticent, laconic, tongue-tied, mute, silent, tight-lipped; guarded, secretive, close, private; distant, remote, aloof, withdrawn, unsociable; informal mum, stand-offish.
– OPPOSITES talkative.

uncomplicated adjective *an uncomplicated computer interface that is truly easy to use:* **simple**, straightforward, clear, accessible, undemanding, unchallenging, unsophisticated, trouble-free, painless, effortless, easy, elementary, idiot-proof, plain sailing; informal a piece of cake, child's

u

play, a cinch, a doddle, a breeze; Brit. informal easy-peasy.
– OPPOSITES complex.

uncompromising adjective *her uncompromising attitude led to clashes with the governor:* **inflexible**, unbending, unyielding, unshakeable, resolute, rigid, hard-line, immovable, intractable, firm, determined, iron-willed, obstinate, stubborn, adamant, obdurate, intransigent, headstrong, pig-headed; Brit. informal bloody-minded.
– OPPOSITES flexible.

unconcerned adjective **1** *he is unconcerned about their responses:* **indifferent**, unmoved, apathetic, uninterested, incurious, dispassionate, heedless, unmindful; cool, lukewarm, unenthusiastic. **2** *she tried to look unconcerned:* **untroubled**, unworried, unruffled, insouciant, nonchalant, blasé, carefree, casual, relaxed, at ease, {cool, calm, and collected}; informal laid-back.
– OPPOSITES interested, anxious.

unconditional adjective *he could count on the unconditional support of the president:* **unquestioning**, unqualified, unreserved, unlimited, unrestricted, wholehearted; complete, total, entire, full, absolute, out-and-out, unequivocal.

unconnected adjective **1** *the earth wire was unconnected:* **detached**, disconnected, loose. **2** *unconnected tasks:* **unrelated**, dissociated, separate, independent, distinct, different, disparate, discrete. **3** *unconnected chains of thought:* **disjointed**, incoherent, disconnected, rambling, wandering, diffuse, disorderly, haphazard, disorganized, garbled, mixed, muddled, aimless.
– OPPOSITES attached, related, coherent.

unconscionable adjective **1** *the unconscionable use of test animals:* **unethical**, amoral, immoral, unprincipled, indefensible, wrong; unscrupulous, unfair, underhand, dishonourable. **2** *we had to wait an unconscionable time:* **excessive**, unreasonable, unwarranted, uncalled for, unfair, inordinate, immoderate, undue, inexcusable, unnecessary, needless; informal over the top, OTT.
– OPPOSITES ethical, acceptable.

unconscious adjective **1** *she made sure he was unconscious:* **insensible**, senseless, insentient, insensate, comatose, inert, knocked out, stunned; motionless, immobile, prostrate; informal out cold, out for the count, dead to the world; Brit. informal spark out. **2** *she was unconscious of the pain:* **heedless**, unmindful, disregarding, oblivious to, insensible to, impervious to, unaffected by, unconcerned by, indifferent to; unaware, unknowing. **3** *an unconscious desire for recognition:* **subconscious**, latent, suppressed, subliminal, sleeping, inherent, instinctive, involuntary, uncontrolled, spontaneous; unintentional, unthinking,

unwitting, inadvertent; informal gut.
– OPPOSITES aware, voluntary.
noun *fantasies raging in the unconscious:* **subconscious**, psyche, ego, id, inner self.

uncontrollable adjective **1** *the crowds were uncontrollable:* **unmanageable**, out of control, ungovernable, wild, unruly, disorderly, recalcitrant, turbulent, disobedient, delinquent, defiant, undisciplined. **2** *his dad flew into an uncontrollable rage:* **ungovernable**, irrepressible, unstoppable, unquenchable; wild, violent, frenzied, furious, mad, hysterical, passionate.
– OPPOSITES compliant.

unconventional adjective *contemporary art employs unconventional techniques and materials:* **unusual**, irregular, unorthodox, unfamiliar, uncommon, unwonted, out of the ordinary, atypical, singular, alternative, different; new, novel, innovative, groundbreaking, pioneering, original, unprecedented; eccentric, idiosyncratic, quirky, odd, strange, bizarre, weird, outlandish, curious; abnormal, anomalous, aberrant, extraordinary; nonconformist, bohemian, avant-garde; informal way out, far out, offbeat, wacky, madcap, zany, hippy; Brit. informal rum; N. Amer. informal kooky, wacko.
– OPPOSITES orthodox.

unconvincing adjective *she felt the story was unconvincing:* **improbable**, unlikely, implausible, incredible, unbelievable, questionable, dubious, doubtful; strained, laboured, far-fetched, unrealistic, fanciful, fantastic; feeble, weak, transparent, poor, lame, ineffectual, half-baked; informal hard to swallow.
– OPPOSITES persuasive.

uncooperative adjective *the authorities were inclined to be uncooperative:* **unhelpful**, awkward, disobliging, recalcitrant, perverse, contrary, stubborn, wilful, stiff-necked, unyielding, unbending, inflexible, immovable, obstructive, difficult, obstreperous, disobedient; Brit. informal bloody-minded.
– OPPOSITES obliging.

uncoordinated adjective *as he ran, his uncoordinated limbs flung out in all directions:* **clumsy**, awkward, blundering, bumbling, lumbering, flat-footed, heavy-handed, graceless, gawky, ungainly, ungraceful; inept, unhandy, unskilful, inexpert, maladroit, bungling; informal butterfingered, cack-handed, ham-fisted; Brit. informal all (fingers and) thumbs; N. Amer. informal klutzy.
– OPPOSITES dexterous.

uncouth adjective *the porters shouted to each other in uncouth tones:* **uncivilized**, uncultured, uncultivated, unrefined, unpolished, unsophisticated, common, low, rough, coarse, crude, loutish, boorish, oafish; churlish, uncivil, rude, impolite, discourteous, disrespectful, unmannerly,

u

bad-mannered, ill-bred, indecorous, vulgar, crass, indelicate; Brit. informal yobbish.
– OPPOSITES refined.

uncover verb **1** *she uncovered the sandwiches:* **expose**, reveal, lay bare; unwrap, unveil; strip, denude. **2** *they uncovered a money-laundering plot:* **detect**, discover, come across, stumble on, chance on, find, turn up, unearth, dig up; expose, bring to light, unmask, unveil, reveal, lay bare, make known, make public, betray, give away; informal blow the whistle on, pull the plug on.

unctuous adjective *an unctuous smile:* **sycophantic**, ingratiating, obsequious, fawning, servile, grovelling, subservient, cringing, humble, hypocritical, insincere, gushing, effusive; glib, smooth, slick, slippery, oily, greasy; informal smarmy, slimy, sucky, soapy.

undaunted adjective *despite the tempest the crews were undaunted:* **unafraid**, undismayed, unflinching, unshrinking, unabashed, fearless, dauntless, intrepid, bold, valiant, brave, courageous, plucky, mettlesome, gritty, indomitable, confident, audacious, daring; informal gutsy, spunky.
– OPPOSITES fearful.

undecided adjective *his father's fate was still undecided:* **unresolved**, uncertain, unsure, unclear, unsettled, indefinite, undetermined, unknown, in the balance, up in the air, debatable, arguable, moot, open to question, doubtful, dubious, borderline, ambiguous, vague; indecisive, irresolute, hesitant, tentative, wavering, vacillating, uncommitted, ambivalent, in two minds; informal iffy.
– OPPOSITES certain.

undefined adjective **1** *some matters are still undefined:* **unspecified**, unexplained, unspecific, indeterminate, unsettled; unclear, woolly, imprecise, inexact, indefinite, vague. **2** *undefined shapes:* **indistinct**, indefinite, formless, indistinguishable, vague, hazy, misty, shadowy, nebulous, blurred, blurry.
– OPPOSITES definite, distinct.

undemonstrative adjective *my grandmother was an undemonstrative woman:* **unemotional**, unaffectionate, impassive, dispassionate, restrained, reserved, unresponsive, uncommunicative, unforthcoming, stiff, guarded, aloof, distant, detached, remote, withdrawn; cool, cold, frosty, frigid; informal stand-offish.

undeniable adjective *the force of his theory is undeniable:* **indisputable**, indubitable, unquestionable, beyond doubt, beyond question, undebatable, incontrovertible, incontestable, irrefutable, unassailable; certain, sure, definite, positive, conclusive, plain, obvious, unmistakable, self-evident, patent, emphatic, categorical, unequivocal.
– OPPOSITES questionable.

under preposition **1** *they hid under a bush:* **beneath**, below, underneath. **2** *the rent is under £250:* **less than**, lower than, below. **3** *branch managers are under the retail director:* **subordinate to**, junior to, inferior to, subservient to, answerable to, responsible to, subject to, controlled by. **4** *our finances are under pressure:* **subject to**, liable to, at the mercy of.
– OPPOSITES above, over.
adverb *coughing and spluttering, she went under:* **down**, lower, below, underneath, beneath; underwater.

underclothes plural noun **underwear**, undergarments, underclothing, underthings, lingerie; informal undies, frillies; Brit. informal smalls.

undercover adjective *they were arrested after a three-year undercover investigation:* **covert**, secret, clandestine, underground, surreptitious, furtive, cloak-and-dagger, hole-and-corner, hugger-mugger, stealthy, hidden, concealed; informal hush-hush, sneaky.
– OPPOSITES overt.

undercurrent noun **1** *dangerous undercurrents in the cove:* **undertow**, underflow, underswell, underset. **2** *the undercurrent of despair in his words:* **undertone**, overtone, suggestion, connotation, intimation, hint, nuance, trace, suspicion, whisper, tinge; feeling, atmosphere, aura, echo; informal vibes.

undercut verb **1** *the firm undercut their rivals:* **charge less than**, undersell, underbid. **2** *his authority was being undercut:* **undermine**, weaken, impair, sap, threaten, subvert, sabotage, ruin, destabilize, wreck.

underdog noun *spectators usually root for the underdog:* **weaker party**, victim, loser, scapegoat; informal little guy, fall guy, stooge.

underestimate verb *his political opponents underestimated his capabilities:* **underrate**, undervalue, do an injustice to, be wrong about, sell short, play down, understate; minimize, de-emphasize, underemphasize, diminish, downgrade, gloss over, trivialize; miscalculate, misjudge, misconstrue, misread.
– OPPOSITES exaggerate.

undergo verb *she had to undergo a ferocious and lengthy cross-examination:* **go through**, experience, undertake, face, submit to, be subjected to, come in for, receive, sustain, endure, brave, bear, tolerate, stand, withstand, weather; Brit. informal wear.

underground adjective **1** *an underground car park:* **subterranean**, buried, sunken, basement. **2** *underground organizations:* **clandestine**, secret, surreptitious, covert, undercover, closet; hole-and-corner, cloak-and-dagger, hugger-mugger, back-alley, hidden, sneaky, furtive; resistance, subversive; informal hush-hush. **3** *the underground art scene:* **alternative**, radical, revolutionary, unconventional, unorthodox,

avant-garde, experimental, innovative.
adverb 1 *the insects live underground:* **below ground**, in the earth. **2** *the rebels went underground:* **into hiding**, into seclusion, undercover.
noun 1 *he took the underground to work:* **underground railway**, metro; N. Amer. subway; Brit. informal tube. **2** *information from the French underground:* **resistance (movement)**; partisans, guerrillas, freedom fighters.

undergrowth noun *she groped her way through the thick undergrowth:* **shrubbery**, vegetation, greenery, ground cover, underwood, brushwood, brush, scrub, covert, thicket, copse; bushes, plants, brambles, herbage; N. Amer. underbrush.

underhand adjective *he was accused of employing underhand tactics:* **deceitful**, dishonest, dishonourable, disreputable, unethical, unprincipled, immoral, unscrupulous, fraudulent, dubious, unfair; treacherous, duplicitous, double-dealing; devious, artful, crafty, conniving, scheming, sly, wily; clandestine, sneaky, furtive, covert, cloak-and-dagger; N. Amer. snide; informal crooked, shady, bent, low-down; Brit. informal dodgy; Austral./NZ informal shonky.
– OPPOSITES honest.

underline verb **1** *she underlined a phrase:* **underscore**, mark, pick out, emphasize, highlight. **2** *the programme underlines the benefits of exercise:* **emphasize**, stress, highlight, accentuate, accent, focus on, spotlight, point up, play up; informal rub in.

underling noun *he dishes out orders to his underlings:* **subordinate**, inferior, junior, minion, lackey, flunkey, menial, retainer, vassal, subject, hireling, servant, henchman, factotum; informal dogsbody, gofer; Brit. informal skivvy.
– OPPOSITES boss.

underlying adjective **1** *the underlying aims of the research:* **fundamental**, basic, primary, prime, central, principal, chief, key, elementary, intrinsic, essential. **2** *an underlying feeling of irritation:* **latent**, repressed, suppressed, unrevealed, undisclosed, unexpressed, concealed, hidden, masked.

undermine verb **1** *their integrity is being undermined:* **subvert**, sabotage, threaten, weaken, compromise, diminish, reduce, impair, mar, spoil, ruin, damage, hurt, injure, cripple, sap, shake; informal drag through the mud. **2** *we undermined the building:* **tunnel under**, dig under, burrow under, sap.
– OPPOSITES strengthen, support.

underprivileged adjective *the charity arranges holidays for underprivileged children:* **needy**, deprived, disadvantaged, poor, destitute, in straitened circumstances, impoverished, poverty-stricken, indigent; Brit. on the breadline; informal on one's uppers, on one's beam-ends.

– OPPOSITES wealthy.

underrate verb *most of us have a tendency to underrate our own skills:* **undervalue**, underestimate, do an injustice to, sell short, play down, understate, minimize, diminish, downgrade, trivialize.
– OPPOSITES exaggerate.

undersized adjective *a skinny, undersized 15-year-old:* **underdeveloped**, stunted, small, short, little, tiny, petite, slight, compact, miniature, mini, diminutive, dwarfish, pygmy; Scottish wee; informal pint-sized, pocket-sized, knee-high to a grasshopper, baby, teeny-weeny, itsy-bitsy.
– OPPOSITES overgrown.

understand verb **1** *he couldn't understand anything we said:* **comprehend**, grasp, take in, see, apprehend, follow, make sense of, fathom; unravel, decipher, interpret; informal work out, figure out, make head or tail of, get one's head around, take on board, get the drift of, catch on to, get; Brit. informal twig, suss (out). **2** *she understood how hard he'd worked:* **appreciate**, recognize, realize, acknowledge, know, be aware of, be conscious of; informal be wise to. **3** *I understand that you wish to go:* **believe**, gather, take it, hear (tell), notice, see, learn; conclude, infer, assume, surmise, fancy.

understandable adjective **1** *make it understandable to the layman:* **comprehensible**, intelligible, coherent, clear, explicit, unambiguous, transparent, plain, straightforward, digestible, user-friendly. **2** *an understandable desire to be happy:* **unsurprising**, expected, predictable, inevitable; reasonable, acceptable, logical, rational, normal, natural; justifiable, justified, defensible, excusable, pardonable, forgivable.

understanding noun **1** *test your understanding of the language:* **comprehension**, apprehension, grasp, mastery, appreciation, assimilation, absorption; knowledge, awareness, insight, skill, expertise, proficiency; informal know-how. **2** *a young man of brilliant understanding:* **intellect**, intelligence, brainpower, brains, judgement, reasoning, mentality; insight, intuition, shrewdness, acumen, sagacity, wisdom, wit; informal nous, savvy, know-how. **3** *it was my understanding that this was free:* **belief**, perception, view, conviction, feeling, opinion, intuition, impression, assumption, supposition. **4** *he treated me with understanding:* **compassion**, sympathy, pity, feeling, concern, consideration, kindness, sensitivity, decency, humanity, charity, goodwill, mercy, tolerance. **5** *we had a tacit understanding:* **agreement**, arrangement, deal, bargain, settlement, pledge, pact, compact, contract, covenant, bond.
– OPPOSITES ignorance, indifference.
adjective *an understanding friend:* **compassionate**, sympathetic, sensitive,

u

considerate, tender, kind, thoughtful, tolerant, patient, forbearing, lenient, merciful, forgiving, humane; approachable, supportive, perceptive.

understate verb *we have been guilty of understating the size of the problem:* **play down**, downplay, underrate, underplay, de-emphasize, trivialize, minimize, diminish, downgrade, brush aside, gloss over; informal soft-pedal, sell short.
– OPPOSITES exaggerate.

understudy noun *he muffed his lines and was often replaced by an understudy:* **stand-in**, substitute, replacement, reserve, fill-in, locum, proxy, backup, relief, standby, stopgap, second, ancillary; informal sub; N. Amer. informal pinch-hitter.

undertake verb *the team were asked to undertake a further project:* **tackle**, take on, assume, shoulder, handle, manage, deal with, be responsible for; engage in, take part in, go about, set about, get down to, get to grips with, embark on; attempt, try, endeavour; informal have a go at.

undertaker noun **funeral director**; N. Amer. mortician.

undertaking noun **1** *a risky undertaking:* **enterprise**, venture, project, campaign, scheme, plan, operation, endeavour, effort, task, activity, pursuit, exploit, business, affair, procedure; mission, quest. **2** *sign this undertaking to comply with the rules:* **pledge**, agreement, promise, oath, covenant, vow, commitment, guarantee, assurance, contract.

undertone noun **1** *he said something in an undertone:* **low voice**, murmur, whisper, mutter. **2** *the story's dark undertones:* **undercurrent**, overtone, suggestion, nuance, vein, atmosphere, aura, tenor, flavour; vibrations.

undervalue verb *the enthusiasm of youth was often undervalued by the older generation:* **underrate**, underestimate, play down, understate, underemphasize, diminish, minimize, downgrade, reduce, brush aside, gloss over, trivialize, hold cheap; informal sell short.

underwater adjective *there are some underwater caves nearby:* **submerged**, immersed, sunken; undersea, submarine.

underwear noun **underclothes**, underclothing, undergarments, underthings, lingerie; informal undies, frillies; Brit. informal smalls.

underworld noun **1** *Osiris, god of the underworld:* **the netherworld**, the nether regions, hell, the abyss; eternal damnation; Gehenna, Tophet, Sheol, Hades; Brit. the other place. **2** *the violent underworld of Southwark:* **criminal world**, gangland; criminals, gangsters; informal mobsters.
– OPPOSITES heaven.

underwrite verb *the company which underwrote the deal has crashed:* **sponsor**, support, back, insure, indemnify, subsidize, pay for, finance, fund; informal foot the bill for; N. Amer. informal bankroll.

undesirable adjective **1** *a mix of medicines may result in undesirable side-effects:* **unpleasant**, disagreeable, nasty, unwelcome, unwanted, unfortunate, infelicitous. **2** *some very undesirable people:* **unpleasant**, disagreeable, obnoxious, nasty, awful, terrible, dreadful, frightful, repulsive, repellent, abhorrent, loathsome, hateful, detestable, deplorable, appalling, insufferable, intolerable, despicable, contemptible, odious, vile, unsavoury; informal ghastly, horrible, horrid; Brit. informal beastly.
– OPPOSITES pleasant, agreeable.

undignified adjective *there was an undignified scramble for seats on the train:* **unseemly**, demeaning, unbecoming, unworthy, unbefitting, degrading, shameful, dishonourable, ignominious, discreditable, ignoble, untoward, unsuitable; scandalous, disgraceful, indecent, low, base; informal infra dig.

undisciplined adjective *the school said that his kid was lazy and undisciplined:* **unruly**, disorderly, disobedient, badly behaved, recalcitrant, wilful, wayward, delinquent, naughty, rebellious, insubordinate, disruptive, errant, out of control, uncontrollable, wild; disorganized, unsystematic, unmethodical, lax, slapdash, slipshod, sloppy; Brit. informal stroppy, bolshie.

undisguised adjective *he regarded her with undisguised affection:* **obvious**, evident, patent, manifest, transparent, overt, unconcealed, unhidden, unmistakable, undeniable, plain, clear, clear-cut, explicit, naked, visible; blatant, flagrant, glaring, bold; informal standing/sticking out a mile.

undisputed adjective *his military pre-eminence was undisputed:* **undoubted**, indubitable, uncontested, incontestable, unchallenged, incontrovertible, unequivocal, undeniable, irrefutable, unmistakable, sure, certain, definite, accepted, acknowledged, recognized.
– OPPOSITES doubtful.

undistinguished adjective *he had an undistinguished career as a lecturer in mathematics:* **unexceptional**, indifferent, run-of-the-mill, middle-of-the-road, ordinary, average, commonplace, mediocre, humdrum, lacklustre, forgettable, uninspired, uneventful, unremarkable, inconsequential, featureless, nondescript, middling, moderate; N. Amer. garden-variety; informal nothing special, no great shakes, nothing to write home about, OK, so-so, bog-standard; Brit. informal common or garden; N. Amer. informal bush-league.
– OPPOSITES extraordinary.

undivided adjective *they need the undivided attention of a sympathetic listener:* **complete**, full, total, whole, entire, absolute, unqualified, unreserved, unmitigated, unbroken, consistent, thorough, exclusive, dedicated; focused, engrossed, absorbed, attentive, committed.

undo verb **1** *he undid another button:* **unfasten**, unbutton, unhook, untie, unlace; unlock, unbolt; loosen, disentangle, extricate, release, detach, free, open; disconnect, disengage, separate. **2** *they will undo a decision by the law lords:* **revoke**, overrule, overturn, repeal, rescind, reverse, countermand, cancel, annul, nullify, invalidate, void, negate. **3** *she undid much of the good work done:* **ruin**, undermine, subvert, overturn, scotch, sabotage, spoil, impair, mar, destroy, wreck, eradicate, obliterate; cancel out, neutralize, thwart, foil, frustrate, hamper, hinder, obstruct; informal blow, put the kibosh on, foul up, muck up; Brit. informal scupper, throw a spanner in the works of; N. Amer. informal rain on someone's parade.
– OPPOSITES fasten, ratify, enhance.

undoing noun **1** *she plotted the king's undoing:* **downfall**, defeat, conquest, deposition, overthrow, ruin, ruination, elimination, end, collapse, failure, debasement; Waterloo. **2** *their complacency was their undoing:* **fatal flaw**, Achilles' heel, weakness, weak point, failing, misfortune, affliction, curse.

undone adjective *some work was left undone:* **unfinished**, incomplete, half-done, unaccomplished, unfulfilled, unconcluded; omitted, neglected, disregarded, ignored; remaining, outstanding, deferred, pending, on ice; informal on the back burner.
– OPPOSITES finished.

undoubted adjective *her undoubted ability:* **undisputed**, unchallenged, unquestioned, indubitable, incontrovertible, irrefutable, incontestable, sure, certain, unmistakable; definite, accepted, acknowledged, recognized.

undoubtedly adverb *they are undoubtedly guilty:* **doubtless**, indubitably, doubtlessly, no doubt, without (a) doubt; unquestionably, indisputably, undeniably, incontrovertibly, clearly, obviously, patently, certainly, definitely, surely, of course, indeed.

undress verb *he undressed and got into bed:* **strip (off)**, disrobe, take off one's clothes; Brit. informal peel off.
■ **in a state of undress** naked, (in the) nude, bare, stripped, unclothed, undressed, in a state of nature; informal in one's birthday suit, in the raw, in the buff, in the nuddy; Brit. informal starkers.

undue adjective *make sure that you can afford the repayments without putting undue strain on your finances:* **excessive**, immoderate, intemperate, inordinate, disproportionate; uncalled for, unneeded, unnecessary, non-essential, needless, unwarranted, unjustified, unreasonable; inappropriate,

unmerited, unsuitable, improper.
– OPPOSITES appropriate.

undulate verb *the land undulates between 200 and 250 feet above sea level:* **rise and fall**, surge, swell, heave, ripple, flow; wind, wobble, oscillate.

undying adjective *his undying devotion to the club:* **abiding**, lasting, enduring, permanent, constant, infinite; unceasing, perpetual, ceaseless, incessant, unending, never-ending; immortal, eternal, deathless.

unearth verb **1** *workmen unearthed an artillery shell:* **dig up**, excavate, exhume, disinter, root out, unbury. **2** *I unearthed an interesting fact:* **discover**, uncover, find, come across, hit on, bring to light, expose, turn up, hunt out, nose out.

unearthly adjective **1** *an unearthly chill in the air:* **other-worldly**, supernatural, preternatural, alien; ghostly, spectral, phantom, mysterious, spine-chilling, hair-raising; uncanny, eerie, strange, weird, unnatural, bizarre; Scottish eldritch; informal spooky, creepy, scary. **2** (informal) *they rose at some unearthly hour:* **unreasonable**, preposterous, abnormal, extraordinary, absurd, ridiculous, unheard of; informal ungodly, unholy.
– OPPOSITES normal, reasonable.

uneasy adjective **1** *the doctor made him feel uneasy:* **worried**, anxious, troubled, disturbed, agitated, nervous, tense, overwrought, edgy, apprehensive, restless, discomfited, perturbed, fearful, uncomfortable, unsettled; informal jittery, nervy. **2** *he had an uneasy feeling:* **worrying**, disturbing, troubling, alarming, dismaying, disquieting, unsettling, disconcerting, upsetting. **3** *the victory ensured an uneasy peace:* **tense**, awkward, strained, fraught; precarious, unstable, insecure.
– OPPOSITES calm, stable.

uneconomic, uneconomical adjective *it was uneconomic for landlords to maintain rent-controlled housing:* **unprofitable**, uncommercial, non-viable, loss-making, worthless; wasteful, inefficient, improvident.

uneducated adjective *the workforce remains largely uneducated and unskilled:* **untaught**, unschooled, untutored, untrained, unread, unscholarly, illiterate, unlettered, ignorant, ill-informed, uninformed; uncouth, unsophisticated, uncultured, unaccomplished, unenlightened, philistine, benighted, backward.
– OPPOSITES learned.

unemotional adjective *professionals should remain detached and unemotional:* **reserved**, undemonstrative, sober, restrained, passionless, emotionless, unsentimental, unexcitable, impassive, phlegmatic, stoical, equable; cold, cool, unfeeling.

unemployed adjective *he lost his job in February and is still unemployed:* **jobless**, out of work, between jobs, unwaged, unoccupied, redundant, laid off; on benefit; Brit. signing on; N. Amer. on welfare; Brit. informal on the dole, resting.

unending adjective *she toiled at unending tasks:* **endless**, never-ending, interminable, perpetual, eternal, ceaseless, incessant, unceasing, non-stop, uninterrupted, continuous, continual, constant, persistent, unbroken, unabating, unremitting, relentless.

unendurable adjective *the heat of the stoves made the kitchen almost unendurable:* **intolerable**, unbearable, insufferable, insupportable, more than flesh and blood can stand.

unenthusiastic adjective *he was unenthusiastic about the proposal:* **indifferent**, apathetic, half-hearted, lukewarm, casual, cool, lacklustre, offhand, unmoved; cursory, perfunctory.
– OPPOSITES keen.

unenviable adjective *he had the unenviable task of trying to reconcile their disparate interests:* **disagreeable**, nasty, unpleasant, undesirable, horrible, thankless; unwanted, unwished-for.

unequal adjective **1** *they are unequal in length:* **different**, dissimilar, unlike, unalike, disparate, unmatched, uneven, irregular, varying, variable. **2** *the unequal distribution of wealth:* **unfair**, unjust, disproportionate, inequitable, biased. **3** *an unequal contest:* **one-sided**, uneven, unfair, ill-matched, unbalanced, lopsided. **4** *she felt unequal to the task:* **inadequate for**, incapable of, unqualified for, unsuited to, incompetent at, not up to; informal not cut out for.
– OPPOSITES identical, fair.

unequalled adjective *an unequalled record of five World Cup victories:* **unbeaten**, matchless, unmatched, unrivalled, unsurpassed, unparalleled, peerless, incomparable, inimitable, second to none, unique.

unequivocal adjective *the report's advice was unequivocal:* **unambiguous**, unmistakable, indisputable, incontrovertible, indubitable, undeniable; clear, clear-cut, plain, explicit, specific, categorical, straightforward, blunt, candid, emphatic, manifest.
– OPPOSITES ambiguous.

unerring adjective *with unerring accuracy he hit the gold:* **unfailing**, infallible, perfect, flawless, faultless, impeccable, unimpeachable; sure, true, assured, deadly; informal sure-fire.

unethical adjective *it is unethical to produce and market a drug which would harm the patient:* **immoral**, amoral, unprincipled, unscrupulous, dishonourable, dishonest, wrong, deceitful, unconscionable, fraudulent, underhand, wicked, evil, corrupt; unprofessional, improper.

uneven adjective **1** *they stumbled over the uneven ground:* **bumpy**, rough, lumpy, stony, rocky, potholed, rutted, pitted, jagged. **2** *uneven teeth:* **irregular**, unequal, unbalanced, lopsided, askew, crooked, asymmetrical, unsymmetrical. **3** *uneven quality:* **inconsistent**, variable, varying, fluctuating, irregular, erratic, patchy. **4** *an uneven contest:* **one-sided**, unequal, unfair, unjust, inequitable, ill-matched, unbalanced.
– OPPOSITES flat, regular, equal.

uneventful adjective *a place where dull people live uneventful lives:* **unexciting**, uninteresting, monotonous, boring, dull, tedious, humdrum, routine, unvaried, ordinary, run-of-the-mill, pedestrian, mundane, predictable.
– OPPOSITES exciting.

unexceptional adjective *an adequate but unexceptional hotel:* **ordinary**, average, typical, everyday, mediocre, run-of-the-mill, middle-of-the-road, indifferent; informal OK, so-so, nothing special, no great shakes, fair-to-middling.

unexpected adjective *he received an unexpected invitation from Professor Dobson:* **unforeseen**, unanticipated, unpredicted, unlooked for, without warning; sudden, abrupt, surprising, out of the blue.

unfailing adjective *his unfailing good humour:* **constant**, reliable, dependable, steadfast, steady; endless, undying, unfading, inexhaustible, boundless, ceaseless.

unfair adjective **1** *the trial was unfair:* **unjust**, inequitable, prejudiced, biased, discriminatory; one-sided, unequal, uneven, unbalanced, partisan. **2** *his comments were unfair:* **undeserved**, unmerited, uncalled for, unreasonable, unjustified; Brit. informal out of order. **3** *unfair play:* **unsporting**, unsportsmanlike, dirty, below the belt, underhand, dishonourable. **4** *you're being very unfair:* **inconsiderate**, thoughtless, insensitive, selfish, mean, unkind, unreasonable.
– OPPOSITES just, justified.

unfaithful adjective **1** *her husband had been unfaithful:* **adulterous**, faithless, fickle, untrue, inconstant; informal cheating, two-timing. **2** *an unfaithful friend:* **disloyal**, treacherous, traitorous, untrustworthy, unreliable, undependable, false, two-faced, double-crossing, deceitful.
– OPPOSITES loyal.

unfaltering adjective *he moved with an unfaltering step:* **steady**, resolute, resolved, firm, steadfast, fixed, decided, unswerving, unwavering, tireless, indefatigable, persistent, unyielding, relentless, unremitting, unrelenting.
– OPPOSITES unsteady.

unfamiliar adjective **1** *an unfamiliar part of the city:* **unknown**, new, strange, foreign, alien. **2** *the unfamiliar sounds:* **unusual**, uncommon, unconventional, novel, different, exotic, unorthodox, odd, peculiar, curious, uncharacteristic, anomalous, out of the ordinary. **3** *investors unfamiliar with the stock market:* **unacquainted**, unused, unaccustomed, unconversant, inexperienced, uninformed, unenlightened, ignorant, new to, a stranger to.

unfashionable adjective *unfashionable clothes:* **out of fashion**, outdated, old-fashioned, outmoded, out of style, dated, unstylish, passé, démodé; informal out, square, out of the ark.

unfasten verb *Ron unfastened his seat belt:* **undo**, open, disconnect, remove, untie, unbutton, unzip, loose, loosen, free, unlock, unbolt.

unfathomable adjective *dark unfathomable eyes:* **inscrutable**, incomprehensible, enigmatic, indecipherable, obscure, esoteric, mysterious, mystifying, deep, profound.
– OPPOSITES penetrable.

unfavourable adjective **1** *his poor turnout received unfavourable comment:* **adverse**, critical, hostile, inimical, unfriendly, unsympathetic, negative; discouraging, disapproving, uncomplimentary, unflattering. **2** *the unfavourable economic climate:* **disadvantageous**, adverse, inauspicious, unpropitious, gloomy; unsuitable, inappropriate, inopportune.
– OPPOSITES positive.

unfeeling adjective *my mother is a cold, unfeeling, and unresponsive woman:* **uncaring**, unsympathetic, unemotional, uncharitable; heartless, hard-hearted, hard, harsh, austere, cold, cold-hearted.
– OPPOSITES compassionate.

unfeigned adjective *he looked at his wife with unfeigned admiration:* **sincere**, genuine, real, true, honest, unaffected, unforced, heartfelt, wholehearted.
– OPPOSITES insincere.

unfettered adjective *the choice between a planned economy and an unfettered market:* **unrestrained**, unrestricted, unconstrained, free, unbridled, unchecked, uncontrolled.
– OPPOSITES restricted.

unfinished adjective **1** *an unfinished essay:* **incomplete**, uncompleted; partial, undone, half-done; imperfect, unpolished, unrefined, sketchy, fragmentary, rough. **2** *the door can be supplied unfinished:* **unpainted**, unvarnished, untreated.
– OPPOSITES complete.

unfit adjective **1** *the film is unfit for children | unfit for duty:* **unsuitable**, unsuited, inappropriate, unequipped, inadequate, not designed; incapable of, unable to do something, not up to, not equal to; informal not cut out for, not up to scratch. **2** *I am unfit:* **unhealthy**, out of condition/shape, in poor condition/shape.
– OPPOSITES suitable.

unflagging adjective *an unflagging*

commitment to the ideals of peace: **tireless**, persistent, dogged, tenacious, determined, resolute, staunch, single-minded, unrelenting, unfaltering, unfailing.
– OPPOSITES inconstant.

unflappable adjective (informal) *I prided myself on being unflappable even in the most chaotic circumstances:* **imperturbable**, unexcitable, cool, calm, {cool, calm, and collected}; self-controlled, cool-headed, level-headed; informal laid-back.
– OPPOSITES excitable.

unflattering adjective **1** *an unflattering review of his new book:* **unfavourable**, uncomplimentary, harsh, unsympathetic, critical, hostile, scathing. **2** *an unflattering dress:* **unattractive**, unbecoming, unsightly, ugly, plain, ill-fitting.
– OPPOSITES complimentary, becoming.

unflinching adjective *they stood together in unflinching determination to win:* **resolute**, determined, single-minded, dogged, resolved, firm, committed, steady, unwavering, unflagging, unswerving, unfaltering, untiring, undaunted, fearless.

unfold verb **1** *May unfolded the map:* **open out**, spread out, flatten, straighten out, unroll. **2** *she unfolded her tale to Joanna:* **narrate**, relate, recount, tell, reveal, disclose, divulge, communicate, report, recite, give an account of. **3** *I watched the events unfold:* **develop**, evolve, happen, take place, occur, transpire, progress.

unforeseen adjective *due to unforeseen circumstances:* **unpredicted**, unexpected, unanticipated, unplanned, unlooked for, not bargained for.
– OPPOSITES expected.

unforgettable adjective *a visit to Morocco is a truly unforgettable experience:* **memorable**, not/never to be forgotten, haunting, catchy; striking, impressive, outstanding, extraordinary, exceptional.
– OPPOSITES unexceptional.

unforgivable adjective *he had committed the unforgivable sin—he had informed on his friends:* **inexcusable**, unpardonable, unjustifiable, indefensible, inexpiable, irremissible.
– OPPOSITES venial.

unfortunate adjective **1** *unfortunate people:* **unlucky**, hapless, out of luck, luckless, wretched, miserable, forlorn, poor, pitiful; informal down on one's luck. **2** *an unfortunate start to our holiday:* **adverse**, disadvantageous, unfavourable, unlucky, unwelcome, unpromising, inauspicious, unpropitious. **3** *an unfortunate remark:* **regrettable**, inappropriate, unsuitable, infelicitous, tactless, injudicious.
– OPPOSITES lucky, auspicious.

unfortunately adverb *unfortunately, all hell broke loose:* **unluckily**, sadly, regrettably, unhappily, alas, sad to say; informal worse luck.

u

unfounded adjective *the article was a piece of unfounded speculation:* **groundless**, baseless, unsubstantiated, unproven, unsupported, uncorroborated, unconfirmed, unverified, unattested, without basis, without foundation, speculative, conjectural.
– OPPOSITES proven.

unfriendly adjective 1 *she directed an unfriendly look at Harold:* **hostile**, disagreeable, antagonistic, aggressive; ill-natured, unpleasant, surly, sour, unamicable, uncongenial; inhospitable, unneighbourly, unwelcoming, unkind, unsympathetic; unsociable, antisocial; aloof, cold, cool, frosty, distant, unapproachable; informal stand-offish, starchy. 2 *unfriendly terrain:* **unfavourable**, disadvantageous, unpropitious, inauspicious, hostile.
– OPPOSITES amiable, favourable.

ungainly adjective *an uncouth man with an ungainly walk:* **awkward**, clumsy, ungraceful, graceless, inelegant, gawky, maladroit, gauche, uncoordinated.
– OPPOSITES graceful.

ungodly adjective 1 *ungodly behaviour:* **unholy**, godless, irreligious, impious, blasphemous, sacrilegious; immoral, corrupt, depraved, sinful, wicked, evil, iniquitous. 2 (informal) *he called at an ungodly hour:* **unreasonable**, unsocial, antisocial; informal unearthly.

ungovernable adjective *the country had become ungovernable:* **uncontrollable**, unmanageable, anarchic, intractable; unruly, disorderly, rebellious, riotous, wild, mutinous, undisciplined.

ungracious adjective *it was ungracious not to thank them:* **rude**, impolite, uncivil, discourteous, ill-mannered, bad-mannered, uncouth, disrespectful, insolent, impertinent, offhand.
– OPPOSITES polite.

ungrateful adjective *she's so rude and ungrateful for everything we do:* **unappreciative**, unthankful, ungracious.
– OPPOSITES thankful.

unguarded adjective 1 *an unguarded frontier:* **undefended**, unprotected, unfortified; vulnerable, insecure, open to attack. 2 *an unguarded remark:* **careless**, ill-considered, incautious, thoughtless, rash, foolhardy, foolish, indiscreet, imprudent, injudicious, ill-judged, insensitive. 3 *in an unguarded moment, Iris had let drop that she was receiving no fee to run the course:* **unwary**, inattentive, off guard, distracted, absent-minded.

unhappiness noun **sadness**, sorrow, dejection, depression, misery, cheerlessness, downheartedness, despondency, despair, desolation, wretchedness, glumness, gloom, gloominess, dolefulness; melancholy, low spirits, mournfulness, woe, heartache,

distress, chagrin, grief, pain; informal the blues.

unhappy adjective 1 *an unhappy childhood:* **sad**, miserable, sorrowful, dejected, despondent, disconsolate, morose, broken-hearted, heartbroken, down, downcast, dispirited, downhearted, depressed, melancholy, mournful, gloomy, glum, despairing, doleful, forlorn, woebegone, woeful, long-faced, joyless, cheerless; informal down in the mouth/dumps, fed up, blue. 2 *in the unhappy event of litigation:* **unfortunate**, unlucky, luckless; ill-starred, ill-fated, doomed; informal jinxed. 3 *I was unhappy with the service I received:* **dissatisfied**, displeased, discontented, disappointed, disgruntled.
– OPPOSITES cheerful.

unharmed adjective 1 *they released the hostage unharmed:* **uninjured**, unhurt, unscathed, safe (and sound), alive and well, in one piece, without a scratch. 2 *the tomb was unharmed:* **undamaged**, unbroken, unmarred, unspoiled, unsullied, unmarked; sound, intact, perfect, unblemished, pristine.
– OPPOSITES injured, damaged.

unhealthy adjective 1 *she was leading a very unhealthy lifestyle:* **harmful**, detrimental, destructive, injurious, damaging, deleterious; malign, noxious, poisonous, insalubrious, baleful. 2 *he had an unhealthy pallor:* **ill-looking**, ill, unwell, in poor health, ailing, sick, sickly, poorly, indisposed, weak, frail, delicate, infirm, washed out, run down, peaky. 3 *an unhealthy obsession with drugs:* **unwholesome**, morbid, macabre, twisted, abnormal, warped, depraved, unnatural; informal sick.

unheard of adjective 1 *such behaviour was unheard of:* **unprecedented**, exceptional, extraordinary, out of the ordinary, unthought of, undreamed of, unbelievable, inconceivable, unimaginable, unthinkable. 2 *a game unheard of in the UK:* **unknown**, unfamiliar, new.
– OPPOSITES common, well known.

unheeded adjective *my protest went unheeded:* **disregarded**, ignored, neglected, overlooked, unnoted, unrecognized.

unhinged adjective *Lydia was unhinged with the shock of bereavement:* **deranged**, demented, unbalanced, out of one's mind, crazed, mad, insane, disturbed; informal crazy, mental, bonkers, batty, loopy, bananas, touched.
– OPPOSITES sane.

unholy adjective 1 *a grin of unholy amusement:* **ungodly**, godless, irreligious, impious, blasphemous, sacrilegious, profane, irreverent; wicked, evil, immoral, corrupt, depraved, sinful. 2 (informal) *she'd had an unholy row with Mama:* **shocking**, dreadful, outrageous, appalling, terrible, horrendous, frightful. 3 *an unholy alliance*

u

between the Fascists and Communists: **unnatural**, unusual, improbable, made in hell.

unhurried adjective *he began opening the drawers of his desk in an unhurried way:* **leisurely**, easy, easy-going, relaxed, slow, deliberate, measured, calm.
–OPPOSITES hasty.

unhygienic adjective *animals are kept in cramped and often unhygienic conditions:* **insanitary**, unsanitary, dirty, filthy, contaminated, unhealthy, unwholesome, insalubrious, polluted, foul.
–OPPOSITES sanitary.

unidentified adjective *he had been followed by unidentified armed men:* **unknown**, unnamed, anonymous, incognito, nameless, unfamiliar, strange.
–OPPOSITES known.

unification noun *the costs of German unification:* **union**, merger, fusion, fusing, amalgamation, coalition, combination, confederation, federation, synthesis, joining.

uniform adjective **1** *a uniform temperature of between 18 and 21 degrees:* **constant**, consistent, steady, invariable, unvarying, unfluctuating, unchanging, stable, static, regular, fixed, even, equal. **2** *cut the vegetables into pieces of uniform size:* **identical**, matching, similar, equal; same, like, homogeneous, consistent.
–OPPOSITES variable.
noun *a soldier in uniform:* **costume**, livery, regalia, suit, ensemble, outfit; regimentals, colours; informal get-up, rig, gear.

uniformity noun **1** *uniformity in tax law:* **constancy**, consistency, conformity, invariability, stability, regularity, evenness, homogeneity, homogeneousness, equality. **2** *there was a dull uniformity about the place:* **monotony**, tedium, tediousness, dullness, dreariness, flatness, sameness.
–OPPOSITES variation, variety.

unify verb *he unified the confederacy into a powerful entity:* **unite**, bring together, join (together), merge, fuse, amalgamate, coalesce, combine, blend, mix, bind, consolidate.
–OPPOSITES separate.

unimaginable adjective *unimaginable riches:* **unthinkable**, inconceivable, incredible, unbelievable, unheard of, unthought of, untold, undreamed of, beyond one's wildest dreams.

unimaginative adjective *the production was plodding and unimaginative:* **uninspired**, uninventive, unoriginal, uncreative, commonplace, pedestrian, mundane, ordinary, routine, humdrum, workaday, run-of-the-mill, hackneyed, trite.

unimpeachable adjective *this was information that I got from an unimpeachable source:* **trustworthy**, reliable, dependable, above suspicion, irreproachable.
–OPPOSITES unreliable.

unimpeded adjective *he had an unimpeded view of them:* **unrestricted**, unhindered, unblocked, unhampered, free, clear.

unimportant adjective *the details are unimportant at this stage:* **insignificant**, inconsequential, trivial, minor, trifling, of little/no importance, of little/no consequence, of no account, irrelevant, peripheral, extraneous, petty, paltry; informal piddling.

uninhabited adjective **1** *much of this land was uninhabited:* **unpopulated**, unpeopled, unsettled. **2** *an uninhabited hut:* **vacant**, empty, unoccupied, untenanted, to let.

uninhibited adjective *uninhibited dancing:* **unrestrained**, unrepressed, abandoned, wild, reckless; unrestricted, uncontrolled, unchecked, intemperate, wanton. **2** *I'm pretty uninhibited in company:* **unreserved**, unrepressed, liberated, unselfconscious, free and easy, relaxed, informal, open, outgoing, extrovert, outspoken, frank, forthright; informal upfront.
–OPPOSITES repressed.

uninspired adjective *an album full of uninspired love songs:* **unimaginative**, uninventive, pedestrian, mundane, unoriginal, commonplace, ordinary, routine, humdrum, run-of-the-mill, hackneyed, trite; spiritless, passionless.

uninspiring adjective *they remained a weak and uninspiring political force:* **boring**, dull, dreary, unexciting, unstimulating; dry, colourless, bland, lacklustre, tedious, humdrum, run-of-the-mill.

unintelligent adjective *he treated me like an erring and somewhat unintelligent son:* **stupid**, ignorant, dense, brainless, mindless, foolish, dull-witted, slow, simple-minded, vacuous, vapid, idiotic, obtuse; informal thick, dim, dumb, dopey, half-witted, dozy.

unintelligible adjective **1** *unintelligible sounds:* **incomprehensible**, indiscernible, mumbled, indistinct, unclear, slurred, inarticulate, incoherent, garbled. **2** *unintelligible graffiti:* **illegible**, indecipherable, unreadable.

unintentional adjective *I assure you, the insult was unintentional:* **unintended**, accidental, inadvertent, involuntary, unwitting, unthinking, unpremeditated, unconscious.
–OPPOSITES deliberate.

uninterested adjective *Derek was uninterested in politics:* **indifferent to**, unconcerned about, uninvolved, apathetic, lukewarm, unenthusiastic.

uninteresting adjective *an uninteresting book about genealogy:* **unexciting**, boring, dull, tiresome, wearisome, tedious, dreary, lifeless, humdrum, colourless, bland, insipid, banal, dry, pedestrian; informal samey.

u

– OPPOSITES exciting.

uninterrupted adjective *ten hours of uninterrupted sleep:* **unbroken**, continuous, continual, undisturbed, untroubled.
– OPPOSITES intermittent.

uninvited adjective **1** *an uninvited guest:* **unasked**, unexpected; unwelcome, unwanted. **2** *uninvited suggestions:* **unsolicited**, unrequested, unsought.

uninviting adjective *the bed looked cold and uninviting:* **unappealing**, unattractive, unappetizing, off-putting; bleak, cheerless, dreary, dismal, depressing, grim, inhospitable.
– OPPOSITES tempting.

union noun **1** *the union of art and nature:* **unification**, uniting, joining, merging, merger, fusion, fusing, amalgamating, amalgamation, coalition, combination, synthesis, blend, blending, mingling. **2** *the crowd moved in union:* **unity**, accord, unison, harmony, agreement, concurrence. **3** *his daughter's union with the prince:* **marriage**, wedding, alliance; coupling, intercourse, copulation. **4** *all employees should have the right to be represented by a union:* **association**, trade union, league, guild, confederation, federation.
– OPPOSITES separation, parting.

unique adjective **1** *each site is unique:* **distinctive**, individual, special, idiosyncratic; single, sole, lone, unrepeated, unrepeatable, solitary, exclusive, rare, uncommon, unusual; informal one-off. **2** *a unique insight into history:* **remarkable**, special, singular, noteworthy, notable, extraordinary; unequalled, unparalleled, unmatched, unsurpassed, incomparable. **3** *species unique to the island:* **peculiar**, specific.

unison
■ **in unison 1** *they lifted their arms in unison:* simultaneously, at (one and) the same time, (all) at once, (all) together. **2** *we are in complete unison:* in agreement, in accord, in harmony, as one.

unit noun **1** *the family is the fundamental unit of society:* **component**, element, constituent, subdivision. **2** *a unit of currency:* **quantity**, measure, denomination. **3** *a guerrilla unit:* **detachment**, contingent, division, company, squadron, corps, regiment, brigade, platoon, battalion; cell, faction.

unite verb **1** *the fight against communism seemed to unite the nation:* **unify**, join, link, connect, combine, amalgamate, fuse, weld, bond, bring together, knit together. **2** *environmentalists and activists united:* **join together**, join forces, combine, band together, ally, cooperate, collaborate, work together, pull together, team up. **3** *he sought to unite comfort with elegance:* **merge**, mix, blend, mingle, combine.
– OPPOSITES divide.

united adjective **1** *a united Germany:* **unified**, integrated, amalgamated, joined, merged; federal, confederate. **2** *the parties must decide on a united response to the proposals:* **common**, shared, joint, combined, communal, cooperative, collective, collaborative, concerted. **3** *they were united in their views:* **in agreement**, agreed, in unison, of the same opinion, like-minded, as one, in accord, in harmony, in unity.

unity noun **1** *European unity:* **union**, unification, integration, amalgamation; coalition, federation, confederation. **2** *unity between opposing factions:* **harmony**, accord, cooperation, collaboration, agreement, consensus, solidarity. **3** *the organic unity of the universe:* **oneness**, singleness, wholeness, uniformity, homogeneity.
– OPPOSITES division, discord.

universal adjective *the universal features of language:* **general**, ubiquitous, comprehensive, common, omnipresent, all-inclusive; global, worldwide, international, widespread.

universally adverb *progress is not always universally welcomed:* **invariably**, always, without exception, in all cases; everywhere, worldwide, globally, internationally; widely, commonly, generally.

universe noun **1** *the physical universe:* **cosmos**, macrocosm, totality; infinity, all existence. **2** *the universe of computer hardware:* **province**, world, sphere, preserve, domain.

university noun **college**, academy, institute; N. Amer. school.

unjust adjective **1** *the attack was unjust:* **biased**, prejudiced, unfair, inequitable, discriminatory, partisan, partial, one-sided. **2** *an unjust law:* **wrongful**, unfair, undeserved, unmerited, unwarranted, uncalled for, unreasonable, unjustifiable, indefensible.
– OPPOSITES fair.

unjustifiable adjective **1** *an unjustifiable extravagance:* **indefensible**, inexcusable, unforgivable, unpardonable, uncalled for, without justification, unwarrantable; excessive, immoderate. **2** *an unjustifiable slur on his character:* **groundless**, unfounded, baseless, unsubstantiated, unconfirmed, uncorroborated.
– OPPOSITES reasonable.

unkempt adjective *a rough-looking youth with long unkempt hair:* **untidy**, messy, scruffy, disordered, dishevelled, disarranged, rumpled, wind-blown, ungroomed, bedraggled, in a mess, messed up; tousled, uncombed; N. Amer. informal mussed up.
– OPPOSITES tidy.

unkind adjective **1** *everyone was being unkind to him:* **uncharitable**, unpleasant, disagreeable, nasty, mean, mean-spirited, cruel, vicious, spiteful, malicious, callous, unsympathetic, unfeeling, uncaring,

u

hurtful, ill-natured, hard-hearted, cold-hearted; unfriendly, uncivil, inconsiderate, insensitive, hostile; informal bitchy, catty; Brit. informal beastly. **2** *unkind weather:* **inclement**, intemperate, rough, severe, filthy.

unkindness noun **nastiness**, unpleasantness, disagreeableness, cruelty, malice, meanness, mean-spiritedness, viciousness, callousness, hard-heartedness, cold-heartedness; unfriendliness, inconsiderateness, hostility; informal bitchiness, cattiness.

unknown adjective **1** *the outcome was unknown:* **undisclosed**, unrevealed, secret; undetermined, undecided, unresolved, unsettled, unsure, unascertained. **2** *the dangers in the unknown country ahead:* **unexplored**, uncharted, unmapped, untravelled, undiscovered. **3** *he was murdered by persons unknown:* **unidentified**, unnamed, nameless, anonymous. **4** *firearms were unknown to the Indians:* **unfamiliar**, unheard of, new, novel, strange. **5** *unknown artists:* **obscure**, unheard of, unsung, minor, insignificant, unimportant, undistinguished.
– OPPOSITES familiar.

unlawful adjective *unlawful imports of drugs:* **illegal**, illicit, illegitimate, against the law; criminal, felonious; prohibited, banned, outlawed, proscribed, forbidden.
– OPPOSITES legal.

unleash verb *we unleashed the dog:* **let loose**, release, (set) free, unloose, untie, untether, unchain.

unlike preposition **1** *England is totally unlike Jamaica:* **different from**, unalike, dissimilar to. **2** *unlike Linda, Chrissy was a bit of a radical:* **in contrast to**, as opposed to.
– OPPOSITES similar to.
  adjective *a meeting of unlike minds:* **dissimilar**, unalike, disparate, contrasting, antithetical, different, diverse, heterogeneous, divergent, at variance, varying, at odds; informal like chalk and cheese.

unlikely adjective **1** *it is unlikely they will ever recover:* **improbable**, doubtful, dubious. **2** *an unlikely story:* **implausible**, improbable, questionable, unconvincing, far-fetched, unrealistic, incredible, unbelievable, inconceivable, unimaginable; informal tall, cock and bull.
– OPPOSITES probable, believable.

unlimited adjective **1** *unlimited supplies of water:* **inexhaustible**, limitless, illimitable, boundless, immeasurable, incalculable, untold, infinite, endless, never-ending. **2** *the ticket gives unlimited travel on city buses:* **unrestricted**, unconstrained, unrestrained, unchecked, unbridled, uncurbed. **3** *the unit will be given unlimited power to curb all environmentally destructive activities:* **total**, unqualified, unconditional, unrestricted, absolute, supreme.
– OPPOSITES finite, restricted.

unload verb **1** *we unloaded the van:* **unpack**, empty. **2** *they unloaded the cases from the lorry:* **remove**, offload, discharge. **3** *the state unloaded its 25 per cent stake:* **sell**, discard, jettison, offload, get rid of, dispose of; palm something off on someone, foist something on someone, fob something off on someone; informal dump, junk, get shot/shut of.

unlock verb *I unlocked the door and led the way in:* **unbolt**, unlatch, unbar, unfasten, open.

unlooked-for adjective *the unlooked-for publicity made his work more saleable:* **unexpected**, unforeseen, unanticipated, unsought, unpredicted, undreamed of, fortuitous, chance, serendipitous.

unloved adjective *Melanie felt lonely and unloved:* **uncared-for**, unwanted, friendless, unvalued; rejected, unwelcome, shunned, spurned, neglected, abandoned.

unlucky adjective **1** *he was unlucky not to score:* **unfortunate**, luckless, out of luck, hapless, ill-fated, ill-starred, unhappy; informal down on one's luck. **2** *an unlucky number:* **unfavourable**, inauspicious, unpropitious, ominous, cursed, ill-fated, ill-omened, disadvantageous, unfortunate.
– OPPOSITES fortunate, favourable.

unmanageable adjective **1** *the huge house was unmanageable:* **troublesome**, awkward, inconvenient; cumbersome, bulky, unwieldy. **2** *his behaviour was becoming unmanageable:* **uncontrollable**, ungovernable, unruly, disorderly, out of hand, difficult, disruptive, undisciplined, wayward; informal stroppy.

unmanly adjective *he was on the verge of tears but did not wish to appear unmanly:* **effeminate**, effete, unmasculine; weak, soft, timid, timorous, limp-wristed; informal sissy, wimpish, wimpy.
– OPPOSITES virile.

unmannerly adjective *a rough, unmannerly soldier:* **rude**, impolite, uncivil, discourteous, bad-mannered, ill-mannered, disrespectful, impertinent, impudent, insolent; uncouth, boorish, oafish, loutish, ill-bred, coarse.
– OPPOSITES polite.

unmarried adjective *an unmarried woman:* **unwed(ded)**, single; spinster; bachelor; unattached, available, eligible, free.

unmatched adjective **1** *a talent for publicity unmatched by any other politician:* **unequalled**, unrivalled, unparalleled, unsurpassed. **2** *they have captured all the subtleties of Beethoven with unmatched clarity and balance:* **peerless**, matchless, without equal, without parallel, incomparable, inimitable, superlative, second to none, in a class of its own.

unmentionable adjective *sex was the unmentionable subject:* **taboo**, censored, forbidden, banned, proscribed, prohibited, not to be spoken of, ineffable, unspeakable,

u

unutterable, unprintable, off limits; informal no go.

unmerciful adjective *he gave me an unmerciful thrashing:* **ruthless**, cruel, harsh, merciless, pitiless, cold-blooded, hard-hearted, callous, brutal, severe, unforgiving, inhumane, inhuman, heartless, unsympathetic, unfeeling.

unmistakable adjective *there was the unmistakable odour of whisky on his breath:* **distinctive**, distinct, telltale, indisputable, indubitable, undoubted; plain, clear, definite, obvious, evident, self-evident, manifest, patent, unambiguous, unequivocal, pronounced, as plain as the nose on your face.

unmitigated adjective *the raid was an unmitigated disaster:* **absolute**, unqualified, categorical, complete, total, downright, outright, utter, out-and-out, undiluted, unequivocal, veritable, perfect, consummate, pure, sheer.

unmoved adjective **1** *he was totally unmoved by her outburst:* **unaffected**, untouched, unimpressed, undismayed, unworried; aloof, cool, cold, dry-eyed; unconcerned, uncaring, indifferent, impassive, unemotional, stoical, phlegmatic, equable; impervious (to), oblivious (to), heedless (of), deaf to. **2** *he remained unmoved on the crucial issues:* **steadfast**, firm, unwavering, unswerving, resolute, decided, resolved, inflexible, unbending, implacable, adamant.

unnatural adjective **1** *the life of a battery hen is completely unnatural:* **abnormal**, unusual, uncommon, extraordinary, strange, freak, odd, peculiar, unorthodox, exceptional, irregular, untypical. **2** *a flash of unnatural colour:* **artificial**, man-made, synthetic, manufactured. **3** *unnatural vice:* **perverted**, warped, twisted, deviant, depraved, degenerate; informal kinky, pervy, sick. **4** *her voice sounded unnatural:* **affected**, artificial, stilted, forced, laboured, strained, false, fake, insincere; informal put on, phoney.
– OPPOSITES normal, genuine.

unnecessary adjective *many people feel that holiday insurance is unnecessary for travel in Britain:* **unneeded**, inessential, not required, uncalled for, useless, unwarranted, unwanted, undesired, dispensable, unimportant, optional, extraneous, expendable, disposable, redundant, pointless, purposeless.
– OPPOSITES essential.

unnerve verb *the bleakness of his gaze unnerved her:* **demoralize**, discourage, dishearten, dispirit, daunt, alarm, frighten, dismay, disconcert, discompose, perturb, upset, discomfit, take aback, unsettle, disquiet, fluster, agitate, shake, ruffle, throw off balance; informal rattle, faze, shake up; Brit. informal put the wind up; N. Amer. informal discombobulate.
– OPPOSITES hearten.

unobtrusive adjective *our staff offer efficient, unobtrusive service:* **inconspicuous**, unnoticeable, low-key, discreet, circumspect, understated, unostentatious.
– OPPOSITES extrovert, conspicuous.

unoccupied adjective **1** *an unoccupied house:* **vacant**, empty, uninhabited; free, available, to let. **2** *unoccupied territory:* **uninhabited**, unpopulated, unpeopled, unsettled. **3** *many young people were unoccupied:* **at leisure**, idle, free, with time on one's hands, at a loose end.
– OPPOSITES inhabited, populated, busy.

unofficial adjective **1** *unofficial figures put the death toll at over 300:* **unauthenticated**, unconfirmed, uncorroborated, unsubstantiated, off the record. **2** *an unofficial committee:* **informal**, casual; unauthorized, unsanctioned, unaccredited.
– OPPOSITES confirmed, formal.

unorthodox adjective **1** *unorthodox views on management:* **unconventional**, unusual, radical, nonconformist, avant-garde, eccentric; informal off the wall, way out, offbeat. **2** *unorthodox religious views:* **heterodox**, heretical, nonconformist, dissenting.
– OPPOSITES conventional.

unpaid adjective **1** *unpaid bills:* **unsettled**, outstanding, due, overdue, owing, owed, payable, undischarged; N. Amer. delinquent, past due. **2** *unpaid charity work:* **voluntary**, volunteer, honorary, unremunerative, unsalaried, pro bono (publico).

unpalatable adjective **1** *unpalatable food:* **unappetizing**, unappealing, unsavoury, inedible, uneatable; disgusting, revolting, nauseating, tasteless, flavourless. **2** *the unpalatable truth:* **disagreeable**, unpleasant, regrettable, unwelcome, lamentable, dreadful, hateful.
– OPPOSITES tasty.

unparalleled adjective *an unparalleled opportunity to change society:* **exceptional**, unique, singular, rare, unequalled, unprecedented, without parallel, without equal; matchless, peerless, unrivalled, unsurpassed, unexcelled, incomparable, second to none.

unperturbed adjective *Daniel was unperturbed by the outburst:* **untroubled**, undisturbed, unworried, unconcerned, unmoved, unflustered, unruffled, undismayed; calm, composed, cool, collected, unemotional, self-possessed, self-assured, level-headed, unfazed, laid-back.

unpleasant adjective **1** *a very unpleasant situation:* **disagreeable**, irksome, troublesome, annoying, irritating, vexatious, displeasing, distressing, nasty, horrible, terrible, awful, dreadful, hateful, miserable, invidious, objectionable, offensive, obnoxious, repugnant, repulsive,

repellent, revolting, disgusting, distasteful, nauseating, unsavoury. **2** *an unpleasant man:* **unlikeable**, unlovable, disagreeable; unfriendly, rude, impolite, obnoxious, nasty, spiteful, mean, mean-spirited; insufferable, unbearable, annoying, irritating. **3** *an unpleasant taste:* **unappetizing**, unpalatable, unsavoury, unappealing, bitter, sour, rancid; disgusting, revolting, nauseating, sickening.
– OPPOSITES agreeable, likeable.

unpolished adjective **1** *unpolished wood:* **unvarnished**, unfinished, untreated, natural. **2** *his unpolished ways:* **unsophisticated**, unrefined, uncultured, uncultivated, coarse, vulgar, crude, rough (and ready), awkward, clumsy, gauche.
– OPPOSITES varnished, sophisticated.

unpopular adjective *he was unpopular at school:* **disliked**, friendless, unliked, unloved; unwelcome, avoided, ignored, rejected, shunned, spurned, cold-shouldered.

unprecedented adjective *an era of warfare on an unprecedented scale:* **unparalleled**, unequalled, unmatched, unrivalled, without parallel, without equal, out of the ordinary, unusual, exceptional, singular, remarkable, unique; unheard of, unknown, new, groundbreaking, revolutionary, pioneering.

unpredictable adjective **1** *unpredictable results:* **unforeseeable**, uncertain, unsure, doubtful, dubious, in the balance, up in the air, arbitrary. **2** *unpredictable behaviour:* **erratic**, moody, volatile, unstable, capricious, temperamental, mercurial, changeable, variable.

unprejudiced adjective **1** *science must start with unprejudiced observation:* **objective**, impartial, unbiased, neutral, non-partisan, detached, disinterested. **2** *unprejudiced attitudes:* **unbiased**, tolerant, non-discriminatory, liberal, broad-minded, unbigoted.
– OPPOSITES partisan, intolerant.

unpremeditated adjective *her unpremeditated reply:* **unplanned**, spontaneous, unprepared, impromptu, spur-of-the-moment, unrehearsed; informal off-the-cuff.
– OPPOSITES planned.

unprepared adjective **1** *we were unprepared for the new VAT regime:* **unready**, off (one's) guard, surprised, taken aback; informal caught napping, caught on the hop. **2** *they are unprepared to support the reforms:* **unwilling**, disinclined, loath, reluctant, resistant, opposed.
– OPPOSITES ready, willing.

unpretentious adjective **1** *he was thoroughly unpretentious:* **unaffected**, modest, unassuming, without airs, natural, straightforward, open, honest, sincere, frank. **2** *an unpretentious hotel:* **simple**, plain, modest, humble, unostentatious, homely, unsophisticated.

unprincipled adjective *he is an unprincipled opportunist:* **immoral**, unethical, unscrupulous, dishonourable, dishonest, deceitful, devious, corrupt, crooked, wicked, evil, villainous, shameless, base, low.
– OPPOSITES ethical.

unproductive adjective **1** *unproductive soil:* **sterile**, barren, infertile, unfruitful, poor. **2** *unproductive meetings:* **fruitless**, futile, vain, idle, useless, worthless, valueless, pointless, ineffective, ineffectual, unprofitable, unrewarding.
– OPPOSITES fruitful.

unprofessional adjective **1** *she was reprimanded for unprofessional conduct:* **improper**, unethical, unprincipled, unscrupulous, dishonourable, disreputable, unseemly, unbecoming, indecorous; informal shady, crooked. **2** *he accused the detectives of being unprofessional:* **amateurish**, amateur, unskilled, unskilful, inexpert, unqualified, inexperienced, incompetent, second-rate, inefficient.

unpromising adjective *they were not deterred by this unpromising start:* **inauspicious**, unfavourable, unpropitious, discouraging, disheartening, gloomy, bleak, black, portentous, ominous, ill-omened.
– OPPOSITES auspicious.

unqualified adjective **1** *an unqualified accountant:* **uncertificated**, unlicensed, untrained, inexperienced. **2** *those unqualified to look after children:* **unsuitable**, unfit, ineligible, incompetent, unable, incapable. **3** *the chairman gave the manager his unqualified support:* **unconditional**, unreserved, unlimited, without reservations, categorical, unequivocal, unambiguous, wholehearted; complete, absolute, downright, undivided, total, utter.

unquestionable adjective *the sincerity of his beliefs is unquestionable:* **indubitable**, undoubted, beyond question, beyond doubt, indisputable, undeniable, irrefutable, incontestable, incontrovertible, unequivocal; certain, sure, definite, self-evident, evident, manifest, obvious, apparent, patent.

unravel verb **1** *he unravelled the strands:* **untangle**, disentangle, separate out, unwind, untwist. **2** *detectives are trying to unravel the mystery:* **solve**, resolve, clear up, puzzle out, get to the bottom of, explain, clarify, make head or tail of; informal figure out, suss (out). **3** *society is starting to unravel:* **fall apart**, fail, collapse, go wrong.
– OPPOSITES entangle.

unreadable adjective **1** *unreadable writing:* **illegible**, hard to read, indecipherable, unintelligible, scrawled, crabbed. **2** *heavy, unreadable novels:* **dull**, tedious, boring, uninteresting, dry, wearisome, difficult, heavy.
– OPPOSITES legible, accessible.

u

unreal adjective *the unreal world of art:* **imaginary**, fictitious, pretend, make-believe, made-up, dreamed-up, mock, false, illusory, mythical, fanciful; hypothetical, theoretical; informal phoney.

unrealistic adjective **1** *it is unrealistic to expect changes overnight:* **impractical**, impracticable, unfeasible, non-viable; unreasonable, irrational, illogical, senseless, silly, foolish, fanciful, idealistic, romantic, starry-eyed. **2** *unrealistic images:* **unlifelike**, non-realistic, unnatural, non-representational, abstract.
– OPPOSITES pragmatic, lifelike.

unreasonable adjective **1** *an unreasonable woman:* **uncooperative**, unhelpful, disobliging, unaccommodating, awkward, contrary, difficult; obstinate, obdurate, wilful, headstrong, pig-headed, intractable, intransigent, inflexible; irrational, illogical, prejudiced, intolerant. **2** *unreasonable demands:* **unacceptable**, preposterous, outrageous; excessive, immoderate, disproportionate, undue, inordinate, intolerable, unjustified, unwarranted, uncalled for.

unrecognizable adjective *with his moustache and beard he is practically unrecognizable:* **unidentifiable**, unknowable; disguised.

unrefined adjective **1** *unrefined clay:* **unprocessed**, untreated, crude, raw, natural, unprepared, unfinished. **2** *unrefined men:* **uncultured**, uncultivated, uncivilized, uneducated, unsophisticated; boorish, oafish, loutish, coarse, vulgar, rude, uncouth.

unrelated adjective **1** *the men had been arrested in unrelated incidents:* **separate**, unconnected, independent, unassociated, distinct, discrete, disparate. **2** *a reason unrelated to my work:* **irrelevant**, immaterial, inapplicable, unconcerned, off the subject, beside the point, not pertinent, not germane.

unrelenting adjective **1** *the unrelenting heat:* **continual**, constant, continuous, relentless, unremitting, unabating, unrelieved, incessant, unceasing, endless, unending, persistent. **2** *an unrelenting opponent:* **implacable**, inflexible, uncompromising, unyielding, unbending, relentless, determined, dogged, tireless, unflagging, unshakeable, unswerving, unwavering.
– OPPOSITES intermittent.

unreliable adjective **1** *unreliable volunteers:* **undependable**, untrustworthy, irresponsible, fickle, capricious, erratic, unpredictable, inconstant, faithless. **2** *unemployment can be an unreliable indicator of the tightness of labour markets:* **questionable**, open to doubt, doubtful, dubious, suspect, unsound, tenuous, fallible; risky, chancy, inaccurate; informal iffy, dicey.

unremitting adjective *their lives were*

little more than unremitting toil: **relentless**, unrelenting, continual, constant, continuous, unabating, unrelieved, sustained, unceasing, ceaseless, endless, unending, persistent, perpetual, interminable.

unrepentant adjective *an unrepentant sinner:* **impenitent**, unrepenting, remorseless, unashamed, unapologetic, unabashed.

unreserved adjective **1** *the Prime Minister has had the unreserved support of the Opposition:* **unconditional**, unqualified, without reservations, unlimited, categorical, unequivocal, unambiguous; absolute, complete, thorough, wholehearted, total, utter, undivided. **2** *an unreserved young man:* **uninhibited**, extrovert, outgoing, unrestrained, open, unconstrained, unselfconscious, outspoken, frank, candid. **3** *unreserved seats:* **unbooked**, unallocated, unoccupied, free, empty, vacant.
– OPPOSITES qualified, reticent.

unresolved adjective *some questions remained unresolved:* **undecided**, unsettled, undetermined, uncertain, open, pending, open to debate/question, doubtful, in doubt, up in the air.
– OPPOSITES decided.

unrest noun *the government was clearly fearful of social unrest:* **disruption**, disturbance, trouble, turmoil, disorder, chaos, anarchy; discord, dissension, dissent, strife, protest, rebellion, uprising, rioting.
– OPPOSITES peace.

unrestrained adjective *a period of unrestrained corruption:* **uncontrolled**, unconstrained, unrestricted, unchecked, unbridled, unlimited, unfettered, uninhibited, unbounded, undisciplined.

unrestricted adjective *open drives provide unrestricted access to the rear of the property:* **unlimited**, open, free, clear, unhindered, unimpeded, unhampered, unchecked, unrestrained, unconstrained, unblocked, unbounded, unconfined, unqualified.
– OPPOSITES limited.

unripe adjective *unripe fruit:* **immature**, unready, green, sour.

unrivalled adjective *an unrivalled collection of rare coins:* **unequalled**, without equal, unparalleled, without parallel, unmatched, unsurpassed, unexcelled, incomparable, beyond compare, inimitable, second to none.

unruffled adjective **1** *an unruffled voice:* **calm**, composed, self-controlled, self-possessed, untroubled, unperturbed, at ease, relaxed, serene, cool, {cool, calm, and collected}, cool-headed, unemotional, equanimous, equable, stoical; informal unfazed. **2** *an unruffled sea:* **tranquil**, calm, smooth, still, flat, motionless, placid, waveless, pacific, like a millpond.

unruly adjective *she was scolding some*

u

unruly children: **disorderly**, rowdy, wild, unmanageable, uncontrollable, disobedient, disruptive, undisciplined, wayward, wilful, headstrong, irrepressible, obstreperous, difficult, intractable, out of hand, recalcitrant; boisterous, lively.
– OPPOSITES disciplined.

unsafe adjective **1** *the building was unsafe:* **dangerous**, risky, perilous, hazardous, life-threatening, high-risk, treacherous, insecure, unsound; harmful, injurious, toxic. **2** *the verdict was unsafe:* **unreliable**, insecure, unsound, questionable, open to question/doubt, doubtful, dubious, suspect, fallible; informal iffy.
– OPPOSITES harmless, secure.

unsaid adjective *you've made me say things much better left unsaid:* **unspoken**, unuttered, unstated, unexpressed, unvoiced, untalked-of, suppressed; tacit, implicit, understood, not spelt out, taken as read, inferred, implied.

unsanitary adjective *the houses themselves are overcrowded and unsanitary:* **unhygienic**, insanitary, dirty, filthy, unclean, contaminated, unhealthy, germ-ridden, disease-ridden, infested, insalubrious, polluted.
– OPPOSITES hygienic.

unsatisfactory adjective *this was a most unsatisfactory outcome:* **disappointing**, dissatisfying, undesirable, disagreeable, displeasing; inadequate, unacceptable, poor, bad, substandard, weak, mediocre, not good enough, not up to par, defective, deficient, imperfect, inferior; informal leaving a lot to be desired, no great shakes, not much cop.

unsavoury adjective **1** *unsavoury portions of food:* **unpalatable**, unappetizing, distasteful, disagreeable, unappealing, unattractive; inedible, uneatable, disgusting, revolting, nauseating, sickening, foul, nasty, vile; tasteless, bland, flavourless; informal yucky. **2** *an unsavoury character:* **disreputable**, unpleasant, disagreeable, nasty, mean, rough; immoral, degenerate, dishonourable, dishonest, unprincipled, unscrupulous, low, villainous; informal shady, crooked.
– OPPOSITES tasty, appetizing.

unscathed adjective *his wife and son were fortunate to escape unscathed:* **unharmed**, unhurt, uninjured, undamaged, in one piece, intact, safe (and sound), unmarked, untouched, unscratched.
– OPPOSITES harmed, injured.

unscrupulous adjective *a crackdown on unscrupulous landlords:* **unprincipled**, unethical, immoral, conscienceless, shameless, reprobate, exploitative, corrupt, dishonest, dishonourable, deceitful, devious, underhand, unsavoury, disreputable, evil, wicked, villainous; informal crooked, shady.

unseat verb **1** *the horse unseated his rider:* **dislodge**, throw, dismount, upset, unhorse.

2 *an attempt to unseat the party leader:* **depose**, oust, remove from office, topple, overthrow, bring down, dislodge, supplant, usurp, overturn, eject.

unseemly adjective *an unseemly squabble:* **indecorous**, improper, unbecoming, unfitting, unbefitting, unworthy, undignified, indiscreet, indelicate, ungentlemanly, unladylike.
– OPPOSITES decorous.

unseen adjective *an unseen sniper:* **hidden**, concealed, obscured, camouflaged, out of sight, imperceptible, undetectable, unnoticeable, unnoticed, unobserved.

unselfish adjective *he always acted from unselfish motives:* **altruistic**, disinterested, selfless, self-denying, self-sacrificing; generous, philanthropic, public-spirited, charitable, benevolent, caring, kind, considerate, noble.

unsettle verb *all this talk of death was unsettling him:* **discompose**, unnerve, upset, disturb, disquiet, perturb, discomfit, disconcert, alarm, dismay, trouble, bother, agitate, fluster, ruffle, shake (up), throw, unbalance, destabilize; informal rattle, faze.

unsettled adjective **1** *an unsettled life:* **aimless**, directionless, purposeless, without purpose; rootless, nomadic. **2** *an unsettled child:* **restless**, restive, fidgety, anxious, worried, troubled, fretful; agitated, ruffled, uneasy, disconcerted, discomposed, unnerved, ill at ease, edgy, on edge, tense, nervous, apprehensive, disturbed, perturbed; informal rattled, fazed. **3** *unsettled weather:* **changeable**, changing, variable, varying, inconstant, inconsistent, ever-changing, erratic, unstable, undependable, unreliable, uncertain, unpredictable, protean. **4** *the question remains unsettled:* **undecided**, to be decided, unresolved, undetermined, uncertain, open to debate, doubtful, in doubt, up in the air, in a state of uncertainty. **5** *the debt remains unsettled:* **unpaid**, payable, outstanding, owing, owed, to be paid, due, undischarged; N. Amer. delinquent, past due. **6** *unsettled areas:* **uninhabited**, unpopulated, unpeopled, desolate, lonely.

unshakeable adjective *they both have an unshakeable confidence in the rightness of their own opinions:* **steadfast**, resolute, staunch, firm, decided, determined, unswerving, unwavering; unyielding, inflexible, dogged, obstinate, persistent, indefatigable, tireless, unflagging, unremitting, unrelenting, relentless.

unsightly adjective *an unsightly concrete church:* **ugly**, unattractive, unprepossessing, unlovely, disagreeable, displeasing, hideous, horrible, repulsive, revolting, offensive, grotesque, monstrous, ghastly.
– OPPOSITES attractive.

unskilful adjective *the furniture had been repaired by an unskilful hand:* **inexpert**, incompetent, inept, unskilled, amateurish,

u

unprofessional, inexperienced, untrained, unpractised; informal ham-fisted, ham-handed, cack-handed.

unskilled adjective *unskilled manual workers:* **untrained**, unqualified; manual, blue-collar, labouring, menial; inexpert, inexperienced, unpractised, amateurish, unprofessional.

unsociable adjective *he was grumpy and unsociable:* **unfriendly**, uncongenial, unneighbourly, unapproachable, introverted, reticent, reserved, withdrawn, aloof, distant, remote, detached, unsocial, antisocial, taciturn, silent, quiet; informal stand-offish.
– OPPOSITES friendly.

unsolicited adjective *he did not take easily to unsolicited advice:* **uninvited**, unsought, unasked for, unrequested.

unsophisticated adjective **1** *she seemed terribly unsophisticated:* **unworldly**, naive, simple, innocent, ignorant, green, immature, callow, inexperienced, childlike, artless, guileless, ingenuous, natural, unaffected, unassuming, unpretentious.
2 *unsophisticated software:* **simple**, crude, basic, rudimentary, primitive, rough and ready; straightforward, uncomplicated, uninvolved.

unsound adjective **1** *the building is structurally unsound:* **rickety**, flimsy, wobbly, unstable, crumbling, damaged, rotten, ramshackle, insubstantial, unsafe, dangerous. **2** *this submission appears unsound:* **untenable**, flawed, defective, faulty, ill-founded, flimsy, unreliable, questionable, dubious, tenuous, suspect, fallacious, fallible; informal iffy. **3** *of unsound mind:* **disordered**, deranged, disturbed, demented, unstable, unbalanced, unhinged, insane; informal touched.
– OPPOSITES strong.

unspeakable adjective **1** *unspeakable delights:* **indescribable**, beyond description, inexpressible, unutterable, indefinable, unimaginable, inconceivable, marvellous, wonderful. **2** *an unspeakable crime:* **dreadful**, awful, appalling, horrific, horrifying, horrendous, abominable, frightful, fearful, shocking, ghastly, gruesome, monstrous, heinous, egregious, deplorable, despicable, execrable, vile.

unspecified adjective *he proposed to resign at an unspecified date:* **unnamed**, unstated, unidentified, undesignated, undefined, unfixed, undecided, undetermined, uncertain; nameless, unknown, indefinite, indeterminate, vague.

unspectacular adjective *he had a steady, unspectacular career:* **unremarkable**, unexceptional, undistinguished, unmemorable; ordinary, average, commonplace, mediocre, run-of-the-mill, indifferent.
– OPPOSITES remarkable.

unspoilt adjective *unspoilt countryside:* **unimpaired**, as good as new/before, perfect, pristine, immaculate, unblemished, unharmed, unflawed, undamaged, untouched, unmarked, untainted.

unspoken adjective *there was an unspoken contract between them:* **unstated**, unexpressed, unuttered, unsaid, unvoiced, unarticulated, undeclared, not spelt out; tacit, implicit, implied, understood, taken as read.
– OPPOSITES explicit.

unstable adjective **1** *icebergs are notoriously unstable:* **unsteady**, rocky, wobbly, rickety, shaky, unsafe, insecure, precarious. **2** *unstable coffee prices:* **changeable**, volatile, variable, fluctuating, irregular, unpredictable, erratic. **3** *he was mentally unstable:* **unbalanced**, of unsound mind, mentally ill, deranged, demented, disturbed, unhinged.
– OPPOSITES steady, firm.

unsteady adjective **1** *she was unsteady on her feet:* **unstable**, rocky, wobbly, rickety, shaky, tottery, doddery, insecure. **2** *an unsteady flow:* **irregular**, uneven, varying, variable, erratic, spasmodic, changeable, changing, fluctuating, inconstant, intermittent, fitful.
– OPPOSITES stable, regular.

unstinted, unstinting adjective *unstinted praise:* **lavish**, liberal, generous, open-handed, ungrudging, unsparing, willingly given, ready, profuse, abundant, ample.

unstudied adjective *he always does it with unstudied grace:* **natural**, easy, unaffected, unforced, uncontrived, unstilted, unpretentious, without airs, artless.

unsubstantiated adjective *there were unsubstantiated allegations of serious misbehaviour:* **unconfirmed**, unsupported, uncorroborated, unverified, unattested, unproven; unfounded, groundless, baseless, without foundation.

unsuccessful adjective **1** *an unsuccessful attempt:* **failed**, without success, abortive, ineffective, fruitless, profitless, unproductive; vain, futile, useless, pointless, worthless. **2** *an unsuccessful business:* **unprofitable**, loss-making. **3** *an unsuccessful candidate:* **failed**, losing, beaten; unlucky, out of luck.

unsuitable adjective **1** *they had been sold an unsuitable product:* **inappropriate**, unsuited, ill-suited, inapt, inapposite, unacceptable, unfitting, unbefitting, incompatible, out of place/keeping. **2** *her comment came at an unsuitable moment:* **inopportune**, infelicitous.
– OPPOSITES appropriate, opportune.

unsullied adjective *he came with an unsullied reputation:* **spotless**, untarnished, unblemished, unspoilt, untainted, impeccable, undamaged, unimpaired, stainless, immaculate, unflawed.

u

– OPPOSITES tarnished.

unsung adjective *one of the finest unsung heroes of the last war:* **unacknowledged**, uncelebrated, unacclaimed, unapplauded, unhailed; neglected, unrecognized, overlooked, forgotten.
– OPPOSITES celebrated.

unsure adjective **1** *she felt very unsure:* **unconfident**, unassertive, insecure, hesitant, diffident, anxious, apprehensive. **2** *Sally was unsure what to do:* **undecided**, irresolute, dithering, equivocating, in two minds, in a quandary. **3** *some teachers are unsure about the proposed strike:* **dubious**, doubtful, sceptical, uncertain, unconvinced. **4** *the date is unsure:* **not fixed**, undecided, uncertain.
– OPPOSITES confident.

unsurpassed adjective *the quality of workmanship is unsurpassed:* **unmatched**, unrivalled, unparalleled, unequalled, matchless, peerless, without equal, inimitable, incomparable, unsurpassable.

unsurprising adjective *his failure to win the leadership of the party was unsurprising:* **predictable**, foreseeable, (only) to be expected, foreseen, anticipated, par for the course; informal inevitable, on the cards.

unsuspecting adjective *anti-personnel mines lie in wait for their unsuspecting victims:* **unsuspicious**, unwary, unaware, unconscious, ignorant, unwitting; trusting, gullible, credulous, ingenuous, naive.
– OPPOSITES wary.

unswerving adjective *she has always demanded unswerving loyalty:* **unwavering**, unfaltering, steadfast, unshakeable, staunch, firm, resolute, stalwart, dedicated, committed, constant, single-minded, dogged, indefatigable, unyielding, unbending, indomitable.

unsympathetic adjective **1** *unsympathetic staff:* **uncaring**, unconcerned, unfeeling, insensitive, unkind, pitiless, heartless, hard-hearted. **2** *the government was unsympathetic to these views:* **opposed**, against, (dead) set against, antagonistic, ill-disposed; informal anti. **3** *an unsympathetic character:* **unlikeable**, disagreeable, unpleasant, objectionable, unsavoury; uncongenial, unfriendly, unneighbourly, unapproachable.
– OPPOSITES caring.

unsystematic adjective *the burial mound was excavated in an unsystematic way:* **unmethodical**, uncoordinated, disorganized, unplanned, indiscriminate; random, inconsistent, irregular, erratic, casual, haphazard, chaotic.

untamed adjective *the untamed wildlife which proliferates in the region:* **wild**, feral, undomesticated, unbroken.

untangle verb **1** *I untangled the fishing tackle:* **disentangle**, unravel, unsnarl, straighten out, untwist, untwine, unknot.

2 *untangling a mystery:* **solve**, find the/an answer to, resolve, puzzle out, fathom, clear up, clarify, get to the bottom of; informal figure out; Brit. informal suss out.

untarnished adjective *the reputation of the school was untarnished:* **unsullied**, unblemished, untainted, impeccable, undamaged, unspoilt, unimpaired, spotless, stainless.

untenable adjective *the Government's position is untenable:* **indefensible**, undefendable, insupportable, unsustainable, unjustified, unjustifiable, flimsy, weak, shaky.

unthinkable adjective *it was unthinkable that John could be dead:* **unimaginable**, inconceivable, unbelievable, incredible, beyond belief, implausible.

unthinking adjective **1** *an unthinking woman:* **thoughtless**, inconsiderate, insensitive; tactless, undiplomatic, indiscreet. **2** *an unthinking remark:* **absent-minded**, heedless, thoughtless, careless, injudicious, imprudent, unwise, foolish, reckless, rash, precipitate; involuntary, inadvertent, unintentional, spontaneous, impulsive, unpremeditated.
– OPPOSITES thoughtful, intentional.

untidy adjective **1** *untidy hair:* **scruffy**, tousled, dishevelled, unkempt, messy, disordered, disarranged, messed up, rumpled, bedraggled, uncombed, ungroomed, straggly, ruffled, tangled, matted, wind-blown; informal mussed up; N. Amer. informal raggedy. **2** *the room was untidy:* **disordered**, messy, in a mess, disorderly, disorganized, in disorder, cluttered, in a muddle, muddled, in chaos, chaotic, haywire, topsy-turvy, in disarray, at sixes and sevens; informal higgledy-piggledy.
– OPPOSITES neat, orderly.

untie verb *she knelt to untie her laces:* **undo**, unknot, unbind, unfasten, unlace, untether, unhitch, unmoor; loose, (set) free, release, let go.

until preposition & conjunction **1** *I was working until midnight:* **(up) till**, up to, up until, as late as; N. Amer. through. **2** *this did not happen until 1998:* **before**, prior to, previous to, up to, up until, (up) till, earlier than.

untimely adjective **1** *an untimely interruption:* **ill-timed**, badly timed, mistimed; inopportune, inappropriate; inconvenient, unwelcome, infelicitous. **2** *his untimely death:* **premature**, (too) early, too soon, before time.
– OPPOSITES opportune.

untiring adjective *an untiring advocate of political and economic reform:* **vigorous**, energetic, determined, resolute, enthusiastic, keen, zealous, spirited, dogged, tenacious, persistent, persevering, staunch; tireless, unflagging, unfailing, unfaltering, unwavering, indefatigable, unrelenting, unswerving.

u

untold adjective **1** *thieves caused untold damage:* **boundless**, measureless, limitless, unlimited, infinite, immeasurable, incalculable. **2** *untold billions have been poured into research:* **countless**, innumerable, endless, limitless, numberless, an infinite number of, without number, uncountable; numerous, many, multiple. **3** *the untold story:* **unreported**, unrecounted, unrevealed, undisclosed, undivulged, unpublished.
– OPPOSITES limited.

untouched adjective **1** *the food was untouched:* **uneaten**, unconsumed, undrunk. **2** *one of the few untouched areas:* **unspoilt**, unmarked, unblemished, unsullied, undefiled, undamaged, unharmed; pristine, natural, immaculate, in perfect condition, unaffected, unchanged, unaltered.

untoward adjective *Tom had noticed nothing untoward:* **unexpected**, unanticipated, unforeseen, unpredictable, unpredicted, surprising, unusual; unwelcome, unfavourable, adverse, unfortunate, infelicitous.

untrained adjective *the system can be utilized quickly by untrained users:* **unskilled**, untaught, unschooled, untutored, unpractised, inexperienced; unqualified, unlicensed, amateur, non-professional.

untried adjective *dealers used their clients as guinea pigs for their untried techniques:* **untested**, unestablished, new, experimental, unattempted, trial, test, pilot, unproven.
– OPPOSITES established.

untroubled adjective *a man untroubled by a guilty conscience:* **unworried**, unperturbed, unconcerned, unruffled, undismayed, unbothered, unagitated, unflustered; insouciant, nonchalant, blasé, carefree, serene, relaxed, at ease, happy-go-lucky; informal laid-back.

untrue adjective **1** *these suggestions are totally untrue:* **false**, untruthful, fabricated, made up, invented, concocted, trumped up; erroneous, wrong, incorrect, inaccurate, fallacious, unsound, unfounded, misguided. **2** *he was untrue to his friends:* **unfaithful**, disloyal, faithless, false, treacherous, traitorous, deceitful, deceiving, duplicitous, double-dealing, insincere, unreliable, undependable, inconstant; informal two-timing.
– OPPOSITES correct, faithful.

untrustworthy adjective *the clubs are vulnerable to untrustworthy treasurers:* **dishonest**, deceitful, double-dealing, treacherous, traitorous, two-faced, duplicitous, dishonourable, unprincipled, unscrupulous, corrupt; unreliable, undependable.
– OPPOSITES reliable.

untruth noun **1** *a patent untruth:* **lie**, falsehood, fib, fabrication, invention, falsification, cock-and-bull story, half-truth, exaggeration; story, myth, piece of fiction; informal tall story, fairy tale, whopper, kidology; Brit. informal porky (pie). **2** *the total untruth of the story:* **falsity**, falsehood, falseness, untruthfulness, fallaciousness, fictitiousness; fabrication, dishonesty, deceit, deceitfulness.

untruthful adjective **1** *the answers may be untruthful:* **false**, untrue, fabricated, made up, invented, trumped up; erroneous, wrong, incorrect, inaccurate, fallacious, fictitious. **2** *an untruthful person:* **lying**, mendacious, dishonest, deceitful, duplicitous, false, double-dealing, two-faced; informal crooked, bent.
– OPPOSITES honest.

untutored adjective *such articles will make little sense to an untutored reader:* **uneducated**, untaught, unschooled, ignorant, unsophisticated, uncultured, unenlightened.
– OPPOSITES educated.

untwist verb *he untwisted the wire and straightened it out:* **untwine**, disentangle, unravel, unsnarl, unwind, unroll, uncoil, unfurl.

unused adjective **1** *the notebook is unused | unused food:* **unutilized**, unemployed, unexploited, not in service; left over, remaining, uneaten, unconsumed, unneeded, not required, to spare, surplus. **2** *he was unused to such directness:* **unaccustomed**, new, a stranger, unfamiliar, unconversant, unacquainted.
– OPPOSITES accustomed.

unusual adjective **1** *the unusual sight of a golden eagle flying over Regents Park:* **uncommon**, abnormal, atypical, unexpected, surprising, unfamiliar, different; strange, odd, curious, out of the ordinary, extraordinary, unorthodox, unconventional, outlandish, singular, peculiar, bizarre; rare, scarce, few and far between, thin on the ground, exceptional, isolated, occasional, infrequent; informal weird, offbeat, way out, freaky. **2** *a man of unusual talent:* **remarkable**, extraordinary, exceptional, singular, particular, outstanding, notable, noteworthy, distinctive, striking, significant, special, unique, unparalleled, prodigious.
– OPPOSITES common.

unutterable adjective **1** *an existence of unutterable boredom:* **indescribable**, beyond description, inexpressible, unspeakable, undefinable, inconceivable; extreme, great, overwhelming; dreadful, awful, appalling, terrible. **2** *unutterable joy:* **marvellous**, wonderful, superb, splendid, unimaginable, profound, deep.

unvarnished adjective **1** *unvarnished wood:* **bare**, unpainted, unpolished, unfinished, untreated. **2** *the unvarnished truth:* **straightforward**, plain, simple, stark; truthful, realistic, candid, honest, frank, forthright, direct, blunt, straight from the shoulder.

unveil verb *the club has unveiled plans for a new 1600-seat stand:* **reveal**, present, disclose, divulge, make known, make public, communicate, publish, broadcast; display, show, exhibit, put on display; release, bring out.

unwanted adjective **1** *an unwanted development:* **unwelcome**, undesirable, undesired, unpopular, unfortunate, unlucky, unfavourable, untoward; unpleasant, disagreeable, displeasing, distasteful, objectionable; regrettable, deplorable, lamentable; unacceptable, intolerable, awful, terrible, wretched, appalling. **2** *tins of unwanted pet food:* **unused**, left over, surplus, superfluous; uneaten, unconsumed, untouched. **3** *an unwanted guest:* **uninvited**, unbidden, unasked, unrequested, unsolicited. **4** *many ageing people feel unwanted:* **friendless**, unloved, uncared-for, forsaken, rejected, shunned; superfluous, useless, unnecessary.
– OPPOSITES welcome.

unwarranted adjective **1** *the criticism is unwarranted:* **unjustified**, unjustifiable, indefensible, inexcusable, unforgivable, unpardonable, uncalled for, unnecessary, unreasonable, unjust, groundless, excessive, immoderate, disproportionate. **2** *an unwarranted invasion of privacy:* **unauthorized**, unsanctioned, unapproved, uncertified, unlicensed; illegal, unlawful, illicit, illegitimate, criminal, actionable.
– OPPOSITES justified.

unwary adjective *accidents can happen to the unwary traveller:* **incautious**, careless, thoughtless, heedless, inattentive, unwatchful, off one's guard.

unwavering adjective *she fixed him with an unwavering stare:* **steady**, fixed, resolute, resolved, firm, steadfast, unswerving, unfaltering, untiring, tireless, indefatigable, unyielding, relentless, unremitting, unrelenting, sustained.
– OPPOSITES unsteady.

unwelcome adjective **1** *I was made to feel unwelcome:* **unwanted**, uninvited. **2** *even a small increase is unwelcome:* **undesirable**, undesired, unpopular, unfortunate, unlucky; disappointing, upsetting, distressing, disagreeable, displeasing; regrettable, deplorable, lamentable.

unwell adjective *he had been unwell for some time:* **ill**, sick, poorly, indisposed, ailing, not (very) well, not oneself, under/below par, peaky, queasy, nauseous; Brit. off colour; informal under the weather, not up to snuff, funny, peculiar, lousy, rough; Brit. informal grotty; Austral./NZ informal crook.

unwholesome adjective **1** *unwholesome air:* **unhealthy**, noxious, poisonous; insalubrious, unhygienic, insanitary; harmful, injurious, detrimental,

destructive, damaging, deleterious, baleful. **2** *unwholesome Web pages:* **improper**, immoral, indecent, corrupting, depraving, salacious.
– OPPOSITES healthy, seemly.

unwieldy adjective *he dragged his big unwieldy sword out of its scabbard:* **cumbersome**, unmanageable, unmanoeuvrable; awkward, clumsy, massive, heavy, hefty, bulky, weighty.
– OPPOSITES manageable.

unwilling adjective **1** *unwilling conscripts:* **reluctant**, unenthusiastic, hesitant, resistant, grudging, involuntary, forced. **2** *he was unwilling to take on that responsibility:* **disinclined**, reluctant, averse, loath; (**be unwilling to do something**) not have the heart to, baulk at, demur at, shy away from, flinch from, shrink from, have qualms about, have misgivings about, have reservations about.
– OPPOSITES keen.

unwillingness adjective **disinclination**, reluctance, hesitation, diffidence, wavering, vacillation, resistance, objection, opposition, doubts, second thoughts, scruples, qualms, misgivings.

unwind verb **1** *Ella unwound the scarf from her neck:* **unroll**, uncoil, unravel, untwine, untwist, disentangle, open (out), straighten (out). **2** *it's a good place to unwind after work:* **relax**, loosen up, ease up/off, slow down, de-stress, unbend, rest, put one's feet up, take it easy; informal wind down, let it all hang out, unbutton; N. Amer. informal hang loose, chill out.

unwise adjective *it would have been unwise to argue:* **injudicious**, ill-advised, imprudent, foolish, silly, inadvisable, impolitic, misguided, foolhardy, irresponsible, rash, hasty, overhasty, reckless.
– OPPOSITES sensible.

unwitting adjective **1** *an unwitting accomplice:* **unknowing**, unconscious, unsuspecting, oblivious, unaware, innocent. **2** *an unwitting mistake:* **unintentional**, unintended, inadvertent, involuntary, unconscious, accidental.
– OPPOSITES conscious.

unwonted adjective *they came running with unwonted energy:* **unusual**, uncommon, unaccustomed, unfamiliar, unprecedented, exceptional, extraordinary, remarkable, singular, surprising.
– OPPOSITES usual.

unworldly adjective **1** *a gauche, unworldly girl:* **naive**, simple, inexperienced, innocent, green, raw, callow, immature, unsophisticated, gullible, ingenuous, artless, guileless, childlike, trusting, credulous. **2** *unworldly beauty:* **unearthly**, otherworldly, ethereal, ghostly, preternatural, supernatural, paranormal, mystical. **3** *an unworldly religious order:* **nonmaterialistic**, spiritualistic, religious.

unworthy adjective **1** *he was unworthy of trust:* **undeserving**, ineligible, unqualified, unfit. **2** *unworthy behaviour:* **unbecoming**, unsuitable, inappropriate, unbefitting, unfitting, unseemly, improper; discreditable, shameful, dishonourable, despicable, ignoble, contemptible, reprehensible.
– OPPOSITES deserving, becoming.

unwritten adjective *there are unwritten rules about what is acceptable dress:* **tacit**, implicit, unvoiced, taken for granted, accepted, recognized, understood; traditional, customary, conventional; oral, verbal, spoken, vocal, word-of-mouth.

unyielding adjective **1** *unyielding spikes of cane:* **stiff**, inflexible, unbending, inelastic, firm, hard, solid, tough, tight, compact, compressed, dense. **2** *an unyielding policy:* **resolute**, inflexible, uncompromising, unbending, unshakeable, unwavering, immovable, intractable, intransigent, rigid, stiff, firm, determined, dogged, obstinate, stubborn, adamant, obdurate, tenacious, relentless, implacable, single-minded.

up-and-coming adjective *up-and-coming young players:* **promising**, budding, rising, on the up and up, with potential; talented, gifted, able.

upbraid verb *she had upbraided him firmly for his deception:* **reprimand**, rebuke, admonish, chastise, chide, reprove, reproach, scold, berate, take to task, lambaste, give someone a piece of one's mind, haul over the coals, lecture; informal tell off, give someone a talking-to, dress down, give someone an earful, rap over the knuckles, bawl out, lay into; Brit. informal tick off, carpet, tear off a strip, give someone what for, give someone a rocket/rollicking; N. Amer. informal chew out, ream out; Austral. informal monster.

upbringing noun *her upbringing had not prepared her for that:* **childhood**, early life, formative years, teaching, instruction, care, bringing-up, rearing.

update verb **1** *security measures are continually updated:* **modernize**, upgrade, bring up to date, improve, overhaul; N. Amer. bring up to code. **2** *I'll update him on today's developments:* **brief**, bring up to date, inform, fill in, tell, notify, apprise, keep posted; informal clue in, put in the picture, bring/keep up to speed.

upgrade verb **1** *there are plans to upgrade the rail system:* **improve**, modernize, update, bring up to date, make better, ameliorate, reform; rehabilitate, recondition, refurbish, renovate; N. Amer. bring up to code. **2** *he was upgraded to a seat in the cabinet:* **promote**, give promotion to, elevate, move up, raise.
– OPPOSITES downgrade, demote.

upheaval noun *the upheaval caused by wartime evacuation:* **disruption**, disturbance, trouble, turbulence, disorder, confusion, turmoil, pandemonium, chaos, mayhem, cataclysm; revolution, change.

uphill adjective **1** *an uphill path:* **upward**, rising, ascending, climbing. **2** *an uphill job:* **arduous**, difficult, hard, tough, taxing, demanding, exacting, stiff, formidable, exhausting, tiring, wearisome, laborious, gruelling, back-breaking, punishing, burdensome, onerous, Herculean; informal no picnic, killing.
– OPPOSITES downhill.

uphold verb **1** *the court upheld his claim for damages:* **confirm**, endorse, sustain, approve, support, back (up), stand by, champion, defend. **2** *they've a tradition to uphold:* **maintain**, sustain, continue, preserve, protect, keep, hold to, keep alive, keep going.
– OPPOSITES overturn, oppose.

upkeep noun **1** *the upkeep of the road:* **maintenance**, repair(s), service, servicing, care, preservation, conservation; running. **2** *the child's upkeep:* **(financial) support**, maintenance, keep, subsistence, care.

uplift verb *she needs something to uplift her spirits:* **boost**, raise, buoy up, lift, cheer up, perk up, enliven, brighten up, lighten, stimulate, inspire, ginger up, revive, restore; informal buck up.

uplifted adjective *his uplifted hand shot to his face:* **raised**, upraised, elevated, upthrust; held high, erect, proud.

uplifting adjective *it's a sweet, uplifting story about an English girl at a mission in India:* **inspiring**, stirring, inspirational, rousing, moving, touching, affecting, cheering, heartening, encouraging.

upper adjective **1** *the upper floor:* **higher**, superior; top. **2** *the upper echelons of the party:* **senior**, superior, higher-level, higher-ranking, top.
– OPPOSITES lower.
▪ **the upper hand** an advantage, the edge, the whip hand, a lead, a head start, ascendancy, superiority, supremacy, sway, control, power, mastery, dominance, command.

upper-class adjective *an upper-class family:* **aristocratic**, noble, of noble birth, patrician, titled, blue-blooded, high-born, well born, elite, landowning, landed, born with a silver spoon in one's mouth; Brit. county, upmarket; informal upper-crust, {huntin', shootin', and fishin'}; Brit. informal posh.

uppermost adjective **1** *the uppermost branches:* **highest**, top, topmost. **2** *their own problems remained uppermost in their minds:* **predominant**, of greatest importance, to the fore, foremost, dominant, principal, chief, main, paramount, major.

upright adjective **1** *an upright position:* **vertical**, perpendicular, plumb, straight (up), straight up and down, bolt upright, erect, on end; on one's feet; Heraldry rampant. **2** *an upright member of*

the community: **honest**, honourable, upstanding, respectable, high-minded, law-abiding, right-minded, worthy, moral, ethical, righteous, decent, good, virtuous, principled, high-principled, of principle, noble, incorruptible.
– OPPOSITES horizontal, dishonourable.

uprising noun *the uprising was put down by the police and the army:* **rebellion**, revolt, insurrection, mutiny, revolution, insurgence, rioting, riot; civil disobedience, unrest, anarchy, fighting in the streets; coup, coup d'état, putsch.

uproar noun **1** *the uproar in the kitchen continued for some time:* **turmoil**, disorder, confusion, chaos, commotion, disturbance, rumpus, tumult, turbulence, mayhem, pandemonium, bedlam, noise, din, clamour, hubbub, racket; shouting, yelling, babel; informal hullabaloo; Brit. informal row. **2** *there was an uproar when he was dismissed:* **outcry**, furore, howl of protest; fuss, commotion, hue and cry, rumpus, ruckus, brouhaha; informal hullabaloo, stink, ructions; Brit. informal row.
– OPPOSITES calm.

uproarious adjective **1** *an uproarious party:* **riotous**, rowdy, noisy, loud, wild, unrestrained, unruly, rip-roaring, rollicking, boisterous; Brit. informal rumbustious; N. Amer. informal rambunctious. **2** *an uproarious joke:* **hilarious**, hysterically funny, too funny for words, rib-tickling; informal priceless, side-splitting, a scream, a hoot.
– OPPOSITES quiet.

uproot verb **1** *don't pick or uproot wild flowers:* **pull up**, root out, deracinate, grub out/up. **2** *a revolution is necessary to uproot the social order:* **eradicate**, get rid of, eliminate, root out, destroy, put an end to, do away with, wipe out, stamp out.
– OPPOSITES plant.

upset verb **1** *the accusation upset her:* **distress**, trouble, perturb, dismay, disturb, discompose, unsettle, disconcert, disquiet, worry, bother, agitate, fluster, throw, ruffle, unnerve, shake; hurt, sadden, grieve. **2** *he upset a tureen of soup:* **knock over**, overturn, upend, tip over, topple (over); spill. **3** *the dam will upset the ecological balance:* **disrupt**, interfere with, disturb, throw out, turn topsy-turvy, throw into confusion, mess up.
noun **1** *a legal dispute will cause worry and upset:* **distress**, trouble, perturbation, dismay, disquiet, worry, bother, agitation; hurt, grief. **2** *a stomach upset:* **disorder**, complaint, ailment, illness, sickness, malady; informal bug; Brit. informal lurgy.
adjective **1** *I was upset by the news:* **distressed**, troubled, perturbed, dismayed, disturbed, unsettled, disconcerted, worried, bothered, anxious, agitated, flustered, ruffled, unnerved, shaken; hurt, saddened, grieved; informal cut up, choked; Brit. informal gutted. **2** *an upset stomach:* **disturbed**,

unsettled, queasy, bad, poorly; informal gippy.
– OPPOSITES unperturbed, calm.

upshot noun *the upshot of this conflict of interests was a compromise:* **result**, end result, consequence, outcome, conclusion; effect, repercussion, reverberations, ramification.
– OPPOSITES cause.

upside down adjective **1** *an upside-down canoe:* **upturned**, upended, wrong side up, overturned, inverted; capsized. **2** *they left the flat upside down:* **in disarray**, in disorder, jumbled up, in a muddle, untidy, disorganized, chaotic, all over the place, in chaos, in confusion, topsy-turvy, at sixes and sevens; informal higgledy-piggledy.

upstanding adjective *an upstanding member of the community:* **honest**, honourable, upright, respectable, high-minded, law-abiding, right-minded, worthy, moral, ethical, righteous, decent, good, virtuous, principled, high-principled, of principle, noble, incorruptible.
– OPPOSITES dishonourable.

upstart noun *these upstarts, they don't know their place:* **parvenu(e)**, arriviste, nouveau riche, vulgarian; status seeker, social climber.

up to date adjective **1** *up-to-date equipment:* **modern**, contemporary, the latest, state-of-the-art, new, present-day, up to the minute; advanced; informal bang up to date, mod. **2** *the newsletter will keep you up to date:* **informed**, up to speed, in the picture, in touch, au fait, au courant, conversant, familiar, knowledgeable, acquainted, aware.
– OPPOSITES out of date, old-fashioned.

upturn noun *an upturn in the economy:* **improvement**, upswing, turn for the better; recovery, revival, rally, resurgence, increase, rise, jump, leap, upsurge, boost, escalation.
– OPPOSITES fall, slump.

upward adjective *an upward trend:* **rising**, on the rise, ascending, climbing, mounting; uphill.
adverb *the smoke drifts upward.* **up**, upwards, uphill; to the top.
– OPPOSITES downward.

upwards adverb *he inched his way upwards:* **up**, upward, uphill; to the top.
– OPPOSITES downward.
■ **upward(s) of** more than, above, over, in excess of, exceeding, beyond.

urban adjective *crime rates are significantly higher in urban areas:* **town**, city, municipal, metropolitan, built-up, inner-city, suburban.
– OPPOSITES rural.

urbane adjective *the urbane and scholarly former information minister:* **suave**, sophisticated, debonair, worldly, cultivated, cultured, civilized; smooth, polished, refined, self-possessed; courteous, polite, civil, well mannered, mannerly, charming, gentlemanly, gallant.
– OPPOSITES uncouth, unsophisticated.

u

urchin noun **ragamuffin**, waif, stray; imp, rascal.

urge verb **1** *she urged him to try again:* **encourage**, exhort, enjoin, press, entreat, implore, call on, appeal to, beg, plead with; egg on, spur, push, pressure, pressurize. **2** *she urged her horse down the lane:* **spur (on)**, force, drive, impel. **3** *I urge caution in interpreting these results:* **advise**, counsel, advocate, recommend.
noun *his urge to travel:* **desire**, wish, need, compulsion, longing, yearning, hankering, craving, appetite, hunger, thirst; fancy, impulse; informal yen, itch.

urgent adjective **1** *the urgent need for more funding:* **acute**, pressing, dire, desperate, critical, serious, grave, intense, crying, burning, compelling, extreme, high-priority, top-priority; life-and-death. **2** *an urgent whisper:* **insistent**, persistent, importunate, earnest, pleading, begging.

urinate verb *one of the symptoms of the disease is a frequent desire to urinate:* **pass water**, relieve oneself; informal spend a penny, have/take a leak, pee, piddle, widdle, have a tinkle; Brit. informal wee, have a Jimmy (Riddle), have a slash; N. Amer. informal take a whizz.

usable adjective *his family owned about one sixth of the usable land in the country:* **ready/fit for use**, able to be used, at someone's disposal, disposable; working, in working order, functioning, functional, serviceable, operational, up and running.

usage noun **1** *energy usage:* **use**, consumption, utilization. **2** *the usage of equipment:* **use**, utilization, operation, manipulation, running, handling. **3** *the intricacies of English usage:* **phraseology**, parlance, idiom, way of speaking/writing, mode of expression; idiolect. **4** *the usages of polite society:* **custom**, practice, habit, tradition, convention, rule, observance; way, procedure, form, wont; (**usages**) mores.

use verb **1** *she used her key to open the front door:* **utilize**, make use of, avail oneself of, employ, work, operate, wield, ply, apply, manoeuvre, manipulate, put to use, put into service. **2** *the court will use its discretion in making an order:* **exercise**, employ, bring into play, practise, apply. **3** *use your troops well and they will not let you down:* **manage**, handle, treat, deal with, behave/act towards, conduct oneself towards. **4** *I couldn't help feeling that she was using me:* **take advantage of**, exploit, manipulate, take liberties with, impose on, abuse; capitalize on, profit from, trade on, milk; informal cash in on, walk all over. **5** *we have used all the available funds:* **consume**, get/go through, exhaust, deplete, expend, spend; waste, fritter away, squander, dissipate.
noun **1** *the use of such weapons:* **utilization**, usage, application, employment, operation, manipulation. **2** *his use of other people for his own ends:* **exploitation**, manipulation;

abuse. **3** *what is the use of that?* **advantage**, benefit, service, utility, usefulness, help, good, gain, avail, profit, value, worth, point, object, purpose, sense, reason. **4** *composers have not found much use for the device:* **need**, necessity, call, demand, requirement.

used adjective *a used car:* **second-hand**, pre-owned, nearly new, old; worn, hand-me-down, handed-down, cast-off; Brit. informal reach-me-down.
– OPPOSITES new.
■ **used to** *I'm used to hard work:* accustomed to, no stranger to, familiar with, at home with, in the habit of, experienced in, versed in, conversant with, acquainted with.

useful adjective **1** *a useful multi-purpose tool:* **functional**, practical, handy, convenient, utilitarian, serviceable, of use, of service; informal nifty. **2** *a useful experience:* **beneficial**, advantageous, helpful, worthwhile, profitable, rewarding, productive, constructive, valuable, fruitful. **3** (informal) *they had some very useful players:* **competent**, capable, able, skilful, skilled, talented, proficient, accomplished, good, handy.
– OPPOSITES useless, disadvantageous, incompetent.

useless adjective **1** *it was useless to try | a piece of useless knowledge:* **futile**, to no avail, in vain, vain, pointless, to no purpose, unavailing, hopeless, ineffectual, ineffective, to no effect, fruitless, unprofitable, profitless, unproductive; broken, kaput. **2** (informal) *he was useless at his job:* **incompetent**, inept, ineffective, incapable, inadequate, hopeless, bad; informal pathetic, a dead loss; Brit. informal pants.
– OPPOSITES useful, beneficial, competent.

usher verb *she ushered him to a window seat:* **escort**, accompany, take, show, see, lead, conduct, guide, steer, shepherd.
noun *ushers showed them to their seats:* **guide**, attendant, escort.
■ **usher something in** *the railways ushered in an era of cheap mass travel:* **herald**, mark the start of, signal, ring in, show in, set the scene for, pave the way for; start, begin, introduce, open the door to, get going, set in motion, get under way, kick off, launch.

usual adjective *his usual route to work:* **habitual**, customary, accustomed, wonted, normal, routine, regular, standard, typical, established, set, settled, stock, conventional, traditional, expected, predictable, familiar; average, general, ordinary, everyday.
– OPPOSITES exceptional.

usually adverb *he usually arrived home about 1 o'clock:* **normally**, generally, habitually, customarily, routinely, typically, ordinarily, commonly, conventionally, traditionally; as a rule, in general, more often than not, in the main, mainly, mostly, for the most part.

usurp verb **1** *Richard usurped the throne:* **seize**, take over, take possession of, take, commandeer, assume. **2** *the Hanoverian* *dynasty had usurped the Stuarts:* **oust**, overthrow, remove, topple, unseat, depose, dethrone; supplant, replace.

utensil noun *kitchen utensils:* **implement**, tool, instrument, device, apparatus, gadget, appliance, contrivance, contraption, aid; informal gizmo.

utilitarian adjective *coal-burning fires have been replaced with utilitarian heaters and radiators:* **practical**, functional, serviceable, useful, sensible, efficient, utility, workaday; plain, unadorned, undecorative.
– OPPOSITES decorative.

utility noun *a study that looks at the utility of using sled dogs rather than snowmobiles:* **usefulness**, use, benefit, value, advantage, advantageousness, help, helpfulness, profitability, practicality, effectiveness, avail, service.

utilize verb *concrete had long been utilized as a bonding and covering material:* **use**, make use of, put to use, employ, avail oneself of, bring/press into service, bring into play, deploy, draw on, exploit.

utmost adjective **1** *a matter of the utmost importance:* **greatest**, highest, maximum, most, uttermost; extreme, supreme, paramount. **2** *the utmost tip of Shetland:* **furthest**, farthest, furthermost, farthermost, extreme, very, uttermost, outermost, endmost.
noun *a plot that stretches credulity to the utmost:* **uttermost**, maximum, limit.

Utopia noun *it may be your idea of Utopia, but it's not mine:* **paradise**, heaven, heaven on earth, Eden, Garden of Eden, Shangri-La, Elysium; idyll, nirvana, ideal place.

Utopian adjective *a Utopian vision of gender equality:* **idealistic**, visionary, romantic, starry-eyed, fanciful, unrealistic; ideal, perfect, paradisal, heavenly, idyllic, blissful, Elysian.

utter[1] adjective *that's utter nonsense:* **complete**, total, absolute, thorough, perfect, downright, out-and-out, outright, thoroughgoing, all-out, sheer, arrant, positive, prize, rank, pure, real, veritable, consummate, categorical, unmitigated, unqualified, unadulterated, unalloyed.

utter[2] verb **1** *he uttered an exasperated snort:* **emit**, let out, give, produce. **2** *he hardly uttered a word:* **say**, speak, voice, express, articulate, pronounce, enunciate, verbalize, vocalize.

utterance noun *the victory was soured by the jingoistic utterances of the commentators:* **remark**, comment, word, statement, observation, declaration, pronouncement.

utterly adverb *he looked utterly ridiculous:* **completely**, totally, absolutely, entirely, wholly, fully, thoroughly, quite, altogether, one hundred per cent, downright, outright, in all respects, unconditionally, perfectly, really, to the hilt, to the core; informal dead.

uttermost adjective & noun. See UTMOST.

U-turn noun *a complete U-turn in economic policy:* **volte-face**, turnaround, about-face, reversal, shift, change of heart, change of mind, backtracking, change of plan; Brit. about-turn.

u

Vv

vacancy noun **1** *there are vacancies for computer technicians:* **opening**, position, situation vacant, post, job, opportunity, place. **2** *Cathy stared into vacancy, seeing nothing:* **empty space**, emptiness, nothingness, void. **3** *a vacancy of mind:* **empty-headedness**, lack of intelligence, brainlessness, vacuousness, vacuity, stupidity.

vacant adjective **1** *a vacant house:* **empty**, unoccupied, available, not in use, free, unfilled; uninhabited, untenanted. **2** *a vacant look:* **blank**, expressionless, unresponsive, emotionless, impassive, uninterested, vacuous, empty, glazed, glassy; unintelligent, dull-witted, dense, brainless, empty-headed.
– OPPOSITES full, occupied, expressive.

vacate verb **1** *he was forced to vacate the premises:* **leave**, move out of, evacuate, quit, depart from; abandon, desert. **2** *he will be vacating his post next year:* **resign from**, leave, stand down from, give up, bow out of, relinquish, retire from; informal quit.
– OPPOSITES occupy, take up.

vacation noun **1** *his summer vacations in France:* **holiday**, trip, tour, break, mini-break; leave, time off, recess, furlough; informal hol, vac. **2** *the squatters' vacation of the occupied land:* **departure**, evacuation, abandonment, desertion.

vacillate verb *I vacillated between teaching and journalism:* **dither**, be indecisive, be undecided, waver, hesitate, be in two minds, blow hot and cold, keep changing one's mind; Brit. haver, hum and haw; informal dilly-dally, shilly-shally.

vacillating adjective **irresolute**, indecisive, dithering, undecided, hesitant, wavering, ambivalent, divided, uncertain, in two minds, blowing hot and cold; informal dilly-dallying, shilly-shallying.
– OPPOSITES resolute.

vacuous adjective *a vacuous smile:* **silly**, inane, unintelligent, foolish, stupid, fatuous, idiotic, brainless, witless, vapid, vacant, empty-headed; informal dumb, gormless, moronic, brain-dead.
– OPPOSITES intelligent.

vacuum noun **1** *people longing to fill the spiritual vacuum in their lives:* **emptiness**, void, nothingness, vacancy. **2** *the political vacuum left by the Emperor's death:* **gap**, space, lacuna, void. **3** (informal) *I use the vacuum for cleaning the rug:* **vacuum cleaner**; Brit. informal vac; trademark Hoover.

vagabond noun. See **VAGRANT** noun.

vagary noun *the vagaries of the weather:* **change**, fluctuation, variation, quirk, peculiarity, oddity, eccentricity, unpredictability, caprice, foible, whim, whimsy, fancy.

vagrant noun *a temporary home for vagrants:* **tramp**, drifter, down-and-out, derelict, beggar, itinerant, wanderer, nomad, traveller, vagabond, transient, homeless person, beachcomber; informal knight of the road; N. Amer. hobo; Austral. bagman; informal bag lady; N. Amer. informal bum.
adjective *vagrant beggars:* **homeless**, drifting, transient, roving, roaming, itinerant, wandering, nomadic, travelling, vagabond, rootless, of no fixed address/abode.

vague adjective **1** *a vague shape:* **indistinct**, indefinite, indeterminate, unclear, ill-defined; hazy, fuzzy, misty, blurred, blurry, out of focus, faint, shadowy, dim, obscure, nebulous, amorphous. **2** *a vague description:* **imprecise**, rough, approximate, inexact, non-specific, generalized, ambiguous, equivocal, hazy, woolly. **3** *they had only vague plans:* **hazy**, uncertain, undecided, unsure, unclear, unsettled, indefinite, indeterminate, unconfirmed, up in the air, speculative. **4** *she was so vague in everyday life:* **absent-minded**, forgetful, dreamy, abstracted, with one's head in the clouds; informal scatty, not with it.
– OPPOSITES clear, precise, certain.

vaguely adverb **1** *she looks vaguely familiar:* **slightly**, a little, a bit, somewhat, rather, in a way; faintly, obscurely; informal sort of, kind of. **2** *he fired his rifle vaguely in our direction:* **roughly**, more or less, approximately. **3** *he smiled vaguely:* **absent-mindedly**, abstractedly, vacantly.
– OPPOSITES very, exactly.

vain adjective **1** *he was vain about his looks:* **conceited**, narcissistic, self-loving, in love with oneself, self-admiring, self-regarding, egotistic, egotistical; proud, arrogant, boastful, cocky, immodest, swaggering; informal big-headed. **2** *a vain attempt:* **futile**, useless, pointless, to no purpose, in vain; ineffective, ineffectual, inefficacious, impotent, unavailing, to no avail, fruitless,

profitless, unproductive, unsuccessful, failed, abortive, for nothing; thwarted, frustrated, foiled.
– OPPOSITES modest, successful.
■ **in vain 1** *they tried in vain to save him:* unsuccessfully, without success, to no avail, to no purpose, fruitlessly. **2** *his efforts were in vain.* See **VAIN** sense 2.

valet noun **manservant**, man, personal attendant, gentleman's gentleman, Jeeves.

valiant adjective *a valiant warrior:* **brave**, courageous, plucky, valorous, intrepid, heroic, gallant, lionhearted, bold, fearless, daring, audacious; unflinching, unshrinking, unafraid, dauntless, undaunted, doughty, indomitable, mettlesome, stout-hearted, spirited; informal game, gutsy, spunky.
– OPPOSITES cowardly.

valid adjective **1** *a valid criticism:* **well founded**, sound, reasonable, rational, logical, justifiable, defensible, viable, bona fide; cogent, effective, powerful, convincing, credible, forceful, strong, weighty. **2** *a valid contract:* **legally binding**, lawful, legal, official, signed and sealed, contractual; in force, in effect, effective.

validate verb **1** *clinical trials now exist to validate this claim:* **prove**, substantiate, corroborate, verify, support, back up, bear out, confirm, justify, vindicate, authenticate. **2** *250 course proposals were validated:* **ratify**, endorse, approve, agree to, accept, authorize, legalize, legitimize, warrant, license, certify, recognize.
– OPPOSITES disprove.

valley noun **dale**, vale; hollow, gully, gorge, ravine, canyon, rift; Brit. combe, dene; N. English clough; Scottish glen, strath.

valour noun *the medals are awarded for acts of valour:* **bravery**, courage, pluck, intrepidity, nerve, daring, fearlessness, audacity, boldness, dauntlessness, stout-heartedness, heroism, backbone, spirit; informal guts, spunk; Brit. informal bottle; N. Amer. informal moxie.
– OPPOSITES cowardice.

valuable adjective **1** *a valuable watch:* **precious**, costly, high-priced, high-cost, expensive, dear; worth its weight in gold, worth a king's ransom, priceless. **2** *a valuable contribution:* **useful**, helpful, beneficial, invaluable, productive, constructive, effective, advantageous, worthwhile, worthy, important.
– OPPOSITES cheap, worthless, useless.

valuables plural noun *valuables may be left in the hotel safe:* **precious items**, costly items, prized possessions, personal effects, treasures.

value noun **1** *houses exceeding £250,000 in value:* **price**, cost, worth; market price, monetary value, face value. **2** *the value of adequate preparation cannot be understated:* **worth**, usefulness, advantage, benefit, gain, profit, good, help, helpfulness, avail; importance, significance. **3** *society's values are passed on to us as children:* **principles**, ethics, moral code, morals, standards, code of behaviour.
verb **1** *his estate was valued at £45,000:* **evaluate**, assess, estimate, appraise, price, put/set a price on. **2** *she valued his opinion:* **think highly of**, have a high opinion of, hold in high regard, rate highly, esteem, set (great) store by, appreciate, respect; prize, cherish, treasure.

valued adjective *a valued friend:* **cherished**, treasured, dear, prized; esteemed, respected, highly regarded.

valueless adjective *the watercolours turned out to be valueless:* **worthless**, of no value, useless, to no purpose, (of) no use, profitless, futile, pointless, vain, in vain, to no avail, to no effect, fruitless, unproductive, idle, ineffective, unavailing.

vanguard noun *women are often in the vanguard of linguistic change:* **forefront**, van, advance guard, spearhead, front, front line, fore, lead, cutting edge; leaders, founders, founding fathers, pioneers, trailblazers, trendsetters, innovators, groundbreakers.
– OPPOSITES rear.

vanish verb **1** *he vanished into the darkness:* **disappear**, be lost to sight/view, become invisible, vanish into thin air, recede from view. **2** *all hope of freedom vanished:* **fade (away)**, evaporate, melt away, come to an end, end, cease to exist, pass away, die out, be no more.
– OPPOSITES appear, materialize.

vanity noun **1** *she had none of the vanity often associated with beautiful women:* **conceit**, narcissism, self-love, self-admiration, self-regard, egotism; pride, arrogance, boastfulness, cockiness, swagger; informal big-headedness. **2** *the vanity of all desires of the will:* **futility**, uselessness, pointlessness, worthlessness, fruitlessness.
– OPPOSITES modesty.

vanquish verb *he successfully vanquished his rival:* **conquer**, defeat, beat, trounce, rout, triumph over, be victorious over, get the better of, worst; overcome, overwhelm, overpower, overthrow, subdue, subjugate, quell, quash, crush, bring someone to their knees; informal lick, hammer, clobber, thrash, demolish, wipe the floor with, make mincemeat of, massacre, slaughter, annihilate; Brit. informal stuff; N. Amer. informal cream, shellac.

vapid adjective *tuneful but vapid musical comedies:* **insipid**, uninspired, colourless, uninteresting, feeble, flat, dull, boring, tedious, tired, unexciting, uninspiring, unimaginative, lifeless, tame, vacuous, bland, trite.
– OPPOSITES lively, colourful.

vapour noun **haze**, mist, steam, condensation; fumes, exhalation, fog, smog, smoke.

V

variable adjective *the wind was variable in direction and strength:* **changeable**, changing, varying, shifting, fluctuating, changeful, irregular, inconstant, inconsistent, fluid, unsteady, unstable, unsettled, fitful, mutable, protean, wavering, vacillating, capricious, fickle, volatile, unpredictable, unreliable; informal up and down.
– OPPOSITES constant.

variance noun *data indicate no variance in church attendance between blue- and white-collar workers:* **difference**, variation, discrepancy, dissimilarity, disagreement, conflict, divergence, deviation, contrast, contradiction, imbalance, incongruity.
■ **at variance 1** *his recollections were at variance with documentary evidence:* inconsistent, at odds, not in keeping, out of keeping, out of line, out of step, in conflict, in disagreement, different, differing, divergent, discrepant, dissimilar, contrary, incompatible, contradictory, irreconcilable, incongruous. **2** *they were at variance with their previous allies:* in disagreement, at odds, at cross purposes, at loggerheads, in conflict, in dispute, at outs, quarrelling.

variant noun *there are a number of variants of the same idea:* **variation**, form, alternative, adaptation, alteration, modification, permutation.
adjective *a variant spelling:* **alternative**, other, different, divergent, derived, modified.

variation noun **1** *regional variations in farming practice:* **difference**, dissimilarity; disparity, contrast, discrepancy, imbalance. **2** *opening times are subject to variation:* **change**, alteration, modification; diversification. **3** *there was very little variation from an understood pattern:* **deviation**, variance, divergence, departure, fluctuation. **4** *hurling is an Irish variation of hockey:* **variant**, form, alternative form; development, adaptation, alteration, diversification, modification.

varied adjective *a varied selection:* **diverse**, assorted, miscellaneous, mixed, sundry, heterogeneous, wide-ranging, multifarious; disparate, motley.

variegated adjective *evergreen shrubs with variegated foliage:* **multicoloured**, particoloured, multicolour, many-coloured, many-hued, polychromatic, colourful, prismatic, rainbow-like, kaleidoscopic; mottled, striated, marbled, streaked, speckled, flecked, dappled; informal splotchy, splodgy.
– OPPOSITES plain, monochrome.

variety noun **1** *the lack of variety in the curriculum:* **diversity**, variation, diversification, multifariousness, heterogeneity, many-sidedness; change, difference. **2** *a wide variety of flowers and shrubs:* **assortment**, miscellany, range, array, collection, selection, mixture, medley,

multiplicity; mixed bag, motley collection, pot-pourri. **3** *fifty varieties of pasta:* **sort**, kind, type, class, category, style, form; make, model, brand; strain, breed, genus.
– OPPOSITES uniformity.

various adjective *dresses of various colours:* **diverse**, different, differing, varied, varying, a variety of, assorted, mixed, sundry, miscellaneous, heterogeneous, disparate, motley.

varnish noun & verb *several coats of varnish | we stripped the floor and varnished it:* **lacquer**, shellac, japan, enamel, glaze; polish.

vary verb **1** *estimates of the development cost vary:* **differ**, be different, be dissimilar. **2** *rates of interest vary over time:* **fluctuate**, rise and fall, go up and down, change, alter, shift, swing. **3** *the diaphragm is used for varying the aperture of the lens:* **modify**, change, alter, adjust, regulate, control, set; diversify. **4** *the routine never varied:* **change**, alter, deviate, differ, fluctuate.

vast adjective *a vast plain full of orchards:* **huge**, extensive, expansive, broad, wide, boundless, immeasurable, limitless, infinite; enormous, immense, great, massive, colossal, tremendous, mighty, prodigious, gigantic, gargantuan, mammoth, monumental; giant, towering, mountainous, titanic, Brobdingnagian; informal jumbo, mega, monster, whopping, humongous, astronomical; Brit. informal ginormous.
– OPPOSITES tiny.

vat noun *a vat of hot tar:* **tub**, tank, cistern, barrel, butt, cask, tun, drum, basin; vessel, receptacle, container, holder, reservoir.

vault¹ noun **1** *the highest Gothic vault in Europe:* **arched roof**, dome, arch. **2** *the vault under the church:* **cellar**, basement, underground chamber; crypt, undercroft, catacomb, burial chamber. **3** *valuables stored in the vault:* **strongroom**, safe deposit, safety deposit.

vault² verb *he vaulted over the gate:* **jump over**, leap over, spring over, bound over; hurdle, clear.

vaunt verb *the much vaunted health-care system:* **boast about**, brag about, make much of, crow about, parade, flaunt; acclaim, praise, extol, celebrate; informal show off about.

veer verb *the car veered to the left and crashed into the van:* **turn**, swerve, swing, sheer, career, weave, wheel; change direction/course, go off course, deviate.

vegetate verb *it is important not to let him vegetate in front of the television:* **do nothing**, idle, languish, laze, lounge, loll; moulder, stagnate; informal veg out, slob out; Brit. informal slummock; N. Amer. informal bum around, lollygag.

vegetation noun **plants**, flora; greenery, foliage, herbage, verdure.

vehemence noun *the vehemence of her*

answer surprised both of them: **passion**, force, forcefulness, ardour, fervour, violence, urgency, strength, vigour, intensity, keenness, enthusiasm, zeal.

vehement adjective **passionate**, forceful, ardent, impassioned, heated, spirited, urgent, fervent, violent, fierce, strong, forcible, powerful, emphatic, vigorous, intense, earnest, keen, enthusiastic, zealous.
– OPPOSITES mild, apathetic.

vehicle noun 1 *a stolen vehicle:* **means of transport**, conveyance; car, automobile, motorcycle, motorbike, van, bus, coach, lorry, truck; N. Amer. informal auto. 2 *a vehicle for the communication of original ideas:* **channel**, medium, means (of expression), agency, agent, instrument, mechanism, organ, apparatus.

veil noun *a thin veil of high cloud made the sun hazy:* **covering**, cover, screen, curtain, mantle, cloak, mask, blanket, shroud, canopy, cloud, pall.
verb *the peak was veiled in mist:* **envelop**, surround, swathe, enfold, cover, conceal, hide, screen, shield, cloak, blanket, shroud; obscure.

veiled adjective *veiled threats:* **disguised**, camouflaged, masked, covert, hidden, concealed, suppressed, underlying, implicit, implied, indirect.
– OPPOSITES overt.

vein noun 1 *a vein in his neck pulsed:* **blood vessel**. 2 *the mineral veins in the rock:* **layer**, lode, seam, stratum, stratification, deposit. 3 *white marble with grey veins:* **streak**, marking, mark, line, stripe, strip, band, thread, strand. 4 *he closes the article in a humorous vein:* **mood**, humour, frame of mind, temper, disposition, attitude, tenor, tone, key, spirit, character, feel, flavour, quality, atmosphere; manner, way, style.

velocity noun *light always travels at a constant velocity:* **speed**, pace, rate, tempo, momentum, impetus; swiftness, rapidity.

venal adjective *the law courts are venal and can take decades to decide a case:* **corrupt**, corruptible, bribable, open to bribery; dishonest, dishonourable, untrustworthy, unscrupulous, unprincipled; mercenary, greedy; informal bent.
– OPPOSITES honourable, honest.

vendetta noun *he was the victim of a political vendetta:* **feud**, blood feud, quarrel, argument, falling-out, dispute, fight, war; bad blood, enmity, rivalry, conflict, strife.

vendor noun *the ice-cream vendors were doing a brisk trade:* **seller**, retailer, purveyor, dealer, trader, tradesman, shopkeeper, merchant, supplier, stockist; huckster, pedlar, hawker; N. Amer. storekeeper.

veneer noun 1 *American cherry wood with a maple veneer:* **surface**, lamination, layer, overlay, facing, covering, finish, exterior. 2 *a veneer of sophistication:* **facade**, front, false front, show, outward display, appearance,

impression, semblance, guise, disguise, mask, masquerade, pretence, camouflage, cover.

venerable adjective *he was a venerable and most pious king:* **respected**, venerated, revered, reverenced, honoured, esteemed, hallowed, august, distinguished, eminent, great.

venerate verb *the Hindus venerate oxen:* **revere**, reverence, worship, hallow, hold sacred, exalt, adore, honour, respect, esteem.

veneration noun **reverence**, worship, adoration, exaltation, devotion, honour, respect, esteem, high regard.

vengeance noun *he demanded vengeance for the murder of his father:* **revenge**, retribution, retaliation, requital, reprisal, satisfaction, an eye for an eye (and a tooth for a tooth).
■ **with a vengeance** vigorously, strenuously, energetically, with a will, with might and main, with all the stops out, for all one is worth, all out, flat out, at full tilt; informal hammer and tongs, like crazy, like mad; Brit. informal like billy-o.

vengeful adjective *Whistler's vengeful creditors were determined to ruin him:* **vindictive**, revengeful, out for revenge, unforgiving, grudge-bearing.
– OPPOSITES forgiving.

venial adjective *venial failings:* **forgivable**, pardonable, excusable, allowable, permissible; slight, minor, unimportant, insignificant, trivial, trifling.
– OPPOSITES unforgivable, mortal.

venom noun 1 *snake venom:* **poison**, toxin. 2 *his voice was full of venom:* **rancour**, malevolence, vitriol, spite, vindictiveness, malice, maliciousness, ill will, animosity, animus, bitterness, antagonism, hostility, bile, hate, hatred; informal bitchiness, cattiness.

venomous adjective 1 *a venomous snake | the spider's venomous bite:* **poisonous**, toxic; dangerous, deadly, lethal, fatal, mortal. 2 *venomous remarks:* **vicious**, spiteful, rancorous, malevolent, vitriolic, vindictive, malicious, poisonous, virulent, bitter, acrimonious, antagonistic, hostile, cruel; informal bitchy, catty.
– OPPOSITES harmless, benevolent.

vent noun *an air vent:* **outlet**, **inlet**, opening, aperture, hole, gap, orifice, space; duct, flue, shaft, well, passage, airway.
verb *demonstrators vented their anger over the military strikes:* **let out**, give vent to, give free rein to, release, pour out, express, give expression to, air, voice, give voice to, ventilate.

ventilate verb 1 *the greenhouse must be properly ventilated:* **air**, aerate, oxygenate, air-condition; freshen, cool. 2 *the workers ventilated their discontent:* **express**, give expression to, air, bring into the open, communicate, voice, give voice to, verbalize,

V

discuss, debate, talk over.

venture noun *a business venture:* **enterprise**, undertaking, project, scheme, operation, endeavour, speculation, plunge, gamble, experiment.
verb **1** *we ventured across the moor:* **set out**, go, travel, journey. **2** *may I venture an opinion?* **put forward**, advance, proffer, offer, air, suggest, submit, propose, moot, ventilate. **3** *I ventured to ask her to come and dine with me:* **dare**, make so bold as, presume; take the liberty of; informal stick one's neck out, go out on a limb.

verbal adjective *he was given a verbal assurance that his application would be approved:* **oral**, spoken, stated, said, verbalized; unwritten.

verbatim adverb *their stories were taped and then transcribed verbatim:* **word for word**, letter for letter, line for line, to the letter, literally, exactly, precisely, closely, faithfully.

verbiage noun *there is plenty of irrelevant verbiage but no real information:* **verbosity**, padding, wordiness, prolixity, long-windedness; Brit. informal waffle.

verbose adjective *verbose articles from amateur authors:* **wordy**, loquacious, garrulous, talkative, voluble; long-winded, lengthy, prolix, tautological, pleonastic, periphrastic, circumlocutory, circuitous, discursive, digressive, rambling; informal mouthy, gabby; Brit. informal waffly.
– OPPOSITES succinct, laconic.

verbosity noun **wordiness**, loquacity, garrulity, talkativeness, volubility; long-windedness, lengthiness, verbiage, prolixity, tautology, circumlocution, discursiveness; Brit. informal waffle.

verdant adjective *the verdant forests of southern Vermont:* **green**, leafy, grassy; lush, rich.

verdict noun *the coroner recorded a verdict of death by misadventure:* **judgement**, adjudication, decision, finding, ruling, resolution, pronouncement, conclusion, opinion.

verge noun **1** *the verge of the lake:* **edge**, border, margin, side, brink, rim, lip; fringe, boundary, perimeter. **2** *Spain was on the verge of an economic crisis:* **brink**, threshold, edge, point.
verb *a degree of caution that verged on the obsessive:* **approach**, border on, be close/near to, be tantamount to; tend towards, approximate to, resemble.

verification noun **confirmation**, substantiation, proof, corroboration, support, attestation, validation, authentication, endorsement.

verify verb *reports of the massacre could not be verified:* **substantiate**, confirm, prove, corroborate, back up, bear out, justify, support, uphold, attest to, testify to, validate, authenticate, endorse, certify.

– OPPOSITES refute.

vernacular noun *he wrote in the vernacular to reach a wider audience:* **everyday language**, colloquial language, conversational language, common parlance; dialect, regional language, regionalisms, patois; informal lingo, local lingo.

versatile adjective *he was versatile enough to play on either wing:* **adaptable**, flexible, all-round, multifaceted, multitalented, resourceful; adjustable, multi-purpose, all-purpose, handy.

verse noun **1** *Elizabethan verse:* **poetry**, versification; poems, balladry, lyrics; blank verse, heroic verse, free verse. **2** *a verse he'd composed to mark my anniversary:* **poem**, lyric, ballad, sonnet, ode, limerick, rhyme, ditty, lay. **3** *a poem with sixty verses:* **stanza**, canto, couplet; strophe.
– OPPOSITES prose.

version noun **1** *his version of events:* **account**, report, statement, description, record, story, rendering, interpretation, explanation, understanding, reading, impression, side. **2** *the English version will be published next year:* **edition**, translation, impression. **3** *they have replaced coal-burning fires with gas versions:* **form**, sort, kind, type, variety, variant.

vertex noun *a line was drawn from the vertex of the figure to the middle of the base:* **apex**, peak, tip, top.

vertical adjective *the manhole lid conceals a vertical shaft:* **upright**, erect, perpendicular, plumb, straight up and down, on end, standing, upstanding, bolt upright, upended.
– OPPOSITES horizontal.

vertigo noun **dizziness**, giddiness, light-headedness, loss of balance.

verve noun *I played most sports with schoolboy verve:* **enthusiasm**, vigour, energy, pep, dynamism, go, elan, vitality, vivacity, buoyancy, liveliness, animation, zest, sparkle, spirit, ebullience, life, brio, gusto, eagerness, keenness, passion, zeal, relish, feeling, ardour, fire; informal zing, zip, vim, pizzazz, oomph.

very adverb *that's very kind of you:* **extremely**, exceedingly, exceptionally, extraordinarily, tremendously, immensely, hugely, intensely, acutely, abundantly, singularly, uncommonly, unusually, decidedly, particularly, supremely, highly, remarkably, really, truly, mightily, most; informal terrifically, awfully, fearfully, terribly, devilishly, majorly, seriously, mega, ultra, damn, damned; Brit. informal ever so, well, hellish, dead, jolly; N. Amer. informal real, mighty, awful, darned.
– OPPOSITES slightly.
adjective **1** *those were his very words:* **exact**, actual, precise. **2** *the very thought of food made her feel ill:* **mere**, simple, pure; sheer.

vessel noun **1** *a fishing vessel:* **boat**, ship, craft, watercraft. **2** *pour the mixture into* *a heatproof vessel:* **container**, receptacle; basin, bowl, pan, pot; urn, cask, barrel, drum, butt, vat.

vest verb *executive power is vested in the President:* **confer on**, entrust to, invest in, bestow on, grant to, give to; endow, lodge, lay, place.

vestibule noun *we sat in a high vestibule between the street and the courtyard:* **entrance hall**, hall, hallway, entrance, porch, portico, foyer, lobby, anteroom, antechamber, waiting room.

vestige noun **1** *the last vestiges of colonialism:* **remnant**, fragment, relic, echo, indication, sign, trace, mark, legacy, reminder; remains. **2** *she showed no vestige of emotion:* **bit**, touch, hint, suggestion, suspicion, shadow, scrap, tinge, speck, shred, jot, iota, whit, scintilla, glimmer; informal smidgen, tad.

vestigial adjective **1** *vestigial limbs:* **rudimentary**, undeveloped; non-functional. **2** *he felt a vestigial flicker of anger from last night:* **remaining**, surviving, residual, leftover, lingering.

vet verb *press releases are vetted by an executive council:* **check**, examine, scrutinize, investigate, inspect, look over, screen, assess, evaluate, appraise; informal check out.
noun *I took the cat to the vet:* **veterinary surgeon**, animal doctor, horse doctor; N. Amer. veterinarian.

veteran noun *a veteran of 16 political campaigns:* **old hand**, past master, doyen; informal old-timer, old stager, old warhorse.
– OPPOSITES novice.
adjective *a veteran diplomat:* **long-serving**, seasoned, old, hardened; adept, expert, well trained, practised, experienced; informal battle-scarred.

veto noun *parliament's right of veto:* **rejection**, dismissal; prohibition, proscription, embargo, ban, interdict; informal thumbs down, red light.
– OPPOSITES approval.
verb *the president vetoed the bill:* **reject**, turn down, throw out, dismiss; prohibit, forbid, interdict, proscribe, disallow, embargo, ban; informal kill, put the kibosh on, give the thumbs down to, give the red light to.
– OPPOSITES approve.

vex verb *Alice was vexed by his remarks:* **annoy**, irritate, anger, infuriate, exasperate, irk, gall, pique, put out, antagonize, get on someone's nerves, ruffle someone's feathers, make someone's hackles rise; Brit. rub up the wrong way; informal aggravate, peeve, miff, rile, nettle, needle, get (to), bug, hack off, get up someone's nose, get someone's goat, get someone's back up, give someone the hump, get someone's dander up; Brit. informal wind up, nark, get on someone's wick; N. Amer. informal tee off, tick off, burn up, rankle.

vexation noun **annoyance**, irritation, exasperation, indignation, anger, crossness,

displeasure, pique, disgruntlement; informal aggravation.

vexatious adjective **annoying**, irritating, infuriating, exasperating, maddening, trying, tiresome, troublesome, bothersome, irksome, vexing, galling; informal aggravating, pesky.

vexed adjective **1** *a vexed expression:* **annoyed**, irritated, cross, angry, infuriated, exasperated, irked, piqued, displeased, put out, disgruntled; informal aggravated, peeved, nettled, miffed, miffy, riled, hacked off, hot under the collar; Brit. informal narked, shirty; N. Amer. informal teed off, ticked off, sore, bent out of shape. **2** *the vexed issue of immigration:* **disputed**, in dispute, contested, in contention, contentious, debated, at issue, controversial, moot; problematic, difficult, knotty, thorny.

viable adjective *the committee came forward with the only viable solution:* **feasible**, workable, practicable, practical, usable, possible, realistic, achievable, attainable, realizable; informal doable.
– OPPOSITES impracticable.

vibrant adjective **1** *a vibrant and passionate woman:* **spirited**, lively, full of life, energetic, vigorous, vital, full of vim and vigour, animated, sparkling, effervescent, vivacious, dynamic, stimulating, exciting, passionate, fiery; informal peppy, feisty. **2** *she was vibrant with excitement:* **quivering**, trembling, shaking, shivering, shuddering, quavering, quaking. **3** *vibrant colours:* **vivid**, bright, striking, brilliant, strong, rich. **4** *his vibrant voice:* **resonant**, sonorous, reverberant, resounding, ringing, echoing; strong, rich, full.
– OPPOSITES lifeless, pale.

vibrate verb **1** *the floor beneath them vibrated:* **quiver**, shake, tremble, shiver, shudder, judder, throb, pulsate; rock, oscillate, swing, sway, move to and fro. **2** *a low rumbling sound began to vibrate through the car:* **reverberate**, resonate, resound, ring, echo.

vibration noun **tremor**, shaking, quivering, quaking, judder, juddering, shuddering, throb, throbbing, pulsation.

vicar noun **minister**, rector, priest, parson, clergyman, clergywoman, cleric, churchman, churchwoman, ecclesiastic, pastor, father, man/woman of the cloth, man/woman of god, curate, chaplain, preacher; Scottish kirkman; N. Amer. dominie; informal reverend, padre, Holy Joe, sky pilot; Austral. informal josser.

vicarious adjective *this catalogue brings vicarious pleasure in luxury living:* **indirect**, second-hand, secondary, derivative, derived, surrogate, substitute; empathetic, empathic.

vice noun **1** *youngsters may be driven to vice:* **immorality**, wrongdoing, wickedness, badness, evil, iniquity, villainy, corruption, misconduct; sin, sinfulness, ungodliness;

depravity, degeneracy, dissolution, dissipation, debauchery, decadence, lechery; crime, transgression. **2** *smoking is my only vice:* **shortcoming**, failing, flaw, fault, defect, weakness, deficiency, limitation, imperfection, blemish, foible, frailty.
– OPPOSITES virtue.

vice versa adverb *dancers can teach actors a lot and vice versa:* **conversely**, inversely, contrariwise; reciprocally.

vicinity noun *she lives in the vicinity:* **neighbourhood**, surrounding area, locality, locale, (local) area, district, region, quarter, zone; environs, surroundings, precincts; N. Amer. vicinage; informal neck of the woods.
■ **in the vicinity of** around, about, nearly, circa, approaching, roughly, something like, more or less; in the region of, in the neighbourhood of, near to, close to; Brit. getting on for.

vicious adjective **1** *a vicious killer:* **brutal**, ferocious, savage, violent, dangerous, ruthless, remorseless, merciless, heartless, callous, cruel, harsh, cold-blooded, inhuman, fierce, barbarous, barbaric, brutish, bloodthirsty, fiendish, sadistic, monstrous, murderous, homicidal. **2** *a vicious hate campaign:* **malicious**, malevolent, malignant, malign, spiteful, vindictive, venomous, poisonous, rancorous, mean, cruel, bitter, acrimonious, hostile, nasty; defamatory, slanderous; informal catty.
– OPPOSITES gentle, kindly.

vicissitude noun *he maintains his sunny disposition despite life's vicissitudes:* **change**, alteration, transition, shift, reversal, downturn; inconstancy, instability, uncertainty, unpredictability, chanciness, fickleness, variability, changeability, fluctuation, vacillation; ups and downs.

victim noun **1** *a victim of crime:* **sufferer**, injured party, casualty; fatality, loss; loser. **2** *the victim of a confidence trick:* **dupe**, stooge, gull, fool; target, prey, quarry, object, subject, focus, recipient; informal sucker, fall guy, chump, muggins, charlie; N. Amer. informal patsy, pigeon, sap. **3** *a sacrificial victim:* **sacrifice**, (burnt) offering, scapegoat.
■ **fall victim to** fall ill with, be stricken with, catch, develop, contract, pick up; succumb to; informal go down with.

victimize verb *he was victimized by cruel practical jokers:* **persecute**, pick on, push around, bully, abuse, discriminate against, ill-treat, mistreat, maltreat, terrorize; exploit, prey on, take advantage of, dupe, cheat, double-cross; informal get at, have it in for, give someone a hard time, hassle, lean on.

victor verb *a disastrous civil war from which no victor can emerge:* **winner**, champion, conqueror, vanquisher, hero; prizewinner, medallist; informal champ, top dog.
– OPPOSITES loser.

victorious adjective *the victorious British team brought the trophy back from Paris:*

triumphant, conquering, vanquishing, winning, champion, successful, top, first.

victory noun *they had won a tremendous victory:* **success**, triumph, conquest, win, favourable result, landslide, coup, vanquishment; mastery, superiority, supremacy; informal walkover, thrashing, trouncing.
– OPPOSITES defeat.

vie verb *restaurants vied with each other to attract custom:* **compete**, contend, contest, struggle, fight, battle, cross swords, lock horns, jockey; war, feud.

view noun **1** *the view from her flat:* **outlook**, prospect, panorama, vista, scene, aspect, perspective, spectacle, sight; scenery, landscape. **2** *we agree with this view:* **opinion**, point of view, viewpoint, belief, judgement, thinking, notion, idea, conviction, persuasion, attitude, feeling, sentiment, concept, hypothesis, theory; stance, standpoint, approach. **3** *the church came into view:* **sight**, perspective, vision, visibility.
verb **1** *they viewed the landscape:* **look at**, eye, observe, gaze at, stare at, ogle, contemplate, regard, scan, survey, inspect, scrutinize; informal check out, get a load of, gawp at; Brit. informal clock; N. Amer. informal eyeball. **2** *the law was viewed as a last resort:* **consider**, regard, look on, see, perceive, judge, deem, reckon.
■ **in view of** considering, bearing in mind, taking into account, on account of, in the light of, owing to, because of, as a result of.
■ **on view** on display, on exhibition, on show.

viewer noun *the new television series has been a smash hit with viewers:* **watcher**, spectator, onlooker, observer; (**viewers**) audience, crowd.

viewpoint noun. See VIEW noun sense 2.

vigilant adjective *there had been a rash of petty thefts and we were warned to be vigilant:* **watchful**, observant, attentive, alert, eagle-eyed, hawk-eyed, on the lookout, on one's toes, on the qui vive; wide awake, on one's guard, cautious, wary, circumspect, heedful, mindful; informal beady-eyed.
– OPPOSITES inattentive.

vigorous adjective **1** *the child was vigorous:* **robust**, healthy, hale and hearty, strong, sturdy, fit; hardy, tough, athletic; bouncing, thriving, flourishing, blooming; energetic, lively, active, perky, spirited, vibrant, vital, zestful; informal peppy, bouncy, in the pink. **2** *a vigorous defence of policy:* **strenuous**, powerful, forceful, spirited, mettlesome, determined, aggressive, eager, zealous, ardent, fervent, vehement, passionate; tough, blunt, hard-hitting; informal punchy.
– OPPOSITES weak, feeble.

vigorously adverb *she pedalled vigorously down the farm track:* **strenuously**, strongly, powerfully, forcefully, energetically, heartily, with might and main, for dear life, for all one is worth, all out, fiercely, hard; informal like mad, like crazy; Brit. informal like billy-o.

vigour noun *they ran with great vigour:* **robustness**, health, hardiness, strength, sturdiness, toughness; bloom, radiance, energy, life, vitality, verve, spirit; zeal, passion, determination, dynamism, zest, pep, drive; informal oomph, get-up-and-go; Brit. informal welly.
– OPPOSITES lethargy.

vile adjective *a vile smell:* **foul**, nasty, unpleasant, bad, disagreeable, horrid, horrible, dreadful, abominable, atrocious, offensive, obnoxious, odious, unsavoury, repulsive, disgusting, distasteful, loathsome, hateful, nauseating, sickening; disgraceful, appalling, shocking, sorry, shabby, shameful, dishonourable, execrable, heinous, abhorrent, deplorable, monstrous, wicked, evil, iniquitous, depraved, debased; contemptible, despicable, reprehensible; informal gross, God-awful, low-down, lousy; Brit. informal beastly.
– OPPOSITES pleasant.

vilify verb *the media vilified several of the election candidates:* **disparage**, denigrate, defame, run down, revile, abuse, speak ill of, criticize, condemn; malign, slander, libel; N. Amer. slur; informal pull apart, lay into, slam, bad-mouth; Brit. informal rubbish, slate; Austral./NZ informal bag, monster.
– OPPOSITES commend.

villain noun *an evil villain bent on destroying and dominating the world:* **criminal**, lawbreaker, offender, felon, convict, malefactor, miscreant, wrongdoer; gangster, gunman, thief, robber; rogue, scoundrel, reprobate, ruffian, hoodlum; informal crook, con, crim, baddy.

villainous adjective *a villainous attack:* **wicked**, evil, iniquitous, sinful, nefarious, vile, foul, monstrous, outrageous, atrocious, abominable, reprehensible, hateful, odious, contemptible, horrible, heinous, egregious; diabolical, fiendish, vicious, murderous; criminal, illicit, unlawful, illegal, lawless; immoral, corrupt, degenerate, sordid, depraved, dishonourable, dishonest, unscrupulous, unprincipled; informal crooked, bent, low-down, dirty, shady.
– OPPOSITES virtuous.

villainy noun **wickedness**, badness, evil, iniquity, wrongdoing, dishonesty, unscrupulousness, roguery, delinquency; crime, vice, criminality, lawlessness, lawbreaking, corruption; Law malfeasance; informal crookedness.

vindicate verb **1** *he was vindicated by the jury:* **acquit**, clear, absolve, exonerate; discharge, liberate, free, redeem; informal let off (the hook). **2** *I had fully vindicated my request:* **justify**, warrant, substantiate, ratify, authenticate, verify, confirm, corroborate, prove, defend, support, back, evidence, endorse.

vindictive adjective *the criticism was both vindictive and personalized:* **vengeful**, revengeful, unforgiving, resentful, acrimonious, bitter; spiteful, mean, rancorous, venomous, malicious, malevolent, nasty, cruel, unkind; informal catty.
– OPPOSITES forgiving.

vintage noun **1** *1986 was a classic vintage:* **year**. **2** *he lost a vintage through frost:* **(grape) harvest**, crop, yield. **3** *furniture of Louis XV vintage:* **period**, era, epoch, time, origin; genre, style, kind, sort, type.
adjective **1** *vintage French wine:* **high-quality**, quality, choice, select, superior, best. **2** *vintage motor vehicles:* **classic**, ageless, timeless; old, antique, heritage, historic. **3** *his reaction was vintage Francis:* **characteristic**, typical, pure.

violate verb **1** *this violates fundamental human rights:* **contravene**, breach, infringe, break, transgress, overstep, disobey, defy, flout; disregard, ignore. **2** *the tomb was violated:* **desecrate**, profane, defile, degrade, debase; damage, vandalize, deface, destroy. **3** *he drugged and then violated her:* **rape**, assault, force oneself on, abuse, molest, interfere with.
– OPPOSITES respect.

violation noun **1** *a violation of human rights:* **contravention**, breach, infringement, infraction, transgression, defiance; neglect. **2** *a violation of their private lives:* **invasion**, breach, infraction; trespass, intrusion, encroachment.

violence noun **1** *police violence:* **brutality**, brute force, ferocity, savagery, cruelty, sadism, barbarity, brutishness. **2** *the violence of the blow:* **forcefulness**, force, power, strength, might, savagery, ferocity, brutality. **3** *the violence of his passion:* **intensity**, severity, strength, force, vehemence, power, potency, fervency, ardency, ferocity, fury.

violent adjective **1** *a violent alcoholic:* **brutal**, vicious, savage, rough, aggressive, threatening, fierce, wild, ferocious; barbarous, barbaric, thuggish, cut-throat, homicidal, murderous, cruel. **2** *a violent blow:* **powerful**, forceful, hard, sharp, smart, strong, vigorous, mighty, hefty; savage, ferocious, brutal, vicious. **3** *violent jealousy:* **intense**, extreme, strong, powerful, vehement, intemperate, unbridled, uncontrollable, ungovernable, inordinate, consuming, passionate.
– OPPOSITES gentle, weak, mild.

virgin noun *she remained a virgin:* **chaste woman**, celibate.
adjective *virgin forest:* **untouched**, unspoilt, untainted, immaculate, pristine, flawless; spotless, unsullied, unpolluted, undefiled, perfect; unchanged, intact; unexplored, uncharted, unmapped.

virginal adjective *her virginal innocence:* **chaste**, virgin, celibate, abstinent;

V

unmarried, unwed, maiden, maidenly; pure, uncorrupted, incorrupt, undefiled, unsullied, innocent.
– OPPOSITES despoiled.

virginity noun *I managed to graduate from high school with my virginity intact:* **chastity**, maidenhood, honour, purity, innocence; celibacy, abstinence; informal cherry.

virile adjective *she liked to read about strong, virile heroes:* **manly**, masculine, male; strong, tough, vigorous, robust, muscular, muscly, brawny, rugged, sturdy, husky; red-blooded, fertile; informal macho, laddish, butch, beefy, hunky.
– OPPOSITES effeminate.

virtual adjective *we drove to the cottage in virtual silence:* **effective**, in effect, near (enough), essential, practical, to all intents and purposes; indirect, implied, implicit, unacknowledged, tacit.

virtually adverb *the huge building was virtually empty:* **almost**, effectively, in effect, all but, more or less, practically, nearly, close to, verging on, just about, as good as, essentially, to all intents and purposes, as near as dammit; roughly, approximately; informal pretty much, pretty well.

virtue noun **1** *the simple virtue of peasant life:* **goodness**, virtuousness, righteousness, morality, integrity, dignity, rectitude, honour, decency, respectability, nobility, worthiness, purity; principles, ethics. **2** *promptness was not one of his virtues:* **good point**, good quality, strong point, asset, forte, attribute, strength, talent. **3** *I can see no virtue in this:* **merit**, advantage, benefit, usefulness, strength, efficacy.
– OPPOSITES vice, failing, disadvantage.
■ **by virtue of** because of, on account of, by dint of, by means of, by way of, via, through, as a result of, as a consequence of, on the strength of, owing to, thanks to, due to, by reason of.

virtuosity noun *the singer has to display extreme virtuosity:* **skill**, skilfulness, mastery, expertise, prowess, proficiency, ability, aptitude; excellence, brilliance, talent, genius, artistry, flair, panache, finesse, wizardry; informal know-how.

virtuoso noun *the pianist is clearly a virtuoso:* **genius**, expert, (past) master, maestro, artist, prodigy, marvel, adept, professional, doyen, veteran; star, champion; informal hotshot, wizard, pro, ace; Brit. informal dab hand.
– OPPOSITES duffer.
adjective *a virtuoso violinist:* **skilful**, expert, accomplished, masterly, master, consummate, proficient, talented, gifted, adept, able, good, competent, capable; impressive, outstanding, exceptional, magnificent, supreme, first-rate, brilliant, excellent; informal superb, mean, ace.
– OPPOSITES incompetent.

virtuous adjective *they were entirely virtuous in their endeavours:* **righteous**, good, moral, ethical, upright, upstanding, high-minded, principled, exemplary; law-abiding, irreproachable, blameless, guiltless, unimpeachable, honest, honourable, reputable, decent, respectable, noble, worthy, meritorious; pure, whiter than white, saintly, angelic; informal squeaky clean.

virulent adjective **1** *virulent herbicides:* **poisonous**, toxic, venomous, noxious, deadly, lethal, fatal, mortal, dangerous, harmful, injurious, pernicious, damaging, destructive. **2** *a virulent epidemic:* **infectious**, infective, contagious, communicable, transmittable, transmissible, spreading, pestilential; informal catching. **3** *a virulent attack on morals:* **vitriolic**, malicious, malevolent, hostile, spiteful, venomous, vicious, vindictive, bitter, rancorous, acrimonious, scathing, caustic, withering, nasty, savage, harsh.
– OPPOSITES harmless, amicable.

viscous adjective *viscous liquid had started to ooze across the floor:* **sticky**, gummy, gluey, adhesive, tacky, adherent, treacly, syrupy; glutinous, gelatinous, thick, viscid, mucous, mucoid, mucilaginous; informal gooey, gloopy; N. Amer. informal gloppy.

visible adjective *light from the fires was visible for many miles:* **perceptible**, perceivable, seeable, observable, noticeable, detectable, discernible; in sight, in/on view, on display; evident, apparent, manifest, transparent, plain, clear, conspicuous, obvious, patent, unmistakable, unconcealed, undisguised, prominent, salient, striking, glaring.

vision noun **1** *her vision was blurred by tears:* **eyesight**, sight, observation, (visual) perception; eyes; view, perspective. **2** *visions of the ancestral pilgrims:* **apparition**, spectre, phantom, ghost, wraith, manifestation; hallucination, illusion, mirage; informal spook. **3** *visions of a better future:* **dream**, daydream, reverie; plan, hope; fantasy, pipe dream, delusion. **4** *his speech lacked vision:* **imagination**, creativity, inventiveness, innovation, inspiration, intuition, perception, insight, foresight, prescience. **5** *Melissa was a vision in lilac:* **beautiful sight**, feast for the eyes, pleasure to behold, delight, dream, beauty, picture, joy, marvel, sensation; informal sight for sore eyes, stunner, knockout, looker, peach; Brit. informal smasher.

visionary adjective *a visionary leader:* **inspired**, imaginative, creative, inventive, ingenious, enterprising, innovative; insightful, perceptive, intuitive, prescient, discerning, shrewd, wise, clever, resourceful; idealistic, romantic, quixotic, dreamy; informal starry-eyed.
noun **1** *a visionary pictured him in hell:* **seer**, mystic, oracle, prophet(ess), soothsayer, augur, diviner, clairvoyant, crystal-gazer;

Scottish spaewife. **2** *a visionary can't run a business effectively:* **dreamer**, daydreamer, idealist, romantic, fantasist, utopian.

visit verb **1** *I visited my dear uncle:* **call on**, pay a visit to, go to see, look in on; stay with, holiday with; stop by, drop by; N. Amer. visit with, go see; informal pop in on, drop in on, look up. **2** *Alex was visiting America:* **stay in**, stop over in, spend time in, holiday in, vacation in; tour, explore, see; informal do. **3** *they were visited with many epidemics:* **afflict**, attack, trouble, torment.
noun **1** *she paid a visit to her mum:* **(social) call**. **2** *a visit to the museum:* **trip to**, tour of, look round; stopover, stay; holiday, break, vacation.

visitation noun **1** *the bishop's pastoral visitations:* **(official) visit**, tour of inspection, survey, examination. **2** *a visitation from God:* **apparition**, vision, appearance, manifestation, materialization. **3** *Jehovah punished them by visitations:* **affliction**, scourge, bane, curse, plague, blight, disaster, tragedy, catastrophe; punishment, retribution, vengeance.

visitor noun **1** *I am expecting a visitor:* **guest**, caller; company. **2** *the monument attracts foreign visitors:* **tourist**, traveller, holidaymaker, day tripper, tripper, vacationer, vacationist, sightseer; pilgrim; foreigner, outsider, stranger, alien; Brit. informal emmet, grockle.

vista noun *there's a marvellous vista from the hotel balcony:* **view**, prospect, panorama, aspect, perspective, spectacle, sight; scenery, landscape.

visual adjective **1** *visual defects:* **optical**, optic, ocular, eye; vision, sight. **2** *a visual indication that the alarm works:* **visible**, perceptible, perceivable, discernible.

visualize verb *it's not easy to visualize the future:* **envisage**, envision, conjure up, picture, call to mind, see, imagine, evoke, dream up, fantasize about, conceptualize, contemplate.

vital adjective **1** *it is vital that action is taken:* **essential**, of the essence, critical, crucial, indispensable, all-important, imperative, mandatory, urgent, pressing, burning, compelling, high-priority; informal earth-shattering, world-shaking. **2** *the vital organs:* **major**, main, chief; essential, necessary. **3** *he is young and vital:* **lively**, energetic, active, sprightly, spry, spirited, vivacious, exuberant, bouncy, enthusiastic, vibrant, zestful, sparkling, dynamic, vigorous, lusty, hale and hearty; informal peppy, spunky, full of beans, bright-eyed and bushy-tailed.
– OPPOSITES unimportant, minor, listless.

vitality noun **liveliness**, life, energy, spirit, vivacity, exuberance, buoyancy, bounce, verve, vim, pep, brio, zest, sparkle, dynamism, passion, fire, vigour, drive; informal get-up-and-go.

vitriolic adjective *he launched a vitriolic attack on the government:* **acrimonious**, rancorous, bitter, caustic, mordant, acerbic, trenchant, virulent, spiteful, savage, venomous, poisonous, malicious, splenetic; nasty, mean, cruel, unkind, harsh, vindictive, scathing, barbed, wounding, sharp, cutting, withering, sarcastic; informal bitchy, catty.

vivacious adjective *she was a pretty and vivacious brunette:* **lively**, spirited, bubbly, ebullient, buoyant, sparkling, light-hearted, jaunty, merry, happy, jolly, full of fun, cheery, cheerful, perky, sunny, breezy, enthusiastic, irrepressible, vibrant, vital, zestful, energetic, dynamic; informal peppy, bouncy, upbeat, chirpy.
– OPPOSITES dull.

vivid adjective **1** *a vivid blue sea:* **bright**, colourful, brilliant, radiant, vibrant, strong, bold, deep, intense, rich, warm. **2** *a vivid account of urban poverty:* **graphic**, evocative, realistic, lifelike, faithful, authentic, clear, detailed, lucid, striking, arresting, impressive, colourful, rich, dramatic, lively, stimulating, interesting, fascinating, scintillating; memorable, powerful, stirring, moving, haunting.
– OPPOSITES dull, vague.

viz. adverb *Article 1 sets out the purpose of the Charter, viz. to ensure the continuation of farming:* **namely**, that is to say, in other words, to wit, specifically; such as, as, like, for instance, for example.

vocabulary noun **1** *she has an extensive vocabulary:* **lexicon**, lexis. **2** *we listed the terms in a vocabulary:* **wordbook**, dictionary, wordfinder, glossary, lexicon, thesaurus.

vocal adjective **1** *vocal sounds:* **vocalized**, voiced, uttered, articulated, oral; spoken, said. **2** *a vocal critic of the government:* **vociferous**, outspoken, forthright, plain-spoken, blunt, frank, candid, open; vehement, vigorous, emphatic, insistent, forceful, zealous, clamorous.

vocation noun *his vocation as a clergyman was not eclipsed by his scientific career:* **calling**, life's work, mission, purpose, function; profession, occupation, career, job, employment, trade, craft, business, line (of work), métier.

vociferous adjective. See VOCAL sense 2.

vogue noun *the skirt is enjoying a new vogue:* **fashion**, trend, fad, fancy, craze, rage, enthusiasm, passion, obsession, mania; fashionableness, popularity, currency, favour; informal trendiness.
■ **in vogue** fashionable, voguish, stylish, modish, up to date, up to the minute, modern, current; prevalent, popular, in favour, in demand, sought-after, all the rage; chic, smart, le dernier cri; informal trendy, hip, cool, big, happening, now, in, with it; N. Amer. informal tony, kicky.

voice noun **1** *she lost her voice:* **power**

V

of speech. **2** *he gave voice to his anger:* **expression**, utterance, verbalization, vocalization. **3** *the voice of the people:* **opinion**, view, feeling, wish, desire, vote, input. **4** *a powerful voice for conservation:* **mouthpiece**, representative, spokesperson, intermediary; forum, vehicle, instrument, channel, organ, agent.
▸verb *they voiced their opposition:* **express**, vocalize, communicate, declare, state, assert, reveal, proclaim, announce, table, air, ventilate, vent; utter, say, speak, articulate; informal come out with.

void noun *the void of space:* **vacuum**, emptiness, nothingness, blankness, vacuity; (empty) space, gap, cavity, chasm, abyss, gulf, pit.
▸verb **1** *the contract was voided:* **invalidate**, annul, nullify; negate, quash, cancel, countermand, repeal, revoke, rescind, retract, withdraw, reverse, undo, abolish. **2** *they voided their bladders:* **evacuate**, empty, drain, clear, purge. **3** *bacteria are voided in the urine:* **eject**, expel, emit, discharge, pass, excrete, exude, eliminate.
– OPPOSITES validate, fill.
▸adjective **1** *vast void spaces:* **empty**, vacant, blank, bare, clear, free, unfilled, unoccupied, uninhabited. **2** *a country void of man or beast:* **devoid of**, empty of, vacant of, bereft of, free from; lacking, wanting, without. **3** *the election was void:* **invalid**, null, ineffective, non-viable, useless, worthless, nugatory.
– OPPOSITES full, occupied, valid.

volatile adjective **1** *a volatile personality:* **unpredictable**, changeable, variable, inconstant, inconsistent, erratic, irregular, unstable, turbulent, blowing hot and cold, varying, shifting, fluctuating, fluid, mutable; mercurial, capricious, whimsical, fickle, flighty, impulsive, temperamental, highly strung, excitable, emotional, fiery, moody, tempestuous. **2** *the atmosphere is too volatile for an election:* **tense**, strained, fraught, uneasy, uncomfortable, charged, explosive, inflammatory, turbulent; informal nail-biting; Brit. informal dodgy. **3** *a volatile organic compound:* **evaporative**, vaporous; explosive, inflammable; unstable, labile.
– OPPOSITES stable, calm.

volition
■ **of one's own volition** *they chose to leave early of their own volition:* of one's own free will, of one's own accord, by choice, by preference; voluntarily, willingly, readily, freely, intentionally, consciously, deliberately, on purpose, purposely; gladly, with pleasure.

volley noun *he fired off a volley of shots from his semi-automatic rifle:* **barrage**, cannonade, battery, bombardment, salvo, fusillade; storm, hail, shower, deluge, torrent; historical broadside.

voluble adjective *Mrs Maddox was as voluble as her husband was silent:*

talkative, loquacious, garrulous, verbose, wordy, chatty, gossipy, effusive, gushing, forthcoming, conversational, communicative, expansive; articulate, fluent; informal mouthy, gabby, gassy, windy.
– OPPOSITES taciturn.

volume noun **1** *a volume from the library:* **book**, publication, tome, hardback, paperback, title; manual, almanac, compendium. **2** *a glass syringe of known volume:* **capacity**, cubic measure, size, magnitude, mass, bulk, extent; dimensions, proportions, measurements. **3** *a huge volume of water:* **quantity**, amount, proportion, measure, mass, bulk. **4** *she turned the volume down:* **loudness**, sound, amplification.

voluminous adjective *he folded his arms into the voluminous sleeves of his robe:* **capacious**, roomy, spacious, ample, full, big, large, generous; billowing, baggy, loose-fitting.

voluntarily adverb *they signed a paper agreeing to leave the country voluntarily:* **of one's own free will**, of one's own accord, of one's own volition, by choice, by preference; willingly, readily, freely, intentionally, deliberately, on purpose, purposely, spontaneously; gladly, with pleasure.

voluntary adjective **1** *attendance is voluntary:* **optional**, discretionary, elective, non-compulsory, volitional. **2** *voluntary work:* **unpaid**, unsalaried, for free, without charge, for nothing; honorary, volunteer.
– OPPOSITES compulsory, paid.

volunteer verb **1** *I volunteered my services:* **offer**, tender, proffer, put forward, put up, venture. **2** *he volunteered as a driver:* **offer one's services**, present oneself, make oneself available.
▸noun *each volunteer was tested three times:* **subject**, participant, case, client, patient; informal guinea pig.

voluptuous adjective **1** *a voluptuous model:* **curvaceous**, shapely, ample, buxom, full-figured, Junoesque, Rubenesque; seductive, alluring, sultry, sensuous, sexy; informal curvy, busty, slinky. **2** *she was voluptuous by nature:* **hedonistic**, sybaritic, epicurean, pleasure-loving, self-indulgent; decadent, intemperate, immoderate, dissolute, sensual, licentious.
– OPPOSITES scrawny, ascetic.

vomit verb **1** *he needed to vomit:* **be sick**, spew, fetch up; heave, retch, reach, gag; N. Amer. get sick; informal throw up, puke, chunder, chuck up, hurl; Brit. informal honk; Scottish informal boke; N. Amer. informal barf, upchuck. **2** *I vomited my breakfast:* **regurgitate**, bring up, spew up, cough up; informal chuck up, throw up, puke; Brit. informal sick up; N. Amer. informal spit up.
▸noun *a coat stained with vomit:* **sick**; informal chunder, puke, spew; N. Amer. informal barf.

voracious adjective *boxer dogs have voracious appetites:* **insatiable**, unquenchable, unappeasable, prodigious, uncontrollable, compulsive, gluttonous, greedy, rapacious; enthusiastic, eager, keen, avid, desirous, hungry, ravenous; informal piggish.

vortex noun *a whirling vortex of buff-coloured smoke:* **whirlwind**, whirlpool, gyre, maelstrom, eddy, swirl.

vote noun **1** *a rigged vote:* **ballot**, poll, election, referendum, plebiscite; show of hands. **2** *in 1918 women got the vote:* **suffrage**, voting rights, franchise, enfranchisement; voice, say.
▶ verb **1** *only half of them voted:* **go to the polls**, cast one's vote. **2** *I vote we have one more game:* **suggest**, propose, recommend, advocate, move, table, submit.
■ **vote someone in** elect, return, select, choose, pick, adopt, appoint, designate, opt for, plump for, decide on.

vouch
■ **vouch for** *I can vouch for the veracity of his story:* **attest to**, confirm, affirm, verify, swear to, testify to, bear out, back up, support, stick up for, corroborate, substantiate, prove, uphold, give credence to, endorse, certify, warrant, validate.

voucher noun *a free travel voucher:* **coupon**, token, ticket, licence, permit, carnet, pass; chit, slip, stub, docket; Brit. informal chitty; N. Amer. informal ducat, comp.

vouchsafe verb **1** *the grace which God had vouchsafed him:* **grant**, give, accord; confer on, bestow on, favour with. **2** *you never vouchsafed that information before:* **disclose**, reveal, divulge, impart, give away, make known, broadcast, air; informal blab, spill; Brit. informal cough. **3** *if he would only vouchsafe to talk with them:* **deign**, condescend, stoop, lower oneself, humble oneself, demean oneself.
– OPPOSITES withhold, conceal.

vow noun *a vow of silence:* **oath**, pledge, promise, bond, covenant, commitment, avowal, profession, affirmation, attestation, assurance, guarantee; word (of honour).
▶ verb *I vowed to do better:* **swear**, pledge, promise, avow, undertake, engage, make a commitment, give one's word, guarantee.

voyage noun *the voyage lasted 120 days:* **journey**, trip, expedition, excursion, tour; hike, trek; pilgrimage, quest, crusade, odyssey; cruise, passage, flight, drive.
▶ verb *he voyaged through Peru:* **travel**, journey, tour, globetrot; sail, steam, cruise, fly, drive; informal gallivant.

vulgar adjective **1** *a vulgar joke:* **rude**, indecent, indelicate, offensive, distasteful, coarse, crude, ribald, risqué, naughty, suggestive, racy, earthy, off colour, bawdy, obscene, lewd, salacious, smutty, dirty, filthy, pornographic, X-rated; informal sleazy, raunchy, blue, locker-room; Brit. informal saucy, close to the bone; N. Amer. informal gamy; euphemistic adult. **2** *the decor was lavish but vulgar:* **tasteless**, crass, tawdry, ostentatious, flamboyant, overdone, showy, gaudy, garish, brassy, kitsch, tinselly, loud; informal flash, flashy, tacky, over the top. **3** *it was vulgar for a woman to whistle:* **impolite**, ill-mannered, unmannerly, indecorous, unseemly, ill-bred, boorish, uncouth, crude, rough; unsophisticated, unrefined, common.
– OPPOSITES tasteful, decorous.

vulnerable adjective **1** *a vulnerable city:* **in danger**, in peril, in jeopardy, at risk, endangered, unsafe, unprotected, unguarded; open to attack, assailable, exposed, wide open; undefended, unfortified, unarmed, defenceless, helpless, pregnable. **2** *he is vulnerable to criticism:* **exposed to**, open to, liable to, prone to, prey to, susceptible to, subject to, an easy target for.
– OPPOSITES resilient.

Ww

wacky adjective (informal). See ECCENTRIC adjective.

wad noun **1** *a wad of cotton wool:* **lump**, clump, mass, plug, pad, hunk, wedge, ball, cake, nugget; bit, piece; Brit. informal wodge. **2** *a wad of dollar bills:* **bundle**, roll, pile, stack, sheaf; N. Amer. bankroll. **3** *a wad of tobacco:* **quid**, twist, plug, chew.
verb *the teddy bear was wadded with cotton:* **stuff**, pad, fill, pack; wrap, cover, cushion.

wadding noun **stuffing**, filling, filler, packing, padding, cushioning, quilting.

waddle verb *he waddled forward to greet her:* **toddle**, dodder, totter, wobble, shuffle; duckwalk.

wade verb **1** *they waded in the icy water:* **paddle**, wallow, dabble, squelch; informal splosh. **2** *I had to wade through some hefty documents:* **plough**, plod, trawl, labour, toil; study, browse; informal slog.
■ **wade in** *police with truncheons waded in:* (informal) set to work, buckle down, go to it, put one's shoulder to the wheel; informal plunge in, dive in, get stuck in, get cracking.

waffle (Brit. informal) verb *they waffled on about the baby:* **prattle**, chatter, babble, ramble, jabber, gibber, gabble, prate, drivel; informal blather; Brit. informal rabbit, witter, natter.
noun *my panic reduced the interview to waffle:* **prattle**, drivel, nonsense, twaddle, gibberish, mumbo-jumbo; informal hot air, poppycock, bunk, hogwash, gobbledegook.

waft verb **1** *smoke wafted through the air:* **drift**, float, glide, whirl, travel. **2** *a breeze wafted the smell towards us:* **convey**, carry, transport, bear; blow, puff.

wag¹ verb **1** *the dog's tail wagged frantically:* **swing**, swish, switch, sway, shake, quiver, twitch, whip; informal waggle. **2** *he wagged his stick at them:* **shake**, wave, wiggle, flourish, brandish.
noun **1** *a feeble wag of her tail:* **swing**, shake, swish, switch, quiver, twitch, whip; informal waggle. **2** *a wag of the finger:* **shake**, flourish, wiggle, wobble, wave; informal waggle.

wag² noun (informal) *he's a bit of a wag.* See JOKER.

wage noun **1** *the farm workers' wages:* **pay**, payment, remuneration, salary, stipend, fee, honorarium; income, revenue; profit, gain, reward; earnings. **2** *the wages of sin is death:* **reward**, recompense, retribution; returns, deserts.
verb *they waged war on the guerrillas:* **engage in**, carry on, conduct, execute, pursue, prosecute, proceed with.

wager noun *a wager of £100:* **bet**, gamble, speculation; stake, pledge, ante; Brit. informal flutter.
verb *I'll wager a pound on the home team:* **bet**, gamble, lay odds, put money on; stake, pledge, risk, venture, hazard, chance; informal punt.

waif noun **ragamuffin**, urchin; foundling, orphan, stray; derogatory guttersnipe.

wail noun *a wail of anguish:* **howl**, bawl, yowl, cry, moan, groan; shriek, scream, yelp.
verb *the children began to wail:* **howl**, weep, cry, sob, moan, groan, keen, lament, yowl, snivel, whimper, whine, bawl, shriek, scream, yelp, caterwaul; Scottish greet; informal blubber, blub.

wait verb **1** *we'll wait in the airport:* **stay (put)**, remain, rest, stop, halt, pause; linger, loiter, dally; informal stick around. **2** *she had to wait until her bags arrived:* **stand by**, hold back, bide one's time, hang fire, mark time, kill time, waste time, kick one's heels, twiddle one's thumbs; informal hold on, hang around, sit tight, hold one's horses. **3** *they were waiting for the kettle to boil:* **await**; anticipate, expect, be ready. **4** *that job will have to wait:* **be postponed**, be delayed, be put off, be deferred; informal be put on the back burner, be put on ice.
noun *there can be a long wait to see a doctor:* **delay**, hold-up, interval, interlude, intermission, pause, break, stay, cessation, suspension, stoppage, halt, interruption, lull, respite, recess, moratorium, hiatus, gap, rest.
■ **wait on someone** *the men ate in silence, waited on by the two girls:* serve, attend to, tend, cater for/to; minister to, take care of, look after, see to.
■ **wait up** *I'll be back late—don't wait up for me:* stay awake, stay up.

waiter, waitress noun *the waiter came to take their order:* **server**, stewardess, steward, attendant, garçon; hostess, host; butler, servant, page; N. Amer. waitperson.

waive verb **1** *he waived his right to a hearing:* **relinquish**, renounce, give up, abandon, surrender, yield, reject, dispense with, abdicate, sacrifice, refuse, turn down, spurn. **2** *the manager waived the rules:* **disregard**, ignore, overlook, set aside, forgo, drop.

wake[1] verb **1** *at 4.30 am Mark woke up:*
awake, waken (up), awaken, rouse oneself,
stir, come to, come round, bestir oneself; get
up, get out of bed. **2** *she woke her husband:*
rouse, arouse, waken; Brit. informal knock up.
3 *the shock woke him up a bit:* **activate**,
stimulate, galvanize, enliven, stir up, spur
on, ginger up, buoy up, invigorate, revitalize;
informal perk up, pep up. **4** *they woke up to
what we were saying:* **realize**, become aware
of, become conscious of, become mindful of.
5 *the name woke an old memory:* **evoke**,
conjure up, rouse, stir, revive, awaken,
rekindle, rejuvenate, stimulate.
– OPPOSITES sleep.
noun *a mourner at a wake:* **vigil**, watch;
funeral.

wake[2] noun *the cruiser's wake:* **backwash**,
wash, slipstream, turbulence; trail, path.
■ **in the wake of** in the aftermath of, after,
subsequent to, following, as a result of, as a
consequence of, on account of, because of,
owing to.

wakeful adjective **1** *he had been wakeful all
night:* **awake**, restless, restive, tossing and
turning. **2** *I was suddenly wakeful:* **alert**,
watchful, vigilant, on the lookout, on one's
guard, attentive, heedful, wary.
– OPPOSITES asleep, inattentive.

waken verb. See WAKE[1] verb senses 1, 2.

Wales noun Cambria; Brit. the Principality.

walk verb **1** *they walked along the road:*
stroll, saunter, amble, trudge, plod, hike,
tramp, trek, march, stride, troop, patrol,
step out, wander, ramble, tread, prowl,
footslog, promenade, roam, traipse; stretch
one's legs; informal mosey, pootle, hoof it;
Brit. informal yomp. **2** *he walked her home:*
accompany, escort, guide, show, see, usher,
take, chaperone, steer, shepherd.
noun **1** *country walks:* **stroll**, saunter, amble,
promenade; ramble, hike, tramp, march;
turn, airing. **2** *her elegant walk:* **gait**, step,
stride, tread. **3** *the riverside walk:* **pathway**,
path, footpath, track, walkway, promenade,
footway, pavement, trail, towpath.
■ **walk all over someone** (informal) be firm
or they'll walk all over you: take advantage
of, impose on, exploit, use, abuse, misuse,
manipulate, take liberties with; informal take
for a ride, run rings around.
■ **walk off/away with** *he walked off with
four awards:* win easily, win hands down,
attain, earn, gain, receive, acquire, secure,
collect, pick up, net; informal bag.
■ **walk of life** class, status, rank, caste,
sphere, arena; profession, career, vocation,
job, occupation, employment, business,
trade, craft; province, field.
■ **walk out 1** *he walked out in a temper:*
leave, depart, get up and go, storm off/out,
flounce out, absent oneself; informal take off.
2 *teachers walked out in protest:* (go on)
strike, stop work; protest, mutiny, revolt;
Brit. informal down tools.
■ **walk out on someone** *he walked out*

on his pregnant girlfriend: desert, abandon,
leave, betray, throw over, jilt, run out on, rat
on; informal chuck, dump, ditch.

walker noun **hiker**, rambler, traveller,
roamer, rover, stroller; pedestrian.

walkout noun *a one-day walkout by 200
workers:* **strike**, stoppage, industrial action;
revolt, rebellion.

walkover noun *away games are never a
walkover:* **easy victory**, rout, landslide;
informal piece of cake, doddle, pushover,
cinch, breeze, picnic, low-hanging fruit,
whitewash; N. Amer. informal duck soup.

wall noun **1** *brick walls:* **barrier**, partition,
enclosure, screen, panel, separator. **2** *an
ancient city wall:* **fortification**, rampart,
barricade, bulwark, stockade. **3** *break down
the walls that stop world trade:* **obstacle**,
barrier, fence; impediment, hindrance,
block, check.
verb **1** *tenements walled in the courtyard:*
enclose, bound, encircle, confine, hem, close
in, shut in, fence in. **2** *the doorway had been
walled up:* **block**, seal, close, brick up.

wallet noun **purse**; N. Amer. billfold,
pocketbook.

wallow verb **1** *buffalo wallowed in the lake:*
loll about/around, lie about/around, splash
about/around; slosh, wade, paddle; informal
splosh. **2** *a ship wallowing in stormy seas:*
roll, lurch, toss, plunge, reel, rock, flounder,
keel, list; labour. **3** *she seems to wallow in
self-pity:* **luxuriate**, bask, take pleasure,
take satisfaction, indulge (oneself), delight,
revel, glory; enjoy, like, love, relish, savour;
informal get a kick out of, get a buzz from.

wan adjective **1** *she looked so wan and frail:*
pale, pallid, ashen, white, grey; anaemic,
colourless, bloodless, waxen, chalky, pasty,
peaky, sickly, washed out, drained, drawn,
ghostly. **2** *the wan light of the moon:* **dim**,
faint, weak, feeble, pale, watery.
– OPPOSITES flushed, bright.

wand noun *a magic wand:* **baton**, stick, staff,
bar, dowel, rod; twig, cane, birch, switch.

wander verb **1** *I wandered around the estate:*
stroll, amble, saunter, walk, dawdle, potter,
ramble, meander; roam, rove, range, drift,
prowl; Scottish & Irish stravaig; informal traipse,
mosey, tootle; Brit. informal mooch. **2** *we are
wandering from the point:* **stray**, depart,
diverge, veer, swerve, deviate, digress, drift,
get sidetracked. **3** *the child wandered off:*
get lost, lose one's way, go astray. **4** *the road
wanders along the shore:* **meander**, wind,
twist, curve, zigzag, bend, snake.
noun *let's go for a wander:* **stroll**, amble,
saunter, walk, potter, ramble, prowl;
promenade; turn, breather, airing; informal
traipse, mosey, tootle; Brit. informal mooch.

wanderer noun *a wanderer in the wilderness:*
traveller, rambler, hiker, migrant,
globetrotter, roamer, rover; itinerant,
rolling stone, bird of passage, nomad; tramp,
drifter, vagabond, vagrant; Brit. informal dosser;

w

N. Amer. informal. **hobo, bum.**

wane verb 1 *the moon is waning:* **decrease**, diminish, dwindle. 2 *their support was waning:* **decline**, diminish, decrease, dwindle, shrink, tail off, ebb, fade (away), lessen, peter out, fall off, recede, slump, flag, weaken, give way, wither, evaporate, die out.
– OPPOSITES wax, grow.
■ **on the wane** declining, decreasing, diminishing, dwindling, shrinking, contracting, tapering off, subsiding, ebbing, fading away, dissolving, petering out, winding down, falling off, on the way out, receding, flagging, melting away, crumbling, withering, disintegrating, evaporating, dying out.

want verb *do you want more coffee?* **desire**, wish for, hope for, fancy, care for, like; long for, yearn for, crave, hanker after, hunger for, thirst for, cry out for, covet; need; informal have a yen for, be dying for.
noun 1 *his want of vigilance:* **lack**, absence, non-existence, unavailability; dearth, deficiency, inadequacy, insufficiency, paucity, shortage, scarcity, deficit. 2 *a time of want:* **need**, neediness, austerity, privation, deprivation, poverty, impoverishment, penury, destitution; famine, drought. 3 *all her wants would be taken care of:* **wish**, desire, demand, longing, yearning, fancy, craving, hankering; need, requirement; informal yen.

wanting adjective 1 *the defences were found wanting:* **deficient**, inadequate, lacking, insufficient, imperfect, unacceptable, flawed, faulty, defective, unsound, substandard, inferior, second-rate, poor, shoddy; Brit. informal not much cop. 2 *the kneecap is wanting in amphibians:* **absent**, missing, lacking, non-existent. 3 *millions were left wanting for food:* **without**, lacking, deprived of, devoid of, bereft of, in need of; deficient in, short on; informal minus.
– OPPOSITES sufficient, present.

wanton adjective 1 *wanton destruction:* **deliberate**, wilful, malicious, spiteful, wicked, cruel; gratuitous, unprovoked, motiveless, arbitrary, groundless, unjustifiable, needless, unnecessary, uncalled for, senseless, pointless, purposeless, meaningless, empty. 2 *a wanton seductress:* **promiscuous**, immoral, immodest, indecent, shameless, unchaste, fast, impure, abandoned, lustful, lecherous, lascivious, libidinous, licentious, dissolute, debauched, degenerate, corrupt, whorish, disreputable.
– OPPOSITES justifiable, chaste.

war noun 1 *the Napoleonic Wars:* **conflict**, warfare, combat, fighting, (military) action, bloodshed, struggle; battle, skirmish, fight, clash, engagement, encounter; offensive, attack, campaign; hostilities; jihad, crusade. 2 *the war against drugs:* **campaign**, crusade, battle, fight, struggle, movement, drive.
– OPPOSITES peace.
verb *rival emperors warred against each other:* **fight**, battle, combat, wage war, take up arms; feud, quarrel, struggle, contend, wrangle, cross swords; attack, engage, take on, skirmish with.

warble verb *larks warbled in the sky:* **trill**, sing, chirp, chirrup, cheep, twitter, tweet, chatter, peep.
noun *a warble pierced the air:* **trill**, song, chirp, chirrup, chirr, cheep, twitter, tweet, chatter, peep, call.

ward noun 1 *the surgical ward:* **room**, department, unit, area. 2 *the most marginal ward in Westminster:* **district**, constituency, division, quarter, zone, parish. 3 *the boy is my ward:* **dependant**, charge, protégé.
■ **ward someone off** *Kelly held out a hand to ward him off:* fend off, repel, repulse, beat back, chase away; informal send packing.
■ **ward something off** 1 *she warded off the blow:* parry, avert, deflect, block; evade, avoid, dodge. 2 *garlic is worn to ward off evil spirits:* rebuff, avert, keep at bay, fend off, stave off, resist, prevent, obstruct, foil, frustrate, thwart, check, stop.

warden noun 1 *the flats have a resident warden:* **superintendent**, caretaker, janitor, porter, custodian, watchman, concierge, doorman. 2 *a game warden:* **ranger**, custodian, keeper, guardian, protector. 3 *he was handcuffed to a warden:* **prison officer**, guard, jailer, warder, wardress, keeper, sentry; informal screw. 4 (Brit.) *the college warden:* **principal**, head, governor, master, mistress, rector, provost, president, director, chancellor; N. Amer. informal prexy.

warder, wardress noun. See WARDEN sense 3.

wardrobe noun 1 *she opened the wardrobe:* **cupboard**, cabinet, locker; N. Amer. closet. 2 *her wardrobe has an outfit for every mood:* **collection of clothes**; garments, attire, outfits; trousseau.

warehouse noun *a furniture warehouse:* **storeroom**, storehouse, store, depot, depository, stockroom; magazine; granary; informal lock-up.

wares plural noun **merchandise**, goods, products, produce, stock, commodities; lines, range.

warfare noun *the reality of modern warfare:* **fighting**, war, combat, conflict, (military) action, hostilities; bloodshed, battles, skirmishes.

warlike adjective *a warlike ruler:* **aggressive**, belligerent, warring, bellicose, pugnacious, combative, bloodthirsty, jingoistic, sabre-rattling; hostile, threatening, quarrelsome; militaristic, militant; informal gung-ho.

warlock noun **sorcerer**, wizard, magus, (black) magician, enchanter.

warm adjective 1 *a warm kitchen:* **hot**, cosy, snug; informal toasty. 2 *a warm day in spring:* **balmy**, summery, sultry, hot,

mild, temperate; sunny, fine. **3** *warm water:* **heated**, tepid, lukewarm. **4** *a warm sweater:* **thick**, chunky, thermal, winter, woolly. **5** *a warm welcome:* **friendly**, cordial, amiable, genial, kind, pleasant, fond; welcoming, hospitable, benevolent, benign, charitable; sincere, genuine, wholehearted, heartfelt, enthusiastic, eager, hearty.
– OPPOSITES cold, chilly, light, hostile.
verb *warm the soup in that pan:* **heat (up)**, reheat, cook; thaw (out), melt; N. Amer. warm over; informal zap; Brit. informal hot up.
– OPPOSITES chill.

■ **warm to/towards 1** *everyone warmed to him:* like, take to, get on (well) with, hit it off with, be on good terms with. **2** *he couldn't warm to the notion:* be enthusiastic about, be supportive of, be excited about.

■ **warm up** *if you don't warm up first you can easily pull a muscle:* limber up, loosen up, stretch, work out, exercise; prepare, rehearse.

■ **warm someone up** *the compère warmed up the crowd:* enliven, liven, stimulate, animate, rouse, stir, excite; informal get going.

warm-blooded adjective *a warm-blooded woman:* **passionate**, ardent, red-blooded, emotional, intense, impetuous, lively, spirited, fiery, tempestuous.
– OPPOSITES reserved.

warmed-up adjective **1** *a warmed-up pasty:* **reheated**; N. Amer. warmed-over. **2** *warmed-up ideas:* **unoriginal**, derivative, imitative, uninspired; copied, plagiarized, rehashed; hackneyed, stale, tired, banal; informal old hat.
– OPPOSITES original.

warm-hearted adjective *she's a very warm-hearted person:* **kind**, warm, big-hearted, tender-hearted, tender, loving, caring, feeling, unselfish, selfless, benevolent, humane, good-natured; friendly, sympathetic, understanding, compassionate, charitable, generous.

warmonger noun *a trigger-happy warmonger:* **militarist**, hawk, jingoist, sabre-rattler, aggressor, belligerent.

warmth noun **1** *the warmth of the fire:* **heat**, warmness, hotness; cosiness. **2** *the warmth of their welcome:* **friendliness**, amiability, geniality, cordiality, kindness, tenderness, fondness; benevolence, charity; enthusiasm, eagerness, ardour, fervour, effusiveness.

warn verb **1** *David warned her that it was too late:* **notify**, alert, apprise, inform, tell, make someone aware, forewarn, remind; informal tip off, put wise. **2** *police are warning galleries to be alert:* **advise**, exhort, urge, counsel, caution.

warning noun **1** *the earthquake came without warning:* **(advance) notice**, forewarning, alert; hint, signal, sign, alarm bells; informal a tip-off. **2** *cigarette packets are required to carry a health warning:* **caution**, notification, information; exhortation; injunction; advice. **3** *a warning of things to come:* **omen**, premonition, foreboding,

prophecy, prediction, forecast, token, portent, signal, sign. **4** *his sentence is a warning to other drunk-drivers:* **example**, deterrent, lesson, caution, exemplar, message, moral. **5** *a further complaint may lead to a written warning:* **admonition**, caution, remonstrance, reprimand, censure; informal dressing-down, talking-to, telling-off.

warp verb **1** *timber which is too dry will warp:* **buckle**, twist, bend, distort, deform, misshape, malform, curve, bow, contort. **2** *he warped the mind of her child:* **corrupt**, twist, pervert, deprave.
– OPPOSITES straighten.

warrant noun **1** *a warrant for his arrest:* **authorization**, order, licence, permit, document; writ, summons, subpoena; mandate, decree, fiat, edict. **2** *a travel warrant:* **voucher**, chit, slip, ticket, coupon, pass.
verb **1** *the charges warranted a severe sentence:* **justify**, vindicate, call for, sanction, validate; permit, authorize; deserve, excuse, account for, legitimize; support, license, approve of; merit, qualify for, rate, be worthy of, be deserving of. **2** *we warrant that the texts do not infringe copyright:* **guarantee**, affirm, swear, promise, vow, pledge, undertake, state, assert, declare, profess, attest; vouch, testify, bear witness.

warranty noun *a three-year warranty:* **guarantee**, assurance, promise, commitment, undertaking, agreement.

warring adjective *envoys for peace are trying to bring the warring factions together:* **opposing**, conflicting, at war, fighting, battling, quarrelling; competing, hostile, rival.

warrior noun *fearsome warriors:* **fighter**, soldier, serviceman, combatant.

wary adjective **1** *he was trained to be wary:* **cautious**, careful, circumspect, on one's guard, chary, alert, on the lookout, on one's toes, on the qui vive; attentive, heedful, watchful, vigilant, observant; informal wide awake. **2** *we are wary of strangers:* **suspicious**, chary, leery, careful, distrustful, mistrustful, sceptical, doubtful, dubious.
– OPPOSITES inattentive, trustful.

wash verb **1** *he washed in the bath:* **clean oneself**, have a wash; bathe, bath, shower, soak, freshen up. **2** *she washed her hands:* **clean**, cleanse, sponge, scrub, wipe, scour; shampoo, lather; sluice, swill, douse, swab, disinfect. **3** *she washed off the blood:* **remove**, expunge, eradicate; sponge off, scrub off, wipe off, rinse off. **4** *the women were washing clothes:* **launder**, clean, rinse. **5** *waves washed against the hull:* **splash**, lap, splosh, dash, break, beat, surge, ripple, roll. **6** *the wreckage was washed up downriver:* **sweep**, carry, convey, transport; deposit. **7** *guilt washed over her:* **affect**, rush through, surge through, course through, flood over, flow over.

W

– OPPOSITES dirty, soil.

noun 1 *she needs a wash:* **clean**, shower, dip, bath, soak. **2** *that shirt should go in the wash:* **laundry**, washing. **3** *antiseptic skin wash:* **lotion**, salve, preparation, rinse, liquid; liniment, embrocation. **4** *the wash of a motor boat:* **backwash**, wake, trail, path. **5** *the wash of the waves on the beach:* **surge**, flow, swell, sweep, rise and fall, roll, splash. **6** *water thinned out the crayon into a wash:* **paint**, stain, film.

■ **wash something away** *about two acres of land has been washed away:* erode, abrade, wear away, eat away, undermine.

■ **wash one's hands of** disown, renounce, reject, forswear, disavow, give up on, turn one's back on, cast aside, abandon.

■ **wash up** wash the dishes, do the dishes, do the washing-up.

waspish adjective *she sounded waspish and impatient:* **irritable**, touchy, testy, cross, snappish, cantankerous, splenetic, short-tempered, bad-tempered, moody, crotchety, crabby, ratty; informal grouchy.

waste verb **1** *he doesn't like to waste money:* **squander**, misspend, misuse, fritter away, throw away, lavish, dissipate, throw around; informal blow, splurge. **2** *kids are wasting away in the streets:* **grow weak**, grow thin, shrink, decline, wilt, fade, flag, deteriorate, degenerate, languish. **3** *the disease wasted his legs:* **emaciate**, atrophy, wither, debilitate, shrivel, shrink, weaken, enfeeble.

– OPPOSITES conserve, thrive.

adjective **1** *waste material:* **unwanted**, excess, superfluous, left over, scrap, useless, worthless; unusable, unprofitable. **2** *waste ground:* **uncultivated**, barren, desert, arid, bare; desolate, void, uninhabited, unpopulated; wild.

noun **1** *a waste of money:* **misuse**, misapplication, misemployment, abuse; extravagance, wastefulness, lavishness. **2** *household waste:* **rubbish**, refuse, litter, debris, dross, junk, detritus, scrap; dregs, scraps; sewage, effluent; N. Amer. garbage, trash. **3** *the frozen wastes of the South Pole:* **desert**, wasteland, wilderness, emptiness, wilds.

■ **lay waste**. See LAY¹.

wasted adjective **1** *it was all wasted effort:* **squandered**, misspent, misdirected, misused, dissipated; pointless, useless, needless, unnecessary. **2** *a wasted opportunity:* **missed**, lost, forfeited, neglected, squandered, bungled; informal down the drain. **3** *I'm wasted in this job:* **underemployed**, underused, too good for; neglected, forgotten, disregarded. **4** *his wasted legs:* **emaciated**, atrophied, withered, shrivelled, weak, frail, shrunken, skeletal, rickety, scrawny, wizened.

wasteful adjective *wasteful use of energy in the home:* **prodigal**, profligate, uneconomical, extravagant, lavish,

excessive, imprudent, improvident; thriftless, spendthrift; needless, useless.

– OPPOSITES frugal.

wasteland noun *he turned the land into a desolate wasteland:* **wilderness**, desert; wilds, wastes, badlands.

watch verb **1** *she watched him as he spoke:* **observe**, view, look at, eye, gaze at, stare at, gape at, peer at; contemplate, survey, keep an eye on; inspect, scrutinize, scan, examine, study, ogle, regard, mark; informal check out, get a load of, recce, eyeball; Brit. informal have a butcher's at. **2** *he was being watched by the police:* **spy on**, keep in sight, track, monitor, survey, follow, keep under surveillance; informal keep tabs on, stake out. **3** *will you watch the kids?* **look after**, mind, keep an eye on, take care of, supervise, tend, attend to. **4** *we stayed to watch the boat:* **guard**, protect, shield, defend, safeguard; cover, patrol, police. **5** *watch what you say:* **be careful**, mind, be aware of, pay attention to, consider, pay heed to.

– OPPOSITES ignore, neglect.

noun **1** *Bill looked at his watch:* **timepiece**, chronometer; wristwatch, pocket watch, stopwatch. **2** *we kept watch on the yacht:* **guard**, vigil, lookout, an eye; observation, surveillance, vigilance.

■ **watch out/it/yourself** be careful, be watchful, be on your guard, beware, be wary, be cautious, mind out, look out, pay attention, take heed, take care, keep an eye open/out, keep one's eyes peeled, be vigilant.

watchdog noun **1** *they use watchdogs to ward off trespassers:* **guard dog**. **2** *a consumer watchdog:* **ombudsman**, monitor, scrutineer, inspector, supervisor; custodian, guardian, protector.

watchful adjective *her mother kept a watchful eye on her:* **observant**, alert, vigilant, attentive, awake, aware, heedful, sharp-eyed, eagle-eyed; on the lookout, on the qui vive, wary, cautious, careful, chary.

watchman noun **security guard**, custodian, warden; sentry, guard, patrolman, lookout, sentinel, scout, watch.

watchword noun *efficiency in all things was the watchword:* **guiding principle**, motto, slogan, maxim, mantra, catchword, catchphrase, byword; informal buzzword.

water noun *a house down by the water:* **sea**, ocean; lake, river.

verb **1** *water the plants:* **sprinkle**, moisten, dampen, wet, spray, splash; soak, douse, souse, drench, saturate; hose (down). **2** *my mouth watered:* **moisten**, become wet, leak; salivate.

■ **hold water** be tenable, ring true, bear scrutiny, make sense, stand up, hold up, be convincing, be plausible, be sound.

■ **water something down 1** *staff had watered down the drinks:* dilute, water, thin (out), weaken; adulterate, doctor, mix; informal cut. **2** *the proposals were watered* *down:* moderate, temper, mitigate, tone down, soften, tame; understate, play down, soft-pedal.

waterfall noun **cascade**, cataract, falls, rapids; N. English force.

waterproof adjective *a waterproof jacket:* **watertight**, water-repellent, water-resistant, damp-proof; impermeable, impervious; rubberized, waxed.
noun (Brit.) *she put on a waterproof:* **raincoat**, anorak, oilskin, cagoule; Brit. mackintosh; Brit. informal mac.

watertight adjective **1** *a watertight container:* **impermeable**, impervious, (hermetically) sealed; waterproof, water-repellent, water-resistant, damp-proof. **2** *a watertight alibi:* **indisputable**, unquestionable, incontrovertible, irrefutable, unassailable, impregnable; foolproof, sound, flawless, airtight, conclusive.
– OPPOSITES leaky, flawed.

watery adjective **1** *a watery discharge:* **liquid**, fluid, aqueous. **2** *a watery meadow:* **wet**, damp, moist, sodden, soggy, squelchy, soft; saturated, waterlogged; boggy, marshy, swampy, miry, muddy. **3** *watery porridge:* **thin**, runny, weak, sloppy, dilute, diluted; tasteless, flavourless, insipid, bland. **4** *the light was watery and grey:* **pale**, wan, faint, weak, feeble; informal wishy-washy. **5** *watery eyes:* **tearful**, teary, weepy, moist, rheumy.
– OPPOSITES dry, thick, bright.

wave verb **1** *he waved his flag furiously:* **move up and down**, move to and fro, wag, shake, swish, sweep, swing, brandish, flourish, wield; flick, flutter; informal waggle. **2** *the grass waved in the breeze:* **ripple**, flutter, undulate, stir, flap, sway, shake, quiver, move. **3** *the waiter waved them over:* **gesture**, gesticulate, signal, beckon, motion.
noun **1** *she gave him a friendly wave:* **gesture**, gesticulation; signal, sign, motion. **2** *he surfs the big waves:* **breaker**, roller, comber, boomer, ripple, white horse; (**waves**) swell, surf, froth; Austral. bombora. **3** *a wave of emigration:* **flow**, rush, surge, flood, stream, tide, deluge, spate. **4** *a wave of self-pity:* **surge**, rush, stab, dart, upsurge; thrill, frisson; feeling. **5** *his hair grew in thick waves:* **curl**, kink, corkscrew, twist, ringlet, coil. **6** *electromagnetic waves:* **vibration**, oscillation, ripple.
■ **wave something aside** he waved aside her protest: dismiss, reject, brush aside, shrug off, disregard, ignore, discount, play down; informal pooh-pooh.
■ **wave someone/something down** he waved down a taxi and drove off: flag down, hail, stop, summon, call, accost.

waver verb **1** *the candlelight wavered in the draught:* **flicker**, quiver, twinkle, glimmer, wink, blink. **2** *his voice wavered:* **falter**, wobble, tremble, quaver. **3** *he wavered between the choices:* **be undecided**, be irresolute, hesitate, dither, equivocate,

vacillate, fluctuate; think twice, change one's mind, blow hot and cold; Brit. haver, hum and haw; informal shilly-shally, sit on the fence.

wavy adjective *the leaf has a wavy edge:* **curly**, curvy, curved, undulating, squiggly, rippled, crinkly, kinked, zigzag.

wax verb *the moon is waxing:* **get bigger**, increase, enlarge.
– OPPOSITES wane.

waxen adjective *the waxen pallor of a corpse:* **pallid**, pale, pasty, wan, ashen, colourless, anaemic, bloodless, washed out, white, grey, whitish, waxy, drained, sickly.
– OPPOSITES ruddy.

way noun **1** *a way of reducing the damage:* **method**, process, procedure, technique, system; plan, strategy, scheme; means, mechanism, approach. **2** *she kissed him in her brisk way:* **manner**, style, fashion, mode; modus operandi, MO. **3** *I've changed my ways:* **practice**, wont, habit, custom, policy, procedure, convention, routine, modus vivendi; trait, attribute, peculiarity, idiosyncrasy; conduct, behaviour, manner, style, nature, personality, temperament, disposition, character. **4** *which way leads home?* **route**, course, direction; road, street, track, path. **5** *I'll go out the back way:* **door**, gate, exit, entrance, entry; route. **6** *a short way downstream:* **distance**, length, stretch, journey; space, interval, span. **7** *April is a long way away:* **time**, stretch, term, span, duration. **8** *a car coming the other way:* **direction**, bearing, course, orientation, line, tack. **9** *in some ways, he may be better off:* **respect**, regard, aspect, facet, sense; detail, point, particular. **10** *the country is in a bad way:* **state**, condition, situation, circumstances, position; predicament, plight; informal shape.
■ **by the way** incidentally, by the by, in passing, en passant.
■ **give way 1** the government gave way and passed the bill: yield, back down, surrender, concede defeat, give in, submit, succumb; acquiesce, agree, assent; informal throw in the towel/sponge, cave in. **2** the door gave way: collapse, give, cave in, fall in, come apart, crumple. **3** grief gave way to guilt: be replaced by, be succeeded by, be followed by, be supplanted by.
■ **on the way** the doctor's on his way: coming, imminent, forthcoming, approaching, impending, close, near, on us; proceeding, en route, in transit.

waylay verb **1** *we were waylaid and robbed:* **ambush**, hold up, attack, assail, rob; informal mug, stick up. **2** *several people waylaid her to chat:* **accost**, detain, intercept, take aside, pounce on, importune; informal buttonhole.

wayward adjective *a wayward child:* **wilful**, headstrong, stubborn, obstinate, obdurate, perverse, contrary, disobedient, insubordinate, undisciplined; rebellious, defiant, uncooperative, recalcitrant, unruly,

wild, unmanageable, erratic; difficult,
impossible.
– OPPOSITES docile.

weak adjective **1** *they are too weak to move:*
frail, feeble, delicate, fragile; infirm,
sick, sickly, debilitated, incapacitated,
ailing, indisposed, decrepit; tired, fatigued,
exhausted; informal weedy. **2** *bats have weak
eyes:* **inadequate**, poor, feeble; defective,
faulty, deficient, imperfect, substandard.
3 *a weak excuse:* **unconvincing**, untenable,
tenuous, implausible, unsatisfactory,
poor, inadequate, feeble, flimsy, lame,
hollow; informal pathetic. **4** *I was too weak
to be a rebel:* **spineless**, craven, cowardly,
pusillanimous, timid; irresolute, indecisive,
ineffectual, inept, effete, meek, tame,
ineffective, impotent, soft, faint-hearted;
informal yellow, weak-kneed, gutless, chicken.
5 *a weak light:* **dim**, pale, wan, faint, feeble,
muted. **6** *a weak voice:* **indistinct**, muffled,
muted, hushed, faint, low. **7** *weak coffee:*
watery, diluted, dilute, watered down, thin,
tasteless, flavourless, bland, insipid, wishy-
washy. **8** *a weak smile:* **unenthusiastic**,
feeble, half-hearted, lame.
– OPPOSITES strong, powerful, convincing,
resolute, bright, loud.

weaken verb **1** *the virus weakened him
terribly:* **enfeeble**, debilitate, incapacitate,
sap, enervate, tire, exhaust, wear out;
wither, cripple, disable. **2** *she tried to
weaken the shock for him:* **reduce**, decrease,
diminish, lessen, moderate, temper, dilute,
blunt, mitigate, soften. **3** *our morale
weakened:* **decrease**, dwindle, diminish,
wane, ebb, subside, peter out, fizzle out, tail
off, decline, falter. **4** *the move weakened her
authority:* **impair**, undermine, compromise;
invalidate, negate, discredit.

weakling noun *a nine-stone weakling:*
milksop, namby-pamby, coward, pushover;
informal wimp, weed, sissy, drip, softie,
doormat, chicken, yellow-belly, scaredy-cat;
N. Amer. informal wuss, pussy.

weakness noun **1** *with old age
came weakness:* **frailty**, feebleness,
enfeeblement, fragility, delicacy;
infirmity, sickness, sickliness, debility,
incapacity, indisposition, decrepitude;
informal weediness. **2** *he has worked on
his weaknesses:* **fault**, flaw, defect,
deficiency, weak point, failing, shortcoming,
imperfection, Achilles' heel. **3** *a weakness
for champagne:* **fondness**, liking, partiality,
preference, love, penchant, soft spot,
predilection, inclination, taste, eye;
enthusiasm, appetite. **4** *the President was
accused of weakness:* **timidity**, cravenness,
cowardliness, pusillanimity; indecision,
irresolution, ineffectuality, ineptitude,
meekness, powerlessness, ineffectiveness,
impotence. **5** *the weakness of this argument:*
untenability, implausibility, poverty,
inadequacy, transparency; flimsiness,
hollowness. **6** *the weakness of the sound:*

indistinctness, mutedness, faintness,
feebleness, lowness; dimness, paleness.

weak-willed adjective *I was too weak-willed
to continue:* **spineless**, weak, irresolute,
indecisive; impressionable, persuadable,
persuasible, submissive, unassertive,
compliant, pusillanimous; informal wimpish,
chicken.

weal noun *blood dripped from a weal on his
shoulders:* **welt**, wound, lesion, swelling;
scar, cicatrix, mark, blemish.

wealth noun **1** *a gentleman of wealth:*
affluence, prosperity, riches, means,
substance, fortune; money, cash,
lucre, capital, treasure, finance; assets,
possessions, resources, funds; property,
stock, reserves, securities, holdings; informal
wherewithal, dough, bread. **2** *a wealth
of information:* **abundance**, profusion,
plethora, mine, store, treasury, bounty,
cornucopia; informal lot, load, heap, mass,
mountain, stack, ton; Brit. informal shedload.
– OPPOSITES poverty, dearth.

wealthy adjective *he enjoyed the company of
wealthy people:* **rich**, affluent, moneyed, well
off, well-to-do, prosperous, comfortable,
propertied; of substance; informal well heeled,
rolling in it, in the money, made of money,
filthy rich, stinking rich, loaded, flush, quids
in; Austral./NZ informal financial.
– OPPOSITES poor.

wear verb **1** *he wore a suit:* **dress in**, be
clothed in, have on, sport; put on, don.
2 *Barbara wore a smile:* **bear**, have (on one's
face), show, display, exhibit; give, put on,
assume. **3** *the bricks have been worn down:*
erode, abrade, rub away, grind away, wash
away, crumble (away), wear down; corrode,
eat away (at), dissolve. **4** *the tyres are
wearing well:* **last**, endure, hold up, bear up,
prove durable. **5** (Brit. informal) *I've asked him
twice, but he won't wear it:* **allow**, permit,
authorize, sanction, condone, indulge,
agree to, approve of; put up with, take,
stand, support; accept, swallow, tolerate,
countenance; informal hack, abide, stomach;
Brit. informal stick.
noun **1** *you won't get much wear out of that:*
use, wearing, service, utility, value; informal
mileage. **2** *evening wear:* **clothes**, clothing,
garments, dress, attire, garb, wardrobe;
informal get-up, gear, togs; Brit. informal kit,
clobber. **3** *the varnish will withstand
wear:* **damage**, friction, erosion, attrition,
abrasion.
■ **wear something down** *he wore
down her resistance:* gradually overcome,
slowly reduce, erode, wear away, exhaust,
undermine.
■ **wear off** *the novelty soon wore off:* fade,
diminish, lessen, dwindle, decrease, wane,
ebb, peter out, fizzle out, pall, disappear,
vanish, run out.
■ **wear on** *the afternoon wore on:* pass,
elapse, proceed, advance, progress, go by,
roll by, march on, slip by/away, fly by/past.

w

■ **wear out** *our stair carpet has worn out:* deteriorate, become worn, wear thin, fray, become threadbare, go into holes, wear through.

■ **wear something out** *he wore out six pairs of walking boots:* go through, use up, consume.

■ **wear someone out** *eventually her exertions wore her out:* fatigue, tire out, weary, exhaust, drain, sap, overtax, enervate, debilitate, jade, prostrate; informal whack, poop, shatter, frazzle, do in; Brit. informal knacker.

wearing adjective *it had been a rather wearing day:* **tiring**, exhausting, wearying, fatiguing, enervating, draining, sapping; demanding, exacting, taxing, arduous, gruelling, punishing, difficult, hard, tough, laborious, strenuous, rigorous.

wearisome adjective. See WEARING.

weary adjective **1** *he was weary after cycling:* **tired**, worn out, exhausted, fatigued, sapped, dog-tired, spent, drained, prostrate, enervated; informal all in, done in, dead beat, ready to drop, bushed, worn to a frazzle, shattered; Brit. informal knackered, whacked; N. Amer. informal pooped, tuckered out. **2** *she was weary of the arguments:* **tired of**, fed up with, bored by, sick of; informal have had it up to here with. **3** *a weary journey:* **tiring**, exhausting, wearying, fatiguing, enervating, draining, sapping, wearing, trying, demanding, taxing, arduous, gruelling, difficult, hard, tough.
– OPPOSITES fresh, keen, refreshing.
verb **1** *she was wearied by her illness:* **tire**, fatigue, wear out, overtire, exhaust, drain, sap, enervate, debilitate, enfeeble, prostrate; informal whack, bush, shatter, frazzle, poop, do in; Brit. informal knacker. **2** *don't risk wearying the reader:* **bore**, tire; irk, irritate, exasperate. **3** *he wearied of the struggle:* **tire of**, become fed up with, become bored by, sicken of; have had enough of.
– OPPOSITES refresh, interest.

weather noun *what's the weather like?* **forecast**, outlook; meteorological conditions, climate, atmospheric pressure, temperature; elements.
verb *we weathered the recession:* **survive**, come through, ride out, pull through; withstand, endure, rise above, surmount, overcome, resist; informal stick out.

weathered adjective *the weathered face of a true countryman:* **weather-beaten**, worn; tanned, bronzed; lined, creased, wrinkled, gnarled.

weave[1] verb **1** *flowers were woven into their hair:* **entwine**, lace, twist, knit, intertwine, braid, plait. **2** *he weaves colourful plots:* **invent**, make up, fabricate, construct, create, contrive, spin; tell, recount, relate.

weave[2] verb *he had to weave his way through the crowds:* **thread**, wind, wend; dodge, zigzag.

web noun **1** *a spider's web:* **mesh**, net, lattice, latticework, lacework, webbing; gauze, gossamer. **2** *a web of friendships:* **network**, nexus, complex, set, chain.

wed verb **1** *they are old enough to wed:* **marry**, get married, become husband and wife; informal tie the knot, walk down the aisle, get spliced, get hitched. **2** *he will wed his girlfriend:* **marry**, take as one's wife/husband, lead to the altar; informal make an honest woman of. **3** *she wedded the two forms of spirituality:* **unite**, unify, join, combine, amalgamate, fuse, integrate, bond, merge.
– OPPOSITES divorce, separate.

wedded adjective **1** *wedded bliss:* **married**, matrimonial, marital, conjugal, nuptial. **2** *he is wedded to his work:* **dedicated to**, devoted to, attached to, fixated on, single-minded about.

wedding noun **marriage (service/rites)**, nuptials, union.

wedge noun **1** *the door was secured by a wedge:* **tapered block**, chock, stop. **2** *a wedge of cheese:* **triangle**, segment, slice, section; chunk, lump, slab, hunk, block, piece.
verb *she wedged her case between two bags:* **squeeze**, cram, jam, ram, force, push, shove; informal stuff, bung.

wedlock noun **marriage**, (holy) matrimony, married state, union.

weed

■ **weed something/someone out** *a good agency will weed out those unsuitable candidates:* isolate, separate out, sort out, sift out, winnow out, filter out, set apart, segregate; eliminate, get rid of, remove; informal lose.

weedy adjective (informal) *a weedy little man:* **puny**, feeble, weak, frail, undersized, slight, skinny; informal pint-sized.

weekly adjective *he was paying off his debt in weekly instalments:* **once a week**; lasting a week.
adverb *the directors meet weekly:* **once a week**, every week, each week, on a weekly basis; by the week, per week, a week.

weep verb *even the toughest soldiers wept:* **cry**, shed tears, sob, snivel, whimper, whine, wail, bawl, keen; Scottish greet; informal boohoo, blub, blubber; Brit. informal grizzle.
noun *you sit and have a weep:* **cry**, sob, snivel, whimper, bawl; informal blub, blubber; Brit. informal grizzle.

weepy adjective *she was weepy when her husband was first admitted to hospital:* **tearful**, close to tears, upset, distressed, sad, unhappy; in tears, crying, weeping, snivelling; informal teary.

weigh verb **1** *she weighs the vegetables:* **measure the weight of**, put on the scales. **2** *he weighed 118 kg:* **have a weight of**, tip the scales at. **3** *the situation weighed heavily on him.* See WEIGH SOMEONE DOWN sense 2. **4** *he has to weigh up the possibilities:* **consider,**

W

contemplate, think about, mull over, chew over, reflect on, ruminate about, muse on; assess, appraise, analyse, investigate, inquire into, look into, examine, review, explore, take stock of. **5** *they need to weigh benefit against risk:* **balance**, evaluate, compare, juxtapose, contrast.
■ **weigh someone down 1** *my fishing gear weighed me down:* burden, saddle, overload, overburden, encumber, hamper, handicap. **2** *the silence weighed me down:* oppress, depress, lie heavy on, burden, cast down, hang over, gnaw at, prey on (one's mind); trouble, worry, bother, disturb, upset, haunt, nag, torment, afflict, plague.

weight noun **1** *she misjudged the weight of the book:* **heaviness**, mass, load, burden, pressure, force; poundage, tonnage. **2** *his recommendation will carry great weight:* **influence**, force, leverage, sway, pull, importance, significance, consequence, value, substance, power, authority; informal clout. **3** *a weight off her mind:* **burden**, load, millstone, albatross, encumbrance; trouble, worry, strain. **4** *the weight of the evidence is against him:* **preponderance**, majority, bulk, body, lion's share, predominance; most, almost all.

weighty adjective **1** *a weighty tome:* **heavy**, thick, bulky, hefty, cumbersome, ponderous. **2** *a weighty subject:* **important**, significant, momentous, consequential, far-reaching, key, major, vital, critical, crucial; serious, grave, solemn. **3** *a weighty responsibility:* **burdensome**, onerous, heavy, oppressive, taxing, troublesome. **4** *weighty arguments:* **compelling**, cogent, strong, forceful, powerful, potent, effective, sound, valid, telling; impressive, persuasive, convincing, influential, authoritative.
– OPPOSITES light, trivial, weak.

weird adjective **1** *weird apparitions:* **uncanny**, eerie, unnatural, supernatural, unearthly, other-worldly, ghostly, mysterious, strange, abnormal, unusual; Scottish eldritch; informal creepy, spooky, freaky. **2** (informal) *a weird sense of humour:* **bizarre**, quirky, outlandish, eccentric, unconventional, unorthodox, idiosyncratic, surreal, crazy, peculiar, odd, strange, queer, freakish, zany, madcap, outré; informal wacky, freaky, way-out, offbeat, off the wall; Brit. informal rum; N. Amer. informal wacko.
– OPPOSITES normal, conventional.

welcome noun *a welcome from the vicar:* **greeting**, salutation; reception, hospitality; the red carpet.
verb **1** *welcome your guests in their own language:* **greet**, salute, receive, meet, usher in. **2** *we welcomed their decision:* **be pleased by**, be glad about, approve of, appreciate, embrace; informal give the thumbs up to.
adjective *welcome news:* **pleasing**, agreeable, encouraging, gratifying, heartening, promising, favourable, pleasant; gladly

received, wanted, appreciated, popular, desirable.

weld verb *they simply welded sheets of metal together:* **fuse**, bond, stick, join, attach, seal, splice, melt, solder.

welfare noun **1** *the welfare of children:* **well-being**, health, comfort, security, safety, protection, prosperity, success, fortune; interest, good. **2** *we cannot claim welfare:* **social security**, (state) benefit, public assistance; pension, credit, support; sick pay, unemployment benefit; Brit. informal the dole.

well¹ adverb **1** *please behave well:* **satisfactorily**, nicely, correctly, properly, fittingly, suitably, appropriately. **2** *they get on well together:* **harmoniously**, agreeably, pleasantly, nicely, happily, amicably, amiably, peaceably; informal famously. **3** *he plays the piano well:* **skilfully**, ably, competently, proficiently, adeptly, deftly, expertly, admirably, excellently. **4** *treat your employees well:* **decently**, fairly, kindly, generously, honestly. **5** *mix the ingredients well:* **thoroughly**, completely; effectively, rigorously, carefully. **6** *I know her quite well:* **intimately**, thoroughly, deeply, profoundly, personally. **7** *they studied the car market well:* **carefully**, closely, attentively, rigorously, in depth, exhaustively, in detail, meticulously, scrupulously, conscientiously, methodically, completely, comprehensively, fully, extensively. **8** *they speak well of him:* **admiringly**, highly, approvingly, favourably, appreciatively, warmly, enthusiastically, glowingly. **9** *she makes enough money to live well:* **comfortably**, in (the lap of) luxury, prosperously. **10** *you may well be right:* **quite possibly**, conceivably, probably; undoubtedly, certainly, unquestionably. **11** *he is well over forty:* **considerably**, very much, a great deal, substantially, easily, comfortably, significantly. **12** *she could well afford it:* **easily**, comfortably, readily, effortlessly.
– OPPOSITES badly, negligently, disparagingly, barely.
adjective **1** *she was completely well again:* **healthy**, fine, fit, robust, strong, vigorous, blooming, thriving, hale and hearty, in good shape, in good condition, in good trim, in fine fettle; informal in the pink. **2** *all is not well:* **satisfactory**, all right, fine, in order, as it should be, acceptable; informal OK, hunky-dory; N. Amer. & Austral./NZ informal jake. **3** *it would be well to tell us in advance:* **advisable**, sensible, prudent, politic, commonsensical, wise, judicious, expedient, recommended, advantageous, beneficial, profitable, desirable; a good idea.
– OPPOSITES poorly, unsatisfactory, inadvisable.
■ **as well** too, also, in addition, additionally, into the bargain, besides, furthermore, moreover, to boot.
■ **as well as** together with, along with,

besides, plus, and, with, on top of, not to mention, to say nothing of, let alone.

well² noun **1** *she drew water from the well:* **borehole**, bore, spring, waterhole. **2** *he's a bottomless well of forgiveness:* **source**, supply, fount, reservoir, mine, fund, treasury.
▸ verb *tears welled from her eyes:* **flow**, spill, stream, run, rush, gush, roll, cascade, flood, spout; seep, trickle; burst, issue.

well advised adjective *you would be well advised to take your time:* **wise**, prudent, sensible.

well balanced adjective. See **BALANCED** senses 1, 2, 3.

well behaved adjective *well-behaved children:* **orderly**, obedient, disciplined, peaceable, docile, controlled, restrained, cooperative, compliant; mannerly, polite, civil, courteous, respectful, proper, decorous, refined, polished.
– OPPOSITES naughty.

well-being noun. See **WELFARE** sense 1.

well bred adjective *she is too well bred to say anything:* **well brought up**, polite, civil, mannerly, courteous, respectful, ladylike, gentlemanly, genteel, cultivated, urbane, proper, refined, polished, well behaved.

well built adjective *he was about six feet tall and well built:* **sturdy**, strapping, brawny, burly, hefty, muscular, muscly, strong, rugged, lusty, Herculean; informal hunky, beefy, husky, hulking.
– OPPOSITES puny.

well dressed adjective *he was always well dressed, regardless of the time of day:* **smart**, fashionable, stylish, chic, modish, elegant, neat, spruce, trim, dapper, besuited; N. Amer. trig; informal snazzy, natty, snappy, sharp; N. Amer. informal spiffy, fly.
– OPPOSITES scruffy.

well founded adjective *they have a well-founded fear of persecution if they are deported:* **justifiable**, justified, warranted, legitimate, defensible, valid, admissible, allowable, understandable, excusable, acceptable, reasonable, sensible, sound.
– OPPOSITES groundless.

well known adjective **1** *well-known principles:* **familiar**, widely known, popular, common, everyday, established. **2** *a well-known family of architects:* **famous**, famed, prominent, notable, renowned, distinguished, eminent, illustrious, celebrated, acclaimed, important.
– OPPOSITES obscure.

well mannered adjective *they were well mannered and eager to please:* **polite**, courteous, civil, mannerly, genteel, decorous, respectful, refined, polished, civilized, urbane, well bred.

well-nigh adverb *policing the coastline all the time was well-nigh impossible:* **almost**, nearly, just about, more or less, practically, virtually, all but, as good as, nearing,

approaching; roughly, approximately; informal pretty much, nigh on.

well off adjective **1** *her family's very well off.* See **WELL-TO-DO**. **2** *the prisoners were relatively well off:* **fortunate**, lucky, comfortable; informal sitting pretty. **3** *the island is not well off for harbours:* **well supplied with**, well stocked with, well furnished with, well equipped with.

well read adjective *he was very well read in this field:* **knowledgeable**, well informed, well versed, erudite, scholarly, literate, educated, cultured, bookish, studious.
– OPPOSITES ignorant.

well spoken adjective *she was very well spoken:* **articulate**, nicely spoken; refined, polite; Brit. informal posh.

well-to-do adjective **wealthy**, rich, affluent, moneyed, well off, prosperous, comfortable, propertied; informal rolling in it, in the money, loaded, well heeled, flush, made of money, quids in, worth a packet, on easy street.

welter noun *a welter of confused sounds:* **confusion**, jumble, tangle, mess, hotchpotch, mishmash, mass.

wend verb *they wended their way across the city:* **meander**, wind one's way, wander, amble, stroll, saunter, drift, roam, swan, traipse, walk; journey, travel; informal mosey, tootle.

west adjective *the Scottish west coast:* **western**, westerly, occidental.

wet adjective **1** *wet clothes:* **damp**, moist, soaked, drenched, saturated, sopping, dripping, soggy; waterlogged, squelchy. **2** *it was cold and wet:* **rainy**, raining, pouring, teeming, showery, drizzly, drizzling; damp. **3** *the paint is still wet:* **sticky**, tacky; fresh. **4** *a wet mortar mix:* **aqueous**, watery, sloppy.
– OPPOSITES dry, fine.
▸ verb *wet the clothes before ironing them:* **dampen**, damp, moisten; sprinkle, spray, splash; soak, saturate, flood, douse, souse, drench.
– OPPOSITES dry.
▸ noun **1** *the wet of his tears:* **wetness**, damp, moisture, moistness, sogginess; wateriness. **2** *the race was held in the wet:* **rain**, drizzle, precipitation; spray, dew, damp.

wharf noun quay, pier, dock, berth, landing, jetty; harbour, dockyard, marina.

wheedle verb *she had wheedled us into employing her brother:* **coax**, cajole, inveigle, induce, entice, charm, tempt, beguile, flatter, persuade, influence, win someone over, bring someone round, convince, prevail on, get round; informal sweet-talk, soft-soap.

wheel verb **1** *she wheeled the trolley away:* **push**, trundle, roll. **2** *the flock of doves wheeled round:* **turn**, go round, circle, orbit.
■ **at/behind the wheel** driving, steering, in the driving seat.

wheeze verb *the illness left her wheezing:* **breathe noisily**, gasp, whistle, hiss, rasp,

W

croak, pant, cough.
noun *she still had a slight wheeze:* **rasp**, croak, whistle, hiss, pant, cough.

whereabouts noun *his whereabouts remain secret:* **location**, position, site, place, situation, spot, point, vicinity; home, address, locale, neighbourhood; bearings, orientation.

wherewithal noun *she had the wherewithal to buy anything which took her fancy:* **money**, cash, capital, finance(s), funds; resources, means, ability, capability; informal dough, bread, loot, readies, necessary, boodle, dibs, ducats; Brit. informal dosh, brass, lolly; N. Amer. informal bucks; US informal greenbacks.

whet verb **1** *he whetted his knife on a stone:* **sharpen**, hone, strop, grind, file. **2** *something to whet your appetite:* **stimulate**, excite, arouse, rouse, kindle, trigger, spark, quicken, stir, inspire, animate, fuel, fire, activate, tempt, galvanize.
– OPPOSITES blunt.

whiff noun **1** *I caught a whiff of perfume:* **faint smell**, trace, sniff, scent, odour, aroma. **2** *the faintest whiff of irony:* **trace**, hint, suggestion, impression, suspicion, soupçon, nuance, intimation, tinge, vein, shred, whisper, air, element, overtone. **3** *whiffs of smoke from the boiler:* **puff**, gust, flurry, breath, draught, waft.

while noun *we chatted for a while:* **time**, spell, stretch, stint, span, interval, period; duration, phase; Brit. informal patch.
verb *tennis helped to while away the time:* **pass**, spend, occupy, use up, kill.

whim noun **1** *she bought it on a whim:* **impulse**, urge, notion, fancy, foible, caprice, conceit, vagary, crotchet, inclination. **2** *human whim:* **capriciousness**, whimsy, caprice, volatility, fickleness, idiosyncrasy.

whimper verb *he was whimpering in pain:* **whine**, cry, sob, moan, snivel, wail, groan; Brit. informal grizzle.
noun *she gave a whimper of protest:* **whine**, cry, sob, moan, bleat, wail, groan.

whimsical adjective **1** *a whimsical sense of humour:* **fanciful**, playful, mischievous, waggish, quaint, curious, droll; eccentric, quirky, idiosyncratic, unconventional, outlandish, queer; informal offbeat, freaky. **2** *the whimsical arbitrariness of autocracy:* **volatile**, capricious, fickle, changeable, unpredictable, variable, erratic, mercurial, mutable, inconstant, inconsistent, unstable, protean.

whine noun **1** *the dog gave a whine:* **whimper**, cry, mewl, howl, yowl. **2** *the whine of the motor:* **hum**, drone. **3** *a whine about the quality of service:* **complaint**, grouse, grumble, murmur; informal gripe, moan, grouch, whinge, bellyache, beef.
verb **1** *a child was whining:* **wail**, whimper, cry, mewl, moan, howl, yowl. **2** *the lift began to whine:* **hum**, drone. **3** *he's always whining*

about something: **complain**, grouse, grouch, grumble, moan, carp, mutter, murmur; informal gripe, bellyache, whinge.

whinge (informal) verb *I whinged about the weather.* See **WHINE** verb sense 3.
noun *his tale is one long whinge.* See **WHINE** noun sense 3.

whip noun *he would use a whip on his dogs:* **lash**, scourge, strap, belt.
verb **1** *he whipped the boy:* **flog**, scourge, flagellate, lash, strap, belt, thrash, beat, tan someone's hide. **2** *whip the cream:* **whisk**, beat. **3** *he whipped his listeners into a frenzy:* **rouse**, stir up, excite, galvanize, electrify, stimulate, inspire, fire up, get someone going, inflame, agitate, goad, provoke.

whirl verb **1** *leaves whirled in eddies of wind:* **rotate**, circle, wheel, turn, revolve, orbit, spin, twirl; Scottish birl. **2** *they whirled past:* **hurry**, race, dash, rush, run, sprint, bolt, dart, gallop, career, charge, shoot, hurtle, hare, fly, speed, scurry; informal tear, belt, pelt, scoot; Brit. informal bomb; N. Amer. informal hightail it. **3** *his mind was whirling:* **spin**, reel, swim.
noun **1** *a whirl of dust:* **swirl**, flurry, eddy. **2** *the mad social whirl:* **hurly-burly**, activity, bustle, rush, flurry, fuss, turmoil, merry-go-round; informal to-do. **3** *Laura's mind was in a whirl:* **spin**, daze, stupor, muddle, jumble; confusion; informal dither.

whirlpool noun **1** *a river full of whirlpools:* **eddy**, vortex, maelstrom; N. Amer. informal suckhole. **2** *the health club has a whirlpool:* spa bath, hot tub; trademark jacuzzi.

whirlwind noun **1** *the building was hit by a whirlwind:* **tornado**, hurricane, typhoon, cyclone, vortex; Austral. willy-willy; N. Amer. informal twister. **2** *a whirlwind of activity:* **maelstrom**, welter, bedlam, mayhem, babel, swirl, tumult, hurly-burly, commotion, confusion; informal madhouse; N. Amer. three-ring circus.
adjective *a whirlwind romance:* **rapid**, lightning, headlong, impulsive, breakneck, meteoric, sudden, swift, fast, quick, speedy; informal quickie.

whisk verb **1** *the cable car will whisk you to the top:* **speed**, hurry, rush, sweep, hurtle, shoot; Scottish informal wheech. **2** *she whisked the cloth away:* **pull**, snatch, pluck, tug, jerk; informal whip, yank; Scottish informal wheech. **3** *he whisked out of sight:* **dash**, rush, race, bolt, dart, gallop, career, charge, shoot, hurtle, hare, fly, speed, zoom, scurry, scuttle, scamper; informal tear, belt, pelt, scoot, zip, whip. **4** *horses whisk their tails:* **flick**, twitch, wave. **5** *whisk the egg yolks:* **whip**, beat, mix.
noun **1** *the horse gave a whisk of its tail:* **flick**, twitch, wave, sweep. **2** *blend the eggs with a whisk:* **beater**, mixer, blender.

whisper verb *Alison whispered in his ear:* **murmur**, mutter, mumble, speak softly, breathe.
– OPPOSITES roar.
noun **1** *she spoke in a whisper:* **murmur**,

mutter, mumble, low voice, undertone. **2** *I heard a whisper that he's left town:* **rumour**, story, report, speculation, insinuation, suggestion, hint; informal buzz. **3** *not a whisper of interest.* See **WHIT**.

whit noun *his death wouldn't have made a whit of difference:* **scrap**, bit, speck, iota, jot, atom, crumb, shred, grain, mite, touch, trace, shadow, suggestion, whisper, suspicion, scintilla; informal smidgen, smidge.

white adjective **1** *a clean white bandage:* **colourless**, unpigmented, bleached, natural; snowy, milky, chalky, ivory. **2** *her face was white with fear:* **pale**, pallid, wan, ashen, bloodless, waxen, chalky, pasty, peaky, washed out, drained, drawn, ghostly, deathly. **3** *white hair:* **snowy**, grey, silver, silvery, hoary, grizzled. **4** *the early white settlers:* **Caucasian**, European. **5** *a whiter than white government:* **virtuous**, moral, ethical, good, righteous, honourable, reputable, wholesome, honest, upright, upstanding, irreproachable; decent, worthy, noble; blameless, spotless, impeccable, unsullied, unblemished, uncorrupted, untainted; informal squeaky clean.
– OPPOSITES black, florid, immoral.

white-collar adjective *white-collar workers:* **clerical**, professional, executive, salaried, office.

whiten verb *snow whitened the mountain tops:* **make white**, make pale, bleach, blanch, lighten, fade.

whitewash noun **1** *the report was a whitewash:* **cover-up**, camouflage, deception, facade, veneer, pretext. **2** *a four-match whitewash:* **walkover**, rout, landslide; informal pushover, cinch, breeze.
– OPPOSITES exposé.
verb *don't whitewash what happened:* **cover up**, sweep under the carpet, hush up, suppress, draw a veil over, conceal, veil, obscure, keep secret; gloss over, downplay, soft-pedal.
– OPPOSITES expose.

whittle verb **1** *he sat whittling a piece of wood.* **pare**, shave, trim, carve, shape, model. **2** *his powers were whittled away:* **erode**, wear away, eat away, reduce, diminish, undermine, weaken, subvert, compromise, impair, impede, hinder, cripple, disable, enfeeble, sap. **3** *the ten teams have been whittled down to six:* **reduce**, cut down, cut back, prune, trim, slim down, pare down, shrink, decrease, diminish.

whole adjective **1** *they refused to publish the whole report:* **entire**, complete, full, unabridged, uncut. **2** *they discovered a whole marble mantelpiece:* **intact**, in one piece, unbroken; undamaged, flawless, faultless, unmarked, perfect.
– OPPOSITES incomplete.
noun **1** *the two movements had been fused into a single whole:* **entity**, unit, body, discrete item, ensemble. **2** *the whole of the year:* **all**, every part, the lot, the sum (total).

■ **on the whole** overall, all in all, all things considered, for the most part, in the main, in general, generally (speaking), as a (general) rule, by and large; normally, usually, more often than not, almost always, most of the time, typically, ordinarily.

wholehearted adjective *you have my wholehearted support:* **committed**, positive, emphatic, devoted, dedicated, enthusiastic, unshakeable, unswerving; unqualified, unreserved, without reservations, unconditional, unequivocal, unmitigated; complete, full, total, absolute.
– OPPOSITES half-hearted.

wholesale adverb *the images were removed wholesale:* **extensively**, on a large scale, comprehensively; indiscriminately, without exception.
– OPPOSITES selectively.
adjective *the wholesale destruction of a city:* **extensive**, widespread, large-scale, wide-ranging, comprehensive, total, mass; indiscriminate.
– OPPOSITES partial.

wholesome adjective **1** *wholesome food:* **healthy**, health-giving, healthful, good (for one), nutritious, nourishing; natural, uncontaminated, organic. **2** *wholesome fun:* **moral**, ethical, good, clean, virtuous, pure, innocent, chaste; uplifting, edifying, proper, correct, decent; informal squeaky clean.

wholly adverb **1** *the measures were wholly inadequate:* **completely**, totally, absolutely, entirely, fully, thoroughly, utterly, quite, perfectly, downright, in every respect, in all respects; informal one hundred per cent. **2** *they rely wholly on you:* **exclusively**, only, solely, purely, alone.

whoop noun & verb *whoops of delight* | *he whooped for joy:* **shout**, cry, call, yell, roar, scream, shriek, screech, cheer; informal holler.

whopper noun (informal) **1** *what a whopper!* **monster**, brute, giant, colossus, mammoth, monstrosity; informal jumbo. **2** *Joseph's story is a whopper.* See **LIE**[1] noun.

whopping adjective (informal). See **HUGE**.

whore noun *the whores on the street.* See **PROSTITUTE** noun.
verb **1** *she spent her life whoring:* **work as a prostitute**, sell one's body, sell oneself; be on the streets; informal be on the game. **2** *the men whored and drank:* **use prostitutes**.

whorehouse noun. See **BROTHEL**.

whorl noun *elegant whorls of wrought iron:* **loop**, coil, hoop, ring, curl, twirl, twist, spiral, helix.

wicked adjective **1** *wicked deeds:* **evil**, sinful, immoral, wrong, morally wrong, wrongful, bad, iniquitous, corrupt, black-hearted, base, mean, vile; villainous, nefarious, erring, foul, monstrous, shocking, outrageous, atrocious, abominable, reprehensible, hateful, detestable, despicable, odious, contemptible, horrible, heinous, egregious, execrable, fiendish, vicious, murderous,

w

barbarous; criminal, illicit, unlawful, illegal, lawless, felonious, dishonest, unscrupulous; informal crooked; Brit. informal beastly. **2** *a wicked sense of humour:* **mischievous**, playful, naughty, impish, roguish, arch, puckish, cheeky. **3** (informal) *Sophie makes wicked cakes.* See **EXCELLENT**.
– OPPOSITES virtuous.

wickedness noun **evil-doing**, evil, sin, sinfulness, iniquity, vileness, baseness, badness, wrongdoing, dishonesty, unscrupulousness, roguery, villainy, viciousness, degeneracy, depravity, immorality, vice, corruption, corruptness, devilry, fiendishness.

wide adjective **1** *a wide river:* **broad**, extensive, spacious, vast, spread out. **2** *their mouths were wide with shock:* **fully open**, agape, wide open. **3** *a wide range of opinion:* **comprehensive**, ample, broad, extensive, large, large-scale, wide-ranging, exhaustive, general, all-inclusive. **4** *his shot was wide:* **off target**, off the mark, wide of the mark/target, inaccurate.
– OPPOSITES narrow.
adverb **1** *he opened his eyes wide:* **fully**, to the fullest/furthest extent, as far/much as possible. **2** *he shot wide:* **off target**, wide of the mark/target, inaccurately.

wide-eyed adjective **1** *the whole class was wide-eyed:* **staring in amazement**, goggle-eyed, open-mouthed, dumbstruck, amazed, surprised, astonished, astounded, stunned, staggered; informal flabbergasted; Brit. informal gobsmacked. **2** *wide-eyed visitors:* **innocent**, naive, impressionable, ingenuous, childlike, credulous, trusting, unquestioning, unsophisticated, gullible.

widen verb **1** *a proposal to widen the motorway:* **broaden**, make/become wider, open up/out, expand, extend, enlarge. **2** *the Party must widen its support:* **increase**, augment, boost, swell, enlarge.

wide open adjective **1** *his eyes were wide open:* **fully open**, open wide, agape. **2** *the championship is wide open:* **unpredictable**, uncertain, unsure, in the balance, up in the air; informal anyone's guess. **3** *they were wide open to attacks:* **vulnerable**, exposed, unprotected, defenceless, undefended, at risk, in danger.

widespread adjective *there is widespread concern about the outcome:* **general**, extensive, universal, common, global, worldwide, international, omnipresent, ubiquitous, across the board, predominant, prevalent, rife, broad, rampant, pervasive.
– OPPOSITES limited.

width noun **1** *the width of the river:* **wideness**, breadth, broadness, thickness, span, diameter, girth. **2** *the width of experience required:* **range**, breadth, compass, scope, span, scale, extent, extensiveness, comprehensiveness.
– OPPOSITES length, narrowness.

wield verb **1** *he was wielding a sword:* **brandish**, flourish, wave, swing; use, employ, handle. **2** *he has wielded power since 1972:* **exercise**, exert, hold, maintain, command, control.

wife noun **spouse**, partner, mate, consort, woman, helpmate, helpmeet, bride; informal old lady, wifey, better half, missus; Brit. informal other half, her indoors, trouble and strife.

wiggle verb *she wiggled her toes:* **jiggle**, wriggle, twitch, shimmy, joggle, wag, wobble, shake, twist, squirm, writhe; informal waggle.

wild adjective **1** *wild animals:* **untamed**, undomesticated, feral; fierce, ferocious, savage. **2** *wild flowers:* **uncultivated**, native, indigenous. **3** *wild tribes:* **primitive**, uncivilized, uncultured; savage, barbarous, barbaric. **4** *wild hill country:* **uninhabited**, unpopulated, uncultivated; rugged, rough, inhospitable, desolate, barren. **5** *a wild night:* **stormy**, squally, tempestuous, turbulent, boisterous. **6** *her wild black hair:* **dishevelled**, tousled, tangled, windswept, untidy, unkempt; N. Amer. mussed up. **7** *wild behaviour:* **uncontrolled**, unrestrained, out of control, undisciplined, unruly, rowdy, disorderly, riotous. **8** *wild with excitement:* **very excited**, delirious, in a frenzy; tumultuous, passionate, vehement, unrestrained. **9** (informal) *I was wild with jealousy:* **distraught**, frantic, beside oneself, in a frenzy, hysterical, deranged, berserk; informal mad, crazy. **10** *Bill's wild schemes:* **madcap**, ridiculous, ludicrous, foolish, stupid, foolhardy, idiotic, absurd, silly, ill-considered, senseless, nonsensical; impractical, impracticable, unworkable; informal crazy, crackpot, cockeyed. **11** *a wild guess:* **random**, arbitrary, haphazard, uninformed.
– OPPOSITES tame, cultivated, calm, disciplined.
■ **run wild 1** *the garden had run wild:* grow unchecked, grow profusely, run riot. **2** *the children are running wild:* run amok, run riot, get out of control, be undisciplined.

wilderness noun **1** *the Siberian wilderness:* **wilds**, wastes, inhospitable region; desert. **2** *a litter-strewn wilderness:* **wasteland**.

wildlife noun **(wild) animals**, fauna.

wilds plural noun *he spent a year in the wilds of Canada:* **remote areas**, wilderness; backwoods; N. Amer. backcountry, backland; Austral./NZ outback, bush, backblocks, booay; N. Amer. informal boondocks, tall timbers.

wiles plural noun *feminine wiles:* **tricks**, ruses, ploys, schemes, dodges, manoeuvres, subterfuges, artifices; guile, artfulness, cunning, craftiness.

wilful adjective **1** *wilful destruction:* **deliberate**, intentional, done on purpose, premeditated, planned, conscious. **2** *a wilful child:* **headstrong**, strong-willed, obstinate,

w

stubborn, pig-headed, recalcitrant, uncooperative, obstreperous, ungovernable, unmanageable; Brit. informal bloody-minded, bolshie; N. Amer. informal balky.
– OPPOSITES accidental, amenable.

will¹ verb *accidents will happen:* **have a tendency to**, are bound to, do.

will² noun **1** *the will to succeed:* **determination**, will power, strength of character, resolution, resolve, resoluteness, single-mindedness, purposefulness, drive, commitment, dedication, doggedness, tenacity, tenaciousness, staying power. **2** *they stayed against their will:* **desire**, wish, preference, inclination, intention, intent. **3** *they believed it to be God's will:* **wish**, desire, decision, choice; decree, command. **4** *his late father's will:* **(last will and) testament**.
verb *do what you will:* **want**, wish, please, see/think fit, think best, like, choose, prefer. **2** *God willed it:* **decree**, order, ordain, command. **3** *she willed the money to her husband:* **bequeath**, leave, hand down, pass on, settle on.
■ **at will** as one pleases, as one thinks fit, to suit oneself, at whim.

willing adjective **1** *I'm willing to give it a try:* **ready**, prepared, disposed, inclined, of a mind, minded; happy, glad, pleased, agreeable, amenable; informal game. **2** *willing help:* **readily given**, willingly given, ungrudging.
– OPPOSITES reluctant.

willingly adverb *Joe had gone with her willingly:* **voluntarily**, of one's own free will, of one's own accord; readily, without reluctance, ungrudgingly, cheerfully, happily, gladly, with pleasure.

willingness noun *many people have expressed a willingness to help:* **readiness**, inclination, will, wish, desire.

willowy adjective *a willowy blonde:* **tall**, slim, slender, svelte, lissom, sylphlike, long-limbed, graceful, lithe; informal slinky.

will power noun. See **WILL²** noun sense 1.

willy-nilly adverb *cars were parked willy-nilly:* **haphazardly**, at random, randomly.

wilt verb **1** *the roses had begun to wilt:* **droop**, sag, become limp, flop; wither, shrivel (up). **2** *wilting in the heat:* **languish**, flag, droop, become listless. **3** *Shelley's happy mood wilted:* **fade**, ebb, wane, evaporate, melt away.
– OPPOSITES flourish.

wily adjective *a wily old rascal:* **shrewd**, clever, sharp, sharp-witted, astute, canny, smart; crafty, cunning, artful, sly, scheming, calculating, devious; informal tricky, foxy.
– OPPOSITES naive.

wimp noun (informal) *don't be such a wimp!* **coward**, namby-pamby, milksop, weakling; informal drip, sissy, weed, wuss, pansy, scaredy-cat, chicken; Brit. informal wet, mummy's boy, big girl's blouse; N. Amer.

informal cupcake, pantywaist, pussy; Austral./NZ informal sook.

win verb **1** *Steve won the race:* **be the victor in**, be the winner of, come first in, take first prize in, triumph in, be successful in. **2** *she was determined to win:* **come first**, be the winner, be victorious, carry/win the day, come out on top, succeed, triumph, prevail. **3** *he won a cash prize:* **secure**, gain, collect, pick up, walk away/off with, carry off; informal land, net, bag, scoop. **4** *Ilona won his heart:* **captivate**, steal.
– OPPOSITES lose.
noun *a 3–0 win:* **victory**, triumph, conquest.
– OPPOSITES defeat.
■ **win someone round/over** *Daisy made heroic efforts to win him round:* persuade, talk round, convince, sway, prevail on.

wince verb *he winced at the pain:* **grimace**, pull a face, flinch, blench, start.
noun *a wince of pain:* **grimace**, flinch, start.

wind¹ noun **1** *the trees were swaying in the wind:* **breeze**, current of air; gale, hurricane; informal blow. **2** *Jez got his wind back:* **breath**; informal puff. **3** *you do talk a lot of wind.* See **HOT AIR**. **4** **flatulence**, gas.
■ **in the wind** *there is trouble in the wind:* on the way, coming, about to happen, in the offing, in the air, on the horizon, approaching, looming, brewing, afoot; informal on the cards.

wind² verb **1** *the road winds up the mountain:* **twist (and turn)**, bend, curve, loop, zigzag, weave, snake. **2** *he wound a towel around his waist:* **wrap**, furl, entwine, lace. **3** *Anne wound the wool into a ball:* **coil**, roll, twist, twine.
■ **wind down** *the campaign was winding down:* draw to a close, come to an end, tail off, slack(en) off, slow down.
■ **wind something down** *a decision was taken to wind down the business:* bring to a close/end, wind up, close down.
■ **wind someone up** *David was winding him up on purpose:* annoy, anger, irritate, exasperate, get on someone's nerves, provoke, goad; Brit. rub up the wrong way; informal aggravate, rile, niggle, bug, put someone's back up, get up someone's nose, hack off; Brit. informal nark; N. Amer. informal ride.
■ **wind something up 1** *Richard wound up the meeting:* conclude, bring to an end/close, end, terminate; informal wrap up. **2** *the company has been wound up:* close (down), dissolve, put into liquidation.

winded adjective *he lay there for a moment, winded:* **out of breath**, breathless, gasping for breath, panting, puffing, puffed out; informal out of puff.

windfall noun *a £43,000 windfall:* **bonanza**, jackpot, pennies from heaven.

winding noun *the windings of the stream:* **twist**, turn, turning, bend, loop, curve, zigzag, meander.
adjective *the winding country roads:* **twisting and turning**, meandering, windy, twisty,

w

bending, curving, zigzag, zigzagging, serpentine, sinuous, snaking.
– OPPOSITES straight.

windpipe noun **trachea**, pharynx; throat.

windswept adjective **1** *the windswept moors:* **exposed**, bleak, bare, desolate. **2** *his windswept hair:* **dishevelled**, tousled, unkempt, wind-blown, untidy; N. Amer. mussed up.

windy adjective **1** *a windy day:* **breezy**, blowy, fresh, blustery, gusty; wild, stormy, squally, tempestuous, boisterous. **2** *a windy hillside:* **windswept**, exposed, open to the elements, bare, bleak.
– OPPOSITES still, sheltered.

wine noun informal plonk, vino, the grape.

wing noun **1** *the east wing of the house:* **part**, section, side; annexe, extension; N. Amer. ell. **2** *the radical wing of the party:* **faction**, camp, caucus, arm, branch, group, section, set, coterie, cabal.
verb **1** *a seagull winged its way over the sea:* **fly**, glide, soar. **2** *the bomb winged past:* **hurtle**, speed, shoot, whizz, zoom, streak, fly. **3** *she was shot at and winged:* **wound**, graze, hit.

wink verb **1** *he winked an eye at her:* **blink**, flutter, bat. **2** *the diamond winked in the moonlight:* **sparkle**, twinkle, flash, glitter, gleam, shine, scintillate.
noun *a wink of light:* **glimmer**, gleam, glint, flash, flicker, twinkle, sparkle.
■ **wink at** *the authorities winked at their illegal trade:* turn a blind eye to, close one's eyes to, ignore, overlook, disregard; connive at, condone, tolerate.

winkle
■ **winkle something out** *Ewan managed to winkle the details out of him:* worm out, prise out, dig out, extract, draw out, obtain, get.

winner noun **victor**, champion, conqueror, vanquisher, hero; medallist; Brit. victor ludorum; informal champ, top dog.
– OPPOSITES loser.

winning adjective **1** *the winning team:* **victorious**, successful, triumphant, vanquishing, conquering; first, top. **2** *a winning smile:* **engaging**, charming, appealing, endearing, sweet, cute, winsome, attractive, pretty, prepossessing, fetching, lovely, adorable, delightful, disarming, captivating.

winnings plural noun *Sanchez collected his winnings from the cashier:* **prize money**, gains, prize, booty, spoils; proceeds, profits, takings, purse.

winnow verb *the dust and chaff is winnowed from the grain:* **separate (out)**, divide, sort out, sift out, filter out; isolate, find, identify; remove, get rid of.

winsome adjective. See WINNING sense 2.

wintry adjective **1** *wintry weather:* **bleak**, cold, chilly, chill, frosty, freezing, icy, snowy, arctic, glacial, bitter, raw; informal nippy; Brit. informal parky. **2** *a wintry smile:* **unfriendly**, unwelcoming, cool, cold, frosty, frigid.
– OPPOSITES summery, warm.

wipe verb **1** *Beth wiped the table:* **rub**, mop, sponge, swab; clean, dry, polish. **2** *he wiped the marks off the window:* **rub off**, clean off, clear up, remove, get rid of, take off, erase, efface. **3** *she wiped the memory from her mind:* **obliterate**, expunge, erase, blot out, blank out.
noun *he gave the table a wipe:* **rub**, mop, sponge, swab; clean, polish.
■ **wipe someone/something out** *soldiers wiped out an entire village:* destroy, annihilate, eradicate, eliminate; slaughter, massacre, kill, exterminate; demolish, raze to the ground; informal take out, zap; N. Amer. informal waste.

wire noun **cable**, lead, flex.

wiry adjective **1** *a wiry man:* **sinewy**, tough, athletic, strong; lean, spare, thin, stringy, skinny. **2** *wiry hair:* **coarse**, rough, strong; curly, wavy.
– OPPOSITES flabby, smooth.

wisdom noun **1** *we questioned the wisdom of the decision:* **sagacity**, intelligence, sense, common sense, shrewdness, astuteness, smartness, judiciousness, judgement, prudence, circumspection; logic, rationale, rationality, soundness, advisability. **2** *the wisdom of the East:* **knowledge**, learning, erudition, scholarship, philosophy; lore.
– OPPOSITES folly.

wise adjective *a wise old man:* **sage**, sagacious, intelligent, clever, learned, knowledgeable, enlightened; astute, smart, shrewd, sharp-witted, canny, knowing; sensible, prudent, discerning, judicious, perceptive, insightful, perspicacious; rational, logical, sound, sane; Brit. informal fly.
– OPPOSITES foolish.

wish verb **1** *I wished for power:* **desire**, want, hope for, covet, dream of, long for, yearn for, crave, hunger for, lust after; aspire to, set one's heart on, seek, fancy, hanker after; informal have a yen for, itch for. **2** *they can do as they wish:* **want**, desire, feel inclined, feel like, care; choose, please, think fit. **3** *I wish you to send them a message:* **want**, desire, require. **4** *I wished him farewell:* **bid**, give.
noun **1** *his wish to own a Mercedes:* **desire**, longing, yearning, inclination, urge, whim, craving, hunger; hope, aspiration, aim, ambition, dream; informal hankering, yen, itch. **2** *she was unwilling to go against her parents' wishes:* **request**, requirement, bidding, instruction, direction, demand, order, command; want, desire; will.

wishy-washy adjective **1** *he's so wishy-washy:* **feeble**, ineffectual, weak, vapid, effete, spineless, limp, namby-pamby, spiritless, indecisive; informal wet, pathetic. **2** *wishy-washy soup:* **watery**, weak, thin; tasteless, flavourless, insipid. **3** *a wishy-washy colour:* **pale**, insipid, pallid, muted.

W

– OPPOSITES strong, tasty, vibrant.

wisp noun *a stray wisp of hair:* **strand**, tendril, lock; scrap, shred, thread.

wispy adjective *her wispy blonde hair:* **thin**, fine, feathery, flyaway.

wistful adjective *his wistful expression:* **nostalgic**, yearning, longing; plaintive, regretful, rueful, melancholy, mournful; pensive, reflective, contemplative.

wit noun **1** *he needed all his wits to escape:* **intelligence**, shrewdness, astuteness, cleverness, canniness, (common) sense, wisdom, sagacity, judgement, acumen, insight; brains, mind; informal nous, gumption, savvy, horse sense; Brit. informal common; N. Amer. informal smarts. **2** *I wanted to bowl him over with my sparkling wit:* **wittiness**, humour, funniness, drollery; repartee, badinage, banter, wordplay; jokes, witticisms, quips, puns. **3** *she's such a wit:* **comedian**, humorist, comic, joker, jokester; informal wag.

witch noun **1** *the witch cast a spell:* **sorceress**, enchantress, hex; Wiccan. **2** (informal) *she's a right old witch:* **hag**, crone, harpy, harridan, she-devil; informal battleaxe.

witchcraft noun **sorcery**, (black) magic, witching, witchery, wizardry, thaumaturgy, spells, incantations; Wicca; Irish pishogue.

witch doctor noun **medicine man**, shaman, healer.

with preposition *she's gone out with her boyfriend:* **accompanied by**, escorted by; alongside, in addition to, as well as.

withdraw verb **1** *she withdrew her hand from his:* **remove**, extract, pull out, take out; take back, take away. **2** *the ban on advertising was withdrawn:* **abolish**, cancel, lift, set aside, end, stop, remove, reverse, revoke, rescind, repeal, annul, void. **3** *she withdrew the allegation:* **retract**, take back, go back on, recant, disavow, disclaim, repudiate, renounce; back down, climb down, backtrack, back-pedal, do a U-turn, eat one's words. **4** *the troops withdrew from the city:* **leave**, pull out of, evacuate, quit, retreat from. **5** *his partner withdrew from the project:* **pull out of**, back out of, bow out of; get cold feet. **6** *they withdrew to their rooms:* **retire**, retreat, adjourn, decamp; leave, depart, absent oneself.
– OPPOSITES insert, introduce, deposit, enter.

withdrawal noun **1** *the withdrawal of subsidies:* **removal**, abolition, cancellation, discontinuation, termination, elimination. **2** *the withdrawal of the troops:* **departure**, pull-out, exit, exodus, evacuation, retreat.

withdrawn adjective *over the last few months he had become very withdrawn:* **introverted**, unsociable, inhibited, uncommunicative, unforthcoming, quiet, reticent, reserved, retiring, private, reclusive; shy, timid; aloof; informal stand-offish.
– OPPOSITES outgoing.

wither verb **1** *the flowers withered in the sun:* **shrivel (up)**, dry up, wilt, droop, go limp, fade, perish. **2** *the muscles in his leg withered:* **waste (away)**, shrivel (up), shrink, atrophy. **3** *her confidence withered:* **diminish**, dwindle, shrink, lessen, fade, ebb, wane; evaporate, disappear.
– OPPOSITES thrive, grow.

withering adjective *a withering look:* **scornful**, contemptuous, scathing, stinging, devastating; humiliating, mortifying.
– OPPOSITES admiring.

withhold verb **1** *he withheld the information:* **hold back**, keep back, refuse to give; retain, hold on to; hide, conceal, keep secret; informal sit on. **2** *she could not withhold her tears:* **suppress**, repress, hold back, fight back, choke back, control, check, restrain, contain.

within preposition **1** *within the prison walls:* **inside**, in, enclosed by, surrounded by; within the bounds of, within the confines of. **2** *within a few hours:* **in less than**, in under, in no more than, after only.
– OPPOSITES outside.

without preposition **1** *thousands were without food:* **lacking**, short of, deprived of, in need of, wanting, needing, requiring. **2** *I don't want to go without you:* **unaccompanied by**, unescorted by; in the absence of.

withstand verb *the company was able to withstand the rigours of the recession:* **resist**, weather, survive, endure, cope with, stand, tolerate, bear, defy, brave, hold out against, bear up against; stand up to, face, confront.

witless adjective *a witless youth:* **foolish**, stupid, unintelligent, idiotic, brainless, mindless; fatuous, inane, half-baked, empty-headed, slow-witted; informal thick, birdbrained, pea-brained, dopey, dim, dim-witted, half-witted, dippy, lamebrained, wooden-headed; Brit. informal daft; Scottish & N. English informal glaikit; N. Amer. informal dumb-ass.

witness noun **1** *witnesses claimed that he started the fight:* **observer**, onlooker, eyewitness, spectator, viewer, watcher; bystander, passer-by. **2** *a whisky bottle was the only witness of his mood:* **evidence**, indication, proof, testimony.
verb **1** *who witnessed the incident?* **see**, observe, watch, view, notice, spot; be present at, attend. **2** *the will is correctly witnessed:* **countersign**, sign, endorse, validate; N. Amer. notarize. **3** *his writings witness an inner toughness:* **attest to**, testify to, bear witness to, confirm, evidence, prove, verify, corroborate, substantiate; show, demonstrate, indicate, reveal, bespeak.

witter verb (Brit. informal). See **GABBLE** verb.

witticism noun **joke**, quip, jest, pun, play on words, bon mot; informal one-liner, gag, funny, crack, wisecrack.

witty adjective *his witty conversation:* **humorous**, amusing, droll, funny, comic,

W

comical; jocular, facetious, waggish; sparkling, scintillating, entertaining; clever, quick-witted.

wizard noun **1** *the wizard cast a spell over them:* **sorcerer**, warlock, magus, (black) magician, enchanter. **2** *a financial wizard:* **genius**, expert, master, virtuoso, maestro, marvel, Wunderkind; informal hotshot, demon, whizz-kid, buff, pro, ace; Brit. informal dab hand; N. Amer. informal maven.

wizardry noun **sorcery**, witchcraft, witchery, witching, (black) magic, enchantment; spells, charms; Irish pishogue.

wizened adjective *his wizened face:* **wrinkled**, lined, creased, shrivelled (up), withered, weather-beaten, shrunken, gnarled.

wobble verb **1** *the table wobbled:* **rock**, teeter, jiggle, sway, see-saw, shake. **2** *he wobbled across to the door:* **teeter**, totter, stagger, lurch. **3** *her voice wobbled:* **tremble**, shake, quiver, quaver, waver.
noun **1** *she stood up with a wobble:* **totter**, teeter, sway. **2** *the operatic wobble in her voice:* **tremor**, quiver, quaver, trembling, vibrato.

wobbly adjective **1** *a wobbly table:* **unsteady**, unstable, shaky, rocky, rickety; unsafe, precarious; uneven, unbalanced; informal wonky. **2** *her legs were a bit wobbly:* **shaky**, quivery, weak, unsteady; informal trembly, like jelly. **3** *I feel so wobbly:* **faint**, dizzy, light-headed, giddy, weak (at the knees), groggy, muzzy; informal woozy.
– OPPOSITES stable.

woe noun **1** *a tale of woe:* **misery**, sorrow, distress, wretchedness, sadness, unhappiness, heartache, heartbreak, despondency, despair, depression, gloom, melancholy; adversity, misfortune, disaster, suffering, hardship. **2** *financial woes:* **trouble**, difficulty, problem, trial, tribulation, misfortune, setback, reverse.
– OPPOSITES joy.

woebegone adjective *her woebegone expression:* **sad**, unhappy, miserable, dejected, disconsolate, forlorn, crestfallen, downcast, glum, gloomy, doleful, downhearted, despondent, melancholy, sorrowful, mournful, woeful, depressed, wretched, desolate; informal down in the mouth, down in the dumps, blue.
– OPPOSITES cheerful.

woeful adjective **1** *her face was woeful.* See **WOEBEGONE**. **2** *a woeful tale:* **tragic**, sad, miserable, cheerless, gloomy, sorry, pitiful, pathetic, traumatic, depressing, heartbreaking, heart-rending, tear-jerking. **3** *the team's woeful performance:* **dreadful**, awful, terrible, atrocious, disgraceful, deplorable, shameful, hopeless, lamentable; substandard, poor, inadequate, inferior, unsatisfactory; informal rotten, appalling, crummy, pathetic, pitiful, lousy, abysmal, dire; Brit. informal duff, chronic, rubbish, pants.
– OPPOSITES cheerful, excellent.

wolf verb *he wolfed down his breakfast:* **devour**, gobble (up), guzzle, gulp down, bolt; informal put away, demolish, shovel down, scoff (down), get outside of; Brit. informal gollop; N. Amer. informal scarf (down/up), snarf (down/up).

woman noun **1** *a woman got out of the car:* **lady**, girl, female; matron; Scottish & N. English lass, lassie; Irish colleen; informal chick, girlie, filly, biddy; Brit. informal bird; Scottish & N. English informal wifie; N. Amer. informal sister, dame, broad, gal, jane; Austral./NZ informal sheila. **2** *he found himself a new woman:* **girlfriend**, sweetheart, partner, significant other, inamorata, lover, mistress, fiancée; wife, spouse; informal bird, fancy woman, missus, better half; Brit. informal other half, Dutch, trouble and strife; Irish informal mot; N. Amer. informal squeeze.

womanhood noun **1** *she was on the brink of womanhood:* **adulthood**, maturity. **2** *she's an ideal of womanhood:* **womanliness**, femininity. **3** *the stereotype of Soviet womanhood:* **women**, womenfolk; womankind, womenkind, woman; the female sex.

womanish adjective *his high womanish voice:* **effeminate**, girlish, girlie, unmanly, unmasculine.
– OPPOSITES manly.

womanizer noun *his reputation as a womanizer:* **philanderer**, Casanova, Don Juan, Romeo, Lothario, ladies' man, playboy, seducer, rake, roué, libertine, lecher; informal skirt-chaser, ladykiller, lech.

womankind noun **women**, woman, the female sex, womenkind, womanhood, womenfolk.

womanly adjective **1** *womanly virtues:* **feminine**, female. **2** *her womanly figure:* **voluptuous**, curvaceous, shapely, ample, Junoesque, Rubenesque, buxom, full-figured; informal curvy, busty.
– OPPOSITES masculine, boyish.

wonder noun **1** *she was speechless with wonder:* **awe**, admiration, wonderment, fascination; surprise, astonishment, amazement. **2** *the wonders of nature:* **marvel**, miracle, phenomenon, sensation, spectacle, beauty; curiosity.
verb **1** *I wondered what was on her mind:* **ponder**, think about, meditate on, reflect on, muse on, speculate about, conjecture; be curious about. **2** *I wonder you were so patient:* **be surprised**, find it surprising. **3** *people wondered at such bravery:* **marvel**, be amazed, be astonished, stand in awe, be dumbfounded, gape, goggle; informal be flabbergasted.

wonderful adjective *I've had a wonderful evening:* **marvellous**, magnificent, superb, glorious, sublime, lovely, delightful; informal super, great, fantastic, terrific, tremendous, sensational, incredible, fabulous, fab, awesome, magic, ace, wicked, far out; Brit.

w

informal smashing, brilliant, brill; N. Amer. informal peachy, dandy, neat; Austral./NZ informal beaut, bonzer.
– OPPOSITES awful.

wont adjective *he was wont to arise at 5.30:* **accustomed**, used, given, inclined.
noun *Paul drove fast, as was his wont:* **custom**, habit, way, practice, convention, rule.

wonted adjective *McTeague had relapsed into his wonted stolidity:* **customary**, habitual, usual, accustomed, familiar, normal, conventional, routine, common.

woo verb **1** *Richard wooed Joan:* **pay court to**, pursue, chase (after). **2** *the party wooed voters with promises:* **seek**, pursue, curry favour with, try to win, try to attract, try to cultivate. **3** *an attempt to woo him out of retirement:* **entice**, tempt, coax, persuade, wheedle; informal sweet-talk.

wood noun **1** *polished wood:* **timber**, planks, planking; logs; N. Amer. lumber. **2** *a walk through the woods:* **forest**, woodland, trees; copse, coppice, grove; Brit. spinney.

wooded adjective *a wooded valley:* **forested**, afforested, tree-covered, woody.

wooden adjective **1** *a wooden door:* **wood**, timber, woody; ligneous. **2** *wooden acting:* **stilted**, stiff, unnatural, awkward, leaden; dry, flat, stodgy, lifeless, passionless, spiritless, soulless. **3** *her face was wooden:* **expressionless**, impassive, poker-faced, emotionless, blank, vacant, unresponsive.

woodland noun *1000 acres of natural woodland:* **woods**, wood, forest, trees.

woodwork noun **carpentry**, joinery.

wool noun **1** *sheep's wool:* **fleece**, hair, coat; floccus. **2** *a sweater made of cream wool:* **yarn**.

woolly adjective **1** *a woolly hat:* **woollen**, wool, fleecy. **2** *a sheep's woolly coat:* **fleecy**, shaggy, hairy, fluffy, flocculent. **3** *woolly generalizations:* **vague**, ill-defined, hazy, unclear, fuzzy, blurry, foggy, nebulous, imprecise, inexact, indefinite; confused, muddled.

woozy adjective (informal). See GROGGY.

word noun **1** *the Italian word for 'ham':* **term**, name, expression, designation, locution, vocable. **2** *his words were meant kindly:* **remark**, comment, observation, statement, utterance, pronouncement. **3** *I've got three weeks to learn the words:* **script**, lyrics, libretto. **4** *I give you my word:* **promise**, word of honour, assurance, guarantee, undertaking; pledge, vow, oath, bond. **5** *I want a word with you:* **talk**, conversation, chat, tête-à-tête, heart-to-heart, one-to-one; discussion, consultation; informal confab, powwow. **6** *there's no word from the hospital:* **news**, information, communication, intelligence; message, report, communiqué, dispatch, bulletin; informal info, gen, dope. **7** *word has it he's turned over a new leaf:* **rumour**, hearsay, talk, gossip; informal the grapevine, the word on the street. **8** *I'm waiting for the word from HQ:* **instruction**, order, command; signal, prompt, cue, tip-off; informal go-ahead, thumbs up, green light. **9** *his word was law:* **command**, order, decree, edict; bidding, will.
verb *the question was carefully worded:* **phrase**, express, put, couch, frame, formulate, style; say, utter.
■ **have words** quarrel, argue, disagree, squabble, bicker, fight, wrangle, dispute, fall out, clash; Brit. informal row.
■ **in a word** briefly, to be brief, in short, in a nutshell, to come to the point, to cut a long story short, not to put too fine a point on it; to sum up, to summarize, in summary.
■ **word for word 1** *they took down the speeches word for word:* **verbatim**, letter for letter, to the letter; exactly, faithfully. **2** *a word-for-word translation:* **verbatim**, literal, exact, direct, accurate, faithful; unadulterated, unabridged.

wording noun *the wording of the question was ambiguous:* **phrasing**, words, phraseology, language, expression, terminology.

wordplay noun *clever wordplay:* **punning**, puns, play on words; wit, witticisms, repartee.

wordy adjective *a wordy speech:* **long-winded**, verbose, prolix, lengthy, protracted, long-drawn-out, rambling, circumlocutory, periphrastic, pleonastic; loquacious, garrulous, voluble; informal windy; Brit. informal waffly.
– OPPOSITES succinct.

work noun **1** *a day's work in the fields:* **labour**, toil, slog, drudgery, exertion, effort, industry, service; informal grind, sweat, elbow grease; Brit. informal graft, fag; Austral./NZ informal yakka. **2** *I'm looking for work:* **employment**, a job, a post, a position, a situation; occupation, profession, career, vocation, calling. **3** *haven't you got any work to do?* **tasks**, jobs, duties, assignments, projects; chores. **4** *works of literature:* **composition**, piece, creation; opus, oeuvre. **5** *this is the work of a radical faction:* **handiwork**, doing, act, deed. **6** *a lifetime spent doing good works:* **deeds**, acts, actions. **7** *the complete works of Shakespeare:* **writings**, oeuvre, canon, output. **8** *a car works:* **factory**, plant, mill, foundry, yard, workshop, shop. **9** *the works of a clock:* **mechanism**, machinery, workings, parts, movement, action; informal insides.
– OPPOSITES leisure.
verb **1** *staff worked late into the night:* **toil**, labour, exert oneself, slave (away); keep at it, keep one's nose to the grindstone; informal slog (away), beaver away, plug away, put one's back into it, knock oneself out, sweat blood; Brit. informal graft, fag. **2** *he worked in education for years:* **be employed**, have a job, earn one's living, do business. **3** *farmers worked the land:* **cultivate**, farm,

W

till, plough. **4** *his car was working perfectly:* **function**, go, run, operate; informal behave. **5** *how do I work this machine?* **operate**, use, handle, control, manipulate, run. **6** *their ploy worked:* **succeed**, work out, turn out well, go as planned, get results, be effective; informal come off, pay off, do the trick; N. Amer. informal turn the trick. **7** *blusher can work miracles:* **bring about**, accomplish, achieve, produce, perform, create, engender, contrive, effect. **8** *he worked the crowd into a frenzy:* **stir (up)**, excite, drive, move, rouse, fire, galvanize; whip up, agitate. **9** *work the mixture into a paste:* **knead**, squeeze, form; mix, stir, blend. **10** *he worked the blade into the padlock:* **manoeuvre**, manipulate, guide, edge. **11** *her mouth worked furiously:* **twitch**, quiver, convulse. **12** *he worked his way through the crowd:* **manoeuvre**, make, thread, wind, weave, wend.
– OPPOSITES rest, fail.

■ **work on someone** *leave him to me—I'll work on him:* persuade, manipulate, influence; coax, cajole, wheedle, soften up; informal twist someone's arm, lean on.

■ **work out 1** *the bill works out at £50:* amount to, add up to, come to, total; Brit. tot up to. **2** *my idea worked out.* See WORK verb sense 6. **3** *things didn't work out the way she planned:* end up, turn out, go, come out, develop; happen, occur; informal pan out. **4** *he works out at the local gym:* exercise, train.

■ **work something out 1** *work out what you can afford:* calculate, compute, reckon up, determine. **2** *I'm trying to work out what she meant:* understand, comprehend, puzzle out, sort out, make sense of, get to the bottom of, make head or tail of, unravel, decipher, decode; informal figure out; Brit. informal suss out. **3** *they worked out a plan:* devise, formulate, draw up, put together, develop, construct, arrange, organize, contrive, concoct; hammer out, negotiate.

■ **work something up** *he couldn't seem to work up any enthusiasm:* stimulate, rouse, raise, arouse, awaken, excite.

workable adjective *a workable solution to the problem:* **practicable**, feasible, viable, possible, achievable; realistic, reasonable, sensible, practical; informal doable.
– OPPOSITES impracticable.

workaday adjective *her workaday life:* **ordinary**, average, run-of-the-mill, middle-of-the-road, conventional, unremarkable, unexceptional, humdrum, undistinguished, commonplace, mundane, pedestrian; routine, everyday, day-to-day; N. Amer. garden-variety; informal bog-standard, nothing to write home about, ten a penny, a dime a dozen; Brit. informal common or garden.
– OPPOSITES exceptional.

worker noun **1** *a strike by 500 workers:* **employee**, member of staff; workman, labourer, hand, operative, operator; proletarian; artisan, craftsman,

craftswoman; wage-earner, breadwinner. **2** (informal) *I got a reputation for being a worker:* **hard worker**, toiler, workhorse; informal busy bee, eager beaver, workaholic; N. Amer. informal wheel horse.

workforce noun *the company has a 9000-strong workforce:* **staff**, employees, personnel, workers, labour force, manpower; human resources; informal liveware.

working adjective **1** *working mothers:* **employed**, in (gainful) employment, in work, waged. **2** *a working waterwheel:* **functioning**, operating, running, active, operational, functional, serviceable; informal up and running. **3** *a working knowledge of contract law:* **sufficient**, adequate, viable; useful, effective.
– OPPOSITES unemployed, faulty.
noun **1** *the working of a carburettor:* **functioning**, operation, running, action, performance. **2** *the workings of a watch:* **mechanism**, machinery, parts, movement, action, works; informal insides.

workman noun **(manual) worker**, labourer, hand, operative, operator; employee; journeyman, artisan.

workmanlike adjective *the team put up a good, workmanlike performance:* **efficient**, competent, professional, proficient, skilful, adept, masterly.

workmanship noun *a long tradition of fine workmanship:* **craftsmanship**, artistry, craft, art, artisanship, handiwork; skill, expertise, technique.

workout noun *a strenuous workout:* **exercise session**, keep-fit session, training session, drill; warm-up; exercises, aerobics.

workshop noun **1** *a car repair workshop:* **factory**, works, plant; garage. **2** *the craftsmen had a chilly workshop:* **workroom**, studio, atelier. **3** *a workshop on combating stress:* **study group**, discussion group, seminar, class.

world noun **1** *he travelled the world:* **earth**, globe, planet, sphere. **2** *life on other worlds:* **planet**, satellite, moon, star, heavenly body, orb. **3** *the academic world:* **sphere**, society, circle, arena, milieu, province, domain, orbit, preserve, realm, field, discipline, area. **4** *she would show the world that she was strong:* **everyone**, everybody, people, mankind, humankind, humanity, the (general) public, the population, the populace, all and sundry, every mother's son, {every Tom, Dick, and Harry}, every man jack. **5** *a world of difference:* **huge amount**, good deal, great deal, abundance, wealth, profusion, mountain; plenty; informal heap, lot, load, ton, masses; Brit. informal shedload. **6** *she renounced the world:* **society**, secular interests, temporal concerns, earthly concerns.

■ **on top of the world** (informal). See OVERJOYED.

■ **out of this world** (informal). See WONDERFUL.

worldly adjective **1** *his youth was wasted on worldly pursuits:* **earthly**, terrestrial, temporal, mundane; mortal, human, material, materialistic, physical, carnal, fleshly, bodily, corporeal, sensual. **2** *a worldly man:* **sophisticated**, experienced, worldly-wise, knowledgeable, knowing, enlightened, shrewd, mature, seasoned, cosmopolitan, urbane, cultivated, cultured.
– OPPOSITES spiritual, naive.

worldwide adjective *a worldwide effort to stop the spread of Aids:* **global**, international, intercontinental, universal; ubiquitous, extensive, widespread, far-reaching, wide-ranging, all-embracing.
– OPPOSITES local.

worn adjective **1** *his hat was worn:* **shabby**, worn out, threadbare, tattered, in tatters, holey, falling to pieces, ragged, frayed, moth-eaten, scruffy, having seen better days; informal tatty, ratty, the worse for wear; N. Amer. informal raggedy. **2** *her face looked worn.* See **WORN OUT** sense 2.
– OPPOSITES smart, fresh.

worn out adjective **1** *a worn-out shirt.* See **WORN** sense 1. **2** *by evening they looked worn out:* **exhausted**, fatigued, tired (out), weary, drained, worn, drawn, wan, sapped, spent; careworn, haggard, hollow-eyed, pinched, pale, peaky; informal all in, done in, dog-tired, dead beat, fit to drop, shattered; Brit. informal knackered; N. Amer. informal pooped, tuckered out. **3** *worn-out ideas:* **obsolete**, antiquated, old, stale, hackneyed, trite, overused, overworked, clichéd, unoriginal, commonplace, pedestrian, prosaic, stock, conventional; informal played out, old hat.
– OPPOSITES smart, fresh.

worried adjective *they kept their fingers crossed but they weren't too worried:* **anxious**, perturbed, troubled, bothered, concerned, upset, distressed, distraught, disquieted, uneasy, fretful, agitated, nervous, edgy, on edge, tense, overwrought, worked up, keyed up, jumpy, stressed; apprehensive, fearful, afraid, frightened, scared; informal uptight, a bundle of nerves, on tenterhooks, jittery, twitchy, in a stew, all of a dither, in a flap, in a sweat, het up, rattled; Brit. informal windy, having kittens; N. Amer. informal antsy, squirrelly.
– OPPOSITES carefree.

worrisome adjective. See **WORRYING**.

worry verb **1** *she worries about his health:* **fret**, be concerned, be anxious, agonize, brood, panic, lose sleep, get worked up; informal get stressed, get in a flap, get in a state, stew, torment oneself. **2** *is something worrying you?* **trouble**, bother, make anxious, disturb, distress, upset, concern, disquiet, fret, agitate, unsettle, perturb, scare, fluster, stress, tax, torment, plague, bedevil; prey on one's mind, weigh down, gnaw at; informal rattle, bug, get to. **3** *a dog*

worried the sheep: **attack**, savage, maul, mutilate, mangle, go for; molest, torment, persecute.
noun **1** *I'm beside myself with worry:* **anxiety**, perturbation, distress, concern, uneasiness, unease, disquiet, fretfulness, restlessness, nervousness, nerves, agitation, edginess, tension, stress; apprehension, fear, dread, trepidation, misgiving, angst; informal butterflies (in the stomach), the willies, the heebie-jeebies. **2** *the rats are a worry:* **problem**, cause for concern; nuisance, pest, plague, trial, trouble, vexation, bane, bugbear; informal pain (in the neck), headache, hassle, stress.

worrying adjective *their financial situation was very worrying:* **alarming**, worrisome, daunting, perturbing, niggling, bothersome, troublesome, unsettling, nerve-racking; distressing, disquieting, upsetting, traumatic, problematic; informal scary, hairy.

worsen verb **1** *insomnia can worsen a patient's distress:* **aggravate**, exacerbate, compound, add to, intensify, increase, magnify, heighten, inflame, augment; informal add fuel to the fire. **2** *the recession worsened:* **deteriorate**, degenerate, decline; informal go downhill, go to pot, go to the dogs, hit the skids, nosedive.
– OPPOSITES improve.

worship noun **1** *the worship of saints:* **reverence**, veneration, adoration, glorification, glory, exaltation; devotion, praise, thanksgiving, homage, honour. **2** *morning worship:* **service**, religious rite, prayer, praise, devotion, religious observance; matins, vespers, evensong. **3** *he contemplated her with worship:* **admiration**, adulation, idolization, lionization, hero-worship.
verb *they worship pagan gods:* **revere**, reverence, venerate, pay homage to, honour, adore, praise, pray to, glorify, exalt, extol; hold dear, cherish, treasure, esteem, adulate, idolize, deify, hero-worship, lionize; informal put on a pedestal.

worst verb *they were worsted by a large and desperate band of armed malefactors:* **defeat**, beat, prevail over, triumph over, trounce, rout, vanquish, conquer, master, overcome, overwhelm, overpower, crush; outdo, outclass, outstrip, surpass; informal thrash, lick, best, clobber, drub, slaughter, murder, wipe out, crucify, demolish, wipe the floor with, take to the cleaners, walk all over, make mincemeat of; Brit. informal stuff; N. Amer. informal shellac, cream.

worth noun **1** *evidence of the rug's worth:* **value**, price, cost; valuation, quotation, estimate. **2** *the intrinsic worth of education:* **benefit**, advantage, use, value, virtue, utility, service, profit, help, aid; desirability, appeal; significance, sense; informal mileage, percentage. **3** *a sense of personal worth:* **worthiness**, merit, value, excellence, calibre, quality, stature, eminence,

w

consequence, importance, significance, distinction.

worthless adjective **1** *the item was worthless:* **valueless**; poor quality, inferior, second-rate, low-grade, cheap, shoddy, tawdry; informal crummy, rubbishy, ten a penny; Brit. informal twopenny-halfpenny; N. Amer. informal nickel-and-dime. **2** *your conclusions are worthless:* **useless**, no use, ineffective, ineffectual, fruitless, unproductive, unavailing, pointless, nugatory, valueless, inadequate, deficient, meaningless, senseless, insubstantial, empty, hollow, trifling, petty, inconsequential, lame, paltry, pathetic; informal a dead loss. **3** *his worthless son:* **good-for-nothing**, ne'er-do-well, useless, despicable, contemptible, low, ignominious, corrupt, villainous, degenerate, shiftless, feckless; informal no-good, lousy.
– OPPOSITES valuable, useful.

worthwhile adjective *everyone felt that the campaign had been worthwhile:* **valuable**, useful, of use, of service, beneficial, rewarding, advantageous, positive, helpful, profitable, gainful, fruitful, productive, constructive, effective, effectual, meaningful, worthy.
– OPPOSITES useless.

worthy adjective *a worthy citizen | a worthy objective:* **virtuous**, righteous, good, moral, upright, upstanding, high-minded, principled, exemplary, honest, honourable, reputable, decent, respectable, noble, meritorious, admirable, praiseworthy, laudable, commendable, creditable, sterling; informal squeaky clean.
– OPPOSITES disreputable.
noun *local worthies:* **dignitary**, personage, grandee, VIP, notable, notability, pillar of society, luminary, leading light, big name; informal heavyweight, bigwig, top dog, big shot, big cheese; N. Amer. informal big wheel, big kahuna.
– OPPOSITES nobody.
■ **be worthy of** deserve, merit, warrant, rate, justify, earn, be entitled to, qualify for.

would-be adjective *would-be actors:* **aspiring**, budding, promising, prospective, potential, hopeful, keen, eager, ambitious; informal wannabe.

wound noun **1** *a chest wound:* **injury**, lesion, cut, gash, laceration, tear, slash; graze, scratch, abrasion; bruise, contusion; Medicine trauma. **2** *the wounds inflicted by the media:* **insult**, blow, slight, offence, affront; hurt, damage, injury, pain, distress, grief, anguish, torment.
verb **1** *he was critically wounded:* **injure**, hurt, harm; maim, mutilate, disable, incapacitate, cripple; lacerate, cut, graze, gash, stab, slash. **2** *her words had wounded him:* **hurt**, scar, damage, injure; insult, slight, offend, affront, distress, disturb, upset, trouble; grieve, sadden, pain, sting, shock, traumatize, torment.

wrangle noun *a wrangle over money:* **argument**, dispute, disagreement, quarrel, falling-out, fight, squabble, altercation, war of words, shouting match, tiff; informal set-to, run-in, slanging match; Brit. informal barney, row, bust-up.
verb *we wrangled over the details:* **argue**, quarrel, bicker, squabble, fall out, have words, disagree, be at odds, fight, battle, feud, clash; informal scrap; Brit. informal row.

wrap verb **1** *she wrapped herself in a towel:* **swathe**, bundle, swaddle, muffle, cloak, enfold, envelop, encase, cover, fold, wind. **2** *I wrapped the vase carefully:* **parcel (up)**, package, pack (up), bundle (up); gift-wrap.
noun *he put a wrap round her:* **shawl**, stole, cloak, cape, mantle, scarf, poncho, pashmina, serape.
■ **wrap up 1** *wrap up well—it's cold:* dress warmly, muffle up. **2** (Brit. informal) *for goodness' sake tell that child to wrap up.* See SHUT UP at SHUT.

wrapper noun **1** *a sweet wrapper:* **wrapping**, packaging, paper, cover, covering; jacket, sheath. **2** (N. Amer.) *she wore a cotton wrapper:* **housecoat**, bathrobe, dressing gown, robe, kimono, peignoir.

wrath noun *he hadn't the nerve to face his mother's wrath:* **anger**, rage, fury, outrage, spleen, vexation, (high) dudgeon, crossness, displeasure, annoyance, irritation.
– OPPOSITES happiness.

wreak verb *these policies would wreak havoc on the British economy:* **inflict**, bestow, mete out, administer, deliver, impose, exact, create, cause, result in, effect, engender, bring about, perpetrate, unleash, vent.

wreath noun *a delicate wreath of roses:* **garland**, circlet, chaplet, crown, festoon, lei; ring, loop, circle.

wreathe verb **1** *a pulpit wreathed in holly:* **festoon**, garland, drape, cover, bedeck, deck, decorate, ornament, adorn. **2** *blue smoke wreathed upwards:* **spiral**, coil, loop, wind, curl, twist, snake, curve.

wreck noun **1** *salvage teams landed on the wreck:* **shipwreck**, sunken ship, derelict; shell, hull. **2** *the wreck of a stolen car:* **wreckage**, debris, remainder, ruins, remains.
verb **1** *he had wrecked her car:* **demolish**, crash, smash up, damage, destroy; vandalize, deface, desecrate, write off; N. Amer. informal trash, total. **2** *his ship was wrecked:* **shipwreck**, sink, capsize, run aground. **3** *the crisis wrecked his plans:* **ruin**, spoil, disrupt, undo, put a stop to, frustrate, blight, crush, quash, dash, destroy, scotch, shatter, devastate, sabotage; informal mess up, screw up, foul up, put paid to, stymie, put the kibosh on, nix; Brit. informal scupper, dish.

wrench noun **1** *she felt a wrench on her shoulders:* **tug**, pull, jerk, jolt, heave; informal yank. **2** *hold the piston with a wrench:* **spanner**, monkey wrench. **3** *leaving was*

an immense wrench: **painful parting**, traumatic event; pang, trauma.
verb **1** he wrenched the gun from her hand: **tug**, pull, jerk, wrest, heave, twist, pluck, grab, seize, snatch, force, prise; N. Amer. pry; informal yank. **2** she wrenched her ankle: **sprain**, twist, turn, strain, rick, crick, pull; injure, hurt.

wrest verb he tried to wrest the broom from Angela's grasp: **wrench**, snatch, seize, grab, prise, pluck, tug, pull, jerk, dislodge; N. Amer. pry; informal yank.

wrestle verb she wrestled with her conscience: **grapple**, fight, struggle, contend, vie, battle, wrangle; scuffle, tussle, brawl; informal scrap.

wretch noun **1** the wretches killed themselves: **poor creature**, poor soul, poor thing, poor unfortunate; informal poor devil, poor beggar. **2** I wouldn't trust the old wretch: **scoundrel**, villain, ruffian, rogue, rascal, reprobate, criminal, miscreant, good-for-nothing; informal heel, creep, louse, rat, swine, dog, lowlife, scumbag.

wretched adjective **1** I felt so wretched without you: **miserable**, unhappy, sad, heartbroken, grief-stricken, sorrowful, distressed, desolate, devastated, despairing, disconsolate, downcast, dejected, crestfallen, cheerless, depressed, melancholy, morose, gloomy, mournful, doleful, dismal, forlorn, woebegone; informal blue. **2** I feel wretched: **ill**, unwell, poorly, sick, below par; Brit. off colour; informal under the weather, out of sorts. **3** their living conditions are wretched: **harsh**, hard, grim, stark, difficult; poor, impoverished; pitiful, pathetic, miserable, cheerless, sordid, shabby, seedy, dilapidated; informal scummy; Brit. informal grotty. **4** the wretched dweller in the shanty town: **unfortunate**, unlucky, luckless, ill-starred, blighted, hapless, poor, pitiable, downtrodden, oppressed. **5** he's a wretched coward: **despicable**, contemptible, reprehensible, base, vile, loathsome, hateful, detestable, odious, ignoble, shameful, shabby, worthless; informal dirty, rotten, low-down, lousy. **6** wretched weather: **terrible**, awful, dire, atrocious, dreadful, bad, poor, lamentable, deplorable; informal God-awful; Brit. informal beastly. **7** (informal) I don't want the wretched money: **damned**, damn, blasted, blessed, flaming, confounded, rotten; Brit. informal flipping, blinking, blooming, bloody.
– OPPOSITES cheerful, well, comfortable, fortunate, excellent.

wriggle verb **1** she tried to hug him but he wriggled: **squirm**, writhe, wiggle, jiggle, jerk, thresh, flounder, flail, twitch, twist and turn; snake, worm, slither. **2** he wriggled out of his responsibilities: **avoid**, shirk, dodge, evade, elude, sidestep; escape from; informal duck.
noun the baby gave a wriggle: **squirm**, jiggle, wiggle, twitch, twist.

wring verb **1** wring out the clothes: **twist**,

squeeze, screw, scrunch, knead, press, mangle. **2** concessions were wrung from the government: **extract**, elicit, force, exact, wrest, wrench, squeeze, milk; informal bleed. **3** his expression wrung her heart: **rend**, tear at, harrow, pierce, stab, wound, rack; distress, pain, hurt.

wrinkle noun fine wrinkles around her mouth: **crease**, fold, pucker, line, crinkle, furrow, ridge, groove; informal crow's feet. verb his coat-tails wrinkled up: **crease**, pucker, gather, line, crinkle, crimp, crumple, rumple, ruck up, scrunch up.

writ noun they were served with a High Court writ: **summons**, subpoena, warrant, arraignment, indictment, citation, court order.

write verb **1** he wrote her name in the book: **put in writing**, write down, put down, jot down, note (down), take down, record, register, log, list; inscribe, sign, scribble, scrawl, pencil. **2** I wrote a poem: **compose**, draft, think up, formulate, compile, pen, dash off, produce. **3** he had her address and promised to write: **correspond**, write a letter, communicate, get in touch, keep in contact; informal drop someone a line.
■ **write someone/something off 1** they have had to write off loans: **forget about**, disregard, give up on, cancel, annul, wipe out. **2** he wrote off his new car: **wreck**, smash up, crash, destroy, demolish, ruin; N. Amer. informal total. **3** who would write off a player of his stature? disregard, dismiss, ignore.

writer noun **author**, wordsmith, man/woman of letters, penman; novelist, essayist, biographer; journalist, columnist, correspondent; scriptwriter, playwright, dramatist, dramaturge, tragedian; poet; informal scribbler, scribe, pen-pusher, hack.

writhe verb she writhed about on the floor in agony: **squirm**, wriggle, thrash, flail, toss, toss and turn, twist, twist and turn, struggle.

writing noun **1** I can't read his writing: **handwriting**, hand, script, print; penmanship, calligraphy, chirography; informal scribble, scrawl. **2** the writings of Gertrude Stein: **works**, compositions, books, publications, oeuvre; papers, articles, essays.

wrong adjective **1** the wrong answer: **incorrect**, mistaken, in error, erroneous, inaccurate, inexact, imprecise, fallacious, wide of the mark, off target, unsound, faulty; informal off beam, out. **2** he knew he had said the wrong thing: **inappropriate**, unsuitable, inapt, inapposite, undesirable; ill-advised, ill-considered, ill-judged, impolitic, injudicious, infelicitous, unfitting, out of keeping, improper; informal out of order. **3** I've done nothing wrong: **illegal**, unlawful, illicit, criminal, dishonest, dishonourable, corrupt; unethical, immoral, bad, wicked, sinful, iniquitous, nefarious, blameworthy, reprehensible; informal crooked. **4** there's something wrong with the engine: **amiss**, awry, out of order, not

right, faulty, defective.
– OPPOSITES right, correct, appropriate, legal.
adverb *she guessed wrong:* **incorrectly**,
wrongly, inaccurately, erroneously,
mistakenly.
noun 1 *the difference between right and
wrong:* **immorality**, sin, sinfulness,
wickedness, evil; unlawfulness, crime,
corruption, villainy, dishonesty, injustice,
wrongdoing, misconduct, transgression.
2 *an attempt to make up for past
wrongs:* **misdeed**, offence, injury, crime,
transgression, peccadillo, sin; injustice,
outrage, atrocity.
– OPPOSITES right.
verb 1 *she was determined to forget the man
who had wronged her:* **ill-use**, mistreat,
do an injustice to, do wrong to, ill-treat,
abuse, harm, hurt, injure; informal do the dirty
on. **2** *perhaps I am wronging him:* **malign**,
misrepresent, do a disservice to, impugn,
defame, slander, libel.
■ **get someone/something wrong**
misunderstand, misinterpret, misconstrue,
mistake, misread, take amiss; get the wrong
idea/impression; informal get the wrong end
of the stick, be barking up the wrong tree.
■ **go wrong 1** *I've gone wrong somewhere:*
make a mistake, make an error, make a
blunder, blunder, miscalculate, trip up;
informal slip up, screw up, make a boo-boo;
Brit. informal boob. **2** *their plans went wrong:*
go awry, go amiss, go off course, fail, be
unsuccessful, fall through, come to nothing;
backfire, misfire, rebound; informal come to
grief, come a cropper, go up in smoke; Brit.
informal go adrift. **3** *the radio's gone wrong:*
break down, malfunction, fail, stop working,
crash, give out; informal be on the blink, conk
out, go kaput; Brit. informal play up, pack up.
■ **in the wrong** to blame, blameworthy,

at fault, reprehensible, responsible,
culpable, answerable, guilty.
wrongdoer noun **offender**, lawbreaker,
criminal, felon, delinquent, villain, culprit,
evil-doer, sinner, transgressor, malefactor,
miscreant, rogue, scoundrel; informal crook,
wrong 'un.
wrongdoing noun *good journalism can
expose wrongdoing:* **crime**, lawbreaking,
lawlessness, criminality, misconduct,
misbehaviour, malpractice, corruption,
immorality, sin, sinfulness, wickedness,
evil, vice, iniquity, villainy; offence, felony,
wrong, misdeed, misdemeanour, fault,
peccadillo, transgression.
wrongful adjective *she's suing the police for
wrongful arrest:* **unjustified**, unwarranted,
unjust, unfair, undue, undeserved,
unreasonable, groundless, indefensible,
inappropriate, improper, unlawful, illegal,
illegitimate.
– OPPOSITES rightful.
wrought up adjective *it was easy to see
that she was wrought up over something:*
agitated, tense, stressed, overwrought,
nervous, on edge, edgy, keyed up, worked
up, jumpy, anxious, nervy, flustered, fretful,
upset; informal in a state, in a stew, het up,
wound up, uptight, in a tizz/tizzy; Brit. informal
strung up; N. Amer. informal spooky, squirrelly.
– OPPOSITES calm.
wry adjective **1** *his wry humour:* **ironic**,
sardonic, satirical, mocking, sarcastic;
dry, droll, witty, humorous. **2** *a wry
expression:* **unimpressed**, displeased,
annoyed, irritated, irked, vexed, piqued,
disgruntled, dissatisfied; informal peeved.
3 *a wry neck:* **twisted**, crooked, contorted,
distorted, deformed, misshapen; Scottish
thrawn.

w

Xx

xenophobic adjective *an unadventurous and xenophobic nation:* **jingoistic**, chauvinistic, flag-waving, excessively nationalistic, isolationist; prejudiced, bigoted, intolerant.

Xerox noun (trademark) *in case you haven't read the article, I enclose a Xerox:* **photocopy**, copy, duplicate, reproduction; trademark photostat.

X-ray noun *an X-ray of her left knee:* **radiograph**, X-ray image/picture/photograph, roentgenogram, radiogram.

Yy

yahoo noun *you're no yahoo, you're too smart:* **boor**, lout, oaf, thug, barbarian, Neanderthal, brute, bully boy; informal clod, roughneck, bruiser; Brit. informal yobbo, yob, oik.

yank (informal) verb *Gilbert yanked open the door to the office:* **jerk**, pull, tug, wrench, rip; snatch, seize.
noun *she gave his hat a sharp yank:* **jerk**, pull, tug, wrench.

yap verb **1** *the dogs yapped about his heels:* **bark**, woof, yelp. **2** (informal) *what are they yapping on about?* See **BABBLE** verb sense 1.

yardstick noun *they ought to appraise their investments against a more realistic yardstick:* **standard**, measure, gauge, scale, guide, guideline, indicator, test, touchstone, barometer, criterion, benchmark, point of reference, model, pattern.

yarn noun *you need to use a fine yarn:* **thread**, cotton, wool, fibre, filament; ply.

yawning adjective *there was a yawning hole where the door had been wrenched off:* **gaping**, wide open, wide, cavernous, deep; huge, great, big.

year noun **twelve-month period**, calendar year.
■ **year in, year out** *we pay the same fixed sum year in, year out:* **repeatedly**, again and again, time and (time) again, time after time, over and over (again), {week in, week out}, {day in, day out}, recurrently, continuously, continually, constantly, habitually, regularly, without a break, unfailingly, always.

yearly adjective *a yearly payment:* **annual**, once a year, every year, each year.
adverb *the guide is published yearly:* **annually**, once a year, per annum, by the year, every year, each year.

yearn verb *she yearned to be with him:* **long**, pine, crave, desire, want, wish, hanker, covet, lust, pant, hunger, thirst, ache, eat one's heart out, have one's heart set on; informal have a yen, itch.

yearning noun *they sometimes feel a yearning for the mountains and the sea:* **longing**, craving, desire, want, wish, hankering, urge, hunger, thirst, appetite, lust, ache; informal yen, itch.

yell verb *he yelled in agony:* **cry out**, call out, call at the top of one's voice, shout, howl, yowl, wail, scream, shriek, screech, yelp, squeal; roar, bawl; informal holler.
noun *a yell of rage:* **cry**, shout, howl, yowl, scream, shriek, screech, yelp, squeal; roar; informal holler.

yellow adjective **flaxen**, golden, gold, blonde, fair; lemon, mustard.

yelp noun & verb *he yelped in pain:* **squeal**, shriek, howl, yowl, yell, cry, shout, yawp; informal holler.

yen noun (informal) *he had a yen for foreign travel:* **hankering**, yearning, longing, craving, urge, desire, want, wish, hunger, thirst, lust, appetite, ache; fancy, inclination; informal itch.

yes adverb *yes, I'll come to your party:* **all right**, very well, of course, by all means, sure, certainly, absolutely, indeed, affirmative, in the affirmative, agreed, roger; Scottish, N. English, & archaic aye; informal yeah, yep, yup, uh-huh, okay, OK, okey-dokey, okey-doke; Brit. informal righto, righty-ho; N. Amer. informal surely.
– OPPOSITES no.

yet adverb **1** *he hasn't made up his mind yet:* **so far**, thus far, as yet, up till/to now, until now. **2** *don't celebrate just yet:* **now**, right now, at this time; already, so soon. **3** *he was doing nothing, yet he appeared purposeful:* **nevertheless**, nonetheless, even so, but, however, still, notwithstanding, despite that, in spite of that, for all that, all the same, just the same, at the same time, be that as it may. **4** *he supplied yet more unsolicited advice:* **even**, still, further, in addition, additionally, besides, into the bargain, to boot.

yield verb **1** *too many projects yield poor returns:* **produce**, bear, give, supply, provide, afford, return, bring in, earn, realize, generate, deliver, pay out. **2** *the nobility had yielded power to the new capitalist class:* **relinquish**, surrender, cede, remit, part with, hand over; make over, bequeath, leave. **3** *the Duke's army was forced to yield:* **surrender**, capitulate, submit, relent, admit defeat, back down, climb down, give in, give up the struggle, lay down one's arms, raise/show the white flag, throw in the towel/sponge. **4** *he yielded to her demands:* **give in to**, give way to, submit to, bow down to, comply with, agree to, consent to, go along with; grant, permit, allow; informal cave in to; formal accede to. **5** *the*

floorboards yielded underfoot: **bend**, give, give way.
– OPPOSITES withhold, resist, defy.
noun *risky investments usually have higher yields:* **profit**, gain, return, dividend, earnings; Brit. informal bunce.

yob, yobbo noun (Brit. informal). See **HOOLIGAN**.

yoke noun **1** *the horses were loosened from the yoke:* **harness**, collar, coupling. **2** *countries struggling under the yoke of imperialism:* **tyranny**, oppression, domination, hegemony, enslavement, servitude, subjugation, subjection, bondage, thrall; bonds, chains, fetters, shackles. **3** *the yoke of marriage:* **bond**, tie, connection, link.
verb **1** *a pair of oxen were yoked together:* **harness**, hitch, couple, tether, fasten, attach, join. **2** *their aim of yoking biology and mechanics:* **unite**, join, link, connect; tie, bind, bond.

yokel noun *the yokels drank cider and pronounced it 'zyder':* **bumpkin**, peasant, provincial, rustic, country cousin, countryman/woman; Irish informal culchie; N. Amer. informal hayseed, hillbilly, hick; Austral. informal bushy.

young adjective **1** *young people:* **youthful**, juvenile; junior, adolescent, teenage; in the springtime of life, in one's salad days. **2** *she's very young for her age:* **immature**, childish, inexperienced, unsophisticated, naive, unworldly; informal wet behind the ears. **3** *the young microbrewery industry:*

fledgling, developing, budding, in its infancy, emerging.
– OPPOSITES old, elderly, mature.
noun **1** *a robin feeding its young:* **offspring**, progeny, family, babies. **2** *the young don't care nowadays:* **young people**, children, boys and girls, youngsters, youth, the younger generation, juveniles, minors; informal kids, young 'uns.

youngster noun *a new magazine for youngsters:* **child**, teenager, adolescent, youth, juvenile, minor, junior; boy, girl; Scottish & N. English lass, lassie; informal lad, kid, whippersnapper, young 'un, teen.

youth noun **1** *he had been a keen sportsman in his youth:* **early years**, young days, teens, teenage years, adolescence, boyhood, girlhood, childhood; minority. **2** *she had kept her youth and beauty:* **youthfulness**, freshness, bloom, vigour, energy. **3** *local youths:* **young man**, boy, juvenile, teenager, adolescent, junior, minor; informal lad, kid. **4** *the youth of the nation:* **young people**, young, younger generation, next generation; informal kids.
– OPPOSITES adulthood, old age.

youthful adjective *people aspiring to remain youthful:* **young-looking**, spry, sprightly, vigorous, active; young, boyish, girlish; fresh-faced, in the springtime of life, in one's salad days.
– OPPOSITES old, elderly.

y

Zz

zany adjective *the film has a zany plot and some peculiar characters:* **eccentric**, peculiar, odd, unconventional, strange, bizarre, weird; mad, crazy, comic, madcap, funny, quirky, idiosyncratic; informal wacky, screwy, nutty, oddball, off the wall; Brit. informal daft; N. Amer. informal kooky, wacko.
– OPPOSITES conventional, sensible.

zeal noun *his zeal for football:* **passion**, ardour, love, fervour, fire, avidity, devotion, enthusiasm, eagerness, keenness, appetite, relish, gusto, vigour, energy, intensity; fanaticism.
– OPPOSITES apathy.

zealot noun *reforming zealots destroyed a vast collection of papers:* **fanatic**, enthusiast, extremist, radical, Young Turk, diehard, activist, militant; bigot, dogmatist, sectarian, partisan; informal fiend, maniac, ultra, nut.

zealous adjective *he is a zealous worker:* **fervent**, ardent, fervid, fanatical, passionate, impassioned, devout, devoted, committed, dedicated, enthusiastic, eager, keen, avid, vigorous, energetic, intense, fierce.
– OPPOSITES apathetic.

zenith noun *the king was at the zenith of his power:* **highest point**, high point, crowning point, height, top, acme, peak, pinnacle, apex, apogee, crown, crest, summit, climax, culmination, prime, meridian.
– OPPOSITES nadir.

zero noun **1** *the sum's wrong—you've left off a zero:* **nought**, nothing, nil, 0; Computing null character. **2** *I rated my chances as zero:* **nothing (at all)**, nil, none; N. English nowt; informal zilch, nix, sweet Fanny Adams, sweet FA; Brit. informal damn all, not a sausage; N. Amer. informal zip, nada, diddly-squat.
■ **zero in on** *different scientists chose to zero in on different diseases:* **focus on**, focus attention on, centre on, concentrate on, home in on, fix on, pinpoint, highlight, spotlight; informal zoom in on.

zero hour noun *as zero hour approached, thirty ships swung into position:* **the appointed time**, the critical moment, the moment of truth, the point/moment of decision, the Rubicon, the crux; informal the crunch.

zest noun **1** *she had a great zest for life:* **enthusiasm**, gusto, relish, appetite, eagerness, keenness, avidity, zeal, fervour, ardour, passion; verve, vigour, liveliness, sparkle, fire, animation, vitality, dynamism, energy, brio, pep, spirit, exuberance, high spirits; informal zing, zip, oomph, vim, pizzazz, get-up-and-go. **2** *I used to try to beat past records to add zest to my monotonous job:* **piquancy**, tang, flavour, savour, taste, spice, spiciness, relish, bite; excitement, interest, an edge; informal kick, punch, zing, oomph. **3** *the zest of an orange:* **rind**, peel, skin.
– OPPOSITES apathy, indifference, blandness.

zigzag adjective *I steered a zigzag course between the trees:* **twisting**, twisty, full of twists and turns, serpentine, meandering, snaking, snaky, winding, crooked.
– OPPOSITES straight.

zing noun (informal). See ZEST sense 1.

zone noun *the immediate vicinity of a radar mast is a dangerous zone:* **area**, sector, section, belt, stretch, region, territory, district, quarter, precinct, locality, neighbourhood, province.

zoom verb (informal). See SPEED verb sense 1.